THE OFFICIAL 2002 PRICE GUIDE TO FOOTBALL CARDS

DR. JAMES BECKETT

TWENTY-FIRST EDITION

HOUSE OF COLLECTIBLES
The Crown Publishing Group • New York

Important Notice: All of the information, including valuations, in this book has been compiled from the most reliable sources, and every effort has been made to eliminate errors and questionable data. Nevertheless, the possibility of error, in a work of such immense scope, always exists. The publisher will not be held responsible for losses that may occur in the purchase, sale, or other transaction of items because of information contained herein. Readers who feel they have discovered errors are invited to *write* and inform us, so they may be corrected in subsequent editions. Those seeking further information on the topics covered in this book are advised to refer to the complete line of *Official Price Guides* published by the House of Collectibles.

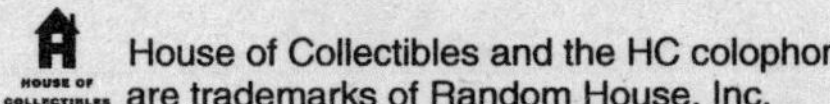

House of Collectibles and the HC colophon are trademarks of Random House, Inc.

Published by:
House of Collectibles
The Crown Publishing Group
New York, New York

Distributed by The Crown Publishing Group,
a division of Random House, Inc.,
New York, and simultaneously in Canada by
Random House of Canada Limited, Toronto.

www.randomhouse.com

Manufactured in the United States of America

ISSN: 0748-1365

ISBN: 0-609-80843-5

10 9 8 7 6 5 4 3 2 1

Twenty First Edition: August 2001

Table of Contents

About the Author

Jim Beckett, the leading authority on sports card values in the United States, maintains a wide range of activities in the world of sports. He possesses one of the finest collections of sportscards and autographs in the world, has made numerous appearances on radio and television. and has been frequently cited in many national publications. He was awarded the first "Special Achievement Award" for Contributions to the Hobby by the National Sports Collectors Convention in 1980, the "Jock-Jaspersen Award" for Hobby Dedication in 1983, and the "Buck Barker, Spirit of the Hobby" Award in 1991.

Dr. Beckett is the author of *Beckett Baseball Card Price Guide, The Official Price Guide to Baseball Cards, The Sport Americana Price Guide to Baseball Collectibles, Beckett Almanac of Baseball Cards and Collectibles, The Sport Americana Baseball Memorabilia and Autograph Price Guide, Beckett Football Card Price Guide, The Official Price Guide to Football Cards, Beckett Hockey Card Price Guide and Alphabetical Checklist, Beckett Basketball Card Price Guide, The Official Price Guide to Basketball Cards,* and *Beckett Baseball Card Alphabetical Checklist.* In addition, he is the founder, publisher, and editor of *Beckett Baseball Card Monthly, Beckett Basketball Card Monthly, Beckett Football Card Monthly, Beckett Hockey Collector, Beckett Sports Collectibles and Autographs,* and *Beckett Racing and Motorsports Marketplace.*

Jim Beckett received his Ph.D. in Statistics from Southern Methodist University in 1975. Prior to starting Beckett Publications in 1984, Dr. Beckett served as an Associate Professor of Statistics at Bowling Green State University and as a Vice President of a consulting firm in Dallas, Texas. He currently resides in Dallas.

How to Use This Book

Isn't it great? Every year this book gets bigger and bigger with all the new sets coming out. But even more exciting is that every year there are more attractive choices and, subsequently, more interest in the cards we love so much. This edition has been enhanced and expanded from the previous edition. The cards you collect — who appears on them, what they look like, where they are from, and (most important to most of you) what their current values are — are enumerated within. Many of the features contained in the other *Beckett Price Guides* have been incorporated into this volume since condition-grading, terminology, and many other aspects of collecting are common to the card hobby in general. We hope you find the book both interesting and useful in your collecting pursuits.

The Beckett Guide has been successful where other attempts have failed because it is complete, current, and valid. This Price Guide contains not just one, but two prices by condition for all the football cards listed. These account for most of the football cards in existence. The prices were added to the card lists just prior to printing and reflect not the author's opinions or desires but the going retail prices for each card, based on the marketplace (sports memorabilia conventions and shows, sportscard shops, hobby papers, current mail-order catalogs, Internet sales, auction results, and other firsthand reporting of actually realized prices).

What is the best price guide available on the market today? Of course card sellers will prefer the price guide with the highest prices, while card buyers will naturally prefer the one with the lowest prices. Accuracy, however, is the true test. Use the price guide used by more collectors and dealers than all the others combined. Look for the Beckett name. I won't put my name on anything I won't stake my reputation on. Not the lowest and not the highest — but the most accurate, with integrity.

To facilitate your use of this book, read the complete introductory section on the following pages before going to the pricing pages. Every collectible field has its own terminology; we've tried to capture most of these terms and definitions in our glossary. Please read carefully the section on grading and the condition of your cards, as you will not be able to determine which price column is appropriate for a given card without first knowing its condition.

Prices in This Guide

Prices found in this guide reflect current retail rates just prior to the printing of this book. They do not reflect the FOR SALE prices of the author, the publisher, the distributors, the advertisers, or any card dealers associated with this guide. No one is obligated in any way to buy, sell, or trade his or her cards based on these prices. The price listings were compiled by the author from actual buy/sell transactions at sports conventions, sportscard shops, buy/sell advertisements in the hobby papers, for-sale prices from dealer catalogs and price lists, and discussions with leading hobbyists in the U.S. and Canada. All prices are in U.S. dollars.

Acknowledgments

A great deal of diligence, hard work, and dedicated effort went into this year's volume. The high standards to which we hold ourselves, however, could not have been met without the expert input and generous amount of time contributed by many people. Our sincere thanks are extended to each and every one of you.

A complete list of these invaluable contributors appears after the Price Guide section.

Introduction

Welcome to the exciting world of sportscard collecting, one of America's most popular avocations. You have made a good choice in buying this book, since it will open up to you the entire panorama of this field in the simplest, most concise way.

The growth of *Beckett Baseball Card Monthly, Beckett Basketball Monthly, Beckett Football Card Monthly, Beckett Hockey Collector, Sports Collectibles & Beckett Racing Monthly* is an indication of the unprecedented popularity of sportscards. Founded in 1984 by Dr. James Beckett, the author of this Price Guide, *Beckett Baseball Card Monthly* contains the most extensive and accepted monthly Price Guide, collectible glossy superstar covers, colorful feature articles, "Hot List," Convention Calendar, tips for beginners, "Readers Write" letters to and responses from the editor, information on errors and varieties, autograph collecting tips, and profiles of the sport's hottest stars. Published every month, BBCM is the hobby's largest paid circulation periodical. The other five magazines were built on the success of BBCM.

So collecting sportscards — while still pursued as a hobby with youthful exuberance by kids in the neighborhood — has also taken on the trappings of an industry, with thousands of full- and part-time card dealers, as well as vendors of supplies, clubs and conventions. In fact, each year since 1980 thousands of hobbyists have assembled for a National Sports Collectors Convention, at which hundreds of dealers have displayed their wares, seminars have been conducted, autographs penned by sports notables, and millions of cards changed hands. The Beckett Guide is the best annual guide available to the exciting world of football cards. Read it and use it. May your enjoyment and your card collection increase in the coming months and years.

How to Collect

Each collection is personal and reflects the individuality of its owner. There are no set rules on how to collect cards. Since card collecting is a hobby or leisure pastime, what you collect, how much you collect, and how much time and money you spend collecting are entirely up to you. The funds you have available for collecting and your own personal taste should determine how you collect. The information and ideas presented here are intended to help you get the most enjoyment from this hobby.

It is impossible to collect every card ever produced. Therefore, beginners as well as intermediate and advanced collectors usually specialize in some way. One of the reasons this hobby is popular is that individual collectors can define and tailor their collecting methods to match their own tastes. To give you some ideas of the various approaches to collecting, we will list some of the more popular areas of specialization.

Many collectors select complete sets from particular years. For example, they may concentrate on assembling complete sets from all the years since their birth or since they became avid sports fans. They may try to collect a card for every player during that specified period of time. Many others wish to acquire only certain players. Usually such players are the superstars of the sport, but occasionally collectors will specialize in all the cards of players who attended a particular college or came from a certain town. Some collectors are only interested in the first cards or Rookie Cards of certain players.

Another fun way to collect cards is by team. Most fans have a favorite team, and it is natural for that loyalty to be translated into a desire for cards of the players on that favorite team. For most of the recent years, team sets (all the cards from a given team for that year) are readily available at a reasonable price. *The Beckett Football Card Alphabetical Checklist* will open up this field to the collector.

Obtaining Cards

Several avenues are open to card collectors. Cards still can be purchased in the traditional way: by the pack at the local discount, grocery, or convenience stores. But there are also thousands of card shops across the country that specialize in selling cards individually or by the pack, box, or set. Another alternative is the thousands of card shows held each month around the country, which feature anywhere from five to 800 tables of sports cards and memorabilia for sale.

For many years, it has been possible to purchase complete sets of cards through mail-order advertisers found in traditional sports media publications, such as *The Sporting News, Football Digest, Street & Smith* yearbooks, and others. These sets also are advertised in the card collecting periodicals. Many collectors will begin by subscribing to at least one of the hobby periodicals, all with good up-to-date information. Another way of obtaining cards and information is through Beckett's website, www.beckett.com.

Most serious card collectors obtain old (and new) cards from one or more of several main sources: (1) trading or buying from other collectors or dealers; (2) responding to sale or auction ads in the hobby publications; (3) buying at a local hobby store; (4) attending sports collectibles shows or conventions; and/or (5) purchasing cards over the Internet.

We advise that you try all four methods since each has its own distinct advantages: (1) trading is a great way to make new friends; (2) hobby periodicals help you keep up with what's going on in the hobby (including when and where the conventions are happening); (3) stores provide the opportunity to enjoy personalized service and consider a great diversity of material in a relaxed sports-oriented atmosphere; and (4) shows allow you to choose from multiple dealers and thousands of cards under one roof in a competitive situation; and (5) the Internet allows one to purchase cards in a convenient manner from almost anywhere in the world.

Preserving Your Cards

Cards are fragile. They must be handled properly in order to retain their value. Careless handling can easily result in creased or bent cards. It is, however, not recommended that tweezers or tongs be used to pick up your cards since such utensils might mar or indent card surfaces and thus reduce those cards' conditions and values. In general, your cards should be handled directly as little as possible. This is sometimes easier to say than to do.

Although there are still many who use custom boxes, storage trays, or even shoe boxes, plastic sheets are the preferred method of many collectors for storing cards. A collection stored in plastic pages in a three-ring album allows you to view your collection at any time without the need to touch the card itself. Cards can also be kept in single holders (of various type and thickness) designed for the enjoyment of each card individually. For a large collection, some collectors may use a combination of the above methods. When purchasing plastic sheets for your cards, be sure that you find the pocket size that fits the cards snugly. Don't put your 1951 Bowman in a sheet designed to fit 1981 Topps.

Most hobby and collectibles shops and virtually all collectors' conventions will have these plastic pages available in quantity for the various sizes offered, or you can purchase them directly from the advertisers in this book. Also, remember that pocket size isn't the only factor to consider when looking for plastic sheets. Other factors such as safety, economy, appearance, availability, or personal preference also may indicate which types of sheets a collector may want to buy.

Damp, sunny and/or hot conditions — no, this is not a weather forecast — are three elements to avoid in extremes if you are interested in preserving your collection. Too much (or too little) humidity can cause gradual deterioration of a card. Direct, bright sun (or fluorescent light) over time will bleach out the color of a card. Extreme heat accelerates the decomposition of the card. On the other hand, many cards have lasted more than 50 years without much scientific intervention. So be cautious, even if the above factors typically present a problem only when present in the extreme. It never hurts to be prudent.

Collecting vs. Investing

Collecting individual players and collecting complete sets are both popular vehicles for investment and speculation. Most investors and speculators stock up on complete sets or on quantities of players they think have good investment potential.

There is obviously no guarantee in this book, or anywhere else for that matter, that cards will outperform the stock market or other investment alternatives in the future. After all, football cards do not pay quarterly dividends and cards cannot be sold at their "current values" as easily as stocks or bonds.

Nevertheless, investors have noticed a favorable long-term trend in the past performance of sports collectibles, and certain cards and sets have outperformed just about any other investment in some years. Many hobbyists maintain that the best investment is and always will be the building of a collection, which traditionally has held up better than outright speculation.

Some of the obvious questions are: Which cards? When to buy? When to sell? The best investment you can make is in your own education. The more you know about your collection and the hobby, the more informed the decisions you will be able to make. We're not selling investment tips. We're selling information about the current value of football cards. It's up to you to use that information to your best advantage.

Terminology

Each hobby has its own language to describe its area of

interest. The terminology traditionally used for trading cards is derived from the American Card Catalog, published in 1960 by Nostalgia Press. That catalog, written by Jefferson Burdick (who is called the "Father of Card Collecting" for his pioneering work), uses letter and number designations for each separate set of cards. The letter used in the ACC designation refers to the generic type of card. While both sport and non-sport issues are classified in the ACC, we shall confine ourselves to the sport issues. The following list defines the letters and their meanings as used by the American Card Catalog, as applied to football cards:

(none) or **N** - 19th Century U.S. Tobacco
F - Food Inserts
H - Advertising
M - Periodicals
N - 19th Century U.S. Tobacco
PC - Postcards
R - Recent Candy and Gum Cards, 1930 to Present
UO - Gas and Oil Inserts
V - Canadian Candy
W - Exhibits, Strip Cards, Team Cards

Following the letter prefix and an optional hyphen are one-, two-, or three-digit numbers, R(-)999. These typically represent the company or entity issuing the cards. In several cases, the ACC number is extended by an additional hyphen and another one- or two-digit numerical suffix. For example, the 1957 Topps regular-series football card issue carries an ACC designation of R415-5. The "R" indicates a Candy or Gum card produced since 1930. The "415" is the ACC designation for the 1957 regular issue (Topps fifth football set).

Like other traditional methods of identification, this system provides order to the process of cataloging cards; however, most serious collectors learn the ACC designation of the popular sets by repetition and familiarity, rather than by attempting to "figure out" what they might or should be. From 1948 forward, collectors and dealers commonly refer to all sets by their year, maker, type of issue, and any other distinguishing characteristic. For example, such a characteristic could be an unusual issue or one of several regular issues put out by a specific maker in a single year. Regional issues are usually referred to by year, maker, and sometimes by title or theme of the set.

Glossary/Legend

Our glossary defines terms frequently used in the card collecting hobby. Many of these terms are also common to other types of sports memorabilia collecting. Some terms may have several meanings depending on use and context.

ACC - Acronym for American Card Catalog.

ACETATE - A transparent plastic.

AFC - American Football Conference.

AFL - American Football League.

AS - All-Star.

ATG - All Time Great card.

AU(TO) - An autographed card.

BRICK - A group or "lot" or cards, usually 50 or more having common characteristics, that is intended to be bought, sold, or traded as a unit.

C - Center.

CB - Cornerback.

CFL - Canadian Football League.

CL - Checklist card. A card that lists in order the cards and players in the set or series. Older checklist cards in Mint condition that have not been checked off are very desirable and command large premiums.

CO - Coach card.

COLLECTOR ISSUE - A set produced for the sake of the card itself, with no product or service sponsor. It derives its name from the fact that most of these sets are produced for sale directly to the hobby market.

COMBINATION CARD - A single card depicting two or more players (not including team cards).

COMMON CARD - The typical card of any set; it has no premium value accruing from subject matter, numerical scarcity, popular demand, or anomaly.

CONVENTION - A large gathering of dealers and collectors at a single location for the purpose of buying, selling, and sometimes trading sports memorabilia items. Conventions are open to the public and sometimes also feature autograph guests, door prizes, films, contests, etc. More commonly called "shows."

COR - Corrected card. A version of an error card that was fixed by the manufacturer.

DB - Defensive back.

DIE-CUT - A card with its stock partially cut. In some cases, after removal or appropriate folding, the remaining part of the card can be made to stand up.

DISC - A circular-shaped card.

DISPLAY SHEET - A clear, plastic page that is punched for insertion into a binder (with standard three-ring spacing) containing pockets for displaying cards. Many different styles of sheets exist with pockets of varying sizes to hold the many differing card formats. The vast majority of current cards measure 2 1/2 by 3 1/2 inches and fit in nine-pocket sheets.

DP - Double Print. A card that was printed in approximately double the quantity compared to other cards in the same series, or draft pick card.

DT - Defensive tackle or Dream Team.

DUFEX - A method of card manufacturing technology patented by Pinnacle Brands, Inc. It involves a refractive quality to a card with a foil coating.

EMBOSSED - A raised surface; features of a card that are projected from a flat background.

ERR - Error card. A card with erroneous information, spelling, or depiction on either side of the card. Most errors are never corrected by the producing card company.

ETCHED - Impressions within the surface of a card.

EXHIBIT - The generic name given to thick-stock, postcard-size cards with single-color, obverse pictures. The name is derived from the Exhibit Supply Co. of Chicago, the principal manufacturer of this type of card. These are also known as Arcade cards since they were found in many arcades.

FB - Fullback.

FDP - First (round) draft pick.

FG - Field goal.

FOIL - A special type of sticker with a metallic-looking surface.

FULL-BLEED - A borderless card; a card containing a photo that encompasses the entire card.

FULL SHEET - A complete sheet of cards that has not been cut into individual cards by the manufacturer. Also called an uncut sheet.

G - Guard.

GLOSS- A card with luster; a shiny finish as in a card with UV coating.

HIGH NUMBER - The cards in the last series of number, in a year in which such higher-numbered cards were printed or distributed in significantly lesser amount than the lower-numbered cards. The high-number designation refers to a scarcity of the high-numbered cards.

HL - Highlight card, for example from the 1978 Topps subset.

HOF - Hall of Fame, or Hall of Famer (also abbreviated HOFer).

HOLOGRAM - A three-dimensional photographic image.

HOR - Horizontal pose on a card as opposed to the standard vertical orientation found on most cards.

IA - In Action card. A special type of card depicting a player in an action photo, such as the 1982 Topps cards.

IL - Inside linebacker.

INSERT - A card of a different type, e.g., a poster, or any other sports collectible contained and sold in the same package along with a card or cards of a major set.

INTERACTIVE - A concept that involves collector participation.

K - Kicker.

KARAT - A unit of measure for the fineness of gold; i.e. 24K.

KP - Kid Picture card.

LAYERING - The separation or peeling of one or more layers of the card stock, usually at the corner of the card. Also see the Condition Guide.

LB - Linebacker.

LID - A circular-shaped card (possibly with tab) that forms the top of the container for the product being promoted.

LL - League leader card. A card depicting the leader or leaders in a specific statistical category from the previous season. Not to be confused with team leader (TL).

LOGO - NFLPA logo on card.

MAJOR SET - A set produced by a national manufacturer of cards, containing a large number of cards. Usually 100 or more different cards comprise a major set.

MEM - Memorial.

METALLIC - A glossy design that enhances card features.

MINI - A small card or stamp (specifically the 1969 Topps Four-in-One football inserts or the 1987 Topps mini football set issued for the United Kingdom).

MVP - Most Valuable Player.

NFLPA - National Football League Players Association.

NO LOGO - No NFLPA logo on card.

NO TR - No trade reference on card.

NPO - No position.

NT - Nose tackle.

OFF - Officials cards.

O-ROY - Offensive Rookie of the Year.

OT - Offensive tackle.

P - Punter.

P1 - First Printing.

P2 - Second Printing.

PACKS - A means with which cards are issued in terms of pack type (wax, cello, foil, rack, etc.) and channels of distribution (hobby, retail, etc.).

PANEL - An extended card that is composed of multiple individual cards.

PARALLEL- A card that is similar in design to its counterpart from a basic set, but offers a distinguishing quality.

PB - Pro Bowl.

PLATINUM - A metallic element used in the process of creating a glossy card.

POY - Player of the Year.

PREMIUM - A card, sometimes on photographic stock, that is purchased or obtained in conjunction with (or redeemed for) another card or product. This term applies mainly to older products, as newer cards distributed in this manner are generally lumped together as peripheral sets.

PREMIUM CARDS - A class of products introduced recently, intended to have higher quality card stock and photography than regular cards, but more limited production and higher cost. Defining what is and isn't a premium card is somewhat subjective.

PRISMATIC/PRISM - A glossy or bright design that refracts or disperses light.

PROMOTIONAL SET - A set, usually containing a small number of cards, issued by a national card producer and distributed in limited quantities or to a select group of people, such as major show attendees or dealers with wholesale accounts. Presumably, the purpose of a promo set is to stir up demand for an upcoming set. Also called a preview, prototype, or test set.

QB - Quarterback.

RARE - A card or series of cards of very limited availability. Unfortunately, "rare" is a subjective term sometimes used indiscriminately. Using the strict definitions, rare cards are harder to obtain than scarce cards.

RB - Record Breaker card or running back.

RC - Rookie Card. A player's first appearance on a regular issue card from one of the major card companies. With a few exceptions, each player has only one RC in any given set. A Rookie Card typically cannot be an All-Star, Highlight, In Action, league leader, Super Action, or team leader card. It can, however, be a coach card or draft pick card.

REDEMPTION - A program established by manufacturers that allows collectors to mail in a special card (usually a random insert) in return for special cards, sets, or other prizes not available through conventional channels.

REFRACTORS - A card that features a design element which enhances (distorts) its color/appearance through deflecting light.

REGIONAL - A card issued and distributed only in a limited geographical area of the country. The producer may or may not be a major, national producer of trading cards. The key is whether the set was distributed nationally in any form or not.

REPLICA - An identical copy or reproduction.

RET - Retired.

REV NEG - Reversed or flopped photo side of the card. This is a major type of error card, but only some are corrected.

ROY - Rookie of the Year.

S - Safety.

SB - Super Bowl.

SCARCE - A card or series of cards of limited availability. This subjective term is sometimes used indiscriminately to promote or hype value. Using strict definitions, scarce cards are easier to obtain than rare cards.

SEMI-HIGH - A card from the next-to-last series of a sequentially issued set. It has more value than an average card and generally less value than a high number. A card is not called a semi-high unless its next-to-last series has an additional premium attached to it.

SERIES - The entire set of cards issued by a particular producer in a particular year, e.g., the 1978 Topps series. Also, within a particular set, series can refer to a group of (consecutively numbered) cards printed at the same time, e.g., the first series of the 1948 Leaf set (#1 through #49).

SET - One each of an entire run of cards of the same type, produced by a particular manufacturer during a single season. In other words, if you have a complete set of 1975 Topps football cards, then you have every card from #1 up to and including #528; i.e., all the different cards that were produced.

SHEEN - Brightness or luster emitted by a card.

SKIP-NUMBERED - A set that has many unissued card numbers between the lowest number in the set and the highest number in the set, e.g., the 1949 Leaf football set contains 49 cards skip-numbered from number 1-144. A major set in which a few numbers were not printed is not considered to be skip-numbered.

SP - Single or Short Print. A card which was printed in lesser quantity compared to the other cards in the same series (also see DP). This term can only be used in a relative sense and in reference to one particular set. For instance, the 1989 Pro Set Pete Rozelle SP is less common than the other cards in that set, but it isn't necessarily scarcer than regular cards of any other set.

SPECIAL CARD - A card that portrays something other than a single player or team; for example, the 1990 Fleer Joe Montana/Jerry Rice Super Bowl

MVPs card #397.

SR - Super Rookie.

STAMP - Adhesive-backed papers depicting a player. The stamp may be individual or in a sheet of many stamps. Moisture must be applied to the adhesive in order for the stamp to be attached to another surface.

STAR CARD - A card that portrays a player of some repute, usually determined by his ability, but sometimes referring to sheer popularity.

STICKER - A card-like item with a removable layer that can be affixed to another surface. Example: 1983 Topps inserts.

STOCK - The cardboard or paper on which the card is printed.

SUPERIMPOSED - To be affixed on top of something, i.e., a player photo over a solid background.

SUPERSTAR CARD - A card that portrays a superstar, e.g., a Hall of Fame member or a player whose current performance may eventually warrant serious Hall of Fame consideration.

TAB - A card portion set off from the rest of the card, usually with perforations, that may be removed without damaging the central character or event depicted by the card.

TC - Team card or team checklist card.

TEAM CARD - A card that depicts an entire team.

THREE-DIMENSIONAL (3D) - A visual image that provides an illusion of depth and perspective.

TL - Team leader card or Top Leader.

TOPICAL - a subset or group of cards that have a common theme, i.e., MVP award winners.

TR - Trade reference on card.

TRANSPARENT - Clear, see-through.

TRIMMED - A card cut down from its original size. Trimmed cards are undesirable to most collectors, and are therefore less valuable than otherwise identical, untrimmed cards. Also see the Condition Guide.

UER - Uncorrected error card.

USFL - United States Football League.

UV - Ultraviolet, a glossy coating used in producing cards.

VAR - Variation card. One of two or more cards from the same series, with the same card number (or player with identical pose, if the series is unnumbered) differing from one another in some aspect, from the printing, stock, or other feature of the card. This is often caused when the manufacturer of the cards notices an error, in a particular card, corrects the error and then resumes the print run. In this case there will be two versions or variations of the same card. Sometimes one of the variations is relatively scarce. Variations also can result from accidental or deliberate design changes, information updates, photo substitutions, etc.

VERT - Vertical pose on a card.

WFL - World Football League.

WLAF - World League of American Football.

WR - Wide receiver.

XRC - Extended Rookie Card. A player's first appearance on a card, but issued in a set that was not distributed nationally nor in packs. In football sets, this term generally refers to the 1984 and 1985 Topps USFL sets.

Understanding Card Values

Determining Value

Why are some cards more valuable than others? Obviously, the economic laws of supply and demand are applicable to card collecting just as they are to any other field where a commodity is bought, sold, or traded in a free, unregulated market.

Supply (the number of cards available on the market) is less than the total number of cards originally produced since attrition diminishes that original quantity. Each year a percentage of cards is typically thrown away, destroyed, or otherwise lost to collectors. This percentage is much, much smaller today than it was in the past because more and more people have become increasingly aware of the value of their cards.

For those who collect only Mint condition cards, the supply of older cards can be quite small indeed. Until recently, collectors were not so conscious of the need to preserve the condition of their cards. For this reason, it is difficult to know exactly how many 1962 Topps are currently available, Mint or otherwise. It is generally accepted that there are fewer 1962 Topps available than 1972, 1982, or 1992 Topps cards. If demand were equal for each of these sets, the law of supply and demand would increase the price for the least available sets.

Demand, however, is never equal for all sets, so price correlations can be complicated. The demand for a card is influenced by many factors. These include: (1) the age of the card; (2) the number of cards printed; (3) the player(s) portrayed on the card; (4) the attractiveness and popularity of the set; and (5) the physical condition of the card.

In general, (1) the older the card, (2) the fewer the number of the cards printed, (3) the more famous, popular and talented the player, (4) the more attractive and popular the set, and (5) the better the condition of the card, the higher the value of the card will be. There are exceptions to all but one of these factors: the condition of the card. Given two cards similar in all respects except condition, the one in the better condition will always be valued higher.

While those guidelines help to establish the value of a card, the countless exceptions and peculiarities make any simple, direct mathematical formula to determine card values impossible.

Regional Variation

Since the market varies from region to region, card prices of local players may be higher. This is known as a regional premium. How significant the premium is — and if there is any premium at all — depends on the local popularity of the team and the player.

The largest regional premiums usually do not apply to superstars, who often are so well known nationwide that the prices of their key cards are too high for local dealers to realize a premium.

Lesser stars often command the strongest premiums. Their popularity is concentrated in their home region, creating local demand that greatly exceeds overall demand.

Regional premiums can apply to popular retired players and sometimes can be found in the areas where the players grew up or starred in college.

A regional discount is the converse of a regional premium. Regional discounts occur when a player has been so popular in his region for so long that local collectors and dealers have accumulated quantities of his cards. The abundant supply may make the cards available in that area at the lowest prices anywhere.

Set Prices

A somewhat paradoxical situation exists in the price of a complete set vs. the combined cost of the individual cards in the set. In nearly every case, the sum of the prices for the individual cards is higher than the cost for the complete set. This is prevalent especially in the cards of the past few years. The reasons for this apparent anomaly stem from the habits of collectors and from the carrying costs to dealers. Today, each card in a set normally is produced in the same quantity as all others in its set.

Many collectors pick up only stars, superstars, and particular teams. As a result, the dealer is left with a shortage of certain player cards and an abundance of others. He therefore incurs an expense in simply "carrying" these less desirable cards in stock. On the other hand, if he sells a complete set, he gets rid of large numbers of cards at one time. For this reason, he generally is willing to receive less money for a complete set. By doing this, he recovers all of his costs and also makes a profit.

Set prices do not include rare card varieties, unless specifically stated. Of course, the prices for sets do include one example of each type for the given set, but this is the least expensive variety.

Scarce Series

Scarce series occur because cards issued before 1973 were made available to the public each year in several series of finite numbers of cards, rather than all cards of the set being available for purchase at one time. At some point during the season, interest in current year cards waned. Consequently, the manufacturers produced smaller numbers of these later-series cards. Nearly all nationwide issues from post World War II manufacturers (1948 to 1972) exhibit these series variations.

In the past, Topps, for example, may have issued series consisting of many different numbers of cards, including 55, 66, 80, 88, 110, and others. However, after 1968, the sheet size generally has been 132. Despite Topps' standardization of the sheet size, the company double-printed one sheet in 1983 and possibly in 1984 and 1985, too. This was apparently an effort to induce collectors to buy more packs.

We are always looking for information or photographs of printing sheets of cards for research. Each year, we try to update the hobby's knowledge of distribution anomalies. Please let us know at the address in this book if you have firsthand knowledge that would be helpful in this pursuit.

Grading Your Cards

Each hobby has its own grading terminology — stamps, coins, comic books, record collecting, etc. Collectors of sports cards are no exception. The one invariable criterion for determining the value of a card is its condition: the better the condition of the card, the more valuable it is. Condition grading, however, is subjective. Individual card dealers and collectors differ in the strictness of their grading, but the stated condition of a card should be determined without regard to whether it is being bought or sold.

No allowance is made for age. A 1952 card is judged by the same standards as a 1992 card. But there are specific sets and cards that are condition, sensitive because of their border color, consistently poor centering, etc. Such cards and sets sometimes command premiums above the listed percentages in Mint condition.

Centering

Current centering terminology uses numbers representing the percentage of border on either side of the main design. Obviously, centering is diminished in importance for borderless cards such as Stadium Club.

Slightly Off-Center (60/40): A slightly off-center card is one that upon close inspection is found to have one border bigger than the opposite border.

This degree once was offensive only to purists, but now some hobbyists try to avoid cards that are anything other than perfectly centered.

Off-Center (70/30): An off-center card has one border that is noticeably more than twice as wide as the opposite border.

Badly Off-Center (80/20 or worse): A badly off-center card has virtually no border on one side of the card.

Miscut: A miscut card actually shows part of the adjacent card in its larger border and consequently a corresponding amount of its card is cut off.

Corner Wear

Corner wear is the most scrutinized grading criteria in the hobby. These are the major categories of corner wear:

Corner with a slight touch of wear: The corner still is sharp, but there is a slight touch of wear showing. On a dark-bordered card, this shows as a dot of white.

Fuzzy corner: The corner still comes to a point, but the point has just begun to fray. A slightly "dinged" corner is considered the same as a fuzzy corner.

Slightly rounded corner: The fraying of the corner has increased to where there is only a hint of a point. Mild layering may be evident. A "dinged" corner is considered the same as a slightly rounded corner.

Rounded corner: The point is completely gone. Some layering is noticeable.

Badly rounded corner: The corner is completely round and rough. Severe layering is evident.

Creases

A third common defect is the crease. The degree of creasing in a card is difficult to show in a drawing or picture. On giving the specific condition of an expensive card for sale, the seller should note any creases additionally. Creases can be categorized as to severity according to the following scale.

Light Crease: A light crease is a crease that is barely noticeable upon close inspection. In fact, when cards are in plastic sheets or holders, a light crease may not be seen (until the card is taken out of the holder). A light crease on the front is much more serious than a light crease on the card back only.

Medium Crease: A medium crease is noticeable when held and studied at arm's length by the naked eye, but does not overly detract from the appearance of the card. It is an obvious crease, but not one that breaks the picture surface of the card.

Heavy Crease: A heavy crease is one that has torn or broken through the card's picture surface, e.g., puts a tear in the photo surface.

Alterations

Deceptive Trimming: This occurs when someone alters the card in order (1) to shave off edge wear, (2) to improve the sharpness of the corners, or (3) to improve centering — obviously their objective is to falsely increase the perceived value of the card to an unsuspecting buyer. The shrinkage usually is evident only if the trimmed card is compared to an adjacent full-sized card or if the trimmed card is itself measured.

Obvious Trimming: Obvious trimming is noticeable and unfortunate. It is usually performed by non-collectors who give no thought to the present or future value of their cards.

Deceptively Retouched Borders: This occurs when the borders (especially on those cards with dark borders) are touched up on the edges and corners with magic marker or crayons of appropriate color in order to make the card appear to be Mint.

Categorization of Defects

Miscellaneous Flaws

The following are common minor flaws that, depending on severity, lower a card's condition by one to four grades and often render it no better than Excellent-Mint: bubbles (lumps in surface), gum and wax stains, diamond cutting (slanted borders), notching, off-centered backs, paper wrinkles, scratched-off cartoons or puzzles on back, rubber band marks, scratches, surface impressions, and warping.

The following are common serious flaws that, depending on severity, lower a card's condition at least four grades and often render it no better than Good: chemical or sun fading, erasure marks, mildew, miscutting (severe off-centering), holes, bleached or retouched borders, tape marks, tears, trimming, water or coffee stains, and writing.

Condition Guide

Grades

Mint (Mt) - A card with no flaws or wear. The card has four perfect corners, 55/45 or better centering from top to bottom and from left to right, original gloss, smooth edges, and original color borders. A Mint card does not have print spots, color, or focus imperfections.

Near Mint-Mint (NrMt-Mt) - A card with one minor flaw. Any one of the following would lower a Mint card to Near Mint-Mint: one corner with a slight touch of wear, barely noticeable print spots, color or focus imperfections. The card must have 60/40 or better centering in both directions, original gloss, smooth edges, and original color borders.

Near Mint (NrMt) - A card with one minor flaw. Any one of the following would lower a Mint card to Near Mint: one fuzzy corner or two to four corners with slight touches of wear, 70/30 to 60/40 centering, slightly rough edges, minor print spots, color or focus imperfections. The card must have original gloss and original color borders.

Excellent-Mint (ExMt) - A card with two or three fuzzy, but not rounded, corners and centering no worse than 80/20. The card may have no more than two of the following: slightly rough edges, very slightly discolored borders, minor print spots, color or focus imperfections. The card must have original gloss.

Excellent (Ex) - A card with four fuzzy but definitely not rounded corners and centering no worse than 80/20. The card may have a small amount of original gloss lost, rough edges, slightly discolored borders and minor print spots, color or focus imperfections.

Very Good (Vg) - A card that has been handled but not abused: slightly rounded corners with slight layering, slight notching on edges, a significant amount of gloss lost from the surface but no scuffing and moderate discoloration of borders. The card may have a few light creases.

Good (G), Fair (F), Poor (P) - A well-worn, mishandled, or abused card: badly rounded and layered corners, scuffing, most or all original gloss missing, seriously discolored borders, moderate or heavy creases, and one or more serious flaws. The grade of Good, Fair, or Poor depends on the severity of wear and flaws. Good, Fair, and Poor cards generally are used only as fillers.

The most widely used grades are defined above. Obviously, many cards will not perfectly fit one of the definitions.

Therefore, categories between the major grades known as in-between grades are used, such as Good to Very Good (G-Vg), Very Good to Excellent (VgEx), and Excellent-Mint to Near Mint (ExMt-NrMt). Such grades indicate a card with all qualities of the lower category but with at least a few qualities of the higher category.

The Beckett Guide lists each card and set in three grades, with the middle grade valued at about 40-45% of the top grade, and the bottom grade valued at about 10-15% of the top grade.

The value of cards that fall between the listed columns can also be calculated using a percentage of the top grade. For example, a card that falls between the top and middle grades (Ex, ExMt, or NrMt in most cases) will generally be valued at anywhere from 50% to 90% of the top grade.

Similarly, a card that falls between the middle and bottom grades (G-Vg, Vg, or VgEx in most cases) will generally be valued at anywhere from 20% to 40% of the top grade.

There are also cases where cards are in better condition than the top grade or worse than the bottom grade. Cards that grade worse than the lowest grade are generally valued at 5-10% of the top grade.

When a card exceeds the top grade by one — such as NrMt-Mt when the top grade is NrMt, or Mint when the top grade is NrMt-Mt — a premium of up to 50% is possible, with 10-20% the usual norm.

When a card exceeds the top grade by two — such as Mint when the top grade is NrMt, or NrMt-Mt when the top grade is ExMt — a premium of 25-50% is the usual norm. But certain condition-sensitive cards or sets, particularly those from the pre-war era, can bring premiums of up to 100% or even more.

Unopened packs, boxes and factory-collated sets are considered Mint in their unknown (and presumed perfect) state. Once opened, however, each card can be graded (and valued) in its own right by taking into account any defects that may be present in spite of the fact that the card has never been handled.

Selling Your Cards

Just about every collector sells cards or will sell cards eventually. Someday you may be interested in selling your duplicates or maybe even your whole collection. You may sell to other collectors, friends, or dealers. You may even sell cards you purchased from a certain dealer back to that same dealer. In any event, it helps to know some of the mechanics of the typical transaction between buyer and seller.

Dealers will buy cards in order to resell them to other collectors who are interested in the cards. Dealers will always pay a higher percentage for items that (in their opinion) can be resold quickly, and a much lower percentage for those items that are perceived as having low demand and hence are slow moving. In either case, dealers must buy at a price that allows for the expense of doing business and a margin for profit.

If you have cards for sale, the best advice we can give is that you get several offers for your cards — either from card shops or at a card show — and take the best offer, all things considered. Note, the "best" offer may not be the one for the highest amount. And remember, if a dealer really wants your cards, he won't let you get away without making his best competitive offer. Another alternative is to place your cards in an auction as one or several lots.

Many people think nothing of going into a department store and paying $15 for an item of clothing for which the store paid $5. But if you were selling your $15 card to a dealer and he offered you $5 for it, you might think his markup unreasonable. To complete the analogy: most department stores (and card dealers) that consistently pay $10 for $15 items eventually go out of business. An exception is when the dealer has lined up a willing buyer for the item(s) you

Centering

Well-centered

Slightly Off-centered

Off-centered

Badly Off-centered

Miscut

are attempting to sell, or if the cards are so hot that it's likely he'll have to hold the cards for only a short period of time.

In those cases, an offer of up to 75% of book value still will allow the dealer to make a reasonable profit considering the short time he will need to hold the merchandise. In general, however, most cards and collections will bring offers in the range of 25 to 50% of retail price. Also consider that most material from the past five to 10 years is plentiful. If that's what you're selling, don't be surprised if your best offer is well below that range.

Interesting Notes

The first card numerically of an issue is the single card most likely to obtain excessive wear. Consequently, you typically will find the price on the #1 card (in NrMt or Mint condition) somewhat higher than might otherwise be the case. Similarly, but to a lesser extent (because normally the less important, reverse side of the card is the one exposed), the last card numerically in an issue also is prone to abnormal wear. This extra wear and tear occurs because the first and last cards are exposed to the elements (human element included) more than any other cards. They are generally end cards in any brick formations, rubber bandings, stackings on wet surfaces, and like activities.

Sports cards have no intrinsic value. The value of a card, like the value of other collectibles, can be determined only by you and your enjoyment in viewing and possessing these cardboard treasures.

Remember, the buyer ultimately determines the price of each card. You are the determining price factor because you have the ability to say "No" to the price of any card by not exchanging your hard-earned money for a given card. When the cost of a trading card exceeds the enjoyment you will receive from it, your answer should be "No." We assess and report the prices. You set them!

We are always interested in receiving the price input of collectors and dealers from around the country. We happily credit major contributors. We welcome your opinions, since your contributions assist us in ensuring a better guide each year. If you would like to join our survey list for the next editions of this book and others authored by Dr. Beckett, please send your name and address to Dr. James Beckett, 15850 Dallas Parkway, Dallas, Texas 75248.

History of Football Cards

Until the 1930s, the only set devoted exclusively to football players was the Mayo N302 set. The first bubblegum issue dedicated entirely to football players did not appear until the National Chicle issue of 1935. Before this, athletes from several sports were pictured in the multi-sport Goudey Sport Kings issue of 1933. In that set, football was represented by three legends whose fame has not diminished through the years: Red Grange, Knute Rockne, and Jim Thorpe.

But it was not until 1948, and the post-war bubblegum boom, that the next football issues appeared. Bowman and Leaf Gum companies both issued football card sets in that year. From this point on, football cards have been issued annually by one company or another up to the present time, with Topps being the only major card producer until 1989, when Pro Set and Score debuted and sparked a football card boom.

Football cards depicting players from the Canadian Football League (CFL) did not appear until Parkhurst issued a 100-card set in 1952. Four years later, Parkhurst issued another CFL set with 50 small cards this time. Topps began issuing CFL sets in 1958 and continued annually until 1965, although from 1961 to 1965 these cards were printed in Canada by O-Pee-Chee. Post Cereal issued two CFL sets in 1962 and 1963; these cards formed the backs of

Corner Wear

The partial cards here have been photographed at 300%. This was done in order to magnify each card's corner wear to such a degree that differences could be shown on a printed page.

This 1985 Topps Fred Quillan card has a fuzzy corner. Notice the extremely slight fraying on the corner.

This 1985 Topps Fred Smerlas card has a slightly rounded corner. Notice that there is no longer a sharp corner but heavy wear.

This 1985 Topps Daryl Turner card has a rounded corner evident by the lack of a sharp point and heavy wear on both edges.

This 1985 Topps Kim Bokamper card displays a badly rounded corner. Notice a large portion of missing cardboard accompanied by heavy wear and excessive fraying.

This 1985 Topps Neil O'Donaghue card displays creases of varying degrees. Light creases (left side of the card) may not break the card's surface, while heavy creases (right side) will.

boxes of Post Cereals distributed in Canada. The O-Pee-Chee company, which has maintained a working relationship with the Topps Gum Company, issued four CFL sets in the years 1968, 1970, 1971, and 1972. Since 1981, the JOGO Novelties Company has been producing a number of CFL sets depicting past and present players.

Returning to American football issues, Bowman resumed its football cards (by then with full-color fronts) from 1950 to 1955. The company twice increased the size of its card during that period. Bowman was unopposed during most of the early 1950s as the sole producer of cards featuring pro football players.

Topps issued its first football card set in 1950 with a group of very small, felt-back cards. In 1951 Topps issued what is referred to as the "Magic Football Card" set. This set of 75 has a scratch-off section on the back which answers a football quiz. Topps did not issue another football set until 1955 when its All-American Football set paid tribute to past college football greats. In January of 1956, Topps Gum Company (of Brooklyn) purchased the Bowman Company (of Philadelphia).

After the purchase, Topps issued sets of National Football League (NFL) players up until 1963. The 1961 Topps football set also included American Football League (AFL) players in the high-number series (133-198). Topps sets from 1964 to 1967 contained AFL players only. From 1968 to the present, Topps has issued a major set of football cards each year.

When the AFL was founded in 1960, Fleer produced a 132-card set of AFL players and coaches. In 1961, Fleer issued a 220-card set (even larger than the Topps issue of that year) featuring players from both the NFL and AFL. Apparently, for that one year, Topps and Fleer tested a reciprocal arrangement, trading the card printing rights to each other's contracted players. The 1962 and 1963 Fleer sets feature only AFL players. Both sets are relatively small at 88 cards each.

Post Cereal issued a 200-card set of National League football players in 1962 which contains numerous scarcities, namely those players appearing on unpopular varieties of Post Cereal. From 1964 to 1967, the Philadelphia Gum company issued four 198-card NFL player sets.

In 1984 and 1985, Topps produced a set for the now defunct United States Football League, in addition to its annual NFL set. The 1984 set in particular is quite scarce, due to both low distribution and the high demand for the extended Rookie Cards of current NFL superstars Jim Kelly and Reggie White, among others.

In 1986, the McDonald's Restaurants generated the most excitement in football cards in many years. McDonald's created a nationwide football card promotion in which customers could receive a card or two per food purchase, upon request. However, the cards distributed were only of the local team, or of the "McDonald's All-Stars" for areas not near NFL cities. Also, each set was produced with four possible color tabs: blue, black, gold, and green. The tab color distributed depended on the week of the promotion. In general, cards with blue tabs are the scarcest, although for some teams the cards with black tabs are the hardest to find. The tabs were intended to be scratched off and removed by customers to be redeemed for food and other prizes, but among collectors, cards with scratched or removed tabs are categorized as having a major defect, and therefore are valued considerably less.

The entire set, including four color tabs for all 29 subsets, totals over 2800 different cards. The hoopla over the McDonald's cards fell off precipitously after 1988, as collector interest shifted to the new 1989 Score and Pro Set issues.

The popularity of football cards has continued to grow since 1986. Topps introduced "Super Rookie" cards in 1987. Card companies other than Topps noticed the burgeoning interest in football cards, resulting in the two landmark 1989 football sets: a 330-card Score issue, and a 440-card Pro Set release. Score later produced a self-contained 110-card supplemental set, while Pro Set printed 100 Series II cards and a 21-card "Final Update" set. Topps, Pro Set, and Score all improved card quality and increased the size of their sets for 1990. That season also marked Fleer's return to football cards and Action Packed's first major set.

In 1991, Pacific, Pro Line, Upper Deck, and Wild Card joined a market that is now at least as competitive as the baseball card market. And the premium card trend that began in baseball cards spilled over to the gridiron in the form of Fleer Ultra, Pro Set Platinum, Score Pinnacle, and Topps Stadium Club sets.

The year 1992 brought even more growth with the debuts of All World, Collectors Edge, GameDay, Playoff, Pro Set Power, SkyBox Impact, and SkyBox Primetime.

The football card market stabilized somewhat in 1993 thanks to an agreement between the long-feuding NFL licensing bodies, NFL Properties and the NFL Players Association. Also helping the stabilization was the emergence of several promising rookies, including Drew Bledsoe, Jerome Bettis, and Rick Mirer. Limited production became the industry buzzword in sports cards, and football was no exception. The result was the success of three new product lines: 1993 Playoff Contenders, 1993 Select, and 1993 SP.

The year 1994 brought further stabilization and limited production. Pro Set and Wild Card dropped out, while no new card companies joined the ranks. However, several new NFL sets were added to the mix by existing manufacturers: Classic NFL Experience, Collector's Choice, Excalibur, Finest, and Sportflics. The new trend centered around multi-level parallel sets and interactive game inserts with parallel prizes. Another strong rookie crop and reported production cutbacks contributed to strong football card sales throughout 1994.

The football card market continued to grow between 1995 and 1998. Many new sets were released by the major manufacturers and a few new players entered the hobby. Companies continued to push the limits of printing technology with issues printed on plastic, leather, cloth, and various metals. Rookie Cards once more came into vogue and the "1-of-1" insert card was born. There are more choices than ever before for the football card collector– most like it that way. In the last couple of years, more changes have occurred in the football card market. The Rookie Card popularity continued but with a twist. Since 1998, many Rookie Cards have been sequentially numbered and/or printed to a shorter supply than other cards in the set they are in.

Also, many companies have begun to issue "game worn jerseys" or certified autographed cards of leading players, both active and retired.

In addition, graded cards, old and new, have revitalized the card market. Many collectors and dealers have been able to trade over Internet services such as eBay or the many different ways cards are available on beckett.com.

While some collectors are frustrated by the changing hobby, others are thrilled because there are more choices than ever for the football card collector – and many of the collectors like it that way.

Additional Reading

Each year Beckett Publications produces comprehensive annual price guides for each of the four major sports: *Beckett Baseball Card Price Guide,*

Beckett Football Card Price Guide, Beckett Basketball Card Price Guide, and *Beckett Hockey Card Price Guide.* The aim of these annual guides is to provide information and accurate pricing on a wide array of sports cards, ranging from main issues by the major card manufacturers to various regional, promotional, and food issues. Also other alphabetical checklists, such as *The Beckett Baseball Card Alphabetical, The Beckett Football Card Alphabetical, The Beckett Basketball Card Alphabetical,* and *The Beckett Hockey Card Price Guide and Alphabetical*, are published to assist the collector in identifying all the cards of any particular player. Our website beckett.com was created to allow our readers with Internet access an avenue for buying and selling cards as well as participating in online auctions and interactive Price Guides. The seasoned collector will find these tools valuable sources of information that will enable him to pursue his hobby interests.

In addition, abridged editions of the Beckett Price Guides have been published for each of the three major sports as part of the House of Collectibles series: *The Official Price Guide to Baseball Cards, The Official Price Guide to Football Cards,* and *The Official Price Guide to Basketball Cards.* Published in a convenient mass-market paperback format, these price guides provide information and accurate pricing on all the main issues by the major card manufacturers.

1990 Action Packed

	MINT	NRMT
COMPLETE SET (280)	15.00	6.75
COMP.FACT.SET (281)	15.00	6.75
❑ 1 Aundray Bruce UER	.10	.05
(Andre on back)		
❑ 2 Scott Case	.10	.05
❑ 3 Tony Casillas	.10	.05
❑ 4 Shawn Collins	.10	.05
❑ 5 Marcus Cotton	.10	.05
❑ 6 Bill Fralic	.10	.05
❑ 7 Tim Green RC	.10	.05
❑ 8 Chris Miller	.50	.23
❑ 9 Deion Sanders	1.25	.55
❑ 10 John Settle	.10	.05
❑ 11 Cornelius Bennett	.25	.11
❑ 12 Shane Conlan	.10	.05
❑ 13 Kent Hull	.10	.05
❑ 14 Jim Kelly	.50	.23
❑ 15 Mark Kelso	.10	.05
❑ 16 Scott Norwood	.10	.05
❑ 17 Andre Reed	.50	.23
❑ 18 Fred Smerlas	.10	.05
❑ 19 Bruce Smith	.50	.23
❑ 20 Thurman Thomas	.50	.23
❑ 21 Neal Anderson UER	.25	.11
(Action note begins"Neil ...")		
❑ 22 Kevin Butler	.10	.05
❑ 23 Richard Dent	.25	.11
❑ 24 Dennis Gentry	.10	.05
❑ 25 Dan Hampton	.25	.11
❑ 26 Jay Hilgenberg	.10	.05
❑ 27 Steve McMichael	.25	.11
❑ 28 Brad Muster	.10	.05
❑ 29 Mike Singletary	.25	.11
❑ 30 Mike Tomczak	.25	.11
❑ 31 James Brooks	.25	.11
❑ 32 Rickey Dixon RC	.10	.05
❑ 33 Boomer Esiason	.25	.11
❑ 34 David Fulcher	.10	.05
❑ 35 Rodney Holman	.10	.05
❑ 36 Tim Krumrie	.10	.05
❑ 37 Tim McGee	.10	.05
❑ 38 Anthony Munoz UER	.25	.11
(Action note says he's blocking Howie Long, but jersey begins with a nine)		
❑ 39 Reggie Williams	.10	.05
❑ 40 Ickey Woods	.10	.05
❑ 41 Thane Gash RC	.10	.05
❑ 42 Mike Johnson	.10	.05
❑ 43 Bernie Kosar	.25	.11
❑ 44 Reggie Langhorne	.10	.05
❑ 45 Clay Matthews	.25	.11
❑ 46 Eric Metcalf	.50	.23
❑ 47 Frank Minnifield	.10	.05
❑ 48 Ozzie Newsome	.25	.11
❑ 49 Webster Slaughter	.25	.11
❑ 50 Felix Wright	.10	.05
❑ 51 Troy Aikman	2.00	.90
❑ 52 James Dixon	.10	.05
❑ 53 Michael Irvin	.50	.23
❑ 54 Jim Jeffcoat	.10	.05
❑ 55 Ed Too Tall Jones	.25	.11
❑ 56 Eugene Lockhart	.10	.05
❑ 57 Danny Noonan	.10	.05
❑ 58 Paul Palmer	.10	.05
❑ 59 Everson Walls	.10	.05
❑ 60 Steve Walsh	.25	.11
❑ 61 Steve Atwater	.10	.05
❑ 62 Tyrone Braxton	.10	.05
❑ 63 John Elway	3.00	1.35
❑ 64 Bobby Humphrey	.10	.05
❑ 65 Mark Jackson	.10	.05
❑ 66 Vance Johnson	.10	.05
❑ 67 Greg Kragen	.10	.05
❑ 68 Karl Mecklenburg	.10	.05
❑ 69 Dennis Smith	.25	.11
❑ 70 David Treadwell	.10	.05
❑ 71 Jim Arnold	.10	.05
❑ 72 Jerry Ball	.10	.05
❑ 73 Bennie Blades	.10	.05
❑ 74 Mel Gray	.25	.11
❑ 75 Richard Johnson	.10	.05
❑ 76 Eddie Murray	.10	.05
❑ 77 Rodney Peete UER	.25	.11
(On back, squeaker misspelled as squeeker)		
❑ 78 Barry Sanders	4.00	1.80
❑ 79 Chris Spielman	.50	.23
❑ 80 Walter Stanley	.10	.05
❑ 81 Dave Brown DB	.10	.05
❑ 82 Brent Fullwood	.10	.05
❑ 83 Tim Harris	.10	.05
❑ 84 Johnny Holland	.10	.05
❑ 85 Don Majkowski	.10	.05
❑ 86 Tony Mandarich	.10	.05
❑ 87 Mark Murphy	.10	.05
❑ 88 Brian Noble UER	.10	.05
(Fumble recovery stats show 9 instead of 7)		
❑ 89 Ken Ruettgers	.10	.05
❑ 90 Sterling Sharpe UER	.50	.23
(Born Glenville, Ga., should be Chicago)		
❑ 91 Ray Childress	.10	.05
❑ 92 Ernest Givins	.25	.11
❑ 93 Alonzo Highsmith	.10	.05
❑ 94 Drew Hill	.10	.05
❑ 95 Bruce Matthews	.25	.11
❑ 96 Bubba McDowell	.10	.05
❑ 97 Warren Moon	.50	.23
❑ 98 Mike Munchak	.10	.05
❑ 99 Allen Pinkett	.10	.05
❑ 100 Mike Rozier	.10	.05
❑ 101 Albert Bentley	.10	.05
❑ 102 Duane Bickett	.10	.05
❑ 103 Bill Brooks	.10	.05
❑ 104 Chris Chandler	.50	.23
❑ 105 Ray Donaldson	.10	.05
❑ 106 Chris Hinton	.10	.05
❑ 107 Andre Rison	.50	.23
❑ 108 Keith Taylor	.10	.05
❑ 109 Clarence Verdin	.10	.05
❑ 110 Fredd Young	.10	.05
❑ 111 Deron Cherry	.10	.05
❑ 112 Steve DeBerg	.10	.05
❑ 113 Dino Hackett	.10	.05
❑ 114 Albert Lewis	.10	.05
❑ 115 Nick Lowery	.10	.05
❑ 116 Christian Okoye	.10	.05
❑ 117 Stephone Paige	.10	.05
❑ 118 Kevin Ross	.10	.05
❑ 119 Derrick Thomas	.50	.23
❑ 120 Mike Webster	.25	.11
❑ 121 Marcus Allen	.50	.23
❑ 122 Eddie Anderson RC	.10	.05
❑ 123 Steve Beuerlein	.25	.11
❑ 124 Tim Brown	.50	.23
❑ 125 Mervyn Fernandez	.10	.05
❑ 126 Willie Gault	.25	.11
❑ 127 Bob Golic	.10	.05
❑ 128 Bo Jackson UER	.60	.25
(Final column in stats has LG, should be TD)		
❑ 129 Howie Long	.25	.11
❑ 130 Greg Townsend	.10	.05
❑ 131 Flipper Anderson	.10	.05
❑ 132 Greg Bell	.10	.05
❑ 133 Robert Delpino	.10	.05
❑ 134 Henry Ellard	.25	.11
❑ 135 Jim Everett	.25	.11
❑ 136 Jerry Gray	.10	.05
❑ 137 Kevin Greene	.50	.23
❑ 138 Tom Newberry	.10	.05
❑ 139 Jackie Slater	.10	.05
❑ 140 Doug Smith	.10	.05
❑ 141 Mark Clayton	.25	.11
❑ 142 Jeff Cross	.10	.05
❑ 143 Mark Duper	.25	.11
❑ 144 Ferrell Edmunds	.10	.05
❑ 145 Jim C.Jensen	.10	.05
❑ 146 Dan Marino	3.00	1.35
❑ 147 John Offerdahl	.10	.05
❑ 148 Louis Oliver	.10	.05
❑ 149 Reggie Roby	.10	.05
❑ 150 Sammie Smith	.10	.05
❑ 151 Joey Browner	.10	.05
❑ 152 Anthony Carter	.25	.11
❑ 153 Chris Doleman	.10	.05
❑ 154 Steve Jordan	.10	.05
❑ 155 Carl Lee	.10	.05
❑ 156 Randall McDaniel	.25	.11
❑ 157 Keith Millard	.10	.05
❑ 158 Herschel Walker	.25	.11
❑ 159 Wade Wilson	.25	.11
❑ 160 Gary Zimmerman	.10	.05
❑ 161 Hart Lee Dykes	.10	.05
❑ 162 Irving Fryar	.50	.23
❑ 163 Steve Grogan	.25	.11
❑ 164 Maurice Hurst RC	.10	.05
❑ 165 Fred Marion	.10	.05
❑ 166 Stanley Morgan	.10	.05
❑ 167 Robert Perryman	.10	.05
❑ 168 John Stephens UER	.10	.05
(Taking handoff from Eason, not Grogan)		
❑ 169 Andre Tippett	.10	.05
❑ 170 Brent Williams	.10	.05
❑ 171 John Fourcade	.10	.05
❑ 172 Bobby Hebert	.10	.05
❑ 173 Dalton Hilliard	.10	.05
❑ 174 Rickey Jackson	.25	.11
❑ 175 Vaughan Johnson	.10	.05
❑ 176 Eric Martin	.10	.05
❑ 177 Robert Massey	.10	.05
❑ 178 Rueben Mayes UER	.10	.05
(Final column in stats has LG, should be TD)		
❑ 179 Sam Mills	.25	.11
❑ 180 Pat Swilling	.25	.11
❑ 181 Ottis Anderson	.25	.11
❑ 182 Carl Banks	.10	.05
❑ 183 Mark Bavaro	.10	.05
❑ 184 Mark Collins	.10	.05
❑ 185 Leonard Marshall	.10	.05
❑ 186 Dave Meggett	.25	.11
❑ 187 Gary Reasons	.10	.05
❑ 188 Phil Simms	.50	.23
❑ 189 Lawrence Taylor	.50	.23
❑ 190 Odessa Turner RC	.10	.05
❑ 191 Kyle Clifton	.10	.05
❑ 192 James Hasty	.10	.05
❑ 193 Johnny Hector	.10	.05
❑ 194 Jeff Lageman	.10	.05
❑ 195 Pat Leahy	.10	.05
❑ 196 Erik McMillan	.10	.05
❑ 197 Ken O'Brien	.10	.05
❑ 198 Mickey Shuler	.10	.05
❑ 199 Al Toon	.25	.11
❑ 200 Jo Jo Townsell	.10	.05
❑ 201 Eric Allen UER	.10	.05
(Card has 24 passes defended, Eagles say 25)		
❑ 202 Jerome Brown	.10	.05
❑ 203 Keith Byars UER	.10	.05
(LG column shows TD's, not longest run)		
❑ 204 Cris Carter	1.25	.55
❑ 205 Wes Hopkins	.10	.05
(Photo from 1985 season)		
❑ 206 Keith Jackson UER	.25	.11
(Born AK, should be AR)		
❑ 207 Seth Joyner	.25	.11
(Photo not from an Eagle home game)		
❑ 208 Mike Quick	.10	.05
(Photo is from a		

pre-1985 game)
❑ 209 Andre Waters .10 .05
❑ 210 Reggie White .50 .23
❑ 211 Rich Camarillo .10 .05
❑ 212 Roy Green .10 .05
❑ 213 Ken Harvey RC .50 .23
❑ 214 Gary Hogeboom .10 .05
❑ 215 Tim McDonald .10 .05
❑ 216 Stump Mitchell .10 .05
❑ 217 Luis Sharpe .10 .05
❑ 218 Vai Sikahema .10 .05
❑ 219 J.T. Smith .10 .05
❑ 220 Ron Wolfley .10 .05
❑ 221 Gary Anderson K .10 .05
❑ 222 Bubby Brister UER .10 .05
(Stats say 0 TD passes in 1989, should be 9)
❑ 223 Merril Hoge .10 .05
❑ 224 Tunch Ilkin .10 .05
❑ 225 Louis Lipps .25 .11
❑ 226 David Little .10 .05
❑ 227 Greg Lloyd .50 .23
❑ 228 Dwayne Woodruff .10 .05
❑ 229 Rod Woodson .50 .23
(AJR patch is from 1988 season, not 1989)
❑ 230 Tim Worley .10 .05
❑ 231 Marion Butts .25 .11
❑ 232 Gill Byrd .10 .05
❑ 233 Burt Grossman .10 .05
❑ 234 Jim McMahon .25 .11
❑ 235 Anthony Miller UER .50 .23
(Text says 76 catches, stats say 75)
❑ 236 Leslie O'Neal UER .25 .11
(Born AK, should be AR)
❑ 237 Gary Plummer .10 .05
❑ 238 Billy Ray Smith .10 .05
(Action note begins,"Bily Ray ...")
❑ 239 Tim Spencer .10 .05
❑ 240 Lee Williams .10 .05
❑ 241 Mike Cofer .10 .05
❑ 242 Roger Craig .25 .11
❑ 243 Charles Haley .25 .11
❑ 244 Ronnie Lott .25 .11
❑ 245 Guy McIntyre .10 .05
❑ 246 Joe Montana 3.00 1.35
❑ 247 Tom Rathman .10 .05
❑ 248 Jerry Rice 2.00 .90
❑ 249 John Taylor .50 .23
❑ 250 Michael Walter .10 .05
❑ 251 Brian Blades .25 .11
❑ 252 Jacob Green .10 .05
❑ 253 Dave Krieg .25 .11
❑ 254 Steve Largent .50 .23
❑ 255 Joe Nash .10 .05
❑ 256 Rufus Porter .10 .05
❑ 257 Eugene Robinson .10 .05
❑ 258 Paul Skansi RC .10 .05
❑ 259 Curt Warner UER .10 .05
(Yards and attempts are reversed in text)
❑ 260 John L. Williams .10 .05
❑ 261 Mark Carrier WR .50 .23
❑ 262 Reuben Davis .10 .05
❑ 263 Harry Hamilton .10 .05
❑ 264 Bruce Hill .10 .05
❑ 265 Donald Igwebuike .10 .05
❑ 266 Eugene Marve .10 .05
❑ 267 Kevin Murphy .10 .05
❑ 268 Mark Robinson .10 .05
❑ 269 Lars Tate .10 .05
❑ 270 Vinny Testaverde .25 .11
❑ 271 Gary Clark .50 .23
❑ 272 Monte Coleman .10 .05
❑ 273 Darrell Green .25 .11
❑ 274 Charles Mann UER .10 .05
(CA is not alphabetized on back)
❑ 275 Wilber Marshall .10 .05
❑ 276 Art Monk .25 .11
❑ 277 Gerald Riggs .10 .05
❑ 278 Mark Rypien .25 .11
❑ 279 Ricky Sanders .10 .05
❑ 280 Alvin Walton .10 .05
❑ NNO Jim Plunkett BR 4.00 1.80
(Braille on card back)

1990 Action Packed Rookie Update

	MINT	NRMT
COMPLETE SET (84)	20.00	9.00
COMP.FACT.SET (84)	20.00	9.00

❑ 1 Jeff George RC 3.00 1.35
❑ 2 Richmond Webb RC .15 .07
❑ 3 James Williams RC .15 .07
❑ 4 Tony Bennett RC .25 .11
❑ 5 Darrell Thompson RC .15 .07
❑ 6 Steve Broussard RC .15 .07
❑ 7 Rodney Hampton RC 1.00 .45
❑ 8 Rob Moore RC 3.00 1.35
❑ 9 Alton Montgomery RC .15 .07
❑ 10 LeRoy Butler RC .50 .23
❑ 11 Anthony Johnson RC .50 .23
❑ 12 Scott Mitchell RC .75 .35
❑ 13 Mike Fox RC .15 .07
❑ 14 Robert Blackmon RC .15 .07
❑ 15 Blair Thomas RC .15 .07
❑ 16 Tony Stargell RC .15 .07
❑ 17 Peter Tom Willis RC .15 .07
❑ 18 Harold Green RC .25 .11
❑ 19 Bernard Clark .15 .07
❑ 20 Aaron Wallace RC .15 .07
❑ 21 Dennis Brown RC .15 .07
❑ 22 Johnny Johnson RC .25 .11
❑ 23 Chris Calloway RC .15 .07
❑ 24 Walter Wilson .15 .07
❑ 25 Dexter Carter RC .15 .07
❑ 26 Percy Snow RC .15 .07
❑ 27 Johnny Bailey RC .15 .07
❑ 28 Mike Bellamy RC .15 .07
❑ 29 Ben Smith RC .15 .07
❑ 30 Mark Carrier DB RC UER .50 .23
(Stats say 54 yards in '89, text has 58)
❑ 31 James Francis RC .15 .07
❑ 32 Lamar Lathon RC .25 .11
❑ 33 Bern Brostek RC .15 .07
❑ 34 Emmitt Smith RC UER 10.00 4.50
(Career yardage on back is 4232, should be 3928)
❑ 35 Andre Collins RC UER .15 .07
(Born '86, should be '66)
❑ 36 Alexander Wright RC .15 .07
❑ 37 Fred Barnett RC .50 .23
❑ 38 Junior Seau RC 3.00 1.35
❑ 39 Cortez Kennedy RC .50 .23
❑ 40 Terry Wooden RC .15 .07
❑ 41 Eric Davis RC .25 .11
❑ 42 Fred Washington RC .15 .07
❑ 43 Reggie Cobb RC .15 .07
❑ 44 Andre Ware RC .25 .11
❑ 45 Anthony Smith RC .15 .07
❑ 46 Shannon Sharpe RC 8.00 3.60
❑ 47 Harlon Barnett RC .15 .07
❑ 48 Greg McMurtry RC .15 .07
❑ 49 Stacey Simmons RC .15 .07
❑ 50 Calvin Williams RC .25 .11
❑ 51 Anthony Thompson RC .15 .07
❑ 52 Ricky Proehl RC .25 .11
❑ 53 Tony Jones RC .25 .11
❑ 54 Ray Agnew RC .15 .07
❑ 55 Tommy Hodson RC .15 .07
❑ 56 Ron Cox RC .15 .07
❑ 57 Leroy Hoard RC 1.00 .45
❑ 58 Eric Green RC UER .25 .11
(Back photo reversed)
❑ 59 Barry Foster RC .25 .11
❑ 60 Keith McCants RC .15 .07
❑ 61 Oliver Barnett RC .15 .07
❑ 62 Chris Warren RC 1.00 .45
❑ 63 Pat Terrell RC .15 .07
❑ 64 Renaldo Turnbull RC .15 .07
❑ 65 Chris Chandler .50 .23
❑ 66 Everson Walls .15 .07
❑ 67 Alonzo Highsmith .15 .07
❑ 68 Gary Anderson RB .15 .07
❑ 69 Fred Smerlas .15 .07
❑ 70 Jim McMahon .25 .11
❑ 71 Curt Warner .15 .07
❑ 72 Stanley Morgan .15 .07
❑ 73 Dave Waymer .15 .07
❑ 74 Billy Joe Tolliver .15 .07
❑ 75 Tony Eason .15 .07
❑ 76 Max Montoya .15 .07
❑ 77 Greg Bell .15 .07
❑ 78 Dennis McKinnon .15 .07
❑ 79 Raymond Clayborn .15 .07
❑ 80 Broderick Thomas .15 .07
❑ 81 Timm Rosenbach .15 .07
❑ 82 Tim McKyer .15 .07
❑ 83 Andre Rison .50 .23
❑ 84 Randall Cunningham .50 .23

1991 Action Packed

	MINT	NRMT
COMPLETE SET (280)	15.00	6.75
COMP.FACT.SET (291)	20.00	9.00

❑ 1 Steve Broussard .10 .05
❑ 2 Scott Case .10 .05
❑ 3 Brian Jordan .20 .09
❑ 4 Darion Conner .10 .05
❑ 5 Tim Green .10 .05
❑ 6 Chris Miller .20 .09
❑ 7 Andre Rison .20 .09
❑ 8 Mike Rozier .10 .05
❑ 9 Deion Sanders 1.00 .45
❑ 10 Jessie Tuggle .10 .05
❑ 11 Leonard Smith .10 .05
❑ 12 Shane Conlan .10 .05
❑ 13 Kent Hull .10 .05
❑ 14 Keith McKeller .10 .05
❑ 15 James Lofton .20 .09
❑ 16 Andre Reed .20 .09
❑ 17 Bruce Smith .40 .18
❑ 18 Darryl Talley .10 .05
❑ 19 Steve Tasker .20 .09
❑ 20 Thurman Thomas .40 .18
❑ 21 Neal Anderson .20 .09
❑ 22 Trace Armstrong .10 .05
❑ 23 Mark Bortz .10 .05
❑ 24 Mark Carrier DB .20 .09
❑ 25 Wendell Davis .10 .05
❑ 26 Richard Dent .20 .09
❑ 27 Jim Harbaugh .40 .18
❑ 28 Jay Hilgenberg .10 .05
❑ 29 Brad Muster .10 .05
❑ 30 Mike Singletary .20 .09

	No.	Player		
❑	31	Harold Green	.10	.05
❑	32	James Brooks	.10	.05
❑	33	Eddie Brown	.10	.05
❑	34	Boomer Esiason	.20	.09
❑	35	James Francis	.10	.05
❑	36	David Fulcher	.10	.05
❑	37	Rodney Holman	.10	.05
❑	38	Tim McGee	.10	.05
❑	39	Anthony Munoz	.20	.09
❑	40	Ickey Woods	.10	.05
❑	41	Rob Burnett RC	.20	.09
❑	42	Thane Gash	.10	.05
❑	43	Mike Johnson	.10	.05
❑	44	Brian Brennan	.10	.05
❑	45	Reggie Langhorne	.10	.05
❑	46	Kevin Mack	.10	.05
❑	47	Clay Matthews	.20	.09
❑	48	Eric Metcalf	.20	.09
❑	49	Anthony Pleasant	.10	.05
❑	50	Ozzie Newsome	.20	.09
❑	51	Troy Aikman	1.50	.70
❑	52	Issiac Holt	.10	.05
❑	53	Michael Irvin	.40	.18
❑	54	Jimmie Jones	.10	.05
❑	55	Eugene Lockhart	.10	.05
❑	56	Kelvin Martin	.10	.05
❑	57	Ken Norton Jr.	.40	.18
❑	58	Jay Novacek	.40	.18
❑	59	Emmitt Smith	4.00	1.80
❑	60	Daniel Stubbs	.10	.05
❑	61	Steve Atwater	.10	.05
❑	62	Michael Brooks	.10	.05
❑	63	John Elway	2.50	1.10
❑	64	Simon Fletcher	.10	.05
❑	65	Bobby Humphrey	.10	.05
❑	66	Mark Jackson	.10	.05
❑	67	Vance Johnson	.10	.05
❑	68	Karl Mecklenburg	.10	.05
❑	69	Dennis Smith	.10	.05
❑	70	Greg Kragen UER (NT, not DT)	.10	.05
❑	71	Jerry Ball	.10	.05
❑	72	Lomas Brown	.10	.05
❑	73	Robert Clark	.10	.05
❑	74	Michael Cofer	.10	.05
❑	75	Mel Gray	.10	.05
❑	76	Richard Johnson	.10	.05
❑	77	Rodney Peete	.20	.09
❑	78	Barry Sanders	3.00	1.35
❑	79	Chris Spielman	.20	.09
❑	80	Andre Ware	.20	.09
❑	81	Matt Brock RC	.10	.05
❑	82	LeRoy Butler	.20	.09
❑	83	Tim Harris	.10	.05
❑	84	Perry Kemp	.10	.05
❑	85	Don Majkowski	.10	.05
❑	86	Mark Murphy	.10	.05
❑	87	Brian Noble	.10	.05
❑	88	Sterling Sharpe	.40	.18
❑	89	Darrell Thompson	.10	.05
❑	90	Ed West	.10	.05
❑	91	Ray Childress	.10	.05
❑	92	Ernest Givins	.20	.09
❑	93	Drew Hill	.10	.05
❑	94	Haywood Jeffires	.20	.09
❑	95	Richard Johnson RC	.10	.05
❑	96	Sean Jones	.20	.09
❑	97	Bruce Matthews	.20	.09
❑	98	Warren Moon	.40	.18
❑	99	Mike Munchak	.10	.05
❑	100	Lorenzo White	.10	.05
❑	101	Albert Bentley	.10	.05
❑	102	Duane Bickett	.10	.05
❑	103	Bill Brooks	.10	.05
❑	104	Jeff George	.40	.18
❑	105	Jon Hand	.10	.05
❑	106	Jeff Herrod	.10	.05
❑	107	Jessie Hester	.10	.05
❑	108	Mike Prior UER (Did not play in '86)	.10	.05
❑	109	Rohn Stark	.10	.05
❑	110	Clarence Verdin	.10	.05
❑	111	Steve DeBerg	.10	.05
❑	112	Dan Saleaumua UER (NT, not DT)	.10	.05
❑	113	Albert Lewis	.10	.05
❑	114	Nick Lowery	.10	.05
❑	115	Christian Okoye	.10	.05
❑	116	Stephone Paige	.10	.05
❑	117	Kevin Ross	.10	.05
❑	118	Dino Hackett	.10	.05
❑	119	Derrick Thomas UER (Drafted in '89, not '90)	.40	.18
❑	120	Barry Word UER (Bio says 1105 yards, stats say 1015)	.10	.05
❑	121	Marcus Allen	.40	.18
❑	122	Mervyn Fernandez UER (Drafted by Raiders)	.10	.05
❑	123	Willie Gault	.10	.05
❑	124	Bo Jackson	.50	.23
❑	125	Terry McDaniel	.10	.05
❑	126	Don Mosebar	.10	.05
❑	127	Jay Schroeder	.10	.05
❑	128	Greg Townsend UER (B in DeBerg not in caps)	.10	.05
❑	129	Aaron Wallace	.10	.05
❑	130	Steve Wisniewski	.10	.05
❑	131	Flipper Anderson	.10	.05
❑	132	Henry Ellard	.20	.09
❑	133	Jim Everett	.20	.09
❑	134	Cleveland Gary	.10	.05
❑	135	Jerry Gray	.10	.05
❑	136	Kevin Greene	.40	.18
❑	137	Buford McGee	.10	.05
❑	138	Vince Newsome	.10	.05
❑	139	Jackie Slater	.10	.05
❑	140	Frank Stams	.10	.05
❑	141	Jeff Cross	.10	.05
❑	142	Mark Duper	.20	.09
❑	143	Ferrell Edmunds	.10	.05
❑	144	Dan Marino	2.50	1.10
❑	145	Louis Oliver	.10	.05
❑	146	John Offerdahl	.10	.05
❑	147	Tony Paige	.10	.05
❑	148	Sammie Smith	.10	.05
❑	149	Richmond Webb	.10	.05
❑	150	Jarvis Williams	.10	.05
❑	151	Joey Browner	.10	.05
❑	152	Anthony Carter	.20	.09
❑	153	Chris Doleman	.10	.05
❑	154	Hassan Jones	.10	.05
❑	155	Steve Jordan	.10	.05
❑	156	Carl Lee	.10	.05
❑	157	Randall McDaniel	.10	.05
❑	158	Mike Merriweather	.10	.05
❑	159	Herschel Walker	.20	.09
❑	160	Wade Wilson	.20	.09
❑	161	Ray Agnew	.10	.05
❑	162	Bruce Armstrong	.10	.05
❑	163	Marv Cook	.10	.05
❑	164	Hart Lee Dykes	.10	.05
❑	165	Irving Fryar	.20	.09
❑	166	Tommy Hodson	.10	.05
❑	167	Ronnie Lippett	.10	.05
❑	168	Fred Marion	.10	.05
❑	169	John Stephens	.10	.05
❑	170	Brent Williams	.10	.05
❑	171A	Morten Andersen ERR (Back photo has white emblem, should be black)	.10	.05
❑	171B	Morten Andersen COR	.10	.05
❑	172A	Gene Atkins ERR (Back photo has white emblem, should be black)	.10	.05
❑	172B	Gene Atkins COR	.10	.05
❑	173A	Craig Heyward ERR (Back photo has white emblem, should be black)	.20	.09
❑	173B	Craig Heyward COR	.20	.09
❑	174A	Rickey Jackson ERR (Back photo has white emblem, should be black)	.10	.05
❑	174B	Rickey Jackson COR	.10	.05
❑	175A	Vaughan Johnson ERR (Back photo has white emblem, should be black)	.10	.05
❑	175B	Vaughan Johnson COR	.10	.05
❑	176A	Eric Martin ERR (Back photo has white emblem, should be black)	.10	.05
❑	176B	Eric Martin COR	.10	.05
❑	177A	Rueben Mayes ERR (Back photo has white emblem, should be black; would have been fifth season, not sixth)	.10	.05
❑	177B	Rueben Mayes COR	.10	.05
❑	178A	Pat Swilling ERR (Back photo has white emblem, should be black)	.20	.09
❑	178B	Pat Swilling COR	.20	.09
❑	179A	Renaldo Turnbull ERR (Back photo has white emblem, should be black)	.20	.09
❑	179B	Renaldo Turnbull COR	.20	.09
❑	180A	Steve Walsh ERR (Back photo has white emblem, should be black)	.10	.05
❑	180B	Steve Walsh COR	.10	.05
❑	181	Ottis Anderson	.20	.09
❑	182	Rodney Hampton	.40	.18
❑	183	Jeff Hostetler	.40	.18
❑	184	Pepper Johnson	.10	.05
❑	185	Sean Landeta	.10	.05
❑	186	Dave Meggett	.20	.09
❑	187	Bart Oates	.10	.05
❑	188	Phil Simms	.40	.18
❑	189	Lawrence Taylor	.40	.18
❑	190	Reyna Thompson	.10	.05
❑	191	Brad Baxter	.10	.05
❑	192	Dennis Byrd	.10	.05
❑	193	Kyle Clifton	.10	.05
❑	194	James Hasty	.10	.05
❑	195	Pat Leahy	.10	.05
❑	196	Erik McMillan	.10	.05
❑	197	Rob Moore	.40	.18
❑	198	Ken O'Brien	.10	.05
❑	199	Mark Boyer	.10	.05
❑	200	Al Toon	.20	.09
❑	201	Fred Barnett	.40	.18
❑	202	Jerome Brown	.10	.05
❑	203	Keith Byars	.10	.05
❑	204	Randall Cunningham	.40	.18
❑	205	Wes Hopkins	.10	.05
❑	206	Keith Jackson	.20	.09
❑	207	Seth Joyner	.20	.09
❑	208	Heath Sherman	.10	.05
❑	209	Reggie White	.40	.18
❑	210	Calvin Williams	.20	.09
❑	211	Roy Green	.10	.05
❑	212	Ken Harvey UER (Tackling Rodney Hampton, not Howard Cross)	.20	.09
❑	213	Luis Sharpe	.10	.05
❑	214	Ernie Jones	.10	.05
❑	215	Tim McDonald	.10	.05
❑	216	Freddie Joe Nunn	.10	.05
❑	217	Ricky Proehl	.10	.05
❑	218	Timm Rosenbach	.10	.05
❑	219	Anthony Thompson	.10	.05
❑	220	Lonnie Young	.10	.05
❑	221	Gary Anderson K	.10	.05
❑	222	Bubby Brister	.10	.05
❑	223	Eric Green	.10	.05
❑	224	Merril Hoge	.10	.05
❑	225	Carnell Lake	.10	.05
❑	226	Louis Lipps	.10	.05
❑	227	David Little	.10	.05
❑	228	Greg Lloyd	.40	.18
❑	229	Gerald Williams	.10	.05
❑	230	Rod Woodson	.40	.18
❑	231	Marion Butts	.10	.05
❑	232	Gill Byrd	.10	.05
❑	233	Burt Grossman	.10	.05
❑	234	Courtney Hall	.10	.05
❑	235	Ronnie Harmon	.10	.05
❑	236	Anthony Miller	.20	.09
❑	237	Leslie O'Neal	.20	.09
❑	238	Junior Seau	.40	.18
❑	239	Billy Joe Tolliver	.10	.05
❑	240	Lee Williams	.10	.05
❑	241	Dexter Carter	.10	.05
❑	242	Kevin Fagan	.10	.05
❑	243	Charles Haley	.20	.09
❑	244	Brent Jones	.40	.18
❑	245	Ronnie Lott	.20	.09

❑ 246 Guy McIntyre .10 .05
❑ 247 Joe Montana 2.50 1.10
❑ 248 Jerry Rice 1.50 .70
❑ 249 John Taylor .20 .09
❑ 250 Roger Craig .20 .09
❑ 251 Brian Blades .20 .09
❑ 252 Derrick Fenner .10 .05
❑ 253 Nesby Glasgow UER .10 .05
('91 was his 13th season, not 12th)
❑ 254 Jacob Green .10 .05
❑ 255 Tommy Kane .10 .05
❑ 256 Dave Krieg .20 .09
❑ 257 Rufus Porter .10 .05
❑ 258 Eugene Robinson .10 .05
❑ 259 Cortez Kennedy .40 .18
❑ 260 John L. Williams .10 .05
❑ 261 Gary Anderson RB .10 .05
❑ 262 Mark Carrier WR .40 .18
❑ 263 Steve Christie .10 .05
❑ 264 Reggie Cobb .10 .05
❑ 265 Paul Gruber .10 .05
❑ 266 Wayne Haddix .10 .05
❑ 267 Bruce Hill .10 .05
❑ 268 Keith McCants .10 .05
❑ 269 Vinny Testaverde .20 .09
❑ 270 Broderick Thomas .10 .05
❑ 271 Earnest Byner .10 .05
❑ 272 Gary Clark .40 .18
❑ 273 Darrell Green .10 .05
❑ 274 Jim Lachey .10 .05
❑ 275 Chip Lohmiller .10 .05
❑ 276 Charles Mann .10 .05
❑ 277 Wilber Marshall .10 .05
❑ 278 Art Monk .20 .09
❑ 279 Mark Rypien .20 .09
❑ 280 Alvin Walton .10 .05
❑ 281 Randall Cunningham BR .40 .18
NFC Passing Leader
❑ 282 Warren Moon BR .40 .18
AFC Passing Leader
❑ 283 Barry Sanders BR 5.00 2.20
NFC Rushing Leader
❑ 284 Thurman Thomas BR .40 .18
AFC Rushing Leader
❑ 285 Jerry Rice BR 2.00 .90
NFC Receiving Leader
❑ 286 Haywood Jeffires BR .10 .05
AFC Receiving Leader
❑ 287 Charles Haley BR .10 .05
NFC Sack Leader
❑ 288 Derrick Thomas BR .20 .09
AFC Sack Leader
❑ 289 NFC Logo Card .10 .05
❑ 290 AFC Logo Card .10 .05
❑ P1 Randall Cunningham 4.00 1.80
Prototype
❑ P2 Emmitt Smith 10.00 4.50
Rookie prototype
(Numbered "R")
❑ NNO Checklist Card .40 .18
(Double fold)
❑ NNO Randall Cunningham 500.00 220.00
(18K Gold Card, serial numbered of 26)

1991 Action Packed Rookie Update

	MINT	NRMT
COMPLETE SET (84)	12.00	5.50
COMP.FACT.SET (84)	12.00	5.50

❑ 1 Herman Moore RC 3.00 1.35
❑ 2 Eric Turner RC .10 .05
❑ 3 Mike Croel RC .05 .02
❑ 4 Alfred Williams RC .05 .02
❑ 5 Stanley Richard RC .05 .02
❑ 6 Russell Maryland RC .25 .11
❑ 7 Pat Harlow RC .05 .02
❑ 8 Alvin Harper RC .25 .11
❑ 9 Mike Pritchard RC .10 .05
❑ 10 Leonard Russell RC .25 .11
❑ 11 Jarrod Bunch RC .05 .02
❑ 12 Dan McGwire RC .05 .02

❑ 13 Bobby Wilson RC .05 .02
❑ 14 Vinnie Clark RC .05 .02
❑ 15 Kelvin Pritchett RC .10 .05
❑ 16 Harvey Williams RC .25 .11
❑ 17 Stan Thomas .05 .02
❑ 18 Todd Marinovich RC .05 .02
❑ 19 Antone Davis RC .05 .02
❑ 20 Greg Lewis RC .05 .02
❑ 21 Brett Favre RC 8.00 3.60
❑ 22 Wesley Carroll RC .05 .02
❑ 23 Ed McCaffrey RC 3.00 1.35
❑ 24 Reggie Barrett .05 .02
❑ 25 Chris Zorich RC .25 .11
❑ 26 Kenny Walker RC .05 .02
❑ 27 Aaron Craver RC .05 .02
❑ 28 Browning Nagle RC .05 .02
❑ 29 Nick Bell RC .05 .02
❑ 30 Anthony Morgan RC .05 .02
❑ 31 Jesse Campbell RC .05 .02
❑ 32 Eric Bieniemy RC .05 .02
❑ 33 Ricky Ervins RC UER .10 .05
(Totals don't add up)
❑ 34 Kanavis McGhee RC .05 .02
❑ 35 Shawn Moore RC .05 .02
❑ 36 Todd Lyght RC .05 .02
❑ 37 Eric Swann RC .25 .11
❑ 38 Henry Jones RC .10 .05
❑ 39 Ted Washington RC .05 .02
❑ 40 Charles McRae RC .05 .02
❑ 41 Randal Hill RC .10 .05
❑ 42 Huey Richardson RC .05 .02
❑ 43 Roman Phifer RC .05 .02
❑ 44 Ricky Watters RC 2.00 .90
❑ 45 Esera Tuaolo RC .05 .02
❑ 46 Michael Jackson RC .25 .11
❑ 47 Shawn Jefferson RC .10 .05
❑ 48 Tim Barnett RC .05 .02
❑ 49 Chuck Webb RC .05 .02
❑ 50 Moe Gardner RC .05 .02
❑ 51 Mo Lewis RC .10 .05
❑ 52 Mike Dumas RC .05 .02
❑ 53 Jon Vaughn RC .05 .02
❑ 54 Jerome Henderson RC .05 .02
❑ 55 Harry Colon RC .05 .02
❑ 56 David Daniels RC .05 .02
❑ 57 Phil Hansen RC .05 .02
❑ 58 Ernie Mills RC .10 .05
❑ 59 John Kasay RC .10 .05
❑ 60 Darren Lewis RC .05 .02
❑ 61 James Joseph RC .05 .02
❑ 62 Robert Wilson RC .05 .02
❑ 63 Lawrence Dawsey RC .10 .05
❑ 64 Mike Jones RC .05 .02
❑ 65 Dave McCloughan .05 .02
❑ 66 Erric Pegram RC .25 .11
❑ 67 Aeneas Williams RC .25 .11
❑ 68 Reggie Johnson RC .05 .02
❑ 69 Todd Scott RC .05 .02
❑ 70 James Jones RC .05 .02
❑ 71 Lamar Rogers RC .05 .02
❑ 72 Darryll Lewis RC .10 .05
❑ 73 Bryan Cox RC .25 .11
❑ 74 Leroy Thompson RC .05 .02
❑ 75 Mark Higgs RC .05 .02
❑ 76 John Friesz .25 .11
❑ 77 Tim McKyer .05 .02
❑ 78 Roger Craig .10 .05
❑ 79 Ronnie Lott .10 .05
❑ 80 Steve Young 1.00 .45
❑ 81 Percy Snow .05 .02
❑ 82 Cornelius Bennett .10 .05
❑ 83 Johnny Johnson .05 .02
❑ 84 Blair Thomas .05 .02

1992 Action Packed

	MINT	NRMT
COMPLETE SET (280)	25.00	11.00
COMP.FACT.SET (292)	30.00	13.50

❑ 1 Steve Broussard .15 .07
❑ 2 Michael Haynes .25 .11
❑ 3 Tim McKyer .15 .07
❑ 4 Chris Miller .25 .11
❑ 5 Andre Rison .25 .11
❑ 6 Jessie Tuggle .15 .07
❑ 7 Mike Pritchard .15 .07
❑ 8 Moe Gardner .15 .07
❑ 9 Brian Jordan .25 .11
❑ 10 Mike Kenn and .15 .07
Chris Hinton
❑ 11 Steve Tasker .25 .11
❑ 12 Cornelius Bennett .25 .11
❑ 13 Shane Conlan .15 .07
❑ 14 Darryl Talley .15 .07
❑ 15 Thurman Thomas .50 .23
❑ 16 James Lofton .25 .11
❑ 17 Don Beebe .15 .07
❑ 18 Jim Ritcher .15 .07
❑ 19 Keith McKeller .15 .07
❑ 20 Nate Odomes .15 .07
❑ 21 Mark Carrier DB .15 .07
❑ 22 Wendell Davis .15 .07
❑ 23 Richard Dent .25 .11
❑ 24 Jim Harbaugh .50 .23
❑ 25 Jay Hilgenberg .15 .07
❑ 26 Steve McMichael .25 .11
❑ 27 Tom Waddle .15 .07
❑ 28 Neal Anderson .15 .07
❑ 29 Brad Muster .15 .07
❑ 30 Shaun Gayle .15 .07
❑ 31 Jim Breech .15 .07
❑ 32 James Brooks .15 .07
❑ 33 James Francis .15 .07
❑ 34 David Fulcher .15 .07
❑ 35 Harold Green .15 .07
❑ 36 Rodney Holman .15 .07
❑ 37 Anthony Munoz .25 .11
❑ 38 Tim Krumrie .15 .07
❑ 39 Tim McGee .15 .07
❑ 40 Eddie Brown .15 .07
❑ 41 Kevin Mack .15 .07
❑ 42 James Jones .15 .07
❑ 43 Vince Newsome .15 .07
❑ 44 Ed King .15 .07
❑ 45 Eric Metcalf .25 .11
❑ 46 Leroy Hoard .25 .11
❑ 47 Stephen Braggs .15 .07
❑ 48 Clay Matthews .25 .11
❑ 49 David Brandon RC .15 .07
❑ 50 Rob Burnett .15 .07
❑ 51 Larry Brown DB .15 .07
❑ 52 Alvin Harper .25 .11
❑ 53 Michael Irvin .50 .23
❑ 54 Ken Norton Jr. .50 .23

❑ 55 Jay Novacek .25 .11
❑ 56 Emmitt Smith 4.00 1.80
❑ 57 Tony Tolbert .15 .07
❑ 58 Nate Newton .25 .11
❑ 59 Steve Beuerlein .15 .07
❑ 60 Tony Casillas .15 .07
❑ 61 Steve Atwater .15 .07
❑ 62 Mike Croel .15 .07
❑ 63 Gaston Green .15 .07
❑ 64 Mark Jackson .15 .07
❑ 65 Greg Kragen .15 .07
❑ 66 Karl Mecklenburg .15 .07
❑ 67 Dennis Smith .15 .07
❑ 68 Steve Sewell .15 .07
❑ 69 John Elway 3.00 1.35
❑ 70 Simon Fletcher .15 .07
❑ 71 Mel Gray .15 .07
❑ 72 Barry Sanders 4.00 1.80
❑ 73 Jerry Ball .15 .07
❑ 74 Bennie Blades .15 .07
❑ 75 Lomas Brown .15 .07
❑ 76 Erik Kramer .25 .11
❑ 77 Chris Spielman .25 .11
❑ 78 Ray Crockett .15 .07
❑ 79 Willie Green .15 .07
❑ 80 Rodney Peete .25 .11
❑ 81 Sterling Sharpe .50 .23
❑ 82 Tony Bennett .15 .07
❑ 83 Chuck Cecil .15 .07
❑ 84 Perry Kemp .15 .07
❑ 85 Brian Noble .15 .07
❑ 86 Darrell Thompson .15 .07
❑ 87 Mike Tomczak .15 .07
❑ 88 Vince Workman .15 .07
❑ 89 Esera Tuaolo .15 .07
❑ 90 Mark Murphy .15 .07
❑ 91 William Fuller .25 .11
❑ 92 Ernest Givins .25 .11
❑ 93 Drew Hill .15 .07
❑ 94 Al Smith .15 .07
❑ 95 Ray Childress .15 .07
❑ 96 Haywood Jeffires .25 .11
❑ 97 Cris Dishman .15 .07
❑ 98 Warren Moon .50 .23
❑ 99 Lamar Lathon .15 .07
❑ 100 Mike Munchak and Bruce Matthews .15 .07
❑ 101 Bill Brooks .15 .07
❑ 102 Duane Bickett .15 .07
❑ 103 Eugene Daniel .15 .07
❑ 104 Jeff Herrod .15 .07
❑ 105 Jessie Hester .15 .07
❑ 106 Donnell Thompson .15 .07
❑ 107 Anthony Johnson .25 .11
❑ 108 Jon Hand .15 .07
❑ 109 Rohn Stark .15 .07
❑ 110 Clarence Verdin .15 .07
❑ 111 Derrick Thomas .50 .23
❑ 112 Steve DeBerg .15 .07
❑ 113 Deron Cherry .15 .07
❑ 114 Chris Martin .15 .07
❑ 115 Christian Okoye .15 .07
❑ 116 Dan Saleaumua .15 .07
❑ 117 Neil Smith .50 .23
❑ 118 Barry Word .15 .07
❑ 119 Tim Barnett .15 .07
❑ 120 Albert Lewis .15 .07
❑ 121 Ronnie Lott .25 .11
❑ 122 Marcus Allen .50 .23
❑ 123 Todd Marinovich .15 .07
❑ 124 Nick Bell .15 .07
❑ 125 Tim Brown .50 .23
❑ 126 Ethan Horton .15 .07
❑ 127 Greg Townsend .15 .07
❑ 128 Jeff Gossett and Jeff Jaeger .15 .07
❑ 129 Scott Davis .15 .07
❑ 130 Steve Wisniewski and Don Mosebar .15 .07
❑ 131 Kevin Greene .50 .23
❑ 132 Roman Phifer .15 .07
❑ 133 Tony Zendejas .15 .07
❑ 134 Pat Terrell .15 .07
❑ 135 Flipper Anderson .15 .07
❑ 136 Robert Delpino .15 .07
❑ 137 Jim Everett .25 .11
❑ 138 Larry Kelm .15 .07
❑ 139 Todd Lyght .15 .07
❑ 140 Henry Ellard .25 .11
❑ 141 Mark Clayton .25 .11
❑ 142 Jeff Cross .15 .07
❑ 143 Mark Duper .15 .07
❑ 144 John Offerdahl .15 .07
❑ 145 Louis Oliver .15 .07
❑ 146 Pete Stoyanovich .15 .07
❑ 147 Richmond Webb .15 .07
❑ 148 Mark Higgs .15 .07
❑ 149 Tony Paige .15 .07
❑ 150 Bryan Cox .25 .11
❑ 151 Anthony Carter .25 .11
❑ 152 Cris Carter 1.00 .45
❑ 153 Rich Gannon .50 .23
❑ 154 Steve Jordan .15 .07
❑ 155 Mike Merriweather .15 .07
❑ 156 Henry Thomas .15 .07
❑ 157 Herschel Walker .25 .11
❑ 158 Randall McDaniel .15 .07
❑ 159 Terry Allen .50 .23
❑ 160 Joey Browner .15 .07
❑ 161 Leonard Russell .25 .11
❑ 162 Bruce Armstrong .15 .07
❑ 163 Vincent Brown .15 .07
❑ 164 Hugh Millen .15 .07
❑ 165 Andre Tippett .15 .07
❑ 166 Jon Vaughn .15 .07
❑ 167 Pat Harlow .15 .07
❑ 168 Marv Cook .15 .07
❑ 169 Irving Fryar .25 .11
❑ 170 Maurice Hurst .15 .07
❑ 171 Pat Swilling .25 .11
❑ 172 Vince Buck .15 .07
❑ 173 Rickey Jackson .15 .07
❑ 174 Sam Mills .15 .07
❑ 175 Bobby Hebert .15 .07
❑ 176 Vaughan Johnson .15 .07
❑ 177 Floyd Turner .15 .07
❑ 178 Fred McAfee RC .15 .07
❑ 179 Morten Andersen .15 .07
❑ 180 Eric Martin .15 .07
❑ 181 Rodney Hampton .50 .23
❑ 182 Pepper Johnson .15 .07
❑ 183 Leonard Marshall .15 .07
❑ 184 Stephen Baker .15 .07
❑ 185 Mark Ingram .15 .07
❑ 186 Dave Meggett .25 .11
❑ 187 Bart Oates .15 .07
❑ 188 Mark Collins .15 .07
❑ 189 Myron Guyton .15 .07
❑ 190 Jeff Hostetler .25 .11
❑ 191 Jeff Lageman .15 .07
❑ 192 Brad Baxter .15 .07
❑ 193 Mo Lewis .15 .07
❑ 194 Chris Burkett .15 .07
❑ 195 James Hasty .15 .07
❑ 196 Rob Moore .25 .11
❑ 197 Kyle Clifton .15 .07
❑ 198 Terance Mathis .25 .11
❑ 199 Marvin Washington .15 .07
❑ 200 Lonnie Young .15 .07
❑ 201 Reggie White .50 .23
❑ 202 Eric Allen .15 .07
❑ 203 Fred Barnett .25 .11
❑ 204 Keith Byars .15 .07
❑ 205 Seth Joyner .25 .11
❑ 206 Clyde Simmons .15 .07
❑ 207 Jerome Brown .15 .07
❑ 208 Wes Hopkins .15 .07
❑ 209 Keith Jackson .25 .11
❑ 210 Calvin Williams .25 .11
❑ 211 Aeneas Williams .25 .11
❑ 212 Ken Harvey .15 .07
❑ 213 Ernie Jones .15 .07
❑ 214 Freddie Joe Nunn .15 .07
❑ 215 Rich Camarillo .15 .07
❑ 216 Johnny Johnson .15 .07
❑ 217 Tim McDonald .15 .07
❑ 218 Eric Swann .25 .11
❑ 219 Eric Hill .15 .07
❑ 220 Anthony Thompson .15 .07
❑ 221 Hardy Nickerson .50 .23
❑ 222 Barry Foster .25 .11
❑ 223 Louis Lipps .15 .07
❑ 224 Greg Lloyd .50 .23
❑ 225 Neil O'Donnell .50 .23
❑ 226 Jerrol Williams .15 .07
❑ 227 Eric Green .15 .07
❑ 228 Rod Woodson .50 .23
❑ 229 Carnell Lake .15 .07
❑ 230 Dwight Stone .15 .07
❑ 231 Marion Butts .15 .07
❑ 232 John Friesz .25 .11
❑ 233 Burt Grossman .15 .07
❑ 234 Ronnie Harmon .15 .07
❑ 235 Gill Byrd .15 .07
❑ 236 Rod Bernstine .15 .07
❑ 237 Courtney Hall .15 .07
❑ 238 Nate Lewis .15 .07
❑ 239 Joe Phillips .15 .07
❑ 240 Henry Rolling .15 .07
❑ 241 Keith Henderson .15 .07
❑ 242 Guy McIntyre .15 .07
❑ 243 Bill Romanowski .15 .07
❑ 244 Don Griffin .15 .07
❑ 245 Dexter Carter .15 .07
❑ 246 Charles Haley .25 .11
❑ 247 Brent Jones .25 .11
❑ 248 John Taylor .25 .11
❑ 249 Steve Young 1.50 .70
❑ 250 Larry Roberts .15 .07
❑ 251 Brian Blades .25 .11
❑ 252 Jacob Green .15 .07
❑ 253 John Kasay .15 .07
❑ 254 Cortez Kennedy .25 .11
❑ 255 Rufus Porter .15 .07
❑ 256 John L. Williams .15 .07
❑ 257 Tommy Kane .15 .07
❑ 258 Eugene Robinson .15 .07
❑ 259 Terry Wooden .15 .07
❑ 260 Chris Warren .50 .23
❑ 261 Lawrence Dawsey .15 .07
❑ 262 Mark Carrier WR .25 .11
❑ 263 Keith McCants .15 .07
❑ 264 Jesse Solomon .15 .07
❑ 265 Vinny Testaverde .25 .11
❑ 266 Ricky Reynolds .15 .07
❑ 267 Broderick Thomas .15 .07
❑ 268 Gary Anderson RB .15 .07
❑ 269 Reggie Cobb .15 .07
❑ 270 Tony Covington .15 .07
❑ 271 Darrell Green .15 .07
❑ 272 Charles Mann .15 .07
❑ 273 Wilber Marshall .15 .07
❑ 274 Gary Clark .50 .23
❑ 275 Chip Lohmiller .15 .07
❑ 276 Earnest Byner .15 .07
❑ 277 Jim Lachey .15 .07
❑ 278 Art Monk .25 .11
❑ 279 Mark Rypien .15 .07
❑ 280 Mark Schlereth RC .15 .07
❑ 281 Mark Rypien BR NFC Passing Yardage Leader .25 .11
❑ 282 Warren Moon BR AFC Passing Yardage Leader .50 .23
❑ 283 Emmitt Smith BR NFC Rushing Leader 2.00 .90
❑ 284 Thurman Thomas BR AFC Rushing Leader .50 .23
❑ 285 Michael Irvin BR NFC Receiving Leader .50 .23
❑ 286 Haywood Jeffires BR AFC Receiving Leader .25 .11
❑ 287 Pat Swilling BR NFC Sack Leader .25 .11
❑ 288 Ronnie Lott BR AFC Interception Leader .50 .23
❑ 289 NFC Logo (Only available in factory sets) .15 .07
❑ 290 AFC Logo (Only available in factory sets) .15 .07
❑ 43G B.Sanders 24K GOLD 10.00 4.50
❑ 44G B.Sanders 24K GOLD 10.00 4.50
❑ NNO Barry Sanders (18K gold card) 2000.00 900.00

1992 Action Packed Rookie Update

	MINT	NRMT
COMPLETE SET (84)	12.00	5.50
❑ 1 Steve Emtman RC	.15	.07
❑ 2 Quentin Coryatt RC	.50	.23
❑ 3 Sean Gilbert RC	.50	.23
❑ 4 John Fina RC	.15	.07
❑ 5 Alonzo Spellman RC	.25	.11
❑ 6 Amp Lee RC	.15	.07
❑ 7 Robert Porcher RC	.15	.07
❑ 8 Jason Hanson RC	.25	.11
❑ 9 Ty Detmer	.50	.23
❑ 10 Ray Roberts RC	.15	.07
❑ 11 Bob Whitfield RC	.15	.07
❑ 12 Greg Skrepenak RC	.15	.07
❑ 13 Vaughn Dunbar RC	.15	.07
❑ 14 Siran Stacy RC	.15	.07
❑ 15 Mark D'Onofrio RC	.15	.07
❑ 16 Tony Sacca RC	.15	.07
❑ 17 Dana Hall RC	.25	.11
❑ 18 Courtney Hawkins RC	.25	.11
❑ 19 Shane Collins RC	.15	.07
❑ 20 Tony Smith RC	.15	.07
❑ 21 Rod Smith RC	.15	.07
❑ 22 Troy Auzenne RC	.15	.07
❑ 23 David Klingler RC	.25	.11
❑ 24 Darryl Williams RC	.15	.07
❑ 25 Carl Pickens RC	2.00	.90
❑ 26 Ricardo McDonald RC	.15	.07
❑ 27 Tommy Vardell RC	.25	.11
❑ 28 Kevin Smith RC	.50	.23
❑ 29 Rodney Culver RC	.15	.07
❑ 30 Jimmy Smith RC	5.00	2.20
❑ 31 Robert Jones RC	.15	.07
❑ 32 Tommy Maddox RC	.15	.07
❑ 33 Shane Dronett RC	.15	.07
❑ 34 Terrell Buckley RC	.15	.07
❑ 35 Santana Dotson RC	.50	.23
❑ 36 Edgar Bennett RC	.75	.35
❑ 37 Ashley Ambrose RC	.25	.11
❑ 38 Dale Carter RC	.50	.23
❑ 39 Chester McGlockton RC	.50	.23
❑ 40 Steve Israel RC	.15	.07
❑ 41 Marc Boutte RC	.15	.07
❑ 42 Marco Coleman RC	.25	.11
❑ 43 Troy Vincent RC	.25	.11
❑ 44 Mark Wheeler RC	.15	.07
❑ 45 Darren Perry RC	.15	.07
❑ 46 Eugene Chung RC	.15	.07
❑ 47 Derek Brown TE RC	.15	.07
❑ 48 Phillippi Sparks RC	.15	.07
❑ 49 Johnny Mitchell RC	.15	.07
❑ 50 Kurt Barber RC	.15	.07
❑ 51 Leon Searcy RC	.25	.11
❑ 52 Chris Mims RC	.25	.11
❑ 53 Keith Jackson	.25	.11
❑ 54 Charles Haley	.25	.11
❑ 55 Dave Krieg	.25	.11
❑ 56 Dan McGwire	.15	.07
❑ 57 Phil Simms	.25	.11
❑ 58 Bobby Humphrey	.15	.07
❑ 59 Jerry Rice	2.50	1.10
❑ 60 Joe Montana	4.00	1.80
❑ 61 Junior Seau	.50	.23
❑ 62 Leslie O'Neal	.25	.11
❑ 63 Anthony Miller	.25	.11
❑ 64 Timm Rosenbach	.15	.07
❑ 65 Herschel Walker	.25	.11
❑ 66 Randal Hill	.15	.07
❑ 67 Randall Cunningham	.50	.23
❑ 68 Al Toon	.25	.11
❑ 69 Browning Nagle	.15	.07
❑ 70 Lawrence Taylor	.50	.23
❑ 71 Dan Marino	4.00	1.80
❑ 72 Eric Dickerson	.25	.11
❑ 73 Harvey Williams	.50	.23
❑ 74 Jeff George	.50	.23
❑ 75 Russell Maryland	.25	.11
❑ 76 Troy Aikman	2.00	.90
❑ 77 Michael Dean Perry	.25	.11
❑ 78 Bernie Kosar	.25	.11
❑ 79 Boomer Esiason	.25	.11
❑ 80 Mike Singletary	.25	.11
❑ 81 Bruce Smith	.50	.23
❑ 82 Andre Reed	.25	.11
❑ 83 Jim Kelly	.50	.23
❑ 84 Deion Sanders	1.00	.45
❑ 84N Deion Sanders Neon orange card	10.00	4.50

1993 Action Packed

	MINT	NRMT
COMPLETE SET (222)	70.00	32.00
COMP.SERIES 1 (162)	45.00	20.00
COMP.SERIES 2 (60)	30.00	13.50
❑ 1 Michael Haynes	.30	.14
❑ 2 Chris Miller	.30	.14
❑ 3 Andre Rison	.30	.14
❑ 4 Jim Kelly	.60	.25
❑ 5 Andre Reed	.30	.14
❑ 6 Thurman Thomas	.60	.25
❑ 7 Jim Harbaugh	.60	.25
❑ 8 Harold Green	.15	.07
❑ 9 David Klingler	.15	.07
❑ 10 Bernie Kosar	.30	.14
❑ 11 Troy Aikman	2.50	1.10
❑ 12 Michael Irvin	.60	.25
❑ 13 Emmitt Smith	4.00	1.80
❑ 14 John Elway	4.00	1.80
❑ 15 Barry Sanders	4.00	1.80
❑ 16 Brett Favre	5.00	2.20
❑ 17 Sterling Sharpe	.60	.25
❑ 18 Ernest Givins	.30	.14
❑ 19 Haywood Jeffires	.30	.14
❑ 20 Warren Moon	.60	.25
❑ 21 Lorenzo White	.15	.07
❑ 22 Jeff George	.60	.25
❑ 23 Joe Montana	4.00	1.80
❑ 24 Jim Everett	.30	.14
❑ 25 Cleveland Gary	.15	.07
❑ 26 Dan Marino	4.00	1.80
❑ 27 Terry Allen	.60	.25
❑ 28 Rodney Hampton	.60	.25
❑ 29 Phil Simms	.30	.14
❑ 30 Fred Barnett	.30	.14
❑ 31 Randall Cunningham	.60	.25
❑ 32 Gary Clark	.30	.14
❑ 33 Barry Foster	.30	.14
❑ 34 Neil O'Donnell	.60	.25
❑ 35 Stan Humphries	.60	.25
❑ 36 Anthony Miller	.30	.14
❑ 37 Jerry Rice	3.00	1.35
❑ 38 Ricky Watters	.60	.25
❑ 39 Steve Young	2.00	.90
❑ 40 Chris Warren	.30	.14
❑ 41 Reggie Cobb	.15	.07
❑ 42 Mark Rypien	.15	.07
❑ 43 Deion Sanders	1.50	.70
❑ 44 Henry Jones	.15	.07
❑ 45 Bruce Smith	.60	.25
❑ 46 Richard Dent	.30	.14
❑ 47 Tommy Vardell	.15	.07
❑ 48 Charles Haley	.30	.14
❑ 49 Ken Norton Jr.	.30	.14
❑ 50 Jay Novacek	.30	.14
❑ 51 Simon Fletcher	.15	.07
❑ 52 Pat Swilling	.15	.07
❑ 53 Tony Bennett	.15	.07
❑ 54 Reggie White	.60	.25
❑ 55 Ray Childress	.15	.07
❑ 56 Quentin Coryatt	.30	.14
❑ 57 Steve Emtman	.15	.07
❑ 58 Derrick Thomas	.60	.25
❑ 59 James Lofton	.30	.14
❑ 60 Marco Coleman	.15	.07
❑ 61 Bryan Cox	.15	.07
❑ 62 Troy Vincent	.15	.07
❑ 63 Chris Doleman	.15	.07
❑ 64 Audray McMillian	.15	.07
❑ 65 Vaughn Dunbar	.15	.07
❑ 66 Rickey Jackson	.15	.07
❑ 67 Lawrence Taylor	.60	.25
❑ 68 Ronnie Lott	.30	.14
❑ 69 Rob Moore	.30	.14
❑ 70 Browning Nagle	.15	.07
❑ 71 Eric Allen	.15	.07
❑ 72 Tim Harris	.15	.07
❑ 73 Clyde Simmons	.15	.07
❑ 74 Steve Beuerlein	.15	.07
❑ 75 Randal Hill	.15	.07
❑ 76 Darren Perry	.15	.07
❑ 77 Rod Woodson	.60	.25
❑ 78 Marion Butts	.15	.07
❑ 79 Chris Mims	.15	.07
❑ 80 Junior Seau	.60	.25
❑ 81 Cortez Kennedy	.30	.14
❑ 82 Santana Dotson	.30	.14
❑ 83 Earnest Byner	.15	.07
❑ 84 Charles Mann	.15	.07
❑ 85 Pierce Holt	.15	.07
❑ 86 Mike Pritchard	.30	.14
❑ 87 Cornelius Bennett	.30	.14
❑ 88 Neal Anderson	.15	.07
❑ 89 Carl Pickens	.60	.25
❑ 90 Eric Metcalf	.30	.14
❑ 91 Michael Dean Perry	.30	.14
❑ 92 Alvin Harper	.30	.14
❑ 93 Robert Jones	.15	.07
❑ 94 Steve Atwater	.15	.07
❑ 95 Rod Bernstine	.15	.07
❑ 96 Herman Moore	1.50	.70
❑ 97 Chris Spielman	.30	.14
❑ 98 Terrell Buckley	.15	.07
❑ 99 Dale Carter	.15	.07
❑ 100 Terry McDaniel	.15	.07
❑ 101 Tim Brown	.60	.25
❑ 102 Gaston Green	.15	.07
❑ 103 Howie Long	.30	.14
❑ 104 Todd Marinovich	.15	.07
❑ 105 Anthony Smith	.15	.07
❑ 106 Flipper Anderson	.15	.07
❑ 107 Henry Ellard	.30	.14
❑ 108 Mark Higgs	.15	.07
❑ 109 Keith Jackson	.30	.14
❑ 110 Irving Fryar	.30	.14
❑ 111 Cris Carter	1.50	.70
❑ 112 Leonard Russell	.30	.14
❑ 113 Wayne Martin	.15	.07
❑ 114 Mark Jackson	.15	.07
❑ 115 Dave Meggett	.15	.07
❑ 116 Brad Baxter	.15	.07
❑ 117 Boomer Esiason	.30	.14
❑ 118 Johnny Johnson	.15	.07
❑ 119 Seth Joyner	.15	.07
❑ 120 Kevin Greene	.60	.25
❑ 121 Greg Lloyd	.60	.25
❑ 122 Brent Jones	.30	.14

No.	Player	Mint	NrMt
❑ 123	Amp Lee	.15	.07
❑ 124	Tim McDonald	.15	.07
❑ 125	Darrell Green	.15	.07
❑ 126	Art Monk	.30	.14
❑ 127	Tony Smith	.15	.07
❑ 128	Bill Brooks	.15	.07
❑ 129	Kenneth Davis	.15	.07
❑ 130	Donnell Woolford	.15	.07
❑ 131	Derrick Fenner	.15	.07
❑ 132	Michael Jackson	.30	.14
❑ 133	Mark Clayton	.15	.07
❑ 134	Al Smith	.15	.07
❑ 135	Curtis Duncan	.15	.07
❑ 136	Rodney Culver	.15	.07
❑ 137	Harvey Williams	.30	.14
❑ 138	Neil Smith	.60	.25
❑ 139	Marcus Allen	.60	.25
❑ 140	Eric Dickerson	.30	.14
❑ 141	Sean Gilbert	.30	.14
❑ 142	Shane Conlan	.15	.07
❑ 143	Todd Scott	.15	.07
❑ 144	Vincent Brown	.15	.07
❑ 145	Andre Tippett	.15	.07
❑ 146	Jon Vaughn	.15	.07
❑ 147	Marv Cook	.15	.07
❑ 148	Morten Andersen	.15	.07
❑ 149	Sam Mills	.15	.07
❑ 150	Mark Collins	.15	.07
❑ 151	Heath Sherman	.15	.07
❑ 152	Johnny Bailey	.15	.07
❑ 153	Eric Green	.15	.07
❑ 154	Ronnie Harmon	.15	.07
❑ 155	Gill Byrd	.15	.07
❑ 156	Leslie O'Neal	.30	.14
❑ 157	Rufus Porter	.15	.07
❑ 158	Eugene Robinson	.15	.07
❑ 159	Broderick Thomas	.15	.07
❑ 160	Lawrence Dawsey	.15	.07
❑ 161	Anthony Munoz	.30	.14
❑ 162	Wilber Marshall	.15	.07
❑ 163	Drew Bledsoe RC	6.00	2.70
❑ 164	Rick Mirer RC	1.00	.45
❑ 165	Garrison Hearst RC	2.00	.90
❑ 166	Marvin Jones RC	.15	.07
❑ 167	John Copeland RC	.30	.14
❑ 168	Eric Curry RC	.15	.07
❑ 169	Curtis Conway RC	1.50	.70
❑ 170	William Roaf RC	.30	.14
❑ 171	Lincoln Kennedy RC	.15	.07
❑ 172	Jerome Bettis RC	2.50	1.10
❑ 173	Dan Williams RC	.15	.07
❑ 174	Patrick Bates RC	.15	.07
❑ 175	Brad Hopkins RC	.15	.07
❑ 176	Steve Everitt RC	.15	.07
❑ 177	W.Simmons RC UER (College touchdowns and yards are in wrong columns)	.15	.07
❑ 178	Tom Carter RC	.30	.14
❑ 179	Ernest Dye RC	.15	.07
❑ 180	Lester Holmes	.15	.07
❑ 181	Irv Smith RC	.15	.07
❑ 182	Robert Smith RC	5.00	2.20
❑ 183	Darrien Gordon RC	.15	.07
❑ 184	Deon Figures RC	.30	.14
❑ 185	Leonard Renfro RC	.15	.07
❑ 186	O.J. McDuffie RC	2.00	.90
❑ 187	Dana Stubblefield RC	.60	.25
❑ 188	Todd Kelly RC	.15	.07
❑ 189	Thomas Smith RC	.30	.14
❑ 190	George Teague RC	.30	.14
❑ 191	Wilber Marshall	.15	.07
❑ 192	Reggie White	.60	.25
❑ 193	Carlton Gray RC	.15	.07
❑ 194	Chris Slade RC	.30	.14
❑ 195	Ben Coleman RC	.15	.07
❑ 196	Ryan McNeil RC	.15	.07
❑ 197	Demetrius DuBose RC	.15	.07
❑ 198	Coleman Rudolph RC	.15	.07
❑ 199	Tony McGee RC	.30	.14
❑ 200	Troy Drayton RC	.30	.14
❑ 201	Natrone Means RC	1.50	.70
❑ 202	Glyn Milburn RC	.60	.25
❑ 203	Chad Brown RC	.30	.14
❑ 204	Reggie Brooks RC	.30	.14
❑ 205	Kevin Williams RC	.60	.25
❑ 206	Micheal Barrow RC	.30	.14
❑ 207	Roosevelt Potts RC	.15	.07
❑ 208	Victor Bailey RC	.15	.07
❑ 209	Qadry Ismail RC	2.00	.90
❑ 210	Vincent Brisby RC	.60	.25
❑ 211	Billy Joe Hobert RC	.60	.25
❑ 212	Lamar Thomas RC	.15	.07
❑ 213	Jason Elam RC	.30	.14
❑ 214	Andre Hastings RC	.60	.25
❑ 215	Terry Kirby RC	.60	.25
❑ 216	Joe Montana	4.00	1.80
❑ 217	Derrick Lassic RC	.15	.07
❑ 218	Mark Brunell RC	8.00	3.60
❑ 219	Vaughn Hebron RC	.15	.07
❑ 220	Troy Brown RC	1.00	.45
❑ 221	Derek Brown RBK RC	.15	.07
❑ 222	Raghib Ismail	.30	.14

1994 Action Packed

	MINT	NRMT
COMPLETE SET (198)	60.00	27.00
COMP.SERIES 1 (120)	40.00	18.00
COMP.SERIES 2 (78)	30.00	13.50

*BRAILLE VERSIONS: 1X to 2X HI COLUMN
*GOLD SIGNATURES: 1.5X to 3X HI COLUMN

No.	Player	Mint	NrMt
❑ 1	Michael Haynes	.40	.18
❑ 2	Andre Rison	.40	.18
❑ 3	Mike Pritchard	.20	.09
❑ 4	Erric Pegram	.20	.09
❑ 5	Deion Sanders	1.25	.55
❑ 6	Jim Kelly	.75	.35
❑ 7	Andre Reed	.40	.18
❑ 8	Thurman Thomas	.75	.35
❑ 9	Bruce Smith	.75	.35
❑ 10	Cornelius Bennett	.40	.18
❑ 11	Nate Odomes	.20	.09
❑ 12	Richard Dent	.40	.18
❑ 13	Donnell Woolford	.20	.09
❑ 14	Harold Green	.20	.09
❑ 15	David Klingler	.20	.09
❑ 16	Eric Metcalf	.40	.18
❑ 17	Michael Dean Perry	.40	.18
❑ 18	Michael Jackson	.40	.18
❑ 19	Vinny Testaverde	.40	.18
❑ 20	Troy Aikman	2.50	1.10
❑ 21	Michael Irvin	.75	.35
❑ 22	Emmitt Smith	4.00	1.80
❑ 23	Jay Novacek	.40	.18
❑ 24	Alvin Harper	.40	.18
❑ 25	Charles Haley	.40	.18
❑ 26	John Elway	5.00	2.20
❑ 27	Shannon Sharpe	.40	.18
❑ 28	Rod Bernstine	.20	.09
❑ 29	Simon Fletcher	.20	.09
❑ 30	Barry Sanders	5.00	2.20
❑ 31	Herman Moore	.75	.35
❑ 32	Pat Swilling	.20	.09
❑ 33	Chris Spielman	.40	.18
❑ 34	Brett Favre	5.00	2.20
❑ 35	Sterling Sharpe UER (Photo on back is Shannon Sharpe)	.75	.35
❑ 36	Reggie White	.75	.35
❑ 37	Jackie Harris	.20	.09
❑ 38	Tony Bennett	.20	.09
❑ 39	LeRoy Butler	.20	.09
❑ 40	Warren Moon	.75	.35
❑ 41	Ernest Givins	.40	.18
❑ 42	Haywood Jeffires	.40	.18
❑ 43	Webster Slaughter	.20	.09
❑ 44	Ray Childress	.20	.09
❑ 45	Gary Brown	.20	.09
❑ 46	Jeff George	.75	.35
❑ 47	Roosevelt Potts	.20	.09
❑ 48	Quentin Coryatt	.20	.09
❑ 49	Joe Montana	5.00	2.20
❑ 50	Derrick Thomas	.75	.35
❑ 51	Neil Smith	.75	.35
❑ 52	Marcus Allen	.75	.35
❑ 53	Willie Davis	.40	.18
❑ 54	Jerome Bettis	.75	.35
❑ 55	Sean Gilbert	.20	.09
❑ 56	Chris Miller	.20	.09
❑ 57	Jeff Hostetler	.40	.18
❑ 58	Tim Brown	.75	.35
❑ 59	Anthony Smith	.20	.09
❑ 60	Greg Townsend	.20	.09
❑ 61	Terry McDaniel	.20	.09
❑ 62	Dan Marino	5.00	2.20
❑ 63	Irving Fryar	.40	.18
❑ 64	Keith Jackson	.20	.09
❑ 65	Terry Kirby	.75	.35
❑ 66	Bryan Cox	.20	.09
❑ 67	Chris Doleman	.20	.09
❑ 68	Cris Carter	1.25	.55
❑ 69	John Randle	.40	.18
❑ 70	Drew Bledsoe	3.00	1.35
❑ 71	Ben Coates	.75	.35
❑ 72	Vincent Brisby	.75	.35
❑ 73	Rickey Jackson	.20	.09
❑ 74	Eric Martin	.20	.09
❑ 75	Renaldo Turnbull	.20	.09
❑ 76	Rodney Hampton	.75	.35
❑ 77	Mike Sherrard	.20	.09
❑ 78	Phil Simms	.40	.18
❑ 79	Keith Hamilton	.20	.09
❑ 80	Rob Moore	.40	.18
❑ 81	Brad Baxter	.20	.09
❑ 82	Boomer Esiason	.40	.18
❑ 83	Johnny Johnson	.20	.09
❑ 84	Ronnie Lott	.40	.18
❑ 85	Randall Cunningham	.75	.35
❑ 86	Herschel Walker	.40	.18
❑ 87	Eric Allen	.20	.09
❑ 88	Clyde Simmons	.20	.09
❑ 89	Seth Joyner	.20	.09
❑ 90	Calvin Williams	.40	.18
❑ 91	Garrison Hearst	.75	.35
❑ 92	Steve Beuerlein	.20	.09
❑ 93	Ricky Proehl	.20	.09
❑ 94	Ronald Moore	.20	.09
❑ 95	Barry Foster	.20	.09
❑ 96	Neil O'Donnell	.75	.35
❑ 97	Eric Green	.20	.09
❑ 98	Rod Woodson	.75	.35
❑ 99	Greg Lloyd	.75	.35
❑ 100	Kevin Greene	.75	.35
❑ 101	Stan Humphries	.75	.35
❑ 102	Anthony Miller	.40	.18
❑ 103	Junior Seau	.75	.35
❑ 104	Leslie O'Neal	.20	.09
❑ 105	Ronnie Harmon	.20	.09
❑ 106	Jerry Rice	2.50	1.10
❑ 107	Ricky Watters	.75	.35
❑ 108	Steve Young	2.00	.90
❑ 109	Brent Jones	.40	.18
❑ 110	John Taylor	.40	.18
❑ 111	Rick Mirer	.75	.35
❑ 112	Chris Warren	.40	.18
❑ 113	Cortez Kennedy	.40	.18
❑ 114	Brian Blades	.40	.18
❑ 115	Eugene Robinson	.20	.09
❑ 116	Reggie Cobb	.20	.09
❑ 117	Hardy Nickerson	.40	.18
❑ 118	Reggie Brooks	.40	.18
❑ 119	Darrell Green	.20	.09
❑ 120	Troy Aikman Back to Back	3.00	1.35
❑ 121	Dan Wilkinson RC	.40	.18
❑ 122	Marshall Faulk RC	6.00	2.70
❑ 123	Heath Shuler RC	.75	.35
❑ 124	Willie McGinest RC	.75	.35
❑ 125	Trev Alberts RC	.40	.18

No.	Player	MINT	NRMT
❑ 126	Trent Dilfer RC	3.00	1.35
❑ 127	Bryant Young RC	.75	.35
❑ 128	Sam Adams RC	.40	.18
❑ 129	Antonio Langham RC	.40	.18
❑ 130	Jamir Miller RC	.20	.09
❑ 131	John Thierry RC	.20	.09
❑ 132	Aaron Glenn RC	.40	.18
❑ 133	Joe Johnson RC	.20	.09
❑ 134	Bernard Williams	.20	.09
❑ 135	Wayne Gandy	.20	.09
❑ 136	Charles Johnson RC	1.25	.55
❑ 137	Dewayne Washington RC	.40	.18
❑ 138	Todd Steussie RC	.40	.18
❑ 139	Tim Bowens RC	.40	.18
❑ 140	Johnnie Morton RC	2.00	.90
❑ 141	Rob Fredrickson RC	.40	.18
❑ 142	Shante Carver RC	.20	.09
❑ 143	Thomas Lewis RC	.40	.18
❑ 144	Greg Hill RC	.75	.35
❑ 145	Henry Ford	.20	.09
❑ 146	Jeff Burris RC	.40	.18
❑ 147	William Floyd RC	.75	.35
❑ 148	Der. Alexander WR RC	1.25	.55
❑ 149	Darnay Scott RC	2.00	.90
❑ 150	Isaac Bruce RC	6.00	2.70
❑ 151	Errict Rhett RC	1.50	.70
❑ 152	Kevin Lee RC	.20	.09
❑ 153	Chuck Levy RC	.20	.09
❑ 154	David Palmer RC	1.25	.55
❑ 155	Ryan Yarborough RC	.20	.09
❑ 156	Charlie Garner RC	2.50	1.10
❑ 157	Mario Bates RC	.75	.35
❑ 158	Bert Emanuel RC	1.25	.55
❑ 159	Bucky Brooks RC	.20	.09
❑ 160	Donnell Bennett RC	.75	.35
❑ 161	Tydus Winans RC	.20	.09
❑ 162	Andre Coleman RC	.20	.09
❑ 163	Calvin Jones RC	.20	.09
❑ 164	LeShon Johnson RC	.40	.18
❑ 165	Doug Brien RC	.20	.09
❑ 166	Byron Bam Morris RC	.75	.35
❑ 167	Lake Dawson RC	.75	.35
❑ 168	Perry Klein RC	.20	.09
❑ 169	Doug Nussmeier RC	.20	.09
❑ 170	Lamont Warren RC	.20	.09
❑ 171	Gus Frerotte RC	1.25	.55
❑ 172	Troy Aikman QC	1.50	.70
❑ 173	Randall Cunningham QC	.75	.35
❑ 174	John Elway QC	2.50	1.10
❑ 175	Jim Everett QC	.20	.09
❑ 176	Drew Bledsoe QC	1.50	.70
❑ 177	Jim Kelly QC	.40	.18
❑ 178	Dan Marino QC	2.50	1.10
❑ 179	Chris Miller QC	.20	.09
❑ 180	Warren Moon QC	.40	.18
❑ 181	Rick Mirer QC	.75	.35
❑ 182	Jeff Hostetler QC	.20	.09
❑ 183	Brett Favre QC	2.50	1.10
❑ 184	Steve Young QC	1.00	.45
❑ 185	Anthony Miller	.40	.18
❑ 186	Michael Haynes	.40	.18
❑ 187	Mike Pritchard	.20	.09
❑ 188	Jeff George	.75	.35
❑ 189	Lewis Tillman	.20	.09
❑ 190	Ken Norton	.40	.18
❑ 191	Erik Kramer	.40	.18
❑ 192	Richard Dent	.40	.18
❑ 193	Rick Mirer GD	.75	.35
❑ 194	Jerome Bettis GD	.75	.35
❑ 195	Reggie Brooks GD	.20	.09
❑ 196	Tom Carter GD	.20	.09
❑ 197	Irv Smith GD	.20	.09
❑ 198	Rocket Ismail GD	.40	.18

1995 Action Packed

		MINT	NRMT
COMPLETE SET (126)		20.00	9.00
❑ 1	Jerry Rice	1.50	.70
❑ 2	Emmitt Smith	2.50	1.10
❑ 3	Drew Bledsoe	1.50	.70
❑ 4	Ben Coates	.25	.11
❑ 5	Jim Everett	.10	.05
❑ 6	Warren Moon	.25	.11

No.	Player	MINT	NRMT
❑ 7	Herman Moore	.50	.23
❑ 8	Deion Sanders	1.00	.45
❑ 9	Rick Mirer	.50	.23
❑ 10	Natrone Means	.50	.23
❑ 11	Jeff Blake RC	1.50	.70
❑ 12	William Floyd	.50	.23
❑ 13	Steve Young	1.25	.55
❑ 14	John Elway	3.00	1.35
❑ 15	Brett Favre	3.00	1.35
❑ 16	Marshall Faulk	.75	.35
❑ 17	Heath Shuler	.50	.23
❑ 18	Ricky Watters	.50	.23
❑ 19	Michael Haynes	.25	.11
❑ 20	Troy Aikman	1.50	.70
❑ 21	Dan Marino	3.00	1.35
❑ 22	Byron Bam Morris	.25	.11
❑ 23	Marcus Allen	.50	.23
❑ 24	Carl Pickens	.50	.23
❑ 25	Rodney Hampton	.25	.11
❑ 26	Dave Brown	.25	.11
❑ 27	Jerome Bettis	.50	.23
❑ 28	Jim Kelly	.50	.23
❑ 29	Andre Reed	.25	.11
❑ 30	Michael Irvin	.50	.23
❑ 31	Barry Sanders	3.00	1.35
❑ 32	Chris Warren	.25	.11
❑ 33	Jeff Hostetler	.25	.11
❑ 34	Alvin Harper	.10	.05
❑ 35	Rob Moore	.10	.05
❑ 36	Steve McNair RC	4.00	1.80
❑ 37	Rashaan Salaam RC	.50	.23
❑ 38	Joey Galloway RC	3.00	1.35
❑ 39	J.J. Stokes RC	.50	.23
❑ 40	Michael Westbrook RC	2.50	1.10
❑ 41	Kerry Collins RC	2.50	1.10
❑ 42	Ki-Jana Carter RC	.50	.23
❑ 43	Boomer Esiason	.25	.11
❑ 44	Chris Spielman	.25	.11
❑ 45	Vinny Testaverde	.25	.11
❑ 46	Kevin Williams WR	.25	.11
❑ 47	Ronnie Harmon	.10	.05
❑ 48	Fred Barnett	.25	.11
❑ 49	Harvey Williams	.10	.05
❑ 50	Reggie White	.50	.23
❑ 51	Brent Jones	.10	.05
❑ 52	Henry Ellard	.25	.11
❑ 53	Cris Carter	.50	.23
❑ 54	Leroy Hoard	.10	.05
❑ 55	Trent Dilfer	.50	.23
❑ 56	Raymont Harris	.10	.05
❑ 57	Garrison Hearst	.50	.23
❑ 58	Lewis Tillman	.10	.05
❑ 59	Mark Brunell	1.50	.70
❑ 60	Bruce Smith	.50	.23
❑ 61	Lake Dawson	.25	.11
❑ 62	Bert Emanuel	.50	.23
❑ 63	Eric Green	.10	.05
❑ 64	Barry Foster	.25	.11
❑ 65	Jeff Graham	.10	.05
❑ 66	Curtis Conway	.50	.23
❑ 67	Herschel Walker	.25	.11
❑ 68	Edgar Bennett	.25	.11
❑ 69	Mario Bates	.50	.23
❑ 70	Irving Fryar	.25	.11
❑ 71	Gary Brown	.10	.05
❑ 72	Cortez Kennedy	.25	.11
❑ 73	John Taylor	.10	.05
❑ 74	Jeff George	.25	.11
❑ 75	Shannon Sharpe	.25	.11
❑ 76	Andre Rison	.25	.11
❑ 77	Mike Sherrard	.10	.05
❑ 78	Errict Rhett	.50	.23
❑ 79	Junior Seau	.50	.23
❑ 80	Willie Davis	.25	.11
❑ 81	Craig Erickson	.10	.05
❑ 82	Torrance Small	.10	.05
❑ 83	Randall Cunningham	.50	.23
❑ 84	Robert Brooks	.50	.23
❑ 85	Terance Mathis	.25	.11
❑ 86	Rod Woodson	.25	.11
❑ 87	Anthony Miller	.25	.11
❑ 88	Stan Humphries	.25	.11
❑ 89	Chris Miller	.10	.05
❑ 90	Steve Beuerlein	.10	.05
❑ 91	Steve Bono	.25	.11
❑ 92	Frank Reich	.10	.05
❑ 93	Cory Fleming	.10	.05
❑ 94	Isaac Bruce	.75	.35
❑ 95	Dave Meggett	.10	.05
❑ 96	Jackie Harris	.10	.05
❑ 97	J.J. Birden	.10	.05
❑ 98	Flipper Anderson	.10	.05
❑ 99	Johnnie Morton	.25	.11
❑ 100	Michael Timpson	.10	.05
❑ 101	Derek Brown RBK	.10	.05
❑ 102	Ricky Ervins	.10	.05
❑ 103	Der.Alexander DE RC	.10	.05
❑ 104	Dave Barr RC	.10	.05
❑ 105	Tony Boselli RC	.50	.23
❑ 106	Kyle Brady RC	.50	.23
❑ 107	Mark Bruener RC	.25	.11
❑ 108	Kevin Carter RC	.50	.23
❑ 109	Neil O'Donnell	.25	.11
❑ 110	Derrick Alexander WR	.50	.23
❑ 111	Charlie Garner	.25	.11
❑ 112	Darnay Scott	.50	.23
❑ 113	Scott Mitchell	.25	.11
❑ 114	Charles Johnson	.25	.11
❑ 115	Greg Hill	.25	.11
❑ 116	Ty Law RC	.25	.11
❑ 117	Frank Sanders RC	1.50	.70
❑ 118	James O. Stewart RC	3.00	1.35
❑ 119	James A.Stewart RC	.10	.05
❑ 120	Kordell Stewart RC	3.00	1.35
❑ 121	Rob Johnson RC	3.00	1.35
❑ 122	John Walsh RC	.10	.05
❑ 123	Stoney Case RC	.50	.23
❑ 124	Tyrone Wheatley RC	2.00	.90
❑ 125	Sherman Williams RC	.10	.05
❑ 126	Ray Zellars RC	.25	.11

1996 Action Packed

		MINT	NRMT
COMPLETE SET (126)		25.00	11.00
❑ 1	Emmitt Smith	3.00	1.35
❑ 2	Dan Marino	4.00	1.80
❑ 3	Isaac Bruce	.60	.25
❑ 4	Eric Zeier	.15	.07
❑ 5	Ben Coates	.30	.14
❑ 6	Jim Kelly	.60	.25
❑ 7	Rodney Hampton	.30	.14
❑ 8	Greg Lloyd	.30	.14
❑ 9	Reggie White	.60	.25

❑ 10	Derrick Thomas	.30	.14
❑ 11	Jerry Rice	2.00	.90
❑ 12	Drew Bledsoe	2.00	.90
❑ 13	Cris Carter	.60	.25
❑ 14	Troy Aikman	2.00	.90
❑ 15	Steve McNair	1.50	.70
❑ 16	Steve Young	1.50	.70
❑ 17	Ricky Watters	.30	.14
❑ 18	Brett Favre	4.00	1.80
❑ 19	Michael Westbrook	.60	.25
❑ 20	Charles Haley	.30	.14
❑ 21	Heath Shuler	.30	.14
❑ 22	Tim Brown	.60	.25
❑ 23	Kerry Collins	.60	.25
❑ 24	Hugh Douglas	.30	.14
❑ 25	Marcus Allen	.60	.25
❑ 26	Steve Bono	.15	.07
❑ 27	Curtis Martin	1.50	.70
❑ 28	Wayne Chrebet	1.00	.45
❑ 29	Dave Brown	.15	.07
❑ 30	James O. Stewart	.30	.14
❑ 31	Chris Sanders	.30	.14
❑ 32	Deion Sanders	1.00	.45
❑ 33	Rodney Thomas	.15	.07
❑ 34	Rashaan Salaam	.60	.25
❑ 35	Curtis Conway	.60	.25
❑ 36	Harvey Williams	.15	.07
❑ 37	William Floyd	.30	.14
❑ 38	Carl Pickens	.60	.25
❑ 39	Herman Moore	.60	.25
❑ 40	Stan Humphries	.30	.14
❑ 41	Orlando Thomas	.15	.07
❑ 42	Bert Emanuel	.30	.14
❑ 43	Yancey Thigpen	.30	.14
❑ 44	Darick Holmes	.15	.07
❑ 45	Mario Bates	.30	.14
❑ 46	Greg Hill	.30	.14
❑ 47	Errict Rhett	.30	.14
❑ 48	Erik Kramer	.15	.07
❑ 49	Garrison Hearst	.30	.14
❑ 50	Jim Everett	.15	.07
❑ 51	Barry Sanders	4.00	1.80
❑ 52	Eric Metcalf	.15	.07
❑ 53	Marshall Faulk	.60	.25
❑ 54	Junior Seau	.30	.14
❑ 55	Bruce Smith	.30	.14
❑ 56	Kordell Stewart	1.25	.55
❑ 57	Edgar Bennett	.30	.14
❑ 58	Joey Galloway	1.25	.55
❑ 59	Jeff Hostetler	.15	.07
❑ 60	Frank Sanders	.30	.14
❑ 61	John Elway	4.00	1.80
❑ 62	Tyrone Wheatley	.30	.14
❑ 63	Jeff George	.30	.14
❑ 64	Ken Norton, Jr.	.15	.07
❑ 65	Bryan Cox	.15	.07
❑ 66	Bryce Paup	.15	.07
❑ 67	Larry Centers	.30	.14
❑ 68	Bernie Parmalee	.15	.07
❑ 69	Jeff Graham	.15	.07
❑ 70	Rick Mirer	.30	.14
❑ 71	Chris Warren	.30	.14
❑ 72	Charlie Garner	.15	.07
❑ 73	Robert Brooks	.60	.25
❑ 74	Jim Harbaugh	.30	.14
❑ 75	Tamarick Vanover	.30	.14
❑ 76	Napoleon Kaufman	.60	.25
❑ 77	Warren Moon	.30	.14
❑ 78	Vincent Brisby	.15	.07
❑ 79	Ki-Jana Carter	.30	.14
❑ 80	Michael Irvin	.60	.25
❑ 81	Trent Dilfer	.60	.25
❑ 82	Byron Bam Morris	.30	.14
❑ 83	Mark Brunell	2.00	.90
❑ 84	Jeff Blake	.60	.25
❑ 85	Kevin Williams	.15	.07
❑ 86	Rod Woodson	.30	.14
❑ 87	Andre Reed	.30	.14
❑ 88	Erric Pegram	.15	.07
❑ 89	Anthony Miller	.30	.14
❑ 90	Gus Frerotte	.60	.25
❑ 91	Quinn Early	.15	.07
❑ 92	Daryl Johnston	.30	.14
❑ 93	Tony Martin	.30	.14
❑ 94	Terrell Davis	5.00	2.20
❑ 95	Brent Jones	.15	.07
❑ 96	Mark Chmura	.30	.14
❑ 97	Kyle Brady	.15	.07
❑ 98	J.J. Stokes	.60	.25
❑ 99	Rodney Peete	.15	.07
❑ 100	Natrone Means	.60	.25
❑ 101	Sherman Williams	.15	.07
❑ 102	Brian Blades	.15	.07
❑ 103	Brett Perriman	.15	.07
❑ 104	Antonio Freeman	1.50	.70
❑ 105	Neil O'Donnell	.30	.14
❑ 106	Craig Heyward	.15	.07
❑ 107	Derek Loville	.15	.07
❑ 108	Jay Novacek	.15	.07
❑ 109	Scott Mitchell	.30	.14
❑ 110	Bill Brooks	.15	.07
❑ 111	Shannon Sharpe	.30	.14
❑ 112	Jake Reed	.30	.14
❑ 113	Derrick Moore	.15	.07
❑ 114	Steve Atwater	.15	.07
❑ 115	Darren Woodson ETS	.30	.14
❑ 116	Junior Seau ETS	.30	.14
❑ 117	Quentin Coryatt ETS	.15	.07
❑ 118	Bruce Smith ETS	.30	.14
❑ 119	Rod Woodson ETS	.30	.14
❑ 120	Charles Haley ETS	.30	.14
❑ 121	Derrick Thomas ETS	.30	.14
❑ 122	Ken Norton, Jr. ETS	.15	.07
❑ 123	Steve Atwater ETS	.15	.07
❑ 124	Greg Lloyd ETS	.30	.14
❑ 125	Reggie White ETS	.60	.25
❑ 126	Bryan Cox ETS	.15	.07

1997 Action Packed

		MINT	NRMT
COMPLETE SET (125)		30.00	13.50
❑ 1	Jerry Rice	2.50	1.10
❑ 2	Troy Aikman	2.50	1.10
❑ 3	Ricky Watters	.40	.18
❑ 4	Dan Marino	5.00	2.20
❑ 5	Emmitt Smith	4.00	1.80
❑ 6	Warren Moon	.75	.35
❑ 7	Rashaan Salaam	.20	.09
❑ 8	Drew Bledsoe	2.50	1.10
❑ 9	Eddie George	2.00	.90
❑ 10	John Elway	5.00	2.20
❑ 11	Robert Brooks	.40	.18
❑ 12	Scott Mitchell	.40	.18
❑ 13	Isaac Bruce	.75	.35
❑ 14	Marshall Faulk	.75	.35
❑ 15	Steve Bono	.40	.18
❑ 16	Barry Sanders	5.00	2.20
❑ 17	Brett Favre	5.00	2.20
❑ 18	Curtis Martin	1.25	.55
❑ 19	Keyshawn Johnson	.75	.35
❑ 20	Dave Brown	.20	.09
❑ 21	Frank Sanders	.40	.18
❑ 22	Gus Frerotte	.20	.09
❑ 23	Eric Metcalf	.40	.18
❑ 24	Thurman Thomas	.75	.35
❑ 25	Steve Young	1.50	.70
❑ 26	Alvin Harper	.20	.09
❑ 27	Mark Brunell	2.50	1.10
❑ 28	Kordell Stewart	1.00	.45
❑ 29	Terry Glenn	.75	.35
❑ 30	Junior Seau	.40	.18
❑ 31	Karim Abdul-Jabbar	.75	.35
❑ 32	Jeff Hostetler	.20	.09
❑ 33	Rodney Hampton	.40	.18
❑ 34	Irving Fryar	.40	.18
❑ 35	Cris Carter	.75	.35
❑ 36	James O.Stewart	.40	.18
❑ 37	Marcus Allen	.75	.35
❑ 38	Napoleon Kaufman	.75	.35
❑ 39	Shannon Sharpe	.40	.18
❑ 40	LeShon Johnson	.20	.09
❑ 41	Tony Banks	.40	.18
❑ 42	Lawrence Phillips	.20	.09
❑ 43	Kerry Collins	.40	.18
❑ 44	Curtis Conway	.40	.18
❑ 45	Jim Harbaugh	.40	.18
❑ 46	Garrison Hearst	.40	.18
❑ 47	Trent Dilfer	.75	.35
❑ 48	Terance Mathis	.40	.18
❑ 49	Jerome Bettis	.75	.35
❑ 50	Chris Sanders	.20	.09
❑ 51	Deion Sanders	.75	.35
❑ 52	Herman Moore	.75	.35
❑ 53	Elvis Grbac	.40	.18
❑ 54	O.J. McDuffie	.40	.18
❑ 55	Ben Coates	.40	.18
❑ 56	Jim Kelly	.75	.35
❑ 57	J.J. Stokes	.40	.18
❑ 58	Terrell Davis	4.00	1.80
❑ 59	Stan Humphries	.40	.18
❑ 60	Carl Pickens	.75	.35
❑ 61	Neil O'Donnell	.40	.18
❑ 62	Edgar Bennett	.40	.18
❑ 63	Yancey Thigpen	.40	.18
❑ 64	Bert Emanuel	.40	.18
❑ 65	Amani Toomer	.40	.18
❑ 66	Jeff Blake	.40	.18
❑ 67	Eddie Kennison	.40	.18
❑ 68	Jason Dunn	.20	.09
❑ 69	Rob Moore	.40	.18
❑ 70	Andre Rison	.40	.18
❑ 71	Vinny Testaverde	.40	.18
❑ 72	Henry Ellard	.20	.09
❑ 73	Dale Carter	.20	.09
❑ 74	Tony Martin	.40	.18
❑ 75	Jim Everett	.20	.09
❑ 76	Joey Galloway	1.00	.45
❑ 77	Mike Alstott	.75	.35
❑ 78	Kevin Hardy	.20	.09
❑ 79	Jake Reed	.40	.18
❑ 80	Tim Brown	.75	.35
❑ 81	Sean Dawkins	.20	.09
❑ 82	Bobby Engram	.40	.18
❑ 83	Michael Irvin	.75	.35
❑ 84	Rickey Dudley	.40	.18
❑ 85	Chris Chandler	.40	.18
❑ 86	Keith Jackson	.20	.09
❑ 87	Muhsin Muhammad	.40	.18
❑ 88	Tamarick Vanover	.40	.18
❑ 89	Chris Warren	.40	.18
❑ 90	Johnnie Morton	.40	.18
❑ 91	Terry Allen	.75	.35
❑ 92	Stanley Pritchett	.20	.09
❑ 93	Charles Johnson	.40	.18
❑ 94	Chris T. Jones	.20	.09
❑ 95	Winslow Oliver	.20	.09
❑ 96	Anthony Miller	.20	.09
❑ 97	Tyrone Wheatley	.40	.18
❑ 98	Robert Smith	.40	.18
❑ 99	Eric Moulds	.75	.35
❑ 100	Hardy Nickerson	.20	.09
❑ 101	Derrick Alexander WR	.40	.18
❑ 102	Michael Haynes	.20	.09
❑ 103	Jamal Anderson	1.50	.70
❑ 104	Marvin Harrison	.75	.35
❑ 105	Antonio Freeman	1.25	.55
❑ 106	Dorsey Levens	.75	.35
❑ 107	Natrone Means	.75	.35
❑ 108	Keenan McCardell	.40	.18
❑ 109	Mark Chmura	.40	.18
❑ 110	Darren Woodson	.20	.09
❑ 111	Brett Favre DD	2.50	1.10
❑ 112	Emmitt Smith DD	2.00	.90
❑ 113	Junior Seau DD	.40	.18
❑ 114	Jerry Rice DD	1.25	.55
❑ 115	Barry Sanders DD	2.50	1.10
❑ 116	Bruce Smith DD	.20	.09
❑ 117	Troy Aikman DD	1.25	.55

Card	MINT	NRMT
❑ 118 Bryan Cox DD	.20	.09
❑ 119 Zach Thomas DD	.40	.18
❑ 120 Reggie White DD	.75	.35
❑ 121 Ben Coates DD	.40	.18
❑ 122 Jerome Bettis DD	.75	.35
❑ 123 Michael Irvin DD	.40	.18
❑ 124 Quentin Coryatt DD	.20	.09
❑ 125 Checklist Card	.20	.09
❑ P4 Jerry Rice Promo Studs Card	5.00	2.20
❑ P28 Kordell Stewart Promo	2.00	.90
❑ P45 Jim Harbaugh Promo	.50	.23

1995 Action Packed Rookies/Stars

	MINT	NRMT
COMPLETE SET (105)	20.00	9.00
❑ 1 Steve Young	1.25	.55
❑ 2 Steve Bono	.25	.11
❑ 3 Natrone Means	.50	.23
❑ 4 Steve Beuerlein	.10	.05
❑ 5 Neil O'Donnell	.25	.11
❑ 6 Marshall Faulk	.75	.35
❑ 7 Ricky Watters	.50	.23
❑ 8 Gary Brown	.10	.05
❑ 9 Jeff Hostetler	.25	.11
❑ 10 Robert Brooks	.50	.23
❑ 11 Johnny Mitchell	.10	.05
❑ 12 Barry Sanders	3.00	1.35
❑ 13 Dave Brown	.25	.11
❑ 14 John Elway	3.00	1.35
❑ 15 Garrison Hearst	.50	.23
❑ 16 Jim Everett	.10	.05
❑ 17 Michael Irvin	.50	.23
❑ 18 Dan Marino	3.00	1.35
❑ 19 Jeff George	.25	.11
❑ 20 Ben Coates	.25	.11
❑ 21 Charles Johnson	.25	.11
❑ 22 Carl Pickens	.50	.23
❑ 23 Deion Sanders	1.00	.45
❑ 24 Errict Rhett	.50	.23
❑ 25 Steve Walsh	.10	.05
❑ 26 Bruce Smith	.50	.23
❑ 27 Andre Rison	.25	.11
❑ 28 Warren Moon	.25	.11
❑ 29 Terry Allen	.25	.11
❑ 30 Desmond Howard	.25	.11
❑ 31 Shannon Sharpe	.25	.11
❑ 32 Dave Krieg	.10	.05
❑ 33 Byron Bam Morris	.25	.11
❑ 34 Rodney Hampton	.25	.11
❑ 35 Scott Mitchell	.25	.11
❑ 36 Alvin Harper	.10	.05
❑ 37 Robert Smith	.50	.23
❑ 38 Troy Aikman	1.50	.70
❑ 39 William Floyd	.50	.23
❑ 40 Randall Cunningham	.50	.23
❑ 41 Mario Bates	.50	.23
❑ 42 Reggie White	.50	.23
❑ 43 Chris Chandler	.25	.11
❑ 44 Erik Kramer	.10	.05
❑ 45 Emmitt Smith	2.50	1.10
❑ 46 Irving Fryar	.25	.11
❑ 47 Jeff Blake RC	1.00	.45
❑ 48 Drew Bledsoe	1.50	.70
❑ 49 Anthony Miller	.25	.11
❑ 50 Marcus Allen	.50	.23
❑ 51 Leroy Hoard	.10	.05
❑ 52 Stan Humphries	.25	.11
❑ 53 Eric Green	.10	.05
❑ 54 Herschel Walker	.25	.11
❑ 55 Junior Seau	.50	.23
❑ 56 Terance Mathis	.25	.11
❑ 57 Boomer Esiason	.25	.11
❑ 58 Lorenzo White	.10	.05
❑ 59 Tim Brown	.50	.23
❑ 60 Brett Favre	3.00	1.35
❑ 61 Craig Erickson	.10	.05
❑ 62 Rod Woodson	.25	.11
❑ 63 Frank Reich	.10	.05
❑ 64 Cris Carter	.50	.23
❑ 65 Jerry Rice	1.50	.70
❑ 66 Greg Hill	.25	.11
❑ 67 Andre Reed	.25	.11
❑ 68 Trent Dilfer	.50	.23
❑ 69 Eric Metcalf	.25	.11
❑ 70 Jim Kelly	.50	.23
❑ 71 Herman Moore	.50	.23
❑ 72 Vinny Testaverde	.25	.11
❑ 73 Jeff Graham	.10	.05
❑ 74 Edgar Bennett	.25	.11
❑ 75 Jerome Bettis	.50	.23
❑ 76 Heath Shuler	.50	.23
❑ 77 Chris Warren	.25	.11
❑ 78 Reggie Brooks	.25	.11
❑ 79 Rick Mirer	.50	.23
❑ 80 Chris Miller	.10	.05
❑ 81 Napoleon Kaufman RC	1.50	.70
❑ 82 Christian Fauria RC	.10	.05
❑ 83 Todd Collins RC	.50	.23
❑ 84 J.J. Stokes RC	.50	.23
❑ 85 Mark Bruener RC	.25	.11
❑ 86 Frank Sanders RC	1.00	.45
❑ 87 Chad May RC	.10	.05
❑ 88 Kordell Stewart RC	2.00	.90
❑ 89 Ki-Jana Carter RC	.50	.23
❑ 90 Curtis Martin RC	2.50	1.10
❑ 91 Sherman Williams RC	.10	.05
❑ 92 Terrell Davis RC	10.00	4.50
❑ 93 Chris Sanders RC	.50	.23
❑ 94 Kyle Brady RC	.50	.23
❑ 95 Tyrone Wheatley RC	1.25	.55
❑ 96 Rodney Thomas RC	.50	.23
❑ 97 James O. Stewart RC	2.00	.90
❑ 98 Kerry Collins RC	1.50	.70
❑ 99 Rashaan Salaam RC	.50	.23
❑ 100 Stoney Case RC	.50	.23
❑ 101 Steve McNair RC	2.50	1.10
❑ 102 Joey Galloway RC	2.00	.90
❑ 103 Michael Westbrook RC	1.50	.70
❑ 104 Eric Zeier RC	.50	.23
❑ 105 Ray Zellars RC	.25	.11

1992 All World

	MINT	NRMT
COMPLETE SET (300)	15.00	6.75
❑ 1 Emmitt Smith LM	.60	.25
❑ 2 Thurman Thomas LM	.10	.05
❑ 3 Deion Sanders LM	.25	.11
❑ 4 Randall Cunningham LM	.10	.05
❑ 5 Michael Irvin LM	.10	.05
❑ 6 Bruce Smith LM	.10	.05
❑ 7 Jeff George LM	.10	.05
❑ 8 Derrick Thomas LM	.10	.05
❑ 9 Andre Rison LM	.25	.11
❑ 10 Troy Aikman LM	.40	.18
❑ 11 Quentin Coryatt RC	.25	.11
❑ 12 Carl Pickens RC	.60	.25
❑ 13 Steve Emtman RC	.10	.05
❑ 14 Derek Brown TE RC	.10	.05
❑ 15 Desmond Howard RC	.50	.23
❑ 16 Troy Vincent RC	.05	.02
❑ 17 David Klingler RC	.10	.05
❑ 18 Vaughn Dunbar RC	.05	.02
❑ 19 Terrell Buckley RC	.10	.05
❑ 20 Jimmy Smith RC	3.00	1.35
❑ 21 Marquez Pope RC	.05	.02
❑ 22 Kurt Barber RC	.05	.02
❑ 23 Robert Harris RC	.05	.02
❑ 24 Tony Sacca RC	.05	.02
❑ 25 Alonzo Spellman RC	.25	.11
❑ 26 Shane Collins RC	.05	.02
❑ 27 Chris Mims RC	.10	.05
❑ 28 Siran Stacy RC	.05	.02
❑ 29 Edgar Bennett RC	.25	.11
❑ 30 Sean Gilbert RC	.10	.05
❑ 31 Eugene Chung RC	.05	.02
❑ 32 Levon Kirkland RC	.05	.02
❑ 33 Chuck Smith RC	.05	.02
❑ 34 Chester McGlockton RC	.10	.05
❑ 35 Ashley Ambrose RC	.10	.05
❑ 36 Phillippi Sparks RC	.05	.02
❑ 37 Darryl Williams RC	.10	.05
❑ 38 Tracy Scroggins RC	.05	.02
❑ 39 Mike Gaddis RC	.05	.02
❑ 40 Tony Brooks RC	.05	.02
❑ 41 Steve Israel RC	.05	.02
❑ 42 Patrick Rowe RC	.05	.02
❑ 43 Shane Dronett RC	.05	.02
❑ 44 Mike Pawlawski RC	.25	.11
❑ 45 Dale Carter RC	.10	.05
❑ 46 Tyji Armstrong RC	.05	.02
❑ 47 Kevin Smith RC	.10	.05
❑ 48 Courtney Hawkins RC	.10	.05
❑ 49 Marco Coleman RC	.10	.05
❑ 50 Tommy Vardell RC	.10	.05
❑ 51 Ray Ethridge RC	.05	.02
❑ 52 Robert Porcher RC	.10	.05
❑ 53 Todd Collins RC	.05	.02
❑ 54 Robert Jones RC	.10	.05
❑ 55 Tommy Maddox RC	.10	.05
❑ 56 Dana Hall RC	.10	.05
❑ 57 Leon Searcy RC	.10	.05
❑ 58 Robert Brooks RC	.75	.35
❑ 59 Darren Woodson RC	.25	.11
❑ 60 Jeremy Lincoln RC	.05	.02
❑ 61 Sean Jones	.10	.05
❑ 62 Howie Long	.25	.11
❑ 63 Rich Gannon	.25	.11
❑ 64 Keith Byars	.05	.02
❑ 65 John Taylor	.10	.05
❑ 66 Burt Grossman	.05	.02
❑ 67 Chris Hinton	.05	.02
❑ 68 Brad Muster	.05	.02
❑ 69 Cris Dishman	.05	.02
❑ 70 Russell Maryland	.10	.05
❑ 71 Harvey Williams	.10	.05
❑ 72 Broderick Thomas	.05	.02
❑ 73 Louis Lipps	.05	.02
❑ 74 Erik Kramer	.05	.02
❑ 75 David Fulcher	.05	.02
❑ 76 Andre Tippett	.05	.02
❑ 77 Timm Rosenbach	.05	.02
❑ 78 Mark Rypien	.10	.05
❑ 79 James Lofton	.10	.05
❑ 80 Dan Saleaumua	.05	.02
❑ 81 John L. Williams	.05	.02
❑ 82 Kevin Fagan	.05	.02
❑ 83 Flipper Anderson	.05	.02
❑ 84 Michael Dean Perry	.10	.05
❑ 85 Mark Higgs	.05	.02
❑ 86 Pat Swilling	.10	.05
❑ 87 Pierce Holt	.05	.02
❑ 88 John Elway	1.25	.55
❑ 89 Bill Brooks	.10	.05
❑ 90 Rob Moore	.10	.05
❑ 91 Junior Seau	.25	.11
❑ 92 Wendell Davis	.05	.02

Card	Mint	Nrmt
❑ 93 Brian Noble	.05	.02
❑ 94 Ernest Givins	.10	.05
❑ 95 Phil Simms	.10	.05
❑ 96 Eric Dickerson	.10	.05
❑ 97 Bennie Blades	.05	.02
❑ 98 Gary Anderson RB	.05	.02
❑ 99 Erric Pegram	.05	.02
❑ 100 Hart Lee Dykes	.05	.02
❑ 101 Charles Haley	.10	.05
❑ 102 Bruce Smith	.25	.11
❑ 103 Nick Lowery	.05	.02
❑ 104 Webster Slaughter	.05	.02
❑ 105 Ray Childress	.10	.05
❑ 106 Gene Atkins	.05	.02
❑ 107 Bruce Armstrong	.05	.02
❑ 108 Anthony Miller	.25	.11
❑ 109 Eric Thomas	.05	.02
❑ 110 Greg Townsend	.05	.02
❑ 111 Anthony Carter	.10	.05
❑ 112 James Hasty	.05	.02
❑ 113 Chris Miller	.05	.02
❑ 114 Sammie Smith	.05	.02
❑ 115 Bubby Brister	.10	.05
❑ 116 Mark Clayton	.10	.05
❑ 117 Richard Johnson	.05	.02
❑ 118 Bernie Kosar	.10	.05
❑ 119 Lionel Washington	.05	.02
❑ 120 Gary Clark	.10	.05
❑ 121 Anthony Munoz	.25	.11
❑ 122 Brent Jones	.10	.05
❑ 123 Thurman Thomas	.25	.11
❑ 124 Lee Williams	.05	.02
❑ 125 Jessie Hester	.05	.02
❑ 126 Andre Ware	.10	.05
❑ 127 Patrick Hunter	.05	.02
❑ 128 Erik Howard	.05	.02
❑ 129 Keith Jackson	.10	.05
❑ 130 Troy Aikman	.75	.35
❑ 131 Mike Singletary	.10	.05
❑ 132 Carnell Lake	.10	.05
❑ 133 Jeff Hostetler	.10	.05
❑ 134 Alonzo Highsmith	.05	.02
❑ 135 Vaughan Johnson	.05	.02
❑ 136 Louis Oliver	.05	.02
❑ 137 Mel Gray	.10	.05
❑ 138 Al Toon	.10	.05
❑ 139 Bubba McDowell	.05	.02
❑ 140 Ronnie Lott	.10	.05
❑ 141 Deion Sanders	.50	.23
❑ 142 Jim Harbaugh	.25	.11
❑ 143 Gary Zimmerman	.05	.02
❑ 144 Ernie Jones	.05	.02
❑ 145 Cortez Kennedy	.10	.05
❑ 146 Jeff Cross	.05	.02
❑ 147 Floyd Turner UER (Bio says he was drafted in 4th round)	.05	.02
❑ 148 Mike Tomczak	.10	.05
❑ 149 Lorenzo White	.05	.02
❑ 150 Mark Carrier DB	.05	.02
❑ 151 John Stephens	.05	.02
❑ 152 Jerry Rice	.75	.35
❑ 153 Jim Kelly	.25	.11
❑ 154 Al Smith	.05	.02
❑ 155 Duane Bickett	.05	.02
❑ 156 Brett Perriman	.25	.11
❑ 157 Boomer Esiason	.10	.05
❑ 158 Neil Smith	.25	.11
❑ 159 Eddie Anderson	.05	.02
❑ 160 Browning Nagle	.05	.02
❑ 161 John Friesz	.10	.05
❑ 162 Robert Delpino	.05	.02
❑ 163 Darren Lewis	.05	.02
❑ 164 Roger Craig	.10	.05
❑ 165 Keith McCants	.05	.02
❑ 166 Stephone Paige	.05	.02
❑ 167 Steve Broussard	.05	.02
❑ 168 Gaston Green	.05	.02
❑ 169 Ethan Horton	.05	.02
❑ 170 Lewis Billups	.05	.02
❑ 171 Mike Merriweather	.05	.02
❑ 172 Randall Cunningham	.25	.11
❑ 173 Leonard Marshall	.05	.02
❑ 174 Jay Novacek	.10	.05
❑ 175 Irving Fryar	.10	.05
❑ 176 Randal Hill	.05	.02
❑ 177 Keith Henderson	.05	.02
❑ 178 Brad Baxter	.05	.02
❑ 179 William Fuller	.10	.05
❑ 180 Leslie O'Neal	.10	.05
❑ 181 Steve Smith	.05	.02
❑ 182 Joe Montana UER (Born 1956, not 1965)	1.25	.55
❑ 183 Eric Green	.10	.05
❑ 184 Rodney Peete	.10	.05
❑ 185 Lawrence Dawsey	.10	.05
❑ 186 Brian Mitchell	.10	.05
❑ 187 Rickey Jackson	.05	.02
❑ 188 Christian Okoye	.10	.05
❑ 189 David Wyman	.05	.02
❑ 190 Jessie Tuggle	.05	.02
❑ 191 Ronnie Harmon	.10	.05
❑ 192 Andre Reed	.25	.11
❑ 193 Chris Doleman	.10	.05
❑ 194 Leroy Hoard	.05	.02
❑ 195 Mark Ingram	.05	.02
❑ 196 Willie Gault	.05	.02
❑ 197 Eugene Lockhart	.05	.02
❑ 198 Jim Everett	.10	.05
❑ 199 Doug Smith	.05	.02
❑ 200 Clarence Verdin	.05	.02
❑ 201 Steve Bono RC	.25	.11
❑ 202 Mark Vlasic	.05	.02
❑ 203 Fred Barnett	.10	.05
❑ 204 Henry Thomas	.05	.02
❑ 205 Shaun Gayle	.05	.02
❑ 206 Rod Bernstine	.05	.02
❑ 207 Harold Green	.10	.05
❑ 208 Dan McGwire	.05	.02
❑ 209 Marv Cook	.05	.02
❑ 210 Emmitt Smith	1.50	.70
❑ 211 Merril Hoge	.05	.02
❑ 212 Darion Conner	.05	.02
❑ 213 Mike Sherrard	.10	.05
❑ 214 Jeff George	.25	.11
❑ 215 Craig Heyward	.05	.02
❑ 216 Henry Ellard	.10	.05
❑ 217 Lawrence Taylor	.25	.11
❑ 218 Jerry Ball	.05	.02
❑ 219 Tom Rathman	.05	.02
❑ 220 Warren Moon	.25	.11
❑ 221 Ricky Proehl	.05	.02
❑ 222 Sterling Sharpe	.25	.11
❑ 223 Earnest Byner	.05	.02
❑ 224 Jay Schroeder	.05	.02
❑ 225 Vance Johnson	.05	.02
❑ 226 Cornelius Bennett	.10	.05
❑ 227 Ken O'Brien	.05	.02
❑ 228 Ferrell Edmunds	.05	.02
❑ 229 Eric Allen	.05	.02
❑ 230 Derrick Thomas	.25	.11
❑ 231 Cris Carter	.50	.23
❑ 232 Jon Vaughn	.05	.02
❑ 233 Eric Metcalf	.10	.05
❑ 234 William Perry	.10	.05
❑ 235 Vinny Testaverde	.10	.05
❑ 236 Chip Banks	.05	.02
❑ 237 Brian Blades	.10	.05
❑ 238 Calvin Williams	.05	.02
❑ 239 Andre Rison	.25	.11
❑ 240 Neil O'Donnell	.10	.05
❑ 241 Michael Irvin	.25	.11
❑ 242 Gary Plummer	.05	.02
❑ 243 Nick Bell	.05	.02
❑ 244 Ray Crockett	.05	.02
❑ 245 Sam Mills	.05	.02
❑ 246 Haywood Jeffires	.05	.02
❑ 247 Steve Young	.60	.25
❑ 248 Martin Bayless	.05	.02
❑ 249 Dan Marino	1.25	.55
❑ 250 Carl Banks	.05	.02
❑ 251 Keith McKeller	.05	.02
❑ 252 Aaron Wallace	.05	.02
❑ 253 Lamar Lathon	.05	.02
❑ 254 Derrick Fenner	.05	.02
❑ 255 Vai Sikahema	.05	.02
❑ 256 Keith Sims	.05	.02
❑ 257 Rohn Stark	.05	.02
❑ 258 Reggie Roby	.05	.02
❑ 259 Tony Zendejas	.05	.02
❑ 260 Harris Barton	.05	.02
❑ 261 Checklist 1-100	.05	.02
❑ 262 Checklist 101-200	.05	.02
❑ 263 Checklist 201-300	.05	.02
❑ 264 Rookies Checklist	.05	.02
❑ 265 Greats Checklist	.05	.02
❑ 266 Joe Namath GG	.25	.11
❑ 267 Joe Namath GG	.25	.11
❑ 268 Joe Namath GG	.25	.11
❑ 269 Joe Namath GG	.25	.11
❑ 270 Joe Namath GG	.25	.11
❑ 271 Jim Brown GG	.25	.11
❑ 272 Jim Brown GG	.25	.11
❑ 273 Jim Brown GG	.25	.11
❑ 274 Jim Brown GG	.25	.11
❑ 275 Jim Brown GG	.25	.11
❑ 276 Vince Lombardi GG	.25	.11
❑ 277 Jim Thorpe GG	.05	.02
❑ 278 Tom Fears GG	.05	.02
❑ 279 John Henry Johnson GG	.05	.02
❑ 280 Gale Sayers GG	.10	.05
❑ 281 Willie Brown GG	.05	.02
❑ 282 Doak Walker GG	.05	.02
❑ 283 Dick Lane GG	.05	.02
❑ 284 Otto Graham GG	.10	.05
❑ 285 Hugh McElhenny GG	.05	.02
❑ 286 Roger Staubach GG	.25	.11
❑ 287 Steve Largent GG	.25	.11
❑ 288 Otis Taylor GG	.05	.02
❑ 289 Sam Huff GG	.05	.02
❑ 290 Harold Carmichael GG	.05	.02
❑ 291 Steve Van Buren GG	.05	.02
❑ 292 Gino Marchetti GG	.05	.02
❑ 293 Tony Dorsett GG	.10	.05
❑ 294 Leo Nomellini GG	.05	.02
❑ 295 Jack Lambert GG	.05	.02
❑ 296 Joe Theismann GG	.10	.05
❑ 297 Bobby Layne GG	.05	.02
❑ 298 John Stallworth GG	.05	.02
❑ 299 Paul Hornung GG	.10	.05
❑ 300 Don Maynard GG	.05	.02
❑ A1 Desmond Howard AU (Certified autograph)	40.00	18.00
❑ A2 Jim Brown AU (Certified autograph)	100.00	45.00
❑ A3 Joe Namath AU (Certified autograph)	120.00	55.00
❑ P1 Desmond Howard (Promo; Numbered P)	1.00	.45
❑ TRI Desmond Howard, Jim Brown, Joe Namath (Triplefolder)	3.00	1.35

1998 Aurora

	MINT	NRMT
COMPLETE SET (200)	70.00	32.00
❑ 1 Rob Moore	.40	.18
❑ 2 Jake Plummer	1.50	.70
❑ 3 Frank Sanders	.40	.18
❑ 4 Eric Swann	.20	.09
❑ 5 Jamal Anderson	.75	.35
❑ 6 Chris Chandler	.40	.18
❑ 7 Byron Hanspard	.40	.18
❑ 8 Terance Mathis	.40	.18
❑ 9 O.J. Santiago	.20	.09
❑ 10 Chuck Smith	.20	.09
❑ 11 Jessie Tuggle	.20	.09

❑ 12 Jay Graham	.20	.09
❑ 13 Jim Harbaugh	.40	.18
❑ 14 Michael Jackson	.20	.09
❑ 15 Pat Johnson RC	2.50	1.10
❑ 16 Jermaine Lewis	.40	.18
❑ 17 Errict Rhett	.40	.18
❑ 18 Rod Woodson	.40	.18
❑ 19 Quinn Early	.20	.09
❑ 20 Andre Reed	.40	.18
❑ 21 Antowain Smith	.75	.35
❑ 22 Bruce Smith	.40	.18
❑ 23 Thurman Thomas	.75	.35
❑ 24 Ted Washington	.20	.09
❑ 25 Michael Bates	.20	.09
❑ 26 Rae Carruth	.40	.18
❑ 27 Kerry Collins	.40	.18
❑ 28 Fred Lane	.40	.18
❑ 29 Wesley Walls	.40	.18
❑ 30 Edgar Bennett	.20	.09
❑ 31 Curtis Conway	.40	.18
❑ 32 Curtis Enis RC	2.50	1.10
❑ 33 Walt Harris	.20	.09
❑ 34 Erik Kramer	.20	.09
❑ 35 Barry Minter	.20	.09
❑ 36 Jeff Blake	.40	.18
❑ 37 Corey Dillon	1.25	.55
❑ 38 Carl Pickens	.75	.35
❑ 39 Darnay Scott	.40	.18
❑ 40 Troy Aikman	2.00	.90
❑ 41 Michael Irvin	.75	.35
❑ 42 Deion Sanders	.75	.35
❑ 43 Emmitt Smith	3.00	1.35
❑ 44 Chris Warren	.40	.18
❑ 45 Terrell Davis	3.00	1.35
❑ 46 John Elway	4.00	1.80
❑ 47 Brian Griese RC	6.00	2.70
❑ 48 Ed McCaffrey	.40	.18
❑ 49 John Mobley	.20	.09
❑ 50 Shannon Sharpe	.40	.18
❑ 51 Neil Smith	.40	.18
❑ 52 Rod Smith WR	.40	.18
❑ 53 Stephen Boyd	.20	.09
❑ 54 Scott Mitchell	.40	.18
❑ 55 Herman Moore	.75	.35
❑ 56 Johnnie Morton	.40	.18
❑ 57 Robert Porcher	.20	.09
❑ 58 Barry Sanders	4.00	1.80
❑ 59 Robert Brooks	.40	.18
❑ 60 Mark Chmura	.40	.18
❑ 61 Brett Favre	4.00	1.80
❑ 62 Antonio Freeman	.75	.35
❑ 63 Vonnie Holliday RC	2.50	1.10
❑ 64 Dorsey Levens	.75	.35
❑ 65 Ross Verba	.20	.09
❑ 66 Reggie White	.75	.35
❑ 67 Elijah Alexander	.20	.09
❑ 68 Ken Dilger	.20	.09
❑ 69 Marshall Faulk	.75	.35
❑ 70 Marvin Harrison	.40	.18
❑ 71 Peyton Manning RC	15.00	6.75
❑ 72 Bryan Barker	.20	.09
❑ 73 Mark Brunell	1.50	.70
❑ 74 Keenan McCardell	.40	.18
❑ 75 Jimmy Smith	.40	.18
❑ 76 James Stewart	.40	.18
❑ 77 Derrick Alexander WR	.40	.18
❑ 78 Kimble Anders	.40	.18
❑ 79 Donnell Bennett	.20	.09
❑ 80 Elvis Grbac	.40	.18
❑ 81 Andre Rison	.40	.18
❑ 82 Rashaan Shehee RC	2.50	1.10
❑ 83 Derrick Thomas	.40	.18
❑ 84 Karim Abdul-Jabbar	.75	.35
❑ 85 Trace Armstrong	.20	.09
❑ 86 Charles Jordan	.20	.09
❑ 87 Dan Marino	4.00	1.80
❑ 88 O.J. McDuffie	.40	.18
❑ 89 Zach Thomas	.40	.18
❑ 90 Cris Carter	.75	.35
❑ 91 Charles Evans	.20	.09
❑ 92 Andrew Glover	.20	.09
❑ 93 Brad Johnson	.75	.35
❑ 94 Randy Moss RC	15.00	6.75
❑ 95 John Randle	.40	.18
❑ 96 Jake Reed	.40	.18
❑ 97 Robert Smith	.75	.35
❑ 98 Bruce Armstrong	.20	.09
❑ 99 Drew Bledsoe	1.50	.70
❑ 100 Ben Coates	.40	.18
❑ 101 Robert Edwards RC	3.00	1.35
❑ 102 Terry Glenn	.75	.35
❑ 103 Willie McGinest	.20	.09
❑ 104 Sedrick Shaw	.20	.09
❑ 105 Tony Simmons RC	2.50	1.10
❑ 106 Chris Slade	.20	.09
❑ 107 Billy Joe Hobert	.20	.09
❑ 108 Qadry Ismail	.20	.09
❑ 109 Heath Shuler	.20	.09
❑ 110 Lamar Smith	.40	.18
❑ 111 Ray Zellars	.20	.09
❑ 112 Tiki Barber	.40	.18
❑ 113 Chris Calloway	.20	.09
❑ 114 Ike Hilliard	.40	.18
❑ 115 Joe Jurevicius RC	2.50	1.10
❑ 116 Danny Kanell	.40	.18
❑ 117 Amani Toomer	.40	.18
❑ 118 Charles Way	.20	.09
❑ 119 Tyrone Wheatley	.40	.18
❑ 120 Wayne Chrebet	.75	.35
❑ 121 John Elliott	.20	.09
❑ 122 Glenn Foley	.40	.18
❑ 123 Scott Frost	.40	.18
❑ 124 Aaron Glenn	.20	.09
❑ 125 Keyshawn Johnson	.75	.35
❑ 126 Curtis Martin	.75	.35
❑ 127 Vinny Testaverde	.40	.18
❑ 128 Tim Brown	.75	.35
❑ 129 Rickey Dudley	.20	.09
❑ 130 Jeff George	.40	.18
❑ 131 James Jett	.40	.18
❑ 132 Napoleon Kaufman	.75	.35
❑ 133 Darrell Russell	.20	.09
❑ 134 Charles Woodson RC	2.50	1.10
❑ 135 James Darling RC	.20	.09
❑ 136 Koy Detmer	.75	.35
❑ 137 Irving Fryar	.40	.18
❑ 138 Charlie Garner	.20	.09
❑ 139 Bobby Hoying	.40	.18
❑ 140 Chad Lewis	.20	.09
❑ 141 Duce Staley	1.50	.70
❑ 142 Kevin Turner	.20	.09
❑ 143 Jerome Bettis	.75	.35
❑ 144 Will Blackwell	.20	.09
❑ 145 Mark Bruener	.20	.09
❑ 146 Dermontti Dawson	.20	.09
❑ 147 Charles Johnson	.20	.09
❑ 148 Levon Kirkland	.20	.09
❑ 149 Tim Lester	.20	.09
❑ 150 Kordell Stewart	.75	.35
❑ 151 Tony Banks	.40	.18
❑ 152 Isaac Bruce	.75	.35
❑ 153 Robert Holcombe RC	1.50	.70
❑ 154 Eddie Kennison	.40	.18
❑ 155 Amp Lee	.20	.09
❑ 156 Jerald Moore	.20	.09
❑ 157 Charlie Jones	.20	.09
❑ 158 Freddie Jones	.20	.09
❑ 159 Ryan Leaf RC	4.00	1.80
❑ 160 Natrone Means	.75	.35
❑ 161 Junior Seau	.40	.18
❑ 162 Bryan Still	.20	.09
❑ 163 Marc Edwards	.20	.09
❑ 164 Merton Hanks	.20	.09
❑ 165 Garrison Hearst	.75	.35
❑ 166 Terrell Owens	.75	.35
❑ 167 Jerry Rice	2.00	.90
❑ 168 J.J. Stokes	.40	.18
❑ 169 Bryant Young	.20	.09
❑ 170 Steve Young	1.25	.55
❑ 171 Chad Brown	.20	.09
❑ 172 Joey Galloway	.75	.35
❑ 173 Walter Jones	.20	.09
❑ 174 Cortez Kennedy	.20	.09
❑ 175 Jon Kitna	1.25	.55
❑ 176 James McKnight	.20	.09
❑ 177 Warren Moon	.75	.35
❑ 178 Michael Sinclair	.20	.09
❑ 179 Mike Alstott	.75	.35
❑ 180 Reidel Anthony	.40	.18
❑ 181 Derrick Brooks	.20	.09
❑ 182 Trent Dilfer	.75	.35
❑ 183 Warrick Dunn	.75	.35
❑ 184 Hardy Nickerson	.20	.09
❑ 185 Warren Sapp	.40	.18
❑ 186 Willie Davis	.20	.09
❑ 187 Eddie George	1.50	.70
❑ 188 Steve McNair	.75	.35
❑ 189 Jon Runyan	.20	.09
❑ 190 Chris Sanders	.20	.09
❑ 191 Frank Wycheck	.20	.09
❑ 192 Stephen Alexander RC	2.50	1.10
❑ 193 Terry Allen	.75	.35
❑ 194 Stephen Davis	.20	.09
❑ 195 Cris Dishman	.20	.09
❑ 196 Gus Frerotte	.20	.09
❑ 197 Darrell Green	.40	.18
❑ 198 Skip Hicks RC	2.50	1.10
❑ 199 Dana Stubblefield	.20	.09
❑ 200 Michael Westbrook	.40	.18
❑ S1 Warrick Dunn Sample	1.00	.45

1999 Aurora

	MINT	NRMT
COMPLETE SET (150)	50.00	22.00
❑ 1 David Boston RC	3.00	1.35
❑ 2 Larry Centers	.15	.07
❑ 3 Rob Moore	.30	.14
❑ 4 Adrian Murrell	.30	.14
❑ 5 Jake Plummer	1.00	.45
❑ 6 Jamal Anderson	1.00	.45
❑ 7 Chris Chandler	.30	.14
❑ 8 Tim Dwight	.50	.23
❑ 9 Terance Mathis	.30	.14
❑ 10 O.J. Santiago	.15	.07
❑ 11 Priest Holmes	.50	.23
❑ 12 Michael Jackson	.15	.07
❑ 13 Jermaine Lewis	.30	.14
❑ 14 Ray Lewis	.30	.14
❑ 15 Michael McCrary	.15	.07
❑ 16 Doug Flutie	.60	.25
❑ 17 Eric Moulds	.50	.23
❑ 18 Peerless Price RC	2.00	.90
❑ 19 Antowain Smith	.50	.23
❑ 20 Bruce Smith	.30	.14
❑ 21 Steve Beuerlein	.15	.07
❑ 22 Tim Biakabutuka	.30	.14
❑ 23 Kevin Greene	.15	.07
❑ 24 Muhsin Muhammad	.30	.14
❑ 25 Wesley Walls	.30	.14
❑ 26 Curtis Conway	.30	.14
❑ 27 Bobby Engram	.30	.14
❑ 28 Curtis Enis	.50	.23
❑ 29 Erik Kramer	.15	.07
❑ 30 Cade McNown RC	2.00	.90
❑ 31 Jeff Blake	.30	.14
❑ 32 Corey Dillon	.50	.23
❑ 33 Carl Pickens	.30	.14
❑ 34 Darnay Scott	.15	.07
❑ 35 Akili Smith RC	3.00	1.35
❑ 36 Tim Couch RC	6.00	2.70
❑ 37 Ty Detmer	.30	.14
❑ 38 Kevin Johnson RC	3.00	1.35
❑ 39 Terry Kirby	.15	.07
❑ 40 Troy Aikman	1.25	.55
❑ 41 Michael Irvin	.30	.14
❑ 42 Rocket Ismail	.30	.14
❑ 43 Deion Sanders	.50	.23
❑ 44 Emmitt Smith	1.25	.55

❑ 45 Bubby Brister	.15	.07
❑ 46 Terrell Davis	1.25	.55
❑ 47 Brian Griese	1.00	.45
❑ 48 Ed McCaffrey	.30	.14
❑ 49 Shannon Sharpe	.30	.14
❑ 50 Rod Smith	.30	.14
❑ 51 Charlie Batch	1.00	.45
❑ 52 Sedrick Irvin RC	.50	.23
❑ 53 Herman Moore	.50	.23
❑ 54 Johnnie Morton	.30	.14
❑ 55 Barry Sanders	2.00	.90
❑ 56 Robert Brooks	.30	.14
❑ 57 Brett Favre	2.00	.90
❑ 58 Antonio Freeman	.50	.23
❑ 59 Dorsey Levens	.50	.23
❑ 60 Derrick Mayes	.15	.07
❑ 61 Marvin Harrison	.50	.23
❑ 62 Edgerrin James RC	10.00	4.50
❑ 63 Peyton Manning	2.00	.90
❑ 64 Jerome Pathon	.15	.07
❑ 65 Tavian Banks	.15	.07
❑ 66 Mark Brunell	.75	.35
❑ 67 Keenan McCardell	.30	.14
❑ 68 Jimmy Smith	.30	.14
❑ 69 Fred Taylor	1.25	.55
❑ 70 Derrick Alexander	.30	.14
❑ 71 Kimble Anders	.30	.14
❑ 72 Mike Cloud RC	1.50	.70
❑ 73 Elvis Grbac	.30	.14
❑ 74 Andre Rison	.30	.14
❑ 75 Karim Abdul-Jabbar	.30	.14
❑ 76 James Johnson RC	1.50	.70
❑ 77 Dan Marino	2.00	.90
❑ 78 O.J. McDuffie	.30	.14
❑ 79 Lamar Thomas	.15	.07
❑ 80 Cris Carter	.50	.23
❑ 81 Daunte Culpepper RC	10.00	4.50
❑ 82 Randall Cunningham	.50	.23
❑ 83 Randy Moss	2.00	.90
❑ 84 John Randle	.30	.14
❑ 85 Robert Smith	.50	.23
❑ 86 Drew Bledsoe	.75	.35
❑ 87 Ben Coates	.30	.14
❑ 88 Kevin Faulk RC	2.50	1.10
❑ 89 Terry Glenn	.50	.23
❑ 90 Ty Law	.15	.07
❑ 91 Cam Cleeland	.15	.07
❑ 92 Andre Hastings	.15	.07
❑ 93 Billy Joe Hobert	.15	.07
❑ 94 Ricky Williams RC	6.00	2.70
❑ 95 Tiki Barber	.15	.07
❑ 96 Kent Graham	.15	.07
❑ 97 Ike Hilliard	.15	.07
❑ 98 Charles Way	.15	.07
❑ 99 Wayne Chrebet	.30	.14
❑ 100 Keyshawn Johnson	.50	.23
❑ 101 Curtis Martin	.50	.23
❑ 102 Vinny Testaverde	.30	.14
❑ 103 Dedric Ward	.15	.07
❑ 104 Tim Brown	.50	.23
❑ 105 Rickey Dudley	.15	.07
❑ 106 James Jett	.30	.14
❑ 107 Napoleon Kaufman	.50	.23
❑ 108 Charles Woodson	.50	.23
❑ 109 Jeff Graham	.15	.07
❑ 110 Charles Johnson	.15	.07
❑ 111 Donovan McNabb RC	6.00	2.70
❑ 112 Duce Staley	.50	.23
❑ 113 Jerome Bettis	.50	.23
❑ 114 Troy Edwards RC	2.00	.90
❑ 115 Courtney Hawkins	.15	.07
❑ 116 Kordell Stewart	.50	.23
❑ 117 Amos Zereoue RC	1.50	.70
❑ 118 Isaac Bruce	.50	.23
❑ 119 Marshall Faulk	.50	.23
❑ 120 Joe Germaine RC	1.50	.70
❑ 121 Torry Holt RC	4.00	1.80
❑ 122 Amp Lee	.15	.07
❑ 123 Charlie Jones	.15	.07
❑ 124 Ryan Leaf	.50	.23
❑ 125 Natrone Means	.30	.14
❑ 126 Junior Seau	.30	.14
❑ 127 Garrison Hearst	.30	.14
❑ 128 Terrell Owens	.50	.23
❑ 129 Jerry Rice	1.25	.55
❑ 130 J.J. Stokes	.30	.14
❑ 131 Steve Young	.75	.35
❑ 132 Chad Brown	.15	.07
❑ 133 Joey Galloway	.50	.23
❑ 134 Brock Huard RC	2.50	1.10
❑ 135 Jon Kitna	.50	.23
❑ 136 Ricky Watters	.30	.14
❑ 137 Mike Alstott	.50	.23
❑ 138 Reidel Anthony	.30	.14
❑ 139 Trent Dilfer	.30	.14
❑ 140 Warrick Dunn	.50	.23
❑ 141 Jacquez Green	.30	.14
❑ 142 Shaun King RC	3.00	1.35
❑ 143 Eddie George	.60	.25
❑ 144 Steve McNair	.50	.23
❑ 145 Yancey Thigpen	.15	.07
❑ 146 Frank Wycheck	.15	.07
❑ 147 Champ Bailey RC	2.00	.90
❑ 148 Skip Hicks	.50	.23
❑ 149 Brad Johnson	.50	.23
❑ 150 Michael Westbrook	.30	.14
❑ AU1 Terrell Owens AUTO/197	50.00	22.00

2000 Aurora

	MINT	NRMT
COMPLETE SET (150)	30.00	13.50
COMP.PINSTRIPE SET (50)	50.00	22.00
❑ 1 David Boston	.50	.23
❑ 2 Thomas Jones RC	1.50	.70
❑ 3 Rob Moore	.25	.11
❑ 4 Jake Plummer	.50	.23
❑ 5 Frank Sanders	.25	.11
❑ 6 Jamal Anderson	.50	.23
❑ 7 Chris Chandler	.25	.11
❑ 8 Tim Dwight	.50	.23
❑ 9 Doug Johnson RC	1.00	.45
❑ 10 Tony Banks	.25	.11
❑ 11 Qadry Ismail	.15	.07
❑ 12 Jamal Lewis RC	5.00	2.20
❑ 13 Chris Redman RC	2.00	.90
❑ 14 Travis Taylor RC	1.25	.55
❑ 15 Doug Flutie	.60	.25
❑ 16 Rob Johnson	.25	.11
❑ 17 Eric Moulds	.50	.23
❑ 18 Peerless Price	.50	.23
❑ 19 Antowain Smith	.25	.11
❑ 20 Steve Beuerlein	.25	.11
❑ 21 Tim Biakabutuka	.25	.11
❑ 22 Patrick Jeffers	.50	.23
❑ 23 Muhsin Muhammad	.25	.11
❑ 24 Curtis Enis	.25	.11
❑ 25 Cade McNown	.50	.23
❑ 26 Marcus Robinson	.50	.23
❑ 27 Dez White RC	.75	.35
❑ 28 Corey Dillon	.50	.23
❑ 29 Ron Dugans RC	.75	.35
❑ 30 Darnay Scott	.25	.11
❑ 31 Akili Smith	.50	.23
❑ 32 Peter Warrick RC	3.00	1.35
❑ 33 Tim Couch	1.00	.45
❑ 34 JaJuan Dawson RC	1.00	.45
❑ 35 Kevin Johnson	.50	.23
❑ 36 Dennis Northcutt RC	1.25	.55
❑ 37 Travis Prentice RC	1.50	.70
❑ 38 Troy Aikman	1.25	.55
❑ 39 Rocket Ismail	.25	.11
❑ 40 Emmitt Smith	1.25	.55
❑ 41 Jason Tucker	.15	.07
❑ 42 Terrell Davis	1.25	.55
❑ 43 Olandis Gary	.50	.23
❑ 44 Brian Griese	.60	.25
❑ 45 Ed McCaffrey	.50	.23
❑ 46 Rod Smith	.25	.11
❑ 47 Charlie Batch	.50	.23
❑ 48 Germane Crowell	.25	.11
❑ 49 Reuben Droughns RC	1.00	.45
❑ 50 Herman Moore	.25	.11
❑ 51 Barry Sanders	1.50	.70
❑ 52 Brett Favre	2.00	.90
❑ 53 Bubba Franks RC	1.25	.55
❑ 54 Antonio Freeman	.50	.23
❑ 55 Dorsey Levens	.25	.11
❑ 56 Bill Schroeder	.25	.11
❑ 57 Marvin Harrison	.50	.23
❑ 58 Edgerrin James	2.00	.90
❑ 59 Peyton Manning	1.50	.70
❑ 60 Terrence Wilkins	.50	.23
❑ 61 Mark Brunell	.75	.35
❑ 62 Keenan McCardell	.25	.11
❑ 63 Jimmy Smith	.25	.11
❑ 64 R.Jay Soward RC	1.00	.45
❑ 65 Shyrone Stith RC	1.00	.45
❑ 66 Fred Taylor	.60	.25
❑ 67 Derrick Alexander	.25	.11
❑ 68 Donnell Bennett	.15	.07
❑ 69 Tony Gonzalez	.25	.11
❑ 70 Elvis Grbac	.25	.11
❑ 71 Sylvester Morris RC	2.00	.90
❑ 72 Damon Huard	.50	.23
❑ 73 James Johnson	.25	.11
❑ 74 Dan Marino	2.00	.90
❑ 75 Tony Martin	.25	.11
❑ 76 O.J. McDuffie	.25	.11
❑ 77 Quinton Spotwood RC	.75	.35
❑ 78 Cris Carter	.50	.23
❑ 79 Daunte Culpepper	1.00	.45
❑ 80 Randy Moss	1.50	.70
❑ 81 Robert Smith	.50	.23
❑ 82 Troy Walters RC	1.00	.45
❑ 83 Drew Bledsoe	.75	.35
❑ 84 Tom Brady RC	1.00	.45
❑ 85 Kevin Faulk	.25	.11
❑ 86 Terry Glenn	.25	.11
❑ 87 J.R. Redmond RC	1.25	.55
❑ 88 Marc Bulger RC	1.00	.45
❑ 89 Sherrod Gideon RC	.75	.35
❑ 90 Keith Poole	.15	.07
❑ 91 Ricky Williams	1.25	.55
❑ 92 Kerry Collins	.25	.11
❑ 93 Ron Dayne RC	3.00	1.35
❑ 94 Ike Hilliard	.25	.11
❑ 95 Amani Toomer	.15	.07
❑ 96 Wayne Chrebet	.25	.11
❑ 97 Laveranues Coles RC	1.50	.70
❑ 98 Curtis Martin	.50	.23
❑ 99 Chad Pennington RC	3.00	1.35
❑ 100 Vinny Testaverde	.25	.11
❑ 101 Tim Brown	.50	.23
❑ 102 Rich Gannon	.25	.11
❑ 103 Napoleon Kaufman	.25	.11
❑ 104 Jerry Porter RC	1.00	.45
❑ 105 Tyrone Wheatley	.25	.11
❑ 106 Charles Johnson	.25	.11
❑ 107 Donovan McNabb	.75	.35
❑ 108 Todd Pinkston RC	1.00	.45
❑ 109 Duce Staley	.50	.23
❑ 110 Jerome Bettis	.50	.23
❑ 111 Plaxico Burress RC	2.00	.90
❑ 112 Troy Edwards	.25	.11
❑ 113 Richard Huntley	.15	.07
❑ 114 Tee Martin RC	1.50	.70
❑ 115 Kordell Stewart	.50	.23
❑ 116 Isaac Bruce	.50	.23
❑ 117 Trung Canidate RC	1.00	.45
❑ 118 Marshall Faulk	.60	.25
❑ 119 Torry Holt	.50	.23
❑ 120 Kurt Warner	2.00	.90
❑ 121 Jermaine Fazande	.15	.07
❑ 122 Trevor Gaylor RC	.75	.35
❑ 123 Jim Harbaugh	.25	.11
❑ 124 Junior Seau	.25	.11
❑ 125 Giovanni Carmazzi RC	1.25	.55
❑ 126 Charlie Garner	.25	.11

❑ 127	Terrell Owens	.50	.23
❑ 128	Jerry Rice	1.25	.55
❑ 129	J.J. Stokes	.25	.11
❑ 130	Steve Young	.75	.35
❑ 131	Shaun Alexander RC	2.50	1.10
❑ 132	Christian Fauria	.15	.07
❑ 133	Jon Kitna	.50	.23
❑ 134	Derrick Mayes	.25	.11
❑ 135	Ricky Watters	.15	.07
❑ 136	Mike Alstott	.50	.23
❑ 137	Warrick Dunn	.50	.23
❑ 138	Jacquez Green	.25	.11
❑ 139	Joe Hamilton RC	1.25	.55
❑ 140	Shaun King	.75	.35
❑ 141	Eddie George	.60	.25
❑ 142	Jevon Kearse	.50	.23
❑ 143	Steve McNair	.50	.23
❑ 144	Yancey Thigpen	.15	.07
❑ 145	Frank Wycheck	.15	.07
❑ 146	Albert Connell	.15	.07
❑ 147	Stephen Davis	.50	.23
❑ 148	Todd Husak RC	.75	.35
❑ 149	Brad Johnson	.50	.23
❑ 150	Michael Westbrook	.25	.11
❑ S1	Jon Kitna Sample	1.00	.45

1997 Black Diamond

	MINT	NRMT
COMPLETE SET (180)	300.00	135.00
COMP.SERIES 1 (90)	25.00	11.00
COMMON CARD (1-90)	.20	.09
COMMON DOUBLE (91-150)	1.25	.55
COMMON TRIPLE (151-180)	5.00	2.20

❑ 1	Alfred Williams	.20	.09
❑ 2	Alvin Harper	.20	.09
❑ 3	Andre Hastings	.20	.09
❑ 4	Andre Reed	.40	.18
❑ 5	Anthony Johnson	.20	.09
❑ 6	Anthony Miller	.20	.09
❑ 7	Byron Bam Morris	.20	.09
❑ 8	Bobby Hebert	.20	.09
❑ 9	Bobby Taylor	.20	.09
❑ 10	Boomer Esiason	.40	.18
❑ 11	Brett Perriman	.20	.09
❑ 12	Brian Blades	.20	.09
❑ 13	Bryan Cox	.20	.09
❑ 14	Bryant Young	.20	.09
❑ 15	Bryce Paup	.20	.09
❑ 16	Carnell Lake	.20	.09
❑ 17	Cedric Jones	.20	.09
❑ 18	Chad Brown	.20	.09
❑ 19	Charlie Garner	.20	.09
❑ 20	Chris Chandler	.40	.18
❑ 21	Cornelius Bennett	.20	.09
❑ 22	Cortez Kennedy	.20	.09
❑ 23	Cris Carter	.75	.35
❑ 24	Dale Carter	.20	.09
❑ 25	Daryl Gardener	.20	.09
❑ 26	Derrick Alexander WR	.40	.18
❑ 27	Derrick Mayes	.40	.18
❑ 28	Don Beebe	.20	.09
❑ 29	Eric Allen	.20	.09
❑ 30	Eric Moulds	.75	.35
❑ 31	Errict Rhett	.20	.09
❑ 32	Frank Sanders	.40	.18
❑ 33	Glyn Milburn	.20	.09
❑ 34	Henry Ellard	.20	.09
❑ 35	Jamal Anderson	1.25	.55
❑ 36	James O. Stewart	.40	.18
❑ 37	Jason Dunn	.20	.09
❑ 38	Jerry Rice	3.00	1.35
❑ 39	Jim Everett	.20	.09
❑ 40	Jim Kelly	.75	.35
❑ 41	Joey Galloway	1.00	.45
❑ 42	John Carney	.20	.09
❑ 43	John Elway	5.00	2.20
❑ 44	John Randle	.40	.18
❑ 45	Karim Abdul-Jabbar	.75	.35
❑ 46	Keenan McCardell	.40	.18
❑ 47	Ken Dilger	.20	.09
❑ 48	Ken Norton	.20	.09
❑ 49	Ki-Jana Carter	.20	.09
❑ 50	Kordell Stewart	1.00	.45
❑ 51	Lawrence Phillips	.20	.09
❑ 52	Leslie O'Neal	.20	.09
❑ 53	Mark Chmura	.40	.18
❑ 54	Marshall Faulk	.75	.35
❑ 55	Michael Haynes	.20	.09
❑ 56	Michael Irvin	.75	.35
❑ 57	Michael Jackson	.40	.18
❑ 58	Michael Westbrook	.40	.18
❑ 59	Mike Tomczak	.20	.09
❑ 60	Napoleon Kaufman	.75	.35
❑ 61	Neil O'Donnell	.40	.18
❑ 62	Neil Smith	.40	.18
❑ 63	O.J. McDuffie	.40	.18
❑ 64	Orlando Thomas	.20	.09
❑ 65	Rashaan Salaam	.20	.09
❑ 66	Regan Upshaw	.20	.09
❑ 67	Rick Mirer	.20	.09
❑ 68	Rob Moore	.40	.18
❑ 69	Ronnie Harmon	.20	.09
❑ 70	Sam Mills	.20	.09
❑ 71	Sean Dawkins	.20	.09
❑ 72	Shawn Jefferson	.20	.09
❑ 73	Stan Humphries	.40	.18
❑ 74	Stepfret Williams	.20	.09
❑ 75	Stephen Davis	2.00	.90
❑ 76	Steve Atwater	.20	.09
❑ 77	Terance Mathis	.40	.18
❑ 78	Terrell Fletcher	.20	.09
❑ 79	Terry Glenn	.75	.35
❑ 80	Terry McDaniel	.20	.09
❑ 81	Tony McGee	.20	.09
❑ 82	Trent Dilfer	.75	.35
❑ 83	Troy Drayton	.20	.09
❑ 84	Ty Detmer	.40	.18
❑ 85	Tyrone Hughes	.20	.09
❑ 86	Walt Harris	.20	.09
❑ 87	Wayne Chrebet	.75	.35
❑ 88	Wesley Walls	.40	.18
❑ 89	Willie Davis	.20	.09
❑ 90	Willie McGinest	.20	.09
❑ 91	Adrian Murrell	3.00	1.35
❑ 92	Alex Molden	1.25	.55
❑ 93	Alex Van Dyke	2.00	.90
❑ 94	Andre Coleman	1.25	.55
❑ 95	Ben Coates	3.00	1.35
❑ 96	Bobby Engram	2.00	.90
❑ 97	Bruce Smith	3.00	1.35
❑ 98	Charles Johnson	3.00	1.35
❑ 99	Chris Sanders	3.00	1.35
❑ 100	Chris T. Jones	3.00	1.35
❑ 101	Chris Warren	2.00	.90
❑ 102	Darnay Scott	3.00	1.35
❑ 103	Dave Brown	2.00	.90
❑ 104	Derrick Thomas	3.00	1.35
❑ 105	Drew Bledsoe	10.00	4.50
❑ 106	Edgar Bennett	3.00	1.35
❑ 107	Emmitt Smith	15.00	6.75
❑ 108	Eric Bjornson	1.25	.55
❑ 109	Eric Metcalf	3.00	1.35
❑ 110	Garrison Hearst	2.00	.90
❑ 111	Gus Frerotte	2.00	.90
❑ 112	Hardy Nickerson	1.25	.55
❑ 113	Herman Moore	3.00	1.35
❑ 114	Hugh Douglas	1.25	.55
❑ 115	Irving Fryar	2.00	.90
❑ 116	J.J. Stokes	2.00	.90
❑ 117	Jake Reed	2.00	.90
❑ 118	Jeff Hostetler	2.00	.90
❑ 119	Jeff Lewis	2.00	.90
❑ 120	Jim Harbaugh	2.00	.90
❑ 121	Johnnie Morton	2.00	.90
❑ 122	Jonathan Ogden	1.25	.55
❑ 123	Kevin Carter	2.00	.90
❑ 124	Kevin Greene	2.00	.90
❑ 125	Kevin Hardy	2.00	.90
❑ 126	Leeland McElroy	2.00	.90
❑ 127	Mike Alstott	3.00	1.35
❑ 128	Muhsin Muhammad	3.00	1.35
❑ 129	Natrone Means	2.00	.90
❑ 130	Quentin Coryatt	1.25	.55
❑ 131	Ray Lewis	2.00	.90
❑ 132	Ray Zellars	1.25	.55
❑ 133	Rickey Dudley	2.00	.90
❑ 134	Ricky Watters	2.00	.90
❑ 135	Robert Smith	3.00	1.35
❑ 136	Scott Mitchell	2.00	.90
❑ 137	Sean Gilbert	1.25	.55
❑ 138	Shannon Sharpe	2.00	.90
❑ 139	Simeon Rice	2.00	.90
❑ 140	Stanley Pritchett	1.25	.55
❑ 141	Steve McNair	5.00	2.20
❑ 142	Steve Young	8.00	3.60
❑ 143	Tamarick Vanover	2.00	.90
❑ 144	Terry Allen	2.00	.90
❑ 145	Thurman Thomas	3.00	1.35
❑ 146	Tony Banks	3.00	1.35
❑ 147	Tony Martin	2.00	.90
❑ 148	Tyrone Wheatley	3.00	1.35
❑ 149	Vinny Testaverde	2.00	.90
❑ 150	Zach Thomas	3.00	1.35
❑ 151	Amani Toomer	8.00	3.60
❑ 152	Barry Sanders	30.00	13.50
❑ 153	Bobby Hoying	8.00	3.60
❑ 154	Brett Favre	30.00	13.50
❑ 155	Carl Pickens	8.00	3.60
❑ 156	Curtis Conway	8.00	3.60
❑ 157	Curtis Martin	12.00	5.50
❑ 158	Dan Marino	30.00	13.50
❑ 159	Deion Sanders	8.00	3.60
❑ 160	Eddie George	15.00	6.75
❑ 161	Eddie Kennison	5.00	2.20
❑ 162	Elvis Grbac	8.00	3.60
❑ 163	Isaac Bruce	8.00	3.60
❑ 164	Jeff Blake	5.00	2.20
❑ 165	Jerome Bettis	8.00	3.60
❑ 166	Junior Seau	5.00	2.20
❑ 167	Kerry Collins	5.00	2.20
❑ 168	Keyshawn Johnson	8.00	3.60
❑ 169	Larry Centers	5.00	2.20
❑ 170	Marcus Allen	8.00	3.60
❑ 171	Mark Brunell	15.00	6.75
❑ 172	Marvin Harrison	8.00	3.60
❑ 173	Reggie White	8.00	3.60
❑ 174	Rodney Hampton	5.00	2.20
❑ 175	Terrell Davis	25.00	11.00
❑ 176	Tim Brown	8.00	3.60
❑ 177	Todd Collins	5.00	2.20
❑ 178	Troy Aikman	15.00	6.75
❑ 179	Tim Biakabutuka	5.00	2.20
❑ 180	Warren Moon	8.00	3.60
❑ BD1	Troy Aikman Promo	2.00	.90

1998 Black Diamond

	MINT	NRMT
COMPLETE SET (150)	40.00	18.00

❑ 1	Kent Graham	.20	.09
❑ 2	Darrell Russell	.20	.09
❑ 3	Jim Harbaugh	.40	.18

❑ 4 Cornelius Bennett .20 .09
❑ 5 Troy Vincent .20 .09
❑ 6 Natrone Means .75 .35
❑ 7 Michael Jackson .20 .09
❑ 8 Will Blackwell .20 .09
❑ 9 Greg Hill .20 .09
❑ 10 Andre Reed .40 .18
❑ 11 Darren Bennett .20 .09
❑ 12 Dan Marino 4.00 1.80
❑ 13 Tim Biakabutuka .40 .18
❑ 14 Terrell Owens .75 .35
❑ 15 Cris Carter .75 .35
❑ 16 Darnell Autry .20 .09
❑ 17 Joey Galloway .75 .35
❑ 18 Terry Glenn .75 .35
❑ 19 Ki-Jana Carter .20 .09
❑ 20 Isaac Bruce .75 .35
❑ 21 Shawn Jefferson .20 .09
❑ 22 Michael Irvin .75 .35
❑ 23 Warren Sapp .40 .18
❑ 24 Dave Brown .20 .09
❑ 25 Terrell Davis 3.00 1.35
❑ 26 Frank Wycheck .20 .09
❑ 27 Neil O'Donnell .40 .18
❑ 28 Scott Mitchell .40 .18
❑ 29 Michael Westbrook .40 .18
❑ 30 Tim Brown .75 .35
❑ 31 Antonio Freeman .75 .35
❑ 32 Jake Plummer 1.50 .70
❑ 33 Irving Fryar .40 .18
❑ 34 Quentin Coryatt .20 .09
❑ 35 Jamal Anderson .75 .35
❑ 36 Jerome Bettis .75 .35
❑ 37 Keenan McCardell .40 .18
❑ 38 Derrick Alexander WR .40 .18
❑ 39 Stan Humphries .20 .09
❑ 40 Andre Rison .40 .18
❑ 41 Bruce Smith .40 .18
❑ 42 Garrison Hearst .75 .35
❑ 43 Zach Thomas .40 .18
❑ 44 Rae Carruth .40 .18
❑ 45 Kevin Greene .40 .18
❑ 46 Robert Smith .75 .35
❑ 47 Curtis Conway .40 .18
❑ 48 Christian Fauria .20 .09
❑ 49 Curtis Martin .75 .35
❑ 50 Dan Wilkinson .20 .09
❑ 51 Eddie Kennison .40 .18
❑ 52 Mark Fields .20 .09
❑ 53 Anthony Miller .20 .09
❑ 54 Mike Alstott .75 .35
❑ 55 Tiki Barber .40 .18
❑ 56 Neil Smith .40 .18
❑ 57 Gus Frerotte .20 .09
❑ 58 Adrian Murrell .40 .18
❑ 59 Johnnie Morton .40 .18
❑ 60 O.J. McDuffie .40 .18
❑ 61 Napoleon Kaufman .75 .35
❑ 62 Robert Brooks .40 .18
❑ 63 Byron Hanspard .40 .18
❑ 64 Ty Detmer .40 .18
❑ 65 Mark Brunell 1.50 .70
❑ 66 Byron Bam Morris .20 .09
❑ 67 Kordell Stewart .75 .35
❑ 68 Elvis Grbac .40 .18
❑ 69 Antowain Smith .75 .35
❑ 70 Junior Seau .40 .18
❑ 71 Tony Gonzalez .20 .09
❑ 72 Anthony Johnson .20 .09
❑ 73 Steve Young 1.25 .55
❑ 74 Brian Manning .20 .09
❑ 75 Erik Kramer .20 .09
❑ 76 Warren Moon .75 .35
❑ 77 Torrian Gray .20 .09
❑ 78 Carl Pickens .75 .35
❑ 79 Tony Banks .40 .18
❑ 80 Willie McGinest .20 .09
❑ 81 Deion Sanders .75 .35
❑ 82 Warrick Dunn .75 .35
❑ 83 Danny Wuerffel .40 .18
❑ 84 Rod Smith WR .40 .18
❑ 85 Steve McNair .75 .35
❑ 86 Danny Kanell .40 .18
❑ 87 Herman Moore .75 .35
❑ 88 Brian Mitchell .20 .09
❑ 89 James Farrior .20 .09
❑ 90 Reggie White .75 .35
❑ 91 Simeon Rice .40 .18
❑ 92 James Jett .40 .18
❑ 93 Marshall Faulk .75 .35
❑ 94 Chris Chandler .40 .18
❑ 95 Mike Mamula .20 .09
❑ 96 Jimmy Smith .40 .18
❑ 97 Jamie Sharper .20 .09
❑ 98 Carnell Lake .20 .09
❑ 99 Marcus Allen .75 .35
❑ 100 Thurman Thomas .75 .35
❑ 101 Freddie Jones .20 .09
❑ 102 Karim Abdul-Jabbar .75 .35
❑ 103 Kerry Collins .40 .18
❑ 104 Jerry Rice 2.00 .90
❑ 105 Brad Johnson .75 .35
❑ 106 Raymont Harris .20 .09
❑ 107 Lamar Smith .40 .18
❑ 108 Drew Bledsoe 1.50 .70
❑ 109 Corey Dillon 1.25 .55
❑ 110 Lawrence Phillips .20 .09
❑ 111 Heath Shuler .20 .09
❑ 112 Emmitt Smith 3.00 1.35
❑ 113 Reidel Anthony .40 .18
❑ 114 Ike Hilliard .40 .18
❑ 115 Shannon Sharpe .40 .18
❑ 116 Chris Sanders .20 .09
❑ 117 Keyshawn Johnson .75 .35
❑ 118 Barry Sanders 4.00 1.80
❑ 119 Cris Dishman .20 .09
❑ 120 Jeff George .40 .18
❑ 121 Dorsey Levens .75 .35
❑ 122 Rob Moore .40 .18
❑ 123 Ricky Watters .40 .18
❑ 124 Marvin Harrison .40 .18
❑ 125 Vinny Testaverde .40 .18
❑ 126 Charles Johnson .20 .09
❑ 127 Renaldo Wynn .20 .09
❑ 128 Todd Collins QB .20 .09
❑ 129 Tony Martin .40 .18
❑ 130 Derrick Thomas .40 .18
❑ 131 Wesley Walls .40 .18
❑ 132 Rod Woodson .40 .18
❑ 133 Troy Drayton .20 .09
❑ 134 Bryan Cox .20 .09
❑ 135 Shawn Springs .20 .09
❑ 136 Jake Reed .40 .18
❑ 137 Jeff Blake .40 .18
❑ 138 Craig Heyward .20 .09
❑ 139 Ben Coates .40 .18
❑ 140 Troy Aikman 2.00 .90
❑ 141 Trent Dilfer .75 .35
❑ 142 Troy Davis .20 .09
❑ 143 John Elway 4.00 1.80
❑ 144 Eddie George 1.50 .70
❑ 145 Rodney Hampton .40 .18
❑ 146 Ed McCaffrey .40 .18
❑ 147 Terry Allen .75 .35
❑ 148 Wayne Chrebet .75 .35
❑ 149 Brett Favre 4.00 1.80
❑ 150 Daryl Johnston .40 .18

1998 Black Diamond Rookies

	MINT	NRMT
COMPLETE SET (120)	100.00	45.00
COMMON ROOKIE (91-120)	1.50	.70

❑ 1 Jake Plummer 1.00 .45
❑ 2 Adrian Murrell .30 .14
❑ 3 Frank Sanders .30 .14
❑ 4 Jamal Anderson .60 .25
❑ 5 Chris Chandler .30 .14
❑ 6 Tony Martin .30 .14
❑ 7 Jim Harbaugh .30 .14
❑ 8 Errict Rhett .30 .14
❑ 9 Michael Jackson .15 .07
❑ 10 Rob Johnson .30 .14
❑ 11 Antowain Smith .60 .25
❑ 12 Thurman Thomas .60 .25
❑ 13 Fred Lane .30 .14
❑ 14 Kerry Collins .15 .07
❑ 15 Rae Carruth .30 .14
❑ 16 Erik Kramer .15 .07
❑ 17 Edgar Bennett .15 .07
❑ 18 Curtis Conway .30 .14
❑ 19 Corey Dillon 1.00 .45
❑ 20 Neil O'Donnell .30 .14
❑ 21 Carl Pickens .60 .25
❑ 22 Troy Aikman 1.50 .70
❑ 23 Emmitt Smith 2.50 1.10
❑ 24 Deion Sanders .60 .25
❑ 25 John Elway 3.00 1.35
❑ 26 Terrell Davis 2.50 1.10
❑ 27 Rod Smith .30 .14
❑ 28 Barry Sanders 3.00 1.35
❑ 29 Johnnie Morton .30 .14
❑ 30 Herman Moore .60 .25
❑ 31 Brett Favre 3.00 1.35
❑ 32 Antonio Freeman .60 .25
❑ 33 Dorsey Levens .60 .25
❑ 34 Marshall Faulk .60 .25
❑ 35 Marvin Harrison .30 .14
❑ 36 Zack Crockett .15 .07
❑ 37 Mark Brunell 1.25 .55
❑ 38 Jimmy Smith .30 .14
❑ 39 Keenan McCardell .30 .14
❑ 40 Elvis Grbac .30 .14
❑ 41 Andre Rison .30 .14
❑ 42 Derrick Alexander .30 .14
❑ 43 Dan Marino 3.00 1.35
❑ 44 Karim Abdul-Jabbar .60 .25
❑ 45 Zach Thomas .30 .14
❑ 46 Brad Johnson .60 .25
❑ 47 Cris Carter .60 .25
❑ 48 Robert Smith .60 .25
❑ 49 Drew Bledsoe 1.25 .55
❑ 50 Terry Glenn .60 .25
❑ 51 Ben Coates .30 .14
❑ 52 Danny Wuerffel .30 .14
❑ 53 Lamar Smith .30 .14
❑ 54 Sean Dawkins .15 .07
❑ 55 Danny Kanell .30 .14
❑ 56 Tiki Barber .30 .14
❑ 57 Ike Hilliard .30 .14
❑ 58 Curtis Martin .60 .25
❑ 59 Vinny Testaverde .30 .14
❑ 60 Keyshawn Johnson .60 .25
❑ 61 Napoleon Kaufman .60 .25
❑ 62 Jeff George .30 .14
❑ 63 Tim Brown .60 .25
❑ 64 Bobby Hoying .30 .14
❑ 65 Charlie Garner .15 .07
❑ 66 Duce Staley 1.00 .45
❑ 67 Kordell Stewart .60 .25
❑ 68 Jerome Bettis .60 .25
❑ 69 Charles Johnson .15 .07
❑ 70 Tony Banks .30 .14
❑ 71 Isaac Bruce .60 .25
❑ 72 Eddie Kennison .30 .14
❑ 73 Natrone Means .60 .25
❑ 74 Bryan Still .15 .07
❑ 75 Junior Seau .30 .14
❑ 76 Steve Young 1.00 .45
❑ 77 Jerry Rice 1.50 .70
❑ 78 Garrison Hearst .60 .25
❑ 79 Ricky Watters .30 .14
❑ 80 Joey Galloway .60 .25
❑ 81 Warren Moon .15 .07
❑ 82 Warrick Dunn .60 .25
❑ 83 Trent Dilfer .60 .25
❑ 84 Bert Emanuel .30 .14
❑ 85 Steve McNair .60 .25
❑ 86 Eddie George 1.25 .55

	MINT	NRMT
❑ 87 Yancey Thigpen	.15	.07
❑ 88 Leslie Shepherd	.15	.07
❑ 89 Terry Allen	.60	.25
❑ 90 Michael Westbrook	.30	.14
❑ 91 Peyton Manning RC	20.00	9.00
❑ 92 Jacquez Green RC	4.00	1.80
❑ 93 Fred Taylor RC	8.00	3.60
❑ 94 Terry Fair RC	2.50	1.10
❑ 95 Pat Johnson RC	4.00	1.80
❑ 96 Corey Chavous RC	1.50	.70
❑ 97 Randy Moss RC	20.00	9.00
❑ 98 Curtis Enis RC	4.00	1.80
❑ 99 Rashaan Shehee RC	2.50	1.10
❑ 100 Kevin Dyson RC	4.00	1.80
❑ 101 Shaun Williams RC	1.50	.70
❑ 102 Grant Wistrom RC	1.50	.70
❑ 103 John Avery RC	4.00	1.80
❑ 104 Brian Griese RC	10.00	4.50
❑ 105 Ryan Leaf RC	6.00	2.70
❑ 106 Jerome Pathon RC	2.50	1.10
❑ 107 Sam Cowart RC	1.50	.70
❑ 108 Germane Crowell RC	5.00	2.20
❑ 109 Ahman Green RC	6.00	2.70
❑ 110 Greg Ellis RC	1.50	.70
❑ 111 Robert Holcombe RC	4.00	1.80
❑ 112 Marcus Nash RC	4.00	1.80
❑ 113 Duane Starks RC	1.50	.70
❑ 114 Andre Wadsworth RC	2.50	1.10
❑ 115 Takeo Spikes RC	2.50	1.10
❑ 116 Eric Brown RC	1.50	.70
❑ 117 Robert Edwards RC	5.00	2.20
❑ 118 Charlie Batch RC	8.00	3.60
❑ 119 Mikhael Ricks RC	2.50	1.10
❑ 120 Charles Woodson RC	4.00	1.80
❑ S13 Dan Marino SAMPLE	2.00	.90

1999 Black Diamond

	MINT	NRMT
COMPLETE SET (150)	120.00	55.00
COMP.SET w/o SPs (110)	20.00	9.00
COMMON ROOKIE (111-150)	2.00	.90

	MINT	NRMT
❑ 1 Adrian Murrell	.40	.18
❑ 2 Jake Plummer	1.50	.70
❑ 3 Rob Moore	.40	.18
❑ 4 Frank Sanders	.40	.18
❑ 5 Jamal Anderson	.75	.35
❑ 6 Terance Mathis	.40	.18
❑ 7 Chris Chandler	.40	.18
❑ 8 Tim Dwight	.75	.35
❑ 9 Jermaine Lewis	.40	.18
❑ 10 Priest Holmes	.75	.35
❑ 11 Peter Boulware	.20	.09
❑ 12 Doug Flutie	1.00	.45
❑ 13 Antowain Smith	.75	.35
❑ 14 Eric Moulds	.75	.35
❑ 15 Bruce Smith	.40	.18
❑ 16 Rae Carruth	.40	.18
❑ 17 Muhsin Muhammad	.40	.18
❑ 18 Wesley Walls	.40	.18
❑ 19 Tim Biakabutuka	.40	.18
❑ 20 Curtis Enis	.75	.35
❑ 21 Curtis Conway	.40	.18
❑ 22 Bobby Engram	.40	.18
❑ 23 Damay Scott	.20	.09
❑ 24 Corey Dillon	.75	.35
❑ 25 Jeff Blake	.40	.18
❑ 26 Ty Detmer	.40	.18
❑ 27 Terry Kirby	.20	.09
❑ 28 Leslie Shepherd	.20	.09
❑ 29 Emmitt Smith	2.00	.90
❑ 30 Troy Aikman	2.00	.90
❑ 31 Michael Irvin	.40	.18
❑ 32 Rocket Ismail	.40	.18
❑ 33 Brian Griese	1.50	.70
❑ 34 Terrell Davis	2.00	.90
❑ 35 Shannon Sharpe	.40	.18
❑ 36 Rod Smith	.40	.18
❑ 37 Barry Sanders	3.00	1.35
❑ 38 Herman Moore	.75	.35
❑ 39 Charlie Batch	1.50	.70
❑ 40 Johnnie Morton	.40	.18
❑ 41 Brett Favre	3.00	1.35
❑ 42 Dorsey Levens	.75	.35
❑ 43 Antonio Freeman	.75	.35
❑ 44 Mark Chmura	.20	.09
❑ 45 Peyton Manning	3.00	1.35
❑ 46 Jerome Pathon	.20	.09
❑ 47 Marvin Harrison	.75	.35
❑ 48 Fred Taylor	2.00	.90
❑ 49 Mark Brunell	1.25	.55
❑ 50 Jimmy Smith	.40	.18
❑ 51 Keenan McCardell	.40	.18
❑ 52 Andre Rison	.40	.18
❑ 53 Elvis Grbac	.40	.18
❑ 54 Derrick Alexander WR	.40	.18
❑ 55 Tony Gonzalez	.40	.18
❑ 56 Dan Marino	3.00	1.35
❑ 57 Oronde Gadsden	.20	.09
❑ 58 O.J. McDuffie	.40	.18
❑ 59 Randy Moss	3.00	1.35
❑ 60 Randall Cunningham	.75	.35
❑ 61 Cris Carter	.75	.35
❑ 62 Robert Smith	.75	.35
❑ 63 Drew Bledsoe	1.25	.55
❑ 64 Terry Glenn	.75	.35
❑ 65 Ben Coates	.40	.18
❑ 66 Billy Joe Hobert	.20	.09
❑ 67 Eddie Kennison	.40	.18
❑ 68 Cam Cleeland	.20	.09
❑ 69 Gary Brown	.20	.09
❑ 70 Ike Hilliard	.20	.09
❑ 71 Amani Toomer	.20	.09
❑ 72 Vinny Testaverde	.40	.18
❑ 73 Keyshawn Johnson	.75	.35
❑ 74 Curtis Martin	.75	.35
❑ 75 Wayne Chrebet	.40	.18
❑ 76 Tim Brown	.75	.35
❑ 77 Rickey Dudley	.20	.09
❑ 78 Napoleon Kaufman	.75	.35
❑ 79 Charles Woodson	.75	.35
❑ 80 Duce Staley	.75	.35
❑ 81 Doug Pederson	.20	.09
❑ 82 Charles Johnson	.20	.09
❑ 83 Kordell Stewart	.75	.35
❑ 84 Jerome Bettis	.75	.35
❑ 85 Courtney Hawkins	.20	.09
❑ 86 Isaac Bruce	.75	.35
❑ 87 Marshall Faulk	.75	.35
❑ 88 Trent Green	.40	.18
❑ 89 Jim Harbaugh	.40	.18
❑ 90 Junior Seau	.40	.18
❑ 91 Natrone Means	.40	.18
❑ 92 Lawrence Phillips	.40	.18
❑ 93 Steve Young	1.25	.55
❑ 94 Terrell Owens	.75	.35
❑ 95 Jerry Rice	2.00	.90
❑ 96 Jon Kitna	.75	.35
❑ 97 Ricky Watters	.40	.18
❑ 98 Joey Galloway	.75	.35
❑ 99 Shawn Springs	.20	.09
❑ 100 Warrick Dunn	.75	.35
❑ 101 Trent Dilfer	.40	.18
❑ 102 Reidel Anthony	.40	.18
❑ 103 Mike Alstott	.75	.35
❑ 104 Steve McNair	.75	.35
❑ 105 Eddie George	1.00	.45
❑ 106 Kevin Dyson	.40	.18
❑ 107 Yancey Thigpen	.20	.09
❑ 108 Michael Westbrook	.40	.18
❑ 109 Brad Johnson	.75	.35
❑ 110 Skip Hicks	.75	.35
❑ 111 Tim Couch RC	15.00	6.75
❑ 112 Akili Smith RC	8.00	3.60
❑ 113 Ricky Williams RC	15.00	6.75
❑ 114 Donovan McNabb RC	15.00	6.75
❑ 115 Edgerrin James RC	20.00	9.00
❑ 116 Cade McNown RC	5.00	2.20
❑ 117 Daunte Culpepper RC	20.00	9.00
❑ 118 Shaun King RC	8.00	3.60
❑ 119 Brock Huard RC	6.00	2.70
❑ 120 Joe Germaine RC	4.00	1.80
❑ 121 Troy Edwards RC	5.00	2.20
❑ 122 Champ Bailey RC	5.00	2.20
❑ 123 Kevin Faulk RC	6.00	2.70
❑ 124 David Boston RC	8.00	3.60
❑ 125 Kevin Johnson RC	8.00	3.60
❑ 126 Torry Holt RC	10.00	4.50
❑ 127 James Johnson RC	4.00	1.80
❑ 128 Peerless Price RC	5.00	2.20
❑ 129 D'Wayne Bates RC	3.00	1.35
❑ 130 Cecil Collins RC	4.00	1.80
❑ 131 Na Brown RC	4.00	1.80
❑ 132 Rob Konrad RC	4.00	1.80
❑ 133 Joel Makovicka RC	4.00	1.80
❑ 134 Dameane Douglas RC	3.00	1.35
❑ 135 Scott Covington RC	4.00	1.80
❑ 136 Daylon McCutcheon RC	2.00	.90
❑ 137 Chris Claiborne RC	2.00	.90
❑ 138 Karsten Bailey RC	3.00	1.35
❑ 139 Mike Cloud RC	4.00	1.80
❑ 140 Sean Bennett RC	4.00	1.80
❑ 141 Jermaine Fazande RC	4.00	1.80
❑ 142 Chris McAlister RC	3.00	1.35
❑ 143 Ebenezer Ekuban RC	3.00	1.35
❑ 144 Jeff Paulk RC	3.00	1.35
❑ 145 Jim Kleinsasser RC	4.00	1.80
❑ 146 Bobby Collins RC	4.00	1.80
❑ 147 Andy Katzenmoyer RC	4.00	1.80
❑ 148 Jevon Kearse RC	8.00	3.60
❑ 149 Amos Zereoue RC	4.00	1.80
❑ 150 Sedrick Irvin RC	4.00	1.80
❑ WPBD Walter Payton (Game Jersey AUTO/34)	2000.00	900.00

2000 Black Diamond

	MINT	NRMT
❑ 1 Jake Plummer	.60	.25
❑ 2 David Boston	.60	.25
❑ 3 Frank Sanders	.30	.14
❑ 4 Tim Dwight	.60	.25
❑ 5 Chris Chandler	.30	.14
❑ 6 Jamal Anderson	.60	.25
❑ 7 Shawn Jefferson	.15	.07
❑ 8 Terance Mathis	.30	.14
❑ 9 Qadry Ismail	.30	.14
❑ 10 Tony Banks	.30	.14
❑ 11 Shannon Sharpe	.30	.14
❑ 12 Peerless Price	.60	.25
❑ 13 Rob Johnson	.30	.14
❑ 14 Eric Moulds	.60	.25
❑ 15 Antowain Smith	.30	.14
❑ 16 Muhsin Muhammad	.30	.14
❑ 17 Patrick Jeffers	.60	.25
❑ 18 Steve Beuerlein	.15	.07
❑ 19 Tim Biakabutuka	.30	.14
❑ 20 Cade McNown	.60	.25
❑ 21 Marcus Robinson	.60	.25
❑ 22 Eddie Kennison	.30	.14
❑ 23 Bobby Engram	.30	.14

❑ 24 Akili Smith .60 .25
❑ 25 Corey Dillon .60 .25
❑ 26 Darnay Scott .30 .14
❑ 27 Tim Couch 1.25 .55
❑ 28 Kevin Johnson .60 .25
❑ 29 Errict Rhett .30 .14
❑ 30 Troy Aikman 1.50 .70
❑ 31 Emmitt Smith 1.50 .70
❑ 32 Rocket Ismail .30 .14
❑ 33 Joey Galloway .60 .25
❑ 34 Terrell Davis 1.50 .70
❑ 35 Olandis Gary .60 .25
❑ 36 Brian Griese .75 .35
❑ 37 Ed McCaffrey .60 .25
❑ 38 Rod Smith .30 .14
❑ 39 Charlie Batch .60 .25
❑ 40 Germane Crowell .30 .14
❑ 41 Johnnie Morton .30 .14
❑ 42 James Stewart .30 .14
❑ 43 Brett Favre 2.50 1.10
❑ 44 Antonio Freeman .60 .25
❑ 45 Dorsey Levens .30 .14
❑ 46 Peyton Manning 2.00 .90
❑ 47 Edgerrin James 2.50 1.10
❑ 48 Marvin Harrison .60 .25
❑ 49 Terrence Wilkins .60 .25
❑ 50 Mark Brunell 1.00 .45
❑ 51 Fred Taylor .75 .35
❑ 52 Jimmy Smith .30 .14
❑ 53 Keenan McCardell .30 .14
❑ 54 Elvis Grbac .30 .14
❑ 55 Tony Gonzalez .30 .14
❑ 56 Derrick Alexander .30 .14
❑ 57 James Johnson .30 .14
❑ 58 Tony Martin .30 .14
❑ 59 Damon Huard .60 .25
❑ 60 Oronde Gadsden .30 .14
❑ 61 Randy Moss 2.00 .90
❑ 62 Robert Smith .60 .25
❑ 63 Cris Carter .60 .25
❑ 64 Daunte Culpepper 1.25 .55
❑ 65 Drew Bledsoe 1.00 .45
❑ 66 Terry Glenn .30 .14
❑ 67 Sean Morey RC .15 .07
❑ 68 Ricky Williams 1.50 .70
❑ 69 Keith Poole .15 .07
❑ 70 Jake Reed .30 .14
❑ 71 Jeff Blake .30 .14
❑ 72 Kerry Collins .30 .14
❑ 73 Amani Toomer .30 .14
❑ 74 Joe Montgomery .15 .07
❑ 75 Ike Hilliard .30 .14
❑ 76 Ray Lucas .60 .25
❑ 77 Curtis Martin .60 .25
❑ 78 Vinny Testaverde .30 .14
❑ 79 Wayne Chrebet .30 .14
❑ 80 Tim Brown .60 .25
❑ 81 Rich Gannon .30 .14
❑ 82 Tyrone Wheatley .30 .14
❑ 83 Rickey Dudley .15 .07
❑ 84 Napoleon Kaufman .30 .14
❑ 85 Duce Staley .60 .25
❑ 86 Donovan McNabb 1.00 .45
❑ 87 Torrance Small .15 .07
❑ 88 Charles Johnson .30 .14
❑ 89 Kent Graham .15 .07
❑ 90 Troy Edwards .30 .14
❑ 91 Jerome Bettis .60 .25
❑ 92 Kordell Stewart .60 .25
❑ 93 Marshall Faulk .75 .35
❑ 94 Kurt Warner 2.50 1.10
❑ 95 Torry Holt .60 .25
❑ 96 Isaac Bruce .60 .25
❑ 97 Jermaine Fazande .15 .07
❑ 98 Ryan Leaf .60 .25
❑ 99 Jeff Graham .15 .07
❑ 100 Moses Moreno .15 .07
❑ 101 Jerry Rice 1.50 .70
❑ 102 Terrell Owens .60 .25
❑ 103 Jeff Garcia .60 .25
❑ 104 Ricky Watters .15 .07
❑ 105 Jon Kitna .60 .25
❑ 106 Derrick Mayes .30 .14
❑ 107 Charlie Rogers .15 .07
❑ 108 Warrick Dunn .60 .25
❑ 109 Shaun King 1.00 .45

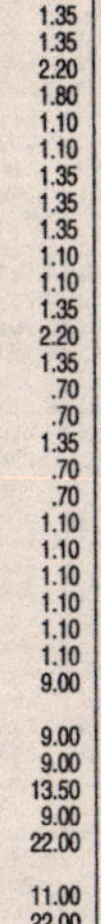

❑ 110 Mike Alstott .60 .25
❑ 111 Keyshawn Johnson .60 .25
❑ 112 Eddie George .75 .35
❑ 113 Steve McNair .60 .25
❑ 114 Kevin Dyson .30 .14
❑ 115 Kevin Daft .15 .07
❑ 116 Jevon Kearse .60 .25
❑ 117 Brad Johnson .60 .25
❑ 118 Stephen Davis .60 .25
❑ 119 Michael Westbrook .30 .14
❑ 120 Jeff George .30 .14
❑ 121 Kwame Cavil RC 2.50 1.10
❑ 122 Corey Moore RC 2.50 1.10
❑ 123 Sebastian Janikowski RC 3.00 1.35
❑ 124 Troy Walters RC 3.00 1.35
❑ 125 Mike Anderson RC 20.00 9.00
❑ 126 Tom Brady RC 3.00 1.35
❑ 127 Spergon Wynn RC 3.00 1.35
❑ 128 Tim Rattay RC 5.00 2.20
❑ 129 Giovanni Carmazzi RC 4.00 1.80
❑ 130 Chris Cole RC 2.50 1.10
❑ 131 Demario Brown RC 2.50 1.10
❑ 132 Chris Coleman RC 3.00 1.35
❑ 133 Michael Wiley RC 3.00 1.35
❑ 134 JaJuan Dawson RC 3.00 1.35
❑ 135 Deon Dyer RC 2.50 1.10
❑ 136 Trevor Gaylor RC 2.50 1.10
❑ 137 Todd Husak RC 3.00 1.35
❑ 138 Darrell Jackson RC 5.00 2.20
❑ 139 Erron Kinney RC 3.00 1.35
❑ 140 Anthony Lucas RC 1.50 .70
❑ 141 Rondell Mealey RC 1.50 .70
❑ 142 Chad Morton RC 3.00 1.35
❑ 143 Leon Murray RC 1.50 .70
❑ 144 Mareno Philyaw RC 1.50 .70
❑ 145 Gari Scott RC 2.50 1.10
❑ 146 Paul Smith RC 2.50 1.10
❑ 147 Terrelle Smith RC 2.50 1.10
❑ 148 Shyrone Stith RC 2.50 1.10
❑ 149 Bashir Yamini RC 2.50 1.10
❑ 150 Windrell Hayes RC 2.50 1.10
❑ 151 Courtney Brown JSY RC 20.00 9.00
❑ 152 Corey Simon JSY RC 20.00 9.00
❑ 153 R.Jay Soward JSY RC 20.00 9.00
❑ 154 Chris Redman JSY RC 30.00 13.50
❑ 155 Joe Hamilton JSY RC 20.00 9.00
❑ 156 Chad Pennington JSY RC 50.00 22.00
❑ 157 Tee Martin JSY RC 25.00 11.00
❑ 158 Ron Dayne JSY RC 50.00 22.00
❑ 159 Shaun Alexander JSY RC 40.00 18.00
❑ 160 Thomas Jones JSY RC 25.00 11.00
❑ 161 Reuben Droughns JSY RC 20.00 9.00
❑ 162 Jamal Lewis JSY RC 80.00 36.00
❑ 163 J.R. Redmond JSY RC 20.00 9.00
❑ 164 Travis Prentice JSY RC 25.00 11.00
❑ 165 Trung Canidate JSY RC 20.00 9.00
❑ 166 Brian Urlacher JSY RC 60.00 27.00
❑ 167 Anthony Becht JSY RC 20.00 9.00
❑ 168 Bubba Franks JSY RC 20.00 9.00
❑ 169 Peter Warrick JSY RC 50.00 22.00
❑ 170 Plaxico Burress JSY RC 30.00 13.50
❑ 171 Sylvester Morris JSY RC 30.00 13.50
❑ 172 Dez White JSY RC 12.00 5.50
❑ 173 Travis Taylor JSY RC 20.00 9.00
❑ 174 Todd Pinkston JSY RC 20.00 9.00
❑ 175 Dennis Northcutt JSY RC 20.00 9.00
❑ 176 Jerry Porter JSY RC 20.00 9.00
❑ 177 Laveranues Coles JSY RC 25.00 11.00
❑ 178 Danny Farmer JSY RC 20.00 9.00
❑ 179 Curtis Keaton JSY RC 12.00 5.50
❑ 180 Ron Dugans JSY RC 12.00 5.50

1948 Bowman

	NRMT	VG-E
COMPLETE SET (108)	6000.00	2700.00
COMMON 1/4/7/-/-/-	20.00	9.00
COMMON 2/5/8/-/-/-	25.00	11.00
COMMON SP 3/6/9 /-/-/-	100.00	45.00
WRAPPER (1-CENT)	200.00	90.00

❑ 1 Joe Tereshinski RC 150.00 38.00
❑ 2 Larry Olsonoski 25.00 11.00
❑ 3 John Lujack SP RC 350.00 160.00
❑ 4 Ray Poole 20.00 9.00
❑ 5 Bill DeCorrevont 25.00 11.00
❑ 6 Paul Briggs SP 100.00 45.00
❑ 7 Steve Van Buren RC 150.00 70.00
❑ 8 Kenny Washington RC 60.00 27.00
❑ 9 Nolan Luhn SP 100.00 45.00
❑ 10 Chris Iversen 20.00 9.00
❑ 11 Jack Wiley 25.00 11.00
❑ 12 Charley Conerly RC SP 350.00 160.00
❑ 13 Hugh Taylor RC 25.00 11.00
❑ 14 Frank Seno 25.00 11.00
❑ 15 Gil Bouley SP 100.00 45.00
❑ 16 Tommy Thompson RC 35.00 16.00
❑ 17 Charley Trippi RC 100.00 45.00
❑ 18 Vince Banonis SP 100.00 45.00
❑ 19 Art Faircloth 20.00 9.00
❑ 20 Clyde Goodnight 25.00 11.00
❑ 21 Bill Chipley SP 100.00 45.00
❑ 22 Sammy Baugh RC 500.00 220.00
❑ 23 Don Kindt 25.00 11.00
❑ 24 John Koniszewski SP 100.00 45.00
❑ 25 Pat McHugh 20.00 9.00
❑ 26 Bob Waterfield RC 200.00 90.00
❑ 27 Tony Compagno SP 100.00 45.00
❑ 28 Paul Governali RC 25.00 11.00
❑ 29 Pat Harder RC 60.00 27.00
❑ 30 Vic Lindskog SP 100.00 45.00
❑ 31 Salvatore Rosato 20.00 9.00
❑ 32 John Mastrangelo 25.00 11.00
❑ 33 Fred Gehrke SP 100.00 45.00
❑ 34 Bosh Pritchard 20.00 9.00
❑ 35 Mike Micka 25.00 11.00
❑ 36 Bulldog Turner RC SP 250.00 110.00
❑ 37 Len Younce 20.00 9.00
❑ 38 Pat West 25.00 11.00
❑ 39 Russ Thomas SP 100.00 45.00
❑ 40 James Peebles 20.00 9.00
❑ 41 Bob Skoglund 25.00 11.00
❑ 42 Walt Stickle SP 100.00 45.00
❑ 43 Whitey Wistert RC 25.00 11.00
❑ 44 Paul Christman RC 60.00 27.00
❑ 45 Jay Rhodemyre SP 100.00 45.00
❑ 46 Tony Minisi 20.00 9.00
❑ 47 Bob Mann 25.00 11.00
❑ 48 Mal Kutner RC SP 110.00 50.00
❑ 49 Dick Poillon 20.00 9.00
❑ 50 Charles Cherundolo 25.00 11.00
❑ 51 Gerald Cowhig SP 100.00 45.00
❑ 52 Neill Armstrong RC 25.00 11.00
❑ 53 Frank Maznicki 25.00 11.00
❑ 54 John Sanchez SP 100.00 45.00
❑ 55 Frank Reagan 20.00 9.00
❑ 56 Jim Hardy 25.00 11.00
❑ 57 John Badaczewski SP 100.00 45.00
❑ 58 Robert Nussbaumer 20.00 9.00
❑ 59 Marvin Pregulman 25.00 11.00
❑ 60 Elbert Nickel RC SP 125.00 55.00
❑ 61 Alex Wojciechowicz RC 125.00 55.00
❑ 62 Walt Schlinkman 25.00 11.00
❑ 63 Pete Pihos RC SP 225.00 100.00
❑ 64 Joseph Sulaitis 20.00 9.00
❑ 65 Mike Holovak RC 50.00 22.00
❑ 66 Cecil Souders SP 100.00 45.00
❑ 67 Paul McKee 20.00 9.00
❑ 68 Bill Moore 25.00 11.00
❑ 69 Frank Minini SP 100.00 45.00
❑ 70 Jack Ferrante 20.00 9.00
❑ 71 Les Horvath RC 50.00 22.00

- ❑ 72 Ted Fritsch Sr. RC SP 110.00 50.00
- ❑ 73 Tex Coulter RC 25.00 11.00
- ❑ 74 Boley Dancewicz 25.00 11.00
- ❑ 75 Dante Mangani SP 100.00 45.00
- ❑ 76 James Hefti 20.00 9.00
- ❑ 77 Paul Sarringhaus 25.00 11.00
- ❑ 78 Joe Scott SP 100.00 45.00
- ❑ 79 Bucko Kilroy RC 25.00 11.00
- ❑ 80 Bill Dudley RC 125.00 55.00
- ❑ 81 Marshall Goldberg RC SP 110.00 50.00
- ❑ 82 John Cannady 20.00 9.00
- ❑ 83 Perry Moss 25.00 11.00
- ❑ 84 Harold Crisler RC SP 110.00 50.00
- ❑ 85 Bill Gray 20.00 9.00
- ❑ 86 John Clement 25.00 11.00
- ❑ 87 Dan Sandifer SP 100.00 45.00
- ❑ 88 Ben Kish 20.00 9.00
- ❑ 89 Herbert Banta 25.00 11.00
- ❑ 90 Bill Garnaas SP 100.00 45.00
- ❑ 91 Jim White 20.00 9.00
- ❑ 92 Frank Barzilauskas 25.00 11.00
- ❑ 93 Vic Sears SP 100.00 45.00
- ❑ 94 John Adams 20.00 9.00
- ❑ 95 George McAfee RC 100.00 45.00
- ❑ 96 Ralph Heywood SP 100.00 45.00
- ❑ 97 Joe Muha 20.00 9.00
- ❑ 98 Fred Enke 25.00 11.00
- ❑ 99 Harry Gilmer RC SP 175.00 80.00
- ❑ 100 Bill Miklich 20.00 9.00
- ❑ 101 Joe Gottlieb 25.00 11.00
- ❑ 102 Bud Angsman SP RC 110.00 50.00
- ❑ 103 Tom Farmer 20.00 9.00
- ❑ 104 Bruce Smith RC 60.00 27.00
- ❑ 105 Bob Cifers SP 100.00 45.00
- ❑ 106 Ernie Steele 20.00 9.00
- ❑ 107 Sid Luckman RC 250.00 110.00
- ❑ 108 Buford Ray SP RC 350.00 90.00

1950 Bowman

	NRMT	VG-E
COMPLETE SET (144)	4000.00	1800.00
WRAPPER (5-CENT)	150.00	70.00

- ❑ 1 Doak Walker 250.00 45.00
- ❑ 2 John Greene 25.00 11.00
- ❑ 3 Bob Nowasky 25.00 11.00
- ❑ 4 Jonathan Jenkins 25.00 11.00
- ❑ 5 Y.A. Tittle RC 250.00 110.00
- ❑ 6 Lou Groza RC 175.00 80.00
- ❑ 7 Alex Agase RC 30.00 13.50
- ❑ 8 Mac Speedie RC 50.00 22.00
- ❑ 9 Tony Canadeo RC 90.00 40.00
- ❑ 10 Larry Craig 25.00 11.00
- ❑ 11 Ted Fritsch Sr. 30.00 13.50
- ❑ 12 Joe Goldring 25.00 11.00
- ❑ 13 Martin Ruby 25.00 11.00
- ❑ 14 George Taliaferro 30.00 13.50
- ❑ 15 Tank Younger RC 50.00 22.00
- ❑ 16 Glenn Army Davis RC 125.00 55.00
- ❑ 17 Bob Waterfield 125.00 55.00
- ❑ 18 Val Jansante 25.00 11.00
- ❑ 19 Joe Geri 25.00 11.00
- ❑ 20 Jerry Nuzum 25.00 11.00
- ❑ 21 Elmer Bud Angsman 25.00 11.00
- ❑ 22 Billy Dewell 25.00 11.00
- ❑ 23 Steve Van Buren 90.00 40.00
- ❑ 24 Cliff Patton 25.00 11.00
- ❑ 25 Bosh Pritchard 25.00 11.00
- ❑ 26 John Lujack 75.00 34.00
- ❑ 27 Sid Luckman 125.00 55.00
- ❑ 28 Bulldog Turner 60.00 27.00
- ❑ 29 Bill Dudley 60.00 27.00
- ❑ 30 Hugh Taylor 30.00 13.50
- ❑ 31 George Thomas 25.00 11.00
- ❑ 32 Ray Poole 25.00 11.00
- ❑ 33 Travis Tidwell 25.00 11.00
- ❑ 34 Gail Bruce 25.00 11.00
- ❑ 35 Joe Perry RC 175.00 80.00
- ❑ 36 Frankie Albert RC 40.00 18.00
- ❑ 37 Bobby Layne 200.00 90.00
- ❑ 38 Leon Hart 40.00 18.00
- ❑ 39 Bob Hoernschemeyer RC 30.00 13.50
- ❑ 40 Dick Barwegan RC 25.00 11.00
- ❑ 41 Adrian Burk RC 30.00 13.50
- ❑ 42 Barry French 25.00 11.00
- ❑ 43 Marion Motley RC 200.00 90.00
- ❑ 44 Jim Martin 30.00 13.50
- ❑ 45 Otto Graham RC 450.00 200.00
- ❑ 46 Al Baldwin 25.00 11.00
- ❑ 47 Larry Coutre 25.00 11.00
- ❑ 48 John Rauch 25.00 11.00
- ❑ 49 Sam Tamburo 25.00 11.00
- ❑ 50 Mike Swistowicz 25.00 11.00
- ❑ 51 Tom Fears RC 125.00 55.00
- ❑ 52 Elroy Hirsch RC 175.00 80.00
- ❑ 53 Dick Huffman 25.00 11.00
- ❑ 54 Bob Gage 25.00 11.00
- ❑ 55 Buddy Tinsley 25.00 11.00
- ❑ 56 Bill Blackburn 25.00 11.00
- ❑ 57 John Cochran 25.00 11.00
- ❑ 58 Bill Fischer 25.00 11.00
- ❑ 59 Whitey Wistert 30.00 13.50
- ❑ 60 Clyde Scott 25.00 11.00
- ❑ 61 Walter Barnes 25.00 11.00
- ❑ 62 Bob Perina 25.00 11.00
- ❑ 63 Bill Wightkin 25.00 11.00
- ❑ 64 Bob Goode 25.00 11.00
- ❑ 65 Al Demao 25.00 11.00
- ❑ 66 Harry Gilmer 30.00 13.50
- ❑ 67 Bill Austin 25.00 11.00
- ❑ 68 Joe Scott 25.00 11.00
- ❑ 69 Tex Coulter 30.00 13.50
- ❑ 70 Paul Salata 25.00 11.00
- ❑ 71 Emil Sitko RC 30.00 13.50
- ❑ 72 Bill Johnson 25.00 11.00
- ❑ 73 Don Doll RC 25.00 11.00
- ❑ 74 Dan Sandifer 25.00 11.00
- ❑ 75 John Panelli 25.00 11.00
- ❑ 76 Bill Leonard 25.00 11.00
- ❑ 77 Bob Kelly 25.00 11.00
- ❑ 78 Dante Lavelli RC 125.00 55.00
- ❑ 79 Tony Adamle 30.00 13.50
- ❑ 80 Dick Wildung 25.00 11.00
- ❑ 81 Tobin Rote RC 40.00 18.00
- ❑ 82 Paul Burris 25.00 11.00
- ❑ 83 Lowell Tew 25.00 11.00
- ❑ 84 Barney Poole 25.00 11.00
- ❑ 85 Fred Naumetz 25.00 11.00
- ❑ 86 Dick Hoerner 25.00 11.00
- ❑ 87 Bob Reinhard 25.00 11.00
- ❑ 88 Howard Hartley RC 25.00 11.00
- ❑ 89 Darrell Hogan RC 25.00 11.00
- ❑ 90 Jerry Shipkey 25.00 11.00
- ❑ 91 Frank Tripucka 30.00 13.50
- ❑ 92 Garrard Ramsey RC 25.00 11.00
- ❑ 93 Pat Harder 30.00 13.50
- ❑ 94 Vic Sears 25.00 11.00
- ❑ 95 Tommy Thompson 30.00 13.50
- ❑ 96 Bucko Kilroy 30.00 13.50
- ❑ 97 George Connor 50.00 22.00
- ❑ 98 Fred Morrison 25.00 11.00
- ❑ 99 Jim Keane 25.00 11.00
- ❑ 100 Sammy Baugh 250.00 110.00
- ❑ 101 Harry Ulinski 25.00 11.00
- ❑ 102 Frank Spaniel 25.00 11.00
- ❑ 103 Charley Conerly 90.00 40.00
- ❑ 104 Dick Hensley 25.00 11.00
- ❑ 105 Eddie Price 25.00 11.00
- ❑ 106 Ed Carr 25.00 11.00
- ❑ 107 Leo Nomellini 75.00 34.00
- ❑ 108 Verl Lillywhite 25.00 11.00
- ❑ 109 Wallace Triplett 25.00 11.00
- ❑ 110 Joe Watson 25.00 11.00
- ❑ 111 Cloyce Box RC 30.00 13.50
- ❑ 112 Billy Stone 25.00 11.00
- ❑ 113 Earl Murray 25.00 11.00
- ❑ 114 Chet Mutryn RC 30.00 13.50
- ❑ 115 Ken Carpenter 30.00 13.50
- ❑ 116 Lou Rymkus RC 30.00 13.50
- ❑ 117 Dub Jones RC 30.00 13.50
- ❑ 118 Clayton Tonnemaker 25.00 11.00
- ❑ 119 Walt Schlinkman 25.00 11.00
- ❑ 120 Billy Grimes 25.00 11.00
- ❑ 121 George Ratterman RC 30.00 13.50
- ❑ 122 Bob Mann 25.00 11.00
- ❑ 123 Buddy Young RC 40.00 18.00
- ❑ 124 Jack Zilly 25.00 11.00
- ❑ 125 Tom Kalmanir 25.00 11.00
- ❑ 126 Frank Sinkovitz 25.00 11.00
- ❑ 127 Elbert Nickel 30.00 13.50
- ❑ 128 Jim Finks RC 60.00 27.00
- ❑ 129 Charley Trippi 60.00 27.00
- ❑ 130 Tom Wham 25.00 11.00
- ❑ 131 Ventan Yablonski 25.00 11.00
- ❑ 132 Chuck Bednarik 100.00 45.00
- ❑ 133 Joe Muha 25.00 11.00
- ❑ 134 Pete Pihos 60.00 27.00
- ❑ 135 Washington Serini 25.00 11.00
- ❑ 136 George Gulyanics 25.00 11.00
- ❑ 137 Ken Kavanaugh 30.00 13.50
- ❑ 138 Howie Livingston 25.00 11.00
- ❑ 139 Joe Tereshinski 25.00 11.00
- ❑ 140 Jim White 25.00 11.00
- ❑ 141 Gene Roberts 25.00 11.00
- ❑ 142 Bill Swiacki 30.00 13.50
- ❑ 143 Norm Standlee 25.00 11.00
- ❑ 144 Knox Ramsey RC 100.00 25.00

1951 Bowman

	NRMT	VG-E
COMPLETE SET (144)	3500.00	1600.00
WRAPPER (1-CENT)	150.00	70.00
WRAPPER (5-CENT)	200.00	90.00

- ❑ 1 Weldon Humble RC 75.00 19.00
- ❑ 2 Otto Graham 200.00 90.00
- ❑ 3 Mac Speedie 35.00 16.00
- ❑ 4 Norm Van Brocklin RC 300.00 135.00
- ❑ 5 Woodley Lewis RC 25.00 11.00
- ❑ 6 Tom Fears 50.00 22.00
- ❑ 7 George Musacco 20.00 9.00
- ❑ 8 George Taliaferro 25.00 11.00
- ❑ 9 Barney Poole 20.00 9.00
- ❑ 10 Steve Van Buren 60.00 27.00
- ❑ 11 Whitey Wistert 25.00 11.00
- ❑ 12 Chuck Bednarik 80.00 36.00
- ❑ 13 Bulldog Turner 50.00 22.00
- ❑ 14 Bob Williams 20.00 9.00
- ❑ 15 John Lujack 60.00 27.00
- ❑ 16 Roy Rebel Steiner 20.00 9.00
- ❑ 17 Jug Girard 25.00 11.00
- ❑ 18 Bill Neal 20.00 9.00
- ❑ 19 Travis Tidwell 20.00 9.00
- ❑ 20 Tom Landry RC 525.00 240.00
- ❑ 21 Arnie Weinmeister RC 60.00 27.00
- ❑ 22 Joe Geri 20.00 9.00
- ❑ 23 Bill Walsh RC 25.00 11.00
- ❑ 24 Fran Rogel 20.00 9.00
- ❑ 25 Doak Walker 60.00 27.00
- ❑ 26 Leon Hart 35.00 16.00
- ❑ 27 Thurman McGraw 20.00 9.00
- ❑ 28 Buster Ramsey 20.00 9.00
- ❑ 29 Frank Tripucka 35.00 16.00

❑ 30	Don Paul	20.00	9.00
❑ 31	Alex Loyd	20.00	9.00
❑ 32	Y.A. Tittle	135.00	60.00
❑ 33	Verl Lillywhite	20.00	9.00
❑ 34	Sammy Baugh	175.00	80.00
❑ 35	Chuck Drazenovich	20.00	9.00
❑ 36	Bob Goode	20.00	9.00
❑ 37	Horace Gillom	25.00	11.00
❑ 38	Lou Rymkus	25.00	11.00
❑ 39	Ken Carpenter	20.00	9.00
❑ 40	Bob Waterfield	75.00	34.00
❑ 41	Vitamin Smith RC	25.00	11.00
❑ 42	Glenn Army Davis	60.00	27.00
❑ 43	Dan Edwards	20.00	9.00
❑ 44	John Rauch	20.00	9.00
❑ 45	Zollie Toth	20.00	9.00
❑ 46	Pete Pihos	60.00	27.00
❑ 47	Russ Craft	20.00	9.00
❑ 48	Walter Barnes	20.00	9.00
❑ 49	Fred Morrison	20.00	9.00
❑ 50	Ray Bray	20.00	9.00
❑ 51	Ed Sprinkle RC	25.00	11.00
❑ 52	Floyd Reid	20.00	9.00
❑ 53	Billy Grimes	20.00	9.00
❑ 54	Ted Fritsch Sr.	25.00	11.00
❑ 55	Al DeRogatis	25.00	11.00
❑ 56	Charley Conerly	75.00	34.00
❑ 57	Jon Baker	20.00	9.00
❑ 58	Tom McWilliams	20.00	9.00
❑ 59	Jerry Shipkey	20.00	9.00
❑ 60	Lynn Chandnois RC	25.00	11.00
❑ 61	Don Doll	20.00	9.00
❑ 62	Lou Creekmur	50.00	22.00
❑ 63	Bob Hoernschemeyer	25.00	11.00
❑ 64	Tom Wham	20.00	9.00
❑ 65	Bill Fischer	20.00	9.00
❑ 66	Robert Nussbaumer	20.00	9.00
❑ 67	Gordy Soltau RC	20.00	9.00
❑ 68	Visco Grgich	20.00	9.00
❑ 69	John Strzykalski RC	20.00	9.00
❑ 70	Pete Stout	20.00	9.00
❑ 71	Paul Lipscomb	20.00	9.00
❑ 72	Harry Gilmer	35.00	16.00
❑ 73	Dante Lavelli	50.00	22.00
❑ 74	Dub Jones	25.00	11.00
❑ 75	Lou Groza	75.00	34.00
❑ 76	Elroy Hirsch	75.00	34.00
❑ 77	Tom Kalmanir	20.00	9.00
❑ 78	Jack Zilly	20.00	9.00
❑ 79	Bruce Alford	20.00	9.00
❑ 80	Art Weiner	20.00	9.00
❑ 81	Brad Ecklund	20.00	9.00
❑ 82	Bosh Pritchard	20.00	9.00
❑ 83	John Green	20.00	9.00
❑ 84	Ebert Van Buren	20.00	9.00
❑ 85	Julie Rykovich	20.00	9.00
❑ 86	Fred Davis	20.00	9.00
❑ 87	John Hoffman	20.00	9.00
❑ 88	Tobin Rote	25.00	11.00
❑ 89	Paul Burris	20.00	9.00
❑ 90	Tony Canadeo	50.00	22.00
❑ 91	Emlen Tunnell RC	100.00	45.00
❑ 92	Otto Schnellbacher RC	20.00	9.00
❑ 93	Ray Poole	20.00	9.00
❑ 94	Darrell Hogan	20.00	9.00
❑ 95	Frank Sinkovitz	20.00	9.00
❑ 96	Ernie Stautner	75.00	34.00
❑ 97	Elmer Bud Angsman	20.00	9.00
❑ 98	Jack Jennings	20.00	9.00
❑ 99	Jerry Groom	20.00	9.00
❑ 100	John Prchlik	20.00	9.00
❑ 101	J. Robert Smith	20.00	9.00
❑ 102	Bobby Layne	135.00	60.00
❑ 103	Frankie Albert	35.00	16.00
❑ 104	Gail Bruce	20.00	9.00
❑ 105	Joe Perry	75.00	34.00
❑ 106	Leon Heath	20.00	9.00
❑ 107	Ed Quirk	20.00	9.00
❑ 108	Hugh Taylor	25.00	11.00
❑ 109	Marion Motley	100.00	45.00
❑ 110	Tony Adamle	20.00	9.00
❑ 111	Alex Agase	25.00	11.00
❑ 112	Tank Younger	35.00	16.00
❑ 113	Bob Boyd	20.00	9.00
❑ 114	Jerry Williams	20.00	9.00
❑ 115	Joe Golding	20.00	9.00
❑ 116	Sherman Howard	20.00	9.00
❑ 117	John Wozniak	20.00	9.00
❑ 118	Frank Reagan	20.00	9.00
❑ 119	Vic Sears	20.00	9.00
❑ 120	Clyde Scott	20.00	9.00
❑ 121	George Gulyanics	20.00	9.00
❑ 122	Bill Wightkin	20.00	9.00
❑ 123	Chuck Hunsinger	20.00	9.00
❑ 124	Jack Cloud	20.00	9.00
❑ 125	Abner Wimberly	20.00	9.00
❑ 126	Dick Wildung	20.00	9.00
❑ 127	Eddie Price	20.00	9.00
❑ 128	Joe Scott	20.00	9.00
❑ 129	Jerry Nuzum	20.00	9.00
❑ 130	Jim Finks	35.00	16.00
❑ 131	Bob Gage	20.00	9.00
❑ 132	Bill Swiacki	25.00	11.00
❑ 133	Joe Watson	20.00	9.00
❑ 134	Ollie Cline	20.00	9.00
❑ 135	Jack Lininger	20.00	9.00
❑ 136	Fran Polsfoot	20.00	9.00
❑ 137	Charley Trippi	50.00	22.00
❑ 138	Ventan Yablonski	20.00	9.00
❑ 139	Emil Sitko	20.00	9.00
❑ 140	Leo Nomellini	60.00	27.00
❑ 141	Norm Standlee	20.00	9.00
❑ 142	Eddie Saenz	20.00	9.00
❑ 143	Al Demao	20.00	9.00
❑ 144	Bill Dudley	150.00	38.00
❑ NNO	Darrell Hogan Proof	125.00	275.00
❑ NNO	Johnny Lujack Proof	300.00	55.00
❑ NNO	Bob Gage Proof	125.00	55.00

1952 Bowman Large

	NRMT	VG-E
COMPLETE SET (144)	12500.00	5600.00
COMMON CARD (1-72)	35.00	16.00
COMMON CARD (73-144)	40.00	18.00
WRAPPER (5-CENT)	60.00	27.00

❑ 1	Norm Van Brocklin	500.00	125.00
❑ 2	Otto Graham	300.00	135.00
❑ 3	Doak Walker	75.00	34.00
❑ 4	Steve Owen CO RC	75.00	34.00
❑ 5	Frankie Albert	50.00	22.00
❑ 6	Laurie Niemi	35.00	16.00
❑ 7	Chuck Hunsinger	35.00	16.00
❑ 8	Ed Modzelewski	50.00	22.00
❑ 9	Joe Spencer SP	75.00	34.00
❑ 10	Chuck Bednarik SP	300.00	135.00
❑ 11	Barney Poole	35.00	16.00
❑ 12	Charley Trippi	75.00	34.00
❑ 13	Tom Fears	75.00	34.00
❑ 14	Paul Brown CO RC	250.00	110.00
❑ 15	Leon Hart	50.00	22.00
❑ 16	Frank Gifford RC	500.00	220.00
❑ 17	Y.A. Tittle	300.00	135.00
❑ 18	Charlie Justice SP	175.00	80.00
❑ 19	George Connor SP	175.00	80.00
❑ 20	Lynn Chandnois	35.00	16.00
❑ 21	Billy Howton RC	50.00	22.00
❑ 22	Kenneth Snyder	35.00	16.00
❑ 23	Gino Marchetti RC	250.00	110.00
❑ 24	John Karras	35.00	16.00
❑ 25	Tank Younger	50.00	22.00
❑ 26	Tommy Thompson LB	35.00	16.00
❑ 27	Bob Miller SP RC	300.00	135.00
❑ 28	Kyle Rote RC SP	175.00	80.00
❑ 29	Hugh McElhenny RC	250.00	110.00
❑ 30	Sammy Baugh	350.00	160.00
❑ 31	Jim Dooley RC	45.00	20.00
❑ 32	Ray Mathews	35.00	16.00
❑ 33	Fred Cone	35.00	16.00
❑ 34	Al Pollard	35.00	16.00
❑ 35	Brad Ecklund	35.00	16.00
❑ 36	John Lee Hancock SP RC	350.00	160.00
❑ 37	Elroy Hirsch SP	200.00	90.00
❑ 38	Keever Jankovich	35.00	16.00
❑ 39	Emlen Tunnell	75.00	34.00
❑ 40	Steve Dowden	35.00	16.00
❑ 41	Claude Hipps	35.00	16.00
❑ 42	Norm Standlee	35.00	16.00
❑ 43	Dick Todd CO	35.00	16.00
❑ 44	Babe Parilli	50.00	22.00
❑ 45	Steve Van Buren SP	300.00	135.00
❑ 46	Art Donovan RC SP	350.00	160.00
❑ 47	Bill Fischer	35.00	16.00
❑ 48	George Halas CO RC	275.00	125.00
❑ 49	Jerrell Price	35.00	16.00
❑ 50	John Sandusky RC	35.00	16.00
❑ 51	Ray Beck	35.00	16.00
❑ 52	Jim Martin	45.00	20.00
❑ 53	Joe Bach CO UER (Misspelled Back)	35.00	16.00
❑ 54	Glen Christian SP	75.00	34.00
❑ 55	Andy Davis SP	75.00	34.00
❑ 56	Tobin Rote	45.00	20.00
❑ 57	Wayne Millner CO RC	90.00	40.00
❑ 58	Zollie Toth	35.00	16.00
❑ 59	Jack Jennings	35.00	16.00
❑ 60	Bill McColl	35.00	16.00
❑ 61	Les Richter RC	45.00	20.00
❑ 62	Walt Michaels RC	45.00	20.00
❑ 63	Charley Conerly SP	600.00	275.00
❑ 64	Howard Hartley SP	75.00	34.00
❑ 65	Jerome Smith	35.00	16.00
❑ 66	James Clark	35.00	16.00
❑ 67	Dick Logan	35.00	16.00
❑ 68	Wayne Robinson	35.00	16.00
❑ 69	James Hammond	35.00	16.00
❑ 70	Gene Schroeder	35.00	16.00
❑ 71	Tex Coulter	45.00	20.00
❑ 72	John Schweder SP RC	600.00	275.00
❑ 73	Vitamin Smith SP	150.00	70.00
❑ 74	Joe Campanella RC	40.00	18.00
❑ 75	Joe Kuharich CO RC	50.00	22.00
❑ 76	Herman Clark	40.00	18.00
❑ 77	Dan Edwards	40.00	18.00
❑ 78	Bobby Layne	250.00	110.00
❑ 79	Bob Hoernschemeyer	50.00	22.00
❑ 80	John Carr Blount	40.00	18.00
❑ 81	John Kastan RC SP	150.00	70.00
❑ 82	Harry Minarik RC SP	150.00	70.00
❑ 83	Joe Perry	100.00	45.00
❑ 84	Ray(Buddy) Parker CO RC	50.00	22.00
❑ 85	Andy Robustelli RC	200.00	90.00
❑ 86	Dub Jones	50.00	22.00
❑ 87	Mal Cook	40.00	18.00
❑ 88	Billy Stone	40.00	18.00
❑ 89	George Taliaferro	50.00	22.00
❑ 90	Thomas Johnson RC SP	150.00	70.00
❑ 91	Leon Heath SP	100.00	45.00
❑ 92	Pete Pihos	100.00	45.00
❑ 93	Fred Benners	40.00	18.00
❑ 94	George Tarasovic	40.00	18.00
❑ 95	Lawr. (Buck) Shaw CO RC	40.00	18.00
❑ 96	Bill Wightkin	40.00	18.00
❑ 97	John Wozniak	40.00	18.00
❑ 98	Bobby Dillon RC	50.00	22.00
❑ 99	Joe Stydahar CO SP RC	650.00	300.00
❑ 100	Dick Alban RC SP	150.00	70.00
❑ 101	Arnie Weinmeister	60.00	27.00
❑ 102	Bobby Cross	40.00	18.00
❑ 103	Don Paul	40.00	18.00
❑ 104	Buddy Young	60.00	27.00
❑ 105	Lou Groza	125.00	55.00
❑ 106	Ray Pelfrey	40.00	18.00
❑ 107	Maurice Nipp	40.00	18.00
❑ 108	Hubert Johnston SP RC	650.00	300.00
❑ 109	Volney Quinlan RC SP	100.00	45.00
❑ 110	Jack Simmons	40.00	18.00
❑ 111	George Ratterman	50.00	22.00
❑ 112	John Badaczewski	40.00	18.00
❑ 113	Bill Reichardt	40.00	18.00

❑ 114 Art Weiner 40.00 18.00
❑ 115 Keith Flowers 40.00 18.00
❑ 116 Russ Craft 40.00 18.00
❑ 117 Jim O'Donahue RC SP 150.00 70.00
❑ 118 Darrell Hogan SP 100.00 45.00
❑ 119 Frank Ziegler 40.00 18.00
❑ 120 Deacon Dan Towler 60.00 27.00
❑ 121 Fred Williams 40.00 18.00
❑ 122 Jimmy Phelan CO 40.00 18.00
❑ 123 Eddie Price 40.00 18.00
❑ 124 Chet Ostrowski 40.00 18.00
❑ 125 Leo Nomellini 100.00 45.00
❑ 126 Steve Romanik SP RC 300.00 135.00
❑ 127 Ollie Matson RC SP 300.00 135.00
❑ 128 Dante Lavelli 90.00 40.00
❑ 129 Jack Christiansen RC 175.00 80.00
❑ 130 Dom Moselle 40.00 18.00
❑ 131 John Rapacz 40.00 18.00
❑ 132 Chuck Ortmann UER 40.00 18.00
(Avg. gain 9.4, should be 4.8)
❑ 133 Bob Williams 40.00 18.00
❑ 134 Chuck Ulrich 40.00 18.00
❑ 135 G.Ronzani CO SP RC 650.00 300.00
❑ 136 Bert Rechichar SP 100.00 45.00
❑ 137 Bob Waterfield 125.00 55.00
❑ 138 Bobby Walston RC 50.00 22.00
❑ 139 Jerry Shipkey 40.00 18.00
❑ 140 Yale Lary RC 175.00 80.00
❑ 141 Gordy Soltau 40.00 18.00
❑ 142 Tom Landry 600.00 275.00
❑ 143 John Papit 40.00 18.00
❑ 144 Jim Lansford SP RC 3000.00 750.00

1952 Bowman Small

	NRMT	VG-E
COMPLETE SET (144)	5000.00	2200.00
COMMON CARD (1-72)	25.00	11.00
COMMON CARD (73-144)	30.00	13.50
WRAPPER (1-CENT)	50.00	22.00

❑ 1 Norm Van Brocklin 350.00 90.00
❑ 2 Otto Graham 175.00 80.00
❑ 3 Doak Walker 60.00 27.00
❑ 4 Steve Owen CO RC 60.00 27.00
❑ 5 Frankie Albert 35.00 16.00
❑ 6 Laurie Niemi 25.00 11.00
❑ 7 Chuck Hunsinger 25.00 11.00
❑ 8 Ed Modzelewski 35.00 16.00
❑ 9 Joe Spencer 25.00 11.00
❑ 10 Chuck Bednarik 75.00 34.00
❑ 11 Barney Poole 25.00 11.00
❑ 12 Charley Trippi 60.00 27.00
❑ 13 Tom Fears 60.00 27.00
❑ 14 Paul Brown CO RC 150.00 70.00
❑ 15 Leon Hart 35.00 16.00
❑ 16 Frank Gifford RC 400.00 180.00
❑ 17 Y.A. Tittle 125.00 55.00
❑ 18 Charlie Justice 45.00 20.00
❑ 19 George Connor 35.00 16.00
❑ 20 Lynn Chandnois 25.00 11.00
❑ 21 Billy Howton RC 40.00 18.00
❑ 22 Kenneth Snyder 25.00 11.00
❑ 23 Gino Marchetti RC 125.00 55.00
❑ 24 John Karras 25.00 11.00
❑ 25 Tank Younger 35.00 16.00
❑ 26 Tommy Thompson 25.00 11.00
❑ 27 Bob Miller 25.00 11.00
❑ 28 Kyle Rote RC 50.00 22.00
❑ 29 Hugh McElhenny RC 175.00 80.00
❑ 30 Sammy Baugh 250.00 110.00
❑ 31 Jim Dooley RC 30.00 13.50
❑ 32 Ray Mathews 25.00 11.00
❑ 33 Fred Cone 25.00 11.00
❑ 34 Al Pollard 25.00 11.00
❑ 35 Brad Ecklund 25.00 11.00
❑ 36 John Lee Hancock 25.00 11.00
❑ 37 Elroy Hirsch 60.00 27.00
❑ 38 Keever Jankovich 25.00 11.00
❑ 39 Emlen Tunnell 50.00 22.00
❑ 40 Steve Dowden 25.00 11.00
❑ 41 Claude Hipps 25.00 11.00
❑ 42 Norm Standlee 25.00 11.00
❑ 43 Dick Todd CO 25.00 11.00
❑ 44 Babe Parilli 35.00 16.00
❑ 45 Steve Van Buren 75.00 34.00
❑ 46 Art Donovan RC 200.00 90.00
❑ 47 Bill Fischer 25.00 11.00
❑ 48 George Halas CO RC 200.00 90.00
❑ 49 Jerrell Price 25.00 11.00
❑ 50 John Sandusky RC 25.00 11.00
❑ 51 Ray Beck 25.00 11.00
❑ 52 Jim Martin 30.00 13.50
❑ 53 Joe Bach CO UER 25.00 11.00
(Misspelled Back)
❑ 54 Glen Christian 25.00 11.00
❑ 55 Andy Davis 25.00 11.00
❑ 56 Tobin Rote 30.00 13.50
❑ 57 Wayne Millner CO RC 50.00 22.00
❑ 58 Zollie Toth 25.00 11.00
❑ 59 Jack Jennings 25.00 11.00
❑ 60 Bill McColl 25.00 11.00
❑ 61 Les Richter RC 30.00 13.50
❑ 62 Walt Michaels RC 30.00 13.50
❑ 63 Charley Conerly 60.00 27.00
❑ 64 Howard Hartley 25.00 11.00
❑ 65 Jerome Smith 25.00 11.00
❑ 66 James Clark 25.00 11.00
❑ 67 Dick Logan 25.00 11.00
❑ 68 Wayne Robinson 25.00 11.00
❑ 69 James Hammond 25.00 11.00
❑ 70 Gene Schroeder 25.00 11.00
❑ 71 Tex Coulter 30.00 13.50
❑ 72 John Schweder 25.00 11.00
❑ 73 Vitamin Smith 35.00 16.00
❑ 74 Joe Campanella RC 30.00 13.50
❑ 75 Joe Kuharich CO RC 35.00 16.00
❑ 76 Herman Clark 30.00 13.50
❑ 77 Dan Edwards 30.00 13.50
❑ 78 Bobby Layne 150.00 70.00
❑ 79 Bob Hoernschemeyer 35.00 16.00
❑ 80 John Carr Blount 30.00 13.50
❑ 81 John Kastan RC 30.00 13.50
❑ 82 Harry Minarik 30.00 13.50
❑ 83 Joe Perry 75.00 34.00
❑ 84 Ray(Buddy) Parker CO RC 35.00 16.00
❑ 85 Andy Robustelli RC 125.00 55.00
❑ 86 Dub Jones 35.00 16.00
❑ 87 Mal Cook 30.00 13.50
❑ 88 Billy Stone 30.00 13.50
❑ 89 George Taliaferro 35.00 16.00
❑ 90 Thomas Johnson RC 30.00 13.50
❑ 91 Leon Heath 30.00 13.50
❑ 92 Pete Pihos 50.00 22.00
❑ 93 Fred Benners 30.00 13.50
❑ 94 George Tarasovic 30.00 13.50
❑ 95 Lawr. (Buck) Shaw CO RC 30.00 13.50
❑ 96 Bill Wightkin 30.00 13.50
❑ 97 John Wozniak 30.00 13.50
❑ 98 Bobby Dillon RC 35.00 16.00
❑ 99 Joe Stydahar CO RC 45.00 20.00
❑ 100 Dick Alban RC 30.00 13.50
❑ 101 Arnie Weinmeister 40.00 18.00
❑ 102 Bobby Cross 30.00 13.50
❑ 103 Don Paul 30.00 13.50
❑ 104 Buddy Young 40.00 18.00
❑ 105 Lou Groza 75.00 34.00
❑ 106 Ray Pelfrey 30.00 13.50
❑ 107 Maurice Nipp 30.00 13.50
❑ 108 Hubert Johnston 30.00 13.50
❑ 109 Volney Quinlan RC 30.00 13.50
❑ 110 Jack Simmons 30.00 13.50
❑ 111 George Ratterman 35.00 16.00
❑ 112 John Badaczewski 30.00 13.50
❑ 113 Bill Reichardt 30.00 13.50
❑ 114 Art Weiner 30.00 13.50
❑ 115 Keith Flowers 30.00 13.50
❑ 116 Russ Craft 30.00 13.50
❑ 117 Jim O'Donahue RC 30.00 13.50
❑ 118 Darrell Hogan 30.00 13.50
❑ 119 Frank Ziegler 30.00 13.50
❑ 120 Deacon Dan Towler 40.00 18.00
❑ 121 Fred Williams 30.00 13.50
❑ 122 Jimmy Phelan CO 30.00 13.50
❑ 123 Eddie Price 30.00 13.50
❑ 124 Chet Ostrowski 30.00 13.50
❑ 125 Leo Nomellini 75.00 34.00
❑ 126 Steve Romanik 30.00 13.50
❑ 127 Ollie Matson RC 125.00 55.00
❑ 128 Dante Lavelli 60.00 27.00
❑ 129 Jack Christiansen RC 80.00 36.00
❑ 130 Dom Moselle 30.00 13.50
❑ 131 John Rapacz 30.00 13.50
❑ 132 Chuck Ortmann UER 30.00 13.50
(Avg. gain 9.4, should be 4.8)
❑ 133 Bob Williams 30.00 13.50
❑ 134 Chuck Ulrich 30.00 13.50
❑ 135 Gene Ronzani CO RC 30.00 13.50
❑ 136 Bert Rechichar 35.00 16.00
❑ 137 Bob Waterfield 75.00 34.00
❑ 138 Bobby Walston RC 35.00 16.00
❑ 139 Jerry Shipkey 30.00 13.50
❑ 140 Yale Lary RC 80.00 36.00
❑ 141 Gordy Soltau 30.00 13.50
❑ 142 Tom Landry 400.00 180.00
❑ 143 John Papit 30.00 13.50
❑ 144 Jim Lansford RC 175.00 45.00

1953 Bowman

	NRMT	VG-E
COMPLETE SET (96)	3400.00	1500.00
WRAPPER (5-CENT)	175.00	80.00

❑ 1 Eddie LeBaron RC 120.00 30.00
❑ 2 John Dottley 30.00 13.50
❑ 3 Babe Parilli 35.00 16.00
❑ 4 Bucko Kilroy 35.00 16.00
❑ 5 Joe Tereshinski 30.00 13.50
❑ 6 Doak Walker 75.00 34.00
❑ 7 Fran Polsfoot 30.00 13.50
❑ 8 Sisto Averno 30.00 13.50
❑ 9 Marion Motley 75.00 34.00
❑ 10 Pat Brady 30.00 13.50
❑ 11 Norm Van Brocklin 125.00 55.00
❑ 12 Bill McColl 30.00 13.50
❑ 13 Jerry Groom 30.00 13.50
❑ 14 Al Pollard 30.00 13.50
❑ 15 Dante Lavelli 50.00 22.00
❑ 16 Eddie Price 30.00 13.50
❑ 17 Charley Trippi 50.00 22.00
❑ 18 Elbert Nickel 35.00 16.00
❑ 19 George Taliaferro 35.00 16.00
❑ 20 Charley Conerly 75.00 34.00
❑ 21 Bobby Layne 125.00 55.00
❑ 22 Elroy Hirsch 75.00 34.00
❑ 23 Jim Finks 40.00 18.00
❑ 24 Chuck Bednarik 75.00 34.00
❑ 25 Kyle Rote 40.00 18.00
❑ 26 Otto Graham 175.00 80.00

❑ 27 Harry Gilmer 35.00 16.00
❑ 28 Tobin Rote........ 35.00 16.00
❑ 29 Billy Stone........ 30.00 13.50
❑ 30 Buddy Young........ 40.00 18.00
❑ 31 Leon Hart 40.00 18.00
❑ 32 Hugh McElhenny........ 75.00 34.00
❑ 33 Dale Samuels 30.00 13.50
❑ 34 Lou Creekmur 50.00 22.00
❑ 35 Tom Catlin........ 30.00 13.50
❑ 36 Tom Fears........ 60.00 27.00
❑ 37 George Connor 40.00 18.00
❑ 38 Bill Walsh C........ 30.00 13.50
❑ 39 Leo Sanford SP........ 45.00 20.00
❑ 40 Horace Gillom 35.00 16.00
❑ 41 John Schweder SP 45.00 20.00
❑ 42 Tom O'Connell 30.00 13.50
❑ 43 Frank Gifford SP 450.00 200.00
❑ 44 Frank Continetti SP...... 45.00 20.00
❑ 45 John Olszewski SP 45.00 20.00
❑ 46 Dub Jones........ 35.00 16.00
❑ 47 Don Paul SP 45.00 20.00
❑ 48 Gerald Weatherly 30.00 13.50
❑ 49 Fred Bruney SP........ 45.00 20.00
❑ 50 Jack Scarbath 30.00 13.50
❑ 51 John Karras........ 30.00 13.50
❑ 52 Al Conway........ 30.00 13.50
❑ 53 Emlen Tunnell SP 125.00 55.00
❑ 54 Gern Nagler SP........ 45.00 20.00
❑ 55 Kenneth Snyder SP...... 45.00 20.00
❑ 56 Y.A. Tittle........ 125.00 55.00
❑ 57 John Rapacz SP 45.00 20.00
❑ 58 Harley Sewell SP 45.00 20.00
❑ 59 Don Bingham 30.00 13.50
❑ 60 Darrell Hogan 30.00 13.50
❑ 61 Tony Curcillo 30.00 13.50
❑ 62 Ray Renfro RC SP 50.00 22.00
❑ 63 Leon Heath 30.00 13.50
❑ 64 Tex Coulter SP 45.00 20.00
❑ 65 Dewayne Douglas........ 30.00 13.50
❑ 66 J. Robert Smith SP 45.00 20.00
❑ 67 Bob McChesney SP 45.00 20.00
❑ 68 Dick Alban SP........ 45.00 20.00
❑ 69 Andy Kozar 30.00 13.50
❑ 70 Merwin Hodel SP 45.00 20.00
❑ 71 Thurman McGraw 30.00 13.50
❑ 72 Cliff Anderson 30.00 13.50
❑ 73 Pete Pihos........ 50.00 22.00
❑ 74 Julie Rykovich 30.00 13.50
❑ 75 John Kreamcheck SP .. 45.00 20.00
❑ 76 Lynn Chandnois 30.00 13.50
❑ 77 Cloyce Box SP 45.00 20.00
❑ 78 Ray Mathews 30.00 13.50
❑ 79 Bobby Walston 35.00 16.00
❑ 80 Jim Dooley 30.00 13.50
❑ 81 Pat Harder SP........ 45.00 20.00
❑ 82 Jerry Shipkey 30.00 13.50
❑ 83 Bobby Thomason RC .. 30.00 13.50
❑ 84 Hugh Taylor........ 35.00 16.00
❑ 85 George Ratterman 35.00 16.00
❑ 86 Don Stonesifer 30.00 13.50
❑ 87 John Williams SP 45.00 20.00
❑ 88 Leo Nomellini 50.00 22.00
❑ 89 Frank Ziegler........ 30.00 13.50
❑ 90 Don Paul UER........ 30.00 13.50
(19th in punt returns, should be 9th) Chicago Cardinals
❑ 91 Tom Dublinski 30.00 13.50
❑ 92 Ken Carpenter........ 30.00 13.50
❑ 93 Ted Marchibroda RC.... 40.00 18.00
❑ 94 Chuck Drazenovich...... 30.00 13.50
❑ 95 Lou Groza SP 125.00 55.00
❑ 96 William Cross SP RC 100.00 25.00

1954 Bowman

	NRMT	VG-E
COMPLETE SET (128)	1700.00	750.00
COMMON CARD (1-64)	5.00	2.20
COMMON SP (65-96)	25.00	11.00
COMMON CARD (97-128)	5.00	2.20
WRAPPER (1-CENT)	15.00	6.75
WRAPPER (5-CENT)	30.00	13.50

❑ 1 Ray Mathews 30.00 7.50
❑ 2 John Huzvar 5.00 2.20

❑ 3 Jack Scarbath 5.00 2.20
❑ 4 Doug Atkins RC........ 50.00 22.00
❑ 5 Bill Stits 5.00 2.20
❑ 6 Joe Perry........ 30.00 13.50
❑ 7 Kyle Rote........ 15.00 6.75
❑ 8 Norm Van Brocklin 50.00 22.00
❑ 9 Pete Pihos........ 20.00 9.00
❑ 10 Babe Parilli 8.00 3.60
❑ 11 Zeke Bratkowski RC 25.00 11.00
❑ 12 Ollie Matson 25.00 11.00
❑ 13 Pat Brady 5.00 2.20
❑ 14 Fred Enke 5.00 2.20
❑ 15 Harry Ulinski 5.00 2.20
❑ 16 Bob Garrett 5.00 2.20
❑ 17 Bill Bowman 5.00 2.20
❑ 18 Leo Rucka........ 5.00 2.20
❑ 19 John Cannady........ 5.00 2.20
❑ 20 Tom Fears........ 25.00 11.00
❑ 21 Norm Willey........ 5.00 2.20
❑ 22 Floyd Reid........ 5.00 2.20
❑ 23 George Blanda RC 175.00 80.00
❑ 24 Don Doheney 5.00 2.20
❑ 25 John Schweder 5.00 2.20
❑ 26 Bert Rechichar 5.00 2.20
❑ 27 Harry Dowda 5.00 2.20
❑ 28 John Sandusky 5.00 2.20
❑ 29 Les Bingaman RC........ 15.00 6.75
❑ 30 Joe Arenas 5.00 2.20
❑ 31 Ray Wietecha RC 5.00 2.20
❑ 32 Elroy Hirsch........ 30.00 13.50
❑ 33 Harold Giancanelli........ 5.00 2.20
❑ 34 Billy Howton 8.00 3.60
❑ 35 Fred Morrison 5.00 2.20
❑ 36 Bobby Cavazos........ 5.00 2.20
❑ 37 Darrell Hogan 5.00 2.20
❑ 38 Buddy Young........ 8.00 3.60
❑ 39 Charlie Justice........ 20.00 9.00
❑ 40 Otto Graham 75.00 34.00
❑ 41 Doak Walker 30.00 13.50
❑ 42 Y.A. Tittle........ 60.00 27.00
❑ 43 Buford Long........ 5.00 2.20
❑ 44 Volney Quinlan 5.00 2.20
❑ 45 Bobby Thomason 5.00 2.20
❑ 46 Fred Cone 5.00 2.20
❑ 47 Gerald Weatherly 5.00 2.20
❑ 48 Don Stonesifer 5.00 2.20
❑ 49 Lynn Chandnois 5.00 2.20
❑ 50 George Taliaferro 5.00 2.20
❑ 51 Dick Alban........ 5.00 2.20
❑ 52 Lou Groza 30.00 13.50
❑ 53 Bobby Layne........ 60.00 27.00
❑ 54 Hugh McElhenny........ 40.00 18.00
❑ 55 Frank Gifford UER...... 100.00 45.00
(Avg. gain 7.83, should be 3.1)
❑ 56 Leon McLaughlin........ 5.00 2.20
❑ 57 Chuck Bednarik........ 40.00 18.00
❑ 58 Art Hunter 5.00 2.20
❑ 59 Bill McColl 5.00 2.20
❑ 60 Charley Trippi 20.00 9.00
❑ 61 Jim Finks........ 15.00 6.75
❑ 62 Bill Lange 5.00 2.20
❑ 63 Laurie Niemi 5.00 2.20
❑ 64 Ray Renfro 8.00 3.60
❑ 65 Dick Chapman........ 25.00 11.00
❑ 66 Bob Hantla 25.00 11.00
❑ 67 Ralph Starkey 25.00 11.00
❑ 68 Don Paul 25.00 11.00
❑ 69 Kenneth Snyder 25.00 11.00
❑ 70 Tobin Rote........ 30.00 13.50
❑ 71 Art DeCarlo 25.00 11.00
❑ 72 Tom Keane 25.00 11.00
❑ 73 Hugh Taylor........ 30.00 13.50
❑ 74 Warren Lahr RC 25.00 11.00
❑ 75 Jim Neal 25.00 11.00
❑ 76 Leo Nomellini 60.00 27.00
❑ 77 Dick Yelvington 25.00 11.00
❑ 78 Les Richter 30.00 13.50
❑ 79 Bucko Kilroy 30.00 13.50
❑ 80 John Martinkovic........ 25.00 11.00
❑ 81 Dale Dodrill RC 25.00 11.00
❑ 82 Ken Jackson 25.00 11.00
❑ 83 Paul Lipscomb........ 25.00 11.00
❑ 84 John Bauer 25.00 11.00
❑ 85 Lou Creekmur 50.00 22.00
❑ 86 Eddie Price 25.00 11.00
❑ 87 Kenneth Farragut 25.00 11.00
❑ 88 Dave Hanner RC........ 30.00 13.50
❑ 89 Don Boll........ 25.00 11.00
❑ 90 Chet Hanulak 25.00 11.00
❑ 91 Thurman McGraw 25.00 11.00
❑ 92 Don Heinrich RC 30.00 13.50
❑ 93 Dan McKown........ 25.00 11.00
❑ 94 Bob Fleck 25.00 11.00
❑ 95 Jerry Hilgenberg 25.00 11.00
❑ 96 Bill Walsh 25.00 11.00
❑ 97A Tom Finnin ERR 60.00 27.00
❑ 97B Tom Finnan COR 8.00 3.60
❑ 98 Paul Barry 5.00 2.20
❑ 99 Chick Jagade 5.00 2.20
❑ 100 Jack Christiansen 20.00 9.00
❑ 101 Gordy Soltau 5.00 2.20
❑ 102 Emlen Tunnell 20.00 9.00
❑ 103 Stan West 5.00 2.20
❑ 104 Jerry Williams 5.00 2.20
❑ 105 Veryl Switzer 5.00 2.20
❑ 106 Billy Stone 5.00 2.20
❑ 107 Jerry Watford........ 5.00 2.20
❑ 108 Elbert Nickel 8.00 3.60
❑ 109 Ed Sharkey 5.00 2.20
❑ 110 Steve Meilinger 5.00 2.20
❑ 111 Dante Lavelli 20.00 9.00
❑ 112 Leon Hart 15.00 6.75
❑ 113 Charley Conerly 30.00 13.50
❑ 114 Richard Lemmon........ 5.00 2.20
❑ 115 Al Carmichael 5.00 2.20
❑ 116 George Connor 20.00 9.00
❑ 117 John Olszewski 5.00 2.20
❑ 118 Ernie Stautner 25.00 11.00
❑ 119 Ray Smith 5.00 2.20
❑ 120 Neil Worden 5.00 2.20
❑ 121 Jim Dooley 5.00 2.20
❑ 122 Arnold Galiffa 5.00 2.20
❑ 123 Kline Gilbert........ 5.00 2.20
❑ 124 Bob Hoernschemeyer .. 8.00 3.60
❑ 125 Wilford Whizzer White RC 15.00 6.75
(Not the Supreme Court Justice)
❑ 126 Art Spinney 5.00 2.20
❑ 127 Joe Koch 5.00 2.20
❑ 128 John Lattner RC 80.00 20.00

1955 Bowman

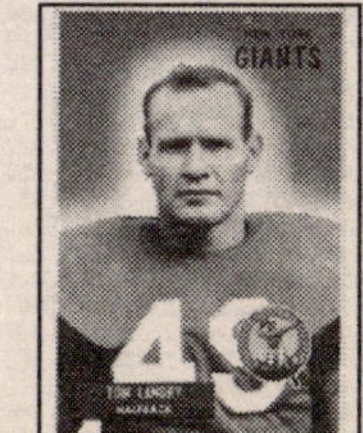

	NRMT	VG-E
COMPLETE SET (160)	1600.00	700.00
COMMON CARD (1-64)	5.00	2.20

COMMON CARD (65-160)	8.00	3.60
WRAPPER (1-CENT)	200.00	90.00
WRAPPER (5-CENT)	75.00	34.00
❑ 1 Doak Walker	60.00	15.00
❑ 2 Mike McCormack RC	30.00	13.50
❑ 3 John Olszewski	5.00	2.20
❑ 4 Dorne Dibble	5.00	2.20
❑ 5 Lindon Crow	5.00	2.20
❑ 6 Hugh Taylor UER	8.00	3.60
(First word in bio should be Bones)		
❑ 7 Frank Gifford	75.00	34.00
❑ 8 Alan Ameche RC	35.00	16.00
❑ 9 Don Stonesifer	5.00	2.20
❑ 10 Pete Pihos	15.00	6.75
❑ 11 Bill Austin	5.00	2.20
❑ 12 Dick Alban	5.00	2.20
❑ 13 Bobby Walston	8.00	3.60
❑ 14 Len Ford RC	35.00	16.00
❑ 15 Jug Girard	5.00	2.20
❑ 16 Charley Conerly	25.00	11.00
❑ 17 Volney Peters	5.00	2.20
❑ 18 Max Boydston	5.00	2.20
❑ 19 Leon Hart	12.00	5.50
❑ 20 Bert Rechichar	5.00	2.20
❑ 21 Lee Riley	5.00	2.20
❑ 22 Johnny Carson	5.00	2.20
❑ 23 Harry Thompson	5.00	2.20
❑ 24 Ray Wietecha	5.00	2.20
❑ 25 Ollie Matson	25.00	11.00
❑ 26 Eddie LeBaron	15.00	6.75
❑ 27 Jack Simmons	5.00	2.20
❑ 28 Jack Christiansen	15.00	6.75
❑ 29 Bucko Kilroy	8.00	3.60
❑ 30 Tom Keane	5.00	2.20
❑ 31 Dave Leggett	5.00	2.20
❑ 32 Norm Van Brocklin	35.00	16.00
❑ 33 Harlon Hill RC	8.00	3.60
❑ 34 Robert Haner	5.00	2.20
❑ 35 Veryl Switzer	5.00	2.20
❑ 36 Dick Stanfel RC	12.00	5.50
❑ 37 Lou Groza	25.00	11.00
❑ 38 Tank Younger	12.00	5.50
❑ 39 Dick Flanagan	5.00	2.20
❑ 40 Jim Dooley	5.00	2.20
❑ 41 Ray Collins	5.00	2.20
❑ 42 John Henry Johnson RC	40.00	18.00
❑ 43 Tom Fears	15.00	6.75
❑ 44 Joe Perry	25.00	11.00
❑ 45 Gene Brito RC	5.00	2.20
❑ 46 Bill Johnson	5.00	2.20
❑ 47 Deacon Dan Towler	12.00	5.50
❑ 48 Dick Moegle	8.00	3.60
❑ 49 Kline Gilbert	5.00	2.20
❑ 50 Les Gobel	5.00	2.20
❑ 51 Ray Krouse	5.00	2.20
❑ 52 Pat Summerall RC	75.00	34.00
❑ 53 Ed Brown RC	12.00	5.50
❑ 54 Lynn Chandnois	5.00	2.20
❑ 55 Joe Heap	5.00	2.20
❑ 56 John Hoffman	5.00	2.20
❑ 57 Howard Ferguson	5.00	2.20
❑ 58 Bobby Watkins	5.00	2.20
❑ 59 Charlie Ane	5.00	2.20
❑ 60 Ken MacAfee E RC	8.00	3.60
❑ 61 Ralph Guglielmi RC	8.00	3.60
❑ 62 George Blanda	60.00	27.00
❑ 63 Kenneth Snyder	5.00	2.20
❑ 64 Chet Ostrowski	5.00	2.20
❑ 65 Buddy Young	15.00	6.75
❑ 66 Gordy Soltau	8.00	3.60
❑ 67 Eddie Bell	8.00	3.60
❑ 68 Ben Agajanian RC	12.00	5.50
❑ 69 Tom Dahms	8.00	3.60
❑ 70 Jim Ringo RC	50.00	22.00
❑ 71 Bobby Layne	75.00	34.00
❑ 72 Y.A. Tittle	75.00	34.00
❑ 73 Bob Gaona	8.00	3.60
❑ 74 Tobin Rote	12.00	5.50
❑ 75 Hugh McElhenny	30.00	13.50
❑ 76 John Kreamcheck	8.00	3.60
❑ 77 Al Dorow	12.00	5.50
❑ 78 Bill Wade	15.00	6.75
❑ 79 Dale Dodrill	8.00	3.60
❑ 80 Chuck Drazenovich	8.00	3.60
❑ 81 Billy Wilson RC	12.00	5.50
❑ 82 Les Richter	12.00	5.50
❑ 83 Pat Brady	8.00	3.60
❑ 84 Bob Hoernschemeyer	12.00	5.50
❑ 85 Joe Arenas	8.00	3.60
❑ 86 Len Szafaryn UER	8.00	3.60
(Listed as Ben on front)		
❑ 87 Rick Casares RC	20.00	9.00
❑ 88 Leon McLaughlin	8.00	3.60
❑ 89 Charley Toogood	8.00	3.60
❑ 90 Tom Bettis	8.00	3.60
❑ 91 John Sandusky	8.00	3.60
❑ 92 Bill Wightkin	8.00	3.60
❑ 93 Darrel Brewster	8.00	3.60
❑ 94 Marion Campbell	15.00	6.75
❑ 95 Floyd Reid	8.00	3.60
❑ 96 Chick Jagade	8.00	3.60
❑ 97 George Taliaferro	8.00	3.60
❑ 98 Carlton Massey	8.00	3.60
❑ 99 Fran Rogel	8.00	3.60
❑ 100 Alex Sandusky	8.00	3.60
❑ 101 Bob St. Clair RC	35.00	16.00
❑ 102 Al Carmichael	8.00	3.60
❑ 103 Carl Taseff RC	8.00	3.60
❑ 104 Leo Nomellini	25.00	11.00
❑ 105 Tom Scott	8.00	3.60
❑ 106 Ted Marchibroda	15.00	6.75
❑ 107 Art Spinney	8.00	3.60
❑ 108 Wayne Robinson	8.00	3.60
❑ 109 Jim Ricca	8.00	3.60
❑ 110 Lou Ferry	8.00	3.60
❑ 111 Roger Zatkoff	8.00	3.60
❑ 112 Lou Creekmur	15.00	6.75
❑ 113 Kenny Konz	8.00	3.60
❑ 114 Doug Eggers	8.00	3.60
❑ 115 Bobby Thomason	8.00	3.60
❑ 116 Bill McPeak	8.00	3.60
❑ 117 William Brown	8.00	3.60
❑ 118 Royce Womble	8.00	3.60
❑ 119 Frank Gatski RC	30.00	13.50
❑ 120 Jim Finks	15.00	6.75
❑ 121 Andy Robustelli	25.00	11.00
❑ 122 Bobby Dillon	8.00	3.60
❑ 123 Leo Sanford	8.00	3.60
❑ 124 Elbert Nickel	12.00	5.50
❑ 125 Wayne Hansen	8.00	3.60
❑ 126 Buck Lansford	8.00	3.60
❑ 127 Gern Nagler	8.00	3.60
❑ 128 Jim Salsbury	8.00	3.60
❑ 129 Dale Atkeson RC	8.00	3.60
❑ 130 John Schweder	8.00	3.60
❑ 131 Dave Hanner	12.00	5.50
❑ 132 Eddie Price	8.00	3.60
❑ 133 Vic Janowicz	20.00	9.00
❑ 134 Ernie Stautner	25.00	11.00
❑ 135 James Parmer	8.00	3.60
❑ 136 Emlen Tunnell UER	20.00	9.00
(Misspelled Tunnel on card front)		
❑ 137 Kyle Rote UER	15.00	6.75
(Longest gain 1.8 yards, should be 18 yards)		
❑ 138 Norm Willey	8.00	3.60
❑ 139 Charley Trippi	20.00	9.00
❑ 140 Billy Howton	12.00	5.50
❑ 141 Bobby Clatterbuck	8.00	3.60
❑ 142 Bob Boyd	8.00	3.60
❑ 143 Bob Toneff RC UER	12.00	5.50
(name misspelled Toneoff)		
❑ 144 Jerry Helluin	8.00	3.60
❑ 145 Adrian Burk	8.00	3.60
❑ 146 Walt Michaels	12.00	5.50
❑ 147 Zollie Toth	8.00	3.60
❑ 148 Frank Varrichione RC	8.00	3.60
❑ 149 Dick Bielski	8.00	3.60
❑ 150 George Ratterman	12.00	5.50
❑ 151 Mike Jarmoluk	8.00	3.60
❑ 152 Tom Landry	200.00	90.00
❑ 153 Ray Renfro	12.00	5.50
❑ 154 Zeke Bratkowski	12.00	5.50
❑ 155 Jerry Norton	8.00	3.60
❑ 156 Maurice Bassett	8.00	3.60
❑ 157 Volney Quinlan	8.00	3.60
❑ 158 Chuck Bednarik	30.00	13.50
❑ 159 Don Colo	8.00	3.60
❑ 160 L.G. Dupre RC	40.00	10.00

1991 Bowman

	MINT	NRMT
COMPLETE SET (561)	12.00	5.50
COMP.FACT.SET (561)	12.00	5.50
❑ 1 Jeff George RS	.25	.11
❑ 2 Richmond Webb RS	.04	.02
❑ 3 Emmitt Smith RS	1.00	.45
❑ 4 Mark Carrier DB RS UER	.04	.02
(Chambers was rookie in '73, not '74)		
❑ 5 Steve Christie RS	.04	.02
❑ 6 Keith Sims RS	.04	.02
❑ 7 Rob Moore RS UER	.25	.11
(Yards misspelled as yarders on back)		
❑ 8 Johnny Johnson RS	.04	.02
❑ 9 Eric Green RS	.04	.02
❑ 10 Ben Smith RS	.04	.02
❑ 11 Tory Epps RS	.04	.02
❑ 12 Andre Rison	.10	.05
❑ 13 Shawn Collins	.04	.02
❑ 14 Chris Hinton	.04	.02
❑ 15 Deion Sanders UER	.40	.18
(Bio says he played for Georgia, College listed should be Florida State)		
❑ 16 Darion Conner	.04	.02
❑ 17 Michael Haynes	.25	.11
❑ 18 Chris Miller	.10	.05
❑ 19 Jessie Tuggle	.04	.02
❑ 20 Scott Fulhage	.04	.02
❑ 21 Bill Fralic	.04	.02
❑ 22 Floyd Dixon	.04	.02
❑ 23 Oliver Barnett	.04	.02
❑ 24 Mike Rozier	.04	.02
❑ 25 Tory Epps	.04	.02
❑ 26 Tim Green	.04	.02
❑ 27 Steve Broussard	.04	.02
❑ 28 Bruce Pickens RC	.04	.02
❑ 29 Mike Pritchard RC	.25	.11
❑ 30 Andre Reed	.10	.05
❑ 31 Darryl Talley	.04	.02
❑ 32 Nate Odomes	.04	.02
❑ 33 Jamie Mueller	.04	.02
❑ 34 Leon Seals	.04	.02
❑ 35 Keith McKeller	.04	.02
❑ 36 Al Edwards	.04	.02
❑ 37 Butch Rolle	.04	.02
❑ 38 Jeff Wright RC	.04	.02
❑ 39 Will Wolford	.04	.02
❑ 40 James Williams	.04	.02
❑ 41 Kent Hull	.04	.02
❑ 42 James Lofton	.10	.05
❑ 43 Frank Reich	.10	.05
❑ 44 Bruce Smith	.25	.11
❑ 45 Thurman Thomas	.25	.11
❑ 46 Leonard Smith	.04	.02
❑ 47 Shane Conlan	.04	.02
❑ 48 Steve Tasker	.10	.05
❑ 49 Ray Bentley	.04	.02
❑ 50 Cornelius Bennett	.10	.05
❑ 51 Stan Thomas	.04	.02
❑ 52 Shaun Gayle	.04	.02
❑ 53 Wendell Davis	.04	.02
❑ 54 James Thornton	.04	.02
❑ 55 Mark Carrier DB	.10	.05

❑ 56	Richard Dent	.10	.05
❑ 57	Ron Morris	.04	.02
❑ 58	Mike Singletary	.10	.05
❑ 59	Jay Hilgenberg	.04	.02
❑ 60	Donnell Woolford	.04	.02
❑ 61	Jim Covert	.04	.02
❑ 62	Jim Harbaugh	.25	.11
❑ 63	Neal Anderson	.10	.05
❑ 64	Brad Muster	.04	.02
❑ 65	Kevin Butler	.04	.02
❑ 66	Trace Armstrong UER (Bio says 80 tackles in '90, stats say 82)	.04	.02
❑ 67	Ron Cox	.04	.02
❑ 68	Peter Tom Willis	.04	.02
❑ 69	Johnny Bailey	.04	.02
❑ 70	Mark Bortz UER (Bio has 6th round, but was 8th round)	.04	.02
❑ 71	Chris Zorich RC	.25	.11
❑ 72	Lamar Rogers RC	.04	.02
❑ 73	David Grant UER (Listed as DE, but should be NT)	.04	.02
❑ 74	Lewis Billups	.04	.02
❑ 75	Harold Green	.10	.05
❑ 76	Ickey Woods	.04	.02
❑ 77	Eddie Brown	.04	.02
❑ 78	David Fulcher	.04	.02
❑ 79	Anthony Munoz	.10	.05
❑ 80	Carl Zander	.04	.02
❑ 81	Rodney Holman	.04	.02
❑ 82	James Brooks	.10	.05
❑ 83	Tim McGee	.04	.02
❑ 84	Boomer Esiason	.10	.05
❑ 85	Leon White	.04	.02
❑ 86	James Francis UER (Ron is CB, card says he's LB)	.04	.02
❑ 87	Mitchell Price RC	.04	.02
❑ 88	Ed King RC	.04	.02
❑ 89	Eric Turner RC	.10	.05
❑ 90	Rob Burnett RC	.10	.05
❑ 91	Leroy Hoard	.10	.05
❑ 92	Kevin Mack UER (Height 6-2, should be 6-0)	.04	.02
❑ 93	Thane Gash UER (Comma omitted after name in bio)	.04	.02
❑ 94	Gregg Rakoczy	.04	.02
❑ 95	Clay Matthews	.10	.05
❑ 96	Eric Metcalf	.10	.05
❑ 97	Stephen Braggs	.04	.02
❑ 98	Frank Minnifield	.04	.02
❑ 99	Reggie Langhorne	.04	.02
❑ 100	Mike Johnson	.04	.02
❑ 101	Brian Brennan	.04	.02
❑ 102	Anthony Pleasant	.04	.02
❑ 103	Godfrey Myles RC UER (Vertical misspelled as verticle)	.04	.02
❑ 104	Russell Maryland RC	.25	.11
❑ 105	James Washington RC	.04	.02
❑ 106	Nate Newton	.10	.05
❑ 107	Jimmie Jones	.04	.02
❑ 108	Jay Novacek	.25	.11
❑ 109	Alexander Wright	.04	.02
❑ 110	Jack Del Rio	.04	.02
❑ 111	Jim Jeffcoat	.04	.02
❑ 112	Mike Saxon	.04	.02
❑ 113	Troy Aikman	.75	.35
❑ 114	Issiac Holt	.04	.02
❑ 115	Ken Norton	.25	.11
❑ 116	Kelvin Martin	.04	.02
❑ 117	Emmitt Smith	2.00	.90
❑ 118	Ken Willis	.04	.02
❑ 119	Daniel Stubbs	.04	.02
❑ 120	Michael Irvin	.25	.11
❑ 121	Danny Noonan	.04	.02
❑ 122	Alvin Harper RC UER (Drafted in first round, not second)	.25	.11
❑ 123	Reggie Johnson RC	.04	.02
❑ 124	Vance Johnson	.04	.02
❑ 125	Steve Atwater	.04	.02
❑ 126	Greg Kragen	.04	.02
❑ 127	John Elway	1.25	.55
❑ 128	Simon Fletcher	.04	.02
❑ 129	Wymon Henderson	.04	.02
❑ 130	Ricky Nattiel	.04	.02
❑ 131	Shannon Sharpe	.50	.23
❑ 132	Ron Holmes	.04	.02
❑ 133	Karl Mecklenburg	.04	.02
❑ 134	Bobby Humphrey	.04	.02
❑ 135	Clarence Kay	.04	.02
❑ 136	Dennis Smith	.04	.02
❑ 137	Jim Juriga	.04	.02
❑ 138	Melvin Bratton	.04	.02
❑ 139	Mark Jackson UER (Apostrophe placed in front of longest)	.04	.02
❑ 140	Michael Brooks	.04	.02
❑ 141	Alton Montgomery	.04	.02
❑ 142	Mike Croel RC	.04	.02
❑ 143	Mel Gray	.10	.05
❑ 144	Michael Cofer	.04	.02
❑ 145	Jeff Campbell	.04	.02
❑ 146	Dan Owens	.04	.02
❑ 147	Robert Clark UER (Drafted in '87, not '89)	.04	.02
❑ 148	Jim Arnold	.04	.02
❑ 149	William White	.04	.02
❑ 150	Rodney Peete	.10	.05
❑ 151	Jerry Ball	.04	.02
❑ 152	Bennie Blades	.04	.02
❑ 153	Barry Sanders UER (Drafted in '89, not '88)	1.50	.70
❑ 154	Andre Ware	.10	.05
❑ 155	Lomas Brown	.04	.02
❑ 156	Chris Spielman	.10	.05
❑ 157	Kelvin Pritchett RC	.10	.05
❑ 158	Herman Moore RC	2.00	.90
❑ 159	Chris Jacke	.04	.02
❑ 160	Tony Mandarich	.04	.02
❑ 161	Perry Kemp	.04	.02
❑ 162	Johnny Holland	.04	.02
❑ 163	Mark Lee	.04	.02
❑ 164	Anthony Dilweg	.04	.02
❑ 165	Scott Stephen RC	.04	.02
❑ 166	Ed West	.04	.02
❑ 167	Mark Murphy	.04	.02
❑ 168	Darrell Thompson	.04	.02
❑ 169	James Campen RC	.04	.02
❑ 170	Jeff Query	.04	.02
❑ 171	Brian Noble	.04	.02
❑ 172	Sterling Sharpe UER (Card says he gained 3314 yards in 1990)	.25	.11
❑ 173	Robert Brown	.04	.02
❑ 174	Tim Harris	.04	.02
❑ 175	LeRoy Butler	.10	.05
❑ 176	Don Majkowski	.04	.02
❑ 177	Vinnie Clark RC	.04	.02
❑ 178	Esera Tuaolo RC	.04	.02
❑ 179	Lorenzo White UER (Bio says 3rd year, actually 4th year)	.04	.02
❑ 180	Warren Moon	.25	.11
❑ 181	Sean Jones	.10	.05
❑ 182	Curtis Duncan	.04	.02
❑ 183	Al Smith	.04	.02
❑ 184	Richard Johnson RC	.04	.02
❑ 185	Tony Jones	.10	.05
❑ 186	Bubba McDowell	.04	.02
❑ 187	Bruce Matthews	.10	.05
❑ 188	Ray Childress	.04	.02
❑ 189	Haywood Jeffires	.10	.05
❑ 190	Ernest Givins	.10	.05
❑ 191	Mike Munchak	.04	.02
❑ 192	Greg Montgomery	.04	.02
❑ 193	Cody Carlson RC	.04	.02
❑ 194	Johnny Meads	.04	.02
❑ 195	Drew Hill UER (Age listed as 24, should be 34)	.04	.02
❑ 196	Mike Dumas RC	.04	.02
❑ 197	Darryll Lewis RC	.10	.05
❑ 198	Rohn Stark	.04	.02
❑ 199	Clarence Verdin UER (Played 2 seasons in USFL, not one)	.04	.02
❑ 200	Mike Prior	.04	.02
❑ 201	Eugene Daniel	.04	.02
❑ 202	Dean Biasucci	.04	.02
❑ 203	Jeff Herrod	.04	.02
❑ 204	Keith Taylor	.04	.02
❑ 205	Jon Hand	.04	.02
❑ 206	Pat Beach	.04	.02
❑ 207	Duane Bickett	.04	.02
❑ 208	Jessie Hester UER (Bio confuses Hester's NFL history)	.04	.02
❑ 209	Chip Banks	.04	.02
❑ 210	Ray Donaldson	.04	.02
❑ 211	Bill Brooks	.04	.02
❑ 212	Jeff George	.25	.11
❑ 213	Tony Siragusa RC	.10	.05
❑ 214	Albert Bentley	.04	.02
❑ 215	Joe Valerio	.04	.02
❑ 216	Chris Martin	.04	.02
❑ 217	Christian Okoye	.04	.02
❑ 218	Stephone Paige	.04	.02
❑ 219	Percy Snow	.04	.02
❑ 220	David Szott	.04	.02
❑ 221	Derrick Thomas	.25	.11
❑ 222	Todd McNair	.04	.02
❑ 223	Albert Lewis	.04	.02
❑ 224	Neil Smith	.25	.11
❑ 225	Barry Word	.04	.02
❑ 226	Robb Thomas	.04	.02
❑ 227	John Alt	.04	.02
❑ 228	Jonathan Hayes	.04	.02
❑ 229	Kevin Ross	.04	.02
❑ 230	Nick Lowery	.04	.02
❑ 231	Tim Grunhard	.04	.02
❑ 232	Dan Saleaumua	.04	.02
❑ 233	Steve DeBerg	.04	.02
❑ 234	Harvey Williams RC	.25	.11
❑ 235	Nick Bell RC UER (Lives in Nevada, not California)	.04	.02
❑ 236	Mervyn Fernandez UER (Drafted in '83, not FA '87 as on card)	.04	.02
❑ 237	Howie Long	.10	.05
❑ 238	Marcus Allen	.25	.11
❑ 239	Eddie Anderson	.04	.02
❑ 240	Ethan Horton	.04	.02
❑ 241	Lionel Washington	.04	.02
❑ 242	Steve Wisniewski UER (Drafted, should be traded to)	.04	.02
❑ 243	Bo Jackson UER (Drafted by Raiders, should say drafted by Tampa Bay in '86)	.30	.14
❑ 244	Greg Townsend	.04	.02
❑ 245	Jeff Jaeger	.04	.02
❑ 246	Aaron Wallace	.04	.02
❑ 247	Garry Lewis	.04	.02
❑ 248	Steve Smith	.04	.02
❑ 249	Willie Gault UER ('90 stats 839 yards, should be 985)	.04	.02
❑ 250	Scott Davis	.04	.02
❑ 251	Jay Schroeder	.04	.02
❑ 252	Don Mosebar	.04	.02
❑ 253	Todd Marinovich RC	.04	.02
❑ 254	Irv Pankey	.04	.02
❑ 255	Flipper Anderson	.04	.02
❑ 256	Tom Newberry	.04	.02
❑ 257	Kevin Greene	.25	.11
❑ 258	Mike Wilcher	.04	.02
❑ 259	Bern Brostek	.04	.02
❑ 260	Buford McGee	.04	.02
❑ 261	Cleveland Gary	.04	.02
❑ 262	Jackie Slater	.04	.02
❑ 263	Henry Ellard	.10	.05
❑ 264	Alvin Wright	.04	.02
❑ 265	Darryl Henley RC	.04	.02
❑ 266	Damone Johnson RC	.04	.02
❑ 267	Frank Stams	.04	.02
❑ 268	Jerry Gray	.04	.02
❑ 269	Jim Everett	.10	.05
❑ 270	Pat Terrell	.04	.02

- ❑ 271 Todd Lyght RC .04 .02
- ❑ 272 Aaron Cox .04 .02
- ❑ 273 Barry Sanders LL .60 .25
  Rushing Leader
- ❑ 274 Jerry Rice LL .40 .18
  Receiving Leader
- ❑ 275 Derrick Thomas LL .25 .11
  Sack Leader
- ❑ 276 Mark Carrier DB LL .10 .05
  Interception Leader
- ❑ 277 Warren Moon LL .25 .11
  Passing Yardage Leader
- ❑ 278 Randall Cunningham LL .10 .05
  Rushing Average Leader
- ❑ 279 Nick Lowery LL .04 .02
  Scoring Leader
- ❑ 280 Clarence Verdin LL .04 .02
  Punt Return Leader
- ❑ 281 Thurman Thomas LL .25 .11
  Yards From Scrimmage Leader
- ❑ 282 Mike Horan LL .04 .02
  Punting Average Leader
- ❑ 283 Flipper Anderson LL .04 .02
  Receiving Average Leader
- ❑ 284 John Offerdahl .04 .02
- ❑ 285 Dan Marino UER 1.25 .55
  (2637 yards gained, should be 3563)
- ❑ 286 Mark Clayton .10 .05
- ❑ 287 Tony Paige .04 .02
- ❑ 288 Keith Sims .04 .02
- ❑ 289 Jeff Cross .04 .02
- ❑ 290 Pete Stoyanovich .04 .02
- ❑ 291 Ferrell Edmunds .04 .02
- ❑ 292 Reggie Roby .04 .02
- ❑ 293 Louis Oliver .04 .02
- ❑ 294 Jarvis Williams .04 .02
- ❑ 295 Sammie Smith .04 .02
- ❑ 296 Richmond Webb .04 .02
- ❑ 297 J.B. Brown .04 .02
- ❑ 298 Jim C.Jensen .04 .02
- ❑ 299 Mark Duper .10 .05
- ❑ 300 David Griggs .04 .02
- ❑ 301 Randal Hill RC .10 .05
- ❑ 302 Aaron Craver RC .04 .02
  (See also 320)
- ❑ 303 Keith Millard .04 .02
- ❑ 304 Steve Jordan .04 .02
- ❑ 305 Anthony Carter .10 .05
- ❑ 306 Mike Merriweather .04 .02
- ❑ 307 Audray McMillian RC UER .04 .02
  (Front Audray, back Audrey)
- ❑ 308 Randall McDaniel .04 .02
- ❑ 309 Gary Zimmerman .04 .02
- ❑ 310 Carl Lee .04 .02
- ❑ 311 Reggie Rutland .04 .02
- ❑ 312 Hassan Jones .04 .02
- ❑ 313 Kirk Lowdermilk UER .04 .02
  (Reversed negative)
- ❑ 314 Herschel Walker .10 .05
- ❑ 315 Chris Doleman .04 .02
- ❑ 316 Joey Browner .04 .02
- ❑ 317 Wade Wilson .10 .05
- ❑ 318 Henry Thomas .04 .02
- ❑ 319 Rich Gannon .25 .11
- ❑ 320 Al Noga UER .04 .02
  (Numbered incorrectly as 302 on card)
- ❑ 321 Pat Harlow RC .04 .02
- ❑ 322 Bruce Armstrong .04 .02
- ❑ 323 Maurice Hurst .04 .02
- ❑ 324 Brent Williams .04 .02
- ❑ 325 Chris Singleton .04 .02
- ❑ 326 Jason Staurovsky .04 .02
- ❑ 327 Marvin Allen .04 .02
- ❑ 328 Hart Lee Dykes .04 .02
- ❑ 329 Johnny Rembert .04 .02
- ❑ 330 Andre Tippett .04 .02
- ❑ 331 Greg McMurtry .04 .02
- ❑ 332 John Stephens .04 .02
- ❑ 333 Ray Agnew .04 .02
- ❑ 334 Tommy Hodson .04 .02
- ❑ 335 Ronnie Lippett .04 .02
- ❑ 336 Marv Cook .04 .02
- ❑ 337 Tommy Barnhardt RC .04 .02
- ❑ 338 Dalton Hilliard .04 .02
- ❑ 339 Sam Mills .04 .02
- ❑ 340 Morten Andersen .04 .02
- ❑ 341 Stan Brock .04 .02
- ❑ 342 Brett Maxie .04 .02
- ❑ 343 Steve Walsh .04 .02
- ❑ 344 Vaughan Johnson .04 .02
- ❑ 345 Rickey Jackson .04 .02
- ❑ 346 Renaldo Turnbull .04 .02
- ❑ 347 Joel Hilgenberg .04 .02
- ❑ 348 Toi Cook RC .04 .02
- ❑ 349 Robert Massey .04 .02
- ❑ 350 Pat Swilling .10 .05
- ❑ 351 Eric Martin .04 .02
- ❑ 352 Rueben Mayes UER .04 .02
  (Bio says 2nd round, should be 3rd)
- ❑ 353 Vince Buck .04 .02
- ❑ 354 Brett Perriman .25 .11
- ❑ 355 Wesley Carroll RC .04 .02
- ❑ 356 Jarrod Bunch RC .04 .02
- ❑ 357 Pepper Johnson .04 .02
- ❑ 358 Dave Meggett .10 .05
- ❑ 359 Mark Collins .04 .02
- ❑ 360 Sean Landeta .04 .02
- ❑ 361 Maurice Carthon .04 .02
- ❑ 362 Mike Fox UER .04 .02
  (Listed as DE, should say DT)
- ❑ 363 Jeff Hostetler .10 .05
- ❑ 364 Phil Simms .10 .05
- ❑ 365 Leonard Marshall .04 .02
- ❑ 366 Gary Reasons .04 .02
- ❑ 367 Rodney Hampton .25 .11
- ❑ 368 Greg Jackson RC .04 .02
- ❑ 369 Jumbo Elliott .04 .02
- ❑ 370 Bob Kratch RC .04 .02
- ❑ 371 Lawrence Taylor .25 .11
- ❑ 372 Erik Howard .04 .02
- ❑ 373 Carl Banks .04 .02
- ❑ 374 Stephen Baker .04 .02
- ❑ 375 Mark Ingram .10 .05
- ❑ 376 Browning Nagle RC .04 .02
- ❑ 377 Jeff Lageman .04 .02
- ❑ 378 Ken O'Brien .04 .02
- ❑ 379 Al Toon .10 .05
- ❑ 380 Joe Prokop .04 .02
- ❑ 381 Tony Stargell .04 .02
- ❑ 382 Blair Thomas .04 .02
- ❑ 383 Erik McMillan .04 .02
- ❑ 384 Dennis Byrd .04 .02
- ❑ 385 Freeman McNeil .04 .02
- ❑ 386 Brad Baxter .04 .02
- ❑ 387 Mark Boyer .04 .02
- ❑ 388 Terance Mathis .10 .05
- ❑ 389 Jim Sweeney .04 .02
- ❑ 390 Kyle Clifton .04 .02
- ❑ 391 Pat Leahy .04 .02
- ❑ 392 Rob Moore .25 .11
- ❑ 393 James Hasty .04 .02
- ❑ 394 Blaise Bryant .04 .02
- ❑ 395A Jesse Campbell RC ERR 1.00 .45
  (Photo actually Dan McGwire; see 509)
- ❑ 395B Jesse Campbell RC COR .04 .02
- ❑ 396 Keith Jackson .10 .05
- ❑ 397 Jerome Brown .04 .02
- ❑ 398 Keith Byars .04 .02
- ❑ 399 Seth Joyner .10 .05
- ❑ 400 Mike Bellamy .04 .02
- ❑ 401 Fred Barnett .25 .11
- ❑ 402 Reggie Singletary RC .04 .02
- ❑ 403 Reggie White .25 .11
- ❑ 404 Randall Cunningham .25 .11
- ❑ 405 Byron Evans .04 .02
- ❑ 406 Wes Hopkins .04 .02
- ❑ 407 Ben Smith .04 .02
- ❑ 408 Roger Ruzek .04 .02
- ❑ 409 Eric Allen UER .04 .02
  (Comparative misspelled as comparate)
- ❑ 410 Anthony Toney UER .04 .02
  (Heath Sherman was rookie in '89, not '90)
- ❑ 411 Clyde Simmons .04 .02
- ❑ 412 Andre Waters .04 .02
- ❑ 413 Calvin Williams .10 .05
- ❑ 414 Eric Swann RC .25 .11
- ❑ 415 Eric Hill .04 .02
- ❑ 416 Tim McDonald .04 .02
- ❑ 417 Luis Sharpe .04 .02
- ❑ 418 Ernie Jones UER .04 .02
  (Photo actually Steve Jordan)
- ❑ 419 Ken Harvey .10 .05
- ❑ 420 Ricky Proehl .04 .02
- ❑ 421 Johnny Johnson .04 .02
- ❑ 422 Anthony Bell .04 .02
- ❑ 423 Timm Rosenbach .04 .02
- ❑ 424 Rich Camarillo .04 .02
- ❑ 425 Walter Reeves .04 .02
- ❑ 426 Freddie Joe Nunn .04 .02
- ❑ 427 Anthony Thompson UER .04 .02
  (40 touchdowns, sic)
- ❑ 428 Bill Lewis .04 .02
- ❑ 429 Jim Wahler RC .04 .02
- ❑ 430 Cedric Mack .04 .02
- ❑ 431 Michael Jones RC .04 .02
- ❑ 432 Ernie Mills RC .10 .05
- ❑ 433 Tim Worley .04 .02
- ❑ 434 Greg Lloyd .25 .11
- ❑ 435 Dermontti Dawson .04 .02
- ❑ 436 Louis Lipps .04 .02
- ❑ 437 Eric Green .04 .02
- ❑ 438 Donald Evans .04 .02
- ❑ 439 D.J. Johnson .04 .02
- ❑ 440 Tunch Ilkin .04 .02
- ❑ 441 Bubby Brister .04 .02
- ❑ 442 Chris Calloway .04 .02
- ❑ 443 David Little .04 .02
- ❑ 444 Thomas Everett .04 .02
- ❑ 445 Carnell Lake .04 .02
- ❑ 446 Rod Woodson .25 .11
- ❑ 447 Gary Anderson K .04 .02
- ❑ 448 Merril Hoge .04 .02
- ❑ 449 Gerald Williams .04 .02
- ❑ 450 Eric Moten RC .04 .02
- ❑ 451 Marion Butts .10 .05
- ❑ 452 Leslie O'Neal .10 .05
- ❑ 453 Ronnie Harmon .04 .02
- ❑ 454 Gill Byrd .04 .02
- ❑ 455 Junior Seau .25 .11
- ❑ 456 Nate Lewis RC .04 .02
- ❑ 457 Leo Goeas .04 .02
- ❑ 458 Burt Grossman .04 .02
- ❑ 459 Courtney Hall .04 .02
- ❑ 460 Anthony Miller .10 .05
- ❑ 461 Gary Plummer .04 .02
- ❑ 462 Billy Joe Tolliver .04 .02
- ❑ 463 Lee Williams .04 .02
- ❑ 464 Arthur Cox .04 .02
- ❑ 465 John Kidd UER .04 .02
  (Stron gleg, sic)
- ❑ 466 Frank Cornish .04 .02
- ❑ 467 John Carney .04 .02
- ❑ 468 Eric Bieniemy RC .04 .02
- ❑ 469 Don Griffin .04 .02
- ❑ 470 Jerry Rice .75 .35
- ❑ 471 Keith DeLong .04 .02
- ❑ 472 John Taylor .10 .05
- ❑ 473 Brent Jones .25 .11
- ❑ 474 Pierce Holt .04 .02
- ❑ 475 Kevin Fagan .04 .02
- ❑ 476 Bill Romanowski .04 .02
- ❑ 477 Dexter Carter .04 .02
- ❑ 478 Guy McIntyre .04 .02
- ❑ 479 Joe Montana 1.25 .55
- ❑ 480 Charles Haley .10 .05
- ❑ 481 Mike Cofer .04 .02
- ❑ 482 Jesse Sapolu .04 .02
- ❑ 483 Eric Davis .04 .02
- ❑ 484 Mike Sherrard .04 .02
- ❑ 485 Steve Young .75 .35
- ❑ 486 Darryl Pollard .04 .02
- ❑ 487 Tom Rathman .04 .02
- ❑ 488 Michael Carter .04 .02
- ❑ 489 Ricky Watters RC 1.50 .70
- ❑ 490 John Johnson RC .04 .02
- ❑ 491 Eugene Robinson .04 .02
- ❑ 492 Andy Heck .04 .02
- ❑ 493 John L. Williams .04 .02

❑ 494 Norm Johnson .04 .02
❑ 495 David Wyman .04 .02
❑ 496 Derrick Fenner UER .04 .02
(Drafted in '88, should be '89)
❑ 497 Rick Donnelly .04 .02
❑ 498 Tony Woods .04 .02
❑ 499 Derek Loville RC UER .04 .02
(Ahmad Rashad is misspelled Ahmed)
❑ 500 Dave Krieg .10 .05
❑ 501 Joe Nash .04 .02
❑ 502 Brian Blades .10 .05
❑ 503 Cortez Kennedy .25 .11
❑ 504 Jeff Bryant .04 .02
❑ 505 Tommy Kane .04 .02
❑ 506 Travis McNeal .04 .02
❑ 507 Terry Wooden .04 .02
❑ 508 Chris Warren .25 .11
❑ 509A Dan McGwire RC ERR .04 .02
(Photo actually Jesse Campbell; see 395)
❑ 509B Dan McGwire COR RC .04 .02
❑ 510 Mark Robinson .04 .02
❑ 511 Ron Hall .04 .02
❑ 512 Paul Gruber .04 .02
❑ 513 Harry Hamilton .04 .02
❑ 514 Keith McCants .04 .02
❑ 515 Reggie Cobb .04 .02
❑ 516 Steve Christie UER .04 .02
(Listed as Californian, should be Canadian)
❑ 517 Broderick Thomas .04 .02
❑ 518 Mark Carrier WR .25 .11
❑ 519 Vinny Testaverde .10 .05
❑ 520 Ricky Reynolds .04 .02
❑ 521 Jesse Anderson .04 .02
❑ 522 Reuben Davis .04 .02
❑ 523 Wayne Haddix .04 .02
❑ 524 Gary Anderson RB UER .04 .02
(Photo actually Don Mosebar)
❑ 525 Bruce Hill .04 .02
❑ 526 Kevin Murphy .04 .02
❑ 527 Lawrence Dawsey RC .10 .05
❑ 528 Ricky Ervins RC .10 .05
❑ 529 Charles Mann .04 .02
❑ 530 Jim Lachey .04 .02
❑ 531 Mark Rypien UER .10 .05
(No stat for percentage; 2,0703 yards, sic)
❑ 532 Darrell Green .04 .02
❑ 533 Stan Humphries .25 .11
❑ 534 Jeff Bostic UER .04 .02
(Age listed as 32 in stats and 33 in bio)
❑ 535 Earnest Byner .04 .02
❑ 536 Art Monk UER .10 .05
(Bio says 718 receptions, should be 730)
❑ 537 Don Warren .04 .02
❑ 538 Darryl Grant .04 .02
❑ 539 Wilber Marshall .04 .02
❑ 540 Kurt Gouveia RC .04 .02
❑ 541 Markus Koch .04 .02
❑ 542 Andre Collins .04 .02
❑ 543 Chip Lohmiller .04 .02
❑ 544 Alvin Walton .04 .02
❑ 545 Gary Clark .25 .11
❑ 546 Ricky Sanders .04 .02
❑ 547 Redskins vs. Eagles .04 .02
(Gary Clark)
❑ 548 Bengals vs. Oilers .04 .02
(Cody Carlson)
❑ 549 Dolphins vs. Chiefs .04 .02
(Mark Clayton)
❑ 550 Bears vs. Saints UER .04 .02
(Neal Anderson; Name misspelled Andersen on back)
❑ 551 Bills vs. Dolphins .10 .05
(Thurman Thomas)
❑ 552 49ers vs. Redskins .04 .02
(Line play)
❑ 553 Giants vs. Bears .04 .02
(Ottis Anderson)
❑ 554 Raiders vs. Bengals .10 .05
(Bo Jackson)
❑ 555 AFC Championship .04 .02
(Andre Reed)
❑ 556 NFC Championship .04 .02
(Jeff Hostetler)
❑ 557 Super Bowl XXV .04 .02
(Ottis Anderson)
❑ 558 Checklist 1-140 .04 .02
❑ 559 Checklist 141-280 .04 .02
❑ 560 Checklist 281-420 UER .04 .02
(301 Randall Hill)
❑ 561 Checklist 421-561 UER .04 .02

1992 Bowman

	MINT	NRMT
COMPLETE SET (573)	100.00	45.00

❑ 1 Reggie White 1.00 .45
❑ 2 Johnny Meads .25 .11
❑ 3 Chip Lohmiller .25 .11
❑ 4 James Lofton .50 .23
❑ 5 Ray Horton .25 .11
❑ 6 Rich Moran .25 .11
❑ 7 Howard Cross .25 .11
❑ 8 Mike Horan .25 .11
❑ 9 Erik Kramer .50 .23
❑ 10 Steve Wisniewski .25 .11
❑ 11 Michael Haynes .50 .23
❑ 12 Donald Evans .25 .11
❑ 13 Michael Irvin FOIL 1.00 .45
❑ 14 Gary Zimmerman .25 .11
❑ 15 John Friesz .50 .23
❑ 16 Mark Carrier WR 1.00 .45
❑ 17 Mark Duper .25 .11
❑ 18 James Thornton .25 .11
❑ 19 Jon Hand .25 .11
❑ 20 Sterling Sharpe 1.00 .45
❑ 21 Jacob Green .25 .11
❑ 22 Wesley Carroll .25 .11
❑ 23 Clay Matthews .50 .23
❑ 24 Kevin Greene 1.00 .45
❑ 25 Brad Baxter .25 .11
❑ 26 Don Griffin .25 .11
❑ 27 Robert Delpino FOIL SP 1.50 .70
❑ 28 Lee Johnson .25 .11
❑ 29 Jim Wahler .25 .11
❑ 30 Leonard Russell .50 .23
❑ 31 Eric Moore .25 .11
❑ 32 Dino Hackett .25 .11
❑ 33 Simon Fletcher .25 .11
❑ 34 Al Edwards .25 .11
❑ 35 Brad Edwards .25 .11
❑ 36 James Joseph .25 .11
❑ 37 Rodney Peete .50 .23
❑ 38 Ricky Reynolds .25 .11
❑ 39 Eddie Anderson .25 .11
❑ 40 Ken Clarke .25 .11
❑ 41 Tony Bennett FOIL .50 .23
❑ 42 Larry Brown DB .25 .11
❑ 43 Ray Childress .25 .11
❑ 44 Mike Kenn .25 .11
❑ 45 Vestee Jackson .25 .11
❑ 46 Neil O'Donnell 1.00 .45
❑ 47 Bill Brooks .25 .11
❑ 48 Kevin Butler .25 .11
❑ 49 Joe Phillips .25 .11
❑ 50 Cortez Kennedy .50 .23
❑ 51 Rickey Jackson .25 .11
❑ 52 Vinnie Clark .25 .11
❑ 53 Michael Jackson .50 .23
❑ 54 Ernie Jones .25 .11
❑ 55 Tom Newberry .25 .11
❑ 56 Pat Harlow .25 .11
❑ 57 Craig Taylor .25 .11
❑ 58 Joe Prokop .25 .11
❑ 59 Warren Moon FOIL SP 2.00 .90
❑ 60 Jeff Lageman .25 .11
❑ 61 Neil Smith .50 .23
❑ 62 Jim Jeffcoat .25 .11
❑ 63 Bill Fralic .25 .11
❑ 64 Mark Schlereth RC .25 .11
❑ 65 Keith Byars .25 .11
❑ 66 Jeff Hostetler .50 .23
❑ 67 Joey Browner .25 .11
❑ 68 Bobby Hebert FOIL SP 1.50 .70
❑ 69 Keith Sims .25 .11
❑ 70 Warren Moon 1.00 .45
❑ 71 Pio Sagapolutele RC .25 .11
❑ 72 Cornelius Bennett .50 .23
❑ 73 Greg Davis .25 .11
❑ 74 Ronnie Harmon .25 .11
❑ 75 Ron Hall .25 .11
❑ 76 Howie Long .50 .23
❑ 77 Greg Lewis .25 .11
❑ 78 Carnell Lake .25 .11
❑ 79 Ray Crockett .25 .11
❑ 80 Tom Waddle .25 .11
❑ 81 Vincent Brown .25 .11
❑ 82 Bill Brooks FOIL .50 .23
❑ 83 John L. Williams .25 .11
❑ 84 Floyd Turner .25 .11
❑ 85 Scott Radecic .25 .11
❑ 86 Anthony Munoz .50 .23
❑ 87 Lonnie Young .25 .11
❑ 88 Dexter Carter .25 .11
❑ 89 Tony Zendejas .25 .11
❑ 90 Tim Jorden .25 .11
❑ 91 LeRoy Butler .25 .11
❑ 92 Richard Brown RC .25 .11
❑ 93 Erric Pegram .50 .23
❑ 94 Sean Landeta .25 .11
❑ 95 Clyde Simmons .25 .11
❑ 96 Martin Mayhew .25 .11
❑ 97 Jarvis Williams .25 .11
❑ 98 Barry Word .25 .11
❑ 99 John Taylor FOIL .50 .23
❑ 100 Emmitt Smith 10.00 4.50
❑ 101 Leon Seals .25 .11
❑ 102 Marion Butts .25 .11
❑ 103 Mike Merriweather .25 .11
❑ 104 Ernest Givins .50 .23
❑ 105 Wymon Henderson .25 .11
❑ 106 Robert Wilson .25 .11
❑ 107 Bobby Hebert .25 .11
❑ 108 Terry McDaniel .25 .11
❑ 109 Jerry Ball .25 .11
❑ 110 John Taylor .50 .23
❑ 111 Rob Moore .50 .23
❑ 112 Thurman Thomas FOIL 1.00 .45
❑ 113 Checklist 1-115 .25 .11
❑ 114 Brian Blades .50 .23
❑ 115 Larry Kelm .25 .11
❑ 116 James Francis .25 .11
❑ 117 Rod Woodson 1.00 .45
❑ 118 Trace Armstrong .25 .11
❑ 119 Eugene Daniel .25 .11
❑ 120 Andre Tippett .25 .11
❑ 121 Chris Jacke .25 .11
❑ 122 Jessie Tuggle .25 .11
❑ 123 Chris Chandler 1.00 .45
❑ 124 Tim Johnson .25 .11
❑ 125 Mark Collins .25 .11
❑ 126 Aeneas Williams FOIL SP 1.50 .70
❑ 127 James Jones .25 .11
❑ 128 George Jamison .25 .11
❑ 129 Deron Cherry .25 .11
❑ 130 Mark Clayton .50 .23
❑ 131 Keith DeLong .25 .11
❑ 132 Marcus Allen 1.00 .45
❑ 133 Joe Walter RC .25 .11
❑ 134 Reggie Rutland .25 .11

❑ 135 Kent Hull .25 .11
❑ 136 Jeff Feagles .25 .11
❑ 137 Ronnie Lott FOIL SP 2.00 .90
❑ 138 Henry Rolling .25 .11
❑ 139 Gary Anderson RB .25 .11
❑ 140 Morten Andersen .25 .11
❑ 141 Cris Dishman .25 .11
❑ 142 David Treadwell .25 .11
❑ 143 Kevin Gogan .25 .11
❑ 144 James Hasty .25 .11
❑ 145 Robert Delpino .25 .11
❑ 146 Patrick Hunter .25 .11
❑ 147 Gary Anderson K .25 .11
❑ 148 Chip Banks .25 .11
❑ 149 Dan Fike .25 .11
❑ 150 Chris Miller .50 .23
❑ 151 Hugh Millen .25 .11
❑ 152 Courtney Hall .25 .11
❑ 153 Gary Clark .50 .23
❑ 154 Michael Brooks .25 .11
❑ 155 Jay Hilgenberg .25 .11
❑ 156 Tim McDonald .25 .11
❑ 157 Andre Tippett FOIL .50 .23
❑ 158 Doug Riesenberg .25 .11
❑ 159 Bill Maas .25 .11
❑ 160 Fred Barnett .50 .23
❑ 161 Pierce Holt .25 .11
❑ 162 Brian Noble .25 .11
❑ 163 Harold Green .25 .11
❑ 164 Joel Hilgenberg .25 .11
❑ 165 Mervyn Fernandez .25 .11
❑ 166 John Offerdahl .25 .11
❑ 167 Shane Conlan .25 .11
❑ 168 Mark Higgs FOIL SP 1.50 .70
❑ 169 Bubba McDowell .25 .11
❑ 170 Barry Sanders 8.00 3.60
❑ 171 Larry Roberts .25 .11
❑ 172 Herschel Walker .50 .23
❑ 173 Steve McMichael .50 .23
❑ 174 Kelly Stouffer .25 .11
❑ 175 Louis Lipps .25 .11
❑ 176 Jim Everett .50 .23
❑ 177 Tony Tolbert .25 .11
❑ 178 Mike Baab .25 .11
❑ 179 Eric Swann .50 .23
❑ 180 Emmitt Smith FOIL SP 15.00 6.75
❑ 181 Tim Brown 1.00 .45
❑ 182 Dennis Smith .25 .11
❑ 183 Moe Gardner .25 .11
❑ 184 Derrick Walker .25 .11
❑ 185 Reyna Thompson .25 .11
❑ 186 Esera Tuaolo .25 .11
❑ 187 Jeff Wright .25 .11
❑ 188 Mark Rypien .25 .11
❑ 189 Quinn Early .50 .23
❑ 190 Christian Okoye .25 .11
❑ 191 Keith Jackson .50 .23
❑ 192 Doug Smith .25 .11
❑ 193 John Elway FOIL 10.00 4.50
❑ 194 Reggie Cobb .25 .11
❑ 195 Reggie Roby .25 .11
❑ 196 Clarence Verdin .25 .11
❑ 197 Jim Breech .25 .11
❑ 198 Jim Sweeney .25 .11
❑ 199 Marv Cook .25 .11
❑ 200 Ronnie Lott .50 .23
❑ 201 Mel Gray .50 .23
❑ 202 Maury Buford .25 .11
❑ 203 Lorenzo Lynch .25 .11
❑ 204 Jesse Sapolu .25 .11
❑ 205 Steve Jordan .25 .11
❑ 206 Don Majkowski .25 .11
❑ 207 Flipper Anderson .25 .11
❑ 208 Ed King .25 .11
❑ 209 Tony Woods .25 .11
❑ 210 Ron Heller .25 .11
❑ 211 Greg Kragen .25 .11
❑ 212 Scott Case .25 .11
❑ 213 Tommy Barnhardt .25 .11
❑ 214 Charles Mann .25 .11
❑ 215 David Griggs .25 .11
❑ 216 Kenneth Davis FOIL SP 1.50 .70
❑ 217 Lamar Lathon .25 .11
❑ 218 Nate Odomes .25 .11
❑ 219 Vinny Testaverde .50 .23
❑ 220 Rod Bernstine .25 .11
❑ 221 Barry Sanders FOIL 12.00 5.50
❑ 222 Carlton Haselrig RC .25 .11
❑ 223 Steve Beuerlein .25 .11
❑ 224 John Alt .25 .11
❑ 225 Pepper Johnson .25 .11
❑ 226 Checklist 116-230 .25 .11
❑ 227 Irv Eatman .25 .11
❑ 228 Greg Townsend .25 .11
❑ 229 Mark Jackson .25 .11
❑ 230 Robert Blackmon .25 .11
❑ 231 Terry Allen 1.50 .70
❑ 232 Bennie Blades .25 .11
❑ 233 Sam Mills FOIL 1.00 .45
❑ 234 Richmond Webb .25 .11
❑ 235 Richard Dent .50 .23
❑ 236 Alonzo Mitz RC .25 .11
❑ 237 Steve Young 5.00 2.20
❑ 238 Pat Swilling .50 .23
❑ 239 James Campen .25 .11
❑ 240 Earnest Byner .25 .11
❑ 241 Pat Terrell .25 .11
❑ 242 Carwell Gardner .25 .11
❑ 243 Charles McRae .25 .11
❑ 244 Vince Newsome .25 .11
❑ 245 Eric Hill .25 .11
❑ 246 Steve Young FOIL 5.00 2.20
❑ 247 Nate Lewis .25 .11
❑ 248 William Fuller .50 .23
❑ 249 Andre Waters .25 .11
❑ 250 Dean Biasucci .25 .11
❑ 251 Andre Rison .50 .23
❑ 252 Brent Williams .25 .11
❑ 253 Todd McNair .25 .11
❑ 254 Jeff Davidson RC .25 .11
❑ 255 Art Monk .50 .23
❑ 256 Kirk Lowdermilk .25 .11
❑ 257 Bob Golic .25 .11
❑ 258 Michael Irvin 1.00 .45
❑ 259 Eric Green .25 .11
❑ 260 David Fulcher FOIL .50 .23
❑ 261 Damone Johnson .25 .11
❑ 262 Marc Spindler .25 .11
❑ 263 Alfred Williams .25 .11
❑ 264 Donnie Elder .25 .11
❑ 265 Keith McKeller .25 .11
❑ 266 Steve Bono RC 1.50 .70
❑ 267 Jumbo Elliott .25 .11
❑ 268 Randy Hilliard RC .25 .11
❑ 269 Rufus Porter .25 .11
❑ 270 Neal Anderson .25 .11
❑ 271 Dalton Hilliard .25 .11
❑ 272 Michael Zordich RC .25 .11
❑ 273 Cornelius Bennett FOIL .50 .23
❑ 274 Louie Aguiar RC .25 .11
❑ 275 Aaron Craver .25 .11
❑ 276 Tony Bennett .25 .11
❑ 277 Terry Wooden .25 .11
❑ 278 Mike Munchak .25 .11
❑ 279 Chris Hinton .25 .11
❑ 280 John Elway 6.00 2.70
❑ 281 Randall McDaniel .25 .11
❑ 282 Brad Baxter FOIL .50 .23
❑ 283 Wes Hopkins .25 .11
❑ 284 Scott Davis .25 .11
❑ 285 Mark Tuinei .25 .11
❑ 286 Broderick Thompson .25 .11
❑ 287 Henry Ellard .50 .23
❑ 288 Adrian Cooper .25 .11
❑ 289 Don Warren .25 .11
❑ 290 Rodney Hampton 1.00 .45
❑ 291 Kevin Ross .25 .11
❑ 292 Mark Carrier DB .25 .11
❑ 293 Ian Beckles .25 .11
❑ 294 Gene Atkins .25 .11
❑ 295 Mark Rypien FOIL .50 .23
❑ 296 Eric Metcalf .50 .23
❑ 297 Howard Ballard .25 .11
❑ 298 Nate Newton .50 .23
❑ 299 Dan Owens .25 .11
❑ 300 Tim McGee .25 .11
❑ 301 Greg McMurtry .25 .11
❑ 302 Walter Reeves .25 .11
❑ 303 Jeff Herrod .25 .11
❑ 304 Darren Comeaux .25 .11
❑ 305 Pete Stoyanovich .25 .11
❑ 306 Johnny Holland .25 .11
❑ 307 Jay Novacek .50 .23
❑ 308 Steve Broussard .25 .11
❑ 309 Darrell Green .25 .11
❑ 310 Sam Mills .25 .11
❑ 311 Tim Barnett .25 .11
❑ 312 Steve Atwater .25 .11
❑ 313 Tom Waddle FOIL .50 .23
❑ 314 Felix Wright .25 .11
❑ 315 Sean Jones .50 .23
❑ 316 Jim Harbaugh 1.00 .45
❑ 317 Eric Allen .25 .11
❑ 318 Don Mosebar .25 .11
❑ 319 Rob Taylor .25 .11
❑ 320 Terance Mathis .50 .23
❑ 321 Leroy Hoard .50 .23
❑ 322 Kenneth Davis .25 .11
❑ 323 Guy McIntyre .25 .11
❑ 324 Deron Cherry FOIL .50 .23
❑ 325 Tunch Ilkin .25 .11
❑ 326 Willie Green .25 .11
❑ 327 Darryl Henley .25 .11
❑ 328 Shawn Jefferson .25 .11
❑ 329 Greg Jackson .25 .11
❑ 330 John Roper .25 .11
❑ 331 Bill Lewis .25 .11
❑ 332 Rodney Holman .25 .11
❑ 333 Bruce Armstrong .25 .11
❑ 334 Robb Thomas .25 .11
❑ 335 Alvin Harper .50 .23
❑ 336 Brian Jordan .50 .23
❑ 337 Morten Andersen FOIL .50 .23
❑ 338 Dermontti Dawson .25 .11
❑ 339 Checklist 231-345 .25 .11
❑ 340 Louis Oliver .25 .11
❑ 341 Paul McJulien RC .25 .11
❑ 342 Karl Mecklenburg .25 .11
❑ 343 Lawrence Dawsey .50 .23
❑ 344 Kyle Clifton .25 .11
❑ 345 Jeff Bostic .25 .11
❑ 346 Cris Carter 1.50 .70
❑ 347 Al Smith .25 .11
❑ 348 Mark Kelso .25 .11
❑ 349 Art Monk FOIL 1.00 .45
❑ 350 Michael Carter .25 .11
❑ 351 Ethan Horton .25 .11
❑ 352 Andy Heck .25 .11
❑ 353 Gill Fenerty .25 .11
❑ 354 David Brandon RC .25 .11
❑ 355 Anthony Johnson 1.00 .45
❑ 356 Mike Golic .25 .11
❑ 357 Ferrell Edmunds .25 .11
❑ 358 Dennis Gibson .25 .11
❑ 359 Gill Byrd .25 .11
❑ 360 Todd Lyght .25 .11
❑ 361 Jayice Pearson RC .25 .11
❑ 362 John Rade .25 .11
❑ 363 Keith Van Horne .25 .11
❑ 364 John Kasay .25 .11
❑ 365 Brod. Thomas FOIL SP 1.50 .70
❑ 366 Ken Harvey .25 .11
❑ 367 Rich Gannon 1.00 .45
❑ 368 Darrell Thompson .25 .11
❑ 369 Jon Vaughn .25 .11
❑ 370 Jesse Solomon .25 .11
❑ 371 Erik McMillan .25 .11
❑ 372 Bruce Matthews .25 .11
❑ 373 Wilber Marshall .25 .11
❑ 374 Brian Blades FOIL SP 1.50 .70
❑ 375 Vance Johnson .25 .11
❑ 376 Eddie Brown .25 .11
❑ 377 Don Beebe .25 .11
❑ 378 Brent Jones .50 .23
❑ 379 Matt Bahr .25 .11
❑ 380 Dwight Stone .25 .11
❑ 381 Tony Casillas .25 .11
❑ 382 Jay Schroeder .25 .11
❑ 383 Byron Evans .25 .11
❑ 384 Dan Saleaumua .25 .11
❑ 385 Wendell Davis .25 .11
❑ 386 Ron Holmes .25 .11
❑ 387 George Thomas RC .25 .11
❑ 388 Ray Berry .25 .11
❑ 389 Eric Martin .25 .11
❑ 390 Kevin Mack .25 .11
❑ 391 Natu Tuatagaloa RC .25 .11
❑ 392 Bill Romanowski .25 .11

❑ 393 Nick Bell FOIL SP .... 1.50 .70
❑ 394 Grant Feasel .... .25 .11
❑ 395 Eugene Lockhart............ .25 .11
❑ 396 Lorenzo White............... .25 .11
❑ 397 Mike Farr....................... .25 .11
❑ 398 Eric Bieniemy .... .25 .11
❑ 399 Kevin Murphy .... .25 .11
❑ 400 Luis Sharpe................... .25 .11
❑ 401 Jessie Tuggle FOIL SP 1.50 .70
❑ 402 Cleveland Gary .... .25 .11
❑ 403 Tony Mandarich .... .25 .11
❑ 404 Bryan Cox....................... .50 .23
❑ 405 Marvin Washington .... .25 .11
❑ 406 Fred Stokes.................... .25 .11
❑ 407 Duane Bickett .... .25 .11
❑ 408 Leonard Marshall .... .25 .11
❑ 409 Barry Foster .... .50 .23
❑ 410 Thurman Thomas .... 1.00 .45
❑ 411 Willie Gault .... .50 .23
❑ 412 Vinson Smith RC............ .25 .11
❑ 413 Mark Bortz...................... .25 .11
❑ 414 Johnny Johnson .... .25 .11
❑ 415 Rodney Hampton FOIL 1.00 .45
❑ 416 Steve Wallace .... .25 .11
❑ 417 Fuad Reveiz .... .25 .11
❑ 418 Derrick Thomas............. .50 .23
❑ 419 Jackie Harris RC.......... 1.00 .45
❑ 420 Derek Russell .... .25 .11
❑ 421 David Grant................... .25 .11
❑ 422 Tommy Kane.................. .25 .11
❑ 423 Stan Brock..................... .25 .11
❑ 424 Haywood Jeffires........... .50 .23
❑ 425 Broderick Thomas.......... .25 .11
❑ 426 John Kidd .... .25 .11
❑ 427 S.McCarthy FOIL RC .... .50 .23
❑ 428 Jim Arnold...................... .25 .11
❑ 429 Scott Fulhage .... .25 .11
❑ 430 Jackie Slater .... .25 .11
❑ 431 Scott Galbraith RC .... .25 .11
❑ 432 Roger Ruzek.................. .25 .11
❑ 433 Irving Fryar .... .50 .23
❑ 434A Der. Thomas FOIL ERR 1.00 .45
(Misnumbered 494)
❑ 434B Der. Thomas FOIL COR 1.00 .45
(Numbered 434)
❑ 435 D.J. Johnson .... .25 .11
❑ 436 Jim C.Jensen .... .25 .11
❑ 437 James Washington .... .25 .11
❑ 438 Phil Hansen................... .25 .11
❑ 439 Rohn Stark .... .25 .11
❑ 440 Jarrod Bunch................. .25 .11
❑ 441 Todd Marinovich .... .25 .11
❑ 442 Brett Perriman.............. 1.00 .45
❑ 443 Eugene Robinson .... .25 .11
❑ 444 Robert Massey .... .25 .11
❑ 445 Nick Lowery................... .25 .11
❑ 446 Rickey Dixon .... .25 .11
❑ 447 Jim Lachey .... .25 .11
❑ 448 Johnny Hector FOIL ...... .50 .23
❑ 449 Gary Plummer............... .25 .11
❑ 450 Robert Brown .... .25 .11
❑ 451 Gaston Green .... .25 .11
❑ 452 Checklist 346-459 .... .25 .11
❑ 453 Darion Conner............... .25 .11
❑ 454 Mike Cofer..................... .25 .11
❑ 455 Craig Heyward .... .50 .23
❑ 456 Anthony Carter .... .50 .23
❑ 457 Pat Coleman RC............ .25 .11
❑ 458 Jeff Bryant..................... .25 .11
❑ 459 Mark Gunn RC .... .25 .11
❑ 460 Stan Thomas................. .25 .11
❑ 461 Simon Fletcher FOIL SP 1.50 .70
❑ 462 Ray Agnew .... .25 .11
❑ 463 Jessie Hester .... .25 .11
❑ 464 Rob Burnett.................... .25 .11
❑ 465 Mike Croel...................... .25 .11
❑ 466 Mike Pitts....................... .25 .11
❑ 467 Darryl Talley .... .25 .11
❑ 468 Rich Camarillo............... .25 .11
❑ 469 Reggie White FOIL ...... 1.00 .45
❑ 470 Nick Bell .... .25 .11
❑ 471 Tracy Hayworth RC........ .25 .11
❑ 472 Eric Thomas .... .25 .11
❑ 473 Paul Gruber................... .25 .11
❑ 474 David Richards .... .25 .11
❑ 475 T.J. Turner..................... .25 .11
❑ 476 Mark Ingram .... .25 .11
❑ 477 Tim Grunhard .... .25 .11
❑ 478 Marion Butts FOIL.......... .50 .23
❑ 479 Tom Rathman .... .25 .11
❑ 480 Brian Mitchell................. .50 .23
❑ 481 Bryce Paup .... 1.00 .45
❑ 482 Mike Pritchard................ .50 .23
❑ 483 Ken Norton Jr. .... .50 .23
❑ 484 Roman Phifer .... .25 .11
❑ 485 Greg Lloyd.................. 1.00 .45
❑ 486 Brett Maxie .... .25 .11
❑ 487 Richard Dent FOIL SP 1.50 .70
❑ 488 Curtis Duncan .... .25 .11
❑ 489 Chris Burkett .... .25 .11
❑ 490 Travis McNeal .... .25 .11
❑ 491 Carl Lee......................... .25 .11
❑ 492 Clarence Kay................. .25 .11
❑ 493 Tom Thayer.................... .25 .11
❑ 494 Erik Kramer FOIL SP .. 2.00 .90
(See also 434A)
❑ 495 Perry Kemp.................... .25 .11
❑ 496 Jeff Jaeger .... .25 .11
❑ 497 Eric Sanders .... .25 .11
❑ 498 Burt Grossman .... .25 .11
❑ 499 Ben Smith .... .25 .11
❑ 500 Keith McCants............... .25 .11
❑ 501 John Stephens .... .25 .11
❑ 502 John Rienstra .... .25 .11
❑ 503 Jim Ritcher .... .25 .11
❑ 504 Harris Barton................. .25 .11
❑ 505 Andre Rison FOIL SP .. 2.00 .90
❑ 506 Chris Martin................... .25 .11
❑ 507 Freddie Joe Nunn .... .25 .11
❑ 508 Mark Higgs .... .25 .11
❑ 509 Norm Johnson............... .25 .11
❑ 510 Stephen Baker .... .25 .11
❑ 511 Ricky Sanders............... .25 .11
❑ 512 Ray Donaldson .... .25 .11
❑ 513 David Fulcher .... .25 .11
❑ 514 Gerald Williams............. .25 .11
❑ 515 Toi Cook .... .25 .11
❑ 516 Chris Warren .... 1.00 .45
❑ 517 Jeff Gossett................... .25 .11
❑ 518 Ken Lanier..................... .25 .11
❑ 519 H.Jeffires FOIL SP ...... 2.00 .90
❑ 520 Kevin Glover .... .25 .11
❑ 521 Mo Lewis........................ .25 .11
❑ 522 Bern Brostek.................. .25 .11
❑ 523 Bo Orlando RC .... .25 .11
❑ 524 Mike Saxon .... .25 .11
❑ 525 Seth Joyner................... .50 .23
❑ 526 John Carney .... .25 .11
❑ 527 Jeff Cross .... .25 .11
❑ 528 G.Anderson K FOIL SP 1.50 .70
❑ 529 Chuck Cecil................... .25 .11
❑ 530 Tim Green .... .25 .11
❑ 531 Kevin Porter .... .25 .11
❑ 532 Chris Spielman .... .50 .23
❑ 533 Willie Drewrey............... .25 .11
❑ 534 Chris Singleton UER ...... .25 .11
(Card has wrong score for Super Bowl XX)
❑ 535 Matt Stover .... .25 .11
❑ 536 Andre Collins................. .25 .11
❑ 537 Erik Howard................... .25 .11
❑ 538 Steve Tasker................. .50 .23
❑ 539 Anthony Thompson........ .25 .11
❑ 540 Charles Haley .... .50 .23
❑ 541 Mike Merriweather FOIL .50 .23
❑ 542 Henry Thomas................ .25 .11
❑ 543 Scott Stephen .... .25 .11
❑ 544 Bruce Kozerski .... .25 .11
❑ 545 Tim McKyer.................... .25 .11
❑ 546 Chris Doleman .... .25 .11
❑ 547 Riki Ellison..................... .25 .11
❑ 548 Mike Prior .... .25 .11
❑ 549 Dwayne Harper.............. .25 .11
❑ 550 Bubby Brister................. .25 .11
❑ 551 Dave Meggett .... .50 .23
❑ 552 Greg Montgomery.......... .25 .11
❑ 553 Kevin Mack FOIL........... .50 .23
❑ 554 Mark Stepnoski .... .50 .23
❑ 555 Kenny Walker .... .25 .11
❑ 556 Eric Moten .... .25 .11
❑ 557 Michael Stewart............. .25 .11
❑ 558 Calvin Williams .... .50 .23
❑ 559 Johnny Hector............... .25 .11
❑ 560 Tony Paige .... .25 .11
❑ 561 Tim Newton.................... .25 .11
❑ 562 Brad Muster................... .25 .11
❑ 563 Aeneas Williams .... .50 .23
❑ 564 Herman Moore 3.00 1.35
❑ 565 Checklist 460-573 .... .25 .11
❑ 566 Jerome Henderson .... .25 .11
❑ 567 Danny Copeland .... .25 .11
❑ 568 Alexander Wright FOIL .. .50 .23
❑ 569 Tim Harris .... .25 .11
❑ 570 Jonathan Hayes .... .25 .11
❑ 571 Tony Jones .... .25 .11
❑ 572 Carlton Bailey RC .... .50 .23
❑ 573 Vaughan Johnson.......... .25 .11

1993 Bowman

	MINT	NRMT
COMPLETE SET (423)	40.00	18.00

❑ 1 Troy Aikman FOIL........... 3.00 1.35
❑ 2 John Parrella RC.............. .20 .09
❑ 3 Dana Stubblefield RC .... .75 .35
❑ 4 Mark Higgs .... .20 .09
❑ 5 Tom Carter RC .... .40 .18
❑ 6 Nate Lewis .... .20 .09
❑ 7 Vaughn Hebron RC........... .20 .09
❑ 8 Ernest Givins.................... .40 .18
❑ 9 Vince Buck .... .20 .09
❑ 10 Levon Kirkland .... .20 .09
❑ 11 J.J. Birden...................... .20 .09
❑ 12 Steve Jordan.................. .20 .09
❑ 13 Simon Fletcher .... .20 .09
❑ 14 Willie Green.................... .20 .09
❑ 15 Pepper Johnson .... .20 .09
❑ 16 Roger Harper RC .... .20 .09
❑ 17 Rob Moore .... .40 .18
❑ 18 David Lang .... .20 .09
❑ 19 David Klingler .... .20 .09
❑ 20 Garrison Hearst FOIL RC 2.00 .90
❑ 21 Anthony Johnson .... .40 .18
❑ 22 Eric Curry FOIL RC......... .20 .09
❑ 23 Nolan Harrison .... .20 .09
❑ 24 Earl Dotson RC .... .20 .09
❑ 25 Leonard Russell .... .40 .18
❑ 26 Doug Riesenberg .... .20 .09
❑ 27 Dwayne Harper............... .20 .09
❑ 28 Richard Dent .... .40 .18
❑ 29 Victor Bailey RC .... .20 .09
❑ 30 Junior Seau.................... .75 .35
❑ 31 Steve Tasker.................. .40 .18
❑ 32 Kurt Gouveia .... .20 .09
❑ 33 Renaldo Turnbull UER .... .20 .09
(Listed as wide receiver)
❑ 34 Dale Carter .... .20 .09
❑ 35 Russell Maryland........... .20 .09
❑ 36 Dana Hall .... .20 .09
❑ 37 Marco Coleman.............. .20 .09
❑ 38 Greg Montgomery.......... .20 .09
❑ 39 Deon Figures RC .... .40 .18
❑ 40 Troy Drayton RC............. .40 .18
❑ 41 Eric Metcalf .... .40 .18
❑ 42 Michael Husted RC......... .20 .09
❑ 43 Harry Newsome .... .20 .09
❑ 44 Kelvin Pritchett .... .20 .09
❑ 45 Andre Rison FOIL........... .35 .16
❑ 46 John Copeland RC .... .40 .18

❑ 47 Greg Biekert RC .20 .09
❑ 48 Johnny Johnson .20 .09
❑ 49 Chuck Cecil .20 .09
❑ 50 Rick Mirer FOIL RC 1.50 .70
❑ 51 Rod Bernstine .20 .09
❑ 52 Steve McMichael .40 .18
❑ 53 Roosevelt Potts RC .20 .09
❑ 54 Mike Sherrard .20 .09
❑ 55 Terrell Buckley .20 .09
❑ 56 Eugene Chung .20 .09
❑ 57 Kimble Anders RC 1.00 .45
❑ 58 Daryl Johnston .75 .35
❑ 59 Harris Barton .20 .09
❑ 60 Thurman Thomas FOIL .75 .35
❑ 61 Eric Martin .20 .09
❑ 62 Reggie Brooks FOIL RC .40 .18
❑ 63 Eric Bieniemy .20 .09
❑ 64 John Offerdahl .20 .09
❑ 65 Wilber Marshall .20 .09
❑ 66 Mark Carrier WR .40 .18
❑ 67 Merril Hoge .20 .09
❑ 68 Cris Carter 1.25 .55
❑ 69 Marty Thompson RC .20 .09
❑ 70 Randall Cunningham FOIL .75 .35
❑ 71 Winston Moss .20 .09
❑ 72 Doug Pelfrey RC .20 .09
❑ 73 Jackie Slater .20 .09
❑ 74 Pierce Holt .20 .09
❑ 75 Hardy Nickerson .40 .18
❑ 76 Chris Burkett .20 .09
❑ 77 Michael Brandon .20 .09
❑ 78 Tom Waddle .20 .09
❑ 79 Walter Reeves .20 .09
❑ 80 Lawrence Taylor FOIL .75 .35
❑ 81 Wayne Simmons RC .20 .09
❑ 82 Brent Williams .20 .09
❑ 83 Shannon Sharpe .75 .35
❑ 84 Robert Blackmon .20 .09
❑ 85 Keith Jackson .40 .18
❑ 86 A.J. Johnson .20 .09
❑ 87 Ryan McNeil RC .20 .09
❑ 88 Michael Dean Perry .40 .18
❑ 89 Russell Copeland RC .40 .18
❑ 90 Sam Mills .20 .09
❑ 91 Courtney Hall .20 .09
❑ 92 Gino Torretta RC .40 .18
❑ 93 Artie Smith RC .20 .09
❑ 94 David Whitmore .20 .09
❑ 95 Charles Haley .40 .18
❑ 96 Rod Woodson .75 .35
❑ 97 Lorenzo White .20 .09
❑ 98 Tom Scott RC .20 .09
❑ 99 Tyji Armstrong .20 .09
❑ 100 Boomer Esiason .40 .18
❑ 101 Rocket Ismail FOIL .40 .18
❑ 102 Mark Carrier DB .20 .09
❑ 103 Broderick Thompson .20 .09
❑ 104 Bob Whitfield .20 .09
❑ 105 Ben Coleman RC .20 .09
❑ 106 Jon Vaughn .20 .09
❑ 107 Marcus Buckley RC .20 .09
❑ 108 Cleveland Gary .20 .09
❑ 109 Ashley Ambrose .20 .09
❑ 110 Reggie White FOIL .75 .35
❑ 111 Arthur Marshall RC .20 .09
❑ 112 Greg McMurtry .20 .09
❑ 113 Mike Johnson .20 .09
❑ 114 Tim McGee .20 .09
❑ 115 John Carney .20 .09
❑ 116 Neil Smith .75 .35
❑ 117 Mark Stepnoski .20 .09
❑ 118 Don Beebe .20 .09
❑ 119 Scott Mitchell .75 .35
❑ 120 Randall McDaniel .20 .09
❑ 121 Chidi Ahanotu RC .20 .09
❑ 122 Ray Childress .20 .09
❑ 123 Tony McGee RC .40 .18
❑ 124 Marc Boutte .20 .09
❑ 125 Ronnie Lott .40 .18
❑ 126 Jason Elam RC .75 .35
❑ 127 Martin Harrison RC .20 .09
❑ 128 Leonard Renfro RC .20 .09
❑ 129 Jessie Armstead RC .40 .18
❑ 130 Quentin Coryatt .40 .18
❑ 131 Luis Sharpe .20 .09
❑ 132 Bill Maas .20 .09
❑ 133 Jesse Solomon .20 .09
❑ 134 Kevin Greene .75 .35
❑ 135 Derek Brown RBK RC .40 .18
❑ 136 Greg Townsend .20 .09
❑ 137 Neal Anderson .20 .09
❑ 138 John L. Williams .20 .09
❑ 139 Vincent Brisby RC .75 .35
❑ 140 Barry Sanders FOIL 6.00 2.70
❑ 141 Charles Mann .20 .09
❑ 142 Ken Norton .40 .18
❑ 143 Eric Moten .20 .09
❑ 144 John Alt .20 .09
❑ 145 Dan Footman RC .20 .09
❑ 146 Bill Brooks .20 .09
❑ 147 James Thornton .20 .09
❑ 148 Martin Mayhew .20 .09
❑ 149 Andy Harmon .40 .18
❑ 150 Dan Marino FOIL 6.00 2.70
❑ 151 Micheal Barrow RC .40 .18
❑ 152 Flipper Anderson .20 .09
❑ 153 Jackie Harris .20 .09
❑ 154 Todd Kelly RC .20 .09
❑ 155 Dan Williams RC .20 .09
❑ 156 Harold Green .20 .09
❑ 157 David Treadwell .20 .09
❑ 158 Chris Doleman .20 .09
❑ 159 Eric Hill .20 .09
❑ 160 Lincoln Kennedy RC .20 .09
❑ 161 Devon McDonald RC .20 .09
❑ 162 Natrone Means RC 2.00 .90
❑ 163 Rick Hamilton RC .20 .09
❑ 164 Kelvin Martin .20 .09
❑ 165 Jeff Hostetler .40 .18
❑ 166 Mark Brunell RC 8.00 3.60
❑ 167 Tim Barnett .20 .09
❑ 168 Ray Crockett .20 .09
❑ 169 William Perry .40 .18
❑ 170 Michael Irvin .75 .35
❑ 171 Marvin Washington .20 .09
❑ 172 Irving Fryar .40 .18
❑ 173 Scott Sisson RC .20 .09
❑ 174 Gary Anderson K .20 .09
❑ 175 Bruce Smith .75 .35
❑ 176 Clyde Simmons .20 .09
❑ 177 Russell White RC .40 .18
❑ 178 Irv Smith RC .20 .09
❑ 179 Mark Wheeler .20 .09
❑ 180 Warren Moon .75 .35
❑ 181 Del Speer RC .20 .09
❑ 182 Henry Thomas .20 .09
❑ 183 Keith Kartz .20 .09
❑ 184 Ricky Ervins .20 .09
❑ 185 Phil Simms .40 .18
❑ 186 Tim Brown .75 .35
❑ 187 Willis Peguese .20 .09
❑ 188 Rich Moran .20 .09
❑ 189 Robert Jones .20 .09
❑ 190 Craig Heyward .40 .18
❑ 191 Ricky Watters .75 .35
❑ 192 Stan Humphries .75 .35
❑ 193 Larry Webster .20 .09
❑ 194 Brad Baxter .20 .09
❑ 195 Randal Hill .20 .09
❑ 196 Robert Porcher .20 .09
❑ 197 Patrick Robinson RC .20 .09
❑ 198 Ferrell Edmunds .20 .09
❑ 199 Melvin Jenkins .20 .09
❑ 200 Joe Montana FOIL 6.00 2.70
❑ 201 Marv Cook .20 .09
❑ 202 Henry Ellard .40 .18
❑ 203 Calvin Williams .40 .18
❑ 204 Craig Erickson .40 .18
❑ 205 Steve Atwater .20 .09
❑ 206 Najee Mustafaa .20 .09
❑ 207 Darryl Talley .20 .09
❑ 208 Jarrod Bunch .20 .09
❑ 209 Tim McDonald .20 .09
❑ 210 Patrick Bates RC .20 .09
❑ 211 Sean Jones .20 .09
❑ 212 Leslie O'Neal .40 .18
❑ 213 Mike Golic .20 .09
❑ 214 Mark Clayton .20 .09
❑ 215 Leonard Marshall .20 .09
❑ 216 Curtis Conway RC 2.00 .90
❑ 217 Andre Hastings RC .75 .35
❑ 218 Barry Word .20 .09
❑ 219 Will Wolford .20 .09
❑ 220 Desmond Howard .40 .18
❑ 221 Rickey Jackson .20 .09
❑ 222 Alvin Harper .40 .18
❑ 223 William White .20 .09
❑ 224 Steve Broussard .20 .09
❑ 225 Aeneas Williams .20 .09
❑ 226 Michael Brooks .20 .09
❑ 227 Reggie Cobb .20 .09
❑ 228 Derrick Walker .20 .09
❑ 229 Marcus Allen .75 .35
❑ 230 Jerry Ball .20 .09
❑ 231 J.B. Brown .20 .09
❑ 232 Terry McDaniel .20 .09
❑ 233 LeRoy Butler .20 .09
❑ 234 Kyle Clifton .20 .09
❑ 235 Henry Jones .20 .09
❑ 236 Shane Conlan .20 .09
❑ 237 Michael Bates RC .20 .09
❑ 238 Vincent Brown .20 .09
❑ 239 William Fuller .20 .09
❑ 240 Ricardo McDonald .20 .09
❑ 241 Gary Zimmerman .20 .09
❑ 242 Fred Barnett .40 .18
❑ 243 Elvis Grbac RC 6.00 2.70
❑ 244 Myron Baker RC .20 .09
❑ 245 Steve Emtman .20 .09
❑ 246 Mike Compton RC .20 .09
❑ 247 Mark Jackson .20 .09
❑ 248 Santo Stephens RC .20 .09
❑ 249 Tommie Agee .20 .09
❑ 250 Broderick Thomas .20 .09
❑ 251 Fred Baxter RC .20 .09
❑ 252 Andre Collins .20 .09
❑ 253 Ernest Dye RC .20 .09
❑ 254 Raylee Johnson RC .20 .09
❑ 255 Rickey Dixon .20 .09
❑ 256 Ron Heller .20 .09
❑ 257 Joel Steed .20 .09
❑ 258 Everett Lindsay RC .20 .09
❑ 259 Tony Smith .20 .09
❑ 260 Sterling Sharpe UER .75 .35
(Edgar Bennett is pictured on front)
❑ 261 Tommy Vardell .20 .09
❑ 262 Morten Andersen .20 .09
❑ 263 Eddie Robinson .20 .09
❑ 264 Jerome Bettis RC 3.00 1.35
❑ 265 Alonzo Spellman .20 .09
❑ 266 Harvey Williams .40 .18
❑ 267 Jason Belser RC .20 .09
❑ 268 Derek Russell .20 .09
❑ 269 Derrick Lassic RC .20 .09
❑ 270 Steve Young FOIL 3.00 1.35
❑ 271 Adrian Murrell RC 1.50 .70
❑ 272 Lewis Tillman .20 .09
❑ 273 O.J. McDuffie RC 2.50 1.10
❑ 274 Marty Carter .20 .09
❑ 275 Ray Seals .20 .09
❑ 276 Earnest Byner .20 .09
❑ 277 Marion Butts .20 .09
❑ 278 Chris Spielman .40 .18
❑ 279 Carl Pickens .75 .35
❑ 280 Drew Bledsoe FOIL RC 6.00 2.70
❑ 281 Mark Kelso .20 .09
❑ 282 Eugene Robinson .20 .09
❑ 283 Eric Allen .20 .09
❑ 284 Ethan Horton .20 .09
❑ 285 Greg Lloyd .75 .35
❑ 286 Anthony Carter .40 .18
❑ 287 Edgar Bennett .75 .35
❑ 288 Bobby Hebert .20 .09
❑ 289 Haywood Jeffires .40 .18
❑ 290 Glyn Milburn RC .75 .35
❑ 291 Bernie Kosar .40 .18
❑ 292 Jumbo Elliott .20 .09
❑ 293 Jessie Hester .20 .09
❑ 294 Bront Jones .40 .18
❑ 295 Carl Banks .20 .09
❑ 296 Brian Washington .20 .09
❑ 297 Steve Beuerlein .20 .09
❑ 298 John Lynch RC 1.25 .55
❑ 299 Troy Vincent .20 .09
❑ 300 Emmitt Smith FOIL 5.00 2.20
❑ 301 Chris Zorich .20 .09
❑ 302 Wade Wilson .20 .09
❑ 303 Darrien Gordon RC .20 .09

❑ 304 Fred Stokes .20 .09
❑ 305 Nick Lowery .20 .09
❑ 306 Rodney Peete .20 .09
❑ 307 Chris Warren .40 .18
❑ 308 Herschel Walker .40 .18
❑ 309 Aundray Bruce .20 .09
❑ 310 Barry Foster FOIL .40 .18
❑ 311 George Teague RC .40 .18
❑ 312 Darryl Williams .20 .09
❑ 313 Thomas Smith RC .40 .18
❑ 314 Dennis Brown .20 .09
❑ 315 Marvin Jones FOIL RC .40 .18
❑ 316 Andre Tippett .20 .09
❑ 317 Demetrius DuBose RC .20 .09
❑ 318 Kirk Lowdermilk .20 .09
❑ 319 Shane Dronett .20 .09
❑ 320 Terry Kirby RC .75 .35
❑ 321 Qadry Ismail RC 2.50 1.10
❑ 322 Lorenzo Lynch .20 .09
❑ 323 Willie Drewrey .20 .09
❑ 324 Jessie Tuggle .20 .09
❑ 325 Leroy Hoard .40 .18
❑ 326 Mark Collins .20 .09
❑ 327 Darrell Green .20 .09
❑ 328 Anthony Miller .40 .18
❑ 329 Brad Muster .20 .09
❑ 330 Jim Kelly FOIL .75 .35
❑ 331 Sean Gilbert .40 .18
❑ 332 Tim McKyer .20 .09
❑ 333 Scott Mersereau .20 .09
❑ 334 Willie Davis .75 .35
❑ 335 Brett Favre FOIL 6.00 2.70
❑ 336 Kevin Gogan .20 .09
❑ 337 Jim Harbaugh .75 .35
❑ 338 James Trapp RC .20 .09
❑ 339 Pete Stoyanovich .20 .09
❑ 340 Jerry Rice FOIL 3.00 1.35
❑ 341 Gary Anderson RB .20 .09
❑ 342 Carlton Gray RC .20 .09
❑ 343 Dermontti Dawson .20 .09
❑ 344 Ray Buchanan RC .20 .09
❑ 345 Derrick Fenner .20 .09
❑ 346 Dennis Smith .20 .09
❑ 347 Todd Rucci RC .20 .09
❑ 348 Seth Joyner .20 .09
❑ 349 Jim McMahon .20 .09
❑ 350 Rodney Hampton .75 .35
❑ 351 Al Smith .20 .09
❑ 352 Steve Everitt RC .20 .09
❑ 353 Vinnie Clark .20 .09
❑ 354 Eric Swann .40 .18
❑ 355 Brian Mitchell .40 .18
❑ 356 Will Shields RC .20 .09
❑ 357 Cornelius Bennett .40 .18
❑ 358 Darrin Smith RC .40 .18
❑ 359 Chris Mims .20 .09
❑ 360 Blair Thomas .20 .09
❑ 361 Dennis Gibson .20 .09
❑ 362 Santana Dotson .40 .18
❑ 363 Mark Ingram .20 .09
❑ 364 Don Mosebar .20 .09
❑ 365 Ty Detmer .75 .35
❑ 366 Bob Christian RC .20 .09
❑ 367 Adrian Hardy .20 .09
❑ 368 Vaughan Johnson .20 .09
❑ 369 Jim Everett .40 .18
❑ 370 Ricky Sanders .20 .09
❑ 371 Jonathan Hayes .20 .09
❑ 372 Bruce Matthews .20 .09
❑ 373 Darren Drozdov RC .75 .35
❑ 374 Scott Brumfield RC .20 .09
❑ 375 Cortez Kennedy .40 .18
❑ 376 Tim Harris .20 .09
❑ 377 Neil O'Donnell .75 .35
❑ 378 Robert Smith RC 6.00 2.70
❑ 379 Mike Caldwell RC .20 .09
❑ 380 Burt Grossman .20 .09
❑ 381 Corey Miller .20 .09
❑ 382 Kevin Williams FOIL RC .40 .18
❑ 383 Ken Harvey .20 .09
❑ 384 Greg Robinson RC .20 .09
❑ 385 Harold Alexander RC .20 .09
❑ 386 Andre Reed .40 .18
❑ 387 Reggie Langhorne .20 .09
❑ 388 Courtney Hawkins .20 .09
❑ 389 James Hasty .20 .09
❑ 390 Pat Swilling .20 .09
❑ 391 Chris Slade RC .40 .18
❑ 392 Keith Byars .20 .09
❑ 393 Dalton Hilliard .20 .09
❑ 394 David Williams .20 .09
❑ 395 Terry Obee RC .20 .09
❑ 396 Heath Sherman .20 .09
❑ 397 John Taylor .40 .18
❑ 398 Irv Eatman .20 .09
❑ 399 Johnny Holland .20 .09
❑ 400 John Elway FOIL 6.00 2.70
❑ 401 Clay Matthews .40 .18
❑ 402 Dave Meggett .20 .09
❑ 403 Eric Green .20 .09
❑ 404 Bryan Cox .20 .09
❑ 405 Jay Novacek .40 .18
❑ 406 Kenneth Davis .20 .09
❑ 407 Lamar Thomas RC .20 .09
❑ 408 Lance Gunn RC .20 .09
❑ 409 Audray McMillian .20 .09
❑ 410 Derrick Thomas FOIL .75 .35
❑ 411 Rufus Porter .20 .09
❑ 412 Coleman Rudolph RC .20 .09
❑ 413 Mark Rypien .20 .09
❑ 414 Duane Bickett .20 .09
❑ 415 Chris Singleton .20 .09
❑ 416 Mitch Lyons RC .20 .09
❑ 417 Bill Fralic .20 .09
❑ 418 Gary Plummer .20 .09
❑ 419 Ricky Proehl .20 .09
❑ 420 Howie Long .40 .18
❑ 421 Willie Roaf FOIL RC .75 .35
❑ 422 Checklist 1-212 .20 .09
❑ 423 Checklist 213-423 .20 .09

1994 Bowman

	MINT	NRMT
COMPLETE SET (390)	60.00	27.00

❑ 1 Dan Wilkinson RC .40 .18
❑ 2 Marshall Faulk RC 20.00 9.00
❑ 3 Heath Shuler RC .75 .35
❑ 4 Willie McGinest RC .75 .35
❑ 5 Trent Dilfer RC 5.00 2.20
❑ 6 Brent Jones .40 .18
❑ 7 Sam Adams RC .40 .18
❑ 8 Randy Baldwin .20 .09
❑ 9 Jamir Miller RC .20 .09
❑ 10 John Thierry RC .20 .09
❑ 11 Aaron Glenn RC .40 .18
❑ 12 Joe Johnson RC .20 .09
❑ 13 Bernard Williams RC .20 .09
❑ 14 Wayne Gandy RC .20 .09
❑ 15 Aaron Taylor RC .20 .09
❑ 16 Charles Johnson RC 1.25 .55
❑ 17 Dewayne Washington RC .40 .18
❑ 18 Bernie Kosar .40 .18
❑ 19 Johnnie Morton RC 2.00 .90
❑ 20 Rob Fredrickson RC .40 .18
❑ 21 Shante Carver RC .20 .09
❑ 22 Thomas Lewis RC .40 .18
❑ 23 Greg Hill RC .75 .35
❑ 24 Cris Dishman .20 .09
❑ 25 Jeff Burris RC .40 .18
❑ 26 Isaac Davis RC .20 .09
❑ 27 Bert Emanuel RC 1.50 .70
❑ 28 Allen Aldridge RC .20 .09
❑ 29 Kevin Lee RC .20 .09
❑ 30 Chris Brantley RC .20 .09
❑ 31 Rich Braham RC .20 .09
❑ 32 Ricky Watters .75 .35
❑ 33 Quentin Coryatt .20 .09
❑ 34 Hardy Nickerson .40 .18
❑ 35 Johnny Johnson .20 .09
❑ 36 Ken Harvey .20 .09
❑ 37 Chris Zorich .20 .09
❑ 38 Chris Warren .40 .18
❑ 39 David Palmer RC 1.50 .70
❑ 40 Chris Miller .20 .09
❑ 41 Ken Ruettgers .20 .09
❑ 42 Joe Panos RC .20 .09
❑ 43 Mario Bates RC .75 .35
❑ 44 Harry Colon .20 .09
❑ 45 Barry Foster .20 .09
❑ 46 Steve Tasker .40 .18
❑ 47 Richmond Webb .20 .09
❑ 48 James Folston RC .20 .09
❑ 49 Erik Williams .20 .09
❑ 50 Rodney Hampton .75 .35
❑ 51 Derek Russell .20 .09
❑ 52 Greg Montgomery .20 .09
❑ 53 Anthony Phillips .20 .09
❑ 54 Andre Coleman RC .20 .09
❑ 55 Gary Brown .20 .09
❑ 56 Neil Smith .75 .35
❑ 57 Myron Baker .20 .09
❑ 58 Sean Dawkins RC .75 .35
❑ 59 Marvin Washington .20 .09
❑ 60 Steve Beuerlein .20 .09
❑ 61 Brenston Buckner RC .20 .09
❑ 62 William Gaines RC .20 .09
❑ 63 LeShon Johnson RC .40 .18
❑ 64 Errict Rhett RC 2.50 1.10
❑ 65 Jim Everett .40 .18
❑ 66 Desmond Howard .40 .18
❑ 67 Jack Del Rio .20 .09
❑ 68 Isaac Bruce RC 20.00 9.00
❑ 69 Van Malone RC .20 .09
❑ 70 Jim Kelly .75 .35
❑ 71 Leon Lett .20 .09
❑ 72 Greg Robinson .20 .09
❑ 73 Ryan Yarborough RC .20 .09
❑ 74 Terry Wooden .20 .09
❑ 75 Eric Allen .20 .09
❑ 76 Ernest Givins .40 .18
❑ 77 Marcus Spears RC .20 .09
❑ 78 Thomas Randolph RC .20 .09
❑ 79 Willie Clark RC .20 .09
❑ 80 John Elway 5.00 2.20
❑ 81 Aubrey Beavers RC .20 .09
❑ 82 Jeff Cothran RC .20 .09
❑ 83 Norm Johnson .20 .09
❑ 84 Donnell Bennett RC .75 .35
❑ 85 Phillippi Sparks .20 .09
❑ 86 Scott Mitchell .75 .35
❑ 87 Bucky Brooks RC .20 .09
❑ 88 Courtney Hawkins .20 .09
❑ 89 Kevin Greene .75 .35
❑ 90 Doug Nussmeier RC .20 .09
❑ 91 Floyd Turner .20 .09
❑ 92 Anthony Newman .20 .09
❑ 93 Vinny Testaverde .40 .18
❑ 94 Ronnie Lott .40 .18
❑ 95 Troy Aikman 2.50 1.10
❑ 96 John Taylor .40 .18
❑ 97 Henry Ellard .40 .18
❑ 98 Carl Lee .20 .09
❑ 99 Terry McDaniel .20 .09
❑ 100 Joe Montana 5.00 2.20
❑ 101 David Klingler .20 .09
❑ 102 Bruce Walker RC .20 .09
❑ 103 Rick Cunningham RC .20 .09
❑ 104 Robert Delpino .20 .09
❑ 105 Mark Ingram .20 .09
❑ 106 Leslie O'Neal .20 .09
❑ 107 Darrell Thompson .20 .09
❑ 108 Dave Meggett .20 .09
❑ 109 Chris Gardocki .20 .09
❑ 110 Andre Rison .40 .18
❑ 111 Kelvin Martin .20 .09
❑ 112 Marcus Robertson .20 .09
❑ 113 Jason Gildon RC .20 .09
❑ 114 Mel Gray .20 .09

❑ 115 Tommy Vardell .20 .09
❑ 116 Dexter Carter .20 .09
❑ 117 Scottie Graham RC .40 .18
❑ 118 Horace Copeland .20 .09
❑ 119 Cornelius Bennett .40 .18
❑ 120 Chris Maumalanga RC .20 .09
❑ 121 Mo Lewis .20 .09
❑ 122 Toby Wright RC .20 .09
❑ 123 George Hegamin RC .20 .09
❑ 124 Chip Lohmiller .20 .09
❑ 125 Calvin Jones RC .20 .09
❑ 126 Steve Shine .20 .09
❑ 127 Chuck Levy RC .20 .09
❑ 128 Sam Mills .20 .09
❑ 129 Terance Mathis .40 .18
❑ 130 Randall Cunningham .75 .35
❑ 131 John Fina .20 .09
❑ 132 Reggie White .75 .35
❑ 133 Tom Waddle .20 .09
❑ 134 Chris Calloway .20 .09
❑ 135 Kevin Mawae RC .20 .09
❑ 136 Lake Dawson RC .75 .35
❑ 137 Alai Kalaniuvalu .20 .09
❑ 138 Tom Nalen .20 .09
❑ 139 Cody Carlson .20 .09
❑ 140 Dan Marino 5.00 2.20
❑ 141 Harris Barton .20 .09
❑ 142 Don Mosebar .20 .09
❑ 143 Romeo Bandison .20 .09
❑ 144 Bruce Smith .75 .35
❑ 145 Warren Moon .75 .35
❑ 146 David Lutz .20 .09
❑ 147 Dermontti Dawson .20 .09
❑ 148 Ricky Proehl .20 .09
❑ 149 Lou Benfatti RC .20 .09
❑ 150 Craig Erickson .20 .09
❑ 151 Sean Gilbert .20 .09
❑ 152 Zefross Moss .20 .09
❑ 153 Darnay Scott RC 2.00 .90
❑ 154 Courtney Hall .20 .09
❑ 155 Brian Mitchell .20 .09
❑ 156 Joe Burch RC UER .20 .09
❑ 157 Terry Mickens .20 .09
❑ 158 Jay Novacek .40 .18
❑ 159 Chris Gedney .20 .09
❑ 160 Bruce Matthews .20 .09
❑ 161 Marlo Perry RC .20 .09
❑ 162 Vince Buck .20 .09
❑ 163 Michael Bates .20 .09
❑ 164 Willie Davis .40 .18
❑ 165 Mike Pritchard .20 .09
❑ 166 Doug Riesenberg .20 .09
❑ 167 Herschel Walker .40 .18
❑ 168 Tim Ruddy RC .20 .09
❑ 169 William Floyd RC .75 .35
❑ 170 John Randle .40 .18
❑ 171 Winston Moss .20 .09
❑ 172 Thurman Thomas .75 .35
❑ 173 Eric England RC .20 .09
❑ 174 Vincent Brisby .75 .35
❑ 175 Greg Lloyd .75 .35
❑ 176 Paul Gruber .20 .09
❑ 177 Brad Ottis RC .20 .09
❑ 178 George Teague .20 .09
❑ 179 Willie Jackson RC 1.00 .45
❑ 180 Barry Sanders 5.00 2.20
❑ 181 Brian Washington .20 .09
❑ 182 Michael Jackson .40 .18
❑ 183 Jason Mathews RC .20 .09
❑ 184 Chester McGlockton .20 .09
❑ 185 Tydus Winans RC .20 .09
❑ 186 Michael Haynes .40 .18
❑ 187 Erik Kramer .40 .18
❑ 188 Chris Doleman .20 .09
❑ 189 Haywood Jeffires .40 .18
❑ 190 Larry Whigham RC .20 .09
❑ 191 Shawn Jefferson .20 .09
❑ 192 Pete Stoyanovich .20 .09
❑ 193 Rod Bernstine .20 .09
❑ 194 William Thomas .20 .09
❑ 195 Marcus Allen .75 .35
❑ 196 Dave Brown .40 .18
❑ 197 Harold Bishop RC .20 .09
❑ 198 Lorenzo Lynch .20 .09
❑ 199 Dwight Stone .20 .09
❑ 200 Jerry Rice 2.50 1.10
❑ 201 Rocket Ismail .40 .18
❑ 202 LeRoy Butler .20 .09
❑ 203 Glenn Parker .20 .09
❑ 204 Bruce Armstrong .20 .09
❑ 205 Shane Conlan .20 .09
❑ 206 Russell Maryland .20 .09
❑ 207 Herman Moore .75 .35
❑ 208 Eric Martin .20 .09
❑ 209 John Friesz .40 .18
❑ 210 Boomer Esiason .40 .18
❑ 211 Jim Harbaugh .75 .35
❑ 212 Harold Green .20 .09
❑ 213 Perry Klein RC .20 .09
❑ 214 Eric Metcalf .40 .18
❑ 215 Steve Everitt .20 .09
❑ 216 Victor Bailey .20 .09
❑ 217 Lincoln Kennedy .20 .09
❑ 218 Glyn Milburn .40 .18
❑ 219 John Copeland .20 .09
❑ 220 Drew Bledsoe 3.00 1.35
❑ 221 Kevin Williams .40 .18
❑ 222 Roosevelt Potts .20 .09
❑ 223 Troy Drayton .20 .09
❑ 224 Terry Kirby .75 .35
❑ 225 Ronald Moore .20 .09
❑ 226 Tyrone Hughes .40 .18
❑ 227 Wayne Simmons .20 .09
❑ 228 Tony McGee .20 .09
❑ 229 Derek Brown RBK .20 .09
❑ 230 Jason Elam .20 .09
❑ 231 Qadry Ismail .75 .35
❑ 232 O.J. McDuffie .75 .35
❑ 233 Mike Caldwell .20 .09
❑ 234 Reggie Brooks .40 .18
❑ 235 Rick Mirer .75 .35
❑ 236 Steve Tovar .20 .09
❑ 237 Patrick Robinson .20 .09
❑ 238 Tom Carter .20 .09
❑ 239 Ben Coates .75 .35
❑ 240 Jerome Bettis .75 .35
❑ 241 Garrison Hearst .75 .35
❑ 242 Natrone Means .75 .35
❑ 243 Dana Stubblefield .75 .35
❑ 244 Willie Roaf .20 .09
❑ 245 Cortez Kennedy .40 .18
❑ 246 Todd Steussie RC .40 .18
❑ 247 Pat Coleman .20 .09
❑ 248 David Wyman .20 .09
❑ 249 Jeremy Lincoln .20 .09
❑ 250 Carlester Crumpler .20 .09
❑ 251 Dale Carter .20 .09
❑ 252 Corey Raymond RC .20 .09
❑ 253 Bryan Cox .20 .09
❑ 254 Charlie Garner RC 5.00 2.20
❑ 255 Jeff Hostetler .40 .18
❑ 256 Shane Bonham RC .20 .09
❑ 257 Thomas Everett .20 .09
❑ 258 John Jackson .20 .09
❑ 259 Terry Irving RC .20 .09
❑ 260 Corey Sawyer .20 .09
❑ 261 Rob Waldrop .20 .09
❑ 262 Curtis Conway .75 .35
❑ 263 Winfred Tubbs RC .40 .18
❑ 264 Sean Jones .20 .09
❑ 265 James Washington .20 .09
❑ 266 Lonnie Johnson RC .20 .09
❑ 267 Rob Moore .40 .18
❑ 268 Flipper Anderson .20 .09
❑ 269 Jon Hand .20 .09
❑ 270 Joe Patton RC .20 .09
❑ 271 Howard Ballard .20 .09
❑ 272 Fernando Smith RC .20 .09
❑ 273 Jessie Tuggle .20 .09
❑ 274 John Alt .20 .09
❑ 275 Corey Miller .20 .09
❑ 276 Gus Frerotte RC 1.50 .70
❑ 277 Jeff Cross .20 .09
❑ 278 Kevin Smith .20 .09
❑ 279 Corey Louchiey RC .20 .09
❑ 280 Micheal Barrow .20 .09
❑ 281 Jim Flanigan RC .40 .18
❑ 282 Calvin Williams .40 .18
❑ 283 Jeff Jaeger .20 .09
❑ 284 John Reece RC .20 .09
❑ 285 Jason Hanson .20 .09
❑ 286 Kurt Haws RC .20 .09
❑ 287 Eric Davis .20 .09
❑ 288 Maurice Hurst .20 .09
❑ 289 Kirk Lowdermilk .20 .09
❑ 290 Rod Woodson .75 .35
❑ 291 Andre Reed .40 .18
❑ 292 Vince Workman .20 .09
❑ 293 Wayne Martin .20 .09
❑ 294 Keith Lyle RC .20 .09
❑ 295 Brett Favre 5.00 2.20
❑ 296 Doug Brien RC .20 .09
❑ 297 Junior Seau .75 .35
❑ 298 Randall McDaniel .20 .09
❑ 299 Johnny Mitchell .20 .09
❑ 300 Emmitt Smith 4.00 1.80
❑ 301 Michael Brooks .20 .09
❑ 302 Steve Jackson .20 .09
❑ 303 Jeff George .75 .35
❑ 304 Irving Fryar .40 .18
❑ 305 Derrick Thomas .75 .35
❑ 306 Dante Jones .20 .09
❑ 307 Darrell Green .20 .09
❑ 308 Mark Bavaro .20 .09
❑ 309 Eugene Robinson .20 .09
❑ 310 Shannon Sharpe .40 .18
❑ 311 Michael Timpson .20 .09
❑ 312 Kevin Mitchell RC .20 .09
❑ 313 Stevon Moore .20 .09
❑ 314 Eric Swann .40 .18
❑ 315 James Bostic RC .75 .35
❑ 316 Robert Brooks .75 .35
❑ 317 Pete Pierson RC .20 .09
❑ 318 Jim Sweeney .20 .09
❑ 319 Anthony Smith .20 .09
❑ 320 Rohn Stark .20 .09
❑ 321 Gary Anderson K .20 .09
❑ 322 Robert Porcher .20 .09
❑ 323 Darryl Talley .20 .09
❑ 324 Stan Humphries .75 .35
❑ 325 Shelly Hammonds RC .20 .09
❑ 326 Jim McMahon .20 .09
❑ 327 Lamont Warren RC .20 .09
❑ 328 Chris Penn RC .20 .09
❑ 329 Tony Woods .20 .09
❑ 330 Raymont Harris RC .75 .35
❑ 331 Mitch Davis RC .20 .09
❑ 332 Michael Irvin .75 .35
❑ 333 Kent Graham .40 .18
❑ 334 Brian Blades .40 .18
❑ 335 Lomas Brown .20 .09
❑ 336 Willie Drewrey .20 .09
❑ 337 Russell Freeman .20 .09
❑ 338 Eric Zomalt RC .20 .09
❑ 339 Santana Dotson .40 .18
❑ 340 Sterling Sharpe .40 .18
❑ 341 Ray Crittenden RC .20 .09
❑ 342 Perry Carter RC .20 .09
❑ 343 Austin Robbins .20 .09
❑ 344 Mike Wells RC .20 .09
❑ 345 Toddrick McIntosh RC .20 .09
❑ 346 Mark Carrier WR .40 .18
❑ 347 Eugene Daniel .20 .09
❑ 348 Tre Johnson RC .20 .09
❑ 349 D.J. Johnson .20 .09
❑ 350 Steve Young 2.00 .90
❑ 351 Jim Pyne RC .20 .09
❑ 352 Jocelyn Borgella RC .20 .09
❑ 353 Pat Carter .20 .09
❑ 354 Sam Rogers RC .20 .09
❑ 355 Jason Sehorn RC 1.00 .45
❑ 356 Darren Carrington .20 .09
❑ 357 Lamar Smith RC 15.00 6.75
❑ 358 James Burton RC .20 .09
❑ 359 Darrin Smith .20 .09
❑ 360 Marco Coleman .20 .09
❑ 361 Webster Slaughter .20 .09
❑ 362 Lewis Tillman .20 .09
❑ 363 David Alexander .20 .09
❑ 364 Bradford Banta RC .20 .09
❑ 365 Ernic Pegram .20 .09
❑ 366 Mike Fox .20 .09
❑ 367 Jeff Lageman .20 .09
❑ 368 Kurt Gouveia .20 .09
❑ 369 Tim Brown .75 .35
❑ 370 Seth Joyner .20 .09
❑ 371 Irv Eatman .20 .09
❑ 372 Dorsey Levens RC 10.00 4.50

Card	MINT	NRMT
❑ 373 Anthony Pleasant	.20	.09
❑ 374 Henry Jones	.20	.09
❑ 375 Cris Carter	1.25	.55
❑ 376 Morten Andersen	.20	.09
❑ 377 Neil O'Donnell	.75	.35
❑ 378 Tyronne Drakeford RC	.20	.09
❑ 379 John Carney	.20	.09
❑ 380 Vincent Brown	.20	.09
❑ 381 J.J. Birden	.20	.09
❑ 382 Chris Spielman	.40	.18
❑ 383 Mark Bortz	.20	.09
❑ 384 Ray Childress	.20	.09
❑ 385 Carlton Bailey	.20	.09
❑ 386 Charles Haley	.40	.18
❑ 387 Shane Dronett	.20	.09
❑ 388 Jon Vaughn	.20	.09
❑ 389 Checklist 1-195	.20	.09
❑ 390 Checklist 196-390	.20	.09

1995 Bowman

	MINT	NRMT
COMPLETE SET (357)	100.00	45.00
❑ 1 Ki-Jana Carter RC	.75	.35
❑ 2 Tony Boselli RC	.75	.35
❑ 3 Steve McNair RC	8.00	3.60
❑ 4 Michael Westbrook RC	5.00	2.20
❑ 5 Kerry Collins RC	5.00	2.20
❑ 6 Kevin Carter RC	.75	.35
❑ 7 Mike Mamula RC	.40	.18
❑ 8 Joey Galloway RC	6.00	2.70
❑ 9 Kyle Brady RC	.40	.18
❑ 10 J.J. Stokes RC	.75	.35
❑ 11 Derrick Alexander DE RC	.20	.09
❑ 12 Warren Sapp RC	1.50	.70
❑ 13 Mark Fields RC	.20	.09
❑ 14 Ruben Brown RC	.20	.09
❑ 15 Ellis Johnson RC	.20	.09
❑ 16 Hugh Douglas RC	.75	.35
❑ 17 Mike Pelton RC	.20	.09
❑ 18 Napoleon Kaufman RC	5.00	2.20
❑ 19 James O. Stewart RC	6.00	2.70
❑ 20 Luther Elliss RC	.20	.09
❑ 21 Rashaan Salaam RC	.75	.35
❑ 22 Tyrone Poole RC	.40	.18
❑ 23 Ty Law RC	.40	.18
❑ 24 Korey Stringer RC	.20	.09
❑ 25 Billy Milner RC	.20	.09
❑ 26 Devin Bush RC	.20	.09
❑ 27 Mark Bruener RC	.40	.18
❑ 28 Derrick Brooks RC	.75	.35
❑ 29 Blake Brockermeyer RC	.20	.09
❑ 30 Alundis Brice RC	.20	.09
❑ 31 Trezelle Jenkins RC	.20	.09
❑ 32 Craig Newsome RC	.20	.09
❑ 33 Fred Barnett	.30	.14
❑ 34 Ray Childress	.15	.07
❑ 35 Chris Miller	.15	.07
❑ 36 Charles Haley	.30	.14
❑ 37 Ray Crittenden	.15	.07
❑ 38 Gus Frerotte	.60	.25
❑ 39 Jeff George	.30	.14
❑ 40 Dan Marino	3.00	1.35
❑ 41 Shawn Lee	.15	.07
❑ 42 Herman Moore	.60	.25
❑ 43 Chris Calloway	.15	.07
❑ 44 Jeff Graham	.15	.07
❑ 45 Ray Buchanan	.15	.07
❑ 46 Doug Pelfrey	.15	.07
❑ 47 Lake Dawson	.30	.14
❑ 48 Glenn Parker	.15	.07
❑ 49 Terry McDaniel	.15	.07
❑ 50 Rod Woodson	.30	.14
❑ 51 Santana Dotson	.15	.07
❑ 52 Anthony Miller	.30	.14
❑ 53 Bo Orlando	.15	.07
❑ 54 David Palmer	.30	.14
❑ 55 William Floyd	.60	.25
❑ 56 Edgar Bennett	.30	.14
❑ 57 Jeff Blake RC	3.00	1.35
❑ 58 Anthony Pleasant	.15	.07
❑ 59 Quinn Early	.30	.14
❑ 60 Bobby Houston	.15	.07
❑ 61 Terrell Fletcher RC	.20	.09
❑ 62 Gary Brown	.15	.07
❑ 63 Dwayne Sabb	.15	.07
❑ 64 Roman Phifer	.15	.07
❑ 65 Sherman Williams RC	.20	.09
❑ 66 Roosevelt Potts	.15	.07
❑ 67 Darnay Scott	.60	.25
❑ 68 Charlie Garner	.30	.14
❑ 69 Bert Emanuel	.60	.25
❑ 70 Herschel Walker	.30	.14
❑ 71 Lorenzo Styles RC	.20	.09
❑ 72 Andre Coleman	.15	.07
❑ 73 Tyronne Drakeford	.15	.07
❑ 74 Jay Novacek	.30	.14
❑ 75 Raymont Harris	.15	.07
❑ 76 Tamarick Vanover RC	.40	.18
❑ 77 Tom Carter	.15	.07
❑ 78 Eric Green	.15	.07
❑ 79 Patrick Hunter	.15	.07
❑ 80 Jeff Hostetler	.30	.14
❑ 81 Robert Blackmon	.15	.07
❑ 82 Anthony Cook RC	.20	.09
❑ 83 Craig Erickson	.15	.07
❑ 84 Glyn Milburn	.15	.07
❑ 85 Greg Lloyd	.30	.14
❑ 86 Brent Jones	.15	.07
❑ 87 Barrett Brooks RC	.20	.09
❑ 88 Alvin Harper	.15	.07
❑ 89 Sean Jones	.15	.07
❑ 90 Cris Carter	.60	.25
❑ 91 Russell Copeland	.15	.07
❑ 92 Frank Sanders RC	3.00	1.35
❑ 93 Mo Lewis	.15	.07
❑ 94 Michael Haynes	.30	.14
❑ 95 Andre Rison	.30	.14
❑ 96 Jesse James RC	.20	.09
❑ 97 Stan Humphries	.30	.14
❑ 98 James Hasty	.15	.07
❑ 99 Ricardo McDonald	.15	.07
❑ 100 Jerry Rice	1.50	.70
❑ 101 Chris Hudson RC	.20	.09
❑ 102 Dave Meggett	.15	.07
❑ 103 Brian Mitchell	.15	.07
❑ 104 Mike Johnson	.15	.07
❑ 105 Kordell Stewart RC	6.00	2.70
❑ 106 Michael Brooks	.15	.07
❑ 107 Steve Walsh	.15	.07
❑ 108 Eric Metcalf	.30	.14
❑ 109 Ricky Watters	.60	.25
❑ 110 Brett Favre	3.00	1.35
❑ 111 Aubrey Beavers	.15	.07
❑ 112 Brian Williams LB RC	.20	.09
❑ 113 Eugene Robinson	.15	.07
❑ 114 Matt O'Dwyer RC	.20	.09
❑ 115 Micheal Barrow	.15	.07
❑ 116 Rocket Ismail	.30	.14
❑ 117 Scott Gragg RC	.20	.09
❑ 118 Leon Lett	.15	.07
❑ 119 Reggie Roby	.15	.07
❑ 120 Marshall Faulk	1.00	.45
❑ 121 Jack Jackson RC	.20	.09
❑ 122 Keith Byars	.15	.07
❑ 123 Eric Hill	.15	.07
❑ 124 Todd Sauerbrun RC	.20	.09
❑ 125 Dexter Carter	.15	.07
❑ 126 Vinny Testaverde	.30	.14
❑ 127 Shane Conlan	.15	.07
❑ 128 Terrance Shaw RC	.20	.09
❑ 129 Willie Roaf	.15	.07
❑ 130 Jim Kelly	.60	.25
❑ 131 Neil O'Donnell	.30	.14
❑ 132 Ray McElroy RC	.20	.09
❑ 133 Ed McDaniel	.15	.07
❑ 134 Brian Gelzheiser RC	.20	.09
❑ 135 Marcus Allen	.60	.25
❑ 136 Carl Pickens	.60	.25
❑ 137 Mike Verstegen RC	.20	.09
❑ 138 Chris Mims	.15	.07
❑ 139 Darryl Pounds RC	.20	.09
❑ 140 Emmitt Smith	2.50	1.10
❑ 141 Mike Frederick RC	.20	.09
❑ 142 Henry Ellard	.30	.14
❑ 143 Willie McGinest	.30	.14
❑ 144 Michael Roan RC	.20	.09
❑ 145 Chris Spielman	.30	.14
❑ 146 Darryl Talley	.15	.07
❑ 147 Randall Cunningham	.60	.25
❑ 148 Andrew Greene RC	.20	.09
❑ 149 George Teague	.15	.07
❑ 150 Tyrone Hughes	.30	.14
❑ 151 Ron Davis RC	.20	.09
❑ 152 Stevon Moore	.15	.07
❑ 153 Merton Hanks	.15	.07
❑ 154 Darren Perry	.15	.07
❑ 155 Dave Brown	.30	.14
❑ 156 Mike Morton RC	.20	.09
❑ 157 Seth Joyner	.15	.07
❑ 158 Bryan Cox	.15	.07
❑ 159 Corey Fuller RC	.20	.09
❑ 160 John Elway	3.00	1.35
❑ 161 Dewayne Washington	.30	.14
❑ 162 Chris Warren	.30	.14
❑ 163 Jeff Kopp RC	.20	.09
❑ 164 Sean Dawkins	.30	.14
❑ 165 Mark Carrier DB	.15	.07
❑ 166 Andre Hastings	.30	.14
❑ 167 Derek West RC	.20	.09
❑ 168 Glenn Montgomery	.15	.07
❑ 169 Trent Dilfer	.60	.25
❑ 170 Rob Johnson RC	6.00	2.70
❑ 171 Todd Scott	.15	.07
❑ 172 Charles Johnson	.30	.14
❑ 173 Kez McCorvey RC	.20	.09
❑ 174 Rob Fredrickson	.15	.07
❑ 175 Corey Sawyer	.15	.07
❑ 176 Brett Perriman	.30	.14
❑ 177 Ken Dilger RC	.75	.35
❑ 178 Dana Stubblefield	.60	.25
❑ 179 Eric Allen	.15	.07
❑ 180 Drew Bledsoe	1.50	.70
❑ 181 Tyrone Davis RC	.20	.09
❑ 182 Reggie Brooks	.30	.14
❑ 183 Dale Carter	.30	.14
❑ 184 William Henderson RC	.40	.18
❑ 185 Reggie White	.60	.25
❑ 186 Lorenzo White	.15	.07
❑ 187 Leslie O'Neal	.30	.14
❑ 188 Stoney Case RC	.75	.35
❑ 189 Jeff Burris	.15	.07
❑ 190 Leroy Hoard	.15	.07
❑ 191 Thomas Randolph	.15	.07
❑ 192 Rodney Thomas RC	.40	.18
❑ 193 Quentin Coryatt	.30	.14
❑ 194 Terry Wooden	.15	.07
❑ 195 David Sloan RC	.40	.18
❑ 196 Bernie Parmalee	.30	.14
❑ 197 Zack Crockett RC	.20	.09
❑ 198 Troy Aikman	1.50	.70
❑ 199 Bruce Smith	.60	.25
❑ 200 Eric Zeier RC	.75	.35
❑ 201 Anthony Smith	.15	.07
❑ 202 Jake Reed	.30	.14
❑ 203 Hardy Nickerson	.15	.07
❑ 204 Patrick Riley RC	.20	.09
❑ 205 Bruce Matthews	.15	.07
❑ 206 Larry Centers	.30	.14
❑ 207 Troy Drayton	.15	.07
❑ 208 John Burrough RC	.20	.09
❑ 209 Jason Elam	.15	.07
❑ 210 Donnell Woolford	.15	.07
❑ 211 Sam Shade RC	.20	.09
❑ 212 Kevin Greene	.30	.14
❑ 213 Ronald Moore	.15	.07
❑ 214 Shane Hannah RC	.20	.09
❑ 215 Jim Everett	.15	.07
❑ 216 Scott Mitchell	.30	.14

	Card	Mint	NrMt
❑	217 Antonio Freeman RC	8.00	3.60
❑	218 Tony McGee	.15	.07
❑	219 Clay Matthews	.30	.14
❑	220 Neil Smith	.30	.14
❑	221 Mark Williams FOIL	.40	.18
❑	222 Derrick Graham FOIL	.40	.18
❑	223 Mike Hollis FOIL	.40	.18
❑	224 Darion Conner FOIL	.40	.18
❑	225 Steve Beuerlein FOIL	.40	.18
❑	226 Rod Smith DB FOIL	.40	.18
❑	227 James Williams FOIL	.40	.18
❑	228 Bob Christian FOIL	.40	.18
❑	229 Jeff Lageman FOIL	.40	.18
❑	230 Frank Reich FOIL	.40	.18
❑	231 Harry Colon FOIL	.40	.18
❑	232 Carlton Bailey FOIL	.40	.18
❑	233 Mickey Washington FOIL	.40	.18
❑	234 Shawn Bouwens FOIL	.40	.18
❑	235 Don Beebe FOIL	.40	.18
❑	236 Kelvin Pritchett FOIL	.40	.18
❑	237 Tommy Barnhardt FOIL	.40	.18
❑	238 Mike Dumas FOIL	.40	.18
❑	239 Brett Maxie FOIL	.40	.18
❑	240 Desmond Howard FOIL	.40	.18
❑	241 Sam Mills FOIL	.40	.18
❑	242 Keith Goganious FOIL	.40	.18
❑	243 Bubba McDowell FOIL	.40	.18
❑	244 Vinnie Clark FOIL	.40	.18
❑	245 Lamar Lathon FOIL	.40	.18
❑	246 Bryan Barker FOIL	.40	.18
❑	247 Darren Carrington FOIL	.40	.18
❑	248 Jay Barker RC	.20	.09
❑	249 Eric Davis	.15	.07
❑	250 Heath Shuler	.60	.25
❑	251 Donta Jones RC	.20	.09
❑	252 LeRoy Butler	.15	.07
❑	253 Michael Zordich	.15	.07
❑	254 Cortez Kennedy	.30	.14
❑	255 Brian DeMarco RC	.20	.09
❑	256 Randal Hill	.15	.07
❑	257 Michael Irvin	.60	.25
❑	258 Natrone Means	.60	.25
❑	259 Linc Harden RC	.20	.09
❑	260 Jerome Bettis	.60	.25
❑	261 Tony Bennett	.15	.07
❑	262 Dameian Jeffries RC	.20	.09
❑	263 Cornelius Bennett	.30	.14
❑	264 Chris Zorich	.15	.07
❑	265 Bobby Taylor RC	.40	.18
❑	266 Terrell Buckley	.15	.07
❑	267 Troy Dumas RC	.20	.09
❑	268 Rodney Hampton	.30	.14
❑	269 Steve Everitt	.15	.07
❑	270 Mel Gray	.15	.07
❑	271 Antonio Armstrong RC	.20	.09
❑	272 Jim Harbaugh	.30	.14
❑	273 Gary Clark	.15	.07
❑	274 Tau Pupua RC	.20	.09
❑	275 Warren Moon	.30	.14
❑	276 Corey Croom	.15	.07
❑	277 Tony Berti RC	.20	.09
❑	278 Shannon Sharpe	.30	.14
❑	279 Boomer Esiason	.30	.14
❑	280 Aeneas Williams	.15	.07
❑	281 Lethon Flowers RC	.20	.09
❑	282 Derek Brown TE	.15	.07
❑	283 Charlie Williams RC	.20	.09
❑	284 Dan Wilkinson	.30	.14
❑	285 Mike Sherrard	.15	.07
❑	286 Evan Pilgrim RC	.20	.09
❑	287 Kimble Anders	.30	.14
❑	288 Greg Jefferson RC	.20	.09
❑	289 Ken Norton	.30	.14
❑	290 Terance Mathis	.30	.14
❑	291 Torey Hunter RC	.20	.09
❑	292 Ken Harvey	.15	.07
❑	293 Irving Fryar	.30	.14
❑	294 Michael Reed RC	.20	.09
❑	295 Andre Reed	.30	.14
❑	296 Vencie Glenn	.15	.07
❑	297 Corey Swinson	.15	.07
❑	298 Harvey Williams	.15	.07
❑	299 Willie Davis	.30	.14
❑	300 Barry Sanders	3.00	1.35
❑	301 Curtis Martin RC	8.00	3.60
❑	302 Johnny Mitchell	.15	.07
❑	303 Daryl Johnston	.30	.14
❑	304 Lorenzo Lynch	.15	.07
❑	305 Christian Fauria RC	.40	.18
❑	306 Sean Gilbert	.30	.14
❑	307 Ray Zellars RC	.40	.18
❑	308 William Strong RC	.20	.09
❑	309 Jack Del Rio	.15	.07
❑	310 Junior Seau	.60	.25
❑	311 Justin Armour RC	.40	.18
❑	312 Eric Bjornson RC	.40	.18
❑	313 Vincent Brown	.15	.07
❑	314 Darius Holland RC	.20	.09
❑	315 Chad May RC	.20	.09
❑	316 Simon Fletcher	.15	.07
❑	317 Roell Preston RC	.75	.35
❑	318 John Thierry	.15	.07
❑	319 Orlando Thomas RC	.20	.09
❑	320 Zach Wiegert RC	.20	.09
❑	321 Derrick Alexander WR	.60	.25
❑	322 Chris Cowart RC	.20	.09
❑	323 Chris Sanders RC	.75	.35
❑	324 Robert Brooks	.60	.25
❑	325 Todd Collins RC	.75	.35
❑	326 Ken Irvin RC	.20	.09
❑	327 Erric Pegram	.30	.14
❑	328 Damien Covington RC	.20	.09
❑	329 Brendan Stai RC	.20	.09
❑	330 James A.Stewart RC	.20	.09
❑	331 Jessie Tuggle	.15	.07
❑	332 Marco Coleman	.15	.07
❑	333 Steve Young	1.25	.55
❑	334 Greg Hill	.30	.14
❑	335 Darryl Williams	.15	.07
❑	336 Calvin Williams	.30	.14
❑	337 Cris Dishman	.15	.07
❑	338 Anthony Morgan	.15	.07
❑	339 Renaldo Turnbull	.15	.07
❑	340 Rick Mirer	.60	.25
❑	341 Tim Brown	.60	.25
❑	342 Dennis Gibson	.15	.07
❑	343 Brad Baxter	.15	.07
❑	344 Henry Jones	.15	.07
❑	345 Johnny Bailey	.15	.07
❑	346 Rocket Ismail	.30	.14
❑	347 Richmond Webb	.15	.07
❑	348 Robert Jones	.15	.07
❑	349 Garrison Hearst	.60	.25
❑	350 Errict Rhett	.60	.25
❑	351 Steve Atwater	.15	.07
❑	352 Joe Cain	.15	.07
❑	353 Ben Coates	.30	.14
❑	354 Aaron Glenn	.15	.07
❑	355 Antonio Langham	.15	.07
❑	356 Eugene Daniel	.15	.07
❑	357 Tim Bowens	.15	.07

1998 Bowman

		MINT	NRMT
	COMPLETE SET (220)	50.00	22.00
❑	1 Peyton Manning RC	20.00	9.00
❑	2 Keith Brooking RC	2.00	.90
❑	3 Duane Starks RC	1.50	.70
❑	4 Takeo Spikes RC	2.00	.90
❑	5 Andre Wadsworth RC	2.00	.90
❑	6 Greg Ellis RC	1.50	.70
❑	7 Brian Griese RC	10.00	4.50
❑	8 Germane Crowell RC	4.00	1.80
❑	9 Jerome Pathon RC	2.00	.90
❑	10 Ryan Leaf RC	5.00	2.20
❑	11 Fred Taylor RC	8.00	3.60
❑	12 Robert Edwards RC	3.00	1.35
❑	13 Grant Wistrom RC	1.50	.70
❑	14 Robert Holcombe RC	2.50	1.10
❑	15 Tim Dwight RC	3.00	1.35
❑	16 Jacquez Green RC	3.00	1.35
❑	17 Marcus Nash RC	2.50	1.10
❑	18 Jason Peter RC	1.50	.70
❑	19 Anthony Simmons RC	1.50	.70
❑	20 Curtis Enis RC	2.50	1.10
❑	21 John Avery RC	2.50	1.10
❑	22 Pat Johnson RC	2.00	.90
❑	23 Joe Jurevicius RC	2.00	.90
❑	24 Brian Simmons RC	1.50	.70
❑	25 Kevin Dyson RC	3.00	1.35
❑	26 Skip Hicks RC	2.50	1.10
❑	27 Hines Ward RC	2.00	.90
❑	28 Tavian Banks RC	2.00	.90
❑	29 Ahman Green RC	5.00	2.20
❑	30 Tony Simmons RC	2.00	.90
❑	31 Charles Johnson	.15	.07
❑	32 Freddie Jones	.15	.07
❑	33 Joey Galloway	.60	.25
❑	34 Tony Banks	.30	.14
❑	35 Jake Plummer	1.25	.55
❑	36 Reidel Anthony	.30	.14
❑	37 Steve McNair	.60	.25
❑	38 Michael Westbrook	.30	.14
❑	39 Chris Sanders	.15	.07
❑	40 Isaac Bruce	.60	.25
❑	41 Charlie Garner	.15	.07
❑	42 Wayne Chrebet	.60	.25
❑	43 Michael Strahan	.15	.07
❑	44 Brad Johnson	.60	.25
❑	45 Mike Alstott	.60	.25
❑	46 Tony Gonzalez	.15	.07
❑	47 Johnnie Morton	.30	.14
❑	48 Darnay Scott	.30	.14
❑	49 Rae Carruth	.30	.14
❑	50 Terrell Davis	2.50	1.10
❑	51 Jermaine Lewis	.30	.14
❑	52 Frank Sanders	.30	.14
❑	53 Byron Hanspard	.30	.14
❑	54 Gus Frerotte	.15	.07
❑	55 Terry Glenn	.60	.25
❑	56 J.J. Stokes	.30	.14
❑	57 Will Blackwell	.15	.07
❑	58 Keyshawn Johnson	.60	.25
❑	59 Tiki Barber	.30	.14
❑	60 Dorsey Levens	.60	.25
❑	61 Zach Thomas	.30	.14
❑	62 Corey Dillon	1.00	.45
❑	63 Antowain Smith	.60	.25
❑	64 Michael Sinclair	.15	.07
❑	65 Rod Smith	.30	.14
❑	66 Trent Dilfer	.60	.25
❑	67 Warren Sapp	.30	.14
❑	68 Charles Way	.15	.07
❑	69 Tamarick Vanover	.15	.07
❑	70 Drew Bledsoe	1.25	.55
❑	71 John Mobley	.15	.07
❑	72 Kerry Collins	.30	.14
❑	73 Peter Boulware	.15	.07
❑	74 Simeon Rice	.30	.14
❑	75 Eddie George	1.25	.55
❑	76 Fred Lane	.30	.14
❑	77 Jamal Anderson	.60	.25
❑	78 Antonio Freeman	.60	.25
❑	79 Jason Sehorn	.30	.14
❑	80 Curtis Martin	.60	.25
❑	81 Bobby Hoying	.30	.14
❑	82 Garrison Hearst	.60	.25
❑	83 Glenn Foley	.30	.14
❑	84 Danny Kanell	.30	.14
❑	85 Kordell Stewart	.60	.25
❑	86 O.J. McDuffie	.30	.14
❑	87 Marvin Harrison	.30	.14
❑	88 Bobby Engram	.30	.14
❑	89 Chris Slade	.15	.07
❑	90 Warrick Dunn	.60	.25
❑	91 Ricky Watters	.30	.14
❑	92 Rickey Dudley	.15	.07
❑	93 Terrell Owens	.60	.25

❑ 94 Karim Abdul-Jabbar .60 .25
❑ 95 Napoleon Kaufman .60 .25
❑ 96 Darrell Green .30 .14
❑ 97 Levon Kirkland .15 .07
❑ 98 Jeff George .30 .14
❑ 99 Andre Hastings .15 .07
❑ 100 John Elway 3.00 1.35
❑ 101 John Randle .30 .14
❑ 102 Andre Rison .30 .14
❑ 103 Keenan McCardell .30 .14
❑ 104 Marshall Faulk .60 .25
❑ 105 Emmitt Smith 2.50 1.10
❑ 106 Robert Brooks .30 .14
❑ 107 Scott Mitchell .30 .14
❑ 108 Shannon Sharpe .30 .14
❑ 109 Deion Sanders .60 .25
❑ 110 Jerry Rice 1.50 .70
❑ 111 Erik Kramer .15 .07
❑ 112 Michael Jackson .15 .07
❑ 113 Aeneas Williams .15 .07
❑ 114 Terry Allen .60 .25
❑ 115 Steve Young 1.00 .45
❑ 116 Warren Moon .60 .25
❑ 117 Junior Seau .30 .14
❑ 118 Jerome Bettis .60 .25
❑ 119 Irving Fryar .30 .14
❑ 120 Barry Sanders 3.00 1.35
❑ 121 Tim Brown .60 .25
❑ 122 Chad Brown .15 .07
❑ 123 Ben Coates .30 .14
❑ 124 Robert Smith .60 .25
❑ 125 Brett Favre 3.00 1.35
❑ 126 Derrick Thomas .30 .14
❑ 127 Reggie White .60 .25
❑ 128 Troy Aikman 1.50 .70
❑ 129 Jeff Blake .30 .14
❑ 130 Mark Brunell 1.25 .55
❑ 131 Curtis Conway .30 .14
❑ 132 Wesley Walls .30 .14
❑ 133 Thurman Thomas .60 .25
❑ 134 Chris Chandler .30 .14
❑ 135 Dan Marino 3.00 1.35
❑ 136 Larry Centers .15 .07
❑ 137 Shawn Jefferson .15 .07
❑ 138 Andre Reed .30 .14
❑ 139 Jake Reed .30 .14
❑ 140 Cris Carter .60 .25
❑ 141 Elvis Grbac .30 .14
❑ 142 Mark Chmura .30 .14
❑ 143 Michael Irvin .60 .25
❑ 144 Carl Pickens .60 .25
❑ 145 Herman Moore .60 .25
❑ 146 Marvin Jones .15 .07
❑ 147 Terance Mathis .30 .14
❑ 148 Rob Moore .30 .14
❑ 149 Bruce Smith .30 .14
❑ 150 Rob Johnson CL .15 .07
❑ 151 Leslie Shepherd .15 .07
❑ 152 Chris Spielman .15 .07
❑ 153 Tony McGee .15 .07
❑ 154 Kevin Smith .15 .07
❑ 155 Bill Romanowski .15 .07
❑ 156 Stephen Boyd .15 .07
❑ 157 James Stewart .30 .14
❑ 158 Jason Taylor .15 .07
❑ 159 Troy Drayton .15 .07
❑ 160 Mark Fields .15 .07
❑ 161 Jessie Armstead .15 .07
❑ 162 James Jett .30 .14
❑ 163 Bobby Taylor .15 .07
❑ 164 Kimble Anders .30 .14
❑ 165 Jimmy Smith .30 .14
❑ 166 Quentin Coryatt .15 .07
❑ 167 Bryant Westbrook .15 .07
❑ 168 Neil Smith .30 .14
❑ 169 Darren Woodson .15 .07
❑ 170 Ray Buchanan .15 .07
❑ 171 Earl Holmes .15 .07
❑ 172 Ray Lewis .60 .25
❑ 173 Steve Broussard .15 .07
❑ 174 Derrick Brooks .15 .07
❑ 175 Ken Harvey .15 .07
❑ 176 Darryll Lewis .15 .07
❑ 177 Derrick Rodgers .15 .07
❑ 178 James McKnight .15 .07
❑ 179 Cris Dishman .15 .07
❑ 180 Hardy Nickerson .15 .07
❑ 181 Charles Woodson RC 3.00 1.35
❑ 182 Randy Moss RC 20.00 9.00
❑ 183 Stephen Alexander RC 2.00 .90
❑ 184 Samari Rolle RC 1.50 .70
❑ 185 Jamie Duncan RC 1.50 .70
❑ 186 Lance Schulters RC 1.50 .70
❑ 187 Tony Parrish RC 1.50 .70
❑ 188 Corey Chavous RC 1.50 .70
❑ 189 Jammi German RC 1.50 .70
❑ 190 Sam Cowart RC 1.50 .70
❑ 191 Donald Hayes RC 2.50 1.10
❑ 192 R.W. McQuarters RC 1.50 .70
❑ 193 Az-Zahir Hakim RC 2.50 1.10
❑ 194 C.Fuamatu-Ma'Afala RC 2.00 .90
❑ 195 Allen Rossum RC 2.00 .90
❑ 196 Jon Ritchie RC 2.00 .90
❑ 197 Blake Spence RC 1.50 .70
❑ 198 Brian Alford RC 2.00 .90
❑ 199 Fred Weary RC 1.50 .70
❑ 200 Rod Rutledge RC 1.50 .70
❑ 201 Michael Myers RC 1.50 .70
❑ 202 Rashaan Shehee RC 2.00 .90
❑ 203 Donovin Darius RC 1.50 .70
❑ 204 E.G. Green RC 2.00 .90
❑ 205 Vonnie Holliday RC 2.00 .90
❑ 206 Charlie Batch RC 8.00 3.60
❑ 207 Michael Pittman RC 2.50 1.10
❑ 208 Artrell Hawkins RC 1.50 .70
❑ 209 Jonathan Quinn RC 2.00 .90
❑ 210 Kailee Wong RC 1.50 .70
❑ 211 DeShea Townsend RC 1.50 .70
❑ 212 Patrick Surtain RC 1.50 .70
❑ 213 Brian Kelly RC 1.50 .70
❑ 214 Tebucky Jones RC 1.50 .70
❑ 215 Pete Gonzalez RC 1.50 .70
❑ 216 Shaun Williams RC 1.50 .70
❑ 217 Scott Frost RC 2.00 .90
❑ 218 Leonard Little RC 1.50 .70
❑ 219 Alonzo Mayes RC 1.50 .70
❑ 220 Cordell Taylor RC 1.50 .70

1999 Bowman

	MINT	NRMT
COMPLETE SET (220)	50.00	22.00

❑ 1 Dan Marino 2.50 1.10
❑ 2 Michael Westbrook .30 .14
❑ 3 Yancey Thigpen .15 .07
❑ 4 Tony Martin .30 .14
❑ 5 Michael Strahan .15 .07
❑ 6 Dedric Ward .15 .07
❑ 7 Joey Galloway .60 .25
❑ 8 Bobby Engram .30 .14
❑ 9 Frank Sanders .30 .14
❑ 10 Jake Plummer 1.25 .55
❑ 11 Eddie Kennison .30 .14
❑ 12 Curtis Martin .60 .25
❑ 13 Chris Spielman .15 .07
❑ 14 Trent Dilfer .30 .14
❑ 15 Tim Biakabutuka .30 .14
❑ 16 Elvis Grbac .30 .14
❑ 17 Charlie Batch 1.25 .55
❑ 18 Takeo Spikes .15 .07
❑ 19 Tony Banks .30 .14
❑ 20 Doug Flutie .75 .35
❑ 21 Ty Law .15 .07
❑ 22 Isaac Bruce .60 .25
❑ 23 James Jett .30 .14
❑ 24 Kent Graham .15 .07
❑ 25 Derrick Mayes .15 .07
❑ 26 Amani Toomer .15 .07
❑ 27 Ray Lewis .30 .14
❑ 28 Shawn Springs .15 .07
❑ 29 Warren Sapp .15 .07
❑ 30 Jamal Anderson .60 .25
❑ 31 Byron Bam Morris .15 .07
❑ 32 Johnnie Morton .15 .07
❑ 33 Terance Mathis .15 .07
❑ 34 Terrell Davis 1.50 .70
❑ 35 John Randle .30 .14
❑ 36 Vinny Testaverde .15 .07
❑ 37 Junior Seau .30 .14
❑ 38 Reidel Anthony .30 .14
❑ 39 Brad Johnson .15 .07
❑ 40 Emmitt Smith 1.50 .70
❑ 41 Mo Lewis .15 .07
❑ 42 Terry Glenn .60 .25
❑ 43 Dorsey Levens .60 .25
❑ 44 Thurman Thomas .30 .14
❑ 45 Rob Moore .30 .14
❑ 46 Corey Dillon .60 .25
❑ 47 Jessie Armstead .15 .07
❑ 48 Marshall Faulk .60 .25
❑ 49 Charles Woodson .15 .07
❑ 50 John Elway 2.50 1.10
❑ 51 Kevin Dyson .30 .14
❑ 52 Tony Simmons .15 .07
❑ 53 Keenan McCardell .30 .14
❑ 54 O.J. Santiago .15 .07
❑ 55 Jermaine Lewis .30 .14
❑ 56 Herman Moore .60 .25
❑ 57 Gary Brown .15 .07
❑ 58 Jim Harbaugh .30 .14
❑ 59 Mike Alstott .60 .25
❑ 60 Brett Favre 2.50 1.10
❑ 61 Tim Brown .60 .25
❑ 62 Steve McNair .60 .25
❑ 63 Ben Coates .30 .14
❑ 64 Jerome Pathon .15 .07
❑ 65 Ray Buchanan .15 .07
❑ 66 Troy Aikman 1.50 .70
❑ 67 Andre Reed .30 .14
❑ 68 Bubby Brister .15 .07
❑ 69 Karim Abdul-Jabbar .30 .14
❑ 70 Peyton Manning 2.50 1.10
❑ 71 Charles Johnson .15 .07
❑ 72 Natrone Means .30 .14
❑ 73 Michael Sinclair .15 .07
❑ 74 Skip Hicks .30 .14
❑ 75 Derrick Alexander .30 .14
❑ 76 Wayne Chrebet .30 .14
❑ 77 Rod Smith .30 .14
❑ 78 Carl Pickens .30 .14
❑ 79 Adrian Murrell .30 .14
❑ 80 Fred Taylor 1.50 .70
❑ 81 Eric Moulds .60 .25
❑ 82 Lawrence Phillips .30 .14
❑ 83 Marvin Harrison .60 .25
❑ 84 Cris Carter .60 .25
❑ 85 Ike Hilliard .15 .07
❑ 86 Hines Ward .15 .07
❑ 87 Terrell Owens .60 .25
❑ 88 Ricky Proehl .15 .07
❑ 89 Bert Emanuel .30 .14
❑ 90 Randy Moss 2.50 1.10
❑ 91 Aaron Glenn .15 .07
❑ 92 Robert Smith .60 .25
❑ 93 Andre Hastings .15 .07
❑ 94 Jake Reed .30 .14
❑ 95 Curtis Enis .60 .25
❑ 96 Andre Wadsworth .15 .07
❑ 97 Ed McCaffrey .30 .14
❑ 98 Zach Thomas .30 .14
❑ 99 Kerry Collins .30 .14
❑ 100 Drew Bledsoe 1.00 .45
❑ 101 Germane Crowell .30 .14
❑ 102 Bryan Still .15 .07
❑ 103 Chad Brown .15 .07
❑ 104 Jacquez Green .15 .07
❑ 105 Garrison Hearst .30 .14
❑ 106 Napoleon Kaufman .60 .25
❑ 107 Ricky Watters .30 .14

❑ 108 O.J. McDuffie	.30	.14
❑ 109 Keyshawn Johnson	.60	.25
❑ 110 Jerome Bettis	.60	.25
❑ 111 Duce Staley	.60	.25
❑ 112 Curtis Conway	.30	.14
❑ 113 Chris Chandler	.30	.14
❑ 114 Marcus Nash	.30	.14
❑ 115 Stephen Alexander	.15	.07
❑ 116 Darnay Scott	.15	.07
❑ 117 Bruce Smith	.30	.14
❑ 118 Priest Holmes	.60	.25
❑ 119 Mark Brunell	1.00	.45
❑ 120 Jerry Rice	1.50	.70
❑ 121 Randall Cunningham	.60	.25
❑ 122 Scott Mitchell	.15	.07
❑ 123 Antonio Freeman	.60	.25
❑ 124 Kordell Stewart	.60	.25
❑ 125 Jon Kitna	.60	.25
❑ 126 Ahman Green	.30	.14
❑ 127 Warrick Dunn	.60	.25
❑ 128 Robert Brooks	.30	.14
❑ 129 Derrick Thomas	.30	.14
❑ 130 Steve Young	1.00	.45
❑ 131 Peter Boulware	.15	.07
❑ 132 Michael Irvin	.30	.14
❑ 133 Shannon Sharpe	.15	.07
❑ 134 Jimmy Smith	.30	.14
❑ 135 John Avery	.30	.14
❑ 136 Fred Lane	.30	.14
❑ 137 Trent Green	.30	.14
❑ 138 Andre Rison	.30	.14
❑ 139 Antowain Smith	.15	.07
❑ 140 Eddie George	.75	.35
❑ 141 Jeff Blake	.30	.14
❑ 142 Rocket Ismail	.30	.14
❑ 143 Rickey Dudley	.15	.07
❑ 144 Courtney Hawkins	.15	.07
❑ 145 Mikhael Ricks	.15	.07
❑ 146 J.J. Stokes	.30	.14
❑ 147 Levon Kirkland	.15	.07
❑ 148 Deion Sanders	.60	.25
❑ 149 Barry Sanders	2.50	1.10
❑ 150 Tiki Barber	.15	.07
❑ 151 David Boston RC	4.00	1.80
❑ 152 Chris McAlister RC	1.50	.70
❑ 153 Peerless Price RC	2.50	1.10
❑ 154 D'Wayne Bates RC	1.50	.70
❑ 155 Cade McNown RC	2.50	1.10
❑ 156 Akili Smith RC	4.00	1.80
❑ 157 Kevin Johnson RC	4.00	1.80
❑ 158 Tim Couch RC	8.00	3.60
❑ 159 Sedrick Irvin RC	2.00	.90
❑ 160 Chris Claiborne RC	.75	.35
❑ 161 Edgerrin James RC	12.00	5.50
❑ 162 Mike Cloud RC	2.00	.90
❑ 163 Cecil Collins RC	2.00	.90
❑ 164 James Johnson RC	2.00	.90
❑ 165 Rob Konrad RC	2.00	.90
❑ 166 Daunte Culpepper RC	12.00	5.50
❑ 167 Kevin Faulk RC	3.00	1.35
❑ 168 Donovan McNabb RC	8.00	3.60
❑ 169 Troy Edwards RC	2.50	1.10
❑ 170 Amos Zereoue RC	2.00	.90
❑ 171 Karsten Bailey RC	1.50	.70
❑ 172 Brock Huard RC	3.00	1.35
❑ 173 Joe Germaine RC	2.00	.90
❑ 174 Torry Holt RC	5.00	2.20
❑ 175 Shaun King RC	4.00	1.80
❑ 176 Jevon Kearse RC	4.00	1.80
❑ 177 Champ Bailey RC	2.50	1.10
❑ 178 Ebenezer Ekuban RC	1.50	.70
❑ 179 Andy Katzenmoyer	2.00	.90
❑ 180 Antoine Winfield RC	1.50	.70
❑ 181 Jermaine Fazande RC	2.00	.90
❑ 182 Ricky Williams RC	8.00	3.60
❑ 183 Joel Makovicka RC	2.00	.90
❑ 184 Reginald Kelly RC	.75	.35
❑ 185 Brandon Stokley RC	2.00	.90
❑ 186 L.C. Stevens RC	.75	.35
❑ 187 Marty Booker RC	2.00	.90
❑ 188 Jerry Azumah	2.00	.90
❑ 189 Ted White RC	1.50	.70
❑ 190 Scott Covington RC	2.00	.90
❑ 191 Tim Alexander RC	.75	.35
❑ 192 Darrin Chiaverini RC	1.50	.70
❑ 193 Dat Nguyen RC	2.00	.90
❑ 194 Wane McGarity RC	1.50	.70
❑ 195 Al Wilson RC	2.00	.90
❑ 196 Travis McGriff RC	2.00	.90
❑ 197 Stacey Mack RC	2.00	.90
❑ 198 Antuan Edwards RC	.75	.35
❑ 199 Aaron Brooks RC	8.00	3.60
❑ 200 De'Mond Parker RC	2.00	.90
❑ 201 Jed Weaver RC	.75	.35
❑ 202 Madre Hill RC	.75	.35
❑ 203 Jim Kleinsasser RC	2.00	.90
❑ 204 Michael Bishop RC	2.50	1.10
❑ 205 Michael Basnight RC	1.50	.70
❑ 206 Sean Bennett RC	2.00	.90
❑ 207 Dameane Douglas RC	1.50	.70
❑ 208 Na Brown RC	2.00	.90
❑ 209 Patrick Kerney RC	.75	.35
❑ 210 Malcolm Johnson RC	1.50	.70
❑ 211 Dre Bly RC	1.50	.70
❑ 212 Terry Jackson RC	1.50	.70
❑ 213 Eugene Baker RC	.75	.35
❑ 214 Autry Denson RC	2.00	.90
❑ 215 Darnell McDonald	2.00	.90
❑ 216 Charlie Rogers RC	1.50	.70
❑ 217 Joe Montgomery RC	2.00	.90
❑ 218 Cecil Martin RC	1.50	.70
❑ 219 Larry Parker RC	1.50	.70
❑ 220 Mike Peterson RC	2.00	.90

2000 Bowman

	MINT	NRMT
COMPLETE SET (240)	50.00	22.00
❑ 1 Eddie George	.60	.25
❑ 2 Ike Hilliard	.25	.11
❑ 3 Terrell Owens	.50	.23
❑ 4 James Stewart	.25	.11
❑ 5 Joey Galloway	.50	.23
❑ 6 Jake Reed	.25	.11
❑ 7 Derrick Alexander	.25	.11
❑ 8 Jeff George	.25	.11
❑ 9 Kerry Collins	.25	.11
❑ 10 Tony Gonzalez	.25	.11
❑ 11 Marcus Robinson	.50	.23
❑ 12 Charles Woodson	.25	.11
❑ 13 Germane Crowell	.25	.11
❑ 14 Yancey Thigpen	.15	.07
❑ 15 Tony Martin	.25	.11
❑ 16 Frank Sanders	.25	.11
❑ 17 Napoleon Kaufman	.25	.11
❑ 18 Jay Fiedler	.50	.23
❑ 19 Patrick Jeffers	.50	.23
❑ 20 Steve McNair	.50	.23
❑ 21 Herman Moore	.25	.11
❑ 22 Tim Brown	.50	.23
❑ 23 Olandis Gary	.50	.23
❑ 24 Corey Dillon	.50	.23
❑ 25 Warren Sapp	.25	.11
❑ 26 Curtis Enis	.25	.11
❑ 27 Vinny Testaverde	.25	.11
❑ 28 Tim Biakabutuka	.25	.11
❑ 29 Kevin Johnson	.50	.23
❑ 30 Charlie Batch	.50	.23
❑ 31 Jermaine Fazande	.15	.07
❑ 32 Shaun King	.75	.35
❑ 33 Errict Rhett	.25	.11
❑ 34 O.J. McDuffie	.25	.11
❑ 35 Bruce Smith	.25	.11
❑ 36 Antonio Freeman	.50	.23
❑ 37 Tim Couch	1.00	.45
❑ 38 Duce Staley	.50	.23
❑ 39 Jeff Blake	.25	.11
❑ 40 Jim Harbaugh	.25	.11
❑ 41 Jeff Graham	.15	.07
❑ 42 Drew Bledsoe	.75	.35
❑ 43 Mike Alstott	.50	.23
❑ 44 Terance Mathis	.25	.11
❑ 45 Antowain Smith	.25	.11
❑ 46 Johnnie Morton	.25	.11
❑ 47 Chris Chandler	.25	.11
❑ 48 Keith Poole	.25	.11
❑ 49 Ricky Watters	.25	.11
❑ 50 Darnay Scott	.25	.11
❑ 51 Damon Huard	.50	.23
❑ 52 Peerless Price	.50	.23
❑ 53 Brian Griese	.60	.25
❑ 54 Frank Wycheck	.15	.07
❑ 55 Kevin Dyson	.25	.11
❑ 56 Junior Seau	.25	.11
❑ 57 Curtis Conway	.25	.11
❑ 58 Jamal Anderson	.50	.23
❑ 59 Jim Miller	.15	.07
❑ 60 Rob Johnson	.15	.07
❑ 61 Mark Brunell	.75	.35
❑ 62 Wayne Chrebet	.25	.11
❑ 63 James Johnson	.25	.11
❑ 64 Sean Dawkins	.15	.07
❑ 65 Stephen Davis	.50	.23
❑ 66 Daunte Culpepper	1.00	.45
❑ 67 Doug Flutie	.60	.25
❑ 68 Pete Mitchell	.15	.07
❑ 69 Bill Schroeder	.15	.07
❑ 70 Terrence Wilkins	.50	.23
❑ 71 Cade McNown	.50	.23
❑ 72 Muhsin Muhammad	.25	.11
❑ 73 E.G. Green	.15	.07
❑ 74 Edgerrin James	2.00	.90
❑ 75 Troy Edwards	.25	.11
❑ 76 Terry Glenn	.25	.11
❑ 77 Tony Banks	.25	.11
❑ 78 Derrick Mayes	.25	.11
❑ 79 Curtis Martin	.50	.23
❑ 80 Kordell Stewart	.50	.23
❑ 81 Amani Toomer	.25	.11
❑ 82 Dorsey Levens	.25	.11
❑ 83 Brad Johnson	.50	.23
❑ 84 Ed McCaffrey	.50	.23
❑ 85 Charlie Garner	.25	.11
❑ 86 Brett Favre	2.00	.90
❑ 87 J.J. Stokes	.25	.11
❑ 88 Steve Young	.75	.35
❑ 89 Jonathan Linton	.15	.07
❑ 90 Isaac Bruce	.50	.23
❑ 91 Shawn Jefferson	.15	.07
❑ 92 Rod Smith	.25	.11
❑ 93 Champ Bailey	.25	.11
❑ 94 Ricky Williams	1.25	.55
❑ 95 Priest Holmes	.25	.11
❑ 96 Corey Bradford	.25	.11
❑ 97 Eric Moulds	.50	.23
❑ 98 Warrick Dunn	.50	.23
❑ 99 Jevon Kearse	.50	.23
❑ 100 Albert Connell	.15	.07
❑ 101 Az-Zahir Hakim	.15	.07
❑ 102 Marvin Harrison	.50	.23
❑ 103 Qadry Ismail	.25	.11
❑ 104 Oronde Gadsden	.25	.11
❑ 105 Rob Moore	.25	.11
❑ 106 Marshall Faulk	.60	.25
❑ 107 Steve Beuerlein	.15	.07
❑ 108 Torry Holt	.50	.23
❑ 109 Donovan McNabb	.75	.35
❑ 110 Rich Gannon	.25	.11
❑ 111 Jerome Bettis	.50	.23
❑ 112 Peyton Manning	1.50	.70
❑ 113 Cris Carter	.50	.23
❑ 114 Jake Plummer	.50	.23
❑ 115 Kent Graham	.15	.07
❑ 116 Keenan McCardell	.25	.11
❑ 117 Tim Dwight	.50	.23
❑ 118 Fred Taylor	.60	.25
❑ 119 Jerry Rice	1.25	.55
❑ 120 Michael Westbrook	.25	.11
❑ 121 Kurt Warner	2.00	.90

No.	Player	Mint	Nrmt
❑ 122	Jimmy Smith	.25	.11
❑ 123	Emmitt Smith	1.25	.55
❑ 124	Terrell Davis	1.25	.55
❑ 125	Randy Moss	1.50	.70
❑ 126	Akili Smith	.50	.23
❑ 127	Rocket Ismail	.25	.11
❑ 128	Jon Kitna	.50	.23
❑ 129	Elvis Grbac	.25	.11
❑ 130	Wesley Walls	.15	.07
❑ 131	Torrance Small	.15	.07
❑ 132	Tyrone Wheatley	.25	.11
❑ 133	Carl Pickens	.25	.11
❑ 134	Zach Thomas	.25	.11
❑ 135	Jacquez Green	.25	.11
❑ 136	Robert Smith	.50	.23
❑ 137	Keyshawn Johnson	.50	.23
❑ 138	Matthew Hatchette	.15	.07
❑ 139	Troy Aikman	1.25	.55
❑ 140	Charles Johnson	.25	.11
❑ 141	Terry Battle EP	.50	.23
❑ 142	Pepe Pearson EP RC	1.00	.45
❑ 143	Cory Sauter EP	.50	.23
❑ 144	Brian Shay EP	.50	.23
❑ 145	Marcus Crandell EP RC	.50	.23
❑ 146	Danny Wuerffel EP	.60	.25
❑ 147	L.C. Stevens EP	.50	.23
❑ 148	Ted White EP	.50	.23
❑ 149	Matt Lytle EP RC	.60	.25
❑ 150	Vershan Jackson EP RC	.50	.23
❑ 151	Mario Bailey EP	.50	.23
❑ 152	Darryl Daniel EP RC	.60	.25
❑ 153	Sean Morey EP RC	.60	.25
❑ 154	Jim Kubiak EP RC	.60	.25
❑ 155	Aaron Stecker EP RC	1.00	.45
❑ 156	Damon Dunn EP RC	.60	.25
❑ 157	Kevin Daft EP	.50	.23
❑ 158	Corey Thomas EP	.50	.23
❑ 159	Deon Mitchell EP RC	.60	.25
❑ 160	Todd Floyd EP RC	.50	.23
❑ 161	Norman Miller EP RC	.50	.23
❑ 162	Jeremaine Copeland EP	.50	.23
❑ 163	Michael Blair EP	.50	.23
❑ 164	Ron Powlus EP RC	1.50	.70
❑ 165	Pat Barnes EP	.60	.25
❑ 166	Dez White RC	.75	.35
❑ 167	Trung Canidate RC	1.00	.45
❑ 168	Thomas Jones RC	1.50	.70
❑ 169	Courtney Brown RC	1.25	.55
❑ 170	Jamal Lewis RC	6.00	2.70
❑ 171	Chris Redman RC	2.00	.90
❑ 172	Ron Dayne RC	3.00	1.35
❑ 173	Chad Pennington RC	3.00	1.35
❑ 174	Plaxico Burress RC	2.00	.90
❑ 175	R.Jay Soward RC	1.00	.45
❑ 176	Travis Taylor RC	1.25	.55
❑ 177	Shaun Alexander RC	2.50	1.10
❑ 178	Brian Urlacher RC	3.00	1.35
❑ 179	Danny Farmer RC	1.00	.45
❑ 180	Tee Martin RC	1.50	.70
❑ 181	Sylvester Morris RC	2.00	.90
❑ 182	Curtis Keaton RC	.75	.35
❑ 183	Peter Warrick RC	3.00	1.35
❑ 184	Anthony Becht RC	1.00	.45
❑ 185	Travis Prentice RC	1.50	.70
❑ 186	J.R. Redmond RC	1.25	.55
❑ 187	Bubba Franks RC	1.25	.55
❑ 188	Ron Dugans RC	.75	.35
❑ 189	Reuben Droughns RC	1.00	.45
❑ 190	Corey Simon RC	1.25	.55
❑ 191	Joe Hamilton RC	1.25	.55
❑ 192	Laveranues Coles RC	1.50	.70
❑ 193	Todd Pinkston RC	1.00	.45
❑ 194	Jerry Porter RC	1.00	.45
❑ 195	Dennis Northcutt RC	1.25	.55
❑ 196	Tim Rattay RC	1.50	.70
❑ 197	Giovanni Carmazzi RC	1.25	.55
❑ 198	Mareno Philyaw RC	.50	.23
❑ 199	Avion Black RC	.75	.35
❑ 200	Chafie Fields RC	.75	.35
❑ 201	Rondell Mealey RC	.50	.23
❑ 202	Troy Walters RC	1.00	.45
❑ 203	Frank Moreau RC	1.00	.45
❑ 204	Vaughn Sanders RC	.50	.23
❑ 205	Sherrod Gideon RC	.50	.23
❑ 206	Doug Chapman RC	2.00	.90
❑ 207	Marcus Knight RC	.50	.23
❑ 208	Jamel White RC	1.00	.45
❑ 209	Windrell Hayes RC	.75	.35
❑ 210	Reggie Jones RC	1.00	.45
❑ 211	Jarious Jackson RC	1.00	.45
❑ 212	Ronney Jenkins RC	.75	.35
❑ 213	Quinton Spotwood RC	.50	.23
❑ 214	Rob Morris RC	.75	.35
❑ 215	Gari Scott RC	.75	.35
❑ 216	Kevin Thompson RC	1.00	.45
❑ 217	Trevor Insley RC	.50	.23
❑ 218	Frank Murphy RC	.50	.23
❑ 219	Patrick Pass RC	.75	.35
❑ 220	Mike Anderson RC	6.00	2.70
❑ 221	Derrius Thompson RC	.75	.35
❑ 222	John Abraham RC	.75	.35
❑ 223	Dante Hall RC	.75	.35
❑ 224	Chad Morton RC	1.00	.45
❑ 225	Ahmed Plummer RC	1.00	.45
❑ 226	Julian Peterson RC	.75	.35
❑ 227	Mike Green RC	.75	.35
❑ 228	Michael Wiley RC	1.00	.45
❑ 229	Spergon Wynn RC	1.00	.45
❑ 230	Trevor Gaylor RC	.75	.35
❑ 231	Doug Johnson RC	1.00	.45
❑ 232	Marc Bulger RC	1.00	.45
❑ 233	Ron Dixon RC	1.25	.55
❑ 234	Aaron Shea RC	.60	.25
❑ 235	Thomas Hamner RC	.75	.35
❑ 236	Tom Brady RC	1.00	.45
❑ 237	Deltha O'Neal RC	.75	.35
❑ 238	Todd Husak RC	1.00	.45
❑ 239	Erron Kinney RC	1.00	.45
❑ 240	JaJuan Dawson RC	1.00	.45

1998 Bowman Chrome

		MINT	NRMT
	COMPLETE SET (220)	250.00	110.00
❑ 1	Peyton Manning RC	50.00	22.00
❑ 2	Keith Brooking RC	5.00	2.20
❑ 3	Duane Starks RC	3.00	1.35
❑ 4	Takeo Spikes RC	5.00	2.20
❑ 5	Andre Wadsworth RC	5.00	2.20
❑ 6	Greg Ellis RC	3.00	1.35
❑ 7	Brian Griese RC	25.00	11.00
❑ 8	Germane Crowell RC	12.00	5.50
❑ 9	Jerome Pathon RC	5.00	2.20
❑ 10	Ryan Leaf RC	12.00	5.50
❑ 11	Fred Taylor RC	20.00	9.00
❑ 12	Robert Edwards RC	10.00	4.50
❑ 13	Grant Wistrom RC	3.00	1.35
❑ 14	Robert Holcombe RC	8.00	3.60
❑ 15	Tim Dwight RC	10.00	4.50
❑ 16	Jacquez Green RC	10.00	4.50
❑ 17	Marcus Nash RC	8.00	3.60
❑ 18	Jason Peter RC	3.00	1.35
❑ 19	Anthony Simmons RC	3.00	1.35
❑ 20	Curtis Enis RC	8.00	3.60
❑ 21	John Avery RC	8.00	3.60
❑ 22	Pat Johnson RC	5.00	2.20
❑ 23	Joe Jurevicius RC	5.00	2.20
❑ 24	Brian Simmons RC	3.00	1.35
❑ 25	Kevin Dyson RC	10.00	4.50
❑ 26	Skip Hicks RC	8.00	3.60
❑ 27	Hines Ward RC	5.00	2.20
❑ 28	Tavian Banks RC	5.00	2.20
❑ 29	Ahman Green RC	12.00	5.50
❑ 30	Tony Simmons RC	5.00	2.20
❑ 31	Charles Johnson	.25	.11
❑ 32	Freddie Jones	.25	.11
❑ 33	Joey Galloway	1.00	.45
❑ 34	Tony Banks	.50	.23
❑ 35	Jake Plummer	2.00	.90
❑ 36	Reidel Anthony	.50	.23
❑ 37	Steve McNair	1.00	.45
❑ 38	Michael Westbrook	.50	.23
❑ 39	Chris Sanders	.25	.11
❑ 40	Isaac Bruce	.25	.11
❑ 41	Charlie Garner	.25	.11
❑ 42	Wayne Chrebet	1.00	.45
❑ 43	Michael Strahan	.25	.11
❑ 44	Brad Johnson	1.00	.45
❑ 45	Mike Alstott	.25	.11
❑ 46	Tony Gonzalez	.25	.11
❑ 47	Johnnie Morton	.50	.23
❑ 48	Darnay Scott	.50	.23
❑ 49	Rae Carruth	.50	.23
❑ 50	Terrell Davis	4.00	1.80
❑ 51	Jermaine Lewis	.50	.23
❑ 52	Frank Sanders	.50	.23
❑ 53	Byron Hanspard	.50	.23
❑ 54	Gus Frerotte	.25	.11
❑ 55	Terry Glenn	1.00	.45
❑ 56	J.J. Stokes	.50	.23
❑ 57	Will Blackwell	.25	.11
❑ 58	Keyshawn Johnson	1.00	.45
❑ 59	Tiki Barber	.50	.23
❑ 60	Dorsey Levens	1.00	.45
❑ 61	Zach Thomas	.50	.23
❑ 62	Corey Dillon	1.50	.70
❑ 63	Antowain Smith	1.00	.45
❑ 64	Michael Sinclair	.25	.11
❑ 65	Rod Smith	.50	.23
❑ 66	Trent Dilfer	1.00	.45
❑ 67	Warren Sapp	.50	.23
❑ 68	Charles Way	.25	.11
❑ 69	Tamarick Vanover	.25	.11
❑ 70	Drew Bledsoe	2.00	.90
❑ 71	John Mobley	.25	.11
❑ 72	Kerry Collins	.50	.23
❑ 73	Peter Boulware	.25	.11
❑ 74	Simeon Rice	.50	.23
❑ 75	Eddie George	2.00	.90
❑ 76	Fred Lane	.50	.23
❑ 77	Jamal Anderson	1.00	.45
❑ 78	Antonio Freeman	1.00	.45
❑ 79	Jason Sehorn	.50	.23
❑ 80	Curtis Martin	1.00	.45
❑ 81	Bobby Hoying	.50	.23
❑ 82	Garrison Hearst	1.00	.45
❑ 83	Glenn Foley	.50	.23
❑ 84	Danny Kanell	.50	.23
❑ 85	Kordell Stewart	1.00	.45
❑ 86	O.J. McDuffie	.50	.23
❑ 87	Marvin Harrison	.50	.23
❑ 88	Bobby Engram	.50	.23
❑ 89	Chris Slade	.25	.11
❑ 90	Warrick Dunn	1.00	.45
❑ 91	Ricky Watters	.50	.23
❑ 92	Rickey Dudley	.25	.11
❑ 93	Terrell Owens	1.00	.45
❑ 94	Karim Abdul-Jabbar	1.00	.45
❑ 95	Napoleon Kaufman	1.00	.45
❑ 96	Darrell Green	.50	.23
❑ 97	Levon Kirkland	.25	.11
❑ 98	Jeff George	.50	.23
❑ 99	Andre Hastings	.25	.11
❑ 100	John Elway	5.00	2.20
❑ 101	John Randle	.50	.23
❑ 102	Andre Rison	.50	.23
❑ 103	Keenan McCardell	.50	.23
❑ 104	Marshall Faulk	1.00	.45
❑ 105	Emmitt Smith	4.00	1.80
❑ 106	Robert Brooks	.50	.23
❑ 107	Scott Mitchell	.50	.23
❑ 108	Shannon Sharpe	.50	.23
❑ 109	Deion Sanders	1.00	.45
❑ 110	Jerry Rice	2.50	1.10
❑ 111	Erik Kramer	.25	.11
❑ 112	Michael Jackson	.25	.11
❑ 113	Aeneas Williams	.25	.11
❑ 114	Terry Allen	1.00	.45
❑ 115	Steve Young	1.50	.70
❑ 116	Warren Moon	1.00	.45
❑ 117	Junior Seau	.50	.23
❑ 118	Jerome Bettis	1.00	.45
❑ 119	Irving Fryar	.50	.23
❑ 120	Barry Sanders	5.00	2.20
❑ 121	Tim Brown	.25	.11
❑ 122	Chad Brown	.25	.11
❑ 123	Ben Coates	.50	.23
❑ 124	Robert Smith	1.00	.45
❑ 125	Brett Favre	5.00	2.20
❑ 126	Derrick Thomas	.50	.23
❑ 127	Reggie White	1.00	.45
❑ 128	Troy Aikman	2.50	1.10
❑ 129	Jeff Blake	.50	.23
❑ 130	Mark Brunell	2.00	.90
❑ 131	Curtis Conway	.50	.23
❑ 132	Wesley Walls	.50	.23
❑ 133	Thurman Thomas	1.00	.45

No.	Player	Mint	Nrmt
134	Chris Chandler	.50	.23
135	Dan Marino	5.00	2.20
136	Larry Centers	.25	.11
137	Shawn Jefferson	.25	.11
138	Andre Reed	.50	.23
139	Jake Reed	.50	.23
140	Cris Carter	1.00	.45
141	Elvis Grbac	.50	.23
142	Mark Chmura	.50	.23
143	Michael Irvin	1.00	.45
144	Carl Pickens	1.00	.45
145	Herman Moore	1.00	.45
146	Marvin Jones	.25	.11
147	Terance Mathis	.50	.23
148	Rob Moore	.50	.23
149	Bruce Smith	.50	.23
150	Rob Johnson CL	.25	.11
151	Leslie Shepherd	.25	.11
152	Chris Spielman	.25	.11
153	Tony McGee	.25	.11
154	Kevin Smith	.25	.11
155	Bill Romanowski	.25	.11
156	Stephen Boyd	.25	.11
157	James Stewart	.50	.23
158	Jason Taylor	.25	.11
159	Troy Drayton	.25	.11
160	Mark Fields	.25	.11
161	Jessie Armstead	.25	.11
162	James Jett	.50	.23
163	Bobby Taylor	.25	.11
164	Kimble Anders	.50	.23
165	Jimmy Smith	.50	.23
166	Quentin Coryatt	.25	.11
167	Bryant Westbrook	.25	.11
168	Neil Smith	.50	.23
169	Darren Woodson	.25	.11
170	Ray Buchanan	.25	.11
171	Earl Holmes	.25	.11
172	Ray Lewis	1.00	.45
173	Steve Broussard	.25	.11
174	Derrick Brooks	.25	.11
175	Ken Harvey	.25	.11
176	Darryll Lewis	.25	.11
177	Derrick Rodgers	.25	.11
178	James McKnight	.25	.11
179	Cris Dishman	.25	.11
180	Hardy Nickerson	.25	.11
181	Charles Woodson RC	10.00	4.50
182	Randy Moss RC	50.00	22.00
183	Stephen Alexander RC	5.00	2.20
184	Samari Rolle RC	3.00	1.35
185	Jamie Duncan RC	3.00	1.35
186	Lance Schulters RC	3.00	1.35
187	Tony Parrish RC	3.00	1.35
188	Corey Chavous RC	3.00	1.35
189	Jammi German RC	3.00	1.35
190	Sam Cowart RC	3.00	1.35
191	Donald Hayes RC	8.00	3.60
192	R.W. McQuarters RC	3.00	1.35
193	Az-Zahir Hakim RC	8.00	3.60
194	C.Fuamatu-Ma'afala RC	5.00	2.20
195	Allen Rossum RC	3.00	1.35
196	Jon Ritchie RC	5.00	2.20
197	Blake Spence RC	3.00	1.35
198	Brian Alford RC	5.00	2.20
199	Fred Weary RC	3.00	1.35
200	Rod Rutledge RC	3.00	1.35
201	Michael Myers RC	3.00	1.35
202	Rashaan Shehee RC	5.00	2.20
203	Donovin Darius RC	3.00	1.35
204	E.G. Green RC	5.00	2.20
205	Vonnie Holliday RC	5.00	2.20
206	Charlie Batch RC	15.00	6.75
207	Michael Pittman RC	8.00	3.60
208	Artrell Hawkins RC	3.00	1.35
209	Jonathan Quinn RC	5.00	2.20
210	Kailee Wong RC	3.00	1.35
211	Deshea Townsend RC	3.00	1.35
212	Patrick Surtain RC	3.00	1.35
213	Brian Kelly RC	3.00	1.35
214	Tebucky Jones RC	3.00	1.35
215	Pete Gonzalez RC	3.00	1.35
216	Shaun Williams RC	3.00	1.35
217	Scott Frost RC	5.00	2.20
218	Leonard Little RC	3.00	1.35
219	Alonzo Mayes RC	3.00	1.35
220	Cordell Taylor RC	3.00	1.35

1999 Bowman Chrome

	MINT	NRMT
COMPLETE SET (220)	200.00	90.00

No.	Player	Mint	Nrmt
1	Dan Marino	4.00	1.80
2	Michael Westbrook	.50	.23
3	Yancey Thigpen	.25	.11
4	Tony Martin	.50	.23
5	Michael Strahan	.25	.11
6	Dedric Ward	.25	.11
7	Joey Galloway	1.00	.45
8	Bobby Engram	.50	.23
9	Frank Sanders	.50	.23
10	Jake Plummer	1.50	.70
11	Eddie Kennison	.50	.23
12	Curtis Martin	1.00	.45
13	Chris Spielman	.25	.11
14	Trent Dilfer	.50	.23
15	Tim Biakabutuka	.50	.23
16	Elvis Grbac	.50	.23
17	Charlie Batch	2.00	.90
18	Takeo Spikes	.25	.11
19	Tony Banks	.50	.23
20	Doug Flutie	1.25	.55
21	Ty Law	.25	.11
22	Isaac Bruce	1.00	.45
23	James Jett	.50	.23
24	Kent Graham	.25	.11
25	Derrick Mayes	.25	.11
26	Amani Toomer	.25	.11
27	Ray Lewis	.50	.23
28	Shawn Springs	.25	.11
29	Warren Sapp	.25	.11
30	Jamal Anderson	1.00	.45
31	Byron Bam Morris	.25	.11
32	Johnnie Morton	.25	.11
33	Terance Mathis	.25	.11
34	Terrell Davis	2.50	1.10
35	John Randle	.50	.23
36	Vinny Testaverde	.25	.11
37	Junior Seau	.50	.23
38	Reidel Anthony	.50	.23
39	Brad Johnson	.25	.11
40	Emmitt Smith	2.50	1.10
41	Mo Lewis	.25	.11
42	Terry Glenn	1.00	.45
43	Dorsey Levens	1.00	.45
44	Thurman Thomas	.50	.23
45	Rob Moore	.50	.23
46	Corey Dillon	1.00	.45
47	Jessie Armstead	.25	.11
48	Marshall Faulk	1.00	.45
49	Charles Woodson	.25	.11
50	John Elway	4.00	1.80
51	Kevin Dyson	.50	.23
52	Tony Simmons	.25	.11
53	Keenan McCardell	.50	.23
54	O.J. Santiago	.25	.11
55	Jermaine Lewis	.50	.23
56	Herman Moore	.25	.11
57	Gary Brown	.25	.11
58	Jim Harbaugh	.50	.23
59	Mike Alstott	1.00	.45
60	Brett Favre	4.00	1.80
61	Tim Brown	1.00	.45
62	Steve McNair	.25	.11
63	Ben Coates	.50	.23
64	Jerome Pathon	.25	.11
65	Ray Buchanan	.25	.11
66	Troy Aikman	2.50	1.10
67	Andre Reed	.50	.23
68	Bubby Brister	.25	.11
69	Karim Abdul-Jabbar	.50	.23
70	Peyton Manning	4.00	1.80
71	Charles Johnson	.25	.11
72	Natrone Means	.50	.23
73	Michael Sinclair	.25	.11
74	Skip Hicks	.50	.23
75	Derrick Alexander	.25	.11
76	Wayne Chrebet	.50	.23
77	Rod Smith	.50	.23
78	Carl Pickens	.50	.23
79	Adrian Murrell	.50	.23
80	Fred Taylor	2.50	1.10
81	Eric Moulds	1.00	.45
82	Lawrence Phillips	.50	.23
83	Marvin Harrison	1.00	.45
84	Cris Carter	1.00	.45
85	Ike Hilliard	.25	.11
86	Hines Ward	.25	.11
87	Terrell Owens	1.00	.45
88	Ricky Proehl	.25	.11
89	Bert Emanuel	.50	.23
90	Randy Moss	4.00	1.80
91	Aaron Glenn	.25	.11
92	Robert Smith	1.00	.45
93	Andre Hastings	.25	.11
94	Jake Reed	.50	.23
95	Curtis Enis	1.00	.45
96	Andre Wadsworth	.25	.11
97	Ed McCaffrey	.50	.23
98	Zach Thomas	.50	.23
99	Kerry Collins	.50	.23
100	Drew Bledsoe	1.50	.70
101	Germane Crowell	.50	.23
102	Bryan Still	.25	.11
103	Chad Brown	.25	.11
104	Jacquez Green	.25	.11
105	Garrison Hearst	.50	.23
106	Napoleon Kaufman	1.00	.45
107	Ricky Watters	.50	.23
108	O.J. McDuffie	.50	.23
109	Keyshawn Johnson	1.00	.45
110	Jerome Bettis	1.00	.45
111	Duce Staley	1.00	.45
112	Curtis Conway	.50	.23
113	Chris Chandler	.50	.23
114	Marcus Nash	.50	.23
115	Stephen Alexander	.25	.11
116	Darnay Scott	.50	.23
117	Bruce Smith	.50	.23
118	Priest Holmes	1.00	.45
119	Mark Brunell	1.50	.70
120	Jerry Rice	2.50	1.10
121	Randall Cunningham	1.00	.45
122	Scott Mitchell	.25	.11
123	Antonio Freeman	1.00	.45
124	Kordell Stewart	1.00	.45
125	Jon Kitna	1.00	.45
126	Ahman Green	.50	.23
127	Warrick Dunn	1.00	.45
128	Robert Brooks	.50	.23
129	Derrick Thomas	.50	.23
130	Steve Young	1.50	.70
131	Peter Boulware	.25	.11
132	Michael Irvin	.50	.23
133	Shannon Sharpe	.50	.23
134	Jimmy Smith	.50	.23
135	John Avery	.50	.23
136	Fred Lane	.50	.23
137	Trent Green	.50	.23
138	Andre Rison	.50	.23
139	Antowain Smith	1.00	.45
140	Eddie George	1.25	.55
141	Jeff Blake	.50	.23
142	Rocket Ismail	.50	.23
143	Rickey Dudley	.25	.11
144	Courtney Hawkins	.25	.11
145	Mikhael Ricks	.25	.11

❑ 146 J.J. Stokes .50 .23
❑ 147 Levon Kirkland .25 .11
❑ 148 Deion Sanders 1.00 .45
❑ 149 Barry Sanders 4.00 1.80
❑ 150 Tiki Barber .25 .11
❑ 151 David Boston RC 8.00 3.60
❑ 152 Chris McAlister RC 2.50 1.10
❑ 153 Peerless Price RC 5.00 2.20
❑ 154 D'Wayne Bates RC 2.50 1.10
❑ 155 Cade McNown RC 5.00 2.20
❑ 156 Akili Smith RC 8.00 3.60
❑ 157 Kevin Johnson RC 8.00 3.60
❑ 158 Tim Couch RC 15.00 6.75
❑ 159 Sedrick Irvin RC 3.00 1.35
❑ 160 Chris Claiborne RC 1.50 .70
❑ 161 Edgerrin James RC 20.00 9.00
❑ 162 Mike Cloud RC 3.00 1.35
❑ 163 Cecil Collins RC 3.00 1.35
❑ 164 James Johnson RC 3.00 1.35
❑ 165 Rob Konrad RC 3.00 1.35
❑ 166 Daunte Culpepper RC 20.00 9.00
❑ 167 Kevin Faulk RC 6.00 2.70
❑ 168 Donovan McNabb RC 15.00 6.75
❑ 169 Troy Edwards RC 5.00 2.20
❑ 170 Amos Zereoue RC 3.00 1.35
❑ 171 Karsten Bailey RC 2.50 1.10
❑ 172 Brock Huard RC 6.00 2.70
❑ 173 Joe Germaine RC 3.00 1.35
❑ 174 Torry Holt RC 10.00 4.50
❑ 175 Shaun King RC 8.00 3.60
❑ 176 Jevon Kearse RC 8.00 3.60
❑ 177 Champ Bailey RC 5.00 2.20
❑ 178 Ebenezer Ekuban RC 2.50 1.10
❑ 179 Andy Katzenmoyer RC 3.00 1.35
❑ 180 Antoine Winfield RC 2.50 1.10
❑ 181 Jermaine Fazande RC 3.00 1.35
❑ 182 Ricky Williams RC 15.00 6.75
❑ 183 Joel Makovicka RC 3.00 1.35
❑ 184 Reginald Kelly RC 2.50 1.10
❑ 185 Brandon Stokley RC 3.00 1.35
❑ 186 L.C. Stevens RC 1.50 .70
❑ 187 Marty Booker RC 3.00 1.35
❑ 188 Jerry Azumah RC 2.50 1.10
❑ 189 Ted White RC 2.50 1.10
❑ 190 Scott Covington RC 3.00 1.35
❑ 191 Tim Alexander RC 1.50 .70
❑ 192 Darrin Chiaverini RC 2.50 1.10
❑ 193 Dat Nguyen RC 3.00 1.35
❑ 194 Wane McGarity RC 2.50 1.10
❑ 195 Al Wilson RC 3.00 1.35
❑ 196 Travis McGriff RC 2.50 1.10
❑ 197 Stacey Mack RC 3.00 1.35
❑ 198 Antuan Edwards RC 1.50 .70
❑ 199 Aaron Brooks RC 15.00 6.75
❑ 200 De'Mond Parker RC 3.00 1.35
❑ 201 Jed Weaver RC 1.50 .70
❑ 202 Madre Hill RC 2.50 1.10
❑ 203 Jim Kleinsasser RC 3.00 1.35
❑ 204 Michael Bishop RC 5.00 2.20
❑ 205 Michael Basnight RC 2.50 1.10
❑ 206 Sean Bennett RC 2.50 1.10
❑ 207 Dameane Douglas RC 2.50 1.10
❑ 208 Na Brown RC 3.00 1.35
❑ 209 Patrick Kerney RC 2.50 1.10
❑ 210 Malcolm Johnson RC 2.50 1.10
❑ 211 Dre Bly RC 2.50 1.10
❑ 212 Terry Jackson RC 2.50 1.10
❑ 213 Eugene Baker RC 1.50 .70
❑ 214 Autry Denson RC 3.00 1.35
❑ 215 Darnell McDonald RC 3.00 1.35
❑ 216 Charlie Rogers RC 2.50 1.10
❑ 217 Joe Montgomery RC 3.00 1.35
❑ 218 Cecil Martin RC 2.50 1.10
❑ 219 Larry Parker RC 2.50 1.10
❑ 220 Mike Peterson RC 2.50 1.10

2000 Bowman Chrome

	MINT	NRMT
COMPLETE SET (270)	2000.00	900.00

❑ 1 Eddie George 1.00 .45
❑ 2 Ike Hilliard .40 .18
❑ 3 Terrell Owens .75 .35
❑ 4 James Stewart .40 .18
❑ 5 Joey Galloway .75 .35

❑ 6 Jake Reed .25 .11
❑ 7 Derrick Alexander .40 .18
❑ 8 Jeff George .40 .18
❑ 9 Kerry Collins .40 .18
❑ 10 Tony Gonzalez .40 .18
❑ 11 Marcus Robinson .75 .35
❑ 12 Charles Woodson .40 .18
❑ 13 Germane Crowell .40 .18
❑ 14 Yancey Thigpen .25 .11
❑ 15 Tony Martin .25 .11
❑ 16 Frank Sanders .40 .18
❑ 17 Napoleon Kaufman .40 .18
❑ 18 Jay Fiedler .75 .35
❑ 19 Patrick Jeffers .75 .35
❑ 20 Steve McNair .75 .35
❑ 21 Herman Moore .40 .18
❑ 22 Tim Brown .75 .35
❑ 23 Olandis Gary .75 .35
❑ 24 Corey Dillon .75 .35
❑ 25 Warren Sapp .40 .18
❑ 26 Curtis Enis .40 .18
❑ 27 Vinny Testaverde .40 .18
❑ 28 Tim Biakabutuka .40 .18
❑ 29 Kevin Johnson .75 .35
❑ 30 Charlie Batch .75 .35
❑ 31 Jermaine Fazande .40 .18
❑ 32 Shaun King 1.25 .55
❑ 33 Errict Rhett .40 .18
❑ 34 O.J. McDuffie .40 .18
❑ 35 Bruce Smith .40 .18
❑ 36 Antonio Freeman .75 .35
❑ 37 Tim Couch 1.50 .70
❑ 38 Duce Staley .75 .35
❑ 39 Jeff Blake .40 .18
❑ 40 Jim Harbaugh .40 .18
❑ 41 Jeff Graham .25 .11
❑ 42 Drew Bledsoe 1.25 .55
❑ 43 Mike Alstott .75 .35
❑ 44 Terance Mathis .40 .18
❑ 45 Antowain Smith .40 .18
❑ 46 Johnnie Morton .40 .18
❑ 47 Chris Chandler .40 .18
❑ 48 Keith Poole .25 .11
❑ 49 Ricky Watters .40 .18
❑ 50 Darnay Scott .25 .11
❑ 51 Damon Huard .40 .18
❑ 52 Peerless Price .75 .35
❑ 53 Brian Griese 1.00 .45
❑ 54 Frank Wycheck .40 .18
❑ 55 Kevin Dyson .40 .18
❑ 56 Junior Seau .40 .18
❑ 57 Curtis Conway .40 .18
❑ 58 Jamal Anderson .75 .35
❑ 59 Jim Miller .25 .11
❑ 60 Rob Johnson .40 .18
❑ 61 Mark Brunell 1.25 .55
❑ 62 Wayne Chrebet .40 .18
❑ 63 James Johnson .40 .18
❑ 64 Sean Dawkins .25 .11
❑ 65 Stephen Davis .75 .35
❑ 66 Daunte Culpepper 1.50 .70
❑ 67 Doug Flutie 1.00 .45
❑ 68 Pete Mitchell .25 .11
❑ 69 Bill Schroeder .25 .11
❑ 70 Terrence Wilkins .75 .35
❑ 71 Cade McNown .75 .35
❑ 72 Muhsin Muhammad .40 .18
❑ 73 E.G. Green .25 .11
❑ 74 Edgerrin James 3.00 1.35
❑ 75 Troy Edwards .40 .18
❑ 76 Terry Glenn .40 .18
❑ 77 Tony Banks .40 .18
❑ 78 Derrick Mayes .40 .18
❑ 79 Curtis Martin .75 .35
❑ 80 Kordell Stewart .75 .35
❑ 81 Amani Toomer .40 .18
❑ 82 Dorsey Levens .40 .18
❑ 83 Brad Johnson .75 .35
❑ 84 Ed McCaffrey .75 .35
❑ 85 Charlie Garner .40 .18
❑ 86 Brett Favre 3.00 1.35
❑ 87 J.J. Stokes .40 .18
❑ 88 Steve Young 1.25 .55
❑ 89 Jonathan Linton .25 .11
❑ 90 Isaac Bruce .75 .35
❑ 91 Shawn Jefferson .25 .11
❑ 92 Rod Smith .40 .18
❑ 93 Champ Bailey .40 .18
❑ 94 Ricky Williams 2.00 .90
❑ 95 Priest Holmes .40 .18
❑ 96 Corey Bradford .40 .18
❑ 97 Eric Moulds .75 .35
❑ 98 Warrick Dunn .75 .35
❑ 99 Jevon Kearse .75 .35
❑ 100 Albert Connell .25 .11
❑ 101 Az-Zahir Hakim .25 .11
❑ 102 Marvin Harrison .75 .35
❑ 103 Qadry Ismail .40 .18
❑ 104 Oronde Gadsden .40 .18
❑ 105 Rob Moore .40 .18
❑ 106 Marshall Faulk 1.00 .45
❑ 107 Steve Beuerlein .40 .18
❑ 108 Torry Holt .75 .35
❑ 109 Donovan McNabb 1.25 .55
❑ 110 Rich Gannon .40 .18
❑ 111 Jerome Bettis .75 .35
❑ 112 Peyton Manning 2.50 1.10
❑ 113 Cris Carter .75 .35
❑ 114 Jake Plummer .75 .35
❑ 115 Kent Graham .25 .11
❑ 116 Keenan McCardell .40 .18
❑ 117 Tim Dwight .75 .35
❑ 118 Fred Taylor 1.00 .45
❑ 119 Jerry Rice 2.00 .90
❑ 120 Michael Westbrook .40 .18
❑ 121 Kurt Warner 3.00 1.35
❑ 122 Jimmy Smith .40 .18
❑ 123 Emmitt Smith 2.00 .90
❑ 124 Terrell Davis 2.00 .90
❑ 125 Randy Moss 2.50 1.10
❑ 126 Akili Smith .75 .35
❑ 127 Rocket Ismail .40 .18
❑ 128 Jon Kitna .75 .35
❑ 129 Elvis Grbac .40 .18
❑ 130 Wesley Walls .25 .11
❑ 131 Torrance Small .25 .11
❑ 132 Tyrone Wheatley .40 .18
❑ 133 Carl Pickens .25 .11
❑ 134 Zach Thomas .40 .18
❑ 135 Jacquez Green .40 .18
❑ 136 Robert Smith .75 .35
❑ 137 Keyshawn Johnson .75 .35
❑ 138 Matthew Hatchette .25 .11
❑ 139 Troy Aikman 2.00 .90
❑ 140 Charles Johnson .40 .18
❑ 141 Terry Battle EP 1.00 .45
❑ 142 Pepe Pearson EP RC 2.00 .90
❑ 143 Cory Sauter EP 1.00 .45
❑ 144 Brian Shay EP 1.00 .45
❑ 145 Marcus Crandell EP RC 1.00 .45
❑ 146 Danny Wuerffel EP 1.50 .70
❑ 147 L.C. Stevens EP 1.00 .45
❑ 148 Ted White EP 1.00 .45
❑ 149 Matt Lytle EP RC 1.50 .70
❑ 150 Vershan Jackson EP RC 1.00 .45
❑ 151 Mario Bailey EP 1.00 .45
❑ 152 Darryl Daniel EP RC 1.50 .70
❑ 153 Sean Morey EP RC 1.50 .70
❑ 154 Jim Kubiak EP RC 1.50 .70
❑ 155 Aaron Stecker EP RC 2.00 .90
❑ 156 Damon Dunn EP RC 1.50 .70
❑ 157 Kevin Daft EP 1.00 .45
❑ 158 Corey Thomas EP 1.00 .45

❑ 159 Deon Mitchell EP RC 1.50 .70
❑ 160 Todd Floyd EP RC 1.00 .45
❑ 161 Norman Miller EP RC 1.00 .45
❑ 162 Jeremaine Copeland EP 1.00 .45
❑ 163 Michael Blair EP 1.00 .45
❑ 164 Ron Powlus EP RC 3.00 1.35
❑ 165 Pat Barnes EP 1.50 .70
❑ 166 Dez White RC 3.00 1.35
❑ 167 Trung Canidate RC SP 50.00 22.00
❑ 168 Thomas Jones RC SP 80.00 36.00
❑ 169 Courtney Brown RC SP 50.00 22.00
❑ 170 Jamal Lewis RC SP 200.00 90.00
❑ 171 Chris Redman RC SP 100.00 45.00
❑ 172 Ron Dayne RC SP 120.00 55.00
❑ 173 Chad Pennington RC SP 120.00 55.00
❑ 174 Plaxico Burress RC SP 100.00 45.00
❑ 175 R.Jay Soward RC SP 50.00 22.00
❑ 176 Travis Taylor RC SP 60.00 27.00
❑ 177 Shaun Alexander RC SP 100.00 45.00
❑ 178 Brian Urlacher RC 15.00 6.75
❑ 179 Danny Farmer RC 4.00 1.80
❑ 180 Tee Martin RC SP 80.00 36.00
❑ 181 Sylvester Morris RC SP 80.00 36.00
❑ 182 Curtis Keaton RC 3.00 1.35
❑ 183 Peter Warrick RC SP 120.00 55.00
❑ 184 Anthony Becht RC 4.00 1.80
❑ 185 Travis Prentice RC SP 50.00 22.00
❑ 186 J.R. Redmond RC SP 50.00 22.00
❑ 187 Bubba Franks RC SP 50.00 22.00
❑ 188 Ron Dugans RC SP 40.00 18.00
❑ 189 Reuben Droughns RC 4.00 1.80
❑ 190 Corey Simon RC 5.00 2.20
❑ 191 Joe Hamilton RC 5.00 2.20
❑ 192 Laveranues Coles RC 6.00 2.70
❑ 193 Todd Pinkston RC SP 50.00 22.00
❑ 194 Jerry Porter RC SP 40.00 18.00
❑ 195 Dennis Northcutt RC 5.00 2.20
❑ 196 Tim Rattay RC 6.00 2.70
❑ 197 Giovanni Carmazzi RC 5.00 2.20
❑ 198 Mareno Philyaw RC 2.00 .90
❑ 199 Avion Black RC 3.00 1.35
❑ 200 Chafie Fields RC 3.00 1.35
❑ 201 Rondell Mealey RC 2.00 .90
❑ 202 Troy Walters RC 4.00 1.80
❑ 203 Frank Moreau RC 4.00 1.80
❑ 204 Vaughn Sanders RC 2.00 .90
❑ 205 Sherrod Gideon RC 2.00 .90
❑ 206 Doug Chapman RC 8.00 3.60
❑ 207 Marcus Knight RC 2.00 .90
❑ 208 Jamel White RC 4.00 1.80
❑ 209 Windrell Hayes RC 3.00 1.35
❑ 210 Reggie Jones RC 4.00 1.80
❑ 211 Jarious Jackson RC 4.00 1.80
❑ 212 Ronney Jenkins RC 3.00 1.35
❑ 213 Quinton Spotwood RC 2.00 .90
❑ 214 Rob Morris RC 3.00 1.35
❑ 215 Gari Scott RC 3.00 1.35
❑ 216 Kevin Thompson RC 4.00 1.80
❑ 217 Trevor Insley RC 2.00 .90
❑ 218 Frank Murphy RC 2.00 .90
❑ 219 Patrick Pass RC 3.00 1.35
❑ 220 Mike Anderson RC 20.00 9.00
❑ 221 Derrius Thompson RC 3.00 1.35
❑ 222 John Abraham RC 3.00 1.35
❑ 223 Dante Hall RC 3.00 1.35
❑ 224 Chad Morton RC 4.00 1.80
❑ 225 Ahmed Plummer RC 4.00 1.80
❑ 226 Julian Peterson RC 3.00 1.35
❑ 227 Mike Green RC 3.00 1.35
❑ 228 Michael Wiley RC 4.00 1.80
❑ 229 Spergon Wynn RC 4.00 1.80
❑ 230 Trevor Gaylor RC 3.00 1.35
❑ 231 Doug Johnson RC 4.00 1.80
❑ 232 Marc Bulger RC 4.00 1.80
❑ 233 Ron Dixon RC 5.00 2.20
❑ 234 Aaron Shea RC 1.50 .70
❑ 235 Thomas Hamner RC 3.00 1.35
❑ 236 Tom Brady RC 4.00 1.80
❑ 237 Deltha O'Neal RC 3.00 1.35
❑ 238 Todd Husak RC 4.00 1.80
❑ 239 Erron Kinney RC 4.00 1.80
❑ 240 JaJuan Dawson RC 4.00 1.80
❑ 241 Nick Williams .75 .35
❑ 242 Deon Grant RC 2.00 .90
❑ 243 Brad Hoover RC 10.00 4.50
❑ 244 Kamil Loud .75 .35
❑ 245 Rashard Anderson RC 3.00 1.35
❑ 246 Clint Stoerner RC 8.00 3.60
❑ 247 Antwan Harris RC 2.00 .90
❑ 248 Jason Webster RC 2.00 .90
❑ 249 Kevin McDougal RC 3.00 1.35
❑ 250 Tony Scott RC 2.00 .90
❑ 251 Thabiti Davis RC 3.00 1.35
❑ 252 Ian Gold RC 3.00 1.35
❑ 253 Sammy Morris RC 5.00 2.20
❑ 254 Raynoch Thompson RC 3.00 1.35
❑ 255 Jeremy McDaniel .75 .35
❑ 256 Terrelle Smith RC 3.00 1.35
❑ 257 Deon Dyer RC 3.00 1.35
❑ 258 Na'il Diggs RC 4.00 1.80
❑ 259 Brandon Short RC 3.00 1.35
❑ 260 Mike Brown RC 4.00 1.80
❑ 261 John Engelberger RC 3.00 1.35
❑ 262 Rogers Beckett RC 3.00 1.35
❑ 263 JaJuan Seider RC 2.00 .90
❑ 264 Desmond Kitchings RC 3.00 1.35
❑ 265 Reggie Davis RC 3.00 1.35
❑ 266 Corey Moore RC 3.00 1.35
❑ 267 Cornelius Griffin RC 3.00 1.35
❑ 268 Stockar McDougle RC 2.00 .90
❑ 269 James Williams RC 3.00 1.35
❑ 270 Darrell Jackson RC 5.00 2.20

1995 Bowman's Best

	MINT	NRMT
COMPLETE SET (180)	150.00	70.00

❑ R1 Ki-Jana Carter RC 2.00 .90
❑ R2 Tony Boselli RC 2.00 .90
❑ R3 Steve McNair RC 12.00 5.50
❑ R4 Michael Westbrook RC 8.00 3.60
❑ R5 Kerry Collins RC 8.00 3.60
❑ R6 Kevin Carter RC 2.00 .90
❑ R7 Mike Mamula RC 1.00 .45
❑ R8 Joey Galloway RC 10.00 4.50
❑ R9 Kyle Brady RC 1.00 .45
❑ R10 Ray McElroy RC .50 .23
❑ R11 Derrick Alexander DE RC .50 .23
❑ R12 Warren Sapp RC 3.00 1.35
❑ R13 Mark Fields RC .50 .23
❑ R14 Ruben Brown RC .50 .23
❑ R15 Ellis Johnson RC .50 .23
❑ R16 Hugh Douglas RC 2.00 .90
❑ R17 Alundis Brice RC .50 .23
❑ R18 Napoleon Kaufman RC 8.00 3.60
❑ R19 James O. Stewart RC 10.00 4.50
❑ R20 Luther Elliss RC .50 .23
❑ R21 Rashaan Salaam RC 2.00 .90
❑ R22 Tyrone Poole RC 1.00 .45
❑ R23 Ty Law RC 1.00 .45
❑ R24 Korey Stringer RC .50 .23
❑ R25 Billy Milner RC .50 .23
❑ R26 Roell Preston RC 2.00 .90
❑ R27 Mark Bruener RC 1.00 .45
❑ R28 Derrick Brooks RC .50 .23
❑ R29 Blake Brockermeyer RC .50 .23
❑ R30 Mike Frederick RC .50 .23
❑ R31 Trezelle Jenkins RC .50 .23
❑ R32 Craig Newsome RC .50 .23
❑ R33 Matt O'Dwyer RC .50 .23
❑ R34 Terrance Shaw RC .50 .23
❑ R35 Anthony Cook RC .50 .23
❑ R36 Darick Holmes RC .50 .23
❑ R37 Cory Raymer RC .50 .23
❑ R38 Zach Wiegert RC .50 .23
❑ R39 Sam Shade RC .50 .23
❑ R40 Brian DeMarco RC .50 .23
❑ R41 Ron Davis RC .50 .23
❑ R42 Orlando Thomas RC .50 .23
❑ R43 Derek West RC .50 .23
❑ R44 Ray Zellars RC 1.00 .45
❑ R45 Todd Collins RC 2.00 .90
❑ R46 Linc Harden RC .50 .23
❑ R47 Frank Sanders RC 5.00 2.20
❑ R48 Ken Dilger RC 1.00 .45
❑ R49 Barrett Robbins RC .50 .23
❑ R50 Bobby Taylor RC 1.00 .45
❑ R51 Terrell Fletcher RC .50 .23
❑ R52 Jack Jackson RC .50 .23
❑ R53 Jeff Kopp RC .50 .23
❑ R54 Brendan Stai RC .50 .23
❑ R55 Corey Fuller RC .50 .23
❑ R56 Todd Sauerbrun RC .50 .23
❑ R57 Dameian Jeffries RC .50 .23
❑ R58 Troy Dumas RC .50 .23
❑ R59 Charlie Williams RC .50 .23
❑ R60 Kordell Stewart RC 10.00 4.50
❑ R61 Jay Barker RC .50 .23
❑ R62 Jesse James RC .50 .23
❑ R63 Shane Hannah RC .50 .23
❑ R64 Rob Johnson RC 10.00 4.50
❑ R65 Darius Holland RC .50 .23
❑ R66 William Henderson .30 .14
❑ R67 Chris Sanders RC 2.00 .90
❑ R68 Darryl Pounds RC .50 .23
❑ R69 Melvin Tuten RC .50 .23
❑ R70 David Sloan RC 1.00 .45
❑ R71 Chris Hudson RC .50 .23
❑ R72 William Strong RC .50 .23
❑ R73 Brian Williams LB RC .50 .23
❑ R74 Curtis Martin RC 12.00 5.50
❑ R75 Mike Verstegen RC .50 .23
❑ R76 Justin Armour RC 1.00 .45
❑ R77 Lorenzo Styles RC .50 .23
❑ R78 Oliver Gibson RC .50 .23
❑ R79 Zack Crockett RC .50 .23
❑ R80 Tau Pupua RC .50 .23
❑ R81 Tamarick Vanover RC 1.00 .45
❑ R82 Steve McLaughlin RC .50 .23
❑ R83 Sean Harris RC .50 .23
❑ R84 Eric Zeier RC 2.00 .90
❑ R85 Rodney Young RC .50 .23
❑ R86 Chad May RC .50 .23
❑ R87 Evan Pilgrim RC .50 .23
❑ R88 James A.Stewart RC .50 .23
❑ R89 Torey Hunter RC .50 .23
❑ R90 Antonio Freeman RC 12.00 5.50
❑ V1 Rob Moore .30 .14
❑ V2 Craig Heyward .60 .25
❑ V3 Jim Kelly 1.25 .55
❑ V4 John Kasay .30 .14
❑ V5 Jeff Graham .30 .14
❑ V6 Jeff Blake RC 5.00 2.20
❑ V7 Antonio Langham .30 .14
❑ V8 Troy Aikman 3.00 1.35
❑ V9 Simon Fletcher .30 .14
❑ V10 Barry Sanders 6.00 2.70
❑ V11 Edgar Bennett .60 .25
❑ V12 Ray Childress .30 .14
❑ V13 Ray Buchanan .30 .14
❑ V14 Desmond Howard .60 .25
❑ V15 Dale Carter .60 .25
❑ V16 Troy Vincent .30 .14
❑ V17 David Palmer .60 .25
❑ V18 Ben Coates .60 .25
❑ V19 Derek Brown TE .30 .14
❑ V20 Dave Brown .60 .25
❑ V21 Mo Lewis .30 .14
❑ V22 Harvey Williams .30 .14
❑ V23 Randall Cunningham 1.25 .55
❑ V24 Kevin Greene .60 .25
❑ V25 Junior Seau 1.25 .55
❑ V26 Merton Hanks .30 .14
❑ V27 Cortez Kennedy .60 .25
❑ V28 Troy Drayton .30 .14
❑ V29 Hardy Nickerson .30 .14
❑ V30 Brian Mitchell .30 .14
❑ V31 Raymont Harris .30 .14
❑ V32 Keith Goganious .30 .14

❑ V33 Andre Reed .60 .25
❑ V34 Terance Mathis .60 .25
❑ V35 Garrison Hearst 1.25 .55
❑ V36 Glyn Milburn .30 .14
❑ V37 Emmitt Smith 5.00 2.20
❑ V38 Vinny Testaverde .60 .25
❑ V39 Darnay Scott 1.25 .55
❑ V40 Mickey Washington .30 .14
❑ V41 Craig Erickson .30 .14
❑ V42 Chris Chandler 1.25 .55
❑ V43 Brett Favre 6.00 2.70
❑ V44 Scott Mitchell .60 .25
❑ V45 Chris Slade .60 .25
❑ V46 Warren Moon .60 .25
❑ V47 Dan Marino 6.00 2.70
❑ V48 Greg Hill .60 .25
❑ V49 Rocket Ismail .60 .25
❑ V50 Bobby Houston .30 .14
❑ V51 Rodney Hampton .60 .25
❑ V52 Jim Everett .30 .14
❑ V53 Rick Mirer 1.25 .55
❑ V54 Steve Young 2.50 1.10
❑ V55 Dennis Gibson .30 .14
❑ V56 Rod Woodson .60 .25
❑ V57 Calvin Williams .60 .25
❑ V58 Tom Carter .30 .14
❑ V59 Trent Dilfer 1.25 .55
❑ V60 Shane Conlan .30 .14
❑ V61 Cornelius Bennett .60 .25
❑ V62 Eric Metcalf .60 .25
❑ V63 Frank Reich .30 .14
❑ V64 Eric Hill .30 .14
❑ V65 Erik Kramer .30 .14
❑ V66 Michael Irvin 1.25 .55
❑ V67 Tony McGee .30 .14
❑ V68 Andre Rison .60 .25
❑ V69 Shannon Sharpe .60 .25
❑ V70 Quentin Coryatt .60 .25
❑ V71 Robert Brooks 1.25 .55
❑ V72 Steve Beuerlein .30 .14
❑ V73 Herman Moore 1.25 .55
❑ V74 Jack Del Rio .30 .14
❑ V75 Dave Meggett .30 .14
❑ V76 Pete Stoyanovich .30 .14
❑ V77 Neil Smith .60 .25
❑ V78 Corey Miller .30 .14
❑ V79 Tim Brown 1.25 .55
❑ V80 Tyrone Hughes .60 .25
❑ V81 Boomer Esiason .60 .25
❑ V82 Natrone Means 1.25 .55
❑ V83 Chris Warren .60 .25
❑ V84 Byron Bam Morris .60 .25
❑ V85 Jerry Rice 3.00 1.35
❑ V86 Michael Zordich .30 .14
❑ V87 Errict Rhett 1.25 .55
❑ V88 Henry Ellard .60 .25
❑ V89 Chris Miller .30 .14
❑ V90 John Elway 6.00 2.70

1996 Bowman's Best

	MINT	NRMT
COMPLETE SET (180)	80.00	36.00

❑ 1 Emmitt Smith 3.00 1.35
❑ 2 Kordell Stewart 1.00 .45
❑ 3 Mark Chmura .40 .18
❑ 4 Sean Dawkins .20 .09
❑ 5 Steve Young 1.50 .70
❑ 6 Tamarick Vanover .40 .18
❑ 7 Scott Mitchell .40 .18
❑ 8 Aaron Hayden .20 .09
❑ 9 William Thomas .20 .09
❑ 10 Dan Marino 4.00 1.80
❑ 11 Curtis Conway .75 .35
❑ 12 Steve Atwater .20 .09
❑ 13 Derrick Brooks .20 .09
❑ 14 Rick Mirer .40 .18
❑ 15 Mark Brunell 2.00 .90
❑ 16 Garrison Hearst .40 .18
❑ 17 Eric Turner .20 .09
❑ 18 Mark Carrier WR .20 .09
❑ 19 Darnay Scott .40 .18
❑ 20 Steve McNair 1.25 .55
❑ 21 Jim Everett .20 .09
❑ 22 Wayne Chrebet 1.00 .45
❑ 23 Ben Coates .40 .18
❑ 24 Harvey Williams .20 .09
❑ 25 Michael Westbrook .75 .35
❑ 26 Kevin Carter .20 .09
❑ 27 Dave Brown .20 .09
❑ 28 Jake Reed .40 .18
❑ 29 Thurman Thomas .75 .35
❑ 30 Jeff George .40 .18
❑ 31 Carnell Lake .20 .09
❑ 32 J.J. Stokes .75 .35
❑ 33 Jay Novacek .20 .09
❑ 34 Brett Perriman .20 .09
❑ 35 Robert Brooks .75 .35
❑ 36 Neil Smith .20 .09
❑ 37 Chris Zorich .20 .09
❑ 38 Micheal Barrow .20 .09
❑ 39 Quentin Coryatt .20 .09
❑ 40 Kerry Collins .75 .35
❑ 41 Aeneas Williams .20 .09
❑ 42 James O.Stewart .40 .18
❑ 43 Warren Moon .40 .18
❑ 44 Willie McGinest .20 .09
❑ 45 Rodney Hampton .40 .18
❑ 46 Jeff Hostetler .20 .09
❑ 47 Darrell Green .20 .09
❑ 48 Warren Sapp .20 .09
❑ 49 Troy Drayton .20 .09
❑ 50 Junior Seau .40 .18
❑ 51 Mike Mamula .20 .09
❑ 52 Antonio Langham .20 .09
❑ 53 Eric Metcalf .20 .09
❑ 54 Adrian Murrell .75 .35
❑ 55 Joey Galloway 1.00 .45
❑ 56 Anthony Miller .40 .18
❑ 57 Carl Pickens .75 .35
❑ 58 Bruce Smith .40 .18
❑ 59 Merton Hanks .20 .09
❑ 60 Troy Aikman 2.00 .90
❑ 61 Erik Kramer .20 .09
❑ 62 Tyrone Poole .20 .09
❑ 63 Michael Jackson .40 .18
❑ 64 Rob Moore .40 .18
❑ 65 Marcus Allen .75 .35
❑ 66 Orlando Thomas .20 .09
❑ 67 Dave Meggett .20 .09
❑ 68 Trent Dilfer .75 .35
❑ 69 Herman Moore .75 .35
❑ 70 Brett Favre 4.00 1.80
❑ 71 Blaine Bishop .20 .09
❑ 72 Eric Allen .20 .09
❑ 73 Bernie Parmalee .20 .09
❑ 74 Kyle Brady .20 .09
❑ 75 Terry McDaniel .20 .09
❑ 76 Rodney Peete .20 .09
❑ 77 Yancey Thigpen .40 .18
❑ 78 Stan Humphries .40 .18
❑ 79 Craig Heyward .20 .09
❑ 80 Rashaan Salaam .75 .35
❑ 81 Shannon Sharpe .40 .18
❑ 82 Jim Harbaugh .40 .18
❑ 83 Vinnie Clark .20 .09
❑ 84 Steve Bono .20 .09
❑ 85 Drew Bledsoe 2.00 .90
❑ 86 Ken Norton .20 .09
❑ 87 Brian Mitchell .20 .09
❑ 88 Hardy Nickerson .20 .09
❑ 89 Todd Lyght .20 .09
❑ 90 Barry Sanders 4.00 1.80
❑ 91 Robert Blackmon .20 .09
❑ 92 Larry Centers .40 .18
❑ 93 Jim Kelly .75 .35
❑ 94 Lamar Lathon .20 .09
❑ 95 Cris Carter .75 .35
❑ 96 Hugh Douglas .40 .18
❑ 97 Michael Strahan .20 .09
❑ 98 Lee Woodall .20 .09
❑ 99 Michael Irvin .75 .35
❑ 100 Marshall Faulk .75 .35
❑ 101 Terance Mathis .20 .09
❑ 102 Eric Zeier .20 .09
❑ 103 Marty Carter .20 .09
❑ 104 Steve Tovar .20 .09
❑ 105 Isaac Bruce .75 .35
❑ 106 Tony Martin .40 .18
❑ 107 Dale Carter .20 .09
❑ 108 Terry Kirby .40 .18
❑ 109 Tyrone Hughes .20 .09
❑ 110 Bryce Paup .20 .09
❑ 111 Errict Rhett .40 .18
❑ 112 Ricky Watters .40 .18
❑ 113 Chris Chandler .40 .18
❑ 114 Edgar Bennett .40 .18
❑ 115 John Elway 4.00 1.80
❑ 116 Sam Mills .20 .09
❑ 117 Seth Joyner .20 .09
❑ 118 Jeff Lageman .20 .09
❑ 119 Chris Calloway .20 .09
❑ 120 Curtis Martin 1.25 .55
❑ 121 Ken Harvey .20 .09
❑ 122 Eugene Daniel .20 .09
❑ 123 Tim Brown .75 .35
❑ 124 Mo Lewis .20 .09
❑ 125 Jeff Blake .75 .35
❑ 126 Jessie Tuggle .20 .09
❑ 127 Vinny Testaverde .40 .18
❑ 128 Chris Warren .40 .18
❑ 129 Terrell Davis 5.00 2.20
❑ 130 Greg Lloyd .40 .18
❑ 131 Deion Sanders 1.00 .45
❑ 132 Derrick Thomas .40 .18
❑ 133 Darryll Lewis .20 .09
UER back Daryl Lewis
❑ 134 Reggie White .75 .35
❑ 135 Jerry Rice 2.00 .90
❑ 136 Tony Banks RC 5.00 2.20
❑ 137 Derrick Mayes RC 2.50 1.10
❑ 138 Leeland McElroy RC 1.25 .55
❑ 139 Bryan Still RC .60 .25
❑ 140 Tim Biakabutuka RC 3.00 1.35
❑ 141 Rickey Dudley RC 1.25 .55
❑ 142 Tory James RC .30 .14
❑ 143 Lawyer Milloy RC .30 .14
❑ 144 Mike Ulufale RC .30 .14
❑ 145 Bobby Engram RC 1.25 .55
❑ 146 Willie Anderson RC .30 .14
❑ 147 Terrell Owens RC 15.00 6.75
❑ 148 Jonathan Ogden RC .30 .14
❑ 149 Darrius Johnson RC .30 .14
❑ 150 Kevin Hardy RC 1.25 .55
❑ 151 Simeon Rice RC 1.25 .55
❑ 152 Alex Molden RC .30 .14
❑ 153 Cedric Jones RC .30 .14
❑ 154 Duane Clemons RC .30 .14
❑ 155 Karim Abdul-Jabbar RC 2.50 1.10
❑ 156 Dedric Mathis RC .30 .14
❑ 157 John Michels RC .30 .14
❑ 158 Winslow Oliver RC .30 .14
❑ 159 Stepfret Williams RC .30 .14
❑ 160 Eddie Kennison RC 1.25 .55
❑ 161 Marcus Coleman RC .30 .14
❑ 162 Tedy Bruschi RC .30 .14
❑ 163 Detron Smith RC .30 .14
❑ 164 Ray Lewis RC 15.00 6.75
❑ 165 Marvin Harrison RC 12.00 5.50
❑ 166 Je'rod Cherry RC .30 .14
❑ 167 Jerris McPhail RC .30 .14
❑ 168 Eric Moulds RC 10.00 4.50
❑ 169 Walt Harris RC .30 .14
❑ 170 Eddie George RC 20.00 9.00
❑ 171 Jermaine Lewis RC 2.50 1.10
❑ 172 Jeff Lewis RC 1.50 .70
❑ 173 Ray Mickens RC .30 .14
❑ 174 Amani Toomer RC 5.00 2.20

		MINT	NRMT
❑ 175	Zach Thomas RC	3.00	1.35
❑ 176	Lawrence Phillips RC	.60	.25
❑ 177	John Mobley RC	.30	.14
❑ 178	Anthony Dorsett RC	.30	.14
❑ 179	DeRon Jenkins	.20	.09
❑ 180	Keyshawn Johnson RC	12.00	5.50

1997 Bowman's Best

	MINT	NRMT
COMPLETE SET (125)	40.00	18.00

		MINT	NRMT
❑ 1	Brett Favre	4.00	1.80
❑ 2	Larry Centers	.40	.18
❑ 3	Trent Dilfer	.75	.35
❑ 4	Rodney Hampton	.40	.18
❑ 5	Wesley Walls	.40	.18
❑ 6	Jerome Bettis	.75	.35
❑ 7	Keyshawn Johnson	.75	.35
❑ 8	Keenan McCardell	.40	.18
❑ 9	Terry Allen	.75	.35
❑ 10	Troy Aikman	2.00	.90
❑ 11	Tony Banks	.40	.18
❑ 12	Ty Detmer	.40	.18
❑ 13	Chris Chandler	.40	.18
❑ 14	Marshall Faulk	.75	.35
❑ 15	Heath Shuler	.20	.09
❑ 16	Stan Humphries	.40	.18
❑ 17	Bryan Cox	.20	.09
❑ 18	Chris Spielman	.20	.09
❑ 19	Derrick Thomas	.40	.18
❑ 20	Steve Young	1.25	.55
❑ 21	Desmond Howard	.40	.18
❑ 22	Jeff Blake	.40	.18
❑ 23	Michael Jackson	.40	.18
❑ 24	Cris Carter	.75	.35
❑ 25	Joey Galloway	1.00	.45
❑ 26	Simeon Rice	.40	.18
❑ 27	Reggie White	.75	.35
❑ 28	Dave Brown	.20	.09
❑ 29	Mike Alstott	.75	.35
❑ 30	Emmitt Smith	3.00	1.35
❑ 31	Anthony Johnson	.20	.09
❑ 32	Mark Brunell	2.00	.90
❑ 33	Ricky Watters	.40	.18
❑ 34	Terrell Davis	3.00	1.35
❑ 35	Ben Coates	.40	.18
❑ 36	Gus Frerotte	.20	.09
❑ 37	Andre Reed	.40	.18
❑ 38	Isaac Bruce	.75	.35
❑ 39	Junior Seau	.40	.18
❑ 40	Eddie George	2.00	.90
❑ 41	Adrian Murrell	.40	.18
❑ 42	Jake Reed	.40	.18
❑ 43	Karim Abdul-Jabbar	.75	.35
❑ 44	Scott Mitchell	.40	.18
❑ 45	Ki-Jana Carter	.20	.09
❑ 46	Curtis Conway	.40	.18
❑ 47	Jim Harbaugh	.40	.18
❑ 48	Tim Brown	.75	.35
❑ 49	Mario Bates	.20	.09
❑ 50	Jerry Rice	2.00	.90
❑ 51	Byron Bam Morris	.20	.09
❑ 52	Marcus Allen	.75	.35
❑ 53	Errict Rhett	.20	.09
❑ 54	Steve McNair	1.00	.45
❑ 55	Kerry Collins	.40	.18
❑ 56	Bert Emanuel	.40	.18
❑ 57	Curtis Martin	1.00	.45
❑ 58	Bryce Paup	.20	.09
❑ 59	Brad Johnson	1.00	.45
❑ 60	John Elway	4.00	1.80
❑ 61	Natrone Means	.75	.35
❑ 62	Deion Sanders	.75	.35
❑ 63	Tony Martin	.40	.18
❑ 64	Michael Westbrook	.40	.18
❑ 65	Chris Calloway	.20	.09
❑ 66	Antonio Freeman	1.00	.45
❑ 67	Rob Johnson	.75	.35
❑ 68	Kent Graham	.20	.09
❑ 69	O.J. McDuffie	.40	.18
❑ 70	Barry Sanders	4.00	1.80
❑ 71	Chris Warren	.40	.18
❑ 72	Kordell Stewart	1.00	.45
❑ 73	Thurman Thomas	.75	.35
❑ 74	Marvin Harrison	.75	.35
❑ 75	Carl Pickens	.75	.35
❑ 76	Brent Jones	.40	.18
❑ 77	Irving Fryar	.40	.18
❑ 78	Neil O'Donnell	.40	.18
❑ 79	Elvis Grbac	.40	.18
❑ 80	Drew Bledsoe	2.00	.90
❑ 81	Shannon Sharpe	.40	.18
❑ 82	Vinny Testaverde	.40	.18
❑ 83	Chris Sanders	.20	.09
❑ 84	Herman Moore	.75	.35
❑ 85	Jeff George	.40	.18
❑ 86	Bruce Smith	.40	.18
❑ 87	Robert Smith	.40	.18
❑ 88	Kevin Hardy	.20	.09
❑ 89	Kevin Greene	.40	.18
❑ 90	Dan Marino	4.00	1.80
❑ 91	Michael Irvin	.75	.35
❑ 92	Garrison Hearst	.40	.18
❑ 93	Lake Dawson	.20	.09
❑ 94	Lawrence Phillips	.20	.09
❑ 95	Terry Glenn	.75	.35
❑ 96	Jake Plummer RC	8.00	3.60
❑ 97	Byron Hanspard RC	.75	.35
❑ 98	Bryant Westbrook RC	.20	.09
❑ 99	Troy Davis RC	.75	.35
❑ 100	Danny Wuerffel RC	2.50	1.10
❑ 101	Tony Gonzalez RC	4.00	1.80
❑ 102	Jim Druckenmiller RC	.75	.35
❑ 103	Kevin Lockett RC	.40	.18
❑ 104	Renaldo Wynn RC	.20	.09
❑ 105	James Farrior RC	.20	.09
❑ 106	Rae Carruth RC	.75	.35
❑ 107	Tom Knight RC	.20	.09
❑ 108	Corey Dillon RC	8.00	3.60
❑ 109	Kenny Holmes RC	.75	.35
❑ 110	Orlando Pace RC	.75	.35
❑ 111	Reidel Anthony RC	2.50	1.10
❑ 112	Chad Scott RC	.20	.09
❑ 113	Antowain Smith RC	3.00	1.35
❑ 114	David LaFleur RC	1.50	.70
❑ 115	Yatil Green RC	.40	.18
❑ 116	Darrell Russell RC	.20	.09
❑ 117	Joey Kent RC	.75	.35
❑ 118	Darnell Autry RC	.40	.18
❑ 119	Peter Boulware RC	.40	.18
❑ 120	Shawn Springs RC	.40	.18
❑ 121	Ike Hilliard RC	2.50	1.10
❑ 122	Dwayne Rudd RC	.75	.35
❑ 123	Reinard Wilson RC	.20	.09
❑ 124	Michael Booker RC	.20	.09
❑ 125	Warrick Dunn RC	4.00	1.80

1998 Bowman's Best

	MINT	NRMT
COMPLETE SET (125)	100.00	45.00

		MINT	NRMT
❑ 1	Emmitt Smith	3.00	1.35
❑ 2	Reggie White	.75	.35
❑ 3	Jake Plummer	1.50	.70
❑ 4	Ike Hilliard	.20	.09
❑ 5	Isaac Bruce	.20	.09
❑ 6	Trent Dilfer	.75	.35
❑ 7	Ricky Watters	.40	.18
❑ 8	Jeff George	.40	.18
❑ 9	Wayne Chrebet	.75	.35
❑ 10	Brett Favre	4.00	1.80

		MINT	NRMT
❑ 11	Terry Allen	.75	.35
❑ 12	Bert Emanuel	.20	.09
❑ 13	Andre Reed	.40	.18
❑ 14	Andre Rison	.40	.18
❑ 15	Jeff Blake	.40	.18
❑ 16	Steve McNair	.75	.35
❑ 17	Joey Galloway	.75	.35
❑ 18	Irving Fryar	.40	.18
❑ 19	Dorsey Levens	.75	.35
❑ 20	Jerry Rice	2.00	.90
❑ 21	Kerry Collins	.40	.18
❑ 22	Michael Jackson	.20	.09
❑ 23	Kordell Stewart	.75	.35
❑ 24	Junior Seau	.40	.18
❑ 25	Jimmy Smith	.40	.18
❑ 26	Michael Westbrook	.40	.18
❑ 27	Eddie George	1.50	.70
❑ 28	Cris Carter	.75	.35
❑ 29	Jason Sehorn	.40	.18
❑ 30	Warrick Dunn	.75	.35
❑ 31	Garrison Hearst	.75	.35
❑ 32	Erik Kramer	.20	.09
❑ 33	Chris Chandler	.40	.18
❑ 34	Michael Irvin	.75	.35
❑ 35	Marshall Faulk	.75	.35
❑ 36	Warren Moon	.75	.35
❑ 37	Rickey Dudley	.20	.09
❑ 38	Drew Bledsoe	1.50	.70
❑ 39	Antowain Smith	.75	.35
❑ 40	Terrell Davis	3.00	1.35
❑ 41	Gus Frerotte	.20	.09
❑ 42	Robert Brooks	.40	.18
❑ 43	Tony Banks	.40	.18
❑ 44	Terrell Owens	.75	.35
❑ 45	Edgar Bennett	.20	.09
❑ 46	Rob Moore	.40	.18
❑ 47	J.J. Stokes	.40	.18
❑ 48	Yancey Thigpen	.20	.09
❑ 49	Elvis Grbac	.40	.18
❑ 50	John Elway	4.00	1.80
❑ 51	Charles Johnson	.20	.09
❑ 52	Karim Abdul-Jabbar	.75	.35
❑ 53	Carl Pickens	.75	.35
❑ 54	Peter Boulware	.20	.09
❑ 55	Chris Warren	.20	.09
❑ 56	Terance Mathis	.40	.18
❑ 57	Andre Hastings	.20	.09
❑ 58	Jake Reed	.40	.18
❑ 59	Mike Alstott	.20	.09
❑ 60	Mark Brunell	1.50	.70
❑ 61	Herman Moore	.75	.35
❑ 62	Troy Aikman	2.00	.90
❑ 63	Fred Lane	.40	.18
❑ 64	Rod Smith	.40	.18
❑ 65	Terry Glenn	.75	.35
❑ 66	Jerome Bettis	.75	.35
❑ 67	Derrick Thomas	.40	.18
❑ 68	Marvin Harrison	.40	.18
❑ 69	Adrian Murrell	.20	.09
❑ 70	Curtis Martin	.75	.35
❑ 71	Bobby Hoying	.40	.18
❑ 72	Darrell Green	.40	.18
❑ 73	Sean Dawkins	.20	.09
❑ 74	Robert Smith	.75	.35
❑ 75	Antonio Freeman	.75	.35
❑ 76	Scott Mitchell	.40	.18
❑ 77	Curtis Conway	.40	.18

Card	Mint	NrMt
78 Rae Carruth	.40	.18
79 Jamal Anderson	.75	.35
80 Dan Marino	4.00	1.80
81 Brad Johnson	.75	.35
82 Danny Kanell	.40	.18
83 Charlie Garner	.20	.09
84 Rob Johnson	.40	.18
85 Natrone Means	.75	.35
86 Tim Brown	.75	.35
87 Keyshawn Johnson	.75	.35
88 Ben Coates	.40	.18
89 Derrick Alexander	.40	.18
90 Steve Young	1.25	.55
91 Shannon Sharpe	.40	.18
92 Corey Dillon	1.25	.55
93 Bruce Smith	.40	.18
94 Errict Rhett	.40	.18
95 Jim Harbaugh	.20	.09
96 Napoleon Kaufman	.75	.35
97 Glenn Foley	.40	.18
98 Tony Gonzalez	.20	.09
99 Keenan McCardell	.40	.18
100 Barry Sanders	4.00	1.80
101 Charles Woodson RC	5.00	2.20
102 Tim Dwight RC	5.00	2.20
103 Marcus Nash RC	4.00	1.80
104 Joe Jurevicius RC	3.00	1.35
105 Jacquez Green RC	5.00	2.20
106 Kevin Dyson RC	5.00	2.20
107 Keith Brooking RC	3.00	1.35
108 Andre Wadsworth RC	3.00	1.35
109 Randy Moss RC	25.00	11.00
110 Robert Edwards RC	5.00	2.20
111 Pat Johnson RC	3.00	1.35
112 Peyton Manning RC	25.00	11.00
113 Duane Starks RC	2.00	.90
114 Grant Wistrom RC	2.00	.90
115 Anthony Simmons RC	2.00	.90
116 Takeo Spikes RC	3.00	1.35
117 Tony Simmons RC	3.00	1.35
118 Jerome Pathon RC	3.00	1.35
119 Ryan Leaf RC	8.00	3.60
120 Skip Hicks RC	4.00	1.80
121 Curtis Enis RC	4.00	1.80
122 Germane Crowell RC	6.00	2.70
123 John Avery RC	3.00	1.35
124 Hines Ward RC	3.00	1.35
125 Fred Taylor RC	10.00	4.50

1999 Bowman's Best

	MINT	NRMT
COMPLETE SET (133)	80.00	36.00
1 Randy Moss	3.00	1.35
2 Skip Hicks	.40	.18
3 Robert Smith	.75	.35
4 Drew Bledsoe	1.25	.55
5 Tim Brown	.75	.35
6 Marshall Faulk	.75	.35
7 Terance Mathis	.40	.18
8 Sean Dawkins	.20	.09
9 Ed McCaffrey	.40	.18
10 Jamal Anderson	.75	.35
11 Antonio Freeman	.75	.35
12 Terry Kirby	.40	.18
13 Vinny Testaverde	.40	.18
14 Eddie George	1.00	.45
15 Ricky Watters	.40	.18
16 Johnnie Morton	.40	.18
17 Natrone Means	.40	.18
18 Terry Glenn	.75	.35
19 Michael Westbrook	.40	.18
20 Doug Flutie	1.00	.45
21 Jake Plummer	1.25	.55
22 Darnay Scott	.40	.18
23 Andre Rison	.40	.18
24 Jon Kitna	.75	.35
25 Dan Marino	3.00	1.35
26 Ike Hilliard	.40	.18
27 Warrick Dunn	.75	.35
28 Jerome Bettis	.75	.35
29 Curtis Conway	.40	.18
30 Emmitt Smith	2.00	.90
31 Jimmy Smith	.40	.18
32 Isaac Bruce	.75	.35
33 Jerry Rice	2.00	.90
34 Curtis Martin	.75	.35
35 Steve McNair	.75	.35
36 Jeff Blake	.40	.18
37 Rob Moore	.40	.18
38 Dorsey Levens	.75	.35
39 Terrell Davis	2.00	.90
40 John Elway	3.00	1.35
41 Trent Dilfer	.40	.18
42 Joey Galloway	.75	.35
43 Keyshawn Johnson	.75	.35
44 O.J. McDuffie	.40	.18
45 Fred Taylor	2.00	.90
46 Andre Reed	.40	.18
47 Frank Sanders	.40	.18
48 Keenan McCardell	.40	.18
49 Elvis Grbac	.40	.18
50 Barry Sanders	3.00	1.35
51 Terrell Owens	.75	.35
52 Trent Green	.40	.18
53 Brad Johnson	.75	.35
54 Rich Gannon	.40	.18
55 Randall Cunningham	.75	.35
56 Tony Martin	.40	.18
57 Rod Smith	.40	.18
58 Eric Moulds	.75	.35
59 Yancey Thigpen	.20	.09
60 Brett Favre	3.00	1.35
61 Cris Carter	.75	.35
62 Marvin Harrison	.75	.35
63 Chris Chandler	.40	.18
64 Antowain Smith	.75	.35
65 Carl Pickens	.40	.18
66 Shannon Sharpe	.40	.18
67 Mike Alstott	.75	.35
68 J.J. Stokes	.40	.18
69 Ben Coates	.40	.18
70 Peyton Manning	3.00	1.35
71 Duce Staley	.75	.35
72 Michael Irvin	.40	.18
73 Tim Biakabutuka	.40	.18
74 Priest Holmes	.75	.35
75 Steve Young	1.25	.55
76 Jerome Pathon	.40	.18
77 Wayne Chrebet	.75	.35
78 Bert Emanuel	.20	.09
79 Curtis Enis	.75	.35
80 Mark Brunell	1.25	.55
81 Herman Moore	.75	.35
82 Corey Dillon	.75	.35
83 Jim Harbaugh	.40	.18
84 Gary Brown	.20	.09
85 Kordell Stewart	.75	.35
86 Garrison Hearst	.40	.18
87 Rocket Ismail	.40	.18
88 Charlie Batch	1.50	.70
89 Napoleon Kaufman	.75	.35
90 Troy Aikman	2.00	.90
91 Brett Favre BP	1.50	.70
92 Randy Moss BP	1.50	.70
93 Terrell Davis BP	1.00	.45
94 Barry Sanders BP	1.50	.70
95 Peyton Manning BP	1.50	.70
96 Troy Edwards BP	1.00	.45
97 Cade McNown BP	1.00	.45
98 Edgerrin James BP	6.00	2.70
99 Torry Holt BP	1.25	.55
100 Tim Couch BP	2.50	1.10
101 Chris Claiborne RC	1.50	.70
102 Brock Huard RC	3.00	1.35
103 Amos Zereoue RC	2.00	.90
104 Sedrick Irvin RC	2.00	.90
105 Kevin Faulk RC	3.00	1.35
106 Ebenezer Ekuban RC	1.50	.70
107 Daunte Culpepper RC	12.00	5.50
108 Rob Konrad RC	2.00	.90
109 James Johnson RC	2.00	.90
110 Kurt Warner RC	15.00	6.75
111 Mike Cloud RC	2.00	.90
112 Andy Katzenmoyer RC	2.00	.90
113 Jevon Kearse RC	4.00	1.80
114 Akili Smith RC	4.00	1.80
115 Edgerrin James RC	12.00	5.50
116 Cecil Collins RC	2.00	.90
117 Chris McAlister RC	2.00	.90
118 Donovan McNabb RC	8.00	3.60
119 Kevin Johnson RC	4.00	1.80
120 Torry Holt RC	5.00	2.20
121 Antoine Winfield RC	1.50	.70
122 Michael Bishop RC	2.50	1.10
123 Joe Germaine RC	2.00	.90
124 David Boston RC	4.00	1.80
125 D'Wayne Bates RC	1.50	.70
126 Champ Bailey RC	2.50	1.10
127 Cade McNown RC	2.50	1.10
128 Shaun King RC	4.00	1.80
129 Peerless Price RC	2.50	1.10
130 Troy Edwards RC	2.50	1.10
131 Karsten Bailey RC	2.00	.90
132 Tim Couch RC	8.00	3.60
133 Ricky Williams RC	8.00	3.60
C1 Rookie Class Photo	8.00	3.60

2000 Bowman's Best

	MINT	NRMT
COMPLETE SET (150)	500.00	220.00
1 Troy Edwards	.30	.14
2 Kurt Warner	2.50	1.10
3 Steve McNair	.60	.25
4 Terry Glenn	.30	.14
5 Charlie Batch	.60	.25
6 Patrick Jeffers	.60	.25
7 Jake Plummer	.60	.25
8 Derrick Alexander	.30	.14
9 Joey Galloway	.60	.25
10 Tony Banks	.30	.14
11 Robert Smith	.60	.25
12 Jerry Rice	1.50	.70
13 Jeff Garcia	.60	.25
14 Michael Westbrook	.30	.14
15 Curtis Conway	.30	.14
16 Brian Griese	.75	.35
17 Peyton Manning	2.00	.90
18 Daunte Culpepper	1.25	.55
19 Frank Sanders	.30	.14
20 Muhsin Muhammad	.30	.14
21 Corey Dillon	.60	.25
22 Brett Favre	2.50	1.10
23 Warrick Dunn	.60	.25
24 Tim Brown	.60	.25
25 Kerry Collins	.30	.14
26 Brad Johnson	.60	.25
27 Rocket Ismail	.30	.14
28 Jamal Anderson	.60	.25

❑ 29 Jimmy Smith .30 .14
❑ 30 Torry Holt .60 .25
❑ 31 Duce Staley .60 .25
❑ 32 Drew Bledsoe 1.00 .45
❑ 33 Jerome Bettis .60 .25
❑ 34 Keyshawn Johnson .60 .25
❑ 35 Fred Taylor .75 .35
❑ 36 Akili Smith .60 .25
❑ 37 Rob Johnson .30 .14
❑ 38 Elvis Grbac .30 .14
❑ 39 Antonio Freeman .60 .25
❑ 40 Curtis Enis .60 .25
❑ 41 Terance Mathis .30 .14
❑ 42 Terrell Davis 1.50 .70
❑ 43 Randy Moss 2.00 .90
❑ 44 Jon Kitna .60 .25
❑ 45 Curtis Martin .60 .25
❑ 46 Terrell Owens .30 .14
❑ 47 Robert Smith .60 .25
❑ 48 Albert Connell .15 .07
❑ 49 Edgerrin James 2.50 1.10
❑ 50 Tony Gonzalez .30 .14
❑ 51 Eric Moulds .60 .25
❑ 52 Natrone Means .30 .14
❑ 53 Carl Pickens .30 .14
❑ 54 Mark Brunell 1.00 .45
❑ 55 Rob Moore .30 .14
❑ 56 Marshall Faulk .75 .35
❑ 57 Stephen Davis .60 .25
❑ 58 Rich Gannon .30 .14
❑ 59 Ricky Williams 1.50 .70
❑ 60 Emmitt Smith 1.50 .70
❑ 61 Germane Crowell .30 .14
❑ 62 Doug Flutie .75 .35
❑ 63 O.J. McDuffie .30 .14
❑ 64 Chris Chandler .30 .14
❑ 65 Qadry Ismail .30 .14
❑ 66 Tim Couch 1.25 .55
❑ 67 James Stewart .30 .14
❑ 68 Marvin Harrison .60 .25
❑ 69 Cris Carter .60 .25
❑ 70 Cade McNown .60 .25
❑ 71 Marcus Robinson .60 .25
❑ 72 Steve Beuerlein .30 .14
❑ 73 Jevon Kearse .60 .25
❑ 74 Eddie George .75 .35
❑ 75 Donovan McNabb 1.00 .45
❑ 76 Jeff Blake .30 .14
❑ 77 Wayne Chrebet .30 .14
❑ 78 Kordell Stewart .60 .25
❑ 79 Steve Young 1.00 .45
❑ 80 Mike Alstott .60 .25
❑ 81 Ricky Watters .15 .07
❑ 82 Charlie Garner .30 .14
❑ 83 Troy Aikman 1.50 .70
❑ 84 Dorsey Levens .30 .14
❑ 85 Ike Hilliard .30 .14
❑ 86 Shaun King 1.00 .45
❑ 87 Isaac Bruce .60 .25
❑ 88 Tyrone Wheatley .30 .14
❑ 89 Amani Toomer .30 .14
❑ 90 Ed McCaffrey .60 .25
❑ 91 Edgerrin James 1.50 .70
Marshall Faulk
❑ 92 Drew Bledsoe .60 .25
Brad Johnson
❑ 93 Jimmy Smith 1.25 .55
Randy Moss
❑ 94 Eddie George .30 .14
Stephen Davis
❑ 95 Mark Brunell 1.00 .45
Troy Aikman
❑ 96 Marvin Harrison .30 .14
Cris Carter
❑ 97 Curtis Martin 1.00 .45
Emmitt Smith
❑ 98 Tim Brown .30 .14
Isaac Bruce
❑ 99 Fred Taylor .75 .35
Ricky Williams
❑ 100 Kurt Warner 1.50 .70
Peyton Manning
❑ 101 Shaun Alexander RC 20.00 9.00
❑ 102 Thomas Jones RC 12.00 5.50
❑ 103 Courtney Brown RC 10.00 4.50
❑ 104 Curtis Keaton RC 6.00 2.70
❑ 105 Jerry Porter RC 8.00 3.60
❑ 106 Corey Simon RC 10.00 4.50
❑ 107 Dez White RC 6.00 2.70
❑ 108 Jamal Lewis RC 40.00 18.00
❑ 109 Ron Dayne RC 25.00 11.00
❑ 110 R.Jay Soward RC 8.00 3.60
❑ 111 Tee Martin RC 12.00 5.50
❑ 112 Brian Urlacher RC 25.00 11.00
❑ 113 Reuben Droughns RC 8.00 3.60
❑ 114 Travis Taylor RC 10.00 4.50
❑ 115 Plaxico Burress RC 15.00 6.75
❑ 116 Chad Pennington RC 25.00 11.00
❑ 117 Sylvester Morris RC 15.00 6.75
❑ 118 Ron Dugans RC 6.00 2.70
❑ 119 Joe Hamilton RC 10.00 4.50
❑ 120 Chris Redman RC 15.00 6.75
❑ 121 Trung Canidate RC 8.00 3.60
❑ 122 J.R. Redmond RC 10.00 4.50
❑ 123 Danny Farmer RC 8.00 3.60
❑ 124 Todd Pinkston RC 8.00 3.60
❑ 125 Dennis Northcutt RC 10.00 4.50
❑ 126 Laveranues Coles RC 12.00 5.50
❑ 127 Bubba Franks RC 10.00 4.50
❑ 128 Travis Prentice RC 12.00 5.50
❑ 129 Peter Warrick RC 25.00 11.00
❑ 130 Anthony Becht RC 8.00 3.60
❑ 131 Ike Charlton RC 4.00 1.80
❑ 132 Shaun Ellis RC 6.00 2.70
❑ 133 Sean Morey RC 6.00 2.70
❑ 134 Sebastian Janikowski RC 8.00 3.60
❑ 135 Aaron Stecker RC 8.00 3.60
❑ 136 Ronney Jenkins RC 6.00 2.70
❑ 137 Jamel White RC 8.00 3.60
❑ 138 Nick Williams 4.00 1.80
❑ 139 Andy McCullough 4.00 1.80
❑ 140 Kevin Daft 4.00 1.80
❑ 141 Thomas Hamner RC 6.00 2.70
❑ 142 Tim Rattay RC 12.00 5.50
❑ 143 Spergon Wynn RC 8.00 3.60
❑ 144 Brandon Short RC 6.00 2.70
❑ 145 Chad Morton RC 8.00 3.60
❑ 146 Gari Scott RC 6.00 2.70
❑ 147 Frank Murphy RC 4.00 1.80
❑ 148 James Williams RC 6.00 2.70
❑ 149 Windrell Hayes RC 6.00 2.70
❑ 150 Doug Johnson RC 8.00 3.60

2000 Bowman Reserve

	MINT	NRMT
❑ 1 Chad Pennington RC	60.00	27.00
❑ 2 Shaun Alexander RC	50.00	22.00
❑ 3 Thomas Jones RC	30.00	13.50
❑ 4 Courtney Brown RC	25.00	11.00
❑ 5 Curtis Keaton RC	15.00	6.75
❑ 6 Jerry Porter RC	20.00	9.00
❑ 7 Jamal Lewis RC	100.00	45.00
❑ 8 Ron Dayne RC	50.00	22.00
❑ 9 R.Jay Soward RC	20.00	9.00
❑ 10 Tee Martin RC	30.00	13.50
❑ 11 Travis Taylor RC	25.00	11.00
❑ 12 Plaxico Burress RC	40.00	18.00
❑ 13 Giovanni Carmazzi RC	25.00	11.00
❑ 14 Sylvester Morris RC	40.00	18.00
❑ 15 Chris Redman RC	40.00	18.00
❑ 16 Trung Canidate RC	20.00	9.00
❑ 17 J.R. Redmond RC	25.00	11.00
❑ 18 Bubba Franks RC	25.00	11.00
❑ 19 Travis Prentice RC	30.00	13.50
❑ 20 Peter Warrick RC	50.00	22.00
❑ 21 Frank Sanders	.50	.23
❑ 22 Edgerrin James	4.00	1.80
❑ 23 Marcus Robinson	1.00	.45
❑ 24 Mike Alstott	1.00	.45
❑ 25 Jerry Rice	2.50	1.10
❑ 26 Marshall Faulk	1.25	.55
❑ 27 Brad Johnson	1.00	.45
❑ 28 Elvis Grbac	.50	.23
❑ 29 Wayne Chrebet	.50	.23
❑ 30 Akili Smith	1.00	.45
❑ 31 Rob Johnson	.50	.23
❑ 32 Brett Favre	4.00	1.80
❑ 33 Ricky Williams	2.50	1.10
❑ 34 Donovan McNabb	1.50	.70
❑ 35 Cris Carter	1.00	.45
❑ 36 Ricky Watters	.30	.14
❑ 37 Steve McNair	2.00	.90
❑ 38 Stephen Davis	1.00	.45
❑ 39 Fred Taylor	1.25	.55
❑ 40 Rocket Ismail	.50	.23
❑ 41 Terry Glenn	.50	.23
❑ 42 Ed McCaffrey	1.00	.45
❑ 43 Patrick Jeffers	1.00	.45
❑ 44 Jake Plummer	1.00	.45
❑ 45 Doug Flutie	1.25	.55
❑ 46 Terrell Davis	2.50	1.10
❑ 47 Marvin Harrison	1.00	.45
❑ 48 Amani Toomer	.50	.23
❑ 49 Tyrone Wheatley	.50	.23
❑ 50 Charlie Garner	.50	.23
❑ 51 Jevon Kearse	1.00	.45
❑ 52 Michael Westbrook	.50	.23
❑ 53 Eddie George	1.25	.55
❑ 54 Robert Smith	1.00	.45
❑ 55 Keyshawn Johnson	1.00	.45
❑ 56 Torry Holt	1.00	.45
❑ 57 Jon Kitna	1.00	.45
❑ 58 Curtis Conway	.50	.23
❑ 59 Jeff Garcia	1.00	.45
❑ 60 Randy Moss	3.00	1.35
❑ 61 Jimmy Smith	.50	.23
❑ 62 James Stewart	.50	.23
❑ 63 Troy Aikman	2.50	1.10
❑ 64 Cade McNown	1.00	.45
❑ 65 Natrone Means	.50	.23
❑ 66 Jamal Anderson	1.00	.45
❑ 67 Warrick Dunn	1.00	.45
❑ 68 Kordell Stewart	1.00	.45
❑ 69 Duce Staley	1.00	.45
❑ 70 Rich Gannon	.50	.23
❑ 71 Curtis Martin	1.00	.45
❑ 72 Kerry Collins	.50	.23
❑ 73 Jeff Blake	.50	.23
❑ 74 Drew Bledsoe	1.50	.70
❑ 75 Kevin Dyson	.50	.23
❑ 76 Tony Gonzalez	.50	.23
❑ 77 Mark Brunell	1.50	.70
❑ 78 Peyton Manning	3.00	1.35
❑ 79 Dorsey Levens	.50	.23
❑ 80 Germane Crowell	.50	.23
❑ 81 Brian Griese	1.25	.55
❑ 82 Steve Beuerlein	.50	.23
❑ 83 Eric Moulds	1.00	.45
❑ 84 Tony Banks	.50	.23
❑ 85 Chris Chandler	.50	.23
❑ 86 Isaac Bruce	1.00	.45
❑ 87 Terrell Owens	1.00	.45
❑ 88 Jerome Bettis	1.00	.45
❑ 89 Daunte Culpepper	2.00	.90
❑ 90 Emmitt Smith	2.50	1.10
❑ 91 Curtis Enis	1.00	.45
❑ 92 Shaun King	1.25	.55
❑ 93 Tim Brown	1.00	.45
❑ 94 Antonio Freeman	1.00	.45
❑ 95 Charlie Batch	1.00	.45
❑ 96 Tim Couch	2.00	.90
❑ 97 Corey Dillon	1.00	.45
❑ 98 Muhsin Muhammad	.50	.23
❑ 99 Joey Galloway	1.00	.45
❑ 100 Kurt Warner	4.00	1.80
❑ 101 David Boston	1.00	.45
❑ 102 Rod Smith	.30	.14
❑ 103 Derrick Mayes	.50	.23
❑ 104 Tony Martin	.50	.23

❑	105 Darnay Scott	.50	.23
❑	106 Joe Horn	.50	.23
❑	107 Troy Edwards	.50	.23
❑	108 James Johnson	.50	.23
❑	109 Vinny Testaverde	.50	.23
❑	110 Qadry Ismail	.50	.23
❑	111 Andre Reed	.50	.23
❑	112 Zach Thomas	.50	.23
❑	113 Ike Hilliard	.50	.23
❑	114 Herman Moore	.50	.23
❑	115 Kevin Johnson	1.00	.45
❑	116 Shawn Jefferson	.30	.14
❑	117 Terance Mathis	.50	.23
❑	118 Peerless Price	1.00	.45
❑	119 Bert Emanuel	.30	.14
❑	120 Terrence Wilkins	1.00	.45
❑	121 Mike Anderson RC	100.00	45.00
❑	122 Dez White RC	15.00	6.75
❑	123 Todd Pinkston RC	20.00	9.00
❑	124 Reuben Droughns RC	20.00	9.00
❑	125 Danny Farmer RC	20.00	9.00

1994 Collector's Choice

		MINT	NRMT
	COMPLETE SET (384)	20.00	9.00
❑	1 Antonio Langham RC	.10	.05
❑	2 Aaron Glenn RC	.10	.05
❑	3 Sam Adams RC	.10	.05
❑	4 Dewayne Washington RC	.10	.05
❑	5 Dan Wilkinson RC	.10	.05
❑	6 Bryant Young RC	.25	.11
❑	7 Aaron Taylor RC	.05	.02
❑	8 Willie McGinest RC	.10	.05
❑	9 Trev Alberts RC	.10	.05
❑	10 Jamir Miller RC	.05	.02
❑	11 John Thierry RC	.05	.02
❑	12 Heath Shuler RC	.25	.11
❑	13 Trent Dilfer RC	2.00	.90
❑	14 Marshall Faulk RC	4.00	1.80
❑	15 Greg Hill RC	.25	.11
❑	16 William Floyd RC	.25	.11
❑	17 Chuck Levy RC	.05	.02
❑	18 Charlie Garner RC	1.50	.70
❑	19 Mario Bates RC	.25	.11
❑	20 Donnell Bennett RC	.25	.11
❑	21 LeShon Johnson RC	.10	.05
❑	22 Calvin Jones RC	.05	.02
❑	23 Darnay Scott RC	.75	.35
❑	24 Charles Johnson RC	.40	.18
❑	25 Johnnie Morton RC	.25	.11
❑	26 Shante Carver RC	.05	.02
❑	27 Derrick Alexander WR RC	.50	.23
❑	28 David Palmer RC	.50	.23
❑	29 Ryan Yarborough RC	.05	.02
❑	30 Errict Rhett RC	1.00	.45
❑	31 James Washington I93	.05	.02
❑	32 Sterling Sharpe I93	.05	.02
❑	33 Drew Bledsoe I93	.40	.18
❑	34 Eric Allen I93	.05	.02
❑	35 Jerome Bettis I93	.10	.05
❑	36 Joe Montana I93	.60	.25
❑	37 John Carney I93	.05	.02
❑	38 Emmitt Smith I93	.50	.23
❑	39 Chris Warren I93	.25	.11
❑	40 Reggie Brooks I93	.05	.02
❑	41 Gary Brown I93	.05	.02
❑	42 Tim Brown I93	.10	.05
❑	43 Eric Pegram I93	.05	.02
❑	44 Ronald Moore I93	.05	.02
❑	45 Jerry Rice I93	.40	.18
❑	46 Ricky Watters TE	.25	.11
❑	47 Joe Montana TE	.60	.25
❑	48 Reggie Brooks TE	.05	.02
❑	49 Rick Mirer TE	.25	.11
❑	50 Rocket Ismail TE	.10	.05
❑	51 Curtis Conway TE	.10	.05
❑	52 Junior Seau TE	.25	.11
❑	53 Mark Carrier DB TE	.05	.02
❑	54 Ronnie Lott TE	.10	.05
❑	55 Marcus Allen TE	.25	.11
❑	56 Michael Irvin TE	.25	.11
❑	57 Bennie Blades	.05	.02
❑	58 Randal Hill	.05	.02
❑	59 Brian Blades	.10	.05
❑	60 Russell Maryland	.05	.02
❑	61 Jim Kelly	.25	.11
❑	62 Arthur Marshall	.05	.02
❑	63 Webster Slaughter	.05	.02
❑	64 Dave Krieg	.10	.05
❑	65 Steve Jordan	.05	.02
❑	66 Neil O'Donnell	.25	.11
❑	67 Andre Reed	.10	.05
❑	68 Mike Croel	.05	.02
❑	69 Al Smith	.05	.02
❑	70 Joe Montana	1.50	.70
❑	71 Randall McDaniel	.05	.02
❑	72 Greg Lloyd	.25	.11
❑	73 Thomas Smith	.05	.02
❑	74 Glyn Milburn	.10	.05
❑	75 Lorenzo White	.05	.02
❑	76 Neil Smith	.25	.11
❑	77 John Randle	.10	.05
❑	78 Rod Woodson	.25	.11
❑	79 Russell Maryland	.05	.02
❑	80 Rodney Peete	.05	.02
❑	81 Jackie Harris	.05	.02
❑	82 James Jett	.05	.02
❑	83 Rodney Hampton	.25	.11
❑	84 Bill Romanowski	.05	.02
❑	85 Ken Norton Jr.	.10	.05
❑	86 Barry Sanders	1.50	.70
❑	87 Johnny Holland	.05	.02
❑	88 Terry McDaniel	.05	.02
❑	89 Greg Jackson	.05	.02
❑	90 Dana Stubblefield	.25	.11
❑	91 Jay Novacek	.10	.05
❑	92 Chris Spielman	.10	.05
❑	93 Ken Ruettgers	.05	.02
❑	94 Greg Robinson	.05	.02
❑	95 Mark Jackson	.05	.02
❑	96 John Taylor	.10	.05
❑	97 Roger Harper	.05	.02
❑	98 Jerry Ball	.05	.02
❑	99 Keith Byars	.05	.02
❑	100 Morten Andersen	.05	.02
❑	101 Eric Allen	.05	.02
❑	102 Marion Butts	.05	.02
❑	103 Michael Haynes	.10	.05
❑	104 Rob Burnett	.05	.02
❑	105 Marco Coleman	.05	.02
❑	106 Derek Brown RBK	.05	.02
❑	107 Andy Harmon	.05	.02
❑	108 Darren Carrington	.05	.02
❑	109 Bobby Hebert	.05	.02
❑	110 Mark Carrier WR	.10	.05
❑	111 Bryan Cox	.05	.02
❑	112 Toi Cook	.05	.02
❑	113 Tim Harris	.05	.02
❑	114 John Friesz	.10	.05
❑	115 Neal Anderson	.05	.02
❑	116 Jerome Bettis	.25	.11
❑	117 Bruce Armstrong	.05	.02
❑	118 Brad Baxter	.05	.02
❑	119 Johnny Bailey	.05	.02
❑	120 Brian Blades	.10	.05
❑	121 Mark Carrier DB	.05	.02
❑	122 Shane Conlan	.05	.02
❑	123 Drew Bledsoe	.75	.35
❑	124 Chris Burkett	.05	.02
❑	125 Steve Beuerlein	.05	.02
❑	126 Ferrell Edmunds	.05	.02
❑	127 Curtis Conway	.25	.11
❑	128 Troy Drayton	.05	.02
❑	129 Vincent Brown	.05	.02
❑	130 Boomer Esiason	.10	.05
❑	131 Larry Centers	.25	.11
❑	132 Carlton Gray	.05	.02
❑	133 Chris Miller	.05	.02
❑	134 Eric Metcalf	.10	.05
❑	135 Mark Higgs	.05	.02
❑	136 Tyrone Hughes	.10	.05
❑	137 Randall Cunningham	.25	.11
❑	138 Ronnie Harmon	.05	.02
❑	139 Andre Rison	.10	.05
❑	140 Eric Turner	.05	.02
❑	141 Terry Kirby	.25	.11
❑	142 Eric Martin	.05	.02
❑	143 Seth Joyner	.05	.02
❑	144 Stan Humphries	.25	.11
❑	145 Deion Sanders	.40	.18
❑	146 Vinny Testaverde	.10	.05
❑	147 Dan Marino	1.50	.70
❑	148 Renaldo Turnbull	.05	.02
❑	149 Herschel Walker	.10	.05
❑	150 Anthony Miller	.10	.05
❑	151 Richard Dent	.10	.05
❑	152 Jim Everett	.10	.05
❑	153 Ben Coates	.25	.11
❑	154 Jeff Lageman	.05	.02
❑	155 Garrison Hearst	.25	.11
❑	156 Kelvin Martin	.05	.02
❑	157 Dante Jones	.05	.02
❑	158 Sean Gilbert	.05	.02
❑	159 Leonard Russell	.05	.02
❑	160 Ronnie Lott	.10	.05
❑	161 Randal Hill	.05	.02
❑	162 Rick Mirer	.25	.11
❑	163 Alonzo Spellman	.05	.02
❑	164 Todd Lyght	.05	.02
❑	165 Chris Slade	.05	.02
❑	166 Johnny Mitchell	.05	.02
❑	167 Ronald Moore	.05	.02
❑	168 Eugene Robinson	.05	.02
❑	169 Chris Hinton	.05	.02
❑	170 Dan Footman	.05	.02
❑	171 Keith Jackson	.05	.02
❑	172 Rickey Jackson	.05	.02
❑	173 Heath Sherman	.05	.02
❑	174 Chris Mims	.05	.02
❑	175 Eric Pegram	.05	.02
❑	176 Leroy Hoard	.05	.02
❑	177 O.J. McDuffie	.25	.11
❑	178 Wayne Martin	.05	.02
❑	179 Clyde Simmons	.05	.02
❑	180 Leslie O'Neal	.05	.02
❑	181 Mike Pritchard	.05	.02
❑	182 Michael Jackson	.10	.05
❑	183 Scott Mitchell	.25	.11
❑	184 Lorenzo Neal	.05	.02
❑	185 William Thomas	.05	.02
❑	186 Junior Seau UER (Career tackles 322, but add up to 451)	.25	.11
❑	187 Chris Gedney	.05	.02
❑	188 Tim Lester	.05	.02
❑	189 Sam Gash	.05	.02
❑	190 Johnny Johnson	.05	.02
❑	191 Chuck Cecil	.05	.02
❑	192 Cortez Kennedy	.10	.05
❑	193 Jim Harbaugh	.25	.11
❑	194 Roman Phifer	.05	.02
❑	195 Pat Harlow	.05	.02
❑	196 Rob Moore	.10	.05
❑	197 Gary Clark	.10	.05
❑	198 Jon Vaughn	.05	.02
❑	199 Craig Heyward	.10	.05
❑	200 Michael Stewart	.05	.02
❑	201 Greg McMurtry	.05	.02
❑	202 Brian Washington	.05	.02
❑	203 Ken Harvey	.05	.02
❑	204 Chris Warren	.10	.05
❑	205 Bruce Smith	.25	.11
❑	206 Tom Rouen	.05	.02
❑	207 Cris Dishman	.05	.02
❑	208 Keith Cash	.05	.02
❑	209 Carlos Jenkins	.05	.02
❑	210 Levon Kirkland	.05	.02
❑	211 Pete Metzelaars	.05	.02

❑ 212 Shannon Sharpe .10 .05
❑ 213 Cody Carlson .05 .02
❑ 214 Derrick Thomas .25 .11
❑ 215 Emmitt Smith 1.25 .55
❑ 216 Robert Porcher .05 .02
❑ 217 Sterling Sharpe .10 .05
❑ 218 Anthony Smith .05 .02
❑ 219 Mike Sherrard .05 .02
❑ 220 Tom Rathman .05 .02
❑ 221 Nate Newton .05 .02
❑ 222 Pat Swilling .05 .02
❑ 223 George Teague .05 .02
❑ 224 Greg Townsend .05 .02
❑ 225 Eric Guliford RC .05 .02
❑ 226 Leroy Thompson .05 .02
❑ 227 Thurman Thomas .25 .11
❑ 228 Dan Williams .05 .02
❑ 229 Bubba McDowell .05 .02
❑ 230 Tracy Simien .05 .02
❑ 231 Scottie Graham RC .10 .05
❑ 232 Eric Green .05 .02
❑ 233 Phil Simms .10 .05
❑ 234 Ricky Watters .25 .11
❑ 235 Kevin Williams .10 .05
❑ 236 Brett Perriman .10 .05
❑ 237 Reggie White .25 .11
❑ 238 Steve Wisniewski .05 .02
❑ 239 Mark Collins .05 .02
❑ 240 Steve Young .75 .35
❑ 241 Steve Tovar .05 .02
❑ 242 Jason Belser .05 .02
❑ 243 Ray Seals .05 .02
❑ 244 Earnest Byner .05 .02
❑ 245 Ricky Proehl .05 .02
❑ 246 Rich Miano .05 .02
❑ 247 Alfred Williams .05 .02
❑ 248 Ray Buchanan UER .05 .02
(Buchannan on front)
❑ 249 Hardy Nickerson .10 .05
❑ 250 Brad Edwards .05 .02
❑ 251 Jerrol Williams .05 .02
❑ 252 Marvin Washington .05 .02
❑ 253 Tony McGee .05 .02
❑ 254 Jeff George .25 .11
❑ 255 Ron Hall .05 .02
❑ 256 Tim Johnson .05 .02
❑ 257 Willie Roaf .05 .02
❑ 258 Corwin Brown RC .05 .02
❑ 259 Ricardo McDonald .05 .02
❑ 260 Jeff Herrod .05 .02
❑ 261 Demetrius DuBose .05 .02
❑ 262 Ricky Sanders .05 .02
❑ 263 John L. Williams .05 .02
❑ 264 John Lynch .10 .05
❑ 265 Lance Gunn .05 .02
❑ 266 Jessie Hester .05 .02
❑ 267 Mark Wheeler .05 .02
❑ 268 Chip Lohmiller .05 .02
❑ 269 Eric Swann .10 .05
❑ 270 Byron Evans .05 .02
❑ 271 Gary Plummer .05 .02
❑ 272 Roger Duffy RC .05 .02
❑ 273 Irv Smith .05 .02
❑ 274 Todd Collins .05 .02
❑ 275 Robert Blackmon .05 .02
❑ 276 Reggie Roby .05 .02
❑ 277 Russell Copeland .05 .02
❑ 278 Simon Fletcher .05 .02
❑ 279 Ernest Givins .10 .05
❑ 280 Tim Barnett .05 .02
❑ 281 Chris Doleman .05 .02
❑ 282 Jeff Graham .05 .02
❑ 283 Kenneth Davis .05 .02
❑ 284 Vance Johnson .05 .02
❑ 285 Haywood Jeffires .10 .05
❑ 286 Todd McNair .05 .02
❑ 287 Daryl Johnston .10 .05
❑ 288 Ryan McNeil .05 .02
❑ 289 Terrell Buckley .05 .02
❑ 290 Ethan Horton .05 .02
❑ 291 Corey Miller .05 .02
❑ 292 Marc Logan .05 .02
❑ 293 Lincoln Coleman RC .05 .02
❑ 294 Derrick Moore .05 .02
❑ 295 LeRoy Butler .05 .02
❑ 296 Jeff Hostetler .10 .05
❑ 297 Qadry Ismail .25 .11
❑ 298 Andre Hastings .10 .05
❑ 299 Henry Jones .05 .02
❑ 300 John Elway 1.50 .70
❑ 301 Warren Moon .25 .11
❑ 302 Willie Davis .10 .05
❑ 303 Vencie Glenn .05 .02
❑ 304 Kevin Greene .25 .11
❑ 305 Marcus Buckley .05 .02
❑ 306 Tim McDonald .05 .02
❑ 307 Michael Irvin .25 .11
❑ 308 Herman Moore .25 .11
❑ 309 Brett Favre 1.50 .70
❑ 310 Rocket Ismail .10 .05
❑ 311 Jarrod Bunch .05 .02
❑ 312 Don Beebe .05 .02
❑ 313 Steve Atwater .05 .02
❑ 314 Gary Brown .05 .02
❑ 315 Marcus Allen .25 .11
❑ 316 Terry Allen .10 .05
❑ 317 Chad Brown .05 .02
❑ 318 Cornelius Bennett .10 .05
❑ 319 Rod Bernstine .05 .02
❑ 320 Greg Montgomery .05 .02
❑ 321 Kimble Anders .10 .05
❑ 322 Charles Haley .10 .05
❑ 323 Mol Gray .05 .02
❑ 324 Edgar Bennett .25 .11
❑ 325 Eddie Anderson .05 .02
❑ 326 Derek Brown TE .05 .02
❑ 327 Steve Bono .10 .05
❑ 328 Alvin Harper .10 .05
❑ 329 Willie Green .05 .02
❑ 330 Robert Brooks .25 .11
❑ 331 Patrick Bates .05 .02
❑ 332 Anthony Carter .10 .05
❑ 333 Barry Foster .05 .02
❑ 334 Bill Brooks .05 .02
❑ 335 Jason Elam .05 .02
❑ 336 Ray Childress .05 .02
❑ 337 J.J. Birden .05 .02
❑ 338 Cris Carter .40 .18
❑ 339 Deon Figures .05 .02
❑ 340 Carlton Bailey .05 .02
❑ 341 Brent Jones .10 .05
❑ 342 Troy Aikman UER .75 .35
(Stats on back has 60 Int., should be 66)
❑ 343 Rodney Holman .05 .02
❑ 344 Tony Bennett .05 .02
❑ 345 Tim Brown .25 .11
❑ 346 Michael Brooks .05 .02
❑ 347 Martin Harrison .05 .02
❑ 348 Jerry Rice .75 .35
❑ 349 John Copeland .05 .02
❑ 350 Kerry Cash .05 .02
❑ 351 Reggie Cobb .05 .02
❑ 352 Brian Mitchell .05 .02
❑ 353 Derrick Fenner .05 .02
❑ 354 Roosevelt Potts .05 .02
❑ 355 Courtney Hawkins .05 .02
❑ 356 Carl Banks .05 .02
❑ 357 Harold Green .05 .02
❑ 358 Steve Emtman .05 .02
❑ 359 Santana Dotson .10 .05
❑ 360 Reggie Brooks .10 .05
❑ 361 Terry Obee .05 .02
❑ 362 David Klingler .05 .02
❑ 363 Quentin Coryatt .05 .02
❑ 364 Craig Erickson .05 .02
❑ 365 Desmond Howard .10 .05
❑ 366 Carl Pickens .25 .11
❑ 367 Lawrence Dawsey .05 .02
❑ 368 Henry Ellard .10 .05
❑ 369 Shaun Gayle .05 .02
❑ 370 David Lang .05 .02
❑ 371 Anthony Johnson .10 .05
❑ 372 Darnell Walker RC .05 .02
❑ 373 Pepper Johnson .05 .02
❑ 374 Kurt Gouveia .05 .02
❑ 375 Louis Oliver .05 .02
❑ 376 Lincoln Kennedy .05 .02
❑ 377 Anthony Pleasant .05 .02
❑ 378 Irving Fryar .10 .05
❑ 379 Carolina Panthers .25 .11
Expansion Team Card
❑ 380 Jacksonville Jaguars .05 .02
Expansion Team Card
❑ 381 Checklist UER .10 .05
Sterling Sharpe
(Front has 193-288 and back has Sharp; should be Sharpe)
❑ 382 Dan Marino ART .25 .11
Checklist Card
❑ 383 Jerry Rice ART UER .25 .11
Checklist Card
(Front has 289-384)
❑ 384 Joe Montana ART UER .25 .11
Checklist Card
(Front has 1-96)
Joe Montana
❑ P19 Joe Montana Promo 2.00 .90

1995 Collector's Choice

	MINT	NRMT
COMPLETE SET (348)	20.00	9.00

❑ 1 Ki-Jana Carter RC .25 .11
❑ 2 Tony Boselli RC .25 .11
❑ 3 Steve McNair RC 2.50 1.10
❑ 4 Michael Westbrook RC 1.25 .55
❑ 5 Kerry Collins RC 1.25 .55
❑ 6 Kevin Carter RC .25 .11
❑ 7 Mike Mamula RC .10 .05
❑ 8 Joey Galloway RC 2.00 .90
❑ 9 Kyle Brady RC .25 .11
❑ 10 J.J. Stokes RC .25 .11
❑ 11 Derrick Alexander DE RC .05 .02
❑ 12 Warren Sapp RC .50 .23
❑ 13 Mark Fields RC .05 .02
❑ 14 Tyrone Wheatley RC 1.00 .45
❑ 15 Napoleon Kaufman RC 1.25 .55
❑ 16 James O. Stewart RC 1.50 .70
❑ 17 Luther Elliss RC .05 .02
❑ 18 Rashaan Salaam RC .25 .11
❑ 19 Ty Law RC .10 .05
❑ 20 Mark Bruener RC .10 .05
❑ 21 Derrick Brooks RC .25 .11
❑ 22 Christian Fauria RC .05 .02
❑ 23 Ray Zellars RC .10 .05
❑ 24 Todd Collins RC .25 .11
❑ 25 Sherman Williams RC .05 .02
❑ 26 Frank Sanders RC .75 .35
❑ 27 Rodney Thomas RC .25 .11
❑ 28 Rob Johnson RC 1.50 .70
❑ 29 Steve Stenstrom RC .05 .02
❑ 30 James A.Stewart RC .05 .02
❑ 31 Barry Sanders DYK .60 .25
❑ 32 Marshall Faulk DYK .25 .11
❑ 33 Darnay Scott DYK .25 .11
❑ 34 Joe Montana DYK .60 .25
❑ 35 Michael Irvin DYK .10 .05
❑ 36 Jerry Rice DYK .40 .18
❑ 37 Errict Rhett DYK .25 .11
❑ 38 Drew Bledsoe DYK .40 .18
❑ 39 Dan Marino DYK .60 .25
❑ 40 Terance Mathis DYK .05 .02
❑ 41 Natrone Means DYK .25 .11
❑ 42 Tim Brown DYK .10 .05
❑ 43 Steve Young DYK .30 .14
❑ 44 Mel Gray DYK .05 .02
❑ 45 Jerome Bettis DYK .25 .11
❑ 46 Aeneas Williams DYK .05 .02

❑ 47 Charlie Garner DYK .10 .05
❑ 48 Deion Sanders DYK .25 .11
❑ 49 Ken Harvey DYK .05 .02
❑ 50 Emmitt Smith DYK .50 .23
❑ 51 Andre Reed .10 .05
❑ 52 Sean Dawkins .10 .05
❑ 53 Irving Fryar .10 .05
❑ 54 Vincent Brisby .05 .02
❑ 55 Rob Moore .05 .02
❑ 56 Carl Pickens .25 .11
❑ 57 Vinny Testaverde .10 .05
❑ 58 Webster Slaughter .05 .02
❑ 59 Eric Green .05 .02
❑ 60 Anthony Miller .10 .05
❑ 61 Lake Dawson .10 .05
❑ 62 Tim Brown .25 .11
❑ 63 Stan Humphries .10 .05
❑ 64 Rick Mirer .25 .11
❑ 65 Gary Clark .05 .02
❑ 66 Troy Aikman .75 .35
❑ 67 Mike Sherrard .05 .02
❑ 68 Fred Barnett .10 .05
❑ 69 Henry Ellard .10 .05
❑ 70 Terry Allen .10 .05
❑ 71 Jeff Graham .05 .02
❑ 72 Herman Moore .25 .11
❑ 73 Brett Favre 1.50 .70
❑ 74 Trent Dilfer .25 .11
❑ 75 Derek Brown RBK .05 .02
❑ 76 Andre Rison .10 .05
❑ 77 Flipper Anderson .05 .02
❑ 78 Jerry Rice UER .75 .35
(Career totals are all wrong)
❑ 79 Thurman Thomas .25 .11
❑ 80 Marshall Faulk .40 .18
❑ 81 O.J. McDuffie .25 .11
❑ 82 Ben Coates .10 .05
❑ 83 Johnny Mitchell .05 .02
❑ 84 Darnay Scott .25 .11
❑ 85 Derrick Alexander WR .25 .11
❑ 86 Micheal Barrow UER .05 .02
(Name spelled Michael on both sides)
❑ 87 Charles Johnson .10 .05
❑ 88 John Elway 1.50 .70
❑ 89 Willie Davis .10 .05
❑ 90 James Jett .10 .05
❑ 91 Mark Seay .10 .05
❑ 92 Brian Blades .10 .05
❑ 93 Ricky Proehl .05 .02
❑ 94 Charles Haley .10 .05
❑ 95 Chris Calloway .05 .02
❑ 96 Calvin Williams .10 .05
❑ 97 Ethan Horton .05 .02
❑ 98 Cris Carter .25 .11
❑ 99 Curtis Conway .25 .11
❑ 100 Lomas Brown .05 .02
❑ 101 Edgar Bennett .10 .05
❑ 102 Craig Erickson .05 .02
❑ 103 Jim Everett .05 .02
❑ 104 Terance Mathis .10 .05
❑ 105 Wayne Gandy .05 .02
❑ 106 Brent Jones .05 .02
❑ 107 Bruce Smith .25 .11
❑ 108 Roosevelt Potts .05 .02
❑ 109 Dan Marino 1.50 .70
❑ 110 Michael Timpson .05 .02
❑ 111 Boomer Esiason .10 .05
❑ 112 David Klingler .10 .05
❑ 113 Eric Metcalf .10 .05
❑ 114 Lorenzo White .05 .02
❑ 115 Neil O'Donnell .10 .05
❑ 116 Shannon Sharpe .10 .05
❑ 117 Joe Montana 1.50 .70
❑ 118 Jeff Hostetler .10 .05
❑ 119 Ronnie Harmon .05 .02
❑ 120 Chris Warren .10 .05
❑ 121 Randal Hill .05 .02
❑ 122 Alvin Harper .05 .02
❑ 123 Dave Brown .10 .05
❑ 124 Randall Cunningham .25 .11
❑ 125 Heath Shuler .25 .11
❑ 126 Jake Reed .10 .05
❑ 127 Donnell Woolford .05 .02
❑ 128 Scott Mitchell .10 .05
❑ 129 Reggie White .25 .11
❑ 130 Lawrence Dawsey .05 .02
❑ 131 Michael Haynes .10 .05
❑ 132 Bert Emanuel .25 .11
❑ 133 Troy Drayton .05 .02
❑ 134 Merton Hanks .05 .02
❑ 135 Jim Kelly .25 .11
❑ 136 Tony Bennett .05 .02
❑ 137 Terry Kirby .10 .05
❑ 138 Drew Bledsoe .75 .35
❑ 139 Johnny Johnson .05 .02
❑ 140 Dan Wilkinson .10 .05
❑ 141 Leroy Hoard .05 .02
❑ 142 Gary Brown .05 .02
❑ 143 Barry Foster .10 .05
❑ 144 Shane Dronett .05 .02
❑ 145 Marcus Allen .25 .11
❑ 146 Harvey Williams .05 .02
❑ 147 Tony Martin .10 .05
❑ 148 Rod Stephens .05 .02
❑ 149 Ronald Moore .05 .02
❑ 150 Michael Irvin .25 .11
❑ 151 Rodney Hampton .10 .05
❑ 152 Herschel Walker .10 .05
❑ 153 Reggie Brooks .10 .05
❑ 154 Qadry Ismail .10 .05
❑ 155 Chris Zorich .05 .02
❑ 156 Barry Sanders 1.50 .70
❑ 157 Sean Jones .05 .02
❑ 158 Errict Rhett .25 .11
❑ 159 Tyrone Hughes .10 .05
❑ 160 Jeff George .10 .05
❑ 161 Chris Miller .05 .02
❑ 162 Steve Young .60 .25
❑ 163 Cornelius Bennett .10 .05
❑ 164 Trev Alberts .05 .02
❑ 165 J.B. Brown .05 .02
❑ 166 Marion Butts .05 .02
❑ 167 Aaron Glenn .05 .02
❑ 168 James Francis .05 .02
❑ 169 Eric Turner .05 .02
❑ 170 Darryll Lewis .05 .02
❑ 171 John L. Williams .05 .02
❑ 172 Simon Fletcher .05 .02
❑ 173 Neil Smith .10 .05
❑ 174 Chester McGlockton .10 .05
❑ 175 Natrone Means .25 .11
❑ 176 Michael Sinclair .05 .02
❑ 177 Larry Centers .10 .05
❑ 178 Daryl Johnston .10 .05
❑ 179 Dave Meggett .05 .02
❑ 180 Greg Jackson .05 .02
❑ 181 Ken Harvey .05 .02
❑ 182 Warren Moon .10 .05
❑ 183 Steve Walsh .05 .02
❑ 184 Chris Spielman .10 .05
❑ 185 Bryce Paup .25 .11
❑ 186 Courtney Hawkins .05 .02
❑ 187 Willie Roaf .05 .02
❑ 188 Chris Doleman .05 .02
❑ 189 Jerome Bettis .25 .11
❑ 190 Ricky Watters .25 .11
❑ 191 Henry Jones .05 .02
❑ 192 Quentin Coryatt .10 .05
❑ 193 Bryan Cox .05 .02
❑ 194 Kevin Turner .05 .02
❑ 195 Siupeli Malamala .05 .02
❑ 196 Louis Oliver .05 .02
❑ 197 Rob Burnett .05 .02
❑ 198 Cris Dishman .05 .02
❑ 199 Byron Bam Morris .10 .05
❑ 200 Ray Crockett .05 .02
❑ 201 Jon Vaughn .05 .02
❑ 202 Nolan Harrison .05 .02
❑ 203 Leslie O'Neal .10 .05
❑ 204 Sam Adams .05 .02
❑ 205 Eric Swann .10 .05
❑ 206 Jay Novacek .10 .05
❑ 207 Keith Hamilton .05 .02
❑ 208 Charlie Garner .10 .05
❑ 209 Tom Carter .05 .02
❑ 210 Henry Thomas .05 .02
❑ 211 Lewis Tillman .05 .02
❑ 212 Pat Swilling .05 .02
❑ 213 Terrell Buckley .05 .02
❑ 214 Hardy Nickerson .05 .02
❑ 215 Mario Bates .25 .11
❑ 216 D.J. Johnson .05 .02
❑ 217 Robert Young .05 .02
❑ 218 Dana Stubblefield .25 .11
❑ 219 Jeff Burris .05 .02
❑ 220 Floyd Turner .05 .02
❑ 221 Troy Vincent .05 .02
❑ 222 Willie McGinest .10 .05
❑ 223 James Hasty .05 .02
❑ 224 Jeff Blake RC .75 .35
❑ 225 Stevon Moore .05 .02
❑ 226 Ernest Givins .05 .02
❑ 227 Greg Lloyd .10 .05
❑ 228 Steve Atwater .05 .02
❑ 229 Dale Carter .10 .05
❑ 230 Terry McDaniel .05 .02
❑ 231 John Carney .05 .02
❑ 232 Cortez Kennedy .10 .05
❑ 233 Clyde Simmons .05 .02
❑ 234 Emmitt Smith 1.25 .55
❑ 235 Thomas Lewis .10 .05
❑ 236 William Fuller .05 .02
❑ 237 Ricky Ervins .05 .02
❑ 238 John Randle .10 .05
❑ 239 John Thierry .05 .02
❑ 240 Mel Gray .05 .02
❑ 241 George Teague .05 .02
❑ 242 Charles Wilson Bucs .05 .02
(See '95 Coll.Choice Update #U170)
❑ 243 Joe Johnson .05 .02
❑ 244 Chuck Smith .05 .02
❑ 245 Sean Gilbert .10 .05
❑ 246 Bryant Young .10 .05
❑ 247 Bucky Brooks .05 .02
❑ 248 Ray Buchanan .05 .02
❑ 249 Tim Bowens .05 .02
❑ 250 Vincent Brown .05 .02
❑ 251 Marcus Turner .05 .02
❑ 252 Derrick Fenner .05 .02
❑ 253 Antonio Langham .05 .02
❑ 254 Cody Carlson .05 .02
❑ 255 Kevin Greene .10 .05
❑ 256 Leonard Russell .05 .02
❑ 257 Donnell Bennett .10 .05
❑ 258 Rocket Ismail .10 .05
❑ 259 Alfred Pupunu RC .05 .02
❑ 260 Eugene Robinson .05 .02
❑ 261 Seth Joyner .05 .02
❑ 262 Darren Woodson .10 .05
❑ 263 Phillippi Sparks .05 .02
❑ 264 Andy Harmon .05 .02
❑ 265 Brian Mitchell .05 .02
❑ 266 Fuad Reveiz .05 .02
❑ 267 Mark Carrier DB .05 .02
❑ 268 Johnnie Morton .10 .05
❑ 269 LeShon Johnson .10 .05
❑ 270 Eric Curry .05 .02
❑ 271 Quinn Early .10 .05
❑ 272 Elbert Shelley .05 .02
❑ 273 Roman Phifer .05 .02
❑ 274 Ken Norton Jr. .10 .05
❑ 275 Steve Tasker .10 .05
❑ 276 Jim Harbaugh .10 .05
❑ 277 Aubrey Beavers .05 .02
❑ 278 Chris Slade .10 .05
❑ 279 Mo Lewis .05 .02
❑ 280 Alfred Williams .05 .02
❑ 281 Michael Dean Perry UER .05 .02
(Misspelled Micheal)
❑ 282 Marcus Robertson .05 .02
❑ 283 Rod Woodson .10 .05
❑ 284 Glyn Milburn .05 .02
❑ 285 Greg Hill .10 .05
❑ 286 Rob Fredrickson .05 .02
❑ 287 Junior Seau .25 .11
❑ 288 Rick Tuten .05 .02
❑ 289 Aeneas Williams .05 .02
❑ 290 Darrin Smith .05 .02
❑ 291 John Booty .05 .02
❑ 292 Eric Allen .05 .02
❑ 293 Reggie Roby .05 .02
❑ 294 David Palmer .10 .05
❑ 295 Trace Armstrong .05 .02
❑ 296 Dave Krieg UER .05 .02
(Misspelled Kreig on front)
❑ 297 Robert Brooks .25 .11
❑ 298 Brad Culpepper .05 .02

		MINT	NRMT
❑ 299	Wayne Martin	.05	.02
❑ 300	Craig Heyward	.10	.05
❑ 301	Isaac Bruce	.40	.18
❑ 302	Deion Sanders	.40	.18
❑ 303	Matt Darby	.05	.02
❑ 304	Kirk Lowdermilk	.05	.02
❑ 305	Bernie Parmalee	.10	.05
❑ 306	Leroy Thompson	.05	.02
❑ 307	Ronnie Lott	.10	.05
❑ 308	Steve Tovar	.05	.02
❑ 309	Michael Jackson	.10	.05
❑ 310	Al Smith	.05	.02
❑ 311	Chad Brown	.10	.05
❑ 312	Elijah Alexander	.05	.02
❑ 313	Kimble Anders	.10	.05
❑ 314	Anthony Smith	.05	.02
❑ 315	Andre Coleman	.05	.02
❑ 316	Terry Wooden	.05	.02
❑ 317	Garrison Hearst	.25	.11
❑ 318	Russell Maryland	.05	.02
❑ 319	Michael Brooks	.05	.02
❑ 320	Bernard Williams	.05	.02
❑ 321	Andre Collins	.05	.02
❑ 322	Dewayne Washington	.10	.05
❑ 323	Raymont Harris	.05	.02
❑ 324	Brett Perriman	.10	.05
❑ 325	LeRoy Butler	.05	.02
❑ 326	Santana Dotson	.05	.02
❑ 327	Irv Smith	.05	.02
❑ 328	Ron George	.05	.02
❑ 329	Marquez Pope	.05	.02
❑ 330	William Floyd	.25	.11
❑ 331	Mickey Washington	.05	.02
❑ 332	Keith Goganious	.05	.02
❑ 333	Derek Brown TE	.05	.02
❑ 334	Steve Beuerlein UER (Name spelled Beuerlien on front)	.05	.02
❑ 335	Reggie Cobb	.05	.02
❑ 336	Jeff Lageman	.05	.02
❑ 337	Kelvin Martin	.05	.02
❑ 338	Darren Carrington	.05	.02
❑ 339	Mark Carrier WR	.10	.05
❑ 340	Willie Green	.05	.02
❑ 341	Frank Reich	.05	.02
❑ 342	Don Beebe	.05	.02
❑ 343	Lamar Lathon	.05	.02
❑ 344	Tim McKyer	.05	.02
❑ 345	Pete Metzelaars	.05	.02
❑ 346	Vernon Turner	.05	.02
❑ 347	Dan Marino Checklist 1-174	.25	.11
❑ 348	Joe Montana Checklist 175-348	.25	.11
❑ PC1	Joe Montana Promo (Crash the Game promo)	1.00	.45
❑ P1	Joe Montana Promo	1.00	.45

1995 Collector's Choice Update

		MINT	NRMT
COMPLETE SET (225)		18.00	8.00
❑ U1	Roell Preston RC	.05	.02
❑ U2	Lorenzo Styles RC	.05	.02
❑ U3	Todd Collins	.25	.11
❑ U4	Darick Holmes RC	.10	.05
❑ U5	Justin Armour RC	.05	.02
❑ U6	Tony Cline RC	.05	.02
❑ U7	Tyrone Poole	.10	.05
❑ U8	Kerry Collins	.75	.35
❑ U9	Sean Harris	.05	.02
❑ U10	Steve Stenstrom	.05	.02
❑ U11	Rashaan Salaam	.25	.11
❑ U12	Ki-Jana Carter	.25	.11
❑ U13	Craig Powell	.05	.02
❑ U14	Eric Zeier RC	.25	.11
❑ U15	Ernest Hunter	.05	.02
❑ U16	Sherman Williams	.05	.02
❑ U17	Terrell Davis RC	10.00	4.50
❑ U18	Luther Elliss	.05	.02
❑ U19	Craig Newsome	.05	.02
❑ U20	Steve McNair	1.25	.55
❑ U21	Chris Sanders RC	.25	.11
❑ U22	Rodney Thomas	.25	.11
❑ U23	Ellis Johnson RC	.05	.02
❑ U24	Ken Dilger RC	.10	.05
❑ U25	Zack Crockett RC	.05	.02
❑ U26	Tony Boselli	.25	.11
❑ U27	Rob Johnson	1.00	.45
❑ U28	James O. Stewart	1.00	.45
❑ U29	Tamarick Vanover RC	.25	.11
❑ U30	Napoleon Kaufman	.75	.35
❑ U31	Kevin Carter	.25	.11
❑ U32	Steve McLaughlin	.05	.02
❑ U33	Lovell Pinkney	.05	.02
❑ U34	Pete Mitchell RC	.25	.11
❑ U35	James A.Stewart	.05	.02
❑ U36	Chad May RC	.05	.02
❑ U37	Derrick Alexander DE	.05	.02
❑ U38	Curtis Martin RC	2.50	1.10
❑ U39	Will Moore RC	.05	.02
❑ U40	Ty Law	.10	.05
❑ U41	Ray Zellars	.10	.05
❑ U42	Mark Fields	.05	.02
❑ U43	Tyrone Wheatley	.25	.11
❑ U44	Kyle Brady	.25	.11
❑ U45	Mike Mamula	.10	.05
❑ U46	Bobby Taylor RC	.10	.05
❑ U47	Chris T.Jones RC	.25	.11
❑ U48	Frank Sanders	.60	.25
❑ U49	Stoney Case RC	.25	.11
❑ U50	Mark Bruener	.10	.05
❑ U51	Kordell Stewart RC	2.00	.90
❑ U52	Jimmy Oliver	.05	.02
❑ U53	Terrance Shaw RC	.05	.02
❑ U54	Terrell Fletcher RC	.05	.02
❑ U55	J.J. Stokes	.25	.11
❑ U56	Christian Fauria	.05	.02
❑ U57	Joey Galloway	1.00	.45
❑ U58	Warren Sapp	.10	.05
❑ U59	Derrick Brooks	.10	.05
❑ U60	Michael Westbrook	.75	.35
❑ U61	Emmitt Smith K	.75	.35
❑ U62	Barry Sanders K	1.00	.45
❑ U63	Marshall Faulk K	.30	.14
❑ U64	Troy Aikman K	.50	.23
❑ U65	Steve Young K	.40	.18
❑ U66	Junior Seau K	.25	.11
❑ U67	John Elway K	1.00	.45
❑ U68	Dan Marino K	1.00	.45
❑ U69	Drew Bledsoe K	.50	.23
❑ U70	Errict Rhett K	.25	.11
❑ U71	Natrone Means K	.25	.11
❑ U72	Deion Sanders K	.30	.14
❑ U73	Brett Favre K	1.00	.45
❑ U74	Cris Carter K	.25	.11
❑ U75	Ben Coates K	.10	.05
❑ U76	Jerome Bettis K	.25	.11
❑ U77	Reggie White K	.25	.11
❑ U78	Stan Humphries K	.05	.02
❑ U79	Michael Westbrook K	.25	.11
❑ U80	Steve McNair K	.75	.35
❑ U81	Kevin Greene K	.10	.05
❑ U82	Joey Galloway K	.50	.23
❑ U83	Napoleon Kaufman K	.50	.23
❑ U84	Jerry Rice K	.50	.23
❑ U85	Andre Rison K	.10	.05
❑ U86	Eric Metcalf K	.10	.05
❑ U87	Kerry Collins K	.25	.11
❑ U88	Chris Warren K	.10	.05
❑ U89	Irving Fryar K	.10	.05
❑ U90	Michael Irvin K	.25	.11
❑ U91	Don Beebe	.05	.02
❑ U92	Pete Metzelaars	.05	.02
❑ U93	Mark Carrier	.05	.02
❑ U94	Frank Reich	.05	.02
❑ U95	Randy Baldwin	.05	.02
❑ U96	Bob Christian	.05	.02
❑ U97	John Kasay	.05	.02
❑ U98	Lamar Lathon	.05	.02
❑ U99	Sam Mills	.10	.05
❑ U100	Carlton Bailey	.05	.02
❑ U101	Darion Conner	.05	.02
❑ U102	Blake Brockermeyer	.05	.02
❑ U103	Gerald Williamss	.05	.02
❑ U104	Willie Green	.05	.02
❑ U105	Derrick Moore	.05	.02
❑ U106	Desmond Howard	.10	.05
❑ U107	Harry Colon	.05	.02
❑ U108	Steve Beuerlein	.05	.02
❑ U109	Reggie Cobb	.05	.02
❑ U110	Jeff Lageman	.05	.02
❑ U111	Mark Brunell UER (Name spelled Brunnell on front)	1.25	.55
❑ U112	Darren Carrington	.05	.02
❑ U113	Brian DeMarco	.10	.05
❑ U114	Ernest Givins	.05	.02
❑ U115	Le'shai Maston	.05	.02
❑ U116	Willie Jackson	.10	.05
❑ U117	Keith Goganious	.05	.02
❑ U118	Kelvin Pritchett	.05	.02
❑ U119	Ryan Christopherson	.05	.02
❑ U120	Bryan Schwartz	.05	.02
❑ U121	Dave Krieg UER (Name spelled Kreig on fron)	.05	.02
❑ U122	Darryl Talley	.05	.02
❑ U123	Bryce Paup	.25	.11
❑ U124	Anthony Johnson	.10	.05
❑ U125	Eric Bieniemy	.05	.02
❑ U126	Andre Rison	.10	.05
❑ U127	Rodney Peete	.05	.02
❑ U128	Aaron Craver	.05	.02
❑ U129	Henry Thomas	.05	.02
❑ U130	Antonio Freeman RC	2.50	1.10
❑ U131	Chris Chandler	.10	.05
❑ U132	Craig Erickson	.05	.02
❑ U133	Roell Preston	.05	.02
❑ U134	Brian Washington	.05	.02
❑ U135	Eric Green	.05	.02
❑ U136	Broderick Thomas	.05	.02
❑ U137	Dave Meggett	.05	.02
❑ U138	Eric Allen	.05	.02
❑ U139	Herschel Walker	.10	.05
❑ U140	Dexter Carter	.05	.02
❑ U141	Kerry Cash	.05	.02
❑ U142	Kelvin Martin	.05	.02
❑ U143	Erric Pegram	.10	.05
❑ U144	Bo Orlando	.05	.02
❑ U145	Ricky Ervins	.05	.02
❑ U146	John Friesz	.10	.05
❑ U147	Alexander Wright	.05	.02
❑ U148	Alvin Harper	.05	.02
❑ U149	Gus Frerotte	.25	.11
❑ U150	Duval Love	.05	.02
❑ U151	Eric Metcalf	.10	.05
❑ U152	Ruben Brown RC	.05	.02
❑ U153	Marty Carter	.05	.02
❑ U154	James Joseph	.05	.02
❑ U155	Hugh Douglas RC	.25	.11
❑ U156	Wade Wilson	.05	.02
❑ U157	Britt Hager	.05	.02
❑ U158	Mark Schlereth	.05	.02
❑ U159	Cory Schlesinger UER (Name spelled Corey)	.05	.02
❑ U160	Mark Ingram	.05	.02
❑ U161	Mark Stepnoski	.05	.02
❑ U162	Flipper Anderson	.05	.02
❑ U163	Donta Jones	.05	.02
❑ U164	James Hasty	.05	.02
❑ U165	Gary Clark	.05	.02
❑ U166	David Sloan RC	.10	.05
❑ U167	Jeff Dellenbach	.05	.02
❑ U168	Rufus Porter	.05	.02
❑ U169	Mike Croel	.05	.02
❑ U170	Charles Wilson UER Card number 242 (See '95 Coll.Choice #242)	.05	.02
❑ U171	Pat Swilling	.05	.02
❑ U172	Kurt Gouveia	.05	.02
❑ U173	Norm Johnson	.05	.02

❑ U174 Shaun Gayle .05 .02
❑ U175 Marquez Pope .05 .02
❑ U176 Tyronne Stowe .05 .02
❑ U177 Anthony Parker .05 .02
❑ U178 Kenneth Gant .05 .02
❑ U179 James Washington .05 .02
❑ U180 Rob Moore .05 .02
❑ U181 Alundis Brice .05 .02
❑ U182 Lamont Warren .05 .02
❑ U183 Michael Timpson .05 .02
❑ U184 Lorenzo White .05 .02
❑ U185 Charlie Williams RC .05 .02
❑ U186 Ed McCaffrey .10 .05
❑ U187 James Jones .05 .02
❑ U188 Derrick Fenner .05 .02
❑ U189 Mel Gray .05 .02
❑ U190 James Williams LB .05 .02
❑ U191 Jeff Criswell .05 .02
❑ U192 Randal Hill .05 .02
❑ U193 Terry Allen .10 .05
❑ U194 Joel Smeenge .05 .02
❑ U195 Ricky Watters .25 .11
❑ U196 Don Sasa .05 .02
❑ U197 Steve Bono .10 .05
❑ U198 Steve Broussard .05 .02
❑ U199 Carlos Jenkins .05 .02
❑ U200 Reggie Roby .05 .02
❑ U201 Stanley Richard .05 .02
❑ U202 Vince Workman .05 .02
❑ U203 Eric Guliford .05 .02
❑ U204 Lionel Washington .05 .02
❑ U205 Brian Williams LB .05 .02
❑ U206 Ronnie Lott .10 .05
❑ U207 Corey Harris .05 .02
❑ U208 Harlon Barnett .05 .02
❑ U209 Bubby Brister .05 .02
❑ U210 Darren Bennett .10 .05
❑ U211 Winston Moss .05 .02
❑ U212 Leonard Russell .05 .02
❑ U213 Ron Davis .05 .02
❑ U214 Curtis Whitley .05 .02
❑ U215 Webster Slaughter .05 .02
❑ U216 Korey Stringer .05 .02
❑ U217 Don Davey .05 .02
❑ U218 Mark Rypien .05 .02
❑ U219 Chad Cota .05 .02
❑ U220 Tim Ruddy .05 .02
❑ U221 Corey Fuller .05 .02
❑ U222 Mike Dumas .05 .02
❑ U223 Eddie Murray .05 .02
❑ U224 Dan Marino CL .50 .23
U1-U114
❑ U225 Dan Marino CL UER .50 .23
U115-U225
front reads U115-U228
❑ P1 Michael Westbrook Promo .75 .35
Numbered CUS1
❑ P2 Dan Marino Promo 1.00 .45
Stick-um card, blankbacked
❑ P3 Dan Marino Promo .75 .35
Michael Westbrook
Tim Brown
Stick-um card, blankbacked

1996 Collector's Choice

	MINT	NRMT
COMPLETE SET (375)	25.00	11.00
COMP.FACT.SET (395)	30.00	13.50

❑ 1 Keyshawn Johnson RC 1.50 .70
❑ 2 Kevin Hardy RC .30 .14
❑ 3 Simeon Rice RC .30 .14
❑ 4 Jonathan Ogden RC .10 .05
❑ 5 Cedric Jones RC .10 .05
❑ 6 Lawrence Phillips RC .30 .14
❑ 7 Tim Biakabutuka RC .60 .25
❑ 8 Terry Glenn RC 1.00 .45
❑ 9 Rickey Dudley RC .30 .14
❑ 10 Regan Upshaw RC .10 .05
❑ 11 Walt Harris RC .10 .05
❑ 12 Eddie George RC 2.50 1.10
❑ 13 John Mobley RC .10 .05
❑ 14 Duane Clemons RC .10 .05
❑ 15 Marvin Harrison RC 2.00 .90
❑ 16 Daryl Gardener RC .10 .05
❑ 17 Pete Kendall RC .10 .05
❑ 18 Marcus Jones RC .10 .05
❑ 19 Eric Moulds RC 1.50 .70
❑ 20 Ray Lewis RC 2.00 .90
❑ 21 Alex Van Dyke RC .20 .09
❑ 22 Leeland McElroy RC .30 .14
❑ 23 Mike Alstott RC 1.25 .55
❑ 24 Lawyer Milloy RC .10 .05
❑ 25 Marco Battaglia RC .10 .05
❑ 26 Je'rod Cherry RC .10 .05
❑ 27 Israel Ifeanyi RC .10 .05
❑ 28 Bobby Engram RC .30 .14
❑ 29 Jason Dunn RC .20 .09
❑ 30 Derrick Mayes RC .60 .25
❑ 31 Stepfret Williams RC .20 .09
❑ 32 Bobby Hoying RC .30 .14
❑ 33 Karim Abdul-Jabbar RC .50 .23
❑ 34 Danny Kanell RC .30 .14
❑ 35 Chris Darkins RC .10 .05
❑ 36 Charlie Jones RC .30 .14
❑ 37 Tedy Bruschi RC .10 .05
❑ 38 Stanley Pritchett RC .20 .09
❑ 39 Donnie Edwards RC .10 .05
❑ 40 Jeff Lewis RC .40 .18
❑ 41 Stephen Davis RC 2.50 1.10
❑ 42 Winslow Oliver RC .10 .05
❑ 43 Mercury Hayes RC .10 .05
❑ 44 Jon Runyan RC .10 .05
❑ 45 Steve Taneyhill RC .10 .05
❑ 46 Eric Metcalf SR .10 .05
❑ 47 Bryce Paup SR .10 .05
❑ 48 Kerry Collins SR .30 .14
❑ 49 Rashaan Salaam SR .20 .09
❑ 50 Carl Pickens SR .30 .14
❑ 51 Emmitt Smith SR .50 .23
❑ 52 Michael Irvin SR .20 .09
❑ 53 Troy Aikman SR .40 .18
❑ 54 Terrell Davis SR 1.00 .45
❑ 55 John Elway SR .75 .35
❑ 56 Herman Moore SR .30 .14
❑ 57 Brett Favre SR .75 .35
❑ 58 Rodney Thomas SR .10 .05
❑ 59 Jim Harbaugh SR .20 .09
❑ 60 Mark Brunell SR .40 .18
❑ 61 Marcus Allen SR .30 .14
❑ 62 Tamarick Vanover SR .20 .09
❑ 63 Steve Bono SR .10 .05
❑ 64 Dan Marino SR .75 .35
❑ 65 Warren Moon SR .10 .05
❑ 66 Curtis Martin SR .30 .14
❑ 67 Tyrone Hughes SR .10 .05
❑ 68 Rodney Hampton SR .10 .05
❑ 69 Hugh Douglas SR .10 .05
❑ 70 Tim Brown SR .20 .09
❑ 71 Ricky Watters SR .20 .09
❑ 72 Kordell Stewart SR .30 .14
❑ 73 Andre Coleman SR .10 .05
❑ 74 Jerry Rice SR .40 .18
❑ 75 Joey Galloway SR .30 .14
❑ 76 Isaac Bruce SR .30 .14
❑ 77 Errict Rhett SR .20 .09
❑ 78 Michael Westbrook SR .30 .14
❑ 79 Brian Mitchell SR .10 .05
❑ 80 Aeneas Williams .10 .05
❑ 81 Andre Reed .20 .09
❑ 82 Brett Maxie .10 .05
❑ 83 Jim Flanigan .10 .05
❑ 84 Jeff Blake .30 .14
❑ 85 Mike Frederick .10 .05
❑ 86 Michael Irvin .30 .14
❑ 87 Aaron Craver .10 .05
❑ 88 Barry Sanders 1.50 .70
❑ 89 Travis Jervey RC .30 .14
❑ 90 Chris Sanders .20 .09
❑ 91 Marshall Faulk .30 .14
❑ 92 Bryan Schwartz .10 .05
❑ 93 Tamarick Vanover .20 .09
❑ 94 Troy Vincent .10 .05
❑ 95 Robert Smith .20 .09
❑ 96 Drew Bledsoe .75 .35
❑ 97 Quinn Early .10 .05
❑ 98 Wayne Chrebet .40 .18
❑ 99 Tim Brown .30 .14
❑ 100 Charlie Garner .10 .05
❑ 101 Yancey Thigpen .20 .09
❑ 102 Isaac Bruce .30 .14
❑ 103 Natrone Means .30 .14
❑ 104 Jerry Rice .75 .35
❑ 105 Chris Warren .20 .09
❑ 106 Errict Rhett .20 .09
❑ 107 Heath Shuler .20 .09
❑ 108 Eric Swann .10 .05
❑ 109 Jeff George .20 .09
❑ 110 Steve Tasker .10 .05
❑ 111 Sam Mills .10 .05
❑ 112 Jeff Graham .10 .05
❑ 113 Carl Pickens .30 .14
❑ 114 Vinny Testaverde .20 .09
❑ 115 Emmitt Smith 1.25 .55
❑ 116 John Elway 1.50 .70
❑ 117 Henry Thomas .10 .05
❑ 118 LeRoy Butler .10 .05
❑ 119 Blaine Bishop .10 .05
❑ 120 Floyd Turner .10 .05
❑ 121 Jeff Lageman .10 .05
❑ 122 Kimble Anders .20 .09
❑ 123 Bryan Cox .10 .05
❑ 124 Qadry Ismail .10 .05
❑ 125 Ted Johnson RC .10 .05
❑ 126 Wesley Walls .20 .09
❑ 127 Rodney Hampton .20 .09
❑ 128 Adrian Murrell .30 .14
❑ 129 Daryl Hobbs RC .10 .05
❑ 130 Ricky Watters .20 .09
❑ 131 Carnell Lake .10 .05
❑ 132 Toby Wright .10 .05
❑ 133 Darren Bennett .10 .05
❑ 134 J.J. Stokes .30 .14
❑ 135 Eugene Robinson .10 .05
❑ 136 Eric Curry .10 .05
❑ 137 Tom Carter .10 .05
❑ 138 Dave Krieg .10 .05
❑ 139 Eric Metcalf .10 .05
❑ 140 Bill Brooks .10 .05
❑ 141 Pete Metzelaars .10 .05
❑ 142 Kevin Butler .10 .05
❑ 143 John Copeland .10 .05
❑ 144 Keenan McCardell .30 .14
❑ 145 Larry Brown .10 .05
❑ 146 Jason Elam .10 .05
❑ 147 Willie Clay .10 .05
❑ 148 Robert Brooks .30 .14
❑ 149 Chris Chandler .20 .09
❑ 150 Quentin Coryatt .10 .05
❑ 151 Pete Mitchell .20 .09
❑ 152 Martin Bayless .10 .05
❑ 153 Pete Stoyanovich .10 .05
❑ 154 Cris Carter .30 .14
❑ 155 Jimmy Hitchcock RC .10 .05
❑ 156 Mario Bates .20 .09
❑ 157 Mike Sherrard .10 .05
❑ 158 Boomer Esiason .20 .09
❑ 159 Chester McGlockton .10 .05
❑ 160 Bobby Taylor .10 .05
❑ 161 Kordell Stewart .40 .18
❑ 162 Kevin Carter .10 .05
❑ 163 Junior Seau .20 .09
❑ 164 Derek Loville .10 .05
❑ 165 Brian Blades .10 .05
❑ 166 Jackie Harris .10 .05
❑ 167 Michael Westbrook .30 .14
❑ 168 Rob Moore .20 .09
❑ 169 Jessie Tuggle .10 .05
❑ 170 Darick Holmes .10 .05
❑ 171 Tim McKyer .10 .05

Card	Player	MINT	NRMT
❑ 172	Erik Kramer	.10	.05
❑ 173	Harold Green	.10	.05
❑ 174	Stevon Moore	.10	.05
❑ 175	Deion Sanders	.40	.18
❑ 176	Anthony Miller	.20	.09
❑ 177	Herman Moore	.30	.14
❑ 178	Brett Favre	1.50	.70
❑ 179	Rodney Thomas	.10	.05
❑ 180	Ken Dilger	.20	.09
❑ 181	Mark Brunell	.75	.35
❑ 182	Marcus Allen	.30	.14
❑ 183	Dan Marino	1.50	.70
❑ 184	John Randle	.20	.09
❑ 185	Ben Coates	.20	.09
❑ 186	Tyrone Hughes	.10	.05
❑ 187	Dave Brown	.10	.05
❑ 188	Johnny Mitchell	.10	.05
❑ 189	Harvey Williams	.10	.05
❑ 190	Andy Harmon	.10	.05
❑ 191	Kevin Greene	.20	.09
❑ 192	D'Marco Farr	.10	.05
❑ 193	Andre Coleman	.10	.05
❑ 194	Bryant Young	.20	.09
❑ 195	Rick Mirer	.20	.09
❑ 196	Horace Copeland	.10	.05
❑ 197	Leslie Shepherd	.10	.05
❑ 198	Jamir Miller	.10	.05
❑ 199	Bert Emanuel	.20	.09
❑ 200	Steve Christie	.10	.05
❑ 201	Kerry Collins	.30	.14
❑ 202	Rashaan Salaam	.30	.14
❑ 203	Steve Tovar	.10	.05
❑ 204	Michael Jackson	.20	.09
❑ 205	Kevin Williams	.10	.05
❑ 206	Glyn Milburn	.10	.05
❑ 207	Johnnie Morton	.20	.09
❑ 208	Antonio Freeman	.50	.23
❑ 209	Cris Dishman	.10	.05
❑ 210	Ellis Johnson	.10	.05
❑ 211	Cedric Tillman	.10	.05
❑ 212	Steve Bono	.10	.05
❑ 213	Eric Green	.10	.05
❑ 214	David Palmer	.10	.05
❑ 215	Vincent Brisby	.10	.05
❑ 216	Michael Haynes	.10	.05
❑ 217	Chris Calloway	.10	.05
❑ 218	Kyle Brady	.10	.05
❑ 219	Terry McDaniel	.10	.05
❑ 220	Calvin Williams	.10	.05
❑ 221	Greg Lloyd	.20	.09
❑ 222	Jerome Bettis	.30	.14
❑ 223	Stan Humphries	.20	.09
❑ 224	Lee Woodall	.10	.05
❑ 225	Robert Blackmon	.10	.05
❑ 226	Warren Sapp	.10	.05
❑ 227	Brian Mitchell	.10	.05
❑ 228	Garrison Hearst	.20	.09
❑ 229	Terance Mathis	.10	.05
❑ 230	Bryce Paup	.10	.05
❑ 231	Derrick Moore	.10	.05
❑ 232	Curtis Conway	.30	.14
❑ 233	Darnay Scott	.20	.09
❑ 234	Andre Rison	.20	.09
❑ 235	Jay Novacek	.10	.05
❑ 236	Terrell Davis	2.00	.90
❑ 237	David Sloan	.10	.05
❑ 238	Reggie White	.30	.14
❑ 239	Todd McNair	.10	.05
❑ 240	Ray Buchanan	.10	.05
❑ 241	Steve Beuerlein	.10	.05
❑ 242	Dan Saleaumua	.10	.05
❑ 243	Bernie Parmalee	.10	.05
❑ 244	Warren Moon	.20	.09
❑ 245	Ty Law	.10	.05
❑ 246	Torrance Small	.10	.05
❑ 247	Phillippi Sparks	.10	.05
❑ 248	Mo Lewis	.10	.05
❑ 249	Jeff Hostetler	.10	.05
❑ 250	Rodney Peete	.10	.05
❑ 251	Byron Bam Morris	.20	.09
❑ 252	Chris Miller	.10	.05
❑ 253	Tony Martin	.20	.09
❑ 254	Eric Davis	.10	.05
❑ 255	Joey Galloway	.40	.18
❑ 256	Derrick Brooks	.10	.05
❑ 257	Ken Harvey	.10	.05
❑ 258	Frank Sanders	.20	.09
❑ 259	Morten Andersen	.10	.05
❑ 260	Marlon Kerner	.10	.05
❑ 261	Mark Carrier WR	.10	.05
❑ 262	Mark Carrier DB	.10	.05
❑ 263	Tony McGee	.10	.05
❑ 264	Eric Zeier	.10	.05
❑ 265	Darren Woodson	.20	.09
❑ 266	Shannon Sharpe	.20	.09
❑ 267	Brett Perriman	.10	.05
❑ 268	Edgar Bennett	.20	.09
❑ 269	Darryll Lewis	.10	.05
❑ 270	Jim Harbaugh	.20	.09
❑ 271	Desmond Howard	.20	.09
❑ 272	Derrick Thomas	.20	.09
❑ 273	Irving Fryar	.20	.09
❑ 274	Jake Reed	.20	.09
❑ 275	Curtis Martin	.50	.23
❑ 276	Eric Allen	.10	.05
❑ 277	Thomas Lewis	.10	.05
❑ 278	Hugh Douglas	.20	.09
❑ 279	Pat Swilling	.10	.05
❑ 280	William Thomas	.10	.05
❑ 281	Norm Johnson	.10	.05
❑ 282	Roman Phifer	.10	.05
❑ 283	Chris Mims	.10	.05
❑ 284	Steve Young	.60	.25
❑ 285	Cortez Kennedy	.10	.05
❑ 286	Trent Dilfer	.30	.14
❑ 287	Terry Allen	.20	.09
❑ 288	Clyde Simmons	.10	.05
❑ 289	Craig Heyward	.10	.05
❑ 290	Jim Kelly	.30	.14
❑ 291	Tyrone Poole	.10	.05
❑ 292	Chris Zorich	.10	.05
❑ 293	Dan Wilkinson	.10	.05
❑ 294	Antonio Langham	.10	.05
❑ 295	Troy Aikman	.75	.35
❑ 296	Steve Atwater	.10	.05
❑ 297	Scott Mitchell	.20	.09
❑ 298	Mark Chmura	.20	.09
❑ 299	Steve McNair	.50	.23
❑ 300	Tony Bennett	.10	.05
❑ 301	Willie Jackson	.10	.05
❑ 302	Neil Smith	.10	.05
❑ 303	Terry Kirby	.20	.09
❑ 304	Orlando Thomas	.10	.05
❑ 305	Willie McGinest	.10	.05
❑ 306	Wayne Martin	.10	.05
❑ 307	Michael Brooks	.10	.05
❑ 308	Marvin Washington	.10	.05
❑ 309	Nolan Harrison	.10	.05
❑ 310	William Fuller	.10	.05
❑ 311	Willie Williams	.10	.05
❑ 312	Troy Drayton	.10	.05
❑ 313	Shawn Lee	.10	.05
❑ 314	Ken Norton	.10	.05
❑ 315	Terry Wooden	.10	.05
❑ 316	Hardy Nickerson	.10	.05
❑ 317	Gus Frerotte	.30	.14
❑ 318	Oscar McBride	.10	.05
❑ 319	Merton Hanks	.10	.05
❑ 320	Justin Armour	.10	.05
❑ 321	Willie Green	.10	.05
❑ 322	Roger Jones RC	.10	.05
❑ 323	Leroy Hoard	.10	.05
❑ 324	Chris Boniol	.10	.05
❑ 325	Jason Hanson	.10	.05
❑ 326	Sean Jones	.10	.05
❑ 327	Roosevelt Potts	.10	.05
❑ 328	Greg Hill	.20	.09
❑ 329	O.J. McDuffie	.20	.09
❑ 330	Amp Lee	.10	.05
❑ 331	Chris Slade	.10	.05
❑ 332	Jim Everett	.10	.05
❑ 333	Tyrone Wheatley	.20	.09
❑ 334	Charles Wilson	.10	.05
❑ 335	Napoleon Kaufman	.30	.14
❑ 336	Fred Barnett	.10	.05
❑ 337	Neil O'Donnell	.20	.09
❑ 338	Sean Gilbert	.10	.05
❑ 339	Aaron Hayden RC	.10	.05
❑ 340	Brent Jones	.10	.05
❑ 341	Christian Fauria	.10	.05
❑ 342	Alvin Harper	.10	.05
❑ 343	Henry Ellard	.10	.05
❑ 344	Willie Davis	.10	.05
❑ 345	Charles Haley	.20	.09
❑ 346	Chris Jacke	.10	.05
❑ 347	Allen Aldridge	.10	.05
❑ 348	Jeff Herrod	.10	.05
❑ 349	Rocket Ismail	.10	.05
❑ 350	Leslie O'Neal	.10	.05
❑ 351	Marquez Pope	.10	.05
❑ 352	Brock Marion	.10	.05
❑ 353	Ernie Mills	.10	.05
❑ 354	Larry Centers	.20	.09
❑ 355	Chris Doleman	.10	.05
❑ 356	Bruce Smith	.20	.09
❑ 357	John Kasay	.10	.05
❑ 358	Donnell Woolford	.10	.05
❑ 359	David Dunn	.10	.05
❑ 360	Eric Turner	.10	.05
❑ 361	Sherman Williams	.10	.05
❑ 362	Chris Spielman	.10	.05
❑ 363	Craig Newsome	.10	.05
❑ 364	Sean Dawkins	.10	.05
❑ 365	James O. Stewart	.20	.09
❑ 366	Dale Carter	.10	.05
❑ 367	Marco Coleman	.10	.05
❑ 368	Dave Meggett	.10	.05
❑ 369	Irv Smith	.10	.05
❑ 370	Mike Mamula	.10	.05
❑ 371	Erric Pegram	.10	.05
❑ 372	Dana Stubblefield	.20	.09
❑ 373	Terrance Shaw	.10	.05
❑ 374	Jerry Rice CL	.30	.14
❑ 375	Dan Marino CL	.40	.18
❑ P1	Jerry Rice Promo Base brand card #801	1.00	.45
❑ P2	Dan Marino Promo Crash the Game April 1	1.00	.45

1996 Collector's Choice Update

	MINT	NRMT
COMPLETE SET (200)	15.00	6.75

Card	Player	MINT	NRMT
❑ U1	Zach Thomas RC	.60	.25
❑ U2	Simeon Rice	.20	.09
❑ U3	Jonathan Ogden	.10	.05
❑ U4	Eric Moulds	.30	.14
❑ U5	Tim Biakabutuka	.30	.14
❑ U6	Walt Harris	.10	.05
❑ U7	Willie Anderson	.10	.05
❑ U8	Ricky Whittle	.10	.05
❑ U9	John Mobley	.10	.05
❑ U10	Reggie Brown	.10	.05
❑ U11	John Michels	.10	.05
❑ U12	Eddie George	1.50	.70
❑ U13	Marvin Harrison	1.25	.55
❑ U14	Kevin Hardy	.20	.09
❑ U15	Kavika Pittman	.10	.05
❑ U16	Daryl Gardener	.10	.05
❑ U17	Duane Clemons	.10	.05
❑ U18	Terry Glenn	.60	.25
❑ U19	Alex Molden RC	.10	.05
❑ U20	Cedric Jones	.10	.05
❑ U21	Keyshawn Johnson	.75	.35
❑ U22	Rickey Dudley	.30	.14
❑ U23	Jason Dunn	.10	.05
❑ U24	Jamain Stephens	.10	.05
❑ U25	Lawrence Phillips	.30	.14

U26 Bryan Still RC	.30	.14
U27 Israel Ifeanyi	.10	.05
U28 Pete Kendall	.10	.05
U29 Regan Upshaw	.10	.05
U30 Andre Johnson	.10	.05
U31 Leeland McElroy	.30	.14
U32 Ray Lewis	1.00	.45
U33 Sean Moran	.10	.05
U34 Muhsin Muhammad RC	.50	.23
U35 Bobby Engram	.30	.14
U36 Marco Battaglia	.10	.05
U37 Stepfret Williams	.10	.05
U38 Jeff Lewis	.25	.11
U39 Derrick Mayes	.20	.09
U40 Reggie Tongue	.10	.05
U41 Tory James	.10	.05
U42 Tony Banks RC	1.00	.45
U43 Tedy Bruschi	.10	.05
U44 Mike Alstott	.60	.25
U45 Anthony Dorsett	.10	.05
U46 Tony Brackens RC	.20	.09
U47 Bryant Mix	.10	.05
U48 Karim Abdul-Jabbar	.30	.14
U49 Moe Williams RC	.20	.09
U50 Lawyer Milloy	.10	.05
U51 Je'rod Cherry	.10	.05
U52 Amani Toomer RC	.50	.23
U53 Alex Van Dyke	.20	.09
U54 Lance Johnstone	.10	.05
U55 Bobby Hoying	.30	.14
U56 Jon Witman RC	.20	.09
U57 Eddie Kennison RC	.30	.14
U58 Brian Roche RC	.10	.05
U59 Terrell Owens RC	2.00	.90
U60 Stephen Davis	1.50	.70
U61 Jeff George FP	.20	.09
U62 Darick Holmes FP	.10	.05
U63 Kerry Collins FP	.30	.14
U64 Rashaan Salaam FP	.20	.09
U65 Jeff Blake FP	.20	.09
U66 Emmitt Smith FP	.75	.35
U67 Troy Aikman FP	.50	.23
U68 John Elway FP	1.00	.45
U69 Terrell Davis FP	1.25	.55
U70 Barry Sanders FP	1.00	.45
U71 Herman Moore FP	.30	.14
U72 Brett Favre FP	1.00	.45
U73 Robert Brooks FP	.20	.09
U74 Steve McNair FP	.50	.23
U75 Marshall Faulk FP	.20	.09
U76 Marcus Allen FP	.30	.14
U77 Dan Marino FP	1.00	.45
U78 Warren Moon FP	.10	.05
U79 Drew Bledsoe FP	.50	.23
U80 Curtis Martin FP	.40	.18
U81 Mario Bates FP	.20	.09
U82 Tim Brown FP	.20	.09
U83 Charlie Garner FP	.10	.05
U84 Kordell Stewart FP	.40	.18
U85 Isaac Bruce FP	.30	.14
U86 Tony Martin FP	.10	.05
U87 Jerry Rice FP	.50	.23
U88 J.J. Stokes FP	.30	.14
U89 Joey Galloway FP	.50	.23
U90 Errict Rhett FP	.20	.09
U91 Mike Pritchard	.10	.05
U92 Jerome Bettis	.30	.14
U93 Winslow Oliver	.10	.05
U94 David Klingler	.10	.05
U95 Lawrence Dawsey	.10	.05
U96 Charlie Jones	.20	.09
U97 Dave Krieg	.10	.05
U98 Chris Spielman	.10	.05
U99 Stanley Pritchett	.10	.05
U100 Sean Gilbert	.10	.05
U101 Tommy Vardell	.10	.05
U102 DeRon Jenkins	.10	.05
U103 Larry Bowie	.10	.05
U104 Kyle Wachholtz	.10	.05
U105 Brady Smith	.10	.05
U106 Steve Walsh	.10	.05
U107 Wesley Walls	.20	.09
U108 Kevin Ross	.10	.05
U109 Willie Clay	.10	.05
U110 Olanda Truitt	.10	.05
U111 Calvin Williams	.10	.05
U112 Chris Doleman	.10	.05
U113 Irving Fryar	.20	.09
U114 Jimmy Spencer	.10	.05
U115 Reggie Barlow RC	.10	.05
U116 Reggie Brown	.10	.05
U117 Dixon Edwards	.10	.05
U118 Haywood Jeffires	.10	.05
U119 Santana Dotson	.10	.05
U120 Herschel Walker	.20	.09
U121 Darryl Williams	.10	.05
U122 Bryan Cox	.10	.05
U123 Lamar Thomas	.10	.05
U124 Hendrick Lusk	.10	.05
U125 Jahine Arnold RC	.10	.05
U126 Boomer Esiason	.20	.09
U127 Willie Davis	.10	.05
U128 Pete Stoyanovich	.10	.05
U129 Bill Romanowski	.10	.05
U130 Tim McKyer	.10	.05
U131 Patrick Sapp	.10	.05
U132 Natrone Means	.30	.14
U133 Quinn Early	.10	.05
U134 Leslie O'Neal	.10	.05
U135 Mark Seay	.10	.05
U136 Pete Metzelaars	.10	.05
U137 Jay Leeuwenburg UER (Name misspelled ...berg)	.10	.05
U138 Buster Owens	.10	.05
U139 Todd McNair	.10	.05
U140 Eugene Robinson	.10	.05
U141 Sean Salisbury	.10	.05
U142 Eddie Robinson	.10	.05
U143 Jerris McPhail	.10	.05
U144 Ray Farmer RC	.10	.05
U145 Garrison Hearst	.20	.09
U146 Leonard Russell	.10	.05
U147 Roy Barker	.10	.05
U148 Larry Brown	.10	.05
U149 Webster Slaughter	.10	.05
U150 Roman Oben	.10	.05
U151 LeShon Johnson	.10	.05
U152 Patrick Bates	.10	.05
U153 I.Uwaezuoke RC UER (Uwaezoke on back)	.30	.14
U154 Scott Slutzker	.10	.05
U155 John Jurkovic	.10	.05
U156 Brian Milne	.10	.05
U157 Mike Sherrard	.10	.05
U158 Neil O'Donnell	.20	.09
U159 Roger Harper	.10	.05
U160 Desmond Howard	.20	.09
U161 Alfred Williams	.10	.05
U162 Ronnie Harmon	.10	.05
U163 Sammie Burroughs RC	.10	.05
U164 Keenan McCardell	.30	.14
U165 Shane Dronett	.10	.05
U166 Jeff Graham	.10	.05
U167 Bill Brooks	.10	.05
U168 Shawn Jefferson	.10	.05
U169 Detron Smith	.10	.05
U170 Danny Kanell	.30	.14
U171 Jevon Langford	.10	.05
U172 Russell Maryland	.10	.05
U173 Scott Milanovich RC	.30	.14
U174 Eric Davis	.10	.05
U175 Ernie Conwell	.10	.05
U176 Kurt Gouveia	.10	.05
U177 Andre Rison	.20	.09
U178 Harold Green	.10	.05
U179 Frank Reich	.10	.05
U180 Glyn Milburn	.10	.05
U181 Nilo Silvan	.10	.05
U182 Cornelius Bennett	.10	.05
U183 Freddie Solomon	.10	.05
U184 Pat Terrell	.10	.05
U185 Miles Macik	.10	.05
U186 Bo Orlando	.10	.05
U187 Kelvin Martin	.10	.05
U188 Todd Kinchen	.10	.05
U189 Reggie Brooks	.10	.05
U190 Steve Beuerlein UER (Name misspelled Beurlein)	.10	.05
U191 Marco Coleman	.10	.05
U192 Johnny Johnson	.10	.05
U193 Dedric Mathis	.10	.05
U194 Leon Searcy	.10	.05
U195 Kevin Greene	.20	.09
U196 Daniel Stubbs	.10	.05
U197 Ray Mickens	.10	.05
U198 Devin Wyman	.10	.05
U199 Lorenzo Lynch	.10	.05
U200 Checklist Card (Jerry Rice and Dan Marino ghosted images)	.30	.14

1997 Collector's Choice

	MINT	NRMT
COMPLETE SET (565)	35.00	16.00
COMP.SERIES 1 (310)	20.00	9.00
COMP.FACT.SER.1(330)	30.00	13.50
COMP.SERIES 2 (255)	15.00	6.75
1 Orlando Pace RC	.40	.18
2 Darrell Russell RC	.10	.05
3 Shawn Springs RC	.20	.09
4 Peter Boulware RC	.20	.09
5 Bryant Westbrook RC	.10	.05
6 Tom Knight RC	.10	.05
7 Ike Hilliard RC	.75	.35
8 James Farrior RC	.10	.05
9 Chris Naeole RC	.10	.05
10 Michael Booker RC	.10	.05
11 Warrick Dunn RC UER (No card number on back)	1.25	.55
12 Tony Gonzalez RC	1.25	.55
13 Reinard Wilson RC	.10	.05
14 Yatil Green RC	.20	.09
15 Reidel Anthony RC	.75	.35
16 Kenard Lang RC	.10	.05
17 Kenny Holmes RC	.40	.18
18 Tarik Glenn RC	.10	.05
19 Dwayne Rudd RC	.40	.18
20 Renaldo Wynn RC	.10	.05
21 David LaFleur RC	.20	.09
22 Antowain Smith RC	1.00	.45
23 Jim Druckenmiller RC	.40	.18
24 Rae Carruth RC	.40	.18
25 Jared Tomich RC	.10	.05
26 Chris Canty RC	.10	.05
27 Jake Plummer RC	2.50	1.10
28 Troy Davis RC	.40	.18
29 Sedrick Shaw RC	.40	.18
30 Jamie Sharper RC	.20	.09
31 Tiki Barber RC	1.25	.55
32 Byron Hanspard RC	.40	.18
33 Darnell Autry RC	.20	.09
34 Corey Dillon RC	2.50	1.10
35 Joey Kent RC	.40	.18
36 Nathan Davis RC	.10	.05
37 Will Blackwell RC	.40	.18
38 Kim Herring RC	.10	.05
39 Pat Barnes RC	.40	.18
40 Kevin Lockett RC	.20	.09
41 Trevor Pryce RC	.10	.05
42 Matt Russell RC	.10	.05
43 Greg Jones RC	.10	.05
44 Antonio Anderson RC	.10	.05
45 George Jones RC	.20	.09
46 Steve Young NG	.40	.18
47 Jerry Rice NG	.50	.23
48 Curtis Conway NG	.10	.05
49 Jeff Blake NG	.20	.09
50 Carl Pickens NG	.20	.09

51 Bruce Smith NG .10 .05
52 John Elway NG 1.00 .45
53 Terrell Davis NG .75 .35
54 Shannon Sharpe NG .10 .05
55 Junior Seau NG .10 .05
56 Darren Bennett NG .10 .05
57 Jim Harbaugh NG .20 .09
58 Marshall Faulk NG .40 .18
59 Emmitt Smith NG .75 .35
60 Troy Aikman NG .50 .23
61 Deion Sanders NG .40 .18
62 Dan Marino NG 1.00 .45
63 Ricky Watters NG .10 .05
64 Mark Brunell NG .50 .23
65 Keenan McCardell NG .10 .05
66 Keyshawn Johnson NG .40 .18
67 Barry Sanders NG 1.00 .45
68 Herman Moore NG .20 .09
69 Eddie George NG .50 .23
70 Steve McNair NG .40 .18
71 Brett Favre NG 1.00 .45
72 Reggie White NG .20 .09
73 Edgar Bennett NG .10 .05
74 Kerry Collins NG .20 .09
75 Kevin Greene NG .10 .05
76 Drew Bledsoe NG .50 .23
77 Terry Glenn NG .20 .09
78 Curtis Martin NG .40 .18
79 Jeff Hostetler NG .10 .05
80 Napoleon Kaufman NG .40 .18
81 Isaac Bruce NG .40 .18
82 Terry Allen NG .20 .09
83 Joey Galloway NG .40 .18
84 Kordell Stewart NG .40 .18
85 Jerome Bettis NG .40 .18
86 Dana Stubblefield .10 .05
87 Merton Hanks .10 .05
88 Terrell Owens .40 .18
89 Brent Jones .20 .09
90 Ken Norton Jr. .10 .05
91 Jerry Rice 1.00 .45
92 Terry Kirby .20 .09
93 Bryant Young .10 .05
94 Raymont Harris .10 .05
95 Jeff Jaeger .10 .05
96 Curtis Conway .20 .09
97 Walt Harris .10 .05
98 Bobby Engram .20 .09
99 Donnell Woolford .10 .05
100 Rashaan Salaam .10 .05
101 Jeff Blake .20 .09
102 Tony McGee .10 .05
103 Ashley Ambrose .10 .05
104 Dan Wilkinson .10 .05
105 Jevon Langford .10 .05
106 Darnay Scott .20 .09
107 David Dunn .10 .05
108 Eric Moulds .40 .18
109 Darick Holmes .10 .05
110 Thurman Thomas .40 .18
111 Quinn Early .10 .05
112 Jim Kelly .40 .18
113 Bryce Paup .10 .05
114 Bruce Smith .20 .09
115 Todd Collins .10 .05
116 Tory James .10 .05
117 Anthony Miller .10 .05
118 Terrell Davis 1.50 .70
119 Tyrone Braxton .10 .05
120 John Mobley .10 .05
121 Bill Romanowski .10 .05
122 Vaughn Hebron .10 .05
123 Mike Alstott .40 .18
124 Errict Rhett .10 .05
125 Trent Dilfer .40 .18
126 Courtney Hawkins .10 .05
127 Hardy Nickerson .10 .05
128 Donnie Abraham RC .40 .18
129 Regan Upshaw .10 .05
130 Kent Graham .10 .05
131 Rob Moore .20 .09
132 Simeon Rice .20 .09
133 LeShon Johnson .10 .05
134 Frank Sanders .20 .09
135 Leeland McElroy .10 .05
136 Seth Joyner .10 .05
137 Andre Coleman .10 .05
138 Stan Humphries .20 .09
139 Charlie Jones .20 .09
140 Junior Seau .20 .09
141 Rodney Harrison .10 .05
142 Darrien Gordon .10 .05
143 Terrell Fletcher .10 .05
144 Tamarick Vanover .20 .09
145 Greg Hill .10 .05
146 Marcus Allen .40 .18
147 Lake Dawson .10 .05
148 Dale Carter .10 .05
149 Kimble Anders .20 .09
150 Chris Penn .10 .05
151 Sean Dawkins .10 .05
152 Ken Dilger .10 .05
153 Marvin Harrison .40 .18
154 Jeff Herrod .10 .05
155 Jim Harbaugh .20 .09
156 Cary Blanchard .10 .05
157 Aaron Bailey .10 .05
158 Deion Sanders .40 .18
159 Jim Schwantz RC .10 .05
160 Michael Irvin .40 .18
161 Herschel Walker .20 .09
162 Emmitt Smith 1.50 .70
163 Chris Boniol .10 .05
164 Eric Bjornson .10 .05
165 Karim Abdul-Jabbar .40 .18
166 O.J. McDuffie .20 .09
167 Troy Drayton .10 .05
168 Zach Thomas .20 .09
169 Irving Spikes .10 .05
170 Shane Burton .10 .05
171 Stanley Pritchett .10 .05
172 Ty Detmer .20 .09
173 Chris T. Jones .10 .05
174 Troy Vincent .10 .05
175 Brian Dawkins .10 .05
176 Irving Fryar .20 .09
177 Charlie Garner .10 .05
178 Bobby Taylor .10 .05
179 Jamal Anderson .60 .25
180 Terance Mathis .20 .09
181 Craig Heyward .10 .05
182 Cornelius Bennett .10 .05
183 Jessie Tuggle .10 .05
184 Devin Bush .10 .05
185 Dave Brown .10 .05
186 Danny Kanell .20 .09
187 Rodney Hampton .20 .09
188 Tyrone Wheatley .20 .09
189 Amani Toomer .20 .09
190 Phillippi Sparks .10 .05
191 Thomas Lewis .10 .05
192 Jimmy Smith .20 .09
193 Pete Mitchell .10 .05
194 Natrone Means .40 .18
195 Mark Brunell 1.00 .45
196 Kevin Hardy .10 .05
197 Tony Brackens .10 .05
198 Aaron Beasley .10 .05
199 Chris Hudson .10 .05
200 Wayne Chrebet .40 .18
201 Keyshawn Johnson .40 .18
202 Adrian Murrell .20 .09
203 Neil O'Donnell .20 .09
204 Hugh Douglas .10 .05
205 Mo Lewis .10 .05
206 Glenn Foley .10 .05
207 Aaron Glenn .10 .05
208 Johnnie Morton .20 .09
209 Reggie Brown LB .20 .09
210 Barry Sanders 2.00 .90
211 Glyn Milburn .10 .05
212 Bennie Blades .10 .05
213 Steve McNair .50 .23
214 Frank Wycheck .10 .05
215 Chris Sanders .10 .05
216 Blaine Bishop .10 .05
217 Willie Davis .10 .05
218 Darryll Lewis .10 .05
219 Marcus Robertson .10 .05
220 Robert Brooks .20 .09
221 Antonio Freeman .50 .23
222 Keith Jackson .10 .05
223 Mark Chmura .20 .09
224 Brett Favre 2.00 .90
225 Sean Jones .10 .05
226 Reggie White .40 .18
227 LeRoy Butler .10 .05
228 Craig Newsome .10 .05
229 Wesley Walls .20 .09
230 Mark Carrier WR .10 .05
231 Muhsin Muhammad .20 .09
232 John Kasay .10 .05
233 Anthony Johnson .10 .05
234 Kerry Collins .20 .09
235 Kevin Greene .20 .09
236 Sam Mills .10 .05
237 Ben Coates .20 .09
238 Terry Glenn .40 .18
239 Willie McGinest .10 .05
240 Ted Johnson .10 .05
241 Lawyer Milloy .10 .05
242 Drew Bledsoe 1.00 .45
243 Willie Clay .10 .05
244 Chris Slade .10 .05
245 Tim Brown .40 .18
246 Daryl Hobbs .10 .05
247 Rickey Dudley .20 .09
248 Joe Aska .10 .05
249 Chester McGlockton .10 .05
250 Rob Fredrickson .10 .05
251 Terry McDaniel .10 .05
252 Tony Banks .20 .09
253 Lawrence Phillips .10 .05
254 Isaac Bruce .40 .18
255 Eddie Kennison .20 .09
256 Kevin Carter .10 .05
257 Roman Phifer .10 .05
258 Keith Lyle .10 .05
259 Vinny Testaverde .20 .09
260 Derrick Alexander WR .20 .09
261 Ray Lewis .20 .09
262 Jermaine Lewis .40 .18
263 Byron Bam Morris .10 .05
264 Stevon Moore .10 .05
265 Antonio Langham .10 .05
266 Brian Mitchell .10 .05
267 Henry Ellard .10 .05
268 Leslie Shepherd .10 .05
269 Michael Westbrook .20 .09
270 Jamie Asher .10 .05
271 Ken Harvey .10 .05
272 Gus Frerotte .10 .05
273 Michael Haynes .10 .05
274 Ray Zellars .10 .05
275 Jim Everett .10 .05
276 Tyrone Hughes .10 .05
277 Joe Johnson .10 .05
278 Eric Allen .10 .05
279 Brady Smith .10 .05
280 Mario Bates .10 .05
281 Torrance Small .10 .05
282 John Friesz .10 .05
283 Brian Blades .10 .05
284 Chris Warren .20 .09
285 Joey Galloway .50 .23
286 Michael Sinclair .10 .05
287 Lamar Smith .40 .18
288 Mike Pritchard .10 .05
289 Jerome Bettis .40 .18
290 Charles Johnson .20 .09
291 Mike Tomczak .10 .05
292 Levon Kirkland .10 .05
293 Carnell Lake .10 .05
294 Erric Pegram .10 .05
295 Kordell Stewart .50 .23
296 Greg Lloyd .10 .05
297 Dixon Edwards .10 .05
298 Cris Carter .40 .18
299 Brad Johnson .50 .23
300 Qadry Ismail .20 .09
301 John Randle .20 .09
302 Orlanda Thomas .10 .05
303 Dewayne Washington .10 .05
304 Jake Reed .20 .09
305 Derrick Alexander DE .10 .05
306 Eddie George CL .40 .18
307 Dan Marino CL .40 .18
308 Curtis Martin CL .20 .09

	No.	Card		
❑	309	Troy Aikman CL	.40	.18
❑	310	Marcus Allen CL	.40	.18
❑	311	Jim Druckenmiller	.40	.18
❑	312	Greg Clark RC	.10	.05
❑	313	Darnell Autry	.20	.09
❑	314	Reinard Wilson	.10	.05
❑	315	Corey Dillon	1.00	.45
❑	316	Antowain Smith	.50	.23
❑	317	Trevor Pryce	.10	.05
❑	318	Warrick Dunn	.50	.23
❑	319	Reidel Anthony	.50	.23
❑	320	Jake Plummer	1.50	.70
❑	321	Tom Knight	.10	.05
❑	322	Freddie Jones RC	.20	.09
❑	323	Tony Gonzalez	.50	.23
❑	324	Pat Barnes	.20	.09
❑	325	Kevin Lockett	.20	.09
❑	326	Tarik Glenn	.10	.05
❑	327	David LaFleur	.20	.09
❑	328	Antonio Anderson	.10	.05
❑	329	Yatil Green	.20	.09
❑	330	Jason Taylor RC	.10	.05
❑	331	Brian Manning RC	.10	.05
❑	332	Michael Booker	.10	.05
❑	333	Byron Hanspard	.40	.18
❑	334	Ike Hilliard	.40	.18
❑	335	Tiki Barber	.50	.23
❑	336	Renaldo Wynn	.10	.05
❑	337	Damon Jones RC	.10	.05
❑	338	James Farrior	.10	.05
❑	339	Dedric Ward RC	.75	.35
❑	340	Bryant Westbrook	.10	.05
❑	341	Joey Kent	.40	.18
❑	342	Kenny Holmes	.10	.05
❑	343	Darren Sharper RC	.20	.09
❑	344	Rae Carruth	.20	.09
❑	345	Chris Canty	.10	.05
❑	346	Darrell Russell	.10	.05
❑	347	Orlando Pace	.40	.18
❑	348	Peter Boulware	.20	.09
❑	349	Kenard Lang	.10	.05
❑	350	Danny Wuerffel RC	.60	.25
❑	351	Troy Davis	.40	.18
❑	352	Shawn Springs	.20	.09
❑	353	Walter Jones RC	.10	.05
❑	354	Will Blackwell	.40	.18
❑	355	Dwayne Rudd	.10	.05
❑	356	49ers BB	.10	.05
		Jerry Rice		
		Steve Young		
		Ken Norton		
		Jim Druckenmiller		
		Bryant Young		
❑	357	Bears BB	.10	.05
		Bobby Engram		
		Rick Mirer		
		Raymont Harris		
		Curtis Conway		
		Bryan Cox		
❑	358	Bengals BB	.10	.05
		Ki-Jana Carter		
		Jeff Blake		
		Carl Pickens		
		Dan Wilkinson		
		Darnay Scott		
❑	359	Bills BB	.10	.05
		Thurman Thomas		
		Todd Collins		
		Antowain Smith		
		Bruce Smith		
		Chris Spielman		
❑	360	Broncos BB	.10	.05
		Terrell Davis		
		John Elway		
		Shannon Sharpe		
		Neil Smith		
		Rod Smith WR		
❑	361	Buccaneers BB	.10	.05
		Warrick Dunn		
		Trent Dilfer		
		Errict Rhett		
		Hardy Nickerson		
		Reidel Anthony		
❑	362	Cardinals BB	.10	.05
		Frank Sanders		
		Eric Swann		
		Jake Plummer		
		Kent Graham		
		Rob Moore		
❑	363	Chargers BB	.10	.05
		Tony Martin		
		Stan Humphries		
		Junior Seau		
		Eric Metcalf		
		Freddie Jones		
❑	364	Chiefs BB	.10	.05
		Marcus Allen		
		Kevin Lockett		
		Tony Gonzalez		
		Pat Barnes		
		Elvis Grbac		
		Derrick Thomas		
		Eric Hill		
❑	365	Colts BB	.10	.05
		Marvin Harrison		
		Jim Harbaugh		
		Marshall Faulk		
		Quentin Coryatt		
		Sean Dawkins		
❑	366	Cowboys BB	.10	.05
		Emmitt Smith		
		Troy Aikman		
		Deion Sanders		
		Michael Irvin		
		David LaFleur		
❑	367	Dolphins BB	.10	.05
		Dan Marino		
		Troy Drayton		
		Karim Abdul-Jabbar		
		Zach Thomas		
		O.J. McDuffie		
❑	368	Eagles BB	.10	.05
		Chris T. Jones		
		Ricky Watters		
		Ty Detmer		
		Irving Fryar		
		Mike Mamula		
❑	369	Falcons BB	.10	.05
		Byron Hanspard		
		Jamal Anderson		
		Cornelius Bennett		
		Ray Buchanan		
		Terence Mathis		
❑	370	Giants BB	.10	.05
		Ike Hilliard		
		Dave Brown		
		Rodney Hampton		
		Tyrone Wheatley		
		Phillippi Sparks		
❑	371	Jaguars BB	.10	.05
		Keenan McCardell		
		Mark Brunell		
		Kevin Hardy		
		Renaldo Wynn		
		Natrone Means		
❑	372	Jets BB	.10	.05
		Keyshawn Johnson		
		Neil O'Donnell		
		James Farrior		
		Adrian Murrell		
		Wayne Chrebet		
❑	373	Lions BB	.10	.05
		Barry Sanders		
		Bryant Westbrook		
		Herman Moore		
		Johnnie Morton		
		Scott Mitchell		
❑	374	Oilers BB	.10	.05
		Eddie George		
		Steve McNair		
		Joey Kent		
		Chris Sanders		
		Blaine Bishop		
❑	375	Packers BB	.40	.18
		Robert Brooks		
		Brett Favre		
		Reggie White		
		Dorsey Levens		
		Derrick Mayes		
❑	376	Panthers BB	.10	.05
		Tim Biakabutuka		
		Kerry Collins		
		Rae Carruth		
		Sam Mills		
		Anthony Johnson		
❑	377	Patriots BB	.10	.05
		Terry Glenn		
		Drew Bledsoe		
		Curtis Martin		
		Willie McGinest		
		Ben Coates		
❑	378	Raiders BB	.10	.05
		Tim Brown		
		Jeff George		
		Napoleon Kaufman		
		Darrell Russell		
		Desmond Howard		
❑	379	Rams BB	.10	.05
		Eddie Kennison		
		Tony Banks		
		Isaac Bruce		
		Orlando Pace		
		Lawrence Phillips		
❑	380	Ravens BB	.10	.05
		Vinny Testaverde		
		Peter Boulware		
		Michael Jackson		
		Byron Bam Morris		
		Derrick Alexander WR		
❑	381	Redskins BB	.10	.05
		Brian Mitchell		
		Gus Frerotte		
		Terry Allen		
		Sean Gilbert		
		Michael Westbrook		
❑	382	Saints BB	.10	.05
		Heath Shuler		
		Daryl Hobbs		
		Troy Davis		
		Wayne Martin		
		Mario Bates		
❑	383	Seahawks BB	.10	.05
		Joey Galloway		
		Chris Warren		
		Shawn Springs		
		Cortez Kennedy		
		Warren Moon		
❑	384	Steelers BB	.10	.05
		Jerome Bettis		
		Kordell Stewart		
		Greg Lloyd		
		Charles Johnson		
		Will Blackwell		
❑	385	Vikings BB	.20	.09
		Jake Reed		
		Cris Carter		
		Brad Johnson		
		Robert Smith		
		John Randle		
❑	386	William Floyd	.20	.09
❑	387	Steve Young	.60	.25
❑	388	Lee Woodall	.10	.05
❑	389	J.J. Stokes	.20	.09
❑	390	Marc Edwards	.10	.05
❑	391	Rod Woodson	.20	.09
❑	392	Jim Schwantz	.10	.05
❑	393	Garrison Hearst	.20	.09
❑	394	Rick Mirer	.10	.05
❑	395	Alonzo Spellman	.10	.05
❑	396	Tom Carter	.10	.05
❑	397	Bryan Cox	.10	.05
❑	398	John Allred RC	.10	.05
❑	399	Ricky Proehl	.10	.05
❑	400	Tyrone Hughes	.10	.05
❑	401	Carl Pickens	.40	.18
❑	402	Tremain Mack RC	.10	.05
❑	403	Boomer Esiason	.20	.09
❑	404	Ki-Jana Carter	.10	.05
❑	405	Steve Tovar	.10	.05
❑	406	Billy Joe Hobert	.20	.09
❑	407	Andre Reed	.20	.09
❑	408	Marcellus Wiley RC	.10	.05
❑	409	Steve Tasker	.10	.05
❑	410	Chris Spielman	.10	.05
❑	411	Alfred Williams	.10	.05
❑	412	John Elway	2.00	.90
❑	413	Shannon Sharpe	.20	.09
❑	414	Steve Atwater	.10	.05

No.	Player	MINT	NRMT
❑ 415	Neil Smith	.20	.09
❑ 416	Darrien Gordon	.10	.05
❑ 417	Jeff Lewis	.10	.05
❑ 418	Flipper Anderson	.10	.05
❑ 419	Willie Green	.10	.05
❑ 420	Jackie Harris	.10	.05
❑ 421	Steve Walsh	.10	.05
❑ 422	Anthony Parker	.10	.05
❑ 423	Ronde Barber RC	.10	.05
❑ 424	Warren Sapp	.20	.09
❑ 425	Aeneas Williams	.10	.05
❑ 426	Larry Centers	.20	.09
❑ 427	Eric Swann	.10	.05
❑ 428	Kevin Williams	.10	.05
❑ 429	Darren Bennett	.10	.05
❑ 430	Tony Martin	.20	.09
❑ 431	John Carney	.10	.05
❑ 432	Jim Everett	.10	.05
❑ 433	William Fuller	.10	.05
❑ 434	Latario Rachal RC	.10	.05
❑ 435	Erric Pegram	.10	.05
❑ 436	Eric Metcalf	.20	.09
❑ 437	Jerome Woods	.10	.05
❑ 438	Derrick Thomas	.20	.09
❑ 439	Elvis Grbac	.20	.09
❑ 440	Terry Wooden	.10	.05
❑ 441	Andre Rison	.20	.09
❑ 442	Brett Perriman	.10	.05
❑ 443	Paul Justin	.10	.05
❑ 444	Robert Blackmon	.10	.05
❑ 445	Carlton Gray	.10	.05
❑ 446	Chris Gardocki	.10	.05
❑ 447	Marshall Faulk	.40	.18
❑ 448	Sammie Burroughs	.10	.05
❑ 449	Quentin Coryatt	.10	.05
❑ 450	Troy Aikman	1.00	.45
❑ 451	Daryl Johnston	.20	.09
❑ 452	Tony Tolbert	.10	.05
❑ 453	Brock Marion	.10	.05
❑ 454	Billy Davis RC	.10	.05
❑ 455	Stepfret Williams	.10	.05
❑ 456	Anthony Miller	.10	.05
❑ 457	Dan Marino	2.00	.90
❑ 458	Jerris McPhail	.10	.05
❑ 459	Terrell Buckley	.10	.05
❑ 460	Daryl Gardener	.10	.05
❑ 461	George Teague	.10	.05
❑ 462	Derrick Rodgers RC	.10	.05
❑ 463	Fred Barnett	.10	.05
❑ 464	Darrin Smith	.10	.05
❑ 465	Michael Timpson	.10	.05
❑ 466	Jon Harris	.10	.05
❑ 467	Jason Dunn	.10	.05
❑ 468	Bobby Hoying	.20	.09
❑ 469	Ricky Watters	.20	.09
❑ 470	Derrick Witherspoon	.10	.05
❑ 471	Chris Chandler	.20	.09
❑ 472	Ray Buchanan	.10	.05
❑ 473	Michael Haynes	.10	.05
❑ 474	O.J. Santiago RC	.40	.18
❑ 475	Morten Andersen	.10	.05
❑ 476	Bert Emanuel	.20	.09
❑ 477	Chris Calloway	.10	.05
❑ 478	Jason Sehorn	.20	.09
❑ 479	John Jurkovic	.10	.05
❑ 480	Keenan McCardell	.20	.09
❑ 481	James O. Stewart	.20	.09
❑ 482	Rob Johnson	.40	.18
❑ 483	Mike Logan RC	.10	.05
❑ 484	Deon Figures	.10	.05
❑ 485	Kyle Brady	.10	.05
❑ 486	Alex Van Dyke	.10	.05
❑ 487	Jeff Graham	.10	.05
❑ 488	Jason Hanson	.10	.05
❑ 489	Herman Moore	.40	.18
❑ 490	Scott Mitchell	.20	.09
❑ 491	Tommy Vardell	.10	.05
❑ 492	Derrick Mason RC	1.00	.45
❑ 493	Rodney Thomas	.10	.05
❑ 494	Ronnie Harmon	.10	.05
❑ 495	Eddie George	1.00	.45
❑ 496	Edgar Bennett	.20	.09
❑ 497	William Henderson	.10	.05
❑ 498	Dorsey Levens	.40	.18
❑ 499	Gilbert Brown	.10	.05
❑ 500	Steve Bono	.20	.09

No.	Player	MINT	NRMT
❑ 501	Derrick Mayes	.20	.09
❑ 502	Fred Lane RC	.40	.18
❑ 503	Ernie Mills	.10	.05
❑ 504	Tim Biakabutuka	.20	.09
❑ 505	Michael Bates	.10	.05
❑ 506	Winslow Oliver	.10	.05
❑ 507	Ty Law	.10	.05
❑ 508	Shawn Jefferson	.10	.05
❑ 509	Vincent Brisby	.10	.05
❑ 510	Henry Thomas	.10	.05
❑ 511	Tedy Bruschi	.10	.05
❑ 512	Curtis Martin	.50	.23
❑ 513	Jeff George	.20	.09
❑ 514	Desmond Howard	.20	.09
❑ 515	Napoleon Kaufman	.40	.18
❑ 516	Kenny Shedd RC	.10	.05
❑ 517	Russell Maryland	.10	.05
❑ 518	Lance Johnstone	.10	.05
❑ 519	Eric Turner	.10	.05
❑ 520	Dexter McLeon RC	.10	.05
❑ 521	Craig Heyward	.10	.05
❑ 522	Ryan McNeil	.10	.05
❑ 523	Mark Rypien	.10	.05
❑ 524	Mike Jones LB	.10	.05
❑ 525	Jamie Sharper	.10	.05
❑ 526	Tony Siragusa	.10	.05
❑ 527	Michael Jackson	.20	.09
❑ 528	Floyd Turner	.10	.05
❑ 529	Eric Green	.10	.05
❑ 530	Michael McCrary	.10	.05
❑ 531	Jay Graham RC	.40	.18
❑ 532	Terry Allen	.40	.18
❑ 533	Sean Gilbert	.10	.05
❑ 534	Scott Turner	.10	.05
❑ 535	Cris Dishman	.10	.05
❑ 536	Darrell Green	.20	.09
❑ 537	Stephen Davis	.50	.23
❑ 538	Alvin Harper	.10	.05
❑ 539	Daryl Hobbs	.10	.05
❑ 540	Wayne Martin	.10	.05
❑ 541	Heath Shuler	.10	.05
❑ 542	Andre Hastings	.10	.05
❑ 543	Jared Tomich	.10	.05
❑ 544	Nicky Savoie RC	.10	.05
❑ 545	Cortez Kennedy	.10	.05
❑ 546	Warren Moon	.40	.18
❑ 547	Chad Brown	.10	.05
❑ 548	Willie Williams	.10	.05
❑ 549	Bennie Blades	.10	.05
❑ 550	Darren Perry	.10	.05
❑ 551	Mark Bruener	.10	.05
❑ 552	Yancey Thigpen	.20	.09
❑ 553	Courtney Hawkins	.10	.05
❑ 554	Chad Scott	.10	.05
❑ 555	George Jones	.20	.09
❑ 556	Robert Tate RC	.10	.05
❑ 557	Torrian Gray RC	.10	.05
❑ 558	Robert Griffith	.10	.05
❑ 559	Leroy Hoard	.10	.05
❑ 560	Robert Smith	.20	.09
❑ 561	Randall Cunningham	.40	.18
❑ 562	Darrell Russell CL	.10	.05
❑ 563	Troy Aikman CL	.40	.18
❑ 564	Dan Marino CL	.40	.18
❑ 565	Jim Druckenmiller CL	.40	.18

1992 Collector's Edge

	MINT	NRMT
COMPLETE SET (250)	25.00	11.00
COMP.SERIES 1 (175)	15.00	6.75
COMP.FACT.SER.1 (175)	15.00	6.75
COMP.SERIES 2 (75)	10.00	4.50
COMP.FACT.SER.2 (75)	12.00	5.50

No.	Player	MINT	NRMT
❑ 1	Chris Miller	.20	.09
❑ 2	Steve Broussard	.10	.05
❑ 3	Mike Pritchard	.20	.09
❑ 4	Tim Green	.10	.05
❑ 5	Andre Rison	.20	.09
❑ 6	Deion Sanders	1.00	.45
❑ 7	Jim Kelly	.40	.18
❑ 8	James Lofton	.20	.09
❑ 9	Andre Reed	.20	.09
❑ 10	Bruce Smith	.40	.18
❑ 11	Thurman Thomas	.40	.18
❑ 12	Cornelius Bennett	.20	.09
❑ 13	Jim Harbaugh	.40	.18
❑ 14	William Perry	.20	.09
❑ 15	Mike Singletary	.20	.09
❑ 16	Mark Carrier DB	.10	.05
❑ 17	Kevin Butler	.10	.05
❑ 18	Tom Waddle	.10	.05
❑ 19	Boomer Esiason	.20	.09
❑ 20	David Fulcher	.10	.05
❑ 21	Anthony Munoz	.20	.09
❑ 22	Tim McGee	.10	.05
❑ 23	Harold Green	.10	.05
❑ 24	Rickey Dixon	.10	.05
❑ 25	Bernie Kosar	.20	.09
❑ 26	Michael Dean Perry	.20	.09
❑ 27	Mike Baab	.10	.05
❑ 28	Brian Brennan	.10	.05
❑ 29	Michael Jackson	.20	.09
❑ 30	Eric Metcalf	.20	.09
❑ 31	Troy Aikman	2.50	1.10
❑ 32	Emmitt Smith	5.00	2.20
❑ 33	Michael Irvin	.40	.18
❑ 34	Jay Novacek	.20	.09
❑ 35	Issiac Holt	.10	.05
❑ 36	Ken Norton	.40	.18
❑ 37	John Elway	4.00	1.80
❑ 38	Gaston Green	.10	.05
❑ 39	Charles Dimry	.10	.05
❑ 40	Vance Johnson	.10	.05
❑ 41	Dennis Smith	.10	.05
❑ 42	David Treadwell	.10	.05
❑ 43	Michael Young	.10	.05
❑ 44	Bennie Blades	.10	.05
❑ 45	Mel Gray	.20	.09
❑ 46	Andre Ware	.10	.05
❑ 47	Rodney Peete	.20	.09
❑ 48	Toby Caston RC	.10	.05
❑ 49	Herman Moore	1.00	.45
❑ 50	Brian Noble	.10	.05
❑ 51	Sterling Sharpe	.40	.18
❑ 52	Mike Tomczak	.10	.05
❑ 53	Vinnie Clark	.10	.05
❑ 54	Tony Mandarich	.10	.05
❑ 55	Ed West	.10	.05
❑ 56	Warren Moon	.40	.18
❑ 57	Ray Childress	.10	.05
❑ 58	Haywood Jeffires	.20	.09
❑ 59	Al Smith	.10	.05
❑ 60	Cris Dishman	.10	.05
❑ 61	Ernest Givins	.20	.09
❑ 62	Richard Johnson	.10	.05
❑ 63	Eric Dickerson	.20	.09
❑ 64	Jessie Hester	.10	.05
❑ 65	Rohn Stark	.10	.05
❑ 66	Clarence Verdin	.10	.05
❑ 67	Dean Biasucci	.10	.05
❑ 68	Duane Bickett	.10	.05
❑ 69	Jeff George	.40	.18
❑ 70	Christian Okoye	.10	.05
❑ 71	Derrick Thomas	.40	.18
❑ 72	Stephone Paige	.10	.05
❑ 73	Dan Saleaumua	.10	.05
❑ 74	Deron Cherry	.10	.05
❑ 75	Kevin Ross	.10	.05
❑ 76	Barry Word	.10	.05
❑ 77	Ronnie Lott	.20	.09
❑ 78	Greg Townsend	.10	.05
❑ 79	Willie Gault	.20	.09

No.	Player	Mint	NrMt
❑ 80	Howie Long	.20	.09
❑ 81	Winston Moss	.10	.05
❑ 82	Steve Smith	.10	.05
❑ 83	Jay Schroeder	.10	.05
❑ 84	Jim Everett	.20	.09
❑ 85	Flipper Anderson	.10	.05
❑ 86	Henry Ellard	.20	.09
❑ 87	Tony Zendejas	.10	.05
❑ 88	Robert Delpino	.10	.05
❑ 89	Pat Terrell	.10	.05
❑ 90	Dan Marino	4.00	1.80
❑ 91	Mark Clayton	.20	.09
❑ 92	Jim C.Jensen	.10	.05
❑ 93	Reggie Roby	.10	.05
❑ 94	Sammie Smith	.10	.05
❑ 95	Tony Martin	.40	.18
❑ 96	Jeff Cross	.10	.05
❑ 97	Anthony Carter	.20	.09
❑ 98	Chris Doleman	.10	.05
❑ 99	Wade Wilson	.20	.09
❑ 100	Cris Carter	.75	.35
❑ 101	Mike Merriweather	.10	.05
❑ 102	Gary Zimmerman	.10	.05
❑ 103	Chris Singleton	.10	.05
❑ 104	Bruce Armstrong	.10	.05
❑ 105	Marv Cook	.10	.05
❑ 106	Andre Tippett	.10	.05
❑ 107	Tommy Hodson	.10	.05
❑ 108	Greg McMurtry	.10	.05
❑ 109	Jon Vaughn	.10	.05
❑ 110	Vaughan Johnson	.10	.05
❑ 111	Craig Heyward	.20	.09
❑ 112	Floyd Turner	.10	.05
❑ 113	Pat Swilling	.20	.09
❑ 114	Rickey Jackson	.10	.05
❑ 115	Steve Walsh	.10	.05
❑ 116	Phil Simms	.20	.09
❑ 117	Carl Banks	.10	.05
❑ 118	Mark Ingram	.10	.05
❑ 119	Bart Oates	.10	.05
❑ 120	Lawrence Taylor	.40	.18
❑ 121	Jeff Hostetler	.20	.09
❑ 122	Rob Moore	.20	.09
❑ 123	Ken O'Brien	.10	.05
❑ 124	Bill Pickel	.10	.05
❑ 125	Irv Eatman	.10	.05
❑ 126	Browning Nagle	.10	.05
❑ 127	Al Toon	.20	.09
❑ 128	Randall Cunningham	.40	.18
❑ 129	Eric Allen	.10	.05
❑ 130	Mike Golic	.10	.05
❑ 131	Fred Barnett	.40	.18
❑ 132	Keith Byars	.10	.05
❑ 133	Calvin Williams	.20	.09
❑ 134	Randal Hill	.10	.05
❑ 135	Ricky Proehl	.10	.05
❑ 136	Lance Smith	.10	.05
❑ 137	Ernie Jones	.10	.05
❑ 138	Timm Rosenbach	.10	.05
❑ 139	Anthony Thompson	.10	.05
❑ 140	Bubby Brister	.10	.05
❑ 141	Merril Hoge	.10	.05
❑ 142	Louis Lipps	.10	.05
❑ 143	Eric Green	.10	.05
❑ 144	Gary Anderson K	.10	.05
❑ 145	Neil O'Donnell	.40	.18
❑ 146	Rod Bernstine	.10	.05
❑ 147	John Friesz	.20	.09
❑ 148	Anthony Miller	.20	.09
❑ 149	Junior Seau	.40	.18
❑ 150	Leslie O'Neal	.20	.09
❑ 151	Nate Lewis	.10	.05
❑ 152	Steve Young	2.00	.90
❑ 153	Kevin Fagan	.10	.05
❑ 154	Charles Haley	.20	.09
❑ 155	Tom Rathman	.10	.05
❑ 156	Jerry Rice	2.50	1.10
❑ 157	John Taylor	.20	.09
❑ 158	Brian Blades	.20	.09
❑ 159	Patrick Hunter	.10	.05
❑ 160	Cortez Kennedy	.20	.09
❑ 161	Vann McElroy	.10	.05
❑ 162	Dan McGwire	.10	.05
❑ 163	John L. Williams	.10	.05
❑ 164	Gary Anderson RB	.10	.05
❑ 165	Broderick Thomas	.10	.05
❑ 166	Vinny Testaverde	.20	.09
❑ 167	Lawrence Dawsey	.20	.09
❑ 168	Paul Gruber	.10	.05
❑ 169	Keith McCants	.10	.05
❑ 170	Mark Rypien	.10	.05
❑ 171	Gary Clark	.40	.18
❑ 172	Earnest Byner	.10	.05
❑ 173	Brian Mitchell	.20	.09
❑ 174	Monte Coleman	.10	.05
❑ 175	Joe Jacoby	.10	.05
❑ 176	Tommy Vardell RC	.20	.09
❑ 177	Troy Vincent RC	.20	.09
❑ 178	Robert Jones RC	.10	.05
❑ 179	Marc Boutte RC	.10	.05
❑ 180	Marco Coleman RC	.20	.09
❑ 181	Chris Mims RC	.20	.09
❑ 182	Tony Casillas	.10	.05
❑ 182X	Ray Roberts Large X on front	50.00	22.00
❑ 183	Shane Dronett RC	.10	.05
❑ 184	Sean Gilbert RC	.40	.18
❑ 185	Siran Stacy RC	.10	.05
❑ 186	Tommy Maddox RC	.10	.05
❑ 187	Steve Israel RC	.10	.05
❑ 188	Brad Muster	.10	.05
❑ 188X	Casey Weldon large X on front	50.00	22.00
❑ 189	Shane Collins RC	.10	.05
❑ 190	Terrell Buckley RC	.10	.05
❑ 191	Eugene Chung RC	.10	.05
❑ 192	Leon Searcy RC	.20	.09
❑ 193	Chuck Smith RC	.10	.05
❑ 194	Patrick Rowe RC	.10	.05
❑ 195	Bill Johnson RC	.10	.05
❑ 196	Gerald Dixon RC	.10	.05
❑ 197	Robert Porcher RC	.20	.09
❑ 198	Tracy Scroggins RC	.10	.05
❑ 199	Jason Hanson RC	.20	.09
❑ 200	Corey Harris RC	.10	.05
❑ 201	Eddie Robinson RC	.10	.05
❑ 202	Steve Emtman RC	.10	.05
❑ 203	Ashley Ambrose RC	.20	.09
❑ 204	Greg Skrepenak RC	.10	.05
❑ 205	Todd Collins RC	.10	.05
❑ 206	Derek Brown TE RC	.10	.05
❑ 207	Kurt Barber RC	.10	.05
❑ 208	Tony Sacca RC	.10	.05
❑ 209	Mark Wheeler RC	.10	.05
❑ 210	Kevin Smith RC	.40	.18
❑ 211	John Fina RC	.10	.05
❑ 212	Johnny Mitchell RC	.10	.05
❑ 213	Dale Carter RC	.40	.18
❑ 214	Bob Spitulski RC	.10	.05
❑ 215	Phillippi Sparks RC	.10	.05
❑ 216	Levon Kirkland RC	.10	.05
❑ 217	Mike Sherrard	.10	.05
❑ 218	Marquez Pope RC	.10	.05
❑ 219	Courtney Hawkins RC	.20	.09
❑ 220	Tyji Armstrong RC	.10	.05
❑ 221	Keith Jackson	.20	.09
❑ 222	Clayton Holmes RC	.10	.05
❑ 223	Quentin Coryatt RC	.40	.18
❑ 224	Troy Auzenne RC	.10	.05
❑ 225	David Klingler RC	.20	.09
❑ 226	Darryl Williams RC	.10	.05
❑ 227	Carl Pickens RC	1.25	.55
❑ 228	Jimmy Smith RC	5.00	2.20
❑ 229	Chester McGlockton RC	.40	.18
❑ 230	Robert Brooks RC	2.00	.90
❑ 231	Alonzo Spellman RC	.20	.09
❑ 232	Darren Woodson RC	.40	.18
❑ 233	Lewis Billups	.10	.05
❑ 234	Edgar Bennett RC	.75	.35
❑ 235	Vaughn Dunbar RC	.10	.05
❑ 236	Steve Bono RC	.40	.18
❑ 237	Clarence Kay	.10	.05
❑ 238	Chris Hinton	.10	.05
❑ 239	Jimmie Jones	.10	.05
❑ 240	Vai Sikahema	.10	.05
❑ 241	Russell Maryland	.20	.09
❑ 241X	Bobby Humphrey large X on front	50.00	22.00
❑ 242	Neal Anderson	.10	.05
❑ 242X	Mark Bavaro large X on front	50.00	22.00
❑ 243	Charles Mann	.10	.05
❑ 244	Hugh Millen	.10	.05
❑ 245	Roger Craig	.20	.09
❑ 246	Rich Gannon	.40	.18
❑ 247	Ricky Ervins	.10	.05
❑ 247X	Marion Butts large X on front	50.00	22.00
❑ 248	Leonard Marshall	.10	.05
❑ 249	Eric Dickerson	.20	.09
❑ 250	Joe Montana	4.00	1.80
❑ RU1	Terrell Buckley Prototype	2.00	.90
❑ RU2	Tommy Maddox Prototype	2.00	.90
❑ AU37	John Elway (2,500 signed)	80.00	36.00
❑ AU77	Ronnie Lott Bonus (2,500 signed)	15.00	6.75
❑ AU123	Ken O'Brien (2,500 signed)	8.00	3.60

1993 Collector's Edge

	MINT	NRMT
COMPLETE SET (325)	20.00	9.00
COMP.SERIES 1 (250)	10.00	4.50
COMP.SERIES 2 (75)	10.00	4.50

No.	Player	Mint	NrMt
❑ 1	Falcons Team Photo	.05	.02
❑ 2	Michael Haynes	.10	.05
❑ 3	Chris Miller	.10	.05
❑ 4	Mike Pritchard	.10	.05
❑ 5	Andre Rison	.10	.05
❑ 6	Deion Sanders	.50	.23
❑ 7	Chuck Smith	.05	.02
❑ 8	Drew Hill	.05	.02
❑ 9	Bobby Hebert	.05	.02
❑ 10	Bills Team Photo	.05	.02
❑ 11	Matt Darby	.05	.02
❑ 12	John Fina	.05	.02
❑ 13	Jim Kelly	.25	.11
❑ 14	Marvcus Patton RC	.05	.02
❑ 15	Andre Reed	.10	.05
❑ 16	Thurman Thomas	.25	.11
❑ 17	James Lofton	.10	.05
❑ 18	Bruce Smith	.25	.11
❑ 19	Bears Team Photo	.05	.02
❑ 20	Neal Anderson	.05	.02
❑ 21	Troy Auzenne	.05	.02
❑ 22	Jim Harbaugh	.25	.11
❑ 23	Alonzo Spellman	.05	.02
❑ 24	Tom Waddle	.05	.02
❑ 25	Darren Lewis	.05	.02
❑ 26	Wendell Davis	.05	.02
❑ 27	Will Furrer	.05	.02
❑ 28	Bengals Team Photo	.05	.02
❑ 29	David Klingler	.05	.02
❑ 30	Ricardo McDonald	.05	.02
❑ 31	Carl Pickens	.25	.11
❑ 32	Harold Green	.05	.02
❑ 33	Anthony Munoz	.10	.05
❑ 34	Darryl Williams	.05	.02
❑ 35	Browns Team Photo	.05	.02
❑ 36	Michael Jackson	.10	.05
❑ 37	Pio Sagapolutele	.05	.02
❑ 38	Tommy Vardell	.05	.02
❑ 39	Bernie Kosar	.10	.05
❑ 40	Michael Dean Perry	.10	.05
❑ 41	Bill Johnson	.05	.02

❑ 42 Vinny Testaverde	.10	.05
❑ 43 Cowboys Team Photo	.05	.02
❑ 44 Troy Aikman	.75	.35
❑ 45 Alvin Harper	.10	.05
❑ 46 Michael Irvin	.25	.11
❑ 47 Russell Maryland	.05	.02
❑ 48 Emmitt Smith	1.50	.70
❑ 49 Kenneth Gant	.05	.02
❑ 50 Jay Novacek	.10	.05
❑ 51 Robert Jones	.05	.02
❑ 52 Clayton Holmes	.05	.02
❑ 53 Broncos Team Photo	.05	.02
❑ 54 Mike Croel	.05	.02
❑ 55 Shane Dronett	.05	.02
❑ 56 Kenny Walker	.05	.02
❑ 57 Tommy Maddox	.05	.02
❑ 58 Dennis Smith	.05	.02
❑ 59 John Elway	1.50	.70
❑ 60 Karl Mecklenburg	.05	.02
❑ 61 Steve Atwater	.05	.02
❑ 62 Vance Johnson	.05	.02
❑ 63 Lions Team Photo	.05	.02
❑ 64 Barry Sanders	1.50	.70
❑ 65 Andre Ware	.05	.02
❑ 66 Pat Swilling	.05	.02
❑ 67 Jason Hanson	.05	.02
❑ 68 Willie Green	.05	.02
❑ 69 Herman Moore	.50	.23
❑ 70 Rodney Peete	.05	.02
❑ 71 Erik Kramer	.10	.05
❑ 72 Robert Porcher	.05	.02
❑ 73 Packers Team Photo	.05	.02
❑ 74 Terrell Buckley	.05	.02
❑ 75 Reggie White	.25	.11
❑ 76 Brett Favre	2.00	.90
❑ 77 Don Majkowski	.05	.02
❑ 78 Edgar Bennett	.25	.11
❑ 79 Ty Detmer	.25	.11
❑ 80 Sanjay Beach	.05	.02
❑ 81 Sterling Sharpe	.25	.11
❑ 82 Oilers Team Photo	.05	.02
❑ 83 Gary Brown	.05	.02
❑ 84 Ernest Givins	.10	.05
❑ 85 Haywood Jeffires	.10	.05
❑ 86 Corey Harris	.05	.02
❑ 87 Warren Moon	.25	.11
❑ 88 Eddie Robinson	.05	.02
❑ 89 Lorenzo White	.05	.02
❑ 90 Bo Orlando	.05	.02
❑ 91 Colts Team Photo	.05	.02
❑ 92 Quentin Coryatt	.10	.05
❑ 93 Steve Emtman	.05	.02
❑ 94 Jeff George	.25	.11
❑ 95 Jessie Hester	.05	.02
❑ 96 Rohn Stark	.05	.02
❑ 97 Ashley Ambrose	.05	.02
❑ 98 John Baylor	.05	.02
❑ 99 Chiefs Team Photo	.05	.02
❑ 100 Tim Barnett	.05	.02
❑ 101 Derrick Thomas	.25	.11
❑ 102 Barry Word	.05	.02
❑ 103 Dale Carter	.05	.02
❑ 104 Jayice Pearson	.05	.02
❑ 105 Tracy Simien	.05	.02
❑ 106 Harvey Williams	.10	.05
❑ 107 Dave Krieg	.10	.05
❑ 108 Christian Okoye	.05	.02
❑ 109 Joe Montana	1.50	.70
❑ 110 Dolphins Team Photo	.05	.02
❑ 111 J.B. Brown	.05	.02
❑ 112 Marco Coleman	.05	.02
❑ 113 Dan Marino	1.50	.70
❑ 114 Mark Clayton	.05	.02
❑ 115 Mark Higgs	.05	.02
❑ 116 Bryan Cox	.05	.02
❑ 117 Chuck Klingbeil	.05	.02
❑ 118 Troy Vincent	.05	.02
❑ 119 Keith Jackson	.10	.05
❑ 120 Bruce Alexander	.05	.02
❑ 121 Vikings Team Photo	.05	.02
❑ 122 Terry Allen	.25	.11
❑ 123 Rich Gannon	.25	.11
❑ 124 Todd Scott	.05	.02
❑ 125 Cris Carter	.50	.23
❑ 126 Sean Salisbury	.05	.02
❑ 127 Jack Del Rio	.05	.02
❑ 128 Chris Doleman	.05	.02
❑ 129 Anthony Carter	.10	.05
❑ 130 Patriots Team Photo	.05	.02
❑ 131 Eugene Chung	.05	.02
❑ 132 Todd Collins	.05	.02
❑ 133 Tommy Hodson	.05	.02
❑ 134 Leonard Russell	.10	.05
❑ 135 Jon Vaughn	.05	.02
❑ 136 Andre Tippett	.05	.02
❑ 137 Saints Team Photo	.05	.02
❑ 138 Wesley Carroll	.05	.02
❑ 139 Richard Cooper	.05	.02
❑ 140 Vaughn Dunbar	.05	.02
❑ 141 Fred McAfee	.05	.02
❑ 142 Torrance Small	.05	.02
❑ 143 Steve Walsh	.05	.02
❑ 144 Vaughan Johnson	.05	.02
❑ 145 Giants Team Photo	.05	.02
❑ 146 Jarrod Bunch	.05	.02
❑ 147 Phil Simms	.10	.05
❑ 148 Carl Banks	.05	.02
❑ 149 Lawrence Taylor	.25	.11
❑ 150 Rodney Hampton	.25	.11
❑ 151 Phillippi Sparks	.05	.02
❑ 152 Derek Brown TE	.05	.02
❑ 153 Jets Team Photo	.05	.02
❑ 154 Boomer Esiason	.10	.05
❑ 155 Johnny Mitchell	.05	.02
❑ 156 Rob Moore	.10	.05
❑ 157 Ronnie Lott	.10	.05
❑ 158 Browning Nagle	.05	.02
❑ 159 Johnny Johnson	.05	.02
❑ 160 Dwayne White	.05	.02
❑ 161 Blair Thomas	.05	.02
❑ 162 Eagles Team Photo	.05	.02
❑ 163 Randall Cunningham	.25	.11
❑ 164 Fred Barnett	.10	.05
❑ 165 Siran Stacy	.05	.02
❑ 166 Keith Byars	.05	.02
❑ 167 Calvin Williams	.10	.05
❑ 168 Jeff Sydner	.05	.02
❑ 169 Tommy Jeter	.05	.02
❑ 170 Andre Waters	.05	.02
❑ 171 Phoenix Team Photo	.05	.02
❑ 172 Steve Beuerlein	.05	.02
❑ 173 Randal Hill	.05	.02
❑ 174 Timm Rosenbach	.05	.02
❑ 175 Ed Cunningham	.05	.02
❑ 176 Walter Reeves	.05	.02
❑ 177 Michael Zordich	.05	.02
❑ 178 Gary Clark	.10	.05
❑ 179 Ken Harvey	.05	.02
❑ 180 Steelers Team Photo	.05	.02
❑ 181 Barry Foster	.10	.05
❑ 182 Neil O'Donnell	.25	.11
❑ 183 Leon Searcy	.05	.02
❑ 184 Bubby Brister	.05	.02
❑ 185 Merril Hoge	.05	.02
❑ 186 Joel Steed	.05	.02
❑ 187 Raiders Team Photo	.05	.02
❑ 188 Nick Bell	.05	.02
❑ 189 Eric Dickerson	.10	.05
❑ 190 Nolan Harrison	.05	.02
❑ 191 Todd Marinovich	.05	.02
❑ 192 Greg Skrepenak	.05	.02
❑ 193 Howie Long	.10	.05
❑ 194 Jay Schroeder	.05	.02
❑ 195 Chester McGlockton	.10	.05
❑ 196 Rams Team Photo	.05	.02
❑ 197 Jim Everett	.10	.05
❑ 198 Sean Gilbert	.10	.05
❑ 199 Steve Israel	.05	.02
❑ 200 Marc Boutte	.05	.02
❑ 201 Joe Milinichik	.05	.02
❑ 202 Henry Ellard	.10	.05
❑ 203 Jackie Slater	.05	.02
❑ 204 Chargers Team Photo	.05	.02
❑ 205 Eric Bieniemy	.05	.02
❑ 206 Marion Butts	.05	.02
❑ 207 Nate Lewis	.05	.02
❑ 208 Junior Seau	.25	.11
❑ 209 Steve Hendrickson	.05	.02
❑ 210 Chris Mims	.05	.02
❑ 211 Harry Swayne	.05	.02
❑ 212 Marquez Pope	.05	.02
❑ 213 Donald Frank	.05	.02
❑ 214 Anthony Miller	.10	.05
❑ 215 Seahawks Team Photo	.05	.02
❑ 216 Cortez Kennedy	.10	.05
❑ 217 Dan McGwire	.05	.02
❑ 218 Kelly Stouffer	.05	.02
❑ 219 Chris Warren	.10	.05
❑ 220 Brian Blades	.10	.05
❑ 221 Rod Stephens RC	.05	.02
❑ 222 49ers Team Photo	.05	.02
❑ 223 Jerry Rice	1.00	.45
❑ 224 Ricky Watters	.25	.11
❑ 225 Steve Young	.75	.35
❑ 226 Tom Rathman	.05	.02
❑ 227 Dana Hall	.05	.02
❑ 228 Amp Lee	.05	.02
❑ 229 Brian Bollinger	.05	.02
❑ 230 Keith DeLong	.05	.02
❑ 231 John Taylor	.10	.05
❑ 232 Buccaneers Team Photo	.05	.02
❑ 233 Tyji Armstrong	.05	.02
❑ 234 Lawrence Dawsey	.05	.02
❑ 235 Mark Wheeler	.05	.02
❑ 236 Vince Workman	.05	.02
❑ 237 Reggie Cobb	.05	.02
❑ 238 Tony Mayberry	.05	.02
❑ 239 Marty Carter	.05	.02
❑ 240 Courtney Hawkins	.05	.02
❑ 241 Ray Seals	.05	.02
❑ 242 Mark Carrier WR	.10	.05
❑ 243 Redskins Team Photo	.05	.02
❑ 244 Mark Rypien	.05	.02
❑ 245 Ricky Ervins	.05	.02
❑ 246 Gerald Riggs	.05	.02
❑ 247 Art Monk	.10	.05
❑ 248 Mark Schlereth	.05	.02
❑ 249 Monte Coleman	.05	.02
❑ 250 Wilber Marshall	.05	.02
❑ 251 Ben Coleman RC	.05	.02
❑ 252 Curtis Conway RC	.40	.18
❑ 253 Ernest Dye RC	.05	.02
❑ 254 Todd Kelly RC	.05	.02
❑ 255 Patrick Bates RC	.05	.02
❑ 256 George Teague RC	.10	.05
❑ 257 Mark Brunell RC	2.50	1.10
❑ 258 Adrian Hardy	.05	.02
❑ 259 Dana Stubblefield RC	.25	.11
❑ 260 William Roaf RC	.10	.05
❑ 261 Irv Smith RC	.05	.02
❑ 262 Drew Bledsoe RC	2.00	.90
❑ 263 Dan Williams RC	.05	.02
❑ 264 Jerry Ball	.05	.02
❑ 265 Mark Clayton	.05	.02
❑ 266 John Stephens	.05	.02
❑ 267 Reggie White	.25	.11
❑ 268 Jeff Hostetler	.10	.05
❑ 269 Boomer Esiason	.10	.05
❑ 270 Wade Wilson	.05	.02
❑ 271 Steve Beuerlein	.05	.02
❑ 272 Tim McDonald	.05	.02
❑ 273 Craig Heyward	.10	.05
❑ 274 Everson Walls	.05	.02
❑ 275 Stan Humphries	.25	.11
❑ 276 Carl Banks	.05	.02
❑ 277 Brad Muster	.05	.02
❑ 278 Tim Harris	.05	.02
❑ 279 Gary Clark	.10	.05
❑ 280 Joe Milinichik	.05	.02
❑ 281 Leonard Marshall	.05	.02
❑ 282 Joe Montana	1.50	.70
❑ 283 Rod Bernstine	.05	.02
❑ 284 Mark Carrier WR	.10	.05
❑ 285 Michael Brooks	.05	.02
❑ 286 Marvin Jones RC	.05	.02
❑ 287 John Copeland RC	.10	.05
❑ 288 Eric Curry RC	.05	.02
❑ 289 Steve Everitt RC	.05	.02
❑ 290 Tom Carter RC	.10	.05
❑ 291 Deon Figures RC	.10	.05
❑ 292A Leonard Renfro RC	.05	.02
❑ 292B Leonard Renfro RC	.05	.02
❑ 293 Thomas Smith RC	.10	.05
❑ 294 Carlton Gray RC	.05	.02
❑ 295 Demetrius DuBose RC	.05	.02
❑ 296 Coleman Rudolph RC	.05	.02
❑ 297 John Parrella RC	.05	.02
❑ 298 Glyn Milburn RC	.25	.11

❑ 299 Reggie Brooks RC .10 .05
❑ 300 Garrison Hearst RC .50 .23
❑ 301 John Elway 1.50 .70
❑ 302 Brad Hopkins RC .05 .02
❑ 303 Darrien Gordon RC UER .05 .02
(Card states he was drafted 12th instead of 22nd)
❑ 304 Robert Smith RC 2.00 .90
❑ 305 Chris Slade RC .10 .05
❑ 306 Ryan McNeil RC .05 .02
❑ 307 Micheal Barrow RC .10 .05
❑ 308 Roosevelt Potts RC .05 .02
❑ 309 Qadry Ismail RC .50 .23
❑ 310 Reggie Freeman RC .05 .02
❑ 311 Vincent Brisby RC .25 .11
❑ 312 Rick Mirer RC .30 .14
❑ 313 Billy Joe Hobert RC .25 .11
❑ 314 Natrone Means RC .40 .18
❑ 315 Gary Zimmerman .05 .02
❑ 316 Bobby Hebert .05 .02
❑ 317 Don Beebe .05 .02
❑ 318 Wilber Marshall .05 .02
❑ 319 Marcus Allen .25 .11
❑ 320 Ronnie Lott .10 .05
❑ 321 Ricky Sanders .05 .02
❑ 322 Charles Mann .05 .02
❑ 323 Simon Fletcher .05 .02
❑ 324 Johnny Johnson .05 .02
❑ 325 Gary Plummer .05 .02
❑ 326 Carolina Panthers Insert 25.00 11.00
❑ M326 Carolina Panthers Send Away 4.00 1.80
❑ M327 Jacksonville Jaguars Send Away 4.00 1.80
❑ PRO1 John Elway AUTO/3000 60.00 27.00

1994 Collector's Edge

	MINT	NRMT
COMPLETE SET (200)	15.00	6.75

❑ 1 Mike Pritchard .05 .02
❑ 2 Erric Pegram .05 .02
❑ 3 Michael Haynes .10 .05
❑ 4 Bobby Hebert .05 .02
❑ 5 Deion Sanders .50 .23
❑ 6 Andre Rison .10 .05
❑ 7 Don Beebe .05 .02
❑ 8 Mark Kelso .05 .02
❑ 9 Darryl Talley .05 .02
❑ 10 Cornelius Bennett .10 .05
❑ 11 Jim Kelly .25 .11
❑ 12 Andre Reed .10 .05
❑ 13 Bruce Smith .25 .11
❑ 14 Thurman Thomas .25 .11
❑ 15 Craig Heyward .10 .05
❑ 16 Chris Zorich .05 .02
❑ 17 Alonzo Spellman .05 .02
❑ 18 Tom Waddle .05 .02
❑ 19 Neal Anderson .05 .02
❑ 20 Kevin Butler .05 .02
❑ 21 Curtis Conway .25 .11
❑ 22 Richard Dent .10 .05
❑ 23 Jim Harbaugh .25 .11
❑ 24 Derrick Fenner .05 .02
❑ 25 Harold Green .05 .02
❑ 26 David Klingler .05 .02
❑ 27 Daniel Stubbs .05 .02
❑ 28 Alfred Williams .05 .02
❑ 29 John Copeland .05 .02
❑ 30 Mark Carrier WR .10 .05
❑ 31 Michael Jackson .10 .05
❑ 32 Eric Metcalf .10 .05
❑ 33 Vinny Testaverde .10 .05
❑ 34 Tommy Vardell .05 .02
❑ 35 Alvin Harper .10 .05
❑ 36 Ken Norton Jr. .10 .05
❑ 37 Tony Casillas .05 .02
❑ 38 Leon Lett .05 .02
❑ 39 Jay Novacek .10 .05
❑ 40 Kevin Smith .05 .02
❑ 41 Troy Aikman 1.00 .45
❑ 42 Michael Irvin .25 .11
❑ 43 Russell Maryland .05 .02
❑ 44 Emmitt Smith 1.50 .70
❑ 45 Robert Delpino .05 .02
❑ 46 Simon Fletcher .05 .02
❑ 47 Greg Kragen .05 .02
❑ 48 Arthur Marshall .05 .02
❑ 49 Steve Atwater .05 .02
❑ 50 Rod Bernstine .05 .02
❑ 51 John Elway 2.00 .90
❑ 52 Glyn Milburn .10 .05
❑ 53 Shannon Sharpe .10 .05
❑ 54 Bennie Blades .05 .02
❑ 55 Mel Gray .05 .02
❑ 56 Herman Moore .25 .11
❑ 57 Pat Swilling .05 .02
❑ 58 Chris Spielman .10 .05
❑ 59 Rodney Peete .05 .02
❑ 60 Andre Ware .05 .02
❑ 61 Brett Perriman .10 .05
❑ 62 Erik Kramer .10 .05
❑ 63 Barry Sanders 2.00 .90
❑ 64 Mark Clayton .05 .02
❑ 65 Chris Jacke .05 .02
❑ 66 Terrell Buckley .05 .02
❑ 67 Ty Detmer .10 .05
❑ 68 Sanjay Beach .05 .02
❑ 69 Brian Noble .05 .02
❑ 70 Edgar Bennett .25 .11
❑ 71 Brett Favre 2.00 .90
❑ 72 Sterling Sharpe .10 .05
❑ 73 Reggie White .25 .11
❑ 74 Ernest Givins .10 .05
❑ 75 Al Del Greco .05 .02
❑ 76 Cris Dishman .05 .02
❑ 77 Curtis Duncan .05 .02
❑ 78 Webster Slaughter .05 .02
❑ 79 Spencer Tillman .05 .02
❑ 80 Warren Moon .25 .11
❑ 81 Wilber Marshall .05 .02
❑ 82 Haywood Jeffires .10 .05
❑ 83 Lorenzo White .05 .02
❑ 84 Gary Brown .05 .02
❑ 85 Reggie Langhorne .05 .02
❑ 86 Dean Biasucci .05 .02
❑ 87 Steve Emtman .05 .02
❑ 88 Jessie Hester .05 .02
❑ 89 Quentin Coryatt .05 .02
❑ 90 Roosevelt Potts .05 .02
❑ 91 Jeff George .25 .11
❑ 92 Nick Lowery .05 .02
❑ 93 Willie Davis .10 .05
❑ 94 Joe Montana 2.00 .90
❑ 95 Neil Smith .25 .11
❑ 96 Marcus Allen .25 .11
❑ 97 Derrick Thomas .25 .11
❑ 98 Greg Townsend .05 .02
❑ 99 Willie Gault .05 .02
❑ 100 Ethan Horton .05 .02
❑ 101 Jeff Hostetler .10 .05
❑ 102 Tim Brown .25 .11
❑ 103 Rocket Ismail .10 .05
❑ 104 Shane Conlan .05 .02
❑ 105 Henry Ellard .10 .05
❑ 106 T.J. Rubley .05 .02
❑ 107 Sean Gilbert .05 .02
❑ 108 Troy Drayton .05 .02
❑ 109 Jerome Bettis .25 .11
❑ 110 Terry Kirby .25 .11
❑ 111 Mark Ingram .05 .02
❑ 112 John Offerdahl .05 .02
❑ 113 Louis Oliver .05 .02
❑ 114 Irving Fryar .10 .05
❑ 115 Dan Marino 2.00 .90
❑ 116 Keith Jackson .05 .02
❑ 117 O.J. McDuffie .25 .11
❑ 118 Jim McMahon .05 .02
❑ 119 Sean Salisbury .05 .02
❑ 120 Randall McDaniel .05 .02
❑ 121 Jack Del Rio .05 .02
❑ 122 Cris Carter .50 .23
❑ 123 Chris Doleman .05 .02
❑ 124 John Randle .05 .02
❑ 125 Vincent Brisby .25 .11
❑ 126 Greg McMurtry .05 .02
❑ 127 Drew Bledsoe 1.00 .45
❑ 128 Leonard Russell .05 .02
❑ 129 Michael Brooks .05 .02
❑ 130 Mark Jackson .05 .02
❑ 131 Pepper Johnson .05 .02
❑ 132 Doug Riesenberg .05 .02
❑ 133 Phil Simms .10 .05
❑ 134 Rodney Hampton .25 .11
❑ 135 Leonard Marshall .05 .02
❑ 136 Rob Moore .10 .05
❑ 137 Chris Burkett .05 .02
❑ 138 Boomer Esiason .10 .05
❑ 139 Johnny Johnson .05 .02
❑ 140 Ronnie Lott .10 .05
❑ 141 Brad Muster .05 .02
❑ 142 Renaldo Turnbull .05 .02
❑ 143 Willie Roaf .05 .02
❑ 144 Rickey Jackson .05 .02
❑ 145 Morten Andersen .05 .02
❑ 146 Vaughn Dunbar .05 .02
❑ 147 Wade Wilson .05 .02
❑ 148 Eric Martin .05 .02
❑ 149 Seth Joyner .05 .02
❑ 150 Calvin Williams .10 .05
❑ 151 Vai Sikahema .05 .02
❑ 152 Herschel Walker .10 .05
❑ 153 Eric Allen .05 .02
❑ 154 Fred Barnett .10 .05
❑ 155 Randall Cunningham .25 .11
❑ 156 Steve Beuerlein .05 .02
❑ 157 Gary Clark .10 .05
❑ 158 Anthony Edwards .05 .02
❑ 159 Randal Hill .05 .02
❑ 160 Freddie Joe Nunn .05 .02
❑ 161 Garrison Hearst .25 .11
❑ 162 Ricky Proehl .05 .02
❑ 163 Eric Green .05 .02
❑ 164 Levon Kirkland .05 .02
❑ 165 Joel Steed .05 .02
❑ 166 Deon Figures .05 .02
❑ 167 Leroy Thompson .05 .02
❑ 168 Barry Foster .05 .02
❑ 169 Neil O'Donnell .25 .11
❑ 170 Junior Seau .25 .11
❑ 171 Leslie O'Neal .05 .02
❑ 172 Stan Humphries .25 .11
❑ 173 Marion Butts .05 .02
❑ 174 Anthony Miller .10 .05
❑ 175 Natrone Means .25 .11
❑ 176 Odessa Turner .05 .02
❑ 177 Dana Stubblefield .25 .11
❑ 178 John Taylor .10 .05
❑ 179 Ricky Watters .25 .11
❑ 180 Steve Young .75 .35
❑ 181 Jerry Rice 1.00 .45
❑ 182 Tom Rathman .05 .02
❑ 183 Brian Blades .10 .05
❑ 184 Patrick Hunter .05 .02
❑ 185 Rick Mirer .25 .11
❑ 186 Chris Warren .10 .05
❑ 187 Cortez Kennedy .10 .05
❑ 188 Reggie Cobb .05 .02
❑ 189 Craig Erickson .05 .02
❑ 190 Hardy Nickerson .10 .05
❑ 191 Lawrence Dawsey .05 .02
❑ 192 Broderick Thomas .05 .02
❑ 193 Ricky Sanders .05 .02
❑ 194 Carl Banks .05 .02
❑ 195 Ricky Ervins .05 .02
❑ 196 Darrell Green .05 .02
❑ 197 Mark Rypien .05 .02

		MINT	NRMT
❑ 198	Desmond Howard	.10	.05
❑ 199	Art Monk	.10	.05
❑ 200	Reggie Brooks	.10	.05
❑ P1	Sh.Sharpe Prototype Numbered 53	1.00	.45

1995 Collector's Edge

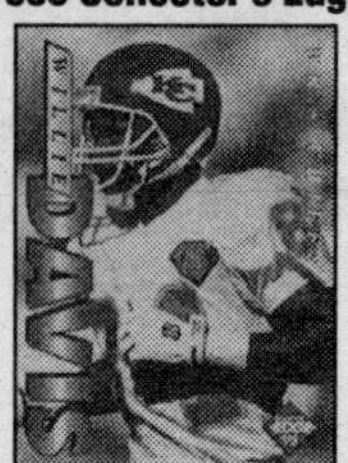

		MINT	NRMT
COMPLETE SET (205)		20.00	9.00
❑ 1	Anthony Edwards	.05	.02
❑ 2	Garrison Hearst	.25	.11
❑ 3	Seth Joyner	.05	.02
❑ 4	Dave Krieg	.05	.02
❑ 5	Chuck Levy	.05	.02
❑ 6	Rob Moore	.05	.02
❑ 7	J.J. Birden	.05	.02
❑ 8	Jeff George	.10	.05
❑ 9	Craig Heyward	.10	.05
❑ 10	Norm Johnson	.05	.02
❑ 11	Terance Mathis	.10	.05
❑ 12	Eric Metcalf	.10	.05
❑ 13	Chuck Smith	.05	.02
❑ 14	Darryl Talley	.05	.02
❑ 15	Cornelius Bennett	.10	.05
❑ 16	Steve Christie	.05	.02
❑ 17	Kenneth Davis	.05	.02
❑ 18	Phil Hansen	.05	.02
❑ 19	Jim Kelly	.25	.11
❑ 20	Bryce Paup	.25	.11
❑ 21	Andre Reed	.10	.05
❑ 22	Bruce Smith	.25	.11
❑ 23	Eric Ball	.05	.02
❑ 24	Don Beebe	.05	.02
❑ 25	Mark Carrier WR	.10	.05
❑ 26	Tim McKyer	.05	.02
❑ 27	Pete Metzelaars	.05	.02
❑ 28	Sam Mills	.10	.05
❑ 29	Jack Trudeau	.05	.02
❑ 30	Mark Carrier DB	.05	.02
❑ 31	Curtis Conway	.25	.11
❑ 32	Erik Kramer	.05	.02
❑ 33	Lewis Tillman	.05	.02
❑ 34	Michael Timpson	.05	.02
❑ 35	Steve Walsh	.05	.02
❑ 36	Chris Zorich	.05	.02
❑ 37	Jeff Blake RC	.75	.35
❑ 38	Harold Green	.05	.02
❑ 39	David Klingler	.10	.05
❑ 40	Carl Pickens	.25	.11
❑ 41	Tom Waddle	.05	.02
❑ 42	Dan Wilkinson	.10	.05
❑ 43	Leroy Hoard	.05	.02
❑ 44	Michael Jackson	.10	.05
❑ 45	Antonio Langham	.05	.02
❑ 46	Andre Rison	.10	.05
❑ 47	Vinny Testaverde	.10	.05
❑ 48	Eric Turner	.05	.02
❑ 49	Tommy Vardell	.05	.02
❑ 50	Troy Aikman	1.00	.45
❑ 51	Charles Haley	.10	.05
❑ 52	Michael Irvin	.25	.11
❑ 53	Daryl Johnston	.10	.05
❑ 54	Leon Lett	.05	.02
❑ 55	Jay Novacek	.10	.05
❑ 56	Emmitt Smith	1.50	.70
❑ 57	Kevin Williams WR	.10	.05
❑ 58	Steve Atwater	.05	.02
❑ 59	John Elway	2.00	.90
❑ 60	Simon Fletcher	.05	.02
❑ 61	Glyn Milburn	.05	.02
❑ 62	Anthony Miller	.10	.05
❑ 63	Leonard Russell	.05	.02
❑ 64	Shannon Sharpe	.10	.05
❑ 65	Scott Mitchell	.10	.05
❑ 66	Herman Moore	.25	.11
❑ 67	Johnnie Morton	.10	.05
❑ 68	Brett Perriman	.10	.05
❑ 69	Barry Sanders	2.00	.90
❑ 70	Edgar Bennett	.10	.05
❑ 71	Brett Favre	2.00	.90
❑ 72	Mark Ingram	.05	.02
❑ 73	Chris Jacke	.05	.02
❑ 74	Guy McIntyre	.05	.02
❑ 75	Reggie White	.25	.11
❑ 76	Gary Brown	.05	.02
❑ 77	Ernest Givins	.05	.02
❑ 78	Mel Gray	.05	.02
❑ 79	Haywood Jeffires	.05	.02
❑ 80	Webster Slaughter	.05	.02
❑ 81	Craig Erickson	.05	.02
❑ 82	Marshall Faulk	.40	.18
❑ 83	Jim Harbaugh	.10	.05
❑ 84	Roosevelt Potts	.05	.02
❑ 85	Floyd Turner	.05	.02
❑ 86	Steve Beuerlein	.05	.02
❑ 87	Reggie Cobb	.05	.02
❑ 88	Jeff Lageman	.05	.02
❑ 89	Mazio Royster	.05	.02
❑ 90	Marcus Allen	.25	.11
❑ 91	Steve Bono	.10	.05
❑ 92	Willie Davis	.10	.05
❑ 93	Lake Dawson	.10	.05
❑ 94	Ronnie Lott	.10	.05
❑ 95	Eric Martin	.05	.02
❑ 96	Chris Penn	.05	.02
❑ 97	Tim Brown	.25	.11
❑ 98	Derrick Fenner	.05	.02
❑ 99	Rob Fredrickson	.05	.02
❑ 100	Nolan Harrison	.05	.02
❑ 101	Jeff Hostetler	.10	.05
❑ 102	Rocket Ismail	.10	.05
❑ 103	James Jett	.10	.05
❑ 104	Chester McGlockton	.10	.05
❑ 105	Anthony Smith	.05	.02
❑ 106	Harvey Williams	.05	.02
❑ 107	Jerome Bettis	.25	.11
❑ 108	Troy Drayton	.05	.02
❑ 109	Chris Miller	.05	.02
❑ 110	Robert Young	.05	.02
❑ 111	Keith Byars	.05	.02
❑ 112	Gary Clark	.05	.02
❑ 113	Bryan Cox	.05	.02
❑ 114	Jeff Cross	.05	.02
❑ 115	Irving Fryar	.10	.05
❑ 116	Randal Hill	.05	.02
❑ 117	Terry Kirby	.10	.05
❑ 118	Dan Marino	2.00	.90
❑ 119	O.J. McDuffie	.25	.11
❑ 120	Bernie Parmalee	.10	.05
❑ 121	Terry Allen	.10	.05
❑ 122	Cris Carter	.25	.11
❑ 123	Qadry Ismail	.10	.05
❑ 124	Warren Moon	.10	.05
❑ 125	John Randle	.10	.05
❑ 126	Jake Reed	.10	.05
❑ 127	Fuad Reveiz	.05	.02
❑ 128	Broderick Thomas	.05	.02
❑ 129	Drew Bledsoe	1.00	.45
❑ 130	Vincent Brisby	.05	.02
❑ 131	Ben Coates	.10	.05
❑ 132	Dave Meggett	.05	.02
❑ 133	Chris Slade	.10	.05
❑ 134	Leroy Thompson	.05	.02
❑ 135	Eric Allen	.05	.02
❑ 136	Mario Bates	.25	.11
❑ 137	Quinn Early	.05	.02
❑ 138	Jim Everett	.05	.02
❑ 139	Michael Haynes	.10	.05
❑ 140	Torrance Small	.05	.02
❑ 141	Dave Brown	.10	.05
❑ 142	Chris Calloway	.05	.02
❑ 143	Keith Hamilton	.05	.02
❑ 144	Rodney Hampton	.10	.05
❑ 145	Mike Sherrard	.05	.02
❑ 146	David Treadwell	.05	.02
❑ 147	Herschel Walker	.10	.05
❑ 148	Boomer Esiason	.10	.05
❑ 149	Erik Howard	.05	.02
❑ 150	Johnny Johnson	.05	.02
❑ 151	Mo Lewis	.05	.02
❑ 152	Johnny Mitchell	.05	.02
❑ 153	Fred Barnett	.10	.05
❑ 154	Randall Cunningham	.25	.11
❑ 155	William Fuller	.05	.02
❑ 156	Charlie Garner	.10	.05
❑ 157	Greg Jackson	.05	.02
❑ 158	Ricky Watters	.25	.11
❑ 159	Calvin Williams	.10	.05
❑ 160	Barry Foster	.10	.05
❑ 161	Kevin Greene	.10	.05
❑ 162	Greg Lloyd	.10	.05
❑ 163	Byron Bam Morris	.10	.05
❑ 164	Neil O'Donnell	.10	.05
❑ 165	Erric Pegram	.10	.05
❑ 166	John L. Williams	.05	.02
❑ 167	Rod Woodson	.10	.05
❑ 168	John Carney	.05	.02
❑ 169	Stan Humphries	.10	.05
❑ 170	Natrone Means	.25	.11
❑ 171	Chris Mims	.05	.02
❑ 172	Leslie O'Neal	.10	.05
❑ 173	Alfred Pupunu RC	.05	.02
❑ 174	Junior Seau	.25	.11
❑ 175	Mark Seay	.10	.05
❑ 176	William Floyd	.25	.11
❑ 177	Jerry Rice	1.00	.45
❑ 178	Deion Sanders	.60	.25
❑ 179	Dana Stubblefield	.25	.11
❑ 180	John Taylor	.05	.02
❑ 181	Steve Young	.75	.35
❑ 182	Bryant Young	.10	.05
❑ 183	Brian Blades	.10	.05
❑ 184	Cortez Kennedy	.10	.05
❑ 185	Kelvin Martin	.05	.02
❑ 186	Rick Mirer	.25	.11
❑ 187	Ricky Proehl	.05	.02
❑ 188	Michael Sinclair	.05	.02
❑ 189	Chris Warren	.10	.05
❑ 190	Trent Dilfer	.25	.11
❑ 191	Alvin Harper	.05	.02
❑ 192	Jackie Harris	.05	.02
❑ 193	Hardy Nickerson	.05	.02
❑ 194	Errict Rhett	.25	.11
❑ 195	Reggie Roby	.05	.02
❑ 196	Henry Ellard	.10	.05
❑ 197	Ricky Ervins	.05	.02
❑ 198	Darrell Green	.05	.02
❑ 199	Brian Mitchell	.05	.02
❑ 200	Heath Shuler	.25	.11
❑ 201	Checklist	.05	.02
❑ 202	Checklist	.05	.02
❑ 203	Checklist	.05	.02
❑ 204	Checklist	.05	.02
❑ 205	Checklist	.05	.02
❑ P1	Natrone Means Promo	.50	.23
❑ P2	Chris Warren Promo	.50	.23

1995 Collector's Edge Instant Replay

	MINT	NRMT
COMPLETE SET (51)	15.00	6.75
1 Jeff George	.10	.05
2 Eric Metcalf	.10	.05
3 Jim Kelly	.20	.09
4 Jeff Blake RC	.75	.35
5 Andre Rison	.10	.05
6 Troy Aikman	.75	.35
7 Michael Irvin	.20	.09
8 Emmitt Smith	1.25	.55
9 John Elway	1.50	.70
10 Terrell Davis RC	8.00	3.60
11 Herman Moore	.20	.09
12 Barry Sanders	1.50	.70
13 Brett Favre	1.50	.70
14 Marshall Faulk	.30	.14
15 Steve Beuerlein	.05	.02
16 Steve Bono	.10	.05
17 Tim Brown	.20	.09
18 Jeff Hostetler	.10	.05
19 Jerome Bettis	.20	.09
20 Dan Marino	1.50	.70
21 Cris Carter	.20	.09
22 Drew Bledsoe	.75	.35
23 Ben Coates	.10	.05
24 Randall Cunningham	.20	.09
25 Terry Kirby	.10	.05
26 Ricky Watters	.20	.09
27 Kyle Brady	.20	.09
28 Byron Bam Morris	.10	.05
29 Neil O'Donnell	.10	.05
30 Natrone Means	.20	.09
31 Junior Seau	.20	.09
32 William Floyd	.20	.09
33 Jerry Rice	.75	.35
34 Deion Sanders	.50	.23
35 Steve Young	.60	.25
36 Rick Mirer	.20	.09
37 Chris Warren	.10	.05
38 Trent Dilfer	.20	.09
39 Errict Rhett	.20	.09
40 Heath Shuler	.20	.09
41 Ki-Jana Carter RC	.20	.09
42 Kerry Collins RC	1.25	.55
43 Steve McNair RC	2.00	.90
44 Rashaan Salaam RC	.20	.09
45 James O. Stewart RC	1.50	.70
46 J.J. Stokes RC	.20	.09
47 Tyrone Wheatley RC	1.00	.45
48 Joey Galloway RC	1.50	.70
49 Napoleon Kaufman RC	1.25	.55
50 Michael Westbrook RC	1.25	.55
NNO Checklist Card	.05	.02

1996 Collector's Edge

	MINT	NRMT
COMPLETE SET (250)	20.00	9.00
1 Larry Centers	.20	.09
2 Garrison Hearst	.20	.09
3 Dave Krieg	.10	.05
4 Rob Moore	.20	.09
5 Frank Sanders	.20	.09
6 Eric Swann	.10	.05
7 Morten Andersen	.10	.05
8 Chris Doleman	.10	.05
9 Bert Emanuel	.20	.09
10 Jeff George	.20	.09
11 Craig Heyward	.10	.05
12 Terance Mathis	.10	.05
13 Clay Matthews	.10	.05
14 Eric Metcalf	.10	.05
15 Bill Brooks	.10	.05
16 Todd Collins	.20	.09
17 Russell Copeland	.10	.05
18 Jim Kelly	.40	.18
19 Bryce Paup	.10	.05
20 Andre Reed	.20	.09
21 Bruce Smith	.20	.09
22 Mark Carrier WR	.10	.05
23 Kerry Collins	.40	.18
24 Willie Green	.10	.05
25 Eric Guliford	.10	.05
26 Brett Maxie	.10	.05
27 Tim McKyer	.10	.05
28 Derrick Moore	.10	.05
29 Curtis Conway	.40	.18
30 Jim Flanigan	.10	.05
31 Jeff Graham	.10	.05
32 Robert Green	.10	.05
33 Erik Kramer	.10	.05
34 Rashaan Salaam	.40	.18
35 Alonzo Spellman	.10	.05
36 Donnell Woolford	.10	.05
37 Chris Zorich	.10	.05
38 Eric Bieniemy	.10	.05
39 Jeff Blake	.40	.18
40 Ki-Jana Carter	.20	.09
41 John Copeland	.10	.05
42 Harold Green	.10	.05
43 Tony McGee	.10	.05
44 Carl Pickens	.40	.18
45 Darnay Scott	.20	.09
46 Bracey Walker	.10	.05
47 Dan Wilkinson	.10	.05
48 Rob Burnett	.10	.05
49 Leroy Hoard	.10	.05
50 Ernest Hunter	.10	.05
51 Michael Jackson	.20	.09
52 Stevon Moore	.10	.05
53 Anthony Pleasant	.10	.05
54 Andre Rison	.20	.09
55 Vinny Testaverde	.20	.09
56 Eric Zeier	.10	.05
57 Troy Aikman	1.00	.45
58 Bill Bates	.20	.09
59 Shante Carver	.10	.05
60 Michael Irvin	.40	.18
61 Daryl Johnston	.20	.09
62 Jay Novacek	.10	.05
63 Deion Sanders	.60	.25
64 Emmitt Smith	1.50	.70
65 Sherman Williams	.10	.05
66 Terrell Davis	2.50	1.10
67 John Elway	2.00	.90
68 Ed McCaffrey	.20	.09
69 Glyn Milburn	.10	.05
70 Anthony Miller	.20	.09
71 Michael Dean Perry	.10	.05
72 Shannon Sharpe	.20	.09
73 Willie Clay	.10	.05
74 Scott Mitchell	.20	.09
75 Herman Moore	.40	.18
76 Johnnie Morton	.20	.09
77 Brett Perriman	.10	.05
78 Barry Sanders	2.00	.90
79 Tracy Scroggins	.10	.05
80 Edgar Bennett	.20	.09
81 Robert Brooks	.40	.18
82 Brett Favre	2.00	.90
83 Dorsey Levens	.40	.18
84 Craig Newsome	.10	.05
85 Wayne Simmons	.10	.05
86 Reggie White	.40	.18
87 Chris Chandler	.20	.09
88 Anthony Cook	.10	.05
89 Mel Gray	.10	.05
90 Haywood Jeffires	.10	.05
91 Darryll Lewis	.10	.05
92 Steve McNair	.75	.35
93 Todd McNair	.10	.05
94 Rodney Thomas	.10	.05
95 Trev Alberts	.10	.05
96 Tony Bennett	.10	.05
97 Quentin Coryatt	.10	.05
98 Sean Dawkins	.10	.05
99 Ken Dilger	.20	.09
100 Marshall Faulk	.40	.18
101 Jim Harbaugh	.20	.09
102 Ronald Humphrey	.10	.05
103 Floyd Turner	.10	.05
104 Steve Beuerlein	.10	.05
105 Tony Boselli	.10	.05
106 Mark Brunell	1.00	.45
107 Willie Jackson	.10	.05
108 Jeff Lageman	.10	.05
109 James O. Stewart	.20	.09
110 Cedric Tillman	.10	.05
111 Marcus Allen	.40	.18
112 Kimble Anders	.20	.09
113 Steve Bono	.10	.05
114 Dale Carter	.10	.05
115 Willie Davis	.10	.05
116 Lake Dawson	.10	.05
117 Dan Saleaumua	.10	.05
118 Neil Smith	.10	.05
119 Derrick Thomas	.20	.09
120 Tamarick Vanover	.20	.09
121 Marco Coleman	.10	.05
122 Bryan Cox	.10	.05
123 Steve Emtman	.10	.05
124 Irving Fryar	.20	.09
125 Eric Green	.10	.05
126 Terry Kirby	.20	.09
127 Dan Marino	2.00	.90
128 O.J. McDuffie	.20	.09
129 Bernie Parmalee	.10	.05
130 Troy Vincent	.10	.05
131 Cris Carter	.40	.18
132 Jack Del Rio	.10	.05
133 Qadry Ismail	.10	.05
134 Amp Lee	.10	.05
135 Warren Moon	.20	.09
136 John Randle	.20	.09
137 Jake Reed	.20	.09
138 Robert Smith	.20	.09
139 Drew Bledsoe	1.00	.45
140 Vincent Brisby	.10	.05
141 Ben Coates	.20	.09
142 Curtis Martin	.75	.35
143 Dave Meggett	.10	.05
144 Will Moore	.10	.05
145 Chris Slade	.10	.05
146 Mario Bates	.20	.09
147 Quinn Early	.10	.05
148 Jim Everett	.10	.05
149 Michael Haynes	.10	.05
150 Tyrone Hughes	.10	.05
151 Wayne Martin	.10	.05
152 Renaldo Turnbull	.10	.05
153 Dave Brown	.10	.05
154 Chris Calloway	.10	.05
155 Rodney Hampton	.20	.09
156 Mike Sherrard	.10	.05
157 Michael Strahan	.10	.05
158 Herschel Walker	.20	.09
159 Tyrone Wheatley	.20	.09
160 Kyle Brady	.10	.05
161 Wayne Chrebet	.60	.25
162 Hugh Douglas	.20	.09
163 Adrian Murrell	.40	.18
164 Todd Scott	.10	.05
165 Charles Wilson	.10	.05
166 Tim Brown	.40	.18
167 Aundray Bruce	.10	.05
168 Andrew Glover	.10	.05
169 Jeff Hostetler	.10	.05
170 Napoleon Kaufman	.40	.18
171 Terry McDaniel	.10	.05
172 Chester McGlockton	.10	.05
173 Pat Swilling	.10	.05
174 Harvey Williams	.10	.05
175 Fred Barnett	.10	.05
176 Randall Cunningham	.40	.18
177 William Fuller	.10	.05
178 Charlie Garner	.10	.05
179 Andy Harmon	.10	.05
180 Rodney Peete	.10	.05

Card	MINT	NRMT
❑ 181 Ricky Watters	.20	.09
❑ 182 Calvin Williams	.10	.05
❑ 183 Chad Brown	.10	.05
❑ 184 Kevin Greene	.20	.09
❑ 185 Greg Lloyd	.20	.09
❑ 186 Byron Bam Morris	.20	.09
❑ 187 Neil O'Donnell	.20	.09
❑ 188 Erric Pegram	.10	.05
❑ 189 Kordell Stewart	.60	.25
❑ 190 Yancey Thigpen	.20	.09
❑ 191 Rod Woodson	.20	.09
❑ 192 Darren Bennett	.10	.05
❑ 193 Ronnie Harmon	.10	.05
❑ 194 Stan Humphries	.20	.09
❑ 195 Tony Martin	.20	.09
❑ 196 Natrone Means	.40	.18
❑ 197 Leslie O'Neal	.10	.05
❑ 198 Junior Seau	.20	.09
❑ 199 Mark Seay	.10	.05
❑ 200 William Floyd	.20	.09
❑ 201 Merton Hanks	.10	.05
❑ 202 Brent Jones	.10	.05
❑ 203 Derek Loville	.10	.05
❑ 204 Ken Norton, Jr.	.10	.05
❑ 205 Gary Plummer	.10	.05
❑ 206 Jerry Rice	1.00	.45
❑ 207 J.J. Stokes	.40	.18
❑ 208 Dana Stubblefield	.20	.09
❑ 209 John Taylor	.10	.05
❑ 210 Bryant Young	.20	.09
❑ 211 Steve Young	.75	.35
❑ 212 Brian Blades	.10	.05
❑ 213 Joey Galloway	.60	.25
❑ 214 Carlton Gray	.10	.05
❑ 215 Cortez Kennedy	.10	.05
❑ 216 Rick Mirer	.20	.09
❑ 217 Chris Warren	.20	.09
❑ 218 Jerome Bettis	.40	.18
❑ 219 Isaac Bruce	.40	.18
❑ 220 Troy Drayton	.10	.05
❑ 221 D'Marco Farr	.10	.05
❑ 222 Sean Gilbert	.10	.05
❑ 223 Chris Miller	.10	.05
❑ 224 Roman Phifer	.10	.05
❑ 225 Trent Dilfer	.40	.18
❑ 226 Santana Dotson	.10	.05
❑ 227 Alvin Harper	.10	.05
❑ 228 Jackie Harris	.10	.05
❑ 229 John Lynch	.20	.09
❑ 230 Hardy Nickerson	.10	.05
❑ 231 Errict Rhett	.20	.09
❑ 232 Warren Sapp	.10	.05
❑ 233 Terry Allen	.20	.09
❑ 234 Henry Ellard	.10	.05
❑ 235 Gus Frerotte	.40	.18
❑ 236 Ken Harvey	.10	.05
❑ 237 Brian Mitchell	.10	.05
❑ 238 Heath Shuler	.20	.09
❑ 239 James Washington	.10	.05
❑ 240 Michael Westbrook	.40	.18
❑ 241 Checklist	.10	.05
❑ 242 Checklist	.10	.05
❑ 243 Checklist	.10	.05
❑ 244 Checklist	.10	.05
❑ 245 Checklist	.10	.05
❑ 246 Checklist	.10	.05
❑ 247 Checklist	.10	.05
❑ 248 Checklist	.10	.05
❑ 249 Checklist	.10	.05
❑ 250 Checklist	.10	.05
❑ PR1 Eddie George Promo (Die cut Crucibles promo)	.50	.23

1996 Collector's Edge Advantage

	MINT	NRMT
COMPLETE SET (150)	25.00	11.00
❑ 1 Drew Bledsoe	1.25	.55
❑ 2 Chris Warren	.25	.11
❑ 3 Eddie George RC	4.00	1.80
❑ 4 Barry Sanders	2.50	1.10
❑ 5 Scott Mitchell	.25	.11
❑ 6 Carl Pickens	.50	.23

Card	MINT	NRMT
❑ 7 Tim Brown	.50	.23
❑ 8 John Elway	2.50	1.10
❑ 9 Michael Westbrook	.50	.23
❑ 10 Cris Carter	.50	.23
❑ 11 Troy Aikman	1.25	.55
❑ 12 Ben Coates	.25	.11
❑ 13 Brett Favre	2.50	1.10
❑ 14 Marshall Faulk	.50	.23
❑ 15 Steve Young	1.00	.45
❑ 16 Terrell Davis	3.00	1.35
❑ 17 Keyshawn Johnson RC	2.50	1.10
❑ 18 Mario Bates	.25	.11
❑ 19 Steve McNair	1.00	.45
❑ 20 Kerry Collins	.50	.23
❑ 21 Natrone Means	.50	.23
❑ 22 Kordell Stewart	.75	.35
❑ 23 Jeff George	.25	.11
❑ 24 Rick Mirer	.25	.11
❑ 25 Herman Moore	.50	.23
❑ 26 Rodney Peete	.15	.07
❑ 27 Isaac Bruce	.50	.23
❑ 28 Errict Rhett	.25	.11
❑ 29 Jerry Rice	1.25	.55
❑ 30 Rashaan Salaam	.50	.23
❑ 31 Eric Metcalf	.15	.07
❑ 32 Jim Kelly	.50	.23
❑ 33 Jerome Bettis	.50	.23
❑ 34 Deion Sanders	.75	.35
❑ 35 J.J. Stokes	.50	.23
❑ 36 Neil O'Donnell	.25	.11
❑ 37 Marcus Allen	.50	.23
❑ 38 Thurman Thomas	.50	.23
❑ 39 Dan Marino	2.50	1.10
❑ 40 Rickey Dudley RC	.50	.23
❑ 41 Napoleon Kaufman	.50	.23
❑ 42 Kyle Brady	.15	.07
❑ 43 Emmitt Smith	2.00	.90
❑ 44 Tyrone Wheatley	.25	.11
❑ 45 Jeff Blake	.50	.23
❑ 46 Reggie White	.50	.23
❑ 47 Joey Galloway	.75	.35
❑ 48 Antonio Langham	.15	.07
❑ 49 Craig Heyward	.15	.07
❑ 50 Curtis Martin	1.00	.45
❑ 51 Karim Abdul-Jabbar RC	.75	.35
❑ 52 Antonio Freeman	1.00	.45
❑ 53 Ki-Jana Carter	.25	.11
❑ 54 Willie Davis	.15	.07
❑ 55 Jim Everett	.15	.07
❑ 56 Gus Frerotte	.50	.23
❑ 57 Daryl Gardener RC	.15	.07
❑ 58 Charles Haley	.25	.11
❑ 59 Michael Irvin	.50	.23
❑ 60 Keith Jackson	.15	.07
❑ 61 Cortez Kennedy	.15	.07
❑ 62 Greg Lloyd	.25	.11
❑ 63 Tony Martin	.25	.11
❑ 64 Ken Norton Jr.	.15	.07
❑ 65 Bobby Hoying RC	.75	.35
❑ 66 Bryce Paup	.15	.07
❑ 67 Jake Reed	.25	.11
❑ 68 Frank Sanders	.25	.11
❑ 69 Vinny Testaverde	.25	.11
❑ 70 Regan Upshaw RC	.15	.07
❑ 71 Tamarick Vanover	.25	.11
❑ 72 Walt Harris RC	.15	.07
❑ 73 John Randle	.25	.11
❑ 74 Ricky Watters	.25	.11
❑ 75 Terry Allen	.25	.11
❑ 76 Edgar Bennett	.25	.11
❑ 77 Larry Centers	.25	.11
❑ 78 Chris Penn	.15	.07
❑ 79 Bobby Engram RC	.50	.23
❑ 80 Irving Fryar	.25	.11
❑ 81 Charlie Garner	.15	.07
❑ 82 Rodney Hampton	.25	.11
❑ 83 Michael Jackson	.25	.11
❑ 84 O.J. McDuffie	.25	.11
❑ 85 Shannon Sharpe	.25	.11
❑ 86 Aaron Hayden	.15	.07
❑ 87 Muhsin Muhammad RC	1.00	.45
❑ 88 Rod Woodson	.25	.11
❑ 89 Levon Kirkland	.15	.07
❑ 90 Chad Brown	.15	.07
❑ 91 Junior Seau	.25	.11
❑ 92 Terry Kirby	.25	.11
❑ 93 Zach Thomas RC	.75	.35
❑ 94 Harvey Williams	.15	.07
❑ 95 Robert Brooks	.50	.23
❑ 96 Darrell Green	.15	.07
❑ 97 Chester McGlockton	.15	.07
❑ 98 Neil Smith	.15	.07
❑ 99 Eric Swann	.15	.07
❑ 100 Mike Alstott RC	1.50	.70
❑ 101 Tim Biakabutuka RC	.75	.35
❑ 102 Mark Brunell	1.25	.55
❑ 103 Chris Doleman	.15	.07
❑ 104 Sean Gilbert	.15	.07
❑ 105 Jim Harbaugh	.25	.11
❑ 106 Chris T. Jones	.25	.11
❑ 107 Tyrone Hughes	.15	.07
❑ 108 Amani Toomer RC	1.00	.45
❑ 109 Larry Brown	.15	.07
❑ 110 Kevin Greene	.25	.11
❑ 111 John Mobley	.15	.07
❑ 112 Danny Kanell RC	.50	.23
❑ 113 Kevin Hardy RC	.50	.23
❑ 114 Brett Perriman	.15	.07
❑ 115 Simeon Rice RC	.50	.23
❑ 116 Chris Sanders	.25	.11
❑ 117 Dave Brown	.15	.07
❑ 118 Bryan Cox	.15	.07
❑ 119 Yancey Thigpen	.25	.11
❑ 120 Terance Mathis	.15	.07
❑ 121 Warren Moon	.25	.11
❑ 122 Derrick Thomas	.25	.11
❑ 123 Trent Dilfer	.50	.23
❑ 124 Terry Glenn RC	1.25	.55
❑ 125 Jeff Hostetler	.15	.07
❑ 126 Leeland McElroy RC	.50	.23
❑ 127 Hardy Nickerson	.15	.07
❑ 128 Steve Bono	.15	.07
❑ 129 Stanley Pritchett RC	.25	.11
❑ 130 Dana Stubblefield	.25	.11
❑ 131 Andre Coleman	.15	.07
❑ 132 Anthony Miller	.25	.11
❑ 133 Stan Humphries	.25	.11
❑ 134 Robert Smith	.25	.11
❑ 135 Curtis Conway	.50	.23
❑ 136 Darick Holmes	.15	.07
❑ 137 Pat Swilling	.15	.07
❑ 138 Andre Rison	.25	.11
❑ 139 Erik Kramer	.15	.07
❑ 140 Jason Dunn RC	.25	.11
❑ 141 Torrance Small	.15	.07
❑ 142 Cedric Jones RC	.15	.07
❑ 143 Derek Loville	.15	.07
❑ 144 Brian Mitchell	.15	.07
❑ 145 Eric Moulds RC	2.00	.90
❑ 146 James O.Stewart	.25	.11
❑ 147 Bruce Smith	.25	.11
❑ 148 Keenan McCardell	.50	.23
❑ 149 Warren Sapp	.15	.07
❑ 150 Marvin Harrison RC	3.00	1.35

1998 Collector's Edge Advantage

	MINT	NRMT
COMPLETE SET (200)	80.00	36.00
COMP.SHORT SET (180)	60.00	27.00

❑ 1 Larry Centers .30 .14
❑ 2 Kent Graham .30 .14
❑ 3 LeShon Johnson .30 .14
❑ 4 Leeland McElroy .30 .14
❑ 5 Jake Plummer 2.00 .90
❑ 6 Jamal Anderson 1.00 .45
❑ 7 Chris Chandler .50 .23
❑ 8 Bert Emanuel .50 .23
❑ 9 Byron Hanspard .50 .23
❑ 10 O.J. Santiago .30 .14
❑ 11 Derrick Alexander WR .50 .23
❑ 12 Peter Boulware .30 .14
❑ 13 Eric Green .30 .14
❑ 14 Michael Jackson .30 .14
❑ 15 Byron Bam Morris .30 .14
❑ 16 Vinny Testaverde .50 .23
❑ 17 Todd Collins .30 .14
❑ 18 Quinn Early .30 .14
❑ 19 Jim Kelly 1.00 .45
❑ 20 Andre Reed .50 .23
❑ 21 Antowain Smith 1.00 .45
❑ 22 Steve Tasker .30 .14
❑ 23 Thurman Thomas 1.00 .45
❑ 24 Steve Beuerlein .30 .14
❑ 25 Rae Carruth .50 .23
❑ 26 Kerry Collins .50 .23
❑ 27 Anthony Johnson .30 .14
❑ 28 Ernie Mills .30 .14
❑ 29 Wesley Walls .50 .23
❑ 30 Curtis Conway .50 .23
❑ 31 Bobby Engram .50 .23
❑ 32 Raymont Harris .30 .14
❑ 33 Erik Kramer .30 .14
❑ 34 Rick Mirer .30 .14
❑ 35 Darnay Scott .50 .23
❑ 36 Tony McGee .30 .14
❑ 37 Jeff Blake .50 .23
❑ 38 Corey Dillon 1.50 .70
❑ 39 Carl Pickens 1.00 .45
❑ 40 Troy Aikman 2.50 1.10
❑ 41 Billy Davis .30 .14
❑ 42 David LaFleur .30 .14
❑ 43 Anthony Miller .30 .14
❑ 44 Emmitt Smith 4.00 1.80
❑ 45 Herschel Walker .50 .23
❑ 46 Sherman Williams .30 .14
❑ 47 Flipper Anderson .30 .14
❑ 48 Terrell Davis 4.00 1.80
❑ 49 Jason Elam .30 .14
❑ 50 John Elway 5.00 2.20
❑ 51 Darrien Gordon .30 .14
❑ 52 Ed McCaffrey .50 .23
❑ 53 Shannon Sharpe .50 .23
❑ 54 Neil Smith .50 .23
❑ 55 Rod Smith WR .50 .23
❑ 56 Maa Tanuvasa .30 .14
❑ 57 Glyn Milburn .30 .14
❑ 58 Scott Mitchell .50 .23
❑ 59 Herman Moore 1.00 .45
❑ 60 Johnnie Morton .50 .23
❑ 61 Barry Sanders 5.00 2.20
❑ 62 Tommy Vardell .30 .14
❑ 63 Bryant Westbrook .30 .14
❑ 64 Robert Brooks .50 .23
❑ 65 Mark Chmura .50 .23
❑ 66 Brett Favre 5.00 2.20
❑ 67 Antonio Freeman 1.00 .45
❑ 68 Dorsey Levens 1.00 .45
❑ 69 Bill Schroeder RC 4.00 1.80
❑ 70 Marshall Faulk 1.00 .45
❑ 71 Jim Harbaugh .50 .23
❑ 72 Marvin Harrison .50 .23
❑ 73 Derek Brown TE .30 .14
❑ 74 Mark Brunell 2.00 .90
❑ 75 Rob Johnson .50 .23
❑ 76 Keenan McCardell .50 .23
❑ 77 Natrone Means 1.00 .45
❑ 78 Jimmy Smith .50 .23
❑ 79 James O.Stewart .50 .23
❑ 80 Marcus Allen 1.00 .45
❑ 81 Pat Barnes .30 .14
❑ 82 Tony Gonzalez .30 .14
❑ 83 Elvis Grbac .50 .23
❑ 84 Greg Hill .30 .14
❑ 85 Kevin Lockett .30 .14
❑ 86 Andre Rison .50 .23
❑ 87 Karim Abdul-Jabbar 1.00 .45
❑ 88 Fred Barnett .30 .14
❑ 89 Troy Drayton .30 .14
❑ 90 Dan Marino 5.00 2.20
❑ 91 Irving Spikes .30 .14
❑ 92 Cris Carter 1.00 .45
❑ 93 Matthew Hatchette .30 .14
❑ 94 Brad Johnson 1.00 .45
❑ 95 Jake Reed .50 .23
❑ 96 Robert Smith 1.00 .45
❑ 97 Drew Bledsoe 2.00 .90
❑ 98 Keith Byars .30 .14
❑ 99 Ben Coates .50 .23
❑ 100 Terry Glenn 1.00 .45
❑ 101 Shawn Jefferson .30 .14
❑ 102 Curtis Martin 1.00 .45
❑ 103 Dave Meggett .30 .14
❑ 104 Troy Davis .30 .14
❑ 105 Danny Wuerffel .50 .23
❑ 106 Ray Zellars .30 .14
❑ 107 Tiki Barber .50 .23
❑ 108 Rodney Hampton .50 .23
❑ 109 Ike Hilliard .50 .23
❑ 110 Danny Kanell .50 .23
❑ 111 Tyrone Wheatley .50 .23
❑ 112 Kyle Brady .30 .14
❑ 113 Wayne Chrebet 1.00 .45
❑ 114 Aaron Glenn .30 .14
❑ 115 Jeff Graham .30 .14
❑ 116 Keyshawn Johnson 1.00 .45
❑ 117 Adrian Murrell .50 .23
❑ 118 Neil O'Donnell .50 .23
❑ 119 Heath Shuler .30 .14
❑ 120 Tim Brown 1.00 .45
❑ 121 Rickey Dudley .30 .14
❑ 122 Jeff George .50 .23
❑ 123 Desmond Howard .50 .23
❑ 124 James Jett .50 .23
❑ 125 Napoleon Kaufman 1.00 .45
❑ 126 Chad Levitt RC .30 .14
❑ 127 Darrell Russell .30 .14
❑ 128 Ty Detmer .50 .23
❑ 129 Irving Fryar .50 .23
❑ 130 Charlie Garner .30 .14
❑ 131 Kevin Turner .30 .14
❑ 132 Ricky Watters .50 .23
❑ 133 Jerome Bettis 1.00 .45
❑ 134 Will Blackwell .30 .14
❑ 135 Mark Bruener .30 .14
❑ 136 Charles Johnson .30 .14
❑ 137 George Jones .30 .14
❑ 138 Kordell Stewart 1.00 .45
❑ 139 Yancey Thigpen .30 .14
❑ 140 Gary Brown .30 .14
❑ 141 Jim Everett .30 .14
❑ 142 Terrell Fletcher .30 .14
❑ 143 Stan Humphries .30 .14
❑ 144 Freddie Jones .30 .14
❑ 145 Tony Martin .50 .23
❑ 146 Jim Druckenmiller .50 .23
❑ 147 Garrison Hearst 1.00 .45
❑ 148 Brent Jones .30 .14
❑ 149 Terrell Owens 1.00 .45
❑ 150 Jerry Rice 2.50 1.10
❑ 151 J.J. Stokes .50 .23
❑ 152 Steve Young 1.50 .70
❑ 153 Steve Broussard .30 .14
❑ 154 Joey Galloway 1.00 .45
❑ 155 Jon Kitna 1.50 .70
❑ 156 Warren Moon 1.00 .45
❑ 157 Shawn Springs .30 .14
❑ 158 Chris Warren .50 .23
❑ 159 Tony Banks .50 .23
❑ 160 Isaac Bruce 1.00 .45
❑ 161 Eddie Kennison .50 .23
❑ 162 Orlando Pace .30 .14
❑ 163 Lawrence Phillips .30 .14
❑ 164 Mike Alstott 1.00 .45
❑ 165 Reidel Anthony .50 .23
❑ 166 Horace Copeland .30 .14
❑ 167 Trent Dilfer 1.00 .45
❑ 168 Warrick Dunn 1.00 .45
❑ 169 Hardy Nickerson .30 .14
❑ 170 Karl Williams .30 .14
❑ 171 Eddie George 2.00 .90
❑ 172 Ronnie Harmon .30 .14
❑ 173 Joey Kent .50 .23
❑ 174 Steve McNair 1.00 .45
❑ 175 Chris Sanders .30 .14
❑ 176 Terry Allen 1.00 .45
❑ 177 Jamie Asher .30 .14
❑ 178 Stephen Davis .30 .14
❑ 179 Gus Frerotte .30 .14
❑ 180 Leslie Shepherd .30 .14
❑ 181 Victor Riley RC .25 .11
❑ 182 Curtis Enis RC 1.00 .45
❑ 183 Brian Griese RC 3.00 1.35
❑ 184 Eric Brown RC .25 .11
❑ 185 Jacquez Green RC 1.25 .55
❑ 186 Andre Wadsworth RC .50 .23
❑ 187 Ryan Leaf RC 2.00 .90
❑ 188 Rashaan Shehee RC .50 .23
❑ 189 Peyton Manning RC 8.00 3.60
❑ 190 Flozell Adams RC .25 .11
❑ 191 Fred Taylor RC 2.50 1.10
❑ 192 Charlie Batch RC 2.50 1.10
❑ 193 Kevin Dyson RC 1.25 .55
❑ 194 Charles Woodson RC 1.25 .55
❑ 195 Ahman Green RC 2.00 .90
❑ 196 Randy Moss RC 8.00 3.60
❑ 197 Robert Edwards RC .60 .25
❑ 198 Reidel Anthony .50 .23
❑ 199 Jerome Pathon RC .50 .23
❑ 200 Samari Rolle RC .25 .11

1999 Collector's Edge Advantage

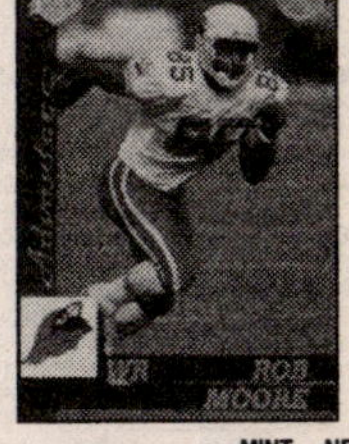

	MINT	NRMT
COMPLETE SET (190)	50.00	22.00

❑ 1 Larry Centers .15 .07
❑ 2 Rob Moore .30 .14
❑ 3 Adrian Murrell .30 .14
❑ 4 Jake Plummer 1.25 .55
❑ 5 Frank Sanders .30 .14
❑ 6 Jamal Anderson .60 .25
❑ 7 Chris Chandler .30 .14
❑ 8 Tim Dwight .60 .25
❑ 9 Tony Martin .30 .14
❑ 10 Terance Mathis .30 .14
❑ 11 O.J. Santiago .15 .07
❑ 12 Jim Harbaugh .30 .14
❑ 13 Priest Holmes .60 .25
❑ 14 Jermaine Lewis .30 .14
❑ 15 Rod Woodson .30 .14
❑ 16 Eric Zeier .30 .14
❑ 17 Doug Flutie .75 .35
❑ 18 Sam Gash .15 .07
❑ 19 Rob Johnson .30 .14
❑ 20 Eric Moulds .60 .25
❑ 21 Andre Reed .30 .14
❑ 22 Antowain Smith .60 .25
❑ 23 Bruce Smith .30 .14
❑ 24 Thurman Thomas .30 .14
❑ 25 Steve Beuerlein .30 .14
❑ 26 Kevin Greene .30 .14
❑ 27 Rocket Ismail .30 .14
❑ 28 Fred Lane .30 .14
❑ 29 Muhsin Muhammad .30 .14
❑ 30 Edgar Bennett .15 .07
❑ 31 Curtis Conway .30 .14
❑ 32 Bobby Engram .30 .14
❑ 33 Curtis Enis .60 .25

❑ 34 Erik Kramer .30 .14
❑ 35 Jeff Blake .30 .14
❑ 36 Corey Dillon .60 .25
❑ 37 Neil O'Donnell .30 .14
❑ 38 Carl Pickens .30 .14
❑ 39 Takeo Spikes .15 .07
❑ 40 Troy Aikman 1.50 .70
❑ 41 Billy Davis .15 .07
❑ 42 Michael Irvin .30 .14
❑ 43 Deion Sanders .60 .25
❑ 44 Emmitt Smith 1.50 .70
❑ 45 Darren Woodson .15 .07
❑ 46 Bubby Brister .30 .14
❑ 47 Terrell Davis 1.50 .70
❑ 48 John Elway 2.50 1.10
❑ 49 Ed McCaffrey .30 .14
❑ 50 Bill Romanowski .15 .07
❑ 51 Shannon Sharpe .30 .14
❑ 52 Rod Smith .30 .14
❑ 53 Charlie Batch 1.25 .55
❑ 54 Germane Crowell .30 .14
❑ 55 Herman Moore .60 .25
❑ 56 Johnnie Morton .30 .14
❑ 57 Barry Sanders 2.50 1.10
❑ 58 Robert Brooks .30 .14
❑ 59 Brett Favre 2.50 1.10
❑ 60 Antonio Freeman .60 .25
❑ 61 Darick Holmes .15 .07
❑ 62 Dorsey Levens .60 .25
❑ 63 Roell Preston .15 .07
❑ 64 Marshall Faulk .60 .25
❑ 65 E.G.Green .15 .07
❑ 66 Marvin Harrison .60 .25
❑ 67 Peyton Manning 2.50 1.10
❑ 68 Jerome Pathon .15 .07
❑ 69 Mark Brunell 1.00 .45
❑ 70 Kevin Hardy .15 .07
❑ 71 Keenan McCardell .30 .14
❑ 72 Jimmy Smith .30 .14
❑ 73 Fred Taylor 1.50 .70
❑ 74 Alvis Whitted .15 .07
❑ 75 Kimble Anders .30 .14
❑ 76 Donnell Bennett .15 .07
❑ 77 Rich Gannon .30 .14
❑ 78 Elvis Grbac .30 .14
❑ 79 Byron Bam Morris .15 .07
❑ 80 Andre Rison .30 .14
❑ 81 Karim Abdul-Jabbar .30 .14
❑ 82 John Avery .15 .07
❑ 83 Oronde Gadsden .15 .07
❑ 84 Sam Madison .15 .07
❑ 85 Dan Marino 2.50 1.10
❑ 86 O.J. McDuffie .30 .14
❑ 87 Zach Thomas .30 .14
❑ 88 Cris Carter .60 .25
❑ 89 Randall Cunningham .60 .25
❑ 90 Brad Johnson .60 .25
❑ 91 Randy Moss 2.50 1.10
❑ 92 John Randle .30 .14
❑ 93 Jake Reed .30 .14
❑ 94 Robert Smith .60 .25
❑ 95 Drew Bledsoe 1.00 .45
❑ 96 Ben Coates .30 .14
❑ 97 Robert Edwards .30 .14
❑ 98 Terry Glenn .60 .25
❑ 99 Ty Law .15 .07
❑ 100 Cam Cleeland .15 .07
❑ 101 Kerry Collins .30 .14
❑ 102 Gary Brown .15 .07
❑ 103 Kent Graham .15 .07
❑ 104 Ike Hilliard .30 .14
❑ 105 Joe Jurevicius .15 .07
❑ 106 Danny Kanell .15 .07
❑ 107 Wayne Chrebet .30 .14
❑ 108 Aaron Glenn .15 .07
❑ 109 Keyshawn Johnson .60 .25
❑ 110 Curtis Martin .60 .25
❑ 111 Vinny Testaverde .30 .14
❑ 112 Tim Brown .60 .25
❑ 113 Jeff George .30 .14
❑ 114 James Jett .30 .14
❑ 115 Napoleon Kaufman .60 .25
❑ 116 Charles Woodson .60 .25
❑ 117 Koy Detmer .15 .07
❑ 118 Duce Staley .60 .25
❑ 119 Jerome Bettis .60 .25
❑ 120 Charles Johnson .30 .14
❑ 121 Kordell Stewart .60 .25
❑ 122 Tony Banks .30 .14
❑ 123 Isaac Bruce .60 .25
❑ 124 June Henley RC .15 .07
❑ 125 Ryan Leaf .60 .25
❑ 126 Natrone Means .30 .14
❑ 127 Mikhael Ricks .15 .07
❑ 128 Craig Whelihan .15 .07
❑ 129 Garrison Hearst .30 .14
❑ 130 Terrell Owens .60 .25
❑ 131 Jerry Rice 1.50 .70
❑ 132 J.J.Stokes .30 .14
❑ 133 Steve Young 1.00 .45
❑ 134 Joey Galloway .60 .25
❑ 135 Ahman Green .30 .14
❑ 136 Jon Kitna .60 .25
❑ 137 Ricky Watters .30 .14
❑ 138 Mike Alstott .60 .25
❑ 139 Reidel Anthony .30 .14
❑ 140 Trent Dilfer .30 .14
❑ 141 Warrick Dunn .60 .25
❑ 142 Jacquez Green .30 .14
❑ 143 Kevin Dyson .30 .14
❑ 144 Eddie George .75 .35
❑ 145 Steve McNair .60 .25
❑ 146 Yancey Thigpen .15 .07
❑ 147 Terry Allen .30 .14
❑ 148 Trent Green .30 .14
❑ 149 Skip Hicks .60 .25
❑ 150 Michael Westbrook .30 .14
❑ 151 Rahim Abdullah RC 1.25 .55
❑ 152 Champ Bailey RC 2.00 .90
❑ 153 Marlon Barnes RC 1.25 .55
❑ 154 D'Wayne Bates RC 1.25 .55
❑ 155 Michael Bishop RC 2.00 .90
❑ 156 Dre' Bly RC 1.25 .55
❑ 157 David Boston RC 2.50 1.10
❑ 158 Chris Claiborne RC .75 .35
❑ 159 Tim Couch RC 5.00 2.20
❑ 160 Daunte Culpepper RC 10.00 4.50
❑ 161 Autry Denson RC 1.50 .70
❑ 162 Jared DeVries RC 1.25 .55
❑ 163 Troy Edwards RC 2.00 .90
❑ 164 Kris Farris RC .75 .35
❑ 165 Kevin Faulk RC 2.50 1.10
❑ 166 Martin Gramatica RC .75 .35
❑ 167 Torry Holt RC 4.00 1.80
❑ 168 Brock Huard RC 2.50 1.10
❑ 169 Sedrick Irvin RC 1.50 .70
❑ 170 Edgerrin James RC 10.00 4.50
❑ 171 James Johnson RC 1.50 .70
❑ 172 Kevin Johnson RC 2.50 1.10
❑ 173 Andy Katzenmoyer RC 1.50 .70
❑ 174 Jevon Kearse RC 2.50 1.10
❑ 175 Shaun King RC 3.00 1.35
❑ 176 Rob Konrad RC 1.25 .55
❑ 177 Chris McAlister RC 1.25 .55
❑ 178 Darnell McDonald RC 1.50 .70
❑ 179 Donovan McNabb RC 6.00 2.70
❑ 180 Cade McNown RC 2.00 .90
❑ 181 Dat Nguyen RC 1.50 .70
❑ 182 Peerless Price RC 2.00 .90
❑ 183 Akili Smith RC 2.50 1.10
❑ 184 Tai Streets RC 1.50 .70
❑ 185 Cuncho Brown RC UER 1.25 .55
(Photo is actually Courtney Brown)
❑ 186 Ricky Williams RC 6.00 2.70
❑ 187 Craig Yeast RC 1.25 .55
❑ 188 Amos Zereoue RC 1.50 .70
❑ 189 Checklist .15 .07
❑ 190 Checklist .15 .07

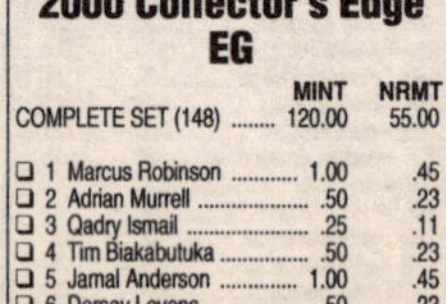

2000 Collector's Edge EG

	MINT	NRMT
COMPLETE SET (148)	120.00	55.00

❑ 1 Marcus Robinson 1.00 .45
❑ 2 Adrian Murrell .50 .23
❑ 3 Qadry Ismail .25 .11
❑ 4 Tim Biakabutuka .50 .23
❑ 5 Jamal Anderson 1.00 .45
❑ 6 Dorsey Levens .50 .23

❑ 7 Robert Smith 1.00 .45
❑ 8 Tony Banks .50 .23
❑ 9 Yancey Thigpen .25 .11
❑ 10 Elvis Grbac .50 .23
❑ 11 Sedrick Irvin .25 .11
❑ 12 Rob Johnson .50 .23
❑ 13 Frank Sanders .50 .23
❑ 14 Rich Gannon .50 .23
❑ 15 Steve Beuerlein .50 .23
❑ 16 James Stewart .50 .23
❑ 17 Ricky Watters .50 .23
❑ 18 Curtis Enis .50 .23
❑ 19 Eddie Kennison .25 .11
❑ 20 Kerry Collins .50 .23
❑ 21 Ray Lucas 1.00 .45
❑ 22 Carl Pickens .50 .23
❑ 23 Natrone Means .25 .11
❑ 24 Daunte Culpepper 2.00 .90
❑ 25 Karim Abdul-Jabbar .50 .23
❑ 26 David Boston 1.00 .45
❑ 27 Rocket Ismail .50 .23
❑ 28 Jacquez Green .50 .23
❑ 29 Kevin Dyson .50 .23
❑ 30 Chris Chandler .50 .23
❑ 31 Brian Griese 1.25 .55
❑ 32 Charlie Garner .50 .23
❑ 33 Wayne Chrebet .50 .23
❑ 34 Mike Alstott 1.00 .45
❑ 35 Germane Crowell .50 .23
❑ 36 Michael Cloud .25 .11
❑ 37 Antowain Smith .50 .23
❑ 38 Jeff George .50 .23
❑ 39 Antonio Freeman 1.00 .45
❑ 40 Champ Bailey
❑ 41 Terrence Wilkins 1.00 .45
❑ 42 Junior Seau .50 .23
❑ 43 Jimmy Smith .50 .23
❑ 44 Greg Hill .25 .11
❑ 45 Tyrone Wheatley .50 .23
❑ 46 Tony Gonzalez .50 .23
❑ 47 Rod Smith .50 .23
❑ 48 Damon Huard 1.00 .45
❑ 49 Jerome Bettis 1.00 .45
❑ 50 Cris Carter 1.00 .45
❑ 51 Darnay Scott .50 .23
❑ 52 Ike Hilliard .50 .23
❑ 53 Errict Rhett .50 .23
❑ 54 Tim Brown 1.00 .45
❑ 55 Terry Glenn .50 .23
❑ 56 Jeff Blake .50 .23
❑ 57 Terance Mathis .50 .23
❑ 58 Duce Staley 1.00 .45
❑ 59 Amani Toomer .25 .11
❑ 60 Terry Allen .50 .23
❑ 61 Corey Dillon 1.00 .45
❑ 62 Kordell Stewart 1.00 .45
❑ 63 Az-Zahir Hakim .50 .23
❑ 64 Jim Harbaugh .50 .23
❑ 65 Bill Schroeder .50 .23
❑ 66 O.J. McDuffie .50 .23
❑ 67 Keenan McCardell .50 .23
❑ 68 Terrell Owens 1.00 .45
❑ 69 Joey Galloway 1.00 .45
❑ 70 Derrick Alexander .50 .23
❑ 71 Ed McCaffrey 1.00 .45
❑ 72 Reidel Anthony .25 .11
❑ 73 Michael Irvin .50 .23

❑ 74 Herman Moore	.50	.23
❑ 75 Joe Montgomery	.25	.11
❑ 76 Muhsin Muhammad	.50	.23
❑ 77 Charles Johnson	.50	.23
❑ 78 Michael Westbrook	.50	.23
❑ 79 Jevon Kearse	1.00	.45
❑ 80 Courtney Brown RC	2.50	1.10
❑ 81 Shaun Alexander RC	5.00	2.20
❑ 82 R.Jay Soward RC	2.00	.90
❑ 83 Sylvester Morris RC	4.00	1.80
❑ 84 Giovanni Carmazzi RC	2.50	1.10
❑ 85 J.R. Redmond RC	2.50	1.10
❑ 86 Sherrod Gideon RC	1.50	.70
❑ 87 Tee Martin RC	3.00	1.35
❑ 88 Dennis Northcutt RC	2.50	1.10
❑ 89 Troy Walters RC	2.00	.90
❑ 90 Joe Hamilton RC	2.50	1.10
❑ 91 Reuben Droughns RC	2.00	.90
❑ 92 Trung Canidate RC	2.00	.90
❑ 94 Tim Rattay RC	3.00	1.35
❑ 95 Jerry Porter RC	2.00	.90
❑ 96 Michael Wiley RC	2.00	.90
❑ 97 Anthony Lucas RC	1.50	.70
❑ 98 Danny Farmer RC	2.00	.90
❑ 99 Travis Prentice RC	3.00	1.35
❑ 100 Dez White RC	1.50	.70
❑ 101 Chad Pennington RC	6.00	2.70
❑ 102 Chris Redman RC	4.00	1.80
❑ 103 Thomas Jones RC	3.00	1.35
❑ 104 Ron Dayne RC	6.00	2.70
❑ 105 Jamal Lewis RC	10.00	4.50
❑ 106 Shyrone Stith RC	2.00	.90
❑ 107 Peter Warrick RC	6.00	2.70
❑ 108 Plaxico Burress RC	4.00	1.80
❑ 109 Travis Taylor RC	2.50	1.10
❑ 110A LaVar Arrington RC	80.00	36.00
❑ 110B LaVar Arrington RC Red	45.00	20.00
❑ 111 Terrell Davis	2.50	1.10
❑ 112 Dan Marino	4.00	1.80
❑ 113 Brad Johnson	1.00	.45
❑ 114 Isaac Bruce	1.00	.45
❑ 115 Eric Moulds	1.00	.45
❑ 116 Olandis Gary	1.00	.45
❑ 117 Drew Bledsoe	1.50	.70
❑ 118 Steve Young	1.50	.70
❑ 119 Keyshawn Johnson	1.00	.45
❑ 120 Emmitt Smith	2.50	1.10
❑ 121 Warrick Dunn	1.00	.45
❑ 122 Doug Flutie	1.25	.55
❑ 123 Troy Edwards	.50	.23
❑ 124 Brett Favre	4.00	1.80
❑ 125 Charlie Batch	1.00	.45
❑ 126 Curtis Martin	1.00	.45
❑ 127 Stephen Davis	1.00	.45
❑ 128 Troy Aikman	2.50	1.10
❑ 129 Fred Taylor	1.25	.55
❑ 130 Jerry Rice	2.50	1.10
❑ 131 Jon Kitna	1.00	.45
❑ 132 Steve McNair	1.00	.45
❑ 133 Jake Plummer	1.00	.45
❑ 134 Donovan McNabb	1.50	.70
❑ 135 Ricky Williams	2.50	1.10
❑ 136 Torry Holt	1.00	.45
❑ 137 James Johnson	.50	.23
❑ 138 Kevin Johnson	1.00	.45
❑ 139 Akili Smith	1.00	.45
❑ 140 Cade McNown	1.00	.45
❑ 141 Eddie George	1.25	.55
❑ 142 Shaun King	1.50	.70
❑ 143 Marshall Faulk	1.25	.55
❑ 144 Kurt Warner	4.00	1.80
❑ 145 Randy Moss	3.00	1.35
❑ 146 Mark Brunell	1.50	.70
❑ 147 Marvin Harrison	1.00	.45
❑ 148 Edgerrin James	4.00	1.80
❑ 149 Tim Couch	2.00	.90
❑ 150 Peyton Manning	3.00	1.35

1997 Collector's Edge Extreme

	MINT	NRMT
COMPLETE SET (180)	20.00	9.00
❑ 1 Larry Centers	.20	.09
❑ 2 Leeland McElroy	.10	.05
❑ 3 Jake Plummer RC	2.50	1.10
❑ 4 Simeon Rice	.20	.09
❑ 5 Eric Swann	.10	.05
❑ 6 Jamal Anderson	.60	.25
❑ 7 Bert Emanuel	.20	.09
❑ 8 Byron Hanspard RC	.40	.18
❑ 9 Derrick Alexander WR UER (Derek on back)	.20	.09
❑ 10 Peter Boulware RC	.20	.09
❑ 11 Michael Jackson	.20	.09
❑ 12 Ray Lewis	.20	.09
❑ 13 Vinny Testaverde	.20	.09
❑ 14 Todd Collins	.10	.05
❑ 15 Eric Moulds	.40	.18
❑ 16 Bryce Paup UER (Numbered 122 on back)	.10	.05
❑ 17 Andre Reed	.20	.09
❑ 18 Bruce Smith	.20	.09
❑ 19 Antowain Smith RC	1.00	.45
❑ 20 Chris Spielman	.10	.05
❑ 21 Thurman Thomas	.40	.18
❑ 22 Tim Biakabutuka	.20	.09
❑ 23 Rae Carruth RC	.40	.18
❑ 24 Kerry Collins	.20	.09
❑ 25 Anthony Johnson	.10	.05
❑ 26 Lamar Lathon	.10	.05
❑ 27 Muhsin Muhammad	.20	.09
❑ 28 Darnell Autry RC	.20	.09
❑ 29 Curtis Conway	.20	.09
❑ 30 Bryan Cox	.10	.05
❑ 31 Bobby Engram	.20	.09
❑ 32 Walt Harris	.10	.05
❑ 33 Erik Kramer	.10	.05
❑ 34 Rashaan Salaam	.10	.05
❑ 35 Jeff Blake	.20	.09
❑ 36 Ki-Jana Carter	.10	.05
❑ 37 Corey Dillon RC	2.50	1.10
❑ 38 Carl Pickens	.40	.18
❑ 39 Troy Aikman	1.00	.45
❑ 40 Dexter Coakley RC	.10	.05
❑ 41 Michael Irvin	.40	.18
❑ 42 Daryl Johnston	.20	.09
❑ 43 David LaFleur RC	.20	.09
❑ 44 Anthony Miller	.10	.05
❑ 45 Deion Sanders	.40	.18
❑ 46 Emmitt Smith	1.50	.70
❑ 47 Broderick Thomas	.10	.05
❑ 48 Terrell Davis	1.50	.70
❑ 49 John Elway	2.00	.90
❑ 50 John Mobley	.10	.05
❑ 51 Shannon Sharpe	.20	.09
❑ 52 Neil Smith	.20	.09
❑ 53 Checklist	.10	.05
❑ 54 Scott Mitchell	.20	.09
❑ 55 Herman Moore	.40	.18
❑ 56 Barry Sanders	2.00	.90
❑ 57 Edgar Bennett	.20	.09
❑ 58 Robert Brooks	.20	.09
❑ 59 Mark Chmura	.20	.09
❑ 60 Brett Favre	2.00	.90
❑ 61 Antonio Freeman	.50	.23
❑ 62 Dorsey Levens	.40	.18
❑ 63 Reggie White	.40	.18
❑ 64 Eddie George	1.00	.45
❑ 65 Darryll Lewis	.10	.05
❑ 66 Steve McNair	.50	.23
❑ 67 Chris Sanders	.10	.05
❑ 68 Marshall Faulk	.40	.18
❑ 69 Jim Harbaugh	.20	.09
❑ 70 Marvin Harrison	.40	.18
❑ 71 Tony Brackens	.10	.05
❑ 72 Mark Brunell	1.00	.45
❑ 73 Kevin Hardy	.10	.05
❑ 74 Rob Johnson	.40	.18
❑ 75 Keenan McCardell	.20	.09
❑ 76 Natrone Means	.40	.18
❑ 77 Jimmy Smith	.20	.09
❑ 78 Marcus Allen	.40	.18
❑ 79 Pat Barnes RC	.40	.18
❑ 80 Tony Gonzalez RC UER (Gonzalez on back)	1.25	.55
❑ 81 Elvis Grbac	.20	.09
❑ 82 Brett Perriman	.10	.05
❑ 83 Andre Rison	.20	.09
❑ 84 Derrick Thomas	.20	.09
❑ 85 Tamarick Vanover	.20	.09
❑ 86 Karim Abdul-Jabbar	.40	.18
❑ 87 Fred Barnett	.10	.05
❑ 88 Terrell Buckley	.10	.05
❑ 89 Yatil Green RC	.20	.09
❑ 90 Dan Marino	2.00	.90
❑ 91 O.J. McDuffie	.20	.09
❑ 92 Jason Taylor	.10	.05
❑ 93 Zach Thomas	.20	.09
❑ 94 Cris Carter	.40	.18
❑ 95 Brad Johnson	.50	.23
❑ 96 John Randle	.20	.09
❑ 97 Jake Reed	.20	.09
❑ 98 Robert Smith	.20	.09
❑ 99 Drew Bledsoe	1.00	.45
❑ 100 Chris Canty RC	.10	.05
❑ 101 Ben Coates	.20	.09
❑ 102 Terry Glenn	.40	.18
❑ 103 Ty Law	.10	.05
❑ 104 Curtis Martin	.50	.23
❑ 105 Willie McGinest	.10	.05
❑ 106 Troy Davis RC	.40	.18
❑ 107 Wayne Martin	.10	.05
❑ 108 Heath Shuler	.10	.05
❑ 109 Danny Wuerffel RC	.60	.25
❑ 110 Ray Zellars	.10	.05
❑ 111 Tiki Barber RC	1.25	.55
❑ 112 Dave Brown	.10	.05
❑ 113 Checklist	.10	.05
❑ 114 Ike Hilliard RC	.75	.35
❑ 115 Jason Sehorn	.20	.09
❑ 116 Amani Toomer	.20	.09
❑ 117 Tyrone Wheatley	.20	.09
❑ 118 Hugh Douglas	.10	.05
❑ 119 Aaron Glenn	.10	.05
❑ 120 Jeff Graham	.10	.05
❑ 121 Keyshawn Johnson	.40	.18
❑ 122 Adrian Murrell	.20	.09
❑ 123 Neil O'Donnell	.20	.09
❑ 124 Tim Brown	.40	.18
❑ 125 Jeff George	.20	.09
❑ 126 Desmond Howard	.20	.09
❑ 127 Napoleon Kaufman	.40	.18
❑ 128 Chester McGlockton	.10	.05
❑ 129 Darrell Russell RC	.10	.05
❑ 130 Ty Detmer	.20	.09
❑ 131 Irving Fryar	.20	.09
❑ 132 Chris T. Jones	.10	.05
❑ 133 Ricky Watters	.20	.09
❑ 134 Jerome Bettis	.40	.18
❑ 135 Charles Johnson	.20	.09
❑ 136 George Jones RC	.20	.09
❑ 137 Greg Lloyd	.10	.05
❑ 138 Kordell Stewart	.50	.23
❑ 139 Yancey Thigpen	.20	.09
❑ 140 Jim Everett	.10	.05
❑ 141 Stan Humphries	.20	.09
❑ 142 Tony Martin	.20	.09
❑ 143 Eric Metcalf	.20	.09
❑ 144 Junior Seau	.20	.09
❑ 145 Jim Druckenmiller RC	.40	.18
❑ 146 Kevin Greene	.20	.09
❑ 147 Garrison Hearst	.20	.09
❑ 148 Terry Kirby	.20	.09
❑ 149 Terrell Owens	.40	.18
❑ 150 Jerry Rice	1.00	.45
❑ 151 Dana Stubblefield	.10	.05
❑ 152 Rod Woodson	.20	.09

Card	MINT	NRMT
153 Bryant Young	.10	.05
154 Steve Young	.60	.25
155 Chad Brown	.10	.05
156 John Friesz	.10	.05
157 Joey Galloway	.50	.23
158 Cortez Kennedy	.10	.05
159 Warren Moon	.40	.18
160 Shawn Springs RC	.20	.09
161 Chris Warren	.20	.09
162 Tony Banks	.20	.09
163 Isaac Bruce	.40	.18
164 Eddie Kennison	.20	.09
165 Keith Lyle	.10	.05
166 Orlando Pace RC	.40	.18
167 Lawrence Phillips	.10	.05
168 Checklist	.10	.05
169 Mike Alstott	.40	.18
170 Reidel Anthony RC	.75	.35
171 Warrick Dunn RC	1.25	.55
172 Hardy Nickerson	.10	.05
173 Errict Rhett	.10	.05
174 Warren Sapp	.20	.09
175 Terry Allen	.40	.18
176 Gus Frerotte	.10	.05
177 Sean Gilbert	.10	.05
178 Ken Harvey	.10	.05
179 Jeff Hostetler	.10	.05
180 Michael Westbrook	.20	.09

1998 Collector's Edge First Place

	MINT	NRMT
COMPLETE SET (250)	60.00	27.00
1 Karim Abdul-Jabbar	.60	.25
2 Flozell Adams RC	.75	.35
3 Troy Aikman	1.50	.70
4 Robert Smith	.60	.25
5 Stephen Alexander RC	1.00	.45
6 Harold Shaw RC	1.00	.45
7 Marcus Allen	.60	.25
8 Terry Allen	.60	.25
9 Mike Alstott	.60	.25
10 Jamal Anderson	.60	.25
11 Reidel Anthony	.30	.14
12 Jamie Asher	.15	.07
13 Darnell Autry	.15	.07
14 Phil Savoy RC	1.00	.45
15 Jon Ritchie RC	1.00	.45
16 Tony Banks	.30	.14
17 Tiki Barber	.30	.14
18 Pat Barnes	.15	.07
19 Charlie Batch RC	4.00	1.80
20 Mikhael Ricks RC	1.00	.45
21 Jerome Bettis	.60	.25
22 Tim Biakabutuka	.30	.14
23 Roosevelt Blackmon RC	.75	.35
24 Jeff Blake	.30	.14
25 Drew Bledsoe	1.25	.55
26 Tony Boselli	.15	.07
27 Peter Boulware	.15	.07
28 Tony Brackens	.15	.07
29 Corey Bradford RC	4.00	1.80
30 Michael Pittman RC	2.00	.90
31 Keith Brooking RC	1.00	.45
32 Robert Brooks	.30	.14
33 Derrick Brooks	.15	.07
34 Ken Oxendine RC	.75	.35
35 R.W. McQuarters RC	.75	.35
36 Tim Brown	.60	.25
37 Chad Brown	.15	.07
38 Isaac Bruce	.60	.25
39 Mark Brunell	1.25	.55
40 Chris Canty	.15	.07
41 Mark Carrier	.15	.07
42 Rae Carruth	.30	.14
43 Ki-Jana Carter	.15	.07
44 Cris Carter	.60	.25
45 Larry Centers	.15	.07
46 Corey Chavous RC	.75	.35
47 Mark Chmura	.30	.14
48 Cameron Cleeland RC	1.00	.45
49 Dexter Coakley	.15	.07
50 Ben Coates	.30	.14
51 Jonathan Linton RC	2.00	.90
52 Todd Collins	.15	.07
53 Kerry Collins	.30	.14
54 Tebucky Jones RC	.75	.35
55 Curtis Conway	.30	.14
56 Sam Cowart RC	.75	.35
57 Bryan Cox	.15	.07
58 Randall Cunningham	.60	.25
59 Terrell Davis	2.50	1.10
60 Troy Davis	.15	.07
61 Pat Johnson RC	1.00	.45
62 Trent Dilfer	.60	.25
63 Vonnie Holliday RC	1.00	.45
64 Corey Dillon	1.00	.45
65 Hugh Douglas	.15	.07
66 Jim Druckenmiller	.30	.14
67 Warrick Dunn	.60	.25
68 Robert Edwards RC	2.50	1.10
69 Greg Ellis RC	.75	.35
70 John Elway	3.00	1.35
71 Bert Emanuel	.30	.14
72 Bobby Engram	.30	.14
73 Curtis Enis RC	2.00	.90
74 Marshall Faulk	.60	.25
75 Brett Favre	3.00	1.35
76 Doug Flutie	.60	.25
77 Glenn Foley	.30	.14
78 Antonio Freeman	.60	.25
79 Gus Frerotte	.15	.07
80 John Friesz	.15	.07
81 Irving Fryar	.30	.14
82 Joey Galloway	.60	.25
83 Rich Gannon	.30	.14
84 Charlie Garner	.15	.07
85 Jeff George	.30	.14
86 Eddie George	1.25	.55
87 Sean Gilbert	.15	.07
88 Terry Glenn	.60	.25
89 Aaron Glenn	.15	.07
90 Tony Gonzalez	.15	.07
91 Jeff Graham	.15	.07
92 Elvis Grbac	.30	.14
93 Jacquez Green RC	2.50	1.10
94 Kevin Greene	.30	.14
95 Brian Griese RC UER	5.00	2.20
96 Byron Hanspard	.30	.14
97 Jim Harbaugh	.30	.14
98 Kevin Hardy	.15	.07
99 Walt Harris	.15	.07
100 Marvin Harrison	.30	.14
101 Rodney Harrison	.30	.14
102 Jeff Hartings RC	.75	.35
103 Ken Harvey	.15	.07
104 Garrison Hearst	.60	.25
105 Ike Hilliard	.30	.14
106 Jeff Hostetler	.15	.07
107 Bobby Hoying	.30	.14
108 Michael Jackson	.15	.07
109 Anthony Johnson	.15	.07
110 Brad Johnson	.60	.25
111 Keyshawn Johnson	.60	.25
112 Charles Johnson	.15	.07
113 Daryl Johnston	.30	.14
114 Chris Jones	.15	.07
115 George Jones	.15	.07
116 Donald Hayes RC	2.00	.90
117 Danny Kanell	.30	.14
118 Napoleon Kaufman	.60	.25
119 Cortez Kennedy	.15	.07
120 Eddie Kennison	.30	.14
121 Levon Kirkland	.15	.07
122 Jon Kitna	1.00	.45
123 Erik Kramer	.15	.07
124 David LaFleur	.15	.07
125 Lamar Lathon	.15	.07
126 Ty Law	.15	.07
127 Ryan Leaf RC	3.00	1.35
128 Dorsey Levens	.60	.25
129 Ray Lewis	.60	.25
130 Darryll Lewis	.15	.07
131 Matt Hasselbeck RC	25.00	11.00
132 Greg Lloyd	.15	.07
133 Kevin Lockett	.15	.07
134 Keith Lyle	.15	.07
135 Peyton Manning RC	12.00	5.50
136 Dan Marino	3.00	1.35
137 Wayne Martin	.15	.07
138 Ahman Green RC	3.00	1.35
139 Tony Martin	.30	.14
140 E.G. Green RC	1.00	.45
141 Derrick Mayes	.30	.14
142 Ed McCaffrey	.30	.14
143 Keenan McCardell	.30	.14
144 O.J. McDuffie	.30	.14
145 Leeland McElroy	.15	.07
146 Willie McGinest	.15	.07
147 Chester McGlockton	.15	.07
148 Steve McNair	.60	.25
149 Natrone Means	.60	.25
150 Eric Metcalf	.15	.07
151 Anthony Miller	.15	.07
152 Rick Mirer	.15	.07
153 Scott Mitchell	.30	.14
154 John Mobley	.15	.07
155 Warren Moon	.60	.25
156 Herman Moore	.60	.25
157 Randy Moss RC	12.00	5.50
158 Eric Moulds	.60	.25
159 Muhsin Muhammad	.30	.14
160 Adrian Murrell	.30	.14
161 Marcus Nash RC	2.00	.90
162 Hardy Nickerson	.15	.07
163 Ken Norton	.15	.07
164 Neil O'Donnell	.30	.14
165 Terrell Owens	.60	.25
166 Orlando Pace	.15	.07
167 Jammi German RC	.75	.35
168 Erric Pegram	.15	.07
169 Jason Peter RC	.75	.35
170 Carl Pickens	.60	.25
171 Jake Plummer	1.25	.55
172 John Randle	.30	.14
173 Andre Reed	.30	.14
174 Jake Reed	.30	.14
175 Errict Rhett	.30	.14
176 Simeon Rice	.30	.14
177 Jerry Rice	1.50	.70
178 Andre Rison	.30	.14
179 Darrell Russell	.15	.07
180 Rashaan Salaam	.15	.07
181 Deion Sanders	.60	.25
182 Barry Sanders	3.00	1.35
183 Chris Sanders	.15	.07
184 Warren Sapp	.30	.14
185 Junior Seau	.30	.14
186 Jason Sehorn	.30	.14
187 Shannon Sharpe	.30	.14
188 Sedrick Shaw	.15	.07
189 Heath Shuler	.15	.07
190 Chris Floyd RC	.75	.35
191 Terry Fair RC	1.00	.45
192 Kevin Dyson RC	2.50	1.10
193 Torrance Small	.15	.07
194 Antowain Smith	.60	.25
195 Bruce Smith	.30	.14
196 Tarik Smith RC	1.00	.45
197 Emmitt Smith	2.50	1.10
198 Neil Smith	.30	.14
199 Jimmy Smith	.30	.14
200 Chris Spielman	.15	.07
201 Danny Wuerffel	.30	.14
202 Irving Spikes	.15	.07
203 Shawn Springs	.15	.07
204 Duane Starks RC	.75	.35

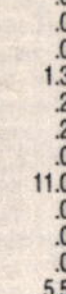

❑ 205 Kordell Stewart .60 .25
❑ 206 J.J. Stokes .30 .14
❑ 207 Eric Swann .15 .07
❑ 208 Steve Tasker .15 .07
❑ 209 Tim Dwight RC 2.50 1.10
❑ 210 Jason Taylor .15 .07
❑ 211 Vinny Testaverde .30 .14
❑ 212 Thurman Thomas .60 .25
❑ 213 Broderick Thomas .15 .07
❑ 214 Derrick Thomas .30 .14
❑ 215 Zach Thomas .30 .14
❑ 216 Germane Crowell RC 3.00 1.35
❑ 217 Amani Toomer .30 .14
❑ 218 Tamarick Vanover .15 .07
❑ 219 Ross Verba .15 .07
❑ 220 Andre Wadsworth RC 1.00 .45
❑ 221 Ray Zellars .15 .07
❑ 222 Chris Warren .30 .14
❑ 223 Steve Young 1.00 .45
❑ 224 Tyrone Wheatley .30 .14
❑ 225 Reggie White .60 .25
❑ 226 John Avery RC 2.00 .90
❑ 227 Charles Woodson RC 2.50 1.10
❑ 228 Takeo Spikes RC 1.00 .45
❑ 229 Bryant Young .15 .07
❑ 230 Tavian Banks RC .30 .14
❑ 231 Fred Beasley RC .75 .35
❑ 232 Chris Ruhman RC .75 .35
❑ CK1A Broncos Logo CL .10 .05
❑ CK1B Steelers Logo CL .10 .05
❑ CK2A 49ers Logo CL .10 .05
❑ CK2B Panthers Logo CL .10 .05
❑ CK3A Giants Logo CL .10 .05
❑ CK3B Packers Logo CL .10 .05
❑ CK4A Colts Logo CL .10 .05
❑ CK4B Dolphins Logo CL .10 .05
❑ CK5A Chargers Logo CL .10 .05
❑ CK5B Vikings Logo Cl .10 .05
❑ CK6A Patriots Logo Cl .10 .05
❑ CK6B Raiders Logo CL .10 .05
❑ CK7A Buccaneers Logo CL .10 .05
❑ CK7B Cowboys Logo CL .10 .05
❑ CK8A Bills Logo CL .10 .05
❑ CK8B Lions Logo CL .10 .05
❑ CK9A Chiefs Logo CL .10 .05
❑ CK9B Seahawks Logo CL .10 .05

1999 Collector's Edge First Place

	MINT	NRMT
COMPLETE SET (200)	50.00	22.00

❑ 1 Adrian Murrell .30 .14
❑ 2 Rob Moore .30 .14
❑ 3 Jake Plummer 1.25 .55
❑ 4 Simeon Rice .15 .07
❑ 5 Frank Sanders .30 .14
❑ 6 Jamal Anderson .60 .25
❑ 7 Chris Calloway .15 .07
❑ 8 Chris Chandler .30 .14
❑ 9 Tim Dwight .60 .25
❑ 10 Terance Mathis .30 .14
❑ 11 Jessie Tuggle .15 .07
❑ 12 Tony Banks .30 .14
❑ 13 Priest Holmes .60 .25
❑ 14 Jermaine Lewis .30 .14
❑ 15 Scott Mitchell .15 .07
❑ 16 Doug Flutie .75 .35
❑ 17 Eric Moulds .60 .25
❑ 18 Andre Reed .30 .14
❑ 19 Antowain Smith .60 .25
❑ 20 Bruce Smith .30 .14
❑ 21 Thurman Thomas .30 .14
❑ 22 Steve Beuerlein .15 .07
❑ 23 Tim Biakabutuka .30 .14
❑ 24 Kevin Greene .15 .07
❑ 25 Muhsin Muhammad .30 .14
❑ 26 Edgar Bennett .15 .07
❑ 27 Curtis Conway .30 .14
❑ 28 Bobby Engram .30 .14
❑ 29 Curtis Enis .60 .25
❑ 30 Erik Kramer .15 .07
❑ 31 Jeff Blake .30 .14
❑ 32 Corey Dillon .60 .25
❑ 33 Carl Pickens .30 .14
❑ 34 Darnay Scott .15 .07
❑ 35 Takeo Spikes .15 .07
❑ 36 Ty Detmer .15 .07
❑ 37 Terry Kirby .15 .07
❑ 38 Leslie Shepherd .15 .07
❑ 39 Chris Spielman .15 .07
❑ 40 Troy Aikman 1.50 .70
❑ 41 Michael Irvin .30 .14
❑ 42 Rocket Ismail .30 .14
❑ 43 Ernie Mills .15 .07
❑ 44 Deion Sanders .60 .25
❑ 45 Emmitt Smith 1.50 .70
❑ 46 Chris Warren .15 .07
❑ 47 Bubba Brister .15 .07
❑ 48 Terrell Davis 1.50 .70
❑ 49 Brian Griese 1.25 .55
❑ 50 Ed McCaffrey .30 .14
❑ 51 Shannon Sharpe .30 .14
❑ 52 Rod Smith .30 .14
❑ 53 Charlie Batch 1.25 .55
❑ 54 Terry Fair .15 .07
❑ 55 Herman Moore .60 .25
❑ 56 Johnnie Morton .30 .14
❑ 57 Barry Sanders 2.50 1.10
❑ 58 Santana Dotson .15 .07
❑ 59 Brett Favre 2.50 1.10
❑ 60 Mark Chmura .15 .07
❑ 61 Antonio Freeman .60 .25
❑ 62 Dorsey Levens .60 .25
❑ 63 Derrick Mayes .30 .14
❑ 64 Marvin Harrison .60 .25
❑ 65 Peyton Manning 2.50 1.10
❑ 66 Jerome Pathon .15 .07
❑ 67 Mark Brunell 1.00 .45
❑ 68 Keenan McCardell .30 .14
❑ 69 Jimmy Smith .30 .14
❑ 70 Fred Taylor 1.50 .70
❑ 71 Derrick Alexander WR .30 .14
❑ 72 Kimble Anders .30 .14
❑ 73 Elvis Grbac .30 .14
❑ 74 Warren Moon .60 .25
❑ 75 Byron Bam Morris .15 .07
❑ 76 Andre Rison .30 .14
❑ 77 Karim Abdul-Jabbar .30 .14
❑ 78 Dan Marino 2.50 1.10
❑ 79 Tony Martin .30 .14
❑ 80 O.J. McDuffie .30 .14
❑ 81 Zach Thomas .30 .14
❑ 82 Cris Carter .60 .25
❑ 83 Randall Cunningham .60 .25
❑ 84 Jeff George .30 .14
❑ 85 Randy Moss 2.50 1.10
❑ 86 Jake Reed .30 .14
❑ 87 Robert Smith .60 .25
❑ 88 Drew Bledsoe 1.00 .45
❑ 89 Ben Coates .30 .14
❑ 90 Terry Glenn .60 .25
❑ 91 Ty Law .15 .07
❑ 92 Shawn Jefferson .15 .07
❑ 93 Cameron Cleeland .15 .07
❑ 94 Andre Hastings .15 .07
❑ 95 Billy Joe Hobert .15 .07
❑ 96 Eddie Kennison .30 .14
❑ 97 Gary Brown .15 .07
❑ 98 Kerry Collins .30 .14
❑ 99 Kent Graham .15 .07
❑ 100 Ike Hilliard .15 .07
❑ 101 Joe Jurevicius .15 .07
❑ 102 Wayne Chrebet .30 .14
❑ 103 Aaron Glenn .15 .07
❑ 104 Keyshawn Johnson .60 .25
❑ 105 Mo Lewis .15 .07
❑ 106 Curtis Martin .60 .25
❑ 107 Vinny Testaverde .30 .14
❑ 108 Tim Brown .60 .25
❑ 109 Rich Gannon .30 .14
❑ 110 James Jett .30 .14
❑ 111 Napoleon Kaufman .60 .25
❑ 112 Charles Woodson .60 .25
❑ 113 Koy Detmer .15 .07
❑ 114 Charles Johnson .15 .07
❑ 115 Duce Staley .60 .25
❑ 116 Jerome Bettis .60 .25
❑ 117 Courtney Hawkins .15 .07
❑ 118 Levon Kirkland .15 .07
❑ 119 Kordell Stewart .60 .25
❑ 120 Isaac Bruce .60 .25
❑ 121 Marshall Faulk .60 .25
❑ 122 Trent Green .30 .14
❑ 123 Amp Lee .15 .07
❑ 124 Jim Harbaugh .30 .14
❑ 125 Bryan Still .15 .07
❑ 126 Freddie Jones .15 .07
❑ 127 Mikhael Ricks .15 .07
❑ 128 Natrone Means .30 .14
❑ 129 Junior Seau .30 .14
❑ 130 Lawrence Phillips .30 .14
❑ 131 Terrell Owens .60 .25
❑ 132 Jerry Rice 1.50 .70
❑ 133 J.J. Stokes .30 .14
❑ 134 Steve Young 1.00 .45
❑ 135 Joey Galloway .60 .25
❑ 136 Jon Kitna .60 .25
❑ 137 Ricky Watters .30 .14
❑ 138 Mike Alstott .60 .25
❑ 139 Reidel Anthony .30 .14
❑ 140 Trent Dilfer .30 .14
❑ 141 Warrick Dunn .60 .25
❑ 142 Kevin Dyson .30 .14
❑ 143 Eddie George .75 .35
❑ 144 Steve McNair .60 .25
❑ 145 Frank Wycheck .15 .07
❑ 146 Skip Hicks .60 .25
❑ 147 Brad Johnson .60 .25
❑ 148 Michael Westbrook .30 .14
❑ 149 Checklist Card .15 .07
❑ 150 Checklist Card .15 .07
❑ 151 David Boston RC 2.50 1.10
❑ 152 Patrick Kerney RC .60 .25
❑ 153 Chris McAlister RC 1.00 .45
❑ 154 Peerless Price RC 1.50 .70
❑ 155 Antoine Winfield RC 1.00 .45
❑ 156 D'Wayne Bates RC 1.00 .45
❑ 157 Cade McNown RC 1.50 .70
❑ 158 Akili Smith RC 2.50 1.10
❑ 159 Rahim Abdullah RC 1.00 .45
❑ 160 Tim Couch RC 4.00 1.80
❑ 161 Kevin Johnson RC 2.50 1.10
❑ 162 Ebenezer Ekuban RC 1.00 .45
❑ 163 Dat Nguyen RC 1.25 .55
❑ 164 Al Wilson RC 1.00 .45
❑ 165 Chris Claiborne RC .60 .25
❑ 166 Sedrick Irvin RC 1.25 .55
❑ 167 Antuan Edwards RC 1.00 .45
❑ 168 Aaron Brooks RC 5.00 2.20
❑ 169 De'Mond Parker RC 1.25 .55
❑ 170 Edgerrin James RC 8.00 3.60
❑ 171 Fernando Bryant RC 1.00 .45
❑ 172 Mike Cloud RC 1.25 .55
❑ 173 John Tait RC .60 .25
❑ 174 Cecil Collins RC 1.25 .55
❑ 175 James Johnson RC 1.25 .55
❑ 176 Rob Konrad RC 1.25 .55
❑ 177 Daunte Culpepper RC 8.00 3.60
❑ 178 Jim Kleinsasser RC 1.25 .55
❑ 179 Brock Huard RC 2.00 .90
❑ 180 Michael Bishop RC 1.50 .70
❑ 181 Kevin Faulk RC 2.00 .90
❑ 182 Andy Katzenmoyer RC 1.25 .55
❑ 183 Ricky Williams RC 5.00 2.20
❑ 184 Joe Montgomery RC 1.25 .55
❑ 185 Donovan McNabb RC 5.00 2.20
❑ 186 Troy Edwards RC 1.50 .70

Card	MINT	NRMT
❑ 187 Amos Zereoue RC	1.25	.55
❑ 188 Joe Germaine RC	1.25	.55
❑ 189 Torry Holt RC	3.00	1.35
❑ 190 Jermaine Fazande RC	1.25	.55
❑ 191 Reggie McGrew RC	1.00	.45
❑ 192 Karsten Bailey RC	1.00	.45
❑ 193 Lamar King RC	.60	.25
❑ 194 Autry Denson RC	1.25	.55
❑ 195 Martin Gramatica RC	.60	.25
❑ 196 Shaun King RC	2.50	1.10
❑ 197 Darnell McDonald RC	1.25	.55
❑ 198 Anthony McFarland RC	1.25	.55
❑ 199 Jevon Kearse RC	2.50	1.10
❑ 200 Champ Bailey RC	1.50	.70
❑ 201 Kurt Warner RC/500	400.00	180.00
❑ 201P Kurt Warner Promo	50.00	22.00

1999 Collector's Edge Fury

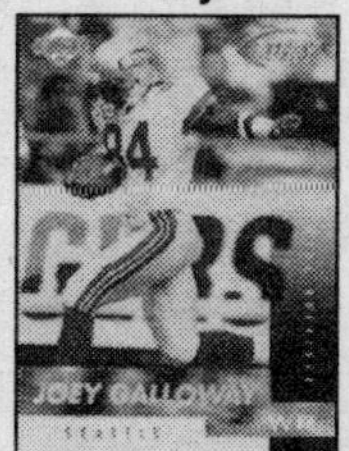

	MINT	NRMT
COMPLETE SET (200)	40.00	18.00
❑ 1 Checklist Card 1	.15	.07
❑ 2 Checklist Card 2	.15	.07
❑ 3 Karim Abdul-Jabbar	.30	.14
❑ 4 Troy Aikman	1.50	.70
❑ 5 Derrick Alexander WR	.30	.14
❑ 6 Mike Alstott	.60	.25
❑ 7 Jamal Anderson	.60	.25
❑ 8 Reidel Anthony	.30	.14
❑ 9 Tiki Barber	.15	.07
❑ 10 Charlie Batch	1.25	.55
❑ 11 Edgar Bennett	.15	.07
❑ 12 Jerome Bettis	.60	.25
❑ 13 Steve Beuerlein	.15	.07
❑ 14 Tim Biakabutuka	.30	.14
❑ 15 Jeff Blake	.30	.14
❑ 16 Drew Bledsoe	1.00	.45
❑ 17 Bubby Brister	.15	.07
❑ 18 Robert Brooks	.30	.14
❑ 19 Gary Brown	.15	.07
❑ 20 Tim Brown	.60	.25
❑ 21 Isaac Bruce	.60	.25
❑ 22 Mark Brunell	1.00	.45
❑ 23 Chris Calloway	.15	.07
❑ 24 Cris Carter	.60	.25
❑ 25 Larry Centers	.15	.07
❑ 26 Chris Chandler	.30	.14
❑ 27 Wayne Chrebet	.30	.14
❑ 28 Cam Cleeland	.15	.07
❑ 29 Kerry Collins	.30	.14
❑ 30 Curtis Conway	.30	.14
❑ 31 Germane Crowell	.30	.14
❑ 32 Randall Cunningham	.60	.25
❑ 33 Terrell Davis	1.50	.70
❑ 34 Koy Detmer	.15	.07
❑ 35 Ty Detmer	.30	.14
❑ 36 Trent Dilfer	.30	.14
❑ 37 Corey Dillon	.60	.25
❑ 38 Warrick Dunn	.60	.25
❑ 39 Tim Dwight	.60	.25
❑ 40 Kevin Dyson	.30	.14
❑ 41 John Elway	2.50	1.10
❑ 42 Bobby Engram	.30	.14
❑ 43 Curtis Enis	.60	.25
❑ 44 Terry Fair	.15	.07
❑ 45 Marshall Faulk	.60	.25
❑ 46 Brett Favre	2.50	1.10
❑ 47 Doug Flutie	.75	.35
❑ 48 Antonio Freeman	.60	.25
❑ 49 Joey Galloway	.60	.25
❑ 50 Rich Gannon	.30	.14
❑ 51 Eddie George	.75	.35
❑ 52 Jeff George	.30	.14
❑ 53 Terry Glenn	.60	.25
❑ 54 Elvis Grbac	.30	.14
❑ 55 Ahman Green	.30	.14
❑ 56 Jacquez Green	.15	.07
❑ 57 Trent Green	.30	.14
❑ 58 Kevin Greene	.15	.07
❑ 59 Brian Griese	1.25	.55
❑ 60 Az-Zahir Hakim	.15	.07
❑ 61 Jim Harbaugh	.30	.14
❑ 62 Marvin Harrison	.60	.25
❑ 63 Courtney Hawkins	.15	.07
❑ 64 Garrison Hearst	.30	.14
❑ 65 Ike Hilliard	.15	.07
❑ 66 Billy Joe Hobert	.15	.07
❑ 67 Priest Holmes	.60	.25
❑ 68 Michael Irvin	.30	.14
❑ 69 Rocket Ismail	.30	.14
❑ 70 Shawn Jefferson	.15	.07
❑ 71 James Jett	.30	.14
❑ 72 Brad Johnson	.60	.25
❑ 73 Charles Johnson	.15	.07
❑ 74 Keyshawn Johnson	.60	.25
❑ 75 Pat Johnson	.15	.07
❑ 76 Joe Jurevicius	.15	.07
❑ 77 Napoleon Kaufman	.60	.25
❑ 78 Eddie Kennison	.30	.14
❑ 79 Terry Kirby	.15	.07
❑ 80 Jon Kitna	.60	.25
❑ 81 Erik Kramer	.15	.07
❑ 82 Fred Lane	.30	.14
❑ 83 Ty Law	.15	.07
❑ 84 Ryan Leaf	.60	.25
❑ 85 Amp Lee	.15	.07
❑ 86 Dorsey Levens	.60	.25
❑ 87 Jermaine Lewis	.30	.14
❑ 88 Sam Madison	.15	.07
❑ 89 Peyton Manning	2.50	1.10
❑ 90 Dan Marino	2.50	1.10
❑ 91 Curtis Martin	.60	.25
❑ 92 Tony Martin	.30	.14
❑ 93 Terance Mathis	.30	.14
❑ 94 Ed McCaffrey	.30	.14
❑ 95 Keenan McCardell	.30	.14
❑ 96 O.J. McDuffie	.30	.14
❑ 97 Steve McNair	.60	.25
❑ 98 Natrone Means	.30	.14
❑ 99 Herman Moore	.60	.25
❑ 100 Rob Moore	.30	.14
❑ 101 Byron Bam Morris	.15	.07
❑ 102 Johnnie Morton	.15	.07
❑ 103 Randy Moss	2.50	1.10
❑ 104 Eric Moulds	.60	.25
❑ 105 Muhsin Muhammad	.30	.14
❑ 106 Adrian Murrell	.30	.14
❑ 107 Terrell Owens	.60	.25
❑ 108 Jerome Pathon	.15	.07
❑ 109 Carl Pickens	.30	.14
❑ 110 Jake Plummer	1.25	.55
❑ 111 Andre Reed	.30	.14
❑ 112 Jake Reed	.30	.14
❑ 113 Jerry Rice	1.50	.70
❑ 114 Mikhael Ricks	.15	.07
❑ 115 Andre Rison	.30	.14
❑ 116 Barry Sanders	2.50	1.10
❑ 117 Deion Sanders	.60	.25
❑ 118 Frank Sanders	.30	.14
❑ 119 O.J. Santiago	.15	.07
❑ 120 Darnay Scott	.15	.07
❑ 121 Junior Seau	.30	.14
❑ 122 Shannon Sharpe	.30	.14
❑ 123 Leslie Shepherd	.15	.07
❑ 124 Antowain Smith	.60	.25
❑ 125 Bruce Smith	.30	.14
❑ 126 Emmitt Smith	1.50	.70
❑ 127 Jimmy Smith	.30	.14
❑ 128 Robert Smith	.60	.25
❑ 129 Rod Smith	.30	.14
❑ 130 Chris Spielman	.15	.07
❑ 131 Takeo Spikes	.15	.07
❑ 132 Duce Staley	.60	.25
❑ 133 Kordell Stewart	.60	.25
❑ 134 Bryan Still	.15	.07
❑ 135 J.J. Stokes	.30	.14
❑ 136 Fred Taylor	1.50	.70
❑ 137 Vinny Testaverde	.30	.14
❑ 138 Yancey Thigpen	.15	.07
❑ 139 Thurman Thomas	.30	.14
❑ 140 Zach Thomas	.30	.14
❑ 141 Amani Toomer	.15	.07
❑ 142 Hines Ward	.15	.07
❑ 143 Chris Warren	.15	.07
❑ 144 Ricky Watters	.30	.14
❑ 145 Michael Westbrook	.30	.14
❑ 146 Alvis Whitted	.15	.07
❑ 147 Charles Woodson	.60	.25
❑ 148 Rod Woodson	.30	.14
❑ 149 Frank Wycheck	.15	.07
❑ 150 Steve Young	1.00	.45
❑ 151 Rahim Abdullah RC	1.00	.45
❑ 152 Champ Bailey RC	2.00	.90
❑ 153 D'Wayne Bates RC	1.00	.45
❑ 154 Michael Bishop RC	2.00	.90
❑ 155 Dre' Bly RC	1.00	.45
❑ 156 David Boston RC	3.00	1.35
❑ 157 Fernando Bryant RC	1.00	.45
❑ 158 Chris Claiborne RC	.50	.23
❑ 159 Mike Cloud RC	1.50	.70
❑ 160 Cecil Colliins RC	1.50	.70
❑ 161 Tim Couch RC	5.00	2.20
❑ 162 Daunte Culpepper RC	10.00	4.50
❑ 163 Antuan Edwards RC	.50	.23
❑ 164 Troy Edwards RC	2.00	.90
❑ 165 Ebenezer Ekuban RC	1.00	.45
❑ 166 Kevin Faulk RC	2.50	1.10
❑ 167 Joe Germaine RC	1.50	.70
❑ 168 Aaron Gibson RC	.50	.23
❑ 169 Martin Gramatica RC	.50	.23
❑ 170 Torry Holt RC	4.00	1.80
❑ 171 Brock Huard RC	2.50	1.10
❑ 172 Sedrick Irvin RC	1.50	.70
❑ 173 Edgerrin James RC	10.00	4.50
❑ 174 James Johnson RC	1.50	.70
❑ 175 Kevin Johnson RC	3.00	1.35
❑ 176 Andy Katzenmoyer RC	1.50	.70
❑ 177 Jevon Kearse RC	3.00	1.35
❑ 178 Patrick Kerney RC	.50	.23
❑ 179 Lamar King RC	.50	.23
❑ 180 Shaun King RC	3.00	1.35
❑ 181 Jim Kleinsasser RC	1.50	.70
❑ 182 Rob Konrad RC	1.00	.45
❑ 183 Chris McAlister RC	1.00	.45
❑ 184 Anthony McFarland RC	1.50	.70
❑ 185 Karsten Bailey RC	1.00	.45
❑ 186 Donovan McNabb RC	6.00	2.70
❑ 187 Cade McNown RC	2.00	.90
❑ 188 Joe Montgomery RC	1.50	.70
❑ 189 Dat Nguyen RC	1.50	.70
❑ 190 Luke Petitgout RC	.50	.23
❑ 191 Peerless Price RC	2.00	.90
❑ 192 Akili Smith RC	3.00	1.35
❑ 193 Matt Stinchcomb RC	.50	.23
❑ 194 John Tait RC	.50	.23
❑ 195 Jermaine Fazande RC	1.50	.70
❑ 196 Ricky Williams RC	6.00	2.70
❑ 197 Al Wilson RC	1.00	.45
❑ 198 Antoine Winfield RC	1.00	.45
❑ 199 Damien Woody RC	.50	.23
❑ 200 Amos Zereoue RC	1.50	.70

1997 Collector's Edge Masters

	MINT	NRMT
COMPLETE SET (270)	40.00	18.00
❑ 1 Cardinals Flag	.50	.23
❑ 2 Larry Centers	.40	.18
❑ 3 Rob Moore	.40	.18
❑ 4 Frank Sanders	.40	.18
❑ 5 Eric Swann	.20	.09
❑ 6 Falcons Flag	.50	.23
❑ 7 Morten Andersen UER (Misspelled Morton)	.20	.09
❑ 8 Bert Emanuel	.40	.18

❑ 9 Jeff George .40 .18
❑ 10 Craig Heyward .20 .09
❑ 11 Terance Mathis .40 .18
❑ 12 Clay Matthews .20 .09
❑ 13 Eric Metcalf .40 .18
❑ 14 Ravens Flag .50 .23
❑ 15 Rob Burnett .20 .09
❑ 16 Leroy Hoard .20 .09
❑ 17 Ernest Hunter .20 .09
❑ 18 Michael Jackson .40 .18
❑ 19 Stevon Moore .20 .09
❑ 20 Anthony Pleasant .20 .09
❑ 21 Vinny Testaverde .40 .18
❑ 22 Eric Zeier .40 .18
❑ 23 Bills Flag .50 .23
❑ 24 Todd Collins .20 .09
❑ 25 Russell Copeland .20 .09
❑ 26 Quinn Early .20 .09
❑ 27 Jim Kelly .75 .35
❑ 28 Bryce Paup .20 .09
❑ 29 Andre Reed .40 .18
❑ 30 Bruce Smith .40 .18
❑ 31 Panthers Flag .50 .23
❑ 32 Steve Beuerlein .20 .09
❑ 33 Mark Carrier WR .20 .09
❑ 34 Kerry Collins .40 .18
❑ 35 Willie Green .20 .09
❑ 36 Kevin Greene .40 .18
❑ 37 Eric Guliford .20 .09
❑ 38 Brett Maxie .20 .09
❑ 39 Tim McKyer .20 .09
❑ 40 Derrick Moore .20 .09
❑ 41 Bears Flag .50 .23
❑ 42 Curtis Conway .40 .18
❑ 43 Bryan Cox .20 .09
❑ 44 Jim Flanigan .20 .09
❑ 45 Robert Green .20 .09
❑ 46 Erik Kramer .20 .09
❑ 47 Dave Krieg .20 .09
❑ 48 Rashaan Salaam .20 .09
❑ 49 Alonzo Spellman .20 .09
❑ 50 Donnell Woolford .20 .09
❑ 51 Chris Zorich .20 .09
❑ 52 Bengals Flag .50 .23
❑ 53 Eric Bieniemy .20 .09
❑ 54 Jeff Blake .40 .18
❑ 55 Ki-Jana Carter .20 .09
❑ 56 John Copeland .20 .09
❑ 57 Garrison Hearst .40 .18
❑ 58 Tony McGee .20 .09
❑ 59 Carl Pickens .75 .35
❑ 60 Darnay Scott .40 .18
❑ 61 Bracey Walker .20 .09
❑ 62 Dan Wilkinson .20 .09
❑ 63 Cowboys Flag .50 .23
❑ 64 Troy Aikman 2.00 .90
❑ 65 Bill Bates .40 .18
❑ 66 Shante Carver .20 .09
❑ 67 Michael Irvin .75 .35
❑ 68 Daryl Johnston .40 .18
❑ 69 Jay Novacek .20 .09
❑ 70 Deion Sanders .75 .35
❑ 71 Emmitt Smith 3.00 1.35
❑ 72 Herschel Walker .40 .18
❑ 73 Sherman Williams .20 .09
❑ 74 Broncos Flag .50 .23
❑ 75 Terrell Davis 3.00 1.35
❑ 76 John Elway 4.00 1.80
❑ 77 Ed McCaffrey .40 .18
❑ 78 Anthony Miller .20 .09
❑ 79 Michael Dean Perry .20 .09
❑ 80 Shannon Sharpe .40 .18
❑ 81 Mike Sherrard .20 .09
❑ 82 Lions Flag .50 .23
❑ 83 Scott Mitchell .40 .18
❑ 84 Glyn Milburn .20 .09
❑ 85 Herman Moore .75 .35
❑ 86 Johnnie Morton .40 .18
❑ 87 Brett Perriman .20 .09
❑ 88 Barry Sanders 4.00 1.80
❑ 89 Tracy Scroggins .20 .09
❑ 90 Packers Flag .50 .23
❑ 91 Edgar Bennett .40 .18
❑ 92 Robert Brooks .40 .18
❑ 93 Santana Dotson .20 .09
❑ 94 Brett Favre 4.00 1.80
❑ 95 Dorsey Levens .75 .35
❑ 96 Craig Newsome .20 .09
❑ 97 Wayne Simmons .20 .09
❑ 98 Reggie White .75 .35
❑ 99 Oilers Flag .50 .23
❑ 100 Chris Chandler .40 .18
❑ 101 Anthony Cook .20 .09
❑ 102 Willie Davis .20 .09
❑ 103 Mel Gray .20 .09
❑ 104 Ronnie Harmon .20 .09
❑ 105 Darryll Lewis .20 .09
❑ 106 Steve McNair 1.25 .55
❑ 107 Todd McNair .20 .09
❑ 108 Rodney Thomas .20 .09
❑ 109 Colts Flag .50 .23
❑ 110 Trev Alberts .20 .09
❑ 111 Tony Bennett .20 .09
❑ 112 Quentin Coryatt .20 .09
❑ 113 Sean Dawkins .20 .09
❑ 114 Ken Dilger .20 .09
❑ 115 Marshall Faulk .75 .35
❑ 116 Jim Harbaugh UER .40 .18
numbered 115 on back
❑ 117 Ronald Humphrey .20 .09
❑ 118 Floyd Turner .20 .09
❑ 119 Jaguars Flag .50 .23
❑ 120 Tony Boselli .20 .09
❑ 121 Mark Brunell 2.00 .90
❑ 122 Willie Jackson .20 .09
❑ 123 Jeff Lageman .20 .09
❑ 124 Natrone Means .75 .35
❑ 125 Andre Rison .40 .18
❑ 126 James O.Stewart .40 .18
❑ 127 Cedric Tillman .20 .09
❑ 128 Chiefs Flag .50 .23
❑ 129 Marcus Allen .75 .35
❑ 130 Kimble Anders .40 .18
❑ 131 Steve Bono .40 .18
❑ 132 Dale Carter .20 .09
❑ 133 Lake Dawson .20 .09
❑ 134 Dan Saleaumua .20 .09
❑ 135 Neil Smith .40 .18
❑ 136 Derrick Thomas .40 .18
❑ 137 Tamarick Vanover .40 .18
❑ 138 Dolphins Flag .50 .23
❑ 139 Fred Barnett .20 .09
❑ 140 Steve Emtman .20 .09
❑ 141 Eric Green .20 .09
❑ 142 Dan Marino 4.00 1.80
❑ 143 O.J. McDuffie .40 .18
❑ 144 Bernie Parmalee .20 .09
❑ 145 Vikings Flag .50 .23
❑ 146 Cris Carter .75 .35
❑ 147 Jack Del Rio .20 .09
❑ 148 Qadry Ismail .40 .18
❑ 149 Amp Lee .20 .09
❑ 150 Warren Moon .75 .35
❑ 151 John Randle .40 .18
❑ 152 Jake Reed .40 .18
❑ 153 Robert Smith .40 .18
❑ 154 Patriots Flag .50 .23
❑ 155 Drew Bledsoe 2.00 .90
❑ 156 Vincent Brisby .20 .09
❑ 157 Willie Clay .20 .09
❑ 158 Ben Coates .40 .18
❑ 159 Curtis Martin 1.25 .55
❑ 160 Dave Meggett .20 .09
❑ 161 Will Moore .20 .09
❑ 162 Chris Slade .20 .09
❑ 163 Saints Flag .50 .23
❑ 164 Mario Bates .20 .09
❑ 165 Jim Everett .20 .09
❑ 166 Michael Haynes .20 .09
❑ 167 Tyrone Hughes .20 .09
❑ 168 Haywood Jeffires .20 .09
❑ 169 Wayne Martin .20 .09
❑ 170 Renaldo Turnbull .20 .09
❑ 171 Giants Flag .50 .23
❑ 172 Dave Brown .20 .09
❑ 173 Chris Calloway .20 .09
❑ 174 Rodney Hampton .40 .18
(See card 259)
❑ 175 Michael Strahan .20 .09
❑ 176 Tyrone Wheatley .40 .18
❑ 177 Jets Flag .50 .23
❑ 178 Kyle Brady .20 .09
❑ 179 Wayne Chrebet .75 .35
❑ 180 Hugh Douglas .20 .09
❑ 181 Jeff Graham .20 .09
❑ 182 Adrian Murrell .40 .18
❑ 183 Neil O'Donnell .40 .18
❑ 184 Raiders Flag .50 .23
❑ 185 Tim Brown .75 .35
❑ 186 Aundray Bruce .20 .09
❑ 187 Andrew Glover .20 .09
❑ 188 Jeff Hostetler .20 .09
❑ 189 Napoleon Kaufman .75 .35
❑ 190 Terry McDaniel .20 .09
❑ 191 Chester McGlockton .20 .09
❑ 192 Pat Swilling .20 .09
❑ 193 Harvey Williams .20 .09
❑ 194 Eagles Flag .50 .23
❑ 195 Randall Cunningham .75 .35
❑ 196 Irving Fryar .40 .18
❑ 197 William Fuller .20 .09
❑ 198 Charlie Garner .20 .09
❑ 199 Andy Harmon .20 .09
❑ 200 Rodney Peete .20 .09
❑ 201 Mark Seay .20 .09
❑ 202 Troy Vincent .20 .09
❑ 203 Ricky Watters .40 .18
❑ 204 Calvin Williams .20 .09
❑ 205 Steelers Flag .50 .23
❑ 206 Jerome Bettis .75 .35
❑ 207 Chad Brown .20 .09
❑ 208 Greg Lloyd .20 .09
❑ 209 Byron Bam Morris .20 .09
❑ 210 Erric Pegram .20 .09
❑ 211 Kordell Stewart 1.00 .45
❑ 212 Yancey Thigpen .40 .18
❑ 213 Rod Woodson .40 .18
❑ 214 Chargers Flag .50 .23
❑ 215 Darren Bennett .20 .09
❑ 216 Marco Coleman .20 .09
❑ 217 Stan Humphries .40 .18
❑ 218 Tony Martin .40 .18
❑ 219 Junior Seau .40 .18
❑ 220 49ers Flag .50 .23
❑ 221 Chris Doleman .20 .09
❑ 222 William Floyd .40 .18
❑ 223 Merton Hanks .20 .09
❑ 224 Brent Jones .40 .18
❑ 225 Terry Kirby .40 .18
❑ 226 Derek Loville .20 .09
❑ 227 Ken Norton Jr. .20 .09
❑ 228 Gary Plummer .20 .09
❑ 229 Jerry Rice 2.00 .90
❑ 230 J.J. Stokes .40 .18
❑ 231 Dana Stubblefield .20 .09
❑ 232 John Taylor .20 .09
❑ 233 Bryant Young .20 .09
❑ 234 Steve Young 1.50 .70
❑ 235 Seahawks Flag .50 .23
❑ 236 Brian Blades .20 .09
❑ 237 Joey Galloway 1.00 .45
❑ 238 Carlton Gray .20 .09
❑ 239 Cortez Kennedy .20 .09
❑ 240 Rick Mirer .20 .09
❑ 241 Chris Warren .40 .18
❑ 242 Rams Flag .50 .23
❑ 243 Isaac Bruce .75 .35
❑ 244 Troy Drayton .20 .09
❑ 245 D'Marco Farr .20 .09

Card	MINT	NRMT
❑ 246 Harold Green	.20	.09
❑ 247 Chris Miller	.20	.09
❑ 248 Leslie O'Neal	.20	.09
❑ 249 Roman Phifer	.20	.09
❑ 250 Buccaneers Flag	.50	.23
❑ 251 Trent Dilfer	.75	.35
❑ 252 Alvin Harper	.20	.09
❑ 253 Jackie Harris	.20	.09
❑ 254 John Lynch	.40	.18
❑ 255 Hardy Nickerson	.20	.09
❑ 256 Errict Rhett	.20	.09
❑ 257 Warren Sapp	.40	.18
❑ 258 Todd Scott	.20	.09
❑ 259 Charles Wilson UER (Numbered 174 on back)	.20	.09
❑ 260 Redskins Flag	.50	.23
❑ 261 Terry Allen	.75	.35
❑ 262 Bill Brooks	.20	.09
❑ 263 Henry Ellard	.20	.09
❑ 264 Gus Frerotte	.20	.09
❑ 265 Sean Gilbert	.20	.09
❑ 266 Ken Harvey	.20	.09
❑ 267 Brian Mitchell	.20	.09
❑ 268 Heath Shuler	.20	.09
❑ 269 James Washington	.20	.09
❑ 270 Michael Westbrook	.40	.18

1998 Collector's Edge Masters

	MINT	NRMT
COMPLETE SET (199)	250.00	110.00
❑ 1 Rob Moore	.60	.25
❑ 2 Adrian Murrell	.60	.25
❑ 3 Jake Plummer	2.50	1.10
❑ 4 Michael Pittman RC	4.00	1.80
❑ 5 Frank Sanders	.60	.25
❑ 6 Andre Wadsworth RC	4.00	1.80
❑ 7 Jamal Anderson	1.25	.55
❑ 8 Chris Chandler	.60	.25
❑ 9 Tim Dwight RC	6.00	2.70
❑ 10 Tony Martin	.60	.25
❑ 11 Terance Mathis	.60	.25
❑ 12 Ken Oxendine RC	1.50	.70
❑ 13 Jim Harbaugh	.60	.25
❑ 14 Priest Holmes RC	6.00	2.70
❑ 15 Michael Jackson	.30	.14
❑ 16 Pat Johnson RC	4.00	1.80
❑ 17 Jermaine Lewis	.60	.25
❑ 18 Eric Zeier	.60	.25
❑ 19 Doug Flutie	1.50	.70
❑ 20 Rob Johnson	.60	.25
❑ 21 Eric Moulds	1.25	.55
❑ 22 Andre Reed	.60	.25
❑ 23 Antowain Smith	1.25	.55
❑ 24 Bruce Smith	.60	.25
❑ 25 Thurman Thomas	1.25	.55
❑ 26 Steve Beuerlein	.30	.14
❑ 27 Kevin Greene	.60	.25
❑ 29 Rocket Ismail	.30	.14
❑ 30 Fred Lane	.60	.25
❑ 31 Muhsin Muhammad	.60	.25
❑ 32 Edgar Bennett	.30	.14
❑ 33 Curtis Conway	.60	.25
❑ 34 Bobby Engram	.60	.25
❑ 35 Curtis Enis RC	5.00	2.20
❑ 36 Erik Kramer	.30	.14
❑ 37 Chris Penn	.30	.14
❑ 38 Jeff Blake	.60	.25
❑ 39 Corey Dillon	2.00	.90
❑ 40 Neil O'Donnell	.60	.25
❑ 41 Carl Pickens	1.25	.55
❑ 42 Darnay Scott	.60	.25
❑ 43 Damon Gibson RC	1.50	.70
❑ 44 Troy Aikman	3.00	1.35
❑ 45 Billy Davis	.30	.14
❑ 46 Michael Irvin	1.25	.55
❑ 47 Ernie Mills	.30	.14
❑ 48 Deion Sanders	1.25	.55
❑ 49 Emmitt Smith	5.00	2.20
❑ 50 Chris Warren	.60	.25
❑ 51 Bubby Brister	.30	.14
❑ 52 Terrell Davis	5.00	2.20
❑ 53 John Elway	6.00	2.70
❑ 54 Brian Griese RC	12.00	5.50
❑ 55 Ed McCaffrey	.60	.25
❑ 56 Marcus Nash RC	4.00	1.80
❑ 57 Shannon Sharpe	.60	.25
❑ 58 Rod Smith	.60	.25
❑ 59 Charlie Batch RC	10.00	4.50
❑ 60 Germane Crowell RC	8.00	3.60
❑ 61 Scott Mitchell	.60	.25
❑ 62 Johnnie Morton	.60	.25
❑ 63 Herman Moore	1.25	.55
❑ 64 Barry Sanders	6.00	2.70
❑ 65 Robert Brooks	.60	.25
❑ 66 Brett Favre	6.00	2.70
❑ 67 Antonio Freeman	1.25	.55
❑ 68 Raymont Harris	.30	.14
❑ 69 Dorsey Levens	1.25	.55
❑ 70 Reggie White	1.25	.55
❑ 71 Marshall Faulk	1.25	.55
❑ 72 Marvin Harrison	.60	.25
❑ 73 Peyton Manning RC	25.00	11.00
❑ 74 Jerome Pathon RC	4.00	1.80
❑ 75 Tavian Banks RC	4.00	1.80
❑ 76 Mark Brunell	2.50	1.10
❑ 77 Keenan McCardell	.60	.25
❑ 78 Jimmy Smith	.60	.25
❑ 79 Fred Taylor RC	10.00	4.50
❑ 80 Derrick Alexander	.60	.25
❑ 81 Donnell Bennett	.30	.14
❑ 82 Rich Gannon	.60	.25
❑ 83 Elvis Grbac	.60	.25
❑ 84 Andre Rison	.60	.25
❑ 85 Rashaan Shehee RC	4.00	1.80
❑ 86 Karim Abdul-Jabbar	1.25	.55
❑ 87 John Avery RC	4.00	1.80
❑ 88 Oronde Gadsden RC	4.00	1.80
❑ 89 Dan Marino	6.00	2.70
❑ 90 O.J. McDuffie	.60	.25
❑ 91 Zach Thomas	.60	.25
❑ 92 Cris Carter	1.25	.55
❑ 93 Randall Cunningham	1.25	.55
❑ 94 Brad Johnson	1.25	.55
❑ 95 Randy Moss RC	25.00	11.00
❑ 96 Jake Reed	.60	.25
❑ 97 Robert Smith	1.25	.55
❑ 98 Drew Bledsoe	2.50	1.10
❑ 99 Ben Coates	.60	.25
❑ 100 Robert Edwards RC	5.00	2.20
❑ 101 Terry Glenn	1.25	.55
❑ 102 Shawn Jefferson	.30	.14
❑ 103 Ty Law	.30	.14
❑ 104 Cameron Cleeland RC	4.00	1.80
❑ 105 Kerry Collins	.60	.25
❑ 106 Sean Dawkins	.30	.14
❑ 107 Andre Hastings	.30	.14
❑ 108 Lamar Smith	.60	.25
❑ 109 Danny Wuerffel	.60	.25
❑ 110 Gary Brown	.30	.14
❑ 111 Chris Calloway	.30	.14
❑ 112 Ike Hilliard	.60	.25
❑ 113 Joe Jurevicius RC	4.00	1.80
❑ 114 Danny Kanell	.60	.25
❑ 115 Wayne Chrebet	1.25	.55
❑ 116 Glenn Foley	.60	.25
❑ 117 Keyshawn Johnson	1.25	.55
❑ 118 Leon Johnson	.30	.14
❑ 119 Curtis Martin	1.25	.55
❑ 120 Vinny Testaverde	.60	.25
❑ 121 Tim Brown	1.25	.55
❑ 122 Jeff George	.60	.25
❑ 123 James Jett	.60	.25
❑ 124 Napoleon Kaufman	1.25	.55
❑ 125 Charles Woodson RC	6.00	2.70
❑ 126 Irving Fryar	.60	.25
❑ 127 Jeff Graham	.30	.14
❑ 128 Bobby Hoying	.60	.25
❑ 129 Duce Staley	2.50	1.10
❑ 130 Jerome Bettis	1.25	.55
❑ 131 C.Fuamatu-Ma'afala RC	4.00	1.80
❑ 132 Courtney Hawkins	.30	.14
❑ 133 Charles Johnson	.30	.14
❑ 134 Kordell Stewart	1.25	.55
❑ 135 Hines Ward RC	4.00	1.80
❑ 136 Tony Banks	.60	.25
❑ 137 Isaac Bruce	1.25	.55
❑ 138 Robert Holcombe RC	4.00	1.80
❑ 139 Eddie Kennison	.60	.25
❑ 140 Ryan Leaf RC	8.00	3.60
❑ 141 Natrone Means	1.25	.55
❑ 142 Mikhael Ricks RC	4.00	1.80
❑ 143 Junior Seau	.60	.25
❑ 144 Bryan Still	.30	.14
❑ 145 Garrison Hearst	1.25	.55
❑ 146 R.W. McQuarters RC	1.50	.70
❑ 147 Terrell Owens	1.25	.55
❑ 148 Jerry Rice	3.00	1.35
❑ 149 J.J. Stokes	.60	.25
❑ 150 Steve Young	2.00	.90
❑ 151 Joey Galloway	1.25	.55
❑ 152 Ahman Green RC	8.00	3.60
❑ 153 Warren Moon	1.25	.55
❑ 154 Shawn Springs	.30	.14
❑ 155 Ricky Watters	.60	.25
❑ 156 Mike Alstott	1.25	.55
❑ 157 Reidel Anthony	.60	.25
❑ 158 Trent Dilfer	1.25	.55
❑ 159 Warrick Dunn	1.25	.55
❑ 160 Jacquez Green RC	6.00	2.70
❑ 161 Kevin Dyson RC	6.00	2.70
❑ 162 Eddie George	2.50	1.10
❑ 163 Steve McNair	1.25	.55
❑ 164 Yancey Thigpen	.30	.14
❑ 165 Frank Wycheck	.30	.14
❑ 166 Terry Allen	1.25	.55
❑ 167 Gus Frerotte	.30	.14
❑ 168 Trent Green	1.50	.70
❑ 169 Skip Hicks RC	4.00	1.80
❑ 170 Michael Westbrook	.60	.25
❑ 171 Jamal Anderson SM	1.25	.55
❑ 172 Carl Pickens SM	1.25	.55
❑ 173 Deion Sanders SM	1.25	.55
❑ 174 Emmitt Smith SM	3.00	1.35
❑ 175 Terrell Davis SM	3.00	1.35
❑ 176 John Elway SM	4.00	1.80
❑ 177 Charlie Batch SM	5.00	2.20
❑ 178 Herman Moore SM	1.25	.55
❑ 179 Barry Sanders SM	4.00	1.80
❑ 180 Brett Favre SM	4.00	1.80
❑ 181 Antonio Freeman SM	.60	.25
❑ 182 Marshall Faulk SM	1.25	.55
❑ 183 Peyton Manning SM	15.00	6.75
❑ 184 Mark Brunell SM	1.25	.55
❑ 185 Dan Marino SM	4.00	1.80
❑ 186 Randy Moss SM	15.00	6.75
❑ 187 Drew Bledsoe SM	1.25	.55
❑ 188 Robert Edwards SM	1.50	.70
❑ 189 Curtis Martin SM	1.25	.55
❑ 190 Charles Woodson SM	2.50	1.10
❑ 191 Jerome Bettis SM	1.25	.55
❑ 192 Robert Holcombe SM	1.25	.55
❑ 193 Ryan Leaf SM	3.00	1.35
❑ 194 Natrone Means SM	1.25	.55
❑ 195 Jerry Rice SM	2.00	.90
❑ 196 Steve Young SM	1.25	.55
❑ 197 Warrick Dunn SM	1.25	.55
❑ 198 Eddie George SM	1.25	.55
❑ 199 Peyton Manning CL	6.00	2.70
❑ 200 Ryan Leaf CL	2.50	1.10

1999 Collector's Edge Masters

	MINT	NRMT
COMPLETE SET (200)	500.00	220.00
❑ 1 David Boston RC	12.00	5.50

	Card	Mint	NrMt
❑	2 Mac Cody RC	5.00	2.20
❑	3 Chris Greisen RC	6.00	2.70
❑	4 Joel Makovicka RC	6.00	2.70
❑	5 Adrian Murrell	.50	.23
❑	6 Jake Plummer	1.50	.70
❑	7 Frank Sanders	.50	.23
❑	8 Jamal Anderson	1.00	.45
❑	9 Chris Chandler	.50	.23
❑	10 Reginald Kelly RC	5.00	2.20
❑	11 Patrick Kerney RC	5.00	2.20
❑	12 Terance Mathis	.50	.23
❑	13 Jeff Paulk RC	5.00	2.20
❑	14 Stoney Case	.25	.11
❑	15 Qadry Ismail	.25	.11
❑	16 Chris McAlister RC	5.00	2.20
❑	17 Errict Rhett	.25	.11
❑	18 Brandon Stokley RC	6.00	2.70
❑	19 Doug Flutie	1.25	.55
❑	20 Kamil Loud RC	5.00	2.20
❑	21 Eric Moulds	1.00	.45
❑	22 Peerless Price RC	8.00	3.60
❑	23 Andre Reed	.50	.23
❑	24 Antowain Smith	1.00	.45
❑	25 Antoine Winfield RC	5.00	2.20
❑	26 Steve Beuerlein	.50	.23
❑	27 Tim Biakabutuka	.50	.23
❑	28 Dameyune Craig RC	6.00	2.70
❑	29 Patrick Jeffers RC	15.00	6.75
❑	30 Muhsin Muhammad	.50	.23
❑	31 D'Wayne Bates RC	5.00	2.20
❑	32 Marty Booker RC	6.00	2.70
❑	33 Bobby Engram	.25	.11
❑	34 Curtis Enis	1.00	.45
❑	35 Ty Hallock RC	5.00	2.20
❑	36 Shane Matthews	1.00	.45
❑	37 Cade McNown RC	8.00	3.60
❑	38 Marcus Robinson	2.00	.90
❑	39 Scott Covington RC	6.00	2.70
❑	40 Corey Dillon	1.00	.45
❑	41 Damon Griffin RC	5.00	2.20
❑	42 Carl Pickens	.50	.23
❑	43 Darnay Scott	.50	.23
❑	44 Akili Smith RC	12.00	5.50
❑	45 Craig Yeast RC	5.00	2.20
❑	46 Darrin Chiaverini RC	6.00	2.70
❑	47 Tim Couch RC	20.00	9.00
❑	48 Phil Dawson RC	5.00	2.20
❑	49 Kevin Johnson RC	12.00	5.50
❑	50 Terry Kirby	.25	.11
❑	51 Wali Rainer RC	5.00	2.20
❑	52 Troy Aikman	2.50	1.10
❑	53 Ebenezer Ekuban RC	5.00	2.20
❑	54 Michael Irvin	.50	.23
❑	55 Rocket Ismail	.50	.23
❑	56 Wane McGarity RC	5.00	2.20
❑	57 Dat Nguyen RC	6.00	2.70
❑	58 Deion Sanders	1.00	.45
❑	59 Emmitt Smith	2.50	1.10
❑	60 Byron Chamberlain	.50	.23
❑	61 Andre Cooper RC	5.00	2.20
❑	62 Terrell Davis	2.50	1.10
❑	63 Olandis Gary RC	12.00	5.50
❑	64 Brian Griese	2.00	.90
❑	65 Ed McCaffrey	.50	.23
❑	66 Travis McGriff RC	5.00	2.20
❑	67 Shannon Sharpe	.50	.23
❑	68 Rod Smith	.50	.23
❑	69 Al Wilson RC	6.00	2.70
❑	70 Charlie Batch	2.00	.90
❑	71 Chris Claiborne RC	3.00	1.35
❑	72 Germane Crowell	.50	.23
❑	73 Greg Hill	.25	.11
❑	74 Sedrick Irvin RC	6.00	2.70
❑	75 Herman Moore	1.00	.45
❑	76 Johnnie Morton	.50	.23
❑	77 Barry Sanders	4.00	1.80
❑	78 Aaron Brooks RC	20.00	9.00
❑	79 Antuan Edwards RC	5.00	2.20
❑	80 Brett Favre	4.00	1.80
❑	81 Antonio Freeman	1.00	.45
❑	82 Dorsey Levens	1.00	.45
❑	83 Bill Schroeder	1.00	.45
❑	84 E.G. Green	.25	.11
❑	85 Marvin Harrison	1.00	.45
❑	86 Edgerrin James RC	30.00	13.50
❑	87 Peyton Manning	4.00	1.80
❑	88 Mark Brunell	1.50	.70
❑	89 Jay Fiedler RC	10.00	4.50
❑	90 Keenan McCardell	.50	.23
❑	91 Jimmy Smith	.50	.23
❑	92 James Stewart	.50	.23
❑	93 Fred Taylor	2.50	1.10
❑	94 Derrick Alexander WR	.50	.23
❑	95 Mike Cloud RC	6.00	2.70
❑	96 Elvis Grbac	.50	.23
❑	97 Byron Bam Morris	.25	.11
❑	98 Andre Rison	.50	.23
❑	99 Cecil Collins RC	6.00	2.70
❑	100 Damon Huard	2.50	1.10
❑	101 James Johnson RC	6.00	2.70
❑	102 Rob Konrad RC	6.00	2.70
❑	103 Dan Marino	4.00	1.80
❑	104 O.J. McDuffie	.50	.23
❑	105 Cris Carter	1.00	.45
❑	106 Daunte Culpepper RC	30.00	13.50
❑	107 Randall Cunningham	1.00	.45
❑	108 Jeff George	.50	.23
❑	109 Jim Kleinsasser RC	6.00	2.70
❑	110 Randy Moss	4.00	1.80
❑	111 Robert Smith	1.00	.45
❑	112 Terry Allen	.50	.23
❑	113 Michael Bishop RC	8.00	3.60
❑	114 Drew Bledsoe	1.50	.70
❑	115 Kevin Faulk RC	10.00	4.50
❑	116 Terry Glenn	1.00	.45
❑	117 Andy Katzenmoyer RC	6.00	2.70
❑	118 Billy Joe Hobert	.25	.11
❑	119 Eddie Kennison	.50	.23
❑	120 Ricky Williams RC	25.00	11.00
❑	121 Tiki Barber	.50	.23
❑	122 Sean Bennett RC	5.00	2.20
❑	123 Gary Brown	.25	.11
❑	124 Kent Graham	.25	.11
❑	125 Ike Hilliard	.25	.11
❑	126 Joe Montgomery RC	6.00	2.70
❑	127 Amani Toomer	.25	.11
❑	128 Wayne Chrebet	1.00	.45
❑	129 Keyshawn Johnson	1.00	.45
❑	130 Curtis Martin	1.00	.45
❑	131 Ray Lucas RC	5.00	2.20
❑	132 Vinny Testaverde	.50	.23
❑	133 Tim Brown	1.00	.45
❑	134 Tony Bryant RC	5.00	2.20
❑	135 Scott Dreisbach RC	6.00	2.70
❑	136 Rich Gannon	.50	.23
❑	137 Tyrone Wheatley	1.00	.45
❑	138 Charles Woodson	1.00	.45
❑	139 Na Brown RC	6.00	2.70
❑	140 Charles Johnson	.25	.11
❑	141 Cecil Martin RC	5.00	2.20
❑	142 Donovan McNabb RC	25.00	11.00
❑	143 Doug Pederson	.25	.11
❑	144 Duce Staley	1.00	.45
❑	145 Jerome Bettis	1.00	.45
❑	146 Kris Brown RC	5.00	2.20
❑	147 Troy Edwards RC	8.00	3.60
❑	148 Kordell Stewart	1.00	.45
❑	149 Hines Ward	.25	.11
❑	150 Amos Zereoue RC	6.00	2.70
❑	151 Dre' Bly RC	5.00	2.20
❑	152 Isaac Bruce	1.00	.45
❑	153 Marshall Faulk	1.00	.45
❑	154 Joe Germaine RC	6.00	2.70
❑	155 Az-Zahir Hakim	.25	.11
❑	156 Torry Holt RC	15.00	6.75
❑	157 Kurt Warner RC	60.00	27.00
❑	158 Justin Watson RC	5.00	2.20
❑	159 Jermaine Fazande RC	6.00	2.70
❑	160 Jeff Graham	.25	.11
❑	161 Jim Harbaugh	.50	.23
❑	162 Steve Heiden RC	3.00	1.35
❑	163 Erik Kramer	.25	.11
❑	164 Natrone Means	.50	.23
❑	165 Mikhael Ricks	.25	.11
❑	166 Junior Seau	.50	.23
❑	167 Jeff Garcia RC	40.00	18.00
❑	168 Charlie Garner	.50	.23
❑	169 Terry Jackson RC	5.00	2.20
❑	170 Terrell Owens	1.00	.45
❑	171 Jerry Rice	2.50	1.10
❑	172 Steve Young	1.50	.70
❑	173 Karsten Bailey RC	6.00	2.70
❑	174 Joey Galloway	1.00	.45
❑	175 Brock Huard RC	6.00	2.70
❑	176 Jon Kitna	1.00	.45
❑	177 Derrick Mayes	.50	.23
❑	178 Charlie Rogers RC	5.00	2.20
❑	179 Ricky Watters	.50	.23
❑	180 Rabih Abdullah RC	5.00	2.20
❑	181 Mike Alstott	1.00	.45
❑	182 Reidel Anthony	.50	.23
❑	183 Trent Dilfer	.50	.23
❑	184 Warrick Dunn	1.00	.45
❑	185 Martin Gramatica RC	3.00	1.35
❑	186 Shaun King RC	12.00	5.50
❑	187 Darnell McDonald RC	5.00	2.20
❑	188 Yo Murphy RC	5.00	2.20
❑	189 Kevin Daft RC	6.00	2.70
❑	190 Kevin Dyson	.50	.23
❑	191 Eddie George	1.25	.55
❑	192 Jevon Kearse RC	12.00	5.50
❑	193 Steve McNair	1.00	.45
❑	194 Yancey Thigpen	.25	.11
❑	195 Champ Bailey RC	8.00	3.60
❑	196 Albert Connell	.25	.11
❑	197 Stephen Davis	1.00	.45
❑	198 Skip Hicks	.50	.23
❑	199 Brad Johnson	1.00	.45
❑	200 Michael Westbrook	.50	.23

2000 Collector's Edge Masters

		MINT	NRMT
❑	1 David Boston	1.50	.70
❑	2 Michael Pittman	.50	.23
❑	3 Jake Plummer	1.50	.70
❑	4 Frank Sanders	.75	.35
❑	5 Jamal Anderson	1.50	.70
❑	6 Chris Chandler	.75	.35
❑	7 Tim Dwight	1.50	.70
❑	8 Shawn Jefferson	.50	.23
❑	9 Terance Mathis	.75	.35
❑	10 Tony Banks	.75	.35
❑	11 Trent Dilfer	.75	.35
❑	12 Priest Holmes	.75	.35
❑	13 Qadry Ismail	.75	.35
❑	14 Jermaine Lewis	.75	.35
❑	15 Shannon Sharpe	.75	.35
❑	16 Doug Flutie	2.00	.90
❑	17 Rob Johnson	.75	.35

Card	Player	MINT	NRMT
❑ 18	Jeremy McDaniel	.75	.35
❑ 19	Eric Moulds	1.50	.70
❑ 20	Peerless Price	.75	.35
❑ 21	Antowain Smith	.75	.35
❑ 22	Steve Beuerlein	.75	.35
❑ 23	Tim Biakabutuka	.75	.35
❑ 24	Dialleo Burks RC	.75	.35
❑ 25	Dameyune Craig	.50	.23
❑ 26	Donald Hayes	.50	.23
❑ 27	Patrick Jeffers	1.50	.70
❑ 28	Muhsin Muhammad	.75	.35
❑ 29	Reggie White	1.50	.70
❑ 30	Bobby Engram	.75	.35
❑ 31	Curtis Enis	.75	.35
❑ 32	Eddie Kennison	.50	.23
❑ 33	Cade McNown	1.50	.70
❑ 34	Marcus Robinson	1.50	.70
❑ 35	Corey Dillon	1.50	.70
❑ 36	James Hundon	.50	.23
❑ 37	Scott Mitchell	.50	.23
❑ 38	Tony McGee	.50	.23
❑ 39	Akili Smith	1.50	.70
❑ 40	Craig Yeast	.50	.23
❑ 41	Darrin Chiaverini	.50	.23
❑ 42	Tim Couch	3.00	1.35
❑ 43	Kevin Johnson	1.50	.70
❑ 44	Errict Rhett	.75	.35
❑ 45	Troy Aikman	4.00	1.80
❑ 46	Randall Cunningham	1.50	.70
❑ 47	Joey Galloway	1.50	.70
❑ 48	Rocket Ismail	.75	.35
❑ 49	James McKnight	.50	.23
❑ 50	Dat Nguyen	.50	.23
❑ 51	Emmitt Smith	4.00	1.80
❑ 52	Chris Warren	.50	.23
❑ 53	Robert Brooks	.75	.35
❑ 54	Terrell Davis	4.00	1.80
❑ 55	Gus Frerotte	.50	.23
❑ 56	Olandis Gary	1.50	.70
❑ 57	Brian Griese	2.00	.90
❑ 58	Ed McCaffrey	1.50	.70
❑ 59	Rod Smith	.75	.35
❑ 60	Charlie Batch	1.50	.70
❑ 61	Germane Crowell	.75	.35
❑ 62	Sedrick Irvin	.50	.23
❑ 63	Herman Moore	.75	.35
❑ 64	Johnnie Morton	.75	.35
❑ 65	James Stewart	.75	.35
❑ 66	Corey Bradford	.75	.35
❑ 67	Brett Favre	6.00	2.70
❑ 68	Antonio Freeman	1.50	.70
❑ 69	Matt Hasselbeck	.50	.23
❑ 70	Dorsey Levens	.75	.35
❑ 71	Bill Schroeder	.75	.35
❑ 72	Ken Dilger	.50	.23
❑ 73	E.G. Green	.50	.23
❑ 74	Marvin Harrison	1.50	.70
❑ 75	Edgerrin James	6.00	2.70
❑ 76	Peyton Manning	5.00	2.20
❑ 77	Jerome Pathon	.75	.35
❑ 78	Terrence Wilkins	1.50	.70
❑ 79	Kyle Brady	.50	.23
❑ 80	Mark Brunell	2.50	1.10
❑ 81	Kevin Hardy	.50	.23
❑ 82	Stacey Mack	.50	.23
❑ 83	Keenan McCardell	.75	.35
❑ 84	Jimmy Smith	.75	.35
❑ 85	Fred Taylor	2.00	.90
❑ 86	Derrick Alexander	.75	.35
❑ 87	Mike Cloud	.50	.23
❑ 88	Tony Gonzalez	.75	.35
❑ 89	Elvis Grbac	.75	.35
❑ 90	Kevin Lockett	.50	.23
❑ 91	Tony Richardson RC	.50	.23
❑ 92	Jay Fiedler	1.50	.70
❑ 93	Oronde Gadsden	.75	.35
❑ 94	Damon Huard	.75	.35
❑ 95	Rob Konrad	.50	.23
❑ 96	James Johnson	.75	.35
❑ 97	Tony Martin	.75	.35
❑ 98	O.J. McDuffie	.75	.35
❑ 99	Lamar Smith	.75	.35
❑ 100	Thurman Thomas	.75	.35
❑ 101	Todd Bouman	.50	.23
❑ 102	Bubby Brister	.50	.23
❑ 103	Cris Carter	1.50	.70
❑ 104	Daunte Culpepper	3.00	1.35
❑ 105	Matthew Hatchette	.50	.23
❑ 106	Randy Moss	5.00	2.20
❑ 107	Robert Smith	1.50	.70
❑ 108	Moe Williams	.50	.23
❑ 109	Michael Bishop	.75	.35
❑ 110	Drew Bledsoe	2.50	1.10
❑ 111	Troy Brown	.50	.23
❑ 112	Kevin Faulk	.75	.35
❑ 113	Terry Glenn	.75	.35
❑ 114	Andy Katzenmoyer	.50	.23
❑ 115	Tony Simmons	.50	.23
❑ 116	Jeff Blake	.75	.35
❑ 117	Aaron Brooks	1.50	.70
❑ 118	Jake Delhomme RC	1.50	.70
❑ 119	Joe Horn	.75	.35
❑ 120	Jake Reed	.75	.35
❑ 121	Ricky Williams	4.00	1.80
❑ 122	Tiki Barber	.75	.35
❑ 123	Kerry Collins	.75	.35
❑ 124	Ike Hilliard	.75	.35
❑ 125	Amani Toomer	.75	.35
❑ 126	Wayne Chrebet	.75	.35
❑ 127	Ray Lucas	.75	.35
❑ 128	Curtis Martin	1.50	.70
❑ 129	Vinny Testaverde	.75	.35
❑ 130	Dedric Ward	.50	.23
❑ 131	Tim Brown	1.50	.70
❑ 132	Rickey Dudley	.50	.23
❑ 133	Rich Gannon	.75	.35
❑ 134	James Jett	.50	.23
❑ 135	Napoleon Kaufman	.75	.35
❑ 136	Tyrone Wheatley	.75	.35
❑ 137	Charles Woodson	.75	.35
❑ 138	Charles Johnson	.75	.35
❑ 139	Donovan McNabb	2.50	1.10
❑ 140	Torrance Small	.50	.23
❑ 141	Duce Staley	1.50	.70
❑ 142	Jerome Bettis	1.50	.70
❑ 143	Troy Edwards	.75	.35
❑ 144	Kent Graham	.50	.23
❑ 145	Richard Huntley	.50	.23
❑ 146	Kordell Stewart	1.50	.70
❑ 147	Amos Zereoue	.50	.23
❑ 148	Isaac Bruce	1.50	.70
❑ 149	Kevin Carter	.50	.23
❑ 150	Marshall Faulk	2.00	.90
❑ 151	Trent Green	.75	.35
❑ 152	Az-Zahir Hakim	.50	.23
❑ 153	Robert Holcombe	.50	.23
❑ 154	Torry Holt	1.50	.70
❑ 155	Kurt Warner	6.00	2.70
❑ 156	Kenny Bynum	.50	.23
❑ 157	Robert Chancey	.50	.23
❑ 158	Curtis Conway	.75	.35
❑ 159	Jermaine Fazande	.50	.23
❑ 160	Jeff Graham	.50	.23
❑ 161	Jim Harbaugh	.75	.35
❑ 162	Ryan Leaf	1.50	.70
❑ 163	Junior Seau	.75	.35
❑ 164	Jeff Garcia	1.50	.70
❑ 165	Charlie Garner	.75	.35
❑ 166	Terrell Owens	1.50	.70
❑ 167	Jerry Rice	4.00	1.80
❑ 168	J.J. Stokes	.75	.35
❑ 169	Karsten Bailey	.50	.23
❑ 170	Sean Dawkins	.50	.23
❑ 171	Brock Huard	.75	.35
❑ 172	Jon Kitna	1.50	.70
❑ 173	Derrick Mayes	.75	.35
❑ 174	Ricky Watters	.50	.23
❑ 175	Rabih Abdullah	.50	.23
❑ 176	Mike Alstott	1.50	.70
❑ 177	Reidel Anthony	.50	.23
❑ 178	Warrick Dunn	1.50	.70
❑ 179	Jacquez Green	.75	.35
❑ 180	Keyshawn Johnson	1.50	.70
❑ 181	Shaun King	2.50	1.10
❑ 182	Warren Sapp	.75	.35
❑ 183	Kevin Dyson	.75	.35
❑ 184	Eddie George	2.00	.90
❑ 185	Jevon Kearse	1.50	.70
❑ 186	Steve McNair	1.50	.70
❑ 187	Neil O'Donnell	.50	.23
❑ 188	Carl Pickens	.75	.35
❑ 189	Yancey Thigpen	.50	.23
❑ 190	Frank Wycheck	.50	.23
❑ 191	Champ Bailey	.75	.35
❑ 192	Larry Centers	.50	.23
❑ 193	Albert Connell	.50	.23
❑ 194	Stephen Davis	1.50	.70
❑ 195	Jeff George	.75	.35
❑ 196	Brad Johnson	1.50	.70
❑ 197	Deion Sanders	1.50	.70
❑ 198	Bruce Smith	.75	.35
❑ 199	James Thrash	.50	.23
❑ 200	Michael Westbrook	.75	.35
❑ 201	Thomas Jones RC	10.00	4.50
❑ 202	Jamal Lewis RC	30.00	13.50
❑ 203	Chris Redman RC	12.00	5.50
❑ 204	Travis Taylor RC	8.00	3.60
❑ 205	Avion Black RC	5.00	2.20
❑ 206	Kwame Cavil RC	5.00	2.20
❑ 207	Sammy Morris RC	8.00	3.60
❑ 208	Brian Urlacher RC	20.00	9.00
❑ 209	Dez White RC	5.00	2.20
❑ 210	Ron Dugans RC	5.00	2.20
❑ 211	Danny Farmer RC	6.00	2.70
❑ 212	Curtis Keaton RC	5.00	2.20
❑ 213	Peter Warrick RC	20.00	9.00
❑ 214	Courtney Brown RC	8.00	3.60
❑ 215	JaJuan Dawson RC	6.00	2.70
❑ 216	Dennis Northcutt RC	8.00	3.60
❑ 217	Travis Prentice RC	10.00	4.50
❑ 218	Spergon Wynn RC	6.00	2.70
❑ 219	Michael Wiley RC	6.00	2.70
❑ 220	Mike Anderson RC	30.00	13.50
❑ 221	Chris Cole RC	5.00	2.20
❑ 222	Deltha O'Neal RC	5.00	2.20
❑ 223	Reuben Droughns RC	6.00	2.70
❑ 224	Bubba Franks RC	8.00	3.60
❑ 225	Charles Lee RC	3.00	1.35
❑ 226	Rob Morris RC	5.00	2.20
❑ 227	R.Jay Soward RC	6.00	2.70
❑ 228	Shyrone Stith RC	5.00	2.20
❑ 229	Frank Moreau RC	6.00	2.70
❑ 230	Sylvester Morris RC	12.00	5.50
❑ 231	J.R. Redmond RC	8.00	3.60
❑ 232	Chad Morton RC	6.00	2.70
❑ 233	Ron Dayne RC	20.00	9.00
❑ 234	Ron Dixon RC	8.00	3.60
❑ 235	Anthony Becht RC	6.00	2.70
❑ 236	Laveranues Coles RC	10.00	4.50
❑ 237	Chad Pennington RC	20.00	9.00
❑ 238	Sebastian Janikowski RC	6.00	2.70
❑ 239	Jerry Porter RC	6.00	2.70
❑ 240	Todd Pinkston RC	6.00	2.70
❑ 241	Gari Scott RC	5.00	2.20
❑ 242	Corey Simon RC	8.00	3.60
❑ 243	Plaxico Burress RC	12.00	5.50
❑ 244	Tee Martin RC	10.00	4.50
❑ 245	Trung Canidate RC	6.00	2.70
❑ 246	Trevor Gaylor RC	5.00	2.20
❑ 247	Giovanni Carmazzi RC	8.00	3.60
❑ 248	Tim Rattay RC	10.00	4.50
❑ 249	Shaun Alexander RC	15.00	6.75
❑ 250	Joe Hamilton RC	8.00	3.60

1998 Collector's Edge Odyssey

	MINT	NRMT
COMPLETE SET (250)	400.00	180.00
COMMON CARD (1-150)	.10	.05

Card		
COMMON CARD (151-200)	.60	.25
COMMON CARD (201-230)	.75	.35
COMMON CARD (231-250)	2.50	1.10
❑ 1 Terance Mathis	.20	.09
❑ 2 Tony Martin	.20	.09
❑ 3 Chris Chandler	.20	.09
❑ 4 Jamal Anderson	.40	.18
❑ 5 Jake Plummer	.75	.35
❑ 6 Adrian Murrell	.20	.09
❑ 7 Rob Moore	.20	.09
❑ 8 Frank Sanders	.20	.09
❑ 9 Larry Centers	.10	.05
❑ 10 Andre Wadsworth RC	2.00	.90
❑ 11 Jim Harbaugh	.20	.09
❑ 12 Errict Rhett	.20	.09
❑ 13 Jermaine Lewis	.20	.09
❑ 14 Michael Jackson	.10	.05
❑ 15 Eric Zeier	.20	.09
❑ 16 Rob Johnson	.20	.09
❑ 17 Antowain Smith	.40	.18
❑ 18 Andre Reed	.20	.09
❑ 19 Bruce Smith	.20	.09
❑ 20 Doug Flutie	.40	.18
❑ 21 Thurman Thomas	.40	.18
❑ 22 Kerry Collins	.20	.09
❑ 23 Fred Lane	.20	.09
❑ 24 Muhsin Muhammad	.20	.09
❑ 25 Rae Carruth	.20	.09
❑ 26 Rocket Ismail	.10	.05
❑ 27 Kevin Greene	.20	.09
❑ 28 Curtis Enis RC	2.00	.90
❑ 29 Curtis Conway	.20	.09
❑ 30 Erik Kramer	.10	.05
❑ 31 Edgar Bennett	.10	.05
❑ 32 Neil O'Donnell	.20	.09
❑ 33 Jeff Blake	.20	.09
❑ 34 Carl Pickens	.40	.18
❑ 35 Corey Dillon	.50	.23
❑ 36 Troy Aikman	1.00	.45
❑ 37 Jason Garrett RC	.10	.05
❑ 38 Emmitt Smith	1.50	.70
❑ 39 Deion Sanders	.40	.18
❑ 40 Michael Irvin	.40	.18
❑ 41 Chris Warren	.20	.09
❑ 42 John Elway	2.00	.90
❑ 43 Terrell Davis	1.50	.70
❑ 44 Shannon Sharpe	.20	.09
❑ 45 Rod Smith WR	.20	.09
❑ 46 Marcus Nash RC	2.00	.90
❑ 47 Brian Griese RC	5.00	2.20
❑ 48 Barry Sanders	2.00	.90
❑ 49 Herman Moore	.40	.18
❑ 50 Scott Mitchell	.20	.09
❑ 51 Johnnie Morton	.20	.09
❑ 52 Rashaan Shehee RC	2.00	.90
❑ 53 Charlie Batch RC	4.00	1.80
❑ 54 Brett Favre	2.00	.90
❑ 55 Dorsey Levens	.40	.18
❑ 56 Antonio Freeman	.40	.18
❑ 57 Reggie White	.40	.18
❑ 58 Robert Brooks	.20	.09
❑ 59 Raymont Harris	.10	.05
❑ 60 Peyton Manning RC	12.00	5.50
❑ 61 Marshall Faulk	.40	.18
❑ 62 Jerome Pathon RC	2.00	.90
❑ 63 Marvin Harrison	.20	.09
❑ 64 Mark Brunell	.75	.35
❑ 65 Fred Taylor RC	4.00	1.80
❑ 66 Jimmy Smith	.20	.09
❑ 67 James Stewart	.20	.09
❑ 68 Keenan McCardell	.20	.09
❑ 69 Andre Rison	.20	.09
❑ 70 Elvis Grbac	.20	.09
❑ 71 Donnell Bennett	.10	.05
❑ 72 Rich Gannon	.20	.09
❑ 73 Derrick Thomas	.20	.09
❑ 74 Dan Marino	2.00	.90
❑ 75 Karim Abdul-Jabbar UER	.40	.18
no first name on cardfront		
❑ 76 John Avery RC	2.00	.90
UER photo Karim Abdul-Jabbar		
❑ 77 O.J. McDuffie	.20	.09
❑ 78 Oronde Gadsden RC	2.00	.90
❑ 79 Zach Thomas	.20	.09
❑ 80 Randy Moss RC	12.00	5.50
❑ 81 Cris Carter	.40	.18
❑ 82 Jake Reed	.20	.09
❑ 83 Robert Smith	.40	.18
❑ 84 Brad Johnson	.40	.18
❑ 85 Drew Bledsoe	.75	.35
❑ 86 Robert Edwards RC	2.50	1.10
❑ 87 Terry Glenn	.40	.18
❑ 88 Troy Brown	.10	.05
❑ 89 Shawn Jefferson	.10	.05
❑ 90 Danny Wuerffel	.20	.09
❑ 91 Dana Stubblefield	.10	.05
❑ 92 Derrick Alexander	.20	.09
❑ 93 Ray Zellars	.10	.05
❑ 94 Andre Hastings	.10	.05
❑ 95 Danny Kanell	.20	.09
❑ 96 Tiki Barber	.20	.09
❑ 97 Ike Hilliard	.20	.09
❑ 98 Charles Way	.10	.05
❑ 99 Chris Calloway	.10	.05
❑ 100 Curtis Martin	.40	.18
❑ 101 Glenn Foley	.20	.09
❑ 102 Vinny Testaverde	.20	.09
❑ 103 Keyshawn Johnson	.40	.18
❑ 104 Wayne Chrebet	.40	.18
❑ 105 Leon Johnson	.10	.05
❑ 106 Jeff George	.20	.09
❑ 107 Charles Woodson RC	2.50	1.10
❑ 108 Tim Brown	.40	.18
❑ 109 James Jett	.20	.09
❑ 110 Napoleon Kaufman	.40	.18
❑ 111 Charlie Garner	.10	.05
❑ 112 Bobby Hoying	.20	.09
❑ 113 Duce Staley	1.00	.45
❑ 114 Irving Fryar	.20	.09
❑ 115 Kordell Stewart	.40	.18
❑ 116 Jerome Bettis	.40	.18
❑ 117 Charles Johnson	.10	.05
❑ 118 Randall Cunningham	.40	.18
❑ 119 Courtney Hawkins	.10	.05
❑ 120 Tony Banks	.20	.09
❑ 121 Isaac Bruce	.40	.18
❑ 122 Robert Holcombe RC	2.00	.90
❑ 123 Eddie Kennison	.20	.09
❑ 124 Ryan Leaf RC	3.00	1.35
❑ 125 Mikhael Ricks RC	2.00	.90
❑ 126 Natrone Means	.40	.18
❑ 127 Junior Seau	.20	.09
❑ 128 Jerry Rice	1.00	.45
❑ 129 Terrell Owens	.40	.18
❑ 130 Garrison Hearst	.40	.18
❑ 131 Steve Young	.50	.23
❑ 132 J.J. Stokes	.20	.09
❑ 133 Warren Moon	.40	.18
❑ 134 Joey Galloway	.40	.18
❑ 135 Ricky Watters	.20	.09
❑ 136 Ahman Green RC	3.00	1.35
❑ 137 Trent Dilfer	.40	.18
❑ 138 Mike Alstott	.40	.18
❑ 139 Warrick Dunn	.40	.18
❑ 140 Reidel Anthony	.20	.09
❑ 141 Jacquez Green RC	2.50	1.10
❑ 142 Steve McNair	.40	.18
❑ 143 Eddie George	.75	.35
❑ 144 Yancey Thigpen	.10	.05
❑ 145 Kevin Dyson RC	2.50	1.10
❑ 146 Trent Green	.60	.25
❑ 147 Gus Frerotte	.10	.05
❑ 148 Terry Allen	.40	.18
❑ 149 Michael Westbrook	.20	.09
❑ 150 Jim Druckenmiller	.20	.09
❑ 151 Jake Plummer 2Q	1.25	.55
❑ 152 Adrian Murrell 2Q	.60	.25
❑ 153 Rob Johnson 2Q	.60	.25
❑ 154 Antowain Smith 2Q	.60	.25
❑ 155 Kerry Collins 2Q	.60	.25
❑ 156 Curtis Enis 2Q	3.00	1.35
❑ 157 Carl Pickens 2Q	.60	.25
❑ 158 Corey Dillon 2Q	.75	.35
❑ 159 Troy Aikman 2Q	1.50	.70
❑ 160 Emmitt Smith 2Q	2.00	.90
❑ 161 Deion Sanders 2Q	.60	.25
❑ 162 Michael Irvin 2Q	.60	.25
❑ 163 John Elway 2Q	3.00	1.35
❑ 164 Terrell Davis 2Q	2.00	.90
❑ 165 Shannon Sharpe 2Q	.60	.25
❑ 166 Rod Smith 2Q	.60	.25
❑ 167 Barry Sanders 2Q	3.00	1.35
❑ 168 Herman Moore 2Q	.60	.25
❑ 169 Brett Favre 2Q	3.00	1.35
❑ 170 Dorsey Levens 2Q	.60	.25
❑ 171 Antonio Freeman 2Q	.60	.25
❑ 172 Peyton Manning 2Q	15.00	6.75
❑ 173 Marshall Faulk 2Q	.60	.25
❑ 174 Mark Brunell 2Q	1.00	.45
❑ 175 Fred Taylor 2Q	5.00	2.20
❑ 176 Dan Marino 2Q	3.00	1.35
❑ 177 Randy Moss 2Q	15.00	6.75
❑ 178 Cris Carter 2Q	.60	.25
❑ 179 Drew Bledsoe 2Q	1.00	.45
❑ 180 Robert Edwards 2Q	2.00	.90
❑ 181 Curtis Martin 2Q	.60	.25
❑ 182 Napoleon Kaufman 2Q	.60	.25
❑ 183 Kordell Stewart 2Q	.60	.25
❑ 184 Jerome Bettis 2Q	.60	.25
❑ 185 Tony Banks 2Q	.60	.25
❑ 186 Isaac Bruce 2Q	.60	.25
❑ 187 Ryan Leaf 2Q	5.00	2.20
❑ 188 Natrone Means 2Q	.60	.25
❑ 189 Jerry Rice 2Q	1.50	.70
❑ 190 Terrell Owens 2Q	.60	.25
❑ 191 Garrison Hearst 2Q	.60	.25
❑ 192 Steve Young 2Q	.75	.35
❑ 193 Warren Moon 2Q	.60	.25
❑ 194 Joey Galloway 2Q	.60	.25
❑ 195 Trent Dilfer 2Q	.60	.25
❑ 196 Mike Alstott 2Q	.60	.25
❑ 197 Warrick Dunn 2Q	.60	.25
❑ 198 Steve McNair 2Q	.60	.25
❑ 199 Eddie George 2Q	1.00	.45
❑ 200 Terry Allen 2Q	.60	.25
❑ 201 Jake Plummer 3Q	1.50	.70
❑ 202 Curtis Enis 3Q	4.00	1.80
❑ 203 Carl Pickens 3Q	.75	.35
❑ 204 Corey Dillon 3Q	1.00	.45
❑ 205 Troy Aikman 3Q	2.00	.90
❑ 206 Emmitt Smith 3Q	3.00	1.35
❑ 207 John Elway 3Q	4.00	1.80
❑ 208 Terrell Davis 3Q	3.00	1.35
❑ 209 Barry Sanders 3Q	4.00	1.80
❑ 210 Brett Favre 3Q	4.00	1.80
❑ 211 Antonio Freeman 3Q	.75	.35
❑ 212 Peyton Manning 3Q	20.00	9.00
❑ 213 Mark Brunell 3Q	1.50	.70
❑ 214 Fred Taylor 3Q	6.00	2.70
❑ 215 Dan Marino 3Q	4.00	1.80
❑ 216 Randy Moss 3Q	20.00	9.00
❑ 217 Drew Bledsoe 3Q	1.50	.70
❑ 218 Robert Edwards 3Q	2.50	1.10
❑ 219 Curtis Martin 3Q	.75	.35
❑ 220 Kordell Stewart 3Q	.75	.35
❑ 221 Jerome Bettis 3Q	.75	.35
❑ 222 Tony Banks 3Q	.75	.35
❑ 223 Ryan Leaf 3Q	6.00	2.70
❑ 224 Jerry Rice 3Q	2.00	.90
❑ 225 Steve Young 3Q	1.00	.45
❑ 226 Warren Moon 3Q	.75	.35
❑ 227 Trent Dilfer 3Q	.75	.35
❑ 228 Warrick Dunn 3Q	.75	.35
❑ 229 Steve McNair 3Q	.75	.35
❑ 230 Eddie George 3Q	1.50	.70
❑ 231 Curtis Enis 4Q	6.00	2.70
❑ 232 Carl Pickens 4Q	2.50	1.10
❑ 233 Troy Aikman 4Q	6.00	2.70
❑ 234 Emmitt Smith 4Q	10.00	4.50
❑ 235 John Elway 4Q	12.00	5.50
❑ 236 Terrell Davis 4Q	10.00	4.50
❑ 237 Barry Sanders 4Q	12.00	5.50
❑ 238 Brett Favre 4Q	12.00	5.50
❑ 239 Peyton Manning 4Q	30.00	13.50
❑ 240 Fred Taylor 4Q	10.00	4.50
❑ 241 Dan Marino 4Q	12.00	5.50
❑ 242 Randy Moss 4Q	30.00	13.50
❑ 243 Drew Bledsoe 4Q	5.00	2.20
❑ 244 Kordell Stewart 4Q	2.50	1.10
❑ 245 Jerome Bettis 4Q	2.50	1.10
❑ 246 Ryan Leaf 4Q	10.00	4.50
❑ 247 Jerry Rice 4Q	6.00	2.70
❑ 248 Steve Young 4Q	4.00	1.80
❑ 249 Warren Moon 4Q	2.50	1.10
❑ 250 Eddie George 4Q	5.00	2.20

1999 Collector's Edge Odyssey

	MINT	NRMT
COMPLETE SET (193)	150.00	70.00
COMP.SET w/o SP's (148)	40.00	18.00
COMMON CARD (1-149)	.15	.07
COMMON CARD (151-170)	1.00	.45
COMMON CARD (171-185)	3.00	1.35
COMMON CARD (186-195)	5.00	2.20

Card	MINT	NRMT
☐ 1 Checklist Card	.15	.07
☐ 2 Checklist Card	.15	.07
☐ 3 David Boston RC	2.00	.90
☐ 4 Rob Moore	.30	.14
☐ 5 Adrian Murrell	.30	.14
☐ 6 Jake Plummer	1.00	.45
☐ 7 Frank Sanders	.30	.14
☐ 8 Jamal Anderson	.60	.25
☐ 9 Chris Calloway	.15	.07
☐ 10 Chris Chandler	.30	.14
☐ 11 Tim Dwight	.60	.25
☐ 12 Terance Mathis	.30	.14
☐ 13 Tony Banks	.30	.14
☐ 14 Priest Holmes	.60	.25
☐ 15 Jermaine Lewis	.30	.14
☐ 16 Chris McAlister RC	1.00	.45
☐ 17 Scott Mitchell	.30	.14
☐ 18 Doug Flutie	.75	.35
☐ 19 Eric Moulds	.60	.25
☐ 20 Peerless Price RC	1.25	.55
☐ 21 Andre Reed SP Pulled from packout, embossed player profile on cardfront)	200.00	90.00
☐ 22 Antowain Smith	.60	.25
☐ 23 Antoine Winfield RC	.75	.35
☐ 24 Steve Beuerlein	.30	.14
☐ 25 Tim Biakabutuka	.30	.14
☐ 26 Rae Carruth	.15	.07
☐ 27 Muhsin Muhammad	.30	.14
☐ 28 D'Wayne Bates RC	.75	.35
☐ 29 Bobby Engram	.30	.14
☐ 30 Curtis Enis	.60	.25
☐ 31 Shane Matthews	.60	.25
☐ 32 Cade McNown RC	1.25	.55
☐ 33 Jeff Blake	.30	.14
☐ 34 Corey Dillon	.60	.25
☐ 35 Carl Pickens	.30	.14
☐ 36 Darnay Scott	.30	.14
☐ 37 Akili Smith RC	2.00	.90
☐ 38 Tim Couch RC	4.00	1.80
☐ 39 Kevin Johnson RC	2.00	.90
☐ 40 Terry Kirby	.30	.14
☐ 41 Leslie Shepherd	.15	.07
☐ 42 Troy Aikman	1.50	.70
☐ 43 Michael Irvin	.30	.14
☐ 44 Rocket Ismail	.30	.14
☐ 45 Deion Sanders	.60	.25
☐ 46 Emmitt Smith	1.50	.70
☐ 47 Bubby Brister	.30	.14
☐ 48 Terrell Davis	1.50	.70
☐ 49 Brian Griese	1.25	.55
☐ 50 Ed McCaffrey	.30	.14
☐ 51 Shannon Sharpe	.30	.14
☐ 52 Rod Smith	.30	.14
☐ 53 Charlie Batch	1.25	.55
☐ 54 Chris Claiborne RC	1.00	.45
☐ 56 Herman Moore	.60	.25
☐ 57 Johnnie Morton	.30	.14
☐ 58 Ron Rivers	.15	.07
☐ 59 Brett Favre	2.50	1.10
☐ 60 Mark Chmura	.30	.14
☐ 61 Antonio Freeman	.60	.25
☐ 62 Dorsey Levens	.60	.25
☐ 63 E.G. Green	.15	.07
☐ 64 Marvin Harrison	.60	.25
☐ 65 Edgerrin James RC	6.00	2.70
☐ 66 Peyton Manning	2.50	1.10
☐ 67 Mark Brunell	1.00	.45
☐ 68 Keenan McCardell	.30	.14
☐ 69 Jimmy Smith	.30	.14
☐ 70 Fred Taylor	1.50	.70
☐ 71 Derrick Alexander WR	.30	.14
☐ 72 Kimble Anders	.30	.14
☐ 73 Mike Cloud RC	1.00	.45
☐ 74 Elvis Grbac	.30	.14
☐ 75 Andre Rison	.30	.14
☐ 76 Karim Abdul-Jabbar	.30	.14
☐ 77 Cecil Collins RC	.75	.35
☐ 78 James Johnson RC	1.00	.45
☐ 79 Rob Konrad RC	1.00	.45
☐ 80 Dan Marino	2.50	1.10
☐ 81 O.J. McDuffie	.30	.14
☐ 82 Cris Carter	.60	.25
☐ 83 Daunte Culpepper RC	6.00	2.70
☐ 84 Randall Cunningham	.60	.25
☐ 85 Randy Moss	2.50	1.10
☐ 86 Jake Reed	.30	.14
☐ 87 Robert Smith	.60	.25
☐ 88 Terry Allen	.30	.14
☐ 89 Drew Bledsoe	1.00	.45
☐ 90 Ben Coates	.15	.07
☐ 91 Kevin Faulk RC	1.50	.70
☐ 92 Terry Glenn	.60	.25
☐ 93 Andy Katzenmoyer RC	1.00	.45
☐ 94 Cameron Cleeland	.15	.07
☐ 95 Billy Joe Hobert	.15	.07
☐ 96 Eddie Kennison	.30	.14
☐ 97 Ricky Williams RC	4.00	1.80
☐ 98 Sean Bennett RC	1.00	.45
☐ 99 Gary Brown	.15	.07
☐ 100 Kerry Collins	.30	.14
☐ 101 Kent Graham	.15	.07
☐ 102 Ike Hilliard	.30	.14
☐ 103 Wayne Chrebet	.60	.25
☐ 104 Keyshawn Johnson	.60	.25
☐ 105 Curtis Martin	.60	.25
☐ 106 Rick Mirer	.30	.14
☐ 107 Tim Brown	.60	.25
☐ 108 Rich Gannon	.30	.14
☐ 109 Napoleon Kaufman	.60	.25
☐ 110 Charles Woodson	.60	.25
☐ 111 Charles Johnson	.15	.07
☐ 112 Donovan McNabb RC	4.00	1.80
☐ 113 Doug Pederson	.30	.14
☐ 114 Duce Staley	.60	.25
☐ 115 Jerome Bettis	.60	.25
☐ 116 Troy Edwards RC	1.25	.55
☐ 117 Kordell Stewart	.60	.25
☐ 118 Amos Zereoue RC	1.00	.45
☐ 119 Isaac Bruce	.60	.25
☐ 120 Marshall Faulk	.60	.25
☐ 121 Joe Germaine RC	1.00	.45
☐ 122 Torry Holt RC	2.50	1.10
☐ 123 Kurt Warner RC	15.00	6.75
☐ 124 Jim Harbaugh	.30	.14
☐ 125 Erik Kramer	.15	.07
☐ 126 Natrone Means	.30	.14
☐ 127 Junior Seau	.30	.14
☐ 128 Terrell Owens	.60	.25
☐ 129 Lawrence Phillips	.30	.14
☐ 130 Jerry Rice	1.50	.70
☐ 131 J.J. Stokes	.30	.14
☐ 132 Steve Young	1.00	.45
☐ 133 Karsten Bailey RC	1.00	.45
☐ 134 Joey Galloway	.60	.25
☐ 135 Brock Huard RC	1.50	.70
☐ 136 Jon Kitna	.60	.25
☐ 137 Ricky Watters	.30	.14
☐ 138 Reidel Anthony	.15	.07
☐ 139 Trent Dilfer	.30	.14
☐ 140 Warrick Dunn	.60	.25
☐ 141 Shaun King RC	2.00	.90
☐ 142 Jevon Kearse RC	2.00	.90
☐ 143 Kevin Dyson	.30	.14
☐ 144 Eddie George	.75	.35
☐ 145 Steve McNair	.60	.25
☐ 146 Champ Bailey RC	1.25	.55
☐ 147 Stephen Davis	.60	.25
☐ 148 Skip Hicks	.30	.14
☐ 149 Brad Johnson	.60	.25
☐ 150 Michael Westbrook	.30	.14
☐ 151 Chris McAlister 2Q	1.00	.45
☐ 152 Peerless Price 2Q	1.50	.70
☐ 153 Antoine Winfield 2Q	1.00	.45
☐ 154 D'Wayne Bates 2Q	1.00	.45
☐ 155 Kevin Johnson 2Q	2.50	1.10
☐ 156 Chris Claiborne 2Q	1.00	.45
☐ 157 Sedrick Irvin 2Q	.15	.07
☐ 158 Mike Cloud 2Q	1.25	.55
☐ 159 Cecil Collins 2Q	.15	.07
☐ 160 James Johnson 2Q	1.25	.55
☐ 161 Rob Konrad 2Q	1.25	.55
☐ 162 Daunte Culpepper 2Q	5.00	2.20
☐ 163 Andy Katzenmoyer 2Q	1.25	.55
☐ 164 Amos Zereoue 2Q	1.25	.55
☐ 165 Joe Germaine 2Q	1.25	.55
☐ 166 Karsten Bailey 2Q	1.25	.55
☐ 167 Brock Huard 2Q	2.00	.90
☐ 168 Shaun King 2Q	2.50	1.10
☐ 169 Jevon Kearse 2Q	2.50	1.10
☐ 170 Champ Bailey 2Q	1.50	.70
☐ 171 Jake Plummer 3Q	3.00	1.35
☐ 172 Doug Flutie 3Q	3.00	1.35
☐ 173 Troy Aikman 3Q	5.00	2.20
☐ 174 Emmitt Smith 3Q	5.00	2.20
☐ 175 Terrell Davis 3Q	5.00	2.20
☐ 176 Barry Sanders 3Q	8.00	3.60
☐ 177 Brett Favre 3Q	8.00	3.60
☐ 178 Peyton Manning 3Q	8.00	3.60
☐ 179 Mark Brunell 3Q	3.00	1.35
☐ 180 Fred Taylor 3Q	5.00	2.20
☐ 181 Dan Marino 3Q	8.00	3.60
☐ 182 Randy Moss 3Q	8.00	3.60
☐ 183 Drew Bledsoe 3Q	3.00	1.35
☐ 184 Jerry Rice 3Q	5.00	2.20
☐ 185 Steve Young 3Q	3.00	1.35
☐ 186 David Boston 4Q	8.00	3.60
☐ 187 Cade McNown 4Q	6.00	2.70
☐ 188 Akili Smith 4Q	8.00	3.60
☐ 189 Tim Couch 4Q	15.00	6.75
☐ 190 Edgerrin James 4Q	25.00	11.00
☐ 191 Kevin Faulk 4Q	5.00	2.20
☐ 192 Ricky Williams 4Q	15.00	6.75
☐ 193 Donovan McNabb 4Q	15.00	6.75
☐ 194 Troy Edwards 4Q	5.00	2.20
☐ 195 Torry Holt 4Q	10.00	4.50

2000 Collector's Edge Odyssey

	MINT	NRMT
COMPLETE SET (190)	400.00	180.00

Card	MINT	NRMT
☐ 1 David Boston	.60	.25
☐ 2 Jake Plummer	.60	.25
☐ 3 Frank Sanders	.30	.14
☐ 4 Jamal Anderson	.60	.25
☐ 5 Chris Chandler	.30	.14
☐ 6 Terance Mathis	.30	.14
☐ 7 Tony Banks	.30	.14
☐ 8 Qadry Ismail	.30	.14

❑ 9 Doug Flutie .75 .35
❑ 10 Rob Johnson .30 .14
❑ 11 Eric Moulds .60 .25
❑ 12 Peerless Price .60 .25
❑ 13 Antowain Smith .30 .14
❑ 14 Steve Beuerlein .15 .07
❑ 15 Tim Biakabutuka .30 .14
❑ 16 Muhsin Muhammad .30 .14
❑ 17 Curtis Enis .30 .14
❑ 18 Cade McNown .60 .25
❑ 19 Marcus Robinson .60 .25
❑ 20 Corey Dillon .60 .25
❑ 21 Akili Smith .60 .25
❑ 22 Tim Couch 1.25 .55
❑ 23 Kevin Johnson .60 .25
❑ 24 Errict Rhett .30 .14
❑ 25 Troy Aikman 1.50 .70
❑ 26 Joey Galloway .60 .25
❑ 27 Rocket Ismail .30 .14
❑ 28 Emmitt Smith 1.50 .70
❑ 29 Terrell Davis 1.50 .70
❑ 30 Olandis Gary .60 .25
❑ 31 Brian Griese .75 .35
❑ 32 Ed McCaffrey .60 .25
❑ 33 Charlie Batch .60 .25
❑ 34 Germane Crowell .30 .14
❑ 35 Herman Moore .30 .14
❑ 36 James Stewart .30 .14
❑ 37 Brett Favre 2.50 1.10
❑ 38 Antonio Freeman .60 .25
❑ 39 Dorsey Levens .30 .14
❑ 40 Marvin Harrison .60 .25
❑ 41 Edgerrin James 2.50 1.10
❑ 42 Peyton Manning 2.00 .90
❑ 43 Terrence Wilkins .60 .25
❑ 44 Mark Brunell 1.00 .45
❑ 45 Keenan McCardell .30 .14
❑ 46 Jimmy Smith .30 .14
❑ 47 Fred Taylor .75 .35
❑ 48 Mike Cloud .15 .07
❑ 49 Tony Gonzalez .30 .14
❑ 50 Elvis Grbac .30 .14
❑ 51 Damon Huard .60 .25
❑ 52 James Johnson .30 .14
❑ 53 Tony Martin .30 .14
❑ 54 Cris Carter .60 .25
❑ 55 Daunte Culpepper 1.25 .55
❑ 56 Randy Moss 2.00 .90
❑ 57 Robert Smith .60 .25
❑ 58 Drew Bledsoe 1.00 .45
❑ 59 Terry Glenn .30 .14
❑ 60 Jeff Blake .30 .14
❑ 61 Ricky Williams 1.25 .55
❑ 62 Kerry Collins .30 .14
❑ 63 Ike Hilliard .30 .14
❑ 64 Amani Toomer .30 .14
❑ 65 Wayne Chrebet .30 .14
❑ 66 Curtis Martin .60 .25
❑ 67 Vinny Testaverde .30 .14
❑ 68 Tim Brown .60 .25
❑ 69 Rich Gannon .30 .14
❑ 70 Donovan McNabb 1.00 .45
❑ 71 Duce Staley .60 .25
❑ 72 Jerome Bettis .60 .25
❑ 73 Troy Edwards .30 .14
❑ 74 Kordell Stewart .60 .25
❑ 75 Isaac Bruce .60 .25
❑ 76 Marshall Faulk .75 .35
❑ 77 Torry Holt .60 .25
❑ 78 Kurt Warner 2.50 1.10
❑ 79 Jermaine Fazande .15 .07
❑ 80 Jim Harbaugh .30 .14
❑ 81 Jeff Garcia .60 .25
❑ 82 Charlie Garner .30 .14
❑ 83 Terrell Owens .60 .25
❑ 84 Jerry Rice 1.50 .70
❑ 85 Jon Kitna .60 .25
❑ 86 Derrick Mayes .30 .14
❑ 87 Ricky Watters .30 .14
❑ 88 Mike Alstott .60 .25
❑ 89 Warrick Dunn .60 .25
❑ 90 Keyshawn Johnson .60 .25
❑ 91 Shaun King 1.00 .45
❑ 92 Kevin Dyson .30 .14
❑ 93 Eddie George .75 .35
❑ 94 Jevon Kearse .60 .25
❑ 95 Steve McNair .60 .25
❑ 96 Carl Pickens .30 .14
❑ 97 Champ Bailey .30 .14
❑ 98 Stephen Davis .60 .25
❑ 99 Brad Johnson .60 .25
❑ 100 Michael Westbrook .30 .14
❑ 101 Thomas Jones RC 12.00 5.50
❑ 102 Doug Johnson RC 8.00 3.60
❑ 103 Mareno Philyaw RC 4.00 1.80
❑ 104 Jamal Lewis RC 40.00 18.00
❑ 105 Chris Redman RC 15.00 6.75
❑ 106 Travis Taylor RC 10.00 4.50
❑ 107 Kwame Cavil RC 6.00 2.70
❑ 108 Sammy Morris RC 10.00 4.50
❑ 109 Frank Murphy RC 4.00 1.80
❑ 110 Brian Urlacher RC 25.00 11.00
❑ 111 Dez White RC 6.00 2.70
❑ 112 Ron Dugans RC 6.00 2.70
❑ 113 Curtis Keaton RC 6.00 2.70
❑ 114 Peter Warrick RC 25.00 11.00
❑ 115 Courtney Brown RC 10.00 4.50
❑ 116 JaJuan Dawson RC 8.00 3.60
❑ 117 Dennis Northcutt RC 10.00 4.50
❑ 118 Travis Prentice RC 12.00 5.50
❑ 119 Michael Wiley RC 8.00 3.60
❑ 120 Mike Anderson RC 40.00 18.00
❑ 121 Chris Cole RC 6.00 2.70
❑ 122 Jarious Jackson RC 8.00 3.60
❑ 123 Deltha O'Neal RC 6.00 2.70
❑ 124 Reuben Droughns RC 8.00 3.60
❑ 125 Bubba Franks RC 10.00 4.50
❑ 126 Anthony Lucas RC 4.00 1.80
❑ 127 Rondell Mealey RC 4.00 1.80
❑ 128 Rob Morris RC 6.00 2.70
❑ 129 R.Jay Soward RC 8.00 3.60
❑ 130 Shyrone Stith RC 6.00 2.70
❑ 131 Frank Moreau RC 8.00 3.60
❑ 132 Sylvester Morris RC 15.00 6.75
❑ 133 Doug Chapman RC 15.00 6.75
❑ 134 J.R. Redmond RC 10.00 4.50
❑ 135 Marc Bulger RC 8.00 3.60
❑ 136 Sherrod Gideon RC 4.00 1.80
❑ 137 Terrelle Smith RC 6.00 2.70
❑ 138 Ron Dayne RC 25.00 11.00
❑ 139 Anthony Becht RC 8.00 3.60
❑ 140 Laveranues Coles RC 12.00 5.50
❑ 141 Shaun Ellis RC 6.00 2.70
❑ 142 Chad Pennington RC 25.00 11.00
❑ 143 Sebastian Janikowski RC 8.00 3.60
❑ 144 Jerry Porter RC 8.00 3.60
❑ 145 Todd Pinkston RC 8.00 3.60
❑ 146 Gari Scott RC 6.00 2.70
❑ 147 Corey Simon RC 10.00 4.50
❑ 148 Plaxico Burress RC 15.00 6.75
❑ 149 Danny Farmer RC 8.00 3.60
❑ 150 Tee Martin RC 12.00 5.50
❑ 151 Trung Canidate RC 8.00 3.60
❑ 152 Trevor Gaylor RC 6.00 2.70
❑ 153 Giovanni Carmazzi RC 10.00 4.50
❑ 154 John Engelberger RC 6.00 2.70
❑ 155 Ahmed Plummer RC 8.00 3.60
❑ 156 Tim Rattay RC 12.00 5.50
❑ 157 Shaun Alexander RC 20.00 9.00
❑ 158 Joe Hamilton RC 10.00 4.50
❑ 159 Keith Bulluck RC 6.00 2.70
❑ 160 Todd Husak RC 8.00 3.60
❑ 161 Cade McNown SV 8.00 3.60
❑ 162 Tim Couch SV 3.00 1.35
❑ 163 Terrell Davis SV 4.00 1.80
❑ 164 Brett Favre SV 6.00 2.70
❑ 165 Edgerrin James SV 5.00 2.20
❑ 166 Peyton Manning SV 5.00 2.20
❑ 167 Daunte Culpepper SV 3.00 1.35
❑ 168 Randy Moss SV 5.00 2.20
❑ 169 Ricky Williams SV 4.00 1.80
❑ 170 Kurt Warner SV 6.00 2.70
❑ 171 Cade McNown LV 1.50 .70
❑ 172 Akili Smith LV 1.50 .70
❑ 173 Tim Couch LV 3.00 1.35
❑ 174 Troy Aikman LV 4.00 1.80
❑ 175 Emmitt Smith LV 4.00 1.80
❑ 176 Terrell Davis LV 4.00 1.80
❑ 177 Brett Favre LV 6.00 2.70
❑ 178 Edgerrin James LV 5.00 2.20
❑ 179 Peyton Manning LV 5.00 2.20
❑ 180 Mark Brunell LV 2.50 1.10
❑ 181 Daunte Culpepper LV 3.00 1.35
❑ 182 Randy Moss LV 5.00 2.20
❑ 183 Drew Bledsoe LV 2.50 1.10
❑ 184 Ricky Williams LV 4.00 1.80
❑ 185 Donovan McNabb LV 1.50 .70
❑ 186 Torry Holt LV 1.50 .70
❑ 187 Kurt Warner LV 6.00 2.70
❑ 188 Shaun King LV 1.50 .70
❑ 189 Eddie George LV 1.50 .70
❑ 190 Steve McNair LV 1.50 .70

1996 CE President's Reserve

	MINT	NRMT
COMPLETE SET (400)	70.00	32.00
COMP.SERIES 1 (200)	40.00	18.00
COMP.SERIES 2 (200)	30.00	13.50

❑ 1 Larry Centers .50 .23
❑ 2 Frank Sanders .50 .23
❑ 3 Clyde Simmons .25 .11
❑ 4 Eric Swann .50 .23
❑ 5 Morten Andersen .25 .11
❑ 6 Lester Archambeau .25 .11
❑ 7 J.J. Birden .25 .11
❑ 8 Bert Emanuel .50 .23
❑ 9 Jumpy Geathers .25 .11
❑ 10 Jeff George .50 .23
❑ 11 Craig Heyward .25 .11
❑ 12 Bill Brooks .25 .11
❑ 13 Steve Christie .25 .11
❑ 14 Todd Collins .50 .23
❑ 15 Darick Holmes .50 .23
❑ 16 Andre Reed .50 .23
❑ 17 Bryce Paup .50 .23
❑ 18 Bruce Smith 1.00 .45
❑ 19 Blake Brockermeyer .25 .11
❑ 20 Mark Carrier .25 .11
❑ 21 Kerry Collins 1.00 .45
❑ 22 Darion Conner .25 .11
❑ 23 Eric Guliford .25 .11
❑ 24 Lamar Lathon .25 .11
❑ 25 Derrick Moore .25 .11
❑ 26 Frank Reich .25 .11
❑ 27 Kevin Butler .25 .11
❑ 28 Tony Carter .25 .11
❑ 29 Curtis Conway 1.00 .45
❑ 30 Robert Green .25 .11
❑ 31 Jay Leeuwenburg .25 .11
❑ 32 Alonzo Spellman .25 .11
❑ 33 Chris Zorich .25 .11
❑ 34 Eric Bieniemy .25 .11
❑ 35 Jeff Blake 1.00 .45
❑ 36 Tony McGee .25 .11
❑ 37 Carl Pickens 1.00 .45
❑ 38 Rob Burnett .25 .11
❑ 39 Earnest Byner .25 .11
❑ 40 Michael Jackson .50 .23
❑ 41 Antonio Langham .25 .11
❑ 42 Anthony Pleasant .25 .11
❑ 43 Vinny Testaverde .50 .23
❑ 44 Troy Aikman 2.50 1.10
❑ 45 Larry Allen .25 .11
❑ 46 Bill Bates .50 .23
❑ 47 Chris Boniol .25 .11
❑ 48 Charles Haley .50 .23
❑ 49 Michael Irvin 1.00 .45

Card		
❑ 50 Robert Jones	.25	.11
❑ 51 Leon Lett	.25	.11
❑ 52 Russell Maryland	.25	.11
❑ 53 Nate Newton	.25	.11
❑ 54 Deion Sanders	1.50	.70
❑ 55 Sherman Williams	.25	.11
❑ 56 Darren Woodson	.50	.23
❑ 57 Aaron Craver	.25	.11
❑ 58 Terrell Davis	6.00	2.70
❑ 59 Jason Elam	.25	.11
❑ 60 Simon Fletcher	.25	.11
❑ 61 Anthony Miller	.50	.23
❑ 62 Shannon Sharpe	.50	.23
❑ 63 Tracy Scroggins	.25	.11
❑ 64 Antonio London	.25	.11
❑ 65 Scott Mitchell	.50	.23
❑ 66 Johnnie Morton	.50	.23
❑ 67 Barry Sanders	5.00	2.20
❑ 68 Edgar Bennett	.50	.23
❑ 69 Mark Chmura	.50	.23
❑ 70 Brett Favre	5.00	2.20
❑ 71 Mark Ingram	.25	.11
❑ 72 Dorsey Levens	1.00	.45
❑ 73 Wayne Simmons	.25	.11
❑ 74 Gary Brown	.25	.11
❑ 75 Anthony Cook	.25	.11
❑ 76 Al Del Greco	.25	.11
❑ 77 Haywood Jeffires	.25	.11
❑ 78 Steve McNair	2.00	.90
❑ 79 Rodney Thomas	.25	.11
❑ 80 Trev Alberts	.25	.11
❑ 81 Quentin Coryatt	.25	.11
❑ 82 Ken Dilger	.50	.23
❑ 83 Jim Harbaugh	.50	.23
❑ 84 Floyd Turner	.25	.11
❑ 85 Lamont Warren	.25	.11
❑ 86 Steve Beuerlein	.25	.11
❑ 87 Mark Brunell	2.50	1.10
❑ 88 Eugene Chung	.25	.11
❑ 89 Jeff Lageman	.25	.11
❑ 90 Willie Jackson	.50	.23
❑ 91 Kimble Anders	.25	.11
❑ 92 Steve Bono	.50	.23
❑ 93 Derrick Thomas	.50	.23
❑ 94 Willie Davis	.50	.23
❑ 95 Greg Hill	.50	.23
❑ 96 Neil Smith	.50	.23
❑ 97 Tamarick Vanover	1.00	.45
❑ 98 James Hasty	.25	.11
❑ 99 Gary Clark	.25	.11
❑ 100 Marco Coleman	.25	.11
❑ 101 Steve Emtman	.25	.11
❑ 102 Irving Fryar	.50	.23
❑ 103 Randal Hill	.25	.11
❑ 104 Terry Kirby	.50	.23
❑ 105 Dan Marino	5.00	2.20
❑ 106 Cris Carter	1.00	.45
❑ 107 Jack Del Rio	.25	.11
❑ 108 David Palmer	.50	.23
❑ 109 Jake Reed	.50	.23
❑ 110 Robert Smith	.50	.23
❑ 111 Korey Stringer	.25	.11
❑ 112 Orlando Thomas	.25	.11
❑ 113 Drew Bledsoe	2.50	1.10
❑ 114 Vincent Brisby	.25	.11
❑ 115 Ted Johnson RC	.25	.11
❑ 116 Curtis Martin	2.00	.90
❑ 117 Chris Slade	.25	.11
❑ 118 Jim Dombrowski	.25	.11
❑ 119 William Roaf	.25	.11
❑ 120 Quinn Early	.25	.11
❑ 121 Wesley Walls	.50	.23
❑ 122 Wayne Martin	.25	.11
❑ 123 Irv Smith	.25	.11
❑ 124 Torrance Small	.25	.11
❑ 125 Dave Brown	.50	.23
❑ 126 Chris Calloway	.25	.11
❑ 127 Jumbo Elliott	.25	.11
❑ 128 Rodney Hampton	.50	.23
❑ 129 Tyrone Wheatley	.50	.23
❑ 130 Kyle Brady	.50	.23
❑ 131 Hugh Douglas	.50	.23
❑ 132 Todd Scott	.25	.11
❑ 133 Adrian Murrell	.50	.23
❑ 134 Wayne Chrebet	1.50	.70
❑ 135 Aundray Bruce	.25	.11
❑ 136 Andrew Glover	.25	.11
❑ 137 Daryl Hobbs RC	.25	.11
❑ 138 Napoleon Kaufman	1.00	.45
❑ 139 Chester McGlockton	.25	.11
❑ 140 Rob Fredrickson	.25	.11
❑ 141 Guy McIntyre	.25	.11
❑ 142 Bobby Taylor	.50	.23
❑ 143 Fred Barnett	.50	.23
❑ 144 William Fuller	.25	.11
❑ 145 Rodney Peete	.25	.11
❑ 146 Daniel Stubbs	.25	.11
❑ 147 Charlie Garner	.25	.11
❑ 148 Myron Bell	.25	.11
❑ 149 Rod Woodson	.50	.23
❑ 150 Charles Johnson	.50	.23
❑ 151 Ernie Mills	.25	.11
❑ 152 Levon Kirkland	.25	.11
❑ 153 Carnell Lake	.25	.11
❑ 154 Kevin Greene	.50	.23
❑ 155 Neil O'Donnell	.50	.23
❑ 156 Erric Pegram	.50	.23
❑ 157 Ray Seals	.25	.11
❑ 158 Willie Williams	.25	.11
❑ 159 Kordell Stewart	1.50	.70
❑ 160 Yancey Thigpen	.50	.23
❑ 161 Darren Bennett	.50	.23
❑ 162 Andre Coleman	.25	.11
❑ 163 Aaron Hayden RC	1.00	.45
❑ 164 Tony Martin	.50	.23
❑ 165 Chris Mims	.25	.11
❑ 166 Shawn Lee	.25	.11
❑ 167 Junior Seau	1.00	.45
❑ 168 Merton Hanks	.25	.11
❑ 169 Rickey Jackson	.25	.11
❑ 170 Derek Loville	.25	.11
❑ 171 Gary Plummer	.25	.11
❑ 172 J.J. Stokes	1.00	.45
❑ 173 John Taylor	.25	.11
❑ 174 Bryant Young	.50	.23
❑ 175 Antonio Edwards RC	.50	.23
❑ 176 Joey Galloway	1.50	.70
❑ 177 Carlton Gray	.25	.11
❑ 178 Rick Mirer	.50	.23
❑ 179 Winston Moss	.25	.11
❑ 180 Jerome Bettis	1.00	.45
❑ 181 Troy Drayton	.25	.11
❑ 182 Wayne Gandy	.25	.11
❑ 183 Sean Gilbert	.25	.11
❑ 184 Jessie Hester	.25	.11
❑ 185 Sean Landeta	.25	.11
❑ 186 Roman Phifer	.25	.11
❑ 187 Alberto White	.25	.11
❑ 188 Santana Dotson	.25	.11
❑ 189 Jerry Ellison RC	.25	.11
❑ 190 Jackie Harris	.25	.11
❑ 191 Courtney Hawkins	.25	.11
❑ 192 Horace Copeland	.25	.11
❑ 193 Hardy Nickerson	.25	.11
❑ 194 Warren Sapp	.25	.11
❑ 195 Terry Allen	.50	.23
❑ 196 Henry Ellard	.50	.23
❑ 197 Gus Frerotte	1.00	.45
❑ 198 John Gesek	.25	.11
❑ 199 Jim Lachey	.25	.11
❑ 200 Brian Mitchell	.25	.11
❑ 201 Garrison Hearst	.50	.23
❑ 202 Dave Krieg	.25	.11
❑ 203 Rob Moore	.25	.11
❑ 204 Aeneas Williams	.25	.11
❑ 205 Chris Doleman	.25	.11
❑ 206 Terance Mathis	.25	.11
❑ 207 Clay Matthews	.50	.23
❑ 208 Eric Metcalf	.50	.23
❑ 209 Jessie Tuggle	.25	.11
❑ 210 Cornelius Bennett	.50	.23
❑ 211 Ruben Brown	.25	.11
❑ 212 Russell Copeland	.25	.11
❑ 213 Phil Hansen	.25	.11
❑ 214 Jim Kelly	1.00	.45
❑ 215 Don Beebe	.25	.11
❑ 216 Willie Green	.25	.11
❑ 217 Howard Griffith	.25	.11
❑ 218 John Kasay	.25	.11
❑ 219 Brett Maxie	.25	.11
❑ 220 Tim McKyer	.25	.11
❑ 221 Sam Mills	.50	.23
❑ 222 Jim Flanigan	.25	.11
❑ 223 Jeff Graham	.25	.11
❑ 224 Erik Kramer	.25	.11
❑ 225 Rashaan Salaam	1.00	.45
❑ 226 Steve Walsh	.25	.11
❑ 227 Donnell Woolford	.25	.11
❑ 228 Ki-Jana Carter	.50	.23
❑ 229 John Copeland	.25	.11
❑ 230 Harold Green	.25	.11
❑ 231 Doug Pelfrey	.25	.11
❑ 232 Darnay Scott	.50	.23
❑ 233 Bracey Walker	.25	.11
❑ 234 Dan Wilkinson	.25	.11
❑ 235 Leroy Hoard	.25	.11
❑ 236 Ernest Hunter UER name spelled Earnest	.25	.11
❑ 237 Keenan McCardell	1.00	.45
❑ 238 Stevon Moore	.25	.11
❑ 239 Andre Rison	.50	.23
❑ 240 Eric Zeier	.50	.23
❑ 241 Larry Brown	.25	.11
❑ 242 Shante Carver	.25	.11
❑ 243 Chad Hennings	.50	.23
❑ 244 John Jett	.25	.11
❑ 245 Daryl Johnston	.50	.23
❑ 246 Derek Kennard	.25	.11
❑ 247 Brock Marion	.25	.11
❑ 248 Jay Novacek	.50	.23
❑ 249 Emmitt Smith	4.00	1.80
❑ 250 Tony Tolbert	.25	.11
❑ 251 Mark Tuinei	.25	.11
❑ 252 Erik Williams	.25	.11
❑ 253 Kevin Williams	.25	.11
❑ 254 John Elway	5.00	2.20
❑ 255 Ed McCaffrey	.50	.23
❑ 256 Glyn Milburn	.25	.11
❑ 257 Michael Dean Perry	.25	.11
❑ 258 Mike Pritchard	.25	.11
❑ 259 Willie Clay	.25	.11
❑ 260 Jason Hanson	.25	.11
❑ 261 Herman Moore	1.00	.45
❑ 262 Brett Perriman	.50	.23
❑ 263 Lomas Brown	.25	.11
❑ 264 Chris Spielman	.50	.23
❑ 265 Henry Thomas	.25	.11
❑ 266 Robert Brooks	1.00	.45
❑ 267 Sean Jones	.25	.11
❑ 268 John Jurkovic	.25	.11
❑ 269 Anthony Morgan	.25	.11
❑ 270 Craig Newsome	.25	.11
❑ 271 Reggie White	1.00	.45
❑ 272 Chris Chandler	.50	.23
❑ 273 Mel Gray	.25	.11
❑ 274 Darryll Lewis	.25	.11
❑ 275 Bruce Matthews	.25	.11
❑ 276 Todd McNair	.25	.11
❑ 277 Chris Sanders	.50	.23
❑ 278 Mark Stepnoski	.25	.11
❑ 279 Ashley Ambrose	.25	.11
❑ 280 Tony Bennett	.25	.11
❑ 281 Zack Crockett	.25	.11
❑ 282 Sean Dawkins	.25	.11
❑ 283 Marshall Faulk	1.00	.45
❑ 284 Ronald Humphrey	.25	.11
❑ 285 Tony Siragusa	.25	.11
❑ 286 Roosevelt Potts	.25	.11
❑ 287 Bryan Barker	.25	.11
❑ 288 Tony Boselli	.50	.23
❑ 289 Keith Goganious	.25	.11
❑ 290 Desmond Howard	.50	.23
❑ 291 Don Davey	.25	.11
❑ 292 Corey Mayfield	.25	.11
❑ 293 James O. Stewart	.50	.23
❑ 294 Cedric Tillman	.25	.11
❑ 295 Marcus Allen	1.00	.45
❑ 296 Dale Carter	.25	.11
❑ 297 Lake Dawson	.50	.23
❑ 298 Darren Mickell	.25	.11
❑ 299 Dan Saleaumua	.25	.11
❑ 300 Webster Slaughter	.25	.11
❑ 301 Keith Cash	.25	.11
❑ 302 Bryan Cox	.25	.11
❑ 303 Jeff Cross	.25	.11
❑ 304 Eric Green	.25	.11
❑ 305 O.J. McDuffie	.50	.23
❑ 306 Bernie Parmalee	.25	.11

❑ 307 Billy Milner .25 .11
❑ 308 Pete Stoyanovich .25 .11
❑ 309 Troy Vincent .25 .11
❑ 310 Qadry Ismail .50 .23
❑ 311 Amp Lee .25 .11
❑ 312 Warren Moon .50 .23
❑ 313 Scottie Graham .25 .11
❑ 314 John Randle .50 .23
❑ 315 Fuad Reveiz .25 .11
❑ 316 Broderick Thomas .25 .11
❑ 317 Ben Coates .50 .23
❑ 318 Willie McGinest .25 .11
❑ 319 Dave Meggett .25 .11
❑ 320 Will Moore .25 .11
❑ 321 Dave Wohlabaugh .25 .11
❑ 322 Mario Bates .50 .23
❑ 323 Jim Everett .25 .11
❑ 324 Tyrone Hughes .25 .11
❑ 325 Vaughn Dunbar .25 .11
❑ 326 Renaldo Turnbull .25 .11
❑ 327 Michael Haynes .50 .23
❑ 328 Mike Sherrard .25 .11
❑ 329 Michael Strahan .25 .11
❑ 330 Herschel Walker .50 .23
❑ 331 Charles Wilson .25 .11
❑ 332 Otis Smith RC .25 .11
❑ 333 Mo Lewis .25 .11
❑ 334 Marvin Washington .25 .11
❑ 335 Tim Brown .50 .23
❑ 336 Greg Skrepenak .25 .11
❑ 337 Kevin Gogan .25 .11
❑ 338 Jeff Hostetler .50 .23
❑ 339 Terry McDaniel .25 .11
❑ 340 Anthony Smith .25 .11
❑ 341 Pat Swilling .25 .11
❑ 342 Harvey Williams .25 .11
❑ 343 Tom Hutton RC .25 .11
❑ 344 Mike Mamula .25 .11
❑ 345 Randall Cunningham 1.00 .45
❑ 346 Ricky Watters .50 .23
❑ 347 Andy Harmon .25 .11
❑ 348 William Thomas .25 .11
❑ 349 Calvin Williams 1.00 .45
❑ 350 Mark Bruener .25 .11
❑ 351 Dermontti Dawson .25 .11
❑ 352 Greg Lloyd .50 .23
❑ 353 Norm Johnson .25 .11
❑ 354 Byron Bam Morris .50 .23
❑ 355 Thomas Newberry .25 .11
❑ 356 Darren Perry .25 .11
❑ 357 Rohn Stark .25 .11
❑ 358 Joel Steed .25 .11
❑ 359 Brendan Stai UER .25 .11
(Name spelled Brenden)
❑ 360 Justin Strzelczyk RC .25 .11
❑ 361 Leon Searcy .25 .11
❑ 362 Chad Brown .50 .23
❑ 363 John Carney .25 .11
❑ 364 Rodney Culver .50 .23
❑ 365 Ronnie Harmon .25 .11
❑ 366 Stan Humphries .50 .23
❑ 367 Leslie O'Neal .25 .11
❑ 368 Natrone Means 1.00 .45
❑ 369 Mark Seay .25 .11
❑ 370 William Floyd .50 .23
❑ 371 Brent Jones .25 .11
❑ 372 Tim McDonald .25 .11
❑ 373 Ken Norton, Jr. .50 .23
❑ 374 Jerry Rice 2.50 1.10
❑ 375 Dana Stubblefield .50 .23
❑ 376 Steve Young 2.00 .90
❑ 377 Brian Blades .50 .23
❑ 378 Cortez Kennedy .50 .23
❑ 379 Michael Sinclair .25 .11
❑ 380 Lamar Smith 1.00 .45
❑ 381 Chris Warren .50 .23
❑ 382 Johnny Bailey .25 .11
❑ 383 Isaac Bruce 1.00 .45
❑ 384 Kevin Carter .50 .23
❑ 385 Shane Conlan .25 .11
❑ 386 D'Marco Farr .25 .11
❑ 387 Todd Kinchen .25 .11
❑ 388 Chris Miller .25 .11
❑ 389 Lonnie Marts .25 .11
❑ 390 Trent Dilfer .50 .23
❑ 391 Alvin Harper .25 .11
❑ 392 John Lynch .50 .23
❑ 393 Errict Rhett .50 .23
❑ 394 Darnell Stephens RC .25 .11
❑ 395 Ken Harvey .25 .11
❑ 396 Eddie Murray .25 .11
❑ 397 Heath Shuler 1.00 .45
❑ 398 Matt Turk RC .25 .11
❑ 399 Michael Westbrook 1.00 .45
❑ 400 James Washington .25 .11

1998 CE Supreme Season Review

	MINT	NRMT
COMPLETE SET (200)	70.00	32.00
COMP.SET w/o SPs (200)	25.00	11.00

❑ 1 Larry Centers .25 .11
❑ 2 Jake Plummer 1.50 .70
❑ 3 Simeon Rice .50 .23
❑ 4 Cardinals Draft Pick .10 .05
❑ 4A Andre Wadsworth RC 1.00 .45
❑ 4B Michael Pittman RC 1.50 .70
❑ 5 Jamal Anderson 1.00 .45
❑ 6 Bert Emanuel .50 .23
❑ 7 Byron Hanspard .50 .23
❑ 8 Falcons Draft Pick .10 .05
❑ 8A Jammi German RC 1.00 .45
❑ 8B Keith Brooking RC 1.00 .45
❑ 9 Derrick Alexander WR .50 .23
❑ 10 Peter Boulware .25 .11
❑ 11 Michael Jackson .25 .11
❑ 12 Ray Lewis 1.00 .45
❑ 13 Vinny Testaverde .50 .23
❑ 14 Ravens Draft Pick .10 .05
❑ 14A Duane Starks RC 1.00 .45
❑ 14B Pat Johnson RC 1.00 .45
❑ 15 Todd Collins .25 .11
❑ 16 Jim Kelly 1.00 .45
❑ 17 Andre Reed .50 .23
❑ 18 Antowain Smith 1.00 .45
❑ 19 Bruce Smith .50 .23
❑ 20 Thurman Thomas 1.00 .45
❑ 21 Bills Draft Pick .10 .05
❑ 21A Jonathan Linton RC 1.00 .45
❑ 22 Tim Biakabutuka .50 .23
❑ 23 Rae Carruth .50 .23
❑ 24 Kerry Collins .50 .23
❑ 25 Anthony Johnson .25 .11
❑ 26 Lamar Lathon .25 .11
❑ 27 Panthers Draft Pick .10 .05
❑ 27A Jason Peters RC 1.00 .45
❑ 27B Donald Hayes RC 1.50 .70
❑ 28 Curtis Conway .50 .23
❑ 29 Bryan Cox .25 .11
❑ 30 Bobby Engram .50 .23
❑ 31 Erik Kramer .25 .11
❑ 32 Rick Mirer .25 .11
❑ 33 Rashaan Salaam .25 .11
❑ 34 Bears Draft Pick .10 .05
❑ 34A Curtis Enis RC 2.00 .90
❑ 35 Jeff Blake .50 .23
❑ 36 Ki-Jana Carter .25 .11
❑ 37 Corey Dillon 1.25 .55
❑ 38 Carl Pickens 1.00 .45
❑ 39 Bengals Draft Pick .10 .05
❑ 39A Takeo Spikes RC 1.00 .45
❑ 39B Brian Simmons RC 1.00 .45
❑ 40 Troy Aikman 2.00 .90
❑ 41 Daryl Johnston .50 .23
❑ 42 David LaFleur .25 .11
❑ 43 Anthony Miller .25 .11
❑ 44 Deion Sanders 1.00 .45
❑ 45 Emmitt Smith 3.00 1.35
❑ 46 Broderick Thomas .25 .11
❑ 47 Cowboys Draft Pick .10 .05
❑ 47A Greg Ellis RC 1.00 .45
❑ 48 Terrell Davis 3.00 1.35
❑ 49 John Elway 4.00 1.80
❑ 50 Ed McCaffrey .50 .23
❑ 51 John Mobley .25 .11
❑ 52 Bill Romanowski .25 .11
❑ 53 Shannon Sharpe .50 .23
❑ 54 Neil Smith .50 .23
❑ 55 Rod Smith WR .50 .23
❑ 56 Maa Tanuvasa .25 .11
❑ 57 Broncos Draft Pick .10 .05
❑ 57A Marcus Nash RC 1.50 .70
❑ 57B Brian Griese RC 6.00 2.70
❑ 58 Scott Mitchell .50 .23
❑ 59 Herman Moore 1.00 .45
❑ 60 Barry Sanders 4.00 1.80
❑ 61 Lions Draft Pick .10 .05
❑ 61A Jamaal Alexander RC 1.00 .45
❑ 61B Chris Liwienski RC 1.00 .45
❑ 61C Terry Fair RC 1.00 .45
❑ 61D Germane Crowell RC 3.00 1.35
❑ 61E Charlie Batch RC 4.00 1.80
❑ 62 Robert Brooks .50 .23
❑ 63 Mark Chmura .50 .23
❑ 64 Brett Favre 4.00 1.80
❑ 65 Antonio Freeman 1.00 .45
❑ 66 Dorsey Levens 1.00 .45
❑ 67 Derrick Mayes .50 .23
❑ 68 Ross Verba .25 .11
❑ 69 Reggie White 1.00 .45
❑ 70 Packers Draft Pick .50 .23
❑ 70A Vonnie Holliday RC 1.00 .45
❑ 70B Roosevelt Blackmon RC 1.00 .45
❑ 71 Marshall Faulk 1.00 .45
❑ 72 Jim Harbaugh .50 .23
❑ 73 Marvin Harrison .50 .23
❑ 74 Colts Draft Pick .10 .05
❑ 74A E.G. Green RC 1.50 .70
❑ 74B Peyton Manning RC 15.00 6.75
❑ 75 Tony Brackens .25 .11
❑ 76 Mark Brunell 1.50 .70
❑ 77 Rob Johnson .50 .23
❑ 78 Keenan McCardell .50 .23
❑ 79 Natrone Means 1.00 .45
❑ 80 Jimmy Smith .50 .23
❑ 81 Jaguars Draft Pick .10 .05
❑ 81A Tavian Banks RC 1.50 .70
❑ 82 Marcus Allen 1.00 .45
❑ 83 Tony Gonzalez .25 .11
❑ 84 Elvis Grbac .50 .23
❑ 85 Derrick Thomas .50 .23
❑ 86 Tamarick Vanover .25 .11
❑ 87 Chiefs Draft Pick .10 .05
❑ 87A Rashaan Shehee RC 1.50 .70
❑ 88 Karim Abdul-Jabbar 1.00 .45
❑ 89 Fred Barnett .25 .11
❑ 90 Dan Marino 4.00 1.80
❑ 91 O.J. McDuffie .50 .23
❑ 92 Brett Perriman .25 .11
❑ 93 Irving Spikes .25 .11
❑ 94 Zach Thomas .50 .23
❑ 95 Dolphins Draft Pick .10 .05
❑ 95A John Avery RC 1.00 .45
❑ 96 Cris Carter 1.00 .45
❑ 97 Brad Johnson 1.00 .45
❑ 98 John Randle .50 .23
❑ 99 Jake Reed .50 .23
❑ 100 Robert Smith 1.00 .45
❑ 101 Vikings Draft Pick .10 .05
❑ 101A Randy Moss RC 15.00 6.75
❑ 102 Drew Bledsoe 1.50 .70
❑ 103 Chris Canty .25 .11
❑ 104 Ben Coates .50 .23
❑ 105 Terry Glenn 1.00 .45
❑ 106 Curtis Martin 1.00 .45
❑ 107 Willie McGinest .25 .11
❑ 108 Sedrick Shaw .25 .11
❑ 109 Patriots Draft Pick .10 .05

Card		
❑ 109A Chris Floyd RC	1.00	.45
❑ 109B Tebucky Jones RC	1.00	.45
❑ 109C Harold Shaw RC	1.00	.45
❑ 110 Mario Bates	.50	.23
❑ 111 Heath Shuler	.25	.11
❑ 112 Danny Wuerffel	.50	.23
❑ 113 Saints Draft Pick	.10	.05
❑ 113A Cameron Cleeland RC	1.00	.45
❑ 114 Ray Zellars	.25	.11
❑ 115 Tiki Barber	.50	.23
❑ 116 Dave Brown	.25	.11
❑ 117 Ike Hilliard	.50	.23
❑ 118 Danny Kanell	.50	.23
❑ 119 Jason Sehorn	.50	.23
❑ 120 Amani Toomer	.50	.23
❑ 121 Giants Draft Pick	.10	.05
❑ 121A Shaun Williams RC	1.00	.45
❑ 121B Joe Jurevicius RC	1.50	.70
❑ 121C Brian Alford RC	1.00	.45
❑ 122 Wayne Chrebet	1.00	.45
❑ 123 Hugh Douglas	.25	.11
❑ 124 Jeff Graham	.25	.11
❑ 125 Keyshawn Johnson	1.00	.45
❑ 126 Adrian Murrell	.50	.23
❑ 127 Neil O'Donnell	.50	.23
❑ 128 Jets Draft Pick	.10	.05
❑ 128A Scott Frost RC	1.00	.45
❑ 129 Tim Brown	1.00	.45
❑ 130 Jeff George	.50	.23
❑ 131 Desmond Howard	.50	.23
❑ 132 Napoleon Kaufman	1.00	.45
❑ 133 Darrell Russell	.25	.11
❑ 134 Raiders Draft Pick	.10	.05
❑ 134A Charles Woodson RC	2.50	1.10
❑ 135 Ty Detmer	.50	.23
❑ 136 Irving Fryar	.50	.23
❑ 137 Bobby Hoying	.50	.23
❑ 138 Chris T. Jones	.25	.11
❑ 139 Ricky Watters	.50	.23
❑ 140 Eagles Draft Pick	.10	.05
❑ 140A Allen Rossum RC	1.00	.45
❑ 141 Jerome Bettis	1.00	.45
❑ 142 Charles Johnson	.25	.11
❑ 143 George Jones	.25	.11
❑ 144 Greg Lloyd	.25	.11
❑ 145 Kordell Stewart	1.00	.45
❑ 146 Yancey Thigpen	.25	.11
❑ 147 Steelers Draft Pick	.10	.05
❑ 147A C.Fuamatu-Ma'afala RC	1.00	.45
❑ 148 Stan Humphries	.25	.11
❑ 149 Tony Martin	.50	.23
❑ 150 Eric Metcalf	.25	.11
❑ 151 Junior Seau	.50	.23
❑ 152 Chargers Draft Pick	.10	.05
❑ 152A Ryan Leaf RC	3.00	1.35
❑ 153 Jim Druckenmiller	.50	.23
❑ 154 William Floyd	.25	.11
❑ 155 Kevin Greene	.50	.23
❑ 156 Garrison Hearst	1.00	.45
❑ 157 Ken Norton	.25	.11
❑ 158 Terrell Owens	1.00	.45
❑ 159 Jerry Rice	2.00	.90
❑ 160 J.J. Stokes	.50	.23
❑ 161 Dana Stubblefield	.25	.11
❑ 162 Rod Woodson	.50	.23
❑ 163 Bryant Young	.25	.11
❑ 164 Steve Young	1.25	.55
❑ 165 49ers Draft Pick	.25	.11
❑ 165A Fred Beasley RC	1.00	.45
❑ 165B R.W. McQuarters RC	1.00	.45
❑ 165C Chris Ruhman RC	1.00	.45
❑ 166 Steve Broussard	.25	.11
❑ 167 Chad Brown	.25	.11
❑ 168 Joey Galloway	1.00	.45
❑ 169 Jon Kitna	1.25	.55
❑ 170 Warren Moon	1.00	.45
❑ 171 Chris Warren	.50	.23
❑ 172 Seahawks Draft Pick	.10	.05
❑ 172A Ahman Green RC	3.00	1.35
❑ 173 Tony Banks	.50	.23
❑ 174 Isaac Bruce	1.00	.45
❑ 175 Eddie Kennison	.50	.23
❑ 176 Keith Lyle	.25	.11
❑ 177 Lawrence Phillips	.25	.11
❑ 178 Rams Draft Pick	.10	.05
❑ 178A Robert Holcombe RC	1.50	.70
❑ 179 Mike Alstott	1.00	.45
❑ 180 Reidel Anthony	.50	.23
❑ 181 Trent Dilfer	1.00	.45
❑ 182 Warrick Dunn	1.00	.45
❑ 183 Hardy Nickerson	.25	.11
❑ 184 Errict Rhett	.50	.23
❑ 185 Warren Sapp	.50	.23
❑ 186 Bucs Draft Pick	.10	.05
❑ 186A Jacquez Green RC	2.50	1.10
❑ 187 Eddie George	1.50	.70
❑ 188 Darryll Lewis	.25	.11
❑ 189 Steve McNair	1.00	.45
❑ 190 Chris Sanders	.25	.11
❑ 191 Oilers Draft Pick	.10	.05
❑ 191A Kevin Dyson RC	2.50	1.10
❑ 192 Terry Allen	1.00	.45
❑ 193 Jamie Asher	.25	.11
❑ 194 Stephen Davis	.25	.11
❑ 195 Gus Frerotte	.25	.11
❑ 196 Sean Gilbert	.25	.11
❑ 197 Ken Harvey	.25	.11
❑ 198 Jeff Hostetler	.25	.11
❑ 199 Michael Westbrook	.50	.23
❑ 200 Redskins Draft Pick	.10	.05
❑ 200A Stephen Alexander RC	1.50	.70
❑ 200B Mike Sellers RC	1.00	.45

1999 Collector's Edge Supreme

	MINT	NRMT
COMPLETE SET (170)	300.00	135.00
COMP.SET w/o #166 (169)	100.00	45.00
❑ 1 Randy Moss CL	1.25	.55
❑ 2 Peyton Manning CL	.60	.25
❑ 3 Rob Moore	.30	.14
❑ 4 Adrian Murrell	.30	.14
❑ 5 Jake Plummer	1.25	.55
❑ 6 Andre Wadsworth	.15	.07
❑ 7 Jamal Anderson	.60	.25
❑ 8 Chris Chandler	.30	.14
❑ 9 Tony Martin	.30	.14
❑ 10 Terence Mathis	.30	.14
❑ 11 Jim Harbaugh	.30	.14
❑ 12 Priest Holmes	.60	.25
❑ 13 Jermaine Lewis	.30	.14
❑ 14 Eric Zeier	.15	.07
❑ 15 Doug Flutie	.60	.25
❑ 16 Eric Moulds	.60	.25
❑ 17 Andre Reed	.30	.14
❑ 18 Antowain Smith	.60	.25
❑ 19 Steve Beuerlein	.15	.07
❑ 20 Kevin Greene	.15	.07
❑ 21 Rocket Ismail	.30	.14
❑ 22 Fred Lane	.15	.07
❑ 23 Edgar Bennett	.15	.07
❑ 24 Curtis Conway	.30	.14
❑ 25 Curtis Enis	.60	.25
❑ 26 Erik Kramer	.15	.07
❑ 27 Corey Dillon	.60	.25
❑ 28 Neil O'Donnell	.15	.07
❑ 29 Carl Pickens	.30	.14
❑ 30 Darnay Scott	.15	.07
❑ 31 Troy Aikman	1.50	.70
❑ 32 Michael Irvin	.30	.14
❑ 33 Deion Sanders	.60	.25
❑ 34 Emmitt Smith	1.50	.70
❑ 35 Chris Warren	.15	.07
❑ 36 Terrell Davis	1.50	.70
❑ 37 John Elway	2.50	1.10
❑ 38 Ed McCaffrey	.30	.14
❑ 39 Shannon Sharpe	.30	.14
❑ 40 Rod Smith	.30	.14
❑ 41 Charlie Batch	1.25	.55
❑ 42 Herman Moore	.60	.25
❑ 43 Johnnie Morton	.15	.07
❑ 44 Barry Sanders	2.50	1.10
❑ 45 Robert Brooks	.30	.14
❑ 46 Brett Favre	2.50	1.10
❑ 47 Antonio Freeman	.60	.25
❑ 48 Darick Holmes	.15	.07
❑ 49 Dorsey Levens	.60	.25
❑ 50 Reggie White	.15	.07
❑ 51 Marshall Faulk	.60	.25
❑ 52 Marvin Harrison	.60	.25
❑ 53 Peyton Manning	2.50	1.10
❑ 54 Jerome Pathon	.15	.07
❑ 55 Tavian Banks	.15	.07
❑ 56 Mark Brunell	1.00	.45
❑ 57 Keenan McCardell	.30	.14
❑ 58 Fred Taylor	1.50	.70
❑ 59 Derrick Alexander	.15	.07
❑ 60 Donnell Bennett	.15	.07
❑ 61 Rich Gannon	.30	.14
❑ 62 Andre Rison	.30	.14
❑ 63 Karim Abdul-Jabbar	.30	.14
❑ 64 John Avery	.30	.14
❑ 65 Oronde Gadsden	.15	.07
❑ 66 Dan Marino	2.50	1.10
❑ 67 O.J. McDuffie	.30	.14
❑ 68 Cris Carter	.60	.25
❑ 69 Randall Cunningham	.60	.25
❑ 70 Brad Johnson	.60	.25
❑ 71 Randy Moss	3.00	1.35
❑ 72 Jake Reed	.30	.14
❑ 73 Robert Smith	.60	.25
❑ 74 Drew Bledsoe	1.00	.45
❑ 75 Ben Coates	.30	.14
❑ 76 Robert Edwards	.30	.14
❑ 77 Terry Glenn	.60	.25
❑ 78 Cameron Cleeland	.15	.07
❑ 79 Kerry Collins	.30	.14
❑ 80 Sean Dawkins	.15	.07
❑ 81 Lamar Smith	.30	.14
❑ 82 Gary Brown	.15	.07
❑ 83 Chris Calloway	.15	.07
❑ 84 Danny Kanell	.15	.07
❑ 85 Ike Hilliard	.15	.07
❑ 86 Wayne Chrebet	.30	.14
❑ 87 Keyshawn Johnson	.60	.25
❑ 88 Curtis Martin	.60	.25
❑ 89 Vinny Testaverde	.30	.14
❑ 90 Tim Brown	.60	.25
❑ 91 Jeff George	.30	.14
❑ 92 Napoleon Kaufman	.60	.25
❑ 93 Charles Woodson	.60	.25
❑ 94 Irving Fryar	.30	.14
❑ 95 Bobby Hoying	.30	.14
❑ 96 Duce Staley	.60	.25
❑ 97 Jerome Bettis	.60	.25
❑ 98 Courtney Hawkins	.15	.07
❑ 99 Charles Johnson	.15	.07
❑ 100 Kordell Stewart	.60	.25
❑ 101 Hines Ward	.30	.14
❑ 102 Tony Banks	.30	.14
❑ 103 Isaac Bruce	.60	.25
❑ 104 Robert Holcombe	.30	.14
❑ 105 Ryan Leaf	.60	.25
❑ 106 Natrone Means	.30	.14
❑ 107 Mikhael Ricks	.15	.07
❑ 108 Junior Seau	.30	.14
❑ 109 Garrison Hearst	.30	.14
❑ 110 Terrell Owens	.60	.25
❑ 111 Jerry Rice	1.50	.70
❑ 112 J.J. Stokes	.30	.14
❑ 113 Steve Young	1.00	.45
❑ 114 Joey Galloway	.60	.25
❑ 115 Jon Kitna	.60	.25
❑ 116 Warren Moon	.60	.25
❑ 117 Ricky Watters	.30	.14
❑ 118 Mike Alstott	.60	.25
❑ 119 Reidel Anthony	.30	.14
❑ 120 Warrick Dunn	.60	.25

Card		
❑ 121 Trent Dilfer	.30	.14
❑ 122 Jacquez Green	.30	.14
❑ 123 Kevin Dyson	.30	.14
❑ 124 Eddie George	.75	.35
❑ 125 Steve McNair	.60	.25
❑ 126 Frank Wycheck	.15	.07
❑ 127 Terry Allen	.30	.14
❑ 128 Trent Green	.30	.14
❑ 129 Skip Hicks	.60	.25
❑ 130 Michael Westbrook	.30	.14
❑ 131 Rahim Abdullah RC	1.50	.70
❑ 132 Champ Bailey RC	2.50	1.10
❑ 133 Marlon Barnes RC	1.50	.70
❑ 134 D'Wayne Bates RC	1.50	.70
❑ 135 Michael Bishop RC	2.50	1.10
❑ 136 Dre' Bly RC	1.50	.70
❑ 137 David Boston RC	4.00	1.80
❑ 138 Cuncho Brown RC UER (Photo is actually Courtney Brown)	1.50	.70
❑ 139 Na Brown RC	2.50	1.10
❑ 140 Tony Bryant RC	1.50	.70
❑ 141 Tim Couch RC ERR (Text on back reads "already sent")	60.00	27.00
❑ 141TC Tim Couch RC COR (Card number reads "TC")	15.00	6.75
❑ 142 Chris Claiborne RC	1.00	.45
❑ 143 Daunte Culpepper RC	10.00	4.50
❑ 144 Jared DeVries RC	1.50	.70
❑ 145 Troy Edwards RC UER	2.50	1.10
❑ 146 Kris Farris RC	1.00	.45
❑ 147 Kevin Faulk RC	3.00	1.35
❑ 148 Joe Germaine RC	2.50	1.10
❑ 149 Aaron Gibson RC	1.00	.45
❑ 150 Torry Holt RC	5.00	2.20
❑ 151 Brock Huard RC	3.00	1.35
❑ 152 Sedrick Irvin RC	2.50	1.10
❑ 153 James Johnson RC	2.50	1.10
❑ 154 Kevin Johnson RC	4.00	1.80
❑ 155 Andy Katzenmoyer RC	2.50	1.10
❑ 156 Jevon Kearse RC	4.00	1.80
❑ 157 Shaun King RC	4.00	1.80
❑ 158 Rob Konrad RC	1.50	.70
❑ 159 Chris McAlister RC	1.50	.70
❑ 160 Darnell McDonald RC	2.50	1.10
❑ 161 Donovan McNabb RC	6.00	2.70
❑ 162 Cade McNown RC	2.50	1.10
❑ 163 Peerless Price RC	2.50	1.10
❑ 164 Akili Smith RC	4.00	1.80
❑ 165 Matt Stinchcomb RC	1.00	.45
❑ 166A Michael Wiley (Pink tint on card front)	250.00	110.00
❑ 166B Edgerrin James RC (Issue via mail redemption)	60.00	27.00
❑ 167 Ricky Williams RC	6.00	2.70
❑ 168 Antoine Winfield RC	1.50	.70
❑ 169 Craig Yeast RC	1.50	.70
❑ 170 Amos Zereoue RC	2.50	1.10

2000 Collector's Edge Supreme

	MINT	NRMT
COMPLETE SET (190)	150.00	70.00
COMP.SET w/o SP's (150)	20.00	9.00
❑ 1 David Boston	.50	.23
❑ 2 Adrian Murrell	.20	.09
❑ 3 Michael Pittman	.10	.05
❑ 4 Jake Plummer	.50	.23
❑ 5 Frank Sanders	.20	.09
❑ 6 Jamal Anderson	.50	.23
❑ 7 Chris Chandler	.20	.09
❑ 8 Terance Mathis	.20	.09
❑ 9 Justin Armour	.10	.05
❑ 10 Tony Banks	.20	.09
❑ 11 Qadry Ismail	.10	.05
❑ 12 Errict Rhett	.20	.09
❑ 13 Doug Flutie	.60	.25
❑ 14 Eric Moulds	.50	.23
❑ 15 Peerless Price	.50	.23
❑ 16 Andre Reed	.20	.09
❑ 17 Antowain Smith	.20	.09
❑ 18 Steve Beuerlein	.20	.09
❑ 19 Tim Biakabutuka	.20	.09
❑ 20 Muhsin Muhammad	.20	.09
❑ 21 Wesley Walls	.10	.05
❑ 22 Bobby Engram	.10	.05
❑ 23 Curtis Enis	.20	.09
❑ 24 Shane Matthews	.20	.09
❑ 25 Cade McNown	.50	.23
❑ 26 Jim Miller	.10	.05
❑ 27 Marcus Robinson	.50	.23
❑ 28 Corey Dillon	.50	.23
❑ 29 Carl Pickens	.20	.09
❑ 30 Darnay Scott	.20	.09
❑ 31 Akili Smith	.50	.23
❑ 32 Karim Abdul-Jabbar	.20	.09
❑ 33 Tim Couch	1.00	.45
❑ 34 Kevin Johnson	.50	.23
❑ 35 Troy Aikman	1.25	.55
❑ 36 Michael Irvin	.20	.09
❑ 37 Rocket Ismail	.20	.09
❑ 38 Deion Sanders	.50	.23
❑ 39 Emmitt Smith	1.25	.55
❑ 40 Terrell Davis	1.25	.55
❑ 41 Olandis Gary	.50	.23
❑ 42 Brian Griese	.60	.25
❑ 43 Ed McCaffrey	.50	.23
❑ 44 Rod Smith	.20	.09
❑ 45 Charlie Batch	.50	.23
❑ 46 Germane Crowell	.20	.09
❑ 47 Greg Hill	.10	.05
❑ 48 Sedrick Irvin	.10	.05
❑ 49 Herman Moore	.20	.09
❑ 50 Johnnie Morton	.20	.09
❑ 51 Corey Bradford	.20	.09
❑ 52 Brett Favre	2.00	.90
❑ 53 Antonio Freeman	.50	.23
❑ 54 Dorsey Levens	.20	.09
❑ 55 Bill Schroeder	.20	.09
❑ 56 E.G. Green	.10	.05
❑ 57 Marvin Harrison	.50	.23
❑ 58 Edgerrin James	2.00	.90
❑ 59 Peyton Manning	1.50	.70
❑ 60 Terrence Wilkins	.50	.23
❑ 61 Mark Brunell	.75	.35
❑ 62 Keenan McCardell	.20	.09
❑ 63 Jimmy Smith	.20	.09
❑ 64 James Stewart	.20	.09
❑ 65 Fred Taylor	.60	.25
❑ 66 Derrick Alexander	.20	.09
❑ 67 Donnell Bennett	.10	.05
❑ 68 Mike Cloud	.10	.05
❑ 69 Tony Gonzalez	.20	.09
❑ 70 Elvis Grbac	.20	.09
❑ 71 Damon Huard	.50	.23
❑ 72 James Johnson	.20	.09
❑ 73 Rob Konrad	.10	.05
❑ 74 Dan Marino	2.00	.90
❑ 75 Tony Martin	.20	.09
❑ 76 O.J. McDuffie	.20	.09
❑ 77 Cris Carter	.50	.23
❑ 78 Daunte Culpepper	1.00	.45
❑ 79 Jeff George	.20	.09
❑ 80 Randy Moss	1.50	.70
❑ 81 Robert Smith	.50	.23
❑ 82 Terry Allen	.20	.09
❑ 83 Drew Bledsoe	.75	.35
❑ 84 Kevin Faulk	.20	.09
❑ 85 Terry Glenn	.20	.09
❑ 86 Shawn Jefferson	.10	.05
❑ 87 Billy Joe Hobert	.10	.05
❑ 88 Eddie Kennison	.20	.09
❑ 89 Billy Joe Tolliver	.10	.05
❑ 90 Ricky Williams	1.25	.55
❑ 91 Tiki Barber	.20	.09
❑ 92 Gary Brown	.10	.05
❑ 93 Kent Graham	.10	.05
❑ 94 Ike Hilliard	.20	.09
❑ 95 Amani Toomer	.10	.05
❑ 96 Wayne Chrebet	.20	.09
❑ 97 Keyshawn Johnson	.50	.23
❑ 98 Ray Lucas	.50	.23
❑ 99 Curtis Martin	.50	.23
❑ 100 Vinny Testaverde	.20	.09
❑ 101 Tim Brown	.50	.23
❑ 102 Rich Gannon	.20	.09
❑ 103 James Jett	.10	.05
❑ 104 Napoleon Kaufman	.20	.09
❑ 105 Tyrone Wheatley	.20	.09
❑ 106 Charles Johnson	.20	.09
❑ 107 Donovan McNabb	.75	.35
❑ 108 Duce Staley	.50	.23
❑ 109 Jerome Bettis	.50	.23
❑ 110 Troy Edwards	.20	.09
❑ 111 Kordell Stewart	.50	.23
❑ 112 Hines Ward	.10	.05
❑ 113 Isaac Bruce	.50	.23
❑ 114 Marshall Faulk	.60	.25
❑ 115 Az-Zahir Hakim	.20	.09
❑ 116 Torry Holt	.50	.23
❑ 117 Kurt Warner	2.00	.90
❑ 118 Jeff Graham	.10	.05
❑ 119 Jim Harbaugh	.20	.09
❑ 120 Freddie Jones	.10	.05
❑ 121 Natrone Means	.10	.05
❑ 122 Junior Seau	.20	.09
❑ 123 Jeff Garcia	.50	.23
❑ 124 Charlie Garner	.20	.09
❑ 125 Terrell Owens	.50	.23
❑ 126 Jerry Rice	1.25	.55
❑ 127 Steve Young	.75	.35
❑ 128 Sean Dawkins	.10	.05
❑ 129 Joey Galloway	.50	.23
❑ 130 Jon Kitna	.50	.23
❑ 131 Derrick Mayes	.20	.09
❑ 132 Ricky Watters	.20	.09
❑ 133 Mike Alstott	.50	.23
❑ 134 Reidel Anthony	.10	.05
❑ 135 Trent Dilfer	.20	.09
❑ 136 Warrick Dunn	.50	.23
❑ 137 Jacquez Green	.20	.09
❑ 138 Shaun King	.75	.35
❑ 139 Kevin Dyson	.20	.09
❑ 140 Eddie George	.60	.25
❑ 141 Jevon Kearse	.50	.23
❑ 142 Steve McNair	.50	.23
❑ 143 Yancey Thigpen	.10	.05
❑ 144 Champ Bailey	.20	.09
❑ 145 Albert Connell	.10	.05
❑ 146 Stephen Davis	.50	.23
❑ 147 Brad Johnson	.50	.23
❑ 148 Michael Westbrook	.20	.09
❑ 149 Checklist	.10	.05
❑ 150 Checklist	.10	.05
❑ 151 Sylvester Morris RC (Issued via redemption)	8.00	3.60
❑ 152 Peter Warrick RC	20.00	9.00
❑ 153 Chad Pennington RC	20.00	9.00
❑ 154 Courtney Brown RC	8.00	3.60
❑ 155 Thomas Jones RC	10.00	4.50
❑ 156 Chris Redman RC	12.00	5.50
❑ 157 R.Jay Soward RC	6.00	2.70
❑ 158 Jamal Lewis RC	30.00	13.50
❑ 159 Shaun Alexander RC	15.00	6.75
❑ 160 Travis Taylor RC	8.00	3.60
❑ 161 Ron Dayne RC	20.00	9.00
❑ 162 Travis Prentice RC	10.00	4.50
❑ 163 Plaxico Burress RC	15.00	6.75
❑ 164 J.R. Redmond RC	8.00	3.60
❑ 165 Sherrod Gideon RC	4.00	1.80
❑ 166 Dez White RC	5.00	2.20
❑ 167 Chafie Fields RC	5.00	2.20
❑ 168 Brandon Short RC (Issued via redemption)	8.00	3.60
❑ 169 Reuben Droughns RC	6.00	2.70
❑ 170 Trung Canidate RC	6.00	2.70
❑ 171 Keith Bulluck RC (Issued via redemption)	8.00	3.60

Card	MINT	NRMT
❑ 172 Doug Johnson RC (Issued via redemption)	6.00	2.70
❑ 173 Shyrone Stith RC	6.00	2.70
❑ 174 Michael Wiley RC	6.00	2.70
❑ 175 Bubba Franks RC	8.00	3.60
❑ 176 Tom Brady RC	6.00	2.70
❑ 177. Anthony Lucas RC	6.00	2.70
❑ 178 Danny Farmer RC	6.00	2.70
❑ 179 Rob Morris RC	6.00	2.70
❑ 180 Dennis Northcutt RC	8.00	3.60
❑ 181 Troy Walters RC	6.00	2.70
❑ 182 Giovanni Carmazzi RC	8.00	3.60
❑ 183 Tee Martin RC	10.00	4.50
❑ 184 Joe Hamilton RC	8.00	3.60
❑ 185 Tim Rattay RC	10.00	4.50
❑ 186 Sebastian Janikowski RC	6.00	2.70
❑ 187 Na'il Diggs RC	6.00	2.70
❑ 188 Todd Husak RC (Issued via redemption)	6.00	2.70
❑ 189 Jerry Porter RC	6.00	2.70
❑ 190 Brian Urlacher RC (Issued via redemption)	20.00	9.00
❑ 59A P.Manning AUTO/300	70.00	32.00

2000 Collector's Edge T3

	MINT	NRMT
COMP.SET w/o SP's (150)	30.00	13.50
❑ 1 David Boston	.60	.25
❑ 2 Rob Moore	.30	.14
❑ 3 Michael Pittman	.20	.09
❑ 4 Jake Plummer	.60	.25
❑ 5 Frank Sanders	.30	.14
❑ 6 Jamal Anderson	.60	.25
❑ 7 Chris Chandler	.30	.14
❑ 8 Tim Dwight	.60	.25
❑ 9 Shawn Jefferson	.20	.09
❑ 10 Terance Mathis	.30	.14
❑ 11 Tony Banks	.30	.14
❑ 12 Priest Holmes	.30	.14
❑ 13 Qadry Ismail	.20	.09
❑ 14 Shannon Sharpe	.30	.14
❑ 15 Doug Flutie	.75	.35
❑ 16 Rob Johnson	.30	.14
❑ 17 Eric Moulds	.60	.25
❑ 18 Peerless Price	.60	.25
❑ 19 Antowain Smith	.30	.14
❑ 20 Steve Beuerlein	.30	.14
❑ 21 Tim Biakabutuka	.30	.14
❑ 22 Muhsin Muhammad	.30	.14
❑ 23 Patrick Jeffers	.60	.25
❑ 24 Wesley Walls	.20	.09
❑ 25 Bobby Engram	.20	.09
❑ 26 Curtis Enis	.30	.14
❑ 27 Cade McNown	.60	.25
❑ 28 Marcus Robinson	.60	.25
❑ 29 Corey Dillon	.60	.25
❑ 30 Carl Pickens	.30	.14
❑ 31 Darnay Scott	.30	.14
❑ 32 Akili Smith	.60	.25
❑ 33 Tim Couch	1.25	.55
❑ 34 Kevin Johnson	.60	.25
❑ 35 Errict Rhett	.30	.14
❑ 36 Troy Aikman	1.50	.70
❑ 37 Joey Galloway	.60	.25
❑ 38 Rocket Ismail	.30	.14
❑ 39 Emmitt Smith	1.50	.70
❑ 40 Chris Warren	.20	.09
❑ 41 Terrell Davis	1.50	.70
❑ 42 Olandis Gary	.60	.25
❑ 43 Brian Griese	.75	.35
❑ 44 Ed McCaffrey	.60	.25
❑ 45 Rod Smith	.30	.14
❑ 46 Charlie Batch	.60	.25
❑ 47 Germane Crowell	.30	.14
❑ 48 Sedrick Irvin	.20	.09
❑ 49 Herman Moore	.30	.14
❑ 50 Johnnie Morton	.30	.14
❑ 51 James Stewart	.30	.14
❑ 52 Brett Favre	2.50	1.10
❑ 53 Antonio Freeman	.60	.25
❑ 54 Dorsey Levens	.30	.14
❑ 55 Bill Schroeder	.30	.14
❑ 56 Ken Dilger	.20	.09
❑ 57 Marvin Harrison	.60	.25
❑ 58 Edgerrin James	2.50	1.10
❑ 59 Peyton Manning	2.00	.90
❑ 60 Terrence Wilkins	.60	.25
❑ 61 Mark Brunell	1.00	.45
❑ 62 Keenan McCardell	.30	.14
❑ 63 Jimmy Smith	.30	.14
❑ 64 Fred Taylor	.75	.35
❑ 65 Derrick Alexander	.30	.14
❑ 66 Donnell Bennett	.20	.09
❑ 67 Mike Cloud	.20	.09
❑ 68 Tony Gonzalez	.30	.14
❑ 69 Elvis Grbac	.30	.14
❑ 70 Tony Richardson RC	.30	.14
❑ 71 Damon Huard	.60	.25
❑ 72 James Johnson	.30	.14
❑ 73 Rob Konrad	.20	.09
❑ 74 Tony Martin	.30	.14
❑ 75 O.J. McDuffie	.30	.14
❑ 76 Cris Carter	.60	.25
❑ 77 Daunte Culpepper	1.25	.55
❑ 78 Randy Moss	2.00	.90
❑ 79 Robert Smith	.60	.25
❑ 80 Drew Bledsoe	1.00	.45
❑ 81 Kevin Faulk	.30	.14
❑ 82 Terry Glenn	.30	.14
❑ 83 Willie McGinest	.20	.09
❑ 84 Tony Simmons	.20	.09
❑ 85 Jeff Blake	.30	.14
❑ 86 Jake Reed	.30	.14
❑ 87 Ricky Williams	1.50	.70
❑ 88 Kerry Collins	.30	.14
❑ 89 Ike Hilliard	.30	.14
❑ 90 Joe Montgomery	.20	.09
❑ 91 Amani Toomer	.20	.09
❑ 92 Wayne Chrebet	.30	.14
❑ 93 Ray Lucas	.60	.25
❑ 94 Curtis Martin	.60	.25
❑ 95 Vinny Testaverde	.30	.14
❑ 96 Tim Brown	.60	.25
❑ 97 Rich Gannon	.30	.14
❑ 98 James Jett	.20	.09
❑ 99 Napoleon Kaufman	.30	.14
❑ 100 Tyrone Wheatley	.30	.14
❑ 101 Charles Woodson	.30	.14
❑ 102 Charles Johnson	.30	.14
❑ 103 Donovan McNabb	1.00	.45
❑ 104 Duce Staley	.60	.25
❑ 105 Jerome Bettis	.60	.25
❑ 106 Troy Edwards	.30	.14
❑ 107 Kent Graham	.20	.09
❑ 108 Kordell Stewart	.60	.25
❑ 109 Hines Ward	.20	.09
❑ 110 Isaac Bruce	.60	.25
❑ 111 Kevin Carter	.20	.09
❑ 112 Marshall Faulk	.75	.35
❑ 113 Trent Green	.20	.09
❑ 114 Az-Zahir Hakim	.30	.14
❑ 115 Torry Holt	.60	.25
❑ 116 Kurt Warner	2.50	1.10
❑ 117 Curtis Conway	.30	.14
❑ 118 Jermaine Fazande	.20	.09
❑ 119 Jeff Graham	.20	.09
❑ 120 Jim Harbaugh	.30	.14
❑ 121 Junior Seau	.30	.14
❑ 122 Jeff Garcia	.60	.25
❑ 123 Charlie Garner	.30	.14
❑ 124 Garrison Hearst	.30	.14
❑ 125 Terrell Owens	.60	.25
❑ 126 Jerry Rice	1.50	.70
❑ 127 Steve Young	1.00	.45
❑ 128 Sean Dawkins	.20	.09
❑ 129 Jon Kitna	.60	.25
❑ 130 Derrick Mayes	.30	.14
❑ 131 Ricky Watters	.30	.14
❑ 132 Mike Alstott	.60	.25
❑ 133 Warrick Dunn	.60	.25
❑ 134 Jacquez Green	.30	.14
❑ 135 Keyshawn Johnson	.60	.25
❑ 136 Shaun King	1.00	.45
❑ 137 Warren Sapp	.30	.14
❑ 138 Kevin Dyson	.30	.14
❑ 139 Eddie George	.75	.35
❑ 140 Jevon Kearse	.60	.25
❑ 141 Steve McNair	.60	.25
❑ 142 Yancey Thigpen	.20	.09
❑ 143 Frank Wycheck	.20	.09
❑ 144 Champ Bailey	.30	.14
❑ 145 Larry Centers	.20	.09
❑ 146 Albert Connell	.20	.09
❑ 147 Stephen Davis	.60	.25
❑ 148 Jeff George	.30	.14
❑ 149 Brad Johnson	.60	.25
❑ 150 Michael Westbrook	.30	.14
❑ 151 Thomas Jones RC	25.00	11.00
❑ 152 Doug Johnson RC	15.00	6.75
❑ 153 Mareno Philyaw RC	8.00	3.60
❑ 154 Jamal Lewis RC	80.00	36.00
❑ 155 Chris Redman RC	30.00	13.50
❑ 156 Travis Taylor RC	20.00	9.00
❑ 157 Kwame Cavil RC	12.00	5.50
❑ 158 Sammy Morris RC	20.00	9.00
❑ 159 Deon Grant RC	8.00	3.60
❑ 160 Frank Murphy RC	8.00	3.60
❑ 161 Brian Urlacher RC	50.00	22.00
❑ 162 Dez White RC	12.00	5.50
❑ 163 Ron Dugans RC	12.00	5.50
❑ 164 Curtis Keaton RC	12.00	5.50
❑ 165 Peter Warrick RC	50.00	22.00
❑ 166 Courtney Brown RC	20.00	9.00
❑ 167 JaJuan Dawson RC	15.00	6.75
❑ 168 Dennis Northcutt RC	20.00	9.00
❑ 169 Travis Prentice RC	25.00	11.00
❑ 170 Michael Wiley RC	15.00	6.75
❑ 171 Mike Anderson RC	80.00	36.00
❑ 172 Chris Cole RC	12.00	5.50
❑ 173 Jarious Jackson RC	15.00	6.75
❑ 174 Deltha O'Neal RC	12.00	5.50
❑ 175 Reuben Droughns RC	15.00	6.75
❑ 176 Na'il Diggs RC	15.00	6.75
❑ 177 Bubba Franks RC	20.00	9.00
❑ 178 Anthony Lucas RC	8.00	3.60
❑ 179 Rondell Mealey RC	8.00	3.60
❑ 180 Dan Kendra RC	8.00	3.60
❑ 181 Rob Morris RC	15.00	6.75
❑ 182 R.Jay Soward RC	15.00	6.75
❑ 183 Shyrone Stith RC	15.00	6.75
❑ 184 William Bartee RC	12.00	5.50
❑ 185 Frank Moreau RC	15.00	6.75
❑ 186 Sylvester Morris RC	30.00	13.50
❑ 187 Deon Dyer RC	12.00	5.50
❑ 188 Quinton Spotwood RC	8.00	3.60
❑ 189 Doug Chapman RC	30.00	13.50
❑ 190 Troy Walters RC	15.00	6.75
❑ 191 J.R. Redmond RC	20.00	9.00
❑ 192 Marc Bulger RC	15.00	6.75
❑ 193 Sherrod Gideon RC	8.00	3.60
❑ 194 Darren Howard RC	12.00	5.50
❑ 195 Chad Morton RC	15.00	6.75
❑ 196 Terrelle Smith RC	12.00	5.50
❑ 197 Ron Dayne RC	50.00	22.00
❑ 198 John Abraham RC	12.00	5.50
❑ 199 Anthony Becht RC	15.00	6.75
❑ 200 Laveranues Coles RC	25.00	11.00
❑ 201 Shaun Ellis RC	12.00	5.50
❑ 202 Chad Pennington RC	40.00	18.00
❑ 203 Sebastian Janikowski RC	15.00	6.75
❑ 204 Jerry Porter RC	15.00	6.75
❑ 205 Todd Pinkston RC	15.00	6.75
❑ 206 Corey Simon RC	20.00	9.00
❑ 207 Plaxico Burress RC	30.00	13.50
❑ 208 Danny Farmer RC	15.00	6.75
❑ 209 Tee Martin RC	25.00	11.00
❑ 210 Hank Poteat RC	12.00	5.50

No.	Player	MINT	NRMT
211	Trung Canidate RC	15.00	6.75
212	Jacoby Shepherd RC	12.00	5.50
213	Trevor Gaylor RC	12.00	5.50
214	Giovanni Carmazzi RC	20.00	9.00
215	John Engelberger RC	12.00	5.50
216	Chafie Fields RC	12.00	5.50
217	Julian Peterson RC	12.00	5.50
218	Ahmed Plummer RC	15.00	6.75
219	Tim Rattay RC	25.00	11.00
220	Shaun Alexander RC	40.00	18.00
221	Joe Hamilton RC	20.00	9.00
222	Keith Bulluck RC	12.00	5.50
223	Erron Kinney RC	15.00	6.75
224	Todd Husak RC	15.00	6.75
225	Chris Samuels RC	12.00	5.50

1999 Collector's Edge Triumph

		MINT	NRMT
	COMPLETE SET (180)	60.00	27.00
1	Jamal Anderson	.60	.25
2	Jerome Bettis	.60	.25
3	Terrell Davis	1.50	.70
4	Corey Dillon	.60	.25
5	Warrick Dunn	.60	.25
6	Marshall Faulk	.60	.25
7	Eddie George	.75	.35
8	Garrison Hearst	.30	.14
9	Skip Hicks	.60	.25
10	Napoleon Kaufman	.60	.25
11	Dorsey Levens	.60	.25
12	Curtis Martin	.60	.25
13	Natrone Means	.30	.14
14	Adrian Murrell	.30	.14
15	Barry Sanders	2.50	1.10
16	Antowain Smith	.60	.25
17	Emmitt Smith	1.50	.70
18	Robert Smith	.60	.25
19	Fred Taylor	1.50	.70
20	Ricky Watters	.30	.14
21	Cameron Cleeland	.15	.07
22	Ben Coates	.30	.14
23	Shannon Sharpe	.30	.14
24	Frank Wycheck	.15	.07
25	Derrick Alexander WR	.30	.14
26	Reidel Anthony	.30	.14
27	Robert Brooks	.30	.14
28	Tim Brown	.60	.25
29	Cris Carter	.60	.25
30	Wayne Chrebet	.30	.14
31	Curtis Conway	.30	.14
32	Tim Dwight	.60	.25
33	Kevin Dyson	.30	.14
34	Antonio Freeman	.60	.25
35	Joey Galloway	.60	.25
36	Terry Glenn	.60	.25
37	Marvin Harrison	.60	.25
38	Ike Hilliard	.15	.07
39	Michael Irvin	.30	.14
40	Keyshawn Johnson	.60	.25
41	Jermaine Lewis	.30	.14
42	Terance Mathis	.30	.14
43	Ed McCaffrey	.30	.14
44	Keenan McCardell	.30	.14
45	O.J. McDuffie	.30	.14
46	Herman Moore	.60	.25
47	Rob Moore	.30	.14
48	Randy Moss	2.50	1.10
49	Eric Moulds	.60	.25
50	Muhsin Muhammad	.30	.14
51	Terrell Owens	.60	.25
52	Jerome Pathon	.15	.07
53	Carl Pickens	.30	.14
54	Andre Reed	.30	.14
55	Jake Reed	.30	.14
56	Jerry Rice	1.50	.70
57	Andre Rison	.30	.14
58	Jimmy Smith	.30	.14
59	Rod Smith WR	.30	.14
60	Michael Westbrook	.30	.14
61	Morten Andersen	.15	.07
62	Gary Anderson	.15	.07
63	Doug Brien	.15	.07
64	Chris Boniol	.15	.07
65	John Carney	.15	.07
66	Steve Christie	.15	.07
67	Richie Cunningham	.15	.07
68	Brad Daluiso	.15	.07
69	AL Del Greco	.15	.07
70	Jason Elam	.15	.07
71	John Hall	.15	.07
72	Jason Hanson	.15	.07
73	Mike Hollis	.15	.07
74	Norm Johnson	.15	.07
75	Olindo Mare	.15	.07
76	Doug Pelfrey	.15	.07
77	Wade Richey	.15	.07
78	Pete Stoyanovich	.15	.07
79	Mike Vanderjagt	.15	.07
80	Adam Vinatieri	.15	.07
81	Ray Buchanan	.15	.07
82	Jim Flanigan	.15	.07
83	Darrell Green	.15	.07
84	Kevin Greene	.15	.07
85	Ty Law	.15	.07
86	Ken Norton Jr.	.15	.07
87	John Randle	.30	.14
88	Bill Romanowski	.15	.07
89	Deion Sanders	.60	.25
90	Junior Seau	.30	.14
91	Michael Sinclair	.15	.07
92	Bruce Smith	.30	.14
93	Takeo Spikes	.15	.07
94	Michael Strahan	.15	.07
95	Derrick Thomas	.30	.14
96	Zach Thomas	.30	.14
97	Andre Wadsworth	.15	.07
98	Charles Woodson	.60	.25
99	Checklist Card	.15	.07
100	Checklist Card	.15	.07
101	Troy Aikman	1.50	.70
102	Tony Banks	.30	.14
103	Charlie Batch	1.25	.55
104	Steve Beuerlein	.15	.07
105	Jeff Blake	.30	.14
106	Drew Bledsoe	1.00	.45
107	Bubby Brister	.15	.07
108	Mark Brunell	1.00	.45
109	Chris Chandler	.30	.14
110	Kerry Collins	.30	.14
111	Randall Cunningham	.60	.25
112	Koy Detmer	.15	.07
113	Ty Detmer	.15	.07
114	Trent Dilfer	.30	.14
115	John Elway	2.50	1.10
116	Brett Favre	2.50	1.10
117	Doug Flutie	.75	.35
118	Rich Gannon	.30	.14
119	Jeff Garcia RC	8.00	3.60
120	Jeff George	.30	.14
121	Jon Kitna	.60	.25
122	Elvis Grbac	.30	.14
123	Brian Griese	1.25	.55
124	Trent Green	.30	.14
125	Jim Harbaugh	.30	.14
126	Billy Joe Hobert	.15	.07
127	Brad Johnson	.60	.25
128	Rob Johnson	.30	.14
129	Jon Kitna	.60	.25
130	Erik Kramer	.15	.07
131	Ryan Leaf	.60	.25
132	Peyton Manning	2.50	1.10
133	Dan Marino	2.50	1.10
134	Steve McNair	.60	.25
135	Scott Mitchell	.15	.07
136	Warren Moon	.60	.25
137	Jake Plummer	1.25	.55
138	Kordell Stewart	.60	.25
139	Vinny Testaverde	.30	.14
140	Steve Young	1.00	.45
141	Champ Bailey RC	2.00	.90
142	Karsten Bailey RC	1.00	.45
143	D'Wayne Bates RC	1.50	.70
144	David Boston RC	3.00	1.35
145	Cuncho Brown RC	1.00	.45
146	Dat Nguyen RC	1.50	.70
147	Chris Claiborne RC	.50	.23
148	Mike Cloud RC	1.50	.70
149	Cecil Collins RC	1.50	.70
150	Tim Couch RC	5.00	2.20
151	Daunte Culpepper RC	10.00	4.50
152	Autry Denson RC	1.50	.70
153	Troy Edwards RC	2.00	.90
154	Ebenezor Ekuban RC	1.00	.45
155	Kevin Faulk RC	2.50	1.10
156	Jermaine Fazande RC	1.50	.70
157	Joe Germaine RC	1.50	.70
158	Martin Gramatica RC	.50	.23
159	Torry Holt RC	4.00	1.80
160	Brock Huard RC	2.50	1.10
161	Sedrick Irvin RC	1.50	.70
162	Edgerrin James RC	10.00	4.50
163	James Johnson RC	1.50	.70
164	Kevin Johnson RC	3.00	1.35
165	Andy Katzenmoyer RC	1.50	.70
166	Jevon Kearse RC	3.00	1.35
167	Patrick Kerney RC	.50	.23
168	Shaun King RC	3.00	1.35
169	Jim Kleinsasser RC	1.50	.70
170	Rob Konrad RC	1.50	.70
171	Chris McAlister RC	1.00	.45
172	Donovan McNabb RC	6.00	2.70
173	Cade McNown RC	2.00	.90
174	Joe Montgomery RC	1.50	.70
175	Peerless Price RC	2.00	.90
176	Akili Smith RC	3.00	1.35
177	Ricky Williams RC	6.00	2.70
178	Larry Parker RC	1.00	.45
179	Antoine Winfield RC	1.00	.45
180	Amos Zereoue RC	1.50	.70

1995 Crown Royale

		MINT	NRMT
	COMPLETE SET (144)	80.00	36.00
1	Lake Dawson	.75	.35
2	Steve Beuerlein	.40	.18
3	Jake Reed	.75	.35
4	Jim Everett	.40	.18
5	Sean Dawkins	.75	.35
6	Jeff Hostetler	.75	.35
7	Marshall Faulk	2.50	1.10
8	Jeff Blake RC	4.00	1.80
9	Dave Brown	.75	.35
10	Frank Reich	.40	.18
11	Rocket Ismail	.75	.35
12	Jerry Jones OWN UER (Built is spelled bulit)	1.50	.70
13	Dan Marino	8.00	3.60

❑ 14 Ricky Watters 1.50 .70
❑ 15 Herman Moore 1.50 .70
❑ 16 Daryl Johnston .75 .35
❑ 17 Craig Erickson .40 .18
❑ 18 Alexander Wright .40 .18
❑ 19 Reggie White 1.50 .70
❑ 20 Andre Rison .75 .35
❑ 21 Fred Barnett .75 .35
❑ 22 Tyrone Wheatley RC 5.00 2.20
❑ 23 Charles Johnson .75 .35
❑ 24 Rashaan Salaam RC 1.50 .70
❑ 25 Mark Brunell 4.00 1.80
❑ 26 Derek Loville .40 .18
❑ 27 Garrison Hearst 1.50 .70
❑ 28 Ken Norton Jr. .75 .35
❑ 29 Kerry Collins RC 6.00 2.70
❑ 30 Isaac Bruce 2.50 1.10
❑ 31 Andre Reed .75 .35
❑ 32 Leon Lett .40 .18
❑ 33 Deion Sanders 2.50 1.10
❑ 34 Terance Mathis .75 .35
❑ 35 Tim Bowens .40 .18
❑ 36 Shannon Sharpe .75 .35
❑ 37 Quinn Early .75 .35
❑ 38 Jerry Rice 4.00 1.80
❑ 39 Bruce Smith 1.50 .70
❑ 40 Drew Bledsoe 4.00 1.80
❑ 41 Alvin Harper .40 .18
❑ 42 Jim Kelly 1.50 .70
❑ 43 Napoleon Kaufman RC 6.00 2.70
❑ 44 Errict Rhett 1.50 .70
❑ 45 Henry Ellard .75 .35
❑ 46 Barry Sanders 8.00 3.60
❑ 47 Vincent Brisby .40 .18
❑ 48 Chris Zorich .40 .18
❑ 49 Zack Crockett RC .40 .18
❑ 50 Haywood Jeffires .40 .18
❑ 51 Byron Bam Morris .75 .35
❑ 52 John Kasay .40 .18
❑ 53 Scott Mitchell .75 .35
❑ 54 Boomer Esiason .75 .35
❑ 55 Eric Metcalf .75 .35
❑ 56 Kevin Greene .75 .35
❑ 57 Courtney Hawkins .40 .18
❑ 58 Johnny Johnson .40 .18
❑ 59 Larry Centers .75 .35
❑ 60 Leroy Hoard .40 .18
❑ 61 Lorenzo White .40 .18
❑ 62 Chris Spielman .75 .35
❑ 63 Carl Pickens 1.50 .70
❑ 64 Steve Young 3.00 1.35
❑ 65 Trent Dilfer 1.50 .70
❑ 66 Erik Kramer .40 .18
❑ 67 Cortez Kennedy .75 .35
❑ 68 Ray Childress .40 .18
❑ 69 Rick Mirer 1.50 .70
❑ 70 Kevin Williams WR .75 .35
❑ 71 Joey Galloway RC 8.00 3.60
❑ 72 Dan Wilkinson .75 .35
❑ 73 Antonio Freeman RC 10.00 4.50
❑ 74 Curtis Conway 1.50 .70
❑ 75 Troy Aikman 4.00 1.80
❑ 76 Natrone Means 1.50 .70
❑ 77 Jeff George .75 .35
❑ 78 Curtis Martin RC 10.00 4.50
❑ 79 William Floyd 1.50 .70
❑ 80 Anthony Miller .75 .35
❑ 81 Greg Hill .75 .35
❑ 82 Craig Heyward .75 .35
❑ 83 Brian Mitchell .40 .18
❑ 84 Anthony Carter .75 .35
❑ 85 Jerome Bettis 1.50 .70
❑ 86 Jim Harbaugh .75 .35
❑ 87 Harvey Williams .40 .18
❑ 88 Tony Martin .75 .35
❑ 89 Rob Moore .40 .18
❑ 90 Neil O'Donnell .75 .35
❑ 91 Cris Carter 1.50 .70
❑ 92 Warren Sapp RC 3.00 1.35
❑ 93 Terry Allen .75 .35
❑ 94 Michael Irvin 1.50 .70
❑ 95 Heath Shuler 1.50 .70
❑ 96 Cornelius Bennett .75 .35
❑ 97 Randy Baldwin .40 .18
❑ 98 Vince Workman .40 .18
❑ 99 Irving Fryar .75 .35
❑ 100 Randall Cunningham 1.50 .70
❑ 101 James O. Stewart RC 8.00 3.60
❑ 102 Stan Humphries .75 .35
❑ 103 Mario Bates 1.50 .70
❑ 104 Ben Coates .75 .35
❑ 105 Charlie Garner .75 .35
❑ 106 Todd Collins RC 1.50 .70
❑ 107 Tim Brown 1.50 .70
❑ 108 Edgar Bennett .75 .35
❑ 109 J.J. Stokes RC 1.50 .70
❑ 110 Michael Timpson .40 .18
❑ 111 Junior Seau 1.50 .70
❑ 112 Bernie Parmalee .75 .35
❑ 113 Willie McGinest .75 .35
❑ 114 David Dunn RC .40 .18
❑ 115 Kyle Brady RC 1.50 .70
❑ 116 Vinny Testaverde .75 .35
❑ 117 Ernest Givins .40 .18
❑ 118 Eric Zeier RC 1.50 .70
❑ 119 Michael Jackson .75 .35
❑ 120 Chad May RC .40 .18
❑ 121 Dave Krieg .40 .18
❑ 122 Rodney Hampton .75 .35
❑ 123 Darnay Scott 1.50 .70
❑ 124 Chris Miller .40 .18
❑ 125 Emmitt Smith 6.00 2.70
❑ 126 Steve McNair RC 10.00 4.50
❑ 127 Warren Moon .75 .35
❑ 128 Robert Brooks 1.50 .70
❑ 129 Bert Emanuel 1.50 .70
❑ 130 John Elway 8.00 3.60
❑ 131 Chris Warren .75 .35
❑ 132 Herschel Walker .75 .35
❑ 133 Terry Kirby .75 .35
❑ 134 Michael Westbrook RC 6.00 2.70
❑ 135 Kordell Stewart RC 8.00 3.60
❑ 136 Terrell Davis RC 15.00 6.75
❑ 137 Desmond Howard .75 .35
❑ 138 Rodney Thomas RC 1.50 .70
❑ 139 Brett Favre 8.00 3.60
❑ 140 Ray Zellars RC .75 .35
❑ 141 Marcus Allen 1.50 .70
❑ 142 Gus Frerotte 1.50 .70
❑ 143 Steve Bono .75 .35
❑ 144 Aaron Craver .40 .18
❑ P144 Natrone Means Promo 2.00 .90
Jumbo card 7" by 9 3/4"

1996 Crown Royale

	MINT	NRMT
COMPLETE SET (144)	80.00	36.00

❑ 1 Dan Marino 10.00 4.50
❑ 2 Frank Sanders 1.00 .45
❑ 3 Bobby Engram RC 2.00 .90
❑ 4 Cornelius Bennett .60 .25
❑ 5 Steve Bono .60 .25
❑ 6 Aaron Hayden RC .60 .25
❑ 7 Leroy Hoard .60 .25
❑ 8 Brett Perriman .60 .25
❑ 9 Irv Smith .60 .25
❑ 10 Jim Kelly 2.00 .90
❑ 11 Rodney Thomas .60 .25
❑ 12 Eric Bieniemy .60 .25
❑ 13 Darnay Scott 1.00 .45
❑ 14 Ki-Jana Carter 1.00 .45
❑ 15 Kerry Collins 2.00 .90
❑ 16 Shannon Sharpe 1.00 .45
❑ 17 Michael Westbrook 2.00 .90
❑ 18 Steve McNair 4.00 1.80
❑ 19 Tony Banks RC 6.00 2.70
❑ 20 Rashaan Salaam 2.00 .90
❑ 21 Terrell Fletcher .60 .25
❑ 22 Michael Timpson .60 .25
❑ 23 Bobby Hoying RC 2.50 1.10
❑ 24 Quinn Early .60 .25
❑ 25 Warren Moon 1.00 .45
❑ 26 Tommy Vardell .60 .25
❑ 27 Marvin Harrison RC 12.00 5.50
❑ 28 Lake Dawson .60 .25
❑ 29 Karim Abdul-Jabbar RC 3.00 1.35
❑ 30 Chris Warren 1.00 .45
❑ 31 Heath Shuler 1.00 .45
❑ 32 Bert Emanuel 1.00 .45
❑ 33 Howard Griffith RC .60 .25
❑ 34 Alex Van Dyke RC 1.00 .45
❑ 35 Isaac Bruce 2.00 .90
❑ 36 Mark Brunell 5.00 2.20
❑ 37 Winslow Oliver RC .60 .25
❑ 38 O.J. McDuffie 1.00 .45
❑ 39 Terrell Owens RC 12.00 5.50
❑ 40 Jerry Rice 5.00 2.20
❑ 41 Henry Ellard .60 .25
❑ 42 Chris Sanders 1.00 .45
❑ 43 Craig Heyward .60 .25
❑ 44 Eddie Kennison RC 2.00 .90
❑ 45 Terrell Davis 10.00 4.50
❑ 46 Rodney Hampton 1.00 .45
❑ 47 Bryan Still RC 2.00 .90
❑ 48 Tim Brown 2.00 .90
❑ 49 Keyshawn Johnson RC 10.00 4.50
❑ 50 Barry Sanders 10.00 4.50
❑ 51 Terry Allen 1.00 .45
❑ 52 Sean Dawkins .60 .25
❑ 53 Bryce Paup .60 .25
❑ 54 Brett Favre 10.00 4.50
❑ 55 Deion Sanders 3.00 1.35
❑ 56 Kevin Hardy RC 2.00 .90
❑ 57 Kevin Williams .60 .25
❑ 58 Jeff George 1.00 .45
❑ 59 Tim Biakabutuka RC 5.00 2.20
❑ 60 Drew Bledsoe 5.00 2.20
❑ 61 Michael Jackson 1.00 .45
❑ 62 James O. Stewart 1.00 .45
❑ 63 Mario Bates 1.00 .45
❑ 64 Daryl Johnston 1.00 .45
❑ 65 Herman Moore 2.00 .90
❑ 66 Ben Coates 1.00 .45
❑ 67 Terry Glenn RC 6.00 2.70
❑ 68 Robert Smith 1.00 .45
❑ 69 Irving Fryar 1.00 .45
❑ 70 Napoleon Kaufman 2.00 .90
❑ 71 Rickey Dudley RC 2.00 .90
❑ 72 Bernie Parmalee .60 .25
❑ 73 Kyle Brady .60 .25
❑ 74 Neil O'Donnell 1.00 .45
❑ 75 Lawrence Phillips RC 2.00 .90
❑ 76 Hardy Nickerson .60 .25
❑ 77 John Elway 10.00 4.50
❑ 78 Pete Mitchell 1.00 .45
❑ 79 Jason Dunn RC 1.00 .45
❑ 80 Reggie White 2.00 .90
❑ 81 J.J. Stokes 2.00 .90
❑ 82 Jake Reed 1.00 .45
❑ 83 Yancey Thigpen 1.00 .45
❑ 84 Jonathan Ogden RC .60 .25
❑ 85 Larry Centers 1.00 .45
❑ 86 Scott Mitchell 1.00 .45
❑ 87 Eric Zeier .60 .25
❑ 88 Anthony Miller 1.00 .45
❑ 89 Brian Blades .60 .25
❑ 90 Cris Carter 2.00 .90
❑ 91 Kordell Stewart 3.00 1.35
❑ 92 Charles Way RC 2.00 .90
❑ 93 Jeff Hostetler .60 .25
❑ 94 Brad Johnson 5.00 2.20
❑ 95 Marcus Allen 2.00 .90
❑ 96 Errict Rhett 1.00 .45
❑ 97 Stan Humphries 1.00 .45
❑ 98 Michael Haynes .60 .25
❑ 99 Curtis Martin 4.00 1.80
❑ 100 Troy Aikman 5.00 2.20
❑ 101 Earnest Byner .60 .25

❑ 102 Vincent Brisby .60 .25
❑ 103 Zack Crockett .60 .25
❑ 104 Haywood Jeffires .60 .25
❑ 105 Joey Galloway 3.00 1.35
❑ 106 Carl Pickens 2.00 .90
❑ 107 Leeland McElroy RC 2.00 .90
❑ 108 Adrian Murrell 2.00 .90
❑ 109 Joe Horn RC/C 12.00 5.50
❑ 110 Steve Young 4.00 1.80
❑ 111 Andre Rison 1.00 .45
❑ 112 Jim Everett .60 .25
❑ 113 Jamie Asher RC 1.00 .45
❑ 114 Steve Walsh .60 .25
❑ 115 Robert Brooks 2.00 .90
❑ 116 Eric Moulds RC 8.00 3.60
❑ 117 Edgar Bennett 1.00 .45
❑ 118 Greg Lloyd 1.00 .45
❑ 119 Jerris McPhail RC .60 .25
❑ 120 Marshall Faulk 2.00 .90
❑ 121 Dave Brown .60 .25
❑ 122 Harvey Williams .60 .25
❑ 123 Trent Dilfer 2.00 .90
❑ 124 Eddie George RC 15.00 6.75
❑ 125 Jeff Blake 2.00 .90
❑ 126 Mark Chmura 1.00 .45
❑ 127 Boomer Esiason 1.00 .45
❑ 128 Jim Harbaugh 1.00 .45
❑ 129 Bryan Cox .60 .25
❑ 130 Ricky Watters 1.00 .45
❑ 131 Amani Toomer RC 6.00 2.70
❑ 132 Jim Miller .60 .25
❑ 133 Cortez Kennedy .60 .25
❑ 134 Courtney Hawkins .60 .25
❑ 135 Junior Seau 1.00 .45
❑ 136 Tamarick Vanover 1.00 .45
❑ 137 Jerome Bettis 2.00 .90
❑ 138 Chris Calloway .60 .25
❑ 139 Rick Mirer 1.00 .45
❑ 140 Thurman Thomas 2.00 .90
❑ 141 Sheddrick Wilson RC .60 .25
❑ 142 Charlie Garner .60 .25
❑ 143 Erik Kramer .60 .25
❑ 144 Emmitt Smith 8.00 3.60

1997 Crown Royale

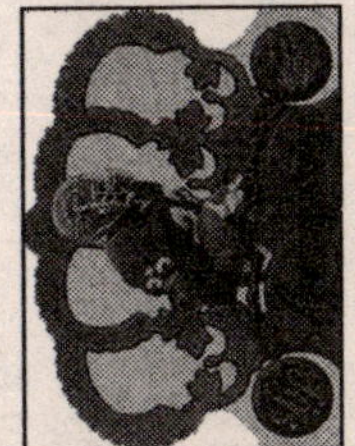

	MINT	NRMT
COMPLETE SET (144)	150.00	70.00

❑ 1 Larry Centers .75 .35
❑ 2 Kent Graham .50 .23
❑ 3 LeShon Johnson .50 .23
❑ 4 Leeland McElroy .50 .23
❑ 5 Jake Plummer RC 12.00 5.50
❑ 6 Jamal Anderson 2.50 1.10
❑ 7 Chris Chandler .75 .35
❑ 8 Byron Hanspard RC 1.50 .70
❑ 9 O.J. Santiago RC 1.50 .70
❑ 10 Derrick Alexander WR .75 .35
❑ 11 Jay Graham RC 1.50 .70
❑ 12 Michael Jackson .75 .35
❑ 13 Vinny Testaverde .75 .35
❑ 14 Todd Collins .50 .23
❑ 15 Jay Riemersma RC .50 .23
❑ 16 Antowain Smith RC 5.00 2.20
❑ 17 Steve Tasker .50 .23
❑ 18 Thurman Thomas 1.50 .70
❑ 19 Rae Carruth RC 1.50 .70
❑ 20 Kerry Collins .75 .35
❑ 21 Anthony Johnson .50 .23
❑ 22 Fred Lane RC 1.50 .70
❑ 23 Muhsin Muhammad .75 .35
❑ 24 Wesley Walls .75 .35
❑ 25 Darnell Autry RC .75 .35
❑ 26 Raymont Harris .50 .23
❑ 27 Erik Kramer .50 .23
❑ 28 Rick Mirer .50 .23
❑ 29 Rashaan Salaam .50 .23
❑ 30 Jeff Blake .75 .35
❑ 31 Ki-Jana Carter .50 .23
❑ 32 Corey Dillon RC 12.00 5.50
❑ 33 Carl Pickens 1.50 .70
❑ 34 Troy Aikman 4.00 1.80
❑ 35 Michael Irvin 1.50 .70
❑ 36 Daryl Johnston .75 .35
❑ 37 David LaFleur RC 2.00 .90
❑ 38 Deion Sanders 1.50 .70
❑ 39 Emmitt Smith 6.00 2.70
❑ 40 Terrell Davis 6.00 2.70
❑ 41 John Elway 8.00 3.60
❑ 42 Ed McCaffrey .75 .35
❑ 43 Shannon Sharpe .75 .35
❑ 44 Neil Smith .75 .35
❑ 45 Scott Mitchell .75 .35
❑ 46 Herman Moore 1.50 .70
❑ 47 Johnnie Morton .75 .35
❑ 48 Barry Sanders 8.00 3.60
❑ 49 Robert Brooks .75 .35
❑ 50 Mark Chmura .75 .35
❑ 51 Brett Favre 8.00 3.60
❑ 52 Antonio Freeman 2.50 1.10
❑ 53 Dorsey Levens 1.50 .70
❑ 54 Reggie White 1.50 .70
❑ 55 Ken Dilger .50 .23
❑ 56 Marshall Faulk 1.50 .70
❑ 57 Jim Harbaugh .75 .35
❑ 58 Marvin Harrison 1.50 .70
❑ 59 Mark Brunell 4.00 1.80
❑ 60 Rob Johnson 1.50 .70
❑ 61 Keenan McCardell .75 .35
❑ 62 Natrone Means 1.50 .70
❑ 63 Jimmy Smith .75 .35
❑ 64 Marcus Allen 1.50 .70
❑ 65 Tony Gonzalez RC 6.00 2.70
❑ 66 Elvis Grbac .75 .35
❑ 67 Greg Hill .50 .23
❑ 68 Tamarick Vanover .75 .35
❑ 69 Karim Abdul-Jabbar 1.50 .70
❑ 70 Fred Barnett .50 .23
❑ 71 Dan Marino 8.00 3.60
❑ 72 O.J. McDuffie .75 .35
❑ 73 Jerris McPhail .50 .23
❑ 74 Cris Carter 1.50 .70
❑ 75 Randall Cunningham 1.50 .70
❑ 76 Brad Johnson 1.50 .70
❑ 77 Jake Reed .75 .35
❑ 78 Robert Smith .75 .35
❑ 79 Drew Bledsoe 4.00 1.80
❑ 80 Ben Coates .75 .35
❑ 81 Terry Glenn 1.50 .70
❑ 82 Curtis Martin 2.50 1.10
❑ 83 Troy Davis RC 1.50 .70
❑ 84 Heath Shuler .50 .23
❑ 85 Irv Smith .50 .23
❑ 86 Danny Wuerffel RC 2.50 1.10
❑ 87 Tiki Barber RC 6.00 2.70
❑ 88 Dave Brown .50 .23
❑ 89 Rodney Hampton .75 .35
❑ 90 Ike Hilliard RC 4.00 1.80
❑ 91 Amani Toomer .75 .35
❑ 92 Wayne Chrebet 1.50 .70
❑ 93 Keyshawn Johnson 1.50 .70
❑ 94 Adrian Murrell .75 .35
❑ 95 Neil O'Donnell .75 .35
❑ 96 Dedric Ward RC 4.00 1.80
❑ 97 Tim Brown 1.50 .70
❑ 98 Jeff George .75 .35
❑ 99 Desmond Howard .75 .35
❑ 100 Napoleon Kaufman 1.50 .70
❑ 101 Ty Detmer .75 .35
❑ 102 Irving Fryar .75 .35
❑ 103 Bobby Hoying .75 .35
❑ 104 Ricky Watters .75 .35
❑ 105 Jerome Bettis 1.50 .70
❑ 106 Will Blackwell RC 1.50 .70
❑ 107 Charles Johnson .75 .35
❑ 108 George Jones RC .75 .35
❑ 109 Kordell Stewart 2.00 .90
❑ 110 Tony Banks .75 .35
❑ 111 Isaac Bruce 1.50 .70
❑ 112 Eddie Kennison .75 .35
❑ 113 Lawrence Phillips .50 .23
❑ 114 Jim Everett .50 .23
❑ 115 Stan Humphries .75 .35
❑ 116 Freddie Jones .75 .35
❑ 117 Tony Martin .75 .35
❑ 118 Junior Seau .75 .35
❑ 119 Jim Druckenmiller RC 1.50 .70
❑ 120 Garrison Hearst .75 .35
❑ 121 Brent Jones .75 .35
❑ 122 Terrell Owens 1.50 .70
❑ 123 Jerry Rice 4.00 1.80
❑ 124 Steve Young 3.00 1.35
❑ 125 Chad Brown .50 .23
❑ 126 Joey Galloway 2.00 .90
❑ 127 Jon Kitna RC 15.00 6.75
❑ 128 Warren Moon 1.50 .70
❑ 129 Chris Warren .75 .35
❑ 130 Mike Alstott 1.50 .70
❑ 131 Reidel Anthony RC 4.00 1.80
❑ 132 Trent Dilfer 1.50 .70
❑ 133 Warrick Dunn RC 6.00 2.70
❑ 134 Karl Williams RC 1.50 .70
❑ 135 Willie Davis .50 .23
❑ 136 Eddie George 4.00 1.80
❑ 137 Joey Kent RC 1.50 .70
❑ 138 Steve McNair 2.50 1.10
❑ 139 Chris Sanders .50 .23
❑ 140 Terry Allen 1.50 .70
❑ 141 Jamie Asher .50 .23
❑ 142 Stephen Davis 4.00 1.80
❑ 143 Henry Ellard .50 .23
❑ 144 Gus Frerotte .50 .23
❑ S1 Mark Brunell Sample 1.00 .45

1998 Crown Royale

	MINT	NRMT
COMPLETE SET (144)	120.00	55.00

❑ 1 Larry Centers .40 .18
❑ 2 Rob Moore .75 .35
❑ 3 Adrian Murrell .75 .35
❑ 4 Jake Plummer 2.50 1.10
❑ 5 Jamal Anderson 1.50 .70
❑ 6 Chris Chandler .75 .35
❑ 7 Tim Dwight RC 4.00 1.80
❑ 8 Tony Martin .75 .35
❑ 9 Jay Graham .40 .18
❑ 10 Pat Johnson RC 2.50 1.10
❑ 11 Jermaine Lewis .75 .35
❑ 12 Eric Zeier .75 .35
❑ 13 Rob Johnson .75 .35
❑ 14 Eric Moulds 1.50 .70
❑ 15 Antowain Smith 1.50 .70
❑ 16 Bruce Smith .75 .35
❑ 17 Steve Beuerlein .40 .18
❑ 18 Anthony Johnson .40 .18
❑ 19 Fred Lane .75 .35
❑ 20 Muhsin Muhammad .75 .35
❑ 21 Curtis Conway .75 .35
❑ 22 Curtis Enis RC 3.00 1.35

❑ 23 Erik Kramer .40 .18
❑ 24 Tony Parrish RC 1.50 .70
❑ 25 Corey Dillon 2.50 1.10
❑ 26 Neil O'Donnell .75 .35
❑ 27 Carl Pickens 1.50 .70
❑ 28 Takeo Spikes RC 2.50 1.10
❑ 29 Troy Aikman 4.00 1.80
❑ 30 Michael Irvin 1.50 .70
❑ 31 Deion Sanders 1.50 .70
❑ 32 Emmitt Smith 6.00 2.70
❑ 33 Chris Warren .75 .35
❑ 34 Terrell Davis 6.00 2.70
❑ 35 John Elway 8.00 3.60
❑ 36 Brian Griese RC 12.00 5.50
❑ 37 Ed McCaffrey .75 .35
❑ 38 Shannon Sharpe .75 .35
❑ 39 Rod Smith WR .75 .35
❑ 40 Charlie Batch RC 10.00 4.50
❑ 41 Herman Moore 1.50 .70
❑ 42 Johnnie Morton .75 .35
❑ 43 Barry Sanders 8.00 3.60
❑ 44 Bryant Westbrook .40 .18
❑ 45 Robert Brooks .75 .35
❑ 46 Brett Favre 8.00 3.60
❑ 47 Antonio Freeman 1.50 .70
❑ 48 Raymont Harris .40 .18
❑ 49 Vonnie Holliday RC 2.50 1.10
❑ 50 Reggie White 1.50 .70
❑ 51 Marshall Faulk 1.50 .70
❑ 52 E.G. Green RC 2.50 1.10
❑ 53 Marvin Harrison .75 .35
❑ 54 Peyton Manning RC 25.00 11.00
❑ 55 Jerome Pathon RC 4.00 1.80
❑ 56 Tavian Banks RC .75 .35
❑ 57 Mark Brunell 3.00 1.35
❑ 58 Keenan McCardell .75 .35
❑ 59 Jimmy Smith .75 .35
❑ 60 Fred Taylor RC 10.00 4.50
❑ 61 Derrick Alexander WR .75 .35
❑ 62 Tony Gonzalez .40 .18
❑ 63 Elvis Grbac .75 .35
❑ 64 Andre Rison .75 .35
❑ 65 Rashaan Shehee RC 2.50 1.10
❑ 66 Derrick Thomas .75 .35
❑ 67 Karim Abdul-Jabbar 1.50 .70
❑ 68 John Avery RC 3.00 1.35
❑ 69 Oronde Gadsden RC 2.50 1.10
❑ 70 Dan Marino 8.00 3.60
❑ 71 O.J. McDuffie .75 .35
❑ 72 Cris Carter 1.50 .70
❑ 73 Randall Cunningham 1.50 .70
❑ 74 Brad Johnson 1.50 .70
❑ 75 Randy Moss RC 25.00 11.00
❑ 76 John Randle .75 .35
❑ 77 Jake Reed .75 .35
❑ 78 Robert Smith 1.50 .70
❑ 79 Drew Bledsoe 3.00 1.35
❑ 80 Robert Edwards RC 4.00 1.80
❑ 81 Terry Glenn 1.50 .70
❑ 82 Tebucky Jones RC 1.50 .70
❑ 83 Tony Simmons RC 2.50 1.10
❑ 84 Mark Fields .40 .18
❑ 85 Andre Hastings .40 .18
❑ 86 Danny Wuerffel .75 .35
❑ 87 Ray Zellars .40 .18
❑ 88 Tiki Barber .75 .35
❑ 89 Ike Hilliard .75 .35
❑ 90 Joe Jurevicius RC 2.50 1.10
❑ 91 Danny Kanell .75 .35
❑ 92 Wayne Chrebet 1.50 .70
❑ 93 Glenn Foley .75 .35
❑ 94 Keyshawn Johnson 1.50 .70
❑ 95 Leon Johnson .40 .18
❑ 96 Curtis Martin 1.50 .70
❑ 97 Tim Brown 1.50 .70
❑ 98 Jeff George .75 .35
❑ 99 Napoleon Kaufman 1.50 .70
❑ 100 Jon Ritchie RC 2.50 1.10
❑ 101 Charles Woodson RC 4.00 1.80
❑ 102 Irving Fryar .75 .35
❑ 103 Bobby Hoying .75 .35
❑ 104 Allen Rossum RC 1.50 .70
❑ 105 Duce Staley 3.00 1.35
❑ 106 Jerome Bettis 1.50 .70
❑ 107 C.Fuamatu-Ma'afala RC 2.50 1.10
❑ 108 Charles Johnson .40 .18
❑ 109 Levon Kirkland .40 .18
❑ 110 Kordell Stewart 1.50 .70
❑ 111 Hines Ward RC 2.50 1.10
❑ 112 Tony Banks .75 .35
❑ 113 Tony Horne RC 1.50 .70
❑ 114 Eddie Kennison .75 .35
❑ 115 Amp Lee .40 .18
❑ 116 Freddie Jones .40 .18
❑ 117 Ryan Leaf RC 8.00 3.60
❑ 118 Natrone Means 1.50 .70
❑ 119 Mikhael Ricks RC 2.50 1.10
❑ 120 Bryan Still .40 .18
❑ 121 Marc Edwards .40 .18
❑ 122 Garrison Hearst 1.50 .70
❑ 123 Terrell Owens 1.50 .70
❑ 124 Jerry Rice 4.00 1.80
❑ 125 J.J. Stokes .75 .35
❑ 126 Steve Young 2.50 1.10
❑ 127 Joey Galloway 1.50 .70
❑ 128 Ahman Green RC 8.00 3.60
❑ 129 Warren Moon 1.50 .70
❑ 130 Ricky Watters .75 .35
❑ 131 Mike Alstott 1.50 .70
❑ 132 Trent Dilfer 1.50 .70
❑ 133 Warrick Dunn 1.50 .70
❑ 134 Jacquez Green RC 4.00 1.80
❑ 135 Warren Sapp .75 .35
❑ 136 Kevin Dyson RC 4.00 1.80
❑ 137 Eddie George 3.00 1.35
❑ 138 Steve McNair 1.50 .70
❑ 139 Yancey Thigpen .40 .18
❑ 140 Stephen Alexander RC 2.50 1.10
❑ 141 Terry Allen 1.50 .70
❑ 142 Trent Green 2.00 .90
❑ 143 Skip Hicks RC 3.00 1.35
❑ 144 Michael Westbrook .75 .35

1999 Crown Royale

	MINT	NRMT
COMPLETE SET (144)	150.00	70.00

❑ 1 David Boston RC 8.00 3.60
❑ 2 Chris Greisen RC 3.00 1.35
❑ 3 Rob Moore .75 .35
❑ 4 Jake Plummer 3.00 1.35
❑ 5 Frank Sanders .75 .35
❑ 6 Jamal Anderson 1.50 .70
❑ 7 Chris Chandler .75 .35
❑ 8 Tim Dwight 1.50 .70
❑ 9 Byron Hanspard .75 .35
❑ 10 Stoney Case .40 .18
❑ 11 Priest Holmes 1.50 .70
❑ 12 Jermaine Lewis .75 .35
❑ 13 Chris McAlister RC 3.00 1.35
❑ 14 Brandon Stokley RC 4.00 1.80
❑ 15 Doug Flutie 2.00 .90
❑ 16 Eric Moulds 1.50 .70
❑ 17 Peerless Price RC 5.00 2.20
❑ 18 Antowain Smith 1.50 .70
❑ 19 Steve Beuerlein .40 .18
❑ 20 Tim Biakabutuka .75 .35
❑ 21 Muhsin Muhammad .75 .35
❑ 22 Curtis Conway .75 .35
❑ 23 Curtis Enis 1.50 .70
❑ 24 Shane Matthews .75 .35
❑ 25 Cade McNown RC 5.00 2.20
❑ 26 Marcus Robinson 3.00 1.35
❑ 27 Jeff Blake .75 .35
❑ 28 Scott Covington RC 4.00 1.80
❑ 29 Corey Dillon 1.50 .70
❑ 30 Damon Griffin RC 3.00 1.35
❑ 31 Carl Pickens .75 .35
❑ 32 Akili Smith RC 8.00 3.60
❑ 33 Tim Couch RC 12.00 5.50
❑ 34 Kevin Johnson RC 8.00 3.60
❑ 35 Terry Kirby .40 .18
❑ 36 Leslie Shepherd .40 .18
❑ 37 Troy Aikman 4.00 1.80
❑ 38 Rocket Ismail .40 .18
❑ 39 Wane McGarity RC 3.00 1.35
❑ 40 Deion Sanders 1.50 .70
❑ 41 Emmitt Smith 4.00 1.80
❑ 42 Terrell Davis 4.00 1.80
❑ 43 Brian Griese 3.00 1.35
❑ 44 Ed McCaffrey .75 .35
❑ 45 Shannon Sharpe .75 .35
❑ 46 Rod Smith .75 .35
❑ 47 Charlie Batch 3.00 1.35
❑ 48 Germane Crowell .75 .35
❑ 49 Sedrick Irvin RC 4.00 1.80
❑ 50 Herman Moore 1.50 .70
❑ 51 Barry Sanders 6.00 2.70
❑ 52 Brett Favre 6.00 2.70
❑ 53 Antonio Freeman 1.50 .70
❑ 54 Matt Hasselbeck 2.00 .90
❑ 55 Dorsey Levens 1.50 .70
❑ 56 Basil Mitchell RC 3.00 1.35
❑ 57 E.G. Green .40 .18
❑ 58 Marvin Harrison 1.50 .70
❑ 59 Edgerrin James RC 20.00 9.00
❑ 60 Peyton Manning 6.00 2.70
❑ 61 Terrence Wilkins RC 10.00 4.50
❑ 62 Mark Brunell 2.50 1.10
❑ 63 Keenan McCardell .75 .35
❑ 64 Jimmy Smith .75 .35
❑ 65 Fred Taylor 4.00 1.80
❑ 66 Derrick Alexander WR .75 .35
❑ 67 Elvis Grbac .75 .35
❑ 68 Warren Moon .40 .18
❑ 69 Larry Parker RC 3.00 1.35
❑ 70 Andre Rison .75 .35
❑ 71 Cecil Collins RC 3.00 1.35
❑ 72 Damon Huard 4.00 1.80
❑ 73 James Johnson RC 4.00 1.80
❑ 74 Rob Konrad RC 3.00 1.35
❑ 75 Dan Marino 6.00 2.70
❑ 76 O.J. McDuffie .75 .35
❑ 77 Cris Carter 1.50 .70
❑ 78 Daunte Culpepper RC 20.00 9.00
❑ 79 Randall Cunningham 1.50 .70
❑ 80 Randy Moss UER 6.00 2.70
(card actually #81)
❑ 81 Robert Smith .40 .18
❑ 82 Michael Bishop RC 5.00 2.20
❑ 83 Drew Bledsoe 2.50 1.10
❑ 84 Ben Coates .75 .35
❑ 85 Kevin Faulk RC 6.00 2.70
❑ 86 Terry Glenn 1.50 .70
❑ 87 Billy Joe Hobert .40 .18
❑ 88 Eddie Kennison .75 .35
❑ 89 Keith Poole .40 .18
❑ 90 Ricky Williams RC 12.00 5.50
❑ 91 Sean Bennett RC 3.00 1.35
❑ 92 Kerry Collins .75 .35
❑ 93 Pete Mitchell .40 .18
❑ 94 Amani Toomer .40 .18
❑ 95 Wayne Chrebet .75 .35
❑ 96 Keyshawn Johnson 1.50 .70
❑ 97 Curtis Martin 1.50 .70
❑ 98 Tim Brown 1.50 .70
❑ 99 Scott Dreisbach RC 3.00 1.35
❑ 100 Rich Gannon .75 .35
❑ 101 Napoleon Kaufman 1.50 .70
❑ 102 Tyrone Wheatley .75 .35
❑ 103 Duce Staley 1.50 .70
❑ 104 Charles Johnson .40 .18
❑ 105 Donovan McNabb RC 12.00 5.50
❑ 106 Torrance Small .40 .18
❑ 107 Jed Weaver RC 3.00 1.35
❑ 108 Jerome Bettis 1.50 .70
❑ 109 Troy Edwards RC 5.00 2.20
❑ 110 Kordell Stewart 1.50 .70
❑ 111 Amos Zereoue RC 4.00 1.80

	Card	MINT	NRMT
❑	112 Isaac Bruce	1.50	.70
❑	113 Marshall Faulk	1.50	.70
❑	114 Joe Germaine RC	4.00	1.80
❑	115 Torry Holt RC	10.00	4.50
❑	116 Kurt Warner RC	25.00	11.00
❑	117 Jim Harbaugh	.75	.35
❑	118 Erik Kramer	.40	.18
❑	119 Natrone Means	.75	.35
❑	120 Junior Seau	.75	.35
❑	121 Jeff Garcia RC	15.00	6.75
❑	122 Terrell Owens	1.50	.70
❑	123 Jerry Rice	4.00	1.80
❑	124 J.J. Stokes	.75	.35
❑	125 Steve Young	2.50	1.10
❑	126 Sean Dawkins	.40	.18
❑	127 Brock Huard RC	6.00	2.70
❑	128 Jon Kitna	1.50	.70
❑	129 Derrick Mayes	.75	.35
❑	130 Charlie Rogers RC	3.00	1.35
❑	131 Ricky Watters	.75	.35
❑	132 Mike Alstott	1.50	.70
❑	133 Trent Dilfer	.75	.35
❑	134 Warrick Dunn	1.50	.70
❑	135 Eric Zeier	.75	.35
❑	136 Kevin Daft RC	3.00	1.35
❑	137 Kevin Dyson	.75	.35
❑	138 Eddie George	2.00	.90
❑	139 Steve McNair	1.50	.70
❑	140 Neil O'Donnell	.75	.35
❑	141 Champ Bailey RC	5.00	2.20
❑	142 Albert Connell	.40	.18
❑	143 Stephen Davis	1.50	.70
❑	144 Brad Johnson	1.50	.70

2000 Crown Royale

	MINT	NRMT
COMPLETE SET (144)	120.00	55.00

	Card	MINT	NRMT
❑	1 Rob Moore	.40	.18
❑	2 Jake Plummer	.75	.35
❑	3 Frank Sanders	.40	.18
❑	4 Jamal Anderson	.75	.35
❑	5 Chris Chandler	.40	.18
❑	6 Tim Dwight	.75	.35
❑	7 Tony Banks	.40	.18
❑	8 Priest Holmes	.40	.18
❑	9 Qadry Ismail	.20	.09
❑	10 Doug Flutie	1.00	.45
❑	11 Rob Johnson	.40	.18
❑	12 Eric Moulds	.75	.35
❑	13 Peerless Price	.75	.35
❑	14 Steve Beuerlein	.40	.18
❑	15 Patrick Jeffers	.75	.35
❑	16 Muhsin Muhammad	.40	.18
❑	17 Curtis Enis	.40	.18
❑	18 Cade McNown	.75	.35
❑	19 Marcus Robinson	.75	.35
❑	20 Corey Dillon	.75	.35
❑	21 Darnay Scott	.40	.18
❑	22 Akili Smith	.75	.35
❑	23 Karim Abdul-Jabbar	.40	.18
❑	24 Tim Couch	1.50	.70
❑	25 Kevin Johnson	.75	.35
❑	26 Troy Aikman	2.00	.90
❑	27 Joey Galloway	.75	.35
❑	28 Emmitt Smith	2.00	.90
❑	29 Terrell Davis	2.00	.90
❑	30 Olandis Gary	.75	.35
❑	31 Brian Griese	1.00	.45
❑	32 Ed McCaffrey	.75	.35
❑	33 Charlie Batch	.75	.35
❑	34 Herman Moore	.40	.18
❑	35 Barry Sanders	2.50	1.10
❑	36 James Stewart	.40	.18
❑	37 Brett Favre	3.00	1.35
❑	38 Antonio Freeman	.75	.35
❑	39 Dorsey Levens	.40	.18
❑	40 Marvin Harrison	.75	.35
❑	41 Edgerrin James	3.00	1.35
❑	42 Peyton Manning	2.50	1.10
❑	43 Mark Brunell	1.25	.55
❑	44 Keenan McCardell	.40	.18
❑	45 Jimmy Smith	.40	.18
❑	46 Fred Taylor	1.00	.45
❑	47 Derrick Alexander	.40	.18
❑	48 Tony Gonzalez	.40	.18
❑	49 Elvis Grbac	.40	.18
❑	50 Damon Huard	.75	.35
❑	51 James Johnson	.40	.18
❑	52 Dan Marino	3.00	1.35
❑	53 O.J. McDuffie	.40	.18
❑	54 Cris Carter	.75	.35
❑	55 Daunte Culpepper	1.50	.70
❑	56 Jeff George	.40	.18
❑	57 Randy Moss	2.50	1.10
❑	58 Robert Smith	.75	.35
❑	59 Drew Bledsoe	1.25	.55
❑	60 Terry Glenn	.40	.18
❑	61 Lawyer Milloy	.20	.09
❑	62 Jeff Blake	.40	.18
❑	63 Keith Poole	.20	.09
❑	64 Ricky Williams	2.00	.90
❑	65 Kerry Collins	.40	.18
❑	66 Ike Hilliard	.40	.18
❑	67 Amani Toomer	.20	.09
❑	68 Wayne Chrebet	.40	.18
❑	69 Keyshawn Johnson	.75	.35
❑	70 Ray Lucas	.75	.35
❑	71 Curtis Martin	.75	.35
❑	72 Vinny Testaverde	.40	.18
❑	73 Tim Brown	.75	.35
❑	74 Rich Gannon	.40	.18
❑	75 Napoleon Kaufman	.40	.18
❑	76 Tyrone Wheatley	.40	.18
❑	77 Donovan McNabb	1.25	.55
❑	78 Torrance Small	.20	.09
❑	79 Duce Staley	.75	.35
❑	80 Jerome Bettis	.75	.35
❑	81 Troy Edwards	.40	.18
❑	82 Kordell Stewart	.75	.35
❑	83 Issac Bruce	.75	.35
❑	84 Marshall Faulk	1.00	.45
❑	85 Torry Holt	.75	.35
❑	86 Kurt Warner	3.00	1.35
❑	87 Jim Harbaugh	.40	.18
❑	88 Jermaine Fazande	.20	.09
❑	89 Junior Seau	.40	.18
❑	90 Charlie Garner	.40	.18
❑	91 Terrell Owens	.75	.35
❑	92 Jerry Rice	2.00	.90
❑	93 Steve Young	1.25	.55
❑	94 Sean Dawkins	.20	.09
❑	95 Jon Kitna	.75	.35
❑	96 Derrick Mayes	.40	.18
❑	97 Ricky Watters	.40	.18
❑	98 Mike Alstott	.75	.35
❑	99 Warrick Dunn	.75	.35
❑	100 Jacquez Green	.40	.18
❑	101 Shaun King	1.25	.55
❑	102 Kevin Dyson	.40	.18
❑	103 Eddie George	1.00	.45
❑	104 Jevon Kearse	.75	.35
❑	105 Steve McNair	.75	.35
❑	106 Stephen Davis	.75	.35
❑	107 Brad Johnson	.75	.35
❑	108 Michael Westbrook	.40	.18
❑	109 Shaun Alexander RC	6.00	2.70
❑	110 Tom Brady RC	2.50	1.10
❑	111 Marc Bulger RC	2.50	1.10
❑	112 Plaxico Burress RC	5.00	2.20
❑	113 Giovanni Carmazzi RC	3.00	1.35
❑	114 Kwame Cavil RC	2.00	.90
❑	115 Chris Cole RC	2.00	.90
❑	116 Chris Coleman RC	2.50	1.10
❑	117 Laveranues Coles RC	4.00	1.80
❑	118 Ron Dayne RC	8.00	3.60
❑	119 Reuben Droughns RC	2.50	1.10
❑	120 Ron Dugans RC	2.00	.90
❑	121 Danny Farmer RC	2.50	1.10
❑	122 Chafie Fields RC	2.00	.90
❑	123 Joe Hamilton RC	3.00	1.35
❑	124 Todd Husak RC	2.50	1.10
❑	125 Darrell Jackson RC	4.00	1.80
❑	126 Thomas Jones RC	4.00	1.80
❑	127 Jamal Lewis RC	12.00	5.50
❑	128 Tee Martin RC	4.00	1.80
❑	129 Rondell Mealey RC	1.25	.55
❑	130 Sylvester Morris RC	5.00	2.20
❑	131 Chad Morton RC	2.50	1.10
❑	132 Dennis Northcutt RC	3.00	1.35
❑	133 Chad Pennington RC	8.00	3.60
❑	134 Travis Prentice RC	4.00	1.80
❑	135 Tim Rattay RC	4.00	1.80
❑	136 Chris Redman RC	5.00	2.20
❑	137 J.R. Redmond RC	3.00	1.35
❑	138 R.Jay Soward RC	2.50	1.10
❑	139 Shyrone Stith RC	2.50	1.10
❑	140 Travis Taylor RC	3.00	1.35
❑	141 Troy Walters RC	2.50	1.10
❑	142 Peter Warrick RC	8.00	3.60
❑	143 Dez White RC	2.00	.90
❑	144 Michael Wiley RC	2.50	1.10
❑	S1 Jon Kitna Sample	2.00	.90

2000 Dominion

	MINT	NRMT
COMPLETE SET (243)	30.00	13.50

	Card	MINT	NRMT
❑	1 Tim Couch	.75	.35
❑	2 Byron Hanspard	.10	.05
❑	3 Jay Riemersma	.10	.05
❑	4 Cade McNown	.40	.18
❑	5 Darnay Scott	.20	.09
❑	6 Emmitt Smith	1.00	.45
❑	7 Rod Smith	.20	.09
❑	8 James Stewart	.20	.09
❑	9 Marvin Harrison	.40	.18
❑	10 Keenan McCardell	.20	.09
❑	11 Andre Rison	.10	.05
❑	12 Jeff George	.20	.09
❑	13 Terry Glenn	.20	.09
❑	14 Cam Cleeland	.10	.05
❑	15 Curtis Martin	.40	.18
❑	16 Troy Edwards	.20	.09
❑	17 Mikhael Ricks	.10	.05
❑	18 Joey Galloway	.40	.18
❑	19 Az-Zahir Hakim	.20	.09
❑	20 Mike Alstott	.40	.18
❑	21 Samari Rolle	.10	.05
❑	22 Michael Pittman	.10	.05
❑	23 Tony Banks	.20	.09
❑	24 Bruce Smith	.20	.09
❑	25 Curtis Enis	.20	.09
❑	26 Jake Plummer	.40	.18
❑	27 Darren Woodson	.10	.05
❑	28 Bill Romanowski	.10	.05
❑	29 Antonio Freeman	.40	.18

❑ 30 Terrence Wilkins .40 .18
❑ 31 Kevin Hardy .10 .05
❑ 32 Peerless Price .40 .18
❑ 33 Cris Carter .40 .18
❑ 34 Willie McGinest .10 .05
❑ 35 Kerry Collins .20 .09
❑ 36 Bryan Cox .10 .05
❑ 37 Tyrone Wheatley .20 .09
❑ 38 Jason Sehorn .10 .05
❑ 39 Jerry Rice 1.00 .45
❑ 40 Christian Fauria .10 .05
❑ 41 Kevin Carter .10 .05
❑ 42 John Lynch .10 .05
❑ 43 Brad Johnson .40 .18
❑ 44 David Boston .40 .18
❑ 45 Peter Boulware .10 .05
❑ 46 Muhsin Muhammad .20 .09
❑ 47 Bobby Engram .20 .09
❑ 48 Kevin Johnson .40 .18
❑ 49 Charlie Batch .40 .18
❑ 50 Dorsey Levens .20 .09
❑ 51 Cornelius Bennett .10 .05
❑ 52 Kyle Brady .10 .05
❑ 53 Damon Huard .40 .18
❑ 54 Robert Smith .40 .18
❑ 55 Ty Law .10 .05
❑ 56 Amani Toomer .20 .09
❑ 57 Aaron Glenn .10 .05
❑ 58 Donovan McNabb .60 .25
❑ 59 Levon Kirkland .10 .05
❑ 60 Terrell Owens .40 .18
❑ 61 Sam Adams .10 .05
❑ 62 London Fletcher RC .10 .05
❑ 63 Steve McNair .40 .18
❑ 64 Stephen Davis .40 .18
❑ 65 Daunte Culpepper .75 .35
❑ 66 Andre Wadsworth .10 .05
❑ 67 Priest Holmes .20 .09
❑ 68 Patrick Jeffers .40 .18
❑ 69 Walt Harris .10 .05
❑ 70 Darrin Chiaverini .10 .05
❑ 71 Dat Nguyen .10 .05
❑ 72 Robert Porcher .10 .05
❑ 73 Bill Schroeder .20 .09
❑ 74 Tyrone Poole .10 .05
❑ 75 Bryce Paup .10 .05
❑ 76 O.J. McDuffie .20 .09
❑ 77 Jake Reed .20 .09
❑ 78 Ike Hilliard .20 .09
❑ 79 Victor Green .10 .05
❑ 80 Duce Staley .40 .18
❑ 81 Amos Zereoue .10 .05
❑ 82 Charlie Garner .20 .09
❑ 83 Shawn Springs .10 .05
❑ 84 Shaun King .60 .25
❑ 85 Eddie George .50 .23
❑ 86 Michael Westbrook .20 .09
❑ 87 Ricky Williams 1.00 .45
❑ 88 Chris Chandler .20 .09
❑ 89 Chris McAlister .10 .05
❑ 90 Steve Beuerlein .20 .09
❑ 91 Marty Booker .10 .05
❑ 92 Karim Abdul-Jabbar .20 .09
❑ 93 Brian Griese .50 .23
❑ 94 Germane Crowell .20 .09
❑ 95 Mark Chmura .10 .05
❑ 96 E.G. Green .10 .05
❑ 97 Elvis Grbac .20 .09
❑ 98 Tony Martin .20 .09
❑ 99 John Randle .20 .09
❑ 100 Michael Strahan .10 .05
❑ 101 Tim Brown .40 .18
❑ 102 Torrance Small .10 .05
❑ 103 Junior Seau .20 .09
❑ 104 Bryant Young .10 .05
❑ 105 Kurt Warner 1.50 .70
❑ 106 Trent Dilfer .20 .09
❑ 107 Kevin Dyson .20 .09
❑ 108 Stephen Alexander .10 .05
❑ 109 Tim Dwight .40 .18
❑ 110 Rob Johnson .20 .09
❑ 111 Tim Biakabutuka .20 .09
❑ 112 Akili Smith .40 .18
❑ 113 Terry Kirby .10 .05
❑ 114 Terrell Davis 1.00 .45
❑ 115 Herman Moore .20 .09
❑ 116 Vonnie Holliday .10 .05
❑ 117 Mark Brunell .60 .25
❑ 118 Derrick Alexander .20 .09
❑ 119 Oronde Gadsden .20 .09
❑ 120 Ed McDaniel .10 .05
❑ 121 Eddie Kennison .20 .09
❑ 122 Jessie Armstead .10 .05
❑ 123 Charles Woodson .20 .09
❑ 124 Troy Vincent .10 .05
❑ 125 Jeff Garcia .40 .18
❑ 126 Marshall Faulk .50 .23
❑ 127 Jacquez Green .20 .09
❑ 128 Frank Wycheck .10 .05
❑ 129 Champ Bailey .20 .09
❑ 130 Natrone Means .10 .05
❑ 131 Jamal Anderson .40 .18
❑ 132 Doug Flutie .50 .23
❑ 133 Michael Bates .10 .05
❑ 134 Corey Dillon .40 .18
❑ 135 Corey Fuller .10 .05
❑ 136 Olandis Gary .40 .18
❑ 137 Johnnie Morton .20 .09
❑ 138 Peyton Manning 1.25 .55
❑ 139 Fred Taylor .50 .23
❑ 140 Tony Gonzalez .20 .09
❑ 141 Zach Thomas .20 .09
❑ 142 Drew Bledsoe .60 .25
❑ 143 Keith Poole .10 .05
❑ 144 Vinny Testaverde .20 .09
❑ 145 Rich Gannon .20 .09
❑ 146 Jeremiah Trotter RC .40 .18
❑ 147 Freddie Jones .10 .05
❑ 148 Jon Kitna .40 .18
❑ 149 Isaac Bruce .40 .18
❑ 150 Warrick Dunn .40 .18
❑ 151 Yancey Thigpen .10 .05
❑ 152 Darrell Green .10 .05
❑ 153 Terance Mathis .20 .09
❑ 154 Eric Moulds .40 .18
❑ 155 Wesley Walls .10 .05
❑ 156 Carl Pickens .20 .09
❑ 157 Troy Aikman 1.00 .45
❑ 158 Dwayne Carswell .10 .05
❑ 159 David Sloan .10 .05
❑ 160 Edgerrin James 1.50 .70
❑ 161 Jimmy Smith .20 .09
❑ 162 Tamarick Vanover .10 .05
❑ 163 Sam Madison .10 .05
❑ 164 Tony Simmons .10 .05
❑ 165 Andre Hastings .10 .05
❑ 166 Keyshawn Johnson .40 .18
❑ 167 Napoleon Kaufman .20 .09
❑ 168 Hines Ward .10 .05
❑ 169 Jeff Graham .10 .05
❑ 170 Derrick Mayes .20 .09
❑ 171 Torry Holt .40 .18
❑ 172 Blaine Bishop .10 .05
❑ 173 Rob Moore .20 .09
❑ 174 Pat Johnson .10 .05
❑ 175 Antowain Smith .20 .09
❑ 176 Marcus Robinson .40 .18
❑ 177 Takeo Spikes .10 .05
❑ 178 Rocket Ismail .20 .09
❑ 179 Ed McCaffrey .40 .18
❑ 180 Brett Favre 1.50 .70
❑ 181 Ken Dilger .10 .05
❑ 182 Carnell Lake .10 .05
❑ 183 Cris Dishman .10 .05
❑ 184 Randy Moss 1.25 .55
❑ 185 Lawyer Milloy .10 .05
❑ 186 Jake Delhomme RC .60 .25
❑ 187 Wayne Chrebet .20 .09
❑ 188 Darrell Russell .10 .05
❑ 189 Jerome Bettis .40 .18
❑ 190 Steve Young .60 .25
❑ 191 Ricky Watters .20 .09
❑ 192 Grant Wistrom .10 .05
❑ 193 Warren Sapp .20 .09
❑ 194 Jevon Kearse .40 .18
❑ 195 James Jett .10 .05
❑ 196 Courtney Brown RC .75 .35
❑ 197 Peter Warrick RC 2.00 .90
❑ 198 Thomas Jones RC 1.00 .45
❑ 199 Sylvester Morris RC 1.25 .55
❑ 200 Chad Pennington RC 2.00 .90
❑ 201 Ron Dayne RC 2.00 .90
❑ 202 Todd Pinkston RC .60 .25
❑ 203 Deon Dyer RC .40 .18
❑ 204 Chris Redman RC 1.25 .55
❑ 205 Jerry Porter RC .60 .25
❑ 206 Michael Wiley RC .60 .25
❑ 207 J.R. Redmond RC .75 .35
❑ 208 Dennis Northcutt RC .75 .35
❑ 209 Gari Scott RC .40 .18
❑ 210 Anthony Lucas RC .40 .18
❑ 211 Danny Farmer RC .60 .25
❑ 212 Marcus Knight RC .40 .18
❑ 213 Plaxico Burress RC 1.25 .55
❑ 215 Bubba Franks RC .75 .35
❑ 216 Shaun Alexander RC 1.50 .70
❑ 217 Dez White RC .40 .18
❑ 218 Mareno Philyaw RC .40 .18
❑ 219 Travis Taylor RC .75 .35
❑ 220 Kwame Cavil RC .40 .18
❑ 221 Jamal Lewis RC 3.00 1.35
❑ 222 Sebastian Janikowski RC .60 .25
❑ 223 Shyrone Stith RC .60 .25
❑ 224 Ron Dugans RC .40 .18
❑ 225 Darrell Jackson RC 1.00 .45
❑ 227 Tee Martin RC 1.00 .45
❑ 228 Tim Rattay RC 1.00 .45
❑ 229 Marc Bulger RC .60 .25
❑ 230 Doug Johnson RC .60 .25
❑ 231 Joe Hamilton RC .75 .35
Todd Husak RC
❑ 232 Travis Prentice RC 1.00 .45
R.Jay Soward RC
❑ 233 Trung Canidate RC .60 .25
Reuben Droughns RC
❑ 234 Giovanni Carmazzi RC .75 .35
Tom Brady RC
❑ 235 Laveranues Coles RC 1.00 .45
Chafie Fields RC
❑ 236 Jarious Jackson RC .60 .25
Sherrod Gideon RC
❑ 237 Troy Walters RC .60 .25
Erron Kinney RC
❑ 238 Ronell Mealey RC .40 .18
Joey Goodspeed RC
❑ 239 Anthony Becht RC .60 .25
Quinton Spotwood RC
❑ 240 Deltha O'Neal RC .40 .18
Na'il Diggs RC
❑ 241 Corey Simon RC .75 .35
Chris Hovan RC
❑ 242 Brian Urlacher RC 2.00 .90
Corey Moore RC
❑ 243 Keith Bulluck RC .60 .25
Rob Morris RC
❑ 244 Raynoch Thompson RC .40 .18
Deon Grant RC
❑ 245 John Abraham RC .40 .18
Shaun Ellis RC
❑ P1 Tim Couch Promo 2.00 .90

1996 Donruss

	MINT	NRMT
COMPLETE SET (240)	20.00	9.00
❑ 1 Barry Sanders	2.00	.90
❑ 2 Flipper Anderson	.10	.05
❑ 3 Ben Coates	.20	.09

❑ 4 Rob Johnson .40 .18
❑ 5 Rodney Hampton .20 .09
❑ 6 Desmond Howard .20 .09
❑ 7 Craig Heyward .10 .05
❑ 8 Alvin Harper .10 .05
❑ 9 Todd Collins .20 .09
❑ 10 Ken Norton Jr. .10 .05
❑ 11 Stan Humphries .20 .09
❑ 12 Aeneas Williams .10 .05
❑ 13 Jeff Hostetler .10 .05
❑ 14 Frank Sanders .20 .09
❑ 15 J.J. Birden .10 .05
❑ 16 Bryce Paup .10 .05
❑ 17 Bill Brooks .10 .05
❑ 18 Kevin Williams .10 .05
❑ 19 Boomer Esiason .20 .09
❑ 20 O.J. McDuffie .20 .09
❑ 21 Eric Swann .10 .05
❑ 22 Neil Smith .10 .05
❑ 23 Charlie Garner .10 .05
❑ 24 Greg Lloyd .20 .09
❑ 25 Willie Jackson .10 .05
❑ 26 Shawn Jefferson .10 .05
❑ 27 Rodney Peete .10 .05
❑ 28 Michael Westbrook .40 .18
❑ 29 J.J. Stokes .40 .18
❑ 30 Troy Aikman 1.00 .45
❑ 31 Sean Dawkins .10 .05
❑ 32 Larry Centers .20 .09
❑ 33 Herschel Walker .20 .09
❑ 34 Stoney Case .10 .05
❑ 35 Kevin Greene .20 .09
❑ 36 Quinn Early .10 .05
❑ 37 Fred Barnett .10 .05
❑ 38 Andre Coleman .10 .05
❑ 39 Mark Chmura .20 .09
❑ 40 Adrian Murrell .40 .18
❑ 41 Roosevelt Potts .10 .05
❑ 42 Jay Novacek .10 .05
❑ 43 Derrick Alexander WR .20 .09
❑ 44 Ken Dilger .20 .09
❑ 45 Rob Moore .20 .09
❑ 46 Cris Carter .40 .18
❑ 47 Jeff Blake .40 .18
❑ 48 Derek Loville .10 .05
❑ 49 Tyrone Wheatley .20 .09
❑ 50 Terrell Fletcher .10 .05
❑ 51 Sherman Williams .10 .05
❑ 52 Justin Armour .10 .05
❑ 53 Kordell Stewart .60 .25
❑ 54 Tim Brown .40 .18
❑ 55 Kevin Carter .10 .05
❑ 56 Andre Rison .20 .09
❑ 57 James O.Stewart .20 .09
❑ 58 Brent Jones .10 .05
❑ 59 Erik Kramer .10 .05
❑ 60 Floyd Turner .10 .05
❑ 61 Ricky Watters .20 .09
❑ 62 Hardy Nickerson .10 .05
❑ 63 Aaron Craver .10 .05
❑ 64 Dave Krieg .10 .05
❑ 65 Warren Moon .20 .09
❑ 66 Wayne Chrebet .50 .23
❑ 67 Napoleon Kaufman .40 .18
❑ 68 Terance Mathis .10 .05
❑ 69 Chad May .10 .05
❑ 70 Andre Reed .20 .09
❑ 71 Reggie White .40 .18
❑ 72 Brett Favre 2.00 .90
❑ 73 Chris Zorich .10 .05
❑ 74 Kerry Collins .75 .35
❑ 75 Herman Moore .40 .18
❑ 76 Yancey Thigpen .20 .09
❑ 77 Glenn Foley .20 .09
❑ 78 Quentin Coryatt .10 .05
❑ 79 Terry Kirby .20 .09
❑ 80 Edgar Bennett .20 .09
❑ 81 Mark Brunell 1.00 .45
❑ 82 Heath Shuler .20 .09
❑ 83 Gus Frerotte .40 .18
❑ 84 Deion Sanders .60 .25
❑ 85 Calvin Williams .10 .05
❑ 86 Junior Seau .20 .09
❑ 87 Jim Kelly .40 .18
❑ 88 Daryl Johnston .20 .09
❑ 89 Irving Fryar .20 .09
❑ 90 Brian Blades .10 .05
❑ 91 Willie Davis .10 .05
❑ 92 Jerome Bettis .40 .18
❑ 93 Marcus Allen .40 .18
❑ 94 Jeff Graham .10 .05
❑ 95 Rick Mirer .20 .09
❑ 96 Harvey Williams .10 .05
❑ 97 Steve Atwater .10 .05
❑ 98 Carl Pickens .40 .18
❑ 99 Darick Holmes .10 .05
❑ 100 Bruce Smith .20 .09
❑ 101 Vinny Testaverde .20 .09
❑ 102 Thurman Thomas .40 .18
❑ 103 Drew Bledsoe 1.00 .45
❑ 104 Bernie Parmalee .10 .05
❑ 105 Greg Hill .20 .09
❑ 106 Steve McNair .75 .35
❑ 107 Andre Hastings .10 .05
❑ 108 Eric Metcalf .10 .05
❑ 109 Kimble Anders .20 .09
❑ 110 Stevo Tasker .10 .05
❑ 111 Mark Carrier WR .10 .05
❑ 112 Jerry Rice 1.00 .45
❑ 113 Joey Galloway .60 .25
❑ 114 Robert Smith .20 .09
❑ 115 Hugh Douglas .20 .09
❑ 116 Willie McGinest .10 .05
❑ 117 Terrell Davis 2.50 1.10
❑ 118 Cortez Kennedy .10 .05
❑ 119 Marshall Faulk .40 .18
❑ 120 Michael Haynes .10 .05
❑ 121 Isaac Bruce .40 .18
❑ 122 Brian Mitchell .10 .05
❑ 123 Bryan Cox .10 .05
❑ 124 Tamarick Vanover .20 .09
❑ 125 William Floyd .20 .09
❑ 126 Chris Chandler .20 .09
❑ 127 Carnell Lake .10 .05
❑ 128 Aaron Bailey .10 .05
❑ 129 Darnay Scott .20 .09
❑ 130 Darren Woodson .20 .09
❑ 131 Ernie Mills .10 .05
❑ 132 Charles Haley .20 .09
❑ 133 Rocket Ismail .10 .05
❑ 134 Bert Emanuel .20 .09
❑ 135 Lake Dawson .10 .05
❑ 136 Jake Reed .20 .09
❑ 137 Dave Brown .10 .05
❑ 138 Steve Bono .10 .05
❑ 139 Terry Allen .20 .09
❑ 140 Errict Rhett .20 .09
❑ 141 Rod Woodson .20 .09
❑ 142 Charles Johnson .10 .05
❑ 143 Emmitt Smith 1.50 .70
❑ 144 Ki-Jana Carter .20 .09
❑ 145 Garrison Hearst .20 .09
❑ 146 Rashaan Salaam .40 .18
❑ 147 Tony Boselli .10 .05
❑ 148 Derrick Thomas .20 .09
❑ 149 Mark Seay .10 .05
❑ 150 Derrick Alexander DE .10 .05
❑ 151 Christian Fauria .10 .05
❑ 152 Aaron Hayden .10 .05
❑ 153 Chris Warren .20 .09
❑ 154 Dave Meggett .10 .05
❑ 155 Jeff George .20 .09
❑ 156 Jackie Harris .10 .05
❑ 157 Michael Irvin .40 .18
❑ 158 Scott Mitchell .20 .09
❑ 159 Trent Dilfer .40 .18
❑ 160 Kyle Brady .10 .05
❑ 161 Dan Marino 2.00 .90
❑ 162 Curtis Martin .75 .35
❑ 163 Mario Bates .20 .09
❑ 164 Erric Pegram .10 .05
❑ 165 Eric Zeier .10 .05
❑ 166 Rodney Thomas .10 .05
❑ 167 Neil O'Donnell .20 .09
❑ 168 Warren Sapp .10 .05
❑ 169 Jim Harbaugh .20 .09
❑ 170 Henry Ellard .10 .05
❑ 171 Anthony Miller .20 .09
❑ 172 Derrick Moore .10 .05
❑ 173 John Elway 2.00 .90
❑ 174 Vincent Brisby .10 .05
❑ 175 Antonio Freeman .75 .35
❑ 176 Chris Sanders .20 .09
❑ 177 Steve Young .75 .35
❑ 178 Shannon Sharpe .20 .09
❑ 179 Brett Perriman .10 .05
❑ 180 Orlando Thomas .10 .05
❑ 181 Eric Bjornson .10 .05
❑ 182 Natrone Means .40 .18
❑ 183 Jim Everett .10 .05
❑ 184 Curtis Conway .40 .18
❑ 185 Robert Brooks .40 .18
❑ 186 Tony Martin .20 .09
❑ 187 Mark Carrier DB .10 .05
❑ 188 LeShon Johnson .10 .05
❑ 189 Bernie Kosar .10 .05
❑ 190 Ray Zellars .10 .05
❑ 191 Steve Walsh .10 .05
❑ 192 Craig Erickson .10 .05
❑ 193 Tommy Maddox .10 .05
❑ 194 Leslie O'Neal .10 .05
❑ 195 Harold Green .10 .05
❑ 196 Steve Beuerlein .10 .05
❑ 197 Ronald Moore .10 .05
❑ 198 Leslie Shepherd .10 .05
❑ 199 Leroy Hoard .10 .05
❑ 200 Michael Jackson .20 .09
❑ 201 Will Moore .10 .05
❑ 202 Ricky Ervins .10 .05
❑ 203 Keith Jennings .10 .05
❑ 204 Eric Green .10 .05
❑ 205 Mark Rypien .10 .05
❑ 206 Torrance Small .10 .05
❑ 207 Sean Gilbert .10 .05
❑ 208 Mike Alstott RC 1.50 .70
❑ 209 Willie Anderson RC .10 .05
❑ 210 Alex Molden RC .10 .05
❑ 211 Jonathan Ogden RC .10 .05
❑ 212 Stepfret Williams RC .20 .09
❑ 213 Jeff Lewis RC .50 .23
❑ 214 Regan Upshaw RC .10 .05
❑ 215 Daryl Gardener RC .10 .05
❑ 216 Danny Kanell RC .40 .18
❑ 217 John Mobley RC .10 .05
❑ 218 Reggie Brown LB RC .10 .05
❑ 219 Muhsin Muhammad RC .75 .35
❑ 220 Kevin Hardy RC .40 .18
❑ 221 Stanley Pritchett RC .20 .09
❑ 222 Cedric Jones RC .10 .05
❑ 223 Marco Battaglia RC .10 .05
❑ 224 Duane Clemons RC .10 .05
❑ 225 Jerald Moore RC .40 .18
❑ 226 Simeon Rice RC .40 .18
❑ 227 Chris Darkins RC .10 .05
❑ 228 Bobby Hoying RC .50 .23
❑ 229 Stephen Davis RC 2.50 1.10
❑ 230 Walt Harris RC .10 .05
❑ 231 Jermane Mayberry RC .10 .05
❑ 232 Tony Brackens RC .20 .09
❑ 233 Eric Moulds RC 2.00 .90
❑ 234 Alex Van Dyke RC .20 .09
❑ 235 Marvin Harrison RC 2.00 .90
❑ 236 Rickey Dudley RC .40 .18
❑ 237 Terrell Owens RC 2.50 1.10
❑ 238 Jerry Rice .40 .18
Checklist Card
❑ 239 Dan Marino .40 .18
Checklist Card
❑ 240 Emmitt Smith .40 .18
Checklist Card

1997 Donruss

	MINT	NRMT
COMPLETE SET (230)	20.00	9.00
❑ 1 Dan Marino	2.00	.90
❑ 2 Brett Favre	2.00	.90
❑ 3 Emmitt Smith	1.50	.70
❑ 4 Eddie George	1.00	.45
❑ 5 Karim Abdul-Jabbar	.30	.14
❑ 6 Terrell Davis	1.50	.70
❑ 7 Curtis Martin	.50	.23
❑ 8 Drew Bledsoe	1.00	.45
❑ 9 Jerry Rice	1.00	.45
❑ 10 Troy Aikman	1.00	.45
❑ 11 Barry Sanders	2.00	.90
❑ 12 Mark Brunell	1.00	.45

❑ 13 Kerry Collins .20 .09
❑ 14 Steve Young .60 .25
❑ 15 Kordell Stewart .50 .23
❑ 16 Eddie Kennison .20 .09
❑ 17 Terry Glenn .30 .14
❑ 18 John Elway 2.00 .90
❑ 19 Joey Galloway .50 .23
❑ 20 Deion Sanders .30 .14
❑ 21 Keyshawn Johnson .30 .14
❑ 22 Lawrence Phillips .10 .05
❑ 23 Ricky Watters .20 .09
❑ 24 Marvin Harrison .30 .14
❑ 25 Bobby Engram .20 .09
❑ 26 Marshall Faulk .30 .14
❑ 27 Carl Pickens .30 .14
❑ 28 Isaac Bruce .30 .14
❑ 29 Herman Moore .30 .14
❑ 30 Jerome Bettis .30 .14
❑ 31 Rashaan Salaam .10 .05
❑ 32 Errict Rhett .10 .05
❑ 33 Tim Biakabutuka .20 .09
❑ 34 Robert Brooks .20 .09
❑ 35 Antonio Freeman .50 .23
❑ 36 Steve McNair .50 .23
❑ 37 Jeff Blake .20 .09
❑ 38 Tony Banks .20 .09
❑ 39 Terrell Owens .30 .14
❑ 40 Eric Moulds .30 .14
❑ 41 Leeland McElroy .10 .05
❑ 42 Chris Sanders .10 .05
❑ 43 Thurman Thomas .30 .14
❑ 44 Bruce Smith .20 .09
❑ 45 Reggie White .30 .14
❑ 46 Chris Warren .20 .09
❑ 47 J.J. Stokes .20 .09
❑ 48 Ben Coates .20 .09
❑ 49 Tim Brown .30 .14
❑ 50 Marcus Allen .30 .14
❑ 51 Michael Irvin .30 .14
❑ 52 William Floyd .20 .09
❑ 53 Ken Dilger .10 .05
❑ 54 Bobby Taylor .10 .05
❑ 55 Keenan McCardell .20 .09
❑ 56 Raymont Harris .10 .05
❑ 57 Keith Byars .10 .05
❑ 58 O.J. McDuffie .20 .09
❑ 59 Robert Smith .20 .09
❑ 60 Bert Emanuel .20 .09
❑ 61 Rick Mirer .10 .05
❑ 62 Vinny Testaverde .20 .09
❑ 63 Kyle Brady .10 .05
❑ 64 Mark Bruener .10 .05
❑ 65 Neil O'Donnell .20 .09
❑ 66 Anthony Johnson .10 .05
❑ 67 Ken Norton .10 .05
❑ 68 Warren Sapp .20 .09
❑ 69 Amani Toomer .20 .09
❑ 70 Simeon Rice .20 .09
❑ 71 Kevin Hardy .10 .05
❑ 72 Junior Seau .20 .09
❑ 73 Neil Smith .20 .09
❑ 74 LeShon Johnson .10 .05
❑ 75 Quinn Early .10 .05
❑ 76 Andre Reed .20 .09
❑ 77 Jake Reed .20 .09
❑ 78 Elvis Grbac .20 .09
❑ 79 Tyrone Wheatley .20 .09
❑ 80 Adrian Murrell .20 .09
❑ 81 Fred Barnett .10 .05
❑ 82 Darrell Green .20 .09
❑ 83 Stan Humphries .20 .09
❑ 84 Troy Drayton .10 .05
❑ 85 Steve Atwater .10 .05
❑ 86 Quentin Coryatt .10 .05
❑ 87 Dan Wilkinson .10 .05
❑ 88 Scott Mitchell .20 .09
❑ 89 Willie McGinest .10 .05
❑ 90 Kevin Smith .10 .05
❑ 91 Gus Frerotte .10 .05
❑ 92 Byron Bam Morris .10 .05
❑ 93 Darick Holmes .10 .05
❑ 94 Zach Thomas .20 .09
❑ 95 Tom Carter .10 .05
❑ 96 Cortez Kennedy .10 .05
❑ 97 Kevin Williams .10 .05
❑ 98 Michael Haynes .10 .05
❑ 99 Lamont Warren .10 .05
❑ 100 Jeff Graham .10 .05
❑ 101 Alex Van Dyke .10 .05
❑ 102 Jim Everett .10 .05
❑ 103 Chris Chandler .20 .09
❑ 104 Qadry Ismail .20 .09
❑ 105 Ray Zellars .10 .05
❑ 106 Chris T. Jones .10 .05
❑ 107 Charlie Garner .10 .05
❑ 108 Bobby Hoying .20 .09
❑ 109 Mark Chmura .20 .09
❑ 110 Cris Carter .30 .14
❑ 111 Darnay Scott .20 .09
❑ 112 Anthony Miller .10 .05
❑ 113 Desmond Howard .20 .09
❑ 114 Terance Mathis .20 .09
❑ 115 Rodney Hampton .20 .09
❑ 116 Napoleon Kaufman .30 .14
❑ 117 Jim Harbaugh .20 .09
❑ 118 Shannon Sharpe .20 .09
❑ 119 Irving Fryar .20 .09
❑ 120 Garrison Hearst .20 .09
❑ 121 Terry Allen .30 .14
❑ 122 Larry Centers .20 .09
❑ 123 Sean Dawkins .10 .05
❑ 124 Jeff George .20 .09
❑ 125 Tony Martin .20 .09
❑ 126 Mike Alstott .30 .14
❑ 127 Rickey Dudley .20 .09
❑ 128 Kevin Carter .10 .05
❑ 129 Derrick Alexander WR .20 .09
❑ 130 Greg Lloyd .10 .05
❑ 131 Bryce Paup .10 .05
❑ 132 Derrick Thomas .20 .09
❑ 133 Greg Hill .10 .05
❑ 134 Jamal Anderson .60 .25
❑ 135 Curtis Conway .20 .09
❑ 136 Frank Sanders .20 .09
❑ 137 Brett Perriman .10 .05
❑ 138 Edgar Bennett .20 .09
❑ 139 Wayne Chrebet .30 .14
❑ 140 Natrone Means .30 .14
❑ 141 Eric Metcalf .20 .09
❑ 142 Trent Dilfer .30 .14
❑ 143 Terry Kirby .20 .09
❑ 144 Johnnie Morton .20 .09
❑ 145 Dale Carter .10 .05
❑ 146 Michael Westbrook .20 .09
❑ 147 Stanley Pritchett .10 .05
❑ 148 Todd Collins .10 .05
❑ 149 Tamarick Vanover .20 .09
❑ 150 Kevin Greene .20 .09
❑ 151 Lamar Lathon .10 .05
❑ 152 Muhsin Muhammad .20 .09
❑ 153 Dorsey Levens .30 .14
❑ 154 Rod Woodson .20 .09
❑ 155 Brent Jones .20 .09
❑ 156 Michael Jackson .20 .09
❑ 157 Shawn Jefferson .10 .05
❑ 158 Kimble Anders .20 .09
❑ 159 Sean Gilbert .10 .05
❑ 160 Carnell Lake .10 .05
❑ 161 Darren Woodson .10 .05
❑ 162 Dave Meggett .10 .05
❑ 163 Henry Ellard .10 .05
❑ 164 Eric Swann .10 .05
❑ 165 Tony Boselli .10 .05
❑ 166 Daryl Johnston .20 .09
❑ 167 Willie Jackson .10 .05
❑ 168 Wesley Walls .20 .09
❑ 169 Mario Bates .10 .05
❑ 170 Lake Dawson .10 .05
❑ 171 Mike Mamula .10 .05
❑ 172 Ed McCaffrey .20 .09
❑ 173 Tony Brackens .10 .05
❑ 174 Craig Heyward .10 .05
❑ 175 Harvey Williams .10 .05
❑ 176 Dave Brown .10 .05
❑ 177 Aaron Glenn .10 .05
❑ 178 Jeff Hostetler .10 .05
❑ 179 Alvin Harper .10 .05
❑ 180 Ty Detmer .20 .09
❑ 181 James Jett .20 .09
❑ 182 James O.Stewart .20 .09
❑ 183 Warren Moon .30 .14
❑ 184 Herschel Walker .20 .09
❑ 185 Ki-Jana Carter .10 .05
❑ 186 Leslie O'Neal .10 .05
❑ 187 Danny Kanell .20 .09
❑ 188 Eric Bjornson .10 .05
❑ 189 Alex Molden .10 .05
❑ 190 Bryant Young .10 .05
❑ 191 Merton Hanks .10 .05
❑ 192 Heath Shuler .10 .05
❑ 193 Brian Blades .10 .05
❑ 194 Steve Bono .20 .09
❑ 195 Wayne Simmons .10 .05
❑ 196 Warrick Dunn RC 1.25 .55
❑ 197 Peter Boulware RC .20 .09
❑ 198 David LaFleur RC .20 .09
❑ 199 Shawn Springs RC .20 .09
❑ 200 Reidel Anthony RC .75 .35
❑ 201 Jim Druckenmiller RC .30 .14
❑ 202 Orlando Pace RC .30 .14
❑ 203 Yatil Green RC .20 .09
❑ 204 Bryant Westbrook RC .10 .05
❑ 205 Tiki Barber RC 1.25 .55
❑ 206 James Farrior RC .10 .05
❑ 207 Rae Carruth RC .30 .14
❑ 208 Danny Wuerffel RC .60 .25
❑ 209 Corey Dillon RC 2.50 1.10
❑ 210 Ike Hilliard RC .75 .35
❑ 211 Tony Gonzalez RC 1.25 .55
❑ 212 Antowain Smith RC 1.00 .45
❑ 213 Pat Barnes RC .30 .14
❑ 214 Troy Davis RC .30 .14
❑ 215 Byron Hanspard RC .30 .14
❑ 216 Joey Kent RC .30 .14
❑ 217 Jake Plummer RC 2.50 1.10
❑ 218 Kenny Holmes RC .30 .14
❑ 219 Darnell Autry RC .20 .09
❑ 220 Darrell Russell RC .10 .05
❑ 221 Walter Jones RC .10 .05
❑ 222 Dwayne Rudd RC .30 .14
❑ 223 Tom Knight RC .10 .05
❑ 224 Kevin Lockett RC .20 .09
❑ 225 Will Blackwell RC .30 .14
❑ 226 Dan Marino .40 .18
Checklist back
❑ 227 Brett Favre .40 .18
Checklist back
❑ 228 Emmitt Smith .30 .14
Checklist back
❑ 229 Barry Sanders .30 .14
Checklist back
❑ 230 Jerry Rice .25 .11
Checklist back
❑ P1 Drew Bledsoe 1.00 .45
(Ad back promo)
❑ P2 Mark Brunell 1.00 .45
(Ad back promo)
❑ P3 Barry Sanders 1.50 .70
(Ad back promo)

1999 Donruss

	MINT	NRMT
COMPLETE SET (200)	150.00	70.00
COMP.SET w/o SP's (150)	20.00	9.00

❑ 1 Jake Plummer .75 .35
❑ 2 Rob Moore .25 .11

❑ 3 Adrian Murrell .25 .11
❑ 4 Frank Sanders .25 .11
❑ 5 Jamal Anderson .50 .23
❑ 6 Tim Dwight .25 .11
❑ 7 Terance Mathis .25 .11
❑ 8 Chris Chandler .25 .11
❑ 9 Byron Hanspard .25 .11
❑ 10 Priest Holmes .50 .23
❑ 11 Jermaine Lewis .25 .11
❑ 12 Errict Rhett .25 .11
❑ 13 Doug Flutie .60 .25
❑ 14 Eric Moulds .50 .23
❑ 15 Antowain Smith .50 .23
❑ 16 Thurman Thomas .25 .11
❑ 17 Andre Reed .25 .11
❑ 18 Bruce Smith .25 .11
❑ 19 Tim Biakabutuka .25 .11
❑ 20 Rae Carruth .25 .11
❑ 21 Muhsin Muhammad .25 .11
❑ 22 Curtis Enis .50 .23
❑ 23 Curtis Conway .25 .11
❑ 24 Bobby Engram .25 .11
❑ 25 Corey Dillon .50 .23
❑ 26 Carl Pickens .25 .11
❑ 27 Jeff Blake .25 .11
❑ 28 Darnay Scott .25 .11
❑ 29 Ty Detmer .25 .11
❑ 30 Leslie Shepherd .15 .07
❑ 31 Emmitt Smith 1.25 .55
❑ 32 Troy Aikman 1.25 .55
❑ 33 Michael Irvin .25 .11
❑ 34 Deion Sanders .50 .23
❑ 35 Rocket Ismail .25 .11
❑ 36 John Elway 2.00 .90
❑ 37 Terrell Davis 1.25 .55
❑ 38 Ed McCaffrey .25 .11
❑ 39 Shannon Sharpe .25 .11
❑ 40 Rod Smith .25 .11
❑ 41 Bubby Brister .15 .07
❑ 42 Brian Griese 1.00 .45
❑ 43 Barry Sanders 2.00 .90
❑ 44 Charlie Batch 1.00 .45
❑ 45 Herman Moore .50 .23
❑ 46 Germane Crowell .25 .11
❑ 47 Johnnie Morton .25 .11
❑ 48 Ron Rivers .15 .07
❑ 49 Brett Favre 2.00 .90
❑ 50 Antonio Freeman .50 .23
❑ 51 Dorsey Levens .50 .23
❑ 52 Mark Chmura .15 .07
❑ 53 Corey Bradford .50 .23
❑ 54 Bill Schroeder .50 .23
❑ 55 Peyton Manning 2.00 .90
❑ 56 Marvin Harrison .50 .23
❑ 57 E.G. Green .15 .07
❑ 58 Fred Taylor 1.25 .55
❑ 59 Mark Brunell .75 .35
❑ 60 Tavian Banks .15 .07
❑ 61 Jimmy Smith .25 .11
❑ 62 Keenan McCardell .25 .11
❑ 63 Warren Moon .50 .23
❑ 64 Derrick Alexander WR .25 .11
❑ 65 Byron Bam Morris .15 .07
❑ 66 Elvis Grbac .25 .11
❑ 67 Andre Rison .25 .11
❑ 68 Dan Marino 2.00 .90
❑ 69 Karim Abdul-Jabbar .25 .11
❑ 70 O.J. McDuffie .25 .11
❑ 71 Tony Martin .15 .07
❑ 72 Randy Moss 2.00 .90
❑ 73 Cris Carter .50 .23
❑ 74 Randall Cunningham .50 .23
❑ 75 Robert Smith .50 .23
❑ 76 Jeff George .25 .11
❑ 77 Jake Reed .25 .11
❑ 78 Terry Allen .25 .11
❑ 79 Drew Bledsoe .75 .35
❑ 80 Terry Glenn .50 .23
❑ 81 Ben Coates .25 .11
❑ 82 Tony Simmons .15 .07
❑ 83 Cam Cleeland .15 .07
❑ 84 Eddie Kennison .25 .11
❑ 85 Kerry Collins .15 .07
❑ 86 Ike Hilliard .15 .07
❑ 87 Gary Brown .15 .07
❑ 88 Joe Jurevicius .15 .07
❑ 89 Kent Graham .15 .07
❑ 90 Wayne Chrebet .25 .11
❑ 91 Keyshawn Johnson .50 .23
❑ 92 Curtis Martin .50 .23
❑ 93 Vinny Testaverde .25 .11
❑ 94 Tim Brown .50 .23
❑ 95 Napoleon Kaufman .50 .23
❑ 96 Charles Woodson .50 .23
❑ 97 Tyrone Wheatley .25 .11
❑ 98 Rich Gannon .25 .11
❑ 99 Charles Johnson .15 .07
❑ 100 Duce Staley .50 .23
❑ 101 Kordell Stewart .50 .23
❑ 102 Jerome Bettis .50 .23
❑ 103 Hines Ward .15 .07
❑ 104 Ryan Leaf .50 .23
❑ 105 Natrone Means .25 .11
❑ 106 Jim Harbaugh .25 .11
❑ 107 Junior Seau .25 .11
❑ 108 Mikhael Ricks .15 .07
❑ 109 Jerry Rice 1.25 .55
❑ 110 Steve Young .75 .35
❑ 111 Garrison Hearst .25 .11
❑ 112 Terrell Owens .50 .23
❑ 113 Lawrence Phillips .25 .11
❑ 114 J.J. Stokes .25 .11
❑ 115 Sean Dawkins .15 .07
❑ 116 Derrick Mayes .15 .07
❑ 117 Joey Galloway .50 .23
❑ 118 Jon Kitna .50 .23
❑ 119 Ahman Green .25 .11
❑ 120 Ricky Watters .25 .11
❑ 121 Isaac Bruce .50 .23
❑ 122 Marshall Faulk .50 .23
❑ 123 Az-Zahir Hakim .15 .07
❑ 124 Warrick Dunn .50 .23
❑ 125 Mike Alstott .50 .23
❑ 126 Trent Dilfer .25 .11
❑ 127 Reidel Anthony .25 .11
❑ 128 Jacquez Green .25 .11
❑ 129 Warren Sapp .25 .11
❑ 130 Eddie George .60 .25
❑ 131 Steve McNair .50 .23
❑ 132 Kevin Dyson .25 .11
❑ 133 Yancey Thigpen .15 .07
❑ 134 Frank Wycheck .15 .07
❑ 135 Stephen Davis .50 .23
❑ 136 Brad Johnson .50 .23
❑ 137 Skip Hicks .25 .11
❑ 138 Michael Westbrook .25 .11
❑ 139 Darrell Green .15 .07
❑ 140 Albert Connell .15 .07
❑ 141 Tim Couch RC 6.00 2.70
❑ 142 Donovan McNabb RC 6.00 2.70
❑ 143 Akili Smith RC 4.00 1.80
❑ 144 Edgerrin James RC 10.00 4.50
❑ 145 Ricky Williams RC 6.00 2.70
❑ 146 Torry Holt RC 5.00 2.20
❑ 147 Champ Bailey RC 2.50 1.10
❑ 148 David Boston RC 4.00 1.80
❑ 149 Andy Katzenmoyer RC 2.00 .90
❑ 150 Chris McAlister RC 1.50 .70
❑ 151 Daunte Culpepper RC 10.00 4.50
❑ 152 Cade McNown RC 2.50 1.10
❑ 153 Troy Edwards RC 2.50 1.10
❑ 154 Kevin Johnson RC 4.00 1.80
❑ 155 James Johnson RC 2.00 .90
❑ 156 Rob Konrad RC 1.50 .70
❑ 157 Jim Kleinsasser RC 2.00 .90
❑ 158 Kevin Faulk RC 3.00 1.35
❑ 159 Joe Montgomery RC 2.00 .90
❑ 160 Shaun King RC 4.00 1.80
❑ 161 Peerless Price RC 2.50 1.10
❑ 162 Mike Cloud RC 2.00 .90
❑ 163 Jermaine Fazande RC 2.00 .90
❑ 164 D'Wayne Bates RC 1.50 .70
❑ 165 Brock Huard RC 3.00 1.35
❑ 166 Marty Booker RC 2.00 .90
❑ 167 Karsten Bailey RC 2.00 .90
❑ 168 Shawn Bryson RC 2.00 .90
❑ 169 Jeff Paulk RC 1.50 .70
❑ 170 Travis McGriff RC 1.50 .70
❑ 171 Amos Zereoue RC 2.00 .90
❑ 172 Craig Yeast RC 1.50 .70
❑ 173 Joe Germaine RC 2.00 .90
❑ 174 Dameane Douglas RC 1.50 .70
❑ 175 Brandon Stokley RC 2.00 .90
❑ 176 Larry Parker RC 1.50 .70
❑ 177 Joel Makovicka RC 2.00 .90
❑ 178 Wane McGarity RC 1.50 .70
❑ 179 Na Brown RC 2.00 .90
❑ 180 Cecil Collins RC 2.00 .90
❑ 181 Nick Williams RC 1.50 .70
❑ 182 Charlie Rogers RC 1.50 .70
❑ 183 Darrin Chiaverini RC 2.00 .90
❑ 184 Terry Jackson RC 1.50 .70
❑ 185 De'Mond Parker RC 1.50 .70
❑ 186 Sedrick Irvin RC 2.00 .90
❑ 187 MarTay Jenkins RC 1.50 .70
❑ 188 Kurt Warner RC 20.00 9.00
❑ 189 Michael Bishop RC 2.50 1.10
❑ 190 Sean Bennett RC 1.50 .70
❑ 191 Jamal Anderson CL .15 .07
❑ 192 Eric Moulds CL .15 .07
❑ 193 Terrell Davis CL .50 .23
❑ 194 John Elway CL .75 .35
❑ 195 Barry Sanders CL .75 .35
❑ 196 Peyton Manning CL .75 .35
❑ 197 Fred Taylor CL .50 .23
❑ 198 Dan Marino CL .75 .35
❑ 199 Randy Moss CL .75 .35
❑ 200 Terrell Owens CL .15 .07

1999 Donruss Elite

	MINT	NRMT
COMPLETE SET (200)	200.00	90.00
COMP.SET w/o SP's (160)	30.00	13.50
COMMON CARD (1-100)	.25	.11
COMMON CARD (101-200)	.50	.23
COMMON ROOKIE (161-200)	3.00	1.35

❑ 1 Warren Moon 1.00 .45
❑ 2 Terry Allen .50 .23
❑ 3 Jeff George .50 .23
❑ 4 Brett Favre 4.00 1.80
❑ 5 Rob Moore .50 .23
❑ 6 Bubby Brister .25 .11
❑ 7 John Elway 4.00 1.80
❑ 8 Troy Aikman 2.50 1.10
❑ 9 Steve McNair 1.00 .45
❑ 10 Charlie Batch 2.00 .90
❑ 11 Elvis Grbac .50 .23
❑ 12 Trent Dilfer .50 .23
❑ 13 Kerry Collins .50 .23

❑ 14 Neil O'Donnell .25 .11
❑ 15 Tony Simmons .25 .11
❑ 16 Ryan Leaf 1.00 .45
❑ 17 Bobby Hoying .50 .23
❑ 18 Marvin Harrison 1.00 .45
❑ 19 Keyshawn Johnson 1.00 .45
❑ 20 Cris Carter 1.00 .45
❑ 21 Deion Sanders 1.00 .45
❑ 22 Emmitt Smith 2.50 1.10
❑ 23 Antowain Smith 1.00 .45
❑ 24 Terry Fair .25 .11
❑ 25 Robert Holcombe .50 .23
❑ 26 Napoleon Kaufman 1.00 .45
❑ 27 Eddie George 1.25 .55
❑ 28 Corey Dillon 1.00 .45
❑ 29 Adrian Murrell .50 .23
❑ 30 Charles Way .25 .11
❑ 31 Amp Lee .25 .11
❑ 32 Ricky Watters .50 .23
❑ 33 Gary Brown .25 .11
❑ 34 Thurman Thomas .50 .23
❑ 35 Pat Johnson .25 .11
❑ 36 Jerome Bettis 1.00 .45
❑ 37 Muhsin Muhammad .50 .23
❑ 38 Kimble Anders .50 .23
❑ 39 Curtis Enis 1.00 .45
❑ 40 Mike Alstott 1.00 .45
❑ 41 Charles Johnson .25 .11
❑ 42 Chris Warren .25 .11
❑ 43 Tony Banks .50 .23
❑ 44 Leroy Hoard .25 .11
❑ 45 Chris Fuamatu-Ma'afala .. .25 .11
❑ 46 Michael Irvin 1.00 .45
❑ 47 Robert Edwards .50 .23
❑ 48 Hines Ward .25 .11
❑ 49 Trent Green .50 .23
❑ 50 Eric Zeier .25 .11
❑ 51 Sean Dawkins .25 .11
❑ 52 Yancey Thigpen .25 .11
❑ 53 Jacquez Green .50 .23
❑ 54 Zach Thomas .50 .23
❑ 55 Junior Seau .50 .23
❑ 56 Darnay Scott .25 .11
❑ 57 Kent Graham .25 .11
❑ 58 O.J. Santiago .25 .11
❑ 59 Tony Gonzalez .50 .23
❑ 60 Ty Detmer .25 .11
❑ 61 Albert Connell .25 .11
❑ 62 James Jett .50 .23
❑ 63 Bert Emanuel .50 .23
❑ 64 Derrick Alexander WR .50 .23
❑ 65 Wesley Walls .50 .23
❑ 66 Jake Reed .50 .23
❑ 67 Randall Cunningham 1.00 .45
❑ 68 Leslie Shepherd .25 .11
❑ 69 Mark Chmura .25 .11
❑ 70 Bobby Engram .50 .23
❑ 71 Rickey Dudley .25 .11
❑ 72 Darick Holmes .25 .11
❑ 73 Andre Reed .50 .23
❑ 74 Az-Zahir Hakim .25 .11
❑ 75 Cameron Cleeland .25 .11
❑ 76 Lamar Thomas .25 .11
❑ 77 Oronde Gadsden .25 .11
❑ 78 Ben Coates .50 .23
❑ 79 Bruce Smith .50 .23
❑ 80 Jerry Rice 2.50 1.10
❑ 81 Tim Brown 1.00 .45
❑ 82 Michael Westbrook .50 .23
❑ 83 J.J. Stokes .50 .23
❑ 84 Shannon Sharpe .50 .23
❑ 85 Reidel Anthony .50 .23
❑ 86 Antonio Freeman 1.00 .45
❑ 87 Keenan McCardell .50 .23
❑ 88 Terry Glenn 1.00 .45
❑ 89 Andre Rison .50 .23
❑ 90 Neil Smith .50 .23
❑ 91 Terrance Mathis .50 .23
❑ 92 Rocket Ismail .50 .23
❑ 93 Byron Bam Morris .25 .11
❑ 94 Ike Hilliard .25 .11
❑ 95 Eddie Kennison .50 .23
❑ 96 Tavian Banks .50 .23
❑ 97 Yatil Green .25 .11
❑ 98 Frank Wycheck .25 .11
❑ 99 Warren Sapp .25 .11
❑ 100 Germane Crowell .50 .23
❑ 101 Curtis Martin 2.00 .90
❑ 102 John Avery 1.00 .45
❑ 103 Eric Moulds 2.00 .90
❑ 104 Randy Moss 10.00 4.50
❑ 105 Terrell Owens 2.00 .90
❑ 106 Vinny Testaverde 1.00 .45
❑ 107 Doug Flutie 2.50 1.10
❑ 108 Mark Brunell 3.00 1.35
❑ 109 Isaac Bruce 2.00 .90
❑ 110 Kordell Stewart 2.00 .90
❑ 111 Drew Bledsoe 3.00 1.35
❑ 112 Chris Chandler 1.00 .45
❑ 113 Dan Marino 8.00 3.60
❑ 114 Brian Griese 3.00 1.35
❑ 115 Carl Pickens 1.00 .45
❑ 116 Jake Plummer 4.00 1.80
❑ 117 Natrone Means 1.00 .45
❑ 118 Peyton Manning 10.00 4.50
❑ 119 Garrison Hearst 2.00 .90
❑ 120 Barry Sanders 8.00 3.60
❑ 121 Steve Young 3.00 1.35
❑ 122 Rashaan Shehee .50 .23
❑ 123 Ed McCaffrey 1.00 .45
❑ 124 Charles Woodson 2.00 .90
❑ 125 Dorsey Levens 2.00 .90
❑ 126 Robert Smith 2.00 .90
❑ 127 Greg Hill .50 .23
❑ 128 Fred Taylor 5.00 2.20
❑ 129 Marcus Nash 1.00 .45
❑ 130 Terrell Davis 5.00 2.20
❑ 131 Ahman Green 1.00 .45
❑ 132 Jamal Anderson 2.00 .90
❑ 133 Karim Abdul-Jabbar 1.00 .45
❑ 134 Jermaine Lewis 1.00 .45
❑ 135 Jerome Pathon 1.00 .45
❑ 136 Brad Johnson 2.00 .90
❑ 137 Herman Moore 2.00 .90
❑ 138 Tim Dwight 2.00 .90
❑ 139 Johnnie Morton .50 .23
❑ 140 Marshall Faulk 2.00 .90
❑ 141 Frank Sanders 1.00 .45
❑ 142 Kevin Dyson 1.00 .45
❑ 143 Curtis Conway 1.00 .45
❑ 144 Derrick Mayes .50 .23
❑ 145 O.J. McDuffie 1.00 .45
❑ 146 Joe Jurevicius .50 .23
❑ 147 Jon Kitna 2.00 .90
❑ 148 Joey Galloway 2.00 .90
❑ 149 Jimmy Smith 1.00 .45
❑ 150 Skip Hicks 1.00 .45
❑ 151 Rod Smith 1.00 .45
❑ 152 Duce Staley 2.00 .90
❑ 153 James Stewart .50 .23
❑ 154 Rob Johnson 1.00 .45
❑ 155 Mikhael Ricks .50 .23
❑ 156 Wayne Chrebet 1.00 .45
❑ 157 Robert Brooks 1.00 .45
❑ 158 Tim Biakabutuka 1.00 .45
❑ 159 Priest Holmes 2.00 .90
❑ 160 Warrick Dunn 2.00 .90
❑ 161 Champ Bailey RC 5.00 2.20
❑ 162 D'Wayne Bates RC 4.00 1.80
❑ 163 Michael Bishop RC 5.00 2.20
❑ 164 David Boston RC 8.00 3.60
❑ 165 Na Brown RC 5.00 2.20
❑ 166 Chris Claiborne RC 3.00 1.35
❑ 167 Joe Montgomery RC 5.00 2.20
❑ 168 Mike Cloud RC 5.00 2.20
❑ 169 Travis McGriff RC 5.00 2.20
❑ 170 Tim Couch RC 12.00 5.50
❑ 171 Daunte Culpepper RC 20.00 9.00
❑ 172 Autry Denson RC 5.00 2.20
❑ 173 Jermaine Fazande RC 5.00 2.20
❑ 174 Troy Edwards RC 5.00 2.20
❑ 175 Kevin Faulk RC 6.00 2.70
❑ 176 Dee Miller RC 4.00 1.80
❑ 177 Brock Huard RC 6.00 2.70
❑ 178 Torry Holt RC 10.00 4.50
❑ 179 Sedrick Irvin RC 5.00 2.20
❑ 180 Edgerrin James RC 20.00 9.00
❑ 181 Joe Germaine RC 5.00 2.20
❑ 182 James Johnson RC 5.00 2.20
❑ 183 Kevin Johnson RC 8.00 3.60
❑ 184 Andy Katzenmoyer RC 5.00 2.20
❑ 185 Jevon Kearse RC 8.00 3.60
❑ 186 Shaun King RC 8.00 3.60
❑ 187 Rob Konrad RC 5.00 2.20
❑ 188 Jim Kleinsasser RC 5.00 2.20
❑ 189 Chris McAlister RC 4.00 1.80
❑ 190 Donovan McNabb RC 12.00 5.50
❑ 191 Cade McNown RC 5.00 2.20
❑ 192 De'Mond Parker RC 2.00 .90
❑ 193 Craig Yeast RC 4.00 1.80
❑ 194 Shawn Bryson RC 5.00 2.20
❑ 195 Peerless Price RC 5.00 2.20
❑ 196 Darnell McDonald RC 5.00 2.20
❑ 197 Akili Smith RC 8.00 3.60
❑ 198 Tai Streets RC 5.00 2.20
❑ 199 Ricky Williams RC 12.00 5.50
❑ 200 Amos Zereoue RC 5.00 2.20

2000 Donruss Elite

	MINT	NRMT
COMPLETE SET (200)	500.00	220.00
COMMON CARD (1-100)	.20	.09
COMMON CARD (101-125)	1.00	.45

❑ 1 Jake Plummer .75 .35
❑ 2 David Boston .75 .35
❑ 3 Rob Moore .40 .18
❑ 4 Chris Chandler .40 .18
❑ 5 Tim Dwight .75 .35
❑ 6 Terance Mathis .40 .18
❑ 7 Jamal Anderson .75 .35
❑ 8 Priest Holmes .40 .18
❑ 9 Tony Banks .40 .18
❑ 10 Shannon Sharpe .40 .18
❑ 11 Qadry Ismail .20 .09
❑ 12 Eric Moulds .75 .35
❑ 13 Doug Flutie 1.00 .45
❑ 14 Antowain Smith .40 .18
❑ 15 Peerless Price .75 .35
❑ 16 Muhsin Muhammad .40 .18
❑ 17 Tim Biakabutuka .40 .18
❑ 18 Patrick Jeffers .75 .35
❑ 19 Steve Beuerlein .40 .18
❑ 20 Wesley Walls .20 .09
❑ 21 Curtis Enis .40 .18
❑ 22 Marcus Robinson .75 .35
❑ 23 Carl Pickens .40 .18
❑ 24 Corey Dillon .75 .35
❑ 25 Akili Smith .75 .35
❑ 26 Darnay Scott .40 .18
❑ 27 Kevin Johnson .75 .35
❑ 28 Errict Rhett .40 .18
❑ 29 Emmitt Smith 2.00 .90
❑ 30 Deion Sanders .75 .35
❑ 31 Troy Aikman 2.00 .90
❑ 32 Joey Galloway .75 .35
❑ 33 Michael Irvin .40 .18
❑ 34 Rocket Ismail .40 .18
❑ 35 Jason Tucker .40 .18
❑ 36 Ed McCaffrey .75 .35
❑ 37 Rod Smith .40 .18
❑ 38 Brian Griese 1.00 .45
❑ 39 Terrell Davis 2.00 .90
❑ 40 Olandis Gary .75 .35
❑ 41 Charlie Batch .75 .35
❑ 42 Johnnie Morton .40 .18
❑ 43 Herman Moore .40 .18
❑ 44 James Stewart .40 .18
❑ 45 Dorsey Levens .40 .18

❑ 46 Antonio Freeman .75 .35
❑ 47 Brett Favre 3.00 1.35
❑ 48 Bill Schroeder .40 .18
❑ 49 Peyton Manning 2.50 1.10
❑ 50 Keenan McCardell .40 .18
❑ 51 Fred Taylor 1.00 .45
❑ 52 Jimmy Smith .40 .18
❑ 53 Elvis Grbac .40 .18
❑ 54 Tony Gonzalez .40 .18
❑ 55 Derrick Alexander .40 .18
❑ 56 Dan Marino 3.00 1.35
❑ 57 Tony Martin .40 .18
❑ 58 James Johnson .40 .18
❑ 59 Damon Huard .75 .35
❑ 60 Thurman Thomas .40 .18
❑ 61 Robert Smith .75 .35
❑ 62 Randall Cunningham .75 .35
❑ 63 Jeff George .40 .18
❑ 64 Terry Glenn .40 .18
❑ 65 Drew Bledsoe 1.25 .55
❑ 66 Jeff Blake .40 .18
❑ 67 Amani Toomer .40 .18
❑ 68 Kerry Collins .40 .18
❑ 69 Joe Montgomery .20 .09
❑ 70 Vinny Testaverde .40 .18
❑ 71 Ray Lucas .75 .35
❑ 72 Keyshawn Johnson .75 .35
❑ 73 Wayne Chrebet .40 .18
❑ 74 Napoleon Kaufman .40 .18
❑ 75 Tim Brown .75 .35
❑ 76 Rich Gannon .40 .18
❑ 77 Duce Staley .75 .35
❑ 78 Kordell Stewart .75 .35
❑ 79 Jerome Bettis .75 .35
❑ 80 Troy Edwards .40 .18
❑ 81 Natrone Means .20 .09
❑ 82 Curtis Conway .40 .18
❑ 83 Jim Harbaugh .40 .18
❑ 84 Junior Seau .40 .18
❑ 85 Jermaine Fazande .20 .09
❑ 86 Terrell Owens .75 .35
❑ 87 Charlie Garner .40 .18
❑ 88 Steve Young 1.25 .55
❑ 89 Jeff Garcia .75 .35
❑ 90 Derrick Mayes .40 .18
❑ 91 Ricky Watters .40 .18
❑ 92 Az-Zahir Hakim .40 .18
❑ 93 Torry Holt .75 .35
❑ 94 Warren Sapp .40 .18
❑ 95 Mike Alstott .75 .35
❑ 96 Warrick Dunn .75 .35
❑ 97 Kevin Dyson .40 .18
❑ 98 Bruce Smith .40 .18
❑ 99 Albert Connell .20 .09
❑ 100 Michael Westbrook .40 .18
❑ 101 Cade McNown .75 .35
❑ 102 Tim Couch 4.00 1.80
❑ 103 John Elway 8.00 3.60
❑ 104 Barry Sanders 6.00 2.70
❑ 105 Germane Crowell 1.00 .45
❑ 106 Marvin Harrison 2.00 .90
❑ 107 Edgerrin James 8.00 3.60
❑ 108 Mark Brunell 3.00 1.35
❑ 109 Randy Moss 6.00 2.70
❑ 110 Cris Carter 2.00 .90
❑ 111 Daunte Culpepper 4.00 1.80
❑ 112 Ricky Williams 5.00 2.20
❑ 113 Curtis Martin 2.00 .90
❑ 114 Donovan McNabb 3.00 1.35
❑ 115 Jerry Rice 5.00 2.20
❑ 116 Jon Kitna 2.00 .90
❑ 117 Isaac Bruce 2.00 .90
❑ 118 Marshall Faulk 2.50 1.10
❑ 119 Kurt Warner 8.00 3.60
❑ 120 Shaun King 3.00 1.35
❑ 121 Eddie George 2.50 1.10
❑ 122 Steve McNair 2.00 .90
❑ 123 Jevon Kearse 2.00 .90
❑ 124 Stephen Davis 2.00 .90
❑ 125 Brad Johnson 2.00 .90
❑ 126 Mike Anderson RC 50.00 22.00
❑ 127 Peter Warrick RC 20.00 9.00
❑ 128 Courtney Brown RC 8.00 3.60
❑ 129 Plaxico Burress RC 12.00 5.50
❑ 130 Corey Simon RC 8.00 3.60
❑ 131 Thomas Jones RC 10.00 4.50
❑ 132 Travis Taylor RC 8.00 3.60
❑ 133 Shaun Alexander RC 15.00 6.75
❑ 134 Deon Grant RC 3.00 1.35
❑ 135 Chris Redman RC 12.00 5.50
❑ 136 Chad Pennington RC 20.00 9.00
❑ 137 Jamal Lewis RC 40.00 18.00
❑ 138 Brian Urlacher RC 20.00 9.00
❑ 139 Keith Bulluck RC 6.00 2.70
❑ 140 Bubba Franks RC 8.00 3.60
❑ 141 Dez White RC 5.00 2.20
❑ 142 Na'il Diggs RC 6.00 2.70
❑ 143 Ahmed Plummer RC 6.00 2.70
❑ 144 Ron Dayne RC 20.00 9.00
❑ 145 Shaun Ellis RC 5.00 2.20
❑ 146 Sylvester Morris RC 12.00 5.50
❑ 147 Deltha O'Neal RC 5.00 2.20
❑ 148 Raynoch Thompson RC 5.00 2.20
❑ 149 R.Jay Soward RC 6.00 2.70
❑ 150 Mario Edwards RC 3.00 1.35
❑ 151 John Engelberger RC 5.00 2.20
❑ 152 D.Goodrich RC 6.00 2.70
❑ 153 Sherrod Gideon RC 3.00 1.35
❑ 154 John Abraham RC 5.00 2.20
❑ 155 Ben Kelly RC EXCH 6.00 2.70
❑ 156 Travis Prentice RC 10.00 4.50
❑ 157 Darrell Jackson RC 10.00 4.50
❑ 158 Giovanni Carmazzi RC 8.00 3.60
❑ 159 Anthony Lucas RC 3.00 1.35
❑ 160 Danny Farmer RC 6.00 2.70
❑ 161 Dennis Northcutt RC 8.00 3.60
❑ 162 Troy Walters RC 6.00 2.70
❑ 163 Laveranues Coles RC 10.00 4.50
❑ 164 Tee Martin RC 10.00 4.50
❑ 165 J.R. Redmond RC 8.00 3.60
❑ 166 Tim Rattay RC 10.00 4.50
❑ 167 Jerry Porter RC 6.00 2.70
❑ 168 Sebastian Janikowski RC 6.00 2.70
❑ 169 Michael Wiley RC 6.00 2.70
❑ 170 Reuben Droughns RC 6.00 2.70
❑ 171 Trung Canidate RC 6.00 2.70
❑ 172 Shyrone Stith RC 6.00 2.70
❑ 173 Chris Hovan RC 5.00 2.20
❑ 174 Brandon Short RC 6.00 2.70
❑ 175 Mark Roman RC 6.00 2.70
❑ 176 Trevor Gaylor RC 5.00 2.20
❑ 177 Chris Cole RC 5.00 2.20
❑ 178 Hank Poteat RC 5.00 2.20
❑ 179 Darren Howard RC 5.00 2.20
❑ 180 Rob Morris RC 6.00 2.70
❑ 181 Spergon Wynn RC 6.00 2.70
❑ 182 Marc Bulger RC 6.00 2.70
❑ 183 Tom Brady RC 6.00 2.70
❑ 184 Todd Husak RC 6.00 2.70
❑ 185 Gari Scott RC 5.00 2.20
❑ 186 Erron Kinney RC 5.00 2.20
❑ 187 Julian Peterson RC 5.00 2.20
❑ 188 Sammy Morris RC 8.00 3.60
❑ 189 Rondell Mealey RC 3.00 1.35
❑ 190 Doug Chapman RC 12.00 5.50
❑ 191 Ron Dugans RC 5.00 2.20
❑ 192 Deon Dyer RC 5.00 2.20
❑ 193 Fred Robbins RC 3.00 1.35
❑ 194 Ike Charlton RC 6.00 2.70
❑ 195 Mareno Philyaw RC 3.00 1.35
❑ 196 Thomas Hamner RC 6.00 2.70
❑ 197 Jarious Jackson RC 6.00 2.70
❑ 198 Anthony Becht RC 6.00 2.70
❑ 199 Joe Hamilton RC 8.00 3.60
❑ 200 Todd Pinkston RC 6.00 2.70

1997 Donruss Preferred

	MINT	NRMT
COMPLETE SET (150)	400.00	180.00
COMP.BRONZE SET (80)	30.00	13.50
COMMON BRONZE	.30	.14
COMMON SILVER	2.50	1.10
COMMON GOLD	4.00	1.80

❑ 1 Emmitt Smith P 20.00 9.00
❑ 2 Steve Young G 10.00 4.50
❑ 3 Cris Carter S 4.00 1.80
❑ 4 Tim Biakabutuka B .50 .23
❑ 5 Brett Favre P 25.00 11.00
❑ 6 Troy Aikman G 12.00 5.50
❑ 7 Eddie Kennison S 4.00 1.80

❑ 8 Ben Coates B .50 .23
❑ 9 Dan Marino P 25.00 11.00
❑ 10 Deion Sanders G 6.00 2.70
❑ 11 Curtis Conway S 4.00 1.80
❑ 12 Jeff George B .50 .23
❑ 13 Barry Sanders P 25.00 11.00
❑ 14 Kerry Collins G .50 .23
❑ 15 Marvin Harrison S 4.00 1.80
❑ 16 Bobby Engram B .50 .23
❑ 17 Jerry Rice P 15.00 6.75
❑ 18 Kordell Stewart G 8.00 3.60
❑ 19 Tony Banks S 4.00 1.80
❑ 20 Jim Harbaugh B .50 .23
❑ 21 Mark Brunell P 12.00 5.50
❑ 22 Steve McNair G 10.00 4.50
❑ 23 Terrell Owens S 8.00 3.60
❑ 24 Raymont Harris B .30 .14
❑ 25 Curtis Martin P 10.00 4.50
❑ 26 Karim Abdul-Jabbar G 6.00 2.70
❑ 27 Joey Galloway S 5.00 2.20
❑ 28 Bobby Hoying B .50 .23
❑ 29 Terrell Davis P 20.00 9.00
❑ 30 Terry Glenn G 4.00 1.80
❑ 31 Antonio Freeman S 6.00 2.70
❑ 32 Brad Johnson B 1.00 .45
❑ 33 Drew Bledsoe P 12.00 5.50
❑ 34 John Elway G 25.00 11.00
❑ 35 Herman Moore G 6.00 2.70
❑ 36 Robert Brooks S 4.00 1.80
❑ 37 Rod Smith B .75 .35
❑ 38 Eddie George P 12.00 5.50
❑ 39 Keyshawn Johnson G 6.00 2.70
❑ 40 Greg Hill S 2.50 1.10
❑ 41 Scott Mitchell B .50 .23
❑ 42 Muhsin Muhammad B .50 .23
❑ 43 Isaac Bruce G 6.00 2.70
❑ 44 Jeff Blake S 4.00 1.80
❑ 45 Neil O'Donnell B .50 .23
❑ 46 Jimmy Smith B .50 .23
❑ 47 Jerome Bettis G 6.00 2.70
❑ 48 Terry Allen S 4.00 1.80
❑ 49 Andre Reed B .50 .23
❑ 50 Frank Sanders B .50 .23
❑ 51 Tim Brown G 6.00 2.70
❑ 52 Thurman Thomas S 4.00 1.80
❑ 53 Heath Shuler B .30 .14
❑ 54 Vinny Testaverde B .50 .23
❑ 55 Marcus Allen S 4.00 1.80
❑ 56 Napoleon Kaufman B .75 .35
❑ 57 Derrick Alexander WR B .50 .23
❑ 58 Carl Pickens G 4.00 1.80
❑ 59 Marshall Faulk S 4.00 1.80
❑ 60 Mike Alstott B .75 .35
❑ 61 Jamal Anderson B 2.00 .90
❑ 62 Ricky Watters G 4.00 1.80
❑ 63 Dorsey Levens S 4.00 1.80
❑ 64 Todd Collins B .30 .14
❑ 65 Trent Dilfer B .75 .35
❑ 66 Natrone Means S 4.00 1.80
❑ 67 Gus Frerotte B .30 .14
❑ 68 Irving Fryar B .50 .23
❑ 69 Adrian Murrell S 4.00 1.80
❑ 70 Rodney Hampton B .50 .23
❑ 71 Garrison Hearst B .50 .23
❑ 72 Reggie White S 4.00 1.80
❑ 73 Anthony Johnson B .30 .14
❑ 74 Tony Martin B .50 .23

❑ 75 Chris Sanders S 2.50 1.10
❑ 76 O.J. McDuffie B .50 .23
❑ 77 Leeland McElroy B .30 .14
❑ 78 Ki-Jana Carter S 4.00 1.80
❑ 79 Anthony Miller B .30 .14
❑ 80 Johnnie Morton B .50 .23
❑ 81 Robert Smith S .50 .23
❑ 82 Brett Perriman B .30 .14
❑ 83 Errict Rhett B .30 .14
❑ 84 Michael Irvin S 4.00 1.80
❑ 85 Darnay Scott B .50 .23
❑ 86 Shannon Sharpe B .50 .23
❑ 87 Lawrence Phillips S 4.00 1.80
❑ 88 Bruce Smith B .50 .23
❑ 89 James O.Stewart B .50 .23
❑ 90 J.J. Stokes B .50 .23
❑ 91 Chris Warren B .50 .23
❑ 92 Daryl Johnston B .50 .23
❑ 93 Andre Rison B .50 .23
❑ 94 Rashaan Salaam B .30 .14
❑ 95 Amani Toomer B .50 .23
❑ 96 Warrick Dunn G RC 20.00 9.00
❑ 97 Tiki Barber S RC 10.00 4.50
❑ 98 Peter Boulware B RC .50 .23
❑ 99 Ike Hilliard G RC 12.00 5.50
❑ 100 Antowain Smith S RC 8.00 3.60
❑ 101 Yatil Green S RC 4.00 1.80
❑ 102 Tony Gonzalez B RC 5.00 2.20
❑ 103 Reidel Anthony G RC 12.00 5.50
❑ 104 Troy Davis S RC 4.00 1.80
❑ 105 Rae Carruth S RC 2.50 1.10
❑ 106 David LaFleur B RC .75 .35
❑ 107 Jim Druckenmiller G RC 4.00 1.80
❑ 108 Joey Kent S RC 4.00 1.80
❑ 109 Byron Hanspard S RC 4.00 1.80
❑ 110 Darrell Russell B RC .30 .14
❑ 111 Danny Wuerffel S RC 4.00 1.80
❑ 112 Jake Plummer S RC 15.00 6.75
❑ 113 Jay Graham B RC .75 .35
❑ 114 Corey Dillon S RC 15.00 6.75
❑ 115 Orlando Pace B RC .75 .35
❑ 116 Pat Barnes S RC 4.00 1.80
❑ 117 Shawn Springs B RC .50 .23
❑ 118 Troy Aikman NT B 2.00 .90
❑ 119 Drew Bledsoe NT B 2.00 .90
❑ 120 Mark Brunell NT B 2.00 .90
❑ 121 Kerry Collins NT B .50 .23
❑ 122 Terrell Davis NT B 3.00 1.35
❑ 123 Jerome Bettis NT B .75 .35
❑ 124 Brett Favre NT B 4.00 1.80
❑ 125 Eddie George NT B 2.00 .90
❑ 126 Terry Glenn NT B .75 .35
❑ 127 Karim Abdul-Jabbar NT B .75 .35
❑ 128 Keyshawn Johnson NT B .75 .35
❑ 129 Dan Marino NT B 4.00 1.80
❑ 130 Curtis Martin NT B 1.00 .45
❑ 131 Natrone Means NT B .75 .35
❑ 132 Herman Moore NT S 4.00 1.80
❑ 133 Jerry Rice NT B 2.00 .90
❑ 134 Barry Sanders NT B 4.00 1.80
❑ 135 Deion Sanders NT B .75 .35
❑ 136 Emmitt Smith NT B 3.00 1.35
❑ 137 Kordell Stewart NT B 1.00 .45
❑ 138 Steve Young NT B 1.50 .70
❑ 139 Carl Pickens NT S 4.00 1.80
❑ 140 Isaac Bruce NT S 4.00 1.80
❑ 141 Steve McNair NT S 5.00 2.20
❑ 142 John Elway NT S 10.00 4.50
❑ 143 Cris Carter NT B .50 .23
❑ 144 Tim Brown NT B .50 .23
❑ 145 Ricky Watters NT B .30 .14
❑ 146 Robert Brooks NT B .50 .23
❑ 147 Jeff Blake NT B .50 .23
❑ 148 Tiki Barber CL B .50 .23
❑ 149 Jim Druckenmiller CL B .75 .35
❑ 150 Warrick Dunn CL B 1.00 .45

1999 Donruss Preferred QBC

	MINT	NRMT
COMPLETE SET (120)	150.00	70.00
COMP.BRONZE SET (45)	25.00	11.00
COMMON BRONZE (1-45)	.15	.07
COMMON SILVER (46-80)	.50	.23

COMMON GOLD (81-105)	1.00	.45
COMMON PLATINUM (106-120)	3.00	1.35

❑ 1 Troy Aikman B 1.50 .70
❑ 2 Tony Banks B .30 .14
❑ 3 Jeff Blake B .30 .14
❑ 4 Drew Bledsoe B 1.00 .45
❑ 5 Bubby Brister B .15 .07
❑ 6 Chris Chandler B .30 .14
❑ 7 Kerry Collins B .30 .14
❑ 8 Randall Cunningham B .60 .25
❑ 9 Terrell Davis B 1.50 .70
❑ 10 Trent Dilfer B .30 .14
❑ 11 John Elway B 2.50 1.10
❑ 12 Boomer Esiason B .15 .07
❑ 13 Jim Everett B .15 .07
❑ 14 Brett Favre B 2.50 1.10
❑ 15 Doug Flutie B .60 .25
❑ 16 Gus Frerotte B .15 .07
❑ 17 Jeff George B .30 .14
❑ 18 Elvis Grbac B .30 .14
❑ 19 Jim Harbaugh B .30 .14
❑ 20 Michael Irvin B .30 .14
❑ 21 Brad Johnson B .60 .25
❑ 22 Keyshawn Johnson B .60 .25
❑ 23 Danny Kanell B .15 .07
❑ 24 Jim Kelly B .15 .07
❑ 25 Bernie Kosar B .15 .07
❑ 26 Erik Kramer B .15 .07
❑ 27 Ryan Leaf B .60 .25
❑ 28 Peyton Manning B 2.50 1.10
❑ 29 Dan Marino B 2.50 1.10
❑ 30 Donovan McNabb B RC 5.00 2.20
❑ 31 Steve McNair B .60 .25
❑ 32 Cade McNown B RC 1.50 .70
❑ 33 Scott Mitchell B .15 .07
❑ 34 Warren Moon B .60 .25
❑ 35 Neil O'Donnell B .30 .14
❑ 36 Jake Plummer B 1.25 .55
❑ 37 Jerry Rice B 1.50 .70
❑ 38 Barry Sanders B 2.50 1.10
❑ 39 Junior Seau B .30 .14
❑ 40 Phil Simms B .15 .07
❑ 41 Kordell Stewart B .60 .25
❑ 42 Vinny Testaverde B .30 .14
❑ 43 Ricky Williams B RC 5.00 2.20
❑ 44 Steve Young B 1.00 .45
❑ 45 Dan Marino B 3.00 1.35
Brett Favre B
John Elway B
❑ 46 Troy Aikman S 2.50 1.10
❑ 47 Tony Banks S .30 .14
❑ 48 Drew Bledsoe S 1.50 .70
❑ 49 Bubby Brister S .15 .07
❑ 50 Chris Chandler S .30 .14
❑ 51 Kerry Collins S .30 .14
❑ 52 Randall Cunningham S 1.00 .45
❑ 53 Terrell Davis S 2.50 1.10
❑ 54 Trent Dilfer S .30 .14
❑ 55 John Elway S 4.00 1.80
❑ 56 Boomer Esiason S .15 .07
❑ 57 Brett Favre S 4.00 1.80
❑ 58 Doug Flutie S 1.25 .55
❑ 59 Elvis Grbac S .30 .14
❑ 60 Jim Harbaugh S 1.00 .45
❑ 61 Michael Irvin S .30 .14
❑ 62 Brad Johnson S 1.00 .45
❑ 63 Keyshawn Johnson S 1.00 .45
❑ 64 Jim Kelly S 1.00 .45
❑ 65 Ryan Leaf S 1.00 .45
❑ 66 Peyton Manning S 4.00 1.80
❑ 67 Dan Marino S 4.00 1.80
❑ 68 Donovan McNabb S 8.00 3.60
❑ 69 Steve McNair S 1.00 .45
❑ 70 Cade McNown S 3.00 1.35
❑ 71 Warren Moon S 1.00 .45
❑ 72 Jake Plummer S 2.00 .90
❑ 73 Jerry Rice S 2.50 1.10
❑ 74 Barry Sanders S 4.00 1.80
❑ 75 Junior Seau S .30 .14
❑ 76 Phil Simms S .15 .07
❑ 77 Kordell Stewart S 1.00 .45
❑ 78 Vinny Testaverde S .30 .14
❑ 79 Ricky Williams S 8.00 3.60
❑ 80 Steve Young S 1.50 .70
❑ 81 Troy Aikman G 5.00 2.20
❑ 82 Drew Bledsoe G 3.00 1.35
❑ 83 Bubby Brister G .15 .07
❑ 84 Chris Chandler G .30 .14
❑ 85 Randall Cunningham G 2.00 .90
❑ 86 Terrell Davis G 6.00 2.70
❑ 87 John Elway G 8.00 3.60
❑ 88 Brett Favre G 8.00 3.60
❑ 89 Doug Flutie G 2.50 1.10
❑ 90 Brad Johnson G 2.00 .90
❑ 91 Keyshawn Johnson G 2.00 .90
❑ 92 Ryan Leaf G 2.00 .90
❑ 93 Peyton Manning G 8.00 3.60
❑ 94 Dan Marino G 8.00 3.60
❑ 95 Donovan McNabb G 15.00 6.75
❑ 96 Steve McNair G 2.00 .90
❑ 97 Cade McNown G 6.00 2.70
❑ 98 Warren Moon G 2.00 .90
❑ 99 Jake Plummer G 4.00 1.80
❑ 100 Jerry Rice G 5.00 2.20
❑ 101 Barry Sanders G 8.00 3.60
❑ 102 Kordell Stewart G 2.00 .90
❑ 103 Vinny Testaverde G .30 .14
❑ 104 Ricky Williams G 15.00 6.75
❑ 105 Steve Young G 3.00 1.35
❑ 106 Troy Aikman P 8.00 3.60
❑ 107 Drew Bledsoe P 5.00 2.20
❑ 108 Terrell Davis P 8.00 3.60
❑ 109 John Elway P 12.00 5.50
❑ 110 Brett Favre P 12.00 5.50
❑ 111 Keyshawn Johnson P 3.00 1.35
❑ 112 Peyton Manning P 12.00 5.50
❑ 113 Dan Marino P 12.00 5.50
❑ 114 Donovan McNabb P 20.00 9.00
❑ 115 Cade McNown P 8.00 3.60
❑ 116 Jake Plummer P 6.00 2.70
❑ 117 Jerry Rice P 8.00 3.60
❑ 118 Barry Sanders P 12.00 5.50
❑ 119 Kordell Stewart P 3.00 1.35
❑ 120 Ricky Williams P 20.00 9.00

2000 Donruss Preferred

	MINT	NRMT
COMPLETE SET (103)	25.00	11.00

❑ 1 Jake Plummer .40 .18
❑ 2 Chris Chandler .25 .11
❑ 3 Trent Dilfer .25 .11
❑ 4 Doug Flutie .50 .23

Card	MINT	NRMT
❑ 5 Cade McNown	.40	.18
❑ 6 Michael Irvin	.25	.11
❑ 7 Troy Aikman	1.00	.45
❑ 8 Terrell Davis	1.00	.45
❑ 9 John Elway	1.50	.70
❑ 10 Brett Favre	1.50	.70
❑ 11 Peyton Manning	1.00	.45
❑ 12 Warren Moon	.40	.18
❑ 13 Randall Cunningham	.40	.18
❑ 14 Drew Bledsoe	.60	.25
❑ 15 Ricky Williams	.75	.35
❑ 16 Kerry Collins	.25	.11
❑ 17 Vinny Testaverde	.25	.11
❑ 18 Donovan McNabb	.60	.25
❑ 19 Jim Harbaugh	.25	.11
❑ 20 Jerry Rice	1.00	.45
❑ 21 Steve Young	.60	.25
❑ 22 Keyshawn Johnson	.40	.18
❑ 23 Neil O'Donnell	.25	.11
❑ 24 Steve McNair	.40	.18
❑ 25 Brad Johnson	.40	.18
❑ 26 Jeff George	.25	.11
❑ 27 Dan Marino	1.50	.70
❑ 28 Jim Kelly	.40	.18
❑ 29 Barry Sanders	1.25	.55
❑ 30 Phil Simms	.25	.11
❑ 31 Gus Frerotte	.25	.11
❑ 32 Elvis Grbac	.25	.11
❑ 33 Jeff Blake	.25	.11
❑ 34 Kordell Stewart	.40	.18
❑ 35 Tony Banks	.25	.11
❑ 36 Doug Flutie C	.50	.23
❑ 37 Cade McNown C	.40	.18
❑ 38 Troy Aikman C	1.00	.45
❑ 39 Terrell Davis C	1.00	.45
❑ 40 John Elway C	1.50	.70
❑ 41 Brett Favre C	1.50	.70
❑ 42 Peyton Manning C	1.00	.45
❑ 43 Drew Bledsoe C	.60	.25
❑ 44 Ricky Williams C	.75	.35
❑ 45 Kerry Collins C	.25	.11
❑ 46 Vinny Testaverde C	.25	.11
❑ 47 Donovan McNabb C	.60	.25
❑ 48 Kordell Stewart C	.40	.18
❑ 49 Ryan Leaf C	.40	.18
❑ 50 Jerry Rice C	1.00	.45
❑ 51 Steve Young C	.60	.25
❑ 52 Keyshawn Johnson C	.40	.18
❑ 53 Steve McNair C	.40	.18
❑ 54 Jeff George C	.25	.11
❑ 55 Dan Marino C	1.50	.70
❑ 56 Jim Kelly C	.40	.18
❑ 57 Barry Sanders C	1.25	.55
❑ 58 Bernie Kosar C	.25	.11
❑ 59 Chris Chandler C	.25	.11
❑ 60 Jim Everett C	.25	.11
❑ 61 Jake Plummer HS	.40	.18
❑ 62 Cade McNown HS	.50	.23
❑ 63 Troy Aikman HS	1.00	.45
❑ 64 Ricky Williams HS	.75	.35
❑ 65 Donovan McNabb HS	.60	.25
❑ 66 Steve Young HS	.60	.25
❑ 67 Brad Johnson HS	.40	.18
❑ 68 Kerry Collins HS	.25	.11
❑ 69 Ryan Leaf HS	.40	.18
❑ 70 Drew Bledsoe HS	.60	.25
❑ 71 Jake Plummer PS	.40	.18
❑ 72 Chris Chandler PS	.25	.11
❑ 73 Michael Irvin PS	.25	.11
❑ 74 Troy Aikman PS	1.00	.45
❑ 75 Terrell Davis PS	1.00	.45
❑ 76 John Elway PS	1.50	.70
❑ 77 Brett Favre PS	1.50	.70
❑ 78 Peyton Manning PS	1.00	.45
❑ 79 Drew Bledsoe PS	.60	.25
❑ 80 Junior Seau PS	.25	.11
❑ 81 Jerry Rice PS	1.00	.45
❑ 82 Steve Young PS	.60	.25
❑ 83 Keyshawn Johnson PS	.40	.18
❑ 84 Steve McNair PS	.40	.18
❑ 85 Brad Johnson PS	.40	.18
❑ 86 Dan Marino PS	1.50	.70
❑ 87 Jim Kelly PS	.40	.18
❑ 88 Barry Sanders PS	1.25	.55
❑ 89 Phil Simms PS	.25	.11
❑ 90 Boomer Esiason PS	.25	.11
❑ 91 Jake Plummer OF	.40	.18
❑ 92 Chris Chandler OF	.25	.11
❑ 93 Bubby Brister OF	.25	.11
❑ 94 Cade McNown OF	.50	.23
❑ 95 Jim Harbaugh OF	.25	.11
❑ 96 Peyton Manning OF	1.00	.45
❑ 97 Donovan McNabb OF	.60	.25
❑ 98 Jim Kelly OF	.40	.18
❑ 99 Brad Johnson OF	.40	.18
❑ 100 Kordell Stewart OF	.40	.18
❑ 101 Rob Johnson SP	1.00	.45
❑ 102 Jevon Kearse SP	1.00	.45
❑ 103 Rich Gannon SP	1.00	.45

1997 E-X2000

	MINT	NRMT
COMPLETE SET (60)	50.00	22.00
❑ 1 Jake Plummer RC	20.00	9.00
❑ 2 Jamal Anderson	2.00	.90
❑ 3 Rae Carruth RC	.60	.25
❑ 4 Kerry Collins	.60	.25
❑ 5 Darnell Autry RC	1.25	.55
❑ 6 Rashaan Salaam	.30	.14
❑ 7 Troy Aikman	3.00	1.35
❑ 8 Deion Sanders	1.25	.55
❑ 9 Emmitt Smith	5.00	2.20
❑ 10 Herman Moore	1.25	.55
❑ 11 Barry Sanders	6.00	2.70
❑ 12 Mark Chmura	.60	.25
❑ 13 Brett Favre	6.00	2.70
❑ 14 Antonio Freeman	2.00	.90
❑ 15 Reggie White	1.25	.55
❑ 16 Cris Carter	1.25	.55
❑ 17 Brad Johnson	1.50	.70
❑ 18 Troy Davis RC	.60	.25
❑ 19 Danny Wuerffel RC	3.00	1.35
❑ 20 Dave Brown	.30	.14
❑ 21 Ike Hilliard RC	4.00	1.80
❑ 22 Ty Detmer	.60	.25
❑ 23 Ricky Watters	.60	.25
❑ 24 Tony Banks	.60	.25
❑ 25 Eddie Kennison	.60	.25
❑ 26 Jim Druckenmiller RC	1.25	.55
❑ 27 Jerry Rice	3.00	1.35
❑ 28 Steve Young	2.00	.90
❑ 29 Trent Dilfer	1.25	.55
❑ 30 Warrick Dunn RC	8.00	3.60
❑ 31 Terry Allen	1.25	.55
❑ 32 Gus Frerotte	.30	.14
❑ 33 Vinny Testaverde	.60	.25
❑ 34 Antowain Smith RC	5.00	2.20
❑ 35 Thurman Thomas	1.25	.55
❑ 36 Jeff Blake	.60	.25
❑ 37 Carl Pickens	1.25	.55
❑ 38 Terrell Davis	5.00	2.20
❑ 39 John Elway	6.00	2.70
❑ 40 Eddie George	3.00	1.35
❑ 41 Steve McNair	2.00	.90
❑ 42 Marshall Faulk	1.25	.55
❑ 43 Marvin Harrison	1.25	.55
❑ 44 Mark Brunell	3.00	1.35
❑ 45 Marcus Allen	1.25	.55
❑ 46 Elvis Grbac	.60	.25
❑ 47 Karim Abdul-Jabbar	1.25	.55
❑ 48 Dan Marino	6.00	2.70
❑ 49 Drew Bledsoe	3.00	1.35
❑ 50 Terry Glenn	1.25	.55
❑ 51 Curtis Martin	2.00	.90
❑ 52 Keyshawn Johnson	1.25	.55
❑ 53 Tim Brown	1.25	.55
❑ 54 Jeff George	.60	.25
❑ 55 Jerome Bettis	1.25	.55
❑ 56 Kordell Stewart	1.50	.70
❑ 57 Stan Humphries	.60	.25
❑ 58 Junior Seau	.60	.25
❑ 59 Joey Galloway	1.50	.70
❑ 60 Chris Warren	.60	.25

1998 E-X2001

	MINT	NRMT
COMPLETE SET (60)	80.00	36.00
❑ 1 Kordell Stewart	.75	.35
❑ 2 Steve Young	2.00	.90
❑ 3 Mark Brunell	2.50	1.10
❑ 4 Brett Favre	6.00	2.70
❑ 5 Barry Sanders	6.00	2.70
❑ 6 Warrick Dunn	.75	.35
❑ 7 Jerry Rice	3.00	1.35
❑ 8 Dan Marino	6.00	2.70
❑ 9 Emmitt Smith	5.00	2.20
❑ 10 John Elway	6.00	2.70
❑ 11 Eddie George	2.50	1.10
❑ 12 Jake Plummer	2.00	.90
❑ 13 Terrell Davis	5.00	2.20
❑ 14 Curtis Martin	.75	.35
❑ 15 Troy Aikman	3.00	1.35
❑ 16 Terry Glenn	.75	.35
❑ 17 Mike Alstott	.75	.35
❑ 18 Drew Bledsoe	2.50	1.10
❑ 19 Keyshawn Johnson	.75	.35
❑ 20 Dorsey Levens	.75	.35
❑ 21 Elvis Grbac	.40	.18
❑ 22 Ricky Watters	.40	.18
❑ 23 Robert Smith	.75	.35
❑ 24 Trent Dilfer	.75	.35
❑ 25 Joey Galloway	.75	.35
❑ 26 Rob Moore	.40	.18
❑ 27 Steve McNair	.75	.35
❑ 28 Jim Harbaugh	.40	.18
❑ 29 Troy Davis	.20	.09
❑ 30 Rob Johnson	.40	.18
❑ 31 Shannon Sharpe	.40	.18
❑ 32 Jerome Bettis	.75	.35
❑ 33 Tim Brown	.75	.35
❑ 34 Kerry Collins	.40	.18
❑ 35 Garrison Hearst	.75	.35
❑ 36 Antonio Freeman	.75	.35
❑ 37 Charlie Garner	.20	.09
❑ 38 Glenn Foley	.40	.18
❑ 39 Yatil Green	.20	.09
❑ 40 Tiki Barber	.40	.18
❑ 41 Bobby Hoying	.40	.18
❑ 42 Corey Dillon	2.00	.90
❑ 43 Antowain Smith	.75	.35
❑ 44 Robert Edwards RC	5.00	2.20
❑ 45 Jammi German RC	2.00	.90
❑ 46 Ahman Green RC	8.00	3.60
❑ 47 Hines Ward RC	2.00	.90
❑ 48 Skip Hicks RC	4.00	1.80
❑ 49 Brian Griese RC	12.00	5.50
❑ 50 Charlie Batch RC	10.00	4.50
❑ 51 Jacquez Green RC	6.00	2.70

Card	MINT	NRMT
❑ 52 John Avery RC	.40	.18
❑ 53 Kevin Dyson RC	6.00	2.70
❑ 54 Peyton Manning RC	25.00	11.00
❑ 55 Randy Moss RC	25.00	11.00
❑ 56 Ryan Leaf RC	8.00	3.60
❑ 57 Curtis Enis RC	5.00	2.20
❑ 58 Charles Woodson RC	6.00	2.70
❑ 59 Robert Holcombe RC	.40	.18
❑ 60 Fred Taylor RC	10.00	4.50
❑ NNO Checklist Card 1	.20	.09
❑ NNO Checklist Card 2	.20	.09

1999 E-X Century

	MINT	NRMT
COMPLETE SET (90)	150.00	70.00
COMP.SET w/o SP's (60)	40.00	18.00

Card	MINT	NRMT
❑ 1 Keyshawn Johnson	1.00	.45
❑ 2 Natrone Means	.50	.23
❑ 3 Antonio Freeman	1.00	.45
❑ 4 Muhsin Muhammad	.50	.23
❑ 5 Curtis Martin	1.00	.45
❑ 6 Chris Chandler	.50	.23
❑ 7 Priest Holmes	1.00	.45
❑ 8 Vinny Testaverde	.50	.23
❑ 9 Tim Brown	1.00	.45
❑ 10 Eddie George	1.25	.55
❑ 11 Brad Johnson	1.00	.45
❑ 12 Mike Alstott	1.00	.45
❑ 13 Dorsey Levens	1.00	.45
❑ 14 Jamal Anderson	1.00	.45
❑ 15 Herman Moore	1.00	.45
❑ 16 Brett Favre	4.00	1.80
❑ 17 John Elway	4.00	1.80
❑ 18 Steve Young	1.50	.70
❑ 19 Warrick Dunn	1.00	.45
❑ 20 Fred Taylor	2.50	1.10
❑ 21 Charlie Batch	2.00	.90
❑ 22 Jimmy Smith	.50	.23
❑ 23 Steve McNair	1.00	.45
❑ 24 Jerry Rice	2.50	1.10
❑ 25 Dan Marino	4.00	1.80
❑ 26 Jake Plummer	2.00	.90
❑ 27 Marshall Faulk	1.00	.45
❑ 28 Garrison Hearst	.50	.23
❑ 29 Terrell Davis	2.50	1.10
❑ 30 Barry Sanders	4.00	1.80
❑ 31 Carl Pickens	.50	.23
❑ 32 Jerome Bettis	1.00	.45
❑ 33 Scott Mitchell	.25	.11
❑ 34 Duce Staley	1.00	.45
❑ 35 Robert Smith	1.00	.45
❑ 36 Wayne Chrebet	.50	.23
❑ 37 Steve Beuerlein	.25	.11
❑ 38 Elvis Grbac	.50	.23
❑ 39 Troy Aikman	2.50	1.10
❑ 40 Emmitt Smith	2.50	1.10
❑ 41 Joey Galloway	1.00	.45
❑ 42 Ryan Leaf	1.00	.45
❑ 43 Skip Hicks	1.00	.45
❑ 44 Cris Carter	1.00	.45
❑ 45 Shannon Sharpe	.50	.23
❑ 46 Mark Brunell	1.50	.70
❑ 47 Kerry Collins	.50	.23
❑ 48 Corey Dillon	1.00	.45
❑ 49 Kordell Stewart	1.00	.45
❑ 50 Randy Moss	4.00	1.80
❑ 51 Jon Kitna	1.00	.45
❑ 52 Deion Sanders	1.00	.45
❑ 53 Rod Smith	.50	.23
❑ 54 Drew Bledsoe	1.50	.70
❑ 55 Terrell Owens	1.00	.45
❑ 56 Napoleon Kaufman	1.00	.45
❑ 57 Trent Green	.50	.23
❑ 58 Ricky Watters	.50	.23
❑ 59 Randall Cunningham	1.00	.45
❑ 60 Peyton Manning	4.00	1.80
❑ 61 Tim Couch RC	15.00	6.75
❑ 62 Amos Zereoue RC	4.00	1.80
❑ 63 Cade McNown RC	5.00	2.20
❑ 64 Donovan McNabb RC	15.00	6.75
❑ 65 Ricky Williams RC	15.00	6.75
❑ 66 Daunte Culpepper RC	25.00	11.00
❑ 67 Troy Edwards RC	5.00	2.20
❑ 68 Peerless Price RC	5.00	2.20
❑ 69 Edgerrin James RC	25.00	11.00
❑ 70 Champ Bailey RC	5.00	2.20
❑ 71 Akili Smith RC	8.00	3.60
❑ 72 Kevin Johnson RC	8.00	3.60
❑ 73 Cecil Collins RC	4.00	1.80
❑ 74 David Boston RC	8.00	3.60
❑ 75 Torry Holt RC	10.00	4.50
❑ 76 James Johnson RC	4.00	1.80
❑ 77 Na Brown RC	4.00	1.80
❑ 78 Rob Konrad RC	3.00	1.35
❑ 79 Mike Cloud RC	4.00	1.80
❑ 80 Craig Yeast RC	3.00	1.35
❑ 81 Brock Huard RC	6.00	2.70
❑ 82 Chris McAlister RC	3.00	1.35
❑ 83 Shaun King RC	8.00	3.60
❑ 84 Wane McGarity RC	3.00	1.35
❑ 85 Joe Germaine RC	4.00	1.80
❑ 86 D'Wayne Bates RC	4.00	1.80
❑ 87 Kevin Faulk RC	6.00	2.70
❑ 88 Antoine Winfield RC	3.00	1.35
❑ 89 Reginald Kelly RC	2.00	.90
❑ 90 Antuan Edwards RC	2.00	.90
❑ P1 Jake Plummer Promo	1.00	.45

2000 E-X

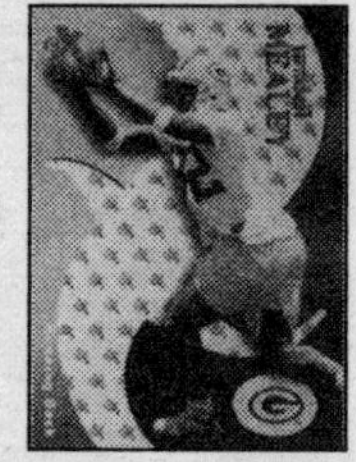

	MINT	NRMT
COMPLETE SET (150)	500.00	220.00
COMP.SET w/o SP's (100)	15.00	6.75

Card	MINT	NRMT
❑ 1 Tim Couch	1.25	.55
❑ 2 Daunte Culpepper	1.25	.55
❑ 3 Jake Reed	.30	.14
❑ 4 Donovan McNabb	1.00	.45
❑ 5 Terry Glenn	.30	.14
❑ 6 Vinny Testaverde	.30	.14
❑ 7 Michael Westbrook	.30	.14
❑ 8 Errict Rhett	.30	.14
❑ 9 Joey Galloway	.60	.25
❑ 10 O.J. McDuffie	.30	.14
❑ 11 Rob Johnson	.30	.14
❑ 12 Warren Sapp	.30	.14
❑ 13 Brian Griese	.75	.35
❑ 14 Derrick Mayes	.30	.14
❑ 15 Ike Hilliard	.30	.14
❑ 16 Kevin Dyson	.30	.14
❑ 17 Shannon Sharpe	.30	.14
❑ 18 Cade McNown	.60	.25
❑ 19 Damon Huard	.60	.25
❑ 20 James Stewart	.30	.14
❑ 21 Kevin Johnson	.60	.25
❑ 22 Muhsin Muhammad	.30	.14
❑ 23 Shaun King	1.00	.45
❑ 24 Corey Dillon	.60	.25
❑ 25 Fred Taylor	.75	.35
❑ 26 Peyton Manning	2.00	.90
❑ 27 Steve McNair	.60	.25
❑ 28 Tim Brown	.60	.25
❑ 29 Brad Johnson	.60	.25
❑ 30 Edgerrin James	2.50	1.10
❑ 31 Germane Crowell	.30	.14
❑ 32 Kordell Stewart	.60	.25
❑ 33 Randy Moss	2.00	.90
❑ 34 Tony Banks	.30	.14
❑ 35 Akili Smith	.60	.25
❑ 36 Charlie Batch	.60	.25
❑ 37 Duce Staley	.60	.25
❑ 38 Jerome Bettis	.60	.25
❑ 39 Rich Gannon	.30	.14
❑ 40 Steve Young	1.00	.45
❑ 41 Tony Gonzalez	.30	.14
❑ 42 Curtis Martin	.60	.25
❑ 43 Eddie George	.75	.35
❑ 44 Marshall Faulk	.75	.35
❑ 45 Troy Edwards	.30	.14
❑ 46 Curtis Enis	.30	.14
❑ 47 Jake Plummer	.60	.25
❑ 48 Jon Kitna	.60	.25
❑ 49 Qadry Ismail	.30	.14
❑ 50 Terrell Davis	1.50	.70
❑ 51 Troy Aikman	1.50	.70
❑ 52 Elvis Grbac	.30	.14
❑ 53 Jeff Blake	.30	.14
❑ 54 Kurt Warner	2.50	1.10
❑ 55 Ricky Watters	.30	.14
❑ 56 Torry Holt	.60	.25
❑ 57 Brett Favre	2.50	1.10
❑ 58 Chris Chandler	.30	.14
❑ 59 Eric Moulds	.60	.25
❑ 60 Jimmy Smith	.30	.14
❑ 61 Ricky Williams	1.50	.70
❑ 62 Antonio Freeman	.60	.25
❑ 63 Curtis Conway	.30	.14
❑ 64 Emmitt Smith	1.50	.70
❑ 65 Kerry Collins	.30	.14
❑ 66 Marvin Harrison	.60	.25
❑ 67 Tyrone Wheatley	.30	.14
❑ 68 Charlie Garner	.30	.14
❑ 69 Derrick Alexander	.30	.14
❑ 70 Jamal Anderson	.60	.25
❑ 71 Mike Alstott	.60	.25
❑ 72 Ryan Leaf	.60	.25
❑ 73 Tim Biakabutuka	.30	.14
❑ 74 Amani Toomer	.30	.14
❑ 75 Dorsey Levens	.30	.14
❑ 76 Frank Sanders	.30	.14
❑ 77 Junior Seau	.30	.14
❑ 78 Steve Beuerlein	.15	.07
❑ 79 Wayne Chrebet	.30	.14
❑ 80 Carl Pickens	.30	.14
❑ 81 Drew Bledsoe	1.00	.45
❑ 82 Isaac Bruce	.60	.25
❑ 83 Marcus Robinson	.60	.25
❑ 84 Stephen Davis	.60	.25
❑ 85 Cris Carter	.60	.25
❑ 86 Ed McCaffrey	.60	.25
❑ 87 Jerry Rice	1.50	.70
❑ 88 Mark Brunell	1.00	.45
❑ 89 Peerless Price	.60	.25
❑ 90 Terance Mathis	.30	.14
❑ 91 Tony Martin	.30	.14
❑ 92 Jevon Kearse	.60	.25
❑ 93 Robert Smith	.60	.25
❑ 94 Rob Moore	.30	.14
❑ 95 Charles Johnson	.30	.14
❑ 96 Doug Flutie	.75	.35
❑ 97 Sean Dawkins	.15	.07
❑ 98 Keenan McCardell	.30	.14
❑ 99 Bill Schroeder	.15	.07
❑ 100 Rod Smith	.30	.14
❑ 101 Peter Warrick RC	30.00	13.50
❑ 102 Corey Simon RC	12.00	5.50
❑ 103 Danny Farmer RC	10.00	4.50
❑ 104 Jamal Lewis RC	50.00	22.00
❑ 105 Jerry Porter RC	10.00	4.50
❑ 106 Joe Hamilton RC	12.00	5.50

		MINT	NRMT
❑ 107	Marc Bulger RC	10.00	4.50
❑ 108	R.Jay Soward RC	10.00	4.50
❑ 109	Ron Dugans RC	8.00	3.60
❑ 110	Shaun Alexander RC	25.00	11.00
❑ 111	Travis Prentice RC	15.00	6.75
❑ 112	Anthony Becht RC	10.00	4.50
❑ 113	Bubba Franks RC	12.00	5.50
❑ 114	Chris Redman RC	20.00	9.00
❑ 115	Dennis Northcutt RC	12.00	5.50
❑ 116	Dez White RC	8.00	3.60
❑ 117	Gari Scott RC	8.00	3.60
❑ 118	Mareno Philyaw RC	5.00	2.20
❑ 119	Ron Dayne RC	30.00	13.50
❑ 120	Shyrone Stith RC	8.00	3.60
❑ 121	Tee Martin RC	15.00	6.75
❑ 122	Tom Brady RC	10.00	4.50
❑ 123	Trung Canidate RC	10.00	4.50
❑ 124	Chad Pennington RC	30.00	13.50
❑ 125	Chris Cole RC	8.00	3.60
❑ 126	Courtney Brown RC	12.00	5.50
❑ 127	Doug Chapman RC	20.00	9.00
❑ 128	Giovanni Carmazzi RC	12.00	5.50
❑ 129	J.R. Redmond RC	12.00	5.50
❑ 130	Michael Wiley RC	10.00	4.50
❑ 131	Reuben Droughns RC	10.00	4.50
❑ 132	Terrelle Smith RC	8.00	3.60
❑ 133	Thomas Jones RC	15.00	6.75
❑ 134	Travis Taylor RC	12.00	5.50
❑ 135	Anthony Lucas RC	5.00	2.20
❑ 136	Curtis Keaton RC	8.00	3.60
❑ 137	Frank Moreau RC	10.00	4.50
❑ 138	Darrell Jackson RC	15.00	6.75
❑ 139	Laveranues Coles RC	15.00	6.75
❑ 140	Brian Urlacher RC	30.00	13.50
❑ 141	Plaxico Burress RC	20.00	9.00
❑ 142	Sammy Morris RC	12.00	5.50
❑ 143	Sylvester Morris RC	20.00	9.00
❑ 144	Tim Rattay RC	15.00	6.75
❑ 145	Todd Pinkston RC	10.00	4.50
❑ 146	Troy Walters RC	10.00	4.50
❑ 147	Sebastian Janikowski RC	10.00	4.50
❑ 148	JaJuan Dawson RC	10.00	4.50
❑ 149	Trevor Gaylor RC	8.00	3.60
❑ 150	Rondell Mealey RC	5.00	2.20

1994 Excalibur

	MINT	NRMT
COMPLETE SET (75)	25.00	11.00

		MINT	NRMT
❑ 1	Bobby Hebert	.25	.11
❑ 2	Deion Sanders	1.25	.55
❑ 3	Andre Rison	.50	.23
❑ 4	Cornelius Bennett	.50	.23
❑ 5	Jim Kelly	.75	.35
❑ 6	Andre Reed	.50	.23
❑ 7	Bruce Smith	.75	.35
❑ 8	Thurman Thomas	.75	.35
❑ 9	Curtis Conway	.75	.35
❑ 10	Richard Dent	.50	.23
❑ 11	Jim Harbaugh	.75	.35
❑ 12	Troy Aikman	2.50	1.10
❑ 13	Michael Irvin	.75	.35
❑ 14	Russell Maryland	.25	.11
❑ 15	Emmitt Smith	4.00	1.80
❑ 16	Steve Atwater	.25	.11
❑ 17	Rod Bernstine	.25	.11
❑ 18	John Elway	5.00	2.20
❑ 19	Glyn Milburn	.50	.23
❑ 20	Shannon Sharpe	.50	.23
❑ 21	Barry Sanders	5.00	2.20
❑ 22	Edgar Bennett	.75	.35
❑ 23	Brett Favre	5.00	2.20
❑ 24	Sterling Sharpe	.50	.23
❑ 25	Reggie White	.75	.35
❑ 26	Warren Moon	.75	.35
❑ 27	Wilber Marshall	.25	.11
❑ 28	Haywood Jeffires	.50	.23
❑ 29	Lorenzo White	.25	.11
❑ 30	Quentin Coryatt	.25	.11
❑ 31	Roosevelt Potts	.25	.11
❑ 32	Jeff George	.75	.35
❑ 33	Joe Montana	5.00	2.20
❑ 34	Neil Smith	.75	.35
❑ 35	Marcus Allen	.75	.35
❑ 36	Derrick Thomas	.75	.35
❑ 37	Jeff Hostetler	.50	.23
❑ 38	Tim Brown	.75	.35
❑ 39	Rocket Ismail	.50	.23
❑ 40	Randall Cunningham	.75	.35
❑ 41	Jerome Bettis	.75	.35
❑ 42	Dan Marino	5.00	2.20
❑ 43	Keith Jackson	.25	.11
❑ 44	O.J. McDuffie	.75	.35
❑ 45	Drew Bledsoe	2.50	1.10
❑ 46	Leonard Russell	.25	.11
❑ 47	Wade Wilson	.25	.11
❑ 48	Eric Martin	.25	.11
❑ 49	Phil Simms	.50	.23
❑ 50	Gary Brown RB	.75	.35
❑ 51	Rodney Hampton	.75	.35
❑ 52	Boomer Esiason	.50	.23
❑ 53	Johnny Johnson	.25	.11
❑ 54	Ronnie Lott	.50	.23
❑ 55	Fred Barnett	.50	.23
❑ 56	Leroy Thompson	.25	.11
❑ 57	Barry Foster	.25	.11
❑ 58	Neil O'Donnell	.75	.35
❑ 59	Stan Humphries	.75	.35
❑ 60	Marion Butts	.25	.11
❑ 61	Anthony Miller	.50	.23
❑ 62	Natrone Means	.75	.35
❑ 63	Dana Stubblefield	.75	.35
❑ 64	John Taylor	.50	.23
❑ 65	Ricky Watters	.75	.35
❑ 66	Steve Young	2.00	.90
❑ 67	Jerry Rice	2.50	1.10
❑ 68	Tom Rathman	.25	.11
❑ 69	Rick Mirer	.75	.35
❑ 70	Chris Warren	.50	.23
❑ 71	Cortez Kennedy	.50	.23
❑ 72	Mark Rypien	.25	.11
❑ 73	Desmond Howard	.50	.23
❑ 74	Art Monk	.50	.23
❑ 75	Reggie Brooks	.50	.23

1995 Excalibur

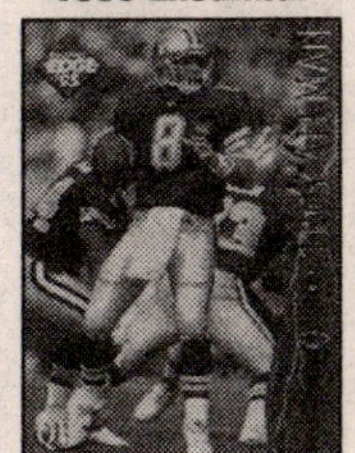

	MINT	NRMT
COMPLETE SET (150)	30.00	13.50
COMP.SERIES 1 (75)	15.00	6.75
COMP.SERIES 2 (75)	15.00	6.75

		MINT	NRMT
❑ 1	Gary Clark	.15	.07
❑ 2	Randal Hill	.15	.07
❑ 3	Anthony Edwards	.15	.07
❑ 4	Terance Mathis	.30	.14
❑ 5	Erric Pegram	.30	.14
❑ 6	Jeff George	.30	.14
❑ 7	Pete Metzelaars	.15	.07
❑ 8	Jim Kelly	.50	.23
❑ 9	Andre Reed	.30	.14
❑ 10	Lewis Tillman	.15	.07
❑ 11	Curtis Conway	.50	.23
❑ 12	Steve Walsh	.15	.07
❑ 13	Derrick Fenner	.15	.07
❑ 14	Harold Green	.15	.07
❑ 15	Michael Jackson	.30	.14
❑ 16	Eric Metcalf	.30	.14
❑ 17	Antonio Langham	.15	.07
❑ 18	Troy Aikman	2.00	.90
❑ 19	Alvin Harper	.15	.07
❑ 20	Jay Novacek	.30	.14
❑ 21	John Elway	4.00	1.80
❑ 22	Glyn Milburn	.15	.07
❑ 23	Steve Atwater	.15	.07
❑ 24	Mel Gray	.15	.07
❑ 25	Herman Moore	.50	.23
❑ 26	Scott Mitchell	.30	.14
❑ 27	Guy McIntyre	.15	.07
❑ 28	Edgar Bennett	.30	.14
❑ 29	Sterling Sharpe	.30	.14
❑ 30	Gary Brown	.15	.07
❑ 31	Haywood Jeffires	.15	.07
❑ 32	Marshall Faulk	.75	.35
❑ 33	Roosevelt Potts	.15	.07
❑ 34	Marcus Allen	.50	.23
❑ 35	Willie Davis	.30	.14
❑ 36	Lake Dawson	.30	.14
❑ 37	Jeff Hostetler	.30	.14
❑ 38	Rocket Ismail	.30	.14
❑ 39	Troy Drayton	.15	.07
❑ 40	Jerome Bettis	.50	.23
❑ 41	Dan Marino	4.00	1.80
❑ 42	Mark Ingram	.15	.07
❑ 43	O.J. McDuffie	.50	.23
❑ 44	Warren Moon	.30	.14
❑ 45	Qadry Ismail	.30	.14
❑ 46	Jake Reed	.30	.14
❑ 47	Ben Coates	.30	.14
❑ 48	Vincent Brisby	.15	.07
❑ 49	Michael Timpson	.15	.07
❑ 50	Brad Daluiso	.15	.07
❑ 51	Rodney Hampton	.30	.14
❑ 52	Chris Calloway	.15	.07
❑ 53	Rob Moore	.15	.07
❑ 54	Boomer Esiason	.30	.14
❑ 55	Michael Haynes	.30	.14
❑ 56	Vaughn Dunbar	.15	.07
❑ 57	Calvin Williams	.30	.14
❑ 58	Herschel Walker	.30	.14
❑ 59	Charlie Garner	.30	.14
❑ 60	Neil O'Donnell	.30	.14
❑ 61	Deon Figures	.15	.07
❑ 62	Byron Bam Morris	.30	.14
❑ 63	Junior Seau	.50	.23
❑ 64	Leslie O'Neal	.30	.14
❑ 65	Natrone Means	.50	.23
❑ 66	Jerry Rice	2.00	.90
❑ 67	Deion Sanders	1.25	.55
❑ 68	William Floyd	.50	.23
❑ 69	Chris Warren	.30	.14
❑ 70	Cortez Kennedy	.30	.14
❑ 71	Hardy Nickerson	.15	.07
❑ 72	Craig Erickson	.15	.07
❑ 73	Heath Shuler	.50	.23
❑ 74	Reggie Brooks	.30	.14
❑ 75	Henry Ellard	.30	.14
❑ 76	Garrison Hearst	.50	.23
❑ 77	Steve Beuerlein	.15	.07
❑ 78	Seth Joyner	.15	.07
❑ 79	Andre Rison	.30	.14
❑ 80	Norm Johnson	.15	.07
❑ 81	Craig Heyward	.30	.14
❑ 82	Darryl Talley	.15	.07
❑ 83	Kenneth Davis	.15	.07
❑ 84	Bruce Smith	.50	.23
❑ 85	Tom Waddle	.15	.07
❑ 86	Erik Kramer	.15	.07
❑ 87	Carl Pickens	.50	.23
❑ 88	Dan Wilkinson	.30	.14
❑ 89	Jeff Blake RC	1.00	.45

❑ 90 Vinny Testaverde	.30	.14
❑ 91 Tommy Vardell	.15	.07
❑ 92 Leroy Hoard	.15	.07
❑ 93 Emmitt Smith	3.00	1.35
❑ 94 Michael Irvin	.50	.23
❑ 95 Daryl Johnston	.30	.14
❑ 96 Shannon Sharpe	.30	.14
❑ 97 Anthony Miller	.30	.14
❑ 98 Leonard Russell	.15	.07
❑ 99 Barry Sanders	4.00	1.80
❑ 100 Brett Perriman	.30	.14
❑ 101 Johnnie Morton	.30	.14
❑ 102 Brett Favre	4.00	1.80
❑ 103 Bryce Paup	.50	.23
❑ 104 Ernest Givins	.15	.07
❑ 105 Webster Slaughter	.15	.07
❑ 106 Jim Harbaugh	.30	.14
❑ 107 Joe Montana	4.00	1.80
❑ 108 J.J. Birden	.15	.07
❑ 109 Steve Bono	.30	.14
❑ 110 James Jett	.30	.14
❑ 111 Tim Brown	.50	.23
❑ 112 Rob Fredrickson	.15	.07
❑ 113 Chris Miller	.15	.07
❑ 114 Bernie Parmalee	.30	.14
❑ 115 Terry Kirby	.30	.14
❑ 116 Bryan Cox	.15	.07
❑ 117 Irving Fryar	.30	.14
❑ 118 Terry Allen	.30	.14
❑ 119 Cris Carter	.50	.23
❑ 120 Fuad Reveiz	.15	.07
❑ 121 Drew Bledsoe	2.00	.90
❑ 122 Greg McMurtry	.20	.09
❑ 123 Dave Brown	.30	.14
❑ 124 Dave Meggett	.15	.07
❑ 125 Johnny Johnson	.15	.07
❑ 126 Ronnie Lott	.30	.14
❑ 127 Johnny Mitchell	.15	.07
❑ 128 Eric Martin	.15	.07
❑ 129 Jim Everett	.15	.07
❑ 130 Randall Cunningham	.50	.23
❑ 131 Eric Allen	.15	.07
❑ 132 Fred Barnett	.30	.14
❑ 133 Barry Foster	.30	.14
❑ 134 Kevin Greene	.30	.14
❑ 135 Eric Green	.15	.07
❑ 136 Stan Humphries	.30	.14
❑ 137 Mark Seay	.30	.14
❑ 138 Alfred Pupunu RC	.15	.07
❑ 139 Steve Young	1.50	.70
❑ 140 John Taylor	.15	.07
❑ 141 Ricky Watters	.50	.23
❑ 142 Brian Blades	.30	.14
❑ 143 Rick Mirer	.50	.23
❑ 144 Cortez Kennedy	.30	.14
❑ 145 Jackie Harris	.15	.07
❑ 146 Errict Rhett	.50	.23
❑ 147 Trent Dilfer	.50	.23
❑ 148 Brian Mitchell	.15	.07
❑ 149 Ricky Ervins	.15	.07
❑ 150 Darrell Green	.15	.07

1997 Excalibur

	MINT	NRMT
COMPLETE SET (150)	60.00	27.00
❑ 1 Larry Centers	.50	.23
❑ 2 Leeland McElroy	.25	.11
❑ 3 Simeon Rice	.50	.23
❑ 4 Eric Swann	.25	.11
❑ 5 Jamal Anderson	2.00	.90
❑ 6 Bert Emanuel	.50	.23
❑ 7 Eric Metcalf	.50	.23
❑ 8 Ray Lewis	.50	.23
❑ 9 Derrick Alexander WR	.50	.23
❑ 10 Michael Jackson	.50	.23
❑ 11 Vinny Testaverde	.50	.23
❑ 12 Todd Collins	.25	.11
❑ 13 Jim Kelly	1.00	.45
❑ 14 Eric Moulds	1.00	.45
❑ 15 Andre Reed	.50	.23
❑ 16 Bruce Smith	.50	.23
❑ 17 Thurman Thomas	1.00	.45
❑ 18 Tim Biakabutuka	.50	.23
❑ 19 Kerry Collins	.50	.23
❑ 20 Kevin Greene	.50	.23
❑ 21 Anthony Johnson	.25	.11
❑ 22 Lamar Lathon	.25	.11
❑ 23 Muhsin Muhammad	.50	.23
❑ 24 Curtis Conway	.50	.23
❑ 25 Bryan Cox	.25	.11
❑ 26 Walt Harris	.25	.11
❑ 27 Erik Kramer	.25	.11
❑ 28 Rick Mirer	.25	.11
❑ 29 Rashaan Salaam	.25	.11
❑ 30 Jeff Blake	.50	.23
❑ 31 Ki-Jana Carter	.25	.11
❑ 32 Carl Pickens	1.00	.45
❑ 33 Troy Aikman	3.00	1.35
❑ 34 Michael Irvin	1.00	.45
❑ 35 Daryl Johnston	.50	.23
❑ 36 Emmitt Smith	5.00	2.20
❑ 37 Broderick Thomas	.25	.11
❑ 38 Terrell Davis	5.00	2.20
❑ 39 John Elway	6.00	2.70
❑ 40 Anthony Miller	.25	.11
❑ 41 John Mobley	.25	.11
❑ 42 Shannon Sharpe	.50	.23
❑ 43 Neil Smith	.50	.23
❑ 44 Scott Mitchell	.50	.23
❑ 45 Herman Moore	1.00	.45
❑ 46 Brett Perriman	.25	.11
❑ 47 Barry Sanders	6.00	2.70
❑ 48 Edgar Bennett	.50	.23
❑ 49 Robert Brooks	.50	.23
❑ 50 Brett Favre	6.00	2.70
❑ 51 Antonio Freeman	1.50	.70
❑ 52 Dorsey Levens	1.00	.45
❑ 53 Reggie White	1.00	.45
❑ 54 Eddie George	4.00	1.80
❑ 55 Darryll Lewis	.25	.11
❑ 56 Steve McNair	1.50	.70
❑ 57 Chris Sanders	.25	.11
❑ 58 Marshall Faulk	1.00	.45
❑ 59 Jim Harbaugh	.50	.23
❑ 60 Marvin Harrison	1.00	.45
❑ 61 Jimmy Smith	.50	.23
❑ 62 Tony Brackens	.25	.11
❑ 63 Mark Brunell	3.00	1.35
❑ 64 Kevin Hardy	.25	.11
❑ 65 Keenan McCardell	.50	.23
❑ 66 Natrone Means	1.00	.45
❑ 67 Marcus Allen	1.00	.45
❑ 68 Elvis Grbac	.50	.23
❑ 69 Derrick Thomas	.50	.23
❑ 70 Tamarick Vanover	.50	.23
❑ 71 Karim Abdul-Jabbar	1.00	.45
❑ 72 Terrell Buckley	.25	.11
❑ 73 Irving Fryar	.50	.23
❑ 74 Dan Marino	6.00	2.70
❑ 75 O.J. McDuffie	.50	.23
❑ 76 Zach Thomas	.50	.23
❑ 77 Terry Kirby	.50	.23
❑ 78 Cris Carter	1.00	.45
❑ 79 Brad Johnson	1.25	.55
❑ 80 John Randle	.50	.23
❑ 81 Jake Reed	.50	.23
❑ 82 Robert Smith	.50	.23
❑ 83 Drew Bledsoe	3.00	1.35
❑ 84 Ben Coates	.50	.23
❑ 85 Terry Glenn	1.00	.45
❑ 86 Ty Law	.25	.11
❑ 87 Curtis Martin	1.50	.70
❑ 88 Willie McGinest	.25	.11
❑ 89 Mario Bates	.25	.11
❑ 90 Jim Everett	.25	.11
❑ 91 Wayne Martin	.25	.11
❑ 92 Heath Shuler	.25	.11
❑ 93 Torrance Small	.25	.11
❑ 94 Ray Zellars	.25	.11
❑ 95 Dave Brown	.25	.11
❑ 96 Jason Sehorn	.50	.23
❑ 97 Amani Toomer	.50	.23
❑ 98 Tyrone Wheatley	.50	.23
❑ 99 Hugh Douglas	.25	.11
❑ 100 Aaron Glenn	.25	.11
❑ 101 Jeff Graham	.25	.11
❑ 102 Keyshawn Johnson	1.00	.45
❑ 103 Adrian Murrell	.50	.23
❑ 104 Neil O'Donnell	.50	.23
❑ 105 Tim Brown	1.00	.45
❑ 106 Jeff George	.50	.23
❑ 107 Jeff Hostetler	.25	.11
❑ 108 Napoleon Kaufman	1.00	.45
❑ 109 Chester McGlockton	.25	.11
❑ 110 Fred Barnett	.25	.11
❑ 111 Ty Detmer	.50	.23
❑ 112 Chris T. Jones	.25	.11
❑ 113 Ricky Watters	.50	.23
❑ 114 Bobby Engram	.50	.23
❑ 115 Jerome Bettis	1.00	.45
❑ 116 Charles Johnson	.50	.23
❑ 117 Greg Lloyd	.25	.11
❑ 118 Kordell Stewart	1.25	.55
❑ 119 Yancey Thigpen	.50	.23
❑ 120 Rod Woodson	.50	.23
❑ 121 Stan Humphries	.50	.23
❑ 122 Tony Martin	.50	.23
❑ 123 Leonard Russell	.25	.11
❑ 124 Junior Seau	.50	.23
❑ 125 Chad Brown	.25	.11
❑ 126 John Friesz	.25	.11
❑ 127 Joey Galloway	1.25	.55
❑ 128 Cortez Kennedy	.25	.11
❑ 129 Warren Moon	1.00	.45
❑ 130 Chris Warren	.50	.23
❑ 131 Garrison Hearst	.50	.23
❑ 132 Terrell Owens	1.00	.45
❑ 133 Jerry Rice	3.00	1.35
❑ 134 Dana Stubblefield	.25	.11
❑ 135 Bryant Young	.25	.11
❑ 136 Steve Young	2.00	.90
❑ 137 Tony Banks	.50	.23
❑ 138 Isaac Bruce	1.00	.45
❑ 139 Eddie Kennison	.50	.23
❑ 140 Keith Lyle	.25	.11
❑ 141 Lawrence Phillips	.25	.11
❑ 142 Mike Alstott	1.00	.45
❑ 143 Hardy Nickerson	.25	.11
❑ 144 Errict Rhett	.25	.11
❑ 145 Warren Sapp	.50	.23
❑ 146 Gus Frerotte	.25	.11
❑ 147 Sean Gilbert	.25	.11
❑ 148 Ken Harvey	.25	.11
❑ 149 Terry Allen	1.00	.45
❑ 150 Michael Westbrook	.50	.23

1994 Finest

	MINT	NRMT
COMPLETE SET (220)	50.00	22.00
❑ 1 Emmitt Smith	6.00	2.70

❑ 2	Calvin Williams	.60	.25
❑ 3	Mark Collins	.30	.14
❑ 4	Steve McMichael	.60	.25
❑ 5	Jim Kelly	1.25	.55
❑ 6	Michael Dean Perry	.60	.25
❑ 7	Wayne Simmons	.30	.14
❑ 8	Rocket Ismail	.60	.25
❑ 9	Mark Rypien	.30	.14
❑ 10	Brian Blades	.60	.25
❑ 11	Barry Word	.30	.14
❑ 12	Jerry Rice	4.00	1.80
❑ 13	Derrick Fenner	.30	.14
❑ 14	Karl Mecklenburg	.30	.14
❑ 15	Reggie Cobb	.30	.14
❑ 16	Eric Swann	.60	.25
❑ 17	Neil Smith	1.25	.55
❑ 18	Barry Foster	.30	.14
❑ 19	Willie Roaf	.30	.14
❑ 20	Troy Drayton	.30	.14
❑ 21	Warren Moon	1.25	.55
❑ 22	Richmond Webb	.30	.14
❑ 23	Anthony Miller	.60	.25
❑ 24	Chris Slade	.30	.14
❑ 25	Mel Gray	.30	.14
❑ 26	Ronnie Lott	.60	.25
❑ 27	Andre Rison	.60	.25
❑ 28	Jeff George	1.25	.55
❑ 29	John Copeland	.30	.14
❑ 30	Derrick Thomas	1.25	.55
❑ 31	Sterling Sharpe	.60	.25
❑ 32	Chris Doleman	.30	.14
❑ 33	Monte Coleman	.30	.14
❑ 34	Mark Bavaro	.30	.14
❑ 35	Kevin Williams	.60	.25
❑ 36	Eric Metcalf	.60	.25
❑ 37	Brent Jones	.60	.25
❑ 38	Steve Tasker	.60	.25
❑ 39	Dave Meggett	.30	.14
❑ 40	Howie Long	.60	.25
❑ 41	Rick Mirer	1.25	.55
❑ 42	Jerome Bettis	1.50	.70
❑ 43	Marion Butts	.30	.14
❑ 44	Barry Sanders	8.00	3.60
❑ 45	Jason Elam	.30	.14
❑ 46	Broderick Thomas	.30	.14
❑ 47	Derek Brown RBK	.30	.14
❑ 48	Lorenzo White	.30	.14
❑ 49	Neil O'Donnell	1.25	.55
❑ 50	Chris Burkett	.30	.14
❑ 51	John Offerdahl	.30	.14
❑ 52	Rohn Stark	.30	.14
❑ 53	Neal Anderson	.30	.14
❑ 54	Steve Beuerlein	.30	.14
❑ 55	Bruce Armstrong	.30	.14
❑ 56	Lincoln Kennedy	.30	.14
❑ 57	Darrell Green	.30	.14
❑ 58	Ricardo McDonald	.30	.14
❑ 59	Chris Warren	.60	.25
❑ 60	Mark Jackson	.30	.14
❑ 61	Pepper Johnson	.30	.14
❑ 62	Chris Spielman	.60	.25
❑ 63	Marcus Allen	1.25	.55
❑ 64	Jim Everett	.60	.25
❑ 65	Greg Townsend	.30	.14
❑ 66	Cris Carter	1.50	.70
❑ 67	Don Beebe	.30	.14
❑ 68	Reggie Langhorne	.30	.14
❑ 69	Randall Cunningham	1.25	.55
❑ 70	Johnny Holland	.30	.14
❑ 71	Morten Andersen	.30	.14
❑ 72	Leonard Marshall	.30	.14
❑ 73	Keith Jackson	.30	.14
❑ 74	Leslie O'Neal	.30	.14
❑ 75	Hardy Nickerson	.60	.25
❑ 76	Dan Williams	.30	.14
❑ 77	Steve Young	3.00	1.35
❑ 78	Deon Figures	.30	.14
❑ 79	Michael Irvin	1.25	.55
❑ 80	Luis Sharpe	.30	.14
❑ 81	Andre Tippett	.30	.14
❑ 82	Ricky Sanders	.30	.14
❑ 83	Erric Pegram	.30	.14
❑ 84	Albert Lewis	.30	.14
❑ 85	Anthony Blaylock	.30	.14
❑ 86	Pat Swilling	.30	.14
❑ 87	Duane Bickett	.30	.14
❑ 88	Myron Guyton	.30	.14
❑ 89	Clay Matthews	.30	.14
❑ 90	Jim McMahon	.30	.14
❑ 91	Bruce Smith	1.25	.55
❑ 92	Reggie White	1.25	.55
❑ 93	Shannon Sharpe	.60	.25
❑ 94	Rickey Jackson	.30	.14
❑ 95	Ronnie Harmon	.30	.14
❑ 96	Terry McDaniel	.30	.14
❑ 97	Bryan Cox	.30	.14
❑ 98	Webster Slaughter	.30	.14
❑ 99	Boomer Esiason	.60	.25
❑ 100	Tim Krumrie	.30	.14
❑ 101	Cortez Kennedy	.60	.25
❑ 102	Henry Ellard	.60	.25
❑ 103	Clyde Simmons	.30	.14
❑ 104	Craig Erickson	.30	.14
❑ 105	Eric Green	.30	.14
❑ 106	Gary Clark	.60	.25
❑ 107	Jay Novacek	.60	.25
❑ 108	Dana Stubblefield	1.25	.55
❑ 109	Mike Johnson	.30	.14
❑ 110	Ray Crockett	.30	.14
❑ 111	Leonard Russell	.30	.14
❑ 112	Robert Smith	2.00	.90
❑ 113	Art Monk	.60	.25
❑ 114	Ray Childress	.30	.14
❑ 115	O.J. McDuffie	1.25	.55
❑ 116	Tim Brown	1.25	.55
❑ 117	Kevin Ross	.30	.14
❑ 118	Richard Dent	.60	.25
❑ 119	John Elway	8.00	3.60
❑ 120	James Hasty	.30	.14
❑ 121	Gary Plummer	.30	.14
❑ 122	Pierce Holt	.30	.14
❑ 123	Eric Martin	.30	.14
❑ 124	Brett Favre	8.00	3.60
❑ 125	Cornelius Bennett	.60	.25
❑ 126	Jessie Hester	.30	.14
❑ 127	Lewis Tillman	.30	.14
❑ 128	Qadry Ismail	1.25	.55
❑ 129	Jay Schroeder	.30	.14
❑ 130	Curtis Conway	1.25	.55
❑ 131	Santana Dotson	.60	.25
❑ 132	Nick Lowery	.30	.14
❑ 133	Lomas Brown	.30	.14
❑ 134	Reggie Roby	.30	.14
❑ 135	John L. Williams	.30	.14
❑ 136	Vinny Testaverde	.60	.25
❑ 137	Seth Joyner	.30	.14
❑ 138	Ethan Horton	.30	.14
❑ 139	Jackie Slater	.30	.14
❑ 140	Rod Bernstine	.30	.14
❑ 141	Rob Moore	.60	.25
❑ 142	Dan Marino	8.00	3.60
❑ 143	Ken Harvey	.30	.14
❑ 144	Ernest Givins	.60	.25
❑ 145	Russell Maryland	.30	.14
❑ 146	Drew Bledsoe	5.00	2.20
❑ 147	Kevin Greene	1.25	.55
❑ 148	Bobby Hebert	.30	.14
❑ 149	Junior Seau	1.25	.55
❑ 150	Tim McDonald	.30	.14
❑ 151	Thurman Thomas	1.25	.55
❑ 152	Phil Simms	.60	.25
❑ 153	Terrell Buckley	.30	.14
❑ 154	Sam Mills	.30	.14
❑ 155	Anthony Carter	.60	.25
❑ 156	Kelvin Martin	.30	.14
❑ 157	Shane Conlan	.30	.14
❑ 158	Irving Fryar	.60	.25
❑ 159	Demetrius DuBose	.30	.14
❑ 160	David Klingler	.30	.14
❑ 161	Herman Moore	1.25	.55
❑ 162	Jeff Hostetler	.60	.25
❑ 163	Tommy Vardell	.30	.14
❑ 164	Craig Heyward	.60	.25
❑ 165	Wilber Marshall	.30	.14
❑ 166	Quentin Coryatt	.30	.14
❑ 167	Glyn Milburn	.60	.25
❑ 168	Fred Barnett	.60	.25
❑ 169	Charles Haley	.60	.25
❑ 170	Carl Banks	.30	.14
❑ 171	Ricky Proehl	.30	.14
❑ 172	Joe Montana	8.00	3.60
❑ 173	Johnny Mitchell	.30	.14
❑ 174	Andre Reed	.60	.25
❑ 175	Marco Coleman	.30	.14
❑ 176	Vaughan Johnson	.30	.14
❑ 177	Carl Pickens	1.25	.55
❑ 178	Dwight Stone	.30	.14
❑ 179	Ricky Watters	1.25	.55
❑ 180	Michael Haynes	.60	.25
❑ 181	Roger Craig	.60	.25
❑ 182	Cleveland Gary	.30	.14
❑ 183	Steve Emtman	.30	.14
❑ 184	Patrick Bates	.30	.14
❑ 185	Mark Carrier WR	.60	.25
❑ 186	Brad Hopkins	.30	.14
❑ 187	Dennis Smith	.30	.14
❑ 188	Natrone Means	1.25	.55
❑ 189	Michael Jackson	.60	.25
❑ 190	Ken Norton Jr.	.60	.25
❑ 191	Carlton Gray	.30	.14
❑ 192	Edgar Bennett	1.25	.55
❑ 193	Lawrence Taylor	1.25	.55
❑ 194	Marv Cook	.30	.14
❑ 195	Eric Curry	.30	.14
❑ 196	Victor Bailey	.30	.14
❑ 197	Ryan McNeil	.30	.14
❑ 198	Rod Woodson	1.25	.55
❑ 199	Earnest Byner	.30	.14
❑ 200	Marvin Jones	.30	.14
❑ 201	Thomas Smith	.30	.14
❑ 202	Troy Aikman	4.00	1.80
❑ 203	Audray McMillian	.30	.14
❑ 204	Wade Wilson	.30	.14
❑ 205	George Teague	.30	.14
❑ 206	Deion Sanders	2.00	.90
❑ 207	Will Shields	.30	.14
❑ 208	John Taylor	.60	.25
❑ 209	Jim Harbaugh	1.25	.55
❑ 210	Micheal Barrow	.30	.14
❑ 211	Harold Green	.30	.14
❑ 212	Steve Everitt	.30	.14
❑ 213	Flipper Anderson	.30	.14
❑ 214	Rodney Hampton	1.25	.55
❑ 215	Steve Atwater	.30	.14
❑ 216	James Trapp	.30	.14
❑ 217	Terry Kirby	1.25	.55
❑ 218	Garrison Hearst	2.50	1.10
❑ 219	Jeff Bryant	.30	.14
❑ 220	Roosevelt Potts	.30	.14

1995 Finest

	MINT	NRMT
COMPLETE SET (275)	80.00	36.00
COMP.SERIES 1 (165)	20.00	9.00
COMP.SERIES 2 (110)	60.00	27.00
COMMON CARD (1-275)	.25	.11

❑ 1	Natrone Means	1.25	.55
❑ 2	Dave Meggett	.25	.11
❑ 3	Tim Bowens	.25	.11
❑ 4	Jay Novacek	.60	.25
❑ 5	Michael Jackson	.60	.25
❑ 6	Calvin Williams	.60	.25
❑ 7	Neil Smith	.60	.25
❑ 8	Chris Gardocki	.25	.11
❑ 9	Jeff Burris	.25	.11
❑ 10	Warren Moon	.60	.25
❑ 11	Gary Anderson K	.25	.11
❑ 12	Bert Emanuel	1.25	.55

❑ 13 Rick Tuten .25 .11
❑ 14 Steve Wallace .25 .11
❑ 15 Marion Butts .25 .11
❑ 16 Johnnie Morton .60 .25
❑ 17 Rob Moore .25 .11
❑ 18 Wayne Gandy .25 .11
❑ 19 Quentin Coryatt .60 .25
❑ 20 Richmond Webb .25 .11
❑ 21 Errict Rhett 1.25 .55
❑ 22 Joe Johnson .25 .11
❑ 23 Gary Brown .25 .11
❑ 24 Jeff Hostetler .60 .25
❑ 25 Larry Centers .60 .25
❑ 26 Tom Carter .25 .11
❑ 27 Steve Atwater .25 .11
❑ 28 Doug Pelfrey .25 .11
❑ 29 Bryce Paup 1.25 .55
❑ 30 Erik Williams .25 .11
❑ 31 Henry Jones .25 .11
❑ 32 Stanley Richard .25 .11
❑ 33 Marcus Allen 1.25 .55
❑ 34 Antonio Langham .25 .11
❑ 35 Lewis Tillman .25 .11
❑ 36 Thomas Randolph .25 .11
❑ 37 Byron Bam Morris .60 .25
❑ 38 David Palmer .60 .25
❑ 39 Ricky Watters 1.25 .55
❑ 40 Brett Perriman .60 .25
❑ 41 Will Wolford .25 .11
❑ 42 Burt Grossman .25 .11
❑ 43 Vincent Brisby .25 .11
❑ 44 Ronnie Lott .60 .25
❑ 45 Brian Blades .60 .25
❑ 46 Brent Jones .25 .11
❑ 47 Anthony Newman .25 .11
❑ 48 Willie Roaf .25 .11
❑ 49 Paul Gruber .25 .11
❑ 50 Jeff George .60 .25
❑ 51 Jamir Miller .25 .11
❑ 52 Anthony Miller .60 .25
❑ 53 Darrell Green .25 .11
❑ 54 Steve Wisniewski .25 .11
❑ 55 Dan Wilkinson .60 .25
❑ 56 Brett Favre 5.00 2.20
❑ 57 Leslie O'Neal .60 .25
❑ 58 Keith Byars .25 .11
❑ 59 James Washington .25 .11
❑ 60 Andre Reed .60 .25
❑ 61 Ken Norton Jr. .60 .25
❑ 62 John Randle .60 .25
❑ 63 Lake Dawson .60 .25
❑ 64 Greg Montgomery .25 .11
❑ 65 Erric Pegram .60 .25
❑ 66 Steve Everitt .25 .11
❑ 67 Chris Brantley .25 .11
❑ 68 Rod Woodson .60 .25
❑ 69 Eugene Robinson .25 .11
❑ 70 Dave Brown .60 .25
❑ 71 Ricky Reynolds .25 .11
❑ 72 Rohn Stark .25 .11
❑ 73 Randal Hill .25 .11
❑ 74 Brian Washington .25 .11
❑ 75 Heath Shuler 1.25 .55
❑ 76 Darion Conner .25 .11
❑ 77 Terry McDaniel .25 .11
❑ 78 Al Del Greco .25 .11
❑ 79 Allen Aldridge .25 .11
❑ 80 Trace Armstrong .25 .11
❑ 81 Darnay Scott 1.25 .55
❑ 82 Charlie Garner .60 .25
❑ 83 Harold Bishop .25 .11
❑ 84 Reggie White 1.25 .55
❑ 85 Shawn Jefferson .25 .11
❑ 86 Irving Spikes .60 .25
❑ 87 Mel Gray .25 .11
❑ 88 D.J. Johnson .25 .11
❑ 89 Daryl Johnston .60 .25
❑ 90 Joe Montana 5.00 2.20
❑ 91 Michael Strahan .60 .25
❑ 92 Robert Blackmon .25 .11
❑ 93 Ryan Yarborough .60 .25
❑ 94 Terry Allen .60 .25
❑ 95 Michael Haynes .60 .25
❑ 96 Jim Harbaugh .60 .25
❑ 97 Micheal Barrow .25 .11
❑ 98 John Thierry .25 .11
❑ 99 Seth Joyner .25 .11
❑ 100 Deion Sanders 2.00 .90
❑ 101 Eric Turner .25 .11
❑ 102 LeShon Johnson .60 .25
❑ 103 John Copeland .25 .11
❑ 104 Cornelius Bennett .60 .25
❑ 105 Sean Gilbert .60 .25
❑ 106 Herschel Walker .60 .25
❑ 107 Henry Ellard .60 .25
❑ 108 Neil O'Donnell .60 .25
❑ 109 Charles Wilson .25 .11
❑ 110 Willie McGinest .60 .25
❑ 111 Tim Brown 1.25 .55
❑ 112 Simon Fletcher .25 .11
❑ 113 Broderick Thomas .25 .11
❑ 114 Tom Waddle .25 .11
❑ 115 Jessie Tuggle .25 .11
❑ 116 Maurice Hurst .25 .11
❑ 117 Aubrey Beavers .25 .11
❑ 118 Donnell Bennett .60 .25
❑ 119 Shante Carver .25 .11
❑ 120 Eric Metcalf .60 .25
❑ 121 John Carney .25 .11
❑ 122 Thomas Lewis .60 .25
❑ 123 Johnny Mitchell .25 .11
❑ 124 Trent Dilfer 1.25 .55
❑ 125 Marshall Faulk 2.50 1.10
❑ 126 Ernest Givins .25 .11
❑ 127 Aeneas Williams .25 .11
❑ 128 Bucky Brooks .25 .11
❑ 129 Todd Steussie .25 .11
❑ 130 Randall Cunningham 1.25 .55
❑ 131 Reggie Brooks .60 .25
❑ 132 Morten Andersen .25 .11
❑ 133 James Jett .60 .25
❑ 134 George Teague .25 .11
❑ 135 John Taylor .25 .11
❑ 136 Charles Johnson .60 .25
❑ 137 Isaac Bruce 2.50 1.10
❑ 138 Jason Elam .25 .11
❑ 139 Carl Pickens 1.25 .55
❑ 140 Chris Warren .60 .25
❑ 141 Bruce Armstrong .25 .11
❑ 142 Mark Carrier DB .25 .11
❑ 143 Irving Fryar .60 .25
❑ 144 Van Malone .25 .11
❑ 145 Charles Haley .60 .25
❑ 146 Chris Calloway .25 .11
❑ 147 J.J. Birden .25 .11
❑ 148 Tony Bennett .25 .11
❑ 149 Lincoln Kennedy .25 .11
❑ 150 Stan Humphries .60 .25
❑ 151 Hardy Nickerson .25 .11
❑ 152 Randall McDaniel .25 .11
❑ 153 Marcus Robertson .25 .11
❑ 154 Ronald Moore .25 .11
❑ 155 Thurman Thomas 1.25 .55
❑ 156 Tommy Vardell .25 .11
❑ 157 Ken Ruettgers .25 .11
❑ 158 Rob Fredrickson .25 .11
❑ 159 Johnny Bailey .25 .11
❑ 160 Greg Lloyd .60 .25
❑ 161 David Alexander .25 .11
❑ 162 Kevin Mawae .25 .11
❑ 163 Derek Brown RBK .25 .11
❑ 164 William Floyd 1.25 .55
❑ 165 Aaron Glenn .25 .11
❑ 166 Joey Galloway RC 12.00 5.50
❑ 167 Troy Drayton .25 .11
❑ 168 Dermontti Dawson .60 .25
❑ 169 Ronald Moore .25 .11
❑ 170 Dan Marino 5.00 2.20
❑ 171 Dennis Gibson .25 .11
❑ 172 Raymont Harris .25 .11
❑ 173 Shannon Sharpe .60 .25
❑ 174 Kevin Williams .60 .25
❑ 175 Jim Everett .25 .11
❑ 176 Rocket Ismail .60 .25
❑ 177 Mark Fields .25 .11
❑ 178 George Koonce .25 .11
❑ 179 Chris Hudson .25 .11
❑ 180 Jerry Rice 2.50 1.10
❑ 181 Dewayne Washington .60 .25
❑ 182 Dale Carter .60 .25
❑ 183 Pete Stoyanovich .25 .11
❑ 184 Blake Brockermeyer .25 .11
❑ 185 Troy Aikman 2.50 1.10
❑ 186 Jeff Blake RC 3.00 1.35
❑ 187 Troy Vincent .25 .11
❑ 188 Lamar Lathon .25 .11
❑ 189 Tony Boselli 1.25 .55
❑ 190 Emmitt Smith 4.00 1.80
❑ 191 Bobby Houston .25 .11
❑ 192 Edgar Bennett .60 .25
❑ 193 Derrick Brooks RC 1.50 .70
❑ 194 Ricky Proehl .25 .11
❑ 195 Rodney Hampton .60 .25
❑ 196 Dave Krieg .25 .11
❑ 197 Vinny Testaverde .60 .25
❑ 198 Erik Kramer .25 .11
❑ 199 Ben Coates .60 .25
❑ 200 Steve Young 2.00 .90
❑ 201 Glyn Milburn .25 .11
❑ 202 Bryan Cox .25 .11
❑ 203 Luther Elliss .25 .11
❑ 204 Mark McMillian .25 .11
❑ 205 Jerome Bettis 1.25 .55
❑ 206 Craig Heyward .60 .25
❑ 207 Ray Buchanan .25 .11
❑ 208 Kimble Anders .60 .25
❑ 209 Kevin Greene .60 .25
❑ 210 Eric Allen .25 .11
❑ 211 Ricardo McDonald .25 .11
❑ 212 Ruben Brown RC .40 .18
❑ 213 Harvey Williams .25 .11
❑ 214 Broderick Thomas .25 .11
❑ 215 Frank Reich .25 .11
❑ 216 Frank Sanders RC UER 5.00 2.20
(Plays Wide Receiver,
Defensive Record on Back)
❑ 217 Craig Newsome .25 .11
❑ 218 Merton Hanks .25 .11
❑ 219 Chris Miller .25 .11
❑ 220 John Elway 5.00 2.20
❑ 221 Ernest Givins .25 .11
❑ 222 Boomer Esiason .60 .25
❑ 223 Reggie Roby .25 .11
❑ 224 Qadry Ismail .60 .25
❑ 225 Ki-Jana Carter RC 1.50 .70
❑ 226 Leon Lett .25 .11
❑ 227 Eric Hill .25 .11
❑ 228 Scott Mitchell .60 .25
❑ 229 Craig Erickson .25 .11
❑ 230 Drew Bledsoe 2.50 1.10
❑ 231 Sean Landeta .25 .11
❑ 232 Barrett Brooks .25 .11
❑ 233 Brian Mitchell .25 .11
❑ 234 Tyrone Poole .60 .25
❑ 235 Desmond Howard .60 .25
❑ 236 Wayne Simmons .25 .11
❑ 237 Michael Westbrook RC 8.00 3.60
❑ 238 Quinn Early .60 .25
❑ 239 Willie Davis .60 .25
❑ 240 Rashaan Salaam RC 1.50 .70
❑ 241 Devin Bush .25 .11
❑ 242 Dana Stubblefield 1.25 .55
❑ 243 Dexter Carter .25 .11
❑ 244 Shane Conlan .25 .11
❑ 245 Keith Elias RC .25 .11
❑ 246 Robert Brooks 1.25 .55
❑ 247 Garrison Hearst 1.25 .55
❑ 248 Eric Zeier RC 1.50 .70
❑ 249 Nate Newton .60 .25
❑ 250 Barry Sanders 5.00 2.20
❑ 251 Dave Meggett .25 .11
❑ 252 Courtney Hawkins .25 .11
❑ 253 Cortez Kennedy .60 .25
❑ 254 Mario Bates 1.25 .55
❑ 255 Junior Seau 1.25 .55
❑ 256 Brian Washington .25 .11
❑ 257 Darius Holland .25 .11
❑ 258 Jeff Graham .25 .11
❑ 259 Rob Moore .25 .11
❑ 260 Andre Rison .60 .25
❑ 261 Kerry Collins RC 8.00 3.60
❑ 262 Roosevelt Potts .25 .11
❑ 263 Cris Carter 1.25 .55
❑ 264 Curtis Martin RC 12.00 5.50
❑ 265 Rick Mirer 1.25 .55
❑ 266 Mo Lewis .25 .11
❑ 267 Mike Sherrard .25 .11
❑ 268 Herman Moore 1.25 .55

❑ 269 Eric Metcalf	.60	.25
❑ 270 Ray Childress	.25	.11
❑ 271 Chris Slade	.60	.25
❑ 272 Michael Irvin	1.25	.55
❑ 273 Jim Kelly	1.25	.55
❑ 274 Terance Mathis	.60	.25
❑ 275 LeRoy Butler	.25	.11

1996 Finest

	MINT	NRMT
COMPLETE SET (359)	700.00	325.00
COMP.SERIES 1 (191)	400.00	180.00
COMP.SERIES 2 (168)	300.00	135.00
COMP.BRONZE SER.1 (110)	40.00	18.00
COMP.BRONZE SER.2 (110)	40.00	18.00
COMMON BRONZE	.30	.14
COMMON GOLD	1.50	.70
COMMON SILVER	.75	.35

❑ B2 Jay Novacek B	.60	.25
❑ B3 Ray Buchanan B	.30	.14
❑ B5 Phil Hansen B	.30	.14
❑ B6 Mike Mamula B	.30	.14
❑ B9 Bernie Parmalee B	.30	.14
❑ B10 Herman Moore B	1.00	.45
❑ B11 Shawn Jefferson B	.30	.14
❑ B12 Chris Doleman B	.30	.14
❑ B13 Erik Kramer B	.60	.25
❑ B15 Orlando Thomas B	.30	.14
❑ B16 Terrell Davis B	10.00	4.50
❑ B18 Roman Phifer B	.30	.14
❑ B19 Trent Dilfer B	.60	.25
❑ B21 Darnay Scott B	.60	.25
❑ B22 Steve McNair B	5.00	2.20
❑ B23 Lamar Lathon B	.30	.14
❑ B26 Thomas Randolph B	.30	.14
❑ B27 Michael Jackson B	.60	.25
❑ B28 Seth Joyner B	.30	.14
❑ B29 Jeff Lageman B	.30	.14
❑ B30 Darryl Williams B	.30	.14
❑ B32 Erric Pegram B	.60	.25
❑ B34 Sean Dawkins B	.60	.25
❑ B38 Dan Saleaumua B UER (Card misnumbered 28)	.30	.14
❑ B39 Henry Thomas B	.30	.14
❑ B43 Pat Swilling B	.30	.14
❑ B44 Marty Carter B	.30	.14
❑ B45 Anthony Miller B	.60	.25
❑ B48 Chris Warren B	.60	.25
❑ B49 Derek Brown RBK B	.30	.14
❑ B51 Blaine Bishop B	.30	.14
❑ B52 Jake Reed B	.60	.25
❑ B55 Vencie Glenn B	.30	.14
❑ B58 Derrick Alexander WR B	.60	.25
❑ B64 Jessie Tuggle B	.30	.14
❑ B65 Terrance Shaw B	.30	.14
❑ B66 David Sloan B	.60	.25
❑ B68 Brent Jones B	.30	.14
❑ B70 William Thomas B	.30	.14
❑ B71 Robert Smith B	.60	.25
❑ B72 Wayne Simmons B	.30	.14
❑ B73 Jim Harbaugh B	.60	.25
❑ B76 Wayne Chrebet B	2.00	.90
❑ B77 Chris Hudson B	.30	.14
❑ B79 Stevon Moore B	.30	.14
❑ B80 Chris Calloway B	.30	.14
❑ B81 Tom Carter B	.30	.14
❑ B82 Dave Meggett B	.30	.14
❑ B83 Sam Mills B	.60	.25
❑ B86 Renaldo Turnbull B	.30	.14
❑ B87 Derrick Brooks B	.30	.14
❑ B89 Eugene Robinson B	.30	.14
❑ B91 Rodney Thomas B	.30	.14
❑ B92 Dan Wilkinson B	.30	.14
❑ B93 Mark Fields B	.30	.14
❑ B94 Warren Sapp B	.30	.14
❑ B95 Curtis Martin B	5.00	2.20
❑ B97 Ray Crockett B	.30	.14
❑ B98 Ed McDaniel B	.30	.14
❑ B101 Craig Heyward B	.30	.14
❑ B102 Ellis Johnson B	.30	.14
❑ B104 O.J. McDuffie B	.60	.25
❑ B105 J.J. Stokes B	1.00	.45
❑ B106 Mo Lewis B	.30	.14
❑ B108 Rob Moore B	.30	.14
❑ B110 Tyrone Wheatley B	.60	.25
❑ B111 Ken Harvey B	.30	.14
❑ B113 Willie Green B	.30	.14
❑ B114 Willie Davis B	.60	.25
❑ B115 Andy Harmon B	.30	.14
❑ B117 Bryan Cox B	.30	.14
❑ B119 Bert Emanuel B	.60	.25
❑ B120 Greg Lloyd B	.60	.25
❑ B122 Willie Jackson B	.60	.25
❑ B123 Lorenzo Lynch B	.30	.14
❑ B124 Pepper Johnson B	.30	.14
❑ B128 Tyrone Poole B	.30	.14
❑ B129 Neil Smith B	.60	.25
❑ B130 Eddie Robinson B	.30	.14
❑ B131 Bryce Paup B	.60	.25
❑ B134 Troy Aikman B	5.00	2.20
❑ B136 Chris Sanders B	.60	.25
❑ B138 Jim Everett B	.30	.14
❑ B139 Frank Sanders B	.60	.25
❑ B141 Cortez Kennedy B	.60	.25
❑ B143 Derrick Alexander DE B	.30	.14
❑ B144 Rob Fredrickson B	.30	.14
❑ B145 Chris Zorich B	.30	.14
❑ B146 Devin Bush B	.30	.14
❑ B149 Troy Vincent B	.30	.14
❑ B151 Deion Sanders B	2.50	1.10
❑ B152 James O. Stewart B	.60	.25
❑ B156 Lawrence Dawsey B	.30	.14
❑ B157 Robert Brooks B	1.00	.45
❑ B158 Rashaan Salaam B	1.00	.45
❑ B161 Tim Brown B	.60	.25
❑ B162 Brendan Stai B	.30	.14
❑ B163 Sean Gilbert B	.30	.14
❑ B169 Calvin Williams B	.60	.25
❑ B171 Ruben Brown B	.30	.14
❑ B172 Eric Green B	.30	.14
❑ B175 Jerry Rice B	5.00	2.20
❑ B176 Bruce Smith B	1.00	.45
❑ B177 Mark Bruener B	.30	.14
❑ B179 Lamont Warren B	.30	.14
❑ B180 Tamarick Vanover B	1.00	.45
❑ B182 Scott Mitchell B	.60	.25
❑ B186 Terry Wooden B	.30	.14
❑ B187 Ken Norton B	.60	.25
❑ B188 Jeff Herrod B	.30	.14
❑ B192 Gus Frerotte B	1.00	.45
❑ B194 Brett Maxie B	.30	.14
❑ B198 Eddie Kennison B RC	1.25	.55
❑ B201 Marcus Jones B RC	.30	.14
❑ B202 Terry Allen B	.60	.25
❑ B203 Leroy Hoard B	.30	.14
❑ B205 Reggie White B	1.00	.45
❑ B206 Larry Centers B	.60	.25
❑ B208 Vincent Brisby B	.30	.14
❑ B209 Michael Timpson B	.30	.14
❑ B211 John Mobley B RC	.30	.14
❑ B212 Clay Matthews B	.60	.25
❑ B213 Shannon Sharpe B	.60	.25
❑ B214 Tony Bennett B	.30	.14
❑ B216 Mickey Washington B	.30	.14
❑ B217 Fred Barnett B	.60	.25
❑ B218 Michael Haynes B	.60	.25
❑ B219 Stan Humphries B	.60	.25
❑ B221 Winston Moss B	.30	.14
❑ B222 Tim Biakabutuka B RC	3.00	1.35
❑ B223 Leeland McElroy B RC	1.25	.55
❑ B224 Vinnie Clark B	.30	.14
❑ B225 Keyshawn Johnson B RC	8.00	3.60
❑ B228 Tony Woods B	.30	.14
❑ B231 Anthony Pleasant B	.30	.14
❑ B232 Jeff George B	.60	.25
❑ B233 Curtis Conway B	1.00	.45
❑ B235 Jeff Lewis B RC	.75	.35
❑ B236 Edgar Bennett B	.60	.25
❑ B237 Regan Upshaw B RC	.30	.14
❑ B238 William Fuller B	.30	.14
❑ B241 Willie Anderson B RC	.30	.14
❑ B242 Derrick Thomas B	.60	.25
❑ B243 Marvin Harrison B RC	10.00	4.50
❑ B244 Darion Conner B	.30	.14
❑ B245 Antonio Langham B	.30	.14
❑ B246 Rodney Peete B	.30	.14
❑ B247 Tim McDonald B	.30	.14
❑ B248 Robert Jones B	.30	.14
❑ B251 Mark Carrier DB B	.30	.14
❑ B252 Stephen Grant B	.30	.14
❑ B254 Jeff Hostetler B	.60	.25
❑ B255 Darrell Green B	.30	.14
❑ B261 Eric Swann B	.60	.25
❑ B263 Irv Smith B	.30	.14
❑ B264 Tim McKyer B	.30	.14
❑ B266 Sean Jones B	.30	.14
❑ B271 Yancey Thigpen B	.60	.25
❑ B273 Quentin Coryatt B	.30	.14
❑ B274 Hardy Nickerson B	.30	.14
❑ B275 Ricardo McDonald B	.30	.14
❑ B277 Robert Blackmon B	.30	.14
❑ B279 Alonzo Spellman B	.30	.14
❑ B281 Rickey Dudley B RC	1.25	.55
❑ B282 Joe Cain B	.30	.14
❑ B284 John Randle B	.60	.25
❑ B286 Vinny Testaverde B	.60	.25
❑ B289 Henry Jones B	.30	.14
❑ B290 Simeon Rice B RC	1.25	.55
❑ B295 Leslie O'Neal B	.30	.14
❑ B297 Greg Hill B	.60	.25
❑ B301 Eric Metcalf B	.60	.25
❑ B303 Jerome Woods B RC	.30	.14
❑ B306 Anthony Smith B	.30	.14
❑ B307 Darren Perry B	.30	.14
❑ B311 James Hasty B	.30	.14
❑ B312 Cris Carter B	1.00	.45
❑ B314 Lawrence Phillips B RC	.60	.25
❑ B317 Aeneas Williams B	.30	.14
❑ B318 Eric Hill B	.30	.14
❑ B319 Kevin Hardy B RC	1.25	.55
❑ B321 Chris Chandler B	.60	.25
❑ B322 Rocket Ismail B	.60	.25
❑ B323 Anthony Parker B	.30	.14
❑ B324 John Thierry B	.30	.14
❑ B325 Micheal Barrow B	.30	.14
❑ B326 Henry Ford B	.30	.14
❑ B327 Aaron Hayden B RC	.30	.14
❑ B328 Terance Mathis B	.30	.14
❑ B329 Kirk Pointer B RC	.30	.14
❑ B330 Ray Mickens B RC	.30	.14
❑ B331 J.Mayberry B RC	.30	.14
❑ B332 Mario Bates B	.60	.25
❑ B333 Carlton Gray B	.30	.14
❑ B334 Derek Loville B	.30	.14
❑ B335 Mike Alstott B RC	6.00	2.70
❑ B336 Eric Guliford B	.30	.14
❑ B337 Marvcus Patton B	.30	.14
❑ B338 Terrell Owens B RC	10.00	4.50
❑ B339 Lance Johnstone B RC	.30	.14
❑ B340 Lake Dawson B	.60	.25
❑ B341 Winslow Oliver B RC	.30	.14
❑ B342 Adrian Murrell B	.60	.25
❑ B343 Jason Belser B	.30	.14
❑ B344 Brian Dawkins B RC	.30	.14
❑ B345 Reggie Brown B RC	.30	.14
❑ B346 Shaun Gayle B	.30	.14
❑ B347 Tony Brackens B RC	1.25	.55
❑ B348 Thomas Lewis B	.30	.14
❑ B349 Kelvin Pritchett B	.30	.14
❑ B350 Bobby Engram B RC	1.25	.55
❑ B351 Moe Williams B RC	.60	.25
❑ B352 Thomas Smith B	.30	.14
❑ B353 Dexter Carter B	.30	.14
❑ B354 Qadry Ismail B	.60	.25
❑ B355 Marco Battaglia B RC	.30	.14
❑ B356 Levon Kirkland B	.30	.14
❑ B357 Eric Allen B	.30	.14
❑ B358 Bobby Hoying B RC	2.50	1.10

❑ B359 Checklist B .30 .14
❑ G1 Kordell Stewart G 8.00 3.60
❑ G7 Kimble Anders G 1.50 .70
❑ G8 Merton Hanks G 1.50 .70
❑ G17 Rick Mirer G 3.00 1.35
❑ G33 Craig Newsome G 1.50 .70
❑ G36 Bryce Paup G 3.00 1.35
❑ G40 Dan Marino G 20.00 9.00
❑ G42 Andre Coleman G 1.50 .70
❑ G47 Kevin Carter G 1.50 .70
❑ G60 Mark Brunell G 12.00 5.50
❑ G61 David Palmer G 3.00 1.35
❑ G75 Carnell Lake G 1.50 .70
❑ G96 Joey Galloway G 8.00 3.60
❑ G112 Melvin Tuten G 1.50 .70
❑ G121 Aaron Glenn G 1.50 .70
❑ G132 Brett Favre G 20.00 9.00
❑ G133 Ken Dilger G 3.00 1.35
❑ G140 Barry Sanders G 20.00 9.00
❑ G142 Glyn Milburn G 1.50 .70
❑ G148 Brett Perriman G 3.00 1.35
❑ G160 Kerry Collins G 5.00 2.20
❑ G164 Lee Woodall G 1.50 .70
❑ G173 Marshall Faulk G 5.00 2.20
❑ G178 Troy Aikman G 12.00 5.50
❑ G190 Drew Bledsoe G 12.00 5.50
❑ G191 Checklist G 1.50 .70
❑ G193 Michael Irvin G 5.00 2.20
❑ G196 Warren Moon G 3.00 1.35
❑ G200 Steve Young G 10.00 4.50
❑ G207 Alex Van Dyke G RC 3.00 1.35
❑ G220 Cris Carter G 5.00 2.20
❑ G230 John Elway G 20.00 9.00
❑ G234 Charles Haley G 3.00 1.35
❑ G240 Jim Kelly G 5.00 2.20
❑ G250 Rodney Hampton G 3.00 1.35
❑ G256 Erric Rhett G 3.00 1.35
❑ G257 Alex Molden G 1.50 .70
❑ G260 Kevin Hardy G 3.00 1.35
❑ G267 Bryant Young G 3.00 1.35
❑ G268 Jeff Blake G 5.00 2.20
❑ G270 Keyshawn Johnson G 8.00 3.60
❑ G278 Junior Seau G 5.00 2.20
❑ G285 Terry Kirby G 3.00 1.35
❑ G293 Hugh Douglas G 3.00 1.35
❑ G296 Reggie White G 5.00 2.20
❑ G298 Elvis Grbac G 5.00 2.20
❑ G300 Emmitt Smith G 15.00 6.75
❑ G309 Ricky Watters G 3.00 1.35
❑ S4 Brett Favre S 15.00 6.75
❑ S14 Chester McGlockton S .75 .35
❑ S20 Tyrone Hughes S .75 .35
❑ S24 Ty Law S .75 .35
❑ S25 Brian Mitchell S .75 .35
❑ S31 Darren Woodson S 1.50 .70
❑ S35 Brian Mitchell S .75 .35
❑ S37 Dana Stubblefield S 1.50 .70
❑ S41 Kerry Collins S 3.00 1.35
❑ S46 Orlando Thomas S .75 .35
❑ S50 Jerry Rice S 8.00 3.60
❑ S53 Willie McGinest S .75 .35
❑ S54 Blake Brockermeyer S .75 .35
❑ S56 Michael Westbrook S 3.00 1.35
❑ S57 Garrison Hearst S 3.00 1.35
❑ S59 Kyle Brady S 1.50 .70
❑ S62 Tim Brown S 1.50 .70
❑ S63 Jeff Graham S .75 .35
❑ S67 Dan Marino S 15.00 6.75
❑ S69 Tamarick Vanover S 3.00 1.35
❑ S74 Daryl Johnston S 1.50 .70
❑ S78 Frank Sanders S 1.50 .70
❑ S84 Darryll Lewis S .75 .35
❑ S85 Carl Pickens S 3.00 1.35
❑ S88 Jerome Bettis S 3.00 1.35
❑ S90 Terrell Davis S 15.00 6.75
❑ S99 Napoleon Kaufman S 3.00 1.35
❑ S100 Rashaan Salaam S 3.00 1.35
❑ S103 Barry Sanders S 15.00 6.75
❑ S107 Tony Boselli S 1.50 .70
❑ S109 Eric Zeier S 1.50 .70
❑ S116 Bruce Smith S 3.00 1.35
❑ S118 Zack Crockett S .75 .35
❑ S125 Joey Galloway S 6.00 2.70
❑ S126 Heath Shuler S 3.00 1.35
❑ S127 Curtis Martin S 8.00 3.60
❑ S135 Greg Lloyd S 1.50 .70
❑ S137 Marshall Faulk S 3.00 1.35
❑ S147 Tyrone Poole S .75 .35
❑ S150 J.J. Stokes S 3.00 1.35
❑ S153 Drew Bledsoe S 8.00 3.60
❑ S154 Terry McDaniel S .75 .35
❑ S155 Terrell Fletcher S .75 .35
❑ S159 Dave Brown S .75 .35
❑ S165 Jim Harbaugh S 1.50 .70
❑ S166 Larry Brown S .75 .35
❑ S167 Neil Smith S 1.50 .70
❑ S168 Herman Moore S 3.00 1.35
❑ S170 Deion Sanders S 5.00 2.20
❑ S174 Mark Chmura S 1.50 .70
❑ S181 Chris Warren S 1.50 .70
❑ S183 Robert Brooks S 3.00 1.35
❑ S184 Steve McNair S 8.00 3.60
❑ S185 Kordell Stewart S 6.00 2.70
❑ S189 Charlie Garner S .75 .35
❑ S195 Harvey Williams S .75 .35
❑ S197 Jeff George S 1.50 .70
❑ S199 Ricky Watters S 1.50 .70
❑ S204 Steve Bono S 1.50 .70
❑ S210 Jeff Blake S 3.00 1.35
❑ S215 Phillippi Sparks S .75 .35
❑ S226 William Floyd S 1.50 .70
❑ S227 Troy Drayton S .75 .35
❑ S229 Rodney Hampton S 1.50 .70
❑ S239 Duane Clemons S RC .75 .35
❑ S249 Curtis Conway S 3.00 1.35
❑ S253 John Mobley S .75 .35
❑ S258 Chris Slade S .75 .35
❑ S259 Derrick Thomas S 1.50 .70
❑ S262 Eric Metcalf S 1.50 .70
❑ S265 Emmitt Smith S 12.00 5.50
❑ S269 Jeff Hostetler S 1.50 .70
❑ S272 Thurman Thomas S 3.00 1.35
❑ S276 Steve Atwater S .75 .35
❑ S280 Isaac Bruce S 3.00 1.35
❑ S283 Neil O'Donnell S 1.50 .70
❑ S287 Jim Kelly S 3.00 1.35
❑ S288 Lawrence Phillips S 3.00 1.35
❑ S291 Terance Mathis S .75 .35
❑ S292 Erric Rhett S 1.50 .70
❑ S294 Santo Stephens S .75 .35
❑ S299 Walt Harris S RC .75 .35
❑ S302 Jamir Miller S .75 .35
❑ S304 Ben Coates S 1.50 .70
❑ S305 Marcus Allen S 3.00 1.35
❑ S308 Jonathan Ogden S RC .75 .35
❑ S310 John Elway S 15.00 6.75
❑ S313 Irving Fryar S 1.50 .70
❑ S315 Junior Seau S 3.00 1.35
❑ S316 Alex Molden S RC .75 .35
❑ S320 Steve Young S 6.00 2.70

1997 Finest

	MINT	NRMT
COMPLETE SET (350)	800.00	350.00
COMP.SERIES 1 SET (175)	400.00	180.00
COMP.SERIES 2 SET (175)	400.00	180.00
COMP.BRONZE SER.1 (100)	30.00	13.50
COMP.BRONZE SER.2 (100)	50.00	22.00
COMMON BRONZE	.30	.14
COMMON SILVER	.60	.25
COMMON GOLD	1.50	.70

❑ 1 Mark Brunell B 4.00 1.80
❑ 2 Chris Slade B .30 .14
❑ 3 Chris Doleman B .30 .14
❑ 4 Chris Hudson B .30 .14
❑ 5 Karim Abdul-Jabbar B 1.25 .55
❑ 6 Darren Perry B .30 .14
❑ 7 Daryl Johnston B .60 .25
❑ 8 Rob Moore B UER .60 .25
(Listed as uncommon)
❑ 9 Robert Smith B .60 .25
❑ 10 Terry Allen B 1.25 .55
❑ 11 Jason Dunn B .30 .14
❑ 12 Henry Thomas B .30 .14
❑ 13 Rod Stephens B .30 .14
❑ 14 Ray Mickens B .30 .14
❑ 15 Ty Detmer B .60 .25
❑ 16 Fred Barnett B .30 .14
❑ 17 Derrick Alexander WR B .60 .25
❑ 18 Marcus Robertson B .30 .14
❑ 19 Robert Blackmon B .30 .14
❑ 20 Isaac Bruce B 1.25 .55
❑ 21 Chester McGlockton B .30 .14
❑ 22 Stan Humphries B .60 .25
❑ 23 Lonnie Marts B .30 .14
❑ 24 Jason Sehorn B .60 .25
❑ 25 Bobby Engram B UER .60 .25
(Listed as uncommon)
❑ 26 Brett Perriman B UER .30 .14
(Listed as uncommon)
❑ 27 Stevon Moore B .30 .14
❑ 28 Jamal Anderson B 2.00 .90
❑ 29 Wayne Martin B .30 .14
❑ 30 Michael Irvin B UER 1.25 .55
(Listed as uncommon)
❑ 31 Thomas Smith B .30 .14
❑ 32 Tony Brackens B .30 .14
❑ 33 Eric Davis B .30 .14
❑ 34 James O.Stewart B .60 .25
❑ 35 Ki-Jana Carter B .30 .14
❑ 36 Ken Norton B .30 .14
❑ 37 William Thomas B .30 .14
❑ 38 Tim Brown B 1.25 .55
❑ 39 Lawrence Phillips B .30 .14
❑ 40 Ricky Watters B .60 .25
❑ 41 Tony Bennett B .30 .14
❑ 42 Jessie Armstead B .30 .14
❑ 43 Trent Dilfer B 1.25 .55
❑ 44 Rodney Hampton B .60 .25
❑ 45 Sam Mills B .30 .14
❑ 46 Rodney Harrison B .30 .14
❑ 47 Rob Fredrickson B .30 .14
❑ 48 Eric Hill B .30 .14
❑ 49 Bennie Blades B .30 .14
❑ 50 Eddie George B 4.00 1.80
❑ 51 Dave Brown B .30 .14
❑ 52 Raymont Harris B .30 .14
❑ 53 Steve Tovar B .30 .14
❑ 54 Thurman Thomas B 1.25 .55
❑ 55 Leeland McElroy B .30 .14
❑ 56 Brian Mitchell B UER .30 .14
(Listed as uncommon)
❑ 57 Eric Allen B .30 .14
❑ 58 Vinny Testaverde B .60 .25
❑ 59 Marvin Washington B .30 .14
❑ 60 Junior Seau B .60 .25
❑ 61 Bert Emanuel B .60 .25
❑ 62 Kevin Carter B .30 .14
❑ 63 Mark Carrier DB B .30 .14
❑ 64 Andre Coleman B .30 .14
❑ 65 Chris Warren B .60 .25
❑ 66 Aeneas Williams B .30 .14
❑ 67 Eugene Robinson B .30 .14
❑ 68 Darren Woodson B .30 .14
❑ 69 Anthony Johnson B .30 .14
❑ 70 Terry Glenn B 1.25 .55
❑ 71 Troy Vincent B .30 .14
❑ 72 John Copeland B .30 .14
❑ 73 Warren Sapp B .60 .25
❑ 74 Bobby Hebert B .30 .14
❑ 75 Jeff Hostetler B .30 .14
❑ 76 Willie Davis B .30 .14
❑ 77 Mickey Washington B .30 .14
❑ 78 Cortez Kennedy B .30 .14
❑ 79 Michael Strahan B .30 .14
❑ 80 Jerome Bettis B 1.25 .55
❑ 81 Andre Hastings B UER .30 .14
(Listed as uncommon)
❑ 82 Simeon Rice B .60 .25

❑ 83 Cornelius Bennett B .... .30 .14
❑ 84 Napoleon Kaufman B .... 1.25 .55
❑ 85 Jim Harbaugh B .... .60 .25
❑ 86 Aaron Hayden B .... .30 .14
❑ 87 Gus Frerotte B............... .30 .14
❑ 88 Jeff Blake B..................... .60 .25
❑ 89 Anthony Miller B UER ...... .30 .14
(Listed as uncommon)
❑ 90 Deion Sanders B........... 1.25 .55
❑ 91 Curtis Conway B .... .60 .25
❑ 92 William Floyd B .... .60 .25
❑ 93 Eric Moulds B UER .... 1.25 .55
(Listed as uncommon)
❑ 94 Mel Gray B .... .30 .14
❑ 95 Andre Rison B UER .... .60 .25
(Listed as uncommon)
❑ 96 Eugene Daniel B............. .30 .14
❑ 97 Jason Belser B .... .30 .14
❑ 98 Mike Mamula B .... .30 .14
❑ 99 Jim Everett B.................... .30 .14
❑ 100 Checklist B .... .30 .14
❑ 101 Drew Bledsoe S 6.00 2.70
❑ 102 Shannon Sharpe S ...... 1.25 .55
❑ 103 Ken Harvey S .... .60 .25
❑ 104 Isaac Bruce S 2.50 1.10
❑ 105 Terry Allen S................ 2.50 1.10
❑ 106 Lawyer Milloy S............. .60 .25
❑ 107 Ashley Ambrose S.......... .60 .25
❑ 108 Alfred Williams S........... .60 .25
❑ 109 Hugh Douglas S .... .60 .25
❑ 110 Junior Seau S .... 1.25 .55
❑ 111 Kordell Stewart S 4.00 1.80
❑ 112 Adrian Murrell S .... 1.25 .55
❑ 113 Byron Bam Morris S ...... .60 .25
❑ 114 Terrell Buckley S........... .60 .25
❑ 115 Dan Marino S 12.00 5.50
❑ 116 Willie Clay S .... .60 .25
❑ 117 Neil Smith S .... 1.25 .55
❑ 118 Blaine Bishop S............. .60 .25
❑ 119 John Mobley S .... .60 .25
❑ 120 Herman Moore S.......... 2.50 1.10
❑ 121 Keyshawn Johnson S .. 2.50 1.10
❑ 122 Boomer Esiason S ...... 1.25 .55
❑ 123 Marshall Faulk S 2.50 1.10
❑ 124 Keith Jackson S .... .60 .25
❑ 125 Ricky Watters S............ 1.25 .55
❑ 126 Carl Pickens S............ 1.25 .55
❑ 127 Cris Carter S 2.50 1.10
❑ 128 Mike Alstott S 2.50 1.10
❑ 129 Simeon Rice S .... 1.25 .55
❑ 130 Troy Aikman S............. 6.00 2.70
❑ 131 Tamarick Vanover S .... 1.25 .55
❑ 132 Marquez Pope S .... .60 .25
❑ 133 Winslow Oliver S........... .60 .25
❑ 134 Edgar Bennett S .... 1.25 .55
❑ 135 Dave Meggett S .... .60 .25
❑ 136 Marcus Allen S 2.50 1.10
❑ 137 Jerry Rice S................. 6.00 2.70
❑ 138 Steve Atwater S .... .60 .25
❑ 139 Tim McDonald S .... .60 .25
❑ 140 Barry Sanders S 12.00 5.50
❑ 141 Eddie George S........... 8.00 3.60
❑ 142 Wesley Walls S............. .60 .25
❑ 143 Jerome Bettis S.......... 2.50 1.10
❑ 144 Kevin Greene S........... 1.25 .55
❑ 145 Terrell Davis S........... 12.00 5.50
❑ 146 Gus Frerotte S............ 1.25 .55
❑ 147 Joey Galloway S 4.00 1.80
❑ 148 Vinny Testaverde S...... 1.25 .55
❑ 149 Hardy Nickerson S .... .60 .25
❑ 150 Brett Favre S 12.00 5.50
❑ 151 Desmond Howard G .... 1.50 .70
❑ 152 Keyshawn Johnson G .. 5.00 2.20
❑ 153 Tony Banks G 5.00 2.20
❑ 154 Chris Spielman G .... 1.50 .70
❑ 155 Reggie White G........... 5.00 2.20
❑ 156 Zach Thomas G 5.00 2.20
❑ 157 Carl Pickens G 3.00 1.35
❑ 158 Karim Abdul-Jabbar G.. 5.00 2.20
❑ 159 Chad Brown G............. 1.50 .70
❑ 160 Kerry Collins G 3.00 1.35
❑ 161 Marvin Harrison G........ 5.00 2.20
❑ 162 Steve Young G 8.00 3.60
❑ 163 Deion Sanders G.......... 5.00 2.20
❑ 164 Trent Dilfer G.............. 5.00 2.20
❑ 165 Barry Sanders G 20.00 9.00
❑ 166 Cris Carter G................ 5.00 2.20
❑ 167 Keenan McCardell G.... 3.00 1.35
❑ 168 Terry Glenn G 5.00 2.20
❑ 169 Emmitt Smith G......... 15.00 6.75
❑ 170 John Elway G 20.00 9.00
❑ 171 Jerry Rice G 10.00 4.50
❑ 172 Troy Aikman G 10.00 4.50
❑ 173 Curtis Martin G 8.00 3.60
❑ 174 Darrell Green G........... 1.50 .70
❑ 175 Mark Brunell G 10.00 4.50
❑ 176 Corey Dillon B RC 12.00 5.50
❑ 177 Tyrone Poole B .... .30 .14
❑ 178 Anthony Pleasant B........ .30 .14
❑ 179 Frank Sanders B........... .60 .25
❑ 180 Troy Aikman B............. 3.00 1.35
❑ 181 Bill Romanowski B .... .30 .14
❑ 182 Ty Law B........................ .30 .14
❑ 183 Orlando Thomas B .... .30 .14
❑ 184 Quentin Coryatt B .... .30 .14
❑ 185 Kenny Holmes B RC .... 1.50 .70
❑ 186 Bryant Young B.............. .30 .14
❑ 187 Michael Sinclair B .... .30 .14
❑ 188 Mike Tomczak B .... .30 .14
❑ 189 Bobby Taylor B .... .30 .14
❑ 190 Brett Favre B............... 6.00 2.70
❑ 191 Kent Graham B .... .30 .14
❑ 192 Jessie Tuggle B............. .30 .14
❑ 193 Jimmy Smith B .... .60 .25
❑ 194 Greg Hill B..................... .30 .14
❑ 195 Yatil Green B RC .... 1.00 .45
❑ 196 Mark Fields B .... .30 .14
❑ 197 Phillippi Sparks B .... .30 .14
❑ 198 Aaron Glenn B............... .30 .14
❑ 199 Pat Swilling B .... .30 .14
❑ 200 Barry Sanders B 6.00 2.70
❑ 201 Mark Chmura B.............. .60 .25
❑ 202 Marco Coleman B .... .30 .14
❑ 203 Merton Hanks B .... .30 .14
❑ 204 Brian Blades B .... .30 .14
❑ 205 Errict Rhett B................ .30 .14
❑ 206 Henry Ellard B............... .30 .14
❑ 207 Andre Reed B .... .60 .25
❑ 208 Bryan Cox B .... .30 .14
❑ 209 Darnay Scott B .... .60 .25
❑ 210 John Elway B 6.00 2.70
❑ 211 Glyn Milburn B............... .30 .14
❑ 212 Don Beebe B................. .30 .14
❑ 213 Kevin Lockett B RC .... 1.00 .45
❑ 214 Dorsey Levens B.......... 1.25 .55
❑ 215 Kordell Stewart B .... 1.50 .70
❑ 216 Larry Centers B............. .60 .25
❑ 217 Cris Carter B .... 1.25 .55
❑ 218 Willie McGinest B .... .30 .14
❑ 219 Renaldo Wynn B RC...... .40 .18
❑ 220 Jerry Rice B................ 3.00 1.35
❑ 221 Reidel Anthony B RC .. 4.00 1.80
❑ 222 Mark Carrier WR B .... .30 .14
❑ 223 Quinn Early B .... .30 .14
❑ 224 Chris Sanders B .... .30 .14
❑ 225 Shawn Springs B RC .. 1.00 .45
❑ 226 Kevin Smith B .... .30 .14
❑ 227 Ben Coates B .... .60 .25
❑ 228 Tyrone Wheatley B .... .60 .25
❑ 229 Antonio Freeman B...... 2.00 .90
❑ 230 Dan Marino B 6.00 2.70
❑ 231 Dwayne Rudd B RC .... 1.50 .70
❑ 232 Leslie O'Neal B .... .30 .14
❑ 233 Brent Jones B .... .60 .25
❑ 234 Jake Plummer B RC.. 12.00 5.50
❑ 235 Kerry Collins B .... .60 .25
❑ 236 Rashaan Salaam B........ .30 .14
❑ 237 Tyrone Braxton B .... .30 .14
❑ 238 Herman Moore B.......... 1.25 .55
❑ 239 Keyshawn Johnson B .. 1.25 .55
❑ 240 Drew Bledsoe B 3.00 1.35
❑ 241 Rickey Dudley B .... .60 .25
❑ 242 Antowain Smith B RC.. 5.00 2.20
❑ 243 Jeff Lageman B.............. .30 .14
❑ 244 Chris T. Jones B .... .30 .14
❑ 245 Steve Young B .... 2.00 .90
❑ 246 Eddie Robinson B .... .30 .14
❑ 247 Chad Cota B .... .30 .14
❑ 248 Michael Jackson B .... .60 .25
❑ 249 Robert Porcher B .... .30 .14
❑ 250 Reggie White B........... 1.25 .55
❑ 251 Carnell Lake B............... .30 .14
❑ 252 Chris Calloway B............ .30 .14
❑ 253 Terance Mathis B .... .60 .25
❑ 254 Carl Pickens B............ 1.25 .55
❑ 255 Curtis Martin B .... 2.00 .90
❑ 256 Jeff Graham B................ .30 .14
❑ 257 Regan Upshaw B RC .... .40 .18
❑ 258 Sean Gilbert B................ .30 .14
❑ 259 Will Blackwell B RC .... 1.00 .45
❑ 260 Emmitt Smith B 5.00 2.20
❑ 261 Reinard Wilson B RC .... .40 .18
❑ 262 Darrell Russell B RC...... .40 .18
❑ 263 Wayne Chrebet B .... .60 .25
❑ 264 Kevin Hardy B .... .30 .14
❑ 265 Shannon Sharpe B .... .60 .25
❑ 266 Harvey Williams B.......... .30 .14
❑ 267 John Randle B................ .60 .25
❑ 268 Tim Bowens B................ .30 .14
❑ 269 Tony Gonzalez B RC .. 6.00 2.70
❑ 270 Warrick Dunn B RC 6.00 2.70
❑ 271 Sean Dawkins B .... .30 .14
❑ 272 Darryll Lewis B .... .30 .14
❑ 273 Alonzo Spellman B .... .30 .14
❑ 274 Mark Collins B................ .30 .14
❑ 275 Checklist Card B .... .30 .14
❑ 276 Pat Barnes S RC 3.00 1.35
❑ 277 Dana Stubblefield S .... 1.25 .55
❑ 278 Dan Wilkinson S .... .60 .25
❑ 279 Bryce Paup S .... .60 .25
❑ 280 Kerry Collins S .... 1.25 .55
❑ 281 Derrick Brooks S............ .60 .25
❑ 282 Walter Jones S .... .60 .25
❑ 283 Terry McDaniel S .... .60 .25
❑ 284 James Farrior S RC ...... .60 .25
❑ 285 Curtis Martin S 5.00 2.20
❑ 286 O.J. McDuffie S........... 1.25 .55
❑ 287 Natrone Means S 2.50 1.10
❑ 288 Bryant Westbrook S RC 1.25 .55
❑ 289 Peter Boulware S RC .. 2.50 1.10
❑ 290 Emmitt Smith S 10.00 4.50
❑ 291 Joey Kent S RC 2.50 1.10
❑ 292 Eddie Kennison S .... 1.25 .55
❑ 293 LeRoy Butler S .... .60 .25
❑ 294 Dale Carter S .... .60 .25
❑ 295 Jim Druckenmiller S RC 2.50 1.10
❑ 296 Byron Hanspard S RC 2.50 1.10
❑ 297 Jeff Blake S.................. 1.25 .55
❑ 298 Levon Kirkland S............ .60 .25
❑ 299 Michael Westbrook S .. 1.25 .55
❑ 300 John Elway S 12.00 5.50
❑ 301 Lamar Lathon S.............. .60 .25
❑ 302 Ray Lewis S .... .60 .25
❑ 303 Steve McNair S........... 5.00 2.20
❑ 304 Shawn Springs S......... 1.25 .55
❑ 305 Karim Abdul-Jabbar S.. 1.25 .55
❑ 306 Orlando Pace S RC 2.50 1.10
❑ 307 Scott Mitchell S .... .60 .25
❑ 308 Walt Harris S.................. .60 .25
❑ 309 Bruce Smith S............. 1.25 .55
❑ 310 Reggie White S........... 2.50 1.10
❑ 311 Eric Swann S................. .60 .25
❑ 312 Derrick Thomas S .... 1.25 .55
❑ 313 Tony Martin S .... 1.25 .55
❑ 314 Darrell Russell S RC.... 1.25 .55
❑ 315 Mark Brunell S............. 6.00 2.70
❑ 316 Trent Dilfer S.............. 2.50 1.10
❑ 317 Irving Fryar S................. .60 .25
❑ 318 Amani Toomer S.......... 1.25 .55
❑ 319 Jake Reed S .... 1.25 .55
❑ 320 Steve Young S 5.00 2.20
❑ 321 Troy Davis S RC .... 1.25 .55
❑ 322 Jim Harbaugh S .... 1.25 .55
❑ 323 Neil O'Donnell S .... .60 .25
❑ 324 Terry Glenn S 2.50 1.10
❑ 325 Deion Sanders S......... 2.50 1.10
❑ 326 Gus Frerotte G 3.00 1.35
❑ 327 Tom Knight G RC 3.00 1.35
❑ 328 Peter Boulware G 3.00 1.35
❑ 329 Jerome Bettis G 5.00 2.20
❑ 330 Orlando Pace G 5.00 2.20
❑ 331 Darnell Autry G RC 3.00 1.35
❑ 332 Ike Hilliard G RC 12.00 5.50
❑ 333 David LaFleur G RC.... 3.00 1.35
❑ 334 Jim Harbaugh G 3.00 1.35
❑ 335 Eddie George G 12.00 5.50
❑ 336 Vinny Testaverde G 3.00 1.35
❑ 337 Terry Allen G................ 3.00 1.35

		MINT	NRMT
❑ 338	Jim Druckenmiller G	5.00	2.20
❑ 339	Ricky Watters G	3.00	1.35
❑ 340	Brett Favre G	20.00	9.00
❑ 341	Simeon Rice G	3.00	1.35
❑ 342	Shannon Sharpe G	3.00	1.35
❑ 343	Kordell Stewart G	6.00	2.70
❑ 344	Isaac Bruce G	5.00	2.20
❑ 345	Drew Bledsoe G	10.00	4.50
❑ 346	Jeff Blake G	3.00	1.35
❑ 347	Herman Moore G	5.00	2.20
❑ 348	Junior Seau G	3.00	1.35
❑ 349	Rae Carruth G RC	3.00	1.35
❑ 350	Dan Marino G	20.00	9.00
❑ P5	K.Abdul-Jabbar Promo	1.50	.70
❑ P32	Tony Brackens Promo	1.50	.70
❑ P45	Sam Mills Promo	1.50	.70
❑ P70	Terry Glenn Promo	1.50	.70
❑ P87	Gus Frerotte Promo	1.50	.70

1998 Finest

	MINT	NRMT
COMPLETE SET (270)	120.00	55.00
COMP.SERIES 1 (150)	80.00	36.00
COMP.SERIES 2 (120)	40.00	18.00

		MINT	NRMT
❑ 1	John Elway	5.00	2.20
❑ 2	Terance Mathis	.50	.23
❑ 3	Jermaine Lewis	.50	.23
❑ 4	Fred Lane	.50	.23
❑ 5	Simeon Rice	.50	.23
❑ 6	David Dunn	.25	.11
❑ 7	Dexter Coakley	.25	.11
❑ 8	Carl Pickens	1.00	.45
❑ 9	Antonio Freeman	1.00	.45
❑ 10	Herman Moore	1.00	.45
❑ 11	Kevin Hardy	.25	.11
❑ 12	Tony Gonzalez	.25	.11
❑ 13	O.J. McDuffie	.50	.23
❑ 14	David Palmer	.25	.11
❑ 15	Lawyer Milloy	.25	.11
❑ 16	Danny Kanell	.50	.23
❑ 17	Randal Hill	.25	.11
❑ 18	Chris Slade	.25	.11
❑ 19	Charlie Garner	.25	.11
❑ 20	Mark Brunell	2.00	.90
❑ 21	Donnell Woolford	.25	.11
❑ 22	Freddie Jones	.25	.11
❑ 23	Ken Norton	.25	.11
❑ 24	Tony Banks	.50	.23
❑ 25	Isaac Bruce	1.00	.45
❑ 26	Willie Davis	.25	.11
❑ 27	Cris Dishman	.25	.11
❑ 28	Aeneas Williams	.25	.11
❑ 29	Michael Booker	.25	.11
❑ 30	Cris Carter	1.00	.45
❑ 31	Michael McCrary	.25	.11
❑ 32	Eric Moulds	1.00	.45
❑ 33	Rae Carruth	.50	.23
❑ 34	Bobby Engram	.50	.23
❑ 35	Jeff Blake	.50	.23
❑ 36	Deion Sanders	1.00	.45
❑ 37	Rod Smith	.50	.23
❑ 38	Bryant Westbrook	.25	.11
❑ 39	Mark Chmura	.50	.23
❑ 40	Tim Brown	1.00	.45
❑ 41	Bobby Taylor	.25	.11
❑ 42	James Stewart	.50	.23
❑ 43	Kimble Anders	.50	.23
❑ 44	Karim Abdul-Jabbar	1.00	.45
❑ 45	Willie McGinest	.25	.11
❑ 46	Jessie Armstead	.25	.11
❑ 47	Brad Johnson	1.00	.45
❑ 48	Greg Lloyd	.25	.11
❑ 49	Stephen Davis	.25	.11
❑ 50	Jerome Bettis	1.00	.45
❑ 51	Warren Sapp	.50	.23
❑ 52	Horace Copeland	.25	.11
❑ 53	Chad Brown	.25	.11
❑ 54	Chris Canty	.25	.11
❑ 55	Robert Smith	1.00	.45
❑ 56	Pete Mitchell	.25	.11
❑ 57	Aaron Bailey	.25	.11
❑ 58	Robert Porcher	.25	.11
❑ 59	John Mobley	.25	.11
❑ 60	Tony Martin	.50	.23
❑ 61	Michael Irvin	1.00	.45
❑ 62	Charles Way	.25	.11
❑ 63	Raymont Harris	.25	.11
❑ 64	Chuck Smith	.25	.11
❑ 65	Larry Centers	.25	.11
❑ 66	Greg Hill	.25	.11
❑ 67	Kenny Holmes	.25	.11
❑ 68	John Lynch	.50	.23
❑ 69	Michael Sinclair	.25	.11
❑ 70	Steve Young	1.50	.70
❑ 71	Michael Strahan	.25	.11
❑ 72	Levon Kirkland	.25	.11
❑ 73	Rickey Dudley	.25	.11
❑ 74	Marcus Allen	1.00	.45
❑ 75	John Randle	.50	.23
❑ 76	Erik Kramer	.25	.11
❑ 77	Neil Smith	.50	.23
❑ 78	Byron Hanspard	.50	.23
❑ 79	Quinn Early	.25	.11
❑ 80	Warren Moon	1.00	.45
❑ 81	William Thomas	.25	.11
❑ 82	Ben Coates	.50	.23
❑ 83	Lake Dawson	.25	.11
❑ 84	Steve McNair	1.00	.45
❑ 85	Gus Frerotte	.25	.11
❑ 86	Rodney Harrison	.50	.23
❑ 87	Reggie White	1.00	.45
❑ 88	Derrick Thomas	.50	.23
❑ 89	Dale Carter	.25	.11
❑ 90	Warrick Dunn	1.00	.45
❑ 91	Will Blackwell	.25	.11
❑ 92	Troy Vincent	.25	.11
❑ 93	Johnnie Morton	.50	.23
❑ 94	David LaFleur	.25	.11
❑ 95	Tony McGee	.25	.11
❑ 96	Lonnie Johnson	.25	.11
❑ 97	Thurman Thomas	1.00	.45
❑ 98	Chris Chandler	.50	.23
❑ 99	Jamal Anderson	1.00	.45
❑ 100	Checklist	.25	.11
❑ 101	Marshall Faulk	1.00	.45
❑ 102	Chris Calloway	.25	.11
❑ 103	Chris Spielman	.25	.11
❑ 104	Zach Thomas	.50	.23
❑ 105	Jeff George	.50	.23
❑ 106	Darrell Russell	.25	.11
❑ 107	Darryll Lewis	.25	.11
❑ 108	Reidel Anthony	.50	.23
❑ 109	Terrell Owens	1.00	.45
❑ 110	Rob Moore	.50	.23
❑ 111	Darrell Green	.50	.23
❑ 112	Merton Hanks	.25	.11
❑ 113	Shawn Jefferson	.25	.11
❑ 114	Chris Sanders	.25	.11
❑ 115	Scott Mitchell	.50	.23
❑ 116	Vaughn Hebron	.25	.11
❑ 117	Ed McCaffrey	.50	.23
❑ 118	Bruce Smith	.50	.23
❑ 119	Peter Boulware	.25	.11
❑ 120	Brett Favre	5.00	2.20
❑ 121	Peyton Manning RC	30.00	13.50
❑ 122	Brian Griese RC	12.00	5.50
❑ 123	Tavian Banks RC	3.00	1.35
❑ 124	Duane Starks RC	2.00	.90
❑ 125	Robert Holcombe RC	4.00	1.80
❑ 126	Brian Simmons RC	2.00	.90
❑ 127	Skip Hicks RC	4.00	1.80
❑ 128	Keith Brooking RC	3.00	1.35
❑ 129	Ahman Green RC	10.00	4.50
❑ 130	Jerome Pathon RC	3.00	1.35
❑ 131	Curtis Enis RC	5.00	2.20
❑ 132	Grant Wistrom RC	2.00	.90
❑ 133	Germane Crowell RC	8.00	3.60
❑ 134	Jacquez Green RC	6.00	2.70
❑ 135	Randy Moss RC	30.00	13.50
❑ 136	Jason Peter RC	2.00	.90
❑ 137	John Avery RC	4.00	1.80
❑ 138	Takeo Spikes RC	3.00	1.35
❑ 139	Pat Johnson RC	3.00	1.35
❑ 140	Andre Wadsworth RC	3.00	1.35
❑ 141	Fred Taylor RC	10.00	4.50
❑ 142	Charles Woodson RC	6.00	2.70
❑ 143	Marcus Nash RC	4.00	1.80
❑ 144	Robert Edwards RC	5.00	2.20
❑ 145	Kevin Dyson RC	6.00	2.70
❑ 146	Joe Jurevicius RC	3.00	1.35
❑ 147	Anthony Simmons RC	2.00	.90
❑ 148	Hines Ward RC	3.00	1.35
❑ 149	Greg Ellis RC	2.00	.90
❑ 150	Ryan Leaf RC	10.00	4.50
❑ 151	Jerry Rice	2.50	1.10
❑ 152	Tony Martin	.50	.23
❑ 153	Checklist	.25	.11
❑ 154	Rob Johnson	.50	.23
❑ 155	Shannon Sharpe	.50	.23
❑ 156	Bert Emanuel	.50	.23
❑ 157	Eric Metcalf	.25	.11
❑ 158	Natrone Means	1.00	.45
❑ 159	Derrick Alexander	.50	.23
❑ 160	Emmitt Smith	4.00	1.80
❑ 161	Jeff Burris	.25	.11
❑ 162	Chris Warren	.50	.23
❑ 163	Corey Fuller	.25	.11
❑ 164	Courtney Hawkins	.25	.11
❑ 165	James McKnight	.25	.11
❑ 166	Shawn Springs	.25	.11
❑ 167	Wayne Martin	.25	.11
❑ 168	Michael Westbrook	.50	.23
❑ 169	Michael Jackson	.25	.11
❑ 170	Dan Marino	5.00	2.20
❑ 171	Amp Lee	.25	.11
❑ 172	James Jett	.50	.23
❑ 173	Ty Law	.25	.11
❑ 174	Kerry Collins	.50	.23
❑ 175	Robert Brooks	.50	.23
❑ 176	Blaine Bishop	.25	.11
❑ 177	Stephen Boyd	.25	.11
❑ 178	Keyshawn Johnson	1.00	.45
❑ 179	Deon Figures	.25	.11
❑ 180	Allen Aldridge	.25	.11
❑ 181	Corey Miller	.25	.11
❑ 182	Chad Lewis	.25	.11
❑ 183	Derrick Rodgers	.25	.11
❑ 184	Troy Drayton	.25	.11
❑ 185	Darren Woodson	.25	.11
❑ 186	Ken Dilger	.25	.11
❑ 187	Elvis Grbac	.50	.23
❑ 188	Terrell Fletcher	.25	.11
❑ 189	Frank Sanders	.50	.23
❑ 190	Curtis Martin	1.00	.45
❑ 191	Derrick Brooks	.25	.11
❑ 192	Darrien Gordon	.25	.11
❑ 193	Andre Reed	.50	.23
❑ 194	Darnay Scott	.50	.23
❑ 195	Curtis Conway	.50	.23
❑ 196	Tim McDonald	.25	.11
❑ 197	Sean Dawkins	.25	.11
❑ 198	Napoleon Kaufman	1.00	.45
❑ 199	Willie Clay	.25	.11
❑ 200	Terrell Davis	4.00	1.80
❑ 201	Wesley Walls	.50	.23
❑ 202	Santana Dotson	.25	.11
❑ 203	Frank Wycheck	.25	.11
❑ 204	Wayne Chrebet	1.00	.45
❑ 205	Andre Rison	.50	.23
❑ 206	Jason Sehorn	.50	.23
❑ 207	Jessie Tuggle	.25	.11
❑ 208	Kevin Turner	.25	.11
❑ 209	Jason Taylor	.25	.11
❑ 210	Yancey Thigpen	.25	.11
❑ 211	Jake Reed	.50	.23
❑ 212	Carnell Lake	.25	.11
❑ 213	Joey Galloway	1.00	.45
❑ 214	Andre Hastings	.25	.11

❑ 215 Terry Allen 1.00 .45
❑ 216 Jim Harbaugh .50 .23
❑ 217 Tony Banks .50 .23
❑ 218 Greg Clark .25 .11
❑ 219 Corey Dillon 1.50 .70
❑ 220 Troy Aikman 2.50 1.10
❑ 221 Antowain Smith 1.00 .45
❑ 222 Steve Atwater .25 .11
❑ 223 Trent Dilfer 1.00 .45
❑ 224 Junior Seau .50 .23
❑ 225 Garrison Hearst 1.00 .45
❑ 226 Eric Allen .25 .11
❑ 227 Chad Cota .25 .11
❑ 228 Vinny Testaverde .50 .23
❑ 229 Duce Staley 2.00 .90
❑ 230 Drew Bledsoe 2.00 .90
❑ 231 Charles Johnson .25 .11
❑ 232 Jake Plummer 2.00 .90
❑ 233 Errict Rhett .50 .23
❑ 234 Doug Evans .25 .11
❑ 235 Phillippi Sparks .25 .11
❑ 236 Ashley Ambrose .25 .11
❑ 237 Bryan Cox .25 .11
❑ 238 Kevin Smith .25 .11
❑ 239 Hardy Nickerson .25 .11
❑ 240 Terry Glenn 1.00 .45
❑ 241 Lee Woodall .25 .11
❑ 242 Andre Coleman .25 .11
❑ 243 Michael Bates .25 .11
❑ 244 Mark Fields .25 .11
❑ 245 Eddie Kennison .50 .23
❑ 246 Dana Stubblefield .25 .11
❑ 247 Bobby Hoying .50 .23
❑ 248 Mo Lewis .25 .11
❑ 249 Derrick Mayes .50 .23
❑ 250 Eddie George 2.00 .90
❑ 251 Mike Alstott 1.00 .45
❑ 252 J.J. Stokes .50 .23
❑ 253 Adrian Murrell .50 .23
❑ 254 Kevin Greene .50 .23
❑ 255 LeRoy Butler .25 .11
❑ 256 Glenn Foley .50 .23
❑ 257 Jimmy Smith .50 .23
❑ 258 Tiki Barber .50 .23
❑ 259 Irving Fryar .50 .23
❑ 260 Ricky Watters .50 .23
❑ 261 Jeff Graham .25 .11
❑ 262 Kordell Stewart 1.00 .45
❑ 263 Rod Woodson .50 .23
❑ 264 Leslie Shepherd .25 .11
❑ 265 Ryan McNeil .25 .11
❑ 266 Ike Hilliard .50 .23
❑ 267 Keenan McCardell .50 .23
❑ 268 Marvin Harrison .50 .23
❑ 269 Dorsey Levens 1.00 .45
❑ 270 Barry Sanders 5.00 2.20

1999 Finest

	MINT	NRMT
COMPLETE SET (175)	100.00	45.00
COMP.SET w/o SPs (124)	30.00	13.50
COMMON CARD (1-124)	.20	.09
COMMON CARD (125-146)	1.25	.55
COMMON ROOKIE (147-175)	2.50	1.10

❑ 1 Peyton Manning 3.00 1.35
❑ 2 Priest Holmes .75 .35
❑ 3 Kordell Stewart .75 .35
❑ 4 Shannon Sharpe .40 .18
❑ 5 Andre Rison .40 .18
❑ 6 Rickey Dudley .20 .09
❑ 7 Duce Staley .75 .35
❑ 8 Randall Cunningham .75 .35
❑ 9 Warrick Dunn .75 .35
❑ 10 Dan Marino 3.00 1.35
❑ 11 Kevin Greene .20 .09
❑ 12 Garrison Hearst .40 .18
❑ 13 Eric Moulds .75 .35
❑ 14 Marvin Harrison .75 .35
❑ 15 Eddie George 1.00 .45
❑ 16 Vinny Testaverde .40 .18
❑ 17 Brad Johnson .75 .35
❑ 18 Derrick Thomas .40 .18
❑ 19 Chris Chandler .40 .18
❑ 20 Troy Aikman 2.00 .90
❑ 21 Terance Mathis .40 .18
❑ 22 Terrell Owens .75 .35
❑ 23 Junior Seau .40 .18
❑ 24 Cris Carter .75 .35
❑ 25 Fred Taylor 2.00 .90
❑ 26 Adrian Murrell .40 .18
❑ 27 Terry Glenn .75 .35
❑ 28 Rod Smith .40 .18
❑ 29 Darnay Scott .40 .18
❑ 30 Brett Favre 3.00 1.35
❑ 31 Cam Cleeland .20 .09
❑ 32 Ricky Watters .40 .18
❑ 33 Derrick Alexander .40 .18
❑ 34 Bruce Smith .40 .18
❑ 35 Steve McNair .75 .35
❑ 36 Wayne Chrebet .40 .18
❑ 37 Herman Moore .75 .35
❑ 38 Bert Emanuel .40 .18
❑ 39 Michael Irvin .40 .18
❑ 40 Steve Young 1.25 .55
❑ 41 Napoleon Kaufman .75 .35
❑ 42 Tim Biakabutuka .40 .18
❑ 43 Isaac Bruce .75 .35
❑ 44 J.J. Stokes .40 .18
❑ 45 Antonio Freeman .75 .35
❑ 46 John Randle .40 .18
❑ 47 Frank Sanders .40 .18
❑ 48 O.J. McDuffie .40 .18
❑ 49 Keenan McCardell .40 .18
❑ 50 Randy Moss 3.00 1.35
❑ 51 Ed McCaffrey .40 .18
❑ 52 Yancey Thigpen .20 .09
❑ 53 Curtis Conway .40 .18
❑ 54 Mike Alstott .75 .35
❑ 55 Deion Sanders .75 .35
❑ 56 Dorsey Levens .75 .35
❑ 57 Joey Galloway .75 .35
❑ 58 Natrone Means .40 .18
❑ 59 Tim Brown .75 .35
❑ 60 Jerry Rice 2.00 .90
❑ 61 Robert Smith .75 .35
❑ 62 Carl Pickens .40 .18
❑ 63 Ben Coates .40 .18
❑ 64 Jerome Bettis .75 .35
❑ 65 Corey Dillon .75 .35
❑ 66 Curtis Martin .75 .35
❑ 67 Jimmy Smith .40 .18
❑ 68 Keyshawn Johnson .75 .35
❑ 69 Charlie Batch 1.50 .70
❑ 70 Jamal Anderson .75 .35
❑ 71 Mark Brunell 1.25 .55
❑ 72 Antowain Smith .75 .35
❑ 73 Aeneas Williams .20 .09
❑ 74 Wesley Walls .40 .18
❑ 75 Jake Plummer 1.50 .70
❑ 76 Oronde Gadsden .20 .09
❑ 77 Gary Brown .20 .09
❑ 78 Peter Boulware .20 .09
❑ 79 Stephen Alexander .20 .09
❑ 80 Barry Sanders 3.00 1.35
❑ 81 Warren Sapp .40 .18
❑ 82 Michael Sinclair .20 .09
❑ 83 Freddie Jones .20 .09
❑ 84 Ike Hilliard .20 .09
❑ 85 Jake Reed .40 .18
❑ 86 Tim Dwight .75 .35
❑ 87 Johnnie Morton .40 .18
❑ 88 Robert Brooks .40 .18
❑ 89 Rocket Ismail .40 .18
❑ 90 Emmitt Smith 2.00 .90
❑ 91 Ricky Proehl .20 .09
❑ 92 James Jett .40 .18
❑ 93 Karim Abdul-Jabbar .40 .18
❑ 94 Mark Chmura .20 .09
❑ 95 Andre Reed .40 .18
❑ 96 Michael Westbrook .40 .18
❑ 97 Michael Strahan .20 .09
❑ 98 Chad Brown .20 .09
❑ 99 Trent Dilfer .40 .18
❑ 100 Terrell Davis 2.00 .90
❑ 101 Aaron Glenn .20 .09
❑ 102 Skip Hicks .40 .18
❑ 103 Tony Gonzalez .40 .18
❑ 104 Ty Law .20 .09
❑ 105 Jermaine Lewis .40 .18
❑ 106 Ray Lewis .40 .18
❑ 107 Zach Thomas .40 .18
❑ 108 Reidel Anthony .40 .18
❑ 109 Levon Kirkland .20 .09
❑ 110 Drew Bledsoe 1.25 .55
❑ 111 Bobby Engram .40 .18
❑ 112 Jerome Pathon .20 .09
❑ 113 Muhsin Muhammad .40 .18
❑ 114 Vonnie Holliday .20 .09
❑ 115 Bill Romanowski .20 .09
❑ 116 Marshall Faulk .75 .35
❑ 117 Ty Detmer .40 .18
❑ 118 Mo Lewis .20 .09
❑ 119 Charles Woodson .75 .35
❑ 120 Doug Flutie 1.00 .45
❑ 121 Jon Kitna .75 .35
❑ 122 Courtney Hawkins .20 .09
❑ 123 Trent Green .40 .18
❑ 124 John Elway 3.00 1.35
❑ 125 Barry Sanders GM 5.00 2.20
❑ 126 Brett Favre GM 5.00 2.20
❑ 127 Curtis Martin GM 1.25 .55
❑ 128 Dan Marino GM 5.00 2.20
❑ 129 Eddie George GM 1.50 .70
❑ 130 Emmitt Smith GM 5.00 2.20
❑ 131 Jamal Anderson GM 1.25 .55
❑ 132 Jerry Rice GM 3.00 1.35
❑ 133 John Elway GM 5.00 2.20
❑ 134 Terrell Davis GM 3.00 1.35
❑ 135 Troy Aikman GM 3.00 1.35
❑ 136 Skip Hicks SN .75 .35
❑ 137 Charles Woodson SN .75 .35
❑ 138 Charlie Batch SN 2.50 1.10
❑ 139 Curtis Enis SN 1.25 .55
❑ 140 Fred Taylor SN 3.00 1.35
❑ 141 Jake Plummer SN 2.50 1.10
❑ 142 Peyton Manning SN 5.00 2.20
❑ 143 Randy Moss SN 5.00 2.20
❑ 144 Corey Dillon SN 1.25 .55
❑ 145 Priest Holmes SN 1.25 .55
❑ 146 Warrick Dunn SN 1.25 .55
❑ 147 Jevon Kearse RC 6.00 2.70
❑ 148 Chris Claiborne RC 2.50 1.10
❑ 149 Akili Smith RC 6.00 2.70
❑ 150 Brock Huard RC 5.00 2.20
❑ 151 Daunte Culpepper RC 15.00 6.75
❑ 152 Edgerrin James RC 15.00 6.75
❑ 153 Cecil Collins RC 4.00 1.80
❑ 154 Kevin Faulk RC 5.00 2.20
❑ 155 Amos Zereoue RC 4.00 1.80
❑ 156 James Johnson RC 4.00 1.80
❑ 157 Sedrick Irvin RC 4.00 1.80
❑ 158 Ricky Williams RC 12.00 5.50
❑ 159 Mike Cloud RC 3.00 1.35
❑ 160 Chris McAlister 2.50 1.10
❑ 161 Rob Konrad RC 3.00 1.35
❑ 162 Champ Bailey RC 4.00 1.80
❑ 163 Ebenezer Ekuban RC 3.00 1.35
❑ 164 Tim Couch RC 10.00 4.50
❑ 165 Cade McNown RC 4.00 1.80
❑ 166 Donovan McNabb RC 12.00 5.50
❑ 167 Joe Germaine RC 4.00 1.80
❑ 168 Shaun King RC 6.00 2.70
❑ 169 Peerless Price RC 4.00 1.80
❑ 170 Kevin Johnson RC 6.00 2.70
❑ 171 Troy Edwards RC 4.00 1.80
❑ 172 Karsten Bailey RC 2.50 1.10
❑ 173 David Boston RC 6.00 2.70
❑ 174 D'Wayne Bates RC 3.00 1.35
❑ 175 Torry Holt RC 8.00 3.60

2000 Finest

	MINT	NRMT
COMPLETE SET (205)	500.00	220.00

Card	MINT	NRMT
❑ 1 Tim Dwight	.60	.25
❑ 2 Cade McNown	.60	.25
❑ 3 Drew Bledsoe	1.00	.45
❑ 4 Torry Holt	.60	.25
❑ 5 Derrick Mayes	.30	.14
❑ 6 Vinny Testaverde	.30	.14
❑ 7 Patrick Jeffers	.60	.25
❑ 8 Dorsey Levens	.30	.14
❑ 9 James Johnson	.30	.14
❑ 10 Champ Bailey	.30	.14
❑ 11 Jeff George	.30	.14
❑ 12 Shawn Jefferson	.20	.09
❑ 13 Terrence Wilkins	.60	.25
❑ 14 J.J. Stokes	.30	.14
❑ 15 Doug Flutie	.75	.35
❑ 16 Corey Dillon	.60	.25
❑ 17 Rod Smith	.30	.14
❑ 18 Jimmy Smith	.30	.14
❑ 19 Amani Toomer	.30	.14
❑ 20 Curtis Conway	.30	.14
❑ 21 Brad Johnson	.60	.25
❑ 22 Edgerrin James	2.50	1.10
❑ 23 Derrick Alexander	.30	.14
❑ 24 Terrell Owens	.60	.25
❑ 25 Kurt Warner	2.50	1.10
❑ 26 Frank Sanders	.30	.14
❑ 27 Tony Banks	.30	.14
❑ 28 Troy Aikman	1.50	.70
❑ 29 Curtis Enis	.30	.14
❑ 30 Eddie George	.75	.35
❑ 31 Bill Schroeder	.30	.14
❑ 32 Kent Graham	.20	.09
❑ 33 Mike Alstott	.60	.25
❑ 34 Steve Young	1.00	.45
❑ 35 Jacquez Green	.30	.14
❑ 36 Frank Wycheck	.20	.09
❑ 37 Kerry Collins	.30	.14
❑ 38 Stephen Davis	.60	.25
❑ 39 Tony Gonzalez	.30	.14
❑ 40 Tyrone Wheatley	.30	.14
❑ 41 Brett Favre	2.50	1.10
❑ 42 Joey Galloway	.60	.25
❑ 43 Terrell Davis	1.50	.70
❑ 44 Marvin Harrison	.60	.25
❑ 45 Zach Thomas	.30	.14
❑ 46 Jerry Rice	1.50	.70
❑ 47 Keyshawn Johnson	.60	.25
❑ 48 Rob Johnson	.30	.14
❑ 49 Rocket Ismail	.30	.14
❑ 50 Elvis Grbac	.30	.14
❑ 51 Warrick Dunn	.60	.25
❑ 52 Jevon Kearse	.60	.25
❑ 53 Albert Connell	.20	.09
❑ 54 Muhsin Muhammad	.30	.14
❑ 55 Carl Pickens	.30	.14
❑ 56 Peyton Manning	2.00	.90
❑ 57 Daunte Culpepper	1.25	.55
❑ 58 Ike Hilliard	.30	.14
❑ 59 Steve McNair	.60	.25
❑ 60 Sean Dawkins	.20	.09
❑ 61 Steve Beuerlein	.30	.14
❑ 62 Priest Holmes	.30	.14
❑ 63 Jim Harbaugh	.30	.14
❑ 64 Germane Crowell	.30	.14
❑ 65 Cris Carter	.60	.25
❑ 66 Jamal Anderson	.60	.25
❑ 67 Kevin Johnson	.60	.25
❑ 68 Herman Moore	.30	.14
❑ 69 Ricky Williams	1.50	.70
❑ 70 Rich Gannon	.30	.14
❑ 71 Isaac Bruce	.60	.25
❑ 72 Peerless Price	.60	.25
❑ 73 Az-Zahir Hakim	.30	.14
❑ 74 Mark Brunell	1.00	.45
❑ 75 Rob Moore	.30	.14
❑ 76 Antowain Smith	.30	.14
❑ 77 Tim Biakabutuka	.30	.14
❑ 78 Ed McCaffrey	.60	.25
❑ 79 Tony Martin	.30	.14
❑ 80 Marcus Robinson	.60	.25
❑ 81 Kevin Dyson	.30	.14
❑ 82 Wesley Walls	.20	.09
❑ 83 Chris Chandler	.30	.14
❑ 84 Keenan McCardell	.30	.14
❑ 85 Napoleon Kaufman	.30	.14
❑ 86 Emmitt Smith	1.50	.70
❑ 87 James Stewart	.30	.14
❑ 88 Tim Brown	.60	.25
❑ 89 Ricky Watters	.30	.14
❑ 90 Johnnie Morton	.30	.14
❑ 91 Jake Plummer	.60	.25
❑ 92 Olandis Gary	.60	.25
❑ 93 Jerome Bettis	.60	.25
❑ 94 Terry Glenn	.30	.14
❑ 95 Kordell Stewart	.60	.25
❑ 96 Charlie Garner	.30	.14
❑ 97 Yancey Thigpen	.20	.09
❑ 98 Michael Westbrook	.30	.14
❑ 99 Bobby Engram	.30	.14
❑ 100 Eric Moulds	.60	.25
❑ 101 Darnay Scott	.30	.14
❑ 102 Antonio Freeman	.60	.25
❑ 103 Wayne Chrebet	.30	.14
❑ 104 Akili Smith	.60	.25
❑ 105 Jeff Blake	.30	.14
❑ 106 Curtis Martin	.60	.25
❑ 107 Errict Rhett	.30	.14
❑ 108 Damon Huard	.60	.25
❑ 109 Jeff Graham	.20	.09
❑ 110 Terance Mathis	.30	.14
❑ 111 Jon Kitna	.60	.25
❑ 112 Tim Couch	1.25	.55
❑ 113 Fred Taylor	.75	.35
❑ 114 Qadry Ismail	.20	.09
❑ 115 Donovan McNabb	1.00	.45
❑ 116 Charles Johnson	.30	.14
❑ 117 Troy Edwards	.30	.14
❑ 118 Shaun King	1.00	.45
❑ 119 Charlie Batch	.60	.25
❑ 120 Robert Smith	.60	.25
❑ 121 Marshall Faulk	.75	.35
❑ 122 Brian Griese	.75	.35
❑ 123 O.J. McDuffie	.30	.14
❑ 124 Randy Moss	2.00	.90
❑ 125 Duce Staley	.60	.25
❑ 126 Peter Warrick RC	30.00	13.50
❑ 127 Dez White RC	8.00	3.60
❑ 128 Ron Dayne RC	30.00	13.50
❑ 129 J.R. Redmond RC	12.00	5.50
❑ 130 Thomas Jones RC	15.00	6.75
❑ 131 Plaxico Burress RC	20.00	9.00
❑ 132 Reuben Droughns RC	10.00	4.50
❑ 133 Shaun Alexander RC	25.00	11.00
❑ 134 Ron Dugans RC	8.00	3.60
❑ 135 Travis Prentice RC	15.00	6.75
❑ 136 Joe Hamilton RC	12.00	5.50
❑ 137 Curtis Keaton RC	8.00	3.60
❑ 138 Chris Redman RC	20.00	9.00
❑ 139 Chad Pennington RC	30.00	13.50
❑ 140 Travis Taylor RC	12.00	5.50
❑ 141 Bubba Franks RC	12.00	5.50
❑ 142 Dennis Northcutt RC	12.00	5.50
❑ 143 Jerry Porter RC	10.00	4.50
❑ 144 Sylvester Morris RC	20.00	9.00
❑ 145 Anthony Becht RC	10.00	4.50
❑ 146 Trung Canidate RC	10.00	4.50
❑ 147 Jamal Lewis RC	50.00	22.00
❑ 148 R.Jay Soward RC	10.00	4.50
❑ 149 Tee Martin RC	15.00	6.75
❑ 150 Courtney Brown RC	12.00	5.50
❑ 151 Brian Urlacher RC	30.00	13.50
❑ 152 Danny Farmer RC	10.00	4.50
❑ 153 Laveranues Coles RC	15.00	6.75
❑ 154 Todd Pinkston RC	10.00	4.50
❑ 155 Corey Simon RC	12.00	5.50
❑ 156 Spergon Wynn RC	10.00	4.50
❑ 157 Tim Rattay RC	15.00	6.75
❑ 158 Todd Husak RC	10.00	4.50
❑ 159 Aaron Shea RC	8.00	3.60
❑ 160 Giovanni Carmazzi RC	12.00	5.50
❑ 161 Trevor Gaylor RC	8.00	3.60
❑ 162 JaJuan Dawson RC	10.00	4.50
❑ 163 Jarious Jackson RC	10.00	4.50
❑ 164 Chris Samuels RC	8.00	3.60
❑ 165 Rob Morris RC	8.00	3.60
❑ 166 Peter Warrick Randy Moss	4.00	1.80
❑ 167 Randy Moss Peter Warrick	4.00	1.80
❑ 168 Travis Prentice Stephen Davis	2.00	.90
❑ 169 Stephen Davis Travis Prentice	2.00	.90
❑ 170 Chris Redman Kurt Warner	4.00	1.80
❑ 171 Kurt Warner Chris Redman	4.00	1.80
❑ 172 Sylvester Morris Jimmy Smith	2.50	1.10
❑ 173 Jimmy Smith Sylvester Morris	2.50	1.10
❑ 174 Chad Pennington Peyton Manning	3.00	1.35
❑ 175 Peyton Manning Chad Pennington	4.00	1.80
❑ 176 R.Jay Soward Marvin Harrison	2.00	.90
❑ 177 Marvin Harrison R.Jay Soward	2.00	.90
❑ 178 Ron Dayne Jamal Anderson	3.00	1.35
❑ 179 Jamal Anderson Ron Dayne	3.00	1.35
❑ 180 Shaun Alexander Eddie George	2.50	1.10
❑ 181 Eddie George Shaun Alexander	2.50	1.10
❑ 182 Courtney Brown Bruce Smith	2.00	.90
❑ 183 Bruce Smith Courtney Brown	2.00	.90
❑ 184 Jamal Lewis Edgerrin James	5.00	2.20
❑ 185 Edgerrin James Jamal Lewis	5.00	2.20
❑ 186 Trung Canidate Emmitt Smith	3.00	1.35
❑ 187 Emmitt Smith Trung Canidate	3.00	1.35
❑ 188 Travis Taylor Cris Carter	2.00	.90
❑ 189 Cris Carter Travis Taylorr	2.00	.90
❑ 190 Curtis Keaton Marshall Faulk	2.50	1.10
❑ 191 Marshall Faulk Curtis Keaton	2.50	1.10
❑ 192 Plaxico Burress Jerry Rice	3.00	1.35
❑ 193 Jerry Rice Plaxico Burress	3.00	1.35
❑ 194 Thomas Jones Terrell Davis	3.00	1.35
❑ 195 Terrell Davis Thomas Jones	3.00	1.35
❑ 196 Peyton Manning GM	5.00	2.20
❑ 197 Randy Moss GM	5.00	2.20
❑ 198 Terrell Davis GM	4.00	1.80
❑ 199 Marshall Faulk GM	1.50	.70
❑ 200 Edgerrin James GM	5.00	2.20
❑ 201 Emmitt Smith GM	4.00	1.80
❑ 202 Ricky Williams GM	3.00	1.35
❑ 203 Kurt Warner GM	5.00	2.20
❑ 204 Eddie George GM	1.50	.70
❑ 205 Brett Favre GM	6.00	2.70

1995 Flair

	MINT	NRMT
COMPLETE SET (220)	30.00	13.50
❑ 1 Larry Centers	.40	.18
❑ 2 Garrison Hearst	.75	.35
❑ 3 Seth Joyner	.20	.09
❑ 4 Dave Krieg	.20	.09
❑ 5 Rob Moore	.20	.09
❑ 6 Frank Sanders RC (Wearing 18 on front, Wearing 81 on back)	1.50	.70
❑ 7 Eric Swann	.40	.18
❑ 8 Devin Bush	.20	.09
❑ 9 Chris Doleman	.20	.09
❑ 10 Bert Emanuel	.75	.35
❑ 11 Jeff George	.40	.18
❑ 12 Craig Heyward	.40	.18
❑ 13 Terance Mathis	.40	.18
❑ 14 Eric Metcalf	.40	.18
❑ 15 Cornelius Bennett	.40	.18
❑ 16 Jeff Burris	.20	.09
❑ 17 Todd Collins RC	.75	.35
❑ 18 Russell Copeland	.20	.09
❑ 19 Jim Kelly	.75	.35
❑ 20 Andre Reed	.40	.18
❑ 21 Bruce Smith	.75	.35
❑ 22 Don Beebe	.20	.09
❑ 23 Mark Carrier	.40	.18
❑ 24 Kerry Collins RC	2.50	1.10
❑ 25 Barry Foster	.40	.18
❑ 26 Pete Metzelaars	.20	.09
❑ 27 Tyrone Poole	.40	.18
❑ 28 Frank Reich	.20	.09
❑ 29 Curtis Conway	.75	.35
❑ 30 Chris Gedney	.20	.09
❑ 31 Jeff Graham	.20	.09
❑ 32 Raymont Harris	.20	.09
❑ 33 Erik Kramer	.20	.09
❑ 34 Rashaan Salaam RC	.75	.35
❑ 35 Lewis Tillman	.20	.09
❑ 36 Michael Timpson	.20	.09
❑ 37 Jeff Blake RC	1.50	.70
❑ 38 Ki-Jana Carter RC	.75	.35
❑ 39 Tony McGee	.20	.09
❑ 40 Carl Pickens	.75	.35
❑ 41 Corey Sawyer	.20	.09
❑ 42 Darnay Scott	.75	.35
❑ 43 Dan Wilkinson	.40	.18
❑ 44 Derrick Alexander	.75	.35
❑ 45 Leroy Hoard	.20	.09
❑ 46 Michael Jackson	.40	.18
❑ 47 Antonio Langham	.20	.09
❑ 48 Andre Rison	.40	.18
❑ 49 Vinny Testaverde	.40	.18
❑ 50 Eric Turner	.20	.09
❑ 51 Troy Aikman	2.00	.90
❑ 52 Charles Haley	.40	.18
❑ 53 Michael Irvin	.75	.35
❑ 54 Daryl Johnston	.40	.18
❑ 55 Leon Lett	.20	.09
❑ 56 Jay Novacek	.40	.18
❑ 57 Emmitt Smith	3.00	1.35
❑ 58 Kevin Williams WR	.40	.18
❑ 59 Steve Atwater	.20	.09
❑ 60 Rod Bernstine	.20	.09
❑ 61 John Elway	4.00	1.80
❑ 62 Glyn Milburn	.20	.09
❑ 63 Anthony Miller	.40	.18
❑ 64 Mike Pritchard	.20	.09
❑ 65 Shannon Sharpe	.40	.18
❑ 66 Scott Mitchell	.40	.18
❑ 67 Herman Moore	.75	.35
❑ 68 Johnnie Morton	.40	.18
❑ 69 Brett Perriman	.40	.18
❑ 70 Barry Sanders	4.00	1.80
❑ 71 Chris Spielman	.40	.18
❑ 72 Edgar Bennett	.40	.18
❑ 73 Robert Brooks	.75	.35
❑ 74 Brett Favre	4.00	1.80
❑ 75 LeShon Johnson	.40	.18
❑ 76 Sean Jones	.20	.09
❑ 77 George Teague	.20	.09
❑ 78 Reggie White	.75	.35
❑ 79 Micheal Barrow	.20	.09
❑ 80 Gary Brown	.20	.09
❑ 81 Mel Gray	.20	.09
❑ 82 Haywood Jeffires	.20	.09
❑ 83 Steve McNair RC	4.00	1.80
❑ 84 Rodney Thomas RC	.75	.35
❑ 85 Trev Alberts	.20	.09
❑ 86 Flipper Anderson	.20	.09
❑ 87 Tony Bennett	.20	.09
❑ 88 Quentin Coryatt	.40	.18
❑ 89 Sean Dawkins	.40	.18
❑ 90 Craig Erickson	.20	.09
❑ 91 Marshall Faulk	1.25	.55
❑ 92 Steve Beuerlein	.20	.09
❑ 93 Tony Boselli RC	.75	.35
❑ 94 Reggie Cobb	.20	.09
❑ 95 Ernest Givins	.20	.09
❑ 96 Desmond Howard	.40	.18
❑ 97 Jeff Lageman	.20	.09
❑ 98 James O. Stewart RC	3.00	1.35
❑ 99 Marcus Allen	.75	.35
❑ 100 Steve Bono	.40	.18
❑ 101 Dale Carter	.40	.18
❑ 102 Willie Davis	.40	.18
❑ 103 Lake Dawson	.40	.18
❑ 104 Greg Hill	.40	.18
❑ 105 Neil Smith	.40	.18
❑ 106 Tim Bowens	.20	.09
❑ 107 Bryan Cox	.20	.09
❑ 108 Irving Fryar	.40	.18
❑ 109 Eric Green	.20	.09
❑ 110 Terry Kirby	.40	.18
❑ 111 Dan Marino	4.00	1.80
❑ 112 O.J. McDuffie	.75	.35
❑ 113 Bernie Parmalee	.40	.18
❑ 114 Derrick Alexander RC	.20	.09
❑ 115 Cris Carter	.75	.35
❑ 116 Qadry Ismail	.40	.18
❑ 117 Warren Moon	.40	.18
❑ 118 Jake Reed	.40	.18
❑ 119 Robert Smith	.75	.35
❑ 120 Dewayne Washington	.40	.18
❑ 121 Drew Bledsoe	2.00	.90
❑ 122 Vincent Brisby	.20	.09
❑ 123 Ben Coates	.40	.18
❑ 124 Curtis Martin RC	4.00	1.80
❑ 125 Willie McGinest	.40	.18
❑ 126 Dave Meggett	.20	.09
❑ 127 Chris Slade UER 126	.40	.18
❑ 128 Eric Allen	.20	.09
❑ 129 Mario Bates	.75	.35
❑ 130 Jim Everett	.20	.09
❑ 131 Michael Haynes	.40	.18
❑ 132 Tyrone Hughes	.40	.18
❑ 133 Renaldo Turnbull	.20	.09
❑ 134 Ray Zellars RC	.40	.18
❑ 135 Michael Brooks	.20	.09
❑ 136 Dave Brown	.40	.18
❑ 137 Rodney Hampton	.40	.18
❑ 138 Thomas Lewis	.40	.18
❑ 139 Mike Sherrard	.20	.09
❑ 140 Herschel Walker	.40	.18
❑ 141 Tyrone Wheatley RC	2.00	.90
❑ 142 Kyle Brady RC	.75	.35
❑ 143 Boomer Esiason	.40	.18
❑ 144 Aaron Glenn	.20	.09
❑ 145 Mo Lewis	.20	.09
❑ 146 Johnny Mitchell	.20	.09
❑ 147 Ronald Moore	.20	.09
❑ 148 Joe Aska	.40	.18
❑ 149 Tim Brown	.75	.35
❑ 150 Jeff Hostetler	.40	.18
❑ 151 Rocket Ismail	.40	.18
❑ 152 Napoleon Kaufman RC	2.50	1.10
❑ 153 Chester McGlockton	.40	.18
❑ 154 Harvey Williams	.20	.09
❑ 155 Fred Barnett	.40	.18
❑ 156 Randall Cunningham	.75	.35
❑ 157 Charlie Garner	.40	.18
❑ 158 Mike Mamula RC	.40	.18
❑ 159 Kevin Turner	.20	.09
❑ 160 Ricky Watters	.75	.35
❑ 161 Calvin Williams	.40	.18
❑ 162 Mark Bruener RC	.40	.18
❑ 163 Kevin Greene	.40	.18
❑ 164 Charles Johnson	.40	.18
❑ 165 Greg Lloyd	.40	.18
❑ 166 Byron Bam Morris	.40	.18
❑ 167 Neil O'Donnell	.40	.18
❑ 168 Kordell Stewart RC	3.00	1.35
❑ 169 John L. Williams	.20	.09
❑ 170 Rod Woodson	.40	.18
❑ 171 Jerome Bettis	.75	.35
❑ 172 Isaac Bruce	1.25	.55
❑ 173 Kevin Carter RC	.75	.35
❑ 174 Troy Drayton	.20	.09
❑ 175 Sean Gilbert	.40	.18
❑ 176 Carlos Jenkins	.20	.09
❑ 177 Todd Lyght	.20	.09
❑ 178 Chris Miller	.20	.09
❑ 179 Andre Coleman	.20	.09
❑ 180 Stan Humphries	.40	.18
❑ 181 Shawn Jefferson	.20	.09
❑ 182 Natrone Means	.75	.35
❑ 183 Leslie O'Neal	.40	.18
❑ 184 Junior Seau	.75	.35
❑ 185 Mark Seay	.40	.18
❑ 186 William Floyd	.75	.35
❑ 187 Merton Hanks	.20	.09
❑ 188 Brent Jones	.20	.09
❑ 189 Ken Norton	.40	.18
❑ 190 Jerry Rice	2.00	.90
❑ 191 Deion Sanders	1.00	.45
❑ 192 J.J. Stokes RC	.75	.35
❑ 193 Dana Stubblefield	.75	.35
❑ 194 Steve Young	1.50	.70
❑ 195 Sam Adams	.20	.09
❑ 196 Brian Blades	.40	.18
❑ 197 Joey Galloway RC	3.00	1.35
❑ 198 Cortez Kennedy	.40	.18
❑ 199 Rick Mirer	.75	.35
❑ 200 Chris Warren	.40	.18
❑ 201 Derrick Brooks RC	.75	.35
❑ 202 Lawrence Dawsey	.20	.09
❑ 203 Trent Dilfer	.75	.35
❑ 204 Alvin Harper	.20	.09
❑ 205 Jackie Harris	.20	.09
❑ 206 Courtney Hawkins	.20	.09
❑ 207 Hardy Nickerson	.20	.09
❑ 208 Errict Rhett	.75	.35
❑ 209 Warren Sapp RC	1.25	.55
❑ 210 Terry Allen	.40	.18
❑ 211 Tom Carter	.20	.09
❑ 212 Henry Ellard	.40	.18
❑ 213 Darrell Green	.20	.09
❑ 214 Brian Mitchell	.20	.09
❑ 215 Heath Shuler	.75	.35
❑ 216 Michael Westbrook RC	2.50	1.10
❑ 217 Tydus Winans	.20	.09
❑ 218 Checklist	.20	.09
❑ 219 Checklist	.20	.09
❑ 220 Checklist	.40	.18
❑ S1 Michael Irvin Sample	1.25	.55

1997 Flair Showcase Row 2

	MINT	NRMT
COMPLETE SET (120)	40.00	18.00
COMMON CARD (1-40)	.20	.09
COMMON CARD (41-80)	.25	.11
COMMON CARD (81-120)	.20	.09
❑ 1 Jerry Rice	2.00	.90

❑ 2 Mark Brunell 2.00 .90
❑ 3 Eddie Kennison .40 .18
❑ 4 Brett Favre 4.00 1.80
❑ 5 Karim Abdul-Jabbar .75 .35
❑ 6 David LaFleur RC .75 .35
❑ 7 John Elway 4.00 1.80
❑ 8 Troy Aikman 2.00 .90
❑ 9 Steve McNair 1.25 .55
❑ 10 Kordell Stewart 1.00 .45
❑ 11 Drew Bledsoe 2.00 .90
❑ 12 Kerry Collins .40 .18
❑ 13 Dan Marino 4.00 1.80
❑ 14 Steve Young 1.25 .55
❑ 15 Marvin Harrison .75 .35
❑ 16 Lawrence Phillips .20 .09
❑ 17 Jeff Blake .40 .18
❑ 18 Yatil Green RC .40 .18
❑ 19 Jake Plummer RC 8.00 3.60
❑ 20 Barry Sanders 4.00 1.80
❑ 21 Deion Sanders .75 .35
❑ 22 Emmitt Smith 3.00 1.35
❑ 23 Rae Carruth RC .75 .35
❑ 24 Chris Warren .40 .18
❑ 25 Terry Glenn .75 .35
❑ 26 Jim Druckenmiller RC .75 .35
❑ 27 Eddie George 2.50 1.10
❑ 28 Curtis Martin 1.25 .55
❑ 29 Warrick Dunn RC 4.00 1.80
❑ 30 Terrell Davis 3.00 1.35
❑ 31 Rashaan Salaam .20 .09
❑ 32 Marcus Allen .75 .35
❑ 33 Jeff George .40 .18
❑ 34 Thurman Thomas .75 .35
❑ 35 Keyshawn Johnson .75 .35
❑ 36 Jerome Bettis .75 .35
❑ 37 Larry Centers .40 .18
❑ 38 Tony Banks .40 .18
❑ 39 Marshall Faulk .75 .35
❑ 40 Mike Alstott .75 .35
❑ 41 Elvis Grbac .40 .18
❑ 42 Errict Rhett .20 .09
❑ 43 Edgar Bennett .40 .18
❑ 44 Jim Harbaugh .40 .18
❑ 45 Antonio Freeman 1.50 .70
❑ 46 Tiki BarbeR RC 4.00 1.80
❑ 47 Tim Biakabutuka .40 .18
❑ 48 Joey Galloway 1.25 .55
❑ 49 Tony Gonzalez RC 4.00 1.80
❑ 50 Keenan McCardell .40 .18
❑ 51 Darnay Scott .40 .18
❑ 52 Brad Johnson 1.50 .70
❑ 53 Herman Moore .75 .35
❑ 54 Reidel Anthony RC 2.50 1.10
❑ 55 Junior Seau .40 .18
❑ 56 Ricky Watters .40 .18
❑ 57 Amani Toomer .40 .18
❑ 58 Andre Reed .40 .18
❑ 59 Antowain Smith RC 3.00 1.35
❑ 60 Ike Hilliard RC 2.50 1.10
❑ 61 Byron Hanspard RC 1.00 .45
❑ 62 Robert Smith .40 .18
❑ 63 Gus Frerotte .20 .09
❑ 64 Charles Way .40 .18
❑ 65 Trent Dilfer .75 .35
❑ 66 Adrian Murrell .40 .18
❑ 67 Stan Humphries .40 .18
❑ 68 Robert Brooks .40 .18
❑ 69 Jamal Anderson 2.50 1.10
❑ 70 Natrone Means .75 .35
❑ 71 John Friesz .20 .09
❑ 72 Ki-Jana Carter .20 .09
❑ 73 Marc Edwards RC .20 .09
❑ 74 Michael Westbrook .40 .18
❑ 75 Neil O'Donnell .40 .18
❑ 76 Scott Mitchell .40 .18
❑ 77 Wesley Walls .40 .18
❑ 78 Bruce Smith .40 .18
❑ 79 Corey Dillon RC 8.00 3.60
❑ 80 Wayne Chrebet .75 .35
❑ 81 Tony Martin .40 .18
❑ 82 Jimmy Smith .40 .18
❑ 83 Terry Allen .75 .35
❑ 84 Shannon Sharpe .40 .18
❑ 85 Derrick Alexander WR .40 .18
❑ 86 Garrison Hearst .40 .18
❑ 87 Tamarick Vanover .40 .18
❑ 88 Michael Irvin .75 .35
❑ 89 Mark Chmura .40 .18
❑ 90 Bert Emanuel .40 .18
❑ 91 Eric Metcalf .40 .18
❑ 92 Reggie White .75 .35
❑ 93 Carl Pickens .75 .35
❑ 94 Chris Sanders .20 .09
❑ 95 Frank Sanders .40 .18
❑ 96 Desmond Howard .40 .18
❑ 97 Michael Jackson .40 .18
❑ 98 Tim Brown .75 .35
❑ 99 O.J. McDuffie .40 .18
❑ 100 Mario Bates .20 .09
❑ 101 Warren Moon .75 .35
❑ 102 Curtis Conway .40 .18
❑ 103 Irving Fryar .40 .18
❑ 104 Isaac Bruce .75 .35
❑ 105 Cris Carter .75 .35
❑ 106 Chris Chandler .40 .18
❑ 107 Charles Johnson .40 .18
❑ 108 Kevin Lockett RC .75 .35
❑ 109 Rob Moore .40 .18
❑ 110 Napoleon Kaufman .75 .35
❑ 111 Henry Ellard .20 .09
❑ 112 Vinny Testaverde .40 .18
❑ 113 Rick Mirer .20 .09
❑ 114 Ty Detmer .40 .18
❑ 115 Todd Collins .20 .09
❑ 116 Jake Reed .40 .18
❑ 117 Dave Brown .20 .09
❑ 118 Dedric Ward RC 2.50 1.10
❑ 119 Heath Shuler .20 .09
❑ 120 Ben Coates .40 .18
❑ S1 Rae Carruth Sample .25 .11
(Three card strip)

1998 Flair Showcase Row 3

	MINT	NRMT
COMPLETE SET (80)	80.00	36.00
COMMON CARD (1-40)	.20	.09
COMMON CARD (41-60)	.30	.14
COMMON CARD (61-80)	.40	.18

❑ 1 Brett Favre 3.00 1.35
❑ 2 Emmitt Smith 2.50 1.10
❑ 3 Peyton Manning RC 12.00 5.50
❑ 4 Mark Brunell 1.25 .55
❑ 5 Randy Moss RC 12.00 5.50
❑ 6 Jerry Rice 1.50 .70
❑ 7 John Elway 3.00 1.35
❑ 8 Troy Aikman 1.50 .70
❑ 9 Warrick Dunn .75 .35
❑ 10 Kordell Stewart .75 .35
❑ 11 Drew Bledsoe 1.25 .55
❑ 12 Eddie George 1.25 .55
❑ 13 Dan Marino 3.00 1.35
❑ 14 Antowain Smith .75 .35
❑ 15 Curtis Enis RC 2.00 .90
❑ 16 Jake Plummer 1.25 .55
❑ 17 Steve Young 1.00 .45
❑ 18 Ryan Leaf RC 4.00 1.80
❑ 19 Terrell Davis 2.50 1.10
❑ 20 Barry Sanders 3.00 1.35
❑ 21 Corey Dillon 1.00 .45
❑ 22 Fred Taylor RC 5.00 2.20
❑ 23 Herman Moore .75 .35
❑ 24 Marshall Faulk .75 .35
❑ 25 John Avery RC .40 .18
❑ 26 Terry Glenn .75 .35
❑ 27 Keyshawn Johnson .75 .35
❑ 28 Charles Woodson RC 2.00 .90
❑ 29 Garrison Hearst .75 .35
❑ 30 Steve McNair .75 .35
❑ 31 Deion Sanders .75 .35
❑ 32 Robert Holcombe RC .40 .18
❑ 33 Jerome Bettis .75 .35
❑ 34 Robert Edwards RC 2.50 1.10
❑ 35 Skip Hicks RC 2.00 .90
❑ 36 Marcus Nash RC 2.00 .90
❑ 37 Fred Lane .40 .18
❑ 38 Kevin Dyson RC 2.00 .90
❑ 39 Dorsey Levens .75 .35
❑ 40 Jacquez Green RC 2.00 .90
❑ 41 Shannon Sharpe .50 .23
❑ 42 Michael Irvin 1.00 .45
❑ 43 Jim Harbaugh .50 .23
❑ 44 Curtis Martin 1.00 .45
❑ 45 Bobby Hoying .50 .23
❑ 46 Trent Dilfer 1.00 .45
❑ 47 Yancey Thigpen .30 .14
❑ 48 Warren Moon 1.00 .45
❑ 49 Danny Kanell .50 .23
❑ 50 Rob Johnson .50 .23
❑ 51 Carl Pickens 1.00 .45
❑ 52 Scott Mitchell .50 .23
❑ 53 Tim Brown 1.00 .45
❑ 54 Tony Banks 1.00 .45
❑ 55 Jamal Anderson 1.00 .45
❑ 56 Kerry Collins .50 .23
❑ 57 Elvis Grbac .50 .23
❑ 58 Mike Alstott 1.00 .45
❑ 59 Glenn Foley .50 .23
❑ 60 Brad Johnson 1.00 .45
❑ 61 Robert Brooks .75 .35
❑ 62 Irving Fryar .75 .35
❑ 63 Natrone Means 1.50 .70
❑ 64 Rae Carruth .75 .35
❑ 65 Isaac Bruce 1.50 .70
❑ 66 Andre Rison .75 .35
❑ 67 Jeff George .75 .35
❑ 68 Charles Way .40 .18
❑ 69 Derrick Alexander .75 .35
❑ 70 Michael Jackson .40 .18
❑ 71 Rob Moore .75 .35
❑ 72 Ricky Watters .75 .35
❑ 73 Curtis Conway .75 .35
❑ 74 Antonio Freeman 1.50 .70
❑ 75 Jimmy Smith .75 .35
❑ 76 Troy Davis .40 .18
❑ 77 Robert Smith 1.50 .70
❑ 78 Terry Allen 1.50 .70
❑ 79 Joey Galloway 1.50 .70
❑ 80 Charles Johnson .40 .18
❑ NNO Checklist Card .20 .09

1999 Flair Showcase

	MINT	NRMT
COMPLETE SET (192)	800.00	350.00
COMP.SET w/o SPs (160)	50.00	22.00

❑ 1 Troy Aikman PW 2.00 .90
❑ 2 Jamal Anderson PW .20 .09

❑ 3 Charlie Batch PW .... 1.50 .70
❑ 4 Jerome Bettis PW .... .20 .09
❑ 5 Drew Bledsoe PW .... 1.25 .55
❑ 6 Mark Brunell PW .... 1.25 .55
❑ 7 Randall Cunningham PW .. .75 .35
❑ 8 Terrell Davis PW .... 2.00 .90
❑ 9 Corey Dillon PW .... .75 .35
❑ 10 Warrick Dunn PW .... .75 .35
❑ 11 Curtis Enis PW .... .75 .35
❑ 12 Marshall Faulk PW .... .75 .35
❑ 13 Brett Favre PW 3.00 1.35
❑ 14 Doug Flutie PW .... 1.00 .45
❑ 15 Eddie George PW .... 1.00 .45
❑ 16 Brian Griese PW .... 1.50 .70
❑ 17 Keyshawn Johnson PW .. .75 .35
❑ 18 Peyton Manning PW 3.00 1.35
❑ 19 Dan Marino PW 3.00 1.35
❑ 20 Curtis Martin PW .... .75 .35
❑ 21 Steve McNair PW .... .75 .35
❑ 22 Randy Moss PW 3.00 1.35
❑ 23 Terrell Owens PW .... .75 .35
❑ 24 Jake Plummer PW .... 1.50 .70
❑ 25 Jerry Rice PW .... 2.00 .90
❑ 26 Barry Sanders PW 3.00 1.35
❑ 27 Antowain Smith PW .... .75 .35
❑ 28 Emmitt Smith PW .... 2.00 .90
❑ 29 Kordell Stewart PW .... .75 .35
❑ 30 J.J. Stokes PW .... .40 .18
❑ 31 Fred Taylor PW .... 2.00 .90
❑ 32 Steve Young PW .... 1.25 .55
❑ 33 Troy Aikman PN .... 2.00 .90
❑ 34 Mike Alstott PN .... .75 .35
❑ 35 Jamal Anderson PN .... .75 .35
❑ 36 Charlie Batch PN .... 1.50 .70
❑ 37 Jerome Bettis PN .... .75 .35
❑ 38 Drew Bledsoe PN .... 1.25 .55
❑ 39 Mark Brunell PN .... 1.25 .55
❑ 40 Cris Carter PN .... .75 .35
❑ 41 Mark Chmura PN .... .20 .09
❑ 42 Wayne Chrebet PN .... .40 .18
❑ 43 Kerry Collins PN .... .20 .09
❑ 44 Randall Cunningham PN.. .75 .35
❑ 45 Terrell Davis PN .... 2.00 .90
❑ 46 Trent Dilfer PN .... .40 .18
❑ 47 Corey Dillon PN .... .75 .35
❑ 48 Warrick Dunn PN .... .75 .35
❑ 49 Kevin Dyson PN .... .40 .18
❑ 50 Curtis Enis PN .... .75 .35
❑ 51 Marshall Faulk PN .... .75 .35
❑ 52 Brett Favre PN 3.00 1.35
❑ 53 Doug Flutie PN .... 1.00 .45
❑ 54 Antonio Freeman PN .... .75 .35
❑ 55 Eddie George PN .... 1.00 .45
❑ 56 Terry Glenn PN .... .75 .35
❑ 57 Tony Gonzalez PN .... .40 .18
❑ 58 Elvis Grbac PN .... .40 .18
❑ 59 Jacquez Green PN .... .40 .18
❑ 60 Brian Griese PN .... 1.50 .70
❑ 61 Marvin Harrison PN .... .75 .35
❑ 62 Garrison Hearst PN .... .40 .18
❑ 63 Skip Hicks PN .... .40 .18
❑ 64 Priest Holmes PN .... .75 .35
❑ 65 Michael Irvin PN .... .40 .18
❑ 66 Brad Johnson PN .... .40 .18
❑ 67 Keyshawn Johnson PN.... .75 .35
❑ 68 Napoleon Kaufman PN .... .75 .35
❑ 69 Dorsey Levens PN .... .75 .35
❑ 70 Peyton Manning PN 3.00 1.35
❑ 71 Dan Marino PN 3.00 1.35
❑ 72 Curtis Martin PN .... .75 .35
❑ 73 Ed McCaffrey PN .... .40 .18
❑ 74 Keenan McCardell PN...... .40 .18
❑ 75 O.J. McDuffie PN .... .40 .18
❑ 76 Steve McNair PN .... .75 .35
❑ 77 Scott Mitchell PN .... .20 .09
❑ 78 Randy Moss PN 3.00 1.35
❑ 79 Eric Moulds PN .... .75 .35
❑ 80 Terrell Owens PN .... .75 .35
❑ 81 Lawrence Phillips PN ...... .40 .18
❑ 82 Jake Plummer PN .... 1.50 .70
❑ 83 Jerry Rice PN .... 2.00 .90
❑ 84 Andre Rison PN .... .40 .18
❑ 85 Barry Sanders PN 3.00 1.35
❑ 86 Shannon Sharpe PN .... .40 .18
❑ 87 Antowain Smith PN .... .75 .35
❑ 88 Emmitt Smith PN .... 2.00 .90
❑ 89 Rod Smith PN .... .40 .18
❑ 90 Duce Staley PN .... .75 .35
❑ 91 Kordell Stewart PN .... .75 .35
❑ 92 J.J. Stokes PN .... .40 .18
❑ 93 Fred Taylor PN .... 2.00 .90
❑ 94 Vinny Testaverde PN ...... .40 .18
❑ 95 Ricky Watters PN .... .40 .18
❑ 96 Steve Young PN .... 1.25 .55
❑ 97 Mike Alstott .... .75 .35
❑ 98 Jamal Anderson .... .75 .35
❑ 99 Charlie Batch .... 1.50 .70
❑ 100 Jerome Bettis .... .75 .35
❑ 101 Tim Biakabutuka .... .40 .18
❑ 102 Drew Bledsoe .... 1.25 .55
❑ 103 Tim Brown .... .75 .35
❑ 104 Mark Brunell .... 1.25 .55
❑ 105 Cris Carter .... .75 .35
❑ 106 Chris Chandler .... .40 .18
❑ 107 Mark Chmura .... .20 .09
❑ 108 Wayne Chrebet .... .40 .18
❑ 109 Ben Coates .... .40 .18
❑ 110 Kerry Collins .... .40 .18
❑ 111 Randall Cunningham...... .75 .35
❑ 112 Trent Dilfer .... .40 .18
❑ 113 Corey Dillon .... .75 .35
❑ 114 Warrick Dunn .... .75 .35
❑ 115 Kevin Dyson .... .40 .18
❑ 116 Curtis Enis .... .75 .35
❑ 117 Marshall Faulk .... .75 .35
❑ 118 Doug Flutie .... 1.00 .45
❑ 119 Antonio Freeman .... .75 .35
❑ 120 Joey Galloway .... .75 .35
❑ 121 Rich Gannon .... .40 .18
❑ 122 Eddie George .... 1.00 .45
❑ 123 Terry Glenn .... .75 .35
❑ 124 Tony Gonzalez .... .40 .18
❑ 125 Elvis Grbac .... .40 .18
❑ 126 Jacquez Green .... .40 .18
❑ 127 Brian Griese .... 1.50 .70
❑ 128 Marvin Harrison .... .75 .35
❑ 129 Garrison Hearst .... .40 .18
❑ 130 Skip Hicks .... .40 .18
❑ 131 Priest Holmes .... .75 .35
❑ 132 Michael Irvin .... .40 .18
❑ 133 Brad Johnson .... .40 .18
❑ 134 Napoleon Kaufman .... .75 .35
❑ 135 Terry Kirby .... .20 .09
❑ 136 Dorsey Levens .... .75 .35
❑ 137 Curtis Martin .... .75 .35
❑ 138 Ed McCaffrey .... .40 .18
❑ 139 Keenan McCardell .... .40 .18
❑ 140 O.J. McDuffie .... .40 .18
❑ 141 Steve McNair .... .75 .35
❑ 142 Natrone Means .... .40 .18
❑ 143 Scott Mitchell .... .20 .09
❑ 144 Herman Moore .... .75 .35
❑ 145 Eric Moulds .... .75 .35
❑ 146 Terrell Owens .... .75 .35
❑ 147 Lawrence Phillips .... .40 .18
❑ 148 Jerry Rice .... 2.00 .90
❑ 149 Andre Rison .... .40 .18
❑ 150 Deion Sanders .... .75 .35
❑ 151 Shannon Sharpe .... .40 .18
❑ 152 Antowain Smith .... .75 .35
❑ 153 Rod Smith .... .40 .18
❑ 154 Duce Staley .... .75 .35
❑ 155 Kordell Stewart .... .75 .35
❑ 156 J.J. Stokes .... .40 .18
❑ 157 Vinny Testaverde .... .40 .18
❑ 158 Yancey Thigpen .... .20 .09
❑ 159 Ricky Watters .... .40 .18
❑ 160 Steve Young .... 1.25 .55
❑ 161 Troy Aikman SP 12.00 5.50
❑ 162 Champ Bailey RC 20.00 9.00
❑ 163 Karsten Bailey RC 12.00 5.50
❑ 164 D'Wayne Bates RC 12.00 5.50
❑ 165 David Boston RC 30.00 13.50
❑ 166 Mike Cloud RC 15.00 6.75
❑ 167 Cecil Collins RC 15.00 6.75
❑ 168 Tim Couch RC 80.00 36.00
❑ 169 Daunte Culpepper RC 120.00 55.00
❑ 170 Terrell Davis SP 12.00 5.50
❑ 171 Troy Edwards RC 25.00 11.00
❑ 172 Kevin Faulk RC 20.00 9.00
❑ 173 Brett Favre SP 20.00 9.00
❑ 174 Torry Holt RC 40.00 18.00
❑ 175 Sedrick Irvin RC 15.00 6.75
❑ 176 Edgerrin James RC .. 120.00 55.00
❑ 177 James Johnson RC 15.00 6.75
❑ 178 Kevin Johnson RC 25.00 11.00
❑ 179 Keyshawn Johnson SP 5.00 2.20
❑ 180 Peyton Manning SP .. 20.00 9.00
❑ 181 Dan Marino SP 20.00 9.00
❑ 182 Donovan McNabb RC 80.00 36.00
❑ 183 Cade McNown RC 30.00 13.50
❑ 184 Joe Montgomery RC .. 15.00 6.75
❑ 185 Randy Moss SP 20.00 9.00
❑ 186 Jake Plummer SP 10.00 4.50
❑ 187 Peerless Price RC...... 20.00 9.00
❑ 188 Barry Sanders SP 20.00 9.00
❑ 189 Akili Smith RC 25.00 11.00
❑ 190 Emmitt Smith SP 12.00 5.50
❑ 191 Fred Taylor SP 12.00 5.50
❑ 192 Ricky Williams RC...... 80.00 36.00

1960 Fleer

	NRMT	VG-E
COMPLETE SET (132)	750.00	350.00
WRAPPER (5-CENT)	25.00	11.00

❑ 1 Harvey White RC 20.00 5.00
❑ 2 Tom Corky Tharp 3.50 1.55
❑ 3 Dan McGrew 3.50 1.55
❑ 4 Bob White 3.50 1.55
❑ 5 Dick Jamieson 3.50 1.55
❑ 6 Sam Salerno 3.50 1.55
❑ 7 Sid Gillman CO RC 20.00 9.00
❑ 8 Ben Preston 3.50 1.55
❑ 9 George Blanch 3.50 1.55
❑ 10 Bob Stransky 3.50 1.55
❑ 11 Fran Curci 3.50 1.55
❑ 12 George Shirkey 3.50 1.55
❑ 13 Paul Larson 3.50 1.55
❑ 14 John Stolte 3.50 1.55
❑ 15 Serafino(Foge) Fazio RC 5.00 2.20
❑ 16 Tom Dimitroff 3.50 1.55
❑ 17 Elbert Dubenion RC 12.00 5.50
❑ 18 Hogan Wharton 3.50 1.55
❑ 19 Tom O'Connell 3.50 1.55
❑ 20 Sammy Baugh CO 50.00 22.00
❑ 21 Tony Sardisco 3.50 1.55
❑ 22 Alan Cann 3.50 1.55
❑ 23 Mike Hudock 3.50 1.55
❑ 24 Bill Atkins 3.50 1.55

Card	NRMT	VG-E
❑ 25 Charlie Jackson	3.50	1.55
❑ 26 Frank Tripucka	6.00	2.70
❑ 27 Tony Teresa	3.50	1.55
❑ 28 Joe Amstutz	3.50	1.55
❑ 29 Bob Fee	3.50	1.55
❑ 30 Jim Baldwin	3.50	1.55
❑ 31 Jim Yates	3.50	1.55
❑ 32 Don Flynn	3.50	1.55
❑ 33 Ken Adamson	3.50	1.55
❑ 34 Ron Drzewiecki	3.50	1.55
❑ 35 J.W. Slack	3.50	1.55
❑ 36 Bob Yates	3.50	1.55
❑ 37 Gary Cobb	3.50	1.55
❑ 38 Jacky Lee RC	5.00	2.20
❑ 39 Jack Spikes RC	5.00	2.20
❑ 40 Jim Padgett	3.50	1.55
❑ 41 Jack Larscheid RC	3.50	1.55
❑ 42 Bob Reifsnyder RC	3.50	1.55
❑ 43 Fran Rogel	3.50	1.55
❑ 44 Ray Moss	3.50	1.55
❑ 45 Tony Banfield RC	5.00	2.20
❑ 46 George Herring	3.50	1.55
❑ 47 Willie Smith	3.50	1.55
❑ 48 Buddy Allen	3.50	1.55
❑ 49 Bill Brown	3.50	1.55
❑ 50 Ken Ford	3.50	1.55
❑ 51 Billy Kinard	3.50	1.55
❑ 52 Buddy Mayfield	3.50	1.55
❑ 53 Bill Krisher	3.50	1.55
❑ 54 Frank Bernardi	3.50	1.55
❑ 55 Lou Saban CO RC	5.00	2.20
❑ 56 Gene Cockrell	3.50	1.55
❑ 57 Sam Sanders	3.50	1.55
❑ 58 George Blanda	50.00	22.00
❑ 59 Sherrill Headrick RC	5.00	2.20
❑ 60 Carl Larpenter	3.50	1.55
❑ 61 Gene Prebola	3.50	1.55
❑ 62 Dick Chorovich	3.50	1.55
❑ 63 Bob McNamara	3.50	1.55
❑ 64 Tom Saidock	3.50	1.55
❑ 65 Willie Evans	3.50	1.55
❑ 66 Billy Cannon RC UER (Hometown: Istruma, should be Istrouma)	18.00	8.00
❑ 67 Sam McCord	3.50	1.55
❑ 68 Mike Simmons	3.50	1.55
❑ 69 Jim Swink RC	5.00	2.20
❑ 70 Don Hitt	3.50	1.55
❑ 71 Gerhard Schwedes	3.50	1.55
❑ 72 Thurlow Cooper	3.50	1.55
❑ 73 Abner Haynes RC	18.00	8.00
❑ 74 Billy Shoemake	3.50	1.55
❑ 75 Marv Lasater	3.50	1.55
❑ 76 Paul Lowe RC	15.00	6.75
❑ 77 Bruce Hartman	3.50	1.55
❑ 78 Blanche Martin	3.50	1.55
❑ 79 Gene Grabosky	3.50	1.55
❑ 80 Lou Rymkus CO	5.00	2.20
❑ 81 Chris Burford RC	8.00	3.60
❑ 82 Don Allen	3.50	1.55
❑ 83 Bob Nelson	3.50	1.55
❑ 84 Jim Woodard	3.50	1.55
❑ 85 Tom Rychlec	3.50	1.55
❑ 86 Bob Cox	3.50	1.55
❑ 87 Jerry Cornelison	3.50	1.55
❑ 88 Jack Work	3.50	1.55
❑ 89 Sam DeLuca	3.50	1.55
❑ 90 Rommie Loudd	3.50	1.55
❑ 91 Teddy Edmondson	3.50	1.55
❑ 92 Buster Ramsey CO	3.50	1.55
❑ 93 Doug Asad	3.50	1.55
❑ 94 Jimmy Harris	3.50	1.55
❑ 95 Larry Cundiff	3.50	1.55
❑ 96 Richie Lucas RC	6.00	2.70
❑ 97 Don Norwood	3.50	1.55
❑ 98 Larry Grantham RC	5.00	2.20
❑ 99 Bill Mathis RC	6.00	2.70
❑ 100 Mel Branch RC	5.00	2.20
❑ 101 Marvin Terrell	3.50	1.55
❑ 102 Charlie Flowers	3.50	1.55
❑ 103 John McMullan	3.50	1.55
❑ 104 Charlie Kaaihue	3.50	1.55
❑ 105 Joe Schaffer	3.50	1.55
❑ 106 Al Day	3.50	1.55
❑ 107 Johnny Carson	3.50	1.55
❑ 108 Alan Goldstein	3.50	1.55
❑ 109 Doug Cline	3.50	1.55
❑ 110 Al Carmichael	3.50	1.55
❑ 111 Bob Dee	3.50	1.55
❑ 112 John Bredice	3.50	1.55
❑ 113 Don Floyd	3.50	1.55
❑ 114 Ronnie Cain	3.50	1.55
❑ 115 Stan Flowers	3.50	1.55
❑ 116 Hank Stram CO RC	50.00	22.00
❑ 117 Bob Dougherty	3.50	1.55
❑ 118 Ron Mix RC	40.00	18.00
❑ 119 Roger Ellis	3.50	1.55
❑ 120 Elvin Caldwell	3.50	1.55
❑ 121 Bill Kimber	3.50	1.55
❑ 122 Jim Matheny	3.50	1.55
❑ 123 Curley Johnson RC	3.50	1.55
❑ 124 Jack Kemp RC	275.00	125.00
❑ 125 Ed Denk	3.50	1.55
❑ 126 Jerry McFarland	3.50	1.55
❑ 127 Dan Lanphear	3.50	1.55
❑ 128 Paul Maguire RC	18.00	8.00
❑ 129 Ray Collins	3.50	1.55
❑ 130 Ron Burton RC	6.00	2.70
❑ 131 Eddie Erdelatz CO	3.50	1.55
❑ 132 Ron Beagle RC !	15.00	3.70

1961 Fleer

	NRMT	VG-E
COMPLETE SET (220)	1600.00	700.00
COMMON CARD (1-132)	4.00	1.80
COMMON CARD (133-220)	6.00	2.70
WRAPPER (5-CENT, SER.1)	25.00	11.00
WRAPPER (5-CENT, SER.2)	30.00	13.50

Card	NRMT	VG-E
❑ 1 Ed Brown	15.00	3.70
❑ 2 Rick Casares	6.00	2.70
❑ 3 Willie Galimore	6.00	2.70
❑ 4 Jim Dooley	4.00	1.80
❑ 5 Harlon Hill	4.00	1.80
❑ 6 Stan Jones	7.00	3.10
❑ 7 J.C. Caroline	4.00	1.80
❑ 8 Joe Fortunato	4.00	1.80
❑ 9 Doug Atkins	8.00	3.60
❑ 10 Milt Plum	6.00	2.70
❑ 11 Jim Brown	125.00	55.00
❑ 12 Bobby Mitchell	10.00	4.50
❑ 13 Ray Renfro	6.00	2.70
❑ 14 Gern Nagler	4.00	1.80
❑ 15 Jim Shofner	4.00	1.80
❑ 16 Vince Costello	4.00	1.80
❑ 17 Galen Fiss	4.00	1.80
❑ 18 Walt Michaels	6.00	2.70
❑ 19 Bob Gain	4.00	1.80
❑ 20 Mal Hammack	4.00	1.80
❑ 21 Frank Mestnick	4.00	1.80
❑ 22 Bobby Joe Conrad	6.00	2.70
❑ 23 John David Crow	6.00	2.70
❑ 24 Sonny Randle RC	6.00	2.70
❑ 25 Don Gillis	4.00	1.80
❑ 26 Jerry Norton	4.00	1.80
❑ 27 Bill Stacy	4.00	1.80
❑ 28 Leo Sugar	4.00	1.80
❑ 29 Frank Fuller	4.00	1.80
❑ 30 John Unitas	60.00	27.00
❑ 31 Alan Ameche	7.00	3.10
❑ 32 Lenny Moore	15.00	6.75
❑ 33 Raymond Berry	15.00	6.75
❑ 34 Jim Mutscheller	4.00	1.80
❑ 35 Jim Parker	7.00	3.10
❑ 36 Bill Pellington	4.00	1.80
❑ 37 Gino Marchetti	10.00	4.50
❑ 38 Gene Lipscomb	7.00	3.10
❑ 39 Art Donovan	15.00	6.75
❑ 40 Eddie LeBaron	6.00	2.70
❑ 41 Don Meredith RC	150.00	70.00
❑ 42 Don McIlhenny	4.00	1.80
❑ 43 L.G. Dupre	4.00	1.80
❑ 44 Fred Dugan	4.00	1.80
❑ 45 Billy Howton	6.00	2.70
❑ 46 Duane Putnam	4.00	1.80
❑ 47 Gene Cronin	4.00	1.80
❑ 48 Jerry Tubbs	4.00	1.80
❑ 49 Clarence Peaks	4.00	1.80
❑ 50 Ted Dean RC	4.00	1.80
❑ 51 Tommy McDonald	7.00	3.10
❑ 52 Bill Barnes	4.00	1.80
❑ 53 Pete Retzlaff	6.00	2.70
❑ 54 Bobby Walston	4.00	1.80
❑ 55 Chuck Bednarik	12.00	5.50
❑ 56 Maxie Baughan RC	6.00	2.70
❑ 57 Bob Pellegrini	4.00	1.80
❑ 58 Jesse Richardson	4.00	1.80
❑ 59 John Brodie RC	50.00	22.00
❑ 60 J.D. Smith RB	6.00	2.70
❑ 61 Ray Norton RC	4.00	1.80
❑ 62 Monty Stickles RC	4.00	1.80
❑ 63 Bob St. Clair	7.00	3.10
❑ 64 Dave Baker	4.00	1.80
❑ 65 Abe Woodson	4.00	1.80
❑ 66 Matt Hazeltine	4.00	1.80
❑ 67 Leo Nomellini	10.00	4.50
❑ 68 Charley Conerly	10.00	4.50
❑ 69 Kyle Rote	7.00	3.10
❑ 70 Jack Stroud	4.00	1.80
❑ 71 Roosevelt Brown	7.00	3.10
❑ 72 Jim Patton	4.00	1.80
❑ 73 Erich Barnes	4.00	1.80
❑ 74 Sam Huff	15.00	6.75
❑ 75 Andy Robustelli	10.00	4.50
❑ 76 Dick Modzelewski	4.00	1.80
❑ 77 Roosevelt Grier	7.00	3.10
❑ 78 Earl Morrall	7.00	3.10
❑ 79 Jim Ninowski	4.00	1.80
❑ 80 Nick Pietrosante RC	6.00	2.70
❑ 81 Howard Cassady	6.00	2.70
❑ 82 Jim Gibbons	4.00	1.80
❑ 83 Gail Cogdill RC	6.00	2.70
❑ 84 Dick Lane	7.00	3.10
❑ 85 Yale Lary	7.00	3.10
❑ 86 Joe Schmidt	8.00	3.60
❑ 87 Darris McCord	4.00	1.80
❑ 88 Bart Starr	60.00	27.00
❑ 89 Jim Taylor	50.00	22.00
❑ 90 Paul Hornung	55.00	25.00
❑ 91 Tom Moore RC	8.00	3.60
❑ 92 Boyd Dowler RC	15.00	6.75
❑ 93 Max McGee	7.00	3.10
❑ 94 Forrest Gregg	8.00	3.60
❑ 95 Jerry Kramer	10.00	4.50
❑ 96 Jim Ringo	8.00	3.60
❑ 97 Bill Forester	6.00	2.70
❑ 98 Frank Ryan	6.00	2.70
❑ 99 Ollie Matson	12.00	5.50
❑ 100 Jon Arnett	6.00	2.70
❑ 101 Dick Bass RC	6.00	2.70
❑ 102 Jim Phillips	4.00	1.80
❑ 103 Del Shofner	6.00	2.70
❑ 104 Art Hunter	4.00	1.80
❑ 105 Lindon Crow	4.00	1.80
❑ 106 Les Richter	6.00	2.70
❑ 107 Lou Michaels	4.00	1.80
❑ 108 Ralph Guglielmi	4.00	1.80
❑ 109 Don Bosseler	4.00	1.80
❑ 110 John Olszewski	4.00	1.80
❑ 111 Bill Anderson	4.00	1.80
❑ 112 Joe Walton	4.00	1.80
❑ 113 Jim Schrader	4.00	1.80
❑ 114 Gary Glick	4.00	1.80
❑ 115 Ralph Felton	4.00	1.80
❑ 116 Bob Toneff	4.00	1.80
❑ 117 Bobby Layne	40.00	18.00
❑ 118 John Henry Johnson	7.00	3.10
❑ 119 Tom Tracy	6.00	2.70
❑ 120 Jimmy Orr RC	7.00	3.10

	NRMT	VG-E
❑ 121 John Nisby	4.00	1.80
❑ 122 Dean Derby	4.00	1.80
❑ 123 John Reger	4.00	1.80
❑ 124 George Tarasovic	4.00	1.80
❑ 125 Ernie Stautner	10.00	4.50
❑ 126 George Shaw	4.00	1.80
❑ 127 Hugh McElhenny	12.00	5.50
❑ 128 Dick Haley	4.00	1.80
❑ 129 Dave Middleton	4.00	1.80
❑ 130 Perry Richards	4.00	1.80
❑ 131 Gene Johnson	4.00	1.80
❑ 132 Don Joyce	4.00	1.80
❑ 133 Johnny Green	8.00	3.60
❑ 134 Wray Carlton RC	8.00	3.60
❑ 135 Richie Lucas	8.00	3.60
❑ 136 Elbert Dubenion	8.00	3.60
❑ 137 Tom Rychlec	6.00	2.70
❑ 138 Mack Yoho	6.00	2.70
❑ 139 Phil Blazer	6.00	2.70
❑ 140 Dan McGrew	6.00	2.70
❑ 141 Bill Atkins	6.00	2.70
❑ 142 Archie Matsos RC	6.00	2.70
❑ 143 Gene Grabosky	6.00	2.70
❑ 144 Frank Tripucka	10.00	4.50
❑ 145 Al Carmichael	6.00	2.70
❑ 146 Bob McNamara	6.00	2.70
❑ 147 Lionel Taylor RC	15.00	6.75
❑ 148 Eldon Danenhauer	6.00	2.70
❑ 149 Willie Smith	6.00	2.70
❑ 150 Carl Larpenter	6.00	2.70
❑ 151 Ken Adamson	6.00	2.70
❑ 152 Goose Gonsoulin RC	10.00	4.50
❑ 153 Joe Young	6.00	2.70
❑ 154 Gordy Molz	6.00	2.70
❑ 155 Jack Kemp	200.00	90.00
❑ 156 Charlie Flowers	6.00	2.70
❑ 157 Paul Lowe	10.00	4.50
❑ 158 Don Norton	6.00	2.70
❑ 159 Howard Clark	6.00	2.70
❑ 160 Paul Maguire	15.00	6.75
❑ 161 Ernie Wright RC	8.00	3.60
❑ 162 Ron Mix	15.00	6.75
❑ 163 Fred Cole	6.00	2.70
❑ 164 Jim Sears	6.00	2.70
❑ 165 Volney Peters	6.00	2.70
❑ 166 George Blanda	45.00	20.00
❑ 167 Jacky Lee	8.00	3.60
❑ 168 Bob White	6.00	2.70
❑ 169 Doug Cline	6.00	2.70
❑ 170 Dave Smith	6.00	2.70
❑ 171 Billy Cannon	15.00	6.75
❑ 172 Bill Groman	6.00	2.70
❑ 173 Al Jamison	6.00	2.70
❑ 174 Jim Norton	6.00	2.70
❑ 175 Dennit Morris	6.00	2.70
❑ 176 Don Floyd	6.00	2.70
❑ 177 Butch Songin	6.00	2.70
❑ 178 Billy Lott	6.00	2.70
❑ 179 Ron Burton	10.00	4.50
❑ 180 Jim Colclough	6.00	2.70
❑ 181 Charley Leo	6.00	2.70
❑ 182 Walt Cudzik	6.00	2.70
❑ 183 Fred Bruney	6.00	2.70
❑ 184 Ross O'Hanley	6.00	2.70
❑ 185 Tony Sardisco	6.00	2.70
❑ 186 Harry Jacobs	6.00	2.70
❑ 187 Bob Dee	6.00	2.70
❑ 188 Tom Flores RC	30.00	13.50
❑ 189 Jack Larscheid	6.00	2.70
❑ 190 Dick Christy	6.00	2.70
❑ 191 Alan Miller RC	6.00	2.70
❑ 192 James Smith	6.00	2.70
❑ 193 Gerald Burch	6.00	2.70
❑ 194 Gene Prebola	6.00	2.70
❑ 195 Alan Goldstein	6.00	2.70
❑ 196 Don Manoukian	6.00	2.70
❑ 197 Jim Otto RC	60.00	27.00
❑ 198 Wayne Crow	6.00	2.70
❑ 199 Cotton Davidson RC	8.00	3.60
❑ 200 Randy Duncan RC*/C	8.00	3.60
❑ 201 Jack Spikes	8.00	3.60
❑ 202 Johnny Robinson RC	15.00	6.75
❑ 203 Abner Haynes	15.00	6.75
❑ 204 Chris Burford	8.00	3.60
❑ 205 Bill Krisher	6.00	2.70
❑ 206 Marvin Terrell	6.00	2.70
❑ 207 Jimmy Harris	6.00	2.70
❑ 208 Mel Branch	8.00	3.60
❑ 209 Paul Miller	6.00	2.70
❑ 210 Al Dorow	6.00	2.70
❑ 211 Dick Jamieson	6.00	2.70
❑ 212 Pete Hart	6.00	2.70
❑ 213 Bill Shockley	6.00	2.70
❑ 214 Dewey Bohling	6.00	2.70
❑ 215 Don Maynard RC	80.00	36.00
❑ 216 Bob Mischak	6.00	2.70
❑ 217 Mike Hudock	6.00	2.70
❑ 218 Bob Reifsnyder	6.00	2.70
❑ 219 Tom Saidock	6.00	2.70
❑ 220 Sid Youngelman	20.00	5.00

1962 Fleer

	NRMT	VG-E
COMPLETE SET (88)	900.00	400.00
WRAPPER (5-CENT)	200.00	90.00

	NRMT	VG-E
❑ 1 Billy Lott	16.00	4.00
❑ 2 Ron Burton	10.00	4.50
❑ 3 Gino Cappelletti RC	15.00	6.75
❑ 4 Babe Parilli	10.00	4.50
❑ 5 Jim Colclough	7.00	3.10
❑ 6 Tony Sardisco	7.00	3.10
❑ 7 Walt Cudzik	7.00	3.10
❑ 8 Bob Dee	7.00	3.10
❑ 9 Tommy Addison RC	8.00	3.60
❑ 10 Harry Jacobs	7.00	3.10
❑ 11 Ross O'Hanley	7.00	3.10
❑ 12 Art Baker	7.00	3.10
❑ 13 Johnny Green	7.00	3.10
❑ 14 Elbert Dubenion	10.00	4.50
❑ 15 Tom Rychlec	7.00	3.10
❑ 16 Billy Shaw RC	18.00	8.00
❑ 17 Ken Rice	7.00	3.10
❑ 18 Bill Atkins	7.00	3.10
❑ 19 Richie Lucas	8.00	3.60
❑ 20 Archie Matsos	7.00	3.10
❑ 21 Laverne Torczon	7.00	3.10
❑ 22 Warren Rabb	7.00	3.10
❑ 23 Jack Spikes	8.00	3.60
❑ 24 Cotton Davidson	8.00	3.60
❑ 25 Abner Haynes	15.00	6.75
❑ 26 Jimmy Saxton	7.00	3.10
❑ 27 Chris Burford	8.00	3.60
❑ 28 Bill Miller	7.00	3.10
❑ 29 Sherrill Headrick	8.00	3.60
❑ 30 E.J. Holub RC	8.00	3.60
❑ 31 Jerry Mays RC	10.00	4.50
❑ 32 Mel Branch	8.00	3.60
❑ 33 Paul Rochester	7.00	3.10
❑ 34 Frank Tripucka	10.00	4.50
❑ 35 Gene Mingo	7.00	3.10
❑ 36 Lionel Taylor	12.00	5.50
❑ 37 Ken Adamson	7.00	3.10
❑ 38 Eldon Danenhauer	7.00	3.10
❑ 39 Goose Gonsoulin	10.00	4.50
❑ 40 Gordy Holz	7.00	3.10
❑ 41 Bud McFadin	8.00	3.60
❑ 42 Jim Stinnette	7.00	3.10
❑ 43 Bob Hudson	7.00	3.10
❑ 44 George Herring	7.00	3.10
❑ 45 Charley Tolar RC	7.00	3.10
❑ 46 George Blanda	50.00	22.00
❑ 47 Billy Cannon	15.00	6.75
❑ 48 Charlie Hennigan RC	15.00	6.75
❑ 49 Bill Groman	7.00	3.10
❑ 50 Al Jamison	7.00	3.10
❑ 51 Tony Banfield	7.00	3.10
❑ 52 Jim Norton	7.00	3.10
❑ 53 Dennit Morris	7.00	3.10
❑ 54 Don Floyd	7.00	3.10
❑ 55 Ed Husmann UER (Misspelled Hussman on both sides)	7.00	3.10
❑ 56 Robert Brooks	7.00	3.10
❑ 57 Al Dorow	7.00	3.10
❑ 58 Dick Christy	7.00	3.10
❑ 59 Don Maynard	50.00	22.00
❑ 60 Art Powell	10.00	4.50
❑ 61 Mike Hudock	7.00	3.10
❑ 62 Bill Mathis	8.00	3.60
❑ 63 Butch Songin	7.00	3.10
❑ 64 Larry Grantham	7.00	3.10
❑ 65 Nick Mumley	7.00	3.10
❑ 66 Tom Saidock	7.00	3.10
❑ 67 Alan Miller	7.00	3.10
❑ 68 Tom Flores	15.00	6.75
❑ 69 Bob Coolbaugh	7.00	3.10
❑ 70 George Fleming	7.00	3.10
❑ 71 Wayne Hawkins RC	8.00	3.60
❑ 72 Jim Otto	35.00	16.00
❑ 73 Wayne Crow	7.00	3.10
❑ 74 Fred Williamson RC	25.00	11.00
❑ 75 Tom Louderback	7.00	3.10
❑ 76 Volney Peters	7.00	3.10
❑ 77 Charley Powell	7.00	3.10
❑ 78 Don Norton	7.00	3.10
❑ 79 Jack Kemp	250.00	110.00
❑ 80 Paul Lowe	10.00	4.50
❑ 81 Dave Kocourek	7.00	3.10
❑ 82 Ron Mix	15.00	6.75
❑ 83 Ernie Wright	10.00	4.50
❑ 84 Dick Harris	7.00	3.10
❑ 85 Bill Hudson	7.00	3.10
❑ 86 Ernie Ladd RC	25.00	11.00
❑ 87 Earl Faison RC	8.00	3.60
❑ 88 Ron Nery	18.00	4.50

1963 Fleer

	NRMT	VG-E
COMPLETE SET (88)	1800.00	800.00
WRAPPER (5-CENT)	125.00	55.00

	NRMT	VG-E
❑ 1 Larry Garron RC	20.00	5.00
❑ 2 Babe Parilli	10.00	4.50
❑ 3 Ron Burton	12.00	5.50
❑ 4 Jim Colclough	8.00	3.60
❑ 5 Gino Cappelletti	12.00	5.50
❑ 6 Charles Long RC SP	150.00	70.00
❑ 7 Bill Neighbors RC	8.00	3.60
❑ 8 Dick Felt	8.00	3.60
❑ 9 Tommy Addison	8.00	3.60
❑ 10 Nick Buoniconti RC	75.00	34.00
❑ 11 Larry Eisenhauer RC	8.00	3.60
❑ 12 Bill Mathis	8.00	3.60
❑ 13 Lee Grosscup RC	10.00	4.50
❑ 14 Dick Christy	8.00	3.60
❑ 15 Don Maynard	50.00	22.00
❑ 16 Alex Kroll RC	8.00	3.60
❑ 17 Bob Mischak	8.00	3.60
❑ 18 Dainard Paulson	8.00	3.60

❑ 19 Lee Riley 8.00 3.60
❑ 20 Larry Grantham 10.00 4.50
❑ 21 Hubert Bobo 8.00 3.60
❑ 22 Nick Mumley 8.00 3.60
❑ 23 Cookie Gilchrist RC**/C 45.00 20.00
❑ 24 Jack Kemp 250.00 110.00
❑ 25 Wray Carlton 8.00 3.60
❑ 26 Elbert Dubenion 10.00 4.50
❑ 27 Ernie Warlick 8.00 3.60
❑ 28 Billy Shaw 15.00 6.75
❑ 29 Ken Rice 8.00 3.60
❑ 30 Booker Edgerson 8.00 3.60
❑ 31 Ray Abruzzese 8.00 3.60
❑ 32 Mike Stratton RC 12.00 5.50
❑ 33 Tom Sestak RC 10.00 4.50
❑ 34 Charley Tolar 8.00 3.60
❑ 35 Dave Smith 8.00 3.60
❑ 36 George Blanda 55.00 25.00
❑ 37 Billy Cannon 15.00 6.75
❑ 38 Charlie Hennigan 10.00 4.50
❑ 39 Bob Talamini RC 8.00 3.60
❑ 40 Jim Norton 8.00 3.60
❑ 41 Tony Banfield 8.00 3.60
❑ 42 Doug Cline 8.00 3.60
❑ 43 Don Floyd 8.00 3.60
❑ 44 Ed Husmann 8.00 3.60
❑ 45 Curtis McClinton RC 15.00 6.75
❑ 46 Jack Spikes 10.00 4.50
❑ 47 Len Dawson RC 225.00 100.00
❑ 48 Abner Haynes 15.00 6.75
❑ 49 Chris Burford 10.00 4.50
❑ 50 Fred Arbanas RC 12.00 5.50
❑ 51 Johnny Robinson 10.00 4.50
❑ 52 E.J. Holub 10.00 4.50
❑ 53 Sherrill Headrick 10.00 4.50
❑ 54 Mel Branch 10.00 4.50
❑ 55 Jerry Mays 10.00 4.50
❑ 56 Cotton Davidson 10.00 4.50
❑ 57 Clem Daniels RC 15.00 6.75
❑ 58 Bo Roberson 8.00 3.60
❑ 59 Art Powell 12.00 5.50
❑ 60 Bob Coolbaugh 8.00 3.60
❑ 61 Wayne Hawkins 8.00 3.60
❑ 62 Jim Otto 30.00 13.50
❑ 63 Fred Williamson 12.00 5.50
❑ 64 Bob Dougherty SP 150.00 70.00
❑ 65 Dalva Allen 8.00 3.60
❑ 66 Chuck McMurtry 8.00 3.60
❑ 67 Gerry McDougall 8.00 3.60
❑ 68 Tobin Rote 10.00 4.50
❑ 69 Paul Lowe 12.00 5.50
❑ 70 Keith Lincoln RC 40.00 18.00
❑ 71 Dave Kocourek 8.00 3.60
❑ 72 Lance Alworth RC 200.00 90.00
❑ 73 Ron Mix 25.00 11.00
❑ 74 Charley McNeil RC 8.00 3.60
❑ 75 Emil Karas 8.00 3.60
❑ 76 Ernie Ladd 20.00 9.00
❑ 77 Earl Faison 8.00 3.60
❑ 78 Jim Stinnette 8.00 3.60
❑ 79 Frank Tripucka 12.00 5.50
❑ 80 Don Stone 8.00 3.60
❑ 81 Bob Scarpitto 8.00 3.60
❑ 82 Lionel Taylor 12.00 5.50
❑ 83 Jerry Tarr 8.00 3.60
❑ 84 Eldon Danenhauer 8.00 3.60
❑ 85 Goose Gonsoulin 10.00 4.50
❑ 86 Jim Fraser 8.00 3.60
❑ 87 Chuck Gavin 8.00 3.60
❑ 88 Bud McFadin 20.00 5.00
❑ NNO Checklist Card SP 350.00 90.00

1990 Fleer

MINT NRMT
COMPLETE SET (400) 7.50 3.40

❑ 1 Harris Barton .04 .02
❑ 2 Chet Brooks .04 .02
❑ 3 Michael Carter .04 .02
❑ 4 Mike Cofer UER .04 .02
(FGA and FGM columns switched)
❑ 5 Roger Craig .10 .05
❑ 6 Kevin Fagan RC .04 .02
❑ 7 Charles Haley UER .10 .05
(Fumble recoveries should be 2 in '86 and 5 career, card says 1 and 4)
❑ 8 Pierce Holt RC .04 .02
❑ 9 Ronnie Lott .10 .05
❑ 10A Joe Montana ERR 1.25 .55
(31,054 TD's)
❑ 10B Joe Montana COR 1.25 .55
(216 TD's)
❑ 11 Bubba Paris .04 .02
❑ 12 Tom Rathman .04 .02
❑ 13 Jerry Rice .75 .35
❑ 14 John Taylor .25 .11
❑ 15 Keena Turner .04 .02
❑ 16 Michael Walter .04 .02
❑ 17 Steve Young .50 .23
❑ 18 Steve Atwater .04 .02
❑ 19 Tyrone Braxton .04 .02
❑ 20 Michael Brooks RC .04 .02
❑ 21 John Elway 1.25 .55
❑ 22 Simon Fletcher .04 .02
❑ 23 Bobby Humphrey .04 .02
❑ 24 Mark Jackson .04 .02
❑ 25 Vance Johnson .04 .02
❑ 26 Greg Kragen .04 .02
❑ 27 Ken Lanier RC .04 .02
❑ 28 Karl Mecklenburg .04 .02
❑ 29 Orson Mobley RC .04 .02
❑ 30 Steve Sewell .04 .02
❑ 31 Dennis Smith .04 .02
❑ 32 David Treadwell .04 .02
❑ 33 Flipper Anderson .04 .02
❑ 34 Greg Bell .04 .02
❑ 35 Henry Ellard .10 .05
❑ 36 Jim Everett .10 .05
❑ 37 Jerry Gray .04 .02
❑ 38 Kevin Greene .25 .11
❑ 39 Pete Holohan .04 .02
❑ 40 LeRoy Irvin .04 .02
❑ 41 Mike Lansford .04 .02
❑ 42 Buford McGee RC .04 .02
❑ 43 Tom Newberry .04 .02
❑ 44 Vince Newsome RC .04 .02
❑ 45 Jackie Slater .04 .02
❑ 46 Mike Wilcher .04 .02
❑ 47 Matt Bahr .04 .02
❑ 48 Brian Brennan .04 .02
❑ 49 Thane Gash RC .04 .02
❑ 50 Mike Johnson .04 .02
❑ 51 Bernie Kosar .10 .05
❑ 52 Reggie Langhorne .04 .02
❑ 53 Tim Manoa .04 .02
❑ 54 Clay Matthews .10 .05
❑ 55 Eric Metcalf .25 .11
❑ 56 Frank Minnifield .04 .02
❑ 57 Gregg Rakoczy RC UER .04 .02
(First line of text calls him Greg)
❑ 58 Webster Slaughter .10 .05
❑ 59 Bryan Wagner .04 .02
❑ 60 Felix Wright .04 .02
❑ 61 Raul Allegre .04 .02
❑ 62 Ottis Anderson UER .10 .05
(Stats say 9.317 yards, should be 9,317)
❑ 63 Carl Banks .04 .02
❑ 64 Mark Bavaro .04 .02
❑ 65 Maurice Carthon .04 .02
❑ 66 Mark Collins UER .04 .02
(Total fumble recoveries should be 5, not 3)
❑ 67 Jeff Hostetler RC .25 .11
❑ 68 Erik Howard .04 .02
❑ 69 Pepper Johnson .04 .02
❑ 70 Sean Landeta .04 .02
❑ 71 Lionel Manuel .04 .02
❑ 72 Leonard Marshall .04 .02
❑ 73 Dave Meggett .10 .05
❑ 74 Bart Oates .04 .02
❑ 75 Doug Riesenberg RC .04 .02
❑ 76 Phil Simms .10 .05
❑ 77 Lawrence Taylor .25 .11
❑ 78 Eric Allen .04 .02
❑ 79 Jerome Brown .04 .02
❑ 80 Keith Byars .04 .02
❑ 81 Cris Carter .50 .23
❑ 82A Byron Evans RC ERR .15 .07
(Should be 83 according to checklist)
❑ 82B Randall Cunningham .15 .07
❑ 83A Ron Heller RC ERR .15 .07
(Should be 84 according to checklist)
❑ 83B Byron Evans COR RC .15 .07
❑ 84 Ron Heller RC .04 .02
❑ 85 Terry Hoage RC .04 .02
❑ 86 Keith Jackson .10 .05
❑ 87 Seth Joyner .10 .05
❑ 88 Mike Quick .04 .02
❑ 89 Mike Schad .04 .02
❑ 90 Clyde Simmons .04 .02
❑ 91 John Teltschik .04 .02
❑ 92 Anthony Toney .04 .02
❑ 93 Reggie White .25 .11
❑ 94 Ray Berry .04 .02
❑ 95 Joey Browner .04 .02
❑ 96 Anthony Carter .10 .05
❑ 97 Chris Doleman .04 .02
❑ 98 Rick Fenney .04 .02
❑ 99 Rich Gannon RC 2.00 .90
❑ 100 Hassan Jones .04 .02
❑ 101 Steve Jordan .04 .02
❑ 102 Rich Karlis .04 .02
❑ 103 Andre Ware RC .25 .11
❑ 104 Kirk Lowdermilk .04 .02
❑ 105 Keith Millard .04 .02
❑ 106 Scott Studwell .04 .02
❑ 107 Herschel Walker .10 .05
❑ 108 Wade Wilson .10 .05
❑ 109 Gary Zimmerman .04 .02
❑ 110 Don Beebe .10 .05
❑ 111 Cornelius Bennett .10 .05
❑ 112 Shane Conlan .04 .02
❑ 113 Jim Kelly .25 .11
❑ 114 Scott Norwood UER .04 .02
(FGA and FGM columns switched)
❑ 115 Mark Kelso UER .04 .02
(Some stats added wrong on back)
❑ 116 Larry Kinnebrew .04 .02
❑ 117 Pete Metzelaars .04 .02
❑ 118 Scott Radecic .04 .02
❑ 119 Andre Reed .25 .11
❑ 120 Jim Ritcher RC .04 .02
❑ 121 Bruce Smith .25 .11
❑ 122 Leonard Smith .04 .02
❑ 123 Art Still .04 .02
❑ 124 Thurman Thomas .25 .11
❑ 125 Steve Brown .04 .02
❑ 126 Ray Childress .04 .02
❑ 127 Ernest Givins .10 .05
❑ 128 John Grimsley .04 .02
❑ 129 Alonzo Highsmith .04 .02
❑ 130 Drew Hill .04 .02
❑ 131 Bruce Matthews .10 .05
❑ 132 Johnny Meads .04 .02
❑ 133 Warren Moon UER .25 .11
(186 completions in '87 and 1341 career, should be 184 and 1339)

	No.	Player		
❑	134	Mike Munchak	.04	.02
❑	135	Mike Rozier	.04	.02
❑	136	Dean Steinkuhler	.04	.02
❑	137	Lorenzo White	.04	.02
❑	138	Tony Zendejas	.04	.02
❑	139	Gary Anderson K	.04	.02
❑	140	Bubby Brister	.04	.02
❑	141	Thomas Everett	.04	.02
❑	142	Derek Hill	.04	.02
❑	143	Merril Hoge	.04	.02
❑	144	Tim Johnson	.04	.02
❑	145	Louis Lipps	.10	.05
❑	146	David Little	.04	.02
❑	147	Greg Lloyd	.25	.11
❑	148	Mike Mularkey	.04	.02
❑	149	John Rienstra RC	.04	.02
❑	150	Gerald Williams RC UER (Tackles and fumble recovery headers are switched)	.04	.02
❑	151	Keith Willis UER (Tackles and fumble recovery headers are switched)	.04	.02
❑	152	Rod Woodson	.25	.11
❑	153	Tim Worley	.04	.02
❑	154	Gary Clark	.25	.11
❑	155	Darryl Grant	.04	.02
❑	156	Darrell Green	.10	.05
❑	157	Joe Jacoby	.04	.02
❑	158	Jim Lachey	.04	.02
❑	159	Chip Lohmiller	.04	.02
❑	160	Charles Mann	.04	.02
❑	161	Wilber Marshall	.04	.02
❑	162	Mark May	.04	.02
❑	163	Ralf Mojsiejenko	.04	.02
❑	164	Art Monk UER (No explanation of How Acquired)	.10	.05
❑	165	Gerald Riggs	.10	.05
❑	166	Mark Rypien	.10	.05
❑	167	Ricky Sanders	.04	.02
❑	168	Don Warren	.04	.02
❑	169	Robert Brown RC	.04	.02
❑	170	Blair Bush	.04	.02
❑	171	Brent Fullwood	.04	.02
❑	172	Tim Harris	.04	.02
❑	173	Chris Jacke	.04	.02
❑	174	Perry Kemp	.04	.02
❑	175	Don Majkowski	.04	.02
❑	176	Tony Mandarich	.04	.02
❑	177	Mark Murphy	.04	.02
❑	178	Brian Noble	.04	.02
❑	179	Ken Ruettgers	.04	.02
❑	180	Sterling Sharpe	.25	.11
❑	181	Ed West RC	.04	.02
❑	182	Keith Woodside	.04	.02
❑	183	Morten Andersen	.04	.02
❑	184	Stan Brock	.04	.02
❑	185	Jim Dombrowski RC	.04	.02
❑	186	John Fourcade	.04	.02
❑	187	Bobby Hebert	.04	.02
❑	188	Craig Heyward	.10	.05
❑	189	Dalton Hilliard	.04	.02
❑	190	Rickey Jackson	.10	.05
❑	191	Buford Jordan	.04	.02
❑	192	Eric Martin	.04	.02
❑	193	Robert Massey	.04	.02
❑	194	Sam Mills	.10	.05
❑	195	Pat Swilling	.10	.05
❑	196	Jim Wilks	.04	.02
❑	197	John Alt RC	.04	.02
❑	198	Walker Lee Ashley	.04	.02
❑	199	Steve DeBerg	.04	.02
❑	200	Leonard Griffin	.04	.02
❑	201	Albert Lewis	.04	.02
❑	202	Nick Lowery	.04	.02
❑	203	Bill Maas	.04	.02
❑	204	Pete Mandley	.04	.02
❑	205	Chris Martin RC	.04	.02
❑	206	Christian Okoye	.04	.02
❑	207	Stephone Paige	.04	.02
❑	208	Kevin Porter RC	.04	.02
❑	209	Derrick Thomas	.25	.11
❑	210	Lewis Billups	.04	.02
❑	211	James Brooks	.10	.05
❑	212	Jason Buck	.04	.02
❑	213	Rickey Dixon RC	.04	.02
❑	214	Boomer Esiason	.10	.05
❑	215	David Fulcher	.04	.02
❑	216	Rodney Holman	.04	.02
❑	217	Lee Johnson	.04	.02
❑	218	Tim Krumrie	.04	.02
❑	219	Tim McGee	.04	.02
❑	220	Anthony Munoz	.10	.05
❑	221	Bruce Reimers RC	.04	.02
❑	222	Leon White	.04	.02
❑	223	Ickey Woods	.04	.02
❑	224	Harvey Armstrong RC	.04	.02
❑	225	Michael Ball RC	.04	.02
❑	226	Chip Banks	.04	.02
❑	227	Pat Beach	.04	.02
❑	228	Duane Bickett	.04	.02
❑	229	Bill Brooks	.04	.02
❑	230	Jon Hand	.04	.02
❑	231	Andre Rison	.25	.11
❑	232	Rohn Stark	.04	.02
❑	233	Donnell Thompson	.04	.02
❑	234	Jack Trudeau	.04	.02
❑	235	Clarence Verdin	.04	.02
❑	236	Mark Clayton	.10	.05
❑	237	Jeff Cross	.04	.02
❑	238	Jeff Dellenbach RC	.04	.02
❑	239	Mark Duper	.10	.05
❑	240	Ferrell Edmunds	.04	.02
❑	241	Hugh Green UER (Back says Traded '86, should be '85)	.04	.02
❑	242	E.J. Junior	.04	.02
❑	243	Marc Logan	.04	.02
❑	244	Dan Marino	1.25	.55
❑	245	John Offerdahl	.04	.02
❑	246	Reggie Roby	.04	.02
❑	247	Sammie Smith	.04	.02
❑	248	Pete Stoyanovich	.04	.02
❑	249	Marcus Allen	.25	.11
❑	250	Eddie Anderson RC	.04	.02
❑	251	Steve Beuerlein	.10	.05
❑	252	Mike Dyal	.04	.02
❑	253	Mervyn Fernandez	.04	.02
❑	254	Bob Golic	.04	.02
❑	255	Mike Harden	.04	.02
❑	256	Bo Jackson	.30	.14
❑	257	Howie Long UER (Born Sommerville, should be Somerville)	.10	.05
❑	258	Don Mosebar	.04	.02
❑	259	Jay Schroeder	.04	.02
❑	260	Steve Smith	.04	.02
❑	261	Greg Townsend	.04	.02
❑	262	Lionel Washington	.04	.02
❑	263	Brian Blades	.10	.05
❑	264	Jeff Bryant	.04	.02
❑	265	Grant Feasel RC	.04	.02
❑	266	Jacob Green	.04	.02
❑	267	James Jefferson	.04	.02
❑	268	Norm Johnson	.04	.02
❑	269	Dave Krieg UER (Misspelled Kreig on card front)	.10	.05
❑	270	Travis McNeal	.04	.02
❑	271	Joe Nash	.04	.02
❑	272	Rufus Porter	.04	.02
❑	273	Kelly Stouffer	.04	.02
❑	274	John L. Williams	.04	.02
❑	275	Jim Arnold	.04	.02
❑	276	Jerry Ball	.04	.02
❑	277	Bennie Blades	.04	.02
❑	278	Lomas Brown	.04	.02
❑	279	Michael Cofer	.04	.02
❑	280	Bob Gagliano	.04	.02
❑	281	Richard Johnson	.04	.02
❑	282	Eddie Murray	.04	.02
❑	283	Rodney Peete	.10	.05
❑	284	Barry Sanders	1.50	.70
❑	285	Eric Sanders	.04	.02
❑	286	Chris Spielman	.25	.11
❑	287	Eric Williams RC	.04	.02
❑	288	Neal Anderson	.10	.05
❑	289A	Kevin Butler ERR/ERR (Listed as Punter on front and back)	.25	.11
❑	289B	Kevin Butler COR/ERR (Listed as Placekicker on front and Punter on back)	.25	.11
❑	289C	Kevin Butler ERR/COR (Listed as Punter on front and Placekicker on back)	.25	.11
❑	289D	Kevin Butler COR/COR (Listed as Placekicker on front and back)	.04	.02
❑	290	Jim Covert	.04	.02
❑	291	Richard Dent	.10	.05
❑	292	Dennis Gentry	.04	.02
❑	293	Jim Harbaugh	.25	.11
❑	294	Jay Hilgenberg	.04	.02
❑	295	Vestee Jackson	.04	.02
❑	296	Steve McMichael	.10	.05
❑	297	Ron Morris	.04	.02
❑	298	Brad Muster	.04	.02
❑	299	Mike Singletary	.10	.05
❑	300	James Thornton UER (Missing birthdate)	.04	.02
❑	301	Mike Tomczak	.10	.05
❑	302	Keith Van Horne	.04	.02
❑	303	Chris Bahr UER ('86 FGA and FGM stats are reversed)	.04	.02
❑	304	Martin Bayless RC	.04	.02
❑	305	Marion Butts	.10	.05
❑	306	Gill Byrd	.04	.02
❑	307	Arthur Cox	.04	.02
❑	308	Burt Grossman	.04	.02
❑	309	Jamie Holland	.04	.02
❑	310	Jim McMahon	.10	.05
❑	311	Anthony Miller	.25	.11
❑	312	Leslie O'Neal	.10	.05
❑	313	Billy Ray Smith	.04	.02
❑	314	Tim Spencer	.04	.02
❑	315	Broderick Thompson RC	.04	.02
❑	316	Lee Williams	.04	.02
❑	317	Bruce Armstrong	.04	.02
❑	318	Tim Goad RC	.04	.02
❑	319	Steve Grogan	.10	.05
❑	320	Roland James	.04	.02
❑	321	Cedric Jones	.04	.02
❑	322	Fred Marion	.04	.02
❑	323	Stanley Morgan	.04	.02
❑	324	Robert Perryman (Back says Robert, front says Bob)	.04	.02
❑	325	Johnny Rembert	.04	.02
❑	326	Ed Reynolds	.04	.02
❑	327	Kenneth Sims	.04	.02
❑	328	John Stephens	.04	.02
❑	329	Danny Villa RC	.04	.02
❑	330	Robert Awalt	.04	.02
❑	331	Anthony Bell	.04	.02
❑	332	Rich Camarillo	.04	.02
❑	333	Earl Ferrell	.04	.02
❑	334	Roy Green	.10	.05
❑	335	Gary Hogeboom	.04	.02
❑	336	Cedric Mack	.04	.02
❑	337	Freddie Joe Nunn	.04	.02
❑	338	Luis Sharpe	.04	.02
❑	339	Vai Sikahema	.04	.02
❑	340	J.T. Smith	.04	.02
❑	341	Tom Tupa RC	.04	.02
❑	342	Percy Snow RC	.04	.02
❑	343	Mark Carrier WR	.25	.11
❑	344	Randy Grimes	.04	.02
❑	345	Paul Gruber	.04	.02
❑	346	Ron Hall	.04	.02
❑	347	Jeff George RC	1.00	.45
❑	348	Bruce Hill UER (Photo on back is actually Jerry Bell)	.04	.02
❑	349	William Howard UER (Yards rec. says 284, should be 285)	.04	.02
❑	350	Donald Igwebuike	.04	.02
❑	351	Chris Mohr RC	.04	.02
❑	352	Winston Moss RC	.04	.02
❑	353	Ricky Reynolds	.04	.02
❑	354	Mark Robinson	.04	.02
❑	355	Lars Tate	.04	.02

Card	MINT	NRMT
❑ 356 Vinny Testaverde	.10	.05
❑ 357 Broderick Thomas	.04	.02
❑ 358 Troy Benson	.04	.02
❑ 359 Jeff Criswell RC	.04	.02
❑ 360 Tony Eason	.04	.02
❑ 361 James Hasty	.04	.02
❑ 362 Johnny Hector	.04	.02
❑ 363 Bobby Humphery UER (Photo on back is actually Bobby Humphrey)	.04	.02
❑ 364 Pat Leahy	.04	.02
❑ 365 Erik McMillan	.04	.02
❑ 366 Freeman McNeil	.04	.02
❑ 367 Ken O'Brien	.04	.02
❑ 368 Ron Stallworth	.04	.02
❑ 369 Al Toon	.10	.05
❑ 370 Blair Thomas RC	.04	.02
❑ 371 Aundray Bruce	.04	.02
❑ 372 Tony Casillas	.04	.02
❑ 373 Shawn Collins	.04	.02
❑ 374 Evan Cooper	.04	.02
❑ 375 Bill Fralic	.04	.02
❑ 376 Scott Funhage	.04	.02
❑ 377 Mike Gann	.04	.02
❑ 378 Ron Heller	.04	.02
❑ 379 Keith Jones	.04	.02
❑ 380 Mike Kenn	.04	.02
❑ 381 Chris Miller	.25	.11
❑ 382 Deion Sanders UER (Stats say no '89 fumble recoveries, should be 1)	.50	.23
❑ 383 John Settle	.04	.02
❑ 384 Troy Aikman	.75	.35
❑ 385 Bill Bates	.10	.05
❑ 386 Willie Broughton	.04	.02
❑ 387 Steve Folsom	.04	.02
❑ 388 Ray Horton UER (Extra line after career totals)	.04	.02
❑ 389 Michael Irvin	.25	.11
❑ 390 Jim Jeffcoat	.04	.02
❑ 391 Eugene Lockhart	.04	.02
❑ 392 Kelvin Martin RC	.04	.02
❑ 393 Nate Newton	.10	.05
❑ 394 Mike Saxon UER (6 career blocked kicks, stats add up to 4)	.04	.02
❑ 395 Derrick Shepard	.04	.02
❑ 396 Steve Walsh UER (Yards Passing 50.2; Percentage and yards data are switched)	.10	.05
❑ 397 Super Bowl MVP's (Jerry Rice and Joe Montana) HOR	.75	.35
❑ 398 Checklist Card UER (Card 103 not listed)	.04	.02
❑ 399 Checklist Card UER (Bengals misspelled)	.04	.02
❑ 400 Checklist Card	.04	.02

1990 Fleer Update

	MINT	NRMT
COMP.FACT.SET (120)	25.00	11.00

Card	MINT	NRMT
❑ U1 Albert Bentley	.08	.04
❑ U2 Dean Biasucci	.08	.04
❑ U3 Ray Donaldson	.08	.04
❑ U4 Jeff George	4.00	1.80
❑ U5 Ray Agnew RC	.08	.04
❑ U6 Greg McMurtry RC	.08	.04
❑ U7 Chris Singleton RC	.08	.04
❑ U8 James Francis RC	.08	.04
❑ U9 Harold Green RC	.30	.14
❑ U10 John Elliott	.08	.04
❑ U11 Rodney Hampton RC	1.00	.45
❑ U12 Gary Reasons	.08	.04
❑ U13 Lewis Tillman	.08	.04
❑ U14 Everson Walls	.08	.04
❑ U15 David Alexander RC	.08	.04
❑ U16 Jim McMahon	.15	.07
❑ U17 Ben Smith RC	.08	.04
❑ U18 Andre Waters	.08	.04
❑ U19 Calvin Williams RC	.15	.07
❑ U20 Earnest Byner	.08	.04
❑ U21 Andre Collins RC	.08	.04
❑ U22 Russ Grimm	.08	.04
❑ U23 Stan Humphries RC	.30	.14
❑ U24 Martin Mayhew RC	.08	.04
❑ U25 Barry Foster RC	.30	.14
❑ U26 Eric Green RC	.15	.07
❑ U27 Tunch Ilkin	.08	.04
❑ U28 Hardy Nickerson	.15	.07
❑ U29 Jerrol Williams	.08	.04
❑ U30 Mike Baab	.08	.04
❑ U31 Leroy Hoard RC	1.00	.45
❑ U32 Eddie Johnson RC	.08	.04
❑ U33 William Fuller	.15	.07
❑ U34 Haywood Jeffires RC	.30	.14
❑ U35 Don Maggs RC	.08	.04
❑ U36 Allen Pinkett	.08	.04
❑ U37 Robert Awalt	.08	.04
❑ U38 Dennis McKinnon	.08	.04
❑ U39 Ken Norton RC	.15	.07
❑ U40 Emmitt Smith RC	25.00	11.00
❑ U41 Alexander Wright RC	.08	.04
❑ U42 Eric Hill	.08	.04
❑ U43 Johnny Johnson RC	.15	.07
❑ U44 Timm Rosenbach	.08	.04
❑ U45 Anthony Thompson RC	.08	.04
❑ U46 Dexter Carter RC	.08	.04
❑ U47 Eric Davis RC UER (Listed as WR on front, DB on back)	.15	.07
❑ U48 Keith DeLong	.08	.04
❑ U49 Brent Jones RC	.30	.14
❑ U50 Darryl Pollard RC	.08	.04
❑ U51 Steve Wallace RC	.30	.14
❑ U52 Bern Brostek RC	.08	.04
❑ U53 Aaron Cox	.08	.04
❑ U54 Cleveland Gary	.08	.04
❑ U55 Fred Strickland RC	.08	.04
❑ U56 Pat Terrell RC	.08	.04
❑ U57 Steve Broussard RC	.08	.04
❑ U58 Scott Case	.08	.04
❑ U59 Brian Jordan RC	.15	.07
❑ U60 Andre Rison	.30	.14
❑ U61 Kevin Haverdink	.08	.04
❑ U62 Rueben Mayes	.08	.04
❑ U63 Steve Walsh	.15	.07
❑ U64 Greg Bell	.08	.04
❑ U65 Tim Brown	.30	.14
❑ U66 Willie Gault	.15	.07
❑ U67 Vance Mueller RC	.08	.04
❑ U68 Bill Pickel	.08	.04
❑ U69 Aaron Wallace RC	.08	.04
❑ U70 Glenn Parker RC	.08	.04
❑ U71 Frank Reich	.30	.14
❑ U72 Leon Seals RC	.08	.04
❑ U73 Darryl Talley	.08	.04
❑ U74 Brad Baxter RC	.08	.04
❑ U75 Jeff Criswell	.08	.04
❑ U76 Jeff Lageman	.08	.04
❑ U77 Rob Moore RC	4.00	1.80
❑ U78 Blair Thomas	.15	.07
❑ U79 Louis Oliver	.08	.04
❑ U80 Tony Paige	.08	.04
❑ U81 Richmond Webb RC	.08	.04
❑ U82 Robert Blackmon RC	.08	.04
❑ U83 Derrick Fenner RC	.08	.04
❑ U84 Andy Heck	.08	.04
❑ U85 Cortez Kennedy RC	.30	.14
❑ U86 Terry Wooden RC	.08	.04
❑ U87 Jeff Donaldson	.08	.04
❑ U88 Tim Grunhard RC	.08	.04
❑ U89 Emile Harry RC	.08	.04
❑ U90 Dan Saleaumua	.08	.04
❑ U91 Percy Snow	.08	.04
❑ U92 Andre Ware	.30	.14
❑ U93 Darrell Fullington RC	.08	.04
❑ U94 Mike Merriweather	.08	.04
❑ U95 Henry Thomas	.08	.04
❑ U96 Robert Brown	.08	.04
❑ U97 LeRoy Butler RC	.30	.14
❑ U98 Anthony Dilweg	.08	.04
❑ U99 Darrell Thompson RC	.08	.04
❑ U100 Keith Woodside	.08	.04
❑ U101 Gary Plummer	.08	.04
❑ U102 Junior Seau RC	4.00	1.80
❑ U103 Billy Joe Tolliver	.08	.04
❑ U104 Mark Vlasic	.08	.04
❑ U105 Gary Anderson RB	.08	.04
❑ U106 Ian Beckles RC	.08	.04
❑ U107 Reggie Cobb RC	.08	.04
❑ U108 Keith McCants RC	.08	.04
❑ U109 Mark Bortz RC	.08	.04
❑ U110 Maury Buford	.08	.04
❑ U111 Mark Carrier DB RC	.30	.14
❑ U112 Dan Hampton	.15	.07
❑ U113 William Perry	.15	.07
❑ U114 Ron Rivera	.08	.04
❑ U115 Lemuel Stinson	.08	.04
❑ U116 Melvin Bratton RC	.08	.04
❑ U117 Gary Kubiak RC	.08	.04
❑ U118 Alton Montgomery RC	.08	.04
❑ U119 Ricky Nattiel	.08	.04
❑ U120 Checklist 1-132	.08	.04

1991 Fleer

	MINT	NRMT
COMPLETE SET (432)	8.00	3.60

Card	MINT	NRMT
❑ 1 Shane Conlan	.04	.02
❑ 2 John Davis RC	.04	.02
❑ 3 Kent Hull	.04	.02
❑ 4 James Lofton	.10	.05
❑ 5 Keith McKeller	.04	.02
❑ 6 Scott Norwood	.04	.02
❑ 7 Nate Odomes	.04	.02
❑ 8 Andre Reed	.10	.05
❑ 9 Jim Ritcher	.04	.02
❑ 10 Leon Seals	.04	.02
❑ 11 Bruce Smith	.25	.11
❑ 12 Leonard Smith	.04	.02
❑ 13 Steve Tasker	.10	.05
❑ 14 Thurman Thomas	.25	.11
❑ 15 Lewis Billups	.04	.02
❑ 16 James Brooks	.10	.05
❑ 17 Eddie Brown	.04	.02
❑ 18 Carl Carter	.04	.02
❑ 19 Boomer Esiason	.10	.05
❑ 20 James Francis	.04	.02
❑ 21 David Fulcher	.04	.02
❑ 22 Harold Green	.10	.05
❑ 23 Rodney Holman	.04	.02
❑ 24 Bruce Kozerski	.04	.02
❑ 25 Tim McGee	.04	.02
❑ 26 Anthony Munoz	.10	.05
❑ 27 Bruce Reimers	.04	.02
❑ 28 Ickey Woods	.04	.02

❑ 29 Carl Zander .04 .02
❑ 30 Mike Baab .04 .02
❑ 31 Brian Brennan .04 .02
❑ 32 Rob Burnett RC .10 .05
❑ 33 Paul Farren .04 .02
❑ 34 Thane Gash .04 .02
❑ 35 David Grayson .04 .02
❑ 36 Mike Johnson .04 .02
❑ 37 Reggie Langhorne .04 .02
❑ 38 Kevin Mack .04 .02
❑ 39 Eric Metcalf .10 .05
❑ 40 Frank Minnifield .04 .02
❑ 41 Gregg Rakoczy .04 .02
❑ 42 Felix Wright .04 .02
❑ 43 Steve Atwater .04 .02
❑ 44 Michael Brooks .04 .02
❑ 45 John Elway 1.25 .55
❑ 46 Simon Fletcher .04 .02
❑ 47 Bobby Humphrey .04 .02
❑ 48 Mark Jackson .04 .02
❑ 49 Keith Kartz .04 .02
❑ 50 Clarence Kay .04 .02
❑ 51 Greg Kragen .04 .02
❑ 52 Karl Mecklenburg .04 .02
❑ 53 Warren Powers .04 .02
❑ 54 Dennis Smith .04 .02
❑ 55 Jim Szymanski .04 .02
❑ 56 David Treadwell .04 .02
❑ 57 Michael Young .04 .02
❑ 58 Ray Childress .04 .02
❑ 59 Curtis Duncan .04 .02
❑ 60 William Fuller .10 .05
❑ 61 Ernest Givins .10 .05
❑ 62 Drew Hill .04 .02
❑ 63 Haywood Jeffires .10 .05
❑ 64 Richard Johnson .04 .02
❑ 65 Sean Jones .10 .05
❑ 66 Don Maggs .04 .02
❑ 67 Bruce Matthews .10 .05
❑ 68 Johnny Meads .04 .02
❑ 69 Greg Montgomery .04 .02
❑ 70 Warren Moon .25 .11
❑ 71 Mike Munchak .04 .02
❑ 72 Allen Pinkett .04 .02
❑ 73 Lorenzo White .04 .02
❑ 74 Pat Beach .04 .02
❑ 75 Albert Bentley .04 .02
❑ 76 Dean Biasucci .04 .02
❑ 77 Duane Bickett .04 .02
❑ 78 Bill Brooks .04 .02
❑ 79 Sam Clancy .04 .02
❑ 80 Ray Donaldson .04 .02
❑ 81 Jeff George .25 .11
❑ 82 Alan Grant .04 .02
❑ 83 Jessie Hester .04 .02
❑ 84 Jeff Herrod .04 .02
❑ 85 Rohn Stark .04 .02
❑ 86 Jack Trudeau .04 .02
❑ 87 Clarence Verdin .04 .02
❑ 88 John Alt .04 .02
❑ 89 Steve DeBerg .04 .02
❑ 90 Tim Grunhard .04 .02
❑ 91 Dino Hackett .04 .02
❑ 92 Jonathan Hayes .04 .02
❑ 93 Albert Lewis .04 .02
❑ 94 Nick Lowery .04 .02
❑ 95 Bill Maas UER .04 .02
(Back photo actually
David Szott)
❑ 96 Christian Okoye .04 .02
❑ 97 Stephone Paige .04 .02
❑ 98 Kevin Porter .04 .02
❑ 99 David Szott .04 .02
❑ 100 Derrick Thomas .25 .11
❑ 101 Barry Word .04 .02
❑ 102 Marcus Allen .25 .11
❑ 103 Thomas Benson .04 .02
❑ 104 Tim Brown .25 .11
❑ 105 Riki Ellison .04 .02
❑ 106 Mervyn Fernandez .04 .02
❑ 107 Willie Gault .10 .05
❑ 108 Bob Golic .04 .02
❑ 109 Ethan Horton .04 .02
❑ 110 Bo Jackson .30 .14
❑ 111 Howie Long .10 .05
❑ 112 Don Mosebar .04 .02
❑ 113 Jerry Robinson .04 .02
❑ 114 Jay Schroeder .04 .02
❑ 115 Steve Smith .04 .02
❑ 116 Greg Townsend .04 .02
❑ 117 Steve Wisniewski .04 .02
❑ 118 Mark Clayton .10 .05
❑ 119 Mark Duper .10 .05
❑ 120 Ferrell Edmunds .04 .02
❑ 121 Hugh Green .04 .02
❑ 122 David Griggs .04 .02
❑ 123 Jim C. Jensen .04 .02
❑ 124 Dan Marino 1.25 .55
❑ 125 Tim McKyer .04 .02
❑ 126 John Offerdahl .04 .02
❑ 127 Louis Oliver .04 .02
❑ 128 Tony Paige .04 .02
❑ 129 Reggie Roby .04 .02
❑ 130 Keith Sims .04 .02
❑ 131 Sammie Smith .04 .02
❑ 132 Pete Stoyanovich .04 .02
❑ 133 Richmond Webb .04 .02
❑ 134 Bruce Armstrong .04 .02
❑ 135 Vincent Brown .04 .02
❑ 136 Hart Lee Dykes .04 .02
❑ 137 Irving Fryar .10 .05
❑ 138 Tim Goad .04 .02
❑ 139 Tommy Hodson .04 .02
❑ 140 Maurice Hurst .04 .02
❑ 141 Ronnie Lippett .04 .02
❑ 142 Greg McMurtry .04 .02
❑ 143 Ed Reynolds .04 .02
❑ 144 John Stephens .04 .02
❑ 145 Andre Tippett .04 .02
❑ 146 Danny Villa .04 .02
(Old photo wearing
retired number)
❑ 147 Brad Baxter .04 .02
❑ 148 Kyle Clifton .04 .02
❑ 149 Jeff Criswell .04 .02
❑ 150 James Hasty .04 .02
❑ 151 Jeff Lageman .04 .02
❑ 152 Pat Leahy .04 .02
❑ 153 Rob Moore .25 .11
❑ 154 Al Toon .10 .05
❑ 155 Gary Anderson K .04 .02
❑ 156 Bubby Brister .04 .02
❑ 157 Chris Calloway .04 .02
❑ 158 Donald Evans .04 .02
❑ 159 Eric Green .04 .02
❑ 160 Bryan Hinkle .04 .02
❑ 161 Merril Hoge .04 .02
❑ 162 Tunch Ilkin .04 .02
❑ 163 Louis Lipps .04 .02
❑ 164 David Little .04 .02
❑ 165 Mike Mularkey .04 .02
❑ 166 Gerald Williams .04 .02
❑ 167 Warren Williams .04 .02
❑ 168 Rod Woodson .25 .11
❑ 169 Tim Worley .04 .02
❑ 170 Martin Bayless .04 .02
❑ 171 Marion Butts .10 .05
❑ 172 Gill Byrd .04 .02
❑ 173 Frank Cornish .04 .02
❑ 174 Arthur Cox .04 .02
❑ 175 Burt Grossman .04 .02
❑ 176 Anthony Miller .10 .05
❑ 177 Leslie O'Neal .10 .05
❑ 178 Gary Plummer .04 .02
❑ 179 Junior Seau .25 .11
❑ 180 Billy Joe Tolliver .04 .02
❑ 181 Derrick Walker RC .04 .02
❑ 182 Lee Williams .04 .02
❑ 183 Robert Blackmon .04 .02
❑ 184 Brian Blades .10 .05
❑ 185 Grant Feasel .04 .02
❑ 186 Derrick Fenner .04 .02
❑ 187 Andy Heck .04 .02
❑ 188 Norm Johnson .04 .02
❑ 189 Tommy Kane .04 .02
❑ 190 Cortez Kennedy .25 .11
❑ 191 Dave Krieg .10 .05
❑ 192 Travis McNeal .04 .02
❑ 193 Eugene Robinson .04 .02
❑ 194 Chris Warren .25 .11
❑ 195 John L. Williams .04 .02
❑ 196 Steve Broussard .04 .02
❑ 197 Scott Case .04 .02
❑ 198 Shawn Collins .04 .02
❑ 199 Darion Conner UER .04 .02
(Player on back 8
is not Conner 56)
❑ 200 Tory Epps .04 .02
❑ 201 Bill Fralic .04 .02
❑ 202 Michael Haynes .25 .11
❑ 203 Chris Hinton .04 .02
❑ 204 Keith Jones .04 .02
❑ 205 Brian Jordan .10 .05
❑ 206 Mike Kenn .04 .02
❑ 207 Chris Miller .10 .05
❑ 208 Andre Rison .10 .05
❑ 209 Mike Rozier .04 .02
❑ 210 Deion Sanders .40 .18
❑ 211 Gary Wilkins .04 .02
❑ 212 Neal Anderson .10 .05
❑ 213 Trace Armstrong .04 .02
❑ 214 Mark Bortz .04 .02
❑ 215 Kevin Butler .04 .02
❑ 216 Mark Carrier DB .10 .05
❑ 217 Wendell Davis .04 .02
❑ 218 Richard Dent .10 .05
❑ 219 Dennis Gentry .04 .02
❑ 220 Jim Harbaugh .25 .11
❑ 221 Jay Hilgenberg .04 .02
❑ 222 Steve McMichael .10 .05
❑ 223 Ron Morris .04 .02
❑ 224 Brad Muster .04 .02
❑ 225 Mike Singletary .10 .05
❑ 226 James Thornton .04 .02
❑ 227 Tommie Agee .04 .02
❑ 228 Troy Aikman .75 .35
❑ 229 Jack Del Rio .04 .02
❑ 230 Issiac Holt .04 .02
❑ 231 Ray Horton .04 .02
❑ 232 Jim Jeffcoat .04 .02
❑ 233 Eugene Lockhart .04 .02
❑ 234 Kelvin Martin .04 .02
❑ 235 Nate Newton .10 .05
❑ 236 Mike Saxon .04 .02
❑ 237 Emmitt Smith 2.00 .90
❑ 238A Daniel Stubbs .10 .05
(Danny on back)
❑ 238B Danny Stubbs .10 .05
(Daniel on back)
❑ 239 Jim Arnold .04 .02
❑ 240 Jerry Ball .04 .02
❑ 241 Bennie Blades .04 .02
❑ 242 Lomas Brown .04 .02
❑ 243 Robert Clark .04 .02
❑ 244 Mike Cofer .04 .02
❑ 245 Mel Gray .10 .05
❑ 246 Rodney Peete .10 .05
❑ 247 Barry Sanders 1.50 .70
❑ 248 Andre Ware .10 .05
❑ 249 Matt Brock RC .04 .02
❑ 250 Robert Brown .04 .02
❑ 251 Anthony Dilweg .04 .02
❑ 252 Johnny Holland .04 .02
❑ 253 Tim Harris .04 .02
❑ 254 Chris Jacke .04 .02
❑ 255 Perry Kemp .04 .02
❑ 256 Don Majkowski UER .04 .02
(1990 attempts should
be 264, not 265)
❑ 257 Tony Mandarich .04 .02
❑ 258 Mark Murphy .04 .02
❑ 259 Brian Noble .04 .02
❑ 260 Jeff Query .04 .02
❑ 261 Sterling Sharpe .25 .11
❑ 262 Ed West .04 .02
❑ 263 Keith Woodside .04 .02
❑ 264 Flipper Anderson .04 .02
❑ 265 Aaron Cox .04 .02
❑ 266 Henry Ellard .10 .05
❑ 267 Jim Everett .10 .05
❑ 268 Cleveland Gary .04 .02
❑ 269 Kevin Greene .25 .11
❑ 270 Pete Holohan .04 .02
❑ 271 Mike Lansford .04 .02
❑ 272 Duval Love RC .04 .02
❑ 273 Buford McGee .04 .02
❑ 274 Tom Newberry .04 .02
❑ 275 Jackie Slater .04 .02

❑	276 Frank Stams	.04	.02
❑	277 Alfred Anderson	.04	.02
❑	278 Joey Browner	.04	.02
❑	279 Anthony Carter	.10	.05
❑	280 Chris Doleman	.04	.02
❑	281 Rick Fenney	.04	.02
❑	282 Rich Gannon	.25	.11
❑	283 Hassan Jones	.04	.02
❑	284 Steve Jordan	.04	.02
❑	285 Carl Lee	.04	.02
❑	286 Randall McDaniel	.04	.02
❑	287 Keith Millard	.04	.02
❑	288 Herschel Walker	.10	.05
❑	289 Wade Wilson	.10	.05
❑	290 Gary Zimmerman	.04	.02
❑	291 Morten Andersen	.04	.02
❑	292 Jim Dombrowski	.04	.02
❑	293 Gill Fenerty	.04	.02
❑	294 Craig Heyward	.10	.05
❑	295 Dalton Hilliard	.04	.02
❑	296 Rickey Jackson	.04	.02
❑	297 Vaughan Johnson	.04	.02
❑	298 Eric Martin	.04	.02
❑	299 Robert Massey	.04	.02
❑	300 Rueben Mayes	.04	.02
❑	301 Sam Mills	.04	.02
❑	302 Brett Perriman	.25	.11
❑	303 Pat Swilling	.10	.05
❑	304 Steve Walsh	.04	.02
❑	305 Ottis Anderson	.10	.05
❑	306 Matt Bahr	.04	.02
❑	307 Mark Bavaro	.04	.02
❑	308 Maurice Carthon	.04	.02
❑	309 Mark Collins	.04	.02
❑	310 John Elliott	.04	.02
❑	311 Rodney Hampton	.25	.11
❑	312 Jeff Hostetler	.10	.05
❑	313 Erik Howard	.04	.02
❑	314 Pepper Johnson	.04	.02
❑	315 Sean Landeta	.04	.02
❑	316 Dave Meggett	.10	.05
❑	317 Bart Oates	.04	.02
❑	318 Phil Simms	.10	.05
❑	319 Lawrence Taylor	.25	.11
❑	320 Reyna Thompson	.04	.02
❑	321 Everson Walls	.04	.02
❑	322 Eric Allen	.04	.02
❑	323 Fred Barnett	.25	.11
❑	324 Jerome Brown	.04	.02
❑	325 Keith Byars	.04	.02
❑	326 Randall Cunningham	.25	.11
❑	327 Byron Evans	.04	.02
❑	328 Ron Heller	.04	.02
❑	329 Keith Jackson	.10	.05
❑	330 Seth Joyner	.10	.05
❑	331 Heath Sherman	.04	.02
❑	332 Clyde Simmons	.04	.02
❑	333 Ben Smith	.04	.02
❑	334 Anthony Toney	.04	.02
❑	335 Andre Waters	.04	.02
❑	336 Reggie White	.25	.11
❑	337 Calvin Williams	.10	.05
❑	338 Anthony Bell	.04	.02
❑	339 Rich Camarillo	.04	.02
❑	340 Roy Green	.04	.02
❑	341 Tim Jorden RC	.04	.02
❑	342 Cedric Mack	.04	.02
❑	343 Dexter Manley	.04	.02
❑	344 Freddie Joe Nunn	.04	.02
❑	345 Ricky Proehl	.04	.02
❑	346 Tootie Robbins	.04	.02
❑	347 Timm Rosenbach	.04	.02
❑	348 Luis Sharpe	.04	.02
❑	349 Vai Sikahema	.04	.02
❑	350 Anthony Thompson	.04	.02
❑	351 Lonnie Young	.04	.02
❑	352 Dexter Carter	.04	.02
❑	353 Mike Cofer	.04	.02
❑	354 Kevin Fagan	.04	.02
❑	355 Don Griffin	.04	.02
❑	356 Charles Haley UER (Total fumbles should be 6, not 5)	.10	.05
❑	357 Pierce Holt	.04	.02
❑	358 Brent Jones	.25	.11
❑	359 Guy McIntyre	.04	.02
❑	360 Joe Montana	1.25	.55
❑	361 Darryl Pollard	.04	.02
❑	362 Tom Rathman	.04	.02
❑	363 Jerry Rice	.75	.35
❑	364 Bill Romanowski	.04	.02
❑	365 John Taylor	.10	.05
❑	366 Steve Wallace UER (Listed as a DL on front of card)	.10	.05
❑	367 Steve Young	.75	.35
❑	368 Gary Anderson RB	.04	.02
❑	369 Ian Beckles	.04	.02
❑	370 Mark Carrier WR	.25	.11
❑	371 Reggie Cobb	.04	.02
❑	372 Reuben Davis	.04	.02
❑	373 Randy Grimes	.04	.02
❑	374 Wayne Haddix	.04	.02
❑	375 Ron Hall	.04	.02
❑	376 Harry Hamilton	.04	.02
❑	377 Bruce Hill	.04	.02
❑	378 Keith McCants	.04	.02
❑	379 Bruce Perkins	.04	.02
❑	380 Vinny Testaverde UER (Misspelled Vinnie on card front)	.10	.05
❑	381 Broderick Thomas	.04	.02
❑	382 Jeff Bostic	.04	.02
❑	383 Earnest Byner	.04	.02
❑	384 Gary Clark	.25	.11
❑	385 Darryl Grant	.04	.02
❑	386 Darrell Green	.04	.02
❑	387 Stan Humphries	.25	.11
❑	388 Jim Lachey	.04	.02
❑	389 Charles Mann	.04	.02
❑	390 Wilber Marshall	.04	.02
❑	391 Art Monk	.10	.05
❑	392 Gerald Riggs	.04	.02
❑	393 Mark Rypien	.10	.05
❑	394 Ricky Sanders	.04	.02
❑	395 Don Warren	.04	.02
❑	396 Bruce Smith HIT	.10	.05
❑	397 Reggie White HIT	.10	.05
❑	398 Lawrence Taylor HIT	.10	.05
❑	399 David Fulcher HIT	.04	.02
❑	400 Derrick Thomas HIT	.10	.05
❑	401 Mark Carrier DB HIT	.04	.02
❑	402 Mike Singletary HIT	.10	.05
❑	403 Charles Haley HIT	.04	.02
❑	404 Jeff Cross HIT	.04	.02
❑	405 Leslie O'Neal HIT	.10	.05
❑	406 Tim Harris HIT	.04	.02
❑	407 Steve Atwater HIT	.04	.02
❑	408 Joe Montana LL UER (4th on yardage list, not 3rd)	.50	.23
❑	409 Randall Cunningham LL	.10	.05
❑	410 Warren Moon LL	.10	.05
❑	411 Andre Rison LL UER (Card incorrectly numbered as 412 and Michigan State misspelled as Stage)	.10	.05
❑	412 Haywood Jeffires LL (See number 411)	.10	.05
❑	413 Stephone Paige LL	.04	.02
❑	414 Phil Simms LL	.10	.05
❑	415 Barry Sanders LL	.60	.25
❑	416 Bo Jackson LL	.10	.05
❑	417 Thurman Thomas LL	.10	.05
❑	418 Emmitt Smith LL	1.00	.45
❑	419 John L. Williams LL	.04	.02
❑	420 Nick Bell RP RC	.04	.02
❑	421 Eric Bieniemy RP RC	.04	.02
❑	422 Mike Dumas RP RC UER (Returned interception vs. Purdue, not Michigan State)	.04	.02
❑	423 Russell Maryland RP RC	.25	.11
❑	424 Derek Russell RP RC	.04	.02
❑	425 Chris Smith RP RC UER (Bengals misspelled as Bengels)	.04	.02
❑	426 Mike Stonebreaker RP	.04	.02
❑	427 Pat Tyrance RP	.04	.02
❑	428 Kenny Walker RP RC (How Acquired has a different style)	.04	.02
❑	429 Checklist 1-108 UER (David Grayson misspelled as Graysor)	.04	.02
❑	430 Checklist 109-216	.04	.02
❑	431 Checklist 217-324	.04	.02
❑	432 Checklist 325-432	.04	.02

1992 Fleer

		MINT	NRMT
	COMPLETE SET (480)	10.00	4.50
❑	1 Steve Broussard	.04	.02
❑	2 Rick Bryan	.04	.02
❑	3 Scott Case	.04	.02
❑	4 Tory Epps	.04	.02
❑	5 Bill Fralic	.04	.02
❑	6 Moe Gardner	.04	.02
❑	7 Michael Haynes	.10	.05
❑	8 Chris Hinton	.04	.02
❑	9 Brian Jordan	.10	.05
❑	10 Mike Kenn	.04	.02
❑	11 Tim McKyer	.04	.02
❑	12 Chris Miller	.10	.05
❑	13 Erric Pegram	.10	.05
❑	14 Mike Pritchard	.10	.05
❑	15 Andre Rison	.10	.05
❑	16 Jessie Tuggle	.04	.02
❑	17 Carlton Bailey RC	.10	.05
❑	18 Howard Ballard	.04	.02
❑	19 Don Beebe	.04	.02
❑	20 Cornelius Bennett	.10	.05
❑	21 Shane Conlan	.04	.02
❑	22 Kent Hull	.04	.02
❑	23 Mark Kelso	.04	.02
❑	24 James Lofton	.10	.05
❑	25 Keith McKeller	.04	.02
❑	26 Scott Norwood	.04	.02
❑	27 Nate Odomes	.04	.02
❑	28 Frank Reich	.10	.05
❑	29 Jim Ritcher	.04	.02
❑	30 Leon Seals	.04	.02
❑	31 Darryl Talley	.04	.02
❑	32 Steve Tasker	.10	.05
❑	33 Thurman Thomas	.25	.11
❑	34 Will Wolford	.04	.02
❑	35 Neal Anderson	.04	.02
❑	36 Trace Armstrong	.04	.02
❑	37 Mark Carrier DB	.04	.02
❑	38 Richard Dent	.10	.05
❑	39 Shaun Gayle	.04	.02
❑	40 Jim Harbaugh	.25	.11
❑	41 Jay Hilgenberg	.04	.02
❑	42 Darren Lewis	.04	.02
❑	43 Steve McMichael	.10	.05
❑	44 Brad Muster	.04	.02
❑	45 William Perry	.10	.05
❑	46 John Roper	.04	.02
❑	47 Lemuel Stinson	.04	.02
❑	48 Stan Thomas	.04	.02
❑	49 Keith Van Horne	.04	.02
❑	50 Tom Waddle	.04	.02
❑	51 Donnell Woolford	.04	.02
❑	52 Chris Zorich	.10	.05
❑	53 Eddie Brown	.04	.02
❑	54 James Francis	.04	.02
❑	55 David Fulcher	.04	.02
❑	56 David Grant	.04	.02

❑ 57 Harold Green .04 .02
❑ 58 Rodney Holman .04 .02
❑ 59 Lee Johnson .04 .02
❑ 60 Tim Krumrie .04 .02
❑ 61 Anthony Munoz .10 .05
❑ 62 Joe Walter RC .04 .02
❑ 63 Mike Baab .04 .02
❑ 64 Stephen Braggs .04 .02
❑ 65 Richard Brown RC .04 .02
❑ 66 Dan Fike .04 .02
❑ 67 Scott Galbraith RC .04 .02
❑ 68 Randy Hilliard RC .04 .02
❑ 69 Michael Jackson .10 .05
❑ 70 Tony Jones .04 .02
❑ 71 Ed King .04 .02
❑ 72 Kevin Mack .04 .02
❑ 73 Clay Matthews .10 .05
❑ 74 Eric Metcalf .10 .05
❑ 75 Vince Newsome .04 .02
❑ 76 John Rienstra .04 .02
❑ 77 Steve Beuerlein .04 .02
❑ 78 Larry Brown DB .04 .02
❑ 79 Tony Casillas .04 .02
❑ 80 Alvin Harper .10 .05
❑ 81 Issiac Holt .04 .02
❑ 82 Ray Horton .04 .02
❑ 83 Michael Irvin .25 .11
❑ 84 Daryl Johnston .25 .11
❑ 85 Kelvin Martin .04 .02
❑ 86 Nate Newton .10 .05
❑ 87 Ken Norton .25 .11
❑ 88 Jay Novacek .10 .05
❑ 89 Emmitt Smith 1.50 .70
❑ 90 Vinson Smith RC .04 .02
❑ 91 Mark Stepnoski .10 .05
❑ 92 Steve Atwater .04 .02
❑ 93 Mike Croel .04 .02
❑ 94 John Elway 1.25 .55
❑ 95 Simon Fletcher .04 .02
❑ 96 Gaston Green .04 .02
❑ 97 Mark Jackson .04 .02
❑ 98 Keith Kartz .04 .02
❑ 99 Greg Kragen .04 .02
❑ 100 Greg Lewis .04 .02
❑ 101 Karl Mecklenburg .04 .02
❑ 102 Derek Russell .04 .02
❑ 103 Steve Sewell .04 .02
❑ 104 Dennis Smith .04 .02
❑ 105 David Treadwell .04 .02
❑ 106 Kenny Walker .04 .02
❑ 107 Doug Widell .04 .02
❑ 108 Michael Young .04 .02
❑ 109 Jerry Ball .04 .02
❑ 110 Bennie Blades .04 .02
❑ 111 Lomas Brown .04 .02
❑ 112 Scott Conover RC .04 .02
❑ 113 Ray Crockett .04 .02
❑ 114 Mike Farr .04 .02
❑ 115 Mel Gray .10 .05
❑ 116 Willie Green .04 .02
❑ 117 Tracy Hayworth RC .04 .02
❑ 118 Erik Kramer .10 .05
❑ 119 Herman Moore .50 .23
❑ 120 Dan Owens .04 .02
❑ 121 Rodney Peete .10 .05
❑ 122 Brett Perriman .25 .11
❑ 123 Barry Sanders 1.50 .70
❑ 124 Chris Spielman .10 .05
❑ 125 Marc Spindler .04 .02
❑ 126 Tony Bennett .04 .02
❑ 127 Matt Brock .04 .02
❑ 128 LeRoy Butler .04 .02
❑ 129 Johnny Holland .04 .02
❑ 130 Perry Kemp .04 .02
❑ 131 Don Majkowski .04 .02
❑ 132 Mark Murphy .04 .02
❑ 133 Brian Noble .04 .02
❑ 134 Bryce Paup .25 .11
❑ 135 Sterling Sharpe .25 .11
❑ 136 Scott Stephen .04 .02
❑ 137 Darrell Thompson .04 .02
❑ 138 Mike Tomczak .04 .02
❑ 139 Esera Tuaolo .04 .02
❑ 140 Keith Woodside .04 .02
❑ 141 Ray Childress .04 .02
❑ 142 Cris Dishman .04 .02
❑ 143 Curtis Duncan .04 .02
❑ 144 John Flannery .04 .02
❑ 145 William Fuller .10 .05
❑ 146 Ernest Givins .10 .05
❑ 147 Haywood Jeffires .10 .05
❑ 148 Sean Jones .10 .05
❑ 149 Lamar Lathon .04 .02
❑ 150 Bruce Matthews .04 .02
❑ 151 Bubba McDowell .04 .02
❑ 152 Johnny Meads .04 .02
❑ 153 Warren Moon .25 .11
❑ 154 Mike Munchak .04 .02
❑ 155 Al Smith .04 .02
❑ 156 Doug Smith .04 .02
❑ 157 Lorenzo White .04 .02
❑ 158 Michael Ball .04 .02
❑ 159 Chip Banks .04 .02
❑ 160 Duane Bickett .04 .02
❑ 161 Bill Brooks .04 .02
❑ 162 Ken Clark .04 .02
❑ 163 Jon Hand .04 .02
❑ 164 Jeff Herrod .04 .02
❑ 165 Jessie Hester .04 .02
❑ 166 Scott Radecic .04 .02
❑ 167 Rohn Stark .04 .02
❑ 168 Clarence Verdin .04 .02
❑ 169 John Alt .04 .02
❑ 170 Tim Barnett .04 .02
❑ 171 Tim Grunhard .04 .02
❑ 172 Dino Hackett .04 .02
❑ 173 Jonathan Hayes .04 .02
❑ 174 Bill Maas .04 .02
❑ 175 Chris Martin .04 .02
❑ 176 Christian Okoye .04 .02
❑ 177 Stephone Paige .04 .02
❑ 178 Jayice Pearson RC .04 .02
❑ 179 Kevin Porter .04 .02
❑ 180 Kevin Ross .04 .02
❑ 181 Dan Saleaumua .04 .02
❑ 182 Tracy Simien RC .04 .02
❑ 183 Neil Smith .25 .11
❑ 184 Derrick Thomas .25 .11
❑ 185 Robb Thomas .04 .02
❑ 186 Mark Vlasic .04 .02
❑ 187 Barry Word .04 .02
❑ 188 Marcus Allen .25 .11
❑ 189 Eddie Anderson .04 .02
❑ 190 Nick Bell .04 .02
❑ 191 Tim Brown .25 .11
❑ 192 Scott Davis .04 .02
❑ 193 Riki Ellison .04 .02
❑ 194 Mervyn Fernandez .04 .02
❑ 195 Willie Gault .10 .05
❑ 196 Jeff Gossett .04 .02
❑ 197 Ethan Horton .04 .02
❑ 198 Jeff Jaeger .04 .02
❑ 199 Howie Long .10 .05
❑ 200 Ronnie Lott .10 .05
❑ 201 Todd Marinovich .04 .02
❑ 202 Don Mosebar .04 .02
❑ 203 Jay Schroeder .04 .02
❑ 204 Greg Townsend .04 .02
❑ 205 Lionel Washington .04 .02
❑ 206 Steve Wisniewski .04 .02
❑ 207 Flipper Anderson .04 .02
❑ 208 Bern Brostek .04 .02
❑ 209 Robert Delpino .04 .02
❑ 210 Henry Ellard .10 .05
❑ 211 Jim Everett .10 .05
❑ 212 Cleveland Gary .04 .02
❑ 213 Kevin Greene .25 .11
❑ 214 Darryl Henley .04 .02
❑ 215 Damone Johnson .04 .02
❑ 216 Larry Kelm .04 .02
❑ 217 Todd Lyght .04 .02
❑ 218 Jackie Slater .04 .02
❑ 219 Michael Stewart .04 .02
❑ 220 Pat Terrell UER .04 .02
(1991 stats have 74
tackles, text has 64)
❑ 221 Robert Young .04 .02
❑ 222 Mark Clayton .10 .05
❑ 223 Bryan Cox .10 .05
❑ 224 Aaron Craver .04 .02
❑ 225 Jeff Cross .04 .02
❑ 226 Mark Duper .04 .02
❑ 227 Harry Galbreath .04 .02
❑ 228 David Griggs .04 .02
❑ 229 Mark Higgs .04 .02
❑ 230 Vestee Jackson .04 .02
❑ 231 John Offerdahl .04 .02
❑ 232 Louis Oliver .04 .02
❑ 233 Tony Paige .04 .02
❑ 234 Reggie Roby .04 .02
❑ 235 Sammie Smith .04 .02
❑ 236 Pete Stoyanovich .04 .02
❑ 237 Richmond Webb .04 .02
❑ 238 Terry Allen .25 .11
❑ 239 Ray Berry .04 .02
❑ 240 Joey Browner .04 .02
❑ 241 Anthony Carter .10 .05
❑ 242 Cris Carter .50 .23
❑ 243 Chris Doleman .04 .02
❑ 244 Rich Gannon .25 .11
❑ 245 Tim Irwin .04 .02
❑ 246 Steve Jordan .04 .02
❑ 247 Carl Lee .04 .02
❑ 248 Randall McDaniel .04 .02
❑ 249 Mike Merriweather .04 .02
❑ 250 Harry Newsome .04 .02
❑ 251 John Randle .10 .05
❑ 252 Henry Thomas .04 .02
❑ 253 Herschel Walker .10 .05
❑ 254 Ray Agnew .04 .02
❑ 255 Bruce Armstrong .04 .02
❑ 256 Vincent Brown .04 .02
❑ 257 Marv Cook .04 .02
❑ 258 Irving Fryar .10 .05
❑ 259 Pat Harlow .04 .02
❑ 260 Tommy Hodson .04 .02
❑ 261 Maurice Hurst .04 .02
❑ 262 Ronnie Lippett .04 .02
❑ 263 Eugene Lockhart .04 .02
❑ 264 Greg McMurtry .04 .02
❑ 265 Hugh Millen .04 .02
❑ 266 Leonard Russell .10 .05
❑ 267 Andre Tippett .04 .02
❑ 268 Brent Williams .04 .02
❑ 269 Morten Andersen .04 .02
❑ 270 Gene Atkins .04 .02
❑ 271 Wesley Carroll .04 .02
❑ 272 Jim Dombrowski .04 .02
❑ 273 Quinn Early .10 .05
❑ 274 Gill Fenerty .04 .02
❑ 275 Bobby Hebert .04 .02
❑ 276 Joel Hilgenberg .04 .02
❑ 277 Rickey Jackson .04 .02
❑ 278 Vaughan Johnson .04 .02
❑ 279 Eric Martin .04 .02
❑ 280 Brett Maxie .04 .02
❑ 281 Fred McAfee RC .04 .02
❑ 282 Sam Mills .04 .02
❑ 283 Pat Swilling .10 .05
❑ 284 Floyd Turner .04 .02
❑ 285 Steve Walsh .04 .02
❑ 286 Frank Warren .04 .02
❑ 287 Stephen Baker .04 .02
❑ 288 Maurice Carthon .04 .02
❑ 289 Mark Collins .04 .02
❑ 290 John Elliott .04 .02
❑ 291 Myron Guyton .04 .02
❑ 292 Rodney Hampton .25 .11
❑ 293 Jeff Hostetler .10 .05
❑ 294 Mark Ingram .04 .02
❑ 295 Pepper Johnson .04 .02
❑ 296 Sean Landeta .04 .02
❑ 297 Leonard Marshall .04 .02
❑ 298 Dave Meggett .10 .05
❑ 299 Bart Oates .04 .02
❑ 300 Phil Simms .10 .05
❑ 301 Reyna Thompson .04 .02
❑ 302 Lewis Tillman .04 .02
❑ 303 Brad Baxter .04 .02
❑ 304 Kyle Clifton .04 .02
❑ 305 James Hasty .04 .02
❑ 306 Joe Kelly .04 .02
❑ 307 Jeff Lageman .04 .02
❑ 308 Mo Lewis .04 .02
❑ 309 Erik McMillan .04 .02
❑ 310 Rob Moore .10 .05
❑ 311 Tony Stargell .04 .02
❑ 312 Jim Sweeney .04 .02

No.	Player	MINT	NRMT
313	Marvin Washington	.04	.02
314	Lonnie Young	.04	.02
315	Eric Allen	.04	.02
316	Fred Barnett	.25	.11
317	Jerome Brown	.04	.02
318	Keith Byars	.04	.02
319	Wes Hopkins	.04	.02
320	Keith Jackson	.10	.05
321	James Joseph	.04	.02
322	Seth Joyner	.10	.05
323	Jeff Kemp	.04	.02
324	Roger Ruzek	.04	.02
325	Clyde Simmons	.04	.02
326	William Thomas	.04	.02
327	Reggie White	.25	.11
328	Calvin Williams	.10	.05
329	Rich Camarillo	.04	.02
330	Ken Harvey	.04	.02
331	Eric Hill	.04	.02
332	Johnny Johnson	.04	.02
333	Ernie Jones	.04	.02
334	Tim Jorden	.04	.02
335	Tim McDonald	.04	.02
336	Freddie Joe Nunn	.04	.02
337	Luis Sharpe	.04	.02
338	Eric Swann	.10	.05
339	Aeneas Williams	.10	.05
340	Gary Anderson K	.04	.02
341	Bubby Brister	.04	.02
342	Adrian Cooper	.04	.02
343	Barry Foster	.10	.05
344	Eric Green	.04	.02
345	Bryan Hinkle	.04	.02
346	Tunch Ilkin	.04	.02
347	Carnell Lake	.04	.02
348	Louis Lipps	.04	.02
349	David Little	.04	.02
350	Greg Lloyd	.25	.11
351	Neil O'Donnell	.25	.11
352	Dwight Stone	.04	.02
353	Rod Woodson	.25	.11
354	Rod Bernstine	.04	.02
355	Eric Bieniemy	.04	.02
356	Marion Butts	.04	.02
357	Gill Byrd	.04	.02
358	John Friesz	.10	.05
359	Burt Grossman	.04	.02
360	Courtney Hall	.04	.02
361	Ronnie Harmon	.04	.02
362	Shawn Jefferson	.04	.02
363	Nate Lewis	.04	.02
364	Craig McEwen RC	.04	.02
365	Eric Moten	.04	.02
366	Joe Phillips	.04	.02
367	Gary Plummer	.04	.02
368	Henry Rolling	.04	.02
369	Broderick Thompson	.04	.02
370	Harris Barton	.04	.02
371	Steve Bono RC	.25	.11
372	Todd Bowles	.04	.02
373	Dexter Carter	.04	.02
374	Michael Carter	.04	.02
375	Mike Cofer	.04	.02
376	Keith DeLong	.04	.02
377	Charles Haley	.10	.05
378	Merton Hanks	.10	.05
379	Tim Harris	.04	.02
380	Brent Jones	.10	.05
381	Guy McIntyre	.04	.02
382	Tom Rathman	.04	.02
383	Bill Romanowski	.04	.02
384	Jesse Sapolu	.04	.02
385	John Taylor	.10	.05
386	Steve Young	.60	.25
387	Robert Blackmon	.04	.02
388	Brian Blades	.10	.05
389	Jacob Green	.04	.02
390	Dwayne Harper	.04	.02
391	Andy Heck	.04	.02
392	Tommy Kane	.04	.02
393	John Kasay	.04	.02
394	Cortez Kennedy	.10	.05
395	Bryan Millard	.04	.02
396	Rufus Porter	.04	.02
397	Eugene Robinson	.04	.02
398	John L. Williams	.04	.02
399	Terry Wooden	.04	.02
400	Gary Anderson RB	.04	.02
401	Ian Beckles	.04	.02
402	Mark Carrier WR	.10	.05
403	Reggie Cobb	.04	.02
404	Lawrence Dawsey	.10	.05
405	Ron Hall	.04	.02
406	Keith McCants	.04	.02
407	Charles McRae	.04	.02
408	Tim Newton	.04	.02
409	Jesse Solomon	.04	.02
410	Vinny Testaverde	.10	.05
411	Broderick Thomas	.04	.02
412	Robert Wilson	.04	.02
413	Jeff Bostic	.04	.02
414	Earnest Byner	.04	.02
415	Gary Clark	.25	.11
416	Andre Collins	.04	.02
417	Brad Edwards	.04	.02
418	Kurt Gouveia	.04	.02
419	Darrell Green	.04	.02
420	Joe Jacoby	.04	.02
421	Jim Lachey	.04	.02
422	Chip Lohmiller	.04	.02
423	Charles Mann	.04	.02
424	Wilber Marshall	.04	.02
425	Ron Middleton RC	.04	.02
426	Brian Mitchell	.10	.05
427	Art Monk UER (Born in 1967, should say 1957)	.10	.05
428	Mark Rypien	.04	.02
429	Ricky Sanders	.04	.02
430	Mark Schlereth RC	.04	.02
431	Fred Stokes	.04	.02
432	Edgar Bennett RC	.25	.11
433	Brian Bollinger RC	.04	.02
434	Joe Bowden RC	.04	.02
435	Terrell Buckley RC	.04	.02
436	Willie Clay RC	.04	.02
437	Steve Gordon RC	.04	.02
438	Keith Hamilton RC	.10	.05
439	Carlos Huerta	.04	.02
440	Matt LaBounty RC	.04	.02
441	Amp Lee RC	.04	.02
442	Ricardo McDonald RC	.04	.02
443	Chris Mims RC	.10	.05
444	Michael Mooney RC	.04	.02
445	Patrick Rowe RC	.04	.02
446	Leon Searcy RC	.10	.05
447	Siran Stacy RC	.04	.02
448	Kevin Turner RC	.04	.02
449	Tommy Vardell RC	.10	.05
450	Bob Whitfield RC	.04	.02
451	Darryl Williams RC	.04	.02
452	Thurman Thomas LL	.10	.05
453	Emmitt Smith LL UER (Thr at start of second paragraph should be the)	.75	.35
454	Haywood Jeffires LL	.04	.02
455	Michael Irvin LL	.10	.05
456	Mark Clayton LL	.04	.02
457	Barry Sanders LL	.60	.25
458	Pete Stoyanovich LL	.04	.02
459	Chip Lohmiller LL	.04	.02
460	William Fuller LL	.04	.02
461	Pat Swilling LL	.04	.02
462	Ronnie Lott LL	.04	.02
463	Ray Crockett LL	.04	.02
464	Tim McKyer LL	.04	.02
465	Aeneas Williams LL	.04	.02
466	Rod Woodson LL	.10	.05
467	Mel Gray LL	.04	.02
468	Nate Lewis LL	.04	.02
469	Steve Young LL	.30	.14
470	Reggie Roby LL	.04	.02
471	John Elway PV	.60	.25
472	Ronnie Lott PV	.04	.02
473	Art Monk PV UER (Born in 1967, should say 1957)	.04	.02
474	Warren Moon PV	.10	.05
475	Emmitt Smith PV	.75	.35
476	Thurman Thomas PV	.10	.05
477	Checklist 1-120	.04	.02
478	Checklist 121-240	.04	.02
479	Checklist 241-360	.04	.02
480	Checklist 361-480	.04	.02

1993 Fleer

	MINT	NRMT
COMPLETE SET (500)	20.00	9.00

No.	Player	MINT	NRMT
1	Dan Saleaumua	.05	.02
2	Bryan Cox	.05	.02
3	Dermontti Dawson	.05	.02
4	Michael Jackson	.10	.05
5	Calvin Williams	.10	.05
6	Terry McDaniel	.05	.02
7	Jack Del Rio	.05	.02
8	Steve Atwater	.05	.02
9	Ernie Jones	.05	.02
10	Brad Muster (Signed with New Orleans Saints)	.05	.02
11	Harold Green	.05	.02
12	Eric Bieniemy	.05	.02
13	Eric Dorsey	.05	.02
14	Fred Barnett	.10	.05
15	Cleveland Gary	.05	.02
16	Darion Conner	.05	.02
17	Jerry Ball (Traded to Cleveland Browns)	.05	.02
18	Tony Casillas	.05	.02
19	Brian Blades	.10	.05
20	Tony Bennett	.05	.02
21	Reggie Cobb	.05	.02
22	Kurt Gouveia	.05	.02
23	Greg McMurtry	.05	.02
24	Kyle Clifton	.05	.02
25	Trace Armstrong	.05	.02
26	Terry Allen	.25	.11
27	Steve Bono	.25	.11
28	Barry Word	.05	.02
29	Mark Duper	.05	.02
30	Nate Newton	.10	.05
31	Will Wolford (Signed with Indianapolis Colts)	.05	.02
32	Curtis Duncan	.05	.02
33	Nick Bell	.05	.02
34	Don Beebe	.05	.02
35	Mike Croel	.05	.02
36	Rich Camarillo	.05	.02
37	Wade Wilson (Signed with New Orleans Saints)	.05	.02
38	John Taylor	.10	.05
39	Marion Butts	.05	.02
40	Rodney Hampton	.25	.11
41	Seth Joyner	.05	.02
42	Wilber Marshall	.05	.02
43	Bobby Hebert (Signed with Atlanta Falcons)	.05	.02
44	Bennie Blades	.05	.02
45	Thomas Everett	.05	.02
46	Ricky Sanders	.05	.02
47	Matt Brock	.05	.02
48	Lawrence Dawsey	.05	.02
49	Brad Edwards	.05	.02
50	Vincent Brown	.05	.02

	No.	Card		
❑	51	Jeff Lageman	.05	.02
❑	52	Mark Carrier DB	.05	.02
❑	53	Cris Carter	.50	.23
❑	54	Brent Jones	.10	.05
❑	55	Barry Foster	.10	.05
❑	56	Derrick Thomas	.25	.11
❑	57	Scott Zolak	.05	.02
❑	58	Mark Stepnoski	.05	.02
❑	59	Eric Metcalf	.10	.05
❑	60	Al Smith	.05	.02
❑	61	Ronnie Harmon	.05	.02
❑	62	Cornelius Bennett	.10	.05
❑	63	Karl Mecklenburg	.05	.02
❑	64	Chris Chandler	.10	.05
❑	65	Toi Cook	.05	.02
❑	66	Tim Krumrie	.05	.02
❑	67	Gill Byrd	.05	.02
❑	68	Mark Jackson	.05	.02
		(Signed with		
		New York Giants)		
❑	69	Tim Harris	.05	.02
		(Signed with		
		Philadelphia Eagles)		
❑	70	Shane Conlan	.05	.02
		(Signed with		
		Los Angeles Rams)		
❑	71	Moe Gardner	.05	.02
❑	72	Lomas Brown	.05	.02
❑	73	Charles Haley	.10	.05
❑	74	Mark Rypien	.05	.02
❑	75	LeRoy Butler	.05	.02
❑	76	Steve DeBerg	.05	.02
❑	77	Darrell Green	.05	.02
❑	78	Marv Cook	.05	.02
❑	79	Chris Burkett	.05	.02
❑	80	Richard Dent	.10	.05
❑	81	Roger Craig	.10	.05
❑	82	Amp Lee	.05	.02
❑	83	Eric Green	.05	.02
❑	84	Willie Davis	.25	.11
❑	85	Mark Higgs	.05	.02
❑	86	Carlton Haselrig	.05	.02
❑	87	Tommy Vardell	.05	.02
❑	88	Haywood Jeffires	.10	.05
❑	89	Tim Brown	.25	.11
❑	90	Randall McDaniel	.05	.02
❑	91	John Elway	1.50	.70
❑	92	Ken Harvey	.05	.02
❑	93	Joel Hilgenberg	.05	.02
❑	94	Steve Wallace	.05	.02
❑	95	Stan Humphries	.25	.11
❑	96	Greg Jackson	.05	.02
❑	97	Clyde Simmons	.05	.02
❑	98	Jim Everett	.10	.05
❑	99	Michael Haynes	.10	.05
❑	100	Mel Gray	.10	.05
❑	101	Alvin Harper	.10	.05
❑	102	Art Monk	.10	.05
❑	103	Brett Favre	2.00	.90
❑	104	Keith McCants	.05	.02
❑	105	Charles Mann	.05	.02
❑	106	Leonard Russell	.10	.05
❑	107	Mo Lewis	.05	.02
❑	108	Shaun Gayle	.05	.02
❑	109	Chris Doleman	.05	.02
❑	110	Tim McDonald	.05	.02
		(Signed with		
		San Francisco 49ers)		
❑	111	Louis Oliver	.05	.02
❑	112	Greg Lloyd	.25	.11
❑	113	Chip Banks	.05	.02
❑	114	Sean Jones	.05	.02
❑	115	Ethan Horton	.05	.02
❑	116	Kenneth Davis	.05	.02
❑	117	Simon Fletcher	.05	.02
❑	118	Johnny Johnson	.05	.02
		(Traded to		
		New York Jets)		
❑	119	Vaughan Johnson	.05	.02
❑	120	Derrick Fenner	.05	.02
❑	121	Nate Lewis	.05	.02
❑	122	Pepper Johnson	.05	.02
❑	123	Heath Sherman	.05	.02
❑	124	Darryl Henley	.05	.02
❑	125	Pierce Holt	.05	.02
		(Signed with		
		Atlanta Falcons)		
❑	126	Herman Moore	.50	.23
❑	127	Michael Irvin	.25	.11
❑	128	Tommy Kane	.05	.02
❑	129	Jackie Harris	.05	.02
❑	130	Hardy Nickerson	.10	.05
		(Signed with		
		Tampa Bay Buccaneers)		
❑	131	Chip Lohmiller	.05	.02
❑	132	Andre Tippett	.05	.02
❑	133	Leonard Marshall	.05	.02
		(Signed with		
		New York Jets)		
❑	134	Craig Heyward	.10	.05
		(Signed with		
		Chicago Bears)		
❑	135	Anthony Carter	.10	.05
❑	136	Tom Rathman	.05	.02
❑	137	Lorenzo White	.05	.02
❑	138	Nick Lowery	.05	.02
❑	139	John Offerdahl	.05	.02
❑	140	Neil O'Donnell	.25	.11
❑	141	Clarence Verdin	.05	.02
❑	142	Ernest Givins	.10	.05
❑	143	Todd Marinovich	.05	.02
❑	144	Jeff Wright	.05	.02
❑	145	Michael Brooks	.05	.02
❑	146	Freddie Joe Nunn	.05	.02
❑	147	William Perry	.10	.05
❑	148	Daniel Stubbs	.05	.02
❑	149	Morten Andersen	.05	.02
❑	150	Dave Meggett	.05	.02
❑	151	Andre Waters	.05	.02
❑	152	Todd Lyght	.05	.02
❑	153	Chris Miller	.10	.05
❑	154	Rodney Peete	.05	.02
❑	155	Jim Jeffcoat	.05	.02
❑	156	Cortez Kennedy	.10	.05
❑	157	Johnny Holland	.05	.02
❑	158	Ricky Reynolds	.05	.02
❑	159	Kevin Greene	.25	.11
		(Signed with		
		Pittsburgh Steelers)		
❑	160	Jeff Herrod	.05	.02
❑	161	Bruce Matthews	.05	.02
❑	162	Anthony Smith	.05	.02
❑	163	Henry Jones	.05	.02
❑	164	Rob Burnett	.05	.02
❑	165	Eric Swann	.10	.05
❑	166	Tom Waddle	.05	.02
❑	167	Alfred Williams	.05	.02
❑	168	Darren Carrington RC	.05	.02
❑	169	Mike Sherrard	.05	.02
		(Signed with		
		New York Giants)		
❑	170	Frank Reich	.10	.05
❑	171	Anthony Newman RC	.05	.02
❑	172	Mike Pritchard	.10	.05
❑	173	Andre Ware	.05	.02
❑	174	Daryl Johnston	.25	.11
❑	175	Rufus Porter	.05	.02
❑	176	Reggie White	.25	.11
		(Signed with		
		Green Bay Packers)		
❑	177	Charles Mincy RC	.05	.02
❑	178	Pete Stoyanovich	.05	.02
❑	179	Rod Woodson	.25	.11
❑	180	Anthony Johnson	.10	.05
❑	181	Cody Carlson	.05	.02
❑	182	Gaston Green	.05	.02
		(Traded to		
		Los Angeles Raiders)		
❑	183	Audray McMillian	.05	.02
❑	184	Mike Johnson	.05	.02
❑	185	Aeneas Williams	.05	.02
❑	186	Jarrod Bunch	.05	.02
❑	187	Dennis Smith	.05	.02
❑	188	Quinn Early	.10	.05
❑	189	James Hasty	.05	.02
❑	190	Darryl Talley	.05	.02
❑	191	Jon Vaughn	.05	.02
❑	192	Andre Rison	.10	.05
❑	193	Kelvin Pritchett	.05	.02
❑	194	Ken Norton Jr.	.10	.05
❑	195	Chris Warren	.10	.05
❑	196	Sterling Sharpe	.25	.11
❑	197	Christian Okoye	.05	.02
❑	198	Richmond Webb	.05	.02
❑	199	James Francis	.05	.02
❑	200	Reggie Langhorne	.05	.02
❑	201	J.J. Birden	.05	.02
❑	202	Aaron Wallace	.05	.02
❑	203	Henry Thomas	.05	.02
❑	204	Clay Matthews	.10	.05
❑	205	Robert Massey	.05	.02
❑	206	Donnell Woolford	.05	.02
❑	207	Ricky Watters	.25	.11
❑	208	Wayne Martin	.05	.02
❑	209	Rob Moore	.10	.05
❑	210	Steve Tasker	.10	.05
❑	211	Jackie Slater	.05	.02
❑	212	Steve Young	.75	.35
❑	213	Barry Sanders	1.50	.70
❑	214	Jay Novacek	.10	.05
❑	215	Eugene Robinson	.05	.02
❑	216	Duane Bickett	.05	.02
❑	217	Broderick Thomas	.05	.02
❑	218	David Fulcher	.05	.02
❑	219	Rohn Stark	.05	.02
❑	220	Warren Moon	.25	.11
❑	221	Steve Wisniewski	.05	.02
❑	222	Nate Odomes	.05	.02
❑	223	Shannon Sharpe	.25	.11
❑	224	Byron Evans	.05	.02
❑	225	Mark Collins	.05	.02
❑	226	Rod Bernstine	.05	.02
		(Signed with		
		Denver Broncos)		
❑	227	Sam Mills	.05	.02
❑	228	Marvin Washington	.05	.02
❑	229	Thurman Thomas	.25	.11
❑	230	Brent Williams	.05	.02
❑	231	Jessie Tuggle	.05	.02
❑	232	Chris Spielman	.10	.05
❑	233	Emmitt Smith	1.50	.70
❑	234	John L. Williams	.05	.02
❑	235	Jeff Cross	.05	.02
❑	236	Chris Doleman AW	.05	.02
❑	237	John Elway AW	.75	.35
❑	238	Barry Foster AW	.05	.02
❑	239	Cortez Kennedy AW	.05	.02
❑	240	Steve Young AW	.40	.18
❑	241	Barry Foster LL	.05	.02
❑	242	Warren Moon LL	.05	.02
❑	243	Sterling Sharpe LL	.05	.02
❑	244	Emmitt Smith LL	.75	.35
❑	245	Thurman Thomas LL	.10	.05
❑	246	Michael Irvin PV	.10	.05
❑	247	Steve Young PV	.40	.18
❑	248	Barry Foster PV	.05	.02
❑	249	Checklist	.05	.02
		Teams Atlanta		
		through Detroit		
❑	250	Checklist	.05	.02
		Teams Detroit		
		through Miami		
❑	251	Checklist	.05	.02
		Teams Minnesota		
		through Pittsburgh		
❑	252	Checklist	.05	.02
		Teams Pittsburgh		
		through Washington		
		and Specials		
❑	253	Troy Aikman AW	.40	.18
❑	254	Jason Hanson AW	.05	.02
❑	255	Carl Pickens AW	.25	.11
❑	256	Santana Dotson AW	.05	.02
❑	257	Dale Carter AW	.05	.02
❑	258	Clyde Simmons LL	.05	.02
❑	259	Audray McMillian LL	.05	.02
❑	260	Henry Jones LL	.05	.02
❑	261	Deion Sanders LL	.25	.11
❑	262	Haywood Jeffires LL	.05	.02
❑	263	Deion Sanders PV	.25	.11
❑	264	Andre Reed PV	.10	.05
❑	265	Vince Workman	.05	.02
		(Signed with		
		Tampa Bay Buccaneers)		
❑	266	Robert Brown	.05	.02
❑	267	Ray Agnew	.05	.02
❑	268	Ronnie Lott	.10	.05
		(Signed with		

New York Jets)
❑ 269 Wesley Carroll .05 .02
❑ 270 John Randle .10 .05
❑ 271 Rodney Culver .05 .02
❑ 272 David Alexander .05 .02
❑ 273 Troy Aikman .75 .35
❑ 274 Bernie Kosar .10 .05
❑ 275 Scott Case .05 .02
❑ 276 Dan McGwire .05 .02
❑ 277 John Alt .05 .02
❑ 278 Dan Marino 1.50 .70
❑ 279 Santana Dotson .10 .05
❑ 280 Johnny Mitchell .05 .02
❑ 281 Alonzo Spellman .05 .02
❑ 282 Adrian Cooper .05 .02
❑ 283 Gary Clark .10 .05
(Signed with
Phoenix Cardinals)
❑ 284 Vance Johnson .05 .02
❑ 285 Eric Martin .05 .02
❑ 286 Jesse Solomon .05 .02
❑ 287 Carl Banks .05 .02
❑ 288 Harris Barton .05 .02
❑ 289 Jim Harbaugh .25 .11
❑ 290 Bubba McDowell .05 .02
❑ 291 Anthony McDowell RC .05 .02
❑ 292 Terrell Buckley .05 .02
❑ 293 Bruce Armstrong .05 .02
❑ 294 Kurt Barber .05 .02
❑ 295 Reginald Jones .05 .02
❑ 296 Steve Jordan .05 .02
❑ 297 Kerry Cash .05 .02
❑ 298 Ray Crockett .05 .02
❑ 299 Keith Byars .05 .02
❑ 300 Russell Maryland .05 .02
❑ 301 Johnny Bailey .05 .02
❑ 302 Vinnie Clark .05 .02
(Traded to
Atlanta Falcons)
❑ 303 Terry Wooden .05 .02
❑ 304 Harvey Williams .10 .05
❑ 305 Marco Coleman .05 .02
❑ 306 Mark Wheeler .05 .02
❑ 307 Greg Townsend .05 .02
❑ 308 Tim McGee .05 .02
(Signed with
Washington Redskins)
❑ 309 Donald Evans .05 .02
❑ 310 Randal Hill .05 .02
❑ 311 Kenny Walker .05 .02
❑ 312 Dalton Hilliard .05 .02
❑ 313 Howard Ballard .05 .02
❑ 314 Phil Simms .10 .05
❑ 315 Jerry Rice 1.00 .45
❑ 316 Courtney Hall .05 .02
❑ 317 Darren Lewis .05 .02
❑ 318 Greg Montgomery .05 .02
❑ 319 Paul Gruber .05 .02
❑ 320 George Koonce RC .05 .02
❑ 321 Eugene Chung .05 .02
❑ 322 Mike Brim .05 .02
❑ 323 Patrick Hunter .05 .02
❑ 324 Todd Scott .05 .02
❑ 325 Steve Emtman .05 .02
❑ 326 Andy Harmon RC .10 .05
❑ 327 Larry Brown DB .05 .02
❑ 328 Chuck Cecil .05 .02
(Signed with
Phoenix Cardinals)
❑ 329 Tim McKyer .05 .02
❑ 330 Jeff Bryant .05 .02
❑ 331 Tim Barnett .05 .02
❑ 332 Irving Fryar .10 .05
(Traded to
Miami Dolphins)
❑ 333 Tyji Armstrong .05 .02
❑ 334 Brad Baxter .05 .02
❑ 335 Shane Collins .05 .02
❑ 336 Jeff Graham .10 .05
❑ 337 Ricky Proehl .05 .02
❑ 338 Tommy Maddox .05 .02
❑ 339 Jim Dombrowski .05 .02
❑ 340 Bill Brooks .05 .02
(Signed with
Buffalo Bills)
❑ 341 Dave Brown RC .25 .11
❑ 342 Eric Davis .05 .02
❑ 343 Leslie O'Neal .10 .05
❑ 344 Jim Morrissey .05 .02
❑ 345 Mike Munchak .05 .02
❑ 346 Ron Hall .05 .02
❑ 347 Brian Noble .05 .02
❑ 348 Chris Singleton .05 .02
❑ 349 Boomer Esiason UER .10 .05
(Signed with
New York Jets)
(Card front notes he was
signed instead of traded)
❑ 350 Ray Roberts .05 .02
❑ 351 Gary Zimmerman .05 .02
❑ 352 Quentin Coryatt .10 .05
❑ 353 Willie Green .05 .02
❑ 354 Randall Cunningham .25 .11
❑ 355 Kevin Smith .10 .05
❑ 356 Michael Dean Perry .10 .05
❑ 357 Tim Green .05 .02
❑ 358 Dwayne Harper .05 .02
❑ 359 Dale Carter .05 .02
❑ 360 Keith Jackson .10 .05
❑ 361 Martin Mayhew .05 .02
(Signed with
Tampa Bay Buccaneers)
❑ 362 Brian Washington .05 .02
❑ 363 Earnest Byner .05 .02
❑ 364 D.J. Johnson .05 .02
❑ 365 Timm Rosenbach .05 .02
❑ 366 Doug Widell .05 .02
❑ 367 Vaughn Dunbar .05 .02
❑ 368 Phil Hansen .05 .02
❑ 369 Mike Fox .05 .02
❑ 370 Dana Hall .05 .02
❑ 371 Junior Seau .25 .11
❑ 372 Steve McMichael .10 .05
❑ 373 Eddie Robinson .05 .02
❑ 374 Milton Mack RC .05 .02
❑ 375 Mike Prior .05 .02
(Signed with
Green Bay Packers)
❑ 376 Jerome Henderson .05 .02
❑ 377 Scott Mersereau .05 .02
❑ 378 Neal Anderson .05 .02
❑ 379 Harry Newsome .05 .02
❑ 380 John Baylor .05 .02
❑ 381 Bill Fralic .05 .02
(Signed with
Detroit Lions)
❑ 382 Mark Bavaro .05 .02
(Signed with
Philadelphia Eagles)
❑ 383 Robert Jones .05 .02
❑ 384 Tyronne Stowe .05 .02
❑ 385 Deion Sanders .50 .23
❑ 386 Robert Blackmon .05 .02
❑ 387 Neil Smith .25 .11
❑ 388 Mark Ingram .05 .02
(Signed with
Miami Dolphins)
❑ 389 Mark Carrier WR .10 .05
(Signed with
Cleveland Browns)
❑ 390 Browning Nagle .05 .02
❑ 391 Ricky Ervins .05 .02
❑ 392 Carnell Lake .05 .02
❑ 393 Luis Sharpe .05 .02
❑ 394 Greg Kragen .05 .02
❑ 395 Tommy Barnhardt .05 .02
❑ 396 Mark Kelso .05 .02
❑ 397 Kent Graham RC .25 .11
❑ 398 Bill Romanowski .05 .02
❑ 399 Anthony Miller .10 .05
❑ 400 John Roper .05 .02
❑ 401 Lamar Rogers .05 .02
❑ 402 Troy Auzenne .05 .02
❑ 403 Webster Slaughter .05 .02
❑ 404 David Brandon .05 .02
❑ 405 Chris Hinton .05 .02
❑ 406 Andy Heck .05 .02
❑ 407 Tracy Simien .05 .02
❑ 408 Troy Vincent .05 .02
❑ 409 Jason Hanson .05 .02
❑ 410 Rod Jones RC .05 .02
❑ 411 Al Noga .05 .02
(Signed with
Washington Redskins)
❑ 412 Ernie Mills .05 .02
❑ 413 Willie Gault .05 .02
❑ 414 Henry Ellard .10 .05
❑ 415 Rickey Jackson .05 .02
❑ 416 Bruce Smith .25 .11
❑ 417 Derek Brown TE .05 .02
❑ 418 Kevin Fagan .05 .02
❑ 419 Gary Plummer .05 .02
❑ 420 Wendell Davis .05 .02
❑ 421 Craig Thompson .05 .02
❑ 422 Wes Hopkins .05 .02
❑ 423 Ray Childress .05 .02
❑ 424 Pat Harlow .05 .02
❑ 425 Howie Long .10 .05
❑ 426 Shane Dronett .05 .02
❑ 427 Sean Salisbury .05 .02
❑ 428 Dwight Hollier RC .05 .02
❑ 429 Brett Perriman .25 .11
❑ 430 Donald Hollas RC .05 .02
❑ 431 Jim Lachey .05 .02
❑ 432 Darren Perry .05 .02
❑ 433 Lionel Washington .05 .02
❑ 434 Sean Gilbert .10 .05
❑ 435 Gene Atkins .05 .02
❑ 436 Jim Kelly .25 .11
❑ 437 Ed McCaffrey .10 .05
❑ 438 Don Griffin .05 .02
❑ 439 Jerrol Williams .05 .02
(Signed with
San Diego Chargers)
❑ 440 Bryce Paup .25 .11
❑ 441 Darryl Williams .05 .02
❑ 442 Vai Sikahema .05 .02
❑ 443 Cris Dishman .05 .02
❑ 444 Kevin Mack .05 .02
❑ 445 Winston Moss .05 .02
❑ 446 Tyrone Braxton .05 .02
❑ 447 Mike Merriweather .05 .02
❑ 448 Tony Paige .05 .02
❑ 449 Robert Porcher .05 .02
❑ 450 Ricardo McDonald .05 .02
❑ 451 Danny Copeland .05 .02
❑ 452 Tony Tolbert .05 .02
❑ 453 Eric Dickerson .10 .05
❑ 454 Flipper Anderson .05 .02
❑ 455 Dave Krieg .10 .05
❑ 456 Brad Lamb RC .05 .02
❑ 457 Bart Oates .05 .02
❑ 458 Guy McIntyre .05 .02
❑ 459 Stanley Richard .05 .02
❑ 460 Edgar Bennett .25 .11
❑ 461 Pat Carter .05 .02
❑ 462 Eric Allen .05 .02
❑ 463 William Fuller .05 .02
❑ 464 James Jones .05 .02
❑ 465 Chester McGlockton .10 .05
❑ 466 Charles Dimry .05 .02
❑ 467 Tim Grunhard .05 .02
❑ 468 Jarvis Williams .05 .02
❑ 469 Tracy Scroggins .05 .02
❑ 470 David Klingler .05 .02
❑ 471 Andre Collins .05 .02
❑ 472 Erik Williams .05 .02
❑ 473 Eddie Anderson .05 .02
❑ 474 Marc Boutte .05 .02
❑ 475 Joe Montana 1.50 .70
❑ 476 Andre Reed .10 .05
❑ 477 Lawrence Taylor .25 .11
❑ 478 Jeff George .25 .11
❑ 479 Chris Mims .05 .02
❑ 480 Ken Ruettgers .05 .02
❑ 481 Roman Phifer .05 .02
❑ 482 William Thomas .05 .02
❑ 483 Lamar Lathon .05 .02
❑ 484 Vinny Testaverde .10 .05
(Signed with
Cleveland Browns)
❑ 485 Mike Kenn .05 .02
❑ 486 Greg Lewis .05 .02
❑ 487 Chris Martin .05 .02
(Traded to
Los Angeles Rams)
❑ 488 Maurice Hurst .05 .02
❑ 489 Pat Swilling .05 .02

		MINT	NRMT
	(Traded to Detroit Lions)		
❑ 490	Carl Pickens	.25	.11
❑ 491	Tony Smith	.05	.02
❑ 492	James Washington	.05	.02
❑ 493	Jeff Hostetler	.10	.05
	(Signed with Los Angeles Raiders)		
❑ 494	Jeff Chadwick	.05	.02
❑ 495	Kevin Ross	.05	.02
❑ 496	Jim Ritcher	.05	.02
❑ 497	Jessie Hester	.05	.02
❑ 498	Burt Grossman	.05	.02
❑ 499	Keith Van Horne	.05	.02
❑ 500	Gerald Robinson	.05	.02
❑ P1	Promo Panel	5.00	2.20
	Steve Young Kenny Walker Chip Lohmiller Kevin Greene Craig Heyward Ernie Jones Emmitt Smith Keith Byars		

1994 Fleer

		MINT	NRMT
COMPLETE SET (480)		20.00	9.00
❑ 1	Michael Bankston	.05	.02
❑ 2	Steve Beuerlein	.05	.02
❑ 3	John Booty	.05	.02
❑ 4	Rich Camarillo	.05	.02
❑ 5	Chuck Cecil	.05	.02
❑ 6	Larry Centers	.25	.11
❑ 7	Gary Clark	.10	.05
❑ 8	Garrison Hearst	.25	.11
❑ 9	Eric Hill	.05	.02
❑ 10	Randal Hill	.05	.02
❑ 11	Ronald Moore	.05	.02
❑ 12	Ricky Proehl	.05	.02
❑ 13	Luis Sharpe	.05	.02
❑ 14	Clyde Simmons	.05	.02
❑ 15	Tyronne Stowe	.05	.02
❑ 16	Eric Swann	.10	.05
❑ 17	Aeneas Williams	.05	.02
❑ 18	Darion Conner	.05	.02
❑ 19	Moe Gardner	.05	.02
❑ 20	Jumpy Geathers	.05	.02
❑ 21	Jeff George	.25	.11
❑ 22	Roger Harper	.05	.02
❑ 23	Bobby Hebert	.05	.02
❑ 24	Pierce Holt	.05	.02
❑ 25	D.J. Johnson	.05	.02
❑ 26	Mike Kenn	.05	.02
❑ 27	Lincoln Kennedy	.05	.02
❑ 28	Erric Pegram	.05	.02
❑ 29	Mike Pritchard	.05	.02
❑ 30	Andre Rison	.10	.05
❑ 31	Deion Sanders	.50	.23
❑ 32	Tony Smith	.05	.02
❑ 33	Jesse Solomon	.05	.02
❑ 34	Jessie Tuggle	.05	.02
❑ 35	Don Beebe	.05	.02
❑ 36	Cornelius Bennett	.10	.05
❑ 37	Bill Brooks	.05	.02
❑ 38	Kenneth Davis	.05	.02
❑ 39	John Fina	.05	.02
❑ 40	Phil Hansen	.05	.02
❑ 41	Kent Hull	.05	.02
❑ 42	Henry Jones	.05	.02
❑ 43	Jim Kelly	.25	.11
❑ 44	Pete Metzelaars	.05	.02
❑ 45	Marvcus Patton	.05	.02
❑ 46	Andre Reed	.10	.05
❑ 47	Frank Reich	.10	.05
❑ 48	Bruce Smith	.25	.11
❑ 49	Thomas Smith	.05	.02
❑ 50	Darryl Talley	.05	.02
❑ 51	Steve Tasker	.10	.05
❑ 52	Thurman Thomas	.25	.11
❑ 53	Jeff Wright	.05	.02
❑ 54	Neal Anderson	.05	.02
❑ 55	Trace Armstrong	.05	.02
❑ 56	Troy Auzenne	.05	.02
❑ 57	Joe Cain RC	.05	.02
❑ 58	Mark Carrier DB	.05	.02
❑ 59	Curtis Conway	.25	.11
❑ 60	Richard Dent	.10	.05
❑ 61	Shaun Gayle	.05	.02
❑ 62	Andy Heck	.05	.02
❑ 63	Dante Jones	.05	.02
❑ 64	Erik Kramer	.10	.05
❑ 65	Steve McMichael	.10	.05
❑ 66	Terry Obee	.05	.02
❑ 67	Vinson Smith	.05	.02
❑ 68	Alonzo Spellman	.05	.02
❑ 69	Tom Waddle	.05	.02
❑ 70	Donnell Woolford	.05	.02
❑ 71	Tim Worley	.05	.02
❑ 72	Chris Zorich	.05	.02
❑ 73	Mike Brim	.05	.02
❑ 74	John Copeland	.05	.02
❑ 75	Derrick Fenner	.05	.02
❑ 76	James Francis	.05	.02
❑ 77	Harold Green	.05	.02
❑ 78	Rod Jones	.05	.02
❑ 79	David Klingler	.05	.02
❑ 80	Bruce Kozerski	.05	.02
❑ 81	Tim Krumrie	.05	.02
❑ 82	Ricardo McDonald	.05	.02
❑ 83	Tim McGee	.05	.02
❑ 84	Tony McGee	.05	.02
❑ 85	Louis Oliver	.05	.02
❑ 86	Carl Pickens	.25	.11
❑ 87	Jeff Query	.05	.02
❑ 88	Daniel Stubbs	.05	.02
❑ 89	Steve Tovar	.05	.02
❑ 90	Alfred Williams	.05	.02
❑ 91	Darryl Williams	.05	.02
❑ 92	Rob Burnett	.05	.02
❑ 93	Mark Carrier WR	.10	.05
❑ 94	Leroy Hoard	.05	.02
❑ 95	Michael Jackson	.10	.05
❑ 96	Mike Johnson	.05	.02
❑ 97	Pepper Johnson	.05	.02
❑ 98	Tony Jones	.05	.02
❑ 99	Clay Matthews	.05	.02
❑ 100	Eric Metcalf	.10	.05
❑ 101	Stevon Moore	.05	.02
❑ 102	Michael Dean Perry	.10	.05
❑ 103	Anthony Pleasant	.05	.02
❑ 104	Vinny Testaverde	.10	.05
❑ 105	Eric Turner	.05	.02
❑ 106	Tommy Vardell	.05	.02
❑ 107	Troy Aikman	1.00	.45
❑ 108	Larry Brown DB	.05	.02
❑ 109	Dixon Edwards	.05	.02
❑ 110	Charles Haley	.10	.05
❑ 111	Alvin Harper	.10	.05
❑ 112	Michael Irvin	.25	.11
❑ 113	Jim Jeffcoat	.05	.02
❑ 114	Daryl Johnston	.10	.05
❑ 115	Leon Lett	.05	.02
❑ 116	Russell Maryland	.05	.02
❑ 117	Nate Newton	.05	.02
❑ 118	Ken Norton Jr.	.10	.05
❑ 119	Jay Novacek	.10	.05
❑ 120	Darrin Smith	.05	.02
❑ 121	Emmitt Smith	1.50	.70
❑ 122	Kevin Smith	.05	.02
❑ 123	Mark Stepnoski	.05	.02
❑ 124	Tony Tolbert	.05	.02
❑ 125	Erik Williams	.05	.02
❑ 126	Kevin Williams	.10	.05
❑ 127	Darren Woodson	.10	.05
❑ 128	Steve Atwater	.05	.02
❑ 129	Rod Bernstine	.05	.02
❑ 130	Ray Crockett	.05	.02
❑ 131	Mike Croel	.05	.02
❑ 132	Robert Delpino	.05	.02
❑ 133	Shane Dronett	.05	.02
❑ 134	Jason Elam	.05	.02
❑ 135	John Elway	2.00	.90
❑ 136	Simon Fletcher	.05	.02
❑ 137	Greg Kragen	.05	.02
❑ 138	Karl Mecklenburg	.05	.02
❑ 139	Glyn Milburn	.10	.05
❑ 140	Anthony Miller	.10	.05
❑ 141	Derek Russell	.05	.02
❑ 142	Shannon Sharpe	.10	.05
❑ 143	Dennis Smith	.05	.02
❑ 144	Dan Williams	.05	.02
❑ 145	Gary Zimmerman	.05	.02
❑ 146	Bennie Blades	.05	.02
❑ 147	Lomas Brown	.05	.02
❑ 148	Bill Fralic	.05	.02
❑ 149	Mel Gray	.05	.02
❑ 150	Willie Green	.05	.02
❑ 151	Jason Hanson	.05	.02
❑ 152	Robert Massey	.05	.02
❑ 153	Ryan McNeil	.05	.02
❑ 154	Scott Mitchell	.25	.11
❑ 155	Derrick Moore	.05	.02
❑ 156	Herman Moore	.25	.11
❑ 157	Brett Perriman	.10	.05
❑ 158	Robert Porcher	.05	.02
❑ 159	Kelvin Pritchett	.05	.02
❑ 160	Barry Sanders	2.00	.90
❑ 161	Tracy Scroggins	.05	.02
❑ 162	Chris Spielman	.10	.05
❑ 163	Pat Swilling	.05	.02
❑ 164	Edgar Bennett	.25	.11
❑ 165	Robert Brooks	.25	.11
❑ 166	Terrell Buckley	.05	.02
❑ 167	LeRoy Butler	.05	.02
❑ 168	Brett Favre	2.00	.90
❑ 169	Harry Galbreath	.05	.02
❑ 170	Jackie Harris	.05	.02
❑ 171	Johnny Holland	.05	.02
❑ 172	Chris Jacke	.05	.02
❑ 173	George Koonce	.05	.02
❑ 174	Bryce Paup	.25	.11
❑ 175	Ken Ruettgers	.05	.02
❑ 176	Sterling Sharpe	.10	.05
❑ 177	Wayne Simmons	.05	.02
❑ 178	George Teague	.05	.02
❑ 179	Darrell Thompson	.05	.02
❑ 180	Reggie White	.25	.11
❑ 181	Gary Brown	.05	.02
❑ 182	Cody Carlson	.05	.02
❑ 183	Ray Childress	.05	.02
❑ 184	Cris Dishman	.05	.02
❑ 185	Ernest Givins	.10	.05
❑ 186	Haywood Jeffires	.10	.05
❑ 187	Sean Jones	.05	.02
❑ 188	Lamar Lathon	.05	.02
❑ 189	Bruce Matthews	.05	.02
❑ 190	Bubba McDowell	.05	.02
❑ 191	Glenn Montgomery	.05	.02
❑ 192	Greg Montgomery	.05	.02
❑ 193	Warren Moon	.25	.11
❑ 194	Bo Orlando	.05	.02
❑ 195	Marcus Robertson	.05	.02
❑ 196	Eddie Robinson	.05	.02
❑ 197	Webster Slaughter	.05	.02
❑ 198	Lorenzo White	.05	.02
❑ 199	John Baylor	.05	.02
❑ 200	Jason Belser	.05	.02
❑ 201	Tony Bennett	.05	.02
❑ 202	Dean Biasucci	.05	.02
❑ 203	Ray Buchanan	.05	.02
❑ 204	Kerry Cash	.05	.02
❑ 205	Quentin Coryatt	.05	.02
❑ 206	Eugene Daniel	.05	.02
❑ 207	Steve Emtman	.05	.02
❑ 208	Jon Hand	.05	.02
❑ 209	Jim Harbaugh	.25	.11
❑ 210	Jeff Herrod	.05	.02

❑ 211 Anthony Johnson .10 .05
❑ 212 Roosevelt Potts .05 .02
❑ 213 Rohn Stark .05 .02
❑ 214 Will Wolford .05 .02
❑ 215 Marcus Allen .25 .11
❑ 216 John Alt .05 .02
❑ 217 Kimble Anders .10 .05
❑ 218 J.J. Birden .05 .02
❑ 219 Dale Carter .05 .02
❑ 220 Keith Cash .05 .02
❑ 221 Tony Casillas .05 .02
❑ 222 Willie Davis .10 .05
❑ 223 Tim Grunhard .05 .02
❑ 224 Nick Lowery .05 .02
❑ 225 Charles Mincy .05 .02
❑ 226 Joe Montana 2.00 .90
❑ 227 Dan Saleaumua .05 .02
❑ 228 Tracy Simien .05 .02
❑ 229 Neil Smith .25 .11
❑ 230 Derrick Thomas .25 .11
❑ 231 Eddie Anderson .05 .02
❑ 232 Tim Brown .25 .11
❑ 233 Nolan Harrison .05 .02
❑ 234 Jeff Hostetler .10 .05
❑ 235 Rocket Ismail .10 .05
❑ 236 Jeff Jaeger .05 .02
❑ 237 James Jett .05 .02
❑ 238 Joe Kelly .05 .02
❑ 239 Albert Lewis .05 .02
❑ 240 Terry McDaniel .05 .02
❑ 241 Chester McGlockton .05 .02
❑ 242 Winston Moss .05 .02
❑ 243 Gerald Perry .05 .02
❑ 244 Greg Robinson .05 .02
❑ 245 Anthony Smith .05 .02
❑ 246 Steve Smith .05 .02
❑ 247 Greg Townsend .05 .02
❑ 248 Lionel Washington .05 .02
❑ 249 Steve Wisniewski .05 .02
❑ 250 Alexander Wright .05 .02
❑ 251 Flipper Anderson .05 .02
❑ 252 Jerome Bettis .25 .11
❑ 253 Marc Boutte .05 .02
❑ 254 Shane Conlan .05 .02
❑ 255 Troy Drayton .05 .02
❑ 256 Henry Ellard .10 .05
❑ 257 Sean Gilbert .05 .02
❑ 258 Nate Lewis .05 .02
❑ 259 Todd Lyght .05 .02
❑ 260 Chris Miller .05 .02
❑ 261 Anthony Newman .05 .02
❑ 262 Roman Phifer .05 .02
❑ 263 Henry Rolling .05 .02
❑ 264 T.J. Rubley RC .05 .02
❑ 265 Jackie Slater .05 .02
❑ 266 Fred Stokes .05 .02
❑ 267 Robert Young .05 .02
❑ 268 Gene Atkins .05 .02
❑ 269 J.B. Brown .05 .02
❑ 270 Keith Byars .05 .02
❑ 271 Marco Coleman .05 .02
❑ 272 Bryan Cox .05 .02
❑ 273 Jeff Cross .05 .02
❑ 274 Irving Fryar .10 .05
❑ 275 Mark Higgs .05 .02
❑ 276 Dwight Hollier .05 .02
❑ 277 Mark Ingram .05 .02
❑ 278 Keith Jackson .05 .02
❑ 279 Terry Kirby .25 .11
❑ 280 Bernie Kosar .10 .05
❑ 281 Dan Marino 2.00 .90
❑ 282 O.J. McDuffie .25 .11
❑ 283 Keith Sims .05 .02
❑ 284 Pete Stoyanovich .05 .02
❑ 285 Troy Vincent .05 .02
❑ 286 Richmond Webb .05 .02
❑ 287 Terry Allen .10 .05
❑ 288 Anthony Carter .10 .05
❑ 289 Cris Carter .50 .23
❑ 290 Jack Del Rio .05 .02
❑ 291 Chris Doleman .05 .02
❑ 292 Vencie Glenn .05 .02
❑ 293 Scottie Graham RC .10 .05
❑ 294 Chris Hinton .05 .02
❑ 295 Qadry Ismail .25 .11
❑ 296 Carlos Jenkins .05 .02
❑ 297 Steve Jordan .05 .02
❑ 298 Carl Lee .05 .02
❑ 299 Randall McDaniel .05 .02
❑ 300 John Randle .10 .05
❑ 301 Todd Scott .05 .02
❑ 302 Robert Smith .25 .11
❑ 303 Fred Strickland .05 .02
❑ 304 Henry Thomas .05 .02
❑ 305 Bruce Armstrong .05 .02
❑ 306 Harlon Barnett .05 .02
❑ 307 Drew Bledsoe 1.25 .55
❑ 308 Vincent Brown .05 .02
❑ 309 Ben Coates .25 .11
❑ 310 Todd Collins .05 .02
❑ 311 Myron Guyton .05 .02
❑ 312 Pat Harlow .05 .02
❑ 313 Maurice Hurst .05 .02
❑ 314 Leonard Russell .05 .02
❑ 315 Chris Slade .05 .02
❑ 316 Michael Timpson .05 .02
❑ 317 Andre Tippett .05 .02
❑ 318 Morten Andersen .05 .02
❑ 319 Derek Brown RBK .05 .02
❑ 320 Vince Buck .05 .02
❑ 321 Toi Cook .05 .02
❑ 322 Quinn Early .10 .05
❑ 323 Jim Everett .10 .05
❑ 324 Michael Haynes .10 .05
❑ 325 Tyrone Hughes .10 .05
❑ 326 Rickey Jackson .05 .02
❑ 327 Vaughan Johnson .05 .02
❑ 328 Eric Martin .05 .02
❑ 329 Wayne Martin .05 .02
❑ 330 Sam Mills .05 .02
❑ 331 Willie Roaf .05 .02
❑ 332 Irv Smith .05 .02
❑ 333 Keith Taylor .05 .02
❑ 334 Renaldo Turnbull .05 .02
❑ 335 Carlton Bailey .05 .02
❑ 336 Michael Brooks .05 .02
❑ 337 Jarrod Bunch .05 .02
❑ 338 Chris Calloway .05 .02
❑ 339 Mark Collins .05 .02
❑ 340 Howard Cross .05 .02
❑ 341 Stacey Dillard RC .05 .02
❑ 342 John Elliott .05 .02
❑ 343 Rodney Hampton .25 .11
❑ 344 Greg Jackson .05 .02
❑ 345 Mark Jackson .05 .02
❑ 346 Dave Meggett .05 .02
❑ 347 Corey Miller .05 .02
❑ 348 Mike Sherrard .05 .02
❑ 349 Phil Simms .10 .05
❑ 350 Lewis Tillman .05 .02
❑ 351 Brad Baxter .05 .02
❑ 352 Kyle Clifton .05 .02
❑ 353 Boomer Esiason .10 .05
❑ 354 James Hasty .05 .02
❑ 355 Bobby Houston .05 .02
❑ 356 Johnny Johnson .05 .02
❑ 357 Jeff Lageman .05 .02
❑ 358 Mo Lewis .05 .02
❑ 359 Ronnie Lott .10 .05
❑ 360 Leonard Marshall .05 .02
❑ 361 Johnny Mitchell .05 .02
❑ 362 Rob Moore .10 .05
❑ 363 Eric Thomas .05 .02
❑ 364 Brian Washington .05 .02
❑ 365 Marvin Washington .05 .02
❑ 366 Eric Allen .05 .02
❑ 367 Fred Barnett .10 .05
❑ 368 Bubby Brister .05 .02
❑ 369 Randall Cunningham .25 .11
❑ 370 Byron Evans .05 .02
❑ 371 William Fuller .05 .02
❑ 372 Andy Harmon .05 .02
❑ 373 Seth Joyner .05 .02
❑ 374 William Perry .10 .05
❑ 375 Leonard Renfro .05 .02
❑ 376 Heath Sherman .05 .02
❑ 377 Ben Smith .05 .02
❑ 378 William Thomas .05 .02
❑ 379 Herschel Walker .10 .05
❑ 380 Calvin Williams .10 .05
❑ 381 Chad Brown .05 .02
❑ 382 Dermontti Dawson .05 .02
❑ 383 Deon Figures .05 .02
❑ 384 Barry Foster .05 .02
❑ 385 Jeff Graham .05 .02
❑ 386 Eric Green .05 .02
❑ 387 Kevin Greene .25 .11
❑ 388 Carlton Haselrig .05 .02
❑ 389 Levon Kirkland .05 .02
❑ 390 Carnell Lake .05 .02
❑ 391 Greg Lloyd .25 .11
❑ 392 Neil O'Donnell .25 .11
❑ 393 Darren Perry .05 .02
❑ 394 Dwight Stone .05 .02
❑ 395 Leroy Thompson .05 .02
❑ 396 Rod Woodson .25 .11
❑ 397 Marion Butts .05 .02
❑ 398 John Carney .05 .02
❑ 399 Darren Carrington .05 .02
❑ 400 Burt Grossman .05 .02
❑ 401 Courtney Hall .05 .02
❑ 402 Ronnie Harmon .05 .02
❑ 403 Stan Humphries .25 .11
❑ 404 Shawn Jefferson .05 .02
❑ 405 Vance Johnson .05 .02
❑ 406 Chris Mims .05 .02
❑ 407 Leslie O'Neal .05 .02
❑ 408 Stanley Richard .05 .02
❑ 409 Junior Seau .25 .11
❑ 410 Harris Barton .05 .02
❑ 411 Dennis Brown .05 .02
❑ 412 Eric Davis .05 .02
❑ 413 Merton Hanks .10 .05
❑ 414 John Johnson .05 .02
❑ 415 Brent Jones .10 .05
❑ 416 Marc Logan .05 .02
❑ 417 Tim McDonald .05 .02
❑ 418 Gary Plummer .05 .02
❑ 419 Tom Rathman .05 .02
❑ 420 Jerry Rice 1.00 .45
❑ 421 Bill Romanowski .05 .02
❑ 422 Jesse Sapolu .05 .02
❑ 423 Dana Stubblefield .25 .11
❑ 424 John Taylor .10 .05
❑ 425 Steve Wallace .05 .02
❑ 426 Ted Washington .05 .02
❑ 427 Ricky Watters .25 .11
❑ 428 Troy Wilson RC .05 .02
❑ 429 Steve Young .75 .35
❑ 430 Howard Ballard .05 .02
❑ 431 Michael Bates .05 .02
❑ 432 Robert Blackmon .05 .02
❑ 433 Brian Blades .10 .05
❑ 434 Ferrell Edmunds .05 .02
❑ 435 Carlton Gray .05 .02
❑ 436 Patrick Hunter .05 .02
❑ 437 Cortez Kennedy .10 .05
❑ 438 Kelvin Martin .05 .02
❑ 439 Rick Mirer .25 .11
❑ 440 Nate Odomes .05 .02
❑ 441 Ray Roberts .05 .02
❑ 442 Eugene Robinson .05 .02
❑ 443 Rod Stephens .05 .02
❑ 444 Chris Warren .10 .05
❑ 445 John L. Williams .05 .02
❑ 446 Terry Wooden .05 .02
❑ 447 Marty Carter .05 .02
❑ 448 Reggie Cobb .05 .02
❑ 449 Lawrence Dawsey .05 .02
❑ 450 Santana Dotson .10 .05
❑ 451 Craig Erickson .05 .02
❑ 452 Thomas Everett .05 .02
❑ 453 Paul Gruber .05 .02
❑ 454 Courtney Hawkins .05 .02
❑ 455 Martin Mayhew .05 .02
❑ 456 Hardy Nickerson .10 .05
❑ 457 Ricky Reynolds .05 .02
❑ 458 Vince Workman .05 .02
❑ 459 Reggie Brooks .10 .05
❑ 460 Earnest Byner .05 .02
❑ 461 Andre Collins .05 .02
❑ 462 Brad Edwards .05 .02
❑ 463 Kurt Gouveia .05 .02
❑ 464 Darrell Green .05 .02
❑ 465 Ken Harvey .05 .02
❑ 466 Ethan Horton .05 .02
❑ 467 A.J. Johnson .05 .02
❑ 468 Tim Johnson .05 .02

❑ 469 Jim Lachey	.05	.02
❑ 470 Chip Lohmiller	.05	.02
❑ 471 Art Monk	.10	.05
❑ 472 Sterling Palmer RC	.05	.02
❑ 473 Mark Rypien	.05	.02
❑ 474 Ricky Sanders	.05	.02
❑ 475 Checklist 1-106	.05	.02
❑ 476 Checklist 107-214	.05	.02
❑ 477 Checklist 215-317	.05	.02
❑ 478 Checklist 318-409	.05	.02
❑ 479 Checklist 410-480/Inserts	.05	.02
❑ 480 Inserts Checklist	.05	.02
❑ P244 Jerome Bettis Promo Numbered 244	1.00	.45

1995 Fleer

	MINT	NRMT
COMPLETE SET (400)	20.00	9.00
❑ 1 Michael Bankston	.10	.05
❑ 2 Larry Centers	.20	.09
❑ 3 Gary Clark	.10	.05
❑ 4 Eric Hill	.10	.05
❑ 5 Seth Joyner	.10	.05
❑ 6 Dave Krieg	.10	.05
❑ 7 Lorenzo Lynch	.10	.05
❑ 8 Jamir Miller	.10	.05
❑ 9 Ronald Moore	.10	.05
❑ 10 Ricky Proehl	.10	.05
❑ 11 Clyde Simmons	.10	.05
❑ 12 Eric Swann	.20	.09
❑ 13 Aeneas Williams	.10	.05
❑ 14 J.J. Birden	.10	.05
❑ 15 Chris Doleman	.10	.05
❑ 16 Bert Emanuel	.30	.14
❑ 17 Jumpy Geathers	.10	.05
❑ 18 Jeff George	.20	.09
❑ 19 Roger Harper	.10	.05
❑ 20 Craig Heyward	.20	.09
❑ 21 Pierce Holt	.10	.05
❑ 22 D.J. Johnson	.10	.05
❑ 23 Terance Mathis	.20	.09
❑ 24 Clay Matthews	.20	.09
❑ 25 Andre Rison	.20	.09
❑ 26 Chuck Smith	.10	.05
❑ 27 Jessie Tuggle	.10	.05
❑ 28 Cornelius Bennett	.20	.09
❑ 29 Bucky Brooks	.10	.05
❑ 30 Jeff Burris	.10	.05
❑ 31 Russell Copeland	.10	.05
❑ 32 Matt Darby	.10	.05
❑ 33 Phil Hansen	.10	.05
❑ 34 Henry Jones	.10	.05
❑ 35 Jim Kelly	.30	.14
❑ 36 Mark Maddox RC	.10	.05
❑ 37 Bryce Paup	.30	.14
❑ 38 Andre Reed	.20	.09
❑ 39 Bruce Smith	.30	.14
❑ 40 Darryl Talley	.10	.05
❑ 41 Dewell Brewer RC	.10	.05
❑ 42 Mike Fox	.10	.05
❑ 43 Eric Guliford	.10	.05
❑ 44 Lamar Lathon	.10	.05
❑ 45 Pete Metzelaars	.10	.05
❑ 46 Sam Mills	.20	.09
❑ 47 Frank Reich	.10	.05
❑ 48 Rod Smith DB	.20	.09
❑ 49 Jack Trudeau	.10	.05
❑ 50 Trace Armstrong	.10	.05
❑ 51 Joe Cain	.10	.05
❑ 52 Mark Carrier DB	.10	.05
❑ 53 Curtis Conway	.30	.14
❑ 54 Shaun Gayle	.10	.05
❑ 55 Jeff Graham	.10	.05
❑ 56 Raymont Harris	.10	.05
❑ 57 Erik Kramer	.10	.05
❑ 58 Lewis Tillman	.10	.05
❑ 59 Tom Waddle	.10	.05
❑ 60 Steve Walsh	.10	.05
❑ 61 Donnell Woolford	.10	.05
❑ 62 Chris Zorich	.10	.05
❑ 63 Jeff Blake RC	1.00	.45
❑ 64 Mike Brim	.10	.05
❑ 65 Steve Broussard	.10	.05
❑ 66 James Francis	.10	.05
❑ 67 Ricardo McDonald	.10	.05
❑ 68 Tony McGee	.10	.05
❑ 70 Darnay Scott	.30	.14
❑ 71 Steve Tovar	.10	.05
❑ 72 Dan Wilkinson	.20	.09
❑ 73 Alfred Williams	.10	.05
❑ 74 Darryl Williams	.10	.05
❑ 75 Derrick Alexander WR	.30	.14
❑ 76 Randy Baldwin	.10	.05
❑ 77 Carl Banks	.10	.05
❑ 78 Rob Burnett	.10	.05
❑ 79 Steve Everitt	.10	.05
❑ 80 Leroy Hoard	.10	.05
❑ 81 Michael Jackson	.20	.09
❑ 82 Pepper Johnson	.10	.05
❑ 83 Tony Jones	.10	.05
❑ 84 Antonio Langham	.10	.05
❑ 85 Eric Metcalf	.20	.09
❑ 86 Stevon Moore	.10	.05
❑ 87 Anthony Pleasant	.10	.05
❑ 88 Vinny Testaverde	.20	.09
❑ 89 Eric Turner	.10	.05
❑ 90 Troy Aikman	1.00	.45
❑ 91 Charles Haley	.20	.09
❑ 92 Michael Irvin	.30	.14
❑ 93 Daryl Johnston	.20	.09
❑ 94 Robert Jones	.10	.05
❑ 95 Leon Lett	.10	.05
❑ 96 Russell Maryland	.10	.05
❑ 97 Nate Newton	.20	.09
❑ 98 Jay Novacek	.20	.09
❑ 99 Darrin Smith	.10	.05
❑ 100 Emmitt Smith	1.50	.70
❑ 101 Kevin Smith	.10	.05
❑ 102 Erik Williams	.10	.05
❑ 103 Kevin Williams WR	.20	.09
❑ 104 Darren Woodson	.20	.09
❑ 105 Elijah Alexander	.10	.05
❑ 106 Steve Atwater	.10	.05
❑ 107 Ray Crockett	.10	.05
❑ 108 Shane Dronett	.10	.05
❑ 109 Jason Elam	.10	.05
❑ 110 John Elway	2.00	.90
❑ 111 Simon Fletcher	.10	.05
❑ 112 Glyn Milburn	.10	.05
❑ 113 Anthony Miller	.20	.09
❑ 114 Michael Dean Perry	.10	.05
❑ 115 Mike Pritchard	.10	.05
❑ 116 Derek Russell	.10	.05
❑ 117 Leonard Russell	.10	.05
❑ 118 Shannon Sharpe	.20	.09
❑ 119 Gary Zimmerman	.10	.05
❑ 120 Bennie Blades	.10	.05
❑ 121 Lomas Brown	.10	.05
❑ 122 Willie Clay	.10	.05
❑ 123 Mike Johnson	.10	.05
❑ 124 Robert Massey	.10	.05
❑ 125 Scott Mitchell	.20	.09
❑ 126 Herman Moore	.30	.14
❑ 127 Brett Perriman	.20	.09
❑ 128 Robert Porcher	.10	.05
❑ 129 Barry Sanders	2.00	.90
❑ 130 Chris Spielman	.20	.09
❑ 131 Henry Thomas	.10	.05
❑ 132 Edgar Bennett	.20	.09
❑ 134 LeRoy Butler	.10	.05
❑ 135 Brett Favre	2.00	.90
❑ 136 Sean Jones	.10	.05
❑ 137 John Jurkovic	.10	.05
❑ 138 George Koonce	.10	.05
❑ 139 Wayne Simmons	.10	.05
❑ 140 George Teague	.10	.05
❑ 141 Reggie White	.30	.14
❑ 142 Micheal Barrow	.10	.05
❑ 143 Gary Brown	.10	.05
❑ 144 Cody Carlson	.10	.05
❑ 145 Ray Childress	.10	.05
❑ 146 Cris Dishman	.10	.05
❑ 147 Ernest Givins	.10	.05
❑ 148 Mel Gray	.10	.05
❑ 149 Darryll Lewis	.10	.05
❑ 150 Bruce Matthews	.10	.05
❑ 151 Marcus Robertson	.10	.05
❑ 152 Webster Slaughter	.10	.05
❑ 153 Al Smith	.10	.05
❑ 154 Mark Stepnoski	.10	.05
❑ 155 Trev Alberts	.10	.05
❑ 156 Flipper Anderson	.10	.05
❑ 157 Jason Belser	.10	.05
❑ 158 Tony Bennett	.10	.05
❑ 159 Ray Buchanan	.10	.05
❑ 160 Quentin Coryatt	.20	.09
❑ 161 Sean Dawkins	.20	.09
❑ 162 Steve Emtman	.10	.05
❑ 163 Marshall Faulk	.50	.23
❑ 164 Stephen Grant RC	.10	.05
❑ 165 Jim Harbaugh	.20	.09
❑ 166 Jeff Herrod	.10	.05
❑ 167 Tony Siragusa	.10	.05
❑ 168 Steve Beuerlein	.10	.05
❑ 169 Darren Carrington	.10	.05
❑ 170 Reggie Cobb	.10	.05
❑ 171 Kelvin Martin	.10	.05
❑ 172 Kelvin Pritchett	.10	.05
❑ 173 Joel Smeenge	.10	.05
❑ 174 James Williams	.10	.05
❑ 175 Marcus Allen	.30	.14
❑ 176 Kimble Anders	.20	.09
❑ 177 Dale Carter	.20	.09
❑ 178 Mark Collins	.10	.05
❑ 179 Willie Davis	.20	.09
❑ 180 Lake Dawson	.20	.09
❑ 181 Greg Hill	.20	.09
❑ 182 Darren Mickell	.10	.05
❑ 183 Joe Montana	2.00	.90
❑ 184 Tracy Simien	.10	.05
❑ 185 Neil Smith	.20	.09
❑ 186 William White	.10	.05
❑ 187 Greg Biekert	.10	.05
❑ 188 Tim Brown	.30	.14
❑ 189 Rob Fredrickson	.10	.05
❑ 190 Andrew Glover RC	.10	.05
❑ 191 Nolan Harrison	.10	.05
❑ 192 Jeff Hostetler	.20	.09
❑ 193 Rocket Ismail	.20	.09
❑ 194 Terry McDaniel	.10	.05
❑ 195 Chester McGlockton	.20	.09
❑ 196 Winston Moss	.10	.05
❑ 197 Anthony Smith	.10	.05
❑ 198 Harvey Williams	.10	.05
❑ 199 Steve Wisniewski	.10	.05
❑ 200 Johnny Bailey	.10	.05
❑ 201 Jerome Bettis	.30	.14
❑ 202 Isaac Bruce	.50	.23
❑ 203 Shane Conlan	.10	.05
❑ 204 Troy Drayton	.10	.05
❑ 205 Sean Gilbert	.20	.09
❑ 206 Jessie Hester	.10	.05
❑ 207 Jimmie Jones	.10	.05
❑ 208 Todd Lyght	.10	.05
❑ 209 Chris Miller	.10	.05
❑ 210 Roman Phifer	.10	.05
❑ 211 Marquez Pope	.10	.05
❑ 212 Robert Young	.10	.05
❑ 213 Gene Atkins	.10	.05
❑ 214 Aubrey Beavers	.10	.05
❑ 215 Tim Bowens	.10	.05
❑ 216 Bryan Cox	.10	.05
❑ 217 Jeff Cross	.10	.05
❑ 218 Irving Fryar	.20	.09
❑ 219 Eric Green	.10	.05
❑ 220 Mark Ingram	.10	.05
❑ 221 Terry Kirby	.20	.09
❑ 222 Dan Marino	2.00	.90

❑ 223 O.J. McDuffie .30 .14
❑ 224 Bernie Parmalee .20 .09
❑ 225 Keith Sims .10 .05
❑ 226 Irving Spikes .20 .09
❑ 227 Michael Stewart .10 .05
❑ 228 Troy Vincent .10 .05
❑ 229 Richmond Webb .10 .05
❑ 230 Terry Allen .20 .09
❑ 231 Cris Carter .30 .14
❑ 232 Jack Del Rio .10 .05
❑ 233 Vencie Glenn .10 .05
❑ 234 Qadry Ismail .20 .09
❑ 235 Carlos Jenkins .10 .05
❑ 236 Ed McDaniel .10 .05
❑ 237 Randall McDaniel .10 .05
❑ 238 Warren Moon .20 .09
❑ 239 Anthony Parker .10 .05
❑ 240 John Randle .20 .09
❑ 241 Jake Reed .20 .09
❑ 242 Fuad Reveiz .10 .05
❑ 243 Broderick Thomas .10 .05
❑ 244 Dewayne Washington .20 .09
❑ 245 Bruce Armstrong .10 .05
❑ 246 Drew Bledsoe 1.00 .45
❑ 247 Vincent Brisby .10 .05
❑ 248 Vincent Brown .10 .05
❑ 249 Marion Butts .10 .05
❑ 250 Ben Coates .20 .09
❑ 251 Tim Goad .10 .05
❑ 252 Myron Guyton .10 .05
❑ 253 Maurice Hurst .10 .05
❑ 254 Mike Jones .10 .05
❑ 255 Willie McGinest .20 .09
❑ 256 Dave Meggett .10 .05
❑ 257 Ricky Reynolds .10 .05
❑ 258 Chris Slade .20 .09
❑ 259 Michael Timpson .10 .05
❑ 260 Mario Bates .30 .14
❑ 261 Derek Brown RBK .10 .05
❑ 262 Darion Conner .10 .05
❑ 263 Quinn Early .20 .09
❑ 264 Jim Everett .10 .05
❑ 265 Michael Haynes .20 .09
❑ 266 Tyrone Hughes .20 .09
❑ 267 Joe Johnson .10 .05
❑ 268 Wayne Martin .10 .05
❑ 269 Willie Roaf .10 .05
❑ 270 Irv Smith .10 .05
❑ 271 Jimmy Spencer .10 .05
❑ 272 Winfred Tubbs .10 .05
❑ 273 Renaldo Turnbull .10 .05
❑ 274 Michael Brooks .10 .05
❑ 275 Dave Brown .20 .09
❑ 276 Chris Calloway .10 .05
❑ 277 Jesse Campbell .10 .05
❑ 278 Howard Cross .10 .05
❑ 279 John Elliott .10 .05
❑ 280 Keith Hamilton .10 .05
❑ 281 Rodney Hampton .20 .09
❑ 282 Thomas Lewis .20 .09
❑ 283 Thomas Randolph .10 .05
❑ 284 Mike Sherrard .10 .05
❑ 285 Michael Strahan .20 .09
❑ 286 Brad Baxter .10 .05
❑ 287 Tony Casillas .10 .05
❑ 288 Kyle Clifton .10 .05
❑ 289 Boomer Esiason .20 .09
❑ 290 Aaron Glenn .10 .05
❑ 291 Bobby Houston .10 .05
❑ 292 Johnny Johnson .10 .05
❑ 293 Jeff Lageman .10 .05
❑ 294 Mo Lewis .10 .05
❑ 295 Johnny Mitchell .10 .05
❑ 296 Rob Moore .10 .05
❑ 297 Marcus Turner .10 .05
❑ 298 Marvin Washington .10 .05
❑ 299 Eric Allen .10 .05
❑ 300 Fred Barnett .20 .09
❑ 301 Randall Cunningham .30 .14
❑ 302 Byron Evans .10 .05
❑ 303 William Fuller .10 .05
❑ 304 Charlie Garner .20 .09
❑ 305 Andy Harmon .10 .05
❑ 306 Greg Jackson .10 .05
❑ 307 Bill Romanowski .10 .05
❑ 308 William Thomas .10 .05
❑ 309 Herschel Walker .20 .09
❑ 310 Calvin Williams .20 .09
❑ 311 Michael Zordich .10 .05
❑ 312 Chad Brown .20 .09
❑ 313 Dermontti Dawson .20 .09
❑ 314 Barry Foster .20 .09
❑ 315 Kevin Greene .20 .09
❑ 316 Charles Johnson .20 .09
❑ 317 Levon Kirkland .10 .05
❑ 318 Carnell Lake .10 .05
❑ 319 Greg Lloyd .20 .09
❑ 320 Byron Bam Morris .20 .09
❑ 321 Neil O'Donnell .20 .09
❑ 322 Darren Perry .10 .05
❑ 323 Ray Seals .10 .05
❑ 324 John L. Williams .10 .05
❑ 325 Rod Woodson .20 .09
❑ 326 John Carney .10 .05
❑ 327 Andre Coleman .10 .05
❑ 328 Courtney Hall .10 .05
❑ 329 Ronnie Harmon .10 .05
❑ 330 Dwayne Harper .10 .05
❑ 331 Stan Humphries .20 .09
❑ 332 Shawn Jefferson .10 .05
❑ 333 Tony Martin .20 .09
❑ 334 Natrone Means .30 .14
❑ 335 Chris Mims .10 .05
❑ 336 Leslie O'Neal .20 .09
❑ 337 Alfred Pupunu RC .10 .05
❑ 338 Junior Seau .30 .14
❑ 339 Mark Seay .20 .09
❑ 340 Eric Davis .10 .05
❑ 341 William Floyd .30 .14
❑ 342 Merton Hanks .10 .05
❑ 343 Rickey Jackson .10 .05
❑ 344 Brent Jones .10 .05
❑ 345 Tim McDonald .10 .05
❑ 346 Ken Norton Jr. .20 .09
❑ 347 Gary Plummer .10 .05
❑ 348 Jerry Rice 1.00 .45
❑ 349 Deion Sanders .40 .18
❑ 350 Jesse Sapolu .10 .05
❑ 351 Dana Stubblefield .30 .14
❑ 352 John Taylor .10 .05
❑ 353 Steve Wallace .10 .05
❑ 354 Ricky Watters .30 .14
❑ 355 Lee Woodall .10 .05
❑ 356 Bryant Young .20 .09
❑ 357 Steve Young .75 .35
❑ 358 Sam Adams .10 .05
❑ 359 Howard Ballard .10 .05
❑ 360 Robert Blackmon .10 .05
❑ 361 Brian Blades .20 .09
❑ 362 Carlton Gray .10 .05
❑ 363 Cortez Kennedy .20 .09
❑ 364 Rick Mirer .30 .14
❑ 365 Eugene Robinson .10 .05
❑ 366 Chris Warren .20 .09
❑ 367 Terry Wooden .10 .05
❑ 368 Brad Culpepper .10 .05
❑ 369 Lawrence Dawsey .10 .05
❑ 370 Trent Dilfer .30 .14
❑ 371 Santana Dotson .10 .05
❑ 372 Craig Erickson .10 .05
❑ 373 Thomas Everett .10 .05
❑ 374 Paul Gruber .10 .05
❑ 375 Alvin Harper .10 .05
❑ 376 Jackie Harris .10 .05
❑ 377 Courtney Hawkins .10 .05
❑ 378 Martin Mayhew .10 .05
❑ 379 Hardy Nickerson .10 .05
❑ 380 Errict Rhett .30 .14
❑ 381 Charles Wilson .10 .05
❑ 382 Reggie Brooks .20 .09
❑ 383 Tom Carter .10 .05
❑ 384 Andre Collins .10 .05
❑ 385 Henry Ellard .20 .09
❑ 386 Ricky Ervins .10 .05
❑ 387 Darrell Green .10 .05
❑ 388 Ken Harvey .10 .05
❑ 389 Brian Mitchell .10 .05
❑ 390 Stanley Richard .10 .05
❑ 391 Heath Shuler .30 .14
❑ 392 Rod Stephens .10 .05
❑ 393 Tyronne Stowe .10 .05
❑ 394 Tydus Winans .10 .05
❑ 395 Tony Woods .10 .05
❑ 396 Checklist (1-104) .10 .05
❑ 397 Checklist (105-212) .10 .05
❑ 398 Checklist (213-298) .10 .05
❑ 399 Checklist (299-400) .10 .05
❑ 400 Checklist (Inserts) .10 .05
❑ P1 Promo Panel 2.50 1.10
Reggie Brooks
Jerome Bettis
Rick Mirer

1996 Fleer

	MINT	NRMT
COMPLETE SET (200)	20.00	9.00

❑ 1 Garrison Hearst .20 .09
❑ 2 Rob Moore .20 .09
❑ 3 Frank Sanders .20 .09
❑ 4 Eric Swann .10 .05
❑ 5 Aeneas Williams .10 .05
❑ 6 Jeff George .20 .09
❑ 7 Craig Heyward .10 .05
❑ 8 Terance Mathis .10 .05
❑ 9 Eric Metcalf .10 .05
❑ 10 Michael Jackson .20 .09
❑ 11 Andre Rison .20 .09
❑ 12 Vinny Testaverde .20 .09
❑ 13 Eric Turner .10 .05
❑ 14 Darick Holmes .10 .05
❑ 15 Jim Kelly .30 .14
❑ 16 Bryce Paup .10 .05
❑ 17 Bruce Smith .20 .09
❑ 18 Thurman Thomas .30 .14
❑ 19 Kerry Collins .30 .14
❑ 20 Lamar Lathon .10 .05
❑ 21 Derrick Moore .10 .05
❑ 22 Tyrone Poole .10 .05
❑ 23 Curtis Conway .30 .14
❑ 24 Bryan Cox .10 .05
❑ 25 Erik Kramer .10 .05
❑ 26 Rashaan Salaam .30 .14
❑ 27 Jeff Blake .30 .14
❑ 28 Ki-Jana Carter .20 .09
❑ 29 Carl Pickens .30 .14
❑ 30 Darnay Scott .20 .09
❑ 31 Troy Aikman .75 .35
❑ 32 Charles Haley .20 .09
❑ 33 Michael Irvin .30 .14
❑ 34 Daryl Johnston .20 .09
❑ 35 Jay Novacek .10 .05
❑ 36 Deion Sanders .40 .18
❑ 37 Emmitt Smith 1.25 .55
❑ 38 Steve Atwater .10 .05
❑ 39 Terrell Davis 2.00 .90
❑ 40 John Elway 1.50 .70
❑ 41 Anthony Miller .20 .09
❑ 42 Shannon Sharpe .20 .09
❑ 43 Scott Mitchell .20 .09
❑ 44 Herman Moore .30 .14
❑ 45 Johnnie Morton .20 .09
❑ 46 Brett Perriman .10 .05
❑ 47 Barry Sanders 1.50 .70
❑ 48 Edgar Bennett .20 .09
❑ 49 Robert Brooks .30 .14
❑ 50 Mark Chmura .20 .09
❑ 51 Brett Favre 1.50 .70
❑ 52 Reggie White .30 .14

❑ 53	Mel Gray	.10	.05
❑ 54	Steve McNair	.50	.23
❑ 55	Chris Sanders	.20	.09
❑ 56	Rodney Thomas	.10	.05
❑ 57	Quentin Coryatt	.10	.05
❑ 58	Sean Dawkins	.10	.05
❑ 59	Ken Dilger	.20	.09
❑ 60	Marshall Faulk	.30	.14
❑ 61	Jim Harbaugh	.20	.09
❑ 62	Tony Boselli	.10	.05
❑ 63	Mark Brunell	.75	.35
❑ 64	Natrone Means	.30	.14
❑ 65	James O.Stewart	.20	.09
❑ 66	Marcus Allen	.30	.14
❑ 67	Steve Bono	.10	.05
❑ 68	Neil Smith	.10	.05
❑ 69	Derrick Thomas	.20	.09
❑ 70	Tamarick Vanover	.20	.09
❑ 71	Fred Barnett	.10	.05
❑ 72	Eric Green	.10	.05
❑ 73	Dan Marino	1.50	.70
❑ 74	O.J. McDuffie	.20	.09
❑ 75	Bernie Parmalee	.10	.05
❑ 76	Cris Carter	.30	.14
❑ 77	Qadry Ismail	.10	.05
❑ 78	Warren Moon	.20	.09
❑ 79	Jake Reed	.20	.09
❑ 80	Robert Smith	.20	.09
❑ 81	Drew Bledsoe	.75	.35
❑ 82	Vincent Brisby	.10	.05
❑ 83	Ben Coates	.20	.09
❑ 84	Curtis Martin	.50	.23
❑ 85	Dave Meggett	.10	.05
❑ 86	Mario Bates	.20	.09
❑ 87	Jim Everett	.10	.05
❑ 88	Michael Haynes	.10	.05
❑ 89	Renaldo Turnbull	.10	.05
❑ 90	Dave Brown	.10	.05
❑ 91	Rodney Hampton	.20	.09
❑ 92	Thomas Lewis	.10	.05
❑ 93	Tyrone Wheatley	.20	.09
❑ 94	Kyle Brady	.10	.05
❑ 95	Hugh Douglas	.20	.09
❑ 96	Aaron Glenn	.10	.05
❑ 97	Jeff Graham	.10	.05
❑ 98	Adrian Murrell	.30	.14
❑ 99	Neil O'Donnell	.20	.09
❑ 100	Tim Brown	.30	.14
❑ 101	Jeff Hostetler	.10	.05
❑ 102	Napoleon Kaufman	.30	.14
❑ 103	Chester McGlockton	.10	.05
❑ 104	Harvey Williams	.10	.05
❑ 105	William Fuller	.10	.05
❑ 106	Charlie Garner	.10	.05
❑ 107	Ricky Watters	.20	.09
❑ 108	Calvin Williams	.10	.05
❑ 109	Jerome Bettis	.30	.14
❑ 110	Greg Lloyd	.20	.09
❑ 111	Byron Bam Morris	.20	.09
❑ 112	Kordell Stewart	.40	.18
❑ 113	Yancey Thigpen	.20	.09
❑ 114	Rod Woodson	.20	.09
❑ 115	Isaac Bruce	.30	.14
❑ 116	Troy Drayton	.10	.05
❑ 117	Leslie O'Neal	.10	.05
❑ 118	Steve Walsh	.10	.05
❑ 119	Marco Coleman	.10	.05
❑ 120	Aaron Hayden	.10	.05
❑ 121	Stan Humphries	.20	.09
❑ 122	Junior Seau	.20	.09
❑ 123	William Floyd	.20	.09
❑ 124	Brent Jones	.10	.05
❑ 125	Ken Norton	.10	.05
❑ 126	Jerry Rice	.75	.35
❑ 127	J.J. Stokes	.30	.14
❑ 128	Steve Young	.60	.25
❑ 129	Brian Blades	.10	.05
❑ 130	Joey Galloway	.40	.18
❑ 131	Rick Mirer	.20	.09
❑ 132	Chris Warren	.20	.09
❑ 133	Trent Dilfer	.30	.14
❑ 134	Alvin Harper	.10	.05
❑ 135	Hardy Nickerson	.10	.05
❑ 136	Errict Rhett	.20	.09
❑ 137	Terry Allen	.20	.09
❑ 138	Henry Ellard	.10	.05
❑ 139	Heath Shuler	.20	.09
❑ 140	Michael Westbrook	.30	.14
❑ 141	Karim Abdul-Jabbar RC	.50	.23
❑ 142	Mike Alstott RC	1.25	.55
❑ 143	Marco Battaglia RC	.10	.05
❑ 144	Tim Biakabutuka RC	.60	.25
❑ 145	Tony Brackens RC	.20	.09
❑ 146	Duane Clemons RC	.10	.05
❑ 147	Ernie Conwell RC	.10	.05
❑ 148	Chris Darkins RC	.10	.05
❑ 149	Stephen Davis RC	2.50	1.10
❑ 150	Brian Dawkins RC	.10	.05
❑ 151	Rickey Dudley RC	.30	.14
❑ 152	Jason Dunn RC	.20	.09
❑ 153	Bobby Engram RC	.30	.14
❑ 154	Daryl Gardener RC	.10	.05
❑ 155	Eddie George RC	2.50	1.10
❑ 156	Terry Glenn RC	1.00	.45
❑ 157	Kevin Hardy RC	.30	.14
❑ 158	Walt Harris RC	.10	.05
❑ 159	Marvin Harrison RC	2.00	.90
❑ 160	Bobby Hoying RC	.40	.18
❑ 161	Keyshawn Johnson RC	1.50	.70
❑ 162	Cedric Jones RC	.10	.05
❑ 163	Marcus Jones RC	.10	.05
❑ 164	Eddie Kennison RC	.30	.14
❑ 165	Ray Lewis RC	2.00	.90
❑ 166	Derrick Mayes RC	.50	.23
❑ 167	Leeland McElroy RC	.30	.14
❑ 168	Johnny McWilliams RC	.20	.09
❑ 169	John Mobley RC	.10	.05
❑ 170	Alex Molden RC	.10	.05
❑ 171	Eric Moulds RC	1.50	.70
❑ 172	Muhsin Muhammad RC	.75	.35
❑ 173	Jonathan Ogden RC	.10	.05
❑ 174	Lawrence Phillips RC	.30	.14
❑ 175	Stanley Pritchett RC	.20	.09
❑ 176	Simeon Rice RC	.30	.14
❑ 177	Bryan Still RC	.30	.14
❑ 178	Amani Toomer RC	.75	.35
❑ 179	Regan Upshaw RC	.10	.05
❑ 180	Alex Van Dyke RC	.20	.09
❑ 181	Barry Sanders PFW	.75	.35
❑ 182	Marcus Allen PFW	.30	.14
❑ 183	Bryce Paup PFW	.10	.05
❑ 184	Jerry Rice PFW	.40	.18
❑ 185	Desmond Howard PFW Bob Christian	.20	.09
❑ 186	Leon Lett PFW	.10	.05
❑ 187	Brett Favre PFW	.75	.35
❑ 188	Greg Lloyd PFW Derrick Thomas	.10	.05
❑ 189	Jeff Blake PFW	.20	.09
❑ 190	Emmitt Smith PFW	.60	.25
❑ 191	John Elway PFW Jeff Hostetler	.40	.18
❑ 192	Chiefs PFW	.10	.05
❑ 193	Marshall Faulk PFW	.20	.09
❑ 194	Troy Aikman PFW Steve Young	.40	.18
❑ 195	Dan Marino PFW	.75	.35
❑ 196	Donta Jones PFW	.10	.05
❑ 197	Jim Kelly PFW	.30	.14
❑ 198	Checklist	.10	.05
❑ 199	Checklist	.10	.05
❑ 200	Checklist	.10	.05
❑ P1	Promo Sheet William Floyd Trent Dilfer Brett Favre	4.00	1.80

1997 Fleer

	MINT	NRMT
COMPLETE SET (450)	40.00	18.00

❑ 1	Mark Brunell	1.50	.70
❑ 2	Andre Reed	.30	.14
❑ 3	Darrell Green	.30	.14
❑ 4	Mario Bates	.15	.07
❑ 5	Eddie George	1.50	.70
❑ 6	Cris Carter	.50	.23
❑ 7	Terrell Owens	.50	.23
❑ 8	Bill Romanowski	.15	.07
❑ 9	Isaac Bruce	.50	.23
❑ 10	Eric Curry	.15	.07
❑ 11	Danny Kanell	.30	.14
❑ 12	Ki-Jana Carter	.15	.07
❑ 13	Antonio Freeman	1.25	.55
❑ 14	Ricky Watters	.30	.14
❑ 15	Ty Law	.15	.07
❑ 16	Alonzo Spellman	.15	.07
❑ 17	Kordell Stewart	.60	.25
❑ 18	Jerry Rice	1.50	.70
❑ 19	Derrick Alexander WR	.30	.14
❑ 20	Barry Sanders	3.00	1.35
❑ 21	Keyshawn Johnson	.50	.23
❑ 22	Emmitt Smith	2.50	1.10
❑ 23	Ricky Proehl	.15	.07
❑ 24	Daryl Gardener	.15	.07
❑ 25	Dan Saleaumua	.15	.07
❑ 26	Kevin Greene	.30	.14
❑ 27	Junior Seau	.30	.14
❑ 28	Randall McDaniel	.15	.07
❑ 29	Marshall Faulk	.50	.23
❑ 30	Lorenzo Lynch	.15	.07
❑ 31	Terance Mathis	.30	.14
❑ 32	Warren Sapp	.30	.14
❑ 33	Chris Sanders	.15	.07
❑ 34	Tom Carter	.15	.07
❑ 35	Aeneas Williams	.15	.07
❑ 36	Lawrence Phillips	.15	.07
❑ 37	John Elway	3.00	1.35
❑ 38	Stanley Richard	.15	.07
❑ 39	Darryl Williams	.15	.07
❑ 40	Phillippi Sparks	.15	.07
❑ 41	Tedy Bruschi	.15	.07
❑ 42	Merton Hanks	.15	.07
❑ 43	Ray Lewis	.60	.25
❑ 44	Erik Williams	.15	.07
❑ 45	Jason Gildon	.15	.07
❑ 46	George Koonce	.15	.07
❑ 47	Louis Oliver	.15	.07
❑ 48	Muhsin Muhammad	.30	.14
❑ 49	Daryl Hobbs	.15	.07
❑ 50	Terry Glenn	.50	.23
❑ 51	Marvin Harrison	.50	.23
❑ 52	Brian Dawkins	.15	.07
❑ 53	Dale Carter	.15	.07
❑ 54	Alex Molden	.15	.07
❑ 55	Raymont Harris	.15	.07
❑ 56	Jeff Burris	.15	.07
❑ 57	Don Beebe	.15	.07
❑ 58	Jamir Miller	.15	.07
❑ 59	Carl Pickens	.50	.23
❑ 60	Antonio London	.15	.07
❑ 61	Courtney Hall	.15	.07
❑ 62	Derrick Brooks	.15	.07
❑ 63	Chris Boniol	.15	.07
❑ 64	Jeff Lageman	.15	.07
❑ 65	Roy Barker	.15	.07
❑ 66	Devin Bush	.15	.07
❑ 67	Aaron Glenn	.15	.07
❑ 68	Wayne Simmons	.15	.07
❑ 69	Steve Atwater	.15	.07
❑ 70	Jimmie Jones	.15	.07
❑ 71	Mark Carrier WR	.15	.07
❑ 72	Chris Chandler	.30	.14
❑ 73	Andy Harmon	.15	.07
❑ 74	John Friesz	.15	.07
❑ 75	Karim Abdul-Jabbar	.50	.23
❑ 76	Levon Kirkland	.15	.07
❑ 77	Torrance Small	.15	.07

No.	Player		
78	Harvey Williams	.15	.07
79	Chris Calloway	.15	.07
80	Vinny Testaverde	.30	.14
81	Bryant Young	.15	.07
82	Ray Buchanan	.15	.07
83	Robert Smith	.30	.14
84	Robert Brooks	.30	.14
85	Ray Crockett	.15	.07
86	Bennie Blades	.15	.07
87	Mark Carrier DB	.15	.07
88	Mike Tomczak	.15	.07
89	Darick Holmes	.15	.07
90	Drew Bledsoe	1.50	.70
91	Darren Woodson	.15	.07
92	Dan Wilkinson	.15	.07
93	Charles Way	.30	.14
94	Ray Farmer	.15	.07
95	Marcus Allen	.50	.23
96	Marco Coleman	.15	.07
97	Zach Thomas	.30	.14
98	Wesley Walls	.30	.14
99	Frank Wycheck	.15	.07
100	Troy Aikman	1.50	.70
101	Clyde Simmons	.15	.07
102	Courtney Hawkins	.15	.07
103	Chuck Smith	.15	.07
104	Neil O'Donnell	.30	.14
105	Kevin Carter	.15	.07
106	Chris Slade	.15	.07
107	Jessie Armstead	.15	.07
108	Sean Dawkins	.15	.07
109	Robert Blackmon	.15	.07
110	Kevin Smith	.15	.07
111	Lonnie Johnson	.15	.07
112	Craig Newsome	.15	.07
113	Jonathan Ogden	.15	.07
114	Chris Zorich	.15	.07
115	Tim Brown	.50	.23
116	Fred Barnett	.15	.07
117	Michael Haynes	.15	.07
118	Eric Hill	.15	.07
119	Ronnie Harmon	.15	.07
120	Sean Gilbert	.15	.07
121	Derrick Alexander DE	.15	.07
122	Derrick Thomas	.30	.14
123	Tyrone Wheatley	.30	.14
124	Cortez Kennedy	.15	.07
125	Jeff George	.30	.14
126	Chad Cota	.15	.07
127	Gary Zimmerman	.15	.07
128	Johnnie Morton	.30	.14
129	Chad Brown	.15	.07
130	Marvcus Patton	.15	.07
131	James O.Stewart	.30	.14
132	Terry Kirby	.30	.14
133	Chris Mims	.15	.07
134	William Thomas	.15	.07
135	Steve Tasker	.15	.07
136	Jason Belser	.15	.07
137	Bryan Cox	.15	.07
138	Jessie Tuggle	.15	.07
139	Ashley Ambrose	.15	.07
140	Mark Chmura	.30	.14
141	Jeff Hostetler	.15	.07
142	Rich Owens	.15	.07
143	Willie Davis	.15	.07
144	Hardy Nickerson	.15	.07
145	Curtis Martin	.75	.35
146	Ken Norton	.15	.07
147	Victor Green	.15	.07
148	Anthony Miller	.15	.07
149	John Kasay	.15	.07
150	O.J. McDuffie	.30	.14
151	Darren Perry	.15	.07
152	Luther Elliss	.15	.07
153	Greg Hill	.15	.07
154	John Randle	.30	.14
155	Stephen Grant	.15	.07
156	Leon Lett	.15	.07
157	Darrien Gordon	.15	.07
158	Ray Zellars	.15	.07
159	Michael Jackson	.30	.14
160	Leslie O'Neal	.15	.07
161	Bruce Smith	.30	.14
162	Santana Dotson	.15	.07
163	Bobby Hebert	.15	.07
164	Keith Hamilton	.15	.07
165	Tony Boselli	.15	.07
166	Alfred Williams	.15	.07
167	Ty Detmer	.30	.14
168	Chester McGlockton	.15	.07
169	William Floyd	.30	.14
170	Bruce Matthews	.15	.07
171	Simeon Rice	.30	.14
172	Scott Mitchell	.30	.14
173	Ricardo McDonald	.15	.07
174	Tyrone Poole	.15	.07
175	Greg Lloyd	.15	.07
176	Bruce Armstrong	.15	.07
177	Erik Kramer	.15	.07
178	Kimble Anders	.30	.14
179	Lamar Smith	.50	.23
180	Tony Tolbert	.15	.07
181	Joe Aska	.15	.07
182	Eric Allen	.15	.07
183	Eric Turner	.15	.07
184	Brad Johnson	.75	.35
185	Tony Martin	.30	.14
186	Mike Mamula	.15	.07
187	Irving Spikes	.15	.07
188	Keith Jackson	.15	.07
189	Carlton Bailey	.15	.07
190	Tyrone Braxton	.15	.07
191	Chad Bratzke	.15	.07
192	Adrian Murrell	.30	.14
193	Roman Phifer	.15	.07
194	Todd Collins	.15	.07
195	Chris Warren	.30	.14
196	Kevin Hardy	.15	.07
197	Rick Mirer	.15	.07
198	Cornelius Bennett	.15	.07
199	Jimmy Hitchcock	.15	.07
200	Michael Irvin	.50	.23
201	Quentin Coryatt	.15	.07
202	Reggie White	.50	.23
203	Larry Centers	.30	.14
204	Rodney Thomas	.15	.07
205	Dana Stubblefield	.15	.07
206	Rod Woodson	.30	.14
207	Rhett Hall	.15	.07
208	Steve Tovar	.15	.07
209	Michael Westbrook	.30	.14
210	Steve Wisniewski	.15	.07
211	Carlester Crumpler	.15	.07
212	Elvis Grbac	.30	.14
213	Tim Bowens	.15	.07
214	Robert Porcher	.15	.07
215	John Carney	.15	.07
216	Anthony Newman	.15	.07
217	Earnest Byner	.15	.07
218	Dewayne Washington	.15	.07
219	Willie Green	.15	.07
220	Terry Allen	.50	.23
221	William Fuller	.15	.07
222	Al Del Greco	.15	.07
223	Trent Dilfer	.50	.23
224	Michael Dean Perry	.15	.07
225	Larry Allen	.15	.07
226	Mark Bruener	.15	.07
227	Clay Matthews	.15	.07
228	Reuben Brown	.15	.07
229	Edgar Bennett	.30	.14
230	Neil Smith	.30	.14
231	Ken Harvey	.15	.07
232	Kyle Brady	.15	.07
233	Corey Miller	.15	.07
234	Tony Siragusa	.15	.07
235	Todd Sauerbrun	.15	.07
236	Daniel Stubbs	.15	.07
237	Robb Thomas	.15	.07
238	Jimmy Smith	.30	.14
239	Marquez Pope	.15	.07
240	Tim Biakabutuka	.30	.14
241	Jamie Asher	.15	.07
242	Steve McNair	.75	.35
243	Harold Green	.15	.07
244	Frank Sanders	.30	.14
245	Joe Johnson	.15	.07
246	Eric Bieniemy	.15	.07
247	Kevin Turner	.15	.07
248	Rickey Dudley	.30	.14
249	Orlando Thomas	.15	.07
250	Dan Marino	3.00	1.35
251	Deion Sanders	.50	.23
252	Dan Williams	.15	.07
253	Sam Gash	.15	.07
254	Lonnie Marts	.15	.07
255	Mo Lewis	.15	.07
256	Charles Johnson	.30	.14
257	Chris Jacke	.15	.07
258	Keenan McCardell	.30	.14
259	Donnell Woolford	.15	.07
260	Terrance Shaw	.15	.07
261	Jason Dunn	.15	.07
262	Willie McGinest	.15	.07
263	Ken Dilger	.15	.07
264	Keith Lyle	.15	.07
265	Antonio Langham	.15	.07
266	Carlton Gray	.15	.07
267	LeShon Johnson	.15	.07
268	Thurman Thomas	.50	.23
269	Jesse Campbell	.15	.07
270	Carnell Lake	.15	.07
271	Cris Dishman	.15	.07
272	Kevin Williams	.15	.07
273	Troy Brown	.15	.07
274	William Roaf	.15	.07
275	Terrell Davis	2.50	1.10
276	Herman Moore	.50	.23
277	Walt Harris	.15	.07
278	Mark Collins	.15	.07
279	Bert Emanuel	.30	.14
280	Qadry Ismail	.30	.14
281	Phil Hansen	.15	.07
282	Steve Young	1.00	.45
283	Michael Sinclair	.15	.07
284	Jeff Graham	.15	.07
285	Sam Mills	.15	.07
286	Terry McDaniel	.15	.07
287	Eugene Robinson	.15	.07
288	Tony Bennett	.15	.07
289	Daryl Johnston	.30	.14
290	Eric Swann	.15	.07
291	Byron Bam Morris	.15	.07
292	Thomas Lewis	.15	.07
293	Terrell Fletcher	.15	.07
294	Gus Frerotte	.15	.07
295	Stanley Pritchett	.15	.07
296	Mike Alstott	.50	.23
297	Will Shields	.15	.07
298	Errict Rhett	.15	.07
299	Garrison Hearst	.30	.14
300	Kerry Collins	.30	.14
301	Darryll Lewis	.15	.07
302	Chris T. Jones	.15	.07
303	Yancey Thigpen	.30	.14
304	Jackie Harris	.15	.07
305	Steve Christie	.15	.07
306	Gilbert Brown	.15	.07
307	Terry Wooden	.15	.07
308	Pete Mitchell	.15	.07
309	Tim McDonald	.15	.07
310	Jake Reed	.30	.14
311	Ed McCaffrey	.30	.14
312	Chris Doleman	.15	.07
313	Eric Metcalf	.30	.14
314	Ricky Reynolds	.15	.07
315	David Sloan	.15	.07
316	Marvin Washington	.15	.07
317	Herschel Walker	.30	.14
318	Michael Timpson	.15	.07
319	Blaine Bishop	.15	.07
320	Irv Smith	.15	.07
321	Seth Joyner	.15	.07
322	Terrell Buckley	.15	.07
323	Michael Strahan	.15	.07
324	Sam Adams	.15	.07
325	Leslie Shepherd	.15	.07
326	James Jett	.30	.14
327	Anthony Pleasant	.15	.07
328	Lee Woodall	.15	.07
329	Shannon Sharpe	.30	.14
330	Jamal Anderson	1.00	.45
331	Andre Hastings	.15	.07
332	Troy Vincent	.15	.07
333	Sean LaChapelle	.15	.07
334	Winslow Oliver	.15	.07
335	Sean Jones	.15	.07

- ❑ 336 Darnay Scott .30 .14
- ❑ 337 Todd Lyght .15 .07
- ❑ 338 Leonard Russell .15 .07
- ❑ 339 Nate Newton .15 .07
- ❑ 340 Zack Crockett .15 .07
- ❑ 341 Amp Lee .15 .07
- ❑ 342 Bobby Engram .30 .14
- ❑ 343 Mike Hollis .15 .07
- ❑ 344 Rodney Hampton .30 .14
- ❑ 345 Mel Gray .15 .07
- ❑ 346 Van Malone .15 .07
- ❑ 347 Aaron Craver .15 .07
- ❑ 348 Jim Everett .15 .07
- ❑ 349 Trace Armstrong .15 .07
- ❑ 350 Pat Swilling .15 .07
- ❑ 351 Brent Jones .30 .14
- ❑ 352 Chris Spielman .15 .07
- ❑ 353 Brett Perriman .15 .07
- ❑ 354 Brian Kinchen .15 .07
- ❑ 355 Joey Galloway .60 .25
- ❑ 356 Henry Ellard .15 .07
- ❑ 357 Ben Coates .30 .14
- ❑ 358 Dorsey Levens .50 .23
- ❑ 359 Charlie Garner .15 .07
- ❑ 360 Erric Pegram .15 .07
- ❑ 361 Anthony Johnson .15 .07
- ❑ 362 Rashaan Salaam .15 .07
- ❑ 363 Jeff Blake .30 .14
- ❑ 364 Kent Graham .15 .07
- ❑ 365 Broderick Thomas .15 .07
- ❑ 366 Richmond Webb .15 .07
- ❑ 367 Alfred Pupunu .15 .07
- ❑ 368 Mark Stepnoski .15 .07
- ❑ 369 David Dunn .15 .07
- ❑ 370 Bobby Houston .15 .07
- ❑ 371 Anthony Parker .15 .07
- ❑ 372 Quinn Early .15 .07
- ❑ 373 LeRoy Butler .15 .07
- ❑ 374 Kurt Gouveia .15 .07
- ❑ 375 Greg Biekert .15 .07
- ❑ 376 Jim Harbaugh .30 .14
- ❑ 377 Eric Bjornson .15 .07
- ❑ 378 Craig Heyward .15 .07
- ❑ 379 Steve Bono .30 .14
- ❑ 380 Tony Banks .30 .14
- ❑ 381 John Mobley .15 .07
- ❑ 382 Irving Fryar .30 .14
- ❑ 383 Dermontti Dawson .15 .07
- ❑ 384 Eric Davis .15 .07
- ❑ 385 Natrone Means .50 .23
- ❑ 386 Jason Sehorn .30 .14
- ❑ 387 Michael McCrary .15 .07
- ❑ 388 Corwin Brown .15 .07
- ❑ 389 Kevin Glover .15 .07
- ❑ 390 Jerris McPhail .15 .07
- ❑ 391 Bobby Taylor .15 .07
- ❑ 392 Tony McGee .15 .07
- ❑ 393 Curtis Conway .30 .14
- ❑ 394 Napoleon Kaufman .50 .23
- ❑ 395 Brian Blades .15 .07
- ❑ 396 Richard Dent .15 .07
- ❑ 397 Dave Brown .15 .07
- ❑ 398 Stan Humphries .30 .14
- ❑ 399 Stevon Moore .15 .07
- ❑ 400 Brett Favre 3.00 1.35
- ❑ 401 Jerome Bettis .50 .23
- ❑ 402 Darrin Smith .15 .07
- ❑ 403 Chris Penn .15 .07
- ❑ 404 Rob Moore .30 .14
- ❑ 405 Micheal Barrow .15 .07
- ❑ 406 Tony Brackens .15 .07
- ❑ 407 Wayne Martin .15 .07
- ❑ 408 Warren Moon .50 .23
- ❑ 409 Jason Elam .15 .07
- ❑ 410 J.J. Birden .15 .07
- ❑ 411 Hugh Douglas .15 .07
- ❑ 412 Lamar Lathon .15 .07
- ❑ 413 John Kidd .15 .07
- ❑ 414 Bryce Paup .15 .07
- ❑ 415 Shawn Jefferson .15 .07
- ❑ 416 Leeland McElroy SS .15 .07
- ❑ 417 Elbert Shelley SS .15 .07
- ❑ 418 Jermaine Lewis SS .30 .14
- ❑ 419 Eric Moulds SS .50 .23
- ❑ 420 Michael Bates SS .15 .07
- ❑ 421 John Mangum SS .15 .07
- ❑ 422 Corey Sawyer SS .15 .07
- ❑ 423 Jim Schwantz SS RC .15 .07
- ❑ 424 Rod Smith WR SS .50 .23
- ❑ 425 Glyn Milburn SS .15 .07
- ❑ 426 Desmond Howard SS .30 .14
- ❑ 427 John Henry Mills SS RC .15 .07
- ❑ 428 Cary Blanchard SS RC .15 .07
- ❑ 429 Chris Hudson SS .15 .07
- ❑ 430 Tamarick Vanover SS .30 .14
- ❑ 431 Kirby Dar Dar SS RC .30 .14
- ❑ 432 David Palmer SS .15 .07
- ❑ 433 Dave Meggett SS .15 .07
- ❑ 434 Tyrone Hughes SS .15 .07
- ❑ 435 Amani Toomer SS .30 .14
- ❑ 436 Wayne Chrebet SS .30 .14
- ❑ 437 Carl Kidd SS RC .15 .07
- ❑ 438 Derrick Witherspoon SS .15 .07
- ❑ 439 Jahine Arnold SS .15 .07
- ❑ 440 Andre Coleman SS .15 .07
- ❑ 441 Jeff Wilkins SS .15 .07
- ❑ 442 Jay Bellamy SS RC .15 .07
- ❑ 443 Eddie Kennison SS .30 .14
- ❑ 444 Nilo Silvan SS .15 .07
- ❑ 445 Brian Mitchell SS .15 .07
- ❑ 446 Garrison Hearst .30 .14
  Checklist back
- ❑ 447 Napoleon Kaufman .50 .23
  Checklist back
- ❑ 448 Brian Mitchell .15 .07
  Checklist back
- ❑ 449 Rodney Hampton .15 .07
  Checklist back
- ❑ 450 Edgar Bennett .15 .07
  Checklist back
- ❑ S1 Mark Chmura Sample 1.00 .45
- ❑ AU1 Reggie White AUTO 125.00 55.00
  (Numbered of 80)

1998 Fleer

	MINT	NRMT
COMPLETE SET (250)	40.00	18.00

- ❑ 1 Brett Favre 2.00 .90
- ❑ 2 Barry Sanders 2.00 .90
- ❑ 3 John Elway 2.00 .90
- ❑ 4 Emmitt Smith 1.50 .70
- ❑ 5 Dan Marino 2.00 .90
- ❑ 6 Eddie George .75 .35
- ❑ 7 Jerry Rice 1.00 .45
- ❑ 8 Jake Plummer .75 .35
- ❑ 9 Joey Galloway .40 .18
- ❑ 10 Mike Alstott .40 .18
- ❑ 11 Brian Mitchell .10 .05
- ❑ 12 Keyshawn Johnson .40 .18
- ❑ 13 Jerald Moore .10 .05
- ❑ 14 Randal Hill .10 .05
- ❑ 15 Byron Hanspard .20 .09
- ❑ 16 Jeff George .20 .09
- ❑ 17 Terry Glenn .40 .18
- ❑ 18 Jerome Bettis .40 .18
- ❑ 19 Curtis Conway .20 .09
- ❑ 20 Fred Lane .20 .09
- ❑ 21 Isaac Bruce .40 .18
- ❑ 22 Tiki Barber .20 .09
- ❑ 23 Bobby Hoying .20 .09
- ❑ 24 Marcus Allen .40 .18
- ❑ 25 Dana Stubblefield .10 .05
- ❑ 26 Peter Boulware .10 .05
- ❑ 27 John Randle .20 .09
- ❑ 28 Jason Sehorn .20 .09
- ❑ 29 Rod Smith .20 .09
- ❑ 30 Michael Sinclair .10 .05
- ❑ 31 Marshall Faulk .40 .18
- ❑ 32 Karl Williams .10 .05
- ❑ 33 Kordell Stewart .40 .18
- ❑ 34 Corey Dillon .60 .25
- ❑ 35 Bryant Young .10 .05
- ❑ 36 Charlie Garner .10 .05
- ❑ 37 Andre Reed .20 .09
- ❑ 38 Ray Buchanan .10 .05
- ❑ 39 Brett Perriman .10 .05
- ❑ 40 Leon Lett .10 .05
- ❑ 41 Keenan McCardell .20 .09
- ❑ 42 Eric Swann .10 .05
- ❑ 43 Leslie Shepherd .10 .05
- ❑ 44 Curtis Martin .40 .18
- ❑ 45 Andre Rison .20 .09
- ❑ 46 Keith Lyle .10 .05
- ❑ 47 Rae Carruth .20 .09
- ❑ 48 William Henderson .10 .05
- ❑ 49 Sean Dawkins .10 .05
- ❑ 50 Terrell Davis 1.50 .70
- ❑ 51 Tim Brown .40 .18
- ❑ 52 Willie McGinest .10 .05
- ❑ 53 Jermaine Lewis .20 .09
- ❑ 54 Ricky Watters .20 .09
- ❑ 55 Freddie Jones .10 .05
- ❑ 56 Robert Smith .40 .18
- ❑ 57 Reidel Anthony .20 .09
- ❑ 58 James Stewart .20 .09
- ❑ 59 Earl Holmes RC .50 .23
- ❑ 60 Dale Carter .10 .05
- ❑ 61 Michael Irvin .40 .18
- ❑ 62 Jason Taylor .10 .05
- ❑ 63 Eric Metcalf .10 .05
- ❑ 64 LeRoy Butler .10 .05
- ❑ 65 Jamal Anderson .40 .18
- ❑ 66 Jamie Asher .10 .05
- ❑ 67 Chris Sanders .10 .05
- ❑ 68 Warren Sapp .20 .09
- ❑ 69 Ray Zellars .10 .05
- ❑ 70 Carl Pickens .40 .18
- ❑ 71 Garrison Hearst .40 .18
- ❑ 72 Eddie Kennison .20 .09
- ❑ 73 John Mobley .10 .05
- ❑ 74 Rob Johnson .20 .09
- ❑ 75 William Thomas .10 .05
- ❑ 76 Drew Bledsoe .75 .35
- ❑ 77 Micheal Barrow .10 .05
- ❑ 78 Jim Harbaugh .20 .09
- ❑ 79 Terry McDaniel .10 .05
- ❑ 80 Johnnie Morton .20 .09
- ❑ 81 Danny Kanell .20 .09
- ❑ 82 Larry Centers .10 .05
- ❑ 83 Courtney Hawkins .10 .05
- ❑ 84 Tony Brackens .10 .05
- ❑ 85 Tony Gonzalez .10 .05
- ❑ 86 Aaron Glenn .10 .05
- ❑ 87 Cris Carter .40 .18
- ❑ 88 Chuck Smith .10 .05
- ❑ 89 Tamarick Vanover .10 .05
- ❑ 90 Karim Abdul-Jabbar .40 .18
- ❑ 91 Bryant Westbrook .10 .05
- ❑ 92 Mike Pritchard .10 .05
- ❑ 93 Darren Woodson .10 .05
- ❑ 94 Wesley Walls .20 .09
- ❑ 95 Tony Banks .20 .09
- ❑ 96 Michael Westbrook .20 .09
- ❑ 97 Shannon Sharpe .20 .09
- ❑ 98 Jeff Blake .20 .09
- ❑ 99 Terrell Owens .40 .18
- ❑ 100 Warrick Dunn .40 .18
- ❑ 101 Levon Kirkland .10 .05
- ❑ 102 Frank Wycheck .10 .05
- ❑ 103 Gus Frerotte .10 .05
- ❑ 104 Simeon Rice .20 .09
- ❑ 105 Shawn Jefferson .10 .05
- ❑ 106 Irving Fryar .20 .09
- ❑ 107 Michael McCrary .10 .05
- ❑ 108 Robert Brooks .20 .09
- ❑ 109 Chris Chandler .20 .09
- ❑ 110 Junior Seau .20 .09
- ❑ 111 O.J. McDuffie .20 .09

		MINT	NRMT
❑ 112	Glenn Foley	.20	.09
❑ 113	Darryl Williams	.10	.05
❑ 114	Elvis Grbac	.20	.09
❑ 115	Napoleon Kaufman	.40	.18
❑ 116	Anthony Miller	.10	.05
❑ 117	Troy Davis	.10	.05
❑ 118	Charles Way	.10	.05
❑ 119	Scott Mitchell	.20	.09
❑ 120	Ken Harvey	.10	.05
❑ 121	Tyrone Hughes	.10	.05
❑ 122	Mark Brunell	.75	.35
❑ 123	David Palmer	.10	.05
❑ 124	Rob Moore	.20	.09
❑ 125	Kerry Collins	.20	.09
❑ 126	Will Blackwell	.10	.05
❑ 127	Ray Crockett	.10	.05
❑ 128	Leslie O'Neal	.10	.05
❑ 129	Antowain Smith	.40	.18
❑ 130	Carlester Crumpler	.10	.05
❑ 131	Michael Jackson	.10	.05
❑ 132	Trent Dilfer	.40	.18
❑ 133	Dan Williams	.10	.05
❑ 134	Dorsey Levens	.40	.18
❑ 135	Ty Law	.10	.05
❑ 136	Rickey Dudley	.10	.05
❑ 137	Jessie Tuggle	.10	.05
❑ 138	Darrien Gordon	.10	.05
❑ 139	Kevin Turner	.10	.05
❑ 140	Willie Davis	.10	.05
❑ 141	Zach Thomas	.20	.09
❑ 142	Tony McGee	.10	.05
❑ 143	Dexter Coakley	.10	.05
❑ 144	Troy Brown	.10	.05
❑ 145	Leeland McElroy	.10	.05
❑ 146	Michael Strahan	.10	.05
❑ 147	Ken Dilger	.10	.05
❑ 148	Bryce Paup	.10	.05
❑ 149	Herman Moore	.40	.18
❑ 150	Reggie White	.40	.18
❑ 151	Dewayne Washington	.10	.05
❑ 152	Natrone Means	.40	.18
❑ 153	Ben Coates	.20	.09
❑ 154	Bert Emanuel	.20	.09
❑ 155	Steve Young	.60	.25
❑ 156	Jimmy Smith	.20	.09
❑ 157	Darrell Green	.20	.09
❑ 158	Troy Aikman	1.00	.45
❑ 159	Greg Hill	.10	.05
❑ 160	Raymont Harris	.10	.05
❑ 161	Troy Drayton	.10	.05
❑ 162	Stevon Moore	.10	.05
❑ 163	Warren Moon	.40	.18
❑ 164	Wayne Martin	.10	.05
❑ 165	Jason Gildon	.10	.05
❑ 166	Chris Calloway	.10	.05
❑ 167	Aeneas Williams	.10	.05
❑ 168	Michael Bates	.10	.05
❑ 169	Hugh Douglas	.10	.05
❑ 170	Brad Johnson	.40	.18
❑ 171	Bruce Smith	.20	.09
❑ 172	Neil Smith	.20	.09
❑ 173	James McKnight	.10	.05
❑ 174	Robert Porcher	.10	.05
❑ 175	Merton Hanks	.10	.05
❑ 176	Ki-Jana Carter	.10	.05
❑ 177	Mo Lewis	.10	.05
❑ 178	Chester McGlockton	.10	.05
❑ 179	Zack Crockett	.10	.05
❑ 180	Derrick Thomas	.20	.09
❑ 181	J.J. Stokes	.20	.09
❑ 182	Derrick Rodgers	.10	.05
❑ 183	Daryl Johnston	.20	.09
❑ 184	Chris Penn	.10	.05
❑ 185	Steve Atwater	.10	.05
❑ 186	Amp Lee	.10	.05
❑ 187	Frank Sanders	.20	.09
❑ 188	Chris Slade	.10	.05
❑ 189	Mark Chmura	.20	.09
❑ 190	Kimble Anders	.20	.09
❑ 191	Charles Johnson	.10	.05
❑ 192	William Floyd	.10	.05
❑ 193	Jay Graham	.10	.05
❑ 194	Hardy Nickerson	.10	.05
❑ 195	Terry Allen	.40	.18
❑ 196	James Jett	.20	.09
❑ 197	Jessie Armstead	.10	.05
❑ 198	Yancey Thigpen	.20	.09
❑ 199	Terance Mathis	.20	.09
❑ 200	Steve McNair	.40	.18
❑ 201	Wayne Chrebet	.40	.18
❑ 202	Jamir Miller	.10	.05
❑ 203	Duce Staley	.75	.35
❑ 204	Deion Sanders	.40	.18
❑ 205	Carnell Lake	.10	.05
❑ 206	Ed McCaffrey	.20	.09
❑ 207	Shawn Springs	.10	.05
❑ 208	Tony Martin	.20	.09
❑ 209	Jerris McPhail	.10	.05
❑ 210	Darnay Scott	.20	.09
❑ 211	Jake Reed	.20	.09
❑ 212	Adrian Murrell	.20	.09
❑ 213	Quinn Early	.10	.05
❑ 214	Marvin Harrison	.20	.09
❑ 215	Ryan McNeil	.10	.05
❑ 216	Derrick Alexander	.20	.09
❑ 217	Ray Lewis	.40	.18
❑ 218	Antonio Freeman	.40	.18
❑ 219	Dwayne Rudd	.10	.05
❑ 220	Muhsin Muhammad	.20	.09
❑ 221	Kevin Hardy	.10	.05
❑ 222	Andre Hastings	.10	.05
❑ 223	John Avery RC	1.25	.55
❑ 224	Keith Brooking RC	.75	.35
❑ 225	Kevin Dyson RC	2.00	.90
❑ 226	Robert Edwards RC	1.50	.70
❑ 227	Greg Ellis RC	.50	.23
❑ 228	Curtis Enis RC	1.50	.70
❑ 229	Terry Fair RC	.75	.35
❑ 230	Ahman Green RC	3.00	1.35
❑ 231	Jacquez Green RC	2.00	.90
❑ 232	Brian Griese RC	4.00	1.80
❑ 233	Skip Hicks RC	1.25	.55
❑ 234	Ryan Leaf RC	3.00	1.35
❑ 235	Peyton Manning RC	10.00	4.50
❑ 236	R.W. McQuarters RC	.50	.23
❑ 237	Randy Moss RC	10.00	4.50
❑ 238	Marcus Nash RC	1.25	.55
❑ 239	Anthony Simmons RC	.50	.23
❑ 240	Brian Simmons RC	.50	.23
❑ 241	Takeo Spikes RC	.75	.35
❑ 242	Duane Starks RC	.50	.23
❑ 243	Fred Taylor RC	3.00	1.35
❑ 244	Andre Wadsworth RC	.75	.35
❑ 245	Shaun Williams RC	.50	.23
❑ 246	Grant Wistrom RC	.50	.23
❑ 247	Charles Woodson RC	2.00	.90
❑ 248	Checklist	.10	.05
❑ 249	Checklist	.10	.05
❑ 250	Checklist	.10	.05

1999 Fleer

		MINT	NRMT
COMPLETE SET (300)		40.00	18.00
❑ 1	Randy Moss	1.50	.70
❑ 2	Peyton Manning	1.50	.70
❑ 3	Barry Sanders	1.50	.70
❑ 4	Terrell Davis	1.00	.45
❑ 5	Brett Favre	1.50	.70
❑ 6	Fred Taylor	1.00	.45
❑ 7	Jake Plummer	.75	.35
❑ 8	John Elway	1.50	.70
❑ 9	Emmitt Smith	1.00	.45
❑ 10	Kerry Collins	.20	.09
❑ 11	Peter Boulware	.10	.05
❑ 12	Jamal Anderson	.40	.18
❑ 13	Doug Flutie	.50	.23
❑ 14	Michael Bates	.10	.05
❑ 15	Corey Dillon	.40	.18
❑ 16	Curtis Conway	.20	.09
❑ 17	Ty Detmer	.20	.09
❑ 18	Robert Brooks	.20	.09
❑ 19	Dale Carter	.10	.05
❑ 20	Charlie Batch	.75	.35
❑ 21	Ken Dilger	.10	.05
❑ 22	Troy Aikman	1.00	.45
❑ 23	Tavian Banks	.10	.05
❑ 24	Cris Carter	.40	.18
❑ 25	Derrick Alexander WR	.20	.09
❑ 26	Chris Bordano RC	.10	.05
❑ 27	Karim Abdul-Jabbar	.20	.09
❑ 28	Jessie Armstead	.10	.05
❑ 29	Drew Bledsoe	.60	.25
❑ 30	Brian Dawkins	.10	.05
❑ 31	Wayne Chrebet	.20	.09
❑ 32	Garrison Hearst	.20	.09
❑ 33	Eric Allen	.10	.05
❑ 34	Tony Banks	.20	.09
❑ 35	Jerome Bettis	.40	.18
❑ 36	Stephen Alexander	.10	.05
❑ 37	Rodney Harrison	.10	.05
❑ 38	Mike Alstott	.40	.18
❑ 39	Chad Brown	.10	.05
❑ 40	Johnny McWilliams	.10	.05
❑ 41	Kevin Dyson	.20	.09
❑ 42	Keith Brooking	.10	.05
❑ 43	Jim Harbaugh	.20	.09
❑ 44	Bobby Engram	.20	.09
❑ 45	John Holecek	.10	.05
❑ 46	Steve Beuerlein	.10	.05
❑ 47	Tony McGee	.10	.05
❑ 48	Greg Ellis	.10	.05
❑ 49	Corey Fuller	.10	.05
❑ 50	Stephen Boyd	.10	.05
❑ 51	Marshall Faulk	.40	.18
❑ 52	Leroy Butler	.10	.05
❑ 53	Reggie Barlow	.10	.05
❑ 54	Randall Cunningham	.40	.18
❑ 55	Aeneas Williams	.10	.05
❑ 56	Kimble Anders	.20	.09
❑ 57	Cam Cleeland	.10	.05
❑ 58	John Avery	.20	.09
❑ 59	Gary Brown	.10	.05
❑ 60	Ben Coates	.20	.09
❑ 61	Koy Detmer	.10	.05
❑ 62	Bryan Cox	.10	.05
❑ 63	Edgar Bennett	.10	.05
❑ 64	Tim Brown	.40	.18
❑ 65	Isaac Bruce	.40	.18
❑ 66	Eddie George	.50	.23
❑ 67	Reidel Anthony	.20	.09
❑ 68	Charlie Jones	.10	.05
❑ 69	Terry Allen	.20	.09
❑ 70	Joey Galloway	.40	.18
❑ 71	Jamir Miller	.10	.05
❑ 72	Will Blackwell	.10	.05
❑ 73	Ray Buchanan	.10	.05
❑ 74	Priest Holmes	.40	.18
❑ 75	Michael Irvin	.20	.09
❑ 76	Jonathan Linton	.10	.05
❑ 77	Curtis Enis	.40	.18
❑ 78	Neil O'Donnell	.20	.09
❑ 79	Tim Biakabutuka	.20	.09
❑ 80	Terry Kirby	.10	.05
❑ 81	Germane Crowell	.20	.09
❑ 82	Jason Elam	.10	.05
❑ 83	Mark Chmura	.10	.05
❑ 84	Marvin Harrison	.40	.18
❑ 85	Jimmy Hitchcock	.10	.05
❑ 86	Tony Brackens	.10	.05
❑ 87	Sean Dawkins	.10	.05
❑ 88	Tony Gonzalez	.20	.09
❑ 89	Kent Graham	.10	.05
❑ 90	Oronde Gadsden	.10	.05
❑ 91	Hugh Douglas	.10	.05
❑ 92	Robert Edwards	.20	.09
❑ 93	R.W. McQuarters	.10	.05
❑ 94	Aaron Glenn	.10	.05
❑ 95	Kevin Carter	.10	.05

❑ 96 Rickey Dudley .10 .05
❑ 97 Derrick Brooks .10 .05
❑ 98 Mark Bruener .10 .05
❑ 99 Darrell Green .10 .05
❑ 100 Jessie Tuggle .10 .05
❑ 101 Freddie Jones .10 .05
❑ 102 Rob Moore .20 .09
❑ 103 Ahman Green .20 .09
❑ 104 Chris Chandler .20 .09
❑ 105 Steve McNair .40 .18
❑ 106 Kevin Greene .10 .05
❑ 107 Jermaine Lewis .20 .09
❑ 108 Erik Kramer .10 .05
❑ 109 Eric Moulds .40 .18
❑ 110 Terry Fair .10 .05
❑ 111 Carl Pickens .20 .09
❑ 112 La'Roi Glover .10 .05
❑ 113 Chris Spielman .10 .05
❑ 114 Leroy Hoard .10 .05
❑ 115 Mark Brunell .60 .25
❑ 116 Patrick Jeffers RC 3.00 1.35
❑ 117 Elvis Grbac .20 .09
❑ 118 Ike Hilliard .10 .05
❑ 119 Sam Madison .10 .05
❑ 120 Terrell Owens .40 .18
❑ 121 Rich Gannon .20 .09
❑ 122 Skip Hicks .40 .18
❑ 123 Eric Green .10 .05
❑ 124 Trent Dilfer .20 .09
❑ 125 Terry Glenn .40 .18
❑ 126 Trent Green .20 .09
❑ 127 Charles Johnson .10 .05
❑ 128 Adrian Murrell .20 .09
❑ 129 Jason Gildon .10 .05
❑ 130 Tim Dwight .40 .18
❑ 131 Ryan Leaf .40 .18
❑ 132 Rocket Ismail .20 .09
❑ 133 Jon Kitna .40 .18
❑ 134 Alonzo Mayes .10 .05
❑ 135 Yancey Thigpen .10 .05
❑ 136 David LaFleur .10 .05
❑ 137 Ray Lewis .20 .09
❑ 138 Herman Moore .40 .18
❑ 139 Brian Griese .75 .35
❑ 140 Antonio Freeman .40 .18
❑ 141 Darnay Scott .10 .05
❑ 142 Ed McDaniel .10 .05
❑ 143 Andre Reed .20 .09
❑ 144 Andre Hastings .10 .05
❑ 145 Chris Warren .10 .05
❑ 146 Kevin Hardy .10 .05
❑ 147 Joe Jurevicius .10 .05
❑ 148 Jerome Pathon .10 .05
❑ 149 Duce Staley .40 .18
❑ 150 Dan Marino 1.50 .70
❑ 151 Jerry Rice 1.00 .45
❑ 152 Byron Bam Morris .10 .05
❑ 153 Az-Zahir Hakim .10 .05
❑ 154 Ty Law .10 .05
❑ 155 Warrick Dunn .40 .18
❑ 156 Keyshawn Johnson .40 .18
❑ 157 Brian Mitchell .10 .05
❑ 158 James Jett .20 .09
❑ 159 Fred Lane .10 .05
❑ 160 Courtney Hawkins .10 .05
❑ 161 Andre Wadsworth .10 .05
❑ 162 Natrone Means .20 .09
❑ 163 Andrew Glover .10 .05
❑ 164 Anthony Simmons .10 .05
❑ 165 Leon Lett .10 .05
❑ 166 Frank Wycheck .10 .05
❑ 167 Barry Minter .10 .05
❑ 168 Michael McCrary .10 .05
❑ 169 Johnnie Morton .20 .09
❑ 170 Jay Riemersma .10 .05
❑ 171 Vonnie Holliday .10 .05
❑ 172 Brian Simmons .10 .05
❑ 173 Joe Johnson .10 .05
❑ 174 Ed McCaffrey .20 .09
❑ 175 Jason Sehorn .10 .05
❑ 176 Keenan McCardell .20 .09
❑ 177 Bobby Taylor .10 .05
❑ 178 Andre Rison .20 .09
❑ 179 Greg Hill .10 .05
❑ 180 O.J. McDuffie .20 .09
❑ 181 Darren Woodson .10 .05
❑ 182 Willie McGinest .10 .05
❑ 183 J.J. Stokes .20 .09
❑ 184 Leon Johnson .10 .05
❑ 185 Bert Emanuel .20 .09
❑ 186 Napoleon Kaufman .40 .18
❑ 187 Leslie Shepherd .10 .05
❑ 188 Levon Kirkland .10 .05
❑ 189 Simeon Rice .10 .05
❑ 190 Mikhael Ricks .10 .05
❑ 191 Robert Smith .40 .18
❑ 192 Michael Sinclair .10 .05
❑ 193 Muhsin Muhammad .20 .09
❑ 194 Duane Starks .10 .05
❑ 195 Terance Mathis .20 .09
❑ 196 Antowain Smith .40 .18
❑ 197 Tony Parrish .10 .05
❑ 198 Takeo Spikes .10 .05
❑ 199 Ernie Mills .10 .05
❑ 200 John Mobley .10 .05
❑ 202 Pete Mitchell .10 .05
❑ 203 Darick Holmes .10 .05
❑ 204 Derrick Thomas .20 .09
❑ 205 David Palmer .10 .05
❑ 206 Jason Taylor .10 .05
❑ 207 Sammy Knight .10 .05
❑ 208 Dwayne Rudd .10 .05
❑ 209 Lawyer Milloy .10 .05
❑ 210 Michael Strahan .10 .05
❑ 211 Mo Lewis .10 .05
❑ 212 William Thomas .10 .05
❑ 213 Darrell Russell .10 .05
❑ 214 Brad Johnson .40 .18
❑ 215 Kordell Stewart .40 .18
❑ 216 Robert Holcombe .20 .09
❑ 217 Junior Seau .20 .09
❑ 218 Jacquez Green .20 .09
❑ 219 Shawn Springs .10 .05
❑ 220 Michael Westbrook .20 .09
❑ 221 Rod Woodson .20 .09
❑ 222 Frank Sanders .20 .09
❑ 223 Bruce Smith .20 .09
❑ 224 Eugene Robinson .10 .05
❑ 225 Bill Romanowski .10 .05
❑ 226 Wesley Walls .20 .09
❑ 227 Jimmy Smith .20 .09
❑ 228 Deion Sanders .40 .18
❑ 229 Lamar Thomas .10 .05
❑ 230 Dorsey Levens .40 .18
❑ 231 Tony Simmons .10 .05
❑ 232 John Randle .20 .09
❑ 233 Curtis Martin .40 .18
❑ 234 Bryant Young .10 .05
❑ 235 Charles Woodson .40 .18
❑ 236 Charles Way .10 .05
❑ 237 Zach Thomas .20 .09
❑ 238 Ricky Proehl .10 .05
❑ 239 Ricky Watters .20 .09
❑ 240 Hardy Nickerson .10 .05
❑ 241 Shannon Sharpe .20 .09
❑ 242 O.J. Santiago .10 .05
❑ 243 Vinny Testaverde .20 .09
❑ 244 Roell Preston .10 .05
❑ 245 James Stewart .20 .09
❑ 246 Jake Reed .20 .09
❑ 247 Steve Young .60 .25
❑ 248 Shaun Williams .10 .05
❑ 249 Rod Smith .20 .09
❑ 250 Warren Sapp .20 .09
❑ 251 Champ Bailey RC 1.50 .70
❑ 252 Karsten Bailey RC .75 .35
❑ 253 D'Wayne Bates RC 1.25 .55
❑ 254 Michael Bishop RC 1.50 .70
❑ 255 David Boston RC 2.50 1.10
❑ 256 Na Brown RC 1.25 .55
❑ 257 Fernando Bryant RC .75 .35
❑ 258 Shawn Bryson RC 1.25 .55
❑ 259 Darrin Chiaverini RC .75 .35
❑ 260 Chris Claiborne RC .40 .18
❑ 261 Mike Cloud RC 1.25 .55
❑ 262 Cecil Collins RC 1.25 .55
❑ 263 Tim Couch RC 4.00 1.80
❑ 264 Scott Covington RC 1.25 .55
❑ 265 Daunte Culpepper RC 8.00 3.60
❑ 266 Antuan Edwards RC .40 .18
❑ 267 Troy Edwards RC 1.50 .70
❑ 268 Ebenezer Ekuban RC .75 .35
❑ 269 Kevin Faulk RC 2.00 .90
❑ 270 Jermaine Fazande RC 1.25 .55
❑ 271 Joe Germaine RC 1.25 .55
❑ 272 Martin Gramatica RC .40 .18
❑ 273 Torry Holt RC 3.00 1.35
❑ 274 Brock Huard RC 2.00 .90
❑ 275 Sedrick Irvin RC 1.25 .55
❑ 276 Sheldon Jackson RC .75 .35
❑ 277 Edgerrin James RC 8.00 3.60
❑ 278 James Johnson RC 1.25 .55
❑ 279 Kevin Johnson RC 2.50 1.10
❑ 280 Malcolm Johnson RC .75 .35
❑ 281 Andy Katzenmoyer RC 1.25 .55
❑ 282 Jevon Kearse RC 2.50 1.10
❑ 283 Patrick Kerney RC .40 .18
❑ 284 Shaun King RC 2.50 1.10
❑ 285 Jim Kleinsasser RC 1.25 .55
❑ 286 Rob Konrad RC 1.25 .55
❑ 287 Chris McAlister RC .75 .35
❑ 288 Donovan McNabb RC 5.00 2.20
❑ 289 Cade McNown RC 1.50 .70
❑ 290 Dee Miller RC .75 .35
❑ 291 Joe Montgomery RC 1.25 .55
❑ 292 De'Mond Parker RC 1.25 .55
❑ 293 Peerless Price RC 1.50 .70
❑ 294 Akili Smith RC 2.50 1.10
❑ 295 Justin Swift RC .40 .18
❑ 296 Jerame Tuman RC .75 .35
❑ 297 Ricky Williams RC 5.00 2.20
❑ 298 Antoine Winfield .75 .35
❑ 299 Craig Yeast RC .75 .35
❑ 300 Amos Zereoue RC 1.25 .55
❑ P6 Fred Taylor Promo 1.00 .45

2000 Fleer

	MINT	NRMT
COMPLETE SET (400)	60.00	27.00

❑ 1 Kevin Johnson .40 .18
❑ 2 Chris Chandler .20 .09
❑ 3 Peerless Price .40 .18
❑ 4 Andre Rison .10 .05
❑ 5 Curtis Enis .20 .09
❑ 6 Tim Couch .75 .35
❑ 7 Brian Dawkins .10 .05
❑ 8 Akili Smith .40 .18
❑ 9 Kevin Faulk .20 .09
❑ 10 Joey Galloway .40 .18
❑ 11 Bill Romanowski .10 .05
❑ 12 Charlie Batch .40 .18
❑ 13 Terrence Wilkins .40 .18
❑ 14 Kevin Hardy .10 .05
❑ 15 Cade McNown .40 .18
❑ 16 Elvis Grbac .20 .09
❑ 17 Cris Carter .40 .18
❑ 18 Willie McGinest .10 .05
❑ 19 Michael Bishop .10 .05
❑ 20 Lee Woodall .10 .05
❑ 21 Jake Reed .20 .09
❑ 22 Bryan Cox .10 .05
❑ 23 Chris Sanders .10 .05
❑ 24 Tavian Banks .10 .05
❑ 25 Levon Kirkland .10 .05
❑ 26 James Hundon .10 .05
❑ 27 Junior Seau .20 .09
❑ 28 Darren Woodson .10 .05
❑ 29 Kevin Carter .10 .05

	#	Player		
❑	30	Joe Jurevicius	.10	.05
❑	31	John Lynch	.10	.05
❑	32	Steve McNair	.40	.18
❑	33	Jake Plummer	.40	.18
❑	34	Antonio Freeman	.40	.18
❑	35	Peter Boulware	.10	.05
❑	36	Brad Johnson	.40	.18
❑	37	Bobby Engram	.20	.09
❑	38	David Boston	.40	.18
❑	39	Jason Tucker	.20	.09
❑	40	Troy Brown	.10	.05
❑	41	Brian Griese	.50	.23
❑	42	Dorsey Levens	.20	.09
❑	43	Cornelius Bennett	.10	.05
❑	44	Donovan McNabb	.60	.25
❑	45	Rob Johnson	.20	.09
❑	46	Robert Smith	.40	.18
❑	47	Stanley Pritchett	.10	.05
❑	48	Tedy Bruschi	.10	.05
❑	49	Dan Marino	1.50	.70
❑	50	Amani Toomer	.20	.09
❑	51	Aaron Glenn	.10	.05
❑	52	Rickey Dudley	.10	.05
❑	53	Tim Brown	.40	.18
❑	54	Jim Harbaugh	.20	.09
❑	55	Terrell Owens	.40	.18
❑	56	Jason Sehorn	.10	.05
❑	57	Cortez Kennedy	.10	.05
❑	58	London Fletcher RC	.20	.09
❑	59	Simeon Rice	.10	.05
❑	60	Shaun King	.60	.25
❑	61	Stephen Davis	.40	.18
❑	62	Andre Wadsworth	.10	.05
❑	63	Kyle Brady	.10	.05
❑	64	Priest Holmes	.20	.09
❑	65	Patrick Jeffers	.40	.18
❑	66	Barry Minter	.10	.05
❑	67	Curtis Martin	.40	.18
❑	68	Darrin Chiaverini	.10	.05
❑	69	Robert Thomas	.20	.09
❑	70	Samari Rolle	.10	.05
❑	71	Robert Porcher	.10	.05
❑	72	Jerry Rice	1.00	.45
❑	73	Bill Schroeder	.20	.09
❑	74	Chad Bratzke	.10	.05
❑	75	Tony Brackens	.10	.05
❑	76	O.J. McDuffie	.20	.09
❑	77	John Randle	.20	.09
❑	78	Michael Pittman	.10	.05
❑	79	Drew Bledsoe	.60	.25
❑	80	Ike Hilliard	.20	.09
❑	81	Victor Green	.10	.05
❑	82	Duce Staley	.40	.18
❑	83	Bruce Smith	.20	.09
❑	84	Amos Zereoue	.10	.05
❑	85	Charlie Garner	.20	.09
❑	86	Shawn Springs	.10	.05
❑	87	Kurt Warner	1.50	.70
❑	88	Eddie George	.50	.23
❑	89	Michael Westbrook	.20	.09
❑	90	Dexter Coakley	.10	.05
❑	91	Rob Moore	.20	.09
❑	92	Duane Starks	.10	.05
❑	93	Steve Beuerlein	.20	.09
❑	94	Marty Booker	.10	.05
❑	95	Karim Abdul-Jabbar	.20	.09
❑	96	Troy Aikman	1.00	.45
❑	97	Germane Crowell	.20	.09
❑	98	Matt Hasselbeck	.10	.05
❑	99	E.G. Green	.10	.05
❑	100	Mark Brunell	.60	.25
❑	101	Tony Martin	.20	.09
❑	102	Darrell Green	.10	.05
❑	103	Ricky Williams	1.00	.45
❑	104	Michael Strahan	.10	.05
❑	105	Vinny Testaverde	.20	.09
❑	106	Charles Johnson	.20	.09
❑	107	Hines Ward	.10	.05
❑	108	Bryant Young	.10	.05
❑	109	Mo Lewis	.10	.05
❑	110	Greg Clark	.10	.05
❑	111	Jon Kitna	.40	.18
❑	112	Jacquez Green	.20	.09
❑	113	Kevin Dyson	.20	.09
❑	114	Stephen Alexander	.10	.05
❑	115	Cam Cleeland	.10	.05
❑	116	Keith Poole	.10	.05
❑	117	Az-Zahir Hakim	.20	.09
❑	118	Tim Dwight	.40	.18
❑	119	Corey Bradford	.10	.05
❑	120	Carlos Emmons	.10	.05
❑	121	Trent Dilfer	.20	.09
❑	122	Lance Schulters	.10	.05
❑	123	Byron Hanspard	.10	.05
❑	124	Tim Biakabutuka	.20	.09
❑	125	Eddie Kennison	.20	.09
❑	126	Terry Kirby	.10	.05
❑	127	Mike McKenzie	.10	.05
❑	128	Fred Beasley	.10	.05
❑	129	Chad Brown	.10	.05
❑	130	Terrell Davis	1.00	.45
❑	131	Herman Moore	.20	.09
❑	132	Vonnie Holliday	.10	.05
❑	133	Jim Miller	.10	.05
❑	134	Peyton Manning	1.25	.55
❑	135	Derrick Alexander	.20	.09
❑	136	Oronde Gadsden	.20	.09
❑	137	Robert Griffith	.10	.05
❑	138	Troy Edwards	.20	.09
❑	139	Damon Huard	.40	.18
❑	140	Jessie Armstead	.10	.05
❑	141	Charles Woodson	.20	.09
❑	142	Troy Vincent	.10	.05
❑	143	Natrone Means	.10	.05
❑	144	Jeff Garcia	.40	.18
❑	145	Terry Glenn	.20	.09
❑	146	Marshall Faulk	.50	.23
❑	147	Pat Johnson	.10	.05
❑	148	Frank Wycheck	.10	.05
❑	149	Champ Bailey	.20	.09
❑	150	Jamal Anderson	.40	.18
❑	151	Doug Flutie	.50	.23
❑	152	Michael Bates	.10	.05
❑	153	Corey Dillon	.40	.18
❑	154	Keith McKenzie	.10	.05
❑	155	Orpheus Roye	.10	.05
❑	156	Olandis Gary	.40	.18
❑	157	Johnnie Morton	.20	.09
❑	158	Brett Favre	1.50	.70
❑	159	Adrian Murrell	.10	.05
❑	160	Fred Taylor	.50	.23
❑	161	Tony Gonzalez	.20	.09
❑	162	Zach Thomas	.20	.09
❑	163	Randy Moss	1.25	.55
❑	164	Marcus Robinson	.40	.18
❑	165	Tiki Barber	.10	.05
❑	166	Rich Gannon	.20	.09
❑	167	Jeremiah Trotter RC	.40	.18
❑	168	Jermaine Fazande	.10	.05
❑	169	Steve Young	.60	.25
❑	170	Isaac Bruce	.40	.18
❑	171	Warrick Dunn	.40	.18
❑	172	Yancey Thigpen	.10	.05
❑	173	Rod Smith	.20	.09
❑	174	Albert Connell	.10	.05
❑	175	Freddie Jones	.10	.05
❑	176	Terance Mathis	.20	.09
❑	177	Eric Moulds	.40	.18
❑	178	Brian Mitchell	.10	.05
❑	179	Wesley Walls	.10	.05
❑	180	Carl Pickens	.20	.09
❑	181	Errict Rhett	.20	.09
❑	182	Madre Hill	.10	.05
❑	183	Jason Elam	.10	.05
❑	184	Greg Ellis	.10	.05
❑	185	David Sloan	.10	.05
❑	186	Edgerrin James	1.50	.70
❑	187	Jimmy Smith	.20	.09
❑	188	Tony Richardson RC	.20	.09
❑	189	James Hasty	.10	.05
❑	190	Sam Madison	.10	.05
❑	191	Tony Simmons	.10	.05
❑	192	Andre Hastings	.10	.05
❑	193	Keyshawn Johnson	.40	.18
❑	194	Na Brown	.10	.05
❑	195	Napoleon Kaufman	.20	.09
❑	196	Torrance Small	.10	.05
❑	197	Curtis Conway	.20	.09
❑	198	Jeff Graham	.10	.05
❑	199	Jason Hanson	.10	.05
❑	200	Derrick Mayes	.20	.09
❑	201	Torry Holt	.40	.18
❑	202	Warren Sapp	.20	.09
❑	203	Kimble Anders	.10	.05
❑	204	Blaine Bishop	.10	.05
❑	205	Leroy Hoard	.10	.05
❑	206	Larry Centers	.10	.05
❑	207	O.J. Santiago	.10	.05
❑	208	Antowain Smith	.20	.09
❑	209	Chuck Smith	.10	.05
❑	210	Takeo Spikes	.10	.05
❑	211	Rocket Ismail	.20	.09
❑	212	Ed McCaffrey	.40	.18
❑	213	Karsten Bailey	.10	.05
❑	214	Terry Fair	.10	.05
❑	215	Ken Dilger	.10	.05
❑	216	Jamie Martin	.10	.05
❑	217	Cris Dishman	.10	.05
❑	218	Jay Fiedler	.20	.09
❑	219	Lawyer Milloy	.10	.05
❑	220	Jake Delhomme RC	.75	.35
❑	221	Wayne Chrebet	.20	.09
❑	222	Darrell Russell	.10	.05
❑	223	Christian Fauria	.10	.05
❑	224	Jerome Bettis	.40	.18
❑	225	Ryan Leaf	.40	.18
❑	226	Ricky Watters	.20	.09
❑	227	Keenan McCardell	.20	.09
❑	228	Grant Wistrom	.10	.05
❑	229	Jevon Kearse	.40	.18
❑	230	Frank Sanders	.20	.09
❑	231	Shannon Sharpe	.20	.09
❑	232	Jonathan Linton	.10	.05
❑	233	Alonzo Mayes	.10	.05
❑	234	Jason Garrett	.10	.05
❑	235	Kordell Stewart	.40	.18
❑	236	David LaFleur	.10	.05
❑	237	Kenny Bynum	.10	.05
❑	238	Byron Chamberlain	.10	.05
❑	239	Tyrone Davis	.10	.05
❑	240	Jerome Pathon	.20	.09
❑	241	Alvis Whitted	.10	.05
❑	242	Kevin Lockett	.10	.05
❑	243	Matthew Hatchette	.10	.05
❑	244	Rod Woodson	.20	.09
❑	245	Joe Horn	.20	.09
❑	246	Ronnie Powell	.10	.05
❑	247	Dedric Ward	.10	.05
❑	248	James Johnson	.20	.09
❑	249	James Jett	.10	.05
❑	250	Bobby Shaw RC	1.00	.45
❑	251	J.J. Stokes	.20	.09
❑	252	Paul Shields RC	.10	.05
❑	253	Sean Dawkins	.10	.05
❑	254	Hardy Nickerson	.10	.05
❑	255	Stephen Boyd	.10	.05
❑	256	Chris Warren	.10	.05
❑	257	Kerry Collins	.20	.09
❑	258	Isaac Byrd	.10	.05
❑	259	Bobby Hoying	.10	.05
❑	260	Daunte Culpepper	.75	.35
❑	261	Moe Williams	.10	.05
❑	262	Kamil Loud	.10	.05
❑	263	Derrick Brooks	.10	.05
❑	264	Jay Riemersma	.10	.05
❑	265	Ray Lucas	.40	.18
❑	266	Jason Gildon	.10	.05
❑	267	James Stewart	.20	.09
❑	268	Marcellus Wiley	.10	.05
❑	269	Craig Yeast	.10	.05
❑	270	Michael Basnight	.10	.05
❑	271	Tyrone Wheatley	.20	.09
❑	272	Martin Gramatica	.10	.05
❑	273	Phillip Daniels RC	.20	.09
❑	274	Richard Huntley	.10	.05
❑	275	Muhsin Muhammad	.20	.09
❑	276	Todd Lyght	.10	.05
❑	277	Carlester Crumpler	.10	.05
❑	278	Jeff Lewis	.10	.05
❑	279	Jeff George	.20	.09
❑	280	Jeff Blake	.20	.09
❑	281	Michael McCrary	.10	.05
❑	282	Shawn Jefferson	.10	.05
❑	283	Mark Bruener	.10	.05
❑	284	Donnie Abraham	.10	.05
❑	285	Yatil Green	.10	.05
❑	286	Jermaine Lewis	.10	.05
❑	287	Rob Fredrickson	.10	.05

❑ 288 Thurman Thomas .... .20 .09
❑ 289 Kent Graham.................. .10 .05
❑ 290 Darnay Scott .... .20 .09
❑ 291 Tony Graziani .... .10 .05
❑ 292 Qadry Ismail .... .10 .05
❑ 293 Aeneas Williams .... .10 .05
❑ 294 Marvin Harrison.............. .40 .18
❑ 295 Jimmy Hitchcock .... .10 .05
❑ 296 Bob Christian.................. .10 .05
❑ 297 Pete Mitchell .... .10 .05
❑ 298 Mike Alstott .... .40 .18
❑ 299 Emmitt Smith............... 1.00 .45
❑ 300 Trevor Pryce .... .10 .05
❑ 301 Tony Banks..................... .20 .09
❑ 302 Mikhael Ricks .... .10 .05
❑ 303 Randall Cunningham....... .40 .18
❑ 304 Thomas Jones RC ...... 1.25 .55
❑ 305 Mark Simoneau RC........ .75 .35
❑ 306 Jamal Lewis RC 4.00 1.80
❑ 307 Kwame Cavil RC............ .60 .25
❑ 308 Rashard Anderson RC .. .60 .25
❑ 309 Brian Urlacher RC 2.50 1.10
❑ 310 Peter Warrick RC 2.50 1.10
❑ 311 Courtney Brown RC .... 1.00 .45
❑ 312 Michael Wiley RC .... .75 .35
❑ 313 Chris Cole RC .... .60 .25
❑ 314 Reuben Droughns RC..... .75 .35
❑ 315 Bubba Franks RC .... 1.00 .45
❑ 316 Rob Morris RC .... .60 .25
❑ 317 R.Jay Soward RC .... .75 .35
❑ 318 Sylvester Morris RC .... 1.50 .70
❑ 319 Ben Kelly RC.................. .40 .18
❑ 320 Doug Chapman RC...... 1.50 .70
❑ 321 J.R. Redmond RC .... 1.00 .45
❑ 322 Darren Howard RC .... .60 .25
❑ 323 Ron Dayne RC 2.50 1.10
❑ 324 Chad Pennington RC .. 2.50 1.10
❑ 325 Jerry Porter RC .... .75 .35
❑ 326 Corey Simon RC .... 1.00 .45
❑ 327 Plaxico Burress RC...... 1.50 .70
❑ 328 Trung Canidate RC......... .75 .35
❑ 329 Rogers Beckett RC .... .60 .25
❑ 330 Giovanni Carmazzi RC 1.00 .45
❑ 331 Shaun Alexander RC .. 2.00 .90
❑ 332 Joe Hamilton RC.......... 1.00 .45
❑ 333 Keith Bulluck RC............ .60 .25
❑ 334 Todd Husak RC.............. .75 .35
❑ 335 Darwin Walker RC.......... .60 .25
Raynoch Thompson RC
❑ 336 Mareno Philyaw RC .... .40 .18
Anthony Midget RC
❑ 337 Chris Redman RC........ 1.25 .55
Travis Taylor RC
❑ 338 Sammy Morris RC........ 1.25 .55
Avion Black RC
❑ 339 Deon Grant RC .... .40 .18
Alvin McKinley RC
❑ 340 Dez White RC .... .60 .25
Frank Murphy RC
❑ 341 Curtis Keaton RC .... 1.00 .45
Ron Dugans RC
❑ 342 Travis Prentice RC ...... 1.25 .55
Dennis Northcutt RC
❑ 343 Orantes Grant RC .... .40 .18
Dwayne Goodrich RC
❑ 344 Deltha O'Neal RC .... .60 .25
Ian Gold RC
❑ 345 Stockar McDougle RC..... .40 .18
Barrett Green RC
❑ 346 Anthony Lucas RC .... .60 .25
Na'il Diggs RC
❑ 347 Marcus Washington RC .40 .18
Don Kendra RC
❑ 348 T.J. Slaughter RC .... .60 .25
Shyrone Stith RC
❑ 349 William Bartee RC.......... .60 .25
Frank Moreau RC
❑ 350 Deon Dyer RC................ .60 .25
Todd Wade RC
❑ 351 Chris Hovan RC .... .75 .35
Troy Walters RC
❑ 352 David Stachelski RC ...... .75 .35
Tom Brady RC
❑ 353 Marc Bulger RC.............. .75 .35
Terrelle Smith RC
❑ 354 Cornelius Griffin RC .... 1.00 .45
Ron Dixon RC
❑ 355 Laveranues Coles RC.. 1.00 .45
Anthony Becht RC
❑ 356 Sebastian Janikowski RC .75 .35
Shane Lechler RC
❑ 357 Todd Pinkston RC.......... .75 .35
Gari Scott RC
❑ 358 Danny Farmer RC........ 1.25 .55
Tee Martin RC
❑ 359 Brian Young RC .... .60 .25
Jacoby Shepherd RC
❑ 360 JaJuan Seider RC.......... .60 .25
Trevor Gaylor RC
❑ 361 Tim Rattay RC............. 1.25 .55
Chafie Fields RC
❑ 362 Darrell Jackson RC ...... 1.00 .45
James Williams RC
❑ 363 Nate Webster RC .... .40 .18
James Whalen RC
❑ 364 Erron Kinney RC .... .75 .35
Chris Coleman RC
❑ 365 Chris Samuels RC.......... .60 .25
Leon Murray RC
❑ 366 Arizona Cardinals IA ...... .20 .09
Jake Plummer
❑ 367 Atlanta Falcons IA.......... .20 .09
Chris Chandler
Jamal Anderson
❑ 368 Baltimore Ravens IA ...... .10 .05
Peter Boulware
❑ 369 Buffalo Bills IA................ .20 .09
Doug Flutie
❑ 370 Carolina Panthers IA...... .20 .09
Steve Beuerlein
❑ 371 Chicago Bears IA .... .20 .09
Cade McNown
❑ 372 Cincinnati Bengals IA .... .20 .09
Corey Dillon
❑ 373 Cleveland Browns IA...... .40 .18
Tim Couch
❑ 374 Dallas Cowboys IA .... .50 .23
Emmitt Smith
❑ 375 Denver Broncos IA .... .20 .09
Olandis Gary
❑ 376 Detroit Lions IA .... .20 .09
Charlie Batch
❑ 377 Green Bay Packers IA.... .20 .09
Dorsey Levens
❑ 378 Indianapolis Colts IA ...... .60 .25
Edgerrin James
❑ 379 Jacksonville Jaguars IA.. .10 .05
Tony Brackens
❑ 380 Kansas City Chiefs IA .... .10 .05
Elvis Grbac
❑ 381 Miami Dolphins IA .... .75 .35
Dan Marino
❑ 382 Minnesota Vikings IA...... .20 .09
Robert Smith
❑ 383 New England Patriots IA .20 .09
Drew Bledsoe
❑ 384 New Orleans Saints IA .. .40 .18
Ricky Williams
❑ 385 New York Giants IA........ .10 .05
Jessie Armstead
❑ 386 New York Jets IA............ .20 .09
Curtis Martin
❑ 387 Oakland Raiders IA........ .20 .09
Napoleon Kaufman
❑ 388 Philadelphia Eagles IA .. .20 .09
Donovan McNabb
❑ 389 Pittsburgh Steelers IA .... .20 .09
Jerome Bettis
❑ 390 St. Louis Rams IA .... .20 .09
Marshall Faulk
❑ 391 San Diego Chargers IA .. .10 .05
Jermaine Fazande
❑ 392 San Francisco 49ers IA.. .20 .09
Charlie Garner
❑ 393 Seattle Seahawks IA...... .10 .05
Cortez Kennedy
❑ 394 Tampa Bay Bucs IA ...... .20 .09
Mike Alstott
❑ 395 Tennessee Titans IA...... .20 .09
Steve McNair
❑ 396 Washington Redskins IA .20 .09
Stephen Davis
❑ 397 Tim Couch CL................ .40 .18
❑ 398 Peyton Manning CL......... .60 .25
❑ 399 Kurt Warner CL .... .75 .35
❑ 400 Randy Moss CL.............. .60 .25

2000 Fleer Glossy

	MINT	NRMT
COMP.FACT.SET (406)........	100.00	45.00
COMP.SET w/o SP's (400)......	60.00	27.00

*1-400 STARS: .8X TO 2X BASIC CARDS
*304-365 ROOK: 1X TO 2.5X BASIC CARDS

❑ 401 JaJuan Dawson RC 8.00 3.60
❑ 402 Mike Anderson RC 50.00 22.00
❑ 403 Windrell Hayes RC 6.00 2.70
❑ 404 Shockmain Davis RC .. 6.00 2.70
❑ 405 Dante Hall RC 6.00 2.70
❑ 406 Charles Lee RC............ 4.00 1.80
❑ 407 Maurice Smith RC........ 6.00 2.70
❑ 408 Obafemi Ayanbadejo RC 8.00 3.60
❑ 409 Travis Taylor 5.00 2.20
❑ 410 Dez White 3.00 1.35
❑ 411 Sammy Morris............... 5.00 2.20
❑ 412 Darrell Jackson 6.00 2.70
❑ 413 Todd Pinkston 4.00 1.80
❑ 414 Ron Dixon 5.00 2.20
❑ 415 Frank Moreau 4.00 1.80
❑ 416 James Williams 3.00 1.35
❑ 417 Lenzie Jackson RC 6.00 2.70
❑ 418 Chad Morton RC 8.00 3.60
❑ 419 Matt Lytle RC 6.00 2.70
❑ 420 Travis Prentice 6.00 2.70
❑ 421 Laveranues Coles 6.00 2.70
❑ 422 Clint Stoerner RC 20.00 9.00
❑ 423 Karon Coleman RC...... 6.00 2.70
❑ 424 Ron Dugans 3.00 1.35
❑ 425 Dennis Northcutt 5.00 2.20
❑ 426 Herbert Goodman RC .. 6.00 2.70
❑ 427 Dane Looker RC 6.00 2.70
❑ 428 Mike Brown RC 8.00 3.60
❑ 429 Derrius Thompson RC 6.00 2.70
❑ 430 Danny Farmer............... 4.00 1.80
❑ 431 Bashir Yamini RC 6.00 2.70
❑ 432 Trevor Gaylor 3.00 1.35
❑ 433 Erron Kinney RC.......... 8.00 3.60
❑ 434 James Hodgins RC 6.00 2.70
❑ 435 Aaron Shea RC............ 8.00 3.60
❑ 436 Patrick Pass RC 6.00 2.70
❑ 437 Terrelle Smith 3.00 1.35
❑ 438 Avion Black 3.00 1.35
❑ 439 Deltha O'Neal 3.00 1.35
❑ 440 Chris Coleman .... 2.00 .90
❑ 441 Reggie Jones RC 8.00 3.60
❑ 442 Shyrone Stith................ 3.00 1.35
❑ 443 Aaron Stecker RC 8.00 3.60
❑ 444 Chris Redman 8.00 3.60
❑ 445 Curtis Keaton 3.00 1.35
❑ 446 Jamel White RC 8.00 3.60
❑ 447 Troy Walters 4.00 1.80
❑ 448 Spergon Wynn 4.00 1.80
❑ 449 Ronney Jenkins RC 6.00 2.70
❑ 450 Doug Johnson RC........ 8.00 3.60

1998 Fleer Brilliants

	MINT	NRMT
COMPLETE SET (150)	150.00	70.00

❑ 1 John Elway 5.00 2.20

❑ 2 Curtis Conway	.50	.23
❑ 3 Danny Wuerffel	.50	.23
❑ 4 Emmitt Smith	4.00	1.80
❑ 5 Marvin Harrison	.50	.23
❑ 6 Antowain Smith	1.00	.45
❑ 7 James Stewart	.50	.23
❑ 8 Junior Seau	.50	.23
❑ 9 Herman Moore	1.00	.45
❑ 10 Drew Bledsoe	2.00	.90
❑ 11 Rae Carruth	.50	.23
❑ 12 Trent Dilfer	1.00	.45
❑ 13 Derrick Alexander	.50	.23
❑ 14 Ike Hilliard	.50	.23
❑ 15 Bruce Smith	.50	.23
❑ 16 Warren Moon	1.00	.45
❑ 17 Jermaine Lewis	.50	.23
❑ 18 Mike Alstott	1.00	.45
❑ 19 Robert Brooks	.50	.23
❑ 20 Jerome Bettis	1.00	.45
❑ 21 Brett Favre	5.00	2.20
❑ 22 Garrison Hearst	1.00	.45
❑ 23 Neil O'Donnell	.50	.23
❑ 24 Joey Galloway	1.00	.45
❑ 25 Barry Sanders	5.00	2.20
❑ 26 Donnell Bennett	.25	.11
❑ 27 Jamal Anderson	1.00	.45
❑ 28 Isaac Bruce	1.00	.45
❑ 29 Chris Chandler	.50	.23
❑ 30 Kordell Stewart	1.00	.45
❑ 31 Corey Dillon	1.50	.70
❑ 32 Troy Aikman	2.50	1.10
❑ 33 Frank Sanders	.50	.23
❑ 34 Cris Carter	1.00	.45
❑ 35 Greg Hill	.25	.11
❑ 36 Tony Martin	.50	.23
❑ 37 Shannon Sharpe	.50	.23
❑ 38 Wayne Chrebet	1.00	.45
❑ 39 Trent Green	1.25	.55
❑ 40 Warrick Dunn	1.00	.45
❑ 41 Michael Irvin	1.00	.45
❑ 42 Eddie George	2.00	.90
❑ 43 Carl Pickens	1.00	.45
❑ 44 Wesley Walls	.50	.23
❑ 45 Steve McNair	1.00	.45
❑ 46 Bert Emanuel	.50	.23
❑ 47 Terry Glenn	1.00	.45
❑ 48 Elvis Grbac	.50	.23
❑ 49 Charles Way	.25	.11
❑ 50 Steve Young	1.50	.70
❑ 51 Deion Sanders	1.00	.45
❑ 52 Keyshawn Johnson	1.00	.45
❑ 53 Kerry Collins	.50	.23
❑ 54 O.J. McDuffie	.50	.23
❑ 55 Ricky Watters	.50	.23
❑ 56 Derrick Thomas	.50	.23
❑ 57 Antonio Freeman	1.00	.45
❑ 58 Jake Plummer	2.00	.90
❑ 59 Andre Reed	.50	.23
❑ 60 Jerry Rice	2.50	1.10
❑ 61 Dorsey Levens	1.00	.45
❑ 62 Eddie Kennison	.50	.23
❑ 63 Marshall Faulk	1.00	.45
❑ 64 Michael Jackson	.25	.11
❑ 65 Karim Abdul-Jabbar	1.00	.45
❑ 66 Andre Rison	.50	.23
❑ 67 Glenn Foley	.50	.23
❑ 68 Jake Reed	.50	.23
❑ 69 Tony Banks	.50	.23
❑ 70 Dan Marino	5.00	2.20
❑ 71 Bryan Still	.25	.11
❑ 72 Tim Brown	1.00	.45
❑ 73 Charles Johnson	.25	.11
❑ 74 Jeff George	.50	.23
❑ 75 Jimmy Smith	.50	.23
❑ 76 Ben Coates	.50	.23
❑ 77 Rob Moore	.50	.23
❑ 78 Johnnie Morton	.50	.23
❑ 79 Peter Boulware	.25	.11
❑ 80 Curtis Martin	1.00	.45
❑ 81 James McKnight	.25	.11
❑ 82 Danny Kanell	.50	.23
❑ 83 Brad Johnson	1.00	.45
❑ 84 Amani Toomer	.50	.23
❑ 85 Terry Allen	1.00	.45
❑ 86 Rod Smith	.50	.23
❑ 87 Keenan McCardell	.50	.23
❑ 88 Leslie Shepherd	.25	.11
❑ 89 Irving Fryar	.50	.23
❑ 90 Terrell Davis	4.00	1.80
❑ 91 Robert Smith	1.00	.45
❑ 92 Duce Staley	2.00	.90
❑ 93 Rickey Dudley	.25	.11
❑ 94 Bobby Hoying	.50	.23
❑ 95 Terrell Owens	1.00	.45
❑ 96 Fred Lane	.50	.23
❑ 97 Natrone Means	1.00	.45
❑ 98 Yancey Thigpen	.25	.11
❑ 99 Reggie White	1.00	.45
❑ 100 Mark Brunell	2.00	.90
❑ 101 Ahman Green RC	6.00	2.70
❑ 102 Skip Hicks RC	3.00	1.35
❑ 103 Hines Ward RC	2.50	1.10
❑ 104 Marcus Nash RC	3.00	1.35
❑ 105 Terry Hardy RC	1.50	.70
❑ 106 Pat Johnson RC	2.50	1.10
❑ 107 Tremayne Stephens RC	1.50	.70
❑ 108 Joe Jurevicius RC	2.50	1.10
❑ 109 Moses Moreno RC	2.50	1.10
❑ 110 Charles Woodson RC	5.00	2.20
❑ 111 Kevin Dyson RC	5.00	2.20
❑ 112 Alvis Whitted RC	1.50	.70
❑ 113 Michael Pittman RC	3.00	1.35
❑ 114 Stephen Alexander RC	2.50	1.10
❑ 115 Tavian Banks RC	2.50	1.10
❑ 116 John Avery RC	3.00	1.35
❑ 117 Keith Brooking RC	2.50	1.10
❑ 118 Jerome Pathon RC	2.50	1.10
❑ 119 Terry Fair RC	2.50	1.10
❑ 120 Peyton Manning RC	25.00	11.00
❑ 121 R.W. McQuarters RC	1.50	.70
❑ 122 Charlie Batch RC	8.00	3.60
❑ 123 Jonathan Quinn RC	2.50	1.10
❑ 124 C.Fuamatu-Ma'afala RC	2.50	1.10
❑ 125 Jacquez Green RC	5.00	2.20
❑ 126 Germane Crowell RC	8.00	3.60
❑ 127 Oronde Gadsden RC	3.00	1.35
❑ 128 Koy Detmer	3.00	1.35
❑ 129 Robert Holcombe RC	3.00	1.35
❑ 130 Curtis Enis RC	4.00	1.80
❑ 131 Brian Griese RC	10.00	4.50
❑ 132 Tony Simmons RC	2.50	1.10
❑ 133 Vonnie Holliday RC	2.50	1.10
❑ 134 Alonzo Mayes RC	1.50	.70
❑ 135 Jon Ritchie RC	2.50	1.10
❑ 136 Robert Edwards RC	5.00	2.20
❑ 137 Mike Vanderjagt RC	1.50	.70
❑ 138 Jonathan Linton RC	3.00	1.35
❑ 139 Fred Taylor RC	8.00	3.60
❑ 140 Randy Moss RC	25.00	11.00
❑ 141 Rod Rutledge RC	1.50	.70
❑ 142 Andre Wadsworth RC	2.50	1.10
❑ 143 Rashaan Shehee RC	2.50	1.10
❑ 144 Shaun Williams RC	1.50	.70
❑ 145 Mikhael Ricks RC	2.50	1.10
❑ 146 Wade Richey RC	1.50	.70
❑ 147 Carlos King RC	1.50	.70
❑ 148 Tim Dwight RC	5.00	2.20
❑ 149 Scott Frost RC	2.50	1.10
❑ 150 Ryan Leaf RC	6.00	2.70

1999 Fleer Focus

	MINT	NRMT
COMPLETE SET (175)	400.00	180.00
COMP.SET w/o SP's (100)	40.00	18.00
❑ 1 Randy Moss	3.00	1.35
❑ 2 Andre Rison	.40	.18
❑ 3 Ed McCaffrey	.40	.18
❑ 4 Jerry Rice	2.00	.90
❑ 5 Tim Biakabutuka	.40	.18
❑ 6 Wayne Chrebet	.40	.18
❑ 7 Deion Sanders	.75	.35
❑ 8 Ricky Watters	.40	.18
❑ 9 Skip Hicks	.40	.18
❑ 10 Charlie Batch	1.50	.70
❑ 11 Joey Galloway	.75	.35
❑ 12 Stephen Alexander	.20	.09
❑ 13 Curtis Conway	.40	.18
❑ 14 Garrison Hearst	.40	.18
❑ 15 Kerry Collins	.40	.18
❑ 16 Cris Carter	.75	.35
❑ 17 Eddie George	1.00	.45
❑ 18 Eric Moulds	.75	.35
❑ 19 Vinny Testaverde	.40	.18
❑ 20 Curtis Enis	.75	.35
❑ 21 Gary Brown	.20	.09
❑ 22 Junior Seau	.40	.18
❑ 23 Kevin Dyson	.40	.18
❑ 24 Jeff Blake	.40	.18
❑ 25 Herman Moore	.75	.35
❑ 26 Natrone Means	.40	.18
❑ 27 Terry Glenn	.75	.35
❑ 28 Fred Taylor	2.00	.90
❑ 29 Ben Coates	.40	.18
❑ 30 Corey Dillon	.75	.35
❑ 31 Eddie Kennison	.40	.18
❑ 32 Byron Bam Morris	.20	.09
❑ 33 Doug Pederson	.20	.09
❑ 34 Jamal Anderson	.75	.35
❑ 35 Michael Westbrook	.40	.18
❑ 36 Peyton Manning	3.00	1.35
❑ 37 Carl Pickens	.40	.18
❑ 38 Drew Bledsoe	1.50	.70
❑ 39 Jim Harbaugh	.40	.18
❑ 40 Kurt Warner RC	12.00	5.50
❑ 41 Mark Chmura	.20	.09
❑ 42 Hines Ward	.20	.09
❑ 43 Terry Kirby	.20	.09
❑ 44 Brett Favre	3.00	1.35
❑ 45 Kordell Stewart	.75	.35
❑ 46 Leslie Shepherd	.20	.09
❑ 47 Marshall Faulk	.75	.35
❑ 48 Troy Aikman	2.00	.90
❑ 49 Isaac Bruce	.75	.35
❑ 50 Michael Irvin	.40	.18
❑ 51 Robert Smith	.40	.18
❑ 52 Dorsey Levens	.75	.35
❑ 53 Duce Staley	.75	.35
❑ 54 Jake Plummer	1.25	.55
❑ 55 Adrian Murrell	.40	.18
❑ 56 Antonio Freeman	.75	.35
❑ 57 Jerome Bettis	.40	.18
❑ 58 Elvis Grbac	.40	.18
❑ 59 Keyshawn Johnson	.75	.35
❑ 60 Steve Beuerlein	.20	.09
❑ 61 Yancey Thigpen	.20	.09
❑ 62 Doug Flutie	1.00	.45
❑ 63 Jacquez Green	.40	.18
❑ 64 Jimmy Smith	.40	.18
❑ 65 Tim Brown	.75	.35
❑ 66 Jason Sehorn	.20	.09
❑ 67 Muhsin Muhammad	.40	.18
❑ 68 Shannon Sharpe	.40	.18
❑ 69 Terrell Owens	.75	.35
❑ 70 Keenan McCardell	.40	.18
❑ 71 Rich Gannon	.40	.18
❑ 72 Scott Mitchell	.20	.09
❑ 73 Warrick Dunn	.75	.35
❑ 74 Brad Johnson	.40	.18
❑ 75 Charles Johnson	.20	.09
❑ 76 Chris Chandler	.40	.18
❑ 77 Marcus Pollard	.20	.09
❑ 78 Mike Alstott	.75	.35
❑ 79 Bubby Brister	.40	.18
❑ 80 Jon Kitna	.75	.35
❑ 81 Randall Cunningham	.75	.35
❑ 82 Antowain Smith	.75	.35
❑ 83 Curtis Martin	.75	.35
❑ 84 Steve McNair	.75	.35
❑ 85 Tony Gonzalez	.40	.18
❑ 86 O.J. McDuffie	.40	.18

Card	Player	Mint	NrMt
❑ 87	Steve Young	1.25	.55
❑ 88	Terrell Davis	2.00	.90
❑ 89	Mark Brunell	1.25	.55
❑ 90	Napoleon Kaufman	.75	.35
❑ 91	Priest Holmes	.75	.35
❑ 92	Trent Dilfer	.40	.18
❑ 93	Brian Griese	1.50	.70
❑ 94	J.J. Stokes	.40	.18
❑ 95	Karim Abdul-Jabbar	.40	.18
❑ 96	Barry Sanders	3.00	1.35
❑ 97	Dan Marino	3.00	1.35
❑ 98	Emmitt Smith	2.00	.90
❑ 99	Marvin Harrison	.75	.35
❑ 100	Rod Smith	.40	.18
❑ 101	Champ Bailey RC	4.00	1.80
❑ 102	Fernando Bryant RC	2.00	.90
❑ 103	Chris Claiborne RC	1.25	.55
❑ 104	Antuan Edwards RC	2.00	.90
❑ 105	Martin Gramatica RC	1.25	.55
❑ 106	Andy Katzenmoyer RC	3.00	1.35
❑ 107	Jevon Kearse RC	6.00	2.70
❑ 108	Chris McAlister RC	2.00	.90
❑ 109	Al Wilson RC	2.00	.90
❑ 110	Antoine Winfield RC	2.00	.90
❑ 111	Karsten Bailey RC	4.00	1.80
❑ 112	D'Wayne Bates RC	3.00	1.35
❑ 113	Marty Booker RC	5.00	2.20
❑ 114	David Boston RC	10.00	4.50
❑ 115	Na Brown RC	4.00	1.80
❑ 116	Desmond Clark RC	3.00	1.35
❑ 117	Dameane Douglas RC	3.00	1.35
❑ 118	Donald Driver RC	4.00	1.80
❑ 119	Troy Edwards RC	6.00	2.70
❑ 120	Torry Holt RC	12.00	5.50
❑ 121	Kevin Johnson RC	10.00	4.50
❑ 122	Reginald Kelly RC	3.00	1.35
❑ 123	Jimmy Kleinsasser RC	4.00	1.80
❑ 124	Jeremy McDaniel RC	5.00	2.20
❑ 125	Darnell McDonald RC	4.00	1.80
❑ 126	Travis McGriff RC	3.00	1.35
❑ 127	Billy Miller RC	3.00	1.35
❑ 128	Dee Miller RC	4.00	1.80
❑ 129	Peerless Price RC	6.00	2.70
❑ 130	Troy Smith RC	3.00	1.35
❑ 131	Brandon Stokley RC	5.00	2.20
❑ 132	Wane McGarity RC	3.00	1.35
❑ 133	Mark Campbell RC	3.00	1.35
❑ 134	Jerame Tuman RC	3.00	1.35
❑ 135	Craig Yeast RC	3.00	1.35
❑ 136	Jerry Azumah RC	6.00	2.70
❑ 137	Marlon Barnes RC	6.00	2.70
❑ 138	Michael Basnight RC	6.00	2.70
❑ 139	Shawn Bryson RC	8.00	3.60
❑ 140	Mike Cloud RC	8.00	3.60
❑ 141	Cecil Collins RC	4.00	1.80
❑ 142	Autry Denson RC	8.00	3.60
❑ 143	Kevin Faulk RC	10.00	4.50
❑ 144	Jermaine Fazande RC	8.00	3.60
❑ 145	Jim Finn RC	4.00	1.80
❑ 146	Madre Hill RC	6.00	2.70
❑ 147	Sedrick Irvin RC	8.00	3.60
❑ 148	Terry Jackson RC	6.00	2.70
❑ 149	Edgerrin James RC	40.00	18.00
❑ 150	James Johnson RC	8.00	3.60
❑ 151	Rob Konrad RC	8.00	3.60
❑ 152	Joel Makovicka RC	8.00	3.60
❑ 153	Cecil Martin RC	8.00	3.60
❑ 154	Joe Montgomery RC	8.00	3.60
❑ 155	De'Mond Parker RC	8.00	3.60
❑ 156	Sirr Parker RC	6.00	2.70
❑ 157	Jeff Paulk RC	6.00	2.70
❑ 158	Nick Williams RC	6.00	2.70
❑ 159	Ricky Williams RC	30.00	13.50
❑ 160	Amos Zereoue RC	8.00	3.60
❑ 161	Michael Bishop RC	10.00	4.50
❑ 162	Aaron Brooks RC	30.00	13.50
❑ 163	Tim Couch RC	30.00	13.50
❑ 164	Scott Covington RC	10.00	4.50
❑ 165	Daunte Culpepper RC	40.00	18.00
❑ 166	Kevin Daft RC	8.00	3.60
❑ 167	Joe Germaine RC	10.00	4.50
❑ 168	Chris Greisen RC	8.00	3.60
❑ 169	Brock Huard RC	12.00	5.50
❑ 170	Shaun King RC	15.00	6.75
❑ 171	Cory Sauter RC	8.00	3.60
❑ 172	Donovan McNabb RC	30.00	13.50
❑ 173	Cade McNown RC	12.00	5.50
❑ 174	Chad Plummer RC	6.00	2.70
❑ 175	Akili Smith RC	25.00	11.00
❑ P1	Promo Sheet (SBXXXIV NFL Experience) NFLX1 Kurt Warner NFLX2 Jamal Anderson NFLX3 Edgerrin James NFLX4 Peyton Manning NFLX5 Randy Moss NFLX6 Dan Marino	4.00	1.80

2000 Fleer Focus

Card	Player	MINT	NRMT
❑ 1	Tim Couch	1.00	.45
❑ 2	Germane Crowell	.25	.11
❑ 3	Curtis Martin	.50	.23
❑ 4	Samari Rolle	.15	.07
❑ 5	Brian Griese	.60	.25
❑ 6	Kerry Collins	.25	.11
❑ 7	Jevon Kearse	.50	.23
❑ 8	Rocket Ismail	.25	.11
❑ 9	Cam Cleeland	.15	.07
❑ 10	Warrick Dunn	.50	.23
❑ 11	Carl Pickens	.25	.11
❑ 12	Cris Carter	.50	.23
❑ 13	Mike Pritchard	.15	.07
❑ 14	Corey Dillon	.50	.23
❑ 15	Randy Moss	1.50	.70
❑ 16	Derrick Mayes	.25	.11
❑ 17	Marcus Robinson	.50	.23
❑ 18	Thurman Thomas	.25	.11
❑ 19	J.J. Stokes	.25	.11
❑ 20	Muhsin Muhammad	.25	.11
❑ 21	Derrick Alexander	.25	.11
❑ 22	Curtis Conway	.25	.11
❑ 23	Qadry Ismail	.25	.11
❑ 24	Ken Dilger	.15	.07
❑ 25	Troy Edwards	.25	.11
❑ 26	Shawn Jefferson	.15	.07
❑ 27	Terrence Wilkins	.50	.23
❑ 28	Duce Staley	.50	.23
❑ 29	Aeneas Williams	.15	.07
❑ 30	Antonio Freeman	.50	.23
❑ 31	Tim Brown	.50	.23
❑ 32	Darrell Green	.15	.07
❑ 33	Herman Moore	.25	.11
❑ 34	Vinny Testaverde	.25	.11
❑ 35	Yancey Thigpen	.15	.07
❑ 36	Emmitt Smith	1.25	.55
❑ 37	Ricky Williams	1.25	.55
❑ 38	Keyshawn Johnson	.50	.23
❑ 39	Eddie Kennison	.15	.07
❑ 40	Zach Thomas	.25	.11
❑ 41	Shawn Springs	.15	.07
❑ 42	Wesley Walls	.15	.07
❑ 43	Andre Rison	.15	.07
❑ 44	Jerry Rice	1.25	.55
❑ 45	Rob Johnson	.25	.11
❑ 46	Keenan McCardell	.25	.11
❑ 47	Ryan Leaf	.50	.23
❑ 48	Michael McCrary	.15	.07
❑ 49	Marvin Harrison	.50	.23
❑ 50	Donovan McNabb	.75	.35
❑ 51	Curtis Enis	.25	.11
❑ 52	Tony Martin	.25	.11
❑ 53	Jeff Garcia	.50	.23
❑ 54	Tim Biakabutuka	.25	.11
❑ 55	Tony Gonzalez	.25	.11
❑ 56	Jim Harbaugh	.25	.11
❑ 57	Peerless Price	.50	.23
❑ 58	Fred Taylor	.60	.25
❑ 59	Kordell Stewart	.50	.23
❑ 60	Chris Chandler	.25	.11
❑ 61	Bill Schroeder	.25	.11
❑ 62	Charles Woodson	.25	.11
❑ 63	Terance Mathis	.25	.11
❑ 64	Brett Favre	2.00	.90
❑ 65	Rickey Dudley	.15	.07
❑ 66	Rob Moore	.25	.11
❑ 67	Charlie Batch	.50	.23
❑ 68	Wayne Chrebet	.25	.11
❑ 69	Jeff George	.25	.11
❑ 70	Olandis Gary	.50	.23
❑ 71	Amani Toomer	.25	.11
❑ 72	Kevin Dyson	.25	.11
❑ 73	Darrin Chiaverini	.15	.07
❑ 74	Willie McGinest	.15	.07
❑ 75	Ricky Proehl	.15	.07
❑ 76	Craig Yeast	.15	.07
❑ 77	Dwayne Rudd	.15	.07
❑ 78	Marshall Faulk	.60	.25
❑ 79	Bobby Engram	.25	.11
❑ 80	Jay Fiedler	.50	.23
❑ 81	Jon Kitna	.50	.23
❑ 82	Patrick Jeffers	.50	.23
❑ 83	James Johnson	.15	.07
❑ 84	Charlie Garner	.25	.11
❑ 85	Eric Moulds	.50	.23
❑ 86	Mark Brunell	.75	.35
❑ 87	Richard Huntley	.15	.07
❑ 88	Frank Sanders	.25	.11
❑ 89	Robert Porcher	.15	.07
❑ 90	Aaron Glenn	.15	.07
❑ 91	Stephen Davis	.50	.23
❑ 92	Ed McCaffrey	.50	.23
❑ 93	Pete Mitchell	.15	.07
❑ 94	Frank Wycheck	.15	.07
❑ 95	David LaFleur	.15	.07
❑ 96	Jake Delhomme RC	.50	.23
❑ 97	John Lynch	.15	.07
❑ 98	Michael Pittman	.15	.07
❑ 99	Andy Katzenmoyer	.15	.07
❑ 100	Isaac Bruce	.50	.23
❑ 101	Terry Kirby	.15	.07
❑ 102	Kevin Faulk	.25	.11
❑ 103	Kevin Carter	.25	.11
❑ 104	Darnay Scott	.25	.11
❑ 105	Robert Smith	.50	.23
❑ 106	Brian Mitchell	.15	.07
❑ 107	Shane Matthews	.15	.07
❑ 108	O.J. McDuffie	.25	.11
❑ 109	Bryant Young	.15	.07
❑ 110	Jay Riemersma	.15	.07
❑ 111	Elvis Grbac	.25	.11
❑ 112	Jermaine Fazande	.15	.07
❑ 113	Jonathan Linton	.15	.07
❑ 114	Kyle Brady	.15	.07
❑ 115	Junior Seau	.25	.11
❑ 116	Shannon Sharpe	.25	.11
❑ 117	Jerome Pathon	.25	.11
❑ 118	Jerome Bettis	.50	.23
❑ 119	O.J. Santiago	.15	.07
❑ 120	Ahman Green	.25	.11
❑ 121	Troy Vincent	.15	.07
❑ 122	David Boston	.50	.23
❑ 123	James Stewart	.25	.11
❑ 124	Ray Lucas	.50	.23
❑ 125	Brad Johnson	.50	.23
❑ 126	Rod Smith	.25	.11
❑ 127	Joe Jurevicius	.15	.07
❑ 128	Eddie George	.60	.25
❑ 129	Darren Woodson	.15	.07
❑ 130	Jake Reed	.25	.11
❑ 131	Mike Alstott	.50	.23
❑ 132	Leslie Shepherd	.15	.07
❑ 133	Terry Glenn	.25	.11
❑ 134	Az-Zahir Hakim	.25	.11
❑ 135	Alonzo Mayes	.15	.07
❑ 136	Sam Madison	.15	.07
❑ 137	Ricky Watters	.15	.07
❑ 138	Antowain Smith	.25	.11
❑ 139	Jimmy Smith	.25	.11

	Card	Mint	Nrmt
❑	140 Hines Ward	.15	.07
❑	141 Priest Holmes	.15	.07
❑	142 Edgerrin James	2.00	.90
❑	143 Charles Johnson	.25	.11
❑	144 Jamal Anderson	.50	.23
❑	145 Dorsey Levens	.25	.11
❑	146 Rich Gannon	.25	.11
❑	147 Champ Bailey	.25	.11
❑	148 Bill Romanowski	.15	.07
❑	149 Jason Sehorn	.15	.07
❑	150 Steve McNair	.50	.23
❑	151 Jermaine Lewis	.25	.11
❑	152 Cornelius Bennett	.15	.07
❑	153 Torrance Small	.15	.07
❑	154 Tim Dwight	.50	.23
❑	155 Corey Bradford	.25	.11
❑	156 Napoleon Kaufman	.25	.11
❑	157 Jake Plummer	.50	.23
❑	158 David Sloan	.15	.07
❑	159 Dedric Ward	.15	.07
❑	160 Michael Westbrook	.25	.11
❑	161 Terrell Davis	1.25	.55
❑	162 Ike Hilliard	.25	.11
❑	163 Derrick Brooks	.15	.07
❑	164 Greg Ellis	.15	.07
❑	165 Keith Poole	.15	.07
❑	166 Jacquez Green	.25	.11
❑	167 Joey Galloway	.50	.23
❑	168 Lawyer Milloy	.15	.07
❑	169 Warren Sapp	.25	.11
❑	170 Takeo Spikes	.15	.07
❑	171 John Randle	.25	.11
❑	172 Torry Holt	.50	.23
❑	173 Cade McNown	.50	.23
❑	174 Damon Huard	.50	.23
❑	175 Terrell Owens	.50	.23
❑	176 Steve Beuerlein	.25	.11
❑	177 Tony Richardson RC	.25	.11
❑	178 Jeff Graham	.25	.11
❑	179 Doug Flutie	.60	.25
❑	180 Kevin Hardy	.15	.07
❑	181 Mark Bruener	.15	.07
❑	182 Tony Banks	.25	.11
❑	183 Peyton Manning	1.50	.70
❑	184 Hugh Douglas	.15	.07
❑	185 Simeon Rice	.15	.07
❑	186 Terry Fair	.15	.07
❑	187 James Jett	.15	.07
❑	188 Albert Connell	.15	.07
❑	189 Troy Aikman	1.50	.70
❑	190 Jeff Blake	.25	.11
❑	191 Shaun King	.75	.35
❑	192 Kevin Johnson	.50	.23
❑	193 Drew Bledsoe	.75	.35
❑	194 Kurt Warner	2.00	.90
❑	195 Akili Smith	.50	.23
❑	196 Daunte Culpepper	1.00	.45
❑	197 Sean Dawkins	.15	.07
❑	198 Natrone Means	.15	.07
❑	199 Kimble Anders	.15	.07
❑	200 Steve Young	.75	.35
❑	201 Courtney Brown RC	5.00	2.20
❑	202 Chris Samuels RC	3.00	1.35
❑	203 Corey Simon RC	5.00	2.20
❑	204 Deon Grant RC	3.00	1.35
❑	205 Darren Howard RC	3.00	1.35
❑	206 Rob Morris RC	4.00	1.80
❑	207 Ahmed Plummer RC	4.00	1.80
❑	208 Anthony Becht RC	4.00	1.80
❑	209 Brian Urlacher RC	12.00	5.50
❑	210 Shaun Ellis RC	3.00	1.35
❑	211 Bubba Franks RC	5.00	2.20
❑	212 Plaxico Burress RC	15.00	6.75
❑	213 R.Jay Soward RC	8.00	3.60
❑	214 Dez White RC	8.00	3.60
❑	215 Peter Warrick RC	30.00	13.50
❑	216 Jerry Porter RC	8.00	3.60
❑	217 Ron Dugans RC	8.00	3.60
❑	218 Laveranues Coles RC	12.00	5.50
❑	219 Travis Taylor RC	10.00	4.50
❑	220 Anthony Lucas RC	6.00	2.70
❑	221 Sylvester Morris RC	15.00	6.75
❑	222 Dennis Northcutt RC	10.00	4.50
❑	223 Chafie Fields RC	8.00	3.60
❑	224 Danny Farmer RC	8.00	3.60
❑	225 Chris Cole RC	6.00	2.70
❑	226 Sherrod Gideon RC	6.00	2.70
❑	227 Todd Pinkston RC	8.00	3.60
❑	228 Gari Scott RC	8.00	3.60
❑	229 Darrell Jackson RC	12.00	5.50
❑	230 JaJuan Dawson RC	8.00	3.60
❑	231 Trevor Gaylor RC	6.00	2.70
❑	232 Bashir Yamini RC	6.00	2.70
❑	233 Quinton Spotwood RC	6.00	2.70
❑	234 Michael Wiley RC	6.00	2.70
❑	235 Ron Dayne RC	25.00	11.00
❑	236 Thomas Jones RC	10.00	4.50
❑	237 Jamal Lewis RC	40.00	18.00
❑	238 Travis Prentice RC	10.00	4.50
❑	239 J.R. Redmond RC	8.00	3.60
❑	240 Trung Canidate RC	6.00	2.70
❑	241 Shaun Alexander RC	12.00	5.50
❑	242 Frank Murphy RC	4.00	1.80
❑	243 Shyrone Stith RC	6.00	2.70
❑	244 Rondell Mealey RC	4.00	1.80
❑	245 Terrelle Smith RC	5.00	2.20
❑	246 Reuben Droughns RC	6.00	2.70
❑	247 Chad Morton RC	6.00	2.70
❑	248 Mike Anderson RC	40.00	18.00
❑	249 Paul Smith RC	5.00	2.20
❑	250 Curtis Keaton RC	5.00	2.20
❑	251 Jarious Jackson RC	5.00	2.20
❑	252 Marc Bulger RC	5.00	2.20
❑	253 Tee Martin RC	8.00	3.60
❑	254 Todd Husak RC	5.00	2.20
❑	255 Joe Hamilton RC	6.00	2.70
❑	256 Doug Johnson RC	8.00	3.60
❑	257 Giovanni Carmazzi RC	6.00	2.70
❑	258 Chris Redman RC	10.00	4.50
❑	259 Tim Rattay RC	8.00	3.60
❑	260 Chad Pennington RC	12.00	5.50
❑	P1 Tim Couch Promo	2.00	.90

2000 Fleer Gamers

	MINT	NRMT
COMPLETE SET (150)	100.00	45.00
COMP.SET w/o SPs (100)	20.00	9.00

	Card	Mint	Nrmt
❑	1 Edgerrin James	2.50	1.10
❑	2 Tim Couch	1.25	.55
❑	3 Cris Carter	.60	.25
❑	4 Rich Gannon	.30	.14
❑	5 Akili Smith	.60	.25
❑	6 Muhsin Muhammad	.30	.14
❑	7 Dorsey Levens	.30	.14
❑	8 Dedric Ward	.15	.07
❑	9 Jevon Kearse	.60	.25
❑	10 Peerless Price	.60	.25
❑	11 Mike Alstott	.60	.25
❑	12 Michael Strahan	.15	.07
❑	13 Stephen Davis	.60	.25
❑	14 Rob Moore	.30	.14
❑	15 James Stewart	.30	.14
❑	16 Robert Smith	.60	.25
❑	17 Napoleon Kaufman	.30	.14
❑	18 Peyton Manning	2.00	.90
❑	19 Keyshawn Johnson	.60	.25
❑	20 Tony Martin	.30	.14
❑	21 Jermaine Fazande	.15	.07
❑	22 Jamal Anderson	.60	.25
❑	23 Ed McCaffrey	.60	.25
❑	24 Drew Bledsoe	1.00	.45
❑	25 Duce Staley	.60	.25
❑	26 Warrick Dunn	.60	.25
❑	27 Chris Chandler	.30	.14
❑	28 Olandis Gary	.60	.25
❑	29 Terry Glenn	.30	.14
❑	30 Donovan McNabb	1.00	.45
❑	31 Torry Holt	.60	.25
❑	32 Tim Dwight	.60	.25
❑	33 Terrell Davis	1.50	.70
❑	34 Tony Simmons	.15	.07
❑	35 Jerome Bettis	.60	.25
❑	36 Az-Zahir Hakim	.30	.14
❑	37 Darrin Chiaverini	.15	.07
❑	38 Fred Taylor	.75	.35
❑	39 Jon Kitna	.60	.25
❑	40 Tony Banks	.30	.14
❑	41 Brian Griese	.75	.35
❑	42 Jeff Blake	.30	.14
❑	43 Kordell Stewart	.60	.25
❑	44 Isaac Bruce	.60	.25
❑	45 Shannon Sharpe	.30	.14
❑	46 Rocket Ismail	.30	.14
❑	47 Ricky Williams	1.50	.70
❑	48 Marshall Faulk	.75	.35
❑	49 Qadry Ismail	.15	.07
❑	50 Joey Galloway	.60	.25
❑	51 Jake Reed	.30	.14
❑	52 Kurt Warner	2.50	1.10
❑	53 Cade McNown	.60	.25
❑	54 Herman Moore	.30	.14
❑	55 Curtis Martin	.60	.25
❑	56 Steve McNair	.60	.25
❑	57 Tim Biakabutuka	.30	.14
❑	58 Brett Favre	2.50	1.10
❑	59 Wayne Chrebet	.30	.14
❑	60 Eddie George	.75	.35
❑	61 Troy Aikman	1.50	.70
❑	62 Jimmy Smith	.30	.14
❑	63 Derrick Mayes	.30	.14
❑	64 Emmitt Smith	1.50	.70
❑	65 Mark Brunell	1.00	.45
❑	66 Ricky Watters	.30	.14
❑	67 Marcus Robinson	.60	.25
❑	68 Randy Moss	2.00	.90
❑	69 Troy Edwards	.30	.14
❑	70 Carl Pickens	.30	.14
❑	71 Damon Huard	.60	.25
❑	72 Mikhael Ricks	.15	.07
❑	73 David Boston	.60	.25
❑	74 Charlie Batch	.60	.25
❑	75 Randall Cunningham	.60	.25
❑	76 Tim Brown	.60	.25
❑	77 Shaun King	1.00	.45
❑	78 Darnay Scott	.30	.14
❑	79 Derrick Alexander	.30	.14
❑	80 Steve Young	1.00	.45
❑	81 Kevin Johnson	.60	.25
❑	82 Elvis Grbac	.30	.14
❑	83 Tai Streets	.15	.07
❑	84 Steve Beuerlein	.30	.14
❑	85 Antonio Freeman	.60	.25
❑	86 Vinny Testaverde	.30	.14
❑	87 Brad Johnson	.60	.25
❑	88 Curtis Enis	.30	.14
❑	89 Jay Fiedler	.30	.14
❑	90 Junior Seau	.30	.14
❑	91 Eric Moulds	.60	.25
❑	92 Jake Plummer	.60	.25
❑	93 Amani Toomer	.30	.14
❑	94 Champ Bailey	.30	.14
❑	95 Germane Crowell	.30	.14
❑	96 Tony Gonzalez	.30	.14
❑	97 Jerry Rice	1.50	.70
❑	98 Rob Johnson	.30	.14
❑	99 Marvin Harrison	.60	.25
❑	100 Kerry Collins	.30	.14
❑	101 Thomas Jones RC	4.00	1.80
❑	102 Jarious Jackson RC	2.50	1.10
❑	103 R.Jay Soward RC	2.50	1.10
❑	104 Trung Canidate RC	2.50	1.10
❑	105 Travis Taylor RC	3.00	1.35
❑	106 Giovanni Carmazzi RC	3.00	1.35
❑	107 Jerry Porter RC	2.50	1.10
❑	108 Chris Redman RC	5.00	2.20
❑	109 Tee Martin RC	4.00	1.80
❑	110 Dez White RC	2.00	.90
❑	111 Danny Farmer RC	2.50	1.10

	Card	Mint	NRMT
❑	112 Brian Urlacher RC	8.00	3.60
❑	113 Reuben Droughns RC	2.50	1.10
❑	114 Marc Bulger RC	2.50	1.10
❑	115 Peter Warrick RC	8.00	3.60
❑	116 Plaxico Burress RC	5.00	2.20
❑	117 Ron Dugans RC	2.00	.90
❑	118 Gari Scott RC	2.00	.90
❑	119 Curtis Keaton RC	2.00	.90
❑	120 Corey Simon RC	3.00	1.35
❑	121 Rob Morris RC	2.00	.90
❑	122 Chad Morton RC	2.50	1.10
❑	123 Hank Poteat RC	2.00	.90
❑	124 Ahmed Plummer RC	2.50	1.10
❑	125 Bashir Yamini RC	2.00	.90
❑	126 J.R. Redmond RC	3.00	1.35
❑	127 Travis Prentice RC	4.00	1.80
❑	128 Todd Pinkston RC	2.50	1.10
❑	129 Courtney Brown RC	3.00	1.35
❑	130 Laveranues Coles RC	4.00	1.80
❑	131 Jamal Lewis RC	12.00	5.50
❑	132 Tim Rattay RC	4.00	1.80
❑	133 Anthony Becht RC	2.50	1.10
❑	134 Chris Cole RC	2.00	.90
❑	135 Ron Dayne RC	8.00	3.60
❑	136 Sylvester Morris RC	5.00	2.20
❑	137 Joe Hamilton RC	3.00	1.35
❑	138 Dennis Northcutt RC	3.00	1.35
❑	139 Doug Johnson RC	2.50	1.10
❑	140 Shyrone Stith RC	2.00	.90
❑	141 Darrell Jackson RC	4.00	1.80
❑	142 Michael Wiley RC	2.50	1.10
❑	143 Chad Pennington RC	8.00	3.60
❑	144 Bubba Franks RC	3.00	1.35
❑	145 Shaun Alexander RC	6.00	2.70

1997 Fleer Goudey

		MINT	NRMT
	COMPLETE SET (150)	15.00	6.75
❑	1 Michael Jackson	.20	.09
❑	2 Ray Lewis	.40	.18
❑	3 Vinny Testaverde	.20	.09
❑	4 Eric Turner	.10	.05
❑	5 Jim Kelly	.30	.14
❑	6 Bryce Paup	.10	.05
❑	7 Andre Reed	.20	.09
❑	8 Bruce Smith	.20	.09
❑	9 Thurman Thomas	.30	.14
❑	10 Jeff Blake	.20	.09
❑	11 Ki-Jana Carter	.10	.05
❑	12 Carl Pickens	.30	.14
❑	13 Darnay Scott	.20	.09
❑	14 Terrell Davis	1.50	.70
❑	15 John Elway	2.00	.90
❑	16 Anthony Miller	.10	.05
❑	17 John Mobley	.10	.05
❑	18 Shannon Sharpe	.20	.09
❑	19 Chris Chandler	.20	.09
❑	20 Eddie George	1.00	.45
❑	21 Steve McNair	.50	.23
❑	22 Chris Sanders	.10	.05
❑	23 Quentin Coryatt	.10	.05
❑	24 Sean Dawkins	.10	.05
❑	25 Ken Dilger	.10	.05
❑	26 Marshall Faulk	.30	.14
❑	27 Jim Harbaugh	.20	.09
❑	28 Marvin Harrison	.30	.14
❑	29 Tony Brackens	.10	.05
❑	30 Mark Brunell	1.00	.45
❑	31 Kevin Hardy	.10	.05
❑	32 Keenan McCardell	.20	.09
❑	33 James O.Stewart	.20	.09
❑	34 Marcus Allen	.30	.14
❑	35 Steve Bono	.20	.09
❑	36 Dale Carter	.10	.05
❑	37 Neil Smith	.20	.09
❑	38 Derrick Thomas	.20	.09
❑	39 Tamarick Vanover	.20	.09
❑	40 Karim Abdul-Jabbar	.30	.14
❑	41 Dan Marino	2.00	.90
❑	42 O.J. McDuffie	.20	.09
❑	43 Stanley Pritchett	.10	.05
❑	44 Zach Thomas	.20	.09
❑	45 Drew Bledsoe	1.00	.45
❑	46 Ben Coates	.20	.09
❑	47 Terry Glenn	.30	.14
❑	48 Shawn Jefferson	.10	.05
❑	49 Curtis Martin	.50	.23
❑	50 Dave Meggett	.10	.05
❑	51 Hugh Douglas	.10	.05
❑	52 Keyshawn Johnson	.30	.14
❑	53 Adrian Murrell	.20	.09
❑	54 Tim Brown	.30	.14
❑	55 Rickey Dudley	.20	.09
❑	56 Jeff Hostetler	.10	.05
❑	57 Napoleon Kaufman	.30	.14
❑	58 Chester McGlockton	.10	.05
❑	59 Jerome Bettis	.30	.14
❑	60 Andre Hastings	.10	.05
❑	61 Greg Lloyd	.10	.05
❑	62 Kordell Stewart	.40	.18
❑	63 Yancey Thigpen	.20	.09
❑	64 Rod Woodson	.20	.09
❑	65 Andre Coleman	.10	.05
❑	66 Stan Humphries	.20	.09
❑	67 Tony Martin	.20	.09
❑	68 Leonard Russell	.10	.05
❑	69 Junior Seau	.20	.09
❑	70 Brian Blades	.10	.05
❑	71 Joey Galloway	.40	.18
❑	72 Chris Warren	.20	.09
❑	73 Larry Centers	.20	.09
❑	74 Leeland McElroy	.10	.05
❑	75 Simeon Rice	.20	.09
❑	76 Frank Sanders	.20	.09
❑	77 Eric Swann	.10	.05
❑	78 Jamal Anderson	.60	.25
❑	79 Bert Emanuel	.20	.09
❑	80 Terance Mathis	.20	.09
❑	81 Eric Metcalf	.20	.09
❑	82 Tim Biakabutuka	.20	.09
❑	83 Kerry Collins	.20	.09
❑	84 Kevin Greene	.20	.09
❑	85 Muhsin Muhammad	.20	.09
❑	86 Wesley Walls	.20	.09
❑	87 Curtis Conway	.20	.09
❑	88 Bryan Cox	.10	.05
❑	89 Walt Harris	.10	.05
❑	90 Erik Kramer	.10	.05
❑	91 Rashaan Salaam	.10	.05
❑	92 Troy Aikman	1.00	.45
❑	93 Michael Irvin	.30	.14
❑	94 Daryl Johnston	.20	.09
❑	95 Leon Lett	.10	.05
❑	96 Deion Sanders	.30	.14
❑	97 Emmitt Smith	1.50	.70
❑	98 Scott Mitchell	.20	.09
❑	99 Herman Moore	.30	.14
❑	100 Johnnie Morton	.20	.09
❑	101 Brett Perriman	.10	.05
❑	102 Barry Sanders	2.00	.90
❑	103 Edgar Bennett	.20	.09
❑	104 Robert Brooks	.20	.09
❑	105 Brett Favre	2.00	.90
❑	106 Antonio Freeman	.50	.23
❑	107 Keith Jackson	.10	.05
❑	108 Reggie White	.30	.14
❑	109 Cris Carter	.30	.14
❑	110 Warren Moon	.30	.14
❑	111 John Randle	.20	.09
❑	112 Jake Reed	.20	.09
❑	113 Robert Smith	.20	.09
❑	114 Jim Everett	.10	.05
❑	115 Michael Haynes	.10	.05
❑	116 Alex Molden	.10	.05
❑	117 Ray Zellars	.10	.05
❑	118 Chris Calloway	.10	.05
❑	119 Rodney Hampton	.20	.09
❑	120 Phillippi Sparks	.10	.05
❑	121 Amani Toomer	.20	.09
❑	122 Ty Detmer	.20	.09
❑	123 Jason Dunn	.10	.05
❑	124 Irving Fryar	.20	.09
❑	125 Chris T. Jones	.10	.05
❑	126 Ricky Watters	.20	.09
❑	127 Tony Banks	.20	.09
❑	128 Isaac Bruce	.30	.14
❑	129 Eddie Kennison	.20	.09
❑	130 Lawrence Phillips	.10	.05
❑	131 Merton Hanks	.10	.05
❑	132 Terry Kirby	.20	.09
❑	133 Ken Norton	.10	.05
❑	134 Jerry Rice	1.00	.45
❑	135 J.J. Stokes	.20	.09
❑	136 Steve Young	.60	.25
❑	137 Alvin Harper	.10	.05
❑	138 Jackie Harris	.10	.05
❑	139 Hardy Nickerson	.10	.05
❑	140 Errict Rhett	.10	.05
❑	141 Terry Allen	.30	.14
❑	142 Henry Ellard	.10	.05
❑	143 Gus Frerotte	.10	.05
❑	144 Brian Mitchell	.10	.05
❑	145 Michael Westbrook	.20	.09
❑	146 Chuck Bednarik	.20	.09
❑	146AU Chuck Bednarik (Signed Card)	60.00	27.00
❑	147 Y.A. Tittle	.20	.09
❑	147AU Y.A. Tittle (Signed Card)	60.00	27.00
❑	148 Checklist	.10	.05
❑	149 Checklist	.10	.05
❑	150 Checklist	.10	.05
❑	P1 Brett Favre Promo (Unnumbered base card)	2.00	.90

1997 Fleer Goudey II

		MINT	NRMT
	COMPLETE SET (150)	20.00	9.00
	SAYERS AUTO/40 (1/40/150)	120.00	55.00
	SAYERS RARE TRADITION	8.00	3.60
❑	1 Gale Sayers SP	.50	.23
❑	2 Vinny Testaverde	.20	.09
❑	3 Jeff George	.20	.09
❑	4 Brett Favre	2.00	.90
❑	5 Eddie Kennison	.20	.09
❑	6 Ken Norton	.10	.05
❑	7 John Elway	2.00	.90
❑	8 Troy Aikman	1.00	.45
❑	9 Steve McNair	.50	.23
❑	10 Kordell Stewart	.40	.18
❑	11 Drew Bledsoe	1.00	.45
❑	12 Kerry Collins	.20	.09
❑	13 Dan Marino	2.00	.90
❑	14 Brad Johnson	.50	.23
❑	15 Todd Collins	.10	.05
❑	16 Ki-Jana Carter	.10	.05
❑	17 Pat Barnes RC	.30	.14
❑	18 Aeneas Williams	.10	.05

❑ 19	Keyshawn Johnson	.30	.14
❑ 20	Barry Sanders	2.00	.90
❑ 21	Tiki Barber RC	1.25	.55
❑ 22	Emmitt Smith	1.50	.70
❑ 23	Kevin Hardy RC	.10	.05
❑ 24	Mario Bates	.10	.05
❑ 25	Ricky Watters	.20	.09
❑ 26	Chris Canty RC	.10	.05
❑ 27	Eddie George	1.00	.45
❑ 28	Curtis Martin	.50	.23
❑ 29	Adrian Murrell	.20	.09
❑ 30	Terrell Davis	1.50	.70
❑ 31	Rashaan Salaam	.10	.05
❑ 32	Marcus Allen	.30	.14
❑ 33	Karim Abdul-Jabbar	.30	.14
❑ 34	Thurman Thomas	.30	.14
❑ 35	Marvin Harrison	.30	.14
❑ 36	Jerome Bettis	.30	.14
❑ 37	Larry Centers	.20	.09
❑ 38	Stan Humphries	.20	.09
❑ 39	Lawrence Phillips	.10	.05
❑ 40	Gale Sayers SP	.50	.23
❑ 41	Henry Ellard	.10	.05
❑ 42	Chris Warren	.20	.09
❑ 43	Robert Brooks	.20	.09
❑ 44	Sedrick Shaw RC	.30	.14
❑ 45	Muhsin Muhammad	.20	.09
❑ 46	Napoleon Kaufman	.30	.14
❑ 47	Reidel Anthony RC	.75	.35
❑ 48	Jamal Anderson	.60	.25
❑ 49	Scott Mitchell	.20	.09
❑ 50	Mark Brunell	1.00	.45
❑ 51	William Thomas	.10	.05
❑ 52	Bryan Cox	.10	.05
❑ 53	Carl Pickens	.30	.14
❑ 54	Chris Spielman	.10	.05
❑ 55	Junior Seau	.20	.09
❑ 56	Hardy Nickerson	.10	.05
❑ 57	Dwayne Rudd RC	.30	.14
❑ 58	Peter Boulware RC	.20	.09
❑ 59	Jim Druckenmiller RC	.30	.14
❑ 60	Michael Westbrook	.20	.09
❑ 61	Shawn Springs RC	.20	.09
❑ 62	Zach Thomas	.20	.09
❑ 63	David LaFleur RC	.20	.09
❑ 64	Darrell Russell RC	.10	.05
❑ 65	Jake Plummer RC	2.50	1.10
❑ 66	Tim Biakabutuka	.20	.09
❑ 67	Tyrone Wheatley	.20	.09
❑ 68	Elvis Grbac	.20	.09
❑ 69	Antonio Freeman	.50	.23
❑ 70	Wayne Chrebet	.30	.14
❑ 71	Walter Jones RC	.10	.05
❑ 72	Marshall Faulk	.30	.14
❑ 73	Jason Dunn	.10	.05
❑ 74	Darnay Scott	.20	.09
❑ 75	Errict Rhett	.10	.05
❑ 76	Orlando Pace RC	.30	.14
❑ 77	Natrone Means	.30	.14
❑ 78	Bruce Smith	.20	.09
❑ 79	Jamie Sharper RC	.20	.09
❑ 80	Jerry Rice	1.00	.45
❑ 81	Tim Brown	.30	.14
❑ 82	Brian Mitchell	.10	.05
❑ 83	Andre Reed	.20	.09
❑ 84	Herman Moore	.30	.14
❑ 85	Rob Moore	.20	.09
❑ 86	Rae Carruth RC	.30	.14
❑ 87	Bert Emanuel	.20	.09
❑ 88	Michael Irvin	.30	.14
❑ 89	Mark Chmura	.20	.09
❑ 90	Tony Brackens	.10	.05
❑ 91	Kevin Greene	.20	.09
❑ 92	Reggie White	.30	.14
❑ 93	Derrick Thomas	.20	.09
❑ 94	Troy Davis RC	.30	.14
❑ 95	Greg Lloyd	.10	.05
❑ 96	Cortez Kennedy	.10	.05
❑ 97	Simeon Rice	.20	.09
❑ 98	Terrell Owens	.30	.14
❑ 99	Hugh Douglas	.10	.05
❑ 100	Terry Glenn	.30	.14
❑ 101	Jim Harbaugh	.20	.09
❑ 102	Shannon Sharpe	.20	.09
❑ 103	Joey Kent RC	.30	.14
❑ 104	Jeff Blake	.20	.09
❑ 105	Terry Allen	.30	.14
❑ 106	Cris Carter	.30	.14
❑ 107	Amani Toomer	.20	.09
❑ 108	Derrick Alexander WR	.20	.09
❑ 109	Darnell Autry RC	.20	.09
❑ 110	Irving Fryar	.20	.09
❑ 111	Bryant Westbrook RC	.10	.05
❑ 112	Tony Banks	.20	.09
❑ 113	Michael Booker RC	.10	.05
❑ 114	Yatil Green RC	.20	.09
❑ 115	James Farrior RC	.10	.05
❑ 116	Warrick Dunn RC	1.25	.55
❑ 117	Greg Hill	.10	.05
❑ 118	Tony Martin	.20	.09
❑ 119	Chris Sanders	.10	.05
❑ 120	Charles Johnson	.20	.09
❑ 121	John Mobley	.10	.05
❑ 122	Keenan McCardell	.20	.09
❑ 123	Willie McGinest	.10	.05
❑ 124	O.J. McDuffie	.20	.09
❑ 125	Deion Sanders	.30	.14
❑ 126	Curtis Conway	.20	.09
❑ 127	Desmond Howard	.20	.09
❑ 128	Johnnie Morton	.20	.09
❑ 129	Ike Hilliard RC	.75	.35
❑ 130	Gus Frerotte	.10	.05
❑ 131	Tom Knight	.10	.05
❑ 132	Sean Dawkins	.10	.05
❑ 133	Isaac Bruce	.30	.14
❑ 134	Wesley Walls	.20	.09
❑ 135	Danny Wuerffel RC	.50	.23
❑ 136	Tony Gonzalez RC	1.25	.55
❑ 137	Ben Coates	.20	.09
❑ 138	Joey Galloway	.40	.18
❑ 139	Michael Jackson	.20	.09
❑ 140	Steve Young	.60	.25
❑ 141	Corey Dillon RC	2.50	1.10
❑ 142	Jake Reed	.20	.09
❑ 143	Edgar Bennett	.20	.09
❑ 144	Ty Detmer	.20	.09
❑ 145	Darrell Green	.20	.09
❑ 146	Antowain Smith RC	1.00	.45
❑ 147	Mike Alstott	.30	.14
❑ 148	Checklist	.10	.05
❑ 149	Checklist	.10	.05
❑ 150	Gale Sayers SP	.50	.23
❑ P92	Reggie White Promo (Printed on white stock)	.50	.23

2000 Fleer Greats of the Game

	MINT	NRMT
COMP.SET w/o SP's (100)	25.00	11.00

❑ 1	Terry Bradshaw	2.50	1.10
❑ 2	Paul Hornung	.60	.25
❑ 3	Tony Dorsett	.50	.23
❑ 4	L.C. Greenwood	.25	.11
❑ 5	Ozzie Newsome	.15	.07
❑ 6	Michael Irvin	.25	.11
❑ 7	Art Donovan	.25	.11
❑ 8	Don Maynard	.25	.11
❑ 9	Bobby Mitchell	.25	.11
❑ 10	Bob Lilly	.25	.11
❑ 11	Earl Morrall	.15	.07
❑ 12	Harvey Martin	.15	.07
❑ 13	Dan Fouts	.50	.23
❑ 14	Joe Theismann	.50	.23
❑ 15	Roger Staubach	2.50	1.10
❑ 16	Otto Graham	.60	.25
❑ 17	Cliff Branch	.25	.11
❑ 18	Sonny Jurgensen	.25	.11
❑ 19	Eric Dickerson	.25	.11
❑ 20	Lee Roy Selmon	.25	.11
❑ 21	Roger Craig	.25	.11
❑ 22	Raymond Berry	.25	.11
❑ 23	Bob Hayes	.25	.11
❑ 24	Steve Largent	.50	.23
❑ 25	Lenny Moore	.25	.11
❑ 26	Chuck Bednarik	.25	.11
❑ 27	Ken Stabler	2.00	.90
❑ 28	William Perry	.15	.07
❑ 29	Joe Greene	.25	.11
❑ 30	Joe Namath	2.50	1.10
❑ 31	Jim Kelly	.50	.23
❑ 32	Steve Young	.75	.35
❑ 33	Randy White	.25	.11
❑ 34	Lawrence Taylor	.25	.11
❑ 35	Franco Harris	.50	.23
❑ 36	Marcus Allen	.50	.23
❑ 37	Mike Singletary	.15	.07
❑ 38	Fran Tarkenton	1.25	.55
❑ 39	Mel Renfro	.15	.07
❑ 40	Len Dawson	.50	.23
❑ 41	Carl Eller	.15	.07
❑ 42	Chuck Foreman	.15	.07
❑ 43	Gino Marchetti	.15	.07
❑ 44	Jim Marshall	.15	.07
❑ 45	Jack Ham	.25	.11
❑ 46	Mercury Morris	.15	.07
❑ 47	Anthony Munoz	.25	.11
❑ 48	Herschel Walker	.15	.07
❑ 49	Drew Pearson	.25	.11
❑ 50	John Elway	2.50	1.10
❑ 51	George Blanda	.25	.11
❑ 52	Earl Campbell	.50	.23
❑ 53	Bart Starr	2.00	.90
❑ 54	Dan Marino	2.50	1.10
❑ 55	Johnny Unitas	2.00	.90
❑ 56	Sammy Baugh	.50	.23
❑ 57	Steve Van Buren	.25	.11
❑ 58	Mel Blount	.25	.11
❑ 59	Fred Biletnikoff	.25	.11
❑ 60	John Brodie	.15	.07
❑ 61	Daryle Lamonica	.15	.07
❑ 62	James Lofton	.15	.07
❑ 63	Ronnie Lott	.25	.11
❑ 64	Gale Sayers	1.25	.55
❑ 65	Art Monk	.25	.11
❑ 66	Jim Plunkett	.25	.11
❑ 67	Charlie Joiner	.25	.11
❑ 68	Deacon Jones	.25	.11
❑ 69	Paul Warfield	.50	.23
❑ 70	Jim Otto	.25	.11
❑ 71	Billy Kilmer	.25	.11
❑ 72	Archie Manning	.25	.11
❑ 73	Alex Karras	.25	.11
❑ 74	Tom Matte	.15	.07
❑ 75	Jay Novacek	.15	.07
❑ 76	Charley Taylor	.25	.11
❑ 77	Sam Huff	.25	.11
❑ 78	Jack Lambert	.25	.11
❑ 79	Mike Ditka	1.00	.45
❑ 80	Frank Gifford	.50	.23
❑ 81	Jim Thorpe	.50	.23
❑ 82	Walter Payton	3.00	1.35
❑ 83	Doak Walker	.15	.07
❑ 84	Sid Luckman	.25	.11
❑ 85	Bronko Nagurski	.50	.23
❑ 86	Alan Ameche	.15	.07
❑ 87	Merlin Olsen	.25	.11
❑ 88	Dick Butkus	1.25	.55
❑ 89	Elroy Hirsch	.25	.11
❑ 90	Max McGee	.15	.07
❑ 91	Ray Nitschke	.25	.11
❑ 92	Phil Simms	.25	.11
❑ 93	Vince Lombardi CC	1.25	.55
❑ 94	Tom Landry CC	.75	.35
❑ 95	Bill Walsh CC	.25	.11
❑ 96	Mike Ditka CC	.50	.23
❑ 97	Jimmy Johnson CC	.25	.11
❑ 98	Chuck Noll CC	.25	.11
❑ 99	Dan Reeves CC	.25	.11

❑ 100	Don Shula CC	.50	.23
❑ 101	Peter Warrick RC	25.00	11.00
❑ 102	Thomas Jones RC	12.00	5.50
❑ 103	Jamal Lewis RC	40.00	18.00
❑ 104	Chad Pennington RC	25.00	11.00
❑ 105	Chris Redman RC	15.00	6.75
❑ 106	Ron Dayne RC	25.00	11.00
❑ 107	Trung Canidate RC	8.00	3.60
❑ 108	Shaun Alexander RC	20.00	9.00
❑ 109	Plaxico Burress RC	15.00	6.75
❑ 110	J.R. Redmond RC	10.00	4.50
❑ 111	Travis Taylor RC	10.00	4.50
❑ 112	Dez White RC	6.00	2.70
❑ 113	Todd Pinkston RC	8.00	3.60
❑ 114	Laveranues Coles RC	12.00	5.50
❑ 115	Dennis Northcutt RC	10.00	4.50
❑ 116	Jerry Porter RC	8.00	3.60
❑ 117	R.Jay Soward RC	8.00	3.60
❑ 118	Sylvester Morris RC	15.00	6.75
❑ 119	Ron Dugans RC	6.00	2.70
❑ 120	Travis Prentice RC	12.00	5.50
❑ 121	Tee Martin RC	12.00	5.50
❑ 122	James Williams RC	6.00	2.70
❑ 123	Trevor Gaylor RC	6.00	2.70
❑ 124	Shyrone Stith RC	6.00	2.70
❑ 125	Frank Moreau RC	8.00	3.60
❑ 126	Kwame Cavil RC	6.00	2.70
❑ 127	Ron Dixon RC	10.00	4.50
❑ 128	Darrell Jackson RC	12.00	5.50
❑ 129	Sammy Morris RC	10.00	4.50
❑ 130	JaJuan Dawson RC	8.00	3.60
❑ 131	Doug Johnson RC	25.00	11.00
❑ 132	Brian Urlacher RC	80.00	36.00
❑ 133	Brad Hoover RC	40.00	18.00
❑ 134	Mike Anderson AUTO RC	175.00	80.00

1999 Fleer Mystique

	MINT	NRMT
COMPLETE SET (160)	600.00	275.00
COMP.SHORT SET (100)	50.00	22.00

❑ 1	Terrell Davis SP	4.00	1.80
❑ 2	Jerome Bettis SP	1.50	.70
❑ 3	J.J. Stokes	.50	.23
❑ 4	Frank Wycheck	.25	.11
❑ 5	O.J. McDuffie	.50	.23
❑ 6	Johnnie Morton	.50	.23
❑ 7	Marshall Faulk SP	1.50	.70
❑ 8	Ryan Leaf	1.00	.45
❑ 9	Sean Dawkins	.25	.11
❑ 10	Brett Favre SP	6.00	2.70
❑ 11	Steve Young SP	2.50	1.10
❑ 12	Jimmy Smith	.50	.23
❑ 13	Isaac Bruce	1.00	.45
❑ 14	Trent Dilfer	.50	.23
❑ 15	Brian Mitchell	.25	.11
❑ 16	Kordell Stewart SP	1.50	.70
❑ 17	Herman Moore	1.00	.45
❑ 18	Troy Aikman SP	4.00	1.80
❑ 19	Cris Carter	1.00	.45
❑ 20	Barry Sanders SP	6.00	2.70
❑ 21	Tony Gonzalez	.50	.23
❑ 22	Skip Hicks	.50	.23
❑ 23	Steve McNair SP	1.50	.70
❑ 24	Brad Johnson	.50	.23
❑ 25	Mark Chmura	.25	.11
❑ 26	Randall Cunningham SP	1.50	.70
❑ 27	Jerry Rice SP	4.00	1.80
❑ 28	Jamie Asher	.25	.11
❑ 29	Brian Griese SP	3.00	1.35
❑ 30	Peyton Manning SP	6.00	2.70
❑ 31	Keith Poole	.25	.11
❑ 32	Wayne Chrebet	.50	.23
❑ 33	Rich Gannon	.50	.23
❑ 34	Michael Irvin	.50	.23
❑ 35	Yancey Thigpen	.25	.11
❑ 36	Corey Dillon	1.00	.45
❑ 37	Steve Beuerlein	.25	.11
❑ 38	Terry Kirby	.25	.11
❑ 39	Jacquez Green	.50	.23
❑ 40	Mark Brunell SP	2.50	1.10
❑ 41	Rickey Dudley	.25	.11
❑ 42	Shannon Sharpe	.50	.23
❑ 43	Andre Rison	.50	.23
❑ 44	Chris Chandler	.50	.23
❑ 45	Fred Taylor SP	4.00	1.80
❑ 46	Kerry Collins	.50	.23
❑ 47	Antowain Smith SP	1.50	.70
❑ 48	Wesley Walls	.25	.11
❑ 49	Rob Moore	.50	.23
❑ 50	Dan Marino SP	6.00	2.70
❑ 51	Robert Smith	1.00	.45
❑ 52	Keenan McCardell	.50	.23
❑ 53	Joey Galloway	1.00	.45
❑ 54	Fred Lane	.25	.11
❑ 55	Napoleon Kaufman	1.00	.45
❑ 56	Curtis Martin	1.00	.45
❑ 57	Rod Smith	.50	.23
❑ 58	Curtis Conway	.50	.23
❑ 59	Kevin Dyson	.50	.23
❑ 60	Warrick Dunn SP	1.50	.70
❑ 61	Ahman Green	.50	.23
❑ 62	Duce Staley	1.00	.45
❑ 63	Emmitt Smith SP	4.00	1.80
❑ 64	Adrian Murrell	.50	.23
❑ 65	Dorsey Levens	1.00	.45
❑ 66	Drew Bledsoe SP	2.50	1.10
❑ 67	Ed McCaffrey	.50	.23
❑ 68	Natrone Means	.50	.23
❑ 69	Deion Sanders	1.00	.45
❑ 70	Keyshawn Johnson SP	1.50	.70
❑ 71	Antonio Freeman	1.00	.45
❑ 72	James Stewart	.50	.23
❑ 73	Ben Coates	.50	.23
❑ 74	Priest Holmes	1.00	.45
❑ 75	Jake Reed	.50	.23
❑ 76	Mike Alstott	1.00	.45
❑ 77	Vinny Testaverde	.50	.23
❑ 78	Ricky Watters	.50	.23
❑ 79	Garrison Hearst	.50	.23
❑ 80	Junior Seau	.50	.23
❑ 81	Tim Brown	1.00	.45
❑ 82	Jamal Anderson	1.00	.45
❑ 83	Robert Brooks	.50	.23
❑ 84	Marc Edwards	.25	.11
❑ 85	Curtis Enis	1.00	.45
❑ 86	Doug Flutie	1.25	.55
❑ 87	Terry Glenn	.25	.11
❑ 88	Charlie Batch SP	3.00	1.35
❑ 89	Marvin Harrison	1.00	.45
❑ 90	Jake Plummer SP	3.00	1.35
❑ 91	Terrell Owens	1.00	.45
❑ 92	Scott Mitchell	.25	.11
❑ 93	Tim Dwight	.50	.23
❑ 94	Eddie George SP	2.00	.90
❑ 95	Ike Hilliard	.25	.11
❑ 96	Robert Holcombe	.25	.11
❑ 97	Charles Johnson	.25	.11
❑ 98	Eric Moulds	1.00	.45
❑ 99	Michael Westbrook	.50	.23
❑ 100	Randy Moss SP	6.00	2.70
❑ 101	Tim Couch RC	25.00	11.00
❑ 102	Donovan McNabb RC	30.00	13.50
❑ 103	Akili Smith RC	15.00	6.75
❑ 104	Cade McNown RC	10.00	4.50
❑ 105	Daunte Culpepper RC	50.00	22.00
❑ 106	Ricky Williams RC	30.00	13.50
❑ 107	Edgerrin James RC	50.00	22.00
❑ 108	Kevin Faulk RC	12.00	5.50
❑ 109	Torry Holt RC	20.00	9.00
❑ 110	David Boston RC	15.00	6.75
❑ 111	Chris Claiborne RC	4.00	1.80
❑ 112	Mike Cloud RC	8.00	3.60
❑ 113	Joe Germaine RC	8.00	3.60
❑ 114	Cecil Collins RC	8.00	3.60
❑ 115	Tim Alexander RC	4.00	1.80
❑ 116	Brandon Stokley RC	8.00	3.60
❑ 117	Lamarr Glenn RC	4.00	1.80
❑ 118	Shawn Bryson RC	8.00	3.60
❑ 119	Jeff Paulk RC	6.00	2.70
❑ 120	Kevin Johnson RC	15.00	6.75
❑ 121	Charlie Rogers RC	6.00	2.70
❑ 122	Joe Montgomery RC	8.00	3.60
❑ 123	Travis McGriff RC	6.00	2.70
❑ 124	Dee Miller RC	6.00	2.70
❑ 125	Rob Konrad RC	8.00	3.60
❑ 126	Peerless Price RC	10.00	4.50
❑ 127	D'Wayne Bates RC	6.00	2.70
❑ 128	Craig Yeast RC	6.00	2.70
❑ 129	Malcolm Johnson RC	6.00	2.70
❑ 130	Brock Huard RC	12.00	5.50
❑ 131	Sedrick Irvin RC	1.50	.70
❑ 132	Troy Smith RC	6.00	2.70
❑ 133	Troy Edwards RC	10.00	4.50
❑ 134	Al Wilson RC	6.00	2.70
❑ 135	Terry Jackson RC	6.00	2.70
❑ 136	Dameane Douglas RC	6.00	2.70
❑ 137	Amos Zereoue RC	8.00	3.60
❑ 138	Shaun King RC	15.00	6.75
❑ 139	James Johnson RC	8.00	3.60
❑ 140	Jermaine Fazande RC	8.00	3.60
❑ 141	Autry Denson RC	8.00	3.60
❑ 142	Darran Hall RC	6.00	2.70
❑ 143	Na Brown RC	8.00	3.60
❑ 144	Mike Lucky RC	4.00	1.80
❑ 145	Karsten Bailey RC	6.00	2.70
❑ 146	Kevin Daft RC	6.00	2.70
❑ 147	Sean Bennett RC	8.00	3.60
❑ 148	Madre Hill RC	4.00	1.80
❑ 149	Michael Bishop RC	10.00	4.50
❑ 150	Scott Covington RC	8.00	3.60
❑ 151	Randy Moss STAR	15.00	6.75
❑ 152	Fred Taylor STAR	10.00	4.50
❑ 153	Brett Favre STAR	15.00	6.75
❑ 154	Dan Marino STAR	15.00	6.75
❑ 155	Terrell Davis STAR	10.00	4.50
❑ 156	Barry Sanders STAR	15.00	6.75
❑ 157	Emmitt Smith STAR	10.00	4.50
❑ 158	Jake Plummer STAR	8.00	3.60
❑ 159	Warrick Dunn STAR	4.00	1.80
❑ 160	Troy Aikman STAR	10.00	4.50
❑ P86	Doug Flutie Promo	1.25	.55

2000 Fleer Mystique

	MINT	NRMT
COMPLETE SET (145)	300.00	135.00
COMP.SET w/o SP's (100)	15.00	6.75

❑ 1	Tim Couch	1.50	.70
❑ 2	Edgerrin James	3.00	1.35
❑ 3	Terrell Davis	2.00	.90
❑ 4	Eddie George	1.00	.45
❑ 5	Jevon Kearse	.75	.35
❑ 6	Mike Alstott	.75	.35
❑ 7	Tony Martin	.40	.18
❑ 8	Jermaine Fazande	.20	.09
❑ 9	Akili Smith	.75	.35
❑ 10	Damon Huard	.75	.35
❑ 11	Kordell Stewart	.75	.35

❑ 12 Peyton Manning 2.50 1.10
❑ 13 Michael Westbrook .40 .18
❑ 14 Tim Biakabutuka .40 .18
❑ 15 Curtis Martin .75 .35
❑ 16 Shaun King 1.25 .55
❑ 17 Jamal Anderson .75 .35
❑ 18 Terry Allen .40 .18
❑ 19 Sean Dawkins .20 .09
❑ 20 Muhsin Muhammad .40 .18
❑ 21 Vinny Testaverde .40 .18
❑ 22 Warren Sapp .40 .18
❑ 23 Wesley Walls .40 .18
❑ 24 Mark Brunell 1.25 .55
❑ 25 Tim Brown .75 .35
❑ 26 Kevin Dyson .40 .18
❑ 27 Curtis Enis .40 .18
❑ 28 Keenan McCardell .40 .18
❑ 29 Rich Gannon .40 .18
❑ 30 Jermaine Lewis .40 .18
❑ 31 Johnnie Morton .40 .18
❑ 32 Kerry Collins .40 .18
❑ 33 Az-Zahir Hakim .20 .09
❑ 34 Cade McNown .75 .35
❑ 35 Jimmy Smith .40 .18
❑ 36 Tyrone Wheatley .40 .18
❑ 37 Marcus Robinson .75 .35
❑ 38 Fred Taylor 1.00 .45
❑ 39 Donovan McNabb 1.25 .55
❑ 40 Steve McNair .75 .35
❑ 41 Corey Dillon .75 .35
❑ 42 Tony Gonzalez .40 .18
❑ 43 Duce Staley .75 .35
❑ 44 Albert Connell .20 .09
❑ 45 Isaac Bruce .75 .35
❑ 46 Troy Aikman 2.00 .90
❑ 47 Charlie Garner .40 .18
❑ 48 Kevin Johnson .75 .35
❑ 49 Cris Carter .75 .35
❑ 50 Ryan Leaf .75 .35
❑ 51 Doug Flutie 1.00 .45
❑ 52 Brett Favre 3.00 1.35
❑ 53 Joe Montgomery .20 .09
❑ 54 Torry Holt .75 .35
❑ 55 Jonathan Linton .20 .09
❑ 56 Antonio Freeman .75 .35
❑ 57 Amani Toomer .40 .18
❑ 58 Kurt Warner 3.00 1.35
❑ 59 Jake Plummer .75 .35
❑ 60 Rob Johnson .40 .18
❑ 61 Randy Moss 2.50 1.10
❑ 62 Jerry Rice 2.00 .90
❑ 63 Chris Chandler .40 .18
❑ 64 Joey Galloway .75 .35
❑ 65 Olandis Gary .40 .18
❑ 66 Drew Bledsoe 1.25 .55
❑ 67 Steve Beuerlein .20 .09
❑ 68 Marvin Harrison .75 .35
❑ 69 Keyshawn Johnson .75 .35
❑ 70 Warrick Dunn .75 .35
❑ 71 Tim Dwight .75 .35
❑ 72 Brian Griese 1.00 .45
❑ 73 Terry Glenn .40 .18
❑ 74 Jon Kitna .75 .35
❑ 75 Qadry Ismail .40 .18
❑ 76 Germane Crowell .40 .18
❑ 77 Ricky Williams 2.00 .90
❑ 78 Marshall Faulk 1.00 .45
❑ 79 Karim Abdul-Jabbar .40 .18
❑ 80 James Johnson .20 .09
❑ 81 Hines Ward .20 .09
❑ 82 Frank Sanders .40 .18
❑ 83 Emmitt Smith 2.00 .90
❑ 84 Robert Smith .75 .35
❑ 85 Steve Young 1.25 .55
❑ 86 Damay Scott .40 .18
❑ 87 Tamarick Vanover .20 .09
❑ 88 Troy Edwards .40 .18
❑ 89 Brad Johnson .75 .35
❑ 90 Tony Banks .40 .18
❑ 91 Charlie Batch .75 .35
❑ 92 Jeff Blake .40 .18
❑ 93 Ricky Watters .40 .18
❑ 94 Carl Pickens .40 .18
❑ 95 Elvis Grbac .40 .18
❑ 96 Jerome Bettis .75 .35
❑ 97 Eric Moulds .75 .35
❑ 98 Dorsey Levens .40 .18
❑ 99 Wayne Chrebet .40 .18
❑ 100 Stephen Davis .75 .35
❑ 101 Shaun Alexander RC 12.00 5.50
❑ 102 Sebastian Janikowski RC 6.00 2.70
❑ 103 Tom Brady RC 6.00 2.70
❑ 104 Courtney Brown RC 6.00 2.70
❑ 105 Marc Bulger RC 6.00 2.70
❑ 106 Plaxico Burress RC 10.00 4.50
❑ 107 Trung Canidate RC 6.00 2.70
❑ 108 Giovanni Carmazzi RC 6.00 2.70
❑ 109 Trevor Gaylor RC 5.00 2.20
❑ 110 Laveranues Coles RC 8.00 3.60
❑ 111 Ron Dayne RC 15.00 6.75
❑ 112 Reuben Droughns RC 6.00 2.70
❑ 113 Danny Farmer RC 6.00 2.70
❑ 114 Chafie Fields RC 5.00 2.20
❑ 115 Bubba Franks RC 6.00 2.70
❑ 116 Sherrod Gideon RC 3.00 1.35
❑ 117 Joe Hamilton RC 6.00 2.70
❑ 118 Chris Cole RC 5.00 2.20
❑ 119 Darrell Jackson RC 8.00 3.60
❑ 120 Thomas Jones RC 8.00 3.60
❑ 121 Jamal Lewis RC 25.00 11.00
❑ 122 Anthony Lucas RC 3.00 1.35
❑ 123 Tee Martin RC 8.00 3.60
❑ 124 Frank Murphy RC 3.00 1.35
❑ 125 Rondell Mealey RC 3.00 1.35
❑ 126 Sylvester Morris RC 10.00 4.50
❑ 127 Dennis Northcutt RC 6.00 2.70
❑ 128 Chad Pennington RC 15.00 6.75
❑ 129 Travis Prentice RC 8.00 3.60
❑ 130 Tim Rattay RC 8.00 3.60
❑ 131 Chris Redman RC 10.00 4.50
❑ 132 J.R. Redmond RC 6.00 2.70
❑ 133 R.Jay Soward RC 6.00 2.70
❑ 134 Quinton Spotwood RC 3.00 1.35
❑ 135 Shyrone Stith RC 5.00 2.20
❑ 136 Travis Taylor RC 8.00 3.60
❑ 137 Troy Walters RC 6.00 2.70
❑ 138 Peter Warrick RC 15.00 6.75
❑ 139 Dez White RC 5.00 2.20
❑ 140 Michael Wiley RC 6.00 2.70
❑ 141 Jerry Porter RC 6.00 2.70
❑ 142 Mareno Philyaw RC 3.00 1.35
❑ 143 Anthony Becht RC 6.00 2.70
❑ 144 JaJuan Dawson RC 6.00 2.70
❑ 145 Ron Dugans RC 6.00 2.70

2000 Fleer Showcase

	MINT	NRMT
COMP.SET w/o SP's (100)	25.00	11.00

❑ 1 Tim Couch 1.25 .55
❑ 2 Deion Sanders .60 .25
❑ 3 Damay Scott .30 .14
❑ 4 Brett Favre 2.50 1.10
❑ 5 Mark Brunell 1.00 .45
❑ 6 Randy Moss 2.00 .90
❑ 7 Tyrone Wheatley .30 .14
❑ 8 Isaac Bruce .60 .25
❑ 9 Eddie George .75 .35
❑ 10 Troy Aikman 1.50 .70
❑ 11 Charlie Batch .60 .25
❑ 12 Marvin Harrison .60 .25
❑ 13 Terry Glenn .30 .14
❑ 14 Charles Johnson .30 .14
❑ 15 Jerry Rice 1.50 .70
❑ 16 Kurt Warner 2.50 1.10
❑ 17 Kevin Johnson .60 .25
❑ 18 Jay Fiedler .60 .25
❑ 19 Vinny Testaverde .30 .14
❑ 20 Curtis Enis .60 .25
❑ 21 Elvis Grbac .30 .14
❑ 22 Kordell Stewart .60 .25
❑ 23 Jamal Anderson .60 .25
❑ 24 Dorsey Levens .30 .14
❑ 25 Derrick Mayes .30 .14
❑ 26 Marcus Robinson .60 .25
❑ 27 Cam Cleeland .15 .07
❑ 28 Charlie Garner .30 .14
❑ 29 Germane Crowell .30 .14
❑ 30 Cade McNown .60 .25
❑ 31 Tony Gonzalez .30 .14
❑ 32 Shaun King 1.00 .45
❑ 33 Wayne Chrebet .30 .14
❑ 34 Muhsin Muhammad .30 .14
❑ 35 Olandis Gary .60 .25
❑ 36 Ray Lewis .30 .14
❑ 37 Terrell Davis 1.50 .70
❑ 38 Steve Beuerlein .30 .14
❑ 39 James Stewart .30 .14
❑ 40 Jon Kitna .60 .25
❑ 41 Tim Biakabutuka .30 .14
❑ 42 Ryan Leaf .60 .25
❑ 43 Mike Alstott .60 .25
❑ 44 Yancey Thigpen .15 .07
❑ 45 Champ Bailey .30 .14
❑ 46 Peerless Price .60 .25
❑ 47 Ken Dilger .15 .07
❑ 48 Derrick Alexander .30 .14
❑ 49 Drew Bledsoe 1.00 .45
❑ 50 Jerome Bettis .60 .25
❑ 51 Jermaine Fazande .15 .07
❑ 52 Joey Galloway .60 .25
❑ 53 Jeff Blake .30 .14
❑ 54 Emmitt Smith 1.50 .70
❑ 55 Ricky Williams 1.50 .70
❑ 56 Marshall Faulk .75 .35
❑ 57 Stephen Davis .60 .25
❑ 58 Rob Johnson .30 .14
❑ 59 Brian Griese .75 .35
❑ 60 Damon Huard .60 .25
❑ 61 Jevon Kearse .60 .25
❑ 62 Doug Flutie .75 .35
❑ 63 Curtis Martin .60 .25
❑ 64 Torry Holt .60 .25
❑ 65 David Boston .60 .25
❑ 66 Cris Carter .60 .25
❑ 67 Jason Sehorn .15 .07
❑ 68 Keyshawn Johnson .60 .25
❑ 69 Chris Chandler .30 .14
❑ 70 Antonio Freeman .60 .25
❑ 71 Kerry Collins .30 .14
❑ 72 Akili Smith .60 .25
❑ 73 Troy Edwards .30 .14
❑ 74 Tim Dwight .60 .25
❑ 75 Donovan McNabb 1.00 .45
❑ 76 Tony Banks .30 .14
❑ 77 Ed McCaffrey .60 .25
❑ 78 Errict Rhett .15 .07
❑ 79 Fred Taylor .75 .35
❑ 80 Terrell Owens .60 .25
❑ 81 Steve McNair .60 .25
❑ 82 Rob Moore .30 .14
❑ 83 Jimmy Smith .30 .14
❑ 84 Daunte Culpepper 1.25 .55
❑ 85 Carl Pickens .30 .14
❑ 86 Moses Moreno .15 .07
❑ 87 Brad Johnson .60 .25
❑ 88 Jake Plummer .60 .25
❑ 89 Edgerrin James 2.50 1.10
❑ 90 Zach Thomas .30 .14
❑ 91 Rich Gannon .30 .14
❑ 92 Warrick Dunn .60 .25
❑ 93 Shannon Sharpe .30 .14
❑ 94 Peyton Manning 2.00 .90
❑ 95 Keenan McCardell .30 .14
❑ 96 Tony Simmons .15 .07
❑ 97 Duce Staley .60 .25
❑ 98 Corey Dillon .60 .25
❑ 99 Tim Brown .60 .25
❑ 100 Ricky Watters .15 .07

Card	Mint	NrMt
❑ 101 Peter Warrick RC	30.00	13.50
❑ 102 Shaun Alexander RC	30.00	13.50
❑ 103 Anthony Becht RC	12.00	5.50
❑ 104 Courtney Brown RC	15.00	6.75
❑ 105 Plaxico Burress RC	25.00	11.00
❑ 106 Trung Canidate RC	12.00	5.50
❑ 107 Giovanni Carmazzi RC	15.00	6.75
❑ 108 Laveranues Coles RC	20.00	9.00
❑ 109 Ron Dayne RC	40.00	18.00
❑ 110 Reuben Droughns RC	12.00	5.50
❑ 111 Danny Farmer RC	12.00	5.50
❑ 112 Bubba Franks RC	15.00	6.75
❑ 113 Thomas Jones RC	20.00	9.00
❑ 114 Jamal Lewis RC	80.00	36.00
❑ 115 Sylvester Morris RC	25.00	11.00
❑ 116 Chad Pennington RC	40.00	18.00
❑ 117 Travis Prentice RC	20.00	9.00
❑ 118 J.R. Redmond RC	15.00	6.75
❑ 119 R.Jay Soward RC	12.00	5.50
❑ 120 Dez White RC	12.00	5.50
❑ 121 Sebastian Janikowski RC	6.00	2.70
❑ 122 Todd Pinkston RC	6.00	2.70
❑ 123 Marc Bulger RC	6.00	2.70
❑ 124 Ron Dugans RC	5.00	2.20
❑ 125 Joe Hamilton RC	8.00	3.60
❑ 126 Curtis Keaton RC	5.00	2.20
❑ 127 Tee Martin RC	10.00	4.50
❑ 128 Dennis Northcutt RC	8.00	3.60
❑ 129 Corey Simon RC	8.00	3.60
❑ 130 Chris Redman RC	12.00	5.50
❑ 131 Brian Urlacher RC	20.00	9.00
❑ 132 Travis Taylor RC	8.00	3.60
❑ 133 Michael Wiley RC	6.00	2.70
❑ 134 Tim Rattay RC	10.00	4.50
❑ 135 Jerry Porter RC	6.00	2.70
❑ 136 Tom Brady RC	6.00	2.70
❑ 137 Deon Dyer RC	5.00	2.20
❑ 138 Mareno Philyaw RC	3.00	1.35
❑ 139 Shaun Ellis RC	5.00	2.20
❑ 140 John Abraham RC	5.00	2.20
❑ 141 Ahmed Plummer RC	6.00	2.70
❑ 142 Chris Hovan RC	5.00	2.20
❑ 143 Rob Morris RC	5.00	2.20
❑ 144 Keith Bulluck RC	5.00	2.20
❑ 145 JaJuan Dawson RC	6.00	2.70
❑ 146 Chris Cole RC	5.00	2.20
❑ 147 Chafie Fields RC	3.00	1.35
❑ 148 Darrell Jackson RC	10.00	4.50
❑ 149 Marcus Knight RC	3.00	1.35
❑ 150 Gari Scott RC	5.00	2.20
❑ 151 Kwame Cavil RC	5.00	2.20
❑ 152 Frank Moreau RC	6.00	2.70
❑ 153 Doug Chapman RC	12.00	5.50
❑ 154 Erron Kinney RC	6.00	2.70
❑ 155 Ron Dixon RC	8.00	3.60
❑ 156 Ben Kelly RC	3.00	1.35
❑ 157 Bashir Yamini RC	5.00	2.20
❑ 158 Anthony Lucas RC	3.00	1.35
❑ 159 Avion Black RC	5.00	2.20
❑ 160 Ian Gold RC	5.00	2.20

1994 Images

	MINT	NRMT
COMPLETE SET (125)	40.00	18.00

Card	Mint	NrMt
❑ 1 Emmitt Smith	3.00	1.35
❑ 2 Reggie White	.75	.35
❑ 3 Michael Haynes	.40	.18
❑ 4 Chris Warren	.40	.18
❑ 5 Jeff George	.75	.35
❑ 6 Sean Gilbert	.20	.09
❑ 7 Ricky Watters	.75	.35
❑ 8 Eric Metcalf	.40	.18
❑ 9 Randall Cunningham	.75	.35
❑ 10 Tim Brown	.75	.35
❑ 11 Trent Dilfer RC	3.00	1.35
❑ 12 Marshall Faulk RC	6.00	2.70
❑ 13 David Klingler	.20	.09
❑ 14 Barry Foster	.20	.09
❑ 15 John Elway	4.00	1.80
❑ 16 Joe Montana	4.00	1.80
❑ 17 Rodney Hampton	.75	.35
❑ 18 Todd Steussie RC	.40	.18
❑ 19 Bruce Smith	.75	.35
❑ 20 Wayne Gandy RC	.20	.09
❑ 21 Anthony Miller	.40	.18
❑ 22 Reggie Brooks	.40	.18
❑ 23 Johnny Johnson	.20	.09
❑ 24 Byron Bam Morris RC	.75	.35
❑ 25 Drew Bledsoe	2.50	1.10
❑ 26 Jeff Hostetler	.40	.18
❑ 27 Alvin Harper	.40	.18
❑ 28 Cris Carter	1.00	.45
❑ 29 Bert Emanuel RC	1.25	.55
❑ 30 Errict Rhett RC	1.50	.70
❑ 31 Scott Mitchell	.75	.35
❑ 32 Deion Sanders	1.00	.45
❑ 33 Lewis Tillman	.20	.09
❑ 34 Tim Bowens RC	.40	.18
❑ 35 Charles Haley	.40	.18
❑ 36 Stan Humphries	.75	.35
❑ 37 Haywood Jeffires	.40	.18
❑ 38 Andre Reed	.40	.18
❑ 39 Charles Johnson RC	1.25	.55
❑ 40 Ronald Moore	.20	.09
❑ 41 Jim Everett	.40	.18
❑ 42 Greg Hill RC	.75	.35
❑ 43 Thurman Thomas	.75	.35
❑ 44 Willie McGinest RC	.75	.35
❑ 45 Aaron Glenn RC	.40	.18
❑ 46 Erric Pegram	.20	.09
❑ 47 Terry Kirby	.75	.35
❑ 48 Warren Moon	.75	.35
❑ 49 Clyde Simmons	.20	.09
❑ 50 Eric Turner	.20	.09
❑ 51 Heath Shuler RC	.75	.35
❑ 52 Rickey Jackson	.20	.09
❑ 53 Johnnie Morton RC	2.00	.90
❑ 54 Charlie Garner RC	2.50	1.10
❑ 55 Mark Collins	.20	.09
❑ 56 Mike Pritchard	.20	.09
❑ 57 Bryant Young RC	.75	.35
❑ 58 Joe Johnson RC	.20	.09
❑ 59 Erik Kramer	.40	.18
❑ 60 Barry Sanders	4.00	1.80
❑ 61 Rod Woodson	.75	.35
❑ 62 Dave Brown	.40	.18
❑ 63 Gary Brown	.20	.09
❑ 64 Brett Favre	4.00	1.80
❑ 65 Isaac Bruce RC	6.00	2.70
❑ 66 Boomer Esiason	.40	.18
❑ 67 Jim Harbaugh	.75	.35
❑ 68 Jackie Harris	.20	.09
❑ 69 Art Monk	.40	.18
❑ 70 Jamir Miller RC	.20	.09
❑ 71 Neil O'Donnell	.75	.35
❑ 72 Neil Smith	.75	.35
❑ 73 Junior Seau	.75	.35
❑ 74 Jerome Bettis	.75	.35
❑ 75 Bernard Williams RC	.20	.09
❑ 76 Jeff Burris RC	.40	.18
❑ 77 Henry Ellard	.40	.18
❑ 78 Reggie Cobb	.20	.09
❑ 79 Shante Carver RC	.20	.09
❑ 80 Terry Allen	.40	.18
❑ 81 Cortez Kennedy	.40	.18
❑ 82 Trev Alberts RC	.40	.18
❑ 83 Michael Irvin	.75	.35
❑ 84 Herschel Walker	.40	.18
❑ 85 Dan Marino	4.00	1.80
❑ 86 Dave Meggett	.20	.09
❑ 87 Herman Moore	.75	.35
❑ 88 Darnay Scott RC	2.00	.90
❑ 89 Dewayne Washington RC	.40	.18
❑ 90 Rob Fredrickson RC	.40	.18
❑ 91 Rick Mirer	.75	.35
❑ 92 Thomas Lewis RC	.40	.18
❑ 93 Chris Miller	.20	.09
❑ 94 Marion Butts	.20	.09
❑ 95 Sam Adams RC	.40	.18
❑ 96 Jerry Rice	2.00	.90
❑ 97 Ben Coates	.75	.35
❑ 98 David Palmer RC	1.25	.55
❑ 99 Antonio Langham RC	.40	.18
❑ 100 Curtis Conway	.75	.35
❑ 101 Derrick Thomas	.75	.35
❑ 102 Ken Norton Jr.	.40	.18
❑ 103 Ronnie Lott	.40	.18
❑ 104 Sterling Sharpe	.40	.18
❑ 105 Troy Aikman	2.00	.90
❑ 106 Shannon Sharpe	.40	.18
❑ 107 Natrone Means	.75	.35
❑ 108 Derek Brown RBK	.20	.09
❑ 109 Dan Wilkinson RC	.40	.18
❑ 110 Andre Rison	.40	.18
❑ 111 Quentin Coryatt	.20	.09
❑ 112 Cody Carlson	.20	.09
❑ 113 William Floyd RC	.75	.35
❑ 114 Marcus Allen	.75	.35
❑ 115 Steve Young	1.50	.70
❑ 116 Jim Kelly	.75	.35
❑ 117 LeShon Johnson RC	.40	.18
❑ 118 Irving Fryar	.40	.18
❑ 119 Carl Pickens	.75	.35
❑ 120 Keith Jackson	.20	.09
❑ 121 John Thierry RC	.20	.09
❑ 122 Vinny Testaverde	.40	.18
❑ 123 Der.Alexander WR RC	1.25	.55
❑ 124 Seth Joyner	.20	.09
❑ 125 Checklist	.20	.09
❑ IF1 Emmitt Smith Promo (Numbered IF1)	2.50	1.10
❑ TP1 Drew Bledsoe NFL Experience Throwbacks preview card	50.00	22.00
❑ NNO Emmitt Smith NFL Experience Sneak Preview card	10.00	4.50

1995 Images Limited

	MINT	NRMT
COMPLETE SET (125)	25.00	11.00

Card	Mint	NrMt
❑ 1 Emmitt Smith	2.00	.90
❑ 2 Steve Young	1.00	.45
❑ 3 Drew Bledsoe	1.25	.55
❑ 4 Dan Marino	2.50	1.10
❑ 5 John Elway	2.50	1.10
❑ 6 Barry Sanders	2.50	1.10
❑ 7 Brett Favre	2.50	1.10
❑ 8 Troy Aikman	1.25	.55
❑ 9 Jim Kelly	.40	.18
❑ 10 Marshall Faulk	.60	.25
❑ 11 Jerry Rice	1.25	.55
❑ 12 Warren Moon	.20	.09
❑ 13 Jim Everett	.10	.05
❑ 14 Rodney Hampton	.20	.09
❑ 15 Jeff Hostetler	.20	.09
❑ 16 Errict Rhett	.40	.18
❑ 17 Jerome Bettis	.40	.18

❑ 18 Byron Bam Morris	.20	.09
❑ 19 Randall Cunningham	.40	.18
❑ 20 Rick Mirer	.40	.18
❑ 21 Natrone Means	.40	.18
❑ 22 Jeff George	.20	.09
❑ 23 Garrison Hearst	.40	.18
❑ 24 Michael Irvin	.40	.18
❑ 25 Cris Carter	.40	.18
❑ 26 Irving Fryar	.20	.09
❑ 27 Jeff Blake RC	1.00	.45
❑ 28 Bruce Smith	.40	.18
❑ 29 Shannon Sharpe	.20	.09
❑ 30 Steve Beuerlein	.10	.05
❑ 31 Stan Humphries	.20	.09
❑ 32 Chris Warren	.20	.09
❑ 33 Ben Coates	.20	.09
❑ 34 Boomer Esiason	.20	.09
❑ 35 Trent Dilfer	.40	.18
❑ 36 Chris Miller	.10	.05
❑ 37 Dave Brown	.20	.09
❑ 38 Herman Moore	.40	.18
❑ 39 Anthony Miller	.20	.09
❑ 40 Andre Reed	.20	.09
❑ 41 Reggie White	.40	.18
❑ 42 Darnay Scott	.40	.18
❑ 43 Erik Kramer	.10	.05
❑ 44 Leroy Hoard	.10	.05
❑ 45 Fred Barnett	.20	.09
❑ 46 Junior Seau	.40	.18
❑ 47 Vinny Testaverde	.20	.09
❑ 48 Gus Frerotte	.40	.18
❑ 49 William Floyd	.40	.18
❑ 50 Mo Lewis	.10	.05
❑ 51 Tim Brown	.40	.18
❑ 52 Greg Lloyd	.20	.09
❑ 53 Chester McGlockton	.20	.09
❑ 54 Heath Shuler	.40	.18
❑ 55 Rod Woodson	.20	.09
❑ 56 Don Beebe	.10	.05
❑ 57 Carl Pickens	.40	.18
❑ 58 Charles Haley	.20	.09
❑ 59 Steve Bono	.20	.09
❑ 60 Harvey Williams	.10	.05
❑ 61 Greg Hill	.20	.09
❑ 62 Eric Metcalf	.20	.09
❑ 63 Mario Bates	.40	.18
❑ 64 Terry Allen	.20	.09
❑ 65 Michael Timpson	.10	.05
❑ 66 Mark Stepnoski	.10	.05
❑ 67 Jeff Lageman	.10	.05
❑ 68 Robert Smith	.40	.18
❑ 69 Eric Allen	.10	.05
❑ 70 Ricky Watters	.40	.18
❑ 71 Derek Loville	.10	.05
❑ 72 Bernie Parmalee	.20	.09
❑ 73 Bryce Paup	.40	.18
❑ 74 Frank Reich	.10	.05
❑ 75 Henry Thomas	.10	.05
❑ 76 Craig Erickson	.10	.05
❑ 77 Eric Green	.10	.05
❑ 78 Dave Meggett	.10	.05
❑ 79 Deion Sanders	.75	.35
❑ 80 Herschel Walker	.20	.09
❑ 81 Andre Rison	.20	.09
❑ 82 Ki-Jana Carter RC	.40	.18
❑ 83 Tony Boselli RC	.40	.18
❑ 84 Steve McNair RC	3.00	1.35
❑ 85 Michael Westbrook RC	1.50	.70
❑ 86 Kerry Collins RC	1.50	.70
❑ 87 Kevin Carter RC	.40	.18
❑ 88 Warren Sapp RC	.75	.35
❑ 89 Joey Galloway RC	2.50	1.10
❑ 90 J.J. Stokes RC	.40	.18
❑ 92 Kyle Brady RC	.40	.18
❑ 93 Napoleon Kaufman RC	1.50	.70
❑ 94 Tyrone Wheatley RC	1.25	.55
❑ 95 Mike Mamula RC	.20	.09
❑ 96 Desmond Howard	.20	.09
❑ 97 James O. Stewart RC	2.00	.90
❑ 98 Craig Newsome RC	.10	.05
❑ 99 Ty Law RC	.20	.09
❑ 100 Ellis Johnson RC	.10	.05
❑ 101 Hugh Douglas RC	.40	.18
❑ 102 Mark Bruener RC	.20	.09
❑ 103 Tyrone Poole	.20	.09
❑ 104 Luther Elliss	.10	.05
❑ 105 Mark Fields	.10	.05
❑ 106 Frank Sanders RC	1.00	.45
❑ 107 Rashaan Salaam RC	.40	.18
❑ 108 Craig Powell	.10	.05
❑ 109 Sherman Williams RC	.10	.05
❑ 110 Chad May RC	.10	.05
❑ 111 Rob Johnson RC	2.00	.90
❑ 112 Todd Collins RC	.40	.18
❑ 113 Terrell Davis RC	10.00	4.50
❑ 114 Eric Zeier RC	.40	.18
❑ 115 Curtis Martin RC	3.00	1.35
❑ 116 Kordell Stewart RC	2.50	1.10
❑ 117 Troy Vincent	.10	.05
❑ 118 Ray Zellars RC	.20	.09
❑ 119 Dave Krieg	.10	.05
❑ 120 Mike Sherrard	.10	.05
❑ 121 Willie Davis	.10	.05
❑ 122 Robert Brooks	.20	.09
❑ 123 Chris Sanders RC	.20	.09
❑ 124 Checklist #1 Drew Bledsoe	.40	.18
❑ 125 Checklist #2 Emmitt Smith	.60	.25
❑ LT1 Drew Bledsoe Promo (Numbered LT1, ad back)	1.50	.70

2000 Impact

	MINT	NRMT
❑ 1 Kurt Warner	1.50	.70
❑ 2 Dan Marino	1.50	.70
❑ 3 Sedrick Irvin	.10	.05
❑ 4 Chris Redman RC	1.25	.55
❑ 5 Robert Smith	.40	.18
❑ 6 Amani Toomer	.10	.05
❑ 7 Richard Huntley	.10	.05
❑ 8 Ahman Green	.20	.09
❑ 9 Fred Lane	.10	.05
❑ 10 Eddie George	.50	.23
❑ 11 Rocket Ismail	.20	.09
❑ 12 Shannon Sharpe	.20	.09
❑ 13 Shawn Jefferson	.10	.05
❑ 14 Michael Wiley RC	.60	.25
❑ 15 Jeff Graham	.10	.05
❑ 16 Steve Beuerlein	.20	.09
❑ 17 Tim Biakabutuka	.20	.09
❑ 18 Chris Watson	.10	.05
❑ 19 Kevin Faulk	.20	.09
❑ 20 Emmitt Smith	1.00	.45
❑ 21 Plaxico Burress RC	1.25	.55
❑ 22 Hines Ward	.10	.05
❑ 23 Jacquez Green	.20	.09
❑ 24 Doug Flutie	.50	.23
❑ 25 Leslie Shepherd	.10	.05
❑ 26 Johnnie Morton	.20	.09
❑ 27 Tom Brady RC	.20	.09
❑ 28 Jeff George	.20	.09
❑ 29 Derrick Mason	.20	.09
❑ 30 Marshall Faulk	.50	.23
❑ 31 Derrick Mayes	.20	.09
❑ 32 Jerome Bettis	.40	.18
❑ 33 Adrian Murrell	.20	.09
❑ 34 Curtis Enis	.20	.09
❑ 35 Kimble Anders	.10	.05
❑ 36 Travis Prentice RC	1.00	.45
❑ 37 Curtis Martin	.40	.18
❑ 38 Ronnie Powell	.10	.05
❑ 39 Steve Christie	.10	.05
❑ 40 Brett Favre	1.50	.70
❑ 41 Michael Bates	.10	.05
❑ 42 Rondell Mealey RC	.40	.18
❑ 43 Randall Cunningham	.40	.18
❑ 44 Kerry Collins	.20	.09
❑ 45 William Thomas	.10	.05
❑ 46 Ricky Watters	.20	.09
❑ 47 Marvin Harrison	.40	.18
❑ 48 Corey Bradford	.20	.09
❑ 49 Terry Kirby	.10	.05
❑ 50 Troy Aikman	1.00	.45
❑ 51 Cris Carter	.40	.18
❑ 52 Jamal Lewis RC	3.00	1.35
❑ 53 Duce Staley	.40	.18
❑ 54 Isaac Bruce	.40	.18
❑ 55 Yancey Thigpen	.10	.05
❑ 56 R.Jay Soward RC	.60	.25
❑ 57 Jermaine Lewis	.10	.05
❑ 58 Zach Thomas	.20	.09
❑ 59 Sylvester Morris RC	1.25	.55
❑ 60 Steve McNair	.40	.18
❑ 61 Tiki Barber	.20	.09
❑ 62 Torrance Small	.10	.05
❑ 63 Champ Bailey	.20	.09
❑ 64 Tim Dwight	.40	.18
❑ 65 Willie Jackson	.10	.05
❑ 66 Edgerrin James	1.50	.70
❑ 67 Ron Dayne RC	2.00	.90
❑ 68 Rich Gannon	.20	.09
❑ 69 Junior Seau	.20	.09
❑ 70 Warren Sapp	.20	.09
❑ 71 Rob Johnson	.20	.09
❑ 72 Antonio Freeman	.40	.18
❑ 73 O.J. McDuffie	.20	.09
❑ 74 Tamarick Vanover	.10	.05
❑ 75 Courtney Brown RC	.75	.35
❑ 76 Donovan McNabb	.60	.25
❑ 77 Az-Zahir Hakim	.20	.09
❑ 78 Albert Connell	.10	.05
❑ 79 Qadry Ismail	.10	.05
❑ 80 Terrell Davis	1.00	.45
❑ 81 Dorsey Levens	.20	.09
❑ 82 Tony Martin	.20	.09
❑ 83 Laveranues Coles RC	1.00	.45
❑ 84 Karim Abdul-Jabbar	.20	.09
❑ 85 Charles Johnson	.20	.09
❑ 86 Torry Holt	.40	.18
❑ 87 Stephen Davis	.40	.18
❑ 88 Tony Banks	.20	.09
❑ 89 Akili Smith	.40	.18
❑ 90 Tim Couch	.75	.35
❑ 91 Bill Schroeder	.20	.09
❑ 92 Andre Hastings	.10	.05
❑ 93 Eddie Kennison	.10	.05
❑ 94 Randy Moss	1.25	.55
❑ 95 Tony Horne	.10	.05
❑ 96 Sherrod Gideon RC	.40	.18
❑ 97 Wesley Walls	.10	.05
❑ 98 Brian Griese	.50	.23
❑ 99 Jake Delhomme RC	.40	.18
❑ 100 Peyton Manning	1.25	.55
❑ 101 Brad Johnson	.40	.18
❑ 102 Trung Canidate RC	.20	.09
❑ 103 Freddie Jones	.10	.05
❑ 104 Muhsin Muhammad	.20	.09
❑ 105 Eric Moulds	.40	.18
❑ 106 Ed McCaffrey	.40	.18
❑ 107 Joe Montgomery	.10	.05
❑ 108 Olandis Gary	.40	.18
❑ 109 J.J. Stokes	.10	.05
❑ 110 Ricky Williams	1.00	.45
❑ 111 Jim Harbaugh	.20	.09
❑ 112 Mike Alstott	.40	.18
❑ 113 Errict Rhett	.20	.09
❑ 114 Terance Mathis	.10	.05
❑ 115 Kevin Johnson	.40	.18
❑ 116 Tremain Mack	.10	.05
❑ 117 Peter Warrick RC	2.00	.90
❑ 118 Lamont Warren	.10	.05
❑ 119 Damon Huard	.40	.18
❑ 120 Cade McNown	.40	.18
❑ 121 Natrone Means	.10	.05
❑ 122 Ken Oxendine	.10	.05
❑ 123 J.R. Redmond RC	.75	.35
❑ 124 Ken Dilger	.10	.05

❑ 125 James Johnson	.20	.09
❑ 126 Napoleon Kaufman	.20	.09
❑ 127 Ryan Leaf	.40	.18
❑ 128 Michael Westbrook	.20	.09
❑ 129 Mario Bates	.10	.05
❑ 130 Jake Plummer	.40	.18
❑ 131 James Jett	.10	.05
❑ 132 Darnay Scott	.20	.09
❑ 133 Curtis Conway	.20	.09
❑ 134 Fred Taylor	.50	.23
❑ 135 Wayne Chrebet	.20	.09
❑ 136 Sean Dawkins	.10	.05
❑ 138 Keenan McCardell	.20	.09
❑ 139 Donnell Bennett	.10	.05
❑ 140 Jerry Rice	1.00	.45
❑ 141 Vinny Testaverde	.20	.09
❑ 142 Chad Pennington RC	2.00	.90
❑ 143 Jonathan Linton	.10	.05
❑ 144 Herman Moore	.20	.09
❑ 145 David Patten	.10	.05
❑ 146 Troy Edwards	.20	.09
❑ 147 Jon Kitna	.40	.18
❑ 148 Jimmy Smith	.20	.09
❑ 149 Tee Martin RC	1.00	.45
❑ 150 Jevon Kearse	.40	.18
❑ 151 Frank Sanders	.10	.05
❑ 152 Marcus Robinson	.40	.18
❑ 153 Mike Hollis	.10	.05
❑ 154 Frank Wycheck	.10	.05
❑ 155 Tim Rattay RC	1.00	.45
❑ 156 Dedric Ward	.10	.05
❑ 157 Terrell Owens	.40	.18
❑ 158 Chris Chandler	.20	.09
❑ 159 Damon Griffin	.10	.05
❑ 160 Mike Vanderjagt	.10	.05
❑ 161 Elvis Grbac	.10	.05
❑ 162 Rickey Dudley	.10	.05
❑ 163 Jeff Garcia	.40	.18
❑ 164 Thomas Jones RC	1.00	.45
❑ 165 Tyrone Wheatley	.20	.09
❑ 166 Rod Smith	.20	.09
❑ 167 Bubba Franks RC	.75	.35
❑ 168 Chris Warren	.10	.05
❑ 169 Anthony Lucas RC	.10	.05
❑ 170 Terry Glenn	.20	.09
❑ 171 John Carney	.10	.05
❑ 172 Warrick Dunn	.40	.18
❑ 173 Shaun Alexander RC	1.50	.70
❑ 174 David Boston	.40	.18
❑ 175 Bobby Engram	.10	.05
❑ 176 Travis Taylor RC	.75	.35
❑ 177 Derrick Alexander	.20	.09
❑ 178 Keyshawn Johnson	.40	.18
❑ 179 Steve Young	.60	.25
❑ 180 Deion Sanders	.40	.18
❑ 181 Charlie Batch	.40	.18
❑ 182 Drew Bledsoe	.60	.25
❑ 183 Reuben Droughns RC	.60	.25
❑ 184 Ray Lucas	.40	.18
❑ 185 Shaun King	.60	.25
❑ 186 Jamal Anderson	.40	.18
❑ 187 Corey Dillon	.40	.18
❑ 188 Joe Hamilton RC	.75	.35
❑ 189 Terrence Wilkins	.40	.18
❑ 190 Mark Brunell	.60	.25
❑ 191 Tony Gonzalez	.20	.09
❑ 192 Tim Brown	.40	.18
❑ 193 Charlie Garner	.20	.09
❑ 194 Antowain Smith	.20	.09
❑ 195 David LaFleur	.10	.05
❑ 196 Germane Crowell	.20	.09
❑ 197 Terry Allen	.20	.09
❑ 198 Marc Bulger RC	.20	.09
❑ 199 Kevin Dyson	.20	.09
❑ 200 Kordell Stewart	.40	.18

1996 Laser View

	MINT	NRMT
COMPLETE SET (40)	40.00	18.00
❑ 1 Jim Kelly	1.25	.55
❑ 2 Troy Aikman	3.00	1.35
❑ 3 Michael Irvin	1.25	.55
❑ 4 Emmitt Smith	5.00	2.20

❑ 5 John Elway	6.00	2.70
❑ 6 Barry Sanders	6.00	2.70
❑ 7 Brett Favre	6.00	2.70
❑ 8 Jim Harbaugh	.60	.25
❑ 9 Dan Marino	6.00	2.70
❑ 10 Warren Moon	.60	.25
❑ 11 Drew Bledsoe	3.00	1.35
❑ 12 Jim Everett	.30	.14
❑ 13 Jeff Hostetler	.30	.14
❑ 14 Neil O'Donnell	.60	.25
❑ 15 Junior Seau	.60	.25
❑ 16 Jerry Rice	3.00	1.35
❑ 17 Steve Young	2.50	1.10
❑ 18 Rick Mirer	.60	.25
❑ 19 Boomer Esiason	.60	.25
❑ 20 Bernie Kosar	.30	.14
❑ 21 Heath Shuler	.60	.25
❑ 22 Dave Brown	.30	.14
❑ 23 Jeff Blake	1.25	.55
❑ 24 Kerry Collins	1.25	.55
❑ 25 Kordell Stewart	1.50	.70
❑ 26 Scott Mitchell	.60	.25
❑ 27 Kerry Collins PE	1.25	.55
❑ 28 Troy Aikman PE	2.00	.90
❑ 29 Kordell Stewart PE	1.25	.55
❑ 30 Michael Irvin PE	.60	.25
❑ 31 Emmitt Smith PE	3.00	1.35
❑ 32 John Elway PE	4.00	1.80
❑ 33 Barry Sanders PE	4.00	1.80
❑ 34 Brett Favre PE	4.00	1.80
❑ 35 Dan Marino PE	4.00	1.80
❑ 36 Drew Bledsoe PE	2.00	.90
❑ 37 Neil O'Donnell PE	.60	.25
❑ 38 Jerry Rice PE	2.00	.90
❑ 39 Steve Young PE	2.00	.90
❑ 40 Jeff Blake PE	.60	.25
❑ P5 John Elway Promo	3.00	1.35

1948 Leaf

	NRMT	VG-E
COMPLETE SET (98)	6000.00	2700.00
COMMON CARD (1-49)	30.00	13.50
COMMON CARD (50-98)	120.00	55.00
WRAPPER (5-CENT)	160.00	70.00
❑ 1 Sid Luckman RC	400.00	100.00
❑ 2 Steve Suhey	30.00	13.50
❑ 3A Bulldog Turner RC	110.00	50.00
(Red background)		
❑ 3B Bulldog Turner RC	110.00	50.00
(White background)		
❑ 4 Doak Walker RC	200.00	90.00
❑ 5 Levi Jackson RC	40.00	18.00
❑ 6 Bobby Layne RC UER	350.00	160.00
(Name spelled Bobbie on front)		
❑ 7 Bill Fischer	30.00	13.50
❑ 8A Vince Banonis	30.00	13.50
(White name on front)		
❑ 8B Vince Banonis	30.00	13.50
(Black name on front)		
❑ 9 Tommy Thompson RC	40.00	18.00
❑ 10 Perry Moss	30.00	13.50
❑ 11 Terry Brennan RC	40.00	18.00
❑ 12A William Swiacki RC	30.00	13.50
(White name on front)		
❑ 12B William Swiacki RC	30.00	13.50
(Black name on front)		
❑ 13 Johnny Lujack RC	200.00	90.00
❑ 14A Mal Kutner RC	30.00	13.50
(White name on front)		
❑ 14B Mal Kutner RC	30.00	13.50
(Black name on front)		
❑ 15 Charlie Justice RC	90.00	40.00
❑ 16 Pete Pihos RC	110.00	50.00
❑ 17A Kenny Washington RC	55.00	25.00
(White name on front)		
❑ 17B Kenny Washington RC	55.00	25.00
(Black name on front)		
❑ 18 Harry Gilmer RC	50.00	22.00
❑ 19A George McAfee RC ERR	125.00	55.00
(Listed as Gorgeous George on front)		
❑ 19B George McAfee COR RC	110.00	50.00
❑ 20 George Taliaferro RC	40.00	18.00
❑ 21 Paul Christman RC	50.00	22.00
❑ 22 Steve Van Buren RC	250.00	110.00
❑ 23 Ken Kavanaugh RC	40.00	18.00
❑ 24 Jim Martin RC	40.00	18.00
❑ 25 Elmer Bud Angsman RC	40.00	18.00
❑ 26 Bob Waterfield RC	250.00	110.00
❑ 27A Fred Davis	30.00	13.50
(Yellow background)		
❑ 27B Fred Davis	30.00	13.50
(White background)		
❑ 28 Whitey Wistert RC	40.00	18.00
❑ 29 Charley Trippi RC	110.00	50.00
❑ 30 Paul Governali RC	40.00	18.00
❑ 31 Tom McWilliams	30.00	13.50
❑ 32 Leroy Zimmerman	30.00	13.50
❑ 33 Pat Harder RC UER	55.00	25.00
(Misspelled Harber on front)		
❑ 34 Sammy Baugh RC	600.00	275.00
❑ 35 Ted Fritsch Sr. RC	40.00	18.00
❑ 36 Bill Dudley RC	110.00	50.00
❑ 37 George Connor RC	90.00	40.00
❑ 38 Frank Dancewicz	30.00	13.50
❑ 39 Billy Dewell	30.00	13.50
❑ 40 John Nolan	30.00	13.50
❑ 41A Harry Szulborski	30.00	13.50
(Yellow jersey)		
❑ 41B Harry Szulborski	30.00	13.50
(Orange jersey)		
❑ 42 Tex Coulter RC	40.00	18.00
❑ 43A Robert Nussbaumer	30.00	13.50
(Maroon Jersey)		
❑ 43B Robert Nussbaumer	30.00	13.50
(Red Jersey)		
❑ 44 Bob Mann	30.00	13.50
❑ 45 Jim White	30.00	13.50
❑ 46 Jack Jacobs	30.00	13.50
❑ 47 John Clement	30.00	13.50
❑ 48 Frank Reagan	30.00	13.50
❑ 49 Frank Tripucka RC	45.00	20.00
❑ 50 John Rauch RC	120.00	55.00
❑ 51 Mike Dimitro	120.00	55.00
❑ 52 Leo Nomellini RC	400.00	180.00
❑ 53 Charley Conerly RC	400.00	180.00
❑ 54 Chuck Bednarik RC	450.00	200.00
❑ 55 Chick Jagade	120.00	55.00
❑ 56 Bob Folsom RC	140.00	65.00
❑ 57 Gene Rossides RC	140.00	65.00
❑ 58 Art Weiner	120.00	55.00
❑ 59 Alex Sarkistian	120.00	55.00
❑ 60 Dick Harris	120.00	55.00
❑ 61 Len Younce	120.00	55.00
❑ 62 Gene Derricotte	120.00	55.00
❑ 63 Roy Rebel Steiner	120.00	55.00

❑ 64 Frank Seno	120.00	55.00
❑ 65 Bob Hendren RC	120.00	55.00
❑ 66 Jack Cloud	120.00	55.00
❑ 67 Harrell Collins	120.00	55.00
❑ 68 Clyde LeForce	120.00	55.00
❑ 69 Larry Joe	120.00	55.00
❑ 70 Phil O'Reilly	120.00	55.00
❑ 71 Paul Campbell	120.00	55.00
❑ 72 Ray Evans	120.00	55.00
❑ 73 Jackie Jensen RC UER (Spelled Jackey on card front)	350.00	160.00
❑ 74 Russ Steger	120.00	55.00
❑ 75 Tony Minisi	120.00	55.00
❑ 76 Clayton Tonnemaker	120.00	55.00
❑ 77 George Savitsky	120.00	55.00
❑ 78 Clarence Self	120.00	55.00
❑ 79 Rod Franz	120.00	55.00
❑ 80 Jim Youle	120.00	55.00
❑ 81 Billy Bye	120.00	55.00
❑ 82 Fred Enke	120.00	55.00
❑ 83 Fred Folger	120.00	55.00
❑ 84 Jug Girard RC	140.00	65.00
❑ 85 Joe Scott	120.00	55.00
❑ 86 Bob Demoss	120.00	55.00
❑ 87 Dave Templeton	120.00	55.00
❑ 88 Herb Siegert	120.00	55.00
❑ 89 Bucky O'Conner	120.00	55.00
❑ 90 Joe Whisler	120.00	55.00
❑ 91 Leon Hart RC	200.00	90.00
❑ 92 Earl Banks	120.00	55.00
❑ 93 Frank Aschenbrenner	120.00	55.00
❑ 94 John Goldsberry	120.00	55.00
❑ 95 Porter Payne	120.00	55.00
❑ 96 Pete Perini	120.00	55.00
❑ 97 Jay Rhodemyre	120.00	55.00
❑ 98 Al DiMarco RC	250.00	60.00

1949 Leaf

	NRMT	VG-E
COMPLETE SET (49)	2200.00	1000.00
WRAPPER (5-CENT)	300.00	135.00

❑ 1 Bob Hendren	80.00	20.00
❑ 2 Joe Scott	25.00	11.00
❑ 3 Frank Reagan	25.00	11.00
❑ 4 John Rauch	25.00	11.00
❑ 7 Bill Fischer	25.00	11.00
❑ 9 Elmer Bud Angsman	35.00	16.00
❑ 10 Billy Dewell	25.00	11.00
❑ 13 Tommy Thompson	35.00	16.00
❑ 15 Sid Luckman	125.00	55.00
❑ 16 Charley Trippi	55.00	25.00
❑ 17 Bob Mann	25.00	11.00
❑ 19 Paul Christman	35.00	16.00
❑ 22 Bill Dudley	55.00	25.00
❑ 23 Clyde LeForce	25.00	11.00
❑ 26 Sammy Baugh	300.00	135.00
❑ 28 Pete Pihos	70.00	32.00
❑ 31 Tex Coulter	35.00	16.00
❑ 32 Mal Kutner	35.00	16.00
❑ 35 Whitey Wistert	35.00	16.00
❑ 37 Ted Fritsch Sr.	35.00	16.00
❑ 38 Vince Banonis	25.00	11.00
❑ 39 Jim White	25.00	11.00
❑ 40 George Connor	55.00	25.00
❑ 41 George McAfee	55.00	25.00
❑ 43 Frank Tripucka	35.00	16.00
❑ 47 Fred Enke	25.00	11.00
❑ 49 Charley Conerly	100.00	45.00
❑ 51 Ken Kavanaugh	35.00	16.00
❑ 52 Bob Demoss	25.00	11.00
❑ 56 John Lujack	100.00	45.00
❑ 57 Jim Youle	25.00	11.00
❑ 62 Harry Gilmer	35.00	16.00
❑ 65 Robert Nussbaumer	25.00	11.00
❑ 67 Bobby Layne	175.00	80.00
❑ 70 Herb Siegert	25.00	11.00
❑ 74 Tony Minisi	25.00	11.00
❑ 79 Steve Van Buren	125.00	55.00
❑ 81 Perry Moss	25.00	11.00
❑ 89 Bob Waterfield	100.00	45.00
❑ 90 Jack Jacobs	25.00	11.00
❑ 95 Kenny Washington	45.00	20.00
❑ 101 Pat Harder UER (Misspelled Harber on front)	35.00	16.00
❑ 110 Bill Swiacki	35.00	16.00
❑ 118 Fred Davis	25.00	11.00
❑ 126 Jay Rhodemyre	25.00	11.00
❑ 127 Frank Seno	25.00	11.00
❑ 134 Chuck Bednarik	150.00	70.00
❑ 144 George Savitsky	25.00	11.00
❑ 150 Bulldog Turner	150.00	38.00

1996 Leaf

	MINT	NRMT
COMPLETE SET (190)	20.00	9.00

❑ 1 Troy Aikman	1.00	.45
❑ 2 Ricky Watters	.20	.09
❑ 3 Robert Brooks	.40	.18
❑ 4 Ki-Jana Carter	.20	.09
❑ 5 Drew Bledsoe	1.00	.45
❑ 6 Eric Swann	.10	.05
❑ 7 Hardy Nickerson	.10	.05
❑ 8 Tony Martin	.20	.09
❑ 9 Garrison Hearst	.20	.09
❑ 10 Bernie Parmalee	.10	.05
❑ 11 Neil Smith	.10	.05
❑ 12 Aaron Craver	.10	.05
❑ 13 Rashaan Salaam	.40	.18
❑ 14 Greg Hill	.20	.09
❑ 15 Charlie Garner	.10	.05
❑ 16 Kimble Anders	.20	.09
❑ 17 Steve McNair	.75	.35
❑ 18 Neil O'Donnell	.20	.09
❑ 19 Greg Lloyd	.20	.09
❑ 20 Warren Moon	.20	.09
❑ 21 Bernie Kosar	.10	.05
❑ 22 Derrick Thomas	.20	.09
❑ 23 Andre Hastings	.10	.05
❑ 24 Wayne Chrebet	.60	.25
❑ 25 Mark Seay	.10	.05
❑ 26 Eric Metcalf	.10	.05
❑ 27 Shawn Jefferson	.10	.05
❑ 28 Napoleon Kaufman	.40	.18
❑ 29 Steve Walsh	.10	.05
❑ 30 Derrick Alexander DE	.10	.05
❑ 31 Rodney Peete	.10	.05
❑ 32 Terance Mathis	.10	.05
❑ 33 Michael Westbrook	.40	.18
❑ 34 Kevin Carter	.10	.05
❑ 35 Aaron Hayden RC	.10	.05
❑ 36 J.J. Stokes	.40	.18
❑ 37 Andre Reed	.20	.09
❑ 38 Chris Warren	.20	.09
❑ 39 Jerry Rice	1.00	.45
❑ 40 Ben Coates	.20	.09
❑ 41 Reggie White	.40	.18
❑ 42 Joey Galloway	.60	.25
❑ 43 Sean Dawkins	.10	.05
❑ 44 Brett Favre	2.00	.90
❑ 45 Jeff George	.20	.09
❑ 46 Robert Smith	.20	.09
❑ 47 Ken Dilger	.20	.09
❑ 48 Larry Centers	.20	.09
❑ 49 Jackie Harris	.10	.05
❑ 50 Hugh Douglas	.20	.09
❑ 51 Herschel Walker	.20	.09
❑ 52 Kerry Collins	.40	.18
❑ 53 Michael Irvin	.40	.18
❑ 54 Willie McGinest	.10	.05
❑ 55 Herman Moore	.40	.18
❑ 56 Leroy Hoard	.10	.05
❑ 57 Scott Mitchell	.20	.09
❑ 58 Terrell Davis	2.50	1.10
❑ 59 Kevin Greene	.20	.09
❑ 60 Yancey Thigpen	.20	.09
❑ 61 Kevin Smith	.10	.05
❑ 62 Trent Dilfer	.40	.18
❑ 63 Cortez Kennedy	.10	.05
❑ 64 Carnell Lake	.10	.05
❑ 65 Quinn Early	.10	.05
❑ 66 Kyle Brady	.10	.05
❑ 67 Marshall Faulk	.40	.18
❑ 68 Fred Barnett	.10	.05
❑ 69 Quentin Coryatt	.10	.05
❑ 70 Dan Marino	2.00	.90
❑ 71 Junior Seau	.20	.09
❑ 72 Andre Coleman	.10	.05
❑ 73 Terry Kirby	.20	.09
❑ 74 Curtis Martin	.75	.35
❑ 75 Isaac Bruce	.40	.18
❑ 76 Mark Chmura	.20	.09
❑ 77 Edgar Bennett	.20	.09
❑ 78 Mario Bates	.20	.09
❑ 79 Eric Zeier	.10	.05
❑ 80 Adrian Murrell	.40	.18
❑ 81 Mark Brunell	1.00	.45
❑ 82 Mark Rypien	.10	.05
❑ 83 Erric Pegram	.10	.05
❑ 84 Bryan Cox	.10	.05
❑ 85 Heath Shuler	.20	.09
❑ 86 Lake Dawson	.10	.05
❑ 87 O.J. McDuffie	.20	.09
❑ 88 Emmitt Smith	1.50	.70
❑ 89 Jim Harbaugh	.20	.09
❑ 90 Aaron Bailey	.10	.05
❑ 91 Jim Kelly	.40	.18
❑ 92 Rodney Hampton	.20	.09
❑ 93 Cris Carter	.40	.18
❑ 94 Henry Ellard	.10	.05
❑ 95 Darnay Scott	.20	.09
❑ 96 Daryl Johnston	.20	.09
❑ 97 Tamarick Vanover	.20	.09
❑ 98 Jeff Blake	.40	.18
❑ 99 Anthony Miller	.20	.09
❑ 100 Darren Woodson	.20	.09
❑ 101 Irving Fryar	.20	.09
❑ 102 Craig Hayward	.10	.05
❑ 103 Derek Loville	.10	.05
❑ 104 Ernie Mills	.10	.05
❑ 105 Brian Blades	.10	.05
❑ 106 Gus Frerotte	.40	.18
❑ 107 Alvin Harper	.10	.05
❑ 108 Tyrone Wheatley	.20	.09
❑ 109 John Elway	2.00	.90
❑ 110 Charles Haley	.20	.09
❑ 111 Terrell Fletcher	.10	.05
❑ 112 Vincent Brisby	.10	.05
❑ 113 Jerome Bettis	.40	.18
❑ 114 Barry Sanders	2.00	.90
❑ 115 Ken Norton Jr.	.10	.05
❑ 116 Sherman Williams	.10	.05
❑ 117 Antonio Freeman	.75	.35
❑ 118 Bert Emanuel	.20	.09
❑ 119 Marcus Allen	.40	.18
❑ 120 Stan Humphries	.20	.09
❑ 121 Chris Sanders	.20	.09
❑ 122 Jeff Graham	.10	.05
❑ 123 Jay Novacek	.10	.05
❑ 124 Aeneas Williams	.10	.05
❑ 125 Kordell Stewart	.60	.25
❑ 126 Steve Young	.75	.35

❑ 127 Jake Reed	.20	.09
❑ 128 Rick Mirer	.20	.09
❑ 129 Jeff Hostetler	.10	.05
❑ 130 Tim Brown	.40	.18
❑ 131 Shannon Sharpe	.20	.09
❑ 132 Dave Brown	.10	.05
❑ 133 Harvey Williams	.10	.05
❑ 134 Rodney Thomas	.10	.05
❑ 135 Frank Sanders	.20	.09
❑ 136 Brett Perriman	.10	.05
❑ 137 Steve Bono	.10	.05
❑ 138 Steve Atwater	.10	.05
❑ 139 Andre Rison	.20	.09
❑ 140 Orlando Thomas	.10	.05
❑ 141 Terry Allen	.20	.09
❑ 142 Carl Pickens	.40	.18
❑ 143 William Floyd	.20	.09
❑ 144 Bryce Paup	.10	.05
❑ 145 James O. Stewart	.20	.09
❑ 146 Eric Bjornson	.10	.05
❑ 147 Errict Rhett	.20	.09
❑ 148 Darick Holmes	.10	.05
❑ 149 Brian Mitchell	.10	.05
❑ 150 Brent Jones	.10	.05
❑ 151 Natrone Means	.40	.18
❑ 152 Rod Woodson	.20	.09
❑ 153 Bruce Smith	.20	.09
❑ 154 Deion Sanders	.60	.25
❑ 155 Kevin Williams	.10	.05
❑ 156 Erik Kramer	.10	.05
❑ 157 Jim Everett	.10	.05
❑ 158 Vinny Testaverde	.20	.09
❑ 159 Boomer Esiason	.20	.09
❑ 160 Leslie O'Neal	.10	.05
❑ 161 Curtis Conway	.40	.18
❑ 162 Thurman Thomas	.40	.18
❑ 163 Tony Brackens RC	.20	.09
❑ 164 Stepfret Williams RC	.20	.09
❑ 165 Alex Van Dyke RC	.20	.09
❑ 166 Cedric Jones RC	.10	.05
❑ 167 Stanley Pritchett RC	.20	.09
❑ 168 Willie Anderson RC	.10	.05
❑ 169 Regan Upshaw RC	.10	.05
❑ 170 Daryl Gardener RC	.10	.05
❑ 171 Alex Molden RC	.10	.05
❑ 172 John Mobley RC	.10	.05
❑ 173 Danny Kanell RC	.40	.18
❑ 174 Marco Battaglia RC	.10	.05
❑ 175 Simeon Rice RC	.40	.18
❑ 176 Tony Banks RC	1.25	.55
❑ 177 Stephen Davis RC	2.50	1.10
❑ 178 Walt Harris RC	.10	.05
❑ 179 Amani Toomer RC	1.00	.45
❑ 180 Derrick Mayes RC	.75	.35
❑ 181 Jeff Lewis RC	.50	.23
❑ 182 Chris Darkins RC	.10	.05
❑ 183 Rickey Dudley RC	.40	.18
❑ 184 Jonathan Ogden RC	.10	.05
❑ 185 Mike Alstott RC	1.50	.70
❑ 186 Eric Moulds RC	2.00	.90
❑ 187 Karim Abdul-Jabbar RC	.60	.25
❑ 188 Jerry Rice Checklist Card	.40	.18
❑ 189 Dan Marino Checklist Card	.40	.18
❑ 190 Emmitt Smith Checklist Card	.40	.18

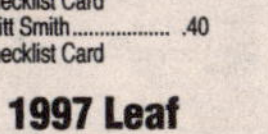

1997 Leaf

	MINT	NRMT
COMPLETE SET (200)	25.00	11.00

❑ 1 Steve Young	.75	.35
❑ 2 Brett Favre	2.50	1.10
❑ 3 Barry Sanders	2.50	1.10
❑ 4 Drew Bledsoe	1.25	.55
❑ 5 Troy Aikman	1.25	.55
❑ 6 Kerry Collins	.25	.11
❑ 7 Dan Marino	2.50	1.10
❑ 8 Jerry Rice	1.25	.55
❑ 9 John Elway	2.50	1.10
❑ 10 Emmitt Smith	2.00	.90
❑ 11 Tony Banks	.25	.11
❑ 12 Gus Frerotte	.10	.05
❑ 13 Elvis Grbac	.25	.11

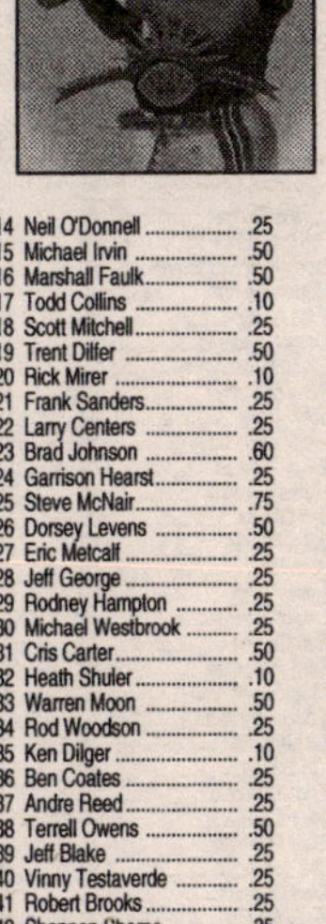

❑ 14 Neil O'Donnell	.25	.11
❑ 15 Michael Irvin	.50	.23
❑ 16 Marshall Faulk	.50	.23
❑ 17 Todd Collins	.10	.05
❑ 18 Scott Mitchell	.25	.11
❑ 19 Trent Dilfer	.50	.23
❑ 20 Rick Mirer	.10	.05
❑ 21 Frank Sanders	.25	.11
❑ 22 Larry Centers	.25	.11
❑ 23 Brad Johnson	.60	.25
❑ 24 Garrison Hearst	.25	.11
❑ 25 Steve McNair	.75	.35
❑ 26 Dorsey Levens	.50	.23
❑ 27 Eric Metcalf	.25	.11
❑ 28 Jeff George	.25	.11
❑ 29 Rodney Hampton	.25	.11
❑ 30 Michael Westbrook	.25	.11
❑ 31 Cris Carter	.50	.23
❑ 32 Heath Shuler	.10	.05
❑ 33 Warren Moon	.50	.23
❑ 34 Rod Woodson	.25	.11
❑ 35 Ken Dilger	.10	.05
❑ 36 Ben Coates	.25	.11
❑ 37 Andre Reed	.25	.11
❑ 38 Terrell Owens	.50	.23
❑ 39 Jeff Blake	.25	.11
❑ 40 Vinny Testaverde	.25	.11
❑ 41 Robert Brooks	.25	.11
❑ 42 Shannon Sharpe	.25	.11
❑ 43 Terry Allen	.50	.23
❑ 44 Terance Mathis	.25	.11
❑ 45 Bobby Engram	.25	.11
❑ 46 Rickey Dudley	.25	.11
❑ 47 Alex Molden	.10	.05
❑ 48 Lawrence Phillips	.10	.05
❑ 49 Curtis Martin	.75	.35
❑ 50 Jim Harbaugh	.25	.11
❑ 51 Wayne Chrebet	.50	.23
❑ 52 Quentin Coryatt	.10	.05
❑ 53 Eddie George	1.00	.45
❑ 54 Michael Jackson	.25	.11
❑ 55 Greg Lloyd	.10	.05
❑ 56 Natrone Means	.50	.23
❑ 57 Marcus Allen	.50	.23
❑ 58 Desmond Howard	.25	.11
❑ 59 Stan Humphries	.25	.11
❑ 60 Reggie White	.50	.23
❑ 61 Brett Perriman	.10	.05
❑ 62 Warren Sapp	.25	.11
❑ 63 Adrian Murrell	.25	.11
❑ 64 Mark Brunell	1.25	.55
❑ 65 Carl Pickens	.50	.23
❑ 66 Kordell Stewart	.60	.25
❑ 67 Ricky Watters	.25	.11
❑ 68 Tyrone Wheatley	.25	.11
❑ 69 Stanley Pritchett	.10	.05
❑ 70 Kevin Greene	.25	.11
❑ 71 Karim Abdul-Jabbar	.50	.23
❑ 72 Ki-Jana Carter	.10	.05
❑ 73 Rashaan Salaam	.10	.05
❑ 74 Simeon Rice	.25	.11
❑ 75 Napoleon Kaufman	.50	.23
❑ 76 Muhsin Muhammad	.25	.11
❑ 77 Bruce Smith	.25	.11
❑ 78 Eric Moulds	.50	.23
❑ 79 O.J. McDuffie	.25	.11
❑ 80 Danny Kanell	.25	.11
❑ 81 Harvey Williams	.10	.05
❑ 82 Greg Hill	.10	.05
❑ 83 Terrell Davis	2.00	.90
❑ 84 Dan Wilkinson	.10	.05
❑ 85 Yancey Thigpen	.25	.11
❑ 86 Darrell Green	.25	.11
❑ 87 Tamarick Vanover	.25	.11
❑ 88 Mike Alstott	.50	.23
❑ 89 Johnnie Morton	.25	.11
❑ 90 Dale Carter	.10	.05
❑ 91 Jerome Bettis	.50	.23
❑ 92 James O.Stewart	.25	.11
❑ 93 Irving Fryar	.25	.11
❑ 94 Junior Seau	.25	.11
❑ 95 Sean Dawkins	.10	.05
❑ 96 J.J. Stokes	.25	.11
❑ 97 Tim Biakabutuka	.25	.11
❑ 98 Bert Emanuel	.25	.11
❑ 99 Eddie Kennison	.25	.11
❑ 100 Ray Zellars	.10	.05
❑ 101 Dave Brown	.10	.05
❑ 102 Leeland McElroy	.10	.05
❑ 103 Chris Warren	.25	.11
❑ 104 Byron Bam Morris	.10	.05
❑ 105 Thurman Thomas	.50	.23
❑ 106 Kyle Brady	.10	.05
❑ 107 Anthony Miller	.10	.05
❑ 108 Derrick Thomas	.25	.11
❑ 109 Mark Chmura	.25	.11
❑ 110 Deion Sanders	.50	.23
❑ 111 Eric Swann	.10	.05
❑ 112 Amani Toomer	.25	.11
❑ 113 Raymont Harris	.10	.05
❑ 114 Jake Reed	.25	.11
❑ 115 Bryant Young	.10	.05
❑ 116 Keenan McCardell	.25	.11
❑ 117 Herman Moore	.50	.23
❑ 118 Errict Rhett	.10	.05
❑ 119 Henry Ellard	.10	.05
❑ 120 Bobby Hoying	.25	.11
❑ 121 Robert Smith	.25	.11
❑ 122 Keyshawn Johnson	.50	.23
❑ 123 Zach Thomas	.25	.11
❑ 124 Charlie Garner	.10	.05
❑ 125 Terry Kirby	.25	.11
❑ 126 Darren Woodson	.10	.05
❑ 127 Darnay Scott	.25	.11
❑ 128 Chris Sanders	.10	.05
❑ 129 Charles Johnson	.25	.11
❑ 130 Joey Galloway	.60	.25
❑ 131 Curtis Conway	.25	.11
❑ 132 Isaac Bruce	.50	.23
❑ 133 Bobby Taylor	.10	.05
❑ 134 Jamal Anderson	.60	.25
❑ 135 Ken Norton	.10	.05
❑ 136 Darick Holmes	.10	.05
❑ 137 Tony Brackens	.10	.05
❑ 138 Tony Martin	.25	.11
❑ 139 Antonio Freeman	.75	.35
❑ 140 Neil Smith	.25	.11
❑ 141 Terry Glenn	.50	.23
❑ 142 Marvin Harrison	.50	.23
❑ 143 Daryl Johnston	.25	.11
❑ 144 Tim Brown	.50	.23
❑ 145 Kimble Anders	.25	.11
❑ 146 Derrick Alexander WR	.25	.11
❑ 147 LeShon Johnson	.10	.05
❑ 148 Anthony Johnson	.10	.05
❑ 149 Leslie Shepherd	.10	.05
❑ 150 Chris T. Jones	.10	.05
❑ 151 Edgar Bennett	.25	.11
❑ 152 Ty Detmer	.25	.11
❑ 153 Ike Hilliard RC	1.00	.45
❑ 154 Jim Druckenmiller RC	.50	.23
❑ 155 Warrick Dunn RC	1.50	.70
❑ 156 Yatil Green RC	.25	.11
❑ 157 Reidel Anthony RC	1.00	.45
❑ 158 Antowain Smith RC	1.25	.55
❑ 159 Rae Carruth RC	.50	.23
❑ 160 Tiki Barber RC	1.50	.70
❑ 161 Byron Hanspard RC	.50	.23
❑ 162 Jake Plummer RC	3.00	1.35
❑ 163 Joey Kent RC	.50	.23
❑ 164 Corey Dillon RC	3.00	1.35
❑ 165 Kevin Lockett RC	.25	.11
❑ 166 Will Blackwell RC	.50	.23

❑ 167 Troy Davis RC .50 .23
❑ 168 James Farrior RC .10 .05
❑ 169 Danny Wuerffel RC .75 .35
❑ 170 Pat Barnes RC .50 .23
❑ 171 Darnell Autry RC .25 .11
❑ 172 Tom Knight RC .10 .05
❑ 173 David LaFleur RC .25 .11
❑ 174 Tony Gonzalez RC 1.50 .70
❑ 175 Kenny Holmes RC .50 .23
❑ 176 Reinard Wilson RC .10 .05
❑ 177 Renaldo Wynn RC .10 .05
❑ 178 Bryant Westbrook RC .10 .05
❑ 179 Darrell Russell RC .10 .05
❑ 180 Orlando Pace RC .50 .23
❑ 181 Shawn Springs RC .25 .11
❑ 182 Peter Boulware RC .25 .11
❑ 183 Dan Marino L 1.25 .55
❑ 184 Brett Favre L 1.25 .55
❑ 185 Emmitt Smith L 1.00 .45
❑ 186 Eddie George L .50 .23
❑ 187 Curtis Martin L .25 .11
❑ 188 Tim Brown L .25 .11
❑ 189 Mark Brunell L .60 .25
❑ 190 Isaac Bruce L .25 .11
❑ 191 Deion Sanders L .25 .11
❑ 192 John Elway L 1.25 .55
❑ 193 Jerry Rice L .60 .25
❑ 194 Barry Sanders L 1.25 .55
❑ 195 Herman Moore L .25 .11
❑ 196 Carl Pickens L .25 .11
❑ 197 Karim Abdul-Jabbar L .25 .11
❑ 198 Drew Bledsoe CL .50 .23
❑ 199 Troy Aikman CL .50 .23
❑ 200 Terrell Davis CL .50 .23

1999 Leaf Certified

	MINT	NRMT
COMPLETE SET (225)	300.00	135.00
COMP.SET w/o RCs 175)	60.00	27.00
COMMON CARD (1-100)	.20	.09
COMMON CARD (101-150)	.60	.25
COMMON CARD (151-175)	1.00	.45
COMMON ROOKIE (176-225)	4.00	1.80

❑ 1 Simeon Rice .20 .09
❑ 2 Frank Sanders .40 .18
❑ 3 Andre Wadsworth .20 .09
❑ 4 Larry Centers .20 .09
❑ 5 Byron Hanspard .20 .09
❑ 6 Terance Mathis .40 .18
❑ 7 O.J. Santiago .20 .09
❑ 8 Chris Calloway .20 .09
❑ 9 Michael Jackson .20 .09
❑ 10 Rod Woodson .40 .18
❑ 11 Pat Johnson .20 .09
❑ 12 Rob Johnson .40 .18
❑ 13 Andre Reed .40 .18
❑ 14 Tim Biakabutuka .40 .18
❑ 15 Rae Carruth .40 .18
❑ 16 Fred Lane .20 .09
❑ 17 Muhsin Muhammad .40 .18
❑ 18 Wesley Walls .40 .18
❑ 19 Edgar Bennett .20 .09
❑ 20 Curtis Conway .40 .18
❑ 21 Bobby Engram .40 .18
❑ 22 Jeff Blake .40 .18
❑ 23 Darnay Scott .20 .09
❑ 24 Ty Detmer .40 .18
❑ 25 Sedrick Shaw .20 .09
❑ 26 Leslie Shepherd .20 .09
❑ 27 Terry Kirby .20 .09
❑ 28 Chris Warren .20 .09
❑ 29 Rocket Ismail .40 .18
❑ 30 Marcus Nash .40 .18
❑ 31 Neil Smith .40 .18
❑ 32 Bubby Brister .20 .09
❑ 33 Brian Griese 2.00 .90
❑ 34 Germane Crowell .40 .18
❑ 35 Johnnie Morton .40 .18
❑ 36 Gus Frerotte .20 .09
❑ 37 Robert Brooks .40 .18
❑ 38 Mark Chmura .20 .09
❑ 39 Derrick Mayes .20 .09
❑ 40 Jerome Pathon .20 .09
❑ 41 Jimmy Smith .40 .18
❑ 42 James Stewart .40 .18
❑ 43 Tavian Banks .20 .09
❑ 44 Derrick Alexander WR .40 .18
❑ 45 Kimble Anders .40 .18
❑ 46 Elvis Grbac .40 .18
❑ 47 Derrick Thomas .40 .18
❑ 48 Byron Bam Morris .20 .09
❑ 49 Tony Gonzalez .40 .18
❑ 50 John Avery .40 .18
❑ 51 Tyrone Wheatley .40 .18
❑ 52 Zach Thomas .40 .18
❑ 53 Lamar Thomas .20 .09
❑ 54 Jeff George .40 .18
❑ 55 John Randle .40 .18
❑ 56 Jake Reed .40 .18
❑ 57 Leroy Hoard .20 .09
❑ 58 Robert Edwards .40 .18
❑ 59 Ben Coates .40 .18
❑ 60 Tony Simmons .20 .09
❑ 61 Shawn Jefferson .20 .09
❑ 62 Eddie Kennison .40 .18
❑ 63 Lamar Smith .40 .18
❑ 64 Tiki Barber .20 .09
❑ 65 Kerry Collins .40 .18
❑ 66 Ike Hilliard .20 .09
❑ 67 Gary Brown .20 .09
❑ 68 Joe Jurevicius .20 .09
❑ 69 Kent Graham .20 .09
❑ 70 Dedric Ward .20 .09
❑ 71 Terry Allen .40 .18
❑ 72 Neil O'Donnell .40 .18
❑ 73 Desmond Howard .40 .18
❑ 74 James Jett .40 .18
❑ 75 Jon Ritchie .20 .09
❑ 76 Rickey Dudley .20 .09
❑ 77 Charles Johnson .20 .09
❑ 78 Chris Fuamatu-Ma'afala .20 .09
❑ 79 Hines Ward .20 .09
❑ 80 Ryan Leaf .75 .35
❑ 81 Jim Harbaugh .40 .18
❑ 82 Junior Seau .40 .18
❑ 83 Mikhael Ricks .20 .09
❑ 84 J.J. Stokes .40 .18
❑ 85 Ahman Green .40 .18
❑ 86 Tony Banks .40 .18
❑ 87 Robert Holcombe .40 .18
❑ 88 Az-Zahir Hakim .20 .09
❑ 89 Greg Hill .20 .09
❑ 90 Trent Green .40 .18
❑ 91 Eric Zeier .20 .09
❑ 92 Reidel Anthony .40 .18
❑ 93 Bert Emanuel .40 .18
❑ 94 Warren Sapp .20 .09
❑ 95 Kevin Dyson .40 .18
❑ 96 Yancey Thigpen .20 .09
❑ 97 Frank Wycheck .20 .09
❑ 98 Michael Westbrook .40 .18
❑ 99 Albert Connell .20 .09
❑ 100 Darrell Green .20 .09
❑ 101 Rob Moore .40 .18
❑ 102 Adrian Murrell .40 .18
❑ 103 Jake Plummer 2.50 1.10
❑ 104 Chris Chandler .40 .18
❑ 105 Jamal Anderson 1.25 .55
❑ 106 Tim Dwight 1.25 .55
❑ 107 Jermaine Lewis 1.25 .55
❑ 108 Priest Holmes 1.25 .55
❑ 109 Bruce Smith 1.25 .55
❑ 110 Eric Moulds 1.25 .55
❑ 111 Antowain Smith 1.25 .55
❑ 112 Curtis Enis 1.25 .55
❑ 113 Corey Dillon 1.25 .55
❑ 114 Michael Irvin 1.25 .55
❑ 115 Ed McCaffrey 1.25 .55
❑ 116 Shannon Sharpe 1.25 .55
❑ 117 Terrell Davis 3.00 1.35
❑ 118 Charlie Batch 2.00 .90
❑ 119 Antonio Freeman 1.25 .55
❑ 120 Dorsey Levens 1.25 .55
❑ 121 Marvin Harrison 1.25 .55
❑ 122 Peyton Manning 5.00 2.20
❑ 123 Keenan McCardell 1.25 .55
❑ 124 Fred Taylor 3.00 1.35
❑ 125 Andre Rison 1.25 .55
❑ 126 O.J. McDuffie 1.25 .55
❑ 127 Karim Abdul-Jabbar 1.25 .55
❑ 128 Randy Moss 5.00 2.20
❑ 129 Terry Glenn 1.25 .55
❑ 130 Vinny Testaverde 1.25 .55
❑ 131 Keyshawn Johnson 1.25 .55
❑ 132 Curtis Martin 1.25 .55
❑ 133 Wayne Chrebet 1.25 .55
❑ 134 Napoleon Kaufman 1.25 .55
❑ 135 Charles Woodson 1.25 .55
❑ 136 Duce Staley 1.25 .55
❑ 137 Kordell Stewart 1.25 .55
❑ 138 Terrell Owens 1.25 .55
❑ 139 Ricky Watters 1.25 .55
❑ 140 Joey Galloway 1.25 .55
❑ 141 Jon Kitna .75 .35
❑ 142 Isaac Bruce 1.25 .55
❑ 143 Jacquez Green 1.25 .55
❑ 144 Warrick Dunn 1.25 .55
❑ 145 Mike Alstott 1.25 .55
❑ 146 Trent Dilfer 1.25 .55
❑ 147 Steve McNair 1.25 .55
❑ 148 Eddie George 1.50 .70
❑ 149 Skip Hicks 1.25 .55
❑ 150 Brad Johnson 1.25 .55
❑ 151 Doug Flutie 2.50 1.10
❑ 152 Thurman Thomas 1.25 .55
❑ 153 Carl Pickens 1.25 .55
❑ 154 Emmitt Smith 5.00 2.20
❑ 155 Troy Aikman 5.00 2.20
❑ 156 Deion Sanders 1.25 .55
❑ 157 John Elway 8.00 3.60
❑ 158 Rod Smith 1.25 .55
❑ 159 Barry Sanders 8.00 3.60
❑ 160 Herman Moore 2.00 .90
❑ 161 Brett Favre 8.00 3.60
❑ 162 Mark Brunell 3.00 1.35
❑ 163 Warren Moon 2.00 .90
❑ 164 Dan Marino 8.00 3.60
❑ 165 Randall Cunningham 2.00 .90
❑ 166 Robert Smith 2.00 .90
❑ 167 Cris Carter 2.00 .90
❑ 168 Drew Bledsoe 3.00 1.35
❑ 169 Tim Brown 2.00 .90
❑ 170 Jerome Bettis 2.00 .90
❑ 171 Natrone Means 1.25 .55
❑ 172 Jerry Rice 5.00 2.20
❑ 173 Steve Young 3.00 1.35
❑ 174 Garrison Hearst 2.00 .90
❑ 175 Marshall Faulk 2.00 .90
❑ 176 David Boston RC 12.00 5.50
❑ 177 Jeff Paulk RC 6.00 2.70
❑ 178 Reginald Kelly RC 4.00 1.80
❑ 179 Scott Covington RC 8.00 3.60
❑ 180 Chris McAlister RC 6.00 2.70
❑ 181 Shawn Bryson RC 8.00 3.60
❑ 182 Peerless Price RC 10.00 4.50
❑ 183 Cade McNown RC 8.00 3.60
❑ 184 Michael Bishop RC 10.00 4.50
❑ 185 D'Wayne Bates RC 6.00 2.70
❑ 186 Marty Booker RC 8.00 3.60
❑ 187 Akili Smith RC 12.00 5.50
❑ 188 Craig Yeast RC 6.00 2.70
❑ 189 Tim Couch RC 15.00 6.75
❑ 190 Kevin Johnson RC 12.00 5.50
❑ 191 Wane McGarity RC 6.00 2.70
❑ 192 Olandis Gary RC 12.00 5.50
❑ 193 Travis McGriff RC 8.00 3.60
❑ 194 Sedrick Irvin RC 8.00 3.60
❑ 195 Chris Claiborne RC 4.00 1.80

- ❑ 196 De'Mond Parker RC 8.00 3.60
- ❑ 197 Dee Miller RC 6.00 2.70
- ❑ 198 Edgerrin James RC.... 30.00 13.50
- ❑ 199 Mike Cloud RC 8.00 3.60
- ❑ 200 Larry Parker RC 6.00 2.70
- ❑ 201 Cecil Collins RC 4.00 1.80
- ❑ 202 James Johnson RC...... 8.00 3.60
- ❑ 203 Rob Konrad RC.......... 8.00 3.60
- ❑ 204 Daunte Culpepper RC 25.00 11.00
- ❑ 205 Jim Kleinsasser RC...... 8.00 3.60
- ❑ 206 Kevin Faulk RC 10.00 4.50
- ❑ 207 Andy Katzenmoyer RC 8.00 3.60
- ❑ 208 Ricky Williams RC...... 20.00 9.00
- ❑ 209 Joe Montgomery RC 8.00 3.60
- ❑ 210 Sean Bennett RC 8.00 3.60
- ❑ 211 Dameane Douglas RC 8.00 3.60
- ❑ 212 Donovan McNabb RC 20.00 9.00
- ❑ 213 Na Brown RC 8.00 3.60
- ❑ 214 Amos Zereoue RC 8.00 3.60
- ❑ 215 Troy Edwards RC 10.00 4.50
- ❑ 216 Jermaine Fazande RC 8.00 3.60
- ❑ 217 Tai Streets RC.......... 8.00 3.60
- ❑ 218 Brock Huard RC 10.00 4.50
- ❑ 219 Charlie Rogers RC 6.00 2.70
- ❑ 220 Karsten Bailey RC........ 6.00 2.70
- ❑ 221 Joe Germaine RC 8.00 3.60
- ❑ 222 Torry Holt RC 12.00 5.50
- ❑ 223 Shaun King RC 10.00 4.50
- ❑ 224 Jevon Kearse RC 12.00 5.50
- ❑ 225 Champ Bailey RC 10.00 4.50

2000 Leaf Certified

	MINT	NRMT
COMPLETE SET (250)	1000.00	450.00
COMMON CARD (1-100)........	.20	.09
COMMON CARD (101-150)........	.30	.14
COMMON ROOKIE (151-190)..	3.00	1.35
COMMON ROOKIE (191-220)..	4.00	1.80

- ❑ 1 Frank Sanders.................. .20 .09
- ❑ 2 Rob Moore .... .20 .09
- ❑ 3 Simeon Rice .... .20 .09
- ❑ 4 David Boston...................... .75 .35
- ❑ 5 Tim Dwight .... .75 .35
- ❑ 6 Jamal Anderson .... .75 .35
- ❑ 7 Chris Chandler .... .20 .09
- ❑ 8 Terance Mathis .... .20 .09
- ❑ 9 Priest Holmes .... .20 .09
- ❑ 10 Rod Woodson .... .40 .18
- ❑ 11 Tony Banks .... .20 .09
- ❑ 12 Jermaine Lewis .... .20 .09
- ❑ 13 Shannon Sharpe .... .20 .09
- ❑ 14 Qadry Ismail .... .20 .09
- ❑ 15 Doug Flutie .... 1.00 .45
- ❑ 16 Antowain Smith .... .40 .18
- ❑ 17 Peerless Price................. .75 .35
- ❑ 18 Rob Johnson.................... .20 .09
- ❑ 19 Muhsin Muhammad......... .20 .09
- ❑ 20 Wesley Walls.................... .20 .09
- ❑ 21 Tim Biakabutuka .... .20 .09
- ❑ 22 Steve Beuerlein................ .20 .09
- ❑ 23 Patrick Jeffers .... .20 .09
- ❑ 24 Natrone Means .... .20 .09
- ❑ 25 Curtis Enis....................... .40 .18
- ❑ 26 Bobby Engram .... .20 .09
- ❑ 27 Marcus Robinson .... .75 .35
- ❑ 28 Eddie Kennison................ .20 .09
- ❑ 29 Marty Booker.................... .20 .09
- ❑ 30 Darnay Scott .... .20 .09
- ❑ 31 Carl Pickens .... .20 .09
- ❑ 32 Karim Abdul-Jabbar .... .20 .09
- ❑ 33 Errict Rhett .... .20 .09
- ❑ 34 Darrin Chiaverini .... .20 .09
- ❑ 35 Randall Cunningham........ .20 .09
- ❑ 36 Michael Irvin .... .20 .09
- ❑ 37 Rocket Ismail.................... .20 .09
- ❑ 38 Ed McCaffrey .... .75 .35
- ❑ 39 Rod Smith .... .20 .09
- ❑ 40 Herman Moore .... .40 .18
- ❑ 41 Johnnie Morton .... .20 .09
- ❑ 42 James Stewart .... .20 .09
- ❑ 43 Bill Schroeder .... .20 .09
- ❑ 44 Ahman Green .... .20 .09
- ❑ 45 Terrence Wilkins .... .75 .35
- ❑ 46 Keenan McCardell............ .20 .09
- ❑ 47 Derrick Alexander .... .20 .09
- ❑ 48 Elvis Grbac .... .20 .09
- ❑ 49 Tony Gonzalez .... .20 .09
- ❑ 50 O.J. McDuffie .... .20 .09
- ❑ 51 Tony Martin .... .20 .09
- ❑ 52 James Johnson................ .20 .09
- ❑ 53 Thurman Thomas .... .20 .09
- ❑ 54 Jay Fiedler........................ .75 .35
- ❑ 55 Damon Huard .... .20 .09
- ❑ 56 Leroy Hoard .... .20 .09
- ❑ 57 Terry Glenn .... .40 .18
- ❑ 58 Kevin Faulk .... .20 .09
- ❑ 59 Jeff Blake .... .20 .09
- ❑ 60 Jake Reed......................... .20 .09
- ❑ 61 Amani Toomer.................. .20 .09
- ❑ 62 Kerry Collins .... .20 .09
- ❑ 63 Ike Hilliard .... .20 .09
- ❑ 64 Joe Montgomery .... .20 .09
- ❑ 65 Vinny Testaverde .... .20 .09
- ❑ 66 Wayne Chrebet................. .20 .09
- ❑ 67 Ray Lucas......................... .75 .35
- ❑ 68 Napoleon Kaufman .... .40 .18
- ❑ 69 Charles Woodson .... .20 .09
- ❑ 70 Tyrone Wheatley.............. .20 .09
- ❑ 71 Rich Gannon .... .40 .18
- ❑ 72 Duce Staley....................... .75 .35
- ❑ 73 Kordell Stewart .... .75 .35
- ❑ 74 Jerome Bettis .... .75 .35
- ❑ 75 Troy Edwards .... .20 .09
- ❑ 76 Junior Seau .... .20 .09
- ❑ 77 Jim Harbaugh .... .20 .09
- ❑ 78 Curtis Conway.................. .20 .09
- ❑ 79 Jermaine Fazande .... .20 .09
- ❑ 80 Terrell Owens .... .75 .35
- ❑ 81 Charlie Garner.................. .20 .09
- ❑ 82 Garrison Hearst................ .20 .09
- ❑ 83 Jeff Garcia........................ .75 .35
- ❑ 84 Derrick Mayes .... .20 .09
- ❑ 85 Az-Zahir Hakim .... .20 .09
- ❑ 86 Mike Alstott .... .75 .35
- ❑ 87 Warrick Dunn .... .75 .35
- ❑ 88 Jacquez Green .... .20 .09
- ❑ 89 Warren Sapp.................... .20 .09
- ❑ 90 Yancey Thigpen .... .20 .09
- ❑ 91 Kevin Dyson .... .20 .09
- ❑ 92 Frank Wycheck .... .20 .09
- ❑ 93 Jevon Kearse .... .75 .35
- ❑ 94 Adrian Murrell................... .20 .09
- ❑ 95 Bruce Smith...................... .20 .09
- ❑ 96 Michael Westbrook .... .20 .09
- ❑ 97 Albert Connell .... .20 .09
- ❑ 98 Champ Bailey .... .40 .18
- ❑ 99 Jeff George .... .20 .09
- ❑ 100 Deion Sanders .... .75 .35
- ❑ 101 Jake Plummer .... 1.25 .55
- ❑ 102 Eric Moulds .... 1.25 .55
- ❑ 103 Cade McNown............... .75 .35
- ❑ 104 Corey Dillon................. 1.25 .55
- ❑ 105 Akili Smith .... 1.25 .55
- ❑ 106 Tim Couch..................... 2.50 1.10
- ❑ 107 Kevin Johnson.............. 1.25 .55
- ❑ 108 Emmitt Smith................ 3.00 1.35
- ❑ 109 Troy Aikman 3.00 1.35
- ❑ 110 Joey Galloway.............. 1.25 .55
- ❑ 111 John Elway 5.00 2.20
- ❑ 112 Terrell Davis 3.00 1.35
- ❑ 113 Olandis Gary .... 1.25 .55
- ❑ 114 Brian Griese .... 1.50 .70
- ❑ 115 Charlie Batch............... 1.25 .55
- ❑ 116 Barry Sanders 4.00 1.80
- ❑ 117 Germane Crowell .... .60 .25
- ❑ 118 Brett Favre 5.00 2.20
- ❑ 119 Dorsey Levens .... .40 .18
- ❑ 120 Antonio Freeman.......... 1.25 .55
- ❑ 121 Peyton Manning 4.00 1.80
- ❑ 122 Edgerrin James............ 5.00 2.20
- ❑ 123 Marvin Harrison........... 1.25 .55
- ❑ 124 Mark Brunell .... 2.00 .90
- ❑ 125 Fred Taylor .... 1.50 .70
- ❑ 126 Jimmy Smith .... .60 .25
- ❑ 127 Dan Marino 5.00 2.20
- ❑ 128 Randy Moss 4.00 1.80
- ❑ 129 Daunte Culpepper........ 2.50 1.10
- ❑ 130 Cris Carter.................... 1.25 .55
- ❑ 131 Robert Smith .... 1.25 .55
- ❑ 132 Drew Bledsoe .... 2.00 .90
- ❑ 133 Ricky Williams.............. 3.00 1.35
- ❑ 134 Curtis Martin .... 1.25 .55
- ❑ 135 Tim Brown.................... 1.25 .55
- ❑ 136 Donovan McNabb .... 2.00 .90
- ❑ 137 Jerry Rice 3.00 1.35
- ❑ 138 Steve Young .... 2.00 .90
- ❑ 139 Jon Kitna .... 1.25 .55
- ❑ 140 Ricky Watters .... .30 .14
- ❑ 141 Kurt Warner.................. 5.00 2.20
- ❑ 142 Marshall Faulk.............. 1.50 .70
- ❑ 143 Torry Holt .... 1.25 .55
- ❑ 144 Isaac Bruce .... 1.25 .55
- ❑ 145 Shaun King .... 2.00 .90
- ❑ 146 Keyshawn Johnson...... 1.25 .55
- ❑ 147 Eddie George .... 1.50 .70
- ❑ 148 Steve McNair................ 1.25 .55
- ❑ 149 Stephen Davis.............. 1.25 .55
- ❑ 150 Brad Johnson .... 1.25 .55
- ❑ 151 Rogers Beckett RC 5.00 2.20
- ❑ 152 Erik Flowers RC 6.00 2.70
- ❑ 153 Demario Brown RC 5.00 2.20
- ❑ 154 Doug Johnson RC........ 6.00 2.70
- ❑ 155 Deon Grant RC 3.00 1.35
- ❑ 156 Ian Gold RC 5.00 2.20
- ❑ 157 Brian Urlacher RC...... 20.00 9.00
- ❑ 158 Frank Murphy RC 3.00 1.35
- ❑ 159 James Whalen RC 3.00 1.35
- ❑ 160 JaJuan Dawson RC 6.00 2.70
- ❑ 161 William Bartee RC........ 5.00 2.20
- ❑ 162 Aaron Shea RC............. .60 .25
- ❑ 163 Deltha O'Neal RC 5.00 2.20
- ❑ 164 Jarious Jackson RC 6.00 2.70
- ❑ 165 Muneer Moore RC......... 3.00 1.35
- ❑ 166 Hank Poteat RC 5.00 2.20
- ❑ 167 Jacoby Shepherd RC .. 3.00 1.35
- ❑ 168 Ben Kelly RC................ 3.00 1.35
- ❑ 169 Orantes Grant RC 3.00 1.35
- ❑ 170 Chris Hovan RC 5.00 2.20
- ❑ 171 Leon Murray RC 3.00 1.35
- ❑ 172 Marc Bulger RC........... 6.00 2.70
- ❑ 173 Chad Morton RC 6.00 2.70
- ❑ 174 Na'il Diggs RC............. 5.00 2.20
- ❑ 175 Shaun Ellis RC 5.00 2.20
- ❑ 176 John Abraham RC........ 5.00 2.20
- ❑ 177 Fred Robbins RC 3.00 1.35
- ❑ 178 Marcus Knight RC........ 3.00 1.35
- ❑ 179 Thomas Hamner RC 5.00 2.20
- ❑ 180 Cornelius Griffin RC 5.00 2.20
- ❑ 181 Raynoch Thompson RC 5.00 2.20
- ❑ 182 Paul Smith RC.............. 5.00 2.20
- ❑ 183 Ahmed Plummer RC 6.00 2.70
- ❑ 184 John Engelberger RC .. 5.00 2.20
- ❑ 185 Darren Howard RC 5.00 2.20
- ❑ 186 Corey Moore RC.......... 5.00 2.20
- ❑ 187 Joe Hamilton RC.......... 8.00 3.60
- ❑ 188 Rob Morris RC 5.00 2.20
- ❑ 189 Keith Bulluck RC.......... 5.00 2.20
- ❑ 190 Todd Husak RC............ 6.00 2.70
- ❑ 191 Mareno Philyaw RC 4.00 1.80
- ❑ 192 Kwame Cavil RC.......... 6.00 2.70
- ❑ 193 Sammy Morris RC...... 10.00 4.50
- ❑ 194 Avion Black RC 6.00 2.70
- ❑ 195 Bashir Yamini RC 6.00 2.70
- ❑ 196 Curtis Keaton RC 6.00 2.70
- ❑ 197 Mike Anderson RC 50.00 22.00
- ❑ 198 Bubba Franks RC 10.00 4.50
- ❑ 199 Anthony Lucas RC 4.00 1.80
- ❑ 200 Rondell Mealey RC...... 4.00 1.80

❑ 201	Terrelle Smith RC	6.00	2.70
❑ 202	Frank Moreau RC	8.00	3.60
❑ 203	Deon Dyer RC	6.00	2.70
❑ 204	Quinton Spotwood RC	4.00	1.80
❑ 205	Troy Walters RC	15.00	6.75
❑ 206	Doug Chapman RC	15.00	6.75
❑ 207	Tom Brady RC	8.00	3.60
❑ 208	Sherrod Gideon RC	4.00	1.80
❑ 209	Ron Dixon RC	10.00	4.50
❑ 210	Anthony Becht RC	8.00	3.60
❑ 211	James Williams RC	6.00	2.70
❑ 212	Sebastian Janikowski RC	8.00	3.60
❑ 213	Corey Simon RC	10.00	4.50
❑ 214	Gari Scott RC	6.00	2.70
❑ 215	Dante Hall RC	6.00	2.70
❑ 216	Tim Rattay RC	12.00	5.50
❑ 217	Chafie Fields RC	6.00	2.70
❑ 218	Trung Canidate RC	8.00	3.60
❑ 219	Chris Coleman RC	8.00	3.60
❑ 220	Erron Kinney RC	8.00	3.60
❑ 221	Thomas Jones RC	25.00	11.00
❑ 222	Travis Taylor RC	20.00	9.00
❑ 223	Chris Redman RC	30.00	13.50
❑ 224	Jamal Lewis RC	60.00	27.00
❑ 225	Dez White RC	12.00	5.50
❑ 226	Peter Warrick RC	40.00	18.00
❑ 227	Ron Dugans RC	12.00	5.50
❑ 228	Courtney Brown RC	20.00	9.00
❑ 229	Travis Prentice RC	25.00	11.00
❑ 230	Dennis Northcutt RC	20.00	9.00
❑ 231	Michael Wiley RC	15.00	6.75
❑ 232	Chris Cole RC	12.00	5.50
❑ 233	Reuben Droughns RC	15.00	6.75
❑ 234	R.Jay Soward RC	15.00	6.75
❑ 235	Shyrone Stith RC	12.00	5.50
❑ 236	Sylvester Morris RC	30.00	13.50
❑ 237	J.R. Redmond RC	20.00	9.00
❑ 238	Ron Dayne RC	40.00	18.00
❑ 239	Chad Pennington RC	50.00	22.00
❑ 240	Laveranues Coles RC	25.00	11.00
❑ 241	Jerry Porter RC	15.00	6.75
❑ 242	Todd Pinkston RC	15.00	6.75
❑ 243	Plaxico Burress RC	30.00	13.50
❑ 244	Danny Farmer RC	15.00	6.75
❑ 245	Tee Martin RC	25.00	11.00
❑ 246	Trevor Gaylor RC	12.00	5.50
❑ 247	Giovanni Carmazzi RC	20.00	9.00
❑ 248	Darrell Jackson RC	25.00	11.00
❑ 249	Shaun Alexander RC	40.00	18.00
❑ 250	Chris Samuels RC	12.00	5.50

2000 Leaf Limited

		MINT	NRMT
COMP.SET w/o SPs (200)		120.00	55.00
❑ 1	Ben Coates	.60	.25
❑ 2	Joe Horn	.60	.25
❑ 3	Jonathan Linton	.60	.25
❑ 4	Derrick Mason	.75	.35
❑ 5	Ray Lucas	1.00	.45
❑ 6	Brock Huard	.75	.35
❑ 7	Frank Wycheck	.60	.25
❑ 8	Michael Strahan	.60	.25
❑ 9	Jessie Armstead	.60	.25
❑ 10	Stephen Alexander	.60	.25
❑ 11	Larry Centers	.60	.25
❑ 12	Michael Pittman	.60	.25
❑ 13	Priest Holmes	.75	.35
❑ 14	Jermaine Lewis	.75	.35
❑ 15	Jay Riemersma	.60	.25
❑ 16	Wesley Walls	.60	.25
❑ 17	Curtis Enis	.75	.35
❑ 18	Bobby Engram	.75	.35
❑ 19	Jim Miller	.60	.25
❑ 20	Eddie Kennison	.75	.35
❑ 21	Errict Rhett	.60	.25
❑ 22	Chris Warren	.60	.25
❑ 23	Byron Chamberlain	.60	.25
❑ 24	Desmond Howard	.60	.25
❑ 25	Lamar Smith	.75	.35
❑ 26	Robert Porcher	.60	.25
❑ 27	Corey Bradford	.75	.35
❑ 28	Donald Driver	.60	.25
❑ 29	Ahman Green	.75	.35
❑ 30	Ken Dilger	.60	.25
❑ 31	James McKnight	.60	.25
❑ 32	Kimble Anders	.60	.25
❑ 33	Zach Thomas	.75	.35
❑ 34	James Johnson	.75	.35
❑ 35	Lawyer Milloy	.60	.25
❑ 36	Ty Law	.60	.25
❑ 37	Willie McGinest	.60	.25
❑ 38	Jason Sehorn	.75	.35
❑ 39	Andre Rison	.60	.25
❑ 40	Rickey Dudley	.60	.25
❑ 41	Patrick Jeffers	1.00	.45
❑ 42	Darrell Russell	.60	.25
❑ 43	Charles Johnson	.75	.35
❑ 44	Michael Westbrook	.75	.35
❑ 45	Levon Kirkland	.60	.25
❑ 46	Ryan Leaf	1.00	.45
❑ 47	Sean Dawkins	.60	.25
❑ 48	Todd Lyght	.60	.25
❑ 49	Kevin Carter	.60	.25
❑ 50	Neil O'Donnell	.60	.25
❑ 51	Randall Cunningham	1.25	.55
❑ 52	Oronde Gadsden	1.00	.45
❑ 53	O.J. McDuffie	1.00	.45
❑ 54	Jake Reed	1.00	.45
❑ 55	Brian Mitchell	.75	.35
❑ 56	Kordell Stewart	1.25	.55
❑ 57	Derrick Mayes	1.00	.45
❑ 58	Az-Zahir Hakim	.75	.35
❑ 59	Jacquez Green	1.00	.45
❑ 60	Andre Reed	1.00	.45
❑ 61	Deion Sanders	1.25	.55
❑ 62	Frank Sanders	1.00	.45
❑ 63	Rob Moore	1.00	.45
❑ 64	Shawn Jefferson	.75	.35
❑ 65	Pat Johnson	.75	.35
❑ 66	Peter Boulware	.75	.35
❑ 67	Donald Hayes	.75	.35
❑ 68	Marty Booker	.75	.35
❑ 69	Leslie Shepherd	.75	.35
❑ 70	Jason Tucker	1.00	.45
❑ 71	Johnnie Morton	1.00	.45
❑ 72	Germane Crowell	1.00	.45
❑ 73	Herman Moore	1.00	.45
❑ 74	Bill Schroeder	1.00	.45
❑ 75	E.G. Green	.75	.35
❑ 76	Jerome Pathon	1.00	.45
❑ 77	Tony Brackens	.75	.35
❑ 78	Tony Richardson	.75	.35
❑ 79	Sam Madison	.75	.35
❑ 80	Jeff George	1.00	.45
❑ 81	Matthew Hatchette	.75	.35
❑ 82	Kevin Faulk	1.00	.45
❑ 83	Jeff Blake	1.00	.45
❑ 84	Ike Hilliard	1.00	.45
❑ 85	Napoleon Kaufman	1.00	.45
❑ 86	Charles Woodson	1.00	.45
❑ 87	Na Brown	.75	.35
❑ 88	Hines Ward	.75	.35
❑ 89	Troy Edwards	1.00	.45
❑ 90	Curtis Conway	1.00	.45
❑ 91	Junior Seau	1.00	.45
❑ 92	Jim Harbaugh	1.00	.45
❑ 93	J.J. Stokes	1.00	.45
❑ 94	Jon Kitna	1.25	.55
❑ 95	Reidel Anthony	.75	.35
❑ 96	Warrick Dunn	1.25	.55
❑ 97	Carl Pickens	1.00	.45
❑ 98	Yancey Thigpen	.75	.35
❑ 99	Albert Connell	.75	.35
❑ 100	Irving Fryar	.75	.35
❑ 101	Qadry Ismail	1.25	.55
❑ 102	Shannon Sharpe	1.25	.55
❑ 103	Joey Galloway	1.50	.70
❑ 104	Ed McCaffrey	1.50	.70
❑ 105	Rod Smith	1.25	.55
❑ 106	Terrell Owens	1.50	.70
❑ 107	Warren Sapp	1.25	.55
❑ 108	Jevon Kearse	1.50	.70
❑ 109	Bruce Smith	1.25	.55
❑ 110	Champ Bailey	1.25	.55
❑ 111	David Boston	1.50	.70
❑ 112	Tim Dwight	1.50	.70
❑ 113	Terance Mathis	1.25	.55
❑ 114	Tony Banks	1.25	.55
❑ 115	Shawn Bryson	1.00	.45
❑ 116	Peerless Price	1.50	.70
❑ 117	Muhsin Muhammad	1.25	.55
❑ 118	Tim Biakabutuka	1.25	.55
❑ 119	Steve Beuerlein	1.25	.55
❑ 120	Corey Dillon	1.50	.70
❑ 121	Kevin Johnson	1.50	.70
❑ 122	Rocket Ismail	1.25	.55
❑ 123	Charlie Batch	1.50	.70
❑ 124	James Stewart	1.25	.55
❑ 125	Terrence Wilkins	1.50	.70
❑ 126	Keenan McCardell	1.25	.55
❑ 127	Mark Brunell	2.50	1.10
❑ 128	Fred Taylor	2.00	.90
❑ 129	Derrick Alexander	1.25	.55
❑ 130	Tony Gonzalez	1.25	.55
❑ 131	Warren Moon	1.50	.70
❑ 132	Thurman Thomas	1.25	.55
❑ 133	Tony Martin	1.25	.55
❑ 134	Jay Fiedler	1.50	.70
❑ 135	John Randle	1.25	.55
❑ 136	Troy Brown	1.00	.45
❑ 137	Amani Toomer	1.25	.55
❑ 138	Kerry Collins	1.25	.55
❑ 139	Tiki Barber	1.25	.55
❑ 140	Wayne Chrebet	1.25	.55
❑ 141	Tyrone Wheatley	1.25	.55
❑ 142	Duce Staley	1.50	.70
❑ 143	Jermaine Fazande	1.00	.45
❑ 144	Charlie Garner	1.25	.55
❑ 145	Torry Holt	1.50	.70
❑ 146	Mike Alstott	1.50	.70
❑ 147	Shaun King	2.50	1.10
❑ 148	Darrell Green	1.00	.45
❑ 149	Brad Johnson	1.50	.70
❑ 150	Olandis Gary	1.50	.70
❑ 151	Jake Plummer	2.00	.90
❑ 152	Chris Chandler	1.50	.70
❑ 153	Jamal Anderson	2.00	.90
❑ 154	Eric Moulds	2.00	.90
❑ 155	Doug Flutie	2.50	1.10
❑ 156	Rob Johnson	1.50	.70
❑ 157	Marcus Robinson	2.00	.90
❑ 158	Cade McNown	2.00	.90
❑ 159	Akili Smith	2.00	.90
❑ 160	Tim Couch	4.00	1.80
❑ 161	Emmitt Smith	5.00	2.20
❑ 162	Troy Aikman	5.00	2.20
❑ 163	Brian Griese	2.50	1.10
❑ 164	John Elway	8.00	3.60
❑ 165	Terrell Davis	5.00	2.20
❑ 166	Dorsey Levens	1.50	.70
❑ 167	Antonio Freeman	2.00	.90
❑ 168	Brett Favre	8.00	3.60
❑ 169	Marvin Harrison	2.00	.90
❑ 170	Peyton Manning	6.00	2.70
❑ 171	Edgerrin James	8.00	3.60
❑ 172	Jimmy Smith	1.50	.70
❑ 173	Elvis Grbac	1.50	.70
❑ 174	Dan Marino	8.00	3.60
❑ 175	Randy Moss	6.00	2.70
❑ 176	Cris Carter	2.00	.90
❑ 177	Robert Smith	2.00	.90
❑ 178	Daunte Culpepper	4.00	1.80
❑ 179	Terry Glenn	1.50	.70
❑ 180	Drew Bledsoe	3.00	1.35
❑ 181	Ricky Williams	5.00	2.20
❑ 182	Jake Delhomme RC	4.00	1.80
❑ 183	Curtis Martin	2.00	.90
❑ 184	Vinny Testaverde	1.50	.70

❑	185 Tim Brown	2.00	.90
❑	186 Rich Gannon	1.50	.70
❑	187 Donovan McNabb	3.00	1.35
❑	188 Jerome Bettis	2.00	.90
❑	189 Bobby Shaw RC	6.00	2.70
❑	190 Jerry Rice	5.00	2.20
❑	191 Steve Young	3.00	1.35
❑	192 Jeff Garcia	2.00	.90
❑	193 Ricky Watters	1.25	.55
❑	194 Isaac Bruce	2.00	.90
❑	195 Marshall Faulk	2.50	1.10
❑	196 Kurt Warner	8.00	3.60
❑	197 Keyshawn Johnson	2.00	.90
❑	198 Eddie George	2.50	1.10
❑	199 Steve McNair	2.00	.90
❑	200 Stephen Davis	2.00	.90
❑	201 Bobby Brooks RC	4.00	1.80
❑	202 Cornelius Griffin RC	5.00	2.20
❑	203 Danny Clark RC	4.00	1.80
❑	204 Pat Dennis RC	5.00	2.20
❑	205 Tommy Hendricks RC	4.00	1.80
❑	206 Fred Jones RC	4.00	1.80
❑	207 Isaiah Kacyvenski RC	4.00	1.80
❑	208 Keith Miller RC	4.00	1.80
❑	209 Andre O' Neal RC	4.00	1.80
❑	210 Justin Snow RC	4.00	1.80
❑	211 Armegis Spearman RC	5.00	2.20
❑	212 Lester Towns RC	4.00	1.80
❑	213 Antonio Wilson RC	4.00	1.80
❑	214 Greg Wesley RC	5.00	2.20
❑	215 Jabari Issa RC	4.00	1.80
❑	216 Darwin Walker RC	4.00	1.80
❑	217 Reggie Grimes RC	4.00	1.80
❑	218 Rian Lindell RC	4.00	1.80
❑	219 Chris Combs RC	4.00	1.80
❑	220 Rashard Anderson RC	5.00	2.20
❑	221 Erik Flowers RC	6.00	2.70
❑	222 Corey Moore RC	5.00	2.20
❑	223 Rob Meier RC	4.00	1.80
❑	224 John Milem RC	4.00	1.80
❑	225 Jeremiah Parker RC	4.00	1.80
❑	226 Neil Rackers RC	4.00	1.80
❑	227 Josh Taves RC	6.00	2.70
❑	228 Mao Tosi RC	4.00	1.80
❑	229 Gary Berry RC	4.00	1.80
❑	230 Matt Bowen RC	4.00	1.80
❑	231 Ralph Brown RC	4.00	1.80
❑	232 Tony Darden RC	4.00	1.80
❑	233 Arturo Freeman RC	4.00	1.80
❑	234 David Gibson RC	4.00	1.80
❑	235 Demario Brown RC	5.00	2.20
❑	236 Deveron Harper RC	4.00	1.80
❑	237 Johnnie Harris RC	4.00	1.80
❑	238 Marcus Knight RC	4.00	1.80
❑	239 Ronnie Heard RC	5.00	2.20
❑	240 Eric Johnson RC	5.00	2.20
❑	241 John Keith RC	4.00	1.80
❑	242 Anthony Malbrough RC	4.00	1.80
❑	243 Anthony Mitchell RC	4.00	1.80
❑	244 Aric Morris RC	4.00	1.80
❑	245 Bobby Myers RC	4.00	1.80
❑	246 Erik Olson RC	6.00	2.70
❑	247 Lewis Sanders RC	4.00	1.80
❑	248 Tony Scott RC	4.00	1.80
❑	249 David Terrell RC	4.00	1.80
❑	250 Travares Tillman RC	4.00	1.80
❑	251 David Stachelski RC	6.00	2.70
❑	252 Darren Howard RC	6.00	2.70
❑	253 Frank Chamberlin RC	5.00	2.20
❑	254 Na'il Diggs RC	8.00	3.60
❑	255 Orantes Grant RC	5.00	2.20
❑	256 Barrett Green RC	5.00	2.20
❑	257 Kory Minor RC	5.00	2.20
❑	258 Deon Grant RC	5.00	2.20
❑	259 Mark Simoneau RC	8.00	3.60
❑	260 Raynoch Thompson RC	6.00	2.70
❑	261 Kenyatta Wright RC	5.00	2.20
❑	262 Marcus Bell RC	5.00	2.20
❑	263 Jack Golden RC	5.00	2.20
❑	264 Thomas Hamner RC	6.00	2.70
❑	265 Sekou Sanyika RC	5.00	2.20
❑	266 Marcus Washington RC	6.00	2.70
❑	267 Tim Seder RC	6.00	2.70
❑	268 Paul Edinger RC	8.00	3.60
❑	269 Michael Boireau RC	5.00	2.20
❑	270 Byron Frisch RC	5.00	2.20
❑	271 Ketric Sanford RC	5.00	2.20
❑	272 Frank Murphy RC	5.00	2.20
❑	273 Robaire Smith RC	5.00	2.20
❑	274 Adalius Thomas RC	5.00	2.20
❑	275 William Bartee RC	6.00	2.70
❑	276 Robert Bean RC	6.00	2.70
❑	277 Tyrone Carter RC	6.00	2.70
❑	278 Ike Charlton RC	5.00	2.20
❑	279 Mario Edwards RC	5.00	2.20
❑	280 Dwayne Goodrich RC	5.00	2.20
❑	281 Michael Hawthorne RC	5.00	2.20
❑	282 Kareem Larrimore RC	6.00	2.70
❑	283 Mark Roman RC	5.00	2.20
❑	284 Jacoby Shepherd RC	5.00	2.20
❑	285 Jason Webster RC	5.00	2.20
❑	286 Jimmy Wyrick RC	5.00	2.20
❑	287 Rashidi Barnes RC	5.00	2.20
❑	288 David Barrett RC	5.00	2.20
❑	289 Ainsley Battles RC	5.00	2.20
❑	290 Lamar Chapman RC	6.00	2.70
❑	291 Todd Franz RC	5.00	2.20
❑	292 Michael Green RC	5.00	2.20
❑	293 Antwan Harris RC	5.00	2.20
❑	294 Brandon Jennings RC	5.00	2.20
❑	295 Darrick Vaughn RC	5.00	2.20
❑	296 David Macklin RC	5.00	2.20
❑	297 Bobby Brown RC	5.00	2.20
❑	298 Reggie Stephens RC	5.00	2.20
❑	299 Kenoy Kennedy RC	5.00	2.20
❑	300 Raion Hill RC	6.00	2.70
❑	301 Windrell Hayes RC	10.00	4.50
❑	302 DaShon Polk RC	8.00	3.60
❑	303 Tywan Mitchell RC	10.00	4.50
❑	304 Casey Crawford RC	8.00	3.60
❑	305 Hank Poteat RC	10.00	4.50
❑	306 Mondriel Fulcher RC	8.00	3.60
❑	307 Cory Geason RC	8.00	3.60
❑	308 James Hill RC	8.00	3.60
❑	309 Brian Jennings RC	8.00	3.60
❑	310 John Jones RC	10.00	4.50
❑	311 Anthony Lucas RC	8.00	3.60
❑	312 Mike Leach RC	8.00	3.60
❑	313 Dustin Lyman RC	8.00	3.60
❑	314 Derek Rackley RC	8.00	3.60
❑	315 Sebastian Janikowski RC	12.00	5.50
❑	316 Brad St.Louis RC	8.00	3.60
❑	317 Jay Tant RC	8.00	3.60
❑	318 Austin Wheatley RC	8.00	3.60
❑	319 Jermaine Wiggins RC	8.00	3.60
❑	320 Todd Yoder RC	10.00	4.50
❑	321 Deon Dyer RC	10.00	4.50
❑	322 Jim Finn RC	10.00	4.50
❑	323 Herbert Goodman RC	10.00	4.50
❑	324 Mike Green RC	10.00	4.50
❑	325 Dante Hall RC	10.00	4.50
❑	326 Thabiti Davis RC	10.00	4.50
❑	327 Kevin Houser RC	10.00	4.50
❑	328 Jonas Lewis RC	10.00	4.50
❑	329 Chad Morton RC	12.00	5.50
❑	330 Patrick Pass RC	10.00	4.50
❑	331 Maurice Smith RC	10.00	4.50
❑	332 Paul Smith RC	10.00	4.50
❑	333 Terrelle Smith RC	10.00	4.50
❑	334 Craig Walendy RC	10.00	4.50
❑	335 Jamel White RC	12.00	5.50
❑	336 Jarious Jackson RC	12.00	5.50
❑	337 Matt Lytle RC	10.00	4.50
❑	338 Ron Powlus RC	20.00	9.00
❑	339 Ian Gold RC	10.00	4.50
❑	340 Brandon Short RC	10.00	4.50
❑	341 T.J. Slaughter RC	8.00	3.60
❑	342 Nate Webster RC	8.00	3.60
❑	343 John Engelberger RC	10.00	4.50
❑	344 Rogers Beckett RC	10.00	4.50
❑	345 Mike Brown RC	12.00	5.50
❑	346 Anthony Wright RC	25.00	11.00
❑	347 Danny Farmer RC	12.00	5.50
❑	348 Clint Stoerner RC	15.00	6.75
❑	349 Julian Peterson RC	10.00	4.50
❑	350 Ahmed Plummer RC	12.00	5.50
❑	351 Avion Black RC	12.00	5.50
❑	352 Kwame Cavil RC	12.00	5.50
❑	353 Chris Cole RC	12.00	5.50
❑	354 Chris Coleman RC	10.00	4.50
❑	355 Trevor Gaylor RC	12.00	5.50
❑	356 Damon Hodge RC	12.00	5.50
❑	357 Darrell Jackson RC	40.00	18.00
❑	358 Reggie Jones RC	15.00	6.75
❑	359 Charles Lee RC	10.00	4.50
❑	360 Jerry Porter RC	15.00	6.75
❑	361 Bobby Shaw	12.00	5.50
❑	362 Ron Dugans RC	12.00	5.50
❑	363 James Williams RC	12.00	5.50
❑	364 Bashir Yamini RC	12.00	5.50
❑	365 Anthony Becht RC	15.00	6.75
❑	366 Erron Kinney RC	15.00	6.75
❑	367 Aaron Shea RC	12.00	5.50
❑	368 Chris Samuels RC	12.00	5.50
❑	369 Trung Canidate RC	15.00	6.75
❑	370 Obafemi Ayanbadejo RC	15.00	6.75
❑	371 Doug Chapman RC	40.00	18.00
❑	372 Ronney Jenkins RC	12.00	5.50
❑	373 Curtis Keaton RC	12.00	5.50
❑	374 Kevin McDougal RC	12.00	5.50
❑	375 Frank Moreau RC	15.00	6.75
❑	376 Aaron Stecker RC	15.00	6.75
❑	377 Shyrone Stith RC	12.00	5.50
❑	378 Tom Brady RC	15.00	6.75
❑	379 Giovanni Carmazzi RC	20.00	9.00
❑	380 Joe Hamilton RC	20.00	9.00
❑	381 Todd Husak RC	15.00	6.75
❑	382 Doug Johnson RC	15.00	6.75
❑	383 Tee Martin RC	25.00	11.00
❑	384 Chad Pennington RC	80.00	36.00
❑	385 Tim Rattay RC	25.00	11.00
❑	386 Chris Redman RC	50.00	22.00
❑	387 Billy Volek RC	12.00	5.50
❑	388 Spergon Wynn RC	15.00	6.75
❑	389 John Abraham RC	12.00	5.50
❑	390 Keith Bulluck RC	12.00	5.50
❑	391 Rob Morris RC	12.00	5.50
❑	392 JaJuan Dawson RC	15.00	6.75
❑	393 Chris Hovan RC	12.00	5.50
❑	394 Shaun Ellis RC	12.00	5.50
❑	395 Deltha O'Neal RC	12.00	5.50
❑	396 Gari Scott RC	12.00	5.50
❑	397 Dialleo Burks RC	12.00	5.50
❑	398 Shockmain Davis RC	12.00	5.50
❑	399 Brad Hoover RC	40.00	18.00
❑	400 Brian Finneran RC	12.00	5.50
❑	401 Sylvester Morris RC/750	40.00	18.00
❑	402 Dennis Northcutt RC/500	30.00	13.50
❑	403 Todd Pinkston RC/1000	20.00	9.00
❑	404 Larry Foster RC/500	25.00	11.00
❑	405 R.Jay Soward RC/1000	25.00	11.00
❑	406 Travis Taylor RC/250	60.00	27.00
❑	407 Peter Warrick RC/1000	80.00	36.00
❑	408 Dez White RC/1000	20.00	9.00
❑	409 Ron Dayne RC/1000	80.00	36.00
❑	410 Thomas Jones RC/500	40.00	18.00
❑	411 Jamal Lewis RC/1000	120.00	55.00
❑	412 Sammy Morris RC/500	30.00	13.50
❑	413 Travis Prentice RC/500	40.00	18.00
❑	414 J.R. Redmond RC/250	60.00	27.00
❑	415 Michael Wiley RC/1000	20.00	9.00
❑	416 Laveranues Coles RC/250	60.00	27.00
❑	417 Bubba Franks RC/500	30.00	13.50
❑	418 Mike Anderson RC/250	250.00	110.00
❑	419 Plaxico Burress RC/250	100.00	45.00
❑	420 Ron Dixon RC/1000	25.00	11.00
❑	421 Troy Walters RC/1000	20.00	9.00
❑	422 Shaun Alexander RC/1000	60.00	27.00
❑	423 Brian Urlacher RC/1000	60.00	27.00
❑	424 Corey Simon RC/1000	20.00	9.00
❑	425 Courtney Brown RC/500	40.00	18.00

1998 Leaf Rookies and Stars

		MINT	NRMT
	COMPLETE SET (300)	400.00	180.00
❑	1 Keyshawn Johnson	.50	.23
❑	2 Marvin Harrison	.25	.11
❑	3 Eddie Kennison	.25	.11
❑	4 Bryant Young	.15	.07
❑	5 Darren Woodson	.15	.07
❑	6 Tyrone Wheatley	.25	.11
❑	7 Michael Westbrook	.25	.11

❑ 8 Charles Way .15 .07
❑ 9 Ricky Watters .25 .11
❑ 10 Chris Warren .25 .11
❑ 11 Wesley Walls .25 .11
❑ 12 Tamarick Vanover .15 .07
❑ 13 Zach Thomas .25 .11
❑ 14 Derrick Thomas .25 .11
❑ 15 Yancey Thigpen .15 .07
❑ 16 Vinny Testaverde .25 .11
❑ 17 Dana Stubblefield .15 .07
❑ 18 J.J. Stokes .25 .11
❑ 19 James Stewart .25 .11
❑ 20 Jeff George .25 .11
❑ 21 John Randle .25 .11
❑ 22 Gary Brown .15 .07
❑ 23 Ed McCaffrey .25 .11
❑ 24 James Jett .25 .11
❑ 25 Rob Johnson .25 .11
❑ 26 Daryl Johnston .25 .11
❑ 27 Jermaine Lewis .25 .11
❑ 28 Tony Martin .25 .11
❑ 29 Derrick Mayes .25 .11
❑ 30 Keenan McCardell .25 .11
❑ 31 O.J. McDuffie .25 .11
❑ 32 Chris Chandler .25 .11
❑ 33 Doug Flutie .60 .25
❑ 34 Scott Mitchell .25 .11
❑ 35 Warren Moon .50 .23
❑ 36 Rob Moore .25 .11
❑ 37 Johnnie Morton .25 .11
❑ 38 Neil O'Donnell .25 .11
❑ 39 Rich Gannon .25 .11
❑ 40 Andre Reed .25 .11
❑ 41 Jake Reed .25 .11
❑ 42 Errict Rhett .25 .11
❑ 43 Simeon Rice .25 .11
❑ 44 Andre Rison .25 .11
❑ 45 Eric Moulds .50 .23
❑ 46 Frank Sanders .25 .11
❑ 47 Darnay Scott .25 .11
❑ 48 Junior Seau .25 .11
❑ 49 Shannon Sharpe .25 .11
❑ 50 Bruce Smith .25 .11
❑ 51 Jimmy Smith .25 .11
❑ 52 Robert Smith .50 .23
❑ 53 Derrick Alexander .25 .11
❑ 54 Kimble Anders .25 .11
❑ 55 Jamal Anderson .50 .23
❑ 56 Mario Bates .25 .11
❑ 57 Edgar Bennett .15 .07
❑ 58 Tim Biakabutuka .25 .11
❑ 59 Ki-Jana Carter .15 .07
❑ 60 Larry Centers .15 .07
❑ 61 Mark Chmura .25 .11
❑ 62 Wayne Chrebet .50 .23
❑ 63 Ben Coates .25 .11
❑ 64 Curtis Conway .25 .11
❑ 65 Randall Cunningham .50 .23
❑ 66 Rickey Dudley .15 .07
❑ 67 Bert Emanuel .25 .11
❑ 68 Bobby Engram .25 .11
❑ 69 William Floyd .15 .07
❑ 70 Irving Fryar .25 .11
❑ 71 Elvis Grbac .25 .11
❑ 72 Kevin Greene .25 .11
❑ 73 Jim Harbaugh .25 .11
❑ 74 Raymont Harris .15 .07
❑ 75 Garrison Hearst .50 .23
❑ 76 Greg Hill .15 .07
❑ 77 Desmond Howard .25 .11
❑ 78 Bobby Hoying .25 .11
❑ 79 Michael Jackson .15 .07
❑ 80 Terry Allen .50 .23
❑ 81 Jerome Bettis .50 .23
❑ 82 Jeff Blake .25 .11
❑ 83 Robert Brooks .25 .11
❑ 84 Tim Brown .50 .23
❑ 85 Isaac Bruce .50 .23
❑ 86 Cris Carter .50 .23
❑ 87 Ty Detmer .25 .11
❑ 88 Trent Dilfer .50 .23
❑ 89 Marshall Faulk .50 .23
❑ 90 Antonio Freeman .50 .23
❑ 91 Gus Frerotte .15 .07
❑ 92 Joey Galloway .50 .23
❑ 93 Michael Irvin .50 .23
❑ 94 Brad Johnson .50 .23
❑ 95 Danny Kanell .25 .11
❑ 96 Napoleon Kaufman .50 .23
❑ 97 Dorsey Levens .50 .23
❑ 98 Natrone Means .50 .23
❑ 99 Herman Moore .50 .23
❑ 100 Adrian Murrell .25 .11
❑ 101 Carl Pickens .50 .23
❑ 102 Rod Smith .25 .11
❑ 103 Thurman Thomas .50 .23
❑ 104 Reggie White .50 .23
❑ 105 Jim Druckenmiller .25 .11
❑ 106 Antowain Smith .50 .23
❑ 107 Reidel Anthony .25 .11
❑ 108 Ike Hilliard .25 .11
❑ 109 Rae Carruth .25 .11
❑ 110 Troy Davis .15 .07
❑ 111 Terance Mathis .25 .11
❑ 112 Brett Favre 2.50 1.10
❑ 113 Dan Marino 2.50 1.10
❑ 114 Emmitt Smith 2.00 .90
❑ 115 Barry Sanders 2.50 1.10
❑ 116 Eddie George 1.00 .45
❑ 117 Drew Bledsoe 1.00 .45
❑ 118 Troy Aikman 1.25 .55
❑ 119 Terrell Davis 2.00 .90
❑ 120 John Elway 2.50 1.10
❑ 121 Mark Brunell 1.00 .45
❑ 122 Jerry Rice 1.25 .55
❑ 123 Kordell Stewart .50 .23
❑ 124 Steve McNair .50 .23
❑ 125 Curtis Martin .50 .23
❑ 126 Steve Young .75 .35
❑ 127 Kerry Collins .25 .11
❑ 128 Terry Glenn .50 .23
❑ 129 Deion Sanders .50 .23
❑ 130 Mike Alstott .50 .23
❑ 131 Tony Banks .25 .11
❑ 132 Karim Abdul-Jabbar .50 .23
❑ 133 Terrell Owens .50 .23
❑ 134 Yatil Green .15 .07
❑ 135 Tony Gonzalez .15 .07
❑ 136 Byron Hanspard .25 .11
❑ 137 David LaFleur .15 .07
❑ 138 Danny Wuerffel .25 .11
❑ 139 Tiki Barber .25 .11
❑ 140 Peter Boulware .15 .07
❑ 141 Will Blackwell .15 .07
❑ 142 Warrick Dunn .50 .23
❑ 143 Corey Dillon .75 .35
❑ 144 Jake Plummer 1.00 .45
❑ 145 Neil Smith .25 .11
❑ 146 Charles Johnson .15 .07
❑ 147 Fred Lane .25 .11
❑ 148 Dan Wilkinson .15 .07
❑ 149 Ken Norton .15 .07
❑ 150 Stephen Davis .15 .07
❑ 151 Gilbert Brown .15 .07
❑ 152 Kenny Bynum RC .15 .07
❑ 153 Derrick Cullors .25 .11
❑ 154 Charlie Garner .15 .07
❑ 155 Jeff Graham .15 .07
❑ 156 Warren Sapp .25 .11
❑ 157 Jerald Moore .15 .07
❑ 158 Sean Dawkins .15 .07
❑ 159 Charlie Jones .15 .07
❑ 160 Kevin Lockett .15 .07
❑ 161 James McKnight .15 .07
❑ 162 Chris Penn .15 .07
❑ 163 Leslie Shepherd .15 .07
❑ 164 Karl Williams .15 .07
❑ 165 Mark Bruener .15 .07
❑ 166 Ernie Conwell .15 .07
❑ 167 Ken Dilger .15 .07
❑ 168 Troy Drayton .15 .07
❑ 169 Freddie Jones .15 .07
❑ 170 Dale Carter .15 .07
❑ 171 Charles Woodson RC 12.00 5.50
❑ 172 Alonzo Mayes RC 2.50 1.10
❑ 173 Andre Wadsworth RC 5.00 2.20
❑ 174 Grant Wistrom RC 2.50 1.10
❑ 175 Greg Ellis RC 2.50 1.10
❑ 176 Chris Howard RC 5.00 2.20
❑ 177 Keith Brooking RC 5.00 2.20
❑ 178 Takeo Spikes RC 5.00 2.20
❑ 179 Anthony Simmons RC 2.50 1.10
❑ 180 Brian Simmons RC 2.50 1.10
❑ 181 Sam Cowart RC 2.50 1.10
❑ 182 Ken Oxendine RC 2.50 1.10
❑ 183 Vonnie Holliday RC 5.00 2.20
❑ 184 Terry Fair RC 5.00 2.20
❑ 185 Shaun Williams RC 2.50 1.10
❑ 186 Tremayne Stephens RC 2.50 1.10
❑ 187 Duane Starks RC 2.50 1.10
❑ 188 Jason Peter RC 2.50 1.10
❑ 189 Tebucky Jones RC 2.50 1.10
❑ 190 Donovin Darius RC 2.50 1.10
❑ 191 R.W. McQuarters RC 2.50 1.10
❑ 192 Corey Chavous RC 2.50 1.10
❑ 193 Cameron Cleeland RC 5.00 2.20
❑ 194 Stephen Alexander RC 5.00 2.20
❑ 195 Rod Rutledge RC 2.50 1.10
❑ 196 Scott Frost RC 5.00 2.20
❑ 197 Fred Beasley RC 2.50 1.10
❑ 198 Dorian Boose RC 2.50 1.10
❑ 199 Randy Moss RC 80.00 36.00
❑ 200 Jacquez Green RC 12.00 5.50
❑ 201 Marcus Nash RC 8.00 3.60
❑ 202 Hines Ward RC 5.00 2.20
❑ 203 Kevin Dyson RC 12.00 5.50
❑ 204 E.G. Green RC 5.00 2.20
❑ 205 Germane Crowell RC 15.00 6.75
❑ 206 Joe Jurevicius RC 5.00 2.20
❑ 207 Tony Simmons RC 5.00 2.20
❑ 208 Tim Dwight RC 12.00 5.50
❑ 209 Az-Zahir Hakim RC 8.00 3.60
❑ 210 Jerome Pathon RC 5.00 2.20
❑ 211 Pat Johnson RC 5.00 2.20
❑ 212 Mikhael Ricks RC 5.00 2.20
❑ 213 Donald Hayes RC 8.00 3.60
❑ 214 Jammi German RC 2.50 1.10
❑ 215 Larry Shannon RC 2.50 1.10
❑ 216 Brian Alford RC 5.00 2.20
❑ 217 Curtis Enis RC 10.00 4.50
❑ 218 Fred Taylor RC 25.00 11.00
❑ 219 Robert Edwards RC 10.00 4.50
❑ 220 Ahman Green RC 15.00 6.75
❑ 221 Tavian Banks RC 5.00 2.20
❑ 222 Skip Hicks RC 8.00 3.60
❑ 223 Robert Holcombe RC 8.00 3.60
❑ 224 John Avery RC 8.00 3.60
❑ 225 C.Fuamatu-Ma'afala RC 5.00 2.20
❑ 226 Michael Pittman RC 8.00 3.60
❑ 227 Rashaan Shehee RC 5.00 2.20
❑ 228 Jonathan Linton RC 8.00 3.60
❑ 229 Jon Ritchie RC 5.00 2.20
❑ 230 Chris Floyd RC 2.50 1.10
❑ 231 Wilmont Perry RC 2.50 1.10
❑ 232 Raymond Priester RC 2.50 1.10
❑ 233 Peyton Manning RC 80.00 36.00
❑ 234 Ryan Leaf RC 15.00 6.75
❑ 235 Brian Griese RC 30.00 13.50
❑ 236 Jeff Ogden RC 8.00 3.60
❑ 237 Charlie Batch RC 20.00 9.00
❑ 238 Moses Moreno RC 5.00 2.20
❑ 239 Jonathan Quinn RC 5.00 2.20
UER back Jonathon
❑ 240 Flozell Adams RC 2.50 1.10
❑ 241 Brett Favre PT 12.00 5.50
❑ 242 Dan Marino PT 12.00 5.50
❑ 243 Emmitt Smith PT 10.00 4.50
❑ 244 Barry Sanders PT 12.00 5.50
❑ 245 Eddie George PT 5.00 2.20

Card	Player	MINT	NRMT
❑ 246	Drew Bledsoe PT	5.00	2.20
❑ 247	Troy Aikman PT	6.00	2.70
❑ 248	Terrell Davis PT	10.00	4.50
❑ 249	John Elway PT	12.00	5.50
❑ 250	Carl Pickens PT	2.50	1.10
❑ 251	Jerry Rice PT	6.00	2.70
❑ 252	Kordell Stewart PT	2.50	1.10
❑ 253	Steve McNair PT	2.50	1.10
❑ 254	Curtis Martin PT	2.50	1.10
❑ 255	Steve Young PT	4.00	1.80
❑ 256	Herman Moore PT	2.50	1.10
❑ 257	Dorsey Levens PT	2.50	1.10
❑ 258	Deion Sanders PT	2.50	1.10
❑ 259	Napoleon Kaufman PT	2.50	1.10
❑ 260	Warrick Dunn PT	2.50	1.10
❑ 261	Corey Dillon PT	4.00	1.80
❑ 262	Jerome Bettis PT	2.50	1.10
❑ 263	Tim Brown PT	2.50	1.10
❑ 264	Cris Carter PT	2.50	1.10
❑ 265	Antonio Freeman PT	2.50	1.10
❑ 266	Randy Moss PT	20.00	9.00
❑ 267	Curtis Enis PT	5.00	2.20
❑ 268	Fred Taylor PT	8.00	3.60
❑ 269	Robert Edwards PT	3.00	1.35
❑ 270	Peyton Manning PT	20.00	9.00
❑ 271	Barry Sanders TL	1.25	.55
❑ 272	Eddie George TL	.50	.23
❑ 273	Troy Aikman TL	.60	.25
❑ 274	Mark Brunell TL	.50	.23
❑ 275	Kordell Stewart TL	.50	.23
❑ 276	Tim Biakabutuka TL	.15	.07
❑ 277	Terry Glenn TL	.15	.07
❑ 278	Mike Alstott TL	.15	.07
❑ 279	Tony Banks TL	.15	.07
❑ 280	Karim Abdul-Jabbar TL	.15	.07
❑ 281	Terrell Owens TL	.25	.11
❑ 282	Byron Hanspard TL	.15	.07
❑ 283	Jake Plummer TL	.60	.25
❑ 284	Terry Allen TL	.15	.07
❑ 285	Jeff Blake TL	.15	.07
❑ 286	Brad Johnson TL	.15	.07
❑ 287	Danny Kanell TL	.15	.07
❑ 288	Natrone Means TL	.15	.07
❑ 289	Rod Smith TL	.15	.07
❑ 290	Thurman Thomas TL	.15	.07
❑ 291	Reggie White TL	.15	.07
❑ 292	Troy Davis TL	.15	.07
❑ 293	Curtis Conway TL	.15	.07
❑ 294	Irving Fryar TL	.15	.07
❑ 295	Jim Harbaugh TL	.15	.07
❑ 296	Andre Rison TL	.15	.07
❑ 297	Ricky Watters TL	.15	.07
❑ 298	Keyshawn Johnson TL	.15	.07
❑ 299	Jeff George TL	.15	.07
❑ 300	Marshall Faulk TL	.25	.11

1999 Leaf Rookies and Stars

	MINT	NRMT
COMPLETE SET (300)	350.00	160.00
COMP.SET w/o SP's (200)	30.00	13.50

Card	Player	MINT	NRMT
❑ 1	Frank Sanders	.25	.11
❑ 2	Adrian Murrell	.25	.11
❑ 3	Rob Moore	.25	.11
❑ 4	Simeon Rice	.15	.07
❑ 5	Michael Pittman	.15	.07
❑ 6	Jake Plummer	.75	.35
❑ 7	Chris Chandler	.25	.11
❑ 8	Tim Dwight	.25	.11
❑ 9	Chris Calloway	.15	.07
❑ 10	Terance Mathis	.25	.11
❑ 11	Jamal Anderson	.50	.23
❑ 12	Byron Hanspard	.25	.11
❑ 13	O.J. Santiago	.15	.07
❑ 14	Ken Oxendine	.15	.07
❑ 15	Priest Holmes	.15	.07
❑ 16	Scott Mitchell	.15	.07
❑ 17	Tony Banks	.25	.11
❑ 18	Patrick Johnson	.15	.07
❑ 19	Rod Woodson	.25	.11
❑ 20	Jermaine Lewis	.25	.11
❑ 21	Errict Rhett	.25	.11
❑ 22	Stoney Case	.15	.07
❑ 23	Andre Reed	.25	.11
❑ 24	Eric Moulds	.25	.11
❑ 25	Rob Johnson	.25	.11
❑ 26	Doug Flutie	.60	.25
❑ 27	Bruce Smith	.25	.11
❑ 28	Jay Riemersma	.15	.07
❑ 29	Antowain Smith	.15	.07
❑ 30	Thurman Thomas	.25	.11
❑ 31	Jonathan Linton	.15	.07
❑ 32	Muhsin Muhammad	.25	.11
❑ 33	Rae Carruth	.25	.11
❑ 34	Wesley Walls	.25	.11
❑ 35	Fred Lane	.25	.11
❑ 36	Kevin Greene	.15	.07
❑ 37	Tim Biakabutuka	.25	.11
❑ 38	Curtis Enis	.50	.23
❑ 39	Shane Matthews	.25	.11
❑ 40	Bobby Engram	.25	.11
❑ 41	Curtis Conway	.25	.11
❑ 42	Marcus Robinson	1.25	.55
❑ 43	Darnay Scott	.15	.07
❑ 44	Carl Pickens	.25	.11
❑ 45	Corey Dillon	.50	.23
❑ 46	Jeff Blake	.25	.11
❑ 47	Terry Kirby	.15	.07
❑ 48	Ty Detmer	.25	.11
❑ 49	Leslie Shepherd	.15	.07
❑ 50	Karim Abdul-Jabbar	.25	.11
❑ 51	Emmitt Smith	1.25	.55
❑ 52	Deion Sanders	.50	.23
❑ 53	Michael Irvin	.25	.11
❑ 54	Rocket Ismail	.25	.11
❑ 55	David LaFleur	.15	.07
❑ 56	Troy Aikman	1.25	.55
❑ 57	Ed McCaffrey	.25	.11
❑ 58	Rod Smith	.25	.11
❑ 59	Shannon Sharpe	.25	.11
❑ 60	Brian Griese	1.00	.45
❑ 61	John Elway	2.00	.90
❑ 62	Bubby Brister	.15	.07
❑ 63	Neil Smith	.25	.11
❑ 64	Terrell Davis	1.25	.55
❑ 65	John Avery	.25	.11
❑ 66	Derek Loville	.15	.07
❑ 67	Ron Rivers	.15	.07
❑ 68	Herman Moore	.50	.23
❑ 69	Johnnie Morton	.25	.11
❑ 70	Charlie Batch	1.00	.45
❑ 71	Barry Sanders	2.00	.90
❑ 72	Germane Crowell	.25	.11
❑ 73	Greg Hill	.15	.07
❑ 74	Gus Frerotte	.25	.11
❑ 75	Corey Bradford	.15	.07
❑ 76	Dorsey Levens	.50	.23
❑ 77	Antonio Freeman	.50	.23
❑ 78	Mark Chmura	.15	.07
❑ 79	Brett Favre	2.00	.90
❑ 80	Bill Schroeder	.25	.11
❑ 81	Matt Hasselbeck	.60	.25
❑ 82	E.G. Green	.15	.07
❑ 83	Ken Dilger	.15	.07
❑ 84	Jerome Pathon	.15	.07
❑ 85	Marvin Harrison	.50	.23
❑ 86	Peyton Manning	2.00	.90
❑ 87	Tavian Banks	.15	.07
❑ 88	Keenan McCardell	.25	.11
❑ 89	Mark Brunell	.75	.35
❑ 90	Fred Taylor	1.25	.55
❑ 91	Jimmy Smith	.25	.11
❑ 92	James Stewart	.25	.11
❑ 93	Kyle Brady	.15	.07
❑ 94	Derrick Thomas	.25	.11
❑ 95	Rashaan Shehee	.15	.07
❑ 96	Derrick Alexander WR	.25	.11
❑ 97	Byron Bam Morris	.15	.07
❑ 98	Andre Rison	.25	.11
❑ 99	Elvis Grbac	.25	.11
❑ 100	Tony Gonzalez	.25	.11
❑ 101	Donnell Bennett	.15	.07
❑ 102	Warren Moon	.50	.23
❑ 103	Zach Thomas	.25	.11
❑ 104	Oronde Gadsden	.15	.07
❑ 105	Dan Marino	2.00	.90
❑ 106	O.J. McDuffie	.25	.11
❑ 107	Tony Martin	.25	.11
❑ 108	Randy Moss	2.00	.90
❑ 109	Cris Carter	.50	.23
❑ 110	Robert Smith	.50	.23
❑ 111	Randall Cunningham	.50	.23
❑ 112	Jake Reed	.25	.11
❑ 113	John Randle	.25	.11
❑ 114	Leroy Hoard	.15	.07
❑ 115	Jeff George	.25	.11
❑ 116	Ty Law	.15	.07
❑ 117	Shawn Jefferson	.15	.07
❑ 118	Troy Brown	.15	.07
❑ 119	Robert Edwards	.15	.07
❑ 120	Tony Simmons	.15	.07
❑ 121	Terry Glenn	.50	.23
❑ 122	Ben Coates	.25	.11
❑ 123	Drew Bledsoe	.75	.35
❑ 124	Terry Allen	.25	.11
❑ 125	Cameron Cleeland	.15	.07
❑ 126	Eddie Kennison	.25	.11
❑ 127	Amani Toomer	.15	.07
❑ 128	Kerry Collins	.25	.11
❑ 129	Joe Jurevicius	.15	.07
❑ 130	Tiki Barber	.15	.07
❑ 131	Ike Hilliard	.15	.07
❑ 132	Michael Strahan	.15	.07
❑ 133	Gary Brown	.15	.07
❑ 134	Jason Sehorn	.15	.07
❑ 135	Curtis Martin	.50	.23
❑ 136	Vinny Testaverde	.25	.11
❑ 137	Dedric Ward	.15	.07
❑ 138	Keyshawn Johnson	.50	.23
❑ 139	Wayne Chrebet	.25	.11
❑ 140	Tyrone Wheatley	.25	.11
❑ 141	Napoleon Kaufman	.50	.23
❑ 142	Tim Brown	.50	.23
❑ 143	Rickey Dudley	.15	.07
❑ 144	Jon Ritchie	.15	.07
❑ 145	James Jett	.15	.07
❑ 146	Rich Gannon	.25	.11
❑ 147	Charles Woodson	.50	.23
❑ 148	Charles Johnson	.15	.07
❑ 149	Duce Staley	.50	.23
❑ 150	Will Blackwell	.15	.07
❑ 151	Kordell Stewart	.50	.23
❑ 152	Jerome Bettis	.50	.23
❑ 153	Hines Ward	.15	.07
❑ 154	Richard Huntley	.50	.23
❑ 155	Natrone Means	.25	.11
❑ 156	Mikhael Ricks	.15	.07
❑ 157	Junior Seau	.25	.11
❑ 158	Jim Harbaugh	.25	.11
❑ 159	Ryan Leaf	.50	.23
❑ 160	Erik Kramer	.15	.07
❑ 161	Terrell Owens	.50	.23
❑ 162	J.J. Stokes	.25	.11
❑ 163	Lawrence Phillips	.25	.11
❑ 164	Charlie Garner	.25	.11
❑ 165	Jerry Rice	1.25	.55
❑ 166	Garrison Hearst	.25	.11
❑ 167	Steve Young	.75	.35
❑ 168	Derrick Mayes	.25	.11
❑ 169	Ahman Green	.25	.11
❑ 170	Joey Galloway	.50	.23
❑ 171	Ricky Watters	.25	.11
❑ 172	Jon Kitna	.50	.23
❑ 173	Sean Dawkins	.15	.07
❑ 174	Az-Zahir Hakim	.15	.07
❑ 175	Robert Holcombe	.15	.07
❑ 176	Isaac Bruce	.50	.23
❑ 177	Amp Lee	.15	.07

❑ 178 Marshall Faulk .50 .23
❑ 179 Trent Green .25 .11
❑ 180 Eric Zeier .25 .11
❑ 181 Bert Emanuel .25 .11
❑ 182 Jacquez Green .25 .11
❑ 183 Reidel Anthony .25 .11
❑ 184 Warren Sapp .15 .07
❑ 185 Mike Alstott .50 .23
❑ 186 Warrick Dunn .50 .23
❑ 187 Trent Dilfer .50 .23
❑ 188 Neil O'Donnell .25 .11
❑ 189 Eddie George .60 .25
❑ 190 Yancey Thigpen .15 .07
❑ 191 Steve McNair .50 .23
❑ 192 Kevin Dyson .25 .11
❑ 193 Frank Wycheck .15 .07
❑ 194 Stephen Davis .50 .23
❑ 195 Stephen Alexander .15 .07
❑ 196 Darrell Green .15 .07
❑ 197 Skip Hicks .25 .11
❑ 198 Brad Johnson .50 .23
❑ 199 Michael Westbrook .25 .11
❑ 200 Albert Connell .15 .07
❑ 201 David Boston RC 10.00 4.50
❑ 202 Joel Makovicka RC 3.00 1.35
❑ 203 Chris Greisen RC 3.00 1.35
❑ 204 Jeff Paulk RC 2.50 1.10
❑ 205 Reginald Kelly RC 2.50 1.10
❑ 206 Chris McAlister RC 2.50 1.10
❑ 207 Brandon Stokley RC 3.00 1.35
❑ 208 Antoine Winfield RC 2.50 1.10
❑ 209 Bobby Collins RC 3.00 1.35
❑ 210 Peerless Price RC 5.00 2.20
❑ 211 Shawn Bryson RC 3.00 1.35
❑ 212 Sheldon Jackson RC 2.50 1.10
❑ 213 Kamil Loud RC 2.50 1.10
❑ 214 D'Wayne Bates RC 2.50 1.10
❑ 215 Jerry Azumah RC 2.50 1.10
❑ 216 Marty Booker RC 3.00 1.35
❑ 217 Cade McNown RC 8.00 3.60
❑ 218 James Allen RC 8.00 3.60
❑ 219 Nick Williams RC 2.50 1.10
❑ 220 Akili Smith RC 10.00 4.50
❑ 221 Craig Yeast RC 2.50 1.10
❑ 222 Damon Griffen RC 2.50 1.10
❑ 223 Scott Covington RC 3.00 1.35
❑ 224 Michael Basnight RC 2.50 1.10
❑ 225 Ronnie Powell RC 2.50 1.10
❑ 226 Rahim Abdullah RC 2.50 1.10
❑ 227 Tim Couch RC 15.00 6.75
❑ 228 Kevin Johnson RC 10.00 4.50
❑ 229 Darrin Chiaverini RC 3.00 1.35
❑ 230 Mark Campbell RC 2.50 1.10
❑ 231 Mike Lucky RC 2.50 1.10
❑ 232 Robert Thomas RC 2.50 1.10
❑ 233 Ebenezer Ekuban RC 2.50 1.10
❑ 234 Dat Nguyen RC 3.00 1.35
❑ 235 Wane McGarity RC 2.50 1.10
❑ 236 Jason Tucker RC 5.00 2.20
❑ 237 Olandis Gary RC 10.00 4.50
❑ 238 Al Wilson RC 3.00 1.35
❑ 239 Travis McGriff RC 2.50 1.10
❑ 240 Desmond Clark RC 2.50 1.10
❑ 241 Andre Cooper RC 2.50 1.10
❑ 242 Chris Watson RC 1.50 .70
❑ 243 Sedrick Irvin RC 3.00 1.35
❑ 244 Chris Claiborne RC 1.50 .70
❑ 245 Cory Sauter RC 2.50 1.10
❑ 246 Brock Olivo RC 2.50 1.10
❑ 247 De'Mond Parker RC 3.00 1.35
❑ 248 Aaron Brooks RC 20.00 9.00
❑ 249 Antuan Edwards RC 2.50 1.10
❑ 250 Basil Mitchell RC 2.50 1.10
❑ 251 Terrence Wilkins RC 12.00 5.50
❑ 252 Edgerrin James RC 30.00 13.50
❑ 253 Fernando Bryant RC 2.50 1.10
❑ 254 Mike Cloud RC 3.00 1.35
❑ 255 Larry Parker RC 2.50 1.10
❑ 256 Rob Konrad RC 3.00 1.35
❑ 257 Cecil Collins RC 3.00 1.35
❑ 258 James Johnson RC 3.00 1.35
❑ 259 Jim Kleinsasser RC 3.00 1.35
❑ 260 Daunte Culpepper RC 30.00 13.50
❑ 261 Michael Bishop RC 5.00 2.20
❑ 262 Andy Katzenmoyer RC 3.00 1.35
❑ 263 Kevin Faulk RC 6.00 2.70
❑ 264 Brett Bech RC 2.50 1.10
❑ 265 Ricky Williams RC 20.00 9.00
❑ 266 Sean Bennett RC 2.50 1.10
❑ 267 Joe Montgomery RC 3.00 1.35
❑ 268 Dan Campbell RC 1.50 .70
❑ 269 Ray Lucas RC 6.00 2.70
❑ 270 Scott Dreisbach RC 3.00 1.35
❑ 271 Jed Weaver RC 1.50 .70
❑ 272 Dameane Douglas RC 2.50 1.10
❑ 273 Cecil Martin RC 2.50 1.10
❑ 274 Donovan McNabb RC 20.00 9.00
❑ 275 Na Brown RC 3.00 1.35
❑ 276 Jerame Tuman RC 2.50 1.10
❑ 277 Amos Zereoue RC 3.00 1.35
❑ 278 Troy Edwards RC 5.00 2.20
❑ 279 Jermaine Fazande RC 3.00 1.35
❑ 280 Steve Heiden RC 1.50 .70
❑ 281 Jeff Garcia RC 20.00 9.00
❑ 282 Terry Jackson RC 2.50 1.10
❑ 283 Charlie Rogers RC 2.50 1.10
❑ 284 Brock Huard RC 6.00 2.70
❑ 285 Karsten Bailey RC 3.00 1.35
❑ 286 Lamar King RC 1.50 .70
❑ 287 Justin Watson RC 2.50 1.10
❑ 288 Kurt Warner RC 50.00 22.00
❑ 289 Torry Holt RC 12.00 5.50
❑ 290 Joe Germaine RC 3.00 1.35
❑ 291 Dre' Bly RC 2.50 1.10
❑ 292 Martin Gramatica RC 1.50 .70
❑ 293 Rabih Abdullah RC 2.50 1.10
❑ 294 Shaun King RC 10.00 4.50
❑ 295 Anthony McFarland RC 2.50 1.10
❑ 296 Darnell McDonald RC 2.50 1.10
❑ 297 Kevin Daft RC 3.00 1.35
❑ 298 Jevon Kearse RC 10.00 4.50
❑ 299 Mike Sellers .15 .07
❑ 300 Champ Bailey RC 5.00 2.20

2000 Leaf Rookies and Stars

	MINT	NRMT
COMP.SET w/o SP's (100)	15.00	6.75

❑ 1 Jake Plummer .50 .23
❑ 2 David Boston .50 .23
❑ 3 Tim Dwight .50 .23
❑ 4 Jamal Anderson .50 .23
❑ 5 Chris Chandler .25 .11
❑ 6 Tony Banks .25 .11
❑ 7 Qadry Ismail .25 .11
❑ 8 Eric Moulds .50 .23
❑ 9 Doug Flutie .60 .25
❑ 10 Lamar Smith .25 .11
❑ 11 Peerless Price .50 .23
❑ 12 Rob Johnson .25 .11
❑ 13 Reggie White .50 .23
❑ 14 Muhsin Muhammad .25 .11
❑ 15 Steve Beuerlein .25 .11
❑ 16 Cade McNown .50 .23
❑ 17 Derrick Alexander .25 .11
❑ 18 Marcus Robinson .50 .23
❑ 19 Corey Dillon .50 .23
❑ 20 Akili Smith .50 .23
❑ 21 Tim Couch 1.00 .45
❑ 22 Kevin Johnson .50 .23
❑ 23 Emmitt Smith 1.25 .55
❑ 24 Troy Aikman 1.25 .55
❑ 25 Joey Galloway .50 .23
❑ 26 Rocket Ismail .25 .11
❑ 27 John Elway 2.00 .90
❑ 28 Terrell Davis 1.25 .55
❑ 29 Brian Griese .60 .25
❑ 30 Olandis Gary .50 .23
❑ 31 Ed McCaffrey .50 .23
❑ 32 Rod Smith .25 .11
❑ 33 Barry Sanders 1.50 .70
❑ 34 Charlie Batch .50 .23
❑ 35 Germane Crowell .25 .11
❑ 36 James Stewart .25 .11
❑ 37 Brett Favre 2.00 .90
❑ 38 Dorsey Levens .25 .11
❑ 39 Antonio Freeman .50 .23
❑ 40 Peyton Manning 1.50 .70
❑ 41 Edgerrin James 1.50 .70
❑ 42 Marvin Harrison .50 .23
❑ 43 Fred Taylor .60 .25
❑ 44 Mark Brunell .75 .35
❑ 45 Jimmy Smith .25 .11
❑ 46 Elvis Grbac .25 .11
❑ 47 Tony Gonzalez .25 .11
❑ 48 Dan Marino 2.00 .90
❑ 49 Joe Horn .25 .11
❑ 50 Jay Fiedler .50 .23
❑ 51 James Allen .25 .11
❑ 52 Randy Moss 1.50 .70
❑ 53 Daunte Culpepper 1.00 .45
❑ 54 Cris Carter .50 .23
❑ 55 Robert Smith .50 .23
❑ 56 Drew Bledsoe .75 .35
❑ 57 Terry Glenn .50 .23
❑ 58 Ricky Williams 1.00 .45
❑ 59 Amani Toomer .25 .11
❑ 60 Kerry Collins .25 .11
❑ 61 Curtis Martin .50 .23
❑ 62 Vinny Testaverde .25 .11
❑ 63 Wayne Chrebet .25 .11
❑ 64 Tim Brown .50 .23
❑ 65 Tyrone Wheatley .25 .11
❑ 66 Rich Gannon .25 .11
❑ 67 Donovan McNabb .75 .35
❑ 68 Duce Staley .50 .23
❑ 69 Jerome Bettis .50 .23
❑ 70 Donald Hayes .15 .07
❑ 71 Junior Seau .25 .11
❑ 72 Jermaine Fazande .15 .07
❑ 73 Jerry Rice 1.25 .55
❑ 74 Steve Young .75 .35
❑ 75 Terrell Owens .50 .23
❑ 76 Charlie Garner .25 .11
❑ 77 Jeff Garcia .50 .23
❑ 78 Tim Biakabutuka .25 .11
❑ 79 Tiki Barber .25 .11
❑ 80 Ricky Watters .25 .11
❑ 81 Kurt Warner 2.00 .90
❑ 82 Marshall Faulk .60 .25
❑ 83 Isaac Bruce .50 .23
❑ 84 Torry Holt .50 .23
❑ 85 Mike Alstott .50 .23
❑ 86 Warrick Dunn .50 .23
❑ 87 Shaun King .75 .35
❑ 88 Keyshawn Johnson .50 .23
❑ 89 Warren Sapp .25 .11
❑ 90 Eddie George .60 .25
❑ 91 Jevon Kearse .50 .23
❑ 92 Steve McNair .50 .23
❑ 93 Carl Pickens .25 .11
❑ 94 Deion Sanders .50 .23
❑ 95 Stephen Davis .50 .23
❑ 96 Brad Johnson .50 .23
❑ 97 Bruce Smith .25 .11
❑ 98 Michael Westbrook .25 .11
❑ 99 Albert Connell .15 .07
❑ 100 Jeff George .25 .11
❑ 101 Thomas Jones RC 20.00 9.00
❑ 102 Bashir Yamini RC 10.00 4.50
❑ 103 Jamal Lewis RC 80.00 36.00
❑ 104 Travis Taylor RC 15.00 6.75
❑ 105 Chris Redman RC 25.00 11.00
❑ 106 Avion Black RC 10.00 4.50
❑ 107 Sammy Morris RC 15.00 6.75
❑ 108 Dez White RC 10.00 4.50
❑ 109 Peter Warrick RC 50.00 22.00
❑ 110 Ron Dugans RC 10.00 4.50

❑ 111 Curtis Keaton RC 10.00 4.50
❑ 112 Danny Farmer RC 12.00 5.50
❑ 113 Courtney Brown RC 15.00 6.75
❑ 114 Dennis Northcutt RC 15.00 6.75
❑ 115 Travis Prentice RC 20.00 9.00
❑ 116 JaJuan Dawson RC 12.00 5.50
❑ 117 Spergon Wynn RC 12.00 5.50
❑ 118 Michael Wiley RC 12.00 5.50
❑ 119 Chris Cole RC 10.00 4.50
❑ 120 Mike Anderson RC 80.00 36.00
❑ 121 Muneer Moore RC 6.00 2.70
❑ 122 Reuben Droughns RC 12.00 5.50
❑ 123 Bubba Franks RC 15.00 6.75
❑ 124 Anthony Lucas RC 6.00 2.70
❑ 125 Charles Lee RC 6.00 2.70
❑ 126 R.Jay Soward RC 12.00 5.50
❑ 127 Shyrone Stith RC 10.00 4.50
❑ 128 Sylvester Morris RC 25.00 11.00
❑ 129 Frank Moreau RC 12.00 5.50
❑ 130 Dante Hall RC 10.00 4.50
❑ 131 Doug Chapman RC 25.00 11.00
❑ 132 Troy Walters RC 12.00 5.50
❑ 133 J.R. Redmond RC 15.00 6.75
❑ 134 Tom Brady RC 12.00 5.50
❑ 135 Terrelle Smith RC 10.00 4.50
❑ 136 Chad Morton RC 12.00 5.50
❑ 137 Ron Dayne RC 50.00 22.00
❑ 138 Ron Dixon RC 15.00 6.75
❑ 139 Chad Pennington RC 40.00 18.00
❑ 140 Anthony Becht RC 12.00 5.50
❑ 141 Laveranues Coles RC 20.00 9.00
❑ 142 Windrell Hayes RC 10.00 4.50
❑ 143 Sebastian Janikowski RC 12.00 5.50
❑ 144 Jerry Porter RC 12.00 5.50
❑ 145 Corey Simon RC 15.00 6.75
❑ 146 Todd Pinkston RC 12.00 5.50
❑ 147 Gari Scott RC 10.00 4.50
❑ 148 Plaxico Burress RC 25.00 11.00
❑ 149 Tee Martin RC 20.00 9.00
❑ 150 Trevor Gaylor RC 10.00 4.50
❑ 151 Ronney Jenkins RC 10.00 4.50
❑ 152 Giovanni Carmazzi RC 15.00 6.75
❑ 153 Tim Rattay RC 20.00 9.00
❑ 154 Shaun Alexander RC 30.00 13.50
❑ 155 Darrell Jackson RC 15.00 6.75
❑ 156 James Williams RC 10.00 4.50
❑ 157 Trung Canidate RC 12.00 5.50
❑ 158 Joe Hamilton RC 15.00 6.75
❑ 159 Erron Kinney RC 12.00 5.50
❑ 160 Todd Husak RC 12.00 5.50
❑ 161 Raynoch Thompson RC 10.00 4.50
❑ 162 Darwin Walker RC 6.00 2.70
❑ 163 Jay Tant RC 6.00 2.70
❑ 164 Doug Johnson RC 12.00 5.50
❑ 165 Robert Bean RC 10.00 4.50
❑ 166 Mark Simoneau RC 12.00 5.50
❑ 167 John Jones RC 10.00 4.50
❑ 168 Obafemi Ayanbadejo RC 12.00 5.50
❑ 169 Mike Brown RC 12.00 5.50
❑ 170 Shockmain Davis RC 10.00 4.50
❑ 171 Erik Flowers RC 12.00 5.50
❑ 172 Corey Moore RC 10.00 4.50
❑ 173 Drew Haddad RC 6.00 2.70
❑ 174 Kwame Cavil RC 10.00 4.50
❑ 175 Pat Dennis RC 10.00 4.50
❑ 176 Rashard Anderson RC 10.00 4.50
❑ 177 Brian Finneran RC 10.00 4.50
❑ 178 Na'il Diggs RC 12.00 5.50
❑ 179 Marc Bulger RC 12.00 5.50
❑ 180 Mondriel Fulcher RC 6.00 2.70
❑ 181 Dwayne Carswell 6.00 2.70
❑ 182 Brian Urlacher RC 40.00 18.00
❑ 183 Paul Edinger RC 12.00 5.50
❑ 184 Karon Coleman RC 10.00 4.50
❑ 185 Aaron Shea RC 10.00 4.50
❑ 186 Fabien Bownes RC 10.00 4.50
❑ 187 Damon Hodge RC 10.00 4.50
❑ 188 Dwayne Goodrich RC 6.00 2.70
❑ 189 Clint Stoerner RC 25.00 11.00
❑ 190 James Whalen RC 6.00 2.70
❑ 191 Deltha O'Neal RC 10.00 4.50
❑ 192 Ian Gold RC 10.00 4.50
❑ 193 Kenoy Kennedy RC 6.00 2.70
❑ 194 Jarious Jackson RC 12.00 5.50
❑ 195 Leroy Fields RC 6.00 2.70
❑ 196 Barrett Green RC 6.00 2.70
❑ 197 Joey Jamison RC 6.00 2.70
❑ 198 Rondell Mealey RC 6.00 2.70
❑ 199 Rob Morris RC 10.00 4.50
❑ 200 Marcus Washington RC 10.00 4.50
❑ 201 Trevor Insley RC 6.00 2.70
❑ 202 Jamel White RC 12.00 5.50
❑ 203 Kevin McDougal RC 10.00 4.50
❑ 204 Ibn Green RC 6.00 2.70
❑ 205 T.J. Slaughter RC 6.00 2.70
❑ 206 Emanuel Smith RC 10.00 4.50
❑ 207 Herbert Goodman RC 10.00 4.50
❑ 208 William Bartee RC 10.00 4.50
❑ 209 Orantes Grant RC 6.00 2.70
❑ 210 Brad Hoover RC 25.00 11.00
❑ 211 Deon Dyer RC 10.00 4.50
❑ 212 Jonas Lewis RC 10.00 4.50
❑ 213 Chris Hovan RC 10.00 4.50
❑ 214 Fred Robbins RC 6.00 2.70
❑ 215 Michael Boireau RC 6.00 2.70
❑ 216 Giles Cole RC 6.00 2.70
❑ 217 Dave Stachelski RC 10.00 4.50
❑ 218 Patrick Pass RC 10.00 4.50
❑ 219 Darren Howard RC 10.00 4.50
❑ 220 Austin Wheatley RC 6.00 2.70
❑ 221 Kevin Houser RC 10.00 4.50
❑ 222 Rian Lindell RC 6.00 2.70
❑ 223 Jake Delhomme RC 12.00 5.50
❑ 224 Cornelius Griffin RC 10.00 4.50
❑ 225 Shaun Ellis RC 10.00 4.50
❑ 226 John Abraham RC 10.00 4.50
❑ 227 Travares Tillman RC 6.00 2.70
❑ 228 Julian Peterson RC 10.00 4.50
❑ 229 Marcus Knight RC 6.00 2.70
❑ 230 Thomas Hamner RC 10.00 4.50
❑ 231 Hank Poteat RC 10.00 4.50
❑ 232 Neil Rackers RC 6.00 2.70
❑ 233 Bobby Shaw RC 15.00 6.75
❑ 234 Rogers Beckett RC 10.00 4.50
❑ 235 Reggie Jones RC 12.00 5.50
❑ 236 Tim Seder RC 10.00 4.50
❑ 237 Durell Price RC 6.00 2.70
❑ 238 Ahmed Plummer RC 12.00 5.50
❑ 239 John Engelberger RC 10.00 4.50
❑ 240 Paul Smith RC 10.00 4.50
❑ 241 Chafie Fields RC 10.00 4.50
❑ 242 Kevin Feterik RC 12.00 5.50
❑ 243 Jacoby Shepherd RC 6.00 2.70
❑ 244 Nate Webster RC 6.00 2.70
❑ 245 Ketric Sanford RC 6.00 2.70
❑ 246 Tavarus Hogans RC 6.00 2.70
❑ 247 Keith Bulluck RC 10.00 4.50
❑ 248 Mike Green RC 10.00 4.50
❑ 249 Chris Coleman RC 12.00 5.50
❑ 250 Demario Brown RC 10.00 4.50
❑ 251 Billy Volek RC 10.00 4.50
❑ 252 Mareno Philyaw RC 6.00 2.70
❑ 253 Ethan Howell RC 6.00 2.70
❑ 254 Chris Samuels RC 10.00 4.50
❑ 255 Brandon Short RC 10.00 4.50
❑ 256 Maurice Smith RC 10.00 4.50
❑ 257 Frank Murphy RC 6.00 2.70
❑ 258 Darrick Vaughn RC 6.00 2.70
❑ 259 Payton Williams RC 6.00 2.70
❑ 260 JaJuan Seider RC 6.00 2.70
❑ 261 Antonio Banks EP RC 2.00 .90
❑ 262 Jonathan Brown EP RC 2.00 .90
❑ 263 Ontiwaun Carter EP RC 2.00 .90
❑ 264 Jeremaine Copeland EP 2.00 .90
❑ 265 Ralph Dawkins EP RC 3.00 1.35
❑ 266 Marques Douglas EP RC 2.00 .90
❑ 267 Kevin Drake EP RC 2.00 .90
❑ 268 Damon Dunn EP RC 3.00 1.35
❑ 269 Todd Floyd EP RC 2.00 .90
❑ 270 Tony Graziani EP 3.00 1.35
❑ 271 Derrick Ham EP RC 3.00 1.35
❑ 272 Duane Hawthorne EP RC 3.00 1.35
❑ 273 Alonzo Johnson EP RC 2.00 .90
❑ 274 Mark Kacmarynski EP RC 2.00 .90
❑ 275 Eric Kresser EP 2.00 .90
❑ 276 Jim Kubiak EP RC 3.00 1.35
❑ 277 Blaine McElmurry EP RC 2.00 .90
❑ 278 Scott Milanovich EP 3.00 1.35
❑ 279 Norman Miller EP RC 2.00 .90
❑ 280 Sean Morey EP RC 3.00 1.35
❑ 281 Jeff Ogden EP 3.00 1.35
❑ 282 Pepe Pearson EP RC 3.00 1.35
❑ 283 Ron Powlus EP RC 8.00 3.60
❑ 284 Jason Shelley EP RC 2.00 .90
❑ 285 Ben Snell EP RC 2.00 .90
❑ 286 Aaron Stecker EP RC 4.00 1.80
❑ 287 L.C. Stevens EP 2.00 .90
❑ 288 Mike Sutton EP RC 2.00 .90
❑ 289 Damian Vaughn EP RC 2.00 .90
❑ 290 Ted White EP 2.00 .90
❑ 291 Marcus Crandell EP RC 2.00 .90
❑ 292 Darryl Daniel EP RC 3.00 1.35
❑ 293 Jesse Haynes EP 2.00 .90
❑ 294 Matt Lytle EP RC 3.00 1.35
❑ 295 Deon Mitchell EP RC 3.00 1.35
❑ 296 Kendrick Nord EP RC 2.00 .90
❑ 297 Ronnie Powell EP 2.00 .90
❑ 298 Selucio Sanford EP RC 3.00 1.35
❑ 299 Corey Thomas EP 2.00 .90
❑ 300 Vershan Jackson EP RC 2.00 .90
❑ 301 First QB 125.00 55.00
❑ 302 Second QB 50.00 22.00
❑ 303 Third QB 25.00 11.00
❑ 304 Fourth QB 25.00 11.00
❑ 305 Fifth QB 25.00 11.00
❑ 306 First RB 60.00 27.00
❑ 307 Second RB 50.00 22.00
❑ 308 Third RB 30.00 13.50
❑ 309 Fourth RB 25.00 11.00
❑ 310 Fifth RB 25.00 11.00
❑ 311 First WR 30.00 13.50
❑ 312 Second WR 25.00 11.00
❑ 313 Third WR 20.00 9.00
❑ 314 Fourth WR 15.00 6.75
❑ 315 Fifth WR 12.00 5.50
❑ 316 First DEF 20.00 9.00
❑ 317 Second DEF 12.00 5.50
❑ 318 Third DEF 10.00 4.50
❑ 319 Fourth DEF 10.00 4.50
❑ 320 Fifth DEF 10.00 4.50

1995 Metal

	MINT	NRMT
COMPLETE SET (200)	20.00	9.00

❑ 1 Garrison Hearst .40 .18
❑ 2 Seth Joyner .10 .05
❑ 3 Dave Krieg .10 .05
❑ 4 Lorenzo Lynch .10 .05
❑ 5 Rob Moore .10 .05
❑ 6 Eric Swann .20 .09
❑ 7 Aeneas Williams .10 .05
❑ 8 Chris Doleman .10 .05
❑ 9 Bert Emanuel .40 .18
❑ 10 Jeff George .20 .09
❑ 11 Craig Heyward .20 .09
❑ 12 Terance Mathis .20 .09
❑ 13 Eric Metcalf .20 .09
❑ 14 Cornelius Bennett .20 .09
❑ 15 Bucky Brooks .10 .05
❑ 16 Jeff Burris .10 .05
❑ 17 Jim Kelly .40 .18
❑ 18 Andre Reed .20 .09
❑ 19 Bruce Smith .40 .18
❑ 20 Don Beebe .10 .05
❑ 21 Kerry Collins RC 1.50 .70
❑ 22 Barry Foster .20 .09
❑ 23 Lamar Lathon .10 .05
❑ 24 Sam Mills .20 .09

❑ 25 Tyrone Poole RC .20 .09
❑ 26 Frank Reich .10 .05
❑ 27 Joe Cain .10 .05
❑ 28 Curtis Conway .40 .18
❑ 29 Jeff Graham .10 .05
❑ 30 Erik Kramer .10 .05
❑ 31 Rashaan Salaam RC .40 .18
❑ 32 Lewis Tillman .10 .05
❑ 33 Chris Zorich .10 .05
❑ 34 Jeff Blake RC 1.00 .45
❑ 35 Ki-Jana Carter RC .40 .18
❑ 36 Carl Pickens .40 .18
❑ 37 Corey Sawyer .10 .05
❑ 38 Darnay Scott .40 .18
❑ 39 Dan Wilkinson .20 .09
❑ 40 Darryl Williams .10 .05
❑ 41 Derrick Alexander WR .40 .18
❑ 42 Leroy Hoard .10 .05
❑ 43 Michael Jackson .20 .09
❑ 44 Antonio Langham .10 .05
❑ 45 Andre Rison .20 .09
❑ 46 Vinny Testaverde .20 .09
❑ 47 Eric Turner .10 .05
❑ 48 Troy Aikman 1.00 .45
❑ 49 Charles Haley .20 .09
❑ 50 Michael Irvin .40 .18
❑ 51 Daryl Johnston .20 .09
❑ 52 Jay Novacek .20 .09
❑ 53 Emmitt Smith 1.50 .70
❑ 54 Kevin Williams WR .20 .09
❑ 55 Steve Atwater .10 .05
❑ 56 Rod Bernstine .10 .05
❑ 57 John Elway 2.00 .90
❑ 58 Glyn Milburn .10 .05
❑ 59 Anthony Miller .20 .09
❑ 60 Mike Pritchard .10 .05
❑ 61 Shannon Sharpe .20 .09
❑ 62 Mike Johnson .10 .05
❑ 63 Scott Mitchell .20 .09
❑ 64 Herman Moore .40 .18
❑ 65 Brett Perriman .20 .09
❑ 66 Barry Sanders 2.00 .90
❑ 67 Chris Spielman .20 .09
❑ 68 Edgar Bennett .20 .09
❑ 69 Robert Brooks .40 .18
❑ 70 Brett Favre 2.00 .90
❑ 71 LeShon Johnson .20 .09
❑ 72 George Koonce .10 .05
❑ 73 Reggie White .40 .18
❑ 74 Gary Brown .10 .05
❑ 75 Cris Dishman .10 .05
❑ 76 Mel Gray .10 .05
❑ 77 Steve McNair RC 4.00 1.80
❑ 78 Webster Slaughter .10 .05
❑ 79 Rodney Thomas RC .40 .18
❑ 80 Trev Alberts .10 .05
❑ 81 Quentin Coryatt .20 .09
❑ 82 Sean Dawkins .20 .09
❑ 83 Craig Erickson .10 .05
❑ 84 Marshall Faulk .60 .25
❑ 85 Stephen Grant RC .10 .05
❑ 86 Steve Beuerlein .10 .05
❑ 87 Tony Boselli RC .40 .18
❑ 88 Desmond Howard .20 .09
❑ 89 James O. Stewart RC 2.50 1.10
❑ 90 Marcus Allen .40 .18
❑ 91 Kimble Anders .20 .09
❑ 92 Steve Bono .20 .09
❑ 93 Lake Dawson .20 .09
❑ 94 Greg Hill .20 .09
❑ 95 Neil Smith .20 .09
❑ 96 William White .10 .05
❑ 97 Tim Bowens .10 .05
❑ 98 Bryan Cox .10 .05
❑ 99 Irving Fryar .20 .09
❑ 100 Eric Green .10 .05
❑ 101 Dan Marino 2.00 .90
❑ 102 O.J. McDuffie .40 .18
❑ 103 Bernie Parmalee .20 .09
❑ 104 Cris Carter .40 .18
❑ 105 Jack Del Rio .10 .05
❑ 106 Rocket Ismail .20 .09
❑ 107 Warren Moon .20 .09
❑ 108 Jake Reed .20 .09
❑ 109 Dewayne Washington .20 .09
❑ 110 Bruce Armstrong .10 .05
❑ 111 Drew Bledsoe 1.00 .45
❑ 112 Vincent Brisby .10 .05
❑ 113 Ben Coates .20 .09
❑ 114 Willie McGinest .20 .09
❑ 115 Dave Meggett .10 .05
❑ 116 Chris Slade .20 .09
❑ 117 Mario Bates .40 .18
❑ 118 Quinn Early .20 .09
❑ 119 Jim Everett .10 .05
❑ 120 Michael Haynes .20 .09
❑ 121 Tyrone Hughes .20 .09
❑ 122 Renaldo Turnbull .10 .05
❑ 123 Ray Zellers RC .20 .09
❑ 124 Dave Brown .20 .09
❑ 125 Chris Calloway .10 .05
❑ 126 Rodney Hampton .20 .09
❑ 127 Thomas Lewis .20 .09
❑ 128 Phillippi Sparks .10 .05
❑ 129 Tyrone Wheatley RC 1.25 .55
❑ 130 Kyle Brady RC .40 .18
❑ 131 Boomer Esiason .20 .09
❑ 132 Aaron Glenn .10 .05
❑ 133 Bobby Houston .10 .05
❑ 134 Mo Lewis .10 .05
❑ 135 Johnny Mitchell .10 .05
❑ 136 Ronald Moore .10 .05
❑ 137 Greg Biekert .10 .05
❑ 138 Tim Brown .40 .18
❑ 139 Jeff Hostetler .20 .09
❑ 140 Rocket Ismail .20 .09
❑ 141 Napoleon Kaufman RC 1.50 .70
❑ 142 Chester McGlockton .20 .09
❑ 143 Harvey Williams .10 .05
❑ 144 Fred Barnett .20 .09
❑ 145 Randall Cunningham .40 .18
❑ 146 William Fuller .10 .05
❑ 147 Charlie Garner .20 .09
❑ 148 Andy Harmon .10 .05
❑ 149 Ricky Watters .40 .18
❑ 150 Calvin Williams .20 .09
❑ 151 Kevin Greene .20 .09
❑ 152 Charles Johnson .20 .09
❑ 153 Greg Lloyd .20 .09
❑ 154 Byron Bam Morris .20 .09
❑ 155 Neil O'Donnell .20 .09
❑ 156 Darren Perry .10 .05
❑ 157 Rod Woodson .20 .09
❑ 158 Jerome Bettis .40 .18
❑ 159 Isaac Bruce .60 .25
❑ 160 Troy Drayton .10 .05
❑ 161 Sean Gilbert .20 .09
❑ 162 Todd Lyght .10 .05
❑ 163 Chris Miller .10 .05
❑ 164 Andre Coleman .10 .05
❑ 165 Stan Humphries .20 .09
❑ 166 Shawn Jefferson .10 .05
❑ 167 Natrone Means .40 .18
❑ 168 Leslie O'Neal .20 .09
❑ 169 Junior Seau .40 .18
❑ 170 Mark Seay .20 .09
❑ 171 William Floyd .40 .18
❑ 172 Merton Hanks .10 .05
❑ 173 Brent Jones .10 .05
❑ 174 Jerry Rice 1.00 .45
❑ 175 Deion Sanders UER .60 .25
(Card lists him as a linebacker)
❑ 176 J.J. Stokes RC .40 .18
❑ 177 Lee Woodall .10 .05
❑ 178 Bryant Young .20 .09
❑ 179 Steve Young .75 .35
❑ 180 Brian Blades .20 .09
❑ 181 Joey Galloway RC 3.00 1.35
❑ 182 Cortez Kennedy .20 .09
❑ 183 Kevin Mawae .10 .05
❑ 184 Rick Mirer .40 .18
❑ 185 Chris Warren .20 .09
❑ 186 Lawrence Dawsey .10 .05
❑ 187 Trent Dilfer .40 .18
❑ 188 Paul Gruber .10 .05
❑ 189 Hardy Nickerson .10 .05
❑ 190 Errict Rhett .40 .18
❑ 191 Warren Sapp RC .75 .35
❑ 192 Tom Carter .10 .05
❑ 193 Henry Ellard .20 .09
❑ 194 Darrell Green .10 .05
❑ 195 Brian Mitchell .10 .05
❑ 196 Heath Shuler .40 .18
❑ 197 Michael Westbrook RC 1.50 .70
❑ 198 Checklist 1-96 .10 .05
❑ 199 Checklist 97-200 .10 .05
❑ 200 Checklist Inserts .10 .05
❑ S1 Trent Dilfer Sample 1.00 .45

1996 Metal

	MINT	NRMT
COMPLETE SET (150)	25.00	11.00

❑ 1 Garrison Hearst .20 .09
❑ 2 Rob Moore .20 .09
❑ 3 Frank Sanders .20 .09
❑ 4 Eric Swann .10 .05
❑ 5 Jeff George .20 .09
❑ 6 Craig Heyward .10 .05
❑ 7 Terance Mathis .10 .05
❑ 8 Eric Metcalf .10 .05
❑ 9 Derrick Alexander WR .20 .09
❑ 10 Andre Rison .20 .09
❑ 11 Vinny Testaverde .20 .09
❑ 12 Eric Turner .10 .05
❑ 13 Jim Kelly .40 .18
❑ 14 Bryce Paup .10 .05
❑ 15 Bruce Smith .20 .09
❑ 16 Thurman Thomas .40 .18
❑ 17 Bob Christian .10 .05
❑ 18 Kerry Collins .40 .18
❑ 19 Lamar Lathon .10 .05
❑ 20 Tyrone Poole .10 .05
❑ 21 Curtis Conway .40 .18
❑ 22 Bryan Cox .10 .05
❑ 23 Erik Kramer .10 .05
❑ 24 Rashaan Salaam .40 .18
❑ 25 Jeff Blake .40 .18
❑ 26 Ki-Jana Carter .20 .09
❑ 27 Carl Pickens .40 .18
❑ 28 Darnay Scott .20 .09
❑ 29 Troy Aikman 1.00 .45
❑ 30 Michael Irvin .40 .18
❑ 31 Daryl Johnston .20 .09
❑ 32 Deion Sanders .60 .25
❑ 33 Emmitt Smith 1.50 .70
❑ 34 Terrell Davis 3.00 1.35
❑ 35 John Elway 2.00 .90
❑ 36 Anthony Miller .20 .09
❑ 37 Shannon Sharpe .20 .09
❑ 38 Scott Mitchell .20 .09
❑ 39 Herman Moore .40 .18
❑ 40 Brett Perriman .10 .05
❑ 41 Barry Sanders 2.00 .90
❑ 42 Edgar Bennett .20 .09
❑ 43 Robert Brooks .40 .18
❑ 44 Mark Chmura .20 .09
❑ 45 Brett Favre 2.00 .90
❑ 46 Reggie White .40 .18
❑ 47 Mel Gray .10 .05
❑ 48 Steve McNair .75 .35
❑ 49 Chris Sanders .20 .09
❑ 50 Rodney Thomas .10 .05
❑ 51 Quentin Coryatt .10 .05
❑ 52 Sean Dawkins .10 .05
❑ 53 Ken Dilger .20 .09
❑ 54 Marshall Faulk .40 .18
❑ 55 Jim Harbaugh .20 .09
❑ 56 Tony Boselli .10 .05

- ❑ 57 Mark Brunell 1.00 .45
- ❑ 58 Natrone Means .40 .18
- ❑ 59 James O.Stewart .20 .09
- ❑ 60 Marcus Allen .40 .18
- ❑ 61 Steve Bono .10 .05
- ❑ 62 Neil Smith .10 .05
- ❑ 63 Tamarick Vanover .20 .09
- ❑ 64 Eric Green .10 .05
- ❑ 65 Terry Kirby .20 .09
- ❑ 66 Dan Marino 2.00 .90
- ❑ 67 O.J. McDuffie .20 .09
- ❑ 68 Cris Carter .40 .18
- ❑ 69 Qadry Ismail .10 .05
- ❑ 70 Warren Moon .20 .09
- ❑ 71 Jake Reed .20 .09
- ❑ 72 Drew Bledsoe 1.00 .45
- ❑ 73 Ben Coates .20 .09
- ❑ 74 Curtis Martin .75 .35
- ❑ 75 Dave Meggett .10 .05
- ❑ 76 Mario Bates .20 .09
- ❑ 77 Jim Everett .10 .05
- ❑ 78 Michael Haynes .10 .05
- ❑ 79 Tyrone Hughes .10 .05
- ❑ 80 Dave Brown .10 .05
- ❑ 81 Rodney Hampton .20 .09
- ❑ 82 Thomas Lewis .10 .05
- ❑ 83 Tyrone Wheatley .20 .09
- ❑ 84 Kyle Brady .10 .05
- ❑ 85 Hugh Douglas .20 .09
- ❑ 86 Adrian Murrell .40 .18
- ❑ 87 Neil O'Donnell .20 .09
- ❑ 88 Tim Brown .40 .18
- ❑ 89 Jeff Hostetler .10 .05
- ❑ 90 Napoleon Kaufman .40 .18
- ❑ 91 Harvey Williams .10 .05
- ❑ 92 Charlie Garner .10 .05
- ❑ 93 Rodney Peete .10 .05
- ❑ 94 Ricky Watters .20 .09
- ❑ 95 Calvin Williams .10 .05
- ❑ 96 Jerome Bettis .40 .18
- ❑ 97 Greg Lloyd .20 .09
- ❑ 98 Kordell Stewart .60 .25
- ❑ 99 Yancey Thigpen .20 .09
- ❑ 100 Rod Woodson .20 .09
- ❑ 101 Isaac Bruce .40 .18
- ❑ 102 Kevin Carter .10 .05
- ❑ 103 Steve Walsh .10 .05
- ❑ 104 Aaron Hayden .10 .05
- ❑ 105 Stan Humphries .20 .09
- ❑ 106 Junior Seau .20 .09
- ❑ 107 William Floyd .20 .09
- ❑ 108 Brent Jones .10 .05
- ❑ 109 Jerry Rice 1.00 .45
- ❑ 110 J.J. Stokes .40 .18
- ❑ 111 Steve Young .75 .35
- ❑ 112 Brian Blades .10 .05
- ❑ 113 Joey Galloway .60 .25
- ❑ 114 Rick Mirer .20 .09
- ❑ 115 Chris Warren .20 .09
- ❑ 116 Trent Dilfer .40 .18
- ❑ 117 Alvin Harper .10 .05
- ❑ 118 Hardy Nickerson .10 .05
- ❑ 119 Errict Rhett .20 .09
- ❑ 120 Terry Allen .20 .09
- ❑ 121 Brian Mitchell .10 .05
- ❑ 122 Heath Shuler .20 .09
- ❑ 123 Michael Westbrook .40 .18
- ❑ 124 Karim Abdul-Jabbar RC .60 .25
- ❑ 125 Tim Biakabutuka RC .75 .35
- ❑ 126 Duane Clemons RC .10 .05
- ❑ 127 Stephen Davis RC 4.00 1.80
- ❑ 128 Rickey Dudley RC .40 .18
- ❑ 129 Bobby Engram RC .40 .18
- ❑ 130 Daryl Gardener RC .10 .05
- ❑ 131 Eddie George RC 4.00 1.80
- ❑ 132 Terry Glenn RC 1.25 .55
- ❑ 133 Kevin Hardy RC .40 .18
- ❑ 134 Walt Harris RC .10 .05
- ❑ 135 Marvin Harrison RC 2.50 1.10
- ❑ 136 Keyshawn Johnson RC 2.00 .90
- ❑ 137 Cedric Jones RC .10 .05
- ❑ 138 Eddie Kennison RC .40 .18
- ❑ 139 Sam Manuel RC .10 .05
  Sean Manuel RC
- ❑ 140 Leeland McElroy RC .40 .18
- ❑ 141 Ray Mickens RC .10 .05
- ❑ 142 Jonathan Ogden RC .10 .05
- ❑ 143 Lawrence Phillips RC .40 .18
- ❑ 144 Kavika Pittman RC .10 .05
- ❑ 145 Simeon Rice RC .40 .18
- ❑ 146 Regan Upshaw RC .10 .05
- ❑ 147 Alex Van Dyke RC .20 .09
- ❑ 148 Stepfret Williams RC .20 .09
- ❑ 149 Checklist .10 .05
- ❑ 150 Checklist .10 .05
- ❑ P1 Promo Sheet 2.50 1.10
  Brett Favre
  Trent Dilfer
  Dave Meggett

1997 Metal Universe

	MINT	NRMT
COMPLETE SET (200)	20.00	9.00

- ❑ 1 Terry Glenn .40 .18
- ❑ 2 Terry Kirby .20 .09
- ❑ 3 Thomas Lewis .10 .05
- ❑ 4 Tim Biakabutuka .20 .09
- ❑ 5 Tim Brown .40 .18
- ❑ 6 Todd Collins .10 .05
- ❑ 7 Tony Banks .20 .09
- ❑ 8 Tony Brackens .10 .05
- ❑ 9 Tony Martin .20 .09
- ❑ 10 Trent Dilfer .40 .18
- ❑ 11 Troy Aikman 1.00 .45
- ❑ 12 Ty Detmer .20 .09
- ❑ 13 Tyrone Wheatley .20 .09
- ❑ 14 Vinny Testaverde .20 .09
- ❑ 15 Wayne Chrebet .40 .18
- ❑ 16 Wesley Walls .20 .09
- ❑ 17 William Floyd .20 .09
- ❑ 18 Willie McGinest .10 .05
- ❑ 19 Yancey Thigpen .20 .09
- ❑ 20 Zach Thomas .20 .09
- ❑ 21 Terry Allen .40 .18
- ❑ 22 Terrell Owens .40 .18
- ❑ 23 Terrell Davis 1.50 .70
- ❑ 24 Terance Mathis .20 .09
- ❑ 25 Ted Johnson .10 .05
- ❑ 26 Tamarick Vanover .20 .09
- ❑ 27 Steve Young .75 .35
- ❑ 28 Steve McNair .75 .35
- ❑ 29 Stan Humphries .20 .09
- ❑ 30 Simeon Rice .20 .09
- ❑ 31 Shannon Sharpe .20 .09
- ❑ 32 Sean Jones .10 .05
- ❑ 33 Scott Mitchell .20 .09
- ❑ 34 Sam Mills .10 .05
- ❑ 35 Rodney Hampton .20 .09
- ❑ 36 Rod Woodson .20 .09
- ❑ 37 Robert Smith .20 .09
- ❑ 38 Rob Moore .20 .09
- ❑ 39 Ricky Watters .20 .09
- ❑ 40 Rickey Dudley .20 .09
- ❑ 41 Rick Mirer .10 .05
- ❑ 42 Reggie White .40 .18
- ❑ 43 Ray Zellars .10 .05
- ❑ 44 Ray Lewis .50 .23
- ❑ 45 Rashaan Salaam .10 .05
- ❑ 46 Quentin Coryatt .10 .05
- ❑ 47 Qadry Ismail .20 .09
- ❑ 48 O.J. McDuffie .20 .09
- ❑ 49 Nilo Silvan .10 .05
- ❑ 50 Neil Smith .20 .09
- ❑ 51 Neil O'Donnell .20 .09
- ❑ 52 Natrone Means .40 .18
- ❑ 53 Napoleon Kaufman .40 .18
- ❑ 54 Mike Tomczak .10 .05
- ❑ 55 Mike Alstott .40 .18
- ❑ 56 Michael Westbrook .20 .09
- ❑ 57 Michael Jackson .20 .09
- ❑ 58 Michael Irvin .40 .18
- ❑ 59 Michael Haynes .10 .05
- ❑ 60 Michael Bates .10 .05
- ❑ 61 Mel Gray .10 .05
- ❑ 62 Marvin Harrison .40 .18
- ❑ 63 Marshall Faulk .40 .18
- ❑ 64 Mark Brunell 1.00 .45
- ❑ 65 Mario Bates .10 .05
- ❑ 66 Marcus Allen .40 .18
- ❑ 67 Lorenzo Neal .10 .05
- ❑ 68 Levon Kirkland .10 .05
- ❑ 69 Leonard Russell .10 .05
- ❑ 70 Leeland McElroy .10 .05
- ❑ 71 Lawyer Milloy .10 .05
- ❑ 72 Lawrence Phillips .10 .05
- ❑ 73 Larry Centers .20 .09
- ❑ 74 Lamar Lathon .10 .05
- ❑ 75 Kordell Stewart .60 .25
- ❑ 76 Kimble Anders .20 .09
- ❑ 77 Ki-Jana Carter .10 .05
- ❑ 78 Keyshawn Johnson .40 .18
- ❑ 79 Kevin Turner .10 .05
- ❑ 80 Jermaine Lewis .40 .18
- ❑ 81 Jerome Bettis .40 .18
- ❑ 82 Jerris McPhail .10 .05
- ❑ 83 Joey Galloway .60 .25
- ❑ 84 Jerry Rice 1.00 .45
- ❑ 85 Jim Everett .10 .05
- ❑ 86 Jimmy Smith .20 .09
- ❑ 87 Jim Harbaugh .20 .09
- ❑ 88 John Elway 2.00 .90
- ❑ 89 John Friesz .10 .05
- ❑ 90 John Mobley .10 .05
- ❑ 91 Johnnie Morton .20 .09
- ❑ 92 Junior Seau .20 .09
- ❑ 93 Karim Abdul-Jabbar .40 .18
- ❑ 94 Keenan McCardell .20 .09
- ❑ 95 Ken Dilger .10 .05
- ❑ 96 Ken Norton .10 .05
- ❑ 97 Kent Graham .10 .05
- ❑ 98 Kerry Collins .20 .09
- ❑ 99 Kevin Greene .20 .09
- ❑ 100 Kevin Hardy .10 .05
- ❑ 101 Jeff Lewis .10 .05
- ❑ 102 Jeff George .20 .09
- ❑ 103 Jeff Graham .10 .05
- ❑ 104 Jeff Blake .20 .09
- ❑ 105 Jason Sehorn .20 .09
- ❑ 106 Jason Dunn .10 .05
- ❑ 107 Jamie Asher .10 .05
- ❑ 108 Jamal Anderson .75 .35
- ❑ 109 Jake Reed .20 .09
- ❑ 110 Isaac Bruce .40 .18
- ❑ 111 Irving Fryar .20 .09
- ❑ 112 Iheanyi Uwaezuoke .20 .09
- ❑ 113 Hugh Douglas .10 .05
- ❑ 114 Herman Moore .40 .18
- ❑ 115 Harvey Williams .10 .05
- ❑ 116 Hardy Nickerson .10 .05
- ❑ 117 Gus Frerotte .10 .05
- ❑ 118 Greg Hill .10 .05
- ❑ 119 Glyn Milburn .10 .05
- ❑ 120 Frank Wycheck .10 .05
- ❑ 121 Frank Sanders .20 .09
- ❑ 122 Errict Rhett .10 .05
- ❑ 123 Erik Kramer .10 .05
- ❑ 124 Eric Moulds .40 .18
- ❑ 125 Eric Metcalf .20 .09
- ❑ 126 Emmitt Smith 1.50 .70
- ❑ 127 Edgar Bennett .20 .09
- ❑ 128 Eddie Kennison .20 .09
- ❑ 129 Eddie George 1.00 .45
- ❑ 130 Drew Bledsoe 1.00 .45
- ❑ 131 Dorsey Levens .40 .18
- ❑ 132 Desmond Howard .20 .09
- ❑ 133 Derrick Thomas .20 .09
- ❑ 134 Derrick Alexander WR .20 .09
- ❑ 135 Deion Sanders .40 .18

❑ 136 Dave Brown	.10	.05
❑ 137 Daryl Johnston	.20	.09
❑ 138 Darnay Scott	.20	.09
❑ 139 Darick Holmes	.10	.05
❑ 140 Dan Marino	2.00	.90
❑ 141 Curtis Martin	.75	.35
❑ 142 Curtis Conway	.20	.09
❑ 143 Cris Carter	.40	.18
❑ 144 Chris Warren	.20	.09
❑ 145 Chris T. Jones	.10	.05
❑ 146 Chris Slade	.10	.05
❑ 147 Chris Sanders	.10	.05
❑ 148 Chester McGlockton	.10	.05
❑ 149 Charlie Jones	.20	.09
❑ 150 Charles Way	.20	.09
❑ 151 Carl Pickens	.40	.18
❑ 152 Bryan Still	.10	.05
❑ 153 Bruce Smith	.20	.09
❑ 154 Brian Mitchell	.10	.05
❑ 155 Brett Perriman	.10	.05
❑ 156 Brett Favre	2.00	.90
❑ 157 Brad Johnson	.60	.25
❑ 158 Thurman Thomas	.40	.18
❑ 159 Bobby Engram	.20	.09
❑ 160 Bert Emanuel	.20	.09
❑ 161 Ben Coates	.20	.09
❑ 162 Barry Sanders	2.00	.90
❑ 163 Byron Bam Morris	.10	.05
❑ 164 Ashley Ambrose	.10	.05
❑ 165 Antonio Freeman	.75	.35
❑ 166 Anthony Miller	.10	.05
❑ 167 Anthony Johnson	.10	.05
❑ 168 Andre Rison	.20	.09
❑ 169 Andre Reed	.20	.09
❑ 170 Alex Molden	.10	.05
❑ 171 Aeneas Williams	.10	.05
❑ 172 Adrian Murrell	.20	.09
❑ 173 Aaron Hayden	.10	.05
❑ 174 Darnell Autry RC	.20	.09
❑ 175 Orlando Pace RC	.40	.18
❑ 176 Darrell Russell RC	.10	.05
❑ 177 Peter Boulware RC	.20	.09
❑ 178 Shawn Springs RC	.20	.09
❑ 179 Bryant Westbrook RC	.10	.05
❑ 180 Dwayne Rudd RC	.40	.18
❑ 181 Rae Carruth RC	.40	.18
❑ 182 Troy Davis RC	.40	.18
❑ 183 Antowain Smith RC	1.50	.70
❑ 184 James Farrior RC	.10	.05
❑ 185 Walter Jones RC	.10	.05
❑ 186 Sam Madison RC	.40	.18
❑ 187 Tom Knight RC	.10	.05
❑ 188 Reidel Anthony RC	1.00	.45
❑ 189 Warrick Dunn RC	2.00	.90
❑ 190 Reinard Wilson RC	.10	.05
❑ 191 Tyrus McCloud RC	.10	.05
❑ 192 Michael Booker RC	.10	.05
❑ 193 Tony Gonzalez RC	2.00	.90
❑ 194 Pat Barnes RC	.40	.18
❑ 195 Tiki Barber RC	2.00	.90
❑ 196 Sedrick Shaw RC	.40	.18
❑ 197 Corey Dillon RC	4.00	1.80
❑ 198 Danny Wuerffel RC	1.00	.45
❑ 199 Checklist (1-152)	.10	.05
❑ 200 Checklist 153-200/inserts	.10	.05
❑ S1 Terrell Davis Sample	2.00	.90

1998 Metal Universe

	MINT	NRMT
COMPLETE SET (200)	40.00	18.00
❑ 1 Jerry Rice	1.00	.45
❑ 2 Muhsin Muhammad	.20	.09
❑ 3 Ed McCaffrey	.20	.09
❑ 4 Brett Favre	2.00	.90
❑ 5 Troy Brown	.10	.05
❑ 6 Brad Johnson	.40	.18
❑ 7 John Elway	2.00	.90
❑ 8 Herman Moore	.40	.18
❑ 9 O.J. McDuffie	.20	.09
❑ 10 Tim Brown	.40	.18
❑ 11 Byron Hanspard	.20	.09
❑ 12 Rae Carruth	.20	.09
❑ 13 Rod Smith WR	.20	.09

❑ 14 John Randle	.20	.09
❑ 15 Karim Abdul-Jabbar	.40	.18
❑ 16 Bobby Hoying	.20	.09
❑ 17 Steve Young	.50	.23
❑ 18 Andre Hastings	.10	.05
❑ 19 Chidi Ahanotu	.10	.05
❑ 20 Barry Sanders	2.00	.90
❑ 21 Bruce Smith	.20	.09
❑ 22 Kimble Anders	.20	.09
❑ 23 Troy Davis	.10	.05
❑ 24 Jamal Anderson	.40	.18
❑ 25 Curtis Conway	.20	.09
❑ 26 Mark Chmura	.20	.09
❑ 27 Reggie White	.40	.18
❑ 28 Jake Reed	.20	.09
❑ 29 Willie McGinest	.10	.05
❑ 30 Terrell Davis	1.50	.70
❑ 31 Joey Galloway	.40	.18
❑ 32 Leslie Shepherd	.10	.05
❑ 33 Peter Boulware	.10	.05
❑ 34 Chad Lewis	.10	.05
❑ 35 Marcus Allen	.40	.18
❑ 36 Randal Hill	.10	.05
❑ 37 Jerome Bettis	.40	.18
❑ 38 William Floyd	.10	.05
❑ 39 Warren Moon	.40	.18
❑ 40 Mike Alstott	.40	.18
❑ 41 Jay Graham	.10	.05
❑ 42 Emmitt Smith	1.50	.70
❑ 43 James O. Stewart	.20	.09
❑ 44 Charlie Garner	.10	.05
❑ 45 Merton Hanks	.10	.05
❑ 46 Shawn Springs	.10	.05
❑ 47 Chris Calloway	.10	.05
❑ 48 Larry Centers	.10	.05
❑ 49 Michael Jackson	.10	.05
❑ 50 Deion Sanders	.40	.18
❑ 51 Jimmy Smith	.20	.09
❑ 52 Jason Sehorn	.20	.09
❑ 53 Charles Johnson	.10	.05
❑ 54 Garrison Hearst	.40	.18
❑ 55 Chris Warren	.20	.09
❑ 56 Warren Sapp	.20	.09
❑ 57 Corey Dillon	.50	.23
❑ 58 Marvin Harrison	.20	.09
❑ 59 Chris Sanders	.10	.05
❑ 60 Jamie Asher	.10	.05
❑ 61 Yancey Thigpen	.10	.05
❑ 62 Freddie Jones	.10	.05
❑ 63 Rob Moore	.20	.09
❑ 64 Jermaine Lewis	.20	.09
❑ 65 Michael Irvin	.40	.18
❑ 66 Natrone Means	.40	.18
❑ 67 Charles Way	.10	.05
❑ 68 Terry Kirby	.10	.05
❑ 69 Tony Banks	.20	.09
❑ 70 Steve McNair	.40	.18
❑ 71 Vinny Testaverde	.20	.09
❑ 72 Dexter Coakley	.10	.05
❑ 73 Keenan McCardell	.20	.09
❑ 74 Glenn Foley	.20	.09
❑ 75 Isaac Bruce	.40	.18
❑ 76 Terry Allen	.40	.18
❑ 77 Todd Collins	.10	.05
❑ 78 Troy Aikman	1.00	.45
❑ 79 Damon Jones	.10	.05
❑ 80 Leon Johnson	.10	.05
❑ 81 James Jett	.20	.09
❑ 82 Frank Wycheck	.10	.05
❑ 83 Andre Reed	.20	.09
❑ 84 Derrick Alexander WR	.20	.09
❑ 85 Jason Taylor	.10	.05
❑ 86 Wayne Chrebet	.40	.18
❑ 87 Napoleon Kaufman	.40	.18
❑ 88 Eddie George	.75	.35
❑ 89 Ernie Conwell	.10	.05
❑ 90 Antowain Smith	.40	.18
❑ 91 Johnnie Morton	.20	.09
❑ 92 Jerris McPhail	.10	.05
❑ 93 Cris Carter	.40	.18
❑ 94 Danny Kanell	.20	.09
❑ 95 Stan Humphries	.10	.05
❑ 96 Terrell Owens	.40	.18
❑ 97 Willie Davis	.10	.05
❑ 98 David Dunn	.10	.05
❑ 99 Tony Brackens	.10	.05
❑ 100 Kordell Stewart	.40	.18
❑ 101 Rodney Thomas	.10	.05
❑ 102 Keyshawn Johnson	.40	.18
❑ 103 Carl Pickens	.40	.18
❑ 104 Mark Brunell	.75	.35
❑ 105 Jeff George	.20	.09
❑ 106 Bert Emanuel	.20	.09
❑ 107 Wesley Walls	.20	.09
❑ 108 Bryant Westbrook	.10	.05
❑ 109 Dorsey Levens	.40	.18
❑ 110 Drew Bledsoe	.75	.35
❑ 111 Adrian Murrell	.20	.09
❑ 112 Aeneas Williams	.10	.05
❑ 113 Raymont Harris	.10	.05
❑ 114 Tony Gonzalez	.10	.05
❑ 115 Sean Dawkins	.10	.05
❑ 116 Billy Joe Hobert	.10	.05
❑ 117 James McKnight	.10	.05
❑ 118 Reidel Anthony	.20	.09
❑ 119 Terance Mathis	.20	.09
❑ 120 Darrien Gordon	.10	.05
❑ 121 Dale Carter	.10	.05
❑ 122 Duce Staley	.75	.35
❑ 123 Jerald Moore	.10	.05
❑ 124 Eric Swann	.10	.05
❑ 125 Antonio Freeman	.40	.18
❑ 126 Chris Penn	.10	.05
❑ 127 Ken Dilger	.10	.05
❑ 128 Robert Smith	.40	.18
❑ 129 Tiki Barber	.20	.09
❑ 130 Mark Bruener	.10	.05
❑ 131 Junior Seau	.20	.09
❑ 132 Trent Dilfer	.40	.18
❑ 133 Gus Frerotte	.10	.05
❑ 134 Jake Plummer	.75	.35
❑ 135 Jeff Blake	.20	.09
❑ 136 Jim Harbaugh	.20	.09
❑ 137 Michael Strahan	.10	.05
❑ 138 Gary Brown	.10	.05
❑ 139 Tony Martin	.20	.09
❑ 140 Stephen Davis	.10	.05
❑ 141 Thurman Thomas	.40	.18
❑ 142 Scott Mitchell	.20	.09
❑ 143 Dan Marino	2.00	.90
❑ 144 David Palmer	.10	.05
❑ 145 J.J. Stokes	.20	.09
❑ 146 Chris Chandler	.20	.09
❑ 147 Darnell Autry	.10	.05
❑ 148 Robert Brooks	.20	.09
❑ 149 Derrick Mayes	.20	.09
❑ 150 Curtis Martin	.40	.18
❑ 151 Steve Broussard	.10	.05
❑ 152 Eddie Kennison UER ('97 stats incorrect)	.20	.09
❑ 153 Kerry Collins	.20	.09
❑ 154 Shannon Sharpe	.20	.09
❑ 155 Andre Rison	.20	.09
❑ 156 Dwayne Rudd	.10	.05
❑ 157 Orlando Pace	.10	.05
❑ 158 Terry Glenn	.40	.18
❑ 159 Frank Sanders	.20	.09
❑ 160 Ricky Proehl	.10	.05
❑ 161 Marshall Faulk	.40	.18
❑ 162 Irving Fryar	.20	.09
❑ 163 Courtney Hawkins	.10	.05
❑ 164 Eric Metcalf	.10	.05
❑ 165 Warrick Dunn	.40	.18

❑ 166 Cris Dishman .10 .05
❑ 167 Fred Lane .20 .09
❑ 168 John Mobley .10 .05
❑ 169 Elvis Grbac .20 .09
❑ 170 Ben Coates .20 .09
❑ 171 Rickey Dudley .10 .05
❑ 172 Ricky Watters .20 .09
❑ 173 Alonzo Mayes RC .75 .35
❑ 174 Andre Wadsworth RC .. 1.50 .70
❑ 175 Brian Simmons RC .75 .35
❑ 176 Charles Woodson RC .. 2.00 .90
❑ 177 Curtis Enis RC 1.50 .70
❑ 178 Fred Taylor RC 3.00 1.35
❑ 179 Germane Crowell RC .. 2.50 1.10
❑ 180 Greg Ellis RC .75 .35
❑ 181 Jacquez Green RC 2.00 .90
❑ 182 Jason Peter RC .75 .35
❑ 183 John Dutton RC .75 .35
❑ 184 Kevin Dyson RC 2.00 .90
❑ 185 Kivuusama Mays RC .75 .35
❑ 186 Marcus Nash RC 1.50 .70
❑ 187 Michael Myers RC .75 .35
❑ 188 Ahman Green RC 2.50 1.10
❑ 189 Peyton Manning RC .. 10.00 4.50
❑ 190 Randy Moss RC 10.00 4.50
❑ 191 Robert Edwards RC 2.00 .90
❑ 192 Robert Holcombe RC .. 1.50 .70
❑ 193 Ryan Leaf RC 2.50 1.10
❑ 194 Takeo Spikes RC 1.50 .70
❑ 195 Tavian Banks RC 1.50 .70
❑ 196 Tim Dwight RC 2.00 .90
❑ 197 Vonnie Holliday RC 1.50 .70
❑ 198 Dorsey Levens CL .20 .09
❑ 199 Jerry Rice CL .40 .18
❑ 200 Dan Marino CL .75 .35

1999 Metal Universe

	MINT	NRMT
COMPLETE SET (250)	40.00	18.00

❑ 1 Eric Moulds .40 .18
❑ 2 David Palmer .10 .05
❑ 3 Ricky Watters .20 .09
❑ 4 Antonio Freeman .40 .18
❑ 5 Hugh Douglas .10 .05
❑ 6 Johnnie Morton .20 .09
❑ 7 Corey Fuller .10 .05
❑ 8 J.J. Stokes .20 .09
❑ 9 Keith Poole .10 .05
❑ 10 Steve Beuerlein .10 .05
❑ 11 Keenan McCardell .20 .09
❑ 12 Carl Pickens .20 .09
❑ 13 Mark Bruener .10 .05
❑ 14 Warren Sapp .20 .09
❑ 15 Rich Gannon .20 .09
❑ 16 Bruce Smith .20 .09
❑ 17 Mark Chmura .10 .05
❑ 18 Drew Bledsoe .60 .25
❑ 19 Charles Woodson .40 .18
❑ 20 Ahman Green .20 .09
❑ 21 Ricky Proehl .10 .05
❑ 22 Corey Dillon .40 .18
❑ 23 Terry Fair .10 .05
❑ 24 Mark Brunell .60 .25
❑ 25 Leroy Hoard .10 .05
❑ 26 La'Roi Glover .10 .05
❑ 27 Tim Brown .40 .18
❑ 28 Kevin Turner .10 .05
❑ 29 Terrell Owens .40 .18
❑ 30 Mike Alstott .40 .18
❑ 31 Rob Moore .20 .09
❑ 32 Troy Aikman 1.00 .45
❑ 33 Derrick Alexander .10 .05
❑ 34 Chris Calloway .10 .05
❑ 35 Kordell Stewart .40 .18
❑ 36 Reidel Anthony .20 .09
❑ 37 Michael Westbrook .20 .09
❑ 38 Ray Lewis .20 .09
❑ 39 Alonzo Mayes .10 .05
❑ 40 Rod Smith .20 .09
❑ 41 Reggie Barlow .10 .05
❑ 42 Sean Dawkins .10 .05
❑ 43 Duce Staley .40 .18
❑ 44 R.W. McQuarters .10 .05
❑ 45 Robert Holcombe .20 .09
❑ 46 Priest Holmes .40 .18
❑ 47 Erik Kramer .10 .05
❑ 48 Shannon Sharpe .20 .09
❑ 49 Mike Vanderjagt .10 .05
❑ 50 Cris Carter .40 .18
❑ 51 Billy Joe Tolliver .10 .05
❑ 52 Vinny Testaverde .20 .09
❑ 53 Antonio Langham .10 .05
❑ 54 Damon Gibson .10 .05
❑ 55 Garrison Hearst .20 .09
❑ 56 Brad Johnson .40 .18
❑ 57 Randall Cunningham .40 .18
❑ 58 Jim Harbaugh .20 .09
❑ 59 Curtis Enis .40 .18
❑ 60 Bill Romanowski .10 .05
❑ 61 Marcus Pollard .10 .05
❑ 62 Zach Thomas .20 .09
❑ 63 Cameron Cleeland .10 .05
❑ 64 Curtis Martin .40 .18
❑ 65 Charlie Garner .20 .09
❑ 66 Jerris McPhail .10 .05
❑ 67 Jon Kitna .40 .18
❑ 68 Chris Chandler .20 .09
❑ 69 Emmitt Smith 1.00 .45
❑ 70 Andre Rison .20 .09
❑ 71 Wayne Chrebet .20 .09
❑ 72 Mikhael Ricks .10 .05
❑ 73 Yancey Thigpen .10 .05
❑ 74 Peter Boulware .10 .05
❑ 75 Bobby Engram .20 .09
❑ 76 John Mobley .10 .05
❑ 77 Peyton Manning 1.50 .70
❑ 78 O.J. McDuffie .20 .09
❑ 79 Tony Simmons .10 .05
❑ 80 Mo Lewis .10 .05
❑ 81 Bryan Still .10 .05
❑ 82 Eugene Robinson .10 .05
❑ 83 Curtis Conway .20 .09
❑ 84 Ed McCaffrey .20 .09
❑ 85 Marvin Harrison .40 .18
❑ 86 Dan Marino 1.50 .70
❑ 87 Ty Law .10 .05
❑ 88 Leon Johnson .10 .05
❑ 89 Junior Seau .20 .09
❑ 90 Terance Mathis .20 .09
❑ 91 Wesley Walls .20 .09
❑ 92 John Elway 1.50 .70
❑ 93 Marshall Faulk .40 .18
❑ 94 Oronde Gadsden .10 .05
❑ 95 Keyshawn Johnson .40 .18
❑ 96 Muhsin Muhammad .20 .09
❑ 97 Dorsey Levens .40 .18
❑ 98 Shawn Jefferson .10 .05
❑ 99 Rocket Ismail .20 .09
❑ 100 Vonnie Holliday .10 .05
❑ 101 Terry Glenn .40 .18
❑ 102 Shawn Springs .10 .05
❑ 103 Tim Dwight .40 .18
❑ 104 Terrell Davis 1.00 .45
❑ 105 Karim Abdul-Jabbar .20 .09
❑ 106 Bryan Cox .10 .05
❑ 107 Steve McNair .40 .18
❑ 108 Tony Martin .20 .09
❑ 109 Jason Elam .10 .05
❑ 110 John Avery .20 .09
❑ 111 Aaron Glenn .10 .05
❑ 112 Eddie George .50 .23
❑ 113 Larry Centers .10 .05
❑ 114 Darnay Scott .10 .05
❑ 115 Jimmy Smith .20 .09
❑ 116 Tiki Barber .10 .05
❑ 117 Charles Johnson .10 .05
❑ 118 Mike Archie RC .20 .09
❑ 119 Adrian Murrell .20 .09
❑ 120 Dexter Coakley .10 .05
❑ 121 Dale Carter .10 .05
❑ 122 Kent Graham .10 .05
❑ 123 Hines Ward .10 .05
❑ 124 Greg Hill .10 .05
❑ 125 Skip Hicks .20 .09
❑ 126 Doug Flutie .50 .23
❑ 127 Leslie Shepherd .10 .05
❑ 128 Neil O'Donnell .20 .09
❑ 129 Herman Moore .40 .18
❑ 130 Kevin Hardy .10 .05
❑ 131 Randy Moss 1.50 .70
❑ 132 Andre Hastings .10 .05
❑ 133 Rickey Dudley .10 .05
❑ 134 Jerome Bettis .40 .18
❑ 135 Jerry Rice 1.00 .45
❑ 136 Jake Plummer .75 .35
❑ 137 Billy Davis .10 .05
❑ 138 Tony Gonzalez .20 .09
❑ 139 Ike Hilliard .10 .05
❑ 140 Freddie Jones .10 .05
❑ 141 Isaac Bruce .40 .18
❑ 142 Darrell Green .10 .05
❑ 143 Trent Green .20 .09
❑ 144 Jamal Anderson .40 .18
❑ 145 Deion Sanders .40 .18
❑ 146 Byron Bam Morris .10 .05
❑ 147 Charles Way .10 .05
❑ 148 Natrone Means .20 .09
❑ 149 Frank Wycheck .10 .05
❑ 150 Brett Favre 1.50 .70
❑ 151 Michael Bates .10 .05
❑ 152 Ben Coates .20 .09
❑ 153 Koy Detmer .10 .05
❑ 154 Eddie Kennison .20 .09
❑ 155 Eric Metcalf .10 .05
❑ 156 Takeo Spikes .10 .05
❑ 157 Fred Taylor 1.00 .45
❑ 158 Gary Brown .10 .05
❑ 159 Levon Kirkland .10 .05
❑ 160 Trent Dilfer .20 .09
❑ 161 Antowain Smith .40 .18
❑ 162 Robert Brooks .20 .09
❑ 163 Robert Smith .40 .18
❑ 164 Napoleon Kaufman .40 .18
❑ 165 Chad Brown .10 .05
❑ 166 Warrick Dunn .40 .18
❑ 167 Joey Galloway .40 .18
❑ 168 Frank Sanders .20 .09
❑ 169 Michael Irvin .20 .09
❑ 170 Elvis Grbac .20 .09
❑ 171 Michael Strahan .10 .05
❑ 172 Ryan Leaf .40 .18
❑ 173 Stephen Alexander .10 .05
❑ 174 Andre Reed .20 .09
❑ 175 Barry Sanders 1.50 .70
❑ 176 Jake Reed .20 .09
❑ 177 James Jett .20 .09
❑ 178 Steve Young .60 .25
❑ 179 Jermaine Lewis .20 .09
❑ 180 Charlie Batch .75 .35
❑ 181 Jacquez Green .20 .09
❑ 182 Kevin Dyson .20 .09
❑ 183 Roell Preston PD .10 .05
❑ 184 Randall Cunningham PD .40 .18
❑ 185 Charlie Batch PD .40 .18
❑ 186 Kordell Stewart PD .40 .18
❑ 187 Bennie Thompson PD .10 .05
❑ 188 Deion Sanders PD .40 .18
❑ 189 Jake Plummer PD .50 .23
❑ 190 Eric Moulds PD .40 .18
❑ 191 Derrick Brooks PD .10 .05
❑ 192 Steve McNair PD .40 .18
❑ 193 Ryan Leaf PD .20 .09
❑ 194 Keyshawn Johnson PD .. .40 .18
❑ 195 Eddie George PD .40 .18
❑ 196 Warrick Dunn PD .40 .18
❑ 197 Jessie Tuggle PD .10 .05
❑ 198 Rodney Harrison PD .10 .05
❑ 199 Vinny Testaverde PD .20 .09

		MINT	NRMT
❑ 200	Marshall Faulk PD	.40	.18
❑ 201	Ray Buchanan PD	.10	.05
❑ 202	Garrison Hearst PD	.20	.09
❑ 203	John Randle PD	.20	.09
❑ 204	Drew Bledsoe PD	.40	.18
❑ 205	Sam Gash PD	.10	.05
❑ 206	Troy Aikman PD	.50	.23
❑ 207	Michael McCrary	.10	.05
❑ 208	Chris Claiborne RC	.40	.18
❑ 209	Ricky Williams RC	5.00	2.20
❑ 210	Tim Couch RC	4.00	1.80
❑ 211	Champ Bailey RC	1.50	.70
❑ 212	Torry Holt RC	3.00	1.35
❑ 213	Donovan McNabb RC	5.00	2.20
❑ 214	David Boston RC	2.50	1.10
❑ 215	Chris McAlister RC	.75	.35
❑ 216	Aaron Gibson RC	.10	.05
❑ 217	Daunte Culpepper RC	8.00	3.60
❑ 218	Matt Stinchcomb RC	.40	.18
❑ 219	Edgerrin James RC	8.00	3.60
❑ 220	Jevon Kearse RC	2.50	1.10
❑ 221	Ebenezer Ekuban RC	.75	.35
❑ 222	Kris Farris RC	.40	.18
❑ 223	Chris Terry RC	.40	.18
❑ 224	Cecil Collins RC	1.25	.55
❑ 225	Akili Smith RC	2.50	1.10
❑ 226	Shaun King RC	2.50	1.10
❑ 227	Rahim Abdullah RC	.75	.35
❑ 228	Peerless Price RC	1.50	.70
❑ 229	Antoine Winfield RC	.75	.35
❑ 230	Antuan Edwards RC	.40	.18
❑ 231	Rob Konrad RC	.75	.35
❑ 232	Troy Edwards RC	1.50	.70
❑ 233	John Thornton RC	.40	.18
❑ 234	Fred Vinson RC	.40	.18
❑ 235	Gary Stills RC	.40	.18
❑ 236	Desmond Clark RC	.75	.35
❑ 237	Lamar King RC	.40	.18
❑ 238	Jared DeVries RC	.75	.35
❑ 239	Martin Gramatica RC	.40	.18
❑ 240	Montae Reagor RC	.40	.18
❑ 241	Andy Katzenmoyer RC	1.25	.55
❑ 242	Rufus French RC	.40	.18
❑ 243	D'Wayne Bates RC	.75	.35
❑ 244	Amos Zereoue RC	1.25	.55
❑ 245	Dre' Bly RC	.75	.35
❑ 246	Kevin Johnson RC	2.50	1.10
❑ 247	Cade McNown RC	1.50	.70
❑ 248	Kordell Stewart CL	.40	.18
❑ 249	Deion Sanders CL	.40	.18
❑ 250	Vinny Testaverde CL	.20	.09
❑ P1	Doug Flutie Promo	1.00	.45

2000 Metal

	MINT	NRMT
COMPLETE SET (300)	80.00	36.00
COMP.SET w/o SP's (250)	15.00	6.75

		MINT	NRMT
❑ 1	Tim Couch	.75	.35
❑ 2	Olandis Gary	.40	.18
❑ 3	Andre Hastings	.10	.05
❑ 4	Donovan McNabb	.60	.25
❑ 5	Bobby Engram	.20	.09
❑ 6	Bert Emanuel	.10	.05
❑ 7	Levon Kirkland	.10	.05
❑ 8	Chris Chandler	.20	.09
❑ 9	Herman Moore	.20	.09
❑ 10	Jeff Blake	.20	.09
❑ 11	Cortez Kennedy	.10	.05
❑ 12	Antowain Smith	.20	.09
❑ 13	Marvin Harrison	.40	.18
❑ 14	Bryant Young	.10	.05
❑ 15	Peerless Price	.40	.18
❑ 16	Peyton Manning	1.25	.55
❑ 17	Darrell Russell	.10	.05
❑ 18	Darrell Green	.10	.05
❑ 19	James Allen	.20	.09
❑ 20	Tedy Bruschi	.10	.05
❑ 21	Jon Kitna	.40	.18
❑ 22	Doug Flutie	.50	.23
❑ 23	Bill Schroeder	.20	.09
❑ 24	Curtis Martin	.40	.18
❑ 25	Kevin Lockett	.10	.05
❑ 26	Errict Rhett	.20	.09
❑ 27	Kevin Faulk	.20	.09
❑ 28	J.J. Stokes	.20	.09
❑ 29	Jonathan Linton	.10	.05
❑ 30	Jimmy Smith	.20	.09
❑ 31	Brian Dawkins	.10	.05
❑ 32	Michael Westbrook	.20	.09
❑ 33	Randall Cunningham	.40	.18
❑ 34	Oronde Gadsden	.20	.09
❑ 35	Shawn Springs	.10	.05
❑ 36	Shannon Sharpe	.20	.09
❑ 37	Terrence Wilkins	.40	.18
❑ 38	Aaron Glenn	.10	.05
❑ 39	Torrance Small	.10	.05
❑ 40	Sean Dawkins	.10	.05
❑ 41	Terrell Davis	1.00	.45
❑ 42	Ike Hilliard	.20	.09
❑ 43	Warrick Dunn	.40	.18
❑ 44	Jeremiah Trotter RC	.40	.18
❑ 45	O.J. McDuffie	.20	.09
❑ 46	Richard Huntley	.10	.05
❑ 47	Aeneas Williams	.10	.05
❑ 48	Rocket Ismail	.20	.09
❑ 49	Terry Glenn	.40	.18
❑ 50	Derrick Mayes	.20	.09
❑ 51	Wayne Chrebet	.20	.09
❑ 52	Kevin Dyson	.20	.09
❑ 53	Takeo Spikes	.10	.05
❑ 54	Matthew Hatchette	.10	.05
❑ 55	Shawn Bryson	.10	.05
❑ 56	Qadry Ismail	.20	.09
❑ 57	Jerome Pathon	.20	.09
❑ 58	Rich Gannon	.20	.09
❑ 59	Stephen Davis	.40	.18
❑ 60	Marcus Robinson	.40	.18
❑ 61	Damon Huard	.40	.18
❑ 62	Junior Seau	.20	.09
❑ 63	Curtis Enis	.20	.09
❑ 64	Tony Richardson RC	.10	.05
❑ 65	Troy Edwards	.20	.09
❑ 66	Robert Brooks	.20	.09
❑ 67	Antonio Freeman	.40	.18
❑ 68	Kerry Collins	.20	.09
❑ 69	Jacquez Green	.20	.09
❑ 70	Akili Smith	.40	.18
❑ 71	Zach Thomas	.20	.09
❑ 72	Kordell Stewart	.40	.18
❑ 73	Deion Sanders	.40	.18
❑ 74	David Patten	.10	.05
❑ 75	Drew Bledsoe	.60	.25
❑ 76	Shaun King	.60	.25
❑ 77	Eddie Kennison	.20	.09
❑ 78	Stacey Mack	.10	.05
❑ 79	Jim Harbaugh	.20	.09
❑ 80	Shawn Jefferson	.10	.05
❑ 81	James Stewart	.20	.09
❑ 82	Pete Mitchell	.10	.05
❑ 83	Mike Alstott	.40	.18
❑ 84	Marty Booker	.10	.05
❑ 85	Hardy Nickerson	.10	.05
❑ 86	Charles Johnson	.20	.09
❑ 87	Jeff George	.20	.09
❑ 88	Jermaine Lewis	.20	.09
❑ 89	Edgerrin James	1.50	.70
❑ 90	Rickey Dudley	.10	.05
❑ 91	Eddie George	.50	.23
❑ 92	Darren Woodson	.10	.05
❑ 93	Willie McGinest	.10	.05
❑ 94	Jeff Garcia	.40	.18
❑ 95	Eric Moulds	.40	.18
❑ 96	Tony Brackens	.10	.05
❑ 97	Charles Woodson	.20	.09
❑ 98	Warren Sapp	.20	.09
❑ 99	Corey Dillon	.40	.18
❑ 100	Tony Martin	.20	.09
❑ 101	Bruce Smith	.20	.09
❑ 102	Troy Aikman	1.00	.45
❑ 103	Daunte Culpepper	.75	.35
❑ 104	Christian Fauria	.10	.05
❑ 105	Steve Beuerlein	.20	.09
❑ 106	Fred Taylor	.50	.23
❑ 107	Ricky Watters	.10	.05
❑ 108	Brian Mitchell	.10	.05
❑ 109	Emmitt Smith	1.00	.45
❑ 110	Robert Smith	.40	.18
❑ 111	Jerry Rice	1.00	.45
❑ 112	Priest Holmes	.20	.09
❑ 113	Jay Fiedler	.40	.18
❑ 114	Curtis Conway	.20	.09
❑ 115	Jamal Anderson	.40	.18
❑ 116	E.G. Green	.10	.05
❑ 117	Kent Graham	.10	.05
❑ 118	Frank Wycheck	.10	.05
❑ 119	Jake Plummer	.40	.18
❑ 120	Randy Moss	1.25	.55
❑ 121	Charlie Garner	.20	.09
❑ 122	Frank Sanders	.20	.09
❑ 123	Germane Crowell	.20	.09
❑ 124	Jason Sehorn	.10	.05
❑ 125	Marshall Faulk	.50	.23
❑ 126	David Sloan	.10	.05
❑ 127	Cris Carter	.40	.18
❑ 128	Robert Chancey	.10	.05
❑ 129	Tony Banks	.20	.09
❑ 130	Ken Dilger	.10	.05
❑ 131	Dedric Ward	.10	.05
❑ 132	Yancey Thigpen	.10	.05
❑ 133	Jeremy McDaniel	.20	.09
❑ 134	John Randle	.10	.05
❑ 135	Jerome Bettis	.40	.18
❑ 136	Tim Dwight	.40	.18
❑ 137	Charlie Batch	.40	.18
❑ 138	Mark Brunell	.60	.25
❑ 139	Tyrone Wheatley	.20	.09
❑ 140	Champ Bailey	.20	.09
❑ 141	Brian Griese	.50	.23
❑ 142	Keith Poole	.10	.05
❑ 143	Kurt Warner	1.50	.70
❑ 144	Tim Biakabutuka	.20	.09
❑ 145	Elvis Grbac	.20	.09
❑ 146	Cade McNown	.40	.18
❑ 147	Albert Connell	.10	.05
❑ 148	Donald Driver	.10	.05
❑ 149	Donald Hayes	.10	.05
❑ 150	Terrell Owens	.40	.18
❑ 151	Johnnie Morton	.20	.09
❑ 152	Tiki Barber	.20	.09
❑ 153	Keyshawn Johnson	.40	.18
❑ 154	Carl Pickens	.20	.09
❑ 155	Thurman Thomas	.20	.09
❑ 156	Jeff Graham	.10	.05
❑ 157	Peter Boulware	.10	.05
❑ 158	Brett Favre	1.50	.70
❑ 159	Vinny Testaverde	.20	.09
❑ 160	Derrick Brooks	.20	.09
❑ 161	Wesley Walls	.10	.05
❑ 162	Derrick Alexander	.20	.09
❑ 163	Duce Staley	.40	.18
❑ 164	Troy Brown	.10	.05
❑ 165	Keenan McCardell	.20	.09
❑ 166	James Jett	.10	.05
❑ 167	Simeon Rice	.10	.05
❑ 168	Rod Smith	.20	.09
❑ 169	Ricky Williams	1.00	.45
❑ 170	Az-Zahir Hakim	.10	.05
❑ 171	Muhsin Muhammad	.20	.09
❑ 172	Andre Rison	.10	.05
❑ 173	Tim Brown	.40	.18
❑ 174	Brad Johnson	.40	.18
❑ 175	Darrin Chiaverini	.10	.05
❑ 176	Jake Reed	.20	.09
❑ 177	Kevin Carter	.10	.05
❑ 178	Jay Riemersma	.10	.05
❑ 179	Tony Gonzalez	.20	.09
❑ 180	Hines Ward	.10	.05
❑ 181	David Boston	.40	.18

❑ 182	Ed McCaffrey	.40	.18
❑ 183	Amani Toomer	.10	.05
❑ 184	Torry Holt	.40	.18
❑ 185	Rob Johnson	.20	.09
❑ 186	Kevin Hardy	.10	.05
❑ 187	Napoleon Kaufman	.20	.09
❑ 188	Jevon Kearse	.40	.18
❑ 189	Terance Mathis	.20	.09
❑ 190	Dorsey Levens	.20	.09
❑ 191	Kyle Brady	.10	.05
❑ 192	Steve McNair	.40	.18
❑ 193	Kevin Johnson	.40	.18
❑ 194	Lamar Smith	.20	.09
❑ 195	Ryan Leaf	.40	.18
❑ 196	Rod Woodson	.20	.09
❑ 197	Corey Bradford	.10	.05
❑ 198	Joe Horn	.20	.09
❑ 199	Isaac Bruce	.40	.18
❑ 200	Steve Young Dan Marino	1.50	.70
❑ 201	DeMario Brown RC	1.00	.45
❑ 202	Chad Morton RC	1.25	.55
❑ 203	Quinton Spotwood RC	.60	.25
❑ 204	Mike Anderson RC	6.00	2.70
❑ 205	Jarious Jackson RC	1.25	.55
❑ 206	Hank Poteat RC	1.00	.45
❑ 207	Rogers Beckett RC	1.00	.45
❑ 208	Deon Dyer RC	1.00	.45
❑ 209	Charles Lee RC	.60	.25
❑ 210	Barrett Green RC	.60	.25
❑ 211	T.J. Slaughter RC	.60	.25
❑ 212	Chris Hovan RC	1.00	.45
❑ 213	Mark Simoneau	1.25	.55
❑ 214	Rashard Anderson RC	1.00	.45
❑ 215	Trevor Insley RC	.60	.25
❑ 216	Paul Smith RC	1.00	.45
❑ 217	Doug Johnson RC	1.25	.55
❑ 218	Dwayne Goodrich RC	.60	.25
❑ 219	Julian Peterson RC	1.00	.45
❑ 220	Keith Bulluck RC	1.00	.45
❑ 221	Chris Samuels RC	1.00	.45
❑ 222	Shaun Ellis RC	1.00	.45
❑ 223	Na'il Diggs RC	1.25	.55
❑ 224	William Bartee RC	1.00	.45
❑ 225	John Abraham RC	1.00	.45
❑ 226	Trevor Gaylor RC	1.00	.45
❑ 227	Dante Hall RC	1.00	.45
❑ 228	Marcus Knight RC	.60	.25
❑ 229	Patrick Pass RC	1.00	.45
❑ 230	Bashir Yamini RC	1.00	.45
❑ 231	Deltha O'Neal RC	1.00	.45
❑ 232	Vaughn Sanders RC	.60	.25
❑ 233	Todd Husak RC	1.25	.55
❑ 234	Thomas Hamner RC	1.00	.45
❑ 235	Chafie Fields RC	1.00	.45
❑ 236	Orantes Grant RC	.60	.25
❑ 237	Muneer Moore RC	.60	.25
❑ 238	Kwame Cavil RC	1.00	.45
❑ 239	Spergon Wynn RC	1.25	.55
❑ 240	Leon Murray RC	.60	.25
❑ 241	Rob Morris RC	1.00	.45
❑ 242	Ben Kelly RC	.60	.25
❑ 243	Darren Howard RC	1.00	.45
❑ 244	Raynoch Thompson RC	1.00	.45
❑ 245	Mike Green RC	1.00	.45
❑ 246	Sammy Morris RC	1.50	.70
❑ 247	Ahmed Plummer RC	1.25	.55
❑ 248	Ian Gold RC	1.00	.45
❑ 249	Chris Coleman RC	1.25	.55
❑ 250	Ron Dixon RC	1.50	.70
❑ 251	Peter Warrick RC	6.00	2.70
❑ 252	Joe Hamilton RC	2.50	1.10
❑ 253	Dennis Northcutt RC	2.50	1.10
❑ 254	Laveranues Coles RC	3.00	1.35
❑ 255	Michael Wiley RC	2.00	.90
❑ 256	Plaxico Burress RC	4.00	1.80
❑ 257	Danny Farmer RC	2.00	.90
❑ 258	Aaron Shea RC	1.00	.45
❑ 259	Sebastian Janikowski RC	2.00	.90
❑ 260	Corey Simon RC	2.50	1.10
❑ 261	Frank Murphy RC	1.00	.45
❑ 262	JaJuan Dawson RC	2.00	.90
❑ 263	Ron Dayne RC	6.00	2.70
❑ 264	Tim Rattay RC	3.00	1.35
❑ 265	Troy Walters RC	2.00	.90
❑ 266	J.R. Redmond RC	2.50	1.10
❑ 267	Tom Brady RC	2.00	.90
❑ 268	Jamal Lewis RC	10.00	4.50
❑ 269	Anthony Lucas RC	1.00	.45
❑ 270	Reuben Droughns RC	2.00	.90
❑ 271	James Williams RC	1.50	.70
❑ 272	Shyrone Stith RC	1.50	.70
❑ 273	Jerry Porter RC	2.00	.90
❑ 274	Brian Urlacher RC	6.00	2.70
❑ 275	Avion Black RC	1.50	.70
❑ 276	Thomas Jones RC	3.00	1.35
❑ 277	Chad Pennington RC	6.00	2.70
❑ 278	Travis Prentice RC	3.00	1.35
❑ 279	Chris Redman RC	4.00	1.80
❑ 280	Travis Taylor RC	2.50	1.10
❑ 281	Giovanni Carmazzi RC	2.50	1.10
❑ 282	Sherrod Gideon RC	1.00	.45
❑ 283	Bubba Franks RC	2.50	1.10
❑ 284	Sylvester Morris RC	4.00	1.80
❑ 285	Curtis Keaton RC	1.50	.70
❑ 286	Frank Moreau RC	2.00	.90
❑ 287	Terrelle Smith RC	1.50	.70
❑ 288	Shaun Alexander RC	5.00	2.20
❑ 289	Tee Martin RC	3.00	1.35
❑ 290	R.Jay Soward RC	2.00	.90
❑ 291	Dez White RC	1.50	.70
❑ 292	Trung Canidate RC	2.00	.90
❑ 293	Darrell Jackson RC	2.50	1.10
❑ 294	Marc Bulger RC	2.00	.90
❑ 295	Courtney Brown RC	2.50	1.10
❑ 296	Todd Pinkston RC	2.00	.90
❑ 297	Anthony Becht RC	2.00	.90
❑ 298	Doug Chapman RC	4.00	1.80
❑ 299	Gari Scott RC	1.50	.70
❑ 300	Chris Cole RC	1.50	.70

1991 Pacific

	MINT	NRMT
COMPLETE SET (660)	15.00	6.75
COMP.SERIES 1 (550)	8.00	3.60
COMP.FACT.SER.1 (550)	10.00	4.50
COMP.SERIES 2 (110)	8.00	3.60
COMP.FACT.SER.2 (110)	12.00	5.50
COMP.CHECKLIST SET (5)	15.00	6.75

❑ 1	Deion Sanders	.40	.18
❑ 2	Steve Broussard	.05	.02
❑ 3	Aundray Bruce	.05	.02
❑ 4	Rick Bryan	.05	.02
❑ 5	John Rade	.05	.02
❑ 6	Scott Case	.05	.02
❑ 7	Tony Casillas	.05	.02
❑ 8	Shawn Collins	.05	.02
❑ 9	Darion Conner	.05	.02
❑ 10	Tory Epps	.05	.02
❑ 11	Bill Fralic	.05	.02
❑ 12	Mike Gann	.05	.02
❑ 13	Tim Green UER (Listed as DT, should say DE)	.05	.02
❑ 14	Chris Hinton	.05	.02
❑ 15	Houston Hoover UER (Deion misspelled as Deon on card back)	.05	.02
❑ 16	Chris Miller	.10	.05
❑ 17	Andre Rison	.10	.05
❑ 18	Mike Rozier	.05	.02
❑ 19	Jessie Tuggle	.05	.02
❑ 20	Don Beebe	.05	.02
❑ 21	Ray Bentley	.05	.02
❑ 22	Shane Conlan	.05	.02
❑ 23	Kent Hull	.05	.02
❑ 24	Mark Kelso	.05	.02
❑ 25	James Lofton UER (Photo on front actually Flip Johnson)	.10	.05
❑ 26	Scott Norwood	.05	.02
❑ 27	Andre Reed	.10	.05
❑ 28	Leonard Smith	.05	.02
❑ 29	Bruce Smith	.25	.11
❑ 30	Leon Seals	.05	.02
❑ 31	Darryl Talley	.05	.02
❑ 32	Steve Tasker	.10	.05
❑ 33	Thurman Thomas	.25	.11
❑ 34	James Williams	.05	.02
❑ 35	Will Wolford	.05	.02
❑ 36	Frank Reich	.10	.05
❑ 37	Jeff Wright RC	.05	.02
❑ 38	Neal Anderson	.10	.05
❑ 39	Trace Armstrong	.05	.02
❑ 40	Johnny Bailey UER (Gained 5320 yards in college, should be 6320)	.05	.02
❑ 41	Mark Bortz UER (Johnny Bailey misspelled as Johhny on cardback)	.05	.02
❑ 42	Cap Boso RC	.05	.02
❑ 43	Kevin Butler	.05	.02
❑ 44	Mark Carrier DB	.10	.05
❑ 45	Jim Covert	.05	.02
❑ 46	Wendell Davis	.05	.02
❑ 47	Richard Dent	.10	.05
❑ 48	Shaun Gayle	.05	.02
❑ 49	Jim Harbaugh	.25	.11
❑ 50	Jay Hilgenberg	.05	.02
❑ 51	Brad Muster	.05	.02
❑ 52	William Perry	.10	.05
❑ 53	Mike Singletary UER (No College listed should say Baylor)	.10	.05
❑ 54	Peter Tom Willis	.05	.02
❑ 55	Donnell Woolford	.05	.02
❑ 56	Steve McMichael	.10	.05
❑ 57	Eric Ball	.05	.02
❑ 58	Lewis Billups	.05	.02
❑ 59	Jim Breech	.05	.02
❑ 60	James Brooks	.10	.05
❑ 61	Eddie Brown	.05	.02
❑ 62	Rickey Dixon	.05	.02
❑ 63	Boomer Esiason	.10	.05
❑ 64	James Francis	.05	.02
❑ 65	David Fulcher	.05	.02
❑ 66	David Grant	.05	.02
❑ 67	Harold Green UER (Misplaced apostrophe in Gamecocks)	.05	.02
❑ 68	Rodney Holman	.05	.02
❑ 69	Stanford Jennings	.05	.02
❑ 70A	Tim Krumrie ERR (Misspelled Krumprie on card front)	.50	.23
❑ 70B	Tim Krumrie COR	.30	.14
❑ 71	Tim McGee	.05	.02
❑ 72	Anthony Munoz	.10	.05
❑ 73	Mitchell Price RC	.05	.02
❑ 74	Eric Thomas	.05	.02
❑ 75	Ickey Woods	.05	.02
❑ 76	Mike Baab	.05	.02
❑ 77	Thane Gash	.05	.02
❑ 78	David Grayson	.05	.02
❑ 79	Mike Johnson	.05	.02
❑ 80	Reggie Langhorne	.05	.02
❑ 81	Kevin Mack	.05	.02
❑ 82	Clay Matthews	.10	.05
❑ 83A	Eric Metcalf ERR ("Terry is the son of Terry")	.50	.23
❑ 83B	Eric Metcalf COR ("Eric is the son of Terry")	.30	.14
❑ 84	Frank Minnifield	.05	.02
❑ 85	Mike Oliphant	.05	.02
❑ 86	Mike Pagel	.05	.02
❑ 87	John Talley	.05	.02
❑ 88	Lawyer Tillman	.05	.02
❑ 89	Gregg Rakoczy UER	.05	.02

(Misspelled Greg on
both sides of card)
❑ 90 Bryan Wagner .05 .02
❑ 91 Rob Burnett RC .10 .05
❑ 92 Tommie Agee .05 .02
❑ 93 Troy Aikman UER .75 .35
(4328 yards is career
total not season; text
has him breaking passing
record which is not true)
❑ 94A Bill Bates ERR .50 .23
(Black line on cardfront)
❑ 94B Bill Bates COR .30 .14
(No black line
on cardfront)
❑ 95 Jack Del Rio .05 .02
❑ 96 Issiac Holt UER .05 .02
(Photo on back
actually Timmy Newsome)
❑ 97 Michael Irvin .25 .11
❑ 98 Jim Jeffcoat UER .05 .02
(On back, red line
has Jeff not Jim)
❑ 99 Jimmie Jones .05 .02
❑ 100 Kelvin Martin .05 .02
❑ 101 Nate Newton .10 .05
❑ 102 Danny Noonan .05 .02
❑ 103 Ken Norton Jr. .25 .11
❑ 104 Jay Novacek .25 .11
❑ 105 Mike Saxon .05 .02
❑ 106 Derrick Shepard .05 .02
❑ 107 Emmitt Smith 2.00 .90
❑ 108 Daniel Stubbs .05 .02
❑ 109 Tony Tolbert .05 .02
❑ 110 Alexander Wright .05 .02
❑ 111 Steve Atwater .05 .02
❑ 112 Melvin Bratton .05 .02
❑ 113 Tyrone Braxton UER .05 .02
(Went to North Dakota
State, not South Dakota)
❑ 114 Alphonso Carreker .05 .02
❑ 115 John Elway 1.25 .55
❑ 116 Simon Fletcher .05 .02
❑ 117 Bobby Humphrey .05 .02
❑ 118 Mark Jackson .05 .02
❑ 119 Vance Johnson .05 .02
❑ 120 Greg Kragen UER .05 .02
(Recovered 20 fumbles
in '89, yet 11 in career)
❑ 121 Karl Mecklenburg UER .05 .02
(Misspelled Mecklenberg
on card front)
❑ 122A Orson Mobley ERR .50 .23
(Misspelled Orsen)
❑ 122B Orson Mobley COR .10 .05
❑ 123 Alton Montgomery .05 .02
❑ 124 Ricky Nattiel .05 .02
❑ 125 Steve Sewell .05 .02
❑ 126 Shannon Sharpe .50 .23
❑ 127 Dennis Smith .05 .02
❑ 128A A.Townsend RC ERR .50 .23
(Misspelled Andie
on card front)
❑ 128B A.Townsend COR RC .10 .05
❑ 129 Mike Horan .05 .02
❑ 130 Jerry Ball .05 .02
❑ 131 Bennie Blades .05 .02
❑ 132 Lomas Brown .05 .02
❑ 133 Jeff Campbell UER .05 .02
(No NFL totals line)
❑ 134 Robert Clark .05 .02
❑ 135 Michael Cofer .05 .02
❑ 136 Dennis Gibson .05 .02
❑ 137 Mel Gray .10 .05
❑ 138 LeRoy Irvin UER .05 .02
(Misspelled LEROY;
spent 10 years with
Rams, not 11)
❑ 139 George Jamison RC .05 .02
❑ 140 Richard Johnson .05 .02
❑ 141 Eddie Murray .05 .02
❑ 142 Dan Owens .05 .02
❑ 143 Rodney Peete .10 .05
❑ 144 Barry Sanders 1.50 .70
❑ 145 Chris Spielman .10 .05
❑ 146 Marc Spindler .05 .02
❑ 147 Andre Ware .10 .05
❑ 148 William White .05 .02
❑ 149 Tony Bennett .10 .05
❑ 150 Robert Brown .05 .02
❑ 151 LeRoy Butler .10 .05
❑ 152 Anthony Dilweg .05 .02
❑ 153 Michael Haddix .05 .02
❑ 154 Ron Hallstrom .05 .02
❑ 155 Tim Harris .05 .02
❑ 156 Johnny Holland .05 .02
❑ 157 Chris Jacke .05 .02
❑ 158 Perry Kemp .05 .02
❑ 159 Mark Lee .05 .02
❑ 160 Don Majkowski .05 .02
❑ 161 Tony Mandarich UER .05 .02
(United Stated on back)
❑ 162 Mark Murphy .05 .02
❑ 163 Brian Noble .05 .02
❑ 164 Shawn Patterson .05 .02
❑ 165 Jeff Query .05 .02
❑ 166 Sterling Sharpe .25 .11
❑ 167 Darrell Thompson .05 .02
❑ 168 Ed West .05 .02
❑ 169 Ray Childress UER .05 .02
(Front DE, back DT)
❑ 170A Cris Dishman RC ERR .10 .05
(Misspelled Chris
on both sides)
❑ 170B C.Dishman RC COR/ERR .10 .05
Misspelled Chris
on back only
❑ 170C Cris Dishman RC COR .10 .05
❑ 171 Curtis Duncan .05 .02
❑ 172 William Fuller .10 .05
❑ 173 Ernest Givins UER .10 .05
(Missing a highlight
line on back)
❑ 174 Drew Hill .05 .02
❑ 175A Haywood Jeffires ERR .25 .11
(Misspelled Jeffries
on both sides of card)
❑ 175B Haywood Jeffires COR .25 .11
❑ 176 Sean Jones .10 .05
❑ 177 Lamar Lathon .05 .02
❑ 178 Bruce Matthews .10 .05
❑ 179 Bubba McDowell .05 .02
❑ 180 Johnny Meads .05 .02
❑ 181 Warren Moon UER .25 .11
(Birth listed as '65,
should be '56)
❑ 182 Mike Munchak .05 .02
❑ 183 Allen Pinkett .05 .02
❑ 184 Dean Steinkuhler UER .05 .02
(Oakland, should
be Outland)
❑ 185 Lorenzo White UER .05 .02
(Rout misspelled as
route on card back)
❑ 186A John Grimsley ERR .50 .23
(Misspelled Grimsby)
❑ 186B John Grimsley COR .10 .05
❑ 187 Pat Beach .05 .02
❑ 188 Albert Bentley .05 .02
❑ 189 Dean Biasucci .05 .02
❑ 190 Duane Bickett .05 .02
❑ 191 Bill Brooks .05 .02
❑ 192 Eugene Daniel .05 .02
❑ 193 Jeff George .25 .11
❑ 194 Jon Hand .05 .02
❑ 195 Jeff Herrod .05 .02
❑ 196A Jessie Hester ERR .30 .14
(Misspelled Jesse)
❑ 196B Jessie Hester ERR .10 .05
(Name corrected;
6-year player, not 7;
no NFL total line)
❑ 197 Mike Prior .05 .02
❑ 198 Stacey Simmons .05 .02
❑ 199 Rohn Stark .05 .02
❑ 200 Pat Tomberlin .05 .02
❑ 201 Clarence Verdin .05 .02
❑ 202 Keith Taylor .05 .02
❑ 203 Jack Trudeau .05 .02
❑ 204 Chip Banks .05 .02
❑ 205 John Alt .05 .02
❑ 206 Deron Cherry .05 .02
❑ 207 Steve DeBerg .05 .02
❑ 208 Tim Grunhard .05 .02
❑ 209 Albert Lewis .05 .02
❑ 210 Nick Lowery UER .05 .02
(12 years NFL exp.,
should be 13)
❑ 211 Bill Maas .05 .02
❑ 212 Chris Martin .05 .02
❑ 213 Todd McNair .05 .02
❑ 214 Christian Okoye .05 .02
❑ 215 Stephone Paige .05 .02
❑ 216 Steve Pelluer .05 .02
❑ 217 Kevin Porter .05 .02
❑ 218 Kevin Ross .05 .02
❑ 219 Dan Saleaumua .05 .02
❑ 220 Neil Smith .25 .11
❑ 221 David Szott UER .05 .02
(Listed as Off. Guard)
❑ 222 Derrick Thomas .25 .11
❑ 223 Barry Word .05 .02
❑ 224 Percy Snow .05 .02
❑ 225 Marcus Allen .25 .11
❑ 226 Eddie Anderson UER .05 .02
(Began career with
Seahawks, not Raiders)
❑ 227 Steve Beuerlein UER .10 .05
(Not injured during '90
season, but was inactive)
❑ 228A Tim Brown ERR .25 .11
(No position on card)
❑ 228B Tim Brown COR .25 .11
❑ 229 Scott Davis .05 .02
❑ 230 Mike Dyal .05 .02
❑ 231 Mervyn Fernandez UER .05 .02
(Card says free agent
in '87, but was
drafted in '83)
❑ 232 Willie Gault UER .05 .02
(Text says 60 catches
in '90, stats say 50)
❑ 233 Ethan Horton UER .05 .02
(No height and
weight listings)
❑ 234 Bo Jackson UER .30 .14
(Drafted in '87, not '86)
❑ 235 Howie Long .10 .05
❑ 236 Terry McDaniel .05 .02
❑ 237 Max Montoya .05 .02
❑ 238 Don Mosebar .05 .02
❑ 239 Jay Schroeder .05 .02
❑ 240 Steve Smith .05 .02
❑ 241 Greg Townsend .05 .02
❑ 242 Aaron Wallace .05 .02
❑ 243 Lionel Washington .05 .02
❑ 244A Steve Wisniewski ERR .10 .05
(Misspelled Winsniewski
on both sides;
drafted, should say
traded to)
❑ 244B Steve Wisniewski ERR .75 .35
(Misspelled Winsniewski
on card back)
❑ 244C Steve Wisniewski COR .10 .05
❑ 245 Flipper Anderson .05 .02
❑ 246 Latin Berry RC .05 .02
❑ 247 Robert Delpino .05 .02
❑ 248 Marcus Dupree .05 .02
❑ 249 Henry Ellard .10 .05
❑ 250 Jim Everett .10 .05
❑ 251 Cleveland Gary .05 .02
❑ 252 Jerry Gray .05 .02
❑ 253 Kevin Greene .25 .11
❑ 254 Pete Holohan UER .05 .02
(Photo on back
actually Kevin Greene)
❑ 255 Buford McGee .05 .02
❑ 256 Tom Newberry .05 .02
❑ 257A Irv Pankey ERR .50 .23
(Misspelled as Panky
on both sides of card)
❑ 257B Irv Pankey COR .10 .05
❑ 258 Jackie Slater .05 .02
❑ 259 Doug Smith .05 .02
❑ 260 Frank Stams .05 .02
❑ 261 Michael Stewart .05 .02
❑ 262 Fred Strickland .05 .02

	No.	Card		
❑	263	J.B. Brown UER (No periods after initials on card front)	.05	.02
❑	264	Mark Clayton	.10	.05
❑	265	Jeff Cross	.05	.02
❑	266	Mark Dennis RC	.05	.02
❑	267	Mark Duper	.10	.05
❑	268	Ferrell Edmunds	.05	.02
❑	269	Dan Marino	1.25	.55
❑	270	John Offerdahl	.05	.02
❑	271	Louis Oliver	.05	.02
❑	272	Tony Paige	.05	.02
❑	273	Reggie Roby	.05	.02
❑	274	Sammie Smith (Picture is sideways on the card)	.05	.02
❑	275	Keith Sims	.05	.02
❑	276	Brian Sochia	.05	.02
❑	277	Pete Stoyanovich	.05	.02
❑	278	Richmond Webb	.05	.02
❑	279	Jarvis Williams	.05	.02
❑	280	Tim McKyer	.05	.02
❑	281A	Jim C. Jensen ERR (Misspelled Jenson on card back)	.50	.23
❑	281B	Jim C. Jensen COR (Plays a skill position, not skilled)	.10	.05
❑	282	Scott Secules RC	.05	.02
❑	283	Ray Berry	.05	.02
❑	284	Joey Browner UER (Safetys, sic)	.05	.02
❑	285	Anthony Carter	.10	.05
❑	286A	Cris Carter ERR (Misspelled Chris on both sides)	.50	.23
❑	286B	Cris Carter ERR/COR (Misspelled Chris on card back)	1.50	.70
❑	286C	Cris Carter COR	.50	.23
❑	287	Chris Doleman	.05	.02
❑	288	Mark Dusbabek UER (Front DT, back LB)	.05	.02
❑	289	Hassan Jones	.05	.02
❑	290	Steve Jordan	.05	.02
❑	291	Carl Lee	.05	.02
❑	292	Kirk Lowdermilk	.05	.02
❑	293	Randall McDaniel	.05	.02
❑	294	Mike Merriweather	.05	.02
❑	295A	Keith Millard UER (No position on card)	.20	.09
❑	295B	Keith Millard COR	10.00	4.50
❑	296	Al Noga UER (Card says DT, should say DE)	.05	.02
❑	297	Scott Studwell UER (83 career tackles, but bio says 156 tackles in '81 season)	.05	.02
❑	298	Henry Thomas	.05	.02
❑	299	Herschel Walker	.10	.05
❑	300	Gary Zimmerman	.05	.02
❑	301	Rick Gannon	.25	.11
❑	302	Wade Wilson UER (Led AFC, should say led NFC)	.10	.05
❑	303	Vincent Brown	.05	.02
❑	304	Marv Cook	.05	.02
❑	305	Hart Lee Dykes	.05	.02
❑	306	Irving Fryar	.10	.05
❑	307	Tommy Hodson UER (No NFL totals line)	.05	.02
❑	308	Maurice Hurst	.05	.02
❑	309	Ronnie Lippett UER (On back,reserves should be reserve)	.05	.02
❑	310	Fred Marion	.05	.02
❑	311	Greg McMurtry	.05	.02
❑	312	Johnny Rembert	.05	.02
❑	313	Chris Singleton	.05	.02
❑	314	Ed Reynolds	.05	.02
❑	315	Andre Tippett	.05	.02
❑	316	Garin Veris	.05	.02
❑	317	Brent Williams	.05	.02
❑	318A	John Stephens ERR (Misspelled Stevens on both sides of card)	.10	.05
❑	318B	J.Stephens COR/ERR (Misspelled Stevens on card back)	.75	.35
❑	318C	John Stephens COR	.10	.05
❑	319	Sammy Martin	.05	.02
❑	320	Bruce Armstrong	.05	.02
❑	321A	Morten Andersen ERR (Misspelled Anderson on both sides of card)	.30	.14
❑	321B	M.Andersen ERR/COR (Misspelled Anderson on card back)	.75	.35
❑	321C	Morten Andersen COR	.10	.05
❑	322	Gene Atkins UER (No NFL Exp. line)	.05	.02
❑	323	Vince Buck	.05	.02
❑	324	John Fourcade	.05	.02
❑	325	Kevin Haverdink	.05	.02
❑	326	Bobby Hebert	.05	.02
❑	327	Craig Heyward	.10	.05
❑	328	Dalton Hilliard	.05	.02
❑	329	Rickey Jackson	.05	.02
❑	330A	Vaughan Johnson ERR (Misspelled Vaughn)	.20	.09
❑	330B	Vaughan Johnson COR	10.00	4.50
❑	331	Eric Martin	.05	.02
❑	332	Wayne Martin	.05	.02
❑	333	Rueben Mayes UER (Misspelled Reuben on card back)	.05	.02
❑	334	Sam Mills	.05	.02
❑	335	Brett Perriman	.25	.11
❑	336	Pat Swilling	.10	.05
❑	337	Renaldo Turnbull	.05	.02
❑	338	Lonzell Hill	.05	.02
❑	339	Steve Walsh UER (19 of 20 for 70.3, should be 95 percent)	.05	.02
❑	340	Carl Banks UER (Led defensive in tackles should say defense)	.05	.02
❑	341	Mark Bavaro UER (Weight on back 145, should say 245)	.05	.02
❑	342	Maurice Carthon	.05	.02
❑	343	Pat Harlow RC	.05	.02
❑	344	Eric Dorsey	.05	.02
❑	345	John Elliott	.05	.02
❑	346	Rodney Hampton	.25	.11
❑	347	Jeff Hostetler	.10	.05
❑	348	Erik Howard UER (Listed as DT, should be NT)	.05	.02
❑	349	Pepper Johnson	.05	.02
❑	350A	Sean Landeta ERR (Misspelled Landetta on both sides of card)	.10	.05
❑	350B	Sean Landeta COR	.50	.23
❑	351	Leonard Marshall	.05	.02
❑	352	Dave Meggett	.10	.05
❑	353A	Bart Oates ERR (Misspelled Oats on both sides; misspelled Megget in Did You Know)	.10	.05
❑	353B	Bart Oates COR/ERR (Misspelled Oats on card back; misspelled Megget in Did You Know)	.75	.35
❑	353C	Bart Oates COR (Dave Meggett still misspelled as Megget)	.10	.05
❑	354	Gary Reasons	.05	.02
❑	355	Phil Simms	.10	.05
❑	356	Lawrence Taylor	.25	.11
❑	357	Reyna Thompson	.05	.02
❑	358	Brian Williams OL UER (Front C-G, back G)	.05	.02
❑	359	Matt Bahr	.05	.02
❑	360	Mark Ingram	.10	.05
❑	361	Brad Baxter	.05	.02
❑	362	Mark Boyer	.05	.02
❑	363	Dennis Byrd	.05	.02
❑	364	Dave Cadigan UER (Terance misspelled as Terrance on back)	.05	.02
❑	365	Kyle Clifton	.05	.02
❑	366	James Hasty	.05	.02
❑	367	Joe Kelly UER (Front 50, back 58)	.05	.02
❑	368	Jeff Lageman	.05	.02
❑	369	Pat Leahy UER (Career-best FG in '65, should say '85)	.05	.02
❑	370	Terance Mathis	.10	.05
❑	371	Erik McMillan	.05	.02
❑	372	Rob Moore	.25	.11
❑	373	Ken O'Brien	.05	.02
❑	374	Tony Stargell	.05	.02
❑	375	Jim Sweeney UER (Landetta, sic)	.05	.02
❑	376	Al Toon	.10	.05
❑	377	Johnny Hector	.05	.02
❑	378	Jeff Criswell	.05	.02
❑	379	Mike Haight RC	.05	.02
❑	380	Troy Benson	.05	.02
❑	381	Eric Allen	.05	.02
❑	382	Fred Barnett	.25	.11
❑	383	Jerome Brown	.05	.02
❑	384	Keith Byars	.05	.02
❑	385	Randall Cunningham	.25	.11
❑	386	Byron Evans	.05	.02
❑	387	Wes Hopkins	.05	.02
❑	388	Keith Jackson	.10	.05
❑	389	Seth Joyner UER (Fumble recovery line not aligned)	.10	.05
❑	390	Bobby Wilson RC	.05	.02
❑	391	Heath Sherman	.05	.02
❑	392	Clyde Simmons UER (Listed as DT, should say DE)	.05	.02
❑	393	Ben Smith	.05	.02
❑	394	Andre Waters	.05	.02
❑	395	Reggie White UER (Derrick Thomas holds NFL record with 7 sacks)	.25	.11
❑	396	Calvin Williams	.10	.05
❑	397	Al Harris	.05	.02
❑	398	Anthony Toney	.05	.02
❑	399	Mike Quick	.05	.02
❑	400	Anthony Bell	.05	.02
❑	401	Rich Camarillo	.05	.02
❑	402	Roy Green	.05	.02
❑	403	Ken Harvey	.10	.05
❑	404	Eric Hill	.05	.02
❑	405	Garth Jax RC UER (Should have comma before "the" and after "Cowboys" on card back)	.05	.02
❑	406	Ernie Jones	.05	.02
❑	407A	Cedric Mack ERR (Misspelled Cedrick on card front)	.20	.09
❑	407B	Cedric Mack COR (NFL Exp. line is red instead of black)	10.00	4.50
❑	408	Dexter Manley	.05	.02
❑	409	Tim McDonald	.05	.02
❑	410	Freddie Joe Nunn	.05	.02
❑	411	Ricky Proehl	.05	.02
❑	412	Moe Gardner RC	.05	.02
❑	413	Timm Rosenbach	.05	.02
❑	414	Luis Sharpe UER (Lomiller, sic)	.05	.02
❑	415	Vai Sikahema UER (Front RB, back PR)	.05	.02
❑	416	Anthony Thompson	.05	.02
❑	417	Ron Wolfley UER (Missing NFL fact line under vital stats)	.05	.02
❑	418	Lonnie Young	.05	.02
❑	419	Gary Anderson K	.05	.02
❑	420	Bubby Brister	.05	.02
❑	421	Thomas Everett	.05	.02
❑	422	Eric Green	.05	.02
❑	423	Delton Hall	.05	.02
❑	424	Bryan Hinkle	.05	.02
❑	425	Merril Hoge	.05	.02
❑	426	Carnell Lake	.05	.02

❑ 427 Louis Lipps .05 .02
❑ 428 David Little .05 .02
❑ 429 Greg Lloyd .25 .11
❑ 430 Mike Mularkey .05 .02
❑ 431 Keith Willis UER .05 .02
(No period after C in
L.C. Greenwood on back)
❑ 432 Dwayne Woodruff .05 .02
❑ 433 Rod Woodson UER .25 .11
(No NFL experience
listed on card)
❑ 434 Tim Worley .05 .02
❑ 435 Warren Williams .05 .02
❑ 436 Terry Long UER .05 .02
(Not 5th NFL team,
tied for 7th)
❑ 437 Martin Bayless .05 .02
❑ 438 Jarrod Bunch RC .05 .02
❑ 439 Marion Butts .10 .05
❑ 440 Gill Byrd UER .05 .02
(Pickoffs misspelled
as two words)
❑ 441 Arthur Cox .05 .02
❑ 442 John Friesz .25 .11
❑ 443 Leo Goeas .05 .02
❑ 444 Burt Grossman .05 .02
❑ 445 Courtney Hall UER .05 .02
(In DYK section,
is should be in)
❑ 446 Ronnie Harmon .05 .02
❑ 447 Nate Lewis RC .05 .02
❑ 448 Anthony Miller .10 .05
❑ 449 Leslie O'Neal .10 .05
❑ 450 Gary Plummer .05 .02
❑ 451 Junior Seau .25 .11
❑ 452 Billy Ray Smith .05 .02
❑ 453 Billy Joe Tolliver .05 .02
❑ 454 Broderick Thompson .05 .02
❑ 455 Lee Williams .05 .02
❑ 456 Michael Carter .05 .02
❑ 457 Mike Cofer .05 .02
❑ 458 Kevin Fagan .05 .02
❑ 459 Charles Haley .10 .05
❑ 460 Pierce Holt .05 .02
❑ 461 Johnnie Jackson RC UER .05 .02
(Johnny on front)
❑ 462 Brent Jones .25 .11
❑ 463 Guy McIntyre .05 .02
❑ 464 Joe Montana 1.25 .55
❑ 465A Bubba Paris ERR .10 .05
(Misspelled Parris;
reversed negative)
❑ 465B Bubba Paris ERR/COR .50 .23
(Misspelled Parris;
photo corrected
❑ 465C Bubba Paris COR .10 .05
❑ 466 Tom Rathman UER .05 .02
(Born 10/7/62,
not 11/7/62)
❑ 467 Jerry Rice UER .75 .35
(4th to catch 100,
should say 2nd)
❑ 468 Mike Sherrard .05 .02
❑ 469 John Taylor UER .10 .05
(AL1-Time, sic)
❑ 470 Steve Young .75 .35
❑ 471 Dennis Brown .05 .02
❑ 472 Dexter Carter .05 .02
❑ 473 Bill Romanowski .05 .02
❑ 474 Dave Waymer .05 .02
❑ 475 Robert Blackmon .05 .02
❑ 476 Derrick Fenner .05 .02
❑ 477 Nesby Glasgow UER .05 .02
(Missing total line
for fumbles)
❑ 478 Jacob Green .05 .02
❑ 479 Andy Heck .05 .02
❑ 480 Norm Johnson UER .05 .02
(They own and operate
card store, not run)
❑ 481 Tommy Kane .05 .02
❑ 482 Cortez Kennedy .25 .11
❑ 483A Dave Krieg ERR .20 .09
(Misspelled Kreig
on both sides)
❑ 483B Dave Krieg COR 10.00 4.50
❑ 484 Bryan Millard .05 .02
❑ 485 Joe Nash .05 .02
❑ 486 Rufus Porter .05 .02
❑ 487 Eugene Robinson .05 .02
❑ 488 Mike Tice RC .05 .02
❑ 489 Chris Warren .25 .11
❑ 490 John L. Williams UER .05 .02
(No period after L
on card front)
❑ 491 Terry Wooden .05 .02
❑ 492 Tony Woods .05 .02
❑ 493 Brian Blades .10 .05
❑ 494 Paul Skansi .05 .02
❑ 495 Gary Anderson RB .05 .02
❑ 496 Mark Carrier WR .25 .11
❑ 497 Chris Chandler .25 .11
❑ 498 Steve Christie .05 .02
❑ 499 Reggie Cobb .05 .02
❑ 500 Reuben Davis .05 .02
❑ 501 Willie Drewrey UER .05 .02
(Misspelled Drewery on
both sides of card)
❑ 502 Randy Grimes .05 .02
❑ 503 Paul Gruber .05 .02
❑ 504 Wayne Haddix .05 .02
❑ 505 Ron Hall .05 .02
❑ 506 Harry Hamilton .05 .02
❑ 507 Bruce Hill .05 .02
❑ 508 Eugene Marve .05 .02
❑ 509 Keith McCants .05 .02
❑ 510 Winston Moss .05 .02
❑ 511 Kevin Murphy .05 .02
❑ 512 Mark Robinson .05 .02
❑ 513 Vinny Testaverde .10 .05
❑ 514 Broderick Thomas .05 .02
❑ 515A Jeff Bostic UER .08 .04
(Lomiller, sic;
on back, word "goal"
touches lower border)
❑ 515B Jeff Bostic UER .08 .04
(Lomiller, sic;
on back, word "goal"
is away from border)
❑ 516 Todd Bowles .05 .02
❑ 517 Earnest Byner .05 .02
❑ 518 Gary Clark .25 .11
❑ 519 Craig Erickson RC .25 .11
❑ 520 Darryl Grant .05 .02
❑ 521 Darrell Green .05 .02
❑ 522 Russ Grimm .05 .02
❑ 523 Stan Humphries .25 .11
❑ 524 Joe Jacoby UER .05 .02
(Lomiller, sic)
❑ 525 Jim Lachey .05 .02
❑ 526 Chip Lohmiller .05 .02
❑ 527 Charles Mann .05 .02
❑ 528 Wilber Marshall .05 .02
❑ 529A Art Monk .08 .04
(On back, "y" in history
touches copyright symbol)
❑ 529B Art Monk .08 .04
(On back, "y" in history
is away from symbol)
❑ 530 Tracy Rocker .05 .02
❑ 531 Mark Rypien .10 .05
❑ 532 Ricky Sanders UER .05 .02
(Stats say caught 56,
text says 57)
❑ 533 Alvin Walton UER .05 .02
(Listed as WR,
should be S)
❑ 534 Todd Marinovich RC UER .05 .02
(17 percent, should
be 71 percent)
❑ 535 Mike Dumas RC .05 .02
❑ 536A R.Maryland RC ERR .25 .11
(No highlight line)
❑ 536B R.Maryland RC COR .25 .11
(Highlight line added)
❑ 537 Eric Turner RC UER .10 .05
(Don Rogers misspelled
as Rodgers)
❑ 538 Ernie Mills RC .10 .05
❑ 539 Ed King RC .05 .02
❑ 540 Mike Stonebreaker .05 .02
❑ 541 Chris Zorich RC .25 .11
❑ 542A Mike Croel RC UER .05 .02
(Missing highlight line
under bio notes; front
photo reversed negative;
on back, "y" in weekly
inside copyright)
❑ 542B Mike Croel RC UER .05 .02
(Missing highlight line
under bio notes; front
photo reversed negative;
on back, "y" in weekly
barely touches copyright)
❑ 543 Eric Moten RC .05 .02
❑ 544 Dan McGwire RC .05 .02
❑ 545 Keith Cash RC .05 .02
❑ 546 Kenny Walker RC UER .05 .02
(Drafted 8th round,
not 7th)
❑ 547 Leroy Hoard UER .10 .05
(LeROY on card;
not a draft pick)
❑ 548 Luis Cristobal UER .05 .02
(Front LB, back G)
❑ 549 Stacy Danley .05 .02
❑ 550 Todd Lyght RC .05 .02
❑ 551 Brett Favre RC 5.00 2.20
❑ 552 Mike Pritchard RC .25 .11
❑ 553 Moe Gardner .05 .02
❑ 554 Tim McKyer .05 .02
❑ 555 Erric Pegram RC .25 .11
❑ 556 Norm Johnson .05 .02
❑ 557 Bruce Pickens RC .05 .02
❑ 558 Henry Jones RC .10 .05
❑ 559 Phil Hansen RC .05 .02
❑ 560 Cornelius Bennett .10 .05
❑ 561 Stan Thomas .05 .02
❑ 562 Chris Zorich .10 .05
❑ 563 Anthony Morgan RC .05 .02
❑ 564 Darren Lewis RC .05 .02
❑ 565 Mike Stonebreaker .05 .02
❑ 566 Alfred Williams RC .05 .02
❑ 567 Lamar Rogers RC .05 .02
❑ 568 Erik Wilhelm RC UER .05 .02
(No NFL Experience
line on card back)
❑ 569 Ed King .05 .02
❑ 570 Michael Jackson RC .25 .11
❑ 571 James Jones RC .05 .02
❑ 572 Russell Maryland .25 .11
❑ 573 Dixon Edwards RC .05 .02
❑ 574 Darrick Brownlow RC .05 .02
❑ 575 Larry Brown DB RC .10 .05
❑ 576 Mike Croel .05 .02
❑ 577 Keith Traylor RC .05 .02
❑ 578 Kenny Walker .05 .02
❑ 579 Reggie Johnson RC .05 .02
❑ 580 Herman Moore RC 2.00 .90
❑ 581 Kelvin Pritchett RC .10 .05
❑ 582 Kevin Scott RC .05 .02
❑ 583 Vinnie Clark RC .05 .02
❑ 584 Esera Tuaolo RC .05 .02
❑ 585 Don Davey .05 .02
❑ 586 Blair Kiel RC .05 .02
❑ 587 Mike Dumas .05 .02
❑ 588 Darryll Lewis RC .10 .05
❑ 589 John Flannery RC .05 .02
❑ 590 Kevin Donnalley .05 .02
❑ 591 Shane Curry .05 .02
❑ 592 Mark Vander Poel RC .05 .02
❑ 593 Dave McCloughan .05 .02
❑ 594 Mel Agee RC .05 .02
❑ 595 Kerry Cash RC .05 .02
❑ 596 Harvey Williams RC .25 .11
❑ 597 Joe Valerio .05 .02
❑ 598 Tim Barnett RC UER .05 .02
(Harvey Williams
pictured on front)
❑ 599 Todd Marinovich .10 .05
❑ 600 Nick Bell RC .05 .02
❑ 601 Roger Craig .10 .05
❑ 602 Ronnie Lott .10 .05
❑ 603 Mike Jones RC .05 .02
❑ 604 Todd Lyght .05 .02
❑ 605 Roman Phifer RC .05 .02
❑ 606 David Lang RC .05 .02
❑ 607 Aaron Craver RC .05 .02

❑ 608 Mark Higgs RC	.05	.02
❑ 609 Chris Green	.05	.02
❑ 610 Randy Baldwin RC	.05	.02
❑ 611 Pat Harlow	.05	.02
❑ 612 Leonard Russell RC	.25	.11
❑ 613 Jerome Henderson RC	.05	.02
❑ 614 Scott Zolak RC UER (Bio says drafted in 1984, should be 1991)	.05	.02
❑ 615 Jon Vaughn RC	.05	.02
❑ 616 Harry Colon RC	.05	.02
❑ 617 Wesley Carroll RC	.05	.02
❑ 618 Quinn Early	.10	.05
❑ 619 Reginald Jones RC	.05	.02
❑ 620 Jarrod Bunch	.05	.02
❑ 621 Kanavis McGhee RC	.05	.02
❑ 622 Ed McCaffrey RC	2.00	.90
❑ 623 Browning Nagle RC	.05	.02
❑ 624 Mo Lewis RC	.10	.05
❑ 625 Blair Thomas	.05	.02
❑ 626 Antone Davis RC	.05	.02
❑ 627 Jim McMahon	.10	.05
❑ 628 Scott Kowalkowski RC	.05	.02
❑ 629 Brad Goebel RC	.05	.02
❑ 630 William Thomas RC	.05	.02
❑ 631 Eric Swann RC	.25	.11
❑ 632 Mike Jones RC	.05	.02
❑ 633 Aeneas Williams RC	.25	.11
❑ 634 Dexter Davis RC	.05	.02
❑ 635 Tom Tupa UER (Did play in 1990, but not as QB)	.05	.02
❑ 636 Johnny Johnson	.05	.02
❑ 637 Randal Hill RC	.10	.05
❑ 638 Jeff Graham RC	.25	.11
❑ 639 Ernie Mills	.05	.02
❑ 640 Adrian Cooper RC	.05	.02
❑ 641 Stanley Richard RC	.05	.02
❑ 642 Eric Bieniemy RC	.05	.02
❑ 643 Eric Moten	.05	.02
❑ 644 Shawn Jefferson RC	.10	.05
❑ 645 Ted Washington RC	.05	.02
❑ 646 John Johnson RC	.05	.02
❑ 647 Dan McGwire	.05	.02
❑ 648 Doug Thomas RC	.05	.02
❑ 649 David Daniels RC	.05	.02
❑ 650 John Kasay RC	.10	.05
❑ 651 Jeff Kemp	.05	.02
❑ 652 Charles McRae RC	.05	.02
❑ 653 Lawrence Dawsey RC	.10	.05
❑ 654 Robert Wilson RC	.05	.02
❑ 655 Dexter Manley	.05	.02
❑ 656 Chuck Weatherspoon	.05	.02
❑ 657 Tim Ryan RC	.05	.02
❑ 658 Bobby Wilson	.05	.02
❑ 659 Ricky Ervins RC	.10	.05
❑ 660 Matt Millen	.10	.05

1992 Pacific

	MINT	NRMT
COMPLETE SET (660)	15.00	6.75
COMP.FACT.SET (690)	25.00	11.00
COMP.SERIES 1 (330)	8.00	3.60
COMP.SERIES 2 (330)	8.00	3.60
COMP.CHECKLIST SET (5)	3.00	1.35

❑ 1 Steve Broussard	.04	.02
❑ 2 Darion Conner	.04	.02
❑ 3 Tory Epps	.04	.02
❑ 4 Michael Haynes	.10	.05
❑ 5 Chris Hinton	.04	.02
❑ 6 Mike Kenn	.04	.02
❑ 7 Tim McKyer	.04	.02
❑ 8 Chris Miller	.10	.05
❑ 9 Erric Pegram	.10	.05
❑ 10 Mike Pritchard	.10	.05
❑ 11 Moe Gardner	.04	.02
❑ 12 Tim Green	.04	.02
❑ 13 Norm Johnson	.04	.02
❑ 14 Don Beebe	.04	.02
❑ 15 Cornelius Bennett	.10	.05
❑ 16 Al Edwards	.04	.02
❑ 17 Mark Kelso	.04	.02
❑ 18 James Lofton	.10	.05
❑ 19 Frank Reich	.10	.05
❑ 20 Leon Seals	.04	.02
❑ 21 Darryl Talley	.04	.02
❑ 22 Thurman Thomas	.25	.11
❑ 23 Kent Hull	.04	.02
❑ 24 Jeff Wright	.04	.02
❑ 25 Nate Odomes	.04	.02
❑ 26 Carwell Gardner	.04	.02
❑ 27 Neal Anderson	.04	.02
❑ 28 Mark Carrier DB	.04	.02
❑ 29 Johnny Bailey	.04	.02
❑ 30 Jim Harbaugh	.25	.11
❑ 31 Jay Hilgenberg	.04	.02
❑ 32 William Perry	.10	.05
❑ 33 Wendell Davis	.04	.02
❑ 34 Donnell Woolford	.04	.02
❑ 35 Keith Van Horne	.04	.02
❑ 36 Shaun Gayle	.04	.02
❑ 37 Tom Waddle	.04	.02
❑ 38 Chris Zorich	.10	.05
❑ 39 Tom Thayer	.04	.02
❑ 40 Rickey Dixon	.04	.02
❑ 41 James Francis	.04	.02
❑ 42 David Fulcher	.04	.02
❑ 43 Reggie Rembert	.04	.02
❑ 44 Anthony Munoz	.10	.05
❑ 45 Harold Green	.04	.02
❑ 46 Mitchell Price	.04	.02
❑ 47 Rodney Holman	.04	.02
❑ 48 Bruce Kozerski	.04	.02
❑ 49 Bruce Reimers	.04	.02
❑ 50 Erik Wilhelm	.04	.02
❑ 51 Harlon Barnett	.04	.02
❑ 52 Mike Johnson	.04	.02
❑ 53 Brian Brennan	.04	.02
❑ 54 Ed King	.04	.02
❑ 55 Reggie Langhorne	.04	.02
❑ 56 James Jones	.04	.02
❑ 57 Mike Baab	.04	.02
❑ 58 Dan Fike	.04	.02
❑ 59 Frank Minnifield	.04	.02
❑ 60 Clay Matthews	.10	.05
❑ 61 Kevin Mack	.04	.02
❑ 62 Tony Casillas	.04	.02
❑ 63 Jay Novacek	.10	.05
❑ 64 Larry Brown DB	.04	.02
❑ 65 Michael Irvin	.25	.11
❑ 66 Jack Del Rio	.04	.02
❑ 67 Ken Willis	.04	.02
❑ 68 Emmitt Smith	1.50	.70
❑ 69 Alan Veingrad	.04	.02
❑ 70 John Gesek	.04	.02
❑ 71 Steve Beuerlein	.04	.02
❑ 72 Vinson Smith RC	.04	.02
❑ 73 Steve Atwater	.04	.02
❑ 74 Mike Croel	.04	.02
❑ 75 John Elway	1.25	.55
❑ 76 Gaston Green	.04	.02
❑ 77 Mike Horan	.04	.02
❑ 78 Vance Johnson	.04	.02
❑ 79 Karl Mecklenburg	.04	.02
❑ 80 Shannon Sharpe	.25	.11
❑ 81 David Treadwell	.04	.02
❑ 82 Kenny Walker	.04	.02
❑ 83 Greg Lewis	.04	.02
❑ 84 Shawn Moore	.04	.02
❑ 85 Alton Montgomery	.04	.02
❑ 86 Michael Young	.04	.02
❑ 87 Jerry Ball	.04	.02
❑ 88 Bennie Blades	.04	.02
❑ 89 Mel Gray	.10	.05
❑ 90 Herman Moore	.50	.23
❑ 91 Erik Kramer	.10	.05
❑ 92 Willie Green	.04	.02
❑ 93 George Jamison	.04	.02
❑ 94 Chris Spielman	.10	.05
❑ 95 Kelvin Pritchett	.04	.02
❑ 96 William White	.04	.02
❑ 97 Mike Utley	.10	.05
❑ 98 Tony Bennett	.04	.02
❑ 99 LeRoy Butler	.04	.02
❑ 100 Vinnie Clark	.04	.02
❑ 101 Ron Hallstrom	.04	.02
❑ 102 Chris Jacke	.04	.02
❑ 103 Tony Mandarich	.04	.02
❑ 104 Sterling Sharpe	.25	.11
❑ 105 Don Majkowski	.04	.02
❑ 106 Johnny Holland	.04	.02
❑ 107 Esera Tuaolo	.04	.02
❑ 108 Darrell Thompson	.04	.02
❑ 109 Bubba McDowell	.04	.02
❑ 110 Curtis Duncan	.04	.02
❑ 111 Lamar Lathon	.04	.02
❑ 112 Drew Hill	.04	.02
❑ 113 Bruce Matthews	.04	.02
❑ 114 Bo Orlando RC	.04	.02
❑ 115 Don Maggs	.04	.02
❑ 116 Lorenzo White	.04	.02
❑ 117 Ernest Givins	.10	.05
❑ 118 Tony Jones	.04	.02
❑ 119 Dean Steinkuhler	.04	.02
❑ 120 Dean Biasucci	.04	.02
❑ 121 Duane Bickett	.04	.02
❑ 122 Bill Brooks	.04	.02
❑ 123 Ken Clark	.04	.02
❑ 124 Jessie Hester	.04	.02
❑ 125 Anthony Johnson	.10	.05
❑ 126 Chip Banks	.04	.02
❑ 127 Mike Prior	.04	.02
❑ 128 Rohn Stark	.04	.02
❑ 129 Jeff Herrod	.04	.02
❑ 130 Clarence Verdin	.04	.02
❑ 131 Tim Manoa	.04	.02
❑ 132 Brian Baldinger RC	.04	.02
❑ 133 Tim Barnett	.04	.02
❑ 134 J.J. Birden	.04	.02
❑ 135 Deron Cherry	.04	.02
❑ 136 Steve DeBerg	.04	.02
❑ 137 Nick Lowery	.04	.02
❑ 138 Todd McNair	.04	.02
❑ 139 Christian Okoye	.04	.02
❑ 140 Mark Vlasic	.04	.02
❑ 141 Dan Saleaumua	.04	.02
❑ 142 Neil Smith	.25	.11
❑ 143 Robb Thomas	.04	.02
❑ 144 Eddie Anderson	.04	.02
❑ 145 Nick Bell	.04	.02
❑ 146 Tim Brown	.25	.11
❑ 147 Roger Craig	.10	.05
❑ 148 Jeff Gossett	.04	.02
❑ 149 Ethan Horton	.04	.02
❑ 150 Jamie Holland	.04	.02
❑ 151 Jeff Jaeger	.04	.02
❑ 152 Todd Marinovich	.04	.02
❑ 153 Marcus Allen	.25	.11
❑ 154 Steve Smith	.04	.02
❑ 155 Flipper Anderson	.04	.02
❑ 156 Robert Delpino	.04	.02
❑ 157 Cleveland Gary	.04	.02
❑ 158 Kevin Greene	.25	.11
❑ 159 Dale Hatcher	.04	.02
❑ 160 Duval Love	.04	.02
❑ 161 Ron Brown	.04	.02
❑ 162 Jackie Slater	.04	.02
❑ 163 Doug Smith	.04	.02
❑ 164 Aaron Cox	.04	.02
❑ 165 Larry Kelm	.04	.02
❑ 166 Mark Clayton	.10	.05
❑ 167 Louis Oliver	.04	.02
❑ 168 Mark Higgs	.04	.02
❑ 169 Aaron Craver	.04	.02
❑ 170 Sammie Smith	.04	.02
❑ 171 Tony Paige	.04	.02
❑ 172 Jeff Cross	.04	.02

No.	Player		
❑ 173	David Griggs	.04	.02
❑ 174	Richmond Webb	.04	.02
❑ 175	Vestee Jackson	.04	.02
❑ 176	Jim C. Jensen	.04	.02
❑ 177	Anthony Carter	.10	.05
❑ 178	Cris Carter	.50	.23
❑ 179	Chris Doleman	.04	.02
❑ 180	Rich Gannon	.25	.11
❑ 181	Al Noga	.04	.02
❑ 182	Randall McDaniel	.04	.02
❑ 183	Todd Scott	.04	.02
❑ 184	Henry Thomas	.04	.02
❑ 185	Felix Wright	.04	.02
❑ 186	Gary Zimmerman	.04	.02
❑ 187	Herschel Walker	.10	.05
❑ 188	Vincent Brown	.04	.02
❑ 189	Harry Colon	.04	.02
❑ 190	Irving Fryar	.10	.05
❑ 191	Marv Cook	.04	.02
❑ 192	Leonard Russell	.10	.05
❑ 193	Hugh Millen	.04	.02
❑ 194	Pat Harlow	.04	.02
❑ 195	Jon Vaughn	.04	.02
❑ 196	Ben Coates RC	2.00	.90
❑ 197	Johnny Rembert	.04	.02
❑ 198	Greg McMurtry	.04	.02
❑ 199	Morten Andersen	.04	.02
❑ 200	Tommy Barnhardt	.04	.02
❑ 201	Bobby Hebert	.04	.02
❑ 202	Dalton Hilliard	.04	.02
❑ 203	Sam Mills	.04	.02
❑ 204	Pat Swilling	.10	.05
❑ 205	Rickey Jackson	.04	.02
❑ 206	Stan Brock	.04	.02
❑ 207	Reginald Jones	.04	.02
❑ 208	Gill Fenerty	.04	.02
❑ 209	Eric Martin	.04	.02
❑ 210	Matt Bahr	.04	.02
❑ 211	Rodney Hampton	.25	.11
❑ 212	Jeff Hostetler	.10	.05
❑ 213	Pepper Johnson	.04	.02
❑ 214	Leonard Marshall	.04	.02
❑ 215	Doug Riesenberg	.04	.02
❑ 216	Stephen Baker	.04	.02
❑ 217	Mike Fox	.04	.02
❑ 218	Bart Oates	.04	.02
❑ 219	Everson Walls	.04	.02
❑ 220	Gary Reasons	.04	.02
❑ 221	Jeff Lageman	.04	.02
❑ 222	Joe Kelly	.04	.02
❑ 223	Mo Lewis	.04	.02
❑ 224	Tony Stargell	.04	.02
❑ 225	Jim Sweeney	.04	.02
❑ 226	Freeman McNeil	.04	.02
❑ 227	Brian Washington	.04	.02
❑ 228	Johnny Hector	.04	.02
❑ 229	Terance Mathis	.10	.05
❑ 230	Rob Moore	.10	.05
❑ 231	Brad Baxter	.04	.02
❑ 232	Eric Allen	.04	.02
❑ 233	Fred Barnett	.25	.11
❑ 234	Jerome Brown	.04	.02
❑ 235	Keith Byars	.04	.02
❑ 236	William Thomas	.04	.02
❑ 237	Jessie Small	.04	.02
❑ 238	Robert Drummond	.04	.02
❑ 239	Reggie White	.25	.11
❑ 240	James Joseph	.04	.02
❑ 241	Brad Goebel	.04	.02
❑ 242	Clyde Simmons	.04	.02
❑ 243	Rich Camarillo	.04	.02
❑ 244	Ken Harvey	.04	.02
❑ 245	Garth Jax	.04	.02
❑ 246	Johnny Johnson UER (Photo on back not him)	.04	.02
❑ 247	Mike Jones	.04	.02
❑ 248	Ernie Jones	.04	.02
❑ 249	Tom Tupa	.04	.02
❑ 250	Ron Wolfley	.04	.02
❑ 251	Luis Sharpe	.04	.02
❑ 252	Eric Swann	.10	.05
❑ 253	Anthony Thompson	.04	.02
❑ 254	Gary Anderson K	.04	.02
❑ 255	Dermontti Dawson	.04	.02
❑ 256	Jeff Graham	.25	.11
❑ 257	Eric Green	.04	.02
❑ 258	Louis Lipps	.04	.02
❑ 259	Neil O'Donnell	.25	.11
❑ 260	Rod Woodson	.25	.11
❑ 261	Dwight Stone	.04	.02
❑ 262	Aaron Jones	.04	.02
❑ 263	Keith Willis	.04	.02
❑ 264	Ernie Mills	.04	.02
❑ 265	Martin Bayless	.04	.02
❑ 266	Rod Bernstine	.04	.02
❑ 267	John Carney	.04	.02
❑ 268	John Friesz	.10	.05
❑ 269	Nate Lewis	.04	.02
❑ 270	Shawn Jefferson	.04	.02
❑ 271	Burt Grossman	.04	.02
❑ 272	Eric Moten	.04	.02
❑ 273	Gary Plummer	.04	.02
❑ 274	Henry Rolling	.04	.02
❑ 275	Steve Hendrickson RC	.04	.02
❑ 276	Michael Carter	.04	.02
❑ 277	Steve Bono RC	.25	.11
❑ 278	Dexter Carter	.04	.02
❑ 279	Mike Cofer	.04	.02
❑ 280	Charles Haley	.10	.05
❑ 281	Tom Rathman	.04	.02
❑ 282	Guy McIntyre	.04	.02
❑ 283	John Taylor	.10	.05
❑ 284	Dave Waymer	.04	.02
❑ 285	Steve Wallace	.04	.02
❑ 286	Jamie Williams	.04	.02
❑ 287	Brian Blades	.10	.05
❑ 288	Jeff Bryant	.04	.02
❑ 289	Grant Feasel	.04	.02
❑ 290	Jacob Green	.04	.02
❑ 291	Andy Heck	.04	.02
❑ 292	Kelly Stouffer	.04	.02
❑ 293	John Kasay	.04	.02
❑ 294	Cortez Kennedy	.10	.05
❑ 295	Bryan Millard	.04	.02
❑ 296	Eugene Robinson	.04	.02
❑ 297	Tony Woods	.04	.02
❑ 298	Jesse Anderson UER (Should have Tight End, not TIGHT END)	.04	.02
❑ 299	Gary Anderson RB	.04	.02
❑ 300	Mark Carrier WR	.10	.05
❑ 301	Reggie Cobb	.04	.02
❑ 302	Robert Wilson	.04	.02
❑ 303	Jesse Solomon	.04	.02
❑ 304	Broderick Thomas	.04	.02
❑ 305	Lawrence Dawsey	.10	.05
❑ 306	Charles McRae	.04	.02
❑ 307	Paul Gruber	.04	.02
❑ 308	Vinny Testaverde	.10	.05
❑ 309	Brian Mitchell	.10	.05
❑ 310	Darrell Green	.04	.02
❑ 311	Art Monk	.10	.05
❑ 312	Russ Grimm	.04	.02
❑ 313	Mark Rypien	.04	.02
❑ 314	Bobby Wilson	.04	.02
❑ 315	Wilber Marshall	.04	.02
❑ 316	Gerald Riggs	.04	.02
❑ 317	Chip Lohmiller	.04	.02
❑ 318	Joe Jacoby	.04	.02
❑ 319	Martin Mayhew	.04	.02
❑ 320	Amp Lee RC	.04	.02
❑ 321	Terrell Buckley RC	.04	.02
❑ 322	Tommy Vardell RC	.10	.05
❑ 323	Ricardo McDonald RC	.04	.02
❑ 324	Joe Bowden RC	.04	.02
❑ 325	Darryl Williams RC	.04	.02
❑ 326	Carlos Huerta	.04	.02
❑ 327	Patrick Rowe RC	.04	.02
❑ 328	Siran Stacy RC	.04	.02
❑ 329	Dexter McNabb RC	.04	.02
❑ 330	Willie Clay RC	.04	.02
❑ 331	Oliver Barnett	.04	.02
❑ 332	Aundray Bruce	.04	.02
❑ 333	Ken Tippins RC	.04	.02
❑ 334	Jessie Tuggle	.04	.02
❑ 335	Brian Jordan	.10	.05
❑ 336	Andre Rison	.10	.05
❑ 337	Houston Hoover	.04	.02
❑ 338	Bill Fralic	.04	.02
❑ 339	Pat Chaffey RC	.04	.02
❑ 340	Keith Jones	.04	.02
❑ 341	Jamie Dukes RC	.04	.02
❑ 342	Chris Mohr	.04	.02
❑ 343	John Davis	.04	.02
❑ 344	Ray Bentley	.04	.02
❑ 345	Scott Norwood	.04	.02
❑ 346	Shane Conlan	.04	.02
❑ 347	Steve Tasker	.10	.05
❑ 348	Will Wolford	.04	.02
❑ 349	Gary Baldinger RC	.04	.02
❑ 350	Kirby Jackson	.04	.02
❑ 351	Jamie Mueller	.04	.02
❑ 352	Pete Metzelaars	.04	.02
❑ 353	Richard Dent	.10	.05
❑ 354	Ron Rivera	.04	.02
❑ 355	Jim Morrissey	.04	.02
❑ 356	John Roper	.04	.02
❑ 357	Steve McMichael	.10	.05
❑ 358	Ron Morris	.04	.02
❑ 359	Darren Lewis	.04	.02
❑ 360	Anthony Morgan	.04	.02
❑ 361	Stan Thomas	.04	.02
❑ 362	James Thornton	.04	.02
❑ 363	Brad Muster	.04	.02
❑ 364	Tim Krumrie	.04	.02
❑ 365	Lee Johnson	.04	.02
❑ 366	Eric Ball	.04	.02
❑ 367	Alonzo Mitz RC	.04	.02
❑ 368	David Grant	.04	.02
❑ 369	Lynn James	.04	.02
❑ 370	Lewis Billups	.04	.02
❑ 371	Jim Breech	.04	.02
❑ 372	Alfred Williams	.04	.02
❑ 373	Wayne Haddix	.04	.02
❑ 374	Tim McGee	.04	.02
❑ 375	Michael Jackson	.10	.05
❑ 376	Leroy Hoard	.10	.05
❑ 377	Tony Jones	.04	.02
❑ 378	Vince Newsome	.04	.02
❑ 379	Todd Philcox RC	.04	.02
❑ 380	Eric Metcalf	.10	.05
❑ 381	John Rienstra	.04	.02
❑ 382	Matt Stover	.04	.02
❑ 383	Brian Hansen	.04	.02
❑ 384	Joe Morris	.04	.02
❑ 385	Anthony Pleasant	.04	.02
❑ 386	Mark Stepnoski	.10	.05
❑ 387	Erik Williams	.04	.02
❑ 388	Jimmie Jones	.04	.02
❑ 389	Kevin Gogan	.04	.02
❑ 390	Manny Hendrix RC	.04	.02
❑ 391	Issiac Holt	.04	.02
❑ 392	Ken Norton	.25	.11
❑ 393	Tommie Agee	.04	.02
❑ 394	Alvin Harper	.10	.05
❑ 395	Alexander Wright	.04	.02
❑ 396	Mike Saxon	.04	.02
❑ 397	Michael Brooks	.04	.02
❑ 398	Bobby Humphrey	.04	.02
❑ 399	Ken Lanier	.04	.02
❑ 400	Steve Sewell	.04	.02
❑ 401	Robert Perryman	.04	.02
❑ 402	Wymon Henderson	.04	.02
❑ 403	Keith Kartz	.04	.02
❑ 404	Clarence Kay	.04	.02
❑ 405	Keith Traylor	.04	.02
❑ 406	Doug Widell	.04	.02
❑ 407	Dennis Smith	.04	.02
❑ 408	Marc Spindler	.04	.02
❑ 409	Lomas Brown	.04	.02
❑ 410	Robert Clark	.04	.02
❑ 411	Eric Andolsek	.04	.02
❑ 412	Mike Farr	.04	.02
❑ 413	Ray Crockett	.04	.02
❑ 414	Jeff Campbell	.04	.02
❑ 415	Dan Owens	.04	.02
❑ 416	Jim Arnold	.04	.02
❑ 417	Barry Sanders	1.50	.70
❑ 418	Eddie Murray	.04	.02
❑ 419	Vince Workman	.10	.05
❑ 420	Ed West	.04	.02
❑ 421	Charles Wilson	.04	.02
❑ 422	Perry Kemp	.04	.02
❑ 423	Chuck Cecil	.04	.02
❑ 424	James Campen	.04	.02
❑ 425	Robert Brown	.04	.02
❑ 426	Brian Noble	.04	.02
❑ 427	Rich Moran	.04	.02

❑ 428 Vai Sikahema .04 .02
❑ 429 Allen Rice .04 .02
❑ 430 Haywood Jeffires .10 .05
❑ 431 Warren Moon .25 .11
❑ 432 Greg Montgomery .04 .02
❑ 433 Sean Jones .10 .05
❑ 434 Richard Johnson .04 .02
❑ 435 Al Smith .04 .02
❑ 436 Johnny Meads .04 .02
❑ 437 William Fuller .10 .05
❑ 438 Mike Munchak .04 .02
❑ 439 Ray Childress .04 .02
❑ 440 Cody Carlson .04 .02
❑ 441 Scott Radecic .04 .02
❑ 442 Quintus McDonald RC .04 .02
❑ 443 Eugene Daniel .04 .02
❑ 444 Mark Herrmann RC .04 .02
❑ 445 John Baylor RC .04 .02
❑ 446 Dave McCloughan .04 .02
❑ 447 Mark Vander Poel .04 .02
❑ 448 Randy Dixon .04 .02
❑ 449 Keith Taylor .04 .02
❑ 450 Alan Grant .04 .02
❑ 451 Tony Siragusa .04 .02
❑ 452 Rich Baldinger .04 .02
❑ 453 Derrick Thomas .25 .11
❑ 454 Bill Jones RC .04 .02
❑ 455 Troy Stradford .04 .02
❑ 456 Barry Word .04 .02
❑ 457 Tim Grunhard .04 .02
❑ 458 Chris Martin .04 .02
❑ 459 Jayice Pearson RC .04 .02
❑ 460 Dino Hackett .04 .02
❑ 461 David Lutz .04 .02
❑ 462 Albert Lewis .04 .02
❑ 463 Fred Jones RC .04 .02
❑ 464 Winston Moss .04 .02
❑ 465 Sam Graddy RC .04 .02
❑ 466 Steve Wisniewski .04 .02
❑ 467 Jay Schroeder .04 .02
❑ 468 Ronnie Lott .10 .05
❑ 469 Willie Gault .10 .05
❑ 470 Greg Townsend .04 .02
❑ 471 Max Montoya .04 .02
❑ 472 Howie Long .10 .05
❑ 473 Lionel Washington .04 .02
❑ 474 Riki Ellison .04 .02
❑ 475 Tom Newberry .04 .02
❑ 476 Damone Johnson .04 .02
❑ 477 Pat Terrell .04 .02
❑ 478 Marcus Dupree .04 .02
❑ 479 Todd Lyght .04 .02
❑ 480 Buford McGee .04 .02
❑ 481 Bern Brostek .04 .02
❑ 482 Jim Price .04 .02
❑ 483 Robert Young .04 .02
❑ 484 Tony Zendejas .04 .02
❑ 485 Robert Bailey RC .04 .02
❑ 486 Alvin Wright .04 .02
❑ 487 Pat Carter .04 .02
❑ 488 Pete Stoyanovich .04 .02
❑ 489 Reggie Roby .04 .02
❑ 490 Harry Galbreath .04 .02
❑ 491 Mike McGruder RC**/C .04 .02
❑ 492 J.B. Brown .04 .02
❑ 493 E.J. Junior .04 .02
❑ 494 Ferrell Edmunds .04 .02
❑ 495 Scott Secules .04 .02
❑ 496 Greg Baty RC .04 .02
❑ 497 Mike Iaquaniello .04 .02
❑ 498 Keith Sims .04 .02
❑ 499 John Randle .10 .05
❑ 500 Joey Browner .04 .02
❑ 501 Steve Jordan .04 .02
❑ 502 Darrin Nelson .04 .02
❑ 503 Audray McMillian .04 .02
❑ 504 Harry Newsome .04 .02
❑ 505 Hassan Jones .04 .02
❑ 506 Ray Berry .04 .02
❑ 507 Mike Merriweather .04 .02
❑ 508 Leo Lewis .04 .02
❑ 509 Tim Irwin .04 .02
❑ 510 Kirk Lowdermilk .04 .02
❑ 511 Alfred Anderson .04 .02
❑ 512 Michael Timpson RC .10 .05
❑ 513 Jerome Henderson .04 .02
❑ 514 Andre Tippett .04 .02
❑ 515 Chris Singleton .04 .02
❑ 516 John Stephens .04 .02
❑ 517 Ronnie Lippett .04 .02
❑ 518 Bruce Armstrong .04 .02
❑ 519 Marion Hobby RC .04 .02
❑ 520 Tim Goad .04 .02
❑ 521 Mickey Washington RC .04 .02
❑ 522 Fred Smerlas .04 .02
❑ 523 Wayne Martin .04 .02
❑ 524 Frank Warren .04 .02
❑ 525 Floyd Turner .04 .02
❑ 526 Wesley Carroll .04 .02
❑ 527 Gene Atkins .04 .02
❑ 528 Vaughan Johnson .04 .02
❑ 529 Hoby Brenner .04 .02
❑ 530 Renaldo Turnbull .04 .02
❑ 531 Joel Hilgenberg .04 .02
❑ 532 Craig Heyward .10 .05
❑ 533 Vince Buck .04 .02
❑ 534 Jim Dombrowski .04 .02
❑ 535 Fred McAfee RC .04 .02
❑ 536 Phil Simms .10 .05
❑ 537 Lewis Tillman .04 .02
❑ 538 John Elliott .04 .02
❑ 539 Dave Meggett .10 .05
❑ 540 Mark Collins .04 .02
❑ 541 Ottis Anderson .10 .05
❑ 542 Bobby Abrams RC .04 .02
❑ 543 Sean Landeta .04 .02
❑ 544 Brian Williams OL .04 .02
❑ 545 Erik Howard .04 .02
❑ 546 Mark Ingram .04 .02
❑ 547 Kanavis McGhee .04 .02
❑ 548 Kyle Clifton .04 .02
❑ 549 Marvin Washington .04 .02
❑ 550 Jeff Criswell .04 .02
❑ 551 Dave Cadigan .04 .02
❑ 552 Chris Burkett .04 .02
❑ 553 Erik McMillan .04 .02
❑ 554 James Hasty .04 .02
❑ 555 Louie Aguiar RC .04 .02
❑ 556 Troy Johnson RC .04 .02
❑ 557 Troy Taylor RC .04 .02
❑ 558 Pat Kelly RC .04 .02
❑ 559 Heath Sherman .04 .02
❑ 560 Roger Ruzek .04 .02
❑ 561 Andre Waters .04 .02
❑ 562 Izel Jenkins .04 .02
❑ 563 Keith Jackson .10 .05
❑ 564 Byron Evans .04 .02
❑ 565 Wes Hopkins .04 .02
❑ 566 Rich Miano .04 .02
❑ 567 Seth Joyner .10 .05
❑ 568 Thomas Sanders .04 .02
❑ 569 David Alexander .04 .02
❑ 570 Jeff Kemp .04 .02
❑ 571 Jock Jones RC .04 .02
❑ 572 Craig Patterson RC .04 .02
❑ 573 Robert Massey .04 .02
❑ 574 Bill Lewis .04 .02
❑ 575 Freddie Joe Nunn .04 .02
❑ 576 Aeneas Williams .10 .05
❑ 577 John Jackson .04 .02
❑ 578 Tim McDonald .04 .02
❑ 579 Michael Zordich RC .04 .02
❑ 580 Eric Hill .04 .02
❑ 581 Lorenzo Lynch .04 .02
❑ 582 Vernice Smith RC .04 .02
❑ 583 Greg Lloyd .25 .11
❑ 584 Carnell Lake .04 .02
❑ 585 Hardy Nickerson .10 .05
❑ 586 Delton Hall .04 .02
❑ 587 Gerald Williams .04 .02
❑ 588 Bryan Hinkle .04 .02
❑ 589 Barry Foster .10 .05
❑ 590 Bubby Brister .04 .02
❑ 591 Rick Strom RC .04 .02
❑ 592 David Little .04 .02
❑ 593 Leroy Thompson RC .04 .02
❑ 594 Eric Bieniemy .04 .02
❑ 595 Courtney Hall .04 .02
❑ 596 George Thornton .04 .02
❑ 597 Donnie Elder .04 .02
❑ 598 Billy Ray Smith .04 .02
❑ 599 Gill Byrd .04 .02
❑ 600 Marion Butts .04 .02
❑ 601 Ronnie Harmon .04 .02
❑ 602 Anthony Shelton .04 .02
❑ 603 Mark May .04 .02
❑ 604 Craig McEwen RC .04 .02
❑ 605 Steve Young .60 .25
❑ 606 Keith Henderson .04 .02
❑ 607 Pierce Holt .04 .02
❑ 608 Roy Foster .04 .02
❑ 609 Don Griffin .04 .02
❑ 610 Harry Sydney .04 .02
❑ 611 Todd Bowles .04 .02
❑ 612 Ted Washington .04 .02
❑ 613 Johnnie Jackson .04 .02
❑ 614 Jesse Sapolu .04 .02
❑ 615 Brent Jones .10 .05
❑ 616 Travis McNeal .04 .02
❑ 617 Darrick Brilz RC .04 .02
❑ 618 Terry Wooden .04 .02
❑ 619 Tommy Kane .04 .02
❑ 620 Nesby Glasgow .04 .02
❑ 621 Dwayne Harper .04 .02
❑ 622 Rick Tuten .04 .02
❑ 623 Chris Warren .25 .11
❑ 624 John L. Williams .04 .02
❑ 625 Rufus Porter .04 .02
❑ 626 David Daniels .04 .02
❑ 627 Keith McCants .04 .02
❑ 628 Reuben Davis .04 .02
❑ 629 Mark Royals .04 .02
❑ 630 Marty Carter RC .04 .02
❑ 631 Ian Beckles .04 .02
❑ 632 Ron Hall .04 .02
❑ 633 Eugene Marve .04 .02
❑ 634 Willie Drewrey .04 .02
❑ 635 Tom McHale RC .04 .02
❑ 636 Kevin Murphy .04 .02
❑ 637 Robert Hardy RC .04 .02
❑ 638 Ricky Sanders .04 .02
❑ 639 Gary Clark .25 .11
❑ 640 Andre Collins .04 .02
❑ 641 Brad Edwards .04 .02
❑ 642 Monte Coleman .04 .02
❑ 643 Clarence Vaughn RC .04 .02
❑ 644 Fred Stokes .04 .02
❑ 645 Charles Mann .04 .02
❑ 646 Earnest Byner .04 .02
❑ 647 Jim Lachey .04 .02
❑ 648 Jeff Bostic .04 .02
❑ 649 Chris Mims RC .10 .05
❑ 650 George Williams RC .04 .02
❑ 651 Ed Cunningham RC .04 .02
❑ 652 Tony Smith RC .04 .02
❑ 653 Will Furrer RC .04 .02
❑ 654 Matt Elliott RC .04 .02
❑ 655 Mike Mooney RC .04 .02
❑ 656 Eddie Blake RC .04 .02
❑ 657 Leon Searcy RC .10 .05
❑ 658 Kevin Turner RC .04 .02
❑ 659 Keith Hamilton RC .10 .05
❑ 660 Alan Haller RC .04 .02

1993 Pacific

	MINT	NRMT
COMPLETE SET (440)	20.00	9.00
❑ 1 Emmitt Smith	1.50	.70
❑ 2 Troy Aikman	.75	.35

❑	3 Larry Brown DB	.05	.02
❑	4 Tony Casillas	.05	.02
❑	5 Thomas Everett	.05	.02
❑	6 Alvin Harper	.10	.05
❑	7 Michael Irvin	.25	.11
❑	8 Charles Haley	.10	.05
❑	9 Leon Lett RC	.10	.05
❑	10 Kevin Smith	.10	.05
❑	11 Robert Jones	.05	.02
❑	12 Jimmy Smith	.10	.05
❑	13 Derrick Gainer RC	.05	.02
❑	14 Lin Elliott	.05	.02
❑	15 William Thomas	.05	.02
❑	16 Clyde Simmons	.05	.02
❑	17 Seth Joyner	.05	.02
❑	18 Randall Cunningham	.25	.11
❑	19 Byron Evans	.05	.02
❑	20 Fred Barnett	.10	.05
❑	21 Calvin Williams	.10	.05
❑	22 James Joseph	.05	.02
❑	23 Heath Sherman	.05	.02
❑	24 Siran Stacy	.05	.02
❑	25 Andy Harmon	.10	.05
❑	26 Eric Allen	.05	.02
❑	27 Herschel Walker	.10	.05
❑	28 Vai Sikahema	.05	.02
❑	29 Earnest Byner	.05	.02
❑	30 Jeff Bostic	.05	.02
❑	31 Monte Coleman	.05	.02
❑	32 Ricky Ervins	.05	.02
❑	33 Darrell Green	.05	.02
❑	34 Mark Schlereth	.05	.02
❑	35 Mark Rypien	.05	.02
❑	36 Art Monk	.10	.05
❑	37 Brian Mitchell	.10	.05
❑	38 Chip Lohmiller	.05	.02
❑	39 Charles Mann	.05	.02
❑	40 Shane Collins	.05	.02
❑	41 Jim Lachey	.05	.02
❑	42 Desmond Howard	.10	.05
❑	43 Rodney Hampton	.25	.11
❑	44 Dave Brown RC	.25	.11
❑	45 Mark Collins	.05	.02
❑	46 Jarrod Bunch	.05	.02
❑	47 William Roberts	.05	.02
❑	48 Sean Landeta	.05	.02
❑	49 Lawrence Taylor	.25	.11
❑	50 Ed McCaffrey	.10	.05
❑	51 Bart Oates	.05	.02
❑	52 Pepper Johnson	.05	.02
❑	53 Eric Dorsey	.05	.02
❑	54 Erik Howard	.05	.02
❑	55 Phil Simms	.10	.05
❑	56 Derek Brown TE	.05	.02
❑	57 Johnny Bailey	.05	.02
❑	58 Rich Camarillo	.05	.02
❑	59 Larry Centers RC	.25	.11
❑	60 Chris Chandler	.10	.05
❑	61 Randal Hill	.05	.02
❑	62 Ricky Proehl	.05	.02
❑	63 Freddie Joe Nunn	.05	.02
❑	64 Robert Massey	.05	.02
❑	65 Aeneas Williams	.05	.02
❑	66 Luis Sharpe	.05	.02
❑	67 Eric Swann	.10	.05
❑	68 Timm Rosenbach	.05	.02
❑	69 Anthony Edwards RC	.05	.02
❑	70 Greg Davis	.05	.02
❑	71 Terry Allen	.25	.11
❑	72 Anthony Carter	.10	.05
❑	73 Cris Carter	.50	.23
❑	74 Roger Craig	.10	.05
❑	75 Jack Del Rio	.05	.02
❑	76 Chris Doleman	.05	.02
❑	77 Rich Gannon	.25	.11
❑	78 Hassan Jones	.05	.02
❑	79 Steve Jordan	.05	.02
❑	80 Randall McDaniel	.05	.02
❑	81 Sean Salisbury	.05	.02
❑	82 Harry Newsome	.05	.02
❑	83 Carlos Jenkins	.05	.02
❑	84 Jake Reed	.25	.11
❑	85 Edgar Bennett	.25	.11
❑	86 Tony Bennett	.05	.02
❑	87 Terrell Buckley	.05	.02
❑	88 Ty Detmer	.25	.11
❑	89 Brett Favre	2.00	.90
❑	90 Chris Jacke	.05	.02
❑	91 Sterling Sharpe	.25	.11
❑	92 James Campen	.05	.02
❑	93 Brian Noble	.05	.02
❑	94 Lester Archambeau RC	.05	.02
❑	95 Harry Sydney	.05	.02
❑	96 Corey Harris	.05	.02
❑	97 Don Majkowski	.05	.02
❑	98 Ken Ruettgers	.05	.02
❑	99 Lomas Brown	.05	.02
❑	100 Jason Hanson	.05	.02
❑	101 Robert Porcher	.05	.02
❑	102 Chris Spielman	.10	.05
❑	103 Erik Kramer	.10	.05
❑	104 Tracy Scroggins	.05	.02
❑	105 Rodney Peete	.05	.02
❑	106 Barry Sanders	1.50	.70
❑	107 Herman Moore	.50	.23
❑	108 Brett Perriman	.25	.11
❑	109 Mel Gray	.10	.05
❑	110 Dennis Gibson	.05	.02
❑	111 Bennie Blades	.05	.02
❑	112 Andre Ware	.05	.02
❑	113 Gary Anderson RB	.05	.02
❑	114 Tyji Armstrong	.05	.02
❑	115 Reggie Cobb	.05	.02
❑	116 Marty Carter	.05	.02
❑	117 Lawrence Dawsey	.05	.02
❑	118 Steve DeBerg	.05	.02
❑	119 Ron Hall	.05	.02
❑	120 Courtney Hawkins	.05	.02
❑	121 Broderick Thomas	.05	.02
❑	122 Keith McCants	.05	.02
❑	123 Bruce Reimers	.05	.02
❑	124 Darrick Brownlow	.05	.02
❑	125 Mark Wheeler	.05	.02
❑	126 Ricky Reynolds	.05	.02
❑	127 Neal Anderson	.05	.02
❑	128 Trace Armstrong	.05	.02
❑	129 Mark Carrier DB	.05	.02
❑	130 Richard Dent	.10	.05
❑	131 Wendell Davis	.05	.02
❑	132 Darren Lewis	.05	.02
❑	133 Tom Waddle	.05	.02
❑	134 Jim Harbaugh	.25	.11
❑	135 Steve McMichael	.10	.05
❑	136 William Perry	.10	.05
❑	137 Alonzo Spellman	.05	.02
❑	138 John Roper	.05	.02
❑	139 Peter Tom Willis	.05	.02
❑	140 Dante Jones	.05	.02
❑	141 Harris Barton	.05	.02
❑	142 Michael Carter	.05	.02
❑	143 Eric Davis	.05	.02
❑	144 Dana Hall	.05	.02
❑	145 Amp Lee	.05	.02
❑	146 Don Griffin	.05	.02
❑	147 Jerry Rice	1.00	.45
❑	148 Ricky Watters	.25	.11
❑	149 Steve Young	.75	.35
❑	150 Bill Romanowski	.05	.02
❑	151 Klaus Wilmsmeyer	.05	.02
❑	152 Steve Bono	.25	.11
❑	153 Tom Rathman	.05	.02
❑	154 Odessa Turner	.05	.02
❑	155 Morten Andersen	.05	.02
❑	156 Richard Cooper	.05	.02
❑	157 Toi Cook	.05	.02
❑	158 Quinn Early	.10	.05
❑	159 Vaughn Dunbar	.05	.02
❑	160 Rickey Jackson	.05	.02
❑	161 Wayne Martin	.05	.02
❑	162 Hoby Brenner	.05	.02
❑	163 Joel Hilgenberg	.05	.02
❑	164 Mike Buck	.05	.02
❑	165 Torrance Small	.05	.02
❑	166 Eric Martin	.05	.02
❑	167 Vaughan Johnson	.05	.02
❑	168 Sam Mills	.05	.02
❑	169 Steve Broussard	.05	.02
❑	170 Darion Conner	.05	.02
❑	171 Drew Hill	.05	.02
❑	172 Chris Hinton	.05	.02
❑	173 Chris Miller	.10	.05
❑	174 Tim McKyer	.05	.02
❑	175 Norm Johnson	.05	.02
❑	176 Mike Pritchard	.10	.05
❑	177 Andre Rison	.10	.05
❑	178 Deion Sanders	.50	.23
❑	179 Tony Smith	.05	.02
❑	180 Bruce Pickens	.05	.02
❑	181 Michael Haynes	.10	.05
❑	182 Jessie Tuggle	.05	.02
❑	183 Marc Boutte	.05	.02
❑	184 Don Bracken	.05	.02
❑	185 Bern Brostek	.05	.02
❑	186 Henry Ellard	.10	.05
❑	187 Jim Everett	.10	.05
❑	188 Sean Gilbert	.10	.05
❑	189 Cleveland Gary	.05	.02
❑	190 Todd Kinchen	.05	.02
❑	191 Pat Terrell	.05	.02
❑	192 Jackie Slater	.05	.02
❑	193 David Lang	.05	.02
❑	194 Flipper Anderson	.05	.02
❑	195 Tony Zendejas	.05	.02
❑	196 Roman Phifer	.05	.02
❑	197 Steve Christie	.05	.02
❑	198 Cornelius Bennett	.10	.05
❑	199 Phil Hansen	.05	.02
❑	200 Don Beebe	.05	.02
❑	201 Mark Kelso	.05	.02
❑	202 Bruce Smith	.25	.11
❑	203 Darryl Talley	.05	.02
❑	204 Andre Reed	.10	.05
❑	205 Mike Lodish	.05	.02
❑	206 Jim Kelly	.25	.11
❑	207 Thurman Thomas	.25	.11
❑	208 Kenneth Davis	.05	.02
❑	209 Frank Reich	.10	.05
❑	210 Kent Hull	.05	.02
❑	211 Marco Coleman	.05	.02
❑	212 Bryan Cox	.05	.02
❑	213 Jeff Cross	.05	.02
❑	214 Mark Higgs	.05	.02
❑	215 Keith Jackson	.10	.05
❑	216 Scott Miller	.05	.02
❑	217 John Offerdahl	.05	.02
❑	218 Dan Marino	1.50	.70
❑	219 Keith Sims	.05	.02
❑	220 Chuck Klingbeil	.05	.02
❑	221 Troy Vincent	.05	.02
❑	222 Mike Williams RC	.05	.02
❑	223 Pete Stoyanovich	.05	.02
❑	224 J.B. Brown	.05	.02
❑	225 Ashley Ambrose	.05	.02
❑	226 Jason Belser RC	.05	.02
❑	227 Jeff George	.25	.11
❑	228 Quentin Coryatt	.10	.05
❑	229 Duane Bickett	.05	.02
❑	230 Steve Emtman	.05	.02
❑	231 Anthony Johnson	.10	.05
❑	232 Rohn Stark	.05	.02
❑	233 Jessie Hester	.05	.02
❑	234 Reggie Langhorne	.05	.02
❑	235 Clarence Verdin	.05	.02
❑	236 Dean Biasucci	.05	.02
❑	237 Jack Trudeau	.05	.02
❑	238 Tony Siragusa	.05	.02
❑	239 Chris Burkett	.05	.02
❑	240 Brad Baxter	.05	.02
❑	241 Rob Moore	.10	.05
❑	242 Browning Nagle	.05	.02
❑	243 Jim Sweeney	.05	.02
❑	244 Kurt Barber	.05	.02
❑	245 Siupeli Malamala RC	.05	.02
❑	246 Mike Brim	.05	.02
❑	247 Mo Lewis	.05	.02
❑	248 Johnny Mitchell	.05	.02
❑	249 Ken Whisenhunt RC	.05	.02
❑	250 James Hasty	.05	.02
❑	251 Kyle Clifton	.05	.02
❑	252 Terance Mathis	.10	.05
❑	253 Ray Agnew	.05	.02
❑	254 Eugene Chung	.05	.02
❑	255 Marv Cook	.05	.02
❑	256 Johnny Rembert	.05	.02
❑	257 Maurice Hurst	.05	.02
❑	258 Jon Vaughn	.05	.02
❑	259 Leonard Russell	.10	.05
❑	260 Pat Harlow	.05	.02

❑ 261 Andre Tippett .05 .02
❑ 262 Michael Timpson .05 .02
❑ 263 Greg McMurtry .05 .02
❑ 264 Chris Singleton .05 .02
❑ 265 Reggie Redding RC .05 .02
❑ 266 Walter Stanley .05 .02
❑ 267 Gary Anderson K .05 .02
❑ 268 Merril Hoge .05 .02
❑ 269 Barry Foster .10 .05
❑ 270 Charles Davenport .05 .02
❑ 271 Jeff Graham .10 .05
❑ 272 Adrian Cooper .05 .02
❑ 273 David Little .05 .02
❑ 274 Neil O'Donnell .25 .11
❑ 275 Rod Woodson .25 .11
❑ 276 Ernie Mills .05 .02
❑ 277 Dwight Stone .05 .02
❑ 278 Darren Perry .05 .02
❑ 279 Dermontti Dawson .05 .02
❑ 280 Carlton Haselrig .05 .02
❑ 281 Pat Coleman .05 .02
❑ 282 Ernest Givins .10 .05
❑ 283 Warren Moon .25 .11
❑ 284 Haywood Jeffires .10 .05
❑ 285 Cody Carlson .05 .02
❑ 286 Ray Childress .05 .02
❑ 287 Bruce Matthews .05 .02
❑ 288 Webster Slaughter .05 .02
❑ 289 Bo Orlando .05 .02
❑ 290 Lorenzo White .05 .02
❑ 291 Eddie Robinson .05 .02
❑ 292 Bubba McDowell .05 .02
❑ 293 Bucky Richardson .05 .02
❑ 294 Sean Jones .05 .02
❑ 295 David Brandon .05 .02
❑ 296 Shawn Collins .05 .02
❑ 297 Lawyer Tillman .05 .02
❑ 298 Bob Dahl .05 .02
❑ 299 Kevin Mack .05 .02
❑ 300 Bernie Kosar .10 .05
❑ 301 Tommy Vardell .05 .02
❑ 302 Jay Hilgenberg .05 .02
❑ 303 Michael Dean Perry .10 .05
❑ 304 Michael Jackson .10 .05
❑ 305 Eric Metcalf .10 .05
❑ 306 Rico Smith RC .05 .02
❑ 307 Stevon Moore RC .05 .02
❑ 308 Leroy Hoard .10 .05
❑ 309 Eric Ball .05 .02
❑ 310 Derrick Fenner .05 .02
❑ 311 James Francis .05 .02
❑ 312 Ricardo McDonald .05 .02
❑ 313 Tim Krumrie .05 .02
❑ 314 Carl Pickens .25 .11
❑ 315 David Klingler .05 .02
❑ 316 Donald Hollas RC .05 .02
❑ 317 Harold Green .05 .02
❑ 318 Daniel Stubbs .05 .02
❑ 319 Alfred Williams .05 .02
❑ 320 Darryl Williams .05 .02
❑ 321 Mike Arthur RC .05 .02
❑ 322 Leonard Wheeler .05 .02
❑ 323 Gill Byrd .05 .02
❑ 324 Eric Bieniemy .05 .02
❑ 325 Marion Butts .05 .02
❑ 326 John Carney .05 .02
❑ 327 Stan Humphries .25 .11
❑ 328 Ronnie Harmon .05 .02
❑ 329 Junior Seau .25 .11
❑ 330 Nate Lewis .05 .02
❑ 331 Harry Swayne .05 .02
❑ 332 Leslie O'Neal .10 .05
❑ 333 Eric Moten .05 .02
❑ 334 Blaise Winter RC .05 .02
❑ 335 Anthony Miller .10 .05
❑ 336 Gary Plummer .05 .02
❑ 337 Willie Davis .25 .11
❑ 338 J.J. Birden .05 .02
❑ 339 Tim Barnett .05 .02
❑ 340 Dave Krieg .10 .05
❑ 341 Barry Word .05 .02
❑ 342 Tracy Simien .05 .02
❑ 343 Christian Okoye .05 .02
❑ 344 Todd McNair .05 .02
❑ 345 Dan Saleaumua .05 .02
❑ 346 Derrick Thomas .25 .11
❑ 347 Harvey Williams .10 .05
❑ 348 Kimble Anders RC .25 .11
❑ 349 Tim Grunhard .05 .02
❑ 350 Tony Hargain RC UER .05 .02
(Hargrain on front)
❑ 351 Simon Fletcher .05 .02
❑ 352 John Elway 1.50 .70
❑ 353 Mike Croel .05 .02
❑ 354 Steve Atwater .05 .02
❑ 355 Tommy Maddox .05 .02
❑ 356 Karl Mecklenburg .05 .02
❑ 357 Shane Dronett .05 .02
❑ 358 Kenny Walker .05 .02
❑ 359 Reggie Rivers RC .05 .02
❑ 360 Cedric Tillman RC .05 .02
❑ 361 Arthur Marshall RC .05 .02
❑ 362 Greg Lewis .05 .02
❑ 363 Shannon Sharpe .25 .11
❑ 364 Doug Widell .05 .02
❑ 365 Todd Marinovich .05 .02
❑ 366 Nick Bell .05 .02
❑ 367 Eric Dickerson .10 .05
❑ 368 Max Montoya .05 .02
❑ 369 Winston Moss .05 .02
❑ 370 Howie Long .10 .05
❑ 371 Willie Gault .05 .02
❑ 372 Tim Brown .25 .11
❑ 373 Steve Smith .05 .02
❑ 374 Steve Wisniewski .05 .02
❑ 375 Alexander Wright .05 .02
❑ 376 Ethan Horton .05 .02
❑ 377 Napoleon McCallum .05 .02
❑ 378 Terry McDaniel .05 .02
❑ 379 Patrick Hunter .05 .02
❑ 380 Robert Blackmon .05 .02
❑ 381 John Kasay .05 .02
❑ 382 Cortez Kennedy .10 .05
❑ 383 Andy Heck .05 .02
❑ 384 Bill Hitchcock RC .05 .02
❑ 385 Rick Mirer RC .30 .14
❑ 386 Jeff Bryant .05 .02
❑ 387 Eugene Robinson .05 .02
❑ 388 John L. Williams .05 .02
❑ 389 Chris Warren .10 .05
❑ 390 Rufus Porter .05 .02
❑ 391 Joe Tofflemire RC .05 .02
❑ 392 Dan McGwire .05 .02
❑ 393 Boomer Esiason .10 .05
❑ 394 Brad Muster .05 .02
❑ 395 James Lofton .10 .05
❑ 396 Tim McGee .05 .02
❑ 397 Steve Beuerlein .05 .02
❑ 398 Gaston Green .05 .02
❑ 399 Bill Brooks .05 .02
❑ 400 Ronnie Lott .10 .05
❑ 401 Jay Schroeder .05 .02
❑ 402 Marcus Allen .25 .11
❑ 403 Kevin Greene .25 .11
❑ 404 Kirk Lowdermilk .05 .02
❑ 405 Hugh Millen .05 .02
❑ 406 Pat Swilling .05 .02
❑ 407 Bobby Hebert .05 .02
❑ 408 Carl Banks .05 .02
❑ 409 Jeff Hostetler .10 .05
❑ 410 Leonard Marshall .05 .02
❑ 411 Ken O'Brien .05 .02
❑ 412 Joe Montana 1.50 .70
❑ 413 Reggie White .25 .11
❑ 414 Gary Clark .10 .05
❑ 415 Johnny Johnson .05 .02
❑ 416 Tim McDonald .05 .02
❑ 417 Pierce Holt .05 .02
❑ 418 Gino Torretta RC .10 .05
❑ 419 Glyn Milburn RC .25 .11
❑ 420 O.J. McDuffie RC .50 .23
❑ 421 Coleman Rudolph RC .05 .02
❑ 422 Reggie Brooks RC .10 .05
❑ 423 Garrison Hearst RC .50 .23
❑ 424 Leonard Renfro RC .05 .02
❑ 425 Kevin Williams RC .25 .11
❑ 426 Demetrius DuBose RC .05 .02
❑ 427 Elvis Grbac RC 1.50 .70
❑ 428 Lincoln Kennedy RC .05 .02
❑ 429 Carlton Gray RC .05 .02
❑ 430 Micheal Barrow RC .10 .05
❑ 431 George Teague RC .10 .05
❑ 432 Curtis Conway RC .40 .18
❑ 433 Natrone Means RC .40 .18
❑ 434 Jerome Bettis RC .75 .35
❑ 435 Drew Bledsoe RC 2.00 .90
❑ 436 Robert Smith RC 1.50 .70
❑ 437 Deon Figures RC .10 .05
❑ 438 Qadry Ismail RC .50 .23
❑ 439 Chris Slade RC .10 .05
❑ 440 Dana Stubblefield RC .25 .11

1994 Pacific

	MINT	NRMT
COMPLETE SET (450)	30.00	13.50

❑ 1 Troy Aikman 1.00 .45
❑ 2 Charles Haley .10 .05
❑ 3 Alvin Harper .10 .05
❑ 4 Michael Irvin .25 .11
❑ 5 Jim Jeffcoat .05 .02
❑ 6 Daryl Johnston .10 .05
❑ 7 Robert Jones .05 .02
❑ 8 Brock Marion RC .05 .02
❑ 9 Russell Maryland .05 .02
❑ 10 Ken Norton .10 .05
❑ 11 Jay Novacek .10 .05
❑ 12 Emmitt Smith 1.50 .70
❑ 13 Kevin Smith .05 .02
❑ 14 Tony Tolbert .05 .02
❑ 15 Kevin Williams WR .10 .05
❑ 16 Don Beebe .05 .02
❑ 17 Cornelius Bennett .10 .05
❑ 18 Bill Brooks .05 .02
❑ 19 Steve Christie .05 .02
❑ 20 Russell Copeland .05 .02
❑ 21 Kenneth Davis .05 .02
❑ 22 Kent Hull .05 .02
❑ 23 Jim Kelly .25 .11
❑ 24 Pete Metzelaars .05 .02
❑ 25 Andre Reed .10 .05
❑ 26 Frank Reich .10 .05
❑ 27 Bruce Smith .25 .11
❑ 28 Darryl Talley .05 .02
❑ 29 Steve Tasker .10 .05
❑ 30 Thurman Thomas .25 .11
❑ 31 Steve Bono .10 .05
❑ 32 Dexter Carter .05 .02
❑ 33 Kevin Fagan .05 .02
❑ 34 Dana Hall .05 .02
❑ 35 Brent Jones .10 .05
❑ 36 Amp Lee .05 .02
❑ 37 Marc Logan .05 .02
❑ 38 Tim McDonald .05 .02
❑ 39 Guy McIntyre .05 .02
❑ 40 Tom Rathman .05 .02
❑ 41 Jerry Rice 1.00 .45
❑ 42 Dana Stubblefield .25 .11
❑ 43 Steve Wallace .05 .02
❑ 44 Ricky Watters .25 .11
❑ 45 Steve Young .75 .35
❑ 46 Marcus Allen .25 .11
❑ 47 Kimble Anders .10 .05
❑ 48 Tim Barnett .05 .02
❑ 49 J.J. Birden .05 .02
❑ 50 Dale Carter .05 .02
❑ 51 Jonathan Hayes .05 .02
❑ 52 Dave Krieg .10 .05
❑ 53 Albert Lewis .05 .02

	No.	Player		
❑	54	Nick Lowery	.05	.02
❑	55	Joe Montana	2.00	.90
❑	56	Neil Smith	.25	.11
❑	57	John Stephens	.05	.02
❑	58	Derrick Thomas	.25	.11
❑	59	Harvey Williams	.10	.05
❑	60	Micheal Barrow	.05	.02
❑	61	Gary Brown	.05	.02
❑	62	Cody Carlson	.05	.02
❑	63	Ray Childress	.05	.02
❑	64	Curtis Duncan	.05	.02
❑	65	Ernest Givins	.10	.05
❑	66	Haywood Jeffires	.10	.05
❑	67	Wilber Marshall	.05	.02
❑	68	Bubba McDowell	.05	.02
❑	69	Warren Moon	.25	.11
❑	70	Mike Munchak	.05	.02
❑	71	Marcus Robertson	.05	.02
❑	72	Webster Slaughter	.05	.02
❑	73	Gary Wellman RC	.05	.02
❑	74	Lorenzo White	.05	.02
❑	75	Ray Crockett	.05	.02
❑	76	Jason Hanson	.05	.02
❑	77	Rodney Holman	.05	.02
❑	78	George Jamison	.05	.02
❑	79	Erik Kramer	.10	.05
❑	80	Ryan McNeil	.05	.02
❑	81	Derrick Moore	.05	.02
❑	82	Herman Moore	.25	.11
❑	83	Rodney Peete	.05	.02
❑	84	Brett Perriman	.10	.05
❑	85	Barry Sanders	2.00	.90
❑	86	Chris Spielman	.10	.05
❑	87	Pat Swilling	.05	.02
❑	88	Vernon Turner	.05	.02
❑	89	Andre Ware	.05	.02
❑	90	Michael Brooks	.05	.02
❑	91	Dave Brown	.10	.05
❑	92	Derek Brown TE	.05	.02
❑	93	Jarrod Bunch	.05	.02
❑	94	Chris Calloway	.05	.02
❑	95	Kent Graham	.10	.05
❑	96	Rodney Hampton	.25	.11
❑	97	Mark Jackson	.05	.02
❑	98	Ed McCaffrey	.10	.05
❑	99	Dave Meggett	.05	.02
❑	100	Aaron Pierce	.05	.02
❑	101	Mike Sherrard	.05	.02
❑	102	Phil Simms	.10	.05
❑	103	Lewis Tillman	.05	.02
❑	104	Eddie Anderson	.05	.02
❑	105	Patrick Bates	.05	.02
❑	106	Nick Bell	.05	.02
❑	107	Tim Brown	.25	.11
❑	108	Willie Gault	.05	.02
❑	109	Jeff Gossett	.05	.02
❑	110	Ethan Horton	.05	.02
❑	111	Jeff Hostetler	.10	.05
❑	112	Rocket Ismail	.10	.05
❑	113	Chester McGlockton	.05	.02
❑	114	Anthony Smith	.05	.02
❑	115	Steve Smith	.05	.02
❑	116	Greg Townsend	.05	.02
❑	117	Steve Wisniewski	.05	.02
❑	118	Alexander Wright	.05	.02
❑	119	Steve Atwater	.05	.02
❑	120	Rod Bernstine	.05	.02
❑	121	Mike Croel	.05	.02
❑	122	Shane Dronett	.05	.02
❑	123	Jason Elam	.05	.02
❑	124	John Elway	2.00	.90
❑	125	Brian Habib	.05	.02
❑	126	Rondell Jones	.05	.02
❑	127	Tommy Maddox	.05	.02
❑	128	Karl Mecklenburg	.05	.02
❑	129	Glyn Milburn	.10	.05
❑	130	Derek Russell	.05	.02
❑	131	Shannon Sharpe	.10	.05
❑	132	Dennis Smith	.05	.02
❑	133	Edgar Bennett	.25	.11
❑	134	Tony Bennett	.05	.02
❑	135	Robert Brooks	.25	.11
❑	136	Terrell Buckley	.05	.02
❑	137	LeRoy Butler	.05	.02
❑	138	Mark Clayton	.05	.02
❑	139	Ty Detmer	.10	.05
❑	140	Brett Favre	2.00	.90
❑	141	John Jurkovic RC	.10	.05
❑	142	Bryce Paup	.25	.11
❑	143	Sterling Sharpe	.10	.05
❑	144	George Teague	.05	.02
❑	145	Darrell Thompson	.05	.02
❑	146	Ed West	.05	.02
❑	147	Reggie White	.25	.11
❑	148	Terry Allen	.10	.05
❑	149	Anthony Carter	.10	.05
❑	150	Cris Carter	.50	.23
❑	151	Roger Craig	.10	.05
❑	152	Jack Del Rio	.05	.02
❑	153	Chris Doleman	.05	.02
❑	154	Scottie Graham RC	.10	.05
❑	155	Eric Guliford RC	.05	.02
❑	156	Qadry Ismail	.25	.11
❑	157	Steve Jordan	.05	.02
❑	158	Randall McDaniel	.05	.02
❑	159	Jim McMahon	.05	.02
❑	160	Audray McMillian	.05	.02
❑	161	Sean Salisbury	.05	.02
❑	162	Robert Smith	.25	.11
❑	163	Henry Thomas	.05	.02
❑	164	Gary Anderson K	.05	.02
❑	165	Deon Figures	.05	.02
❑	166	Barry Foster	.05	.02
❑	167	Jeff Graham	.05	.02
❑	168	Kevin Greene	.25	.11
❑	169	Dave Hoffman	.05	.02
❑	170	Merril Hoge	.05	.02
❑	171	Gary Jones	.05	.02
❑	172	Greg Lloyd	.25	.11
❑	173	Ernie Mills	.05	.02
❑	174	Neil O'Donnell	.25	.11
❑	175	Darren Perry	.05	.02
❑	176	Leon Searcy	.05	.02
❑	177	Leroy Thompson	.05	.02
❑	178	Willie Williams	.05	.02
❑	179	Rod Woodson	.25	.11
❑	180	Keith Byars	.05	.02
❑	181	Marco Coleman	.05	.02
❑	182	Bryan Cox	.05	.02
❑	183	Irving Fryar	.10	.05
❑	184	John Grimsley	.05	.02
❑	185	Mark Higgs	.05	.02
❑	186	Mark Ingram	.05	.02
❑	187	Keith Jackson	.05	.02
❑	188	Terry Kirby	.25	.11
❑	189	Dan Marino	2.00	.90
❑	190	O.J. McDuffie	.25	.11
❑	191	Scott Mitchell	.25	.11
❑	192	Pete Stoyanovich	.05	.02
❑	193	Troy Vincent	.05	.02
❑	194	Richmond Webb	.05	.02
❑	195	Brad Baxter	.05	.02
❑	196	Chris Burkett	.05	.02
❑	197	Rob Carpenter	.05	.02
❑	198	Boomer Esiason	.10	.05
❑	199	Johnny Johnson	.05	.02
❑	200	Jeff Lageman	.05	.02
❑	201	Mo Lewis	.05	.02
❑	202	Ronnie Lott	.10	.05
❑	203	Leonard Marshall	.05	.02
❑	204	Terance Mathis	.10	.05
❑	205	Johnny Mitchell	.05	.02
❑	206	Rob Moore	.10	.05
❑	207	Anthony Prior	.05	.02
❑	208	Blair Thomas	.05	.02
❑	209	Brian Washington	.05	.02
❑	210	Eric Bieniemy	.05	.02
❑	211	Marion Butts	.05	.02
❑	212	Gill Byrd	.05	.02
❑	213	John Carney	.05	.02
❑	214	Darren Carrington	.05	.02
❑	215	John Friesz	.10	.05
❑	216	Ronnie Harmon	.05	.02
❑	217	Stan Humphries	.25	.11
❑	218	Nate Lewis	.05	.02
❑	219	Natrone Means	.25	.11
❑	220	Anthony Miller	.10	.05
❑	221	Chris Mims	.05	.02
❑	222	Eric Moten	.05	.02
❑	223	Leslie O'Neal	.05	.02
❑	224	Junior Seau	.25	.11
❑	225	Morten Andersen	.05	.02
❑	226	Gene Atkins	.05	.02
❑	227	Derek Brown RBK	.05	.02
❑	228	Toi Cook	.05	.02
❑	229	Vaughn Dunbar	.05	.02
❑	230	Quinn Early	.10	.05
❑	231	Reggie Freeman	.05	.02
❑	232	Tyrone Hughes	.10	.05
❑	233	Rickey Jackson	.05	.02
❑	234	Eric Martin	.05	.02
❑	235	Sam Mills	.05	.02
❑	236	Brad Muster	.05	.02
❑	237	Torrance Small	.05	.02
❑	238	Irv Smith	.05	.02
❑	239	Wade Wilson	.05	.02
❑	240	Eric Allen	.05	.02
❑	241	Victor Bailey	.05	.02
❑	242	Fred Barnett	.10	.05
❑	243	Mark Bavaro	.05	.02
❑	244	Bubby Brister	.05	.02
❑	245	Randall Cunningham	.25	.11
❑	246	Antone Davis	.05	.02
❑	247	Britt Hager RC	.05	.02
❑	248	Vaughn Hebron	.05	.02
❑	249	James Joseph	.05	.02
❑	250	Seth Joyner	.05	.02
❑	251	Rich Miano	.05	.02
❑	252	Heath Sherman	.05	.02
❑	253	Clyde Simmons	.05	.02
❑	254	Herschel Walker	.10	.05
❑	255	Calvin Williams	.10	.05
❑	256	Jerry Ball	.05	.02
❑	257	Mark Carrier WR	.10	.05
❑	258	Michael Jackson	.10	.05
❑	259	Mike Johnson	.05	.02
❑	260	James Jones	.05	.02
❑	261	Brian Kinchen	.10	.05
❑	262	Clay Matthews	.05	.02
❑	263	Eric Metcalf	.10	.05
❑	264	Stevon Moore	.05	.02
❑	265	Michael Dean Perry	.10	.05
❑	266	Todd Philcox	.05	.02
❑	267	Anthony Pleasant	.05	.02
❑	268	Vinny Testaverde	.10	.05
❑	269	Eric Turner	.05	.02
❑	270	Tommy Vardell	.05	.02
❑	271	Neal Anderson	.05	.02
❑	272	Trace Armstrong	.05	.02
❑	273	Mark Carrier DB	.05	.02
❑	274	Bob Christian	.05	.02
❑	275	Curtis Conway	.25	.11
❑	276	Richard Dent	.10	.05
❑	277	Robert Green	.05	.02
❑	278	Jim Harbaugh	.25	.11
❑	279	Craig Heyward	.10	.05
❑	280	Terry Obee	.05	.02
❑	281	Alonzo Spellman	.05	.02
❑	282	Tom Waddle	.05	.02
❑	283	Peter Tom Willis	.05	.02
❑	284	Donnell Woolford	.05	.02
❑	285	Tim Worley	.05	.02
❑	286	Chris Zorich	.05	.02
❑	287	Steve Broussard	.05	.02
❑	288	Darion Conner	.05	.02
❑	289	Jumpy Geathers	.05	.02
❑	290	Michael Haynes	.10	.05
❑	291	Bobby Hebert	.05	.02
❑	292	Lincoln Kennedy	.05	.02
❑	293	Chris Miller	.05	.02
❑	294	David Mims RC	.05	.02
❑	295	Erric Pegram	.05	.02
❑	296	Mike Pritchard	.05	.02
❑	297	Andre Rison	.10	.05
❑	298	Deion Sanders	.50	.23
❑	299	Chuck Smith	.05	.02
❑	300	Tony Smith	.05	.02
❑	301	Johnny Bailey	.05	.02
❑	302	Steve Beuerlein	.05	.02
❑	303	Chuck Cecil	.05	.02
❑	304	Chris Chandler	.10	.05
❑	305	Gary Clark	.10	.05
❑	306	Rick Cunningham RC	.05	.02
❑	307	Ken Harvey	.05	.02
❑	308	Garrison Hearst	.25	.11
❑	309	Randal Hill	.05	.02
❑	310	Robert Massey	.05	.02
❑	311	Ronald Moore	.05	.02

❑ 312 Ricky Proehl .05 .02
❑ 313 Eric Swann .10 .05
❑ 314 Aeneas Williams .05 .02
❑ 315 Michael Bates .05 .02
❑ 316 Brian Blades .10 .05
❑ 317 Carlton Gray .05 .02
❑ 318 Paul Green RC .05 .02
❑ 319 Patrick Hunter .05 .02
❑ 320 John Kasay .05 .02
❑ 321 Cortez Kennedy .10 .05
❑ 322 Kelvin Martin .05 .02
❑ 323 Dan McGwire .05 .02
❑ 324 Rick Mirer .25 .11
❑ 325 Eugene Robinson .05 .02
❑ 326 Rick Tuten .05 .02
❑ 327 Chris Warren .10 .05
❑ 328 John L. Williams .05 .02
❑ 329 Reggie Cobb .05 .02
❑ 330 Horace Copeland .05 .02
❑ 331 Lawrence Dawsey .05 .02
❑ 332 Santana Dotson .10 .05
❑ 333 Craig Erickson .05 .02
❑ 334 Ron Hall .05 .02
❑ 335 Courtney Hawkins .05 .02
❑ 336 Keith McCants .05 .02
❑ 337 Hardy Nickerson .10 .05
❑ 338 Mazio Royster RC .05 .02
❑ 339 Broderick Thomas .05 .02
❑ 340 Casey Weldon RC .25 .11
❑ 341 Mark Wheeler .05 .02
❑ 342 Vince Workman .05 .02
❑ 343 Flipper Anderson .05 .02
❑ 344 Jerome Bettis .25 .11
❑ 345 Richard Buchanan .05 .02
❑ 346 Shane Conlan .05 .02
❑ 347 Troy Drayton .05 .02
❑ 348 Henry Ellard .10 .05
❑ 349 Jim Everett .10 .05
❑ 350 Cleveland Gary .05 .02
❑ 351 Sean Gilbert .05 .02
❑ 352 David Lang .05 .02
❑ 353 Todd Lyght .05 .02
❑ 354 T.J. Rubley .05 .02
❑ 355 Jackie Slater .05 .02
❑ 356 Russell White .10 .05
❑ 357 Bruce Armstrong .05 .02
❑ 358 Drew Bledsoe 1.25 .55
❑ 359 Vincent Brisby .25 .11
❑ 360 Vincent Brown .05 .02
❑ 361 Ben Coates .25 .11
❑ 362 Marv Cook .05 .02
❑ 363 Ray Crittenden RC .05 .02
❑ 364 Corey Croom RC .05 .02
❑ 365 Pat Harlow .05 .02
❑ 366 Dion Lambert .05 .02
❑ 367 Greg McMurtry .05 .02
❑ 368 Leonard Russell .05 .02
❑ 369 Scott Secules .05 .02
❑ 370 Chris Slade .05 .02
❑ 371 Michael Timpson .05 .02
❑ 372 Kevin Turner .05 .02
❑ 373 Ashley Ambrose .05 .02
❑ 374 Dean Biasucci .05 .02
❑ 375 Duane Bickett .05 .02
❑ 376 Quentin Coryatt .05 .02
❑ 377 Rodney Culver .05 .02
❑ 378 Sean Dawkins RC .25 .11
❑ 379 Jeff George .25 .11
❑ 380 Jeff Herrod .05 .02
❑ 381 Jessie Hester .05 .02
❑ 382 Anthony Johnson .10 .05
❑ 383 Reggie Langhorne .05 .02
❑ 384 Roosevelt Potts .05 .02
❑ 385 William Schultz RC .05 .02
❑ 386 Rohn Stark .05 .02
❑ 387 Clarence Verdin .05 .02
❑ 388 Carl Banks .05 .02
❑ 389 Reggie Brooks .10 .05
❑ 390 Earnest Byner .05 .02
❑ 391 Tom Carter .05 .02
❑ 392 Cary Conklin .05 .02
❑ 393 Pat Eilers RC .05 .02
❑ 394 Ricky Ervins .05 .02
❑ 395 Rich Gannon .25 .11
❑ 396 Darrell Green .05 .02
❑ 397 Desmond Howard .10 .05
❑ 398 Chip Lohmiller .05 .02
❑ 399 Sterling Palmer RC .05 .02
❑ 400 Mark Rypien .05 .02
❑ 401 Ricky Sanders .05 .02
❑ 402 Johnny Thomas .05 .02
❑ 403 John Copeland .05 .02
❑ 404 Derrick Fenner .05 .02
❑ 405 Alex Gordon .05 .02
❑ 406 Harold Green .05 .02
❑ 407 Lance Gunn .05 .02
❑ 408 David Klingler .05 .02
❑ 409 Ricardo McDonald .05 .02
❑ 410 Tim McGee .05 .02
❑ 411 Reggie Rembert .05 .02
❑ 412 Patrick Robinson .05 .02
❑ 413 Jay Schroeder .05 .02
❑ 414 Erik Wilhelm .05 .02
❑ 415 Alfred Williams .05 .02
❑ 416 Darryl Williams .05 .02
❑ 417 Sam Adams RC .10 .05
❑ 418 Mario Bates RC .25 .11
❑ 419 James Bostic RC .25 .11
❑ 420 Bucky Brooks RC .05 .02
❑ 421 Jeff Burris RC .10 .05
❑ 422 Shante Carver RC .05 .02
❑ 423 Jeff Cothran RC .05 .02
❑ 424 Lake Dawson RC .25 .11
❑ 425 Trent Dilfer RC 2.00 .90
❑ 426 Marshall Faulk RC 4.00 1.80
❑ 427 Cory Fleming RC .05 .02
❑ 428 William Floyd RC .25 .11
❑ 429 Glenn Foley RC .25 .11
❑ 430 Rob Fredrickson RC .10 .05
❑ 431 Charlie Garner RC 1.50 .70
❑ 432 Greg Hill RC .25 .11
❑ 433 Charles Johnson RC .40 .18
❑ 434 Calvin Jones RC .05 .02
❑ 435 Jimmy Klingler RC .10 .05
❑ 436 Antonio Langham RC .10 .05
❑ 437 Kevin Lee RC .05 .02
❑ 438 Chuck Levy RC .05 .02
❑ 439 Willie McGinest RC .25 .11
❑ 440 Jamir Miller RC .05 .02
❑ 441 Johnnie Morton RC .25 .11
❑ 442 David Palmer RC .50 .23
❑ 443 Errict Rhett RC 1.00 .45
❑ 444 Cory Sawyer RC .05 .02
❑ 445 Darnay Scott RC .75 .35
❑ 446 Heath Shuler RC .25 .11
❑ 447 Lamar Smith RC 3.00 1.35
❑ 448 Dan Wilkinson RC .10 .05
❑ 449 Bernard Williams RC .05 .02
❑ 450 Bryant Young RC .25 .11
❑ P1 Sterling Sharpe Promo .75 .35
Numbered 000

1995 Pacific

	MINT	NRMT
COMPLETE SET (450)	30.00	13.50

❑ 1 Randy Baldwin .10 .05
❑ 2 Tommy Barnhardt .10 .05
❑ 3 Tim McKyer .10 .05
❑ 4 Sam Mills .20 .09
❑ 5 Brian O'Neal .10 .05
❑ 6 Frank Reich .10 .05
❑ 7 Jack Trudeau .10 .05
❑ 8 Vernon Turner .10 .05
❑ 9 Kerry Collins RC 1.50 .70
❑ 10 Shawn King .10 .05
❑ 11 Steve Beuerlein .10 .05
❑ 12 Derek Brown .10 .05
❑ 13 Reggie Clark .10 .05
❑ 14 Reggie Cobb .10 .05
❑ 15 Desmond Howard .20 .09
❑ 16 Jeff Lageman .10 .05
❑ 17 Kelvin Pritchett .10 .05
❑ 18 Cedric Tillman .10 .05
❑ 19 Tony Boselli RC .30 .14
❑ 20 James O. Stewart RC 2.00 .90
❑ 21 Eric Davis .10 .05
❑ 22 William Floyd .30 .14
❑ 23 Elvis Grbac .30 .14
❑ 24 Brent Jones .10 .05
❑ 25 Ken Norton, Jr. .20 .09
❑ 26 Bart Oates .10 .05
❑ 27 Jerry Rice 1.00 .45
❑ 28 Deion Sanders .40 .18
❑ 29 John Taylor .10 .05
❑ 30 Adam Walker RC .10 .05
❑ 31 Steve Wallace .10 .05
❑ 32 Ricky Watters .30 .14
❑ 33 Lee Woodall .10 .05
❑ 34 Bryant Young .20 .09
❑ 35 Steve Young .75 .35
❑ 36 J.J. Stokes RC .30 .14
❑ 37 Troy Aikman 1.00 .45
❑ 38 Larry Allen .20 .09
❑ 39 Chris Boniol RC .10 .05
❑ 40 Lincoln Coleman .10 .05
❑ 41 Charles Haley .20 .09
❑ 42 Alvin Harper .10 .05
❑ 43 Chad Hennings .20 .09
❑ 44 Michael Irvin .30 .14
❑ 45 Daryl Johnston .20 .09
❑ 46 Leon Lett .10 .05
❑ 47 Nate Newton .20 .09
❑ 48 Jay Novacek .20 .09
❑ 49 Emmitt Smith 1.50 .70
❑ 50 James Washington .10 .05
❑ 51 Kevin Williams .20 .09
❑ 52 Sherman Williams RC .10 .05
❑ 53 Barry Foster .20 .09
❑ 54 Eric Green .10 .05
❑ 55 Kevin Greene .20 .09
❑ 56 Andre Hastings .20 .09
❑ 57 Charles Johnson .20 .09
❑ 58 Greg Lloyd .20 .09
❑ 59 Ernie Mills .10 .05
❑ 60 Byron Bam Morris .20 .09
❑ 61 Neil O'Donnell .20 .09
❑ 62 Darren Perry .10 .05
❑ 63 Yancey Thigpen RC .30 .14
❑ 64 Mike Tomczak .10 .05
❑ 65 John L. Williams .10 .05
❑ 66 Rod Woodson .20 .09
❑ 67 Mark Bruener RC .20 .09
❑ 68 Kordell Stewart RC 2.00 .90
❑ 69 Jeff Brohm RC .10 .05
❑ 70 Andre Coleman .10 .05
❑ 71 Reuben Davis .10 .05
❑ 72 Dennis Gibson .10 .05
❑ 73 Darrien Gordon .10 .05
❑ 74 Stan Humphries .20 .09
❑ 75 Shawn Jefferson .10 .05
❑ 76 Tony Martin .20 .09
❑ 77 Natrone Means .30 .14
❑ 78 Shannon Mitchell .10 .05
❑ 79 Leslie O'Neal .20 .09
❑ 80 Alfred Pupunu .10 .05
❑ 81 Stanley Richard .10 .05
❑ 82 Junior Seau .30 .14
❑ 83 Mark Seay .20 .09
❑ 84 Derrick Alexander WR .30 .14
❑ 85 Carl Banks .10 .05
❑ 86 Isaac Booth .10 .05
❑ 87 Rob Burnett .10 .05
❑ 88 Earnest Byner .10 .05
❑ 89 Steve Everitt .10 .05
❑ 90 Leroy Hoard .10 .05
❑ 91 Pepper Johnson .10 .05
❑ 92 Antonio Langham .10 .05
❑ 93 Eric Metcalf .20 .09

#	Player		
❑ 94	Anthony Pleasant	.10	.05
❑ 95	Frank Stams	.10	.05
❑ 96	Vinny Testaverde	.20	.09
❑ 97	Eric Turner	.10	.05
❑ 98	Mike Miller	.10	.05
❑ 99	Craig Powell	.10	.05
❑ 100	Gene Atkins	.10	.05
❑ 101	Aubrey Beavers	.10	.05
❑ 102	Tim Bowens	.10	.05
❑ 103	Keith Byars	.10	.05
❑ 104	Bryan Cox	.10	.05
❑ 105	Aaron Craver	.10	.05
❑ 106	Jeff Cross	.10	.05
❑ 107	Irving Fryar	.20	.09
❑ 108	Dan Marino	2.00	.90
❑ 109	O.J. McDuffie	.30	.14
❑ 110	Bernie Parmalee	.20	.09
❑ 111	James Saxon	.10	.05
❑ 112	Keith Sims	.10	.05
❑ 113	Irving Spikes	.20	.09
❑ 114	Pete Mitchell RC	.30	.14
❑ 115	Terry Allen	.20	.09
❑ 116	Cris Carter	.30	.14
❑ 117	Adrian Cooper	.10	.05
❑ 118	Bernard Dafney	.10	.05
❑ 119	Jack Del Rio	.10	.05
❑ 120	Vencie Glenn	.10	.05
❑ 121	Qadry Ismail	.20	.09
❑ 122	Carlos Jenkins	.10	.05
❑ 123	Andrew Jordan	.10	.05
❑ 124	Ed McDaniel	.10	.05
❑ 125	Warren Moon	.20	.09
❑ 126	David Palmer	.20	.09
❑ 127	John Randle	.20	.09
❑ 128	Jake Reed	.20	.09
❑ 129	Derrick Alexander DE RC	.10	.05
❑ 130	Chad May RC	.10	.05
❑ 131	Korey Stringer	.10	.05
❑ 132	Bruce Armstrong	.10	.05
❑ 133	Drew Bledsoe	1.00	.45
❑ 134	Vincent Brisby	.10	.05
❑ 135	Troy Brown	.20	.09
❑ 136	Vincent Brown	.10	.05
❑ 137	Marion Butts	.10	.05
❑ 138	Ben Coates	.20	.09
❑ 139	Ray Crittenden	.10	.05
❑ 140	Maurice Hurst	.10	.05
❑ 141	Aaron Jones	.10	.05
❑ 142	Willie McGinest	.20	.09
❑ 143	Marty Moore	.10	.05
❑ 144	Mike Pitts	.10	.05
❑ 145	Leroy Thompson	.10	.05
❑ 146	Michael Timpson	.10	.05
❑ 147	Bennie Blades	.10	.05
❑ 148	Jocelyn Borgella	.10	.05
❑ 149	Anthony Carter	.20	.09
❑ 150	Willie Clay	.10	.05
❑ 151	Mel Gray	.10	.05
❑ 152	Mike Johnson	.10	.05
❑ 153	Dave Krieg	.10	.05
❑ 154	Robert Massey	.10	.05
❑ 155	Scott Mitchell	.20	.09
❑ 156	Herman Moore	.30	.14
❑ 157	Johnnie Morton	.20	.09
❑ 158	Barry Sanders	2.00	.90
❑ 159	Chris Spielman	.20	.09
❑ 160	Broderick Thomas	.10	.05
❑ 161	Cory Schlesinger	.10	.05
❑ 162	Marcus Allen	.30	.14
❑ 163	Donnell Bennett	.20	.09
❑ 164	J.J. Birden	.10	.05
❑ 165	Matt Blundin RC	.10	.05
❑ 166	Steve Bono	.20	.09
❑ 167	Dale Carter	.20	.09
❑ 168	Lake Dawson	.20	.09
❑ 169	Ron Dickerson	.10	.05
❑ 170	Lin Elliott	.10	.05
❑ 171	Jaime Fields	.10	.05
❑ 172	Greg Hill	.20	.09
❑ 173	Danan Hughes	.10	.05
❑ 174	Neil Smith	.20	.09
❑ 175	Steve Stenstrom RC	.10	.05
❑ 176	Edgar Bennett	.20	.09
❑ 177	Robert Brooks	.30	.14
❑ 178	Mark Brunell	1.00	.45
❑ 179	Doug Evans	.10	.05
❑ 180	Brett Favre	2.00	.90
❑ 181	Corey Harris	.10	.05
❑ 182	LeShon Johnson	.20	.09
❑ 183	Sean Jones	.10	.05
❑ 184	Lenny McGill RC	.10	.05
❑ 185	Terry Mickens	.10	.05
❑ 186	Sterling Sharpe	.20	.09
❑ 187	Joe Sims	.10	.05
❑ 188	Darrell Thompson	.10	.05
❑ 189	Reggie White	.30	.14
❑ 190	Craig Newsome RC	.10	.05
❑ 191	Tim Brown	.30	.14
❑ 192	Vince Evans	.10	.05
❑ 193	Rob Fredrickson	.10	.05
❑ 194	Andrew Glover RC	.10	.05
❑ 195	Jeff Hostetler	.20	.09
❑ 196	Rocket Ismail	.20	.09
❑ 197	Jeff Jaeger	.10	.05
❑ 198	James Jett	.20	.09
❑ 199	Chester McGlockton	.20	.09
❑ 200	Don Mosebar	.10	.05
❑ 201	Tom Rathman	.10	.05
❑ 202	Harvey Williams	.10	.05
❑ 203	Steve Wisniewski	.10	.05
❑ 204	Alexander Wright	.10	.05
❑ 205	Napoleon Kaufman RC	1.50	.70
❑ 206	Trace Armstrong	.10	.05
❑ 207	Curtis Conway	.30	.14
❑ 208	Raymont Harris	.10	.05
❑ 209	Erik Kramer	.10	.05
❑ 210	Nate Lewis	.10	.05
❑ 211	Shane Matthews RC	2.00	.90
❑ 212	John Thierry	.10	.05
❑ 213	Lewis Tillman	.10	.05
❑ 214	Tom Waddle	.10	.05
❑ 215	Steve Walsh	.10	.05
❑ 216	James Williams T RC	.10	.05
❑ 217	Donnell Woolford	.10	.05
❑ 218	Chris Zorich	.10	.05
❑ 219	Rashaan Salaam RC	.30	.14
❑ 220	John Booty	.10	.05
❑ 221	Michael Brooks	.10	.05
❑ 222	Dave Brown	.20	.09
❑ 223	Chris Calloway	.10	.05
❑ 224	Gary Downs	.10	.05
❑ 225	Kent Graham	.20	.09
❑ 226	Keith Hamilton	.10	.05
❑ 227	Rodney Hampton	.20	.09
❑ 228	Brian Kozlowski	.10	.05
❑ 229	Thomas Lewis	.20	.09
❑ 230	Dave Meggett	.10	.05
❑ 231	Aaron Pierce	.10	.05
❑ 232	Mike Sherrard	.10	.05
❑ 233	Phillippi Sparks	.10	.05
❑ 234	Tyrone Wheatley RC	1.25	.55
❑ 235	Trev Alberts	.10	.05
❑ 236	Aaron Bailey RC	.10	.05
❑ 237	Jason Belser	.10	.05
❑ 238	Tony Bennett	.10	.05
❑ 239	Kerry Cash	.10	.05
❑ 240	Marshall Faulk	.50	.23
❑ 241	Stephen Grant	.10	.05
❑ 242	Jeff Herrod	.10	.05
❑ 243	Ronald Humphrey	.10	.05
❑ 244	Kirk Lowdermilk	.10	.05
❑ 245	Don Majkowski	.10	.05
❑ 246	Tony McCoy	.10	.05
❑ 247	Floyd Turner	.10	.05
❑ 248	Lamont Warren	.10	.05
❑ 249	Zack Crockett RC	.10	.05
❑ 250	Michael Bankston	.10	.05
❑ 251	Larry Centers	.20	.09
❑ 252	Gary Clark	.10	.05
❑ 253	Ed Cunningham	.10	.05
❑ 254	Garrison Hearst	.30	.14
❑ 255	Eric Hill	.10	.05
❑ 256	Terry Irving	.10	.05
❑ 257	Lorenzo Lynch	.10	.05
❑ 258	Jamir Miller	.10	.05
❑ 259	Ronald Moore	.10	.05
❑ 260	Terry Samuels	.10	.05
❑ 261	Jay Schroeder	.10	.05
❑ 262	Eric Swann	.20	.09
❑ 263	Aeneas Williams	.10	.05
❑ 264	Frank Sanders RC	1.00	.45
❑ 265	Morten Andersen	.10	.05
❑ 266	Mario Bates	.30	.14
❑ 267	Derek Brown RBK	.10	.05
❑ 268	Darion Conner	.10	.05
❑ 269	Quinn Early	.20	.09
❑ 270	Jim Everett	.10	.05
❑ 271	Michael Haynes	.20	.09
❑ 272	Wayne Martin	.10	.05
❑ 273	Derrell Mitchell	.10	.05
❑ 274	Lorenzo Neal	.10	.05
❑ 275	Jimmy Spencer	.10	.05
❑ 276	Winfred Tubbs	.10	.05
❑ 277	Renaldo Turnbull	.10	.05
❑ 278	Jeff Uhlenhake	.10	.05
❑ 279	Steve Atwater	.10	.05
❑ 280	Keith Burns	.10	.05
❑ 281	Butler By'Not'e RC	.20	.09
❑ 282	Jeff Campbell	.10	.05
❑ 283	Derrick Clark RC	.20	.09
❑ 284	Shane Dronett	.10	.05
❑ 285	Jason Elam	.10	.05
❑ 286	John Elway	2.00	.90
❑ 287	Jerry Evans	.10	.05
❑ 288	Karl Mecklenburg	.10	.05
❑ 289	Glyn Milburn	.10	.05
❑ 290	Anthony Miller	.20	.09
❑ 291	Tom Rouen	.10	.05
❑ 292	Leonard Russell	.10	.05
❑ 293	Shannon Sharpe	.20	.09
❑ 294	Steve Russ	.10	.05
❑ 295	Mel Agee	.10	.05
❑ 296	Lester Archambeau	.10	.05
❑ 297	Bert Emanuel	.30	.14
❑ 298	Jeff George	.20	.09
❑ 299	Craig Heyward	.20	.09
❑ 300	Bobby Hebert	.10	.05
❑ 301	D.J. Johnson	.10	.05
❑ 302	Mike Kenn	.10	.05
❑ 303	Terance Mathis	.20	.09
❑ 304	Clay Matthews	.20	.09
❑ 305	Erric Pegram	.20	.09
❑ 306	Andre Rison	.20	.09
❑ 307	Chuck Smith	.10	.05
❑ 308	Jessie Tuggle	.10	.05
❑ 309	Lorenzo Styles RC	.10	.05
❑ 310	Cornelius Bennett	.20	.09
❑ 311	Bill Brooks	.10	.05
❑ 312	Jeff Burris	.10	.05
❑ 313	Carwell Gardner	.10	.05
❑ 314	Kent Hull	.10	.05
❑ 315	Yonel Jourdain	.10	.05
❑ 316	Jim Kelly	.30	.14
❑ 317	Vince Marrow	.10	.05
❑ 318	Pete Metzelaars	.10	.05
❑ 319	Andre Reed	.20	.09
❑ 320	Kurt Schulz RC	.20	.09
❑ 321	Bruce Smith	.30	.14
❑ 322	Darryl Talley	.10	.05
❑ 323	Matt Darby	.10	.05
❑ 324	Justin Armour RC	.10	.05
❑ 325	Todd Collins RC	.30	.14
❑ 326	David Alexander DE	.10	.05
❑ 327	Eric Allen	.10	.05
❑ 328	Fred Barnett	.20	.09
❑ 329	Randall Cunningham	.30	.14
❑ 330	William Fuller	.10	.05
❑ 331	Charlie Garner	.20	.09
❑ 332	Vaughn Hebron	.10	.05
❑ 333	James Joseph	.10	.05
❑ 334	Bill Romanowski	.10	.05
❑ 335	Ken Rose	.10	.05
❑ 336	Jeff Snyder	.10	.05
❑ 337	William Thomas	.10	.05
❑ 338	Herschel Walker	.20	.09
❑ 339	Calvin Williams	.20	.09
❑ 340	Dave Barr RC	.10	.05
❑ 341	Chidi Ahanotu	.10	.05
❑ 342	Barney Bussey	.10	.05
❑ 343	Horace Copeland	.10	.05
❑ 344	Trent Dilfer	.30	.14
❑ 345	Craig Erickson	.10	.05
❑ 346	Paul Gruber	.10	.05
❑ 347	Courtney Hawkins	.10	.05
❑ 348	Lonnie Marts	.10	.05
❑ 349	Martin Mayhew	.10	.05
❑ 350	Hardy Nickerson	.10	.05
❑ 351	Errict Rhett	.30	.14

❑ 352 Lamar Thomas .10 .05
❑ 353 Charles Wilson .10 .05
❑ 354 Vince Workman .10 .05
❑ 355 Derrick Brooks RC .30 .14
❑ 356 Warren Sapp RC .75 .35
❑ 357 Sam Adams .10 .05
❑ 358 Michael Bates .10 .05
❑ 359 Brian Blades .20 .09
❑ 360 Carlton Gray .10 .05
❑ 361 Bill Hitchcock .10 .05
❑ 362 Cortez Kennedy .20 .09
❑ 363 Rick Mirer .30 .14
❑ 364 Eugene Robinson .10 .05
❑ 365 Michael Sinclair .10 .05
❑ 366 Steve Smith .10 .05
❑ 367 Bob Spitulski .10 .05
❑ 368 Rick Tuten .10 .05
❑ 369 Chris Warren .20 .09
❑ 370 Terrence Warren .10 .05
❑ 371 Christian Fauria RC .10 .05
❑ 372 Joey Galloway RC 2.00 .90
❑ 373 Boomer Esiason .20 .09
❑ 374 Aaron Glenn .10 .05
❑ 375 Victor Green RC .10 .05
❑ 376 Johnny Johnson .10 .05
❑ 377 Mo Lewis .10 .05
❑ 378 Ronnie Lott .20 .09
❑ 379 Nick Lowery .10 .05
❑ 380 Johnny Mitchell .10 .05
❑ 381 Rob Moore .10 .05
❑ 382 Adrian Murrell .20 .09
❑ 383 Anthony Prior .10 .05
❑ 384 Brian Washington .10 .05
❑ 385 Matt Willig .10 .05
❑ 386 Kyle Brady RC .30 .14
❑ 387 Flipper Anderson .10 .05
❑ 388 Johnny Bailey .10 .05
❑ 389 Jerome Bettis .30 .14
❑ 390 Isaac Bruce .50 .23
❑ 391 Shane Conlan .10 .05
❑ 392 Troy Drayton .10 .05
❑ 393 D'Marco Farr .10 .05
❑ 394 Jessie Hester .10 .05
❑ 395 Todd Kinchen .10 .05
❑ 396 Ron Middleton .10 .05
❑ 397 Chris Miller .10 .05
❑ 398 Marquez Pope .10 .05
❑ 399 Robert Young .10 .05
❑ 400 Tony Zendejas .10 .05
❑ 401 Kevin Carter RC .30 .14
❑ 402 Reggie Brooks .20 .09
❑ 403 Tom Carter .10 .05
❑ 404 Andre Collins .10 .05
❑ 405 Pat Eilers .10 .05
❑ 406 Henry Ellard .20 .09
❑ 407 Ricky Ervins .10 .05
❑ 408 Gus Frerotte .30 .14
❑ 409 Ken Harvey .10 .05
❑ 410 Jim Lachey .10 .05
❑ 411 Brian Mitchell .10 .05
❑ 412 Reggie Roby .10 .05
❑ 413 Heath Shuler .30 .14
❑ 414 Tyronne Stowe .10 .05
❑ 415 Tydus Winans .10 .05
❑ 416 Cory Raymer .10 .05
❑ 417 Michael Westbrook RC 1.50 .70
❑ 418 Jeff Blake RC 1.00 .45
❑ 419 Steve Broussard .10 .05
❑ 420 Dave Cadigan .10 .05
❑ 421 Jeff Cothran .10 .05
❑ 422 Derrick Fenner .10 .05
❑ 423 James Francis .10 .05
❑ 424 Lee Johnson .10 .05
❑ 425 Louis Oliver .10 .05
❑ 426 Carl Pickens .30 .14
❑ 427 Jeff Query .10 .05
❑ 428 Corey Sawyer .10 .05
❑ 429 Darnay Scott .30 .14
❑ 430 Dan Wilkinson .20 .09
❑ 431 Alfred Williams .10 .05
❑ 432 Ki-Jana Carter RC .30 .14
❑ 433 David Dunn RC .10 .05
❑ 434 John Walsh RC .10 .05
❑ 435 Gary Brown .10 .05
❑ 436 Pat Carter .10 .05
❑ 437 Ray Childress .10 .05
❑ 438 Ernest Givins .10 .05
❑ 439 Haywood Jeffires .10 .05
❑ 440 Lamar Lathon .10 .05
❑ 441 Bruce Matthews .10 .05
❑ 442 Marcus Robertson .10 .05
❑ 443 Eddie Robinson .10 .05
❑ 444 Malcolm Seabron RC .10 .05
❑ 445 Webster Slaughter .10 .05
❑ 446 Al Smith .10 .05
❑ 447 Billy Joe Tolliver .10 .05
❑ 448 Lorenzo White .10 .05
❑ 449 Steve McNair RC 2.50 1.10
❑ 450 Rodney Thomas RC .30 .14
❑ P1 Natrone Means Promo 1.00 .45
❑ P1J Natrone Means Promo 1.00 .45
Jumbo card 7" by 9 3/4"

1996 Pacific

	MINT	NRMT
COMPLETE SET (450)	40.00	18.00

❑ 1 Jeff Feagles .10 .05
❑ 2 Rob Moore .20 .09
❑ 3 Clyde Simmons .10 .05
❑ 4 Mike Buck .10 .05
❑ 5 Aeneas Williams .10 .05
❑ 6 Simeon Rice RC .40 .18
❑ 7 Garrison Hearst .20 .09
❑ 8 Eric Swann .10 .05
❑ 9 Dave Krieg .10 .05
❑ 10 Leeland McElroy RC .40 .18
❑ 11 Oscar McBride .10 .05
❑ 12 Frank Sanders .20 .09
❑ 13 Larry Centers .20 .09
❑ 14 Seth Joyner .10 .05
❑ 15 Stevie Anderson .10 .05
❑ 16 Craig Heyward .10 .05
❑ 17 Devin Bush .10 .05
❑ 18 Eric Metcalf .10 .05
❑ 19 Jeff George .20 .09
❑ 20 Richard Huntley RC 2.00 .90
❑ 21 Jamal Anderson RC 6.00 2.70
❑ 22 Bert Emanuel .20 .09
❑ 23 Terance Mathis .10 .05
❑ 24 Roman Fortin .10 .05
❑ 25 Jessie Tuggle .10 .05
❑ 26 Morten Andersen .10 .05
❑ 27 Chris Doleman .10 .05
❑ 28 D.J. Johnson .10 .05
❑ 29 Kevin Ross .10 .05
❑ 30 Michael Jackson .20 .09
❑ 31 Eric Zeier .10 .05
❑ 32 Jonathan Ogden RC .10 .05
❑ 33 Eric Turner .10 .05
❑ 34 Andre Rison .20 .09
❑ 35 Lorenzo White .10 .05
❑ 36 Earnest Byner .10 .05
❑ 37 Derrick Alexander WR .20 .09
❑ 38 Brian Kinchen .10 .05
❑ 39 Anthony Pleasant .10 .05
❑ 40 Vinny Testaverde .20 .09
❑ 41 Pepper Johnson .10 .05
❑ 42 Frank Hartley .10 .05
❑ 43 Craig Powell .10 .05
❑ 44 Leroy Hoard .10 .05
❑ 45 Kent Hull .10 .05
❑ 46 Bryce Paup .10 .05
❑ 47 Andre Reed .20 .09
❑ 48 Darick Holmes .10 .05
❑ 49 Russell Copeland .10 .05
❑ 50 Jerry Ostroski .10 .05
❑ 51 Chris Green .10 .05
❑ 52 Eric Moulds RC 1.50 .70
❑ 53 Justin Armour .10 .05
❑ 54 Jim Kelly .40 .18
❑ 55 Cornelius Bennett .10 .05
❑ 56 Steve Tasker .10 .05
❑ 57 Thurman Thomas .40 .18
❑ 58 Bruce Smith .20 .09
❑ 59 Todd Collins .20 .09
❑ 60 Shawn King .10 .05
❑ 61 Don Beebe .10 .05
❑ 62 John Kasay .10 .05
❑ 63 Tim McKyer .10 .05
❑ 64 Darion Conner .10 .05
❑ 65 Pete Metzelaars .10 .05
❑ 66 Derrick Moore .10 .05
❑ 67 Blake Brockermeyer .10 .05
❑ 68 Tim Biakabutuka RC .75 .35
❑ 69 Sam Mills .10 .05
❑ 70 Vince Workman .10 .05
❑ 71 Kerry Collins .40 .18
❑ 72 Carlton Bailey .10 .05
❑ 73 Mark Carrier WR .10 .05
❑ 74 Donnell Woolford .10 .05
❑ 75 Walt Harris RC .10 .05
❑ 76 John Thierry .10 .05
❑ 77 Al Fontenot .10 .05
❑ 78 Lewis Tillman .10 .05
❑ 79 Curtis Conway .40 .18
❑ 80 Chris Zorich .10 .05
❑ 81 Mark Carrier DB .10 .05
❑ 82 Bobby Engram RC .40 .18
❑ 83 Alonzo Spellman .10 .05
❑ 84 Rashaan Salaam .40 .18
❑ 85 Michael Timpson .10 .05
❑ 86 Nate Lewis .10 .05
❑ 87 James Williams T .10 .05
❑ 88 Jeff Graham .10 .05
❑ 89 Erik Kramer .10 .05
❑ 90 Willie Anderson .10 .05
❑ 91 Tony McGee .10 .05
❑ 92 Marco Battaglia .10 .05
❑ 93 Dan Wilkinson .10 .05
❑ 94 John Walsh .10 .05
❑ 95 Eric Bieniemy .10 .05
❑ 96 Ricardo McDonald .10 .05
❑ 97 Carl Pickens .40 .18
❑ 98 Kevin Sargent .10 .05
❑ 99 David Dunn .10 .05
❑ 100 Jeff Blake .40 .18
❑ 101 Harold Green .10 .05
❑ 102 James Francis .10 .05
❑ 103 John Copeland .10 .05
❑ 104 Darnay Scott .20 .09
❑ 105 Darren Woodson .20 .09
❑ 106 Jay Novacek .10 .05
❑ 107 Charles Haley .20 .09
❑ 108 Mark Tuinei .10 .05
❑ 109 Michael Irvin .40 .18
❑ 110 Troy Aikman 1.00 .45
❑ 111 Chris Boniol .10 .05
❑ 112 Sherman Williams .10 .05
❑ 113 Deion Sanders .60 .25
❑ 114 Emmitt Smith 1.50 .70
❑ 115 Eric Bjornson .10 .05
❑ 116 Nate Newton .10 .05
❑ 117 Larry Allen .10 .05
❑ 118 Kevin Williams .10 .05
❑ 119 Leon Lett .10 .05
❑ 120 John Mobley .10 .05
❑ 121 Anthony Miller .20 .09
❑ 122 Brian Habib .10 .05
❑ 123 Aaron Craver .10 .05
❑ 124 Glyn Milburn .10 .05
❑ 125 Shannon Sharpe .20 .09
❑ 126 Steve Atwater .10 .05
❑ 127 Jason Elam .10 .05
❑ 128 John Elway 2.00 .90
❑ 129 Reggie Rivers .10 .05
❑ 130 Mike Pritchard .10 .05
❑ 131 Vance Johnson .10 .05
❑ 132 Terrell Davis 2.50 1.10

❑ 133 Tyrone Braxton .10 .05
❑ 134 Ed McCaffrey .20 .09
❑ 135 Brett Perriman .10 .05
❑ 136 Chris Spielman .10 .05
❑ 137 Luther Elliss .10 .05
❑ 138 Johnnie Morton .20 .09
❑ 139 Zefross Moss .10 .05
❑ 140 Barry Sanders 2.00 .90
❑ 141 Lomas Brown .10 .05
❑ 142 Cory Schlesinger .10 .05
❑ 143 Jason Hanson .10 .05
❑ 144 Kevin Glover .10 .05
❑ 145 Ron Rivers RC .40 .18
❑ 146 Aubrey Matthews .10 .05
❑ 147 Reggie Brown LB RC .10 .05
❑ 148 Herman Moore .40 .18
❑ 149 Scott Mitchell .20 .09
❑ 150 Brett Favre 2.00 .90
❑ 151 Sean Jones .10 .05
❑ 152 LeRoy Butler .10 .05
❑ 153 Mark Chmura .20 .09
❑ 154 Derrick Mayes RC .60 .25
❑ 155 Mark Ingram .10 .05
❑ 156 Antonio Freeman .75 .35
❑ 157 Chris Darkins RC .10 .05
❑ 158 Robert Brooks .40 .18
❑ 159 William Henderson .10 .05
❑ 160 George Koonce .10 .05
❑ 161 Craig Newsome .10 .05
❑ 162 Darius Holland .10 .05
❑ 163 George Teague .10 .05
❑ 164 Edgar Bennett .20 .09
❑ 165 Reggie White .40 .18
❑ 166 Micheal Barrow .10 .05
❑ 167 Mel Gray .10 .05
❑ 168 Anthony Dorsett .10 .05
❑ 169 Roderick Lewis .10 .05
❑ 170 Henry Ford .10 .05
❑ 171 Mark Stepnoski .10 .05
❑ 172 Chris Sanders .20 .09
❑ 173 Anthony Cook .10 .05
❑ 174 Eddie Robinson .10 .05
❑ 175 Steve McNair .75 .35
❑ 176 Haywood Jeffires .10 .05
❑ 177 Eddie George RC 3.00 1.35
❑ 178 Marion Butts .10 .05
❑ 179 Malcolm Seabron .10 .05
❑ 180 Rodney Thomas .10 .05
❑ 181 Ken Dilger .20 .09
❑ 182 Zack Crockett .10 .05
❑ 183 Tony Bennett .10 .05
❑ 184 Quentin Coryatt .10 .05
❑ 185 Marshall Faulk .40 .18
❑ 186 Sean Dawkins .10 .05
❑ 187 Jim Harbaugh .20 .09
❑ 188 Eugene Daniel .10 .05
❑ 189 Roosevelt Potts .10 .05
❑ 190 Lamont Warren .10 .05
❑ 191 Will Wolford .10 .05
❑ 192 Tony Siragusa .10 .05
❑ 193 Aaron Bailey .10 .05
❑ 194 Trev Alberts .10 .05
❑ 195 Kevin Hardy .20 .09
❑ 196 Greg Spann .10 .05
❑ 197 Steve Beuerlein .10 .05
❑ 198 Steve Taneyhill .10 .05
❑ 199 Vaughn Dunbar .10 .05
❑ 200 Mark Brunell 1.00 .45
❑ 201 Bernard Carter .10 .05
❑ 202 James O. Stewart .20 .09
❑ 203 Tony Boselli .10 .05
❑ 204 Chris Doering .10 .05
❑ 205 Willie Jackson .10 .05
❑ 206 Tony Brackens RC .20 .09
❑ 207 Ernest Givins .10 .05
❑ 208 Le'Shai Maston .10 .05
❑ 209 Pete Mitchell .20 .09
❑ 210 Desmond Howard .20 .09
❑ 211 Vinnie Clark .10 .05
❑ 212 Jeff Lageman .10 .05
❑ 213 Derrick Walker .10 .05
❑ 214 Dan Saleaumua .10 .05
❑ 215 Derrick Thomas .20 .09
❑ 216 Neil Smith .10 .05
❑ 217 Willie Davis .10 .05
❑ 218 Mark Collins .10 .05
❑ 219 Lake Dawson .10 .05
❑ 220 Greg Hill .20 .09
❑ 221 Anthony Davis .10 .05
❑ 222 Kimble Anders .20 .09
❑ 223 Webster Slaughter .10 .05
❑ 224 Tamarick Vanover .20 .09
❑ 225 Marcus Allen .40 .18
❑ 226 Steve Bono .10 .05
❑ 227 Will Shields .10 .05
❑ 228 Karim Abdul-Jabbar RC .50 .23
❑ 229 Tim Bowens .10 .05
❑ 230 Keith Sims .10 .05
❑ 231 Terry Kirby .20 .09
❑ 232 Gene Atkins .10 .05
❑ 233 Dan Marino 2.00 .90
❑ 234 Richmond Webb .10 .05
❑ 235 Gary Clark .10 .05
❑ 236 O.J. McDuffie .20 .09
❑ 237 Marco Coleman .10 .05
❑ 238 Bernie Parmalee .10 .05
❑ 239 Randal Hill .10 .05
❑ 240 Bryan Cox .10 .05
❑ 241 Irving Fryar .20 .09
❑ 242 Derrick Alexander DE .10 .05
❑ 243 Qadry Ismail .10 .05
❑ 244 Warren Moon .20 .09
❑ 245 Cris Carter .40 .18
❑ 246 Chad May .10 .05
❑ 247 Robert Smith .20 .09
❑ 248 Fuad Reveiz .10 .05
❑ 249 Orlando Thomas .10 .05
❑ 250 Chris Hinton .10 .05
❑ 251 Jack Del Rio .10 .05
❑ 252 Moe Williams RC .20 .09
❑ 253 Roy Barker .10 .05
❑ 254 Jake Reed .20 .09
❑ 255 Adrian Cooper .10 .05
❑ 256 Curtis Martin .75 .35
❑ 257 Ben Coates .20 .09
❑ 258 Drew Bledsoe 1.00 .45
❑ 259 Maurice Hurst .10 .05
❑ 260 Troy Brown .10 .05
❑ 261 Bruce Armstrong .10 .05
❑ 262 Myron Guyton .10 .05
❑ 263 Dave Meggett .10 .05
❑ 264 Terry Glenn RC 1.00 .45
❑ 265 Chris Slade .10 .05
❑ 266 Vincent Brisby .10 .05
❑ 267 Willie McGinest .10 .05
❑ 268 Vincent Brown .10 .05
❑ 269 Will Moore .10 .05
❑ 270 Jay Barker RC .10 .05
❑ 271 Ray Zellars .10 .05
❑ 272 Derek Brown RBK .10 .05
❑ 273 William Roaf .10 .05
❑ 274 Quinn Early .10 .05
❑ 275 Michael Haynes .10 .05
❑ 276 Rufus Porter .10 .05
❑ 277 Renaldo Turnbull .10 .05
❑ 278 Wayne Martin .10 .05
❑ 279 Tyrone Hughes .10 .05
❑ 280 Irv Smith .10 .05
❑ 281 Eric Allen .10 .05
❑ 282 Mark Fields .10 .05
❑ 283 Mario Bates .20 .09
❑ 284 Jim Everett .10 .05
❑ 285 Vince Buck .10 .05
❑ 286 Alex Molden RC .10 .05
❑ 287 Tyrone Wheatley .20 .09
❑ 288 Chris Calloway .10 .05
❑ 289 Jessie Armstead .10 .05
❑ 290 Arthur Marshall .10 .05
❑ 291 Aaron Pierce .10 .05
❑ 292 Dave Brown .10 .05
❑ 293 Rodney Hampton .20 .09
❑ 294 Jumbo Elliott .10 .05
❑ 295 Mike Sherrard .10 .05
❑ 296 Howard Cross .10 .05
❑ 297 Michael Brooks .10 .05
❑ 298 Herschel Walker .20 .09
❑ 299 Danny Kanell RC .40 .18
❑ 300 Keith Elias .10 .05
❑ 301 Bobby Houston .10 .05
❑ 302 Dexter Carter .10 .05
❑ 303 Tony Casillas .10 .05
❑ 304 Kyle Brady .10 .05
❑ 305 Glenn Foley .20 .09
❑ 306 Ronald Moore .10 .05
❑ 307 Ryan Yarborough .10 .05
❑ 308 Aaron Glenn .10 .05
❑ 309 Adrian Murrell .40 .18
❑ 310 Boomer Esiason .20 .09
❑ 311 Kyle Clifton .10 .05
❑ 312 Wayne Chrebet .60 .25
❑ 313 Erik Howard .10 .05
❑ 314 Keyshawn Johnson RC 1.50 .70
❑ 315 Marvin Washington .10 .05
❑ 316 Johnny Mitchell .10 .05
❑ 317 Alex Van Dyke RC .20 .09
❑ 318 Billy Joe Hobert .20 .09
❑ 319 Andrew Glover .10 .05
❑ 320 Vince Evans .10 .05
❑ 321 Chester McGlockton .10 .05
❑ 322 Pat Swilling .10 .05
❑ 323 Rocket Ismail .10 .05
❑ 324 Eddie Anderson .10 .05
❑ 325 Rickey Dudley RC .40 .18
❑ 326 Steve Wisniewski .10 .05
❑ 327 Harvey Williams .10 .05
❑ 328 Napoleon Kaufman .40 .18
❑ 329 Tim Brown .40 .18
❑ 330 Jeff Hostetler .10 .05
❑ 331 Anthony Smith .10 .05
❑ 332 Terry McDaniel .10 .05
❑ 333 Charlie Garner .10 .05
❑ 334 Ricky Watters .20 .09
❑ 335 Brian Dawkins .10 .05
❑ 336 Randall Cunningham .40 .18
❑ 337 Gary Anderson .10 .05
❑ 338 Calvin Williams .10 .05
❑ 339 Chris T. Jones .20 .09
❑ 340 Bobby Hoying RC .50 .23
❑ 341 William Fuller .10 .05
❑ 342 William Thomas .10 .05
❑ 343 Mike Mamula .10 .05
❑ 344 Fred Barnett .10 .05
❑ 345 Rodney Peete .10 .05
❑ 346 Mark McMillian .10 .05
❑ 347 Bobby Taylor .10 .05
❑ 348 Yancey Thigpen .20 .09
❑ 349 Neil O'Donnell .20 .09
❑ 350 Rod Woodson .20 .09
❑ 351 Kordell Stewart .60 .25
❑ 352 Dermontti Dawson .10 .05
❑ 353 Norm Johnson .10 .05
❑ 354 Ernie Mills .10 .05
❑ 355 Byron Bam Morris .20 .09
❑ 356 Mark Bruener .10 .05
❑ 357 Kevin Greene .20 .09
❑ 358 Greg Lloyd .20 .09
❑ 359 Andre Hastings .10 .05
❑ 360 Erric Pegram .10 .05
❑ 361 Carnell Lake .10 .05
❑ 362 Dwayne Harper .10 .05
❑ 363 Ronnie Harmon .10 .05
❑ 364 Leslie O'Neal .10 .05
❑ 365 John Carney .10 .05
❑ 366 Stan Humphries .20 .09
❑ 367 Brian Roche RC .10 .05
❑ 368 Terrell Fletcher .10 .05
❑ 369 Shaun Gayle .10 .05
❑ 370 Alfred Pupunu .10 .05
❑ 371 Shawn Jefferson .10 .05
❑ 372 Junior Seau .20 .09
❑ 373 Mark Seay .10 .05
❑ 374 Aaron Hayden .10 .05
❑ 375 Tony Martin .20 .09
❑ 376 Steve Young .75 .35
❑ 377 J.J. Stokes .40 .18
❑ 378 Jerry Rice 1.00 .45
❑ 379 Derek Loville .10 .05
❑ 380 Lee Woodall .10 .05
❑ 381 Terrell Owens RC 2.00 .90
❑ 382 Elvis Grbac .20 .09
❑ 383 Ricky Ervins .10 .05
❑ 384 Eric Davis .10 .05
❑ 385 Dana Stubblefield .20 .09
❑ 386 Gary Plummer .10 .05
❑ 387 Tim McDonald .10 .05
❑ 388 William Floyd .20 .09
❑ 389 Ken Norton Jr. .10 .05
❑ 390 Merton Hanks .10 .05

Card	Player	Mint	Nrmt
❑ 391	Bart Oates	.10	.05
❑ 392	Brent Jones	.10	.05
❑ 393	Steve Broussard	.10	.05
❑ 394	Robert Blackmon	.10	.05
❑ 395	Rick Tuten	.10	.05
❑ 396	Pete Kendall	.10	.05
❑ 397	John Friesz	.10	.05
❑ 398	Terry Wooden	.10	.05
❑ 399	Rick Mirer	.20	.09
❑ 400	Chris Warren	.20	.09
❑ 401	Joey Galloway	.60	.25
❑ 402	Howard Ballard	.10	.05
❑ 403	Jason Kyle	.10	.05
❑ 404	Kevin Mawae	.10	.05
❑ 405	Mack Strong	.10	.05
❑ 406	Reggie Brown RBK RC	.10	.05
❑ 407	Cortez Kennedy	.10	.05
❑ 408	Sean Gilbert	.10	.05
❑ 409	J.T. Thomas	.10	.05
❑ 410	Shane Conlan	.10	.05
❑ 411	Johnny Bailey	.10	.05
❑ 412	Mark Rypien	.10	.05
❑ 413	Leonard Russell	.10	.05
❑ 414	Troy Drayton	.10	.05
❑ 415	Jerome Bettis	.40	.18
❑ 416	Jessie Hester	.10	.05
❑ 417	Isaac Bruce	.40	.18
❑ 418	Roman Phifer	.10	.05
❑ 419	Todd Kinchen	.10	.05
❑ 420	Alexander Wright	.10	.05
❑ 421	Marcus Jones RC	.10	.05
❑ 422	Horace Copeland	.10	.05
❑ 423	Eric Curry	.10	.05
❑ 424	Courtney Hawkins	.10	.05
❑ 425	Alvin Harper	.10	.05
❑ 426	Derrick Brooks	.10	.05
❑ 427	Errict Rhett	.20	.09
❑ 428	Trent Dilfer	.40	.18
❑ 429	Hardy Nickerson	.10	.05
❑ 430	Brad Culpepper	.10	.05
❑ 431	Warren Sapp	.10	.05
❑ 432	Reggie Roby	.10	.05
❑ 433	Santana Dotson	.10	.05
❑ 434	Jerry Ellison	.10	.05
❑ 435	Lawrence Dawsey	.10	.05
❑ 436	Heath Shuler	.20	.09
❑ 437	Stanley Richard	.20	.09
❑ 438	Rod Stephens	.10	.05
❑ 439	Stephen Davis RC	3.00	1.35
❑ 440	Terry Allen	.20	.09
❑ 441	Michael Westbrook	.40	.18
❑ 442	Ken Harvey	.10	.05
❑ 443	Coleman Bell	.10	.05
❑ 444	Marvcus Patton	.10	.05
❑ 445	Gus Frerotte	.40	.18
❑ 446	Leslie Shepherd	.10	.05
❑ 447	Tom Carter	.10	.05
❑ 448	Brian Mitchell	.10	.05
❑ 449	Darrell Green	.10	.05
❑ 450A	Tony Woods (Issued in packs)	.10	.05
❑ 450B	Chris Warren Promo	.50	.23
❑ CW1	Chris Warren Promo (Gold Crown Die Cut style)	1.00	.45

1997 Pacific

	MINT	NRMT
COMPLETE SET (450)	30.00	13.50

Card	Player	Mint	Nrmt
❑ 1	Lomas Brown	.10	.05
❑ 2	Pat Carter	.10	.05
❑ 3	Larry Centers	.20	.09
❑ 4	Matt Darby	.10	.05
❑ 5	Marcus Dowdell	.10	.05
❑ 6	Aaron Graham	.10	.05
❑ 7	Kent Graham	.10	.05
❑ 8	LeShon Johnson	.10	.05
❑ 9	Seth Joyner	.10	.05
❑ 10	Leeland McElroy	.10	.05
❑ 11	Rob Moore	.20	.09
❑ 12	Simeon Rice	.20	.09
❑ 13	Eric Swann	.10	.05
❑ 14	Aeneas Williams	.10	.05
❑ 15	Morten Andersen	.10	.05
❑ 16	Jamal Anderson	.60	.25
❑ 17	Lester Archambeau	.10	.05
❑ 18	Cornelius Bennett	.10	.05
❑ 19	J.J. Birden	.10	.05
❑ 20	Antone Davis	.10	.05
❑ 21	Bert Emanuel	.20	.09
❑ 22	Travis Hall	.10	.05
❑ 23	Bobby Hebert	.10	.05
❑ 24	Craig Heyward	.10	.05
❑ 25	Terance Mathis	.20	.09
❑ 26	Tim McKyer	.10	.05
❑ 27	Eric Metcalf	.20	.09
❑ 28	Jessie Tuggle	.10	.05
❑ 29	Derrick Alexander WR	.20	.09
❑ 30	Orlando Brown	.10	.05
❑ 31	Rob Burnett	.10	.05
❑ 32	Earnest Byner	.10	.05
❑ 33	Ray Ethridge	.10	.05
❑ 34	Steve Everitt	.10	.05
❑ 35	Carwell Gardner	.10	.05
❑ 36	Michael Jackson	.20	.09
❑ 37	Jermaine Lewis	.40	.18
❑ 38	Stevon Moore	.10	.05
❑ 39	Byron Bam Morris	.10	.05
❑ 40	Jonathan Ogden	.10	.05
❑ 41	Vinny Testaverde	.20	.09
❑ 42	Todd Collins	.10	.05
❑ 43	Russell Copeland	.10	.05
❑ 44	Quinn Early	.10	.05
❑ 45	John Fina	.10	.05
❑ 46	Phil Hansen	.10	.05
❑ 47	Eric Moulds	.40	.18
❑ 48	Bryce Paup	.10	.05
❑ 49	Andre Reed	.20	.09
❑ 50	Kurt Schulz	.10	.05
❑ 51	Bruce Smith	.20	.09
❑ 52	Chris Spielman	.10	.05
❑ 53	Steve Tasker	.10	.05
❑ 54	Thurman Thomas	.40	.18
❑ 55	Carlton Bailey	.10	.05
❑ 56	Michael Bates	.10	.05
❑ 57	Blake Brockermeyer	.10	.05
❑ 58	Mark Carrier WR	.10	.05
❑ 59	Kerry Collins	.20	.09
❑ 60	Eric Davis	.10	.05
❑ 61	Kevin Greene	.20	.09
❑ 62	Rocket Ismail	.20	.09
❑ 63	Anthony Johnson	.10	.05
❑ 64	Shawn King	.10	.05
❑ 65	Greg Kragen	.10	.05
❑ 66	Sam Mills	.10	.05
❑ 67	Tyrone Poole	.10	.05
❑ 68	Wesley Walls	.20	.09
❑ 69	Mark Carrier DB	.10	.05
❑ 70	Curtis Conway	.20	.09
❑ 71	Bobby Engram	.20	.09
❑ 72	Jim Flanigan	.10	.05
❑ 73	Al Fontenot	.10	.05
❑ 74	Raymont Harris	.10	.05
❑ 75	Walt Harris	.10	.05
❑ 76	Andy Heck	.10	.05
❑ 77	Dave Krieg	.10	.05
❑ 78	Rashaan Salaam	.10	.05
❑ 79	Vinson Smith	.10	.05
❑ 80	Alonzo Spellman	.10	.05
❑ 81	Michael Timpson	.10	.05
❑ 82	James Williams	.10	.05
❑ 83	Ashley Ambrose	.10	.05
❑ 84	Eric Bieniemy	.10	.05
❑ 85	Jeff Blake	.20	.09
❑ 86	Ki-Jana Carter	.10	.05

Card	Player	Mint	Nrmt
❑ 87	John Copeland	.10	.05
❑ 88	David Dunn	.10	.05
❑ 89	Jeff Hill	.10	.05
❑ 90	Ricardo McDonald	.10	.05
❑ 91	Tony McGee	.10	.05
❑ 92	Greg Myers	.10	.05
❑ 93	Carl Pickens	.40	.18
❑ 94	Corey Sawyer	.10	.05
❑ 95	Darnay Scott	.20	.09
❑ 96	Dan Wilkinson	.10	.05
❑ 97	Troy Aikman	1.00	.45
❑ 98	Larry Allen	.10	.05
❑ 99	Eric Bjornson	.10	.05
❑ 100	Ray Donaldson	.10	.05
❑ 101	Michael Irvin	.40	.18
❑ 102	Daryl Johnston	.20	.09
❑ 103	Nate Newton	.10	.05
❑ 104	Deion Sanders	.40	.18
❑ 105	Jim Schwantz RC	.10	.05
❑ 106	Emmitt Smith	1.50	.70
❑ 107	Broderick Thomas	.10	.05
❑ 108	Tony Tolbert	.10	.05
❑ 109	Erik Williams	.10	.05
❑ 110	Sherman Williams	.10	.05
❑ 111	Darren Woodson	.10	.05
❑ 112	Steve Atwater	.10	.05
❑ 113	Aaron Craver	.10	.05
❑ 114	Ray Crockett	.10	.05
❑ 115	Terrell Davis	1.50	.70
❑ 116	Jason Elam	.10	.05
❑ 117	John Elway	2.00	.90
❑ 118	Todd Kinchen	.10	.05
❑ 119	Ed McCaffrey	.20	.09
❑ 120	Anthony Miller	.10	.05
❑ 121	John Mobley	.10	.05
❑ 122	Michael Dean Perry	.10	.05
❑ 123	Reggie Rivers	.10	.05
❑ 124	Shannon Sharpe	.20	.09
❑ 125	Alfred Williams	.10	.05
❑ 126	Reggie Brown LB	.20	.09
❑ 127	Luther Elliss	.10	.05
❑ 128	Kevin Glover	.10	.05
❑ 129	Jason Hanson	.10	.05
❑ 130	Pepper Johnson	.10	.05
❑ 131	Glyn Milburn	.10	.05
❑ 132	Scott Mitchell	.20	.09
❑ 133	Herman Moore	.40	.18
❑ 134	Johnnie Morton	.20	.09
❑ 135	Brett Perriman	.10	.05
❑ 136	Robert Porcher	.10	.05
❑ 137	Ron Rivers	.10	.05
❑ 138	Barry Sanders	2.00	.90
❑ 139	Henry Thomas	.10	.05
❑ 140	Don Beebe	.10	.05
❑ 141	Edgar Bennett	.20	.09
❑ 142	Robert Brooks	.20	.09
❑ 143	LeRoy Butler	.10	.05
❑ 144	Mark Chmura	.20	.09
❑ 145	Brett Favre	2.00	.90
❑ 146	Antonio Freeman	.50	.23
❑ 147	Chris Jacke	.10	.05
❑ 148	Travis Jervey	.20	.09
❑ 149	Sean Jones	.10	.05
❑ 150	Dorsey Levens	.40	.18
❑ 151	John Michels	.10	.05
❑ 152	Craig Newsome	.10	.05
❑ 153	Eugene Robinson	.10	.05
❑ 154	Reggie White	.40	.18
❑ 155	Micheal Barrow	.10	.05
❑ 156	Blaine Bishop	.10	.05
❑ 157	Chris Chandler	.20	.09
❑ 158	Anthony Cook	.10	.05
❑ 159	Malcolm Floyd	.10	.05
❑ 160	Eddie George	1.00	.45
❑ 161	Roderick Lewis	.10	.05
❑ 162	Steve McNair	.50	.23
❑ 163	John Henry Mills RC	.10	.05
❑ 164	Derek Russell	.10	.05
❑ 165	Chris Sanders	.10	.05
❑ 166	Mark Stepnoski	.10	.05
❑ 167	Frank Wycheck	.10	.05
❑ 168	Robert Young	.10	.05
❑ 169	Trev Alberts	.10	.05
❑ 170	Aaron Bailey	.10	.05
❑ 171	Tony Bennett	.10	.05
❑ 172	Ray Buchanan	.10	.05

❑ 173 Quentin Coryatt .10 .05
❑ 174 Eugene Daniel .10 .05
❑ 175 Sean Dawkins .10 .05
❑ 176 Ken Dilger .10 .05
❑ 177 Marshall Faulk .40 .18
❑ 178 Jim Harbaugh .20 .09
❑ 179 Marvin Harrison .40 .18
❑ 180 Paul Justin .10 .05
❑ 181 Lamont Warren .10 .05
❑ 182 Bernard Whittington .10 .05
❑ 183 Tony Boselli .10 .05
❑ 184 Tony Brackens .10 .05
❑ 185 Mark Brunell 1.00 .45
❑ 186 Brian DeMarco .10 .05
❑ 187 Rich Griffith .10 .05
❑ 188 Kevin Hardy .10 .05
❑ 189 Willie Jackson .10 .05
❑ 190 Jeff Lageman .10 .05
❑ 191 Keenan McCardell .20 .09
❑ 192 Natrone Means .40 .18
❑ 193 Pete Mitchell .10 .05
❑ 194 Joel Smeenge .10 .05
❑ 195 Jimmy Smith .20 .09
❑ 196 James O.Stewart .20 .09
❑ 197 Marcus Allen .40 .18
❑ 198 John Alt .10 .05
❑ 199 Kimble Anders .20 .09
❑ 200 Steve Bono .20 .09
❑ 201 Vaughn Booker .10 .05
❑ 202 Dale Carter .10 .05
❑ 203 Mark Collins .10 .05
❑ 204 Greg Hill .10 .05
❑ 205 Joe Horn .40 .18
❑ 206 Dan Saleaumua .10 .05
❑ 207 Will Shields .10 .05
❑ 208 Neil Smith .20 .09
❑ 209 Derrick Thomas .20 .09
❑ 210 Tamarick Vanover .20 .09
❑ 211 Karim Abdul-Jabbar .40 .18
❑ 212 Fred Barnett .10 .05
❑ 213 Tim Bowens .10 .05
❑ 214 Kirby Dar Dar RC .20 .09
❑ 215 Troy Drayton .10 .05
❑ 216 Craig Erickson .10 .05
❑ 217 Daryl Gardener .10 .05
❑ 218 Randal Hill .10 .05
❑ 219 Dan Marino 2.00 .90
❑ 220 O.J. McDuffie .20 .09
❑ 221 Bernie Parmalee .10 .05
❑ 222 Stanley Pritchett .10 .05
❑ 223 Daniel Stubbs .10 .05
❑ 224 Zach Thomas .20 .09
❑ 225 Derrick Alexander DE .10 .05
❑ 226 Cris Carter .40 .18
❑ 227 Jeff Christy .10 .05
❑ 228 Qadry Ismail .20 .09
❑ 229 Brad Johnson .50 .23
❑ 230 Andrew Jordan .10 .05
❑ 231 Randall McDaniel .10 .05
❑ 232 David Palmer .10 .05
❑ 233 John Randle .20 .09
❑ 234 Jake Reed .20 .09
❑ 235 Scott Sisson .10 .05
❑ 236 Korey Stringer .10 .05
❑ 237 Darryl Talley .10 .05
❑ 238 Orlando Thomas .10 .05
❑ 239 Bruce Armstrong .10 .05
❑ 240 Drew Bledsoe 1.00 .45
❑ 241 Willie Clay .10 .05
❑ 242 Ben Coates .20 .09
❑ 243 Ferric Collons RC .10 .05
❑ 244 Terry Glenn .40 .18
❑ 245 Jerome Henderson .10 .05
❑ 246 Shawn Jefferson .10 .05
❑ 247 Dietrich Jells .10 .05
❑ 248 Ty Law .10 .05
❑ 249 Curtis Martin .50 .23
❑ 250 Willie McGinest .10 .05
❑ 251 Dave Meggett .10 .05
❑ 252 Lawyer Milloy .10 .05
❑ 253 Chris Slade .10 .05
❑ 254 Je'rod Cherry .10 .05
❑ 255 Jim Everett .10 .05
❑ 256 Mark Fields .10 .05
❑ 257 Michael Haynes .10 .05
❑ 258 Tyrone Hughes .10 .05
❑ 259 Haywood Jeffires .10 .05
❑ 260 Wayne Martin .10 .05
❑ 261 Mark McMillian .10 .05
❑ 262 Rufus Porter .10 .05
❑ 263 William Roaf .10 .05
❑ 264 Torrance Small .10 .05
❑ 265 Renaldo Turnbull .10 .05
❑ 266 Ray Zellars .10 .05
❑ 267 Jessie Armstead .10 .05
❑ 268 Chad Bratzke .10 .05
❑ 269 Dave Brown .10 .05
❑ 270 Chris Calloway .10 .05
❑ 271 Howard Cross .10 .05
❑ 272 Lawrence Dawsey .10 .05
❑ 273 Rodney Hampton .20 .09
❑ 274 Danny Kanell .20 .09
❑ 275 Arthur Marshall .10 .05
❑ 276 Aaron Pierce .10 .05
❑ 277 Phillippi Sparks .10 .05
❑ 278 Amani Toomer .20 .09
❑ 279 Charles Way .20 .09
❑ 280 Richie Anderson .20 .09
❑ 281 Fred Baxter .10 .05
❑ 282 Wayne Chrebet .40 .18
❑ 283 Kyle Clifton .10 .05
❑ 284 Jumbo Elliott .10 .05
❑ 285 Aaron Glenn .10 .05
❑ 286 Jeff Graham .10 .05
❑ 287 Bobby Hamilton RC .10 .05
❑ 288 Keyshawn Johnson .40 .18
❑ 289 Adrian Murrell .20 .09
❑ 290 Neil O'Donnell .20 .09
❑ 291 Webster Slaughter .10 .05
❑ 292 Alex Van Dyke .10 .05
❑ 293 Marvin Washington .10 .05
❑ 294 Joe Aska .10 .05
❑ 295 Jerry Ball .10 .05
❑ 296 Tim Brown .40 .18
❑ 297 Rickey Dudley .20 .09
❑ 298 Pat Harlow .10 .05
❑ 299 Nolan Harrison .10 .05
❑ 300 Billy Joe Hobert .20 .09
❑ 301 James Jett .20 .09
❑ 302 Napoleon Kaufman .40 .18
❑ 303 Lincoln Kennedy .10 .05
❑ 304 Albert Lewis .10 .05
❑ 305 Chester McGlockton .10 .05
❑ 306 Pat Swilling .10 .05
❑ 307 Steve Wisniewski .10 .05
❑ 308 Darion Conner .10 .05
❑ 309 Ty Detmer .20 .09
❑ 310 Jason Dunn .10 .05
❑ 311 Irving Fryar .20 .09
❑ 312 James Fuller .10 .05
❑ 313 William Fuller .10 .05
❑ 314 Charlie Garner .10 .05
❑ 315 Bobby Hoying .20 .09
❑ 316 Tom Hutton .10 .05
❑ 317 Chris T. Jones .10 .05
❑ 318 Mike Mamula .10 .05
❑ 319 Mark Seay .10 .05
❑ 320 Bobby Taylor .10 .05
❑ 321 Ricky Watters .20 .09
❑ 322 Jahine Arnold .10 .05
❑ 323 Jerome Bettis .40 .18
❑ 324 Chad Brown .10 .05
❑ 325 Mark Bruener .10 .05
❑ 326 Andre Hastings .10 .05
❑ 327 Norm Johnson .10 .05
❑ 328 Levon Kirkland .10 .05
❑ 329 Carnell Lake .10 .05
❑ 330 Greg Lloyd .10 .05
❑ 331 Ernie Mills .10 .05
❑ 332 Orpheus Roye RC .10 .05
❑ 333 Kordell Stewart .50 .23
❑ 334 Yancey Thigpen .20 .09
❑ 335 Mike Tomczak .10 .05
❑ 336 Rod Woodson .20 .09
❑ 337 Tony Banks .20 .09
❑ 338 Bern Brostek .10 .05
❑ 339 Isaac Bruce .40 .18
❑ 340 Ernie Conwell .10 .05
❑ 341 Keith Crawford .10 .05
❑ 342 Wayne Gandy .10 .05
❑ 343 Harold Green .10 .05
❑ 344 Carlos Jenkins .10 .05
❑ 345 Jimmie Jones .10 .05
❑ 346 Eddie Kennison .20 .09
❑ 347 Todd Lyght .10 .05
❑ 348 Leslie O'Neal .10 .05
❑ 349 Lawrence Phillips .10 .05
❑ 350 Greg Robinson .10 .05
❑ 351 Darren Bennett .10 .05
❑ 352 Lewis Bush .10 .05
❑ 353 Eric Castle .10 .05
❑ 354 Terrell Fletcher .10 .05
❑ 355 Darrien Gordon .10 .05
❑ 356 Kurt Gouveia .10 .05
❑ 357 Aaron Hayden .10 .05
❑ 358 Stan Humphries .20 .09
❑ 359 Tony Martin .20 .09
❑ 360 Vaughn Parker .10 .05
❑ 361 Brian Roche .10 .05
❑ 362 Leonard Russell .10 .05
❑ 363 Junior Seau .20 .09
❑ 364 Roy Barker .10 .05
❑ 365 Harris Barton .10 .05
❑ 366 Dexter Carter .10 .05
❑ 367 Chris Doleman .10 .05
❑ 368 Tyronne Drakeford .10 .05
❑ 369 Elvis Grbac .20 .09
❑ 370 Derek Loville .10 .05
❑ 371 Tim McDonald .10 .05
❑ 372 Ken Norton .10 .05
❑ 373 Terrell Owens .40 .18
❑ 374 Gary Plummer .10 .05
❑ 375 Jerry Rice 1.00 .45
❑ 376 Dana Stubblefield .10 .05
❑ 377 Lee Woodall .10 .05
❑ 378 Steve Young .60 .25
❑ 379 Robert Blackmon .10 .05
❑ 380 Brian Blades .10 .05
❑ 381 Carlester Crumpler .10 .05
❑ 382 Christian Fauria .10 .05
❑ 383 John Friesz .10 .05
❑ 384 Joey Galloway .50 .23
❑ 385 Derrick Graham .10 .05
❑ 386 Cortez Kennedy .10 .05
❑ 387 Warren Moon .40 .18
❑ 388 Winston Moss .10 .05
❑ 389 Mike Pritchard .10 .05
❑ 390 Michael Sinclair .10 .05
❑ 391 Lamar Smith .40 .18
❑ 392 Chris Warren .20 .09
❑ 393 Chidi Ahanotu .10 .05
❑ 394 Mike Alstott .40 .18
❑ 395 Reggie Brooks .10 .05
❑ 396 Trent Dilfer .40 .18
❑ 397 Jerry Ellison .10 .05
❑ 398 Paul Gruber .10 .05
❑ 399 Alvin Harper .10 .05
❑ 400 Courtney Hawkins .10 .05
❑ 401 Dave Moore .10 .05
❑ 402 Errict Rhett .10 .05
❑ 403 Warren Sapp .20 .09
❑ 404 Nilo Silvan .10 .05
❑ 405 Regan Upshaw .10 .05
❑ 406 Casey Weldon .10 .05
❑ 407 Terry Allen .40 .18
❑ 408 Jamie Asher .10 .05
❑ 409 Bill Brooks .10 .05
❑ 410 Tom Carter .10 .05
❑ 411 Henry Ellard .10 .05
❑ 412 Gus Frerotte .10 .05
❑ 413 Darrell Green .20 .09
❑ 414 Ken Harvey .10 .05
❑ 415 Tre Johnson .10 .05
❑ 416 Brian Mitchell .10 .05
❑ 417 Rich Owens .10 .05
❑ 418 Heath Shuler .10 .05
❑ 419 Michael Westbrook .20 .09
❑ 420 Tony Woods RC .10 .05
❑ 421 Reidel Anthony RC .75 .35
❑ 422 Darnell Autry RC .20 .09
❑ 423 Tiki Barber RC 1.25 .55
❑ 424 Pat Barnes RC .40 .18
❑ 425 Terry Battle RC .10 .05
❑ 426 Will Blackwell RC .40 .18
❑ 427 Peter Boulware RC .20 .09
❑ 428 Rae Carruth RC .40 .18
❑ 429 Troy Davis RC .40 .18
❑ 430 Jim Druckenmiller RC .40 .18

		MINT	NRMT
❑ 431	Warrick Dunn RC	1.25	.55
❑ 432	Marc Edwards RC	.10	.05
❑ 433	James Farrior RC	.10	.05
❑ 434	Yatil Green RC	.20	.09
❑ 435	Byron Hanspard RC	.40	.18
❑ 436	Ike Hilliard RC	.75	.35
❑ 437	David LaFleur RC	.20	.09
❑ 438	Kevin Lockett RC	.20	.09
❑ 439	Sam Madison RC	.40	.18
❑ 440	Brian Manning RC	.20	.09
❑ 441	Orlando Pace RC	.40	.18
❑ 442	Jake Plummer RC	2.50	1.10
❑ 443	Chad Scott RC	.10	.05
❑ 444	Sedrick Shaw RC	.40	.18
❑ 445	Antowain Smith RC	1.00	.45
❑ 446	Shawn Springs RC	.20	.09
❑ 447	Ross Verba RC	.10	.05
❑ 448	Bryant Westbrook RC	.10	.05
❑ 449	Renaldo Wynn RC	.10	.05
❑ 450	Jimmy Johnson CO	.20	.09
❑ S1	Mark Brunell Sample	1.00	.45

1998 Pacific

		MINT	NRMT
COMPLETE SET (450)		70.00	32.00
❑ 1	Mario Bates	.25	.11
❑ 2	Lomas Brown	.15	.07
❑ 3	Larry Centers	.15	.07
❑ 4	Chris Gedney	.15	.07
❑ 5	Terry Irving	.15	.07
❑ 6	Tom Knight	.15	.07
❑ 7	Eric Metcalf	.15	.07
❑ 8	Jamir Miller	.15	.07
❑ 9	Rob Moore	.25	.11
❑ 10	Joe Nedney	.15	.07
❑ 11	Jake Plummer	.75	.35
❑ 12	Simeon Rice	.25	.11
❑ 13	Frank Sanders	.25	.11
❑ 14	Eric Swann	.15	.07
❑ 15	Aeneas Williams	.15	.07
❑ 16	Morten Andersen	.15	.07
❑ 17	Jamal Anderson	.50	.23
❑ 18	Michael Booker	.15	.07
❑ 19	Keith Brooking RC	1.50	.70
❑ 20	Ray Buchanan	.15	.07
❑ 21	Devin Bush	.15	.07
❑ 22	Chris Chandler	.25	.11
❑ 23	Tony Graziani	.15	.07
❑ 24	Harold Green	.15	.07
❑ 25	Byron Hanspard	.25	.11
❑ 26	Todd Kinchen	.15	.07
❑ 27	Tony Martin	.25	.11
❑ 28	Terance Mathis	.25	.11
❑ 29	Eugene Robinson	.15	.07
❑ 30	O.J. Santiago	.15	.07
❑ 31	Chuck Smith	.15	.07
❑ 32	Jessie Tuggle	.15	.07
❑ 33	Bob Whitfield	.15	.07
❑ 34	Peter Boulware	.15	.07
❑ 35	Jay Graham	.15	.07
❑ 36	Eric Green	.15	.07
❑ 37	Jim Harbaugh	.25	.11
❑ 38	Michael Jackson	.15	.07
❑ 39	Jermaine Lewis	.25	.11
❑ 40	Ray Lewis	.50	.23
❑ 41	Michael McCrary	.15	.07
❑ 42	Stevon Moore	.15	.07
❑ 43	Jonathan Ogden	.15	.07
❑ 44	Errict Rhett	.25	.11
❑ 45	Matt Stover	.15	.07
❑ 46	Rod Woodson	.25	.11
❑ 47	Eric Zeier	.25	.11
❑ 48	Ruben Brown	.15	.07
❑ 49	Steve Christie	.15	.07
❑ 50	Quinn Early	.15	.07
❑ 51	John Fina	.15	.07
❑ 52	Doug Flutie	.50	.23
❑ 53	Phil Hansen	.15	.07
❑ 54	Lonnie Johnson	.15	.07
❑ 55	Rob Johnson	.25	.11
❑ 56	Henry Jones	.15	.07
❑ 57	Eric Moulds	.50	.23
❑ 58	Andre Reed	.25	.11
❑ 59	Antowain Smith	.50	.23
❑ 60	Bruce Smith	.25	.11
❑ 61	Thurman Thomas	.50	.23
❑ 62	Ted Washington	.15	.07
❑ 63	Michael Bates	.15	.07
❑ 64	Tim Biakabutuka	.25	.11
❑ 65	Blake Brockermeyer	.15	.07
❑ 66	Mark Carrier	.15	.07
❑ 67	Rae Carruth	.25	.11
❑ 68	Kerry Collins	.25	.11
❑ 69	Doug Evans	.15	.07
❑ 70	William Floyd	.15	.07
❑ 71	Sean Gilbert	.15	.07
❑ 72	Rocket Ismail	.15	.07
❑ 73	John Kasay	.15	.07
❑ 74	Fred Lane	.25	.11
❑ 75	Lamar Lathon	.15	.07
❑ 76	Muhsin Muhammad	.25	.11
❑ 77	Wesley Walls	.25	.11
❑ 78	Edgar Bennett	.15	.07
❑ 79	Tom Carter	.15	.07
❑ 80	Curtis Conway	.25	.11
❑ 81	Bobby Engram	.25	.11
❑ 82	Curtis Enis RC	1.50	.70
❑ 83	Jim Flanigan	.15	.07
❑ 84	Walt Harris	.15	.07
❑ 85	Jeff Jaeger	.15	.07
❑ 86	Erik Kramer	.15	.07
❑ 87	John Mangum	.15	.07
❑ 88	Glyn Milburn	.15	.07
❑ 89	Barry Minter	.15	.07
❑ 90	Chris Penn	.15	.07
❑ 91	Todd Sauerbrun	.15	.07
❑ 92	James Williams	.15	.07
❑ 93	Ashley Ambrose	.15	.07
❑ 94	Willie Anderson	.15	.07
❑ 95	Eric Bieniemy	.15	.07
❑ 96	Jeff Blake	.25	.11
❑ 97	Ki-Jana Carter	.15	.07
❑ 98	John Copeland	.15	.07
❑ 99	Corey Dillon	.75	.35
❑ 100	Tony McGee	.15	.07
❑ 101	Neil O'Donnell	.25	.11
❑ 102	Carl Pickens	.50	.23
❑ 103	Kevin Sargent	.15	.07
❑ 104	Darnay Scott	.25	.11
❑ 105	Takeo Spikes	.25	.11
❑ 106	Troy Aikman	1.25	.55
❑ 107	Larry Allen	.15	.07
❑ 108	Eric Bjornson	.15	.07
❑ 109	Billy Davis	.15	.07
❑ 110	Jason Garrett RC	.15	.07
❑ 111	Michael Irvin	.50	.23
❑ 112	Daryl Johnston	.25	.11
❑ 113	David LaFleur	.15	.07
❑ 114	Everett McIver	.15	.07
❑ 115	Ernie Mills	.15	.07
❑ 116	Nate Newton	.15	.07
❑ 117	Deion Sanders	.50	.23
❑ 118	Emmitt Smith	2.00	.90
❑ 119	Kevin Smith	.15	.07
❑ 120	Erik Williams	.15	.07
❑ 121	Steve Atwater	.15	.07
❑ 122	Tyrone Braxton	.15	.07
❑ 123	Ray Crockett	.15	.07
❑ 124	Terrell Davis	2.00	.90
❑ 125	Jason Elam	.15	.07
❑ 126	John Elway	2.50	1.10
❑ 127	Willie Green	.15	.07
❑ 128	Brian Griese RC	5.00	2.20
❑ 129	Tony Jones	.15	.07
❑ 130	Ed McCaffrey	.25	.11
❑ 131	John Mobley	.15	.07
❑ 132	Tom Nalen	.15	.07
❑ 133	Marcus Nash RC	1.50	.70
❑ 134	Bill Romanowski	.15	.07
❑ 135	Shannon Sharpe	.25	.11
❑ 136	Neil Smith	.25	.11
❑ 137	Rod Smith	.25	.11
❑ 138	Keith Traylor	.15	.07
❑ 139	Stephen Boyd	.15	.07
❑ 140	Mark Carrier DB	.15	.07
❑ 141	Charlie Batch RC	4.00	1.80
❑ 142	Jason Hanson	.15	.07
❑ 143	Scott Mitchell	.25	.11
❑ 144	Herman Moore	.50	.23
❑ 145	Johnnie Morton	.25	.11
❑ 146	Robert Porcher	.15	.07
❑ 147	Ron Rivers	.15	.07
❑ 148	Barry Sanders	2.50	1.10
❑ 149	Tracy Scroggins	.15	.07
❑ 150	David Sloan	.15	.07
❑ 151	Tommy Vardell	.15	.07
❑ 152	Kerwin Waldroup	.15	.07
❑ 153	Bryant Westbrook	.15	.07
❑ 154	Robert Brooks	.25	.11
❑ 155	Gilbert Brown	.15	.07
❑ 156	LeRoy Butler	.15	.07
❑ 157	Mark Chmura	.25	.11
❑ 158	Earl Dotson	.15	.07
❑ 159	Santana Dotson	.15	.07
❑ 160	Brett Favre	2.50	1.10
❑ 161	Antonio Freeman	.50	.23
❑ 162	Raymont Harris	.15	.07
❑ 163	William Henderson	.15	.07
❑ 164	Vonnie Holliday RC	.25	.11
❑ 165	George Koonce	.15	.07
❑ 166	Dorsey Levens	.50	.23
❑ 167	Derrick Mayes	.25	.11
❑ 168	Craig Newsome	.15	.07
❑ 169	Ross Verba	.15	.07
❑ 170	Reggie White	.50	.23
❑ 171	Elijah Alexander	.15	.07
❑ 172	Aaron Bailey	.15	.07
❑ 173	Jason Belser	.15	.07
❑ 174	Robert Blackmon	.15	.07
❑ 175	Zack Crockett	.15	.07
❑ 176	Ken Dilger	.15	.07
❑ 177	Marshall Faulk	.50	.23
❑ 178	Tarik Glenn	.15	.07
❑ 179	Marvin Harrison	.25	.11
❑ 180	Tony Mandarich	.15	.07
❑ 181	Peyton Manning RC	12.00	5.50
❑ 182	Marcus Pollard	.15	.07
❑ 183	Lamont Warren	.15	.07
❑ 184	Tavian Banks RC	.25	.11
❑ 185	Reggie Barlow	.15	.07
❑ 186	Tony Boselli	.15	.07
❑ 187	Tony Brackens	.15	.07
❑ 188	Mark Brunell	1.00	.45
❑ 189	Kevin Hardy	.15	.07
❑ 190	Mike Hollis	.15	.07
❑ 191	Jeff Lageman	.15	.07
❑ 192	Keenan McCardell	.25	.11
❑ 193	Pete Mitchell	.15	.07
❑ 194	Bryce Paup	.15	.07
❑ 195	Leon Searcy	.15	.07
❑ 196	Jimmy Smith	.25	.11
❑ 197	James Stewart	.25	.11
❑ 198	Fred Taylor RC	4.00	1.80
❑ 199	Renaldo Wynn	.15	.07
❑ 200	Derrick Alexander WR	.25	.11
❑ 201	Kimble Anders	.25	.11
❑ 202	Donnell Bennett	.15	.07
❑ 203	Dale Carter	.15	.07
❑ 204	Anthony Davis	.15	.07
❑ 205	Rich Gannon	.25	.11
❑ 206	Tony Gonzalez	.15	.07
❑ 207	Elvis Grbac	.25	.11
❑ 208	James Hasty	.15	.07
❑ 209	Leslie O'Neal	.15	.07
❑ 210	Andre Rison	.25	.11
❑ 211	Rashaan Shehee RC	1.50	.70
❑ 212	Will Shields	.15	.07
❑ 213	Pete Stoyanovich	.15	.07

❑ 214 Derrick Thomas .25 .11
❑ 215 Tamarick Vanover .15 .07
❑ 216 Karim Abdul-Jabbar .50 .23
❑ 217 Trace Armstrong .15 .07
❑ 218 John Avery RC 1.50 .70
❑ 219 Tim Bowens .15 .07
❑ 220 Terrell Buckley .15 .07
❑ 221 Troy Drayton .15 .07
❑ 222 Daryl Gardener .15 .07
❑ 223 Damon Huard RC 12.00 5.50
❑ 224 Charles Jordan .15 .07
❑ 225 Dan Marino 2.50 1.10
❑ 226 O.J. McDuffie .25 .11
❑ 227 Bernie Parmalee .15 .07
❑ 228 Stanley Pritchett .15 .07
❑ 229 Derrick Rodgers .15 .07
❑ 230 Lamar Thomas .15 .07
❑ 231 Zach Thomas .25 .11
❑ 232 Richmond Webb .15 .07
❑ 233 Derrick Alexander DE .15 .07
❑ 234 Jerry Ball .15 .07
❑ 235 Cris Carter .50 .23
❑ 236 Randall Cunningham .50 .23
❑ 237 Charles Evans .15 .07
❑ 238 Corey Fuller .15 .07
❑ 239 Andrew Glover .15 .07
❑ 240 Leroy Hoard .15 .07
❑ 241 Brad Johnson .50 .23
❑ 242 Ed McDaniel .15 .07
❑ 243 Randall McDaniel .15 .07
❑ 244 Randy Moss RC 12.00 5.50
❑ 245 John Randle .25 .11
❑ 246 Jake Reed .25 .11
❑ 247 Dwayne Rudd .15 .07
❑ 248 Robert Smith .50 .23
❑ 249 Bruce Armstrong .15 .07
❑ 250 Drew Bledsoe 1.00 .45
❑ 251 Vincent Brisby .15 .07
❑ 252 Tedy Bruschi .15 .07
❑ 253 Ben Coates .25 .11
❑ 254 Derrick Cullors .25 .11
❑ 255 Terry Glenn .50 .23
❑ 256 Shawn Jefferson .15 .07
❑ 257 Ted Johnson .15 .07
❑ 258 Ty Law .15 .07
❑ 259 Willie McGinest .15 .07
❑ 260 Lawyer Milloy .15 .07
❑ 261 Sedrick Shaw .15 .07
❑ 262 Chris Slade .15 .07
❑ 263 Troy Davis .15 .07
❑ 264 Mark Fields .15 .07
❑ 265 Andre Hastings .15 .07
❑ 266 Billy Joe Hobert .15 .07
❑ 267 Qadry Ismail .15 .07
❑ 268 Tony Johnson .15 .07
❑ 269 Sammy Knight RC .15 .07
❑ 270 Wayne Martin .15 .07
❑ 271 Chris Naeole .15 .07
❑ 272 Keith Poole .15 .07
❑ 273 William Roaf .15 .07
❑ 274 Pio Sagapolutele .15 .07
❑ 275 Danny Wuerffel .25 .11
❑ 276 Ray Zellars .15 .07
❑ 277 Jessie Armstead .15 .07
❑ 278 Tiki Barber .25 .11
❑ 279 Chris Calloway .15 .07
❑ 280 Percy Ellsworth .15 .07
❑ 281 Sam Garnes RC .15 .07
❑ 282 Kent Graham .15 .07
❑ 283 Ike Hilliard .25 .11
❑ 284 Danny Kanell .25 .11
❑ 285 Corey Miller .15 .07
❑ 286 Phillippi Sparks .15 .07
❑ 287 Michael Strahan .15 .07
❑ 288 Amani Toomer .25 .11
❑ 289 Charles Way .15 .07
❑ 290 Tyrone Wheatley .25 .11
❑ 291 Tito Wooten .15 .07
❑ 292 Kyle Brady .15 .07
❑ 293 Keith Byars .15 .07
❑ 294 Wayne Chrebet .50 .23
❑ 295 John Elliott .15 .07
❑ 296 Glenn Foley .25 .11
❑ 297 Aaron Glenn .15 .07
❑ 298 Keyshawn Johnson .50 .23
❑ 299 Curtis Martin .50 .23
❑ 300 Otis Smith .15 .07
❑ 301 Vinny Testaverde .25 .11
❑ 302 Alex Van Dyke .15 .07
❑ 303 Dedric Ward .15 .07
❑ 304 Greg Biekert .15 .07
❑ 305 Tim Brown .50 .23
❑ 306 Rickey Dudley .15 .07
❑ 307 Jeff George .25 .11
❑ 308 Pat Harlow .15 .07
❑ 309 Desmond Howard .25 .11
❑ 310 James Jett .25 .11
❑ 311 Napoleon Kaufman .50 .23
❑ 312 Lincoln Kennedy .15 .07
❑ 313 Russell Maryland .15 .07
❑ 314 Darrell Russell .15 .07
❑ 315 Eric Turner .15 .07
❑ 316 Steve Wisniewski .15 .07
❑ 317 Charles Woodson RC .. 2.00 .90
❑ 318 James Darling RC .15 .07
❑ 319 Jason Dunn .15 .07
❑ 320 Irving Fryar .25 .11
❑ 321 Charlie Garner .15 .07
❑ 322 Jeff Graham .15 .07
❑ 323 Bobby Hoying .25 .11
❑ 324 Chad Lewis .15 .07
❑ 325 Rodney Peete .15 .07
❑ 326 Freddie Solomon .15 .07
❑ 327 Duce Staley 1.00 .45
❑ 328 Bobby Taylor .15 .07
❑ 329 William Thomas .15 .07
❑ 330 Kevin Turner .15 .07
❑ 331 Troy Vincent .15 .07
❑ 332 Jerome Bettis .50 .23
❑ 333 Will Blackwell .15 .07
❑ 334 Mark Bruener .15 .07
❑ 335 Andre Coleman .15 .07
❑ 336 Dermontti Dawson .15 .07
❑ 337 Jason Gildon .15 .07
❑ 338 Courtney Hawkins .15 .07
❑ 339 Charles Johnson .15 .07
❑ 340 Levon Kirkland .15 .07
❑ 341 Carnell Lake .15 .07
❑ 342 Tim Lester .15 .07
❑ 343 Joel Steed .15 .07
❑ 344 Kordell Stewart .50 .23
❑ 345 Will Wolford .15 .07
❑ 346 Tony Banks .25 .11
❑ 347 Isaac Bruce .50 .23
❑ 348 Ernie Conwell .15 .07
❑ 349 D'Marco Farr .15 .07
❑ 350 Wayne Gandy .15 .07
❑ 351 Jerome Pathon RC 1.50 .70
❑ 352 Eddie Kennison .25 .11
❑ 353 Amp Lee .15 .07
❑ 354 Keith Lyle .15 .07
❑ 355 Ryan McNeil .15 .07
❑ 356 Jerald Moore .15 .07
❑ 357 Orlando Pace .15 .07
❑ 358 Roman Phifer .15 .07
❑ 359 David Thompson .15 .07
❑ 360 Darren Bennett .15 .07
❑ 361 John Carney .15 .07
❑ 362 Marco Coleman .15 .07
❑ 363 Terrell Fletcher .15 .07
❑ 364 William Fuller .15 .07
❑ 365 Charlie Jones .15 .07
❑ 366 Freddie Jones .15 .07
❑ 367 Ryan Leaf RC 3.00 1.35
❑ 368 Natrone Means .50 .23
❑ 369 Junior Seau .25 .11
❑ 370 Terrance Shaw .15 .07
❑ 371 Tremayne Stephens RC .15 .07
❑ 372 Bryan Still .15 .07
❑ 373 Aaron Taylor .15 .07
❑ 374 Greg Clark .15 .07
❑ 375 Ty Detmer .25 .11
❑ 376 Jim Druckenmiller .25 .11
❑ 377 Marc Edwards .15 .07
❑ 378 Merton Hanks .15 .07
❑ 379 Garrison Hearst .50 .23
❑ 380 Chuck Levy .15 .07
❑ 381 Ken Norton .15 .07
❑ 382 Terrell Owens .50 .23
❑ 383 Marquez Pope .15 .07
❑ 384 Jerry Rice 1.25 .55
❑ 385 Irv Smith .15 .07
❑ 386 J.J. Stokes .25 .11
❑ 387 Iheanyi Uwaezuoke .15 .07
❑ 388 Bryant Young .15 .07
❑ 389 Steve Young .75 .35
❑ 390 Sam Adams .15 .07
❑ 391 Chad Brown .15 .07
❑ 392 Christian Fauria .15 .07
❑ 393 Joey Galloway .50 .23
❑ 394 Ahman Green RC 3.00 1.35
❑ 395 Walter Jones .15 .07
❑ 396 Cortez Kennedy .15 .07
❑ 397 Jon Kitna .75 .35
❑ 398 James McKnight .15 .07
❑ 399 Warren Moon .50 .23
❑ 400 Mike Pritchard .15 .07
❑ 401 Michael Sinclair .15 .07
❑ 402 Shawn Springs .15 .07
❑ 403 Ricky Watters .25 .11
❑ 404 Darryl Williams .15 .07
❑ 405 Mike Alstott .50 .23
❑ 406 Reidel Anthony .25 .11
❑ 407 Derrick Brooks .15 .07
❑ 408 Brad Culpepper .15 .07
❑ 409 Trent Dilfer .50 .23
❑ 410 Warrick Dunn .50 .23
❑ 411 Bert Emanuel .25 .11
❑ 412 Jacquez Green RC 2.00 .90
❑ 413 Paul Gruber .15 .07
❑ 414 Patrick Hape RC .15 .07
❑ 415 Dave Moore .15 .07
❑ 416 Hardy Nickerson .15 .07
❑ 417 Warren Sapp .25 .11
❑ 418 Robb Thomas .15 .07
❑ 419 Regan Upshaw .15 .07
❑ 420 Karl Williams .15 .07
❑ 421 Blaine Bishop .15 .07
❑ 422 Anthony Cook .15 .07
❑ 423 Willie Davis .15 .07
❑ 424 Al Del Greco .15 .07
❑ 425 Kevin Dyson .50 .23
❑ 426 Henry Ford .15 .07
❑ 427 Eddie George 1.00 .45
❑ 428 Jackie Harris .15 .07
❑ 429 Steve McNair .50 .23
❑ 430 Chris Sanders .15 .07
❑ 431 Mark Stepnoski .15 .07
❑ 432 Yancey Thigpen .15 .07
❑ 433 Barron Wortham .15 .07
❑ 434 Frank Wycheck .15 .07
❑ 435 Stephen Alexander RC 1.50 .70
❑ 436 Terry Allen .50 .23
❑ 437 Jamie Asher .15 .07
❑ 438 Bob Dahl .15 .07
❑ 439 Stephen Davis .15 .07
❑ 440 Cris Dishman .15 .07
❑ 441 Gus Frerotte .15 .07
❑ 442 Darrell Green .25 .11
❑ 443 Trent Green .75 .35
❑ 444 Ken Harvey .15 .07
❑ 445 Skip Hicks RC 1.50 .70
❑ 446 Jeff Hostetler .15 .07
❑ 447 Brian Mitchell .15 .07
❑ 448 Leslie Shepherd .15 .07
❑ 449 Michael Westbrook .25 .11
❑ 450 Dan Wilkinson .15 .07
❑ S1 Warrick Dunn Sample 1.00 .45

1999 Pacific

	MINT	NRMT
COMPLETE SET (450)	100.00	45.00
❑ 1 Mario Bates	.15	.07
❑ 2 Larry Centers	.15	.07
❑ 3 Chris Gedney	.15	.07
❑ 4 Kwamie Lassiter RC	.15	.07
❑ 5 Johnny McWilliams	.15	.07
❑ 6 Eric Metcalf	.15	.07
❑ 7 Rob Moore	.25	.11
❑ 8 Adrian Murrell	.25	.11
❑ 9 Jake Plummer	1.00	.45
❑ 10 Simeon Rice	.15	.07
❑ 11 Frank Sanders	.25	.11
❑ 12 Andre Wadsworth	.15	.07
❑ 13 Aeneas Williams	.15	.07
❑ 14 Michael Pittman	1.00	.45
Ronnie Anderson RC		
❑ 15 Morten Andersen	.15	.07
❑ 16 Jamal Anderson	.50	.23
❑ 17 Lester Archambeau	.15	.07
❑ 18 Chris Chandler	.25	.11
❑ 19 Bob Christian	.15	.07
❑ 20 Steve DeBerg	.15	.07
❑ 21 Tim Dwight	.50	.23
❑ 22 Tony Martin	.25	.11
❑ 23 Terance Mathis	.25	.11
❑ 24 Eugene Robinson	.15	.07
❑ 25 O.J. Santiago	.15	.07
❑ 26 Chuck Smith	.15	.07
❑ 27 Jessie Tuggle	.15	.07
❑ 28 Jammi German	.15	.07
Ken Oxendine		
❑ 29 Peter Boulware	.15	.07
❑ 30 Jay Graham	.15	.07
❑ 31 Jim Harbaugh	.25	.11
❑ 32 Priest Holmes	.50	.23
❑ 33 Michael Jackson	.15	.07
❑ 34 Jermaine Lewis	.25	.11
❑ 35 Ray Lewis	.25	.11
❑ 36 Michael McCrary	.15	.07
❑ 37 Jonathan Ogden	.15	.07
❑ 38 Errict Rhett	.15	.07
❑ 39 James Roe RC	.15	.07
❑ 40 Floyd Turner	.15	.07
❑ 41 Rod Woodson	.25	.11
❑ 42 Eric Zeier	.15	.07
❑ 43 Wally Richardson	.15	.07
Patrick Johnson		
❑ 44 Ruben Brown	.15	.07
❑ 45 Quinn Early	.15	.07
❑ 46 Doug Flutie	.60	.25
❑ 47 Sam Gash	.15	.07
❑ 48 Phil Hansen	.15	.07
❑ 49 Lonnie Johnson	.15	.07
❑ 50 Rob Johnson	.25	.11
❑ 51 Eric Moulds	.50	.23
❑ 52 Andre Reed	.25	.11
❑ 53 Jay Riemersma	.15	.07
❑ 54 Antowain Smith	.50	.23
❑ 55 Bruce Smith	.25	.11
❑ 56 Thurman Thomas	.25	.11
❑ 57 Ted Washington	.15	.07
❑ 58 Jonathan Linton	.15	.07
Kamil Loud RC		
❑ 59 Michael Bates	.15	.07
❑ 60 Steve Beuerlein	.15	.07
❑ 61 Tim Biakabutuka	.25	.11
❑ 62 Mark Carrier WR	.15	.07
❑ 63 Eric Davis	.15	.07
❑ 64 William Floyd	.15	.07
❑ 65 Sean Gilbert	.15	.07
❑ 66 Kevin Greene	.15	.07
❑ 67 Rocket Ismail	.25	.11
❑ 68 Anthony Johnson	.15	.07
❑ 69 Fred Lane	.15	.07
❑ 70 Muhsin Muhammad	.25	.11
❑ 71 Winslow Oliver	.15	.07
❑ 72 Wesley Walls	.25	.11
❑ 73 Dameyune Craig RC	1.50	.70
Shane Matthews		
❑ 74 Edgar Bennett	.15	.07
❑ 75 Curtis Conway	.25	.11
❑ 76 Bobby Engram	.25	.11
❑ 77 Curtis Enis	.50	.23
❑ 78 Ty Hallock RC	.15	.07
❑ 79 Walt Harris	.15	.07
❑ 80 Jeff Jaeger	.15	.07
❑ 81 Erik Kramer	.15	.07
❑ 82 Glyn Milburn	.15	.07
❑ 83 Chris Penn	.15	.07
❑ 84 Steve Stenstrom	.15	.07
❑ 85 Ryan Wetnight	.15	.07
❑ 86 James Allen RC	3.00	1.35
Moses Moreno		
❑ 87 Ashley Ambrose	.15	.07
❑ 88 Brandon Bennett RC	.15	.07
❑ 89 Eric Bieniemy	.15	.07
❑ 90 Jeff Blake	.25	.11
❑ 91 Corey Dillon	.50	.23
❑ 92 Paul Justin	.15	.07
❑ 93 Eric Kresser RC	.15	.07
❑ 94 Tremain Mack	.15	.07
❑ 95 Tony McGee	.15	.07
❑ 96 Neil O'Donnell	.25	.11
❑ 97 Carl Pickens	.25	.11
❑ 98 Darnay Scott	.15	.07
❑ 99 Takeo Spikes	.15	.07
❑ 100 Ty Detmer	.15	.07
❑ 101 Chris Gardocki	.15	.07
❑ 102 Damon Gibson	.15	.07
❑ 103 Antonio Langham	.15	.07
❑ 104 Jerris McPhail	.15	.07
❑ 105 Irv Smith	.15	.07
❑ 106 Freddie Solomon	.15	.07
❑ 107 Scott Milanovich	.15	.07
Fred Brock RC		
❑ 108 Troy Aikman	1.25	.55
❑ 109 Larry Allen	.15	.07
❑ 110 111	.15	.07
❑ 111 Billy Davis	.15	.07
❑ 112 Michael Irvin	.25	.11
❑ 113 David LaFleur	.15	.07
❑ 114 Ernie Mills	.15	.07
❑ 115 Nate Newton	.15	.07
❑ 116 Deion Sanders	.50	.23
❑ 117 Emmitt Smith	1.25	.55
❑ 118 Chris Warren	.15	.07
❑ 119 Bubby Brister	.25	.11
❑ 120 Terrell Davis	1.25	.55
❑ 121 Jason Elam	.15	.07
❑ 122 John Elway	2.00	.90
❑ 123 Willie Green	.15	.07
❑ 124 Howard Griffith	.15	.07
❑ 125 Vaughn Hebron	.15	.07
❑ 126 Ed McCaffrey	.25	.11
❑ 127 John Mobley	.15	.07
❑ 128 Bill Romanowski	.15	.07
❑ 129 Shannon Sharpe	.25	.11
❑ 130 Neil Smith	.25	.11
❑ 131 Rod Smith	.25	.11
❑ 132 Brian Griese	1.00	.45
Marcus Nash		
❑ 133 Charlie Batch	1.00	.45
❑ 134 Stephen Boyd	.15	.07
❑ 135 Mark Carrier DB	.15	.07
❑ 136 Germane Crowell	.25	.11
❑ 137 Terry Fair	.15	.07
❑ 138 Jason Hanson	.15	.07
❑ 139 Greg Jeffries RC	.15	.07
❑ 140 Herman Moore	.50	.23
❑ 141 Johnnie Morton	.25	.11
❑ 142 Robert Porcher	.15	.07
❑ 143 Ron Rivers	.15	.07
❑ 144 Barry Sanders	2.00	.90
❑ 145 Tommy Vardell	.15	.07
❑ 146 Bryant Westbrook	.15	.07
❑ 147 Robert Brooks	.25	.11
❑ 148 LeRoy Butler	.15	.07
❑ 149 Mark Chmura	.15	.07
❑ 150 Tyrone Davis	.15	.07
❑ 151 Brett Favre	2.00	.90
❑ 152 Antonio Freeman	.50	.23
❑ 153 Raymont Harris	.15	.07
❑ 154 Vonnie Holliday	.15	.07
❑ 155 Darick Holmes	.15	.07
❑ 156 Dorsey Levens	.50	.23
❑ 157 Brian Manning	.15	.07
❑ 158 Derrick Mayes	.15	.07
❑ 159 Roell Preston	.15	.07
❑ 160 Jeff Thomason	.15	.07
❑ 161 Tyrone Williams	.15	.07
❑ 162 Corey Bradford	.50	.23
Michael Blair RC		
❑ 163 Aaron Bailey	.15	.07
❑ 164 Ken Dilger	.15	.07
❑ 165 Marshall Faulk	.50	.23
❑ 166 E.G. Green	.15	.07
❑ 167 Marvin Harrison	.50	.23
❑ 168 Craig Heyward	.15	.07
❑ 169 Peyton Manning	2.00	.90
❑ 170 Jerome Pathon	.25	.11
❑ 171 Marcus Pollard	.15	.07
❑ 172 Torrance Small	.15	.07
❑ 173 Mike Vanderjagt	.15	.07
❑ 174 Lamont Warren	.15	.07
❑ 175 Tavian Banks	.25	.11
❑ 176 Reggie Barlow	.15	.07
❑ 177 Tony Boselli	.15	.07
❑ 178 Tony Brackens	.15	.07
❑ 179 Mark Brunell	.75	.35
❑ 180 Kevin Hardy	.15	.07
❑ 181 Damon Jones	.15	.07
❑ 182 Jamie Martin	.15	.07
❑ 183 Keenan McCardell	.25	.11
❑ 184 Pete Mitchell	.15	.07
❑ 185 Bryce Paup	.15	.07
❑ 186 Jimmy Smith	.25	.11
❑ 187 Fred Taylor	1.25	.55
❑ 188 Alvis Whitted	.15	.07
Chris Howard		
❑ 189 Derrick Alexander WR	.25	.11
❑ 190 Kimble Anders	.25	.11
❑ 191 Donnell Bennett	.15	.07
❑ 192 Dale Carter	.15	.07
❑ 193 Rich Gannon	.25	.11
❑ 194 Tony Gonzalez	.25	.11
❑ 195 Elvis Grbac	.25	.11
❑ 196 Joe Horn	.25	.11
❑ 197 Kevin Lockett	.15	.07
❑ 198 Byron Bam Morris	.15	.07
❑ 199 Andre Rison	.25	.11
❑ 200 Derrick Thomas	.25	.11
❑ 201 Tamarick Vanover	.15	.07
❑ 202 Gregory Favors	.15	.07
Rashaan Shehee		
❑ 203 Karim Abdul-Jabbar	.25	.11
❑ 204 Trace Armstrong	.15	.07
❑ 205 John Avery	.25	.11
❑ 206 Lorenzo Bromell RC	.15	.07
❑ 207 Terrell Buckley	.15	.07
❑ 208 Oronde Gadsden	.15	.07
❑ 209 Sam Madison	.15	.07
❑ 210 Dan Marino	2.00	.90
❑ 211 O.J. McDuffie	.25	.11
❑ 212 Ed Perry	.15	.07
❑ 213 Jason Taylor	.15	.07
❑ 214 Lamar Thomas	.15	.07
❑ 215 Zach Thomas	.25	.11
❑ 216 Henry Lusk	1.00	.45
Nate Jacquet RC		
❑ 217 Damon Huard	4.00	1.80
Todd Doxzon RC		
❑ 218 Gary Anderson	.15	.07
❑ 219 Cris Carter	.50	.23
❑ 220 Randall Cunningham	.50	.23
❑ 221 Andrew Glover	.15	.07
❑ 222 Matthew Hatchette	.15	.07
❑ 223 Brad Johnson	.50	.23
❑ 224 Ed McDaniel	.15	.07
❑ 225 Randall McDaniel	.15	.07
❑ 226 Randy Moss	2.00	.90
❑ 227 David Palmer	.15	.07
❑ 228 John Randle	.25	.11
❑ 229 Jake Reed	.25	.11
❑ 230 Robert Smith	.50	.23
❑ 231 Todd Steussie	.15	.07
❑ 232 Stalin Colinet	.15	.07
Kivuusama Mays		
❑ 233 Jay Fiedler RC	10.00	4.50
Todd Bouman RC		
❑ 234 Drew Bledsoe	.75	.35
❑ 235 Troy Brown	.15	.07
❑ 236 Ben Coates	.25	.11
❑ 237 Derrick Cullors	.15	.07
❑ 238 Robert Edwards	.25	.11
❑ 239 Terry Glenn	.50	.23
❑ 240 Shawn Jefferson	.15	.07

	Card	Mint	NrMt
❑	241 Ty Law	.15	.07
❑	242 Lawyer Milloy	.15	.07
❑	243 Lovett Purnell RC	.15	.07
❑	244 Sedrick Shaw	.15	.07
❑	245 Tony Simmons	.15	.07
❑	246 Chris Slade	.15	.07
❑	247 Rod Rutledge Anthony Ladd RC	.15	.07
❑	248 Chris Floyd Harold Shaw	.15	.07
❑	249 Ink Aleaga RC	.15	.07
❑	250 Cameron Cleeland	.25	.11
❑	251 Kerry Collins	.25	.11
❑	252 Troy Davis	.15	.07
❑	253 Sean Dawkins	.15	.07
❑	254 Mark Fields	.15	.07
❑	255 Andre Hastings	.15	.07
❑	256 Sammy Knight	.15	.07
❑	257 Keith Poole	.15	.07
❑	258 William Roaf	.15	.07
❑	259 Lamar Smith	.25	.11
❑	260 Danny Wuerffel	.15	.07
❑	261 Josh Wilcox RC Brett Bech RC	.15	.07
❑	262 Chris Bordano RC Wilmont Perry	.15	.07
❑	263 Jessie Armstead	.15	.07
❑	264 Tiki Barber	.15	.07
❑	265 Chad Bratzke	.15	.07
❑	266 Gary Brown	.15	.07
❑	267 Chris Calloway	.15	.07
❑	268 Howard Cross	.15	.07
❑	269 Kent Graham	.15	.07
❑	270 Ike Hilliard	.15	.07
❑	271 Danny Kanell	.25	.11
❑	272 Michael Strahan	.15	.07
❑	273 Amani Toomer	.15	.07
❑	274 Charles Way	.15	.07
❑	275 Mike Cherry Greg Comella RC	1.50	.70
❑	276 Kyle Brady	.15	.07
❑	277 Keith Byars	.15	.07
❑	278 Chad Cascadden	.15	.07
❑	279 Wayne Chrebet	.25	.11
❑	280 Bryan Cox	.15	.07
❑	281 Glenn Foley	.25	.11
❑	282 Aaron Glenn	.15	.07
❑	283 Keyshawn Johnson	.50	.23
❑	284 Leon Johnson	.15	.07
❑	285 Mo Lewis	.15	.07
❑	286 Curtis Martin	.50	.23
❑	287 Otis Smith	.15	.07
❑	288 Vinny Testaverde	.25	.11
❑	289 Dedric Ward	.15	.07
❑	290 Tim Brown	.50	.23
❑	291 Rickey Dudley	.15	.07
❑	292 Jeff George	.25	.11
❑	293 Desmond Howard	.25	.11
❑	294 James Jett	.25	.11
❑	295 Lance Johnstone	.15	.07
❑	296 Randy Jordan	.15	.07
❑	297 Napoleon Kaufman	.50	.23
❑	298 Lincoln Kennedy	.15	.07
❑	299 Terry Mickens	.15	.07
❑	300 Darrell Russell	.15	.07
❑	301 Harvey Williams	.15	.07
❑	302 Jon Ritchie Charles Woodson	.50	.23
❑	303 Rodney Williams Jermaine Williams	.15	.07
❑	304 Koy Detmer	.15	.07
❑	305 Hugh Douglas	.15	.07
❑	306 Jason Dunn	.15	.07
❑	307 Irving Fryar	.25	.11
❑	308 Charlie Garner	.25	.11
❑	309 Jeff Graham	.15	.07
❑	310 Bobby Hoying	.25	.11
❑	311 Rodney Peete	.15	.07
❑	312 Allen Rossum	.15	.07
❑	313 Duce Staley	.50	.23
❑	314 William Thomas	.15	.07
❑	315 Kevin Turner	.15	.07
❑	316 Kaseem Sinceno RC Corey Walker RC	.15	.07
❑	317 Jahine Arnold	.15	.07
❑	318 Jerome Bettis	.50	.23
❑	319 Will Blackwell	.15	.07
❑	320 Mark Bruener	.15	.07
❑	321 Dermontti Dawson	.15	.07
❑	322 Chris Fuamatu-Ma'afala	.15	.07
❑	323 Courtney Hawkins	.15	.07
❑	324 Richard Huntley	.50	.23
❑	325 Charles Johnson	.15	.07
❑	326 Levon Kirkland	.15	.07
❑	327 Kordell Stewart	.50	.23
❑	328 Hines Ward	.25	.11
❑	329 Dewayne Washington	.15	.07
❑	330 Tony Banks	.25	.11
❑	331 Steve Bono	.15	.07
❑	332 Isaac Bruce	.50	.23
❑	333 June Henley RC	.50	.23
❑	334 Robert Holcombe	.25	.11
❑	335 Mike Jones LB	.15	.07
❑	336 Eddie Kennison	.25	.11
❑	337 Amp Lee	.15	.07
❑	338 Jerald Moore	.15	.07
❑	339 Ricky Proehl	.15	.07
❑	340 J.T. Thomas	.15	.07
❑	341 Derrick Harris Az-Zahir Hakim	.25	.11
❑	342 Roland Williams Grant Wistrom	.15	.07
❑	343 Kurt Warner RC Tony Horne	50.00	22.00
❑	344 Terrell Fletcher	.15	.07
❑	345 Greg Jackson	.15	.07
❑	346 Charlie Jones	.15	.07
❑	347 Freddie Jones	.15	.07
❑	348 Ryan Leaf	.50	.23
❑	349 Natrone Means	.25	.11
❑	350 Mikhael Ricks	.15	.07
❑	351 Junior Seau	.25	.11
❑	352 Bryan Still	.15	.07
❑	353 Tremayne Stephens Ryan Thelwell	.15	.07
❑	354 Greg Clark	.15	.07
❑	355 Marc Edwards	.15	.07
❑	356 Merton Hanks	.15	.07
❑	357 Garrison Hearst	.25	.11
❑	358 R.W. McQuarters	.15	.07
❑	359 Ken Norton Jr.	.15	.07
❑	360 Terrell Owens	.50	.23
❑	361 Jerry Rice	1.25	.55
❑	362 J.J. Stokes	.25	.11
❑	363 Bryant Young	.15	.07
❑	364 Steve Young	.75	.35
❑	365 Chad Brown	.15	.07
❑	366 Christian Fauria	.15	.07
❑	367 Joey Galloway	.50	.23
❑	368 Ahman Green	.25	.11
❑	369 Cortez Kennedy	.15	.07
❑	370 Jon Kitna	.50	.23
❑	371 James McKnight	.15	.07
❑	372 Mike Pritchard	.15	.07
❑	373 Michael Sinclair	.15	.07
❑	374 Shawn Springs	.15	.07
❑	375 Ricky Watters	.25	.11
❑	376 Darryl Williams	.15	.07
❑	377 Robert Wilson Kerry Joseph RC	.15	.07
❑	378 Mike Alstott	.50	.23
❑	379 Reidel Anthony	.25	.11
❑	380 Derrick Brooks	.15	.07
❑	381 Trent Dilfer	.50	.23
❑	382 Warrick Dunn	.50	.23
❑	383 Bert Emanuel	.25	.11
❑	384 Jacquez Green	.25	.11
❑	385 Patrick Hape	.15	.07
❑	386 John Lynch	.15	.07
❑	387 Dave Moore	.15	.07
❑	388 Hardy Nickerson	.15	.07
❑	389 Warren Sapp	.25	.11
❑	390 Karl Williams	.15	.07
❑	391 Blaine Bishop	.15	.07
❑	392 Joe Bowden	.15	.07
❑	393 Isaac Byrd	1.00	.45
❑	394 Willie Davis	.15	.07
❑	395 Al Del Greco	.15	.07
❑	396 Kevin Dyson	.25	.11
❑	397 Eddie George	.60	.25
❑	398 Jackie Harris	.15	.07
❑	399 Dave Krieg	.15	.07
❑	400 Steve McNair	.50	.23
❑	401 Michael Roan	.15	.07
❑	402 Yancey Thigpen	.15	.07
❑	403 Frank Wycheck	.15	.07
❑	404 Derrick Mason Steve Matthews	.25	.11
❑	405 Stephen Alexander	.15	.07
❑	406 Terry Allen	.25	.11
❑	407 Jamie Asher	.15	.07
❑	408 Stephen Davis	.50	.23
❑	409 Darrell Green	.15	.07
❑	410 Trent Green	.25	.11
❑	411 Skip Hicks	.50	.23
❑	412 Brian Mitchell	.15	.07
❑	413 Leslie Shepherd	.15	.07
❑	414 Michael Westbrook	.25	.11
❑	415 Terry Hardy Rabih Abdullah RC	1.00	.45
❑	416 Corey Thomas RC Mike Quinn RC	1.00	.45
❑	417 Jonathan Quinn Kelly Holcomb RC	.15	.07
❑	418 Brian Alford Blake Spence	.15	.07
❑	419 Andy Haase RC Carlos King	.15	.07
❑	420 Karl Hankton James Thrash RC	5.00	2.20
❑	421 Fred Beasley Itula Mili RC	1.25	.55
❑	422 Champ Bailey RC	2.00	.90
❑	423 D'Wayne Bates RC	1.25	.55
❑	424 Michael Bishop RC	2.00	.90
❑	425 David Boston RC	3.00	1.35
❑	426 Shawn Bryson RC	1.50	.70
❑	427 Tim Couch RC	5.00	2.20
❑	428 Scott Covington RC	1.50	.70
❑	429 Daunte Culpepper RC	10.00	4.50
❑	430 Autry Denson RC	1.50	.70
❑	431 Troy Edwards RC	2.00	.90
❑	432 Kevin Faulk RC	2.50	1.10
❑	433 Joe Germaine RC	1.50	.70
❑	434 Torry Holt RC	4.00	1.80
❑	435 Brock Huard RC	2.50	1.10
❑	436 Sedrick Irvin RC	1.50	.70
❑	437 Edgerrin James RC	10.00	4.50
❑	438 Andy Katzenmoyer RC	1.50	.70
❑	439 Shaun King RC	3.00	1.35
❑	440 Rob Konrad RC	1.25	.55
❑	441 Donovan McNabb RC	6.00	2.70
❑	442 Cade McNown RC	2.00	.90
❑	443 Billy Miller RC	1.25	.55
❑	444 Dee Miller RC	1.25	.55
❑	445 Sirr Parker RC	1.25	.55
❑	446 Peerless Price RC	2.00	.90
❑	447 Akili Smith RC	3.00	1.35
❑	448 Tai Streets RC	1.50	.70
❑	449 Ricky Williams RC	6.00	2.70
❑	450 Amos Zereoue RC	1.50	.70
❑	S1 Warrick Dunn Sample	.50	.23

2000 Pacific

		MINT	NRMT
	COMPLETE SET (450)	60.00	27.00
❑	1 Mario Bates	.15	.07
❑	2 David Boston	.50	.23

	No.	Player		
❑	3	Rob Fredrickson	.15	.07
❑	4	Terry Hardy	.15	.07
❑	5	Rob Moore	.25	.11
❑	6	Adrian Murrell	.25	.11
❑	7	Michael Pittman	.15	.07
❑	8	Jake Plummer	.50	.23
❑	9	Simeon Rice	.15	.07
❑	10	Frank Sanders	.25	.11
❑	11	Aeneas Williams	.15	.07
❑	12	Mac Cody	.15	.07
		Andy McCullough		
❑	13	Dennis McKinley RC	.50	.23
		Joel Makovicka		
❑	14	Jamal Anderson	.50	.23
❑	15	Chris Calloway	.15	.07
❑	16	Chris Chandler	.25	.11
❑	17	Bob Christian	.15	.07
❑	18	Tim Dwight	.50	.23
❑	19	Jammi German	.15	.07
❑	20	Ronnie Harris	.15	.07
❑	21	Terance Mathis	.25	.11
❑	22	Ken Oxendine	.15	.07
❑	23	O.J. Santiago	.15	.07
❑	24	Bob Whitfield	.15	.07
❑	25	Eugene Baker	.15	.07
		Reggie Kelly		
❑	26	Justin Armour	.15	.07
❑	27	Tony Banks	.25	.11
❑	28	Peter Boulware	.15	.07
❑	29	Stoney Case	.15	.07
❑	30	Priest Holmes	.25	.11
❑	31	Qadry Ismail	.15	.07
❑	32	Patrick Johnson	.15	.07
❑	33	Michael McCrary	.15	.07
❑	34	Jonathan Ogden	.15	.07
❑	35	Errict Rhett	.25	.11
❑	36	Duane Starks	.15	.07
❑	37	Doug Flutie	.60	.25
❑	38	Rob Johnson	.25	.11
❑	39	Jonathan Linton	.15	.07
❑	40	Eric Moulds	.50	.23
❑	41	Peerless Price	.50	.23
❑	42	Andre Reed	.25	.11
❑	43	Jay Riemersma	.15	.07
❑	44	Antowain Smith	.25	.11
❑	45	Bruce Smith	.25	.11
❑	46	Thurman Thomas	.25	.11
❑	47	Kevin Williams	.15	.07
❑	48	Bobby Collins	.15	.07
		Sheldon Jackson		
❑	49	Michael Bates	.15	.07
❑	50	Steve Beuerlein	.25	.11
❑	51	Tim Biakabutuka	.25	.11
❑	52	Antonio Edwards	.15	.07
❑	53	Donald Hayes	.15	.07
❑	54	Patrick Jeffers	.50	.23
❑	55	Anthony Johnson	.15	.07
❑	56	Jeff Lewis	.15	.07
❑	57	Eric Metcalf	.15	.07
❑	58	Muhsin Muhammad	.25	.11
❑	59	Jason Peter	.15	.07
❑	60	Wesley Walls	.15	.07
❑	61	John Allred	.15	.07
❑	62	Marty Booker	.15	.07
❑	63	Curtis Conway	.25	.11
❑	64	Bobby Engram	.15	.07
❑	65	Curtis Enis	.25	.11
❑	66	Shane Matthews	.25	.11
❑	67	Cade McNown	.50	.23
❑	68	Glyn Milburn	.15	.07
❑	69	Jim Miller	.15	.07
❑	70	Marcus Robinson	.50	.23
❑	71	Ryan Wetnight	.15	.07
❑	72	James Allen	.15	.07
		Macey Brooks		
❑	73	Jeff Blake	.25	.11
❑	74	Corey Dillon	.50	.23
❑	75	Rodney Heath RC	.25	.11
❑	76	Willie Jackson	.15	.07
❑	77	Tremain Mack	.15	.07
❑	78	Tony McGee	.15	.07
❑	79	Carl Pickens	.25	.11
❑	80	Darnay Scott	.25	.11
❑	81	Akili Smith	.50	.23
❑	82	Takeo Spikes	.15	.07
❑	83	Craig Yeast	.15	.07

	No.	Player		
❑	84	Michael Basnight	.15	.07
		Nick Williams		
❑	85	Karim Abdul-Jabbar	.25	.11
❑	86	Darrin Chiaverini	.15	.07
❑	87	Tim Couch	1.00	.45
❑	88	Marc Edwards	.15	.07
❑	89	Kevin Johnson	.50	.23
❑	90	Terry Kirby	.15	.07
❑	91	Daylon McCutcheon	.15	.07
❑	92	Jamir Miller	.15	.07
❑	93	Leslie Shepherd	.15	.07
❑	94	Irv Smith	.15	.07
❑	95	Mark Campbell	.15	.07
		James Dearth		
❑	96	Zola Davis RC	.25	.11
		Damon Dunn RC		
❑	97	Madre Hill	.15	.07
		Tarek Saleh		
❑	98	Troy Aikman	1.25	.55
❑	99	Eric Bjornson	.15	.07
❑	100	Dexter Coakley	.15	.07
❑	101	Greg Ellis	.15	.07
❑	102	Rocket Ismail	.25	.11
❑	103	David LaFleur	.15	.07
❑	104	Ernie Mills	.15	.07
❑	105	Jeff Ogden	.25	.11
❑	106	Ryan Neufeld RC	.25	.11
		Robert Thomas		
❑	107	Deion Sanders	.50	.23
❑	108	Emmitt Smith	1.25	.55
❑	109	Chris Warren	.15	.07
❑	110	Mike Lucky	.25	.11
		Jason Tucker		
❑	111	Byron Chamberlain	.15	.07
❑	112	Terrell Davis	1.25	.55
❑	113	Jason Elam	.15	.07
❑	114	Olandis Gary	.50	.23
❑	115	Brian Griese	.60	.25
❑	116	Ed McCaffrey	.50	.23
❑	117	Trevor Pryce	.15	.07
❑	118	Bill Romanowski	.15	.07
❑	119	Shannon Sharpe	.25	.11
❑	120	Rod Smith	.25	.11
❑	121	Al Wilson	.15	.07
❑	122	Andre Cooper	.15	.07
		Chris Watson		
❑	123	Charlie Batch	.50	.23
❑	124	Stephen Boyd	.15	.07
❑	125	Chris Claiborne	.15	.07
❑	126	Germane Crowell	.25	.11
❑	127	Terry Fair	.15	.07
❑	128	Gus Frerotte	.15	.07
❑	129	Jason Hanson	.15	.07
❑	130	Greg Hill	.15	.07
❑	131	Herman Moore	.25	.11
❑	132	Johnnie Morton	.25	.11
❑	133	Barry Sanders	2.00	.90
❑	134	David Sloan	.15	.07
❑	135	Brock Olivo	.15	.07
		Cory Sauter		
❑	136	Corey Bradford	.25	.11
❑	137	Tyrone Davis	.15	.07
❑	138	Brett Favre	2.00	.90
❑	139	Antonio Freeman	.50	.23
❑	140	Vonnie Holliday	.15	.07
❑	141	Dorsey Levens	.25	.11
❑	142	Keith McKenzie	.15	.07
❑	143	Mike McKenzie	.15	.07
❑	144	Bill Schroeder	.25	.11
❑	145	Jeff Thomason	.15	.07
❑	146	Frank Winters	.15	.07
❑	147	Cornelius Bennett	.15	.07
❑	148	Tony Blevins RC	.25	.11
❑	149	Chad Bratzke	.15	.07
❑	150	Ken Dilger	.15	.07
❑	151	Tarik Glenn	.15	.07
❑	152	E.G. Green	.15	.07
❑	153	Marvin Harrison	.50	.23
❑	154	Edgerrin James	2.00	.90
❑	155	Peyton Manning	1.50	.70
❑	156	Jerome Pathon	.25	.11
❑	157	Marcus Pollard	.15	.07
❑	158	Terrence Wilkins	.50	.23
❑	159	Isaac Jones RC	.50	.23
		Paul Shields RC		
❑	160	Reggie Barlow	.15	.07

	No.	Player		
❑	161	Aaron Beasley	.15	.07
❑	162	Tony Boselli	.15	.07
❑	163	Tony Brackens	.15	.07
❑	164	Kyle Brady	.15	.07
❑	165	Mark Brunell	.75	.35
❑	166	Jay Fiedler	.50	.23
❑	167	Kevin Hardy	.15	.07
❑	168	Carnell Lake	.15	.07
❑	169	Keenan McCardell	.25	.11
❑	170	Jonathan Quinn	.15	.07
❑	171	Jimmy Smith	.25	.11
❑	172	James Stewart	.25	.11
❑	173	Fred Taylor	.60	.25
❑	174	Lenzie Jackson RC	.50	.23
		Stacey Mack		
❑	175	Derrick Alexander	.25	.11
❑	176	Donnell Bennett	.15	.07
❑	177	Donnie Edwards	.15	.07
❑	178	Tony Gonzalez	.25	.11
❑	179	Elvis Grbac	.25	.11
❑	180	James Hasty	.15	.07
❑	181	Joe Horn	.25	.11
❑	182	Lonnie Johnson	.15	.07
❑	183	Kevin Lockett	.15	.07
❑	184	Larry Parker	.15	.07
❑	185	Tony Richardson RC	.25	.11
❑	186	Rashaan Shehee	.15	.07
❑	187	Tamarick Vanover	.15	.07
❑	188	Trace Armstrong	.15	.07
❑	189	Oronde Gadsden	.25	.11
❑	190	Damon Huard	.50	.23
❑	191	Nate Jacquet	.15	.07
❑	192	James Johnson	.25	.11
❑	193	Rob Konrad	.15	.07
❑	194	Sam Madison	.15	.07
❑	195	Dan Marino	2.00	.90
❑	196	Tony Martin	.25	.11
❑	197	O.J. McDuffie	.25	.11
❑	198	Stanley Pritchett	.15	.07
❑	199	Tim Ruddy	.15	.07
❑	200	Patrick Surtain	.15	.07
❑	201	Zach Thomas	.25	.11
❑	202	Cris Carter	.50	.23
❑	203	Duane Clemons	.15	.07
❑	204	Carlester Crumpler	.15	.07
❑	205	Daunte Culpepper	1.00	.45
❑	206	Jeff George	.25	.11
❑	207	Matthew Hatchette	.25	.11
❑	208	Leroy Hoard	.15	.07
❑	209	Randy Moss	1.50	.70
❑	210	John Randle	.25	.11
❑	211	Jake Reed	.25	.11
❑	212	Robert Smith	.50	.23
❑	213	Robert Tate	.15	.07
❑	214	Terry Allen	.25	.11
❑	215	Bruce Armstrong	.15	.07
❑	216	Drew Bledsoe	.75	.35
❑	217	Ben Coates	.15	.07
❑	218	Kevin Faulk	.25	.11
❑	219	Terry Glenn	.25	.11
❑	220	Shawn Jefferson	.15	.07
❑	221	Andy Katzenmoyer	.15	.07
❑	222	Ty Law	.15	.07
❑	223	Willie McGinest	.15	.07
❑	224	Lawyer Milloy	.15	.07
❑	225	Tony Simmons	.15	.07
❑	226	Michael Bishop	.25	.11
		Sean Morey RC		
❑	227	Cameron Cleeland	.15	.07
❑	228	Troy Davis	.15	.07
❑	229	Jake Delhomme RC	.50	.23
❑	230	Andre Hastings	.15	.07
❑	231	Eddie Kennison	.25	.11
❑	232	Wilmont Perry	.15	.07
❑	233	Dino Philyaw	.15	.07
❑	234	Keith Poole	.15	.07
❑	235	William Roaf	.15	.07
❑	236	Billy Joe Tolliver	.15	.07
❑	237	Fred Weary	.15	.07
❑	238	Ricky Williams	1.25	.55
❑	239	P.J. Franklin RC	.50	.23
		Marvin Powell RC		
❑	240	Jessie Armstead	.15	.07
❑	241	Tiki Barber	.25	.11
❑	242	Daniel Campbell	.15	.07
❑	243	Kerry Collins	.25	.11

❑ 244 Percy Ellsworth .15 .07
❑ 245 Kent Graham .15 .07
❑ 246 Ike Hilliard .25 .11
❑ 247 Cedric Jones .15 .07
❑ 248 Bashir Livingston RC .25 .11
❑ 249 Pete Mitchell .15 .07
❑ 250 Michael Strahan .15 .07
❑ 251 Amani Toomer .15 .07
❑ 252 Charles Way .15 .07
❑ 253 Andre Weathers RC .25 .11
❑ 254 Richie Anderson .25 .11
❑ 255 Wayne Chrebet .25 .11
❑ 256 Marcus Coleman .15 .07
❑ 257 Bryan Cox .15 .07
❑ 258 Jason Fabini RC .25 .11
❑ 259 Robert Farmer RC .50 .23
❑ 260 Keyshawn Johnson .50 .23
❑ 261 Ray Lucas .50 .23
❑ 262 Curtis Martin .50 .23
❑ 263 Kevin Mawae .15 .07
❑ 264 Eric Ogbogu .15 .07
❑ 265 Bernie Parmalee .15 .07
❑ 266 Vinny Testaverde .25 .11
❑ 267 Dedric Ward .15 .07
❑ 268 Eric Barton RC .25 .11
❑ 269 Tim Brown .50 .23
❑ 270 Tony Bryant .15 .07
❑ 271 Rickey Dudley .15 .07
❑ 272 Rich Gannon .25 .11
❑ 273 Bobby Hoying .25 .11
❑ 274 James Jett .15 .07
❑ 275 Napoleon Kaufman .25 .11
❑ 276 Jon Ritchie .15 .07
❑ 277 Darrell Russell .15 .07
❑ 278 Kenny Shedd .15 .07
❑ 279 Marquis Walker RC .25 .11
❑ 280 Tyrone Wheatley .25 .11
❑ 281 Charles Woodson .25 .11
❑ 282 Luther Broughton RC .25 .11
❑ 283 Al Harris .15 .07
❑ 284 Greg Jefferson .15 .07
❑ 285 Dietrich Jells .15 .07
❑ 286 Charles Johnson .25 .11
❑ 287 Chad Lewis .15 .07
❑ 288 Mike Mamula .15 .07
❑ 289 Donovan McNabb .75 .35
❑ 290 Doug Pederson .15 .07
❑ 291 Allen Rossum .15 .07
❑ 292 Torrance Small .15 .07
❑ 293 Duce Staley .50 .23
❑ 294 Jerome Bettis .50 .23
❑ 295 Kris Brown .15 .07
❑ 296 Mark Bruener .15 .07
❑ 297 Troy Edwards .25 .11
❑ 298 Jason Gildon .15 .07
❑ 299 Richard Huntley .15 .07
❑ 300 Bobby Shaw RC .60 .25
❑ 301 Scott Shields RC .25 .11
❑ 302 Kordell Stewart .50 .23
❑ 303 Hines Ward .15 .07
❑ 304 Amos Zereoue .15 .07
❑ 305 Matt Cushing RC .25 .11
Jerame Tuman
❑ 306 Pete Gonzalez 4.00 1.80
Anthony Wright RC
❑ 307 Isaac Bruce .50 .23
❑ 308 Kevin Carter .15 .07
❑ 309 Marshall Faulk .60 .25
❑ 310 London Fletcher RC .25 .11
❑ 311 Joe Germaine .15 .07
❑ 312 Az-Zahir Hakim .25 .11
❑ 313 Torry Holt .50 .23
❑ 314 Tony Home .15 .07
❑ 315 Mike Jones LB .15 .07
❑ 316 Dexter McCleon RC .25 .11
❑ 317 Orlando Pace .15 .07
❑ 318 Ricky Proehl .15 .07
❑ 319 Kurt Warner 2.00 .90
❑ 320 Roland Williams .15 .07
❑ 321 Grant Wistrom .15 .07
❑ 322 James Hodgins RC .25 .11
Justin Watson
❑ 323 Jermaine Fazande .15 .07
❑ 324 Jeff Graham .15 .07
❑ 325 Jim Harbaugh .25 .11
❑ 326 Raylee Johnson .15 .07
❑ 327 Charlie Jones .15 .07
❑ 328 Freddie Jones .15 .07
❑ 329 Natrone Means .15 .07
❑ 330 Chris Penn .15 .07
❑ 331 Mikhael Ricks .15 .07
❑ 332 Junior Seau .25 .11
❑ 333 Reggie Davis RC .25 .11
Robert Reed RC
❑ 334 Fred Beasley .15 .07
❑ 335 Brentson Buckner .15 .07
❑ 336 Greg Clark .15 .07
❑ 337 Dave Fiore RC .15 .07
❑ 338 Charlie Garner .25 .11
❑ 339 Mark Harris RC .50 .23
❑ 340 Ramos McDonald RC .25 .11
❑ 341 Terrell Owens .50 .23
❑ 342 Jerry Rice 1.25 .55
❑ 343 Lance Schulters .15 .07
❑ 344 J.J. Stokes .25 .11
❑ 345 Bryant Young .15 .07
❑ 346 Steve Young .75 .35
❑ 347 Jeff Garcia .50 .23
❑ 348 Fabien Bownes RC .25 .11
❑ 349 Chad Brown .15 .07
❑ 350 Reggie Brown .15 .07
❑ 351 Sean Dawkins .15 .07
❑ 352 Christian Fauria .15 .07
❑ 353 Ahman Green .25 .11
❑ 354 Walter Jones .15 .07
❑ 355 Cortez Kennedy .15 .07
❑ 356 Jon Kitna .50 .23
❑ 357 Derrick Mayes .25 .11
❑ 358 Charlie Rogers .15 .07
❑ 359 Shawn Springs .15 .07
❑ 360 Ricky Watters .25 .11
❑ 361 Donne Abraham .15 .07
❑ 362 Mike Alstott .50 .23
❑ 363 Reidel Anthony .15 .07
❑ 364 Ronde Barber .15 .07
❑ 365 Derrick Brooks .15 .07
❑ 366 Warrick Dunn .50 .23
❑ 367 Jacquez Green .25 .11
❑ 368 Marcus Jones .15 .07
❑ 369 Shaun King .75 .35
❑ 370 John Lynch .15 .07
❑ 371 Warren Sapp .25 .11
❑ 372 Steve White RC .15 .07
❑ 373 Martin Gramatica .25 .11
Kevin McLeod RC
❑ 374 Blaine Bishop .15 .07
❑ 375 Al Del Greco .15 .07
❑ 376 Kevin Dyson .25 .11
❑ 377 Eddie George .60 .25
❑ 378 Jevon Kearse .50 .23
❑ 379 Derrick Mason .25 .11
❑ 380 Bruce Matthews .15 .07
❑ 381 Steve McNair .50 .23
❑ 382 Neil O'Donnell .15 .07
❑ 383 Yancey Thigpen .15 .07
❑ 384 Frank Wycheck .15 .07
❑ 385 Devin Daft .15 .07
Larry Brown
❑ 386 Stephen Alexander .15 .07
❑ 387 Champ Bailey .25 .11
❑ 388 Larry Centers .15 .07
❑ 389 Marco Coleman .15 .07
❑ 390 Albert Connell .15 .07
❑ 391 Stephen Davis .50 .23
❑ 392 Irving Fryar .15 .07
❑ 393 Skip Hicks .25 .11
❑ 394 Brad Johnson .50 .23
❑ 395 Michael Westbrook .25 .11
❑ 396 Obafemi Ayanbadejo RC .25 .11
Lennox Gordon RC
❑ 397 Donald Driver .15 .07
Ronnie Powell
❑ 398 Todd Bouman .50 .23
Jeremy Brigham RC
❑ 399 Brock Huard .15 .07
Sherdrick Bonner
❑ 400 Mike Sellers .25 .11
Spencer George RC
❑ 401 Shaun Alexander RC 3.00 1.35
❑ 402 LaVar Arrington RC 5.00 2.20
❑ 403 Tom Brady RC 1.25 .55
❑ 404 Demario Brown RC 1.00 .45
❑ 405 Plaxico Burress RC 2.50 1.10
❑ 406 Trung Canidate RC 1.25 .55
❑ 407 Giovanni Carmazzi RC 1.50 .70
❑ 408 Kwame Cavil RC 1.00 .45
❑ 409 Chrys Chukwuma RC 1.25 .55
❑ 410 Ron Dayne RC 4.00 1.80
❑ 411 Reuben Droughns RC 1.25 .55
❑ 412 Ron Dugans RC 1.00 .45
❑ 413 Deon Dyer RC 1.00 .45
❑ 414 Danny Farmer RC 1.25 .55
❑ 415 Chafie Fields RC 1.00 .45
❑ 416 Trevor Gaylor RC 1.00 .45
❑ 417 Sherrod Gideon RC .60 .25
❑ 418 Joey Goodspeed RC .60 .25
❑ 419 Joe Hamilton RC 1.50 .70
❑ 420 Tony Hartley RC .60 .25
❑ 421 Todd Husak RC 1.25 .55
❑ 422 Trevor Insley RC .60 .25
❑ 423 Thomas Jones RC 2.00 .90
❑ 424 Marcus Knight RC .60 .25
❑ 425 Jamal Lewis RC 6.00 2.70
❑ 426 Anthony Lucas RC 1.50 .70
❑ 427 Tee Martin RC 2.00 .90
❑ 428 Rondell Mealey RC .60 .25
❑ 429 Sylvester Morris RC 2.50 1.10
❑ 430 Chad Morton RC 1.25 .55
❑ 431 Dennis Northcutt RC 1.50 .70
❑ 432 Chad Pennington RC 4.00 1.80
❑ 433 Rodnick Phillips RC .60 .25
❑ 434 Mareno Philyaw RC .60 .25
❑ 435 Jerry Porter RC 1.25 .55
❑ 436 Travis Prentice RC 2.00 .90
❑ 437 Tim Rattay RC 2.00 .90
❑ 438 Chris Redman RC 2.50 1.10
❑ 439 J.R. Redmond RC 1.50 .70
❑ 440 Gari Scott RC 1.00 .45
❑ 441 Keith Smith RC .60 .25
❑ 442 Terrelle Smith RC 1.00 .45
❑ 443 R.Jay Soward RC 1.25 .55
❑ 444 Q.Spotwood RC UER .60 .25
yardage totals reads 3080
❑ 445 Shyrone Stith RC 1.00 .45
❑ 446 Travis Taylor RC 1.50 .70
❑ 447 Troy Walters RC 1.25 .55
❑ 448 Peter Warrick RC 4.00 1.80
❑ 449 Dez White RC 1.00 .45
❑ 450 Michael Wiley RC 1.25 .55

1996 Pacific Dynagon

	MINT	NRMT
COMPLETE SET (144)	80.00	36.00

❑ 1 Larry Centers .75 .35
❑ 2 Garrison Hearst .75 .35
❑ 3 Dave Krieg .40 .18
❑ 4 Frank Sanders .75 .35
❑ 5 Jeff George .75 .35
❑ 6 Craig Heyward .40 .18
❑ 7 Terance Mathis .40 .18
❑ 8 Eric Metcalf .40 .18
❑ 9 Todd Collins .75 .35
❑ 10 Darick Holmes .40 .18
❑ 11 Jim Kelly 1.50 .70
❑ 12 Eric Moulds RC 5.00 2.20
❑ 13 Bryce Paup .40 .18
❑ 14 Thurman Thomas 1.50 .70
❑ 15 Tim Biakabutuka RC 2.50 1.10

Card	MINT	NRMT
❑ 16 Blake Brockermeyer	.40	.18
❑ 17 Mark Carrier WR	.40	.18
❑ 18 Kerry Collins	1.50	.70
❑ 19 Derrick Moore	.40	.18
❑ 20 Bobby Engram RC	1.50	.70
❑ 21 Jeff Graham	.40	.18
❑ 22 Erik Kramer	.40	.18
❑ 23 Rashaan Salaam	1.50	.70
❑ 24 Steve Stenstrom	.40	.18
❑ 25 Chris Zorich	.40	.18
❑ 26 Jeff Blake	1.50	.70
❑ 27 David Dunn	.40	.18
❑ 28 Carl Pickens	1.50	.70
❑ 29 Darnay Scott	.75	.35
❑ 30 Earnest Byner	.40	.18
❑ 31 Leroy Hoard	.40	.18
❑ 32 Keenan McCardell	1.50	.70
❑ 33 Eric Zeier	.40	.18
❑ 34 Troy Aikman	4.00	1.80
❑ 35 Chris Boniol	.40	.18
❑ 36 Michael Irvin	1.50	.70
❑ 37 Daryl Johnston	.75	.35
❑ 38 Deion Sanders	2.50	1.10
❑ 39 Emmitt Smith	6.00	2.70
❑ 40 Stepfret Williams	.40	.18
❑ 41 John Elway	8.00	3.60
❑ 42 Terrell Davis	8.00	3.60
❑ 43 Anthony Miller	.75	.35
❑ 44 Shannon Sharpe	.75	.35
❑ 45 Scott Mitchell	.75	.35
❑ 46 Herman Moore	1.50	.70
❑ 47 Brett Perriman	.40	.18
❑ 48 Barry Sanders	8.00	3.60
❑ 49 Cory Schlesinger	.40	.18
❑ 50 Edgar Bennett	.75	.35
❑ 51 Robert Brooks	1.50	.70
❑ 52 Mark Chmura	.75	.35
❑ 53 Brett Favre	8.00	3.60
❑ 54 Reggie White	1.50	.70
❑ 55 Eddie George RC	10.00	4.50
❑ 56 Steve McNair	3.00	1.35
❑ 57 Chris Sanders	.75	.35
❑ 58 Rodney Thomas	.40	.18
❑ 59 Ben Bronson RC	.40	.18
❑ 60 Zack Crockett	.40	.18
❑ 61 Marshall Faulk	1.50	.70
❑ 62 Jim Harbaugh	.75	.35
❑ 63 Mark Brunell	4.00	1.80
❑ 64 Kevin Hardy RC	1.50	.70
❑ 65 Willie Jackson	.40	.18
❑ 66 Pete Mitchell	.75	.35
❑ 67 James O.Stewart	.75	.35
❑ 68 Marcus Allen	1.50	.70
❑ 69 Steve Bono	.40	.18
❑ 70 Lake Dawson	.40	.18
❑ 71 Neil Smith	.40	.18
❑ 72 Tamarick Vanover	.75	.35
❑ 73 Irving Fryar	.75	.35
❑ 74 Terry Kirby	.75	.35
❑ 75 Dan Marino	8.00	3.60
❑ 76 O.J. McDuffie	.75	.35
❑ 77 Bernie Parmalee	.40	.18
❑ 78 Stanley Pritchett RC	.75	.35
❑ 79 Cris Carter	1.50	.70
❑ 80 Qadry Ismail	.40	.18
❑ 81 Chad May	.40	.18
❑ 82 Warren Moon	.75	.35
❑ 83 Robert Smith	.75	.35
❑ 84 Drew Bledsoe	4.00	1.80
❑ 85 Ben Coates	.75	.35
❑ 86 Terry Glenn RC	3.00	1.35
❑ 87 Curtis Martin	3.00	1.35
❑ 88 Willie McGinest	.40	.18
❑ 89 Mario Bates	.75	.35
❑ 90 Jim Everett	.40	.18
❑ 91 Wayne Martin	.40	.18
❑ 92 Shane Pahukoa RC	.40	.18
❑ 93 Ray Zellars	.40	.18
❑ 94 Dave Brown	.40	.18
❑ 95 Chris Calloway	.40	.18
❑ 96 Rodney Hampton	.75	.35
❑ 97 Tyrone Wheatley	.75	.35
❑ 98 Wayne Chrebet	2.50	1.10
❑ 99 Glenn Foley	.75	.35
❑ 100 Keyshawn Johnson RC	5.00	2.20
❑ 101 Adrian Murrell	1.50	.70
❑ 102 Alex Van Dyke RC	.75	.35
❑ 103 Tim Brown	1.50	.70
❑ 104 Billy Joe Hobert	.75	.35
❑ 105 Rocket Ismail	.40	.18
❑ 106 Napoleon Kaufman	1.50	.70
❑ 107 Harvey Williams	.40	.18
❑ 108 Charlie Garner	.40	.18
❑ 109 Rodney Peete	.40	.18
❑ 110 Ricky Watters	.75	.35
❑ 111 Calvin Williams	.40	.18
❑ 112 Mark Bruener	.40	.18
❑ 113 Kevin Greene	.75	.35
❑ 114 Ernie Mills	.40	.18
❑ 115 Kordell Stewart	2.50	1.10
❑ 116 Yancey Thigpen	.75	.35
❑ 117 Dave Barr	.40	.18
❑ 118 Jerome Bettis	1.50	.70
❑ 119 Isaac Bruce	1.50	.70
❑ 120 Lawrence Phillips RC	1.50	.70
❑ 121 J.T. Thomas	.40	.18
❑ 122 Ronnie Harmon	.40	.18
❑ 123 Aaron Hayden RC	.40	.18
❑ 124 Stan Humphries	.75	.35
❑ 125 Junior Seau	.75	.35
❑ 126 William Floyd	.75	.35
❑ 127 Elvis Grbac	.75	.35
❑ 128 Jerry Rice	4.00	1.80
❑ 129 J.J. Stokes	1.50	.70
❑ 130 Steve Young	3.00	1.35
❑ 131 Joey Galloway	2.50	1.10
❑ 132 Cortez Kennedy	.40	.18
❑ 133 Kevin Mawae	.40	.18
❑ 134 Rick Mirer	.75	.35
❑ 135 Chris Warren	.75	.35
❑ 136 Trent Dilfer	1.50	.70
❑ 137 Jerry Ellison	.40	.18
❑ 138 Alvin Harper	.40	.18
❑ 139 Errict Rhett	.75	.35
❑ 140 Terry Allen	.75	.35
❑ 141 Brian Mitchell	.40	.18
❑ 142 Gus Frerotte	1.50	.70
❑ 143 Michael Westbrook	1.50	.70
❑ 144 Heath Shuler	.75	.35

1997 Pacific Dynagon

	MINT	NRMT
COMPLETE SET (144)	100.00	45.00
❑ 1 Larry Centers	.75	.35
❑ 2 Kent Graham	.40	.18
❑ 3 Leeland McElroy	.40	.18
❑ 4 Frank Sanders	.75	.35
❑ 5 Jamal Anderson	3.00	1.35
❑ 6 Bert Emanuel	.75	.35
❑ 7 Bobby Hebert	.40	.18
❑ 8 Terance Mathis	.75	.35
❑ 9 Eric Metcalf	.75	.35
❑ 10 Derrick Alexander WR	.75	.35
❑ 11 Earnest Byner	.40	.18
❑ 12 Michael Jackson	.75	.35
❑ 13 Vinny Testaverde	.75	.35
❑ 14 Quinn Early	.40	.18
❑ 15 Jim Kelly	1.50	.70
❑ 16 Eric Moulds	1.50	.70
❑ 17 Andre Reed	.75	.35
❑ 18 Bruce Smith	.75	.35
❑ 19 Thurman Thomas	1.50	.70
❑ 20 Tim Biakabutuka	.75	.35
❑ 21 Mark Carrier WR	.40	.18
❑ 22 Kerry Collins	.75	.35
❑ 23 Kevin Greene	.75	.35
❑ 24 Anthony Johnson	.40	.18
❑ 25 Wesley Walls	.75	.35
❑ 26 Curtis Conway	.75	.35
❑ 27 Bobby Engram	.75	.35
❑ 28 Raymont Harris	.40	.18
❑ 29 Dave Krieg	.40	.18
❑ 30 Rashaan Salaam	.40	.18
❑ 31 Jeff Blake	.75	.35
❑ 32 Ki-Jana Carter	.40	.18
❑ 33 Garrison Hearst	.75	.35
❑ 34 Carl Pickens	1.50	.70
❑ 35 Darnay Scott	.75	.35
❑ 36 Troy Aikman	4.00	1.80
❑ 37 Chris Boniol	.40	.18
❑ 38 Michael Irvin	1.50	.70
❑ 39 Deion Sanders	1.50	.70
❑ 40 Emmitt Smith	6.00	2.70
❑ 41 Herschel Walker	.75	.35
❑ 42 Terrell Davis	6.00	2.70
❑ 43 John Elway	8.00	3.60
❑ 44 Ed McCaffrey	.75	.35
❑ 45 Shannon Sharpe	.75	.35
❑ 46 Alfred Williams	.40	.18
❑ 47 Scott Mitchell	.75	.35
❑ 48 Herman Moore	1.50	.70
❑ 49 Brett Perriman	.40	.18
❑ 50 Barry Sanders	8.00	3.60
❑ 51 Edgar Bennett	.75	.35
❑ 52 Robert Brooks	.75	.35
❑ 53 Mark Chmura	.75	.35
❑ 54 Brett Favre	8.00	3.60
❑ 55 Antonio Freeman	2.50	1.10
❑ 56 Desmond Howard	.75	.35
❑ 57 Reggie White	1.50	.70
❑ 58 Chris Chandler	.75	.35
❑ 59 Eddie George	4.00	1.80
❑ 60 James McKeehan	.40	.18
❑ 61 Steve McNair	2.50	1.10
❑ 62 Chris Sanders	.40	.18
❑ 63 Sean Dawkins	.40	.18
❑ 64 Ken Dilger	.40	.18
❑ 65 Marshall Faulk	1.50	.70
❑ 66 Jim Harbaugh	.75	.35
❑ 67 Marvin Harrison	1.50	.70
❑ 68 Tony Boselli	.40	.18
❑ 69 Mark Brunell	4.00	1.80
❑ 70 Keenan McCardell	.75	.35
❑ 71 Natrone Means	1.50	.70
❑ 72 Jimmy Smith	.75	.35
❑ 73 Marcus Allen	1.50	.70
❑ 74 Kimble Anders	.75	.35
❑ 75 Dale Carter	.40	.18
❑ 76 Greg Hill	.40	.18
❑ 77 Derrick Thomas	.75	.35
❑ 78 Tamarick Vanover	.75	.35
❑ 79 Karim Abdul-Jabbar	1.50	.70
❑ 80 Dan Marino	8.00	3.60
❑ 81 O.J. McDuffie	.75	.35
❑ 82 Jerris McPhail	.40	.18
❑ 83 Zach Thomas	.75	.35
❑ 84 Cris Carter	1.50	.70
❑ 85 Brad Johnson	2.00	.90
❑ 86 Jake Reed	.75	.35
❑ 87 Robert Smith	.75	.35
❑ 88 Drew Bledsoe	4.00	1.80
❑ 89 Ben Coates	.75	.35
❑ 90 Terry Glenn	1.50	.70
❑ 91 Curtis Martin	2.50	1.10
❑ 92 Willie McGinest	.40	.18
❑ 93 Jim Everett	.40	.18
❑ 94 Michael Haynes	.40	.18
❑ 95 Haywood Jeffires	.40	.18
❑ 96 Ray Zellars	.40	.18
❑ 97 Dave Brown	.40	.18
❑ 98 Rodney Hampton	.75	.35
❑ 99 Danny Kanell	.75	.35
❑ 100 Thomas Lewis	.40	.18
❑ 101 Wayne Chrebet	1.50	.70
❑ 102 Keyshawn Johnson	1.50	.70
❑ 103 Adrian Murrell	.75	.35
❑ 104 Neil O'Donnell	.75	.35
❑ 105 Tim Brown	1.50	.70

Card	MINT	NRMT
❑ 106 Rickey Dudley	.75	.35
❑ 107 Jeff Hostetler	.40	.18
❑ 108 Napoleon Kaufman	1.50	.70
❑ 109 Ty Detmer	.75	.35
❑ 110 Jason Dunn	.40	.18
❑ 111 Irving Fryar	.75	.35
❑ 112 Chris T. Jones	.40	.18
❑ 113 Ricky Watters	.75	.35
❑ 114 Jerome Bettis	1.50	.70
❑ 115 Chad Brown	.40	.18
❑ 116 Kordell Stewart	2.00	.90
❑ 117 Mike Tomczak	.40	.18
❑ 118 Rod Woodson	.75	.35
❑ 119 Tony Banks	.75	.35
❑ 120 Isaac Bruce	1.50	.70
❑ 121 Eddie Kennison	.75	.35
❑ 122 Lawrence Phillips	.40	.18
❑ 123 Terrell Fletcher	.40	.18
❑ 124 Stan Humphries	.75	.35
❑ 125 Tony Martin	.75	.35
❑ 126 Junior Seau	.75	.35
❑ 127 Elvis Grbac	.75	.35
❑ 128 Terrell Owens	1.50	.70
❑ 129 Ted Popson	.40	.18
❑ 130 Jerry Rice	4.00	1.80
❑ 131 Steve Young	3.00	1.35
❑ 132 John Friesz	.40	.18
❑ 133 Joey Galloway	2.00	.90
❑ 134 Michael McCrary	.40	.18
❑ 135 Lamar Smith	1.50	.70
❑ 136 Chris Warren	.75	.35
❑ 137 Mike Alstott	1.50	.70
❑ 138 Trent Dilfer	1.50	.70
❑ 139 Courtney Hawkins	.40	.18
❑ 140 Errict Rhett	.40	.18
❑ 141 Terry Allen	1.50	.70
❑ 142 Henry Ellard	.40	.18
❑ 143 Gus Frerotte	.40	.18
❑ 144 Leslie Shepherd	.40	.18
❑ C Mark Brunell Sample	2.00	.90

1996 Pacific Gridiron

	MINT	NRMT
COMPLETE SET (125)	40.00	18.00
❑ 1 Larry Centers	.50	.23
❑ 2 Garrison Hearst	.50	.23
❑ 3 Dave Krieg	.25	.11
❑ 4 Frank Sanders	.50	.23
❑ 5 Jamal Anderson RC	12.00	5.50
❑ 6 J.J. Birden	.25	.11
❑ 7 Eric Metcalf	.25	.11
❑ 8 Jeff George	.50	.23
❑ 9 Cornelius Bennett	.25	.11
❑ 10 Todd Collins	.50	.23
❑ 11 Darick Holmes	.25	.11
❑ 12 Jim Kelly	1.00	.45
❑ 13 Bryce Paup	.25	.11
❑ 14 Bob Christian	.25	.11
❑ 15 Kerry Collins	1.00	.45
❑ 16 Pete Metzelaars	.25	.11
❑ 17 Derrick Moore	.25	.11
❑ 18 Curtis Conway	1.00	.45
❑ 19 Jim Flanigan	.25	.11
❑ 20 Erik Kramer	.25	.11
❑ 21 Rashaan Salaam	1.00	.45
❑ 22 Eric Bieniemy	.25	.11
❑ 23 Jeff Blake	1.00	.45
❑ 24 Tony McGee	.25	.11
❑ 25 Darnay Scott	.50	.23
❑ 26 Vashone Adams	.25	.11
❑ 27 Leroy Hoard	.25	.11
❑ 28 Andre Rison	.50	.23
❑ 29 Tommy Vardell	.25	.11
❑ 30 Troy Aikman	3.00	1.35
❑ 31 Michael Irvin	1.00	.45
❑ 32 Daryl Johnston	.50	.23
❑ 33 Deion Sanders	1.50	.70
❑ 34 Emmitt Smith	5.00	2.20
❑ 35 Terrell Davis	6.00	2.70
❑ 36 John Elway	6.00	2.70
❑ 37 Ed McCaffrey	.50	.23
❑ 38 Anthony Miller	.50	.23
❑ 39 Scott Mitchell	.50	.23
❑ 40 Brett Perriman	.25	.11
❑ 41 Barry Sanders	6.00	2.70
❑ 42 Chris Spielman	.25	.11
❑ 43 Edgar Bennett	.50	.23
❑ 44 Robert Brooks	1.00	.45
❑ 45 Brett Favre	6.00	2.70
❑ 46 Antonio Freeman	3.00	1.35
❑ 47 Reggie White	1.00	.45
❑ 48 Haywood Jeffires	.25	.11
❑ 49 Steve McNair	3.00	1.35
❑ 50 Rodney Thomas	.25	.11
❑ 51 Frank Wycheck	.25	.11
❑ 52 Ashley Ambrose	.25	.11
❑ 53 Mark Brunell	3.00	1.35
❑ 54 Ken Dilger	.50	.23
❑ 55 Marshall Faulk	1.00	.45
❑ 56 Jim Harbaugh	.50	.23
❑ 57 Tony Boselli	.25	.11
❑ 58 Pete Mitchell	.50	.23
❑ 59 James O.Stewart	1.00	.45
❑ 60 Marcus Allen	1.00	.45
❑ 61 Steve Bono	.25	.11
❑ 62 Lake Dawson	.25	.11
❑ 63 Tamarick Vanover	.50	.23
❑ 64 Bryan Cox	.25	.11
❑ 65 Dan Marino	6.00	2.70
❑ 66 O.J. McDuffie	.50	.23
❑ 67 Bernie Parmalee	.25	.11
❑ 68 Cris Carter	1.00	.45
❑ 69 Rocket Ismail	.25	.11
❑ 70 Warren Moon	.50	.23
❑ 71 Robert Smith	.50	.23
❑ 72 Drew Bledsoe	3.00	1.35
❑ 73 Vincent Brisby	.25	.11
❑ 74 Ben Coates	.50	.23
❑ 75 Curtis Martin	3.00	1.35
❑ 76 Mario Bates	.50	.23
❑ 77 Derek Brown RBK	.25	.11
❑ 78 Jim Everett	.25	.11
❑ 79 Dave Brown	.25	.11
❑ 80 Chris Calloway	.25	.11
❑ 81 Rodney Hampton	.50	.23
❑ 82 Tyrone Wheatley	.50	.23
❑ 83 Kyle Brady	.25	.11
❑ 84 Wayne Chrebet	1.50	.70
❑ 85 Adrian Murrell	1.00	.45
❑ 86 Tim Brown	1.00	.45
❑ 87 Rob Carpenter	.25	.11
❑ 88 Charlie Garner	.25	.11
❑ 89 Daryl Hobbs RC	.25	.11
❑ 90 Napoleon Kaufman	1.00	.45
❑ 91 Rodney Peete	.25	.11
❑ 92 Ricky Watters	.50	.23
❑ 93 Calvin Williams	.25	.11
❑ 94 Kevin Greene	.50	.23
❑ 95 Greg Lloyd	.50	.23
❑ 96 Neil O'Donnell	.50	.23
❑ 97 Erric Pegram	.25	.11
❑ 98 Kordell Stewart	2.00	.90
❑ 99 Yancey Thigpen	.50	.23
❑ 100 Rod Woodson	.50	.23
❑ 101 Isaac Bruce	1.00	.45
❑ 102 Jerome Bettis	1.00	.45
❑ 103 J.T. Thomas	.25	.11
❑ 104 Ronnie Harmon	.25	.11
❑ 105 Aaron Hayden RC	.25	.11
❑ 106 Stan Humphries	.50	.23
❑ 107 Alfred Pupunu	.25	.11
❑ 108 William Floyd	.50	.23
❑ 109 Brent Jones	.25	.11
❑ 110 Jerry Rice	3.00	1.35
❑ 111 J.J. Stokes	1.00	.45
❑ 112 John Taylor	.25	.11
❑ 113 Steve Young	2.00	.90
❑ 114 Harvey Williams	.25	.11
❑ 115 John Friesz	.25	.11
❑ 116 Joey Galloway	1.00	.45
❑ 117 Cortez Kennedy	.25	.11
❑ 118 Rick Mirer	.50	.23
❑ 119 Chris Warren	.50	.23
❑ 120 Trent Dilfer	1.00	.45
❑ 121 Alvin Harper	.25	.11
❑ 122 Errict Rhett	.50	.23
❑ 123 Terry Allen	.50	.23
❑ 124 Gus Frerotte	1.00	.45
❑ 125 Michael Westbrook	1.00	.45
❑ S1 Chris Warren Sample	1.00	.45

1996 Pacific Invincible

	MINT	NRMT
COMPLETE SET (150)	80.00	36.00
❑ 1 Larry Centers	1.00	.45
❑ 2 Garrison Hearst	1.00	.45
❑ 3 Seth Joyner	.60	.25
❑ 4 Simeon Rice RC	2.00	.90
❑ 5 Eric Swann	.60	.25
❑ 6 Bert Emanuel	1.00	.45
❑ 7 Jeff George	1.00	.45
❑ 8 Craig Heyward	.60	.25
❑ 9 Terance Mathis	.60	.25
❑ 10 Eric Metcalf	.60	.25
❑ 11 Derrick Alexander WR	1.00	.45
❑ 12 Leroy Hoard	.60	.25
❑ 13 Andre Rison	1.00	.45
❑ 14 Tommy Vardell	.60	.25
❑ 15 Eric Zeier	.60	.25
❑ 16 Jim Kelly	2.00	.90
❑ 17 Eric Moulds RC	6.00	2.70
❑ 18 Bryce Paup	.60	.25
❑ 19 Bruce Smith	1.00	.45
❑ 20 Thurman Thomas	2.00	.90
❑ 21 Tim Biakabutuka RC	3.00	1.35
❑ 22 Blake Brockermeyer	.60	.25
❑ 23 Kerry Collins	2.00	.90
❑ 24 Howard Griffith	.60	.25
❑ 25 Lamar Lathon	.60	.25
❑ 26 Mark Carrier DB	.60	.25
❑ 27 Curtis Conway	2.00	.90
❑ 28 Erik Kramer	.60	.25
❑ 29 Rashaan Salaam	2.00	.90
❑ 30 Alonzo Spellman	.60	.25
❑ 31 Jeff Blake SP (Braille card back)	5.00	2.20
❑ 32 Harold Green	.60	.25
❑ 33 Carl Pickens	2.00	.90
❑ 34 Darnay Scott	1.00	.45
❑ 35 Dan Wilkinson	.60	.25
❑ 36 Troy Aikman	3.00	1.35
❑ 37 Jay Novacek	.60	.25
❑ 38 Deion Sanders	2.00	.90
❑ 39 Emmitt Smith	5.00	2.20
❑ 40 Kevin Williams	.60	.25
❑ 41 Terrell Davis	6.00	2.70
❑ 42 John Elway	6.00	2.70
❑ 43 Anthony Miller	1.00	.45

❑ 44 Michael Dean Perry	.60	.25
❑ 45 Shannon Sharpe	1.00	.45
❑ 46 Scott Mitchell	1.00	.45
❑ 47 Herman Moore	2.00	.90
❑ 48 Brett Perriman	.60	.25
❑ 49 Barry Sanders	6.00	2.70
❑ 50 Chris Spielman	.60	.25
❑ 51 Edgar Bennett	1.00	.45
❑ 52 Robert Brooks	2.00	.90
❑ 53 Brett Favre	6.00	2.70
❑ 54 Derrick Mayes RC	3.00	1.35
❑ 55 Reggie White	2.00	.90
❑ 56 Eddie George RC	10.00	4.50
❑ 57 Haywood Jeffires	.60	.25
❑ 58 Steve McNair	2.50	1.10
❑ 59 Chris Sanders	1.00	.45
❑ 60 Rodney Thomas	.60	.25
❑ 61 Tony Bennett	.60	.25
❑ 62 Quentin Coryatt	.60	.25
❑ 63 Ken Dilger	1.00	.45
❑ 64 Marshall Faulk	2.00	.90
❑ 65 Jim Harbaugh	1.00	.45
❑ 66 Tony Boselli	.60	.25
❑ 67 Mark Brunell	3.00	1.35
❑ 68 Kevin Hardy RC	2.00	.90
❑ 69 Desmond Howard	1.00	.45
❑ 70 James O.Stewart	1.00	.45
❑ 71 Marcus Allen	2.00	.90
❑ 72 Steve Bono	.60	.25
❑ 73 Neil Smith	.60	.25
❑ 74 Derrick Thomas	1.00	.45
❑ 75 Tamarick Vanover	1.00	.45
❑ 76 Karim Abdul-Jabbar RC	2.50	1.10
❑ 77 Irving Fryar	1.00	.45
❑ 78 Eric Green	.60	.25
❑ 79 Dan Marino	6.00	2.70
❑ 80 Bernie Parmalee	.60	.25
❑ 81 Cris Carter	2.00	.90
❑ 82 Warren Moon	1.00	.45
❑ 83 Jake Reed	1.00	.45
❑ 84 Robert Smith	1.00	.45
❑ 85 Moe Williams RC	1.00	.45
❑ 86 Drew Bledsoe	3.00	1.35
❑ 87 Ben Coates	1.00	.45
❑ 88 Terry Glenn RC	4.00	1.80
❑ 89 Curtis Martin	2.50	1.10
❑ 90 Dave Meggett	.60	.25
❑ 91 Mario Bates	1.00	.45
❑ 92 Jim Everett	.60	.25
❑ 93 Michael Haynes	.60	.25
❑ 94 Torrance Small	.60	.25
❑ 95 Ray Zellars	.60	.25
❑ 96 Kyle Brady	.60	.25
❑ 97 Wayne Chrebet	1.50	.70
❑ 98 Keyshawn Johnson RC	6.00	2.70
❑ 99 Adrian Murrell	2.00	.90
❑ 100 Alex Van Dyke RC	1.00	.45
❑ 101 Michael Brooks	.60	.25
❑ 102 Dave Brown	.60	.25
❑ 103 Chris Calloway	.60	.25
❑ 104 Rodney Hampton	1.00	.45
❑ 105 Amani Toomer RC	4.00	1.80
❑ 106 Tyrone Wheatley	1.00	.45
❑ 107 Tim Brown	2.00	.90
❑ 108 Rickey Dudley RC	2.00	.90
❑ 109 Billy Joe Hobert	1.00	.45
❑ 110 Rocket Ismail	.60	.25
❑ 111 Napoleon Kaufman	2.00	.90
❑ 112 Harvey Williams	.60	.25
❑ 113 Charlie Garner	.60	.25
❑ 114 Bobby Hoying RC	2.50	1.10
❑ 115 Rodney Peete	.60	.25
❑ 116 Ricky Watters	1.00	.45
❑ 117 Greg Lloyd	1.00	.45
❑ 118 Erric Pegram	.60	.25
❑ 119 Kordell Stewart	2.00	.90
❑ 120 Yancey Thigpen	1.00	.45
❑ 121 Jon Witman RC	1.00	.45
❑ 122 Aaron Hayden	.60	.25
❑ 123 Stan Humphries	1.00	.45
❑ 124 Tony Martin	1.00	.45
❑ 125 Leslie O'Neal	.60	.25
❑ 126 Junior Seau	1.00	.45
❑ 127 Jerome Bettis	2.00	.90
❑ 128 Isaac Bruce	2.00	.90
❑ 129 Ernie Conwell RC	.60	.25
❑ 130 Lawrence Phillips RC	2.00	.90
❑ 131 William Floyd	1.00	.45
❑ 132 Terrell Owens RC	8.00	3.60
❑ 133 Jerry Rice	3.00	1.35
❑ 134 J.J. Stokes	2.00	.90
❑ 135 Steve Young	2.50	1.10
❑ 136 Brian Blades	.60	.25
❑ 137 Christian Fauria	.60	.25
❑ 138 Joey Galloway	2.00	.90
❑ 139 Rick Mirer	1.00	.45
❑ 140 Chris Warren	1.00	.45
❑ 141 Horace Copeland	.60	.25
❑ 142 Trent Dilfer	2.00	.90
❑ 143 Alvin Harper	.60	.25
❑ 144 Dave Moore	.60	.25
❑ 145 Errict Rhett	1.00	.45
❑ 146 Terry Allen	1.00	.45
❑ 147 Gus Frerotte	2.00	.90
❑ 148 Brian Mitchell	.60	.25
❑ 149 Heath Shuler	1.00	.45
❑ 150 Michael Westbrook	2.00	.90
❑ P1 Chris Warren Promo (Pro Bowl styled card)	1.50	.70

1997 Pacific Invincible

	MINT	NRMT
COMPLETE SET (150)	100.00	45.00
❑ 1 Larry Centers	.60	.25
❑ 2 Kent Graham	.40	.18
❑ 3 LeShon Johnson	.40	.18
❑ 4 Leeland McElroy	.40	.18
❑ 5 Jake Plummer RC	10.00	4.50
❑ 6 Frank Sanders	.60	.25
❑ 7 Morten Andersen	.40	.18
❑ 8 Jamal Anderson	2.50	1.10
❑ 9 Bert Emanuel	.60	.25
❑ 10 Bobby Hebert	.40	.18
❑ 11 Roell Preston	.40	.18
❑ 12 Derrick Alexander WR	.60	.25
❑ 13 Michael Jackson	.60	.25
❑ 14 Byron Bam Morris	.40	.18
❑ 15 Vinny Testaverde	.60	.25
❑ 16 Todd Collins	.40	.18
❑ 17 Andre Reed	.60	.25
❑ 18 Antowain Smith RC	5.00	2.20
❑ 19 Steve Tasker	.40	.18
❑ 20 Thurman Thomas	1.25	.55
❑ 21 Tim Biakabutuka	.60	.25
❑ 22 Rae Carruth RC	1.25	.55
❑ 23 Kerry Collins	.60	.25
❑ 24 Kevin Greene	.60	.25
❑ 25 Anthony Johnson	.40	.18
❑ 26 Wesley Walls	.60	.25
❑ 27 Darnell Autry RC	.60	.25
❑ 28 Curtis Conway	.60	.25
❑ 29 Raymont Harris	.40	.18
❑ 30 Rashaan Salaam	.40	.18
❑ 31 Jeff Blake	.60	.25
❑ 32 Ki-Jana Carter	.40	.18
❑ 33 David Dunn	.40	.18
❑ 34 Carl Pickens	1.25	.55
❑ 35 Darnay Scott	.60	.25
❑ 36 Troy Aikman	3.00	1.35
❑ 37 Michael Irvin	1.25	.55
❑ 38 Deion Sanders	1.25	.55
❑ 39 Emmitt Smith	5.00	2.20
❑ 40 Herschel Walker	.60	.25
❑ 41 Kevin Williams	.40	.18
❑ 42 Steve Atwater	.40	.18
❑ 43 Terrell Davis	5.00	2.20
❑ 44 John Elway	6.00	2.70
❑ 45 Ed McCaffrey	.60	.25
❑ 46 Shannon Sharpe	.60	.25
❑ 47 Scott Mitchell	.60	.25
❑ 48 Herman Moore	1.25	.55
❑ 49 Brett Perriman	.40	.18
❑ 50 Barry Sanders	6.00	2.70
❑ 51 Edgar Bennett	.60	.25
❑ 52 Robert Brooks	.60	.25
❑ 53 Brett Favre	6.00	2.70
❑ 54 Antonio Freeman	1.50	.70
❑ 55 Dorsey Levens	1.25	.55
❑ 56 Reggie White	1.25	.55
❑ 57 Eddie George	3.00	1.35
❑ 58 Steve McNair	1.50	.70
❑ 59 Chris Sanders	.60	.25
❑ 60 Sean Dawkins	.40	.18
❑ 61 Marshall Faulk	1.25	.55
❑ 62 Jim Harbaugh	.60	.25
❑ 63 Marvin Harrison	1.25	.55
❑ 64 Brian Stablein	.40	.18
❑ 65 Mark Brunell	3.00	1.35
❑ 66 Keenan McCardell	.60	.25
❑ 67 Natrone Means	1.25	.55
❑ 68 Pete Mitchell	.40	.18
❑ 69 Jimmy Smith	.60	.25
❑ 70 Marcus Allen	1.25	.55
❑ 71 Kimble Anders	.60	.25
❑ 72 Greg Hill	.40	.18
❑ 73 Kevin Lockett RC	.60	.25
❑ 74 Derrick Thomas	.60	.25
❑ 75 Tamarick Vanover	.60	.25
❑ 76 Karim Abdul-Jabbar	1.25	.55
❑ 77 Yatil Green RC	.60	.25
❑ 78 Randal Hill	.40	.18
❑ 79 Dan Marino	6.00	2.70
❑ 80 Stanley Pritchett	.40	.18
❑ 81 Irving Spikes	.40	.18
❑ 82 Cris Carter	1.25	.55
❑ 83 Brad Johnson	1.50	.70
❑ 84 Robert Smith	.60	.25
❑ 85 Darryl Talley	.40	.18
❑ 86 Drew Bledsoe	3.00	1.35
❑ 87 Ben Coates	.60	.25
❑ 88 Terry Glenn	1.25	.55
❑ 89 Curtis Martin	1.50	.70
❑ 90 Sedrick Shaw RC	1.25	.55
❑ 91 Mario Bates	.40	.18
❑ 92 Troy Davis RC	1.25	.55
❑ 93 Jim Everett	.40	.18
❑ 94 Michael Haynes	.40	.18
❑ 95 Tiki Barber RC	5.00	2.20
❑ 96 Dave Brown	.40	.18
❑ 97 Rodney Hampton	.60	.25
❑ 98 Ike Hilliard RC	3.00	1.35
❑ 99 Danny Kanell	.60	.25
❑ 100 Wayne Chrebet	1.25	.55
❑ 101 Keyshawn Johnson	1.25	.55
❑ 102 Adrian Murrell	.60	.25
❑ 103 Neil O'Donnell	.60	.25
❑ 104 Alex Van Dyke	.40	.18
❑ 105 Joe Aska	.40	.18
❑ 106 Tim Brown	1.25	.55
❑ 107 Rickey Dudley	.60	.25
❑ 108 Napoleon Kaufman	1.25	.55
❑ 109 Carl Kidd RC	.40	.18
❑ 110 Ty Detmer	.60	.25
❑ 111 Jason Dunn	.40	.18
❑ 112 Irving Fryar	.60	.25
❑ 113 Bobby Hoying	.60	.25
❑ 114 Ricky Watters	.60	.25
❑ 115 Jerome Bettis	1.25	.55
❑ 116 Charles Johnson	.60	.25
❑ 117 Greg Lloyd	.40	.18
❑ 118 Kordell Stewart	1.50	.70
❑ 119 Rod Woodson	.60	.25
❑ 120 Tony Banks	.60	.25
❑ 121 Isaac Bruce	1.25	.55
❑ 122 Eddie Kennison	.60	.25
❑ 123 Lawrence Phillips	.40	.18
❑ 124 Stan Humphries	.60	.25
❑ 125 Tony Martin	.60	.25

	MINT	NRMT
❑ 126 Corey Dillon RC	10.00	4.50
❑ 127 Leonard Russell	.40	.18
❑ 128 Junior Seau	.60	.25
❑ 129 Jim Druckenmiller RC	1.25	.55
❑ 130 Marc Edwards RC	.60	.25
❑ 131 Ken Norton Jr.	.40	.18
❑ 132 Terrell Owens	1.25	.55
❑ 133 Jerry Rice	3.00	1.35
❑ 134 Iheanyi Uwaezuoke	.60	.25
❑ 135 Steve Young	2.00	.90
❑ 136 John Friesz	.40	.18
❑ 137 Joey Galloway	1.50	.70
❑ 138 Warren Moon	1.25	.55
❑ 139 Todd Peterson	.40	.18
❑ 140 Chris Warren	.60	.25
❑ 141 Mike Alstott	1.25	.55
❑ 142 Reidel Anthony RC	3.00	1.35
❑ 143 Trent Dilfer	1.25	.55
❑ 144 Warrick Dunn RC	5.00	2.20
❑ 145 Errict Rhett	.40	.18
❑ 146 Terry Allen	1.25	.55
❑ 147 Henry Ellard	.40	.18
❑ 148 Gus Frerotte	.40	.18
❑ 149 Brian Mitchell	.40	.18
❑ 150 Leslie Shepherd	.40	.18
❑ S1 Mark Brunell Sample	3.00	1.35

1996 Pacific Litho-Cel

	MINT	NRMT
COMPLETE SET (100)	80.00	36.00
ALL CARDS PRICED AS PAIRS..		
SINGLE CARDS: HALF VALUE....		
❑ 1 Kent Graham	.30	.14
❑ 2 LeShon Johnson	.30	.14
❑ 3 Leeland McElroy RC	1.25	.55
❑ 4 Frank Sanders	.60	.25
❑ 5 Jamal Anderson RC	10.00	4.50
❑ 6 Cornelius Bennett	.30	.14
❑ 7 Bobby Hebert	.30	.14
❑ 8 Earnest Byner	.30	.14
❑ 9 Michael Jackson	.60	.25
❑ 10 Vinny Testaverde	.60	.25
❑ 11 Jim Kelly	1.25	.55
❑ 12 Andre Reed	.60	.25
❑ 13 Bruce Smith	.60	.25
❑ 14 Thurman Thomas	1.25	.55
❑ 15 Kerry Collins	1.25	.55
❑ 16 Lamar Lathon	.30	.14
❑ 17 Kevin Greene	.60	.25
❑ 18 Bobby Engram RC	1.25	.55
❑ 19 Erik Kramer	.30	.14
❑ 20 Rashaan Salaam	1.25	.55
❑ 21 Jeff Blake	1.25	.55
❑ 22 Garrison Hearst	.60	.25
❑ 23 Carl Pickens	1.25	.55
❑ 24 Darnay Scott	.60	.25
❑ 25 Troy Aikman	3.00	1.35
❑ 26 Eric Bjornson	.30	.14
❑ 27 Deion Sanders	1.50	.70
❑ 28 Emmitt Smith	5.00	2.20
❑ 29 Terrell Davis	8.00	3.60
❑ 30 John Elway	6.00	2.70
❑ 31 Anthony Miller	.60	.25
❑ 32 John Mobley	.30	.14
❑ 33 Scott Mitchell	.60	.25
❑ 34 Herman Moore	1.25	.55
❑ 35 Brett Perriman	.30	.14
❑ 36 Barry Sanders	6.00	2.70
❑ 37 Edgar Bennett	.60	.25
❑ 38 Robert Brooks	1.25	.55
❑ 39 Brett Favre	6.00	2.70
❑ 40 Reggie White	1.25	.55
❑ 41 Chris Chandler	.60	.25
❑ 42 Eddie George RC	8.00	3.60
❑ 43 Steve McNair	2.50	1.10
❑ 44 Chris Sanders	.60	.25
❑ 45 Ken Dilger	.60	.25
❑ 46 Marshall Faulk	1.25	.55
❑ 47 Jim Harbaugh	.60	.25
❑ 48 Mark Brunell	3.00	1.35
❑ 49 Keenan McCardell	1.25	.55
❑ 50 James O.Stewart	.60	.25
❑ 51 Marcus Allen	1.25	.55
❑ 52 Steve Bono	.30	.14
❑ 53 Greg Hill	.60	.25
❑ 54 Tamarick Vanover	.60	.25
❑ 55 Karim Abdul-Jabbar RC	1.50	.70
❑ 56 Dan Marino	6.00	2.70
❑ 57 Zach Thomas RC	2.00	.90
❑ 58 Cris Carter	1.25	.55
❑ 59 Warren Moon	.60	.25
❑ 60 Robert Smith	.60	.25
❑ 61 Drew Bledsoe	3.00	1.35
❑ 62 Terry Glenn RC	2.50	1.10
❑ 63 Curtis Martin	2.50	1.10
❑ 64 Mario Bates	.60	.25
❑ 65 Jim Everett	.30	.14
❑ 66 Haywood Jeffires	.30	.14
❑ 67 Dave Brown	.30	.14
❑ 68 Rodney Hampton	.60	.25
❑ 69 Amani Toomer RC	2.50	1.10
❑ 70 Adrian Murrell	1.25	.55
❑ 71 Neil O'Donnell	.60	.25
❑ 72 Alex Van Dyke RC	.60	.25
❑ 73 Tim Brown	1.25	.55
❑ 74 Jeff Hostetler	.30	.14
❑ 75 Napoleon Kaufman	1.25	.55
❑ 76 Irving Fryar	.60	.25
❑ 77 Chris T. Jones	.60	.25
❑ 78 Ricky Watters	.60	.25
❑ 79 Jerome Bettis	1.25	.55
❑ 80 Kordell Stewart	2.00	.90
❑ 81 Tony Banks RC	2.50	1.10
❑ 82 Eddie Kennison RC	1.25	.55
❑ 83 Lawrence Phillips RC	1.25	.55
❑ 84 Stan Humphries	.60	.25
❑ 85 Tony Martin	.60	.25
❑ 86 Leonard Russell	.30	.14
❑ 87 Junior Seau	.60	.25
❑ 88 Jerry Rice	3.00	1.35
❑ 89 J.J. Stokes	1.25	.55
❑ 90 Tommy Vardell	.30	.14
❑ 91 Steve Young	2.00	.90
❑ 92 Joey Galloway	2.00	.90
❑ 93 Rick Mirer	.60	.25
❑ 94 Chris Warren	.60	.25
❑ 95 Mike Alstott RC	3.00	1.35
❑ 96 Trent Dilfer	1.25	.55
❑ 97 Nilo Silvan	.30	.14
❑ 98 Terry Allen	.60	.25
❑ 99 Gus Frerotte	1.25	.55
❑ 100 Michael Westbrook	1.25	.55
❑ P1 Chris Warren Promo Blue Litho Card	1.00	.45
❑ P2 Chris Warren Promo Red Litho Card	1.00	.45
❑ P3 Chris Warren Promo Blue Cel Card	1.00	.45
❑ P4 Chris Warren Promo Red Cel Card	1.00	.45

1998 Pacific Omega

	MINT	NRMT
COMPLETE SET (250)	40.00	18.00
❑ 1 Larry Centers	.10	.05
❑ 2 Rob Moore	.25	.11
❑ 3 Michael Pittman RC	1.50	.70
❑ 4 Jake Plummer	1.00	.45
❑ 5 Simeon Rice	.25	.11
❑ 6 Frank Sanders	.25	.11

	MINT	NRMT
❑ 7 Eric Swann	.10	.05
❑ 8 Morten Andersen	.10	.05
❑ 9 Jamal Anderson	.50	.23
❑ 10 Chris Chandler	.25	.11
❑ 11 Harold Green	.10	.05
❑ 12 Byron Hanspard	.25	.11
❑ 13 Terance Mathis	.25	.11
❑ 14 O.J. Santiago	.10	.05
❑ 15 Peter Boulware	.10	.05
❑ 16 Jay Graham	.10	.05
❑ 17 Eric Green	.10	.05
❑ 18 Michael Jackson	.10	.05
❑ 19 Jermaine Lewis	.25	.11
❑ 20 Ray Lewis	.50	.23
❑ 21 Jonathan Ogden	.10	.05
❑ 22 Eric Zeier	.25	.11
❑ 23 Steve Christie	.10	.05
❑ 24 Todd Collins	.10	.05
❑ 25 Quinn Early	.10	.05
❑ 26 Eric Moulds	.50	.23
❑ 27 Andre Reed	.25	.11
❑ 28 Antowain Smith	.50	.23
❑ 29 Bruce Smith	.25	.11
❑ 30 Thurman Thomas	.50	.23
❑ 31 Ted Washington	.10	.05
❑ 32 Michael Bates	.10	.05
❑ 33 Tim Biakabutuka	.25	.11
❑ 34 Mark Carrier	.10	.05
❑ 35 Rae Carruth	.25	.11
❑ 36 Kerry Collins	.25	.11
❑ 37 Kevin Greene	.25	.11
❑ 38 Fred Lane	.25	.11
❑ 39 Muhsin Muhammad	.25	.11
❑ 40 Wesley Walls	.25	.11
❑ 41 Curtis Conway	.25	.11
❑ 42 Bobby Engram	.25	.11
❑ 43 Curtis Enis RC	1.50	.70
❑ 44 Walt Harris	.10	.05
❑ 45 Erik Kramer	.10	.05
❑ 46 Chris Penn	.10	.05
❑ 47 Ryan Wetnight RC	.10	.05
❑ 48 Jeff Blake	.25	.11
❑ 49 Ki-Jana Carter	.10	.05
❑ 50 John Copeland	.10	.05
❑ 51 Corey Dillon	.75	.35
❑ 52 Tony McGee	.10	.05
❑ 53 Carl Pickens	.50	.23
❑ 54 Darnay Scott	.25	.11
❑ 55 Takeo Spikes RC	.75	.35
❑ 56 Troy Aikman	1.25	.55
❑ 57 Eric Bjornson	.10	.05
❑ 58 Greg Ellis RC	.50	.23
❑ 59 Michael Irvin	.50	.23
❑ 60 Daryl Johnston	.25	.11
❑ 61 David LaFleur	.10	.05
❑ 62 Deion Sanders	.50	.23
❑ 63 Emmitt Smith	2.00	.90
❑ 64 Herschel Walker	.25	.11
❑ 65 Nicky Sualua RC	.25	.11
❑ 66 Steve Atwater	.10	.05
❑ 67 Terrell Davis	2.00	.90
❑ 68 John Elway	2.50	1.10
❑ 69 Brian Griese RC	5.00	2.20
❑ 70 Ed McCaffrey	.25	.11
❑ 71 John Mobley	.10	.05
❑ 72 Marcus Nash RC	1.50	.70
❑ 73 Shannon Sharpe	.25	.11

❑ 74 Neil Smith .25 .11
❑ 75 Rod Smith .25 .11
❑ 76 Charlie Batch RC 4.00 1.80
❑ 77 Germane Crowell RC 2.50 1.10
❑ 78 Jason Hanson .10 .05
❑ 79 Scott Mitchell .25 .11
❑ 80 Herman Moore .50 .23
❑ 81 Johnnie Morton .25 .11
❑ 82 Barry Sanders 2.50 1.10
❑ 83 Tommy Vardell .10 .05
❑ 84 Robert Brooks .25 .11
❑ 85 Gilbert Brown .10 .05
❑ 86 LeRoy Butler .10 .05
❑ 87 Mark Chmura .25 .11
❑ 88 Brett Favre 2.50 1.10
❑ 89 Antonio Freeman .50 .23
❑ 90 William Henderson .10 .05
❑ 91 Vonnie Holliday RC .75 .35
❑ 92 Dorsey Levens .50 .23
❑ 93 Reggie White .50 .23
❑ 94 Aaron Bailey .10 .05
❑ 95 Quentin Coryatt .10 .05
❑ 96 Zack Crockett .10 .05
❑ 97 Ken Dilger .10 .05
❑ 98 Marshall Faulk .50 .23
❑ 99 E.G. Green RC .75 .35
❑ 100 Marvin Harrison .25 .11
❑ 101 Peyton Manning RC .. 12.00 5.50
❑ 102 Jerome Pathon RC 1.50 .70
❑ 103 Tavian Banks RC 1.50 .70
❑ 104 Tony Boselli .10 .05
❑ 105 Tony Brackens .10 .05
❑ 106 Mark Brunell 1.00 .45
❑ 107 Kevin Hardy .10 .05
❑ 108 Keenan McCardell .25 .11
❑ 109 Pete Mitchell .10 .05
❑ 110 Jimmy Smith .25 .11
❑ 111 James Stewart .25 .11
❑ 112 Fred Taylor RC 4.00 1.80
❑ 113 Kimble Anders .25 .11
❑ 114 Dale Carter .10 .05
❑ 115 Tony Gonzalez .10 .05
❑ 116 Elvis Grbac .25 .11
❑ 117 Donnell Bennett .10 .05
❑ 118 Andre Rison .25 .11
❑ 119 Rashaan Shehee RC .75 .35
❑ 120 Derrick Thomas .25 .11
❑ 121 Tamarick Vanover .10 .05
❑ 122 Karim Abdul-Jabbar .50 .23
❑ 123 John Avery RC 1.50 .70
❑ 124 Troy Drayton .10 .05
❑ 125 John Dutton RC .50 .23
❑ 126 Craig Erickson .10 .05
❑ 127 Dan Marino 2.50 1.10
❑ 128 O.J. McDuffie .25 .11
❑ 129 Jerris McPhail .10 .05
❑ 130 Stanley Pritchett .10 .05
❑ 131 Larry Shannon RC .50 .23
❑ 132 Zach Thomas .25 .11
❑ 133 Cris Carter .50 .23
❑ 134 Randall Cunningham .50 .23
❑ 135 Andrew Glover .10 .05
❑ 136 Brad Johnson .50 .23
❑ 137 Randall McDaniel .10 .05
❑ 138 David Palmer .10 .05
❑ 139 John Randle .25 .11
❑ 140 Jake Reed .25 .11
❑ 141 Robert Smith .50 .23
❑ 142 Drew Bledsoe 1.00 .45
❑ 143 Ben Coates .25 .11
❑ 144 Robert Edwards RC 2.00 .90
❑ 145 Terry Glenn .50 .23
❑ 146 Shawn Jefferson .10 .05
❑ 147 Willie McGinest .10 .05
❑ 148 Tony Simmons RC .75 .35
❑ 149 Chris Slade .10 .05
❑ 150 Troy Davis .10 .05
❑ 151 Mark Fields .10 .05
❑ 152 Andre Hastings .10 .05
❑ 153 Billy Joe Hobert .10 .05
❑ 154 William Roaf .10 .05
❑ 155 Heath Shuler .10 .05
❑ 156 Danny Wuerffel .25 .11
❑ 157 Ray Zellars .10 .05
❑ 158 Jessie Armstead .10 .05
❑ 159 Tiki Barber .25 .11
❑ 160 Chris Calloway .10 .05
❑ 161 Mike Cherry .10 .05
❑ 162 Danny Kanell .25 .11
❑ 163 Amani Toomer .25 .11
❑ 164 Charles Way .10 .05
❑ 165 Tyrone Wheatley .25 .11
❑ 166 Kyle Brady .10 .05
❑ 167 Wayne Chrebet .50 .23
❑ 168 Glenn Foley .25 .11
❑ 169 Scott Frost RC .75 .35
❑ 170 Keyshawn Johnson .50 .23
❑ 171 Leon Johnson .10 .05
❑ 172 Alex Van Dyke .10 .05
❑ 173 Dedric Ward .10 .05
❑ 174 Tim Brown .50 .23
❑ 175 Rickey Dudley .10 .05
❑ 176 Jeff George .25 .11
❑ 177 Desmond Howard .25 .11
❑ 178 James Jett .25 .11
❑ 179 Napoleon Kaufman .50 .23
❑ 180 Darrell Russell .10 .05
❑ 181 Charles Woodson RC .. 2.00 .90
❑ 182 Jason Dunn .10 .05
❑ 183 Irving Fryar .25 .11
❑ 184 Charlie Garner .10 .05
❑ 185 Bobby Hoying .25 .11
❑ 186 Chris T. Jones .10 .05
❑ 187 Michael Timpson .10 .05
❑ 188 Kevin Turner .10 .05
❑ 189 Jerome Bettis .50 .23
❑ 190 Will Blackwell .10 .05
❑ 191 Mark Bruener .10 .05
❑ 192 Charles Johnson .10 .05
❑ 193 George Jones .10 .05
❑ 194 Levon Kirkland .10 .05
❑ 195 Kordell Stewart .50 .23
❑ 196 Hines Ward RC 1.50 .70
❑ 197 Tony Banks .25 .11
❑ 198 Isaac Bruce .50 .23
❑ 199 Ernie Conwell .10 .05
❑ 200 Robert Holcombe RC .. 1.50 .70
❑ 201 Eddie Kennison .25 .11
❑ 202 Amp Lee .10 .05
❑ 203 Orlando Pace .10 .05
❑ 204 Charlie Jones .10 .05
❑ 205 Freddie Jones .10 .05
❑ 206 Ryan Leaf RC 3.00 1.35
❑ 207 Natrone Means .50 .23
❑ 208 Junior Seau .25 .11
❑ 209 Bryan Still .10 .05
❑ 210 Greg Clark .10 .05
❑ 211 Jim Druckenmiller .25 .11
❑ 212 Marc Edwards .10 .05
❑ 213 Garrison Hearst .50 .23
❑ 214 Terrell Owens .50 .23
❑ 215 Jerry Rice 1.25 .55
❑ 216 J.J. Stokes .25 .11
❑ 217 Bryant Young .10 .05
❑ 218 Steve Young .75 .35
❑ 219 Chad Brown .10 .05
❑ 220 Joey Galloway .50 .23
❑ 221 Cortez Kennedy .10 .05
❑ 222 Jon Kitna .75 .35
❑ 223 James McKnight .10 .05
❑ 224 Warren Moon .50 .23
❑ 225 Michael Sinclair .10 .05
❑ 226 Ricky Watters .25 .11
❑ 227 Mike Alstott .50 .23
❑ 228 Reidel Anthony .25 .11
❑ 229 Derrick Brooks .10 .05
❑ 230 Trent Dilfer .50 .23
❑ 231 Warrick Dunn .50 .23
❑ 232 Dave Moore .10 .05
❑ 233 Hardy Nickerson .10 .05
❑ 234 Warren Sapp .25 .11
❑ 235 Karl Williams .10 .05
❑ 236 Willie Davis .10 .05
❑ 237 Kevin Dyson RC 2.00 .90
❑ 238 Eddie George 1.00 .45
❑ 239 Derrick Mason .25 .11
❑ 240 Steve McNair .50 .23
❑ 241 Chris Sanders .10 .05
❑ 242 Frank Wycheck .10 .05
❑ 243 Terry Allen .50 .23
❑ 244 Jamie Asher .10 .05
❑ 245 Gus Frerotte .10 .05
❑ 246 Darrell Green .25 .11
❑ 247 Skip Hicks RC 1.50 .70
❑ 248 Brian Mitchell .10 .05
❑ 249 Leslie Shepherd .10 .05
❑ 250 Michael Westbrook .25 .11

1999 Pacific Omega

	MINT	NRMT
COMPLETE SET (250)	40.00	18.00

❑ 1 Mario Bates .15 .07
❑ 2 David Boston RC 2.50 1.10
❑ 3 Rob Moore .25 .11
❑ 4 Adrian Murrell .25 .11
❑ 5 Jake Plummer 1.00 .45
❑ 6 Frank Sanders .25 .11
❑ 7 Aeneas Williams .15 .07
❑ 8 Joel Makovicka RC 1.25 .55
Lonnie Shelton RC
❑ 9 Jamal Anderson .50 .23
❑ 10 Ray Buchanan .15 .07
❑ 11 Chris Chandler .25 .11
❑ 12 Tim Dwight .50 .23
❑ 13 Byron Hanspard .15 .07
❑ 14 Terance Mathis .25 .11
❑ 15 O.J. Santiago .15 .07
❑ 16 Danny Kanell .15 .07
Chris Calloway
❑ 17 Peter Boulware .15 .07
❑ 18 Priest Holmes .25 .11
❑ 19 Patrick Johnson .15 .07
❑ 20 Jermaine Lewis .25 .11
❑ 21 Ray Lewis .25 .11
❑ 22 Michael McCrary .15 .07
❑ 23 Jonathan Ogden .15 .07
❑ 24 Tony Banks .15 .07
Scott Mitchell
❑ 25 Doug Flutie .60 .25
❑ 26 Rob Johnson .25 .11
❑ 27 Eric Moulds .50 .23
❑ 28 Andre Reed .25 .11
❑ 29 Antowain Smith .50 .23
❑ 30 Bruce Smith .25 .11
❑ 31 Kevin Williams .15 .07
❑ 32 Shawn Bryson RC 1.50 .70
Peerless Price RC
❑ 33 Steve Beuerlein .15 .07
❑ 34 Tim Biakabutuka .25 .11
❑ 35 Rae Carruth .25 .11
❑ 36 Dameyune Craig RC 2.00 .90
❑ 37 William Floyd .15 .07
❑ 38 Kevin Greene .15 .07
❑ 39 Muhsin Muhammad .25 .11
❑ 40 Wesley Walls .25 .11
❑ 41 Edgar Bennett .15 .07
❑ 42 Robert Chancey RC 1.50 .70
❑ 43 Curtis Conway .25 .11
❑ 44 Bobby Engram .25 .11
❑ 45 Curtis Enis .50 .23
❑ 46 Cade McNown RC 1.50 .70
❑ 47 Ryan Wetnight .15 .07
❑ 48 D'Wayne Bates RC 1.00 .45
Marty Booker RC
❑ 49 Jeff Blake .25 .11
❑ 50 Scott Covington RC 1.25 .55
❑ 51 Corey Dillon .50 .23
❑ 52 James Hundon .25 .11

❑ 53 Carl Pickens	.25	.11
❑ 54 Darnay Scott	.15	.07
❑ 55 Akili Smith RC	2.50	1.10
❑ 56 Craig Yeast RC	1.00	.45
❑ 57 Tim Couch RC	4.00	1.80
❑ 58 Ty Detmer	.25	.11
❑ 59 Marc Edwards	.15	.07
❑ 60 Kevin Johnson RC	2.50	1.10
❑ 61 Terry Kirby	.15	.07
❑ 62 Sedrick Shaw	.15	.07
❑ 63 Leslie Shepherd	.15	.07
❑ 64 Darrin Chiaverini RC	.50	.23
Daylon McCutcheon RC		
❑ 65 Troy Aikman	1.25	.55
❑ 66 Michael Irvin	.25	.11
❑ 67 David LaFleur	.15	.07
❑ 68 Wane McGarity RC	1.25	.55
❑ 69 Ernie Mills	.15	.07
❑ 70 Deion Sanders	.50	.23
❑ 71 Emmitt Smith	1.25	.55
❑ 72 Rocket Ismail	.15	.07
James McKnight		
❑ 73 Bubby Brister	.15	.07
❑ 74 Byron Chamberlain RC	1.00	.45
❑ 75 Terrell Davis	1.25	.55
❑ 76 Olandis Gary RC	2.50	1.10
❑ 77 Brian Griese	1.00	.45
❑ 78 Ed McCaffrey	.25	.11
❑ 79 Shannon Sharpe	.25	.11
❑ 80 Rod Smith	.25	.11
❑ 81 Travis McGriff RC	1.00	.45
Al Wilson RC		
❑ 82 Charlie Batch	1.00	.45
❑ 83 Chris Claiborne RC	.50	.23
❑ 84 Germane Crowell	.25	.11
❑ 85 Terry Fair	.15	.07
❑ 86 Sedrick Irvin RC	1.25	.55
❑ 87 Herman Moore	.50	.23
❑ 88 Johnnie Morton	.25	.11
❑ 89 Barry Sanders	2.00	.90
❑ 90 Mark Chmura	.15	.07
❑ 91 Brett Favre	2.00	.90
❑ 92 Antonio Freeman	.50	.23
❑ 93 Desmond Howard	.25	.11
❑ 94 Dorsey Levens	.50	.23
❑ 95 Derrick Mayes	.15	.07
❑ 96 Bill Schroeder	.50	.23
❑ 97 Aaron Brooks RC	4.00	1.80
Dee Miller RC		
❑ 98 E.G. Green	.15	.07
❑ 99 Marvin Harrison	.50	.23
❑ 100 Edgerrin James RC	8.00	3.60
❑ 101 Peyton Manning	2.00	.90
❑ 102 Jerome Pathon	.15	.07
❑ 103 Marcus Pollard	.15	.07
❑ 104 Ken Dilger	.15	.07
❑ 105 Derrick Alexander WR	.25	.11
❑ 106 Reggie Barlow	.15	.07
❑ 107 Tony Boselli	.15	.07
❑ 108 Mark Brunell	.75	.35
❑ 109 George Jones	.15	.07
❑ 110 Keenan McCardell	.25	.11
❑ 111 Jimmy Smith	.25	.11
❑ 112 James Stewart	.25	.11
❑ 113 Fred Taylor	1.25	.55
❑ 114 Kimble Anders	.25	.11
❑ 115 Mike Cloud RC	1.25	.55
❑ 116 Tony Gonzalez	.25	.11
❑ 117 Elvis Grbac	.25	.11
❑ 118 Byron Bam Morris	.15	.07
❑ 119 Andre Rison	.25	.11
❑ 120 Derrick Thomas	.25	.11
❑ 121 Karim Abdul-Jabbar	.25	.11
❑ 122 Oronde Gadsden	.15	.07
❑ 123 James Johnson RC	1.25	.55
❑ 124 Rob Konrad RC	1.25	.55
❑ 125 Dan Marino	2.00	.90
❑ 126 O.J. McDuffie	.25	.11
❑ 127 Lamar Thomas	.15	.07
❑ 128 Zach Thomas	.25	.11
❑ 129 Cris Carter	.50	.23
❑ 130 Daunte Culpepper RC	8.00	3.60
❑ 131 Randall Cunningham	.50	.23
❑ 132 Matthew Hatchette	.15	.07
❑ 133 Leroy Hoard	.15	.07
❑ 134 David Palmer	.15	.07
❑ 135 John Randle	.25	.11
❑ 136 Randy Moss	2.00	.90
❑ 137 Robert Smith	.50	.23
❑ 138 Drew Bledsoe	.75	.35
❑ 139 Ben Coates	.25	.11
❑ 140 Kevin Faulk RC	2.00	.90
❑ 141 Terry Glenn	.50	.23
❑ 142 Shawn Jefferson	.15	.07
❑ 143 Ty Law	.15	.07
❑ 144 Tony Simmons	.15	.07
❑ 145 Michael Bishop RC	1.50	.70
Andy Katzenmoyer RC		
❑ 146 Cameron Cleeland	.15	.07
❑ 147 Andre Hastings	.15	.07
❑ 148 Billy Joe Hobert	.15	.07
❑ 149 Joe Johnson	.15	.07
❑ 150 Keith Poole	.15	.07
❑ 151 William Roaf	.15	.07
❑ 152 Billy Joe Tolliver	.15	.07
❑ 153 Ricky Williams RC	5.00	2.20
❑ 154 Tiki Barber	.15	.07
❑ 155 Gary Brown	.15	.07
❑ 156 Kent Graham	.15	.07
❑ 157 Ike Hilliard	.15	.07
❑ 158 David Patten	.15	.07
❑ 159 Jason Sehorn	.15	.07
❑ 160 Amani Toomer	.15	.07
❑ 161 Joe Montgomery RC	1.25	.55
Luke Petitgout RC		
❑ 162 Wayne Chrebet	.25	.11
❑ 163 Bryan Cox	.15	.07
❑ 164 Aaron Glenn	.15	.07
❑ 165 Keyshawn Johnson	.50	.23
❑ 166 Leon Johnson	.15	.07
❑ 167 Curtis Martin	.50	.23
❑ 168 Vinny Testaverde	.25	.11
❑ 169 Dedric Ward	.15	.07
❑ 170 Tim Brown	.50	.23
❑ 171 Rickey Dudley	.15	.07
❑ 172 James Jett	.25	.11
❑ 173 Napoleon Kaufman	.50	.23
❑ 174 Jon Ritchie	.15	.07
❑ 175 Darrell Russell	.15	.07
❑ 176 Charles Woodson	.50	.23
❑ 177 Rich Gannon	.25	.11
Heath Shuler		
❑ 178 Hugh Douglas	.15	.07
❑ 179 Donovan McNabb RC	5.00	2.20
❑ 180 Allen Rossum	.15	.07
❑ 181 Duce Staley	.25	.11
❑ 182 Kevin Turner	.15	.07
❑ 183 Charles Johnson	.15	.07
Doug Pederson		
❑ 184 Barry Gardner RC	1.00	.45
Cecil Martin RC		
❑ 185 Jerome Bettis	.50	.23
❑ 186 Mark Bruener	.15	.07
❑ 187 Troy Edwards RC	1.50	.70
❑ 188 Courtney Hawkins	.15	.07
❑ 189 Levon Kirkland	.15	.07
❑ 190 Kordell Stewart	.50	.23
❑ 191 Hines Ward	.15	.07
❑ 192 Malcolm Johnson RC	1.25	.55
Amos Zereoue RC		
❑ 193 Greg Clark	.15	.07
❑ 194 Terrell Fletcher	.15	.07
❑ 195 Charlie Jones	.15	.07
❑ 196 Cecil Collins RC	1.25	.55
❑ 197 Natrone Means	.25	.11
❑ 198 Mikhael Ricks	.15	.07
❑ 199 Junior Seau	.25	.11
❑ 200 Bryan Still	.15	.07
❑ 201 Ryan Thelwell	.15	.07
❑ 202 Garrison Hearst	.25	.11
❑ 203 Terry Jackson RC	1.00	.45
❑ 204 R.W. McQuarters	.15	.07
❑ 205 Terrell Owens	.50	.23
❑ 206 Jerry Rice	1.25	.55
❑ 207 J.J. Stokes	.25	.11
❑ 208 Lawrence Phillips	.15	.07
Tommy Vardell		
❑ 209 Steve Young	.75	.35
❑ 210 Karsten Bailey RC	1.00	.45
❑ 211 Chad Brown	.15	.07
❑ 212 Christian Fauria	.15	.07
❑ 213 Joey Galloway	.50	.23
❑ 214 Ahman Green	.25	.11
❑ 215 Brock Huard RC	2.00	.90
❑ 216 Cortez Kennedy	.15	.07
❑ 217 Jon Kitna	.50	.23
❑ 218 Ricky Watters	.25	.11
❑ 219 Isaac Bruce	.50	.23
❑ 220 Az-Zahir Hakim	.15	.07
❑ 221 June Henley RC	.15	.07
❑ 222 Greg Hill	.15	.07
❑ 223 Torry Holt RC	3.00	1.35
❑ 224 Amp Lee	.15	.07
❑ 225 Ricky Proehl	.15	.07
❑ 226 Marshall Faulk	.50	.23
Trent Green		
❑ 227 Mike Alstott	.50	.23
❑ 228 Reidel Anthony	.25	.11
❑ 229 Trent Dilfer	.25	.11
❑ 230 Warrick Dunn	.50	.23
❑ 231 Bert Emanuel	.25	.11
❑ 232 Jacquez Green	.25	.11
❑ 233 Warren Sapp	.15	.07
❑ 234 Shaun King RC	2.50	1.10
Anthony McFarland RC		
❑ 235 Mike Archie RC	.50	.23
❑ 236 Kevin Dyson	.25	.11
❑ 237 Eddie George	.60	.25
❑ 238 Derrick Mason	.25	.11
❑ 239 Steve McNair	.50	.23
❑ 240 Yancey Thigpen	.15	.07
❑ 241 Frank Wycheck	.15	.07
❑ 242 Darran Hall	2.00	.90
Jevon Kearse RC		
❑ 243 Stephen Alexander	.15	.07
❑ 244 Champ Bailey RC	1.50	.70
❑ 245 Stephen Davis	.50	.23
❑ 246 Skip Hicks	.25	.11
❑ 247 James Thrash RC	4.00	1.80
❑ 248 Michael Westbrook	.25	.11
❑ 249 Dan Wilkinson	.15	.07
❑ 250 Brad Johnson	.50	.23
Larry Centers		

2000 Pacific Omega

	MINT	NRMT
COMP.SET w/o SP's (150)	20.00	9.00
❑ 1 David Boston	.50	.23
❑ 2 Dave Brown	.15	.07
❑ 3 Rob Moore	.25	.11
❑ 4 Jake Plummer	.50	.23
❑ 5 Simeon Rice	.15	.07
❑ 6 Frank Sanders	.25	.11
❑ 7 Jamal Anderson	.50	.23
❑ 8 Chris Chandler	.25	.11
❑ 9 Tim Dwight	.50	.23
❑ 10 Terance Mathis	.25	.11
❑ 11 Tony Banks	.25	.11
❑ 12 Peter Boulware	.15	.07
❑ 13 Priest Holmes	.25	.11
❑ 14 Qadry Ismail	.25	.11
❑ 15 Doug Flutie	.60	.25
❑ 16 Rob Johnson	.25	.11
❑ 17 Jonathan Linton	.15	.07
❑ 18 Eric Moulds	.50	.23
❑ 19 Peerless Price	.50	.23
❑ 20 Antowain Smith	.50	.23
❑ 21 Steve Beuerlein	.15	.07

❑ 22 Tim Biakabutuka .25 .11
❑ 23 Patrick Jeffers .50 .23
❑ 24 Muhsin Muhammad .25 .11
❑ 25 Wesley Walls .25 .11
❑ 26 Bobby Engram .25 .11
❑ 27 Curtis Enis .25 .11
❑ 28 Cade McNown .50 .23
❑ 29 Marcus Robinson .50 .23
❑ 30 Willie Anderson .15 .07
❑ 31 Michael Basnight .15 .07
❑ 32 Corey Dillon .50 .23
❑ 33 Akili Smith .50 .23
❑ 34 Tim Couch 1.00 .45
❑ 35 Kevin Johnson .50 .23
❑ 36 Wali Rainer .15 .07
❑ 37 Troy Aikman 1.25 .55
❑ 38 Dexter Coakley .15 .07
❑ 39 Rocket Ismail .25 .11
❑ 40 Emmitt Smith 1.25 .55
❑ 41 Chris Warren .15 .07
❑ 42 Terrell Davis 1.25 .55
❑ 43 Olandis Gary .50 .23
❑ 44 Brian Griese .60 .25
❑ 45 Ed McCaffrey .50 .23
❑ 46 Rod Smith .25 .11
❑ 47 Charlie Batch .50 .23
❑ 48 Germane Crowell .25 .11
❑ 49 Herman Moore .25 .11
❑ 50 Johnnie Morton .25 .11
❑ 51 Barry Sanders 1.50 .70
❑ 52 Corey Bradford .25 .11
❑ 53 Brett Favre 2.00 .90
❑ 54 Antonio Freeman .50 .23
❑ 55 Dorsey Levens .25 .11
❑ 56 Bill Schroeder .25 .11
❑ 57 Ken Dilger .15 .07
❑ 58 Marvin Harrison .50 .23
❑ 59 Edgerrin James 2.00 .90
❑ 60 Peyton Manning 1.50 .70
❑ 61 Jerome Pathon .25 .11
❑ 62 Terrence Wilkins .50 .23
❑ 63 Mark Brunell .75 .35
❑ 64 Keenan McCardell .25 .11
❑ 65 Jimmy Smith .25 .11
❑ 66 Fred Taylor .60 .25
❑ 67 Derrick Alexander .25 .11
❑ 68 Donnell Bennett .15 .07
❑ 69 Tony Gonzalez .25 .11
❑ 70 Elvis Grbac .25 .11
❑ 71 Tony Richardson RC .15 .07
❑ 72 Oronde Gadsden .25 .11
❑ 73 Damon Huard .50 .23
❑ 74 James Johnson .25 .11
❑ 75 Dan Marino 2.00 .90
❑ 76 Tony Martin .25 .11
❑ 77 O.J. McDuffie .25 .11
❑ 78 Cris Carter .50 .23
❑ 79 Daunte Culpepper 1.00 .45
❑ 80 Randy Moss 1.50 .70
❑ 81 Robert Smith .50 .23
❑ 82 Drew Bledsoe .75 .35
❑ 83 Kevin Faulk .25 .11
❑ 84 Terry Glenn .25 .11
❑ 85 P.J. Franklin RC .25 .11
❑ 86 Keith Poole .25 .11
❑ 87 Ricky Williams 1.25 .55
❑ 88 Tiki Barber .25 .11
❑ 89 Kerry Collins .25 .11
❑ 90 Ike Hilliard .25 .11
❑ 91 Amani Toomer .25 .11
❑ 92 Wayne Chrebet .25 .11
❑ 93 Ray Lucas .50 .23
❑ 94 Curtis Martin .50 .23
❑ 95 Vinny Testaverde .25 .11
❑ 96 Tim Brown .50 .23
❑ 97 Rich Gannon .25 .11
❑ 98 James Jett .15 .07
❑ 99 Napoleon Kaufman .25 .11
❑ 100 Tyrone Wheatley .25 .11
❑ 101 Charles Woodson .25 .11
❑ 102 Brian Dawkins .15 .07
❑ 103 Charles Johnson .25 .11
❑ 104 Donovan McNabb .75 .35
❑ 105 Torrance Small .15 .07
❑ 106 Duce Staley .50 .23
❑ 107 Jerome Bettis .50 .23
❑ 108 Troy Edwards .25 .11
❑ 109 Richard Huntley .15 .07
❑ 110 Kordell Stewart .50 .23
❑ 111 Hines Ward .15 .07
❑ 112 Isaac Bruce .50 .23
❑ 113 Marshall Faulk .60 .25
❑ 114 Az-Zahir Hakim .25 .11
❑ 115 Torry Holt .50 .23
❑ 116 Tony Horne .15 .07
❑ 117 Kurt Warner 2.00 .90
❑ 118 Jermaine Fazande .15 .07
❑ 119 Jeff Graham .15 .07
❑ 120 Jim Harbaugh .25 .11
❑ 121 Mikhael Ricks .15 .07
❑ 122 Junior Seau .25 .11
❑ 123 Jeff Garcia .50 .23
❑ 124 Charlie Garner .25 .11
❑ 125 Terrell Owens .50 .23
❑ 126 Jerry Rice 1.25 .55
❑ 127 J.J. Stokes .25 .11
❑ 128 Jon Kitna .50 .23
❑ 129 Derrick Mayes .25 .11
❑ 130 Charlie Rogers .15 .07
❑ 131 Shawn Springs .15 .07
❑ 132 Ricky Watters .25 .11
❑ 133 Mike Alstott .50 .23
❑ 134 Reidel Anthony .15 .07
❑ 135 Warrick Dunn .50 .23
❑ 136 Jacquez Green .25 .11
❑ 137 Shaun King .75 .35
❑ 138 Warren Sapp .25 .11
❑ 139 Kevin Dyson .25 .11
❑ 140 Eddie George .60 .25
❑ 141 Jevon Kearse .50 .23
❑ 142 Steve McNair .50 .23
❑ 143 Yancey Thigpen .15 .07
❑ 144 Frank Wycheck .15 .07
❑ 145 Champ Bailey .25 .11
❑ 146 Larry Centers .15 .07
❑ 147 Albert Connell .15 .07
❑ 148 Stephen Davis .50 .23
❑ 149 Brad Johnson .50 .23
❑ 150 Michael Westbrook .25 .11
❑ 151 Thomas Jones RC 20.00 9.00
❑ 152 Jay Tant RC 6.00 2.70
❑ 153 Doug Johnson RC 12.00 5.50
❑ 154 Mareno Philyaw RC 6.00 2.70
❑ 155 Jamal Lewis RC 60.00 27.00
❑ 156 Chris Redman RC 25.00 11.00
❑ 157 Travis Taylor RC 15.00 6.75
❑ 158 Kwame Cavil RC 10.00 4.50
❑ 159 Corey Moore RC 10.00 4.50
❑ 160 Deon Grant RC 6.00 2.70
❑ 161 Frank Murphy RC 6.00 2.70
❑ 162 Dez White RC 10.00 4.50
❑ 163 Ron Dugans RC 10.00 4.50
❑ 164 Tony Hartley RC 6.00 2.70
❑ 165 Curtis Keaton RC 10.00 4.50
❑ 166 Peter Warrick RC 40.00 18.00
❑ 167 Courtney Brown RC 15.00 6.75
❑ 168 JaJuan Dawson RC 12.00 5.50
❑ 169 Dennis Northcutt RC 15.00 6.75
❑ 170 Travis Prentice RC 20.00 9.00
❑ 171 Aaron Shea RC 10.00 4.50
❑ 172 Michael Wiley RC 12.00 5.50
❑ 173 Chris Cole RC 10.00 4.50
❑ 174 Jarious Jackson RC 12.00 5.50
❑ 175 Deltha O'Neal RC 10.00 4.50
❑ 176 Reuben Droughns RC 12.00 5.50
❑ 177 Bubba Franks RC 15.00 6.75
❑ 178 Anthony Lucas RC 6.00 2.70
❑ 179 Rondell Mealey RC 6.00 2.70
❑ 180 Ibn Green RC 6.00 2.70
❑ 181 Kevin McDougal RC 10.00 4.50
❑ 182 R.Jay Soward RC 12.00 5.50
❑ 183 Shyrone Stith RC 10.00 4.50
❑ 184 Dante Hall RC 10.00 4.50
❑ 185 Frank Moreau RC 12.00 5.50
❑ 186 Sylvester Morris RC 25.00 11.00
❑ 187 Deon Dyer RC 10.00 4.50
❑ 188 Ben Kelly RC 6.00 2.70
❑ 189 Quinton Spotwood RC 6.00 2.70
❑ 190 Troy Walters RC 12.00 5.50
❑ 191 Tom Brady RC 12.00 5.50
❑ 192 J.R. Redmond RC 15.00 6.75
❑ 193 David Stachelski RC 10.00 4.50
❑ 194 Marc Bulger RC 12.00 5.50
❑ 195 Sherrod Gideon RC 6.00 2.70
❑ 196 Chad Morton RC 12.00 5.50
❑ 197 Ron Dayne RC 40.00 18.00
❑ 198 Anthony Becht RC 12.00 5.50
❑ 199 Laveranues Coles RC 20.00 9.00
❑ 200 Chad Pennington RC 40.00 18.00
❑ 201 Sebastian Janikowski RC 12.00 5.50
❑ 202 Marcus Knight RC 6.00 2.70
❑ 203 Jerry Porter RC 12.00 5.50
❑ 204 Todd Pinkston RC 12.00 5.50
❑ 205 Gari Scott RC 10.00 4.50
❑ 206 Plaxico Burress RC 25.00 11.00
❑ 207 Danny Farmer RC 12.00 5.50
❑ 208 Tee Martin RC 20.00 9.00
❑ 209 Hank Poteat RC 10.00 4.50
❑ 210 Trung Canidate RC 12.00 5.50
❑ 211 Patrick Batteaux RC 6.00 2.70
❑ 212 Trevor Gaylor RC 10.00 4.50
❑ 213 Ronney Jenkins RC 10.00 4.50
❑ 214 Terrence McCaskey RC 6.00 2.70
❑ 215 JaJuan Seider RC 6.00 2.70
❑ 216 Giovanni Carmazzi RC 15.00 6.75
❑ 217 Chafie Fields RC 10.00 4.50
❑ 218 Jonas Lewis RC 10.00 4.50
❑ 219 Tim Rattay RC 20.00 9.00
❑ 220 Shaun Alexander RC 30.00 13.50
❑ 221 Darrell Jackson RC 20.00 9.00
❑ 222 James Williams RC 10.00 4.50
❑ 223 Joe Hamilton RC 15.00 6.75
❑ 224 Erron Kinney RC 12.00 5.50
❑ 225 Todd Husak RC 12.00 5.50
❑ 226 Plaxico Burress 10.00 4.50
Danny Farmer
❑ 227 Ron Dayne 15.00 6.75
Joe Hamilton
❑ 228 Peter Warrick 15.00 6.75
Ron Dugans
❑ 229 Thomas Jones 8.00 3.60
Curtis Keaton
❑ 230 Shaun Alexander 12.00 5.50
Reuben Droughns
❑ 231 Travis Taylor 8.00 3.60
Darrell Jackson
❑ 232 Giovanni Carmazzi 6.00 2.70
Tim Rattay
❑ 233 Trung Canidate 6.00 2.70
J.R. Redmond
❑ 234 Sylvester Morris 10.00 4.50
R.Jay Soward
❑ 235 Travis Prentice 8.00 3.60
Trevor Gaylor
❑ 236 Todd Pinkston 5.00 2.20
Sherrod Gideon
❑ 237 Frank Murphy 5.00 2.20
Dez White
❑ 238 Chris Redman 10.00 4.50
Tom Brady
❑ 239 Jamal Lewis 20.00 9.00
Tee Martin
❑ 240 Rondell Mealey 4.00 1.80
Shyrone Stith
❑ 241 Michael Wiley 5.00 2.20
Chad Morton
❑ 242 Laveranues Coles 6.00 2.70
Sebastian Janikowski
❑ 243 Troy Walters 5.00 2.20
Todd Husak
❑ 244 Marc Bulger 5.00 2.20
Jerry Porter
❑ 245 Mareno Philyaw 5.00 2.20
Doug Johnson
❑ 246 Dennis Northcutt 6.00 2.70
Courtney Brown
❑ 247 Jarious Jackson 5.00 2.20
Chris Cole
❑ 248 JaJuan Dawson 5.00 2.20
Gari Scott
❑ 249 Quinton Spotwood 2.50 1.10
Chafie Fields
❑ 250 Chad Pennington 15.00 6.75
James Williams

1997 Pacific Philadelphia

	MINT	NRMT
COMPLETE SET (330)	30.00	13.50
❑ 1 Kevin Butler	.10	.05
❑ 2 Larry Centers	.20	.09
❑ 3 Kent Graham	.10	.05
❑ 4 Leeland McElroy	.10	.05
❑ 5 Ronald McKinnon RC	.10	.05
❑ 6 Johnny McWilliams	.10	.05
❑ 7 Brad Otis	.10	.05
❑ 8 Frank Sanders	.20	.09
❑ 9 Rob Selby	.10	.05
❑ 10 Cedric Smith	.10	.05
❑ 11 Joe Staysniak	.10	.05
❑ 12 Cornelius Bennett	.10	.05
❑ 13 David Brandon	.10	.05
❑ 14 Tyrone Brown	.10	.05
❑ 15 John Burrough	.10	.05
❑ 16 Browning Nagle	.10	.05
❑ 17 Dan Owens	.10	.05
❑ 18 Anthony Phillips	.10	.05
❑ 19 Roell Preston	.10	.05
❑ 20 Darnell Walker	.10	.05
❑ 21 Bob Whitfield	.10	.05
❑ 22 Mike Zandofsky	.10	.05
❑ 23 Vashone Adams	.10	.05
❑ 24 Derrick Alexander WR	.20	.09
❑ 25 Harold Bishop	.10	.05
❑ 26 Jeff Blackshear	.10	.05
❑ 27 Donny Brady	.10	.05
❑ 28 Mike Frederick	.10	.05
❑ 29 Tim Goad	.10	.05
❑ 30 DeRon Jenkins	.10	.05
❑ 31 Ray Lewis	.50	.23
❑ 32 Rick Lyle	.10	.05
❑ 33 Byron Bam Morris	.10	.05
❑ 34 Chris Brantley	.10	.05
❑ 35 Jeff Burris	.10	.05
❑ 36 Todd Collins	.10	.05
❑ 37 Rob Coons	.10	.05
❑ 38 Corbin Lacina	.10	.05
❑ 39 Emanuel Martin	.10	.05
❑ 40 Marlo Perry	.10	.05
❑ 41 Shawn Price	.10	.05
❑ 42 Thomas Smith	.10	.05
❑ 43 Matt Stevens	.10	.05
❑ 44 Thurman Thomas	.40	.18
❑ 45 Jay Barker	.10	.05
❑ 46 Tim Biakabutuka	.20	.09
❑ 47 Kerry Collins	.20	.09
❑ 48 Matt Elliott	.10	.05
❑ 49 Howard Griffith	.10	.05
❑ 50 Anthony Johnson	.10	.05
❑ 51 John Kasay	.10	.05
❑ 52 Muhsin Muhammad	.20	.09
❑ 53 Winslow Oliver	.10	.05
❑ 54 Walter Rasby	.10	.05
❑ 55 Gerald Williams	.10	.05
❑ 56 Mark Butterfield	.10	.05
❑ 57 Bryan Cox	.10	.05
❑ 58 Mike Faulkerson	.10	.05
❑ 59 Paul Grasmanis	.10	.05
❑ 60 Robert Green	.10	.05
❑ 61 Jack Jackson	.10	.05
❑ 62 Bobby Neely	.10	.05
❑ 63 Todd Perry	.10	.05
❑ 64 Evan Pilgrim	.10	.05
❑ 65 Octus Polk	.10	.05
❑ 66 Rashaan Salaam	.10	.05
❑ 67 Willie Anderson	.10	.05
❑ 68 Jeff Blake	.20	.09
❑ 69 Scott Brumfield	.10	.05
❑ 70 Jeff Cothran	.10	.05
❑ 71 Gerald Dixon	.10	.05
❑ 72 Garrison Hearst	.20	.09
❑ 73 James Hundon RC	.40	.18
❑ 74 Brian Milne	.10	.05
❑ 75 Troy Sadowski	.10	.05
❑ 76 Tom Tumulty	.10	.05
❑ 77 Kimo von Oelhoffen	.10	.05
❑ 78 Troy Aikman	1.00	.45
❑ 79 Dale Hellestrae	.10	.05
❑ 80 Roger Harper	.10	.05
❑ 81 Michael Irvin	.40	.18
❑ 82 John Jett	.10	.05
❑ 83 Kelvin Martin	.10	.05
❑ 84 Deion Sanders	.40	.18
❑ 85 Darrin Smith	.10	.05
❑ 86 Emmitt Smith	1.50	.70
❑ 87 Herschel Walker	.20	.09
❑ 88 Charlie Williams	.10	.05
❑ 89 Glenn Cadrez	.10	.05
❑ 90 Dwayne Carswell RC	.40	.18
❑ 91 Terrell Davis	1.50	.70
❑ 92 David Diaz-infante	.10	.05
❑ 93 John Elway	2.00	.90
❑ 94 Harald Hasselbach	.10	.05
❑ 95 Tory James	.10	.05
❑ 96 Bill Musgrave	.10	.05
❑ 97 Ralph Tamm	.10	.05
❑ 98 Maa Tanuvasa RC	.10	.05
❑ 99 Gary Zimmerman	.10	.05
❑ 100 Shane Bonham	.10	.05
❑ 101 Stephen Boyd	.10	.05
❑ 102 Jeff Hartings RC	.10	.05
❑ 103 Hessley Hempstead	.10	.05
❑ 104 Scott Kowalkowski	.10	.05
❑ 105 Herman Moore	.40	.18
❑ 106 Barry Sanders	2.00	.90
❑ 107 Tony Semple	.10	.05
❑ 108 Ryan Stewart	.10	.05
❑ 109 Mike Wells	.10	.05
❑ 110 Richard Woodley	.10	.05
❑ 111 Brett Favre	2.00	.90
❑ 112 Bernardo Harris	.10	.05
❑ 113 Keith McKenzie	.10	.05
❑ 114 Terry Mickens	.10	.05
❑ 115 Doug Pederson RC	.50	.23
❑ 116 Jeff Thomason RC	.10	.05
❑ 117 Adam Timmerman	.10	.05
❑ 118 Reggie White	.40	.18
❑ 119 Bruce Wilkerson	.10	.05
❑ 120 Gabe Wilkins RC	.10	.05
❑ 121 Tyrone Williams RC	.10	.05
❑ 122 Al Del Greco	.10	.05
❑ 123 Anthony Dorsett	.10	.05
❑ 124 Josh Evans	.10	.05
❑ 125 Eddie George	1.00	.45
❑ 126 Lemanski Hall	.10	.05
❑ 127 Ronnie Harmon	.10	.05
❑ 128 Steve McNair	.60	.25
❑ 129 Michael Roan	.10	.05
❑ 130 Marcus Robertson	.10	.05
❑ 131 Jon Runyan	.10	.05
❑ 132 Chris Sanders	.10	.05
❑ 133 Kerwin Bell	.10	.05
❑ 134 Marshall Faulk	.40	.18
❑ 135 Clif Groce	.10	.05
❑ 136 Jim Harbaugh	.20	.09
❑ 137 Marvin Harrison	.40	.18
❑ 138 Eric Mahlum	.10	.05
❑ 139 Tony Mandarich	.10	.05
❑ 140 Dedric Mathis	.10	.05
❑ 141 Marcus Pollard	.10	.05
❑ 142 Scott Slutzker	.10	.05
❑ 143 Mark Stock	.10	.05
❑ 144 Bucky Brooks	.10	.05
❑ 145 Mark Brunell	1.00	.45
❑ 146 Kendricke Bullard	.10	.05
❑ 147 Randy Jordan	.10	.05
❑ 148 Jeff Kopp	.10	.05
❑ 149 Le'Shai Maston	.10	.05
❑ 150 Keenan McCardell	.20	.09
❑ 151 Clyde Simmons	.10	.05
❑ 152 Jimmy Smith	.20	.09
❑ 153 Rich Tylski	.10	.05
❑ 154 Dave Widell	.10	.05
❑ 155 Marcus Allen	.40	.18
❑ 156 Keith Cash	.10	.05
❑ 157 Donnie Edwards	.10	.05
❑ 158 Trezelle Jenkins	.10	.05
❑ 159 Sean LaChapelle	.10	.05
❑ 160 Greg Manusky	.10	.05
❑ 161 Steve Matthews	.10	.05
❑ 162 Pellom McDaniels	.10	.05
❑ 163 Chris Penn	.10	.05
❑ 164 Danny Villa	.10	.05
❑ 165 Jerome Woods	.10	.05
❑ 166 Karim Abdul-Jabbar	.40	.18
❑ 167 John Bock	.10	.05
❑ 168 O.J. Brigance	.10	.05
❑ 169 Norman Hand	.10	.05
❑ 170 Anthony Harris	.10	.05
❑ 171 Larry Izzo	.10	.05
❑ 172 Charles Jordan	.10	.05
❑ 173 Dan Marino	2.00	.90
❑ 174 Everett McIver	.10	.05
❑ 175 Joe Nedney	.10	.05
❑ 176 Robert Wilson RC	.10	.05
❑ 177 David Dixon	.10	.05
❑ 178 Charles Evans	.10	.05
❑ 179 Hunter Goodwin RC	.10	.05
❑ 180 Ben Hanks	.10	.05
❑ 181 Warren Moon	.40	.18
❑ 182 Harold Morrow	.10	.05
❑ 183 Fernando Smith	.10	.05
❑ 184 Robert Smith	.20	.09
❑ 185 Sean Vanhorse	.10	.05
❑ 186 Jay Walker	.10	.05
❑ 187 Dewayne Washington	.10	.05
❑ 188 Moe Williams	.10	.05
❑ 189 Mike Bartrum	.10	.05
❑ 190 Drew Bledsoe	1.00	.45
❑ 191 Troy Brown	.10	.05
❑ 192 Chad Eaton	.10	.05
❑ 193 Sam Gash	.10	.05
❑ 194 Mike Gisler	.10	.05
❑ 195 Curtis Martin	.60	.25
❑ 196 David Richards	.10	.05
❑ 197 Todd Rucci	.10	.05
❑ 198 Chris Sullivan	.10	.05
❑ 199 Adam Vinatieri	.10	.05
❑ 200 Doug Brien	.10	.05
❑ 201 Derek Brown RBK	.10	.05
❑ 202 Lee DeRamus	.10	.05
❑ 203 Jim Everett	.10	.05
❑ 204 Mercury Hayes	.10	.05
❑ 205 Joe Johnson	.10	.05
❑ 206 Henry Lusk RC	.10	.05
❑ 207 Andy McCollum	.10	.05
❑ 208 Alex Molden	.10	.05
❑ 209 Ray Zellars	.10	.05
❑ 210 Marcus Buckley	.10	.05
❑ 211 Doug Coleman RC	.10	.05
❑ 212 Percy Ellsworth	.10	.05
❑ 213 Rodney Hampton	.20	.09
❑ 214 Brian Saxton	.10	.05
❑ 215 Jason Sehorn	.20	.09
❑ 216 Stan White	.10	.05
❑ 217 Corey Widmer	.10	.05
❑ 218 Rodney Young	.10	.05
❑ 219 Rob Zatechka	.10	.05
❑ 220 Henry Bailey	.10	.05
❑ 221 Chad Cascadden RC	.10	.05
❑ 222 Wayne Chrebet	.40	.18
❑ 223 Tyrone Davis	.10	.05
❑ 224 Kwame Ellis	.10	.05
❑ 225 Glenn Foley	.20	.09
❑ 226 Erik Howard	.10	.05
❑ 227 Gary Jones	.10	.05
❑ 228 Adrian Murrell	.20	.09
❑ 229 Marc Spindler	.10	.05
❑ 230 Lonnie Young	.10	.05
❑ 231 Eric Zomalt	.10	.05
❑ 232 Tim Brown	.40	.18
❑ 233 Aundray Bruce	.10	.05
❑ 234 Darren Carrington	.10	.05

❑ 235 Rick Cunningham .10 .05
❑ 236 Rob Hornberg .10 .05
❑ 237 Jeff Hostetler .10 .05
❑ 238 Lorenzo Lynch .10 .05
❑ 239 Barrett Robbins .10 .05
❑ 240 Dan Turk .10 .05
❑ 241 Harvey Williams .10 .05
❑ 242 Brian Dawkins .10 .05
❑ 243 Ty Detmer .20 .09
❑ 244 Troy Drake .10 .05
❑ 245 Rhett Hall .10 .05
❑ 246 Joe Panos .10 .05
❑ 247 Johnny Thomas .10 .05
❑ 248 Kevin Turner .10 .05
❑ 249 Ricky Watters .20 .09
❑ 250 Derrick Witherspoon RC .10 .05
❑ 251 Sylvester Wright .10 .05
❑ 252 Jerome Bettis .40 .18
❑ 253 Carlos Emmons RC .10 .05
❑ 254 Jason Gildon .10 .05
❑ 255 Jonathan Hayes .10 .05
❑ 256 Kevin Henry .10 .05
❑ 257 Jerry Olsavsky .10 .05
❑ 258 Erric Pegram .10 .05
❑ 259 Brendan Stai .10 .05
❑ 260 Justin Strzelczyk .10 .05
❑ 261 Mike Tomczak .10 .05
❑ 262 Tony Banks .20 .09
❑ 263 Hayward Clay .10 .05
❑ 264 Percell Gaskins .10 .05
❑ 265 Eddie Kennison .20 .09
❑ 266 Aaron Laing .10 .05
❑ 267 Keith Lyle .10 .05
❑ 268 Jamie Martin .20 .09
❑ 269 Lawrence Phillips .10 .05
❑ 270 Zach Wiegert .10 .05
❑ 271 Toby Wright .10 .05
❑ 272 Darren Bennett .10 .05
❑ 273 Tony Berti .10 .05
❑ 274 Freddie Bradley .10 .05
❑ 275 Joe Cocozzo .10 .05
❑ 276 Andre Coleman .10 .05
❑ 277 Marco Coleman .10 .05
❑ 278 Rodney Harrison .10 .05
❑ 279 David Hendrix .10 .05
❑ 280 Leonard Russell .10 .05
❑ 281 Sean Salisbury .10 .05
❑ 282 Dennis Brown .10 .05
❑ 283 Chris Dalman .10 .05
❑ 284 Brent Jones .20 .09
❑ 285 Sean Manuel .10 .05
❑ 286 Marquez Pope .10 .05
❑ 287 Jerry Rice 1.00 .45
❑ 288 Kirk Scrafford .10 .05
❑ 289 Iheanyi Uwaezuoke .20 .09
❑ 290 Tommy Vardell .10 .05
❑ 291 Steve Young .60 .25
❑ 292 James Atkins .10 .05
❑ 293 T.J. Cunningham .10 .05
❑ 294 Stan Gelbaugh .10 .05
❑ 295 James Logan .10 .05
❑ 296 James McKnight RC 2.50 1.10
❑ 297 Rick Mirer .10 .05
❑ 298 Todd Peterson .10 .05
❑ 299 Fred Thomas .10 .05
❑ 300 Rick Tuten .10 .05
❑ 301 Chris Warren .20 .09
❑ 302 Donnie Abraham RC .40 .18
❑ 303 Trent Dilfer .40 .18
❑ 304 Kenneth Gant .10 .05
❑ 305 Jeff Gooch .20 .09
❑ 306 Courtney Hawkins .10 .05
❑ 307 Tyoka Jackson .10 .05
❑ 308 Melvin Johnson RC .10 .05
❑ 309 Lonnie Marts .10 .05
❑ 310 Hardy Nickerson .10 .05
❑ 311 Errict Rhett .10 .05
❑ 312 Terry Allen .40 .18
❑ 313 Flipper Anderson .10 .05
❑ 314 William Bell .10 .05
❑ 315 Scott Blanton .10 .05
❑ 316 Leomont Evans .10 .05
❑ 317 Gus Frerotte .10 .05
❑ 318 Darryl Morrison .10 .05
❑ 319 Matt Turk .10 .05
❑ 320 Jeff Uhlenhake .10 .05
❑ 321 Bryan Walker .10 .05
❑ 322 Mark Brunell LL .50 .23
❑ 323 Barry Sanders LL 1.00 .45
❑ 324 Isaac Bruce LL .40 .18
❑ 325 Terry Allen LL .20 .09
❑ 326 Steve Young LL .40 .18
❑ 327 Jerry Rice LL .50 .23
❑ 328 Ricky Watters LL .20 .09
❑ 329 Kevin Greene LL .10 .05
❑ 330 Brett Favre LL 1.00 .45
❑ S1 Mark Brunell Promo 2.00 .90
(Marked "Sample" on back)

1993 Pacific Prisms

	MINT	NRMT
COMPLETE SET (109)	50.00	22.00

❑ 1 Chris Miller .75 .35
❑ 2 Mike Pritchard .75 .35
❑ 3 Andre Rison .75 .35
❑ 4 Deion Sanders 2.50 1.10
❑ 5 Tony Smith .40 .18
❑ 6 Jim Kelly 1.50 .70
❑ 7 Andre Reed .75 .35
❑ 8 Thurman Thomas 1.50 .70
❑ 9 Neal Anderson .40 .18
❑ 10 Jim Harbaugh 1.50 .70
❑ 11 Donnell Woolford .40 .18
❑ 12 David Klingler .40 .18
❑ 13 Carl Pickens 1.50 .70
❑ 14 Alfred Williams .40 .18
❑ 15 Michael Jackson .75 .35
❑ 16 Bernie Kosar .75 .35
❑ 17 Tommy Vardell .40 .18
❑ 18 Troy Aikman 4.00 1.80
❑ 19 Alvin Harper .75 .35
❑ 20 Michael Irvin 1.50 .70
❑ 21 Russell Maryland .40 .18
❑ 22 Emmitt Smith 8.00 3.60
❑ 23 John Elway 8.00 3.60
❑ 24 Tommy Maddox .40 .18
❑ 25 Shannon Sharpe 1.50 .70
❑ 26 Herman Moore 3.00 1.35
❑ 27 Rodney Peete .40 .18
❑ 28 Barry Sanders 8.00 3.60
❑ 29 Pat Swilling .40 .18
❑ 30 Terrell Buckley .40 .18
❑ 31 Brett Favre 10.00 4.50
❑ 32 Sterling Sharpe 1.50 .70
❑ 33 Reggie White 1.50 .70
❑ 34 Ernest Givins .75 .35
❑ 35 Haywood Jeffires .75 .35
❑ 36 Warren Moon 1.50 .70
❑ 37 Lorenzo White .40 .18
❑ 38 Steve Emtman .40 .18
❑ 39 Jeff George 1.50 .70
❑ 40 Reggie Langhorne .40 .18
❑ 41 Dale Carter .40 .18
❑ 42 Joe Montana 8.00 3.60
❑ 43 Derrick Thomas 1.50 .70
❑ 44 Barry Word .40 .18
❑ 45 Nick Bell .40 .18
❑ 46 Eric Dickerson .75 .35
❑ 47 Jeff Jaeger .40 .18
❑ 48 Jerome Bettis RC 3.00 1.35
❑ 49 Henry Ellard .75 .35
❑ 50 Jim Everett .75 .35
❑ 51 Cleveland Gary .40 .18
❑ 52 Marco Coleman .40 .18
❑ 53 Mark Higgs .40 .18
❑ 54 Keith Jackson .75 .35
❑ 55 Dan Marino 8.00 3.60
❑ 56 Troy Vincent .40 .18
❑ 57 Terry Allen 1.50 .70
❑ 58 Jack Del Rio .40 .18
❑ 59 Sean Salisbury .40 .18
❑ 60 Robert Smith RC 6.00 2.70
❑ 61 Drew Bledsoe RC 8.00 3.60
❑ 62 Marv Cook .40 .18
❑ 63 Irving Fryar .75 .35
❑ 64 Leonard Russell .75 .35
❑ 65 Andre Tippett .40 .18
❑ 66 Morten Andersen .40 .18
❑ 67 Vaughn Dunbar .40 .18
❑ 68 Eric Martin .40 .18
❑ 69 David Brown RC 1.50 .70
❑ 70 Rodney Hampton 1.50 .70
❑ 71 Phil Simms .75 .35
❑ 72 Lawrence Taylor 1.50 .70
❑ 73 Ronnie Lott .75 .35
❑ 74 Johnny Mitchell .40 .18
❑ 75 Rob Moore .75 .35
❑ 76 Browning Nagle .40 .18
❑ 77 Fred Barnett .75 .35
❑ 78 Randall Cunningham 1.50 .70
❑ 79 Herschel Walker .75 .35
❑ 80 Gary Clark .75 .35
❑ 81 Ken Harvey .40 .18
❑ 82 Garrison Hearst RC 2.50 1.10
❑ 83 Ricky Proehl .40 .18
❑ 84 Barry Foster .75 .35
❑ 85 Ernie Mills .40 .18
❑ 86 Neil O'Donnell 1.50 .70
❑ 87 Stan Humphries 1.50 .70
❑ 88 Leslie O'Neal .75 .35
❑ 89 Junior Seau 1.50 .70
❑ 90 Amp Lee .40 .18
❑ 91 Jerry Rice 5.00 2.20
❑ 92 Ricky Watters 1.50 .70
❑ 93 Steve Young 4.00 1.80
❑ 94 Cortez Kennedy .75 .35
❑ 95 Rick Mirer RC 2.00 .90
❑ 96 Eugene Robinson .40 .18
❑ 97 Chris Warren .75 .35
❑ 98 John L. Williams .40 .18
❑ 99 Reggie Cobb .40 .18
❑ 100 Lawrence Dawsey .40 .18
❑ 101 Santana Dotson .75 .35
❑ 102 Courtney Hawkins .40 .18
❑ 103 Reggie Brooks RC .75 .35
❑ 104 Ricky Ervins .40 .18
❑ 105 Desmond Howard .75 .35
❑ 106 Art Monk .75 .35
❑ 107 Mark Rypien .40 .18
❑ 108 Ricky Sanders .40 .18
❑ NNO Checklist Card .40 .18
❑ P22 Emmitt Smith Promo 10.00 4.50
❑ P61 Drew Bledsoe Promo 4.00 1.80

1994 Pacific Prisms

	MINT	NRMT
COMPLETE SET (128)	60.00	27.00

❑ 1 Troy Aikman UER 4.00 1.80

(Text on back indicates he led Cowboys to victory in Super Bowl XXV. The Giants won SB XXV)

❑ 2 Marcus Allen 1.25 .55
❑ 3 Morten Andersen .40 .18
❑ 4 Fred Barnett .75 .35
❑ 5 Mario Bates RC 1.25 .55
❑ 6 Edgar Bennett 1.25 .55
❑ 7 Rod Bernstine .40 .18
❑ 8 Jerome Bettis 1.25 .55
❑ 9 Steve Beuerlein .40 .18
❑ 10 Brian Blades .75 .35
❑ 11 Drew Bledsoe 4.00 1.80
❑ 12 Vincent Brisby .75 .35
❑ 13 Reggie Brooks .75 .35
❑ 14 Derek Brown RBK .40 .18
❑ 15 Gary Brown .40 .18
❑ 16 Tim Brown .75 .35
❑ 17 Marion Butts .40 .18
❑ 18 Keith Byars .40 .18
❑ 19 Cody Carlson .40 .18
❑ 20 Anthony Carter .75 .35
❑ 21 Tom Carter .40 .18
❑ 22 Gary Clark .75 .35
❑ 23 Ben Coates 1.25 .55
❑ 24 Reggie Cobb .40 .18
❑ 25 Curtis Conway .75 .35
❑ 26 John Copeland .40 .18
❑ 27 Randall Cunningham 1.25 .55
❑ 28 Willie Davis .75 .35
❑ 29 Sean Dawkins RC 1.25 .55
❑ 30 Lawrence Dawsey .40 .18
❑ 31 Richard Dent .75 .35
❑ 32 Trent Dilfer RC 5.00 2.20
❑ 33 Troy Drayton .40 .18
❑ 34 Vaughn Dunbar .40 .18
❑ 35 Henry Ellard .75 .35
❑ 36 John Elway 8.00 3.60
❑ 37 Craig Erickson .40 .18
❑ 38 Boomer Esiason .75 .35
❑ 39 Marshall Faulk RC 10.00 4.50
❑ 40 Brett Favre 8.00 3.60
❑ 41 William Floyd RC 1.25 .55
❑ 42 Glenn Foley RC 1.25 .55
❑ 43 Barry Foster .40 .18
❑ 44 Irving Fryar .75 .35
❑ 45 Jeff George 1.25 .55
❑ 46 Scottie Graham RC .75 .35
❑ 47 Rodney Hampton .75 .35
❑ 48 Jim Harbaugh 1.25 .55
❑ 49 Alvin Harper .75 .35
❑ 50 Courtney Hawkins .40 .18
❑ 51 Garrison Hearst 1.25 .55
❑ 52 Vaughn Hebron .40 .18
❑ 53 Greg Hill RC 1.25 .55
❑ 54 Jeff Hostetler .75 .35
❑ 55 Michael Irvin 1.25 .55
❑ 56 Qadry Ismail .75 .35
❑ 57 Rocket Ismail .75 .35
❑ 58 Anthony Johnson .75 .35
❑ 59 Charles Johnson RC 2.00 .90
❑ 60 Johnny Johnson .40 .18
❑ 61 Brent Jones .75 .35
❑ 62 Kyle Clifton .40 .18
❑ 63 Jim Kelly .75 .35
❑ 64 Cortez Kennedy .75 .35
❑ 65 Terry Kirby 1.25 .55
❑ 66 David Klingler .40 .18
❑ 67 Erik Kramer .75 .35
❑ 68 Reggie Langhorne .40 .18
❑ 69 Chuck Levy RC .40 .18
❑ 70 Dan Marino 8.00 3.60
❑ 71 O.J. McDuffie 1.25 .55
❑ 72 Natrone Means 1.25 .55
❑ 73 Eric Metcalf .75 .35
❑ 74 Glyn Milburn .75 .35
❑ 75 Anthony Miller .75 .35
❑ 76 Rick Mirer 1.25 .55
❑ 77 Johnny Mitchell .40 .18
❑ 78 Scott Mitchell 1.25 .55
❑ 79 Joe Montana 8.00 3.60
❑ 80 Warren Moon .75 .35
❑ 81 Derrick Moore .40 .18
❑ 82 Herman Moore 1.25 .55
❑ 83 Rob Moore .75 .35
❑ 84 Ronald Moore .40 .18
❑ 85 Johnnie Morton RC 4.00 1.80
❑ 86 Neil O'Donnell .75 .35
❑ 87 David Palmer RC 2.00 .90
❑ 88 Erric Pegram .40 .18
❑ 89 Carl Pickens 1.25 .55
❑ 90 Anthony Pleasant .40 .18
❑ 91 Roosevelt Potts .40 .18
❑ 92 Mike Pritchard .40 .18
❑ 93 Andre Reed .75 .35
❑ 94 Errict Rhett RC 2.50 1.10
❑ 95 Jerry Rice 4.00 1.80
❑ 96 Andre Rison .75 .35
❑ 97 Greg Robinson .40 .18
❑ 98 T.J. Rubley RC .40 .18
❑ 99 Leonard Russell .40 .18
❑ 100 Barry Sanders 8.00 3.60
❑ 101 Deion Sanders 2.50 1.10
❑ 102 Ricky Sanders .40 .18
❑ 103 Junior Seau .75 .35
❑ 104 Shannon Sharpe .75 .35
❑ 105 Sterling Sharpe .75 .35
❑ 106 Heath Shuler RC 1.25 .55
❑ 107 Phil Simms .75 .35
❑ 108 Webster Slaughter .40 .18
❑ 109 Bruce Smith 1.25 .55
❑ 110 Emmitt Smith 8.00 3.60
❑ 111 Irv Smith .40 .18
❑ 112 Robert Smith 1.25 .55
❑ 113 Vinny Testaverde .75 .35
❑ 114 Derrick Thomas .75 .35
❑ 115 Thurman Thomas .75 .35
❑ 116 Leroy Thompson .40 .18
❑ 117 Lewis Tillman .40 .18
❑ 118 Michael Timpson .40 .18
❑ 119 Herschel Walker .75 .35
❑ 120 Chris Warren .75 .35
❑ 121 Ricky Watters 1.25 .55
❑ 122 Lorenzo White .40 .18
❑ 123 Reggie White 1.25 .55
❑ 124 Dan Wilkinson RC .75 .35
❑ 125 Kevin Williams .75 .35
❑ 126 Steve Young 3.00 1.35
❑ CL1 Checklist 1 .30 .14
❑ CL2 Checklist 2 .30 .14
❑ S1 Sterling Sharpe Promo 1.00 .45
(Numbered S-1)

1995 Pacific Prisms

		MINT	NRMT
COMPLETE SET (216)		80.00	36.00
COMP.SERIES 1 (108)		50.00	22.00
COMP.SERIES 2 (108)		50.00	22.00

❑ 1 Chuck Levy .25 .11
❑ 2 Ronald Moore .25 .11
❑ 3 Jay Schroeder .25 .11
❑ 4 Bert Emanuel 1.00 .45
❑ 5 Terance Mathis .50 .23
❑ 6 Andre Rison .50 .23
❑ 7 Bucky Brooks .25 .11
❑ 8 Jeff Burris .25 .11
❑ 9 Jim Kelly 1.00 .45
❑ 10 Lewis Tillman .25 .11
❑ 11 Steve Walsh .25 .11
❑ 12 Chris Zorich .25 .11
❑ 13 Jeff Blake RC 3.00 1.35
❑ 14 Steve Broussard .25 .11
❑ 15 Jeff Cothran .25 .11
❑ 16 Earnset Byner .25 .11
❑ 17 Leroy Hoard .25 .11
❑ 18 Vinny Testaverde .50 .23
❑ 19 Troy Aikman 3.00 1.35
❑ 20 Alvin Harper .25 .11
❑ 21 Leon Lett .25 .11
❑ 22 Jay Novacek .50 .23
❑ 23 John Elway 6.00 2.70
❑ 24 Karl Mecklenburg .25 .11
❑ 25 Leonard Russell .25 .11
❑ 26 Mel Gray .25 .11
❑ 27 Dave Krieg .25 .11
❑ 28 Barry Sanders 6.00 2.70
❑ 29 Chris Spielman .50 .23
❑ 30 Robert Brooks 1.00 .45
❑ 31 LeShon Johnson .50 .23
❑ 32 Sterling Sharpe .50 .23
❑ 33 Ernest Givins .25 .11
❑ 34 Billy Joe Tolliver .25 .11
❑ 35 Lorenzo White .25 .11
❑ 36 Charles Arbuckle .25 .11
❑ 37 Sean Dawkins .50 .23
❑ 38 Marshall Faulk 1.50 .70
❑ 39 Marcus Allen 1.00 .45
❑ 40 Donnell Bennett .50 .23
❑ 41 Matt Blundin RC .25 .11
❑ 42 Greg Hill .50 .23
❑ 43 Tim Brown 1.00 .45
❑ 44 Billy Joe Hobert .50 .23
❑ 45 Rocket Ismail .50 .23
❑ 46 James Jett .50 .23
❑ 47 Tim Bowens .25 .11
❑ 48 Irving Fryar .50 .23
❑ 49 O.J. McDuffie 1.00 .45
❑ 50 Irving Spikes .50 .23
❑ 51 Terry Allen .50 .23
❑ 52 Cris Carter 1.00 .45
❑ 53 Amp Lee .25 .11
❑ 54 Drew Bledsoe 3.00 1.35
❑ 55 Willie McGinest .50 .23
❑ 56 Leroy Thompson .25 .11
❑ 57 Michael Timpson .25 .11
❑ 58 Michael Haynes .50 .23
❑ 59 Derrell Mitchell RC .25 .11
❑ 60 Dave Brown .50 .23
❑ 61 Thomas Lewis .50 .23
❑ 62 Dave Meggett .25 .11
❑ 63 Boomer Esiason .50 .23
❑ 64 Aaron Glenn .25 .11
❑ 65 Ronnie Lott .50 .23
❑ 66 Randall Cunningham 1.00 .45
❑ 67 Charlie Garner .50 .23
❑ 68 Herschel Walker .50 .23
❑ 69 Barry Foster .50 .23
❑ 70 Charles Johnson .50 .23
❑ 71 Jim Miller RC 2.00 .90
❑ 72 Rod Woodson .50 .23
❑ 73 Andre Coleman .25 .11
❑ 74 Natrone Means 1.00 .45
❑ 75 Shannon Mitchell RC .25 .11
❑ 76 Junior Seau 1.00 .45
❑ 77 Elvis Grbac 1.00 .45
❑ 78 Deion Sanders 2.00 .90
❑ 79 Adam Walker RC .25 .11
❑ 80 Ricky Watters 1.00 .45
❑ 81 Michael Bates .25 .11
❑ 82 Brian Blades .50 .23
❑ 83 Eugene Robinson .25 .11
❑ 84 Chris Warren .50 .23
❑ 85 Jerome Bettis 1.00 .45
❑ 86 Troy Drayton .25 .11
❑ 87 Chris Miller .25 .11
❑ 88 Trent Dilfer 1.00 .45
❑ 89 Hardy Nickerson .25 .11
❑ 90 Errict Rhett 1.00 .45
❑ 91 Henry Ellard .50 .23
❑ 92 Gus Frerotte 1.00 .45
❑ 93 Ricky Ervins .25 .11
❑ 94 Dave Barr RC .25 .11
❑ 95 Kyle Brady RC 1.00 .45
❑ 96 Mark Bruener RC .50 .23
❑ 97 Ki-Jana Carter RC 1.00 .45
❑ 98 Kerry Collins RC 5.00 2.20
❑ 99 Joey Galloway RC 8.00 3.60
❑ 100 Napoleon Kaufman RC 5.00 2.20

Card	MINT	NRMT
❑ 101 Steve McNair RC	10.00	4.50
❑ 102 Craig Newsome RC	.25	.11
❑ 103 Rashaan Salaam RC	1.00	.45
❑ 104 Kordell Stewart RC	8.00	3.60
❑ 105 J.J. Stokes RC	1.00	.45
❑ 106 Rodney Thomas RC	1.00	.45
❑ 107 Michael Westbrook RC	5.00	2.20
❑ 108 Tyrone Wheatley RC	4.00	1.80
❑ 109 Larry Centers	.50	.23
❑ 110 Garrison Hearst	1.00	.45
❑ 111 Jamir Miller	.25	.11
❑ 112 Jeff George	.50	.23
❑ 113 Craig Heyward	.50	.23
❑ 114 Cornelius Bennett	.50	.23
❑ 115 Andre Reed	.50	.23
❑ 116 Randy Baldwin	.25	.11
❑ 117 Tommy Barnhardt	.25	.11
❑ 118 Sam Mills	.50	.23
❑ 119 Brian O'Neal	.25	.11
❑ 120 Frank Reich	.25	.11
❑ 121 Tony Smith	.25	.11
❑ 122 Lawyer Tillman	.25	.11
❑ 123 Jack Trudeau	.25	.11
❑ 124 Vernon Turner	.25	.11
❑ 125 Curtis Conway	1.00	.45
❑ 126 Erik Kramer	.25	.11
❑ 127 Nate Lewis	.25	.11
❑ 128 Carl Pickens	1.00	.45
❑ 129 Darnay Scott	1.00	.45
❑ 130 Dan Wilkinson	.50	.23
❑ 131 Derrick Alexander WR	1.00	.45
❑ 132 Carl Banks	.25	.11
❑ 133 Michael Irvin	1.00	.45
❑ 134 Emmitt Smith	5.00	2.20
❑ 135 Kevin Williams WR	.50	.23
❑ 136 Glyn Milburn	.25	.11
❑ 137 Anthony Miller	.50	.23
❑ 138 Shannon Sharpe	.50	.23
❑ 139 Scott Mitchell	.50	.23
❑ 140 Herman Moore	1.00	.45
❑ 141 Edgar Bennett	.50	.23
❑ 142 Brett Favre	6.00	2.70
❑ 143 Reggie White	1.00	.45
❑ 144 Gary Brown	.25	.11
❑ 145 Haywood Jeffires	.25	.11
❑ 146 Webster Slaughter	.25	.11
❑ 147 Craig Erickson	.25	.11
❑ 148 Paul Justin	.25	.11
❑ 149 Lamont Warren	.25	.11
❑ 150 Steve Beuerlein	.25	.11
❑ 151 Derek Brown TE	.25	.11
❑ 152 Mark Brunell	3.00	1.35
❑ 153 Reggie Cobb	.25	.11
❑ 154 Desmond Howard	.50	.23
❑ 155 Kelvin Pritchett	.25	.11
❑ 156 James O. Stewart RC	8.00	3.60
❑ 157 Cedric Tillman	.25	.11
❑ 158 Kimble Anders	.50	.23
❑ 159 Lake Dawson	.50	.23
❑ 160 Keith Byars	.25	.11
❑ 161 Dan Marino	6.00	2.70
❑ 162 Bernie Parmalee	.50	.23
❑ 163 Qadry Ismail	.50	.23
❑ 164 Warren Moon	.50	.23
❑ 165 Jake Reed	.50	.23
❑ 166 Marion Butts	.25	.11
❑ 167 Ben Coates	.50	.23
❑ 168 Mario Bates	1.00	.45
❑ 169 Quinn Early	.50	.23
❑ 170 Jim Everett	.25	.11
❑ 171 Rodney Hampton	.50	.23
❑ 172 Mike Horan	.25	.11
❑ 173 Mike Sherrard	.25	.11
❑ 174 Johnny Johnson	.25	.11
❑ 175 Adrian Murrell	1.00	.45
❑ 176 Andrew Glover RC	.25	.11
❑ 177 Jeff Hostetler	.50	.23
❑ 178 Harvey Williams	.25	.11
❑ 179 Fred Barnett	.50	.23
❑ 180 Vaughn Hebron	.25	.11
❑ 181 Jeff Sydner	.25	.11
❑ 182 Kevin Greene	.50	.23
❑ 183 Byron Bam Morris	.50	.23
❑ 184 Neil O'Donnell	.50	.23
❑ 185 Stan Humphries	.50	.23
❑ 186 Tony Martin	.50	.23
❑ 187 Mark Seay	.50	.23
❑ 188 William Floyd	1.00	.45
❑ 189 Rickey Jackson	.25	.11
❑ 190 Jerry Rice	3.00	1.35
❑ 191 Steve Young	2.50	1.10
❑ 192 Cortez Kennedy	.50	.23
❑ 193 Rick Mirer	1.00	.45
❑ 194 Jessie Hester	.25	.11
❑ 195 Curtis Martin RC	10.00	4.50
❑ 196 Horace Copeland	.25	.11
❑ 197 Charles Wilson	.25	.11
❑ 198 Reggie Brooks	.50	.23
❑ 199 Brian Mitchell	.25	.11
❑ 200 Heath Shuler	1.00	.45
❑ 201 Justin Armour RC	.25	.11
❑ 202 Jay Barker RC	.25	.11
❑ 203 Zack Crockett RC	.25	.11
❑ 204 Christian Fauria RC	.25	.11
❑ 205 Antonio Freeman RC	10.00	4.50
❑ 206 Chad May RC	.25	.11
❑ 207 Frank Sanders RC	3.00	1.35
❑ 208 Steve Stenstrom RC	.25	.11
❑ 209 Lorenzo Styles RC	.25	.11
❑ 210 Sherman Williams RC	.25	.11
❑ 211 Ray Zellars RC	.50	.23
❑ 212 Eric Zeier RC	1.00	.45
❑ 213 Joey Galloway	3.00	1.35
❑ 214 Napoleon Kaufman	2.50	1.10
❑ 215 Rashaan Salaam	1.00	.45
❑ 216 J.J. Stokes	1.00	.45
❑ NNO Steve Beuerlein EE	2.00	.90
❑ NNO Barry Foster EE	2.00	.90
❑ AU9 John Elway AUTO 1994 Gems of the Crown signed card	150.00	70.00
❑ P1 Natrone Means Promo Silver foil	1.00	.45
❑ P2 Natrone Means Promo Gold foil	1.00	.45

1999 Pacific Prisms

	MINT	NRMT
COMPLETE SET (150)	80.00	36.00
❑ 1 David Boston RC	4.00	1.80
❑ 2 Rob Moore	.40	.18
❑ 3 Adrian Murrell	.40	.18
❑ 4 Jake Plummer	1.50	.70
❑ 5 Frank Sanders	.40	.18
❑ 6 Jamal Anderson	.75	.35
❑ 7 Chris Chandler	.40	.18
❑ 8 Tim Dwight	.40	.18
❑ 9 Terance Mathis	.40	.18
❑ 10 Peter Boulware	.20	.09
❑ 11 Priest Holmes	.75	.35
❑ 12 Pat Johnson	.20	.09
❑ 13 Jermaine Lewis	.40	.18
❑ 14 Doug Flutie	1.00	.45
❑ 15 Eric Moulds	.75	.35
❑ 16 Peerless Price RC	2.50	1.10
❑ 17 Antowain Smith	.75	.35
❑ 18 Bruce Smith	.40	.18
❑ 19 Steve Beuerlein	.20	.09
❑ 20 Tim Biakabutuka	.40	.18
❑ 21 Muhsin Muhammad	.40	.18
❑ 22 Wesley Walls	.40	.18
❑ 23 Edgar Bennett	.20	.09
❑ 24 Curtis Conway	.40	.18
❑ 25 Bobby Engram	.40	.18
❑ 26 Curtis Enis	.75	.35
❑ 27 Cade McNown RC	2.50	1.10
❑ 28 Jeff Blake	.40	.18
❑ 29 Scott Covington RC	2.00	.90
❑ 30 Corey Dillon	.75	.35
❑ 31 Carl Pickens	.75	.35
❑ 32 Akili Smith RC	4.00	1.80
❑ 33 Craig Yeast RC	1.50	.70
❑ 34 Tim Couch RC	6.00	2.70
❑ 35 Ty Detmer	.40	.18
❑ 36 Kevin Johnson RC	4.00	1.80
❑ 37 Terry Kirby	.20	.09
❑ 38 Leslie Shepherd	.20	.09
❑ 39 Troy Aikman	2.00	.90
❑ 40 Michael Irvin	.40	.18
❑ 41 Deion Sanders	.75	.35
❑ 42 Emmitt Smith	2.00	.90
❑ 43 Bubby Brister	.20	.09
❑ 44 Terrell Davis	2.00	.90
❑ 45 Brian Griese	1.50	.70
❑ 46 Ed McCaffrey	.40	.18
❑ 47 Shannon Sharpe	.40	.18
❑ 48 Rod Smith	.40	.18
❑ 49 Charlie Batch	1.50	.70
❑ 50 Germane Crowell	.40	.18
❑ 51 Sedrick Irvin RC	2.00	.90
❑ 52 Herman Moore	.75	.35
❑ 53 Johnnie Morton	.40	.18
❑ 54 Barry Sanders	3.00	1.35
❑ 55 Mark Chmura	.20	.09
❑ 56 Brett Favre	3.00	1.35
❑ 57 Antonio Freeman	.75	.35
❑ 58 Dorsey Levens	.75	.35
❑ 59 Ken Dilger	.20	.09
❑ 60 Marvin Harrison	.75	.35
❑ 61 Edgerrin James RC	12.00	5.50
❑ 62 Peyton Manning	3.00	1.35
❑ 63 Jerome Pathon	.20	.09
❑ 64 Mark Brunell	1.25	.55
❑ 65 Keenan McCardell	.40	.18
❑ 66 Jimmy Smith	.40	.18
❑ 67 Fred Taylor	2.00	.90
❑ 68 Derrick Alexander	.40	.18
❑ 69 Mike Cloud RC	1.50	.70
❑ 70 Tony Gonzalez	.40	.18
❑ 71 Elvis Grbac	.40	.18
❑ 72 Andre Rison	.40	.18
❑ 73 Cecil Collins RC	2.00	.90
❑ 74 Oronde Gadsden	.40	.18
❑ 75 James Johnson RC	2.00	.90
❑ 76 Dan Marino	3.00	1.35
❑ 77 O.J. McDuffie	.40	.18
❑ 78 Lamar Thomas	.20	.09
❑ 79 Cris Carter	.75	.35
❑ 80 Daunte Culpepper RC	12.00	5.50
❑ 81 Randall Cunningham	.75	.35
❑ 82 Matthew Hatchette	.20	.09
❑ 83 Randy Moss	3.00	1.35
❑ 84 John Randle	.40	.18
❑ 85 Robert Smith	.75	.35
❑ 86 Drew Bledsoe	1.25	.55
❑ 87 Ben Coates	.40	.18
❑ 88 Kevin Faulk RC	3.00	1.35
❑ 89 Terry Glenn	.75	.35
❑ 90 Shawn Jefferson	.20	.09
❑ 91 Cam Cleeland	.20	.09
❑ 92 Billy Joe Hobert	.20	.09
❑ 93 Keith Poole	.20	.09
❑ 94 Ricky Williams RC	8.00	3.60
❑ 95 Gary Brown	.20	.09
❑ 96 Kent Graham	.20	.09
❑ 97 Ike Hilliard	.20	.09
❑ 98 Amani Toomer	.20	.09
❑ 99 Wayne Chrebet	.40	.18
❑ 100 Keyshawn Johnson	.75	.35
❑ 101 Curtis Martin	.75	.35
❑ 102 Vinny Testaverde	.40	.18
❑ 103 Tim Brown	.75	.35
❑ 104 James Jett	.40	.18
❑ 105 Napoleon Kaufman	.75	.35
❑ 106 Charles Woodson	.75	.35
❑ 107 Koy Detmer	.20	.09
❑ 108 Donovan McNabb RC	8.00	3.60
❑ 109 Duce Staley	.75	.35

❑ 110 Kevin Turner .... .20 .09
❑ 111 Jerome Bettis .... .75 .35
❑ 112 Mark Bruener .... .20 .09
❑ 113 Troy Edwards RC 2.50 1.10
❑ 114 Levon Kirkland .... .20 .09
❑ 115 Kordell Stewart .... .75 .35
❑ 116 Amos Zereoue RC ...... 2.00 .90
❑ 117 Isaac Bruce .... .75 .35
❑ 118 Marshall Faulk .... .75 .35
❑ 119 Joe Germaine RC .... 2.00 .90
❑ 120 Trent Green .... .40 .18
❑ 121 Torry Holt RC 5.00 2.20
❑ 122 Ryan Leaf .... .75 .35
❑ 123 Natrone Means .... .40 .18
❑ 124 Mikhael Ricks .... .20 .09
❑ 125 Junior Seau .... .40 .18
❑ 126 Garrison Hearst .... .40 .18
❑ 127 Terrell Owens .... .75 .35
❑ 128 Jerry Rice .... 2.00 .90
❑ 129 J.J. Stokes .... .40 .18
❑ 130 Steve Young .... 1.25 .55
❑ 131 Chad Brown .... .20 .09
❑ 132 Joey Galloway .... .75 .35
❑ 133 Brock Huard RC 3.00 1.35
❑ 134 Jon Kitna .... .75 .35
❑ 135 Ricky Watters .... .40 .18
❑ 136 Mike Alstott .... .75 .35
❑ 137 Reidel Anthony .... .40 .18
❑ 138 Trent Dilfer .... .40 .18
❑ 139 Warrick Dunn .... .75 .35
❑ 140 Jacquez Green .... .40 .18
❑ 141 Shaun King RC 4.00 1.80
❑ 142 Darnell McDonald RC .. 1.50 .70
❑ 143 Eddie George .... 1.00 .45
❑ 144 Steve McNair .... .75 .35
❑ 145 Yancey Thigpen .... .20 .09
❑ 146 Frank Wycheck .... .20 .09
❑ 147 Champ Bailey RC 2.50 1.10
❑ 148 Albert Connell .... .20 .09
❑ 149 Skip Hicks .... .40 .18
❑ 150 Michael Westbrook .... .20 .09

2000 Pacific Prism Prospects

	MINT	NRMT
COMP.SET w/o SP's (100)......	25.00	11.00

❑ 1 David Boston .... .60 .25
❑ 2 Jake Plummer .... .60 .25
❑ 3 Jamal Anderson .... .60 .25
❑ 4 Chris Chandler .... .30 .14
❑ 5 Tim Dwight .... .60 .25
❑ 6 Terance Mathis .... .30 .14
❑ 7 Tony Banks .... .30 .14
❑ 8 Priest Holmes .... .30 .14
❑ 9 Doug Flutie .... .75 .35
❑ 10 Rob Johnson .... .30 .14
❑ 11 Eric Moulds .... .60 .25
❑ 12 Antowain Smith .... .30 .14
❑ 13 Steve Beuerlein .... .30 .14
❑ 14 Tim Biakabutuka .... .30 .14
❑ 15 Muhsin Muhammad .... .30 .14
❑ 16 Bobby Engram .... .30 .14
❑ 17 Curtis Enis .... .60 .25
❑ 18 Cade McNown .... .60 .25
❑ 19 Marcus Robinson .... .60 .25
❑ 20 Corey Dillon .... .60 .25
❑ 21 Akili Smith .... .60 .25
❑ 22 Tim Couch .... 1.25 .55
❑ 23 Kevin Johnson .... .60 .25
❑ 24 Troy Aikman .... 1.50 .70
❑ 25 Joey Galloway .... .60 .25
❑ 26 Rocket Ismail .... .30 .14
❑ 27 Emmitt Smith .... 1.50 .70
❑ 28 Terrell Davis .... 1.50 .70
❑ 29 Olandis Gary .... .60 .25
❑ 30 Brian Griese .... .75 .35
❑ 31 Charlie Batch .... .60 .25
❑ 32 Herman Moore .... .30 .14
❑ 33 Johnnie Morton .... .30 .14
❑ 34 Brett Favre 2.50 1.10
❑ 35 Antonio Freeman .... .60 .25
❑ 36 Dorsey Levens .... .30 .14
❑ 37 Marvin Harrison .... .60 .25
❑ 38 Edgerrin James 2.50 1.10
❑ 39 Peyton Manning .... 2.00 .90
❑ 40 Mark Brunell .... 1.00 .45
❑ 41 Keenan McCardell .... .30 .14
❑ 42 Jimmy Smith .... .30 .14
❑ 43 Fred Taylor .... .75 .35
❑ 44 Donnell Bennett .... .15 .07
❑ 45 Tony Gonzalez .... .30 .14
❑ 46 Elvis Grbac .... .30 .14
❑ 47 Damon Huard .... .60 .25
❑ 48 James Johnson .... .30 .14
❑ 49 Cris Carter .... .60 .25
❑ 50 Daunte Culpepper .... 1.25 .55
❑ 51 Randy Moss .... 2.00 .90
❑ 52 Robert Smith .... .60 .25
❑ 53 Drew Bledsoe .... 1.00 .45
❑ 54 Kevin Faulk .... .30 .14
❑ 55 Terry Glenn .... .30 .14
❑ 56 Jeff Blake .... .30 .14
❑ 57 Ricky Williams .... 1.50 .70
❑ 58 Kerry Collins .... .30 .14
❑ 59 Ike Hilliard .... .30 .14
❑ 60 Amani Toomer .... .30 .14
❑ 61 Wayne Chrebet .... .30 .14
❑ 62 Curtis Martin .... .60 .25
❑ 63 Vinny Testaverde .... .30 .14
❑ 64 Tim Brown .... .60 .25
❑ 65 Rich Gannon .... .30 .14
❑ 66 Napoleon Kaufman .... .30 .14
❑ 67 Tyrone Wheatley .... .30 .14
❑ 68 Donovan McNabb .... 1.00 .45
❑ 69 Duce Staley .... .60 .25
❑ 70 Jerome Bettis .... .60 .25
❑ 71 Troy Edwards .... .30 .14
❑ 72 Kordell Stewart .... .60 .25
❑ 73 Isaac Bruce .... .60 .25
❑ 74 Torry Holt .... .60 .25
❑ 75 Marshall Faulk .... .75 .35
❑ 76 Kurt Warner 2.50 1.10
❑ 77 Jermaine Fazande .... .15 .07
❑ 78 Jim Harbaugh .... .30 .14
❑ 79 Ryan Leaf .... .60 .25
❑ 80 Junior Seau .... .30 .14
❑ 81 Jeff Garcia .... .60 .25
❑ 82 J.J. Stokes .... .30 .14
❑ 83 Terrell Owens .... .60 .25
❑ 84 Jerry Rice .... 1.50 .70
❑ 85 Jon Kitna .... .60 .25
❑ 86 Derrick Mayes .... .30 .14
❑ 87 Ricky Watters .... .15 .07
❑ 88 Mike Alstott .... .60 .25
❑ 89 Warrick Dunn .... .60 .25
❑ 90 Jacquez Green .... .30 .14
❑ 91 Shaun King .... 1.00 .45
❑ 92 Eddie George .... .75 .35
❑ 93 Jevon Kearse .... .60 .25
❑ 94 Steve McNair .... .60 .25
❑ 95 Carl Pickens .... .30 .14
❑ 96 Stephen Davis .... .60 .25
❑ 97 Jeff George .... .30 .14
❑ 98 Brad Johnson .... .60 .25
❑ 99 Deion Sanders .... .60 .25
❑ 100 Michael Westbrook .... .30 .14
❑ 101 Jabari Issa RC 4.00 1.80
❑ 102 Thomas Jones RC 12.00 5.50
❑ 103 Sekou Sanyika RC 4.00 1.80
❑ 104 Jay Tant RC 4.00 1.80
❑ 105 Raynoch Thompson RC 6.00 2.70
❑ 106 Doug Johnson RC 8.00 3.60
❑ 107 Mark Simoneau RC...... 8.00 3.60
❑ 108 Jamal Lewis RC 40.00 18.00
❑ 109 Chris Redman RC...... 15.00 6.75
❑ 110 Travis Taylor RC........ 10.00 4.50
❑ 111 Kwame Cavil RC.......... 6.00 2.70
❑ 112 Corey Moore RC.......... 6.00 2.70
❑ 113 Rashard Anderson RC 6.00 2.70
❑ 114 Lester Towns RC 4.00 1.80
❑ 115 Paul Edinger RC 8.00 3.60
❑ 116 Brian Urlacher RC...... 25.00 11.00
❑ 117 Dez White RC 6.00 2.70
❑ 118 Ron Dugans RC 6.00 2.70
❑ 119 Danny Farmer RC........ 8.00 3.60
❑ 120 Curtis Keaton RC 6.00 2.70
❑ 121 Peter Warrick RC 25.00 11.00
❑ 122 Courtney Brown RC .. 10.00 4.50
❑ 123 Lamar Chapman RC 6.00 2.70
❑ 124 JaJuan Dawson RC 8.00 3.60
❑ 125 Dennis Northcutt RC .. 10.00 4.50
❑ 126 Travis Prentice RC 12.00 5.50
❑ 127 Aaron Shea RC 6.00 2.70
❑ 128 Spergon Wynn RC 8.00 3.60
❑ 129 Dwayne Goodrich RC .. 4.00 1.80
❑ 130 Orantes Grant RC........ 4.00 1.80
❑ 131 Kareem Larrimore RC .. 6.00 2.70
❑ 132 Michael Wiley RC 8.00 3.60
❑ 133 Mike Anderson RC 40.00 18.00
❑ 134 Chris Cole RC 6.00 2.70
❑ 135 Jarious Jackson RC 8.00 3.60
❑ 136 Jerry Johnson RC........ 4.00 1.80
❑ 137 Kenoy Kennedy RC...... 4.00 1.80
❑ 138 Deltha O'Neal RC 6.00 2.70
❑ 139 Reuben Droughns RC.. 8.00 3.60
❑ 140 Barrett Green RC 4.00 1.80
❑ 141 Bubba Franks RC 10.00 4.50
❑ 142 Kevin McDougal RC 6.00 2.70
❑ 143 Marcus Washington RC 6.00 2.70
❑ 144 T.J. Slaughter RC 4.00 1.80
❑ 145 R.Jay Soward RC 8.00 3.60
❑ 146 Shyrone Stith RC 6.00 2.70
❑ 147 William Bartee RC........ 6.00 2.70
❑ 148 Dante Hall RC 6.00 2.70
❑ 149 Frank Moreau RC 8.00 3.60
❑ 150 Sylvester Morris RC .. 15.00 6.75
❑ 151 Deon Dyer RC 6.00 2.70
❑ 152 Ben Kelly RC 4.00 1.80
❑ 153 Tyrone Carter RC 6.00 2.70
❑ 154 Doug Chapman RC...... 15.00 6.75
❑ 155 Troy Walters RC 8.00 3.60
❑ 156 Tom Brady RC 8.00 3.60
❑ 157 Patrick Pass RC 6.00 2.70
❑ 158 J.R. Redmond RC...... 10.00 4.50
❑ 159 Marc Bulger RC.......... 8.00 3.60
❑ 160 Darren Howard RC 6.00 2.70
❑ 161 Chad Morton RC 8.00 3.60
❑ 162 Mareno Philyaw RC 4.00 1.80
❑ 163 Terrelle Smith RC 6.00 2.70
❑ 164 Ralph Brown RC 4.00 1.80
❑ 165 Ron Dayne RC 25.00 11.00
❑ 166 Brandon Short RC........ 6.00 2.70
❑ 167 John Abraham RC........ 6.00 2.70
❑ 168 Anthony Becht RC........ 8.00 3.60
❑ 169 Laveranues Coles RC 12.00 5.50
❑ 170 Shaun Ellis RC 6.00 2.70
❑ 171 Chad Pennington RC 25.00 11.00
❑ 172 Sebastian Janikowski RC 8.00 3.60
❑ 173 Jerry Porter RC 8.00 3.60
❑ 174 Todd Pinkston RC........ 8.00 3.60
❑ 175 Gari Scott RC 6.00 2.70
❑ 176 Corey Simon RC 10.00 4.50
❑ 177 Plaxico Burress RC 15.00 6.75
❑ 178 Tee Martin RC.......... 12.00 5.50
❑ 179 Hank Poteat RC 6.00 2.70
❑ 180 Rogers Beckett RC 6.00 2.70
❑ 181 Trevor Gaylor RC 6.00 2.70
❑ 182 Ronney Jenkins RC 6.00 2.70
❑ 183 Giovanni Carmazzi RC 10.00 4.50
❑ 184 Chafie Fields RC.......... 6.00 2.70
❑ 185 Ahmed Plummer RC 8.00 3.60
❑ 186 Tim Rattay RC.......... 12.00 5.50
❑ 187 Jeff Ulbrich RC 4.00 1.80
❑ 188 Shaun Alexander RC 20.00 9.00
❑ 189 Darrell Jackson RC 12.00 5.50
❑ 190 Rodnick Phillips RC...... 4.00 1.80
❑ 191 James Williams RC 6.00 2.70
❑ 192 Trung Canidate RC 8.00 3.60

		MINT	NRMT
❑ 193	Joe Hamilton RC	10.00	4.50
❑ 194	DeMario Brown RC	6.00	2.70
❑ 195	Keith Bulluck RC	6.00	2.70
❑ 196	Chris Coleman RC	8.00	3.60
❑ 197	Erron Kinney RC	8.00	3.60
❑ 198	Billy Volek RC	6.00	2.70
❑ 199	Todd Husak RC	8.00	3.60
❑ 200	Chris Samuels RC	6.00	2.70

2000 Pacific Private Stock

		MINT	NRMT
COMP.SET w/o SP's (100)		25.00	11.00
❑ 1	Rob Moore	.40	.18
❑ 2	Jake Plummer	.75	.35
❑ 3	Frank Sanders	.40	.18
❑ 4	Jamal Anderson	.75	.35
❑ 5	Chris Chandler	.40	.18
❑ 6	Tim Dwight	.75	.35
❑ 7	Tony Banks	.40	.18
❑ 8	Priest Holmes	.40	.18
❑ 9	Doug Flutie	1.00	.45
❑ 10	Rob Johnson	.40	.18
❑ 11	Eric Moulds	.75	.35
❑ 12	Antowain Smith	.40	.18
❑ 13	Steve Beuerlein	.20	.09
❑ 14	Tim Biakabutuka	.40	.18
❑ 15	Patrick Jeffers	.75	.35
❑ 16	Muhsin Muhammad	.40	.18
❑ 17	Curtis Enis	.40	.18
❑ 18	Cade McNown	.75	.35
❑ 19	Marcus Robinson	.75	.35
❑ 20	Corey Dillon	.75	.35
❑ 21	Akili Smith	.75	.35
❑ 22	Tim Couch	1.25	.55
❑ 23	Kevin Johnson	.75	.35
❑ 24	Troy Aikman	2.00	.90
❑ 25	Rocket Ismail	.40	.18
❑ 26	Emmitt Smith	2.00	.90
❑ 27	Terrell Davis	2.00	.90
❑ 28	Olandis Gary	.75	.35
❑ 29	Brian Griese	1.00	.45
❑ 30	Ed McCaffrey	.40	.18
❑ 31	Charlie Batch	.75	.35
❑ 32	Germane Crowell	.40	.18
❑ 33	Herman Moore	.40	.18
❑ 34	Barry Sanders	2.50	1.10
❑ 35	Brett Favre	3.00	1.35
❑ 36	Antonio Freeman	.75	.35
❑ 37	Dorsey Levens	.40	.18
❑ 38	Marvin Harrison	.75	.35
❑ 39	Edgerrin James	3.00	1.35
❑ 40	Peyton Manning	2.50	1.10
❑ 41	Terrence Wilkins	.75	.35
❑ 42	Mark Brunell	1.25	.55
❑ 43	Keenan McCardell	.40	.18
❑ 44	Jimmy Smith	.40	.18
❑ 45	Fred Taylor	1.00	.45
❑ 46	Derrick Alexander	.40	.18
❑ 47	Donnell Bennett	.20	.09
❑ 48	Tony Gonzalez	.40	.18
❑ 49	Elvis Grbac	.40	.18
❑ 50	Damon Huard	.75	.35
❑ 51	James Johnson	.40	.18
❑ 52	Dan Marino	3.00	1.35
❑ 53	O.J. McDuffie	.40	.18
❑ 54	Cris Carter	.75	.35
❑ 55	Daunte Culpepper	1.50	.70
❑ 56	Randy Moss	2.50	1.10
❑ 57	Robert Smith	.75	.35
❑ 58	Drew Bledsoe	1.25	.55
❑ 59	Kevin Faulk	.40	.18
❑ 60	Terry Glenn	.40	.18
❑ 61	Keith Poole	.40	.18
❑ 62	Ricky Williams	2.00	.90
❑ 63	Kerry Collins	.40	.18
❑ 64	Ike Hilliard	.40	.18
❑ 65	Amani Toomer	.40	.18
❑ 66	Wayne Chrebet	.40	.18
❑ 67	Ray Lucas	.75	.35
❑ 68	Curtis Martin	.75	.35
❑ 69	Tim Brown	.75	.35
❑ 70	Rich Gannon	.40	.18
❑ 71	Napoleon Kaufman	.40	.18
❑ 72	Donovan McNabb	1.25	.55
❑ 73	Duce Staley	.75	.35
❑ 74	Jerome Bettis	.75	.35
❑ 75	Troy Edwards	.40	.18
❑ 76	Kordell Stewart	.75	.35
❑ 77	Isaac Bruce	.75	.35
❑ 78	Marshall Faulk	1.00	.45
❑ 79	Torry Holt	.75	.35
❑ 80	Kurt Warner	3.00	1.35
❑ 81	Jermaine Fazande	.20	.09
❑ 82	Jim Harbaugh	.40	.18
❑ 83	Junior Seau	.40	.18
❑ 84	Charlie Garner	.40	.18
❑ 85	Terrell Owens	.75	.35
❑ 86	Jerry Rice	2.00	.90
❑ 87	Jon Kitna	.75	.35
❑ 88	Derrick Mayes	.40	.18
❑ 89	Ricky Watters	.40	.18
❑ 90	Mike Alstott	.75	.35
❑ 91	Warrick Dunn	.75	.35
❑ 92	Jacquez Green	.40	.18
❑ 93	Shaun King	1.25	.55
❑ 94	Eddie George	1.00	.45
❑ 95	Jevon Kearse	.75	.35
❑ 96	Steve McNair	.75	.35
❑ 97	Yancey Thigpen	.20	.09
❑ 98	Stephen Davis	.75	.35
❑ 99	Brad Johnson	.75	.35
❑ 100	Michael Westbrook	.40	.18
❑ 101	Thomas Jones RC	50.00	22.00
❑ 102	Doug Johnson RC	30.00	13.50
❑ 103	Mareno Philyaw RC	15.00	6.75
❑ 104	Jamal Lewis RC	200.00	90.00
❑ 105	Chris Redman RC	60.00	27.00
❑ 106	Travis Taylor RC	40.00	18.00
❑ 107	Frank Murphy RC	15.00	6.75
❑ 108	Dez White RC	25.00	11.00
❑ 109	Ron Dugans RC	25.00	11.00
❑ 110	Curtis Keaton RC	25.00	11.00
❑ 111	Peter Warrick RC	100.00	45.00
❑ 112	Courtney Brown RC	40.00	18.00
❑ 113	JaJuan Dawson RC	30.00	13.50
❑ 114	Dennis Northcutt RC	40.00	18.00
❑ 115	Travis Prentice RC	50.00	22.00
❑ 116	Michael Wiley RC	30.00	13.50
❑ 117	Chris Cole RC	25.00	11.00
❑ 118	Jarious Jackson RC	30.00	13.50
❑ 119	Reuben Droughns RC	30.00	13.50
❑ 120	Bubba Franks RC	40.00	18.00
❑ 121	Anthony Lucas RC	15.00	6.75
❑ 122	Rondell Mealey RC	15.00	6.75
❑ 123	R.Jay Soward RC	30.00	13.50
❑ 124	Shyrone Stith RC	25.00	11.00
❑ 125	Sylvester Morris RC	60.00	27.00
❑ 126	Quinton Spotwood RC	15.00	6.75
❑ 127	Troy Walters RC	30.00	13.50
❑ 128	Tom Brady RC	30.00	13.50
❑ 129	J.R. Redmond RC	40.00	18.00
❑ 130	Marc Bulger RC	30.00	13.50
❑ 131	Sherrod Gideon RC	15.00	6.75
❑ 132	Ron Dayne RC	100.00	45.00
❑ 133	Anthony Becht RC	30.00	13.50
❑ 134	Laveranues Coles RC	50.00	22.00
❑ 135	Chad Pennington RC	100.00	45.00
❑ 136	Sebastian Janikowski RC	30.00	13.50
❑ 137	Jerry Porter RC	30.00	13.50
❑ 138	Todd Pinkston RC	30.00	13.50
❑ 139	Gari Scott RC	25.00	11.00
❑ 140	Plaxico Burress RC	60.00	27.00
❑ 141	Danny Farmer RC	30.00	13.50
❑ 142	Tee Martin RC	50.00	22.00
❑ 143	Trung Canidate RC	30.00	13.50
❑ 144	Trevor Gaylor RC	25.00	11.00
❑ 145	Giovanni Carmazzi RC	40.00	18.00
❑ 146	Tim Rattay RC	50.00	22.00
❑ 147	Shaun Alexander RC	80.00	36.00
❑ 148	Darrell Jackson RC	50.00	22.00
❑ 149	Joe Hamilton RC	40.00	18.00
❑ 150	Todd Husak RC	30.00	13.50
❑ S1	Jon Kitna Sample	1.00	.45

2000 Pacific Vanguard

		MINT	NRMT
COMPLETE SET (150)		1000.00	450.00
❑ 1	Tony Banks	.40	.18
❑ 2	Priest Holmes	.40	.18
❑ 3	Qadry Ismail	.30	.14
❑ 4	Doug Flutie	1.00	.45
❑ 5	Rob Johnson	.40	.18
❑ 6	Eric Moulds	.75	.35
❑ 7	Peerless Price	.75	.35
❑ 8	Antowain Smith	.40	.18
❑ 9	Corey Dillon	.75	.35
❑ 10	Darnay Scott	.40	.18
❑ 11	Akili Smith	.75	.35
❑ 12	Tim Couch	1.50	.70
❑ 13	Kevin Johnson	.75	.35
❑ 14	Terry Kirby	.30	.14
❑ 15	Terrell Davis	2.00	.90
❑ 16	Olandis Gary	.75	.35
❑ 17	Brian Griese	1.00	.45
❑ 18	Ed McCaffrey	.75	.35
❑ 19	Rod Smith	.40	.18
❑ 20	Marvin Harrison	.75	.35
❑ 21	Edgerrin James	3.00	1.35
❑ 22	Peyton Manning	2.50	1.10
❑ 23	Terrence Wilkins	.75	.35
❑ 24	Mark Brunell	1.25	.55
❑ 25	Keenan McCardell	.40	.18
❑ 26	Jimmy Smith	.40	.18
❑ 27	Fred Taylor	1.00	.45
❑ 28	Derrick Alexander	.40	.18
❑ 29	Donnell Bennett	.30	.14
❑ 30	Tony Gonzalez	.40	.18
❑ 31	Elvis Grbac	.40	.18
❑ 32	Damon Huard	.75	.35
❑ 33	James Johnson	.40	.18
❑ 34	Dan Marino	3.00	1.35
❑ 35	Tony Martin	.40	.18
❑ 36	O.J. McDuffie	.40	.18
❑ 37	Drew Bledsoe	1.25	.55
❑ 38	Kevin Faulk	.40	.18
❑ 39	Terry Glenn	.40	.18
❑ 40	Wayne Chrebet	.40	.18
❑ 41	Ray Lucas	.75	.35
❑ 42	Curtis Martin	.75	.35
❑ 43	Vinny Testaverde	.40	.18
❑ 44	Tim Brown	.75	.35
❑ 45	Rich Gannon	.40	.18
❑ 46	Napoleon Kaufman	.40	.18
❑ 47	Tyrone Wheatley	.40	.18
❑ 48	Jerome Bettis	.75	.35
❑ 49	Troy Edwards	.40	.18
❑ 50	Richard Huntley	.30	.14

Card	Mint	NrMt
❑ 51 Kordell Stewart	.75	.35
❑ 52 Jermaine Fazande	.30	.14
❑ 53 Jim Harbaugh	.40	.18
❑ 54 Mikhael Ricks	.30	.14
❑ 55 Junior Seau	.40	.18
❑ 56 Brock Huard	.75	.35
❑ 57 Jon Kitna	.75	.35
❑ 58 Derrick Mayes	.40	.18
❑ 59 Ricky Watters	.40	.18
❑ 60 Eddie George	1.00	.45
❑ 61 Jevon Kearse	.75	.35
❑ 62 Steve McNair	.75	.35
❑ 63 Yancey Thigpen	.30	.14
❑ 64 David Boston	.75	.35
❑ 65 Rob Moore	.40	.18
❑ 66 Jake Plummer	.75	.35
❑ 67 Frank Sanders	.40	.18
❑ 68 Jamal Anderson	.75	.35
❑ 69 Chris Chandler	.40	.18
❑ 70 Tim Dwight	.75	.35
❑ 71 Terance Mathis	.40	.18
❑ 72 Steve Beuerlein	.40	.18
❑ 73 Tim Biakabutuka	.40	.18
❑ 74 Patrick Jeffers	.75	.35
❑ 75 Muhsin Muhammad	.40	.18
❑ 76 Bobby Engram	.30	.14
❑ 77 Curtis Enis	.40	.18
❑ 78 Cade McNown	.75	.35
❑ 79 Marcus Robinson	.75	.35
❑ 80 Troy Aikman	2.00	.90
❑ 81 Rocket Ismail	.40	.18
❑ 82 Emmitt Smith	2.00	.90
❑ 83 Jason Tucker	.30	.14
❑ 84 Chris Warren	.30	.14
❑ 85 Charlie Batch	.75	.35
❑ 86 Germane Crowell	.40	.18
❑ 87 Herman Moore	.40	.18
❑ 88 Johnnie Morton	.40	.18
❑ 89 Barry Sanders	2.50	1.10
❑ 90 Brett Favre	3.00	1.35
❑ 91 Antonio Freeman	.75	.35
❑ 92 Dorsey Levens	.40	.18
❑ 93 Bill Schroeder	.40	.18
❑ 94 Cris Carter	.75	.35
❑ 95 Daunte Culpepper	1.50	.70
❑ 96 Randy Moss	2.50	1.10
❑ 97 Robert Smith	.75	.35
❑ 98 Cam Cleeland	.30	.14
❑ 99 Keith Poole	.30	.14
❑ 100 Ricky Williams	2.00	.90
❑ 101 Tiki Barber	.40	.18
❑ 102 Kerry Collins	.40	.18
❑ 103 Ike Hilliard	.40	.18
❑ 104 Amani Toomer	.30	.14
❑ 105 Charles Johnson	.40	.18
❑ 106 Donovan McNabb	1.25	.55
❑ 107 Torrance Small	.30	.14
❑ 108 Duce Staley	.75	.35
❑ 109 Isaac Bruce	.75	.35
❑ 110 Marshall Faulk	1.00	.45
❑ 111 Torry Holt	.75	.35
❑ 112 Kurt Warner	3.00	1.35
❑ 113 Charlie Garner	.40	.18
❑ 114 Terrell Owens	.75	.35
❑ 115 Jerry Rice	2.00	.90
❑ 116 J.J. Stokes	.40	.18
❑ 117 Steve Young	1.25	.55
❑ 118 Mike Alstott	.75	.35
❑ 119 Reidel Anthony	.30	.14
❑ 120 Warrick Dunn	.75	.35
❑ 121 Jacquez Green	.40	.18
❑ 122 Shaun King	1.25	.55
❑ 123 Stephen Davis	.75	.35
❑ 124 Brad Johnson	.75	.35
❑ 125 Michael Westbrook	.40	.18
❑ 126 Thomas Jones RC	30.00	13.50
❑ 127 Jamal Lewis RC	100.00	45.00
❑ 128 Chris Redman RC	40.00	18.00
❑ 129 Travis Taylor RC	25.00	11.00
❑ 130 Dez White RC	20.00	9.00
❑ 131 Ron Dugans RC	20.00	9.00
❑ 132 Peter Warrick RC	60.00	27.00
❑ 133 Dennis Northcutt RC	25.00	11.00
❑ 134 Travis Prentice RC	30.00	13.50
❑ 135 Reuben Droughns RC	15.00	6.75
❑ 136 R.Jay Soward RC	20.00	9.00
❑ 137 Sylvester Morris RC	40.00	18.00
❑ 138 Troy Walters RC	20.00	9.00
❑ 139 Tom Brady RC	15.00	6.75
❑ 140 J.R. Redmond RC	25.00	11.00
❑ 141 Marc Bulger RC	15.00	6.75
❑ 142 Ron Dayne RC	60.00	27.00
❑ 143 Laveranues Coles RC	30.00	13.50
❑ 144 Chad Pennington RC	60.00	27.00
❑ 145 Jerry Porter RC	20.00	9.00
❑ 146 Plaxico Burress RC	40.00	18.00
❑ 147 Trung Canidate RC	15.00	6.75
❑ 148 Giovanni Carmazzi RC	25.00	11.00
❑ 149 Shaun Alexander RC	50.00	22.00
❑ 150 Todd Husak RC	15.00	6.75
❑ S1 Jon Kitna Sample	2.50	1.10

1998 Paramount

	MINT	NRMT
COMPLETE SET (250)	40.00	18.00
❑ 1 Larry Centers	.10	.05
❑ 2 Chris Gedney	.10	.05
❑ 3 Rob Moore	.20	.09
❑ 4 Jake Plummer	.75	.35
❑ 5 Simeon Rice	.20	.09
❑ 6 Frank Sanders	.20	.09
❑ 7 Mark Smith DE	.10	.05
❑ 8 Eric Swann	.10	.05
❑ 9 Jamal Anderson	.40	.18
❑ 10 Chris Chandler	.20	.09
❑ 11 Bert Emanuel	.20	.09
❑ 12 Tony Graziani	.10	.05
❑ 13 Byron Hanspard	.20	.09
❑ 14 Terance Mathis	.20	.09
❑ 15 O.J. Santiago	.10	.05
❑ 16 Chuck Smith	.10	.05
❑ 17 Derrick Alexander WR	.20	.09
❑ 18 Peter Boulware	.10	.05
❑ 19 Jay Graham	.10	.05
❑ 20 Priest Holmes RC	6.00	2.70
❑ 21 Michael Jackson	.10	.05
❑ 22 Byron Bam Morris	.10	.05
❑ 23 Vinny Testaverde	.20	.09
❑ 24 Eric Zeier	.20	.09
❑ 25 Todd Collins	.10	.05
❑ 26 Quinn Early	.10	.05
❑ 27 Bryce Paup	.10	.05
❑ 28 Andre Reed	.20	.09
❑ 29 Jay Riemersma	.10	.05
❑ 30 Antowain Smith	.40	.18
❑ 31 Bruce Smith	.20	.09
❑ 32 Thurman Thomas	.40	.18
❑ 33 Michael Bates	.10	.05
❑ 34 Mark Carrier WR	.10	.05
❑ 35 Rae Carruth	.20	.09
❑ 36 Kerry Collins	.20	.09
❑ 37 Fred Lane	.20	.09
❑ 38 Lamar Lathon	.10	.05
❑ 39 Muhsin Muhammad	.20	.09
❑ 40 Wesley Walls	.20	.09
❑ 41 Darnell Autry	.10	.05
❑ 42 Curtis Conway	.20	.09
❑ 43 Raymont Harris	.10	.05
❑ 44 Tyrone Hughes	.10	.05
❑ 45 Chris Penn	.10	.05
❑ 46 Ricky Proehl	.10	.05
❑ 47 Steve Stenstrom	.10	.05
❑ 48 Ryan Wetnight RC	.10	.05
❑ 49 Jeff Blake	.20	.09
❑ 50 Ki-Jana Carter	.10	.05
❑ 51 Corey Dillon	.50	.23
❑ 52 David Dunn	.10	.05
❑ 53 Boomer Esiason	.10	.05
❑ 54 Brian Milne	.10	.05
❑ 55 Carl Pickens	.40	.18
❑ 56 Darnay Scott	.20	.09
❑ 57 Troy Aikman	1.00	.45
❑ 58 Eric Bjornson	.10	.05
❑ 59 Michael Irvin	.40	.18
❑ 60 Daryl Johnston	.20	.09
❑ 61 Anthony Miller	.10	.05
❑ 62 Deion Sanders	.40	.18
❑ 63 Emmitt Smith	1.50	.70
❑ 64 Omar Stoutmire RC	.10	.05
❑ 65 Sherman Williams	.10	.05
❑ 66 Terrell Davis	1.50	.70
❑ 67 John Elway	2.00	.90
❑ 68 Darrien Gordon	.10	.05
❑ 69 Ed McCaffrey	.20	.09
❑ 70 Bill Romanowski	.10	.05
❑ 71 Shannon Sharpe	.20	.09
❑ 72 Neil Smith	.20	.09
❑ 73 Rod Smith WR	.20	.09
❑ 74 Maa Tanuvasa	.10	.05
❑ 75 Tommie Boyd	.10	.05
❑ 76 Glyn Milburn	.10	.05
❑ 77 Scott Mitchell	.20	.09
❑ 78 Herman Moore	.40	.18
❑ 79 Johnnie Morton	.20	.09
❑ 80 Robert Porcher	.10	.05
❑ 81 Barry Sanders	2.00	.90
❑ 82 Bryant Westbrook	.10	.05
❑ 83 Robert Brooks	.20	.09
❑ 84 LeRoy Butler	.10	.05
❑ 85 Mark Chmura	.20	.09
❑ 86 Brett Favre	2.00	.90
❑ 87 Antonio Freeman	.40	.18
❑ 88 Dorsey Levens	.40	.18
❑ 89 Eugene Robinson	.10	.05
❑ 90 Bill Schroeder RC	6.00	2.70
❑ 91 Reggie White	.40	.18
❑ 92 Aaron Bailey	.10	.05
❑ 93 Quentin Coryatt	.10	.05
❑ 94 Zack Crockett	.10	.05
❑ 95 Sean Dawkins	.10	.05
❑ 96 Ken Dilger	.10	.05
❑ 97 Marshall Faulk	.40	.18
❑ 98 Jim Harbaugh	.20	.09
❑ 99 Marvin Harrison	.20	.09
❑ 100 Bryan Barker	.10	.05
❑ 101 Tony Boselli	.10	.05
❑ 102 Tony Brackens	.10	.05
❑ 103 Mark Brunell	.75	.35
❑ 104 Mike Hollis	.10	.05
❑ 105 Keenan McCardell	.20	.09
❑ 106 Natrone Means	.40	.18
❑ 107 Jimmy Smith	.20	.09
❑ 108 James Stewart	.20	.09
❑ 109 Marcus Allen	.40	.18
❑ 110 Kimble Anders	.20	.09
❑ 111 Dale Carter	.10	.05
❑ 112 Tony Gonzalez	.10	.05
❑ 113 Elvis Grbac	.20	.09
❑ 114 Greg Hill	.10	.05
❑ 115 Andre Rison	.20	.09
❑ 116 Will Shields	.10	.05
❑ 117 Derrick Thomas	.20	.09
❑ 118 Karim Abdul-Jabbar	.40	.18
❑ 119 Trace Armstrong	.10	.05
❑ 120 Damon Huard RC	12.00	5.50
❑ 121 Charles Jordan	.10	.05
❑ 122 Dan Marino	2.00	.90
❑ 123 O.J. McDuffie	.20	.09
❑ 124 Irving Spikes	.10	.05
❑ 125 Zach Thomas	.20	.09
❑ 126 Cris Carter	.40	.18
❑ 127 Charles Woodson RC	2.00	.90
❑ 128 Brad Johnson	.40	.18
❑ 129 Randall McDaniel	.10	.05
❑ 130 John Randle	.20	.09
❑ 131 Jake Reed	.20	.09
❑ 132 Robert Smith	.40	.18
❑ 133 Todd Steussie	.10	.05

❑ 134 Bruce Armstrong .10 .05
❑ 135 Drew Bledsoe .75 .35
❑ 136 Ben Coates .20 .09
❑ 137 Derrick Cullors RC .20 .09
❑ 138 Terry Glenn .40 .18
❑ 139 Shawn Jefferson .10 .05
❑ 140 Curtis Martin .40 .18
❑ 141 Chris Slade .10 .05
❑ 142 Larry Whigham .10 .05
❑ 143 Troy Davis .10 .05
❑ 144 Andre Hastings .10 .05
❑ 145 Randal Hill .10 .05
❑ 146 Sammy Knight RC .10 .05
❑ 147 William Roaf .10 .05
❑ 148 Heath Shuler .10 .05
❑ 149 Danny Wuerffel .20 .09
❑ 150 Ray Zellars .10 .05
❑ 151 Jessie Armstead .10 .05
❑ 152 Tiki Barber .20 .09
❑ 153 Chris Calloway .10 .05
❑ 154 Danny Kanell .20 .09
❑ 155 David Patten RC .40 .18
❑ 156 Michael Strahan .10 .05
❑ 157 Charles Way .10 .05
❑ 158 Tyrone Wheatley .20 .09
❑ 159 Kyle Brady .10 .05
❑ 160 Wayne Chrebet .40 .18
❑ 161 Glenn Foley .20 .09
❑ 162 Aaron Glenn .10 .05
❑ 163 Leon Johnson .10 .05
❑ 164 Adrian Murrell .20 .09
❑ 165 Neil O'Donnell .20 .09
❑ 166 Dedric Ward .10 .05
❑ 167 Tim Brown .40 .18
❑ 168 Rickey Dudley .10 .05
❑ 169 Jeff George .20 .09
❑ 170 Desmond Howard .20 .09
❑ 171 James Jett .20 .09
❑ 172 Napoleon Kaufman .40 .18
❑ 173 Chester McGlockton .10 .05
❑ 174 Darrell Russell .10 .05
❑ 175 Ty Detmer .20 .09
❑ 176 Irving Fryar .20 .09
❑ 177 Charlie Garner .10 .05
❑ 178 Bobby Hoying .20 .09
❑ 179 Chad Lewis .10 .05
❑ 180 Duce Staley .75 .35
❑ 181 Kevin Turner .10 .05
❑ 182 Ricky Watters .20 .09
❑ 183 Jerome Bettis .40 .18
❑ 184 Will Blackwell .10 .05
❑ 185 Charles Johnson .10 .05
❑ 186 George Jones .10 .05
❑ 187 Levon Kirkland .10 .05
❑ 188 Carnell Lake .10 .05
❑ 189 Kordell Stewart .40 .18
❑ 190 Yancey Thigpen .10 .05
❑ 191 Tony Banks .20 .09
❑ 192 Isaac Bruce .40 .18
❑ 193 Ernie Conwell .10 .05
❑ 194 Craig Heyward .10 .05
❑ 195 Eddie Kennison .20 .09
❑ 196 Amp Lee .10 .05
❑ 197 Orlando Pace .10 .05
❑ 198 Torrance Small .10 .05
❑ 199 Gary Brown .10 .05
❑ 200 Kenny Bynum RC .10 .05
❑ 201 Freddie Jones .10 .05
❑ 202 Tony Martin .20 .09
❑ 203 Eric Metcalf .10 .05
❑ 204 Junior Seau .20 .09
❑ 205 Craig Whelihan RC .10 .05
❑ 206 William Floyd .10 .05
❑ 207 Merton Hanks .10 .05
❑ 208 Garrison Hearst .40 .18
❑ 209 Brent Jones .10 .05
❑ 210 Terrell Owens .40 .18
❑ 211 Jerry Rice 1.00 .45
❑ 212 J.J. Stokes .20 .09
❑ 213 Rod Woodson .20 .09
❑ 214 Steve Young .50 .23
❑ 215 Steve Broussard .10 .05
❑ 216 Joey Galloway .40 .18
❑ 217 Cortez Kennedy .10 .05
❑ 218 Jon Kitna .50 .23
❑ 219 James McKnight .10 .05
❑ 220 Warren Moon .40 .18
❑ 221 Michael Sinclair .10 .05
❑ 222 Ryan Leaf RC 2.50 1.10
❑ 223 Darryl Williams .10 .05
❑ 224 Mike Alstott .40 .18
❑ 225 Reidel Anthony .20 .09
❑ 226 Derrick Brooks .10 .05
❑ 227 Horace Copeland .10 .05
❑ 228 Trent Dilfer .40 .18
❑ 229 Warrick Dunn .40 .18
❑ 230 Hardy Nickerson .10 .05
❑ 231 Warren Sapp .20 .09
❑ 232 Karl Williams .10 .05
❑ 233 Blaine Bishop .10 .05
❑ 234 Willie Davis .10 .05
❑ 235 Eddie George .75 .35
❑ 236 Derrick Mason .20 .09
❑ 237 Bruce Matthews .10 .05
❑ 238 Steve McNair .40 .18
❑ 239 Chris Sanders .10 .05
❑ 240 Rodney Thomas .10 .05
❑ 241 Frank Wycheck .10 .05
❑ 242 Terry Allen .40 .18
❑ 243 Jamie Asher .10 .05
❑ 244 Larry Bowie .10 .05
❑ 245 Albert Connell .10 .05
❑ 246 Stephen Davis .10 .05
❑ 247 Gus Frerotte .10 .05
❑ 248 Ken Harvey .10 .05
❑ 249 Leslie Shepherd .10 .05
❑ 250 Michael Westbrook .20 .09
❑ S1 Mark Brunell Sample 1.00 .45

1999 Paramount

	MINT	NRMT
COMPLETE SET (250)	50.00	22.00

❑ 1 David Boston RC 2.50 1.10
❑ 2 Larry Centers .10 .05
❑ 3 Joel Makovicka RC 1.25 .55
❑ 4 Eric Metcalf .10 .05
❑ 5 Rob Moore .20 .09
❑ 6 Adrian Murrell .20 .09
❑ 7 Jake Plummer .75 .35
❑ 8 Frank Sanders .20 .09
❑ 9 Aeneas Williams .10 .05
❑ 10 Morten Andersen .10 .05
❑ 11 Jamal Anderson .40 .18
❑ 12 Chris Chandler .20 .09
❑ 13 Tim Dwight .40 .18
❑ 14 Terance Mathis .20 .09
❑ 15 Jeff Paulk RC 1.25 .55
❑ 16 O.J. Santiago .10 .05
❑ 17 Chuck Smith .10 .05
❑ 18 Peter Boulware .10 .05
❑ 19 Priest Holmes .40 .18
❑ 20 Michael Jackson .10 .05
❑ 21 Jermaine Lewis .20 .09
❑ 22 Ray Lewis .20 .09
❑ 23 Michael McCrary .10 .05
❑ 24 Bennie Thompson .10 .05
❑ 25 Rod Woodson .20 .09
❑ 26 Shawn Bryson RC 1.25 .55
❑ 27 Doug Flutie .50 .23
❑ 28 Eric Moulds .40 .18
❑ 29 Peerless Price RC 1.50 .70
❑ 30 Andre Reed .20 .09
❑ 31 Jay Riemersma .10 .05
❑ 32 Antowain Smith .40 .18
❑ 33 Bruce Smith .20 .09
❑ 34 Michael Bates .10 .05
❑ 35 Steve Beuerlein .10 .05
❑ 36 Tim Biakabutuka .20 .09
❑ 37 Kevin Greene .10 .05
❑ 38 Anthony Johnson .10 .05
❑ 39 Fred Lane .10 .05
❑ 40 Muhsin Muhammad .20 .09
❑ 41 Wesley Walls .20 .09
❑ 42 D'Wayne Bates RC .75 .35
❑ 43 Edgar Bennett .10 .05
❑ 44 Marty Booker RC 1.25 .55
❑ 45 Curtis Conway .20 .09
❑ 46 Bobby Engram .20 .09
❑ 47 Curtis Enis .40 .18
❑ 48 Erik Kramer .10 .05
❑ 49 Cade McNown RC 1.50 .70
❑ 50 Jeff Blake .20 .09
❑ 51 Scott Covington RC 1.25 .55
❑ 52 Corey Dillon .40 .18
❑ 53 Quincy Jackson RC .75 .35
❑ 54 Carl Pickens .20 .09
❑ 55 Darnay Scott .10 .05
❑ 56 Akili Smith RC 2.50 1.10
❑ 57 Craig Yeast RC .75 .35
❑ 58 Jerry Ball .10 .05
❑ 59 Darrin Chiaverini RC .75 .35
❑ 60 Tim Couch RC 4.00 1.80
❑ 61 Ty Detmer .20 .09
❑ 62 Kevin Johnson RC 2.50 1.10
❑ 63 Terry Kirby .10 .05
❑ 64 Daylon McCutcheon RC .40 .18
❑ 65 Irv Smith .10 .05
❑ 66 Troy Aikman 1.00 .45
❑ 67 Ebenezer Ekuban RC .75 .35
❑ 68 Michael Irvin .20 .09
❑ 69 Daryl Johnston .10 .05
❑ 70 Wane McGarity RC .75 .35
❑ 71 Dat Nguyen RC 1.25 .55
❑ 72 Deion Sanders .40 .18
❑ 73 Emmitt Smith 1.00 .45
❑ 74 Bubby Brister .10 .05
❑ 75 Terrell Davis 1.00 .45
❑ 76 Jason Elam .10 .05
❑ 77 Olandis Gary RC 2.50 1.10
❑ 78 Brian Griese .75 .35
❑ 79 Ed McCaffrey .20 .09
❑ 80 Travis McGriff RC 1.25 .55
❑ 81 Shannon Sharpe .20 .09
❑ 82 Rod Smith .20 .09
❑ 83 Charlie Batch .75 .35
❑ 84 Chris Claiborne RC .40 .18
❑ 85 Germane Crowell .20 .09
❑ 86 Sedrick Irvin RC 1.25 .55
❑ 87 Herman Moore .40 .18
❑ 88 Johnnie Morton .20 .09
❑ 89 Barry Sanders 1.50 .70
❑ 90 Robert Brooks .20 .09
❑ 91 Aaron Brooks RC 5.00 2.20
❑ 92 Mark Chmura .10 .05
❑ 93 Brett Favre 1.50 .70
❑ 94 Antonio Freeman .40 .18
❑ 95 Vonnie Holliday .10 .05
❑ 96 Dorsey Levens .40 .18
❑ 97 De'Mond Parker RC 1.25 .55
❑ 98 Ken Dilger .10 .05
❑ 99 Marvin Harrison .40 .18
❑ 100 Edgerrin James RC 8.00 3.60
❑ 101 Peyton Manning 1.50 .70
❑ 102 Jerome Pathon .10 .05
❑ 103 Mike Peterson RC .75 .35
❑ 104 Marcus Pollard .10 .05
❑ 105 Tavian Banks .10 .05
❑ 106 Reggie Barlow .10 .05
❑ 107 Tony Boselli .10 .05
❑ 108 Mark Brunell .60 .25
❑ 109 Keenan McCardell .20 .09
❑ 110 Bryce Paup .10 .05
❑ 111 Jimmy Smith .20 .09
❑ 112 Fred Taylor 1.00 .45
❑ 113 Dave Thomas RC .10 .05
❑ 114 Kimble Anders .20 .09
❑ 115 Donnell Bennett .10 .05
❑ 116 Mike Cloud RC 1.25 .55

❑ 117 Tony Gonzalez .20 .09
❑ 118 Elvis Grbac .20 .09
❑ 119 Larry Parker RC .75 .35
❑ 120 Andre Rison .20 .09
❑ 121 Brian Shay RC .75 .35
❑ 122 Karim Abdul-Jabbar .20 .09
❑ 123 Oronde Gadsden .10 .05
❑ 124 James Johnson RC 1.25 .55
❑ 125 Rob Konrad RC .75 .35
❑ 126 Dan Marino 1.50 .70
❑ 127 O.J. McDuffie .20 .09
❑ 128 Zach Thomas .20 .09
❑ 129 Cris Carter .40 .18
❑ 130 Daunte Culpepper RC 8.00 3.60
❑ 131 Randall Cunningham .40 .18
❑ 132 Matthew Hatchette .10 .05
❑ 133 Leroy Hoard .10 .05
❑ 134 Randy Moss 1.50 .70
❑ 135 John Randle .20 .09
❑ 136 Jake Reed .20 .09
❑ 137 Robert Smith .40 .18
❑ 138 Michael Bishop RC 1.50 .70
❑ 139 Drew Bledsoe .60 .25
❑ 140 Ben Coates .20 .09
❑ 141 Kevin Faulk RC 2.00 .90
❑ 142 Terry Glenn .40 .18
❑ 143 Shawn Jefferson .10 .05
❑ 144 Andy Katzenmoyer RC 1.25 .55
❑ 145 Tony Simmons .10 .05
❑ 146 Cuncho Brown RC .75 .35
❑ 147 Cam Cleeland .10 .05
❑ 148 Mark Fields .10 .05
❑ 149 La'Roi Glover .10 .05
❑ 150 Andre Hastings .10 .05
❑ 151 Billy Joe Hobert .10 .05
❑ 152 William Roaf .10 .05
❑ 153 Billy Joe Tolliver .10 .05
❑ 154 Ricky Williams RC 5.00 2.20
❑ 155 Jessie Armstead .10 .05
❑ 156 Tiki Barber .10 .05
❑ 157 Gary Brown .10 .05
❑ 158 Kent Graham .10 .05
❑ 159 Ike Hilliard .10 .05
❑ 160 Joe Montgomery RC 1.25 .55
❑ 161 Amani Toomer .10 .05
❑ 162 Charles Way .10 .05
❑ 163 Wayne Chrebet .20 .09
❑ 164 Bryan Cox .10 .05
❑ 165 Aaron Glenn .10 .05
❑ 166 Keyshawn Johnson .40 .18
❑ 167 Leon Johnson .10 .05
❑ 168 Curtis Martin .40 .18
❑ 169 Vinny Testaverde .20 .09
❑ 170 Dedric Ward .10 .05
❑ 171 Tim Brown .40 .18
❑ 172 Dameane Douglas RC 1.25 .55
❑ 173 Rickey Dudley .10 .05
❑ 174 James Jett .20 .09
❑ 175 Napoleon Kaufman .40 .18
❑ 176 Darrell Russell .10 .05
❑ 177 Harvey Williams .10 .05
❑ 178 Charles Woodson .40 .18
❑ 179 Na Brown RC 1.25 .55
❑ 180 Hugh Douglas .10 .05
❑ 181 Cecil Martin RC .75 .35
❑ 182 Donovan McNabb RC 5.00 2.20
❑ 183 Duce Staley .40 .18
❑ 184 Kevin Turner .10 .05
❑ 185 Jerome Bettis .40 .18
❑ 186 Troy Edwards RC 1.50 .70
❑ 187 Jason Gildon .10 .05
❑ 188 Courtney Hawkins .10 .05
❑ 189 Malcolm Johnson RC .75 .35
❑ 190 Kordell Stewart .40 .18
❑ 191 Jerame Tuman RC .75 .35
❑ 192 Amos Zereoue RC 1.25 .55
❑ 193 Isaac Bruce .40 .18
❑ 194 Kevin Carter .10 .05
❑ 195 Jeremaine Copeland RC .75 .35
❑ 196 Joe Germaine RC 1.25 .55
❑ 197 Az-Zahir Hakim .10 .05
❑ 198 Torry Holt RC 3.00 1.35
❑ 199 Amp Lee .10 .05
❑ 200 Ricky Proehl .10 .05
❑ 201 Charlie Jones .10 .05
❑ 202 Freddie Jones .10 .05
❑ 203 Ryan Leaf .40 .18
❑ 204 Natrone Means .20 .09
❑ 205 Mikhael Ricks .10 .05
❑ 206 Junior Seau .20 .09
❑ 207 Bryan Still .10 .05
❑ 208 Garrison Hearst .20 .09
❑ 209 Terry Jackson RC .75 .35
❑ 210 R.W. McQuarters .10 .05
❑ 211 Ken Norton Jr. .10 .05
❑ 212 Terrell Owens .40 .18
❑ 213 Jerry Rice 1.00 .45
❑ 214 J.J. Stokes .20 .09
❑ 215 Tai Streets RC 1.25 .55
❑ 216 Steve Young .60 .25
❑ 217 Karsten Bailey RC .75 .35
❑ 218 Chad Brown .10 .05
❑ 219 Joey Galloway .40 .18
❑ 220 Ahman Green .20 .09
❑ 221 Brock Huard RC 2.00 .90
❑ 222 Cortez Kennedy .10 .05
❑ 223 Jon Kitna .40 .18
❑ 224 Shawn Springs .10 .05
❑ 225 Ricky Watters .20 .09
❑ 226 Mike Alstott .40 .18
❑ 227 Reidel Anthony .20 .09
❑ 228 Trent Dilfer .20 .09
❑ 229 Warrick Dunn .40 .18
❑ 230 Bert Emanuel .20 .09
❑ 231 Martin Gramatica RC .40 .18
❑ 232 Jacquez Green .20 .09
❑ 233 Shaun King RC 2.50 1.10
❑ 234 Anthony McFarland RC 1.25 .55
❑ 235 Warren Sapp .20 .09
❑ 236 Willie Davis .10 .05
❑ 237 Kevin Dyson .20 .09
❑ 238 Eddie George .50 .23
❑ 239 Darran Hall RC .75 .35
❑ 240 Jackie Harris .10 .05
❑ 241 Steve McNair .40 .18
❑ 242 Yancey Thigpen .10 .05
❑ 243 Frank Wycheck .10 .05
❑ 244 Stephen Alexander .10 .05
❑ 245 Champ Bailey RC 1.50 .70
❑ 246 Stephen Davis .40 .18
❑ 247 Darrell Green .10 .05
❑ 248 Skip Hicks .40 .18
❑ 249 Brian Mitchell .10 .05
❑ 250 Michael Westbrook .20 .09

2000 Paramount

	MINT	NRMT
COMPLETE SET (249)	40.00	18.00

❑ 1 David Boston .40 .18
❑ 2 Thomas Jones RC 1.25 .55
❑ 3 Rob Moore .20 .09
❑ 4 Jake Plummer .40 .18
❑ 5 Simeon Rice .10 .05
❑ 6 Frank Sanders .20 .09
❑ 7 Raynoch Thompson RC .20 .09
❑ 8 Jamal Anderson .40 .18
❑ 9 Chris Chandler .20 .09
❑ 10 Bob Christian .10 .05
❑ 11 Tim Dwight .40 .18
❑ 12 Byron Hanspard .10 .05
❑ 13 Terance Mathis .20 .09
❑ 14 Mareno Philyaw RC .60 .25
❑ 15 Tony Banks .20 .09
❑ 16 Priest Holmes .20 .09
❑ 17 Qadry Ismail .10 .05
❑ 18 Pat Johnson .10 .05
❑ 19 Jamal Lewis RC 2.50 1.10
❑ 20 Chris Redman RC 1.50 .70
❑ 21 Shannon Sharpe .20 .09
❑ 22 Travis Taylor RC 1.00 .45
❑ 23 Erik Flowers RC 1.00 .45
❑ 24 Doug Flutie .50 .23
❑ 25 Rob Johnson .20 .09
❑ 26 Jonathan Linton .10 .05
❑ 27 Corey Moore RC .60 .25
❑ 28 Eric Moulds .40 .18
❑ 29 Peerless Price .40 .18
❑ 30 Jay Riemersma .10 .05
❑ 31 Antowain Smith .20 .09
❑ 32 Rashard Anderson RC .60 .25
❑ 33 Steve Beuerlein .20 .09
❑ 34 Tim Biakabutuka .20 .09
❑ 35 Donald Hayes .10 .05
❑ 36 Patrick Jeffers .40 .18
❑ 37 Jeff Lewis .10 .05
❑ 38 Muhsin Muhammad .20 .09
❑ 39 Wesley Walls .10 .05
❑ 40 Bobby Engram .20 .09
❑ 41 Curtis Enis .20 .09
❑ 42 Cade McNown .40 .18
❑ 43 Jim Miller .10 .05
❑ 44 Marcus Robinson .40 .18
❑ 45 Brian Urlacher RC 2.50 1.10
❑ 46 Dez White RC .60 .25
❑ 47 Michael Basnight .10 .05
❑ 48 Corey Dillon .40 .18
❑ 49 Ron Dugans RC .60 .25
❑ 50 Willie Jackson .10 .05
❑ 51 Darnay Scott .20 .09
❑ 52 Akili Smith .40 .18
❑ 53 Peter Warrick RC 2.50 1.10
❑ 54 Courtney Brown RC 1.00 .45
❑ 55 Darrin Chiaverini .10 .05
❑ 56 Tim Couch .75 .35
❑ 57 Kevin Johnson .40 .18
❑ 58 Terry Kirby .10 .05
❑ 59 Dennis Northcutt RC 1.00 .45
❑ 60 Travis Prentice RC 1.25 .55
❑ 61 Leslie Shepherd .10 .05
❑ 62 Troy Aikman 1.00 .45
❑ 63 Joey Galloway .40 .18
❑ 64 Rocket Ismail .20 .09
❑ 65 David LaFleur .10 .05
❑ 66 Emmitt Smith 1.00 .45
❑ 67 Jason Tucker .20 .09
❑ 68 Chris Warren .10 .05
❑ 69 Michael Wiley RC .75 .35
❑ 70 Desmond Clark .10 .05
❑ 71 Chris Cole RC .60 .25
❑ 72 Terrell Davis 1.00 .45
❑ 73 Olandis Gary .40 .18
❑ 74 Brian Griese .50 .23
❑ 75 Jarious Jackson RC .75 .35
❑ 76 Ed McCaffrey .40 .18
❑ 77 Deltha O'Neal RC .60 .25
❑ 78 Rod Smith .20 .09
❑ 79 Charlie Batch .40 .18
❑ 80 Germane Crowell .20 .09
❑ 81 Reuben Droughns RC .75 .35
❑ 82 Terry Fair .10 .05
❑ 83 Herman Moore .20 .09
❑ 84 Johnnie Morton .20 .09
❑ 85 Barry Sanders 1.25 .55
❑ 86 James Stewart .20 .09
❑ 87 Corey Bradford .20 .09
❑ 88 Tyrone Davis .10 .05
❑ 89 Brett Favre 1.50 .70
❑ 90 Bubba Franks RC 1.00 .45
❑ 91 Antonio Freeman .40 .18
❑ 92 Matt Hasselbeck .10 .05
❑ 93 Dorsey Levens .20 .09
❑ 94 Anthony Lucas RC .60 .25
❑ 95 Bill Schroeder .20 .09
❑ 96 Ken Dilger .10 .05
❑ 97 E.G. Green .10 .05
❑ 98 Marvin Harrison .40 .18
❑ 99 Edgerrin James 1.50 .70
❑ 100 Peyton Manning 1.25 .55

	Card	NRMT	VG-E
❑	101 Jerome Pathon	.20	.09
❑	102 Marcus Washington RC	.75	.35
❑	103 Terrence Wilkins	.40	.18
❑	104 Kyle Brady	.10	.05
❑	105 Mark Brunell	.60	.25
❑	106 Kevin Hardy	.10	.05
❑	107 Keenan McCardell	.20	.09
❑	108 Jimmy Smith	.20	.09
❑	109 R.Jay Soward RC	.75	.35
❑	110 Shyrone Stith RC	.60	.25
❑	111 Fred Taylor	.50	.23
❑	112 Alvis Whitted	.10	.05
❑	113 Derrick Alexander	.20	.09
❑	114 Kimble Anders	.10	.05
❑	115 Donnell Bennett	.10	.05
❑	116 Tony Gonzalez	.20	.09
❑	117 Elvis Grbac	.20	.09
❑	118 Kevin Lockett	.10	.05
❑	119 Sylvester Morris RC	1.50	.70
❑	120 Tony Richardson RC	.20	.09
❑	121 Deon Dyer RC	.60	.25
❑	122 Oronde Gadsden	.20	.09
❑	123 Damon Huard	.40	.18
❑	124 James Johnson	.10	.05
❑	125 Dan Marino	1.50	.70
❑	126 Tony Martin	.20	.09
❑	127 O.J. McDuffie	.20	.09
❑	128 Zach Thomas	.20	.09
❑	129 Cris Carter	.40	.18
❑	130 Daunte Culpepper	.75	.35
❑	131 Leroy Hoard	.10	.05
❑	132 Chris Hovan RC	.60	.25
❑	133 Randy Moss	1.25	.55
❑	134 John Randle	.20	.09
❑	135 Robert Smith	.40	.18
❑	136 Troy Walters RC	.75	.35
❑	137 Drew Bledsoe	.60	.25
❑	138 Tom Brady RC	.75	.35
❑	139 Troy Brown	.10	.05
❑	140 Kevin Faulk	.10	.05
❑	141 Terry Glenn	.20	.09
❑	142 J.R. Redmond RC	1.00	.45
❑	143 Tony Simmons	.10	.05
❑	144 David Stachelski RC	.60	.25
❑	145 Jeff Blake	.20	.09
❑	146 Marc Bulger RC	.75	.35
❑	147 Cam Cleeland	.10	.05
❑	148 Sherrod Gideon RC	.60	.25
❑	149 Darren Howard RC	.60	.25
❑	150 Chad Morton RC	.75	.35
❑	151 Keith Poole	.10	.05
❑	152 Ricky Williams	1.00	.45
❑	153 Tiki Barber	.20	.09
❑	154 Kerry Collins	.20	.09
❑	155 Ron Dayne RC	2.50	1.10
❑	156 Ike Hilliard	.20	.09
❑	157 Joe Jurevicius	.10	.05
❑	158 Pete Mitchell	.10	.05
❑	159 Joe Montgomery	.10	.05
❑	160 Amani Toomer	.20	.09
❑	161 John Abraham RC	.60	.25
❑	162 Anthony Becht RC	.75	.35
❑	163 Wayne Chrebet	.20	.09
❑	164 Laveranues Coles RC	1.25	.55
❑	165 Ray Lucas	.40	.18
❑	166 Curtis Martin	.40	.18
❑	167 Chad Pennington RC	2.50	1.10
❑	168 Vinny Testaverde	.20	.09
❑	169 Dedric Ward	.20	.09
❑	170 Tim Brown	.40	.18
❑	171 Rich Gannon	.20	.09
❑	172 Bobby Hoying	.20	.09
❑	173 James Jett	.10	.05
❑	174 Napoleon Kaufman	.20	.09
❑	175 Jerry Porter RC	.75	.35
❑	176 Tyrone Wheatley	.20	.09
❑	177 Charles Woodson	.40	.18
❑	178 Dameane Douglas	.10	.05
❑	179 Charles Johnson	.20	.09
❑	180 Donovan McNabb	.60	.25
❑	181 Todd Pinkston RC	.75	.35
❑	182 Gari Scott RC	.60	.25
❑	183 Torrance Small	.10	.05
❑	184 Duce Staley	.40	.18
❑	185 Jerome Bettis	.40	.18
❑	186 Plaxico Burress RC	1.50	.70
❑	187 Troy Edwards	.20	.09
❑	188 Danny Farmer RC	.75	.35
❑	189 Richard Huntley	.10	.05
❑	190 Tee Martin RC	1.25	.55
❑	191 Kordell Stewart	.40	.18
❑	192 Hines Ward	.10	.05
❑	193 Isaac Bruce	.40	.18
❑	194 Trung Canidate RC	.75	.35
❑	195 Marshall Faulk	.50	.23
❑	196 Az-Zahir Hakim	.20	.09
❑	197 Torry Holt	.40	.18
❑	198 Tony Horne	.10	.05
❑	199 Ricky Proehl	.10	.05
❑	200 Kurt Warner	1.50	.70
❑	201 Jermaine Fazande	.10	.05
❑	202 Trevor Gaylor RC	.60	.25
❑	203 Jeff Graham	.10	.05
❑	204 Jim Harbaugh	.20	.09
❑	205 Freddie Jones	.10	.05
❑	206 Mikhael Ricks	.10	.05
❑	207 Junior Seau	.20	.09
❑	208 Fred Beasley	.10	.05
❑	209 Giovanni Carmazzi RC	1.00	.45
❑	210 Jeff Garcia	.40	.18
❑	211 Charlie Garner	.20	.09
❑	212 Terrell Owens	.40	.18
❑	213 Tim Rattay RC	1.25	.55
❑	214 Jerry Rice	1.00	.45
❑	215 J.J. Stokes	.20	.09
❑	216 Steve Young	.60	.25
❑	217 Shaun Alexander RC	2.00	.90
❑	218 Sean Dawkins	.10	.05
❑	219 Darrell Jackson RC	1.25	.55
❑	220 Jon Kitna	.40	.18
❑	221 Derrick Mayes	.20	.09
❑	222 Charlie Rogers	.10	.05
❑	223 Shawn Springs	.10	.05
❑	224 Ricky Watters	.20	.09
❑	225 Mike Alstott	.40	.18
❑	226 Reidel Anthony	.10	.05
❑	227 Warrick Dunn	.40	.18
❑	228 Jacquez Green	.20	.09
❑	229 Joe Hamilton RC	1.00	.45
❑	230 Keyshawn Johnson	.40	.18
❑	231 Shaun King	.60	.25
❑	232 Warren Sapp	.20	.09
❑	233 Keith Bulluck RC	.60	.25
❑	234 Kevin Dyson	.20	.09
❑	235 Eddie George	.50	.23
❑	236 Jevon Kearse	.40	.18
❑	237 Erron Kinney RC	.75	.35
❑	238 Steve McNair	.40	.18
❑	239 Neil O'Donnell	.10	.05
❑	240 Yancy Thigpen	.10	.05
❑	241 Frank Wycheck	.10	.05
❑	243 Champ Bailey	.20	.09
❑	244 Larry Centers	.10	.05
❑	245 Albert Connell	.10	.05
❑	246 Stephen Davis	.40	.18
❑	247 Todd Husak RC	.75	.35
❑	248 Brad Johnson	.40	.18
❑	249 Chris Samuels RC	.60	.25
❑	250 Michael Westbrook	.20	.09

1964 Philadelphia

	NRMT	VG-E
COMPLETE SET (198)	900.00	400.00
WRAPPER (1-CENT)	40.00	18.00
WRAPPER (5-CENT)	15.00	6.75

	Card	NRMT	VG-E
❑	1 Raymond Berry	20.00	9.00
❑	2 Tom Gilburg	2.50	1.10
❑	3 John Mackey RC	30.00	13.50
❑	4 Gino Marchetti	5.00	2.20
❑	5 Jim Martin	2.50	1.10
❑	6 Tom Matte RC	6.00	2.70
❑	7 Jimmy Orr	2.50	1.10
❑	8 Jim Parker	4.00	1.80
❑	9 Bill Pellington	2.50	1.10
❑	10 Alex Sandusky	2.50	1.10
❑	11 Dick Szymanski	2.50	1.10
❑	12 John Unitas	45.00	20.00
❑	13 Baltimore Colts Team Card	3.00	1.35
❑	14 Baltimore Colts Play Card (Don Shula)	35.00	16.00
❑	15 Doug Atkins	5.00	2.20
❑	16 Ron Bull	2.50	1.10
❑	17 Mike Ditka	40.00	18.00
❑	18 Joe Fortunato	2.50	1.10
❑	19 Willie Galimore	3.00	1.35
❑	20 Joe Marconi	2.50	1.10
❑	21 Bennie McRae RC	2.50	1.10
❑	22 Johnny Morris	2.50	1.10
❑	23 Richie Petitbon	2.50	1.10
❑	24 Mike Pyle	2.50	1.10
❑	25 Roosevelt Taylor RC	4.00	1.80
❑	26 Bill Wade	3.00	1.35
❑	27 Chicago Bears Team Card	3.00	1.35
❑	28 Chicago Bears Play Card (George Halas)	12.00	5.50
❑	29 Johnny Brewer	2.50	1.10
❑	30 Jim Brown	80.00	36.00
❑	31 Gary Collins RC	8.00	3.60
❑	32 Vince Costello	2.50	1.10
❑	33 Galen Fiss	2.50	1.10
❑	34 Bill Glass	2.50	1.10
❑	35 Ernie Green RC	3.00	1.35
❑	36 Rich Kreitling	2.50	1.10
❑	37 John Morrow	2.50	1.10
❑	38 Frank Ryan	3.00	1.35
❑	39 Charlie Scales RC	2.50	1.10
❑	40 Dick Schafrath RC	2.50	1.10
❑	41 Cleveland Browns Team Card	3.00	1.35
❑	42 Cleveland Browns Play Card (Blanton Collier)	2.50	1.10
❑	43 Don Bishop	2.50	1.10
❑	44 Frank Clarke RC	3.00	1.35
❑	45 Mike Connelly	2.50	1.10
❑	46 Lee Folkins	2.50	1.10
❑	47 Cornell Green RC	8.00	3.60
❑	48 Bob Lilly	40.00	18.00
❑	49 Amos Marsh	2.50	1.10
❑	50 Tommy McDonald	4.00	1.80
❑	51 Don Meredith	35.00	16.00
❑	52 Pettis Norman RC	3.00	1.35
❑	53 Don Perkins	4.00	1.80
❑	54 Guy Reese	2.50	1.10
❑	55 Dallas Cowboys Team Card	3.00	1.35
❑	56 Dallas Cowboys Play Card (Tom Landry)	15.00	6.75
❑	57 Terry Barr	2.50	1.10
❑	58 Roger Brown	3.00	1.35
❑	59 Gail Cogdill	2.50	1.10
❑	60 John Gordy	2.50	1.10
❑	61 Dick Lane	4.00	1.80
❑	62 Yale Lary	4.00	1.80
❑	63 Dan Lewis	2.50	1.10
❑	64 Darris McCord	2.50	1.10
❑	65 Earl Morrall	3.00	1.35
❑	66 Joe Schmidt	5.00	2.20
❑	67 Pat Studstill RC	3.00	1.35
❑	68 Wayne Walker RC	3.00	1.35
❑	69 Detroit Lions Team Card	3.00	1.35
❑	70 Detroit Lions	2.50	1.10

Card	NRMT	VG-E
Play Card (George Wilson CO)		
❑ 71 Herb Adderley RC	35.00	16.00
❑ 72 Willie Davis RC	30.00	13.50
❑ 73 Forrest Gregg	5.00	2.20
❑ 74 Paul Hornung	35.00	16.00
❑ 75 Hank Jordan	5.00	2.20
❑ 76 Jerry Kramer	6.00	2.70
❑ 77 Tom Moore	3.00	1.35
❑ 78 Jim Ringo UER (Green Bay on front, Philadelphia on back)	5.00	2.20
❑ 79 Bart Starr	40.00	18.00
❑ 80 Jim Taylor	25.00	11.00
❑ 81 Jesse Whittenton RC	3.00	1.35
❑ 82 Willie Wood	8.00	3.60
❑ 83 Green Bay Packers Team Card	6.00	2.70
❑ 84 Green Bay Packers Play Card (Vince Lombardi)	35.00	16.00
❑ 85 Jon Arnett	2.50	1.10
❑ 86 Pervis Atkins RC	2.50	1.10
❑ 87 Dick Bass	3.00	1.35
❑ 88 Carroll Dale	4.00	1.80
❑ 89 Roman Gabriel	6.00	2.70
❑ 90 Ed Meador	2.50	1.10
❑ 91 Merlin Olsen RC	50.00	22.00
❑ 92 Jack Pardee RC	4.00	1.80
❑ 93 Jim Phillips	2.50	1.10
❑ 94 Carver Shannon	2.50	1.10
❑ 95 Frank Varrichione	2.50	1.10
❑ 96 Danny Villanueva	2.50	1.10
❑ 97 Los Angeles Rams Team Card	3.00	1.35
❑ 98 Los Angeles Rams Play Card (Harland Svare)	2.50	1.10
❑ 99 Grady Alderman RC	3.00	1.35
❑ 100 Larry Bowie	2.50	1.10
❑ 101 Bill Brown RC	6.00	2.70
❑ 102 Paul Flatley RC	2.50	1.10
❑ 103 Rip Hawkins	2.50	1.10
❑ 104 Jim Marshall	8.00	3.60
❑ 105 Tommy Mason	3.00	1.35
❑ 106 Jim Prestel	2.50	1.10
❑ 107 Jerry Reichow	2.50	1.10
❑ 108 Ed Sharockman	2.50	1.10
❑ 109 Fran Tarkenton	35.00	16.00
❑ 110 Mick Tingelhoff RC	6.00	2.70
❑ 111 Minnesota Vikings Team Card	3.00	1.35
❑ 112 Minnesota Vikings Play Card (Norm Van Brocklin)	4.00	1.80
❑ 113 Erich Barnes	2.50	1.10
❑ 114 Roosevelt Brown	4.00	1.80
❑ 115 Don Chandler	2.50	1.10
❑ 116 Darrell Dess	2.50	1.10
❑ 117 Frank Gifford	35.00	16.00
❑ 118 Dick James	2.50	1.10
❑ 119 Jim Katcavage	2.50	1.10
❑ 120 John Lovetere	2.50	1.10
❑ 121 Dick Lynch RC	3.00	1.35
❑ 122 Jim Patton	2.50	1.10
❑ 123 Del Shofner	2.50	1.10
❑ 124 Y.A. Tittle	20.00	9.00
❑ 125 New York Giants Team Card	3.00	1.35
❑ 126 New York Giants Play Card (Allie Sherman)	2.50	1.10
❑ 127 Sam Baker	2.50	1.10
❑ 128 Maxie Baughan	2.50	1.10
❑ 129 Timmy Brown	3.00	1.35
❑ 130 Mike Clark	2.50	1.10
❑ 131 Irv Cross RC	3.00	1.35
❑ 132 Ted Dean	2.50	1.10
❑ 133 Ron Goodwin	2.50	1.10
❑ 134 King Hill	2.50	1.10
❑ 135 Clarence Peaks	2.50	1.10
❑ 136 Pete Retzlaff	3.00	1.35
❑ 137 Jim Schrader	2.50	1.10
❑ 138 Norm Snead	3.00	1.35
❑ 139 Philadelphia Eagles Team Card	3.00	1.35
❑ 140 Philadelphia Eagles Play Card (Nick Skorich)	2.50	1.10
❑ 141 Gary Ballman RC	2.50	1.10
❑ 142 Charley Bradshaw	2.50	1.10
❑ 143 Ed Brown	3.00	1.35
❑ 144 John Henry Johnson	4.00	1.80
❑ 145 Joe Krupa	2.50	1.10
❑ 146 Bill Mack	2.50	1.10
❑ 147 Lou Michaels	2.50	1.10
❑ 148 Buzz Nutter	2.50	1.10
❑ 149 Myron Pottios	2.50	1.10
❑ 150 John Reger	2.50	1.10
❑ 151 Mike Sandusky	2.50	1.10
❑ 152 Clendon Thomas	2.50	1.10
❑ 153 Pittsburgh Steelers Team Card	3.00	1.35
❑ 154 Pittsburgh Steelers Play Card (Buddy Parker)	2.50	1.10
❑ 155 Kermit Alexander RC	3.00	1.35
❑ 156 Bernie Casey	3.00	1.35
❑ 157 Dan Colchico	2.50	1.10
❑ 158 Clyde Conner	2.50	1.10
❑ 159 Tommy Davis	2.50	1.10
❑ 160 Matt Hazeltine	2.50	1.10
❑ 161 Jim Johnson RC	15.00	6.75
❑ 162 Don Lisbon RC	2.50	1.10
❑ 163 Lamar McHan	2.50	1.10
❑ 164 Bob St. Clair	4.00	1.80
❑ 165 J.D. Smith	2.50	1.10
❑ 166 Abe Woodson	2.50	1.10
❑ 167 San Francisco 49ers Team Card	3.00	1.35
❑ 168 San Francisco 49ers Play Card (Red Hickey)	2.50	1.10
❑ 169 Garland Boyette UER (Photo on front is not Boyette)	2.50	1.10
❑ 170 Bobby Joe Conrad	3.00	1.35
❑ 171 Bob DeMarco RC	2.50	1.10
❑ 172 Ken Gray RC	2.50	1.10
❑ 173 Jimmy Hill	2.50	1.10
❑ 174 Charlie Johnson UER (Misspelled Charley on both sides)	3.00	1.35
❑ 175 Ernie McMillan	2.50	1.10
❑ 176 Dale Meinert	2.50	1.10
❑ 177 Luke Owens	2.50	1.10
❑ 178 Sonny Randle	2.50	1.10
❑ 179 Joe Robb	2.50	1.10
❑ 180 Bill Stacy	2.50	1.10
❑ 181 St. Louis Cardinals Team Card	3.00	1.35
❑ 182 St. Louis Cardinals Play Card (Wally Lemm)	2.50	1.10
❑ 183 Bill Barnes	2.50	1.10
❑ 184 Don Bosseler	2.50	1.10
❑ 185 Sam Huff	6.00	2.70
❑ 186 Sonny Jurgensen	20.00	9.00
❑ 187 Bob Khayat	2.50	1.10
❑ 188 Riley Mattson	2.50	1.10
❑ 189 Bobby Mitchell	6.00	2.70
❑ 190 John Nisby	2.50	1.10
❑ 191 Vince Promuto	2.50	1.10
❑ 192 Joe Rutgens	2.50	1.10
❑ 193 Lonnie Sanders	2.50	1.10
❑ 194 Jim Steffen	2.50	1.10
❑ 195 Washington Redskins Team Card	3.00	1.35
❑ 196 Washington Redskins Play Card (Bill McPeak)	2.50	1.10
❑ 197 Checklist 1 UER (Dated 1963)	30.00	13.50
❑ 198 Checklist 2 UER (Dated 1963, 174 Charley Johnson should be Charlie)	55.00	25.00

1965 Philadelphia

	NRMT	VG-E
COMPLETE SET (198)	800.00	350.00
WRAPPER (5-CENT)	15.00	6.75
❑ 1 Baltimore Colts Team Card	15.00	6.75
❑ 2 Raymond Berry	8.00	3.60
❑ 3 Bob Boyd	2.00	.90
❑ 4 Wendell Harris	2.00	.90
❑ 5 Jerry Logan	2.00	.90
❑ 6 Tony Lorick	2.00	.90
❑ 7 Lou Michaels	2.00	.90
❑ 8 Lenny Moore	8.00	3.60
❑ 9 Jimmy Orr	3.00	1.35
❑ 10 Jim Parker	4.00	1.80
❑ 11 Dick Szymanski	2.00	.90
❑ 12 John Unitas	40.00	18.00
❑ 13 Bob Vogel RC	2.00	.90
❑ 14 Baltimore Colts Play Card (Don Shula)	20.00	9.00
❑ 15 Chicago Bears Team Card	3.00	1.35
❑ 16 Jon Arnett	2.00	.90
❑ 17 Doug Atkins	5.00	2.20
❑ 18 Rudy Bukich RC	3.00	1.35
❑ 19 Mike Ditka	35.00	13.50
❑ 20 Dick Evey	2.00	.90
❑ 21 Joe Fortunato	2.00	.90
❑ 22 Bobby Joe Green RC	2.00	.90
❑ 23 Johnny Morris	2.00	.90
❑ 24 Mike Pyle	2.00	.90
❑ 25 Roosevelt Taylor	3.00	1.35
❑ 26 Bill Wade	3.00	1.35
❑ 27 Bob Wetoska	2.00	.90
❑ 28 Chicago Bears Play Card (George Halas)	8.00	3.60
❑ 29 Cleveland Browns Team Card	3.00	1.35
❑ 30 Walter Beach	2.00	.90
❑ 31 Jim Brown	75.00	34.00
❑ 32 Gary Collins	3.00	1.35
❑ 33 Bill Glass	2.00	.90
❑ 34 Ernie Green	2.00	.90
❑ 35 Jim Houston RC	2.00	.90
❑ 36 Dick Modzelewski	2.00	.90
❑ 37 Bernie Parrish	2.00	.90
❑ 38 Walter Roberts	2.00	.90
❑ 39 Frank Ryan	3.00	1.35
❑ 40 Dick Schafrath	2.00	.90
❑ 41 Paul Warfield RC	75.00	34.00
❑ 42 Cleveland Browns Play Card (Blanton Collier)	2.00	.90
❑ 43 Dallas Cowboys Team Card UER (Cowboys Dallas on back)	3.00	1.35
❑ 44 Frank Clarke	3.00	1.35
❑ 45 Mike Connelly	2.00	.90
❑ 46 Buddy Dial	2.00	.90
❑ 47 Bob Lilly	30.00	13.50
❑ 48 Tony Liscio RC	2.00	.90
❑ 49 Tommy McDonald	4.00	1.80
❑ 50 Don Meredith	25.00	11.00
❑ 51 Pettis Norman	2.00	.90

❑ 52 Don Perkins 4.00 1.80
❑ 53 Mel Renfro RC 40.00 18.00
❑ 54 Jim Ridlon 2.00 .90
❑ 55 Jerry Tubbs 2.00 .90
❑ 56 Dallas Cowboys 15.00 6.75
Play Card
(Tom Landry)
❑ 57 Detroit Lions 3.00 1.35
Team Card
❑ 58 Terry Barr 2.00 .90
❑ 59 Roger Brown 2.00 .90
❑ 60 Gail Cogdill 2.00 .90
❑ 61 Jim Gibbons 2.00 .90
❑ 62 John Gordy 2.00 .90
❑ 63 Yale Lary 4.00 1.80
❑ 64 Dick LeBeau RC 3.00 1.35
❑ 65 Earl Morrall 3.00 1.35
❑ 66 Nick Pietrosante 2.00 .90
❑ 67 Pat Studstill 2.00 .90
❑ 68 Wayne Walker 3.00 1.35
❑ 69 Tom Watkins 2.00 .90
❑ 70 Detroit Lions 2.00 .90
Play Card
(George Wilson CO)
❑ 71 Green Bay Packers 6.00 2.70
Team Card
❑ 72 Herb Adderley 8.00 3.60
❑ 73 Willie Davis 8.00 3.60
❑ 74 Boyd Dowler 4.00 1.80
❑ 75 Forrest Gregg 5.00 2.20
❑ 76 Paul Hornung 35.00 16.00
❑ 77 Hank Jordan 5.00 2.20
❑ 78 Tom Moore 3.00 1.35
❑ 79 Ray Nitschke 20.00 9.00
❑ 80 Elijah Pitts RC 8.00 3.60
❑ 81 Bart Starr 40.00 18.00
❑ 82 Jim Taylor 20.00 9.00
❑ 83 Willie Wood 6.00 2.70
❑ 84 Green Bay Packers 20.00 9.00
Play Card
(Vince Lombardi)
❑ 85 Los Angeles Rams 3.00 1.35
Team Card
❑ 86 Dick Bass 3.00 1.35
❑ 87 Roman Gabriel 5.00 2.20
❑ 88 Roosevelt Grier 4.00 1.80
❑ 89 Deacon Jones 10.00 4.50
❑ 90 Lamar Lundy RC 4.00 1.80
❑ 91 Marlin McKeever 2.00 .90
❑ 92 Ed Meador 2.00 .90
❑ 93 Bill Munson RC 4.00 1.80
❑ 94 Merlin Olsen 15.00 6.75
❑ 95 Bobby Smith 2.00 .90
❑ 96 Frank Varrichione 2.00 .90
❑ 97 Ben Wilson 2.00 .90
❑ 98 Los Angeles Rams 2.00 .90
Play Card
(Harland Svare)
❑ 99 Minnesota Vikings 3.00 1.35
Team Card
❑ 100 Grady Alderman 2.00 .90
❑ 101 Hal Bedsole RC 2.00 .90
❑ 102 Bill Brown 3.00 1.35
❑ 103 Bill Butler 2.00 .90
❑ 104 Fred Cox RC 3.00 1.35
❑ 105 Carl Eller RC 25.00 11.00
❑ 106 Paul Flatley 2.00 .90
❑ 107 Jim Marshall 6.00 2.70
❑ 108 Tommy Mason 2.00 .90
❑ 109 George Rose 2.00 .90
❑ 110 Fran Tarkenton 25.00 11.00
❑ 111 Mick Tingelhoff 3.00 1.35
❑ 112 Minnesota Vikings 4.00 1.80
Play Card
(Norm Van Brocklin)
❑ 113 New York Giants 3.00 1.35
Team Card
❑ 114 Erich Barnes 2.00 .90
❑ 115 Roosevelt Brown 4.00 1.80
❑ 116 Clarence Childs 2.00 .90
❑ 117 Jerry Hillebrand 2.00 .90
❑ 118 Greg Larson RC 2.00 .90
❑ 119 Dick Lynch 2.00 .90
❑ 120 Joe Morrison RC 4.00 1.80
❑ 121 Lou Slaby 2.00 .90
❑ 122 Aaron Thomas RC 2.00 .90
❑ 123 Steve Thurlow 2.00 .90
❑ 124 Ernie Wheelwright 2.00 .90
❑ 125 Gary Wood RC 2.00 .90
❑ 126 New York Giants 2.00 .90
Play Card
(Allie Sherman)
❑ 127 Philadelphia Eagles 3.00 1.35
Team Card
❑ 128 Sam Baker 2.00 .90
❑ 129 Maxie Baughan 2.00 .90
❑ 130 Timmy Brown 3.00 1.35
❑ 131 Jack Concannon RC 2.00 .90
❑ 132 Irv Cross 3.00 1.35
❑ 133 Earl Gros 2.00 .90
❑ 134 Dave Lloyd 2.00 .90
❑ 135 Floyd Peters RC 2.00 .90
❑ 136 Nate Ramsey 2.00 .90
❑ 137 Pete Retzlaff 3.00 1.35
❑ 138 Jim Ringo 4.00 1.80
❑ 139 Norm Snead 4.00 1.80
❑ 140 Philadelphia Eagles 2.00 .90
Play Card
(Joe Kuharich)
❑ 141 Pittsburgh Steelers 3.00 1.35
Team Card
❑ 142 John Baker 2.00 .90
❑ 143 Gary Ballman 2.00 .90
❑ 144 Charley Bradshaw 2.00 .90
❑ 145 Ed Brown 2.00 .90
❑ 146 Dick Haley 2.00 .90
❑ 147 John Henry Johnson 4.00 1.80
❑ 148 Brady Keys 2.00 .90
❑ 149 Ray Lemek 2.00 .90
❑ 150 Ben McGee 2.00 .90
❑ 151 Clarence Peaks 2.00 .90
❑ 152 Myron Pottios 2.00 .90
❑ 153 Clendon Thomas 2.00 .90
❑ 154 Pittsburgh Steelers 2.00 .90
Play Card
(Buddy Parker)
❑ 155 St. Louis Cardinals 3.00 1.35
Team Card
❑ 156 Jim Bakken RC 3.00 1.35
❑ 157 Joe Childress 2.00 .90
❑ 158 Bobby Joe Conrad 3.00 1.35
❑ 159 Bob DeMarco 2.00 .90
❑ 160 Pat Fischer RC 4.00 1.80
❑ 161 Irv Goode 2.00 .90
❑ 162 Ken Gray 2.00 .90
❑ 163 Charlie Johnson UER 3.00 1.35
(Misspelled Charley
on both sides)
❑ 164 Bill Koman 2.00 .90
❑ 165 Dale Meinert 2.00 .90
❑ 166 Jerry Stovall RC 3.00 1.35
❑ 167 Abe Woodson 2.00 .90
❑ 168 St. Louis Cardinals 2.00 .90
Play Card
(Wally Lemm)
❑ 169 San Francisco 49ers 3.00 1.35
Team Card
❑ 170 Kermit Alexander 2.00 .90
❑ 171 John Brodie 10.00 4.50
❑ 172 Bernie Casey 3.00 1.35
❑ 173 John David Crow 3.00 1.35
❑ 174 Tommy Davis 2.00 .90
❑ 175 Matt Hazeltine 2.00 .90
❑ 176 Jim Johnson 4.00 1.80
❑ 177 Charlie Krueger RC 2.00 .90
❑ 178 Roland Lakes 2.00 .90
❑ 179 George Mira RC 3.00 1.35
❑ 180 Dave Parks RC 3.00 1.35
❑ 181 John Thomas 2.00 .90
❑ 182 San Francisco 49ers 2.00 .90
Play Card
(Jack Christiansen)
❑ 183 Washington Redskins 3.00 1.35
Team Card
❑ 184 Pervis Atkins 2.00 .90
❑ 185 Preston Carpenter 2.00 .90
❑ 186 Angelo Coia 2.00 .90
❑ 187 Sam Huff 6.00 2.70
❑ 188 Sonny Jurgensen 15.00 6.75
❑ 189 Paul Krause RC 20.00 9.00
❑ 190 Jim Martin 2.00 .90
❑ 191 Bobby Mitchell 5.00 2.20
❑ 192 John Nisby 2.00 .90
❑ 193 John Paluck 2.00 .90
❑ 194 Vince Promuto 2.00 .90
❑ 195 Charley Taylor RC 50.00 22.00
❑ 196 Washington Redskins 2.00 .90
Play Card
(Bill McPeak)
❑ 197 Checklist 1 30.00 13.50
❑ 198 Checklist 2 UER 50.00 22.00
(163 Charley Johnson
should be Charlie)

1966 Philadelphia

	NRMT	VG-E
COMPLETE SET (198)	900.00	400.00
WRAPPER (5-CENT)	15.00	6.75

❑ 1 Atlanta Falcons 12.00 5.50
Insignia
❑ 2 Larry Benz 2.00 .90
❑ 3 Dennis Claridge 2.00 .90
❑ 4 Perry Lee Dunn 2.00 .90
❑ 5 Dan Grimm 2.00 .90
❑ 6 Alex Hawkins 2.00 .90
❑ 7 Ralph Heck 2.00 .90
❑ 8 Frank Lasky 2.00 .90
❑ 9 Guy Reese 2.00 .90
❑ 10 Bob Richards 2.00 .90
❑ 11 Ron Smith RC 2.00 .90
❑ 12 Ernie Wheelwright 2.00 .90
❑ 13 Atlanta Falcons 3.00 1.35
Roster
❑ 14 Baltimore Colts 3.00 1.35
Team Card
❑ 15 Raymond Berry 8.00 3.60
❑ 16 Bob Boyd 2.00 .90
❑ 17 Jerry Logan 2.00 .90
❑ 18 John Mackey 6.00 2.70
❑ 19 Tom Matte 4.00 1.80
❑ 20 Lou Michaels 2.00 .90
❑ 21 Lenny Moore 8.00 3.60
❑ 22 Jimmy Orr 2.00 .90
❑ 23 Jim Parker 4.00 1.80
❑ 24 John Unitas 35.00 16.00
❑ 25 Bob Vogel 2.00 .90
❑ 26 Baltimore Colts 4.00 1.80
Play Card
(Lenny Moore
Jim Parker)
❑ 27 Chicago Bears 3.00 1.35
Team Card
❑ 28 Doug Atkins 4.00 1.80
❑ 29 Rudy Bukich 2.00 .90
❑ 30 Ron Bull 2.00 .90
❑ 31 Dick Butkus RC ! 225.00 100.00
❑ 32 Mike Ditka 35.00 16.00
❑ 33 Joe Fortunato 2.00 .90
❑ 34 Bobby Joe Green 2.00 .90
❑ 35 Roger LeClerc 2.00 .90
❑ 36 Johnny Morris 2.00 .90
❑ 37 Mike Pyle 2.00 .90
❑ 38 Gale Sayers RC ! 200.00 90.00
❑ 39 Chicago Bears 35.00 16.00
Play Card
(Gale Sayers)
❑ 40 Cleveland Browns 3.00 1.35
Team Card

	Card	NRMT	VG-E
❑ 41	Jim Brown	70.00	32.00
❑ 42	Gary Collins	3.00	1.35
❑ 43	Ross Fichtner	2.00	.90
❑ 44	Ernie Green	2.00	.90
❑ 45	Gene Hickerson RC	3.00	1.35
❑ 46	Jim Houston	2.00	.90
❑ 47	John Morrow	2.00	.90
❑ 48	Walter Roberts	2.00	.90
❑ 49	Frank Ryan	3.00	1.35
❑ 50	Dick Schafrath	2.00	.90
❑ 51	Paul Wiggin RC	2.00	.90
❑ 52	Cleveland Browns Play Card (Ernie Green sweep)	2.00	.90
❑ 53	Dallas Cowboys Team Card	3.00	1.35
❑ 54	George Andrie RC UER (Text says startling, should be starting)	3.00	1.35
❑ 55	Frank Clarke	3.00	1.35
❑ 56	Mike Connelly	2.00	.90
❑ 57	Cornell Green	4.00	1.80
❑ 58	Bob Hayes RC	45.00	20.00
❑ 59	Chuck Howley RC	18.00	8.00
❑ 60	Bob Lilly	20.00	9.00
❑ 61	Don Meredith	25.00	11.00
❑ 62	Don Perkins	3.00	1.35
❑ 63	Mel Renfro	15.00	6.75
❑ 64	Danny Villanueva	2.00	.90
❑ 65	Dallas Cowboys Play Card (Danny Villanueva)	2.00	.90
❑ 66	Detroit Lions Team Card	3.00	1.35
❑ 67	Roger Brown	2.00	.90
❑ 68	John Gordy	2.00	.90
❑ 69	Alex Karras	10.00	4.50
❑ 70	Dick LeBeau	2.00	.90
❑ 71	Amos Marsh	2.00	.90
❑ 72	Milt Plum	3.00	1.35
❑ 73	Bobby Smith	2.00	.90
❑ 74	Wayne Rasmussen	2.00	.90
❑ 75	Pat Studstill	2.00	.90
❑ 76	Wayne Walker	2.00	.90
❑ 77	Tom Watkins	2.00	.90
❑ 78	Detroit Lions Play Card (George Izo pass)	2.00	.90
❑ 79	Green Bay Packers Team Card	6.00	2.70
❑ 80	Herb Adderley UER (Adderly on back)	6.00	2.70
❑ 81	Lee Roy Caffey RC	4.00	1.80
❑ 82	Don Chandler	3.00	1.35
❑ 83	Willie Davis	6.00	2.70
❑ 84	Boyd Dowler	4.00	1.80
❑ 85	Forrest Gregg	4.00	1.80
❑ 86	Tom Moore	3.00	1.35
❑ 87	Ray Nitschke	15.00	6.75
❑ 88	Bart Starr	40.00	18.00
❑ 89	Jim Taylor	20.00	9.00
❑ 90	Willie Wood	6.00	2.70
❑ 91	Green Bay Packers Play Card (Don Chandler FG)	2.00	.90
❑ 92	Los Angeles Rams Team Card	3.00	1.35
❑ 93	Willie Brown WR	2.00	.90
❑ 94	Dick Bass and Roman Gabriel	4.00	1.80
❑ 95	Bruce Gossett RC (Tom Landry small photo on back)	3.00	1.35
❑ 96	Deacon Jones	6.00	2.70
❑ 97	Tommy McDonald	4.00	1.80
❑ 98	Marlin McKeever	2.00	.90
❑ 99	Aaron Martin	2.00	.90
❑ 100	Ed Meador	2.00	.90
❑ 101	Bill Munson	3.00	1.35
❑ 102	Merlin Olsen	8.00	3.60
❑ 103	Jim Stiger	2.00	.90
❑ 104	Los Angeles Rams Play Card (Willie Brown run)	3.00	1.35
❑ 105	Minnesota Vikings Team Card	3.00	1.35
❑ 106	Grady Alderman	2.00	.90
❑ 107	Bill Brown	3.00	1.35
❑ 108	Fred Cox	2.00	.90
❑ 109	Paul Flatley	2.00	.90
❑ 110	Rip Hawkins	2.00	.90
❑ 111	Tommy Mason	2.00	.90
❑ 112	Ed Sharockman	2.00	.90
❑ 113	Gordon Smith	2.00	.90
❑ 114	Fran Tarkenton	30.00	13.50
❑ 115	Mick Tingelhoff	3.00	1.35
❑ 116	Bobby Walden RC**/C	2.00	.90
❑ 117	Minnesota Vikings Play Card (Bill Brown run)	2.00	.90
❑ 118	New York Giants Team Card	3.00	1.35
❑ 119	Roosevelt Brown	4.00	1.80
❑ 120	Henry Carr RC	3.00	1.35
❑ 121	Clarence Childs	2.00	.90
❑ 122	Tucker Frederickson RC	3.00	1.35
❑ 123	Jerry Hillebrand	2.00	.90
❑ 124	Greg Larson	2.00	.90
❑ 125	Spider Lockhart RC	3.00	1.35
❑ 126	Dick Lynch	2.00	.90
❑ 127	Earl Morrall and Bob Scholtz	3.00	1.35
❑ 128	Joe Morrison	2.00	.90
❑ 129	Steve Thurlow	2.00	.90
❑ 130	New York Giants Play Card (Chuck Mercein over)	2.00	.90
❑ 131	Philadelphia Eagles Team Card	3.00	1.35
❑ 132	Sam Baker	2.00	.90
❑ 133	Maxie Baughan	2.00	.90
❑ 134	Bob Brown OT RC	6.00	2.70
❑ 135	Timmy Brown (Lou Groza small photo on back)	3.00	1.35
❑ 136	Irv Cross	3.00	1.35
❑ 137	Earl Gros	2.00	.90
❑ 138	Ray Poage	2.00	.90
❑ 139	Nate Ramsey	2.00	.90
❑ 140	Pete Retzlaff	3.00	1.35
❑ 141	Jim Ringo (Joe Schmidt small photo on back)	4.00	1.80
❑ 142	Norm Snead (Norm Van Brocklin small photo on back)	4.00	1.80
❑ 143	Philadelphia Eagles Play Card (Earl Gros tackled)	2.00	.90
❑ 144	Pittsburgh Steelers Team Card (Lee Roy Jordan small photo on back)	3.00	1.35
❑ 145	Gary Ballman	2.00	.90
❑ 146	Charley Bradshaw	2.00	.90
❑ 147	Jim Butler	2.00	.90
❑ 148	Mike Clark	2.00	.90
❑ 149	Dick Hoak RC	2.00	.90
❑ 150	Roy Jefferson RC	3.00	1.35
❑ 151	Frank Lambert	2.00	.90
❑ 152	Mike Lind	2.00	.90
❑ 153	Bill Nelsen RC	4.00	1.80
❑ 154	Clarence Peaks	2.00	.90
❑ 155	Clendon Thomas	2.00	.90
❑ 156	Pittsburgh Steelers Play Card (Gary Ballman scores)	2.00	.90
❑ 157	St. Louis Cardinals Team Card	3.00	1.35
❑ 158	Jim Bakken	2.00	.90
❑ 159	Bobby Joe Conrad	3.00	1.35
❑ 160	Willis Crenshaw RC	2.00	.90
❑ 161	Bob DeMarco	2.00	.90
❑ 162	Pat Fischer	3.00	1.35
❑ 163	Charlie Johnson UER (Misspelled Charley on both sides)	3.00	1.35
❑ 164	Dale Meinert	2.00	.90
❑ 165	Sonny Randle	2.00	.90
❑ 166	Sam Silas RC	2.00	.90
❑ 167	Bill Triplett	2.00	.90
❑ 168	Larry Wilson	4.00	1.80
❑ 169	St. Louis Cardinals Play Card (Bill Triplett tackled by Roosevelt Davis and Roger LaLonde)	2.00	.90
❑ 170	San Francisco 49ers Team Card (Vince Lombardi small photo on back)	3.00	1.35
❑ 171	Kermit Alexander	2.00	.90
❑ 172	Bruce Bosley	2.00	.90
❑ 173	John Brodie	6.00	2.70
❑ 174	Bernie Casey	3.00	1.35
❑ 175	John David Crow (Don Shula small photo on back)	4.00	1.80
❑ 176	Tommy Davis	2.00	.90
❑ 177	Jim Johnson	4.00	1.80
❑ 178	Gary Lewis	2.00	.90
❑ 179	Dave Parks	2.00	.90
❑ 180	Walter Rock (Paul Hornung small photo on back)	3.00	1.35
❑ 181	Ken Willard RC (George Halas small photo on back)	4.00	1.80
❑ 182	San Francisco 49ers Play Card (Tommy Davis FG)	2.00	.90
❑ 183	Washington Redskins Team Card	3.00	1.35
❑ 184	Rickie Harris	2.00	.90
❑ 185	Sonny Jurgensen	8.00	3.60
❑ 186	Paul Krause	6.00	2.70
❑ 187	Bobby Mitchell	6.00	2.70
❑ 188	Vince Promuto	2.00	.90
❑ 189	Pat Richter RC (Craig Morton small photo on back)	2.00	.90
❑ 190	Joe Rutgens	2.00	.90
❑ 191	Johnny Sample	2.00	.90
❑ 192	Lonnie Sanders	2.00	.90
❑ 193	Jim Steffen	2.00	.90
❑ 194	Charley Taylor UER (Called Charley and Charlie on card back	15.00	6.75
❑ 195	Washington Redskins Play Card (Dan Lewis tackled by Roger LaLonde)	2.00	.90
❑ 196	Referee Signals	3.00	1.35
❑ 197	Checklist 1	25.00	11.00
❑ 198	Checklist 2 UER (163 Charley Johnson should be Charlie)	50.00	22.00

1967 Philadelphia

	NRMT	VG-E
COMPLETE SET (198)	650.00	300.00
WRAPPER (5-CENT)	15.00	6.75

	Card	NRMT	VG-E
❑ 1	Atlanta Falcons Team Card	10.00	4.50
❑ 2	Junior Coffey RC	3.00	1.35
❑ 3	Alex Hawkins	2.00	.90
❑ 4	Randy Johnson RC	3.00	1.35
❑ 5	Lou Kirouac	2.00	.90

❑ 6 Billy Martin E .... 2.00 .90
❑ 7 Tommy Nobis RC 20.00 9.00
❑ 8 Jerry Richardson RC 4.00 1.80
❑ 9 Marion Rushing .... 2.00 .90
❑ 10 Ron Smith .... 2.00 .90
❑ 11 Ernie Wheelwright UER 2.00 .90
(Misspelled Wheelright on both sides)
❑ 12 Atlanta Falcons .... 2.00 .90
Insignia
❑ 13 Baltimore Colts 3.00 1.35
Team Card
❑ 14 Raymond Berry UER...... 7.00 3.10
(Photo actually Bob Boyd
❑ 15 Bob Boyd .... 2.00 .90
❑ 16 Ordell Braase .... 2.00 .90
❑ 17 Alvin Haymond .... 2.00 .90
❑ 18 Tony Lorick .... 2.00 .90
❑ 19 Lenny Lyles .... 2.00 .90
❑ 20 John Mackey 5.00 2.20
❑ 21 Tom Matte 3.00 1.35
❑ 22 Lou Michaels .... 2.00 .90
❑ 23 John Unitas 30.00 13.50
❑ 24 Baltimore Colts .... 2.00 .90
Insignia
❑ 25 Chicago Bears 3.00 1.35
Team Card
❑ 26 Rudy Bukich UER .... 2.00 .90
(Misspelled Buckich on card back)
❑ 27 Ron Bull .... 2.00 .90
❑ 28 Dick Butkus 75.00 34.00
❑ 29 Mike Ditka 30.00 11.00
❑ 30 Dick Gordon RC 3.00 1.35
❑ 31 Roger LeClerc .... 2.00 .90
❑ 32 Bennie McRae .... 2.00 .90
❑ 33 Richie Petitbon .... 2.00 .90
❑ 34 Mike Pyle .... 2.00 .90
❑ 35 Gale Sayers 75.00 34.00
❑ 36 Chicago Bears .... 2.00 .90
Insignia
❑ 37 Cleveland Browns 3.00 1.35
Team Card
❑ 38 Johnny Brewer .... 2.00 .90
❑ 39 Gary Collins 3.00 1.35
❑ 40 Ross Fichtner .... 2.00 .90
❑ 41 Ernie Green .... 2.00 .90
❑ 42 Gene Hickerson .... 2.00 .90
❑ 43 Leroy Kelly RC 35.00 16.00
❑ 44 Frank Ryan 3.00 1.35
❑ 45 Dick Schafrath .... 2.00 .90
❑ 46 Paul Warfield 18.00 8.00
❑ 47 John Wooten .... 2.00 .90
❑ 48 Cleveland Browns .... 2.00 .90
Insignia
❑ 49 Dallas Cowboys 3.00 1.35
Team Card
❑ 50 George Andrie .... 2.00 .90
❑ 51 Cornell Green 3.00 1.35
❑ 52 Bob Hayes 15.00 6.75
❑ 53 Chuck Howley 4.00 1.80
❑ 54 Lee Roy Jordan RC 20.00 9.00
❑ 55 Bob Lilly 15.00 6.75
❑ 56 Dave Manders RC .... 2.00 .90
❑ 57 Don Meredith 25.00 11.00
❑ 58 Dan Reeves RC 30.00 11.00
❑ 59 Mel Renfro 6.00 2.70
❑ 60 Dallas Cowboys 3.00 1.35
Insignia
❑ 61 Detroit Lions 3.00 1.35
Team Card
❑ 62 Roger Brown 3.00 1.35
❑ 63 Gail Cogdill .... 2.00 .90
❑ 64 John Gordy .... 2.00 .90
❑ 65 Ron Kramer .... 2.00 .90
❑ 66 Dick LeBeau .... 2.00 .90
❑ 67 Mike Lucci RC 4.00 1.80
❑ 68 Amos Marsh .... 2.00 .90
❑ 69 Tom Nowatzke .... 2.00 .90
❑ 70 Pat Studstill .... 2.00 .90
❑ 71 Karl Sweetan .... 2.00 .90
❑ 72 Detroit Lions .... 2.00 .90
Insignia
❑ 73 Green Bay Packers 5.00 2.20
Team Card
❑ 74 Herb Adderley UER 5.00 2.20
(Adderly on back)
❑ 75 Lee Roy Caffey 3.00 1.35
❑ 76 Willie Davis 5.00 2.20
❑ 77 Forrest Gregg 4.00 1.80
❑ 78 Hank Jordan 4.00 1.80
❑ 79 Ray Nitschke 12.00 5.50
❑ 80 Dave Robinson RC 6.00 2.70
❑ 81 Bob Skoronski 3.00 1.35
❑ 82 Bart Starr 30.00 13.50
❑ 83 Willie Wood 5.00 2.20
❑ 84 Green Bay Packers 3.00 1.35
Insignia
❑ 85 Los Angeles Rams 3.00 1.35
Team Card
❑ 86 Dick Bass 3.00 1.35
❑ 87 Maxie Baughan .... 2.00 .90
❑ 88 Roman Gabriel 4.00 1.80
❑ 89 Bruce Gossett .... 2.00 .90
❑ 90 Deacon Jones 5.00 2.20
❑ 91 Tommy McDonald 4.00 1.80
❑ 92 Marlin McKeever .... 2.00 .90
❑ 93 Tom Moore .... 2.00 .90
❑ 94 Merlin Olsen 6.00 2.70
❑ 95 Clancy Williams .... 2.00 .90
❑ 96 Los Angeles Rams .... 2.00 .90
Insignia
❑ 97 Minnesota Vikings 3.00 1.35
Team Card
❑ 98 Grady Alderman .... 2.00 .90
❑ 99 Bill Brown 3.00 1.35
❑ 100 Fred Cox .... 2.00 .90
❑ 101 Paul Flatley .... 2.00 .90
❑ 102 Dale Hackbart RC .... 2.00 .90
❑ 103 Jim Marshall 4.00 1.80
❑ 104 Tommy Mason .... 2.00 .90
❑ 105 Milt Sunde RC .... 2.00 .90
❑ 106 Fran Tarkenton 20.00 8.00
❑ 107 Mick Tingelhoff 3.00 1.35
❑ 108 Minnesota Vikings .... 2.00 .90
Insignia
❑ 109 New York Giants 3.00 1.35
Team Card
❑ 110 Henry Carr .... 2.00 .90
❑ 111 Clarence Childs .... 2.00 .90
❑ 112 Allen Jacobs .... 2.00 .90
❑ 113 Homer Jones RC 3.00 1.35
❑ 114 Tom Kennedy .... 2.00 .90
❑ 115 Spider Lockhart .... 2.00 .90
❑ 116 Joe Morrison .... 2.00 .90
❑ 117 Francis Peay .... 2.00 .90
❑ 118 Jeff Smith .... 2.00 .90
❑ 119 Aaron Thomas .... 2.00 .90
❑ 120 New York Giants .... 2.00 .90
Insignia
❑ 121 New Orleans Saints 3.00 1.35
Insignia
(See also card 132)
❑ 122 Charley Bradshaw .... 2.00 .90
❑ 123 Paul Hornung 25.00 9.00
❑ 124 Elbert Kimbrough .... 2.00 .90
❑ 125 Earl Leggett RC .... 2.00 .90
❑ 126 Obert Logan .... 2.00 .90
❑ 127 Riley Mattson .... 2.00 .90
❑ 128 John Morrow .... 2.00 .90
❑ 129 Bob Scholtz .... 2.00 .90
❑ 130 Dave Whitsell RC .... 2.00 .90
❑ 131 Gary Wood .... 2.00 .90
❑ 132 New Orleans Saints 3.00 1.35
Roster UER
(121 on back)
❑ 133 Philadelphia Eagles...... 3.00 1.35
Team Card
❑ 134 Sam Baker .... 2.00 .90
❑ 135 Bob Brown OT 3.00 1.35
❑ 136 Timmy Brown 3.00 1.35
❑ 137 Earl Gros .... 2.00 .90
❑ 138 Dave Lloyd .... 2.00 .90
❑ 139 Floyd Peters .... 2.00 .90
❑ 140 Pete Retzlaff 3.00 1.35
❑ 141 Joe Scarpati .... 2.00 .90
❑ 142 Norm Snead 3.00 1.35
❑ 143 Jim Skaggs .... 2.00 .90
❑ 144 Philadelphia Eagles...... 2.00 .90
Insignia
❑ 145 Pittsburgh Steelers 3.00 1.35
Team Card
❑ 146 Bill Asbury .... 2.00 .90
❑ 147 John Baker .... 2.00 .90
❑ 148 Gary Ballman .... 2.00 .90
❑ 149 Mike Clark .... 2.00 .90
❑ 150 Riley Gunnels .... 2.00 .90
❑ 151 John Hilton .... 2.00 .90
❑ 152 Roy Jefferson 3.00 1.35
❑ 153 Brady Keys .... 2.00 .90
❑ 154 Ben McGee .... 2.00 .90
❑ 155 Bill Nelsen 3.00 1.35
❑ 156 Pittsburgh Steelers .... 2.00 .90
Insignia
❑ 157 St. Louis Cardinals 3.00 1.35
Team Card
❑ 158 Jim Bakken .... 2.00 .90
❑ 159 Bobby Joe Conrad 3.00 1.35
❑ 160 Ken Gray .... 2.00 .90
❑ 161 Charlie Johnson UER .. 3.00 1.35
(Misspelled Charley on both sides)
❑ 162 Joe Robb .... 2.00 .90
❑ 163 Johnny Roland RC 3.00 1.35
❑ 164 Roy Shivers .... 2.00 .90
❑ 165 Jackie Smith RC 15.00 6.75
❑ 166 Jerry Stovall .... 2.00 .90
❑ 167 Larry Wilson 4.00 1.80
❑ 168 St. Louis Cardinals .... 2.00 .90
Insignia
❑ 169 San Francisco 49ers 3.00 1.35
Team Card
❑ 170 Kermit Alexander .... 2.00 .90
❑ 171 Bruce Bosley .... 2.00 .90
❑ 172 John Brodie 6.00 2.70
❑ 173 Bernie Casey 3.00 1.35
❑ 174 Tommy Davis .... 2.00 .90
❑ 175 Howard Mudd .... 2.00 .90
❑ 176 Dave Parks .... 2.00 .90
❑ 177 John Thomas .... 2.00 .90
❑ 178 Dave Wilcox RC 5.00 2.20
❑ 179 Ken Willard 3.00 1.35
❑ 180 San Francisco 49ers .... 2.00 .90
Insignia
❑ 181 Washington Redskins .. 3.00 1.35
Team Card
❑ 182 Charlie Gogolak RC .... 2.00 .90
❑ 183 Chris Hanburger RC 5.00 2.20
❑ 184 Len Hauss RC 3.00 1.35
❑ 185 Sonny Jurgensen 7.00 3.10
❑ 186 Bobby Mitchell 5.00 2.20
❑ 187 Brig Owens .... 2.00 .90
❑ 188 Jim Shorter .... 2.00 .90
❑ 189 Jerry Smith RC 3.00 1.35
❑ 190 Charley Taylor 8.00 3.60
❑ 191 A.D. Whitfield .... 2.00 .90
❑ 192 Washington Redskins .. 2.00 .90
Insignia
❑ 193 Cleveland Browns 6.00 2.70
Play Card
(Leroy Kelly)
❑ 194 New York Giants .... 2.00 .90
Play Card
(Joe Morrison)
❑ 195 Atlanta Falcons .... 2.00 .90
Play Card
(Ernie Wheelright)
❑ 196 Referee Signals 3.00 1.35
❑ 197 Checklist 1 .... 20.00 9.00
❑ 198 Checklist 2 UER 40.00 18.00
(161 Charley Johnson should be Charlie)

1991 Pinnacle

	MINT	NRMT
COMPLETE SET (415)	20.00	9.00

❑ 1 Warren Moon .... .40 .18
❑ 2 Morten Andersen .... .10 .05
❑ 3 Rohn Stark .... .10 .05
❑ 4 Mark Bortz .... .10 .05
❑ 5 Mark Higgs RC .... .10 .05
❑ 6 Troy Aikman 2.50 1.10
❑ 7 John Elway 4.00 1.80
❑ 8 Neal Anderson .... .20 .09
❑ 9 Chris Doleman .... .10 .05
❑ 10 Jay Schroeder .... .10 .05

❑ 11 Sterling Sharpe .40 .18
❑ 12 Steve DeBerg .10 .05
❑ 13 Ronnie Lott .20 .09
❑ 14 Sean Landeta .10 .05
❑ 15 Jim Everett .20 .09
❑ 16 Jim Breech .10 .05
❑ 17 Barry Foster .20 .09
❑ 18 Mike Merriweather .10 .05
❑ 19 Eric Metcalf .20 .09
❑ 20 Mark Carrier DB .20 .09
❑ 21 James Brooks .20 .09
❑ 22 Nate Odomes .10 .05
❑ 23 Rodney Hampton .40 .18
❑ 24 Chris Miller .20 .09
❑ 25 Roger Craig .20 .09
❑ 26 Louis Oliver .10 .05
❑ 27 Allen Pinkett .10 .05
❑ 28 Bubby Brister .10 .05
❑ 29 Reyna Thompson .10 .05
❑ 30 Issiac Holt .10 .05
❑ 31 Steve Broussard .10 .05
❑ 32 Christian Okoye .10 .05
❑ 33 Dave Meggett .20 .09
❑ 34 Andre Reed .20 .09
❑ 35 Shane Conlan .10 .05
❑ 36 Eric Ball .10 .05
❑ 37 Johnny Bailey .10 .05
❑ 38 Don Majkowski .10 .05
❑ 39 Gerald Williams .10 .05
❑ 40 Kevin Mack .10 .05
❑ 41 Jeff Herrod .10 .05
❑ 42 Emmitt Smith 6.00 2.70
❑ 43 Wendell Davis .10 .05
❑ 44 Lorenzo White .10 .05
❑ 45 Andre Rison .20 .09
❑ 46 Jerry Gray .10 .05
❑ 47 Dennis Smith .10 .05
❑ 48 Gaston Green .10 .05
❑ 49 Dermontti Dawson .10 .05
❑ 50 Jeff Hostetler .20 .09
❑ 51 Nick Lowery .10 .05
❑ 52 Merril Hoge .10 .05
❑ 53 Bobby Hebert .10 .05
❑ 54 Scott Case .10 .05
❑ 55 Jack Del Rio .10 .05
❑ 56 Cornelius Bennett .20 .09
❑ 57 Tony Mandarich .10 .05
❑ 58 Bill Brooks .10 .05
❑ 59 Jessie Tuggle .10 .05
❑ 60 Hugh Millen RC .10 .05
❑ 61 Tony Bennett .20 .09
❑ 62 Cris Dishman RC .10 .05
❑ 63 Darryl Henley RC .10 .05
❑ 64 Duane Bickett .10 .05
❑ 65 Jay Hilgenberg .10 .05
❑ 66 Joe Montana 4.00 1.80
❑ 67 Bill Fralic .10 .05
❑ 68 Sam Mills .10 .05
❑ 69 Bruce Armstrong .10 .05
❑ 70 Dan Marino 4.00 1.80
❑ 71 Jim Lachey .10 .05
❑ 72 Rod Woodson .40 .18
❑ 73 Simon Fletcher .10 .05
❑ 74 Bruce Matthews .20 .09
❑ 75 Howie Long .20 .09
❑ 76 John Friesz .40 .18
❑ 77 Karl Mecklenburg .10 .05
❑ 78 John L. Williams UER .10 .05
(Two photos show
42 Chris Warren)
❑ 79 Rob Burnett RC .20 .09
❑ 80 Anthony Carter .20 .09
❑ 81 Henry Ellard .20 .09
❑ 82 Don Beebe .10 .05
❑ 83 Louis Lipps .10 .05
❑ 84 Greg McMurtry .10 .05
❑ 85 Will Wolford .10 .05
❑ 86 Eric Green .10 .05
❑ 87 Irving Fryar .20 .09
❑ 88 John Offerdahl .10 .05
❑ 89 John Alt .10 .05
❑ 90 Tom Tupa .10 .05
❑ 91 Don Mosebar .10 .05
❑ 92 Jeff George .60 .25
❑ 93 Vinny Testaverde .20 .09
❑ 94 Greg Townsend .10 .05
❑ 95 Derrick Fenner .10 .05
❑ 96 Brian Mitchell .20 .09
❑ 97 Herschel Walker .20 .09
❑ 98 Ricky Proehl .10 .05
❑ 99 Mark Clayton .20 .09
❑ 100 Derrick Thomas .40 .18
❑ 101 Jim Harbaugh .40 .18
❑ 102 Barry Word .10 .05
❑ 103 Jerry Rice 2.50 1.10
❑ 104 Keith Byars .10 .05
❑ 105 Marion Butts .20 .09
❑ 106 Rich Moran .10 .05
❑ 107 Thurman Thomas .40 .18
❑ 108 Stephone Paige .10 .05
❑ 109 D.J. Johnson .10 .05
❑ 110 William Perry .20 .09
❑ 111 Haywood Jeffires .20 .09
❑ 112 Rodney Peete .20 .09
❑ 113 Andy Heck .10 .05
❑ 114 Kevin Ross .10 .05
❑ 115 Michael Carter .10 .05
❑ 116 Tim McKyer .10 .05
❑ 117 Kenneth Davis .10 .05
❑ 118 Richmond Webb .10 .05
❑ 119 Rich Camarillo .10 .05
❑ 120 James Francis .10 .05
❑ 121 Craig Heyward .20 .09
❑ 122 Hardy Nickerson .20 .09
❑ 123 Michael Brooks .10 .05
❑ 124 Fred Barnett .40 .18
❑ 125 Cris Carter 1.25 .55
❑ 126 Brian Jordan .20 .09
❑ 127 Pat Leahy .10 .05
❑ 128 Kevin Greene .40 .18
❑ 129 Trace Armstrong .10 .05
❑ 130 Eugene Lockhart .10 .05
❑ 131 Albert Lewis .10 .05
❑ 132 Ernie Jones .10 .05
❑ 133 Eric Martin .10 .05
❑ 134 Anthony Thompson .10 .05
❑ 135 Tim Krumrie .10 .05
❑ 136 James Lofton .20 .09
❑ 137 John Taylor .20 .09
❑ 138 Jeff Cross .10 .05
❑ 139 Tommy Kane .10 .05
❑ 140 Robb Thomas .10 .05
❑ 141 Gary Anderson K .10 .05
❑ 142 Mark Murphy .10 .05
❑ 143 Rickey Jackson .10 .05
❑ 144 Ken O'Brien .10 .05
❑ 145 Ernest Givins .20 .09
❑ 146 Jessie Hester .10 .05
❑ 147 Deion Sanders 1.00 .45
❑ 148 Keith Henderson RC .10 .05
❑ 149 Chris Singleton .10 .05
❑ 150 Rod Bernstine .10 .05
❑ 151 Quinn Early .20 .09
❑ 152 Boomer Esiason .20 .09
❑ 153 Mike Gann .10 .05
❑ 154 Dino Hackett .10 .05
❑ 155 Perry Kemp .10 .05
❑ 156 Mark Ingram .20 .09
❑ 157 Daryl Johnston 1.00 .45
❑ 158 Eugene Daniel .10 .05
❑ 159 Dalton Hilliard .10 .05
❑ 160 Rufus Porter .10 .05
❑ 161 Tunch Ilkin .10 .05
❑ 162 James Hasty .10 .05
❑ 163 Keith McKeller .10 .05
❑ 164 Heath Sherman .10 .05
❑ 165 Vai Sikahema .10 .05
❑ 166 Pat Terrell .10 .05
❑ 167 Anthony Munoz .20 .09
❑ 168 Brad Edwards RC .10 .05
❑ 169 Tom Rathman .10 .05
❑ 170 Steve McMichael .20 .09
❑ 171 Vaughan Johnson .10 .05
❑ 172 Nate Lewis RC .10 .05
❑ 173 Mark Rypien .20 .09
❑ 174 Rob Moore .60 .25
❑ 175 Tim Green .10 .05
❑ 176 Tony Casillas .10 .05
❑ 177 Jon Hand .10 .05
❑ 178 Todd McNair .10 .05
❑ 179 Toi Cook RC .10 .05
❑ 180 Eddie Brown .10 .05
❑ 181 Mark Jackson .10 .05
❑ 182 Pete Stoyanovich .10 .05
❑ 183 Bryce Paup RC .40 .18
❑ 184 Anthony Miller .20 .09
❑ 185 Dan Saleaumua .10 .05
❑ 186 Guy McIntyre .10 .05
❑ 187 Broderick Thomas .10 .05
❑ 188 Frank Warren .10 .05
❑ 189 Drew Hill .10 .05
❑ 190 Reggie White .40 .18
❑ 191 Chris Hinton .10 .05
❑ 192 David Little .10 .05
❑ 193 David Fulcher .10 .05
❑ 194 Clarence Verdin .10 .05
❑ 195 Junior Seau .60 .25
❑ 196 Blair Thomas .10 .05
❑ 197 Stan Brock .10 .05
❑ 198 Gary Clark .40 .18
❑ 199 Michael Irvin .40 .18
❑ 200 Ronnie Harmon .10 .05
❑ 201 Steve Young 2.50 1.10
❑ 202 Brian Noble .10 .05
❑ 203 Dan Stryzinski .10 .05
❑ 204 Darryl Talley .10 .05
❑ 205 David Alexander .10 .05
❑ 206 Pat Swilling .20 .09
❑ 207 Gary Plummer .10 .05
❑ 208 Robert Delpino .10 .05
❑ 209 Norm Johnson .10 .05
❑ 210 Mike Singletary .20 .09
❑ 211 Anthony Johnson .40 .18
❑ 212 Eric Allen .10 .05
❑ 213 Gill Fenerty .10 .05
❑ 214 Neil Smith .40 .18
❑ 215 Joe Phillips .10 .05
❑ 216 Ottis Anderson .20 .09
❑ 217 LeRoy Butler .20 .09
❑ 218 Ray Childress .10 .05
❑ 219 Rodney Holman .10 .05
❑ 220 Kevin Fagan .10 .05
❑ 221 Bruce Smith .40 .18
❑ 222 Brad Muster .10 .05
❑ 223 Mike Horan .10 .05
❑ 224 Steve Atwater .10 .05
❑ 225 Rich Gannon .60 .25
❑ 226 Anthony Pleasant .10 .05
❑ 227 Steve Jordan .10 .05
❑ 228 Lomas Brown .10 .05
❑ 229 Jackie Slater .10 .05
❑ 230 Brad Baxter .10 .05
❑ 231 Joe Morris .10 .05
❑ 232 Marcus Allen .40 .18
❑ 233 Chris Warren .40 .18
❑ 234 Johnny Johnson .10 .05
❑ 235 Phil Simms .20 .09
❑ 236 Dave Krieg .20 .09
❑ 237 Jim McMahon .20 .09
❑ 238 Richard Dent .20 .09
❑ 239 John Washington RC .10 .05
❑ 240 Sammie Smith .10 .05
❑ 241 Brian Brennan .10 .05
❑ 242 Cortez Kennedy .40 .18
❑ 243 Tim McDonald .10 .05
❑ 244 Charles Haley .20 .09
❑ 245 Joey Browner .10 .05
❑ 246 Eddie Murray .10 .05
❑ 247 Bob Golic .10 .05

No.	Player	Mint	NrMt
248	Myron Guyton	.10	.05
249	Dennis Byrd	.10	.05
250	Barry Sanders	6.00	2.70
251	Clay Matthews	.20	.09
252	Pepper Johnson	.10	.05
253	Eric Swann RC	.40	.18
254	Lamar Lathon	.10	.05
255	Andre Tippett	.10	.05
256	Tom Newberry	.10	.05
257	Kyle Clifton	.10	.05
258	Leslie O'Neal	.20	.09
259	Bubba McDowell	.10	.05
260	Scott Davis	.10	.05
261	Wilber Marshall	.10	.05
262	Marv Cook	.10	.05
263	Jeff Lageman	.10	.05
264	Michael Young	.10	.05
265	Gary Zimmerman	.10	.05
266	Mike Munchak	.10	.05
267	David Treadwell	.10	.05
268	Steve Wisniewski	.10	.05
269	Mark Duper	.20	.09
270	Chris Spielman	.20	.09
271	Brett Perriman	.40	.18
272	Lionel Washington	.10	.05
273	Lawrence Taylor	.40	.18
274	Mark Collins	.10	.05
275	Mark Carrier WR	.40	.18
276	Paul Gruber	.10	.05
277	Earnest Byner	.10	.05
278	Andre Collins	.10	.05
279	Reggie Cobb	.10	.05
280	Art Monk	.20	.09
281	Henry Jones RC	.20	.09
282	Mike Pritchard RC	.40	.18
283	Moe Gardner RC	.10	.05
284	Chris Zorich RC	.40	.18
285	Keith Traylor RC	.10	.05
286	Mike Dumas RC	.10	.05
287	Ed King RC	.10	.05
288	Russell Maryland RC	.40	.18
289	Alfred Williams RC	.10	.05
290	Derek Russell RC	.10	.05
291	Vinnie Clark RC	.10	.05
292	Mike Croel RC	.10	.05
293	Todd Marinovich RC	.10	.05
294	Phil Hansen RC	.10	.05
295	Aaron Craver RC	.10	.05
296	Nick Bell RC	.10	.05
297	Kenny Walker RC	.10	.05
298	Roman Phifer RC	.10	.05
299	Kanavis McGhee RC	.10	.05
300	Ricky Ervins RC	.20	.09
301	Jim Price RC	.10	.05
302	John Johnson RC	.10	.05
303	George Thornton RC	.10	.05
304	Huey Richardson RC	.10	.05
305	Harry Colon RC	.10	.05
306	Antone Davis RC	.10	.05
307	Todd Lyght RC	.10	.05
308	Bryan Cox RC	.40	.18
309	Brad Goebel RC	.10	.05
310	Eric Moten RC	.10	.05
311	John Kasay RC	.20	.09
312	Esera Tuaolo RC	.10	.05
313	Bobby Wilson RC	.10	.05
314	Mo Lewis RC	.20	.09
315	Harvey Williams RC	.40	.18
316	Mike Stonebreaker	.10	.05
317	Charles McRae RC	.10	.05
318	John Flannery RC	.10	.05
319	Ted Washington RC	.10	.05
320	Stanley Richard RC	.10	.05
321	Browning Nagle RC	.10	.05
322	Ed McCaffery RC	5.00	2.20
323	Jeff Graham RC	.40	.18
324	Stan Thomas	.10	.05
325	Lawrence Dawsey RC	.20	.09
326	Eric Bieniemy RC	.10	.05
327	Tim Barnett RC	.10	.05
328	Erric Pegram RC	.40	.18
329	Lamar Rogers RC	.10	.05
330	Ernie Mills RC	.20	.09
331	Pat Harlow RC	.10	.05
332	Greg Lewis RC	.10	.05
333	Jarrod Bunch RC	.10	.05
334	Dan McGwire RC	.10	.05
335	Randal Hill RC	.20	.09
336	Leonard Russell RC	.40	.18
337	Carnell Lake	.10	.05
338	Brian Blades	.20	.09
339	Darrell Green	.10	.05
340	Bobby Humphrey	.10	.05
341	Mervyn Fernandez	.10	.05
342	Ricky Sanders	.10	.05
343	Keith Jackson	.20	.09
344	Carl Banks	.10	.05
345	Gill Byrd	.10	.05
346	Al Toon	.20	.09
347	Stephen Baker	.10	.05
348	Randall Cunningham	.40	.18
349	Flipper Anderson	.10	.05
350	Jay Novacek	.40	.18
351	Steve Young HH vs. Bruce Smith	.40	.18
352	Barry Sanders HH vs. Joey Browner	1.00	.45
353	Joe Montana HH vs. Mark Carrier	.50	.23
354	Thurman Thomas HH vs. Lawrence Taylor	.20	.09
355	Jerry Rice HH vs. Darrell Green	.60	.25
356	Warren Moon TECH	.20	.09
357	Anthony Munoz TECH	.10	.05
358	Barry Sanders TECH	2.50	1.10
359	Jerry Rice TECH	1.25	.55
360	Joey Browner TECH	.10	.05
361	Morten Andersen TECH	.10	.05
362	Sean Landeta TECH	.10	.05
363	Thurman Thomas GW	.40	.18
364	Emmitt Smith GW	3.00	1.35
365	Gaston Green GW	.10	.05
366	Barry Sanders GW	2.50	1.10
367	Christian Okoye GW	.10	.05
368	Earnest Byner GW	.10	.05
369	Neal Anderson GW	.10	.05
370	Herschel Walker GW	.20	.09
371	Rodney Hampton GW	.40	.18
372	Darryl Talley IDOL Ted Hendricks	.10	.05
373	Mark Carrier IDOL Ronnie Lott	.10	.05
374	Jim Breech IDOL Jan Stenerud	.10	.05
375	Rodney Hampton IDOL Ottis Anderson	.10	.05
376	Kevin Mack IDOL Earnest Byner	.10	.05
377	Steve Jordan IDOL Oscar Robertson	.10	.05
378	Boomer Esiason IDOL Bert Jones	.10	.05
379	Steve DeBerg IDOL Roman Gabriel	.20	.09
380	Al Toon IDOL Wesley Walker	.10	.05
381	Ronnie Lott IDOL Charley Taylor	.20	.09
382	Henry Ellard IDOL Bob Hayes	.10	.05
383	Troy Aikman IDOL Roger Staubach	1.25	.55
384	Thurman Thomas IDOL Earl Campbell	.40	.18
385	Dan Marino IDOL Terry Bradshaw	1.50	.70
386	Howie Long IDOL Joe Greene	.20	.09
387	Franco Harris Immaculate Reception	.20	.09
388	Esera Tuaolo	.10	.05
389	Super Bowl XXVI (Super Bowl Records)	.10	.05
390	Charles Mann	.10	.05
391	Kenny Walker	.10	.05
392	Reggie Roby	.10	.05
393	Bruce Pickens RC	.10	.05
394	Ray Childress SIDE	.10	.05
395	Karl Mecklenburg SIDE	.10	.05
396	Dean Biasucci SIDE	.10	.05
397	John Alt SIDE	.10	.05
398	Marcus Allen SIDE	.20	.09
399	John Offerdahl SIDE	.10	.05
400	Richard Tardits SIDE RC	.10	.05
401	Al Toon SIDE	.10	.05
402	Joey Browner SIDE	.10	.05
403	Spencer Tillman SIDE RC	.10	.05
404	Jay Novacek SIDE	.20	.09
405	Stephen Braggs SIDE	.10	.05
406	Mike Tice SIDE RC	.10	.05
407	Kevin Greene SIDE	.20	.09
408	Reggie White SIDE	.20	.09
409	Brian Noble SIDE	.10	.05
410	Bart Oates SIDE	.10	.05
411	Art Monk SIDE	.20	.09
412	Ron Wolfley SIDE	.10	.05
413	Louis Lipps SIDE	.10	.05
414	Dante Jones SIDE RC	.20	.09
415	Kenneth Davis SIDE	.10	.05
P1	Emmitt Smith Promo (Numbered 42; Mentions holdout on back)	25.00	11.00

1992 Pinnacle

	MINT	NRMT
COMPLETE SET (360)	25.00	11.00

No.	Player	Mint	NrMt
1	Reggie White	.50	.23
2	Eric Green	.15	.07
3	Craig Heyward	.30	.14
4	Phil Simms	.30	.14
5	Pepper Johnson	.15	.07
6	Sean Landeta	.15	.07
7	Dino Hackett	.15	.07
8	Andre Ware	.15	.07
9	Ricky Nattiel	.15	.07
10	Jim Price	.15	.07
11	Jim Ritcher	.15	.07
12	Kelly Stouffer	.15	.07
13	Ray Crockett	.15	.07
14	Steve Tasker	.30	.14
15	Barry Sanders	4.00	1.80
16	Pat Swilling	.30	.14
17	Moe Gardner	.15	.07
18	Steve Young	2.00	.90
19	Chris Spielman	.30	.14
20	Richard Dent	.30	.14
21	Anthony Munoz	.30	.14
22	Thurman Thomas	.50	.23
23	Ricky Sanders	.15	.07
24	Steve Atwater	.15	.07
25	Tony Tolbert	.15	.07
26	Haywood Jeffires	.30	.14
27	Duane Bickett	.15	.07
28	Tim McDonald	.15	.07
29	Cris Carter	.75	.35
30	Derrick Thomas	.50	.23
31	Hugh Millen	.15	.07
32	Bart Oates	.15	.07
33	Darryl Talley	.15	.07
34	Marion Butts	.15	.07
35	Pete Stoyanovich	.15	.07
36	Ronnie Lott	.30	.14
37	Simon Fletcher	.15	.07
38	Morten Andersen	.15	.07
39	Clyde Simmons	.15	.07
40	Mark Rypien	.15	.07
41	Henry Ellard	.30	.14

Card	Player	Price	Price
❑ 42	Michael Irvin	.50	.23
❑ 43	Louis Lipps	.15	.07
❑ 44	John L. Williams	.15	.07
❑ 45	Broderick Thomas	.15	.07
❑ 46	Don Majkowski	.15	.07
❑ 47	William Perry	.30	.14
❑ 48	David Fulcher	.15	.07
❑ 49	Tony Bennett	.15	.07
❑ 50	Clay Matthews	.30	.14
❑ 51	Warren Moon	.50	.23
❑ 52	Bruce Armstrong	.15	.07
❑ 53	Bill Brooks	.15	.07
❑ 54	Greg Townsend	.15	.07
❑ 55	Steve Broussard	.15	.07
❑ 56	Mel Gray	.30	.14
❑ 57	Kevin Mack	.15	.07
❑ 58	Emmitt Smith	4.00	1.80
❑ 59	Mike Croel	.15	.07
❑ 60	Brian Mitchell	.30	.14
❑ 61	Bennie Blades	.15	.07
❑ 62	Carnell Lake	.15	.07
❑ 63	Cornelius Bennett	.30	.14
❑ 64	Darrell Thompson	.15	.07
❑ 65	Jessie Hester	.15	.07
❑ 66	Marv Cook	.15	.07
❑ 67	Tim Brown	.50	.23
❑ 68	Mark Duper	.15	.07
❑ 69	Robert Delpino	.15	.07
❑ 70	Eric Martin	.15	.07
❑ 71	Wendell Davis	.15	.07
❑ 72	Vaughan Johnson	.15	.07
❑ 73	Brian Blades	.30	.14
❑ 74	Ed King	.15	.07
❑ 75	Gaston Green	.15	.07
❑ 76	Christian Okoye	.15	.07
❑ 77	Rohn Stark	.15	.07
❑ 78	Kevin Greene	.50	.23
❑ 79	Jay Novacek	.30	.14
❑ 80	Chip Lohmiller	.15	.07
❑ 81	Cris Dishman	.15	.07
❑ 82	Ethan Horton	.15	.07
❑ 83	Pat Harlow	.15	.07
❑ 84	Mark Ingram	.15	.07
❑ 85	Mark Carrier DB	.15	.07
❑ 86	Sam Mills	.15	.07
❑ 87	Mark Higgs	.15	.07
❑ 88	Keith Jackson	.30	.14
❑ 89	Gary Anderson K	.15	.07
❑ 90	Ken Harvey	.15	.07
❑ 91	Anthony Carter	.30	.14
❑ 92	Randall McDaniel	.15	.07
❑ 93	Johnny Johnson	.15	.07
❑ 94	Shane Conlan	.15	.07
❑ 95	Sterling Sharpe	.50	.23
❑ 96	Guy McIntyre	.15	.07
❑ 97	Albert Lewis	.15	.07
❑ 98	Chris Doleman	.15	.07
❑ 99	Andre Rison	.30	.14
❑ 100	Bobby Hebert	.15	.07
❑ 101	Dan Owens	.15	.07
❑ 102	Rodney Hampton	.50	.23
❑ 103	Ernie Jones	.15	.07
❑ 104	Reggie Cobb	.15	.07
❑ 105	Wilber Marshall	.15	.07
❑ 106	Mike Munchak	.15	.07
❑ 107	Cortez Kennedy	.30	.14
❑ 108	Todd Lyght	.15	.07
❑ 109	Burt Grossman	.15	.07
❑ 110	Ferrell Edmunds	.15	.07
❑ 111	Jim Everett	.30	.14
❑ 112	Hardy Nickerson	.30	.14
❑ 113	Andre Tippett	.15	.07
❑ 114	Ronnie Harmon	.15	.07
❑ 115	Andre Waters	.15	.07
❑ 116	Ernest Givins	.30	.14
❑ 117	Eric Hill	.15	.07
❑ 118	Erric Pegram	.30	.14
❑ 119	Jarrod Bunch	.15	.07
❑ 120	Marcus Allen	.50	.23
❑ 121	Barry Foster	.30	.14
❑ 122	Kent Hull	.15	.07
❑ 123	Neal Anderson	.15	.07
❑ 124	Stephen Braggs	.15	.07
❑ 125	Nick Lowery	.15	.07
❑ 126	Jeff Hostetler	.30	.14
❑ 127	Michael Carter	.15	.07
❑ 128	Don Warren	.15	.07
❑ 129	Brad Baxter	.15	.07
❑ 130	John Taylor	.30	.14
❑ 131	Harold Green	.15	.07
❑ 132	Mike Merriweather	.15	.07
❑ 133	Gary Clark	.50	.23
❑ 134	Vince Buck	.15	.07
❑ 135	Dan Saleaumua	.15	.07
❑ 136	Gary Zimmerman	.15	.07
❑ 137	Richmond Webb	.15	.07
❑ 138	Art Monk	.30	.14
❑ 139	Mervyn Fernandez	.15	.07
❑ 140	Mark Jackson	.15	.07
❑ 141	Freddie Joe Nunn	.15	.07
❑ 142	Jeff Lageman	.15	.07
❑ 143	Kenny Walker	.15	.07
❑ 144	Mark Carrier WR	.30	.14
❑ 145	Jon Vaughn	.15	.07
❑ 146	Greg Davis	.15	.07
❑ 147	Bubby Brister	.15	.07
❑ 148	Mo Lewis	.15	.07
❑ 149	Howie Long	.30	.14
❑ 150	Rod Bernstine	.15	.07
❑ 151	Nick Bell	.15	.07
❑ 152	Terry Allen	.50	.23
❑ 153	William Fuller	.30	.14
❑ 154	Dexter Carter	.15	.07
❑ 155	Gene Atkins	.15	.07
❑ 156	Don Beebe	.15	.07
❑ 157	Mark Collins	.15	.07
❑ 158	Jerry Ball	.15	.07
❑ 159	Fred Barnett	.50	.23
❑ 160	Rodney Holman	.15	.07
❑ 161	Stephen Baker	.15	.07
❑ 162	Jeff Graham	.50	.23
❑ 163	Leonard Russell	.30	.14
❑ 164	Jeff Gossett	.15	.07
❑ 165	Vinny Testaverde	.30	.14
❑ 166	Maurice Hurst	.15	.07
❑ 167	Louis Oliver	.15	.07
❑ 168	Jim Morrissey	.15	.07
❑ 169	Greg Kragen	.15	.07
❑ 170	Andre Collins	.15	.07
❑ 171	Dave Meggett	.30	.14
❑ 172	Keith Henderson	.15	.07
❑ 173	Vince Newsome	.15	.07
❑ 174	Chris Hinton	.15	.07
❑ 175	James Hasty	.15	.07
❑ 176	John Offerdahl	.15	.07
❑ 177	Lomas Brown	.15	.07
❑ 178	Neil O'Donnell	.50	.23
❑ 179	Leonard Marshall	.15	.07
❑ 180	Bubba McDowell	.15	.07
❑ 181	Herman Moore	1.25	.55
❑ 182	Rob Moore	.30	.14
❑ 183	Earnest Byner	.15	.07
❑ 184	Keith McCants	.15	.07
❑ 185	Floyd Turner	.15	.07
❑ 186	Steve Jordan	.15	.07
❑ 187	Nate Odomes	.15	.07
❑ 188	Jeff Herrod	.15	.07
❑ 189	Jim Harbaugh	.50	.23
❑ 190	Jessie Tuggle	.15	.07
❑ 191	Al Smith	.15	.07
❑ 192	Lawrence Dawsey	.30	.14
❑ 193	Steve Bono RC	.50	.23
❑ 194	Greg Lloyd	.50	.23
❑ 195	Steve Wisniewski	.15	.07
❑ 196	Larry Kelm	.15	.07
❑ 197	Tommy Kane	.15	.07
❑ 198	Mark Schlereth RC	.15	.07
❑ 199	Ray Childress	.15	.07
❑ 200	Vincent Brown	.15	.07
❑ 201	Rodney Peete	.30	.14
❑ 202	Dennis Smith	.15	.07
❑ 203	Bruce Matthews	.15	.07
❑ 204	Rickey Jackson	.15	.07
❑ 205	Eric Allen	.15	.07
❑ 206	Rich Camarillo	.15	.07
❑ 207	Jim Lachey	.15	.07
❑ 208	Kevin Ross	.15	.07
❑ 209	Irving Fryar	.30	.14
❑ 210	Mark Clayton	.30	.14
❑ 211	Keith Byars	.15	.07
❑ 212	John Elway	3.00	1.35
❑ 213	Harris Barton	.15	.07
❑ 214	Aeneas Williams	.30	.14
❑ 215	Rich Gannon	.50	.23
❑ 216	Toi Cook	.15	.07
❑ 217	Rod Woodson	.50	.23
❑ 218	Gary Anderson RB	.15	.07
❑ 219	Reggie Roby	.15	.07
❑ 220	Karl Mecklenburg	.15	.07
❑ 221	Rufus Porter	.15	.07
❑ 222	Jon Hand	.15	.07
❑ 223	Tim Barnett	.15	.07
❑ 224	Eric Swann	.30	.14
❑ 225	Eugene Robinson	.15	.07
❑ 226	Michael Young	.15	.07
❑ 227	Frank Warren	.15	.07
❑ 228	Mike Kenn	.15	.07
❑ 229	Tim Green	.15	.07
❑ 230	Barry Word	.15	.07
❑ 231	Mike Pritchard	.30	.14
❑ 232	John Kasay	.15	.07
❑ 233	Derek Russell	.15	.07
❑ 234	Jim Breech	.15	.07
❑ 235	Pierce Holt	.15	.07
❑ 236	Tim Krumrie	.15	.07
❑ 237	William Roberts	.15	.07
❑ 238	Erik Kramer	.30	.14
❑ 239	Brett Perriman	.50	.23
❑ 240	Reyna Thompson	.15	.07
❑ 241	Chris Miller	.30	.14
❑ 242	Drew Hill	.15	.07
❑ 243	Curtis Duncan	.15	.07
❑ 244	Seth Joyner	.30	.14
❑ 245	Ken Norton Jr.	.50	.23
❑ 246	Calvin Williams	.30	.14
❑ 247	James Joseph	.15	.07
❑ 248	Bennie Thompson RC	.15	.07
❑ 249	Tunch Ilkin	.15	.07
❑ 250	Brad Edwards	.15	.07
❑ 251	Jeff Jaeger	.15	.07
❑ 252	Gill Byrd	.15	.07
❑ 253	Jeff Feagles	.15	.07
❑ 254	Jamie Dukes RC	.15	.07
❑ 255	Greg McMurtry	.15	.07
❑ 256	Anthony Johnson	.30	.14
❑ 257	Lamar Lathon	.15	.07
❑ 258	John Roper	.15	.07
❑ 259	Lorenzo White	.15	.07
❑ 260	Brian Noble	.15	.07
❑ 261	Chris Singleton	.15	.07
❑ 262	Todd Marinovich	.15	.07
❑ 263	Jay Hilgenberg	.15	.07
❑ 264	Kyle Clifton	.15	.07
❑ 265	Tony Casillas	.15	.07
❑ 266	James Francis	.15	.07
❑ 267	Eddie Anderson	.15	.07
❑ 268	Tim Harris	.15	.07
❑ 269	James Lofton	.30	.14
❑ 270	Jay Schroeder	.15	.07
❑ 271	Ed West	.15	.07
❑ 272	Don Mosebar	.15	.07
❑ 273	Jackie Slater	.15	.07
❑ 274	Fred McAfee RC	.15	.07
❑ 275	Steve Sewell	.15	.07
❑ 276	Charles Mann	.15	.07
❑ 277	Ron Hall	.15	.07
❑ 278	Darrell Green	.15	.07
❑ 279	Jeff Cross	.15	.07
❑ 280	Jeff Wright	.15	.07
❑ 281	Issiac Holt	.15	.07
❑ 282	Dermontti Dawson	.15	.07
❑ 283	Michael Haynes	.30	.14
❑ 284	Tony Mandarich	.15	.07
❑ 285	Leroy Hoard	.30	.14
❑ 286	Darryl Henley	.15	.07
❑ 287	Tim McGee	.15	.07
❑ 288	Willie Gault	.30	.14
❑ 289	Dalton Hilliard	.15	.07
❑ 290	Tim McKyer	.15	.07
❑ 291	Tom Waddle	.15	.07
❑ 292	Eric Thomas	.15	.07
❑ 293	Herschel Walker	.30	.14
❑ 294	Donnell Woolford	.15	.07
❑ 295	James Brooks	.30	.14
❑ 296	Brad Muster	.15	.07
❑ 297	Brent Jones	.30	.14
❑ 298	Erik Howard	.15	.07
❑ 299	Alvin Harper UER	.30	.14

	MINT	NRMT
(Born in Frostproof, not Frostfree)		
□ 300 Joey Browner	.15	.07
□ 301 Jack Del Rio	.15	.07
□ 302 Cleveland Gary	.15	.07
□ 303 Brett Favre	6.00	2.70
□ 304 Freeman McNeil	.15	.07
□ 305 Willie Green	.15	.07
□ 306 Percy Snow	.15	.07
□ 307 Neil Smith	.50	.23
□ 308 Eric Bieniemy	.15	.07
□ 309 Keith Traylor	.15	.07
□ 310 Ernie Mills	.15	.07
□ 311 Will Wolford	.15	.07
□ 312 Robert Young	.15	.07
□ 313 Anthony Smith	.15	.07
□ 314 Robert Porcher RC	.30	.14
□ 315 Leon Searcy RC	.30	.14
□ 316 Amp Lee RC	.15	.07
□ 317 Siran Stacy RC	.15	.07
□ 318 Patrick Rowe RC	.15	.07
□ 319 Chris Mims RC	.30	.14
□ 320 Matt Elliott RC	.15	.07
□ 321 Ricardo McDonald RC	.15	.07
□ 322 Keith Hamilton RC	.30	.14
□ 323 Edgar Bennett RC	.75	.35
□ 324 Chris Hakel RC	.15	.07
□ 325 Dexter McNabb RC	.15	.07
□ 326 Rod Milstead RC	.15	.07
□ 327 Joe Bowden RC	.15	.07
□ 328 Brian Bollinger RC	.15	.07
□ 329 Darryl Williams RC	.15	.07
□ 330 Tommy Vardell RC	.30	.14
□ 331 Glenn Parker SIDE / Mitch Frerotte	.15	.07
□ 332 Herschel Walker SIDE	.15	.07
□ 333 Mike Cofer SIDE	.15	.07
□ 334 Mark Rypien SIDE	.15	.07
□ 335 Andre Rison GW	.30	.14
□ 336 Henry Ellard GW	.15	.07
□ 337 Rob Moore GW	.15	.07
□ 338 Fred Barnett GW	.15	.07
□ 339 Mark Clayton GW	.15	.07
□ 340 Eric Martin GW	.15	.07
□ 341 Irving Fryar GW	.15	.07
□ 342 Tim Brown GW	.30	.14
□ 343 Sterling Sharpe GW	.30	.14
□ 344 Gary Clark GW	.15	.07
□ 345 John Mackey HOF	.15	.07
□ 346 Lem Barney HOF	.15	.07
□ 347 John Riggins HOF	.30	.14
□ 348 Marion Butts IDOL / William Andrews	.15	.07
□ 349 Jeff Lageman IDOL / Jack Lambert	.15	.07
□ 350 Eric Green IDOL / Sam Rutigliano	.15	.07
□ 351 Reggie White IDOL / Bobby Jones	.30	.14
□ 352 Marv Cook IDOL / Dan Gable	.15	.07
□ 353 John Elway IDOL / Roger Staubach	1.25	.55
□ 354 Steve Tasker IDOL / Ed Podolak	.15	.07
□ 355 Nick Lowery IDOL / Jan Stenerud	.15	.07
□ 356 Mark Clayton IDOL / Paul Warfield	.15	.07
□ 357 Warren Moon IDOL / Roman Gabriel	.30	.14
□ 358 Eric Metcalf	.30	.14
□ 359 Charles Haley	.30	.14
□ 360 Terrell Buckley RC	.15	.07
□ P1 Promo Panel / Super Bowl XXVII promo / John Elway / Sterling Sharpe / Warren Moon / Tommy Vardell / Derrick Thomas / Pat Swilling / Neil Smith / Cortez Kennedy	5.00	2.20

1993 Pinnacle

	MINT	NRMT
COMPLETE SET (360)	25.00	11.00
□ 1 Brett Favre	4.00	1.80
□ 2 Tommy Vardell	.10	.05
□ 3 Jarrod Bunch	.10	.05
□ 4 Mike Croel	.10	.05
□ 5 Morten Andersen	.10	.05
□ 6 Barry Foster	.20	.09
□ 7 Chris Spielman	.20	.09
□ 8 Jim Jeffcoat	.10	.05
□ 9 Ken Ruettgers	.10	.05
□ 10 Cris Dishman	.10	.05
□ 11 Ricky Watters	.40	.18
□ 12 Alfred Williams	.10	.05
□ 13 Mark Kelso	.10	.05
□ 14 Moe Gardner	.10	.05
□ 15 Terry Allen	.40	.18
□ 16 Willie Gault	.10	.05
□ 17 Bubba McDowell	.10	.05
□ 18 Brian Mitchell	.20	.09
□ 19 Karl Mecklenburg	.10	.05
□ 20 Jim Everett	.20	.09
□ 21 Bobby Humphrey	.10	.05
□ 22 Tim Krumrie	.10	.05
□ 23 Ken Norton Jr.	.20	.09
□ 24 Wendell Davis	.10	.05
□ 25 Brad Baxter	.10	.05
□ 26 Mel Gray	.20	.09
□ 27 Jon Vaughn	.10	.05
□ 28 James Hasty	.10	.05
□ 29 Chris Warren	.20	.09
□ 30 Tim Harris	.10	.05
□ 31 Eric Metcalf	.20	.09
□ 32 Rob Moore	.20	.09
□ 33 Charles Haley	.20	.09
□ 34 Leonard Marshall	.10	.05
□ 35 Jeff Graham	.20	.09
□ 36 Eugene Robinson	.10	.05
□ 37 Darryl Talley	.10	.05
□ 38 Brent Jones	.20	.09
□ 39 Reggie Roby	.10	.05
□ 40 Bruce Armstrong	.10	.05
□ 41 Audray McMillian	.10	.05
□ 42 Bern Brostek	.10	.05
□ 43 Tony Bennett	.10	.05
□ 44 Albert Lewis	.10	.05
□ 45 Derrick Thomas	.40	.18
□ 46 Cris Carter	.75	.35
□ 47 Richmond Webb	.10	.05
□ 48 Sean Landeta	.10	.05
□ 49 Cleveland Gary	.10	.05
□ 50 Mark Carrier DB	.10	.05
□ 51 Lawrence Dawsey	.10	.05
□ 52 Lamar Lathon	.10	.05
□ 53 Nick Bell	.10	.05
□ 54 Curtis Duncan	.10	.05
□ 55 Irving Fryar	.20	.09
□ 56 Seth Joyner	.10	.05
□ 57 Jay Novacek	.20	.09
□ 58 John L. Williams	.10	.05
□ 59 Amp Lee	.10	.05
□ 60 Marion Butts	.10	.05
□ 61 Clyde Simmons	.10	.05
□ 62 Rich Gannon	.40	.18
□ 63 Anthony Johnson	.20	.09
□ 64 Dave Meggett	.10	.05
□ 65 James Francis	.10	.05
□ 66 Trace Armstrong	.10	.05
□ 67 Mo Lewis	.10	.05
□ 68 Cornelius Bennett	.20	.09
□ 69 Mark Duper	.10	.05
□ 70 Frank Reich	.20	.09
□ 71 Eric Green	.10	.05
□ 72 Bruce Matthews	.10	.05
□ 73 Steve Broussard	.10	.05
□ 74 Anthony Carter	.20	.09
□ 75 Sterling Sharpe	.40	.18
□ 76 Mike Kenn	.10	.05
□ 77 Andre Rison	.20	.09
□ 78 Todd Marinovich	.10	.05
□ 79 Vincent Brown	.10	.05
□ 80 Harold Green	.10	.05
□ 81 Art Monk	.20	.09
□ 82 Reggie Cobb	.10	.05
□ 83 Johnny Johnson	.10	.05
□ 84 Tommy Kane	.10	.05
□ 85 Rohn Stark	.10	.05
□ 86 Steve Tasker	.20	.09
□ 87 Ronnie Harmon	.10	.05
□ 88 Pepper Johnson	.10	.05
□ 89 Hardy Nickerson	.20	.09
□ 90 Alvin Harper	.20	.09
□ 91 Louis Oliver	.10	.05
□ 92 Rod Woodson	.40	.18
□ 93 Sam Mills	.10	.05
□ 94 Randall McDaniel	.10	.05
□ 95 Johnny Holland	.10	.05
□ 96 Jackie Slater	.10	.05
□ 97 Don Mosebar	.10	.05
□ 98 Andre Ware	.10	.05
□ 99 Kelvin Martin	.10	.05
□ 100 Emmitt Smith	3.00	1.35
□ 101 Michael Brooks	.10	.05
□ 102 Dan Saleaumua	.10	.05
□ 103 John Elway	3.00	1.35
□ 104 Henry Jones	.10	.05
□ 105 William Perry	.20	.09
□ 106 James Lofton	.20	.09
□ 107 Carnell Lake	.10	.05
□ 108 Chip Lohmiller	.10	.05
□ 109 Andre Tippett	.10	.05
□ 110 Barry Word	.10	.05
□ 111 Haywood Jeffires	.20	.09
□ 112 Kenny Walker	.10	.05
□ 113 John Randle	.20	.09
□ 114 Donnell Woolford	.10	.05
□ 115 Johnny Bailey	.10	.05
□ 116 Marcus Allen	.40	.18
□ 117 Mark Jackson	.10	.05
□ 118 Ray Agnew	.10	.05
□ 119 Gill Byrd	.10	.05
□ 120 Kyle Clifton	.10	.05
□ 121 Marv Cook	.10	.05
□ 122 Jerry Ball	.10	.05
□ 123 Steve Jordan	.10	.05
□ 124 Shannon Sharpe	.40	.18
□ 125 Brian Blades	.20	.09
□ 126 Rodney Hampton	.40	.18
□ 127 Bobby Hebert	.10	.05
□ 128 Jessie Tuggle	.10	.05
□ 129 Tom Newberry	.10	.05
□ 130 Keith McCants	.10	.05
□ 131 Richard Dent	.20	.09
□ 132 Herman Moore	1.00	.45
□ 133 Michael Irvin	.40	.18
□ 134 Ernest Givins	.20	.09
□ 135 Mark Rypien	.10	.05
□ 136 Leonard Russell	.20	.09
□ 137 Reggie White	.40	.18
□ 138 Thurman Thomas	.40	.18
□ 139 Nick Lowery	.10	.05
□ 140 Al Smith	.10	.05
□ 141 Jackie Harris	.10	.05
□ 142 Duane Bickett	.10	.05
□ 143 Lawyer Tillman	.10	.05
□ 144 Steve Wisniewski	.10	.05
□ 145 Derrick Fenner	.10	.05
□ 146 Harris Barton	.10	.05
□ 147 Rich Camarillo	.10	.05
□ 148 John Offerdahl	.10	.05
□ 149 Mike Johnson	.10	.05

No.	Player	Mint	Nrmt
❑ 150	Ricky Reynolds	.10	.05
❑ 151	Fred Barnett	.20	.09
❑ 152	Nate Newton	.20	.09
❑ 153	Chris Doleman	.10	.05
❑ 154	Todd Scott	.10	.05
❑ 155	Tim McKyer	.10	.05
❑ 156	Ken Harvey	.10	.05
❑ 157	Jeff Feagles	.10	.05
❑ 158	Vince Workman	.10	.05
❑ 159	Bart Oates	.10	.05
❑ 160	Chris Miller	.20	.09
❑ 161	Pete Stoyanovich	.10	.05
❑ 162	Steve Wallace	.10	.05
❑ 163	Dermontti Dawson	.10	.05
❑ 164	Kenneth Davis	.10	.05
❑ 165	Mike Munchak	.10	.05
❑ 166	George Jamison	.10	.05
❑ 167	Christian Okoye	.10	.05
❑ 168	Chris Hinton	.10	.05
❑ 169	Vaughan Johnson	.10	.05
❑ 170	Gaston Green	.10	.05
❑ 171	Kevin Greene	.40	.18
❑ 172	Rob Burnett	.10	.05
❑ 173	Norm Johnson	.10	.05
❑ 174	Eric Hill	.10	.05
❑ 175	Lomas Brown	.10	.05
❑ 176	Chip Banks	.10	.05
❑ 177	Greg Townsend	.10	.05
❑ 178	David Fulcher	.10	.05
❑ 179	Gary Anderson RB	.10	.05
❑ 180	Brian Washington	.10	.05
❑ 181	Brett Perriman	.40	.18
❑ 182	Chris Chandler	.20	.09
❑ 183	Phil Hansen	.10	.05
❑ 184	Mark Clayton	.10	.05
❑ 185	Frank Warren	.10	.05
❑ 186	Tim Brown	.40	.18
❑ 187	Mark Stepnoski	.10	.05
❑ 188	Bryan Cox	.10	.05
❑ 189	Gary Zimmerman	.10	.05
❑ 190	Neil O'Donnell	.40	.18
❑ 191	Anthony Smith	.10	.05
❑ 192	Craig Heyward	.20	.09
❑ 193	Keith Byars	.10	.05
❑ 194	Sean Salisbury	.10	.05
❑ 195	Todd Lyght	.10	.05
❑ 196	Jessie Hester	.10	.05
❑ 197	Rufus Porter	.10	.05
❑ 198	Steve Christie	.10	.05
❑ 199	Nate Lewis	.10	.05
❑ 200	Barry Sanders	3.00	1.35
❑ 201	Michael Haynes	.20	.09
❑ 202	John Taylor	.20	.09
❑ 203	John Friesz	.20	.09
❑ 204	William Fuller	.10	.05
❑ 205	Dennis Smith	.10	.05
❑ 206	Adrian Cooper	.10	.05
❑ 207	Henry Thomas	.10	.05
❑ 208	Gerald Williams	.10	.05
❑ 209	Chris Burkett	.10	.05
❑ 210	Broderick Thomas	.10	.05
❑ 211	Marvin Washington	.10	.05
❑ 212	Bennie Blades	.10	.05
❑ 213	Tony Casillas	.10	.05
❑ 214	Bubby Brister	.10	.05
❑ 215	Don Griffin	.10	.05
❑ 216	Jeff Cross	.10	.05
❑ 217	Derrick Walker	.10	.05
❑ 218	Lorenzo White	.10	.05
❑ 219	Ricky Sanders	.10	.05
❑ 220	Rickey Jackson	.10	.05
❑ 221	Simon Fletcher	.10	.05
❑ 222	Troy Vincent	.10	.05
❑ 223	Gary Clark	.20	.09
❑ 224	Stanley Richard	.10	.05
❑ 225	Dave Krieg	.20	.09
❑ 226	Warren Moon	.40	.18
❑ 227	Reggie Langhorne	.10	.05
❑ 228	Kent Hull	.10	.05
❑ 229	Ferrell Edmunds	.10	.05
❑ 230	Cortez Kennedy	.20	.09
❑ 231	Hugh Millen	.10	.05
❑ 232	Eugene Chung	.10	.05
❑ 233	Rodney Peete	.10	.05
❑ 234	Tom Waddle	.10	.05
❑ 235	David Klingler	.10	.05
❑ 236	Mark Carrier WR	.20	.09
❑ 237	Jay Schroeder	.10	.05
❑ 238	James Jones	.10	.05
❑ 239	Phil Simms	.20	.09
❑ 240	Steve Atwater	.10	.05
❑ 241	Jeff Herrod	.10	.05
❑ 242	Dale Carter	.10	.05
❑ 243	Glenn Cadrez RC	.10	.05
❑ 244	Wayne Martin	.10	.05
❑ 245	Willie Davis	.40	.18
❑ 246	Lawrence Taylor	.40	.18
❑ 247	Stan Humphries	.40	.18
❑ 248	Byron Evans	.10	.05
❑ 249	Wilber Marshall	.10	.05
❑ 250	Michael Bankston RC	.10	.05
❑ 251	Steve McMichael	.20	.09
❑ 252	Brad Edwards	.10	.05
❑ 253	Will Wolford	.10	.05
❑ 254	Paul Gruber	.10	.05
❑ 255	Steve Young	1.50	.70
❑ 256	Chuck Cecil	.10	.05
❑ 257	Pierce Holt	.10	.05
❑ 258	Anthony Miller	.20	.09
❑ 259	Carl Banks	.10	.05
❑ 260	Brad Muster	.10	.05
❑ 261	Clay Matthews	.20	.09
❑ 262	Rod Bernstine	.10	.05
❑ 263	Tim Barnett	.10	.05
❑ 264	Greg Lloyd	.40	.18
❑ 265	Sean Jones	.10	.05
❑ 266	J.J. Birden	.10	.05
❑ 267	Tim McDonald	.10	.05
❑ 268	Charles Mann	.10	.05
❑ 269	Bruce Smith	.40	.18
❑ 270	Sean Gilbert	.20	.09
❑ 271	Ricardo McDonald	.10	.05
❑ 272	Jeff Hostetler	.20	.09
❑ 273	Russell Maryland	.10	.05
❑ 274	Dave Brown RC	.40	.18
❑ 275	Ronnie Lott	.20	.09
❑ 276	Jim Kelly	.40	.18
❑ 277	Joe Montana	3.00	1.35
❑ 278	Eric Allen	.10	.05
❑ 279	Browning Nagle	.10	.05
❑ 280	Neal Anderson	.10	.05
❑ 281	Troy Aikman	1.50	.70
❑ 282	Ed McCaffrey	.20	.09
❑ 283	Robert Jones	.10	.05
❑ 284	Dalton Hilliard	.10	.05
❑ 285	Johnny Mitchell	.10	.05
❑ 286	Jay Hilgenberg	.10	.05
❑ 287	Eric Martin	.10	.05
❑ 288	Steve Emtman	.10	.05
❑ 289	Vaughn Dunbar	.10	.05
❑ 290	Mark Wheeler	.10	.05
❑ 291	Leslie O'Neal	.20	.09
❑ 292	Jerry Rice	2.00	.90
❑ 293	Neil Smith	.40	.18
❑ 294	Kerry Cash	.10	.05
❑ 295	Dan McGwire	.10	.05
❑ 296	Carl Pickens	.40	.18
❑ 297	Terrell Buckley	.10	.05
❑ 298	Randall Cunningham	.40	.18
❑ 299	Santana Dotson	.20	.09
❑ 300	Keith Jackson	.20	.09
❑ 301	Jim Lachey	.10	.05
❑ 302	Dan Marino	3.00	1.35
❑ 303	Lee Williams	.10	.05
❑ 304	Burt Grossman	.10	.05
❑ 305	Kevin Mack	.10	.05
❑ 306	Pat Swilling	.10	.05
❑ 307	Arthur Marshall RC	.10	.05
❑ 308	Jim Harbaugh	.40	.18
❑ 309	Kurt Barber	.10	.05
❑ 310	Harvey Williams	.20	.09
❑ 311	Ricky Ervins	.10	.05
❑ 312	Flipper Anderson	.10	.05
❑ 313	Bernie Kosar	.20	.09
❑ 314	Boomer Esiason	.20	.09
❑ 315	Deion Sanders	1.00	.45
❑ 316	Ray Childress	.10	.05
❑ 317	Howie Long	.20	.09
❑ 318	Henry Ellard	.20	.09
❑ 319	Marco Coleman	.10	.05
❑ 320	Chris Mims	.10	.05
❑ 321	Quentin Coryatt	.20	.09
❑ 322	Jason Hanson	.10	.05
❑ 323	Ricky Proehl	.10	.05
❑ 324	Randal Hill	.10	.05
❑ 325	Vinny Testaverde	.20	.09
❑ 326	Jeff George	.40	.18
❑ 327	Junior Seau	.40	.18
❑ 328	Earnest Byner	.10	.05
❑ 329	Andre Reed	.20	.09
❑ 330	Phillippi Sparks	.10	.05
❑ 331	Kevin Ross	.10	.05
❑ 332	Clarence Verdin	.10	.05
❑ 333	Darryl Henley	.10	.05
❑ 334	Dana Hall	.10	.05
❑ 335	Greg McMurtry	.10	.05
❑ 336	Ron Hall	.10	.05
❑ 337	Darrell Green	.10	.05
❑ 338	Carlton Bailey	.10	.05
❑ 339	Irv Eatman	.10	.05
❑ 340	Greg Kragen	.10	.05
❑ 341	Wade Wilson	.10	.05
❑ 342	Klaus Wilmsmeyer	.10	.05
❑ 343	Derek Brown TE	.10	.05
❑ 344	Erik Williams	.10	.05
❑ 345	Jim McMahon	.10	.05
❑ 346	Mike Sherrard	.10	.05
❑ 347	Mark Bavaro	.10	.05
❑ 348	Anthony Munoz	.20	.09
❑ 349	Eric Dickerson	.20	.09
❑ 350	Steve Beuerlein	.10	.05
❑ 351	Tim McGee	.10	.05
❑ 352	Terry McDaniel	.10	.05
❑ 353	Dan Fouts HOF	.10	.05
❑ 354	Chuck Noll HOF	.20	.09
❑ 355	Bill Walsh HOF RC	.20	.09
❑ 356	Larry Little HOF	.10	.05
❑ 357	Todd Marinovich HH	.10	.05
❑ 358	Jeff George HH	.40	.18
❑ 359	Bernie Kosar HH	.20	.09
❑ 360	Rob Moore HH	.20	.09
❑ NNO	Franco Harris AUTO/3000	30.00	13.50

1994 Pinnacle

	MINT	NRMT
COMPLETE SET (270)	20.00	9.00

No.	Player	Mint	Nrmt
❑ 1	Deion Sanders	.50	.23
❑ 2	Eric Metcalf	.20	.09
❑ 3	Barry Sanders	2.50	1.10
❑ 4	Ernest Givins	.20	.09
❑ 5	Phil Simms	.20	.09
❑ 6	Rod Woodson	.40	.18
❑ 7	Michael Irvin	.40	.18
❑ 8	Cortez Kennedy	.20	.09
❑ 9	Eric Martin	.10	.05
❑ 10	Jeff Hostetler	.20	.09
❑ 11	Sterling Sharpe	.20	.09
❑ 12	John Elway	2.50	1.10
❑ 13	Neal Anderson	.10	.05
❑ 14	Terry Kirby	.40	.18
❑ 15	Jim Everett	.20	.09
❑ 16	Lawrence Dawsey	.10	.05
❑ 17	Kelvin Martin	.10	.05
❑ 18	Tim McGee	.10	.05
❑ 19	Cris Carter	.50	.23
❑ 20	Ronnie Harmon	.10	.05
❑ 21	Jim Kelly	.40	.18

❑ 22 Steve Young 1.00 .45
❑ 23 Johnny Johnson .10 .05
❑ 24 Sean Gilbert .10 .05
❑ 25 Brian Mitchell .10 .05
❑ 26 Carl Pickens .40 .18
❑ 27 Tim Brown .40 .18
❑ 28 Reggie Langhorne .10 .05
❑ 29 Webster Slaughter .10 .05
❑ 30 Alvin Harper .20 .09
❑ 31 Andre Rison .20 .09
❑ 32 Derrick Thomas .40 .18
❑ 33 Irving Fryar .20 .09
❑ 34 Vinny Testaverde .20 .09
❑ 35 Steve Beuerlein .10 .05
❑ 36 Brett Favre 2.50 1.10
❑ 37 Barry Foster .10 .05
❑ 38 Vaughan Johnson .10 .05
❑ 39 Carlton Bailey .10 .05
❑ 40 Steve Emtman .10 .05
❑ 41 Anthony Miller .20 .09
❑ 42 Jeff Cross .10 .05
❑ 43 Trace Armstrong .10 .05
❑ 44 Derek Russell .10 .05
❑ 45 Vincent Brisby .40 .18
❑ 46 Mark Jackson .10 .05
❑ 47 Eugene Robinson .10 .05
❑ 48 John Friesz .20 .09
❑ 49 Scott Mitchell .40 .18
❑ 50 Steve Atwater .10 .05
❑ 51 Ken Norton .20 .09
❑ 52 Vincent Brown .10 .05
❑ 53 Morten Andersen .10 .05
❑ 54 Gary Anderson K .10 .05
❑ 55 Eric Curry .10 .05
❑ 56 Henry Jones .10 .05
❑ 57 Flipper Anderson .10 .05
❑ 58 Pat Swilling .10 .05
❑ 59 Erric Pegram .10 .05
❑ 60 Bruce Matthews .10 .05
❑ 61 Willie Davis .20 .09
❑ 62 O.J. McDuffie .40 .18
❑ 63 Qadry Ismail .40 .18
❑ 64 Anthony Smith .10 .05
❑ 65 Eric Allen .10 .05
❑ 66 Marion Butts .10 .05
❑ 67 Chris Miller .10 .05
❑ 68 Terrell Buckley .10 .05
❑ 69 Thurman Thomas .40 .18
❑ 70 Roosevelt Potts .10 .05
❑ 71 Tony McGee .10 .05
❑ 72 Jason Hanson .10 .05
❑ 73 Victor Bailey .10 .05
❑ 74 Albert Lewis .10 .05
❑ 75 Nate Odomes .10 .05
❑ 76 Ben Coates .40 .18
❑ 77 Warren Moon .40 .18
❑ 78 Derek Brown RBK .10 .05
❑ 79 David Klingler .10 .05
❑ 80 Cleveland Gary .10 .05
❑ 81 Emmitt Smith 2.00 .90
❑ 82 Jay Novacek .20 .09
❑ 83 Dana Stubblefield .40 .18
❑ 84 Michael Brooks .10 .05
❑ 85 James Jett .10 .05
❑ 86 J.J. Birden .10 .05
❑ 87 William Fuller .10 .05
❑ 88 Glyn Milburn .20 .09
❑ 89 Tim Worley .10 .05
❑ 90 Brett Perriman .20 .09
❑ 91 Randall Cunningham .40 .18
❑ 92 Drew Bledsoe 1.25 .55
❑ 93 Jerome Bettis .40 .18
❑ 94 Boomer Esiason .20 .09
❑ 95 Garrison Hearst .40 .18
❑ 96 Bruce Smith .40 .18
❑ 97 Jackie Harris .10 .05
❑ 98 Jeff George .40 .18
❑ 99 Tom Waddle .10 .05
❑ 100 John Copeland .10 .05
❑ 101 Bobby Hebert .10 .05
❑ 102 Joe Montana 2.50 1.10
❑ 103 Herman Moore .40 .18
❑ 104 Rick Mirer .40 .18
❑ 105 Ricky Watters .40 .18
❑ 106 Neil O'Donnell .40 .18
❑ 107 Herschel Walker .20 .09
❑ 108 Rob Moore .20 .09
❑ 109 Reggie Brooks .20 .09
❑ 110 Tommy Vardell .10 .05
❑ 111 Eric Green .10 .05
❑ 112 Stan Humphries .40 .18
❑ 113 Greg Robinson .10 .05
❑ 114 Eric Swann .20 .09
❑ 115 Courtney Hawkins .10 .05
❑ 116 Andre Reed .20 .09
❑ 117 Steve McMichael .20 .09
❑ 118 Gary Brown .10 .05
❑ 119 Terry Allen .20 .09
❑ 120 Dan Marino 2.50 1.10
❑ 121 Gary Clark .20 .09
❑ 122 Chris Warren .20 .09
❑ 123 Pierce Holt .10 .05
❑ 124 Anthony Carter .20 .09
❑ 125 Quentin Coryatt .10 .05
❑ 126 Harold Green .10 .05
❑ 127 Leonard Russell .10 .05
❑ 128 Tim McDonald .10 .05
❑ 129 Chris Spielman .20 .09
❑ 130 Cody Carlson .10 .05
❑ 131 Ronald Moore .10 .05
❑ 132 Renaldo Turnbull .10 .05
❑ 133 Ronnie Lott .20 .09
❑ 134 Natrone Means .40 .18
❑ 135 Keith Byars .10 .05
❑ 136 Henry Ellard .20 .09
❑ 137 Steve Jordan .10 .05
❑ 138 Calvin Williams .20 .09
❑ 139 Brian Blades .20 .09
❑ 140 Michael Jackson .20 .09
❑ 141 Charles Haley .20 .09
❑ 142 Curtis Conway .40 .18
❑ 143 Nick Lowery .10 .05
❑ 144 Bill Brooks .10 .05
❑ 145 Michael Haynes .20 .09
❑ 146 Willie Green .10 .05
❑ 147 Duane Bickett .10 .05
❑ 148 Shannon Sharpe .20 .09
❑ 149 Ricky Proehl .10 .05
❑ 150 Troy Aikman 1.25 .55
❑ 151 Mike Sherrard .10 .05
❑ 152 Reggie Cobb .10 .05
❑ 153 Norm Johnson .10 .05
❑ 154 Neil Smith .40 .18
❑ 155 James Francis .10 .05
❑ 156 Greg McMurtry .10 .05
❑ 157 Greg Townsend .10 .05
❑ 158 Mel Gray .10 .05
❑ 159 Rocket Ismail .20 .09
❑ 160 Leslie O'Neal .10 .05
❑ 161 Johnny Mitchell .10 .05
❑ 162 Brent Jones .20 .09
❑ 163 Chris Doleman .10 .05
❑ 164 Seth Joyner .10 .05
❑ 165 Marco Coleman .10 .05
❑ 166 Mark Higgs .10 .05
❑ 167 John L. Williams .10 .05
❑ 168 Darrell Green .10 .05
❑ 169 Mark Carrier WR .20 .09
❑ 170 Reggie White .40 .18
❑ 171 Darryl Talley .10 .05
❑ 172 Russell Maryland .10 .05
❑ 173 Mark Collins .10 .05
❑ 174 Chris Jacke .10 .05
❑ 175 Richard Dent .20 .09
❑ 176 John Taylor .20 .09
❑ 177 Rodney Hampton .40 .18
❑ 178 Dwight Stone .10 .05
❑ 179 Cornelius Bennett .20 .09
❑ 180 Cris Dishman .10 .05
❑ 181 Jerry Rice 1.25 .55
❑ 182 Rod Bernstine .10 .05
❑ 183 Keith Hamilton .10 .05
❑ 184 Keith Jackson .10 .05
❑ 185 Craig Erickson .10 .05
❑ 186 Marcus Allen .40 .18
❑ 187 Marcus Robertson .10 .05
❑ 188 Junior Seau .40 .18
❑ 189 LeShon Johnson RC .20 .09
❑ 190 Perry Klein RC .10 .05
❑ 191 Bryant Young RC .40 .18
❑ 192 Byron Bam Morris RC .40 .18
❑ 193 Jeff Cothran RC .10 .05
❑ 194 Lamar Smith RC 4.00 1.80
❑ 195 Calvin Jones RC .10 .05
❑ 196 James Bostic RC .40 .18
❑ 197 Dan Wilkinson RC .20 .09
❑ 198 Marshall Faulk RC 5.00 2.20
❑ 199 Heath Shuler RC .40 .18
❑ 200 Willie McGinest RC .40 .18
❑ 201 Trev Alberts RC .20 .09
❑ 202 Trent Dilfer RC 2.50 1.10
❑ 203 Sam Adams RC .20 .09
❑ 204 Charles Johnson RC 1.00 .45
❑ 205 Johnnie Morton RC 1.25 .55
❑ 206 Thomas Lewis RC .20 .09
❑ 207 Greg Hill RC .40 .18
❑ 208 William Floyd RC .40 .18
❑ 209 Der.Alexander WR RC 1.00 .45
❑ 210 Darnay Scott RC 1.25 .55
❑ 211 Lake Dawson RC .40 .18
❑ 212 Errict Rhett RC 1.25 .55
❑ 213 Kevin Lee RC .10 .05
❑ 214 Chuck Levy RC .10 .05
❑ 215 David Palmer RC 1.00 .45
❑ 216 Ryan Yarborough RC .10 .05
❑ 217 Charlie Garner RC 2.00 .90
❑ 218 Mario Bates RC .40 .18
❑ 219 Jamir Miller RC .10 .05
❑ 220 Bucky Brooks RC .10 .05
❑ 221 Donnell Bennett RC .40 .18
❑ 222 Kevin Greene .40 .18
❑ 223 LeRoy Butler .10 .05
❑ 224 Anthony Pleasant .10 .05
❑ 225 Steve Christie .10 .05
❑ 226 Bill Romanowski .10 .05
❑ 227 Darren Carrington .10 .05
❑ 228 Chester McGlockton .10 .05
❑ 229 Jack Del Rio .10 .05
❑ 230 Kevin Smith .10 .05
❑ 231 Chris Zorich .10 .05
❑ 232 Donnell Woolford .10 .05
❑ 233 Tony Casillas .10 .05
❑ 234 Terry McDaniel .10 .05
❑ 235 Ray Childress .10 .05
❑ 236 John Randle .20 .09
❑ 237 Clyde Simmons .10 .05
❑ 238 Dante Jones .10 .05
❑ 239 Karl Mecklenburg .10 .05
❑ 240 Daryl Johnston .20 .09
❑ 241 Hardy Nickerson .20 .09
❑ 242 Jeff Lageman .10 .05
❑ 243 Lewis Tillman .10 .05
❑ 244 Jim McMahon .10 .05
❑ 245 Mike Pritchard .10 .05
❑ 246 Harvey Williams .20 .09
❑ 247 Sean Jones .10 .05
❑ 248 Stevon Moore .10 .05
❑ 249 Pete Metzelaars .10 .05
❑ 250 Mike Johnson .10 .05
❑ 251 Chris Slade .10 .05
❑ 252 Jessie Hester .10 .05
❑ 253 Louis Oliver .10 .05
❑ 254 Ken Harvey .10 .05
❑ 255 Bryan Cox .10 .05
❑ 256 Erik Kramer .20 .09
❑ 257 Andy Harmon .10 .05
❑ 258 Rickey Jackson .10 .05
❑ 259 Mark Carrier DB .10 .05
❑ 260 Greg Lloyd .40 .18
❑ 261 Robert Brooks .40 .18
❑ 262 Dave Brown .20 .09
❑ 263 Dennis Smith .10 .05
❑ 264 Michael Dean Perry .20 .09
❑ 265 Dan Saleaumua .10 .05
❑ 266 Mo Lewis .10 .05
❑ 267 AFC Checklist .10 .05
❑ 268 AFC Checklist .10 .05
❑ 269 NFC Checklist .10 .05
❑ 270 NFC Checklist .10 .05
❑ 271SP Jerry Rice TD King 8.00 3.60
❑ NNO Drew Bledsoe 40.00 18.00
Pinnacle Passer

1995 Pinnacle

	MINT	NRMT
COMPLETE SET (250)	20.00	9.00
❑ 1 Reggie White	.40	.18

❑ 2 Troy Aikman 1.00 .45
❑ 3 Willie Davis .20 .09
❑ 4 Jerry Rice 1.00 .45
❑ 5 Bruce Smith .40 .18
❑ 6 Keith Byars .10 .05
❑ 7 Chris Warren .20 .09
❑ 8 Erik Kramer .10 .05
❑ 9 Leon Lett .10 .05
❑ 10 Greg Lloyd .20 .09
❑ 11 Jackie Harris .10 .05
❑ 12 Irving Fryar .20 .09
❑ 13 Rodney Hampton .20 .09
❑ 14 Michael Irvin .40 .18
❑ 15 Michael Haynes .20 .09
❑ 16 Irving Spikes .20 .09
❑ 17 Calvin Williams .20 .09
❑ 18 Ken Norton Jr. .20 .09
❑ 19 Herman Moore .40 .18
❑ 20 Lewis Tillman .10 .05
❑ 21 Cortez Kennedy .20 .09
❑ 22 Dan Marino 2.00 .90
❑ 23 Erric Pegram .20 .09
❑ 24 Tim Brown .40 .18
❑ 25 Jeff Blake RC 1.00 .45
❑ 26 Brett Favre 2.00 .90
❑ 27 Garrison Hearst .40 .18
❑ 28 Ronnie Harmon .10 .05
❑ 29 Qadry Ismail .20 .09
❑ 30 Ben Coates .20 .09
❑ 31 Deion Sanders .60 .25
❑ 32 John Elway 2.00 .90
❑ 33 Natrone Means .40 .18
❑ 34 Derrick Alexander WR .40 .18
❑ 35 Craig Heyward .20 .09
❑ 36 Jake Reed .20 .09
❑ 37 Steve Walsh .10 .05
❑ 38 John Randle .20 .09
❑ 39 Barry Sanders 2.00 .90
❑ 40 Tydus Winans .10 .05
❑ 41 Thomas Lewis .20 .09
❑ 42 Jim Kelly .40 .18
❑ 43 Gus Frerotte .40 .18
❑ 44 Cris Carter .40 .18
❑ 45 Kevin Williams WR .20 .09
❑ 46 Dave Meggett .10 .05
❑ 47 Pat Swilling .10 .05
❑ 48 Neil O'Donnell .20 .09
❑ 49 Terance Mathis .20 .09
❑ 50 Desmond Howard .20 .09
❑ 51 Bryant Young .20 .09
❑ 52 Stan Humphries .20 .09
❑ 53 Alvin Harper .10 .05
❑ 54 Henry Ellard .20 .09
❑ 55 Jessie Hester .10 .05
❑ 56 Lorenzo White .10 .05
❑ 57 John Friesz .20 .09
❑ 58 Anthony Smith .10 .05
❑ 59 Bert Emanuel .40 .18
❑ 60 Gary Clark .10 .05
❑ 61 Bill Brooks .10 .05
❑ 62 Steve Young .75 .35
❑ 63 Jerome Bettis .40 .18
❑ 64 John Taylor .10 .05
❑ 65 Ricky Proehl .10 .05
❑ 66 Junior Seau .40 .18
❑ 67 Bubby Brister .10 .05
❑ 68 Neil Smith .20 .09
❑ 69 Dan McGwire .10 .05
❑ 70 Brett Perriman .20 .09
❑ 71 Chris Spielman .20 .09
❑ 72 Jeff George .20 .09
❑ 73 Emmitt Smith 1.00 .45
❑ 74 Chris Penn .10 .05
❑ 75 Derrick Fenner .10 .05
❑ 76 Reggie Brooks .20 .09
❑ 77 Chris Chandler .20 .09
❑ 78 Rod Woodson .20 .09
❑ 79 Isaac Bruce .60 .25
❑ 80 Reggie Cobb .10 .05
❑ 81 Bryce Paup .40 .18
❑ 82 Warren Moon .20 .09
❑ 83 Bryan Reeves .10 .05
❑ 84 Lake Dawson .20 .09
❑ 85 Larry Centers .20 .09
❑ 86 Marshall Faulk .60 .25
❑ 87 Jim Harbaugh .20 .09
❑ 88 Ray Childress .10 .05
❑ 89 Eric Metcalf .20 .09
❑ 90 Ernie Mills .10 .05
❑ 91 Lamar Lathon .10 .05
❑ 92 Errict Rhett .40 .18
❑ 93 David Klingler .20 .09
❑ 94 Vincent Brown .10 .05
❑ 95 Andre Rison .20 .09
❑ 96 Brian Mitchell .10 .05
❑ 97 Mark Rypien .10 .05
❑ 98 Eugene Robinson .10 .05
❑ 99 Eric Green .10 .05
❑ 100 Rocket Ismail .20 .09
❑ 101 Flipper Anderson .10 .05
❑ 102 Randall Cunningham .40 .18
❑ 103 Ricky Watters .40 .18
❑ 104 Amp Lee .10 .05
❑ 105 Ernest Givins .10 .05
❑ 106 Daryl Johnston .20 .09
❑ 107 Dave Krieg .10 .05
❑ 108 Dana Stubblefield .40 .18
❑ 109 Torrance Small .10 .05
❑ 110 Yancey Thigpen RC .40 .18
❑ 111 Chester McGlockton .20 .09
❑ 112 Craig Erickson .10 .05
❑ 113 Herschel Walker .20 .09
❑ 114 Mike Sherrard .10 .05
❑ 115 Tony McGee .10 .05
❑ 116 Adrian Murrell .20 .09
❑ 117 Frank Reich .10 .05
❑ 118 Hardy Nickerson .10 .05
❑ 119 Andre Reed .20 .09
❑ 120 Leonard Russell .10 .05
❑ 121 Eric Allen .10 .05
❑ 122 Jeff Hostetler .20 .09
❑ 123 Barry Foster .20 .09
❑ 124 Anthony Miller .20 .09
❑ 125 Shawn Jefferson .10 .05
❑ 126 Richie Anderson RC .40 .18
❑ 127 Steve Bono .20 .09
❑ 128 Seth Joyner .10 .05
❑ 129 Darnay Scott .40 .18
❑ 130 Johnny Mitchell .10 .05
❑ 131 Eric Swann .20 .09
❑ 132 Drew Bledsoe 1.00 .45
❑ 133 Marcus Allen .40 .18
❑ 134 Carl Pickens .40 .18
❑ 135 Michael Brooks .10 .05
❑ 136 John L. Williams .10 .05
❑ 137 Steve Beuerlein .10 .05
❑ 138 Robert Smith .40 .18
❑ 139 O.J. McDuffie .40 .18
❑ 140 Haywood Jeffires .10 .05
❑ 141 Aeneas Williams .10 .05
❑ 142 Rick Mirer .40 .18
❑ 143 William Floyd .40 .18
❑ 144 Fred Barnett .20 .09
❑ 145 Leroy Hoard .10 .05
❑ 146 Terry Kirby .20 .09
❑ 147 Boomer Esiason .20 .09
❑ 148 Ken Harvey .10 .05
❑ 149 Cleveland Gary .10 .05
❑ 150 Brian Blades .20 .09
❑ 151 Eric Turner .10 .05
❑ 152 Vinny Testaverde .20 .09
❑ 153 Ronald Moore UER .10 .05
card pictures Rob Moore
❑ 154 Curtis Conway .40 .18
❑ 155 Johnnie Morton .20 .09
❑ 156 Kenneth Davis .10 .05
❑ 157 Scott Mitchell .20 .09
❑ 158 Sean Gilbert .20 .09
❑ 159 Shannon Sharpe .20 .09
❑ 160 Mark Seay .20 .09
❑ 161 Cornelius Bennett .20 .09
❑ 162 Heath Shuler .40 .18
❑ 163 Byron Bam Morris .20 .09
❑ 164 Robert Brooks .40 .18
❑ 165 Glyn Milburn .10 .05
❑ 166 Gary Brown .10 .05
❑ 167 Jim Everett .10 .05
❑ 168 Steve Atwater .10 .05
❑ 169 Darren Woodson .20 .09
❑ 170 Mark Ingram .10 .05
❑ 171 Donnell Woolford .10 .05
❑ 172 Trent Dilfer .40 .18
❑ 173 Charlie Garner .20 .09
❑ 174 Charles Johnson .20 .09
❑ 175 Mike Pritchard .10 .05
❑ 176 Derek Brown RBK .10 .05
❑ 177 Chris Miller .10 .05
❑ 178 Charles Haley .20 .09
❑ 179 J.J. Birden .10 .05
❑ 180 Jeff Graham .10 .05
❑ 181 Bernie Parmalee .20 .09
❑ 182 Mark Brunell 1.00 .45
❑ 183 Greg Hill .20 .09
❑ 184 Michael Timpson .10 .05
❑ 185 Terry Allen .20 .09
❑ 186 Ricky Ervins .10 .05
❑ 187 Dave Brown .20 .09
❑ 188 Dan Wilkinson .20 .09
❑ 189 Jay Novacek .20 .09
❑ 190 Harvey Williams .10 .05
❑ 191 Mario Bates .40 .18
❑ 192 Steve Young .50 .23
❑ 193 Joe Montana 2.00 .90
❑ 194 Steve Young PP .50 .23
❑ 195 Troy Aikman PP .60 .25
❑ 196 Drew Bledsoe PP .60 .25
❑ 197 Dan Marino PP 1.00 .45
❑ 198 John Elway PP 1.00 .45
❑ 199 Brett Favre PP 1.00 .45
❑ 200 Heath Shuler PP .40 .18
❑ 201 Warren Moon PP .10 .05
❑ 202 Jim Kelly PP .40 .18
❑ 203 Jeff Hostetler PP .20 .09
❑ 204 Rick Mirer PP .20 .09
❑ 205 Dave Brown PP .20 .09
❑ 206 Randall Cunningham PP .20 .09
❑ 207 Neil O'Donnell PP .20 .09
❑ 208 Jim Everett PP .10 .05
❑ 209 Ki-Jana Carter RC .40 .18
❑ 210 Steve McNair RC 2.50 1.10
❑ 211 Michael Westbrook RC 1.50 .70
❑ 212 Kerry Collins RC 1.50 .70
❑ 213 Joey Galloway RC 2.00 .90
❑ 214 Kyle Brady RC .40 .18
❑ 215 J.J. Stokes RC .40 .18
❑ 216 Tyrone Wheatley RC 1.25 .55
❑ 217 Rashaan Salaam RC .40 .18
❑ 218 Napoleon Kaufman RC 1.50 .70
❑ 219 Frank Sanders RC 1.00 .45
❑ 220 Stoney Case RC .40 .18
❑ 221 Todd Collins RC .40 .18
❑ 222 Warren Sapp RC .75 .35
❑ 223 Sherman Williams RC .10 .05
❑ 224 Rob Johnson RC 2.00 .90
❑ 225 Mark Bruener RC .20 .09
❑ 226 Derrick Brooks RC .40 .18
❑ 227 Chad May RC .10 .05
❑ 228 James A.Stewart RC .10 .05
❑ 229 Ray Zellars RC .20 .09
❑ 230 Dave Barr RC .10 .05
❑ 231 Kordell Stewart RC 2.00 .90
❑ 232 Jimmy Oiver RC .10 .05
❑ 233 Tony Boselli RC .40 .18
❑ 234 James O. Stewart RC 2.00 .90
❑ 235 Der. Alexander DE RC .10 .05
❑ 236 Lovell Pinkney RC .10 .05
❑ 237 John Walsh RC .10 .05
❑ 238 Tyrone Davis RC .10 .05
❑ 239 Joe Aska RC .20 .09

		MINT	NRMT
❑ 240	Korey Stringer RC	.10	.05
❑ 241	Hugh Douglas RC	.40	.18
❑ 242	Christian Fauria RC	.10	.05
❑ 243	Terrell Fletcher RC	.10	.05
❑ 244	Dan Marino	.60	.25
❑ 245	Drew Bledsoe	.40	.18
❑ 246	John Elway	.40	.18
❑ 247	Emmitt Smith	.50	.23
❑ 248	Steve Young	.40	.18
❑ 249	Barry Sanders	.60	.25
❑ 250	Jerry Rice CL Junior Seau CL	.40	.18
❑ 251SP	Deion Sanders SP	4.00	1.80

1996 Pinnacle

		MINT	NRMT
COMPLETE SET (200)		20.00	9.00
❑ 1	Emmitt Smith	1.50	.70
❑ 2	Robert Brooks	.40	.18
❑ 3	Joey Galloway	.60	.25
❑ 4	Dan Marino	2.00	.90
❑ 5	Frank Sanders	.20	.09
❑ 6	Cris Carter	.40	.18
❑ 7	Jeff Blake	.40	.18
❑ 8	Steve McNair	.75	.35
❑ 9	Tamarick Vanover	.20	.09
❑ 10	Andre Reed	.20	.09
❑ 11	Junior Seau	.20	.09
❑ 12	Alvin Harper	.10	.05
❑ 13	Trent Dilfer	.40	.18
❑ 14	Kordell Stewart	.60	.25
❑ 15	Kyle Brady	.10	.05
❑ 16	Charles Haley	.20	.09
❑ 17	Greg Lloyd	.20	.09
❑ 18	Mario Bates	.20	.09
❑ 19	Shannon Sharpe	.20	.09
❑ 20	Scott Mitchell	.20	.09
❑ 21	Craig Heyward	.10	.05
❑ 22	Marcus Allen	.40	.18
❑ 23	Curtis Martin	.75	.35
❑ 24	Drew Bledsoe	1.00	.45
❑ 25	Jerry Rice	1.00	.45
❑ 26	Charlie Garner	.10	.05
❑ 27	Michael Irvin	.40	.18
❑ 28	Curtis Conway	.40	.18
❑ 29	Terrell Davis	2.50	1.10
❑ 30	Jeff Hostetler	.10	.05
❑ 31	Neil O'Donnell	.20	.09
❑ 32	Errict Rhett	.20	.09
❑ 33	Stan Humphries	.20	.09
❑ 34	Jeff Graham	.10	.05
❑ 35	Floyd Turner	.10	.05
❑ 36	Vincent Brisby	.10	.05
❑ 37	Steve Young	.75	.35
❑ 38	Carl Pickens	.40	.18
❑ 39	Terance Mathis	.10	.05
❑ 40	Brett Favre	2.00	.90
❑ 41	Ki-Jana Carter	.20	.09
❑ 42	Jim Everett	.10	.05
❑ 43	Marshall Faulk	.40	.18
❑ 44	William Floyd	.20	.09
❑ 45	Deion Sanders	.60	.25
❑ 46	Garrison Hearst	.20	.09
❑ 47	Chris Sanders	.20	.09
❑ 48	Isaac Bruce	.40	.18
❑ 49	Natrone Means	.40	.18
❑ 50	Troy Aikman	1.00	.45
❑ 51	Ben Coates	.20	.09
❑ 52	Tony Martin	.20	.09
❑ 53	Rod Woodson	.20	.09
❑ 54	Edgar Bennett	.20	.09
❑ 55	Eric Zeier	.10	.05
❑ 56	Steve Bono	.10	.05
❑ 57	Tim Brown	.40	.18
❑ 58	Kevin Williams	.10	.05
❑ 59	Erik Kramer	.10	.05
❑ 60	Jim Kelly	.40	.18
❑ 61	Larry Centers	.20	.09
❑ 62	Terrell Fletcher	.10	.05
❑ 63	Michael Westbrook	.40	.18
❑ 64	Kerry Collins	.40	.18
❑ 65	Jay Novacek	.10	.05
❑ 66	J.J. Stokes	.40	.18
❑ 67	John Elway	2.00	.90
❑ 68	Jim Harbaugh	.20	.09
❑ 69	Aeneas Williams	.10	.05
❑ 70	Tyrone Wheatley	.20	.09
❑ 71	Chris Warren	.20	.09
❑ 72	Rodney Thomas	.10	.05
❑ 73	Jeff George	.20	.09
❑ 74	Rick Mirer	.20	.09
❑ 75	Yancey Thigpen	.20	.09
❑ 76	Herman Moore	.40	.18
❑ 77	Gus Frerotte	.40	.18
❑ 78	Anthony Miller	.20	.09
❑ 79	Ricky Watters	.20	.09
❑ 80	Sherman Williams	.10	.05
❑ 81	Hardy Nickerson	.10	.05
❑ 82	Henry Ellard	.10	.05
❑ 83	Aaron Craver	.10	.05
❑ 84	Rodney Peete	.10	.05
❑ 85	Eric Metcalf	.10	.05
❑ 86	Brian Blades	.10	.05
❑ 87	Rob Moore	.20	.09
❑ 88	Kimble Anders	.20	.09
❑ 89	Harvey Williams	.10	.05
❑ 90	Thurman Thomas	.40	.18
❑ 91	Dave Brown	.10	.05
❑ 92	Terry Allen	.20	.09
❑ 93	Ken Norton Jr.	.10	.05
❑ 94	Reggie White	.40	.18
❑ 95	Mark Chmura	.20	.09
❑ 96	Bert Emanuel	.20	.09
❑ 97	Brett Perriman	.10	.05
❑ 98	Antonio Freeman	.75	.35
❑ 99	Brian Mitchell	.10	.05
❑ 100	Orlando Thomas	.10	.05
❑ 101	Aaron Hayden	.10	.05
❑ 102	Quinn Early	.10	.05
❑ 103	Lovell Pinkney	.10	.05
❑ 104	Napoleon Kaufman	.40	.18
❑ 105	Daryl Johnston	.20	.09
❑ 106	Steve Tasker	.10	.05
❑ 107	Brent Jones	.10	.05
❑ 108	Mark Brunell	1.00	.45
❑ 109	Leslie O'Neal	.10	.05
❑ 110	Irving Fryar	.20	.09
❑ 111	Jim Miller	.10	.05
❑ 112	Sean Dawkins	.10	.05
❑ 113	Boomer Esiason	.20	.09
❑ 114	Heath Shuler	.20	.09
❑ 115	Bruce Smith	.20	.09
❑ 116	Russell Maryland	.10	.05
❑ 117	Jake Reed	.20	.09
❑ 118	O.J. McDuffie	.20	.09
❑ 119	Erik Williams	.10	.05
❑ 120	Willie McGinest	.10	.05
❑ 121	Terry Kirby	.20	.09
❑ 122	Fred Barnett	.10	.05
❑ 123	Andre Hastings	.10	.05
❑ 124	Dale Hellestrae	.10	.05
❑ 125	Darren Woodson	.20	.09
❑ 126	Steve Atwater	.10	.05
❑ 127	Quentin Coryatt	.10	.05
❑ 128	Derrick Thomas	.20	.09
❑ 129	Nate Newton	.10	.05
❑ 130	Kevin Greene	.20	.09
❑ 131	Barry Sanders	2.00	.90
❑ 132	Warren Moon	.20	.09
❑ 133	Rashaan Salaam	.40	.18
❑ 134	Rodney Hampton	.20	.09
❑ 135	James O.Stewart	.20	.09
❑ 136	Erric Pegram	.10	.05
❑ 137	Bryan Cox	.10	.05
❑ 138	Adrian Murrell	.40	.18
❑ 139	Robert Smith	.20	.09
❑ 140	Bernie Parmalee	.10	.05
❑ 141	Bryce Paup	.10	.05
❑ 142	Darick Holmes	.10	.05
❑ 143	Hugh Douglas	.20	.09
❑ 144	Ken Dilger	.20	.09
❑ 145	Derek Loville	.10	.05
❑ 146	Horace Copeland	.10	.05
❑ 147	Wayne Chrebet	.60	.25
❑ 148	Andre Coleman	.10	.05
❑ 149	Greg Hill	.20	.09
❑ 150	Eric Swann	.10	.05
❑ 151	Tyrone Hughes	.10	.05
❑ 152	Ernie Mills	.10	.05
❑ 153	Terry Glenn RC	1.25	.55
❑ 154	Cedric Jones RC	.10	.05
❑ 155	Leeland McElroy RC	.40	.18
❑ 156	Bobby Engram RC	.40	.18
❑ 157	Willie Anderson RC	.10	.05
❑ 158	Mike Alstott RC	1.50	.70
❑ 159	Alex Van Dyke RC	.20	.09
❑ 160	Jeff Lewis RC	.50	.23
❑ 161	Keyshawn Johnson RC	2.00	.90
❑ 162	Regan Upshaw RC	.10	.05
❑ 163	Eric Moulds RC	2.00	.90
❑ 164	Tim Biakabutuka RC	.75	.35
❑ 165	Kevin Hardy RC	.40	.18
❑ 166	Marvin Harrison RC	2.50	1.10
❑ 167	Karim Abdul-Jabbar RC	.50	.23
❑ 168	Tony Brackens RC	.20	.09
❑ 169	Stepfret Williams RC	.20	.09
❑ 170	Eddie George RC	4.00	1.80
❑ 171	Lawrence Phillips RC	.40	.18
❑ 172	Danny Kanell RC	.40	.18
❑ 173	Derrick Mayes RC	.75	.35
❑ 174	Daryl Gardener RC	.10	.05
❑ 175	Jonathan Ogden RC	.10	.05
❑ 176	Alex Molden RC	.10	.05
❑ 177	Chris Darkins RC	.10	.05
❑ 178	Stephen Davis RC	4.00	1.80
❑ 179	Rickey Dudley RC	.40	.18
❑ 180	Eddie Kennison RC	.40	.18
❑ 181	Simeon Rice RC	.40	.18
❑ 182	Bobby Hoying RC	.50	.23
❑ 183	Troy Aikman BF6	.50	.23
❑ 184	Emmitt Smith BF6	1.00	.45
❑ 185	Michael Irvin BF6	.20	.09
❑ 186	Deion Sanders BF6	.40	.18
❑ 187	Daryl Johnston BF6	.20	.09
❑ 188	Jay Novacek BF6	.10	.05
❑ 189	Steve Young BF6	.40	.18
❑ 190	Jerry Rice BF6	.50	.23
❑ 191	J.J. Stokes BF6	.40	.18
❑ 192	Ken Norton BF6	.10	.05
❑ 193	William Floyd BF6	.20	.09
❑ 194	Brent Jones BF6	.10	.05
❑ 195	Dan Marino CL	.40	.18
❑ 196	Brett Favre CL	.40	.18
❑ 197	Emmitt Smith CL	.40	.18
❑ 198	Barry Sanders CL	.40	.18
❑ 199	Dan Marino CL Emmitt Smith CL Brett Favre CL Barry Sanders CL	.40	.18
❑ 200	Brett Favre Packer Backer	2.00	.90

1997 Pinnacle

		MINT	NRMT
COMPLETE SET (200)		20.00	9.00
❑ 1	Brett Favre	2.00	.90
❑ 2	Dan Marino	2.00	.90
❑ 3	Emmitt Smith	1.50	.70
❑ 4	Steve Young	.60	.25
❑ 5	Drew Bledsoe	1.00	.45
❑ 6	Eddie George	1.00	.45
❑ 7	Barry Sanders	2.00	.90
❑ 8	Jerry Rice	1.00	.45
❑ 9	John Elway	2.00	.90
❑ 10	Troy Aikman	1.00	.45
❑ 11	Kerry Collins	.20	.09

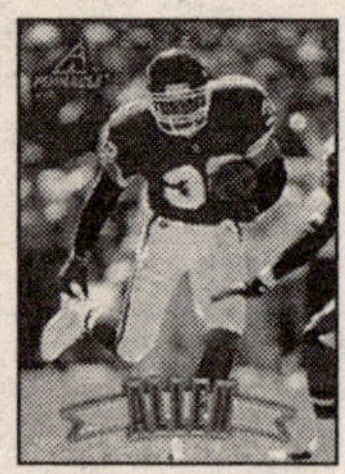

❑ 12 Rick Mirer .10 .05
❑ 13 Jim Harbaugh .20 .09
❑ 14 Elvis Grbac .20 .09
❑ 15 Gus Frerotte .10 .05
❑ 16 Neil O'Donnell .20 .09
❑ 17 Jeff George .20 .09
❑ 18 Kordell Stewart .40 .18
❑ 19 Junior Seau .20 .09
❑ 20 Vinny Testaverde .20 .09
❑ 21 Terry Glenn .30 .14
❑ 22 Anthony Johnson .10 .05
❑ 23 Boomer Esiason .20 .09
❑ 24 Terrell Owens .30 .14
❑ 25 Natrone Means .30 .14
❑ 26 Marcus Allen .30 .14
❑ 27 James Jett .20 .09
❑ 28 Chris T. Jones .10 .05
❑ 29 Stan Humphries .20 .09
❑ 30 Keith Byars .10 .05
❑ 31 John Friesz .10 .05
❑ 32 Mike Alstott .30 .14
❑ 33 Eddie Kennison .20 .09
❑ 34 Eric Moulds .30 .14
❑ 35 Frank Sanders .20 .09
❑ 36 Daryl Johnston .20 .09
❑ 37 Cris Carter .30 .14
❑ 38 Errict Rhett .10 .05
❑ 39 Ben Coates .20 .09
❑ 40 Shannon Sharpe .20 .09
❑ 41 Jamal Anderson .60 .25
❑ 42 Tim Biakabutuka .20 .09
❑ 43 Jeff Blake .20 .09
❑ 44 Michael Irvin .30 .14
❑ 45 Terrell Davis 1.50 .70
❑ 46 Byron Bam Morris .10 .05
❑ 47 Rashaan Salaam .10 .05
❑ 48 Adrian Murrell .20 .09
❑ 49 Ty Detmer .20 .09
❑ 50 Terry Allen .30 .14
❑ 51 Mark Brunell 1.00 .45
❑ 52 O.J. McDuffie .20 .09
❑ 53 Willie McGinest .10 .05
❑ 54 Chris Warren .20 .09
❑ 55 Trent Dilfer .30 .14
❑ 56 Jerome Bettis .30 .14
❑ 57 Tamarick Vanover .20 .09
❑ 58 Ki-Jana Carter .10 .05
❑ 59 Ray Zellars .10 .05
❑ 60 J.J. Stokes .20 .09
❑ 61 Cornelius Bennett .10 .05
❑ 62 Scott Mitchell .20 .09
❑ 63 Tyrone Wheatley .20 .09
❑ 64 Steve McNair .50 .23
❑ 65 Tony Banks .20 .09
❑ 66 James O.Stewart .20 .09
❑ 67 Robert Smith .20 .09
❑ 68 Thurman Thomas .30 .14
❑ 69 Mark Chmura .20 .09
❑ 70 Napoleon Kaufman .30 .14
❑ 71 Ken Norton .10 .05
❑ 72 Herschel Walker .20 .09
❑ 73 Joey Galloway .40 .18
❑ 74 Neil Smith .20 .09
❑ 75 Simeon Rice .20 .09
❑ 76 Michael Jackson .20 .09
❑ 77 Muhsin Muhammad .20 .09
❑ 78 Kevin Hardy .10 .05
❑ 79 Irving Fryar .20 .09
❑ 80 Jeff Hostetler .10 .05
❑ 81 Eric Swann .10 .05
❑ 82 Jim Everett .10 .05
❑ 83 Karim Abdul-Jabbar .30 .14
❑ 84 Garrison Hearst .20 .09
❑ 85 Lawrence Phillips .10 .05
❑ 86 Bryan Cox .10 .05
❑ 87 Larry Centers .20 .09
❑ 88 Wesley Walls .20 .09
❑ 89 Curtis Conway .20 .09
❑ 90 Darnay Scott .20 .09
❑ 91 Anthony Miller .10 .05
❑ 92 Edgar Bennett .20 .09
❑ 93 Willie Green .10 .05
❑ 94 Kent Graham .10 .05
❑ 95 Dave Brown .10 .05
❑ 96 Wayne Chrebet .30 .14
❑ 97 Ricky Watters .20 .09
❑ 98 Tony Martin .20 .09
❑ 99 Warren Moon .30 .14
❑ 100 Curtis Martin .50 .23
❑ 101 Dorsey Levens .30 .14
❑ 102 Jim Pyne .10 .05
❑ 103 Antonio Freeman .50 .23
❑ 104 Leeland McElroy .10 .05
❑ 105 Isaac Bruce .30 .14
❑ 106 Chris Sanders .10 .05
❑ 107 Tim Brown .30 .14
❑ 108 Greg Lloyd .10 .05
❑ 109 Terrell Buckley .10 .05
❑ 110 Deion Sanders .30 .14
❑ 111 Carl Pickens .30 .14
❑ 112 Bobby Engram .20 .09
❑ 113 Andre Reed .20 .09
❑ 114 Terance Mathis .20 .09
❑ 115 Herman Moore .30 .14
❑ 116 Robert Brooks .20 .09
❑ 117 Ken Dilger .10 .05
❑ 118 Keenan McCardell .20 .09
❑ 119 Andre Hastings .10 .05
❑ 120 Willie Davis .10 .05
❑ 121 Bruce Smith .20 .09
❑ 122 Rob Moore .20 .09
❑ 123 Johnnie Morton .20 .09
❑ 124 Sean Dawkins .10 .05
❑ 125 Mario Bates .10 .05
❑ 126 Henry Ellard .10 .05
❑ 127 Derrick Alexander WR .20 .09
❑ 128 Kevin Greene .20 .09
❑ 129 Derrick Thomas .20 .09
❑ 130 Rod Woodson .20 .09
❑ 131 Rodney Hampton .20 .09
❑ 132 Marshall Faulk .30 .14
❑ 133 Michael Westbrook .20 .09
❑ 134 Erik Kramer .10 .05
❑ 135 Todd Collins .10 .05
❑ 136 Bill Romanowski .10 .05
❑ 137 Jake Reed .20 .09
❑ 138 Heath Shuler .10 .05
❑ 139 Keyshawn Johnson .30 .14
❑ 140 Marvin Harrison .30 .14
❑ 141 Andre Rison .20 .09
❑ 142 Zach Thomas .20 .09
❑ 143 Eric Metcalf .20 .09
❑ 144 Amani Toomer .20 .09
❑ 145 Desmond Howard .20 .09
❑ 146 Jimmy Smith .20 .09
❑ 147 Brad Johnson .50 .23
❑ 148 Troy Vincent .10 .05
❑ 149 Bryce Paup .10 .05
❑ 150 Reggie White .30 .14
❑ 151 Jake Plummer RC 2.50 1.10
❑ 152 Darnell Autry RC .20 .09
❑ 153 Tiki Barber RC 1.25 .55
❑ 154 Pat Barnes RC .30 .14
❑ 155 Orlando Pace RC .30 .14
❑ 156 Peter Boulware RC .20 .09
❑ 157 Shawn Springs RC .20 .09
❑ 158 Troy Davis RC .30 .14
❑ 159 Ike Hilliard RC .75 .35
❑ 160 Jim Druckenmiller RC .30 .14
❑ 161 Warrick Dunn RC 1.25 .55
❑ 162 James Farrior RC .10 .05
❑ 163 Tony Gonzalez RC 1.25 .55
❑ 164 Darrell Russell RC .10 .05
❑ 165 Byron Hanspard RC .30 .14
❑ 166 Corey Dillon RC 2.50 1.10
❑ 167 Kenny Holmes RC .30 .14
❑ 168 Walter Jones RC .10 .05
❑ 169 Danny Wuerffel RC .60 .25
❑ 170 Tom Knight RC .10 .05
❑ 171 David LaFleur RC .20 .09
❑ 172 Kevin Lockett RC .20 .09
❑ 173 Will Blackwell RC .30 .14
❑ 174 Reidel Anthony RC .75 .35
❑ 175 Dwayne Rudd RC .30 .14
❑ 176 Yatil Green RC .20 .09
❑ 177 Antowain Smith RC 1.00 .45
❑ 178 Rae Carruth RC .30 .14
❑ 179 Bryant Westbrook RC .10 .05
❑ 180 Reinard Wilson RC .10 .05
❑ 181 Joey Kent RC .30 .14
❑ 182 Renaldo Wynn RC .10 .05
❑ 183 Brett Favre I 1.00 .45
❑ 184 Emmitt Smith I .75 .35
❑ 185 Dan Marino I 1.00 .45
❑ 186 Troy Aikman I .50 .23
❑ 187 Jerry Rice I .50 .23
❑ 188 Drew Bledsoe I .50 .23
❑ 189 Eddie George I .50 .23
❑ 190 Terry Glenn I .20 .09
❑ 191 John Elway I 1.00 .45
❑ 192 Steve Young I .30 .14
❑ 193 Mark Brunell I .50 .23
❑ 194 Barry Sanders I 1.00 .45
❑ 195 Kerry Collins I .20 .09
❑ 196 Curtis Martin I .30 .14
❑ 197 Terrell Davis I .75 .35
❑ 198 Drew Bledsoe .30 .14
Kerry Collins
Dan Marino
Checklist back
❑ 199 Steve Young .10 .05
Jeff George
Mark Brunell
Checklist back
❑ 200 Troy Aikman .10 .05
John Elway
Rick Mirer CL

1997 Pinnacle Certified

	MINT	NRMT
COMPLETE SET (150)	40.00	18.00
❑ 1 Emmitt Smith	3.00	1.35
❑ 2 Dan Marino	4.00	1.80
❑ 3 Brett Favre	4.00	1.80
❑ 4 Steve Young	1.25	.55
❑ 5 Kerry Collins	.40	.18
❑ 6 Troy Aikman	2.00	.90
❑ 7 Drew Bledsoe	2.00	.90
❑ 8 Eddie George	2.50	1.10
❑ 9 Jerry Rice	2.00	.90
❑ 10 John Elway	4.00	1.80
❑ 11 Barry Sanders	4.00	1.80
❑ 12 Mark Brunell	2.00	.90
❑ 13 Elvis Grbac	.40	.18
❑ 14 Tony Banks	.40	.18
❑ 15 Vinny Testaverde	.40	.18
❑ 16 Rick Mirer	.20	.09
❑ 17 Carl Pickens	.75	.35
❑ 18 Deion Sanders	.75	.35

Card	Mint	Nrmt
❏ 19 Terry Glenn	.75	.35
❏ 20 Heath Shuler	.20	.09
❏ 21 Dave Brown	.20	.09
❏ 22 Keyshawn Johnson	.75	.35
❏ 23 Jeff George	.40	.18
❏ 24 Ricky Watters	.40	.18
❏ 25 Kordell Stewart	1.00	.45
❏ 26 Junior Seau	.40	.18
❏ 27 Terrell Owens	.75	.35
❏ 28 Warren Moon	.75	.35
❏ 29 Isaac Bruce	.75	.35
❏ 30 Steve McNair	1.00	.45
❏ 31 Gus Frerotte	.20	.09
❏ 32 Trent Dilfer	.75	.35
❏ 33 Shannon Sharpe	.40	.18
❏ 34 Scott Mitchell	.40	.18
❏ 35 Antonio Freeman	1.00	.45
❏ 36 Jim Harbaugh	.40	.18
❏ 37 Natrone Means	.75	.35
❏ 38 Marcus Allen	.75	.35
❏ 39 Karim Abdul-Jabbar	.75	.35
❏ 40 Tim Biakabutuka	.40	.18
❏ 41 Jeff Blake	.40	.18
❏ 42 Michael Irvin	.75	.35
❏ 43 Herschel Walker	.40	.18
❏ 44 Curtis Martin	1.00	.45
❏ 45 Eddie Kennison	.40	.18
❏ 46 Napoleon Kaufman	.75	.35
❏ 47 Larry Centers	.40	.18
❏ 48 Jamal Anderson	1.25	.55
❏ 49 Derrick Alexander WR	.40	.18
❏ 50 Bruce Smith	.40	.18
❏ 51 Wesley Walls	.40	.18
❏ 52 Rod Smith WR	.75	.35
❏ 53 Keenan McCardell	.40	.18
❏ 54 Robert Brooks	.40	.18
❏ 55 Willie Green	.20	.09
❏ 56 Jake Reed	.40	.18
❏ 57 Joey Galloway	1.00	.45
❏ 58 Eric Metcalf	.40	.18
❏ 59 Chris Sanders	.20	.09
❏ 60 Jeff Hostetler	.20	.09
❏ 61 Kevin Greene	.40	.18
❏ 62 Frank Sanders	.40	.18
❏ 63 Dorsey Levens	.75	.35
❏ 64 Sean Dawkins	.20	.09
❏ 65 Cris Carter	.75	.35
❏ 66 Andre Hastings	.20	.09
❏ 67 Amani Toomer	.40	.18
❏ 68 Adrian Murrell	.40	.18
❏ 69 Ty Detmer	.40	.18
❏ 70 Yancey Thigpen	.40	.18
❏ 71 Jim Everett	.20	.09
❏ 72 Todd Collins	.20	.09
❏ 73 Curtis Conway	.40	.18
❏ 74 Herman Moore	.75	.35
❏ 75 Neil O'Donnell	.40	.18
❏ 76 Rod Woodson	.40	.18
❏ 77 Tony Martin	.40	.18
❏ 78 Kent Graham	.20	.09
❏ 79 Andre Reed	.40	.18
❏ 80 Reggie White	.75	.35
❏ 81 Thurman Thomas	.75	.35
❏ 82 Garrison Hearst	.40	.18
❏ 83 Chris Warren	.40	.18
❏ 84 Wayne Chrebet	.75	.35
❏ 85 Chris T. Jones	.20	.09
❏ 86 Anthony Miller	.20	.09
❏ 87 Chris Chandler	.40	.18
❏ 88 Terrell Davis	4.00	1.80
❏ 89 Mike Alstott	.75	.35
❏ 90 Terry Allen	.75	.35
❏ 91 Jerome Bettis	.75	.35
❏ 92 Stan Humphries	.40	.18
❏ 93 Andre Rison	.40	.18
❏ 94 Marshall Faulk	.75	.35
❏ 95 Erik Kramer	.20	.09
❏ 96 O.J. McDuffie	.40	.18
❏ 97 Robert Smith	.40	.18
❏ 98 Keith Byars	.20	.09
❏ 99 Rodney Hampton	.40	.18
❏ 100 Desmond Howard	.40	.18
❏ 101 Lawrence Phillips	.20	.09
❏ 102 Michael Westbrook	.40	.18
❏ 103 Johnnie Morton	.40	.18
❏ 104 Ben Coates	.40	.18
❏ 105 J.J. Stokes	.40	.18
❏ 106 Terance Mathis	.40	.18
❏ 107 Errict Rhett	.20	.09
❏ 108 Tim Brown	.75	.35
❏ 109 Marvin Harrison	.75	.35
❏ 110 Muhsin Muhammad	.40	.18
❏ 111 Byron Bam Morris	.20	.09
❏ 112 Mario Bates	.20	.09
❏ 113 Jimmy Smith	.40	.18
❏ 114 Irving Fryar	.40	.18
❏ 115 Tamarick Vanover	.40	.18
❏ 116 Brad Johnson	1.00	.45
❏ 117 Rashaan Salaam	.20	.09
❏ 118 Ki-Jana Carter	.20	.09
❏ 119 Tyrone Wheatley	.40	.18
❏ 120 John Friesz	.20	.09
❏ 121 Orlando Pace RC	1.25	.55
❏ 122 Jim Druckenmiller RC	1.25	.55
❏ 123 Byron Hanspard RC	.75	.35
❏ 124 David LaFleur RC	1.25	.55
❏ 125 Reidel Anthony RC	2.50	1.10
❏ 126 Antowain Smith RC	3.00	1.35
❏ 127 Bryant Westbrook RC	.30	.14
❏ 128 Fred Lane RC	1.25	.55
❏ 129 Tiki Barber RC	4.00	1.80
❏ 130 Shawn Springs RC	.60	.25
❏ 131 Ike Hilliard RC	2.50	1.10
❏ 132 James Farrior RC	.30	.14
❏ 133 Darrell Russell RC	.30	.14
❏ 134 Walter Jones RC	.30	.14
❏ 135 Tom Knight RC	.30	.14
❏ 136 Yatil Green RC	.60	.25
❏ 137 Joey Kent RC	.60	.25
❏ 138 Kevin Lockett RC	.60	.25
❏ 139 Troy Davis RC	.60	.25
❏ 140 Darnell Autry RC	.60	.25
❏ 141 Pat Barnes RC	1.25	.55
❏ 142 Rae Carruth RC	.60	.25
❏ 143 Will Blackwell RC	.60	.25
❏ 144 Warrick Dunn RC	4.00	1.80
❏ 145 Corey Dillon RC	8.00	3.60
❏ 146 Dwayne Rudd RC	1.25	.55
❏ 147 Reinard Wilson RC	.30	.14
❏ 148 Peter Boulware RC	1.25	.55
❏ 149 Tony Gonzalez RC	4.00	1.80
❏ 150 Danny Wuerffel RC	1.25	.55

1997 Pinnacle Inscriptions

	MINT	NRMT
COMPLETE SET (50)	20.00	9.00
❏ 1 Mark Brunell	2.00	.90
❏ 2 Steve Young	1.50	.70
❏ 3 Rick Mirer	.20	.09
❏ 4 Brett Favre	4.00	1.80
❏ 5 Tony Banks	.40	.18
❏ 6 Elvis Grbac	.40	.18
❏ 7 John Elway	4.00	1.80
❏ 8 Troy Aikman	2.00	.90
❏ 9 Neil O'Donnell	.40	.18
❏ 10 Kordell Stewart	1.00	.45
❏ 11 Drew Bledsoe	2.00	.90
❏ 12 Kerry Collins	.40	.18
❏ 13 Dan Marino	4.00	1.80
❏ 14 Jeff George	.40	.18
❏ 15 Scott Mitchell	.40	.18
❏ 16 Jim Harbaugh	.40	.18
❏ 17 Dave Brown	.20	.09
❏ 18 Jeff Blake	.40	.18
❏ 19 Trent Dilfer	.75	.35
❏ 20 Barry Sanders	4.00	1.80
❏ 21 Jerry Rice	2.00	.90
❏ 22 Emmitt Smith	3.00	1.35
❏ 23 Vinny Testaverde	.40	.18
❏ 24 Warren Moon	.75	.35
❏ 25 Junior Seau	.40	.18
❏ 26 Gus Frerotte	.20	.09
❏ 27 Heath Shuler	.20	.09
❏ 28 Erik Kramer	.20	.09
❏ 29 Boomer Esiason	.40	.18
❏ 30 Jim Kelly	.75	.35
❏ 31 Mark Brunell TNL	1.25	.55
❏ 32 Steve Young TNL	1.00	.45
❏ 33 Brett Favre TNL	2.50	1.10
❏ 34 Tony Banks TNL	.40	.18
❏ 35 John Elway TNL	2.50	1.10
❏ 36 Troy Aikman TNL	1.25	.55
❏ 37 Kordell Stewart TNL	.75	.35
❏ 38 Drew Bledsoe TNL	1.25	.55
❏ 39 Kerry Collins TNL	.40	.18
❏ 40 Dan Marino TNL	2.50	1.10
❏ 41 Jim Harbaugh TNL	.40	.18
❏ 42 Jeff Blake TNL	.40	.18
❏ 43 Barry Sanders TNL	2.50	1.10
❏ 44 Jerry Rice TNL	1.25	.55
❏ 45 Emmitt Smith TNL	2.00	.90
❏ 46 Rick Mirer TNL	.20	.09
❏ 47 Jeff George TNL	.20	.09
❏ 48 Neil O'Donnell TNL	.40	.18
❏ 49 Elvis Grbac TNL	.40	.18
❏ 50 Scott Mitchell TNL	.20	.09

1997 Pinnacle Inside

	MINT	NRMT
COMPLETE SET (150)	20.00	9.00
❏ 1 Troy Aikman	1.00	.45
❏ 2 Dan Marino	2.00	.90
❏ 3 Barry Sanders	2.00	.90
❏ 4 Drew Bledsoe	1.00	.45
❏ 5 Kerry Collins	.20	.09
❏ 6 Emmitt Smith	1.50	.70
❏ 7 Brett Favre	2.00	.90
❏ 8 John Elway	2.00	.90
❏ 9 Jerry Rice	1.00	.45
❏ 10 Mark Brunell	1.00	.45
❏ 11 Elvis Grbac	.20	.09
❏ 12 Junior Seau	.20	.09
❏ 13 Eddie George	1.00	.45
❏ 14 Steve Young	.60	.25
❏ 15 Terrell Davis	1.50	.70
❏ 16 Thurman Thomas	.30	.14
❏ 17 Deion Sanders	.30	.14
❏ 18 Terrell Owens	.30	.14
❏ 19 Neil O'Donnell	.20	.09
❏ 20 Carl Pickens	.30	.14
❏ 21 Marcus Allen	.30	.14
❏ 22 Ricky Watters	.20	.09
❏ 23 Vinny Testaverde	.20	.09
❏ 24 Kordell Stewart	.40	.18
❏ 25 Tony Banks	.30	.14
❏ 26 Terry Glenn	.30	.14
❏ 27 Todd Collins	.10	.05

❑ 28 Robert Brooks	.20	.09
❑ 29 Heath Shuler	.10	.05
❑ 30 Shannon Sharpe	.20	.09
❑ 31 Michael Westbrook	.20	.09
❑ 32 Reggie White	.30	.14
❑ 33 Brad Johnson	.50	.23
❑ 34 Tamarick Vanover	.20	.09
❑ 35 Larry Centers	.20	.09
❑ 36 Terance Mathis	.20	.09
❑ 37 Hardy Nickerson	.10	.05
❑ 38 Jamal Anderson	.60	.25
❑ 39 Kevin Hardy	.10	.05
❑ 40 Stan Humphries	.20	.09
❑ 41 Chris Warren	.20	.09
❑ 42 Tim Brown	.30	.14
❑ 43 Joey Galloway	.40	.18
❑ 44 Boomer Esiason	.20	.09
❑ 45 Jake Reed	.20	.09
❑ 46 Kent Graham	.10	.05
❑ 47 Marshall Faulk	.30	.14
❑ 48 Sean Dawkins	.10	.05
❑ 49 Dave Brown	.10	.05
❑ 50 Willie Green	.10	.05
❑ 51 Andre Hastings	.10	.05
❑ 52 Erik Kramer	.10	.05
❑ 53 Michael Irvin	.30	.14
❑ 54 Gus Frerotte	.10	.05
❑ 55 Winslow Oliver	.10	.05
❑ 56 Jimmy Smith	.20	.09
❑ 57 Derrick Alexander WR	.20	.09
❑ 58 Adrian Murrell	.20	.09
❑ 59 Ki-Jana Carter	.10	.05
❑ 60 Garrison Hearst	.20	.09
❑ 61 Chris Sanders	.10	.05
❑ 62 Johnnie Morton	.20	.09
❑ 63 Lawrence Phillips	.10	.05
❑ 64 Bobby Engram	.20	.09
❑ 65 Tim Biakabutuka	.20	.09
❑ 66 Anthony Johnson	.10	.05
❑ 67 Keyshawn Johnson	.30	.14
❑ 68 Jeff George	.20	.09
❑ 69 Errict Rhett	.10	.05
❑ 70 Cris Carter	.30	.14
❑ 71 Chris T. Jones	.10	.05
❑ 72 Eric Moulds	.30	.14
❑ 73 Rick Mirer	.10	.05
❑ 74 Keenan McCardell	.20	.09
❑ 75 Simeon Rice	.20	.09
❑ 76 Eddie Kennison	.20	.09
❑ 77 Herman Moore	.30	.14
❑ 78 Jim Harbaugh	.20	.09
❑ 79 Robert Smith	.20	.09
❑ 80 Bruce Smith	.20	.09
❑ 81 John Friesz	.10	.05
❑ 82 Irving Fryar	.20	.09
❑ 83 Edgar Bennett	.20	.09
❑ 84 Ty Detmer	.20	.09
❑ 85 Curtis Conway	.20	.09
❑ 86 Napoleon Kaufman	.30	.14
❑ 87 Tony Martin	.20	.09
❑ 88 Amani Toomer	.20	.09
❑ 89 Willie McGinest	.10	.05
❑ 90 Daryl Johnston	.20	.09
❑ 91 Stanley Pritchett	.10	.05
❑ 92 Chris Chandler	.20	.09
❑ 93 Natrone Means	.30	.14
❑ 94 Kimble Anders	.20	.09
❑ 95 Steve McNair	.50	.23
❑ 96 Curtis Martin	.50	.23
❑ 97 O.J. McDuffie	.20	.09
❑ 98 Ben Coates	.20	.09
❑ 99 Jerome Bettis	.30	.14
❑ 100 Andre Reed	.20	.09
❑ 101 Jeff Blake	.20	.09
❑ 102 Wesley Walls	.20	.09
❑ 103 Warren Moon	.30	.14
❑ 104 Isaac Bruce	.30	.14
❑ 105 Terry Allen	.30	.14
❑ 106 Rodney Hampton	.20	.09
❑ 107 Karim Abdul-Jabbar	.30	.14
❑ 108 Marvin Harrison	.30	.14
❑ 109 Dorsey Levens	.30	.14
❑ 110 Rashaan Salaam	.10	.05
❑ 111 Scott Mitchell	.20	.09
❑ 112 Darnay Scott	.20	.09
❑ 113 Aeneas Williams	.10	.05
❑ 114 Trent Dilfer	.30	.14
❑ 115 Antonio Freeman	.50	.23
❑ 116 Jim Everett	.10	.05
❑ 117 Muhsin Muhammad	.20	.09
❑ 118 Rickey Dudley	.20	.09
❑ 119 Mike Alstott	.30	.14
❑ 120 Jim Druckenmiller RC	.30	.14
❑ 121 Tiki Barber RC	1.25	.55
❑ 122 Ike Hilliard RC	.75	.35
❑ 123 Orlando Pace RC	.30	.14
❑ 124 Jake Plummer RC	2.50	1.10
❑ 125 Yatil Green RC	.20	.09
❑ 126 Byron Hanspard RC	.30	.14
❑ 127 James Farrior RC	.10	.05
❑ 128 Corey Dillon RC	2.50	1.10
❑ 129 Pat Barnes RC	.30	.14
❑ 130 Kenny Holmes RC	.30	.14
❑ 131 Rae Carruth RC	.30	.14
❑ 132 Danny Wuerffel RC	.30	.14
❑ 133 Darnell Autry RC	.20	.09
❑ 134 Reidel Anthony RC	.75	.35
❑ 135 Darrell Russell RC	.10	.05
❑ 136 Will Blackwell RC	.20	.09
❑ 137 Peter Boulware RC	.20	.09
❑ 138 Shawn Springs RC	.20	.09
❑ 139 Joey Kent RC	.30	.14
❑ 140 Troy Davis RC	.20	.09
❑ 141 Antowain Smith RC	1.00	.45
❑ 142 Walter Jones RC	.10	.05
❑ 143 Tony Gonzalez RC	1.25	.55
❑ 144 David LaFleur RC	.30	.14
❑ 145 Warrick Dunn RC	1.25	.55
❑ 146 Bryant Westbrook RC	.10	.05
❑ 147 Dwayne Rudd RC	.30	.14
❑ 148 Tom Knight RC	.10	.05
❑ 149 Kevin Lockett RC	.20	.09
❑ 150 Checklist	.10	.05
❑ P1 Troy Aikman Promo	1.00	.45
❑ P2 Dan Marino Promo	2.00	.90
❑ P7 Brett Favre Promo	2.00	.90

1997 Pinnacle Totally Certified Platinum Red

	MINT	NRMT
COMPLETE SET (150)	200.00	90.00
❑ 1 Emmitt Smith	12.00	5.50
❑ 2 Dan Marino	15.00	6.75
❑ 3 Brett Favre	15.00	6.75
❑ 4 Steve Young	6.00	2.70
❑ 5 Kerry Collins	1.50	.70
❑ 6 Troy Aikman	8.00	3.60
❑ 7 Drew Bledsoe	8.00	3.60
❑ 8 Eddie George	8.00	3.60
❑ 9 Jerry Rice	8.00	3.60
❑ 10 John Elway	15.00	6.75
❑ 11 Barry Sanders	15.00	6.75
❑ 12 Mark Brunell	8.00	3.60
❑ 13 Elvis Grbac	1.50	.70
❑ 14 Tony Banks	1.50	.70
❑ 15 Vinny Testaverde	1.50	.70
❑ 16 Rick Mirer	.75	.35
❑ 17 Carl Pickens	3.00	1.35
❑ 18 Deion Sanders	3.00	1.35
❑ 19 Terry Glenn	3.00	1.35
❑ 20 Heath Shuler	.75	.35
❑ 21 Dave Brown	.75	.35
❑ 22 Keyshawn Johnson	3.00	1.35
❑ 23 Jeff George	1.50	.70
❑ 24 Ricky Watters	1.50	.70
❑ 25 Kordell Stewart	4.00	1.80
❑ 26 Junior Seau	1.50	.70
❑ 27 Terrell Owens	3.00	1.35
❑ 28 Warren Moon	3.00	1.35
❑ 29 Isaac Bruce	3.00	1.35
❑ 30 Steve McNair	4.00	1.80
❑ 31 Gus Frerotte	.75	.35
❑ 32 Trent Dilfer	3.00	1.35
❑ 33 Shannon Sharpe	1.50	.70
❑ 34 Scott Mitchell	1.50	.70
❑ 35 Antonio Freeman	4.00	1.80
❑ 36 Jim Harbaugh	1.50	.70
❑ 37 Natrone Means	3.00	1.35
❑ 38 Marcus Allen	3.00	1.35
❑ 39 Karim Abdul-Jabbar	3.00	1.35
❑ 40 Tim Biakabutuka	1.50	.70
❑ 41 Jeff Blake	1.50	.70
❑ 42 Michael Irvin	3.00	1.35
❑ 43 Herschel Walker	1.50	.70
❑ 44 Curtis Martin	4.00	1.80
❑ 45 Eddie Kennison	1.50	.70
❑ 46 Napoleon Kaufman	3.00	1.35
❑ 47 Larry Centers	1.50	.70
❑ 48 Jamal Anderson	5.00	2.20
❑ 49 Derrick Alexander WR	1.50	.70
❑ 50 Bruce Smith	1.50	.70
❑ 51 Wesley Walls	1.50	.70
❑ 52 Rod Smith WR	3.00	1.35
❑ 53 Keenan McCardell	1.50	.70
❑ 54 Robert Brooks	1.50	.70
❑ 55 Willie Green	.75	.35
❑ 56 Jake Reed	1.50	.70
❑ 57 Joey Galloway	4.00	1.80
❑ 58 Eric Metcalf	1.50	.70
❑ 59 Chris Sanders	.75	.35
❑ 60 Jeff Hostetler	.75	.35
❑ 61 Kevin Greene	1.50	.70
❑ 62 Frank Sanders	1.50	.70
❑ 63 Dorsey Levens	3.00	1.35
❑ 64 Sean Dawkins	.75	.35
❑ 65 Cris Carter	3.00	1.35
❑ 66 Andre Hastings	.75	.35
❑ 67 Amani Toomer	1.50	.70
❑ 68 Adrian Murrell	1.50	.70
❑ 69 Ty Detmer	1.50	.70
❑ 70 Yancey Thigpen	.75	.35
❑ 71 Jim Everett	.75	.35
❑ 72 Todd Collins	.75	.35
❑ 73 Curtis Conway	1.50	.70
❑ 74 Herman Moore	3.00	1.35
❑ 75 Neil O'Donnell	1.50	.70
❑ 76 Rod Woodson	1.50	.70
❑ 77 Tony Martin	1.50	.70
❑ 78 Kent Graham	.75	.35
❑ 79 Andre Reed	1.50	.70
❑ 80 Reggie White	3.00	1.35
❑ 81 Thurman Thomas	3.00	1.35
❑ 82 Garrison Hearst	1.50	.70
❑ 83 Chris Warren	1.50	.70
❑ 84 Wayne Chrebet	3.00	1.35
❑ 85 Chris T. Jones	.75	.35
❑ 86 Anthony Miller	.75	.35
❑ 87 Chris Chandler	1.50	.70
❑ 88 Terrell Davis	12.00	5.50
❑ 89 Mike Alstott	3.00	1.35
❑ 90 Terry Allen	3.00	1.35
❑ 91 Jerome Bettis	3.00	1.35
❑ 92 Stan Humphries	1.50	.70
❑ 93 Andre Rison	1.50	.70
❑ 94 Marshall Faulk	3.00	1.35
❑ 95 Erik Kramer	.75	.35
❑ 96 O.J. McDuffie	1.50	.70
❑ 97 Robert Smith	1.50	.70
❑ 98 Keith Byars	.75	.35
❑ 99 Rodney Hampton	1.50	.70
❑ 100 Desmond Howard	1.50	.70
❑ 101 Lawrence Phillips	.75	.35
❑ 102 Michael Westbrook	1.50	.70
❑ 103 Johnnie Morton	1.50	.70
❑ 104 Ben Coates	1.50	.70
❑ 105 J.J. Stokes	1.50	.70
❑ 106 Terance Mathis	1.50	.70
❑ 107 Errict Rhett	.75	.35

Card	MINT	NRMT
❑ 108 Tim Brown	3.00	1.35
❑ 109 Marvin Harrison	3.00	1.35
❑ 110 Muhsin Muhammad	1.50	.70
❑ 111 Byron Bam Morris	.75	.35
❑ 112 Mario Bates	.75	.35
❑ 113 Jimmy Smith	1.50	.70
❑ 114 Irving Fryar	1.50	.70
❑ 115 Tamarick Vanover	1.50	.70
❑ 116 Brad Johnson	4.00	1.80
❑ 117 Rashaan Salaam	.75	.35
❑ 118 Ki-Jana Carter	.75	.35
❑ 119 Tyrone Wheatley	1.50	.70
❑ 120 John Friesz	.75	.35
❑ 121 Orlando Pace RC	4.00	1.80
❑ 122 Jim Druckenmiller RC	4.00	1.80
❑ 123 Byron Hanspard RC	3.00	1.35
❑ 124 David LaFleur RC	4.00	1.80
❑ 125 Reidel Anthony RC	6.00	2.70
❑ 126 Antowain Smith RC	8.00	3.60
❑ 127 Bryant Westbrook RC	1.00	.45
❑ 128 Fred Lane RC	4.00	1.80
❑ 129 Tiki Barber RC	10.00	4.50
❑ 130 Shawn Springs RC	2.00	.90
❑ 131 Ike Hilliard RC	6.00	2.70
❑ 132 James Farrior RC	1.00	.45
❑ 133 Darrell Russell RC	1.00	.45
❑ 134 Walter Jones RC	1.00	.45
❑ 135 Tom Knight RC	1.00	.45
❑ 136 Yatil Green RC	2.00	.90
❑ 137 Joey Kent RC	2.00	.90
❑ 138 Kevin Lockett RC	2.00	.90
❑ 139 Troy Davis RC	2.00	.90
❑ 140 Darnell Autry RC	2.00	.90
❑ 141 Pat Barnes RC	4.00	1.80
❑ 142 Rae Carruth RC	2.00	.90
❑ 143 Will Blackwell RC	2.00	.90
❑ 144 Warrick Dunn RC	10.00	4.50
❑ 145 Corey Dillon RC	25.00	11.00
❑ 146 Dwayne Rudd RC	4.00	1.80
❑ 147 Reinard Wilson RC	1.00	.45
❑ 148 Peter Boulware RC	4.00	1.80
❑ 149 Tony Gonzalez RC	10.00	4.50
❑ 150 Danny Wuerffel RC	4.00	1.80

1997 Pinnacle X-Press

	MINT	NRMT
COMPLETE SET (150)	20.00	9.00
❑ 1 Drew Bledsoe	1.00	.45
❑ 2 Steve Young	.60	.25
❑ 3 Brett Favre	2.00	.90
❑ 4 John Elway	2.00	.90
❑ 5 Dan Marino	2.00	.90
❑ 6 Jerry Rice	1.00	.45
❑ 7 Tony Banks	.20	.09
❑ 8 Kerry Collins	.20	.09
❑ 9 Mark Brunell	1.00	.45
❑ 10 Troy Aikman	1.00	.45
❑ 11 Barry Sanders	2.00	.90
❑ 12 Elvis Grbac	.20	.09
❑ 13 Eddie George	1.00	.45
❑ 14 Terry Glenn	.30	.14
❑ 15 Kordell Stewart	.40	.18
❑ 16 Junior Seau	.20	.09
❑ 17 Herman Moore	.30	.14
❑ 18 Gus Frerotte	.10	.05
❑ 19 Warren Moon	.30	.14
❑ 20 Emmitt Smith	1.50	.70
❑ 21 Henry Ellard	.10	.05
❑ 22 Rashaan Salaam	.10	.05
❑ 23 Sean Dawkins	.10	.05
❑ 24 Tyrone Wheatley	.20	.09
❑ 25 Lawrence Phillips	.10	.05
❑ 26 Ty Detmer	.20	.09
❑ 27 Vinny Testaverde	.20	.09
❑ 28 Dorsey Levens	.30	.14
❑ 29 Ricky Watters	.20	.09
❑ 30 Natrone Means	.30	.14
❑ 31 Curtis Conway	.20	.09
❑ 32 Larry Centers	.20	.09
❑ 33 Johnnie Morton	.20	.09
❑ 34 Desmond Howard	.20	.09
❑ 35 Marcus Allen	.30	.14
❑ 36 Cris Carter	.30	.14
❑ 37 James O.Stewart	.20	.09
❑ 38 Frank Sanders	.20	.09
❑ 39 Bruce Smith	.20	.09
❑ 40 Carl Pickens	.30	.14
❑ 41 Neil O'Donnell	.20	.09
❑ 42 Trent Dilfer	.30	.14
❑ 43 Rodney Peete	.10	.05
❑ 44 Terance Mathis	.20	.09
❑ 45 Muhsin Muhammad	.20	.09
❑ 46 Jake Reed	.20	.09
❑ 47 Jim Harbaugh	.20	.09
❑ 48 Todd Collins	.10	.05
❑ 49 Ki-Jana Carter	.10	.05
❑ 50 Scott Mitchell	.20	.09
❑ 51 Kevin Hardy	.10	.05
❑ 52 Stanley Pritchett	.10	.05
❑ 53 Dave Brown	.10	.05
❑ 54 Jeff George	.20	.09
❑ 55 Stan Humphries	.20	.09
❑ 56 Isaac Bruce	.30	.14
❑ 57 Eric Moulds	.30	.14
❑ 58 Robert Brooks	.20	.09
❑ 59 Steve McNair	.50	.23
❑ 60 Adrian Murrell	.20	.09
❑ 61 Rodney Hampton	.20	.09
❑ 62 Michael Jackson	.20	.09
❑ 63 Tamarick Vanover	.20	.09
❑ 64 Edgar Bennett	.20	.09
❑ 65 Andre Hastings	.10	.05
❑ 66 Robert Smith	.20	.09
❑ 67 Thurman Thomas	.30	.14
❑ 68 Tim Biakabutuka	.20	.09
❑ 69 Rick Mirer	.10	.05
❑ 70 Deion Sanders	.30	.14
❑ 71 Curtis Martin	.50	.23
❑ 72 Garrison Hearst	.20	.09
❑ 73 Kent Graham	.10	.05
❑ 74 Anthony Johnson	.10	.05
❑ 75 Antonio Freeman	.50	.23
❑ 76 Marshall Faulk	.30	.14
❑ 77 O.J. McDuffie	.20	.09
❑ 78 Heath Shuler	.10	.05
❑ 79 Napoleon Kaufman	.30	.14
❑ 80 Aeneas Williams	.10	.05
❑ 81 Hardy Nickerson	.10	.05
❑ 82 Keenan McCardell	.20	.09
❑ 83 Erik Kramer	.10	.05
❑ 84 Ben Coates	.20	.09
❑ 85 Shannon Sharpe	.20	.09
❑ 86 Tony Martin	.20	.09
❑ 87 Chris Sanders	.10	.05
❑ 88 Jamal Anderson	.60	.25
❑ 89 Karim Abdul-Jabbar	.30	.14
❑ 90 Keyshawn Johnson	.30	.14
❑ 91 Terrell Owens	.30	.14
❑ 92 Michael Irvin	.30	.14
❑ 93 John Friesz	.10	.05
❑ 94 Chris Warren	.20	.09
❑ 95 Errict Rhett	.10	.05
❑ 96 Terry Allen	.30	.14
❑ 97 Michael Westbrook	.20	.09
❑ 98 Simeon Rice	.20	.09
❑ 99 Willie Green	.10	.05
❑ 100 Jerome Bettis	.30	.14
❑ 101 Reggie White	.30	.14
❑ 102 Bert Emanuel	.20	.09
❑ 103 Zach Thomas	.20	.09
❑ 104 Tim Brown	.30	.14
❑ 105 Darnay Scott	.20	.09
❑ 106 Terrell Davis	1.50	.70
❑ 107 Andre Reed	.20	.09
❑ 108 Amani Toomer	.20	.09
❑ 109 Irving Fryar	.20	.09
❑ 110 Joey Galloway	.40	.18
❑ 111 Marvin Harrison	.30	.14
❑ 112 Derrick Alexander WR	.20	.09
❑ 113 Jeff Blake	.20	.09
❑ 114 Brad Johnson	.50	.23
❑ 115 Eddie Kennison	.20	.09
❑ 116 Rae Carruth RC	.30	.14
❑ 117 Tony Gonzalez RC	1.00	.45
❑ 118 Joey Kent RC	.30	.14
❑ 119 Peter Boulware RC	.20	.09
❑ 120 Orlando Pace RC	.30	.14
❑ 121 David LaFleur RC	.20	.09
❑ 122 Darnell Autry RC	.20	.09
❑ 123 Tiki Barber RC	1.00	.45
❑ 124 Troy Davis RC	.30	.14
❑ 125 Jim Druckenmiller RC	.30	.14
❑ 126 Corey Dillon RC	2.00	.90
❑ 127 Ike Hilliard RC	.60	.25
❑ 128 Reidel Anthony RC	.60	.25
❑ 129 Byron Hanspard RC	.30	.14
❑ 130 Antowain Smith RC	.75	.35
❑ 131 Jake Plummer RC	2.00	.90
❑ 132 Warrick Dunn RC	1.00	.45
❑ 133 Bryant Westbrook RC	.10	.05
❑ 134 Darrell Russell RC	.10	.05
❑ 135 Yatil Green RC	.20	.09
❑ 136 Shawn Springs RC	.20	.09
❑ 137 Danny Wuerffel RC	.30	.14
❑ 138 Brett Favre PP	1.00	.45
❑ 139 Emmitt Smith PP	.75	.35
❑ 140 Barry Sanders PP	1.00	.45
❑ 141 Troy Aikman PP	.50	.23
❑ 142 Drew Bledsoe PP	.50	.23
❑ 143 Jerry Rice PP	.50	.23
❑ 144 Dan Marino PP	1.00	.45
❑ 145 John Elway PP	1.00	.45
❑ 146 Kerry Collins PP	.20	.09
❑ 147 Mark Brunell PP	.50	.23
❑ 148 Brett Favre CL	.40	.18
❑ 149 Dan Marino CL	.40	.18
❑ 150 Troy Aikman CL	.30	.14

1992 Playoff

	MINT	NRMT
COMPLETE SET (150)	25.00	11.00
❑ 1 Emmitt Smith	8.00	3.60
❑ 2 Steve Young	3.00	1.35
❑ 3 Jack Del Rio	.25	.11
❑ 4 Bobby Hebert	.25	.11
❑ 5 Shannon Sharpe	.75	.35
❑ 6 Gary Clark	.75	.35
❑ 7 Christian Okoye	.25	.11
❑ 8 Ernest Givins	.40	.18
❑ 9 Mike Horan	.25	.11
❑ 10 Dennis Gentry	.25	.11
❑ 11 Michael Irvin	.75	.35
❑ 12 Eric Floyd	.25	.11
❑ 13 Brent Jones	.40	.18
❑ 14 Anthony Carter	.40	.18
❑ 15 Tony Martin	.75	.35
❑ 16 Greg Lewis UER ("Returning" should be "returned" on back)	.25	.11

Card	Mint	NrMt
❑ 17 Todd McNair	.25	.11
❑ 18 Earnest Byner	.25	.11
❑ 19 Steve Beuerlein	.25	.11
❑ 20 Roger Craig	.40	.18
❑ 21 Mark Higgs	.25	.11
❑ 22 Guy McIntyre	.25	.11
❑ 23 Don Warren	.25	.11
❑ 24 Alvin Harper	.40	.18
❑ 25 Mark Jackson	.25	.11
❑ 26 Chris Doleman	.25	.11
❑ 27 Jesse Sapolu	.25	.11
❑ 28 Tony Tolbert	.25	.11
❑ 29 Wendell Davis	.25	.11
❑ 30 Dan Saleaumua	.25	.11
❑ 31 Jeff Bostic	.25	.11
❑ 32 Jay Novacek	.40	.18
❑ 33 Cris Carter	1.00	.45
❑ 34 Tony Paige	.25	.11
❑ 35 Greg Kragen	.25	.11
❑ 36 Jeff Dellenbach	.25	.11
❑ 37 Keith DeLong	.25	.11
❑ 38 Todd Scott	.25	.11
❑ 39 Jeff Feagles	.25	.11
❑ 40 Mike Saxon	.25	.11
❑ 41 Martin Mayhew	.25	.11
❑ 42 Steve Bono RC	.75	.35
❑ 43 Willie Davis RC	.75	.35
❑ 44 Mark Stepnoski	.40	.18
❑ 45 Harry Newsome	.25	.11
❑ 46 Thane Gash	.25	.11
❑ 47 Gaston Green	.25	.11
❑ 48 James Washington	.25	.11
❑ 49 Kenny Walker	.25	.11
❑ 50 Jeff Davidson RC	.25	.11
❑ 51 Shane Conlan	.25	.11
❑ 52 Richard Dent	.40	.18
❑ 53 Haywood Jeffires	.40	.18
❑ 54 Harry Galbreath	.25	.11
❑ 55 Terry Allen	.75	.35
❑ 56 Tommy Barnhardt	.25	.11
❑ 57 Mike Golic	.25	.11
❑ 58 Dalton Hilliard	.25	.11
❑ 59 Danny Copeland	.25	.11
❑ 60 Jerry Fontenot RC	.25	.11
❑ 61 Kelvin Martin	.25	.11
❑ 62 Mark Kelso	.25	.11
❑ 63 Wymon Henderson	.25	.11
❑ 64 Mark Rypien	.25	.11
❑ 65 Bobby Humphrey	.25	.11
❑ 66 Rich Gannon UER (Tarkington misspelled; Minneapolis instead of Minnesota on back)	.75	.35
❑ 67 Darren Lewis	.25	.11
❑ 68 Barry Foster	.40	.18
❑ 69 Ken Norton Jr.	.75	.35
❑ 70 James Lofton	.40	.18
❑ 71 Trace Armstrong	.25	.11
❑ 72 Vestee Jackson	.25	.11
❑ 73 Clyde Simmons	.25	.11
❑ 74 Brad Muster	.25	.11
❑ 75 Cornelius Bennett	.40	.18
❑ 76 Mike Merriweather	.25	.11
❑ 77 John Elway	4.00	1.80
❑ 78 Herschel Walker	.40	.18
❑ 79 Hassan Jones UER (Minneapolis instead of Minnesota on back)	.25	.11
❑ 80 Jim Harbaugh	.75	.35
❑ 81 Issiac Holt	.25	.11
❑ 82 David Alexander	.25	.11
❑ 83 Brian Mitchell	.40	.18
❑ 84 Mark Tuinei	.25	.11
❑ 85 Tom Rathman	.25	.11
❑ 86 Reggie White	.75	.35
❑ 87 William Perry	.40	.18
❑ 88 Jeff Wright	.25	.11
❑ 89 Keith Kartz	.25	.11
❑ 90 Andre Waters	.25	.11
❑ 91 Darryl Talley	.25	.11
❑ 92 Morten Andersen	.25	.11
❑ 93 Tom Waddle	.25	.11
❑ 94 Felix Wright UER (Minneapolis instead of Minnesota on back)	.25	.11
❑ 95 Keith Jackson	.40	.18
❑ 96 Art Monk	.40	.18
❑ 97 Seth Joyner	.40	.18
❑ 98 Steve McMichael	.40	.18
❑ 99 Thurman Thomas	.75	.35
❑ 100 Warren Moon	.75	.35
❑ 101 Tony Casillas	.25	.11
❑ 102 Vance Johnson	.25	.11
❑ 103 Doug Dawson RC	.25	.11
❑ 104 Bill Maas	.25	.11
❑ 105 Mark Clayton	.40	.18
❑ 106 Hoby Brenner	.25	.11
❑ 107 Gary Anderson K	.25	.11
❑ 108 Marc Logan	.25	.11
❑ 109 Ricky Sanders	.25	.11
❑ 110 Vai Sikahema	.25	.11
❑ 111 Neil Smith	.75	.35
❑ 112 Cody Carlson	.25	.11
❑ 113 Jimmie Jones	.25	.11
❑ 114 Pat Swilling	.40	.18
❑ 115 Neil O'Donnell	.75	.35
❑ 116 Chip Lohmiller	.25	.11
❑ 117 Mike Croel	.25	.11
❑ 118 Pete Metzelaars	.25	.11
❑ 119 Ray Childress	.25	.11
❑ 120 Fred Banks	.25	.11
❑ 121 Derek Kennard	.25	.11
❑ 122 Daryl Johnston	.75	.35
❑ 123 Lorenzo White UER (Minneapolis instead of Minnesota on back)	.25	.11
❑ 124 Hardy Nickerson	.40	.18
❑ 125 Derrick Thomas	.75	.35
❑ 126 Steve Walsh	.25	.11
❑ 127 Doug Widell	.25	.11
❑ 128 Calvin Williams	.40	.18
❑ 129 Tim Harris	.25	.11
❑ 130 Rod Woodson	.75	.35
❑ 131 Craig Heyward	.40	.18
❑ 132 Barry Word	.25	.11
❑ 133 Mark Duper	.25	.11
❑ 134 Tim Johnson	.25	.11
❑ 135 John Gesek	.25	.11
❑ 136 Steve Jackson	.25	.11
❑ 137 Dave Krieg	.40	.18
❑ 138 Barry Sanders UER (Won Heisman in 1988, not 1986)	5.00	2.20
❑ 139 Michael Haynes	.40	.18
❑ 140 Eric Metcalf	.40	.18
❑ 141 Stan Humphries	.75	.35
❑ 142 Sterling Sharpe	.75	.35
❑ 143 Todd Marinovich	.25	.11
❑ 144 Rodney Hampton	.75	.35
❑ 145 Rodney Peete	.40	.18
❑ 146 Darryl Williams RC	.25	.11
❑ 147 Darren Perry RC	.25	.11
❑ 148 Terrell Buckley RC	.25	.11
❑ 149 Amp Lee RC	.25	.11
❑ 150 Ricky Watters	.75	.35

1993 Playoff

	MINT	NRMT
COMPLETE SET (315)	25.00	11.00
❑ 1 Troy Aikman	1.50	.70
❑ 2 Jerry Rice	2.00	.90
❑ 3 Keith Jackson	.20	.09
❑ 4 Sean Gilbert	.20	.09
❑ 5 Jim Kelly	.40	.18
❑ 6 Junior Seau	.40	.18
❑ 7 Deion Sanders	1.00	.45
❑ 8 Joe Montana	3.00	1.35
❑ 9 Terrell Buckley	.10	.05
❑ 10 Emmitt Smith	3.00	1.35
❑ 11 Pete Stoyanovich	.10	.05
❑ 12 Randall Cunningham	.40	.18
❑ 13 Boomer Esiason	.20	.09
❑ 14 Mike Saxon	.10	.05
❑ 15 Chuck Cecil	.10	.05
❑ 16 Vinny Testaverde	.20	.09
❑ 17 Jeff Hostetler	.20	.09
❑ 18 Mark Clayton	.10	.05
❑ 19 Nick Bell	.10	.05
❑ 20 Frank Reich	.20	.09
❑ 21 Henry Ellard	.20	.09
❑ 22 Andre Reed	.20	.09
❑ 23 Mark Ingram	.10	.05
❑ 24 Mike Brim	.10	.05
❑ 25A Bernie Kosar UER (Name spelled Kozar on both sides)	.20	.09
❑ 25B Bernie Kosar COR	.20	.09
❑ 26 Jeff George	.40	.18
❑ 27 Tommy Maddox	.10	.05
❑ 28 Kent Graham RC	.40	.18
❑ 29 David Klingler	.10	.05
❑ 30 Robert Delpino	.10	.05
❑ 31 Kevin Fagan	.10	.05
❑ 32 Mark Bavaro	.10	.05
❑ 33 Harold Green	.10	.05
❑ 34 Shawn McCarthy	.10	.05
❑ 35 Ricky Proehl	.10	.05
❑ 36 Eugene Robinson	.10	.05
❑ 37 Phil Simms	.20	.09
❑ 38 David Lang	.10	.05
❑ 39 Santana Dotson	.20	.09
❑ 40 Brett Perriman	.40	.18
❑ 41 Jim Harbaugh	.40	.18
❑ 42 Keith Byars	.10	.05
❑ 43 Quentin Coryatt	.20	.09
❑ 44 Louis Oliver	.10	.05
❑ 45 Howie Long	.20	.09
❑ 46 Mike Sherrard	.10	.05
❑ 47 Earnest Byner	.10	.05
❑ 48 Neil Smith	.40	.18
❑ 49 Audray McMillian	.10	.05
❑ 50 Vaughn Dunbar	.10	.05
❑ 51 Ronnie Lott	.20	.09
❑ 52 Clyde Simmons	.10	.05
❑ 53 Kevin Scott	.10	.05
❑ 54 Bubby Brister	.10	.05
❑ 55 Randal Hill	.10	.05
❑ 56 Pat Swilling	.10	.05
❑ 57 Steve Beuerlein	.10	.05
❑ 58 Gary Clark	.20	.09
❑ 59 Brian Noble	.10	.05
❑ 60 Leslie O'Neal	.20	.09
❑ 61 Vincent Brown	.10	.05
❑ 62 Edgar Bennett	.40	.18
❑ 63 Anthony Carter	.20	.09
❑ 64 Glenn Cadrez RC UER (Name misspelled Cadez on front)	.10	.05
❑ 65 Dalton Hilliard	.10	.05
❑ 66 James Lofton	.20	.09
❑ 67 Walter Stanley	.10	.05
❑ 68 Tim Harris	.10	.05
❑ 69 Carl Banks	.10	.05
❑ 70 Andre Ware	.10	.05
❑ 71 Karl Mecklenburg	.10	.05
❑ 72 Russell Maryland	.10	.05
❑ 73 Leroy Thompson	.10	.05
❑ 74 Tommy Kane	.10	.05
❑ 75 Dan Marino	3.00	1.35
❑ 76 Darrell Fullington	.10	.05
❑ 77 Jessie Tuggle	.10	.05
❑ 78 Bruce Smith	.40	.18
❑ 79 Neal Anderson	.10	.05
❑ 80 Kevin Mack	.10	.05
❑ 81 Shane Dronett	.10	.05
❑ 82 Nick Lowery	.10	.05
❑ 83 Sheldon White	.10	.05
❑ 84 Flipper Anderson	.10	.05
❑ 85 Jeff Herrod	.10	.05

❑ 86 Dwight Stone .10 .05
❑ 87 Dave Krieg .20 .09
❑ 88 Bryan Cox .10 .05
❑ 89 Greg McMurtry .10 .05
❑ 90 Rickey Jackson .10 .05
❑ 91 Ernie Mills .10 .05
❑ 92 Browning Nagle .10 .05
❑ 93 John Taylor .20 .09
❑ 94 Eric Dickerson .20 .09
❑ 95 Johnny Holland .10 .05
❑ 96 Anthony Miller .20 .09
❑ 97 Fred Barnett .20 .09
❑ 98 Ricky Ervins UER .10 .05
(Name misspelled Rickey on back)
❑ 99 Leonard Russell .20 .09
❑ 100 Lawrence Taylor .40 .18
❑ 101 Tony Casillas .10 .05
❑ 102 John Elway 3.00 1.35
❑ 103 Bennie Blades .10 .05
❑ 104 Harry Sydney .10 .05
❑ 105 Bubba McDowell .10 .05
❑ 106 Todd McNair .10 .05
❑ 107 Steve Smith .10 .05
❑ 108 Jim Everett .20 .09
❑ 109 Bobby Humphrey .10 .05
❑ 110 Rich Gannon .40 .18
❑ 111 Marv Cook .10 .05
❑ 112 Wayne Martin .10 .05
❑ 113 Sean Landeta .10 .05
❑ 114 Brad Baxter UER .10 .05
(Reversed negative on front)
❑ 115 Reggie White .40 .18
❑ 116 Johnny Johnson .10 .05
❑ 117 Jeff Graham .20 .09
❑ 118 Darren Carrington RC .10 .05
❑ 119 Ricky Watters .40 .18
❑ 120 Art Monk UER .20 .09
(Reversed negative on back)
❑ 121 Cornelius Bennett .20 .09
❑ 122 Wade Wilson .10 .05
❑ 123 Daniel Stubbs .10 .05
❑ 124 Brad Muster .10 .05
❑ 125 Mike Tomczak .10 .05
❑ 126 Jay Novacek .20 .09
❑ 127 Shannon Sharpe .40 .18
❑ 128 Rodney Peete .10 .05
❑ 129 Daryl Johnston .40 .18
❑ 130 Warren Moon .40 .18
❑ 131 Willie Gault .10 .05
❑ 132 Tony Martin .40 .18
❑ 133 Terry Allen .40 .18
❑ 134 Hugh Millen .10 .05
❑ 135 Rob Moore .20 .09
❑ 136 Andy Harmon RC .20 .09
❑ 137 Kelvin Martin .10 .05
❑ 138 Rod Woodson .40 .18
❑ 139 Nate Lewis .10 .05
❑ 140 Darryl Talley .10 .05
❑ 141 Guy McIntyre .10 .05
❑ 142 John L. Williams .10 .05
❑ 143 Brad Edwards .10 .05
❑ 144 Trace Armstrong .10 .05
❑ 145 Kenneth Davis .10 .05
❑ 146 Clay Matthews .20 .09
❑ 147 Gaston Green .10 .05
❑ 148 Chris Spielman .20 .09
❑ 149 Cody Carlson .10 .05
❑ 150 Derrick Thomas .40 .18
❑ 151 Terry McDaniel .10 .05
❑ 152 Kevin Greene .40 .18
❑ 153 Roger Craig .20 .09
❑ 154 Craig Heyward .20 .09
❑ 155 Rodney Hampton .40 .18
❑ 156 Heath Sherman .10 .05
❑ 157 Mark Stepnoski .10 .05
❑ 158 Chris Chandler .20 .09
❑ 159 Rod Bernstine .10 .05
❑ 160 Pierce Holt .10 .05
❑ 161 Wilber Marshall .10 .05
❑ 162 Reggie Cobb .10 .05
❑ 163 Tom Rathman .10 .05
❑ 164 Michael Haynes .20 .09
❑ 165 Nate Odomes .10 .05
❑ 166 Tom Waddle .10 .05
❑ 167 Eric Ball .10 .05
❑ 168 Brett Favre UER 4.00 1.80
(Photo of Don Majkowski on back)
❑ 169 Michael Jackson .20 .09
❑ 170 Lorenzo White .10 .05
❑ 171 Cleveland Gary .10 .05
❑ 172 Jay Schroeder .10 .05
❑ 173 Tony Paige .10 .05
❑ 174 Jack Del Rio .10 .05
❑ 175 Jon Vaughn .10 .05
❑ 176 Morten Andersen UER .10 .05
(Misspelled Morton)
❑ 177 Chris Burkett .10 .05
❑ 178 Vai Sikahema .10 .05
❑ 179 Ronnie Harmon .10 .05
❑ 180 Amp Lee .10 .05
❑ 181 Chip Lohmiller .10 .05
❑ 182 Steve Broussard .10 .05
❑ 183 Don Beebe .10 .05
❑ 184 Tommy Vardell .10 .05
❑ 185 Keith Jennings .10 .05
❑ 186 Simon Fletcher .10 .05
❑ 187 Mel Gray .20 .09
❑ 188 Vince Workman .10 .05
❑ 189 Haywood Jeffires .20 .09
❑ 190 Barry Word .10 .05
❑ 191 Ethan Horton .10 .05
❑ 192 Mark Higgs .10 .05
❑ 193 Irving Fryar .20 .09
❑ 194 Charles Haley .20 .09
❑ 195 Steve Bono .40 .18
❑ 196 Mike Golic .10 .05
❑ 197 Gary Anderson K .10 .05
❑ 198 Sterling Sharpe .40 .18
❑ 199 Andre Tippett .10 .05
❑ 200 Thurman Thomas .40 .18
❑ 201 Chris Miller .20 .09
❑ 202 Henry Jones .10 .05
❑ 203 Mo Lewis .10 .05
❑ 204 Marion Butts .10 .05
❑ 205 Mike Johnson .10 .05
❑ 206 Alvin Harper .20 .09
❑ 207 Ray Childress .10 .05
❑ 208 Anthony Johnson .20 .09
❑ 209 Tony Bennett .10 .05
❑ 210 Anthony Newman RC .10 .05
❑ 211 Christian Okoye .10 .05
❑ 212 Marcus Allen .40 .18
❑ 213 Jackie Harris .10 .05
❑ 214 Mark Duper .10 .05
❑ 215 Cris Carter 1.00 .45
❑ 216 John Stephens .10 .05
❑ 217 Barry Sanders 3.00 1.35
❑ 218A Herman Moore ERR 1.25 .55
(First name misspelled Sherman)
❑ 218B Herman Moore COR 2.50 1.10
(Name spelled correctly)
❑ 219 Marvin Washington .10 .05
❑ 220 Calvin Williams .20 .09
❑ 221 John Randle .20 .09
❑ 222 Marco Coleman .10 .05
❑ 223 Eric Martin .10 .05
❑ 224 Dave Meggett .10 .05
❑ 225 Brian Washington .10 .05
❑ 226 Barry Foster .20 .09
❑ 227 Michael Zordich .10 .05
❑ 228 Stan Humphries .40 .18
❑ 229 Mike Cofer .10 .05
❑ 230 Chris Warren .20 .09
❑ 231 Keith McCants .10 .05
❑ 232 Mark Rypien .10 .05
❑ 233 James Francis .10 .05
❑ 234 Andre Rison .20 .09
❑ 235 William Perry .20 .09
❑ 236 Chip Banks .10 .05
❑ 237 Willie Davis .40 .18
❑ 238 Chris Doleman .10 .05
❑ 239 Tim Brown .40 .18
❑ 240 Darren Perry .10 .05
❑ 241 Johnny Bailey .10 .05
❑ 242 Ernest Givins UER .20 .09
(Spelled Givens on back)
❑ 243 John Carney .10 .05
❑ 244 Cortez Kennedy .20 .09
❑ 245 Lawrence Dawsey .10 .05
❑ 246 Martin Mayhew .10 .05
❑ 247 Shane Conlan .10 .05
❑ 248 J.J. Birden .10 .05
❑ 249 Quinn Early .20 .09
❑ 250 Michael Irvin .40 .18
❑ 251 Neil O'Donnell .40 .18
❑ 252 Stan Gelbaugh .10 .05
❑ 253 Drew Hill .10 .05
❑ 254 Wendell Davis .10 .05
❑ 255 Tim Johnson .10 .05
❑ 256 Seth Joyner .10 .05
❑ 257 Derrick Fenner .10 .05
❑ 258 Steve Young 1.50 .70
❑ 259 Jackie Slater .10 .05
❑ 260 Eric Metcalf .20 .09
❑ 261 Rufus Porter .10 .05
❑ 262 Ken Norton Jr. .20 .09
❑ 263 Tim McDonald .10 .05
❑ 264 Mark Jackson .10 .05
❑ 265 Hardy Nickerson .20 .09
❑ 266 Anthony Munoz .20 .09
❑ 267 Mark Carrier WR .20 .09
❑ 268 Mike Pritchard .20 .09
❑ 269 Steve Emtman .10 .05
❑ 270 Ricky Sanders .10 .05
❑ 271 Robert Massey .10 .05
❑ 272 Pete Metzelaars .10 .05
❑ 273 Reggie Langhorne .10 .05
❑ 274 Tim McGee .10 .05
❑ 275 Reggie Rivers RC .10 .05
❑ 276 Jimmie Jones .10 .05
❑ 277 Lorenzo White TB .10 .05
❑ 278 Emmitt Smith TB 2.00 .90
❑ 279 Thurman Thomas TB .40 .18
❑ 280 Barry Sanders TB UER 2.00 .90
(Ten TD's in '92; should be nine)
❑ 281 Rodney Hampton TB .20 .09
❑ 282 Barry Foster TB .20 .09
❑ 283 Troy Aikman PC 1.00 .45
❑ 284 Michael Irvin PC .20 .09
❑ 285 Brett Favre PC 2.50 1.10
❑ 286 Sterling Sharpe PC .20 .09
❑ 287 Steve Young PC 1.00 .45
❑ 288 Jerry Rice PC 1.25 .55
❑ 289 Stan Humphries PC .20 .09
❑ 290 Anthony Miller PC .20 .09
❑ 291 Dan Marino PC 2.00 .90
❑ 292 Keith Jackson PC .10 .05
❑ 293 Patrick Bates RC .10 .05
❑ 294 Jerome Bettis RC 2.50 1.10
❑ 295 Drew Bledsoe RC 6.00 2.70
❑ 296 Tom Carter RC .20 .09
❑ 297 Curtis Conway RC 1.25 .55
❑ 298 John Copeland RC .20 .09
❑ 299 Eric Curry RC .10 .05
❑ 300 Reggie Brooks RC .20 .09
❑ 301 Steve Everitt RC .10 .05
❑ 302 Deon Figures RC .20 .09
❑ 303 Garrison Hearst RC 1.50 .70
❑ 304 Qadry Ismail RC UER 1.50 .70
(Misspelled Quadry on both sides)
❑ 305 Marvin Jones RC .10 .05
❑ 306 Lincoln Kennedy RC .10 .05
❑ 307 O.J. McDuffie RC 1.50 .70
❑ 308 Rick Mirer RC .75 .35
❑ 309 Wayne Simmons RC .10 .05
❑ 310 Irv Smith RC .10 .05
❑ 311 Robert Smith RC 5.00 2.20
❑ 312 Dana Stubblefield RC .40 .18
❑ 313 George Teague RC .20 .09
❑ 314 Dan Williams RC .10 .05
❑ 315 Kevin Williams RC .40 .18
❑ NNO Santa Claus 2.00 .90

1994 Playoff

	MINT	NRMT
COMPLETE SET (336)	30.00	13.50

❑ 1 Joe Montana 4.00 1.80
❑ 2 Derrick Thomas .50 .23
❑ 3 Dan Marino 4.00 1.80
❑ 4 Cris Carter .75 .35
❑ 5 Boomer Esiason .30 .14
❑ 6 Bruce Smith .50 .23
❑ 7 Andre Rison .30 .14
❑ 8 Curtis Conway .50 .23

❑ 9	Michael Irvin	.50	.23
❑ 10	Shannon Sharpe	.30	.14
❑ 11	Pat Swilling	.15	.07
❑ 12	John Parrella	.15	.07
❑ 13	Mel Gray	.15	.07
❑ 14	Ray Childress	.15	.07
❑ 15	Willie Davis	.30	.14
❑ 16	Rocket Ismail	.30	.14
❑ 17	Jim Everett	.30	.14
❑ 18	Mark Higgs	.15	.07
❑ 19	Trace Armstrong	.15	.07
❑ 20	Jim Kelly	.50	.23
❑ 21	Rob Burnett	.15	.07
❑ 22	Jay Novacek	.30	.14
❑ 23	Robert Delpino	.15	.07
❑ 24	Brett Perriman	.30	.14
❑ 25	Troy Aikman	2.00	.90
❑ 26	Reggie White	.50	.23
❑ 27	Lorenzo White	.15	.07
❑ 28	Bubba McDowell	.15	.07
❑ 29	Steve Emtman	.15	.07
❑ 30	Brett Favre	4.00	1.80
❑ 31	Derek Russell	.15	.07
❑ 32	Jeff Hostetler	.30	.14
❑ 33	Henry Ellard	.30	.14
❑ 34	Jack Del Rio	.15	.07
❑ 35	Mike Saxon	.15	.07
❑ 36	Rickey Jackson	.15	.07
❑ 37	Phil Simms	.30	.14
❑ 38	Quinn Early	.30	.14
❑ 39	Russell Copeland	.15	.07
❑ 40	Carl Pickens	.50	.23
❑ 41	Lance Gunn	.15	.07
❑ 42	Bernie Kosar	.30	.14
❑ 43	John Elway	4.00	1.80
❑ 44	George Teague	.15	.07
❑ 45	Nick Lowery	.15	.07
❑ 46	Haywood Jeffires	.30	.14
❑ 47	Will Shields	.15	.07
❑ 48	Daryl Johnston	.30	.14
❑ 49	Pete Metzelaars	.15	.07
❑ 50	Warren Moon	.50	.23
❑ 51	Cornelius Bennett	.30	.14
❑ 52	Vinny Testaverde	.30	.14
❑ 53	John Mangum RC	.15	.07
❑ 54	Tommy Vardell	.15	.07
❑ 55	Lincoln Coleman RC	.15	.07
❑ 56	Karl Mecklenburg	.15	.07
❑ 57	Jackie Harris	.15	.07
❑ 58	Curtis Duncan	.15	.07
❑ 59	Quentin Coryatt	.15	.07
❑ 60	Tim Brown	.50	.23
❑ 61	Irving Fryar	.30	.14
❑ 62	Sean Gilbert	.15	.07
❑ 63	Qadry Ismail	.50	.23
❑ 64	Irv Smith	.15	.07
❑ 65	Mark Jackson	.15	.07
❑ 66	Ronnie Lott	.30	.14
❑ 67	Henry Jones	.15	.07
❑ 68	Horace Copeland	.15	.07
❑ 69	John Copeland	.15	.07
❑ 70	Mark Carrier WR	.30	.14
❑ 71	Michael Jackson	.30	.14
❑ 72	Jason Elam	.15	.07
❑ 73	Rod Bernstine	.15	.07
❑ 74	Wayne Simmons	.15	.07
❑ 75	Cody Carlson	.15	.07
❑ 76	Alexander Wright	.15	.07
❑ 77	Shane Conlan	.15	.07
❑ 78	Keith Jackson	.15	.07
❑ 79	Sean Salisbury	.15	.07
❑ 80	Vaughan Johnson	.15	.07
❑ 81	Rob Moore	.30	.14
❑ 82	Andre Reed	.30	.14
❑ 83	David Klinger	.15	.07
❑ 84	Jim Harbaugh	.50	.23
❑ 85	John Jett RC	.15	.07
❑ 86	Sterling Sharpe	.30	.14
❑ 87	Webster Slaughter	.15	.07
❑ 88	J.J. Birden	.15	.07
❑ 89	O.J. McDuffie	.50	.23
❑ 90	Andre Tippett	.15	.07
❑ 91	Don Beebe	.15	.07
❑ 92	Mark Stepnoski	.15	.07
❑ 93	Neil Smith	.50	.23
❑ 94	Terry Kirby	.50	.23
❑ 95	Wade Wilson	.15	.07
❑ 96	Darryl Talley	.15	.07
❑ 97	Anthony Smith	.15	.07
❑ 98	Willie Roaf	.15	.07
❑ 99	Mo Lewis	.15	.07
❑ 100	James Washington	.15	.07
❑ 101	Nate Odomes	.15	.07
❑ 102	Chris Gedney	.15	.07
❑ 103	Joe Walter	.15	.07
❑ 104	Alvin Harper	.30	.14
❑ 105	Simon Fletcher	.15	.07
❑ 106	Rodney Peete	.15	.07
❑ 107	Terrell Buckley	.15	.07
❑ 108	Jeff George	.50	.23
❑ 109	James Jett	.15	.07
❑ 110	Tony Casillas	.15	.07
❑ 111	Marco Coleman	.15	.07
❑ 112	Anthony Carter	.30	.14
❑ 113	Lincoln Kennedy	.15	.07
❑ 114	Chris Calloway	.15	.07
❑ 115	Randall Cunningham	.50	.23
❑ 116	Steve Beuerlein	.15	.07
❑ 117	Neil O'Donnell	.50	.23
❑ 118	Stan Humphries	.50	.23
❑ 119	John Taylor	.30	.14
❑ 120	Cortez Kennedy	.30	.14
❑ 121	Santana Dotson	.30	.14
❑ 122	Thomas Smith	.15	.07
❑ 123	Kevin Williams	.30	.14
❑ 124	Andre Ware	.15	.07
❑ 125	Ethan Horton	.15	.07
❑ 126	Mike Sherrard	.15	.07
❑ 127	Fred Barnett	.30	.14
❑ 128	Ricky Proehl	.15	.07
❑ 129	Kevin Greene	.50	.23
❑ 130	John Carney	.15	.07
❑ 131	Tim McDonald	.15	.07
❑ 132	Rick Mirer	.50	.23
❑ 133	Blair Thomas	.15	.07
❑ 134	Hardy Nickerson	.30	.14
❑ 135	Heath Sherman	.15	.07
❑ 136	Andre Hastings	.30	.14
❑ 137	Randal Hill	.15	.07
❑ 138	Mike Cofer	.15	.07
❑ 139	Brian Blades	.30	.14
❑ 140	Earnest Byner	.15	.07
❑ 141	Bill Bates	.30	.14
❑ 142	Junior Seau	.50	.23
❑ 143	Johnny Bailey	.15	.07
❑ 144	Dwight Stone	.15	.07
❑ 145	Todd Kelly	.15	.07
❑ 146	Tyrone Montgomery	.15	.07
❑ 147	Herschel Walker	.30	.14
❑ 148	Gary Clark	.30	.14
❑ 149	Eric Green	.15	.07
❑ 150	Steve Young	1.50	.70
❑ 151	Anthony Miller	.30	.14
❑ 152	Dana Stubblefield	.50	.23
❑ 153	Dean Wells RC	.15	.07
❑ 154	Vincent Brisby	.50	.23
❑ 155	Chris Chandler	.30	.14
❑ 156	Clyde Simmons	.15	.07
❑ 157	Rod Woodson	.50	.23
❑ 158	Nate Lewis	.15	.07
❑ 159	Martin Harrison	.15	.07
❑ 160	Kelvin Martin	.15	.07
❑ 161	Craig Erickson	.15	.07
❑ 162	Johnny Mitchell	.15	.07
❑ 163	Calvin Williams	.30	.14
❑ 164	Deon Figures	.15	.07
❑ 165	Tom Rathman	.15	.07
❑ 166	Rick Hamilton	.15	.07
❑ 167	John L. Williams	.15	.07
❑ 168	Demetrius DuBose	.15	.07
❑ 169	Michael Brooks	.15	.07
❑ 170	Marion Butts	.15	.07
❑ 171	Brent Jones	.30	.14
❑ 172	Bobby Hebert	.15	.07
❑ 173	Brad Edwards	.15	.07
❑ 174	David Wyman	.15	.07
❑ 175	Herman Moore	.50	.23
❑ 176	LeRoy Butler	.15	.07
❑ 177	Reggie Langhorne	.15	.07
❑ 178	Dave Krieg	.30	.14
❑ 179	Patrick Bates	.15	.07
❑ 180	Erik Kramer	.30	.14
❑ 181	Troy Drayton	.15	.07
❑ 182	Dave Meggett	.15	.07
❑ 183	Eric Allen	.15	.07
❑ 184	Mark Bavaro	.15	.07
❑ 185	Leslie O'Neal	.15	.07
❑ 186	Jerry Rice	2.00	.90
❑ 187	Desmond Howard	.30	.14
❑ 188	Deion Sanders	.75	.35
❑ 189	Bill Maas	.15	.07
❑ 190	Frank Wycheck RC	2.00	.90
❑ 191	Ernest Givins	.30	.14
❑ 192	Terry McDaniel	.15	.07
❑ 193	Bryan Cox	.15	.07
❑ 194	Guy McIntyre	.15	.07
❑ 195	Pierce Holt	.15	.07
❑ 196	Fred Stokes	.15	.07
❑ 197	Mike Pritchard	.15	.07
❑ 198	Terry Obee	.15	.07
❑ 199	Mark Collins	.15	.07
❑ 200	Drew Bledsoe	2.00	.90
❑ 201	Barry Word	.15	.07
❑ 202	Derrick Lassic	.15	.07
❑ 203	Chris Spielman	.30	.14
❑ 204	John Jurkovic RC	.30	.14
❑ 205	Ken Norton Jr.	.30	.14
❑ 206	Dale Carter	.15	.07
❑ 207	Chris Doleman	.15	.07
❑ 208	Keith Hamilton	.15	.07
❑ 209	Andy Harmon	.15	.07
❑ 210	John Friesz	.30	.14
❑ 211	Steve Bono	.30	.14
❑ 212	Mark Rypien	.15	.07
❑ 213	Ricky Sanders	.15	.07
❑ 214	Michael Haynes	.30	.14
❑ 215	Todd McNair	.15	.07
❑ 216	Leon Lett	.15	.07
❑ 217	Scott Mitchell	.50	.23
❑ 218	Mike Morris RC	.15	.07
❑ 219	Darrin Smith	.15	.07
❑ 220	Jim McMahon	.15	.07
❑ 221	Garrison Hearst	.50	.23
❑ 222	Leroy Thompson	.15	.07
❑ 223	Darren Carrington	.15	.07
❑ 224	Pete Stoyanovich	.15	.07
❑ 225	Chris Miller	.15	.07
❑ 226	Bruce Smith SP	.30	.14
❑ 227	Simon Fletcher SP	.15	.07
❑ 228	Reggie White SP	.50	.23
❑ 229	Neil Smith SP	.50	.23
❑ 230	Chris Doleman SP	.15	.07
❑ 231	Keith Hamilton SP	.15	.07
❑ 232	Dana Stubblefield SP	.15	.07
❑ 233	Eric Pegram GA	.15	.07
❑ 234	Thurman Thomas GA	.50	.23
❑ 235	Lewis Tillman GA	.15	.07
❑ 236	Harold Green GA	.15	.07
❑ 237	Eric Metcalf GA	.30	.14
❑ 238	Emmitt Smith GA	3.00	1.35
❑ 239	Glyn Milburn GA	.30	.14
❑ 240	Barry Sanders GA	4.00	1.80
❑ 241	Edgar Bennett GA	.30	.14
❑ 242	Gary Brown GA	.15	.07
❑ 243	Roosevelt Potts GA	.15	.07
❑ 244	Marcus Allen GA	.50	.23
❑ 245	Greg Robinson GA	.15	.07
❑ 246	Jerome Bettis GA	.50	.23
❑ 247	Keith Byars GA	.15	.07

❑ 248 Robert Smith GA .50 .23
❑ 249 Leonard Russell GA .15 .07
❑ 250 Derek Brown RBK GA .15 .07
❑ 251 Rodney Hampton GA .30 .14
❑ 252 Johnny Johnson GA .15 .07
❑ 253 Vaughn Hebron GA .15 .07
❑ 254 Ronald Moore GA .15 .07
❑ 255 Barry Foster GA .15 .07
❑ 256 Natrone Means GA .50 .23
❑ 257 Ricky Watters GA .50 .23
❑ 258 Chris Warren GA .50 .23
❑ 259 Vince Workman GA .15 .07
❑ 260 Reggie Brooks GA .15 .07
❑ 261 Carolina Panthers Logo .40 .18
❑ 262 Jacksonville Jaguars Logo .40 .18
❑ 263 Troy Aikman SB 1.00 .45
❑ 264 Barry Sanders SB 2.00 .90
❑ 265 Emmitt Smith SB 1.50 .70
❑ 266 Michael Irvin SB .50 .23
❑ 267 Jerry Rice SB 1.00 .45
❑ 268 Shannon Sharpe SB .30 .14
❑ 269 Bob Kratch SB .15 .07
❑ 270 Howard Ballard SB .15 .07
❑ 271 Erik Williams SB .15 .07
❑ 272 Guy McIntyre SB .15 .07
❑ 273 Kelvin Williams SB .30 .14
❑ 274 Mel Gray SB .15 .07
❑ 275 Eddie Murray SB .15 .07
❑ 276 Mark Stepnoski SB .15 .07
❑ 277 Tommy Barnhardt SB .15 .07
❑ 278 Derrick Thomas SB .30 .14
❑ 279 Ken Norton Jr. SB .30 .14
❑ 280 Chris Spielman SB .15 .07
❑ 281 Deion Sanders SB .50 .23
❑ 282 Mark Collins SB .15 .07
❑ 283 Bruce Smith SB .30 .14
❑ 284 Reggie White SB .50 .23
❑ 285 Sean Gilbert SB .15 .07
❑ 286 Cortez Kennedy SB .30 .14
❑ 287 Steve Atwater SB .15 .07
❑ 288 Tim McDonald SB .15 .07
❑ 289 Jerome Bettis SB .30 .14
❑ 290 Dana Stubblefield SB .30 .14
❑ 291 Bert Emanuel RC 1.50 .70
❑ 292 Jeff Burris RC .30 .14
❑ 293 Bucky Brooks RC .15 .07
❑ 294 Dan Wilkinson RC .30 .14
❑ 295 Darnay Scott RC 1.50 .70
❑ 296 Der.Alexander WR RC 1.25 .55
❑ 297 Antonio Langham RC .30 .14
❑ 298 Shante Carver RC .15 .07
❑ 299 Shelby Hill RC .15 .07
❑ 300 Larry Allen RC .30 .14
❑ 301 Johnnie Morton RC 1.50 .70
❑ 302 Van Malone RC .15 .07
❑ 303 Aaron Taylor RC .15 .07
❑ 304 Marshall Faulk RC 5.00 2.20
❑ 305 Eric Mahlum RC .15 .07
❑ 306 Trev Alberts RC .30 .14
❑ 307 Greg Hill RC .50 .23
❑ 308 Donnell Bennett RC .50 .23
❑ 309 Rob Fredrickson RC .30 .14
❑ 310 James Folston RC .15 .07
❑ 311 Isaac Bruce RC 5.00 2.20
❑ 312 Tim Ruddy RC .15 .07
❑ 313 Aubrey Beavers RC .15 .07
❑ 314 David Palmer RC 1.25 .55
❑ 315 Dewayne Washington RC .30 .14
❑ 316 Willie McGinest RC .50 .23
❑ 317 Mario Bates RC .50 .23
❑ 318 Kevin Lee RC .15 .07
❑ 319 Jason Sehorn RC .60 .25
❑ 320 Thomas Randolph RC .15 .07
❑ 321 Ryan Yarborough RC .15 .07
❑ 322 Bernard Williams RC .15 .07
❑ 323 Chuck Levy RC .15 .07
❑ 324 Jamir Miller RC .15 .07
❑ 325 Charles Johnson RC 1.25 .55
❑ 326 Bryant Young RC .50 .23
❑ 327 William Floyd RC .50 .23
❑ 328 Kevin Mitchell RC .15 .07
❑ 329 Sam Adams RC .30 .14
❑ 330 Kevin Mawae RC .15 .07
❑ 331 Errict Rhett RC 1.25 .55
❑ 332 Trent Dilfer RC 2.50 1.10
❑ 333 Heath Shuler RC .50 .23
❑ 334 Aaron Glenn RC .30 .14
❑ 335 Todd Steussie RC .30 .14
❑ 336 Toby Wright RC .15 .07
❑ NNO Gale Sayers Player's Club 5.00 2.20
❑ NNO Gale Sayers AUTO .. signed Player's Club 80.00 36.00

1995 Playoff Absolute

MINT NRMT
COMPLETE SET (200) 20.00 9.00

❑ 1 John Elway 2.00 .90
❑ 2 Reggie White .40 .18
❑ 3 Errict Rhett .40 .18
❑ 4 Deion Sanders .50 .23
❑ 5 Rocket Ismail .20 .09
❑ 6 Jerome Bettis .40 .18
❑ 7 Randall Cunningham .40 .18
❑ 8 Mario Bates .40 .18
❑ 9 Dave Brown .20 .09
❑ 10 Stan Humphries .20 .09
❑ 11 Drew Bledsoe 1.00 .45
❑ 12 Neil O'Donnell .20 .09
❑ 13 Dan Marino 2.00 .90
❑ 14 Larry Centers .20 .09
❑ 15 Craig Heyward .20 .09
❑ 16 Bruce Smith .40 .18
❑ 17 Erik Kramer .10 .05
❑ 18 Jeff Blake RC 1.25 .55
❑ 19 Vinny Testaverde .20 .09
❑ 20 Barry Sanders 2.00 .90
❑ 21 Boomer Esiason .20 .09
❑ 22 Emmitt Smith 1.50 .70
❑ 23 Warren Moon .20 .09
❑ 24 Junior Seau .40 .18
❑ 25 Heath Shuler .40 .18
❑ 26 Jackie Harris .10 .05
❑ 27 Terance Mathis .20 .09
❑ 28 Raymont Harris .10 .05
❑ 29 Jim Kelly .40 .18
❑ 30 Dan Wilkinson .20 .09
❑ 31 Herman Moore .40 .18
❑ 32 Shannon Sharpe .20 .09
❑ 33 Antonio Langham .10 .05
❑ 34 Charles Haley .20 .09
❑ 35 Brett Favre 2.00 .90
❑ 36 Marshall Faulk .75 .35
❑ 37 Neil Smith .20 .09
❑ 38 Harvey Williams .10 .05
❑ 39 Johnny Bailey .10 .05
❑ 40 O.J. McDuffie .40 .18
❑ 41 David Palmer .20 .09
❑ 42 Willie McGinest .20 .09
❑ 43 Quinn Early .20 .09
❑ 44 Johnny Johnson .10 .05
❑ 45 Derek Brown TE .10 .05
❑ 46 Charlie Garner .20 .09
❑ 47 Byron Bam Morris .20 .09
❑ 48 Natrone Means .40 .18
❑ 49 Ken Norton Jr. .20 .09
❑ 50 Troy Aikman 1.00 .45
❑ 51 Reggie Brooks .20 .09
❑ 52 Trent Dilfer .40 .18
❑ 53 Cortez Kennedy .20 .09
❑ 54 Chuck Levy .10 .05
❑ 55 Jeff George .20 .09
❑ 56 Steve Young .75 .35
❑ 57 Lewis Tillman .10 .05
❑ 58 Carl Pickens .40 .18
❑ 59 Brett Perriman .20 .09
❑ 60 Jay Novacek .20 .09
❑ 61 Greg Hill .20 .09
❑ 62 James Jett .20 .09
❑ 63 Terry Kirby .20 .09
❑ 64 Qadry Ismail .20 .09
❑ 65 Ben Coates .20 .09
❑ 66 Kevin Greene .20 .09
❑ 67 Bryant Young .20 .09
❑ 68 Brian Mitchell .10 .05
❑ 69 Steve Walsh .10 .05
❑ 70 Darnay Scott .40 .18
❑ 71 Daryl Johnston .20 .09
❑ 72 Glyn Milburn .10 .05
❑ 73 Tim Brown .40 .18
❑ 74 Isaac Bruce .75 .35
❑ 75 Bernie Parmalee .20 .09
❑ 76 Terry Allen .20 .09
❑ 77 Jim Everett .10 .05
❑ 78 Thomas Lewis .20 .09
❑ 79 Vaughn Hebron .10 .05
❑ 80 Rod Woodson .20 .09
❑ 81 Rick Mirer .40 .18
❑ 82 Dana Stubblefield .40 .18
❑ 83 Bert Emanuel .40 .18
❑ 84 Andre Reed .20 .09
❑ 85 Jeff Graham .10 .05
❑ 86 Johnnie Morton .20 .09
❑ 87 LeShon Johnson .20 .09
❑ 88 Michael Irvin .40 .18
❑ 89 Derrick Alexander WR .40 .18
❑ 90 Lake Dawson .20 .09
❑ 91 Cody Carlson .10 .05
❑ 92 Chris Warren .20 .09
❑ 93 William Floyd .40 .18
❑ 94 Charles Johnson .20 .09
❑ 95 Roosevelt Potts .10 .05
❑ 96 Cris Carter .40 .18
❑ 97 Aaron Glenn .10 .05
❑ 98 Curtis Conway .40 .18
❑ 99 Kevin Williams WR .20 .09
❑ 100 Jerry Rice 1.00 .45
❑ 101 Frank Reich .10 .05
❑ 102 Harold Green .10 .05
❑ 103 Russell Copeland .10 .05
❑ 104 Rob Moore .10 .05
❑ 105 Edgar Bennett .20 .09
❑ 106 Darren Carrington .10 .05
❑ 107 Tommy Maddox .10 .05
❑ 108 Dave Meggett .10 .05
❑ 109 Fred Barnett .20 .09
❑ 110 Mark Seay .20 .09
❑ 111 Gus Frerotte .40 .18
❑ 112 Brent Jones .10 .05
❑ 113 Chris Miller .10 .05
❑ 114 Cedric Tillman .10 .05
❑ 115 Mark Ingram .10 .05
❑ 116 Eric Turner .10 .05
❑ 117 Mark Carrier WR .20 .09
❑ 118 Garrison Hearst .40 .18
❑ 119 Craig Erickson .10 .05
❑ 120 Derek Russell .10 .05
❑ 121 Mike Sherrard .10 .05
❑ 122 Horace Copeland .10 .05
❑ 123 Jack Trudeau .10 .05
❑ 124 Leroy Hoard .10 .05
❑ 125 Gary Brown .10 .05
❑ 126 Mel Gray .10 .05
❑ 127 Steve Beuerlein .10 .05
❑ 128 Marcus Allen .40 .18
❑ 129 Irving Fryar .20 .09
❑ 130 Marion Butts .10 .05
❑ 131 Ricky Watters .40 .18
❑ 132 Tony Martin .20 .09
❑ 133 Lawrence Dawsey .10 .05
❑ 134 Ronnie Harmon .10 .05
❑ 135 Herschel Walker .20 .09
❑ 136 Michael Haynes .20 .09
❑ 137 Eric Green .10 .05
❑ 138 Steve Bono .20 .09
❑ 139 Jamir Miller .10 .05
❑ 140 Rod Smith DB .20 .09

❑ 141 Andre Rison	.20	.09
❑ 142 Eric Metcalf	.20	.09
❑ 143 Michael Timpson	.10	.05
❑ 144 Cornelius Bennett	.20	.09
❑ 145 Sean Dawkins	.20	.09
❑ 146 Scott Mitchell	.20	.09
❑ 147 Ray Childress	.10	.05
❑ 148 Jim Harbaugh	.20	.09
❑ 149 Reggie Cobb	.10	.05
❑ 150 Willie Roaf	.10	.05
❑ 151 Stevie Anderson	.10	.05
❑ 152 Barry Foster	.20	.09
❑ 153 Joe Montana	2.00	.90
❑ 154 David Klingler	.20	.09
❑ 155 Chris Chandler	.20	.09
❑ 156 Carnell Lake	.10	.05
❑ 157 Calvin Williams	.20	.09
❑ 158 Kenneth Davis	.10	.05
❑ 159 Tydus Winans	.10	.05
❑ 160 Sam Adams	.10	.05
❑ 161 Ronald Moore	.10	.05
❑ 162 Vincent Brisby	.10	.05
❑ 163 Alvin Harper	.10	.05
❑ 164 Jake Reed	.20	.09
❑ 165 Jeff Hostetler	.20	.09
❑ 166 Mark Brunell	1.00	.45
❑ 167 Leonard Russell	.10	.05
❑ 168 Greg Truitt	.10	.05
❑ 169 Pete Metzelaars	.10	.05
❑ 170 Dave Krieg	.10	.05
❑ 171 Lorenzo White	.10	.05
❑ 172 Robert Brooks	.40	.18
❑ 173 Willie Davis	.20	.09
❑ 174 Irving Spikes	.20	.09
❑ 175 Rodney Hampton	.20	.09
❑ 176 Erric Pegram	.20	.09
❑ 177 Brian Blades	.20	.09
❑ 178 Shawn Jefferson	.10	.05
❑ 179 Tyrone Poole RC	.20	.09
❑ 180 Rob Johnson RC	4.00	1.80
❑ 181 Ki-Jana Carter RC	.40	.18
❑ 182 Steve McNair RC	5.00	2.20
❑ 183 Michael Westbrook RC	2.50	1.10
❑ 184 Kerry Collins RC	2.50	1.10
❑ 185 Kevin Carter RC	.40	.18
❑ 186 Tony Boselli RC	.40	.18
❑ 187 Joey Galloway RC	4.00	1.80
❑ 188 Kyle Brady RC	.40	.18
❑ 189 J.J. Stokes RC	.40	.18
❑ 190 Warren Sapp RC	.75	.35
❑ 191 Tyrone Wheatley RC	2.00	.90
❑ 192 Napolean Kaufman RC	2.50	1.10
❑ 193 James O. Stewart RC	4.00	1.80
❑ 194 Rashaan Salaam RC	.40	.18
❑ 195 Ray Zellars RC	.20	.09
❑ 196 Todd Collins RC	.40	.18
❑ 197 Sherman Williams RC	.10	.05
❑ 198 Frank Sanders RC	1.25	.55
❑ 199 Terrell Fletcher RC	.10	.05
❑ 200 Chad May RC	.10	.05
❑ DP1G T.Boselli Draft Gold	3.00	1.35
❑ DP1S T.Boselli Draft Silver	2.00	.90
❑ DP2G K.Collins Draft Gold	6.00	2.70
❑ DP2S K.Collins Draft Silver	5.00	2.20

1996 Playoff Absolute

	MINT	NRMT
COMPLETE SET (200)	100.00	45.00
COMP.RED SET (100)	15.00	6.75
COMMON RED CARD (1-100)	.15	.07
COMMON WHITE (101-150)	.50	.23
COMMON BLUE (151-200)	.75	.35

Card	MINT	NRMT
❑ 1 Jim Kelly	.60	.25
❑ 2 Michael Irvin	.60	.25
❑ 3 Jim Harbaugh	.30	.14
❑ 4 Warren Moon	.30	.14
❑ 5 Rick Mirer	.30	.14
❑ 6 Drew Bledsoe	1.50	.70
❑ 7 Steve Young	1.25	.55
❑ 8 Junior Seau	.30	.14
❑ 9 Sherman Williams	.15	.07
❑ 10 Jay Novacek	.15	.07
❑ 11 Bill Brooks	.15	.07
❑ 12 Steve Bono	.15	.07
❑ 13 Leroy Hoard	.15	.07
❑ 14 Willie Jackson	.15	.07
❑ 15 Irving Fryar	.30	.14
❑ 16 Tony McGee	.15	.07
❑ 17 Neil O'Donnell	.30	.14
❑ 18 Fred Barnett	.15	.07
❑ 19 Erric Pegram	.15	.07
❑ 20 Derrick Moore	.15	.07
❑ 21 Johnnie Morton	.30	.14
❑ 22 James Jett	.30	.14
❑ 23 Tim Brown	.60	.25
❑ 24 Kevin Miniefield	.15	.07
❑ 25 Jim McMahon	.15	.07
❑ 26 Brian Blades	.15	.07
❑ 27 Henry Ellard	.15	.07
❑ 28 Calvin Williams	.15	.07
❑ 29 Chris Chandler	.30	.14
❑ 30 Rod Woodson	.30	.14
❑ 31 Ronnie Harmon	.15	.07
❑ 32 Brent Jones	.15	.07
❑ 33 Qadry Ismail	.15	.07
❑ 34 Steve Tasker	.15	.07
❑ 35 Eric Green	.15	.07
❑ 36 Brian Mitchell	.15	.07
❑ 37 Herschel Walker	.30	.14
❑ 38 Sean Dawkins	.15	.07
❑ 39 Bryce Paup	.15	.07
❑ 40 Dorsey Levens	.60	.25
❑ 41 Andre Rison	.30	.14
❑ 42 Lamont Warren	.15	.07
❑ 43 Earnest Byner	.15	.07
❑ 44 Bobby Engram RC	.60	.25
❑ 45 Simeon Rice RC	.60	.25
❑ 46 Michael Jackson	.30	.14
❑ 47 Marvin Harrison RC	3.00	1.35
❑ 48 Thurman Thomas	.60	.25
❑ 49 Charles Haley	.30	.14
❑ 50 Rob Moore	.30	.14
❑ 51 Bryan Cox	.15	.07
❑ 52 Horace Copeland	.15	.07
❑ 53 Rodney Peete	.15	.07
❑ 54 Jeff Graham	.15	.07
❑ 55 Charles Johnson	.15	.07
❑ 56 Natrone Means	.60	.25
❑ 57 Terrell Fletcher	.15	.07
❑ 58 Eric Bieniemy	.15	.07
❑ 59 Karim Abdul-Jabbar RC	.75	.35
❑ 60 Quinn Early	.15	.07
❑ 61 Mark Bruener	.15	.07
❑ 62 Shawn Jefferson	.15	.07
❑ 63 Vinny Testaverde	.30	.14
❑ 64 Derrick Mayes RC	1.00	.45
❑ 65 Mario Bates	.30	.14
❑ 66 J.J. Birden	.15	.07
❑ 67 Eddie Kennison RC	.60	.25
❑ 68 Steve Walsh	.15	.07
❑ 69 Mark Chmura	.30	.14
❑ 70 Mike Sherrard	.15	.07
❑ 71 Boomer Esiason	.30	.14
❑ 72 Alex Van Dyke RC	.30	.14
❑ 73 Jake Reed	.30	.14
❑ 74 Jackie Harris	.15	.07
❑ 75 Mark Rypien	.15	.07
❑ 76 Chris Calloway	.15	.07
❑ 77 Amani Toomer RC	1.25	.55
❑ 78 Terrell Davis	8.00	3.60
❑ 79 Rocket Ismail	.15	.07
❑ 80 Derek Loville	.15	.07
❑ 81 Ben Coates	.30	.14
❑ 82 Kyle Brady	.15	.07
❑ 83 Willie Green	.15	.07
❑ 84 Randall Cunningham	.60	.25
❑ 85 Amp Lee	.15	.07
❑ 86 Bert Emanuel	.30	.14
❑ 87 Jason Dunn RC	.30	.14
❑ 88 Michael Haynes	.15	.07
❑ 89 Robert Green	.15	.07
❑ 90 Willie Davis	.15	.07
❑ 91 O.J. McDuffie	.30	.14
❑ 92 Harold Green	.15	.07
❑ 93 Ken Dilger	.30	.14
❑ 94 Brett Perriman	.15	.07
❑ 95 Eric Zeier	.15	.07
❑ 96 Jerome Bettis	.60	.25
❑ 97 Rickey Dudley RC	.60	.25
❑ 98 Darnay Scott	.30	.14
❑ 99 Mark Brunell	1.50	.70
❑ 100 Christian Fauria	.15	.07
❑ 101 Jeff Blake	2.00	.90
❑ 102 Troy Aikman	5.00	2.20
❑ 103 John Elway	10.00	4.50
❑ 104 Barry Sanders	10.00	4.50
❑ 105 Curtis Conway	2.00	.90
❑ 106 Wayne Chrebet	2.50	1.10
❑ 107 Lake Dawson	1.00	.45
❑ 108 Jerry Rice	5.00	2.20
❑ 109 Kevin Williams	.50	.23
❑ 110 Zack Crockett	.50	.23
❑ 111 Vincent Brisby	.50	.23
❑ 112 Rodney Thomas	.50	.23
❑ 113 Rodney Hampton	1.00	.45
❑ 114 Adrian Murrell	.60	.25
❑ 115 Bruce Smith	2.00	.90
❑ 116 Napoleon Kaufman	2.00	.90
❑ 117 Byron Bam Morris	1.00	.45
❑ 118 Anthony Miller	1.00	.45
❑ 119 Aaron Hayden RC	1.00	.45
❑ 120 Joey Galloway	2.50	1.10
❑ 121 Trent Dilfer	1.00	.45
❑ 122 Stoney Case	.50	.23
❑ 123 Tamarick Vanover	.30	.14
❑ 124 Eric Metcalf	1.00	.45
❑ 125 Marcus Allen	2.00	.90
❑ 126 James O. Stewart	2.00	.90
❑ 127 Charlie Garner	.50	.23
❑ 128 Yancey Thigpen	1.00	.45
❑ 129 William Floyd	1.00	.45
❑ 130 Terry Allen	1.00	.45
❑ 131 Robert Smith	1.00	.45
❑ 132 Todd Kinchen	.50	.23
❑ 133 Gus Frerotte	2.00	.90
❑ 134 Frank Sanders	1.00	.45
❑ 135 Scott Mitchell	1.00	.45
❑ 136 Greg Hill	1.00	.45
❑ 137 Edgar Bennett	1.00	.45
❑ 138 Alvin Harper	.50	.23
❑ 139 Reggie White	2.00	.90
❑ 140 Craig Heyward	.50	.23
❑ 141 Todd Collins	1.00	.45
❑ 142 Ernie Mills	.50	.23
❑ 143 Keyshawn Johnson RC	5.00	2.20
❑ 144 Mark Carrier WR	.50	.23
❑ 145 Robert Brooks	2.00	.90
❑ 146 Bernie Parmalee	.50	.23
❑ 147 Carl Pickens	2.00	.90
❑ 148 Kevin Hardy RC	2.00	.90
❑ 149 Jonathan Ogden RC	2.00	.90
❑ 150 Lawrence Phillips RC	2.00	.90
❑ 151 Emmitt Smith	12.00	5.50
❑ 152 Brett Favre	15.00	6.75
❑ 153 Dan Marino	15.00	6.75
❑ 154 Jim Everett	.75	.35
❑ 155 Dave Brown	1.50	.70
❑ 156 Jeff Hostetler	1.50	.70
❑ 157 Heath Shuler	3.00	1.35
❑ 158 Daryl Johnston	1.50	.70
❑ 159 Terance Mathis	1.50	.70
❑ 160 Curtis Martin	6.00	2.70
❑ 161 Ray Zellars	.75	.35
❑ 162 Ricky Watters	1.50	.70
❑ 163 Chris Warren	1.50	.70
❑ 164 Larry Centers	1.50	.70
❑ 165 Steve McNair	6.00	2.70
❑ 166 Terry Kirby	1.50	.70
❑ 167 Rob Johnson	3.00	1.35

❑ 168 Dave Meggett .75 .35
❑ 169 Antonio Freeman 6.00 2.70
❑ 170 Marshall Faulk 3.00 1.35
❑ 171 Andre Hastings .15 .07
❑ 172 Stan Humphries 1.50 .70
❑ 173 Errict Rhett 1.50 .70
❑ 174 Michael Westbrook 3.00 1.35
❑ 175 Deion Sanders 5.00 2.20
❑ 176 Jeff George 1.50 .70
❑ 177 Cris Carter 3.00 1.35
❑ 178 Chris Sanders 1.50 .70
❑ 179 Ki-Jana Carter 1.50 .70
❑ 180 Kordell Stewart 5.00 2.20
❑ 181 Isaac Bruce 3.00 1.35
❑ 182 Terry Glenn RC 5.00 2.20
❑ 183 Garrison Hearst 1.50 .70
❑ 184 Erik Kramer .75 .35
❑ 185 Leeland McElroy RC 3.00 1.35
❑ 186 Rashaan Salaam 3.00 1.35
❑ 187 Kimble Anders .75 .35
❑ 188 Chad May .75 .35
❑ 189 Tony Martin 1.50 .70
❑ 190 J.J. Stokes 3.00 1.35
❑ 191 Darick Holmes 1.50 .70
❑ 192 Eric Moulds RC 8.00 3.60
❑ 193 Shannon Sharpe 1.50 .70
❑ 194 Tim Biakabutuka RC 4.00 1.80
❑ 195 Eddie George RC 15.00 6.75
❑ 196 Mike Alstott RC 6.00 2.70
❑ 197 Kerry Collins 3.00 1.35
❑ 198 Harvey Williams .75 .35
❑ 199 Herman Moore 3.00 1.35
❑ 200 Tyrone Wheatley 1.50 .70

1997 Playoff Absolute

	MINT	NRMT
COMPLETE SET (200)	100.00	45.00
COMP.GREEN SET (100)	25.00	11.00
COMMON GREEN (1-100)	.10	.05
COMMON BLUE (101-150)	.40	.18
COMMON RED (151-200)	.75	.35

❑ 1 Marcus Allen .45 .20
❑ 2 Eric Bieniemy .10 .05
❑ 3 Jason Dunn .10 .05
❑ 4 Jim Harbaugh .20 .09
❑ 5 Michael Westbrook .20 .09
❑ 6 Tiki Barber RC 1.50 .70
❑ 7 Frank Reich .10 .05
❑ 8 Irving Fryar .20 .09
❑ 9 Courtney Hawkins .10 .05
❑ 10 Eric Zeier .20 .09
❑ 11 Kent Graham .10 .05
❑ 12 Trent Dilfer .45 .20
❑ 13 Neil O'Donnell .20 .09
❑ 14 Reidel Anthony RC 1.00 .45
❑ 15 Jeff Hostetler .10 .05
❑ 16 Lawrence Phillips .10 .05
❑ 17 Dave Brown .10 .05
❑ 18 Mike Tomczak .10 .05
❑ 19 Jake Reed .20 .09
❑ 20 Anthony Miller .10 .05
❑ 21 Eric Metcalf .20 .09
❑ 22 Sedrick Shaw RC .45 .20
❑ 23 Anthony Johnson .10 .05
❑ 24 Mario Bates .10 .05
❑ 25 Dorsey Levens .45 .20
❑ 26 Stan Humphries .20 .09
❑ 27 Ben Coates .20 .09
❑ 28 Tyrone Wheatley .20 .09
❑ 29 Adrian Murrell .20 .09
❑ 30 William Henderson .10 .05
❑ 31 Warrick Dunn RC 1.50 .70
❑ 32 LeShon Johnson .10 .05
❑ 33 James O.Stewart .20 .09
❑ 34 Edgar Bennett .20 .09
❑ 35 Raymont Harris .10 .05
❑ 36 LeRoy Butler .10 .05
❑ 37 Darren Woodson .10 .05
❑ 38 Darnell Autry RC .20 .09
❑ 39 Johnnie Morton .20 .09
❑ 40 William Floyd .20 .09
❑ 41 Terrell Fletcher .10 .05
❑ 42 Leonard Russell .10 .05
❑ 43 Henry Ellard .10 .05
❑ 44 Terrell Owens .45 .20
❑ 45 John Friesz .10 .05
❑ 46 Antowain Smith RC 1.50 .70
❑ 47 Charles Johnson .20 .09
❑ 48 Rickey Dudley .20 .09
❑ 49 Lake Dawson .10 .05
❑ 50 Bert Emanuel .20 .09
❑ 51 Zach Thomas .20 .09
❑ 52 Earnest Byner .10 .05
❑ 53 Yatil Green RC .20 .09
❑ 54 Chris Spielman .10 .05
❑ 55 Muhsin Muhammad .20 .09
❑ 56 Bobby Engram .20 .09
❑ 57 Eric Bjornson .10 .05
❑ 58 Willie Green .10 .05
❑ 59 Derrick Mayes .20 .09
❑ 60 Chris Sanders .10 .05
❑ 61 Jimmy Smith .20 .09
❑ 62 Tony Gonzalez RC 1.50 .70
❑ 63 Rich Gannon .20 .09
❑ 64 Stanley Pritchett .10 .05
❑ 65 Brad Johnson .60 .25
❑ 66 Rodney Peete .10 .05
❑ 67 Sam Gash .10 .05
❑ 68 Chris Calloway .10 .05
❑ 69 Chris T. Jones .10 .05
❑ 70 Will Blackwell RC .45 .20
❑ 71 Mark Bruener .10 .05
❑ 72 Terry Kirby .20 .09
❑ 73 Brian Blades .10 .05
❑ 74 Craig Heyward .10 .05
❑ 75 Jamie Asher .10 .05
❑ 76 Terance Mathis .20 .09
❑ 77 Troy Davis RC .45 .20
❑ 78 Bruce Smith .20 .09
❑ 79 Simeon Rice .20 .09
❑ 80 Fred Barnett .10 .05
❑ 81 Tim Brown .45 .20
❑ 82 James Jett .20 .09
❑ 83 Mark Carrier WR .10 .05
❑ 84 Shawn Jefferson .10 .05
❑ 85 Ken Dilger .10 .05
❑ 86 Rae Carruth RC .45 .20
❑ 87 Keenan McCardell .20 .09
❑ 88 Michael Irvin .45 .20
❑ 89 Mark Chmura .20 .09
❑ 90 Derrick Alexander WR .20 .09
❑ 91 Andre Reed .20 .09
❑ 92 Ed McCaffrey .20 .09
❑ 93 Erik Kramer .10 .05
❑ 94 Albert Connell RC 2.00 .90
❑ 95 Frank Wycheck .10 .05
❑ 96 Zack Crockett .10 .05
❑ 97 Jim Everett .10 .05
❑ 98 Michael Haynes .10 .05
❑ 99 Jeff Graham .10 .05
❑ 100 Brent Jones .20 .09
❑ 101 Troy Aikman 3.00 1.35
❑ 102 Byron Hanspard RC .45 .20
❑ 103 Robert Brooks 1.00 .45
❑ 104 Karim Abdul-Jabbar 1.00 .45
❑ 105 Drew Bledsoe 3.00 1.35
❑ 106 Napoleon Kaufman 1.00 .45
❑ 107 Steve Young 2.50 1.10
❑ 108 Leeland McElroy .10 .05
❑ 109 Jamal Anderson 1.50 .70
❑ 110 David LaFleur RC 1.00 .45
❑ 111 Vinny Testaverde .60 .25
❑ 112 Eric Moulds 1.00 .45
❑ 113 Tim Biakabutuka 1.00 .45
❑ 114 Rick Mirer .60 .25
❑ 115 Jeff Blake 1.00 .45
❑ 116 Jim Schwantz RC .40 .18
❑ 117 Herman Moore 1.00 .45
❑ 118 Ike Hilliard RC 2.50 1.10
❑ 119 Reggie White 1.00 .45
❑ 120 Steve McNair 1.50 .70
❑ 121 Marshall Faulk 1.00 .45
❑ 122 Natrone Means 1.00 .45
❑ 123 Greg Hill .60 .25
❑ 124 O.J. McDuffie .60 .25
❑ 125 Robert Smith .60 .25
❑ 126 Bryant Westbrook RC 1.00 .45
❑ 127 Ray Zellars .40 .18
❑ 128 Rodney Hampton .60 .25
❑ 129 Wayne Chrebet .40 .18
❑ 130 Desmond Howard .60 .25
❑ 131 Ty Detmer .60 .25
❑ 132 Erric Pegram .40 .18
❑ 133 Yancey Thigpen .60 .25
❑ 134 Danny Wuerffel RC .60 .25
❑ 135 Charlie Jones .40 .18
❑ 136 Chris Warren .60 .25
❑ 137 Isaac Bruce 1.00 .45
❑ 138 Errict Rhett .60 .25
❑ 139 Gus Frerotte 1.00 .45
❑ 140 Frank Sanders .60 .25
❑ 141 Todd Collins .60 .25
❑ 142 Jake Plummer RC UER 12.00 5.50
(Height listed at 6'-24")
❑ 143 Damay Scott .60 .25
❑ 144 Rashaan Salaam 1.00 .45
❑ 145 Terrell Davis 6.00 2.70
❑ 146 Scott Mitchell .60 .25
❑ 147 Junior Seau 1.00 .45
❑ 148 Warren Moon .60 .25
❑ 149 Wesley Walls .40 .18
❑ 150 Daryl Johnston .60 .25
❑ 151 Brett Favre 12.00 5.50
❑ 152 Emmitt Smith 10.00 4.50
❑ 153 Dan Marino 12.00 5.50
❑ 154 Larry Centers 1.00 .45
❑ 155 Michael Jackson 1.00 .45
❑ 156 Kerry Collins .20 .09
❑ 157 Curtis Conway 1.00 .45
❑ 158 Peter Boulware RC 1.00 .45
❑ 159 Carl Pickens 1.50 .70
❑ 160 Shannon Sharpe 1.00 .45
❑ 161 Brett Perriman .75 .35
❑ 162 Eddie George 6.00 2.70
❑ 163 Mark Brunell 6.00 2.70
❑ 164 Tamarick Vanover 1.00 .45
❑ 165 Cris Carter 1.50 .70
❑ 166 Corey Dillon RC 12.00 5.50
❑ 167 Curtis Martin 3.00 1.35
❑ 168 Amani Toomer 1.00 .45
❑ 169 Jeff George 1.00 .45
❑ 170 Kordell Stewart 2.50 1.10
❑ 171 Garrison Hearst 1.00 .45
❑ 172 Tony Banks 1.00 .45
❑ 173 Mike Alstott 1.50 .70
❑ 174 Jim Druckenmiller RC .45 .20
❑ 175 Chris Chandler 1.00 .45
❑ 176 Byron Bam Morris .75 .35
❑ 177 Billy Joe Hobert 1.00 .45
❑ 178 Ernie Mills .75 .35
❑ 179 Ki-Jana Carter .75 .35
❑ 180 Deion Sanders 1.50 .70
❑ 181 Ricky Watters 1.00 .45
❑ 182 Shawn Springs RC 1.50 .70
❑ 183 Barry Sanders 12.00 5.50
❑ 184 Antonio Freeman 3.00 1.35
❑ 185 Marvin Harrison 1.50 .70
❑ 186 Elvis Grbac 1.00 .45
❑ 187 Terry Glenn 1.50 .70
❑ 188 Willie Roaf .75 .35
❑ 189 Keyshawn Johnson 1.50 .70
❑ 190 Orlando Pace RC 1.50 .70
❑ 191 Jerome Bettis 1.50 .70
❑ 192 Tony Martin 1.00 .45
❑ 193 Jerry Rice 6.00 2.70
❑ 194 Joey Galloway 2.50 1.10
❑ 195 Terry Allen 1.50 .70
❑ 196 Eddie Kennison 1.00 .45

Card	MINT	NRMT
❑ 197 Thurman Thomas	1.50	.70
❑ 198 Darrell Russell RC	.75	.35
❑ 199 Rob Moore	1.00	.45
❑ 200 John Elway	12.00	5.50

1998 Playoff Absolute Hobby

	MINT	NRMT
COMPLETE SET (200)	150.00	70.00
❑ 1 John Elway	10.00	4.50
❑ 2 Marcus Nash RC	5.00	2.20
❑ 3 Brian Griese RC	12.00	5.50
❑ 4 Terrell Davis	8.00	3.60
❑ 5 Rod Smith WR	1.00	.45
❑ 6 Shannon Sharpe	1.00	.45
❑ 7 Ed McCaffrey	1.00	.45
❑ 8 Brett Favre	10.00	4.50
❑ 9 Dorsey Levens	2.00	.90
❑ 10 Derrick Mayes	1.00	.45
❑ 11 Antonio Freeman	2.00	.90
❑ 12 Robert Brooks	1.00	.45
❑ 13 Mark Chmura	1.00	.45
❑ 14 Reggie White	2.00	.90
❑ 15 Kordell Stewart	2.00	.90
❑ 16 Hines Ward RC	3.00	1.35
❑ 17 Jerome Bettis	2.00	.90
❑ 18 Charles Johnson	.50	.23
❑ 19 Courtney Hawkins	.50	.23
❑ 20 Will Blackwell	.50	.23
❑ 21 Mark Bruener	.50	.23
❑ 22 Steve Young	4.00	1.80
❑ 23 Jim Druckenmiller	1.00	.45
❑ 24 Garrison Hearst	2.00	.90
❑ 25 R.W. McQuarters RC	2.00	.90
❑ 26 Marc Edwards	.50	.23
❑ 27 Irv Smith	.50	.23
❑ 28 Jerry Rice	5.00	2.20
❑ 29 Terrell Owens	2.00	.90
❑ 30 J.J. Stokes	1.00	.45
❑ 31 Elvis Grbac	1.00	.45
❑ 32 Rashaan Shehee RC	3.00	1.35
❑ 33 Donnell Bennett	.50	.23
❑ 34 Kimble Anders	1.00	.45
❑ 35 Ted Popson	.50	.23
❑ 36 Derrick Alexander WR	1.00	.45
❑ 37 Tony Gonzalez	.50	.23
❑ 38 Andre Rison	1.00	.45
❑ 39 Brad Johnson	2.00	.90
❑ 40 Randy Moss RC	25.00	11.00
❑ 41 Robert Smith	2.00	.90
❑ 42 Leroy Hoard	.50	.23
❑ 43 Cris Carter	2.00	.90
❑ 44 Jake Reed	1.00	.45
❑ 45 Drew Bledsoe	4.00	1.80
❑ 46 Tony Simmons RC	3.00	1.35
❑ 47 Chris Floyd RC	2.00	.90
❑ 48 Robert Edwards RC	6.00	2.70
❑ 49 Shawn Jefferson	.50	.23
❑ 50 Ben Coates	1.00	.45
❑ 51 Terry Glenn	2.00	.90
❑ 52 Trent Dilfer	2.00	.90
❑ 53 Jacquez Green RC	6.00	2.70
❑ 54 Warrick Dunn	2.00	.90
❑ 55 Mike Alstott	2.00	.90
❑ 56 Reidel Anthony	1.00	.45
❑ 57 Bert Emanuel	1.00	.45
❑ 58 Warren Sapp	1.00	.45
❑ 59 Charlie Batch RC	10.00	4.50
❑ 60 Germane Crowell RC	10.00	4.50
❑ 61 Scott Mitchell	1.00	.45
❑ 62 Barry Sanders	10.00	4.50
❑ 63 Tommy Vardell	.50	.23
❑ 64 Herman Moore	2.00	.90
❑ 65 Johnnie Morton	1.00	.45
❑ 66 Mark Brunell	4.00	1.80
❑ 67 Jonathan Quinn RC	3.00	1.35
❑ 68 Fred Taylor RC	10.00	4.50
❑ 69 James Stewart	1.00	.45
❑ 70 Jimmy Smith	1.00	.45
❑ 71 Damon Jones	.50	.23
❑ 72 Keenan McCardell	1.00	.45
❑ 73 Dan Marino	10.00	4.50
❑ 74 Larry Shannon RC	2.00	.90
❑ 75 John Avery RC	5.00	2.20
❑ 76 Troy Drayton	.50	.23
❑ 77 Stanley Pritchett	.50	.23
❑ 78 Karim Abdul-Jabbar	2.00	.90
❑ 79 O.J. McDuffie	1.00	.45
❑ 80 Yatil Green	.50	.23
❑ 81 Danny Kanell	1.00	.45
❑ 82 Tiki Barber	1.00	.45
❑ 83 Tyrone Wheatley	1.00	.45
❑ 84 Charles Way	.50	.23
❑ 85 Gary Brown	.50	.23
❑ 86 Brian Alford RC	3.00	1.35
❑ 87 Joe Jurevicius RC	3.00	1.35
❑ 88 Ike Hilliard	1.00	.45
❑ 89 Troy Aikman	5.00	2.20
❑ 90 Deion Sanders	2.00	.90
❑ 91 Emmitt Smith	8.00	3.60
❑ 92 Chris Warren	1.00	.45
❑ 93 Daryl Johnston	1.00	.45
❑ 94 Michael Irvin	2.00	.90
❑ 95 David LaFleur	.50	.23
❑ 96 Kevin Dyson RC	6.00	2.70
❑ 97 Steve McNair	2.00	.90
❑ 98 Eddie George	4.00	1.80
❑ 99 Yancey Thigpen	.50	.23
❑ 100 Frank Wycheck	.50	.23
❑ 101 Glenn Foley	1.00	.45
❑ 102 Vinny Testaverde	1.00	.45
❑ 103 Keyshawn Johnson	2.00	.90
❑ 104 Curtis Martin	2.00	.90
❑ 105 Keith Byars	.50	.23
❑ 106 Scott Frost RC	3.00	1.35
❑ 107 Wayne Chrebet	2.00	.90
❑ 108 Warren Moon	2.00	.90
❑ 109 Ahman Green RC	8.00	3.60
❑ 110 Steve Broussard	.50	.23
❑ 111 Ricky Watters	1.00	.45
❑ 112 Joey Galloway	2.00	.90
❑ 113 Mike Pritchard	.50	.23
❑ 114 Brian Blades	.50	.23
❑ 115 Gus Frerotte	.50	.23
❑ 116 Skip Hicks RC	5.00	2.20
❑ 117 Terry Allen	2.00	.90
❑ 118 Michael Westbrook	1.00	.45
❑ 119 Jamie Asher	.50	.23
❑ 120 Leslie Shepherd	.50	.23
❑ 121 Jeff Blake	1.00	.45
❑ 122 Corey Dillon	3.00	1.35
❑ 123 Carl Pickens	2.00	.90
❑ 124 Tony McGee	.50	.23
❑ 125 Darnay Scott	1.00	.45
❑ 126 Kerry Collins	1.00	.45
❑ 127 Fred Lane	1.00	.45
❑ 128 William Floyd	.50	.23
❑ 129 Rae Carruth	1.00	.45
❑ 130 Wesley Walls	1.00	.45
❑ 131 Muhsin Muhammad	1.00	.45
❑ 132 Jake Plummer	4.00	1.80
❑ 133 Adrian Murrell	1.00	.45
❑ 134 Michael Pittman RC	5.00	2.20
❑ 135 Larry Centers	.50	.23
❑ 136 Frank Sanders	1.00	.45
❑ 137 Rob Moore	1.00	.45
❑ 138 Andre Wadsworth RC	3.00	1.35
❑ 139 Mario Bates	1.00	.45
❑ 140 Chris Chandler	1.00	.45
❑ 141 Byron Hanspard	1.00	.45
❑ 142 Jamal Anderson	2.00	.90
❑ 143 Terance Mathis	1.00	.45
❑ 144 O.J. Santiago	.50	.23
❑ 145 Tony Martin	1.00	.45
❑ 146 Jammi German RC	2.00	.90
❑ 147 Jim Harbaugh	1.00	.45
❑ 148 Errict Rhett	1.00	.45
❑ 149 Michael Jackson	.50	.23
❑ 150 Pat Johnson RC	3.00	1.35
❑ 151 Eric Green	.50	.23
❑ 152 Doug Flutie	2.50	1.10
❑ 153 Rob Johnson	1.00	.45
❑ 154 Antowain Smith	2.00	.90
❑ 155 Bruce Smith	1.00	.45
❑ 156 Eric Moulds	2.00	.90
❑ 157 Andre Reed	1.00	.45
❑ 158 Erik Kramer	.50	.23
❑ 159 Darnell Autry	.50	.23
❑ 160 Edgar Bennett	.50	.23
❑ 161 Curtis Enis RC	5.00	2.20
❑ 162 Curtis Conway	1.00	.45
❑ 163 E.G. Green RC	3.00	1.35
❑ 164 Jerome Pathon RC	3.00	1.35
❑ 165 Peyton Manning RC	25.00	11.00
❑ 166 Marshall Faulk	2.00	.90
❑ 167 Zack Crockett	.50	.23
❑ 168 Ken Dilger	.50	.23
❑ 169 Marvin Harrison	1.00	.45
❑ 170 Danny Wuerffel	1.00	.45
❑ 171 Lamar Smith	1.00	.45
❑ 172 Ray Zellars	.50	.23
❑ 173 Qadry Ismail	.50	.23
❑ 174 Sean Dawkins	.50	.23
❑ 175 Andre Hastings	.50	.23
❑ 176 Jeff George	1.00	.45
❑ 177 Charles Woodson RC	6.00	2.70
❑ 178 Napoleon Kaufman	2.00	.90
❑ 179 Jon Ritchie RC	3.00	1.35
❑ 180 Desmond Howard	1.00	.45
❑ 181 Tim Brown	2.00	.90
❑ 182 James Jett	1.00	.45
❑ 183 Rickey Dudley	.50	.23
❑ 184 Bobby Hoying	1.00	.45
❑ 185 Rodney Peete	.50	.23
❑ 186 Charlie Garner	.50	.23
❑ 187 Irving Fryar	1.00	.45
❑ 188 Chris T. Jones	.50	.23
❑ 189 Jason Dunn	.50	.23
❑ 190 Tony Banks	1.00	.45
❑ 191 Robert Holcombe RC	5.00	2.20
❑ 192 Craig Heyward	.50	.23
❑ 193 Isaac Bruce	2.00	.90
❑ 194 Az-Zahir Hakim RC	5.00	2.20
❑ 195 Eddie Kennison	1.00	.45
❑ 196 Mikhael Ricks RC	3.00	1.35
❑ 197 Ryan Leaf RC	8.00	3.60
❑ 198 Natrone Means	2.00	.90
❑ 199 Junior Seau	1.00	.45
❑ 200 Freddie Jones	.50	.23

1999 Playoff Absolute EXP

	MINT	NRMT
COMPLETE SET (200)	50.00	22.00
❑ 1 Tim Couch RC	4.00	1.80
❑ 2 Donovan McNabb RC	5.00	2.20
❑ 3 Akili Smith RC	2.50	1.10
❑ 4 Edgerrin James RC	8.00	3.60

❑ 5 Ricky Williams RC	5.00	2.20
❑ 6 Torry Holt RC	3.00	1.35
❑ 7 Champ Bailey RC	1.50	.70
❑ 8 David Boston RC	2.50	1.10
❑ 9 Chris Claiborne RC	.50	.23
❑ 10 Chris McAlister RC	.75	.35
❑ 11 Daunte Culpepper RC	8.00	3.60
❑ 12 Cade McNown RC	1.50	.70
❑ 13 Troy Edwards RC	1.50	.70
❑ 14 Kevin Johnson RC	2.50	1.10
❑ 15 James Johnson RC	1.25	.55
❑ 16 Rob Konrad RC	1.25	.55
❑ 17 Jim Kleinsasser RC	1.25	.55
❑ 18 Kevin Faulk RC	2.00	.90
❑ 19 Joe Montgomery RC	1.25	.55
❑ 20 Shaun King RC	2.50	1.10
❑ 21 Peerless Price RC	1.50	.70
❑ 22 Mike Cloud RC	1.25	.55
❑ 23 Jermaine Fazande RC	1.25	.55
❑ 24 D'Wayne Bates RC	1.25	.55
❑ 25 Brock Huard RC	2.00	.90
❑ 26 Marty Booker RC	.75	.35
❑ 27 Karsten Bailey RC	.75	.35
❑ 28 Shawn Bryson RC	1.25	.55
❑ 29 Jeff Paulk RC	1.25	.55
❑ 30 Sedrick Irvin RC	1.25	.55
❑ 31 Craig Yeast RC	.75	.35
❑ 32 Joe Germaine RC	1.25	.55
❑ 33 Dameane Douglas RC	1.25	.55
❑ 34 Brandon Stokley RC	1.25	.55
❑ 35 Larry Parker RC	.75	.35
❑ 36 Wane McGarity RC	1.25	.55
❑ 37 Na Brown RC	1.25	.55
❑ 38 Cecil Collins RC	1.25	.55
❑ 39 Darrin Chiaverini RC	.75	.35
❑ 40 Madre Hill RC	.50	.23
❑ 41 Adrian Murrell	.30	.14
❑ 42 Jake Plummer	1.25	.55
❑ 43 Frank Sanders	.30	.14
❑ 44 Rob Moore	.30	.14
❑ 45 Andre Wadsworth	.15	.07
❑ 46 Simeon Rice	.15	.07
❑ 47 Eric Swann	.15	.07
❑ 48 Terance Mathis	.30	.14
❑ 49 Tim Dwight	.60	.25
❑ 50 Jamal Anderson	.60	.25
❑ 51 Chris Chandler	.30	.14
❑ 52 Chris Calloway	.15	.07
❑ 53 O.J. Santiago	.15	.07
❑ 54 Jermaine Lewis	.30	.14
❑ 55 Priest Holmes	.60	.25
❑ 56 Scott Mitchell	.15	.07
❑ 57 Tony Banks	.30	.14
❑ 58 Rod Woodson	.30	.14
❑ 59 Andre Reed	.30	.14
❑ 60 Thurman Thomas	.30	.14
❑ 61 Bruce Smith	.30	.14
❑ 62 Rob Johnson	.30	.14
❑ 63 Eric Moulds	.60	.25
❑ 64 Doug Flutie	.75	.35
❑ 65 Antowain Smith	.60	.25
❑ 66 Tim Biakabutuka	.30	.14
❑ 67 Muhsin Muhammad	.30	.14
❑ 68 Steve Beuerlein	.15	.07
❑ 69 Bobby Engram	.30	.14
❑ 70 Curtis Conway	.30	.14
❑ 71 Curtis Enis	.60	.25
❑ 72 Edgar Bennett	.15	.07
❑ 73 Jeff Blake	.30	.14
❑ 74 Darnay Scott	.15	.07
❑ 75 Carl Pickens	.30	.14
❑ 76 Corey Dillon	.60	.25
❑ 77 Ty Detmer	.30	.14
❑ 78 Leslie Shepherd	.15	.07
❑ 79 Sedrick Shaw	.15	.07
❑ 80 Rocket Ismail	.30	.14
❑ 81 Emmitt Smith	1.50	.70
❑ 82 Michael Irvin	.30	.14
❑ 83 Troy Aikman	1.50	.70
❑ 84 Deion Sanders	.60	.25
❑ 85 Darren Woodson	.15	.07
❑ 86 Chris Warren	.15	.07
❑ 87 John Elway	2.50	1.10
❑ 88 Brian Griese	1.25	.55
❑ 89 Shannon Sharpe	.30	.14
❑ 90 Terrell Davis	1.50	.70
❑ 91 Bubby Brister	.15	.07
❑ 92 Ed McCaffrey	.30	.14
❑ 93 Rod Smith	.30	.14
❑ 94 Germane Crowell	.30	.14
❑ 95 Johnnie Morton	.30	.14
❑ 96 Barry Sanders	2.50	1.10
❑ 97 Herman Moore	.60	.25
❑ 98 Charlie Batch	1.25	.55
❑ 99 Mark Chmura	.15	.07
❑ 100 Derrick Mayes	.15	.07
❑ 101 Dorsey Levens	.60	.25
❑ 102 Brett Favre	2.50	1.10
❑ 103 Antonio Freeman	.60	.25
❑ 104 Robert Brooks	.30	.14
❑ 105 Desmond Howard	.30	.14
❑ 106 Jerome Pathon	.15	.07
❑ 107 Marvin Harrison	.60	.25
❑ 108 Peyton Manning	2.50	1.10
❑ 109 E.G. Green	.15	.07
❑ 110 Tavian Banks	.15	.07
❑ 111 Keenan McCardell	.30	.14
❑ 112 Jimmy Smith	.30	.14
❑ 113 Mark Brunell	1.00	.45
❑ 114 Fred Taylor	1.50	.70
❑ 115 Byron Bam Morris	.15	.07
❑ 116 Andre Rison	.30	.14
❑ 117 Elvis Grbac	.30	.14
❑ 118 Warren Moon	.60	.25
❑ 119 Tony Gonzalez	.30	.14
❑ 120 Derrick Alexander WR	.30	.14
❑ 121 Rashaan Shehee	.15	.07
❑ 122 Zach Thomas	.30	.14
❑ 123 Oronde Gadsden	.15	.07
❑ 124 Dan Marino	2.50	1.10
❑ 125 Karim Abdul-Jabbar	.30	.14
❑ 126 O.J. McDuffie	.30	.14
❑ 127 Jake Reed	.30	.14
❑ 128 John Randle	.30	.14
❑ 129 Randy Moss	2.50	1.10
❑ 130 Cris Carter	.60	.25
❑ 131 Randall Cunningham	.60	.25
❑ 132 Robert Smith	.60	.25
❑ 133 Terry Glenn	.60	.25
❑ 134 Ben Coates	.30	.14
❑ 135 Drew Bledsoe	1.00	.45
❑ 136 Ty Law	.15	.07
❑ 137 Tony Simmons	.15	.07
❑ 138 Eddie Kennison	.30	.14
❑ 139 Cam Cleeland	.15	.07
❑ 140 Ike Hilliard	.15	.07
❑ 141 Joe Jurevicius	.15	.07
❑ 142 Gary Brown	.15	.07
❑ 143 Kerry Collins	.30	.14
❑ 144 Tiki Barber	.15	.07
❑ 145 Jason Sehorn	.15	.07
❑ 146 Dedric Ward	.15	.07
❑ 147 Vinny Testaverde	.30	.14
❑ 148 Wayne Chrebet	.30	.14
❑ 149 Curtis Martin	.60	.25
❑ 150 Keyshawn Johnson	.60	.25
❑ 151 James Jett	.30	.14
❑ 152 Napoleon Kaufman	.60	.25
❑ 153 Tim Brown	.60	.25
❑ 154 Charles Woodson	.60	.25
❑ 155 Rickey Dudley	.15	.07
❑ 156 Charles Johnson	.15	.07
❑ 157 Duce Staley	.60	.25
❑ 158 Chris Fuamatu-Ma'afala	.15	.07
❑ 159 Jerome Bettis	.60	.25
❑ 160 Kordell Stewart	.60	.25
❑ 161 Levon Kirkland	.15	.07
❑ 162 Hines Ward	.15	.07
❑ 163 Mikhael Ricks	.15	.07
❑ 164 Natrone Means	.30	.14
❑ 165 Ryan Leaf	.60	.25
❑ 166 Jim Harbaugh	.30	.14
❑ 167 Junior Seau	.30	.14
❑ 168 Steve Young	1.00	.45
❑ 169 J.J. Stokes	.30	.14
❑ 170 Terrell Owens	.60	.25
❑ 171 Jerry Rice	1.50	.70
❑ 172 Garrison Hearst	.30	.14
❑ 173 Ricky Watters	.30	.14
❑ 174 Jon Kitna	.60	.25
❑ 175 Joey Galloway	.60	.25
❑ 176 Ahman Green	.30	.14
❑ 177 Isaac Bruce	.60	.25
❑ 178 Marshall Faulk	.60	.25
❑ 179 Trent Green	.30	.14
❑ 180 Amp Lee	.15	.07
❑ 181 Greg Hill	.15	.07
❑ 182 Warren Sapp	.15	.07
❑ 183 Hardy Nickerson	.15	.07
❑ 184 Trent Dilfer	.30	.14
❑ 185 Reidel Anthony	.30	.14
❑ 186 Jacquez Green	.30	.14
❑ 187 Warrick Dunn	.60	.25
❑ 188 Mike Alstott	.60	.25
❑ 189 Kevin Dyson	.30	.14
❑ 190 Eddie George	.75	.35
❑ 191 Yancey Thigpen	.15	.07
❑ 192 Steve McNair	.60	.25
❑ 193 Chris Sanders	.15	.07
❑ 194 Frank Wycheck	.15	.07
❑ 195 Darrell Green	.15	.07
❑ 196 Stephen Alexander	.15	.07
❑ 197 Albert Connell	.15	.07
❑ 198 Michael Westbrook	.30	.14
❑ 199 Brad Johnson	.60	.25
❑ 200 Skip Hicks	.60	.25

1999 Playoff Absolute SSD

	MINT	NRMT
COMPLETE SET (200)	250.00	110.00
❑ 1 Rob Moore	.75	.35
❑ 2 Frank Sanders	.75	.35
❑ 3 Jake Plummer	3.00	1.35
❑ 4 Adrian Murrell	.75	.35
❑ 5 Chris Chandler	.75	.35
❑ 6 Jamal Anderson	1.50	.70
❑ 7 Tim Dwight	1.50	.70
❑ 8 Terance Mathis	.75	.35
❑ 9 Priest Holmes	1.50	.70
❑ 10 Jermaine Lewis	.75	.35
❑ 11 Antowain Smith	1.50	.70
❑ 12 Doug Flutie	2.00	.90
❑ 13 Eric Moulds	1.50	.70
❑ 14 Muhsin Muhammad	.75	.35
❑ 15 Tim Biakabutuka	.75	.35
❑ 16 Curtis Enis	1.50	.70
❑ 17 Curtis Conway	.75	.35
❑ 18 Bobby Engram	.75	.35
❑ 19 Corey Dillon	1.50	.70
❑ 20 Carl Pickens	.75	.35
❑ 21 Darnay Scott	.40	.18
❑ 22 Sedrick Shaw	.40	.18
❑ 23 Leslie Shepherd	.40	.18
❑ 24 Ty Detmer	.75	.35
❑ 25 Deion Sanders	1.50	.70
❑ 26 Troy Aikman	4.00	1.80
❑ 27 Michael Irvin	.75	.35
❑ 28 Emmitt Smith	4.00	1.80
❑ 29 Rocket Ismail	.75	.35
❑ 30 Rod Smith WR	.75	.35
❑ 31 Ed McCaffrey	.75	.35
❑ 32 Bubby Brister	.40	.18
❑ 33 Terrell Davis	4.00	1.80
❑ 34 Shannon Sharpe	.75	.35
❑ 35 Brian Griese	3.00	1.35
❑ 36 John Elway	6.00	2.70
❑ 37 Charlie Batch	3.00	1.35

❑ 38 Herman Moore 1.50 .70
❑ 39 Barry Sanders 6.00 2.70
❑ 40 Johnnie Morton .75 .35
❑ 41 Antonio Freeman 1.50 .70
❑ 42 Brett Favre 6.00 2.70
❑ 43 Dorsey Levens 1.50 .70
❑ 44 Derrick Mayes .75 .35
❑ 45 Mark Chmura .40 .18
❑ 46 Peyton Manning 6.00 2.70
❑ 47 Marvin Harrison 1.50 .70
❑ 48 Jerome Pathon .40 .18
❑ 49 Fred Taylor 4.00 1.80
❑ 50 Mark Brunell 2.50 1.10
❑ 51 Jimmy Smith .75 .35
❑ 52 Keenan McCardell .75 .35
❑ 53 Elvis Grbac .75 .35
❑ 54 Andre Rison .75 .35
❑ 55 Byron Bam Morris .40 .18
❑ 56 O.J. McDuffie .75 .35
❑ 57 Karim Abdul-Jabbar .75 .35
❑ 58 Dan Marino 6.00 2.70
❑ 59 Oronde Gadsden .40 .18
❑ 60 Robert Smith 1.50 .70
❑ 61 Randall Cunningham 1.50 .70
❑ 62 Cris Carter 1.50 .70
❑ 63 Randy Moss 6.00 2.70
❑ 64 Drew Bledsoe 2.50 1.10
❑ 65 Ben Coates .75 .35
❑ 66 Terry Glenn 1.50 .70
❑ 67 Cam Cleeland .40 .18
❑ 68 Eddie Kennison .75 .35
❑ 69 Kerry Collins .75 .35
❑ 70 Gary Brown .40 .18
❑ 71 Joe Jurevicius .40 .18
❑ 72 Ike Hilliard .40 .18
❑ 73 Keyshawn Johnson 1.50 .70
❑ 74 Curtis Martin 1.50 .70
❑ 75 Wayne Chrebet .75 .35
❑ 76 Tim Brown 1.50 .70
❑ 77 Napoleon Kaufman 1.50 .70
❑ 78 James Jett .75 .35
❑ 79 Duce Staley 1.50 .70
❑ 80 Charles Johnson .40 .18
❑ 81 Kordell Stewart 1.50 .70
❑ 82 Jerome Bettis 1.50 .70
❑ 83 Chris Fuamatu-Ma'afala .40 .18
❑ 84 Jim Harbaugh .75 .35
❑ 85 Ryan Leaf 1.50 .70
❑ 86 Natrone Means .75 .35
❑ 87 Mikhael Ricks .40 .18
❑ 88 Garrison Hearst .75 .35
❑ 89 Jerry Rice 4.00 1.80
❑ 90 Terrell Owens 1.50 .70
❑ 91 J.J. Stokes .75 .35
❑ 92 Steve Young 2.50 1.10
❑ 93 Joey Galloway 1.50 .70
❑ 94 Jon Kitna 1.50 .70
❑ 95 Ricky Watters .75 .35
❑ 96 Trent Green .75 .35
❑ 97 Marshall Faulk 1.50 .70
❑ 98 Isaac Bruce 1.50 .70
❑ 99 Mike Alstott 1.50 .70
❑ 100 Warrick Dunn 1.50 .70
❑ 101 Jacquez Green .75 .35
❑ 102 Reidel Anthony .75 .35
❑ 103 Trent Dilfer .75 .35
❑ 104 Steve McNair 1.50 .70
❑ 105 Yancey Thigpen .40 .18
❑ 106 Eddie George 2.00 .90
❑ 107 Kevin Dyson .75 .35
❑ 108 Skip Hicks 1.50 .70
❑ 109 Brad Johnson 1.50 .70
❑ 110 Michael Westbrook .75 .35
❑ 111 Thurman Thomas CA 4.00 1.80
❑ 112 Andre Reed CA 4.00 1.80
❑ 113 Emmitt Smith CA 10.00 4.50
❑ 114 Troy Aikman CA 10.00 4.50
❑ 115 Deion Sanders CA 5.00 2.20
❑ 116 John Elway CA 15.00 6.75
❑ 117 Terrell Davis CA 10.00 4.50
❑ 118 Barry Sanders CA 15.00 6.75
❑ 119 Brett Favre CA 15.00 6.75
❑ 120 Warren Moon CA 5.00 2.20
❑ 121 Dan Marino CA 15.00 6.75
❑ 122 Cris Carter CA 5.00 2.20
❑ 124 Tim Brown CA 5.00 2.20
❑ 125 Jerome Bettis CA 4.00 1.80
❑ 126 Junior Seau CA 4.00 1.80
❑ 127 Jerry Rice CA 10.00 4.50
❑ 127 Vinny Testaverde CA 4.00 1.80
❑ 128 Steve Young CA 6.00 2.70
❑ 129 Eddie George CA 5.00 2.20
❑ 130 Cardinals CL 3.00 1.35
Rob Moore
Jake Plummer
Adrian Murrell
Frank Sanders
David Boston
❑ 131 Falcons CL 3.00 1.35
Jamal Anderson
Chris Chandler
Terance Mathis
Tim Dwight
Jeff Paulk
❑ 132 Ravens CL 3.00 1.35
Priest Holmes
Chris McAllister
Jermaine Lewis
Brandon Stokely
❑ 133 Bills CL 4.00 1.80
Antowain Smith
Thurman Thomas
Shawn Bryson
Doug Flutie
Andre Reed
Eric Moulds
Peerless Price
❑ 134 Panthers CL 3.00 1.35
Tim Biakabutuka
Muhsin Muhammad
❑ 135 Bears CL 3.00 1.35
Curtis Enis
Curtis Conway
Bobby Engram
Cade McNown
Marty Booker
D'Wayne Bates
❑ 136 Bengals CL 4.00 1.80
Corey Dillon
Carl Pickens
Akili Smith
Darnay Scott
Craig Yeast
❑ 137 Browns CL 8.00 3.60
Sedrick Shaw
Tim Couch
Madre Hill
Leslie Shepard
Kevin Johnson
Ty Detmer
Darrin Chiaverini
❑ 138 Cowboys CL 8.00 3.60
Emmitt Smith
Michael Irvin
Deion Sanders
Wane McGarity
Rocket Ismail
Troy Aikman
❑ 139 Broncos CL 8.00 3.60
John Elway
Terrell Davis
Bubby Brister
Ed McCaffrey
Rod Smith
Brian Griese
Shannon Sharpe
❑ 140 Lions CL 8.00 3.60
Barry Sanders
Charlie Batch
Herman Moore
Chris Claiborne
Sedrick Irvin
❑ 141 Packers CL 8.00 3.60
Brett Favre
Dorsey Levens
Derrick Mayes
Mark Chmura
Antonio Freeman
❑ 142 Colts CL 8.00 3.60
Peyton Manning
Jerome Pathon
Marvin Harrison
Edgerrin James
❑ 143 Jaguars CL 4.00 1.80
Mark Brunell
Fred Taylor
Jimmy Smith
Keenan McCardell
❑ 144 Chiefs CL 3.00 1.35
Andre Rison
Elvis Grbac
Warren Moon
Michael Cloud
Byron Bam Morris
Larry Parker
❑ 145 Dolphins CL 4.00 1.80
Dan Marino
Rob Konrad
Cecil Collins
James Johnson
❑ 146 Vikings CL 8.00 3.60
Randy Moss
Robert Smith
Jim Kleinsasser
Randall Cunningham
Cris Carter
Daunte Culpepper
❑ 147 Patriots CL 3.00 1.35
Drew Bledsoe
Terry Glenn
Ben Coates
Kevin Faulk
❑ 148 Saints CL 8.00 3.60
Ricky Williams
Eddie Kennison
Cam Cleeland
❑ 149 Giants CL 3.00 1.35
Kerry Collins
Gary Brown
Joe Jurevicius
Ike Hilliard
Joe Montgomery
❑ 150 Jets CL 4.00 1.80
Keyshawn Johnson
Wayne Chrebet
Curtis Martin
Vinny Testaverde
❑ 151 Raiders CL 4.00 1.80
Tim Brown
Napoleon Kaufman
James Jett
Dameane Douglas
❑ 152 Eagles CL 8.00 3.60
Duce Staley
Donovan McNabb
Na Brown
Charles Johnson
❑ 153 Steelers CL 3.00 1.35
Kordell Stewart
Jerome Bettis
Chris Fuamatu-Ma'afala
Troy Edwards
❑ 154 Chargers CL 3.00 1.35
Jim Harbough
Michael Ricks
Ryan Leaf
Junior Seau
Natrone Means
Jermaine Fazande
❑ 155 49ers CL 8.00 3.60
Steve Young
Jerry Rice
Terrell Owens
J.J. Stokes
❑ 156 Seahawks CL 3.00 1.35
Joey Galloway
Jon Kitna
Ricky Watters
Brock Huard
Karsten Bailey
❑ 157 Rams CL 4.00 1.80
Trent Green
Torry Holt
Marshall Faulk
Isaac Bruce
Joe Germaine
❑ 158 Buccaneers CL 4.00 1.80
Mike Alstott

Card	Mint	NrMt
Warrick Dunn		
Reidel Anthony		
Jacquez Green		
Trent Dilfer		
Shaun King		
❑ 159 Titans CL	4.00	1.80
Eddie George		
Yancy Thigpen		
Kevin Dyson		
Steve McNair		
❑ 160 Redskins CL	4.00	1.80
Brad Johnson		
Champ Bailey		
Skip Hicks		
Michael Westbrook		
❑ 161 Tim Couch RC	8.00	3.60
❑ 162 Donovan McNabb RC	10.00	4.50
❑ 163 Akili Smith RC	5.00	2.20
❑ 164 Edgerrin James RC	15.00	6.75
❑ 165 Ricky Williams RC	10.00	4.50
❑ 166 Torry Holt RC	6.00	2.70
❑ 167 Champ Bailey RC	3.00	1.35
❑ 168 David Boston RC	5.00	2.20
❑ 169 Chris Claiborne RC	1.00	.45
❑ 170 Chris McAlister RC	1.50	.70
❑ 171 Daunte Culpepper RC	15.00	6.75
❑ 172 Cade McNown RC	3.00	1.35
❑ 173 Troy Edwards RC	3.00	1.35
❑ 174 Kevin Johnson RC	5.00	2.20
❑ 175 James Johnson RC	2.50	1.10
❑ 176 Rob Konrad RC	2.50	1.10
❑ 177 Jim Kleinsasser RC	2.50	1.10
❑ 178 Kevin Faulk RC	4.00	1.80
❑ 179 Joe Montgomery RC	2.50	1.10
❑ 180 Shaun King RC	5.00	2.20
❑ 181 Peerless Price RC	3.00	1.35
❑ 182 Mike Cloud RC	2.50	1.10
❑ 183 Jermaine Fazande RC	2.50	1.10
❑ 184 D'Wayne Bates RC	2.50	1.10
❑ 185 Brock Huard RC	4.00	1.80
❑ 186 Marty Booker RC	1.50	.70
❑ 187 Karsten Bailey RC	1.50	.70
❑ 188 Shawn Bryson RC	2.50	1.10
❑ 189 Jeff Paulk RC	2.50	1.10
❑ 190 Sedrick Irvin RC	2.50	1.10
❑ 191 Craig Yeast RC	1.50	.70
❑ 192 Joe Germaine RC	2.50	1.10
❑ 193 Dameane Douglas RC	2.50	1.10
❑ 194 Brandon Stokley RC	2.50	1.10
❑ 195 Larry Parker RC	1.50	.70
❑ 196 Wane McGarity RC	1.50	.70
❑ 197 Na Brown RC	2.50	1.10
❑ 198 Cecil Collins RC	2.50	1.10
❑ 199 Darrin Chiaverini RC	1.50	.70
❑ 200 Madre Hill RC	1.00	.45

2000 Playoff Absolute

	MINT	NRMT
COMPLETE SET (250)	250.00	110.00
❑ 1 Frank Sanders	.30	.14
❑ 2 Rob Moore	.30	.14
❑ 3 Jake Plummer	.60	.25
❑ 4 David Boston	.60	.25
❑ 5 Chris Chandler	.30	.14
❑ 6 Tim Dwight	.60	.25
❑ 7 Terance Mathis	.30	.14
❑ 8 Jamal Anderson	.60	.25
❑ 9 Priest Holmes	.30	.14
❑ 10 Tony Banks	.30	.14
❑ 11 Jermaine Lewis	.15	.07
❑ 12 Qadry Ismail	.15	.07
❑ 13 Brandon Stokley	.15	.07
❑ 14 Shannon Sharpe	.30	.14
❑ 15 Trent Dilfer	.30	.14
❑ 16 Eric Moulds	.60	.25
❑ 17 Doug Flutie	.75	.35
❑ 18 Antowain Smith	.30	.14
❑ 19 Jonathan Linton	.15	.07
❑ 20 Peerless Price	.60	.25
❑ 21 Rob Johnson	.30	.14
❑ 22 Muhsin Muhammad	.30	.14
❑ 23 Wesley Walls	.15	.07
❑ 24 Tim Biakabutuka	.30	.14
❑ 25 Steve Beuerlein	.30	.14
❑ 26 Patrick Jeffers	.60	.25
❑ 27 Natrone Means	.15	.07
❑ 28 Curtis Enis	.30	.14
❑ 29 Bobby Engram	.30	.14
❑ 30 Marcus Robinson	.60	.25
❑ 31 Marty Booker	.15	.07
❑ 32 Cade McNown	.60	.25
❑ 33 Darnay Scott	.30	.14
❑ 34 Carl Pickens	.30	.14
❑ 35 Corey Dillon	.60	.25
❑ 36 Akili Smith	.60	.25
❑ 37 Michael Basnight	.15	.07
❑ 38 Karim Abdul-Jabbar	.30	.14
❑ 39 Tim Couch	1.25	.55
❑ 40 Kevin Johnson	.60	.25
❑ 41 Darrin Chiaverini	.15	.07
❑ 42 Errict Rhett	.30	.14
❑ 43 Emmitt Smith	1.50	.70
❑ 44 Michael Irvin	.30	.14
❑ 45 Rocket Ismail	.30	.14
❑ 46 Troy Aikman	1.50	.70
❑ 47 Jason Tucker	.30	.14
❑ 48 Randall Cunningham	.60	.25
❑ 49 Joey Galloway	.60	.25
❑ 50 Ed McCaffrey	.60	.25
❑ 51 Rod Smith	.30	.14
❑ 52 Brian Griese	.75	.35
❑ 53 John Elway	2.50	1.10
❑ 54 Terrell Davis	1.50	.70
❑ 55 Olandis Gary	.60	.25
❑ 56 Johnnie Morton	.30	.14
❑ 57 Charlie Batch	.60	.25
❑ 58 Barry Sanders	2.00	.90
❑ 59 Germane Crowell	.30	.14
❑ 60 Herman Moore	.30	.14
❑ 61 James Stewart	.30	.14
❑ 62 Corey Bradford	.15	.07
❑ 63 Dorsey Levens	.30	.14
❑ 64 Antonio Freeman	.60	.25
❑ 65 Brett Favre	2.50	1.10
❑ 66 Bill Schroeder	.30	.14
❑ 67 Marvin Harrison	.60	.25
❑ 68 Peyton Manning	1.50	.70
❑ 69 Terrence Wilkins	.60	.25
❑ 70 Edgerrin James	2.50	1.10
❑ 71 Keenan McCardell	.30	.14
❑ 72 Mark Brunell	1.00	.45
❑ 73 Fred Taylor	.75	.35
❑ 74 Jimmy Smith	.30	.14
❑ 75 Elvis Grbac	.30	.14
❑ 76 Tony Gonzalez	.30	.14
❑ 77 Donnell Bennett	.15	.07
❑ 78 Warren Moon	.60	.25
❑ 79 Kimble Anders	.15	.07
❑ 80 Dan Marino	2.50	1.10
❑ 81 O.J. McDuffie	.30	.14
❑ 82 Tony Martin	.30	.14
❑ 83 James Johnson	.30	.14
❑ 84 Thurman Thomas	.30	.14
❑ 85 Randy Moss	1.50	.70
❑ 86 Cris Carter	.60	.25
❑ 87 Robert Smith	.60	.25
❑ 88 Daunte Culpepper	1.25	.55
❑ 89 Terry Glenn	.30	.14
❑ 90 Drew Bledsoe	1.00	.45
❑ 91 Kevin Faulk	.30	.14
❑ 92 Ricky Williams	1.50	.70
❑ 93 Jeff Blake	.30	.14
❑ 94 Jake Reed	.30	.14
❑ 95 Amani Toomer	.30	.14
❑ 96 Kerry Collins	.30	.14
❑ 97 Tiki Barber	.15	.07
❑ 98 Ike Hilliard	.30	.14
❑ 99 Curtis Martin	.60	.25
❑ 100 Vinny Testaverde	.30	.14
❑ 101 Wayne Chrebet	.30	.14
❑ 102 Ray Lucas	.60	.25
❑ 103 Tyrone Wheatley	.30	.14
❑ 104 Napoleon Kaufman	.30	.14
❑ 105 Tim Brown	.60	.25
❑ 106 Rich Gannon	.30	.14
❑ 107 Duce Staley	.60	.25
❑ 108 Donovan McNabb	1.00	.45
❑ 109 Kordell Stewart	.60	.25
❑ 110 Jerome Bettis	.60	.25
❑ 111 Troy Edwards	.30	.14
❑ 112 Junior Seau	.30	.14
❑ 113 Jim Harbaugh	.30	.14
❑ 114 Ryan Leaf	.60	.25
❑ 115 Jermaine Fazande	.15	.07
❑ 116 Curtis Conway	.30	.14
❑ 117 Terrell Owens	.60	.25
❑ 118 Charlie Garner	.30	.14
❑ 119 Jerry Rice	1.50	.70
❑ 120 Steve Young	1.00	.45
❑ 121 Jeff Garcia	.60	.25
❑ 122 Derrick Mayes	.30	.14
❑ 123 Ricky Watters	.30	.14
❑ 124 Jon Kitna	.60	.25
❑ 125 Sean Dawkins	.15	.07
❑ 126 Az-Zahir Hakim	.30	.14
❑ 127 Isaac Bruce	.60	.25
❑ 128 Marshall Faulk	.75	.35
❑ 129 Trent Green	.15	.07
❑ 130 Kurt Warner	2.50	1.10
❑ 131 Torry Holt	.60	.25
❑ 132 Jacquez Green	.30	.14
❑ 133 Warren Sapp	.30	.14
❑ 134 Mike Alstott	.60	.25
❑ 135 Warrick Dunn	.60	.25
❑ 136 Shaun King	1.00	.45
❑ 137 Keyshawn Johnson	.60	.25
❑ 138 Eddie George	.75	.35
❑ 139 Yancey Thigpen	.15	.07
❑ 140 Steve McNair	.60	.25
❑ 141 Kevin Dyson	.30	.14
❑ 142 Frank Wycheck	.15	.07
❑ 143 Jevon Kearse	.60	.25
❑ 144 Stephen Davis	.60	.25
❑ 145 Brad Johnson	.60	.25
❑ 146 Michael Westbrook	.30	.14
❑ 147 Albert Connell	.15	.07
❑ 148 Bruce Smith	.30	.14
❑ 149 Jeff George	.30	.14
❑ 150 Deion Sanders	.60	.25
❑ 151 Peter Warrick RC	12.00	5.50
❑ 152 Courtney Brown RC	5.00	2.20
❑ 153 Plaxico Burress RC	8.00	3.60
❑ 154 Corey Simon RC	6.00	2.70
❑ 155 Thomas Jones RC	6.00	2.70
❑ 156 Travis Taylor RC	5.00	2.20
❑ 157 Shaun Alexander RC	10.00	4.50
❑ 158 Chris Redman RC	8.00	3.60
❑ 159 Chad Pennington RC	12.00	5.50
❑ 160 Jamal Lewis RC	20.00	9.00
❑ 161 Brian Urlacher RC	12.00	5.50
❑ 162 Bubba Franks RC	5.00	2.20
❑ 163 Dez White RC	3.00	1.35
❑ 164 Ahmed Plummer RC	4.00	1.80
❑ 165 Ron Dayne RC	12.00	5.50
❑ 166 Shaun Ellis RC	3.00	1.35
❑ 167 Sylvester Morris RC	8.00	3.60
❑ 168 Deltha O'Neal RC	3.00	1.35
❑ 169 R.Jay Soward RC	4.00	1.80
❑ 170 Sherrod Gideon RC	2.00	.90
❑ 171 John Abraham RC	3.00	1.35
❑ 172 Travis Prentice RC	6.00	2.70
❑ 173 Darrell Jackson RC	6.00	2.70
❑ 174 Giovanni Carmazzi RC	5.00	2.20
❑ 175 Anthony Lucas RC	2.00	.90
❑ 176 Danny Farmer RC	4.00	1.80
❑ 177 Dennis Northcutt RC	5.00	2.20
❑ 178 Troy Walters RC	4.00	1.80
❑ 179 Laveranues Coles RC	6.00	2.70

❑ 180 Kwame Cavil RC 3.00 1.35
❑ 181 Tee Martin RC 6.00 2.70
❑ 182 J.R. Redmond RC 5.00 2.20
❑ 183 Tim Rattay RC 6.00 2.70
❑ 184 Jerry Porter RC 4.00 1.80
❑ 185 Sebastian Janikowski RC 4.00 1.80
❑ 186 Michael Wiley RC 4.00 1.80
❑ 187 Reuben Droughns RC .. 4.00 1.80
❑ 188 Trung Canidate RC 4.00 1.80
❑ 189 Shyrone Stith RC 3.00 1.35
❑ 190 Ian Gold RC 3.00 1.35
❑ 191 Hank Poteat RC 3.00 1.35
❑ 192 Darren Howard RC 3.00 1.35
❑ 193 Rob Morris RC 3.00 1.35
❑ 194 Marc Bulger RC 4.00 1.80
❑ 195 Tom Brady RC 4.00 1.80
❑ 196 Doug Johnson RC 4.00 1.80
❑ 197 Todd Husak RC 4.00 1.80
❑ 198 Gari Scott RC 3.00 1.35
❑ 199 Erron Kinney RC 4.00 1.80
❑ 200 Nate Webster RC .... 2.00 .90
❑ 201 Anthony Becht RC 4.00 1.80
❑ 202 Sammy Morris RC 5.00 2.20
❑ 203 Rondell Mealey RC .... 2.00 .90
❑ 204 Doug Chapman RC 8.00 3.60
❑ 205 Rogers Beckett RC 3.00 1.35
❑ 206 Ron Dugans RC 3.00 1.35
❑ 207 Deon Dyer RC 3.00 1.35
❑ 208 Marcus Knight RC .... 2.00 .90
❑ 209 Thomas Hamner RC 3.00 1.35
❑ 210 Joe Hamilton RC 5.00 2.20
❑ 211 Todd Pinkston RC 4.00 1.80
❑ 212 Chris Cole RC 3.00 1.35
❑ 213 Ron Dixon RC 5.00 2.20
❑ 214 JaJuan Dawson RC 4.00 1.80
❑ 215 Terrelle Smith RC 3.00 1.35
❑ 216 Curtis Keaton RC 3.00 1.35
❑ 217 Keith Bulluck RC 3.00 1.35
❑ 218 John Engelberger RC .. 3.00 1.35
❑ 219 Raynoch Thompson RC 3.00 1.35
❑ 220 Cornelius Griffin RC 3.00 1.35
❑ 221 William Bartee RC 3.00 1.35
❑ 222 Fred Robbins RC .... 2.00 .90
❑ 223 Dwayne Goodrich RC .. 2.00 .90
❑ 224 Deon Grant RC .... 2.00 .90
❑ 225 Jacoby Shepherd RC .. 3.00 1.35
❑ 226 Ben Kelly RC .... 2.00 .90
❑ 227 Corey Moore RC 3.00 1.35
❑ 228 Aaron Shea RC 3.00 1.35
❑ 229 Trevor Gaylor RC 3.00 1.35
❑ 230 Frank Moreau RC 4.00 1.80
❑ 231 Avion Black RC 3.00 1.35
❑ 232 Paul Smith RC 3.00 1.35
❑ 233 Dante Hall RC 3.00 1.35
❑ 234 Muneer Moore RC .... 2.00 .90
❑ 235 James Whalen RC .... 2.00 .90
❑ 236 Chad Morton RC 4.00 1.80
❑ 237 Frank Murphy RC .... 2.00 .90
❑ 238 Mareno Philyaw RC .... 2.00 .90
❑ 239 James Williams RC 3.00 1.35
❑ 240 Mike Anderson RC 20.00 9.00
❑ 241 Jarious Jackson RC 4.00 1.80
❑ 242 Demario Brown RC 3.00 1.35
❑ 243 Chris Coleman RC 4.00 1.80
❑ 244 Rashard Anderson RC 3.00 1.35
❑ 245 John Jones RC 3.00 1.35
❑ 246 Erik Flowers RC 4.00 1.80
❑ 247 JaJuan Seider RC .... 2.00 .90
❑ 248 Leon Murray RC .... 2.00 .90
❑ 249 Bashir Yamini RC 3.00 1.35
❑ 250 Na'il Diggs RC 4.00 1.80

1993 Playoff Contenders

	MINT	NRMT
COMPLETE SET (150)	20.00	9.00

❑ 1 Brett Favre 3.00 1.35
❑ 2 Thurman Thomas .... .40 .18
❑ 3 Barry Word .... .10 .05
❑ 4 Herman Moore .... .75 .35
❑ 5 Reggie Langhorne .... .10 .05
❑ 6 Wilber Marshall .... .10 .05
❑ 7 Ricky Watters .... .40 .18

❑ 8 Marcus Allen .... .40 .18
❑ 9 Jeff Hostetler .... .20 .09
❑ 10 Steve Young .... 1.00 .45
❑ 11 Bobby Hebert .... .10 .05
❑ 12 David Klingler .... .10 .05
❑ 13 Craig Heyward .... .20 .09
❑ 14 Andre Reed .... .20 .09
❑ 15 Tommy Vardell .... .10 .05
❑ 16 Anthony Carter .... .20 .09
❑ 17 Mel Gray .... .20 .09
❑ 18 Dan Marino 2.50 1.10
❑ 19 Haywood Jeffires .... .20 .09
❑ 20 Joe Montana 2.50 1.10
❑ 21 Tim Brown .... .40 .18
❑ 22 Jim McMahon .... .10 .05
❑ 23 Scott Mitchell .... .40 .18
❑ 24 Rickey Jackson .... .10 .05
❑ 25 Troy Aikman .... 1.50 .70
❑ 26 Rodney Hampton .... .40 .18
❑ 27 Fred Barnett .... .20 .09
❑ 28 Gary Clark .... .20 .09
❑ 29 Barry Foster .... .20 .09
❑ 30 Brian Blades .... .20 .09
❑ 31 Tim McDonald .... .10 .05
❑ 32 Kelvin Martin .... .10 .05
❑ 33 Henry Jones .... .10 .05
❑ 34 Erric Pegram .... .20 .09
❑ 35 Don Beebe .... .10 .05
❑ 36 Eric Metcalf .... .20 .09
❑ 37 Charles Haley .... .20 .09
❑ 38 Robert Delpino .... .10 .05
❑ 39 Leonard Russell UER .... .20 .09
(Detroit Lions logo on back)
❑ 40 Jackie Harris .... .10 .05
❑ 41 Ernest Givins .... .20 .09
❑ 42 Willie Davis .... .40 .18
❑ 43 Alexander Wright .... .10 .05
❑ 44 Keith Byars .... .10 .05
❑ 45 Dave Meggett .... .10 .05
❑ 46 Johnny Johnson .... .10 .05
❑ 47 Mark Bavaro .... .10 .05
❑ 48 Seth Joyner .... .10 .05
❑ 49 Junior Seau .... .40 .18
❑ 50 Emmitt Smith 2.50 1.10
❑ 51 Shannon Sharpe .... .40 .18
❑ 52 Rodney Peete .... .10 .05
❑ 53 Andre Rison .... .20 .09
❑ 54 Cornelius Bennett .... .20 .09
❑ 55 Mark Carrier WR .... .20 .09
❑ 56 Mark Clayton .... .10 .05
❑ 57 Warren Moon .... .40 .18
❑ 58 J.J. Birden .... .10 .05
❑ 59 Howie Long .... .20 .09
❑ 60 Irving Fryar .... .20 .09
❑ 61 Mark Jackson .... .10 .05
❑ 62 Eric Martin .... .10 .05
❑ 63 Herschel Walker .... .20 .09
❑ 64 Cortez Kennedy .... .20 .09
❑ 65 Steve Beuerlein .... .10 .05
❑ 66 Jim Kelly .... .40 .18
❑ 67 Bernie Kosar .... .20 .09
❑ 68 Pat Swilling .... .10 .05
❑ 69 Michael Irvin .... .40 .18
❑ 70 Harvey Williams .... .20 .09
❑ 71 Steve Smith .... .10 .05
❑ 72 Wade Wilson .... .10 .05
❑ 73 Phil Simms .... .20 .09
❑ 74 Vinny Testaverde .... .20 .09
❑ 75 Barry Sanders 2.50 1.10
❑ 76 Ken Norton Jr. .... .20 .09
❑ 77 Rod Woodson .... .40 .18
❑ 78 Webster Slaughter .... .10 .05
❑ 79 Derrick Thomas .... .40 .18
❑ 80 Mike Sherrard .... .10 .05
❑ 81 Calvin Williams .... .20 .09
❑ 82 Jay Novacek .... .20 .09
❑ 83 Michael Brooks .... .10 .05
❑ 84 Randall Cunningham .... .40 .18
❑ 85 Chris Warren .... .20 .09
❑ 86 Johnny Mitchell .... .10 .05
❑ 87 Jim Harbaugh .... .40 .18
❑ 88 Rod Bernstine .... .10 .05
❑ 89 John Elway 2.50 1.10
❑ 90 Jerry Rice .... 1.50 .70
❑ 91 Brent Jones .... .20 .09
❑ 92 Cris Carter .... .75 .35
❑ 93 Alvin Harper .... .20 .09
❑ 94 Horace Copeland RC .... .20 .09
❑ 95 Raghib Ismail .... .20 .09
❑ 96 Darrin Smith RC .... .20 .09
❑ 97 Reggie Brooks RC .... .20 .09
❑ 98 Demetrius DuBose RC .... .10 .05
❑ 99 Eric Curry RC .... .10 .05
❑ 100 Rick Mirer RC .... .75 .35
❑ 101 Carlton Gray RC UER .... .10 .05
(Name spelled Grey on front)
❑ 102 Dana Stubblefield RC .... .40 .18
❑ 103 Todd Kelly RC .... .10 .05
❑ 104 Natrone Means RC .... 1.00 .45
❑ 105 Darrien Gordon RC .... .10 .05
❑ 106 Deon Figures RC .... .20 .09
❑ 107 Garrison Hearst RC .... 1.25 .55
❑ 108 Ronald Moore RC .... .20 .09
❑ 109 Leonard Renfro RC .... .10 .05
❑ 110 Lester Holmes .... .10 .05
❑ 111 Vaughn Hebron RC .... .10 .05
❑ 112 Marvin Jones RC .... .10 .05
❑ 113 Irv Smith RC .... .10 .05
❑ 114 Willie Roaf RC .... .20 .09
❑ 115 Derek Brown RBK RC .... .20 .09
❑ 116 Vincent Brisby RC .... .40 .18
❑ 117 Drew Bledsoe RC 3.00 1.35
❑ 118 Gino Torretta RC .... .20 .09
❑ 119 Robert Smith RC 3.00 1.35
❑ 120 Qadry Ismail RC .... 1.25 .55
❑ 121 O.J. McDuffie RC .... 1.25 .55
❑ 122 Terry Kirby RC .... .40 .18
❑ 123 Troy Drayton RC .... .20 .09
❑ 124 Jerome Bettis RC .... 1.50 .70
❑ 125 Patrick Bates RC .... .10 .05
❑ 126 Roosevelt Potts RC .... .10 .05
❑ 127 Tom Carter RC .... .20 .09
❑ 128 Patrick Robinson RC .... .10 .05
❑ 129 Brad Hopkins RC .... .10 .05
❑ 130 George Teague RC .... .20 .09
❑ 131 Wayne Simmons RC .... .10 .05
❑ 132 Mark Brunell RC 4.00 1.80
❑ 133 Ryan McNeil RC .... .10 .05
❑ 134 Dan Williams RC .... .10 .05
❑ 135 Glyn Milburn RC .... .40 .18
❑ 136 Kevin Williams RC .... .40 .18
❑ 137 Derrick Lassic RC .... .10 .05
❑ 138 Steve Everitt RC .... .10 .05
❑ 139 Lance Gunn RC .... .10 .05
❑ 140 John Copeland RC .... .20 .09
❑ 141 Curtis Conway RC .... 1.00 .45
❑ 142 Thomas Smith RC .... .20 .09
❑ 143 Russell Copeland RC .... .20 .09
❑ 144 Lincoln Kennedy RC .... .10 .05
❑ 145 Boomer Esiason CL .... .10 .05
❑ 146 Neil Smith CL .... .10 .05
❑ 147 Jack Del Rio CL .... .10 .05
❑ 148 Morten Andersen CL .... .10 .05
❑ 149 Sterling Sharpe CL .... .20 .09
❑ 150 Reggie White CL .... .20 .09

1994 Playoff Contenders

	MINT	NRMT
COMPLETE SET (120)	20.00	9.00

❑ 1 Drew Bledsoe .... 1.50 .70

❑ 2 Barry Sanders 3.00 1.35
❑ 3 Jerry Rice 1.50 .70
❑ 4 Rod Woodson .40 .18
❑ 5 Irving Fryar .20 .09
❑ 6 Charles Haley .20 .09
❑ 7 Chris Warren .20 .09
❑ 8 Craig Erickson .10 .05
❑ 9 Eric Metcalf .20 .09
❑ 10 Marcus Allen .40 .18
❑ 11 Chris Miller .10 .05
❑ 12 Andre Rison .20 .09
❑ 13 Art Monk .20 .09
❑ 14 Calvin Williams .20 .09
❑ 15 Shannon Sharpe .20 .09
❑ 16 Rodney Hampton .40 .18
❑ 17 Marion Butts .10 .05
❑ 18 John Jurkovic RC .20 .09
❑ 19 Jim Kelly .40 .18
❑ 20 Emmitt Smith 2.50 1.10
❑ 21 Jeff Hostetler .20 .09
❑ 22 Barry Foster .10 .05
❑ 23 Boomer Esiason .20 .09
❑ 24 Jim Harbaugh .40 .18
❑ 25 Joe Montana 3.00 1.35
❑ 26 Jeff George .40 .18
❑ 27 Warren Moon .40 .18
❑ 28 Steve Young 1.25 .55
❑ 29 Randall Cunningham .40 .18
❑ 30 Shawn Jefferson .10 .05
❑ 31 Cortez Kennedy .20 .09
❑ 32 Reggie Brooks .20 .09
❑ 33 Alvin Harper .20 .09
❑ 34 Brent Jones .20 .09
❑ 35 O.J. McDuffie .40 .18
❑ 36 Jerome Bettis .40 .18
❑ 37 Daryl Johnston .20 .09
❑ 38 Herman Moore .40 .18
❑ 39 Dave Meggett .10 .05
❑ 40 Reggie White .40 .18
❑ 41 Junior Seau .40 .18
❑ 42 Dan Marino 3.00 1.35
❑ 43 Scott Mitchell .40 .18
❑ 44 John Elway 3.00 1.35
❑ 45 Troy Aikman 1.50 .70
❑ 46 Terry Allen .20 .09
❑ 47 David Klingler .10 .05
❑ 48 Stan Humphries .40 .18
❑ 49 Rick Mirer .40 .18
❑ 50 Neil O'Donnell .40 .18
❑ 51 Keith Jackson .10 .05
❑ 52 Ricky Watters .40 .18
❑ 53 Dave Brown .20 .09
❑ 54 Neil Smith .40 .18
❑ 55 Johnny Mitchell .10 .05
❑ 56 Jackie Harris .10 .05
❑ 57 Terry Kirby .40 .18
❑ 58 Willie Davis .20 .09
❑ 59 Rob Moore .20 .09
❑ 60 Nate Newton .10 .05
❑ 61 Deion Sanders .75 .35
❑ 62 John Taylor .20 .09
❑ 63 Sterling Sharpe .20 .09
❑ 64 Natrone Means .40 .18
❑ 65 Steve Beuerlein .10 .05
❑ 66 Erik Kramer .20 .09
❑ 67 Qadry Ismail .40 .18
❑ 68 Johnny Johnson .10 .05
❑ 69 Herschel Walker .20 .09
❑ 70 Mark Stepnoski .10 .05
❑ 71 Brett Favre 3.00 1.35
❑ 72 Dana Stubblefield .40 .18
❑ 73 Bruce Smith .40 .18
❑ 74 Leroy Hoard .10 .05
❑ 75 Steve Walsh .10 .05
❑ 76 Jay Novacek .20 .09
❑ 77 Derrick Thomas .40 .18
❑ 78 Keith Byars .10 .05
❑ 79 Ben Coates .40 .18
❑ 80 Lorenzo Neal .10 .05
❑ 81 Ronnie Lott .20 .09
❑ 82 Tim Brown .40 .18
❑ 83 Michael Irvin .40 .18
❑ 84 Ronald Moore .10 .05
❑ 85 Andre Reed .20 .09
❑ 86 James Jett .10 .05
❑ 87 Curtis Conway .40 .18
❑ 88 Bernie Parmalee RC .40 .18
❑ 89 Keith Cash .10 .05
❑ 90 Russell Copeland .10 .05
❑ 91 Kevin Williams .20 .09
❑ 92 Gary Brown .10 .05
❑ 93 Thurman Thomas .40 .18
❑ 94 Jamir Miller RC .10 .05
❑ 95 Bert Emanuel RC 1.25 .55
❑ 96 Bucky Brooks RC .10 .05
❑ 97 Jeff Burris RC .20 .09
❑ 98 Antonio Langham RC .20 .09
❑ 99 Derrick Alexander WR RC 1.25 .55
❑ 100 Dan Wilkinson RC .20 .09
❑ 101 Shante Carver RC .10 .05
❑ 102 Johnnie Morton RC 1.50 .70
❑ 103 LeShon Johnson RC .20 .09
❑ 104 Marshall Faulk RC 5.00 2.20
❑ 105 Greg Hill RC .40 .18
❑ 106 Lake Dawson RC .40 .18
❑ 107 Irving Spikes RC .20 .09
❑ 108 David Palmer RC 1.25 .55
❑ 109 Willie McGinest RC .40 .18
❑ 110 Joe Johnson RC .10 .05
❑ 111 Aaron Glenn RC .20 .09
❑ 112 Charlie Garner RC 2.00 .90
❑ 113 Charles Johnson RC 1.25 .55
❑ 114 Byron Bam Morris RC .40 .18
❑ 115 Bryant Young RC .40 .18
❑ 116 William Floyd RC .40 .18
❑ 117 Trent Dilfer RC 2.50 1.10
❑ 118 Errict Rhett RC 1.25 .55
❑ 119 Heath Shuler RC .40 .18
❑ 120 Gus Frerotte RC 1.25 .55

1995 Playoff Contenders

	MINT	NRMT
COMPLETE SET (150)	25.00	11.00

❑ 1 Steve Young 1.00 .45
❑ 2 Jeff Blake RC 1.00 .45
❑ 3 Rick Mirer .40 .18
❑ 4 Brett Favre 2.50 1.10
❑ 5 Heath Shuler .40 .18
❑ 6 Steve Bono .20 .09
❑ 7 John Elway 2.50 1.10
❑ 8 Troy Aikman 1.25 .55
❑ 9 Rodney Peete .10 .05
❑ 10 Gus Frerotte .40 .18
❑ 11 Drew Bledsoe 1.25 .55
❑ 12 Jim Kelly .40 .18
❑ 13 Dan Marino 2.50 1.10
❑ 14 Errict Rhett .40 .18
❑ 15 Jeff Hostetler .20 .09
❑ 16 Erik Kramer .10 .05
❑ 17 Jim Everett .10 .05
❑ 18 Elvis Grbac .40 .18
❑ 19 Scott Mitchell .20 .09
❑ 20 Barry Sanders 2.50 1.10
❑ 21 Deion Sanders .75 .35
❑ 22 Emmitt Smith 2.00 .90
❑ 23 Garrison Hearst .40 .18
❑ 24 Mario Bates .40 .18
❑ 25 Mark Brunell 1.25 .55
❑ 26 Robert Smith .40 .18
❑ 27 Rodney Hampton .20 .09
❑ 28 Marshall Faulk .75 .35
❑ 29 Greg Hill .20 .09
❑ 30 Bernie Parmalee .20 .09
❑ 31 Natrone Means .40 .18
❑ 32 Marcus Allen .40 .18
❑ 33 Byron Bam Morris .20 .09
❑ 34 Edgar Bennett .20 .09
❑ 35 Vincent Brisby .10 .05
❑ 36 Jerome Bettis .40 .18
❑ 37 Craig Heyward .20 .09
❑ 38 Anthony Miller .20 .09
❑ 39 Curtis Conway .40 .18
❑ 40 William Floyd .40 .18
❑ 41 Chris Warren .20 .09
❑ 42 Terry Kirby .20 .09
❑ 43 Herschel Walker .20 .09
❑ 44 Eric Metcalf .20 .09
❑ 45 Darnay Scott .40 .18
❑ 46 Jackie Harris .10 .05
❑ 47 Dana Stubblefield .40 .18
❑ 48 Daryl Johnston .20 .09
❑ 49 Dave Meggett .10 .05
❑ 50 Ricky Watters .40 .18
❑ 51 Ken Norton .20 .09
❑ 52 Boomer Esiason .20 .09
❑ 53 Lake Dawson .20 .09
❑ 54 Eric Green .10 .05
❑ 55 Junior Seau .40 .18
❑ 56 Yancey Thigpen RC .40 .18
❑ 57 James Jett .20 .09
❑ 58 Leonard Russell .10 .05
❑ 59 Brent Jones .10 .05
❑ 60 Trent Dilfer .40 .18
❑ 61 Terance Mathis .20 .09
❑ 62 Jeff George .20 .09
❑ 63 Alvin Harper .10 .05
❑ 64 Terry Allen .20 .09
❑ 65 Stan Humphries .20 .09
❑ 66 Robert Green .10 .05
❑ 67 Bryce Paup .40 .18
❑ 68 Tamarick Vanover RC .40 .18
❑ 69 Desmond Howard .20 .09
❑ 70 Derek Loville .10 .05
❑ 71 Dave Brown .20 .09
❑ 72 Carl Pickens .40 .18
❑ 73 Gary Clark .10 .05
❑ 74 Gary Brown .10 .05
❑ 75 Brett Perriman .20 .09
❑ 76 Charlie Garner .20 .09
❑ 77 Ben Coates .20 .09
❑ 78 Bruce Smith .40 .18
❑ 79 Erric Pegram .20 .09
❑ 80 Jerry Rice 1.25 .55
❑ 81 Tim Brown .40 .18
❑ 82 John Taylor .10 .05
❑ 83 Will Moore .10 .05
❑ 84 Jay Novacek .20 .09
❑ 85 Kevin Williams .20 .09
❑ 86 Rocket Ismail .20 .09
❑ 87 Robert Brooks .40 .18
❑ 88 Michael Irvin .40 .18
❑ 89 Mark Chmura .40 .18
❑ 90 Shannon Sharpe .20 .09
❑ 91 Henry Ellard .20 .09
❑ 92 Reggie White .40 .18
❑ 93 Isaac Bruce .75 .35
❑ 94 Charles Haley .20 .09
❑ 95 Jake Reed .20 .09

❑ 96 Pete Metzelaars .10 .05
❑ 97 Dave Krieg .10 .05
❑ 98 Tony Martin .20 .09
❑ 99 Charles Jordan RC .20 .09
❑ 100 Bert Emanuel .40 .18
❑ 101 Andre Rison .20 .09
❑ 102 Jeff Graham .10 .05
❑ 103 O.J. McDuffie .40 .18
❑ 104 Randall Cunningham .40 .18
❑ 105 Harvey Williams .10 .05
❑ 106 Cris Carter .40 .18
❑ 107 Irving Fryar .20 .09
❑ 108 Jim Harbaugh .20 .09
❑ 109 Bernie Kosar .10 .05
❑ 110 Charles Johnson .20 .09
❑ 111 Warren Moon .20 .09
❑ 112 Neil O'Donnell .20 .09
❑ 113 Fred Barnett .20 .09
❑ 114 Herman Moore .40 .18
❑ 115 Chris Miller .10 .05
❑ 116 Vinny Testaverde .20 .09
❑ 117 Craig Erickson .10 .05
❑ 118 Qadry Ismail .20 .09
❑ 119 Willie Davis .20 .09
❑ 120 Michael Jackson .20 .09
❑ 121 Stoney Case RC .40 .18
❑ 122 Frank Sanders RC 1.00 .45
❑ 123 Todd Collins RC .40 .18
❑ 124 Kerry Collins RC 1.50 .70
❑ 125 Sherman Williams RC .10 .05
❑ 126 Terrell Davis RC 12.00 5.50
❑ 127 Luther Elliss RC .10 .05
❑ 128 Steve McNair RC 3.00 1.35
❑ 129 Chris Sanders RC .40 .18
❑ 130 Ki-Jana Carter RC .40 .18
❑ 131 Rodney Thomas RC .40 .18
❑ 132 Tony Boselli RC .40 .18
❑ 133 Rob Johnson RC 2.00 .90
❑ 134 James O. Stewart RC 2.00 .90
❑ 135 Chad May RC .10 .05
❑ 136 Eric Bjornson RC .20 .09
❑ 137 Tyrone Wheatley RC 1.25 .55
❑ 138 Kyle Brady RC .40 .18
❑ 139 Curtis Martin RC 3.00 1.35
❑ 140 Eric Zeier RC .40 .18
❑ 141 Ray Zellars RC .20 .09
❑ 142 Napoleon Kaufman RC 1.50 .70
❑ 143 Mike Mamula RC .20 .09
❑ 144 Mark Bruener RC .20 .09
❑ 145 Kordell Stewart RC 2.50 1.10
❑ 146 J.J. Stokes RC .40 .18
❑ 147 Joey Galloway RC 2.50 1.10
❑ 148 Warren Sapp RC .60 .25
❑ 149 Michael Westbrook RC 1.50 .70
❑ 150 Rashaan Salaam RC .40 .18

1996 Playoff Contenders Leather

	MINT	NRMT
COMPLETE SET (100)	300.00	135.00

❑ 1 Brett Favre R 30.00 13.50
❑ 2 Steve Young P 10.00 4.50
❑ 3 Herman Moore P 4.00 1.80
❑ 4 Jim Harbaugh P 2.50 1.10
❑ 5 Curtis Martin R 12.00 5.50
❑ 6 Junior Seau G 1.50 .70
❑ 7 John Elway R 30.00 13.50
❑ 8 Troy Aikman R 15.00 6.75
❑ 9 Terry Allen G 1.50 .70
❑ 10 Kordell Stewart R 10.00 4.50
❑ 11 Drew Bledsoe R 15.00 6.75
❑ 12 Jim Kelly R 6.00 2.70
❑ 13 Dan Marino R 30.00 13.50
❑ 14 Andre Rison G 1.50 .70
❑ 15 Jeff Hostetler G .75 .35
❑ 16 Scott Mitchell G 1.50 .70
❑ 17 Carl Pickens G 2.50 1.10
❑ 18 Larry Centers R 3.00 1.35
❑ 19 Craig Heyward G .75 .35
❑ 20 Barry Sanders R 30.00 13.50
❑ 21 Deion Sanders P 8.00 3.60
❑ 22 Emmitt Smith R 25.00 11.00
❑ 23 Rashaan Salaam P 4.00 1.80
❑ 24 Mario Bates G 1.50 .70
❑ 25 Lawrence Phillips R 3.00 1.35
❑ 26 Napoleon Kaufman P 4.00 1.80
❑ 27 Rodney Hampton G 1.50 .70
❑ 28 Marshall Faulk R 6.00 2.70
❑ 29 Trent Dilfer G 2.50 1.10
❑ 30 Leeland McElroy G 2.50 1.10
❑ 31 Marcus Allen G 2.50 1.10
❑ 32 Ricky Watters R 3.00 1.35
❑ 33 Karim Abdul-Jabbar R 6.00 2.70
❑ 34 Herschel Walker G 1.50 .70
❑ 35 Thurman Thomas G 2.50 1.10
❑ 36 Jerome Bettis G 2.50 1.10
❑ 37 Gus Frerotte P 2.50 1.10
❑ 38 Neil O'Donnell P 2.50 1.10
❑ 39 Rick Mirer G 1.50 .70
❑ 40 Mike Alstott P 8.00 3.60
❑ 41 Vinny Testaverde P 2.50 1.10
❑ 42 Derek Loville G .75 .35
❑ 43 Ben Coates G 1.50 .70
❑ 44 Steve McNair G 4.00 1.80
❑ 45 Bobby Engram G 2.50 1.10
❑ 46 Yancey Thigpen G 1.50 .70
❑ 47 Lake Dawson G .75 .35
❑ 48 Terrell Davis G 10.00 4.50
❑ 49 Kerry Collins P 4.00 1.80
❑ 50 Eric Metcalf G .75 .35
❑ 51 Stanley Pritchett P 1.25 .55
❑ 52 Robert Brooks G 2.50 1.10
❑ 53 Isaac Bruce R 6.00 2.70
❑ 54 Tim Brown G 2.50 1.10
❑ 55 Edgar Bennett G 1.50 .70
❑ 56 Warren Moon G 1.50 .70
❑ 57 Jerry Rice R 15.00 6.75
❑ 58 Michael Westbrook G 2.50 1.10
❑ 59 Keyshawn Johnson R 12.00 5.50
❑ 60 Steve Bono G .75 .35
❑ 61 Derrick Mayes G 1.50 .70
❑ 62 Erik Kramer G .75 .35
❑ 63 Rodney Peete G .75 .35
❑ 64 Eddie Kennison P 4.00 1.80
❑ 65 Derrick Thomas G 1.50 .70
❑ 66 Joey Galloway P 6.00 2.70
❑ 67 Amani Toomer G 3.00 1.35
❑ 68 Reggie White P 4.00 1.80
❑ 69 Heath Shuler R 6.00 2.70
❑ 70 Dave Brown R 2.00 .90
❑ 71 Tony Banks G 2.50 1.10
❑ 72 Chris Warren R 3.00 1.35
❑ 73 J.J. Stokes R 6.00 2.70
❑ 74 Rickey Dudley G 2.50 1.10
❑ 75 Stan Humphries G 1.50 .70
❑ 76 Jason Dunn G .75 .35
❑ 77 Tyrone Wheatley P 4.00 1.80
❑ 78 Jim Everett R 2.00 .90
❑ 79 Cris Carter P 4.00 1.80
❑ 80 Alex Van Dyke G 1.50 .70
❑ 81 O.J. McDuffie G 1.50 .70
❑ 82 Mark Chmura G 1.50 .70
❑ 83 Terry Glenn G 3.00 1.35
❑ 84 Boomer Esiason G 1.50 .70
❑ 85 Bruce Smith G 1.50 .70
❑ 86 Curtis Conway P 4.00 1.80
❑ 87 Ki-Jana Carter G 1.50 .70
❑ 88 Tamarick Vanover G 1.50 .70
❑ 89 Michael Jackson G 1.50 .70
❑ 90 Mark Brunell P 12.00 5.50
❑ 91 Tim Biakabutuka P 5.00 2.20
❑ 92 Anthony Miller P 1.25 .55
❑ 93 Marvin Harrison P 10.00 4.50
❑ 94 Jeff George R 3.00 1.35
❑ 95 Jeff Blake P 4.00 1.80
❑ 96 Eddie George R 15.00 6.75
❑ 97 Eric Moulds G 2.50 1.10
❑ 98 Mike Tomczak P 1.25 .55
❑ 99 Chris Sanders P 2.50 1.10
❑ 100 Chris Chandler G 1.50 .70

1996 Playoff Contenders Open Field Foil

	MINT	NRMT
COMPLETE SET (100)	150.00	70.00

❑ 1 Brett Favre P 12.00 5.50
❑ 2 Steve Young R 10.00 4.50
❑ 3 Herman Moore P 2.50 1.10
❑ 4 Jim Harbaugh G 1.25 .55
❑ 5 Curtis Martin P 6.00 2.70
❑ 6 Junior Seau P 2.50 1.10
❑ 7 John Elway P 12.00 5.50
❑ 8 Troy Aikman R 12.00 5.50
❑ 9 Terry Allen G 1.25 .55
❑ 10 Kordell Stewart P 5.00 2.20
❑ 11 Drew Bledsoe G 5.00 2.20
❑ 12 Jim Kelly G 2.00 .90
❑ 13 Dan Marino R 25.00 11.00
❑ 14 Andre Rison P 1.50 .70
❑ 15 Jeff Hostetler G .75 .35
❑ 16 Scott Mitchell R 3.00 1.35
❑ 17 Carl Pickens G 2.00 .90
❑ 18 Larry Centers G 1.25 .55
❑ 19 Craig Heyward R 1.50 .70
❑ 20 Barry Sanders R 25.00 11.00
❑ 21 Deion Sanders P 4.00 1.80
❑ 22 Emmitt Smith P 10.00 4.50
❑ 23 Rashaan Salaam R 5.00 2.20
❑ 24 Mario Bates P 1.00 .45
❑ 25 Lawrence Phillips P 1.50 .70
❑ 26 Napoleon Kaufman G 2.00 .90
❑ 27 Rodney Hampton G 1.25 .55
❑ 28 Marshall Faulk R 5.00 2.20
❑ 29 Trent Dilfer G 2.00 .90
❑ 30 Leeland McElroy R 5.00 2.20
❑ 31 Marcus Allen G 2.00 .90
❑ 32 Ricky Watters P 1.50 .70
❑ 33 Karim Abdul-Jabbar P 2.50 1.10
❑ 34 Herschel Walker R 3.00 1.35
❑ 35 Thurman Thomas G 2.00 .90
❑ 36 Jerome Bettis G 2.00 .90
❑ 37 Gus Frerotte R 3.00 1.35
❑ 38 Neil O'Donnell G 1.25 .55
❑ 39 Rick Mirer G 1.25 .55
❑ 40 Mike Alstott G 3.00 1.35
❑ 41 Vinny Testaverde G 1.25 .55
❑ 42 Derek Loville G .75 .35
❑ 43 Ben Coates G 1.25 .55
❑ 44 Steve McNair G 4.00 1.80
❑ 45 Bobby Engram R 5.00 2.20
❑ 46 Yancey Thigpen G 1.25 .55
❑ 47 Lake Dawson P 1.00 .45
❑ 48 Terrell Davis G 8.00 3.60
❑ 49 Kerry Collins P 2.50 1.10
❑ 50 Eric Metcalf G .75 .35
❑ 51 Stanley Pritchett G .75 .35

❑ 52 Robert Brooks P	1.50	.70
❑ 53 Isaac Bruce P	2.50	1.10
❑ 54 Tim Brown P	2.50	1.10
❑ 55 Edgar Bennett G	1.25	.55
❑ 56 Warren Moon P	2.50	1.10
❑ 57 Jerry Rice P	6.00	2.70
❑ 58 Michael Westbrook G	2.00	.90
❑ 59 Keyshawn Johnson P	5.00	2.20
❑ 60 Steve Bono G	.75	.35
❑ 61 Derrick Mayes R	5.00	2.20
❑ 62 Erik Kramer G	.75	.35
❑ 63 Rodney Peete G	.75	.35
❑ 64 Eddie Kennison G	2.00	.90
❑ 65 Derrick Thomas G	1.25	.55
❑ 66 Joey Galloway R	6.00	2.70
❑ 67 Amani Toomer R	6.00	2.70
❑ 68 Reggie White R	5.00	2.20
❑ 69 Heath Shuler P	2.50	1.10
❑ 70 Dave Brown G	.75	.35
❑ 71 Tony Banks R	5.00	2.20
❑ 72 Chris Warren G	1.25	.55
❑ 73 J.J. Stokes G	2.00	.90
❑ 74 Rickey Dudley R	5.00	2.20
❑ 75 Stan Humphries G	1.25	.55
❑ 76 Jason Dunn R	1.50	.70
❑ 77 Tyrone Wheatley G	1.25	.55
❑ 78 Jim Everett G	.75	.35
❑ 79 Cris Carter G	2.00	.90
❑ 80 Alex Van Dyke R	3.00	1.35
❑ 81 O.J. McDuffie P	2.50	1.10
❑ 82 Mark Chmura G	1.25	.55
❑ 83 Terry Glenn R	5.00	2.20
❑ 84 Boomer Esiason G	1.25	.55
❑ 85 Bruce Smith G	1.25	.55
❑ 86 Curtis Conway G	1.25	.55
❑ 87 Ki-Jana Carter R	3.00	1.35
❑ 88 Tamarick Vanover P	1.50	.70
❑ 89 Michael Jackson R	3.00	1.35
❑ 90 Mark Brunell G	5.00	2.20
❑ 91 Tim Biakabutuka G	2.00	.90
❑ 92 Anthony Miller G	1.25	.55
❑ 93 Marvin Harrison G	4.00	1.80
❑ 94 Jeff George G	1.25	.55
❑ 95 Jeff Blake G	2.00	.90
❑ 96 Eddie George P	8.00	3.60
❑ 97 Eric Moulds R	8.00	3.60
❑ 98 Mike Tomczak R	1.50	.70
❑ 99 Chris Sanders G	1.25	.55
❑ 100 Chris Chandler G	1.25	.55

1996 Playoff Contenders Pennants

	MINT	NRMT
COMPLETE SET (100)	150.00	70.00
❑ 1 Brett Favre R	30.00	13.50
❑ 2 Steve Young R	12.00	5.50
❑ 3 Herman Moore R	6.00	2.70
❑ 4 Jim Harbaugh R	4.00	1.80
❑ 5 Curtis Martin R	12.00	5.50
❑ 6 Junior Seau G	1.50	.70
❑ 7 John Elway R	30.00	13.50
❑ 8 Troy Aikman P	8.00	3.60
❑ 9 Terry Allen G	1.50	.70
❑ 10 Kordell Stewart R	10.00	4.50
❑ 11 Drew Bledsoe G	8.00	3.60
❑ 12 Jim Kelly P	3.00	1.35
❑ 13 Dan Marino P	15.00	6.75
❑ 14 Andre Rison G	1.50	.70
❑ 15 Jeff Hostetler G	.75	.35
❑ 16 Scott Mitchell G	1.50	.70
❑ 17 Carl Pickens R	6.00	2.70
❑ 18 Larry Centers P	1.00	.45
❑ 19 Craig Heyward G	.75	.35
❑ 20 Barry Sanders P	15.00	6.75
❑ 21 Deion Sanders R	10.00	4.50
❑ 22 Emmitt Smith R	25.00	11.00
❑ 23 Rashaan Salaam R	6.00	2.70
❑ 24 Mario Bates G	1.50	.70
❑ 25 Lawrence Phillips G	2.50	1.10
❑ 26 Napoleon Kaufman G	2.50	1.10
❑ 27 Rodney Hampton G	1.50	.70
❑ 28 Marshall Faulk P	3.00	1.35
❑ 29 Trent Dilfer G	2.50	1.10
❑ 30 Leeland McElroy P	2.00	.90
❑ 31 Marcus Allen P	3.00	1.35
❑ 32 Ricky Watters G	1.50	.70
❑ 33 Karim Abdul-Jabbar G	2.50	1.10
❑ 34 Herschel Walker P	2.00	.90
❑ 35 Thurman Thomas R	6.00	2.70
❑ 36 Jerome Bettis P	3.00	1.35
❑ 37 Gus Frerotte G	2.50	1.10
❑ 38 Neil O'Donnell G	1.50	.70
❑ 39 Rick Mirer G	1.50	.70
❑ 40 Mike Alstott R	8.00	3.60
❑ 41 Vinny Testaverde R	4.00	1.80
❑ 42 Derek Loville G	.75	.35
❑ 43 Ben Coates G	1.50	.70
❑ 44 Steve McNair R	12.00	5.50
❑ 45 Bobby Engram P	3.00	1.35
❑ 46 Yancey Thigpen G	1.50	.70
❑ 47 Lake Dawson G	.75	.35
❑ 48 Terrell Davis P	20.00	9.00
❑ 49 Kerry Collins R	6.00	2.70
❑ 50 Eric Metcalf G	.75	.35
❑ 51 Stanley Pritchett R	2.00	.90
❑ 52 Robert Brooks R	4.00	1.80
❑ 53 Isaac Bruce G	2.50	1.10
❑ 54 Tim Brown G	2.50	1.10
❑ 55 Edgar Bennett P	1.00	.45
❑ 56 Warren Moon G	1.50	.70
❑ 57 Jerry Rice R	15.00	6.75
❑ 58 Michael Westbrook G	2.50	1.10
❑ 59 Keyshawn Johnson G	5.00	2.20
❑ 60 Steve Bono R	.75	.35
❑ 61 Derrick Mayes P	3.00	1.35
❑ 62 Erik Kramer P	1.00	.45
❑ 63 Rodney Peete G	.75	.35
❑ 64 Eddie Kennison G	2.50	1.10
❑ 65 Derrick Thomas G	1.50	.70
❑ 66 Joey Galloway R	10.00	4.50
❑ 67 Amani Toomer P	3.00	1.35
❑ 68 Reggie White G	2.50	1.10
❑ 69 Heath Shuler G	1.50	.70
❑ 70 Dave Brown G	.75	.35
❑ 71 Tony Banks P	3.00	1.35
❑ 72 Chris Warren G	1.50	.70
❑ 73 J.J. Stokes G	2.50	1.10
❑ 74 Rickey Dudley P	3.00	1.35
❑ 75 Stan Humphries G	1.50	.70
❑ 76 Jason Dunn P	1.00	.45
❑ 77 Tyrone Wheatley G	1.50	.70
❑ 78 Jim Everett G	.75	.35
❑ 79 Cris Carter P	3.00	1.35
❑ 80 Alex Van Dyke P	1.00	.45
❑ 81 O.J. McDuffie G	1.50	.70
❑ 82 Mark Chmura P	1.00	.45
❑ 83 Terry Glenn P	3.00	1.35
❑ 84 Boomer Esiason R	4.00	1.80
❑ 85 Bruce Smith G	1.50	.70
❑ 86 Curtis Conway G	1.50	.70
❑ 87 Ki-Jana Carter G	1.50	.70
❑ 88 Tamarick Vanover G	1.50	.70
❑ 89 Michael Jackson G	1.50	.70
❑ 90 Mark Brunell G	8.00	3.60
❑ 91 Tim Biakabutuka R	6.00	2.70
❑ 92 Anthony Miller G	1.50	.70
❑ 93 Marvin Harrison R	10.00	4.50
❑ 94 Jeff George P	2.00	.90
❑ 95 Jeff Blake R	6.00	2.70
❑ 96 Eddie George G	8.00	3.60
❑ 97 Eric Moulds P	5.00	2.20
❑ 98 Mike Tomczak G	.75	.35
❑ 99 Chris Sanders G	1.50	.70
❑ 100 Chris Chandler G	1.50	.70

1997 Playoff Contenders

	MINT	NRMT
COMPLETE SET (150)	80.00	36.00
❑ 1 Kent Graham	.40	.18
❑ 2 Leeland McElroy	.40	.18
❑ 3 Rob Moore	.75	.35
❑ 4 Frank Sanders	.75	.35
❑ 5 Jake Plummer RC	10.00	4.50
❑ 6 Chris Chandler	.75	.35
❑ 7 Bert Emanuel	.75	.35
❑ 8 O.J. Santiago RC	1.50	.70
❑ 9 Byron Hanspard RC	1.50	.70
❑ 10 Vinny Testaverde	.75	.35
❑ 11 Michael Jackson	.75	.35
❑ 12 Earnest Byner	.40	.18
❑ 13 Jermaine Lewis	1.50	.70
❑ 14 Derrick Alexander WR	.75	.35
❑ 15 Jay Graham RC	1.50	.70
❑ 16 Todd Collins	.40	.18
❑ 17 Thurman Thomas	1.50	.70
❑ 18 Bruce Smith	.75	.35
❑ 19 Andre Reed	.75	.35
❑ 20 Quinn Early	.40	.18
❑ 21 Antowain Smith RC	3.00	1.35
❑ 22 Kerry Collins	.75	.35
❑ 23 Tim Biakabutuka	.75	.35
❑ 24 Anthony Johnson	.40	.18
❑ 25 Wesley Walls	.75	.35
❑ 26 Fred Lane RC	1.50	.70
❑ 27 Rae Carruth RC	1.50	.70
❑ 28 Raymont Harris	.40	.18
❑ 29 Rick Mirer	.40	.18
❑ 30 Darnell Autry RC	.75	.35
❑ 31 Jeff Blake	.75	.35
❑ 32 Ki-Jana Carter	.40	.18
❑ 33 Carl Pickens	1.50	.70
❑ 34 Darnay Scott	.75	.35
❑ 35 Corey Dillon RC	8.00	3.60
❑ 36 Troy Aikman	4.00	1.80
❑ 37 Emmitt Smith	6.00	2.70
❑ 38 Michael Irvin	1.50	.70
❑ 39 Deion Sanders	1.50	.70
❑ 40 Anthony Miller	.40	.18
❑ 41 Eric Bjornson	.40	.18
❑ 42 David LaFleur RC	2.00	.90
❑ 43 John Elway	8.00	3.60
❑ 44 Terrell Davis	6.00	2.70
❑ 45 Shannon Sharpe	.75	.35
❑ 46 Ed McCaffrey	.75	.35
❑ 47 Rod Smith WR	1.50	.70
❑ 48 Scott Mitchell	.75	.35
❑ 49 Barry Sanders	8.00	3.60
❑ 50 Herman Moore	1.50	.70
❑ 51 Brett Favre	8.00	3.60
❑ 52 Dorsey Levens	1.50	.70
❑ 53 William Henderson	.40	.18
❑ 54 Derrick Mayes	.75	.35
❑ 55 Antonio Freeman	2.00	.90
❑ 56 Robert Brooks	.75	.35
❑ 57 Mark Chmura	.75	.35
❑ 58 Reggie White	1.50	.70
❑ 59 Darren Sharper RC	.75	.35

		MINT	NRMT
❑ 60	Jim Harbaugh	.75	.35
❑ 61	Marshall Faulk	1.50	.70
❑ 62	Marvin Harrison	1.50	.70
❑ 63	Mark Brunell	4.00	1.80
❑ 64	Natrone Means	1.50	.70
❑ 65	Jimmy Smith	.75	.35
❑ 66	Keenan McCardell	.75	.35
❑ 67	Elvis Grbac	.75	.35
❑ 68	Greg Hill	.40	.18
❑ 69	Marcus Allen	1.50	.70
❑ 70	Andre Rison	.75	.35
❑ 71	Kimble Anders	.75	.35
❑ 72	Tony Gonzalez RC	4.00	1.80
❑ 73	Pat Barnes RC	1.50	.70
❑ 74	Dan Marino	8.00	3.60
❑ 75	Karim Abdul-Jabbar	1.50	.70
❑ 76	Zach Thomas	.75	.35
❑ 77	O.J. McDuffie	.75	.35
❑ 78	Brian Manning RC	.40	.18
❑ 79	Brad Johnson	2.00	.90
❑ 80	Cris Carter	1.50	.70
❑ 81	Jake Reed	.75	.35
❑ 82	Robert Smith	.75	.35
❑ 83	Drew Bledsoe	4.00	1.80
❑ 84	Curtis Martin	2.00	.90
❑ 85	Ben Coates	.75	.35
❑ 86	Terry Glenn	1.50	.70
❑ 87	Shawn Jefferson	.40	.18
❑ 88	Heath Shuler	.40	.18
❑ 89	Mario Bates	.40	.18
❑ 90	Andre Hastings	.40	.18
❑ 91	Troy Davis RC	1.50	.70
❑ 92	Danny Wuerffel RC	2.00	.90
❑ 93	Dave Brown	.40	.18
❑ 94	Chris Calloway	.40	.18
❑ 95	Tiki Barber RC	4.00	1.80
❑ 96	Mike Cherry RC	.40	.18
❑ 97	Neil O'Donnell	.75	.35
❑ 98	Keyshawn Johnson	1.50	.70
❑ 99	Adrian Murrell	.75	.35
❑ 100	Wayne Chrebet	1.50	.70
❑ 101	Dedric Ward RC	2.50	1.10
❑ 102	Leon Johnson RC	.40	.18
❑ 103	Jeff George	.75	.35
❑ 104	Napoleon Kaufman	1.50	.70
❑ 105	Tim Brown	1.50	.70
❑ 106	James Jett	.75	.35
❑ 107	Ty Detmer	.75	.35
❑ 108	Ricky Watters	.75	.35
❑ 109	Irving Fryar	.75	.35
❑ 110	Michael Timpson	.40	.18
❑ 111	Chad Lewis RC	.40	.18
❑ 112	Kordell Stewart	2.00	.90
❑ 113	Jerome Bettis	1.50	.70
❑ 114	Charles Johnson	.75	.35
❑ 115	George Jones RC	.75	.35
❑ 116	Will Blackwell RC	1.50	.70
❑ 117	Stan Humphries	.75	.35
❑ 118	Junior Seau	.75	.35
❑ 119	Freddie Jones RC	.75	.35
❑ 120	Steve Young	2.50	1.10
❑ 121	Jerry Rice	4.00	1.80
❑ 122	Garrison Hearst	.75	.35
❑ 123	William Floyd	.75	.35
❑ 124	Terrell Owens	1.50	.70
❑ 125	J.J. Stokes	.75	.35
❑ 126	Marc Edwards RC	.40	.18
❑ 127	Jim Druckenmiller RC	1.50	.70
❑ 128	Warren Moon	1.50	.70
❑ 129	Chris Warren	.75	.35
❑ 130	Joey Galloway	2.00	.90
❑ 131	Shawn Springs RC	.75	.35
❑ 132	Tony Banks	.75	.35
❑ 133	Lawrence Phillips	.40	.18
❑ 134	Isaac Bruce	1.50	.70
❑ 135	Eddie Kennison	.75	.35
❑ 136	Orlando Pace RC	1.50	.70
❑ 137	Trent Dilfer	1.50	.70
❑ 138	Mike Alstott	1.50	.70
❑ 139	Horace Copeland	.40	.18
❑ 140	Jackie Harris	.40	.18
❑ 141	Warrick Dunn RC	4.00	1.80
❑ 142	Reidel Anthony RC	2.50	1.10
❑ 143	Steve McNair	2.00	.90
❑ 144	Eddie George	4.00	1.80
❑ 145	Chris Sanders	.40	.18
❑ 146	Gus Frerotte	.40	.18
❑ 147	Terry Allen	1.50	.70
❑ 148	Henry Ellard	.40	.18
❑ 149	Leslie Shepherd	.40	.18
❑ 150	Michael Westbrook	.75	.35
❑ S1	Terrell Davis Sample	2.00	.90

1998 Playoff Contenders Leather

	MINT	NRMT
COMPLETE SET (100)	200.00	90.00

		MINT	NRMT
❑ 1	Adrian Murrell	1.00	.45
❑ 2	Michael Pittman	2.50	1.10
❑ 3	Jake Plummer	4.00	1.80
❑ 4	Andre Wadsworth	1.50	.70
❑ 5	Jamal Anderson	2.00	.90
❑ 6	Chris Chandler	1.00	.45
❑ 7	Tim Dwight	4.00	1.80
❑ 8	Pat Johnson	1.50	.70
❑ 9	Jermaine Lewis	1.00	.45
❑ 10	Doug Flutie	2.50	1.10
❑ 11	Antowain Smith	2.00	.90
❑ 12	Muhsin Muhammad	1.00	.45
❑ 13	Bobby Engram	1.00	.45
❑ 14	Curtis Enis	3.00	1.35
❑ 15	Alonzo Mayes	.75	.35
❑ 16	Corey Dillon	3.00	1.35
❑ 17	Carl Pickens	2.00	.90
❑ 18	Troy Aikman	5.00	2.20
❑ 19	Michael Irvin	2.00	.90
❑ 20	Deion Sanders	2.00	.90
❑ 21	Emmitt Smith	8.00	3.60
❑ 22	Terrell Davis	8.00	3.60
❑ 23	John Elway	10.00	4.50
❑ 24	Brian Griese	10.00	4.50
❑ 25	Rod Smith WR	1.00	.45
❑ 26	Charlie Batch	8.00	3.60
❑ 27	Germane Crowell	5.00	2.20
❑ 28	Terry Fair	1.50	.70
❑ 29	Herman Moore	2.00	.90
❑ 30	Barry Sanders	10.00	4.50
❑ 31	Brett Favre	10.00	4.50
❑ 32	Antonio Freeman	2.00	.90
❑ 33	Vonnie Holliday (UER front and back Holiday)	1.50	.70
❑ 34	Reggie White	2.00	.90
❑ 35	Marshall Faulk	2.00	.90
❑ 36	Marvin Harrison	1.00	.45
❑ 37	Peyton Manning	20.00	9.00
❑ 38	Jerome Pathon	1.50	.70
❑ 39	Tavian Banks	1.50	.70
❑ 40	Mark Brunell	4.00	1.80
❑ 41	Keenan McCardell	1.00	.45
❑ 42	Fred Taylor	8.00	3.60
❑ 43	Elvis Grbac	1.00	.45
❑ 44	Andre Rison	1.00	.45
❑ 45	Rashaan Shehee	1.50	.70
❑ 46	Karim Abdul-Jabbar	2.00	.90
❑ 47	John Avery	2.50	1.10
❑ 48	Dan Marino	10.00	4.50
❑ 49	O.J. McDuffie	1.00	.45
❑ 50	Cris Carter	2.00	.90
❑ 51	Brad Johnson	2.00	.90
❑ 52	Randy Moss	20.00	9.00
❑ 53	Robert Smith	2.00	.90
❑ 54	Drew Bledsoe	4.00	1.80
❑ 55	Ben Coates	1.00	.45
❑ 56	Robert Edwards	2.00	.90
❑ 57	Chris Floyd	.75	.35
❑ 58	Terry Glenn	2.00	.90
❑ 59	Cameron Cleeland	1.50	.70
❑ 60	Kerry Collins	1.00	.45
❑ 61	Danny Kanell	1.00	.45
❑ 62	Charles Way	.50	.23
❑ 63	Glenn Foley	1.00	.45
❑ 64	Keyshawn Johnson	2.00	.90
❑ 65	Curtis Martin	2.00	.90
❑ 66	Tim Brown	2.00	.90
❑ 67	Jeff George	1.00	.45
❑ 68	Napoleon Kaufman	2.00	.90
❑ 69	Charles Woodson	4.00	1.80
❑ 70	Irving Fryar	1.00	.45
❑ 71	Bobby Hoying	1.00	.45
❑ 72	Jerome Bettis	2.00	.90
❑ 73	Kordell Stewart	2.00	.90
❑ 74	Hines Ward	1.50	.70
❑ 75	Ryan Leaf	6.00	2.70
❑ 76	Natrone Means	2.00	.90
❑ 77	Mikhael Ricks	1.50	.70
❑ 78	Junior Seau	1.00	.45
❑ 79	Garrison Hearst	2.00	.90
❑ 80	Terrell Owens	2.00	.90
❑ 81	Jerry Rice	5.00	2.20
❑ 82	Steve Young	3.00	1.35
❑ 83	Joey Galloway	2.00	.90
❑ 84	Ahman Green	6.00	2.70
❑ 85	Warren Moon	2.00	.90
❑ 86	Ricky Watters	1.00	.45
❑ 87	Tony Banks	1.00	.45
❑ 88	Isaac Bruce	2.00	.90
❑ 89	Robert Holcombe	2.50	1.10
❑ 90	Mike Alstott	2.00	.90
❑ 91	Trent Dilfer	2.00	.90
❑ 92	Warrick Dunn	2.00	.90
❑ 93	Jacquez Green	4.00	1.80
❑ 94	Kevin Dyson	4.00	1.80
❑ 95	Eddie George	4.00	1.80
❑ 96	Steve McNair	2.00	.90
❑ 97	Yancey Thigpen	.50	.23
❑ 98	Terry Allen	2.00	.90
❑ 99	Skip Hicks	2.50	1.10
❑ 100	Michael Westbrook	1.00	.45

1998 Playoff Contenders Ticket

	MINT	NRMT
COMPLETE SET (99)	3000.00	1350.00
COMP.SET w/o SPs (80)	60.00	27.00

		MINT	NRMT
❑ 1	Rob Moore	.75	.35
❑ 2	Jake Plummer	3.00	1.35
❑ 3	Jamal Anderson	1.50	.70
❑ 4	Terance Mathis	.75	.35
❑ 5	Priest Holmes	12.00	5.50
❑ 6	Michael Jackson	.40	.18
❑ 7	Eric Zeier	.75	.35
❑ 8	Andre Reed	.75	.35
❑ 9	Antowain Smith	1.50	.70
❑ 10	Bruce Smith	.75	.35
❑ 11	Thurman Thomas	1.50	.70
❑ 12	Rocket Ismail	.40	.18
❑ 13	Wesley Walls	.75	.35
❑ 14	Curtis Conway	.75	.35
❑ 15	Jeff Blake	.75	.35

❑ 16 Corey Dillon 2.00 .90
❑ 17 Carl Pickens 1.50 .70
❑ 18 Troy Aikman 4.00 1.80
❑ 19 Michael Irvin 1.50 .70
❑ 20 Ernie Mills .40 .18
❑ 21 Deion Sanders 1.50 .70
❑ 22 Emmitt Smith 6.00 2.70
❑ 23 Terrell Davis 6.00 2.70
❑ 24 John Elway 8.00 3.60
❑ 25 Neil Smith .75 .35
❑ 26 Rod Smith WR .75 .35
❑ 27 Herman Moore 1.50 .70
❑ 28 Johnnie Morton .75 .35
❑ 29 Barry Sanders 8.00 3.60
❑ 30 Robert Brooks .75 .35
❑ 31 Brett Favre 8.00 3.60
❑ 32 Antonio Freeman 1.50 .70
❑ 33 Dorsey Levens 1.50 .70
❑ 34 Reggie White 1.50 .70
❑ 35 Marshall Faulk 1.50 .70
❑ 36 Mark Brunell 3.00 1.35
❑ 37 Jimmy Smith .75 .35
❑ 38 James Stewart .75 .35
❑ 39 Donnell Bennett .40 .18
❑ 40 Andre Rison .75 .35
❑ 41 Derrick Thomas .75 .35
❑ 42 Karim Abdul-Jabbar 1.50 .70
❑ 43 Dan Marino 8.00 3.60
❑ 44 Cris Carter 1.50 .70
❑ 45 Brad Johnson 1.50 .70
❑ 46 Robert Smith 1.50 .70
❑ 47 Drew Bledsoe 3.00 1.35
❑ 48 Terry Glenn 1.50 .70
❑ 49 Lamar Smith .75 .35
❑ 50 Ike Hilliard .75 .35
❑ 51 Danny Kanell .75 .35
❑ 52 Wayne Chrebet 1.50 .70
❑ 53 Keyshawn Johnson 1.50 .70
❑ 54 Curtis Martin 1.50 .70
❑ 55 Tim Brown 1.50 .70
❑ 56 Rickey Dudley .40 .18
❑ 57 Jeff George .75 .35
❑ 58 Napoleon Kaufman 1.50 .70
❑ 59 Irving Fryar .75 .35
❑ 60 Jerome Bettis 1.50 .70
❑ 61 Charles Johnson .40 .18
❑ 62 Kordell Stewart 1.50 .70
❑ 63 Natrone Means 1.50 .70
❑ 64 Bryan Still .40 .18
❑ 65 Garrison Hearst 1.50 .70
❑ 66 Jerry Rice 4.00 1.80
❑ 67 Steve Young 2.00 .90
❑ 68 Joey Galloway 1.50 .70
❑ 69 Warren Moon 1.50 .70
❑ 70 Ricky Watters .75 .35
❑ 71 Isaac Bruce 1.50 .70
❑ 72 Mike Alstott 1.50 .70
❑ 73 Reidel Anthony .75 .35
❑ 74 Trent Dilfer 1.50 .70
❑ 75 Warrick Dunn 1.50 .70
❑ 76 Warren Sapp .75 .35
❑ 77 Eddie George 3.00 1.35
❑ 78 Steve McNair 1.50 .70
❑ 79 Terry Allen 1.50 .70
❑ 80 Gus Frerotte .40 .18
❑ 81 Andre Wadsworth AUTO 25.00 11.00
❑ 82 Tim Dwight AUTO 40.00 18.00
❑ 83 Curtis Enis AUTO/400 80.00 36.00
❑ 85 Charlie Batch AUTO 100.00 45.00
❑ 86 Germane Crowell AUTO 80.00 36.00
❑ 87 Peyton Manning AUTO/200 1200.00 550.00
❑ 88 Jerome Pathon AUTO 40.00 18.00
❑ 89 Fred Taylor AUTO 200.00 90.00
❑ 90 Tavian Banks AUTO 25.00 11.00
❑ 92 Randy Moss AUTO/300 700.00 325.00
❑ 93 Robert Edwards AUTO 60.00 27.00
❑ 94 Hines Ward AUTO 25.00 11.00
❑ 95 Ryan Leaf AUTO/200 100.00 45.00
❑ 96 Mikhael Ricks AUTO 25.00 11.00
❑ 97 Ahman Green AUTO 100.00 45.00
❑ 98 Jacquez Green AUTO 50.00 22.00
❑ 99 Kevin Dyson AUTO 50.00 22.00
❑ 100 Skip Hicks AUTO 25.00 11.00
❑ 103 Chris Fuamatu-Ma'afala AUTO 25.00 11.00

1999 Playoff Contenders SSD

	MINT	NRMT
COMPLETE SET (200)	3200.00	1450.00
COMP.SET w/o RC/PT's (141)	60.00	27.00

❑ 1 Randy Moss 6.00 2.70
❑ 2 Randall Cunningham 1.50 .70
❑ 3 Cris Carter 1.50 .70
❑ 4 Robert Smith 1.50 .70
❑ 5 Jake Reed .75 .35
❑ 6 Albert Connell .40 .18
❑ 7 Jeff George .75 .35
❑ 8 Brett Favre 6.00 2.70
❑ 9 Antonio Freeman 1.50 .70
❑ 10 Dorsey Levens 1.50 .70
❑ 11 Mark Chmura .75 .35
❑ 12 Mike Alstott 1.50 .70
❑ 13 Warrick Dunn 1.50 .70
❑ 14 Trent Dilfer .75 .35
❑ 15 Jacquez Green .40 .18
❑ 16 Reidel Anthony .40 .18
❑ 17 Warren Sapp .75 .35
❑ 18 Amani Toomer .40 .18
❑ 19 Curtis Enis 1.50 .70
❑ 20 Curtis Conway .75 .35
❑ 21 Bobby Engram .75 .35
❑ 22 Barry Sanders 6.00 2.70
❑ 23 Charlie Batch 3.00 1.35
❑ 24 Herman Moore 1.50 .70
❑ 25 Johnnie Morton .75 .35
❑ 26 Greg Hill .40 .18
❑ 27 Germane Crowell .75 .35
❑ 28 Kerry Collins .75 .35
❑ 29 Ike Hilliard .40 .18
❑ 30 Joe Jurevicius .40 .18
❑ 31 Stephen Davis 1.50 .70
❑ 32 Brad Johnson 1.50 .70
❑ 33 Skip Hicks .75 .35
❑ 34 Michael Westbrook .75 .35
❑ 35 Jake Plummer 2.50 1.10
❑ 36 Adrian Murrell .40 .18
❑ 37 Frank Sanders .75 .35
❑ 38 Rob Moore .75 .35
❑ 39 Gary Brown .40 .18
❑ 40 Duce Staley 1.50 .70
❑ 41 Charles Johnson .75 .35
❑ 42 Emmitt Smith 4.00 1.80
❑ 43 Troy Aikman 4.00 1.80
❑ 44 Michael Irvin .75 .35
❑ 45 Deion Sanders 1.50 .70
❑ 46 Rocket Ismail .75 .35
❑ 47 Jerry Rice 4.00 1.80
❑ 48 Terrell Owens 1.50 .70
❑ 49 Steve Young 2.50 1.10
❑ 50 Garrison Hearst .75 .35
❑ 51 J.J. Stokes .75 .35
❑ 52 Lawrence Phillips .75 .35
❑ 53 Jamal Anderson 1.50 .70
❑ 54 Chris Chandler .75 .35
❑ 55 Terance Mathis .75 .35
❑ 56 Tim Dwight 1.50 .70
❑ 57 Charlie Garner .75 .35
❑ 58 Chris Calloway .75 .35
❑ 59 Eddie Kennison .75 .35
❑ 60 Billy Joe Hobert .40 .18
❑ 61 Tim Biakabutuka .75 .35
❑ 62 Muhsin Muhammad .75 .35
❑ 63 Olandis Gary RC/1825 50.00 22.00
❑ 64 Wesley Walls .75 .35
❑ 65 Isaac Bruce 1.50 .70
❑ 66 Marshall Faulk 1.50 .70
❑ 67 Kordell Stewart 1.50 .70
❑ 68 Jerome Bettis 1.50 .70
❑ 69 Hines Ward .40 .18
❑ 70 Corey Dillon 1.50 .70
❑ 71 Carl Pickens .75 .35
❑ 72 Darnay Scott .75 .35
❑ 73 Steve McNair 1.50 .70
❑ 74 Eddie George 2.00 .90
❑ 75 Yancey Thigpen .40 .18
❑ 76 Kevin Dyson .75 .35
❑ 77 Fred Taylor 4.00 1.80
❑ 78 Mark Brunell 2.50 1.10
❑ 79 Jimmy Smith .75 .35
❑ 80 Keenan McCardell .75 .35
❑ 81 James Stewart .75 .35
❑ 82 Jermaine Lewis .75 .35
❑ 83 Priest Holmes 1.50 .70
❑ 84 Stoney Case .40 .18
❑ 85 Errict Rhett .75 .35
❑ 86 Bill Schroeder 1.50 .70
❑ 87 Terry Kirby .40 .18
❑ 88 Leslie Shepherd .40 .18
❑ 89 Terrence Wilkins RC/825 60.00 27.00
❑ 90 Dan Marino 6.00 2.70
❑ 91 O.J. McDuffie .75 .35
❑ 92 Karim Abdul-Jabbar .75 .35
❑ 93 Zach Thomas .75 .35
❑ 94 Terry Allen .75 .35
❑ 95 Tony Martin .75 .35
❑ 96 Drew Bledsoe 2.50 1.10
❑ 97 Terry Glenn 1.50 .70
❑ 98 Ben Coates .75 .35
❑ 99 Tony Simmons .40 .18
❑ 100 Curtis Martin 1.50 .70
❑ 101 Keyshawn Johnson 1.50 .70
❑ 102 Vinny Testaverde .75 .35
❑ 103 Wayne Chrebet 1.50 .70
❑ 104 Peyton Manning 6.00 2.70
❑ 105 Marvin Harrison 1.50 .70
❑ 106 E.G. Green .40 .18
❑ 107 Doug Flutie 2.00 .90
❑ 108 Thurman Thomas .75 .35
❑ 109 Andre Reed .75 .35
❑ 110 Eric Moulds 1.50 .70
❑ 111 Antowain Smith 1.50 .70
❑ 112 Bruce Smith .75 .35
❑ 113 Terrell Davis 4.00 1.80
❑ 114 John Elway 6.00 2.70
❑ 115 Ed McCaffrey .75 .35
❑ 116 Rod Smith .75 .35
❑ 117 Shannon Sharpe .75 .35
❑ 118 Jeff Garcia RC/325 500.00 220.00
❑ 119 Brian Griese 3.00 1.35
❑ 120 Justin Watson RC/325 150.00 70.00
❑ 121 Bubby Brister .75 .35
❑ 122 Ryan Leaf 1.50 .70
❑ 123 Natrone Means .75 .35
❑ 124 Mikhael Ricks .40 .18
❑ 125 Junior Seau .75 .35
❑ 126 Jim Harbaugh .75 .35
❑ 127 Andre Rison .75 .35
❑ 128 Elvis Grbac .75 .35
❑ 129 Bam Morris .40 .18
❑ 130 Rashaan Shehee .40 .18
❑ 131 Warren Moon 1.50 .70
❑ 132 Tony Gonzalez .75 .35
❑ 133 Derrick Alexander .75 .35
❑ 134 Jon Kitna 1.50 .70
❑ 135 Ricky Watters .75 .35
❑ 136 Joey Galloway 1.50 .70
❑ 137 Ahman Green .40 .18
❑ 138 Derrick Mayes .75 .35
❑ 139 Tyrone Wheatley .75 .35
❑ 140 Napoleon Kaufman 1.50 .70
❑ 141 Tim Brown 1.50 .70
❑ 142 Charles Woodson 1.50 .70
❑ 143 Rich Gannon .75 .35
❑ 144 Rickey Dudley .40 .18
❑ 145 Az-Zahir Hakim .40 .18
❑ 146 Kurt Warner RC/1825 400.00 180.00

❑ 147 Sean Bennett RC/1325 15.00 6.75
❑ 148 Brandon Stokley RC/1325 25.00 11.00
❑ 149 Amos Zereoue RC/1325 25.00 11.00
❑ 150 Brock Huard RC/1325 40.00 18.00
❑ 151 Tim Couch RC/1025 175.00 80.00
❑ 152 Ricky Williams RC/725 250.00 110.00
❑ 153 Donovan McNabb RC/525 400.00 180.00
❑ 154 Edgerrin James RC/525 600.00 275.00
❑ 155 Torry Holt RC/1025 100.00 45.00
❑ 156 Daunte Culpepper RC/1025 350.00 160.00
❑ 157 Akili Smith RC/1025 60.00 27.00
❑ 158 Champ Bailey RC/1725 25.00 11.00
❑ 159 Chris Claiborne RC/1825 15.00 6.75
❑ 160A Chris McAlister RC/1825 12.00 5.50
❑ 160B Jason Tucker 25.00 11.00
❑ 161 Troy Edwards RC/1225 30.00 13.50
❑ 162 Jevon Kearse RC/325 150.00 70.00
❑ 163 Darnell McDonald RC/1825 25.00 11.00
❑ 164 David Boston RC/1025 60.00 27.00
❑ 165 Peerless Price RC/1325 30.00 13.50
❑ 166 C.Collins RC/1025 25.00 11.00
❑ 167 Rob Konrad RC/1325 20.00 9.00
❑ 168 Cade McNown RC/1025 60.00 27.00
❑ 169 Shawn Bryson RC/1825 30.00 13.50
❑ 170 Kevin Faulk RC/1325 40.00 18.00
❑ 171 Corby Jones 15.00 6.75
❑ 172A James Johnson RC/1325 15.00 6.75
❑ 172B Patrick Jeffers 40.00 18.00
❑ 173 Autry Denson RC/1825 20.00 9.00
❑ 174 Sedrick Irvin RC/1825 20.00 9.00
❑ 175 Michael Bishop RC/1825 50.00 22.00
❑ 176 Joe Germaine RC/825 35.00 16.00
❑ 177 De'Mond Parker RC/1325 25.00 11.00
❑ 178A Shaun King EXCH RC/1825 80.00 36.00
❑ 178B Jay Fiedler
❑ 178C Ray Lucas
❑ 179 D'Wayne Bates RC/1825 20.00 9.00
❑ 180 Tai Streets RC/1825 35.00 16.00
❑ 181 Na Brown RC/1825 20.00 9.00
❑ 182 Desmond Clark RC/1825 15.00 6.75
❑ 183 Jim Kleinsasser RC/1825 20.00 9.00
❑ 184 Kevin Johnson RC/1325 40.00 18.00
❑ 185 Joe Montgomery RC/1325 20.00 9.00
❑ 186 John Elway PT 10.00 4.50
❑ 187 Dan Marino PT 10.00 4.50
❑ 188 Jerry Rice PT 6.00 2.70
❑ 189 Barry Sanders PT 10.00 4.50
❑ 190 Steve Young PT 4.00 1.80
❑ 191 Doug Flutie PT 3.00 1.35
❑ 192 Troy Aikman PT 6.00 2.70
❑ 193 Drew Bledsoe PT 4.00 1.80
❑ 194 Brett Favre PT 10.00 4.50
❑ 195 Randall Cunningham PT 2.50 1.10
❑ 196 Terrell Davis PT 6.00 2.70
❑ 197 Kordell Stewart PT 2.50 1.10
❑ 198 Keyshawn Johnson PT 2.50 1.10
❑ 199 Jake Plummer PT 4.00 1.80
❑ 200 Peyton Manning PT 10.00 4.50

2000 Playoff Contenders

	MINT	NRMT
COMP.SET w/o SP's (100)	20.00	9.00

❑ 1 David Boston .60 .25
❑ 2 Jake Plummer .60 .25
❑ 3 Chris Chandler .30 .14
❑ 4 Jamal Anderson .60 .25
❑ 5 Tim Dwight .60 .25
❑ 6 Qadry Ismail .30 .14
❑ 7 Tony Banks .30 .14
❑ 8 Lamar Smith .30 .14
❑ 9 Doug Flutie .75 .35
❑ 10 Eric Moulds .60 .25
❑ 11 Peerless Price .60 .25
❑ 12 Rob Johnson .30 .14
❑ 13 Muhsin Muhammad .30 .14
❑ 14 Reggie White .60 .25
❑ 15 Steve Beuerlein .30 .14
❑ 16 Cade McNown .60 .25
❑ 17 Derrick Alexander .30 .14
❑ 18 Marcus Robinson .30 .14
❑ 19 Akili Smith .60 .25
❑ 20 Corey Dillon .60 .25
❑ 21 Kevin Johnson .60 .25
❑ 22 Tim Couch 1.25 .55
❑ 23 Emmitt Smith 1.50 .70
❑ 24 Joey Galloway .60 .25
❑ 25 Rocket Ismail .30 .14
❑ 26 Troy Aikman 1.50 .70
❑ 27 Brian Griese .75 .35
❑ 28 Ed McCaffrey .60 .25
❑ 29 John Elway 2.50 1.10
❑ 30 Olandis Gary .60 .25
❑ 31 Rod Smith .30 .14
❑ 32 Terrell Davis 1.50 .70
❑ 33 Charlie Batch .60 .25
❑ 34 Germane Crowell .30 .14
❑ 35 James Stewart .30 .14
❑ 36 Barry Sanders 2.00 .90
❑ 37 Antonio Freeman .60 .25
❑ 38 Brett Favre 2.50 1.10
❑ 39 Dorsey Levens .30 .14
❑ 40 Edgerrin James 2.50 1.10
❑ 41 Marvin Harrison .60 .25
❑ 42 Peyton Manning 2.00 .90
❑ 43 Fred Taylor .75 .35
❑ 44 Jimmy Smith .30 .14
❑ 45 Mark Brunell 1.00 .45
❑ 46 Elvis Grbac .30 .14
❑ 47 Tony Gonzalez .30 .14
❑ 48 Dan Marino 2.50 1.10
❑ 49 Joe Horn .30 .14
❑ 50 Jay Fiedler .60 .25
❑ 51 Thurman Thomas .30 .14
❑ 52 Cris Carter .60 .25
❑ 53 Daunte Culpepper 1.25 .55
❑ 54 Randy Moss 2.00 .90
❑ 55 Robert Smith .60 .25
❑ 56 Drew Bledsoe 1.00 .45
❑ 57 Terry Glenn .30 .14
❑ 58 Ricky Williams 1.50 .70
❑ 59 Amani Toomer .20 .09
❑ 60 Kerry Collins .30 .14
❑ 61 Curtis Martin .60 .25
❑ 62 Vinny Testaverde .30 .14
❑ 63 Wayne Chrebet .30 .14
❑ 64 Rich Gannon .30 .14
❑ 65 Tim Brown .60 .25
❑ 66 Tyrone Wheatley .30 .14
❑ 67 Donovan McNabb 1.00 .45
❑ 68 Duce Staley .60 .25
❑ 69 Jerome Bettis .60 .25
❑ 70 Jermaine Fazande .20 .09
❑ 71 Junior Seau .30 .14
❑ 72 Donald Hayes .20 .09
❑ 73 Charlie Garner .30 .14
❑ 74 Jeff Garcia .60 .25
❑ 75 Jerry Rice 1.50 .70
❑ 76 Steve Young 1.00 .45
❑ 77 Terrell Owens .60 .25
❑ 78 Tiki Barber .30 .14
❑ 79 Tim Biakabutuka .30 .14
❑ 80 Ricky Watters .20 .09
❑ 81 Isaac Bruce .60 .25
❑ 82 Kurt Warner 2.50 1.10
❑ 83 Marshall Faulk .75 .35
❑ 84 Torry Holt .60 .25
❑ 85 Keyshawn Johnson .60 .25
❑ 86 Mike Alstott .60 .25
❑ 87 Shaun King 1.00 .45
❑ 88 Warren Sapp .30 .14
❑ 89 Warrick Dunn .60 .25
❑ 90 Eddie George .75 .35
❑ 91 Jevon Kearse .60 .25
❑ 92 Steve McNair .60 .25
❑ 93 Carl Pickens .30 .14
❑ 94 Albert Connell .20 .09
❑ 95 Brad Johnson .60 .25
❑ 96 Bruce Smith .30 .14
❑ 97 Deion Sanders .60 .25
❑ 98 Jeff George .30 .14
❑ 99 Michael Westbrook .30 .14
❑ 100 Stephen Davis .60 .25
❑ 101 Courtney Brown RC 100.00 45.00
❑ 102 Corey Simon RC 25.00 11.00
❑ 103 Brian Urlacher RC 80.00 36.00
❑ 104 Deon Grant RC EXCH 10.00 4.50
❑ 105 Peter Warrick RC 120.00 55.00
❑ 106 Jamal Lewis RC 200.00 90.00
❑ 107 Thomas Jones RC EXCH 30.00 13.50
❑ 108 Plaxico Burress RC 40.00 18.00
❑ 109 Travis Taylor RC EXCH 25.00 11.00
❑ 110 Ron Dayne RC 150.00 70.00
❑ 111 Bubba Franks RC 30.00 13.50
❑ 112 Chad Pennington RC 100.00 45.00
❑ 113 Shaun Alexander RC 80.00 36.00
❑ 114 Sylvester Morris RC 40.00 18.00
❑ 115 Mike Anderson RC 100.00 45.00
❑ 116 R.Jay Soward RC 20.00 9.00
❑ 117 Trung Canidate RC 20.00 9.00
❑ 118 Dennis Northcutt RC 25.00 11.00
❑ 119 Todd Pinkston RC 20.00 9.00
❑ 120 Jerry Porter RC 20.00 9.00
❑ 121 Travis Prentice RC EXCH 25.00 11.00
❑ 122 Giovanni Carmazzi RC 25.00 11.00
❑ 123 Ron Dugans RC 15.00 6.75
❑ 124 Dez White RC 15.00 6.75
❑ 125 Chris Cole RC 15.00 6.75
❑ 126 Ron Dixon RC 25.00 11.00
❑ 127 Chris Redman RC 90.00 40.00
❑ 128 J.R. Redmond RC EXCH 25.00 11.00
❑ 129 Laveranues Coles RC 30.00 13.50
❑ 130 JaJuan Dawson RC 20.00 9.00
❑ 131 Darrell Jackson RC 30.00 13.50
❑ 132 Reuben Droughns RC 20.00 9.00
❑ 133 Doug Chapman RC EXCH 40.00 18.00
❑ 134 Curtis Keaton RC EXCH 15.00 6.75
❑ 135 Gari Scott RC 15.00 6.75
❑ 136 Danny Farmer RC 20.00 9.00
❑ 137 Trevor Gaylor RC 15.00 6.75
❑ 138 Avion Black RC 15.00 6.75
❑ 139 Michael Wiley RC 20.00 9.00
❑ 140 Sammy Morris RC 25.00 11.00
❑ 141 Tee Martin RC 30.00 13.50
❑ 142 Troy Walters RC 20.00 9.00
❑ 143 Marc Bulger RC 20.00 9.00
❑ 144 Tom Brady RC 20.00 9.00
❑ 145 Todd Husak RC 20.00 9.00
❑ 146 Tim Rattay RC 30.00 13.50
❑ 147 Jarious Jackson RC EXCH 30.00 13.50
❑ 148 Joe Hamilton RC EXCH 20.00 9.00
❑ 149 Shyrone Stith RC 15.00 6.75
❑ 150 Kwame Cavil RC 15.00 6.75
❑ 151 Antonio Banks ET RC 6.00 2.70
❑ 152 Jonathan Brown ET RC 6.00 2.70
❑ 153 Ontiwaun Carter ET RC 6.00 2.70
❑ 154 Jeremaine Copeland ET 6.00 2.70
❑ 155 Ralph Dawkins ET RC 8.00 3.60
❑ 156 Marques Douglas ET RC 6.00 2.70
❑ 157 Kevin Drake ET RC 6.00 2.70
❑ 158 Damon Dunn ET RC 8.00 3.60
❑ 159 Todd Floyd ET RC 6.00 2.70
❑ 160 Tony Graziani ET 8.00 3.60
❑ 161 Derrick Ham ET RC EXCH 8.00 3.60
❑ 162 Duane Hawthorne ET RC 8.00 3.60

❑ 163 Alonzo Johnson ET RC 6.00 2.70
❑ 164 Mark Kacmarynski ET RC 6.00 2.70
❑ 165 Eric Kresser ET 6.00 2.70
❑ 166 Jim Kubiak ET RC 8.00 3.60
❑ 167 Blaine McElmurry ET RC 6.00 2.70
❑ 168 Scott Milanovich ET 10.00 4.50
❑ 169 Norman Miller ET RC 6.00 2.70
❑ 170 Sean Morey ET RC 8.00 3.60
❑ 171 Jeff Ogden ET 8.00 3.60
❑ 172 Pepe Pearson ET RC 8.00 3.60
❑ 173 Ron Powlus ET RC 15.00 6.75
❑ 174 Jason Shelley ET RC 8.00 3.60
❑ 175 Ben Snell ET RC 8.00 3.60
❑ 176 Aaron Stecker ET RC 8.00 3.60
❑ 177 L.C. Stevens ET 6.00 2.70
❑ 178 Mike Sutton ET RC 6.00 2.70
❑ 179 Damian Vaughn ET RC 6.00 2.70
❑ 180 Ted White ET 6.00 2.70
❑ 181 Marcus Crandell ET RC 10.00 4.50
❑ 182 Darryl Daniel ET RC 8.00 3.60
❑ 183 Jesse Haynes ET 6.00 2.70
❑ 184 Matt Lytle ET RC 8.00 3.60
❑ 185 Deon Mitchell ET RC 8.00 3.60
❑ 186 Kendrick Nord ET RC 6.00 2.70
❑ 187 Ronnie Powell ET EXCH 6.00 2.70
❑ 188 Selucio Sanford ET RC 8.00 3.60
❑ 189 Corey Thomas ET 6.00 2.70
❑ 190 Vershan Jackson ET RC 6.00 2.70
❑ 191 Jake Plummer PT EXCH 20.00 9.00
❑ 192 Jim Kelly PT 50.00 22.00
❑ 193 Bernie Kosar PT 30.00 13.50
❑ 194 Marvin Harrison PT 20.00 9.00
❑ 195 Fred Taylor PT EXCH 30.00 13.50
❑ 196 Kerry Collins PT 25.00 11.00
❑ 197 Kurt Warner PT 100.00 45.00
❑ 198 Jevon Kearse PT EXCH 30.00 13.50
❑ 199 Brad Johnson PT 20.00 9.00
❑ 200 Jeff George PT EXCH 20.00 9.00

1997 Playoff First and Ten

	MINT	NRMT
COMPLETE SET (250)	20.00	9.00

❑ 1 Marcus Allen .30 .14
❑ 2 Eric Bieniemy .10 .05
❑ 3 Jason Dunn .10 .05
❑ 4 Jim Harbaugh .20 .09
❑ 5 Michael Westbrook .20 .09
❑ 6 Tiki Barber RC 1.25 .55
❑ 7 Frank Reich .10 .05
❑ 8 Irving Fryar .20 .09
❑ 9 Courtney Hawkins .10 .05
❑ 10 Eric Zeier .20 .09
❑ 11 Kent Graham .10 .05
❑ 12 Trent Dilfer .30 .14
❑ 13 Neil O'Donnell .20 .09
❑ 14 Reidel Anthony RC .75 .35
❑ 15 Jeff Hostetler .10 .05
❑ 16 Lawrence Phillips .10 .05
❑ 17 Dave Brown .10 .05
❑ 18 Mike Tomczak .10 .05
❑ 19 Jake Reed .20 .09
❑ 20 Anthony Miller .10 .05
❑ 21 Eric Metcalf .20 .09
❑ 22 Sedrick Shaw RC .30 .14
❑ 23 Anthony Johnson .10 .05
❑ 24 Mario Bates .10 .05
❑ 25 Dorsey Levens .30 .14
❑ 26 Stan Humphries .20 .09
❑ 27 Ben Coates .20 .09
❑ 28 Tyrone Wheatley .20 .09
❑ 29 Adrian Murrell .20 .09
❑ 30 William Henderson .10 .05
❑ 31 Warrick Dunn RC 1.25 .55
❑ 32 LeShon Johnson .10 .05
❑ 33 James O.Stewart .20 .09
❑ 34 Edgar Bennett .20 .09
❑ 35 Raymont Harris .10 .05
❑ 36 LeRoy Butler .10 .05
❑ 37 Darren Woodson .10 .05
❑ 38 Darnell Autry RC .20 .09
❑ 39 Johnnie Morton .20 .09
❑ 40 William Floyd .20 .09
❑ 41 Terrell Fletcher .10 .05
❑ 42 Leonard Russell .10 .05
❑ 43 Henry Ellard .10 .05
❑ 44 Terrell Owens .30 .14
❑ 45 John Friesz .10 .05
❑ 46 Antowain Smith RC 1.00 .45
❑ 47 Charles Johnson .20 .09
❑ 48 Rickey Dudley .20 .09
❑ 49 Lake Dawson .10 .05
❑ 50 Bert Emanuel .20 .09
❑ 51 Zach Thomas .20 .09
❑ 52 Earnest Byner .10 .05
❑ 53 Yatil Green RC .20 .09
❑ 54 Chris Spielman .10 .05
❑ 55 Muhsin Muhammad .20 .09
❑ 56 Bobby Engram .20 .09
❑ 57 Eric Bjornson .10 .05
❑ 58 Willie Green .10 .05
❑ 59 Derrick Mayes .20 .09
❑ 60 Chris Sanders .10 .05
❑ 61 Jimmy Smith .20 .09
❑ 62 Tony Gonzalez RC 1.25 .55
❑ 63 Rich Gannon .20 .09
❑ 64 Stanley Pritchett .10 .05
❑ 65 Brad Johnson .50 .23
❑ 66 Rodney Peete .10 .05
❑ 67 Sam Gash .10 .05
❑ 68 Chris Calloway .10 .05
❑ 69 Chris T. Jones .10 .05
❑ 70 Will Blackwell RC .30 .14
❑ 71 Mark Bruener .10 .05
❑ 72 Terry Kirby .20 .09
❑ 73 Brian Blades .10 .05
❑ 74 Craig Heyward .10 .05
❑ 75 Jamie Asher .10 .05
❑ 76 Terance Mathis .20 .09
❑ 77 Troy Davis RC .30 .14
❑ 78 Bruce Smith .20 .09
❑ 79 Simeon Rice .20 .09
❑ 80 Fred Barnett .10 .05
❑ 81 Tim Brown .30 .14
❑ 82 James Jett .20 .09
❑ 83 Mark Carrier WR .10 .05
❑ 84 Shawn Jefferson .10 .05
❑ 85 Ken Dilger .10 .05
❑ 86 Rae Carruth RC .30 .14
❑ 87 Keenan McCardell .20 .09
❑ 88 Michael Irvin .30 .14
❑ 89 Mark Chmura .20 .09
❑ 90 Derrick Alexander WR .20 .09
❑ 91 Andre Reed .20 .09
❑ 92 Ed McCaffrey .20 .09
❑ 93 Erik Kramer .10 .05
❑ 94 Albert Connell RC .75 .35
❑ 95 Frank Wycheck .10 .05
❑ 96 Zack Crockett .10 .05
❑ 97 Jim Everett .10 .05
❑ 98 Michael Haynes .10 .05
❑ 99 Jeff Graham .10 .05
❑ 100 Brent Jones .20 .09
❑ 101 Troy Aikman 1.00 .45
❑ 102 Byron Hanspard RC .30 .14
❑ 103 Robert Brooks .20 .09
❑ 104 Karim Abdul-Jabbar .30 .14
❑ 105 Drew Bledsoe 1.00 .45
❑ 106 Napoleon Kaufman .30 .14
❑ 107 Steve Young .60 .25
❑ 108 Leeland McElroy .10 .05
❑ 109 Jamal Anderson .60 .25
❑ 110 David LaFleur RC .20 .09
❑ 111 Vinny Testaverde .20 .09
❑ 112 Eric Moulds .30 .14
❑ 113 Tim Biakabutuka .20 .09
❑ 114 Rick Mirer .10 .05
❑ 115 Jeff Blake .20 .09
❑ 116 Jim Schwantz RC .10 .05
❑ 117 Herman Moore .30 .14
❑ 118 Ike Hilliard RC .75 .35
❑ 119 Reggie White .30 .14
❑ 120 Steve McNair .50 .23
❑ 121 Marshall Faulk .30 .14
❑ 122 Natrone Means .30 .14
❑ 123 Greg Hill .10 .05
❑ 124 O.J. McDuffie .20 .09
❑ 125 Robert Smith .20 .09
❑ 126 Bryant Westbrook RC .10 .05
❑ 127 Ray Zellars .10 .05
❑ 128 Rodney Hampton .20 .09
❑ 129 Wayne Chrebet .30 .14
❑ 130 Desmond Howard .20 .09
❑ 131 Ty Detmer .20 .09
❑ 132 Erric Pegram .10 .05
❑ 133 Yancey Thigpen .20 .09
❑ 134 Danny Wuerffel RC .30 .14
❑ 135 Charlie Jones .20 .09
❑ 136 Chris Warren .20 .09
❑ 137 Isaac Bruce .30 .14
❑ 138 Errict Rhett .10 .05
❑ 139 Gus Frerotte .10 .05
❑ 140 Frank Sanders .20 .09
❑ 141 Todd Collins .10 .05
❑ 142 Jake Plummer RC 2.50 1.10
❑ 143 Darnay Scott .20 .09
❑ 144 Rashaan Salaam .10 .05
❑ 145 Terrell Davis 1.50 .70
❑ 146 Scott Mitchell .20 .09
❑ 147 Junior Seau .20 .09
❑ 148 Warren Moon .30 .14
❑ 149 Wesley Walls .20 .09
❑ 150 Daryl Johnston .20 .09
❑ 151 Brett Favre 2.00 .90
❑ 152 Emmitt Smith 1.50 .70
❑ 153 Dan Marino 2.00 .90
❑ 154 Larry Centers .20 .09
❑ 155 Michael Jackson .20 .09
❑ 156 Kerry Collins .20 .09
❑ 157 Curtis Conway .20 .09
❑ 158 Peter Boulware RC .20 .09
❑ 159 Carl Pickens .30 .14
❑ 160 Shannon Sharpe .20 .09
❑ 161 Brett Perriman .10 .05
❑ 162 Eddie George 1.00 .45
❑ 163 Mark Brunell 1.00 .45
❑ 164 Tamarick Vanover .20 .09
❑ 165 Cris Carter .30 .14
❑ 166 Corey Dillon RC 2.50 1.10
❑ 167 Curtis Martin .50 .23
❑ 168 Amani Toomer .20 .09
❑ 169 Jeff George .20 .09
❑ 170 Kordell Stewart .40 .18
❑ 171 Garrison Hearst .20 .09
❑ 172 Tony Banks .20 .09
❑ 173 Mike Alstott .30 .14
❑ 174 Jim Druckenmiller RC .30 .14
❑ 175 Chris Chandler .20 .09
❑ 176 Byron Bam Morris .10 .05
❑ 177 Billy Joe Hobert .20 .09
❑ 178 Ernie Mills .10 .05
❑ 179 Ki-Jana Carter .10 .05
❑ 180 Deion Sanders .30 .14
❑ 181 Ricky Watters .20 .09
❑ 182 Shawn Springs RC .20 .09
❑ 183 Barry Sanders 2.00 .90
❑ 184 Antonio Freeman .50 .23
❑ 185 Marvin Harrison .30 .14
❑ 186 Elvis Grbac .20 .09
❑ 187 Terry Glenn .30 .14
❑ 188 Willie Roaf .10 .05
❑ 189 Keyshawn Johnson .30 .14
❑ 190 Orlando Pace RC .30 .14
❑ 191 Jerome Bettis .30 .14
❑ 192 Tony Martin .20 .09
❑ 193 Jerry Rice 1.00 .45
❑ 194 Joey Galloway .40 .18
❑ 195 Terry Allen .30 .14

	#	Player	MINT	NRMT
❑	196	Eddie Kennison	.20	.09
❑	197	Thurman Thomas	.30	.14
❑	198	Darrell Russell RC	.10	.05
❑	199	Rob Moore	.20	.09
❑	200	John Elway	2.00	.90
❑	201	Quinn Early	.10	.05
❑	202	Kevin Greene	.20	.09
❑	203	Robert Green	.10	.05
❑	204	Tony Carter	.10	.05
❑	205	Michael Timpson	.10	.05
❑	206	Kevin Smith	.10	.05
❑	207	Herschel Walker	.20	.09
❑	208	Steve Atwater	.10	.05
❑	209	Tyrone Braxton	.10	.05
❑	210	Willie Davis	.10	.05
❑	211	Lamont Warren	.10	.05
❑	212	Sean Dawkins	.10	.05
❑	213	Dale Carter	.10	.05
❑	214	Kimble Anders	.20	.09
❑	215	Derrick Thomas	.20	.09
❑	216	Chris Penn	.10	.05
❑	217	Irving Spikes	.10	.05
❑	218	Amp Lee	.10	.05
❑	219	Qadry Ismail	.20	.09
❑	220	Dave Meggett	.10	.05
❑	221	Tyrone Hughes	.10	.05
❑	222	Haywood Jeffires	.10	.05
❑	223	Torrance Small	.10	.05
❑	224	Danny Kanell	.20	.09
❑	225	Thomas Lewis	.10	.05
❑	226	Kyle Brady	.10	.05
❑	227	Harvey Williams	.10	.05
❑	228	Bobby Hoying	.20	.09
❑	229	Charlie Garner	.10	.05
❑	230	Andre Hastings	.10	.05
❑	231	Heath Shuler	.10	.05
❑	232	J.J. Stokes	.20	.09
❑	233	Ken Norton	.10	.05
❑	234	Steve Walsh	.10	.05
❑	235	Harold Green	.10	.05
❑	236	Reggie Brooks	.10	.05
❑	237	Robb Thomas	.10	.05
❑	238	Brian Mitchell	.10	.05
❑	239	Bill Brooks	.10	.05
❑	240	Leslie Shepherd	.10	.05
❑	241	Jay Graham RC	.30	.14
❑	242	Kevin Lockett RC	.20	.09
❑	243	Derrick Mason RC	1.25	.55
❑	244	Marc Edwards RC	.10	.05
❑	245	Joey Kent RC	.30	.14
❑	246	Pat Barnes RC	.30	.14
❑	247	Sherman Williams	.10	.05
❑	248	Ray Brown G	.10	.05
❑	249	Stephen Davis	.50	.23
❑	250	Lamar Smith	.30	.14

1996 Playoff Illusions

	MINT	NRMT
COMPLETE SET (120)	50.00	22.00
COMP.SERIES 1 (63)	10.00	4.50
COMP.SERIES 2 (57)	40.00	18.00
COMMON CARD (1-63)	.15	.07
COMMON CARD (64-120)	.30	.14

	#	Player	MINT	NRMT
❑	1	Troy Aikman	1.50	.70
❑	2	Larry Centers	.30	.14
❑	3	Terance Mathis	.15	.07
❑	4	Michael Irvin	.60	.25
❑	5	Jim Kelly	.60	.25
❑	6	Tim Biakabutuka RC	1.25	.55
❑	7	Rashaan Salaam	.60	.25
❑	8	Ki-Jana Carter	.30	.14
❑	9	Anthony Miller	.30	.14
❑	10	Deion Sanders	.75	.35
❑	11	Scott Mitchell	.30	.14
❑	12	Robert Brooks	.60	.25
❑	13	Willie Davis	.15	.07
❑	14	Zack Crockett	.15	.07
❑	15	James O.Stewart	.30	.14
❑	16	Tamarick Vanover	.30	.14
❑	17	Stanley Pritchett	.15	.07
❑	18	Warren Moon	.30	.14
❑	19	Shawn Jefferson	.15	.07
❑	20	Shannon Sharpe	.30	.14
❑	21	Jim Everett	.15	.07
❑	22	Dave Brown	.15	.07
❑	23	Adrian Murrell	.60	.25
❑	24	Rickey Dudley RC	.60	.25
❑	25	Chris T. Jones	.30	.14
❑	26	Andre Hastings	.15	.07
❑	27	Stan Humphries	.30	.14
❑	28	Steve Young	1.25	.55
❑	29	Joey Galloway	1.00	.45
❑	30	Jim Harbaugh	.30	.14
❑	31	Eddie Kennison RC	.60	.25
❑	32	Mike Alstott RC	2.50	1.10
❑	33	Michael Westbrook	.60	.25
❑	34	Leeland McElroy RC	.60	.25
❑	35	Erik Kramer	.15	.07
❑	36	Mark Chmura	.30	.14
❑	37	Cris Carter	.60	.25
❑	38	Ben Coates	.30	.14
❑	39	Wayne Chrebet	1.00	.45
❑	40	Jerome Bettis	.60	.25
❑	41	Tim Brown	.60	.25
❑	42	Jason Dunn RC	.30	.14
❑	43	William Henderson	.15	.07
❑	44	Rick Mirer	.30	.14
❑	45	J.J. Stokes	.60	.25
❑	46	Rodney Peete	.15	.07
❑	47	Neil O'Donnell	.30	.14
❑	48	Tyrone Wheatley	.30	.14
❑	49	Terry Glenn RC	2.00	.90
❑	50	Junior Seau	.30	.14
❑	51	Jake Reed	.30	.14
❑	52	O.J. McDuffie	.30	.14
❑	53	Steve Bono	.15	.07
❑	54	Steve McNair	1.25	.55
❑	55	Antonio Freeman	1.25	.55
❑	56	Johnnie Morton	.30	.14
❑	57	Eric Metcalf	.15	.07
❑	58	Andre Reed	.30	.14
❑	59	Bobby Engram RC	.60	.25
❑	60	Gus Frerotte	.60	.25
❑	61	Jeff Blake	.60	.25
❑	62	Eric Pegram	.15	.07
❑	63	Jeff Hostetler	.15	.07
❑	64	Edgar Bennett	.60	.25
❑	65	Eddie George RC	10.00	4.50
❑	66	Marvin Harrison RC	6.00	2.70
❑	67	LeShon Johnson	.30	.14
❑	68	Jamal Anderson RC	10.00	4.50
❑	69	Thurman Thomas	1.25	.55
❑	70	Barry Sanders	6.00	2.70
❑	71	Muhsin Muhammad RC	4.00	1.80
❑	72	Robert Green	.30	.14
❑	73	Garrison Hearst	.60	.25
❑	74	John Elway	6.00	2.70
❑	75	Herman Moore	1.25	.55
❑	76	Chris Chandler	.30	.14
❑	77	Marshall Faulk	1.25	.55
❑	78	Mark Brunell	3.00	1.35
❑	79	Tony Banks RC	4.00	1.80
❑	80	Terrell Davis	6.00	2.70
❑	81	Marcus Allen	1.25	.55
❑	82	Dan Marino	6.00	2.70
❑	83	Robert Smith	.60	.25
❑	84	Curtis Martin	2.50	1.10
❑	85	Amani Toomer RC	4.00	1.80
❑	86	Napoleon Kaufman	.60	.25
❑	87	Ricky Watters	.60	.25
❑	88	Kordell Stewart	2.00	.90
❑	89	Keyshawn Johnson RC	5.00	2.20
❑	90	Emmitt Smith	5.00	2.20
❑	91	Chris Warren	.60	.25
❑	92	Isaac Bruce	1.25	.55
❑	93	Terry Allen	.60	.25
❑	94	Trent Dilfer	.60	.25
❑	95	Vinny Testaverde	.60	.25
❑	96	Bruce Smith	1.25	.55
❑	97	Kerry Collins	1.25	.55
❑	98	Curtis Conway	1.25	.55
❑	99	Karim Abdul-Jabbar RC	2.50	1.10
❑	100	Brett Favre	6.00	2.70
❑	101	Carl Pickens	1.25	.55
❑	102	Brett Perriman	.30	.14
❑	103	Keith Jackson	.30	.14
❑	104	Drew Bledsoe	3.00	1.35
❑	105	Rodney Hampton	.30	.14
❑	106	Ray Zellars	.30	.14
❑	107	Jeff Graham	.30	.14
❑	108	Irving Fryar	.60	.25
❑	109	Lawrence Phillips RC	1.25	.55
❑	110	Jerry Rice	3.00	1.35
❑	111	Mike Tomczak	.30	.14
❑	112	Tony Martin	.60	.25
❑	113	Brian Blades	.60	.25
❑	114	Bill Brooks	.30	.14
❑	115	Rob Moore	.30	.14
❑	116	Quinn Early	.30	.14
❑	117	Darnay Scott	.60	.25
❑	118	Ken Dilger	.30	.14
❑	119	Derek Loville	.30	.14
❑	120	Reggie White	1.25	.55
❑	P1	Robert Brooks Promo	.75	.35

1998 Playoff Momentum Hobby

	MINT	NRMT
COMPLETE SET (250)	300.00	135.00

	#	Player	MINT	NRMT
❑	1	Jake Plummer	4.00	1.80
❑	2	Eric Metcalf	.60	.25
❑	3	Adrian Murrell	1.25	.55
❑	4	Larry Centers	.60	.25
❑	5	Frank Sanders	1.25	.55
❑	6	Rob Moore	1.25	.55
❑	7	Andre Wadsworth RC	8.00	3.60
❑	8	Chris Chandler	1.25	.55
❑	9	Jamal Anderson	2.00	.90
❑	10	Tony Martin	1.25	.55
❑	11	Terance Mathis	1.25	.55
❑	12	Tim Dwight RC	12.00	5.50
❑	13	Jammi German RC	5.00	2.20
❑	14	O.J. Santiago	.60	.25
❑	15	Jim Harbaugh	1.25	.55
❑	16	Eric Zeier	1.25	.55
❑	17	Duane Starks RC	5.00	2.20
❑	18	Rod Woodson	1.25	.55
❑	19	Errict Rhett	1.25	.55
❑	20	Jay Graham	.60	.25
❑	21	Ray Lewis	2.00	.90
❑	22	Michael Jackson	.60	.25
❑	23	Jermaine Lewis	1.25	.55
❑	24	Pat Johnson RC	8.00	3.60
❑	25	Eric Green	.60	.25
❑	26	Doug Flutie	2.00	.90
❑	27	Rob Johnson	1.25	.55
❑	28	Antowain Smith	2.00	.90
❑	29	Thurman Thomas	2.00	.90

Card	Mint	NrMt
❑ 30 Jonathan Linton RC	10.00	4.50
❑ 31 Bruce Smith	1.25	.55
❑ 32 Eric Moulds	2.00	.90
❑ 33 Kevin Williams	.60	.25
❑ 34 Andre Reed	1.25	.55
❑ 35 Steve Beuerlein	.60	.25
❑ 36 Kerry Collins	1.25	.55
❑ 37 Anthony Johnson	.60	.25
❑ 38 Fred Lane	1.25	.55
❑ 39 William Floyd	.60	.25
❑ 40 Rocket Ismail	.60	.25
❑ 41 Wesley Walls	1.25	.55
❑ 42 Muhsin Muhammad	1.25	.55
❑ 43 Rae Carruth	1.25	.55
❑ 44 Kevin Greene	1.25	.55
❑ 45 Greg Lloyd	.60	.25
❑ 46 Moses Moreno RC	8.00	3.60
❑ 47 Erik Kramer	.60	.25
❑ 48 Edgar Bennett	.60	.25
❑ 49 Curtis Enis RC	12.00	5.50
❑ 50 Curtis Conway	1.25	.55
❑ 51 Bobby Engram	1.25	.55
❑ 52 Alonzo Mayes RC	5.00	2.20
❑ 53 Jeff Blake	1.25	.55
❑ 54 Neil O'Donnell	1.25	.55
❑ 55 Corey Dillon	3.00	1.35
❑ 56 Takeo Spikes RC	8.00	3.60
❑ 57 Carl Pickens	2.00	.90
❑ 58 Tony McGee	.60	.25
❑ 59 Darnay Scott	1.25	.55
❑ 60 Troy Aikman	5.00	2.20
❑ 61 Deion Sanders	2.00	.90
❑ 62 Emmitt Smith	8.00	3.60
❑ 63 Darren Woodson	.60	.25
❑ 64 Chris Warren	1.25	.55
❑ 65 Daryl Johnston	1.25	.55
❑ 66 Ernie Mills	.60	.25
❑ 67 Billy Davis	.60	.25
❑ 68 Michael Irvin	2.00	.90
❑ 69 David LaFleur	.60	.25
❑ 70 John Elway	10.00	4.50
❑ 71 Brian Griese RC	25.00	11.00
❑ 72 Steve Atwater	.60	.25
❑ 73 Terrell Davis	8.00	3.60
❑ 74 Rod Smith	1.25	.55
❑ 75 Marcus Nash RC	10.00	4.50
❑ 76 Shannon Sharpe	1.25	.55
❑ 77 Ed McCaffrey	1.25	.55
❑ 78 Neil Smith	1.25	.55
❑ 79 Charlie Batch RC	20.00	9.00
❑ 80 Germane Crowell RC	20.00	9.00
❑ 81 Scott Mitchell	1.25	.55
❑ 82 Barry Sanders	10.00	4.50
❑ 83 Terry Fair RC	8.00	3.60
❑ 84 Herman Moore	2.00	.90
❑ 85 Johnnie Morton	1.25	.55
❑ 86 Brett Favre	10.00	4.50
❑ 87 Rick Mirer	.60	.25
❑ 88 Dorsey Levens	2.00	.90
❑ 89 William Henderson	.60	.25
❑ 90 Derrick Mayes	1.25	.55
❑ 91 Antonio Freeman	2.00	.90
❑ 92 Robert Brooks	1.25	.55
❑ 93 Mark Chmura	1.25	.55
❑ 94 Vonnie Holliday RC	8.00	3.60
❑ 95 Reggie White	2.00	.90
❑ 96 E.G. Green RC	8.00	3.60
❑ 97 Jerome Pathon RC	8.00	3.60
❑ 98 Peyton Manning RC	50.00	22.00
❑ 99 Marshall Faulk	2.00	.90
❑ 100 Zack Crockett	.60	.25
❑ 101 Ken Dilger	.60	.25
❑ 102 Marvin Harrison	1.25	.55
❑ 103 Mark Brunell	4.00	1.80
❑ 104 Jonathan Quinn RC	8.00	3.60
❑ 105 Tavian Banks RC	8.00	3.60
❑ 106 Fred Taylor RC	20.00	9.00
❑ 107 James Stewart	1.25	.55
❑ 108 Jimmy Smith	1.25	.55
❑ 109 Keenan McCardell	1.25	.55
❑ 110 Elvis Grbac	1.25	.55
❑ 111 Rich Gannon	1.25	.55
❑ 112 Rashaan Shehee RC	8.00	3.60
❑ 113 Donnell Bennett	.60	.25
❑ 114 Kimble Anders	1.25	.55
❑ 115 Derrick Thomas	1.25	.55
❑ 116 Kevin Lockett	.60	.25
❑ 117 Derrick Alexander WR	1.25	.55
❑ 118 Tony Gonzalez	.60	.25
❑ 119 Andre Rison	1.25	.55
❑ 120 Craig Erickson	.60	.25
❑ 121 Dan Marino	10.00	4.50
❑ 122 John Avery RC	10.00	4.50
❑ 123 Karim Abdul-Jabbar	2.00	.90
❑ 124 Zach Thomas	1.25	.55
❑ 125 O.J. McDuffie	1.25	.55
❑ 126 Troy Drayton	.60	.25
❑ 127 Randall Cunningham	2.00	.90
❑ 128 Brad Johnson	2.00	.90
❑ 129 Robert Smith	2.00	.90
❑ 130 Cris Carter	2.00	.90
❑ 131 Randy Moss RC	50.00	22.00
❑ 132 Jake Reed	1.25	.55
❑ 133 John Randle	1.25	.55
❑ 134 Drew Bledsoe	4.00	1.80
❑ 135 Tony Simmons RC	8.00	3.60
❑ 136 Sedrick Shaw	.60	.25
❑ 137 Chris Floyd RC	5.00	2.20
❑ 138 Robert Edwards RC	12.00	5.50
❑ 139 Rod Rutledge RC	5.00	2.20
❑ 140 Shawn Jefferson	.60	.25
❑ 141 Ben Coates	1.25	.55
❑ 142 Terry Glenn	2.00	.90
❑ 143 Heath Shuler	.60	.25
❑ 144 Danny Wuerffel	1.25	.55
❑ 145 Troy Davis	.60	.25
❑ 146 Qadry Ismail	.60	.25
❑ 147 Ray Zellars	.60	.25
❑ 148 Lamar Smith	1.25	.55
❑ 149 Cameron Cleeland RC	8.00	3.60
❑ 150 Sean Dawkins	.60	.25
❑ 151 Andre Hastings	.60	.25
❑ 152 Danny Kanell	1.25	.55
❑ 153 Tiki Barber	1.25	.55
❑ 154 Tyrone Wheatley	1.25	.55
❑ 155 Charles Way	.60	.25
❑ 156 Gary Brown	.60	.25
❑ 157 Shaun Williams RC	5.00	2.20
❑ 158 Chris Calloway	.60	.25
❑ 159 Amani Toomer	1.25	.55
❑ 160 Brian Alford RC	8.00	3.60
❑ 161 Joe Jurevicius RC	8.00	3.60
❑ 162 Ike Hilliard	1.25	.55
❑ 163 Michael Strahan	.60	.25
❑ 164 Glenn Foley	1.25	.55
❑ 165 Vinny Testaverde	1.25	.55
❑ 166 Keyshawn Johnson	2.00	.90
❑ 167 Curtis Martin	2.00	.90
❑ 168 Leon Johnson	.60	.25
❑ 169 Keith Byars	.60	.25
❑ 170 Wayne Chrebet	2.00	.90
❑ 171 Kyle Brady	.60	.25
❑ 172 Dedric Ward	.60	.25
❑ 173 Jeff George	1.25	.55
❑ 174 Charles Woodson RC	12.00	5.50
❑ 175 Napoleon Kaufman	2.00	.90
❑ 176 Jon Ritchie RC	8.00	3.60
❑ 177 Tim Brown	2.00	.90
❑ 178 James Jett	1.25	.55
❑ 179 Rickey Dudley	.60	.25
❑ 180 Bobby Hoying	1.25	.55
❑ 181 Duce Staley	4.00	1.80
❑ 182 Charlie Garner	.60	.25
❑ 183 Irving Fryar	1.25	.55
❑ 184 Jeff Graham	.60	.25
❑ 185 Jason Dunn	.60	.25
❑ 186 Kordell Stewart	2.00	.90
❑ 187 Jerome Bettis	2.00	.90
❑ 188 Andre Coleman	.60	.25
❑ 189 C.Fuamatu-Ma'afala RC	8.00	3.60
❑ 190 Charles Johnson	.60	.25
❑ 191 Hines Ward RC	8.00	3.60
❑ 192 Mark Bruener	.60	.25
❑ 193 Courtney Hawkins	.60	.25
❑ 194 Will Blackwell	.60	.25
❑ 195 Levon Kirkland	.60	.25
❑ 196 Mikhael Ricks RC	8.00	3.60
❑ 197 Ryan Leaf RC	15.00	6.75
❑ 198 Natrone Means	2.00	.90
❑ 199 Junior Seau	1.25	.55
❑ 200 Bryan Still	.60	.25
❑ 201 Freddie Jones	.60	.25
❑ 202 Steve Young	3.00	1.35
❑ 203 Jim Druckenmiller	1.25	.55
❑ 204 Garrison Hearst	2.00	.90
❑ 205 R.W. McQuarters RC	5.00	2.20
❑ 206 Merton Hanks	.60	.25
❑ 207 Marc Edwards	.60	.25
❑ 208 Jerry Rice	5.00	2.20
❑ 209 Terrell Owens	2.00	.90
❑ 210 J.J. Stokes	1.25	.55
❑ 211 Tony Banks	1.25	.55
❑ 212 Robert Holcombe RC	10.00	4.50
❑ 213 Greg Hill	.60	.25
❑ 214 Amp Lee	.60	.25
❑ 215 Jerald Moore	.60	.25
❑ 216 Isaac Bruce	2.00	.90
❑ 217 Az-Zahir Hakim RC	10.00	4.50
❑ 218 Eddie Kennison	1.25	.55
❑ 219 Grant Wistrom RC	5.00	2.20
❑ 220 Warren Moon	2.00	.90
❑ 221 Ahman Green RC	20.00	9.00
❑ 222 Steve Broussard	.60	.25
❑ 223 Ricky Watters	1.25	.55
❑ 224 James McKnight	.60	.25
❑ 225 Joey Galloway	2.00	.90
❑ 226 Mike Pritchard	.60	.25
❑ 227 Trent Dilfer	2.00	.90
❑ 228 Warrick Dunn	2.00	.90
❑ 229 Mike Alstott	2.00	.90
❑ 230 John Lynch	1.25	.55
❑ 231 Jacquez Green RC	12.00	5.50
❑ 232 Reidel Anthony	1.25	.55
❑ 233 Bert Emanuel	1.25	.55
❑ 234 Warren Sapp	1.25	.55
❑ 235 Steve McNair	2.00	.90
❑ 236 Eddie George	4.00	1.80
❑ 237 Chris Sanders	.60	.25
❑ 238 Yancey Thigpen	.60	.25
❑ 239 Willie Davis	.60	.25
❑ 240 Kevin Dyson RC	12.00	5.50
❑ 241 Frank Wycheck	.60	.25
❑ 242 Trent Green	2.50	1.10
❑ 243 Gus Frerotte	.60	.25
❑ 244 Skip Hicks RC	10.00	4.50
❑ 245 Terry Allen	2.00	.90
❑ 246 Stephen Davis	.60	.25
❑ 247 Stephen Alexander RC	8.00	3.60
❑ 248 Michael Westbrook	1.25	.55
❑ 249 Dana Stubblefield SP	2.00	.90
❑ 250 Dan Wilkinson SP	2.00	.90

1999 Playoff Momentum SSD

	MINT	NRMT
COMPLETE SET (200)	300.00	135.00
COMP.SHORT SET (150)	100.00	45.00
COMMON CARD (1-100)	.15	.07
COMMON CARD (101-150)	.25	.11
COMMON ROOKIE (151-200)	2.50	1.10

Card	Mint	NrMt
❑ 1 Rob Moore	.30	.14
❑ 2 Adrian Murrell	.30	.14
❑ 3 Frank Sanders	.30	.14
❑ 4 Andre Wadsworth	.15	.07
❑ 5 Tim Dwight	.60	.25
❑ 6 Terance Mathis	.30	.14
❑ 7 Priest Holmes	.60	.25
❑ 8 Jermaine Lewis	.30	.14

❑ 9 Scott Mitchell .15 .07
❑ 10 Patrick Johnson .15 .07
❑ 11 Tony Banks .30 .14
❑ 12 Thurman Thomas .30 .14
❑ 13 Andre Reed .30 .14
❑ 14 Bruce Smith .30 .14
❑ 15 Tim Biakabutuka .30 .14
❑ 16 Muhsin Muhammad .30 .14
❑ 17 Wesley Walls .30 .14
❑ 18 Rae Carruth .30 .14
❑ 19 Curtis Conway .30 .14
❑ 20 Bobby Engram .30 .14
❑ 21 Jeff Blake .30 .14
❑ 22 Darnay Scott .15 .07
❑ 23 Ty Detmer .30 .14
❑ 24 Leslie Shepherd .15 .07
❑ 25 Sedrick Shaw .15 .07
❑ 26 Michael Irvin .30 .14
❑ 27 Rocket Ismail .30 .14
❑ 28 Ed McCaffrey .30 .14
❑ 29 Marcus Nash .30 .14
❑ 30 Shannon Sharpe .30 .14
❑ 31 Neil Smith .30 .14
❑ 32 Rod Smith .30 .14
❑ 33 Bubby Brister .15 .07
❑ 34 Germane Crowell .30 .14
❑ 35 Johnnie Morton .30 .14
❑ 36 Bill Schroeder .60 .25
❑ 37 Mark Chmura .15 .07
❑ 38 Marvin Harrison .60 .25
❑ 39 E.G. Green .15 .07
❑ 40 Jerome Pathon .15 .07
❑ 41 Keenan McCardell .30 .14
❑ 42 Jimmy Smith .30 .14
❑ 43 Kyle Brady .15 .07
❑ 44 Tavian Banks .15 .07
❑ 45 Warren Moon .60 .25
❑ 46 Derrick Alexander WR .30 .14
❑ 47 Elvis Grbac .30 .14
❑ 48 Andre Rison .30 .14
❑ 49 Byron Bam Morris .15 .07
❑ 50 Rashaan Shehee .15 .07
❑ 51 Karim Abdul-Jabbar .30 .14
❑ 52 John Avery .30 .14
❑ 53 Tony Martin .30 .14
❑ 54 O.J. McDuffie .30 .14
❑ 55 Oronde Gadsden .15 .07
❑ 56 Robert Smith .60 .25
❑ 57 Jeff George .30 .14
❑ 58 Jake Reed .30 .14
❑ 59 Leroy Hoard .15 .07
❑ 60 Terry Allen .30 .14
❑ 61 Terry Glenn .60 .25
❑ 62 Ben Coates .30 .14
❑ 63 Tony Simmons .15 .07
❑ 64 Cameron Cleeland .15 .07
❑ 65 Eddie Kennison .30 .14
❑ 66 Billy Joe Hobert .15 .07
❑ 67 Amani Toomer .15 .07
❑ 68 Kerry Collins .30 .14
❑ 69 Ike Hilliard .15 .07
❑ 70 Gary Brown .15 .07
❑ 71 Joe Jurevicius .15 .07
❑ 72 Wayne Chrebet .30 .14
❑ 73 Vinny Testaverde .30 .14
❑ 74 Charles Woodson .60 .25
❑ 75 James Jett .30 .14
❑ 76 Charles Johnson .15 .07
❑ 77 Duce Staley .60 .25
❑ 78 Hines Ward .15 .07
❑ 79 Jim Harbaugh .30 .14
❑ 80 Ryan Leaf .60 .25
❑ 81 Junior Seau .30 .14
❑ 82 Mikhael Ricks .15 .07
❑ 83 Garrison Hearst .30 .14
❑ 84 J.J. Stokes .30 .14
❑ 85 Lawrence Phillips .30 .14
❑ 86 Derrick Mayes .15 .07
❑ 87 Mike Pritchard .15 .07
❑ 88 Ahman Green .30 .14
❑ 89 Ricky Watters .30 .14
❑ 90 Robert Holcombe .30 .14
❑ 91 Isaac Bruce .60 .25
❑ 92 Trent Dilfer .30 .14
❑ 93 Reidel Anthony .15 .07
❑ 94 Jacquez Green .30 .14
❑ 95 Warren Sapp .15 .07
❑ 96 Kevin Dyson .30 .14
❑ 97 Yancey Thigpen .15 .07
❑ 98 Stephen Davis .60 .25
❑ 99 Irving Fryar .30 .14
❑ 100 Michael Westbrook .30 .14
❑ 101 Jake Plummer 2.00 .90
❑ 102 Jamal Anderson 1.00 .45
❑ 103 Chris Chandler .50 .23
❑ 104 Doug Flutie 1.25 .55
❑ 105 Eric Moulds 1.00 .45
❑ 106 Antowain Smith 1.00 .45
❑ 107 Jonathan Linton .25 .11
❑ 108 Curtis Enis 1.00 .45
❑ 109 Corey Dillon 1.00 .45
❑ 110 Carl Pickens .50 .23
❑ 111 Emmitt Smith 2.50 1.10
❑ 112 Troy Aikman 2.50 1.10
❑ 113 Deion Sanders 1.00 .45
❑ 114 John Elway 4.00 1.80
❑ 115 Terrell Davis 2.50 1.10
❑ 116 Brian Griese 2.00 .90
❑ 117 Barry Sanders 4.00 1.80
❑ 118 Charlie Batch 2.00 .90
❑ 119 Herman Moore 1.00 .45
❑ 120 Brett Favre 4.00 1.80
❑ 121 Antonio Freeman 1.00 .45
❑ 122 Dorsey Levens 1.00 .45
❑ 123 Peyton Manning 4.00 1.80
❑ 124 Fred Taylor 2.50 1.10
❑ 125 Mark Brunell 1.50 .70
❑ 126 Dan Marino 4.00 1.80
❑ 127 Randy Moss 4.00 1.80
❑ 128 Cris Carter 1.00 .45
❑ 129 Randall Cunningham 1.00 .45
❑ 130 Drew Bledsoe 1.50 .70
❑ 131 Keyshawn Johnson 1.00 .45
❑ 132 Curtis Martin 1.00 .45
❑ 133 Tim Brown 1.00 .45
❑ 134 Napoleon Kaufman 1.00 .45
❑ 135 Kordell Stewart 1.00 .45
❑ 136 Jerome Bettis 1.00 .45
❑ 137 Natrone Means .50 .23
❑ 138 Jerry Rice 2.50 1.10
❑ 139 Steve Young 1.50 .70
❑ 140 Terrell Owens 1.00 .45
❑ 141 Joey Galloway 1.00 .45
❑ 142 Jon Kitna .60 .25
❑ 143 Marshall Faulk 1.00 .45
❑ 144 Kurt Warner RC 20.00 9.00
❑ 145 Warrick Dunn 1.00 .45
❑ 146 Mike Alstott 1.00 .45
❑ 147 Eddie George 1.25 .55
❑ 148 Steve McNair 1.00 .45
❑ 149 Brad Johnson 1.00 .45
❑ 150 Skip Hicks 1.00 .45
❑ 151 Tim Couch RC 15.00 6.75
❑ 152 Donovan McNabb RC 15.00 6.75
❑ 153 Akili Smith RC 10.00 4.50
❑ 154 Edgerrin James RC 25.00 11.00
❑ 155 Ricky Williams RC 15.00 6.75
❑ 156 Torry Holt RC 12.00 5.50
❑ 157 Champ Bailey RC 6.00 2.70
❑ 158 David Boston RC 10.00 4.50
❑ 159 Chris Claiborne RC 2.50 1.10
❑ 160 Chris McAlister RC 4.00 1.80
❑ 161 Daunte Culpepper RC 25.00 11.00
❑ 162 Cade McNown RC 6.00 2.70
❑ 163 Troy Edwards RC 6.00 2.70
❑ 164 Jevon Kearse RC 10.00 4.50
❑ 165 Kevin Johnson RC 10.00 4.50
❑ 166 James Johnson RC 5.00 2.20
❑ 167 Reginald Kelly RC 2.50 1.10
❑ 168 Rob Konrad RC 5.00 2.20
❑ 169 Jim Kleinsasser RC 5.00 2.20
❑ 170 Kevin Faulk RC 8.00 3.60
❑ 171 Joe Montgomery RC 5.00 2.20
❑ 172 Shaun King RC 10.00 4.50
❑ 173 Peerless Price RC 6.00 2.70
❑ 174 Mike Cloud RC 5.00 2.20
❑ 175 Jermaine Fazande RC 5.00 2.20
❑ 176 D'Wayne Bates RC 4.00 1.80
❑ 177 Brock Huard RC 8.00 3.60
❑ 178 Marty Booker RC 5.00 2.20
❑ 179 Karsten Bailey RC 4.00 1.80
❑ 180 Shawn Bryson RC 5.00 2.20
❑ 181 Jeff Paulk RC 4.00 1.80
❑ 182 Travis McGriff RC 4.00 1.80
❑ 183 Amos Zereoue RC 5.00 2.20
❑ 184 Craig Yeast RC 4.00 1.80
❑ 185 Joe Germaine RC 5.00 2.20
❑ 186 Dameane Douglas RC 4.00 1.80
❑ 187 Sedrick Irvin RC 5.00 2.20
❑ 188 Brandon Stokley RC 5.00 2.20
❑ 189 Larry Parker RC 4.00 1.80
❑ 190 Sean Bennett RC 5.00 2.20
❑ 191 Wane McGarity RC 4.00 1.80
❑ 192 Olandis Gary RC 10.00 4.50
❑ 193 Na Brown RC 5.00 2.20
❑ 194 Aaron Brooks RC 15.00 6.75
❑ 195 Cecil Collins RC 5.00 2.20
❑ 196 Darrin Chiaverini RC 4.00 1.80
❑ 197 Kevin Daft RC 4.00 1.80
❑ 198 Darnell McDonald RC 5.00 2.20
❑ 199 Joel Makovicka RC 5.00 2.20
❑ 200 Michael Bishop RC 6.00 2.70

2000 Playoff Momentum

	MINT	NRMT
COMP.SET w/o SP's (100)	15.00	6.75

❑ 1 David Boston .50 .23
❑ 2 Jake Plummer .50 .23
❑ 3 Chris Chandler .25 .11
❑ 4 Jamal Anderson .50 .23
❑ 5 Tim Dwight .50 .23
❑ 6 Qadry Ismail .25 .11
❑ 7 Peerless Price .50 .23
❑ 8 Antowain Smith .25 .11
❑ 9 Eric Moulds .50 .23
❑ 10 Rob Johnson .25 .11
❑ 11 Natrone Means .15 .07
❑ 12 Muhsin Muhammad .25 .11
❑ 13 Steve Beuerlein .25 .11
❑ 14 Patrick Jeffers .50 .23
❑ 15 Curtis Enis .25 .11
❑ 16 Cade McNown .50 .23
❑ 17 Marcus Robinson .50 .23
❑ 18 Corey Dillon .50 .23
❑ 19 Akili Smith .50 .23
❑ 20 Carl Pickens .25 .11
❑ 21 Tim Couch 1.00 .45
❑ 22 Kevin Johnson .50 .23
❑ 23 Troy Aikman 1.25 .55
❑ 24 Emmitt Smith 1.25 .55
❑ 25 Joey Galloway .50 .23
❑ 26 Rocket Ismail .25 .11
❑ 27 Olandis Gary .50 .23
❑ 28 John Elway 2.00 .90
❑ 29 Brian Griese .60 .25
❑ 30 Ed McCaffrey .50 .23
❑ 31 Terrell Davis 1.25 .55
❑ 32 Charlie Batch .50 .23
❑ 33 James Stewart .25 .11
❑ 34 Germane Crowell .25 .11
❑ 35 Barry Sanders 1.50 .70
❑ 36 Herman Moore .25 .11
❑ 37 Antonio Freeman .50 .23
❑ 38 Dorsey Levens .25 .11
❑ 39 Brett Favre 2.00 .90
❑ 40 Edgerrin James 2.00 .90
❑ 41 Marvin Harrison .50 .23
❑ 42 Peyton Manning 1.50 .70

	Card	MINT	NRMT
❑	43 Fred Taylor	.60	.25
❑	44 Keenan McCardell	.25	.11
❑	45 Mark Brunell	.75	.35
❑	46 Jimmy Smith	.25	.11
❑	47 Elvis Grbac	.25	.11
❑	48 Tony Gonzalez	.25	.11
❑	49 James Johnson	.25	.11
❑	50 Dan Marino	2.00	.90
❑	51 Thurman Thomas	.25	.11
❑	52 Cris Carter	.50	.23
❑	53 Robert Smith	.50	.23
❑	54 Randy Moss	1.50	.70
❑	55 Daunte Culpepper	1.00	.45
❑	56 Terry Glenn	.25	.11
❑	57 Kevin Faulk	.25	.11
❑	58 Drew Bledsoe	.75	.35
❑	59 Ricky Williams	1.25	.55
❑	60 Amani Toomer	.25	.11
❑	61 Kerry Collins	.25	.11
❑	62 Vinny Testaverde	.25	.11
❑	63 Curtis Martin	.50	.23
❑	64 Rich Gannon	.25	.11
❑	65 Tyrone Wheatley	.25	.11
❑	66 Napoleon Kaufman	.25	.11
❑	67 Tim Brown	.50	.23
❑	68 Duce Staley	.50	.23
❑	69 Donovan McNabb	.75	.35
❑	70 Kordell Stewart	.50	.23
❑	71 Troy Edwards	.50	.23
❑	72 Jerome Bettis	.50	.23
❑	73 Jim Harbaugh	.25	.11
❑	74 Jermaine Fazande	.15	.07
❑	75 Steve Young	.75	.35
❑	76 Charlie Garner	.25	.11
❑	77 Terrell Owens	.50	.23
❑	78 Jerry Rice	1.25	.55
❑	79 Jeff Garcia	.50	.23
❑	80 Ricky Watters	.25	.11
❑	81 Jon Kitna	.50	.23
❑	82 Marshall Faulk	.60	.25
❑	83 Isaac Bruce	.50	.23
❑	84 Torry Holt	.50	.23
❑	85 Kurt Warner	2.00	.90
❑	86 Keyshawn Johnson	.50	.23
❑	87 Warrick Dunn	.50	.23
❑	88 Mike Alstott	.50	.23
❑	89 Warren Sapp	.25	.11
❑	90 Shaun King	.75	.35
❑	91 Eddie George	.60	.25
❑	92 Steve McNair	.50	.23
❑	93 Jevon Kearse	.50	.23
❑	94 Bruce Smith	.25	.11
❑	95 Deion Sanders	.50	.23
❑	96 Albert Connell	.15	.07
❑	97 Michael Westbrook	.25	.11
❑	98 Brad Johnson	.50	.23
❑	99 Jeff George	.25	.11
❑	100 Stephen Davis	.50	.23
❑	101 Peter Warrick RC	30.00	13.50
❑	102 Jamal Lewis RC	60.00	27.00
❑	103 Thomas Jones RC	15.00	6.75
❑	104 Plaxico Burress RC	20.00	9.00
❑	105 Travis Taylor RC	12.00	5.50
❑	106 Ron Dayne RC	30.00	13.50
❑	107 Bubba Franks RC	12.00	5.50
❑	108 Sebastian Janikowski RC	10.00	4.50
❑	109 Chad Pennington RC	30.00	13.50
❑	110 Shaun Alexander RC	25.00	11.00
❑	111 Sylvester Morris RC	20.00	9.00
❑	112 Anthony Becht RC	10.00	4.50
❑	113 R.Jay Soward RC	10.00	4.50
❑	114 Trung Canidate RC	10.00	4.50
❑	115 Dennis Northcutt RC	12.00	5.50
❑	116 Todd Pinkston RC	10.00	4.50
❑	117 Jerry Porter RC	10.00	4.50
❑	118 Travis Prentice RC	15.00	6.75
❑	119 Giovanni Carmazzi RC	12.00	5.50
❑	120 Ron Dugans RC	8.00	3.60
❑	121 Erron Kinney RC	10.00	4.50
❑	122 Dez White RC	8.00	3.60
❑	123 Chris Cole RC	8.00	3.60
❑	124 Ron Dixon RC	12.00	5.50
❑	125 Chris Redman RC	20.00	9.00
❑	126 J.R. Redmond RC	12.00	5.50
❑	127 Laveranues Coles RC	15.00	6.75
❑	128 JaJuan Dawson RC	10.00	4.50
❑	129 Darrell Jackson RC	15.00	6.75
❑	130 Reuben Droughns RC	10.00	4.50
❑	131 Doug Chapman RC	20.00	9.00
❑	132 Terrelle Smith RC	8.00	3.60
❑	133 Curtis Keaton RC	8.00	3.60
❑	134 Gari Scott RC	8.00	3.60
❑	135 Courtney Brown RC	12.00	5.50
❑	136 Corey Simon RC	12.00	5.50
❑	137 Brian Urlacher RC	30.00	13.50
❑	138 Shaun Ellis RC	8.00	3.60
❑	139 John Abraham RC	8.00	3.60
❑	140 Deltha O'Neal RC	8.00	3.60
❑	141 Rashard Anderson RC	8.00	3.60
❑	142 Ahmed Plummer RC	10.00	4.50
❑	143 Chris Hovan RC	8.00	3.60
❑	144 Erik Flowers RC	10.00	4.50
❑	145 Rob Morris RC	8.00	3.60
❑	146 Keith Bulluck RC	8.00	3.60
❑	147 Darren Howard RC	8.00	3.60
❑	148 John Engelberger RC	8.00	3.60
❑	149 Ian Gold RC	8.00	3.60
❑	150 Raynoch Thompson RC	8.00	3.60
❑	151 Cornelius Griffin RC	8.00	3.60
❑	152 Rogers Beckett RC	8.00	3.60
❑	153 Dwayne Goodrich RC	5.00	2.20
❑	154 Barrett Green RC	5.00	2.20
❑	155 Kevin Thompson RC	10.00	4.50
❑	156 Ben Kelly RC	5.00	2.20
❑	157 Danny Farmer RC	10.00	4.50
❑	158 Aaron Shea RC	8.00	3.60
❑	159 Trevor Gaylor RC	8.00	3.60
❑	160 Mike Brown RC	10.00	4.50
❑	161 Frank Moreau RC	10.00	4.50
❑	162 Deon Dyer RC	8.00	3.60
❑	163 Avion Black RC	8.00	3.60
❑	164 Spergon Wynn RC	10.00	4.50
❑	165 Billy Volek RC	8.00	3.60
❑	166 Michael Wiley RC	10.00	4.50
❑	167 Dante Hall RC	8.00	3.60
❑	168 Ronney Jenkins RC	8.00	3.60
❑	169 Sammy Morris RC	12.00	5.50
❑	170 Kevin McDougal RC	8.00	3.60
❑	171 Tee Martin RC	15.00	6.75
❑	172 Troy Walters RC	10.00	4.50
❑	173 Chad Morton RC	10.00	4.50
❑	174 Jamel White RC	10.00	4.50
❑	175 Shockmain Davis RC	8.00	3.60
❑	176 Mario Edwards RC	5.00	2.20
❑	177 Brandon Short RC	8.00	3.60
❑	178 James Williams RC	8.00	3.60
❑	179 Mike Anderson RC	60.00	27.00
❑	180 Tom Brady RC	10.00	4.50
❑	181 Na'il Diggs RC	10.00	4.50
❑	182 Todd Husak RC	10.00	4.50
❑	183 JaJuan Seider RC	5.00	2.20
❑	184 Tim Rattay RC	15.00	6.75
❑	185 Jarious Jackson RC	10.00	4.50
❑	186 Joe Hamilton RC	12.00	5.50
❑	187 Shyrone Stith RC	8.00	3.60
❑	188 Mondriel Fulcher RC	5.00	2.20
❑	189 Bashir Yamini RC	8.00	3.60
❑	190 Herbert Goodman RC	8.00	3.60
❑	191 Mike Green RC	8.00	3.60
❑	192 Demario Brown RC	8.00	3.60
❑	193 Charles Lee RC	5.00	2.20
❑	194 Doug Johnson RC	10.00	4.50
❑	195 Windrell Hayes RC	8.00	3.60
❑	196 Julian Peterson RC	8.00	3.60
❑	197 Kwame Cavil RC	8.00	3.60
❑	198 Hank Poteat RC	8.00	3.60
❑	199 Clint Stoerner RC	15.00	6.75
❑	200 Mark Simoneau RC	10.00	4.50

1998 Playoff Prestige Hobby

		MINT	NRMT
	COMP.HOBBY SET (200)	150.00	70.00
❑	1 John Elway	8.00	3.60
❑	2 Steve Atwater	.40	.18
❑	3 Terrell Davis	6.00	2.70
❑	4 Bill Romanowski	.40	.18
❑	5 Rod Smith	.75	.35
❑	6 Shannon Sharpe	.75	.35

		MINT	NRMT
❑	7 Ed McCaffrey	.75	.35
❑	8 Neil Smith	.75	.35
❑	9 Brett Favre	8.00	3.60
❑	10 Dorsey Levens	1.50	.70
❑	11 LeRoy Butler	.40	.18
❑	12 Antonio Freeman	1.50	.70
❑	13 Robert Brooks	.75	.35
❑	14 Mark Chmura	.75	.35
❑	15 Gilbert Brown	.40	.18
❑	16 Kordell Stewart	1.50	.70
❑	17 Jerome Bettis	1.50	.70
❑	18 Carnell Lake	.40	.18
❑	19 Dermontti Dawson	.40	.18
❑	20 Charles Johnson	.40	.18
❑	21 Greg Lloyd	.40	.18
❑	22 Levon Kirkland	.40	.18
❑	23 Steve Young	2.50	1.10
❑	24 Jim Druckenmiller	.75	.35
❑	25 Garrison Hearst	1.50	.70
❑	26 Merton Hanks	.40	.18
❑	27 Ken Norton	.40	.18
❑	28 Jerry Rice	4.00	1.80
❑	29 Terrell Owens	1.50	.70
❑	30 J.J. Stokes	.75	.35
❑	31 Trent Dilfer	1.50	.70
❑	32 Warrick Dunn	1.50	.70
❑	33 Mike Alstott	1.50	.70
❑	34 Reidel Anthony	.75	.35
❑	35 Warren Sapp	.75	.35
❑	36 Elvis Grbac	.75	.35
❑	37 Kimble Anders	.75	.35
❑	38 Ted Popson	.40	.18
❑	39 Derrick Thomas	.75	.35
❑	40 Tony Gonzalez	.40	.18
❑	41 Andre Rison	.75	.35
❑	42 Derrick Alexander	.75	.35
❑	43 Brad Johnson	1.50	.70
❑	44 Robert Smith	1.50	.70
❑	45 Randall McDaniel	.40	.18
❑	46 Cris Carter	1.50	.70
❑	47 Jake Reed	.75	.35
❑	48 John Randle	.75	.35
❑	49 Drew Bledsoe	3.00	1.35
❑	50 Willie Clay	.40	.18
❑	51 Chris Slade	.40	.18
❑	52 Willie McGinest	.40	.18
❑	53 Shawn Jefferson	.40	.18
❑	54 Ben Coates	.75	.35
❑	55 Terry Glenn	1.50	.70
❑	56 Jason Hanson	.40	.18
❑	57 Scott Mitchell	.75	.35
❑	58 Barry Sanders	8.00	3.60
❑	59 Herman Moore	1.50	.70
❑	60 Johnnie Morton	.75	.35
❑	61 Mark Brunell	3.00	1.35
❑	62 James Stewart	.75	.35
❑	63 Tony Boselli	.40	.18
❑	64 Jimmy Smith	.75	.35
❑	65 Keenan McCardell	.75	.35
❑	66 Dan Marino	8.00	3.60
❑	67 Troy Drayton	.40	.18
❑	68 Bernie Parmalee	.40	.18
❑	69 Karim Abdul-Jabbar	1.50	.70
❑	70 Zach Thomas	.75	.35
❑	71 O.J. McDuffie	.75	.35
❑	72 Tim Bowens	.40	.18
❑	73 Danny Kanell	.75	.35

74 Tiki Barber	.75	.35
75 Tyrone Wheatley	.75	.35
76 Charles Way	.40	.18
77 Jason Sehorn	.75	.35
78 Ike Hilliard	.75	.35
79 Michael Strahan	.40	.18
80 Troy Aikman	4.00	1.80
81 Deion Sanders	1.50	.70
82 Emmitt Smith	6.00	2.70
83 Darren Woodson	.40	.18
84 Daryl Johnston	.75	.35
85 Michael Irvin	1.50	.70
86 David LaFleur	.40	.18
87 Glenn Foley	.75	.35
88 Neil O'Donnell	.75	.35
89 Keyshawn Johnson	1.50	.70
90 Aaron Glenn	.40	.18
91 Wayne Chrebet	1.50	.70
92 Curtis Martin	1.50	.70
93 Steve McNair	1.50	.70
94 Eddie George	3.00	1.35
95 Bruce Matthews	.40	.18
96 Frank Wycheck	.40	.18
97 Yancey Thigpen UER back Yancy	.40	.18
98 Gus Frerotte	.40	.18
99 Terry Allen	1.50	.70
100 Michael Westbrook	.75	.35
101 Jamie Asher	.40	.18
102 Marshall Faulk	1.50	.70
103 Zack Crockett	.40	.18
104 Ken Dilger	.40	.18
105 Marvin Harrison	.75	.35
106 Chris Chandler	.75	.35
107 Byron Hanspard	.75	.35
108 Jamal Anderson	1.50	.70
109 Terance Mathis	.75	.35
110 Peter Boulware	.40	.18
111 Michael Jackson	.40	.18
112 Jim Harbaugh	.75	.35
113 Errict Rhett	.75	.35
114 Antowain Smith	1.50	.70
115 Thurman Thomas	1.50	.70
116 Bruce Smith	.75	.35
117 Doug Flutie	2.00	.90
118 Rob Johnson	.75	.35
119 Kerry Collins	.75	.35
120 Fred Lane	.75	.35
121 Wesley Walls	.75	.35
122 William Floyd	.40	.18
123 Kevin Greene	.75	.35
124 Erik Kramer	.40	.18
125 Darnell Autry	.40	.18
126 Curtis Conway	.75	.35
127 Edgar Bennett	.40	.18
128 Jeff Blake	.75	.35
129 Corey Dillon	2.50	1.10
130 Carl Pickens	1.50	.70
131 Darnay Scott	.75	.35
132 Jake Plummer	3.00	1.35
133 Larry Centers	.40	.18
134 Frank Sanders	.75	.35
135 Rob Moore	.75	.35
136 Adrian Murrell	.75	.35
137 Troy Davis	.40	.18
138 Ray Zellars	.40	.18
139 Willie Roaf	.40	.18
140 Andre Hastings	.40	.18
141 Jeff George	.75	.35
142 Napoleon Kaufman	1.50	.70
143 Desmond Howard	.75	.35
144 Tim Brown	1.50	.70
145 James Jett	.75	.35
146 Rickey Dudley	.40	.18
147 Bobby Hoying	.75	.35
148 Duce Staley	3.00	1.35
149 Charlie Garner	.40	.18
150 Irving Fryar	.75	.35
151 Chris T. Jones	.40	.18
152 Tony Banks	.75	.35
153 Craig Heyward	.40	.18
154 Isaac Bruce	1.50	.70
155 Eddie Kennison	.75	.35
156 Junior Seau	.75	.35
157 Tony Martin	.75	.35
158 Freddie Jones	.40	.18
159 Natrone Means	1.50	.70
160 Warren Moon	1.50	.70
161 Steve Broussard	.40	.18
162 Joey Galloway	1.50	.70
163 Brian Blades	.40	.18
164 Ricky Watters	.75	.35
165 Peyton Manning RC	25.00	11.00
166 Ryan Leaf RC	8.00	3.60
167 Andre Wadsworth RC	3.00	1.35
168 Charles Woodson RC	6.00	2.70
169 Curtis Enis RC	5.00	2.20
170 Fred Taylor RC	10.00	4.50
171 Kevin Dyson RC	6.00	2.70
172 Robert Edwards RC	5.00	2.20
173 Randy Moss RC	25.00	11.00
174 R.W. McQuarters RC	2.00	.90
175 John Avery RC	4.00	1.80
176 Marcus Nash RC	4.00	1.80
177 Jerome Pathon RC	3.00	1.35
178 Jacquez Green RC	6.00	2.70
179 Robert Holcombe RC	4.00	1.80
180 Pat Johnson RC	3.00	1.35
181 Germane Crowell RC	8.00	3.60
182 Tony Simmons RC	3.00	1.35
183 Joe Jurevicius RC	3.00	1.35
184 Mikhael Ricks RC	3.00	1.35
185 Charlie Batch RC	10.00	4.50
186 Jon Ritchie RC	3.00	1.35
187 Scott Frost RC	3.00	1.35
188 Skip Hicks RC	4.00	1.80
189 Brian Alford RC	3.00	1.35
190 E.G. Green RC	3.00	1.35
191 Jammi German RC	2.00	.90
192 Ahman Green RC	8.00	3.60
193 Chris Floyd RC	2.00	.90
194 Larry Shannon RC	2.00	.90
195 Jonathan Quinn RC	3.00	1.35
196 Rashaan Shehee RC	3.00	1.35
197 Brian Griese RC	12.00	5.50
198 Hines Ward RC	3.00	1.35
199 Michael Pittman RC	4.00	1.80
200 Az-Zahir Hakim RC	4.00	1.80

1999 Playoff Prestige EXP

	MINT	NRMT
COMPLETE SET (200)	50.00	22.00
1 Anthony McFarland RC	1.50	.70
2 Al Wilson RC	1.00	.45
3 Jevon Kearse RC	3.00	1.35
4 Aaron Brooks RC	6.00	2.70
5 Travis McGriff RC	1.50	.70
6 Jeff Paulk RC	1.50	.70
7 Shawn Bryson RC	1.50	.70
8 Karsten Bailey RC	1.00	.45
9 Mike Cloud RC	1.50	.70
10 James Johnson RC	1.50	.70
11 Tai Streets RC	1.50	.70
12 Jermaine Fazande RC	1.50	.70
13 Ebenezer Ekuban RC	1.00	.45
14 Joe Montgomery RC	1.50	.70
15 Craig Yeast RC	1.00	.45
16 Joe Germaine RC	1.50	.70
17 Andy Katzenmoyer RC	1.50	.70
18 Kevin Faulk RC	2.50	1.10
19 Chris McAlister RC	1.00	.45
20 Sedrick Irvin RC	1.50	.70
21 Brock Huard RC	2.50	1.10
22 Cade McNown RC	2.00	.90
23 Shaun King RC	3.00	1.35
24 Amos Zereoue RC	1.50	.70
25 Dameane Douglas RC	1.00	.45
26 D'Wayne Bates RC	1.50	.70
27 Kevin Johnson RC	3.00	1.35
28 Rob Konrad RC	1.50	.70
29 Troy Edwards RC	2.00	.90
30 Peerless Price RC	2.00	.90
31 Daunte Culpepper RC	10.00	4.50
32 Akili Smith RC	3.00	1.35
33 David Boston RC	3.00	1.35
34 Chris Claiborne RC	.75	.35
35 Torry Holt RC	4.00	1.80
36 Champ Bailey RC	2.00	.90
37 Edgerrin James RC	10.00	4.50
38 Donovan McNabb RC	6.00	2.70
39 Ricky Williams RC	6.00	2.70
40 Tim Couch RC	5.00	2.20
41 Charles Woodson RP	.75	.35
42 Skip Hicks RP	.75	.35
43 Brian Griese RP	.75	.35
44 Tim Dwight RP	.75	.35
45 Ryan Leaf RP	.40	.18
46 Curtis Enis RP	.75	.35
47 Charlie Batch RP	.75	.35
48 Fred Taylor RP	1.00	.45
49 Peyton Manning RP	1.50	.70
50 Randy Moss RP	1.50	.70
51 Jim Harbaugh	.40	.18
52 Warren Moon	.75	.35
53 Jeff George	.40	.18
54 Rich Gannon	.40	.18
55 Scott Mitchell	.20	.09
56 Kerry Collins	.40	.18
57 Brad Johnson	.75	.35
58 Charles Johnson	.20	.09
59 Chris Calloway	.20	.09
60 Tyrone Wheatley	.40	.18
61 Michael Westbrook	.40	.18
62 Skip Hicks	.75	.35
63 Terry Allen	.40	.18
64 Albert Connell	.20	.09
65 Kevin Dyson	.40	.18
66 Frank Wycheck	.20	.09
67 Yancey Thigpen	.20	.09
68 Steve McNair	.75	.35
69 Eddie George	1.00	.45
70 Eric Zeier	.20	.09
71 Jacquez Green	.40	.18
72 Reidel Anthony	.40	.18
73 Warren Sapp	.40	.18
74 Mike Alstott	.75	.35
75 Warrick Dunn	.75	.35
76 Trent Dilfer	.40	.18
77 Ahman Green	.40	.18
78 Joey Galloway	.75	.35
79 Ricky Watters	.40	.18
80 Jon Kitna	.75	.35
81 Amp Lee	.20	.09
82 Isaac Bruce	.75	.35
83 Robert Holcombe	.40	.18
84 Greg Hill	.20	.09
85 Marshall Faulk	.75	.35
86 Trent Green	.40	.18
87 J.J. Stokes	.40	.18
88 Terrell Owens	.75	.35
89 Jerry Rice	2.00	.90
90 Garrison Hearst	.40	.18
91 Steve Young	1.25	.55
92 Junior Seau	.40	.18
93 Mikhael Ricks	.20	.09
94 Natrone Means	.40	.18
95 Ryan Leaf	.75	.35
96 Courtney Hawkins	.20	.09
97 C.Fuamatu-Ma'afala UER	.20	.09
98 Jerome Bettis	.75	.35
99 Kordell Stewart	.75	.35
100 Bobby Hoying	.40	.18
101 Charlie Garner	.40	.18
102 Duce Staley	.75	.35
103 Charles Woodson	.75	.35
104 James Jett	.40	.18
105 Rickey Dudley	.20	.09

	No.	Player	MINT	NRMT
❑	106	Tim Brown	.75	.35
❑	107	Napoleon Kaufman	.75	.35
❑	108	Wayne Chrebet	.40	.18
❑	109	Keyshawn Johnson	.75	.35
❑	110	Vinny Testaverde	.40	.18
❑	111	Curtis Martin	.75	.35
❑	112	Joe Jurevicius	.20	.09
❑	113	Tiki Barber	.20	.09
❑	114	Ike Hilliard	.20	.09
❑	115	Kent Graham	.20	.09
❑	116	Gary Brown	.20	.09
❑	117	Lamar Smith	.40	.18
❑	118	Eddie Kennison	.40	.18
❑	119	Cam Cleeland	.20	.09
❑	120	Tony Simmons	.20	.09
❑	121	Ben Coates	.40	.18
❑	122	Darick Holmes	.20	.09
❑	123	Terry Glenn	.75	.35
❑	124	Drew Bledsoe	1.25	.55
❑	125	Leroy Hoard	.20	.09
❑	126	Jake Reed	.40	.18
❑	127	Randy Moss	3.00	1.35
❑	128	Cris Carter	.75	.35
❑	129	Robert Smith	.75	.35
❑	130	Randall Cunningham	.75	.35
❑	131	Lamar Thomas	.20	.09
❑	132	John Avery	.40	.18
❑	133	O.J. McDuffie	.40	.18
❑	134	Dan Marino	3.00	1.35
❑	135	Karim Abdul-Jabbar	.40	.18
❑	136	Rashaan Shehee	.20	.09
❑	137	Derrick Alexander WR	.40	.18
❑	138	Byron Bam Morris	.20	.09
❑	139	Andre Rison	.40	.18
❑	140	Elvis Grbac	.40	.18
❑	141	Tavian Banks	.20	.09
❑	142	Keenan McCardell	.40	.18
❑	143	Jimmy Smith	.40	.18
❑	144	Fred Taylor	2.00	.90
❑	145	Mark Brunell	1.25	.55
❑	146	Jerome Pathon	.20	.09
❑	147	Marvin Harrison	.75	.35
❑	148	Peyton Manning	3.00	1.35
❑	149	Robert Brooks	.40	.18
❑	150	Mark Chmura	.20	.09
❑	151	Antonio Freeman	.75	.35
❑	152	Dorsey Levens	.75	.35
❑	153	Brett Favre	3.00	1.35
❑	154	Johnnie Morton	.40	.18
❑	155	Germane Crowell	.40	.18
❑	156	Barry Sanders	3.00	1.35
❑	157	Herman Moore	.75	.35
❑	158	Charlie Batch	1.50	.70
❑	159	Marcus Nash	.40	.18
❑	160	Shannon Sharpe	.40	.18
❑	161	Rod Smith	.40	.18
❑	162	Ed McCaffrey	.40	.18
❑	163	Terrell Davis	2.00	.90
❑	164	John Elway	3.00	1.35
❑	165	Ernie Mills	.20	.09
❑	166	Michael Irvin	.40	.13
❑	167	Deion Sanders	.75	.35
❑	168	Emmitt Smith	2.00	.90
❑	169	Troy Aikman	2.00	.90
❑	170	Chris Spielman	.20	.09
❑	171	Terry Kirby	.20	.09
❑	172	Ty Detmer	.40	.18
❑	173	Leslie Shepherd	.20	.09
❑	174	Darnay Scott	.20	.09
❑	175	Jeff Blake	.40	.18
❑	176	Carl Pickens	.40	.18
❑	177	Corey Dillon	.75	.35
❑	178	Bobby Engram	.40	.18
❑	179	Curtis Conway	.40	.18
❑	180	Curtis Enis	.75	.35
❑	181	Muhsin Muhammad	.40	.18
❑	182	Steve Beuerlein	.20	.09
❑	183	Tim Biakabutuka	.40	.18
❑	184	Bruce Smith	.40	.18
❑	185	Andre Reed	.40	.18
❑	186	Thurman Thomas	.40	.18
❑	187	Eric Moulds	.75	.35
❑	188	Antowain Smith	.75	.35
❑	189	Doug Flutie	1.00	.45
❑	190	Jermaine Lewis	.40	.18
❑	191	Priest Holmes	.75	.35
❑	192	O.J. Santiago	.20	.09
❑	193	Tim Dwight	.75	.35
❑	194	Terance Mathis	.40	.18
❑	195	Chris Chandler	.40	.18
❑	196	Jamal Anderson	.75	.35
❑	197	Rob Moore	.40	.18
❑	198	Frank Sanders	.40	.18
❑	199	Adrian Murrell	.40	.18
❑	200	Jake Plummer	1.50	.70
❑	RR1	Barry Sanders (Run For the Record Insert)	20.00	9.00

1999 Playoff Prestige SSD

		MINT	NRMT
COMPLETE SET (200)		150.00	70.00
COMP.SET w/o SP's (150)		50.00	22.00

	No.	Player	MINT	NRMT
❑	1	Jake Plummer	2.50	1.10
❑	2	Adrian Murrell	.50	.23
❑	3	Frank Sanders	.50	.23
❑	4	Rob Moore	.50	.23
❑	5	Jamal Anderson	1.00	.45
❑	6	Chris Chandler	.50	.23
❑	7	Terance Mathis	.50	.23
❑	8	Tim Dwight	1.00	.45
❑	9	O.J. Santiago	.25	.11
❑	10	Priest Holmes	1.00	.45
❑	11	Jermaine Lewis	.50	.23
❑	12	Doug Flutie	1.25	.55
❑	13	Antowain Smith	1.00	.45
❑	14	Eric Moulds	1.00	.45
❑	15	Thurman Thomas	.50	.23
❑	16	Andre Reed	.50	.23
❑	17	Bruce Smith	.50	.23
❑	18	Tim Biakabutuka	.50	.23
❑	19	Steve Beuerlein	.25	.11
❑	20	Muhsin Muhammad	.50	.23
❑	21	Curtis Enis	1.00	.45
❑	22	Curtis Conway	.50	.23
❑	23	Bobby Engram	.50	.23
❑	24	Corey Dillon	1.00	.45
❑	25	Carl Pickens	.50	.23
❑	26	Jeff Blake	.50	.23
❑	27	Darnay Scott	.25	.11
❑	28	Leslie Shepherd	.25	.11
❑	29	Ty Detmer	.50	.23
❑	30	Terry Kirby	.25	.11
❑	31	Chris Spielman	.25	.11
❑	32	Troy Aikman	3.00	1.35
❑	33	Emmitt Smith	3.00	1.35
❑	34	Deion Sanders	1.00	.45
❑	35	Michael Irvin	.50	.23
❑	36	Ernie Mills	.25	.11
❑	37	John Elway	5.00	2.20
❑	38	Terrell Davis	3.00	1.35
❑	39	Ed McCaffrey	.50	.23
❑	40	Rod Smith	.50	.23
❑	41	Shannon Sharpe	.50	.23
❑	42	Marcus Nash	.50	.23
❑	43	Charlie Batch	2.50	1.10
❑	44	Herman Moore	1.00	.45
❑	45	Barry Sanders	5.00	2.20
❑	46	Germane Crowell	.50	.23
❑	47	Johnnie Morton	.50	.23
❑	48	Brett Favre	5.00	2.20
❑	49	Dorsey Levens	1.00	.45
❑	50	Antonio Freeman	1.00	.45
❑	51	Mark Chmura	.25	.11
❑	52	Robert Brooks	.50	.23
❑	53	Peyton Manning	5.00	2.20
❑	54	Marvin Harrison	1.00	.45
❑	55	Jerome Pathon	.25	.11
❑	56	Mark Brunell	2.00	.90
❑	57	Fred Taylor	3.00	1.35
❑	58	Jimmy Smith	.50	.23
❑	59	Keenan McCardell	.50	.23
❑	60	Tavian Banks	.25	.11
❑	61	Elvis Grbac	.50	.23
❑	62	Andre Rison	.50	.23
❑	63	Byron Bam Morris	.25	.11
❑	64	Derrick Alexander WR	.50	.23
❑	65	Rashaan Shehee	.25	.11
❑	66	Karim Abdul-Jabbar	.50	.23
❑	67	Dan Marino	5.00	2.20
❑	68	O.J. McDuffie	.50	.23
❑	69	John Avery	.50	.23
❑	70	Lamar Thomas	.25	.11
❑	71	Randall Cunningham	1.00	.45
❑	72	Robert Smith	1.00	.45
❑	73	Cris Carter	1.00	.45
❑	74	Randy Moss	5.00	2.20
❑	75	Jake Reed	.50	.23
❑	76	Leroy Hoard	.25	.11
❑	77	Drew Bledsoe	2.00	.90
❑	78	Terry Glenn	1.00	.45
❑	79	Darick Holmes	.25	.11
❑	80	Ben Coates	.50	.23
❑	81	Tony Simmons	.25	.11
❑	82	Cam Cleeland	.25	.11
❑	83	Eddie Kennison	.50	.23
❑	84	Lamar Smith	.50	.23
❑	85	Gary Brown	.25	.11
❑	86	Kent Graham	.25	.11
❑	87	Ike Hilliard	.25	.11
❑	88	Tiki Barber	.25	.11
❑	89	Joe Jurevicius	.25	.11
❑	90	Curtis Martin	1.00	.45
❑	91	Vinny Testaverde	.50	.23
❑	92	Keyshawn Johnson	1.00	.45
❑	93	Wayne Chrebet	.50	.23
❑	94	Napoleon Kaufman	1.00	.45
❑	95	Tim Brown	1.00	.45
❑	96	Rickey Dudley	.25	.11
❑	97	James Jett	.50	.23
❑	98	Charles Woodson	1.00	.45
❑	99	Duce Staley	1.00	.45
❑	100	Charlie Garner	.50	.23
❑	101	Bobby Hoying	.50	.23
❑	102	Kordell Stewart	1.00	.45
❑	103	Jerome Bettis	1.00	.45
❑	104	Chris Fuamatu-Ma'afala	.25	.11
❑	105	Courtney Hawkins	.25	.11
❑	106	Ryan Leaf	1.00	.45
❑	107	Natrone Means	.50	.23
❑	108	Mikhael Ricks	.25	.11
❑	109	Junior Seau	.50	.23
❑	110	Steve Young	2.00	.90
❑	111	Garrison Hearst	.50	.23
❑	112	Jerry Rice	3.00	1.35
❑	113	Terrell Owens	1.00	.45
❑	114	J.J. Stokes	.50	.23
❑	115	Trent Green	.50	.23
❑	116	Marshall Faulk	1.00	.45
❑	117	Greg Hill	.25	.11
❑	118	Robert Holcombe	.50	.23
❑	119	Isaac Bruce	1.00	.45
❑	120	Amp Lee	.25	.11
❑	121	Jon Kitna	1.00	.45
❑	122	Ricky Watters	.50	.23
❑	123	Joey Galloway	1.00	.45
❑	124	Ahman Green	.50	.23
❑	125	Trent Dilfer	.50	.23
❑	126	Warrick Dunn	1.00	.45
❑	127	Mike Alstott	1.00	.45
❑	128	Warren Sapp	.50	.23
❑	129	Reidel Anthony	.50	.23
❑	130	Jacquez Green	.50	.23
❑	131	Eric Zeier	.25	.11
❑	132	Eddie George	1.00	.45
❑	133	Steve McNair	1.00	.45
❑	134	Yancey Thigpen	.25	.11
❑	135	Frank Wycheck	.25	.11

❑ 136 Kevin Dyson	.50	.23
❑ 137 Albert Connell	.25	.11
❑ 138 Terry Allen	.50	.23
❑ 139 Skip Hicks	1.00	.45
❑ 140 Michael Westbrook	.50	.23
❑ 141 Tyrone Wheatley	.50	.23
❑ 142 Chris Calloway	.25	.11
❑ 143 Charles Johnson	.25	.11
❑ 144 Brad Johnson	1.00	.45
❑ 145 Kerry Collins	.50	.23
❑ 146 Scott Mitchell	.25	.11
❑ 147 Rich Gannon	.50	.23
❑ 148 Jeff George	.50	.23
❑ 149 Warren Moon	1.00	.45
❑ 150 Jim Harbaugh	.50	.23
❑ 151 Randy Moss RP	8.00	3.60
❑ 152 Peyton Manning RP	8.00	3.60
❑ 153 Fred Taylor RP	5.00	2.20
❑ 154 Charlie Batch RP	4.00	1.80
❑ 155 Curtis Enis RP	1.50	.70
❑ 156 Ryan Leaf RP	1.50	.70
❑ 157 Tim Dwight RP	1.50	.70
❑ 158 Brian Griese RP	4.00	1.80
❑ 159 Skip Hicks RP	1.50	.70
❑ 160 Charles Woodson RP	1.50	.70
❑ 161 Tim Couch RC	12.00	5.50
❑ 162 Ricky Williams RC	12.00	5.50
❑ 163 Donovan McNabb RC	12.00	5.50
❑ 164 Edgerrin James RC	20.00	9.00
❑ 165 Champ Bailey RC	5.00	2.20
❑ 166 Torry Holt RC	10.00	4.50
❑ 167 Chris Claiborne RC	2.00	.90
❑ 168 David Boston RC	8.00	3.60
❑ 169 Akili Smith RC	8.00	3.60
❑ 170 Daunte Culpepper RC	20.00	9.00
❑ 171 Peerless Price RC	5.00	2.20
❑ 172 Troy Edwards RC	5.00	2.20
❑ 173 Rob Konrad RC	4.00	1.80
❑ 174 Kevin Johnson RC	8.00	3.60
❑ 175 D'Wayne Bates RC	3.00	1.35
❑ 176 Dameane Douglas RC	3.00	1.35
❑ 177 Amos Zereoue RC	4.00	1.80
❑ 178 Shaun King RC	8.00	3.60
❑ 179 Cade McNown RC	5.00	2.20
❑ 180 Brock Huard RC	6.00	2.70
❑ 181 Sedrick Irvin RC	4.00	1.80
❑ 182 Chris McAlister RC	3.00	1.35
❑ 183 Kevin Faulk RC	6.00	2.70
❑ 184 Andy Katzenmoyer RC	4.00	1.80
❑ 185 Joe Germaine RC	4.00	1.80
❑ 186 Craig Yeast RC	3.00	1.35
❑ 187 Joe Montgomery RC	4.00	1.80
❑ 188 Ebenezer Ekuban RC	3.00	1.35
❑ 189 Jermaine Fazande RC	4.00	1.80
❑ 190 Tai Streets RC	4.00	1.80
❑ 191 James Johnson RC	4.00	1.80
❑ 192 Mike Cloud RC	4.00	1.80
❑ 193 Karsten Bailey RC	4.00	1.80
❑ 194 Shawn Bryson RC	4.00	1.80
❑ 195 Jeff Paulk RC	4.00	1.80
❑ 196 Travis McGriff RC	4.00	1.80
❑ 197 Aaron Brooks RC	12.00	5.50
❑ 198 Jevon Kearse RC	8.00	3.60
❑ 199 Al Wilson RC	3.00	1.35
❑ 200 Anthony McFarland RC	4.00	1.80

2000 Playoff Prestige

	MINT	NRMT
COMPLETE SET (300)	500.00	220.00
❑ 1 Frank Sanders	.25	.11
❑ 2 Rob Moore	.25	.11
❑ 3 Michael Pittman	.15	.07
❑ 4 Jake Plummer	.50	.23
❑ 5 David Boston	.50	.23
❑ 6 Chris Chandler	.25	.11
❑ 7 Tim Dwight	.50	.23
❑ 8 Shawn Jefferson	.15	.07
❑ 9 Terance Mathis	.25	.11
❑ 10 Jamal Anderson	.50	.23
❑ 11 Byron Hanspard	.15	.07
❑ 12 Ken Oxendine	.15	.07
❑ 13 Priest Holmes	.25	.11
❑ 14 Tony Banks	.25	.11
❑ 15 Shannon Sharpe	.25	.11
❑ 16 Rod Woodson	.25	.11
❑ 17 Jermaine Lewis	.25	.11
❑ 18 Qadry Ismail	.15	.07
❑ 19 Eric Moulds	.50	.23
❑ 20 Doug Flutie	.60	.25
❑ 21 Jay Riemersma	.15	.07
❑ 22 Antowain Smith	.25	.11
❑ 23 Jonathan Linton	.15	.07
❑ 24 Peerless Price	.50	.23
❑ 25 Rob Johnson	.25	.11
❑ 26 Muhsin Muhammad	.25	.11
❑ 27 Wesley Walls	.15	.07
❑ 28 Tim Biakabutuka	.25	.11
❑ 29 Steve Beuerlein	.25	.11
❑ 30 Patrick Jeffers	.50	.23
❑ 31 Natrone Means	.15	.07
❑ 32 Curtis Enis	.25	.11
❑ 33 Bobby Engram	.25	.11
❑ 34 Marcus Robinson	.50	.23
❑ 35 Marty Booker	.15	.07
❑ 36 Cade McNown	.50	.23
❑ 37 Darnay Scott	.25	.11
❑ 38 Carl Pickens	.25	.11
❑ 39 Corey Dillon	.50	.23
❑ 40 Akili Smith	.50	.23
❑ 41 Michael Basnight	.15	.07
❑ 42 Karim Abdul-Jabbar	.25	.11
❑ 43 Tim Couch	1.00	.45
❑ 44 Kevin Johnson	.50	.23
❑ 45 Darrin Chiaverini	.15	.07
❑ 46 Errict Rhett	.25	.11
❑ 47 Emmitt Smith	1.25	.55
❑ 48 Deion Sanders	.50	.23
❑ 49 Michael Irvin	.25	.11
❑ 50 Rocket Ismail	.25	.11
❑ 51 Troy Aikman	1.25	.55
❑ 52 Jason Tucker	.25	.11
❑ 53 Joey Galloway	.50	.23
❑ 54 David LaFleur	.15	.07
❑ 55 Wane McGarity	.15	.07
❑ 56 Ed McCaffrey	.50	.23
❑ 57 Rod Smith	.25	.11
❑ 58 Brian Griese	.60	.25
❑ 59 John Elway	2.00	.90
❑ 60 Gus Frerotte	.15	.07
❑ 61 Neil Smith	.15	.07
❑ 62 Terrell Davis	1.25	.55
❑ 63 Olandis Gary	.50	.23
❑ 64 Johnnie Morton	.25	.11
❑ 65 Charlie Batch	.50	.23
❑ 66 Barry Sanders	1.50	.70
❑ 67 James Stewart	.25	.11
❑ 68 Germane Crowell	.25	.11
❑ 69 Sedrick Irvin	.15	.07
❑ 70 Herman Moore	.25	.11
❑ 71 Corey Bradford	.25	.11
❑ 72 Dorsey Levens	.25	.11
❑ 73 Antonio Freeman	.50	.23
❑ 74 Brett Favre	2.00	.90
❑ 75 De'Mond Parker	.15	.07
❑ 76 Bill Schroeder	.25	.11
❑ 77 Donald Driver	.15	.07
❑ 78 E.G. Green	.15	.07
❑ 79 Marvin Harrison	.50	.23
❑ 80 Peyton Manning	1.50	.70
❑ 81 Terrence Wilkins	.50	.23
❑ 82 Edgerrin James	2.00	.90
❑ 83 Keenan McCardell	.25	.11
❑ 84 Mark Brunell	.75	.35
❑ 85 Fred Taylor	.60	.25
❑ 86 Jimmy Smith	.25	.11
❑ 87 Derrick Alexander	.25	.11
❑ 88 Andre Rison	.15	.07
❑ 89 Elvis Grbac	.25	.11
❑ 90 Tony Gonzalez	.25	.11
❑ 91 Donnell Bennett	.15	.07
❑ 92 Warren Moon	.50	.23
❑ 93 Kimble Anders	.15	.07
❑ 94 Tony Richardson RC	.25	.11
❑ 95 Jay Fiedler	.50	.23
❑ 96 Zach Thomas	.25	.11
❑ 97 Oronde Gadsden	.25	.11
❑ 98 Dan Marino	2.00	.90
❑ 99 O.J. McDuffie	.25	.11
❑ 100 Tony Martin	.25	.11
❑ 101 James Johnson	.25	.11
❑ 102 Rob Konrad	.15	.07
❑ 103 Damon Huard	.50	.23
❑ 104 Thurman Thomas	.25	.11
❑ 105 Randy Moss	1.50	.70
❑ 106 Cris Carter	.50	.23
❑ 107 Robert Smith	.50	.23
❑ 108 Randall Cunningham	.50	.23
❑ 109 John Randle	.25	.11
❑ 110 Leroy Hoard	.15	.07
❑ 111 Daunte Culpepper	1.00	.45
❑ 112 Matthew Hatchette	.25	.11
❑ 113 Troy Brown	.15	.07
❑ 114 Tony Simmons	.15	.07
❑ 115 Terry Glenn	.25	.11
❑ 116 Ben Coates	.15	.07
❑ 117 Drew Bledsoe	.75	.35
❑ 118 Terry Allen	.25	.11
❑ 119 Kevin Faulk	.15	.07
❑ 120 Ricky Williams	1.25	.55
❑ 121 Jake Delhomme RC	.50	.23
❑ 122 Jake Reed	.25	.11
❑ 123 Jeff Blake	.25	.11
❑ 124 Amani Toomer	.25	.11
❑ 125 Kerry Collins	.25	.11
❑ 126 Tiki Barber	.25	.11
❑ 127 Ike Hilliard	.25	.11
❑ 128 Joe Montgomery	.15	.07
❑ 129 Sean Bennett	.15	.07
❑ 130 Curtis Martin	.50	.23
❑ 131 Vinny Testaverde	.25	.11
❑ 132 Wayne Chrebet	.25	.11
❑ 133 Ray Lucas	.50	.23
❑ 134 Tyrone Wheatley	.25	.11
❑ 135 Napoleon Kaufman	.25	.11
❑ 136 Tim Brown	.50	.23
❑ 137 Rickey Dudley	.15	.07
❑ 138 James Jett	.15	.07
❑ 139 Rich Gannon	.25	.11
❑ 140 Charles Woodson	.25	.11
❑ 141 Duce Staley	.50	.23
❑ 142 Donovan McNabb	.75	.35
❑ 143 Na Brown	.15	.07
❑ 144 Kordell Stewart	.50	.23
❑ 145 Jerome Bettis	.50	.23
❑ 146 Hines Ward	.15	.07
❑ 147 Troy Edwards	.25	.11
❑ 148 Curtis Conway	.25	.11
❑ 149 Junior Seau	.25	.11
❑ 150 Jim Harbaugh	.25	.11
❑ 151 Jermaine Fazande	.15	.07
❑ 152 Terrell Owens	.50	.23
❑ 153 J.J. Stokes	.25	.11
❑ 154 Charlie Garner	.25	.11
❑ 155 Jerry Rice	1.25	.55
❑ 156 Garrison Hearst	.25	.11
❑ 157 Steve Young	.75	.35
❑ 158 Jeff Garcia	.50	.23
❑ 159 Derrick Mayes	.25	.11
❑ 160 Ahman Green	.25	.11
❑ 161 Ricky Watters	.25	.11
❑ 162 Jon Kitna	.50	.23
❑ 163 Karsten Bailey	.15	.07
❑ 164 Sean Dawkins	.15	.07
❑ 165 Az-Zahir Hakim	.25	.11
❑ 166 Isaac Bruce	.50	.23
❑ 167 Marshall Faulk	.60	.25
❑ 168 Trent Green	.25	.11
❑ 169 Kurt Warner	2.00	.90

❑ 170	Torry Holt	.50	.23
❑ 171	Robert Holcombe	.15	.07
❑ 172	Kevin Carter	.15	.07
❑ 173	Keyshawn Johnson	.50	.23
❑ 174	Jacquez Green	.25	.11
❑ 175	Reidel Anthony	.15	.07
❑ 176	Warren Sapp	.25	.11
❑ 177	Mike Alstott	.50	.23
❑ 178	Warrick Dunn	.50	.23
❑ 179	Trent Dilfer	.25	.11
❑ 180	Shaun King	.50	.23
❑ 181	Neil O'Donnell	.15	.07
❑ 182	Eddie George	.60	.25
❑ 183	Yancey Thigpen	.15	.07
❑ 184	Steve McNair	.50	.23
❑ 185	Kevin Dyson	.25	.11
❑ 186	Frank Wycheck	.15	.07
❑ 187	Jevon Kearse	.50	.23
❑ 188	Adrian Murrell	.15	.07
❑ 189	Jeff George	.25	.11
❑ 190	Stephen Davis	.50	.23
❑ 191	Stephen Alexander	.15	.07
❑ 192	Darrell Green	.15	.07
❑ 193	Skip Hicks	.25	.11
❑ 194	Brad Johnson	.50	.23
❑ 195	Michael Westbrook	.25	.11
❑ 196	Albert Connell	.15	.07
❑ 197	Irving Fryar	.15	.07
❑ 198	Bruce Smith	.25	.11
❑ 199	Champ Bailey	.25	.11
❑ 200	Larry Centers	.15	.07
❑ 201	Jake Plummer PP	1.25	.55
❑ 202	Doug Flutie PP	2.00	.90
❑ 203	Eric Moulds PP	1.25	.55
❑ 204	Muhsin Muhammad PP	1.25	.55
❑ 205	Marcus Robinson PP	1.25	.55
❑ 206	Cade McNown PP	1.25	.55
❑ 207	Corey Dillon PP	1.25	.55
❑ 208	Tim Couch PP	2.50	1.10
❑ 209	Kevin Johnson PP	1.25	.55
❑ 210	Emmitt Smith PP	3.00	1.35
❑ 211	Troy Aikman PP	3.00	1.35
❑ 212	Brian Griese PP	1.25	.55
❑ 213	Olandis Gary PP	1.25	.55
❑ 214	Germane Crowell PP	1.25	.55
❑ 215	Brett Favre PP	6.00	2.70
❑ 216	Charlie Batch PP	1.25	.55
❑ 217	Antonio Freeman PP	1.25	.55
❑ 218	Dorsey Levens PP	1.25	.55
❑ 219	Peyton Manning PP	4.00	1.80
❑ 220	Edgerrin James PP	4.00	1.80
❑ 221	Marvin Harrison PP	1.25	.55
❑ 222	Fred Taylor PP	2.00	.90
❑ 223	Mark Brunell PP	2.00	.90
❑ 224	Jimmy Smith PP	1.25	.55
❑ 225	Dan Marino PP	5.00	2.20
❑ 226	Randy Moss PP	4.00	1.80
❑ 227	Cris Carter PP	1.25	.55
❑ 228	Robert Smith PP	1.25	.55
❑ 229	Drew Bledsoe PP	2.00	.90
❑ 230	Terry Glenn PP	1.25	.55
❑ 231	Ricky Williams PP	3.00	1.35
❑ 232	Amani Toomer PP	1.25	.55
❑ 233	Keyshawn Johnson PP	1.25	.55
❑ 234	Curtis Martin PP	1.25	.55
❑ 235	Ray Lucas PP	1.25	.55
❑ 236	Tim Brown PP	1.25	.55
❑ 237	Duce Staley PP	1.25	.55
❑ 238	Donovan McNabb PP	2.00	.90
❑ 239	Jerry Rice PP	3.00	1.35
❑ 240	Jon Kitna PP	1.25	.55
❑ 241	Isaac Bruce PP	1.25	.55
❑ 242	Kurt Warner PP	5.00	2.20
❑ 243	Torry Holt PP	1.25	.55
❑ 244	Mike Alstott PP	1.25	.55
❑ 245	Marshall Faulk PP	1.50	.70
❑ 246	Shaun King PP	2.00	.90
❑ 247	Eddie George PP	1.50	.70
❑ 248	Steve McNair PP	1.25	.55
❑ 249	Stephen Davis PP	1.25	.55
❑ 250	Brad Johnson PP	1.25	.55
❑ 251	Rondell Mealey RC	3.00	1.35
❑ 252	Peter Warrick RC	15.00	6.75
❑ 253	Courtney Brown RC	6.00	2.70
❑ 254	Plaxico Burress RC	10.00	4.50
❑ 255	Corey Simon RC	6.00	2.70
❑ 256	Thomas Jones RC	8.00	3.60
❑ 257	Travis Taylor RC	6.00	2.70
❑ 258	Shaun Alexander RC	12.00	5.50
❑ 259	Chris Redman RC	10.00	4.50
❑ 260	Chad Pennington RC	15.00	6.75
❑ 261	Jamal Lewis RC	30.00	13.50
❑ 262	Bubba Franks RC	6.00	2.70
❑ 263	Dez White RC	4.00	1.80
❑ 264	Ron Dayne RC	15.00	6.75
❑ 265	Sylvester Morris RC	10.00	4.50
❑ 266	R.Jay Soward RC	5.00	2.20
❑ 267	Sherrod Gideon RC	3.00	1.35
❑ 268	Travis Prentice RC	8.00	3.60
❑ 269	Darrell Jackson RC	8.00	3.60
❑ 270	Giovanni Carmazzi RC	6.00	2.70
❑ 271	Anthony Lucas RC	3.00	1.35
❑ 272	Danny Farmer RC	5.00	2.20
❑ 273	Dennis Northcutt RC	6.00	2.70
❑ 274	Troy Walters RC	5.00	2.20
❑ 275	Laveranues Coles RC	8.00	3.60
❑ 276	Tee Martin RC	8.00	3.60
❑ 277	J.R. Redmond RC	6.00	2.70
❑ 278	Jerry Porter RC	5.00	2.20
❑ 279	Sebastian Janikowski RC	5.00	2.20
❑ 280	Michael Wiley RC	5.00	2.20
❑ 281	Reuben Droughns RC	5.00	2.20
❑ 282	Trung Canidate RC	5.00	2.20
❑ 283	Shyrone Stith RC	4.00	1.80
❑ 284	Trevor Gaylor RC	4.00	1.80
❑ 285	Marc Bulger RC	5.00	2.20
❑ 286	Tom Brady RC	5.00	2.20
❑ 287	Todd Husak RC	5.00	2.20
❑ 288	Jarious Jackson RC	5.00	2.20
❑ 289	Terrelle Smith RC	4.00	1.80
❑ 290	Chad Morton RC	5.00	2.20
❑ 291	Chris Cole RC	5.00	2.20
❑ 292	Kwame Cavil RC	4.00	1.80
❑ 293	JaJuan Dawson RC	5.00	2.20
❑ 294	Curtis Keaton RC	4.00	1.80
❑ 295	Tim Rattay RC	8.00	3.60
❑ 296	Joe Hamilton RC	6.00	2.70
❑ 297	Gari Scott RC	4.00	1.80
❑ 298	Mike Anderson RC	30.00	13.50
❑ 299	Ron Dugans RC	4.00	1.80
❑ 300	Todd Pinkston RC	5.00	2.20

1996 Playoff Prime

	MINT	NRMT
COMPLETE SET (200)	100.00	45.00
COMP. BRONZE SET (100)	15.00	6.75
COMMON BRONZE (1-100)	.10	.05
COMMON SILVER (101-150)	.50	.23
COMMON GOLD (151-200)	.75	.35

❑ 1	Brett Favre	3.00	1.35
❑ 2	Jerry Rice	1.50	.70
❑ 3	Troy Aikman	1.50	.70
❑ 4	Bruce Smith	.25	.11
❑ 5	Marshall Faulk	.50	.23
❑ 6	Erik Kramer	.10	.05
❑ 7	Carl Pickens	.50	.23
❑ 8	Anthony Miller	.25	.11
❑ 9	Cris Carter	.50	.23
❑ 10	Todd Kinchen	.10	.05
❑ 11	Stoney Case	.10	.05
❑ 12	Chris Calloway	.10	.05
❑ 13	Andre Rison	.25	.11
❑ 14	Bill Brooks	.10	.05
❑ 15	Shawn Jefferson	.10	.05
❑ 16	Eric Zeier	.10	.05
❑ 17	Yancey Thigpen	.25	.11
❑ 18	Edgar Bennett	.25	.11
❑ 19	Garrison Hearst	.25	.11
❑ 20	Daryl Johnston	.25	.11
❑ 21	Tyrone Wheatley	.25	.11
❑ 22	Darick Holmes	.10	.05
❑ 23	Dave Brown	.10	.05
❑ 24	Leeland McElroy RC	.50	.23
❑ 25	Craig Heyward	.10	.05
❑ 26	Kevin Hardy RC	.50	.23
❑ 27	Scott Mitchell	.25	.11
❑ 28	Willie Green	.10	.05
❑ 29	Vincent Brisby	.10	.05
❑ 30	Mike Tomczak	.10	.05
❑ 31	Luther Elliss	.10	.05
❑ 32	Mike Pritchard	.10	.05
❑ 33	Robert Green	.10	.05
❑ 34	Jeff Graham	.10	.05
❑ 35	Tamarick Vanover	.25	.11
❑ 36	William Floyd	.25	.11
❑ 37	Alvin Harper	.10	.05
❑ 38	Stan Humphries	.25	.11
❑ 39	Herman Moore	.50	.23
❑ 40	Tony Martin	.25	.11
❑ 41	Jonathan Ogden RC	.10	.05
❑ 42	Randall Cunningham	.50	.23
❑ 43	Chris Warren	.25	.11
❑ 44	Bobby Hebert	.10	.05
❑ 45	Jerome Bettis	.50	.23
❑ 46	Joey Galloway	.75	.35
❑ 47	Ernie Mills	.10	.05
❑ 48	Steve McNair	1.00	.45
❑ 49	Karim Abdul-Jabbar RC	.75	.35
❑ 50	Chad May	.10	.05
❑ 51	Jim Everett	.10	.05
❑ 52	Robert Smith	.25	.11
❑ 53	Tony Boselli	.10	.05
❑ 54	William Henderson	.10	.05
❑ 55	Terry Glenn RC UER (Joey Galloway biography on back of card)	1.50	.70
❑ 56	Neil O'Donnell	.25	.11
❑ 57	Chris Chandler	.25	.11
❑ 58	Michael Jackson	.25	.11
❑ 59	Jason Dunn RC	.25	.11
❑ 60	James O. Stewart	.25	.11
❑ 61	Greg Hill	.25	.11
❑ 62	Mark Carrier WR	.10	.05
❑ 63	Bernie Parmalee	.10	.05
❑ 64	Chris Sanders	.25	.11
❑ 65	Jeff Hostetler	.10	.05
❑ 66	Eric Moulds RC	2.50	1.10
❑ 67	James Jett	.25	.11
❑ 68	Henry Ellard	.10	.05
❑ 69	Mario Bates	.25	.11
❑ 70	Natrone Means	.50	.23
❑ 71	Bobby Engram RC	.50	.23
❑ 72	Christian Fauria	.10	.05
❑ 73	Gus Frerotte	.50	.23
❑ 74	Aaron Hayden	.10	.05
❑ 75	Reggie White	.50	.23
❑ 76	Dave Meggett	.10	.05
❑ 77	Harvey Williams	.10	.05
❑ 78	Terance Mathis	.10	.05
❑ 79	Byron Bam Morris	.25	.11
❑ 80	Trent Dilfer	.50	.23
❑ 81	Irving Fryar	.25	.11
❑ 82	Quinn Early	.10	.05
❑ 83	Lake Dawson	.10	.05
❑ 84	Todd Collins	.25	.11
❑ 85	Eric Metcalf	.10	.05
❑ 86	Tim Biakabutuka RC	1.00	.45
❑ 87	Rob Johnson	.50	.23
❑ 88	Charlie Garner	.10	.05
❑ 89	Mike Mamula	.10	.05
❑ 90	Steve Walsh	.10	.05
❑ 91	Charles Haley	.25	.11
❑ 92	Mike Alstott RC	2.00	.90
❑ 93	Wayne Chrebet	.75	.35
❑ 94	Vinny Testaverde	.25	.11
❑ 95	Fred Barnett	.10	.05
❑ 96	Boomer Esiason	.25	.11
❑ 97	Zack Crockett	.10	.05

	MINT	NRMT
❑ 98 Kevin Williams	.10	.05
❑ 99 Eric Bieniemy	.10	.05
❑ 100 Bryan Cox	.10	.05
❑ 101 Larry Centers	1.00	.45
❑ 102 Jeff George	1.00	.45
❑ 103 Bryce Paup	1.00	.45
❑ 104 Kerry Collins	2.00	.90
❑ 105 Derrick Moore	.50	.23
❑ 106 Adrian Murrell	1.00	.45
❑ 107 Harold Green	.50	.23
❑ 108 Ki-Jana Carter	1.00	.45
❑ 109 Sherman Williams	.50	.23
❑ 110 Deion Sanders	4.00	1.80
❑ 111 Emmitt Smith	8.00	3.60
❑ 112 Shannon Sharpe	1.00	.45
❑ 113 Johnnie Morton	1.00	.45
❑ 114 Eddie Kennison RC	2.00	.90
❑ 115 Marvin Harrison RC	8.00	3.60
❑ 116 Amani Toomer RC	2.00	.90
❑ 117 Rickey Dudley RC	2.00	.90
❑ 118 Alex Van Dyke RC	1.00	.45
❑ 119 Dorsey Levens	2.00	.90
❑ 120 Antonio Freeman	4.00	1.80
❑ 121 Willie Davis	1.00	.45
❑ 122 Lamont Warren	.50	.23
❑ 123 Sean Dawkins	.50	.23
❑ 124 Willie Jackson	1.00	.45
❑ 125 Kimble Anders	.50	.23
❑ 126 Dan Marino	10.00	4.50
❑ 127 Terry Kirby	1.00	.45
❑ 128 Amp Lee	.50	.23
❑ 129 Jake Reed	1.00	.45
❑ 130 Curtis Martin	4.00	1.80
❑ 131 Ray Zellars	.50	.23
❑ 132 Herschel Walker	1.00	.45
❑ 133 Mike Sherrard	.50	.23
❑ 134 Kyle Brady	1.00	.45
❑ 135 Rocket Ismail	1.00	.45
❑ 136 Ricky Watters	1.00	.45
❑ 137 Kordell Stewart	3.00	1.35
❑ 138 Andre Hastings	.10	.05
❑ 139 Ronnie Harmon	.50	.23
❑ 140 Terrell Fletcher	.50	.23
❑ 141 J.J. Stokes	2.00	.90
❑ 142 Brent Jones	.50	.23
❑ 143 Tony McGee	.50	.23
❑ 144 Brian Blades	1.00	.45
❑ 145 Isaac Bruce	2.00	.90
❑ 146 Errict Rhett	1.00	.45
❑ 147 Warren Sapp	.50	.23
❑ 148 Horace Copeland	.50	.23
❑ 149 Heath Shuler	2.00	.90
❑ 150 Michael Westbrook	2.00	.90
❑ 151 Frank Sanders	1.50	.70
❑ 152 Rob Moore	.75	.35
❑ 153 Bert Emanuel	1.50	.70
❑ 154 J.J. Birden	.75	.35
❑ 155 Thurman Thomas	2.50	1.10
❑ 156 Jim Kelly	2.50	1.10
❑ 157 Curtis Conway	1.50	.70
❑ 158 Darnay Scott	1.50	.70
❑ 159 Jeff Blake	2.50	1.10
❑ 160 Jay Novacek	1.50	.70
❑ 161 Michael Irvin	2.50	1.10
❑ 162 John Elway	12.00	5.50
❑ 163 Terrell Davis	12.00	5.50
❑ 164 Barry Sanders	10.00	4.50
❑ 165 Brett Perriman	1.50	.70
❑ 166 Keyshawn Johnson RC	6.00	2.70
❑ 167 Eddie George RC	12.00	5.50
❑ 168 Derrick Mayes RC	3.00	1.35
❑ 169 Simeon Rice RC	1.50	.70
❑ 170 Lawrence Phillips RC	1.50	.70
❑ 171 Robert Brooks	1.50	.70
❑ 172 Mark Chmura	1.50	.70
❑ 173 Rodney Thomas	.75	.35
❑ 174 Jim Harbaugh	1.50	.70
❑ 175 Ken Dilger	1.50	.70
❑ 176 Mark Brunell	8.00	3.60
❑ 177 Steve Bono	1.50	.70
❑ 178 Marcus Allen	2.50	1.10
❑ 179 O.J. McDuffie	1.50	.70
❑ 180 Eric Green	.75	.35
❑ 181 Warren Moon	2.50	1.10
❑ 182 Drew Bledsoe	8.00	3.60
❑ 183 Ben Coates	1.50	.70
❑ 184 Michael Haynes	1.50	.70
❑ 185 Rodney Hampton	1.50	.70
❑ 186 Rashaan Salaam	2.50	1.10
❑ 187 Napoleon Kaufman	2.50	1.10
❑ 188 Tim Brown	2.50	1.10
❑ 189 Rodney Peete	.75	.35
❑ 190 Calvin Williams	.75	.35
❑ 191 Erric Pegram	1.50	.70
❑ 192 Mark Bruener	.75	.35
❑ 193 Junior Seau	1.50	.70
❑ 194 Steve Young	6.00	2.70
❑ 195 Derek Loville	.75	.35
❑ 196 Rick Mirer	1.50	.70
❑ 197 Mark Rypien	.75	.35
❑ 198 Jackie Harris	.75	.35
❑ 199 Terry Allen	1.50	.70
❑ 200 Brian Mitchell	.75	.35

1996 Playoff Trophy Contenders

	MINT	NRMT
COMPLETE SET (120)	20.00	9.00
❑ 1 Brett Favre	2.00	.90
❑ 2 Troy Aikman	1.00	.45
❑ 3 Dan Marino	2.00	.90
❑ 4 Emmitt Smith	1.50	.70
❑ 5 Marshall Faulk	.40	.18
❑ 6 Jeff Blake	.40	.18
❑ 7 John Elway	2.00	.90
❑ 8 Steve Young	.75	.35
❑ 9 Curtis Martin	.75	.35
❑ 10 Kordell Stewart	.60	.25
❑ 11 Drew Bledsoe	1.00	.45
❑ 12 Jim Kelly	.40	.18
❑ 13 Steve Bono	.10	.05
❑ 14 Neil O'Donnell	.20	.09
❑ 15 Jeff Hostetler	.10	.05
❑ 16 Jim Harbaugh	.20	.09
❑ 17 Jim Everett	.10	.05
❑ 18 Erric Pegram	.10	.05
❑ 19 Tyrone Wheatley	.20	.09
❑ 20 Barry Sanders	2.00	.90
❑ 21 Deion Sanders	.60	.25
❑ 22 Harvey Williams	.10	.05
❑ 23 Garrison Hearst	.20	.09
❑ 24 Aaron Hayden RC	.10	.05
❑ 25 Dorsey Levens	.40	.18
❑ 26 Napoleon Kaufman	.40	.18
❑ 27 Rodney Hampton	.20	.09
❑ 28 Scott Mitchell	.20	.09
❑ 29 Greg Hill	.20	.09
❑ 30 Charlie Garner	.10	.05
❑ 31 Rashaan Salaam	.40	.18
❑ 32 Errict Rhett	.20	.09
❑ 33 Byron Bam Morris	.20	.09
❑ 34 Edgar Bennett	.20	.09
❑ 35 Jeff George	.20	.09
❑ 36 Rodney Peete	.10	.05
❑ 37 Stan Humphries	.20	.09
❑ 38 Kimble Anders	.20	.09
❑ 39 Natrone Means	.40	.18
❑ 40 Sherman Williams	.10	.05
❑ 41 Eric Metcalf	.10	.05
❑ 42 Chris Warren	.20	.09
❑ 43 Marcus Allen	.40	.18
❑ 44 Bill Brooks	.10	.05
❑ 45 Wayne Chrebet	.60	.25
❑ 46 Irving Fryar	.20	.09
❑ 47 Tony Martin	.20	.09
❑ 48 Daryl Johnston	.20	.09
❑ 49 O.J. McDuffie	.20	.09
❑ 50 Frank Sanders	.20	.09
❑ 51 Ken Norton	.10	.05
❑ 52 Jake Reed	.20	.09
❑ 53 Bert Emanuel	.20	.09
❑ 54 Floyd Turner	.10	.05
❑ 55 Junior Seau	.20	.09
❑ 56 Ernie Mills	.10	.05
❑ 57 Mark Pike	.10	.05
❑ 58 Warren Moon	.20	.09
❑ 59 Mike Mamula	.10	.05
❑ 60 Kerry Collins	.40	.18
❑ 61 Nate Newton	.10	.05
❑ 62 Terry Allen	.20	.09
❑ 63 Bernie Parmalee	.10	.05
❑ 64 James O.Stewart	.20	.09
❑ 65 Isaac Bruce	.40	.18
❑ 66 Lake Dawson	.10	.05
❑ 67 Terance Mathis	.10	.05
❑ 68 Chris Sanders	.20	.09
❑ 69 Anthony Miller	.20	.09
❑ 70 Jay Novacek	.10	.05
❑ 71 Sean Dawkins	.10	.05
❑ 72 J.J. Birden	.10	.05
❑ 73 Calvin Williams	.10	.05
❑ 74 Rick Mirer	.20	.09
❑ 75 Steve McNair	.75	.35
❑ 76 Lamont Warren	.10	.05
❑ 77 Rod Woodson	.20	.09
❑ 78 Larry Brown	.10	.05
❑ 79 Zack Crockett	.10	.05
❑ 80 Jerry Rice	1.00	.45
❑ 81 Tim Brown	.40	.18
❑ 82 Yancey Thigpen	.20	.09
❑ 83 J.J. Stokes	.40	.18
❑ 84 Herman Moore	.40	.18
❑ 85 Kevin Williams	.10	.05
❑ 86 Gus Frerotte	.40	.18
❑ 87 Robert Brooks	.40	.18
❑ 88 Michael Irvin	.40	.18
❑ 89 Steve Tasker	.10	.05
❑ 90 Joey Galloway	.60	.25
❑ 91 Kevin Greene	.20	.09
❑ 92 Reggie White	.40	.18
❑ 93 Cris Carter	.40	.18
❑ 94 Charles Haley	.20	.09
❑ 95 Bryce Paup	.10	.05
❑ 96 Heath Shuler	.20	.09
❑ 97 Eric Zeier	.10	.05
❑ 98 Antonio Freeman	.75	.35
❑ 99 Erik Kramer	.10	.05
❑ 100 Derek Loville	.10	.05
❑ 101 Rodney Thomas	.10	.05
❑ 102 Terrell Davis	2.50	1.10
❑ 103 Ricky Watters	.20	.09
❑ 104 Craig Heyward	.10	.05
❑ 105 Terry Kirby	.20	.09
❑ 106 Bruce Smith	.20	.09
❑ 107 Curtis Conway	.40	.18
❑ 108 Charles Johnson	.10	.05
❑ 109 Brett Perriman	.10	.05
❑ 110 Carl Pickens	.40	.18
❑ 111 Michael Westbrook	.40	.18
❑ 112 Brent Jones	.10	.05
❑ 113 Ken Dilger	.20	.09
❑ 114 Fred Barnett	.10	.05
❑ 115 Mark Bruener	.10	.05
❑ 116 Tamarick Vanover	.20	.09
❑ 117 Quinn Early	.10	.05
❑ 118 Mark Chmura	.20	.09
❑ 119 Andre Hastings	.10	.05
❑ 120 Craig Newsome	.10	.05

1997 Playoff Zone

	MINT	NRMT
COMPLETE SET (150)	25.00	11.00
❑ 1 Brett Favre	2.00	.90
❑ 2 Dorsey Levens	.30	.14
❑ 3 William Henderson	.10	.05
❑ 4 Derrick Mayes	.20	.09

❑ 5 Antonio Freeman	.50	.23
❑ 6 Robert Brooks	.20	.09
❑ 7 Mark Chmura	.20	.09
❑ 8 Reggie White	.30	.14
❑ 9 Randall Cunningham	.30	.14
❑ 10 Brad Johnson	.60	.25
❑ 11 Robert Smith	.20	.09
❑ 12 Cris Carter	.30	.14
❑ 13 Jake Reed	.20	.09
❑ 14 Trent Dilfer	.30	.14
❑ 15 Errict Rhett	.10	.05
❑ 16 Mike Alstott	.30	.14
❑ 17 Scott Mitchell	.20	.09
❑ 18 Barry Sanders	2.00	.90
❑ 19 Herman Moore	.30	.14
❑ 20 Erik Kramer	.10	.05
❑ 21 Rick Mirer	.10	.05
❑ 22 Rashaan Salaam	.10	.05
❑ 23 Troy Aikman	1.00	.45
❑ 24 Deion Sanders	.30	.14
❑ 25 Emmitt Smith	1.50	.70
❑ 26 Daryl Johnston	.20	.09
❑ 27 Anthony Miller	.10	.05
❑ 28 Eric Bjornson	.10	.05
❑ 29 Michael Irvin	.30	.14
❑ 30 Chris T. Jones	.10	.05
❑ 31 Ty Detmer	.20	.09
❑ 32 Ricky Watters	.20	.09
❑ 33 Irving Fryar	.20	.09
❑ 34 Rodney Peete	.10	.05
❑ 35 Jeff Hostetler	.10	.05
❑ 36 Terry Allen	.30	.14
❑ 37 Michael Westbrook	.20	.09
❑ 38 Gus Frerotte	.10	.05
❑ 39 Frank Sanders	.20	.09
❑ 40 Larry Centers	.20	.09
❑ 41 Kent Graham	.10	.05
❑ 42 Dave Brown	.10	.05
❑ 43 Rodney Hampton	.20	.09
❑ 44 Tyrone Wheatley	.20	.09
❑ 45 Chris Calloway	.10	.05
❑ 46 Ernie Mills	.10	.05
❑ 47 Tim Biakabutuka	.20	.09
❑ 48 Anthony Johnson	.10	.05
❑ 49 Wesley Walls	.20	.09
❑ 50 Muhsin Muhammad	.20	.09
❑ 51 Kerry Collins	.20	.09
❑ 52 Terrell Owens	.30	.14
❑ 53 Garrison Hearst	.20	.09
❑ 54 Jerry Rice	1.00	.45
❑ 55 Steve Young	.75	.35
❑ 56 Lawrence Phillips	.10	.05
❑ 57 Isaac Bruce	.30	.14
❑ 58 Eddie Kennison	.20	.09
❑ 59 Tony Banks	.20	.09
❑ 60 Heath Shuler	.10	.05
❑ 61 Andre Hastings	.10	.05
❑ 62 Mario Bates	.10	.05
❑ 63 Chris Chandler	.20	.09
❑ 64 Jamal Anderson	.75	.35
❑ 65 Bert Emanuel	.20	.09
❑ 66 Drew Bledsoe	1.00	.45
❑ 67 Curtis Martin	.50	.23
❑ 68 Ben Coates	.20	.09
❑ 69 Terry Glenn	.30	.14
❑ 70 Dan Marino	2.00	.90
❑ 71 Karim Abdul-Jabbar	.30	.14
❑ 72 Fred Barnett	.10	.05
❑ 73 O.J. McDuffie	.20	.09
❑ 74 Jim Harbaugh	.20	.09
❑ 75 Marshall Faulk	.30	.14
❑ 76 Zack Crockett	.10	.05
❑ 77 Ken Dilger	.10	.05
❑ 78 Marvin Harrison	.30	.14
❑ 79 Keyshawn Johnson	.30	.14
❑ 80 Neil O'Donnell	.20	.09
❑ 81 Adrian Murrell	.20	.09
❑ 82 Wayne Chrebet	.30	.14
❑ 83 Todd Collins	.10	.05
❑ 84 Thurman Thomas	.30	.14
❑ 85 Bruce Smith	.20	.09
❑ 86 Eric Moulds	.30	.14
❑ 87 Rob Johnson	.30	.14
❑ 88 Mark Brunell	1.00	.45
❑ 89 Natrone Means	.30	.14
❑ 90 Jimmy Smith	.20	.09
❑ 91 Keenan McCardell	.20	.09
❑ 92 Kordell Stewart	.40	.18
❑ 93 Jerome Bettis	.30	.14
❑ 94 Charles Johnson	.20	.09
❑ 95 Courtney Hawkins	.10	.05
❑ 96 Greg Lloyd	.10	.05
❑ 97 Ki-Jana Carter	.10	.05
❑ 98 Carl Pickens	.30	.14
❑ 99 Jeff Blake	.20	.09
❑ 100 Steve McNair	.50	.23
❑ 101 Chris Sanders	.10	.05
❑ 102 Eddie George	1.00	.45
❑ 103 Vinny Testaverde	.20	.09
❑ 104 Michael Jackson	.20	.09
❑ 105 Derrick Alexander WR	.20	.09
❑ 106 Willie Green	.10	.05
❑ 107 Shannon Sharpe	.20	.09
❑ 108 Rod Smith WR	.30	.14
❑ 109 Terrell Davis	1.50	.70
❑ 110 John Elway	2.00	.90
❑ 111 Elvis Grbac	.20	.09
❑ 112 Greg Hill	.10	.05
❑ 113 Marcus Allen	.30	.14
❑ 114 Derrick Thomas	.20	.09
❑ 115 Brett Perriman	.10	.05
❑ 116 Andre Rison	.20	.09
❑ 117 Rickey Dudley	.20	.09
❑ 118 Tim Brown	.30	.14
❑ 119 Desmond Howard	.20	.09
❑ 120 Napoleon Kaufman	.30	.14
❑ 121 Jeff George	.20	.09
❑ 122 Warren Moon	.30	.14
❑ 123 John Friesz	.10	.05
❑ 124 Chris Warren	.20	.09
❑ 125 Joey Galloway	.40	.18
❑ 126 Stan Humphries	.20	.09
❑ 127 Tony Martin	.20	.09
❑ 128 Eric Metcalf	.20	.09
❑ 129 Jim Everett	.10	.05
❑ 130 Warrick Dunn RC	1.25	.55
❑ 131 Reidel Anthony RC	.75	.35
❑ 132 Derrick Mason RC	1.00	.45
❑ 133 Joey Kent RC	.30	.14
❑ 134 Will Blackwell RC	.30	.14
❑ 135 Jim Druckenmiller RC	.30	.14
❑ 136 Byron Hanspard RC	.30	.14
❑ 137 John Allred RC	.10	.05
❑ 138 David LaFleur RC	.20	.09
❑ 139 Danny Wuerffel RC	1.00	.45
❑ 140 Tiki Barber RC	1.25	.55
❑ 141 Ike Hilliard RC	.75	.35
❑ 142 Troy Davis RC	.30	.14
❑ 143 Leon Johnson RC	.10	.05
❑ 144 Tony Gonzalez RC	1.25	.55
❑ 145 Jake Plummer RC	4.00	1.80
❑ 146 Antowain Smith RC	1.00	.45
❑ 147 Rae Carruth RC	.30	.14
❑ 148 Darnell Autry RC	.20	.09
❑ 149 Corey Dillon RC	4.00	1.80
❑ 150 Orlando Pace RC	.30	.14

1993 Power Update Prospects

	MINT	NRMT
COMPLETE SET (60)	12.00	5.50

❑ 1 Drew Bledsoe RC	2.00	.90
❑ 2 Rick Mirer RC	.30	.14
❑ 3 Trent Green RC	10.00	4.50
❑ 4 Mark Brunell RC	2.50	1.10
❑ 5 Billy Joe Hobert RC UER (Name spelled Hebert on back)	.25	.11
❑ 6 Ronald Moore RC	.10	.05
❑ 7 Elvis Grbac RC UER (Spelled Grback on both sides)	1.50	.70
❑ 8 Garrison Hearst RC	.50	.23
❑ 9 Jerome Bettis RC	.75	.35
❑ 10 Reggie Brooks RC	.10	.05
❑ 11 Robert Smith RC	1.50	.70
❑ 12 Vaughn Hebron RC	.05	.02
❑ 13 Derek Brown RBK RC	.10	.05
❑ 14 Roosevelt Potts RC	.10	.05
❑ 15 Terry Kirby RC UER (Card says wide receiver; he is a running back)	.10	.05
❑ 16 Glyn Milburn RC	.10	.05
❑ 17 Greg Robinson RC	.05	.02
❑ 18 Natrone Means RC	.40	.18
❑ 19 Curtis Conway RC	.40	.18
❑ 20 James Jett RC	.50	.23
❑ 21 O.J. McDuffie RC	.50	.23
❑ 22 Rocket Ismail	.10	.05
❑ 23 Qadry Ismail RC	.50	.23
❑ 24 Kevin Williams RC	.10	.05
❑ 25 Victor Bailey RC UER (Name spelled Baily on front)	.05	.02
❑ 26 Vincent Brisby RC	.10	.05
❑ 27 Irv Smith RC	.05	.02
❑ 28 Troy Drayton RC	.05	.02
❑ 29 Wayne Simmons RC	.05	.02
❑ 30 Marvin Jones RC	.05	.02
❑ 31 Demetrius DuBose RC	.05	.02
❑ 32 Chad Brown RC	.10	.05
❑ 33 Micheal Barrow RC	.10	.05
❑ 34 Darrin Smith RC	.05	.02
❑ 35 Deon Figures RC	.05	.02
❑ 36 Darrien Gordon RC	.05	.02
❑ 37 Patrick Bates RC	.05	.02
❑ 38 George Teague RC	.05	.02
❑ 39 Lance Gunn RC	.05	.02
❑ 40 Tom Carter RC	.05	.02
❑ 41 Carlton Gray RC	.05	.02
❑ 42 John Copeland RC	.05	.02
❑ 43 Eric Curry RC	.05	.02
❑ 44 Dana Stubblefield RC	.10	.05
❑ 45 Leonard Renfro RC	.05	.02
❑ 46 Dan Williams RC	.05	.02
❑ 47 Todd Kelly RC	.05	.02
❑ 48 Chris Slade RC	.05	.02
❑ 49 Carl Simpson RC UER (Defensive Back spelled Dfensive on back)	.05	.02
❑ 50 Coleman Rudolph RC	.05	.02
❑ 51 Michael Strahan RC	.25	.11
❑ 52 Dan Footman RC	.05	.02
❑ 53 Steve Everitt RC	.05	.02
❑ 54 Will Shields RC	.05	.02
❑ 55 Ben Coleman RC	.05	.02
❑ 56 William Roaf RC	.05	.02
❑ 57 Lincoln Kennedy RC	.05	.02
❑ 58 Brad Hopkins RC	.05	.02
❑ 59 Ernest Dye RC	.05	.02
❑ 60 Jason Elam RC	.10	.05

1993 Pro Line Live

	MINT	NRMT
COMPLETE SET (285)	15.00	6.75
❑ 1 Michael Haynes	.10	.05
❑ 2 Chris Hinton	.05	.02
❑ 3 Pierce Holt	.05	.02
❑ 4 Chris Miller	.10	.05
❑ 5 Mike Pritchard	.10	.05
❑ 6 Andre Rison	.10	.05
❑ 7 Deion Sanders	.50	.23
❑ 8 Jessie Tuggle	.05	.02
❑ 9 Lincoln Kennedy RC	.05	.02
❑ 10 Roger Harper RC	.05	.02
❑ 11 Cornelius Bennett	.10	.05
❑ 12 Henry Jones	.05	.02
❑ 13 Jim Kelly	.25	.11
❑ 14 Bill Brooks	.05	.02
❑ 15 Nate Odomes	.05	.02
❑ 16 Andre Reed	.10	.05
❑ 17 Frank Reich	.10	.05
❑ 18 Bruce Smith	.25	.11
❑ 19 Steve Tasker	.10	.05
❑ 20 Thurman Thomas	.25	.11
❑ 21 Thomas Smith RC	.10	.05
❑ 22 John Parrella RC	.05	.02
❑ 23 Neal Anderson	.05	.02
❑ 24 Mark Carrier DB	.05	.02
❑ 25 Jim Harbaugh	.25	.11
❑ 26 Darren Lewis	.05	.02
❑ 27 Steve McMichael	.10	.05
❑ 28 Alonzo Spellman	.05	.02
❑ 29 Tom Waddle	.05	.02
❑ 30 Curtis Conway RC	.40	.18
❑ 31 Carl Simpson RC	.05	.02
❑ 32 David Fulcher	.05	.02
❑ 33 Harold Green	.05	.02
❑ 34 David Klingler	.05	.02
❑ 35 Tim Krumrie	.05	.02
❑ 36 Carl Pickens	.25	.11
❑ 37 Alfred Williams	.05	.02
❑ 38 Darryl Williams	.05	.02
❑ 39 John Copeland RC	.10	.05
❑ 40 Tony McGee RC	.10	.05
❑ 41 Bernie Kosar	.10	.05
❑ 42 Kevin Mack	.05	.02
❑ 43 Clay Matthews	.10	.05
❑ 44 Eric Metcalf	.10	.05
❑ 45 Michael Dean Perry	.10	.05
❑ 46 Vinny Testaverde	.10	.05
❑ 47 Jerry Ball	.05	.02
❑ 48 Tommy Vardell	.05	.02
❑ 49 Steve Everitt RC	.05	.02
❑ 50 Dan Footman RC	.05	.02
❑ 51 Troy Aikman	.75	.35
❑ 52 Daryl Johnston	.25	.11
❑ 53 Tony Casillas	.05	.02
❑ 54 Charles Haley	.10	.05
❑ 55 Alvin Harper	.10	.05
❑ 56 Michael Irvin	.25	.11
❑ 57 Robert Jones	.05	.02
❑ 58 Russell Maryland	.05	.02
❑ 59 Nate Newton	.10	.05
❑ 60 Ken Norton Jr.	.10	.05
❑ 61 Jay Novacek	.10	.05
❑ 62 Emmitt Smith	1.50	.70
❑ 63 Kevin Smith	.10	.05
❑ 64 Kevin Williams RC	.05	.02
❑ 65 Darrin Smith RC	.10	.05
❑ 66 Steve Atwater	.05	.02
❑ 67 Rod Bernstine	.05	.02
❑ 68 Mike Croel	.05	.02
❑ 69 John Elway	1.50	.70
❑ 70 Tommy Maddox	.05	.02
❑ 71 Karl Mecklenburg	.05	.02
❑ 72 Shannon Sharpe	.25	.11
❑ 73 Dennis Smith	.05	.02
❑ 74 Dan Williams RC	.05	.02
❑ 75 Glyn Milburn RC	.25	.11
❑ 76 Pat Swilling	.05	.02
❑ 77 Bennie Blades	.05	.02
❑ 78 Herman Moore	.50	.23
❑ 79 Rodney Peete	.05	.02
❑ 80 Brett Perriman	.25	.11
❑ 81 Barry Sanders	1.50	.70
❑ 82 Chris Spielman	.10	.05
❑ 83 Andre Ware	.05	.02
❑ 84 Ryan McNeil RC	.05	.02
❑ 85 Antonio London RC	.05	.02
❑ 86 Tony Bennett	.05	.02
❑ 87 Terrell Buckley	.05	.02
❑ 88 Brett Favre	2.00	.90
❑ 89 Brian Noble	.05	.02
❑ 90 Ken O'Brien	.05	.02
❑ 91 Sterling Sharpe	.25	.11
❑ 92 Reggie White	.25	.11
❑ 93 John Stephens	.05	.02
❑ 94 Wayne Simmons RC	.05	.02
❑ 95 George Teague RC	.10	.05
❑ 96 Ray Childress	.05	.02
❑ 97 Curtis Duncan	.05	.02
❑ 98 Ernest Givins	.10	.05
❑ 99 Haywood Jeffires	.10	.05
❑ 100 Bubba McDowell	.05	.02
❑ 101 Warren Moon	.25	.11
❑ 102 Al Smith	.05	.02
❑ 103 Lorenzo White	.05	.02
❑ 104 Brad Hopkins RC	.05	.02
❑ 105 Micheal Barrow RC UER (Name misspelled Michael)	.10	.05
❑ 106 Duane Bickett	.05	.02
❑ 107 Quentin Coryatt	.10	.05
❑ 108 Steve Emtman	.05	.02
❑ 109 Jeff George	.25	.11
❑ 110 Anthony Johnson	.10	.05
❑ 111 Reggie Langhorne	.05	.02
❑ 112 Jack Trudeau	.05	.02
❑ 113 Clarence Verdin	.05	.02
❑ 114 Jessie Hester	.05	.02
❑ 115 Roosevelt Potts RC	.05	.02
❑ 116 Dale Carter	.05	.02
❑ 117 Dave Krieg	.10	.05
❑ 118 Nick Lowery	.05	.02
❑ 119 Christian Okoye	.05	.02
❑ 120 Neil Smith	.25	.11
❑ 121 Derrick Thomas	.25	.11
❑ 122 Harvey Williams	.10	.05
❑ 123 Barry Word	.05	.02
❑ 124 Joe Montana	1.50	.70
❑ 125 Marcus Allen	.25	.11
❑ 126 James Lofton	.10	.05
❑ 127 Nick Bell	.05	.02
❑ 128 Tim Brown	.25	.11
❑ 129 Eric Dickerson	.10	.05
❑ 130 Jeff Hostetler	.10	.05
❑ 131 Howie Long	.10	.05
❑ 132 Todd Marinovich	.05	.02
❑ 133 Greg Townsend	.05	.02
❑ 134 Patrick Bates RC	.05	.02
❑ 135 Billy Joe Hobert RC	.25	.11
❑ 136 Flipper Anderson	.05	.02
❑ 137 Shane Conlan	.05	.02
❑ 138 Henry Ellard	.10	.05
❑ 139 Jim Everett	.10	.05
❑ 140 Cleveland Gary	.05	.02
❑ 141 Sean Gilbert	.10	.05
❑ 142 Todd Lyght	.05	.02
❑ 143 Jerome Bettis RC	.75	.35
❑ 144 Troy Drayton RC	.10	.05
❑ 145 Louis Oliver	.05	.02
❑ 146 Marco Coleman	.05	.02
❑ 147 Bryan Cox	.05	.02
❑ 148 Mark Duper	.05	.02
❑ 149 Irving Fryar	.10	.05
❑ 150 Mark Higgs	.05	.02
❑ 151 Keith Jackson	.10	.05
❑ 152 Dan Marino	1.50	.70
❑ 153 Troy Vincent	.05	.02
❑ 154 Richmond Webb	.05	.02
❑ 155 O.J. McDuffie RC	.50	.23
❑ 156 Terry Kirby RC	.25	.11
❑ 157 Terry Allen	.25	.11
❑ 158 Anthony Carter	.10	.05
❑ 159 Cris Carter	.50	.23
❑ 160 Chris Doleman	.05	.02
❑ 161 Randall McDaniel	.05	.02
❑ 162 Audray McMillian	.05	.02
❑ 163 Henry Thomas	.05	.02
❑ 164 Gary Zimmerman	.05	.02
❑ 165 Robert Smith RC	1.50	.70
❑ 166 Qadry Ismail RC	.50	.23
❑ 167 Vincent Brown	.05	.02
❑ 168 Marv Cook	.05	.02
❑ 169 Greg McMurtry	.05	.02
❑ 170 Jon Vaughn	.05	.02
❑ 171 Leonard Russell	.10	.05
❑ 172 Andre Tippett	.05	.02
❑ 173 Scott Zolak	.05	.02
❑ 174 Drew Bledsoe RC	2.00	.90
❑ 175 Chris Slade RC	.10	.05
❑ 176 Morten Andersen	.05	.02
❑ 177 Vaughn Dunbar	.05	.02
❑ 178 Rickey Jackson	.05	.02
❑ 179 Vaughan Johnson	.05	.02
❑ 180 Eric Martin	.05	.02
❑ 181 Sam Mills	.05	.02
❑ 182 Brad Muster	.05	.02
❑ 183 Willie Roaf RC	.10	.05
❑ 184 Irv Smith RC UER (Birthdate is 7/31/61; should be 9/13/71)	.05	.02
❑ 185 Reggie Freeman RC	.05	.02
❑ 186 Michael Brooks	.05	.02
❑ 187 Dave Brown RC	.25	.11
❑ 188 Rodney Hampton	.25	.11
❑ 189 Pepper Johnson	.05	.02
❑ 190 Ed McCaffrey	.10	.05
❑ 191 Dave Meggett	.05	.02
❑ 192 Bart Oates	.05	.02
❑ 193 Phil Simms	.10	.05
❑ 194 Lawrence Taylor	.25	.11
❑ 195 Michael Strahan RC	.25	.11
❑ 196 Brad Baxter	.05	.02
❑ 197 Johnny Johnson	.05	.02
❑ 198 Boomer Esiason	.10	.05
❑ 199 Ronnie Lott	.10	.05
❑ 200 Johnny Mitchell	.05	.02
❑ 201 Rob Moore	.10	.05
❑ 202 Browning Nagle	.05	.02
❑ 203 Blair Thomas	.05	.02
❑ 204 Marvin Jones RC	.05	.02
❑ 205 Coleman Rudolph RC	.05	.02
❑ 206 Eric Allen	.05	.02
❑ 207 Fred Barnett	.10	.05
❑ 208 Tim Harris	.05	.02
❑ 209 Randall Cunningham	.25	.11
❑ 210 Seth Joyner	.05	.02
❑ 211 Clyde Simmons	.05	.02
❑ 212 Herschel Walker	.10	.05
❑ 213 Calvin Williams	.10	.05
❑ 214 Lester Holmes RC	.05	.02
❑ 215 Leonard Renfro RC	.05	.02
❑ 216 Chris Chandler	.10	.05
❑ 217 Gary Clark	.10	.05
❑ 218 Ken Harvey	.05	.02
❑ 219 Randal Hill	.05	.02
❑ 220 Steve Beuerlein	.05	.02
❑ 221 Ricky Proehl	.05	.02
❑ 222 Timm Rosenbach	.05	.02
❑ 223 Garrison Hearst RC	.50	.23
❑ 224 Ernest Dye RC UER (Birthdate 7/31/61: should be 7/15/71)	.05	.02
❑ 225 Bubby Brister	.05	.02
❑ 226 Dermontti Dawson	.05	.02
❑ 227 Barry Foster	.10	.05
❑ 228 Kevin Greene	.25	.11
❑ 229 Merril Hoge	.05	.02
❑ 230 Greg Lloyd	.25	.11

	Card	Mint	Nrmt
❑	231 Neil O'Donnell	.25	.11
❑	232 Rod Woodson	.25	.11
❑	233 Deon Figures RC	.10	.05
❑	234 Chad Brown RC	.10	.05
❑	235 Marion Butts	.05	.02
❑	236 Gill Byrd	.05	.02
❑	237 Ronnie Harmon	.05	.02
❑	238 Stan Humphries	.25	.11
❑	239 Anthony Miller	.10	.05
❑	240 Leslie O'Neal	.10	.05
❑	241 Stanley Richard	.05	.02
❑	242 Junior Seau	.25	.11
❑	243 Darrien Gordon RC	.05	.02
❑	244 Natrone Means RC	.40	.18
❑	245 Dana Hall	.05	.02
❑	246 Brent Jones	.10	.05
❑	247 Tim McDonald	.05	.02
❑	248 Steve Bono	.25	.11
❑	249 Jerry Rice	1.00	.45
❑	250 John Taylor	.10	.05
❑	251 Ricky Watters	.25	.11
❑	252 Steve Young	.75	.35
❑	253 Dana Stubblefield RC	.25	.11
❑	254 Todd Kelly RC	.05	.02
❑	255 Brian Blades	.10	.05
❑	256 Ferrell Edmunds	.05	.02
❑	257 Stan Gelbaugh	.05	.02
❑	258 Cortez Kennedy	.10	.05
❑	259 Dan McGwire	.05	.02
❑	260 Chris Warren	.10	.05
❑	261 John L. Williams	.05	.02
❑	262 David Wyman	.05	.02
❑	263 Rick Mirer RC	.30	.14
❑	264 Carlton Gray RC	.05	.02
❑	265 Marty Carter	.05	.02
❑	266 Reggie Cobb	.05	.02
❑	267 Lawrence Dawsey	.05	.02
❑	268 Santana Dotson	.10	.05
❑	269 Craig Erickson	.10	.05
❑	270 Paul Gruber	.05	.02
❑	271 Keith McCants	.05	.02
❑	272 Broderick Thomas	.05	.02
❑	273 Eric Curry RC	.05	.02
❑	274 Demetrius DuBose RC	.05	.02
❑	275 Earnest Byner	.05	.02
❑	276 Ricky Ervins	.05	.02
❑	277 Brad Edwards	.05	.02
❑	278 Jim Lachey	.05	.02
❑	279 Charles Mann	.05	.02
❑	280 Carl Banks	.05	.02
❑	281 Art Monk	.10	.05
❑	282 Mark Rypien	.05	.02
❑	283 Ricky Sanders	.05	.02
❑	284 Tom Carter RC	.10	.05
❑	285 Reggie Brooks RC	.10	.05
❑	P1 Troy Aikman Promo (Numbered 51)	1.25	.55
❑	P2 Troy Aikman Promo Tri-Star Prod. Back	1.00	.45

1994 Pro Line Live

	MINT	NRMT
COMPLETE SET (405)	20.00	9.00

	Card	Mint	Nrmt
❑	1 Emmitt Smith	1.25	.55
❑	2 Andre Rison	.10	.05
❑	3 Deion Sanders	.40	.18
❑	4 Jeff George	.25	.11
❑	5 Cornelius Bennett	.10	.05
❑	6 Jim Kelly	.25	.11
❑	7 Andre Reed	.10	.05
❑	8 Bruce Smith	.25	.11
❑	9 Thurman Thomas	.25	.11
❑	10 Mark Carrier DB	.05	.02
❑	11 Curtis Conway	.25	.11
❑	12 Donnell Woolford	.05	.02
❑	13 Chris Zorich	.05	.02
❑	14 Erik Kramer	.10	.05
❑	15 John Copeland	.05	.02
❑	16 Harold Green	.05	.02
❑	17 David Klingler	.05	.02
❑	18 Tony McGee	.05	.02
❑	19 Carl Pickens	.25	.11
❑	20 Michael Jackson	.10	.05
❑	21 Eric Metcalf	.10	.05
❑	22 Michael Dean Perry	.10	.05
❑	23 Vinny Testaverde	.10	.05
❑	24 Eric Turner	.05	.02
❑	25 Tommy Vardell	.05	.02
❑	26 Troy Aikman	.75	.35
❑	27 Charles Haley	.10	.05
❑	28 Michael Irvin	.25	.11
❑	29 Pierce Holt	.05	.02
❑	30 Russell Maryland	.05	.02
❑	31 Erik Williams	.05	.02
❑	32 Thomas Everett	.05	.02
❑	33 Steve Atwater	.05	.02
❑	34 John Elway	1.50	.70
❑	35 Glyn Milburn	.10	.05
❑	36 Shannon Sharpe	.10	.05
❑	37 Anthony Miller	.10	.05
❑	38 Barry Sanders	1.50	.70
❑	39 Chris Spielman	.10	.05
❑	40 Pat Swilling	.05	.02
❑	41 Brett Perriman	.10	.05
❑	42 Herman Moore	.25	.11
❑	43 Scott Mitchell	.25	.11
❑	44 Edgar Bennett	.25	.11
❑	45 Terrell Buckley	.05	.02
❑	46 LeRoy Butler	.05	.02
❑	47 Brett Favre	1.50	.70
❑	48 Jackie Harris	.05	.02
❑	49 Sterling Sharpe	.10	.05
❑	50 Reggie White	.25	.11
❑	51 Gary Brown	.05	.02
❑	52 Cody Carlson	.05	.02
❑	53 Ray Childress	.05	.02
❑	54 Ernest Givins	.10	.05
❑	55 Bruce Matthews	.05	.02
❑	56 Quentin Coryatt	.05	.02
❑	57 Steve Emtman	.05	.02
❑	58 Roosevelt Potts	.05	.02
❑	59 Tony Bennett	.05	.02
❑	60 Marcus Allen	.25	.11
❑	61 Joe Montana	1.50	.70
❑	62 Neil Smith	.25	.11
❑	63 Derrick Thomas	.25	.11
❑	64 Dale Carter	.05	.02
❑	65 Tim Brown	.25	.11
❑	66 Jeff Hostetler	.10	.05
❑	67 Terry McDaniel	.05	.02
❑	68 Chester McGlockton	.05	.02
❑	69 Anthony Smith	.05	.02
❑	70 Albert Lewis	.05	.02
❑	71 Jerome Bettis	.25	.11
❑	72 Shane Conlan	.05	.02
❑	73 Troy Drayton	.05	.02
❑	74 Sean Gilbert	.05	.02
❑	75 Chris Miller	.05	.02
❑	76 Bryan Cox	.05	.02
❑	77 Irving Fryar	.10	.05
❑	78 Keith Jackson	.05	.02
❑	79 Terry Kirby	.25	.11
❑	80 Dan Marino	1.50	.70
❑	81 O.J. McDuffie	.25	.11
❑	82 Terry Allen	.10	.05
❑	83 Cris Carter	.40	.18
❑	84 Chris Doleman	.05	.02
❑	85 Randall McDaniel	.05	.02
❑	86 John Randle	.10	.05
❑	87 Robert Smith	.25	.11
❑	88 Jason Belser	.05	.02
❑	89 Jack Del Rio	.05	.02
❑	90 Vincent Brown	.05	.02
❑	91 Ben Coates	.25	.11
❑	92 Chris Slade	.05	.02
❑	93 Derek Brown RBK	.05	.02
❑	94 Morten Andersen	.05	.02
❑	95 Willie Roaf	.05	.02
❑	96 Irv Smith	.05	.02
❑	97 Tyrone Hughes	.10	.05
❑	98 Michael Haynes	.10	.05
❑	99 Jim Everett	.10	.05
❑	100 Michael Brooks	.05	.02
❑	101 Leroy Thompson	.05	.02
❑	102 Rodney Hampton	.25	.11
❑	103 Dave Meggett	.05	.02
❑	104 Phil Simms	.10	.05
❑	105 Boomer Esiason	.10	.05
❑	106 Johnny Johnson	.05	.02
❑	107 Gary Anderson K	.05	.02
❑	108 Mo Lewis	.05	.02
❑	109 Ronnie Lott	.10	.05
❑	110 Johnny Mitchell	.05	.02
❑	111 Howard Cross	.05	.02
❑	112 Victor Bailey	.05	.02
❑	113 Fred Barnett	.10	.05
❑	114 Randall Cunningham	.25	.11
❑	115 Calvin Williams	.10	.05
❑	116 Steve Beuerlein	.05	.02
❑	117 Gary Clark	.10	.05
❑	118 Ronald Moore	.05	.02
❑	119 Ricky Proehl	.05	.02
❑	120 Eric Swann	.10	.05
❑	121 Barry Foster	.05	.02
❑	122 Kevin Greene	.25	.11
❑	123 Greg Lloyd	.25	.11
❑	124 Neil O'Donnell	.25	.11
❑	125 Rod Woodson	.25	.11
❑	126 Ronnie Harmon	.05	.02
❑	127 Mark Higgs	.05	.02
❑	128 Stan Humphries	.25	.11
❑	129 Leslie O'Neal	.05	.02
❑	130 Chris Mims	.05	.02
❑	131 Stanley Richard	.05	.02
❑	132 Junior Seau	.25	.11
❑	133 Brent Jones	.10	.05
❑	134 Tim McDonald	.05	.02
❑	135 Jerry Rice	.75	.35
❑	136 Dana Stubblefield	.25	.11
❑	137 Ricky Watters	.25	.11
❑	138 Steve Young	.60	.25
❑	139 Cortez Kennedy	.10	.05
❑	140 Rick Mirer	.25	.11
❑	141 Eugene Robinson	.05	.02
❑	142 Chris Warren	.10	.05
❑	143 Nate Odomes	.05	.02
❑	144 Howard Ballard	.05	.02
❑	145 Flipper Anderson	.05	.02
❑	146 Chris Jacke	.05	.02
❑	147 Santana Dotson	.10	.05
❑	148 Craig Erickson	.05	.02
❑	149 Hardy Nickerson	.10	.05
❑	150 Lawrence Dawsey	.05	.02
❑	151 Terry Wooden	.05	.02
❑	152 Ethan Horton	.05	.02
❑	153 John Kasay	.05	.02
❑	154 Desmond Howard	.10	.05
❑	155 Ken Harvey	.05	.02
❑	156 William Fuller	.05	.02
❑	157 Clyde Simmons	.05	.02
❑	158 Randal Hill	.05	.02
❑	159 Garrison Hearst	.25	.11
❑	160 Mike Pritchard	.05	.02
❑	161 Jessie Tuggle	.05	.02
❑	162 Erric Pegram	.05	.02
❑	163 Kevin Ross	.05	.02
❑	164 Bill Brooks	.05	.02
❑	165 Darryl Talley	.05	.02
❑	166 Steve Tasker	.10	.05
❑	167 Pete Stoyanovich	.05	.02
❑	168 Dante Jones	.05	.02
❑	169 Vencie Glenn	.05	.02
❑	170 Tom Waddle	.05	.02
❑	171 Harlon Barnett	.05	.02
❑	172 Trace Armstrong	.05	.02
❑	173 Tim Worley	.05	.02
❑	174 Alfred Williams	.05	.02
❑	175 Louis Oliver	.05	.02

	No.	Player	Mint	NrMt
❑	176	Darryl Williams	.05	.02
❑	177	Clay Matthews	.05	.02
❑	178	Kyle Clifton	.05	.02
❑	179	Alvin Harper	.10	.05
❑	180	Jay Novacek	.10	.05
❑	181	Ken Norton Jr.	.10	.05
❑	182	Kevin Williams	.10	.05
❑	183	Daryl Johnston	.10	.05
❑	184	Rod Bernstine	.05	.02
❑	185	Karl Mecklenburg	.05	.02
❑	186	Dennis Smith	.05	.02
❑	187	Robert Delpino	.05	.02
❑	188	Bennie Blades	.05	.02
❑	189	Jason Hanson	.05	.02
❑	190	Derrick Moore	.05	.02
❑	191	Mark Clayton	.05	.02
❑	192	Webster Slaughter	.05	.02
❑	193	Haywood Jeffires	.10	.05
❑	194	Bubba McDowell	.05	.02
❑	195	Warren Moon	.25	.11
❑	196	Al Smith	.05	.02
❑	197	Bill Romanowski	.05	.02
❑	198	John Carney	.05	.02
❑	199	Kerry Cash	.05	.02
❑	200	Darren Carrington	.05	.02
❑	201	Jeff Lageman	.05	.02
❑	202	Tracy Simien	.05	.02
❑	203	Willie Davis	.10	.05
❑	204	Dan Saleaumua	.05	.02
❑	205	Rocket Ismail	.10	.05
❑	206	James Jett	.05	.02
❑	207	Todd Lyght	.05	.02
❑	208	Roman Phifer	.05	.02
❑	209	Jimmie Jones	.05	.02
❑	210	Jeff Cross	.05	.02
❑	211	Eric Davis	.05	.02
❑	212	Keith Byars	.05	.02
❑	213	Richmond Webb	.05	.02
❑	214	Anthony Carter	.10	.05
❑	215	Henry Thomas	.05	.02
❑	216	Andre Tippett	.05	.02
❑	217	Rickey Jackson	.05	.02
❑	218	Vaughan Johnson	.05	.02
❑	219	Eric Martin	.05	.02
❑	220	Sam Mills	.05	.02
❑	221	Renaldo Turnbull	.05	.02
❑	222	Mark Collins	.05	.02
❑	223	Mike Johnson	.05	.02
❑	224	Rob Moore	.10	.05
❑	225	Seth Joyner	.05	.02
❑	226	Herschel Walker	.10	.05
❑	227	Eric Green	.05	.02
❑	228	Marion Butts	.05	.02
❑	229	John Friesz	.10	.05
❑	230	John Taylor	.10	.05
❑	231	Dexter Carter	.05	.02
❑	232	Brian Blades	.10	.05
❑	233	Reggie Cobb	.05	.02
❑	234	Paul Gruber	.05	.02
❑	235	Ricky Reynolds	.05	.02
❑	236	Vince Workman	.05	.02
❑	237	Darrell Green	.05	.02
❑	238	Jim Lachey	.05	.02
❑	239	James Hasty	.05	.02
❑	240	Howie Long	.10	.05
❑	241	Aeneas Williams	.05	.02
❑	242	Mike Kenn	.05	.02
❑	243	Henry Jones	.05	.02
❑	244	Kenneth Davis	.05	.02
❑	245	Tim Krumrie	.05	.02
❑	246	Derrick Fenner	.05	.02
❑	247	Mark Carrier WR	.10	.05
❑	248	Robert Porcher	.05	.02
❑	249	Darren Woodson	.10	.05
❑	250	Kevin Smith	.05	.02
❑	251	Mark Stepnoski	.05	.02
❑	252	Simon Fletcher	.05	.02
❑	253	Derek Russell	.05	.02
❑	254	Mike Croel	.05	.02
❑	255	Johnny Holland	.05	.02
❑	256	Bryce Paup	.25	.11
❑	257	Cris Dishman	.05	.02
❑	258	Sean Jones	.05	.02
❑	259	Marcus Robertson	.05	.02
❑	260	Steve Jackson	.05	.02
❑	261	Jeff Herrod	.05	.02
❑	262	John Alt	.05	.02
❑	263	Nick Lowery	.05	.02
❑	264	Greg Robinson	.05	.02
❑	265	Alexander Wright	.05	.02
❑	266	Steve Wisniewski	.05	.02
❑	267	Henry Ellard	.10	.05
❑	268	Tracy Scroggins	.05	.02
❑	269	Jackie Slater	.05	.02
❑	270	Troy Vincent	.05	.02
❑	271	Qadry Ismail	.25	.11
❑	272	Steve Jordan	.05	.02
❑	273	Leonard Russell	.05	.02
❑	274	Maurice Hurst	.05	.02
❑	275	Scottie Graham RC	.10	.05
❑	276	Carlton Bailey	.05	.02
❑	277	John Elliott	.05	.02
❑	278	Corey Miller	.05	.02
❑	279	Brad Baxter	.05	.02
❑	280	Brian Washington	.05	.02
❑	281	Tim Harris	.05	.02
❑	282	Byron Evans	.05	.02
❑	283	Dermontti Dawson	.05	.02
❑	284	Carnell Lake	.05	.02
❑	285	Jeff Graham	.05	.02
❑	286	Merton Hanks	.10	.05
❑	287	Harris Barton	.05	.02
❑	288	Guy McIntyre	.05	.02
❑	289	Kelvin Martin	.05	.02
❑	290	John L. Williams	.05	.02
❑	291	Courtney Hawkins	.05	.02
❑	292	Vaughn Hebron	.05	.02
❑	293	Brian Mitchell	.05	.02
❑	294	Andre Collins	.05	.02
❑	295	Art Monk	.10	.05
❑	296	Mark Rypien	.05	.02
❑	297	Ricky Sanders	.05	.02
❑	298	Eric Hill	.05	.02
❑	299	Larry Centers	.25	.11
❑	300	Norm Johnson	.05	.02
❑	301	Pete Metzelaars	.05	.02
❑	302	Ricardo McDonald	.05	.02
❑	303	Stevon Moore	.05	.02
❑	304	Mike Sherrard	.05	.02
❑	305	Andy Harmon	.05	.02
❑	306	Anthony Johnson	.10	.05
❑	307	J.J. Birden	.05	.02
❑	308	Neal Anderson	.05	.02
❑	309	Lewis Tillman	.05	.02
❑	310	Richard Dent	.10	.05
❑	311	Nate Newton	.05	.02
❑	312	Sean Dawkins RC	.25	.11
❑	313	Lawrence Taylor	.25	.11
❑	314	Wilber Marshall	.05	.02
❑	315	Tom Carter	.05	.02
❑	316	Reggie Brooks	.10	.05
❑	317	Eric Curry	.05	.02
❑	318	Horace Copeland	.05	.02
❑	319	Natrone Means	.25	.11
❑	320	Eric Allen	.05	.02
❑	321	Marvin Jones	.05	.02
❑	322	Keith Hamilton	.05	.02
❑	323	Vincent Brisby	.25	.11
❑	324	Drew Bledsoe	1.00	.45
❑	325	Tom Rathman	.05	.02
❑	326	Ed McCaffrey	.10	.05
❑	327	Steve Israel	.05	.02
❑	328	Dan Wilkinson RC	.10	.05
❑	329	Marshall Faulk RC	4.00	1.80
❑	330	Heath Shuler RC	.25	.11
❑	331	Willie McGinest RC	.25	.11
❑	332	Trev Alberts RC	.10	.05
❑	333	Trent Dilfer RC	2.00	.90
❑	334	Bryant Young RC	.25	.11
❑	335	Sam Adams RC	.10	.05
❑	336	Antonio Langham RC	.10	.05
❑	337	Jamir Miller RC	.05	.02
❑	338	John Thierry RC	.05	.02
❑	339	Aaron Glenn RC	.10	.05
❑	340	Joe Johnson RC	.05	.02
❑	341	Bernard Williams RC	.05	.02
❑	342	Wayne Gandy RC	.05	.02
❑	343	Aaron Taylor RC	.05	.02
❑	344	Charles Johnson RC	.50	.23
❑	345	Dewayne Washington RC	.10	.05
❑	346	Todd Steussie RC	.10	.05
❑	347	Tim Bowens RC	.10	.05
❑	348	Johnnie Morton RC	.25	.11
❑	349	Rob Fredrickson RC	.10	.05
❑	350	Shante Carver RC	.05	.02
❑	351	Thomas Lewis RC	.10	.05
❑	352	Greg Hill RC	.25	.11
❑	353	Henry Ford RC	.05	.02
❑	354	Jeff Burris RC	.10	.05
❑	355	William Floyd RC	.25	.11
❑	356	Derrick Alexander WR RC	.50	.23
❑	357	Darnay Scott RC	.75	.35
❑	358	Isaac Bruce RC	4.00	1.80
❑	359	Errict Rhett RC	1.00	.45
❑	360	Kevin Lee RC	.05	.02
❑	361	Chuck Levy RC	.05	.02
❑	362	David Palmer RC	.50	.23
❑	363	Ryan Yarborough RC	.05	.02
❑	364	Charlie Garner RC	1.50	.70
❑	365	Isaac Davis RC	.05	.02
❑	366	Mario Bates RC	.25	.11
❑	367	Bert Emanuel RC	.50	.23
❑	368	Thomas Randolph RC	.05	.02
❑	369	Bucky Brooks RC	.05	.02
❑	370	Allen Aldridge RC	.05	.02
❑	371	Charlie Ward RC 1993 Heisman Trophy Winner	.25	.11
❑	372	Aubrey Beavers RC	.05	.02
❑	373	Donnell Bennett RC	.25	.11
❑	374	Jason Sehorn RC	.30	.14
❑	375	Lonnie Johnson RC	.05	.02
❑	376	Tyronne Drakeford RC	.05	.02
❑	377	Andre Coleman RC	.05	.02
❑	378	Lamar Smith RC	2.00	.90
❑	379	Calvin Jones RC	.05	.02
❑	380	LeShon Johnson RC	.10	.05
❑	381	Byron Bam Morris RC	.25	.11
❑	382	Lake Dawson RC	.25	.11
❑	383	Corey Sawyer RC	.05	.02
❑	384	Willie Jackson RC	.30	.14
❑	385	Perry Klein RC	.05	.02
❑	386	Ronnie Woolfork RC	.05	.02
❑	387	Doug Nussmeier RC	.05	.02
❑	388	Rob Waldrop RC	.05	.02
❑	389	Glenn Foley RC	.25	.11
❑	390	Troy Aikman CC Michael Irvin	.40	.18
❑	391	Steve Young CC Jerry Rice	.40	.18
❑	392	Brett Favre CC Sterling Sharpe	.75	.35
❑	393	Jim Kelly CC Andre Reed	.25	.11
❑	394	John Elway CC Shannon Sharpe	.75	.35
❑	395	Carolina Panthers	.15	.07
❑	396	Jacksonville Jaguars	.15	.07
❑	397	Checklist 1	.05	.02
❑	398	Checklist 2	.05	.02
❑	399	Checklist 3	.05	.02
❑	400	Checklist 4	.05	.02
❑	401	Sterling Sharpe ILL	.10	.05
❑	402	Derrick Thomas ILL	.10	.05
❑	403	Joe Montana ILL	.60	.25
❑	404	Emmitt Smith ILL	.50	.23
❑	405	Barry Sanders ILL	1.00	.45
❑	ES1	Emmitt Smith/15000 Super Bowl MVP	20.00	9.00
❑	JB1	Jerome Bettis ROY	12.00	5.50
❑	P1	Troy Aikman Promo International Sportscard Expo back	1.25	.55
❑	PR1	Emmitt Smith Promo (Numbered PR1)	2.00	.90

1995 Pro Line

			MINT	NRMT
		COMPLETE SET (400)	20.00	9.00
❑	1	Garrison Hearst	.25	.11
❑	2	Anthony Miller	.10	.05
❑	3	Brett Favre	1.50	.70
❑	4	Jessie Hester	.05	.02
❑	5	Mike Fox	.05	.02
❑	6	Jeff Blake RC	.75	.35
❑	7	J.J. Birden	.05	.02

❑ 8 Greg Jackson .05 .02
❑ 9 Leon Lett .05 .02
❑ 10 Bruce Matthews .05 .02
❑ 11 Andre Reed .10 .05
❑ 12 Joe Montana 1.50 .70
❑ 13 Craig Heyward .10 .05
❑ 14 Henry Ellard UER .10 .05
❑ 15 Chris Spielman .10 .05
❑ 16 Tony Woods .05 .02
❑ 17 Carl Banks .05 .02
❑ 18 Eric Zeier RC .25 .11
❑ 19 Michael Brooks .05 .02
❑ 20 Kevin Ross .05 .02
❑ 21 Qadry Ismail .10 .05
❑ 22 Mel Gray .05 .02
❑ 23 Ty Law RC .10 .05
❑ 24 Mark Collins .05 .02
❑ 25 Neil O'Donnell .10 .05
❑ 26 Ellis Johnson RC .05 .02
❑ 27 Rick Mirer .25 .11
❑ 28 Fred Barnett .10 .05
❑ 29 Mike Mamula RC .10 .05
❑ 30 Jim Jeffcoat .05 .02
❑ 31 Reggie Cobb .05 .02
❑ 32 Mark Carrier WR UER .10 .05
(Mark Carrier of the Bears is on front of card)
❑ 33 Darnay Scott .25 .11
❑ 34 Michael Jackson .10 .05
❑ 35 Terrell Buckley .05 .02
❑ 36 Nolan Harrison .05 .02
❑ 37 Thurman Thomas .25 .11
❑ 38 Anthony Smith .05 .02
❑ 39 Phillippi Sparks .05 .02
❑ 40 Cornelius Bennett .10 .05
❑ 41 Robert Young .05 .02
❑ 42 Pierce Holt .05 .02
❑ 43 Greg Lloyd .10 .05
❑ 44 Chad May RC .05 .02
❑ 45 Darrien Gordon .05 .02
❑ 46 Bryan Cox .05 .02
❑ 47 Junior Seau .25 .11
❑ 48 Al Smith .05 .02
❑ 49 Chris Slade .10 .05
❑ 50 Hardy Nickerson .05 .02
❑ 51 Brad Baxter .05 .02
❑ 52 Darryll Lewis .05 .02
❑ 53 Bryant Young .10 .05
❑ 54 Chris Warren .10 .05
❑ 55 Darion Conner .05 .02
❑ 56 Thomas Everett .05 .02
❑ 57 Charles Haley .10 .05
❑ 58 Chris Mims .05 .02
❑ 59 Sean Jones .05 .02
❑ 60 Tamarick Vanover RC .25 .11
❑ 61 Daryl Johnston .10 .05
❑ 62 Rashaan Salaam RC .25 .11
❑ 63 James Hasty .05 .02
❑ 64 Dante Jones .05 .02
❑ 65 Darren Perry UER .05 .02
(Card is numbered as 367)
❑ 66 Troy Drayton .05 .02
❑ 67 Mark Fields RC .05 .02
❑ 68 Brian Williams LB RC .05 .02
❑ 69 Steve Bono UER .10 .05
(Name spelled Bond on card)
❑ 70 Eric Allen .05 .02
❑ 71 Chris Zorich .05 .02
❑ 72 Dave Brown .10 .05
❑ 73 Ken Norton Jr. .10 .05
❑ 74 Wayne Martin .05 .02
❑ 75 Mo Lewis .05 .02
❑ 76 Johnny Mitchell .05 .02
❑ 77 Todd Lyght .05 .02
❑ 78 Erric Pegram .10 .05
❑ 79 Kevin Greene .10 .05
❑ 80 Randal Hill .05 .02
❑ 81 Brett Perriman .10 .05
❑ 82 Mike Sherrard .05 .02
❑ 83 Curtis Conway .25 .11
❑ 84 Mark Tuinei .05 .02
❑ 85 Mark Seay .10 .05
❑ 86 Randy Baldwin .05 .02
❑ 87 Ricky Ervins .05 .02
❑ 88 Chester McGlockton .10 .05
❑ 89 Tyrone Wheatley RC 1.00 .45
❑ 90 Micheal Barrow UER .05 .02
❑ 91 Kenneth Davis .05 .02
❑ 92 Napoleon Kaufman RC 1.25 .55
❑ 93 Webster Slaughter .05 .02
❑ 94 Darren Woodson .10 .05
❑ 95 Pete Stoyanovich .05 .02
❑ 96 Jimmie Jones .05 .02
❑ 97 Craig Erickson .05 .02
❑ 98 Michael Westbrook RC 1.25 .55
❑ 99 Steve McNair RC 2.50 1.10
❑ 100 Errict Rhett .25 .11
❑ 101 Devin Bush RC .05 .02
❑ 102 Dewayne Washington .10 .05
❑ 103 Bart Oates .05 .02
❑ 104 Aaron Pierce .05 .02
❑ 105 Warren Sapp RC .60 .25
❑ 106 Eric Green .05 .02
❑ 107 Glyn Milburn .05 .02
❑ 108 Johnny Johnson .05 .02
❑ 109 Marshall Faulk .40 .18
❑ 110 William Thomas .05 .02
❑ 111 George Koonce .05 .02
❑ 112 Dana Stubblefield .25 .11
❑ 113 Steve Tovar .05 .02
❑ 114 Steve Israel .05 .02
❑ 115 Brent Williams .05 .02
❑ 116 Shane Conlan .05 .02
❑ 117 Winston Moss .05 .02
❑ 118 Nate Newton .10 .05
❑ 119 Michael Irvin .25 .11
❑ 120 Jeff Lageman .05 .02
❑ 121 Ki-Jana Carter RC .25 .11
❑ 122 Dan Marino 1.50 .70
❑ 123 Tony Casillas .05 .02
❑ 124 Kevin Carter RC .25 .11
❑ 125 Warren Moon .10 .05
❑ 126 Byron Bam Morris .10 .05
❑ 127 Ben Coates .10 .05
❑ 128 Michael Bankston .05 .02
❑ 129 Anthony Parker .05 .02
❑ 130 LeRoy Butler .05 .02
❑ 131 Tony Bennett .05 .02
❑ 132 Alvin Harper .05 .02
❑ 133 Tim Brown .25 .11
❑ 134 Tom Carter .05 .02
❑ 135 Lorenzo White .05 .02
❑ 136 Shane Dronett .05 .02
❑ 137 John Elliott UER .05 .02
❑ 138 Korey Stringer .05 .02
❑ 139 Jerry Rice .75 .35
❑ 140 Sherman Williams RC .05 .02
❑ 141 Kevin Turner .05 .02
❑ 142 Randall Cunningham .25 .11
❑ 143 Vinny Testaverde .10 .05
❑ 144 Tim Bowens .05 .02
❑ 145 Russell Maryland .05 .02
❑ 146 Chris Miller .05 .02
❑ 147 Vince Buck .05 .02
❑ 148 Willie Clay .05 .02
❑ 149 Jeff Graham .05 .02
❑ 150 Shannon Sharpe .10 .05
❑ 151 Carnell Lake .05 .02
❑ 152 Mark Bruener RC .10 .05
❑ 153 James Washington .05 .02
❑ 154 Pepper Johnson .05 .02
❑ 155 Bert Emanuel .25 .11
❑ 156 Mark Stepnoski .05 .02
❑ 157 Robert Jones .05 .02
❑ 158 Cris Dishman .05 .02
❑ 159 Henry Jones .05 .02
❑ 160 Henry Thomas .05 .02
❑ 161 John L. Williams .05 .02
❑ 162 Joe Cain .05 .02
❑ 163 Mike Johnson .05 .02
❑ 164 Merton Hanks .05 .02
❑ 165 Deion Sanders .40 .18
❑ 166 William Floyd .25 .11
❑ 167 Leroy Thompson .05 .02
❑ 168 Ray Childress .05 .02
❑ 169 Donnell Woolford .05 .02
❑ 170 Tony Siragusa .05 .02
❑ 171 Chad Brown .10 .05
❑ 172 Stanley Richard .05 .02
❑ 173 Rob Johnson RC 1.50 .70
❑ 174 Derrick Brooks RC .25 .11
❑ 175 Drew Bledsoe .75 .35
❑ 176 Maurice Hurst .05 .02
❑ 177 Ricky Watters .25 .11
❑ 178 Myron Guyton .05 .02
❑ 179 Ricky Proehl .05 .02
❑ 180 Haywood Jeffires .05 .02
❑ 181 Michael Strahan .10 .05
❑ 182 Charles Wilson .05 .02
❑ 183 Mark Carrier DB .05 .02
❑ 184 James O. Stewart RC 1.50 .70
❑ 185 Andy Harmon .05 .02
❑ 186 Ronnie Lott .10 .05
❑ 187 Clay Matthews .10 .05
❑ 188 John Carney .05 .02
❑ 189 Andre Rison .10 .05
❑ 190 Aeneas Williams .05 .02
❑ 191 Alexander Wright .05 .02
❑ 192 Desmond Howard .10 .05
❑ 193 Herman Moore .25 .11
❑ 194 Alfred Williams .05 .02
❑ 195 Tyrone Poole RC .10 .05
❑ 196 Darren Mickell .05 .02
❑ 197 Steve Young .60 .25
❑ 198 Roman Phifer .05 .02
❑ 199 Darrell Green .05 .02
❑ 200 Terry Wooden .05 .02
❑ 201 Chris Calloway .05 .02
❑ 202 Lewis Tillman .05 .02
❑ 203 Cris Carter .25 .11
❑ 204 Jim Everett .05 .02
❑ 205 Adrian Murrell .10 .05
❑ 206 Barry Sanders 1.50 .70
❑ 207 Mario Bates .25 .11
❑ 208 Shawn Lee .05 .02
❑ 209 Charles Mincy .05 .02
❑ 210 Kerry Collins RC 1.25 .55
❑ 211 Steve Walsh .05 .02
❑ 212 Chris Chandler .10 .05
❑ 213 Bennie Blades .05 .02
❑ 214 Kevin Williams WR .10 .05
❑ 215 Jim Kelly .25 .11
❑ 216 Marion Butts .05 .02
❑ 217 Jay Novacek .10 .05
❑ 218 Shawn Jefferson .05 .02
❑ 219 O.J. McDuffie .25 .11
❑ 220 Ray Seals .05 .02
❑ 221 Arthur Marshall .05 .02
❑ 222 Karl Mecklenburg .05 .02
❑ 223 Terance Mathis .10 .05
❑ 224 David Klingler .10 .05
❑ 225 Rod Woodson .10 .05
❑ 226 Quentin Coryatt .10 .05
❑ 227 Leroy Hoard .05 .02
❑ 228 Brian Blades .10 .05
❑ 229 Rob Moore .05 .02
❑ 230 Boomer Esiason .10 .05
❑ 231 Dave Krieg .05 .02
❑ 232 Sterling Sharpe .10 .05
❑ 233 Marcus Allen .25 .11
❑ 234 John Randle .10 .05
❑ 235 Craig Powell .05 .02
❑ 236 John Elway 1.50 .70
❑ 237 Mark Ingram .05 .02
❑ 238 Cortez Kennedy .10 .05
❑ 239 Brent Jones .05 .02
❑ 240 Ken Harvey .05 .02
❑ 241 Keenan McCardell .25 .11
❑ 242 Dan Wilkinson .10 .05

❑ 243 Don Beebe .05 .02
❑ 244 Jack Del Rio .05 .02
❑ 245 Byron Evans .05 .02
❑ 246 Ronald Moore .05 .02
❑ 247 Edgar Bennett .10 .05
❑ 248 William Fuller .05 .02
❑ 249 James Williams .05 .02
❑ 250 Neil Smith .10 .05
❑ 251 Sam Mills .10 .05
❑ 252 Willie McGinest .10 .05
❑ 253 Howard Cross .05 .02
❑ 254 Troy Aikman .75 .35
❑ 255 Herschel Walker .10 .05
❑ 256 Dale Carter .10 .05
❑ 257 Sean Dawkins .10 .05
❑ 258 Greg Hill .10 .05
❑ 259 Stan Humphries .10 .05
❑ 260 Erik Kramer .05 .02
❑ 261 Leslie O'Neal .10 .05
❑ 262 Trezelle Jenkins RC .05 .02
❑ 263 Antonio Langham .05 .02
❑ 264 Bryce Paup .25 .11
❑ 265 Jake Reed .10 .05
❑ 266 Richmond Webb .05 .02
❑ 267 Eric Davis .05 .02
❑ 268 Mark McMillian .05 .02
❑ 269 John Walsh RC .05 .02
❑ 270 Irving Fryar .10 .05
❑ 271 Rocket Ismail .10 .05
❑ 272 Phil Hansen .05 .02
❑ 273 J.J. Stokes RC .25 .11
❑ 274 Craig Newsome RC .05 .02
❑ 275 Leonard Russell .05 .02
❑ 276 Derrick Deese .05 .02
❑ 277 Broderick Thomas .05 .02
❑ 278 Bobby Houston .05 .02
❑ 279 Lamar Lathon .05 .02
❑ 280 Eugene Robinson .05 .02
❑ 281 Dan Saleaumua .05 .02
❑ 282 Kyle Brady RC .25 .11
❑ 283 John Taylor UER .05 .02
(Card lists him as a Tight End)
❑ 284 Tony Boselli RC .25 .11
❑ 285 Seth Joyner .05 .02
❑ 286 Steve Beuerlein .05 .02
❑ 287 Sam Adams .05 .02
❑ 288 Frank Reich .05 .02
❑ 289 Patrick Hunter .05 .02
❑ 290 Sean Gilbert .10 .05
❑ 291 Dermontti Dawson UER .10 .05
❑ 292 Shaun Gayle .05 .02
❑ 293 Vincent Brown .05 .02
❑ 294 Terry Kirby .10 .05
❑ 295 Courtney Hawkins .05 .02
❑ 296 Carl Pickens .25 .11
❑ 297 Luther Elliss RC .05 .02
❑ 298 Steve Atwater .05 .02
❑ 299 James Francis .05 .02
❑ 300 Rob Burnett .05 .02
❑ 301 Keith Hamilton .05 .02
❑ 302 Rob Fredrickson .05 .02
❑ 303 Jerome Bettis .25 .11
❑ 304 Emmitt Smith 1.25 .55
❑ 305 Clyde Simmons .05 .02
❑ 306 Reggie White .25 .11
❑ 307 Rodney Hampton .10 .05
❑ 308 Steve Emtman .05 .02
❑ 309 Hugh Douglas RC .25 .11
❑ 310 Bernie Parmalee .10 .05
❑ 311 Trent Dilfer .25 .11
❑ 312 Flipper Anderson .05 .02
❑ 313 Heath Shuler .25 .11
❑ 314 Rod Smith DB .10 .05
❑ 315 Ray Zellars RC .10 .05
❑ 316 Robert Brooks .25 .11
❑ 317 Lee Woodall .05 .02
❑ 318 Robert Porcher .05 .02
❑ 319 Todd Collins RC .25 .11
❑ 320 Willie Roaf .05 .02
❑ 321 Erik Williams .05 .02
❑ 322 Steve Wisniewski .05 .02
❑ 323 Derrick Alexander .05 .02
DE RC
❑ 324 Frank Warren .05 .02
❑ 325 Kelvin Pritchett .05 .02
❑ 326 Dennis Gibson .05 .02
❑ 327 Jason Belser .05 .02
❑ 328 Vincent Brisby .05 .02
❑ 329 Calvin Williams .10 .05
❑ 330 Derek Brown RBK .05 .02
❑ 331 Blake Brockermeyer .05 .02
❑ 332 Jeff Herrod .05 .02
❑ 333 Darryl Williams .05 .02
❑ 334 Aaron Glenn .05 .02
❑ 335 Eric Metcalf .10 .05
❑ 336 Billy Milner .05 .02
❑ 337 Terry McDaniel .05 .02
❑ 338 Trace Armstrong .05 .02
❑ 339 Yancey Thigpen RC .25 .11
❑ 340 Jackie Harris .05 .02
❑ 341 Jeff George .10 .05
❑ 342 Darryl Talley .05 .02
❑ 343 Marcus Robertson .05 .02
❑ 344 Robert Massey .05 .02
❑ 345 Jessie Tuggle .05 .02
❑ 346 Scott Mitchell .10 .05
❑ 347 Harvey Williams .05 .02
❑ 348 Jack Jackson RC .05 .02
❑ 349 Brian Mitchell .05 .02
❑ 350 Lawrence Dawsey .05 .02
❑ 351 Erik Howard .05 .02
❑ 352 Quinn Early .10 .05
❑ 353 Terry Allen .10 .05
❑ 354 Simon Fletcher .05 .02
❑ 355 Eric Turner .05 .02
❑ 356 Natrone Means .25 .11
❑ 357 Frank Sanders RC .75 .35
❑ 358 Michael Timpson .05 .02
❑ 359 Michael Haynes .10 .05
❑ 360 Ruben Brown RC .05 .02
❑ 361 Troy Vincent UER .05 .02
(Name spelled Vicent on back)
❑ 362 Floyd Turner .05 .02
❑ 363 Larry Centers .10 .05
❑ 364 Eric Swann .10 .05
❑ 365 Albert Lewis .05 .02
❑ 366 Barry Foster .10 .05
❑ 367 Michael Dean Perry .05 .02
❑ 368 Jumpy Geathers UER .05 .02
(Name spelled Jummpy on front)
❑ 369 Kordell Stewart RC 2.00 .90
❑ 370 Chuck Smith .05 .02
❑ 371 Lake Dawson .10 .05
❑ 372 Terry Hoage .05 .02
❑ 373 Jeff Cross .05 .02
❑ 374 Tony McGee .05 .02
❑ 375 Eric Curry .05 .02
❑ 376 Harold Green .05 .02
❑ 377 Eric Hill .05 .02
❑ 378 Ray Buchanan .05 .02
❑ 379 Willie Davis .10 .05
❑ 380 Chris T. Jones RC .25 .11
❑ 381 Martin Mayhew .05 .02
❑ 382 Anthony Pleasant .05 .02
❑ 383 Joey Galloway RC 2.00 .90
❑ 384 Anthony Morgan .05 .02
❑ 385 Harlon Barnett .05 .02
❑ 386 Bruce Smith .25 .11
❑ 387 Jeff Hostetler .10 .05
❑ 388 Randall McDaniel .05 .02
❑ 389 Dave Meggett .05 .02
❑ 390 Bill Romanowski .05 .02
❑ 391 Gary Brown .05 .02
❑ 392 Charles Johnson .10 .05
❑ 393 Chris Doleman .05 .02
❑ 394 Tony Martin .10 .05
❑ 395 Raymont Harris .05 .02
❑ 396 John Copeland .05 .02
❑ 397 Emmitt Smith CL UER .25 .11
(Several wrong names)
❑ 398 Steve Young CL UER .10 .05
(Many wrong names)
❑ 399 Marshall Faulk CL UER .25 .11
(Many wrong names)
❑ 400 Ki-Jana Carter CL UER .10 .05
(Many wrong names)
❑ P1 Marshall Faulk Promo 1.00 .45
GameBreakers card
1995 National Convention back

1995 Pro Line Series 2

	MINT	NRMT
COMPLETE SET (75)	15.00	6.75
❑ 1 Jim Kelly	.25	.11
❑ 2 Steve Walsh	.05	.02
❑ 3 Jeff Blake	.25	.11
❑ 4 Vinny Testaverde	.10	.05
❑ 5 Jeff Hostetler	.10	.05
❑ 6 Dan Marino	2.00	.90
❑ 7 Cris Carter	.25	.11
❑ 8 Drew Bledsoe	1.00	.45
❑ 9 Jim Everett	.05	.02
❑ 10 Neil O'Donnell	.10	.05
❑ 11 Rodney Hampton	.10	.05
❑ 12 Troy Aikman	1.00	.45
❑ 13 John Elway	2.00	.90
❑ 14 Barry Sanders	2.00	.90
❑ 15 Reggie White	.25	.11
❑ 16 Marshall Faulk	.40	.18
❑ 17 Marcus Allen	.25	.11
❑ 18 James O. Stewart	1.00	.45
❑ 19 Randall Cunningham	.25	.11
❑ 20 Natrone Means	.25	.11
❑ 21 Rick Mirer	.25	.11
❑ 22 Jerry Rice	1.00	.45
❑ 23 Errict Rhett	.25	.11
❑ 24 Heath Shuler	.25	.11
❑ 25 Jerome Bettis	.25	.11
❑ 26 Garrison Hearst	.25	.11
❑ 27 Jeff George	.10	.05
❑ 28 Andre Reed	.10	.05
❑ 29 Warren Moon	.10	.05
❑ 30 Ben Coates	.10	.05
❑ 31 Mario Bates	.25	.11
❑ 32 Byron Bam Morris	.10	.05
❑ 33 Dave Brown	.10	.05
❑ 34 Emmitt Smith	1.50	.70
❑ 35 Anthony Miller	.10	.05
❑ 36 Herman Moore	.25	.11
❑ 37 Brett Favre	2.00	.90
❑ 38 Steve Bono	.10	.05
❑ 39 Stan Humphries	.10	.05
❑ 40 Steve Young	.75	.35
❑ 41 Trent Dilfer	.25	.11
❑ 42 Chris Miller	.05	.02
❑ 43 Herschel Walker	.10	.05
❑ 44 Michael Irvin	.25	.11
❑ 45 Junior Seau	.25	.11
❑ 46 Deion Sanders	.60	.25
❑ 47 William Floyd	.25	.11
❑ 48 Ki-Jana Carter	.25	.11
❑ 49 Kerry Collins	.75	.35
❑ 50 Steve McNair	1.25	.55
❑ 51 Tony Boselli	.25	.11
❑ 52 Kyle Brady	.25	.11
❑ 53 Mike Mamula	.10	.05
❑ 54 Warren Sapp	.10	.05
❑ 55 J.J. Stokes	.25	.11
❑ 56 Joey Galloway	1.00	.45
❑ 57 Hugh Douglas	.10	.05
❑ 58 Michael Westbrook	.75	.35
❑ 59 Napoleon Kaufman	.75	.35
❑ 60 Rashaan Salaam	.25	.11
❑ 61 Tyrone Wheatley	.60	.25
❑ 62 Terrell Fletcher RC	.05	.02
❑ 63 Eric Metcalf	.10	.05

❑ 64 Kevin Carter	.25	.11
❑ 65 Andre Rison	.10	.05
❑ 66 Eric Green	.05	.02
❑ 67 Dave Meggett	.05	.02
❑ 68 Ricky Watters	.25	.11
❑ 69 Steve Beuerlein	.05	.02
❑ 70 Craig Erickson	.05	.02
❑ 71 Michael Dean Perry	.05	.02
❑ 72 Alvin Harper	.05	.02
❑ 73 Rob Moore	.05	.02
❑ 74 Frank Reich	.05	.02
❑ 75 Checklist	.10	.05

1996 Pro Line

	MINT	NRMT
COMPLETE SET (350)	25.00	11.00
❑ 1 Troy Aikman	1.00	.45
❑ 2 Steve Young	.75	.35
❑ 3 John Elway	2.00	.90
❑ 4 Jim Kelly	.40	.18
❑ 5 Dan Marino	2.00	.90
❑ 6 Brett Favre	2.00	.90
❑ 7 Kerry Collins	.40	.18
❑ 8 Jeff Blake	.40	.18
❑ 9 Stan Humphries	.20	.09
❑ 10 Steve Bono	.10	.05
❑ 11 Jeff George	.20	.09
❑ 12 Mark Brunell	1.00	.45
❑ 13 Scott Mitchell	.20	.09
❑ 14 Steve McNair	.75	.35
❑ 15 Jeff Hostetler	.10	.05
❑ 16 Jim Everett	.10	.05
❑ 17 Rick Mirer	.20	.09
❑ 18 Boomer Esiason	.20	.09
❑ 19 Neil O'Donnell	.20	.09
❑ 20 Dave Brown	.10	.05
❑ 21 Erik Kramer	.10	.05
❑ 22 Trent Dilfer	.40	.18
❑ 23 Jim Harbaugh	.20	.09
❑ 24 Vinny Testaverde	.20	.09
❑ 25 Thurman Thomas	.40	.18
❑ 26 Rodney Peete	.10	.05
❑ 27 Gus Frerotte	.40	.18
❑ 28 Warren Moon	.20	.09
❑ 29 Eric Zeier	.10	.05
❑ 30 Randall Cunningham	.40	.18
❑ 31 Heath Shuler	.20	.09
❑ 32 John Friesz	.10	.05
❑ 33 Tommy Maddox	.10	.05
❑ 34 Glenn Foley	.20	.09
❑ 35 Drew Bledsoe	1.00	.45
❑ 36 Kordell Stewart	.60	.25
❑ 37 Natrone Means	.40	.18
❑ 38 Errict Rhett	.20	.09
❑ 39 Rashaan Salaam	.40	.18
❑ 40 Emmitt Smith	1.50	.70
❑ 41 Larry Centers	.20	.09
❑ 42 Terrell Davis	2.50	1.10
❑ 43 Marshall Faulk	.40	.18
❑ 44 Rodney Hampton	.20	.09
❑ 45 Byron Bam Morris	.20	.09
❑ 46 Chris Warren	.20	.09
❑ 47 Curtis Martin	.75	.35
❑ 48 Ricky Watters	.20	.09
❑ 49 Marcus Allen	.40	.18
❑ 50 Barry Sanders	2.00	.90
❑ 51 Edgar Bennett	.20	.09
❑ 52 Adrian Murrell	.40	.18
❑ 53 James O. Stewart	.20	.09
❑ 54 Leroy Hoard	.10	.05
❑ 55 Jerome Bettis	.40	.18
❑ 56 Craig Heyward	.10	.05
❑ 57 Harvey Williams	.10	.05
❑ 58 Bernie Parmalee	.10	.05
❑ 59 Garrison Hearst	.20	.09
❑ 60 Terry Allen	.20	.09
❑ 61 Charlie Garner	.10	.05
❑ 62 Dorsey Levens	.40	.18
❑ 63 Derek Loville	.10	.05
❑ 64 Greg Hill	.20	.09
❑ 65 Derrick Moore	.10	.05
❑ 66 Rodney Thomas	.10	.05
❑ 67 Daryl Johnston	.20	.09
❑ 68 Mario Bates	.20	.09
❑ 69 Aaron Hayden RC	.10	.05
❑ 70 Napoleon Kaufman	.40	.18
❑ 71 Terry Kirby	.20	.09
❑ 72 Glyn Milburn	.10	.05
❑ 73 Robert Smith	.20	.09
❑ 74 Ki-Jana Carter	.20	.09
❑ 75 Tyrone Wheatley	.20	.09
❑ 76 Erric Pegram	.10	.05
❑ 77 Brian Mitchell	.10	.05
❑ 78 Vaughn Dunbar	.10	.05
❑ 79 Dave Meggett	.10	.05
❑ 80 Scottie Graham	.10	.05
❑ 81 Darick Holmes	.10	.05
❑ 82 Marion Butts	.10	.05
❑ 83 Harold Green	.10	.05
❑ 84 Zack Crockett	.10	.05
❑ 85 Amp Lee	.10	.05
❑ 86 Lamont Warren	.10	.05
❑ 87 Mark Chmura	.20	.09
❑ 88 Irving Fryar	.20	.09
❑ 89 Tim Brown	.40	.18
❑ 90 Michael Irvin	.40	.18
❑ 91 Tony Martin	.20	.09
❑ 92 Alvin Harper	.10	.05
❑ 93 Darnay Scott	.20	.09
❑ 94 Eric Metcalf	.10	.05
❑ 95 Michael Timpson	.10	.05
❑ 96 Sean Dawkins	.10	.05
❑ 97 Qadry Ismail	.10	.05
❑ 98 Yancey Thigpen	.20	.09
❑ 99 Joey Galloway	.60	.25
❑ 100 Herman Moore	.40	.18
❑ 101 J.J. Stokes	.40	.18
❑ 102 Wayne Chrebet	.60	.25
❑ 103 Ernest Givins	.10	.05
❑ 104 Michael Jackson	.20	.09
❑ 105 Henry Ellard	.10	.05
❑ 106 Thomas Lewis	.10	.05
❑ 107 Anthony Miller	.20	.09
❑ 108 Terance Mathis	.10	.05
❑ 109 Horace Copeland	.10	.05
❑ 110 Rocket Ismail	.10	.05
❑ 111 Quinn Early	.10	.05
❑ 112 Haywood Jeffires	.10	.05
❑ 113 Mark Carrier WR	.10	.05
❑ 114 Brent Jones	.10	.05
❑ 115 Ben Coates	.20	.09
❑ 116 Ken Dilger	.20	.09
❑ 117 Irv Smith	.10	.05
❑ 118 Jay Novacek	.10	.05
❑ 119 Tony McGee	.10	.05
❑ 120 Troy Drayton	.10	.05
❑ 121 Johnny Mitchell	.10	.05
❑ 122 Rob Moore	.20	.09
❑ 123 Kevin Williams WR	.10	.05
❑ 124 O.J. McDuffie	.20	.09
❑ 125 Carl Pickens	.40	.18
❑ 126 Curtis Conway	.40	.18
❑ 127 Ed McCaffrey	.20	.09
❑ 128 Arthur Marshall	.10	.05
❑ 129 Ernie Mills	.10	.05
❑ 130 Cris Carter	.40	.18
❑ 131 Isaac Bruce	.40	.18
❑ 132 Brian Blades	.10	.05
❑ 133 Michael Westbrook	.40	.18
❑ 134 Andre Reed	.20	.09
❑ 135 Andre Rison	.20	.09
❑ 136 Brett Perriman	.10	.05
❑ 137 Willie Jackson	.10	.05
❑ 138 Ryan Yarborough	.10	.05
❑ 139 Chris T. Jones	.20	.09
❑ 140 Jerry Rice	1.00	.45
❑ 141 Lake Dawson	.10	.05
❑ 142 Robert Brooks	.40	.18
❑ 143 Vincent Brisby	.10	.05
❑ 144 Desmond Howard	.20	.09
❑ 145 Johnnie Morton	.20	.09
❑ 146 Steve Tasker	.10	.05
❑ 147 Ty Detmer	.20	.09
❑ 148 Todd Kinchen	.10	.05
❑ 149 Mike Sherrard	.10	.05
❑ 150 Eric Green	.10	.05
❑ 151 Mark Bruener	.10	.05
❑ 152 Kyle Brady	.10	.05
❑ 153 Frank Sanders	.20	.09
❑ 154 Willie Green	.10	.05
❑ 155 Jeff Graham	.10	.05
❑ 156 Bert Emanuel	.20	.09
❑ 157 Courtney Hawkins	.10	.05
❑ 158 Mark Seay	.10	.05
❑ 159 Chris Calloway	.10	.05
❑ 160 John Taylor	.10	.05
❑ 161 Fred Barnett	.10	.05
❑ 162 Tamarick Vanover	.20	.09
❑ 163 Keenan McCardell	.40	.18
❑ 164 Bill Brooks	.10	.05
❑ 165 Alexander Wright	.10	.05
❑ 166 Jake Reed	.20	.09
❑ 167 Floyd Turner	.10	.05
❑ 168 Mike Pritchard	.10	.05
❑ 169 Lawrence Dawsey	.10	.05
❑ 170 Shawn Jefferson	.10	.05
❑ 171 Michael Haynes	.10	.05
❑ 172 Shannon Sharpe	.20	.09
❑ 173 Jackie Harris	.10	.05
❑ 174 Daryl Hobbs RC	.10	.05
❑ 175 Chris Sanders	.20	.09
❑ 176 Willie Davis	.10	.05
❑ 177 Marco Coleman	.10	.05
❑ 178 Pat Swilling	.10	.05
❑ 179 Alonzo Spellman	.10	.05
❑ 180 Simon Fletcher	.10	.05
❑ 181 Sean Gilbert	.10	.05
❑ 182 Tracy Scroggins	.10	.05
❑ 183 Hugh Douglas	.20	.09
❑ 184 Eric Swann	.10	.05
❑ 185 Russell Maryland	.10	.05
❑ 186 Warren Sapp	.10	.05
❑ 187 Jim Flanigan	.10	.05
❑ 188 Cortez Kennedy	.10	.05
❑ 189 Andy Harmon	.10	.05
❑ 190 Dan Saleaumua	.10	.05
❑ 191 Kelvin Pritchett	.10	.05
❑ 192 John Randle	.20	.09
❑ 193 Dan Wilkinson	.10	.05
❑ 194 Chester McGlockton	.10	.05
❑ 195 Leon Lett	.10	.05
❑ 196 Neil Smith	.10	.05
❑ 197 Mike Mamula	.10	.05
❑ 198 Mike Jones	.10	.05
❑ 199 Reggie White	.40	.18
❑ 200 Anthony Pleasant	.10	.05
❑ 201 Phil Hansen	.10	.05
❑ 202 Ray Seals	.10	.05
❑ 203 Tony Bennett	.10	.05
❑ 204 Leslie O'Neal	.10	.05
❑ 205 Jeff Cross	.10	.05
❑ 206 Anthony Cook	.10	.05
❑ 207 Clyde Simmons	.10	.05
❑ 208 Renaldo Turnbull	.10	.05
❑ 209 Charles Haley	.20	.09
❑ 210 John Copeland	.10	.05
❑ 211 John Thierry	.10	.05
❑ 212 Michael Strahan	.10	.05
❑ 213 Jeff Lageman	.10	.05
❑ 214 William Fuller	.10	.05
❑ 215 Rickey Jackson	.10	.05
❑ 216 Wayne Martin	.10	.05
❑ 217 Steve Emtman	.10	.05
❑ 218 Shawn Lee	.10	.05
❑ 219 Chris Zorich	.10	.05
❑ 220 Henry Thomas	.10	.05
❑ 221 Dana Stubblefield	.20	.09
❑ 222 D'Marco Farr	.10	.05

Card	MINT	NRMT
❑ 223 Pierce Holt	.10	.05
❑ 224 Sean Jones	.10	.05
❑ 225 Robert Porcher	.10	.05
❑ 226 Kevin Carter	.10	.05
❑ 227 Chris Doleman	.10	.05
❑ 228 Tony Tolbert	.10	.05
❑ 229 Bruce Smith	.20	.09
❑ 230 Marvin Washington	.10	.05
❑ 231 Blaine Bishop	.10	.05
❑ 232 Bryant Young	.20	.09
❑ 233 Rob Burnett	.10	.05
❑ 234 Lawrence Phillips RC	.40	.18
❑ 235 Trev Alberts	.10	.05
❑ 236 Eric Curry	.10	.05
❑ 237 Anthony Smith	.10	.05
❑ 238 Sam Mills	.10	.05
❑ 239 Seth Joyner	.10	.05
❑ 240 Quentin Coryatt	.10	.05
❑ 241 Levon Kirkland	.10	.05
❑ 242 Cornelius Bennett	.10	.05
❑ 243 Chris Spielman	.10	.05
❑ 244 Mo Lewis	.10	.05
❑ 245 Lee Woodall	.10	.05
❑ 246 Derrick Thomas	.20	.09
❑ 247 Willie McGinest	.10	.05
❑ 248 Terry Wooden	.10	.05
❑ 249 Greg Lloyd	.20	.09
❑ 250 Jack Del Rio	.10	.05
❑ 251 Hardy Nickerson	.10	.05
❑ 252 Micheal Barrow	.10	.05
❑ 253 Lamar Lathon	.10	.05
❑ 254 Bryan Cox	.10	.05
❑ 255 Randy Kirk	.10	.05
❑ 256 Jessie Tuggle	.10	.05
❑ 257 Roman Phifer	.10	.05
❑ 258 Ken Harvey	.10	.05
❑ 259 Junior Seau	.20	.09
❑ 260 Pepper Johnson	.10	.05
❑ 261 Chris Slade	.10	.05
❑ 262 Gary Plummer	.10	.05
❑ 263 Wayne Simmons	.10	.05
❑ 264 Bryce Paup	.10	.05
❑ 265 William Thomas	.10	.05
❑ 266 Kevin Greene	.20	.09
❑ 267 Bobby Engram RC	.40	.18
❑ 268 Ken Norton	.10	.05
❑ 269 Eric Hill	.10	.05
❑ 270 Darion Conner	.10	.05
❑ 271 Tyrone Poole	.10	.05
❑ 272 Cris Dishman	.10	.05
❑ 273 Marcus Jones RC	.10	.05
❑ 274 Rod Woodson	.20	.09
❑ 275 Mark McMillian	.10	.05
❑ 276 Dale Carter	.10	.05
❑ 277 Darrell Green	.10	.05
❑ 278 Donnell Woolford	.10	.05
❑ 279 Troy Vincent	.10	.05
❑ 280 Larry Brown	.10	.05
❑ 281 Aeneas Williams	.10	.05
❑ 282 Eric Allen	.10	.05
❑ 283 Ray Buchanan	.10	.05
❑ 284 Ty Law	.10	.05
❑ 285 Eric Davis	.10	.05
❑ 286 Todd Lyght	.10	.05
❑ 287 Terry McDaniel	.10	.05
❑ 288 Darryll Lewis	.10	.05
❑ 289 Deion Sanders	.60	.25
❑ 290 Phillippi Sparks	.10	.05
❑ 291 Bobby Taylor	.10	.05
❑ 292 Mark Collins	.10	.05
❑ 293 Steve Atwater	.10	.05
❑ 294 Stanley Richard	.20	.09
❑ 295 Stevon Moore	.10	.05
❑ 296 Bennie Blades	.10	.05
❑ 297 Tim McDonald	.10	.05
❑ 298 Shaun Gayle	.10	.05
❑ 299 Darren Woodson	.20	.09
❑ 300 Mark Carrier DB	.10	.05
❑ 301 Carnell Lake	.10	.05
❑ 302 James Washington	.10	.05
❑ 303 LeRoy Butler	.10	.05
❑ 304 Henry Jones	.10	.05
❑ 305 Darryl Williams	.10	.05
❑ 306 Darren Perry	.10	.05
❑ 307 Merton Hanks	.10	.05
❑ 308 Orlando Thomas	.10	.05
❑ 309 Eric Turner	.10	.05
❑ 310 Nate Newton	.10	.05
❑ 311 Steve Wisniewski	.10	.05
❑ 312 Derrick Deese	.10	.05
❑ 313 Larry Allen	.10	.05
❑ 314 Aaron Taylor	.10	.05
❑ 315 Blake Brockermeyer	.10	.05
❑ 316 William Roaf	.10	.05
❑ 317 Jumbo Elliott	.10	.05
❑ 318 Keyshawn Johnson RC	1.50	.70
❑ 319 Karim Abdul-Jabbar RC	.50	.23
❑ 320 Kevin Hardy RC	.40	.18
❑ 321 Duane Clemons RC	.10	.05
❑ 322 Jevon Langford RC	.10	.05
❑ 323 Mike Alstott RC	1.25	.55
❑ 324 Scott Greene RC	.10	.05
❑ 325 Derrick Mayes RC	.60	.25
❑ 326 Chris Doering RC	.10	.05
❑ 327 Amani Toomer RC	.75	.35
❑ 328 Eric Moulds RC	1.50	.70
❑ 329 Alex Molden RC	.10	.05
❑ 330 Lawyer Milloy RC	.20	.09
❑ 331 Daryl Gardener RC	.10	.05
❑ 332 Randall Godfrey RC	.10	.05
❑ 333 Willie Anderson RC	.10	.05
❑ 334 Tony Banks RC	1.00	.45
❑ 335 Jeff Lewis RC	.50	.23
❑ 336 Roman Oben RC	.10	.05
❑ 337 Andre Johnson RC	.10	.05
❑ 338 Brian Roche RC	.10	.05
❑ 339 Johnny McWilliams RC	.20	.09
❑ 340 Alex Van Dyke RC	.20	.09
❑ 341 Ray Mickens RC	.10	.05
❑ 342 Marvin Harrison RC	2.00	.90
❑ 343 Terry Glenn RC	1.00	.45
❑ 344 Tim Biakabutuka RC	.60	.25
❑ 345 Simeon Rice RC	.40	.18
❑ 346 Cedric Jones RC	.10	.05
❑ 347 Eddie George RC	2.50	1.10
❑ 348 Drew Bledsoe Checklist	.40	.18
❑ 349 Emmitt Smith Checklist	.30	.14
❑ 350 Keyshawn Johnson Checklist	.40	.18

1997 Pro Line

	MINT	NRMT
COMPLETE SET (300)	25.00	11.00
❑ 1 Larry Centers	.20	.09
❑ 2 Kent Graham	.10	.05
❑ 3 LeShon Johnson	.10	.05
❑ 4 Leeland McElroy	.10	.05
❑ 5 Rob Moore	.20	.09
❑ 6 Simeon Rice	.20	.09
❑ 7 Frank Sanders	.20	.09
❑ 8 Eric Swann	.10	.05
❑ 9 Aeneas Williams	.10	.05
❑ 10 Jamal Anderson	.60	.25
❑ 11 Cornelius Bennett	.10	.05
❑ 12 Ray Buchanan	.10	.05
❑ 13 Bert Emanuel	.20	.09
❑ 14 Terance Mathis	.20	.09
❑ 15 Eric Metcalf	.20	.09
❑ 16 Jessie Tuggle	.10	.05
❑ 17 Derrick Alexander WR	.20	.09
❑ 18 Earnest Byner	.10	.05
❑ 19 Michael Jackson	.20	.09
❑ 20 Antonio Langham	.10	.05
❑ 21 Ray Lewis	.40	.18
❑ 22 Byron Bam Morris	.10	.05
❑ 23 Jonathan Ogden	.10	.05
❑ 24 Vinny Testaverde	.20	.09
❑ 25 Eric Moulds	.30	.14
❑ 26 Todd Collins	.10	.05
❑ 27 Quinn Early	.10	.05
❑ 28 Phil Hansen	.10	.05
❑ 29 Darick Holmes	.10	.05
❑ 30 Bryce Paup	.10	.05
❑ 31 Andre Reed	.20	.09
❑ 32 Bruce Smith	.20	.09
❑ 33 Chris Spielman	.10	.05
❑ 34 Matt Stevens	.10	.05
❑ 35 Steve Tasker	.10	.05
❑ 36 Thurman Thomas	.30	.14
❑ 37 Mark Carrier WR	.10	.05
❑ 38 Kerry Collins	.20	.09
❑ 39 Tim Biakabutuka	.20	.09
❑ 40 Eric Davis	.10	.05
❑ 41 Kevin Greene	.20	.09
❑ 42 Anthony Johnson	.10	.05
❑ 43 Lamar Lathon	.10	.05
❑ 44 Sam Mills	.10	.05
❑ 45 Wesley Walls	.20	.09
❑ 46 Muhsin Muhammad	.20	.09
❑ 47 Mark Carrier DB	.10	.05
❑ 48 Curtis Conway	.20	.09
❑ 49 Bryan Cox	.10	.05
❑ 50 Bobby Engram	.20	.09
❑ 51 Raymont Harris	.10	.05
❑ 52 Walt Harris	.10	.05
❑ 53 Rick Mirer	.10	.05
❑ 54 Rashaan Salaam	.10	.05
❑ 55 Alonzo Spellman	.10	.05
❑ 56 Ashley Ambrose	.10	.05
❑ 57 Jeff Blake	.20	.09
❑ 58 Ki-Jana Carter	.10	.05
❑ 59 John Copeland	.10	.05
❑ 60 James Francis	.10	.05
❑ 61 Tony McGee	.10	.05
❑ 62 Carl Pickens	.30	.14
❑ 63 Darnay Scott	.20	.09
❑ 64 Steve Tovar	.10	.05
❑ 65 Dan Wilkinson	.10	.05
❑ 66 Troy Aikman	1.00	.45
❑ 67 Eric Bjornson	.10	.05
❑ 68 Michael Irvin	.30	.14
❑ 69 Daryl Johnston	.20	.09
❑ 70 Nate Newton	.10	.05
❑ 71 Deion Sanders	.30	.14
❑ 72 Emmitt Smith	1.50	.70
❑ 73 Kevin Smith	.10	.05
❑ 74 Kevin Williams	.10	.05
❑ 75 Darren Woodson	.10	.05
❑ 76 Mark Tuinei	.10	.05
❑ 77 Steve Atwater	.10	.05
❑ 78 Terrell Davis	1.50	.70
❑ 79 John Elway	2.00	.90
❑ 80 Ed McCaffrey	.20	.09
❑ 81 Anthony Miller	.10	.05
❑ 82 John Mobley	.10	.05
❑ 83 Michael Dean Perry	.10	.05
❑ 84 Shannon Sharpe	.20	.09
❑ 85 Alfred Williams	.10	.05
❑ 86 Reggie Brown LB	.20	.09
❑ 87 Luther Elliss	.10	.05
❑ 88 Scott Mitchell	.20	.09
❑ 89 Herman Moore	.30	.14
❑ 90 Johnnie Morton	.20	.09
❑ 91 Brett Perriman	.10	.05
❑ 92 Robert Porcher	.10	.05
❑ 93 Barry Sanders	2.00	.90
❑ 94 Henry Thomas	.10	.05
❑ 95 Edgar Bennett	.20	.09
❑ 96 Robert Brooks	.20	.09
❑ 97 Gilbert Brown	.10	.05
❑ 98 LeRoy Butler	.10	.05
❑ 99 Mark Chmura	.20	.09
❑ 100 Brett Favre	2.00	.90
❑ 101 Santana Dotson	.10	.05
❑ 102 Antonio Freeman	.50	.23
❑ 103 Dorsey Levens	.30	.14

❑ 104 Wayne Simmons .10 .05
❑ 105 Reggie White .30 .14
❑ 106 Willie Davis .10 .05
❑ 107 Eddie George 1.00 .45
❑ 108 Darryll Lewis .10 .05
❑ 109 Steve McNair .50 .23
❑ 110 Marcus Robertson .10 .05
❑ 111 Chris Sanders .10 .05
❑ 112 Al Smith .10 .05
❑ 113 Tony Bennett .10 .05
❑ 114 Quentin Coryatt .10 .05
❑ 115 Ken Dilger .10 .05
❑ 116 Sean Dawkins .10 .05
❑ 117 Marshall Faulk .30 .14
❑ 118 Jim Harbaugh .20 .09
❑ 119 Marvin Harrison .30 .14
❑ 120 Jeff Herrod .10 .05
❑ 121 Tony Boselli .10 .05
❑ 122 Tony Brackens .10 .05
❑ 123 Mark Brunell 1.00 .45
❑ 124 Kevin Hardy .10 .05
❑ 125 Jeff Lageman .10 .05
❑ 126 Keenan McCardell .20 .09
❑ 127 Natrone Means .30 .14
❑ 128 Eddie Robinson .10 .05
❑ 129 Jimmy Smith .20 .09
❑ 130 James O.Stewart .20 .09
❑ 131 Marcus Allen .30 .14
❑ 132 Dale Carter .10 .05
❑ 133 Mark Collins .10 .05
❑ 134 Lake Dawson .10 .05
❑ 135 Greg Hill .10 .05
❑ 136 Sean LaChapelle .10 .05
❑ 137 Chris Penn .10 .05
❑ 138 Derrick Thomas .20 .09
❑ 139 Tamarick Vanover .20 .09
❑ 140 Elvis Grbac .20 .09
❑ 141 Karim Abdul-Jabbar .30 .14
❑ 142 Fred Barnett .10 .05
❑ 143 Terrell Buckley .10 .05
❑ 144 Daryl Gardener .10 .05
❑ 145 Randal Hill .10 .05
❑ 146 Dan Marino 2.00 .90
❑ 147 O.J. McDuffie .20 .09
❑ 148 Jerris McPhail .10 .05
❑ 149 Zach Thomas .20 .09
❑ 150 Cris Carter .30 .14
❑ 151 Dixon Edwards .10 .05
❑ 152 Leroy Hoard .10 .05
❑ 153 Qadry Ismail .20 .09
❑ 154 Brad Johnson .50 .23
❑ 155 John Randle .20 .09
❑ 156 Jake Reed .20 .09
❑ 157 Robert Smith .20 .09
❑ 158 Orlando Thomas .10 .05
❑ 159 Dewayne Washington .10 .05
❑ 160 Drew Bledsoe 1.00 .45
❑ 161 Tedy Bruschi .10 .05
❑ 162 Willie Clay .10 .05
❑ 163 Ben Coates .20 .09
❑ 164 Terry Glenn .30 .14
❑ 165 Shawn Jefferson .10 .05
❑ 166 Ty Law .10 .05
❑ 167 Curtis Martin .50 .23
❑ 168 Willie McGinest .10 .05
❑ 169 Chris Slade .10 .05
❑ 170 Eric Allen .10 .05
❑ 171 Mario Bates .10 .05
❑ 172 Heath Shuler .10 .05
❑ 173 Michael Haynes .10 .05
❑ 174 Wayne Martin .10 .05
❑ 175 Torrance Small .10 .05
❑ 176 Dave Brown .10 .05
❑ 177 Chris Calloway .10 .05
❑ 178 Rodney Hampton .20 .09
❑ 179 Danny Kanell .20 .09
❑ 180 Thomas Lewis .10 .05
❑ 181 Jason Sehorn .20 .09
❑ 182 Amani Toomer .20 .09
❑ 183 Charles Way .20 .09
❑ 184 Tyrone Wheatley .20 .09
❑ 185 Wayne Chrebet .30 .14
❑ 186 Hugh Douglas .10 .05
❑ 187 Aaron Glenn .10 .05
❑ 188 Jeff Graham .10 .05
❑ 189 Keyshawn Johnson .30 .14
❑ 190 Mo Lewis .10 .05
❑ 191 Adrian Murrell .20 .09
❑ 192 Neil O'Donnell .20 .09
❑ 193 Tim Brown .30 .14
❑ 194 Rickey Dudley .20 .09
❑ 195 Jeff George .20 .09
❑ 196 Napoleon Kaufman .30 .14
❑ 197 Russell Maryland .10 .05
❑ 198 Terry McDaniel .10 .05
❑ 199 Chester McGlockton .10 .05
❑ 200 Desmond Howard .20 .09
❑ 201 Pat Swilling .10 .05
❑ 202 Ty Detmer .20 .09
❑ 203 Jason Dunn .10 .05
❑ 204 Ray Farmer .10 .05
❑ 205 Irving Fryar .20 .09
❑ 206 Chris T. Jones .10 .05
❑ 207 Bobby Taylor .10 .05
❑ 208 William Thomas .10 .05
❑ 209 Hollis Thomas .10 .05
❑ 210 Kevin Turner .10 .05
❑ 211 Ricky Watters .20 .09
❑ 212 Jerome Bettis .30 .14
❑ 213 Andre Hastings .10 .05
❑ 214 Charles Johnson .20 .09
❑ 215 Levon Kirkland .10 .05
❑ 216 Carnell Lake .10 .05
❑ 217 Greg Lloyd .10 .05
❑ 218 Darren Perry .10 .05
❑ 219 Kordell Stewart .40 .18
❑ 220 Rod Woodson .20 .09
❑ 221 Andre Coleman .10 .05
❑ 222 Marco Coleman .10 .05
❑ 223 Leonard Russell .10 .05
❑ 224 Stan Humphries .20 .09
❑ 225 Shawn Lee .10 .05
❑ 226 Tony Martin .20 .09
❑ 227 Chris Mims .10 .05
❑ 228 Junior Seau .20 .09
❑ 229 Chris Doleman .10 .05
❑ 230 William Floyd .20 .09
❑ 231 Merton Hanks .10 .05
❑ 232 Brent Jones .20 .09
❑ 233 Terry Kirby .20 .09
❑ 234 Ken Norton .10 .05
❑ 235 Terrell Owens .30 .14
❑ 236 Jerry Rice 1.00 .45
❑ 237 Bryant Young .10 .05
❑ 238 Steve Young .60 .25
❑ 239 Garrison Hearst .20 .09
❑ 240 Brian Blades .10 .05
❑ 241 Chad Brown .10 .05
❑ 242 John Friesz .10 .05
❑ 243 Joey Galloway .40 .18
❑ 244 Cortez Kennedy .10 .05
❑ 245 Chris Warren .20 .09
❑ 246 Darryl Williams .10 .05
❑ 247 Tony Banks .20 .09
❑ 248 Isaac Bruce .30 .14
❑ 249 Kevin Carter .10 .05
❑ 250 Eddie Kennison .20 .09
❑ 251 Todd Lyght .10 .05
❑ 252 Leslie O'Neal .10 .05
❑ 253 Anthony Parker .10 .05
❑ 254 Roman Phifer .10 .05
❑ 255 Lawrence Phillips .10 .05
❑ 256 Mike Alstott .30 .14
❑ 257 Derrick Brooks .10 .05
❑ 258 Trent Dilfer .30 .14
❑ 259 Jackie Harris .10 .05
❑ 260 Hardy Nickerson .10 .05
❑ 261 Errict Rhett .10 .05
❑ 262 Warren Sapp .20 .09
❑ 263 Terry Allen .30 .14
❑ 264 Jamie Asher .10 .05
❑ 265 Henry Ellard .10 .05
❑ 266 Gus Frerotte .10 .05
❑ 267 Sean Gilbert .10 .05
❑ 268 Darrell Green .20 .09
❑ 269 Ken Harvey .10 .05
❑ 270 Brian Mitchell .10 .05
❑ 271 Michael Westbrook .20 .09
❑ 272 Koy Detmer RC .50 .23
❑ 273 Yatil Green RC .20 .09
❑ 274 Troy Davis RC .30 .14
❑ 275 Darrell Russell RC .10 .05
❑ 276 Warrick Dunn RC 1.25 .55
❑ 277 David LaFleur RC .20 .09
❑ 278 Tony Gonzalez RC 1.25 .55
❑ 279 Jake Plummer RC 2.50 1.10
❑ 280 Antowain Smith RC 1.00 .45
❑ 281 Peter Boulware RC .20 .09
❑ 282 Shawn Springs RC .20 .09
❑ 283 Bryant Westbrook RC .10 .05
❑ 284 Rae Carruth RC .30 .14
❑ 285 Corey Dillon RC 2.50 1.10
❑ 286 Byron Hanspard RC .30 .14
❑ 287 Greg Jones RC .10 .05
❑ 288 Trevor Pryce RC .10 .05
❑ 289 Michael Booker RC .10 .05
❑ 290 Orlando Pace RC .30 .14
❑ 291 James Farrior RC .10 .05
❑ 292 Walter Jones RC .10 .05
❑ 293 Reinard Wilson RC .10 .05
❑ 294 Ike Hilliard RC .75 .35
❑ 295 Kenard Lang RC .10 .05
❑ 296 Reidel Anthony RC .75 .35
❑ 297 Brett Favre .40 .18
Checklist back
❑ 298 Kerry Collins .20 .09
Checklist back
❑ 299 Drew Bledsoe .20 .09
Checklist back
❑ 300 Terrell Davis .30 .14
Checklist back

1997 Pro Line Gems

	MINT	NRMT
COMPLETE SET (100)	20.00	9.00

❑ 1 Brett Favre 2.00 .90
❑ 2 Robert Brooks .20 .09
❑ 3 Reggie White .30 .14
❑ 4 Drew Bledsoe 1.00 .45
❑ 5 Curtis Martin .50 .23
❑ 6 Terry Glenn .30 .14
❑ 7 Kerry Collins .20 .09
❑ 8 Kevin Greene .20 .09
❑ 9 Troy Aikman 1.00 .45
❑ 10 Emmitt Smith 1.50 .70
❑ 11 Deion Sanders .30 .14
❑ 12 John Elway 2.00 .90
❑ 13 Terrell Davis 1.50 .70
❑ 14 Kordell Stewart .40 .18
❑ 15 Jerome Bettis .30 .14
❑ 16 Steve Young .60 .25
❑ 17 Jerry Rice 1.00 .45
❑ 18 Bruce Smith .20 .09
❑ 19 Thurman Thomas .30 .14
❑ 20 Jim Harbaugh .20 .09
❑ 21 Marshall Faulk .30 .14
❑ 22 Marvin Harrison .30 .14
❑ 23 Ricky Watters .20 .09
❑ 24 Seth Joyner .10 .05
❑ 25 Mark Brunell 1.00 .45
❑ 26 Natrone Means .30 .14
❑ 27 Dan Marino 2.00 .90
❑ 28 Zach Thomas .20 .09
❑ 29 Karim Abdul-Jabbar .30 .14
❑ 30 Isaac Bruce .30 .14
❑ 31 Eddie Kennison .20 .09
❑ 32 Tony Banks .20 .09
❑ 33 Tony Martin .20 .09

Card	MINT	NRMT
34 Junior Seau	.20	.09
35 Barry Sanders	2.00	.90
36 Herman Moore	.30	.14
37 Leeland McElroy	.10	.05
38 Jamal Anderson	.30	.14
39 Rick Mirer	.10	.05
40 Rashaan Salaam	.10	.05
41 Vinny Testaverde	.20	.09
42 Elvis Grbac	.20	.09
43 Cris Carter	.30	.14
44 Brad Johnson	.50	.23
45 Keyshawn Johnson	.30	.14
46 Adrian Murrell	.20	.09
47 Joey Galloway	.30	.14
48 Trent Dilfer	.30	.14
49 Gus Frerotte	.10	.05
50 Terry Allen	.30	.14
51 Tim Brown	.30	.14
52 Desmond Howard	.20	.09
53 Jeff George	.20	.09
54 Heath Shuler	.10	.05
55 Steve McNair	.50	.23
56 Eddie George	1.00	.45
57 Jeff Blake	.20	.09
58 Carl Pickens	.30	.14
59 Dave Brown	.10	.05
60 Brett Favre CL	.40	.18
61 Antowain Smith	.30	.14
62 Emmitt Smith PL	.75	.35
63 Terry Glenn PL	.20	.09
64 Herman Moore PL	.20	.09
65 Barry Sanders PL	1.00	.45
66 Derrick Thomas PL	.20	.09
67 Brett Favre PL	1.00	.45
68 Warrick Dunn	.50	.23
69 Emmitt Smith PL	.75	.35
70 Brett Favre CL	.40	.18
71 Orlando Pace RC	.30	.14
72 Darrell Russell RC	.10	.05
73 Shawn Springs RC	.20	.09
74 Warrick Dunn RC	1.25	.55
75 Tiki Barber RC	1.25	.55
76 Tom Knight RC	.10	.05
77 Peter Boulware RC	.20	.09
78 David LaFleur RC	.20	.09
79 Tony Gonzalez RC	1.25	.55
80 Yatil Green RC	.20	.09
81 Ike Hilliard RC	.75	.35
82 James Farrior RC	.10	.05
83 Jim Druckenmiller RC	.30	.14
84 Jon Harris RC	.10	.05
85 Walter Jones RC	.10	.05
86 Reidel Anthony RC	.75	.35
87 Jake Plummer RC	2.50	1.10
88 Reinard Wilson RC	.10	.05
89 Kevin Lockett RC	.20	.09
90 Rae Carruth RC	.30	.14
91 Byron Hanspard RC	.30	.14
92 Renaldo Wynn RC	.10	.05
93 Troy Davis RC	.30	.14
94 Duce Staley RC	6.00	2.70
95 Kenard Lang RC	.10	.05
96 Freddie Jones RC	.20	.09
97 Corey Dillon RC	2.50	1.10
98 Antowain Smith RC	1.00	.45
99 Dwayne Rudd RC	.30	.14
100 Warrick Dunn CL	.30	.14
CR1 Brett Favre Ring (1997 cards produced)	60.00	27.00

1996 Pro Line Intense

	MINT	NRMT
COMPLETE SET (100)	15.00	6.75

Card	MINT	NRMT
1 Kerry Collins	.25	.11
2 Jeff George	.10	.05
3 Mark Brunell	.75	.35
4 Steve McNair	.40	.18
5 Rick Mirer	.10	.05
6 Dave Brown	.05	.02
7 Rashaan Salaam	.05	.02
8 Marshall Faulk	.25	.11
9 Erric Pegram	.05	.02
10 Cris Carter	.25	.11
11 Eric Allen	.05	.02

Card	MINT	NRMT
12 Jim Kelly	.25	.11
13 Jeff Blake	.25	.11
14 Stan Humphries	.10	.05
15 Scott Mitchell	.10	.05
16 Jeff Hostetler	.05	.02
17 Rodney Peete	.05	.02
18 Warren Moon	.10	.05
19 Errict Rhett	.10	.05
20 Terrell Davis	2.00	.90
21 J.J. Stokes	.25	.11
22 Marco Coleman	.05	.02
23 Heath Shuler	.10	.05
24 Duane Clemons RC	.05	.02
25 Amani Toomer RC	.50	.23
26 Leslie O'Neal	.05	.02
27 Tamarick Vanover	.10	.05
28 Steve Bono	.05	.02
29 Jim Everett	.05	.02
30 Erik Kramer	.05	.02
31 Trent Dilfer	.25	.11
32 Jim Harbaugh	.10	.05
33 Vinny Testaverde	.10	.05
34 Rodney Hampton	.10	.05
35 Chris Warren	.10	.05
36 Curtis Martin	.50	.23
37 Eddie Kennison RC	.25	.11
38 Herman Moore	.25	.11
39 Terance Mathis	.05	.02
40 Carl Pickens	.25	.11
41 Isaac Bruce	.25	.11
42 Reggie White	.25	.11
43 Junior Seau	.10	.05
44 Bryce Paup	.05	.02
45 Deion Sanders	.30	.14
46 Thurman Thomas	.25	.11
47 Gus Frerotte	.25	.11
48 Tony Mandarich	.05	.02
49 Michael Irvin	.25	.11
50 Wayne Chrebet	.30	.14
51 Bobby Engram RC	.25	.11
52 Marcus Jones RC	.05	.02
53 Daryl Gardener RC	.05	.02
54 Alex Van Dyke RC	.10	.05
55 Andre Rison	.10	.05
56 Regan Upshaw RC	.05	.02
57 Jason Dunn RC	.10	.05
58 Mark Chmura	.10	.05
59 Ray Lewis RC	1.50	.70
60 Rickey Dudley RC	.25	.11
61 Leeland McElroy RC	.25	.11
62 Derrick Thomas	.10	.05
63 Bobby Hoying RC	.50	.23
64 Robert Brooks	.10	.05
65 Tim Brown	.25	.11
66 Michael Westbrook	.25	.11
67 Jim Miller	.05	.02
68 Aaron Hayden	.05	.02
69 Marcus Allen	.25	.11
70 Troy Aikman	.75	.35
71 Steve Young	.50	.23
72 Neil O'Donnell	.10	.05
73 Drew Bledsoe	.75	.35
74 Emmitt Smith	1.25	.55
75 Ki-Jana Carter	.10	.05
76 Irving Fryar	.10	.05
77 Joey Galloway	.30	.14
78 Russell Maryland	.05	.02
79 Kordell Stewart	.30	.14
80 Barry Sanders	1.50	.70
81 Bryan Cox	.05	.02
82 Keyshawn Johnson RC	1.25	.55
83 Karim Abdul-Jabbar RC	.60	.25
84 Kevin Hardy RC	.25	.11
85 Rodney Thomas	.05	.02
86 John Elway	1.50	.70
87 Dan Marino	1.50	.70
88 Brett Favre	1.50	.70
89 Eric Metcalf	.05	.02
90 Jonathan Ogden RC	.05	.02
91 Eddie George RC	2.00	.90
92 Simeon Rice RC	.25	.11
93 Tim Biakabutuka RC	.30	.14
94 Terry Glenn RC	.75	.35
95 Marvin Harrison RC	1.50	.70
96 Lawrence Phillips RC	.25	.11
97 Natrone Means	.25	.11
98 Jerry Rice	.75	.35
99 Ricky Watters	.10	.05
100 Emmitt Smith Checklist card	.25	.11

1989 Pro Set

	MINT	NRMT
COMPLETE SET (561)	25.00	11.00
COMP.SERIES 1 (440)	6.00	2.70
COMP.SERIES 2 (100)	20.00	9.00
COMP.FINAL FACT.SET (21)	2.00	.90

Card	MINT	NRMT
1 Stacey Bailey	.04	.02
2 Aundray Bruce RC	.04	.02
3 Rick Bryan	.04	.02
4 Bobby Butler	.04	.02
5 Scott Case RC	.04	.02
6 Tony Casillas	.04	.02
7 Floyd Dixon	.04	.02
8 Rick Donnelly	.04	.02
9 Bill Fralic	.04	.02
10 Mike Gann	.04	.02
11 Mike Kenn	.04	.02
12 Chris Miller RC	.25	.11
13 John Rade	.04	.02
14 Gerald Riggs UER (Uniform number is 42 but 43 on back)	.10	.05
15 John Settle RC	.04	.02
16 Marion Campbell CO	.04	.02
17 Cornelius Bennett	.10	.05
18 Derrick Burroughs	.04	.02
19 Shane Conlan	.04	.02
20 Ronnie Harmon	.10	.05
21 Kent Hull RC	.04	.02
22 Jim Kelly	.50	.23
23 Mark Kelso	.04	.02
24 Pete Metzelaars	.04	.02
25 Scott Norwood RC**	.04	.02
26 Andre Reed	.25	.11
27 Fred Smerlas	.04	.02
28 Bruce Smith	.25	.11
29 Leonard Smith	.04	.02
30 Art Still	.04	.02
31 Darryl Talley	.10	.05
32 Thurman Thomas RC	1.00	.45
33 Will Wolford RC	.04	.02
34 Marv Levy CO	.04	.02

❑ 35 Neal Anderson .10 .05
❑ 36 Kevin Butler .04 .02
❑ 37 Jim Covert .04 .02
❑ 38 Richard Dent .10 .05
❑ 39 Dave Duerson .04 .02
❑ 40 Dennis Gentry .04 .02
❑ 41 Dan Hampton .10 .05
❑ 42 Jay Hilgenberg .04 .02
❑ 43 Dennis McKinnon UER .04 .02
(Caught 20 or 21
passes as a rookie)
❑ 44 Jim McMahon .10 .05
❑ 45 Steve McMichael .10 .05
❑ 46 Brad Muster RC .04 .02
❑ 47A William Perry SP 6.00 2.70
❑ 47B Ron Morris RC .04 .02
❑ 48 Ron Rivera .04 .02
❑ 49 Vestee Jackson RC .04 .02
❑ 50 Mike Singletary .10 .05
❑ 51 Mike Tomczak .10 .05
❑ 52 Keith Van Horne RC .04 .02
❑ 53A Mike Ditka CO .25 .11
(No HOF mention
on card front)
❑ 53B Mike Ditka CO .25 .11
(HOF banner on front)
❑ 54 Lewis Billups .04 .02
❑ 55 James Brooks .10 .05
❑ 56 Eddie Brown .04 .02
❑ 57 Jason Buck RC .04 .02
❑ 58 Boomer Esiason .10 .05
❑ 59 David Fulcher .10 .05
❑ 60A Rodney Holman RC .10 .05
(BENGALS on front)
❑ 60B Rodney Holman RC .25 .11
(Bengals on front)
❑ 61 Reggie Williams .04 .02
❑ 62 Joe Kelly RC .04 .02
❑ 63 Tim Krumrie .04 .02
❑ 64 Tim McGee .04 .02
❑ 65 Max Montoya .04 .02
❑ 66 Anthony Munoz .10 .05
❑ 67 Jim Skow .04 .02
❑ 68 Eric Thomas RC .04 .02
❑ 69 Leon White .04 .02
❑ 70 Ickey Woods RC .10 .05
❑ 71 Carl Zander .04 .02
❑ 72 Sam Wyche CO .04 .02
❑ 73 Brian Brennan .04 .02
❑ 74 Earnest Byner .04 .02
❑ 75 Hanford Dixon .04 .02
❑ 76 Mike Pagel .04 .02
❑ 77 Bernie Kosar .10 .05
❑ 78 Reggie Langhorne RC .04 .02
❑ 79 Kevin Mack .04 .02
❑ 80 Clay Matthews .10 .05
❑ 81 Gerald McNeil .04 .02
❑ 82 Frank Minnifield .04 .02
❑ 83 Cody Risien .04 .02
❑ 84 Webster Slaughter .10 .05
❑ 85 Felix Wright .04 .02
❑ 86 Bud Carson CO UER .04 .02
(NFLPA logo on back)
❑ 87 Bill Bates .10 .05
❑ 88 Kevin Brooks .04 .02
❑ 89 Michael Irvin RC 1.25 .55
❑ 90 Jim Jeffcoat .04 .02
❑ 91 Ed Too Tall Jones .10 .05
❑ 92 Eugene Lockhart RC .04 .02
❑ 93 Nate Newton RC .10 .05
❑ 94 Danny Noonan .04 .02
❑ 95 Steve Pelluer .04 .02
❑ 96 Herschel Walker .10 .05
❑ 97 Everson Walls .04 .02
❑ 98 Jimmy Johnson CO RC .10 .05
❑ 99 Keith Bishop .04 .02
❑ 100A John Elway ERR 6.00 2.70
(Drafted 1st Round)
❑ 100B John Elway COR 2.00 .90
(Acquired Trade)
❑ 101 Simon Fletcher RC .04 .02
❑ 102 Mike Harden .04 .02
❑ 103 Mike Horan .04 .02
❑ 104 Mark Jackson .04 .02
❑ 105 Vance Johnson .10 .05
❑ 106 Rulon Jones .04 .02
❑ 107 Clarence Kay .04 .02
❑ 108 Karl Mecklenburg .04 .02
❑ 109 Ricky Nattiel .04 .02
❑ 110 Steve Sewell RC .04 .02
❑ 111 Dennis Smith .10 .05
❑ 112 Gerald Willhite .04 .02
❑ 113 Sammy Winder .04 .02
❑ 114 Dan Reeves CO .04 .02
❑ 115 Jim Arnold .04 .02
❑ 116 Jerry Ball RC .04 .02
❑ 117 Bennie Blades RC .04 .02
❑ 118 Lomas Brown .04 .02
❑ 119 Mike Cofer .04 .02
❑ 120 Garry James .04 .02
❑ 121 James Jones .04 .02
❑ 122 Chuck Long .04 .02
❑ 123 Pete Mandley .04 .02
❑ 124 Eddie Murray .04 .02
❑ 125 Chris Spielman RC .25 .11
❑ 126 Dennis Gibson .04 .02
❑ 127 Wayne Fontes CO .04 .02
❑ 128 John Anderson .04 .02
❑ 129 Brent Fullwood RC .04 .02
❑ 130 Mark Cannon .04 .02
❑ 131 Tim Harris .04 .02
❑ 132 Mark Lee .04 .02
❑ 133 Don Majkowski RC .10 .05
❑ 134 Mark Murphy .04 .02
❑ 135 Brian Noble .04 .02
❑ 136 Ken Ruettgers RC .04 .02
❑ 137 Johnny Holland .04 .02
❑ 138 Randy Wright .04 .02
❑ 139 Lindy Infante CO .04 .02
❑ 140 Steve Brown .04 .02
❑ 141 Ray Childress .04 .02
(Sacking Joe Montana)
❑ 142 Jeff Donaldson .04 .02
❑ 143 Ernest Givins .10 .05
❑ 144 John Grimsley .04 .02
❑ 145 Alonzo Highsmith .04 .02
❑ 146 Drew Hill .04 .02
❑ 147 Robert Lyles .04 .02
❑ 148 Bruce Matthews RC .50 .23
❑ 149 Warren Moon .25 .11
❑ 150 Mike Munchak .04 .02
❑ 151 Allen Pinkett RC .04 .02
❑ 152 Mike Rozier .04 .02
❑ 153 Tony Zendejas .04 .02
❑ 154 Jerry Glanville CO .04 .02
❑ 155 Albert Bentley .04 .02
❑ 156 Dean Biasucci .04 .02
❑ 157 Duane Bickett .04 .02
❑ 158 Bill Brooks .10 .05
❑ 159 Chris Chandler RC 1.00 .45
❑ 160 Pat Beach .04 .02
❑ 161 Ray Donaldson .04 .02
❑ 162 Jon Hand .04 .02
❑ 163 Chris Hinton .04 .02
❑ 164 Rohn Stark .04 .02
❑ 165 Fredd Young .04 .02
❑ 166 Ron Meyer CO .04 .02
❑ 167 Lloyd Burruss .04 .02
❑ 168 Carlos Carson .04 .02
❑ 169 Deron Cherry .10 .05
❑ 170 Irv Eatman .04 .02
❑ 171 Dino Hackett .04 .02
❑ 172 Steve DeBerg .04 .02
❑ 173 Albert Lewis .04 .02
❑ 174 Nick Lowery .04 .02
❑ 175 Bill Maas .04 .02
❑ 176 Christian Okoye .04 .02
❑ 177 Stephone Paige .04 .02
❑ 178 Mark Adickes .04 .02
(Out of alphabetical
sequence for his team)
❑ 179 Kevin Ross RC .10 .05
❑ 180 Neil Smith RC .50 .23
❑ 181 M. Schottenheimer CO .04 .02
❑ 182 Marcus Allen .25 .11
❑ 183 Tim Brown RC 1.50 .70
❑ 184 Willie Gault .10 .05
❑ 185 Bo Jackson .30 .14
❑ 186 Howie Long .10 .05
❑ 187 Vann McElroy .04 .02
❑ 188 Matt Millen .10 .05
❑ 189 Don Mosebar RC .04 .02
❑ 190 Bill Pickel .04 .02
❑ 191 Jerry Robinson UER .04 .02
(Stats show 1 TD, but
text says 2 TD's)
❑ 192 Jay Schroeder .04 .02
❑ 193A Stacey Toran .04 .02
(No mention of death
on card front)
❑ 193B Stacey Toran .50 .23
(1961-1989 banner
on card front)
❑ 194 Mike Shanahan CO .04 .02
❑ 195 Greg Bell .04 .02
❑ 196 Ron Brown .04 .02
❑ 197 Aaron Cox RC .04 .02
❑ 198 Henry Ellard .25 .11
❑ 199 Jim Everett .10 .05
❑ 200 Jerry Gray .04 .02
❑ 201 Kevin Greene .25 .11
❑ 202 Pete Holohan .04 .02
❑ 203 LeRoy Irvin .04 .02
❑ 204 Mike Lansford .04 .02
❑ 205 Tom Newberry RC .04 .02
❑ 206 Mel Owens .04 .02
❑ 207 Jackie Slater .04 .02
❑ 208 Doug Smith .04 .02
❑ 209 Mike Wilcher .04 .02
❑ 210 John Robinson CO .04 .02
❑ 211 John Bosa .04 .02
❑ 212 Mark Brown .04 .02
❑ 213 Mark Clayton .10 .05
❑ 214A Ferrell Edmonds RC .50 .23
(ERR, Misspelled Edmonds
on front and back)
❑ 214B Ferrell Edmonds RC .04 .02
(COR, spelled correctly)
❑ 215 Roy Foster .04 .02
❑ 216 Lorenzo Hampton .04 .02
❑ 217 Jim C. Jensen RC UER .04 .02
(Born Albington,
should be Abington)
❑ 218 William Judson .04 .02
❑ 219 Eric Kumerow RC .04 .02
❑ 220 Dan Marino 2.00 .90
❑ 221 John Offerdahl .04 .02
❑ 222 Fuad Reveiz .04 .02
❑ 223 Reggie Roby .04 .02
❑ 224 Brian Sochia .04 .02
❑ 225 Don Shula CO RC .25 .11
❑ 226 Alfred Anderson .04 .02
❑ 227 Joey Browner .04 .02
❑ 228 Anthony Carter .10 .05
❑ 229 Chris Doleman .10 .05
❑ 230 Hassan Jones RC .04 .02
❑ 231 Steve Jordan .04 .02
❑ 232 Tommy Kramer .04 .02
❑ 233 Carl Lee RC .04 .02
❑ 234 Kirk Lowdermilk RC .04 .02
❑ 235 Randall McDaniel RC .25 .11
❑ 236 Doug Martin .04 .02
❑ 237 Keith Millard .04 .02
❑ 238 Darrin Nelson .04 .02
❑ 239 Jesse Solomon .04 .02
❑ 240 Scott Studwell .04 .02
❑ 241 Wade Wilson .10 .05
❑ 242 Gary Zimmerman .04 .02
❑ 243 Jerry Burns CO .04 .02
❑ 244 Bruce Armstrong RC .04 .02
❑ 245 Raymond Clayborn .04 .02
❑ 246 Reggie Dupard .04 .02
❑ 247 Tony Eason .04 .02
❑ 248 Sean Farrell .04 .02
❑ 249 Doug Flutie .75 .35
❑ 250 Brent Williams RC .04 .02
❑ 251 Roland James .04 .02
❑ 252 Ronnie Lippett .04 .02
❑ 253 Fred Marion .04 .02
❑ 254 Larry McGrew .04 .02
❑ 255 Stanley Morgan .04 .02
❑ 256 Johnny Rembert RC .04 .02
❑ 257 John Stephens RC .04 .02
❑ 258 Andre Tippett .04 .02
❑ 259 Garin Veris .04 .02
❑ 260A Raymond Berry CO .04 .02
(No HOF mention
on card front)

❑ 260B Raymond Berry CO .04 .02
(HOF banner
on card front)
❑ 261 Morten Andersen .04 .02
❑ 262 Hoby Brenner .04 .02
❑ 263 Stan Brock .04 .02
❑ 264 Brad Edelman .04 .02
❑ 265 Jumpy Geathers .04 .02
❑ 266A Bobby Hebert ERR .50 .23
("passers" in 42-0)
❑ 266B Bobby Hebert COR .04 .02
("passes" in 42-0)
❑ 267 Craig Heyward RC .25 .11
❑ 268 Lonzell Hill .04 .02
❑ 269 Dalton Hilliard .04 .02
❑ 270 Rickey Jackson .10 .05
❑ 271 Steve Korte .04 .02
❑ 272 Eric Martin .04 .02
❑ 273 Rueben Mayes .04 .02
❑ 274 Sam Mills .10 .05
❑ 275 Brett Perriman RC .25 .11
❑ 276 Pat Swilling .10 .05
❑ 277 John Tice .04 .02
❑ 278 Jim Mora CO .04 .02
❑ 279 Eric Moore .04 .02
❑ 280 Carl Banks .04 .02
❑ 281 Mark Bavaro .10 .05
❑ 282 Maurice Carthon .04 .02
❑ 283 Mark Collins RC .04 .02
❑ 284 Erik Howard .04 .02
❑ 285 Terry Kinard .04 .02
❑ 286 Sean Landeta .04 .02
❑ 287 Lionel Manuel .04 .02
❑ 288 Leonard Marshall .04 .02
❑ 289 Joe Morris .04 .02
❑ 290 Bart Oates .04 .02
❑ 291 Phil Simms .10 .05
❑ 292 Lawrence Taylor .25 .11
❑ 293 Bill Parcells CO RC .10 .05
❑ 294 Dave Cadigan .04 .02
❑ 295 Kyle Clifton RC .04 .02
❑ 296 Alex Gordon .04 .02
❑ 297 James Hasty RC .04 .02
❑ 298 Johnny Hector .04 .02
❑ 299 Bobby Humphery .04 .02
❑ 300 Pat Leahy .04 .02
❑ 301 Marty Lyons .04 .02
❑ 302 Reggie McElroy RC .04 .02
❑ 303 Erik McMillan RC .04 .02
❑ 304 Freeman McNeil .04 .02
❑ 305 Ken O'Brien .04 .02
❑ 306 Pat Ryan .04 .02
❑ 307 Mickey Shuler .04 .02
❑ 308 Al Toon .10 .05
❑ 309 Jo Jo Townsell .04 .02
❑ 310 Roger Vick .04 .02
❑ 311 Joe Walton CO .04 .02
❑ 312 Jerome Brown .10 .05
❑ 313 Keith Byars .10 .05
❑ 314 Cris Carter RC 2.50 1.10
❑ 315 Randall Cunningham .40 .18
❑ 316 Terry Hoage .04 .02
❑ 317 Wes Hopkins .04 .02
❑ 318 Keith Jackson RC .25 .11
❑ 319 Mike Quick .04 .02
❑ 320 Mike Reichenbach .04 .02
❑ 321 Dave Rimington .04 .02
❑ 322 John Teltschik .04 .02
❑ 323 Anthony Toney .04 .02
❑ 324 Andre Waters .04 .02
❑ 325 Reggie White .25 .11
❑ 326 Luis Zendejas .04 .02
❑ 327 Buddy Ryan CO .04 .02
❑ 328 Robert Awalt .04 .02
❑ 329 Tim McDonald RC .10 .05
❑ 330 Roy Green .10 .05
❑ 331 Neil Lomax .04 .02
❑ 332 Cedric Mack .04 .02
❑ 333 Stump Mitchell .04 .02
❑ 334 Niko Noga RC .04 .02
❑ 335 Jay Novacek RC .25 .11
❑ 336 Freddie Joe Nunn .04 .02
❑ 337 Luis Sharpe .04 .02
❑ 338 Vai Sikahema .04 .02
❑ 339 J.T. Smith .04 .02
❑ 340 Ron Wolfley .04 .02
❑ 341 Gene Stallings CO RC .10 .05
❑ 342 Gary Anderson K .04 .02
❑ 343 Bubby Brister RC .50 .23
❑ 344 Dermontti Dawson RC .10 .05
❑ 345 Thomas Everett RC .04 .02
❑ 346 Delton Hall RC .04 .02
❑ 347 Bryan Hinkle RC .04 .02
❑ 348 Merril Hoge RC .04 .02
❑ 349 Tunch Ilkin RC .04 .02
❑ 350 Aaron Jones RC .04 .02
❑ 351 Louis Lipps .10 .05
❑ 352 David Little .04 .02
❑ 353 Hardy Nickerson RC .25 .11
❑ 354 Rod Woodson RC .50 .23
❑ 355A Chuck Noll RC CO ERR .10 .05
("one of only three")
❑ 355B Chuck Noll RC CO COR .10 .05
("one of only two")
❑ 356 Gary Anderson RB .04 .02
❑ 357 Rod Bernstine RC .04 .02
❑ 358 Gill Byrd .04 .02
❑ 359 Vencie Glenn .04 .02
❑ 360 Dennis McKnight .04 .02
❑ 361 Lionel James .04 .02
❑ 362 Mark Malone .04 .02
❑ 363A Anthony Miller RC ERR .25 .11
(TD total 14.8)
❑ 363B Anthony Miller RC COR .25 .11
(TD total 3)
❑ 364 Ralf Mojsiejenko .04 .02
❑ 365 Leslie O'Neal .10 .05
❑ 366 Jamie Holland RC .04 .02
❑ 367 Lee Williams .04 .02
❑ 368 Dan Henning CO .04 .02
❑ 369 Harris Barton RC .04 .02
❑ 370 Michael Carter .04 .02
❑ 371 Mike Cofer RC .04 .02
(Joe Montana holding)
❑ 372 Roger Craig .25 .11
❑ 373 Riki Ellison RC .04 .02
❑ 374 Jim Fahnhorst .04 .02
❑ 375 John Frank .04 .02
❑ 376 Jeff Fuller .04 .02
❑ 377 Don Griffin .04 .02
❑ 378 Charles Haley .25 .11
❑ 379 Ronnie Lott .10 .05
❑ 380 Tim McKyer .04 .02
❑ 381 Joe Montana 2.00 .90
❑ 382 Tom Rathman .04 .02
❑ 383 Jerry Rice 1.50 .70
❑ 384 John Taylor RC .25 .11
❑ 385 Keena Turner .04 .02
❑ 386 Michael Walter .04 .02
❑ 387 Bubba Paris .04 .02
❑ 388 Steve Young 1.00 .45
❑ 389 G.Seifert CO RC UER .10 .05
(NFLPA logo on back)
❑ 390 Brian Blades RC .25 .11
❑ 391A Brian Bosworth ERR .30 .14
(Seattle on front)
❑ 391B Brian Bosworth COR .10 .05
(Listed by team nick-
name on front)
❑ 392 Jeff Bryant .04 .02
❑ 393 Jacob Green .04 .02
❑ 394 Norm Johnson .04 .02
❑ 395 Dave Krieg .10 .05
❑ 396 Steve Largent .25 .11
❑ 397 Bryan Millard RC .04 .02
❑ 398 Paul Moyer .04 .02
❑ 399 Joe Nash .04 .02
❑ 400 Rufus Porter RC .04 .02
❑ 401 Eugene Robinson RC .04 .02
❑ 402 Bruce Scholtz .04 .02
❑ 403 Kelly Stouffer RC .04 .02
❑ 404A Curt Warner ERR 1.25 .55
("yards 1455")
❑ 404B Curt Warner COR .10 .05
("yards 6074")
❑ 405 John L. Williams .04 .02
❑ 406 Tony Woods RC .04 .02
❑ 407 David Wyman .04 .02
❑ 408 Chuck Knox CO .04 .02
❑ 409 Mark Carrier WR RC .25 .11
❑ 410 Randy Grimes .04 .02
❑ 411 Paul Gruber RC .04 .02
❑ 412 Harry Hamilton .04 .02
❑ 413 Ron Holmes .04 .02
❑ 414 Donald Igwebuike .04 .02
❑ 415 Dan Turk .04 .02
❑ 416 Ricky Reynolds .04 .02
❑ 417 Bruce Hill RC .04 .02
❑ 418 Lars Tate .04 .02
❑ 419 Vinny Testaverde .30 .14
❑ 420 James Wilder .04 .02
❑ 421 Ray Perkins CO .04 .02
❑ 422 Jeff Bostic .04 .02
❑ 423 Kelvin Bryant .04 .02
❑ 424 Gary Clark .25 .11
❑ 425 Monte Coleman .04 .02
❑ 426 Darrell Green .10 .05
❑ 427 Joe Jacoby .04 .02
❑ 428 Jim Lachey .04 .02
❑ 429 Charles Mann .04 .02
❑ 430 Dexter Manley .04 .02
❑ 431 Darryl Grant .04 .02
❑ 432 Mark May RC .04 .02
❑ 433 Art Monk .10 .05
❑ 434 Mark Rypien RC .25 .11
❑ 435 Ricky Sanders .04 .02
❑ 436 Alvin Walton RC .04 .02
❑ 437 Don Warren .04 .02
❑ 438 Jamie Morris .04 .02
❑ 439 Doug Williams .10 .05
❑ 440 Joe Gibbs CO RC .10 .05
❑ 441 Marcus Cotton .04 .02
❑ 442 Joel Williams .04 .02
❑ 443 Joe Devlin .04 .02
❑ 444 Robb Riddick .04 .02
❑ 445 William Perry .10 .05
❑ 446 Thomas Sanders RC .04 .02
❑ 447 Brian Blados .04 .02
❑ 448 Cris Collinsworth .10 .05
❑ 449 Stanford Jennings .04 .02
❑ 450 Barry Krauss UER .04 .02
(Listed as playing for
Indianapolis 1979-88)
❑ 451 Ozzie Newsome .10 .05
❑ 452 Mike Oliphant RC .04 .02
❑ 453 Tony Dorsett .25 .11
❑ 454 Bruce McNorton .04 .02
❑ 455 Eric Dickerson .10 .05
❑ 456 Keith Bostic .04 .02
❑ 457 Sam Clancy RC .04 .02
❑ 458 Jack Del Rio RC .10 .05
❑ 459 Mike Webster .10 .05
❑ 460 Bob Golic .04 .02
❑ 461 Otis Wilson .04 .02
❑ 462 Mike Haynes .10 .05
❑ 463 Greg Townsend .04 .02
❑ 464 Mark Duper .10 .05
❑ 465 E.J. Junior .04 .02
❑ 466 Troy Stradford .04 .02
❑ 467 Mike Merriweather .04 .02
❑ 468 Irving Fryar .25 .11
❑ 469 Vaughan Johnson RC** .04 .02
❑ 470 Pepper Johnson .04 .02
❑ 471 Gary Reasons RC .04 .02
❑ 472 Perry Williams RC .04 .02
❑ 473 Wesley Walker .04 .02
❑ 474 Anthony Bell RC .04 .02
❑ 475 Earl Ferrell .04 .02
❑ 476 Craig Wolfley .04 .02
❑ 477 Billy Ray Smith .04 .02
❑ 478A Jim McMahon .10 .05
(No mention of trade
on card front)
❑ 478B Jim McMahon .10 .05
(Traded banner
on card front)
❑ 478C Jim McMahon 40.00 18.00
(Traded banner
on card front but no
line on back saying
also see card 44)
❑ 479 Eric Wright .04 .02
❑ 480A Earnest Byner .04 .02
(No mention of trade
on card front)
❑ 480B Earnest Byner .30 .14
(Traded banner
on card front)

❑ 480C Earnest Byner 40.00 18.00
(Traded banner on card front but no line on back saying also see card 74)
❑ 481 Russ Grimm .... .04 .02
❑ 482 Wilber Marshall .... .04 .02
❑ 483A Gerald Riggs .... .10 .05
(No mention of trade on card front)
❑ 483B Gerald Riggs .... .30 .14
(Traded banner on card front)
❑ 483C Gerald Riggs 40.00 18.00
(Traded banner on card front but no line on back saying also see card 14)
❑ 484 Brian Davis RC .... .04 .02
❑ 485 Shawn Collins RC .... .04 .02
❑ 486 Deion Sanders RC ...... 2.00 .90
❑ 487 Trace Armstrong RC ...... .04 .02
❑ 488 Donnell Woolford RC .... .10 .05
❑ 489 Eric Metcalf RC .... .25 .11
❑ 490 Troy Aikman RC 6.00 2.70
❑ 491 Steve Walsh RC .... .10 .05
❑ 492 Steve Atwater RC .... .25 .11
❑ 493 B.Humphrey RC UER .... .04 .02
(Jersey 41 on back should be 26)
❑ 494 Barry Sanders RC 10.00 4.50
❑ 495 Tony Mandarich RC ...... .04 .02
❑ 496 David Williams RC .... .04 .02
❑ 497 Andre Rison RC UER .. 1.00 .45
(Jersey number not listed on back)
❑ 498 Derrick Thomas RC...... 1.50 .70
❑ 499 Cleveland Gary RC .... .04 .02
❑ 500 Bill Hawkins RC.............. .04 .02
❑ 501 Louis Oliver RC.............. .10 .05
❑ 502 Sammie Smith RC............ .04 .02
❑ 503 Hart Lee Dykes RC .... .04 .02
❑ 504 Wayne Martin RC .... .04 .02
❑ 505 Brian Williams OL .... .04 .02
❑ 506 Jeff Lageman RC .... .10 .05
❑ 507 Eric Hill RC .... .04 .02
❑ 508 Joe Wolf RC .... .04 .02
❑ 509 Timm Rosenbach RC .... .04 .02
❑ 510 Tom Ricketts .... .04 .02
❑ 511 Tim Worley RC .... .04 .02
❑ 512 Burt Grossman RC .... .04 .02
❑ 513 Keith DeLong RC .... .04 .02
❑ 514 Andy Heck RC................ .04 .02
❑ 515 Broderick Thomas RC.... .25 .11
❑ 516 Don Beebe RC .... .25 .11
❑ 517 James Thornton RC ...... .04 .02
❑ 518 Eric Kattus...................... .04 .02
❑ 519 Bruce Kozerski RC .... .04 .02
❑ 520 Brian Washington RC .... .04 .02
❑ 521 Rodney Peete RC UER.. .25 .11
(Jersey 19 on back, should be 9)
❑ 522 Erik Affholter RC .... .04 .02
❑ 523 Anthony Dilweg RC .... .04 .02
❑ 524 O'Brien Alston .... .04 .02
❑ 525 Mike Elkins .... .04 .02
❑ 526 Jonathan Hayes RC ...... .04 .02
❑ 527 Terry McDaniel RC .... .04 .02
❑ 528 Frank Stams RC .... .04 .02
❑ 529 Darryl Ingram RC .... .04 .02
❑ 530 Henry Thomas................ .04 .02
❑ 531 Eric Coleman DB............ .04 .02
❑ 532 Sheldon White RC.......... .04 .02
❑ 533 Eric Allen RC.................. .25 .11
❑ 534 Robert Drummond.......... .04 .02
❑ 535A Gizmo Williams RC** 10.00 4.50
(Without Scouting Photo on front and "Footbal" misspelled on back)
❑ 535B Gizmo Williams RC** .. .25 .11
(Without Scouting Photo on front but "Canadian Football" on back)
❑ 535C Gizmo Williams RC** .. .04 .02
(With Scouting Photo on card front)
❑ 536 Billy Joe Tolliver RC ...... .04 .02
❑ 537 Daniel Stubbs RC .... .04 .02
❑ 538 Wesley Walls RC .... .40 .18
❑ 539A J.Jefferson RC* ERR .. .30 .14
No Prospect banner on card front
❑ 539B J.Jefferson RC* COR .. .04 .02
Prospect banner on card front
❑ 540 Tracy Rocker.................. .04 .02
❑ 541 Art Shell CO .... .10 .05
❑ 542 Lemuel Stinson RC .... .04 .02
❑ 543 Tyrone Braxton RC UER .04 .02
(Back photo actually Ken Bell)
❑ 544 David Treadwell RC ...... .04 .02
❑ 545 Flipper Anderson RC...... .25 .11
❑ 546 Dave Meggett RC .... .25 .11
❑ 547 Lewis Tillman RC .... .04 .02
❑ 548 Carnell Lake RC .... .25 .11
❑ 549 Marion Butts RC .... .10 .05
❑ 550 Sterling Sharpe RC ...... 1.00 .45
❑ 551 Ezra Johnson .... .04 .02
❑ 552 Clarence Verdin RC** .... .04 .02
❑ 553 M.Fernandez RC**/C .... .04 .02
❑ 554 Ottis Anderson .... .10 .05
❑ 555 Gary Hogeboom .... .04 .02
❑ 556 Paul Palmer TR.............. .04 .02
❑ 557 Jesse Solomon TR .... .04 .02
❑ 558 Chip Banks TR .... .04 .02
❑ 559 Steve Pelluer TR............ .04 .02
❑ 560 Darrin Nelson TR .... .04 .02
❑ 561 Herschel Walker TR ...... .10 .05
❑ CC1 Pete Rozelle SP............ .50 .23
(Commissioner)

1990 Pro Set

	MINT	NRMT
COMPLETE SET (801)	15.00	6.75
COMP.SERIES 1 (377)	6.00	2.70
COMP.SERIES 2 (392)	6.00	2.70
COMP.FINAL SERIES (32)	3.00	1.35
COMP.FINAL FACT. (32)..........	3.00	1.35

❑ 1A Barry Sanders ROY .. 100.00 45.00
(Issued at Hawaii Trade Show in February 1990; no ROY trophy on back)
❑ 1B Barry Sanders UER .... .60 .25
Rookie of the Year (TD total says 14, but adds up to 11)
❑ 2A Joe Montana ERR .... .50 .23
Player of the Year (Jim Kelly's stats in text)
❑ 2B Joe Montana COR .... .50 .23
Player of the Year (Corrected from 3521 yards to 3130)
❑ 3 Lindy Infante UER.............. .04 .02
Coach of the Year (Missing Coach next to Packers)
❑ 4 Warren Moon UER .... .25 .11
Man of the Year (Missing R symbol)
❑ 5 Keith Millard .... .04 .02
Defensive Player of the Year
❑ 6 Derrick Thomas UER .... .25 .11
Defensive Rookie of the Year (No 1989 on front banner of card)
❑ 7 Ottis Anderson .... .10 .05
Comeback Player of the Year
❑ 8 Joe Montana .... .50 .23
Passing Leader
❑ 9 Christian Okoye.................. .04 .02
Rushing Leader
❑ 10 Thurman Thomas .... .25 .11
Total Yardage Leader
❑ 11 Mike Cofer........................ .04 .02
Kick Scoring Leader
❑ 12 Dalton Hilliard UER .... .04 .02
TD Scoring Leader (O.J. Simpson not listed in stats, but is mentioned in text)
❑ 13 Sterling Sharpe .... .25 .11
Receiving Leader
❑ 14 Rich Camarillo.................. .04 .02
Punting Leader
❑ 15A Walter Stanley ERR ...... .50 .23
Punt Return Leader (Jersey on front reads 87, back says 8 or 86)
❑ 15B Walter Stanley COR ...... .04 .02
Punt Return Leader
❑ 16 Rod Woodson .... .25 .11
Kickoff Return Leader
❑ 17 Felix Wright .... .04 .02
Interception Leader
❑ 18A Chris Doleman ERR ...... .50 .23
Sack Leader (Townsent, Jeffcoact)
❑ 18B Chris Doleman COR...... .50 .23
Sack Leader (Townsend, Jeffcoat)
❑ 19A Andre Ware RC .... .10 .05
Heisman Trophy (No drafted stripe on card front)
❑ 19B Andre Ware RC .... .10 .05
Heisman Trophy (Drafted stripe on card front)
❑ 20A Mo Elewonibi RC .... .04 .02
Outland Trophy (No drafted stripe on card front)
❑ 20B Mo Elewonibi RC .... .04 .02
Outland Trophy (Drafted stripe on card front)
❑ 21A Percy Snow.................... .50 .23
Lombardi Award (No drafted stripe on card front)
❑ 21B Percy Snow.................... .04 .02
Lombardi Award (Drafted stripe on card front)
❑ 22A Anthony Thompson RC .04 .02
Maxwell Award (No drafted stripe on card front)
❑ 22B Anthony Thompson RC .04 .02
Maxwell Award (Drafted stripe on card front)
❑ 23 Buck Buchanan................ .04 .02
(Sacking Bart Starr) 1990 HOF Selection
❑ 24 Bob Griese .... .10 .05
1990 HOF Selection
❑ 25A Franco Harris ERR .... .50 .23
1990 HOF Selection (Born 2/7/50)
❑ 25B Franco Harris COR........ .10 .05
1990 HOF Selection

(Born 3/7/50)
❑ 26 Ted Hendricks .04 .02
1990 HOF Selection
❑ 27A Jack Lambert ERR .50 .23
1990 HOF Selection
(Born 7/2/52)
❑ 27B Jack Lambert COR .50 .23
1990 HOF Selection
(Born 7/8/52)
❑ 28 Tom Landry .10 .05
1990 HOF Selection
❑ 29 Bob St.Clair .04 .02
1990 HOF Selection
❑ 30 Aundray Bruce UER .04 .02
(Stats say Falcons)
❑ 31 Tony Casillas UER .04 .02
(Stats say Falcons)
❑ 32 Shawn Collins .04 .02
❑ 33 Marcus Cotton .04 .02
❑ 34 Bill Fralic .04 .02
❑ 35 Chris Miller .10 .05
❑ 36 Deion Sanders UER .50 .23
(Stats say Falcons)
❑ 37 John Settle .04 .02
❑ 38 Jerry Glanville CO .04 .02
❑ 39 Cornelius Bennett .10 .05
❑ 40 Jim Kelly .25 .11
❑ 41 Mark Kelso UER .04 .02
(No fumble rec. in '88;
mentioned in '89)
❑ 42 Scott Norwood .04 .02
❑ 43 Nate Odomes RC .10 .05
❑ 44 Scott Radecic .04 .02
❑ 45 Jim Ritcher RC .04 .02
❑ 46 Leonard Smith .04 .02
❑ 47 Darryl Talley .04 .02
❑ 48 Marv Levy CO .04 .02
❑ 49 Neal Anderson .10 .05
❑ 50 Kevin Butler .04 .02
❑ 51 Jim Covert .04 .02
❑ 52 Richard Dent .10 .05
❑ 53 Jay Hilgenberg .04 .02
❑ 54 Steve McMichael .10 .05
❑ 55 Ron Morris .04 .02
❑ 56 John Roper .04 .02
❑ 57 Mike Singletary .10 .05
❑ 58 Keith Van Horne .04 .02
❑ 59 Mike Ditka CO .25 .11
❑ 60 Lewis Billups .04 .02
❑ 61 Eddie Brown .04 .02
❑ 62 Jason Buck .04 .02
❑ 63A Rickey Dixon RC ERR .50 .23
(Info missing under
bio notes)
❑ 63B Rickey Dixon RC COR .50 .23
❑ 64 Tim McGee .04 .02
❑ 65 Eric Thomas .04 .02
❑ 66 Ickey Woods .04 .02
❑ 67 Carl Zander .04 .02
❑ 68A Sam Wyche CO ERR .50 .23
(Info missing under
bio notes)
❑ 68B Sam Wyche CO COR .50 .23
❑ 69 Paul Farren .04 .02
❑ 70 Thane Gash RC .04 .02
❑ 71 David Grayson .04 .02
❑ 72 Bernie Kosar .10 .05
❑ 73 Reggie Langhorne .04 .02
❑ 74 Eric Metcalf .25 .11
❑ 75A Ozzie Newsome ERR .50 .23
(Born Muscle Shoals)
❑ 75B Ozzie Newsome COR .50 .23
(Born Little Rock)
❑ 75C Cody Risien SP .50 .23
(Withdrawn)
❑ 76 Felix Wright .04 .02
❑ 77 Bud Carson CO .04 .02
❑ 78 Troy Aikman .75 .35
❑ 79 Michael Irvin .25 .11
❑ 80 Jim Jeffcoat .04 .02
❑ 81 Crawford Ker .04 .02
❑ 82 Eugene Lockhart .04 .02
❑ 83 Kelvin Martin RC .04 .02
❑ 84 Ken Norton RC .25 .11
❑ 85 Jimmy Johnson CO .10 .05
❑ 86 Steve Atwater .04 .02
❑ 87 Tyrone Braxton .04 .02
❑ 88 John Elway 1.25 .55
❑ 89 Simon Fletcher .04 .02
❑ 90 Ron Holmes .04 .02
❑ 91 Bobby Humphrey .04 .02
❑ 92 Vance Johnson .04 .02
❑ 93 Ricky Nattiel .04 .02
❑ 94 Dan Reeves CO .04 .02
❑ 95 Jim Arnold .04 .02
❑ 96 Jerry Ball .04 .02
❑ 97 Bennie Blades .04 .02
❑ 98 Lomas Brown .04 .02
❑ 99 Michael Cofer .04 .02
❑ 100 Richard Johnson .04 .02
❑ 101 Eddie Murray .04 .02
❑ 102 Barry Sanders 1.50 .70
❑ 103 Chris Spielman .25 .11
❑ 104 William White RC .04 .02
❑ 105 Eric Williams RC .04 .02
❑ 106 Wayne Fontes CO UER .04 .02
(Says born in MO,
actually born in MA)
❑ 107 Brent Fullwood .04 .02
❑ 108 Ron Hallstrom RC .04 .02
❑ 109 Tim Harris .04 .02
❑ 110A Johnny Holland ERR .50 .23
(No name or position
at top of reverse)
❑ 110B Johnny Holland COR .50 .23
❑ 111A Perry Kemp ERR .50 .23
(Photo on back is
actually Ken Stiles,
wearing gray shirt)
❑ 111B Perry Kemp COR .50 .23
(Wearing green shirt)
❑ 112 Don Majkowski .04 .02
❑ 113 Mark Murphy .04 .02
❑ 114A Sterling Sharpe ERR .25 .11
(Born Glenville, Ga.)
❑ 114B Sterling Sharpe COR .50 .23
(Born Chicago)
❑ 115 Ed West RC .04 .02
❑ 116 Lindy Infante CO .04 .02
❑ 117 Steve Brown .04 .02
❑ 118 Ray Childress .04 .02
❑ 119 Ernest Givins .10 .05
❑ 120 John Grimsley .04 .02
❑ 121 Alonzo Highsmith .04 .02
❑ 122 Drew Hill .04 .02
❑ 123 Bubba McDowell .04 .02
❑ 124 Dean Steinkuhler .04 .02
❑ 125 Lorenzo White .10 .05
❑ 126 Tony Zendejas .04 .02
❑ 127 Jack Pardee CO .04 .02
❑ 128 Albert Bentley .04 .02
❑ 129 Dean Biasucci .04 .02
❑ 130 Duane Bickett .04 .02
❑ 131 Bill Brooks .04 .02
❑ 132 Jon Hand .04 .02
❑ 133 Mike Prior .04 .02
❑ 134A Andre Rison .25 .11
(No mention of trade
on card front)
❑ 134B Andre Rison .25 .11
(Traded banner on card
front; also reissued
with Final Update)
❑ 134C Andre Rison .25 .11
(Traded banner on card
front; message from
Lud Denny on back)
❑ 135 Rohn Stark .04 .02
❑ 136 Donnell Thompson .04 .02
❑ 137 Clarence Verdin .04 .02
❑ 138 Fredd Young .04 .02
❑ 139 Ron Meyer CO .04 .02
❑ 140 John Alt RC .04 .02
❑ 141 Steve DeBerg .04 .02
❑ 142 Irv Eatman .04 .02
❑ 143 Dino Hackett .04 .02
❑ 144 Nick Lowery .04 .02
❑ 145 Bill Maas .04 .02
❑ 146 Stephone Paige .04 .02
❑ 147 Neil Smith .25 .11
❑ 148 Marty Schottenheimer CO .04 .02
❑ 149 Steve Beuerlein .10 .05
❑ 150 Tim Brown .25 .11
❑ 151 Mike Dyal .04 .02
❑ 152A Mervyn Fernandez ERR .75 .35
(Acquired: Free
Agent '87)
❑ 152B Mervyn Fernandez COR .75 .35
(Acquired: Drafted
10th Round, 1983)
❑ 153 Willie Gault .10 .05
❑ 154 Bob Golic .04 .02
❑ 155 Bo Jackson .30 .14
❑ 156 Don Mosebar .04 .02
❑ 157 Steve Smith .04 .02
❑ 158 Greg Townsend .04 .02
❑ 159 Bruce Wilkerson RC .04 .02
❑ 160 Steve Wisniewski .10 .05
(Blocking for Bo Jackson)
❑ 161A Art Shell CO ERR .50 .23
(Born 11/25/46)
❑ 161B Art Shell CO COR .50 .23
(Born 11/26/46;
large HOF print on front)
❑ 161C Art Shell CO COR .50 .23
(Born 11/26/46;
small HOF print on front)
❑ 162 Flipper Anderson .04 .02
❑ 163 Greg Bell UER .04 .02
(Stats have 5 catches,
should be 9)
❑ 164 Henry Ellard .10 .05
❑ 165 Jim Everett .10 .05
❑ 166 Jerry Gray .04 .02
❑ 167 Kevin Greene .25 .11
❑ 168 Pete Holohan .04 .02
❑ 169 Larry Kelm RC .04 .02
❑ 170 Tom Newberry .04 .02
❑ 171 Vince Newsome RC .04 .02
❑ 172 Irv Pankey .04 .02
❑ 173 Jackie Slater .04 .02
❑ 174 Fred Strickland RC .04 .02
❑ 175 Mike Wilcher UER .04 .02
(Fumble rec. number
different from
1989 Pro Set card)
❑ 176 John Robinson CO UER .04 .02
(Stats say Rams,
should say L.A. Rams)
❑ 177 Mark Clayton .10 .05
❑ 178 Roy Foster .04 .02
❑ 179 Harry Galbreath RC .04 .02
❑ 180 Jim C. Jensen .04 .02
❑ 181 Dan Marino 1.25 .55
❑ 182 Louis Oliver .04 .02
❑ 183 Sammie Smith .04 .02
❑ 184 Brian Sochia .04 .02
❑ 185 Don Shula CO .10 .05
❑ 186 Joey Browner .04 .02
❑ 187 Anthony Carter .10 .05
❑ 188 Chris Doleman .04 .02
❑ 189 Steve Jordan .04 .02
❑ 190 Carl Lee .04 .02
❑ 191 Randall McDaniel .10 .05
❑ 192 Mike Merriweather .04 .02
❑ 193 Keith Millard .04 .02
❑ 194 Al Noga .04 .02
❑ 195 Scott Studwell .04 .02
❑ 196 Henry Thomas .04 .02
❑ 197 Herschel Walker .10 .05
❑ 198 Wade Wilson .10 .05
❑ 199 Gary Zimmerman .04 .02
❑ 200 Jerry Burns CO .04 .02
❑ 201 Vincent Brown RC .04 .02
❑ 202 Hart Lee Dykes .04 .02
❑ 203 Sean Farrell .04 .02
❑ 204A Fred Marion .04 .02
(Belt visible on
John Taylor)
❑ 204B Fred Marion .04 .02
(Belt not visible)
❑ 205 Stanley Morgan UER .04 .02
(Text says he reached
10,000 yards fastest;
3 players did it
in 10 seasons)
❑ 206 Eric Sievers RC .04 .02
❑ 207 John Stephens .04 .02

❑ 208 Andre Tippett	.04	.02
❑ 209 Rod Rust CO	.04	.02
❑ 210A Morten Andersen ERR (Card number and name on back in white)	.50	.23
❑ 210B Morten Andersen COR (Card number and name on back in black)	.50	.23
❑ 211 Brad Edelman	.04	.02
❑ 212 John Fourcade	.04	.02
❑ 213 Dalton Hilliard	.04	.02
❑ 214 Rickey Jackson (Forcing Jim Kelly fumble)	.10	.05
❑ 215 Vaughan Johnson	.04	.02
❑ 216A Eric Martin ERR (Card number and name on back in white)	.50	.23
❑ 216B Eric Martin COR (Card number and name on back in black)	.50	.23
❑ 217 Sam Mills	.10	.05
❑ 218 Pat Swilling UER (Total fumble recoveries listed as 4, should be 5)	.10	.05
❑ 219 Frank Warren RC	.04	.02
❑ 220 Jim Wilks	.04	.02
❑ 221A Jim Mora CO ERR (Card number and name on back in white)	.50	.23
❑ 221B Jim Mora CO COR (Card number and name on back in black)	.50	.23
❑ 222 Raul Allegre	.04	.02
❑ 223 Carl Banks	.04	.02
❑ 224 John Elliott	.04	.02
❑ 225 Erik Howard	.04	.02
❑ 226 Pepper Johnson	.04	.02
❑ 227 Leonard Marshall UER (In Super Bowl XXI, George Martin had the safety)	.04	.02
❑ 228 Dave Meggett	.10	.05
❑ 229 Bart Oates	.04	.02
❑ 230 Phil Simms	.10	.05
❑ 231 Lawrence Taylor	.25	.11
❑ 232 Bill Parcells CO	.10	.05
❑ 233 Troy Benson	.04	.02
❑ 234 Kyle Clifton UER (Born: Onley, should be Olney)	.04	.02
❑ 235 Johnny Hector	.04	.02
❑ 236 Jeff Lageman	.04	.02
❑ 237 Pat Leahy	.04	.02
❑ 238 Freeman McNeil	.04	.02
❑ 239 Ken O'Brien	.04	.02
❑ 240 Al Toon	.10	.05
❑ 241 Jo Jo Townsell	.04	.02
❑ 242 Bruce Coslet CO	.04	.02
❑ 243 Eric Allen	.04	.02
❑ 244 Jerome Brown	.04	.02
❑ 245 Keith Byars	.04	.02
❑ 246 Cris Carter	.50	.23
❑ 247 Randall Cunningham	.25	.11
❑ 248 Keith Jackson	.10	.05
❑ 249 Mike Quick (Darrell Green also in photo)	.04	.02
❑ 250 Clyde Simmons	.04	.02
❑ 251 Andre Waters	.04	.02
❑ 252 Reggie White	.25	.11
❑ 253 Buddy Ryan CO	.04	.02
❑ 254 Rich Camarillo	.04	.02
❑ 255 Earl Ferrell (No mention of retirement on card front)	.04	.02
❑ 256 Roy Green	.10	.05
❑ 257 Ken Harvey RC	.25	.11
❑ 258 Ernie Jones RC	.04	.02
❑ 259 Tim McDonald	.04	.02
❑ 260 Timm Rosenbach UER (Born '67, should be '66)	.04	.02
❑ 261 Luis Sharpe	.04	.02
❑ 262 Vai Sikahema	.04	.02
❑ 263 J.T. Smith	.04	.02
❑ 264 Ron Wolfley UER (Born Blaisdel, should be Blasdel)	.04	.02
❑ 265 Joe Bugel CO	.04	.02
❑ 266 Gary Anderson K	.04	.02
❑ 267 Bubby Brister	.04	.02
❑ 268 Merril Hoge	.04	.02
❑ 269 Carnell Lake	.04	.02
❑ 270 Louis Lipps	.10	.05
❑ 271 David Little	.04	.02
❑ 272 Greg Lloyd	.25	.11
❑ 273 Keith Willis	.04	.02
❑ 274 Tim Worley	.04	.02
❑ 275 Chuck Noll CO	.10	.05
❑ 276 Marion Butts	.10	.05
❑ 277 Gill Byrd	.04	.02
❑ 278 Vencie Glenn UER (Sack total should be 2, not 2.5)	.04	.02
❑ 279 Burt Grossman	.04	.02
❑ 280 Gary Plummer	.04	.02
❑ 281 Billy Ray Smith	.04	.02
❑ 282 Billy Joe Tolliver	.04	.02
❑ 283 Dan Henning CO	.04	.02
❑ 284 Harris Barton	.04	.02
❑ 285 Michael Carter	.04	.02
❑ 286 Mike Cofer	.04	.02
❑ 287 Roger Craig	.10	.05
❑ 288 Don Griffin	.04	.02
❑ 289A Charles Haley ERR (Fumble recoveries 1 in '86 and 4 total)	30.00	13.50
❑ 289B Charles Haley COR (Fumble recoveries 2 in '86 and 5 total)	.75	.35
❑ 290 Pierce Holt RC	.04	.02
❑ 291 Ronnie Lott	.10	.05
❑ 292 Guy McIntyre	.04	.02
❑ 293 Joe Montana	1.25	.55
❑ 294 Tom Rathman	.04	.02
❑ 295 Jerry Rice	.75	.35
❑ 296 Jesse Sapolu RC	.04	.02
❑ 297 John Taylor	.10	.05
❑ 298 Michael Walter	.04	.02
❑ 299 George Seifert CO	.10	.05
❑ 300 Jeff Bryant	.04	.02
❑ 301 Jacob Green	.04	.02
❑ 302 Norm Johnson UER (Card shop not in Garden Grove, should say Fullerton)	.04	.02
❑ 303 Bryan Millard	.04	.02
❑ 304 Joe Nash	.04	.02
❑ 305 Eugene Robinson	.04	.02
❑ 306 John L. Williams	.04	.02
❑ 307 David Wyman (NFL EXP is in caps, inconsistent with rest of the set)	.04	.02
❑ 308 Chuck Knox CO	.04	.02
❑ 309 Mark Carrier WR	.25	.11
❑ 310 Paul Gruber	.04	.02
❑ 311 Harry Hamilton	.04	.02
❑ 312 Bruce Hill	.04	.02
❑ 313 Donald Igwebuike	.04	.02
❑ 314 Kevin Murphy	.04	.02
❑ 315 Ervin Randle	.04	.02
❑ 316 Mark Robinson	.04	.02
❑ 317 Lars Tate	.04	.02
❑ 318 Vinny Testaverde	.10	.05
❑ 319A Ray Perkins CO ERR (No name or title at top of reverse)	.75	.35
❑ 319B Ray Perkins CO COR	.04	.02
❑ 320 Earnest Byner	.04	.02
❑ 321 Gary Clark	.25	.11
❑ 322 Darryl Grant	.04	.02
❑ 323 Darrell Green	.10	.05
❑ 324 Jim Lachey	.04	.02
❑ 325 Charles Mann	.04	.02
❑ 326 Wilber Marshall	.04	.02
❑ 327 Ralf Mojsiejenko	.04	.02
❑ 328 Art Monk	.10	.05
❑ 329 Gerald Riggs	.10	.05
❑ 330 Mark Rypien	.10	.05
❑ 331 Ricky Sanders	.04	.02
❑ 332 Alvin Walton	.04	.02
❑ 333 Joe Gibbs CO	.10	.05
❑ 334 Aloha Stadium (Site of Pro Bowl)	.04	.02
❑ 335 Brian Blades PB	.04	.02
❑ 336 James Brooks PB	.04	.02
❑ 337 Shane Conlan PB	.04	.02
❑ 338 Eric Dickerson PB SP (Card withdrawn)	3.00	1.35
❑ 339 Ray Donaldson PB	.04	.02
❑ 340 Ferrell Edmunds PB	.04	.02
❑ 341 Boomer Esiason PB	.04	.02
❑ 342 David Fulcher PB	.04	.02
❑ 343A Chris Hinton PB (No mention of trade on card front)	.50	.23
❑ 343B Chris Hinton PB (Traded banner on card front)	.04	.02
❑ 344 Rodney Holman PB	.04	.02
❑ 345 Kent Hull PB	.04	.02
❑ 346 Tunch Ilkin PB	.04	.02
❑ 347 Mike Johnson PB	.04	.02
❑ 348 Greg Kragen PB	.04	.02
❑ 349 Dave Krieg PB	.10	.05
❑ 350 Albert Lewis PB	.04	.02
❑ 351 Howie Long PB	.10	.05
❑ 352 Bruce Matthews PB	.04	.02
❑ 353 Clay Matthews PB	.04	.02
❑ 354 Erik McMillan PB	.04	.02
❑ 355 Karl Mecklenburg PB	.04	.02
❑ 356 Anthony Miller PB	.04	.02
❑ 357 Frank Minnifield PB	.04	.02
❑ 358 Max Montoya PB	.04	.02
❑ 359 Warren Moon PB	.25	.11
❑ 360 Mike Munchak PB	.04	.02
❑ 361 Anthony Munoz PB	.04	.02
❑ 362 John Offerdahl PB	.04	.02
❑ 363 Christian Okoye PB	.04	.02
❑ 364 Leslie O'Neal PB	.04	.02
❑ 365 Rufus Porter PB UER (TM logo missing)	.04	.02
❑ 366 Andre Reed PB	.10	.05
❑ 367 Johnny Rembert PB	.04	.02
❑ 368 Reggie Roby PB	.04	.02
❑ 369 Kevin Ross PB	.04	.02
❑ 370 Webster Slaughter PB	.04	.02
❑ 371 Bruce Smith PB	.10	.05
❑ 372 Dennis Smith PB	.04	.02
❑ 373 Derrick Thomas PB	.10	.05
❑ 374 Thurman Thomas PB	.25	.11
❑ 375 David Treadwell PB	.04	.02
❑ 376 Lee Williams PB	.04	.02
❑ 377 Rod Woodson PB	.10	.05
❑ 378 Bud Carson CO PB	.04	.02
❑ 379 Eric Allen PB	.04	.02
❑ 380 Neal Anderson PB	.10	.05
❑ 381 Jerry Ball PB	.04	.02
❑ 382 Joey Browner PB	.04	.02
❑ 383 Rich Camarillo PB	.04	.02
❑ 384 Mark Carrier WR PB	.04	.02
❑ 385 Roger Craig PB	.10	.05
❑ 386A R.Cunningham PB (Small print on front)	.50	.23
❑ 386B R.Cunningham PB (Large print on front)	.50	.23
❑ 387 Chris Doleman PB	.04	.02
❑ 388 Henry Ellard PB	.04	.02
❑ 389 Bill Fralic PB	.04	.02
❑ 390 Brent Fullwood PB	.04	.02
❑ 391 Jerry Gray PB	.04	.02
❑ 392 Kevin Greene PB	.10	.05
❑ 393 Tim Harris PB	.04	.02
❑ 394 Jay Hilgenberg PB	.04	.02
❑ 395 Dalton Hilliard PB	.04	.02
❑ 396 Keith Jackson PB	.10	.05
❑ 397 Vaughan Johnson PB	.04	.02
❑ 398 Steve Jordan PB	.04	.02
❑ 399 Carl Lee PB	.04	.02
❑ 400 Ronnie Lott PB	.10	.05
❑ 401 Don Majkowski PB	.04	.02
❑ 402 Charles Mann PB	.04	.02
❑ 403 Randall McDaniel PB	.04	.02
❑ 404 Tim McDonald PB	.04	.02
❑ 405 Guy McIntyre PB	.04	.02
❑ 406 Dave Meggett PB	.04	.02
❑ 407 Keith Millard PB	.04	.02
❑ 408 Joe Montana PB	.50	.23

(Not pictured in Pro Bowl uniform)
❑ 409 Eddie Murray PB .04 .02
❑ 410 Tom Newberry PB .04 .02
❑ 411 Jerry Rice PB .50 .23
❑ 412 Mark Rypien PB .04 .02
❑ 413 Barry Sanders PB .60 .25
❑ 414 Luis Sharpe PB .04 .02
❑ 415 Sterling Sharpe PB .04 .02
❑ 416 Mike Singletary PB .10 .05
❑ 417 Jackie Slater PB .04 .02
❑ 418 Doug Smith PB .04 .02
❑ 419 Chris Spielman PB .04 .02
❑ 420 Pat Swilling PB .04 .02
❑ 421 John Taylor PB .04 .02
❑ 422 Lawrence Taylor PB .10 .05
❑ 423 Reggie White PB .10 .05
❑ 424 Ron Wolfley PB .04 .02
❑ 425 Gary Zimmerman PB .04 .02
❑ 426 John Robinson CO PB .04 .02
❑ 427 Scott Case UER .04 .02
(Front CB, back S)
❑ 428 Mike Kenn .04 .02
❑ 429 Mike Gann .04 .02
❑ 430 Tim Green RC .04 .02
❑ 431 Michael Haynes RC .25 .11
❑ 432 Jessie Tuggle RC UER .04 .02
(Front Jesse, back Jessie)
❑ 433 John Rade .04 .02
❑ 434 Andre Rison .25 .11
❑ 435 Don Beebe .10 .05
❑ 436 Ray Bentley .04 .02
❑ 437 Shane Conlan .04 .02
❑ 438 Kent Hull .04 .02
❑ 439 Pete Metzelaars .04 .02
❑ 440 Andre Reed UER .25 .11
(Vance Johnson also had more catches in '85)
❑ 441 Frank Reich .25 .11
❑ 442 Leon Seals RC .04 .02
❑ 443 Bruce Smith .25 .11
❑ 444 Thurman Thomas .25 .11
❑ 445 Will Wolford .04 .02
❑ 446 Trace Armstrong .04 .02
❑ 447 Mark Bortz RC .04 .02
❑ 448 Tom Thayer RC .04 .02
❑ 449A Dan Hampton ERR .50 .23
(Card back says DE)
❑ 449B Dan Hampton COR 30.00 13.50
(Card back says DT)
❑ 450 Shaun Gayle RC .04 .02
❑ 451 Dennis Gentry .04 .02
❑ 452 Jim Harbaugh .25 .11
❑ 453 Vestee Jackson .04 .02
❑ 454 Brad Muster .04 .02
❑ 455 William Perry .10 .05
❑ 456 Ron Rivera .04 .02
❑ 457 James Thornton .04 .02
❑ 458 Mike Tomczak .10 .05
❑ 459 Donnell Woolford .04 .02
❑ 460 Eric Ball .04 .02
❑ 461 James Brooks .10 .05
❑ 462 David Fulcher .04 .02
❑ 463 Boomer Esiason .10 .05
❑ 464 Rodney Holman .04 .02
❑ 465 Bruce Kozerski .04 .02
❑ 466 Tim Krumrie .04 .02
❑ 467 Anthony Munoz .10 .05
(Type on front smaller compared to other cards)
❑ 468 Brian Blados .04 .02
❑ 469 Mike Baab .04 .02
❑ 470 Brian Brennan .04 .02
❑ 471 Raymond Clayborn .04 .02
❑ 472 Mike Johnson .04 .02
❑ 473 Kevin Mack .04 .02
❑ 474 Clay Matthews .10 .05
❑ 475 Frank Minnifield .04 .02
❑ 476 Gregg Rakoczy RC .04 .02
❑ 477 Webster Slaughter .10 .05
❑ 478 James Dixon .04 .02
❑ 479 Robert Awalt UER .04 .02
(Front 89, back 46)
❑ 480 Dennis McKinnon UER .04 .02
(Front 81, back 85)
❑ 481 Danny Noonan .04 .02
❑ 482 Jesse Solomon .04 .02
❑ 483 Daniel Stubbs UER .04 .02
(Front 66, back 96)
❑ 484 Steve Walsh .10 .05
❑ 485 Michael Brooks RC .04 .02
❑ 486 Mark Jackson .04 .02
❑ 487 Greg Kragen .04 .02
❑ 488 Ken Lanier RC .04 .02
❑ 489 Karl Mecklenburg .04 .02
❑ 490 Steve Sewell .04 .02
❑ 491 Dennis Smith .04 .02
❑ 492 David Treadwell .04 .02
❑ 493 Michael Young RC .04 .02
❑ 494 Robert Clark RC .04 .02
❑ 495 Dennis Gibson .04 .02
❑ 496A Kevin Glover RC ERR .50 .23
(Card back says C/G)
❑ 496B Kevin Glover RC COR .04 .02
(Card back says C)
❑ 497 Mel Gray .10 .05
❑ 498 Rodney Peete .10 .05
❑ 499 Dave Brown DB .04 .02
❑ 500 Jerry Holmes .04 .02
❑ 501 Chris Jacke .04 .02
❑ 502 Alan Veingrad .04 .02
❑ 503 Mark Lee .04 .02
❑ 504 Tony Mandarich .04 .02
❑ 505 Brian Noble .04 .02
❑ 506 Jeff Query .04 .02
❑ 507 Ken Ruettgers .04 .02
❑ 508 Patrick Allen .04 .02
❑ 509 Curtis Duncan .04 .02
❑ 510 William Fuller .10 .05
❑ 511 Haywood Jeffires RC .25 .11
❑ 512 Sean Jones .10 .05
❑ 513 Terry Kinard .04 .02
❑ 514 Bruce Matthews .10 .05
❑ 515 Gerald McNeil .04 .02
❑ 516 Greg Montgomery RC .04 .02
❑ 517 Warren Moon .25 .11
❑ 518 Mike Munchak .04 .02
❑ 519 Allen Pinkett .04 .02
❑ 520 Pat Beach .04 .02
❑ 521 Eugene Daniel .04 .02
❑ 522 Kevin Call .04 .02
❑ 523 Ray Donaldson .04 .02
❑ 524 Jeff Herrod RC .04 .02
❑ 525 Keith Taylor .04 .02
❑ 526 Jack Trudeau .04 .02
❑ 527 Deron Cherry .04 .02
❑ 528 Jeff Donaldson .04 .02
❑ 529 Albert Lewis .04 .02
❑ 530 Pete Mandley .04 .02
❑ 531 Chris Martin RC .04 .02
❑ 532 Christian Okoye .04 .02
❑ 533 Steve Pelluer .04 .02
❑ 534 Kevin Ross .04 .02
❑ 535 Dan Saleaumua .04 .02
❑ 536 Derrick Thomas .25 .11
❑ 537 Mike Webster .10 .05
❑ 538 Marcus Allen .25 .11
❑ 539 Greg Bell .04 .02
❑ 540 Thomas Benson .04 .02
❑ 541 Ron Brown .04 .02
❑ 542 Scott Davis .04 .02
❑ 543 Riki Ellison .04 .02
❑ 544 Jamie Holland .04 .02
❑ 545 Howie Long .10 .05
❑ 546 Terry McDaniel .04 .02
❑ 547 Max Montoya .04 .02
❑ 548 Jay Schroeder .04 .02
❑ 549 Lionel Washington .04 .02
❑ 550 Robert Delpino .04 .02
❑ 551 Bobby Humphery .04 .02
❑ 552 Mike Lansford .04 .02
❑ 553 Michael Stewart RC .04 .02
❑ 554 Doug Smith .04 .02
❑ 555 Curt Warner .04 .02
❑ 556 Alvin Wright RC .04 .02
❑ 557 Jeff Cross .04 .02
❑ 558 Jeff Dellenbach RC .04 .02
❑ 559 Mark Duper .10 .05
❑ 560 Ferrell Edmunds .04 .02
❑ 561 Tim McKyer .04 .02
❑ 562 John Offerdahl .04 .02
❑ 563 Reggie Roby .04 .02
❑ 564 Pete Stoyanovich .04 .02
❑ 565 Alfred Anderson .04 .02
❑ 566 Ray Berry .04 .02
❑ 567 Rick Fenney .04 .02
❑ 568 Rich Gannon RC 2.00 .90
❑ 569 Tim Irwin .04 .02
❑ 570 Hassan Jones .04 .02
❑ 571 Cris Carter .50 .23
❑ 572 Kirk Lowdermilk .04 .02
❑ 573 Reggie Rutland RC .04 .02
❑ 574 Ken Stills .04 .02
❑ 575 Bruce Armstrong .04 .02
❑ 576 Irving Fryar .10 .05
❑ 577 Roland James .04 .02
❑ 578 Robert Perryman .04 .02
❑ 579 Cedric Jones .04 .02
❑ 580 Steve Grogan .10 .05
❑ 581 Johnny Rembert .04 .02
❑ 582 Ed Reynolds .04 .02
❑ 583 Brent Williams .04 .02
❑ 584 Marc Wilson .04 .02
❑ 585 Hoby Brenner .04 .02
❑ 586 Stan Brock .04 .02
❑ 587 Jim Dombrowski RC .04 .02
❑ 588 Joel Hilgenberg RC .04 .02
❑ 589 Robert Massey .04 .02
❑ 590 Floyd Turner .04 .02
❑ 591 Ottis Anderson .10 .05
❑ 592 Mark Bavaro .04 .02
❑ 593 Maurice Carthon .04 .02
❑ 594 Eric Dorsey RC .04 .02
❑ 595 Myron Guyton .04 .02
❑ 596 Jeff Hostetler RC .25 .11
❑ 597 Sean Landeta .04 .02
❑ 598 Lionel Manuel .04 .02
❑ 599 Odessa Turner RC .04 .02
❑ 600 Perry Williams .04 .02
❑ 601 James Hasty .04 .02
❑ 602 Erik McMillan .04 .02
❑ 603 Alex Gordon UER .04 .02
(Reversed photo on back)
❑ 604 Ron Stallworth .04 .02
❑ 605 Byron Evans RC .04 .02
❑ 606 Ron Heller RC .04 .02
❑ 607 Wes Hopkins .04 .02
(Hitting Ottis Anderson)
❑ 608 Mickey Shuler UER .04 .02
(Reversed photo on back)
❑ 609 Seth Joyner .10 .05
❑ 610 Jim McMahon .10 .05
❑ 611 Mike Pitts .04 .02
❑ 612 Izel Jenkins RC .04 .02
❑ 613 Anthony Bell .04 .02
❑ 614 David Galloway .04 .02
❑ 615 Eric Hill .04 .02
❑ 616 Cedric Mack .04 .02
❑ 617 Freddie Joe Nunn .04 .02
❑ 618 Tootie Robbins .04 .02
❑ 619 Tom Tupa RC .04 .02
❑ 620 Joe Wolf .04 .02
❑ 621 Dermontti Dawson .10 .05
❑ 622 Thomas Everett .04 .02
❑ 623 Tunch Ilkin .04 .02
❑ 624 Hardy Nickerson .10 .05
❑ 625 Gerald Williams RC .04 .02
❑ 626 Rod Woodson .25 .11
❑ 627A Rod Bernstine TE ERR .50 .23
❑ 627B Rod Bernstine RB COR .04 .02
❑ 628 Courtney Hall .04 .02
❑ 629 Ronnie Harmon .10 .05
❑ 630A Anthony Miller ERR .25 .11
(Back says WR)
❑ 630B Anthony Miller COR .10 .05
(Back says WR-KR)
❑ 631 Joe Phillips .04 .02
❑ 632A Leslie O'Neal ERR .50 .23
(Listed as LB-DE on front and back)
❑ 632B Leslie O'Neal ERR .15 .07
(Listed as LB-DE on front and LB on back)
❑ 632C Leslie O'Neal COR .10 .05
(Listed as LB on front and back)
❑ 633A David Richards RC ERR .15 .07

(Back says G-T)
☐ 633B D.Richards RC COR.... .15 .07
(Back says G)
☐ 634 Mark Vlasic .04 .02
☐ 635 Lee Williams .04 .02
☐ 636 Chet Brooks .04 .02
☐ 637 Keena Turner .04 .02
☐ 638 Kevin Fagan RC .04 .02
☐ 639 Brent Jones RC .25 .11
☐ 640 Matt Millen .10 .05
☐ 641 Bubba Paris .04 .02
☐ 642 Bill Romanowski RC .30 .14
☐ 643 Fred Smerlas UER .04 .02
(Front 67, back 76)
☐ 644 Dave Waymer .04 .02
☐ 645 Steve Young .50 .23
☐ 646 Brian Blades .10 .05
☐ 647 Andy Heck .04 .02
☐ 648 Dave Krieg .10 .05
☐ 649 Rufus Porter .04 .02
☐ 650 Kelly Stouffer .04 .02
☐ 651 Tony Woods .04 .02
☐ 652 Gary Anderson RB .04 .02
☐ 653 Reuben Davis .04 .02
☐ 654 Randy Grimes .04 .02
☐ 655 Ron Hall .04 .02
☐ 656 Eugene Marve .04 .02
☐ 657A Curt Jarvis ERR .50 .23
(No "Official NFL Card" on front)
☐ 657B Curt Jarvis COR 30.00 13.50
☐ 658 Ricky Reynolds .04 .02
☐ 659 Broderick Thomas .04 .02
☐ 660 Jeff Bostic .04 .02
☐ 661 Todd Bowles RC .04 .02
☐ 662 Ravin Caldwell .04 .02
☐ 663 Russ Grimm UER .04 .02
(Back photo is actually Jeff Bostic)
☐ 664 Joe Jacoby .04 .02
☐ 665 Mark May .04 .02
(Front G, back G/T)
☐ 666 Walter Stanley .04 .02
☐ 667 Don Warren .04 .02
☐ 668 Stan Humphries RC .25 .11
☐ 669A Jeff George SP 1.00 .45
(Illinois uniform; issued in first series)
☐ 669B Jeff George RC 1.00 .45
(Colts uniform; issued in second series)
☐ 670 Blair Thomas RC .10 .05
(No color stripe along line with AFC symbol and Jets logo)
☐ 671 Cortez Kennedy RC UER .25 .11
(No scouting photo line on back)
☐ 672 Keith McCants RC .04 .02
☐ 673 Junior Seau RC 1.00 .45
☐ 674 Mark Carrier DB RC .25 .11
☐ 675 Andre Ware .10 .05
☐ 676 Chris Singleton RC UER .04 .02
(Parsippany High, should be Parsippany Hills High)
☐ 677 Richmond Webb RC .04 .02
☐ 678 Ray Agnew RC .04 .02
☐ 679 Anthony Smith RC .04 .02
☐ 680 James Francis RC .04 .02
☐ 681 Percy Snow .04 .02
☐ 682 Renaldo Turnbull RC .04 .02
☐ 683 Lamar Lathon RC .10 .05
☐ 684 James Williams RC .04 .02
☐ 685 Emmitt Smith RC 4.00 1.80
☐ 686 Tony Bennett RC .25 .11
☐ 687 Darrell Thompson RC .04 .02
☐ 688 Steve Broussard RC .04 .02
☐ 689 Eric Green RC .10 .05
☐ 690 Ben Smith RC .04 .02
☐ 691 Bern Brostek RC UER .04 .02
(Listed as Center but is playing Guard)
☐ 692 Rodney Hampton RC .40 .18
☐ 693 Dexter Carter RC .04 .02
☐ 694 Rob Moore RC 1.00 .45
☐ 695 Alexander Wright RC .04 .02
☐ 696 Darion Conner RC .10 .05
☐ 697 Reggie Rembert RC UER .04 .02
(Missing Scouting Line credit on the front)
☐ 698A Terry Wooden RC ERR .50 .23
(Number on back is 51)
☐ 698B Terry Wooden RC COR .04 .02
(Number on back is 90)
☐ 699 Reggie Cobb RC .04 .02
☐ 700 Anthony Thompson .04 .02
☐ 701 Fred Washington RC .04 .02
(Final Update version mentions his death; this card does not)
☐ 702 Ron Cox RC .04 .02
☐ 703 Robert Blackmon RC .04 .02
☐ 704 Dan Owens RC .04 .02
☐ 705 Anthony Johnson RC .25 .11
☐ 706 Aaron Wallace RC .04 .02
☐ 707 Harold Green RC .25 .11
☐ 708 Keith Sims RC .04 .02
☐ 709 Tim Grunhard RC .04 .02
☐ 710 Jeff Alm RC .04 .02
☐ 711 Carwell Gardner RC .04 .02
☐ 712 Kenny Davidson RC .04 .02
☐ 713 Vince Buck RC .04 .02
☐ 714 Leroy Hoard RC .40 .18
☐ 715 Andre Collins RC .04 .02
☐ 716 Dennis Brown RC .04 .02
☐ 717 LeRoy Butler RC .25 .11
☐ 718A Pat Terrell 41 ERR RC .50 .23
☐ 718B Pat Terrell 37 COR RC .04 .02
☐ 719 Mike Bellamy RC .04 .02
☐ 720 Mike Fox RC .04 .02
☐ 721 Alton Montgomery RC .04 .02
☐ 722 Eric Davis RC .10 .05
☐ 723A Oliver Barnett RC ERR .50 .23
(Front says DT)
☐ 723B Oliver Barnett RC COR .04 .02
(Front says NT)
☐ 724 Houston Hoover RC .04 .02
☐ 725 Howard Ballard RC .04 .02
☐ 726 Keith McKeller RC .04 .02
☐ 727 Wendell Davis RC .04 .02
(Pro Set Prospect in white, not black)
☐ 728 Peter Tom Willis RC .04 .02
☐ 729 Bernard Clark .04 .02
☐ 730 Doug Widell RC .04 .02
☐ 731 Eric Andolsek .04 .02
☐ 732 Jeff Campbell RC .04 .02
☐ 733 Marc Spindler RC .04 .02
☐ 734 Keith Woodside .04 .02
☐ 735 Willis Peguese RC .04 .02
☐ 736 Frank Stams .04 .02
☐ 737 Jeff Uhlenhake .04 .02
☐ 738 Todd Kalis .04 .02
☐ 739 Tommy Hodson RC UER .04 .02
(Born Matthews, should be Mathews)
☐ 740 Greg McMurtry RC .04 .02
☐ 741 Mike Buck RC .04 .02
☐ 742 Kevin Haverdink UER .04 .02
(Jersey says 70, back says 74)
☐ 743A Johnny Bailey RC .10 .05
(Back says 46)
☐ 743B Johnny Bailey RC .10 .05
(Back says 22)
☐ 744A Eric Moore .15 .07
(No Pro Set Prospect on front of card)
☐ 744B Eric Moore 30.00 13.50
(Pro Set Prospect on front of card)
☐ 745 Tony Stargell RC .04 .02
☐ 746 Fred Barnett RC .25 .11
☐ 747 Walter Reeves .04 .02
☐ 748 Derek Hill .04 .02
☐ 749 Quinn Early .25 .11
☐ 750 Ronald Lewis .04 .02
☐ 751 Ken Clark RC .04 .02
☐ 752 Garry Lewis .04 .02
☐ 753 James Lofton .10 .05
☐ 754 Steve Tasker UER .04 .02
(Back says photo is against Raiders, but front shows a Steeler)
☐ 755 Jim Shofner CO .04 .02
☐ 756 Jimmie Jones RC .04 .02
☐ 757 Jay Novacek .25 .11
☐ 758 Jessie Hester RC .04 .02
☐ 759 Barry Word RC .04 .02
☐ 760 Eddie Anderson RC .04 .02
☐ 761 Cleveland Gary .04 .02
☐ 762 Marcus Dupree RC** .04 .02
☐ 763 David Griggs RC .04 .02
☐ 764 Rueben Mayes .04 .02
☐ 765 Stephen Baker .04 .02
☐ 766 R.Thompson RC UER .04 .02
(Front CB, back ST-CB)
☐ 767 Everson Walls .04 .02
☐ 768 Brad Baxter RC .04 .02
☐ 769 Steve Walsh .10 .05
☐ 770 Heath Sherman RC .04 .02
☐ 771 Johnny Johnson RC .10 .05
☐ 772A Dexter Manley 30.00 13.50
(Back mentions substance abuse violation)
☐ 772B Dexter Manley .04 .02
(Bio on back changed; doesn't mention substance abuse violation)
☐ 773 Ricky Proehl RC .10 .05
☐ 774 Frank Cornish .04 .02
☐ 775 Tommy Kane RC .04 .02
☐ 776 Derrick Fenner RC .04 .02
☐ 777 Steve Christie RC .04 .02
☐ 778 Wayne Haddix RC .04 .02
☐ 779 Richard Williamson UER .04 .02
(Experience is misspelled as esperience)
☐ 780 Brian Mitchell RC .25 .11
☐ 781 American Bowl/London .04 .02
Raiders vs. Saints
☐ 782 American Bowl/Berlin .04 .02
Rams vs. Chiefs
☐ 783 American Bowl/Tokyo .04 .02
Broncos vs. Seahawks
☐ 784 American Bowl/Montreal .04 .02
Steelers vs. Patriots
☐ 785A Berlin Wall .75 .35
Paul Tagliabue
("Peered through the Berlin Wall")
☐ 785B Berlin Wall .75 .35
Paul Tagliabue
("Posed at the Berlin Wall")
☐ 786 Raiders Stay in LA .04 .02
(Al Davis RC)
☐ 787 Falcons Back in Black .04 .02
(Jerry Glanville)
☐ 788 NFL Goes International .04 .02
World League Spring Debut
(Number on back is black, Newsreel cards are otherwise white; only Newsreel card with silver borders)
☐ 789 Overseas Appeal .04 .02
(Cheerleaders)
☐ 790 Photo Contest .04 .02
(Mike Mularkey awash)
☐ 791 Photo Contest .04 .02
(Gary Reasons hitting Bobby Humphrey)
☐ 792 Photo Contest .04 .02
(Maurice Hurst covering Drew Hill)
☐ 793 Photo Contest .04 .02
(Ronnie Lott celebrating)
☐ 794 Photo Contest .50 .23
(Felix Wright grabbing Barry Sanders' jersey)
☐ 795 Photo Contest .04 .02
(George Seifert in Gatorade Shower)
☐ 796 Photo Contest .04 .02
(Doug Smith praying)
☐ 797 Photo Contest .04 .02
(Doug Widell keeping cool)
☐ 798 Photo Contest .04 .02
(Todd Bowles covering

Cris Carter)		
❑ 799 Ronnie Lott	.10	.05
(Stay in School)		
❑ 800D Mark Carrier DB	.10	.05
Defensive ROY		
❑ 800O Emmitt Smith	1.25	.55
Offensive ROY		
❑ 1990 Santa Claus SP	.50	.23
(Second series only; No quote mark after Andre Ware)		
❑ CC2 Paul Tagliabue SP	.40	.18
NFL Commissioner (First series only)		
❑ CC3 Joe Robbie Mem SP	.50	.23
(Second series only)		
❑ SC Super Pro SP	.50	.23
(Second series only)		
❑ SC4 Fred Washington UER	.04	.02
(Memorial to his death; word patches repeated in fourth line of text)		
❑ SP1 Payne Stewart SP	1.00	.45
(First series only)		
❑ NNO Lombardi Trophy SP	80.00	36.00
(Hologram: numbered out of 10,000)		
❑ NNO Super Bowl XXIV Logo	.04	.02

1991 Pro Set

	MINT	NRMT
COMPLETE SET (850)	15.00	6.75
COMP.SERIES 1 (405)	7.00	3.10
COMP.SERIES 2 (407)	7.00	3.10
COMP.FINAL FACT. (38)	2.00	.90
❑ 1D Mark Carrier DB	.10	.05
Defensive ROY		
❑ 1O Emmitt Smith	1.00	.45
Offensive ROY		
❑ 3 Joe Montana	.50	.23
NFL Player of the Year		
❑ 4 Art Shell	.10	.05
NFL Coach of the Year		
❑ 5 Mike Singletary	.10	.05
NFL Man of the Year		
❑ 6 Bruce Smith	.10	.05
NFL Defensive Player of the Year		
❑ 7 Barry Word	.05	.02
NFL Comeback Player of the Year		
❑ 8A Jim Kelly	.25	.11
NFL Passing Leader (NFLPA logo on back)		
❑ 8B Jim Kelly	.25	.11
NFL Passing Leader (No NFLPA logo on back)		
❑ 8C Jim Kelly	6.00	2.70
NFL Passing Leader (No NFLPA logo on back but the registered symbol remains)		
❑ 9 Warren Moon	.10	.05
NFL Passing Yardage and TD Leader		
❑ 10 Barry Sanders	.60	.25
NFL Rushing and TD Leader		
❑ 11 Jerry Rice	.40	.18
NFL Receiving and Receiving Yardage Leader		
❑ 12 Jay Novacek	.10	.05
Tight End Leader		
❑ 13 Thurman Thomas	.10	.05
NFL Total Yardage Leader		
❑ 14 Nick Lowery	.05	.02
NFL Scoring Leader, Kickers		
❑ 15 Mike Horan	.05	.02
NFL Punting Leader		
❑ 16 Clarence Verdin	.05	.02
NFL Punt Return Leader		
❑ 17 Kevin Clark RC	.05	.02
NFL Kickoff Return Leader		
❑ 18 Mark Carrier DB	.10	.05
NFL Interception Leader		
❑ 19A Derrick Thomas ERR	10.00	4.50
NFL Sack Leader (Bills helmet on front)		
❑ 19B Derrick Thomas COR	.10	.05
NFL Sack Leader (Chiefs helmet on front)		
❑ 20 Ottis Anderson ML	.10	.05
10000 Career Rushing Yards		
❑ 21 Roger Craig ML	.10	.05
Most Career Receptions by RB		
❑ 22 Art Monk ML	.10	.05
700 Career Receptions		
❑ 23 Chuck Noll ML	.10	.05
200 Victories		
❑ 24 Randall Cunningham ML	.10	.05
Leads team in rushing, fourth straight year UER (586 rushes, should be 486; average 5.9, should be 7.1)		
❑ 25 Dan Marino ML	.50	.23
7th Straight 3000 yard season		
❑ 26 49ers Road Record ML	.05	.02
18 victories in row, still alive		
❑ 27 Earl Campbell HOF	.05	.02
❑ 28 John Hannah HOF	.05	.02
❑ 29 Stan Jones HOF	.05	.02
❑ 30 Tex Schramm HOF	.05	.02
❑ 31 Jan Stenerud HOF	.05	.02
❑ 32 Russell Maryland RC	.10	.05
Outland Winner		
❑ 33 Chris Zorich RC	.10	.05
Lombardi Winner		
❑ 34 Darryll Lewis RC UER	.10	.05
Thorpe Winner (Name misspelled Darryl on card)		
❑ 35 Alfred Williams RC	.05	.02
Butkus Winner		
❑ 36 Raghib(Rocket) Ismail RC	1.00	.45
Walter Camp POY		
❑ 37 Ty Detmer HH RC	.40	.18
❑ 38 Andre Ware HH	.10	.05
❑ 39 Barry Sanders HH	.60	.25
❑ 40 Tim Brown HH UER	.10	.05
(No Official Photo and Stat Card of the NFL~ on card back)		
❑ 41 Vinny Testaverde HH	.10	.05
❑ 42 Bo Jackson HH	.30	.14
❑ 43 Mike Rozier HH	.05	.02
❑ 44 Herschel Walker HH	.10	.05
❑ 45 Marcus Allen HH	.10	.05
❑ 46A James Lofton SB	.10	.05
(NFLPA logo on back)		
❑ 46B James Lofton SB	.10	.05
(No NFLPA logo on back)		
❑ 47A Bruce Smith SB	.10	.05
(Official NFL Card in black letters)		
❑ 47B Bruce Smith SB	.10	.05
(Official NFL Card in white letters)		
❑ 48 Myron Guyton SB	.05	.02
❑ 49 Stephen Baker SB	.05	.02
❑ 50 Mark Ingram SB UER	.05	.02
(First repeated twice on back title)		
❑ 51 Ottis Anderson SB	.10	.05
❑ 52 Thurman Thomas SB	.25	.11
❑ 53 Matt Bahr SB	.05	.02
❑ 54 Scott Norwood SB	.05	.02
❑ 55 Stephen Baker	.05	.02
❑ 56 Carl Banks	.05	.02
❑ 57 Mark Collins	.05	.02
❑ 58 Steve DeOssie	.05	.02
❑ 59 Eric Dorsey	.05	.02
❑ 60 John Elliott	.05	.02
❑ 61 Myron Guyton	.05	.02
❑ 62 Rodney Hampton	.25	.11
❑ 63 Jeff Hostetler	.10	.05
❑ 64 Erik Howard	.05	.02
❑ 65 Mark Ingram	.10	.05
❑ 66 Greg Jackson RC	.05	.02
❑ 67 Leonard Marshall	.05	.02
❑ 68 David Meggett	.10	.05
❑ 69 Eric Moore	.05	.02
❑ 70 Bart Oates	.05	.02
❑ 71 Gary Reasons	.05	.02
❑ 72 Bill Parcells CO	.10	.05
❑ 73 Howard Ballard	.05	.02
❑ 74A Cornelius Bennett	.25	.11
(NFLPA logo on back)		
❑ 74B Cornelius Bennett	.05	.02
(No NFLPA logo on back)		
❑ 75 Shane Conlan	.05	.02
❑ 76 Kent Hull	.05	.02
❑ 77 Kirby Jackson RC	.05	.02
❑ 78A Jim Kelly	.60	.25
(NFLPA logo on back)		
❑ 78B Jim Kelly	.25	.11
(No NFLPA logo on back)		
❑ 79 Mark Kelso	.05	.02
❑ 80 Nate Odomes	.05	.02
❑ 81 Andre Reed	.10	.05
❑ 82 Jim Ritcher	.05	.02
❑ 83 Bruce Smith	.25	.11
❑ 84 Darryl Talley	.05	.02
❑ 85 Steve Tasker	.10	.05
❑ 86 Thurman Thomas	.25	.11
❑ 87 James Williams	.05	.02
❑ 88 Will Wolford	.05	.02
❑ 89 Jeff Wright RC UER	.05	.02
(Went to Central Missouri State, not Central Missouri)		
❑ 90 Marv Levy CO	.05	.02
❑ 91 Steve Broussard	.05	.02
❑ 92A Darion Conner ERR	10.00	4.50
(Drafted 1st round, '99)		
❑ 92B Darion Conner COR	.25	.11
(Drafted 2nd round, '90)		
❑ 93 Bill Fralic	.05	.02
❑ 94 Tim Green	.05	.02
❑ 95 Michael Haynes	.25	.11
❑ 96 Chris Hinton	.05	.02
❑ 97 Chris Miller UER	.10	.05
(Two commas after city in his birth info)		
❑ 98 Deion Sanders UER	.40	.18
(Career TD's 3, but only 2 in yearly stats)		
❑ 99 Jerry Glanville CO	.05	.02
❑ 100 Kevin Butler	.05	.02
❑ 101 Mark Carrier DB	.10	.05
❑ 102 Jim Covert	.05	.02
❑ 103 Richard Dent	.10	.05
❑ 104 Jim Harbaugh	.25	.11
❑ 105 Brad Muster	.05	.02
❑ 106 Lemuel Stinson	.05	.02
❑ 107 Keith Van Horne	.05	.02
❑ 108 Mike Ditka CO UER	.25	.11
(Winning percent in '87 was .733, not .753)		

❑ 109 Lewis Billups .05 .02
❑ 110 James Brooks .10 .05
❑ 111 Boomer Esiason .10 .05
❑ 112 James Francis .05 .02
❑ 113 David Fulcher .05 .02
❑ 114 Rodney Holman .05 .02
❑ 115 Tim McGee .05 .02
❑ 116 Anthony Munoz .10 .05
❑ 117 Sam Wyche CO .05 .02
❑ 118 Paul Farren .05 .02
❑ 119 Thane Gash .05 .02
❑ 120 Mike Johnson .05 .02
❑ 121A Bernie Kosar .10 .05
(NFLPA logo on back)
❑ 121B Bernie Kosar .10 .05
(No NFLPA logo on back)
❑ 122 Clay Matthews .10 .05
❑ 123 Eric Metcalf .10 .05
❑ 124 Frank Minnifield .05 .02
❑ 125A Webster Slaughter .10 .05
(NFLPA logo on back)
❑ 125B Webster Slaughter .10 .05
(No NFLPA logo on back)
❑ 126 Bill Belichick CO .05 .02
❑ 127 Tommie Agee .05 .02
❑ 128 Troy Aikman .75 .35
❑ 129 Jack Del Rio .05 .02
❑ 130 John Gesek RC .05 .02
❑ 131 Issiac Holt .05 .02
❑ 132 Michael Irvin .25 .11
❑ 133 Ken Norton .25 .11
❑ 134 Daniel Stubbs .05 .02
❑ 135 Jimmy Johnson CO .10 .05
❑ 136 Steve Atwater .05 .02
❑ 137 Michael Brooks .05 .02
❑ 138 John Elway 1.25 .55
❑ 139 Wymon Henderson .05 .02
❑ 140 Bobby Humphrey .05 .02
❑ 141 Mark Jackson .05 .02
❑ 142 Karl Mecklenburg .05 .02
❑ 143 Doug Widell .05 .02
❑ 144 Dan Reeves CO .05 .02
❑ 145 Eric Andolsek .05 .02
❑ 146 Jerry Ball .05 .02
❑ 147 Bennie Blades .05 .02
❑ 148 Lomas Brown .05 .02
❑ 149 Robert Clark .05 .02
❑ 150 Michael Cofer .05 .02
❑ 151 Dan Owens .05 .02
❑ 152 Rodney Peete .10 .05
❑ 153 Wayne Fontes CO .05 .02
❑ 154 Tim Harris .05 .02
❑ 155 Johnny Holland .05 .02
❑ 156 Don Majkowski .05 .02
❑ 157 Tony Mandarich .05 .02
❑ 158 Mark Murphy .05 .02
❑ 159 Brian Noble .05 .02
❑ 160 Jeff Query .05 .02
❑ 161 Sterling Sharpe .25 .11
❑ 162 Lindy Infante CO .05 .02
❑ 163 Ray Childress .05 .02
❑ 164 Ernest Givins .10 .05
❑ 165 Richard Johnson .05 .02
❑ 166 Bruce Matthews .10 .05
❑ 167 Warren Moon .25 .11
❑ 168 Mike Munchak .05 .02
❑ 169 Al Smith .05 .02
❑ 170 Lorenzo White .05 .02
❑ 171 Jack Pardee CO .05 .02
❑ 172 Albert Bentley .05 .02
❑ 173 Duane Bickett .05 .02
❑ 174 Bill Brooks .05 .02
❑ 175A Eric Dickerson .40 .18
(NFLPA logo on back)
❑ 175B Eric Dickerson 1.25 .55
(No NFLPA logo on back
and 667 yards rushing
for 1990 in text)
❑ 175C Eric Dickerson .25 .11
(No NFLPA logo on back
and 677 yards rushing
for 1990 in text)
❑ 176 Ray Donaldson .05 .02
❑ 177 Jeff George .25 .11
❑ 178 Jeff Herrod .05 .02
❑ 179 Clarence Verdin .05 .02
❑ 180 Ron Meyer CO .05 .02
❑ 181 John Alt .05 .02
❑ 182 Steve DeBerg .05 .02
❑ 183 Albert Lewis .05 .02
❑ 184 Nick Lowery UER .05 .02
(In his 13th year,
not 12th)
❑ 185 Christian Okoye .05 .02
❑ 186 Stephone Paige .05 .02
❑ 187 Kevin Porter .05 .02
❑ 188 Derrick Thomas .25 .11
❑ 189 Marty Schottenheimer .05 .02
CO
❑ 190 Willie Gault .10 .05
❑ 191 Howie Long .10 .05
❑ 192 Terry McDaniel .05 .02
❑ 193 Jay Schroeder UER .05 .02
(Passing total yards
13863, should be 13683)
❑ 194 Steve Smith .05 .02
❑ 195 Greg Townsend .05 .02
❑ 196 Lionel Washington .05 .02
❑ 197 Steve Wisniewski UER .05 .02
(Back says drafted,
should say traded to)
❑ 198 Art Shell CO .10 .05
❑ 199 Henry Ellard .10 .05
❑ 200 Jim Everett .10 .05
❑ 201 Jerry Gray .05 .02
❑ 202 Kevin Greene .25 .11
❑ 203 Buford McGee .05 .02
❑ 204 Tom Newberry .05 .02
❑ 205 Frank Stams .05 .02
❑ 206 Alvin Wright .05 .02
❑ 207 John Robinson CO .05 .02
❑ 208 Jeff Cross .05 .02
❑ 209 Mark Duper .10 .05
❑ 210 Dan Marino 1.25 .55
❑ 211A Tim McKyer .10 .05
(No Traded box on front)
❑ 211B Tim McKyer .25 .11
(Traded box on front)
❑ 212 John Offerdahl .05 .02
❑ 213 Sammie Smith .05 .02
❑ 214 Richmond Webb .05 .02
❑ 215 Jarvis Williams .05 .02
❑ 216 Don Shula CO .10 .05
❑ 217A Darrell Fullington .10 .05
ERR (No registered
symbol on card back)
❑ 217B Darrell Fullington .10 .05
COR (Registered
symbol on card back)
❑ 218 Tim Irwin .05 .02
❑ 219 Mike Merriweather .05 .02
❑ 220 Keith Millard .05 .02
❑ 221 Al Noga .05 .02
❑ 222 Henry Thomas .05 .02
❑ 223 Wade Wilson .10 .05
❑ 224 Gary Zimmerman .05 .02
❑ 225 Jerry Burns CO .05 .02
❑ 226 Bruce Armstrong .05 .02
❑ 227 Marv Cook .05 .02
❑ 228 Hart Lee Dykes .05 .02
❑ 229 Tommy Hodson .05 .02
❑ 230 Ronnie Lippett .05 .02
❑ 231 Ed Reynolds .05 .02
❑ 232 Chris Singleton .05 .02
❑ 233 John Stephens .05 .02
❑ 234 Dick MacPherson CO .05 .02
❑ 235 Stan Brock .05 .02
❑ 236 Craig Heyward .10 .05
❑ 237 Vaughan Johnson .05 .02
❑ 238 Robert Massey .05 .02
❑ 239 Brett Maxie .05 .02
❑ 240 Rueben Mayes .05 .02
❑ 241 Pat Swilling .10 .05
❑ 242 Renaldo Turnbull .05 .02
❑ 243 Jim Mora CO .05 .02
❑ 244 Kyle Clifton .05 .02
❑ 245 Jeff Criswell .05 .02
❑ 246 James Hasty .05 .02
❑ 247 Erik McMillan .05 .02
❑ 248 Scott Mersereau RC .05 .02
❑ 249 Ken O'Brien .05 .02
❑ 250A Blair Thomas .25 .11
(NFLPA logo on back)
❑ 250B Blair Thomas .10 .05
(No NFLPA logo on back)
❑ 251 Al Toon .10 .05
❑ 252 Bruce Coslet CO .05 .02
❑ 253 Eric Allen .05 .02
❑ 254 Fred Barnett .25 .11
❑ 255 Keith Byars .05 .02
❑ 256 Randall Cunningham .25 .11
❑ 257 Seth Joyner .10 .05
❑ 258 Clyde Simmons .05 .02
❑ 259 Jessie Small .05 .02
❑ 260 Andre Waters .05 .02
❑ 261 Rich Kotite CO .05 .02
❑ 262 Roy Green .05 .02
❑ 263 Ernie Jones .05 .02
❑ 264 Tim McDonald .05 .02
❑ 265 Timm Rosenbach .05 .02
❑ 266 Rod Saddler .05 .02
❑ 267 Luis Sharpe .05 .02
❑ 268 Anthony Thompson UER .05 .02
(Terra Haute should
be Terre Haute)
❑ 269 Marcus Turner RC .05 .02
❑ 270 Joe Bugel CO .05 .02
❑ 271 Gary Anderson K .05 .02
❑ 272 Dermontti Dawson .05 .02
❑ 273 Eric Green .05 .02
❑ 274 Merril Hoge .05 .02
❑ 275 Tunch Ilkin .05 .02
❑ 276 D.J. Johnson .05 .02
❑ 277 Louis Lipps .05 .02
❑ 278 Rod Woodson .25 .11
❑ 279 Chuck Noll CO .10 .05
❑ 280 Martin Bayless .05 .02
❑ 281 Marion Butts UER .10 .05
(2 years exp.,
should be 3)
❑ 282 Gill Byrd .05 .02
❑ 283 Burt Grossman .05 .02
❑ 284 Courtney Hall .05 .02
❑ 285 Anthony Miller .10 .05
❑ 286 Leslie O'Neal .10 .05
❑ 287 Billy Joe Tolliver .05 .02
❑ 288 Dan Henning CO .05 .02
❑ 289 Dexter Carter .05 .02
❑ 290 Michael Carter .05 .02
❑ 291 Kevin Fagan .05 .02
❑ 292 Pierce Holt .05 .02
❑ 293 Guy McIntyre .05 .02
(Joe Montana also in photo)
❑ 294 Tom Rathman .05 .02
❑ 295 John Taylor .10 .05
❑ 296 Steve Young .75 .35
❑ 297 George Seifert CO .10 .05
❑ 298 Brian Blades .10 .05
❑ 299 Jeff Bryant .05 .02
❑ 300 Norm Johnson .05 .02
❑ 301 Tommy Kane .05 .02
❑ 302 Cortez Kennedy UER .25 .11
(Played for Seattle
in '90, not Miami)
❑ 303 Bryan Millard .05 .02
❑ 304 John L. Williams .05 .02
❑ 305 David Wyman .05 .02
❑ 306A Chuck Knox CO ERR .05 .02
(Has NFLPA logo,
but should not)
❑ 306B Chuck Knox CO COR .50 .23
(No NFLPA logo on back)
❑ 307 Gary Anderson RB .05 .02
❑ 308 Reggie Cobb .05 .02
❑ 309 Randy Grimes .05 .02
❑ 310 Harry Hamilton .05 .02
❑ 311 Bruce Hill .05 .02
❑ 312 Eugene Marve .05 .02
❑ 313 Ervin Randle .05 .02
❑ 314 Vinny Testaverde .10 .05
❑ 315 Richard Williamson CO .05 .02
UER (Coach: 1st year,
should be 2nd year)
❑ 316 Earnest Byner .05 .02
❑ 317 Gary Clark .25 .11
❑ 318A Andre Collins .10 .05
(NFLPA logo on back)
❑ 318B Andre Collins .10 .05

(No NFLPA logo on back)
❑ 319 Darryl Grant .05 .02
❑ 320 Chip Lohmiller .05 .02
❑ 321 Martin Mayhew .05 .02
❑ 322 Mark Rypien .10 .05
❑ 323 Alvin Walton .05 .02
❑ 324 Joe Gibbs CO UER .10 .05
(Has registered
symbol but should not)
❑ 325 Jerry Glanville REP .05 .02
❑ 326A John Elway REP 4.00 1.80
(NFLPA logo on back)
❑ 326B John Elway REP 2.00 .90
(No NFLPA logo on back)
❑ 327 Boomer Esiason REP .05 .02
❑ 328A Steve Tasker REP 4.00 1.80
(NFLPA logo on back)
❑ 328B Steve Tasker REP 2.00 .90
(No NFLPA logo on back)
❑ 329 Jerry Rice REP .40 .18
❑ 330 Jeff Rutledge REP .05 .02
❑ 331 K.C. Defense REP .05 .02
❑ 332 49ers Streak REP .05 .02
(Cleveland Gary)
❑ 333 Monday Meeting REP .05 .02
(John Taylor)
❑ 334A Randall Cunningham .05 .02
REP
(NFLPA logo on back)
❑ 334B Randall Cunningham .05 .02
REP
(No NFLPA logo on back)
❑ 335A Bo Jackson and .50 .23
Barry Sanders REP
(NFLPA logo on back)
❑ 335B Bo Jackson and .50 .23
Barry Sanders REP
(No NFLPA logo on back)
❑ 336 Lawrence Taylor REP .25 .11
❑ 337 Warren Moon REP .25 .11
❑ 338 Alan Grant REP .05 .02
❑ 339 Todd McNair REP .05 .02
❑ 340A Miami Dolphins REP .05 .02
(Mark Clayton;
TM symbol on Chiefs
player's shoulder)
❑ 340B Miami Dolphins REP .05 .02
(Mark Clayton;
TM symbol off Chiefs
player's shoulder)
❑ 341A Highest Scoring REP 4.00 1.80
Jim Kelly Passing
(NFLPA logo on back)
❑ 341B Highest Scoring REP 2.00 .90
Jim Kelly Passing
(No NFLPA logo on back)
❑ 342 Matt Bahr REP .05 .02
❑ 343 Robert Tisch NEW .05 .02
(With Wellington Mara)
❑ 344 Sam Jankovich NEW .05 .02
❑ 345 In-the-Grasp NEW .05 .02
(John Elway)
❑ 346 Bo Jackson NEW .10 .05
(Career in Jeopardy)
❑ 347 NFL Teacher of the .05 .02
Year Jack Williams
with Paul Tagliabue
❑ 348 Ronnie Lott NEW .10 .05
(Plan B Free Agent)
❑ 349 Super Bowl XXV .05 .02
Teleclinic NEW (Greg
Gumbel with Warren
Moon, Derrick Thomas,
and Wade Wilson)
❑ 350 W.Houston NEW RC .05 .02
❑ 351 U.S. Troops in .05 .02
Saudia Arabia NEW
(Troops watching TV
with gas masks)
❑ 352 Art McNally OFF .05 .02
❑ 353 Dick Jorgensen OFF .05 .02
❑ 354 Jerry Seeman OFF .05 .02
❑ 355 Jim Tunney OFF .05 .02
❑ 356 Gerry Austin OFF .05 .02
❑ 357 Gene Barth OFF .05 .02
❑ 358 Red Cashion OFF .05 .02
❑ 359 Tom Dooley OFF .05 .02
❑ 360 Johnny Grier OFF .05 .02
❑ 361 Pat Haggerty OFF .05 .02
❑ 362 Dale Hamer OFF .05 .02
❑ 363 Dick Hantak OFF .05 .02
❑ 364 Jerry Markbreit OFF .05 .02
❑ 365 Gordon McCarter OFF .05 .02
❑ 366 Bob McElwee OFF .05 .02
❑ 367 Howard Roe OFF .05 .02
(Illustrations on back
smaller than other
officials' cards)
❑ 368 Tom White OFF .05 .02
❑ 369 Norm Schachter OFF .05 .02
❑ 370A Warren Moon .25 .11
Crack Kills
(Small type on back)
❑ 370B Warren Moon .25 .11
Crack Kills
(Large type on back)
❑ 371A Boomer Esiason .50 .23
Don't Drink
(Small type on back)
❑ 371B Boomer Esiason .10 .05
Don't Drink
(Large type on back)
❑ 372A Troy Aikman .40 .18
Play It Straight
(Small type on back)
❑ 372B Troy Aikman .40 .18
Play It Straight
(Large type on back)
❑ 373A Carl Banks .50 .23
Read
(Small type on back)
❑ 373B Carl Banks .05 .02
Read
(Large type on back)
❑ 374A Jim Everett .50 .23
Study
(Small type on back)
❑ 374B Jim Everett .10 .05
Study
(Large type on back)
❑ 375A Anthony Munoz .10 .05
Quadante en la Escuela
(Dificul; small type)
❑ 375B Anthony Munoz .10 .05
Quadante en la Escuela
(Dificil; small type)
❑ 375C Anthony Munoz .10 .05
Quadante en la Escuela
(Dificil; large type)
❑ 375D Anthony Munoz .10 .05
Quedate en la Escuela
(Large type)
❑ 376A Ray Childress 1.25 .55
Don't Pollute
(Small type on back)
❑ 376B Ray Childress .05 .02
Don't Pollute
(Large type on back)
❑ 377A Charles Mann 1.25 .55
Steroids Destroy
(Small type on back)
❑ 377B Charles Mann .05 .02
Steroids Destroy
(Large type on back)
❑ 378A Jackie Slater 1.25 .55
Keep the Peace
(Small type on back)
❑ 378B Jackie Slater .05 .02
Keep the Peace
(Large type on back)
❑ 379 Jerry Rice NFC .40 .18
❑ 380 Andre Rison NFC .10 .05
❑ 381 Jim Lachey NFC .05 .02
❑ 382 Jackie Slater NFC .05 .02
❑ 383 Randall McDaniel NFC .05 .02
❑ 384 Mark Bortz NFC .05 .02
❑ 385 Jay Hilgenberg NFC .05 .02
❑ 386 Keith Jackson NFC .05 .02
❑ 387 Joe Montana NFC .50 .23
❑ 388 Barry Sanders NFC .60 .25
❑ 389 Neal Anderson NFC .05 .02
❑ 390 Reggie White NFC .25 .11
❑ 391 Chris Doleman NFC .05 .02
❑ 392 Jerome Brown NFC .05 .02
❑ 393 Charles Haley NFC .05 .02
❑ 394 Lawrence Taylor NFC .25 .11
❑ 395 Pepper Johnson NFC .05 .02
❑ 396 Mike Singletary NFC .10 .05
❑ 397 Darrell Green NFC .05 .02
❑ 398 Carl Lee NFC .05 .02
❑ 399 Joey Browner NFC .05 .02
❑ 400 Ronnie Lott NFC .10 .05
❑ 401 Sean Landeta NFC .05 .02
❑ 402 Morten Andersen NFC .05 .02
❑ 403 Mel Gray NFC .05 .02
❑ 404 Reyna Thompson NFC .05 .02
❑ 405 Jimmy Johnson CO NFC .10 .05
❑ 406 Andre Reed AFC .10 .05
❑ 407 Anthony Miller AFC .10 .05
❑ 408 Anthony Munoz AFC .10 .05
❑ 409 Bruce Armstrong AFC .05 .02
❑ 410 Bruce Matthews AFC .05 .02
❑ 411 Mike Munchak AFC .05 .02
❑ 412 Kent Hull AFC .05 .02
❑ 413 Rodney Holman AFC .05 .02
❑ 414 Warren Moon AFC .25 .11
❑ 415 Thurman Thomas AFC .25 .11
❑ 416 Marion Butts AFC .10 .05
❑ 417 Bruce Smith AFC .10 .05
❑ 418 Greg Townsend AFC .05 .02
❑ 419 Ray Childress AFC .05 .02
❑ 420 Derrick Thomas AFC .25 .11
❑ 421 Leslie O'Neal AFC .10 .05
❑ 422 John Offerdahl AFC .05 .02
❑ 423 Shane Conlan AFC .05 .02
❑ 424 Rod Woodson AFC .25 .11
❑ 425 Albert Lewis AFC .05 .02
❑ 426 Steve Atwater AFC .05 .02
❑ 427 David Fulcher AFC .05 .02
❑ 428 Rohn Stark AFC .05 .02
❑ 429 Nick Lowery AFC .05 .02
❑ 430 Clarence Verdin AFC .05 .02
❑ 431 Steve Tasker AFC .05 .02
❑ 432 Art Shell CO AFC .10 .05
❑ 433 Scott Case .05 .02
❑ 434 Tory Epps UER .05 .02
(No TM next to Pro Set
on card back)
❑ 435 Mike Gann UER .05 .02
(Text has 2 fumble
recoveries, stats
say 3)
❑ 436 Brian Jordan UER .10 .05
(No TM next to Pro Set
on card back)
❑ 437 Mike Kenn .05 .02
❑ 438 John Rade .05 .02
❑ 439 Andre Rison .10 .05
❑ 440 Mike Rozier .05 .02
❑ 441 Jessie Tuggle .05 .02
❑ 442 Don Beebe .05 .02
❑ 443 John Davis RC .05 .02
❑ 444 James Lofton .10 .05
❑ 445 Keith McKeller .05 .02
❑ 446 Jamie Mueller .05 .02
❑ 447 Scott Norwood .05 .02
❑ 448 Frank Reich .10 .05
❑ 449 Leon Seals .05 .02
❑ 450 Leonard Smith .05 .02
❑ 451 Neal Anderson .10 .05
❑ 452 Trace Armstrong .05 .02
❑ 453 Mark Bortz .05 .02
❑ 454 Wendell Davis .05 .02
❑ 455 Shaun Gayle .05 .02
❑ 456 Jay Hilgenberg .05 .02
❑ 457 Steve McMichael .10 .05
❑ 458 Mike Singletary .10 .05
❑ 459 Donnell Woolford .05 .02
❑ 460 Jim Breech .05 .02
❑ 461 Eddie Brown .05 .02
❑ 462 Barney Bussey RC .05 .02
❑ 463 Bruce Kozerski .05 .02
❑ 464 Tim Krumrie .05 .02
❑ 465 Bruce Reimers .05 .02
❑ 466 Kevin Walker RC .05 .02
❑ 467 Ickey Woods .05 .02
❑ 468 Carl Zander UER .05 .02
(DOB: 4/12/63, should

be 3/23/63)
❑ 469 Mike Baab .05 .02
❑ 470 Brian Brennan .05 .02
❑ 471 Rob Burnett RC .10 .05
❑ 472 Raymond Clayborn .05 .02
❑ 473 Reggie Langhorne .05 .02
❑ 474 Kevin Mack .05 .02
❑ 475 Anthony Pleasant .05 .02
❑ 476 Joe Morris .05 .02
❑ 477 Dan Fike .05 .02
❑ 478 Ray Horton .05 .02
❑ 479 Jim Jeffcoat .05 .02
❑ 480 Jimmie Jones .05 .02
❑ 481 Kelvin Martin .05 .02
❑ 482 Nate Newton .10 .05
❑ 483 Danny Noonan .05 .02
❑ 484 Jay Novacek .25 .11
❑ 485 Emmitt Smith 2.00 .90
❑ 486 James Washington RC .05 .02
❑ 487 Simon Fletcher .05 .02
❑ 488 Ron Holmes .05 .02
❑ 489 Mike Horan .05 .02
❑ 490 Vance Johnson .05 .02
❑ 491 Keith Kartz .05 .02
❑ 492 Greg Kragen .05 .02
❑ 493 Ken Lanier .05 .02
❑ 494 Warren Powers .05 .02
❑ 495 Dennis Smith .05 .02
❑ 496 Jeff Campbell .05 .02
❑ 497 Ken Dallafior .05 .02
❑ 498 Dennis Gibson .05 .02
❑ 499 Kevin Glover .05 .02
❑ 500 Mel Gray .10 .05
❑ 501 Eddie Murray .05 .02
❑ 502 Barry Sanders 1.50 .70
❑ 503 Chris Spielman .10 .05
❑ 504 William White .05 .02
❑ 505 Matt Brock RC .05 .02
❑ 506 Robert Brown .05 .02
❑ 507 LeRoy Butler .10 .05
❑ 508 James Campen RC .05 .02
❑ 509 Jerry Holmes .05 .02
❑ 510 Perry Kemp .05 .02
❑ 511 Ken Ruettgers .05 .02
❑ 512 Scott Stephen RC .05 .02
❑ 513 Ed West .05 .02
❑ 514 Cris Dishman RC .05 .02
❑ 515 Curtis Duncan .05 .02
❑ 516 Drew Hill UER .05 .02
(Text says 390 catches
and 6368 yards, stats
say 450 and 7715)
❑ 517 Haywood Jeffires .10 .05
❑ 518 Sean Jones .10 .05
❑ 519 Lamar Lathon .05 .02
❑ 520 Don Maggs .05 .02
❑ 521 Bubba McDowell .05 .02
❑ 522 Johnny Meads .05 .02
❑ 523A Chip Banks ERR .50 .23
(No text)
❑ 523B Chip Banks COR .05 .02
❑ 524 Pat Beach .05 .02
❑ 525 Sam Clancy .05 .02
❑ 526 Eugene Daniel .05 .02
❑ 527 Jon Hand .05 .02
❑ 528 Jessie Hester .05 .02
❑ 529A Mike Prior ERR .50 .23
(No textual information)
❑ 529B Mike Prior COR .05 .02
❑ 530 Keith Taylor .05 .02
❑ 531 Donnell Thompson .05 .02
❑ 532 Dino Hackett .05 .02
❑ 533 David Lutz RC .05 .02
❑ 534 Chris Martin .05 .02
❑ 535 Kevin Ross .05 .02
❑ 536 Dan Saleaumua .05 .02
❑ 537 Neil Smith .25 .11
❑ 538 Percy Snow .05 .02
❑ 539 Robb Thomas .05 .02
❑ 540 Barry Word .05 .02
❑ 541 Marcus Allen .25 .11
❑ 542 Eddie Anderson .05 .02
❑ 543 Scott Davis .05 .02
❑ 544 Mervyn Fernandez .05 .02
❑ 545 Ethan Horton .05 .02
❑ 546 Ronnie Lott .10 .05
❑ 547 Don Mosebar .05 .02
❑ 548 Jerry Robinson .05 .02
❑ 549 Aaron Wallace .05 .02
❑ 550 Flipper Anderson .05 .02
❑ 551 Cleveland Gary .05 .02
❑ 552 Damone Johnson RC .05 .02
❑ 553 Duval Love RC .05 .02
❑ 554 Irv Pankey .05 .02
❑ 555 Mike Piel .05 .02
❑ 556 Jackie Slater .05 .02
❑ 557 Michael Stewart .05 .02
❑ 558 Pat Terrell .05 .02
❑ 559 J.B. Brown .05 .02
❑ 560 Mark Clayton .10 .05
❑ 561 Ferrell Edmunds .05 .02
❑ 562 Harry Galbreath .05 .02
❑ 563 David Griggs .05 .02
❑ 564 Jim C. Jensen .05 .02
❑ 565 Louis Oliver .05 .02
❑ 566 Tony Paige .05 .02
❑ 567 Keith Sims .05 .02
❑ 568 Joey Browner .05 .02
❑ 569 Anthony Carter .10 .05
❑ 570 Chris Doleman .05 .02
❑ 571 Rich Gannon UER .25 .11
(Acquired in '87,
not '88 as in text)
❑ 572 Hassan Jones .05 .02
❑ 573 Steve Jordan .05 .02
❑ 574 Carl Lee .05 .02
❑ 575 Randall McDaniel .05 .02
❑ 576 Herschel Walker .10 .05
❑ 577 Ray Agnew .05 .02
❑ 578 Vincent Brown .05 .02
❑ 579 Irving Fryar .10 .05
❑ 580 Tim Goad .05 .02
❑ 581 Maurice Hurst .05 .02
❑ 582 Fred Marion .05 .02
❑ 583 Johnny Rembert .05 .02
❑ 584 Andre Tippett .05 .02
❑ 585 Brent Williams .05 .02
❑ 586 Morten Andersen .05 .02
❑ 587 Toi Cook RC .05 .02
❑ 588 Jim Dombrowski .05 .02
❑ 589 Dalton Hilliard .05 .02
❑ 590 Rickey Jackson .05 .02
❑ 591 Eric Martin .05 .02
❑ 592 Sam Mills .05 .02
❑ 593 Bobby Hebert .05 .02
❑ 594 Steve Walsh .05 .02
❑ 595 Ottis Anderson .10 .05
❑ 596 Pepper Johnson .05 .02
❑ 597 Bob Kratch RC .05 .02
❑ 598 Sean Landeta .05 .02
❑ 599 Doug Riesenberg .05 .02
❑ 600 William Roberts .05 .02
❑ 601 Phil Simms .10 .05
❑ 602 Lawrence Taylor .25 .11
❑ 603 Everson Walls .05 .02
❑ 604 Brad Baxter .05 .02
❑ 605 Dennis Byrd .05 .02
❑ 606 Jeff Lageman .05 .02
❑ 607 Pat Leahy .05 .02
❑ 608 Rob Moore .25 .11
❑ 609 Joe Mott .05 .02
❑ 610 Tony Stargell .05 .02
❑ 611 Brian Washington .05 .02
❑ 612 Marvin Washington RC .05 .02
❑ 613 David Alexander .05 .02
❑ 614 Jerome Brown .05 .02
❑ 615 Byron Evans .05 .02
❑ 616 Ron Heller .05 .02
❑ 617 Wes Hopkins .05 .02
❑ 618 Keith Jackson .10 .05
❑ 619 Heath Sherman .05 .02
❑ 620 Reggie White .25 .11
❑ 621 Calvin Williams .10 .05
❑ 622 Ken Harvey .10 .05
❑ 623 Eric Hill .05 .02
❑ 624 Johnny Johnson .05 .02
❑ 625 Freddie Joe Nunn .05 .02
❑ 626 Ricky Proehl .05 .02
❑ 627 Tootie Robbins .05 .02
❑ 628 Jay Taylor .05 .02
❑ 629 Tom Tupa .05 .02
❑ 630 Jim Wahler RC .05 .02
❑ 631 Bubby Brister .05 .02
❑ 632 Thomas Everett .05 .02
❑ 633 Bryan Hinkle .05 .02
❑ 634 Carnell Lake .05 .02
❑ 635 David Little .05 .02
❑ 636 Hardy Nickerson .10 .05
❑ 637 Gerald Williams .05 .02
❑ 638 Keith Willis .05 .02
❑ 639 Tim Worley .05 .02
❑ 640 Rod Bernstine .05 .02
❑ 641 Frank Cornish .05 .02
❑ 642 Gary Plummer .05 .02
❑ 643 Henry Rolling RC .05 .02
❑ 644 Sam Seale .05 .02
❑ 645 Junior Seau .25 .11
❑ 646 Billy Ray Smith .05 .02
❑ 647 Broderick Thompson .05 .02
❑ 648 Derrick Walker RC .05 .02
❑ 649 Todd Bowles .05 .02
❑ 650 Don Griffin .05 .02
❑ 651 Charles Haley .10 .05
❑ 652 Brent Jones UER .10 .05
(Born in Santa Clara,
not San Jose)
❑ 653 Joe Montana 1.25 .55
❑ 654 Jerry Rice .75 .35
❑ 655 Bill Romanowski .05 .02
❑ 656 Michael Walter .05 .02
❑ 657 Dave Waymer .05 .02
❑ 658 Jeff Chadwick .05 .02
❑ 659 Derrick Fenner .05 .02
❑ 660 Nesby Glasgow .05 .02
❑ 661 Jacob Green .05 .02
❑ 662 Dwayne Harper RC .05 .02
❑ 663 Andy Heck .05 .02
❑ 664 Dave Krieg .10 .05
❑ 665 Rufus Porter .05 .02
❑ 666 Eugene Robinson .05 .02
❑ 667 Mark Carrier WR .25 .11
❑ 668 Steve Christie .05 .02
❑ 669 Reuben Davis .05 .02
❑ 670 Paul Gruber .05 .02
❑ 671 Wayne Haddix .05 .02
❑ 672 Ron Hall .05 .02
❑ 673 Keith McCants UER .05 .02
(Senior All-American,
sic, left school
after junior year)
❑ 674 Ricky Reynolds .05 .02
❑ 675 Mark Robinson .05 .02
❑ 676 Jeff Bostic .05 .02
❑ 677 Darrell Green .05 .02
❑ 678 Markus Koch .05 .02
❑ 679 Jim Lachey .05 .02
❑ 680 Charles Mann .05 .02
❑ 681 Wilber Marshall .05 .02
❑ 682 Art Monk .10 .05
❑ 683 Gerald Riggs .05 .02
❑ 684 Ricky Sanders .05 .02
❑ 685 Ray Handley NEW .05 .02
(Replaces Bill Parcells as
Giants head coach)
❑ 686 NFL announces NEW .05 .02
expansion
❑ 687 Miami gets NEW .05 .02
Super Bowl XXIX
❑ 688 George Young NEW .05 .02
is named NFL Executive
of the Year by
The Sporting News
❑ 689 Five-millionth fan NEW .05 .02
visits Pro Football
Hall of Fame
❑ 690 Sports Illustrated NEW .05 .02
poll finds pro football
is America's Number 1
spectator sport
❑ 691 American Bowl NEW .05 .02
London Theme Art
❑ 692 American Bowl NEW .05 .02
Berlin Theme Art
❑ 693 American Bowl NEW .05 .02
Tokyo Theme Art
❑ 694A Russell Maryland .25 .11
(Says he runs a 4.91
40, card 32 has 4.8)

- ❑ 694B Joe Ferguson LEG .05 .02
- ❑ 695 Carl Hairston LEG .10 .05
- ❑ 696 Dan Hampton LEG .10 .05
- ❑ 697 Mike Haynes LEG .05 .02
- ❑ 698 Marty Lyons LEG .05 .02
- ❑ 699 Ozzie Newsome LEG .10 .05
- ❑ 700 Scott Studwell LEG .05 .02
- ❑ 701 Mike Webster LEG .05 .02
- ❑ 702 Dwayne Woodruff LEG .05 .02
- ❑ 703 Larry Kennan CO .05 .02 London Monarchs
- ❑ 704 Stan Gelbaugh RC LL .10 .05 London Monarchs
- ❑ 705 John Brantley LL .05 .02 Birmingham Fire
- ❑ 706 Danny Lockett LL .05 .02 London Monarchs
- ❑ 707 Anthony Parker RC LL .10 .05 NY/NJ Knights
- ❑ 708 Dan Crossman LL .05 .02 London Monarchs
- ❑ 709 Eric Wilkerson LL .05 .02 NY/NJ Knights
- ❑ 710 Judd Garrett RC LL .05 .02 London Monarchs
- ❑ 711 Tony Baker LL .05 .02 Frankfurt Galaxy
- ❑ 712 1st Place BW PHOTO .05 .02 Randall Cunningham
- ❑ 713 2nd Place BW PHOTO .05 .02 Mark Ingram
- ❑ 714 3rd Place BW PHOTO .05 .02 Pete Holohan Barney Bussey Carl Carter
- ❑ 715 1st Place Color PHOTO .05 .02 Action Sterling Sharpe
- ❑ 716 2nd Place Color PHOTO .05 .02 Action Jim Harbaugh
- ❑ 717 3rd Place Color PHOTO .05 .02 Action Anthony Miller David Fulcher
- ❑ 718 1st Place Color PHOTO .05 .02 Feature Bill Parcells CO Lawrence Taylor
- ❑ 719 2nd Place Color PHOTO .05 .02 Feature Patriotic Crowd
- ❑ 720 3rd Place Color PHOTO .05 .02 Feature Alfredo Roberts
- ❑ 721 Ray Bentley .05 .02 Read And Study
- ❑ 722 Earnest Byner .05 .02 Never Give Up
- ❑ 723 Bill Fralic .05 .02 Steroids Destroy
- ❑ 724 Joe Jacoby .05 .02 Don't Pollute
- ❑ 725 Howie Long .10 .05 Aids Kills
- ❑ 726 Dan Marino .50 .23 School's The Ticket
- ❑ 727 Ron Rivera .05 .02 Leer Y Estudiar
- ❑ 728 Mike Singletary .10 .05 Be The Best
- ❑ 729 Cornelius Bennett .10 .05 Chill
- ❑ 730 Russell Maryland .25 .11
- ❑ 731 Eric Turner RC .10 .05
- ❑ 732 Bruce Pickens RC UER .05 .02 (Wearing 38, but card back lists 39)
- ❑ 733 Mike Croel RC .05 .02
- ❑ 734 Todd Lyght RC .05 .02
- ❑ 735 Eric Swann RC .25 .11
- ❑ 736 Charles McRae RC .05 .02
- ❑ 737 Antone Davis RC .05 .02
- ❑ 738 Stanley Richard RC .05 .02
- ❑ 739 Herman Moore RC 2.00 .90
- ❑ 740 Pat Harlow RC .05 .02
- ❑ 741 Alvin Harper RC .25 .11
- ❑ 742 Mike Pritchard RC .25 .11
- ❑ 743 Leonard Russell RC .25 .11
- ❑ 744 Huey Richardson RC .05 .02
- ❑ 745 Dan McGwire RC .05 .02
- ❑ 746 Bobby Wilson RC .05 .02
- ❑ 747 Alfred Williams .05 .02
- ❑ 748 Vinnie Clark RC .05 .02
- ❑ 749 Kelvin Pritchett RC .10 .05
- ❑ 750 Harvey Williams RC .25 .11
- ❑ 751 Stan Thomas .05 .02
- ❑ 752 Randal Hill RC .10 .05
- ❑ 753 Todd Marinovich RC .05 .02
- ❑ 754 Ted Washington RC .05 .02
- ❑ 755 Henry Jones RC .10 .05
- ❑ 756 Jarrod Bunch RC .05 .02
- ❑ 757 Mike Dumas RC .05 .02
- ❑ 758 Ed King RC .05 .02
- ❑ 759 Reggie Johnson RC .05 .02
- ❑ 760 Roman Phifer RC .05 .02
- ❑ 761 Mike Jones RC .05 .02
- ❑ 762 Brett Favre RC 5.00 2.20
- ❑ 763 Browning Nagle RC .05 .02
- ❑ 764 Esera Tuaolo RC .05 .02
- ❑ 765 George Thornton RC .05 .02
- ❑ 766 Dixon Edwards RC .05 .02
- ❑ 767 Darryll Lewis .10 .05
- ❑ 768 Eric Bieniemy RC .05 .02
- ❑ 769 Shane Curry .05 .02
- ❑ 770 Jerome Henderson RC .05 .02
- ❑ 771 Wesley Carroll RC .05 .02
- ❑ 772 Nick Bell RC .05 .02
- ❑ 773 John Flannery RC .05 .02
- ❑ 774 Ricky Watters RC 1.50 .70
- ❑ 775 Jeff Graham RC .25 .11
- ❑ 776 Eric Moten RC .05 .02
- ❑ 777 Jesse Campbell RC .05 .02
- ❑ 778 Chris Zorich .10 .05
- ❑ 779 Joe Valerio .05 .02
- ❑ 780 Doug Thomas RC .05 .02
- ❑ 781 Lamar Rogers RC UER .05 .02 (No "Official Card of NFL" and TM on card front)
- ❑ 782 John Johnson RC .05 .02
- ❑ 783 Phil Hansen RC .05 .02
- ❑ 784 Kanavis McGhee RC .05 .02
- ❑ 785 Calvin Stephens RC UER .05 .02 (Card says New England, others say New England Patriots)
- ❑ 786 James Jones RC .05 .02
- ❑ 787 Reggie Barrett .05 .02
- ❑ 788 Aeneas Williams RC .25 .11
- ❑ 789 Aaron Craver RC .05 .02
- ❑ 790 Keith Traylor RC .05 .02
- ❑ 791 Godfrey Myles RC .05 .02
- ❑ 792 Mo Lewis RC .10 .05
- ❑ 793 James Richards RC .05 .02
- ❑ 794 Carlos Jenkins RC .05 .02
- ❑ 795 Lawrence Dawsey RC .10 .05
- ❑ 796 Don Davey .05 .02
- ❑ 797 Jake Reed RC .75 .35
- ❑ 798 Dave McCloughan .05 .02
- ❑ 799 Erik Williams RC .10 .05
- ❑ 800 Steve Jackson RC .05 .02
- ❑ 801 Bob Dahl .05 .02
- ❑ 802 Ernie Mills RC .10 .05
- ❑ 803 David Daniels RC .05 .02
- ❑ 804 Rob Selby RC .05 .02
- ❑ 805 Ricky Ervins RC .10 .05
- ❑ 806 Tim Barnett RC .05 .02
- ❑ 807 Chris Gardocki .05 .02
- ❑ 808 Kevin Donnalley .05 .02
- ❑ 809 Robert Wilson RC .05 .02
- ❑ 810 Chuck Webb RC .05 .02
- ❑ 811 Darryl Wren RC .05 .02
- ❑ 812 Ed McCaffrey RC 2.00 .90
- ❑ 813 Shula's 300th Victory .05 .02 NEWS
- ❑ 814 Raiders-49ers sell out Coliseum .05 .02 NEWS
- ❑ 815 NFL International NEWS .05 .02
- ❑ 816 Moe Gardner RC .05 .02
- ❑ 817 Tim McKyer .05 .02
- ❑ 818 Tom Waddle RC .05 .02
- ❑ 819 Michael Jackson RC .25 .11
- ❑ 820 Tony Casillas .05 .02
- ❑ 821 Gaston Green .05 .02
- ❑ 822 Kenny Walker RC .05 .02
- ❑ 823 Willie Green RC .05 .02
- ❑ 824 Erik Kramer RC .40 .18
- ❑ 825 William Fuller .10 .05
- ❑ 826 Allen Pinkett .05 .02
- ❑ 827 Rick Venturi CO .05 .02
- ❑ 828 Bill Maas .05 .02
- ❑ 829 Jeff Jaeger .05 .02
- ❑ 830 Robert Delpino .05 .02
- ❑ 831 Mark Higgs RC .05 .02
- ❑ 832 Reggie Roby .05 .02
- ❑ 833 Terry Allen RC 1.50 .70
- ❑ 834 Cris Carter .50 .23 (No indication when acquired on waivers)
- ❑ 835 John Randle RC .60 .25
- ❑ 836 Hugh Millen RC .05 .02
- ❑ 837 Jon Vaughn RC .05 .02
- ❑ 838 Gill Fenerty .05 .02
- ❑ 839 Floyd Turner .05 .02
- ❑ 840 Irv Eatman .05 .02
- ❑ 841 Lonnie Young .05 .02
- ❑ 842 Jim McMahon .10 .05
- ❑ 843 Randal Hill UER .05 .02 (Traded to Phoenix, not drafted)
- ❑ 844 Barry Foster .10 .05
- ❑ 845 Neil O'Donnell RC 1.00 .45
- ❑ 846 John Friesz UER .25 .11 (Wears 17, not 7)
- ❑ 847 Broderick Thomas .05 .02
- ❑ 848 Brian Mitchell .10 .05
- ❑ 849 Mike Utley RC .10 .05
- ❑ 850 Mike Croel ROY .05 .02
- ❑ SC1 Super Bowl XXVI .25 .11 Theme Art UER (Card says SB 26, should be 25)
- ❑ SC3 Jim Thorpe .75 .35 Pioneers of the Game
- ❑ SC4 Otto Graham .75 .35 Pioneers of the Game
- ❑ SC5 Paul Brown .75 .35 Pioneers of the Game
- ❑ PSS1 Walter Payton .50 .23 and Team 34
- ❑ PSS2 Red Grange .50 .23
- ❑ MVPC25 Ottis Anderson .25 .11 MVP Super Bowl XXV
- ❑ AU336 Lawrence Taylor 175.00 80.00 REP (autographed/500)
- ❑ AU394 Lawrence Taylor 175.00 80.00 PB (autographed/500)
- ❑ AU699 Ozzie Newsome 50.00 22.00 (Certified autograph)
- ❑ AU824 Erik Kramer 50.00 22.00 (Certified autograph)
- ❑ NNO Mini Pro Set Gazette .25 .11
- ❑ NNO Pro Set Gazette .25 .11
- ❑ NNO Santa Claus .50 .23
- ❑ NNO Super Bowl XXV Art .25 .11
- ❑ NNO Super Bowl XXV Logo .25 .11

1991 Pro Set Platinum

	MINT	NRMT
COMPLETE SET (315)	10.00	4.50
COMP.SERIES 1 (150)	4.00	1.80
COMP.SERIES 2 (165)	6.00	2.70
❑ 1 Chris Miller	.10	.05
❑ 2 Andre Rison	.25	.11
❑ 3 Tim Green	.05	.02
❑ 4 Jessie Tuggle	.05	.02
❑ 5 Thurman Thomas	.25	.11
❑ 6 Darryl Talley	.05	.02
❑ 7 Kent Hull	.05	.02
❑ 8 Bruce Smith	.25	.11
❑ 9 Shane Conlan	.05	.02
❑ 10 Jim Harbaugh	.25	.11
❑ 11 Neal Anderson	.10	.05
❑ 12 Mark Bortz	.05	.02
❑ 13 Richard Dent	.10	.05
❑ 14 Steve McMichael	.05	.02
❑ 15 James Brooks	.05	.02
❑ 16 Boomer Esiason	.10	.05
❑ 17 Tim Krumrie	.05	.02
❑ 18 James Francis	.05	.02
❑ 19 Lewis Billups	.05	.02
❑ 20 Eric Metcalf	.25	.11
❑ 21 Kevin Mack	.05	.02
❑ 22 Clay Matthews	.10	.05
❑ 23 Mike Johnson	.05	.02
❑ 24 Troy Aikman	.75	.35
❑ 25 Emmitt Smith	2.00	.90
❑ 26 Daniel Stubbs	.05	.02
❑ 27 Ken Norton	.25	.11
❑ 28 John Elway	1.25	.55
❑ 29 Bobby Humphrey	.05	.02
❑ 30 Simon Fletcher	.05	.02
❑ 31 Karl Mecklenburg	.05	.02
❑ 32 Rodney Peete	.10	.05
❑ 33 Barry Sanders	1.50	.70
❑ 34 Michael Cofer	.05	.02
❑ 35 Jerry Ball	.05	.02
❑ 36 Sterling Sharpe	.25	.11
❑ 37 Tony Mandarich	.05	.02
❑ 38 Brian Noble	.05	.02
❑ 39 Tim Harris	.05	.02
❑ 40 Warren Moon	.10	.05
❑ 41 Ernest Givins UER (Misspelled Givens on card back)	.10	.05
❑ 42 Mike Munchak	.05	.02
❑ 43 Sean Jones	.10	.05
❑ 44 Ray Childress	.10	.05
❑ 45 Jeff George	.25	.11
❑ 46 Albert Bentley	.05	.02
❑ 47 Duane Bickett	.05	.02
❑ 48 Steve DeBerg	.10	.05
❑ 49 Christian Okoye	.10	.05
❑ 50 Neil Smith	.25	.11
❑ 51 Derrick Thomas	.25	.11
❑ 52 Willie Gault	.10	.05
❑ 53 Don Mosebar	.05	.02
❑ 54 Howie Long	.10	.05
❑ 55 Greg Townsend	.05	.02
❑ 56 Terry McDaniel	.10	.05
❑ 57 Jackie Slater	.05	.02
❑ 58 Jim Everett	.10	.05
❑ 59 Cleveland Gary	.05	.02
❑ 60 Mike Piel	.05	.02
❑ 61 Jerry Gray	.05	.02
❑ 62 Dan Marino	1.25	.55
❑ 63 Sammie Smith	.05	.02
❑ 64 Richmond Webb	.05	.02
❑ 65 Louis Oliver	.05	.02
❑ 66 Ferrell Edmunds	.05	.02
❑ 67 Jeff Cross	.05	.02
❑ 68 Wade Wilson	.05	.02
❑ 69 Chris Doleman	.10	.05
❑ 70 Joey Browner	.05	.02
❑ 71 Keith Millard	.05	.02
❑ 72 John Stephens	.05	.02
❑ 73 Andre Tippett	.05	.02
❑ 74 Brent Williams	.05	.02
❑ 75 Craig Heyward	.10	.05
❑ 76 Eric Martin	.05	.02
❑ 77 Pat Swilling	.10	.05
❑ 78 Sam Mills	.10	.05
❑ 79 Jeff Hostetler	.10	.05
❑ 80 Ottis Anderson	.10	.05
❑ 81 Lawrence Taylor	.25	.11
❑ 82 Pepper Johnson	.05	.02
❑ 83 Blair Thomas	.05	.02
❑ 84 Al Toon	.10	.05
❑ 85 Ken O'Brien	.05	.02
❑ 86 Erik McMillan	.05	.02
❑ 87 Dennis Byrd	.10	.05
❑ 88 Randall Cunningham	.25	.11
❑ 89 Fred Barnett	.25	.11
❑ 90 Seth Joyner	.10	.05
❑ 91 Reggie White	.25	.11
❑ 92 Timm Rosenbach	.05	.02
❑ 93 Johnny Johnson	.05	.02
❑ 94 Tim McDonald	.05	.02
❑ 95 Freddie Joe Nunn	.05	.02
❑ 96 Bubby Brister	.10	.05
❑ 97 Gary Anderson K UER (Listed as RB)	.05	.02
❑ 98 Merril Hoge	.05	.02
❑ 99 Keith Willis	.05	.02
❑ 100 Rod Woodson	.25	.11
❑ 101 Billy Joe Tolliver	.05	.02
❑ 102 Marion Butts	.10	.05
❑ 103 Rod Bernstine	.05	.02
❑ 104 Lee Williams	.05	.02
❑ 105 Burt Grossman UER (Photo on back is reversed)	.05	.02
❑ 106 Tom Rathman	.05	.02
❑ 107 John Taylor	.10	.05
❑ 108 Michael Carter	.05	.02
❑ 109 Guy McIntyre	.05	.02
❑ 110 Pierce Holt	.05	.02
❑ 111 John L. Williams	.05	.02
❑ 112 Dave Krieg	.10	.05
❑ 113 Bryan Millard	.05	.02
❑ 114 Cortez Kennedy	.25	.11
❑ 115 Derrick Fenner	.05	.02
❑ 116 Vinny Testaverde	.10	.05
❑ 117 Reggie Cobb	.05	.02
❑ 118 Gary Anderson RB	.05	.02
❑ 119 Bruce Hill	.05	.02
❑ 120 Wayne Haddix	.05	.02
❑ 121 Broderick Thomas	.05	.02
❑ 122 Keith McCants	.05	.02
❑ 123 Andre Collins	.10	.05
❑ 124 Earnest Byner	.05	.02
❑ 125 Jim Lachey	.05	.02
❑ 126 Mark Rypien	.10	.05
❑ 127 Charles Mann	.05	.02
❑ 128 Nick Lowery	.05	.02
❑ 129 Chip Lohmiller	.05	.02
❑ 130 Mike Horan	.05	.02
❑ 131 Rohn Stark	.05	.02
❑ 132 Sean Landeta	.05	.02
❑ 133 Clarence Verdin	.05	.02
❑ 134 Johnny Bailey	.05	.02
❑ 135 Herschel Walker	.10	.05
❑ 136 Bo Jackson PP	.30	.14
❑ 137 Dexter Carter PP	.05	.02
❑ 138 Warren Moon PP	.10	.05
❑ 139 Joe Montana PP	1.25	.55
❑ 140 Jerry Rice PP	.75	.35
❑ 141 Deion Sanders PP	.40	.18
❑ 142 Ronnie Lippett PP	.05	.02
❑ 143 Terance Mathis PP	.25	.11
❑ 144 Gaston Green PP	.05	.02
❑ 145 Dean Biasucci PP	.05	.02
❑ 146 Charles Haley PP	.10	.05
❑ 147 Derrick Thomas PP	.25	.11
❑ 148 Lawrence Taylor PP	.10	.05
❑ 149 Art Shell CO PP	.10	.05
❑ 150 Bill Parcells CO PP	.10	.05
❑ 151 Steve Broussard	.05	.02
❑ 152 Darion Conner	.05	.02
❑ 153 Bill Fralic	.05	.02
❑ 154 Mike Gann	.05	.02
❑ 155 Tim McKyer	.05	.02
❑ 156 Don Beebe UER (4 TD's against Dolphins, should be against Steelers)	.05	.02
❑ 157 Cornelius Bennett	.10	.05
❑ 158 Andre Reed	.25	.11
❑ 159 Leonard Smith	.05	.02
❑ 160 Will Wolford	.05	.02
❑ 161 Mark Carrier DB	.10	.05
❑ 162 Wendell Davis	.05	.02
❑ 163 Jay Hilgenberg	.05	.02
❑ 164 Brad Muster	.05	.02
❑ 165 Mike Singletary	.10	.05
❑ 166 Eddie Brown	.05	.02
❑ 167 David Fulcher	.05	.02
❑ 168 Rodney Holman	.05	.02
❑ 169 Anthony Munoz	.10	.05
❑ 170 Craig Taylor RC	.05	.02
❑ 171 Mike Baab	.05	.02
❑ 172 David Grayson	.05	.02
❑ 173 Reggie Langhorne	.05	.02
❑ 174 Joe Morris	.05	.02
❑ 175 Kevin Gogan RC	.05	.02
❑ 176 Jack Del Rio	.05	.02
❑ 177 Issiac Holt	.05	.02
❑ 178 Michael Irvin	.25	.11
❑ 179 Jay Novacek	.25	.11
❑ 180 Steve Atwater	.05	.02
❑ 181 Mark Jackson	.05	.02
❑ 182 Ricky Nattiel	.05	.02
❑ 183 Warren Powers	.05	.02
❑ 184 Dennis Smith	.05	.02
❑ 185 Bennie Blades	.05	.02
❑ 186 Lomas Brown UER (Spent 6 seasons with Detroit, not 7)	.05	.02
❑ 187 Robert Clark UER (Plan B acquisition in '89, not '90)	.05	.02
❑ 188 Mel Gray	.10	.05
❑ 189 Chris Spielman	.10	.05
❑ 190 Johnny Holland	.05	.02
❑ 191 Don Majkowski	.05	.02
❑ 192 Bryce Paup RC	.25	.11
❑ 193 Darrell Thompson	.05	.02
❑ 194 Ed West UER (Photo on back is reversed)	.05	.02
❑ 195 Cris Dishman RC	.10	.05
❑ 196 Drew Hill	.10	.05
❑ 197 Bruce Matthews	.10	.05
❑ 198 Bubba McDowell	.05	.02
❑ 199 Allen Pinkett	.05	.02
❑ 200 Bill Brooks	.10	.05
❑ 201 Jeff Herrod	.05	.02
❑ 202 Anthony Johnson	.10	.05
❑ 203 Mike Prior	.05	.02
❑ 204 John Alt	.05	.02
❑ 205 Stephone Paige	.05	.02
❑ 206 Kevin Ross	.05	.02
❑ 207 Dan Saleaumua	.05	.02
❑ 208 Barry Word	.05	.02
❑ 209 Marcus Allen	.25	.11
❑ 210 Roger Craig	.10	.05
❑ 211 Ronnie Lott	.10	.05
❑ 212 Winston Moss	.05	.02
❑ 213 Jay Schroeder	.05	.02
❑ 214 Robert Delpino	.05	.02
❑ 215 Henry Ellard	.10	.05
❑ 216 Kevin Greene	.25	.11
❑ 217 Tom Newberry	.05	.02
❑ 218 Michael Stewart	.05	.02
❑ 219 Mark Duper	.10	.05
❑ 220 Mark Higgs RC	.05	.02
❑ 221 John Offerdahl UER (2nd round pick in '86, not 6th)	.05	.02
❑ 222 Keith Sims	.05	.02
❑ 223 Anthony Carter	.10	.05
❑ 224 Cris Carter	.50	.23
❑ 225 Steve Jordan	.05	.02
❑ 226 Randall McDaniel	.05	.02
❑ 227 Al Noga	.05	.02
❑ 228 Ray Agnew	.05	.02
❑ 229 Bruce Armstrong	.05	.02
❑ 230 Irving Fryar	.10	.05
❑ 231 Greg McMurtry	.05	.02
❑ 232 Chris Singleton	.05	.02
❑ 233 Morten Andersen	.05	.02
❑ 234 Vince Buck	.05	.02
❑ 235 Gill Fenerty	.05	.02
❑ 236 Rickey Jackson	.10	.05
❑ 237 Vaughan Johnson	.05	.02

❑ 238 Carl Banks .05 .02

❑ 239 Mark Collins .05 .02

❑ 240 Rodney Hampton .25 .11

❑ 241 David Meggett .10 .05

❑ 242 Bart Oates .05 .02

❑ 243 Kyle Clifton .05 .02

❑ 244 Jeff Lageman .10 .05

❑ 245 Freeman McNeil UER .10 .05
(Drafted in '81, not '80)

❑ 246 Rob Moore .25 .11

❑ 247 Eric Allen .05 .02

❑ 248 Keith Byars .10 .05

❑ 249 Keith Jackson .10 .05

❑ 250 Jim McMahon .10 .05

❑ 251 Andre Waters .05 .02

❑ 252 Ken Harvey .10 .05

❑ 253 Ernie Jones .05 .02

❑ 254 Luis Sharpe .05 .02

❑ 255 Anthony Thompson .05 .02

❑ 256 Tom Tupa .05 .02

❑ 257 Eric Green .10 .05

❑ 258 Barry Foster .10 .05

❑ 259 Bryan Hinkle .05 .02

❑ 260 Tunch Ilkin .05 .02

❑ 261 Louis Lipps .05 .02

❑ 262 Gill Byrd .05 .02

❑ 263 John Friesz .10 .05

❑ 264 Anthony Miller .10 .05

❑ 265 Junior Seau .25 .11

❑ 266 Ronnie Harmon .10 .05

❑ 267 Harris Barton .05 .02

❑ 268 Todd Bowles .05 .02

❑ 269 Don Griffin .05 .02

❑ 270 Bill Romanowski .05 .02

❑ 271 Steve Young .75 .35

❑ 272 Brian Blades .10 .05

❑ 273 Jacob Green .05 .02

❑ 274 Rufus Porter .05 .02

❑ 275 Eugene Robinson .05 .02

❑ 276 Mark Carrier WR .10 .05

❑ 277 Reuben Davis .05 .02

❑ 278 Paul Gruber .05 .02

❑ 279 Gary Clark .25 .11

❑ 280 Darrell Green .10 .05

❑ 281 Wilber Marshall .05 .02

❑ 282 Matt Millen .10 .05

❑ 283 Alvin Walton .05 .02

❑ 284 Joe Gibbs CO UER .10 .05
(NFLPA logo on back)

❑ 285 Don Shula CO UER .10 .05
(NFLPA logo on back)

❑ 286 Larry Brown DB RC .10 .05

❑ 287 Mike Croel RC .05 .02

❑ 288 Antone Davis RC .05 .02

❑ 289 Ricky Ervins RC UER .10 .05
(2nd round choice, should say 3rd)

❑ 290 Brett Favre RC 5.00 2.20

❑ 291 Pat Harlow RC .05 .02

❑ 292 Michael Jackson RC .25 .11

❑ 293 Henry Jones RC .10 .05

❑ 294 Aaron Craver RC .05 .02

❑ 295 Nick Bell RC .05 .02

❑ 296 Todd Lyght RC .10 .05

❑ 297 Todd Marinovich RC .05 .02

❑ 298 Russell Maryland RC .10 .05

❑ 299 Kanavis McGhee RC .05 .02

❑ 300 Dan McGwire RC .10 .05

❑ 301 Charles McRae RC .05 .02

❑ 302 Eric Moten RC .05 .02

❑ 303 Jerome Henderson RC .05 .02

❑ 304 Browning Nagle RC .05 .02

❑ 305 Mike Pritchard RC .25 .11

❑ 306 Stanley Richard RC .10 .05

❑ 307 Randal Hill RC .10 .05

❑ 308 Leonard Russell RC .10 .05

❑ 309 Eric Swann RC .10 .05

❑ 310 Phil Hansen RC .05 .02

❑ 311 Moe Gardner RC .05 .02

❑ 312 Jon Vaughn RC .05 .02

❑ 313 Aeneas Williams RC UER .25 .11
(Misspelled Aaneas on card back)

❑ 314 Alfred Williams RC .05 .02

❑ 315 Harvey Williams RC .25 .11

❑ PM1 Emmitt Smith 250.00 110.00
Platinum metal card

❑ PM2 Paul Brown 80.00 36.00
Platinum metal card

1992 Pro Set

	MINT	NRMT
COMPLETE SET (700)	15.00	6.75
COMP.SERIES 1 (400)	8.00	3.60
COMP.SERIES 2 (300)	8.00	3.60

❑ 1 Mike Croel LL .04 .02
Rookie of the Year

❑ 2 Thurman Thomas LL .25 .11
Player of the Year

❑ 3 Wayne Fontes CO LL .04 .02
Coach of the Year

❑ 4 Anthony Munoz LL .10 .05
Man of the Year

❑ 5 Steve Young LL .30 .14
Passing Leader

❑ 6 Warren Moon LL .10 .05
Passing Yardage Leader

❑ 7 Emmitt Smith LL .60 .25
Rushing Leader

❑ 8 Haywood Jeffires LL .04 .02
Receiving Leader

❑ 9 Marv Cook LL .04 .02
Receiving Leader/TE

❑ 10 Michael Irvin LL .25 .11
Receiving Yardage Leader

❑ 11 Thurman Thomas LL UER .25 .11
Total Yardage Leader
(Total combined yards should be 2,038)

❑ 12 Chip Lohmiller LL UER .04 .02
Scoring Leader
(FG Attempt Totals are off by one)

❑ 13 Barry Sanders LL .60 .25
Scoring Leader TD's

❑ 14 Reggie Roby LL .04 .02
Punting Leader

❑ 15 Mel Gray LL .04 .02
Kickoff/Punt Return Leader

❑ 16 Ronnie Lott LL .10 .05
Interception Leader

❑ 17 Pat Swilling LL .04 .02
Sack Leader

❑ 18 Reggie White LL .10 .05
Defensive MVP

❑ 19 Haywood Jeffires MILE .04 .02
100 Receptions

❑ 20 Pat Leahy MILE .04 .02
300 Field Goals

❑ 21 James Lofton MILE .10 .05
13,000 Yards

❑ 22 Art Monk MILE .10 .05
800 Receptions

❑ 23 Don Shula MILE .10 .05
300 Wins

❑ 24A Nick Lowery MILE ERR .04 .02
9th 100-Point Season
(Says he wears 9)

❑ 24B Nick Lowery MILE COR .04 .02
9th 100-Point Season
(Says he wears 8)

❑ 25 John Elway MILE .50 .23
2,000 Completed Passes

❑ 26 Chicago Bears MILE .04 .02
8 Straight Opening Wins

❑ 27 Marcus Allen MILE .10 .05
2,000 Rushing Attempts

❑ 28 Terrell Buckley DD RC .04 .02

❑ 29 Amp Lee DD RC .04 .02

❑ 30 Chris Mims DD RC .10 .05

❑ 31 Leon Searcy DD RC .10 .05

❑ 32 Jimmy Smith DD RC 3.00 1.35

❑ 33 Siran Stacy DD RC .04 .02

❑ 34 Pete Gogolak INN .04 .02

❑ 35 Cheerleaders INN .04 .02

❑ 36 Houston Astrodome INN .04 .02

❑ 37 Week 1 REPLAY .04 .02
Chiefs 14, Falcons 3
(Christian Okoye)

❑ 38 Week 2 REPLAY .04 .02
Bills 52, Steelers 34
(Don Beebe)

❑ 39 Week 3 REPLAY .04 .02
Bears 20, Giants 17
(Wendell Davis)

❑ 40 Week 4 REPLAY .04 .02
Dolphins 16, Packers 13
(Don Shula CO)

❑ 41 Week 5 REPLAY .04 .02
Raiders 12 49ers 6
(Ronnie Lott)

❑ 42 Week 6 REPLAY .04 .02
Redskins 20, Bears 7
(Art Monk)

❑ 43 Week 7 REPLAY .10 .05
Bills 42, Colts 6
(Thurman Thomas)

❑ 44 Week 8 REPLAY .04 .02
Patriots 26 Vikings 23
(John Stephens)

❑ 45 Week 9 REPLAY UER .04 .02
Vikings 28, Cardinals 0
(Herschel Walker; misspelled Hershel on card back)

❑ 46 Week 10 REPLAY .04 .02
Jets 19 Packers 16
(Chris Burkett)

❑ 47 Week 11 REPLAY .04 .02
Colts 28 Jets 27
(Line play)

❑ 48 Week 12 REPLAY .04 .02
Falcons 43 Buccaneers 7
(Andre Rison)

❑ 49 Week 13 REPLAY .04 .02
Cowboys 24 Redskins 21
(Steve Beuerlein and Michael Irvin)

❑ 50 Week 14 REPLAY .04 .02
Broncos 20 Patriots 3
(Irving Fryar)

❑ 51 Week 15 REPLAY .04 .02
Bills 30 Raiders 27
(Bills' Defense)

❑ 52 Week 16 REPLAY .04 .02
Cowboys 25 Eagles 13
(Kelvin Martin)

❑ 53 Week 17 REPLAY .04 .02
Jets 23 Dolphins 20
(Bruce Coslet CO)

❑ 54 AFC Wild Card REPLAY .04 .02
Chiefs 10 Raiders 6
(Fred Jones)

❑ 55 AFC Wild Card REPLAY .04 .02
Oilers 17 Jets 10
(Oilers' Run-and-Shoot)

❑ 56 NFC Wild Card REPLAY .04 .02
Cowboys 17 Bears 13
(Bill Bates)

❑ 57 NFC Wild Card REPLAY .04 .02
Falcons 27 Saints 20
(Michael Haynes)

❑ 58 AFC Playoff REPLAY .04 .02
Broncos 26 Oilers 24
(Bronco interception)

❑ 59 AFC Playoff REPLAY .10 .05

Bills 37 Chiefs 14
(Thurman Thomas)
❑ 60 NFC Playoff REPLAY .04 .02
Lions 38 Cowboys 6
(Eric Kramer)
❑ 61 NFC Playoff REPLAY .04 .02
Redskins 24 Falcons 7
(Darrell Green)
❑ 62 AFC Champ. REPLAY .04 .02
Bills 10 Broncos 7
(Carlton Bailey)
❑ 63 NFC Champ. REPLAY .04 .02
Redskins 41 Lions 10
(Mark Rypien)
❑ 64 Super Bowl XXVI REPLAY .04 .02
TD Reversed, FG Botched
❑ 65 Super Bowl XXVI REPLAY .04 .02
(Brad) Edwards Picks Off
First of Two
❑ 66 Super Bowl XXVI REPLAY .04 .02
Rypien to Byner, 10-0
❑ 67 Super Bowl XXVI REPLAY .04 .02
Riggs Puts Redskins Up 17-10
❑ 68 Super Bowl XXVI REPLAY .04 .02
Gouveia Interception Buries Bills
❑ 69 Super Bowl XXVI REPLAY .10 .05
Thomas Scores Bills' First TD
❑ 70 Super Bowl XXVI REPLAY .04 .02
Clark Catches Rypien's Second TD
❑ 71 Super Bowl XXVI REPLAY .04 .02
Bills Convert Late Break
❑ 72 Super Bowl XXVI REPLAY .04 .02
Redskins Run Out the Clock
❑ 73 Jeff Bostic .04 .02
❑ 74 Earnest Byner .04 .02
❑ 75 Gary Clark .25 .11
❑ 76 Andre Collins .04 .02
❑ 77 Darrell Green .04 .02
❑ 78 Joe Jacoby .04 .02
❑ 79 Jim Lachey .04 .02
❑ 80 Chip Lohmiller .04 .02
❑ 81 Charles Mann .04 .02
❑ 82 Martin Mayhew .04 .02
❑ 83 Matt Millen .10 .05
❑ 84 Brian Mitchell .10 .05
❑ 85 Art Monk .10 .05
❑ 86 Gerald Riggs .04 .02
❑ 87 Mark Rypien .04 .02
❑ 88 Fred Stokes .04 .02
❑ 89 Bobby Wilson .04 .02
❑ 90 Joe Gibbs CO .10 .05
❑ 91 Howard Ballard .04 .02
❑ 92 Cornelius Bennett UER .10 .05
(Interception total reads 0;
he had 4)
❑ 93 Kenneth Davis .04 .02
❑ 94 Al Edwards .04 .02
❑ 95 Kent Hull .04 .02
❑ 96 Kirby Jackson .04 .02
❑ 97 Mark Kelso .04 .02
❑ 98 James Lofton UER .10 .05
(Says he played in '75
Pro Bowl, but he wasn't
in NFL until 1978)
❑ 99 Keith McKeller .04 .02
❑ 100 Nate Odomes .04 .02
❑ 101 Jim Ritcher .04 .02
❑ 102 Leon Seals .04 .02
❑ 103 Steve Tasker .10 .05
❑ 104 Darryl Talley .04 .02
❑ 105 Thurman Thomas .25 .11
❑ 106 Will Wolford .04 .02
❑ 107 Jeff Wright .04 .02
❑ 108 Marv Levy CO .04 .02
❑ 109 Darion Conner .04 .02
❑ 110 Bill Fralic .04 .02
❑ 111 Moe Gardner .04 .02
❑ 112 Michael Haynes .10 .05
❑ 113 Chris Miller .10 .05
❑ 114 Erric Pegram .10 .05
❑ 115 Bruce Pickens .04 .02
❑ 116 Andre Rison .10 .05
❑ 117 Jerry Glanville CO .04 .02
❑ 118 Neal Anderson .04 .02
❑ 119 Trace Armstrong .04 .02
❑ 120 Wendell Davis .04 .02
❑ 121 Richard Dent .10 .05
❑ 122 Jay Hilgenberg .04 .02
❑ 123 Lemuel Stinson .04 .02
❑ 124 Stan Thomas .04 .02
❑ 125 Tom Waddle .04 .02
❑ 126 Mike Ditka CO .25 .11
❑ 127 James Brooks .10 .05
❑ 128 Eddie Brown .04 .02
❑ 129 David Fulcher .04 .02
❑ 130 Harold Green .04 .02
❑ 131 Tim Krumrie UER .04 .02
(Misspelled Krumerie
on card front)
❑ 132 Anthony Munoz .10 .05
❑ 133 Craig Taylor .04 .02
❑ 134 Eric Thomas .04 .02
❑ 135 David Shula CO RC .04 .02
❑ 136 Mike Baab .04 .02
❑ 137 Brian Brennan .04 .02
❑ 138 Michael Jackson .10 .05
❑ 139 James Jones UER .04 .02
(DL on front, DT on back)
❑ 140 Ed King .04 .02
❑ 141 Clay Matthews .10 .05
❑ 142 Eric Metcalf .10 .05
❑ 143 Joe Morris .04 .02
❑ 144A Bill Belichick CO ERR .10 .05
(No HC next to name
on back)
❑ 144B Bill Belichick CO COR .10 .05
(HC next to name
on back)
❑ 145 Steve Beuerlein .04 .02
❑ 146 Larry Brown DB .04 .02
❑ 147 Ray Horton .04 .02
❑ 148 Ken Norton .25 .11
❑ 149 Mike Saxon .04 .02
❑ 150 Emmitt Smith 1.50 .70
❑ 151 Mark Stepnoski .10 .05
❑ 152 Alexander Wright .04 .02
❑ 153 Jimmy Johnson CO .10 .05
❑ 154 Mike Croel .04 .02
❑ 155 John Elway 1.25 .55
❑ 156 Gaston Green UER .04 .02
(Lists 1991 team as
Rams, but was Broncos)
❑ 157 Wymon Henderson .04 .02
❑ 158 Karl Mecklenburg UER .04 .02
(Card back repeats
Super Bowl XXI)
❑ 159 Warren Powers .04 .02
❑ 160 Steve Sewell UER .04 .02
(Card back repeats
Super Bowl XXI)
❑ 161 Doug Widell .04 .02
❑ 162 Dan Reeves CO .04 .02
❑ 163 Eric Andolsek .04 .02
❑ 164 Jerry Ball .04 .02
❑ 165 Bennie Blades .04 .02
❑ 166 Ray Crockett .04 .02
❑ 167 Willie Green UER .04 .02
(Card back repeats
and in last sentence)
❑ 168 Erik Kramer .10 .05
❑ 169 Barry Sanders 1.50 .70
❑ 170 Chris Spielman UER .04 .02
(Card says named to
Pro Bowl 1989-90,
should say 1989-91)
❑ 171 Wayne Fontes CO .04 .02
❑ 172 Vinnie Clark .04 .02
❑ 173 Tony Mandarich .04 .02
❑ 174 Brian Noble .04 .02
❑ 175 Bryce Paup .25 .11
❑ 176 Sterling Sharpe .25 .11
❑ 177 Darrell Thompson .04 .02
❑ 178 Esera Tuaolo UER .04 .02
(Text has 1 TD via
interception, stats do not)
❑ 179 Ed West .04 .02
❑ 180 Mike Holmgren CO RC .25 .11
❑ 181 Ray Childress .04 .02
❑ 182 Cris Dishman .04 .02
❑ 183 Curtis Duncan .04 .02
❑ 184 William Fuller .10 .05
❑ 185 Lamar Lathon .04 .02
❑ 186 Warren Moon .25 .11
❑ 187 Bo Orlando RC .04 .02
❑ 188 Lorenzo White .04 .02
❑ 189 Jack Pardee CO .04 .02
❑ 190 Chip Banks .04 .02
❑ 191 Dean Biasucci UER .04 .02
(PK on front, K on back)
❑ 192 Bill Brooks .04 .02
❑ 193 Ray Donaldson .04 .02
❑ 194 Jeff Herrod .04 .02
❑ 195 Mike Prior .04 .02
❑ 196 Mark Vander Poel .04 .02
❑ 197 Clarence Verdin .04 .02
❑ 198 Ted Marchibroda CO .04 .02
❑ 199 John Alt .04 .02
❑ 200 Deron Cherry .04 .02
❑ 201 Steve DeBerg .04 .02
❑ 202 Nick Lowery .04 .02
❑ 203 Neil Smith .25 .11
❑ 204 Derrick Thomas .25 .11
❑ 205 Joe Valerio .04 .02
❑ 206 Barry Word .04 .02
❑ 207 Marty Schottenheimer CO .04 .02
❑ 208 Marcus Allen .25 .11
❑ 209 Nick Bell .04 .02
❑ 210 Tim Brown .25 .11
❑ 211 Howie Long .10 .05
❑ 212 Ronnie Lott .10 .05
❑ 213 Todd Marinovich .04 .02
❑ 214 Greg Townsend .04 .02
❑ 215 Steve Wright .04 .02
❑ 216 Art Shell CO .10 .05
❑ 217 Flipper Anderson .04 .02
❑ 218 Robert Delpino .04 .02
❑ 219 Henry Ellard .10 .05
❑ 220 Kevin Greene .25 .11
❑ 221 Todd Lyght .04 .02
❑ 222 Tom Newberry .04 .02
❑ 223 Roman Phifer .04 .02
❑ 224 Michael Stewart .04 .02
❑ 225 Chuck Knox CO .04 .02
❑ 226 Aaron Craver .04 .02
❑ 227 Jeff Cross .04 .02
❑ 228 Mark Duper .04 .02
❑ 229 Ferrell Edmunds .04 .02
❑ 230 Jim C. Jensen .04 .02
❑ 231 Louis Oliver UER .04 .02
(Card has 215 tackles,
but he only had 88)
❑ 232 Reggie Roby .04 .02
❑ 233 Sammie Smith .04 .02
❑ 234 Don Shula CO .10 .05
❑ 235 Joey Browner .04 .02
❑ 236 Anthony Carter .10 .05
❑ 237 Chris Doleman .04 .02
❑ 238 Steve Jordan .04 .02
❑ 239 Kirk Lowdermilk .04 .02
❑ 240 Henry Thomas .04 .02
❑ 241 Herschel Walker .10 .05
❑ 242 Felix Wright .04 .02
❑ 243 Dennis Green CO RC .04 .02
❑ 244 Ray Agnew .04 .02
❑ 245 Marv Cook .04 .02
❑ 246 Irving Fryar UER .10 .05
(WR/KR on front,
WR on back)
❑ 247 Pat Harlow .04 .02
❑ 248 Hugh Millen .04 .02
❑ 249 Leonard Russell .10 .05
❑ 250 Andre Tippett .04 .02
❑ 251 Jon Vaughn .04 .02
❑ 252 Dick MacPherson CO .04 .02
❑ 253 Morten Andersen .04 .02
❑ 254 Bobby Hebert .04 .02
❑ 255 Joel Hilgenberg .04 .02
❑ 256 Vaughan Johnson .04 .02
❑ 257 Sam Mills .04 .02
❑ 258 Pat Swilling .10 .05
❑ 259 Floyd Turner .04 .02
❑ 260 Steve Walsh .04 .02
❑ 261 Jim Mora CO UER .04 .02
(No TM by Pro Set logo)
❑ 262 Stephen Baker .04 .02
❑ 263 Mark Collins .04 .02
❑ 264 Rodney Hampton .25 .11
❑ 265 Jeff Hostetler .10 .05

❑ 266 Erik Howard .04 .02
❑ 267 Sean Landeta .04 .02
❑ 268 Gary Reasons UER .04 .02
(Fumble recovery noted on card, but not in stats)
❑ 269 Everson Walls .04 .02
❑ 270 Ray Handley CO .04 .02
❑ 271 Louis Aguiar RC .04 .02
❑ 272 Brad Baxter .04 .02
❑ 273 Chris Burkett .04 .02
❑ 274 Irv Eatman .04 .02
❑ 275 Jeff Lageman .04 .02
❑ 276 Freeman McNeil .04 .02
❑ 277 Rob Moore .10 .05
❑ 278 Lonnie Young .04 .02
❑ 279 Bruce Coslet CO .04 .02
❑ 280 Jerome Brown .04 .02
❑ 281 Keith Byars .04 .02
❑ 282 Bruce Collie UER .04 .02
(No stats on back)
❑ 283 Keith Jackson .10 .05
❑ 284 James Joseph .04 .02
❑ 285 Seth Joyner .10 .05
❑ 286 Andre Waters .04 .02
❑ 287 Reggie White .25 .11
❑ 288 Rich Kotite CO .04 .02
❑ 289 Rich Camarillo .04 .02
❑ 290 Garth Jax .04 .02
❑ 291 Ernie Jones .04 .02
❑ 292 Tim McDonald .04 .02
❑ 293 Rod Saddler .04 .02
❑ 294 Anthony Thompson UER .04 .02
(NO TD stats for 1991 receiving)
❑ 295 Tom Tupa UER .04 .02
(QB/P on front, QB on back)
❑ 296 Ron Wolfley .04 .02
❑ 297 Joe Bugel CO .04 .02
❑ 298 Gary Anderson K .04 .02
❑ 299 Jeff Graham .25 .11
❑ 300 Eric Green .04 .02
❑ 301 Bryan Hinkle .04 .02
❑ 302 Tunch Ilkin .04 .02
❑ 303 Louis Lipps .04 .02
❑ 304 Neil O'Donnell .25 .11
❑ 305 Rod Woodson .25 .11
❑ 306 Bill Cowher CO RC .10 .05
❑ 307 Eric Bieniemy .04 .02
❑ 308 Marion Butts .04 .02
❑ 309 John Friesz .10 .05
❑ 310 Courtney Hall .04 .02
❑ 311 Ronnie Harmon .04 .02
❑ 312 Henry Rolling .04 .02
❑ 313 Billy Ray Smith .04 .02
❑ 314 George Thornton .04 .02
❑ 315 Bobby Ross CO RC .04 .02
❑ 316 Todd Bowles .04 .02
❑ 317 Michael Carter .04 .02
❑ 318 Don Griffin .04 .02
❑ 319 Charles Haley .10 .05
❑ 320 Brent Jones .10 .05
❑ 321 John Taylor .10 .05
❑ 322 Ted Washington .04 .02
❑ 323 Steve Young .60 .25
❑ 324 George Seifert CO .10 .05
❑ 325 Brian Blades .10 .05
❑ 326 Jacob Green .04 .02
❑ 327 Patrick Hunter .04 .02
❑ 328 Tommy Kane .04 .02
❑ 329 Cortez Kennedy .10 .05
❑ 330 Dave Krieg .10 .05
❑ 331 Rufus Porter .04 .02
❑ 332 John L. Williams .04 .02
❑ 333 Tom Flores CO .04 .02
❑ 334 Gary Anderson RB .04 .02
❑ 335 Mark Carrier WR .10 .05
❑ 336 Reuben Davis .04 .02
❑ 337 Lawrence Dawsey .10 .05
❑ 338 Keith McCants UER .04 .02
(LB on front, DE on back)
❑ 339 Vinny Testaverde .10 .05
❑ 340 Broderick Thomas .04 .02
❑ 341 Robert Wilson .04 .02
❑ 342 Sam Wyche CO .04 .02
❑ 343 1991 Teacher of .04 .02
the Year NEWS
❑ 344 Owners Reject Instant .04 .02
Replay NEWS
❑ 345 NFL Experience .04 .02
Unveiled NEWS
❑ 346 Chuck Noll Retires .10 .05
Tosses Coin NEWS
❑ 347 Isaac Curtis .04 .02
and Tim McGee MN UER
(Birthdates switched)
❑ 348 Drew Pearson .10 .05
Michael Irvin MN
❑ 349 Billy Sims .50 .23
Barry Sanders MN
❑ 350 Ken Stabler .04 .02
Todd Marinovich MN
❑ 351 Craig James .10 .05
Leonard Russell MN
❑ 352 Bob Golic .04 .02
Graffiti
It's a Sign of
Ignorance
❑ 353 Pat Harlow .04 .02
Vote, Let
Your Choice Be Heard
❑ 354 Esera Tuaolo .04 .02
Stand Tall, Be Proud
of Your Heritage
❑ 355 Mark Schlereth RC .04 .02
Save The Environment
Be a Team Player
❑ 356 Trace Armstrong .04 .02
Drug Abuse
Stay in Control
❑ 357 Eric Bieniemy .04 .02
Save a Life
Buckle Up
❑ 358 Bill Romanowski .04 .02
Education
Stay In School
❑ 359 Irv Eatman .04 .02
Exercise
Be Active
❑ 360 Jonathan Hayes .04 .02
Diabetes
Be Your Best
❑ 361 Atlanta Falcons .04 .02
Spirit of the Game
(Helmet)
❑ 362 Chicago Bears .04 .02
Spirit of the Game
(Vintage game photo)
❑ 363 Dallas Cowboys .04 .02
Spirit of the Game
(Mascot)
❑ 364 Detroit Lions .04 .02
Spirit of the Game
(Overhead game photo)
❑ 365 Green Bay Packers .04 .02
Spirit of the Game
(60's huddle)
❑ 366 Los Angeles Rams .04 .02
Spirit of the Game
(Fans)
❑ 367 Minnesota Vikings .04 .02
Spirit of the Game
(Vintage game photo)
❑ 368 New Orleans Saints UER .04 .02
Spirit of the Game
(Fans; Post-season record was 0-3, not 0-2)
❑ 369 New York Giants .04 .02
Spirit of the Game
(Fan's banner)
❑ 370 Philadelphia Eagles .04 .02
Spirit of the Game
(Eric Allen)
❑ 371 Phoenix Cardinals .04 .02
Spirit of the Game
(Fan)
❑ 372 San Francisco 49ers .04 .02
Spirit of the Game
(Tom Rathman)
❑ 373 Tampa Bay Buccaneers .04 .02
Spirit of the Game
(Mascot)
❑ 374 Washington Redskins .04 .02
Spirit of the Game
(Fans)
❑ 375 Steve Atwater PB UER .04 .02
(Photo shows regular game instead of Pro Bowl)
❑ 376 Cornelius Bennett PB .10 .05
❑ 377 Tim Brown PB .10 .05
❑ 378 Marion Butts PB .04 .02
❑ 379 Ray Childress PB .04 .02
(Photo shows regular game instead of Pro Bowl)
❑ 380 Mark Clayton PB .04 .02
❑ 381 Marv Cook PB .04 .02
❑ 382 Cris Dishman PB .04 .02
❑ 383 William Fuller PB .04 .02
❑ 384 Gaston Green PB .04 .02
❑ 385 Jeff Jaeger PB .04 .02
❑ 386 Haywood Jeffires PB .10 .05
❑ 387 James Lofton PB .10 .05
❑ 388 Ronnie Lott PB .10 .05
❑ 389 K.Mecklenburg PB UER .04 .02
(Back and front read ...berg)
❑ 390 Warren Moon PB .10 .05
❑ 391 Anthony Munoz PB .04 .02
❑ 392 Dennis Smith PB .04 .02
❑ 393 Neil Smith PB .10 .05
❑ 394 Darryl Talley PB .04 .02
❑ 395 Derrick Thomas PB .10 .05
❑ 396 Thurman Thomas PB .10 .05
❑ 397 Greg Townsend PB .04 .02
❑ 398 Richmond Webb PB .04 .02
❑ 399 Rod Woodson PB .10 .05
❑ 400 Dan Reeves CO PB .04 .02
❑ 401 Troy Aikman PB .40 .18
❑ 402 Eric Allen PB .04 .02
❑ 403 Bennie Blades PB .04 .02
❑ 404 Lomas Brown PB .04 .02
❑ 405 Mark Carrier DB PB .04 .02
❑ 406 Gary Clark PB .10 .05
❑ 407 Mel Gray PB .04 .02
❑ 408 Darrell Green PB .04 .02
❑ 409 Michael Irvin PB .25 .11
❑ 410 Vaughan Johnson PB .04 .02
❑ 411 Seth Joyner PB .04 .02
❑ 412 Jim Lachey PB .04 .02
❑ 413 Chip Lohmiller PB .04 .02
❑ 414 Charles Mann PB .04 .02
❑ 415 Chris Miller PB .10 .05
❑ 416 Sam Mills PB .04 .02
❑ 417 Bart Oates PB .04 .02
❑ 418 Jerry Rice PB .40 .18
❑ 419 Andre Rison PB .10 .05
❑ 420 Mark Rypien PB .04 .02
❑ 421 Barry Sanders PB .60 .25
❑ 422 Deion Sanders PB .25 .11
❑ 423 Mark Schlereth PB .04 .02
❑ 424 Mike Singletary PB .04 .02
❑ 425 Emmitt Smith PB .60 .25
❑ 426 Pat Swilling PB .04 .02
❑ 427 Reggie White PB .10 .05
❑ 428 Rick Bryan .04 .02
❑ 429 Tim Green .04 .02
❑ 430 Drew Hill .04 .02
❑ 431 Norm Johnson .04 .02
❑ 432 Keith Jones .04 .02
❑ 433 Mike Pritchard .10 .05
❑ 434 Deion Sanders .50 .23
❑ 435 Tony Smith RC .04 .02
❑ 436 Jessie Tuggle .04 .02
❑ 437 Steve Christie .04 .02
❑ 438 Shane Conlan .04 .02
❑ 439 Matt Darby RC .04 .02
❑ 440 John Fina RC .04 .02
❑ 441 Henry Jones .04 .02
❑ 442 Jim Kelly .25 .11
❑ 443 Pete Metzelaars .04 .02
❑ 444 Andre Reed .10 .05
❑ 445 Bruce Smith .25 .11
❑ 446 Troy Auzenne RC .04 .02
❑ 447 Mark Carrier DB .04 .02
❑ 448 Will Furrer RC .04 .02
❑ 449 Jim Harbaugh .25 .11
❑ 450 Brad Muster .04 .02
❑ 451 Darren Lewis .04 .02
❑ 452 Mike Singletary .10 .05

	No.	Player		
❑	453	Alonzo Spellman RC	.10	.05
❑	454	Chris Zorich	.10	.05
❑	455	Jim Breech	.04	.02
❑	456	Boomer Esiason	.10	.05
❑	457	Derrick Fenner	.04	.02
❑	458	James Francis	.04	.02
❑	459	David Klingler RC	.10	.05
❑	460	Tim McGee	.04	.02
❑	461	Carl Pickens RC	.60	.25
❑	462	Alfred Williams	.04	.02
❑	463	Darryl Williams RC	.04	.02
❑	464	Mark Bavaro	.04	.02
❑	465	Jay Hilgenberg	.04	.02
❑	466	Leroy Hoard	.10	.05
❑	467	Bernie Kosar	.10	.05
❑	468	Michael Dean Perry	.10	.05
❑	469	Todd Philcox RC	.04	.02
❑	470	Patrick Rowe RC	.04	.02
❑	471	Tommy Vardell RC	.10	.05
❑	472	Everson Walls	.04	.02
❑	473	Troy Aikman	.75	.35
❑	474	Kenneth Gant RC	.04	.02
❑	475	Charles Haley	.10	.05
❑	476	Michael Irvin	.25	.11
❑	477	Robert Jones RC	.04	.02
❑	478	Russell Maryland	.10	.05
❑	479	Jay Novacek	.10	.05
❑	480	Kevin Smith RC	.25	.11
❑	481	Tony Tolbert	.04	.02
❑	482	Steve Atwater	.04	.02
❑	483	Shane Dronett RC	.04	.02
❑	484	Simon Fletcher	.04	.02
❑	485	Greg Lewis	.04	.02
❑	486	Tommy Maddox RC	.04	.02
❑	487	Shannon Sharpe	.25	.11
❑	488	Dennis Smith	.04	.02
❑	489	Sammie Smith	.04	.02
❑	490	Kenny Walker	.04	.02
❑	491	Lomas Brown	.04	.02
❑	492	Mike Farr	.04	.02
❑	493	Mel Gray	.10	.05
❑	494	Jason Hanson RC	.10	.05
❑	495	Herman Moore	.50	.23
❑	496	Rodney Peete	.10	.05
❑	497	Robert Porcher RC	.10	.05
❑	498	Kelvin Pritchett	.04	.02
❑	499	Andre Ware	.04	.02
❑	500	Sanjay Beach RC	.04	.02
❑	501	Edgar Bennett RC	.25	.11
❑	502	Lewis Billups	.04	.02
❑	503	Terrell Buckley	.04	.02
❑	504	Ty Detmer	.25	.11
❑	505	Brett Favre	2.50	1.10
❑	506	Johnny Holland	.04	.02
❑	507	Dexter McNabb RC	.04	.02
❑	508	Vince Workman	.10	.05
❑	509	Cody Carlson	.04	.02
❑	510	Ernest Givins	.10	.05
❑	511	Jerry Gray	.04	.02
❑	512	Haywood Jeffires	.10	.05
❑	513	Bruce Matthews	.04	.02
❑	514	Bubba McDowell	.04	.02
❑	515	Bucky Richardson RC	.04	.02
❑	516	Webster Slaughter	.04	.02
❑	517	Al Smith	.04	.02
❑	518	Mel Agee	.04	.02
❑	519	Ashley Ambrose RC	.10	.05
❑	520	Kevin Call	.04	.02
❑	521	Ken Clark	.04	.02
❑	522	Quentin Coryatt RC	.25	.11
❑	523	Steve Emtman RC	.04	.02
❑	524	Jeff George	.25	.11
❑	525	Jessie Hester	.04	.02
❑	526	Anthony Johnson	.10	.05
❑	527	Tim Barnett	.04	.02
❑	528	Martin Bayless	.04	.02
❑	529	J.J. Birden	.04	.02
❑	530	Dale Carter RC	.25	.11
❑	531	Dave Krieg	.10	.05
❑	532	Albert Lewis	.04	.02
❑	533	Nick Lowery	.04	.02
❑	534	Christian Okoye	.04	.02
❑	535	Harvey Williams	.25	.11
❑	536	Aundray Bruce	.04	.02
❑	537	Eric Dickerson	.10	.05
❑	538	Willie Gault	.10	.05
❑	539	Ethan Horton	.04	.02
❑	540	Jeff Jaeger	.04	.02
❑	541	Napoleon McCallum	.04	.02
❑	542	Chester McGlockton RC	.25	.11
❑	543	Steve Smith	.04	.02
❑	544	Steve Wisniewski	.04	.02
❑	545	Marc Boutte RC	.04	.02
❑	546	Pat Carter	.04	.02
❑	547	Jim Everett	.10	.05
❑	548	Cleveland Gary	.04	.02
❑	549	Sean Gilbert RC	.25	.11
❑	550	Steve Israel RC	.04	.02
❑	551	Todd Kinchen RC	.04	.02
❑	552	Jackie Slater	.04	.02
❑	553	Tony Zendejas	.04	.02
❑	554	Robert Clark	.04	.02
❑	555	Mark Clayton	.10	.05
❑	556	Marco Coleman RC	.10	.05
❑	557	Bryan Cox	.10	.05
❑	558	Keith Jackson UER (Card says drafted in '88, but acquired as free agent in '92)	.10	.05
❑	559	Dan Marino	1.25	.55
❑	560	John Offerdahl	.04	.02
❑	561	Troy Vincent RC	.10	.05
❑	562	Richmond Webb	.04	.02
❑	563	Terry Allen	.25	.11
❑	564	Cris Carter	.50	.23
❑	565	Roger Craig	.10	.05
❑	566	Rich Gannon	.25	.11
❑	567	Hassan Jones	.04	.02
❑	568	Randall McDaniel	.04	.02
❑	569	Al Noga	.04	.02
❑	570	Todd Scott	.04	.02
❑	571	Van Waiters RC	.04	.02
❑	572	Bruce Armstrong	.04	.02
❑	573	Gene Chilton RC	.04	.02
❑	574	Eugene Chung RC	.04	.02
❑	575	Todd Collins RC	.04	.02
❑	576	Hart Lee Dykes	.04	.02
❑	577	David Howard RC	.04	.02
❑	578	Eugene Lockhart	.04	.02
❑	579	Greg McMurtry	.04	.02
❑	580	Rod Smith DB RC	.04	.02
❑	581	Gene Atkins	.04	.02
❑	582	Vince Buck	.04	.02
❑	583	Wesley Carroll	.04	.02
❑	584	Jim Dombrowski	.04	.02
❑	585	Vaughn Dunbar RC	.04	.02
❑	586	Craig Heyward	.10	.05
❑	587	Dalton Hilliard	.04	.02
❑	588	Wayne Martin	.04	.02
❑	589	Renaldo Turnbull	.04	.02
❑	590	Carl Banks	.04	.02
❑	591	Derek Brown TE RC	.04	.02
❑	592	Jarrod Bunch	.04	.02
❑	593	Mark Ingram	.04	.02
❑	594	Ed McCaffrey	.30	.14
❑	595	Phil Simms	.10	.05
❑	596	Phillippi Sparks RC	.04	.02
❑	597	Lawrence Taylor	.25	.11
❑	598	Lewis Tillman	.04	.02
❑	599	Kyle Clifton	.04	.02
❑	600	Mo Lewis	.04	.02
❑	601	Terance Mathis	.10	.05
❑	602	Scott Mersereau	.04	.02
❑	603	Johnny Mitchell RC	.04	.02
❑	604	Browning Nagle	.04	.02
❑	605	Ken O'Brien	.04	.02
❑	606	Al Toon	.10	.05
❑	607	Marvin Washington	.04	.02
❑	608	Eric Allen	.04	.02
❑	609	Fred Barnett	.25	.11
❑	610	John Booty	.04	.02
❑	611	Randall Cunningham	.25	.11
❑	612	Rich Miano	.04	.02
❑	613	Clyde Simmons	.04	.02
❑	614	Siran Stacy	.04	.02
❑	615	Herschel Walker	.10	.05
❑	616	Calvin Williams	.10	.05
❑	617	Chris Chandler	.25	.11
❑	618	Randal Hill	.04	.02
❑	619	Johnny Johnson	.04	.02
❑	620	Lorenzo Lynch	.04	.02
❑	621	Robert Massey	.04	.02
❑	622	Ricky Proehl	.04	.02
❑	623	Timm Rosenbach	.04	.02
❑	624	Tony Sacca RC	.04	.02
❑	625	Aeneas Williams UER (Name misspelled Aaneas)	.10	.05
❑	626	Bubby Brister	.04	.02
❑	627	Barry Foster	.10	.05
❑	628	Merril Hoge	.04	.02
❑	629	D.J. Johnson	.04	.02
❑	630	David Little	.04	.02
❑	631	Greg Lloyd	.25	.11
❑	632	Ernie Mills	.04	.02
❑	633	Leon Searcy RC	.10	.05
❑	634	Dwight Stone	.04	.02
❑	635	Sam Anno RC	.04	.02
❑	636	Burt Grossman	.04	.02
❑	637	Stan Humphries	.25	.11
❑	638	Nate Lewis	.04	.02
❑	639	Anthony Miller	.10	.05
❑	640	Chris Mims	.25	.11
❑	641	Marquez Pope RC	.04	.02
❑	642	Stanley Richard	.04	.02
❑	643	Junior Seau	.25	.11
❑	644	Brian Bollinger RC	.04	.02
❑	645	Steve Bono RC	.25	.11
❑	646	Dexter Carter	.04	.02
❑	647	Dana Hall RC	.10	.05
❑	648	Amp Lee	.04	.02
❑	649	Joe Montana	1.25	.55
❑	650	Tom Rathman	.04	.02
❑	651	Jerry Rice	.75	.35
❑	652	Ricky Watters	.25	.11
❑	653	Robert Blackmon	.04	.02
❑	654	John Kasay	.04	.02
❑	655	Ronnie Lee RC	.04	.02
❑	656	Dan McGwire	.04	.02
❑	657	Ray Roberts RC	.04	.02
❑	658	Kelly Stouffer	.04	.02
❑	659	Chris Warren	.25	.11
❑	660	Tony Woods	.04	.02
❑	661	David Wyman	.04	.02
❑	662	Reggie Cobb	.04	.02
❑	663A	Steve DeBerg ERR (Career yardage 1455; found in foil packs)	.10	.05
❑	663B	Steve DeBerg COR (Career yardage 31,455; found in jumbo packs)	.10	.05
❑	664	Santana Dotson RC	.25	.11
❑	665	Willie Drewery	.04	.02
❑	666	Paul Gruber	.04	.02
❑	667	Ron Hall	.04	.02
❑	668	Courtney Hawkins RC	.10	.05
❑	669	Charles McRae	.04	.02
❑	670	Ricky Reynolds	.04	.02
❑	671	Monte Coleman	.04	.02
❑	672	Brad Edwards	.04	.02
❑	673	Jumpy Geathers UER (Card says played in New Orleans in '89; should say Washington)	.04	.02
❑	674	Kelly Goodburn	.04	.02
❑	675	Kurt Gouveia	.04	.02
❑	676	Chris Hakel RC	.04	.02
❑	677	Wilber Marshall	.04	.02
❑	678	Ricky Sanders	.04	.02
❑	679	Mark Schlereth	.04	.02
❑	680	Buffalo Bills Spirit of the Game Rich Stadium	.04	.02
❑	681	Cincinnati Bengals Spirit of the Game Boomer Esiason (with tiger cub)	.04	.02
❑	682	Cleveland Browns Spirit of the Game The Dog Pound	.04	.02
❑	683	Denver Broncos Spirit of the Game Bronco Statue	.04	.02
❑	684	Houston Oilers Spirit of the Game "Luv Ya Blue"	.04	.02
❑	685	Indianapolis Colts Spirit of the Game	.04	.02

Hoosier Dome
❑ 686 Kansas City Chiefs .... .04 .02
Spirit of the Game
Mack Lee Hill Award
Mack Lee Hill
Tracy Simien
❑ 687 Los Angeles Raiders...... .04 .02
Spirit of the Game
The Team of the Decades
❑ 688 Miami Dolphins .... .04 .02
Spirit of the Game
Dolphins' helmet
❑ 689 New England Patriots .... .04 .02
Spirit of the Game
Francis J. Kilroy VP
❑ 690 New York Jets............... .04 .02
Spirit of the Game
Team mascot
❑ 691 Pittsburgh Steelers .... .04 .02
Spirit of the Game
Steelers' helmet
❑ 692 San Diego Chargers ...... .04 .02
Spirit of the Game
Charger in parachute
❑ 693 Seattle Seahawks .... .04 .02
Spirit of the Game
Kingdome
❑ 694 Play Smart..................... .04 .02
Stephen Baker
❑ 695 H.Williams Jr. NEWS RC .04 .02
❑ 696 3 Brothers in NFL NEWS .04 .02
Brian Baldinger
Gary Baldinger
Rich Baldinger
❑ 697 Japan Bowl NEWS .... .04 .02
August 2, 1992
❑ 698 Georgia Dome NEWS.... .04 .02
❑ 699 Theme Art NEWS .... .04 .02
Super Bowl XXVII
❑ 700 Mark Rypien NEWS ...... .04 .02
Super Bowl XXVI MVP
❑ AU150 Emmitt Smith AU 200.00 90.00
(Certified autograph)
❑ AU168 Erik Kramer AU 50.00 22.00
(Certified autograph)
❑ NNO Emmitt Smith................ .75 .35
Power Preview Card
❑ NNO Santa Claus................. .50 .23
Spirit of the Season
❑ SC5 Super Bowl XXVI .... .30 .14
Logo card
❑ P1 Cover Card Promo .... 1.00 .45
Hologram, numbered of 2000

1993 Pro Set

	MINT	NRMT
COMPLETE SET (449)	12.00	5.50

❑ 1 Marco Coleman................. .05 .02
Rookie of the Year
❑ 2 Steve Young .... .30 .14
Player of the Year
❑ 3 Mike Holmgren .... .10 .05
Coach of the Year
❑ 4 John Elway .... .75 .35
Man of the Year
❑ 5 Steve Young .... .30 .14
Passing Leader
❑ 6 Dan Marino .... .75 .35
Passing Yardage
❑ 7 Emmitt Smith..................... .75 .35
Rushing Leader
❑ 8 Sterling Sharpe .... .10 .05
Receiving Leader
❑ 9 Jay Novacek .... .10 .05
Receiving TE
❑ 10 Sterling Sharpe .... .10 .05
Receiving Yardage
❑ 11 Thurman Thomas .... .10 .05
Total Yardage
❑ 12 Pete Stoyanovich .... .05 .02
Scoring Leader
❑ 13 Greg Montgomery........... .05 .02
Punting Leader
❑ 14 Johnny Bailey .... .05 .02
Punt Return
❑ 15 Jon Vaughn...................... .05 .02
Kickoff Return
❑ 16 Audray McMillian............. .05 .02
Henry Jones UER
Interception
(Name spelled McMillan on back)
❑ 17 Clyde Simmons............... .05 .02
Sack Leader
❑ 18 Cortez Kennedy .... .05 .02
Defensive MVP
❑ 19 AFC Wildcard .... .05 .02
(Stan Humphries)
❑ 20 AFC Wildcard .... .05 .02
(Don Beebe)
❑ 21 NFC Wildcard .... .05 .02
(Eric Allen)
❑ 22 NFC Wildcard .... .05 .02
(Brian Mitchell)
❑ 23 AFC Divisional................. .05 .02
(Frank Reich)
❑ 24 AFC Divisional................. .75 .35
(Dan Marino)
❑ 25 NFC Divisional .... .50 .23
(Troy Aikman)
❑ 26 NFC Divisional .... .10 .05
(Ricky Watters)
❑ 27 AFC Championship......... .05 .02
(Bruce Smith sacking
(Dan Marino)
❑ 28 NFC Championship......... .05 .02
(Tony Casillas sacking
(Steve Young)
❑ 29 Super Bowl XXVIII Logo .. .05 .02
❑ 30 Troy Aikman .... .75 .35
❑ 31 Thomas Everett............... .05 .02
❑ 32 Charles Haley .... .10 .05
❑ 33 Alvin Harper .... .10 .05
❑ 34 Michael Irvin .... .25 .11
❑ 35 Robert Jones................... .05 .02
❑ 36 Russell Maryland............. .05 .02
❑ 37 Ken Norton .... .10 .05
❑ 38 Jay Novacek .... .10 .05
❑ 39 Emmitt Smith................ 1.50 .70
❑ 40 Darrin Smith RC .... .10 .05
❑ 41 Mark Stepnoski .... .05 .02
❑ 42 Kevin Williams RC........... .25 .11
❑ 43 Daryl Johnston .... .25 .11
❑ 44 Derrick Lassic RC .... .05 .02
❑ 45 Don Beebe .... .05 .02
❑ 46 Cornelius Bennett .... .10 .05
❑ 47 Bill Brooks....................... .05 .02
❑ 48 Kenneth Davis................. .05 .02
❑ 49 Jim Kelly .... .25 .11
❑ 50 Andre Reed..................... .10 .05
❑ 51 Bruce Smith..................... .25 .11
❑ 52 Thomas Smith RC........... .10 .05
❑ 53 Darryl Talley .... .05 .02
❑ 54 Thurman Thomas .... .25 .11
❑ 55 Russell Copeland RC ...... .10 .05
❑ 56 Steve Christie .... .05 .02
❑ 57 Pete Metzelaars .... .05 .02
❑ 58 Frank Reich..................... .10 .05
❑ 59 Henry Jones .... .05 .02
❑ 60 Vinnie Clark..................... .05 .02
❑ 61 Eric Dickerson................. .10 .05
❑ 62 Jumpy Geathers .... .05 .02
❑ 63 Roger Harper RC .... .05 .02
❑ 64 Michael Haynes................ .10 .05
❑ 65 Bobby Hebert .... .05 .02
❑ 66 Lincoln Kennedy RC .... .05 .02
❑ 67 Chris Miller .... .10 .05
❑ 68 Andre Rison .... .10 .05
❑ 69 Deion Sanders .... .50 .23
❑ 70 Jessie Tuggle .... .05 .02
❑ 71 Ron George..................... .05 .02
❑ 72 Erric Pegram.................... .10 .05
❑ 73 Melvin Jenkins................. .05 .02
❑ 74 Pierce Holt....................... .05 .02
❑ 75 Neal Anderson .... .05 .02
❑ 76 Mark Carrier DB .... .05 .02
❑ 77 Curtis Conway RC........... .40 .18
❑ 78 Richard Dent................... .10 .05
❑ 79 Jim Harbaugh .... .25 .11
❑ 80 Craig Heyward .... .10 .05
❑ 81 Darren Lewis................... .05 .02
❑ 82 Alonzo Spellman .... .05 .02
❑ 83 Tom Waddle .... .05 .02
❑ 84 Wendell Davis .... .05 .02
❑ 85 Chris Zorich..................... .05 .02
❑ 86 Carl Simpson RC .... .05 .02
❑ 87 Chris Gedney RC .... .05 .02
❑ 88 Trace Armstrong .... .05 .02
❑ 89 Peter Tom Willis .... .05 .02
❑ 90 John Copeland RC .... .10 .05
❑ 91 Derrick Fenner .... .05 .02
❑ 92 James Francis................. .05 .02
❑ 93 Harold Green................... .05 .02
❑ 94 David Klingler .... .05 .02
❑ 95 Tim Krumrie..................... .05 .02
❑ 96 Tony McGee RC .... .10 .05
❑ 97 Carl Pickens .... .25 .11
❑ 98 Alfred Williams .... .05 .02
❑ 99 Doug Pelfrey RC .... .05 .02
❑ 100 Lance Gunn RC .... .05 .02
❑ 101 Jay Schroeder............... .05 .02
❑ 102 Steve Tovar RC............. .05 .02
❑ 103 Jeff Query .... .05 .02
❑ 104 Ty Parten RC .... .05 .02
❑ 105 Jerry Ball .... .05 .02
❑ 106 Mark Carrier WR .... .10 .05
❑ 107 Rob Burnett................... .05 .02
❑ 108 Michael Jackson .... .10 .05
❑ 109 Mike Johnson .... .05 .02
❑ 110 Bernie Kosar .... .10 .05
❑ 111 Clay Matthews............... .10 .05
❑ 112 Eric Metcalf .... .10 .05
❑ 113 Michael Dean Perry....... .10 .05
❑ 114 Vinny Testaverde .... .10 .05
❑ 115 Eric Turner .... .05 .02
❑ 116 Tommy Vardell .... .05 .02
❑ 117 Leroy Hoard .... .10 .05
❑ 118 Steve Everitt RC .... .05 .02
❑ 119 Everson Walls .... .05 .02
❑ 120 Steve Atwater .... .05 .02
❑ 121 Rod Bernstine .... .05 .02
❑ 122 Mike Croel..................... .05 .02
❑ 123 John Elway .... 1.50 .70
❑ 124 Simon Fletcher .... .05 .02
❑ 125 Glyn Milburn RC .... .25 .11
❑ 126 Reggie Rivers RC .... .05 .02
❑ 127 Shannon Sharpe .... .25 .11
❑ 128 Dennis Smith................. .05 .02
❑ 129 Dan Williams RC .... .05 .02
❑ 130 Rondell Jones RC .... .05 .02
❑ 131 Jason Elam RC .... .10 .05
❑ 132 Arthur Marshall RC .... .05 .02
❑ 133 Gary Zimmerman .... .05 .02
❑ 134 Karl Mecklenburg .... .05 .02
❑ 135 Bennie Blades............... .05 .02
❑ 136 Lomas Brown .... .05 .02
❑ 137 Bill Fralic .... .05 .02
❑ 138 Mel Gray .... .10 .05
❑ 139 Willie Green................... .05 .02
❑ 140 Ryan McNeil RC .... .05 .02
❑ 141 Rodney Peete .... .05 .02
❑ 142 Barry Sanders .... 1.50 .70
❑ 143 Chris Spielman .... .10 .05
❑ 144 Pat Swilling .... .05 .02
❑ 145 Andre Ware.................... .05 .02
❑ 146 Herman Moore .... .50 .23
❑ 147 Tim McKyer.................... .05 .02
❑ 148 Brett Perriman............... .25 .11
❑ 149 Antonio London RC....... .05 .02

❑ 150 Edgar Bennett .25 .11
❑ 151 Terrell Buckley .05 .02
❑ 152 Brett Favre 2.00 .90
❑ 153 Jackie Harris .05 .02
❑ 154 Johnny Holland .05 .02
❑ 155 Sterling Sharpe .25 .11
❑ 156 Tim Hauck .05 .02
❑ 157 George Teague RC .10 .05
❑ 158 Reggie White .25 .11
❑ 159 Mark Clayton .05 .02
❑ 160 Ty Detmer .25 .11
❑ 161 Wayne Simmons RC .05 .02
❑ 162 Mark Brunell RC 2.50 1.10
❑ 163 Tony Bennett .05 .02
❑ 164 Brian Noble .05 .02
❑ 165 Cody Carlson .05 .02
❑ 166 Ray Childress .05 .02
❑ 167 Cris Dishman .05 .02
❑ 168 Curtis Duncan .05 .02
❑ 169 Brad Hopkins RC .05 .02
❑ 170 Haywood Jeffires .10 .05
❑ 171 Wilber Marshall .05 .02
❑ 172 Micheal Barrow RC UER .10 .05
(Name spelled Michael on both sided)
❑ 173 Bubba McDowell .05 .02
❑ 174 Warren Moon .25 .11
❑ 175 Webster Slaughter .05 .02
❑ 176 Travis Hannah RC .05 .02
❑ 177 Lorenzo White .05 .02
❑ 178 Ernest Givins UER .10 .05
(Name spelled Givens on front)
❑ 179 Keith McCants .05 .02
❑ 180 Kerry Cash .05 .02
❑ 181 Quentin Coryatt .10 .05
❑ 182 Kirk Lowdermilk .05 .02
❑ 183 Rodney Culver .05 .02
❑ 184 Rohn Stark .05 .02
❑ 185 Steve Emtman .05 .02
❑ 186 Jeff George .25 .11
❑ 187 Jeff Herrod .05 .02
❑ 188 Reggie Langhorne .05 .02
❑ 189 Roosevelt Potts RC .05 .02
❑ 190 Jack Trudeau .05 .02
❑ 191 Will Wolford .05 .02
❑ 192 Jessie Hester .05 .02
❑ 193 Anthony Johnson .10 .05
❑ 194 Ray Buchanan RC .05 .02
❑ 195 Dale Carter .05 .02
❑ 196 Willie Davis .25 .11
❑ 197 John Alt .05 .02
❑ 198 Joe Montana 1.50 .70
❑ 199 Will Shields RC .05 .02
❑ 200 Neil Smith .25 .11
❑ 201 Derrick Thomas .25 .11
❑ 202 Harvey Williams .10 .05
❑ 203 Marcus Allen .25 .11
❑ 204 J.J. Birden .05 .02
❑ 205 Tim Barnett .05 .02
❑ 206 Albert Lewis .05 .02
❑ 207 Nick Lowery .05 .02
❑ 208 Dave Krieg .10 .05
❑ 209 Keith Cash .05 .02
❑ 210 Patrick Bates RC .05 .02
❑ 211 Nick Bell .05 .02
❑ 212 Tim Brown .25 .11
❑ 213 Willie Gault .05 .02
❑ 214 Ethan Horton .05 .02
❑ 215 Jeff Hostetler .10 .05
❑ 216 Howie Long .10 .05
❑ 217 Greg Townsend .05 .02
❑ 218 Raghib Ismail .10 .05
❑ 219 Alexander Wright .05 .02
❑ 220 Greg Robinson RC .05 .02
❑ 221 Billy Joe Hobert RC .25 .11
❑ 222 Steve Wisniewski .05 .02
❑ 223 Steve Smith .05 .02
❑ 224 Vince Evans .05 .02
❑ 225 Flipper Anderson .05 .02
❑ 226 Jerome Bettis RC .75 .35
❑ 227 Troy Drayton RC .10 .05
❑ 228 Henry Ellard .10 .05
❑ 229 Jim Everett .10 .05
❑ 230 Tony Zendejas .05 .02
❑ 231 Todd Lyght .05 .02
❑ 232 Todd Kinchen .05 .02
❑ 233 Jackie Slater .05 .02
❑ 234 Fred Stokes .05 .02
❑ 235 Russell White RC .10 .05
❑ 236 Cleveland Gary .05 .02
❑ 237 Sean LaChapelle RC .05 .02
❑ 238 Steve Israel .05 .02
❑ 239 Shane Conlan .05 .02
❑ 240 Keith Byars .05 .02
❑ 241 Marco Coleman .05 .02
❑ 242 Bryan Cox .05 .02
❑ 243 Irving Fryar .10 .05
❑ 244 Richmond Webb .05 .02
❑ 245 Mark Higgs .05 .02
❑ 246 Terry Kirby RC .25 .11
❑ 247 Mark Ingram .05 .02
❑ 248 John Offerdahl .05 .02
❑ 249 Keith Jackson .10 .05
❑ 250 Dan Marino 1.50 .70
❑ 251 O.J. McDuffie RC .50 .23
❑ 252 Louis Oliver .05 .02
❑ 253 Pete Stoyanovich .05 .02
❑ 254 Troy Vincent .05 .02
❑ 255 Anthony Carter .10 .05
❑ 256 Cris Carter .50 .23
❑ 257 Roger Craig .10 .05
❑ 258 Jack Del Rio .05 .02
❑ 259 Chris Doleman .05 .02
❑ 260 Barry Word .05 .02
❑ 261 Qadry Ismail RC .50 .23
❑ 262 Jim McMahon .05 .02
❑ 263 Robert Smith RC 1.50 .70
❑ 264 Fred Strickland .05 .02
❑ 265 Randall McDaniel .05 .02
❑ 266 Carl Lee .05 .02
❑ 267 Olanda Truitt RC UER .05 .02
(Name spelled Olanda on front)
❑ 268 Terry Allen .25 .11
❑ 269 Audray McMillian .05 .02
❑ 270 Drew Bledsoe RC 2.00 .90
❑ 271 Eugene Chung .05 .02
❑ 272 Marv Cook .05 .02
❑ 273 Pat Harlow .05 .02
❑ 274 Greg McMurtry .05 .02
❑ 275 Leonard Russell .10 .05
❑ 276 Chris Slade RC .10 .05
❑ 277 Andre Tippett .05 .02
❑ 278 Vincent Brisby RC .25 .11
❑ 279 Ben Coates .50 .23
❑ 280 Sam Gash RC .10 .05
❑ 281 Bruce Armstrong .05 .02
❑ 282 Rod Smith DB .05 .02
❑ 283 Michael Timpson .05 .02
❑ 284 Scott Sisson RC .05 .02
❑ 285 Morten Andersen .05 .02
❑ 286 Reggie Freeman RC .05 .02
❑ 287 Dalton Hilliard .05 .02
❑ 288 Rickey Jackson .05 .02
❑ 289 Vaughan Johnson .05 .02
❑ 290 Eric Martin .05 .02
❑ 291 Sam Mills .05 .02
❑ 292 Brad Muster .05 .02
❑ 293 William Roaf RC .10 .05
❑ 294 Irv Smith RC .05 .02
❑ 295 Wade Wilson .05 .02
❑ 296 Derek Brown RBK RC .10 .05
❑ 297 Quinn Early .10 .05
❑ 298 Steve Walsh .05 .02
❑ 299 Renaldo Turnbull .05 .02
❑ 300 Jessie Armstead RC .10 .05
❑ 301 Carlton Bailey .05 .02
❑ 302 Michael Brooks .05 .02
❑ 303 Rodney Hampton .25 .11
❑ 304 Ed McCaffrey .10 .05
❑ 305 Dave Meggett .05 .02
❑ 306 Bart Oates .05 .02
❑ 307 Mike Sherrard .05 .02
❑ 308 Phil Simms .10 .05
❑ 309 Lawrence Taylor .25 .11
❑ 310 Mark Jackson .05 .02
❑ 311 Jarrod Bunch .05 .02
❑ 312 Howard Cross .05 .02
❑ 313 Michael Strahan RC .25 .11
❑ 314 Marcus Buckley RC .05 .02
❑ 315 Brad Baxter .05 .02
❑ 316 Adrian Murrell RC .40 .18
❑ 317 Boomer Esiason .10 .05
❑ 318 Johnny Johnson .05 .02
❑ 319 Marvin Jones RC .05 .02
❑ 320 Jeff Lageman .05 .02
❑ 321 Ronnie Lott .10 .05
❑ 322 Leonard Marshall .05 .02
❑ 323 Johnny Mitchell .05 .02
❑ 324 Rob Moore .10 .05
❑ 325 Browning Nagle .05 .02
❑ 326 Blair Thomas .05 .02
❑ 327 Brian Washington .05 .02
❑ 328 Terance Mathis .10 .05
❑ 329 Kyle Clifton .05 .02
❑ 330 Eric Allen .05 .02
❑ 331 Victor Bailey RC .05 .02
❑ 332 Fred Barnett .10 .05
❑ 333 Mark Bavaro .05 .02
❑ 334 Randall Cunningham .25 .11
❑ 335 Ken O'Brien .05 .02
❑ 336 Seth Joyner .05 .02
❑ 337 Leonard Renfro RC .05 .02
❑ 338 Heath Sherman .05 .02
❑ 339 Clyde Simmons .05 .02
❑ 340 Herschel Walker .10 .05
❑ 341 Calvin Williams .10 .05
❑ 342 Bubby Brister .05 .02
❑ 343 Vaughn Hebron RC .05 .02
❑ 344 Keith Millard .05 .02
❑ 345 Johnny Bailey .05 .02
❑ 346 Steve Beuerlein .05 .02
❑ 347 Chuck Cecil .05 .02
❑ 348 Larry Centers RC .25 .11
❑ 349 Chris Chandler .10 .05
❑ 350 Ernest Dye RC .05 .02
❑ 351 Garrison Hearst RC .50 .23
❑ 352 Randal Hill .05 .02
❑ 353 John Booty .05 .02
❑ 354 Gary Clark .10 .05
❑ 355 Ronald Moore RC .10 .05
❑ 356 Ricky Proehl .05 .02
❑ 357 Eric Swann .10 .05
❑ 358 Ken Harvey .05 .02
❑ 359 Ben Coleman RC .05 .02
❑ 360 Deon Figures RC .10 .05
❑ 361 Barry Foster .10 .05
❑ 362 Jeff Graham .10 .05
❑ 363 Eric Green .05 .02
❑ 364 Kevin Greene .25 .11
❑ 365 Andre Hastings RC .25 .11
❑ 366 Greg Lloyd .25 .11
❑ 367 Neil O'Donnell .25 .11
❑ 368 Dwight Stone .05 .02
❑ 369 Mike Tomczak .05 .02
❑ 370 Rod Woodson .25 .11
❑ 371 Chad Brown RC .10 .05
❑ 372 Ernie Mills .05 .02
❑ 373 Darren Perry .05 .02
❑ 374 Leon Searcy .05 .02
❑ 375 Marion Butts .05 .02
❑ 376 John Carney .05 .02
❑ 377 Ronnie Harmon .05 .02
❑ 378 Stan Humphries .25 .11
❑ 379 Nate Lewis .05 .02
❑ 380 Natrone Means RC .40 .18
❑ 381 Anthony Miller .10 .05
❑ 382 Chris Mims .05 .02
❑ 383 Leslie O'Neal .10 .05
❑ 384 Joe Cocozzo RC .05 .02
❑ 385 Junior Seau .25 .11
❑ 386 Jerrol Williams .05 .02
❑ 387 John Friesz .10 .05
❑ 388 Darrien Gordon RC .05 .02
❑ 389 Derrick Walker .05 .02
❑ 390 Dana Hall .05 .02
❑ 391 Brent Jones .10 .05
❑ 392 Todd Kelly RC .05 .02
❑ 393 Amp Lee .05 .02
❑ 394 Tim McDonald .05 .02
❑ 395 Jerry Rice 1.00 .45
❑ 396 Dana Stubblefield RC .25 .11
❑ 397 John Taylor .10 .05
❑ 398 Ricky Watters .25 .11
❑ 399 Steve Young .75 .35
❑ 400 Steve Bono .25 .11
❑ 401 Adrian Hardy .05 .02
❑ 402 Tom Rathman .05 .02
❑ 403 Elvis Grbac RC UER 1.50 .70

(Name spelled Grabac on front)
❑ 404 Bill Romanowski .05 .02
❑ 405 Brian Blades .10 .05
❑ 406 Ferrell Edmunds .05 .02
❑ 407 Carlton Gray RC .05 .02
❑ 408 Cortez Kennedy .10 .05
❑ 409 Kelvin Martin .05 .02
❑ 410 Dan McGwire .05 .02
❑ 411 Rick Mirer RC .30 .14
❑ 412 Rufus Porter .05 .02
❑ 413 Chris Warren .10 .05
❑ 414 Jon Vaughn .05 .02
❑ 415 John L. Williams .05 .02
❑ 416 Eugene Robinson .05 .02
❑ 417 Michael McCrary RC .10 .05
❑ 418 Michael Bates RC .05 .02
❑ 419 Stan Gelbaugh .05 .02
❑ 420 Reggie Cobb .05 .02
❑ 421 Eric Curry RC .05 .02
❑ 422 Lawrence Dawsey .05 .02
❑ 423 Santana Dotson .10 .05
❑ 424 Craig Erickson .10 .05
❑ 425 Ron Hall .05 .02
❑ 426 Courtney Hawkins .05 .02
❑ 427 Broderick Thomas .05 .02
❑ 428 Vince Workman .05 .02
❑ 429 Demetrius DuBose RC .. .05 .02
❑ 430 Lamar Thomas RC .05 .02
❑ 431 John Lynch RC .40 .18
❑ 432 Hardy Nickerson .10 .05
❑ 433 Horace Copeland RC .10 .05
❑ 434 Steve DeBerg .05 .02
❑ 435 Joe Jacoby .05 .02
❑ 436 Tom Carter RC .10 .05
❑ 437 Andre Collins .05 .02
❑ 438 Darrell Green .05 .02
❑ 439 Desmond Howard .10 .05
❑ 440 Chip Lohmiller .05 .02
❑ 441 Charles Mann .05 .02
❑ 442 Tim McGee .05 .02
❑ 443 Art Monk .10 .05
❑ 444 Mark Rypien .05 .02
❑ 445 Ricky Sanders .05 .02
❑ 446 Brian Mitchell .10 .05
❑ 447 Reggie Brooks RC .10 .05
❑ 448 Carl Banks .05 .02
❑ 449 Cary Conklin .05 .02
❑ NNO Santa Card 1.50 .70

2000 Quantum Leaf

	MINT	NRMT
COMPLETE SET (350)	175.00	80.00
COMP.SET w/o SP's (300)	25.00	11.00
COMP.ROOKIE UPDATE (31)	20.00	9.00

❑ 1 Frank Sanders .50 .23
❑ 2 Adrian Murrell .50 .23
❑ 3 Rob Moore .50 .23
❑ 4 Simeon Rice .25 .11
❑ 5 Michael Pittman .25 .11
❑ 6 Jake Plummer 1.00 .45
❑ 7 David Boston 1.00 .45
❑ 8 Mario Bates .25 .11
❑ 9 Chris Chandler .50 .23
❑ 10 Tim Dwight 1.00 .45
❑ 11 Chris Calloway .25 .11
❑ 12 Terance Mathis .50 .23
❑ 13 Jamal Anderson 1.00 .45
❑ 14 Byron Hanspard .50 .23
❑ 15 Ken Oxendine .25 .11
❑ 16 Tony Graziani .25 .11
❑ 17 Bob Christian .25 .11
❑ 18 Priest Holmes .50 .23
❑ 19 Tony Banks .50 .23
❑ 20 Patrick Johnson .25 .11
❑ 21 Rod Woodson .50 .23
❑ 22 Jermaine Lewis .25 .11
❑ 23 Errict Rhett .50 .23
❑ 24 Stoney Case .25 .11
❑ 25 Peter Boulware .25 .11
❑ 26 Qadry Ismail .25 .11
❑ 27 Brandon Stokley .25 .11
❑ 28 Andre Reed .50 .23
❑ 29 Eric Moulds 1.00 .45
❑ 30 Doug Flutie 1.25 .55
❑ 31 Bruce Smith .50 .23
❑ 32 Jay Riemersma .25 .11
❑ 33 Antowain Smith .50 .23
❑ 34 Thurman Thomas .50 .23
❑ 35 Jonathan Linton .25 .11
❑ 36 Peerless Price 1.00 .45
❑ 37 Rob Johnson .50 .23
❑ 38 Sam Gash .25 .11
❑ 39 Muhsin Muhammad .50 .23
❑ 40 Wesley Walls .25 .11
❑ 41 Fred Lane .25 .11
❑ 42 Kevin Greene .25 .11
❑ 43 Tim Biakabutuka .50 .23
❑ 44 Steve Beuerlein .50 .23
❑ 45 Donald Hayes .25 .11
❑ 46 Patrick Jeffers 1.00 .45
❑ 47 Curtis Enis .50 .23
❑ 48 Bobby Engram .25 .11
❑ 49 Curtis Conway .50 .23
❑ 50 Marcus Robinson 1.00 .45
❑ 51 Marty Booker .25 .11
❑ 52 Cade McNown 1.00 .45
❑ 53 Shane Matthews .50 .23
❑ 54 Jim Miller .25 .11
❑ 55 Darnay Scott .50 .23
❑ 56 Carl Pickens .50 .23
❑ 57 Corey Dillon 1.00 .45
❑ 58 Jeff Blake .50 .23
❑ 59 Akili Smith 1.00 .45
❑ 60 Michael Basnight .25 .11
❑ 61 Karim Abdul-Jabbar .50 .23
❑ 62 Tim Couch 2.00 .90
❑ 63 Kevin Johnson 1.00 .45
❑ 64 Terry Kirby .25 .11
❑ 65 Ty Detmer .50 .23
❑ 66 Leslie Shepherd .25 .11
❑ 67 Darrin Chiaverini .25 .11
❑ 68 Emmitt Smith 2.50 1.10
❑ 69 Deion Sanders 1.00 .45
❑ 70 Michael Irvin .50 .23
❑ 71 Rocket Ismail .50 .23
❑ 72 Troy Aikman 2.50 1.10
❑ 73 Daryl Johnston .50 .23
❑ 74 Chris Warren .25 .11
❑ 75 Jason Garrett .50 .23
❑ 76 Jason Tucker .50 .23
❑ 77 Lawyer Milloy .25 .11
❑ 78 Dexter Coakley .25 .11
❑ 79 Greg Ellis .25 .11
❑ 80 David LaFleur .25 .11
❑ 81 Todd Lyght .25 .11
❑ 82 Ernie Mills .25 .11
❑ 83 Wane McGarity .25 .11
❑ 84 Chris Brazzell RC .50 .23
❑ 85 Ed McCaffrey 1.00 .45
❑ 86 Rod Smith .50 .23
❑ 87 Shannon Sharpe .50 .23
❑ 88 Brian Griese 1.25 .55
❑ 89 John Elway 4.00 1.80
❑ 90 Neil Smith .50 .23
❑ 91 Terrell Davis 2.50 1.10
❑ 92 Olandis Gary 1.00 .45
❑ 93 Derek Loville .25 .11
❑ 94 John Avery .25 .11
❑ 95 Bubby Brister .25 .11
❑ 96 Byron Chamberlain .25 .11
❑ 97 Dale Carter .25 .11
❑ 98 Johnnie Morton .50 .23
❑ 99 Charlie Batch 1.00 .45
❑ 100 Barry Sanders 3.00 1.35
❑ 101 Germane Crowell .50 .23
❑ 102 Gus Frerotte .25 .11
❑ 103 Desmond Howard .25 .11
❑ 104 Terry Fair .25 .11
❑ 105 Ron Rivers .25 .11
❑ 106 Greg Hill .25 .11
❑ 107 Sedrick Irvin .25 .11
❑ 108 David Sloan .25 .11
❑ 109 Herman Moore .50 .23
❑ 110 Robert Porcher .25 .11
❑ 111 Corey Bradford .50 .23
❑ 112 Dorsey Levens .50 .23
❑ 113 Antonio Freeman 1.00 .45
❑ 114 Brett Favre 4.00 1.80
❑ 115 De'Mond Parker .50 .23
❑ 116 Bill Schroeder .50 .23
❑ 117 Matt Hasselbeck .25 .11
❑ 118 Donald Driver .25 .11
❑ 119 Basil Mitchell .25 .11
❑ 120 E.G. Green .25 .11
❑ 121 Ken Dilger .25 .11
❑ 122 Marvin Harrison 1.00 .45
❑ 123 Peyton Manning 3.00 1.35
❑ 124 Terrence Wilkins 1.00 .45
❑ 125 Edgerrin James 4.00 1.80
❑ 126 Jerome Pathon .50 .23
❑ 127 Marcus Pollard .25 .11
❑ 128 Keenan McCardell .50 .23
❑ 129 Mark Brunell 1.50 .70
❑ 130 Fred Taylor 1.25 .55
❑ 131 Jimmy Smith .50 .23
❑ 132 James Stewart .50 .23
❑ 133 Kyle Brady .25 .11
❑ 134 Tony Brackens .25 .11
❑ 135 Derrick Thomas .50 .23
❑ 136 Rashaan Shehee .25 .11
❑ 137 Derrick Alexander .50 .23
❑ 138 Bam Morris .25 .11
❑ 139 Andre Rison .50 .23
❑ 140 Elvis Grbac .50 .23
❑ 141 Tony Gonzalez .50 .23
❑ 142 Donnell Bennett .25 .11
❑ 143 Warren Moon 1.00 .45
❑ 144 Tamarick Vanover .25 .11
❑ 145 Kimble Anders .25 .11
❑ 146 Tony Richardson RC .50 .23
❑ 147 Zach Thomas .50 .23
❑ 148 Oronde Gadsden .50 .23
❑ 149 Dan Marino 4.00 1.80
❑ 150 O.J. McDuffie .50 .23
❑ 151 Tony Martin .50 .23
❑ 152 Cecil Collins .25 .11
❑ 153 James Johnson .50 .23
❑ 154 Rob Konrad .25 .11
❑ 155 Yatil Green .25 .11
❑ 156 Damon Huard 1.00 .45
❑ 157 Nate Jacquet .25 .11
❑ 158 Stanley Pritchett .25 .11
❑ 159 Sam Madison .25 .11
❑ 160 Randy Moss 3.00 1.35
❑ 161 Cris Carter 1.00 .45
❑ 162 Robert Smith 1.00 .45
❑ 163 Randall Cunningham 1.00 .45
❑ 164 Jake Reed .50 .23
❑ 165 John Randle .50 .23
❑ 166 Leroy Hoard .25 .11
❑ 167 Jeff George .50 .23
❑ 168 Daunte Culpepper 2.00 .90
❑ 169 Matthew Hatchette .50 .23
❑ 170 Robert Tate .25 .11
❑ 171 Ty Law .25 .11
❑ 172 Troy Brown .25 .11
❑ 173 Tony Simmons .25 .11
❑ 174 Terry Glenn .50 .23
❑ 175 Ben Coates .25 .11
❑ 176 Drew Bledsoe 1.50 .70
❑ 177 Terry Allen .50 .23
❑ 178 Kevin Faulk .50 .23
❑ 179 Shawn Jefferson .25 .11
❑ 180 Andy Katzenmoyer .25 .11
❑ 181 Willie McGinest .25 .11
❑ 182 Cameron Cleeland .25 .11
❑ 183 Eddie Kennison .50 .23
❑ 184 Ricky Williams 2.50 1.10

❑ 185 Danny Wuerffel	.50	.23
❑ 186 Brett Bech	.25	.11
❑ 187 Billy Joe Hobert	.25	.11
❑ 188 Jake Delhomme RC	1.00	.45
❑ 189 Wilmont Perry	.25	.11
❑ 190 Keith Poole	.25	.11
❑ 191 Ashley Ambrose	.25	.11
❑ 192 Amani Toomer	.25	.11
❑ 193 Kerry Collins	.50	.23
❑ 194 Tiki Barber	.50	.23
❑ 195 Ike Hilliard	.50	.23
❑ 196 Jason Sehorn	.25	.11
❑ 197 Joe Montgomery	.25	.11
❑ 198 Joe Jurevicius	.25	.11
❑ 199 Michael Strahan	.25	.11
❑ 200 Sean Bennett	.25	.11
❑ 201 Jessie Armstead	.25	.11
❑ 202 Pete Mitchell	.25	.11
❑ 203 Curtis Martin	1.00	.45
❑ 204 Vinny Testaverde	.50	.23
❑ 205 Keyshawn Johnson	1.00	.45
❑ 206 Wayne Chrebet	.50	.23
❑ 207 Ray Lucas	1.00	.45
❑ 208 Tyrone Wheatley	.50	.23
❑ 209 Napoleon Kaufman	.50	.23
❑ 210 Tim Brown	1.00	.45
❑ 211 Rickey Dudley	.25	.11
❑ 212 James Jett	.25	.11
❑ 213 Rich Gannon	.50	.23
❑ 214 Charles Woodson	.50	.23
❑ 215 Zack Crockett	.25	.11
❑ 216 Darrell Russell	.25	.11
❑ 217 Duce Staley	1.00	.45
❑ 218 Donovan McNabb	1.50	.70
❑ 219 Charles Johnson	.50	.23
❑ 220 Dameane Douglas	.25	.11
❑ 221 Doug Pederson	.25	.11
❑ 222 Torrance Small	.25	.11
❑ 223 Troy Vincent	.25	.11
❑ 224 Na Brown	.25	.11
❑ 225 Kordell Stewart	1.00	.45
❑ 226 Jerome Bettis	1.00	.45
❑ 227 Hines Ward	.25	.11
❑ 228 Troy Edwards	.50	.23
❑ 229 Richard Huntley	.25	.11
❑ 230 Mark Bruener	.25	.11
❑ 231 Pete Gonzalez	.25	.11
❑ 232 Levon Kirkland	.25	.11
❑ 233 Bobby Shaw RC	1.25	.55
❑ 234 Amos Zereoue	.25	.11
❑ 235 Natrone Means	.25	.11
❑ 236 Junior Seau	.50	.23
❑ 237 Jim Harbaugh	.50	.23
❑ 238 Ryan Leaf	1.00	.45
❑ 239 Mikhael Ricks	.25	.11
❑ 240 Jermaine Fazande	.25	.11
❑ 241 Jeff Graham	.25	.11
❑ 242 Tremayne Stephens	.25	.11
❑ 243 Terrell Owens	1.00	.45
❑ 244 J.J. Stokes	.50	.23
❑ 245 Charlie Garner	.50	.23
❑ 246 Jerry Rice	2.50	1.10
❑ 247 Garrison Hearst	.50	.23
❑ 248 Steve Young	1.50	.70
❑ 249 Jeff Garcia	1.00	.45
❑ 250 Fred Beasley	.25	.11
❑ 251 Bryant Young	.25	.11
❑ 252 Derrick Mayes	.50	.23
❑ 253 Ahman Green	.50	.23
❑ 254 Joey Galloway	1.00	.45
❑ 255 Ricky Watters	.50	.23
❑ 256 Jon Kitna	1.00	.45
❑ 257 Sean Dawkins	.25	.11
❑ 258 Sam Adams	.25	.11
❑ 259 Christian Fauria	.25	.11
❑ 260 Shawn Springs	.25	.11
❑ 261 Az-Zahir Hakim	.50	.23
❑ 262 Isaac Bruce	1.00	.45
❑ 263 Marshall Faulk	1.25	.55
❑ 264 Trent Green	.50	.23
❑ 265 Kurt Warner	4.00	1.80
❑ 266 Torry Holt	1.00	.45
❑ 267 Robert Holcombe	.25	.11
❑ 268 Kevin Carter	.25	.11
❑ 269 Amp Lee	.25	.11
❑ 270 Roland Williams	.25	.11
❑ 271 Jacquez Green	.50	.23
❑ 272 Reidel Anthony	.25	.11
❑ 273 Warren Sapp	.50	.23
❑ 274 Mike Alstott	1.00	.45
❑ 275 Warrick Dunn	1.00	.45
❑ 276 Trent Dilfer	.50	.23
❑ 277 Shaun King	1.50	.70
❑ 278 Bert Emanuel	.25	.11
❑ 279 Eric Zeier	.25	.11
❑ 280 Neil O'Donnell	.25	.11
❑ 281 Eddie George	1.25	.55
❑ 282 Yancey Thigpen	.25	.11
❑ 283 Steve McNair	1.00	.45
❑ 284 Kevin Dyson	.50	.23
❑ 285 Frank Wycheck	.25	.11
❑ 286 Jevon Kearse	1.00	.45
❑ 287 Bruce Matthews	.25	.11
❑ 288 Lorenzo Neal	.25	.11
❑ 289 Stephen Davis	1.00	.45
❑ 290 Stephen Alexander	.25	.11
❑ 291 Darrell Green	.25	.11
❑ 292 Skip Hicks	.50	.23
❑ 293 Brad Johnson	1.00	.45
❑ 294 Michael Westbrook	.50	.23
❑ 295 Albert Connell	.25	.11
❑ 296 Irving Fryar	.25	.11
❑ 297 Champ Bailey	.50	.23
❑ 298 Larry Centers	.25	.11
❑ 299 Brian Mitchell	.25	.11
❑ 300 James Thrash	1.00	.45
❑ 301 LaVar Arrington RC	10.00	4.50
❑ 302 Peter Warrick RC	8.00	3.60
❑ 303 Courtney Brown RC	3.00	1.35
❑ 304 Plaxico Burress RC	5.00	2.20
❑ 305 Corey Simon RC	3.00	1.35
❑ 306 Thomas Jones RC	4.00	1.80
❑ 307 Travis Taylor RC	3.00	1.35
❑ 308 Shaun Alexander RC	6.00	2.70
❑ 309 Chris Redman RC	5.00	2.20
❑ 310 Chad Pennington RC	8.00	3.60
❑ 311 Jamal Lewis RC	12.00	5.50
❑ 312 Brian Urlacher RC	8.00	3.60
❑ 313 Keith Bulluck RC	2.00	.90
❑ 314 Bubba Franks RC	3.00	1.35
❑ 315 Dez White RC	2.00	.90
❑ 316 Ahmed Plummer RC	2.50	1.10
❑ 317 Ron Dayne RC	8.00	3.60
❑ 318 Shaun Ellis RC	2.00	.90
❑ 319 Sylvester Morris RC	5.00	2.20
❑ 320 Deltha O'Neal RC	2.00	.90
❑ 321 R.Jay Soward RC	2.50	1.10
❑ 322 Sherrod Gideon RC	2.00	.90
❑ 323 John Abraham RC	2.00	.90
❑ 324 Travis Prentice RC	4.00	1.80
❑ 325 Darrell Jackson RC	4.00	1.80
❑ 326 Giovanni Carmazzi RC	3.00	1.35
❑ 327 Anthony Lucas RC	2.00	.90
❑ 328 Danny Farmer RC	2.00	.90
❑ 329 Dennis Northcutt RC	3.00	1.35
❑ 330 Troy Walters RC	2.50	1.10
❑ 331 Laveranues Coles RC	4.00	1.80
❑ 332 Tee Martin RC	4.00	1.80
❑ 333 J.R. Redmond RC	3.00	1.35
❑ 334 Jerry Porter RC	2.50	1.10
❑ 335 Sebastian Janikowski RC	2.00	.90
❑ 336 Michael Wiley RC	2.00	.90
❑ 337 Reuben Droughns RC	2.00	.90
❑ 338 Trung Canidate RC	2.50	1.10
❑ 339 Shyrone Stith RC	2.00	.90
❑ 340 Trevor Gaylor RC	2.00	.90
❑ 341 Rob Morris RC	2.50	1.10
❑ 342 Marc Bulger RC	2.00	.90
❑ 343 Tom Brady RC	2.50	1.10
❑ 344 Todd Husak RC	2.50	1.10
❑ 345 Gari Scott RC	2.00	.90
❑ 346 Erron Kinney RC	2.50	1.10
❑ 347 Julian Peterson RC	2.00	.90
❑ 348 Doug Chapman RC	5.00	2.20
❑ 349 Ron Dugans RC	2.00	.90
❑ 350 Todd Pinkston RC	2.50	1.10
❑ 351 Deon Grant RC	.75	.35
❑ 352 Na'il Diggs RC	2.00	.90
❑ 353 Raynoch Thompson RC	1.25	.55
❑ 354 Mario Edwards RC	.75	.35
❑ 355 John Engelberger RC	1.25	.55
❑ 356 Dwayne Goodrich RC	.75	.35
❑ 357 Ben Kelly RC	.75	.35
❑ 358 Sekou Sanyika RC	.75	.35
❑ 359 Brandon Short RC	1.25	.55
❑ 360 Jabari Issa RC	.75	.35
❑ 361 Darwin Walker RC	.75	.35
❑ 362 Jerry Johnson RC	.75	.35
❑ 363 Robaire Smith RC	.75	.35
❑ 364 Mark Roman RC	.75	.35
❑ 365 Leonardo Carson RC	.75	.35
❑ 366 Mark Simoneau RC	2.50	1.10
❑ 367 Hank Poteat RC	1.25	.55
❑ 368 Darren Howard RC	1.25	.55
❑ 369 David Macklin RC	.75	.35
❑ 370 Adalius Thomas RC	.75	.35
❑ 371 Ralph Brown RC	.75	.35
❑ 372 Mondriel Fulcher RC	.75	.35
❑ 373 Sammy Morris RC	2.50	1.10
❑ 374 Rondell Mealey RC	.75	.35
❑ 375 Deon Dyer RC	1.25	.55
❑ 376 Mareno Philyaw RC	.75	.35
❑ 377 Thomas Hamner RC	1.25	.55
❑ 378 Jarious Jackson RC	2.00	.90
❑ 379 Joe Hamilton RC	2.50	1.10
❑ 380 Tim Rattay RC	3.00	1.35
❑ 381 Chris Hovan RC	1.25	.55
❑ SB1 Kurt Warner MVP	12.00	5.50
❑ SB1A K.Warner MVP Auto/100	120.00	55.00
❑ NFL1 Kurt Warner MVP	12.00	5.50
❑ NFL1A K.Warner MVP Auto/100	120.00	55.00
❑ QLP10 Dan Marino Promo	3.00	1.35

1997 Revolution

	MINT	NRMT
COMPLETE SET (150)	80.00	36.00
❑ 1 Larry Centers	.75	.35
❑ 2 Kent Graham	.50	.23
❑ 3 Leeland McElroy	.50	.23
❑ 4 Rob Moore	.75	.35
❑ 5 Jake Plummer RC	10.00	4.50
❑ 6 Jamal Anderson	2.50	1.10
❑ 7 Bert Emanuel	.75	.35
❑ 8 Byron Hanspard RC	1.50	.70
❑ 9 Terance Mathis	.75	.35
❑ 10 O.J. Santiago RC	1.50	.70
❑ 11 Derrick Alexander WR	.75	.35
❑ 12 Peter Boulware RC	.75	.35
❑ 13 Jay Graham RC	1.50	.70
❑ 14 Michael Jackson	.75	.35
❑ 15 Vinny Testaverde	.75	.35
❑ 16 Todd Collins	.50	.23
❑ 17 Andre Reed	.75	.35
❑ 18 Jay Riemersma	.50	.23
❑ 19 Antowain Smith RC	4.00	1.80
❑ 20 Bruce Smith	.75	.35
❑ 21 Thurman Thomas	1.50	.70
❑ 22 Rae Carruth RC	1.50	.70
❑ 23 Kerry Collins	.75	.35
❑ 24 Anthony Johnson	.50	.23
❑ 25 Muhsin Muhammad	.75	.35
❑ 26 Wesley Walls	.75	.35
❑ 27 Curtis Conway	.75	.35
❑ 28 Bobby Engram	.75	.35
❑ 29 Raymont Harris	.50	.23
❑ 30 Rick Mirer	.50	.23
❑ 31 Rashaan Salaam	.50	.23
❑ 32 Jeff Blake	.75	.35

❑ 33	Corey Dillon RC	10.00	4.50
❑ 34	Carl Pickens	1.50	.70
❑ 35	Darnay Scott	.75	.35
❑ 36	Troy Aikman	4.00	1.80
❑ 37	Michael Irvin	1.50	.70
❑ 38	Daryl Johnston	.75	.35
❑ 39	Deion Sanders	1.50	.70
❑ 40	Emmitt Smith	6.00	2.70
❑ 41	Terrell Davis	6.00	2.70
❑ 42	John Elway	8.00	3.60
❑ 43	Ed McCaffrey	.75	.35
❑ 44	Shannon Sharpe	.75	.35
❑ 45	Neil Smith	.75	.35
❑ 46	Scott Mitchell	.75	.35
❑ 47	Herman Moore	1.50	.70
❑ 48	Johnnie Morton	.75	.35
❑ 49	Barry Sanders	8.00	3.60
❑ 50	Robert Brooks	.75	.35
❑ 51	LeRoy Butler	.50	.23
❑ 52	Brett Favre	8.00	3.60
❑ 53	Antonio Freeman	2.00	.90
❑ 54	Dorsey Levens	1.50	.70
❑ 55	Reggie White	1.50	.70
❑ 56	Sean Dawkins	.50	.23
❑ 57	Ken Dilger	.50	.23
❑ 58	Marshall Faulk	1.50	.70
❑ 59	Jim Harbaugh	.75	.35
❑ 60	Marvin Harrison	1.50	.70
❑ 61	Mark Brunell	4.00	1.80
❑ 62	Keenan McCardell	.75	.35
❑ 63	Natrone Means	1.50	.70
❑ 64	Jimmy Smith	.75	.35
❑ 65	James O.Stewart	.75	.35
❑ 66	Marcus Allen	1.50	.70
❑ 67	Tony Gonzalez RC	5.00	2.20
❑ 68	Elvis Grbac	.75	.35
❑ 69	Greg Hill	.50	.23
❑ 70	Andre Rison	.75	.35
❑ 71	Karim Abdul-Jabbar	1.50	.70
❑ 72	Fred Barnett	.50	.23
❑ 73	Dan Marino	8.00	3.60
❑ 74	O.J. McDuffie	.75	.35
❑ 75	Irving Spikes	.50	.23
❑ 76	Cris Carter	1.50	.70
❑ 77	Matthew Hatchette RC	8.00	3.60
❑ 78	Brad Johnson	2.00	.90
❑ 79	Jake Reed	.75	.35
❑ 80	Robert Smith	.75	.35
❑ 81	Drew Bledsoe	4.00	1.80
❑ 82	Ben Coates	.75	.35
❑ 83	Terry Glenn	1.50	.70
❑ 84	Curtis Martin	2.00	.90
❑ 85	Dave Meggett	.50	.23
❑ 86	Troy Davis RC	1.50	.70
❑ 87	Andre Hastings	.50	.23
❑ 88	Heath Shuler	.50	.23
❑ 89	Irv Smith	.50	.23
❑ 90	Danny Wuerffel RC	1.50	.70
❑ 91	Ray Zellars	.50	.23
❑ 92	Tiki Barber RC	5.00	2.20
❑ 93	Dave Brown	.50	.23
❑ 94	Chris Calloway	.50	.23
❑ 95	Rodney Hampton	.75	.35
❑ 96	Amani Toomer	.75	.35
❑ 97	Wayne Chrebet	1.50	.70
❑ 98	Keyshawn Johnson	1.50	.70
❑ 99	Adrian Murrell	.75	.35
❑ 100	Neil O'Donnell	.75	.35
❑ 101	Dedric Ward RC	3.00	1.35
❑ 102	Tim Brown	1.50	.70
❑ 103	Rickey Dudley	.75	.35
❑ 104	Jeff George	.75	.35
❑ 105	Desmond Howard	.75	.35
❑ 106	Napoleon Kaufman	1.50	.70
❑ 107	Ty Detmer	.75	.35
❑ 108	Jason Dunn	.50	.23
❑ 109	Irving Fryar	.75	.35
❑ 110	Rodney Peete	.50	.23
❑ 111	Ricky Watters	.75	.35
❑ 112	Jerome Bettis	1.50	.70
❑ 113	Will Blackwell RC	1.50	.70
❑ 114	Charles Johnson	.75	.35
❑ 115	Kordell Stewart	2.00	.90
❑ 116	Tony Banks	.75	.35
❑ 117	Isaac Bruce	1.50	.70
❑ 118	Ernie Conwell	.50	.23
❑ 119	Eddie Kennison	.75	.35
❑ 120	Lawrence Phillips	.50	.23
❑ 121	Stan Humphries	.75	.35
❑ 122	Tony Martin	.75	.35
❑ 123	Eric Metcalf	.75	.35
❑ 124	Junior Seau	.75	.35
❑ 125	Jim Druckenmiller RC	1.50	.70
❑ 126	Kevin Greene	.75	.35
❑ 127	Garrison Hearst	.75	.35
❑ 128	Terrell Owens	1.50	.70
❑ 129	Jerry Rice	4.00	1.80
❑ 130	J.J. Stokes	.75	.35
❑ 131	Rod Woodson	.75	.35
❑ 132	Steve Young	2.50	1.10
❑ 133	Joey Galloway	2.00	.90
❑ 134	Cortez Kennedy	.50	.23
❑ 135	Jon Kitna RC	12.00	5.50
❑ 136	Warren Moon	1.50	.70
❑ 137	Chris Warren	.75	.35
❑ 138	Mike Alstott	1.50	.70
❑ 139	Reidel Anthony RC	3.00	1.35
❑ 140	Trent Dilfer	1.50	.70
❑ 141	Warrick Dunn RC	5.00	2.20
❑ 142	Willie Davis	.50	.23
❑ 143	Eddie George	4.00	1.80
❑ 144	Steve McNair	2.00	.90
❑ 145	Chris Sanders	.50	.23
❑ 146	Terry Allen	1.50	.70
❑ 147	Jamie Asher	.50	.23
❑ 148	Henry Ellard	.50	.23
❑ 149	Gus Frerotte	.50	.23
❑ 150	Leslie Shepherd	.50	.23
❑ S1	Mark Brunell Sample	1.00	.45

1998 Revolution

		MINT	NRMT
COMPLETE SET (150)		120.00	55.00
❑ 1	Larry Centers	.40	.18
❑ 2	Leeland McElroy	.40	.18
❑ 3	Rob Moore	.75	.35
❑ 4	Jake Plummer	3.00	1.35
❑ 5	Frank Sanders	.75	.35
❑ 6	Jamal Anderson	1.50	.70
❑ 7	Chris Chandler	.75	.35
❑ 8	Byron Hanspard	.75	.35
❑ 9	Jay Graham	.40	.18
❑ 10	Michael Jackson	.40	.18
❑ 11	Vinny Testaverde	.75	.35
❑ 12	Eric Zeier	.75	.35
❑ 13	Todd Collins	.40	.18
❑ 14	Quinn Early	.40	.18
❑ 15	Andre Reed	.75	.35
❑ 16	Antowain Smith	1.50	.70
❑ 17	Bruce Smith	.75	.35
❑ 18	Thurman Thomas	1.50	.70
❑ 19	Rae Carruth	.75	.35
❑ 20	Kerry Collins	.75	.35
❑ 21	Wesley Walls	.75	.35
❑ 22	Darnell Autry	.40	.18
❑ 23	Curtis Conway	.75	.35
❑ 24	Bobby Engram	.75	.35
❑ 25	Curtis Enis RC	3.00	1.35
❑ 26	Raymont Harris	.40	.18
❑ 27	Jeff Blake	.75	.35
❑ 28	Corey Dillon	2.50	1.10
❑ 29	Carl Pickens	1.50	.70
❑ 30	Darnay Scott	.75	.35
❑ 31	Troy Aikman	4.00	1.80
❑ 32	Michael Irvin	1.50	.70
❑ 33	Deion Sanders	1.50	.70
❑ 34	Emmitt Smith	6.00	2.70
❑ 35	Steve Atwater	.40	.18
❑ 36	Terrell Davis	6.00	2.70
❑ 37	John Elway	8.00	3.60
❑ 38	Brian Griese RC	8.00	3.60
❑ 39	Ed McCaffrey	.75	.35
❑ 40	Marcus Nash RC	3.00	1.35
❑ 41	Shannon Sharpe	.75	.35
❑ 42	Neil Smith	.75	.35
❑ 43	Rod Smith	.75	.35
❑ 44	Charlie Batch RC	6.00	2.70
❑ 45	Germane Crowell RC	5.00	2.20
❑ 46	Scott Mitchell	.75	.35
❑ 47	Herman Moore	1.50	.70
❑ 48	Barry Sanders	8.00	3.60
❑ 49	Robert Brooks	.75	.35
❑ 50	Mark Chmura	.75	.35
❑ 51	Brett Favre	8.00	3.60
❑ 52	Antonio Freeman	1.50	.70
❑ 53	Dorsey Levens	1.50	.70
❑ 54	Aaron Bailey	.40	.18
❑ 55	Ken Dilger	.40	.18
❑ 56	Marshall Faulk	1.50	.70
❑ 57	Marvin Harrison	.75	.35
❑ 58	Peyton Manning RC	20.00	9.00
❑ 59	Tavian Banks RC	.75	.35
❑ 60	Tony Brackens	.40	.18
❑ 61	Mark Brunell	3.00	1.35
❑ 62	Keenan McCardell	.75	.35
❑ 63	Natrone Means	1.50	.70
❑ 64	Jimmy Smith	.75	.35
❑ 65	James Stewart	.75	.35
❑ 66	Fred Taylor RC	6.00	2.70
❑ 67	Tony Gonzalez	.40	.18
❑ 68	Elvis Grbac	.75	.35
❑ 69	Greg Hill	.40	.18
❑ 70	Andre Rison	.75	.35
❑ 71	Derrick Thomas	.75	.35
❑ 72	Karim Abdul-Jabbar	1.50	.70
❑ 73	John Avery RC	3.00	1.35
❑ 74	Troy Drayton	.40	.18
❑ 75	Dan Marino	8.00	3.60
❑ 76	O.J. McDuffie	.75	.35
❑ 77	Cris Carter	1.50	.70
❑ 78	Brad Johnson	1.50	.70
❑ 79	John Randle	.75	.35
❑ 80	Jake Reed	.75	.35
❑ 81	Robert Smith	1.50	.70
❑ 82	Drew Bledsoe	3.00	1.35
❑ 83	Ben Coates	.75	.35
❑ 84	Robert Edwards RC	4.00	1.80
❑ 85	Terry Glenn	1.50	.70
❑ 86	Tony Simmons RC	3.00	1.35
❑ 87	Troy Davis	.40	.18
❑ 88	Heath Shuler	.40	.18
❑ 89	Danny Wuerffel	.75	.35
❑ 90	Ray Zellars	.40	.18
❑ 91	Tiki Barber	.75	.35
❑ 92	Joe Jurevicius RC	3.00	1.35
❑ 93	Danny Kanell	.75	.35
❑ 94	Charles Way	.40	.18
❑ 95	Tyrone Wheatley	.75	.35
❑ 96	Wayne Chrebet	1.50	.70
❑ 97	Glenn Foley	.75	.35
❑ 98	Keyshawn Johnson	1.50	.70
❑ 99	Curtis Martin	1.50	.70
❑ 100	Tim Brown	1.50	.70
❑ 101	Rickey Dudley	.40	.18
❑ 102	Jeff George	.75	.35
❑ 103	Desmond Howard	.75	.35
❑ 104	Napoleon Kaufman	1.50	.70
❑ 105	Charles Woodson RC	4.00	1.80
❑ 106	Jason Dunn	.40	.18
❑ 107	Irving Fryar	.75	.35
❑ 108	Charlie Garner	.40	.18
❑ 109	Bobby Hoying	.75	.35
❑ 110	Jerome Bettis	1.50	.70
❑ 111	Mark Bruener	.40	.18
❑ 112	Charles Johnson	.40	.18
❑ 113	Levon Kirkland	.40	.18
❑ 114	Kordell Stewart	1.50	.70
❑ 115	Hines Ward RC	3.00	1.35

Card	MINT	NRMT
❑ 116 Tony Banks	.75	.35
❑ 117 Isaac Bruce	1.50	.70
❑ 118 Robert Holcombe RC	3.00	1.35
❑ 119 Eddie Kennison	.75	.35
❑ 120 Freddie Jones	.40	.18
❑ 121 Ryan Leaf RC	5.00	2.20
❑ 122 Tony Martin	.75	.35
❑ 123 Junior Seau	.75	.35
❑ 124 Jim Druckenmiller	.75	.35
❑ 125 Garrison Hearst	1.50	.70
❑ 126 Terrell Owens	1.50	.70
❑ 127 Jerry Rice	4.00	1.80
❑ 128 J.J. Stokes	.75	.35
❑ 129 Steve Young	2.50	1.10
❑ 130 Joey Galloway	1.50	.70
❑ 131 Ahman Green RC	5.00	2.20
❑ 132 Cortez Kennedy	.40	.18
❑ 133 Jon Kitna	2.50	1.10
❑ 134 James McKnight	.40	.18
❑ 135 Warren Moon	1.50	.70
❑ 136 Mike Alstott	1.50	.70
❑ 137 Reidel Anthony	.75	.35
❑ 138 Trent Dilfer	1.50	.70
❑ 139 Warrick Dunn	1.50	.70
❑ 140 Warren Sapp	.75	.35
❑ 141 Kevin Dyson RC	4.00	1.80
❑ 142 Eddie George	3.00	1.35
❑ 143 Steve McNair	1.50	.70
❑ 144 Chris Sanders	.40	.18
❑ 145 Frank Wycheck	.40	.18
❑ 146 Stephen Alexander RC	3.00	1.35
❑ 147 Terry Allen	1.50	.70
❑ 148 Gus Frerotte	.40	.18
❑ 149 Skip Hicks RC	3.00	1.35
❑ 150 Michael Westbrook	.75	.35
❑ S1 Warrick Dunn Sample	1.00	.45

1999 Revolution

	MINT	NRMT
COMPLETE SET (175)	100.00	45.00

Card	MINT	NRMT
❑ 1 David Boston SP RC	5.00	2.20
❑ 2 Joel Makovicka RC SP	3.00	1.35
❑ 3 Rob Moore	.50	.23
❑ 4 Adrian Murrell	.50	.23
❑ 5 Jake Plummer	2.00	.90
❑ 6 Frank Sanders	.50	.23
❑ 7 Jamal Anderson	1.00	.45
❑ 8 Chris Chandler	.50	.23
❑ 9 Tim Dwight	1.00	.45
❑ 10 Terance Mathis	.50	.23
❑ 11 Jeff Paulk RC SP	3.00	1.35
❑ 12 O.J. Santiago	.25	.11
❑ 13 Peter Boulware	.25	.11
❑ 14 Priest Holmes	1.00	.45
❑ 15 Michael Jackson	.25	.11
❑ 16 Jermaine Lewis	.50	.23
❑ 17 Doug Flutie	1.25	.55
❑ 18 Eric Moulds	1.00	.45
❑ 19 Peerless Price RC SP	4.00	1.80
❑ 20 Andre Reed	.50	.23
❑ 21 Antowain Smith	1.00	.45
❑ 22 Bruce Smith	.50	.23
❑ 23 Steve Beuerlein	.25	.11
❑ 24 Kevin Greene	.50	.23
❑ 25 Fred Lane	.25	.11
❑ 26 Muhsin Muhammad	.50	.23
❑ 27 Wesley Walls	.50	.23
❑ 28 Marty Booker RC SP	3.00	1.35
❑ 29 Curtis Conway	.50	.23
❑ 30 Bobby Engram	.50	.23
❑ 31 Curtis Enis	1.00	.45
❑ 32 Erik Kramer	.25	.11
❑ 33 Cade McNown SP RC	3.00	1.35
❑ 34 Scott Covington RC	2.50	1.10
❑ 35 Corey Dillon	1.00	.45
❑ 36 Carl Pickens	.50	.23
❑ 37 Darnay Scott	.25	.11
❑ 38 Akili Smith RC	5.00	2.20
❑ 39 Craig Yeast RC SP	2.50	1.10
❑ 40 Darrin Chiaverini RC SP	2.50	1.10
❑ 41 Tim Couch SP RC	8.00	3.60
❑ 42 Ty Detmer	.50	.23
❑ 43 Kevin Johnson SP RC	5.00	2.20
❑ 44 Terry Kirby	.25	.11
❑ 45 D.McCutcheon RC SP	1.50	.70
❑ 46 Irv Smith	.25	.11
❑ 47 Troy Aikman	2.50	1.10
❑ 48 Michael Irvin	.50	.23
❑ 49 Wane McGarity RC SP	2.50	1.10
❑ 50 Dat Nguyen RC SP	3.00	1.35
❑ 51 Deion Sanders	1.00	.45
❑ 52 Emmitt Smith	2.50	1.10
❑ 53 Terrell Davis	2.50	1.10
❑ 54 John Elway	4.00	1.80
❑ 55 Brian Griese	2.00	.90
❑ 56 Ed McCaffrey	.50	.23
❑ 57 Travis McGriff RC SP	3.00	1.35
❑ 58 Shannon Sharpe	.50	.23
❑ 59 Rod Smith WR	.50	.23
❑ 60 Charlie Batch	2.00	.90
❑ 61 Chris Claiborne RC	1.25	.55
❑ 62 Sedrick Irvin RC	2.50	1.10
❑ 63 Herman Moore	1.00	.45
❑ 64 Johnnie Morton	.50	.23
❑ 65 Barry Sanders	4.00	1.80
❑ 66 Aaron Brooks RC SP	12.00	5.50
❑ 67 Mark Chmura	.25	.11
❑ 68 Brett Favre	4.00	1.80
❑ 69 Antonio Freeman	1.00	.45
❑ 70 Dorsey Levens	1.00	.45
❑ 71 De'Mond Parker RC SP	3.00	1.35
❑ 72 Marvin Harrison	1.00	.45
❑ 73 Edgerrin James SP RC	12.00	5.50
❑ 74 Peyton Manning	4.00	1.80
❑ 75 Jerome Pathon	.25	.11
❑ 76 Mike Peterson RC SP	2.50	1.10
❑ 77 Reggie Barlow	.25	.11
❑ 78 Mark Brunell	1.50	.70
❑ 79 Keenan McCardell	.50	.23
❑ 80 Jimmy Smith	.50	.23
❑ 81 Fred Taylor	2.50	1.10
❑ 82 Mike Cloud RC	2.50	1.10
❑ 83 Tony Gonzalez	.50	.23
❑ 84 Elvis Grbac	.50	.23
❑ 85 Larry Parker RC SP	2.50	1.10
❑ 86 Andre Rison	.50	.23
❑ 87 Brian Shay RC SP	2.50	1.10
❑ 88 Karim Abdul-Jabbar	.50	.23
❑ 89 Oronde Gadsden	.25	.11
❑ 90 James Johnson SP RC	2.50	1.10
❑ 91 Rob Konrad RC	2.00	.90
❑ 92 Dan Marino	4.00	1.80
❑ 93 O.J. McDuffie	.50	.23
❑ 94 Cris Carter	1.00	.45
❑ 95 Daunte Culpepper SP RC	12.00	5.50
❑ 96 Randall Cunningham	1.00	.45
❑ 97 Jim Kleinsasser RC SP	2.50	1.10
❑ 98 Randy Moss	4.00	1.80
❑ 99 Jake Reed	.50	.23
❑ 100 Robert Smith	1.00	.45
❑ 101 Drew Bledsoe	1.50	.70
❑ 102 Ben Coates	.50	.23
❑ 103 Kevin Faulk SP RC	4.00	1.80
❑ 104 Terry Glenn	1.00	.45
❑ 105 Shawn Jefferson	.25	.11
❑ 106 A.Katzenmoyer RC SP	3.00	1.35
❑ 107 Cameron Cleeland	.25	.11
❑ 108 Andre Hastings	.25	.11
❑ 109 Billy Joe Tolliver	.25	.11
❑ 110 Ricky Williams RC	10.00	4.50
❑ 111 Gary Brown	.25	.11
❑ 112 Kent Graham	.25	.11
❑ 113 Ike Hilliard	.25	.11
❑ 114 Joe Montgomery RC SP	2.50	1.10
❑ 115 Amani Toomer	.25	.11
❑ 116 Wayne Chrebet	.50	.23
❑ 117 Keyshawn Johnson	1.00	.45
❑ 118 Leon Johnson	.25	.11
❑ 119 Curtis Martin	1.00	.45
❑ 120 Vinny Testaverde	.50	.23
❑ 121 Dedric Ward	.25	.11
❑ 122 Tim Brown	1.00	.45
❑ 123 D.Douglas RC SP	3.00	1.35
❑ 124 Rickey Dudley	.25	.11
❑ 125 James Jett	.50	.23
❑ 126 Napoleon Kaufman	1.00	.45
❑ 127 Charles Woodson	1.00	.45
❑ 128 Na Brown RC SP	3.00	1.35
❑ 129 Cecil Martin RC SP	2.50	1.10
❑ 130 Donovan McNabb SP RC	10.00	4.50
❑ 131 Duce Staley	1.00	.45
❑ 132 Kevin Turner	.25	.11
❑ 133 Jerome Bettis	1.00	.45
❑ 134 Troy Edwards SP RC	3.00	1.35
❑ 135 Courtney Hawkins	.25	.11
❑ 136 Malcolm Johnson RC SP	2.50	1.10
❑ 137 Kordell Stewart	1.00	.45
❑ 138 Jerame Tuman RC SP	2.50	1.10
❑ 139 Amos Zereoue RC	2.50	1.10
❑ 140 Isaac Bruce	1.00	.45
❑ 141 Joe Germaine RC	2.50	1.10
❑ 142 Torry Holt RC SP	8.00	3.60
❑ 143 Amp Lee	.25	.11
❑ 144 Ricky Proehl	.25	.11
❑ 145 Freddie Jones	.25	.11
❑ 146 Ryan Leaf	1.00	.45
❑ 147 Natrone Means	.50	.23
❑ 148 Mikhael Ricks	.25	.11
❑ 149 Garrison Hearst	.50	.23
❑ 150 Terry Jackson RC SP	2.50	1.10
❑ 151 Terrell Owens	1.00	.45
❑ 152 Jerry Rice	2.50	1.10
❑ 153 J.J. Stokes	.50	.23
❑ 154 Steve Young	1.50	.70
❑ 155 Karsten Bailey RC	2.50	1.10
❑ 156 Joey Galloway	1.00	.45
❑ 157 Ahman Green	.50	.23
❑ 158 Brock Huard SP RC	4.00	1.80
❑ 159 Jon Kitna	1.00	.45
❑ 160 Ricky Watters	.50	.23
❑ 161 Mike Alstott	1.00	.45
❑ 162 Reidel Anthony	.50	.23
❑ 163 Trent Dilfer	.50	.23
❑ 164 Warrick Dunn	1.00	.45
❑ 165 Shaun King SP RC	5.00	2.20
❑ 166 Anthony McFarland RC	2.50	1.10
❑ 167 Kevin Dyson	.50	.23
❑ 168 Eddie George	1.25	.55
❑ 169 Darran Hall RC	2.00	.90
❑ 170 Steve McNair	1.00	.45
❑ 171 Frank Wycheck	.25	.11
❑ 172 Stephen Alexander	.25	.11
❑ 173 Champ Bailey	.25	.11
❑ 174 Skip Hicks	1.00	.45
❑ 175 Michael Westbrook	.50	.23

2000 Revolution

	MINT	NRMT
COMP.SET w/o SP's (100)	40.00	18.00

Card	MINT	NRMT
❑ 1 David Boston	1.00	.45
❑ 2 Jake Plummer	1.00	.45
❑ 3 Frank Sanders	.50	.23
❑ 4 Jamal Anderson	1.00	.45
❑ 5 Chris Chandler	.50	.23
❑ 6 Tim Dwight	1.00	.45
❑ 7 Terance Mathis	.50	.23
❑ 8 Tony Banks	.50	.23
❑ 9 Qadry Ismail	.50	.23
❑ 10 Shannon Sharpe	.25	.11
❑ 11 Rob Johnson	.50	.23
❑ 12 Eric Moulds	1.00	.45
❑ 13 Peerless Price	1.00	.45
❑ 14 Antowain Smith	.50	.23
❑ 15 Steve Beuerlein	.50	.23
❑ 16 Tim Biakabutuka	.50	.23
❑ 17 Muhsin Muhammad	.50	.23

❏ 18 Curtis Enis .50 .23
❏ 19 Cade McNown 1.00 .45
❏ 20 Marcus Robinson 1.00 .45
❏ 21 Corey Dillon 1.00 .45
❏ 22 Akili Smith 1.00 .45
❏ 23 Tim Couch 2.00 .90
❏ 24 Kevin Johnson 1.00 .45
❏ 25 Troy Aikman 2.50 1.10
❏ 26 Rocket Ismail .50 .23
❏ 27 Emmitt Smith 2.50 1.10
❏ 28 Terrell Davis 2.50 1.10
❏ 29 Brian Griese 1.25 .55
❏ 30 Ed McCaffrey 1.00 .45
❏ 31 Charlie Batch 1.00 .45
❏ 32 Herman Moore .50 .23
❏ 33 James Stewart .50 .23
❏ 34 Brett Favre 4.00 1.80
❏ 35 Antonio Freeman 1.00 .45
❏ 36 Dorsey Levens .50 .23
❏ 37 Marvin Harrison 1.00 .45
❏ 38 Edgerrin James 4.00 1.80
❏ 39 Peyton Manning 3.00 1.35
❏ 40 Terrence Wilkins 1.00 .45
❏ 41 Mark Brunell 1.50 .70
❏ 42 Keenan McCardell .50 .23
❏ 43 Jimmy Smith .50 .23
❏ 44 Fred Taylor 1.25 .55
❏ 45 Derrick Alexander .50 .23
❏ 46 Tony Gonzalez .50 .23
❏ 47 Elvis Grbac .50 .23
❏ 48 Damon Huard 1.00 .45
❏ 49 James Johnson .50 .23
❏ 50 O.J. McDuffie .50 .23
❏ 51 Cris Carter 1.00 .45
❏ 52 Daunte Culpepper 2.00 .90
❏ 53 Randy Moss 3.00 1.35
❏ 54 Robert Smith 1.00 .45
❏ 55 Drew Bledsoe 1.50 .70
❏ 56 Terry Glenn .50 .23
❏ 57 Jeff Blake .50 .23
❏ 58 Ricky Williams 2.50 1.10
❏ 59 Tiki Barber .50 .23
❏ 60 Kerry Collins .50 .23
❏ 61 Ike Hilliard .50 .23
❏ 62 Amani Toomer .25 .11
❏ 63 Wayne Chrebet .50 .23
❏ 64 Curtis Martin 1.00 .45
❏ 65 Vinny Testaverde .50 .23
❏ 66 Dedric Ward .25 .11
❏ 67 Tim Brown 1.00 .45
❏ 68 Napoleon Kaufman .50 .23
❏ 69 Tyrone Wheatley .50 .23
❏ 70 Charles Johnson .50 .23
❏ 71 Donovan McNabb 1.50 .70
❏ 72 Duce Staley 1.00 .45
❏ 73 Jerome Bettis 1.00 .45
❏ 74 Troy Edwards .50 .23
❏ 75 Kordell Stewart 1.00 .45
❏ 76 Isaac Bruce 1.00 .45
❏ 77 Marshall Faulk 1.25 .55
❏ 78 Az-Zahir Hakim .25 .11
❏ 79 Torry Holt 1.00 .45
❏ 80 Kurt Warner 4.00 1.80
❏ 81 Curtis Conway .50 .23
❏ 82 Jermaine Fazande .25 .11
❏ 83 Ryan Leaf 1.00 .45
❏ 84 Junior Seau .50 .23
❏ 85 Jeff Garcia 1.00 .45
❏ 86 Charlie Garner .50 .23
❏ 87 Terrell Owens 1.00 .45
❏ 88 Jerry Rice 2.50 1.10
❏ 89 Jon Kitna 1.00 .45
❏ 90 Derrick Mayes .50 .23
❏ 91 Ricky Watters .25 .11
❏ 92 Mike Alstott 1.00 .45
❏ 93 Warrick Dunn 1.00 .45
❏ 94 Keyshawn Johnson 1.00 .45
❏ 95 Shaun King 1.50 .70
❏ 96 Eddie George 1.50 .70
❏ 97 Jevon Kearse 1.00 .45
❏ 98 Steve McNair 1.00 .45
❏ 99 Stephen Davis 1.00 .45
❏ 100 Brad Johnson 1.00 .45
❏ 101 Thomas Jones RC 25.00 11.00
❏ 102 Doug Johnson RC 15.00 6.75
❏ 103 Jamal Lewis RC 80.00 36.00
❏ 104 Chris Redman RC 30.00 13.50
❏ 105 Travis Taylor RC 20.00 9.00
❏ 106 Troy Walters RC 15.00 6.75
❏ 107 Kwame Cavil RC 12.00 5.50
❏ 108 Sammy Morris RC 20.00 9.00
❏ 109 Dez White RC 12.00 5.50
❏ 110 Ron Dugans RC 12.00 5.50
❏ 111 Danny Farmer RC 15.00 6.75
❏ 112 Curtis Keaton RC 12.00 5.50
❏ 113 Peter Warrick RC 50.00 22.00
❏ 114 Dennis Northcutt RC 20.00 9.00
❏ 115 Travis Prentice RC 25.00 11.00
❏ 116 Kevin Thompson RC 15.00 6.75
❏ 117 Spergon Wynn RC 15.00 6.75
❏ 118 Michael Wiley RC 15.00 6.75
❏ 119 Mike Anderson RC 80.00 36.00
❏ 120 Chris Cole RC 12.00 5.50
❏ 121 Jarious Jackson RC 15.00 6.75
❏ 122 Charles Lee RC 8.00 3.60
❏ 123 Anthony Lucas RC 8.00 3.60
❏ 124 R.Jay Soward RC 15.00 6.75
❏ 125 Shyrone Stith RC 12.00 5.50
❏ 126 Sylvester Morris RC 30.00 13.50
❏ 127 Doug Chapman RC 30.00 13.50
❏ 128 Tom Brady RC 15.00 6.75
❏ 129 Gari Scott RC 12.00 5.50
❏ 130 J.R. Redmond RC 20.00 9.00
❏ 131 Ron Dayne RC 50.00 22.00
❏ 132 Ron Dixon RC 20.00 9.00
❏ 133 Laveranues Coles RC 25.00 11.00
❏ 134 Ronney Jenkins RC 12.00 5.50
❏ 135 Chad Pennington RC 50.00 22.00
❏ 136 Jerry Porter RC 15.00 6.75
❏ 137 Todd Pinkston RC 15.00 6.75
❏ 138 Plaxico Burress RC 30.00 13.50
❏ 139 Trung Canidate RC 15.00 6.75
❏ 140 Troy Walters RC 15.00 6.75
❏ 141 Giovanni Carmazzi RC 20.00 9.00
❏ 142 Tim Rattay RC 25.00 11.00
❏ 143 Shaun Alexander RC 40.00 18.00
❏ 144 Darrell Jackson RC 25.00 11.00
❏ 145 James Williams RC 12.00 5.50
❏ 146 Joe Hamilton RC 20.00 9.00
❏ 147 Aaron Stecker RC 15.00 6.75
❏ 148 Erron Kinney RC 15.00 6.75
❏ 149 Billy Volek RC 12.00 5.50
❏ 150 Todd Husak RC 15.00 6.75

1989 Score

	MINT	NRMT
COMPLETE SET (330)	140.00	65.00
COMP.FACT.SET (330)	150.00	70.00

❏ 1 Joe Montana 4.00 1.80
❏ 2 Bo Jackson .60 .25
❏ 3 Boomer Esiason .20 .09
❏ 4 Roger Craig .50 .23
❏ 5 Ed Too Tall Jones .20 .09
❏ 6 Phil Simms .20 .09
❏ 7 Dan Hampton .20 .09
❏ 8 John Settle RC .10 .05
❏ 9 Bernie Kosar .20 .09
❏ 10 Al Toon .20 .09
❏ 11 Bubby Brister RC 2.50 1.10
❏ 12 Mark Clayton .20 .09
❏ 13 Dan Marino 4.00 1.80
❏ 14 Joe Morris .10 .05
❏ 15 Warren Moon .50 .23
❏ 16 Chuck Long .10 .05
❏ 17 Mark Jackson .10 .05
❏ 18 Michael Irvin RC 8.00 3.60
❏ 19 Bruce Smith .50 .23
❏ 20 Anthony Carter .20 .09
❏ 21 Charles Haley .50 .23
❏ 22 Dave Duerson .10 .05
❏ 23 Troy Stradford .10 .05
❏ 24 Freeman McNeil .10 .05
❏ 25 Jerry Gray .10 .05
❏ 26 Bill Maas .10 .05
❏ 27 Chris Chandler RC 5.00 2.20
❏ 28 Tom Newberry RC .10 .05
❏ 29 Albert Lewis .10 .05
❏ 30 Jay Schroeder .10 .05
❏ 31 Dalton Hilliard .10 .05
❏ 32 Tony Eason .10 .05
❏ 33 Rick Donnelly UER .10 .05
(229.11 yards per punt)
❏ 34 Herschel Walker .20 .09
❏ 35 Wesley Walker .10 .05
❏ 36 Chris Doleman .20 .09
❏ 37 Pat Swilling .20 .09
❏ 38 Joey Browner .10 .05
❏ 39 Shane Conlan .10 .05
❏ 40 Mike Tomczak .20 .09
❏ 41 Webster Slaughter .20 .09
❏ 42 Ray Donaldson .10 .05
❏ 43 Christian Okoye .10 .05
❏ 44 John Bosa .10 .05
❏ 45 Aaron Cox RC .10 .05
❏ 46 Bobby Hebert .20 .09
❏ 47 Carl Banks .10 .05
❏ 48 Jeff Fuller .10 .05
❏ 49 Gerald Willhite .10 .05
❏ 50 Mike Singletary .20 .09
❏ 51 Stanley Morgan .10 .05
❏ 52 Mark Bavaro .20 .09
❏ 53 Mickey Shuler .10 .05
❏ 54 Keith Millard .10 .05
❏ 55 Andre Tippett .10 .05
❏ 56 Vance Johnson .20 .09
❏ 57 Bennie Blades RC .10 .05
❏ 58 Tim Harris .10 .05
❏ 59 Hanford Dixon .10 .05
❏ 60 Chris Miller RC 1.50 .70
❏ 61 Cornelius Bennett .50 .23
❏ 62 Neal Anderson .20 .09
❏ 63 Ickey Woods RC UER .20 .09
(Jersey is 31 but listed as 30 on card back)
❏ 64 Gary Anderson RB .10 .05
❏ 65 Vaughan Johnson RC** .10 .05
❏ 66 Ronnie Lippett .10 .05
❏ 67 Mike Quick .10 .05
❏ 68 Roy Green .20 .09
❏ 69 Tim Krumrie .10 .05
❏ 70 Mark Malone .10 .05
❏ 71 James Jones .10 .05
❏ 72 Cris Carter RC 20.00 9.00
❏ 73 Ricky Nattiel .10 .05
❏ 74 Jim Arnold UER .10 .05
(238.83 yards per punt)
❏ 75 Randall Cunningham 1.00 .45
❏ 76 John L. Williams .10 .05
❏ 77 Paul Gruber RC .10 .05
❏ 78 Rod Woodson RC 3.00 1.35
❏ 79 Ray Childress .10 .05
❏ 80 Doug Williams .20 .09
❏ 81 Deron Cherry .20 .09
❏ 82 John Offerdahl .10 .05
❏ 83 Louis Lipps .20 .09
❏ 84 Neil Lomax .10 .05
❏ 85 Wade Wilson .20 .09
❏ 86 Tim Brown RC 12.00 5.50
❏ 87 Chris Hinton .10 .05
❏ 88 Stump Mitchell .10 .05
❏ 89 Tunch Ilkin RC .10 .05
❏ 90 Steve Pelluer .10 .05
❏ 91 Brian Noble .10 .05
❏ 92 Reggie White .50 .23
❏ 93 Aundray Bruce RC .10 .05
❏ 94 Garry James .10 .05
❏ 95 Drew Hill .10 .05

❑ 96 Anthony Munoz	.20	.09
❑ 97 James Wilder	.10	.05
❑ 98 Dexter Manley	.10	.05
❑ 99 Lee Williams	.10	.05
❑ 100 Dave Krieg	.20	.09
❑ 101A Keith Jackson RC ERR (Listed as 84 on card back)	.50	.23
❑ 101B Keith Jackson RC COR (Listed as 88 on card back)	.50	.23
❑ 102 Luis Sharpe	.10	.05
❑ 103 Kevin Greene	.50	.23
❑ 104 Duane Bickett	.10	.05
❑ 105 Mark Rypien RC	.50	.23
❑ 106 Curt Warner	.10	.05
❑ 107 Jacob Green	.10	.05
❑ 108 Gary Clark	.50	.23
❑ 109 Bruce Matthews RC	1.00	.45
❑ 110 Bill Fralic	.10	.05
❑ 111 Bill Bates	.20	.09
❑ 112 Jeff Bryant	.10	.05
❑ 113 Charles Mann	.10	.05
❑ 114 Richard Dent	.20	.09
❑ 115 Bruce Hill RC	.10	.05
❑ 116 Mark May RC	.10	.05
❑ 117 Mark Collins RC	.10	.05
❑ 118 Ron Holmes	.10	.05
❑ 119 Scott Case RC	.10	.05
❑ 120 Tom Rathman	.10	.05
❑ 121 Dennis McKinnon	.10	.05
❑ 122A Ricky Sanders ERR (Listed as 46 on card back)	.25	.11
❑ 122B Ricky Sanders COR (Listed as 83 on card back)	.50	.23
❑ 123 Michael Carter	.10	.05
❑ 124 Ozzie Newsome	.20	.09
❑ 125 Irving Fryar UER ("wide reveiver")	.20	.09
❑ 126A Ron Hall RC ERR (Wrong photos on card)	.25	.11
❑ 126B Ron Hall RC COR (Correct photos used)	.50	.23
❑ 127 Clay Matthews	.20	.09
❑ 128 Leonard Marshall	.10	.05
❑ 129 Kevin Mack	.10	.05
❑ 130 Art Monk	.20	.09
❑ 131 Garin Veris	.10	.05
❑ 132 Steve Jordan	.10	.05
❑ 133 Frank Minnifield	.10	.05
❑ 134 Eddie Brown	.10	.05
❑ 135 Stacey Bailey	.10	.05
❑ 136 Rickey Jackson	.20	.09
❑ 137 Henry Ellard	.20	.09
❑ 138 Jim Burt	.10	.05
❑ 139 Jerome Brown	.20	.09
❑ 140 Rodney Holman RC	.10	.05
❑ 141 Sammy Winder	.10	.05
❑ 142 Marcus Cotton	.10	.05
❑ 143 Jim Jeffcoat	.10	.05
❑ 144 Rueben Mayes	.10	.05
❑ 145 Jim McMahon	.20	.09
❑ 146 Reggie Williams	.10	.05
❑ 147 John Anderson	.10	.05
❑ 148 Harris Barton RC	.10	.05
❑ 149 Phillip Epps	.10	.05
❑ 150 Jay Hilgenberg	.10	.05
❑ 151 Earl Ferrell	.10	.05
❑ 152 Andre Reed	.50	.23
❑ 153 Dennis Gentry	.10	.05
❑ 154 Max Montoya	.10	.05
❑ 155 Darrin Nelson	.10	.05
❑ 156 Jeff Chadwick	.10	.05
❑ 157 James Brooks	.20	.09
❑ 158 Keith Bishop	.10	.05
❑ 159 Robert Awalt	.10	.05
❑ 160 Marty Lyons	.10	.05
❑ 161 Johnny Hector	.10	.05
❑ 162 Tony Casillas	.10	.05
❑ 163 Kyle Clifton RC	.10	.05
❑ 164 Cody Risien	.10	.05
❑ 165 Jamie Holland RC	.10	.05
❑ 166 Merril Hoge RC	.10	.05
❑ 167 Chris Spielman RC	1.00	.45
❑ 168 Carlos Carson	.10	.05
❑ 169 Jerry Ball RC	.10	.05
❑ 170 Don Majkowski RC	.20	.09
❑ 171 Everson Walls	.10	.05
❑ 172 Mike Rozier	.10	.05
❑ 173 Matt Millen	.20	.09
❑ 174 Karl Mecklenburg	.10	.05
❑ 175 Paul Palmer	.10	.05
❑ 176 Brian Blades RC UER (Photo on back is reversed negative)	.50	.23
❑ 177 Brent Fullwood RC	.10	.05
❑ 178 Anthony Miller RC	.50	.23
❑ 179 Brian Sochia	.10	.05
❑ 180 Stephen Baker RC	.20	.09
❑ 181 Jesse Solomon	.10	.05
❑ 182 John Grimsley	.10	.05
❑ 183 Timmy Newsome	.10	.05
❑ 184 Steve Sewell RC	.10	.05
❑ 185 Dean Biasucci	.10	.05
❑ 186 Alonzo Highsmith	.10	.05
❑ 187 Randy Grimes	.10	.05
❑ 188A M.Carrier RC WR ERR Photo on back is actually Bruce Hill	1.00	.45
❑ 188B M.Carrier RC WR COR (Wearing helmet in photo on back	1.00	.45
❑ 189 Vann McElroy	.10	.05
❑ 190 Greg Bell	.10	.05
❑ 191 Quinn Early RC	1.50	.70
❑ 192 Lawrence Taylor	.50	.23
❑ 193 Albert Bentley	.10	.05
❑ 194 Ernest Givins	.20	.09
❑ 195 Jackie Slater	.10	.05
❑ 196 Jim Sweeney	.10	.05
❑ 197 Freddie Joe Nunn	.10	.05
❑ 198 Keith Byars	.20	.09
❑ 199 Hardy Nickerson RC	.50	.23
❑ 200 Steve Beuerlein RC	5.00	2.20
❑ 201 Bruce Armstrong RC	.10	.05
❑ 202 Lionel Manuel	.10	.05
❑ 203 J.T. Smith	.10	.05
❑ 204 Mark Ingram RC	.50	.23
❑ 205 Fred Smerlas	.10	.05
❑ 206 Bryan Hinkle RC	.10	.05
❑ 207 Steve McMichael	.20	.09
❑ 208 Nick Lowery	.10	.05
❑ 209 Jack Trudeau	.10	.05
❑ 210 Lorenzo Hampton	.10	.05
❑ 211 Thurman Thomas RC	6.00	2.70
❑ 212 Steve Young	1.50	.70
❑ 213 James Lofton	.50	.23
❑ 214 Jim Covert	.10	.05
❑ 215 Ronnie Lott	.20	.09
❑ 216 Stephone Paige	.10	.05
❑ 217 Mark Duper	.20	.09
❑ 218A Willie Gault ERR (Front photo actually 93 Greg Townsend)	.25	.11
❑ 218B Willie Gault COR (83 clearly visible)	.50	.23
❑ 219 Ken Ruettgers RC	.10	.05
❑ 220 Kevin Ross RC	.20	.09
❑ 221 Jerry Rice	3.00	1.35
❑ 222 Billy Ray Smith	.10	.05
❑ 223 Jim Kelly	1.00	.45
❑ 224 Vinny Testaverde	1.00	.45
❑ 225 Steve Largent	.50	.23
❑ 226 Warren Williams RC	.10	.05
❑ 227 Morten Andersen	.10	.05
❑ 228 Bill Brooks	.20	.09
❑ 229 Reggie Langhorne RC	.10	.05
❑ 230 Pepper Johnson	.10	.05
❑ 231 Pat Leahy	.10	.05
❑ 232 Fred Marion	.10	.05
❑ 233 Gary Zimmerman	.10	.05
❑ 234 Marcus Allen	.50	.23
❑ 235 Gaston Green RC	.10	.05
❑ 236 John Stephens RC	.10	.05
❑ 237 Terry Kinard	.10	.05
❑ 238 John Taylor RC	.50	.23
❑ 239 Brian Bosworth	.20	.09
❑ 240 Anthony Toney	.10	.05
❑ 241 Ken O'Brien	.10	.05
❑ 242 Howie Long	.20	.09
❑ 243 Doug Flutie	2.50	1.10
❑ 244 Jim Everett	.50	.23
❑ 245 Broderick Thomas RC	.50	.23
❑ 246 Deion Sanders RC	12.00	5.50
❑ 247 Donnell Woolford RC	.20	.09
❑ 248 Wayne Martin RC	.10	.05
❑ 249 David Williams RC	.10	.05
❑ 250 Bill Hawkins RC	.10	.05
❑ 251 Eric Hill RC	.10	.05
❑ 252 Burt Grossman RC	.10	.05
❑ 253 Tracy Rocker	.10	.05
❑ 254 Steve Wisniewski RC	.20	.09
❑ 255 Jessie Small RC	.10	.05
❑ 256 David Braxton	.10	.05
❑ 257 Barry Sanders RC	80.00	36.00
❑ 258 Derrick Thomas RC	6.00	2.70
❑ 259 Eric Metcalf RC	1.00	.45
❑ 260 Keith DeLong RC	.10	.05
❑ 261 Hart Lee Dykes RC	.10	.05
❑ 262 Sammie Smith RC	.10	.05
❑ 263 Steve Atwater RC	.50	.23
❑ 264 Eric Ball RC	.10	.05
❑ 265 Don Beebe RC	.50	.23
❑ 266 Brian Williams OL	.10	.05
❑ 267 Jeff Lageman RC	.20	.09
❑ 268 Tim Worley RC	.10	.05
❑ 269 Tony Mandarich RC	.10	.05
❑ 270 Troy Aikman RC	40.00	18.00
❑ 271 Andy Heck RC	.10	.05
❑ 272 Andre Rison RC	5.00	2.20
❑ 273 AFC Championship Bengals over Bills (Ickey Woods and Boomer Esiason)	.10	.05
❑ 274 NFC Championship 49ers over Bears (Joe Montana)	1.00	.45
❑ 275 Super Bowl XXIII 49ers over Bengals (Joe Montana and Jerry Rice)	2.00	.90
❑ 276 Rodney Carter	.10	.05
❑ 277 Mark Jackson, Vance Johnson, and Ricky Nattiel	.10	.05
❑ 278 John L. Williams and Curt Warner	.10	.05
❑ 279 Joe Montana and Jerry Rice	2.00	.90
❑ 280 Roy Green and Neil Lomax	.10	.05
❑ 281 Randall Cunningham and Keith Jackson	.10	.05
❑ 282 Chris Doleman and Keith Millard	.10	.05
❑ 283 Mark Duper and Mark Clayton	.10	.05
❑ 284 Marcus Allen and Bo Jackson	.60	.25
❑ 285 Frank Minnifield AP	.10	.05
❑ 286 Bruce Matthews AP	.20	.09
❑ 287 Joey Browner AP	.10	.05
❑ 288 Jay Hilgenberg AP	.10	.05
❑ 289 Carl Lee AP RC	.10	.05
❑ 290 Scott Norwood AP RC	.10	.05
❑ 291 John Taylor AP	.50	.23
❑ 292 Jerry Rice AP	1.50	.70
❑ 293A Keith Jackson AP ERR (Listed as 84 on card back)	.50	.23
❑ 293B Keith Jackson AP COR (Listed as 88 on card back)	.50	.23
❑ 294 Gary Zimmerman AP	.10	.05
❑ 295 Lawrence Taylor AP	.50	.23
❑ 296 Reggie White AP	.50	.23
❑ 297 Roger Craig AP	.20	.09
❑ 298 Boomer Esiason AP	.20	.09
❑ 299 Cornelius Bennett AP	.20	.09
❑ 300 Mike Horan AP	.10	.05
❑ 301 Deron Cherry AP	.10	.05
❑ 302 Tom Newberry AP	.10	.05
❑ 303 Mike Singletary AP	.20	.09
❑ 304 Shane Conlan AP	.10	.05
❑ 305A Tim Brown ERR AP (Photo on front act-	2.00	.90

ually 80 James Lofton)		
❑ 305B Tim Brown COR AP	2.00	.90
(Dark jersey 81)		
❑ 306 Henry Ellard AP	.20	.09
❑ 307 Bruce Smith AP	.20	.09
❑ 308 Tim Krumrie AP	.10	.05
❑ 309 Anthony Munoz AP	.20	.09
❑ 310 Darrell Green SPEED	.10	.05
❑ 311 Anthony Miller SPEED	.50	.23
❑ 312 Wesley Walker SPEED	.10	.05
❑ 313 Ron Brown SPEED	.10	.05
❑ 314 Bo Jackson SPEED	.60	.25
❑ 315 Phillip Epps SPEED	.10	.05
❑ 316A E.Thomas RC ERR SPEED	.25	.11
(Listed as 31 on card back)		
❑ 316B E.Thomas RC COR SPEED	.50	.23
(Listed as 22 on card back)		
❑ 317 Herschel Walker SPEED	.20	.09
❑ 318 Jacob Green PRED	.10	.05
❑ 319 Andre Tippett PRED	.10	.05
❑ 320 Freddie Joe Nunn PRED	.10	.05
❑ 321 Reggie White PRED	.50	.23
❑ 322 Lawrence Taylor PRED	.50	.23
❑ 323 Greg Townsend PRED	.10	.05
❑ 324 Tim Harris PRED	.10	.05
❑ 325 Bruce Smith PRED	.20	.09
❑ 326 Tony Dorsett RB	.50	.23
❑ 327 Steve Largent RB	.50	.23
❑ 328 Tim Brown RB	2.00	.90
❑ 329 Joe Montana RB	1.50	.70
❑ 330 Tom Landry Tribute	1.00	.45

1989 Score Supplemental

	MINT	NRMT
COMP.FACT.SET (110)	8.00	3.60
❑ 331S Herschel Walker	.40	.18
❑ 332S Allen Pinkett RC	.10	.05
❑ 333S Sterling Sharpe RC	3.00	1.35
❑ 334S Alvin Walton RC	.10	.05
❑ 335S Frank Reich RC	.40	.18
❑ 336S Jim Thornton RC	.10	.05
❑ 337S David Fulcher	.20	.09
❑ 338S Raul Allegre	.10	.05
❑ 339S John Elway	4.00	1.80
❑ 340S Michael Cofer	.10	.05
❑ 341S Jim Skow	.10	.05
❑ 342S Steve DeBerg	.10	.05
❑ 343S M.Fernandez RC**/C	.10	.05
❑ 344S Mike Lansford	.10	.05
❑ 345S Reggie Roby	.10	.05
❑ 346S Raymond Clayborn	.10	.05
❑ 347S Lonzell Hill	.10	.05
❑ 348S Ottis Anderson	.20	.09
❑ 349S Erik McMillan RC	.10	.05
❑ 350S Al Harris	.10	.05
❑ 351S Jack Del Rio RC	.20	.09
❑ 352S Gary Anderson K	.10	.05
❑ 353S Jim McMahon	.20	.09
❑ 354S Keena Turner	.10	.05
❑ 355S Tony Woods RC	.10	.05
❑ 356S Donald Igwebuike	.10	.05
❑ 357S Gerald Riggs	.20	.09
❑ 358S Eddie Murray	.10	.05
❑ 359S Dino Hackett	.10	.05
❑ 360S Brad Muster RC	.10	.05
❑ 361S Paul Palmer	.10	.05
❑ 362S Jerry Robinson	.10	.05
❑ 363S Simon Fletcher RC	.20	.09
❑ 364S Tommy Kramer	.10	.05
❑ 365S Jim C. Jensen RC	.10	.05
❑ 366S Lorenzo White RC	.40	.18
❑ 367S Fredd Young	.10	.05
❑ 368S Ron Jaworski	.10	.05
❑ 369S Mel Owens	.10	.05
❑ 370S Dave Waymer	.10	.05
❑ 371S Sean Landeta	.10	.05
❑ 372S Sam Mills	.20	.09
❑ 373S Todd Blackledge	.10	.05
❑ 374S Jo Jo Townsell	.10	.05
❑ 375S Ron Wolfley	.10	.05
❑ 376S Ralf Mojsiejenko	.10	.05
❑ 377S Eric Wright	.10	.05
❑ 378S Nesby Glasgow	.10	.05
❑ 379S Darryl Talley	.20	.09
❑ 380S Eric Allen RC	.40	.18
❑ 381S Dennis Smith	.20	.09
❑ 382S John Tice	.10	.05
❑ 383S Jesse Solomon	.10	.05
❑ 384S Bo Jackson	1.00	.45
(FB/BB Pose)		
❑ 385S Mike Merriweather	.10	.05
❑ 386S Maurice Carthon	.10	.05
❑ 387S David Grayson	.10	.05
❑ 388S Wilber Marshall	.10	.05
❑ 389S David Wyman	.10	.05
❑ 390S Thomas Everett RC	.10	.05
❑ 391S Alex Gordon	.10	.05
❑ 392S D.J. Dozier	.10	.05
❑ 393S Scott Radecic RC	.10	.05
❑ 394S Eric Thomas	.10	.05
❑ 395S Mike Gann	.10	.05
❑ 396S William Perry	.20	.09
❑ 397S Carl Hairston	.10	.05
❑ 398S Billy Ard	.10	.05
❑ 399S Donnell Thompson	.10	.05
❑ 400S Mike Webster	.20	.09
❑ 401S Scott Davis RC	.10	.05
❑ 402S Sean Farrell	.10	.05
❑ 403S Mike Golic RC	.10	.05
❑ 404S Mike Kenn	.10	.05
❑ 405S Keith Van Horne RC	.10	.05
❑ 406S Bob Golic	.10	.05
❑ 407S Neil Smith RC	2.00	.90
❑ 408S Dermontti Dawson RC	.20	.09
❑ 409S Leslie O'Neal	.20	.09
❑ 410S Matt Bahr	.10	.05
❑ 411S Guy McIntyre RC	.10	.05
❑ 412S Bryan Millard	.10	.05
❑ 413S Joe Jacoby	.10	.05
❑ 414S Rob Taylor RC	.10	.05
❑ 415S Tony Zendejas	.10	.05
❑ 416S Vai Sikahema	.10	.05
❑ 417S Gary Reasons RC	.10	.05
❑ 418S Shawn Collins RC	.10	.05
❑ 419S Mark Green RC	.10	.05
❑ 420S Courtney Hall RC	.10	.05
❑ 421S Bobby Humphrey RC	.10	.05
❑ 422S Myron Guyton RC	.10	.05
❑ 423S Darryl Ingram RC	.10	.05
❑ 424S Chris Jacke RC	.10	.05
❑ 425S Keith Jones RC	.10	.05
❑ 426S Robert Massey RC	.10	.05
❑ 427S Bubba McDowell RC	.40	.18
❑ 428S Dave Meggett RC	.40	.18
❑ 429S Louis Oliver RC	.20	.09
❑ 430S Danny Peebles	.10	.05
❑ 431S Rodney Peete RC	.40	.18
❑ 432S Jeff Query RC	.10	.05
❑ 433S T.Rosenbach RC UER	.10	.05
Photo actually Gary Hogeboom		
❑ 434S Frank Stams RC	.10	.05
❑ 435S Lawyer Tillman RC	.10	.05
❑ 436S Billy Joe Tolliver RC	.10	.05
❑ 437S Floyd Turner RC	.20	.09
❑ 438S Steve Walsh RC	.20	.09
❑ 439S Joe Wolf RC	.10	.05
❑ 440S Trace Armstrong RC	.10	.05

1990 Score

	MINT	NRMT
COMPLETE SET (660)	7.50	3.40
COMP.FACT.SET (665)	10.00	4.50
❑ 1 Joe Montana	1.25	.55
❑ 2 Christian Okoye	.04	.02
❑ 3 Mike Singletary UER	.10	.05
(Text says 146 tackles in '89, should be 151)		
❑ 4 Jim Everett UER	.10	.05
(Text says 415 yards against Saints, should be 454)		
❑ 5 Phil Simms	.10	.05
❑ 6 Brent Fullwood	.04	.02
❑ 7 Bill Fralic	.04	.02
❑ 8 Leslie O'Neal	.10	.05
❑ 9 John Taylor	.25	.11
❑ 10 Bo Jackson	.30	.14
❑ 11 John Stephens	.04	.02
❑ 12 Art Monk	.10	.05
❑ 13 Dan Marino	1.25	.55
❑ 14 John Settle	.04	.02
❑ 15 Don Majkowski	.04	.02
❑ 16 Bruce Smith	.25	.11
❑ 17 Brad Muster	.04	.02
❑ 18 Jason Buck	.04	.02
❑ 19 James Brooks	.10	.05
❑ 20 Barry Sanders	1.50	.70
❑ 21 Troy Aikman	.75	.35
❑ 22 Allen Pinkett	.04	.02
❑ 23 Duane Bickett	.04	.02
❑ 24 Kevin Ross	.04	.02
❑ 25 John Elway	1.25	.55
❑ 26 Jeff Query	.04	.02
❑ 27 Eddie Murray	.04	.02
❑ 28 Richard Dent	.10	.05
❑ 29 Lorenzo White	.04	.02
❑ 30 Eric Metcalf	.25	.11
❑ 31 Jeff Dellenbach RC	.04	.02
❑ 32 Leon White	.04	.02
❑ 33 Jim Jeffcoat	.04	.02
❑ 34 Herschel Walker	.10	.05
❑ 35 Mike Johnson UER	.04	.02
(Front photo actually 51 Eddie Johnson)		
❑ 36 Joe Phillips	.04	.02
❑ 37 Willie Gault	.10	.05
❑ 38 Keith Millard	.04	.02
❑ 39 Fred Marion	.04	.02
❑ 40 Boomer Esiason	.10	.05
❑ 41 Dermontti Dawson	.10	.05
❑ 42 Dino Hackett	.04	.02
❑ 43 Reggie Roby	.04	.02
❑ 44 Roger Vick	.04	.02
❑ 45 Bobby Hebert	.04	.02
❑ 46 Don Beebe	.10	.05
❑ 47 Neal Anderson	.10	.05
❑ 48 Johnny Holland	.04	.02
❑ 49 Bobby Humphery	.04	.02
❑ 50 Lawrence Taylor	.25	.11
❑ 51 Billy Ray Smith	.04	.02
❑ 52 Robert Perryman	.04	.02
❑ 53 Gary Anderson K	.04	.02
❑ 54 Raul Allegre	.04	.02
❑ 55 Pat Swilling	.10	.05

Card	Player	Price	Price
❑ 56	Chris Doleman	.04	.02
❑ 57	Andre Reed	.25	.11
❑ 58	Seth Joyner	.10	.05
❑ 59	Bart Oates	.04	.02
❑ 60	Bernie Kosar	.10	.05
❑ 61	Dave Krieg	.10	.05
❑ 62	Lars Tate	.04	.02
❑ 63	Scott Norwood	.04	.02
❑ 64	Kyle Clifton	.04	.02
❑ 65	Alan Veingrad	.04	.02
❑ 66	Gerald Riggs UER (Text begins Depite, should be Despite)	.10	.05
❑ 67	Tim Worley	.04	.02
❑ 68	Rodney Holman	.04	.02
❑ 69	Tony Zendejas	.04	.02
❑ 70	Chris Miller	.25	.11
❑ 71	Wilber Marshall	.04	.02
❑ 72	Skip McClendon RC	.04	.02
❑ 73	Jim Covert	.04	.02
❑ 74	Sam Mills	.10	.05
❑ 75	Chris Hinton	.04	.02
❑ 76	Irv Eatman	.04	.02
❑ 77	Bubba Paris UER (No draft team mentioned)	.04	.02
❑ 78	John Elliott UER (No draft team mentioned; missing Team/FA status)	.04	.02
❑ 79	Thomas Everett	.04	.02
❑ 80	Steve Smith	.04	.02
❑ 81	Jackie Slater	.04	.02
❑ 82	Kelvin Martin RC	.04	.02
❑ 83	Jo Jo Townsell	.04	.02
❑ 84	Jim C. Jensen	.04	.02
❑ 85	Bobby Humphrey	.04	.02
❑ 86	Mike Dyal	.04	.02
❑ 87	Andre Rison UER (Front 87, back 85)	.25	.11
❑ 88	Brian Sochia	.04	.02
❑ 89	Greg Bell	.04	.02
❑ 90	Dalton Hilliard	.04	.02
❑ 91	Carl Banks	.04	.02
❑ 92	Dennis Smith	.04	.02
❑ 93	Bruce Matthews	.10	.05
❑ 94	Charles Haley	.10	.05
❑ 95	Deion Sanders UER (Reversed photo on back)	.50	.23
❑ 96	Stephone Paige	.04	.02
❑ 97	Marion Butts	.10	.05
❑ 98	Howie Long	.10	.05
❑ 99	Donald Igwebuike	.04	.02
❑ 100	Roger Craig UER (Text says 2 TD's in SB XXIV, should be 1; everything misspelled)	.10	.05
❑ 101	Charles Mann	.04	.02
❑ 102	Fredd Young	.04	.02
❑ 103	Chris Jacke	.04	.02
❑ 104	Scott Case	.04	.02
❑ 105	Warren Moon	.25	.11
❑ 106	Clyde Simmons	.04	.02
❑ 107	Steve Atwater	.04	.02
❑ 108	Morten Andersen	.04	.02
❑ 109	Eugene Marve	.04	.02
❑ 110	Thurman Thomas	.25	.11
❑ 111	Carnell Lake	.04	.02
❑ 112	Jim Kelly	.25	.11
❑ 113	Stanford Jennings	.04	.02
❑ 114	Jacob Green	.04	.02
❑ 115	Karl Mecklenburg	.04	.02
❑ 116	Ray Childress	.04	.02
❑ 117	Erik McMillan	.04	.02
❑ 118	Harry Newsome	.04	.02
❑ 119	James Dixon	.04	.02
❑ 120	Hassan Jones	.04	.02
❑ 121	Eric Allen	.04	.02
❑ 122	Felix Wright	.04	.02
❑ 123	Merril Hoge	.04	.02
❑ 124	Eric Ball	.04	.02
❑ 125	Flipper Anderson	.04	.02
❑ 126	James Jefferson	.04	.02
❑ 127	Tim McDonald	.04	.02
❑ 128	Larry Kinnebrew	.04	.02
❑ 129	Mark Collins	.04	.02
❑ 130	Ickey Woods	.04	.02
❑ 131	Jeff Donaldson UER (Stats say 0 int. and 0 fumble rec., text says 4 and 1)	.04	.02
❑ 132	Rich Camarillo	.04	.02
❑ 133	Melvin Bratton RC	.04	.02
❑ 134A	Kevin Butler (Photo on back has helmet on)	.35	.16
❑ 134B	Kevin Butler (Photo on back has no helmet on)	.50	.23
❑ 135	Albert Bentley	.04	.02
❑ 136A	Vai Sikahema (Photo on back has helmet on)	.35	.16
❑ 136B	Vai Sikahema (Photo on back has no helmet on)	.50	.23
❑ 137	Todd McNair RC	.04	.02
❑ 138	Alonzo Highsmith	.04	.02
❑ 139	Brian Blades	.10	.05
❑ 140	Jeff Lageman	.04	.02
❑ 141	Eric Thomas	.04	.02
❑ 142	Derek Hill	.04	.02
❑ 143	Rick Fenney	.04	.02
❑ 144	Herman Heard	.04	.02
❑ 145	Steve Young	.50	.23
❑ 146	Kent Hull	.04	.02
❑ 147A	Joey Browner (Photo on back looking to side)	.35	.16
❑ 147B	Joey Browner (Photo on back looking up)	.50	.23
❑ 148	Frank Minnifield	.04	.02
❑ 149	Robert Massey	.04	.02
❑ 150	Dave Meggett	.10	.05
❑ 151	Bubba McDowell	.04	.02
❑ 152	Rickey Dixon RC	.04	.02
❑ 153	Ray Donaldson	.04	.02
❑ 154	Alvin Walton	.04	.02
❑ 155	Mike Cofer	.04	.02
❑ 156	Darryl Talley	.04	.02
❑ 157	A.J. Johnson	.04	.02
❑ 158	Jerry Gray	.04	.02
❑ 159	Keith Byars	.04	.02
❑ 160	Andy Heck	.04	.02
❑ 161	Mike Munchak	.04	.02
❑ 162	Dennis Gentry	.04	.02
❑ 163	Timm Rosenbach UER (Born 1967 in Everett, Wa., should be 1966 in Missoula, Mont.)	.04	.02
❑ 164	Randall McDaniel	.10	.05
❑ 165	Pat Leahy	.04	.02
❑ 166	Bubby Brister	.04	.02
❑ 167	Aundray Bruce	.04	.02
❑ 168	Bill Brooks	.04	.02
❑ 169	Eddie Anderson RC	.04	.02
❑ 170	Ronnie Lott	.10	.05
❑ 171	Jay Hilgenberg	.04	.02
❑ 172	Joe Nash	.04	.02
❑ 173	Simon Fletcher	.04	.02
❑ 174	Shane Conlan	.04	.02
❑ 175	Sean Landeta	.04	.02
❑ 176	John Alt RC	.04	.02
❑ 177	Clay Matthews	.10	.05
❑ 178	Anthony Munoz	.10	.05
❑ 179	Pete Holohan	.04	.02
❑ 180	Robert Awalt	.04	.02
❑ 181	Rohn Stark	.04	.02
❑ 182	Vance Johnson	.04	.02
❑ 183	David Fulcher	.04	.02
❑ 184	Robert Delpino	.04	.02
❑ 185	Drew Hill	.04	.02
❑ 186	Reggie Langhorne UER (Stats read 1988, not 1989)	.04	.02
❑ 187	Lonzell Hill	.04	.02
❑ 188	Tom Rathman UER (On back, blocker misspelled)	.04	.02
❑ 189	Greg Montgomery RC	.04	.02
❑ 190	Leonard Smith	.04	.02
❑ 191	Chris Spielman	.25	.11
❑ 192	Tom Newberry	.04	.02
❑ 193	Cris Carter	.50	.23
❑ 194	Kevin Porter RC	.04	.02
❑ 195	Donnell Thompson	.04	.02
❑ 196	Vaughan Johnson	.04	.02
❑ 197	Steve McMichael	.10	.05
❑ 198	Jim Sweeney	.04	.02
❑ 199	Rich Karlis UER (No comma between day and year in birth data)	.04	.02
❑ 200	Jerry Rice	.75	.35
❑ 201	Dan Hampton UER (Card says he's a DE, should be DT)	.10	.05
❑ 202	Jim Lachey	.04	.02
❑ 203	Reggie White	.25	.11
❑ 204	Jerry Ball	.04	.02
❑ 205	Russ Grimm	.04	.02
❑ 206	Tim Green RC	.04	.02
❑ 207	Shawn Collins	.04	.02
❑ 208A	Ralf Mojsiejenko ERR (Chargers stats)	.15	.07
❑ 208B	Ralf Mojsiejenko COR (Redskins stats)	.50	.23
❑ 209	Trace Armstrong	.04	.02
❑ 210	Keith Jackson	.10	.05
❑ 211	Jamie Holland	.04	.02
❑ 212	Mark Clayton	.10	.05
❑ 213	Jeff Cross	.04	.02
❑ 214	Bob Gagliano	.04	.02
❑ 215	Louis Oliver UER (Text says played at Miami, should be Florida as in bio)	.04	.02
❑ 216	Jim Arnold	.04	.02
❑ 217	Robert Clark RC	.04	.02
❑ 218	Gill Byrd	.04	.02
❑ 219	Rodney Peete	.10	.05
❑ 220	Anthony Miller	.25	.11
❑ 221	Steve Grogan	.10	.05
❑ 222	Vince Newsome RC	.04	.02
❑ 223	Thomas Benson	.04	.02
❑ 224	Kevin Murphy	.04	.02
❑ 225	Henry Ellard	.10	.05
❑ 226	Richard Johnson	.04	.02
❑ 227	Jim Skow	.04	.02
❑ 228	Keith Jones	.04	.02
❑ 229	Dave Brown DB	.04	.02
❑ 230	Marcus Allen	.25	.11
❑ 231	Steve Walsh	.10	.05
❑ 232	Jim Harbaugh	.25	.11
❑ 233	Mel Gray	.10	.05
❑ 234	David Treadwell	.04	.02
❑ 235	John Offerdahl	.04	.02
❑ 236	Gary Reasons	.04	.02
❑ 237	Tim Krumrie	.04	.02
❑ 238	Dave Duerson	.04	.02
❑ 239	Gary Clark UER (Stats read 1988, not 1989)	.25	.11
❑ 240	Mark Jackson	.04	.02
❑ 241	Mark Murphy	.04	.02
❑ 242	Jerry Holmes	.04	.02
❑ 243	Tim McGee	.04	.02
❑ 244	Mike Tomczak	.10	.05
❑ 245	Sterling Sharpe UER (Broke 47-yard-old record, should be year)	.25	.11
❑ 246	Bennie Blades	.04	.02
❑ 247	Ken Harvey RC UER (Sacks and fumble recovery listings are switched; disappointing misspelled)	.25	.11
❑ 248	Ron Heller	.04	.02
❑ 249	Louis Lipps	.10	.05
❑ 250	Wade Wilson	.10	.05
❑ 251	Freddie Joe Nunn	.04	.02
❑ 252	Jerome Brown UER ('89 stats show 2 fumble rec., should be 1)	.04	.02
❑ 253	Myron Guyton	.04	.02
❑ 254	Nate Odomes RC	.10	.05
❑ 255	Rod Woodson	.25	.11
❑ 256	Cornelius Bennett	.10	.05
❑ 257	Keith Woodside	.04	.02
❑ 258	Jeff Uhlenhake UER	.04	.02

(Text calls him Ron)
- ❑ 259 Harry Hamilton .04 .02
- ❑ 260 Mark Bavaro .04 .02
- ❑ 261 Vinny Testaverde .10 .05
- ❑ 262 Steve DeBerg .04 .02
- ❑ 263 Steve Wisniewski UER .10 .05 (Drafted by Dallas, not the Raiders)
- ❑ 264 Pete Mandley .04 .02
- ❑ 265 Tim Harris .04 .02
- ❑ 266 Jack Trudeau .04 .02
- ❑ 267 Mark Kelso .04 .02
- ❑ 268 Brian Noble .04 .02
- ❑ 269 Jessie Tuggle RC .04 .02
- ❑ 270 Ken O'Brien .04 .02
- ❑ 271 David Little .04 .02
- ❑ 272 Pete Stoyanovich .04 .02
- ❑ 273 Odessa Turner RC .04 .02
- ❑ 274 Anthony Toney .04 .02
- ❑ 275 Tunch Ilkin .04 .02
- ❑ 276 Carl Lee .04 .02
- ❑ 277 Hart Lee Dykes .04 .02
- ❑ 278 Al Noga .04 .02
- ❑ 279 Greg Lloyd .25 .11
- ❑ 280 Billy Joe Tolliver .04 .02
- ❑ 281 Kirk Lowdermilk .04 .02
- ❑ 282 Earl Ferrell .04 .02
- ❑ 283 Eric Sievers RC .04 .02
- ❑ 284 Steve Jordan .04 .02
- ❑ 285 Burt Grossman .04 .02
- ❑ 286 Johnny Rembert .04 .02
- ❑ 287 Jeff Jaeger RC .04 .02
- ❑ 288 James Hasty .04 .02
- ❑ 289 Tony Mandarich DP .04 .02
- ❑ 290 Chris Singleton RC .04 .02
- ❑ 291 Lynn James RC .04 .02
- ❑ 292 Andre Ware RC .25 .11
- ❑ 293 Ray Agnew RC .04 .02
- ❑ 294 Joel Smeenge RC .04 .02
- ❑ 295 Marc Spindler RC .04 .02
- ❑ 296 Renaldo Turnbull RC .04 .02
- ❑ 297 Reggie Rembert RC .04 .02
- ❑ 298 Jeff Alm RC .04 .02
- ❑ 299 Cortez Kennedy RC .25 .11
- ❑ 300 Blair Thomas RC .10 .05
- ❑ 301 Pat Terrell RC .04 .02
- ❑ 302 Junior Seau RC 1.00 .45
- ❑ 303 Mo Elewonibi RC .04 .02
- ❑ 304 Tony Bennett RC .25 .11
- ❑ 305 Percy Snow RC .04 .02
- ❑ 306 Richmond Webb RC .04 .02
- ❑ 307 R.Hampton RC .40 .18
- ❑ 308 Barry Foster RC .25 .11
- ❑ 309 John Friesz RC .25 .11
- ❑ 310 Ben Smith RC .04 .02
- ❑ 311 Joe Montana HG .50 .23
- ❑ 312 Jim Everett HG .10 .05
- ❑ 313 Mark Rypien HG .10 .05
- ❑ 314 Phil Simms HG UER .10 .05 (Lists him as playing in the AFC)
- ❑ 315 Don Majkowski HG .04 .02
- ❑ 316 Boomer Esiason HG .04 .02
- ❑ 317 Warren Moon HG .25 .11 (Moon on card)
- ❑ 318 Jim Kelly HG .25 .11
- ❑ 319 Bernie Kosar HG UER .10 .05 (Word just is mis-spelled as justs)
- ❑ 320 Dan Marino HG UER .50 .23 (Text says 378 com-pletions in 1984, should be 1986)
- ❑ 321 Christian Okoye GF .04 .02
- ❑ 322 Thurman Thomas GF .25 .11
- ❑ 323 James Brooks GF .10 .05
- ❑ 324 Bobby Humphrey GF .04 .02
- ❑ 325 Barry Sanders GF .60 .25
- ❑ 326 Neal Anderson GF .04 .02
- ❑ 327 Dalton Hilliard GF .04 .02
- ❑ 328 Greg Bell GF .04 .02
- ❑ 329 Roger Craig GF UER .10 .05 (Text says 2 TD's in SB XXIV, should be 1)
- ❑ 330 Bo Jackson GF .30 .14
- ❑ 331 Don Warren .04 .02
- ❑ 332 Rufus Porter .04 .02
- ❑ 333 Sammie Smith .04 .02
- ❑ 334 Lewis Tillman UER .04 .02 (Born 4/16/67, should be 1966)
- ❑ 335 Michael Walter .04 .02
- ❑ 336 Marc Logan .04 .02
- ❑ 337 Ron Hallstrom RC .04 .02
- ❑ 338 Stanley Morgan .04 .02
- ❑ 339 Mark Robinson .04 .02
- ❑ 340 Frank Reich .25 .11
- ❑ 341 Chip Lohmiller .04 .02
- ❑ 342 Steve Beuerlein .10 .05
- ❑ 343 John L. Williams .04 .02
- ❑ 344 Irving Fryar .25 .11
- ❑ 345 Anthony Carter .10 .05
- ❑ 346 Al Toon .10 .05
- ❑ 347 J.T. Smith .04 .02
- ❑ 348 Pierce Holt RC .04 .02
- ❑ 349 Ferrell Edmunds .04 .02
- ❑ 350 Mark Rypien .10 .05
- ❑ 351 Paul Gruber .04 .02
- ❑ 352 Ernest Givins .10 .05
- ❑ 353 Ervin Randle .04 .02
- ❑ 354 Guy McIntyre .04 .02
- ❑ 355 Webster Slaughter .10 .05
- ❑ 356 Reuben Davis .04 .02
- ❑ 357 Rickey Jackson .10 .05
- ❑ 358 Earnest Byner .04 .02
- ❑ 359 Eddie Brown .04 .02
- ❑ 360 Troy Stradford .04 .02
- ❑ 361 Pepper Johnson .04 .02
- ❑ 362 Ravin Caldwell .04 .02
- ❑ 363 Chris Mohr RC .04 .02
- ❑ 364 Jeff Bryant .04 .02
- ❑ 365 Bruce Collie .04 .02
- ❑ 366 Courtney Hall .04 .02
- ❑ 367 Jerry Olsavsky .04 .02
- ❑ 368 David Galloway .04 .02
- ❑ 369 Wes Hopkins .04 .02
- ❑ 370 Johnny Hector .04 .02
- ❑ 371 Clarence Verdin .04 .02
- ❑ 372 Nick Lowery .04 .02
- ❑ 373 Tim Brown .25 .11
- ❑ 374 Kevin Greene .25 .11
- ❑ 375 Leonard Marshall .04 .02
- ❑ 376 Roland James .04 .02
- ❑ 377 Scott Studwell .04 .02
- ❑ 378 Jarvis Williams .04 .02
- ❑ 379 Mike Saxon .04 .02
- ❑ 380 Kevin Mack .04 .02
- ❑ 381 Joe Kelly .04 .02
- ❑ 382 Tom Thayer RC .04 .02
- ❑ 383 Roy Green .10 .05
- ❑ 384 Michael Brooks RC .04 .02
- ❑ 385 Michael Cofer .04 .02
- ❑ 386 Ken Ruettgers .04 .02
- ❑ 387 Dean Steinkuhler .04 .02
- ❑ 388 Maurice Carthon .04 .02
- ❑ 389 Ricky Sanders .04 .02
- ❑ 390 Winston Moss RC .04 .02
- ❑ 391 Tony Woods .04 .02
- ❑ 392 Keith DeLong .04 .02
- ❑ 393 David Wyman .04 .02
- ❑ 394 Vencie Glenn .04 .02
- ❑ 395 Harris Barton .04 .02
- ❑ 396 Bryan Hinkle .04 .02
- ❑ 397 Derek Kennard .04 .02
- ❑ 398 Heath Sherman RC .04 .02
- ❑ 399 Troy Benson .04 .02
- ❑ 400 Gary Zimmerman .04 .02
- ❑ 401 Mark Duper .10 .05
- ❑ 402 Eugene Lockhart .04 .02
- ❑ 403 Tim Manoa .04 .02
- ❑ 404 Reggie Williams .04 .02
- ❑ 405 Mark Bortz RC .04 .02
- ❑ 406 Mike Kenn .04 .02
- ❑ 407 John Grimsley .04 .02
- ❑ 408 Bill Romanowski RC .30 .14
- ❑ 409 Perry Kemp .04 .02
- ❑ 410 Norm Johnson .04 .02
- ❑ 411 Broderick Thomas .04 .02
- ❑ 412 Joe Wolf .04 .02
- ❑ 413 Andre Waters .04 .02
- ❑ 414 Jason Staurovsky .04 .02
- ❑ 415 Eric Martin .04 .02
- ❑ 416 Joe Prokop .04 .02
- ❑ 417 Steve Sewell .04 .02
- ❑ 418 Cedric Jones .04 .02
- ❑ 419 Alphonso Carreker .04 .02
- ❑ 420 Keith Willis .04 .02
- ❑ 421 Bobby Butler .04 .02
- ❑ 422 John Roper .04 .02
- ❑ 423 Tim Spencer .04 .02
- ❑ 424 Jesse Sapolu RC .04 .02
- ❑ 425 Ron Wolfley .04 .02
- ❑ 426 Doug Smith .04 .02
- ❑ 427 William Howard .04 .02
- ❑ 428 Keith Van Horne .04 .02
- ❑ 429 Tony Jordan .04 .02
- ❑ 430 Mervyn Fernandez .04 .02
- ❑ 431 Shaun Gayle RC .04 .02
- ❑ 432 Ricky Nattiel .04 .02
- ❑ 433 Albert Lewis .04 .02
- ❑ 434 Fred Banks RC .04 .02
- ❑ 435 Henry Thomas .04 .02
- ❑ 436 Chet Brooks .04 .02
- ❑ 437 Mark Ingram .10 .05
- ❑ 438 Jeff Gossett .04 .02
- ❑ 439 Mike Wilcher .04 .02
- ❑ 440 Deron Cherry UER .04 .02 (Text says 7 cons. Pro Bowls, but he didn't play in 1989 Pro Bowl)
- ❑ 441 Mike Rozier .04 .02
- ❑ 442 Jon Hand .04 .02
- ❑ 443 Ozzie Newsome .10 .05
- ❑ 444 Sammy Martin .04 .02
- ❑ 445 Luis Sharpe .04 .02
- ❑ 446 Lee Williams .04 .02
- ❑ 447 Chris Martin RC .04 .02
- ❑ 448 Kevin Fagan RC .04 .02
- ❑ 449 Gene Lang .04 .02
- ❑ 450 Greg Townsend .04 .02
- ❑ 451 Robert Lyles .04 .02
- ❑ 452 Eric Hill .04 .02
- ❑ 453 John Teltschik .04 .02
- ❑ 454 Vestee Jackson .04 .02
- ❑ 455 Bruce Reimers .04 .02
- ❑ 456 Butch Rolle RC .04 .02
- ❑ 457 Lawyer Tillman .04 .02
- ❑ 458 Andre Tippett .04 .02
- ❑ 459 James Thornton .04 .02
- ❑ 460 Randy Grimes .04 .02
- ❑ 461 Larry Roberts .04 .02
- ❑ 462 Ron Holmes .04 .02
- ❑ 463 Mike Wise .04 .02
- ❑ 464 Danny Copeland RC .04 .02
- ❑ 465 Bruce Wilkerson RC .04 .02
- ❑ 466 Mike Quick .04 .02
- ❑ 467 Mickey Shuler .04 .02
- ❑ 468 Mike Prior .04 .02
- ❑ 469 Ron Rivera .04 .02
- ❑ 470 Dean Biasucci .04 .02
- ❑ 471 Perry Williams .04 .02
- ❑ 472 Darren Comeaux UER .04 .02 (Front 53, back 52)
- ❑ 473 Freeman McNeil .04 .02
- ❑ 474 Tyrone Braxton .04 .02
- ❑ 475 Jay Schroeder .04 .02
- ❑ 476 Naz Worthen .04 .02
- ❑ 477 Lionel Washington .04 .02
- ❑ 478 Carl Zander .04 .02
- ❑ 479 Al(Bubba) Baker .10 .05
- ❑ 480 Mike Merriweather .04 .02
- ❑ 481 Mike Gann .04 .02
- ❑ 482 Brent Williams .04 .02
- ❑ 483 Eugene Robinson .04 .02
- ❑ 484 Ray Horton .04 .02
- ❑ 485 Bruce Armstrong .04 .02
- ❑ 486 John Fourcade .04 .02
- ❑ 487 Lewis Billups .04 .02
- ❑ 488 Scott Davis .04 .02
- ❑ 489 Kenneth Sims .04 .02
- ❑ 490 Chris Chandler .25 .11
- ❑ 491 Mark Lee .04 .02
- ❑ 492 Johnny Meads .04 .02
- ❑ 493 Tim Irwin .04 .02
- ❑ 494 E.J. Junior .04 .02
- ❑ 495 Hardy Nickerson .10 .05
- ❑ 496 Rob McGovern .04 .02
- ❑ 497 Fred Strickland RC .04 .02

	Card	Mint	NrMt
❑	498 Reggie Rutland RC	.04	.02
❑	499 Mel Owens	.04	.02
❑	500 Derrick Thomas	.25	.11
❑	501 Jerrol Williams	.04	.02
❑	502 Maurice Hurst RC	.04	.02
❑	503 Larry Kelm RC	.04	.02
❑	504 Herman Fontenot	.04	.02
❑	505 Pat Beach	.04	.02
❑	506 Haywood Jeffires RC	.25	.11
❑	507 Neil Smith	.25	.11
❑	508 Cleveland Gary	.04	.02
❑	509 William Perry	.10	.05
❑	510 Michael Carter	.04	.02
❑	511 Walker Lee Ashley	.04	.02
❑	512 Bob Golic	.04	.02
❑	513 Danny Villa RC	.04	.02
❑	514 Matt Millen	.10	.05
❑	515 Don Griffin	.04	.02
❑	516 Jonathan Hayes	.04	.02
❑	517 Gerald Williams RC	.04	.02
❑	518 Scott Fulhage	.04	.02
❑	519 Irv Pankey	.04	.02
❑	520 Randy Dixon RC	.04	.02
❑	521 Terry McDaniel	.04	.02
❑	522 Dan Saleaumua	.04	.02
❑	523 Darrin Nelson	.04	.02
❑	524 Leonard Griffin	.04	.02
❑	525 Michael Ball RC	.04	.02
❑	526 Ernie Jones RC	.04	.02
❑	527 Tony Eason UER (Drafted in 1963, should be 1983)	.04	.02
❑	528 Ed Reynolds	.04	.02
❑	529 Gary Hogeboom	.04	.02
❑	530 Don Mosebar	.04	.02
❑	531 Ottis Anderson	.10	.05
❑	532 Bucky Scribner	.04	.02
❑	533 Aaron Cox	.04	.02
❑	534 Sean Jones	.10	.05
❑	535 Doug Flutie	.50	.23
❑	536 Leo Lewis	.04	.02
❑	537 Art Still	.04	.02
❑	538 Matt Bahr	.04	.02
❑	539 Keena Turner	.04	.02
❑	540 Sammy Winder	.04	.02
❑	541 Mike Webster	.10	.05
❑	542 Doug Riesenberg RC	.04	.02
❑	543 Dan Fike	.04	.02
❑	544 Clarence Kay	.04	.02
❑	545 Jim Burt	.04	.02
❑	546 Mike Horan	.04	.02
❑	547 Al Harris	.04	.02
❑	548 Maury Buford	.04	.02
❑	549 Jerry Robinson	.04	.02
❑	550 Tracy Rocker	.04	.02
❑	551 Karl Mecklenburg CC	.04	.02
❑	552 Lawrence Taylor CC	.25	.11
❑	553 Derrick Thomas CC	.25	.11
❑	554 Mike Singletary CC	.10	.05
❑	555 Tim Harris CC	.04	.02
❑	556 Jerry Rice RM	.50	.23
❑	557 Art Monk RM	.10	.05
❑	558 Mark Carrier WR RM	.10	.05
❑	559 Andre Reed RM	.10	.05
❑	560 Sterling Sharpe RM	.25	.11
❑	561 Herschel Walker GF	.10	.05
❑	562 Ottis Anderson GF	.10	.05
❑	563 Randall Cunningham HG	.10	.05
❑	564 John Elway HG	.50	.23
❑	565 David Fulcher AP	.04	.02
❑	566 Ronnie Lott AP	.10	.05
❑	567 Jerry Gray AP	.04	.02
❑	568 Albert Lewis AP	.04	.02
❑	569 Karl Mecklenburg AP	.04	.02
❑	570 Mike Singletary AP	.10	.05
❑	571 Lawrence Taylor AP	.25	.11
❑	572 Tim Harris AP	.04	.02
❑	573 Keith Millard AP	.04	.02
❑	574 Reggie White AP	.25	.11
❑	575 Chris Doleman AP	.04	.02
❑	576 Dave Meggett AP	.10	.05
❑	577 Rod Woodson AP	.25	.11
❑	578 Sean Landeta AP	.04	.02
❑	579 Eddie Murray AP	.04	.02
❑	580 Barry Sanders AP	.60	.25
❑	581 Christian Okoye AP	.04	.02
❑	582 Joe Montana AP	.50	.23
❑	583 Jay Hilgenberg AP	.04	.02
❑	584 Bruce Matthews AP	.10	.05
❑	585 Tom Newberry AP	.04	.02
❑	586 Gary Zimmerman AP	.04	.02
❑	587 Anthony Munoz AP	.10	.05
❑	588 Keith Jackson AP	.10	.05
❑	589 Sterling Sharpe AP	.25	.11
❑	590 Jerry Rice AP	.50	.23
❑	591 Bo Jackson RB	.30	.14
❑	592 Steve Largent RB	.25	.11
❑	593 Flipper Anderson RB	.04	.02
❑	594 Joe Montana RB	.50	.23
❑	595 Franco Harris HOF	.10	.05
❑	596 Bob St. Clair HOF	.04	.02
❑	597 Tom Landry HOF	.10	.05
❑	598 Jack Lambert HOF	.10	.05
❑	599 Ted Hendricks HOF UER (Int. avg. says 12.8, should be 8.9)	.04	.02
❑	600A Buck Buchanan HOF UER (Drafted in 1983)	.10	.05
❑	600B Buck Buchanan HOF COR (Drafted in 1963)	.10	.05
❑	601 Bob Griese HOF	.10	.05
❑	602 Super Bowl Wrap	.04	.02
❑	603A Vince Lombardi UER Lombardi Legend (Disciplinarian misspelled; no logo for Curtis Mgt. at bottom)	.20	.09
❑	603B Vince Lombardi UER Lombardi Legend (Disciplinarian misspelled; logo for Curtis Mgt. at bottom)	.20	.09
❑	604 Mark Carrier UER (Front 88, back 89)	.10	.05
❑	605 Randall Cunningham	.25	.11
❑	606 Percy Snow C90	.04	.02
❑	607 Andre Ware C90	.25	.11
❑	608 Blair Thomas C90	.10	.05
❑	609 Eric Green C90	.04	.02
❑	610 Reggie Rembert C90	.04	.02
❑	611 Richmond Webb C90	.04	.02
❑	612 Bern Brostek C90	.04	.02
❑	613 James Williams C90	.04	.02
❑	614 Mark Carrier DB C90	.10	.05
❑	615 Renaldo Turnbull C90	.04	.02
❑	616 Cortez Kennedy C90	.10	.05
❑	617 Keith McCants C90	.04	.02
❑	618 Anthony Thompson RC	.04	.02
❑	619 LeRoy Butler RC	.25	.11
❑	620 Aaron Wallace RC	.04	.02
❑	621 Alexander Wright RC	.04	.02
❑	622 Keith McCants RC	.04	.02
❑	623 Jimmie Jones RC UER (January misspelled)	.04	.02
❑	624 Anthony Johnson RC	.25	.11
❑	625 Fred Washington RC	.04	.02
❑	626 Mike Bellamy RC	.04	.02
❑	627 Mark Carrier DB RC	.25	.11
❑	628 Harold Green RC	.25	.11
❑	629 Eric Green RC	.10	.05
❑	630 Andre Collins RC	.04	.02
❑	631 Lamar Lathon RC	.10	.05
❑	632 Terry Wooden RC	.04	.02
❑	633 Jesse Anderson RC	.04	.02
❑	634 Jeff George RC	1.00	.45
❑	635 Carwell Gardner RC	.04	.02
❑	636 Darrell Thompson RC	.04	.02
❑	637 Vince Buck RC	.04	.02
❑	638 Mike Jones TE RC	.04	.02
❑	639 Charles Arbuckle RC	.04	.02
❑	640 Dennis Brown RC	.04	.02
❑	641 James Williams DB RC	.04	.02
❑	642 Bern Brostek RC	.04	.02
❑	643 Darion Conner RC	.10	.05
❑	644 Mike Fox RC	.04	.02
❑	645 Cary Conklin RC	.04	.02
❑	646 Tim Grunhard RC	.04	.02
❑	647 Ron Cox RC	.04	.02
❑	648 Keith Sims RC	.04	.02
❑	649 Alton Montgomery RC	.04	.02
❑	650 Greg McMurtry RC	.04	.02
❑	651 Scott Mitchell RC	.25	.11
❑	652 Tim Ryan DE RC	.04	.02
❑	653 Jeff Mills RC	.04	.02
❑	654 Ricky Proehl RC	.10	.05
❑	655 Steve Broussard RC	.04	.02
❑	656 Peter Tom Willis RC	.04	.02
❑	657 Dexter Carter RC	.04	.02
❑	658 Tony Casillas	.04	.02
❑	659 Joe Morris	.04	.02
❑	660 Greg Kragen	.04	.02
❑	B1 Matt Stover	.25	.11
❑	B2 Demetrius Davis	.04	.02
❑	B3 Ken McMichel	.04	.02
❑	B4 Judd Garrett	.04	.02
❑	B5 Elliott Searcy	.04	.02

1990 Score Supplemental

		MINT	NRMT
	COMP.FACT.SET (110)	120.00	55.00
❑	1T Marcus Dupree RC**	.15	.07
❑	2T Jerry Kauric	.15	.07
❑	3T Everson Walls	.15	.07
❑	4T Elliott Smith	.15	.07
❑	5T Donald Evans RC UER (Misspelled Pittsburg on card back)	.30	.14
❑	6T Jerry Holmes	.15	.07
❑	7T Dan Stryzinski RC	.15	.07
❑	8T Gerald McNeil	.15	.07
❑	9T Rick Tuten RC	.15	.07
❑	10T Mickey Shuler	.15	.07
❑	11T Jay Novacek	.60	.25
❑	12T Eric Williams RC	.15	.07
❑	13T Stanley Morgan	.15	.07
❑	14T Wayne Haddix RC	.15	.07
❑	15T Gary Anderson RB	.15	.07
❑	16T Stan Humphries RC	1.00	.45
❑	17T Raymond Clayborn	.15	.07
❑	18T Mark Boyer RC	.15	.07
❑	19T Dave Waymer	.15	.07
❑	20T Andre Rison	.60	.25
❑	21T Daniel Stubbs	.15	.07
❑	22T Mike Rozier	.15	.07
❑	23T Damian Johnson	.15	.07
❑	24T Don Smith	.15	.07
❑	25T Max Montoya	.15	.07
❑	26T Terry Kinard	.15	.07
❑	27T Herb Welch	.15	.07
❑	28T Cliff Odom	.15	.07
❑	29T John Kidd	.15	.07
❑	30T Barry Word RC	.15	.07
❑	31T Rich Karlis	.15	.07
❑	32T Mike Baab	.15	.07
❑	33T Ronnie Harmon	.30	.14
❑	34T Jeff Donaldson	.15	.07
❑	35T Riki Ellison	.15	.07
❑	36T Steve Walsh	.30	.14
❑	37T Bill Lewis RC	.15	.07
❑	38T Tim McKyer	.15	.07
❑	39T James Wilder	.15	.07
❑	40T Tony Paige	.15	.07
❑	41T Derrick Fenner RC	.15	.07
❑	42T Thane Gash RC	.15	.07

❑ 43T Dave Duerson	.15	.07
❑ 44T Clarence Weathers	.15	.07
❑ 45T Matt Bahr	.15	.07
❑ 46T Alonzo Highsmith	.15	.07
❑ 47T Joe Kelly	.15	.07
❑ 48T Chris Hinton	.15	.07
❑ 49T Bobby Humphery	.15	.07
❑ 50T Greg Bell	.15	.07
❑ 51T Fred Smerlas	.15	.07
❑ 52T Walter Stanley	.15	.07
❑ 53T Jim Skow	.15	.07
❑ 54T Renaldo Turnbull	.15	.07
❑ 55T Bern Brostek	.15	.07
❑ 56T Charles Wilson RC	.15	.07
❑ 57T Keith McCants	.15	.07
❑ 58T Alexander Wright	.30	.14
❑ 59T Ian Beckles RC	.15	.07
❑ 60T Eric Davis RC	.30	.14
❑ 61T Chris Singleton	.15	.07
❑ 62T Rob Moore RC	6.00	2.70
❑ 63T Darion Conner	.30	.14
❑ 64T Tim Grunhard	.15	.07
❑ 65T Junior Seau	5.00	2.20
❑ 66T Tony Stargell RC	.15	.07
❑ 67T Anthony Thompson	.15	.07
❑ 68T Cortez Kennedy	.60	.25
❑ 69T Darrell Thompson	.15	.07
❑ 70T Calvin Williams RC	.60	.25
❑ 71T Rodney Hampton	1.00	.45
❑ 72T Terry Wooden	.15	.07
❑ 73T Leo Goeas RC	.15	.07
❑ 74T Ken Willis	.15	.07
❑ 75T Ricky Proehl	.30	.14
❑ 76T Steve Christie RC	.15	.07
❑ 77T Andre Ware	.60	.25
❑ 78T Jeff George	12.00	5.50
❑ 79T Walter Wilson	.15	.07
❑ 80T Johnny Bailey RC	.15	.07
❑ 81T Harold Green	.30	.14
❑ 82T Mark Carrier	.60	.25
❑ 83T Frank Cornish	.15	.07
❑ 84T James Williams	.15	.07
❑ 85T James Francis RC	.15	.07
❑ 86T Percy Snow	.15	.07
❑ 87T Anthony Johnson	.60	.25
❑ 88T Tim Ryan	.15	.07
❑ 89T Dan Owens RC	.15	.07
❑ 90T Aaron Wallace RC	.15	.07
❑ 91T Steve Broussard	.15	.07
❑ 92T Eric Green	.15	.07
❑ 93T Blair Thomas	.30	.14
❑ 94T Robert Blackmon RC	.15	.07
❑ 95T Alan Grant RC	.15	.07
❑ 96T Andre Collins	.15	.07
❑ 97T Dexter Carter	.15	.07
❑ 98T Reggie Cobb RC	.15	.07
❑ 99T Dennis Brown	.15	.07
❑ 100T Kenny Davidson RC	.15	.07
❑ 101T Emmitt Smith RC	100.00	45.00
❑ 102T Jeff Alm	.15	.07
❑ 103T Alton Montgomery	.15	.07
❑ 104T Tony Bennett	.60	.25
❑ 105T Johnny Johnson RC	.30	.14
❑ 106T Leroy Hoard RC	2.00	.90
❑ 107T Ray Agnew	.15	.07
❑ 108T Richmond Webb	.15	.07
❑ 109T Keith Sims	.15	.07
❑ 110T Barry Foster	.60	.25

1991 Score

	MINT	NRMT
COMPLETE SET (686)	8.00	3.60
COMP.FACT.SET (690)	10.00	4.50

❑ 1 Joe Montana	1.25	.55
❑ 2 Eric Allen	.04	.02
❑ 3 Rohn Stark	.04	.02
❑ 4 Frank Reich	.10	.05
❑ 5 Derrick Thomas	.25	.11
❑ 6 Mike Singletary	.10	.05
❑ 7 Boomer Esiason	.10	.05
❑ 8 Matt Millen	.10	.05
❑ 9 Chris Spielman	.10	.05
❑ 10 Gerald McNeil	.04	.02
❑ 11 Nick Lowery	.04	.02

❑ 12 Randall Cunningham	.25	.11
❑ 13 Marion Butts	.10	.05
❑ 14 Tim Brown	.25	.11
❑ 15 Emmitt Smith	2.00	.90
❑ 16 Rich Camarillo	.04	.02
❑ 17 Mike Merriweather	.04	.02
❑ 18 Derrick Fenner	.04	.02
❑ 19 Clay Matthews	.10	.05
❑ 20 Barry Sanders	1.50	.70
❑ 21 James Brooks	.10	.05
❑ 22 Alton Montgomery	.04	.02
❑ 23 Steve Atwater	.04	.02
❑ 24 Ron Morris	.04	.02
❑ 25 Brad Muster	.04	.02
❑ 26 Andre Rison	.10	.05
❑ 27 Brian Brennan	.04	.02
❑ 28 Leonard Smith	.04	.02
❑ 29 Kevin Butler	.04	.02
❑ 30 Tim Harris	.04	.02
❑ 31 Jay Novacek	.25	.11
❑ 32 Eddie Murray	.04	.02
❑ 33 Keith Woodside	.04	.02
❑ 34 Ray Crockett RC	.04	.02
❑ 35 Eugene Lockhart	.04	.02
❑ 36 Bill Romanowski	.04	.02
❑ 37 Eddie Brown	.04	.02
❑ 38 Eugene Daniel	.04	.02
❑ 39 Scott Fulhage	.04	.02
❑ 40 Harold Green	.10	.05
❑ 41 Mark Jackson	.04	.02
❑ 42 Sterling Sharpe	.25	.11
❑ 43 Mel Gray	.10	.05
❑ 44 Jerry Holmes	.04	.02
❑ 45 Allen Pinkett	.04	.02
❑ 46 Warren Powers	.04	.02
❑ 47 Rodney Peete	.10	.05
❑ 48 Lorenzo White	.04	.02
❑ 49 Dan Owens	.04	.02
❑ 50 James Francis	.04	.02
❑ 51 Ken Norton	.25	.11
❑ 52 Ed West	.04	.02
❑ 53 Andre Reed	.10	.05
❑ 54 John Grimsley	.04	.02
❑ 55 Michael Cofer	.04	.02
❑ 56 Chris Doleman	.04	.02
❑ 57 Pat Swilling	.10	.05
❑ 58 Jessie Tuggle	.04	.02
❑ 59 Mike Johnson	.04	.02
❑ 60 Steve Walsh	.04	.02
❑ 61 Sam Mills	.04	.02
❑ 62 Don Mosebar	.04	.02
❑ 63 Jay Hilgenberg	.04	.02
❑ 64 Cleveland Gary	.04	.02
❑ 65 Andre Tippett	.04	.02
❑ 66 Tom Newberry	.04	.02
❑ 67 Maurice Hurst	.04	.02
❑ 68 Louis Oliver	.04	.02
❑ 69 Fred Marion	.04	.02
❑ 70 Christian Okoye	.04	.02
❑ 71 Marv Cook	.04	.02
❑ 72 Darryl Talley	.04	.02
❑ 73 Rick Fenney	.04	.02
❑ 74 Kelvin Martin	.04	.02
❑ 75 Howie Long	.10	.05
❑ 76 Steve Wisniewski	.04	.02
❑ 77 Karl Mecklenburg	.04	.02
❑ 78 Dan Saleaumua	.04	.02
❑ 79 Ray Childress	.04	.02
❑ 80 Henry Ellard	.10	.05
❑ 81 Ernest Givins UER (3rd on Oilers in receiving, not 4th)	.10	.05
❑ 82 Ferrell Edmunds	.04	.02
❑ 83 Steve Jordan	.04	.02
❑ 84 Tony Mandarich	.04	.02
❑ 85 Eric Martin	.04	.02
❑ 86 Rich Gannon	.25	.11
❑ 87 Irving Fryar	.10	.05
❑ 88 Tom Rathman	.04	.02
❑ 89 Dan Hampton	.10	.05
❑ 90 Barry Word	.04	.02
❑ 91 Kevin Greene	.25	.11
❑ 92 Sean Landeta	.04	.02
❑ 93 Trace Armstrong	.04	.02
❑ 94 Dennis Byrd	.04	.02
❑ 95 Timm Rosenbach	.04	.02
❑ 96 Anthony Toney	.04	.02
❑ 97 Tim Krumrie	.04	.02
❑ 98 Jerry Ball	.04	.02
❑ 99 Tim Green	.04	.02
❑ 100 Bo Jackson	.30	.14
❑ 101 Myron Guyton	.04	.02
❑ 102 Mike Mularkey	.04	.02
❑ 103 Jerry Gray	.04	.02
❑ 104 Scott Stephen RC	.04	.02
❑ 105 Anthony Bell	.04	.02
❑ 106 Lomas Brown	.04	.02
❑ 107 David Little	.04	.02
❑ 108 Brad Baxter	.04	.02
❑ 109 Freddie Joe Nunn	.04	.02
❑ 110 Dave Meggett	.10	.05
❑ 111 Mark Rypien	.10	.05
❑ 112 Warren Williams	.04	.02
❑ 113 Ron Rivera	.04	.02
❑ 114 Terance Mathis	.10	.05
❑ 115 Anthony Munoz	.10	.05
❑ 116 Jeff Bryant	.04	.02
❑ 117 Issiac Holt	.04	.02
❑ 118 Steve Sewell	.04	.02
❑ 119 Tim Newton	.04	.02
❑ 120 Emile Harry	.04	.02
❑ 121 Gary Anderson K	.04	.02
❑ 122 Mark Lee	.04	.02
❑ 123 Alfred Anderson	.04	.02
❑ 124 Anthony Blaylock	.04	.02
❑ 125 Earnest Byner	.04	.02
❑ 126 Bill Maas	.04	.02
❑ 127 Keith Taylor	.04	.02
❑ 128 Cliff Odom	.04	.02
❑ 129 Bob Golic	.04	.02
❑ 130 Bart Oates	.04	.02
❑ 131 Jim Arnold	.04	.02
❑ 132 Jeff Herrod	.04	.02
❑ 133 Bruce Armstrong	.04	.02
❑ 134 Craig Heyward	.10	.05
❑ 135 Joey Browner	.04	.02
❑ 136 Darren Comeaux	.04	.02
❑ 137 Pat Beach	.04	.02
❑ 138 Dalton Hilliard	.04	.02
❑ 139 David Treadwell	.04	.02
❑ 140 Gary Anderson RB	.04	.02
❑ 141 Eugene Robinson	.04	.02
❑ 142 Scott Case	.04	.02
❑ 143 Paul Farren	.04	.02
❑ 144 Gill Fenerty	.04	.02
❑ 145 Tim Irwin	.04	.02
❑ 146 Norm Johnson	.04	.02
❑ 147 Willie Gault	.10	.05
❑ 148 Clarence Verdin	.04	.02
❑ 149 Jeff Uhlenhake	.04	.02
❑ 150 Erik McMillan	.04	.02
❑ 151 Kevin Ross	.04	.02
❑ 152 Pepper Johnson	.04	.02
❑ 153 Bryan Hinkle	.04	.02
❑ 154 Gary Clark	.25	.11
❑ 155 Robert Delpino	.04	.02
❑ 156 Doug Smith	.04	.02
❑ 157 Chris Martin	.04	.02
❑ 158 Ray Berry	.04	.02
❑ 159 Steve Christie	.04	.02
❑ 160 Don Smith	.04	.02
❑ 161 Greg McMurtry	.04	.02
❑ 162 Jack Del Rio	.04	.02

Card	Player		
❑ 163	Floyd Dixon	.04	.02
❑ 164	Buford McGee	.04	.02
❑ 165	Brett Maxie	.04	.02
❑ 166	Morten Andersen	.04	.02
❑ 167	Kent Hull	.04	.02
❑ 168	Skip McClendon	.04	.02
❑ 169	Keith Sims	.04	.02
❑ 170	Leonard Marshall	.04	.02
❑ 171	Tony Woods	.04	.02
❑ 172	Byron Evans	.04	.02
❑ 173	Rob Burnett RC	.10	.05
❑ 174	Tory Epps	.04	.02
❑ 175	Toi Cook RC	.04	.02
❑ 176	John Elliott	.04	.02
❑ 177	Tommie Agee	.04	.02
❑ 178	Keith Van Horne	.04	.02
❑ 179	Dennis Smith	.04	.02
❑ 180	James Lofton	.10	.05
❑ 181	Art Monk	.10	.05
❑ 182	Anthony Carter	.10	.05
❑ 183	Louis Lipps	.04	.02
❑ 184	Bruce Hill	.04	.02
❑ 185	Michael Young	.04	.02
❑ 186	Eric Green	.04	.02
❑ 187	Barney Bussey RC	.04	.02
❑ 188	Curtis Duncan	.04	.02
❑ 189	Robert Awalt	.04	.02
❑ 190	Johnny Johnson	.04	.02
❑ 191	Jeff Cross	.04	.02
❑ 192	Keith McKeller	.04	.02
❑ 193	Robert Brown	.04	.02
❑ 194	Vincent Brown	.04	.02
❑ 195	Calvin Williams	.10	.05
❑ 196	Sean Jones	.10	.05
❑ 197	Willie Drewrey	.04	.02
❑ 198	Bubba McDowell	.04	.02
❑ 199	Al Noga	.04	.02
❑ 200	Ronnie Lott	.10	.05
❑ 201	Warren Moon	.25	.11
❑ 202	Chris Hinton	.04	.02
❑ 203	Jim Sweeney	.04	.02
❑ 204	Wayne Haddix	.04	.02
❑ 205	Tim Jorden RC	.04	.02
❑ 206	Marvin Allen	.04	.02
❑ 207	Jim Morrissey RC	.04	.02
❑ 208	Ben Smith	.04	.02
❑ 209	William White	.04	.02
❑ 210	Jim C. Jensen	.04	.02
❑ 211	Doug Reed	.04	.02
❑ 212	Ethan Horton	.04	.02
❑ 213	Chris Jacke	.04	.02
❑ 214	Johnny Hector	.04	.02
❑ 215	Drew Hill UER (Tied for the NFC lead, should say AFC)	.04	.02
❑ 216	Roy Green	.04	.02
❑ 217	Dean Steinkuhler	.04	.02
❑ 218	Cedric Mack	.04	.02
❑ 219	Chris Miller	.10	.05
❑ 220	Keith Byars	.04	.02
❑ 221	Lewis Billups	.04	.02
❑ 222	Roger Craig	.10	.05
❑ 223	Shaun Gayle	.04	.02
❑ 224	Mike Rozier	.04	.02
❑ 225	Troy Aikman	.75	.35
❑ 226	Bobby Humphrey	.04	.02
❑ 227	Eugene Marve	.04	.02
❑ 228	Michael Carter	.04	.02
❑ 229	Richard Johnson RC	.04	.02
❑ 230	Billy Joe Tolliver	.04	.02
❑ 231	Mark Murphy	.04	.02
❑ 232	John L. Williams	.04	.02
❑ 233	Ronnie Harmon	.04	.02
❑ 234	Thurman Thomas	.25	.11
❑ 235	Martin Mayhew	.04	.02
❑ 236	Richmond Webb	.04	.02
❑ 237	Gerald Riggs UER (Earnest Byner misspelled as Ernest)	.10	.05
❑ 238	Mike Prior	.04	.02
❑ 239	Mike Gann	.04	.02
❑ 240	Alvin Walton	.04	.02
❑ 241	Tim McGee	.04	.02
❑ 242	Bruce Matthews	.10	.05
❑ 243	Johnny Holland	.04	.02
❑ 244	Martin Bayless	.04	.02
❑ 245	Eric Metcalf	.10	.05
❑ 246	John Alt	.04	.02
❑ 247	Max Montoya	.04	.02
❑ 248	Rod Bernstine	.04	.02
❑ 249	Paul Gruber	.04	.02
❑ 250	Charles Haley	.10	.05
❑ 251	Scott Norwood	.04	.02
❑ 252	Michael Haddix	.04	.02
❑ 253	Ricky Sanders	.04	.02
❑ 254	Ervin Randle	.04	.02
❑ 255	Duane Bickett	.04	.02
❑ 256	Mike Munchak	.04	.02
❑ 257	Keith Jones	.04	.02
❑ 258	Riki Ellison	.04	.02
❑ 259	Vince Newsome	.04	.02
❑ 260	Lee Williams	.04	.02
❑ 261	Steve Smith	.04	.02
❑ 262	Sam Clancy	.04	.02
❑ 263	Pierce Holt	.04	.02
❑ 264	Jim Harbaugh	.25	.11
❑ 265	Dino Hackett	.04	.02
❑ 266	Andy Heck	.04	.02
❑ 267	Leo Goeas	.04	.02
❑ 268	Russ Grimm	.04	.02
❑ 269	Gill Byrd	.04	.02
❑ 270	Neal Anderson	.10	.05
❑ 271	Jackie Slater	.04	.02
❑ 272	Joe Nash	.04	.02
❑ 273	Todd Bowles	.04	.02
❑ 274	D.J. Dozier	.04	.02
❑ 275	Kevin Fagan	.04	.02
❑ 276	Don Warren	.04	.02
❑ 277	Jim Jeffcoat	.04	.02
❑ 278	Bruce Smith	.25	.11
❑ 279	Cortez Kennedy	.25	.11
❑ 280	Thane Gash	.04	.02
❑ 281	Perry Kemp	.04	.02
❑ 282	John Taylor	.10	.05
❑ 283	Stephone Paige	.04	.02
❑ 284	Paul Skansi	.04	.02
❑ 285	Shawn Collins	.04	.02
❑ 286	Mervyn Fernandez	.04	.02
❑ 287	Daniel Stubbs	.04	.02
❑ 288	Chip Lohmiller	.04	.02
❑ 289	Brian Blades	.10	.05
❑ 290	Mark Carrier WR	.25	.11
❑ 291	Carl Zander	.04	.02
❑ 292	David Wyman	.04	.02
❑ 293	Jeff Bostic	.04	.02
❑ 294	Irv Pankey	.04	.02
❑ 295	Keith Millard	.04	.02
❑ 296	Jamie Mueller	.04	.02
❑ 297	Bill Fralic	.04	.02
❑ 298	Wendell Davis	.04	.02
❑ 299	Ken Clarke	.04	.02
❑ 300	Wymon Henderson	.04	.02
❑ 301	Jeff Campbell	.04	.02
❑ 302	Cody Carlson RC	.04	.02
❑ 303	Matt Brock RC	.04	.02
❑ 304	Maurice Carthon	.04	.02
❑ 305	Scott Mersereau RC	.04	.02
❑ 306	Steve Wright RC	.04	.02
❑ 307	J.B. Brown	.04	.02
❑ 308	Ricky Reynolds	.04	.02
❑ 309	Darryl Pollard	.04	.02
❑ 310	Donald Evans	.04	.02
❑ 311	Nick Bell RC	.04	.02
❑ 312	Pat Harlow RC	.04	.02
❑ 313	Dan McGwire RC	.04	.02
❑ 314	Mike Dumas RC	.04	.02
❑ 315	Mike Croel RC	.04	.02
❑ 316	Chris Smith RC	.04	.02
❑ 317	Kenny Walker RC	.04	.02
❑ 318	Todd Lyght RC	.04	.02
❑ 319	Mike Stonebreaker	.04	.02
❑ 320	Randall Cunningham 90	.10	.05
❑ 321	Terance Mathis 90	.25	.11
❑ 322	Gaston Green 90	.04	.02
❑ 323	Johnny Bailey 90	.04	.02
❑ 324	Donnie Elder 90	.04	.02
❑ 325	Dwight Stone 90 UER (No '91 copyright on card back)	.04	.02
❑ 326	J.J. Birden 90 RC	.10	.05
❑ 327	Alexander Wright 90	.04	.02
❑ 328	Eric Metcalf 90	.10	.05
❑ 329	Andre Rison TL	.10	.05
❑ 330	Warren Moon TL UER (Not Blanda's record, should be Van Brocklin)	.10	.05
❑ 331	Steve Tasker DT	.04	.02
❑ 332	Mel Gray DT	.10	.05
❑ 333	Nick Lowery DT	.04	.02
❑ 334	Sean Landeta DT	.04	.02
❑ 335	David Fulcher DT	.04	.02
❑ 336	Joey Browner DT	.04	.02
❑ 337	Albert Lewis DT	.04	.02
❑ 338	Rod Woodson DT	.10	.05
❑ 339	Shane Conlan DT	.04	.02
❑ 340	Pepper Johnson DT	.04	.02
❑ 341	Chris Spielman DT	.04	.02
❑ 342	Derrick Thomas DT	.10	.05
❑ 343	Ray Childress DT	.04	.02
❑ 344	Reggie White DT	.10	.05
❑ 345	Bruce Smith DT	.10	.05
❑ 346	Darrell Green	.04	.02
❑ 347	Ray Bentley	.04	.02
❑ 348	Herschel Walker	.10	.05
❑ 349	Rodney Holman	.04	.02
❑ 350	Al Toon	.10	.05
❑ 351	Harry Hamilton	.04	.02
❑ 352	Albert Lewis	.04	.02
❑ 353	Renaldo Turnbull	.04	.02
❑ 354	Junior Seau	.25	.11
❑ 355	Merril Hoge	.04	.02
❑ 356	Shane Conlan	.04	.02
❑ 357	Jay Schroeder	.04	.02
❑ 358	Steve Broussard	.04	.02
❑ 359	Mark Bavaro	.04	.02
❑ 360	Jim Lachey	.04	.02
❑ 361	Greg Townsend	.04	.02
❑ 362	Dave Krieg	.10	.05
❑ 363	Jessie Hester	.04	.02
❑ 364	Steve Tasker	.10	.05
❑ 365	Ron Hall	.04	.02
❑ 366	Pat Leahy	.04	.02
❑ 367	Jim Everett	.10	.05
❑ 368	Felix Wright	.04	.02
❑ 369	Ricky Proehl	.04	.02
❑ 370	Anthony Miller	.10	.05
❑ 371	Keith Jackson	.10	.05
❑ 372	Pete Stoyanovich	.04	.02
❑ 373	Tommy Kane	.04	.02
❑ 374	Richard Johnson	.04	.02
❑ 375	Randall McDaniel	.04	.02
❑ 376	John Stephens	.04	.02
❑ 377	Haywood Jeffires	.10	.05
❑ 378	Rodney Hampton	.25	.11
❑ 379	Tim Grunhard	.04	.02
❑ 380	Jerry Rice	.75	.35
❑ 381	Ken Harvey	.10	.05
❑ 382	Vaughan Johnson	.04	.02
❑ 383	J.T. Smith	.04	.02
❑ 384	Carnell Lake	.04	.02
❑ 385	Dan Marino	1.25	.55
❑ 386	Kyle Clifton	.04	.02
❑ 387	Wilber Marshall	.04	.02
❑ 388	Pete Holohan	.04	.02
❑ 389	Gary Plummer	.04	.02
❑ 390	William Perry	.10	.05
❑ 391	Mark Robinson	.04	.02
❑ 392	Nate Odomes	.04	.02
❑ 393	Ickey Woods	.04	.02
❑ 394	Reyna Thompson	.04	.02
❑ 395	Deion Sanders	.40	.18
❑ 396	Harris Barton	.04	.02
❑ 397	Sammie Smith	.04	.02
❑ 398	Vinny Testaverde	.10	.05
❑ 399	Ray Donaldson	.04	.02
❑ 400	Tim McKyer	.04	.02
❑ 401	Nesby Glasgow	.04	.02
❑ 402	Brent Williams	.04	.02
❑ 403	Rob Moore	.25	.11
❑ 404	Bubby Brister	.04	.02
❑ 405	David Fulcher	.04	.02
❑ 406	Reggie Cobb	.04	.02
❑ 407	Jerome Brown	.04	.02
❑ 408	Erik Howard	.04	.02
❑ 409	Tony Paige	.04	.02
❑ 410	John Elway	1.25	.55
❑ 411	Charles Mann	.04	.02
❑ 412	Luis Sharpe	.04	.02

❑ 413 Hassan Jones .04 .02
❑ 414 Frank Minnifield .04 .02
❑ 415 Steve DeBerg .04 .02
❑ 416 Mark Carrier DB .10 .05
❑ 417 Brian Jordan .10 .05
❑ 418 Reggie Langhorne .04 .02
❑ 419 Don Majkowski .04 .02
❑ 420 Marcus Allen .25 .11
❑ 421 Michael Brooks .04 .02
❑ 422 Vai Sikahema .04 .02
❑ 423 Dermontti Dawson .04 .02
❑ 424 Jacob Green .04 .02
❑ 425 Flipper Anderson .04 .02
❑ 426 Bill Brooks .04 .02
❑ 427 Keith McCants .04 .02
❑ 428 Ken O'Brien .04 .02
❑ 429 Fred Barnett .25 .11
❑ 430 Mark Duper .10 .05
❑ 431 Mark Kelso .04 .02
❑ 432 Leslie O'Neal .10 .05
❑ 433 Ottis Anderson .10 .05
❑ 434 Jesse Sapolu .04 .02
❑ 435 Gary Zimmerman .04 .02
❑ 436 Kevin Porter .04 .02
❑ 437 Anthony Thompson .04 .02
❑ 438 Robert Clark .04 .02
❑ 439 Chris Warren .25 .11
❑ 440 Gerald Williams .04 .02
❑ 441 Jim Skow .04 .02
❑ 442 Rick Donnelly .04 .02
❑ 443 Guy McIntyre .04 .02
❑ 444 Jeff Lageman .04 .02
❑ 445 John Offerdahl .04 .02
❑ 446 Clyde Simmons .04 .02
❑ 447 John Kidd .04 .02
❑ 448 Chip Banks .04 .02
❑ 449 Johnny Meads .04 .02
❑ 450 Rickey Jackson .04 .02
❑ 451 Lee Johnson .04 .02
❑ 452 Michael Irvin .25 .11
❑ 453 Leon Seals .04 .02
❑ 454 Darrell Thompson .04 .02
❑ 455 Everson Walls .04 .02
❑ 456 LeRoy Butler .10 .05
❑ 457 Marcus Dupree .04 .02
❑ 458 Kirk Lowdermilk .04 .02
❑ 459 Chris Singleton .04 .02
❑ 460 Seth Joyner .10 .05
❑ 461 Rueben Mayes UER .04 .02
(Hayes in bio should be Heyward)
❑ 462 Ernie Jones .04 .02
❑ 463 Greg Kragen .04 .02
❑ 464 Bennie Blades .04 .02
❑ 465 Mark Bortz .04 .02
❑ 466 Tony Stargell .04 .02
❑ 467 Mike Cofer .04 .02
❑ 468 Randy Grimes .04 .02
❑ 469 Tim Worley .04 .02
❑ 470 Kevin Mack .04 .02
❑ 471 Wes Hopkins .04 .02
❑ 472 Will Wolford .04 .02
❑ 473 Sam Seale .04 .02
❑ 474 Jim Ritcher .04 .02
❑ 475 Jeff Hostetler .25 .11
❑ 476 Mitchell Price RC .04 .02
❑ 477 Ken Lanier .04 .02
❑ 478 Naz Worthen .04 .02
❑ 479 Ed Reynolds .04 .02
❑ 480 Mark Clayton .10 .05
❑ 481 Matt Bahr .04 .02
❑ 482 Gary Reasons .04 .02
❑ 483 David Szott .04 .02
❑ 484 Barry Foster .10 .05
❑ 485 Bruce Reimers .04 .02
❑ 486 Dean Biasucci .04 .02
❑ 487 Cris Carter .50 .23
❑ 488 Albert Bentley .04 .02
❑ 489 Robert Massey .04 .02
❑ 490 Al Smith .04 .02
❑ 491 Greg Lloyd .25 .11
❑ 492 Steve McMichael UER .10 .05
(Photo on back actually Dan Hampton)
❑ 493 Jeff Wright RC .04 .02
❑ 494 Scott Davis .04 .02
❑ 495 Freeman McNeil .04 .02
❑ 496 Simon Fletcher .04 .02
❑ 497 Terry McDaniel .04 .02
❑ 498 Heath Sherman .04 .02
❑ 499 Jeff Jaeger .04 .02
❑ 500 Mark Collins .04 .02
❑ 501 Tim Goad .04 .02
❑ 502 Jeff George .25 .11
❑ 503 Jimmie Jones .04 .02
❑ 504 Henry Thomas .04 .02
❑ 505 Steve Young .75 .35
❑ 506 William Roberts .04 .02
❑ 507 Neil Smith .25 .11
❑ 508 Mike Saxon .04 .02
❑ 509 Johnny Bailey .04 .02
❑ 510 Broderick Thomas .04 .02
❑ 511 Wade Wilson .10 .05
❑ 512 Hart Lee Dykes .04 .02
❑ 513 Hardy Nickerson .10 .05
❑ 514 Tim McDonald .04 .02
❑ 515 Frank Cornish .04 .02
❑ 516 Jarvis Williams .04 .02
❑ 517 Carl Lee .04 .02
❑ 518 Carl Banks .04 .02
❑ 519 Mike Golic .04 .02
❑ 520 Brian Noble .04 .02
❑ 521 James Hasty .04 .02
❑ 522 Bubba Paris .04 .02
❑ 523 Kevin Walker RC .04 .02
❑ 524 William Fuller .10 .05
❑ 525 Eddie Anderson .04 .02
❑ 526 Roger Ruzek .04 .02
❑ 527 Robert Blackmon .04 .02
❑ 528 Vince Buck .04 .02
❑ 529 Lawrence Taylor .25 .11
❑ 530 Reggie Roby .04 .02
❑ 531 Doug Riesenberg .04 .02
❑ 532 Joe Jacoby .04 .02
❑ 533 Kirby Jackson RC .04 .02
❑ 534 Robb Thomas .04 .02
❑ 535 Don Griffin .04 .02
❑ 536 Andre Waters .04 .02
❑ 537 Marc Logan .04 .02
❑ 538 James Thornton .04 .02
❑ 539 Ray Agnew .04 .02
❑ 540 Frank Stams .04 .02
❑ 541 Brett Perriman .25 .11
❑ 542 Andre Ware .10 .05
❑ 543 Kevin Haverdink .04 .02
❑ 544 Greg Jackson RC .04 .02
❑ 545 Tunch Ilkin .04 .02
❑ 546 Dexter Carter .04 .02
❑ 547 Rod Woodson .25 .11
❑ 548 Donnell Woolford .04 .02
❑ 549 Mark Boyer .04 .02
❑ 550 Jeff Query .04 .02
❑ 551 Burt Grossman .04 .02
❑ 552 Mike Kenn .04 .02
❑ 553 Richard Dent .10 .05
❑ 554 Gaston Green .04 .02
❑ 555 Phil Simms .10 .05
❑ 556 Brent Jones .25 .11
❑ 557 Ronnie Lippett .04 .02
❑ 558 Mike Horan .04 .02
❑ 559 Danny Noonan .04 .02
❑ 560 Reggie White .25 .11
❑ 561 Rufus Porter .04 .02
❑ 562 Aaron Wallace .04 .02
❑ 563 Vance Johnson .04 .02
❑ 564A Aaron Craver RC ERR .04 .02
(No copyright line on back)
❑ 564B Aaron Craver COR RC .04 .02
❑ 565A R.Maryland RC ERR .25 .11
(No copyright line on back)
❑ 565B R.Maryland COR RC .25 .11
❑ 566 Paul Justin RC .04 .02
❑ 567 Walter Dean .04 .02
❑ 568 Herman Moore RC 2.00 .90
❑ 569 Bill Musgrave RC .04 .02
❑ 570 Rob Carpenter RC .04 .02
❑ 571 Greg Lewis RC .04 .02
❑ 572 Ed King RC .04 .02
❑ 573 Ernie Mills RC .10 .05
❑ 574 Jake Reed RC .75 .35
❑ 575 Ricky Watters RC 1.50 .70
❑ 576 Derek Russell RC .04 .02
❑ 577 Shawn Moore RC .04 .02
❑ 578 Eric Bieniemy RC .04 .02
❑ 579 Chris Zorich RC .25 .11
❑ 580 Scott Miller .04 .02
❑ 581 Jarrod Bunch RC .04 .02
❑ 582 Ricky Ervins RC .10 .05
❑ 583 Browning Nagle RC .04 .02
❑ 584 Eric Turner RC .10 .05
❑ 585 William Thomas RC .04 .02
❑ 586 Stanley Richard RC .04 .02
❑ 587 Adrian Cooper RC .04 .02
❑ 588 Harvey Williams RC .25 .11
❑ 589 Alvin Harper RC .25 .11
❑ 590 John Carney .04 .02
❑ 591 Mark Vander Poel RC .04 .02
❑ 592 Mike Pritchard RC .25 .11
❑ 593 Eric Moten RC .04 .02
❑ 594 Moe Gardner RC .04 .02
❑ 595 Wesley Carroll RC .04 .02
❑ 596 Eric Swann RC .25 .11
❑ 597 Joe Kelly .04 .02
❑ 598 Steve Jackson RC .04 .02
❑ 599 Kelvin Pritchett RC .10 .05
❑ 600 Jesse Campbell RC .04 .02
❑ 601 Darryll Lewis RC UER .10 .05
(Name misspelled Darryl)
❑ 602 Howard Griffith .04 .02
❑ 603 Blaise Bryant .04 .02
❑ 604 Vinnie Clark RC .04 .02
❑ 605 Mel Agee RC .04 .02
❑ 606 Bobby Wilson RC .04 .02
❑ 607 Kevin Donnalley .04 .02
❑ 608 Randal Hill RC .10 .05
❑ 609 Stan Thomas .04 .02
❑ 610 Mike Heldt .04 .02
❑ 611 Brett Favre RC 5.00 2.20
❑ 612 L.Dawsey RC UER .10 .05
(Went to Florida State, not Florida)
❑ 613 Dennis Gibson .04 .02
❑ 614 Dean Dingman .04 .02
❑ 615 Bruce Pickens RC .04 .02
❑ 616 Todd Marinovich RC .04 .02
❑ 617 Gene Atkins .04 .02
❑ 618 Marcus Dupree .04 .02
(Comeback Player)
❑ 619 Warren Moon .10 .05
(Man of the Year)
❑ 620 Joe Montana MVP .50 .23
❑ 621 Neal Anderson MVP .04 .02
❑ 622 James Brooks MVP .10 .05
❑ 623 Thurman Thomas MVP .10 .05
❑ 624 Bobby Humphrey MVP .04 .02
❑ 625 Kevin Mack MVP .04 .02
❑ 626 Mark Carrier WR MVP .04 .02
❑ 627 Johnny Johnson MVP .04 .02
❑ 628 Marion Butts MVP .10 .05
❑ 629 Steve DeBerg MVP .04 .02
❑ 630 Jeff George MVP .10 .05
❑ 631 Troy Aikman MVP .40 .18
❑ 632 Dan Marino MVP .50 .23
❑ 633 R.Cunningham MVP .10 .05
❑ 634 Andre Rison MVP .10 .05
❑ 635 Pepper Johnson MVP .04 .02
❑ 636 Pat Leahy MVP .04 .02
❑ 637 Barry Sanders MVP .60 .25
❑ 638 Warren Moon MVP .10 .05
❑ 639 Sterling Sharpe MVP .04 .02
❑ 640 Bruce Armstrong MVP .04 .02
❑ 641 Bo Jackson MVP .10 .05
❑ 642 Henry Ellard MVP .10 .05
❑ 643 Earnest Byner MVP .04 .02
❑ 644 Pat Swilling MVP .04 .02
❑ 645 John L. Williams MVP .04 .02
❑ 646 Rod Woodson MVP .10 .05
❑ 647 Chris Doleman MVP .04 .02
❑ 648 Joey Browner CC .04 .02
❑ 649 Erik McMillan CC .04 .02
❑ 650 David Fulcher CC .04 .02
❑ 651A Ronnie Lott CC ERR .10 .05
(Front 47, back 42)
❑ 651B Ronnie Lott CC COR .10 .05
(Front 47, back 42 is now blacked out)

Card	MINT	NRMT
❑ 652 Louis Oliver CC	.04	.02
❑ 653 Mark Robinson CC	.04	.02
❑ 654 Dennis Smith CC	.04	.02
❑ 655 Reggie White SA	.10	.05
❑ 656 Charles Haley SA	.04	.02
❑ 657 Leslie O'Neal SA	.10	.05
❑ 658 Kevin Greene SA	.10	.05
❑ 659 Dennis Byrd SA	.04	.02
❑ 660 Bruce Smith SA	.10	.05
❑ 661 Derrick Thomas SA	.10	.05
❑ 662 Steve DeBerg TL	.04	.02
❑ 663 Barry Sanders TL	.60	.25
❑ 664 Thurman Thomas TL	.10	.05
❑ 665 Jerry Rice TL	.40	.18
❑ 666 Derrick Thomas TL	.10	.05
❑ 667 Bruce Smith TL	.10	.05
❑ 668 Mark Carrier DB TL	.04	.02
❑ 669 Richard Johnson TL	.04	.02
❑ 670 Jan Stenerud HOF	.04	.02
❑ 671 Stan Jones HOF	.04	.02
❑ 672 John Hannah HOF	.04	.02
❑ 673 Tex Schramm HOF	.04	.02
❑ 674 Earl Campbell HOF	.25	.11
❑ 675 Mark Carrier and Emmitt Smith (Rookies of the Year)	.50	.23
❑ 676 Warren Moon DT	.10	.05
❑ 677 Barry Sanders DT	.60	.25
❑ 678 Thurman Thomas DT	.25	.11
❑ 679 Andre Reed DT	.10	.05
❑ 680 Andre Rison DT	.10	.05
❑ 681 Keith Jackson DT	.04	.02
❑ 682 Bruce Armstrong DT	.04	.02
❑ 683 Jim Lachey DT	.04	.02
❑ 684 Bruce Matthews DT	.04	.02
❑ 685 Mike Munchak DT	.04	.02
❑ 686 Don Mosebar DT	.04	.02
❑ B1 Jeff Hostetler SB	.25	.11
❑ B2 Matt Bahr SB	.04	.02
❑ B3 Ottis Anderson SB	.10	.05
❑ B4 Ottis Anderson SB	.10	.05

1991 Score Supplemental

	MINT	NRMT
COMPLETE FACT.SET (110)	3.00	1.35
❑ 1T Ronnie Lott	.10	.05
❑ 2T Matt Millen	.10	.05
❑ 3T Tim McKyer	.04	.02
❑ 4T Vince Newsome	.04	.02
❑ 5T Gaston Green	.04	.02
❑ 6T Brett Perriman	.25	.11
❑ 7T Roger Craig	.10	.05
❑ 8T Pete Holohan	.04	.02
❑ 9T Tony Zendejas	.04	.02
❑ 10T Lee Williams	.04	.02
❑ 11T Mike Stonebreaker	.04	.02
❑ 12T Felix Wright	.04	.02
❑ 13T Lonnie Young	.04	.02
❑ 14T Hugh Millen RC	.04	.02
❑ 15T Roy Green	.04	.02
❑ 16T Greg Davis RC	.04	.02
❑ 17T Dexter Manley	.04	.02
❑ 18T Ted Washington RC	.04	.02
❑ 19T Norm Johnson	.04	.02
❑ 20T Joe Morris	.04	.02
❑ 21T Robert Perryman	.04	.02
❑ 22T Mike Iaquaniello RC UER (Free agent in '91, not '87)	.04	.02
❑ 23T Gerald Perry RC UER (School should be Southern University A and M)	.04	.02
❑ 24T Zeke Mowatt	.04	.02
❑ 25T Rich Miano RC	.04	.02
❑ 26T Nick Bell	.04	.02
❑ 27T Terry Orr RC	.04	.02
❑ 28T Matt Stover RC	.25	.11
❑ 29T Bubba Paris	.04	.02
❑ 30T Ron Brown	.04	.02
❑ 31T Don Davey	.04	.02
❑ 32T Lee Rouson	.04	.02
❑ 33T Terry Hoage UER (Eaggles, sic)	.04	.02
❑ 34T Tony Covington	.04	.02
❑ 35T John Rienstra	.04	.02
❑ 36T Charles Dimry RC	.04	.02
❑ 37T Todd Marinovich	.04	.02
❑ 38T Winston Moss	.04	.02
❑ 39T Vestee Jackson	.04	.02
❑ 40T Brian Hansen	.04	.02
❑ 41T Irv Eatman	.04	.02
❑ 42T Jarrod Bunch	.04	.02
❑ 43T Kanavis McGhee RC	.04	.02
❑ 44T Vai Sikahema	.04	.02
❑ 45T Charles McRae RC	.04	.02
❑ 46T Quinn Early	.10	.05
❑ 47T Jeff Faulkner RC	.04	.02
❑ 48T William Frizzell RC	.04	.02
❑ 49T John Booty	.04	.02
❑ 50T Tim Harris	.04	.02
❑ 51T Derek Russell	.04	.02
❑ 52T John Flannery RC	.04	.02
❑ 53T Tim Barnett RC	.04	.02
❑ 54T Alfred Williams RC	.04	.02
❑ 55T Dan McGwire	.04	.02
❑ 56T Ernie Mills	.04	.02
❑ 57T Stanley Richard	.04	.02
❑ 58T Huey Richardson RC	.04	.02
❑ 59T Jerome Henderson RC	.04	.02
❑ 60T Bryan Cox RC	.25	.11
❑ 61T Russell Maryland	.10	.05
❑ 62T Reginald Jones RC	.04	.02
❑ 63T Mo Lewis RC	.10	.05
❑ 64T Moe Gardner	.04	.02
❑ 65T Wesley Carroll	.04	.02
❑ 66T Michael Jackson RC	.25	.11
❑ 67T Shawn Jefferson RC	.10	.05
❑ 68T Chris Zorich	.10	.05
❑ 69T Kenny Walker	.04	.02
❑ 70T Erric Pegram RC	.25	.11
❑ 71T Alvin Harper	.25	.11
❑ 72T Harry Colon RC	.04	.02
❑ 73T Scott Miller	.04	.02
❑ 74T Lawrence Dawsey	.10	.05
❑ 75T Phil Hansen RC	.04	.02
❑ 76T Roman Phifer RC	.04	.02
❑ 77T Greg Lewis	.04	.02
❑ 78T Merton Hanks RC	.25	.11
❑ 79T James Jones RC	.04	.02
❑ 80T Vinnie Clark	.04	.02
❑ 81T R.J. Kors	.04	.02
❑ 82T Mike Pritchard	.25	.11
❑ 83T Stan Thomas	.04	.02
❑ 84T Lamar Rogers RC	.04	.02
❑ 85T Erik Williams RC	.10	.05
❑ 86T Keith Traylor RC	.04	.02
❑ 87T Mike Dumas	.04	.02
❑ 88T Mel Agee	.04	.02
❑ 89T Harvey Williams	.25	.11
❑ 90T Todd Lyght	.04	.02
❑ 91T Jake Reed	.40	.18
❑ 92T Pat Harlow	.04	.02
❑ 93T Antone Davis RC	.04	.02
❑ 94T Aeneas Williams RC	.25	.11
❑ 95T Eric Bieniemy	.04	.02
❑ 96T John Kasay RC	.10	.05
❑ 97T Robert Wilson RC	.04	.02
❑ 98T Ricky Ervins	.10	.05
❑ 99T Mike Croel	.04	.02
❑ 100T David Lang RC	.04	.02
❑ 101T Esera Tuaolo RC	.04	.02
❑ 102T Randal Hill	.10	.05
❑ 103T Jon Vaughn RC	.04	.02
❑ 104T Dave McCloughan	.04	.02
❑ 105T David Daniels RC	.04	.02
❑ 106T Eric Moten	.04	.02
❑ 107T Anthony Morgan RC	.04	.02
❑ 108T Ed King	.04	.02
❑ 109T Leonard Russell RC	.10	.05
❑ 110T Aaron Craver	.04	.02

1992 Score

	MINT	NRMT
COMPLETE SET (550)	25.00	11.00
❑ 1 Barry Sanders	2.50	1.10
❑ 2 Pat Swilling	.10	.05
❑ 3 Moe Gardner	.05	.02
❑ 4 Steve Young	1.00	.45
❑ 5 Chris Spielman	.10	.05
❑ 6 Richard Dent	.10	.05
❑ 7 Anthony Munoz	.10	.05
❑ 8 Martin Mayhew	.05	.02
❑ 9 Terry McDaniel	.05	.02
❑ 10 Thurman Thomas	.25	.11
❑ 11 Ricky Sanders	.05	.02
❑ 12 Steve Atwater	.05	.02
❑ 13 Tony Tolbert	.05	.02
❑ 14 Vince Workman	.10	.05
❑ 15 Haywood Jeffires	.10	.05
❑ 16 Duane Bickett	.05	.02
❑ 17 Jeff Uhlenhake	.05	.02
❑ 18 Tim McDonald	.05	.02
❑ 19 Cris Carter	.50	.23
❑ 20 Derrick Thomas	.25	.11
❑ 21 Hugh Millen	.05	.02
❑ 22 Bart Oates	.05	.02
❑ 23 Eugene Robinson	.05	.02
❑ 24 Jerrol Williams	.05	.02
❑ 25 Reggie White	.25	.11
❑ 26 Marion Butts	.05	.02
❑ 27 Jim Sweeney	.05	.02
❑ 28 Tom Newberry	.05	.02
❑ 29 Pete Stoyanovich	.05	.02
❑ 30 Ronnie Lott	.10	.05
❑ 31 Simon Fletcher	.05	.02
❑ 32 Dino Hackett	.05	.02
❑ 33 Morten Andersen	.05	.02
❑ 34 Clyde Simmons	.05	.02
❑ 35 Mark Rypien	.05	.02
❑ 36 Greg Montgomery	.05	.02
❑ 37 Nate Lewis	.05	.02
❑ 38 Henry Ellard	.10	.05
❑ 39 Luis Sharpe	.05	.02
❑ 40 Michael Irvin	.25	.11
❑ 41 Louis Lipps	.05	.02
❑ 42 John L. Williams	.05	.02
❑ 43 Broderick Thomas	.05	.02
❑ 44 Michael Haynes	.10	.05
❑ 45 Don Majkowski	.05	.02
❑ 46 William Perry	.10	.05
❑ 47 David Fulcher	.05	.02
❑ 48 Tony Bennett	.05	.02
❑ 49 Clay Matthews	.10	.05
❑ 50 Warren Moon	.25	.11
❑ 51 Bruce Armstrong	.05	.02
❑ 52 Harry Newsome	.05	.02

❑ 53 Bill Brooks .05 .02
❑ 54 Greg Townsend .05 .02
❑ 55 Tom Rathman .05 .02
❑ 56 Sean Landeta .05 .02
❑ 57 Kyle Clifton .05 .02
❑ 58 Steve Broussard .05 .02
❑ 59 Mark Carrier WR .10 .05
❑ 60 Mel Gray .10 .05
❑ 61 Tim Krumrie .05 .02
❑ 62 Rufus Porter .05 .02
❑ 63 Kevin Mack .05 .02
❑ 64 Todd Bowles .05 .02
❑ 65 Emmitt Smith 2.50 1.10
❑ 66 Mike Croel .05 .02
❑ 67 Brian Mitchell .10 .05
❑ 68 Bennie Blades .05 .02
❑ 69 Carnell Lake .05 .02
❑ 70 Cornelius Bennett .10 .05
❑ 71 Darrell Thompson .05 .02
❑ 72 Wes Hopkins .05 .02
❑ 73 Jessie Hester .05 .02
❑ 74 Irv Eatman .05 .02
❑ 75 Marv Cook .05 .02
❑ 76 Tim Brown .25 .11
❑ 77 Pepper Johnson .05 .02
❑ 78 Mark Duper .05 .02
❑ 79 Robert Delpino .05 .02
❑ 80 Charles Mann .05 .02
❑ 81 Brian Jordan .10 .05
❑ 82 Wendell Davis .05 .02
❑ 83 Lee Johnson .05 .02
❑ 84 Ricky Reynolds .05 .02
❑ 85 Vaughan Johnson .05 .02
❑ 86 Brian Blades .10 .05
❑ 87 Sam Seale .05 .02
❑ 88 Ed King .05 .02
❑ 89 Gaston Green .05 .02
❑ 90 Christian Okoye .05 .02
❑ 91 Chris Jacke .05 .02
❑ 92 Rohn Stark .05 .02
❑ 93 Kevin Greene .25 .11
❑ 94 Jay Novacek .10 .05
❑ 95 Chip Lohmiller .05 .02
❑ 96 Cris Dishman .05 .02
❑ 97 Ethan Horton .05 .02
❑ 98 Pat Harlow .05 .02
❑ 99 Mark Ingram .05 .02
❑ 100 Mark Carrier DB .05 .02
❑ 101 Deron Cherry .05 .02
❑ 102 Sam Mills .05 .02
❑ 103 Mark Higgs .05 .02
❑ 104 Keith Jackson .10 .05
❑ 105 Steve Tasker .10 .05
❑ 106 Ken Harvey .05 .02
❑ 107 Bryan Hinkle .05 .02
❑ 108 Anthony Carter .10 .05
❑ 109 Johnny Hector .05 .02
❑ 110 Randall McDaniel .05 .02
❑ 111 Johnny Johnson .05 .02
❑ 112 Shane Conlan .05 .02
❑ 113 Ray Horton .05 .02
❑ 114 Sterling Sharpe .25 .11
❑ 115 Guy McIntyre .05 .02
❑ 116 Tom Waddle .05 .02
❑ 117 Albert Lewis .05 .02
❑ 118 Riki Ellison .05 .02
❑ 119 Chris Doleman .05 .02
❑ 120 Andre Rison .10 .05
❑ 121 Bobby Hebert .05 .02
❑ 122 Dan Owens .05 .02
❑ 123 Rodney Hampton .25 .11
❑ 124 Ron Holmes .05 .02
❑ 125 Ernie Jones .05 .02
❑ 126 Michael Carter .05 .02
❑ 127 Reggie Cobb .05 .02
❑ 128 Esera Tuaolo .05 .02
❑ 129 Wilber Marshall .05 .02
❑ 130 Mike Munchak .05 .02
❑ 131 Cortez Kennedy .10 .05
❑ 132 Lamar Lathon .05 .02
❑ 133 Todd Lyght .05 .02
❑ 134 Jeff Feagles .05 .02
❑ 135 Burt Grossman .05 .02
❑ 136 Mike Cofer .05 .02
❑ 137 Frank Warren .05 .02
❑ 138 Jarvis Williams .05 .02
❑ 139 Eddie Brown .05 .02
❑ 140 John Elliott .05 .02
❑ 141 Jim Everett .10 .05
❑ 142 Hardy Nickerson .10 .05
❑ 143 Eddie Murray .05 .02
❑ 144 Andre Tippett .05 .02
❑ 145 Heath Sherman .05 .02
❑ 146 Ronnie Harmon .05 .02
❑ 147 Eric Metcalf .10 .05
❑ 148 Tony Martin .25 .11
❑ 149 Chris Burkett .05 .02
❑ 150 Andre Waters .05 .02
❑ 151 Ray Donaldson .05 .02
❑ 152 Paul Gruber .05 .02
❑ 153 Chris Singleton .05 .02
❑ 154 Clarence Kay .05 .02
❑ 155 Ernest Givins .10 .05
❑ 156 Eric Hill .05 .02
❑ 157 Jesse Sapolu .05 .02
❑ 158 Jack Del Rio .05 .02
❑ 159 Erric Pegram .10 .05
❑ 160 Joey Browner .05 .02
❑ 161 Marcus Allen .25 .11
❑ 162 Eric Moten .05 .02
❑ 163 Donnell Thompson .05 .02
❑ 164 Chuck Cecil .05 .02
❑ 165 Matt Millen .10 .05
❑ 166 Barry Foster .10 .05
❑ 167 Kent Hull .05 .02
❑ 168 Tony Jones .05 .02
❑ 169 Mike Prior .05 .02
❑ 170 Neal Anderson .05 .02
❑ 171 Roger Craig .10 .05
❑ 172 Felix Wright .05 .02
❑ 173 James Francis .05 .02
❑ 174 Eugene Lockhart .05 .02
❑ 175 Dalton Hilliard .05 .02
❑ 176 Nick Lowery .05 .02
❑ 177 Tim McKyer .05 .02
❑ 178 Lorenzo White .05 .02
❑ 179 Jeff Hostetler .10 .05
❑ 180 Jackie Harris RC .10 .05
❑ 181 Ken Norton .25 .11
❑ 182 Flipper Anderson .05 .02
❑ 183 Don Warren .05 .02
❑ 184 Brad Baxter .05 .02
❑ 185 John Taylor .10 .05
❑ 186 Harold Green .05 .02
❑ 187 James Washington .05 .02
❑ 188 Aaron Craver .05 .02
❑ 189 Mike Merriweather .05 .02
❑ 190 Gary Clark .25 .11
❑ 191 Vince Buck .05 .02
❑ 192 Cleveland Gary .05 .02
❑ 193 Dan Saleaumua .05 .02
❑ 194 Gary Zimmerman .05 .02
❑ 195 Richmond Webb .05 .02
❑ 196 Gary Plummer .05 .02
❑ 197 Willie Green .05 .02
❑ 198 Chris Warren .25 .11
❑ 199 Mike Pritchard .10 .05
❑ 200 Art Monk .10 .05
❑ 201 Matt Stover .05 .02
❑ 202 Tim Grunhard .05 .02
❑ 203 Mervyn Fernandez .05 .02
❑ 204 Mark Jackson .05 .02
❑ 205 Freddie Joe Nunn .05 .02
❑ 206 Stan Thomas .05 .02
❑ 207 Keith McKeller .05 .02
❑ 208 Jeff Lageman .05 .02
❑ 209 Kenny Walker .05 .02
❑ 210 Dave Krieg .10 .05
❑ 211 Dean Biasucci .05 .02
❑ 212 Herman Moore .50 .23
❑ 213 Jon Vaughn .05 .02
❑ 214 Howard Cross .05 .02
❑ 215 Greg Davis .05 .02
❑ 216 Bubby Brister .05 .02
❑ 217 John Kasay .05 .02
❑ 218 Ron Hall .05 .02
❑ 219 Mo Lewis .05 .02
❑ 220 Eric Green .05 .02
❑ 221 Scott Case .05 .02
❑ 222 Sean Jones .10 .05
❑ 223 Winston Moss .05 .02
❑ 224 Reggie Langhorne .05 .02
❑ 225 Greg Lewis .05 .02
❑ 226 Todd McNair .05 .02
❑ 227 Rod Bernstine .05 .02
❑ 228 Joe Jacoby .05 .02
❑ 229 Brad Muster .05 .02
❑ 230 Nick Bell .05 .02
❑ 231 Terry Allen .25 .11
❑ 232 Cliff Odom .05 .02
❑ 233 Brian Hansen .05 .02
❑ 234 William Fuller .10 .05
❑ 235 Issiac Holt .05 .02
❑ 236 Dexter Carter .05 .02
❑ 237 Gene Atkins .05 .02
❑ 238 Pat Beach .05 .02
❑ 239 Tim McGee .05 .02
❑ 240 Dermontti Dawson .05 .02
❑ 241 Dan Fike .05 .02
❑ 242 Don Beebe .05 .02
❑ 243 Jeff Bostic .05 .02
❑ 244 Mark Collins .05 .02
❑ 245 Steve Sewell .05 .02
❑ 246 Steve Walsh .05 .02
❑ 247 Erik Kramer .10 .05
❑ 248 Scott Norwood .05 .02
❑ 249 Jesse Solomon .05 .02
❑ 250 Jerry Ball .05 .02
❑ 251 Eugene Daniel .05 .02
❑ 252 Michael Stewart .05 .02
❑ 253 Fred Barnett .25 .11
❑ 254 Rodney Holman .05 .02
❑ 255 Stephen Baker .05 .02
❑ 256 Don Griffin .05 .02
❑ 257 Will Wolford .05 .02
❑ 258 Perry Kemp .05 .02
❑ 259 Leonard Russell .10 .05
❑ 260 Jeff Gossett .05 .02
❑ 261 Dwayne Harper .05 .02
❑ 262 Vinny Testaverde .10 .05
❑ 263 Maurice Hurst .05 .02
❑ 264 Tony Casillas .05 .02
❑ 265 Louis Oliver .05 .02
❑ 266 Jim Morrissey .05 .02
❑ 267 Kenneth Davis .05 .02
❑ 268 John Alt .05 .02
❑ 269 Michael Zordich RC .05 .02
❑ 270 Brian Brennan .05 .02
❑ 271 Greg Kragen .05 .02
❑ 272 Andre Collins .05 .02
❑ 273 Dave Meggett .10 .05
❑ 274 Scott Fulhage .05 .02
❑ 275 Tony Zendejas .05 .02
❑ 276 Herschel Walker .10 .05
❑ 277 Keith Henderson .05 .02
❑ 278 Johnny Bailey .05 .02
❑ 279 Vince Newsome .05 .02
❑ 280 Chris Hinton .05 .02
❑ 281 Robert Blackmon .05 .02
❑ 282 James Hasty .05 .02
❑ 283 John Offerdahl .05 .02
❑ 284 Wesley Carroll .05 .02
❑ 285 Lomas Brown .05 .02
❑ 286 Neil O'Donnell .25 .11
❑ 287 Kevin Porter .05 .02
❑ 288 Lionel Washington .05 .02
❑ 289 Carlton Bailey RC .10 .05
❑ 290 Leonard Marshall .05 .02
❑ 291 John Carney .05 .02
❑ 292 Bubba McDowell .05 .02
❑ 293 Nate Newton .10 .05
❑ 294 Dave Waymer .05 .02
❑ 295 Rob Moore .10 .05
❑ 296 Earnest Byner .05 .02
❑ 297 Jason Staurovsky .05 .02
❑ 298 Keith McCants .05 .02
❑ 299 Floyd Turner .05 .02
❑ 300 Steve Jordan .05 .02
❑ 301 Nate Odomes .05 .02
❑ 302 Gerald Riggs .05 .02
❑ 303 Marvin Washington .05 .02
❑ 304 Anthony Thompson .05 .02
❑ 305 Steve DeBerg .05 .02
❑ 306 Jim Harbaugh .25 .11
❑ 307 Larry Brown DB .05 .02
❑ 308 Roger Ruzek .05 .02
❑ 309 Jessie Tuggle .05 .02
❑ 310 Al Smith .05 .02

❑ 311 Mark Kelso .05 .02
❑ 312 Lawrence Dawsey .10 .05
❑ 313 Steve Bono RC .25 .11
❑ 314 Greg Lloyd .25 .11
❑ 315 Steve Wisniewski .05 .02
❑ 316 Gill Fenerty .05 .02
❑ 317 Mark Stepnoski .10 .05
❑ 318 Derek Russell .05 .02
❑ 319 Chris Martin .05 .02
❑ 320 Shaun Gayle .05 .02
❑ 321 Bob Golic .05 .02
❑ 322 Larry Kelm .05 .02
❑ 323 Mike Brim RC .05 .02
❑ 324 Tommy Kane .05 .02
❑ 325 Mark Schlereth RC .05 .02
❑ 326 Ray Childress .05 .02
❑ 327 Richard Brown RC .05 .02
❑ 328 Vincent Brown .05 .02
❑ 329 Mike Farr UER .05 .02
(Back of card refers to him as Mel)
❑ 330 Eric Swann .10 .05
❑ 331 Bill Fralic .05 .02
❑ 332 Rodney Peete .10 .05
❑ 333 Jerry Gray .05 .02
❑ 334 Ray Berry .05 .02
❑ 335 Dennis Smith .05 .02
❑ 336 Jeff Herrod .05 .02
❑ 337 Tony Mandarich .05 .02
❑ 338 Matt Bahr .05 .02
❑ 339 Mike Saxon .05 .02
❑ 340 Bruce Matthews .05 .02
❑ 341 Rickey Jackson .05 .02
❑ 342 Eric Allen .05 .02
❑ 343 Lonnie Young .05 .02
❑ 344 Steve McMichael .10 .05
❑ 345 Willie Gault .10 .05
❑ 346 Barry Word .05 .02
❑ 347 Rich Camarillo .05 .02
❑ 348 Bill Romanowski .05 .02
❑ 349 Jim Lachey .05 .02
❑ 350 Jim Ritcher .05 .02
❑ 351 Irving Fryar .10 .05
❑ 352 Gary Anderson K .05 .02
❑ 353 Henry Rolling .05 .02
❑ 354 Mark Bortz .05 .02
❑ 355 Mark Clayton .10 .05
❑ 356 Keith Woodside .05 .02
❑ 357 Jonathan Hayes .05 .02
❑ 358 Derrick Fenner .05 .02
❑ 359 Keith Byars .05 .02
❑ 360 Drew Hill .05 .02
❑ 361 Harris Barton .05 .02
❑ 362 John Kidd .05 .02
❑ 363 Aeneas Williams .10 .05
❑ 364 Brian Washington .05 .02
❑ 365 John Stephens .05 .02
❑ 366 Norm Johnson .05 .02
❑ 367 Darryl Henley .05 .02
❑ 368 William White .05 .02
❑ 369 Mark Murphy .05 .02
❑ 370 Myron Guyton .05 .02
❑ 371 Leon Seals .05 .02
❑ 372 Rich Gannon .25 .11
❑ 373 Toi Cook .05 .02
❑ 374 Anthony Johnson .10 .05
❑ 375 Rod Woodson .25 .11
❑ 376 Alexander Wright .05 .02
❑ 377 Kevin Butler .05 .02
❑ 378 Neil Smith .25 .11
❑ 379 Gary Anderson RB .05 .02
❑ 380 Reggie Roby .05 .02
❑ 381 Jeff Bryant .05 .02
❑ 382 Ray Crockett .05 .02
❑ 383 Richard Johnson .05 .02
❑ 384 Hassan Jones .05 .02
❑ 385 Karl Mecklenburg .05 .02
❑ 386 Jeff Jaeger .05 .02
❑ 387 Keith Willis .05 .02
❑ 388 Phil Simms .10 .05
❑ 389 Kevin Ross .05 .02
❑ 390 Chris Miller .10 .05
❑ 391 Brian Noble .05 .02
❑ 392 Jamie Dukes RC .05 .02
❑ 393 George Jamison .05 .02
❑ 394 Rickey Dixon .05 .02
❑ 395 Carl Lee .05 .02
❑ 396 Jon Hand .05 .02
❑ 397 Kirby Jackson .05 .02
❑ 398 Pat Terrell .05 .02
❑ 399 Howie Long .10 .05
❑ 400 Michael Young .05 .02
❑ 401 Keith Sims .05 .02
❑ 402 Tommy Barnhardt .05 .02
❑ 403 Greg McMurtry .05 .02
❑ 404 Keith Van Horne .05 .02
❑ 405 Seth Joyner .10 .05
❑ 406 Jim Jeffcoat .05 .02
❑ 407 Courtney Hall .05 .02
❑ 408 Tony Covington .05 .02
❑ 409 Jacob Green .05 .02
❑ 410 Charles Haley .10 .05
❑ 411 Darryl Talley .05 .02
❑ 412 Jeff Cross .05 .02
❑ 413 John Elway 2.00 .90
❑ 414 Donald Evans .05 .02
❑ 415 Jackie Slater .05 .02
❑ 416 John Friesz .10 .05
❑ 417 Anthony Smith .05 .02
❑ 418 Gill Byrd .05 .02
❑ 419 Willie Drewrey .05 .02
❑ 420 Jay Hilgenberg .05 .02
❑ 421 David Treadwell .05 .02
❑ 422 Curtis Duncan .05 .02
❑ 423 Sammie Smith .05 .02
❑ 424 Henry Thomas .05 .02
❑ 425 James Lofton .10 .05
❑ 426 Fred Marion .05 .02
❑ 427 Bryce Paup .25 .11
❑ 428 Michael Timpson RC .10 .05
❑ 429 Reyna Thompson .05 .02
❑ 430 Mike Kenn .05 .02
❑ 431 Bill Maas .05 .02
❑ 432 Quinn Early .10 .05
❑ 433 Everson Walls .05 .02
❑ 434 Jimmie Jones .05 .02
❑ 435 Dwight Stone .05 .02
❑ 436 Harry Colon .05 .02
❑ 437 Don Mosebar .05 .02
❑ 438 Calvin Williams .10 .05
❑ 439 Tom Tupa .05 .02
❑ 440 Darrell Green .05 .02
❑ 441 Eric Thomas .05 .02
❑ 442 Terry Wooden .05 .02
❑ 443 Brett Perriman .25 .11
❑ 444 Todd Marinovich .05 .02
❑ 445 Jim Breech .05 .02
❑ 446 Eddie Anderson .05 .02
❑ 447 Jay Schroeder .05 .02
❑ 448 William Roberts .05 .02
❑ 449 Brad Edwards .05 .02
❑ 450 Tunch Ilkin .05 .02
❑ 451 Ivy Joe Hunter RC .05 .02
❑ 452 Robert Clark .05 .02
❑ 453 Tim Barnett .05 .02
❑ 454 Jarrod Bunch .05 .02
❑ 455 Tim Harris .05 .02
❑ 456 James Brooks .10 .05
❑ 457 Trace Armstrong .05 .02
❑ 458 Michael Brooks .05 .02
❑ 459 Andy Heck .05 .02
❑ 460 Greg Jackson .05 .02
❑ 461 Vance Johnson .05 .02
❑ 462 Kirk Lowdermilk .05 .02
❑ 463 Erik McMillan .05 .02
❑ 464 Scott Mersereau .05 .02
❑ 465 Jeff Wright .05 .02
❑ 466 Mike Tomczak .05 .02
❑ 467 David Alexander .05 .02
❑ 468 Bryan Millard .05 .02
❑ 469 John Randle .10 .05
❑ 470 Joel Hilgenberg .05 .02
❑ 471 Bennie Thompson RC .05 .02
❑ 472 Freeman McNeil .05 .02
❑ 473 Terry Orr RC .05 .02
❑ 474 Mike Horan .05 .02
❑ 475 Leroy Hoard .10 .05
❑ 476 Patrick Rowe RC .05 .02
❑ 477 Siran Stacy RC .05 .02
❑ 478 Amp Lee RC .05 .02
❑ 479 Eddie Blake RC .05 .02
❑ 480 Joe Bowden RC .05 .02
❑ 481 Rod Milstead RC .05 .02
❑ 482 Keith Hamilton RC .10 .05
❑ 483 Darryl Williams RC .05 .02
❑ 484 Robert Porcher RC .10 .05
❑ 485 Ed Cunningham RC .05 .02
❑ 486 Chris Mims RC .10 .05
❑ 487 Chris Hakel RC .05 .02
❑ 488 Jimmy Smith RC 4.00 1.80
❑ 489 Todd Harrison RC .05 .02
❑ 490 Edgar Bennett RC .50 .23
❑ 491 Dexter McNabb RC .05 .02
❑ 492 Leon Searcy RC .10 .05
❑ 493 Tommy Vardell RC .10 .05
❑ 494 Terrell Buckley RC .05 .02
❑ 495 Kevin Turner RC .05 .02
❑ 496 Russ Campbell RC .05 .02
❑ 497 Torrance Small RC .10 .05
❑ 498 Nate Turner RC .05 .02
❑ 499 Cornelius Benton RC .10 .05
❑ 500 Matt Elliott RC .05 .02
❑ 501 Robert Stewart RC .05 .02
❑ 502 Muhammad Shamsid-Deen RC .05 .02
❑ 503 George Williams RC .05 .02
❑ 504 Pumpy Tudors RC .05 .02
❑ 505 Matt LaBounty RC .05 .02
❑ 506 Darryl Hardy RC .05 .02
❑ 507 Derrick Moore RC .10 .05
❑ 508 Willie Clay RC .05 .02
❑ 509 Bob Whitfield RC .05 .02
❑ 510 Ricardo McDonald RC .05 .02
❑ 511 Carlos Huerta RC .05 .02
❑ 512 Selwyn Jones RC .05 .02
❑ 513 Steve Gordon RC .05 .02
❑ 514 Bob Meeks RC .05 .02
❑ 515 Bennie Blades CC .05 .02
❑ 516 Andre Waters CC .05 .02
❑ 517 Bubba McDowell CC .05 .02
❑ 518 Kevin Porter CC .05 .02
❑ 519 Carnell Lake CC .05 .02
❑ 520 Leonard Russell ROY .10 .05
❑ 521 Mike Croel ROY .05 .02
❑ 522 Lawrence Dawsey ROY .05 .02
❑ 523 Moe Gardner ROY .05 .02
❑ 524 Steve Broussard LBM .05 .02
❑ 525 Dave Meggett LBM .05 .02
❑ 526 Darrell Green LBM .05 .02
❑ 527 Tony Jones LBM .05 .02
❑ 528 Barry Sanders LBM 1.25 .55
❑ 529 Pat Swilling SA .05 .02
❑ 530 Reggie White SA .10 .05
❑ 531 William Fuller SA .05 .02
❑ 532 Simon Fletcher SA .05 .02
❑ 533 Derrick Thomas SA .10 .05
❑ 534 Mark Rypien MOY .05 .02
❑ 535 John Mackey HOF .05 .02
❑ 536 John Riggins HOF .10 .05
❑ 537 Lem Barney HOF .05 .02
❑ 538 Shawn McCarthy 90 RC .05 .02
❑ 539 Al Edwards 90 .05 .02
❑ 540 Alexander Wright 90 .05 .02
❑ 541 Ray Crockett 90 .05 .02
❑ 542 Steve Young 90 and John Taylor 90 .25 .11
❑ 543 Nate Lewis 90 .05 .02
❑ 544 Dexter Carter 90 .05 .02
❑ 545 Reggie Rutland 90 .05 .02
❑ 546 Jon Vaughn 90 .05 .02
❑ 547 Chris Martin 90 .05 .02
❑ 548 Warren Moon HL .10 .05
❑ 549 Super Bowl Highlights .05 .02
❑ 550 Robb Thomas .05 .02
❑ NNO Dick Butkus Promo 8.00 3.60

1993 Score

	MINT	NRMT
COMPLETE SET (440)	15.00	6.75
❑ 1 Barry Sanders	1.50	.70
❑ 2 Moe Gardner	.05	.02
❑ 3 Ricky Watters	.25	.11
❑ 4 Todd Lyght	.05	.02
❑ 5 Rodney Hampton	.25	.11
❑ 6 Curtis Duncan	.05	.02
❑ 7 Barry Word	.05	.02

❑ 8 Reggie Cobb	.05	.02
❑ 9 Mike Kenn	.05	.02
❑ 10 Michael Irvin	.25	.11
❑ 11 Bryan Cox	.05	.02
❑ 12 Chris Doleman	.05	.02
❑ 13 Rod Woodson	.25	.11
❑ 14 Emmitt Smith	1.50	.70
❑ 15 Pete Stoyanovich	.05	.02
❑ 16 Steve Young	.75	.35
❑ 17 Randall McDaniel	.05	.02
❑ 18 Cortez Kennedy	.10	.05
❑ 19 Mel Gray	.10	.05
❑ 20 Barry Foster	.10	.05
❑ 21 Tim Brown	.25	.11
❑ 22 Todd McNair	.05	.02
❑ 23 Anthony Johnson	.10	.05
❑ 24 Nate Odomes	.05	.02
❑ 25 Brett Favre	2.00	.90
❑ 26 Jack Del Rio	.05	.02
❑ 27 Terry McDaniel	.05	.02
❑ 28 Haywood Jeffires	.10	.05
❑ 29 Jay Novacek	.10	.05
❑ 30 Wilber Marshall	.05	.02
❑ 31 Richmond Webb	.05	.02
❑ 32 Steve Atwater	.05	.02
❑ 33 James Lofton	.10	.05
❑ 34 Harold Green	.05	.02
❑ 35 Eric Metcalf	.10	.05
❑ 36 Bruce Matthews	.05	.02
❑ 37 Albert Lewis	.05	.02
❑ 38 Jeff Herrod	.05	.02
❑ 39 Vince Workman	.05	.02
❑ 40 John Elway	1.50	.70
❑ 41 Brett Perriman	.25	.11
❑ 42 Jon Vaughn	.05	.02
❑ 43 Terry Allen	.25	.11
❑ 44 Clyde Simmons	.05	.02
❑ 45 Bennie Thompson	.05	.02
❑ 46 Wendell Davis	.05	.02
❑ 47 Bobby Hebert	.05	.02
❑ 48 John Offerdahl	.05	.02
❑ 49 Jeff Graham	.10	.05
❑ 50 Steve Wisniewski	.05	.02
❑ 51 Louis Oliver	.05	.02
❑ 52 Rohn Stark	.05	.02
❑ 53 Cleveland Gary	.05	.02
❑ 54 John Randle	.10	.05
❑ 55 Jim Everett	.10	.05
❑ 56 Donnell Woolford	.05	.02
❑ 57 Pepper Johnson	.05	.02
❑ 58 Irving Fryar	.10	.05
❑ 59 Greg Townsend	.05	.02
❑ 60 Chris Burkett	.05	.02
❑ 61 Johnny Johnson	.05	.02
❑ 62 Ronnie Harmon	.05	.02
❑ 63 Don Griffin	.05	.02
❑ 64 Wayne Martin	.05	.02
❑ 65 John L. Williams	.05	.02
❑ 66 Brad Edwards	.05	.02
❑ 67 Toi Cook	.05	.02
❑ 68 Lawrence Dawsey	.05	.02
❑ 69 Johnny Bailey	.05	.02
❑ 70 Mike Brim	.05	.02
❑ 71 Andre Rison	.10	.05
❑ 72 Cornelius Bennett	.10	.05
❑ 73 Brad Muster	.05	.02
❑ 74 Broderick Thomas	.05	.02
❑ 75 Tom Waddle	.05	.02
❑ 76 Paul Gruber	.05	.02
❑ 77 Jackie Harris	.05	.02
❑ 78 Kenneth Davis	.05	.02
❑ 79 Norm Johnson	.05	.02
❑ 80 Jim Jeffcoat	.05	.02
❑ 81 Chris Warren	.10	.05
❑ 82 Greg Kragen	.05	.02
❑ 83 Ricky Reynolds	.05	.02
❑ 84 Hardy Nickerson	.10	.05
❑ 85 Brian Mitchell	.10	.05
❑ 86 Rufus Porter	.05	.02
❑ 87 Greg Jackson	.05	.02
❑ 88 Seth Joyner	.05	.02
❑ 89 Tim Grunhard	.05	.02
❑ 90 Tim Harris	.05	.02
❑ 91 Sterling Sharpe	.25	.11
❑ 92 Daniel Stubbs	.05	.02
❑ 93 Rob Burnett	.05	.02
❑ 94 Rich Camarillo	.05	.02
❑ 95 Al Smith	.05	.02
❑ 96 Thurman Thomas	.25	.11
❑ 97 Morten Andersen	.05	.02
❑ 98 Reggie White	.25	.11
❑ 99 Gill Byrd	.05	.02
❑ 100 Pierce Holt	.05	.02
❑ 101 Tim McGee	.05	.02
❑ 102 Rickey Jackson	.05	.02
❑ 103 Vince Newsome	.05	.02
❑ 104 Chris Spielman	.10	.05
❑ 105 Tim McDonald	.05	.02
❑ 106 James Francis	.05	.02
❑ 107 Andre Tippett	.05	.02
❑ 108 Sam Mills	.05	.02
❑ 109 Hugh Millen	.05	.02
❑ 110 Brad Baxter	.05	.02
❑ 111 Ricky Sanders	.05	.02
❑ 112 Marion Butts	.05	.02
❑ 113 Fred Barnett	.10	.05
❑ 114 Wade Wilson	.05	.02
❑ 115 Dave Meggett	.05	.02
❑ 116 Kevin Greene	.25	.11
❑ 117 Reggie Langhorne	.05	.02
❑ 118 Simon Fletcher	.05	.02
❑ 119 Tommy Vardell	.05	.02
❑ 120 Darion Conner	.05	.02
❑ 121 Darren Lewis	.05	.02
❑ 122 Charles Mann	.05	.02
❑ 123 David Fulcher	.05	.02
❑ 124 Tommy Kane	.05	.02
❑ 125 Richard Brown	.05	.02
❑ 126 Nate Lewis	.05	.02
❑ 127 Tony Tolbert	.05	.02
❑ 128 Greg Lloyd	.25	.11
❑ 129 Herman Moore	.50	.23
❑ 130 Robert Massey	.05	.02
❑ 131 Chris Jacke	.05	.02
❑ 132 Keith Byars	.05	.02
❑ 133 William Fuller	.05	.02
❑ 134 Rob Moore	.10	.05
❑ 135 Duane Bickett	.05	.02
❑ 136 Jarrod Bunch	.05	.02
❑ 137 Ethan Horton	.05	.02
❑ 138 Leonard Russell	.10	.05
❑ 139 Darryl Henley	.05	.02
❑ 140 Tony Bennett	.05	.02
❑ 141 Harry Newsome	.05	.02
❑ 142 Kelvin Martin	.05	.02
❑ 143 Audray McMillian	.05	.02
❑ 144 Chip Lohmiller	.05	.02
❑ 145 Henry Jones	.05	.02
❑ 146 Rod Bernstine	.05	.02
❑ 147 Darryl Talley	.05	.02
❑ 148 Clarence Verdin	.05	.02
❑ 149 Derrick Thomas	.25	.11
❑ 150 Raleigh McKenzie	.05	.02
❑ 151 Phil Hansen	.05	.02
❑ 152 Lin Elliott RC	.05	.02
❑ 153 Chip Banks	.05	.02
❑ 154 Shannon Sharpe	.25	.11
❑ 155 David Williams	.05	.02
❑ 156 Gaston Green	.05	.02
❑ 157 Trace Armstrong	.05	.02
❑ 158 Todd Scott	.05	.02
❑ 159 Stan Humphries	.25	.11
❑ 160 Christian Okoye	.05	.02
❑ 161 Dennis Smith	.05	.02
❑ 162 Derek Kennard	.05	.02
❑ 163 Melvin Jenkins	.05	.02
❑ 164 Tommy Barnhardt	.05	.02
❑ 165 Eugene Robinson	.05	.02
❑ 166 Tom Rathman	.05	.02
❑ 167 Chris Chandler	.10	.05
❑ 168 Steve Broussard	.05	.02
❑ 169 Wymon Henderson	.05	.02
❑ 170 Bryce Paup	.25	.11
❑ 171 Kent Hull	.05	.02
❑ 172 Willie Davis	.25	.11
❑ 173 Richard Dent	.10	.05
❑ 174 Rodney Peete	.05	.02
❑ 175 Clay Matthews	.10	.05
❑ 176 Erik Williams	.05	.02
❑ 177 Mike Cofer	.05	.02
❑ 178 Mark Kelso	.05	.02
❑ 179 Kurt Gouveia	.05	.02
❑ 180 Keith McCants	.05	.02
❑ 181 Jim Arnold	.05	.02
❑ 182 Sean Jones	.05	.02
❑ 183 Chuck Cecil	.05	.02
❑ 184 Mark Rypien	.05	.02
❑ 185 William Perry	.10	.05
❑ 186 Mark Jackson	.05	.02
❑ 187 Jim Dombrowski	.05	.02
❑ 188 Heath Sherman	.05	.02
❑ 189 Bubba McDowell	.05	.02
❑ 190 Fuad Reveiz	.05	.02
❑ 191 Darren Perry	.05	.02
❑ 192 Karl Mecklenburg	.05	.02
❑ 193 Frank Reich	.10	.05
❑ 194 Tony Casillas	.05	.02
❑ 195 Jerry Ball	.05	.02
❑ 196 Jessie Hester	.05	.02
❑ 197 David Lang	.05	.02
❑ 198 Sean Landeta	.05	.02
❑ 199 Jerry Gray	.05	.02
❑ 200 Mark Higgs	.05	.02
❑ 201 Bruce Armstrong	.05	.02
❑ 202 Vaughan Johnson	.05	.02
❑ 203 Calvin Williams	.10	.05
❑ 204 Leonard Marshall	.05	.02
❑ 205 Mike Munchak	.05	.02
❑ 206 Kevin Ross	.05	.02
❑ 207 Daryl Johnston	.25	.11
❑ 208 Jay Schroeder	.05	.02
❑ 209 Mo Lewis	.05	.02
❑ 210 Carlton Haselrig	.05	.02
❑ 211 Cris Carter	.50	.23
❑ 212 Marv Cook	.05	.02
❑ 213 Mark Duper	.05	.02
❑ 214 Jackie Slater	.05	.02
❑ 215 Mike Prior	.05	.02
❑ 216 Warren Moon	.25	.11
❑ 217 Mike Saxon	.05	.02
❑ 218 Derrick Fenner	.05	.02
❑ 219 Brian Washington	.05	.02
❑ 220 Jessie Tuggle	.05	.02
❑ 221 Jeff Hostetler	.10	.05
❑ 222 Deion Sanders	.50	.23
❑ 223 Neal Anderson	.05	.02
❑ 224 Kevin Mack	.05	.02
❑ 225 Tommy Maddox	.05	.02
❑ 226 Neil Smith	.25	.11
❑ 227 Ronnie Lott	.10	.05
❑ 228 Flipper Anderson	.05	.02
❑ 229 Keith Jackson	.10	.05
❑ 230 Pat Swilling	.05	.02
❑ 231 Carl Banks	.05	.02
❑ 232 Eric Allen	.05	.02
❑ 233 Randal Hill	.05	.02
❑ 234 Burt Grossman	.05	.02
❑ 235 Jerry Rice	1.00	.45
❑ 236 Santana Dotson	.10	.05
❑ 237 Andre Reed	.10	.05
❑ 238 Troy Aikman	.75	.35
❑ 239 Ray Childress	.05	.02
❑ 240 Phil Simms	.10	.05
❑ 241 Steve McMichael	.10	.05
❑ 242 Browning Nagle	.05	.02
❑ 243 Anthony Miller	.10	.05
❑ 244 Earnest Byner	.05	.02
❑ 245 Jay Hilgenberg	.05	.02
❑ 246 Jeff George	.25	.11

❑ 247 Marco Coleman .05 .02
❑ 248 Mark Carrier DB .05 .02
❑ 249 Howie Long .10 .05
❑ 250 Ed McCaffrey .10 .05
❑ 251 Jim Kelly .25 .11
❑ 252 Henry Ellard .10 .05
❑ 253 Joe Montana 1.50 .70
❑ 254 Dale Carter .05 .02
❑ 255 Boomer Esiason .10 .05
❑ 256 Gary Clark .10 .05
❑ 257 Carl Pickens .25 .11
❑ 258 Dave Krieg .10 .05
❑ 259 Russell Maryland .05 .02
❑ 260 Randall Cunningham .25 .11
❑ 261 Leslie O'Neal .10 .05
❑ 262 Vinny Testaverde .10 .05
❑ 263 Ricky Ervins .05 .02
❑ 264 Chris Mims .05 .02
❑ 265 Dan Marino 1.50 .70
❑ 266 Eric Martin .05 .02
❑ 267 Bruce Smith .25 .11
❑ 268 Jim Harbaugh .25 .11
❑ 269 Steve Emtman .05 .02
❑ 270 Ricky Proehl .05 .02
❑ 271 Vaughn Dunbar .05 .02
❑ 272 Junior Seau .25 .11
❑ 273 Sean Gilbert .10 .05
❑ 274 Jim Lachey .05 .02
❑ 275 Dalton Hilliard .05 .02
❑ 276 David Klingler .05 .02
❑ 277 Robert Jones .05 .02
❑ 278 David Treadwell .05 .02
❑ 279 Tracy Scroggins .05 .02
❑ 280 Terrell Buckley .05 .02
❑ 281 Quentin Coryatt .10 .05
❑ 282 Jason Hanson .05 .02
❑ 283 Shane Conlan .05 .02
❑ 284 Guy McIntyre .05 .02
❑ 285 Gary Zimmerman .05 .02
❑ 286 Marty Carter .05 .02
❑ 287 Jim Sweeney .05 .02
❑ 288 Arthur Marshall RC .05 .02
❑ 289 Eugene Chung .05 .02
❑ 290 Mike Pritchard .10 .05
❑ 291 Jim Ritcher .05 .02
❑ 292 Todd Marinovich .05 .02
❑ 293 Courtney Hall .05 .02
❑ 294 Mark Collins .05 .02
❑ 295 Troy Auzenne .05 .02
❑ 296 Aeneas Williams .05 .02
❑ 297 Andy Heck .05 .02
❑ 298 Shaun Gayle .05 .02
❑ 299 Kevin Fagan .05 .02
❑ 300 Carnell Lake .05 .02
❑ 301 Bernie Kosar .10 .05
❑ 302 Maurice Hurst .05 .02
❑ 303 Mike Merriweather .05 .02
❑ 304 Reggie Roby .05 .02
❑ 305 Darryl Williams .05 .02
❑ 306 Jerome Bettis RC .75 .35
❑ 307 Curtis Conway RC .40 .18
❑ 308 Drew Bledsoe RC 2.00 .90
❑ 309 John Copeland RC .10 .05
❑ 310 Eric Curry RC .05 .02
❑ 311 Lincoln Kennedy RC .05 .02
❑ 312 Dan Williams RC .05 .02
❑ 313 Patrick Bates RC .05 .02
❑ 314 Tom Carter RC .10 .05
❑ 315 Garrison Hearst RC .50 .23
❑ 316 Joel Hilgenberg .05 .02
❑ 317 Harris Barton .05 .02
❑ 318 Jeff Lageman .05 .02
❑ 319 Charles Mincy RC .05 .02
❑ 320 Ricardo McDonald .05 .02
❑ 321 Lorenzo White .05 .02
❑ 322 Troy Vincent .05 .02
❑ 323 Bennie Blades .05 .02
❑ 324 Dana Hall .05 .02
❑ 325 Ken Norton Jr. .10 .05
❑ 326 Will Wolford .05 .02
❑ 327 Neil O'Donnell .25 .11
❑ 328 Tracy Simien .05 .02
❑ 329 Darrell Green .05 .02
❑ 330 Kyle Clifton .05 .02
❑ 331 Elbert Shelley RC .05 .02
❑ 332 Jeff Wright .05 .02
❑ 333 Mike Johnson .05 .02
❑ 334 John Gesek .05 .02
❑ 335 Michael Brooks .05 .02
❑ 336 George Jamison .05 .02
❑ 337 Johnny Holland .05 .02
❑ 338 Lamar Lathon .05 .02
❑ 339 Bern Brostek .05 .02
❑ 340 Steve Jordan .05 .02
❑ 341 Gene Atkins .05 .02
❑ 342 Aaron Wallace .05 .02
❑ 343 Adrian Cooper .05 .02
❑ 344 Amp Lee .05 .02
❑ 345 Vincent Brown .05 .02
❑ 346 James Hasty .05 .02
❑ 347 Ron Hall .05 .02
❑ 348 Matt Elliott .05 .02
❑ 349 Tim Krumrie .05 .02
❑ 350 Mark Stepnoski .05 .02
❑ 351 Matt Stover .05 .02
❑ 352 James Washington .05 .02
❑ 353 Marc Spindler .05 .02
❑ 354 Frank Warren .05 .02
❑ 355 Vai Sikahema .05 .02
❑ 356 Dan Saleaumua .05 .02
❑ 357 Mark Clayton .05 .02
❑ 358 Brent Jones .10 .05
❑ 359 Andy Harmon RC .10 .05
❑ 360 Anthony Parker .05 .02
❑ 361 Chris Hinton .05 .02
❑ 362 Greg Montgomery .05 .02
❑ 363 Greg McMurtry .05 .02
❑ 364 Craig Heyward .10 .05
❑ 365 D.J. Johnson .05 .02
❑ 366 Bill Romanowski .05 .02
❑ 367 Steve Christie .05 .02
❑ 368 Art Monk .10 .05
❑ 369 Howard Ballard .05 .02
❑ 370 Andre Collins .05 .02
❑ 371 Alvin Harper .10 .05
❑ 372 Blaise Winter RC .05 .02
❑ 373 Al Del Greco .05 .02
❑ 374 Eric Green .05 .02
❑ 375 Chris Mohr .05 .02
❑ 376 Tom Newberry .05 .02
❑ 377 Cris Dishman .05 .02
❑ 378 Jumpy Geathers .05 .02
❑ 379 Don Mosebar .05 .02
❑ 380 Andre Ware .05 .02
❑ 381 Marvin Washington .05 .02
❑ 382 Bobby Humphrey .05 .02
❑ 383 Marc Logan .05 .02
❑ 384 Lomas Brown .05 .02
❑ 385 Steve Tasker .10 .05
❑ 386 Chris Miller .10 .05
❑ 387 Tony Paige .05 .02
❑ 388 Charles Haley .10 .05
❑ 389 Rich Moran .05 .02
❑ 390 Mike Sherrard .05 .02
❑ 391 Nick Lowery .05 .02
❑ 392 Henry Thomas .05 .02
❑ 393 Keith Sims .05 .02
❑ 394 Thomas Everett .05 .02
❑ 395 Steve Wallace .05 .02
❑ 396 John Carney .05 .02
❑ 397 Tim Johnson .05 .02
❑ 398 Jeff Gossett .05 .02
❑ 399 Anthony Smith .05 .02
❑ 400 Kelvin Pritchett .05 .02
❑ 401 Dermontti Dawson .05 .02
❑ 402 Alfred Williams .05 .02
❑ 403 Michael Haynes .10 .05
❑ 404 Bart Oates .05 .02
❑ 405 Ken Lanier .05 .02
❑ 406 Vencie Glenn .05 .02
❑ 407 John Taylor .10 .05
❑ 408 Nate Newton .10 .05
❑ 409 Mark Carrier WR .10 .05
❑ 410 Ken Harvey .05 .02
❑ 411 Troy Aikman SB .40 .18
❑ 412 Charles Haley SB .05 .02
❑ 413 Warren Moon DT .10 .05
Haywood Jeffires
❑ 414 Henry Jones DT .05 .02
Mark Kelso
❑ 415 Rickey Jackson DT .05 .02
Sam Mills
❑ 416 Clyde Simmons DT .05 .02
Reggie White
❑ 417 Dale Carter ROY .05 .02
❑ 418 Carl Pickens ROY .25 .11
❑ 419 Vaughn Dunbar ROY .05 .02
❑ 420 Santana Dotson ROY .05 .02
❑ 421 Steve Emtman 90 .05 .02
❑ 422 Louis Oliver 90 .05 .02
❑ 423 Carl Pickens 90 .25 .11
❑ 424 Eddie Anderson 90 .05 .02
❑ 425 Deion Sanders 90 .25 .11
❑ 426 Jon Vaughn 90 .05 .02
❑ 427 Darren Lewis 90 .05 .02
❑ 428 Kevin Ross 90 .05 .02
❑ 429 David Brandon 90 .05 .02
❑ 430 Dave Meggett 90 .05 .02
❑ 431 Jerry Rice HL .50 .23
❑ 432 Sterling Sharpe HL .10 .05
❑ 433 Art Monk HL .05 .02
❑ 434 James Lofton HL .05 .02
❑ 435 Lawrence Taylor .10 .05
❑ 436 Bill Walsh HOF RC .10 .05
❑ 437 Chuck Noll HOF .10 .05
❑ 438 Dan Fouts HOF .05 .02
❑ 439 Larry Little HOF .05 .02
❑ 440 Steve Young MOY .40 .18
❑ NNO Dick Butkus AUTO/3000 40.00 18.00

1994 Score

	MINT	NRMT
COMPLETE SET (330)	15.00	6.75

❑ 1 Barry Sanders 1.50 .70
❑ 2 Troy Aikman .75 .35
❑ 3 Sterling Sharpe .10 .05
❑ 4 Deion Sanders .50 .23
❑ 5 Bruce Smith .25 .11
❑ 6 Eric Metcalf .10 .05
❑ 7 John Elway 1.50 .70
❑ 8 Bruce Matthews .05 .02
❑ 9 Rickey Jackson .05 .02
❑ 10 Cortez Kennedy .10 .05
❑ 11 Jerry Rice .75 .35
❑ 12 Stanley Richard .05 .02
❑ 13 Rod Woodson .10 .05
❑ 14 Eric Swann .10 .05
❑ 15 Eric Allen .05 .02
❑ 16 Richard Dent .10 .05
❑ 17 Carl Pickens .25 .11
❑ 18 Rohn Stark .05 .02
❑ 19 Marcus Allen .25 .11
❑ 20 Steve Wisniewski .05 .02
❑ 21 Jerome Bettis .25 .11
❑ 22 Darrell Green .05 .02
❑ 23 Lawrence Dawsey .05 .02
❑ 24 Larry Centers .25 .11
❑ 25 Steve Jordan .05 .02
❑ 26 Johnny Johnson .05 .02
❑ 27 Phil Simms .10 .05
❑ 28 Bruce Armstrong .05 .02
❑ 29 Willie Roaf .05 .02
❑ 30 Andre Rison .10 .05
❑ 31 Henry Jones .05 .02
❑ 32 Warren Moon .25 .11
❑ 33 Sean Gilbert .05 .02
❑ 34 Ben Coates .25 .11
❑ 35 Seth Joyner .05 .02

❑ 36 Ronnie Harmon .05 .02
❑ 37 Quentin Coryatt .05 .02
❑ 38 Ricky Sanders .05 .02
❑ 39 Gerald Williams .05 .02
❑ 40 Emmitt Smith 1.00 .45
❑ 41 Jason Hanson .05 .02
❑ 42 Kevin Smith .05 .02
❑ 43 Irving Fryar .10 .05
❑ 44 Boomer Esiason .10 .05
❑ 45 Darryl Talley .05 .02
❑ 46 Paul Gruber .05 .02
❑ 47 Anthony Smith .05 .02
❑ 48 John Copeland .05 .02
❑ 49 Michael Jackson .10 .05
❑ 50 Shannon Sharpe .10 .05
❑ 51 Reggie White .25 .11
❑ 52 Andre Collins .05 .02
❑ 53 Jack Del Rio .05 .02
❑ 54 John Elliott .05 .02
❑ 55 Kevin Greene .25 .11
❑ 56 Steve Young .60 .25
❑ 57 Erric Pegram .05 .02
❑ 58 Donnell Woolford .05 .02
❑ 59 Darryl Williams .05 .02
❑ 60 Michael Irvin .25 .11
❑ 61 Mel Gray .05 .02
❑ 62 Greg Montgomery .05 .02
❑ 63 Neil Smith .10 .05
❑ 64 Andy Harmon .05 .02
❑ 65 Dan Marino 1.50 .70
❑ 66 Leonard Russell .05 .02
❑ 67 Joe Montana 1.50 .70
❑ 68 John Taylor .10 .05
❑ 69 Cris Dishman .05 .02
❑ 70 Cornelius Bennett .10 .05
❑ 71 Harold Green .05 .02
❑ 72 Anthony Pleasant .05 .02
❑ 73 Dennis Smith .05 .02
❑ 74 Bryce Paup .25 .11
❑ 75 Jeff George .25 .11
❑ 76 Henry Ellard .10 .05
❑ 77 Randall McDaniel .05 .02
❑ 78 Derek Brown RBK .05 .02
❑ 79 Johnny Mitchell .05 .02
❑ 80 Leroy Thompson .05 .02
❑ 81 Junior Seau .10 .05
❑ 82 Kelvin Martin .05 .02
❑ 83 Guy McIntyre .05 .02
❑ 84 Elbert Shelley .05 .02
❑ 85 Louis Oliver .05 .02
❑ 86 Tommy Vardell .05 .02
❑ 87 Jeff Herrod .05 .02
❑ 88 Edgar Bennett .25 .11
❑ 89 Reggie Langhorne .05 .02
❑ 90 Terry Kirby .25 .11
❑ 91 Marcus Robertson .05 .02
❑ 92 Mark Collins .05 .02
❑ 93 Calvin Williams .10 .05
❑ 94 Barry Foster .05 .02
❑ 95 Brent Jones .10 .05
❑ 96 Reggie Cobb .05 .02
❑ 97 Ray Childress .05 .02
❑ 98 Chris Miller .05 .02
❑ 99 John Carney .05 .02
❑ 100 Ricky Proehl .05 .02
❑ 101 Renaldo Turnbull .05 .02
❑ 102 John Randle .10 .05
❑ 103 Flipper Anderson .05 .02
❑ 104 Scottie Graham RC .10 .05
❑ 105 Webster Slaughter .05 .02
❑ 106 Tyrone Hughes .10 .05
❑ 107 Ken Norton Jr. .10 .05
❑ 108 Jim Kelly .25 .11
❑ 109 Michael Haynes .10 .05
❑ 110 Mark Carrier DB .05 .02
❑ 111 Eddie Murray .05 .02
❑ 112 Glyn Milburn .10 .05
❑ 113 Jackie Harris .05 .02
❑ 114 Dean Biasucci .05 .02
❑ 115 Tim Brown .25 .11
❑ 116 Mark Higgs .05 .02
❑ 117 Steve Emtman .05 .02
❑ 118 Clay Matthews .05 .02
❑ 119 Clyde Simmons .05 .02
❑ 120 Howard Ballard .05 .02
❑ 121 Ricky Watters .25 .11
❑ 122 William Fuller .05 .02
❑ 123 Robert Brooks .25 .11
❑ 124 Brian Blades .10 .05
❑ 125 Leslie O'Neal .05 .02
❑ 126 Gary Clark .10 .05
❑ 127 Jim Sweeney .05 .02
❑ 128 Vaughan Johnson .05 .02
❑ 129 Gary Brown .05 .02
❑ 130 Todd Lyght .05 .02
❑ 131 Nick Lowery .05 .02
❑ 132 Ernest Givins .10 .05
❑ 133 Lomas Brown .05 .02
❑ 134 Craig Erickson .05 .02
❑ 135 James Francis .05 .02
❑ 136 Andre Reed .10 .05
❑ 137 Jim Everett .10 .05
❑ 138 Nate Odomes .05 .02
❑ 139 Tom Waddle .05 .02
❑ 140 Stevon Moore .05 .02
❑ 141 Rod Bernstine .05 .02
❑ 142 Brett Favre 1.50 .70
❑ 143 Roosevelt Potts .05 .02
❑ 144 Chester McGlockton .05 .02
❑ 145 LeRoy Butler .05 .02
❑ 146 Charles Haley .10 .05
❑ 147 Rodney Hampton .25 .11
❑ 148 George Teague .05 .02
❑ 149 Gary Anderson K .05 .02
❑ 150 Mark Stepnoski .05 .02
❑ 151 Courtney Hawkins .05 .02
❑ 152 Tim Grunhard .05 .02
❑ 153 David Klingler .05 .02
❑ 154 Erik Williams .05 .02
❑ 155 Herman Moore .25 .11
❑ 156 Daryl Johnston .10 .05
❑ 157 Chris Zorich .05 .02
❑ 158 Shane Conlan .05 .02
❑ 159 Santana Dotson .10 .05
❑ 160 Sam Mills .05 .02
❑ 161 Ronnie Lott .10 .05
❑ 162 Jesse Sapolu .05 .02
❑ 163 Marion Butts .05 .02
❑ 164 Eugene Robinson .05 .02
❑ 165 Mark Schlereth .05 .02
❑ 166 John L. Williams .05 .02
❑ 167 Anthony Miller .10 .05
❑ 168 Rich Camarillo .05 .02
❑ 169 Jeff Lageman .05 .02
❑ 170 Michael Brooks .05 .02
❑ 171 Scott Mitchell .25 .11
❑ 172 Duane Bickett .05 .02
❑ 173 Willie Davis .10 .05
❑ 174 Maurice Hurst .05 .02
❑ 175 Brett Perriman .10 .05
❑ 176 Jay Novacek .10 .05
❑ 177 Terry Allen .10 .05
❑ 178 Pete Metzelaars .05 .02
❑ 179 Erik Kramer .10 .05
❑ 180 Neal Anderson .05 .02
❑ 181 Ethan Horton .05 .02
❑ 182 Tony Bennett .05 .02
❑ 183 Gary Zimmerman .05 .02
❑ 184 Jeff Hostetler .10 .05
❑ 185 Jeff Cross .05 .02
❑ 186 Vincent Brown .05 .02
❑ 187 Herschel Walker .10 .05
❑ 188 Courtney Hall .05 .02
❑ 189 Norm Johnson .05 .02
❑ 190 Hardy Nickerson .10 .05
❑ 191 Greg Townsend .05 .02
❑ 192 Mike Munchak .05 .02
❑ 193 Dante Jones .05 .02
❑ 194 Vinny Testaverde .10 .05
❑ 195 Vance Johnson .05 .02
❑ 196 Chris Jacke .05 .02
❑ 197 Will Wolford .05 .02
❑ 198 Terry McDaniel .05 .02
❑ 199 Bryan Cox .05 .02
❑ 200 Nate Newton .05 .02
❑ 201 Keith Byars .05 .02
❑ 202 Neil O'Donnell .25 .11
❑ 203 Harris Barton .05 .02
❑ 204 Thurman Thomas .25 .11
❑ 205 Jeff Query .05 .02
❑ 206 Russell Maryland .05 .02
❑ 207 Pat Swilling .05 .02
❑ 208 Haywood Jeffires .10 .05
❑ 209 John Alt .05 .02
❑ 210 O.J. McDuffie .25 .11
❑ 211 Keith Sims .05 .02
❑ 212 Eric Martin .05 .02
❑ 213 Kyle Clifton .05 .02
❑ 214 Luis Sharpe .05 .02
❑ 215 Thomas Everett .05 .02
❑ 216 Chris Warren .10 .05
❑ 217 Chris Doleman .05 .02
❑ 218 Tony Jones .05 .02
❑ 219 Karl Mecklenburg .05 .02
❑ 220 Rob Moore .10 .05
❑ 221 Jessie Hester .05 .02
❑ 222 Jeff Jaeger .05 .02
❑ 223 Keith Jackson .05 .02
❑ 224 Mo Lewis .05 .02
❑ 225 Mike Horan .05 .02
❑ 226 Eric Green .05 .02
❑ 227 Jim Ritcher .05 .02
❑ 228 Eric Curry .05 .02
❑ 229 Stan Humphries .25 .11
❑ 230 Mike Johnson .05 .02
❑ 231 Alvin Harper .10 .05
❑ 232 Bennie Blades .05 .02
❑ 233 Cris Carter .50 .23
❑ 234 Morten Andersen .05 .02
❑ 235 Brian Washington .05 .02
❑ 236 Eric Hill .05 .02
❑ 237 Natrone Means .25 .11
❑ 238 Carlton Bailey .05 .02
❑ 239 Anthony Carter .10 .05
❑ 240 Jessie Tuggle .05 .02
❑ 241 Tim Irwin .05 .02
❑ 242 Mark Carrier WR .10 .05
❑ 243 Steve Atwater .05 .02
❑ 244 Sean Jones .05 .02
❑ 245 Bernie Kosar .10 .05
❑ 246 Richmond Webb .05 .02
❑ 247 Dave Meggett .05 .02
❑ 248 Vincent Brisby .25 .11
❑ 249 Fred Barnett .10 .05
❑ 250 Greg Lloyd .25 .11
❑ 251 Tim McDonald .05 .02
❑ 252 Mike Pritchard .05 .02
❑ 253 Greg Robinson .05 .02
❑ 254 Tony McGee .05 .02
❑ 255 Chris Spielman .10 .05
❑ 256 Keith Loneker RC .05 .02
❑ 257 Derrick Thomas .25 .11
❑ 258 Wayne Martin .05 .02
❑ 259 Art Monk .10 .05
❑ 260 Andy Heck .05 .02
❑ 261 Chip Lohmiller .05 .02
❑ 262 Simon Fletcher .05 .02
❑ 263 Ricky Reynolds .05 .02
❑ 264 Chris Hinton .05 .02
❑ 265 Ronald Moore .05 .02
❑ 266 Rocket Ismail .10 .05
❑ 267 Pete Stoyanovich .05 .02
❑ 268 Mark Jackson .05 .02
❑ 269 Randall Cunningham .25 .11
❑ 270 Dermontti Dawson .05 .02
❑ 271 Bill Romanowski .05 .02
❑ 272 Tim Johnson .05 .02
❑ 273 Steve Tasker .05 .02
❑ 274 Keith Hamilton .05 .02
❑ 275 Pierce Holt .05 .02
❑ 276 Heath Shuler RC .25 .11
❑ 277 Marshall Faulk RC 4.00 1.80
❑ 278 Charles Johnson RC .50 .23
❑ 279 Sam Adams RC .10 .05
❑ 280 Trev Alberts RC .10 .05
❑ 281 Der. Alexander WR RC .50 .23
❑ 282 Bryant Young RC .25 .11
❑ 283 Greg Hill RC .25 .11
❑ 284 Darnay Scott RC .75 .35
❑ 285 Willie McGinest RC .25 .11
❑ 286 Thomas Randolph RC .05 .02
❑ 287 Errict Rhett RC 1.00 .45
❑ 288 Lamar Smith RC 2.50 1.10
❑ 289 William Floyd RC .25 .11
❑ 290 Johnnie Morton RC .25 .11
❑ 291 Jamir Miller RC .05 .02
❑ 292 David Palmer RC .50 .23
❑ 293 Dan Wilkinson RC .10 .05

❑ 294 Trent Dilfer RC	2.00	.90
❑ 295 Antonio Langham RC	.10	.05
❑ 296 Chuck Levy RC	.05	.02
❑ 297 John Thierry RC	.05	.02
❑ 298 Kevin Lee RC	.05	.02
❑ 299 Aaron Glenn RC	.10	.05
❑ 300 Charlie Garner RC	1.50	.70
❑ 301 Lonnie Johnson RC	.05	.02
❑ 302 LeShon Johnson RC	.10	.05
❑ 303 Thomas Lewis RC	.10	.05
❑ 304 Ryan Yarborough RC	.05	.02
❑ 305 Mario Bates RC	.25	.11
❑ 306 Buffalo Bills TC	.05	.02
❑ 307 Cincinnati Bengals TC	.05	.02
❑ 308 Cleveland Browns TC	.05	.02
❑ 309 Denver Broncos TC	.05	.02
❑ 310 Houston Oilers TC	.05	.02
❑ 311 Indianapolis Colts TC	.05	.02
❑ 312 Kansas City Chiefs TC	.05	.02
❑ 313 Los Angeles Raiders TC	.05	.02
❑ 314 Miami Dolphins TC	.05	.02
❑ 315 New England Patriots TC	.05	.02
❑ 316 New York Jets TC	.05	.02
❑ 317 Pittsburgh Steelers TC	.05	.02
❑ 318 San Diego Charges TC	.05	.02
❑ 319 Seattle Seahawks TC	.05	.02
❑ 320 Garrison Hearst FF	.25	.11
❑ 321 Drew Bledsoe FF	1.00	.45
❑ 322 Tyrone Hughes FF	.10	.05
❑ 323 James Jett FF	.05	.02
❑ 324 Tom Carter FF	.05	.02
❑ 325 Reggie Brooks FF	.05	.02
❑ 326 Dana Stubblefield FF	.25	.11
❑ 327 Jerome Bettis FF	.10	.05
❑ 328 Chris Slade FF	.05	.02
❑ 329 Rick Mirer FF	.25	.11
❑ 330 Emmitt Smith NFL MVP	.50	.23

1995 Score

	MINT	NRMT
COMPLETE SET (275)	15.00	6.75
❑ 1 Steve Young	.60	.25
❑ 2 Barry Sanders	1.50	.70
❑ 3 Jerry Rice	.75	.35
❑ 4 Marshall Faulk	.40	.18
❑ 5 Terance Mathis	.10	.05
❑ 6 Rod Woodson	.10	.05
❑ 7 Seth Joyner	.05	.02
❑ 8 Michael Timpson	.05	.02
❑ 9 Deion Sanders	.50	.23
❑ 10 Emmitt Smith	1.25	.55
❑ 11 Cris Carter	.25	.11
❑ 12 Jake Reed	.10	.05
❑ 13 Reggie White	.25	.11
❑ 14 Shannon Sharpe	.10	.05
❑ 15 Troy Aikman	.75	.35
❑ 16 Andre Reed	.10	.05
❑ 17 Tyrone Hughes	.10	.05
❑ 18 Sterling Sharpe	.10	.05
❑ 19 Jerome Bettis	.25	.11
❑ 20 Irving Fryar	.10	.05
❑ 21 Warren Moon	.10	.05
❑ 22 Ben Coates	.10	.05
❑ 23 Frank Reich	.05	.02
❑ 24 Henry Ellard	.10	.05
❑ 25 Steve Atwater	.05	.02
❑ 26 Willie Davis	.10	.05
❑ 27 Michael Irvin	.25	.11
❑ 28 Harvey Williams	.05	.02
❑ 29 Aeneas Williams	.05	.02
❑ 30 Errict Rhett	.25	.11
❑ 31 Lorenzo White	.05	.02
❑ 32 John Elway	1.50	.70
❑ 33 Rodney Hampton	.10	.05
❑ 34 Webster Slaughter	.05	.02
❑ 35 Eric Turner	.05	.02
❑ 36 Dan Marino	1.50	.70
❑ 37 Daryl Johnston	.10	.05
❑ 38 Bruce Smith	.25	.11
❑ 39 Ronald Moore	.05	.02
❑ 40 Larry Centers	.10	.05
❑ 41 Curtis Conway	.25	.11
❑ 42 Drew Bledsoe	.75	.35
❑ 43 Quinn Early	.10	.05
❑ 44 Marcus Allen	.25	.11
❑ 45 Andre Rison	.10	.05
❑ 46 Jeff Blake RC	.60	.25
❑ 47 Barry Foster	.10	.05
❑ 48 Antonio Langham	.05	.02
❑ 49 Herman Moore	.25	.11
❑ 50 Flipper Anderson	.05	.02
❑ 51 Rick Mirer	.25	.11
❑ 52 Jay Novacek	.10	.05
❑ 53 Tim Bowens	.05	.02
❑ 54 Carl Pickens	.25	.11
❑ 55 Lewis Tillman	.05	.02
❑ 56 Lawrence Dawsey	.05	.02
❑ 57 Leroy Hoard	.05	.02
❑ 58 Steve Broussard	.05	.02
❑ 59 Dave Krieg	.05	.02
❑ 60 John Taylor	.05	.02
❑ 61 Johnny Mitchell	.05	.02
❑ 62 Jessie Hester	.05	.02
❑ 63 Johnny Bailey	.05	.02
❑ 64 Brett Favre	1.50	.70
❑ 65 Bryce Paup	.25	.11
❑ 66 J.J. Birden	.05	.02
❑ 67 Steve Tasker	.10	.05
❑ 68 Edgar Bennett	.10	.05
❑ 69 Ray Buchanan	.05	.02
❑ 70 Brent Jones	.05	.02
❑ 71 Dave Meggett	.05	.02
❑ 72 Jeff Graham	.05	.02
❑ 73 Michael Brooks	.05	.02
❑ 74 Ricky Ervins	.05	.02
❑ 75 Chris Warren	.10	.05
❑ 76 Natrone Means	.25	.11
❑ 77 Tim Brown	.25	.11
❑ 78 Jim Everett	.05	.02
❑ 79 Chris Calloway	.05	.02
❑ 80 John L. Williams	.05	.02
❑ 81 Chris Chandler	.10	.05
❑ 82 Tim McDonald	.05	.02
❑ 83 Calvin Williams	.10	.05
❑ 84 Tony McGee	.05	.02
❑ 85 Erik Kramer	.05	.02
❑ 86 Eric Green	.05	.02
❑ 87 Nate Newton	.10	.05
❑ 88 Leonard Russell	.05	.02
❑ 89 Jeff George	.10	.05
❑ 90 Raymont Harris	.05	.02
❑ 91 Darnay Scott	.25	.11
❑ 92 Brian Mitchell	.05	.02
❑ 93 Craig Erickson	.05	.02
❑ 94 Cortez Kennedy	.10	.05
❑ 95 Derrick Alexander WR	.25	.11
❑ 96 Charles Haley	.10	.05
❑ 97 Randall Cunningham	.25	.11
❑ 98 Haywood Jeffires	.05	.02
❑ 99 Ronnie Harmon	.05	.02
❑ 100 Dale Carter	.10	.05
❑ 101 Dave Brown	.10	.05
❑ 102 Michael Haynes	.10	.05
❑ 103 Johnny Johnson	.05	.02
❑ 104 William Floyd	.25	.11
❑ 105 Jeff Hostetler	.10	.05
❑ 106 Bernie Parmalee	.10	.05
❑ 107 Mo Lewis	.05	.02
❑ 108 Byron Bam Morris	.10	.05
❑ 109 Vincent Brisby	.05	.02
❑ 110 John Randle	.10	.05
❑ 111 Steve Walsh	.05	.02
❑ 112 Terry Allen	.10	.05
❑ 113 Greg Lloyd	.10	.05
❑ 114 Merton Hanks	.05	.02
❑ 115 Mel Gray	.05	.02
❑ 116 Jim Kelly	.25	.11
❑ 117 Don Beebe	.05	.02
❑ 118 Floyd Turner	.05	.02
❑ 119 Neil Smith	.10	.05
❑ 120 Keith Byars	.05	.02
❑ 121 Rocket Ismail	.10	.05
❑ 122 Leslie O'Neal	.10	.05
❑ 123 Mike Sherrard	.05	.02
❑ 124 Marion Butts	.05	.02
❑ 125 Andre Coleman	.05	.02
❑ 126 Charles Johnson	.10	.05
❑ 127 Derrick Fenner	.05	.02
❑ 128 Vinny Testaverde	.10	.05
❑ 129 Chris Spielman	.10	.05
❑ 130 Bert Emanuel	.25	.11
❑ 131 Craig Heyward	.10	.05
❑ 132 Anthony Miller	.10	.05
❑ 133 Rob Moore	.05	.02
❑ 134 Gary Brown	.05	.02
❑ 135 David Klingler UER (Photo on back is Erik Wilhelm)	.10	.05
❑ 136 Sean Dawkins	.10	.05
❑ 137 Terry McDaniel	.05	.02
❑ 138 Fred Barnett	.10	.05
❑ 139 Bryan Cox	.05	.02
❑ 140 Andrew Jordan	.05	.02
❑ 141 Leroy Thompson	.05	.02
❑ 142 Richmond Webb	.05	.02
❑ 143 Kimble Anders	.10	.05
❑ 144 Mario Bates	.25	.11
❑ 145 Irv Smith	.05	.02
❑ 146 Carnell Lake	.05	.02
❑ 147 Mark Seay	.10	.05
❑ 148 Dana Stubblefield	.25	.11
❑ 149 Kelvin Martin	.05	.02
❑ 150 Pete Metzelaars	.05	.02
❑ 151 Roosevelt Potts	.05	.02
❑ 152 Bubby Brister	.05	.02
❑ 153 Trent Dilfer	.25	.11
❑ 154 Ricky Proehl	.05	.02
❑ 155 Aaron Glenn	.05	.02
❑ 156 Eric Metcalf	.10	.05
❑ 157 Kevin Williams WR	.10	.05
❑ 158 Charlie Garner	.10	.05
❑ 159 Glyn Milburn	.05	.02
❑ 160 Fuad Reveiz	.05	.02
❑ 161 Brett Perriman	.10	.05
❑ 162 Neil O'Donnell	.10	.05
❑ 163 Tony Martin	.10	.05
❑ 164 Sam Adams	.05	.02
❑ 165 John Friesz	.10	.05
❑ 166 Bryant Young	.10	.05
❑ 167 Junior Seau	.25	.11
❑ 168 Ken Harvey	.05	.02
❑ 169 Bill Brooks	.05	.02
❑ 170 Eugene Robinson	.05	.02
❑ 171 Ricky Sanders	.10	.05
❑ 172 Rodney Peete	.05	.02
❑ 173 Boomer Esiason	.10	.05
❑ 174 Reggie Roby	.05	.02
❑ 175 Michael Jackson	.10	.05
❑ 176 Gus Frerotte	.25	.11
❑ 177 Terry Kirby	.10	.05
❑ 178 Jessie Tuggle	.05	.02
❑ 179 Courtney Hawkins	.05	.02
❑ 180 Heath Shuler	.25	.11
❑ 181 Jack Del Rio	.05	.02
❑ 182 O.J. McDuffie	.25	.11
❑ 183 Ricky Watters	.25	.11
❑ 184 Willie Roaf	.05	.02
❑ 185 Glenn Foley	.05	.02
❑ 186 Blair Thomas	.05	.02
❑ 187 Darren Woodson	.10	.05
❑ 188 Kevin Greene	.10	.05
❑ 189 Jeff Burris	.05	.02
❑ 190 Jay Schroeder	.05	.02
❑ 191 Stan Humphries	.10	.05
❑ 192 Irving Spikes	.10	.05
❑ 193 Jim Harbaugh	.10	.05
❑ 194 Robert Brooks	.25	.11
❑ 195 Greg Hill	.10	.05
❑ 196 Herschel Walker	.10	.05
❑ 197 Brian Blades	.10	.05

❑ 198 Mark Ingram	.05	.02
❑ 199 Kevin Turner	.05	.02
❑ 200 Lake Dawson	.10	.05
❑ 201 Alvin Harper	.05	.02
❑ 202 Derek Brown RBK	.05	.02
❑ 203 Qadry Ismail	.10	.05
❑ 204 Reggie Brooks	.10	.05
❑ 205 Steve Young SS	.30	.14
❑ 206 Emmitt Smith SS	.60	.25
❑ 207 Stan Humphries SS	.05	.02
❑ 208 Barry Sanders SS	.75	.35
❑ 209 Marshall Faulk SS	.25	.11
❑ 210 Drew Bledsoe SS	.40	.18
❑ 211 Jerry Rice SS	.40	.18
❑ 212 Tim Brown SS	.10	.05
❑ 213 Cris Carter SS	.25	.11
❑ 214 Dan Marino SS	.75	.35
❑ 215 Troy Aikman SS	.40	.18
❑ 216 Jerome Bettis SS	.10	.05
❑ 217 Deion Sanders SS	.25	.11
❑ 218 Junior Seau SS	.10	.05
❑ 219 John Elway SS	.75	.35
❑ 220 Warren Moon SS	.05	.02
❑ 221 Sterling Sharpe SS	.10	.05
❑ 222 Marcus Allen SS	.25	.11
❑ 223 Michael Irvin SS	.10	.05
❑ 224 Brett Favre SS	.75	.35
❑ 225 Rodney Hampton SS	.05	.02
❑ 226 Dave Brown SS	.10	.05
❑ 227 Ben Coates SS	.10	.05
❑ 228 Jim Kelly SS	.25	.11
❑ 229 Heath Shuler SS	.25	.11
❑ 230 Herman Moore SS	.25	.11
❑ 231 Jeff Hostetler SS	.10	.05
❑ 232 Rick Mirer SS	.10	.05
❑ 233 Byron Bam Morris SS	.10	.05
❑ 234 Terance Mathis SS	.05	.02
❑ 235 John Elway CL Barry Sanders CL	.40	.18
❑ 236 Troy Aikman CL	.25	.11
❑ 237 Jerry Rice CL	.25	.11
❑ 238 Emmitt Smith CL	.25	.11
❑ 239 Steve Young CL	.25	.11
❑ 240 Drew Bledsoe CL	.25	.11
❑ 241 Marshall Faulk CL	.25	.11
❑ 242 Dan Marino CL	.40	.18
❑ 243 Junior Seau CL	.10	.05
❑ 244 Ray Zellars RC	.10	.05
❑ 245 Rob Johnson RC	1.50	.70
❑ 246 Tony Boselli RC	.25	.11
❑ 247 Kevin Carter RC	.25	.11
❑ 248 Steve McNair RC	2.50	1.10
❑ 249 Tyrone Wheatley RC	1.00	.45
❑ 250 Steve Stenstrom RC	.05	.02
❑ 251 Stoney Case RC	.25	.11
❑ 252 Rodney Thomas RC	.25	.11
❑ 253 Michael Westbrook RC	1.25	.55
❑ 254 Der.Alexander DE RC	.05	.02
❑ 255 Kyle Brady RC	.25	.11
❑ 256 Kerry Collins RC	1.25	.55
❑ 257 Rashaan Salaam RC	.25	.11
❑ 258 Frank Sanders RC	.60	.25
❑ 259 John Walsh RC	.05	.02
❑ 260 Sherman Williams RC	.05	.02
❑ 261 Ki-Jana Carter RC	.25	.11
❑ 262 Jack Jackson RC	.05	.02
❑ 263 J.J. Stokes RC	.25	.11
❑ 264 Kordell Stewart RC	2.00	.90
❑ 265 Dave Barr RC	.05	.02
❑ 266 Eddie Goines RC	.05	.02
❑ 267 Warren Sapp RC	.50	.23
❑ 268 James O. Stewart RC	1.50	.70
❑ 269 Joey Galloway RC	2.00	.90
❑ 270 Tyrone Davis RC	.05	.02
❑ 271 Napoleon Kaufman RC	1.25	.55
❑ 272 Mark Bruener RC	.10	.05
❑ 273 Todd Collins RC	.25	.11
❑ 274 Billy Williams RC	.05	.02
❑ 275 James A.Stewart RC	.05	.02
❑ AD3 Steve Young Ad Contest Redemption	3.00	1.35

1996 Score

	MINT	NRMT
COMPLETE SET (275)	15.00	6.75

❑ 1 Emmitt Smith	1.25	.55
❑ 2 Flipper Anderson	.10	.05
❑ 3 Kordell Stewart	.50	.23
❑ 4 Bruce Smith	.20	.09
❑ 5 Marshall Faulk	.40	.18
❑ 6 William Floyd	.20	.09
❑ 7 Darren Woodson	.20	.09
❑ 8 Lake Dawson	.10	.05
❑ 9 Terry Allen	.20	.09
❑ 10 Ki-Jana Carter	.20	.09
❑ 11 Tony Boselli	.10	.05
❑ 12 Christian Fauria	.10	.05
❑ 13 Jeff George	.20	.09
❑ 14 Dan Marino	1.50	.70
❑ 15 Rodney Thomas	.10	.05
❑ 16 Anthony Miller	.20	.09
❑ 17 Chris Sanders	.20	.09
❑ 18 Natrone Means	.40	.18
❑ 19 Curtis Conway	.40	.18
❑ 20 Ben Coates	.20	.09
❑ 21 Alvin Harper	.10	.05
❑ 22 Frank Sanders	.20	.09
❑ 23 Boomer Esiason	.20	.09
❑ 24 Lovell Pinkney	.10	.05
❑ 25 Troy Aikman	.75	.35
❑ 26 Quinn Early	.10	.05
❑ 27 Adrian Murrell	.40	.18
❑ 28 Chris Spielman	.10	.05
❑ 29 Tyrone Wheatley	.20	.09
❑ 30 Tim Brown	.40	.18
❑ 31 Erik Kramer	.10	.05
❑ 32 Warren Moon	.20	.09
❑ 33 Jimmy Oliver	.10	.05
❑ 34 Herman Moore	.40	.18
❑ 35 Quentin Coryatt	.10	.05
❑ 36 Heath Shuler	.20	.09
❑ 37 Jim Kelly	.40	.18
❑ 38 Mike Morris	.10	.05
❑ 39 Harvey Williams	.10	.05
❑ 40 Vinny Testaverde	.20	.09
❑ 41 Steve McNair	.50	.23
❑ 42 Jerry Rice	.75	.35
❑ 43 Darick Holmes	.10	.05
❑ 44 Kyle Brady	.10	.05
❑ 45 Greg Lloyd	.20	.09
❑ 46 Kerry Collins	.40	.18
❑ 47 Willie McGinest	.10	.05
❑ 48 Isaac Bruce	.40	.18
❑ 49 Carnell Lake	.10	.05
❑ 50 Charles Haley	.20	.09
❑ 51 Troy Vincent	.10	.05
❑ 52 Randall Cunningham	.40	.18
❑ 53 Rashaan Salaam	.40	.18
❑ 54 Willie Jackson	.10	.05
❑ 55 Chris Warren	.20	.09
❑ 56 Michael Irvin	.40	.18
❑ 57 Mario Bates	.20	.09
❑ 58 Warren Sapp	.10	.05
❑ 59 John Elway	1.50	.70
❑ 60 Shannon Sharpe	.20	.09
❑ 61 Cornelius Bennett	.10	.05
❑ 62 Robert Brooks	.40	.18
❑ 63 Rodney Hampton	.20	.09
❑ 64 Ken Norton Jr.	.10	.05
❑ 65 Bryce Paup	.10	.05
❑ 66 Eric Swann	.10	.05
❑ 67 Rodney Peete	.10	.05
❑ 68 Larry Centers	.20	.09
❑ 69 Lamont Warren	.10	.05
❑ 70 Jay Novacek	.10	.05
❑ 71 Cris Carter	.40	.18
❑ 72 Terrell Fletcher	.10	.05
❑ 73 Andre Rison	.20	.09
❑ 74 Ricky Watters	.20	.09
❑ 75 Napoleon Kaufman	.40	.18
❑ 76 Reggie White	.40	.18
❑ 77 Yancey Thigpen	.20	.09
❑ 78 Terry Kirby	.20	.09
❑ 79 Deion Sanders	.40	.18
❑ 80 Irving Fryar	.20	.09
❑ 81 Marcus Allen	.40	.18
❑ 82 Carl Pickens	.40	.18
❑ 83 Drew Bledsoe	.75	.35
❑ 84 Eric Metcalf	.10	.05
❑ 85 Robert Smith	.20	.09
❑ 86 Tamarick Vanover	.20	.09
❑ 87 Henry Ellard	.10	.05
❑ 88 Kevin Greene	.20	.09
❑ 89 Mark Brunell	.75	.35
❑ 90 Terrell Davis	2.00	.90
❑ 91 Brian Mitchell	.10	.05
❑ 92 Aaron Bailey	.10	.05
❑ 93 Rocket Ismail	.10	.05
❑ 94 Dave Brown	.10	.05
❑ 95 Rod Woodson	.20	.09
❑ 96 Sean Gilbert	.10	.05
❑ 97 Mark Seay	.10	.05
❑ 98 Zack Crockett	.10	.05
❑ 99 Scott Mitchell	.20	.09
❑ 100 Erric Pegram	.10	.05
❑ 101 David Palmer	.10	.05
❑ 102 Vincent Brisby	.10	.05
❑ 103 Brett Perriman	.10	.05
❑ 104 Jim Everett	.10	.05
❑ 105 Tony Martin	.20	.09
❑ 106 Desmond Howard	.20	.09
❑ 107 Stan Humphries	.20	.09
❑ 108 Bill Brooks	.10	.05
❑ 109 Neil Smith	.10	.05
❑ 110 Michael Westbrook	.40	.18
❑ 111 Herschel Walker	.20	.09
❑ 112 Andre Coleman	.10	.05
❑ 113 Derrick Alexander WR	.20	.09
❑ 114 Jeff Blake	.40	.18
❑ 115 Sherman Williams	.10	.05
❑ 116 James O.Stewart	.20	.09
❑ 117 Hardy Nickerson	.10	.05
❑ 118 Elvis Grbac	.20	.09
❑ 119 Brett Favre	1.50	.70
❑ 120 Mike Sherrard	.10	.05
❑ 121 Edgar Bennett	.20	.09
❑ 122 Calvin Williams	.10	.05
❑ 123 Brian Blades	.10	.05
❑ 124 Jeff Graham	.10	.05
❑ 125 Gary Brown	.10	.05
❑ 126 Bernie Parmalee	.10	.05
❑ 127 Kimble Anders	.20	.09
❑ 128 Hugh Douglas	.20	.09
❑ 129 James A.Stewart	.10	.05
❑ 130 Eric Bjornson	.10	.05
❑ 131 Ken Dilger	.20	.09
❑ 132 Jerome Bettis	.40	.18
❑ 133 Cortez Kennedy	.10	.05
❑ 134 Bryan Cox	.10	.05
❑ 135 Darnay Scott	.20	.09
❑ 136 Bert Emanuel	.20	.09
❑ 137 Steve Bono	.10	.05
❑ 138 Charles Johnson	.10	.05
❑ 139 Glyn Milburn	.10	.05
❑ 140 Derrick Alexander DE	.10	.05
❑ 141 Dave Meggett	.10	.05
❑ 142 Trent Dilfer	.40	.18
❑ 143 Eric Zeier	.10	.05
❑ 144 Jim Harbaugh	.20	.09
❑ 145 Antonio Freeman	.60	.25
❑ 146 Orlando Thomas	.10	.05
❑ 147 Russell Maryland	.10	.05
❑ 148 Chad May	.10	.05
❑ 149 Craig Heyward	.10	.05
❑ 150 Aeneas Williams	.10	.05
❑ 151 Kevin Williams WR	.10	.05
❑ 152 Charlie Garner	.10	.05
❑ 153 J.J. Stokes	.40	.18

❑ 154 Stoney Case .10 .05
❑ 155 Mark Chmura .20 .09
❑ 156 Mark Bruener .10 .05
❑ 157 Derek Loville .10 .05
❑ 158 Justin Armour .10 .05
❑ 159 Brent Jones .10 .05
❑ 160 Aaron Craver .10 .05
❑ 161 Terance Mathis .10 .05
❑ 162 Chris Zorich .10 .05
❑ 163 Glenn Foley .20 .09
❑ 164 Johnny Mitchell .10 .05
❑ 165 Junior Seau .20 .09
❑ 166 Willie Davis .10 .05
❑ 167 Rick Mirer .20 .09
❑ 168 Mike Jones .10 .05
❑ 169 Greg Hill .20 .09
❑ 170 Steve Tasker .10 .05
❑ 171 Tony Bennett .10 .05
❑ 172 Jeff Hostetler .10 .05
❑ 173 Dave Krieg .10 .05
❑ 174 Mark Carrier WR .10 .05
❑ 175 Michael Haynes .10 .05
❑ 176 Chris Chandler .20 .09
❑ 177 Ernie Mills .10 .05
❑ 178 Jake Reed .20 .09
❑ 179 Errict Rhett .20 .09
❑ 180 Garrison Hearst .20 .09
❑ 181 Derrick Thomas .20 .09
❑ 182 Aaron Hayden RC .10 .05
❑ 183 Jackie Harris .10 .05
❑ 184 Curtis Martin .60 .25
❑ 185 Neil O'Donnell .20 .09
❑ 186 Derrick Moore .10 .05
❑ 187 Steve Young .60 .25
❑ 188 Pat Swilling .10 .05
❑ 189 Amp Lee .10 .05
❑ 190 Rob Johnson .40 .18
❑ 191 Todd Collins .20 .09
❑ 192 J.J. Birden .10 .05
❑ 193 O.J. McDuffie .20 .09
❑ 194 Shawn Jefferson .10 .05
❑ 195 Sean Dawkins .10 .05
❑ 196 Fred Barnett .10 .05
❑ 197 Roosevelt Potts .10 .05
❑ 198 Rob Moore .20 .09
❑ 199 Kevin Miniefield .10 .05
❑ 200 Barry Sanders 1.50 .70
❑ 201 Floyd Turner .10 .05
❑ 202 Wayne Chrebet .60 .25
❑ 203 Andre Reed .20 .09
❑ 204 Tyrone Hughes .10 .05
❑ 205 Keenan McCardell .40 .18
❑ 206 Gus Frerotte .40 .18
❑ 207 Daryl Johnston .20 .09
❑ 208 Steve Broussard .10 .05
❑ 209 Steve Atwater .10 .05
❑ 210 Thurman Thomas .40 .18
❑ 211 Andre Hastings .10 .05
❑ 212 Joey Galloway .50 .23
❑ 213 Kevin Carter .10 .05
❑ 214 Keyshawn Johnson RC 1.50 .70
❑ 215 Tony Brackens RC .20 .09
❑ 216 Stepfret Williams RC .20 .09
❑ 217 Mike Alstott RC 1.25 .55
❑ 218 Terry Glenn RC 1.00 .45
❑ 219 Tim Biakabutuka RC .60 .25
❑ 220 Eric Moulds RC 1.50 .70
❑ 221 Jeff Lewis RC .50 .23
❑ 222 Bobby Engram RC .40 .18
❑ 223 Cedric Jones RC .10 .05
❑ 224 Stanley Pritchett RC .20 .09
❑ 225 Kevin Hardy RC .40 .18
❑ 226 Alex Van Dyke RC .20 .09
❑ 227 Willie Anderson RC .10 .05
❑ 228 Regan Upshaw RC .10 .05
❑ 229 Leeland McElroy RC .40 .18
❑ 230 Marvin Harrison RC 2.00 .90
❑ 231 Eddie George RC 2.50 1.10
❑ 232 Lawrence Phillips RC .40 .18
❑ 233 Daryl Gardener RC .10 .05
❑ 234 Alex Molden RC .10 .05
❑ 235 Derrick Mayes RC .60 .25
❑ 236 John Mobley RC .10 .05
❑ 237 Israel Ifeanyi RC .10 .05
❑ 238 Poto Kondall RC .10 .05
❑ 239 Danny Kanell RC .40 .18
❑ 240 Jonathan Ogden RC .10 .05
❑ 241 Reggie Brown LB RC .10 .05
❑ 242 Marcus Jones RC .10 .05
❑ 243 Jon Stark RC .10 .05
❑ 244 Barry Sanders SE .75 .35
❑ 245 Brett Favre SE .75 .35
❑ 246 John Elway SE .75 .35
❑ 247 Dan Marino SE .75 .35
❑ 248 Drew Bledsoe SE .40 .18
❑ 249 Michael Irvin SE .20 .09
❑ 250 Troy Aikman SE .40 .18
❑ 251 Emmitt Smith SE .50 .23
❑ 252 Steve Young SE .40 .18
❑ 253 Jerry Rice SE .40 .18
❑ 254 Jeff Blake SE .20 .09
❑ 255 Tim Brown SE .20 .09
❑ 256 Eric Metcalf SE .10 .05
❑ 257 Rodney Hampton SE .10 .05
❑ 258 Scott Mitchell SE .10 .05
❑ 259 Garrison Hearst SE .20 .09
❑ 260 Larry Centers SE .20 .09
❑ 261 Neil O'Donnell SE .20 .09
❑ 262 Orlando Thomas SE .10 .05
❑ 263 Hugh Douglas SE .10 .05
❑ 264 Bill Brooks SE .10 .05
❑ 265 Harvey Williams SE .10 .05
❑ 266 Charles Haley SE .20 .09
❑ 267 Greg Lloyd SE .20 .09
❑ 268 Daryl Johnston SE .20 .09
❑ 269 Dan Marino CL .30 .14
❑ 270 Jeff Blake CL .20 .09
❑ 271 John Elway CL .40 .18
❑ 272 Emmitt Smith CL .40 .18
❑ 273 Brett Favre CL .30 .14
❑ 274 Jerry Rice CL .40 .18
❑ 275 Dan Marino .40 .18
Jeff Blake
John Elway
Emmitt Smith
Brett Favre
Jerry Rice
Checklist
❑ P1 Barry Sanders Promo 2.00 .90
Dream Team card

1997 Score

	MINT	NRMT
COMPLETE SET (330)	20.00	9.00

❑ 1 John Elway 2.00 .90
❑ 2 Drew Bledsoe 1.00 .45
❑ 3 Brett Favre 2.00 .90
❑ 4 Emmitt Smith 1.50 .70
❑ 5 Kerry Collins .20 .09
❑ 6 Jerry Rice 1.00 .45
❑ 7 Kordell Stewart .40 .18
❑ 8 Barry Sanders 2.00 .90
❑ 9 Dan Marino 2.00 .90
❑ 10 Steve Young .60 .25
❑ 11 Erik Kramer .10 .05
❑ 12 Warren Moon .30 .14
❑ 13 Chris Calloway .10 .05
❑ 14 Doug Evans .10 .05
❑ 15 Darren Woodson .10 .05
❑ 16 Alonzo Spellman .10 .05
❑ 17 Greg Hill .10 .05
❑ 18 Aaron Craver .10 .05
❑ 19 Jeff Hostetler .10 .05
❑ 20 William Thomas .10 .05
❑ 21 Marco Coleman .10 .05
❑ 22 Wayne Simmons .10 .05
❑ 23 Donnell Woolford .10 .05
❑ 24 Vinny Testaverde .20 .09
❑ 25 Ed McCaffrey .20 .09
❑ 26 Jim Everett .10 .05
❑ 27 Gilbert Brown .10 .05
❑ 28 Jason Dunn .10 .05
❑ 29 Stanley Pritchett .10 .05
❑ 30 Joey Galloway .40 .18
❑ 31 Amani Toomer .20 .09
❑ 32 Chris Penn .10 .05
❑ 33 Aeneas Williams .10 .05
❑ 34 Bobby Taylor .10 .05
❑ 35 Bryan Still .10 .05
❑ 36 Ty Law .10 .05
❑ 37 Shannon Sharpe .20 .09
❑ 38 Marty Carter .10 .05
❑ 39 Sam Mills .10 .05
❑ 40 William Floyd .20 .09
❑ 41 Brad Johnson .50 .23
❑ 42 Sean Dawkins .10 .05
❑ 43 Michael Irvin .30 .14
❑ 44 Jeff George .20 .09
❑ 45 Brent Jones .20 .09
❑ 46 Mark Brunell 1.00 .45
❑ 47 Rob Moore .20 .09
❑ 48 Hardy Nickerson .10 .05
❑ 49 Chris Chandler .20 .09
❑ 50 Willie Anderson .10 .05
❑ 51 Isaac Bruce .30 .14
❑ 52 Natrone Means .30 .14
❑ 53 Tony Banks .20 .09
❑ 54 Marshall Faulk .30 .14
❑ 55 Michael Westbrook .20 .09
❑ 56 Bruce Smith .20 .09
❑ 57 Jamal Anderson .60 .25
❑ 58 Jackie Harris .10 .05
❑ 59 Sean Gilbert .10 .05
❑ 60 Ki-Jana Carter .10 .05
❑ 61 Eric Moulds .30 .14
❑ 62 James O.Stewart .20 .09
❑ 63 Jeff Blake .20 .09
❑ 64 O.J. McDuffie .20 .09
❑ 65 Neil Smith .20 .09
❑ 66 Kevin Smith .10 .05
❑ 67 Terry Allen .30 .14
❑ 68 Sean LaChapelle .10 .05
❑ 69 Rashaan Salaam .10 .05
❑ 70 Jeff Graham .10 .05
❑ 71 Mark Carrier WR .10 .05
❑ 72 Allen Aldridge .10 .05
❑ 73 Keenan McCardell .20 .09
❑ 74 Willie McGinest .10 .05
❑ 75 Napoleon Kaufman .30 .14
❑ 76 Jerris McPhail .10 .05
❑ 77 Eric Swann .10 .05
❑ 78 Kimble Anders .20 .09
❑ 79 Charles Johnson .20 .09
❑ 80 Bryan Cox .10 .05
❑ 81 Johnnie Morton .20 .09
❑ 82 Andre Rison .20 .09
❑ 83 Corey Miller .10 .05
❑ 84 Troy Drayton .10 .05
❑ 85 Jim Harbaugh .20 .09
❑ 86 Wesley Walls .20 .09
❑ 87 Bryce Paup .10 .05
❑ 88 Curtis Martin .50 .23
❑ 89 Michael Sinclair .10 .05
❑ 90 Chris T. Jones .10 .05
❑ 91 Jake Reed .20 .09
❑ 92 LeRoy Butler .10 .05
❑ 93 Reggie Tongue .10 .05
❑ 94 Bert Emanuel .20 .09
❑ 95 Stan Humphries .20 .09
❑ 96 Neil O'Donnell .20 .09
❑ 97 Troy Vincent .10 .05
❑ 98 Mike Alstott .30 .14
❑ 99 Chad Cota .10 .05
❑ 100 Marvin Harrison .30 .14
❑ 101 Terrell Owens .30 .14
❑ 102 Dave Brown .10 .05
❑ 103 Harvey Williams .10 .05
❑ 104 Dcomond Howard .20 .09

Card	Mint	NrMt
❑ 105 Carl Pickens	.30	.14
❑ 106 Kent Graham	.10	.05
❑ 107 Michael Bates	.10	.05
❑ 108 Terrell Davis	1.50	.70
❑ 109 Marcus Allen	.30	.14
❑ 110 Ray Zellars	.10	.05
❑ 111 Chris Warren	.20	.09
❑ 112 Phillippi Sparks	.10	.05
❑ 113 Craig Erickson	.10	.05
❑ 114 Eddie George	1.00	.45
❑ 115 Daryl Johnston	.20	.09
❑ 116 Ricky Watters	.20	.09
❑ 117 Tedy Bruschi	.10	.05
❑ 118 Mike Mamula	.10	.05
❑ 119 Ken Harvey	.10	.05
❑ 120 John Randle	.20	.09
❑ 121 Mark Chmura	.20	.09
❑ 122 Sam Gash	.10	.05
❑ 123 John Kasay	.10	.05
❑ 124 Barry Minter	.10	.05
❑ 125 Raymont Harris	.10	.05
❑ 126 Derrick Thomas	.20	.09
❑ 127 Trent Dilfer	.30	.14
❑ 128 Carnell Lake	.10	.05
❑ 129 Brian Dawkins	.10	.05
❑ 130 Tyronne Drakeford	.10	.05
❑ 131 Daryl Gardener	.10	.05
❑ 132 Fred Strickland	.10	.05
❑ 133 Kevin Hardy	.10	.05
❑ 134 Winslow Oliver	.10	.05
❑ 135 Herman Moore	.30	.14
❑ 136 Keith Byars	.10	.05
❑ 137 Harold Green	.10	.05
❑ 138 Ty Detmer	.20	.09
❑ 139 Lamar Thomas	.10	.05
❑ 140 Elvis Grbac	.20	.09
❑ 141 Edgar Bennett	.20	.09
❑ 142 Cornelius Bennett	.10	.05
❑ 143 Tony Tolbert	.10	.05
❑ 144 James Hasty	.10	.05
❑ 145 Ben Coates	.20	.09
❑ 146 Errict Rhett	.10	.05
❑ 147 Jason Sehorn	.20	.09
❑ 148 Michael Jackson	.20	.09
❑ 149 John Mobley	.10	.05
❑ 150 Walt Harris	.10	.05
❑ 151 Terry Kirby	.20	.09
❑ 152 Devin Wyman	.10	.05
❑ 153 Ray Crockett	.10	.05
❑ 154 Quinn Early	.10	.05
❑ 155 Rodney Thomas	.10	.05
❑ 156 Mark Seay	.10	.05
❑ 157 Derrick Alexander WR	.20	.09
❑ 158 Lamar Lathon	.10	.05
❑ 159 Anthony Miller	.10	.05
❑ 160 Shawn Wooden	.10	.05
❑ 161 Antonio Freeman	.50	.23
❑ 162 Cortez Kennedy	.10	.05
❑ 163 Rickey Dudley	.20	.09
❑ 164 Tony Carter	.10	.05
❑ 165 Kevin Williams	.10	.05
❑ 166 Reggie White	.30	.14
❑ 167 Tim Bowens	.10	.05
❑ 168 Roy Barker	.10	.05
❑ 169 Adrian Murrell	.20	.09
❑ 170 Anthony Johnson	.10	.05
❑ 171 Terry Glenn	.30	.14
❑ 172 Jeff Lewis	.10	.05
❑ 173 Dorsey Levens	.30	.14
❑ 174 Willie Jackson	.10	.05
❑ 175 Willie Clay	.10	.05
❑ 176 Richmond Webb	.10	.05
❑ 177 Shawn Lee	.10	.05
❑ 178 Joe Aska	.10	.05
❑ 179 Rod Woodson	.20	.09
❑ 180 Jim Schwantz RC	.10	.05
❑ 181 Alfred Williams	.10	.05
❑ 182 Ferric Collons	.10	.05
❑ 183 Ken Norton Jr.	.10	.05
❑ 184 Rick Mirer	.10	.05
❑ 185 Leeland McElroy	.10	.05
❑ 186 Rodney Hampton	.20	.09
❑ 187 Ted Popson	.10	.05
❑ 188 Fred Barnett	.10	.05
❑ 189 Junior Seau	.20	.09
❑ 190 Micheal Barrow	.10	.05
❑ 191 Corey Widmer	.10	.05
❑ 192 Rodney Peete	.10	.05
❑ 193 Rod Smith WR	.30	.14
❑ 194 Muhsin Muhammad	.20	.09
❑ 195 Keith Jackson	.10	.05
❑ 196 Jimmy Smith	.20	.09
❑ 197 Dave Meggett	.10	.05
❑ 198 Lawrence Phillips	.10	.05
❑ 199 Chad Brown	.10	.05
❑ 200 Darrin Smith	.10	.05
❑ 201 Larry Centers	.20	.09
❑ 202 Kevin Greene	.20	.09
❑ 203 Sherman Williams	.10	.05
❑ 204 Chris Sanders	.10	.05
❑ 205 Shawn Jefferson	.10	.05
❑ 206 Thurman Thomas	.30	.14
❑ 207 Keyshawn Johnson	.30	.14
❑ 208 Bryant Young	.10	.05
❑ 209 Tim Biakabutuka	.20	.09
❑ 210 Troy Aikman	1.00	.45
❑ 211 Quentin Coryatt	.10	.05
❑ 212 Karim Abdul-Jabbar	.30	.14
❑ 213 Brian Blades	.10	.05
❑ 214 Ray Farmer	.10	.05
❑ 215 Simeon Rice	.20	.09
❑ 216 Tyrone Braxton	.10	.05
❑ 217 Jerome Woods	.10	.05
❑ 218 Charles Way	.20	.09
❑ 219 Garrison Hearst	.20	.09
❑ 220 Bobby Engram	.20	.09
❑ 221 Billy Davis RC	.10	.05
❑ 222 Ken Dilger	.10	.05
❑ 223 Robert Smith	.20	.09
❑ 224 John Friesz	.10	.05
❑ 225 Charlie Garner	.10	.05
❑ 226 Jerome Bettis	.30	.14
❑ 227 Darnay Scott	.20	.09
❑ 228 Terance Mathis	.20	.09
❑ 229 Brian Williams LB	.10	.05
❑ 230 Cris Carter	.30	.14
❑ 231 Michael Haynes	.10	.05
❑ 232 Cedric Jones	.10	.05
❑ 233 Danny Kanell	.20	.09
❑ 234 Deion Sanders	.30	.14
❑ 235 Steve Atwater	.10	.05
❑ 236 Jonathan Ogden	.10	.05
❑ 237 Lake Dawson	.10	.05
❑ 238 Eric Allen	.10	.05
❑ 239 Eddie Kennison	.20	.09
❑ 240 Irving Fryar	.20	.09
❑ 241 Michael Strahan	.10	.05
❑ 242 Steve McNair	.50	.23
❑ 243 Terrell Buckley	.10	.05
❑ 244 Merton Hanks	.10	.05
❑ 245 Jessie Armstead	.10	.05
❑ 246 Dana Stubblefield	.10	.05
❑ 247 Brett Perriman	.10	.05
❑ 248 Mark Collins	.10	.05
❑ 249 Willie Roaf	.10	.05
❑ 250 Gus Frerotte	.10	.05
❑ 251 William Fuller	.10	.05
❑ 252 Tamarick Vanover	.20	.09
❑ 253 Scott Mitchell	.20	.09
❑ 254 Eric Metcalf	.20	.09
❑ 255 Herschel Walker	.20	.09
❑ 256 Robert Brooks	.20	.09
❑ 257 Zach Thomas	.20	.09
❑ 258 Alvin Harper	.10	.05
❑ 259 Wayne Chrebet	.30	.14
❑ 260 Bill Romanowski	.10	.05
❑ 261 Willie Green	.10	.05
❑ 262 Dale Carter	.10	.05
❑ 263 Chris Slade	.10	.05
❑ 264 J.J. Stokes	.20	.09
❑ 265 Tim Brown	.30	.14
❑ 266 Eric Davis	.10	.05
❑ 267 Mark Carrier DB	.10	.05
❑ 268 Tony Martin	.20	.09
❑ 269 Tyrone Wheatley	.20	.09
❑ 270 Eugene Robinson	.10	.05
❑ 271 Curtis Conway	.20	.09
❑ 272 Michael Timpson	.10	.05
❑ 273 Orlando Pace RC	.30	.14
❑ 274 Tiki Barber RC	1.25	.55
❑ 275 Byron Hanspard RC	.30	.14
❑ 276 Warrick Dunn RC	1.25	.55
❑ 277 Rae Carruth RC	.30	.14
❑ 278 Bryant Westbrook RC	.10	.05
❑ 279 Antowain Smith RC	1.00	.45
❑ 280 Peter Boulware RC	.20	.09
❑ 281 Reidel Anthony RC	.75	.35
❑ 282 Troy Davis RC	.30	.14
❑ 283 Jake Plummer RC	2.50	1.10
❑ 284 Chris Canty RC	.10	.05
❑ 285 Dwayne Rudd RC	.30	.14
❑ 286 Ike Hilliard RC	.75	.35
❑ 287 Reinard Wilson RC	.10	.05
❑ 288 Corey Dillon RC	2.50	1.10
❑ 289 Tony Gonzalez RC	1.25	.55
❑ 290 Darnell Autry RC	.20	.09
❑ 291 Kevin Lockett RC	.20	.09
❑ 292 Darrell Russell RC	.10	.05
❑ 293 Jim Druckenmiller RC	.30	.14
❑ 294 Simon Mitchell RC	.10	.05
❑ 295 Joey Kent RC	.30	.14
❑ 296 Shawn Springs RC	.20	.09
❑ 297 James Farrior RC	.10	.05
❑ 298 Sedrick Shaw RC	.30	.14
❑ 299 Marcus Harris RC	.10	.05
❑ 300 Danny Wuerffel RC	.60	.25
❑ 301 Marc Edwards RC	.10	.05
❑ 302 Michael Booker RC	.10	.05
❑ 303 David LaFleur RC	.20	.09
❑ 304 Mike Adams WR RC	.10	.05
❑ 305 Pat Barnes RC	.30	.14
❑ 306 George Jones RC	.20	.09
❑ 307 Yatil Green RC	.20	.09
❑ 308 Drew Bledsoe TBP	.50	.23
❑ 309 Troy Aikman TBP	.50	.23
❑ 310 Terrell Davis TBP	.75	.35
❑ 311 Jim Everett TBP	.10	.05
❑ 312 John Elway TBP	1.00	.45
❑ 313 Barry Sanders TBP	1.00	.45
❑ 314 Jim Harbaugh TBP	.20	.09
❑ 315 Steve Young TBP	.30	.14
❑ 316 Dan Marino TBP	1.00	.45
❑ 317 Michael Irvin TBP	.30	.14
❑ 318 Emmitt Smith TBP	.75	.35
❑ 319 Jeff Hostetler TBP	.10	.05
❑ 320 Mark Brunell TBP	.50	.23
❑ 321 Jeff Blake TBP	.30	.14
❑ 322 Scott Mitchell TBP	.10	.05
❑ 323 Boomer Esiason TBP	.20	.09
❑ 324 Jerome Bettis TBP	.30	.14
❑ 325 Warren Moon TBP	.20	.09
❑ 326 Neil O'Donnell TBP	.20	.09
❑ 327 Jim Kelly TBP	.30	.14
❑ 328 Dan Marino CL	.40	.18
❑ 329 John Elway CL		
❑ 330 Drew Bledsoe CL	.40	.18
❑ P1 Troy Aikman (Ad Back Promo)	1.00	.45
❑ P2 Brett Favre (Ad Back Promo)	2.00	.90
❑ P3 Dan Marino (Ad Back Promo)	2.00	.90
❑ P4 Barry Sanders (Ad Back Promo)	1.50	.70

1998 Score

	MINT	NRMT
COMPLETE SET (270)	40.00	18.00
❑ 1 John Elway	2.00	.90

❑ 2	Kordell Stewart	.40	.18
❑ 3	Warrick Dunn	.40	.18
❑ 4	Brad Johnson	.40	.18
❑ 5	Kerry Collins	.20	.09
❑ 6	Danny Kanell	.20	.09
❑ 7	Emmitt Smith	1.50	.70
❑ 8	Jamal Anderson	.40	.18
❑ 9	Jim Harbaugh	.20	.09
❑ 10	Tony Martin	.20	.09
❑ 11	Rod Smith	.20	.09
❑ 12	Dorsey Levens	.40	.18
❑ 13	Steve McNair	.40	.18
❑ 14	Derrick Thomas	.20	.09
❑ 15	Rob Moore	.20	.09
❑ 16	Peter Boulware	.10	.05
❑ 17	Terry Allen	.40	.18
❑ 18	Joey Galloway	.40	.18
❑ 19	Jerome Bettis	.40	.18
❑ 20	Carl Pickens	.40	.18
❑ 21	Napoleon Kaufman	.40	.18
❑ 22	Troy Aikman	1.00	.45
❑ 23	Curtis Conway	.20	.09
❑ 24	Adrian Murrell	.20	.09
❑ 25	Elvis Grbac	.20	.09
❑ 26	Garrison Hearst	.40	.18
❑ 27	Chris Sanders	.10	.05
❑ 28	Scott Mitchell	.20	.09
❑ 29	Junior Seau	.20	.09
❑ 30	Chris Chandler	.20	.09
❑ 31	Kevin Hardy	.10	.05
❑ 32	Terrell Davis	1.50	.70
❑ 33	Keyshawn Johnson	.40	.18
❑ 34	Natrone Means	.40	.18
❑ 35	Antowain Smith	.40	.18
❑ 36	Jake Plummer	.60	.25
❑ 37	Isaac Bruce	.40	.18
❑ 38	Tony Banks	.20	.09
❑ 39	Reidel Anthony	.20	.09
❑ 40	Darren Woodson	.10	.05
❑ 41	Corey Dillon	.50	.23
❑ 42	Antonio Freeman	.40	.18
❑ 43	Eddie George	.75	.35
❑ 44	Yancey Thigpen	.10	.05
❑ 45	Tim Brown	.40	.18
❑ 46	Wayne Chrebet	.40	.18
❑ 47	Andre Rison	.20	.09
❑ 48	Michael Strahan	.10	.05
❑ 49	Deion Sanders	.40	.18
❑ 50	Eric Moulds	.40	.18
❑ 51	Mark Brunell	.75	.35
❑ 52	Rae Carruth	.20	.09
❑ 53	Warren Sapp	.20	.09
❑ 54	Mark Chmura	.20	.09
❑ 55	Darrell Green	.20	.09
❑ 56	Quinn Early	.10	.05
❑ 57	Barry Sanders	2.00	.90
❑ 58	Neil O'Donnell	.20	.09
❑ 59	Tony Brackens	.10	.05
❑ 60	Willie Davis	.10	.05
❑ 61	Shannon Sharpe	.20	.09
❑ 62	Shawn Springs	.10	.05
❑ 63	Tony Gonzalez	.10	.05
❑ 64	Rodney Thomas	.10	.05
❑ 65	Terance Mathis	.20	.09
❑ 66	Brett Favre	2.00	.90
❑ 67	Eric Swann	.10	.05
❑ 68	Kevin Turner	.10	.05
❑ 69	Tyrone Wheatley	.20	.09
❑ 70	Trent Dilfer	.40	.18
❑ 71	Bryan Cox	.10	.05
❑ 72	Lake Dawson	.10	.05
❑ 73	Will Blackwell	.10	.05
❑ 74	Fred Lane	.20	.09
❑ 75	Ty Detmer	.20	.09
❑ 76	Eddie Kennison	.20	.09
❑ 77	Jimmy Smith	.20	.09
❑ 78	Chris Calloway	.10	.05
❑ 79	Shawn Jefferson	.10	.05
❑ 80	Dan Marino	2.00	.90
❑ 81	LeRoy Butler	.10	.05
❑ 82	William Roaf	.10	.05
❑ 83	Rick Mirer	.10	.05
❑ 84	Dermontti Dawson	.10	.05
❑ 85	Errict Rhett	.20	.09
❑ 86	Lamar Thomas	.10	.05
❑ 87	Lamar Lathon	.10	.05
❑ 88	John Randle	.20	.09
❑ 89	Darryl Williams	.10	.05
❑ 90	Keenan McCardell	.20	.09
❑ 91	Erik Kramer	.10	.05
❑ 92	Ken Dilger	.10	.05
❑ 93	Dave Meggett	.10	.05
❑ 94	Jeff Blake	.20	.09
❑ 95	Ed McCaffrey	.20	.09
❑ 96	Charles Johnson	.10	.05
❑ 97	Irving Spikes	.10	.05
❑ 98	Mike Alstott	.40	.18
❑ 99	Vincent Brisby	.10	.05
❑ 100	Michael Westbrook	.20	.09
❑ 101	Rickey Dudley	.10	.05
❑ 102	Bert Emanuel	.20	.09
❑ 103	Daryl Johnston	.20	.09
❑ 104	Lawrence Phillips	.10	.05
❑ 105	Eric Bieniemy	.10	.05
❑ 106	Bryant Westbrook	.10	.05
❑ 107	Rob Johnson	.20	.09
❑ 108	Ray Zellars	.10	.05
❑ 109	Anthony Johnson	.10	.05
❑ 110	Reggie White	.40	.18
❑ 111	Wesley Walls	.20	.09
❑ 112	Amani Toomer	.20	.09
❑ 113	Gary Brown	.10	.05
❑ 114	Brian Blades	.10	.05
❑ 115	Alex Van Dyke	.10	.05
❑ 116	Michael Haynes	.10	.05
❑ 117	Jessie Armstead	.10	.05
❑ 118	James Jett	.20	.09
❑ 119	Troy Drayton	.10	.05
❑ 120	Craig Heyward	.10	.05
❑ 121	Steve Atwater	.10	.05
❑ 122	Tiki Barber	.20	.09
❑ 123	Karim Abdul-Jabbar	.40	.18
❑ 124	Kimble Anders	.20	.09
❑ 125	Frank Sanders	.20	.09
❑ 126	David Sloan	.10	.05
❑ 127	Andre Hastings	.10	.05
❑ 128	Vinny Testaverde	.20	.09
❑ 129	Robert Smith	.40	.18
❑ 130	Horace Copeland	.10	.05
❑ 131	Larry Centers	.10	.05
❑ 132	J.J. Stokes	.20	.09
❑ 133	Ike Hilliard	.20	.09
❑ 134	Muhsin Muhammad	.20	.09
❑ 135	Sean Dawkins	.10	.05
❑ 136	Raymont Harris	.10	.05
❑ 137	Lamar Smith	.20	.09
❑ 138	David Palmer	.10	.05
❑ 139	Steve Young	.50	.23
❑ 140	Bryan Still	.10	.05
❑ 141	Keith Byars	.10	.05
❑ 142	Cris Carter	.40	.18
❑ 143	Charlie Garner	.10	.05
❑ 144	Drew Bledsoe	.75	.35
❑ 145	Simeon Rice	.20	.09
❑ 146	Merton Hanks	.10	.05
❑ 147	Aeneas Williams	.10	.05
❑ 148	Rodney Hampton	.20	.09
❑ 149	Zach Thomas	.20	.09
❑ 150	Mark Bruener	.10	.05
❑ 151	Jason Dunn	.10	.05
❑ 152	Danny Wuerffel	.20	.09
❑ 153	Jim Druckenmiller	.20	.09
❑ 154	Greg Hill	.10	.05
❑ 155	Earnest Byner	.10	.05
❑ 156	Greg Lloyd	.10	.05
❑ 157	John Mobley	.10	.05
❑ 158	Tim Biakabutuka	.20	.09
❑ 159	Terrell Owens	.40	.18
❑ 160	O.J. McDuffie	.20	.09
❑ 161	Glenn Foley	.20	.09
❑ 162	Derrick Brooks	.10	.05
❑ 163	Dave Brown	.10	.05
❑ 164	Ki-Jana Carter	.10	.05
❑ 165	Bobby Hoying	.20	.09
❑ 166	Randal Hill	.10	.05
❑ 167	Michael Irvin	.40	.18
❑ 168	Bruce Smith	.20	.09
❑ 169	Troy Davis	.10	.05
❑ 170	Derrick Mayes	.20	.09
❑ 171	Henry Ellard	.20	.09
❑ 172	Dana Stubblefield	.10	.05
❑ 173	Willie McGinest	.10	.05
❑ 174	Leeland McElroy	.10	.05
❑ 175	Edgar Bennett	.10	.05
❑ 176	Robert Porcher	.10	.05
❑ 177	Randall Cunningham	.40	.18
❑ 178	Jim Everett	.10	.05
❑ 179	Jake Reed	.20	.09
❑ 180	Quentin Coryatt	.10	.05
❑ 181	William Floyd	.10	.05
❑ 182	Jason Sehorn	.20	.09
❑ 183	Carnell Lake	.10	.05
❑ 184	Dexter Coakley	.10	.05
❑ 185	Derrick Alexander WR	.20	.09
❑ 186	Johnnie Morton	.20	.09
❑ 187	Irving Fryar	.20	.09
❑ 188	Warren Moon	.40	.18
❑ 189	Todd Collins	.10	.05
❑ 190	Ken Norton	.10	.05
❑ 191	Terry Glenn	.40	.18
❑ 192	Rashaan Salaam	.10	.05
❑ 193	Jerry Rice	1.00	.45
❑ 194	James O.Stewart	.20	.09
❑ 195	David LaFleur	.10	.05
❑ 196	Eric Green	.10	.05
❑ 197	Gus Frerotte	.10	.05
❑ 198	Willie Green	.10	.05
❑ 199	Marshall Faulk	.40	.18
❑ 200	Brett Perriman	.10	.05
❑ 201	Darnay Scott	.20	.09
❑ 202	Marvin Harrison	.20	.09
❑ 203	Joe Aska	.10	.05
❑ 204	Darrien Gordon	.10	.05
❑ 205	Herman Moore	.40	.18
❑ 206	Curtis Martin	.40	.18
❑ 207	Derek Loville	.10	.05
❑ 208	Dale Carter	.10	.05
❑ 209	Heath Shuler	.10	.05
❑ 210	Jonathan Ogden	.10	.05
❑ 211	Leslie Shepherd	.10	.05
❑ 212	Tony Boselli	.10	.05
❑ 213	Eric Metcalf	.10	.05
❑ 214	Neil Smith	.20	.09
❑ 215	Anthony Miller	.10	.05
❑ 216	Jeff George	.20	.09
❑ 217	Charles Way	.10	.05
❑ 218	Mario Bates	.20	.09
❑ 219	Ben Coates	.20	.09
❑ 220	Michael Jackson	.10	.05
❑ 221	Thurman Thomas	.40	.18
❑ 222	Kyle Brady	.10	.05
❑ 223	Marcus Allen	.40	.18
❑ 224	Robert Brooks	.20	.09
❑ 225	Yatil Green	.10	.05
❑ 226	Byron Hanspard	.20	.09
❑ 227	Andre Reed	.20	.09
❑ 228	Chris Warren	.20	.09
❑ 229	Jackie Harris	.10	.05
❑ 230	Ricky Watters	.20	.09
❑ 231	Bobby Engram	.20	.09
❑ 232	Tamarick Vanover	.10	.05
❑ 233	Peyton Manning RC	10.00	4.50
❑ 234	Curtis Enis RC	1.50	.70
❑ 235	Randy Moss RC	10.00	4.50
❑ 236	Charles Woodson RC	2.00	.90
❑ 237	Robert Edwards RC	1.00	.45
❑ 238	Jacquez Green RC	2.00	.90
❑ 239	Keith Brooking RC	.75	.35
❑ 240	Jerome Pathon RC	.75	.35
❑ 241	Kevin Dyson RC	2.00	.90
❑ 242	Fred Taylor RC	3.00	1.35
❑ 243	Tavian Banks RC	.75	.35
❑ 244	Marcus Nash RC	.75	.35
❑ 245	Brian Griese RC	4.00	1.80
❑ 246	Andre Wadsworth RC	.75	.35
❑ 247	Ahman Green RC	2.50	1.10
❑ 248	Joe Jurevicius RC	.75	.35
❑ 249	Germane Crowell RC	2.50	1.10
❑ 250	Skip Hicks RC	.75	.35
❑ 251	Ryan Leaf RC	2.50	1.10
❑ 252	Hines Ward RC	.75	.35
❑ 253	John Elway OS	1.00	.45
❑ 254	Mark Brunell OS	.40	.18
❑ 255	Brett Favre OS	1.00	.45
❑ 256	Troy Aikman OS	.50	.23
❑ 257	Warrick Dunn OS	.20	.09
❑ 258	Barry Sanders OS	1.00	.45
❑ 259	Eddie George OS	.40	.18

		MINT	NRMT
❑ 260	Kordell Stewart OS	.40	.18
❑ 261	Emmitt Smith OS	.75	.35
❑ 262	Steve Young OS	.40	.18
❑ 263	Terrell Davis OS	.75	.35
❑ 264	Dorsey Levens OS	.20	.09
❑ 265	Dan Marino OS	1.00	.45
❑ 266	Jerry Rice OS	.50	.23
❑ 267	Drew Bledsoe OS	.40	.18
❑ 268	Brett Favre CL	.60	.25
❑ 269	Barry Sanders CL	.60	.25
❑ 270	Terrell Davis CL	.40	.18
❑ 251AU	Ryan Leaf AUTO	80.00	36.00

1999 Score

	MINT	NRMT
COMPLETE SET (275)	135.00	60.00
COMP.SET w/o SP's (220)	15.00	6.75

		MINT	NRMT
❑ 1	Randy Moss	2.00	.90
❑ 2	Randall Cunningham	.50	.23
❑ 3	Cris Carter	.50	.23
❑ 4	Robert Smith	.50	.23
❑ 5	Jake Reed	.25	.11
❑ 6	Leroy Hoard	.15	.07
❑ 7	John Randle	.25	.11
❑ 8	Brett Favre	2.00	.90
❑ 9	Antonio Freeman	.50	.23
❑ 10	Dorsey Levens	.50	.23
❑ 11	Robert Brooks	.25	.11
❑ 12	Derrick Mayes	.25	.11
❑ 13	Mark Chmura	.25	.11
❑ 14	Darick Holmes	.15	.07
❑ 15	Vonnie Holliday	.15	.07
❑ 16	Mike Alstott	.50	.23
❑ 17	Warrick Dunn	.50	.23
❑ 18	Trent Dilfer	.25	.11
❑ 19	Jacquez Green	.25	.11
❑ 20	Reidel Anthony	.25	.11
❑ 21	Warren Sapp	.25	.11
❑ 22	Bert Emanuel	.25	.11
❑ 23	Curtis Enis	.50	.23
❑ 24	Curtis Conway	.25	.11
❑ 25	Bobby Engram	.25	.11
❑ 26	Erik Kramer	.25	.11
❑ 27	Moses Moreno	.15	.07
❑ 28	Edgar Bennett	.15	.07
❑ 29	Barry Sanders	2.00	.90
❑ 30	Charlie Batch	.75	.35
❑ 31	Herman Moore	.50	.23
❑ 32	Johnnie Morton	.25	.11
❑ 33	Germane Crowell	.25	.11
❑ 34	Terry Fair	.15	.07
❑ 35	Gary Brown	.15	.07
❑ 36	Kent Graham	.15	.07
❑ 37	Kerry Collins	.25	.11
❑ 38	Charles Way	.15	.07
❑ 39	Tiki Barber	.15	.07
❑ 40	Ike Hilliard	.15	.07
❑ 41	Joe Jurevicius	.15	.07
❑ 42	Michael Strahan	.15	.07
❑ 43	Jason Sehorn	.15	.07
❑ 44	Brad Johnson	.50	.23
❑ 45	Terry Allen	.25	.11
❑ 46	Skip Hicks	.50	.23
❑ 47	Michael Westbrook	.25	.11
❑ 48	Leslie Shepherd	.15	.07
❑ 49	Stephen Alexander	.15	.07
❑ 50	Albert Connell	.15	.07
❑ 51	Darrell Green	.25	.11
❑ 52	Jake Plummer	1.00	.45
❑ 53	Adrian Murrell	.25	.11
❑ 54	Frank Sanders	.25	.11
❑ 55	Rob Moore	.25	.11
❑ 56	Larry Centers	.15	.07
❑ 57	Simeon Rice	.25	.11
❑ 58	Andre Wadsworth	.15	.07
❑ 59	Duce Staley	.50	.23
❑ 60	Charles Johnson	.15	.07
❑ 61	Charlie Garner	.25	.11
❑ 62	Bobby Hoying	.25	.11
❑ 63	Daryl Johnston	.25	.11
❑ 64	Emmitt Smith	1.25	.55
❑ 65	Troy Aikman	1.25	.55
❑ 66	Michael Irvin	.25	.11
❑ 67	Deion Sanders	.50	.23
❑ 68	Chris Warren	.15	.07
❑ 69	Darren Woodson	.15	.07
❑ 70	Rod Woodson	.25	.11
❑ 71	Travis Jervey	.15	.07
❑ 72	Jerry Rice	1.25	.55
❑ 73	Terrell Owens	.50	.23
❑ 74	Steve Young	.75	.35
❑ 75	Garrison Hearst	.25	.11
❑ 76	J.J. Stokes	.25	.11
❑ 77	Ken Norton	.15	.07
❑ 78	R.W. McQuarters	.15	.07
❑ 79	Bryant Young	.15	.07
❑ 80	Jamal Anderson	.50	.23
❑ 81	Chris Chandler	.25	.11
❑ 82	Terance Mathis	.25	.11
❑ 83	Tim Dwight	.50	.23
❑ 84	O.J. Santiago	.15	.07
❑ 85	Chris Calloway	.15	.07
❑ 86	Keith Brooking	.15	.07
❑ 87	Eddie Kennison	.25	.11
❑ 88	Willie Roaf	.15	.07
❑ 89	Cam Cleeland	.15	.07
❑ 90	Lamar Smith	.25	.11
❑ 91	Sean Dawkins	.15	.07
❑ 92	Tim Biakabutuka	.25	.11
❑ 93	Muhsin Muhammad	.25	.11
❑ 94	Steve Beuerlein	.15	.07
❑ 95	Rae Carruth	.25	.11
❑ 96	Wesley Walls	.25	.11
❑ 97	Kevin Greene	.25	.11
❑ 98	Trent Green	.25	.11
❑ 99	Tony Banks	.25	.11
❑ 100	Greg Hill	.15	.07
❑ 101	Robert Holcombe	.25	.11
❑ 102	Isaac Bruce	.50	.23
❑ 103	Amp Lee	.15	.07
❑ 104	Az-Zahir Hakim	.15	.07
❑ 105	Warren Moon	.50	.23
❑ 106	Jeff George	.25	.11
❑ 107	Rocket Ismail	.25	.11
❑ 108	Kordell Stewart	.50	.23
❑ 109	Jerome Bettis	.50	.23
❑ 110	Courtney Hawkins	.15	.07
❑ 111	Chris Fuamatu-Ma'afala	.15	.07
❑ 112	Levon Kirkland	.15	.07
❑ 113	Hines Ward	.15	.07
❑ 114	Will Blackwell	.15	.07
❑ 115	Corey Dillon	.50	.23
❑ 116	Carl Pickens	.25	.11
❑ 117	Neil O'Donnell	.25	.11
❑ 118	Jeff Blake	.25	.11
❑ 119	Darnay Scott	.15	.07
❑ 120	Takeo Spikes	.15	.07
❑ 121	Steve McNair	.50	.23
❑ 122	Frank Wycheck	.15	.07
❑ 123	Eddie George	.60	.25
❑ 124	Chris Sanders	.15	.07
❑ 125	Yancey Thigpen	.15	.07
❑ 126	Kevin Dyson	.25	.11
❑ 127	Blaine Bishop	.15	.07
❑ 128	Fred Taylor	1.00	.45
❑ 129	Mark Brunell	.75	.35
❑ 130	Jimmy Smith	.25	.11
❑ 131	Keenan McCardell	.25	.11
❑ 132	Kyle Brady	.15	.07
❑ 133	Tavian Banks	.15	.07
❑ 134	James Stewart	.25	.11
❑ 135	Kevin Hardy	.15	.07
❑ 136	Jonathan Quinn	.15	.07
❑ 137	Jermaine Lewis	.25	.11
❑ 138	Priest Holmes	.50	.23
❑ 139	Scott Mitchell	.25	.11
❑ 140	Eric Zeier	.25	.11
❑ 141	Patrick Johnson	.15	.07
❑ 142	Ray Lewis	.25	.11
❑ 143	Terry Kirby	.15	.07
❑ 144	Ty Detmer	.15	.07
❑ 145	Irv Smith	.15	.07
❑ 146	Chris Spielman	.15	.07
❑ 147	Antonio Langham	.15	.07
❑ 148	Dan Marino	2.00	.90
❑ 149	O.J. McDuffie	.25	.11
❑ 150	Oronde Gadsden	.15	.07
❑ 151	Karim Abdul-Jabbar	.25	.11
❑ 152	Yatil Green	.15	.07
❑ 153	Zach Thomas	.25	.11
❑ 154	John Avery	.25	.11
❑ 155	Lamar Thomas	.15	.07
❑ 156	Drew Bledsoe	.75	.35
❑ 157	Terry Glenn	.50	.23
❑ 158	Ben Coates	.25	.11
❑ 159	Shawn Jefferson	.15	.07
❑ 160	Sedrick Shaw	.15	.07
❑ 161	Tony Simmons	.15	.07
❑ 162	Ty Law	.15	.07
❑ 163	Robert Edwards	.25	.11
❑ 164	Curtis Martin	.50	.23
❑ 165	Keyshawn Johnson	.50	.23
❑ 166	Vinny Testaverde	.25	.11
❑ 167	Aaron Glenn	.15	.07
❑ 168	Wayne Chrebet	.25	.11
❑ 169	Dedric Ward	.15	.07
❑ 170	Peyton Manning	2.00	.90
❑ 171	Marshall Faulk	.50	.23
❑ 172	Marvin Harrison	.50	.23
❑ 173	Jerome Pathon	.15	.07
❑ 174	Ken Dilger	.15	.07
❑ 175	E.G. Green	.15	.07
❑ 176	Doug Flutie	.60	.25
❑ 177	Thurman Thomas	.25	.11
❑ 178	Andre Reed	.25	.11
❑ 179	Eric Moulds	.50	.23
❑ 180	Antowain Smith	.50	.23
❑ 181	Bruce Smith	.25	.11
❑ 182	Rob Johnson	.25	.11
❑ 183	Terrell Davis	1.25	.55
❑ 184	John Elway	2.00	.90
❑ 185	Ed McCaffrey	.25	.11
❑ 186	Rod Smith	.25	.11
❑ 187	Shannon Sharpe	.25	.11
❑ 188	Marcus Nash	.25	.11
❑ 189	Brian Griese	.75	.35
❑ 190	Neil Smith	.25	.11
❑ 191	Bubby Brister	.15	.07
❑ 192	Ryan Leaf	.50	.23
❑ 193	Natrone Means	.25	.11
❑ 194	Mikhael Ricks	.15	.07
❑ 195	Junior Seau	.25	.11
❑ 196	Jim Harbaugh	.25	.11
❑ 197	Bryan Still	.15	.07
❑ 198	Freddie Jones	.15	.07
❑ 199	Andre Rison	.25	.11
❑ 200	Elvis Grbac	.25	.11
❑ 201	Byron Bam Morris	.15	.07
❑ 202	Rashaan Shehee	.15	.07
❑ 203	Kimble Anders	.25	.11
❑ 204	Donnell Bennett	.15	.07
❑ 205	Tony Gonzalez	.25	.11
❑ 206	Derrick Alexander WR	.25	.11
❑ 207	Jon Kitna	.50	.23
❑ 208	Ricky Watters	.25	.11
❑ 209	Joey Galloway	.50	.23
❑ 210	Ahman Green	.25	.11
❑ 211	Shawn Springs	.15	.07
❑ 212	Michael Sinclair	.15	.07
❑ 213	Napoleon Kaufman	.50	.23
❑ 214	Tim Brown	.50	.23
❑ 215	Charles Woodson	.50	.23
❑ 216	Harvey Williams	.15	.07
❑ 217	Jon Ritchie	.15	.07
❑ 218	Rich Gannon	.25	.11
❑ 219	Rickey Dudley	.15	.07
❑ 220	James Jett	.25	.11
❑ 221	Tim Couch RC	10.00	4.50

❑ 222 Ricky Williams RC	12.00	5.50
❑ 223 Donovan McNabb RC	12.00	5.50
❑ 224 Edgerrin James RC	15.00	6.75
❑ 225 Torry Holt RC	8.00	3.60
❑ 226 Daunte Culpepper RC	15.00	6.75
❑ 227 Akili Smith RC	6.00	2.70
❑ 228 Champ Bailey RC	4.00	1.80
❑ 229 Chris Claiborne RC	1.25	.55
❑ 230 Chris McAlister RC	2.00	.90
❑ 231 Troy Edwards RC	4.00	1.80
❑ 232 Jevon Kearse RC	6.00	2.70
❑ 233 Shaun King RC	6.00	2.70
❑ 234 David Boston RC	6.00	2.70
❑ 235 Peerless Price RC	4.00	1.80
❑ 236 Cecil Collins RC	3.00	1.35
❑ 237 Rob Konrad RC	2.00	.90
❑ 238 Cade McNown RC UER (College listed as UNLV)	4.00	1.80
❑ 239 Shawn Bryson RC	3.00	1.35
❑ 240 Kevin Faulk RC	5.00	2.20
❑ 241 Scott Covington RC	3.00	1.35
❑ 242 James Johnson RC	3.00	1.35
❑ 243 Mike Cloud RC	3.00	1.35
❑ 244 Aaron Brooks RC	12.00	5.50
❑ 245 Sedrick Irvin RC	3.00	1.35
❑ 246 Amos Zereoue RC	3.00	1.35
❑ 247 Jermaine Fazande RC	3.00	1.35
❑ 248 Joe Germaine RC	3.00	1.35
❑ 249 Brock Huard RC	5.00	2.20
❑ 250 Craig Yeast RC	2.00	.90
❑ 251 Travis McGriff RC	3.00	1.35
❑ 252 D'Wayne Bates RC	2.00	.90
❑ 253 Na Brown RC	3.00	1.35
❑ 254 Tai Streets RC	3.00	1.35
❑ 255 Andy Katzenmoyer RC	3.00	1.35
❑ 256 Kevin Johnson RC	6.00	2.70
❑ 257 Joe Montgomery RC	2.00	.90
❑ 258 Karsten Bailey RC	3.00	1.35
❑ 259 De'Mond Parker RC	3.00	1.35
❑ 260 Reginald Kelly RC	1.25	.55
❑ 261 Eddie George AP	1.50	.70
❑ 262 Jamal Anderson AP	1.50	.70
❑ 263 Barry Sanders AP	6.00	2.70
❑ 264 Fred Taylor AP	3.00	1.35
❑ 265 Keyshawn Johnson AP	1.50	.70
❑ 266 Jerry Rice AP	4.00	1.80
❑ 267 Doug Flutie AP	2.00	.90
❑ 268 Deion Sanders AP	1.50	.70
❑ 269 Randall Cunningham AP	1.50	.70
❑ 270 Steve Young AP	2.50	1.10
❑ 271 John Elway GC Terrell Davis GC	6.00	2.70
❑ 272 Peyton Manning GC Marshall Faulk GC	5.00	2.20
❑ 273 Brett Favre GC Antonio Freeman GC	6.00	2.70
❑ 274 Troy .Aikman GC Emmitt Smith GC	4.00	1.80
❑ 275 Cris Carter GC Randy Moss GC	5.00	2.20

1999 Score Supplemental

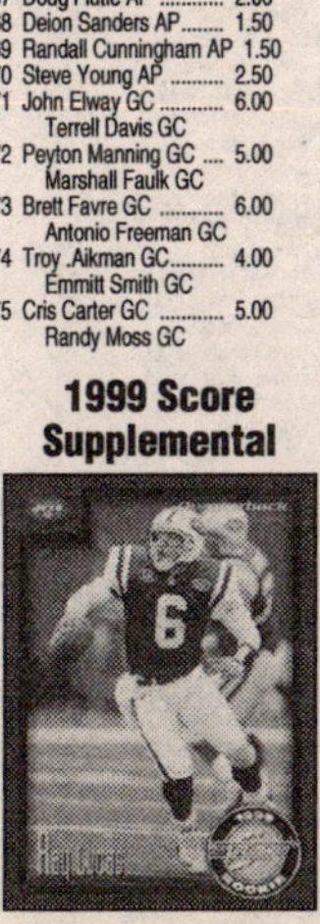

	MINT	NRMT
COMPLETE SET (110)	30.00	13.50
COMP.FACT.SET (110)	30.00	13.50
❑ 1 Chris Greisen RC	1.50	.70
❑ 2 Sherdrick Bonner RC	1.00	.45
❑ 3 Joel Makovicka RC	1.50	.70
❑ 4 Andy McCullough RC	1.00	.45
❑ 5 Jeff Paulk RC	1.00	.45
❑ 6 Brandon Stokley RC	1.50	.70
❑ 7 Sheldon Jackson RC	1.00	.45
❑ 8 Bobby Collins RC	1.50	.70
❑ 9 Kamil Loud RC	1.00	.45
❑ 10 Antoine Winfield RC	1.00	.45
❑ 11 Jerry Azumah RC	1.00	.45
❑ 12 James Allen RC	3.00	1.35
❑ 13 Nick Williams RC	1.00	.45
❑ 14 Michael Basnight RC	1.00	.45
❑ 15 Damon Griffin RC	1.00	.45
❑ 16 Ronnie Powell RC	1.00	.45
❑ 17 Darrin Chiaverini RC	1.50	.70
❑ 18 Mark Campbell RC	1.00	.45
❑ 19 Mike Lucky RC	1.00	.45
❑ 20 Wane McGarity RC	1.00	.45
❑ 21 Jason Tucker RC	2.00	.90
❑ 22 Ebenezer Ekuban RC	1.00	.45
❑ 23 Robert Thomas RC	1.00	.45
❑ 24 Dat Nguyen RC	1.00	.45
❑ 25 Olandis Gary RC	3.00	1.35
❑ 26 Desmond Clark RC	1.00	.45
❑ 27 Andre Cooper RC	1.00	.45
❑ 28 Chris Watson RC	.60	.25
❑ 29 Al Wilson RC	1.50	.70
❑ 30 Cory Sauter RC	1.00	.45
❑ 31 Brock Olivo RC	1.00	.45
❑ 32 Basil Mitchell RC	1.00	.45
❑ 33 Matt Snider RC	.60	.25
❑ 34 Antuan Edwards RC	1.00	.45
❑ 35 Mike McKenzie RC	1.00	.45
❑ 36 Terrence Wilkins RC	4.00	1.80
❑ 37 Fernando Bryant RC	1.00	.45
❑ 38 Larry Parker RC	1.00	.45
❑ 39 Autry Denson RC	1.50	.70
❑ 40 Jim Kleinsasser RC	1.50	.70
❑ 41 Michael Bishop RC	2.00	.90
❑ 42 Andy Katzenmoyer	.15	.07
❑ 43 Brett Bech RC	1.00	.45
❑ 44 Sean Bennett RC	1.50	.70
❑ 45 Dan Campbell RC	.60	.25
❑ 46 Ray Lucas RC	2.00	.90
❑ 47 Scott Dreisbach RC	1.50	.70
❑ 48 Cecil Martin RC	1.00	.45
❑ 49 Dameane Douglas RC	1.00	.45
❑ 50 Jed Weaver RC	1.00	.45
❑ 51 Jerame Tuman RC	1.00	.45
❑ 52 Steve Heiden RC	.60	.25
❑ 53 Jeff Garcia RC	5.00	2.20
❑ 54 Terry Jackson RC	1.00	.45
❑ 55 Charlie Rogers RC	1.00	.45
❑ 56 Lamar King RC	1.00	.45
❑ 57 Kurt Warner RC	15.00	6.75
❑ 58 Dre' Bly RC	1.00	.45
❑ 59 Justin Watson RC	.60	.25
❑ 60 Rabih Abdullah RC	1.00	.45
❑ 61 Martin Gramatica RC	.60	.25
❑ 62 Darnell McDonald RC	1.00	.45
❑ 63 Anthony McFarland RC	1.00	.45
❑ 64 Larry Brown TE RC	.60	.25
❑ 65 Kevin Daft RC	1.00	.45
❑ 66 Mike Sellers	.05	.02
❑ 67 Ken Oxendine	.05	.02
❑ 68 Errict Rhett	.15	.07
❑ 69 Stoney Case	.05	.02
❑ 70 Jonathan Linton	.05	.02
❑ 71 Marcus Robinson	1.00	.45
❑ 72 Shane Matthews	.15	.07
❑ 73 Cade McNown	1.25	.55
❑ 74 Akili Smith	1.50	.70
❑ 75 Karim Abdul-Jabbar	.15	.07
❑ 76 Tim Couch	3.00	1.35
❑ 77 Kevin Johnson	1.50	.70
❑ 78 Ron Rivers	.05	.02
❑ 79 Bill Schroeder	.30	.14
❑ 80 Edgerrin James	5.00	2.20
❑ 81 Cecil Collins	.75	.35
❑ 82 Matthew Hatchette	.05	.02
❑ 83 Daunte Culpepper	5.00	2.20
❑ 84 Ricky Williams	3.00	1.35
❑ 85 Tyrone Wheatley	.30	.14
❑ 86 Donovan McNabb	3.00	1.35
❑ 87 Marshall Faulk	.30	.14
❑ 88 Torry Holt	2.00	.90
❑ 89 Stephen Davis	.30	.14
❑ 90 Brad Johnson	.30	.14
❑ 91 Jake Plummer SS	.50	.23
❑ 92 Emmitt Smith SS	.75	.35
❑ 93 Troy Aikman SS	.75	.35
❑ 94 John Elway SS	1.25	.55
❑ 95 Terrell Davis SS	.75	.35
❑ 96 Barry Sanders SS	1.25	.55
❑ 97 Brett Favre SS	1.25	.55
❑ 98 Antonio Freeman SS	.30	.14
❑ 99 Peyton Manning SS	1.25	.55
❑ 100 Fred Taylor SS	.75	.35
❑ 101 Mark Brunell SS	.50	.23
❑ 102 Dan Marino SS	1.25	.55
❑ 103 Randy Moss SS	1.25	.55
❑ 104 Cris Carter SS	.30	.14
❑ 105 Drew Bledsoe SS	.50	.23
❑ 106 Terry Glenn SS	.30	.14
❑ 107 Keyshawn Johnson SS	.30	.14
❑ 108 Jerry Rice SS	.75	.35
❑ 109 Steve Young SS	.50	.23
❑ 110 Eddie George SS	.40	.18

2000 Score

	MINT	NRMT
COMP.SET w/o SP's (220)	20.00	9.00
❑ 1 Michael Pittman	.15	.07
❑ 2 Jake Plummer	.50	.23
❑ 3 Rob Moore	.25	.11
❑ 4 David Boston	.50	.23
❑ 5 Frank Sanders	.25	.11
❑ 6 Jamal Anderson	.50	.23
❑ 7 Chris Chandler	.25	.11
❑ 8 Tim Dwight	.50	.23
❑ 9 Terance Mathis	.25	.11
❑ 10 Shawn Jefferson	.15	.07
❑ 11 Ashley Ambrose	.15	.07
❑ 12 Peter Boulware	.15	.07
❑ 13 Priest Holmes	.25	.11
❑ 14 Tony Banks	.25	.11
❑ 15 Qadry Ismail	.15	.07
❑ 16 Shannon Sharpe	.25	.11
❑ 17 Rod Woodson	.25	.11
❑ 18 Matt Stover	.15	.07
❑ 19 Michael McCrary	.15	.07
❑ 20 Doug Flutie	.60	.25
❑ 21 Rob Johnson	.25	.11
❑ 22 Eric Moulds	.50	.23
❑ 23 Peerless Price	.50	.23
❑ 24 Jonathan Linton	.15	.07
❑ 25 Antowain Smith	.25	.11
❑ 26 Jay Riemersma	.15	.07
❑ 27 Muhsin Muhammad	.25	.11
❑ 28 Tim Biakabutuka	.25	.11
❑ 29 Patrick Jeffers	.50	.23
❑ 30 Wesley Walls	.15	.07
❑ 31 Steve Beuerlein	.25	.11
❑ 32 John Kasay	.15	.07
❑ 33 Curtis Enis	.25	.11
❑ 34 Cade McNown	.50	.23
❑ 35 Marcus Robinson	.50	.23
❑ 36 Bobby Engram	.15	.07
❑ 37 Eddie Kennison	.15	.07
❑ 38 Akili Smith	.50	.23

❑ 39 Carl Pickens .25 .11
❑ 40 Corey Dillon .50 .23
❑ 41 Darnay Scott .25 .11
❑ 42 Errict Rhett .25 .11
❑ 43 Karim Abdul-Jabbar .25 .11
❑ 44 Tim Couch 1.00 .45
❑ 45 Kevin Johnson .50 .23
❑ 46 Darrin Chiaverini .15 .07
❑ 47 Terry Kirby .15 .07
❑ 48 Jason Tucker .25 .11
❑ 49 Rocket Ismail .25 .11
❑ 50 Joey Galloway .50 .23
❑ 51 Michael Irvin .25 .11
❑ 52 Troy Aikman 1.25 .55
❑ 53 Emmitt Smith 1.25 .55
❑ 54 David LaFleur .15 .07
❑ 55 Trevor Pryce .15 .07
❑ 56 Brian Griese .60 .25
❑ 57 Olandis Gary .50 .23
❑ 58 Terrell Davis 1.25 .55
❑ 59 Rod Smith .25 .11
❑ 60 Ed McCaffrey .50 .23
❑ 61 Gus Frerotte .15 .07
❑ 62 Jason Elam .15 .07
❑ 63 Kavika Pittman .15 .07
❑ 64 James Stewart .25 .11
❑ 65 Charlie Batch .50 .23
❑ 66 Johnnie Morton .25 .11
❑ 67 Herman Moore .25 .11
❑ 68 Germane Crowell .25 .11
❑ 69 Barry Sanders 1.50 .70
❑ 70 Chris Claiborne .15 .07
❑ 71 Brett Favre 2.00 .90
❑ 72 Antonio Freeman .50 .23
❑ 73 Dorsey Levens .25 .11
❑ 74 De'Mond Parker .15 .07
❑ 75 Corey Bradford .25 .11
❑ 76 Basil Mitchell .15 .07
❑ 77 Bill Schroeder .25 .11
❑ 78 Peyton Manning 1.50 .70
❑ 79 Marvin Harrison .50 .23
❑ 80 Terrence Wilkins .50 .23
❑ 81 Edgerrin James 2.00 .90
❑ 82 E.G. Green .15 .07
❑ 83 Chad Bratzke .15 .07
❑ 84 Mark Brunell .75 .35
❑ 85 Fred Taylor .60 .25
❑ 86 Jimmy Smith .25 .11
❑ 87 Keenan McCardell .25 .11
❑ 88 Kevin Hardy .15 .07
❑ 89 Aaron Beasley .15 .07
❑ 90 Elvis Grbac .25 .11
❑ 91 Derrick Alexander .25 .11
❑ 92 Tony Gonzalez .25 .11
❑ 93 Donnell Bennett .15 .07
❑ 94 Warren Moon .50 .23
❑ 95 Andre Rison .25 .11
❑ 96 James Hasty .15 .07
❑ 97 Dan Marino 2.00 .90
❑ 98 Thurman Thomas .25 .11
❑ 99 James Johnson .25 .11
❑ 100 O.J. McDuffie .25 .11
❑ 101 Tony Martin .25 .11
❑ 102 Oronde Gadsden .25 .11
❑ 103 Zach Thomas .25 .11
❑ 104 Sam Madison .15 .07
❑ 105 Jay Fiedler .50 .23
❑ 106 Damon Huard .50 .23
❑ 107 Robert Smith .50 .23
❑ 108 Leroy Hoard .15 .07
❑ 109 Randy Moss 1.50 .70
❑ 110 Cris Carter .50 .23
❑ 111 Daunte Culpepper 1.00 .45
❑ 112 John Randle .25 .11
❑ 113 Randall Cunningham .50 .23
❑ 114 Gary Anderson .15 .07
❑ 115 Drew Bledsoe DP .75 .35
❑ 116 Terry Glenn .25 .11
❑ 117 Kevin Faulk .25 .11
❑ 119 Adam Vinatieri .15 .07
❑ 120 Ty Law .15 .07
❑ 121 Lawyer Milloy .15 .07
❑ 122 Troy Brown .15 .07
❑ 123 Ben Coates .15 .07
❑ 124 Cam Cleeland .15 .07
❑ 125 Jeff Blake .25 .11
❑ 126 Ricky Williams 1.25 .55
❑ 127 Jake Reed .25 .11
❑ 128 Jake Delhomme RC .50 .23
❑ 129 Andrew Glover .15 .07
❑ 130 Keith Poole .15 .07
❑ 131 Joe Horn .25 .11
❑ 132 Kerry Collins .25 .11
❑ 133 Joe Montgomery .15 .07
❑ 134 Sean Bennett .15 .07
❑ 135 Amani Toomer .15 .07
❑ 136 Ike Hilliard .25 .11
❑ 137 Joe Jurevicius .15 .07
❑ 138 Tiki Barber .25 .11
❑ 139 Victor Green .15 .07
❑ 140 Ray Lucas .50 .23
❑ 141 Vinny Testaverde .25 .11
❑ 142 Curtis Martin .50 .23
❑ 143 Wayne Chrebet .25 .11
❑ 144 Tyrone Wheatley .25 .11
❑ 145 Rich Gannon .25 .11
❑ 146 Napoleon Kaufman .25 .11
❑ 147 Tim Brown .15 .07
❑ 148 Rickey Dudley .15 .07
❑ 149 Charles Woodson .50 .23
❑ 150 James Jett .15 .07
❑ 151 Duce Staley .50 .23
❑ 152 Charles Johnson .25 .11
❑ 153 Donovan McNabb .75 .35
❑ 154 Troy Vincent .15 .07
❑ 155 Troy Edwards .25 .11
❑ 156 Jerome Bettis .50 .23
❑ 157 Kordell Stewart .50 .23
❑ 158 Richard Huntley .15 .07
❑ 159 Hines Ward .15 .07
❑ 160 Levon Kirkland .15 .07
❑ 161 Ryan Leaf .50 .23
❑ 162 Jim Harbaugh .25 .11
❑ 163 Jermaine Fazande .15 .07
❑ 164 Natrone Means .15 .07
❑ 165 Junior Seau .25 .11
❑ 166 Curtis Conway .25 .11
❑ 167 Freddie Jones .15 .07
❑ 168 Jeff Graham .15 .07
❑ 169 Terrell Owens .50 .23
❑ 170 Jeff Garcia .50 .23
❑ 171 Jerry Rice 1.25 .55
❑ 172 Steve Young .75 .35
❑ 173 Garrison Hearst .25 .11
❑ 174 Charlie Garner .25 .11
❑ 175 Fred Beasley .15 .07
❑ 176 Bryant Young .15 .07
❑ 177 Derrick Mayes .25 .11
❑ 178 Sean Dawkins .15 .07
❑ 179 Jon Kitna .50 .23
❑ 180 Ricky Watters .25 .11
❑ 181 Charlie Rogers .15 .07
❑ 182 Kurt Warner 2.00 .90
❑ 183 Marshall Faulk .60 .25
❑ 184 Isaac Bruce .50 .23
❑ 185 Az-Zahir Hakim .25 .11
❑ 186 Trent Green .25 .11
❑ 187 Jeff Wilkins .15 .07
❑ 188 Torry Holt .50 .23
❑ 189 London Fletcher RC .25 .11
❑ 190 Robert Holcombe .15 .07
❑ 191 Todd Lyght .15 .07
❑ 192 Keyshawn Johnson .50 .23
❑ 193 Derrick Brooks .15 .07
❑ 194 Warren Sapp .25 .11
❑ 195 Shaun King .75 .35
❑ 196 Warrick Dunn .50 .23
❑ 197 Mike Alstott .50 .23
❑ 198 Jacquez Green .25 .11
❑ 199 Reidel Anthony .15 .07
❑ 200 Martin Gramatica .15 .07
❑ 201 Donnie Abraham .15 .07
❑ 202 Steve McNair .50 .23
❑ 203 Eddie George .60 .25
❑ 204 Jevon Kearse .50 .23
❑ 205 Frank Wycheck .15 .07
❑ 206 Kevin Dyson .25 .11
❑ 207 Yancey Thigpen .15 .07
❑ 208 Al Del Greco .15 .07
❑ 209 Jeff George .25 .11
❑ 210 Adrian Murrell .25 .11
❑ 211 Brad Johnson .50 .23
❑ 212 Stephen Davis .50 .23
❑ 213 Stephen Alexander .15 .07
❑ 214 Michael Westbrook .25 .11
❑ 215 Darrell Green .15 .07
❑ 216 Champ Bailey .50 .23
❑ 217 Albert Connell .15 .07
❑ 218 Larry Centers .15 .07
❑ 219 Bruce Smith .25 .11
❑ 220 Deion Sanders .50 .23
❑ 221 Ricky Williams SS 1.25 .55
❑ 222 Edgerrin James SS 2.00 .90
❑ 223 Tim Couch SS 1.00 .45
❑ 224 Cade McNown SS .60 .25
❑ 225 Olandis Gary SS .60 .25
❑ 226 Torry Holt SS .60 .25
❑ 227 Donovan McNabb SS .75 .35
❑ 228 Shaun King SS .75 .35
❑ 229 Kevin Johnson SS .60 .25
❑ 230 Kurt Warner SS 2.50 1.10
❑ 231 Tony Gonzalez AP .30 .14
❑ 232 Frank Wycheck AP .20 .09
❑ 233 Eddie George AP .75 .35
❑ 234 Mark Brunell AP 1.00 .45
❑ 235 Corey Dillon AP .60 .25
❑ 236 Peyton Manning AP 2.00 .90
❑ 237 Keyshawn Johnson AP .60 .25
❑ 238 Rich Gannon AP .30 .14
❑ 239 Terry Glenn AP .30 .14
❑ 240 Tony Brackens AP .20 .09
❑ 241 Edgerrin James AP 2.00 .90
❑ 242 Tim Brown AP .60 .25
❑ 243 Michael Strahan AP .20 .09
❑ 244 Kurt Warner AP 2.50 1.10
❑ 245 Brad Johnson AP .60 .25
❑ 246 Aeneas Williams AP .20 .09
❑ 247 Marshall Faulk AP .75 .35
❑ 248 Dexter Coakley AP .20 .09
❑ 249 Warren Sapp AP .30 .14
❑ 250 Mike Alstott AP .60 .25
❑ 251 David Sloan AP .20 .09
❑ 252 Cris Carter AP .60 .25
❑ 253 Muhsin Muhammad AP .20 .09
❑ 254 Isaac Bruce AP .60 .25
❑ 255 Wesley Walls AP .20 .09
❑ 256 Steve Beuerlein LL .30 .14
❑ 257 Kurt Warner LL 2.50 1.10
❑ 258 Peyton Manning LL 2.00 .90
❑ 259 Brad Johnson LL .60 .25
❑ 260 Edgerrin James LL 2.00 .90
❑ 261 Curtis Martin LL .60 .25
❑ 262 Stephen Davis LL .60 .25
❑ 263 Emmitt Smith LL 1.50 .70
❑ 264 Marvin Harrison LL .60 .25
❑ 265 Jimmy Smith LL .30 .14
❑ 266 Randy Moss LL 2.00 .90
❑ 267 Marcus Robinson LL .60 .25
❑ 268 Kevin Carter LL .20 .09
❑ 269 Simeon Rice LL .20 .09
❑ 270 Robert Porcher LL .20 .09
❑ 271 Jevon Kearse LL .60 .25
❑ 272 Mike Vanderjagt LL .20 .09
❑ 273 Olindo Mare LL .20 .09
❑ 274 Todd Peterson LL .20 .09
❑ 275 Mike Hollis LL .20 .09
❑ 276 Mike Anderson RC/500 150.00 70.00
❑ 277 Peter Warrick RC 6.00 2.70
❑ 278 Courtney Brown RC 2.50 1.10
❑ 279 Plaxico Burress RC 4.00 1.80
❑ 280 Corey Simon RC 2.50 1.10
❑ 281 Thomas Jones RC 3.00 1.35
❑ 282 Travis Taylor RC 2.50 1.10
❑ 283 Shaun Alexander RC 5.00 2.20
❑ 284 Patrick Pass RC/500 30.00 13.50
❑ 285 Chris Redman RC 4.00 1.80
❑ 286 Chad Pennington RC 6.00 2.70
❑ 287 Jamal Lewis RC 10.00 4.50
❑ 288 Brian Urlacher RC 6.00 2.70
❑ 289 Bubba Franks RC 2.50 1.10
❑ 290 Dez White RC 1.50 .70
❑ 291 Frank Moreau RC/500 30.00 13.50
❑ 292 Ron Dayne RC 6.00 2.70
❑ 293 Sylvester Morris RC 4.00 1.80
❑ 294 R.Jay Soward RC 2.00 .90
❑ 295 Curtis Keaton RC 1.50 .70
❑ 296 Spergon Wynn RC/500 25.00 11.00
❑ 297 Rondell Mealey RC 1.50 .70

	MINT	NRMT
❑ 298 Travis Prentice RC	3.00	1.35
❑ 299 Darrell Jackson RC	3.00	1.35
❑ 300 Giovanni Carmazzi RC	2.50	1.10
❑ 301 Anthony Lucas RC	1.50	.70
❑ 302 Danny Farmer RC	2.00	.90
❑ 303 Dennis Northcutt RC	2.50	1.10
❑ 304 Troy Walters RC	2.00	.90
❑ 305 Laveranues Coles RC	3.00	1.35
❑ 306 Kwame Cavil RC	1.50	.70
❑ 307 Tee Martin RC	3.00	1.35
❑ 308 J.R. Redmond RC	2.50	1.10
❑ 309 Tim Rattay RC	3.00	1.35
❑ 310 Jerry Porter RC	2.00	.90
❑ 311 Michael Wiley RC	2.00	.90
❑ 312 Reuben Droughns RC	2.00	.90
❑ 313 Trung Canidate RC	1.50	.70
❑ 314 Shyrone Stith RC	1.50	.70
❑ 315 Marc Bulger RC	1.50	.70
❑ 316 Tom Brady RC	1.50	.70
❑ 317 Doug Johnson RC	2.00	.90
❑ 318 Todd Husak RC	1.50	.70
❑ 319 Gari Scott RC	2.00	.90
❑ 320 Windrell Hayes RC/500	25.00	11.00
❑ 321 Chris Cole RC	1.50	.70
❑ 322 Sammy Morris RC	2.00	.90
❑ 323 Trevor Gaylor RC	1.50	.70
❑ 324 Jarious Jackson RC	1.50	.70
❑ 325 Doug Chapman RC/500	80.00	36.00
❑ 326 Ron Dugans RC	1.50	.70
❑ 327 Ron Dixon RC/500	25.00	11.00
❑ 328 Joe Hamilton RC	2.50	1.10
❑ 329 Todd Pinkston RC	1.50	.70
❑ 330 Chad Morton RC	2.00	.90

1996 Score Board NFL Lasers

	MINT	NRMT
COMPLETE SET (100)	20.00	9.00
❑ 1 Brett Favre	2.00	.90
❑ 2 Chris Warren	.20	.09
❑ 3 J.J. Stokes	.40	.18
❑ 4 Barry Sanders	2.00	.90
❑ 5 Ben Coates	.20	.09
❑ 6 Bryan Cox	.10	.05
❑ 7 Carl Pickens	.40	.18
❑ 8 Cris Carter	.40	.18
❑ 9 Curtis Martin	.75	.35
❑ 10 Dan Marino	2.00	.90
❑ 11 Dave Brown	.20	.09
❑ 12 Drew Bledsoe	1.00	.45
❑ 13 Edgar Bennett	.20	.09
❑ 14 Herman Moore	.40	.18
❑ 15 Jeff Blake	.40	.18
❑ 16 Jerry Rice	1.00	.45
❑ 17 Jim Kelly	.40	.18
❑ 18 John Elway	2.00	.90
❑ 19 Junior Seau	.40	.18
❑ 20 Kerry Collins	.40	.18
❑ 21 Kordell Stewart	.60	.25
❑ 22 Leonard Russell	.10	.05
❑ 23 Mark Brunell	1.00	.45
❑ 24 Marshall Faulk	.40	.18
❑ 25 Mike Tomczak	.10	.05
❑ 26 Reggie White	.40	.18
❑ 27 Ricky Watters	.20	.09
❑ 28 Rod Woodson	.20	.09
❑ 29 Rodney Peete	.10	.05
❑ 30 Stan Humphries	.20	.09
❑ 31 Steve McNair	.75	.35
❑ 32 Terry Allen	.20	.09
❑ 33 Thurman Thomas	.40	.18
❑ 34 Troy Aikman	1.00	.45
❑ 35 Vinny Testaverde	.20	.09
❑ 36 Chris T. Jones	.40	.18
❑ 37 Deion Sanders	.50	.23
❑ 38 Eric Metcalf	.20	.09
❑ 39 Erik Kramer	.10	.05
❑ 40 Emmitt Smith	1.50	.70
❑ 41 Gus Frerotte	.40	.18
❑ 42 Shannon Sharpe	.20	.09
❑ 43 Jerome Bettis	.40	.18
❑ 44 Jim Harbaugh	.20	.09
❑ 45 Isaac Bruce	.40	.18
❑ 46 Jeff Hostetler	.20	.09
❑ 47 Ki-Jana Carter	.20	.09
❑ 48 Marcus Allen	.40	.18
❑ 49 Neil O'Donnell	.20	.09
❑ 50 Rashaan Salaam	.40	.18
❑ 51 Robert Brooks	.40	.18
❑ 52 Steve Bono	.20	.09
❑ 53 Scott Mitchell	.20	.09
❑ 54 Terrell Davis	2.00	.90
❑ 55 Tim Brown	.20	.09
❑ 56 Troy Vincent	.10	.05
❑ 57 Warren Moon	.20	.09
❑ 58 Tony Martin	.20	.09
❑ 59 Rodney Hampton	.20	.09
❑ 60 Steve Young	.75	.35
❑ 61 Rick Mirer	.20	.09
❑ 62 Mark Chmura	.20	.09
❑ 63 Larry Centers	.20	.09
❑ 64 Ken Dilger	.20	.09
❑ 65 Joey Galloway	.60	.25
❑ 66 Jim Everett	.10	.05
❑ 67 Chris Chandler	.20	.09
❑ 68 James O. Stewart	.40	.18
❑ 69 Robert Smith	.20	.09
❑ 70 Tamarick Vanover	.40	.18
❑ 71 Wayne Chrebet	.60	.25
❑ 72 Keyshawn Johnson RC	1.50	.70
❑ 73 Kevin Hardy RC	.20	.09
❑ 74 Lawrence Phillips RC	.40	.18
❑ 75 Jonathan Ogden RC	.10	.05
❑ 76 Terry Glenn RC	1.00	.45
❑ 77 Tim Biakabutuka RC	.75	.35
❑ 78 Eddie George RC	2.50	1.10
❑ 79 Eric Moulds RC	1.50	.70
❑ 80 John Mobley RC	.10	.05
❑ 81 Amani Toomer RC	.75	.35
❑ 82 Marvin Harrison RC	2.00	.90
❑ 83 Leeland McElroy RC	.40	.18
❑ 84 Rickey Dudley RC	.40	.18
❑ 85 Tony Banks RC	1.00	.45
❑ 86 Zach Thomas RC	.75	.35
❑ 87 Alex Molden RC	.10	.05
❑ 88 Daryl Gardener RC	.20	.09
❑ 89 Jamal Anderson RC	4.00	1.80
❑ 90 Karim Abdul-Jabbar RC	.50	.23
❑ 91 Simeon Rice RC	.40	.18
❑ 92 Walt Harris RC	.10	.05
❑ 93 Bobby Engram RC	.40	.18
❑ 94 Kevin Williams	.10	.05
❑ 95 Sean Gilbert	.10	.05
❑ 96 Kevin Greene	.20	.09
❑ 97 Regan Upshaw RC	.10	.05
❑ 98 Marcus Jones RC	.10	.05
❑ 99 Ray Lewis RC	2.00	.90
❑ 100 Keyshawn Johnson Checklist card	.20	.09
❑ P1 Emmitt Smith Promo Unnumbered Sample card	.75	.35

1993 Select

	MINT	NRMT
COMPLETE SET (200)	20.00	9.00
❑ 1 Steve Young	2.00	.90
❑ 2 Andre Reed	.40	.18
❑ 3 Deion Sanders	1.25	.55
❑ 4 Harold Green	.20	.09
❑ 5 Wendell Davis	.20	.09

	MINT	NRMT
❑ 6 Mike Johnson	.20	.09
❑ 7 Troy Aikman	2.00	.90
❑ 8 Johnny Mitchell	.20	.09
❑ 9 Dale Carter	.20	.09
❑ 10 Bruce Matthews	.20	.09
❑ 11 Terrell Buckley	.20	.09
❑ 12 Steve Emtman	.20	.09
❑ 13 Neil Smith	.75	.35
❑ 14 Tim Brown	.75	.35
❑ 15 Chris Doleman	.20	.09
❑ 16 Dan Marino	4.00	1.80
❑ 17 Terry McDaniel	.20	.09
❑ 18 Neal Anderson	.20	.09
❑ 19 Phil Simms	.40	.18
❑ 20 Jeff Lageman	.20	.09
❑ 21 Jerry Rice	2.50	1.10
❑ 22 Dermontti Dawson	.20	.09
❑ 23 Reggie Cobb	.20	.09
❑ 24 Junior Seau	.75	.35
❑ 25 Darrell Green	.20	.09
❑ 26 Chris Warren	.40	.18
❑ 27 Randall Cunningham	.75	.35
❑ 28 Bruce Smith	.75	.35
❑ 29 Bryan Cox	.20	.09
❑ 30 David Klingler	.20	.09
❑ 31 Chip Lohmiller	.20	.09
❑ 32 Eric Metcalf	.40	.18
❑ 33 Ken Norton Jr.	.40	.18
❑ 34 John Elway	4.00	1.80
❑ 35 Harris Barton	.20	.09
❑ 36 Tim Barnett	.20	.09
❑ 37 Rodney Hampton	.75	.35
❑ 38 Desmond Howard	.40	.18
❑ 39 Tom Rathman	.20	.09
❑ 40 Derrick Thomas	.75	.35
❑ 41 Randal Hill	.20	.09
❑ 42 Steve Wisniewski	.20	.09
❑ 43 Brett Favre	5.00	2.20
❑ 44 Darryl Talley	.20	.09
❑ 45 Shane Conlan	.20	.09
❑ 46 Anthony Miller	.40	.18
❑ 47 Randall McDaniel	.20	.09
❑ 48 Rod Woodson	.75	.35
❑ 49 Eric Martin	.20	.09
❑ 50 Ronnie Lott	.40	.18
❑ 51 Chris Spielman	.40	.18
❑ 52 Vincent Brown	.20	.09
❑ 53 Donnell Woolford	.20	.09
❑ 54 Richmond Webb	.20	.09
❑ 55 Emmitt Smith	3.00	1.35
❑ 56 Haywood Jeffires	.40	.18
❑ 57 Jim Kelly	.75	.35
❑ 58 James Francis	.20	.09
❑ 59 Steve Wallace	.20	.09
❑ 60 Jarrod Bunch	.20	.09
❑ 61 Lawrence Dawsey	.20	.09
❑ 62 Steve Atwater	.20	.09
❑ 63 Art Monk	.40	.18
❑ 64 Eric Green	.20	.09
❑ 65 Lawrence Taylor	.75	.35
❑ 66 Ronnie Harmon	.20	.09
❑ 67 Fred Barnett	.40	.18
❑ 68 Cortez Kennedy	.40	.18
❑ 69 Mark Collins	.20	.09
❑ 70 Howie Long	.40	.18
❑ 71 Jackie Harris	.20	.09
❑ 72 Irving Fryar	.40	.18

❑ 73 Jim Everett	.40	.18
❑ 74 Troy Vincent	.20	.09
❑ 75 Cris Carter	1.00	.45
❑ 76 Boomer Esiason	.40	.18
❑ 77 Sam Mills	.20	.09
❑ 78 Lorenzo White	.20	.09
❑ 79 Andre Rison	.40	.18
❑ 80 Quentin Coryatt	.40	.18
❑ 81 Steve McMichael	.40	.18
❑ 82 Nick Lowery	.20	.09
❑ 83 Michael Irvin	.75	.35
❑ 84 Thurman Thomas	.75	.35
❑ 85 Bill Romanowski	.20	.09
❑ 86 Carl Pickens	.75	.35
❑ 87 Tim McDonald	.20	.09
❑ 88 Bernie Kosar	.40	.18
❑ 89 Greg Lloyd	.75	.35
❑ 90 Barry Sanders	4.00	1.80
❑ 91 Shannon Sharpe	.75	.35
❑ 92 Henry Thomas	.20	.09
❑ 93 Barry Foster	.40	.18
❑ 94 Antone Davis	.20	.09
❑ 95 Stan Humphries	.75	.35
❑ 96 Eric Swann	.40	.18
❑ 97 Mike Pritchard	.40	.18
❑ 98 Reggie White	.75	.35
❑ 99 Jeff Hostetler	.40	.18
❑ 100 Flipper Anderson	.20	.09
❑ 101 Gary Clark	.40	.18
❑ 102 Morten Andersen	.20	.09
❑ 103 Leonard Russell	.40	.18
❑ 104 Chris Hinton	.20	.09
❑ 105 John Stephens	.20	.09
❑ 106 Byron Evans	.20	.09
❑ 107 Warren Moon	.75	.35
❑ 108 Marv Cook	.20	.09
❑ 109 Carlton Gray RC	.20	.09
❑ 110 Jay Novacek	.40	.18
❑ 111 Gary Anderson K	.20	.09
❑ 112 Andre Tippett	.20	.09
❑ 113 Cornelius Bennett	.40	.18
❑ 114 Clyde Simmons	.20	.09
❑ 115 Jeff George	.75	.35
❑ 116 Audray McMillian	.20	.09
❑ 117 Mark Carrier WR	.40	.18
❑ 118 Vaughan Johnson	.20	.09
❑ 119 Kevin Greene	.75	.35
❑ 120 John Taylor	.40	.18
❑ 121 Jerry Ball	.20	.09
❑ 122 Pat Swilling	.20	.09
❑ 123 George Teague RC	.40	.18
❑ 124 Ricky Reynolds	.20	.09
❑ 125 Marcus Allen	.75	.35
❑ 126 Henry Jones	.20	.09
❑ 127 Ricky Watters	.75	.35
❑ 128 Leon Searcy	.20	.09
❑ 129 Chris Miller	.40	.18
❑ 130 Jim Harbaugh	.75	.35
❑ 131 Luis Sharpe	.20	.09
❑ 132 Simon Fletcher	.20	.09
❑ 133 Eric Allen	.20	.09
❑ 134 Carlton Haselrig	.20	.09
❑ 135 Harvey Williams	.40	.18
❑ 136 Leslie O'Neal	.40	.18
❑ 137 Sterling Sharpe	.75	.35
❑ 138 Tim Harris	.20	.09
❑ 139 Mark Rypien	.20	.09
❑ 140 Harry Galbreath	.20	.09
❑ 141 Sean Gilbert	.40	.18
❑ 142 Keith Jackson	.40	.18
❑ 143 Mark Clayton	.20	.09
❑ 144 Guy McIntyre	.20	.09
❑ 145 Jessie Tuggle	.20	.09
❑ 146 Leonard Marshall	.20	.09
❑ 147 Willie Davis	.75	.35
❑ 148 Herman Moore	1.50	.70
❑ 149 Charles Haley	.40	.18
❑ 150 Amp Lee	.20	.09
❑ 151 Gary Zimmerman	.20	.09
❑ 152 Bennie Blades	.20	.09
❑ 153 Pierce Holt	.20	.09
❑ 154 Edgar Bennett	.75	.35
❑ 155 Joe Montana	4.00	1.80
❑ 156 Ted Washington	.20	.09
❑ 157 Hardy Nickerson	.40	.18
❑ 158 Rohn Stark	.20	.09
❑ 159 Brent Jones	.40	.18
❑ 160 Eugene Robinson	.20	.09
❑ 161 Pepper Johnson	.20	.09
❑ 162 Dan Saleaumua	.20	.09
❑ 163 Seth Joyner	.20	.09
❑ 164 Bruce Armstrong	.20	.09
❑ 165 Mike Munchak	.20	.09
❑ 166 Drew Bledsoe RC	6.00	2.70
❑ 167 Curtis Conway RC	1.50	.70
❑ 168 Lincoln Kennedy RC	.20	.09
❑ 169 Dana Stubblefield RC	.75	.35
❑ 170 Wayne Simmons RC	.20	.09
❑ 171 Garrison Hearst RC	2.00	.90
❑ 172 Jerome Bettis RC	2.50	1.10
❑ 173 Eric Curry RC	.20	.09
❑ 174 Natrone Means RC	2.00	.90
❑ 175 Glyn Milburn RC	.75	.35
❑ 176 Marvin Jones RC	.20	.09
❑ 177 O.J. McDuffie RC	2.00	.90
❑ 178 Dan Williams RC	.20	.09
❑ 179 Rick Mirer RC	1.25	.55
❑ 180 John Copeland RC	.40	.18
❑ 181 Willie Roaf RC	.40	.18
❑ 182 Patrick Bates RC	.20	.09
❑ 183 Troy Drayton RC	.40	.18
❑ 184 Vincent Brisby RC	.75	.35
❑ 185 Irv Smith RC	.20	.09
❑ 186 Marion Butts	.20	.09
❑ 187 Wayne Martin	.20	.09
❑ 188 Brian Blades	.40	.18
❑ 189 Mel Gray	.40	.18
❑ 190 Mark Stepnoski	.20	.09
❑ 191 Ernest Givins	.40	.18
❑ 192 Steve Tasker	.40	.18
❑ 193 Tim Grunhard	.20	.09
❑ 194 Stanley Richard	.20	.09
❑ 195 Jeff Wright	.20	.09
❑ 196 Rodney Peete	.20	.09
❑ 197 Tunch Ilkin	.20	.09
❑ 198 Rich Camarillo	.20	.09
❑ 199 Erik Williams	.20	.09
❑ 200 Pete Stoyanovich	.20	.09

1994 Select

	MINT	NRMT
COMPLETE SET (225)	15.00	6.75
❑ 1 Emmitt Smith	2.50	1.10
❑ 2 Bruce Smith	.40	.18
❑ 3 Randall McDaniel	.10	.05
❑ 4 Drew Bledsoe	2.00	.90
❑ 5 Rod Woodson	.40	.18
❑ 6 Richard Dent	.20	.09
❑ 7 Norm Johnson	.10	.05
❑ 8 Jim Everett	.20	.09
❑ 9 Harold Green	.10	.05
❑ 10 John Elway	3.00	1.35
❑ 11 Barry Sanders	3.00	1.35
❑ 12 Sterling Sharpe	.20	.09
❑ 13 Marcus Robertson	.10	.05
❑ 14 Steve Wisniewski	.10	.05
❑ 15 Irving Fryar	.20	.09
❑ 16 Tyrone Hughes	.20	.09
❑ 17 Garrison Hearst	.40	.18
❑ 18 Randall Cunningham	.40	.18
❑ 19 Junior Seau	.40	.18
❑ 20 Rick Mirer	.40	.18
❑ 21 Jerry Rice	1.50	.70
❑ 22 Eric Metcalf	.20	.09
❑ 23 Roosevelt Potts	.10	.05
❑ 24 Neil Smith	.40	.18
❑ 25 Jerome Bettis	.40	.18
❑ 26 Keith Hamilton	.10	.05
❑ 27 Hardy Nickerson	.20	.09
❑ 28 Steve Tasker	.20	.09
❑ 29 Johnny Johnson	.10	.05
❑ 30 Tom Carter	.10	.05
❑ 31 Andre Rison	.20	.09
❑ 32 Cortez Kennedy	.20	.09
❑ 33 Mark Carrier DB	.10	.05
❑ 34 Shannon Sharpe	.20	.09
❑ 35 Eric Swann	.20	.09
❑ 36 Steve Young	1.25	.55
❑ 37 Johnny Mitchell	.10	.05
❑ 38 Dermontti Dawson	.10	.05
❑ 39 Mike Johnson	.10	.05
❑ 40 Troy Aikman	1.50	.70
❑ 41 Pierce Holt	.10	.05
❑ 42 Derrick Thomas	.40	.18
❑ 43 Reggie Cobb	.10	.05
❑ 44 Michael Jackson	.20	.09
❑ 45 Lomas Brown	.10	.05
❑ 46 Jeff Hostetler	.20	.09
❑ 47 Pete Stoyanovich	.10	.05
❑ 48 Reggie White	.40	.18
❑ 49 Quentin Coryatt	.10	.05
❑ 50 Cris Carter	.75	.35
❑ 51 Sean Gilbert	.10	.05
❑ 52 Chris Slade	.10	.05
❑ 53 Ronnie Harmon	.10	.05
❑ 54 Renaldo Turnbull	.10	.05
❑ 55 Fred Barnett	.20	.09
❑ 56 John Elliott	.10	.05
❑ 57 Deion Sanders	.75	.35
❑ 58 John Carney	.10	.05
❑ 59 Louis Oliver	.10	.05
❑ 60 Greg Lloyd	.40	.18
❑ 61 Chris Hinton	.10	.05
❑ 62 Ronald Moore	.10	.05
❑ 63 Vincent Brown	.10	.05
❑ 64 Tony McGee	.10	.05
❑ 65 Erik Williams	.10	.05
❑ 66 Thurman Thomas	.40	.18
❑ 67 Neil O'Donnell	.40	.18
❑ 68 Scott Mitchell	.40	.18
❑ 69 Keith Byars	.10	.05
❑ 70 Henry Ellard	.20	.09
❑ 71 Chris Spielman	.20	.09
❑ 72 LeRoy Butler	.10	.05
❑ 73 Tim Brown	.40	.18
❑ 74 Darrell Green	.10	.05
❑ 75 Bruce Matthews	.10	.05
❑ 76 Stan Humphries	.40	.18
❑ 77 Will Wolford	.10	.05
❑ 78 John Taylor	.20	.09
❑ 79 Joe Montana	3.00	1.35
❑ 80 Chris Warren	.20	.09
❑ 81 Michael Brooks	.10	.05
❑ 82 Vance Johnson	.10	.05
❑ 83 Rob Moore	.20	.09
❑ 84 Herschel Walker	.20	.09
❑ 85 Alvin Harper	.20	.09
❑ 86 Wayne Martin	.10	.05
❑ 87 Leslie O'Neal	.10	.05
❑ 88 Flipper Anderson	.10	.05
❑ 89 Tommy Vardell	.10	.05
❑ 90 Mike Sherrard	.10	.05
❑ 91 Chris Jacke	.10	.05
❑ 92 Jim Kelly	.40	.18
❑ 93 Jeff Graham	.10	.05
❑ 94 Bryan Cox	.10	.05
❑ 95 Michael Irvin	.40	.18
❑ 96 Jeff Lageman	.10	.05
❑ 97 Webster Slaughter	.10	.05
❑ 98 Eugene Robinson	.10	.05
❑ 99 Vencie Glenn	.10	.05
❑ 100 Sean Jones	.10	.05
❑ 101 Calvin Williams	.20	.09
❑ 102 Jim Harbaugh	.40	.18
❑ 103 Eric Curry	.10	.05
❑ 104 Terry Allen	.20	.09
❑ 105 Darryl Williams	.10	.05

No.	Player	MINT	NRMT
❑ 106	Gary Clark	.20	.09
❑ 107	Marcus Allen	.40	.18
❑ 108	Chip Lohmiller	.10	.05
❑ 109	Vaughan Johnson	.10	.05
❑ 110	Herman Moore	.40	.18
❑ 111	Barry Foster	.10	.05
❑ 112	Rocket Ismail	.20	.09
❑ 113	Erric Pegram	.10	.05
❑ 114	Anthony Miller	.20	.09
❑ 115	Shane Conlan	.10	.05
❑ 116	David Klingler	.10	.05
❑ 117	Mark Collins	.10	.05
❑ 118	Tony Bennett	.10	.05
❑ 119	Donnell Woolford	.10	.05
❑ 120	Reggie Brooks	.20	.09
❑ 121	Sam Mills	.10	.05
❑ 122	Greg Montgomery	.10	.05
❑ 123	Kevin Greene	.40	.18
❑ 124	Terry McDaniel	.10	.05
❑ 125	Henry Jones	.10	.05
❑ 126	Ricky Watters	.40	.18
❑ 127	Dan Marino	3.00	1.35
❑ 128	Steve Atwater	.10	.05
❑ 129	Ricky Proehl	.10	.05
❑ 130	Ernest Givins	.20	.09
❑ 131	John L. Williams	.10	.05
❑ 132	John Randle	.20	.09
❑ 133	Jay Novacek	.20	.09
❑ 134	Boomer Esiason	.20	.09
❑ 135	Jessie Hester	.10	.05
❑ 136	Courtney Hawkins	.10	.05
❑ 137	Ben Coates	.40	.18
❑ 138	Stevon Moore	.10	.05
❑ 139	Eric Allen	.10	.05
❑ 140	Jessie Tuggle	.10	.05
❑ 141	Marion Butts	.10	.05
❑ 142	Brett Favre	3.00	1.35
❑ 143	Andre Reed	.20	.09
❑ 144	Rodney Hampton	.40	.18
❑ 145	Keith Sims	.10	.05
❑ 146	Derek Brown RBK	.10	.05
❑ 147	Eric Green	.10	.05
❑ 148	Greg Robinson	.10	.05
❑ 149	Nate Newton	.10	.05
❑ 150	Mark Higgs	.10	.05
❑ 151	Nick Lowery	.10	.05
❑ 152	Craig Erickson	.10	.05
❑ 153	Anthony Carter	.20	.09
❑ 154	Simon Fletcher	.10	.05
❑ 155	Ronnie Lott	.20	.09
❑ 156	Gary Brown	.10	.05
❑ 157	Brent Jones	.20	.09
❑ 158	Jim Sweeney	.10	.05
❑ 159	Robert Brooks	.40	.18
❑ 160	Keith Jackson	.10	.05
❑ 161	Daryl Johnston	.20	.09
❑ 162	Tom Waddle	.10	.05
❑ 163	Eric Martin	.10	.05
❑ 164	Cornelius Bennett	.20	.09
❑ 165	Tim McDonald	.10	.05
❑ 166	Chris Doleman	.10	.05
❑ 167	Gary Zimmerman	.10	.05
❑ 168	Al Smith	.10	.05
❑ 169	Mark Carrier WR	.20	.09
❑ 170	Harris Barton	.10	.05
❑ 171	Ray Childress	.10	.05
❑ 172	Darryl Talley	.10	.05
❑ 173	James Jett	.10	.05
❑ 174	Mark Stepnoski	.10	.05
❑ 175	Jeff Query	.10	.05
❑ 176	Charles Haley	.20	.09
❑ 177	Rod Bernstine	.10	.05
❑ 178	Richmond Webb	.10	.05
❑ 179	Rich Camarillo	.10	.05
❑ 180	Pat Swilling	.10	.05
❑ 181	Chris Miller	.10	.05
❑ 182	Mike Pritchard	.10	.05
❑ 183	Checklist NFC	.10	.05
❑ 184	Natrone Means	.40	.18
❑ 185	Erik Kramer	.20	.09
❑ 186	Clyde Simmons	.10	.05
❑ 187	Checklist AFC/NFC	.10	.05
❑ 188	Warren Moon	.40	.18
❑ 189	Michael Haynes	.20	.09
❑ 190	Terry Kirby	.40	.18
❑ 191	Brian Blades	.20	.09
❑ 192	Haywood Jeffires	.20	.09
❑ 193	Thomas Everett	.10	.05
❑ 194	Morten Andersen	.10	.05
❑ 195	Dana Stubblefield	.40	.18
❑ 196	Ken Norton	.20	.09
❑ 197	Art Monk	.20	.09
❑ 198	Seth Joyner	.10	.05
❑ 199	Heath Shuler RC	.40	.18
❑ 200	Marshall Faulk RC	5.00	2.20
❑ 201	Charles Johnson RC	1.00	.45
❑ 202	Der.Alexander WR RC	1.00	.45
❑ 203	Greg Hill RC	.40	.18
❑ 204	Darnay Scott RC	1.50	.70
❑ 205	Willie McGinest RC	.40	.18
❑ 206	Thomas Randolph RC	.10	.05
❑ 207	Errict Rhett RC	1.00	.45
❑ 208	William Floyd RC	.40	.18
❑ 209	Johnnie Morton RC	1.50	.70
❑ 210	David Palmer RC	1.00	.45
❑ 211	Dan Wilkinson RC	.20	.09
❑ 212	Trent Dilfer RC	2.00	.90
❑ 213	Antonio Langham RC	.20	.09
❑ 214	Chuck Levy RC	.10	.05
❑ 215	John Thierry RC	.10	.05
❑ 216	Kevin Lee RC	.10	.05
❑ 217	Aaron Glenn RC	.20	.09
❑ 218	Charlie Garner RC	1.50	.70
❑ 219	Jeff Burris RC	.20	.09
❑ 220	LeShon Johnson RC	.20	.09
❑ 221	Thomas Lewis RC	.20	.09
❑ 222	Ryan Yarborough RC	.10	.05
❑ 223	Mario Bates RC	.40	.18
❑ 224	Checklist NFC/AFC	.10	.05
❑ 225	Checklist AFC	.10	.05
❑ SR1	Marshall Faulk SR	35.00	16.00
❑ SR2	Dan Wilkinson SR	8.00	3.60

1996 Select

		MINT	NRMT
COMPLETE SET (200)		20.00	9.00
❑ 1	Troy Aikman	1.00	.45
❑ 2	Marshall Faulk	.40	.18
❑ 3	Kordell Stewart	.60	.25
❑ 4	Larry Centers	.20	.09
❑ 5	Tamarick Vanover	.20	.09
❑ 6	Ken Norton Jr.	.10	.05
❑ 7	Steve Tasker	.10	.05
❑ 8	Dan Marino	2.00	.90
❑ 9	Heath Shuler	.20	.09
❑ 10	Anthony Miller	.20	.09
❑ 11	Mario Bates	.20	.09
❑ 12	Natrone Means	.40	.18
❑ 13	Darren Woodson	.20	.09
❑ 14	Chris Sanders	.20	.09
❑ 15	Chris Warren	.20	.09
❑ 16	Eric Metcalf	.10	.05
❑ 17	Quentin Coryatt	.10	.05
❑ 18	Jeff Hostetler	.10	.05
❑ 19	Brett Favre	2.00	.90
❑ 20	Curtis Martin	.75	.35
❑ 21	Floyd Turner	.10	.05
❑ 22	Curtis Conway	.40	.18
❑ 23	Orlando Thomas	.10	.05
❑ 24	Lee Woodall	.10	.05
❑ 25	Darick Holmes	.10	.05
❑ 26	Marcus Allen	.40	.18
❑ 27	Ricky Watters	.20	.09
❑ 28	Herman Moore	.40	.18
❑ 29	Rodney Hampton	.20	.09
❑ 30	Alvin Harper	.10	.05
❑ 31	Jeff Blake	.40	.18
❑ 32	Wayne Chrebet	.60	.25
❑ 33	Jerry Rice	1.00	.45
❑ 34	Dave Krieg	.10	.05
❑ 35	Mark Brunell	1.00	.45
❑ 36	Terry Allen	.20	.09
❑ 37	Emmitt Smith	1.50	.70
❑ 38	Bryan Cox	.10	.05
❑ 39	Tony Martin	.20	.09
❑ 40	John Elway	2.00	.90
❑ 41	Warren Moon	.20	.09
❑ 42	Yancey Thigpen	.20	.09
❑ 43	Jeff George	.20	.09
❑ 44	Rodney Thomas	.10	.05
❑ 45	Joey Galloway	.60	.25
❑ 46	Jim Kelly	.40	.18
❑ 47	Drew Bledsoe	1.00	.45
❑ 48	Greg Lloyd	.20	.09
❑ 49	Michael Irvin	.40	.18
❑ 50	Quinn Early	.10	.05
❑ 51	Brent Jones	.10	.05
❑ 52	Rashaan Salaam	.40	.18
❑ 53	James O.Stewart	.20	.09
❑ 54	Gus Frerotte	.40	.18
❑ 55	Edgar Bennett	.20	.09
❑ 56	Lamont Warren	.10	.05
❑ 57	Napoleon Kaufman	.40	.18
❑ 58	Kevin Williams	.10	.05
❑ 59	Irving Fryar	.20	.09
❑ 60	Trent Dilfer	.40	.18
❑ 61	Eric Zeier	.10	.05
❑ 62	Tyrone Wheatley	.20	.09
❑ 63	Isaac Bruce	.40	.18
❑ 64	Terrell Davis	2.50	1.10
❑ 65	Lake Dawson	.10	.05
❑ 66	Carnell Lake	.10	.05
❑ 67	Kerry Collins	.40	.18
❑ 68	Kyle Brady	.10	.05
❑ 69	Rodney Peete	.10	.05
❑ 70	Carl Pickens	.40	.18
❑ 71	Robert Smith	.20	.09
❑ 72	Rod Woodson	.20	.09
❑ 73	Deion Sanders	.60	.25
❑ 74	Sean Dawkins	.10	.05
❑ 75	William Floyd	.20	.09
❑ 76	Barry Sanders	2.00	.90
❑ 77	Ben Coates	.20	.09
❑ 78	Neil O'Donnell	.20	.09
❑ 79	Bill Brooks	.10	.05
❑ 80	Steve Bono	.10	.05
❑ 81	Jay Novacek	.10	.05
❑ 82	Bernie Parmalee	.10	.05
❑ 83	Derek Loville	.10	.05
❑ 84	Frank Sanders	.20	.09
❑ 85	Robert Brooks	.40	.18
❑ 86	Jim Harbaugh	.20	.09
❑ 87	Rick Mirer	.20	.09
❑ 88	Craig Heyward	.10	.05
❑ 89	Greg Hill	.20	.09
❑ 90	Andre Coleman	.10	.05
❑ 91	Shannon Sharpe	.20	.09
❑ 92	Hugh Douglas	.20	.09
❑ 93	Andre Hastings	.10	.05
❑ 94	Bryce Paup	.10	.05
❑ 95	Jim Everett	.10	.05
❑ 96	Brian Mitchell	.10	.05
❑ 97	Jeff Graham	.10	.05
❑ 98	Steve McNair	.75	.35
❑ 99	Charlie Garner	.10	.05
❑ 100	Willie McGinest	.10	.05
❑ 101	Harvey Williams	.10	.05
❑ 102	Daryl Johnston	.20	.09
❑ 103	Cris Carter	.40	.18
❑ 104	J.J. Stokes	.40	.18
❑ 105	Garrison Hearst	.20	.09
❑ 106	Mark Chmura	.20	.09
❑ 107	Derrick Thomas	.20	.09
❑ 108	Errict Rhett	.20	.09
❑ 109	Terance Mathis	.10	.05
❑ 110	Dave Brown	.10	.05
❑ 111	Erric Pegram	.10	.05
❑ 112	Scott Mitchell	.20	.09

❑	113 Aaron Bailey	.10	.05
❑	114 Stan Humphries	.20	.09
❑	115 Bruce Smith	.20	.09
❑	116 Rob Johnson	.40	.18
❑	117 O.J. McDuffie	.20	.09
❑	118 Brian Blades	.10	.05
❑	119 Steve Atwater	.10	.05
❑	120 Tyrone Hughes	.10	.05
❑	121 Michael Westbrook	.40	.18
❑	122 Ki-Jana Carter	.20	.09
❑	123 Adrian Murrell	.40	.18
❑	124 Steve Young	.75	.35
❑	125 Charles Haley	.20	.09
❑	126 Vincent Brisby	.10	.05
❑	127 Jerome Bettis	.40	.18
❑	128 Erik Kramer	.10	.05
❑	129 Roosevelt Potts	.10	.05
❑	130 Tim Brown	.40	.18
❑	131 Reggie White	.40	.18
❑	132 Jake Reed	.20	.09
❑	133 Junior Seau	.20	.09
❑	134 Stoney Case	.10	.05
❑	135 Kimble Anders	.20	.09
❑	136 Brett Perriman	.10	.05
❑	137 Todd Collins	.20	.09
❑	138 Sherman Williams	.10	.05
❑	139 Hardy Nickerson	.10	.05
❑	140 Ernie Mills	.10	.05
❑	141 Glyn Milburn	.10	.05
❑	142 Terry Kirby	.20	.09
❑	143 Bert Emanuel	.20	.09
❑	144 Aeneas Williams	.10	.05
❑	145 Aaron Craver	.10	.05
❑	146 Jackie Harris	.10	.05
❑	147 Thurman Thomas	.40	.18
❑	148 Aaron Hayden RC	.10	.05
❑	149 Antonio Freeman	.75	.35
❑	150 Kevin Greene	.20	.09
❑	151 Kevin Hardy RC	.40	.18
❑	152 Eric Moulds RC	2.00	.90
❑	153 Tim Biakabutuka RC	.75	.35
❑	154 Keyshawn Johnson RC	2.00	.90
❑	155 Jeff Lewis RC	.50	.23
❑	156 Stepfret Williams RC	.20	.09
❑	157 Tony Brackens RC	.20	.09
❑	158 Mike Alstott RC	1.50	.70
❑	159 Willie Anderson RC	.10	.05
❑	160 Marvin Harrison RC	2.50	1.10
❑	161 Regan Upshaw RC	.10	.05
❑	162 Bobby Engram RC	.40	.18
❑	163 Leeland McElroy RC	.40	.18
❑	164 Alex Van Dyke RC	.20	.09
❑	165 Stanley Pritchett RC	.20	.09
❑	166 Cedric Jones RC	.10	.05
❑	167 Terry Glenn RC	1.25	.55
❑	168 Eddie George RC	4.00	1.80
❑	169 Lawrence Phillips RC	.40	.18
❑	170 Jonathan Ogden RC	.10	.05
❑	171 Danny Kanell RC	.40	.18
❑	172 Alex Molden RC	.10	.05
❑	173 Daryl Gardener RC	.10	.05
❑	174 Derrick Mayes RC	.75	.35
❑	175 Marco Battaglia RC	.10	.05
❑	176 Jon Stark RC	.10	.05
❑	177 Karim Abdul-Jabbar RC	.50	.23
❑	178 Stephen Davis RC	4.00	1.80
❑	179 Rickey Dudley RC	.40	.18
❑	180 Eddie Kennison RC	.40	.18
❑	181 Barry Sanders FF	1.00	.45
❑	182 Brett Favre FF	1.00	.45
❑	183 John Elway FF	1.00	.45
❑	184 Steve Young FF	.40	.18
❑	185 Michael Irvin FF	.20	.09
❑	186 Jerry Rice FF	.50	.23
❑	187 Emmitt Smith FF	.75	.35
❑	188 Isaac Bruce FF	.40	.18
❑	189 Chris Warren FF	.20	.09
❑	190 Errict Rhett FF	.20	.09
❑	191 Herman Moore FF	.40	.18
❑	192 Carl Pickens FF	.40	.18
❑	193 Cris Carter FF	.40	.18
❑	194 Terrell Davis FF	1.25	.55
❑	195 Rodney Thomas FF	.10	.05
❑	196 Dan Marino CL	.40	.18
❑	197 Drew Bledsoe CL	.20	.09
❑	198 Emmitt Smith CL	.40	.18
❑	199 Jerry Rice CL	.40	.18
❑	200 Barry Sanders CL John Elway	.40	.18

1995 Select Certified

		MINT	NRMT
	COMPLETE SET (135)	80.00	36.00
❑	1 Marshall Faulk	2.00	.90
❑	2 Heath Shuler	1.00	.45
❑	3 Garrison Hearst	1.00	.45
❑	4 Errict Rhett	1.00	.45
❑	5 Jeff George	.50	.23
❑	6 Jerome Bettis	1.00	.45
❑	7 Jim Kelly	1.00	.45
❑	8 Rick Mirer	1.00	.45
❑	9 Willie Davis	.50	.23
❑	10 Steve Young	2.50	1.10
❑	11 Erik Kramer	.25	.11
❑	12 Natrone Means	1.00	.45
❑	13 Jeff Blake RC	5.00	2.20
❑	14 Neil O'Donnell	.50	.23
❑	15 Andre Rison	.50	.23
❑	16 Randall Cunningham	1.00	.45
❑	17 Emmitt Smith	5.00	2.20
❑	18 Tim Brown	1.00	.45
❑	19 Shannon Sharpe	.50	.23
❑	20 Boomer Esiason	.50	.23
❑	21 Barry Sanders	6.00	2.70
❑	22 Rodney Hampton	.50	.23
❑	23 Robert Brooks	1.00	.45
❑	24 Jim Everett	.25	.11
❑	25 Gary Brown	.25	.11
❑	26 Drew Bledsoe	3.00	1.35
❑	27 Desmond Howard	.50	.23
❑	28 Cris Carter	1.00	.45
❑	29 Marcus Allen	1.00	.45
❑	30 Dan Marino	6.00	2.70
❑	31 Warren Moon	.50	.23
❑	32 Dave Krieg	.25	.11
❑	33 Ben Coates	.50	.23
❑	34 Terance Mathis	.50	.23
❑	35 Mario Bates	1.00	.45
❑	36 Andre Reed	.50	.23
❑	37 Dave Brown	.50	.23
❑	38 Jeff Graham	.25	.11
❑	39 Johnny Mitchell	.25	.11
❑	40 Carl Pickens	1.00	.45
❑	41 Jeff Hostetler	.50	.23
❑	42 Vinny Testaverde	.50	.23
❑	43 Ricky Watters	1.00	.45
❑	44 Troy Aikman	3.00	1.35
❑	45 Byron Bam Morris	.50	.23
❑	46 John Elway	6.00	2.70
❑	47 Junior Seau	1.00	.45
❑	48 Scott Mitchell	.50	.23
❑	49 Jerry Rice	3.00	1.35
❑	50 Brett Favre	6.00	2.70
❑	51 Chris Warren	.50	.23
❑	52 Chris Chandler	.50	.23
❑	53 Lorenzo White	.25	.11
❑	54 Craig Erickson	.25	.11
❑	55 Alvin Harper	.25	.11
❑	56 Steve Beuerlein	.25	.11
❑	57 Edgar Bennett	.50	.23
❑	58 Steve Bono	.50	.23
❑	59 Eric Green	.25	.11
❑	60 Jake Reed	.50	.23
❑	61 Terry Kirby	.50	.23
❑	62 Vincent Brisby	.25	.11
❑	63 Lake Dawson	.50	.23
❑	64 Torrance Small	.25	.11
❑	65 Mark Brunell	3.00	1.35
❑	66 Haywood Jeffires	.25	.11
❑	67 Flipper Anderson	.25	.11
❑	68 Ronald Moore	.25	.11
❑	69 LeShon Johnson	.50	.23
❑	70 Rocket Ismail	.50	.23
❑	71 Herman Moore	1.00	.45
❑	72 Charlie Garner	.50	.23
❑	73 Anthony Miller	.50	.23
❑	74 Greg Lloyd	.50	.23
❑	75 Michael Irvin	1.00	.45
❑	76 Stan Humphries	.50	.23
❑	77 Leroy Hoard	.25	.11
❑	78 Deion Sanders Card mailed to dealers	3.00	1.35
❑	79 Darnay Scott	1.00	.45
❑	80 Chris Miller	.25	.11
❑	81 Curtis Conway	1.00	.45
❑	82 Trent Dilfer	1.00	.45
❑	83 Bruce Smith	1.00	.45
❑	84 Reggie Brooks	.50	.23
❑	85 Frank Reich	.25	.11
❑	86 Henry Ellard	.50	.23
❑	87 Eric Metcalf	.50	.23
❑	88 Sean Gilbert	.50	.23
❑	89 Larry Centers	.50	.23
❑	90 Ricky Ervins	.25	.11
❑	91 Craig Heyward	.50	.23
❑	92 Rod Woodson	.50	.23
❑	93 Steve Walsh	.25	.11
❑	94 Fred Barnett	.50	.23
❑	95 William Floyd	1.00	.45
❑	96 Harvey Williams	.25	.11
❑	97 Greg Hill	.50	.23
❑	98 Irving Fryar	.50	.23
❑	99 Kevin Williams	.50	.23
❑	100 Herschel Walker	.50	.23
❑	101 Sean Dawkins	.50	.23
❑	102 Michael Haynes	.50	.23
❑	103 Reggie White	1.00	.45
❑	104 Robert Smith	1.00	.45
❑	105 Todd Collins RC	1.00	.45
❑	106 Michael Westbrook RC	10.00	4.50
❑	107 Frank Sanders RC	6.00	2.70
❑	108 Christian Fauria RC	.25	.11
❑	109 Stoney Case RC	1.00	.45
❑	110 Jimmy Oliver RC	.25	.11
❑	111 Mark Bruener RC	.50	.23
❑	112 Rodney Thomas RC	1.00	.45
❑	113 Chris T.Jones RC	1.00	.45
❑	114 James A.Stewart RC	.25	.11
❑	115 Kevin Carter RC	1.00	.45
❑	116 Eric Zeier RC	1.00	.45
❑	117 Curtis Martin RC	12.00	5.50
❑	118 James O. Stewart RC	12.00	5.50
❑	119 Joe Aska RC	.50	.23
❑	120 Ken Dilger RC	.50	.23
❑	121 Tyrone Wheatley RC	6.00	2.70
❑	122 Ray Zellars RC	.50	.23
❑	123 Kyle Brady RC	1.00	.45
❑	124 Chad May RC	.25	.11
❑	125 Napoleon Kaufman RC	10.00	4.50
❑	126 Terrell Davis RC	30.00	13.50
❑	127 Warren Sapp RC	3.00	1.35
❑	128 Sherman Williams RC	.25	.11
❑	129 Kordell Stewart RC	10.00	4.50
❑	130 Ki-Jana Carter RC	1.00	.45
❑	131 Terrell Fletcher RC	.25	.11
❑	132 Rashaan Salaam RC	1.00	.45
❑	133 J.J. Stokes RC	1.00	.45
❑	134 Kerry Collins RC	10.00	4.50
❑	135 Joey Galloway RC	10.00	4.50
❑	P7 Dan Marino Promo Gold Team Card	5.00	2.20
❑	P10 Steve Young Promo	2.00	.90
❑	P44 Troy Aikman Promo	2.50	1.10

1996 Select Certified

	MINT	NRMT
COMPLETE SET (125)	60.00	27.00

Card	MINT	NRMT
❑ 1 Isaac Bruce	.75	.35
❑ 2 Rick Mirer	.40	.18
❑ 3 Jake Reed	.40	.18
❑ 4 Reggie White	.75	.35
❑ 5 Harvey Williams	.20	.09
❑ 6 Jim Everett	.20	.09
❑ 7 Tony Martin	.40	.18
❑ 8 Craig Heyward	.20	.09
❑ 9 Tamarick Vanover	.40	.18
❑ 10 Hugh Douglas	.40	.18
❑ 11 Erik Kramer	.20	.09
❑ 12 Charlie Garner	.20	.09
❑ 13 Erric Pegram	.20	.09
❑ 14 Scott Mitchell	.40	.18
❑ 15 Michael Westbrook	.75	.35
❑ 16 Robert Smith	.40	.18
❑ 17 Kerry Collins	.75	.35
❑ 18 Derek Loville	.20	.09
❑ 19 Jeff Blake	.75	.35
❑ 20 Terry Kirby	.40	.18
❑ 21 Bruce Smith	.40	.18
❑ 22 Stan Humphries	.40	.18
❑ 23 Rodney Thomas	.20	.09
❑ 24 Wayne Chrebet	1.25	.55
❑ 25 Napoleon Kaufman	.75	.35
❑ 26 Marshall Faulk	.75	.35
❑ 27 Emmitt Smith	3.00	1.35
❑ 28 Natrone Means	.75	.35
❑ 29 Neil O'Donnell	.40	.18
❑ 30 Warren Moon	.40	.18
❑ 31 Junior Seau	.40	.18
❑ 32 Chris Sanders	.40	.18
❑ 33 Barry Sanders	4.00	1.80
❑ 34 Jeff Graham	.20	.09
❑ 35 Kordell Stewart	1.25	.55
❑ 36 Jim Harbaugh	.40	.18
❑ 37 Chris Warren	.40	.18
❑ 38 Cris Carter	.75	.35
❑ 39 J.J. Stokes	.75	.35
❑ 40 Tyrone Wheatley	.40	.18
❑ 41 Terrell Davis	5.00	2.20
❑ 42 Mark Brunell	2.00	.90
❑ 43 Steve Young	1.50	.70
❑ 44 Rodney Hampton	.40	.18
❑ 45 Drew Bledsoe	2.00	.90
❑ 46 Larry Centers	.40	.18
❑ 47 Ken Norton Jr.	.20	.09
❑ 48 Deion Sanders	1.25	.55
❑ 49 Alvin Harper	.20	.09
❑ 50 Trent Dilfer	.75	.35
❑ 51 Steve McNair	1.50	.70
❑ 52 Robert Brooks	.75	.35
❑ 53 Edgar Bennett	.40	.18
❑ 54 Troy Aikman	2.00	.90
❑ 55 Dan Marino	4.00	1.80
❑ 56 Steve Bono	.20	.09
❑ 57 Marcus Allen	.75	.35
❑ 58 Rodney Peete	.20	.09
❑ 59 Ben Coates	.40	.18
❑ 60 Yancey Thigpen	.40	.18
❑ 61 Tim Brown	.75	.35
❑ 62 Jerry Rice	2.00	.90
❑ 63 Quinn Early	.20	.09
❑ 64 Ricky Watters	.40	.18
❑ 65 Thurman Thomas	.75	.35
❑ 66 Greg Lloyd	.40	.18
❑ 67 Eric Metcalf	.20	.09
❑ 68 Jeff George	.40	.18
❑ 69 John Elway	4.00	1.80
❑ 70 Frank Sanders	.40	.18
❑ 71 Curtis Conway	.75	.35
❑ 72 Greg Hill	.40	.18
❑ 73 Darick Holmes	.20	.09
❑ 74 Herman Moore	.75	.35
❑ 75 Carl Pickens	.75	.35
❑ 76 Eric Zeier	.20	.09
❑ 77 Curtis Martin	1.50	.70
❑ 78 Rashaan Salaam	.75	.35
❑ 79 Joey Galloway	1.25	.55
❑ 80 Jeff Hostetler	.20	.09
❑ 81 Jim Kelly	.75	.35
❑ 82 Dave Brown	.20	.09
❑ 83 Sean Dawkins	.20	.09
❑ 84 Michael Irvin	.75	.35
❑ 85 Brett Favre	4.00	1.80
❑ 86 Cedric Jones RC	.25	.11
❑ 87 Jeff Lewis RC	.60	.25
❑ 88 Alex Van Dyke RC	.50	.23
❑ 89 Regan Upshaw RC	.25	.11
❑ 90 Karim Abdul-Jabbar RC	2.50	1.10
❑ 91 Marvin Harrison RC	10.00	4.50
❑ 92 Stephen Davis RC	15.00	6.75
❑ 93 Terry Glenn RC	4.00	1.80
❑ 94 Kevin Hardy RC	1.00	.45
❑ 95 Stanley Pritchett RC	.25	.11
❑ 96 Willie Anderson RC	.25	.11
❑ 97 Lawrence Phillips RC	.50	.23
❑ 98 Bobby Hoying RC	2.00	.90
❑ 99 Amani Toomer RC	4.00	1.80
❑ 100 Eddie George RC	15.00	6.75
❑ 101 Stepfret Williams RC	.25	.11
❑ 102 Eric Moulds RC	6.00	2.70
❑ 103 Simeon Rice RC	1.00	.45
❑ 104 John Mobley RC	.25	.11
❑ 105 Keyshawn Johnson RC	6.00	2.70
❑ 106 Daryl Gardener RC	.25	.11
❑ 107 Tony Banks RC	4.00	1.80
❑ 108 Bobby Engram RC	1.00	.45
❑ 109 Jonathan Ogden RC	.25	.11
❑ 110 Eddie Kennison RC	1.00	.45
❑ 111 Danny Kanell RC	1.00	.45
❑ 112 Tony Brackens RC	1.00	.45
❑ 113 Tim Biakabutuka RC	2.50	1.10
❑ 114 Leeland McElroy RC	1.00	.45
❑ 115 Rickey Dudley RC	1.00	.45
❑ 116 Troy Aikman SS	1.00	.45
❑ 117 Brett Favre SS	2.00	.90
❑ 118 Drew Bledsoe SS	1.00	.45
❑ 119 Steve Young SS	.75	.35
❑ 120 Kerry Collins SS	.75	.35
❑ 121 John Elway SS	2.00	.90
❑ 122 Dan Marino SS	2.00	.90
❑ 123 Kordell Stewart SS	.75	.35
❑ 124 Jeff Blake SS	.40	.18
❑ 125 Jim Harbaugh SS	.40	.18

2000 SkyBox

	MINT	NRMT
COMPLETE SET (300)	400.00	180.00
COMP.SET w/o SPs (250)	30.00	13.50

Card	MINT	NRMT
❑ 1 Tim Couch	1.00	.45
❑ 2 Edgerrin James	1.25	.55
❑ 3 Wesley Walls	.15	.07
❑ 4 Brian Griese	.60	.25
❑ 5 Herman Moore	.25	.11
❑ 6 Mark Brunell	.75	.35
❑ 7 John Randle	.25	.11
❑ 8 Victor Green	.15	.07
❑ 9 Michael Sinclair	.15	.07
❑ 10 Jevon Kearse	.50	.23
❑ 11 Peter Boulware	.15	.07
❑ 12 Kevin Johnson	.50	.23
❑ 13 Vonnie Holliday	.15	.07
❑ 14 Jason Taylor	.25	.11
❑ 15 Cam Cleeland	.15	.07
❑ 16 Jeff Graham	.15	.07
❑ 17 Jacquez Green	.25	.11
❑ 18 Chris McAlister	.15	.07
❑ 19 Takeo Spikes	.15	.07
❑ 20 Marvin Harrison	.50	.23
❑ 21 Jay Fiedler	.50	.23
❑ 22 Jake Reed	.25	.11
❑ 23 Jerry Rice	1.25	.55
❑ 24 Shaun King	.75	.35
❑ 25 Donovan McNabb	.75	.35
❑ 26 David Boston	.50	.23
❑ 27 Curtis Enis	.25	.11
❑ 28 Olandis Gary	.50	.23
❑ 29 James Stewart	.25	.11
❑ 30 Jimmy Smith	.25	.11
❑ 31 Randy Moss	1.50	.70
❑ 32 Keyshawn Johnson	.50	.23
❑ 33 Kevin Carter	.15	.07
❑ 34 Stephen Davis	.50	.23
❑ 35 Jay Riemersma	.15	.07
❑ 36 Emmitt Smith	1.25	.55
❑ 37 E.G. Green	.15	.07
❑ 38 Dwayne Rudd	.15	.07
❑ 39 Michael Strahan	.15	.07
❑ 40 Troy Edwards	.25	.11
❑ 41 Derrick Mayes	.25	.11
❑ 42 Eddie George	.60	.25
❑ 43 Bruce Smith	.25	.11
❑ 44 Andre Wadsworth	.15	.07
❑ 45 Bobby Engram	.25	.11
❑ 46 Byron Chamberlain	.15	.07
❑ 47 Antonio Freeman	.50	.23
❑ 48 Hardy Nickerson	.15	.07
❑ 49 Terry Glenn	.25	.11
❑ 50 Wayne Chrebet	.25	.11
❑ 51 London Fletcher RC	.15	.07
❑ 52 Michael Westbrook	.25	.11
❑ 53 Rob Moore	.25	.11
❑ 54 Eddie Kennison	.25	.11
❑ 55 Ed McCaffrey	.50	.23
❑ 56 Dorsey Levens	.25	.11
❑ 57 Andre Rison	.15	.07
❑ 58 Willie McGinest	.15	.07
❑ 59 Tyrone Wheatley	.25	.11
❑ 60 Kurt Warner	2.00	.90
❑ 61 Stephen Alexander	.15	.07
❑ 62 Jessie Tuggle	.15	.07
❑ 63 Jim Miller	.15	.07
❑ 64 Luther Elliss	.15	.07
❑ 65 Bill Schroeder	.25	.11
❑ 66 Elvis Grbac	.25	.11
❑ 67 Ty Law	.15	.07
❑ 68 Tim Brown	.50	.23
❑ 69 Marshall Faulk	.60	.25
❑ 70 Champ Bailey	.25	.11
❑ 71 Charlie Batch	.50	.23
❑ 72 Steve Beuerlein	.25	.11
❑ 73 Rocket Ismail	.25	.11
❑ 74 Kevin Hardy	.15	.07
❑ 75 Zach Thomas	.25	.11
❑ 76 Aaron Glenn	.15	.07
❑ 77 Jerome Bettis	.50	.23
❑ 78 Chris Chandler	.25	.11
❑ 79 Marcus Robinson	.50	.23
❑ 80 Derrick Alexander	.25	.11
❑ 81 Drew Bledsoe	.75	.35
❑ 82 Charles Woodson	.25	.11
❑ 83 Isaac Bruce	.50	.23
❑ 84 Darrell Green	.15	.07
❑ 85 Tim Dwight	.50	.23
❑ 86 Darnay Scott	.25	.11

❑ 87 Chris Claiborne .15 .07
❑ 88 Tony Gonzalez .25 .11
❑ 89 Tony Simmons .15 .07
❑ 90 Rich Gannon .25 .11
❑ 91 Torry Holt .50 .23
❑ 92 Jamal Anderson .50 .23
❑ 93 Akili Smith .50 .23
❑ 94 Germane Crowell .25 .11
❑ 95 Lawyer Milloy .15 .07
❑ 96 Napoleon Kaufman .25 .11
❑ 97 Grant Wistrom .15 .07
❑ 98 Terance Mathis .25 .11
❑ 99 Karim Abdul-Jabbar .25 .11
❑ 100 Kerry Collins .25 .11
❑ 101 Troy Vincent .15 .07
❑ 102 Jermaine Fazande .15 .07
❑ 103 Warren Sapp .25 .11
❑ 104 Tony Banks .25 .11
❑ 105 Darrin Chiaverini .15 .07
❑ 106 Corey Bradford .25 .11
❑ 107 Tony Martin .25 .11
❑ 108 Jeff Blake .25 .11
❑ 109 Torrance Small .15 .07
❑ 110 Freddie Jones .15 .07
❑ 111 Warrick Dunn .50 .23
❑ 112 Tim Biakabutuka .25 .11
❑ 113 Rod Smith .25 .11
❑ 114 Kyle Brady .15 .07
❑ 115 Oronde Gadsden .25 .11
❑ 116 Dedric Ward .25 .11
❑ 117 Mikhael Ricks .15 .07
❑ 118 Bryant Young .15 .07
❑ 119 Michael Bates .15 .07
❑ 120 Junior Seau .25 .11
❑ 121 Bill Romanowski .15 .07
❑ 122 Reggie Barlow .15 .07
❑ 123 Jeff Garcia .50 .23
❑ 124 Peerless Price .50 .23
❑ 125 Jeff George .25 .11
❑ 126 Cornelius Bennett .15 .07
❑ 127 Amani Toomer .25 .11
❑ 128 Charles Johnson .25 .11
❑ 129 Cortez Kennedy .15 .07
❑ 130 Samari Rolle .15 .07
❑ 131 Eric Moulds .50 .23
❑ 132 Joey Galloway .50 .23
❑ 133 Peyton Manning 1.50 .70
❑ 134 Robert Smith .50 .23
❑ 135 Jessie Armstead .15 .07
❑ 136 Will Blackwell .15 .07
❑ 137 Jon Kitna .50 .23
❑ 138 Kevin Dyson .25 .11
❑ 139 Jake Plummer .50 .23
❑ 140 Cade McNown .50 .23
❑ 141 Terrell Davis 1.25 .55
❑ 142 Johnnie Morton .25 .11
❑ 143 Fred Taylor .60 .25
❑ 144 Ed McDaniel .15 .07
❑ 145 Vinny Testaverde .25 .11
❑ 146 Az-Zahir Hakim .25 .11
❑ 147 Brad Johnson .50 .23
❑ 148 Antowain Smith .25 .11
❑ 149 Rob Konrad .15 .07
❑ 150 Sam Cowart .15 .07
❑ 151 Cris Carter .50 .23
❑ 152 Jason Sehorn .15 .07
❑ 153 Levon Kirkland .15 .07
❑ 154 Shawn Springs .15 .07
❑ 155 Frank Wycheck .15 .07
❑ 156 Troy Aikman 1.25 .55
❑ 157 Keenan McCardell .25 .11
❑ 158 Sam Madison .15 .07
❑ 159 Curtis Martin .50 .23
❑ 160 Hines Ward .15 .07
❑ 161 Steve Young .75 .35
❑ 162 Blaine Bishop .15 .07
❑ 163 Shannon Sharpe .25 .11
❑ 164 Michael Pittman .15 .07
❑ 165 Brett Favre 2.00 .90
❑ 166 Damon Huard .50 .23
❑ 167 Keith Poole .15 .07
❑ 168 Curtis Conway .25 .11
❑ 169 Derrick Brooks .15 .07
❑ 170 Duce Staley .50 .23
❑ 171 Rob Johnson .25 .11
❑ 172 Pete Gonzalez .15 .07
❑ 173 Ken Dilger .15 .07
❑ 174 Ike Hilliard .25 .11
❑ 175 Bobby Taylor .15 .07
❑ 176 Ricky Watters .25 .11
❑ 177 Steve McNair .50 .23
❑ 178 Pat Johnson .15 .07
❑ 179 Carl Pickens .25 .11
❑ 180 Terrence Wilkins .50 .23
❑ 181 Rashaan Shehee .15 .07
❑ 182 Ricky Williams 1.25 .55
❑ 183 James Jett .15 .07
❑ 184 Terrell Owens .50 .23
❑ 185 John Lynch .15 .07
❑ 186 Muhsin Muhammad .25 .11
❑ 187 Ryan McNeil .15 .07
❑ 188 Jerome Pathon .25 .11
❑ 189 Daunte Culpepper 1.00 .45
❑ 190 Joe Jurevicius .15 .07
❑ 191 Kordell Stewart .50 .23
❑ 192 Christian Fauria .15 .07
❑ 193 Yancey Thigpen .15 .07
❑ 194 Patrick Jeffers .50 .23
❑ 195 Corey Dillon .50 .23
❑ 196 Tamarick Vanover .15 .07
❑ 197 Doug Flutie .60 .25
❑ 198 Rickey Dudley .15 .07
❑ 199 Charlie Garner .25 .11
❑ 200 Mike Alstott .50 .23
❑ 201 Courtney Brown RC 1.00 .45
❑ 201S Courtney Brown SP 10.00 4.50
❑ 202 Peter Warrick RC 2.50 1.10
❑ 202S Peter Warrick SP 25.00 11.00
❑ 203 Thomas Jones RC 1.25 .55
❑ 203S Thomas Jones SP 12.00 5.50
❑ 204 Sylvester Morris RC 1.50 .70
❑ 204S Sylvester Morris SP 15.00 6.75
❑ 205 Chad Pennington RC 2.50 1.10
❑ 205S Chad Pennington SP 25.00 11.00
❑ 206 Ron Dayne RC 2.50 1.10
❑ 206S Ron Dayne SP 25.00 11.00
❑ 207 Todd Pinkston RC .75 .35
❑ 207S Todd Pinkston SP 8.00 3.60
❑ 208 Todd Husak RC .75 .35
❑ 208S Todd Husak SP 8.00 3.60
❑ 209 Chris Redman RC 1.50 .70
❑ 209S Chris Redman SP 15.00 6.75
❑ 210 Jerry Porter RC .75 .35
❑ 210S Jerry Porter SP 8.00 3.60
❑ 211 Michael Wiley RC .75 .35
❑ 211S Michael Wiley SP 8.00 3.60
❑ 212 J.R. Redmond RC 1.00 .45
❑ 212S J.R. Redmond SP 10.00 4.50
❑ 213 Dennis Northcutt RC 1.00 .45
❑ 213S Dennis Northcutt SP 10.00 4.50
❑ 214 Gari Scott RC .50 .23
❑ 214S Gari Scott SP 5.00 2.20
❑ 215 Bashir Yamini RC .50 .23
❑ 215S Bashir Yamini SP 5.00 2.20
❑ 216 Danny Farmer RC .75 .35
❑ 216S Danny Farmer SP 8.00 3.60
❑ 217 Corey Simon RC 1.00 .45
❑ 217S Corey Simon SP 10.00 4.50
❑ 218 Plaxico Burress RC 1.50 .70
❑ 218S Plaxico Burress SP 15.00 6.75
❑ 219 Chad Morton RC .75 .35
❑ 219S Chad Morton SP 8.00 3.60
❑ 220 Bubba Franks RC 1.00 .45
❑ 220S Bubba Franks SP 10.00 4.50
❑ 221 Shaun Alexander RC 2.00 .90
❑ 221S Shaun Alexander SP 20.00 9.00
❑ 222 Dez White RC .50 .23
❑ 222S Dez White SP 5.00 2.20
❑ 223 Mareno Philyaw RC .50 .23
❑ 223S Mareno Philyaw SP 5.00 2.20
❑ 224 Travis Taylor RC 1.00 .45
❑ 224S Travis Taylor SP 12.00 5.50
❑ 225 Brian Urlacher RC 2.50 1.10
❑ 225S Brian Urlacher SP 25.00 11.00
❑ 226 Jamal Lewis RC 4.00 1.80
❑ 226S Jamal Lewis SP 40.00 18.00
❑ 227 Sherrod Gideon RC .50 .23
❑ 227S Sherrod Gideon SP 5.00 2.20
❑ 228 Shyrone Stith RC .50 .23
❑ 228S Shyrone Stith SP 5.00 2.20
❑ 229 Chris Cole RC .50 .23
❑ 229S Chris Cole SP 5.00 2.20
❑ 230 Darrell Jackson RC 1.25 .55
❑ 230S Darrell Jackson SP 12.00 5.50
❑ 231 Quinton Spotwood RC .50 .23
❑ 231S Quinton Spotwood SP 5.00 2.20
❑ 232 Tee Martin RC 1.25 .55
❑ 232S Tee Martin SP 12.00 5.50
❑ 233 Tim Rattay RC 1.25 .55
❑ 233S Tim Rattay SP 12.00 5.50
❑ 234 Marc Bulger RC .75 .35
❑ 234S Marc Bulger SP 8.00 3.60
❑ 235 Doug Johnson RC .75 .35
❑ 235S Doug Johnson SP 8.00 3.60
❑ 236 Joe Hamilton RC 1.00 .45
❑ 236S Joe Hamilton SP 10.00 4.50
❑ 237 Trevor Gaylor RC .50 .23
❑ 237S Trevor Gaylor SP 5.00 2.20
❑ 238 Travis Prentice RC 1.25 .55
❑ 238S Travis Prentice SP 12.00 5.50
❑ 239 R.Jay Soward RC .75 .35
❑ 239S R.Jay Soward SP 8.00 3.60
❑ 240 Trung Canidate RC .75 .35
❑ 240S Trung Canidate SP 8.00 3.60
❑ 241 Giovanni Carmazzi RC 1.00 .45
❑ 241S Giovanni Carmazzi SP 10.00 4.50
❑ 242 Reuben Droughns RC .75 .35
❑ 242S Reuben Droughns SP 8.00 3.60
❑ 243 Curtis Keaton RC .50 .23
❑ 243S Curtis Keaton SP 5.00 2.20
❑ 244 Laveranues Coles RC 1.25 .55
❑ 244S Laveranues Coles SP 12.00 5.50
❑ 245 Ron Dugans RC .50 .23
❑ 245S Ron Dugans SP 5.00 2.20
❑ 246 Mike Anderson RC 4.00 1.80
❑ 246S Mike Anderson SP 40.00 18.00
❑ 247 Anthony Becht RC .75 .35
❑ 247S Anthony Becht SP 8.00 3.60
❑ 248 Raynoch Thompson RC .50 .23
❑ 248S Raynoch Thompson SP 5.00 2.20
❑ 249 Rob Morris RC .75 .35
❑ 249S Rob Morris SP 8.00 3.60
❑ 250 Chafie Fields RC .50 .23
❑ 250S Chafie Fields SP 5.00 2.20

1999 SkyBox Dominion

	MINT	NRMT
COMPLETE SET (250)	40.00	18.00

❑ 1 Randy Moss 1.50 .70
❑ 2 James Jett .20 .09
❑ 3 Lawyer Milloy .10 .05
❑ 4 Mike Alstott .40 .18
❑ 5 Courtney Hawkins .10 .05
❑ 6 Carl Pickens .20 .09
❑ 7 Marvin Harrison .40 .18
❑ 8 Robert Smith .40 .18
❑ 9 Fred Taylor 1.00 .45
❑ 10 Barry Sanders 1.50 .70
❑ 11 Tony Gonzalez .20 .09
❑ 12 Leroy Hoard .10 .05
❑ 13 Drew Bledsoe .60 .25
❑ 14 Cam Cleeland .10 .05
❑ 15 Steve Atwater .10 .05
❑ 16 Eric Moulds .40 .18
❑ 17 Herman Moore .40 .18
❑ 18 Rickey Dudley .10 .05
❑ 19 Jeff Blake .20 .09
❑ 20 Eddie George .50 .23

❑ 21 Antonio Freeman .40 .18
❑ 22 Stephen Alexander .10 .05
❑ 23 Larry Centers .10 .05
❑ 24 Chris Chandler .20 .09
❑ 25 James Stewart .20 .09
❑ 26 Randall Cunningham .40 .18
❑ 27 Mark Brunell .60 .25
❑ 28 David Palmer .10 .05
❑ 29 Eric Green .10 .05
❑ 30 Terry Glenn .40 .18
❑ 31 Jerry Rice 1.00 .45
❑ 32 Ricky Proehl .10 .05
❑ 33 Tony Banks .20 .09
❑ 34 John Elway 1.50 .70
❑ 35 Johnnie Morton .20 .09
❑ 36 Tony Simmons .10 .05
❑ 37 Jon Kitna .40 .18
❑ 38 Trent Green .20 .09
❑ 39 Peyton Manning 1.50 .70
❑ 40 Emmitt Smith 1.00 .45
❑ 41 Warrick Dunn .40 .18
❑ 42 Jerome Bettis .40 .18
❑ 43 Ricky Watters .20 .09
❑ 44 Rocket Ismail .20 .09
❑ 45 Ryan Leaf .40 .18
❑ 46 Jackie Harris .10 .05
❑ 47 Robert Holcombe .20 .09
❑ 48 Dorsey Levens .40 .18
❑ 49 Duce Staley .40 .18
❑ 50 Brett Favre 1.50 .70
❑ 51 Andre Rison .20 .09
❑ 52 Curtis Conway .20 .09
❑ 53 Mark Chmura .10 .05
❑ 54 Doug Flutie .50 .23
❑ 55 Ernie Mills .10 .05
❑ 56 Jeff George .20 .09
❑ 57 Chris Warren .10 .05
❑ 58 Alonzo Mayes .10 .05
❑ 59 Freddie Jones .10 .05
❑ 60 Shannon Sharpe .20 .09
❑ 61 O.J. Santiago .10 .05
❑ 62 Shawn Springs .10 .05
❑ 63 Kent Graham .10 .05
❑ 64 Muhsin Muhammad .20 .09
❑ 65 Keith Poole .10 .05
❑ 66 Chris Spielman .10 .05
❑ 67 Curtis Enis .40 .18
❑ 68 Lamar Smith .20 .09
❑ 69 Charles Johnson .10 .05
❑ 70 Kerry Collins .20 .09
❑ 71 Charlie Batch .75 .35
❑ 72 Keenan McCardell .20 .09
❑ 73 Ty Detmer .20 .09
❑ 74 Mark Bruener .10 .05
❑ 75 Lamar Thomas .10 .05
❑ 76 Kwamie Lassiter .10 .05
❑ 77 Byron Bam Morris .10 .05
❑ 78 Michael Sinclair .10 .05
❑ 79 Darnay Scott .10 .05
❑ 80 Napoleon Kaufman .40 .18
❑ 81 Ed McCaffrey .20 .09
❑ 82 Reidel Anthony .20 .09
❑ 83 Kevin Greene .10 .05
❑ 84 Michael Irvin .20 .09
❑ 85 Charles Way .10 .05
❑ 86 Tim Brown .40 .18
❑ 87 Johnny McWilliams .10 .05
❑ 88 Brad Johnson .40 .18
❑ 89 Antonio Langham .10 .05
❑ 90 Bruce Smith .20 .09
❑ 91 Reggie Barlow .10 .05
❑ 92 Ty Law .10 .05
❑ 93 Bobby Engram .20 .09
❑ 94 Kimble Anders .20 .09
❑ 95 Dale Carter .10 .05
❑ 96 Jimmy Smith .20 .09
❑ 97 Marc Edwards .10 .05
❑ 98 Ken Dilger .10 .05
❑ 99 Adrian Murrell .20 .09
❑ 100 Terance Mathis .20 .09
❑ 101 Gary Anderson .10 .05
❑ 102 Garrison Hearst .20 .09
❑ 103 Ahman Green .20 .09
❑ 104 Daryl Johnston .10 .05
❑ 105 O.J. McDuffie .20 .09
❑ 106 Matthew Hatchette .10 .05
❑ 107 Chris Doleman .10 .05
❑ 108 Steve McNair .40 .18
❑ 109 Leon Johnson .10 .05
❑ 110 Terrell Davis 1.00 .45
❑ 111 Rob Moore .20 .09
❑ 112 Troy Aikman 1.00 .45
❑ 113 John Avery .20 .09
❑ 114 Frank Wycheck .10 .05
❑ 115 Curtis Martin .40 .18
❑ 116 Jim Harbaugh .20 .09
❑ 117 Sean Dawkins .10 .05
❑ 118 Glenn Foley .20 .09
❑ 119 Warren Sapp .10 .05
❑ 120 R.W. McQuarters .10 .05
❑ 121 Yancey Thigpen .10 .05
❑ 122 Frank Sanders .20 .09
❑ 123 Tim Dwight .40 .18
❑ 124 Pete Mitchell .10 .05
❑ 125 Steve Beuerlein .10 .05
❑ 126 Tyrone Davis .10 .05
❑ 127 Jamie Asher .10 .05
❑ 128 Corey Dillon .40 .18
❑ 129 Doug Pederson .10 .05
❑ 130 Deion Sanders .40 .18
❑ 131 J.J. Stokes .20 .09
❑ 132 Jermaine Lewis .20 .09
❑ 133 Gary Brown .10 .05
❑ 134 Derrick Alexander .10 .05
❑ 135 Tony McGee .10 .05
❑ 136 Kyle Brady .10 .05
❑ 137 Mikhael Ricks .10 .05
❑ 138 Germane Crowell .20 .09
❑ 139 Skip Hicks .40 .18
❑ 140 Ben Coates .20 .09
❑ 141 Will Blackwell .10 .05
❑ 142 Al Del Greco .10 .05
❑ 143 Jake Plummer .75 .35
❑ 144 Marshall Faulk .40 .18
❑ 145 Antowain Smith .40 .18
❑ 146 Corey Fuller .10 .05
❑ 147 Keyshawn Johnson .40 .18
❑ 148 John Randle .20 .09
❑ 149 Terrell Buckley .10 .05
❑ 150 Terry Kirby .10 .05
❑ 151 Robert Brooks .20 .09
❑ 152 Karim Abdul-Jabbar .20 .09
❑ 153 Jason Sehorn .10 .05
❑ 154 Elvis Grbac .20 .09
❑ 155 Andre Reed .20 .09
❑ 156 Ike Hilliard .10 .05
❑ 157 Jamal Anderson .40 .18
❑ 158 Jake Reed .20 .09
❑ 159 Rich Gannon .20 .09
❑ 160 Michael Jackson .10 .05
❑ 161 Bert Emanuel .20 .09
❑ 162 Charles Woodson .40 .18
❑ 163 Ray Lewis .20 .09
❑ 164 Trent Dilfer .20 .09
❑ 165 Oronde Gadsden .10 .05
❑ 166 Wesley Walls .20 .09
❑ 167 Joey Galloway .40 .18
❑ 168 Mo Lewis .10 .05
❑ 169 Darren Woodson .10 .05
❑ 170 Cris Carter .40 .18
❑ 171 Brian Mitchell .10 .05
❑ 172 Tim Biakabutuka .20 .09
❑ 173 Michael Westbrook .20 .09
❑ 174 Dan Marino 1.50 .70
❑ 175 Greg Hill .10 .05
❑ 176 Priest Holmes .40 .18
❑ 177 Fred Lane .10 .05
❑ 178 Isaac Bruce .40 .18
❑ 179 Erik Kramer .10 .05
❑ 180 Steve Young .60 .25
❑ 181 Terry Fair .10 .05
❑ 182 Brian Griese .75 .35
❑ 183 Leslie Shepherd .10 .05
❑ 184 Kordell Stewart .40 .18
❑ 185 Charlie Jones .10 .05
❑ 186 Chris Calloway .10 .05
❑ 187 Wayne Chrebet .20 .09
❑ 188 Natrone Means .20 .09
❑ 189 David LaFleur .10 .05
❑ 190 Rod Smith WR .20 .09
❑ 191 Kevin Dyson .20 .09
❑ 192 Scott Mitchell .10 .05
❑ 193 Andre Wadsworth .10 .05
❑ 194 Vinny Testaverde .20 .09
❑ 195 Az-Zahir Hakim .10 .05
❑ 196 Joe Jurevicius .10 .05
❑ 197 Junior Seau .20 .09
❑ 198 Jason Elam .10 .05
❑ 199 Terrell Owens .40 .18
❑ 200 Jacquez Green .20 .09
❑ 201 Tim Couch RC 4.00 1.80
❑ 202 Donovan McNabb RC 5.00 2.20
❑ 203 Cade McNown RC 1.25 .55
❑ 204 Akili Smith RC 2.00 .90
❑ 205 Kevin Faulk RC 1.50 .70
❑ 206 Sedrick Irvin RC 1.00 .45
❑ 207 Edgerrin James RC 8.00 3.60
❑ 208 Ricky Williams RC 5.00 2.20
❑ 209 D'Wayne Bates RC .75 .35
❑ 210 David Boston RC 2.00 .90
❑ 211 Torry Holt RC 2.50 1.10
❑ 212 Peerless Price RC 1.25 .55
❑ 213 Daunte Culpepper RC 8.00 3.60
❑ 214 Troy Edwards RC 1.25 .55
❑ 215 Rob Konrad RC 1.00 .45
❑ 216 Joe Germaine RC 1.00 .45
❑ 217 James Johnson RC 1.00 .45
❑ 218 Brock Huard RC 1.50 .70
❑ 219 Cecil Collins RC 1.00 .45
❑ 220 Jeff Paulk RC .75 .35
Eugene Baker RC
❑ 221 Marty Booker RC .75 .35
Jim Finn RC
❑ 222 Scott Covington RC 1.00 .45
Nick Williams RC
❑ 223 Kevin Johnson RC 1.50 .70
Darrin Chiaverini RC
❑ 224 Ebenezer Ekuban RC .75 .35
Dat Nguyen RC
❑ 225 Al Wilson RC .50 .23
Chad Plummer RC
❑ 226 Chris Claiborn RC .50 .23
Aaron Gibson RC
❑ 227 Aaron Brooks RC 4.00 1.80
De'Mond Parker RC
❑ 228 John Tait RC .75 .35
Mike Cloud RC
❑ 229 Andy Katzenmoyer RC 1.00 .45
Michael Bishop RC
❑ 230 Joe Montgomery RC .75 .35
Dan Campbell RC
❑ 231 Na Brown RC .75 .35
Cecil Martin RC
❑ 232 Amos Zereoue RC .75 .35
Jerame Tuman RC
❑ 233 Jermaine Fazande RC .75 .35
Steve Heiden RC
❑ 234 Karsten Bailey RC .50 .23
Charlie Rogers RC
❑ 235 Shaun King RC 1.50 .70
Martin Gramatica RC
❑ 236 Jevon Kearse RC 1.50 .70
Kevin Daft RC
❑ 237 Champ Bailey RC 1.00 .45
Tim Alexander RC
❑ 238 Karsten Bailey RC 1.00 .45
Darnell McDonald RC
❑ 239 Lamarr Glenn RC .50 .23
Terry Jackson RC
❑ 240 Troy Smith RC .50 .23
Malcolm Johnson RC
❑ 241 Rondel Menendez RC .50 .23
Craig Yeast RC
❑ 242 Jed Weaver RC .50 .23
James Dearth RC
❑ 243 Joel Makovicka RC 1.00 .45
Shawn Bryson RC
❑ 244 Desmond Clark RC .75 .35
Jim Kleinsasser RC
❑ 245 Sean Bennett RC .75 .35
Autry Denson RC
❑ 246 Billy Miller RC .75 .35
Wane McGarity RC
❑ 247 Mike Lucky RC .50 .23
Justin Swift RC
❑ 248 Travis McGriff RC .75 .35
MarTay Jenkins RC
❑ 249 Donald Driver RC .75 .35

Larry Parker RC
❑ 250 Antoine Winfield RC ...... .50 .23
Dre' Bly RC

1992 SkyBox Impact

	MINT	NRMT
COMPLETE SET (350)	12.00	5.50

❑ 1 Jim Kelly .25 .11
❑ 2 Andre Rison .10 .05
❑ 3 Michael Dean Perry .10 .05
❑ 4 Herman Moore .50 .23
❑ 5 Fred McAfee RC .05 .02
❑ 6 Ricky Proehl .05 .02
❑ 7 Jim Everett .10 .05
❑ 8 Mark Carrier DB .05 .02
❑ 9 Eric Martin .05 .02
❑ 10 John Elway 1.25 .55
❑ 11 Michael Irvin .25 .11
❑ 12 Keith McCants .05 .02
❑ 13 Greg Lloyd .25 .11
❑ 14 Lawrence Taylor .25 .11
❑ 15 Mike Tomczak .05 .02
❑ 16 Cortez Kennedy .10 .05
❑ 17 William Fuller .10 .05
❑ 18 James Lofton .10 .05
❑ 19 Kevin Fagan .05 .02
❑ 20 Bill Brooks .05 .02
❑ 21 Roger Craig UER .10 .05
(Text is about Vikings, but Raiders logo still on card)
❑ 22 Jay Novacek .10 .05
❑ 23 Steve Sewell .05 .02
❑ 24 William Perry UER .10 .05
(Card has him injured for 1988, but he did play)
❑ 25 Jerry Rice .75 .35
❑ 26 James Joseph .05 .02
❑ 27 Timm Rosenbach .05 .02
❑ 28 Pat Terrell .05 .02
❑ 29 Jon Vaughn .05 .02
❑ 30 Steve Walsh .05 .02
❑ 31 James Hasty .05 .02
❑ 32 Dwight Stone .05 .02
❑ 33 Derrick Fenner UER .05 .02
(Text mentions Bengals, but Seahawks logo still on front)
❑ 34 Mark Bortz .05 .02
❑ 35 Dan Saleaumua .05 .02
❑ 36 Sammie Smith UER .05 .02
(Text mentions Broncos, but Dolphins logo still on front)
❑ 37 Antone Davis .05 .02
❑ 38 Steve Young .60 .25
❑ 39 Mike Baab .05 .02
❑ 40 Rick Fenney .05 .02
❑ 41 Chris Hinton .05 .02
❑ 42 Bart Oates .05 .02
❑ 43 Bryan Hinkle .05 .02
❑ 44 James Francis .05 .02
❑ 45 Ray Crockett .05 .02
❑ 46 Eric Dickerson UER .10 .05
(Text mentions Raiders, but Colts logo still on front)
❑ 47 Hart Lee Dykes .05 .02
❑ 48 Percy Snow .05 .02
❑ 49 Ron Hall .05 .02
❑ 50 Warren Moon .25 .11
❑ 51 Ed West .05 .02
❑ 52 Clarence Verdin .05 .02
❑ 53 Eugene Lockhart .05 .02
❑ 54 Andre Reed .10 .05
❑ 55 Kevin Ross .05 .02
❑ 56 Al Noga .05 .02
❑ 57 Wes Hopkins .05 .02
❑ 58 Rufus Porter .05 .02
❑ 59 Brian Mitchell .10 .05
❑ 60 Reggie Roby .05 .02
❑ 61 Rodney Peete .10 .05
❑ 62 Jeff Herrod .05 .02
❑ 63 Anthony Smith .05 .02
❑ 64 Brad Muster .05 .02
❑ 65 Jessie Tuggle .05 .02
❑ 66 Al Smith .05 .02
❑ 67 Jeff Hostetler .10 .05
❑ 68 John L. Williams .05 .02
❑ 69 Paul Gruber .05 .02
❑ 70 Cornelius Bennett .10 .05
❑ 71 William White .05 .02
❑ 72 Tom Rathman .05 .02
❑ 73 Boomer Esiason .10 .05
❑ 74 Neil Smith .25 .11
❑ 75 Sterling Sharpe .25 .11
❑ 76 James Jones .05 .02
❑ 77 David Treadwell .05 .02
❑ 78 Flipper Anderson .05 .02
❑ 79 Eric Allen .05 .02
❑ 80 Joe Jacoby .05 .02
❑ 81 Keith Sims .05 .02
❑ 82 Bubba McDowell .05 .02
❑ 83 Ronnie Lippett .05 .02
❑ 84 Cris Carter .50 .23
❑ 85 Chris Burkett .05 .02
❑ 86 Issiac Holt .05 .02
❑ 87 Duane Bickett .05 .02
❑ 88 Leslie O'Neal .10 .05
❑ 89 Gill Fenerty .05 .02
❑ 90 Pierce Holt .05 .02
❑ 91 Willie Drewrey .05 .02
❑ 92 Brian Blades .10 .05
❑ 93 Tony Martin .25 .11
❑ 94 Jessie Hester .05 .02
❑ 95 John Stephens .05 .02
❑ 96 Keith Willis UER .05 .02
(Text mentions Redskins, but Steelers logo still on front)
❑ 97 Vai Sikahema UER .05 .02
(Text mentions Eagles, but Cardinals logo still on front)
❑ 98 Mark Higgs .05 .02
❑ 99 Steve McMichael .10 .05
❑ 100 Deion Sanders .50 .23
❑ 101 Marvin Washington .05 .02
❑ 102 Ken Norton .25 .11
❑ 103 Barry Word .05 .02
❑ 104 Sean Jones .10 .05
❑ 105 Ronnie Harmon .05 .02
❑ 106 Donnell Woolford .05 .02
❑ 107 Ray Agnew .05 .02
❑ 108 Lemuel Stinson .05 .02
❑ 109 Dennis Smith .05 .02
❑ 110 Lorenzo White .05 .02
❑ 111 Craig Heyward .10 .05
❑ 112 Jeff Query UER .05 .02
(Text mentions Oilers, but Packers logo still on front)
❑ 113 Gary Plummer .05 .02
❑ 114 John Taylor .10 .05
❑ 115 Rohn Stark .05 .02
❑ 116 Tom Waddle .05 .02
❑ 117 Jeff Cross .05 .02
❑ 118 Tim Green .05 .02
❑ 119 Anthony Munoz .10 .05
❑ 120 Mel Gray .10 .05
❑ 121 Ray Donaldson .05 .02
❑ 122 Dennis Byrd .05 .02
❑ 123 Carnell Lake .05 .02
❑ 124 Broderick Thomas .05 .02
❑ 125 Charles Mann .05 .02
❑ 126 Darion Conner .05 .02
❑ 127 John Roper .05 .02
❑ 128 Jack Del Rio UER .05 .02
(Text mentions Vikings, but Cowboys logo still on front)
❑ 129 Rickey Dixon .05 .02
❑ 130 Eddie Anderson .05 .02
❑ 131 Steve Broussard .05 .02
❑ 132 Michael Young .05 .02
❑ 133 Lamar Lathon .05 .02
❑ 134 Rickey Jackson .05 .02
❑ 135 Billy Ray Smith .05 .02
❑ 136 Tony Casillas .05 .02
❑ 137 Ickey Woods .05 .02
❑ 138 Ray Childress .05 .02
❑ 139 Vance Johnson .05 .02
❑ 140 Brett Perriman .25 .11
❑ 141 Calvin Williams .10 .05
❑ 142 Dino Hackett .05 .02
❑ 143 Jacob Green .05 .02
❑ 144 Robert Delpino .05 .02
❑ 145 Marv Cook .05 .02
❑ 146 Dwayne Harper .05 .02
❑ 147 Ricky Ervins .05 .02
❑ 148 Kelvin Martin .05 .02
❑ 149 Leroy Hoard .10 .05
❑ 150 Dan Marino 1.25 .55
❑ 151 Richard Johnson UER .05 .02
(He and Carrier had 2 interceptions, only given credit for 1 on card)
❑ 152 Henry Ellard .10 .05
❑ 153 Al Toon .10 .05
❑ 154 Dermontti Dawson .05 .02
❑ 155 Robert Blackmon .05 .02
❑ 156 Howie Long .10 .05
❑ 157 David Fulcher .05 .02
❑ 158 Mike Merriweather .05 .02
❑ 159 Gary Anderson K .05 .02
❑ 160 John Friesz .10 .05
❑ 161 Eugene Robinson .05 .02
❑ 162 Brad Baxter .05 .02
❑ 163 Bennie Blades .05 .02
❑ 164 Harold Green .05 .02
❑ 165 Ernest Givins .10 .05
❑ 166 Deron Cherry .05 .02
❑ 167 Carl Banks .05 .02
❑ 168 Keith Jackson .10 .05
❑ 169 Pat Leahy .05 .02
❑ 170 Alvin Harper .10 .05
❑ 171 David Little .05 .02
❑ 172 Anthony Carter .10 .05
❑ 173 Willie Gault .10 .05
❑ 174 Bruce Armstrong .05 .02
❑ 175 Junior Seau .25 .11
❑ 176 Eric Metcalf .10 .05
❑ 177 Tony Mandarich .05 .02
❑ 178 Ernie Jones .05 .02
❑ 179 Albert Bentley .05 .02
❑ 180 Mike Pritchard .10 .05
❑ 181 Bubby Brister .05 .02
❑ 182 Vaughan Johnson .05 .02
❑ 183 Robert Clark UER .05 .02
(Text mentions Dolphins, but Seahawks logo on front)
❑ 184 Lawrence Dawsey .10 .05
❑ 185 Eric Green .05 .02
❑ 186 Jay Schroeder .05 .02
❑ 187 Andre Tippett .05 .02
❑ 188 Vinny Testaverde .10 .05
❑ 189 Wendell Davis .05 .02
❑ 190 Russell Maryland .10 .05
❑ 191 Chris Singleton .05 .02
❑ 192 Ken O'Brien .05 .02
❑ 193 Merril Hoge .05 .02
❑ 194 Steve Bono RC .25 .11
❑ 195 Earnest Byner .05 .02
❑ 196 Mike Singletary .10 .05
❑ 197 Gaston Green .05 .02
❑ 198 Mark Carrier WR .10 .05
❑ 199 Harvey Williams .25 .11

❑ 200 Randall Cunningham...... .25 .11
❑ 201 Cris Dishman.................. .05 .02
❑ 202 Greg Townsend.............. .05 .02
❑ 203 Christian Okoye.............. .05 .02
❑ 204 Sam Mills.......................... .05 .02
❑ 205 Kyle Clifton .... .05 .02
❑ 206 Jim Harbaugh .... .25 .11
❑ 207 Anthony Thompson......... .05 .02
❑ 208 Rob Moore .... .10 .05
❑ 209 Irving Fryar .... .10 .05
❑ 210 Derrick Thomas.............. .25 .11
❑ 211 Chris Miller .... .10 .05
❑ 212 Doug Smith .... .05 .02
❑ 213 Michael Haynes.............. .10 .05
❑ 214 Phil Simms .... .10 .05
❑ 215 Charles Haley .... .10 .05
❑ 216 Burt Grossman .... .05 .02
❑ 217 Rod Bernstine .... .05 .02
❑ 218 Louis Lipps .... .05 .02
❑ 219 Dan McGwire UER .... .05 .02
(Actually drafted in
1991, not 1990)
❑ 220 Ethan Horton.................. .05 .02
❑ 221 Michael Carter................ .05 .02
❑ 222 Neil O'Donnell .... .25 .11
❑ 223 Anthony Miller .... .10 .05
❑ 224 Eric Swann .... .10 .05
❑ 225 Thurman Thomas .... .25 .11
❑ 226 Jeff George .... .25 .11
❑ 227 Joe Montana .... 1.25 .55
❑ 228 Leonard Marshall .... .05 .02
❑ 229 Haywood Jeffires........... .10 .05
❑ 230 Mark Clayton.................. .10 .05
❑ 231 Chris Doleman .... .05 .02
❑ 232 Troy Aikman .... .75 .35
❑ 233 Gary Anderson RB .... .05 .02
❑ 234 Pat Swilling .... .10 .05
❑ 235 Ronnie Lott .... .10 .05
❑ 236 Brian Jordan .... .10 .05
❑ 237 Bruce Smith..................... .25 .11
❑ 238 Tony Jones UER .... .05 .02
(Text mentions Falcons,
but Oilers logo
still on front)
❑ 239 Tim McKyer..................... .05 .02
❑ 240 Gary Clark........................ .25 .11
❑ 241 Mitchell Price.................. .05 .02
❑ 242 John Kasay .... .05 .02
❑ 243 Stephone Paige.............. .05 .02
❑ 244 Jeff Wright....................... .05 .02
❑ 245 Shannon Sharpe............. .25 .11
❑ 246 Keith Byars .... .05 .02
❑ 247 Charles Dimry .... .05 .02
❑ 248 Steve Smith..................... .05 .02
❑ 249 Erric Pegram .... .10 .05
❑ 250 Bernie Kosar .... .10 .05
❑ 251 Peter Tom Willis .... .05 .02
❑ 252 Mark Ingram .... .05 .02
❑ 253 Keith McKeller................. .05 .02
❑ 254 Lewis Billups UER.......... .05 .02
(Text mentions Packers,
but Bengals logo
still on front)
❑ 255 Alton Montgomery.......... .05 .02
❑ 256 Jimmie Jones .... .05 .02
❑ 257 Brent Williams .... .05 .02
❑ 258 Gene Atkins...................... .05 .02
❑ 259 Reggie Rutland .... .05 .02
❑ 260 Sam Seale UER .... .05 .02
(Text mentions Raiders,
but Chargers logo
still on back)
❑ 261 Andre Ware..................... .05 .02
❑ 262 Fred Barnett .... .25 .11
❑ 263 Randal Hill....................... .05 .02
❑ 264 Patrick Hunter................. .05 .02
❑ 265 Johnny Rembert UER..... .05 .02
(Card says DNP in 1991,
but he played 12 games)
❑ 266 Monte Coleman............... .05 .02
❑ 267 Aaron Wallace................. .05 .02
❑ 268 Ferrell Edmunds .... .05 .02
❑ 269 Stan Thomas................... .05 .02
❑ 270 Robb Thomas .... .05 .02
❑ 271 Martin Bayless UER ...... .05 .02
(Text mentions Chiefs,
but Chargers logo
still on front)
❑ 272 Dean Biasucci .... .05 .02
❑ 273 Keith Henderson .... .05 .02
❑ 274 Vinnie Clark.................... .05 .02
❑ 275 Emmitt Smith............... 1.50 .70
❑ 276 Mark Rypien .... .05 .02
❑ 277 Atlanta Falcons CL .... .05 .02
Wing and a Prayer
(Michael Haynes)
❑ 278 Buffalo Bills CL .... .10 .05
Machine Gun
(Jim Kelly)
❑ 279 Chicago Bears CL.......... .05 .02
Grizzly
(Tom Waddle)
❑ 280 Cincinnati Bengals CL.... .05 .02
Price is Right
(Mitchell Price)
❑ 281 Cleveland Browns CL .... .05 .02
Coasting
(Bernie Kosar)
❑ 282 Dallas Cowboys CL........ .10 .05
Gunned Down
(Michael Irvin)
❑ 283 Denver Broncos CL........ .50 .23
The Drive II
(John Elway)
❑ 284 Detroit Lions CL .... .05 .02
Lions Roar
(Mel Gray)
❑ 285 Green Bay Packers CL .. .10 .05
Razor Sharpe
(Sterling Sharpe)
❑ 286 Houston Oilers CL.......... .10 .05
Oil's Well
(Warren Moon)
❑ 287 Indianapolis Colts CL .... .10 .05
Whew (Jeff George)
❑ 288 Kansas City Chiefs CL .. .10 .05
Ambush
(Derrick Thomas)
❑ 289 Los Angeles Raiders CL .05 .02
Lott of Defense
(Ronnie Lott)
❑ 290 Los Angeles Rams CL .. .05 .02
Ram It
(Robert Delpino)
❑ 291 Miami Dolphins CL .... .50 .23
Miami Ice
(Dan Marino)
❑ 292 Minnesota Vikings CL .... .25 .11
Purple Blaze
(Cris Carter)
❑ 293 New England Patriots CL .05 .02
Surprise Attack
(Irving Fryar)
❑ 294 New Orleans Saints CL.. .05 .02
Marching In
(Gene Atkins)
❑ 295 New York Giants CL ...... .05 .02
Almost Perfect
(Phil Simms)
❑ 296 New York Jets CL .... .05 .02
Playoff Bound
(Ken O'Brien)
❑ 297 Philadelphia Eagles CL.. .05 .02
Flying High
(Keith Jackson)
❑ 298 Phoenix Cardinals CL ..... .05 .02
Airborne
(Ricky Proehl)
❑ 299 Pittsburgh Steelers CL .. .05 .02
Steel Curtain
(Bryan Hinkle)
❑ 300 San Diego Chargers CL .05 .02
Lightning
(John Friesz)
❑ 301 San Francisco 49ers CL .50 .23
Instant Rice
(Jerry Rice)
❑ 302 Seattle Seahawks CL ..... .05 .02
Defense Never Rests
(Eugene Robinson)
❑ 303 T.Bay Buccaneers CL..... .05 .02
Stunned
Broderick Thomas
❑ 304 Washington Redskins CL .05 .02
Super
(Mark Rypien)
❑ 305 Jim Kelly LL..................... .10 .05
❑ 306 Steve Young LL............... .30 .14
❑ 307 Thurman Thomas LL...... .10 .05
❑ 308 Emmitt Smith LL .... .75 .35
❑ 309 Haywood Jeffires LL ...... .05 .02
❑ 310 Michael Irvin LL.............. .10 .05
❑ 311 William Fuller LL .... .05 .02
❑ 312 Pat Swilling LL................ .05 .02
❑ 313 Ronnie Lott LL................ .05 .02
❑ 314 Deion Sanders LL .... .25 .11
❑ 315 Cornelius Bennett HH .... .05 .02
❑ 316 David Fulcher HH .... .05 .02
❑ 317 Ronnie Lott HH .... .05 .02
❑ 318 Pat Swilling HH .... .05 .02
❑ 319 Lawrence Taylor HH ...... .10 .05
❑ 320 Derrick Thomas HH........ .10 .05
❑ 321 Steve Emtman RC .... .05 .02
❑ 322 Carl Pickens RC .... .60 .25
❑ 323 David Klingler RC .... .10 .05
❑ 324 Dale Carter RC .... .25 .11
❑ 325 Mike Gaddis RC .... .05 .02
❑ 326 Quentin Coryatt RC........ .25 .11
❑ 327 Darryl Williams RC .... .05 .02
❑ 328 Jeremy Lincoln RC .... .05 .02
❑ 329 Robert Jones RC............ .05 .02
❑ 330 Bucky Richardson RC.... .05 .02
❑ 331 Tony Brooks RC .... .05 .02
❑ 332 Alonzo Spellman RC...... .10 .05
❑ 333 Robert Brooks RC .... 1.00 .45
❑ 334 Marco Coleman RC....... .10 .05
❑ 335 Siran Stacy RC UER...... .05 .02
(Misspelled Stacey)
❑ 336 Tommy Maddox RC ...... .05 .02
❑ 337 Steve Israel RC.............. .05 .02
❑ 338 Vaughn Dunbar RC........ .05 .02
❑ 339 Shane Collins RC .... .05 .02
❑ 340 Kevin Smith RC.............. .25 .11
❑ 341 Chris Mims RC .... .10 .05
❑ 342 C.McGlockton RC UER.. .25 .11
(Misspelled McGlokton
on both sides)
❑ 343 Tracy Scroggins RC ...... .05 .02
❑ 344 Howard Dinkins RC........ .05 .02
❑ 345 Levon Kirkland RC .... .05 .02
❑ 346 Terrell Buckley RC .... .05 .02
❑ 347 Marquez Pope RC.......... .05 .02
❑ 348 Phillippi Sparks RC .... .05 .02
❑ 349 Joe Bowden RC .... .05 .02
❑ 350 Edgar Bennett RC.......... .25 .11
❑ SP1 Jim Kelly..................... 8.00 3.60
❑ SP1AU Jim Kelly AUTO.... 50.00 22.00
❑ SP2AU Kelly/Magic AUTO 400.00 180.00

1993 SkyBox Impact

	MINT	NRMT
COMPLETE SET (400)	15.00	6.75

❑ 1 Steve Broussard .... .05 .02
❑ 2 Michael Haynes............... .10 .05
❑ 3 Tony Smith .... .05 .02
❑ 4 Tory Epps .... .05 .02
❑ 5 Chris Hinton .... .05 .02
❑ 6 Bobby Hebert .... .05 .02

❑ 7 Tim McKyer .05 .02
❑ 8 Chris Miller .10 .05
❑ 9 Bruce Pickens .05 .02
❑ 10 Mike Pritchard .10 .05
❑ 11 Andre Rison .10 .05
❑ 12 Deion Sanders .50 .23
❑ 13 Pierce Holt .05 .02
❑ 14 Jessie Tuggle .05 .02
❑ 15 Don Beebe .05 .02
❑ 16 Cornelius Bennett .10 .05
❑ 17 Kenneth Davis .05 .02
❑ 18 Kent Hull .05 .02
❑ 19 Jim Kelly .25 .11
❑ 20 Mark Kelso .05 .02
❑ 21 Keith McKeller UER .05 .02
(Name misspelled McKellar on front)
❑ 22 Andre Reed .10 .05
❑ 23 Jim Ritcher .05 .02
❑ 24 Bruce Smith .25 .11
❑ 25 Thurman Thomas .25 .11
❑ 26 Steve Christie .05 .02
❑ 27 Darryl Talley UER .05 .02
(Name misspelled Darrell on front)
❑ 28 Pete Metzelaars .05 .02
❑ 29 Steve Tasker .10 .05
❑ 30 Henry Jones .05 .02
❑ 31 Neal Anderson .05 .02
❑ 32 Trace Armstrong .05 .02
❑ 33 Mark Bortz .05 .02
❑ 34 Mark Carrier DB .05 .02
❑ 35 Wendell Davis .05 .02
❑ 36 Richard Dent .10 .05
❑ 37 Jim Harbaugh .25 .11
❑ 38 Steve McMichael .10 .05
❑ 39 Craig Heyward .10 .05
❑ 40 William Perry .10 .05
❑ 41 Donnell Woolford .05 .02
❑ 42 Tom Waddle .05 .02
❑ 43 Anthony Morgan .05 .02
❑ 44 Jim Breech .05 .02
❑ 45 David Klingler .05 .02
❑ 46 Derrick Fenner .05 .02
❑ 47 David Fulcher .05 .02
❑ 48 James Francis .05 .02
❑ 49 Harold Green .05 .02
❑ 50 Carl Pickens .25 .11
❑ 51 Jay Schroeder .05 .02
❑ 52 Alex Gordon .05 .02
❑ 53 Eric Ball .05 .02
❑ 54 Eddie Brown .05 .02
❑ 55 Jay Hilgenberg UER .05 .02
(Name misspelled Hilgenburg on front)
❑ 56 Michael Jackson .10 .05
❑ 57 Bernie Kosar .10 .05
❑ 58 Kevin Mack .05 .02
❑ 59 Eric Metcalf .10 .05
❑ 60 Michael Dean Perry .10 .05
❑ 61 Tommy Vardell .05 .02
❑ 62 Leroy Hoard .10 .05
❑ 63 Clay Matthews .10 .05
❑ 64 Vinny Testaverde .10 .05
❑ 65 Mark Carrier WR .10 .05
❑ 66 Troy Aikman .75 .35
❑ 67 Lin Elliott RC UER .05 .02
(Name misspelled Elliot on front)
❑ 68 Thomas Everett .05 .02
❑ 69 Alvin Harper .10 .05
❑ 70 Ray Horton .05 .02
❑ 71 Michael Irvin .25 .11
❑ 72 Russell Maryland .05 .02
❑ 73 Jay Novacek .10 .05
❑ 74 Emmitt Smith 1.50 .70
❑ 75 Tony Casillas .05 .02
❑ 76 Robert Jones .05 .02
❑ 77 Ken Norton Jr. .10 .05
❑ 78 Daryl Johnston .25 .11
❑ 79 Charles Haley .10 .05
❑ 80 Leon Lett RC .10 .05
❑ 81 Steve Atwater .05 .02
❑ 82 Mike Croel .05 .02
❑ 83 John Elway 1.50 .70
❑ 84 Simon Fletcher .05 .02
❑ 85 Vance Johnson .05 .02
❑ 86 Shannon Sharpe .25 .11
❑ 87 Rod Bernstine .05 .02
❑ 88 Robert Delpino .05 .02
❑ 89 Karl Mecklenburg .05 .02
❑ 90 Steve Sewell .05 .02
❑ 91 Tommy Maddox UER .05 .02
(Name misspelled Maddux on front and back)
❑ 92 Arthur Marshall RC .05 .02
❑ 93 Dennis Smith .05 .02
❑ 94 Derek Russell .05 .02
❑ 95 Bennie Blades .05 .02
❑ 96 Michael Cofer .05 .02
❑ 97 Willie Green .05 .02
❑ 98 Herman Moore .50 .23
❑ 99 Rodney Peete .05 .02
❑ 100 Andre Ware .05 .02
❑ 101 Barry Sanders UER 1.50 .70
(Brett Perriman is pictured on front)
❑ 102 Chris Spielman .10 .05
❑ 103 Jason Hanson .05 .02
❑ 104 Mel Gray .10 .05
❑ 105 Pat Swilling .05 .02
❑ 106 Bill Fralic .05 .02
❑ 107 Rodney Holman .05 .02
❑ 108 Brett Favre 2.00 .90
❑ 109 Sterling Sharpe .25 .11
❑ 110 Reggie White .25 .11
❑ 111 Terrell Buckley .05 .02
❑ 112 Sanjay Beach .05 .02
❑ 113 Tony Bennett .05 .02
❑ 114 Jackie Harris .05 .02
❑ 115 Bryce Paup .25 .11
❑ 116 Shawn Patterson .05 .02
❑ 117 John Stephens .05 .02
❑ 118 Cris Dishman .05 .02
❑ 119 Ernest Givins .10 .05
❑ 120 Haywood Jeffires .10 .05
❑ 121 Lamar Lathon .05 .02
❑ 122 Warren Moon .25 .11
❑ 123 Lorenzo White .05 .02
❑ 124 Curtis Duncan .05 .02
❑ 125 Webster Slaughter .05 .02
❑ 126 Cody Carlson .05 .02
❑ 127 Leonard Harris .05 .02
❑ 128 Bruce Matthews .05 .02
❑ 129 Ray Childress .05 .02
❑ 130 Al Smith .05 .02
❑ 131 Jeff George .25 .11
❑ 132 Anthony Johnson .10 .05
❑ 133 Steve Emtman .05 .02
❑ 134 Quentin Coryatt .10 .05
❑ 135 Rodney Culver .05 .02
❑ 136 Jessie Hester .05 .02
❑ 137 Aaron Cox .05 .02
❑ 138 Clarence Verdin .05 .02
❑ 139 Joe Montana 1.50 .70
❑ 140 Dave Krieg .10 .05
❑ 141 Harvey Williams .10 .05
❑ 142 Derrick Thomas .25 .11
❑ 143 Barry Word .05 .02
❑ 144 Christian Okoye .05 .02
❑ 145 Nick Lowery .05 .02
❑ 146 Dale Carter .05 .02
❑ 147 Willie Davis .25 .11
❑ 148 Tim Barnett .05 .02
❑ 149 Neil Smith UER .25 .11
(Name misspelled Neal on front)
❑ 150 Marcus Allen .25 .11
❑ 151 Nick Bell .05 .02
❑ 152 Tim Brown .25 .11
❑ 153 Eric Dickerson .10 .05
❑ 154 Willie Gault .05 .02
❑ 155 Howie Long .10 .05
❑ 156 Gaston Green .05 .02
❑ 157 Chester McGlockton .10 .05
❑ 158 Eddie Anderson .05 .02
❑ 159 Ethan Horton .05 .02
❑ 160 James Lofton .10 .05
❑ 161 Jeff Hostetler .10 .05
❑ 162 Terry McDaniel .05 .02
❑ 163 Flipper Anderson .05 .02
❑ 164 Shane Conlan .05 .02
❑ 165 Jim Everett .10 .05
❑ 166 Henry Ellard .10 .05
❑ 167 Cleveland Gary .05 .02
❑ 168 Todd Lyght .05 .02
❑ 169 Sean Gilbert .10 .05
❑ 170 Jim Price .05 .02
❑ 171 Bill Hawkins .05 .02
❑ 172 Mark Clayton .05 .02
❑ 173 Mark Higgs .05 .02
❑ 174 Dan Marino 1.50 .70
❑ 175 Louis Oliver .05 .02
❑ 176 Reggie Roby .05 .02
❑ 177 Bobby Humphrey .05 .02
❑ 178 Troy Vincent .05 .02
❑ 179 Marco Coleman .05 .02
❑ 180 Aaron Craver .05 .02
❑ 181 Keith Jackson .10 .05
❑ 182 Mark Duper .05 .02
❑ 183 Pete Stoyanovich .05 .02
❑ 184 Irving Fryar .10 .05
❑ 185 Bryan Cox UER .05 .02
(Name misspelled Brian on front and back)
❑ 186 Terry Allen .25 .11
❑ 187 Anthony Carter .10 .05
❑ 188 Cris Carter .50 .23
❑ 189 Chris Doleman .05 .02
❑ 190 Rich Gannon .25 .11
❑ 191 Sean Salisbury .05 .02
❑ 192 Hassan Jones .05 .02
❑ 193 Steve Jordan .05 .02
❑ 194 Roger Craig .10 .05
❑ 195 Todd Scott .05 .02
❑ 196 Esera Tuaolo .05 .02
❑ 197 Ray Agnew .05 .02
❑ 198 Marv Cook .05 .02
❑ 199 Tommy Hodson .05 .02
❑ 200 Chris Singleton .05 .02
❑ 201 Michael Timpson .05 .02
❑ 202 Jon Vaughn ERR .05 .02
(Photo on back is Keith Byars)
❑ 203 Leonard Russell .10 .05
❑ 204 Scott Zolak .05 .02
❑ 205 Reyna Thompson .05 .02
❑ 206 Andre Tippett .05 .02
❑ 207 Morten Andersen UER .05 .02
(Name misspelled Morton Anderson on front)
❑ 208 Wesley Carroll .05 .02
❑ 209 Vince Buck .05 .02
❑ 210 Rickey Jackson .05 .02
❑ 211 Vaughan Johnson UER .05 .02
(Name misspelled Vaughn on front)
❑ 212 Eric Martin .05 .02
❑ 213 Sam Mills .05 .02
❑ 214 Steve Walsh .05 .02
❑ 215 Wade Wilson .05 .02
❑ 216 Vaughn Dunbar .05 .02
❑ 217 Brad Muster .05 .02
❑ 218 Dalton Hilliard .05 .02
❑ 219 Floyd Turner .05 .02
❑ 220 Stephen Baker .05 .02
❑ 221 Mark Jackson .05 .02
❑ 222 Jarrod Bunch .05 .02
❑ 223 Mark Collins .05 .02
❑ 224 Rodney Hampton .25 .11
❑ 225 Phil Simms .10 .05
❑ 226 Pepper Johnson .05 .02
❑ 227 Dave Meggett .05 .02
❑ 228 Derek Brown TE .05 .02
❑ 229 Mike Sherrard .05 .02
❑ 230 Lawrence Taylor .25 .11
❑ 231 Leonard Marshall .05 .02
❑ 232 Brad Baxter .05 .02
❑ 233 Dennis Byrd .05 .02
❑ 234 Ronnie Lott .10 .05
❑ 235 Boomer Esiason .10 .05
❑ 236 Browning Nagle .05 .02
❑ 237 Rob Moore .10 .05
❑ 238 Jeff Lageman .05 .02
❑ 239 Johnny Mitchell .05 .02
❑ 240 Chris Burkett .05 .02

❑ 241 Eric Thomas .05 .02
❑ 242 Johnny Johnson .05 .02
❑ 243 Eric Allen .05 .02
❑ 244 Fred Barnett .10 .05
❑ 245 Keith Byars .05 .02
❑ 246 Randall Cunningham .25 .11
❑ 247 Heath Sherman .05 .02
❑ 248 Calvin Williams .10 .05
❑ 249 Erik McMillan .05 .02
❑ 250 Byron Evans .05 .02
❑ 251 Seth Joyner .05 .02
❑ 252 Vai Sikahema .05 .02
❑ 253 Andre Waters .05 .02
❑ 254 Tim Harris .05 .02
❑ 255 Mark Bavaro .05 .02
❑ 256 Clyde Simmons .05 .02
❑ 257 Steve Beuerlein .05 .02
❑ 258 Randal Hill UER .05 .02
(Name misspelled Randall on front)
❑ 259 Ernie Jones .05 .02
❑ 260 Robert Massey .05 .02
❑ 261 Ricky Proehl UER .05 .02
(Name misspelled Rickey on front)
❑ 262 Aeneas Williams .05 .02
❑ 263 Johnny Bailey .05 .02
❑ 264 Chris Chandler UER .10 .05
(Name misspelled Cris on front)
❑ 265 Anthony Thompson .05 .02
❑ 266 Gary Clark .10 .05
❑ 267 Chuck Cecil .05 .02
❑ 268 Rich Camarillo .05 .02
❑ 269 Neil O'Donnell .25 .11
❑ 270 Gerald Williams .05 .02
❑ 271 Greg Lloyd .25 .11
❑ 272 Eric Green .05 .02
❑ 273 Merril Hoge .05 .02
❑ 274 Ernie Mills .05 .02
❑ 275 Rod Woodson .25 .11
❑ 276 Gary Anderson K .05 .02
❑ 277 Barry Foster .10 .05
❑ 278 Jeff Graham .10 .05
❑ 279 Dwight Stone .05 .02
❑ 280 Kevin Greene .25 .11
❑ 281 Eric Bieniemy .05 .02
❑ 282 Marion Butts .05 .02
❑ 283 Gill Byrd .05 .02
❑ 284 Stan Humphries .25 .11
❑ 285 Anthony Miller .10 .05
❑ 286 Leslie O'Neal .10 .05
❑ 287 Junior Seau .25 .11
❑ 288 Ronnie Harmon .05 .02
❑ 289 Nate Lewis .05 .02
❑ 290 John Kidd .05 .02
❑ 291 Steve Young .75 .35
❑ 292 John Taylor .10 .05
❑ 293 Jerry Rice 1.00 .45
❑ 294 Tim McDonald .05 .02
❑ 295 Brent Jones .10 .05
❑ 296 Tom Rathman .05 .02
❑ 297 Dexter Carter .05 .02
❑ 298 Mike Cofer .05 .02
❑ 299 Ricky Watters .25 .11
❑ 300 Mervyn Fernandez .05 .02
❑ 301 Amp Lee .05 .02
❑ 302 Kevin Fagan .05 .02
❑ 303 Roy Foster .05 .02
❑ 304 Bill Romanowski .05 .02
❑ 305 Brian Blades .10 .05
❑ 306 John L. Williams .05 .02
❑ 307 Tommy Kane .05 .02
❑ 308 John Kasay .05 .02
❑ 309 Chris Warren .10 .05
❑ 310 Rufus Porter .05 .02
❑ 311 Cortez Kennedy .10 .05
❑ 312 Dan McGwire UER .05 .02
(Name misspelled McGuire on front)
❑ 313 Stan Gelbaugh .05 .02
❑ 314 Kelvin Martin .05 .02
❑ 315 Ferrell Edmunds .05 .02
❑ 316 Eugene Robinson .05 .02
❑ 317 Gary Anderson RB .05 .02
❑ 318 Reggie Cobb .05 .02
❑ 319 Lawrence Dawsey .05 .02
❑ 320 Courtney Hawkins .05 .02
❑ 321 Santana Dotson .10 .05
❑ 322 Ron Hall .05 .02
❑ 323 Keith McCants .05 .02
❑ 324 Martin Mayhew .05 .02
❑ 325 Anthony Munoz .10 .05
❑ 326 Steve DeBerg .05 .02
❑ 327 Vince Workman .05 .02
❑ 328 Earnest Byner .05 .02
❑ 329 Ricky Ervins .05 .02
❑ 330 Jim Lachey .05 .02
❑ 331 Chip Lohmiller .05 .02
❑ 332 Ricky Sanders UER .05 .02
(Name misspelled Rickey on front)
❑ 333 Brad Edwards .05 .02
❑ 334 Tim McGee .05 .02
❑ 335 Darrell Green .05 .02
❑ 336 Charles Mann .05 .02
❑ 337 Wilber Marshall .05 .02
❑ 338 Brian Mitchell .10 .05
❑ 339 Art Monk .10 .05
❑ 340 Mark Rypien .05 .02
❑ 341 John Elway C83 .75 .35
❑ 342 Jim Kelly C83 .10 .05
❑ 343 Dan Marino C83 .75 .35
❑ 344 Eric Dickerson C83 .10 .05
❑ 345 Willie Gault C83 .05 .02
❑ 346 Ken O'Brien C83 .05 .02
❑ 347 Darrell Green C83 .05 .02
❑ 348 Richard Dent C83 .05 .02
❑ 349 Karl Mecklenburg C83 .05 .02
❑ 350 Henry Ellard C83 .05 .02
❑ 351 Roger Craig C83 .05 .02
❑ 352 Charles Mann C83 .05 .02
❑ 353 Checklist A UER .05 .02
(Misspellings)
❑ 354 Checklist B UER .05 .02
(Misspellings)
❑ 355 Checklist C UER .05 .02
(Numbering out of order)
❑ 356 Checklist D UER .05 .02
(Misspellings and numbering out of order)
❑ 357 Checklist E UER .05 .02
(Misspelling and numbering out of order)
❑ 358 Checklist F UER .05 .02
(Misspelling and numbering out of order)
❑ 359 Checklist G UER .05 .02
(Misspellings and numbering out of order)
❑ 360 Rookies Checklist UER .05 .02
(Misspelling on 391)
❑ 361 D.Bledsoe IR RC UER 2.00 .90
(Text indicates drafted in '92; should be '93)
❑ 362 Rick Mirer IR RC .30 .14
❑ 363 Garrison Hearst IR RC .50 .23
❑ 364 Marvin Jones IR RC .05 .02
❑ 365 John Copeland IR RC .10 .05
❑ 366 Eric Curry IR RC .05 .02
❑ 367 Curtis Conway IR RC .40 .18
❑ 368 Willie Roaf IR RC .10 .05
❑ 369 Lincoln Kennedy IR RC .05 .02
❑ 370 Jerome Bettis IR RC .75 .35
❑ 371 Dan Williams IR RC .05 .02
❑ 372 Patrick Bates IR RC .05 .02
❑ 373 Brad Hopkins IR RC .05 .02
❑ 374 Steve Everitt IR RC .05 .02
❑ 375 Wayne Simmons IR RC .05 .02
❑ 376 Tom Carter IR RC .10 .05
❑ 377 Ernest Dye IR RC .05 .02
❑ 378 Lester Holmes IR RC .05 .02
❑ 379 Irv Smith IR RC .05 .02
❑ 380 Robert Smith IR RC 1.50 .70
❑ 381 Darrien Gordon IR RC .05 .02
❑ 382 Deon Figures IR RC .10 .05
❑ 383 O.J. McDuffie IR RC .50 .23
❑ 384 Dana Stubblefield IR RC .25 .11
❑ 385 Todd Kelly IR RC .05 .02
❑ 386 Thomas Smith IR RC .10 .05
❑ 387 George Teague IR RC .10 .05
❑ 388 Carlton Gray IR RC .05 .02
❑ 389 Chris Slade IR RC .10 .05
❑ 390 Ben Coleman IR RC .05 .02
❑ 391 Ryan McNeil IR RC UER .05 .02
(Name misspelled McNeill on front)
❑ 392 D.DuBose IR RC .05 .02
❑ 393 Carl Simpson IR RC .05 .02
❑ 394 Coleman Rudolph IR RC .05 .02
❑ 395 Tony McGee IR RC .10 .05
❑ 396 Roger Harper IR RC .05 .02
❑ 397 Troy Drayton IR RC .10 .05
❑ 398 Michael Strahan IR RC .25 .11
❑ 399 Natrone Means IR RC .40 .18
❑ 400 Glyn Milburn IR RC .25 .11

1994 SkyBox Impact

	MINT	NRMT
COMPLETE SET (300)	15.00	6.75

❑ 1 Johnny Bailey .05 .02
❑ 2 Steve Beuerlein .05 .02
❑ 3 Gary Clark .10 .05
❑ 4 Garrison Hearst .25 .11
❑ 5 Ronald Moore .05 .02
❑ 6 Ricky Proehl .05 .02
❑ 7 Eric Swann .10 .05
❑ 8 Aeneas Williams .05 .02
❑ 9 Robert Massey .05 .02
❑ 10 Chuck Cecil .05 .02
❑ 11 Ken Harvey .05 .02
❑ 12 Michael Haynes .10 .05
❑ 13 Tony Smith .05 .02
❑ 14 Bobby Hebert .05 .02
❑ 15 Mike Pritchard .05 .02
❑ 16 Andre Rison .10 .05
❑ 17 Deion Sanders .40 .18
❑ 18 Pierce Holt .05 .02
❑ 19 Erric Pegram .05 .02
❑ 20 Jessie Tuggle .05 .02
❑ 21 Steve Broussard .05 .02
❑ 22 Don Beebe .05 .02
❑ 23 Cornelius Bennett .10 .05
❑ 24 Kenneth Davis .05 .02
❑ 25 Bill Brooks .05 .02
❑ 26 Jim Kelly .25 .11
❑ 27 Andre Reed .10 .05
❑ 28 Bruce Smith .25 .11
❑ 29 Darryl Talley .05 .02
❑ 30 Thurman Thomas .25 .11
❑ 31 Steve Tasker .10 .05
❑ 32 Neal Anderson .05 .02
❑ 33 Mark Carrier DB .05 .02
❑ 34 Richard Dent .10 .05
❑ 35 Jim Harbaugh .25 .11
❑ 36 Chris Gedney .05 .02
❑ 37 Tom Waddle .05 .02
❑ 38 Curtis Conway .25 .11
❑ 39 Dante Jones .05 .02
❑ 40 Donnell Woolford .05 .02
❑ 41 Tim Worley .05 .02
❑ 42 John Copeland .05 .02
❑ 43 David Klingler .05 .02
❑ 44 Derrick Fenner .05 .02
❑ 45 Harold Green .05 .02
❑ 46 Carl Pickens .25 .11
❑ 47 Tony McGee .05 .02
❑ 48 Darryl Williams .05 .02

❑ 49 Steve Everitt .05 .02
❑ 50 Michael Jackson .10 .05
❑ 51 Eric Metcalf .10 .05
❑ 52 Tommy Vardell .05 .02
❑ 53 Vinny Testaverde .10 .05
❑ 54 Mark Carrier WR .10 .05
❑ 55 Michael Dean Perry .10 .05
❑ 56 Eric Turner .05 .02
❑ 57 Troy Aikman .75 .35
❑ 58 Alvin Harper .10 .05
❑ 59 Michael Irvin .25 .11
❑ 60 Leon Lett .05 .02
❑ 61 Russell Maryland .05 .02
❑ 62 Jay Novacek .10 .05
❑ 63 Emmitt Smith 1.25 .55
❑ 64 Ken Norton .10 .05
❑ 65 Charles Haley .10 .05
❑ 66 Daryl Johnston .10 .05
❑ 67 Kevin Smith .05 .02
❑ 68 James Washington .05 .02
❑ 69 Kevin Williams .10 .05
❑ 70 Bernie Kosar .10 .05
❑ 71 Mike Croel .05 .02
❑ 72 John Elway 1.50 .70
❑ 73 Shannon Sharpe .10 .05
❑ 74 Rod Bernstine .05 .02
❑ 75 Simon Fletcher .05 .02
❑ 76 Arthur Marshall .05 .02
❑ 77 Glyn Milburn .10 .05
❑ 78 Dennis Smith .05 .02
❑ 79 Herman Moore .25 .11
❑ 80 Rodney Peete .05 .02
❑ 81 Barry Sanders 1.50 .70
❑ 82 Mel Gray .05 .02
❑ 83 Erik Kramer .10 .05
❑ 84 Pat Swilling .05 .02
❑ 85 Willie Green .05 .02
❑ 86 Chris Spielman .10 .05
❑ 87 Robert Porcher .05 .02
❑ 88 Derrick Moore .05 .02
❑ 89 Edgar Bennett .25 .11
❑ 90 Tony Bennett .05 .02
❑ 91 LeRoy Butler .05 .02
❑ 92 Brett Favre 1.50 .70
❑ 93 Jackie Harris .05 .02
❑ 94 Sterling Sharpe .10 .05
❑ 95 Darrell Thompson .05 .02
❑ 96 Reggie White .25 .11
❑ 97 Terrell Buckley .05 .02
❑ 98 Cris Dishman .05 .02
❑ 99 Ernest Givins .10 .05
❑ 100 Haywood Jeffires .10 .05
❑ 101 Warren Moon .25 .11
❑ 102 Lorenzo White .05 .02
❑ 103 Webster Slaughter .05 .02
❑ 104 Ray Childress .05 .02
❑ 105 Wilber Marshall .05 .02
❑ 106 Gary Brown .05 .02
❑ 107 Marcus Robertson .05 .02
❑ 108 Sean Jones .05 .02
❑ 109 Jeff George .25 .11
❑ 110 Steve Emtman .05 .02
❑ 111 Quentin Coryatt .05 .02
❑ 112 Sean Dawkins RC .25 .11
❑ 113 Jeff Herrod .05 .02
❑ 114 Roosevelt Potts .05 .02
❑ 115 Marcus Allen .25 .11
❑ 116 Kimble Anders .10 .05
❑ 117 Tim Barnett .05 .02
❑ 118 J.J. Birden .05 .02
❑ 119 Dale Carter .05 .02
❑ 120 Willie Davis .10 .05
❑ 121 Nick Lowery .05 .02
❑ 122 Joe Montana 1.50 .70
❑ 123 Kevin Ross .05 .02
❑ 124 Neil Smith .25 .11
❑ 125 Derrick Thomas .25 .11
❑ 126 Keith Cash .05 .02
❑ 127 Tim Brown .25 .11
❑ 128 Rocket Ismail .10 .05
❑ 129 Ethan Horton .05 .02
❑ 130 Jeff Hostetler .10 .05
❑ 131 Patrick Bates .05 .02
❑ 132 Terry McDaniel .05 .02
❑ 133 Anthony Smith .05 .02
❑ 134 Greg Robinson .05 .02
❑ 135 James Jett .05 .02
❑ 136 Alexander Wright .05 .02
❑ 137 Flipper Anderson .05 .02
❑ 138 Shane Conlan .05 .02
❑ 139 Jim Everett .10 .05
❑ 140 Henry Ellard .10 .05
❑ 141 Jerome Bettis .25 .11
❑ 142 Troy Drayton .05 .02
❑ 143 Sean Gilbert .05 .02
❑ 144 Chris Miller .05 .02
❑ 145 Keith Byars .05 .02
❑ 146 Marco Coleman .05 .02
❑ 147 Bryan Cox .05 .02
❑ 148 Irving Fryar .10 .05
❑ 149 Mark Ingram .05 .02
❑ 150 Keith Jackson .05 .02
❑ 151 Terry Kirby .25 .11
❑ 152 Dan Marino 1.50 .70
❑ 153 O.J. McDuffie .25 .11
❑ 154 Scott Mitchell .25 .11
❑ 155 Anthony Carter .10 .05
❑ 156 Cris Carter .40 .18
❑ 157 Chris Doleman .05 .02
❑ 158 Steve Jordan .05 .02
❑ 159 Qadry Ismail .25 .11
❑ 160 Randall McDaniel .05 .02
❑ 161 John Randle .10 .05
❑ 162 Robert Smith .25 .11
❑ 163 Henry Thomas .05 .02
❑ 164 Terry Allen .10 .05
❑ 165 Scottie Graham RC .10 .05
❑ 166 Drew Bledsoe 1.00 .45
❑ 167 Vincent Brown .05 .02
❑ 168 Ben Coates .25 .11
❑ 169 Leonard Russell .05 .02
❑ 170 Andre Tippett .05 .02
❑ 171 Vincent Brisby .25 .11
❑ 172 Michael Timpson .05 .02
❑ 173 Bruce Armstrong .05 .02
❑ 174 Morten Andersen UER .05 .02
(Morton on front)
❑ 175 Derek Brown RBK .05 .02
❑ 176 Quinn Early .10 .05
❑ 177 Rickey Jackson .05 .02
❑ 178 Vaughan Johnson .05 .02
❑ 179 Lorenzo Neal .05 .02
❑ 180 Sam Mills .05 .02
❑ 181 Irv Smith .05 .02
❑ 182 Renaldo Turnbull .05 .02
❑ 183 Wade Wilson .05 .02
❑ 184 Willie Roaf .05 .02
❑ 185 Michael Brooks .05 .02
❑ 186 Mark Jackson .05 .02
❑ 187 Rodney Hampton .25 .11
❑ 188 Phil Simms .10 .05
❑ 189 Dave Meggett .05 .02
❑ 190 Mike Sherrard .05 .02
❑ 191 Chris Calloway .05 .02
❑ 192 Brad Baxter .05 .02
❑ 193 Ronnie Lott .10 .05
❑ 194 Boomer Esiason .10 .05
❑ 195 Rob Moore .10 .05
❑ 196 Johnny Johnson .05 .02
❑ 197 Marvin Jones .05 .02
❑ 198 Mo Lewis .05 .02
❑ 199 Johnny Mitchell .05 .02
❑ 200 Brian Washington .05 .02
❑ 201 Eric Allen .05 .02
❑ 202 Fred Barnett .10 .05
❑ 203 Mark Bavaro .05 .02
❑ 204 Randall Cunningham .25 .11
❑ 205 Vaughn Hebron .05 .02
❑ 206 Seth Joyner .05 .02
❑ 207 Clyde Simmons .05 .02
❑ 208 Herschel Walker .10 .05
❑ 209 Calvin Williams .10 .05
❑ 210 Neil O'Donnell .25 .11
❑ 211 Eric Green .05 .02
❑ 212 Leroy Thompson .05 .02
❑ 213 Rod Woodson .25 .11
❑ 214 Barry Foster .05 .02
❑ 215 Jeff Graham .05 .02
❑ 216 Kevin Greene .25 .11
❑ 217 Deon Figures .05 .02
❑ 218 Greg Lloyd .25 .11
❑ 219 Marion Butts .05 .02
❑ 220 Chris Mims .05 .02
❑ 221 Eric Curry .05 .02
❑ 222 Ronnie Harmon .05 .02
❑ 223 Stan Humphries .25 .11
❑ 224 Nate Lewis .05 .02
❑ 225 Natrone Means .25 .11
❑ 226 Anthony Miller .10 .05
❑ 227 Leslie O'Neal .05 .02
❑ 228 Junior Seau .25 .11
❑ 229 Brent Jones .10 .05
❑ 230 Tim McDonald .05 .02
❑ 231 Tom Rathman .05 .02
❑ 232 Jerry Rice .75 .35
❑ 233 Dana Stubblefield .25 .11
❑ 234 John Taylor .10 .05
❑ 235 Ricky Watters .25 .11
❑ 236 Steve Young .60 .25
❑ 237 Amp Lee .05 .02
❑ 238 Robert Blackmon .05 .02
❑ 239 Brian Blades .10 .05
❑ 240 Cortez Kennedy .10 .05
❑ 241 Kelvin Martin .05 .02
❑ 242 Rick Mirer .25 .11
❑ 243 Eugene Robinson .05 .02
❑ 244 Chris Warren .10 .05
❑ 245 John L. Williams .05 .02
❑ 246 Jon Vaughn .05 .02
❑ 247 Reggie Cobb .05 .02
❑ 248 Horace Copeland .05 .02
❑ 249 Der. Alexander WR RC .50 .23
❑ 250 Santana Dotson .10 .05
❑ 251 Craig Erickson .05 .02
❑ 252 Courtney Hawkins .05 .02
❑ 253 Hardy Nickerson .10 .05
❑ 254 Vince Workman .05 .02
❑ 255 Paul Gruber .05 .02
❑ 256 Reggie Brooks .10 .05
❑ 257 Tom Carter .05 .02
❑ 258 Andre Collins .05 .02
❑ 259 Darrell Green .05 .02
❑ 260 Desmond Howard .10 .05
❑ 261 Tim McGee .05 .02
❑ 262 Brian Mitchell .05 .02
❑ 263 Art Monk .10 .05
❑ 264 John Friesz .10 .05
❑ 265 Ricky Sanders .05 .02
❑ 266 Checklist .05 .02
❑ 267 Checklist .05 .02
❑ 268 Checklist .05 .02
❑ 269 Checklist .05 .02
❑ 270 Checklist .05 .02
❑ 271 Carolina Panthers .15 .07
Logo Card
❑ 272 Jacksonville Jaguars .15 .07
Logo Card
❑ 273 Dan Wilkinson RC .10 .05
❑ 274 Marshall Faulk RC 4.00 1.80
❑ 275 Heath Shuler RC .25 .11
❑ 276 Willie McGinest RC .25 .11
❑ 277 Trev Alberts RC .10 .05
❑ 278 Trent Dilfer RC 2.00 .90
❑ 279 Bryant Young RC .25 .11
❑ 280 Sam Adams RC .10 .05
❑ 281 Antonio Langham RC .10 .05
❑ 282 Jamir Miller RC .05 .02
❑ 283 John Thierry RC .05 .02
❑ 284 Aaron Glenn RC .10 .05
❑ 285 Joe Johnson RC .05 .02
❑ 286 Bernard Williams RC .05 .02
❑ 287 Wayne Gandy RC .05 .02
❑ 288 Aaron Taylor RC .05 .02
❑ 289 Charles Johnson RC .50 .23
❑ 290 Dewayne Washington RC .10 .05
❑ 291 Todd Steussie RC .10 .05
❑ 292 Tim Bowens RC .10 .05
❑ 293 Johnnie Morton RC .25 .11
❑ 294 Rob Frederickson RC .10 .05
❑ 295 Shante Carver RC .05 .02
❑ 296 Thomas Lewis RC .10 .05
❑ 297 Greg Hill RC .25 .11
❑ 298 Henry Ford RC .05 .02
❑ 299 Jeff Burris RC .10 .05
❑ 300 William Floyd RC .25 .11
❑ NNO Carolina Panthers 20.00 9.00
Hologram Logo
❑ P1 Jim Kelly Promo .75 .35

1995 SkyBox Impact

	MINT	NRMT
COMPLETE SET (200)	15.00	6.75

Card	MINT	NRMT
❑ 1 Garrison Hearst	.25	.11
❑ 2 Ronald Moore	.05	.02
❑ 3 Eric Swann	.10	.05
❑ 4 Aeneas Williams	.05	.02
❑ 5 Jeff George	.10	.05
❑ 6 Craig Heyward	.10	.05
❑ 7 Terance Mathis	.10	.05
❑ 8 Andre Rison	.10	.05
❑ 9 Cornelius Bennett	.10	.05
❑ 10 Jim Kelly	.25	.11
❑ 11 Andre Reed	.10	.05
❑ 12 Bruce Smith	.25	.11
❑ 13 Thurman Thomas	.25	.11
❑ 14 Frank Reich	.05	.02
❑ 15 Lamar Lathon	.05	.02
❑ 16 Darion Conner	.05	.02
❑ 17 Randy Baldwin	.05	.02
❑ 18 Don Beebe	.05	.02
❑ 19 Mark Carrier DB	.05	.02
❑ 20 Jeff Graham	.05	.02
❑ 21 Raymont Harris	.05	.02
❑ 22 Alonzo Spellman	.05	.02
❑ 23 Lewis Tillman	.05	.02
❑ 24 Steve Walsh	.05	.02
❑ 25 Jeff Blake RC	.75	.35
❑ 26 Carl Pickens	.25	.11
❑ 27 Darnay Scott	.25	.11
❑ 28 Dan Wilkinson	.10	.05
❑ 29 Derrick Alexander WR	.25	.11
❑ 30 Leroy Hoard	.05	.02
❑ 31 Antonio Langham	.05	.02
❑ 32 Vinny Testaverde	.10	.05
❑ 33 Eric Turner	.05	.02
❑ 34 Troy Aikman	.75	.35
❑ 35 Charles Haley	.10	.05
❑ 36 Alvin Harper	.05	.02
❑ 37 Michael Irvin	.25	.11
❑ 38 Daryl Johnston	.10	.05
❑ 39 Jay Novacek	.10	.05
❑ 40 Leon Lett	.05	.02
❑ 41 Emmitt Smith	1.25	.55
❑ 42 John Elway	1.50	.70
❑ 43 Glyn Milburn	.05	.02
❑ 44 Anthony Miller	.10	.05
❑ 45 Leonard Russell	.05	.02
❑ 46 Shannon Sharpe	.10	.05
❑ 47 Scott Mitchell	.10	.05
❑ 48 Herman Moore	.25	.11
❑ 49 Barry Sanders	1.50	.70
❑ 50 Chris Spielman	.10	.05
❑ 51 Edgar Bennett	.10	.05
❑ 52 Robert Brooks	.25	.11
❑ 53 Brett Favre	1.50	.70
❑ 54 Bryce Paup	.25	.11
❑ 55 Sterling Sharpe	.10	.05
❑ 56 Reggie White	.25	.11
❑ 57 Ray Childress	.05	.02
❑ 58 Haywood Jeffires	.05	.02
❑ 59 Webster Slaughter	.05	.02
❑ 60 Lorenzo White	.05	.02
❑ 61 Trev Alberts	.05	.02
❑ 62 Quentin Coryatt	.10	.05
❑ 63 Sean Dawkins	.10	.05
❑ 64 Marshall Faulk	.40	.18
❑ 65 Jeff Lageman	.05	.02
❑ 66 Steve Beuerlein	.05	.02
❑ 67 Desmond Howard	.10	.05
❑ 68 Kelvin Martin	.05	.02
❑ 69 Reggie Cobb	.05	.02
❑ 70 Marcus Allen	.25	.11
❑ 71 Greg Hill	.10	.05
❑ 72 Joe Montana	1.50	.70
❑ 73 Neil Smith	.10	.05
❑ 74 Derrick Thomas	.10	.05
❑ 75 Tim Brown	.25	.11
❑ 76 Rocket Ismail	.10	.05
❑ 77 Jeff Hostetler	.10	.05
❑ 78 Chester McGlockton	.10	.05
❑ 79 Harvey Williams	.05	.02
❑ 80 Tim Bowens	.05	.02
❑ 81 Irving Fryar	.10	.05
❑ 82 Keith Jackson	.05	.02
❑ 83 Terry Kirby	.10	.05
❑ 84 Dan Marino	1.50	.70
❑ 85 O.J. McDuffie	.25	.11
❑ 86 Bernie Parmalee	.10	.05
❑ 87 Terry Allen	.10	.05
❑ 88 Cris Carter	.25	.11
❑ 89 Qadry Ismail	.10	.05
❑ 90 Warren Moon	.10	.05
❑ 91 Jake Reed	.10	.05
❑ 92 Drew Bledsoe	.75	.35
❑ 93 Vincent Brisby	.05	.02
❑ 94 Ben Coates	.10	.05
❑ 95 Michael Timpson	.05	.02
❑ 96 Jim Everett	.05	.02
❑ 97 Michael Haynes	.10	.05
❑ 98 Willie Roaf	.05	.02
❑ 99 Michael Brooks	.05	.02
❑ 100 Dave Brown	.10	.05
❑ 101 Rodney Hampton	.10	.05
❑ 102 Thomas Lewis	.10	.05
❑ 103 Dave Meggett	.05	.02
❑ 104 Boomer Esiason	.10	.05
❑ 105 Johnny Johnson	.05	.02
❑ 106 Johnny Mitchell	.05	.02
❑ 107 Rob Moore	.05	.02
❑ 108 Fred Barnett	.10	.05
❑ 109 Randall Cunningham	.25	.11
❑ 110 Charlie Garner	.10	.05
❑ 111 Herschel Walker	.10	.05
❑ 112 Barry Foster	.10	.05
❑ 113 Eric Green	.05	.02
❑ 114 Charles Johnson	.10	.05
❑ 115 Greg Lloyd	.10	.05
❑ 116 Byron Bam Morris	.10	.05
❑ 117 Neil O'Donnell	.10	.05
❑ 118 Rod Woodson	.10	.05
❑ 119 Flipper Anderson	.05	.02
❑ 120 Jerome Bettis	.25	.11
❑ 121 Troy Drayton	.05	.02
❑ 122 Sean Gilbert	.10	.05
❑ 123 Ronnie Harmon	.05	.02
❑ 124 Stan Humphries	.10	.05
❑ 125 Shawn Jefferson	.05	.02
❑ 126 Natrone Means	.25	.11
❑ 127 Leslie O'Neal	.10	.05
❑ 128 Junior Seau	.25	.11
❑ 129 William Floyd	.25	.11
❑ 130 Brent Jones	.05	.02
❑ 131 Jerry Rice	.75	.35
❑ 132 Deion Sanders	.50	.23
❑ 133 Dana Stubblefield	.25	.11
❑ 134 Ricky Watters	.25	.11
❑ 135 Bryant Young	.10	.05
❑ 136 Steve Young	.60	.25
❑ 137 Brian Blades	.10	.05
❑ 138 Cortez Kennedy	.10	.05
❑ 139 Rick Mirer	.25	.11
❑ 140 Chris Warren	.10	.05
❑ 141 Horace Copeland	.05	.02
❑ 142 Trent Dilfer	.25	.11
❑ 143 Hardy Nickerson	.05	.02
❑ 144 Errict Rhett	.25	.11
❑ 145 Henry Ellard	.10	.05
❑ 146 Brian Mitchell	.05	.02
❑ 147 Heath Shuler	.25	.11
❑ 148 Tydus Winans	.05	.02
❑ 149 Steve Tasker	.10	.05
❑ 150 Jeff Burris	.05	.02
❑ 151 Tyrone Hughes	.10	.05
❑ 152 Mel Gray	.05	.02
❑ 153 Kevin Williams WR	.10	.05
❑ 154 Andre Coleman	.05	.02
❑ 155 Corey Sawyer	.05	.02
❑ 156 Darrien Gordon	.05	.02
❑ 157 Aaron Glenn	.05	.02
❑ 158 Eric Metcalf	.10	.05
❑ 159 Errict Rhett SS	.25	.11
❑ 160 Marshall Faulk SS	.25	.11
❑ 161 Darnay Scott SS	.25	.11
❑ 162 William Floyd SS	.05	.02
❑ 163 Charlie Garner SS	.10	.05
❑ 164 Heath Shuler SS	.25	.11
❑ 165 Trent Dilfer SS	.25	.11
❑ 166 Willie McGinest SS	.10	.05
❑ 167 Byron Bam Morris SS	.10	.05
❑ 168 Mario Bates SS	.25	.11
❑ 169 Ki-Jana Carter RC	.25	.11
❑ 170 Tony Boselli RC	.25	.11
❑ 171 Steve McNair RC	2.50	1.10
❑ 172 Michael Westbrook RC	1.25	.55
❑ 173 Kerry Collins RC	1.25	.55
❑ 174 Kevin Carter RC	.25	.11
❑ 175 Mike Mamula RC	.10	.05
❑ 176 Joey Galloway RC	2.00	.90
❑ 177 Kyle Brady RC	.25	.11
❑ 178 J.J. Stokes RC	.25	.11
❑ 179 Warren Sapp RC	.50	.23
❑ 180 Rob Johnson RC	1.50	.70
❑ 181 Tyrone Wheatley RC	1.00	.45
❑ 182 Napoleon Kaufman RC	1.25	.55
❑ 183 James O. Stewart RC	1.50	.70
❑ 184 Dino Philyaw RC	.05	.02
❑ 185 Rashaan Salaam RC	.25	.11
❑ 186 Tyrone Poole RC	.10	.05
❑ 187 Ty Law RC	.10	.05
❑ 188 Joe Aska RC	.10	.05
❑ 189 Mark Bruener RC	.10	.05
❑ 190 Derrick Brooks RC	.25	.11
❑ 191 Jack Jackson RC	.05	.02
❑ 192 Ray Zellars RC	.10	.05
❑ 193 Eddie Goines RC	.05	.02
❑ 194 Chris Sanders RC	.25	.11
❑ 195 Charlie Simmons RC	.05	.02
❑ 196 Lee DeRamus RC	.05	.02
❑ 197 Frank Sanders RC	.75	.35
❑ 198 Rodney Thomas RC	.25	.11
❑ 199 Checklist A 1-128	.05	.02
❑ 200 Checklist B 129-200	.05	.02
❑ M1 Brett Favre SkyMotion	35.00	16.00
❑ M2 Brett Favre SkyMotion	35.00	16.00
❑ P1 Promo Sheet	2.50	1.10

Chris Spielman
Ronald Moore
Bernie Parmalee
Tyrone Hughes
Brett Favre Countdown
Bryan Cox Impact Power

1996 SkyBox Impact

	MINT	NRMT
COMPLETE SET (200)	15.00	6.75

Card	MINT	NRMT
❑ 1 Garrison Hearst	.20	.09
❑ 2 Rob Moore	.20	.09

❑ 3 Frank Sanders .20 .09
❑ 4 Eric Swann .10 .05
❑ 5 Aeneas Williams .10 .05
❑ 6 Bert Emanuel .20 .09
❑ 7 Jeff George .20 .09
❑ 8 Craig Heyward .10 .05
❑ 9 Terance Mathis .10 .05
❑ 10 Eric Metcalf .10 .05
❑ 11 Leroy Hoard .10 .05
❑ 12 Michael Jackson .20 .09
❑ 13 Andre Rison .20 .09
❑ 14 Vinny Testaverde .20 .09
❑ 15 Eric Turner .10 .05
❑ 16 Darick Holmes .10 .05
❑ 17 Jim Kelly .30 .14
❑ 18 Bryce Paup .10 .05
❑ 19 Bruce Smith .20 .09
❑ 20 Thurman Thomas .30 .14
❑ 21 Mark Carrier WR .10 .05
❑ 22 Kerry Collins .30 .14
❑ 23 Derrick Moore .10 .05
❑ 24 Tyrone Poole .10 .05
❑ 25 Curtis Conway .30 .14
❑ 26 Jeff Graham .10 .05
❑ 27 Erik Kramer .10 .05
❑ 28 Rashaan Salaam .30 .14
❑ 29 Jeff Blake .30 .14
❑ 30 Ki-Jana Carter .20 .09
❑ 31 Carl Pickens .30 .14
❑ 32 Darnay Scott .20 .09
❑ 33 Troy Aikman .75 .35
❑ 34 Charles Haley .20 .09
❑ 35 Michael Irvin .30 .14
❑ 36 Daryl Johnston .20 .09
❑ 37 Jay Novacek .10 .05
❑ 38 Deion Sanders .40 .18
❑ 39 Emmitt Smith 1.25 .55
❑ 40 Steve Atwater .10 .05
❑ 41 Terrell Davis 2.00 .90
❑ 42 John Elway 1.50 .70
❑ 43 Anthony Miller .20 .09
❑ 44 Shannon Sharpe .20 .09
❑ 45 Scott Mitchell .20 .09
❑ 46 Herman Moore .30 .14
❑ 47 Brett Perriman .10 .05
❑ 48 Barry Sanders 1.50 .70
❑ 49 Edgar Bennett .20 .09
❑ 50 Robert Brooks .30 .14
❑ 51 Mark Chmura .20 .09
❑ 52 Brett Favre 1.50 .70
❑ 53 Reggie White .30 .14
❑ 54 Mel Gray .10 .05
❑ 55 Steve McNair .50 .23
❑ 56 Chris Sanders .20 .09
❑ 57 Rodney Thomas .10 .05
❑ 58 Quentin Coryatt .10 .05
❑ 59 Sean Dawkins .10 .05
❑ 60 Ken Dilger .20 .09
❑ 61 Marshall Faulk .30 .14
❑ 62 Jim Harbaugh .20 .09
❑ 63 Tony Boselli .10 .05
❑ 64 Mark Brunell .75 .35
❑ 65 Keenan McCardell .30 .14
❑ 66 James O.Stewart .20 .09
❑ 67 Marcus Allen .30 .14
❑ 68 Steve Bono .10 .05
❑ 69 Neil Smith .10 .05
❑ 70 Derrick Thomas .20 .09
❑ 71 Tamarick Vanover .20 .09
❑ 72 Bryan Cox .10 .05
❑ 73 Irving Fryar .20 .09
❑ 74 Eric Green .10 .05
❑ 75 Dan Marino 1.50 .70
❑ 76 O.J. McDuffie .20 .09
❑ 77 Bernie Parmalee .10 .05
❑ 78 Cris Carter .30 .14
❑ 79 Qadry Ismail .10 .05
❑ 80 Warren Moon .20 .09
❑ 81 Jake Reed .20 .09
❑ 82 Robert Smith .20 .09
❑ 83 Drew Bledsoe .75 .35
❑ 84 Ben Coates .20 .09
❑ 85 Curtis Martin .50 .23
❑ 86 Willie McGinest .10 .05
❑ 87 Dave Meggett .10 .05
❑ 88 Mario Bates .20 .09
❑ 89 Quinn Early .10 .05
❑ 90 Jim Everett .10 .05
❑ 91 Michael Haynes .10 .05
❑ 92 Renaldo Turnbull .10 .05
❑ 93 Dave Brown .10 .05
❑ 94 Rodney Hampton .20 .09
❑ 95 Thomas Lewis .10 .05
❑ 96 Phillippi Sparks .10 .05
❑ 97 Tyrone Wheatley .20 .09
❑ 98 Kyle Brady .10 .05
❑ 99 Hugh Douglas .20 .09
❑ 100 Mo Lewis .10 .05
❑ 101 Adrian Murrell .30 .14
❑ 102 Tim Brown .30 .14
❑ 103 Jeff Hostetler .10 .05
❑ 104 Rocket Ismail .10 .05
❑ 105 Chester McGlockton .10 .05
❑ 106 Harvey Williams .10 .05
❑ 107 Fred Barnett .10 .05
❑ 108 William Fuller .10 .05
❑ 109 Charlie Garner .10 .05
❑ 110 Rodney Peete .10 .05
❑ 111 Ricky Watters .20 .09
❑ 112 Calvin Williams .10 .05
❑ 113 Byron Bam Morris .20 .09
❑ 114 Neil O'Donnell .20 .09
❑ 115 Erric Pegram .10 .05
❑ 116 Kordell Stewart .40 .18
❑ 117 Yancey Thigpen .20 .09
❑ 118 Rod Woodson .20 .09
❑ 119 Jerome Bettis .30 .14
❑ 120 Isaac Bruce .30 .14
❑ 121 Troy Drayton .10 .05
❑ 122 Leslie O'Neal .10 .05
❑ 123 Aaron Hayden RC .10 .05
❑ 124 Stan Humphries .20 .09
❑ 125 Natrone Means .30 .14
❑ 126 Junior Seau .20 .09
❑ 127 William Floyd .20 .09
❑ 128 Brent Jones .10 .05
❑ 129 Derek Loville .10 .05
❑ 130 Ken Norton .10 .05
❑ 131 Jerry Rice .75 .35
❑ 132 J.J. Stokes .30 .14
❑ 133 Steve Young .60 .25
❑ 134 Brian Blades .10 .05
❑ 135 Joey Galloway .40 .18
❑ 136 Cortez Kennedy .10 .05
❑ 137 Rick Mirer .20 .09
❑ 138 Chris Warren .20 .09
❑ 139 Trent Dilfer .30 .14
❑ 140 Alvin Harper .10 .05
❑ 141 Jackie Harris .10 .05
❑ 142 Hardy Nickerson .10 .05
❑ 143 Errict Rhett .20 .09
❑ 144 Terry Allen .20 .09
❑ 145 Henry Ellard .10 .05
❑ 146 Brian Mitchell .10 .05
❑ 147 Heath Shuler .20 .09
❑ 148 Michael Westbrook .30 .14
❑ 149 Karim Abdul-Jabbar RC .50 .23
❑ 150 Mike Alstott RC 1.25 .55
❑ 151 Marco Battaglia RC .10 .05
❑ 152 Tim Biakabutuka RC .60 .25
❑ 153 Sean Boyd RC .20 .09
❑ 154 Tony Brackens RC .20 .09
❑ 155 Duane Clemons RC .10 .05
❑ 156 Marcus Coleman RC .10 .05
❑ 157 Chris Darkins RC .10 .05
❑ 158 Rickey Dudley RC .30 .14
❑ 159 Jason Dunn RC .20 .09
❑ 160 Bobby Engram RC .30 .14
❑ 161 Daryl Gardener RC .10 .05
❑ 162 Eddie George RC 2.50 1.10
❑ 163 Terry Glenn RC 1.00 .45
❑ 164 Kevin Hardy RC .30 .14
❑ 165 Marvin Harrison RC 2.00 .90
❑ 166 Dietrich Jells RC .10 .05
❑ 167 DeRon Jenkins RC .20 .09
❑ 168 Darrius Johnson RC .10 .05
❑ 169 Keyshawn Johnson RC 1.50 .70
❑ 170 Lance Johnstone RC .20 .09
❑ 171 Cedric Jones RC .10 .05
❑ 172 Marcus Jones RC .10 .05
❑ 173 Danny Kanell RC .30 .14
❑ 174 Eddie Kennison RC .30 .14
❑ 175 Jevon Langford RC .10 .05
❑ 176 Markco Maddox RC .20 .09
❑ 177 Derrick Mayes RC .60 .25
❑ 178 Leeland McElroy RC .30 .14
❑ 179 Dell McGee RC .10 .05
❑ 180 Johnny McWilliams RC .20 .09
❑ 181 Alex Molden RC .10 .05
❑ 182 Eric Moulds RC 1.50 .70
❑ 183 Jonathan Ogden RC .10 .05
❑ 184 Lawrence Phillips RC .30 .14
❑ 185 Simeon Rice RC .30 .14
❑ 186 Amani Toomer RC .75 .35
❑ 187 Regan Upshaw RC .10 .05
❑ 188 Jerome Woods RC .10 .05
❑ 189 Darrell Green I .10 .05
❑ 190 Daryl Johnston I .20 .09
❑ 191 Sam Mills I .10 .05
❑ 192 Earnest Byner I .10 .05
❑ 193 Herschel Walker I .20 .09
❑ 194 Brett Favre HL .30 .14
❑ 195 Brett Favre HL .30 .14
(Card says Pack beat 49ers in Jan 1995; right year is 1996 for that victory)
❑ 196 Brett Favre HL .30 .14
❑ 197 Brett Favre HL .30 .14
❑ 198 Brett Favre HL .30 .14
❑ 199 Checklist .10 .05
❑ 200 Checklist .10 .05
❑ BF1 Brett Favre .50 .23
Expired SkyMotion Exchange Card
❑ BF2 Brett Favre .50 .23
Expired SkyMint Exchange Card
❑ P1 Promo Sheet 2.00 .90
Brett Favre
William Floyd Excelerators
Daryl Johnston Inspirations

1996 SkyBox Impact Rookies

	MINT	NRMT
COMPLETE SET (150)	12.00	5.50

❑ 1 Leeland McElroy RC .20 .09
❑ 2 Johnny McWilliams .05 .02
❑ 3 Simeon Rice RC .20 .09
❑ 4 DeRon Jenkins .05 .02
❑ 5 Jermaine Lewis RC .50 .23
❑ 6 Ray Lewis RC 1.50 .70
❑ 7 Jonathan Ogden .05 .02
❑ 8 Eric Moulds RC UER 1.25 .55
(Card misnumbered 123)
❑ 9 Tim Biakabutuka RC .50 .23
❑ 10 Muhsin Muhammad RC .60 .25
❑ 11 Winslow Oliver .05 .02
❑ 12 Bobby Engram RC .20 .09
❑ 13 Walt Harris .05 .02
❑ 14 Willie Anderson .05 .02
❑ 15 Marco Battaglia .05 .02
❑ 16 Jevon Langford .05 .02
❑ 17 Kavika Pittman .05 .02
❑ 18 Stepfret Williams .05 .02
❑ 19 Tony James .05 .02
❑ 20 Jeff Lewis RC .25 .11
❑ 21 John Mobley .05 .02
❑ 22 Detron Smith .05 .02

❑ 23 Derrick Mayes RC .50 .23
❑ 24 Eddie George RC 2.50 1.10
❑ 25 Marvin Harrison RC 1.50 .70
❑ 26 Dedric Mathis .05 .02
❑ 27 Tony Brackens RC .10 .05
❑ 28 Kevin Hardy RC .20 .09
❑ 29 Jerome Woods .05 .02
❑ 30 Karim Abdul-Jabbar RC .40 .18
❑ 31 Daryl Gardener .05 .02
❑ 32 Jerris McPhail .05 .02
❑ 33 Stanley Pritchett .05 .02
❑ 34 Zach Thomas RC .50 .23
❑ 35 Duane Clemons .05 .02
❑ 36 Moe Williams RC .10 .05
❑ 37 Tedy Bruschi .05 .02
❑ 38 Terry Glenn RC .75 .35
❑ 39 Alex Molden .05 .02
❑ 40 Ricky Whittle .05 .02
❑ 41 Cedric Jones .05 .02
❑ 42 Danny Kanell RC .20 .09
❑ 43 Amani Toomer RC .60 .25
❑ 44 Marcus Coleman .05 .02
❑ 45 Keyshawn Johnson RC 1.25 .55
❑ 46 Ray Mickens .05 .02
❑ 47 Alex Van Dyke RC .10 .05
❑ 48 Rickey Dudley RC .20 .09
❑ 49 Lance Johnstone .05 .02
❑ 50 Brian Dawkins .05 .02
❑ 51 Jason Dunn .05 .02
❑ 52 Ray Farmer .05 .02
❑ 53 Bobby Hoying RC .30 .14
❑ 54 Jermane Mayberry .05 .02
❑ 55 Bryan Still RC .20 .09
❑ 56 Tony Banks RC .75 .35
❑ 57 Ernie Conwell .05 .02
❑ 58 Eddie Kennison RC .20 .09
❑ 59 Jerald Moore RC .20 .09
❑ 60 Lawrence Phillips RC .20 .09
❑ 61 Israel Ifeanyi .05 .02
❑ 62 Terrell Owens RC 1.50 .70
❑ 63 Iheanyi Uwaezuoke RC .20 .09
❑ 64 Mike Alstott RC 1.00 .45
❑ 65 Marcus Jones .05 .02
❑ 66 Nilo Silvan .05 .02
❑ 67 Regan Upshaw .05 .02
❑ 68 Stephen Davis RC 2.50 1.10
❑ 69 Troy Aikman AIR .50 .23
❑ 70 Terry Allen AIR .10 .05
❑ 71 Edgar Bennett AIR .10 .05
❑ 72 Jerome Bettis AIR .10 .05
❑ 73 Drew Bledsoe AIR .50 .23
❑ 74 Tim Brown AIR .10 .05
❑ 75 Mark Brunell AIR .50 .23
❑ 76 Cris Carter AIR .20 .09
❑ 77 Kerry Collins AIR .20 .09
❑ 78 Terrell Davis AIR 1.25 .55
❑ 79 John Elway AIR 1.00 .45
❑ 80 Marshall Faulk AIR .20 .09
❑ 81 Brett Favre AIR 1.00 .45
❑ 82 Joey Galloway AIR .30 .14
❑ 83 Rodney Hampton AIR .05 .02
❑ 84 Jim Harbaugh AIR .10 .05
❑ 85 Michael Irvin AIR .10 .05
❑ 86 Chris T. Jones AIR .20 .09
❑ 87 Napoleon Kaufman AIR .20 .09
❑ 88 Jim Kelly AIR .20 .09
❑ 89 Dan Marino AIR 1.00 .45
❑ 90 Curtis Martin AIR .40 .18
❑ 91 Terance Mathis AIR .05 .02
❑ 92 Steve McNair AIR .40 .18
❑ 93 Anthony Miller AIR .10 .05
❑ 94 Scott Mitchell AIR .05 .02
❑ 95 Herman Moore AIR .20 .09
❑ 96 Brett Perriman AIR .05 .02
❑ 97 Carl Pickens AIR .20 .09
❑ 98 Jerry Rice AIR .50 .23
❑ 99 Andre Rison AIR .10 .05
❑ 100 Rashaan Salaam AIR .10 .05
❑ 101 Barry Sanders AIR 1.00 .45
❑ 102 Chris Sanders AIR .10 .05
❑ 103 Deion Sanders AIR .20 .09
❑ 104 Frank Sanders AIR .10 .05
❑ 105 Bruce Smith AIR .10 .05
❑ 106 Emmitt Smith AIR .75 .35
❑ 107 Robert Smith AIR .10 .05
❑ 108 Kordell Stewart AIR .30 .14
❑ 109 J.J. Stokes AIR .20 .09
❑ 110 Yancey Thigpen AIR .10 .05
❑ 111 Thurman Thomas AIR .10 .05
❑ 112 Eric Turner AIR .05 .02
❑ 113 Tamarick Vanover AIR .10 .05
❑ 114 Chris Warren AIR .10 .05
❑ 115 Ricky Watters AIR .10 .05
❑ 116 Michael Westbrook AIR .20 .09
❑ 117 Reggie White AIR .20 .09
❑ 118 Steve Young AIR .40 .18
❑ 119 Jeff Blake AIR .10 .05
❑ 120 Robert Brooks AIR .10 .05
❑ 121 Isaac Bruce RS .20 .09
❑ 122 Mark Chmura RS .10 .05
❑ 123 Wayne Chrebet RS .30 .14
see card #8
❑ 124 Ben Coates RS .10 .05
❑ 125 Ken Dilger RS .10 .05
❑ 126 Bert Emanuel RS .10 .05
❑ 127 Gus Frerotte RS .20 .09
❑ 128 Kevin Greene RS .10 .05
❑ 129 Erik Kramer RS .05 .02
❑ 130 Greg Lloyd RS .10 .05
❑ 131 Tony Martin RS .05 .02
❑ 132 Brian Mitchell RS .05 .02
❑ 133 Bryce Paup RS .05 .02
❑ 134 Jake Reed RS .10 .05
❑ 135 Errict Rhett RS .10 .05
❑ 136 Yancey Thigpen RS .10 .05
❑ 137 Tamarick Vanover RS .10 .05
❑ 138 Chris Warren RS .10 .05
❑ 139 Marcus Allen RS .20 .09
❑ 140 Jerome Bettis RS .20 .09
❑ 141 Tim Brown RRH .10 .05
❑ 142 Mark Carrier RRH .05 .02
❑ 143 Marshall Faulk RRH .10 .05
❑ 144 Tyrone Hughes RRH .05 .02
❑ 145 Dan Marino RRH 1.00 .45
❑ 146 Curtis Martin RRH .40 .18
❑ 147 Barry Sanders RRH 1.00 .45
❑ 148 Orlando Thomas RRH .05 .02
❑ 149 Checklist (1-107) UER .05 .02
(Card #24 missing from list)
❑ 150 Checklist .05 .02
108-150/inserts
❑ NNO Draft Exchange Card 1.00 .45
Expired 7/22/97

1997 SkyBox Impact

	MINT	NRMT
COMPLETE SET (250)	15.00	6.75

❑ 1 Carl Pickens .30 .14
❑ 2 Ray Lewis .20 .09
❑ 3 Darrell Green .20 .09
❑ 4 Brett Favre 2.00 .90
❑ 5 Todd Collins .10 .05
❑ 6 Errict Rhett .10 .05
❑ 7 John Elway 2.00 .90
❑ 8 Troy Aikman 1.00 .45
❑ 9 Steve McNair .50 .23
❑ 10 Kordell Stewart .40 .18
❑ 11 Drew Bledsoe 1.00 .45
❑ 12 Kerry Collins .20 .09
❑ 13 Dan Marino 2.00 .90
❑ 14 Ricky Watters .20 .09
❑ 15 Marvin Harrison .30 .14
❑ 16 Simeon Rice .20 .09
❑ 17 Qadry Ismail .20 .09
❑ 18 Andre Coleman .10 .05
❑ 19 Keyshawn Johnson .30 .14
❑ 20 Barry Sanders 2.00 .90
❑ 21 Rickey Dudley .20 .09
❑ 22 Emmitt Smith 1.50 .70
❑ 23 Erik Kramer .10 .05
❑ 24 Tony Boselli .10 .05
❑ 25 Steve Young .60 .25
❑ 26 Rod Woodson .20 .09
❑ 27 Eddie George 1.00 .45
❑ 28 Curtis Martin .50 .23
❑ 29 Amani Toomer .20 .09
❑ 30 Terrell Davis 1.50 .70
❑ 31 Jim Everett .10 .05
❑ 32 Marcus Allen .30 .14
❑ 33 Karim Abdul-Jabbar .30 .14
❑ 34 Thurman Thomas .30 .14
❑ 35 Cortez Kennedy .10 .05
❑ 36 Jerome Bettis .30 .14
❑ 37 Kevin Carter .10 .05
❑ 38 Gilbert Brown .10 .05
❑ 39 Bert Emanuel .20 .09
❑ 40 Kyle Brady .10 .05
❑ 41 Trent Dilfer .30 .14
❑ 42 Garrison Hearst .20 .09
❑ 43 Kevin Greene .20 .09
❑ 44 Bryan Cox .10 .05
❑ 45 Desmond Howard .20 .09
❑ 46 Larry Centers .20 .09
❑ 47 Quentin Coryatt .10 .05
❑ 48 Michael Jackson .20 .09
❑ 49 John Randle .20 .09
❑ 50 Mark Brunell 1.00 .45
❑ 51 William Thomas .10 .05
❑ 52 Glyn Milburn .10 .05
❑ 53 Mike Alstott .30 .14
❑ 54 Chris Spielman .10 .05
❑ 55 Junior Seau .20 .09
❑ 56 Brian Blades .10 .05
❑ 57 Lamar Lathon .10 .05
❑ 58 Derrick Thomas .20 .09
❑ 59 Dave Brown .10 .05
❑ 60 Frank Wycheck .10 .05
❑ 61 Chris Slade .10 .05
❑ 62 Neil Smith .20 .09
❑ 63 Ashley Ambrose .10 .05
❑ 64 Alex Molden .10 .05
❑ 65 Edgar Bennett .20 .09
❑ 66 Alvin Harper .10 .05
❑ 67 Jamal Anderson .60 .25
❑ 68 Eddie Kennison .20 .09
❑ 69 Ken Norton .10 .05
❑ 70 Zach Thomas .20 .09
❑ 71 Leeland McElroy .10 .05
❑ 72 Terry Allen .30 .14
❑ 73 Raymont Harris .10 .05
❑ 74 Ken Dilger .10 .05
❑ 75 Jason Dunn .10 .05
❑ 76 Robert Smith .20 .09
❑ 77 William Roaf .10 .05
❑ 78 Bruce Smith .20 .09
❑ 79 Vinny Testaverde .20 .09
❑ 80 Jerry Rice 1.00 .45
❑ 81 Tim Brown .30 .14
❑ 82 James O.Stewart .20 .09
❑ 83 Andre Reed .20 .09
❑ 84 Herman Moore .30 .14
❑ 85 Stan Humphries .20 .09
❑ 86 Chris Warren .20 .09
❑ 87 Tyrone Wheatley .20 .09
❑ 88 Michael Irvin .30 .14
❑ 89 Dan Wilkinson .10 .05
❑ 90 Tony Banks .20 .09
❑ 91 Chester McGlockton .10 .05
❑ 92 Reggie White .30 .14
❑ 93 Elvis Grbac .20 .09
❑ 94 Willie Davis .10 .05
❑ 95 Greg Lloyd .10 .05
❑ 96 Ben Coates .20 .09
❑ 97 Rashaan Salaam .10 .05
❑ 98 Eric Swann .10 .05
❑ 99 Hugh Douglas .10 .05
❑ 100 Henry Ellard .10 .05
❑ 101 Rod Smith WR .30 .14

- ❑ 102 Tim Biakabutuka .20 .09
- ❑ 103 Chad Brown .10 .05
- ❑ 104 Kevin Hardy .10 .05
- ❑ 105 Chris T. Jones .10 .05
- ❑ 106 Antonio Freeman .50 .23
- ❑ 107 Lamont Warren .10 .05
- ❑ 108 Derrick Alexander DE .10 .05
- ❑ 109 Brett Perriman .10 .05
- ❑ 110 Antonio Langham .10 .05
- ❑ 111 Eric Moulds .30 .14
- ❑ 112 O.J. McDuffie .20 .09
- ❑ 113 Eric Metcalf .20 .09
- ❑ 114 Ray Zellars .10 .05
- ❑ 115 Marco Coleman .10 .05
- ❑ 116 Terry Kirby .20 .09
- ❑ 117 Darren Woodson .10 .05
- ❑ 118 Charles Johnson .20 .09
- ❑ 119 Sam Mills .10 .05
- ❑ 120 Rodney Hampton .20 .09
- ❑ 121 Rick Mirer .10 .05
- ❑ 122 Derrick Brooks .10 .05
- ❑ 123 Greg Hill .10 .05
- ❑ 124 John Mobley .10 .05
- ❑ 125 Chris Sanders .10 .05
- ❑ 126 Kent Graham .10 .05
- ❑ 127 Michael Westbrook .20 .09
- ❑ 128 Harvey Williams .10 .05
- ❑ 129 Keenan McCardell .20 .09
- ❑ 130 Neil O'Donnell .20 .09
- ❑ 131 LeRoy Butler .10 .05
- ❑ 132 Willie McGinest .10 .05
- ❑ 133 Ki-Jana Carter .10 .05
- ❑ 134 Robert Jones .10 .05
- ❑ 135 Jim Harbaugh .20 .09
- ❑ 136 Wesley Walls .20 .09
- ❑ 137 Jackie Harris .10 .05
- ❑ 138 Jermaine Lewis .30 .14
- ❑ 139 Jake Reed .20 .09
- ❑ 140 John Friesz .10 .05
- ❑ 141 Jerris McPhail .10 .05
- ❑ 142 Charlie Garner .10 .05
- ❑ 143 Bryce Paup .10 .05
- ❑ 144 Tony Martin .20 .09
- ❑ 145 Shannon Sharpe .20 .09
- ❑ 146 Terrell Owens .30 .14
- ❑ 147 Curtis Conway .20 .09
- ❑ 148 Jamie Asher .10 .05
- ❑ 149 Lawrence Phillips .10 .05
- ❑ 150 Deion Sanders .30 .14
- ❑ 151 Frank Sanders .20 .09
- ❑ 152 Joey Galloway .40 .18
- ❑ 153 Mel Gray .10 .05
- ❑ 154 Robert Brooks .20 .09
- ❑ 155 Jeff George .20 .09
- ❑ 156 Michael Haynes .10 .05
- ❑ 157 Chris Chandler .20 .09
- ❑ 158 Adrian Murrell .20 .09
- ❑ 159 Tamarick Vanover .20 .09
- ❑ 160 Marshall Faulk .30 .14
- ❑ 161 Thomas Lewis .10 .05
- ❑ 162 Ty Detmer .20 .09
- ❑ 163 Darnay Scott .20 .09
- ❑ 164 Byron Bam Morris .10 .05
- ❑ 165 Scott Mitchell .20 .09
- ❑ 166 Brad Johnson .50 .23
- ❑ 167 Dave Meggett .10 .05
- ❑ 168 Bobby Engram .20 .09
- ❑ 169 Natrone Means .30 .14
- ❑ 170 Erric Pegram .10 .05
- ❑ 171 Leonard Russell .10 .05
- ❑ 172 Muhsin Muhammad .20 .09
- ❑ 173 Aeneas Williams .10 .05
- ❑ 174 Fred Barnett .10 .05
- ❑ 175 William Floyd .20 .09
- ❑ 176 Kimble Anders .20 .09
- ❑ 177 Darick Holmes .10 .05
- ❑ 178 Willie Green .10 .05
- ❑ 179 Rodney Thomas .10 .05
- ❑ 180 Derrick Alexander WR .20 .09
- ❑ 181 Sean Dawkins .10 .05
- ❑ 182 Dorsey Levens .30 .14
- ❑ 183 Napoleon Kaufman .30 .14
- ❑ 184 Mario Bates .10 .05
- ❑ 185 Yancey Thigpen .20 .09
- ❑ 186 Johnnie Morton .20 .09
- ❑ 187 Gus Frerotte .10 .05
- ❑ 188 Terance Mathis .20 .09
- ❑ 189 Tyrone Hughes .10 .05
- ❑ 190 Wayne Chrebet .30 .14
- ❑ 191 Tony Brackens .10 .05
- ❑ 192 Hardy Nickerson .10 .05
- ❑ 193 Daryl Johnston .20 .09
- ❑ 194 Irving Fryar .20 .09
- ❑ 195 Jeff Blake .20 .09
- ❑ 196 Charles Way .20 .09
- ❑ 197 Brian Mitchell .10 .05
- ❑ 198 Brent Jones .20 .09
- ❑ 199 Mark Chmura .20 .09
- ❑ 200 Terry Glenn .30 .14
- ❑ 201 Cris Carter .30 .14
- ❑ 202 Steve Atwater .10 .05
- ❑ 203 Rob Moore .20 .09
- ❑ 204 Anthony Johnson .10 .05
- ❑ 205 Warren Moon .30 .14
- ❑ 206 Darrien Gordon .10 .05
- ❑ 207 Isaac Bruce .30 .14
- ❑ 208 Reidel Anthony RC .75 .35
- ❑ 209 Darnell Autry RC .20 .09
- ❑ 210 Tiki Barber RC 1.25 .55
- ❑ 211 Pat Barnes RC .30 .14
- ❑ 212 Terry Battle RC .10 .05
- ❑ 213 Michael Booker RC .10 .05
- ❑ 214 Peter Boulware RC .20 .09
- ❑ 215 Chris Canty RC .10 .05
- ❑ 216 Rae Carruth RC .30 .14
- ❑ 217 Troy Davis RC .30 .14
- ❑ 218 Corey Dillon RC 2.50 1.10
- ❑ 219 Jim Druckenmiller RC .30 .14
- ❑ 220 Warrick Dunn RC 1.25 .55
- ❑ 221 James Farrior RC .10 .05
- ❑ 222 Tarik Glenn RC .10 .05
- ❑ 223 Tony Gonzalez RC 1.25 .55
- ❑ 224 Yatil Green RC .20 .09
- ❑ 225 Byron Hanspard RC .30 .14
- ❑ 226 Ike Hilliard RC .75 .35
- ❑ 227 Kenny Holmes RC .30 .14
- ❑ 228 Walter Jones RC .10 .05
- ❑ 229 Tom Knight RC .10 .05
- ❑ 230 David LaFleur RC .20 .09
- ❑ 231 Kenard Lang RC .10 .05
- ❑ 232 Kevin Lockett RC .20 .09
- ❑ 233 Tremain Mack RC .10 .05
- ❑ 234 Sam Madison RC .30 .14
- ❑ 235 Chris Naeole RC .10 .05
- ❑ 236 Orlando Pace RC .30 .14
- ❑ 237 Jake Plummer RC 2.50 1.10
- ❑ 238 Dwayne Rudd RC .30 .14
- ❑ 239 Darrell Russell RC .10 .05
- ❑ 240 Jamie Sharper RC .20 .09
- ❑ 241 Sedrick Shaw RC .30 .14
- ❑ 242 Antowain Smith RC 1.00 .45
- ❑ 243 Shawn Springs RC .20 .09
- ❑ 244 Bryant Westbrook RC .10 .05
- ❑ 245 Reinard Wilson RC .10 .05
- ❑ 246 Danny Wuerffel RC .60 .25
- ❑ 247 Renaldo Wynn RC .10 .05
- ❑ 248 Checklist .10 .05
- ❑ 249 Checklist .10 .05
- ❑ 250 Checklist .10 .05
- ❑ S1 Karim Abdul-Jabbar Sample Card .30 .14
- ❑ S1AU K.Abdul-Jabbar AUTO 50.00 22.00 (Sample Card Signed; Numbered of 500)

1999 SkyBox Molten Metal

	MINT	NRMT
COMPLETE SET (151)	100.00	45.00
COMP.SET w/o SP's (125)	30.00	13.50

- ❑ 1 Terrell Davis 3.00 1.35
- ❑ 2 Chris Chandler .60 .25
- ❑ 3 Terry Glenn 1.25 .55
- ❑ 4 Jon Kitna 1.25 .55
- ❑ 5 Bubby Brister .60 .25
- ❑ 6 Jermaine Lewis .60 .25
- ❑ 7 Doug Flutie 1.50 .70
- ❑ 8 Napoleon Kaufman 1.25 .55

- ❑ 9 Yancey Thigpen .30 .14
- ❑ 10 Bobby Engram .60 .25
- ❑ 11 Barry Sanders 5.00 2.20
- ❑ 12 Ben Coates .30 .14
- ❑ 13 Joey Galloway 1.25 .55
- ❑ 14 Charlie Batch 2.50 1.10
- ❑ 15 Jerome Bettis 1.25 .55
- ❑ 16 Brad Johnson 1.25 .55
- ❑ 17 Brian Griese 2.50 1.10
- ❑ 18 Jeff Lewis .30 .14
- ❑ 19 Jake Plummer 2.00 .90
- ❑ 20 Mark Brunell 2.00 .90
- ❑ 21 Robert Smith 1.25 .55
- ❑ 22 Steve Young 2.00 .90
- ❑ 23 Derrick Mayes .60 .25
- ❑ 24 Wayne Chrebet 1.25 .55
- ❑ 25 Rich Gannon .60 .25
- ❑ 26 Steve McNair 1.25 .55
- ❑ 27 Charles Johnson .60 .25
- ❑ 28 Stephen Alexander .30 .14
- ❑ 29 Jeff Blake .60 .25
- ❑ 30 Tony Gonzalez .60 .25
- ❑ 31 Eddie Kennison .60 .25
- ❑ 32 Hines Ward .30 .14
- ❑ 33 Isaac Bruce 1.25 .55
- ❑ 34 Peyton Manning 5.00 2.20
- ❑ 35 Doug Pederson .60 .25
- ❑ 36 Stephen Davis 1.25 .55
- ❑ 37 Terance Mathis .60 .25
- ❑ 38 Herman Moore 1.25 .55
- ❑ 39 Fred Taylor 3.00 1.35
- ❑ 40 Courtney Hawkins .30 .14
- ❑ 41 Michael Westbrook .60 .25
- ❑ 42 Vinny Testaverde .60 .25
- ❑ 43 Jacquez Green .30 .14
- ❑ 44 Rocket Ismail .60 .25
- ❑ 45 Curtis Martin 1.25 .55
- ❑ 46 Tim Brown 1.25 .55
- ❑ 47 Kevin Dyson .60 .25
- ❑ 48 Steve Beuerlein .60 .25
- ❑ 49 Adrian Murrell .60 .25
- ❑ 50 Randall Cunningham 1.25 .55
- ❑ 51 Jerry Rice 3.00 1.35
- ❑ 52 Tim Biakabutuka .60 .25
- ❑ 53 Muhsin Muhammad .60 .25
- ❑ 54 Antonio Freeman 1.25 .55
- ❑ 55 Cris Carter 1.25 .55
- ❑ 56 Lawrence Phillips .60 .25
- ❑ 57 Michael Irvin .60 .25
- ❑ 58 Terrell Owens 1.25 .55
- ❑ 59 Warrick Dunn 1.25 .55
- ❑ 60 Leslie Shepherd .30 .14
- ❑ 61 O.J. McDuffie .60 .25
- ❑ 62 Byron Hanspard .60 .25
- ❑ 63 Trent Dilfer .60 .25
- ❑ 64 Eric Moulds 1.25 .55
- ❑ 65 Scott Mitchell .60 .25
- ❑ 66 Marc Edwards .30 .14
- ❑ 67 Dorsey Levens 1.25 .55
- ❑ 68 Dan Marino 5.00 2.20
- ❑ 69 Jason Sehorn .30 .14
- ❑ 70 Junior Seau .60 .25
- ❑ 71 Reidel Anthony .30 .14
- ❑ 72 Rob Moore .60 .25
- ❑ 73 Deion Sanders 1.25 .55
- ❑ 74 Rickey Dudley .30 .14
- ❑ 75 Keyshawn Johnson 1.25 .55

❑ 76	Eddie George	1.50	.70
❑ 77	E.G. Green	.30	.14
❑ 78	Terry Kirby	.60	.25
❑ 79	John Avery	.60	.25
❑ 80	Pete Mitchell	.30	.14
❑ 81	Natrone Means	.60	.25
❑ 82	Mike Alstott	1.25	.55
❑ 83	Carl Pickens	.60	.25
❑ 84	Karim Abdul-Jabbar	.60	.25
❑ 85	Kerry Collins	.60	.25
❑ 86	Erik Kramer	.30	.14
❑ 87	Robert Holcombe	.30	.14
❑ 88	Willie Jackson	.30	.14
❑ 89	Marcus Pollard	.30	.14
❑ 90	Bam Morris	.30	.14
❑ 91	Gary Brown	.30	.14
❑ 92	Freddie Jones	.30	.14
❑ 93	Kurt Warner RC	15.00	6.75
❑ 94	Priest Holmes	1.25	.55
❑ 95	Duce Staley	1.25	.55
❑ 96	Skip Hicks	.60	.25
❑ 97	Frank Sanders	.60	.25
❑ 98	Corey Dillon	1.25	.55
❑ 99	Shannon Sharpe	.60	.25
❑ 100	Randy Moss	5.00	2.20
❑ 101	Sean Dawkins	.30	.14
❑ 102	Marshall Faulk	1.25	.55
❑ 103	Mark Chmura	.30	.14
❑ 104	Keenan McCardell	.60	.25
❑ 105	Jimmy Smith	.60	.25
❑ 106	Jim Harbaugh	.60	.25
❑ 107	Jamal Anderson	1.25	.55
❑ 108	Elvis Grbac	.60	.25
❑ 109	Ed McCaffrey	.60	.25
❑ 110	Drew Bledsoe	2.00	.90
❑ 111	Curtis Conway	.60	.25
❑ 112	Billy Joe Tolliver	.30	.14
❑ 113	J.J. Stokes	.60	.25
❑ 114	Curtis Enis	1.25	.55
❑ 115	Antowain Smith	1.25	.55
❑ 116	Troy Aikman	3.00	1.35
❑ 117	Ricky Watters	.60	.25
❑ 118	Kordell Stewart	1.25	.55
❑ 119	Derrick Alexander	.60	.25
❑ 120	Emmitt Smith	3.00	1.35
❑ 121	Billy Joe Hobert	.30	.14
❑ 122	Johnnie Morton	.60	.25
❑ 123	Rod Smith	.60	.25
❑ 124	Marvin Harrison	1.25	.55
❑ 125	Brett Favre	5.00	2.20
❑ 126	Craig Yeast RC	2.00	.90
❑ 127	Ricky Williams RC	10.00	4.50
❑ 128	Brandon Stokley RC	2.50	1.10
❑ 129	Akili Smith RC	5.00	2.20
❑ 130	Peerless Price RC	3.00	1.35
❑ 131	Joe Montgomery RC	2.50	1.10
❑ 132	Cade McNown RC	3.00	1.35
❑ 133	Donovan McNabb RC	10.00	4.50
❑ 134	Shaun King RC	5.00	2.20
❑ 135	James Johnson RC	2.50	1.10
❑ 136	Kevin Johnson RC	5.00	2.20
❑ 137	Edgerrin James RC	12.00	5.50
❑ 138	Terry Jackson RC	2.00	.90
❑ 139	Sedrick Irvin RC	2.50	1.10
❑ 140	Brock Huard RC	4.00	1.80
❑ 141	Torry Holt RC	6.00	2.70
❑ 142	Amos Zereoue RC	2.50	1.10
❑ 143	Kevin Faulk RC	4.00	1.80
❑ 144	Troy Edwards RC	3.00	1.35
❑ 145	Donald Driver RC	2.00	.90
❑ 146	Daunte Culpepper RC	12.00	5.50
❑ 147	Tim Couch RC	8.00	3.60
❑ 148	Cecil Collins RC	2.00	.90
❑ 149	David Boston RC	5.00	2.20
❑ 150	Champ Bailey RC	3.00	1.35
❑ 151	Olandis Gary RC	6.00	2.70
❑ P133	Donovan McNabb Promo	3.00	1.35

1993 SkyBox Premium

	MINT	NRMT
COMPLETE SET (270)	25.00	11.00

❑ 1	Eric Martin	.10	.05
❑ 2	Earnest Byner	.10	.05

❑ 3	Ricky Proehl	.10	.05
❑ 4	Mark Carrier WR	.20	.09
❑ 5	Shannon Sharpe	.40	.18
❑ 6	Anthony Thompson	.10	.05
❑ 7	Drew Bledsoe RC	4.00	1.80
❑ 8	Tom Carter RC	.20	.09
❑ 9	Ryan McNeil RC	.10	.05
❑ 10	Troy Aikman	1.50	.70
❑ 11	Robert Jones	.10	.05
❑ 12	Rodney Peete	.10	.05
❑ 13	Wendell Davis	.10	.05
❑ 14	Thurman Thomas	.40	.18
❑ 15	John Stephens	.10	.05
❑ 16	Rodney Hampton	.40	.18
❑ 17	Eric Bieniemy	.10	.05
❑ 18	Santana Dotson	.20	.09
❑ 19	Jeff George	.40	.18
❑ 20	John L. Williams	.10	.05
❑ 21	Barry Word	.10	.05
❑ 22	Chris Miller	.20	.09
❑ 23	Jeff Hostetler	.20	.09
❑ 24	Dwight Stone	.10	.05
❑ 25	Brad Baxter	.10	.05
❑ 26	Randall Cunningham	.40	.18
❑ 27	Mark Higgs	.10	.05
❑ 28	Vaughn Dunbar	.10	.05
❑ 29	Ricky Ervins	.10	.05
❑ 30	Johnny Bailey	.10	.05
❑ 31	Michael Jackson	.20	.09
❑ 32	Mike Croel	.10	.05
❑ 33	Steve Young	1.50	.70
❑ 34	Deon Figures RC	.20	.09
❑ 35	Robert Smith RC	3.00	1.35
❑ 36	Irv Smith RC	.10	.05
❑ 37	Charles Haley	.20	.09
❑ 38	Cris Dishman	.10	.05
❑ 39	Barry Sanders	3.00	1.35
❑ 40	Jim Harbaugh	.40	.18
❑ 41	Darryl Talley	.10	.05
❑ 42	Jackie Harris	.10	.05
❑ 43	Phil Simms	.20	.09
❑ 44	Marion Butts	.10	.05
❑ 45	Anthony Munoz	.20	.09
❑ 46	Steve Emtman	.10	.05
❑ 47	Kelvin Martin	.10	.05
❑ 48	Joe Montana	3.00	1.35
❑ 49	Andre Rison	.20	.09
❑ 50	Ethan Horton	.10	.05
❑ 51	Kevin Greene	.40	.18
❑ 52	Browning Nagle	.10	.05
❑ 53	Tim Harris	.10	.05
❑ 54	Keith Byars	.10	.05
❑ 55	Terry Allen	.40	.18
❑ 56	Chip Lohmiller	.10	.05
❑ 57	Robert Massey	.10	.05
❑ 58	Michael Dean Perry	.20	.09
❑ 59	Tommy Maddox	.10	.05
❑ 60	Jerry Rice	2.00	.90
❑ 61	Lincoln Kennedy RC	.10	.05
❑ 62	Jerome Bettis RC	1.50	.70
❑ 63	Coleman Rudolph RC	.10	.05
❑ 64	Emmitt Smith	3.00	1.35
❑ 65	Curtis Duncan	.10	.05
❑ 66	Andre Ware	.10	.05
❑ 67	Neal Anderson	.10	.05
❑ 68	Jim Kelly	.40	.18
❑ 69	Reggie White	.40	.18
❑ 70	Dave Meggett	.10	.05
❑ 71	Junior Seau	.40	.18
❑ 72	Courtney Hawkins	.10	.05
❑ 73	Clarence Verdin	.10	.05
❑ 74	Tommy Kane	.10	.05
❑ 75	Dale Carter	.10	.05
❑ 76	Michael Haynes	.20	.09
❑ 77	Willie Gault	.10	.05
❑ 78	Eric Green	.10	.05
❑ 79	Ronnie Lott	.20	.09
❑ 80	Vai Sikahema	.10	.05
❑ 81	Mark Ingram	.10	.05
❑ 82	Anthony Carter	.20	.09
❑ 83	Mark Rypien	.10	.05
❑ 84	Gary Clark	.20	.09
❑ 85	Bernie Kosar	.20	.09
❑ 86	Cleveland Gary	.10	.05
❑ 87	Tom Rathman	.10	.05
❑ 88	Tony McGee RC	.20	.09
❑ 89	Rick Mirer RC	.75	.35
❑ 90	John Copeland RC	.20	.09
❑ 91	Michael Irvin	.40	.18
❑ 92	Wilber Marshall	.10	.05
❑ 93	Mel Gray	.20	.09
❑ 94	Craig Heyward	.20	.09
❑ 95	Don Beebe	.10	.05
❑ 96	Andre Tippett	.10	.05
❑ 97	Derek Brown TE	.10	.05
❑ 98	Ronnie Harmon	.10	.05
❑ 99	Derrick Fenner	.10	.05
❑ 100	Rodney Culver	.10	.05
❑ 101	Cortez Kennedy	.20	.09
❑ 102	Marcus Allen	.40	.18
❑ 103	Steve Broussard	.10	.05
❑ 104	Tim Brown	.40	.18
❑ 105	Merril Hoge	.10	.05
❑ 106	Chris Burkett	.10	.05
❑ 107	Fred Barnett	.20	.09
❑ 108	Dan Marino	3.00	1.35
❑ 109	Chris Doleman	.10	.05
❑ 110	Art Monk	.20	.09
❑ 111	Ernie Jones	.10	.05
❑ 112	Jay Hilgenberg	.10	.05
❑ 113	Jim Everett	.20	.09
❑ 114	John Taylor	.20	.09
❑ 115	Steve Everitt RC	.10	.05
❑ 116	Carlton Gray RC	.10	.05
❑ 117	Eric Curry RC	.10	.05
❑ 118	Ken Norton Jr.	.20	.09
❑ 119	Lorenzo White	.10	.05
❑ 120	Pat Swilling	.10	.05
❑ 121	William Perry	.20	.09
❑ 122	Brett Favre	4.00	1.80
❑ 123	Jon Vaughn	.10	.05
❑ 124	Mark Jackson	.10	.05
❑ 125	Stan Humphries	.40	.18
❑ 126	Harold Green	.10	.05
❑ 127	Anthony Johnson	.20	.09
❑ 128	Brian Blades	.20	.09
❑ 129	Willie Davis	.40	.18
❑ 130	Bobby Hebert	.10	.05
❑ 131	Terry McDaniel	.10	.05
❑ 132	Jeff Graham	.20	.09
❑ 133	Jeff Lageman	.10	.05
❑ 134	Andre Waters	.10	.05
❑ 135	Steve Walsh	.10	.05
❑ 136	Cris Carter	.75	.35
❑ 137	Tim McGee	.10	.05
❑ 138	Chuck Cecil	.10	.05
❑ 139	John Elway	3.00	1.35
❑ 140	Todd Lyght	.10	.05
❑ 141	Brent Jones	.20	.09
❑ 142	Patrick Bates RC	.10	.05
❑ 143	Darrien Gordon RC	.10	.05
❑ 144	Michael Strahan RC	.40	.18
❑ 145	Jay Novacek	.20	.09
❑ 146	Warren Moon	.40	.18
❑ 147	Rodney Holman	.10	.05
❑ 148	Anthony Morgan	.10	.05
❑ 149	Sterling Sharpe	.40	.18
❑ 150	Leonard Russell	.20	.09
❑ 151	Lawrence Taylor	.40	.18
❑ 152	Leslie O'Neal	.20	.09
❑ 153	Carl Pickens	.40	.18
❑ 154	Aaron Cox	.10	.05
❑ 155	Ferrell Edmunds	.10	.05

❑ 156 Neil O'Donnell	.40	.18
❑ 157 Tony Smith	.10	.05
❑ 158 James Lofton	.20	.09
❑ 159 George Teague RC	.20	.09
❑ 160 Boomer Esiason	.20	.09
❑ 161 Eric Allen	.10	.05
❑ 162 Floyd Turner	.10	.05
❑ 163 Esera Tuaolo	.10	.05
❑ 164 Darrell Green	.10	.05
❑ 165 Steve Beuerlein	.10	.05
❑ 166 Vance Johnson	.10	.05
❑ 167 Flipper Anderson	.10	.05
❑ 168 Ricky Watters	.40	.18
❑ 169 Marvin Jones RC	.10	.05
❑ 170 Dana Stubblefield RC	.40	.18
❑ 171 Willie Roaf RC	.20	.09
❑ 172 Russell Maryland	.10	.05
❑ 173 Ernest Givins	.20	.09
❑ 174 Willie Green	.10	.05
❑ 175 Bruce Smith	.40	.18
❑ 176 Terrell Buckley	.10	.05
❑ 177 Scott Zolak	.10	.05
❑ 178 Mike Sherrard	.10	.05
❑ 179 Lawrence Dawsey	.10	.05
❑ 180 Jay Schroeder	.10	.05
❑ 181 Quentin Coryatt	.20	.09
❑ 182 Harvey Williams	.20	.09
❑ 183 Natrone Means RC	1.00	.45
❑ 184 Eric Dickerson	.20	.09
❑ 185 Gaston Green	.10	.05
❑ 186 Thomas Smith RC	.20	.09
❑ 187 Johnny Johnson	.10	.05
❑ 188 Marco Coleman	.10	.05
❑ 189 Wade Wilson	.10	.05
❑ 190 Rich Gannon	.40	.18
❑ 191 Brian Mitchell	.20	.09
❑ 192 Eric Metcalf	.20	.09
❑ 193 Robert Delpino	.10	.05
❑ 194 Shane Conlan	.10	.05
❑ 195 Dexter Carter	.10	.05
❑ 196 Garrison Hearst RC	1.25	.55
❑ 197 Chris Slade RC	.20	.09
❑ 198 Troy Drayton RC	.20	.09
❑ 199 Lin Elliott	.10	.05
❑ 200 Haywood Jeffires	.20	.09
❑ 201 Herman Moore	1.00	.45
❑ 202 Cornelius Bennett	.20	.09
❑ 203 Mark Clayton	.10	.05
❑ 204 Marv Cook	.10	.05
❑ 205 Stephen Baker	.10	.05
❑ 206 Gary Anderson RB	.10	.05
❑ 207 Eddie Brown	.10	.05
❑ 208 Will Wolford	.10	.05
❑ 209 Derrick Thomas	.40	.18
❑ 210 Seth Joyner	.10	.05
❑ 211 Mike Pritchard	.20	.09
❑ 212 Rod Woodson	.40	.18
❑ 213 Todd Kelly RC	.10	.05
❑ 214 Rob Moore	.20	.09
❑ 215 Keith Jackson	.20	.09
❑ 216 Wesley Carroll	.10	.05
❑ 217 Steve Jordan	.10	.05
❑ 218 Ricky Sanders	.10	.05
❑ 219 Tommy Vardell	.10	.05
❑ 220 Rod Bernstine	.10	.05
❑ 221 Henry Ellard	.20	.09
❑ 222 Amp Lee	.10	.05
❑ 223 O.J. McDuffie RC	1.25	.55
❑ 224 Carl Simpson RC	.10	.05
❑ 225 Dan Williams RC	.10	.05
❑ 226 Thomas Everett	.10	.05
❑ 227 Webster Slaughter	.10	.05
❑ 228 Trace Armstrong	.10	.05
❑ 229 Kenneth Davis	.10	.05
❑ 230 Tony Bennett	.10	.05
❑ 231 Reyna Thompson	.10	.05
❑ 232 Anthony Miller	.20	.09
❑ 233 Reggie Cobb	.10	.05
❑ 234 Mark Duper	.10	.05
❑ 235 Chris Warren	.20	.09
❑ 236 Christian Okoye	.10	.05
❑ 237 Irving Fryar	.20	.09
❑ 238 Deion Sanders	.75	.35
❑ 239 Barry Foster	.20	.09
❑ 240 Ernest Dye RC	.10	.05
❑ 241 Calvin Williams	.20	.09
❑ 242 Louis Oliver	.10	.05
❑ 243 Dalton Hilliard	.10	.05
❑ 244 Roger Craig	.20	.09
❑ 245 Randal Hill	.10	.05
❑ 246 Vinny Testaverde	.20	.09
❑ 247 Steve Atwater	.10	.05
❑ 248 Jim Price	.10	.05
❑ 249 Martin Harrison RC	.10	.05
❑ 250 Curtis Conway RC	1.00	.45
❑ 251 Demetrius DuBose RC	.10	.05
❑ 252 Leonard Renfro RC	.10	.05
❑ 253 Alvin Harper	.20	.09
❑ 254 Leonard Harris	.10	.05
❑ 255 Tom Waddle	.10	.05
❑ 256 Andre Reed	.20	.09
❑ 257 Sanjay Beach	.10	.05
❑ 258 Michael Timpson	.10	.05
❑ 259 Nate Lewis	.10	.05
❑ 260 Steve DeBerg	.10	.05
❑ 261 David Klingler	.10	.05
❑ 262 Dan McGwire	.10	.05
❑ 263 Dave Krieg	.20	.09
❑ 264 Brad Muster	.10	.05
❑ 265 Nick Bell	.10	.05
❑ 266 Checklist 1	.10	.05
❑ 267 Checklist 2	.10	.05
❑ 268 Checklist 3	.10	.05
❑ 269 Checklist 4	.10	.05
❑ 270 Checklist 5	.10	.05
❑ P1 Promo Panel	2.00	.90
Jim Kelly		
Derrick Thomas		
Lawrence Taylor		
Neal Anderson		
Marco Coleman		
Chris Doleman		
❑ P2 Promo Panel	2.00	.90
Lawrence Taylor		
Chris Doleman		
Jim Kelly		
Michael Irvin		
Neal Anderson		
Derrick Thomas		

1994 SkyBox Premium

	MINT	NRMT
COMPLETE SET (200)	20.00	9.00
❑ 1 Steve Beuerlein	.05	.02
❑ 2 Gary Clark	.15	.07
❑ 3 Garrison Hearst	.30	.14
❑ 4 Ronald Moore	.05	.02
❑ 5 Eric Swann	.15	.07
❑ 6 Chuck Cecil	.05	.02
❑ 7 Seth Joyner	.05	.02
❑ 8 Clyde Simmons	.05	.02
❑ 9 Andre Rison	.15	.07
❑ 10 Deion Sanders	.40	.18
❑ 11 Erric Pegram	.05	.02
❑ 12 Steve Broussard	.05	.02
❑ 13 Chris Doleman	.05	.02
❑ 14 Jeff George	.30	.14
❑ 15 Cornelius Bennett	.15	.07
❑ 16 Jim Kelly	.30	.14
❑ 17 Andre Reed	.15	.07
❑ 18 Bruce Smith	.30	.14
❑ 19 Darryl Talley	.05	.02
❑ 20 Thurman Thomas	.30	.14
❑ 21 Mark Carrier DB	.05	.02
❑ 22 Dante Jones	.05	.02
❑ 23 Curtis Conway	.30	.14
❑ 24 Tim Worley	.05	.02
❑ 25 Erik Kramer	.15	.07
❑ 26 John Copeland	.05	.02
❑ 27 David Klingler	.05	.02
❑ 28 Derrick Fenner	.05	.02
❑ 29 Harold Green	.05	.02
❑ 30 Carl Pickens	.30	.14
❑ 31 Tony McGee	.05	.02
❑ 32 Steve Everitt	.05	.02
❑ 33 Michael Jackson	.15	.07
❑ 34 Eric Metcalf	.15	.07
❑ 35 Vinny Testaverde	.15	.07
❑ 36 Michael Dean Perry	.15	.07
❑ 37 Troy Aikman	1.25	.55
❑ 38 Alvin Harper	.15	.07
❑ 39 Michael Irvin	.30	.14
❑ 40 Jay Novacek	.15	.07
❑ 41 Emmitt Smith	2.00	.90
❑ 42 Charles Haley	.15	.07
❑ 43 Daryl Johnston	.15	.07
❑ 44 Kevin Williams	.15	.07
❑ 45 Rodney Peete	.05	.02
❑ 46 John Elway	2.50	1.10
❑ 47 Shannon Sharpe	.15	.07
❑ 48 Rod Bernstine	.05	.02
❑ 49 Glyn Milburn	.15	.07
❑ 50 Mike Pritchard	.05	.02
❑ 51 Anthony Miller	.15	.07
❑ 52 Herman Moore	.30	.14
❑ 53 Barry Sanders	2.50	1.10
❑ 54 Scott Mitchell	.30	.14
❑ 55 Pat Swilling	.05	.02
❑ 56 Willie Green	.05	.02
❑ 57 Edgar Bennett	.30	.14
❑ 58 Brett Favre	2.50	1.10
❑ 59 Sterling Sharpe	.15	.07
❑ 60 Reggie White	.30	.14
❑ 61 Sean Jones	.05	.02
❑ 62 Reggie Cobb	.05	.02
❑ 63 Haywood Jeffires	.15	.07
❑ 64 Lorenzo White	.05	.02
❑ 65 Webster Slaughter	.05	.02
❑ 66 Gary Brown	.05	.02
❑ 67 Steve Emtman	.05	.02
❑ 68 Quentin Coryatt	.05	.02
❑ 69 Sean Dawkins RC	.30	.14
❑ 70 Jim Harbaugh	.30	.14
❑ 71 Tony Bennett	.05	.02
❑ 72 Marcus Allen	.30	.14
❑ 73 Steve Bono	.15	.07
❑ 74 Dale Carter	.05	.02
❑ 75 Joe Montana	2.50	1.10
❑ 76 Neil Smith	.30	.14
❑ 77 Derrick Thomas	.30	.14
❑ 78 Keith Cash	.05	.02
❑ 79 Tim Brown	.30	.14
❑ 80 Rocket Ismail	.15	.07
❑ 81 Jeff Hostetler	.15	.07
❑ 82 Patrick Bates	.05	.02
❑ 83 James Jett	.05	.02
❑ 84 Jerome Bettis	.30	.14
❑ 85 Chris Miller	.05	.02
❑ 86 Marc Boutte	.05	.02
❑ 87 Sean Gilbert	.05	.02
❑ 88 Keith Jackson	.05	.02
❑ 89 Terry Kirby	.30	.14
❑ 90 Dan Marino	2.50	1.10
❑ 91 Bryan Cox	.05	.02
❑ 92 Bernie Kosar	.15	.07
❑ 93 Qadry Ismail	.30	.14
❑ 94 Robert Smith	.30	.14
❑ 95 Terry Allen	.15	.07
❑ 96 Scottie Graham RC	.15	.07
❑ 97 Warren Moon	.30	.14
❑ 98 Drew Bledsoe	1.50	.70
❑ 99 Ben Coates	.30	.14
❑ 100 Leonard Russell	.05	.02
❑ 101 Vincent Brisby	.30	.14
❑ 102 Marion Butts	.05	.02
❑ 103 Morten Andersen	.05	.02
❑ 104 Derek Brown RBK	.05	.02
❑ 105 Michael Haynes	.15	.07

Card	MINT	NRMT
❑ 106 Sam Mills	.05	.02
❑ 107 Lorenzo Neal	.05	.02
❑ 108 Willie Roaf	.05	.02
❑ 109 Jim Everett	.15	.07
❑ 110 Michael Brooks	.05	.02
❑ 111 Rodney Hampton	.30	.14
❑ 112 Dave Brown	.15	.07
❑ 113 Dave Meggett	.05	.02
❑ 114 Ronnie Lott	.15	.07
❑ 115 Boomer Esiason	.15	.07
❑ 116 Rob Moore	.15	.07
❑ 117 Johnny Johnson	.05	.02
❑ 118 Marvin Jones	.05	.02
❑ 119 Johnny Mitchell	.05	.02
❑ 120 Fred Barnett	.15	.07
❑ 121 Randall Cunningham	.30	.14
❑ 122 Herschel Walker	.15	.07
❑ 123 Calvin Williams	.15	.07
❑ 124 Neil O'Donnell	.30	.14
❑ 125 Eric Green	.05	.02
❑ 126 Leroy Thompson	.05	.02
❑ 127 Rod Woodson	.30	.14
❑ 128 Barry Foster	.05	.02
❑ 129 Deon Figures	.05	.02
❑ 130 John L. Williams	.05	.02
❑ 131 Chris Mims	.05	.02
❑ 132 Darrien Gordon	.05	.02
❑ 133 Stan Humphries	.30	.14
❑ 134 Natrone Means	.30	.14
❑ 135 Junior Seau	.30	.14
❑ 136 Brent Jones	.15	.07
❑ 137 Jerry Rice	1.25	.55
❑ 138 Dana Stubblefield	.30	.14
❑ 139 John Taylor	.15	.07
❑ 140 Ricky Watters	.30	.14
❑ 141 Steve Young	1.00	.45
❑ 142 Ken Norton Jr.	.15	.07
❑ 143 Brian Blades	.15	.07
❑ 144 Cortez Kennedy	.15	.07
❑ 145 Kelvin Martin	.05	.02
❑ 146 Rick Mirer	.30	.14
❑ 147 Chris Warren	.15	.07
❑ 148 Eric Curry	.05	.02
❑ 149 Santana Dotson	.15	.07
❑ 150 Craig Erickson	.05	.02
❑ 151 Hardy Nickerson	.15	.07
❑ 152 Paul Gruber	.05	.02
❑ 153 Reggie Brooks	.15	.07
❑ 154 Tom Carter	.05	.02
❑ 155 Desmond Howard	.15	.07
❑ 156 Ken Harvey	.05	.02
❑ 157 Dan Wilkinson RC	.15	.07
❑ 158 Marshall Faulk RC	4.00	1.80
❑ 159 Heath Shuler RC	.30	.14
❑ 160 Willie McGinest RC	.30	.14
❑ 161 Trev Alberts RC	.15	.07
❑ 162 Trent Dilfer RC	2.00	.90
❑ 163 Bryant Young RC	.30	.14
❑ 164 Sam Adams RC	.15	.07
❑ 165 Antonio Langham RC	.15	.07
❑ 166 Jamir Miller RC	.05	.02
❑ 167 John Thierry RC	.05	.02
❑ 168 Aaron Glenn RC	.15	.07
❑ 169 Joe Johnson RC	.05	.02
❑ 170 Bernard Williams RC	.05	.02
❑ 171 Wayne Gandy RC	.05	.02
❑ 172 Aaron Taylor RC	.05	.02
❑ 173 Charles Johnson RC	.75	.35
❑ 174 Dewayne Washington RC	.15	.07
❑ 175 Todd Steussie RC	.15	.07
❑ 176 Tim Bowens RC	.15	.07
❑ 177 Johnnie Morton RC	1.00	.45
❑ 178 Rob Fredrickson	.15	.07
❑ 179 Shante Carver RC	.05	.02
❑ 180 Thomas Lewis RC	.15	.07
❑ 181 Greg Hill RC	.30	.14
❑ 182 Henry Ford RC	.05	.02
❑ 183 Jeff Burris RC	.15	.07
❑ 184 William Floyd RC	.30	.14
❑ 185 Der. Alexander WR RC	.75	.35
❑ 186 Glenn Foley RC	.30	.14
❑ 187 Charlie Garner RC	1.50	.70
❑ 188 Errict Rhett RC	1.00	.45
❑ 189 Chuck Levy RC	.05	.02
❑ 190 Byron Bam Morris RC	.30	.14
❑ 191 Donnell Bennett RC	.30	.14
❑ 192 LeShon Johnson RC	.15	.07
❑ 193 Mario Bates RC	.30	.14
❑ 194 David Palmer RC	.75	.35
❑ 195 Darnay Scott RC	1.00	.45
❑ 196 Lake Dawson RC	.30	.14
❑ 197 Checklist	.05	.02
❑ 198 Checklist	.05	.02
❑ 199 Checklist	.05	.02
❑ 200 Checklist for Inserts	.05	.02
❑ NNO NFL Anniversary Commemorative	.30	.14

1995 SkyBox Premium

	MINT	NRMT
COMPLETE SET (200)	20.00	9.00
❑ 1 Garrison Hearst	.40	.18
❑ 2 Dave Krieg	.10	.05
❑ 3 Rob Moore	.10	.05
❑ 4 Eric Swann	.20	.09
❑ 5 Larry Centers	.20	.09
❑ 6 Jeff George	.20	.09
❑ 7 Craig Heyward	.20	.09
❑ 8 Terance Mathis	.20	.09
❑ 9 Eric Metcalf	.20	.09
❑ 10 Jim Kelly	.40	.18
❑ 11 Andre Reed	.20	.09
❑ 12 Bruce Smith	.40	.18
❑ 13 Cornelius Bennett	.20	.09
❑ 14 Randy Baldwin	.10	.05
❑ 15 Don Beebe	.10	.05
❑ 16 Barry Foster	.20	.09
❑ 17 Lamar Lathon	.10	.05
❑ 18 Frank Reich	.10	.05
❑ 19 Jeff Graham	.10	.05
❑ 20 Raymont Harris	.10	.05
❑ 21 Lewis Tillman	.10	.05
❑ 22 Michael Timpson	.10	.05
❑ 23 Jeff Blake RC	1.25	.55
❑ 24 Carl Pickens	.40	.18
❑ 25 Darnay Scott	.40	.18
❑ 26 Dan Wilkinson	.20	.09
❑ 27 Derrick Alexander WR	.40	.18
❑ 28 Leroy Hoard	.10	.05
❑ 29 Antonio Langham	.10	.05
❑ 30 Andre Rison	.20	.09
❑ 31 Eric Turner	.10	.05
❑ 32 Troy Aikman	1.25	.55
❑ 33 Michael Irvin	.40	.18
❑ 34 Daryl Johnston	.20	.09
❑ 35 Emmitt Smith	2.00	.90
❑ 36 John Elway	2.50	1.10
❑ 37 Glyn Milburn	.10	.05
❑ 38 Anthony Miller	.20	.09
❑ 39 Shannon Sharpe	.20	.09
❑ 40 Scott Mitchell	.20	.09
❑ 41 Herman Moore	.40	.18
❑ 42 Barry Sanders	2.50	1.10
❑ 43 Chris Spielman	.20	.09
❑ 44 Edgar Bennett	.20	.09
❑ 45 Robert Brooks	.40	.18
❑ 46 Brett Favre	2.50	1.10
❑ 47 Reggie White	.40	.18
❑ 48 Mel Gray	.10	.05
❑ 49 Haywood Jeffires	.10	.05
❑ 50 Gary Brown	.10	.05
❑ 51 Craig Erickson	.10	.05
❑ 52 Quentin Coryatt	.20	.09
❑ 53 Sean Dawkins	.20	.09
❑ 54 Marshall Faulk	.60	.25
❑ 55 Steve Beuerlein	.10	.05
❑ 56 Reggie Cobb	.10	.05
❑ 57 Desmond Howard	.20	.09
❑ 58 Ernest Givins	.10	.05
❑ 59 Jeff Lageman	.10	.05
❑ 60 Marcus Allen	.40	.18
❑ 61 Steve Bono	.20	.09
❑ 62 Greg Hill	.20	.09
❑ 63 Willie Davis	.20	.09
❑ 64 Tim Brown	.40	.18
❑ 65 Rocket Ismail	.20	.09
❑ 66 Jeff Hostetler	.20	.09
❑ 67 Chester McGlockton	.20	.09
❑ 68 Tim Bowens	.10	.05
❑ 69 Irving Fryar	.20	.09
❑ 70 Eric Green	.10	.05
❑ 71 Terry Kirby	.20	.09
❑ 72 Dan Marino	2.50	1.10
❑ 73 O.J. McDuffie	.40	.18
❑ 74 Bernie Parmalee	.20	.09
❑ 75 Dewayne Washington	.20	.09
❑ 76 Cris Carter	.40	.18
❑ 77 Qadry Ismail	.20	.09
❑ 78 Warren Moon	.20	.09
❑ 79 Jake Reed	.20	.09
❑ 80 Drew Bledsoe	1.25	.55
❑ 81 Vincent Brisby	.10	.05
❑ 82 Ben Coates	.20	.09
❑ 83 Dave Meggett	.10	.05
❑ 84 Mario Bates	.40	.18
❑ 85 Jim Everett	.10	.05
❑ 86 Michael Haynes	.20	.09
❑ 87 Tyrone Hughes	.20	.09
❑ 88 Dave Brown	.20	.09
❑ 89 Rodney Hampton	.20	.09
❑ 90 Thomas Lewis	.20	.09
❑ 91 Herschel Walker	.20	.09
❑ 92 Mike Sherrard	.10	.05
❑ 93 Boomer Esiason	.20	.09
❑ 94 Aaron Glenn	.10	.05
❑ 95 Johnny Johnson	.10	.05
❑ 96 Johnny Mitchell	.10	.05
❑ 97 Ronald Moore	.10	.05
❑ 98 Fred Barnett	.20	.09
❑ 99 Randall Cunningham	.40	.18
❑ 100 Charlie Garner	.20	.09
❑ 101 Ricky Watters	.40	.18
❑ 102 Calvin Williams	.40	.18
❑ 103 Charles Johnson	.20	.09
❑ 104 Byron Bam Morris	.20	.09
❑ 105 Neil O'Donnell	.20	.09
❑ 106 Rod Woodson	.20	.09
❑ 107 Jerome Bettis	.40	.18
❑ 108 Troy Drayton	.10	.05
❑ 109 Sean Gilbert	.20	.09
❑ 110 Chris Miller	.10	.05
❑ 111 Leonard Russell	.10	.05
❑ 112 Ronnie Harmon	.10	.05
❑ 113 Stan Humphries	.20	.09
❑ 114 Shawn Jefferson	.10	.05
❑ 115 Natrone Means	.40	.18
❑ 116 Junior Seau	.40	.18
❑ 117 William Floyd	.40	.18
❑ 118 Brent Jones	.10	.05
❑ 119 Jerry Rice	1.25	.55
❑ 120 Deion Sanders	.75	.35
❑ 121 Dana Stubblefield	.40	.18
❑ 122 Bryant Young	.20	.09
❑ 123 Steve Young	1.00	.45
❑ 124 Brian Blades	.20	.09
❑ 125 Cortez Kennedy	.20	.09
❑ 126 Rick Mirer	.40	.18
❑ 127 Ricky Proehl	.10	.05
❑ 128 Chris Warren	.20	.09
❑ 129 Horace Copeland	.10	.05
❑ 130 Trent Dilfer	.40	.18
❑ 131 Alvin Harper	.10	.05
❑ 132 Jackie Harris	.10	.05
❑ 133 Hardy Nickerson	.10	.05
❑ 134 Errict Rhett	.40	.18
❑ 135 Henry Ellard	.20	.09
❑ 136 Brian Mitchell	.10	.05
❑ 137 Heath Shuler	.40	.18

❑ 138 Tydus Winans	.10	.05
❑ 139 Brett Favre	1.00	.45
Drew Bledsoe		
❑ 140 Marshall Faulk	.40	.18
William Floyd		
❑ 141 Brett Favre	.75	.35
Trent Dilfer		
❑ 142 Dan Marino	1.00	.45
Brett Favre		
❑ 143 Trent Dilfer	.40	.18
Errict Rhett		
❑ 144 Jerry Rice	.50	.23
Eric Turner		
❑ 145 Andre Rison	.20	.09
Eric Turner		
❑ 146 Barry Sanders	.75	.35
Dave Meggett		
❑ 147 Emmitt Smith	.60	.25
Daryl Johnston		
❑ 148 Steve Young	1.00	.45
Brett Favre		
❑ 149 Emmitt Smith	.60	.25
Errict Rhett		
❑ 150 Marshall Faulk	.75	.35
Barry Sanders		
❑ 151 Jerry Rice	.50	.23
Darnay Scott		
❑ 152 William Floyd	.40	.18
Daryl Johnston		
❑ 153 Dan Marino	.75	.35
Trent Dilfer		
❑ 154 John Elway	.75	.35
Heath Shuler		
❑ 155 Byron Bam Morris	.20	.09
Natrone Means		
❑ 156 Dan Wilkinson	.20	.09
Reggie White		
❑ 157 Mario Bates	.20	.09
Rodney Hampton		
❑ 158 Junior Seau	.40	.18
Marvin Jones		
❑ 159 Ki-Jana Carter RC	.40	.18
❑ 160 Tony Boselli RC	.40	.18
❑ 161 Steve McNair RC	4.00	1.80
❑ 162 Michael Westbrook RC	2.50	1.10
❑ 163 Kerry Collins RC	2.50	1.10
❑ 164 Kevin Carter RC	.40	.18
❑ 165 Mike Mamula RC	.20	.09
❑ 166 Joey Galloway RC	3.00	1.35
❑ 167 Kyle Brady RC	.40	.18
❑ 168 J.J. Stokes RC	.40	.18
❑ 169 Warren Sapp RC	.75	.35
❑ 170 Rob Johnson RC	3.00	1.35
❑ 171 Tyrone Wheatley RC	2.00	.90
❑ 172 Napoleon Kaufman RC	2.50	1.10
❑ 173 James O. Stewart RC	3.00	1.35
❑ 174 Joe Aska RC	.20	.09
❑ 175 Rashaan Salaam RC	.40	.18
❑ 176 Tyrone Poole RC	.20	.09
❑ 177 Ty Law RC	.20	.09
❑ 178 Dino Philyaw RC	.10	.05
❑ 179 Mark Bruener RC	.20	.09
❑ 180 Derrick Brooks RC	.40	.18
❑ 181 Jack Jackson RC	.10	.05
❑ 182 Ray Zellars RC	.20	.09
❑ 183 Eddie Goines RC	.10	.05
❑ 184 Chris Sanders RC	.40	.18
❑ 185 Charlie Simmons RC	.10	.05
❑ 186 Lee DeRamus RC	.10	.05
❑ 187 Frank Sanders RC	1.50	.70
❑ 188 Rodney Thomas RC	.40	.18
❑ 189 Steve Stenstrom RC	.10	.05
❑ 190 Stoney Case RC	.40	.18
❑ 191 Tyrone Davis RC	.10	.05
❑ 192 Kordell Stewart RC	3.00	1.35
❑ 193 Christian Fauria RC	.10	.05
❑ 194 Todd Collins RC	.40	.18
❑ 195 Sherman Williams RC	.10	.05
❑ 196 Lovell Pinkney RC	.10	.05
❑ 197 Eric Zeier RC	.40	.18
❑ 198 Zack Crockett RC	.10	.05
❑ 199 Checklist A	.10	.05
❑ 200 Checklist B	.10	.05
❑ AU36 John Elway AUTO	150.00	70.00
❑ P1 Promo Sheet	2.00	.90
Trent Dilfer Promise		
Eric Turner Quickstrike		
William Floyd		
Dave Meggett		
Daryl Johnston		
Brett Favre		

1996 SkyBox Premium

	MINT	NRMT
COMPLETE SET (250)	20.00	9.00
❑ 1 Larry Centers	.25	.11
❑ 2 Boomer Esiason	.25	.11
❑ 3 Garrison Hearst	.25	.11
❑ 4 Rob Moore	.25	.11
❑ 5 Frank Sanders	.25	.11
❑ 6 Eric Swann	.10	.05
❑ 7 Bert Emanuel	.25	.11
❑ 8 Jeff George	.25	.11
❑ 9 Craig Heyward	.10	.05
❑ 10 Terance Mathis	.10	.05
❑ 11 Eric Metcalf	.10	.05
❑ 12 Derrick Alexander WR	.25	.11
❑ 13 Leroy Hoard	.10	.05
❑ 14 Michael Jackson	.25	.11
❑ 15 Vinny Testaverde	.25	.11
❑ 16 Eric Turner	.10	.05
❑ 17 Darick Holmes	.10	.05
❑ 18 Jim Kelly	.50	.23
❑ 19 Bryce Paup	.10	.05
❑ 20 Andre Reed	.25	.11
❑ 21 Bruce Smith	.25	.11
❑ 22 Thurman Thomas	.50	.23
❑ 23 Tim Tindale RC	.10	.05
❑ 24 Mark Carrier WR	.10	.05
❑ 25 Kerry Collins	.50	.23
❑ 26 Willie Green	.10	.05
❑ 27 Kevin Greene	.25	.11
❑ 28 Tyrone Poole	.10	.05
❑ 29 Curtis Conway	.50	.23
❑ 30 Bryan Cox	.10	.05
❑ 31 Erik Kramer	.10	.05
❑ 32 Nate Lewis	.10	.05
❑ 33 Rashaan Salaam	.50	.23
❑ 34 Alonzo Spellman	.10	.05
❑ 35 Michael Timpson	.10	.05
❑ 36 Jeff Blake	.50	.23
❑ 37 Ki-Jana Carter	.25	.11
❑ 38 David Dunn	.10	.05
❑ 39 Carl Pickens	.50	.23
❑ 40 Darnay Scott	.25	.11
❑ 41 Troy Aikman	1.25	.55
❑ 42 Charles Haley	.25	.11
❑ 43 Michael Irvin	.50	.23
❑ 44 Daryl Johnston	.25	.11
❑ 45 Jay Novacek	.10	.05
❑ 46 Deion Sanders	.75	.35
❑ 47 Emmitt Smith	2.00	.90
❑ 48 Kevin Williams	.10	.05
❑ 49 Steve Atwater	.10	.05
❑ 50 Terrell Davis	3.00	1.35
❑ 51 John Elway	2.50	1.10
❑ 52 Anthony Miller	.25	.11
❑ 53 Shannon Sharpe	.25	.11
❑ 54 Mike Sherrard	.10	.05
❑ 55 Scott Mitchell	.25	.11
❑ 56 Herman Moore	.50	.23
❑ 57 Johnnie Morton	.25	.11
❑ 58 Brett Perriman	.10	.05
❑ 59 Barry Sanders	2.50	1.10
❑ 60 Edgar Bennett	.25	.11
❑ 61 Robert Brooks	.50	.23
❑ 62 Mark Chmura	.25	.11
❑ 63 Brett Favre	2.50	1.10
❑ 64 Antonio Freeman	1.00	.45
❑ 65 Keith Jackson	.10	.05
❑ 66 Reggie White	.50	.23
❑ 67 Chris Chandler	.25	.11
❑ 68 Mel Gray	.10	.05
❑ 69 Steve McNair	1.00	.45
❑ 70 Chris Sanders	.25	.11
❑ 71 Rodney Thomas	.10	.05
❑ 72 Quentin Coryatt	.10	.05
❑ 73 Sean Dawkins	.10	.05
❑ 74 Ken Dilger	.25	.11
❑ 75 Marshall Faulk	.50	.23
❑ 76 Jim Harbaugh	.25	.11
❑ 77 Lamont Warren	.10	.05
❑ 78 Tony Boselli	.10	.05
❑ 79 Mark Brunell	1.25	.55
❑ 80 Willie Jackson	.10	.05
❑ 81 Natrone Means	.50	.23
❑ 82 James O.Stewart	.25	.11
❑ 83 Marcus Allen	.50	.23
❑ 84 Kimble Anders	.25	.11
❑ 85 Steve Bono	.10	.05
❑ 86 Lake Dawson	.10	.05
❑ 87 Neil Smith	.10	.05
❑ 88 Derrick Thomas	.25	.11
❑ 89 Tamarick Vanover	.25	.11
❑ 90 Fred Barnett	.10	.05
❑ 91 Terry Kirby	.25	.11
❑ 92 Dan Marino	2.50	1.10
❑ 93 O.J. McDuffie	.25	.11
❑ 94 Bernie Parmalee	.10	.05
❑ 95 Richmond Webb	.10	.05
❑ 96 Cris Carter	.50	.23
❑ 97 Scottie Graham	.10	.05
❑ 98 Qadry Ismail	.10	.05
❑ 99 Warren Moon	.25	.11
❑ 100 Jake Reed	.25	.11
❑ 101 Robert Smith	.25	.11
❑ 102 Drew Bledsoe	1.25	.55
❑ 103 Vincent Brisby	.10	.05
❑ 104 Ben Coates	.25	.11
❑ 105 Curtis Martin	1.00	.45
❑ 106 Dave Meggett	.10	.05
❑ 107 Chris Slade	.10	.05
❑ 108 Mario Bates	.25	.11
❑ 109 Jim Everett	.10	.05
❑ 110 Michael Haynes	.10	.05
❑ 111 Tyrone Hughes	.10	.05
❑ 112 Renaldo Turnbull	.10	.05
❑ 113 Dave Brown	.10	.05
❑ 114 Chris Calloway	.10	.05
❑ 115 Rodney Hampton	.25	.11
❑ 116 Thomas Lewis	.10	.05
❑ 117 Tyrone Wheatley	.25	.11
❑ 118 Kyle Brady	.10	.05
❑ 119 Hugh Douglas	.25	.11
❑ 120 Aaron Glenn	.10	.05
❑ 121 Jeff Graham	.10	.05
❑ 122 Adrian Murrell	.50	.23
❑ 123 Neil O'Donnell	.25	.11
❑ 124 Tim Brown	.50	.23
❑ 125 Nolan Harrison	.10	.05
❑ 126 Billy Joe Hobert	.25	.11
❑ 127 Jeff Hostetler	.10	.05
❑ 128 Napoleon Kaufman	.50	.23
❑ 129 Chester McGlockton	.10	.05
❑ 130 Harvey Williams	.10	.05
❑ 131 Charlie Garner	.10	.05
❑ 132 Andy Harmon	.10	.05
❑ 133 Chris T. Jones	.25	.11
❑ 134 Mike Mamula	.10	.05
❑ 135 Rodney Peete	.10	.05
❑ 136 Bobby Taylor	.10	.05
❑ 137 Ricky Watters	.25	.11
❑ 138 Jerome Bettis	.50	.23
❑ 139 Greg Lloyd	.25	.11
❑ 140 Jim Miller	.10	.05
❑ 141 Ernie Mills	.10	.05
❑ 142 Kordell Stewart	.75	.35
❑ 143 Yancey Thigpen	.25	.11

❑ 144 Rod Woodson .25 .11
❑ 145 Andre Coleman .10 .05
❑ 146 Terrell Fletcher .10 .05
❑ 147 Aaron Hayden RC .10 .05
❑ 148 Stan Humphries .25 .11
❑ 149 Junior Seau .25 .11
❑ 150 Isaac Bruce .50 .23
❑ 151 Kevin Carter .10 .05
❑ 152 Todd Kinchen .10 .05
❑ 153 Leslie O'Neal .10 .05
❑ 154 Steve Walsh .10 .05
❑ 155 William Floyd .25 .11
❑ 156 Merton Hanks .10 .05
❑ 157 Brent Jones .10 .05
❑ 158 Derek Loville .10 .05
❑ 159 Ken Norton .10 .05
❑ 160 Jerry Rice 1.25 .55
❑ 161 J.J. Stokes .50 .23
❑ 162 Steve Young 1.00 .45
❑ 163 Brian Blades .10 .05
❑ 164 Christian Fauria .10 .05
❑ 165 Joey Galloway .75 .35
❑ 166 Rick Mirer .25 .11
❑ 167 Chris Warren .25 .11
❑ 168 Trent Dilfer .50 .23
❑ 169 Alvin Harper .10 .05
❑ 170 Jackie Harris .10 .05
❑ 171 Hardy Nickerson .10 .05
❑ 172 Errict Rhett .25 .11
❑ 173 Terry Allen .25 .11
❑ 174 Henry Ellard .10 .05
❑ 175 Gus Frerotte .50 .23
❑ 176 Brian Mitchell .10 .05
❑ 177 Heath Shuler .25 .11
❑ 178 Michael Westbrook .50 .23
❑ 179 Karim Abdul-Jabbar RC .60 .25
❑ 180 Mike Alstott RC 1.25 .55
❑ 181 Willie Anderson RC .10 .05
❑ 182 Marco Battaglia RC .10 .05
❑ 183 Tim Biakabutuka RC .75 .35
❑ 184 Tony Brackens RC .25 .11
❑ 185 Duane Clemons RC .10 .05
❑ 186 Marcus Coleman RC .10 .05
❑ 187 Ernie Conwell RC .10 .05
❑ 188 Chris Darkins RC .10 .05
❑ 189 Stephen Davis RC 4.00 1.80
❑ 190 Brian Dawkins RC .10 .05
❑ 191 Rickey Dudley RC .50 .23
❑ 192 Jason Dunn RC .25 .11
❑ 193 Bobby Engram RC .50 .23
❑ 194 Daryl Gardener RC .10 .05
❑ 195 Eddie George RC 4.00 1.80
❑ 196 Terry Glenn RC 1.25 .55
❑ 197 Kevin Hardy RC .50 .23
❑ 198 Walt Harris RC .10 .05
❑ 199 Marvin Harrison RC 2.50 1.10
❑ 200 Bobby Hoying RC .60 .25
❑ 201 Israel Ifeanyi RC .10 .05
❑ 202 DeRon Jenkins RC .10 .05
❑ 203 Keyshawn Johnson RC 2.00 .90
❑ 204 Lance Johnstone RC .10 .05
❑ 205 Cedric Jones RC .10 .05
❑ 206 Marcus Jones RC .10 .05
❑ 207 Eddie Kennison RC .50 .23
❑ 208 Jevon Langford RC .10 .05
❑ 209 Dedric Mathis RC .10 .05
❑ 210 Jermane Mayberry RC .10 .05
❑ 211 Leeland McElroy RC .50 .23
❑ 212 Johnny McWilliams RC .25 .11
❑ 213 Ray Mickens RC .10 .05
❑ 214 John Mobley RC .10 .05
❑ 215 Jerald Moore RC .50 .23
❑ 216 Eric Moulds RC 2.00 .90
❑ 217 Muhsin Muhammad RC 1.00 .45
UER,photo is Tim Biakabutuka)
❑ 218 Jonathan Ogden RC .10 .05
❑ 219 Lawrence Phillips RC .50 .23
❑ 220 Kavika Pittman RC .10 .05
❑ 221 Stanley Pritchett RC .25 .11
❑ 222 Simeon Rice RC .50 .23
❑ 223 Detron Smith RC .10 .05
❑ 224 Bryan Still RC .50 .23
❑ 225 Amani Toomer RC 1.00 .45
❑ 226 Regan Upshaw RC .10 .05
❑ 227 Alex Van Dyke RC .25 .11
❑ 228 Stepfret Williams RC .25 .11
❑ 229 Retrospective .25 .11
Quentin Coryatt
Chester McGlockton
Carl Pickens
Robert Brooks
❑ 230 Retrospective .50 .23
Dale Carter
Edgar Bennett
Drew Bledsoe
Garrison Hearst
❑ 231 Retrospective .25 .11
Natrone Means
Rick Mirer
Jerome Bettis
Robert Smith
❑ 232 Retrospective .25 .11
O.J.McDuffie
Curtis Conway
Marshall Faulk
Greg Hill
❑ 233 Retrospective .25 .11
Heath Shuler
Trent Dilfer
William Floyd
Charles Johnson
❑ 234 Retrospective .25 .11
Errict Rhett
Sean Dawkins
Mario Bates
Ki-Jana Carter
❑ 235 Retrospective .50 .23
Kerry Collins
Steve McNair
Joey Galloway
Rashaan Salaam
❑ 236 Retrospective .50 .23
J.J.Stokes
Michael Westbrook
Kyle Brady
Kordell Stewart
❑ 237 Retrospective .25 .11
Keyshawn Johnson
Eddie George
Leeland McElroy
Lawrence Phillips
❑ 238 Retrospective .25 .11
Bobby Engram
Rickey Dudley
Eric Moulds
Tim Biakabutuka
❑ 239 Panorama Jan.14, 1996 .50 .23
Kordell Stewart
Quentin Coryatt
❑ 240 Panorama Nov.26, 1995 .25 .11
Robert Brooks
❑ 241 Panorama Nov.12, 1995 .10 .05
Henry Jones
Terance Mathis
❑ 242 Panorama Dec.9, 1995 .10 .05
Mark Seay
Alfred Pupunu
❑ 243 Panorama Sept.17, 1995 .25 .11
Robert Brooks
Willie Beamon
❑ 244 Panorama Oct.29, 1995 .10 .05
49ers Halloween
❑ 245 Panorama Oct.15, 1995 .10 .05
❑ 246 Panorama Dec.31, 1995 .25 .11
Zack Crockett
Junior Seau
❑ 247 Panorama Jan.14, 1996 .10 .05
Kevin Williams
Doug Evans
❑ 248 Panorama Nov.19, 1995 .25 .11
Tim Jacobs
Antonio Freeman
❑ 249 Checklist Card 1 .10 .05
❑ 250 Checklist Card 2 .10 .05
❑ P1 Promo Sheet 2.50 1.10
Brett Favre
Leeland McElroy
Kordell Stewart and
Quentin Coryatt Panorama

1997 SkyBox Premium

	MINT	NRMT
COMPLETE SET (250)	35.00	16.00

❑ 1 Brett Favre 2.50 1.10
❑ 2 Michael Bates .15 .07
❑ 3 Jeff Graham .15 .07
❑ 4 Terry Glenn .50 .23
❑ 5 Stephen Davis .60 .25
❑ 6 Wesley Walls .25 .11
❑ 7 Barry Sanders 2.50 1.10
❑ 8 Chris Sanders .15 .07
❑ 9 O.J. McDuffie .25 .11
❑ 10 Ken Dilger .15 .07
❑ 11 Kimble Anders .25 .11
❑ 12 Keenan McCardell .25 .11
❑ 13 Ki-Jana Carter .15 .07
❑ 14 Gary Brown .15 .07
❑ 15 Andre Rison .25 .11
❑ 16 Edgar Bennett .25 .11
❑ 17 Jerome Bettis .50 .23
❑ 18 Ted Johnson .15 .07
❑ 19 John Friesz .15 .07
❑ 20 Tony Brackens .15 .07
❑ 21 Bryan Cox .15 .07
❑ 22 Eric Moulds .50 .23
❑ 23 Johnnie Morton .25 .11
❑ 24 Brad Johnson .60 .25
❑ 25 Byron Bam Morris .15 .07
❑ 26 Anthony Johnson .15 .07
❑ 27 Jim Harbaugh .25 .11
❑ 28 Keyshawn Johnson .50 .23
❑ 29 Cary Blanchard .15 .07
❑ 30 Curtis Conway .25 .11
❑ 31 Herschel Walker .25 .11
❑ 32 Thurman Thomas .50 .23
❑ 33 Frank Sanders .25 .11
❑ 34 Lawrence Phillips .15 .07
❑ 35 Scottie Graham .15 .07
❑ 36 Jim Everett .15 .07
❑ 37 Dale Carter .15 .07
❑ 38 Ashley Ambrose .15 .07
❑ 39 Mark Chmura .25 .11
❑ 40 James O.Stewart .25 .11
❑ 41 John Mobley .15 .07
❑ 42 Terrell Davis 2.00 .90
❑ 43 Ben Coates .25 .11
❑ 44 Jeff George .25 .11
❑ 45 Ty Detmer .25 .11
❑ 46 Isaac Bruce .50 .23
❑ 47 Chris Warren .25 .11
❑ 48 Steve Walsh .15 .07
❑ 49 Bruce Smith .25 .11
❑ 50 Cris Carter .50 .23
❑ 51 Jamal Anderson .75 .35
❑ 52 Tim Biakabutuka .25 .11
❑ 53 Steve Young .75 .35
❑ 54 Eric Turner .15 .07
❑ 55 Jessie Tuggle .15 .07
❑ 56 Chris T. Jones .15 .07
❑ 57 Daryl Johnston .25 .11
❑ 58 Randall Cunningham .50 .23
❑ 59 Trent Dilfer .50 .23
❑ 60 Mark Brunell 1.25 .55
❑ 61 Warren Moon .50 .23
❑ 62 Terry Kirby .25 .11
❑ 63 Eddie George 1.25 .55

❑ 64	Neil Smith	.25	.11
❑ 65	Gilbert Brown	.15	.07
❑ 66	Emmitt Smith	2.00	.90
❑ 67	Chad Brown	.15	.07
❑ 68	Jamie Asher	.15	.07
❑ 69	Willie McGinest	.15	.07
❑ 70	Tim Brown	.50	.23
❑ 71	Quentin Coryatt	.15	.07
❑ 72	Mario Bates	.15	.07
❑ 73	Fred Barnett	.15	.07
❑ 74	Hugh Douglas	.15	.07
❑ 75	Eric Swann	.15	.07
❑ 76	Chris Chandler	.25	.11
❑ 77	Larry Centers	.25	.11
❑ 78	Vinny Testaverde	.25	.11
❑ 79	Jermaine Lewis	.50	.23
❑ 80	Junior Seau	.25	.11
❑ 81	Kevin Greene	.25	.11
❑ 82	Ricky Watters	.25	.11
❑ 83	Billy Davis RC	.15	.07
❑ 84	Michael Westbrook	.25	.11
❑ 85	Charles Way	.25	.11
❑ 86	Andre Reed	.25	.11
❑ 87	Darrell Green	.25	.11
❑ 88	Troy Aikman	1.25	.55
❑ 89	Jim Pyne	.15	.07
❑ 90	Dan Marino	2.50	1.10
❑ 91	Elvis Grbac	.25	.11
❑ 92	Mel Gray	.15	.07
❑ 93	Marcus Allen	.50	.23
❑ 94	Terry Allen	.50	.23
❑ 95	Karim Abdul-Jabbar	.50	.23
❑ 96	Rick Mirer	.15	.07
❑ 97	Bert Emanuel	.25	.11
❑ 98	John Elway	2.50	1.10
❑ 99	Tony Martin	.25	.11
❑ 100	Zach Thomas	.25	.11
❑ 101	Harvey Williams	.15	.07
❑ 102	Jason Sehorn	.25	.11
❑ 103	Lawyer Milloy	.15	.07
❑ 104	Thomas Lewis	.15	.07
❑ 105	Michael Irvin	.50	.23
❑ 106	James Hundon RC	.50	.23
❑ 107	Willie Green	.15	.07
❑ 108	Bobby Engram	.25	.11
❑ 109	Mike Alstott	.50	.23
❑ 110	Greg Lloyd	.15	.07
❑ 111	Shannon Sharpe	.25	.11
❑ 112	Desmond Howard	.25	.11
❑ 113	Jason Elam	.15	.07
❑ 114	Qadry Ismail	.25	.11
❑ 115	William Thomas	.15	.07
❑ 116	Marshall Faulk	.50	.23
❑ 117	Tyrone Wheatley	.25	.11
❑ 118	Tommy Vardell	.15	.07
❑ 119	Rashaan Salaam	.15	.07
❑ 120	Brian Mitchell	.15	.07
❑ 121	Terance Mathis	.25	.11
❑ 122	Dorsey Levens	.50	.23
❑ 123	Todd Collins	.15	.07
❑ 124	Derrick Alexander WR	.25	.11
❑ 125	Stan Humphries	.25	.11
❑ 126	Kordell Stewart	.60	.25
❑ 127	Kent Graham	.15	.07
❑ 128	Yancey Thigpen	.25	.11
❑ 129	Bryan Still	.15	.07
❑ 130	Carl Pickens	.50	.23
❑ 131	Ray Lewis	.60	.25
❑ 132	Curtis Martin	.60	.25
❑ 133	Kerry Collins	.25	.11
❑ 134	Ed McCaffrey	.25	.11
❑ 135	Darick Holmes	.15	.07
❑ 136	Glyn Milburn	.15	.07
❑ 137	Rickey Dudley	.25	.11
❑ 138	Terrell Owens	.50	.23
❑ 139	Kevin Williams	.15	.07
❑ 140	Reggie White	.50	.23
❑ 141	Darnay Scott	.25	.11
❑ 142	Brett Perriman	.15	.07
❑ 143	Neil O'Donnell	.25	.11
❑ 144	Natrone Means	.50	.23
❑ 145	Jerris McPhail	.15	.07
❑ 146	Lamar Lathon	.15	.07
❑ 147	Michael Jackson	.25	.11
❑ 148	Simeon Rice	.25	.11
❑ 149	Greg Hill	.15	.07
❑ 150	Erik Kramer	.15	.07
❑ 151	Quinn Early	.15	.07
❑ 152	Tamarick Vanover	.25	.11
❑ 153	Derrick Thomas	.25	.11
❑ 154	Nilo Silvan	.15	.07
❑ 155	Deion Sanders	.50	.23
❑ 156	Lorenzo Neal	.15	.07
❑ 157	Steve McNair	.60	.25
❑ 158	Levon Kirkland	.15	.07
❑ 159	Bobby Hebert	.15	.07
❑ 160	William Floyd	.25	.11
❑ 161	Leeland McElroy	.15	.07
❑ 162	Chester McGlockton	.15	.07
❑ 163	Michael Haynes	.15	.07
❑ 164	Aeneas Williams	.15	.07
❑ 165	Hardy Nickerson	.15	.07
❑ 166	Ray Zellars	.15	.07
❑ 167	Iheanyi Uwaezuoke	.25	.11
❑ 168	Chris Slade	.15	.07
❑ 169	Herman Moore	.50	.23
❑ 170	Rob Moore	.25	.11
❑ 171	Andre Hastings	.15	.07
❑ 172	Antonio Freeman	.60	.25
❑ 173	Tony Boselli	.15	.07
❑ 174	Drew Bledsoe	1.25	.55
❑ 175	Sam Mills	.15	.07
❑ 176	Robert Smith	.25	.11
❑ 177	Jimmy Smith	.25	.11
❑ 178	Alex Molden	.15	.07
❑ 179	Joey Galloway	.60	.25
❑ 180	Irving Fryar	.25	.11
❑ 181	Wayne Chrebet	.50	.23
❑ 182	Dave Brown	.15	.07
❑ 183	Robert Brooks	.25	.11
❑ 184	Tony Banks	.25	.11
❑ 185	Eric Metcalf	.25	.11
❑ 186	Napoleon Kaufman	.50	.23
❑ 187	Frank Wycheck	.15	.07
❑ 188	Donnell Woolford	.15	.07
❑ 189	Kevin Turner	.15	.07
❑ 190	Eddie Kennison	.25	.11
❑ 191	Cortez Kennedy	.15	.07
❑ 192	Raymont Harris	.15	.07
❑ 193	Ronnie Harmon	.15	.07
❑ 194	Kevin Hardy	.15	.07
❑ 195	Gus Frerotte	.15	.07
❑ 196	Marvin Harrison	.50	.23
❑ 197	Jeff Blake	.25	.11
❑ 198	Mike Tomczak	.15	.07
❑ 199	William Roaf	.15	.07
❑ 200	Jerry Rice	1.25	.55
❑ 201	Jake Reed	.25	.11
❑ 202	Ken Norton	.15	.07
❑ 203	Errict Rhett	.15	.07
❑ 204	Adrian Murrell	.25	.11
❑ 205	Rodney Hampton	.25	.11
❑ 206	Scott Mitchell	.25	.11
❑ 207	Jason Dunn	.15	.07
❑ 208	Mike Adams RC	.15	.07
❑ 209	John Allred RC	.15	.07
❑ 210	Reidel Anthony RC	1.00	.45
❑ 211	Darnell Autry RC	.25	.11
❑ 212	Tiki Barber RC	2.00	.90
❑ 213	Will Blackwell RC	.50	.23
❑ 214	Peter Boulware RC	.25	.11
❑ 215	Macey Brooks RC	.50	.23
❑ 216	Rae Carruth RC	.50	.23
❑ 217	Troy Davis RC	.50	.23
❑ 218	Corey Dillon RC	4.00	1.80
❑ 219	Jim Druckenmiller RC	.50	.23
❑ 220	Warrick Dunn RC	2.00	.90
❑ 221	Marc Edwards RC	.15	.07
❑ 222	James Farrior RC	.15	.07
❑ 223	Tony Gonzalez RC	2.00	.90
❑ 224	Jay Graham RC	.50	.23
❑ 225	Yatil Green RC	.25	.11
❑ 226	Byron Hanspard RC	.50	.23
❑ 227	Ike Hilliard RC	1.00	.45
❑ 228	Leon Johnson RC	.15	.07
❑ 229	Damon Jones RC	.15	.07
❑ 230	Freddie Jones RC	.25	.11
❑ 231	Joey Kent RC	.50	.23
❑ 232	David LaFleur RC	.25	.11
❑ 233	Kevin Lockett RC	.25	.11
❑ 234	Sam Madison RC	.50	.23
❑ 235	Brian Manning RC	.15	.07
❑ 236	Ronnie McAda RC	.15	.07
❑ 237	Orlando Pace RC	.50	.23
❑ 238	Jake Plummer RC	4.00	1.80
❑ 239	Keith Poole RC	.50	.23
❑ 240	Darrell Russell RC	.15	.07
❑ 241	Sedrick Shaw RC	.50	.23
❑ 242	Antowain Smith RC	1.25	.55
❑ 243	Shawn Springs RC	.25	.11
❑ 244	Duce Staley RC	10.00	4.50
❑ 245	Dedric Ward RC	1.25	.55
❑ 246	Bryant Westbrook RC	.15	.07
❑ 247	Danny Wuerffel RC	.75	.35
❑ 248	Checklist	.15	.07
❑ 249	Checklist	.15	.07
❑ 250	Checklist	.15	.07
❑ S1	Terrell Davis Sample	2.00	.90

1998 SkyBox Premium

	MINT	NRMT
COMPLETE SET (250)	150.00	70.00

❑ 1	John Elway	2.50	1.10
❑ 2	Drew Bledsoe	1.00	.45
❑ 3	Antonio Freeman	.50	.23
❑ 4	Merton Hanks	.15	.07
❑ 5	James Jett	.25	.11
❑ 6	Ricky Proehl	.15	.07
❑ 7	Deion Sanders	.50	.23
❑ 8	Frank Sanders	.25	.11
❑ 9	Bruce Smith	.25	.11
❑ 10	Tiki Barber	.25	.11
❑ 11	Isaac Bruce	.50	.23
❑ 12	Mark Brunell	1.00	.45
❑ 13	Quinn Early	.15	.07
❑ 14	Terry Glenn	.50	.23
❑ 15	Darrien Gordon	.15	.07
❑ 16	Keith Byars	.15	.07
❑ 17	Terrell Davis	2.00	.90
❑ 18	Charlie Garner	.15	.07
❑ 19	Eddie Kennison	.25	.11
❑ 20	Keenan McCardell	.25	.11
❑ 21	Eric Moulds	.50	.23
❑ 22	Jimmy Smith	.25	.11
❑ 23	Reidel Anthony	.25	.11
❑ 24	Rae Carruth	.25	.11
❑ 25	Michael Irvin	.50	.23
❑ 26	Dorsey Levens	.50	.23
❑ 27	Derrick Mayes	.25	.11
❑ 28	Adrian Murrell	.25	.11
❑ 29	Dwayne Rudd	.15	.07
❑ 30	Leslie Shepherd	.15	.07
❑ 31	Jamal Anderson	.50	.23
❑ 32	Robert Brooks	.25	.11
❑ 33	Sean Dawkins	.15	.07
❑ 34	Cris Dishman	.15	.07
❑ 35	Rickey Dudley	.15	.07
❑ 36	Bobby Engram	.25	.11
❑ 37	Chester McGlockton	.15	.07
❑ 38	Terrell Owens	.50	.23
❑ 39	Wayne Chrebet	.50	.23
❑ 40	Dexter Coakley	.15	.07
❑ 41	Kerry Collins	.25	.11
❑ 42	Trent Dilfer	.50	.23
❑ 43	Bobby Hoying	.25	.11
❑ 44	Glyn Milburn	.15	.07
❑ 45	Rob Moore	.25	.11
❑ 46	Jake Reed	.25	.11

❑ 47 Dana Stubblefield .15 .07
❑ 48 Reggie White .50 .23
❑ 49 Natrone Means .50 .23
❑ 50 Troy Aikman 1.25 .55
❑ 51 Aaron Bailey .15 .07
❑ 52 William Floyd .15 .07
❑ 53 Eric Metcalf .15 .07
❑ 54 Warrick Dunn .50 .23
❑ 55 Chad Lewis .15 .07
❑ 56 Curtis Martin .50 .23
❑ 57 Tony Martin .25 .11
❑ 58 John Randle .25 .11
❑ 59 Jeff Burris .15 .07
❑ 60 Larry Centers .15 .07
❑ 61 Bert Emanuel .25 .11
❑ 62 Sean Gilbert .15 .07
❑ 63 David Palmer .15 .07
❑ 64 Eric Bieniemy .15 .07
❑ 65 Peter Boulware .15 .07
❑ 66 Charles Johnson .15 .07
❑ 67 Jerris McPhail .15 .07
❑ 68 Scott Mitchell .25 .11
❑ 69 Chris Sanders .15 .07
❑ 70 Ken Dilger .15 .07
❑ 71 Brad Johnson .50 .23
❑ 72 Danny Kanell .25 .11
❑ 73 Fred Lane .25 .11
❑ 74 Warren Sapp .25 .11
❑ 75 Carl Pickens .50 .23
❑ 76 Cris Carter .50 .23
❑ 77 Marshall Faulk .50 .23
❑ 78 Keyshawn Johnson .50 .23
❑ 79 Tony McGee .15 .07
❑ 80 Muhsin Muhammad .25 .11
❑ 81 Kordell Stewart .50 .23
❑ 82 Karl Williams .15 .07
❑ 83 Willie Davis .15 .07
❑ 84 David Dunn .15 .07
❑ 85 Marvin Harrison .25 .11
❑ 86 Michael Jackson .15 .07
❑ 87 John Mobley .15 .07
❑ 88 Shawn Springs .15 .07
❑ 89 Wesley Walls .25 .11
❑ 90 Jermaine Lewis .25 .11
❑ 91 Ed McCaffrey .25 .11
❑ 92 Chris Calloway .15 .07
❑ 93 Lamont Warren .15 .07
❑ 94 Ricky Watters .25 .11
❑ 95 Tony Banks .25 .11
❑ 96 Tony Brackens .15 .07
❑ 97 Gary Brown .15 .07
❑ 98 Howard Griffith .15 .07
❑ 99 Ray Lewis .50 .23
❑ 100 Jeff Blake .25 .11
❑ 101 Charlie Jones .15 .07
❑ 102 Glenn Foley .25 .11
❑ 103 Jay Graham .15 .07
❑ 104 James McKnight .15 .07
❑ 105 Steve McNair .50 .23
❑ 106 Chad Scott .15 .07
❑ 107 Rod Smith WR .25 .11
❑ 108 Jason Taylor .15 .07
❑ 109 Corey Dillon .75 .35
❑ 110 Eddie George 1.00 .45
❑ 111 Jim Harbaugh .25 .11
❑ 112 Warren Moon .50 .23
❑ 113 Shannon Sharpe .25 .11
❑ 114 Darnell Autry .15 .07
❑ 115 Brett Favre 2.50 1.10
❑ 116 Jeff George .25 .11
❑ 117 Tony Gonzalez .15 .07
❑ 118 Garrison Hearst .50 .23
❑ 119 Randal Hill .15 .07
❑ 120 Eric Swann .15 .07
❑ 121 Jamie Asher .15 .07
❑ 122 Tim Brown .50 .23
❑ 123 Stephen Davis .15 .07
❑ 124 Chris Chandler .25 .11
❑ 125 Jerry Rice 1.25 .55
❑ 126 Troy Davis .15 .07
❑ 127 Ronnie Harmon .15 .07
❑ 128 Andre Rison .25 .11
❑ 129 Duce Staley 1.00 .45
❑ 130 Charles Way .15 .07
❑ 131 Bryant Westbrook .15 .07
❑ 132 Mike Alstott .50 .23
❑ 133 Gus Frerotte .15 .07
❑ 134 Travis Jervey .25 .11
❑ 135 Daryl Johnston .25 .11
❑ 136 Jake Plummer 1.00 .45
❑ 137 Junior Seau .25 .11
❑ 138 Robert Smith .50 .23
❑ 139 Thurman Thomas .50 .23
❑ 140 Karim Abdul-Jabbar .50 .23
❑ 141 Jerome Bettis .50 .23
❑ 142 Byron Hanspard .25 .11
❑ 143 Raymont Harris .15 .07
❑ 144 Willie McGinest .15 .07
❑ 145 Barry Sanders 2.50 1.10
❑ 146 Irv Smith .15 .07
❑ 147 Michael Strahan .15 .07
❑ 148 Frank Wycheck .15 .07
❑ 149 Steve Broussard .15 .07
❑ 150 Joey Galloway .50 .23
❑ 151 Courtney Hawkins .15 .07
❑ 152 O.J. McDuffie .25 .11
❑ 153 Herman Moore .50 .23
❑ 154 Chris Penn .15 .07
❑ 155 O.J. Santiago .15 .07
❑ 156 Yancey Thigpen .15 .07
❑ 157 Jason Sehorn .25 .11
❑ 158 Ben Coates .25 .11
❑ 159 Ernie Conwell .15 .07
❑ 160 Dale Carter .15 .07
❑ 161 Jeff Graham .15 .07
❑ 162 Rob Johnson .25 .11
❑ 163 Damon Jones .15 .07
❑ 164 Mark Chmura .25 .11
❑ 165 Curtis Conway .25 .11
❑ 166 Elvis Grbac .25 .11
❑ 167 Andre Hastings .15 .07
❑ 168 Terry Kirby .15 .07
❑ 169 Aeneas Williams .15 .07
❑ 170 Derrick Alexander WR .25 .11
❑ 171 Troy Brown .15 .07
❑ 172 Irving Fryar .25 .11
❑ 173 Jerald Moore .15 .07
❑ 174 Andre Reed .25 .11
❑ 175 James Stewart .25 .11
❑ 176 Chris Warren .25 .11
❑ 177 Will Blackwell .15 .07
❑ 178 Erik Kramer .15 .07
❑ 179 Dan Marino 2.50 1.10
❑ 180 Terance Mathis .25 .11
❑ 181 Johnnie Morton .25 .11
❑ 182 J.J. Stokes .25 .11
❑ 183 Rodney Thomas .15 .07
❑ 184 Steve Young .75 .35
❑ 185 Kimble Anders .25 .11
❑ 186 Napoleon Kaufman .50 .23
❑ 187 Orlando Pace .15 .07
❑ 188 Antowain Smith .50 .23
❑ 189 Emmitt Smith 2.00 .90
❑ 190 Terry Allen .50 .23
❑ 191 Mark Bruener .15 .07
❑ 192 Rodney Harrison .25 .11
❑ 193 Billy Joe Hobert .15 .07
❑ 194 Leon Johnson .15 .07
❑ 195 Freddie Jones .15 .07
❑ 196 John Elway OFA 1.00 .45
❑ 197 Brett Favre OFA .75 .35
Steve Atwater OFA
❑ 198 Brett Favre OFA .75 .35
Steve Atwater OFA
❑ 199 Dorsey Levens OFA .25 .11
Keith Traylor OFA
❑ 200 Packers Offense OFA .50 .23
Broncos Defense OFA
❑ 201 Mark Chmura OFA .15 .07
Tyrone Braxton OFA
❑ 202 Dorsey Levens OFA .25 .11
Steve Atwater OFA
Bill Romanowski OFA
❑ 203 Robert Brooks OFA .25 .11
Ray Crockett OFA
❑ 204 Tim McKyer OFA .15 .07
❑ 205 Allen Aldridge OFA .15 .07
❑ 206 Terrell Davis OFA .75 .35
Rod Smith WR OFA
❑ 207 Bill Romanowski OFA .15 .07
❑ 208 John Elway OFA 1.00 .45
Rod Smith WR OFA
Ed McCaffrey OFA
❑ 209 Ray Crockett OFA .15 .07
❑ 210 John Elway OFA 1.00 .45
❑ 211 Robert Edwards RC 5.00 2.20
❑ 212 Roland Williams RC 2.00 .90
❑ 213 Joe Jurevicius RC 2.50 1.10
❑ 214 Wilmont Perry RC 2.00 .90
❑ 215 Robert Holcombe RC 4.00 1.80
❑ 216 Larry Shannon RC 2.00 .90
❑ 217 Skip Hicks RC 4.00 1.80
❑ 218 Pat Johnson RC 2.50 1.10
❑ 219 Pat Palmer RC 2.00 .90
❑ 220 John Dutton RC 2.00 .90
❑ 221 Az-Zahir Hakim RC 4.00 1.80
❑ 222 Mikhael Ricks RC 2.50 1.10
❑ 223 Rashaan Shehee RC 2.50 1.10
❑ 224 Ryan Leaf RC 8.00 3.60
❑ 225 Alvis Whitted RC 2.00 .90
❑ 226 Marcus Nash RC 4.00 1.80
❑ 227 Fred Taylor RC 10.00 4.50
❑ 228 Hines Ward RC 2.50 1.10
❑ 229 C.Fuamatu-Ma'afala RC 2.50 1.10
❑ 230 Jerome Pathon RC 2.50 1.10
❑ 231 Peyton Manning RC 30.00 13.50
❑ 232 Charles Woodson RC 6.00 2.70
❑ 233 Jon Ritchie RC 2.50 1.10
❑ 234 Scott Frost R RC 2.50 1.10
❑ 235 John Avery RC 4.00 1.80
❑ 236 Jonathan Linton RC 4.00 1.80
❑ 237 Jacquez Green RC 6.00 2.70
❑ 238 Andre Wadsworth RC 2.50 1.10
❑ 239 Cam Quayle RC 2.00 .90
❑ 240 Randy Moss RC 30.00 13.50
❑ 241 Raymond Priester RC 2.00 .90
❑ 242 Donald Hayes RC 4.00 1.80
❑ 243 Brian Griese RC 12.00 5.50
❑ 244 Brian Alford RC 2.50 1.10
❑ 245 Kevin Dyson RC 6.00 2.70
❑ 246 Jammi German RC 2.00 .90
❑ 247 Cameron Cleeland RC 2.50 1.10
❑ 248 Curtis Enis RC 5.00 2.20
❑ 249 Terry Hardy RC 2.00 .90
❑ 250 Tony Simmons RC 2.50 1.10
❑ NNO Checklist Card .15 .07
❑ P136 Jake Plummer Promo 1.50 .70

1999 SkyBox Premium

	MINT	NRMT
COMPLETE SET (290)	350.00	160.00
COMP.SET w/o SPs (250)	50.00	22.00

❑ 1 Randy Moss 2.00 .90
❑ 2 Jamie Asher .15 .07
❑ 3 Joey Galloway .50 .23
❑ 4 Kent Graham .15 .07
❑ 5 Leslie Shepherd .15 .07
❑ 6 Levon Kirkland .15 .07
❑ 7 Marcus Pollard .15 .07
❑ 8 O.J. McDuffie .25 .11
❑ 9 Bill Romanowski .15 .07
❑ 10 Priest Holmes .50 .23
❑ 11 Tim Biakabutuka .25 .11
❑ 12 Duce Staley .50 .23
❑ 13 Isaac Bruce .50 .23
❑ 14 Jay Riemersma .15 .07
❑ 15 Karim Abdul-Jabbar .25 .11
❑ 16 Kevin Dyson .25 .11

❑ 17 Rickey Dudley .15 .07
❑ 18 Rocket Ismail .25 .11
❑ 19 Billy Davis .15 .07
❑ 20 James Jett .25 .11
❑ 21 Jerome Bettis .50 .23
❑ 22 Michael McCrary .15 .07
❑ 23 Michael Westbrook .25 .11
❑ 24 Oronde Gadsden .15 .07
❑ 25 Brad Johnson .50 .23
❑ 26 Shawn Springs .15 .07
❑ 27 Cris Carter .50 .23
❑ 28 Ed McCaffrey .25 .11
❑ 29 Gary Brown .15 .07
❑ 30 Hines Ward .15 .07
❑ 31 Hugh Douglas .15 .07
❑ 32 Jamir Miller .15 .07
❑ 33 Michael Bates .15 .07
❑ 34 Peyton Manning 2.00 .90
❑ 35 Tony Banks .25 .11
❑ 36 Charles Way .15 .07
❑ 37 Charlie Batch 1.00 .45
❑ 38 Jake Reed .25 .11
❑ 39 Mark Brunell .75 .35
❑ 40 Skip Hicks .50 .23
❑ 41 Steve Young .75 .35
❑ 42 Wesley Walls .25 .11
❑ 43 Antonio Langham .15 .07
❑ 44 Antowain Smith .50 .23
❑ 45 Brian Griese 1.00 .45
❑ 46 Jessie Armstead .15 .07
❑ 47 Thurman Thomas .25 .11
❑ 48 Jeff George .25 .11
❑ 49 Jessie Tuggle .15 .07
❑ 50 Jim Harbaugh .25 .11
❑ 51 Marvin Harrison .50 .23
❑ 52 Randall Cunningham .50 .23
❑ 53 Stephen Alexander .15 .07
❑ 54 Tiki Barber .15 .07
❑ 55 Billy Joe Tolliver .15 .07
❑ 56 Bruce Smith .25 .11
❑ 57 Eddie George .60 .25
❑ 58 Eugene Robinson .15 .07
❑ 59 John Elway 2.00 .90
❑ 60 Kent Dilger .15 .07
❑ 61 Rodney Harrison .15 .07
❑ 62 Ty Detmer .25 .11
❑ 63 Andre Reed .25 .11
❑ 64 Dorsey Levens .50 .23
❑ 65 Eddie Kennison .25 .11
❑ 66 Freddie Jones .15 .07
❑ 67 Jacquez Green .25 .11
❑ 68 Jason Elam .15 .07
❑ 69 Marc Edwards .15 .07
❑ 70 Terance Mathis .25 .11
❑ 71 Alonzo Mayes .15 .07
❑ 72 Andre Wadsworth .15 .07
❑ 73 Barry Sanders 2.00 .90
❑ 74 Derrick Alexander .15 .07
❑ 75 Garrison Hearst .25 .11
❑ 76 Leon Johnson .15 .07
❑ 77 Mike Alstott .50 .23
❑ 78 Shawn Jefferson .15 .07
❑ 79 Andre Hastings .15 .07
❑ 80 Eric Moulds .50 .23
❑ 81 Ryan Leaf .50 .23
❑ 82 Takeo Spikes .15 .07
❑ 83 Terrell Davis 1.25 .55
❑ 84 Tim Dwight .50 .23
❑ 85 Trent Dilfer .25 .11
❑ 86 Vonnie Holliday .15 .07
❑ 87 Antonio Freeman .50 .23
❑ 88 Carl Pickens .25 .11
❑ 89 Chris Chandler .25 .11
❑ 90 Dale Carter .15 .07
❑ 91 La'Roi Glover .15 .07
❑ 92 Natrone Means .25 .11
❑ 93 Reidel Anthony .25 .11
❑ 94 Brett Favre 2.00 .90
❑ 95 Bubby Brister .15 .07
❑ 96 Cameron Cleeland .15 .07
❑ 97 Chris Calloway .15 .07
❑ 98 Corey Dillon .50 .23
❑ 99 Greg Hill .15 .07
❑ 100 Vinny Testaverde .25 .11
❑ 101 Trent Green .25 .11
❑ 102 Sam Gash .15 .07
❑ 103 Mikhael Ricks .15 .07
❑ 104 Emmitt Smith 1.25 .55
❑ 105 Doug Flutie .60 .25
❑ 106 Deion Sanders .50 .23
❑ 107 Charles Johnson .15 .07
❑ 108 Byron Bam Morris .15 .07
❑ 109 Andre Rison .25 .11
❑ 110 Doug Pederson .15 .07
❑ 111 Marshall Faulk .50 .23
❑ 112 Tim Brown .50 .23
❑ 113 Warren Sapp .15 .07
❑ 114 Bryan Still .15 .07
❑ 115 Chris Penn .15 .07
❑ 116 Jamal Anderson .50 .23
❑ 117 Keyshawn Johnson .50 .23
❑ 118 Ricky Proehl .15 .07
❑ 119 Robert Brooks .25 .11
❑ 120 Tony Gonzalez .25 .11
❑ 121 Ty Law .15 .07
❑ 122 Elvis Grbac .25 .11
❑ 123 Jeff Blake .25 .11
❑ 124 Mark Chmura .15 .07
❑ 125 Junior Seau .25 .11
❑ 126 Mo Lewis .15 .07
❑ 127 Ray Buchanan .15 .07
❑ 128 Robert Holcombe .25 .11
❑ 129 Tony Simmons .15 .07
❑ 130 David Palmer .15 .07
❑ 131 Ike Hilliard .15 .07
❑ 132 Mike Vanderjagt .15 .07
❑ 133 Rae Carruth .25 .11
❑ 134 Sean Dawkins .15 .07
❑ 135 Shannon Sharpe .25 .11
❑ 136 Curtis Conway .25 .11
❑ 137 Darrell Green .15 .07
❑ 138 Germane Crowell .25 .11
❑ 139 J.J. Stokes .25 .11
❑ 140 Kevin Hardy .15 .07
❑ 141 Rob Moore .25 .11
❑ 142 Robert Smith .50 .23
❑ 143 Wayne Chrebet .25 .11
❑ 144 Yancey Thigpen .15 .07
❑ 145 Jerome Pathon .15 .07
❑ 146 John Mobley .15 .07
❑ 147 Kerry Collins .25 .11
❑ 148 Peter Boulware .15 .07
❑ 149 Matthew Hatchette .15 .07
❑ 150 Kordell Stewart .50 .23
❑ 151 Koy Detmer .15 .07
❑ 152 Sedrick Shaw .15 .07
❑ 153 Steve Beuerlein .15 .07
❑ 154 Zach Thomas .25 .11
❑ 155 Adrian Murrell .25 .11
❑ 156 Bobby Engram .25 .11
❑ 157 Bryan Cox .15 .07
❑ 158 Drew Bledsoe .75 .35
❑ 159 Jerry Rice 1.25 .55
❑ 160 Keenan McCardell .25 .11
❑ 161 Steve McNair .50 .23
❑ 162 Terry Fair .15 .07
❑ 163 Derrick Brooks .15 .07
❑ 164 Eric Green .15 .07
❑ 165 Erik Kramer .15 .07
❑ 166 Frank Sanders .25 .11
❑ 167 Fred Taylor 1.25 .55
❑ 168 Johnnie Morton .25 .11
❑ 169 R.W. McQuarters .15 .07
❑ 170 Terry Glenn .50 .23
❑ 171 Frank Wycheck .15 .07
❑ 172 John Avery .25 .11
❑ 173 Kevin Turner .15 .07
❑ 174 Larry Centers .15 .07
❑ 175 Michael Irvin .25 .11
❑ 176 Rich Gannon .25 .11
❑ 177 Ricky Watters .25 .11
❑ 178 Rodney Thomas .15 .07
❑ 179 Scott Mitchell .15 .07
❑ 180 Chad Brown .15 .07
❑ 181 John Randle .25 .11
❑ 182 Michael Strahan .15 .07
❑ 183 Muhsin Muhammad .25 .11
❑ 184 Reggie Barlow .15 .07
❑ 185 Rod Smith .25 .11
❑ 186 Dan Marino 2.00 .90
❑ 187 Dexter Coakley .15 .07
❑ 188 Jermaine Lewis .25 .11
❑ 189 Jon Kitna .50 .23
❑ 190 Napoleon Kaufman .50 .23
❑ 191 Will Blackwell .15 .07
❑ 192 Aaron Glenn .15 .07
❑ 193 Ben Coates .25 .11
❑ 194 Curtis Enis .50 .23
❑ 195 Herman Moore .50 .23
❑ 196 Jake Plummer 1.00 .45
❑ 197 Jimmy Smith .25 .11
❑ 198 Terrell Owens .50 .23
❑ 199 Warrick Dunn .50 .23
❑ 200 Charles Woodson .50 .23
❑ 201 Ahman Green .25 .11
❑ 202 Mark Bruener .15 .07
❑ 203 Ray Lewis .25 .11
❑ 204 Tony Martin .25 .11
❑ 205 Troy Aikman 1.25 .55
❑ 206 Curtis Martin .50 .23
❑ 207 Darnay Scott .15 .07
❑ 208 Derrick Mayes .15 .07
❑ 209 Keith Poole .15 .07
❑ 210 Warren Moon .50 .23
❑ 211 Chris Claiborne RC .50 .23
❑ 211S Chris Claiborne SP 1.50 .70
❑ 212 Ricky Williams RC 5.00 2.20
❑ 212S Ricky Williams SP 15.00 6.75
❑ 213 Tim Couch RC 5.00 2.20
❑ 213S Tim Couch SP 15.00 6.75
❑ 214 Champ Bailey RC 1.50 .70
❑ 214S Champ Bailey SP 5.00 2.20
❑ 215 Torry Holt RC 3.00 1.35
❑ 215S Torry Holt SP 10.00 4.50
❑ 216 Donovan McNabb RC 5.00 2.20
❑ 216S Donovan McNabb SP 15.00 6.75
❑ 217 David Boston RC 2.50 1.10
❑ 217S David Boston SP 8.00 3.60
❑ 218 Chris McAlister RC .75 .35
❑ 218S Chris McAlister SP 2.50 1.10
❑ 219 Michael Bishop RC 1.50 .70
❑ 219S Michael Bishop SP 5.00 2.20
❑ 220 Daunte Culpepper RC 8.00 3.60
❑ 220S Daunte Culpepper SP 20.00 9.00
❑ 221 Joe Germaine RC 1.25 .55
❑ 221S Joe Germaine SP 4.00 1.80
❑ 222 Edgerrin James RC 8.00 3.60
❑ 222S Edgerrin James SP 20.00 9.00
❑ 223 Jevon Kearse RC 2.50 1.10
❑ 223S Jevon Kearse SP 8.00 3.60
❑ 224 Ebenezer Ekuban RC .75 .35
❑ 224S Ebenezer Ekuban SP 2.50 1.10
❑ 225 Scott Covington RC 1.25 .55
❑ 225S Scott Covington SP 4.00 1.80
❑ 226 Aaron Brooks RC 5.00 2.20
❑ 226S Aaron Brooks SP 15.00 6.75
❑ 227 Cecil Collins RC 1.25 .55
❑ 227S Cecil Collins SP 4.00 1.80
❑ 228 Akili Smith RC 2.50 1.10
❑ 228S Akili Smith SP 8.00 3.60
❑ 229 Shaun King RC 2.50 1.10
❑ 229S Shaun King SP 8.00 3.60
❑ 230 Chad Plummer RC .50 .23
❑ 230S Chad Plummer SP 1.50 .70
❑ 231 Peerless Price RC 1.50 .70
❑ 231S Peerless Price SP 5.00 2.20
❑ 232 Antoine Winfield RC .75 .35
❑ 232S Antoine Winfield SP 2.50 1.10
❑ 233 Antuan Edwards RC .50 .23
❑ 233S Antuan Edwards SP 1.50 .70
❑ 234 Rob Konrad RC 1.25 .55
❑ 234S Rob Konrad SP 4.00 1.80
❑ 235 Troy Edwards RC 1.50 .70
❑ 235S Troy Edwards SP 5.00 2.20
❑ 236 Terry Jackson RC .75 .35
❑ 236S Terry Jackson SP 2.50 1.10
❑ 237 Jim Kleinsasser RC 1.25 .55
❑ 237S Jim Kleinsasser SP 4.00 1.80
❑ 238 Joe Montgomery RC 1.25 .55
❑ 238S Joe Montgomery SP 4.00 1.80
❑ 239 Desmond Clark RC .75 .35
❑ 239S Desmond Clark SP 2.50 1.10
❑ 240 Lamar King RC .50 .23
❑ 240S Lamar King SP 1.50 .70
❑ 241 Dameane Douglas RC .75 .35
❑ 241S Dameane Douglas SP 2.50 1.10
❑ 242 Martin Gramatica RC .50 .23
❑ 242S Martin Gramatica SP 1.50 .70

❑ 243 Jim Finn RC .50 .23
❑ 243S Jim Finn SP 1.50 .70
❑ 244 Andy Katzenmoyer RC 1.25 .55
❑ 244S Andy Katzenmoyer SP 4.00 1.80
❑ 245 Dee Miller RC .75 .35
❑ 245S Dee Miller SP 2.50 1.10
❑ 246 D'Wayne Bates RC 1.25 .55
❑ 246S D'Wayne Bates SP 4.00 1.80
❑ 247 Amos Zereoue RC 1.25 .55
❑ 247S Amos Zereoue SP 4.00 1.80
❑ 248 Karsten Bailey RC .75 .35
❑ 248S Karsten Bailey SP 2.50 1.10
❑ 249 Kevin Johnson RC 2.50 1.10
❑ 249S Kevin Johnson SP 8.00 3.60
❑ 250 Cade McNown RC 1.50 .70
❑ 250S Cade McNown SP 6.00 2.70

1992 SkyBox Prime Time

	MINT	NRMT
COMPLETE SET (360)	25.00	11.00

❑ 1 Deion Sanders 1.00 .45
❑ 2 Shane Collins RC UER .10 .05
(Photo actually Terry Smith; see also number 216)
❑ 3 James Patton RC .10 .05
❑ 4 Reggie Roby .10 .05
❑ 5 Merril Hoge .10 .05
❑ 6 Vinny Testaverde .20 .09
❑ 7 Boomer Esiason .20 .09
❑ 8 Troy Aikman 2.00 .90
❑ 9 Tommy Jeter RC .10 .05
❑ 10 Brent Williams .10 .05
❑ 11 Mark Rypien .10 .05
❑ 12 Jim Kelly .40 .18
❑ 13 Dan Marino 3.00 1.35
❑ 14 Bill Cowher CO RC .20 .09
❑ 15 Leslie O'Neal .20 .09
❑ 16 Joe Montana 3.00 1.35
❑ 17 William Fuller .20 .09
❑ 18 Paul Gruber .10 .05
❑ 19 Bernie Kosar .20 .09
❑ 20 Rickey Jackson .10 .05
❑ 21 Earnest Byner .10 .05
❑ 22 Emmitt Smith 4.00 1.80
❑ 23 Neal Anderson PC .10 .05
❑ 24 Greg Lloyd .40 .18
❑ 25 Ronnie Harmon .10 .05
❑ 26 Ray Donaldson .10 .05
❑ 27 Kevin Ross .10 .05
❑ 28 Irving Fryar .20 .09
❑ 29 John L. Williams .10 .05
❑ 30 Chris Hinton .10 .05
❑ 31 Tracy Scroggins RC .10 .05
❑ 32 Rohn Stark .10 .05
❑ 33 David Fulcher .10 .05
❑ 34 Thurman Thomas .40 .18
❑ 35 Christian Okoye .10 .05
❑ 36 Vaughn Dunbar RC .10 .05
❑ 37 Joel Steed RC .10 .05
❑ 38 James Francis UER .10 .05
(Card number on back is actually 354)
❑ 39 Dermontti Dawson .10 .05
❑ 40 Mark Higgs .10 .05
❑ 41 Flipper Anderson UER .10 .05
5,301 receiving yards in 1991
❑ 42 Ronnie Lott .20 .09
❑ 43 Jim Everett .20 .09
❑ 44 Burt Grossman .10 .05
❑ 45 Charles Haley .20 .09
❑ 46 Ricky Proehl .10 .05
❑ 47 Marquez Pope RC .10 .05
❑ 48 David Treadwell .10 .05
❑ 49 William White .10 .05
❑ 50 John Elway 3.00 1.35
❑ 51 Mark Carrier WR .20 .09
❑ 52 Brian Blades .20 .09
❑ 53 Keith McKeller .10 .05
❑ 54 Art Monk .20 .09
❑ 55 Lamar Lathon .10 .05
❑ 56 Pat Swilling .20 .09
❑ 57 Steve Broussard .10 .05
❑ 58 Derrick Thomas .40 .18
❑ 59 Keith Jackson .20 .09
❑ 60 Leonard Marshall .10 .05
❑ 61 Eric Metcalf UER .40 .18
(Card number on back is actually 350)
❑ 62 Andy Heck .10 .05
❑ 63 Mark Carrier DB .10 .05
❑ 64 Neil O'Donnell .40 .18
❑ 65 Broderick Thomas MVP .10 .05
❑ 66 Eric Kramer .20 .09
❑ 67 Joe Montana PC 1.50 .70
❑ 68 Robert Delpino MVP .10 .05
❑ 69 Steve Israel RC .10 .05
❑ 70 Herman Moore 1.00 .45
❑ 71 Jacob Green .10 .05
❑ 72 Lorenzo White .10 .05
❑ 73 Nick Lowery .10 .05
❑ 74 Eugene Robinson .10 .05
❑ 75 Carl Banks .10 .05
❑ 76 Bruce Smith .40 .18
❑ 77 Mark Rypien MVP .10 .05
❑ 78 Anthony Munoz .20 .09
❑ 79 Clayton Holmes RC .10 .05
❑ 80 Jerry Rice 2.00 .90
❑ 81 Henry Ellard .20 .09
❑ 82 Tim McGee .10 .05
❑ 83 Al Toon .20 .09
❑ 84 Haywood Jeffires .20 .09
❑ 85 Mike Singletary .20 .09
❑ 86 Thurman Thomas PC .20 .09
❑ 87 Jessie Hester .10 .05
❑ 88 Michael Irvin .40 .18
❑ 89 Jack Del Rio .10 .05
❑ 90 Eagles MVP .10 .05
(Seth Joyner listed)
❑ 91 Jeff Herrod .10 .05
❑ 92 Michael Dean Perry .20 .09
❑ 93 Louis Oliver .10 .05
❑ 94 Dan McGwire .10 .05
❑ 95 Cris Carter MVP .20 .09
❑ 96 Dale Carter RC .40 .18
❑ 97 Cornelius Bennett .20 .09
❑ 98 Edgar Bennett RC .50 .23
❑ 99 Steve Young 1.50 .70
❑ 100 Warren Moon .40 .18
❑ 101 Deion Sanders MVP .60 .25
❑ 102 Mel Gray .20 .09
❑ 103 Mark Murphy .10 .05
❑ 104 Jeff George .40 .18
❑ 105 Anthony Miller .20 .09
❑ 106 Tom Rathman .10 .05
❑ 107 Fred McAfee RC .10 .05
❑ 108 Paul Siever RC .10 .05
❑ 109 Lemuel Stinson .10 .05
❑ 110 Vance Johnson .10 .05
❑ 111 Jay Schroeder .10 .05
❑ 112 Calvin Williams .20 .09
❑ 113 Cortez Kennedy .20 .09
❑ 114 Quentin Coryatt RC .40 .18
❑ 115 Ronnie Lippett .10 .05
❑ 116 Brad Baxter .10 .05
❑ 117 Bubba McDowell .10 .05
❑ 118 Cris Carter 1.00 .45
❑ 119 John Stephens .10 .05
❑ 120 James Hasty .10 .05
❑ 121 Bubby Brister .10 .05
❑ 122 Robert Jones RC .10 .05
❑ 123 Sterling Sharpe .40 .18
❑ 124 Jason Hanson RC .20 .09
❑ 125 Sam Mills .10 .05
❑ 126 Ernie Jones .10 .05
❑ 127 Chester McGlockton RC .40 .18
❑ 128 Troy Vincent RC .20 .09
❑ 129 Chuck Smith RC .10 .05
❑ 130 Tim McKyer .10 .05
❑ 131 Tom Newberry .10 .05
❑ 132 Leonard Wheeler RC .10 .05
❑ 133 Patrick Rowe RC .10 .05
❑ 134 Eric Swann .20 .09
❑ 135 Jeremy Lincoln RC .10 .05
❑ 136 Brian Noble .10 .05
❑ 137 Allen Pinkett .10 .05
❑ 138 Carl Pickens RC UER 1.25 .55
(Card number on back is actually 358)
❑ 139 Eric Green .10 .05
❑ 140 Louis Lipps .10 .05
❑ 141 Chris Singleton .10 .05
❑ 142 Gary Clark .40 .18
❑ 143 Tim Green .10 .05
❑ 144 Dennis Green CO RC .10 .05
❑ 145 Gary Anderson K .10 .05
❑ 146 Mark Clayton .20 .09
❑ 147 Kelvin Martin .10 .05
❑ 148 Mike Holmgren CO RC .40 .18
❑ 149 Gaston Green .10 .05
❑ 150 Terrell Buckley RC .10 .05
❑ 151 Robert Brooks RC 2.00 .90
❑ 152 Anthony Smith .10 .05
❑ 153 Jay Novacek .20 .09
❑ 154 Webster Slaughter .10 .05
❑ 155 John Roper .10 .05
❑ 156 Steve Emtman RC .10 .05
❑ 157 Tony Sacca RC .10 .05
❑ 158 Ray Crockett .10 .05
❑ 159 Jerry Rice MVP 1.00 .45
❑ 160 Alonzo Spellman RC .20 .09
❑ 161 Deion Sanders PC .60 .25
❑ 162 Robert Clark .10 .05
❑ 163 Mark Ingram .10 .05
❑ 164 Ricardo McDonald RC .10 .05
❑ 165 Emmitt Smith PC 2.00 .90
❑ 166 Tommy Maddox RC .10 .05
❑ 167 Tom Myslinski RC .10 .05
❑ 168 Packers MVP .10 .05
(Tony Bennett listed)
❑ 169 Ernest Givins .20 .09
❑ 170 Eugene Robinson MVP .10 .05
❑ 171 Roger Craig .20 .09
❑ 172 Irving Fryar MVP .10 .05
❑ 173 Jeff Herrod MVP .10 .05
❑ 174 Chris Mims RC .20 .09
❑ 175 Bart Oates .10 .05
❑ 176 Michael Irvin MVP .40 .18
❑ 177 Lawrence Dawsey .20 .09
❑ 178 Warren Moon MVP .20 .09
❑ 179 Timm Rosenbach .10 .05
❑ 180 Bobby Ross CO RC .10 .05
❑ 181 Chris Burkett MVP .10 .05
❑ 182 Tony Brooks RC .10 .05
❑ 183 Clarence Verdin .10 .05
❑ 184 Bernie Kosar PC .10 .05
❑ 185 Eric Martin .10 .05
❑ 186 Jeff Bryant .10 .05
❑ 187 Carnell Lake .10 .05
❑ 188 Darren Woodson RC .40 .18
❑ 189 Dwayne Harper .10 .05
❑ 190 Bernie Kosar MVP .10 .05
❑ 191 Keith Sims .10 .05
❑ 192 Rich Gannon .40 .18
❑ 193 Broderick Thomas .10 .05
❑ 194 Michael Young .10 .05
❑ 195 Cris Dishman .10 .05
❑ 196 Wes Hopkins .10 .05
❑ 197 Christian Okoye PC .10 .05
❑ 198 David Little .10 .05
❑ 199 Chris Crooms RC .10 .05
❑ 200 Lawrence Taylor .40 .18
❑ 201 Marc Boutte RC .10 .05
❑ 202 Mark Carrier DB PC .10 .05
❑ 203 Keith McCants .10 .05
❑ 204 Dwayne Sabb RC .10 .05
❑ 205 Brian Mitchell .20 .09

❑ 206 Keith Byars .10 .05
❑ 207 Jeff Hostetler .20 .09
❑ 208 Percy Snow .10 .05
❑ 209 Lawrence Taylor MVP .20 .09
❑ 210 Troy Auzenne RC .10 .05
❑ 211 Warren Moon PC .20 .09
❑ 212 Mike Pritchard .20 .09
❑ 213 Eric Dickerson .20 .09
❑ 214 Harvey Williams .40 .18
❑ 215 Phil Simms UER .20 .09
(Misspelled Sims on card front)
❑ 216 Sean Lumpkin RC UER .10 .05
(Card number on back is actually 002)
❑ 217 Marco Coleman RC .20 .09
❑ 218 Phillippi Sparks RC .10 .05
❑ 219 Gerald Dixon RC .10 .05
❑ 220 Steve Walsh .10 .05
❑ 221 Russell Maryland .20 .09
❑ 222 Eddie Anderson .10 .05
❑ 223 Shane Dronett RC .10 .05
❑ 224 Todd Collins RC .10 .05
❑ 225 Leon Searcy RC .20 .09
❑ 226 Andre Rison .20 .09
❑ 227 James Lofton .20 .09
❑ 228 Ken O'Brien .10 .05
❑ 229 Mike Tomczak .10 .05
❑ 230 Nick Bell .10 .05
❑ 231 Ben Smith .10 .05
❑ 232 Wendell Davis MVP .10 .05
❑ 233 Craig Thompson RC .10 .05
❑ 234 Dana Hall RC .20 .09
❑ 235 Larry Webster RC .10 .05
❑ 236 Jerry Rice PC 1.00 .45
❑ 237 Rod Bernstine .10 .05
❑ 238 David Klingler RC .20 .09
❑ 239 Greg Skrepenak RC .10 .05
❑ 240 Mark Wheeler RC .10 .05
❑ 241 Kevin Smith RC .40 .18
❑ 242 Charles Mann .10 .05
❑ 243 Lions MVP .10 .05
(Barry Sanders listed)
❑ 244 Curtis Whitley RC .10 .05
❑ 245 Ronnie Harmon MVP .10 .05
❑ 246 Brent Jones .20 .09
❑ 247 Robert Harris RC .10 .05
❑ 248 Ted Marchibroda CO .10 .05
❑ 249 Willie Gault .20 .09
❑ 250 Siran Stacy RC .10 .05
❑ 251 Dennis Byrd .10 .05
❑ 252 Corey Harris RC .10 .05
❑ 253 Al Noga .10 .05
❑ 254 David Shula CO RC .10 .05
❑ 255 Rob Moore .20 .09
❑ 256 Marv Cook .10 .05
❑ 257 John Elway MVP 1.50 .70
❑ 258 Harold Green .10 .05
❑ 259 Tom Flores CO .10 .05
❑ 260 Andre Reed .20 .09
❑ 261 Anthony Thompson .10 .05
❑ 262 Issiac Holt .10 .05
❑ 263 Mike Evans RC .10 .05
❑ 264 Jimmy Smith RC 5.00 2.20
❑ 265 Anthony Carter .20 .09
❑ 266 Ashley Ambrose RC .20 .09
❑ 267 John Fina RC .10 .05
(Card number on back is actually 357)
❑ 268 Sean Gilbert RC .40 .18
❑ 269 Ken Norton Jr. .40 .18
❑ 270 Barry Word .10 .05
❑ 271 Pat Swilling MVP .10 .05
❑ 272 Dan Marino PC 1.50 .70
❑ 273 David Fulcher MVP .10 .05
❑ 274 William Perry .20 .09
❑ 275 Ed West .10 .05
❑ 276 Gene Atkins .10 .05
❑ 277 Neal Anderson .10 .05
❑ 278 Dino Hackett .10 .05
❑ 279 Greg Townsend .10 .05
❑ 280 Andre Tippett .10 .05
❑ 281 Darryl Williams RC .10 .05
❑ 282 Kurt Barber RC .10 .05
❑ 283 Pat Terrell .10 .05
❑ 284 Derrick Thomas PC .20 .09
❑ 285 Eddie Robinson RC .10 .05
❑ 286 Howie Long .20 .09
❑ 287 Cardinals MVP .10 .05
(Tim McDonald listed)
❑ 288 Thurman Thomas MVP .20 .09
❑ 289 Wendell Davis .10 .05
❑ 290 Jeff Cross .10 .05
❑ 291 Duane Bickett .10 .05
❑ 292 Tony Smith RC .10 .05
❑ 293 Jerry Ball .10 .05
❑ 294 Jessie Tuggle .10 .05
❑ 295 Chris Burkett .10 .05
❑ 296 Eugene Chung RC .10 .05
❑ 297 Chris Miller .20 .09
❑ 298 Albert Bentley .10 .05
❑ 299 Richard Johnson .10 .05
❑ 300 Randall Cunningham .40 .18
❑ 301 Courtney Hawkins RC .20 .09
❑ 302 Ray Childress .10 .05
❑ 303 Rodney Peete .20 .09
❑ 304 Kevin Fagan .10 .05
❑ 305 Ronnie Lott MVP .10 .05
❑ 306 Michael Carter .10 .05
❑ 307 Derrick Thomas MVP .20 .09
❑ 308 Jarvis Williams .10 .05
❑ 309 Greg Lloyd MVP .20 .09
❑ 310 Ethan Horton .10 .05
❑ 311 Ricky Ervins .10 .05
❑ 312 Bennie Blades .10 .05
❑ 313 Troy Aikman PC 1.00 .45
❑ 314 Bruce Armstrong .10 .05
❑ 315 Leroy Hoard .20 .09
❑ 316 Gary Anderson RB .10 .05
❑ 317 Steve McMichael .20 .09
❑ 318 Junior Seau .40 .18
❑ 319 Mark Thomas RC .10 .05
❑ 320 Fred Barnett .40 .18
❑ 321 Mike Merriweather .10 .05
❑ 322 Keith Willis .10 .05
❑ 323 Brett Perriman .40 .18
❑ 324 Michael Haynes .20 .09
❑ 325 Jim Harbaugh .40 .18
❑ 326 Sammie Smith .10 .05
❑ 327 Robert Delpino .10 .05
❑ 328 Tony Mandarich .10 .05
❑ 329 Mark Bortz .10 .05
❑ 330 Ray Etheridge RC UER .10 .05
(Name misspelled Ethridge)
❑ 331 Jarvis Williams PC .10 .05
(Louis Oliver)
❑ 332 Dan Marino MVP 1.50 .70
❑ 333 Dwight Stone .10 .05
❑ 334 Billy Ray Smith .10 .05
❑ 335 Darion Conner .10 .05
❑ 336 Howard Dinkins RC .10 .05
❑ 337 Robert Porcher RC .20 .09
❑ 338 Chris Doleman .10 .05
❑ 339 Alvin Harper .20 .09
❑ 340 John Taylor .20 .09
❑ 341 Ray Agnew .10 .05
❑ 342 Jon Vaughn .10 .05
❑ 343 James Brown RC .10 .05
❑ 344 Michael Irvin PC .40 .18
❑ 345 Neil Smith .20 .09
❑ 346 Vaughan Johnson .10 .05
❑ 347 Checklist .10 .05
❑ 348 Checklist .10 .05
❑ 349 Checklist .10 .05
❑ 350 Checklist .10 .05
(See also number 61)
❑ 351 Checklist .10 .05
❑ 352 Checklist .10 .05
❑ 353 Checklist .10 .05
❑ 354 Checklist .10 .05
(See also number 38)
❑ 355 Checklist .10 .05
❑ 356 Checklist .10 .05
❑ 357 Checklist .10 .05
(See also number 267)
❑ 358 Checklist .10 .05
(See also number 138)
❑ 359 Checklist .10 .05
❑ 360 Checklist .10 .05
❑ H1 Jim Kelly 2.50 1.10
(Flip Hologram)
❑ S1 Steve Emtman .75 .35
Spectra-Etch
("Horse Power"))

1998 SkyBox Thunder

	MINT	NRMT
COMPLETE SET (250)	50.00	22.00
COMMON CARD (1-200)	.10	.05
COMMON CARD (201-225)	.60	.25
COMMON ROOKIE (226-250)	.40	.18

❑ 1 Reggie White .40 .18
❑ 2 Elvis Grbac .20 .09
❑ 3 Ed McCaffrey .20 .09
❑ 4 O.J. McDuffie .20 .09
❑ 5 Scott Mitchell .20 .09
❑ 6 Byron Hanspard .20 .09
❑ 7 John Randle .20 .09
❑ 8 Shawn Jefferson .10 .05
❑ 9 Peter Boulware .10 .05
❑ 10 Karl Williams .10 .05
❑ 11 Napoleon Kaufman .40 .18
(UER front Napolean)
❑ 12 Barry Minter .10 .05
❑ 13 Cris Dishman .10 .05
❑ 14 James Stewart .20 .09
❑ 15 Marcus Robertson .10 .05
❑ 16 Rodney Harrison .20 .09
❑ 17 Michael Barrow .10 .05
(UER front Micheal)
❑ 18 Michael Sinclair .10 .05
❑ 19 Dewayne Washington .10 .05
❑ 20 Phillippi Sparks .10 .05
❑ 21 Ernie Conwell .10 .05
❑ 22 Ken Dilger .10 .05
❑ 23 Johnnie Morton .20 .09
❑ 24 Eric Swann .10 .05
❑ 25 Curtis Conway .20 .09
❑ 26 Duce Staley 1.00 .45
❑ 27 Darrell Green .20 .09
❑ 28 Quinn Early .10 .05
❑ 29 LeRoy Butler .10 .05
❑ 30 Winfred Tubbs .10 .05
❑ 31 Darren Woodson .10 .05
❑ 32 Marcus Allen .40 .18
❑ 33 Glenn Foley .20 .09
❑ 34 Tom Knight .10 .05
❑ 35 Sam Shade .10 .05
❑ 36 James McKnight .10 .05
❑ 37 Leeland McElroy .10 .05
❑ 38 Earl Holmes RC .60 .25
❑ 39 Ryan McNeil .10 .05
❑ 40 Cris Carter .40 .18
❑ 41 Jessie Armstead .10 .05
❑ 42 Bryce Paup .10 .05
❑ 43 Chris Slade .10 .05
❑ 44 Eric Metcalf .10 .05
❑ 45 Jim Harbaugh .20 .09
❑ 46 Terry Kirby .10 .05
❑ 47 Donnie Edwards .10 .05
❑ 48 Darryl Williams .10 .05
❑ 49 Neil Smith .20 .09
❑ 50 Warren Sapp .20 .09
❑ 51 Jason Taylor .10 .05
❑ 52 Irving Fryar .20 .09
❑ 53 Jeff George .20 .09
❑ 54 Yancey Thigpen .10 .05

❑ 55 Ricky Proehl .10 .05
❑ 56 Kevin Greene .20 .09
❑ 57 Joel Steed .10 .05
❑ 58 Larry Allen .10 .05
❑ 59 Thurman Thomas .40 .18
❑ 60 Aaron Glenn .10 .05
❑ 61 Natrone Means .40 .18
❑ 62 Chris Calloway .10 .05
❑ 63 Chuck Smith .10 .05
❑ 64 Chidi Ahanotu .10 .05
❑ 65 Mario Bates .20 .09
❑ 66 Jonathan Ogden .10 .05
❑ 67 Drew Bledsoe CL .40 .18
❑ 68 John Mobley CL .10 .05
❑ 69 Antowain Smith CL .20 .09
❑ 70 Aeneas Williams .10 .05
❑ 71 Brian Williams .10 .05
❑ 72 Derrick Thomas .20 .09
❑ 73 Ted Johnson .10 .05
❑ 74 Troy Drayton .10 .05
❑ 75 Mike Pritchard .10 .05
❑ 76 Darnay Scott .20 .09
❑ 77 James Jett .20 .09
❑ 78 Dwayne Rudd .10 .05
❑ 79 Marvin Harrison .20 .09
❑ 80 Dermontti Dawson .10 .05
❑ 81 Keith Lyle .10 .05
❑ 82 Steve Atwater .10 .05
❑ 83 Tyrone Wheatley .20 .09
❑ 84 Tony Brackens .10 .05
❑ 85 Dale Carter .10 .05
❑ 86 Robert Porcher .10 .05
❑ 87 Merton Hanks .10 .05
❑ 88 Leon Johnson .10 .05
❑ 89 Simeon Rice .20 .09
❑ 90 Robert Brooks .20 .09
❑ 91 William Thomas .10 .05
❑ 92 Wesley Walls .20 .09
❑ 93 Chester McGlockton .10 .05
❑ 94 Chris Chandler .20 .09
❑ 95 Michael Strahan .10 .05
❑ 96 Ray Zellars .10 .05
❑ 97 Dexter Coakley .10 .05
❑ 98 Rob Johnson .20 .09
❑ 99 Eric Green .10 .05
❑ 100 Darrien Gordon .10 .05
❑ 101 Gary Brown .10 .05
❑ 102 Reidel Anthony .20 .09
❑ 103 Keenan McCardell .20 .09
❑ 104 Leslie O'Neal .10 .05
❑ 105 Bryant Westbrook .10 .05
❑ 106 Derrick Alexander .20 .09
❑ 107 Jeff Blake .20 .09
❑ 108 Ben Coates .20 .09
❑ 109 Shawn Springs .10 .05
❑ 110 Robert Smith .40 .18
❑ 111 Karim Abdul-Jabbar .40 .18
❑ 112 Willie Davis .10 .05
❑ 113 Mark Chmura .20 .09
❑ 114 Terry Allen .40 .18
❑ 115 Will Blackwell .10 .05
❑ 116 Jamal Anderson .40 .18
❑ 117 Dana Stubblefield .10 .05
❑ 118 Trent Dilfer .40 .18
❑ 119 Jermaine Lewis .20 .09
❑ 120 Chad Brown .10 .05
❑ 121 Tamarick Vanover .10 .05
❑ 122 Tony Martin .20 .09
❑ 123 Larry Centers .10 .05
❑ 124 J.J. Stokes .20 .09
❑ 125 Danny Kanell .20 .09
❑ 126 Wayne Chrebet .40 .18
❑ 127 Kerry Collins .20 .09
❑ 128 Tony Banks .20 .09
❑ 129 Randal Hill .10 .05
❑ 130 Jimmy Smith .20 .09
❑ 131 Tim Brown .40 .18
❑ 132 Zach Thomas .20 .09
❑ 133 Rod Smith .20 .09
❑ 134 Frank Wycheck .10 .05
❑ 135 Garrison Hearst .40 .18
❑ 136 Bruce Smith .20 .09
❑ 137 Hardy Nickerson .10 .05
❑ 138 Sean Dawkins .10 .05
❑ 139 Willie McGinest .10 .05
❑ 140 Kimble Anders .20 .09
❑ 141 Michael Westbrook .20 .09
❑ 142 Chris Doleman .10 .05
❑ 143 Ricky Watters .20 .09
❑ 144 Levon Kirkland .10 .05
❑ 145 Rob Moore .20 .09
❑ 146 Eddie Kennison .20 .09
❑ 147 Rickey Dudley .10 .05
❑ 148 Jay Graham .10 .05
❑ 149 Brad Johnson .40 .18
❑ 150 Bobby Hoying .20 .09
❑ 151 Sherman Williams .10 .05
❑ 152 Charles Way .10 .05
❑ 153 Adrian Murrell .20 .09
❑ 154 Chris Sanders .10 .05
❑ 155 Greg Hill .10 .05
❑ 156 Rae Carruth .20 .09
❑ 157 Mike Alstott .40 .18
❑ 158 Terance Mathis .20 .09
❑ 159 Antonio Freeman .40 .18
❑ 160 Junior Seau .20 .09
❑ 161 Chris Warren .20 .09
❑ 162 Shannon Sharpe .20 .09
❑ 163 Derrick Rodgers .10 .05
❑ 164 Charles Johnson .10 .05
❑ 165 Marshall Faulk .40 .18
❑ 166 Jamie Asher .10 .05
❑ 167 Michael Jackson .10 .05
❑ 168 Terrell Owens .40 .18
❑ 169 Jason Sehorn .20 .09
❑ 170 Raymont Harris .10 .05
❑ 171 Jake Reed .20 .09
❑ 172 Kevin Hardy .10 .05
❑ 173 Jerald Moore .10 .05
❑ 174 Michael Irvin .40 .18
❑ 175 Freddie Jones .10 .05
❑ 176 Steve McNair .40 .18
❑ 177 Carnell Lake .10 .05
❑ 178 Troy Brown .10 .05
❑ 179 Hugh Douglas .10 .05
❑ 180 Andre Rison .20 .09
❑ 181 Leslie Shepherd .10 .05
❑ 182 Andre Hastings .10 .05
❑ 183 Fred Lane .20 .09
❑ 184 Andre Reed .20 .09
❑ 185 Darrell Russell .10 .05
❑ 186 Frank Sanders .20 .09
❑ 187 Derrick Brooks .10 .05
❑ 188 Charlie Garner .10 .05
❑ 189 Bert Emanuel .20 .09
❑ 190 Terrell Buckley .10 .05
❑ 191 Carl Pickens .40 .18
❑ 192 Tiki Barber .20 .09
❑ 193 Pete Mitchell .10 .05
❑ 194 Gilbert Brown .10 .05
❑ 195 Isaac Bruce .40 .18
❑ 196 Ray Lewis .40 .18
❑ 197 Warren Moon .40 .18
❑ 198 Tony Gonzalez .10 .05
❑ 199 John Mobley .10 .05
❑ 200 Gus Frerotte .10 .05
❑ 201 Brett Favre 3.00 1.35
❑ 202 Terrell Davis 2.50 1.10
❑ 203 Dan Marino 3.00 1.35
❑ 204 Barry Sanders 3.00 1.35
❑ 205 Steve Young .75 .35
❑ 206 Deion Sanders .60 .25
❑ 207 Kordell Stewart .60 .25
❑ 208 Eddie George 1.25 .55
❑ 209 Jake Plummer 1.25 .55
❑ 210 Warrick Dunn .60 .25
❑ 211 John Elway 3.00 1.35
❑ 212 Terry Glenn .60 .25
❑ 213 Mark Brunell 1.25 .55
❑ 214 Corey Dillon .75 .35
❑ 215 Joey Galloway .60 .25
❑ 216 Dorsey Levens .60 .25
❑ 217 Troy Aikman 1.50 .70
❑ 218 Keyshawn Johnson .60 .25
❑ 219 Jerome Bettis .60 .25
❑ 220 Curtis Martin .60 .25
❑ 221 Herman Moore .60 .25
❑ 222 Emmitt Smith 2.50 1.10
❑ 223 Jerry Rice 1.50 .70
❑ 224 Drew Bledsoe 1.25 .55
❑ 225 Antowain Smith .60 .25
❑ 226 Stephen Alexander RC .60 .25
❑ 227 John Avery RC .60 .25
❑ 228 Kevin Dyson RC 2.50 1.10
❑ 229 Robert Edwards RC 1.50 .70
❑ 230 Greg Ellis RC .40 .18
❑ 231 Curtis Enis RC 2.00 .90
❑ 232 C.Fuamatu-Ma'afala RC .60 .25
❑ 233 Ahman Green RC 4.00 1.80
❑ 234 Jacquez Green RC 2.50 1.10
❑ 235 Az-Zahir Hakim RC 1.25 .55
❑ 236 Skip Hicks RC 1.25 .55
❑ 237 Joe Jurevicius RC .60 .25
❑ 238 Ryan Leaf RC 4.00 1.80
❑ 239 Peyton Manning RC 20.00 9.00
❑ 240 Alonzo Mayes RC .40 .18
❑ 241 R.W. McQuarters RC .40 .18
❑ 242 Randy Moss RC 20.00 9.00
❑ 243 Marcus Nash RC 1.25 .55
❑ 244 Jerome Pathon RC .60 .25
❑ 245 Jason Peter RC .40 .18
❑ 246 Brian Simmons RC .40 .18
❑ 247 Takeo Spikes RC .60 .25
❑ 248 Fred Taylor RC 5.00 2.20
❑ 249 Andre Wadsworth RC .60 .25
❑ 250 Charles Woodson RC 2.50 1.10
❑ P162 Shannon Sharpe Promo .75 .35

1993 SP

	MINT	NRMT
COMPLETE SET (270)	100.00	45.00

❑ 1 Curtis Conway FOIL RC 5.00 2.20
❑ 2 John Copeland FOIL RC .75 .35
❑ 3 Kevin Williams FOIL RC 1.50 .70
❑ 4 Dan Williams FOIL RC .75 .35
❑ 5 Patrick Bates FOIL RC .75 .35
❑ 6 Jerome Bettis FOIL RC 10.00 4.50
❑ 7 O.J. McDuffie FOIL RC 8.00 3.60
❑ 8 Robert Smith FOIL RC 20.00 9.00
❑ 9 Drew Bledsoe FOIL RC 50.00 22.00
❑ 10 Irv Smith FOIL RC .75 .35
❑ 11 Marvin Jones FOIL RC .75 .35
❑ 12 Victor Bailey FOIL RC .75 .35
❑ 13 Garrison Hearst FOIL RC 8.00 3.60
❑ 14 Natrone Means FOIL RC 4.00 1.80
❑ 15 Todd Kelly FOIL RC .75 .35
❑ 16 Rick Mirer FOIL RC 4.00 1.80
❑ 17 Eric Curry FOIL RC .75 .35
❑ 18 Reggie Brooks FOIL RC 1.50 .70
❑ 19 Eric Dickerson .50 .23
❑ 20 Roger Harper RC .30 .14
❑ 21 Michael Haynes .50 .23
❑ 22 Bobby Hebert .30 .14
❑ 23 Lincoln Kennedy RC .30 .14
❑ 24 Chris Miller .50 .23
❑ 25 Mike Pritchard .50 .23
❑ 26 Andre Rison .50 .23
❑ 27 Deion Sanders 1.50 .70
❑ 28 Cornelius Bennett .50 .23
❑ 29 Kenneth Davis .30 .14
❑ 30 Henry Jones .30 .14
❑ 31 Jim Kelly 1.00 .45
❑ 32 John Parrella RC .30 .14
❑ 33 Andre Reed .50 .23
❑ 34 Bruce Smith 1.00 .45
❑ 35 Thomas Smith RC .50 .23
❑ 36 Thurman Thomas 1.00 .45
❑ 37 Neal Anderson .30 .14

❑ 38 Myron Baker RC .30 .14
❑ 39 Mark Carrier DB .30 .14
❑ 40 Richard Dent .50 .23
❑ 41 Chris Gedney RC .30 .14
❑ 42 Jim Harbaugh 1.00 .45
❑ 43 Craig Heyward .50 .23
❑ 44 Carl Simpson RC .30 .14
❑ 45 Alonzo Spellman .30 .14
❑ 46 Derrick Fenner .30 .14
❑ 47 Harold Green .30 .14
❑ 48 David Klingler .30 .14
❑ 49 Ricardo McDonald .30 .14
❑ 50 Tony McGee RC .50 .23
❑ 51 Carl Pickens 1.00 .45
❑ 52 Steve Tovar RC .30 .14
❑ 53 Alfred Williams .30 .14
❑ 54 Darryl Williams .30 .14
❑ 55 Jerry Ball .30 .14
❑ 56 Mike Caldwell RC .30 .14
❑ 57 Mark Carrier WR .50 .23
❑ 58 Steve Everitt RC .30 .14
❑ 59 Dan Footman RC .30 .14
❑ 60 Pepper Johnson .30 .14
❑ 61 Bernie Kosar .50 .23
❑ 62 Eric Metcalf .50 .23
❑ 63 Michael Dean Perry .50 .23
❑ 64 Troy Aikman 2.50 1.10
❑ 65 Charles Haley .50 .23
❑ 66 Michael Irvin 1.00 .45
❑ 67 Robert Jones .30 .14
❑ 68 Derrick Lassic RC .30 .14
❑ 69 Russell Maryland .30 .14
❑ 70 Ken Norton Jr. .50 .23
❑ 71 Darrin Smith RC .50 .23
❑ 72 Emmitt Smith 5.00 2.20
❑ 73 Steve Atwater .30 .14
❑ 74 Rod Bernstine .30 .14
❑ 75 Jason Elam RC 1.00 .45
❑ 76 John Elway 5.00 2.20
❑ 77 Simon Fletcher .30 .14
❑ 78 Tommy Maddox .30 .14
❑ 79 Glyn Milburn RC 1.00 .45
❑ 80 Derek Russell .30 .14
❑ 81 Shannon Sharpe 1.00 .45
❑ 82 Bennie Blades .30 .14
❑ 83 Willie Green .30 .14
❑ 84 Antonio London RC .30 .14
❑ 85 Ryan McNeil RC .30 .14
❑ 86 Herman Moore 1.50 .70
❑ 87 Rodney Peete .30 .14
❑ 88 Barry Sanders 5.00 2.20
❑ 89 Chris Spielman .50 .23
❑ 90 Pat Swilling .30 .14
❑ 91 Mark Brunell RC 20.00 9.00
❑ 92 Terrell Buckley .30 .14
❑ 93 Brett Favre 6.00 2.70
❑ 94 Jackie Harris .30 .14
❑ 95 Sterling Sharpe 1.00 .45
❑ 96 John Stephens .30 .14
❑ 97 Wayne Simmons RC .30 .14
❑ 98 George Teague RC .50 .23
❑ 99 Reggie White 1.00 .45
❑ 100 Micheal Barrow RC .50 .23
❑ 101 Cody Carlson .30 .14
❑ 102 Ray Childress .30 .14
❑ 103 Brad Hopkins RC .30 .14
❑ 104 Haywood Jeffires .50 .23
❑ 105 Wilber Marshall .30 .14
❑ 106 Warren Moon 1.00 .45
❑ 107 Webster Slaughter .30 .14
❑ 108 Lorenzo White .30 .14
❑ 109 John Baylor .30 .14
❑ 110 Duane Bickett .30 .14
❑ 111 Quentin Coryatt .50 .23
❑ 112 Steve Emtman .30 .14
❑ 113 Jeff George 1.00 .45
❑ 114 Jessie Hester .30 .14
❑ 115 Anthony Johnson .50 .23
❑ 116 Reggie Langhorne .30 .14
❑ 117 Roosevelt Potts RC .30 .14
❑ 118 Marcus Allen 1.00 .45
❑ 119 J.J. Birden .30 .14
❑ 120 Willie Davis 1.00 .45
❑ 121 Jaime Fields RC .30 .14
❑ 122 Joe Montana 5.00 2.20
❑ 123 Will Shields RC .30 .14
❑ 124 Neil Smith 1.00 .45
❑ 125 Derrick Thomas 1.00 .45
❑ 126 Harvey Williams .50 .23
❑ 127 Tim Brown 1.00 .45
❑ 128 Billy Joe Hobert RC 1.50 .70
❑ 129 Jeff Hostetler .50 .23
❑ 130 Ethan Horton .30 .14
❑ 131 Raghib Ismail .50 .23
❑ 132 Howie Long .50 .23
❑ 133 Terry McDaniel .30 .14
❑ 134 Greg Robinson RC .30 .14
❑ 135 Anthony Smith .30 .14
❑ 136 Flipper Anderson .30 .14
❑ 137 Marc Boutte .30 .14
❑ 138 Shane Conlan .30 .14
❑ 139 Troy Drayton RC .50 .23
❑ 140 Henry Ellard .50 .23
❑ 141 Jim Everett .50 .23
❑ 142 Cleveland Gary .30 .14
❑ 143 Sean Gilbert .50 .23
❑ 144 Robert Young .30 .14
❑ 145 Marco Coleman .30 .14
❑ 146 Bryan Cox .30 .14
❑ 147 Irving Fryar .50 .23
❑ 148 Keith Jackson .50 .23
❑ 149 Terry Kirby RC 1.00 .45
❑ 150 Dan Marino 5.00 2.20
❑ 151 Scott Mitchell 1.00 .45
❑ 152 Louis Oliver .30 .14
❑ 153 Troy Vincent .30 .14
❑ 154 Anthony Carter .50 .23
❑ 155 Cris Carter 1.50 .70
❑ 156 Roger Craig .50 .23
❑ 157 Chris Doleman .30 .14
❑ 158 Qadry Ismail RC 5.00 2.20
❑ 159 Steve Jordan .30 .14
❑ 160 Randall McDaniel .30 .14
❑ 161 Audray McMillian .30 .14
❑ 162 Barry Word .30 .14
❑ 163 Vincent Brown .30 .14
❑ 164 Marv Cook .30 .14
❑ 165 Sam Gash RC .50 .23
❑ 166 Pat Harlow .30 .14
❑ 167 Greg McMurtry .30 .14
❑ 168 Todd Rucci RC .30 .14
❑ 169 Leonard Russell .50 .23
❑ 170 Scott Sisson RC .30 .14
❑ 171 Chris Slade RC .50 .23
❑ 172 Morten Andersen .30 .14
❑ 173 Derek Brown RBK RC .50 .23
❑ 174 Reggie Freeman RC .30 .14
❑ 175 Rickey Jackson .30 .14
❑ 176 Eric Martin .30 .14
❑ 177 Wayne Martin .30 .14
❑ 178 Brad Muster .30 .14
❑ 179 Willie Roaf RC .50 .23
❑ 180 Renaldo Turnbull .30 .14
❑ 181 Derek Brown TE .30 .14
❑ 182 Marcus Buckley RC .30 .14
❑ 183 Jarrod Bunch .30 .14
❑ 184 Rodney Hampton 1.00 .45
❑ 185 Ed McCaffrey .50 .23
❑ 186 Kanavis McGhee .30 .14
❑ 187 Mike Sherrard .30 .14
❑ 188 Phil Simms .50 .23
❑ 189 Lawrence Taylor 1.00 .45
❑ 190 Kurt Barber .30 .14
❑ 191 Boomer Esiason .50 .23
❑ 192 Johnny Johnson .30 .14
❑ 193 Ronnie Lott .50 .23
❑ 194 Johnny Mitchell .30 .14
❑ 195 Rob Moore .50 .23
❑ 196 Adrian Murrell RC 5.00 2.20
❑ 197 Browning Nagle .30 .14
❑ 198 Marvin Washington .30 .14
❑ 199 Eric Allen .30 .14
❑ 200 Fred Barnett .50 .23
❑ 201 Randall Cunningham 1.00 .45
❑ 202 Byron Evans .30 .14
❑ 203 Tim Harris .30 .14
❑ 204 Seth Joyner .30 .14
❑ 205 Leonard Renfro RC .30 .14
❑ 206 Heath Sherman .30 .14
❑ 207 Clyde Simmons .30 .14
❑ 208 Johnny Bailey .30 .14
❑ 209 Steve Beuerlein .30 .14
❑ 210 Chuck Cecil .30 .14
❑ 211 Larry Centers RC 1.50 .70
❑ 212 Gary Clark .50 .23
❑ 213 Ernest Dye RC .30 .14
❑ 214 Ken Harvey .30 .14
❑ 215 Randal Hill .30 .14
❑ 216 Ricky Proehl .30 .14
❑ 217 Deon Figures RC .50 .23
❑ 218 Barry Foster .50 .23
❑ 219 Eric Green .30 .14
❑ 220 Kevin Greene 1.00 .45
❑ 221 Carlton Haselrig .30 .14
❑ 222 Andre Hastings RC 1.00 .45
❑ 223 Greg Lloyd 1.00 .45
❑ 224 Neil O'Donnell 1.00 .45
❑ 225 Rod Woodson 1.00 .45
❑ 226 Marion Butts .30 .14
❑ 227 Darren Carrington RC .30 .14
❑ 228 Darrien Gordon RC .30 .14
❑ 229 Ronnie Harmon .30 .14
❑ 230 Stan Humphries 1.00 .45
❑ 231 Anthony Miller .50 .23
❑ 232 Chris Mims .30 .14
❑ 233 Leslie O'Neal .50 .23
❑ 234 Junior Seau 1.00 .45
❑ 235 Dana Hall .30 .14
❑ 236 Adrian Hardy .30 .14
❑ 237 Brent Jones .50 .23
❑ 238 Tim McDonald .30 .14
❑ 239 Tom Rathman .30 .14
❑ 240 Jerry Rice 3.00 1.35
❑ 241 Dana Stubblefield RC 1.00 .45
❑ 242 Ricky Watters 1.00 .45
❑ 243 Steve Young 2.50 1.10
❑ 244 Brian Blades .50 .23
❑ 245 Ferrell Edmunds .30 .14
❑ 246 Carlton Gray RC .30 .14
❑ 247 Cortez Kennedy .50 .23
❑ 248 Kelvin Martin .30 .14
❑ 249 Dan McGwire .30 .14
❑ 250 Jon Vaughn .30 .14
❑ 251 Chris Warren .50 .23
❑ 252 John L. Williams .30 .14
❑ 253 Reggie Cobb .30 .14
❑ 254 Horace Copeland RC .50 .23
❑ 255 Lawrence Dawsey .30 .14
❑ 256 Demetrius DuBose RC .30 .14
❑ 257 Craig Erickson .50 .23
❑ 258 Courtney Hawkins .30 .14
❑ 259 John Lynch RC 3.00 1.35
❑ 260 Hardy Nickerson .50 .23
❑ 261 Lamar Thomas RC .30 .14
❑ 262 Carl Banks .30 .14
❑ 263 Tom Carter RC .50 .23
❑ 264 Brad Edwards .30 .14
❑ 265 Kurt Gouveia .30 .14
❑ 266 Desmond Howard .50 .23
❑ 267 Charles Mann .30 .14
❑ 268 Art Monk .50 .23
❑ 269 Mark Rypien .30 .14
❑ 270 Ricky Sanders .30 .14
❑ P1 Joe Montana Promo 5.00 2.20
Numbered 19

1994 SP

	MINT	NRMT
COMPLETE SET (200)	60.00	27.00
❑ 1 Dan Wilkinson RC	1.00	.45

❑ 2 Heath Shuler RC .75 .35
❑ 3 Marshall Faulk RC 40.00 18.00
❑ 4 Willie McGinest RC .40 .18
❑ 5 Trent Dilfer RC 6.00 2.70
❑ 6 Bryant Young RC .75 .35
❑ 7 Antonio Langham RC .40 .18
❑ 8 John Thierry RC .40 .18
❑ 9 Aaron Glenn RC .75 .35
❑ 10 Charles Johnson RC 2.00 .90
❑ 11 Dewayne Washington RC .40 .18
❑ 12 Johnnie Morton RC 2.00 .90
❑ 13 Greg Hill RC .75 .35
❑ 14 William Floyd RC .75 .35
❑ 15 Derrick Alexander WR RC 1.50 .70
❑ 16 Darnay Scott RC 2.00 .90
❑ 17 Errict Rhett RC 5.00 2.20
❑ 18 Charlie Garner RC 8.00 3.60
❑ 19 Thomas Lewis RC .40 .18
❑ 20 David Palmer RC 1.50 .70
❑ 21 Andre Reed .30 .14
❑ 22 Thurman Thomas .50 .23
❑ 23 Bruce Smith .50 .23
❑ 24 Jim Kelly .50 .23
❑ 25 Cornelius Bennett .30 .14
❑ 26 Bucky Brooks RC .15 .07
❑ 27 Jeff Burris RC .30 .14
❑ 28 Jim Harbaugh .50 .23
❑ 29 Tony Bennett .15 .07
❑ 30 Quentin Coryatt .15 .07
❑ 31 Floyd Turner .15 .07
❑ 32 Roosevelt Potts .15 .07
❑ 33 Jeff Herrod .15 .07
❑ 34 Irving Fryar .30 .14
❑ 35 Bryan Cox .15 .07
❑ 36 Dan Marino 4.00 1.80
❑ 37 Terry Kirby .50 .23
❑ 38 Michael Stewart .15 .07
❑ 39 Bernie Kosar .30 .14
❑ 40 Aubrey Beavers RC .15 .07
❑ 41 Vincent Brisby .50 .23
❑ 42 Ben Coates .50 .23
❑ 43 Drew Bledsoe 2.50 1.10
❑ 44 Marion Butts .15 .07
❑ 45 Chris Slade .15 .07
❑ 46 Michael Timpson .15 .07
❑ 47 Ray Crittenden RC .15 .07
❑ 48 Rob Moore .30 .14
❑ 49 Johnny Mitchell .15 .07
❑ 50 Art Monk .30 .14
❑ 51 Boomer Esiason .30 .14
❑ 52 Ronnie Lott .30 .14
❑ 53 Ryan Yarborough RC .15 .07
❑ 54 Carl Pickens .50 .23
❑ 55 David Klingler .15 .07
❑ 56 Harold Green .15 .07
❑ 57 John Copeland .15 .07
❑ 58 Louis Oliver .15 .07
❑ 59 Corey Sawyer .15 .07
❑ 60 Michael Jackson .30 .14
❑ 61 Mark Rypien .15 .07
❑ 62 Vinny Testaverde .30 .14
❑ 63 Eric Metcalf .30 .14
❑ 64 Eric Turner .15 .07
❑ 65 Haywood Jeffires .30 .14
❑ 66 Micheal Barrow .15 .07
❑ 67 Cody Carlson .15 .07
❑ 68 Gary Brown .15 .07
❑ 69 Bucky Richardson .15 .07
❑ 70 Al Smith .15 .07
❑ 71 Eric Green .15 .07
❑ 72 Neil O'Donnell .50 .23
❑ 73 Barry Foster .15 .07
❑ 74 Greg Lloyd .50 .23
❑ 75 Rod Woodson .50 .23
❑ 76 Byron Bam Morris RC .50 .23
❑ 77 John L. Williams .15 .07
❑ 78 Anthony Miller .30 .14
❑ 79 Mike Pritchard .15 .07
❑ 80 John Elway 4.00 1.80
❑ 81 Shannon Sharpe .30 .14
❑ 82 Steve Atwater .15 .07
❑ 83 Simon Fletcher .15 .07
❑ 84 Glyn Milburn .30 .14
❑ 85 Mark Collins .15 .07
❑ 86 Keith Cash .15 .07
❑ 87 Willie Davis .30 .14
❑ 88 Joe Montana 4.00 1.80
❑ 89 Marcus Allen .50 .23
❑ 90 Neil Smith .50 .23
❑ 91 Derrick Thomas .50 .23
❑ 92 Tim Brown .50 .23
❑ 93 Jeff Hostetler .30 .14
❑ 94 Terry McDaniel .15 .07
❑ 95 Rocket Ismail .30 .14
❑ 96 Rob Fredrickson RC .30 .14
❑ 97 Harvey Williams .30 .14
❑ 98 Steve Wisniewski .15 .07
❑ 99 Stan Humphries .50 .23
❑ 100 Natrone Means .50 .23
❑ 101 Leslie O'Neal .15 .07
❑ 102 Junior Seau .50 .23
❑ 103 Ronnie Harmon .15 .07
❑ 104 Shawn Jefferson .15 .07
❑ 105 Howard Ballard .15 .07
❑ 106 Rick Mirer .50 .23
❑ 107 Cortez Kennedy .30 .14
❑ 108 Chris Warren .30 .14
❑ 109 Brian Blades .30 .14
❑ 110 Sam Adams RC .30 .14
❑ 111 Gary Clark .30 .14
❑ 112 Steve Beuerlein .15 .07
❑ 113 Ronald Moore .15 .07
❑ 114 Eric Swann .30 .14
❑ 115 Clyde Simmons .15 .07
❑ 116 Seth Joyner .15 .07
❑ 117 Troy Aikman 2.00 .90
❑ 118 Charles Haley .30 .14
❑ 119 Alvin Harper .30 .14
❑ 120 Michael Irvin .50 .23
❑ 121 Daryl Johnston .30 .14
❑ 122 Emmitt Smith 3.00 1.35
❑ 123 Shante Carver RC .15 .07
❑ 124 Dave Brown .30 .14
❑ 125 Rodney Hampton .50 .23
❑ 126 Dave Meggett .15 .07
❑ 127 Chris Calloway .15 .07
❑ 128 Mike Sherrard .15 .07
❑ 129 Carlton Bailey .15 .07
❑ 130 Randall Cunningham .50 .23
❑ 131 William Fuller .15 .07
❑ 132 Eric Allen .15 .07
❑ 133 Calvin Williams .30 .14
❑ 134 Herschel Walker .30 .14
❑ 135 Bernard Williams RC .15 .07
❑ 136 Henry Ellard .30 .14
❑ 137 Ethan Horton .15 .07
❑ 138 Desmond Howard .30 .14
❑ 139 Reggie Brooks .30 .14
❑ 140 John Friesz .30 .14
❑ 141 Tom Carter .15 .07
❑ 142 Terry Allen .30 .14
❑ 143 Adrian Cooper .15 .07
❑ 144 Qadry Ismail .50 .23
❑ 145 Warren Moon .50 .23
❑ 146 Henry Thomas .15 .07
❑ 147 Todd Steussie RC .30 .14
❑ 148 Cris Carter .75 .35
❑ 149 Andy Heck .15 .07
❑ 150 Curtis Conway .50 .23
❑ 151 Erik Kramer .30 .14
❑ 152 Lewis Tillman .15 .07
❑ 153 Dante Jones .15 .07
❑ 154 Alonzo Spellman .15 .07
❑ 155 Herman Moore .50 .23
❑ 156 Broderick Thomas .15 .07
❑ 157 Scott Mitchell .50 .23
❑ 158 Barry Sanders 4.00 1.80
❑ 159 Chris Spielman .30 .14
❑ 160 Pat Swilling .15 .07
❑ 161 Bennie Blades .15 .07
❑ 162 Sterling Sharpe .30 .14
❑ 163 Brett Favre 4.00 1.80
❑ 164 Reggie Cobb .15 .07
❑ 165 Reggie White .50 .23
❑ 166 Sean Jones .15 .07
❑ 167 George Teague .15 .07
❑ 168 LeShon Johnson RC .30 .14
❑ 169 Courtney Hawkins .15 .07
❑ 170 Jackie Harris .15 .07
❑ 171 Craig Erickson .15 .07
❑ 172 Santana Dotson .30 .14
❑ 173 Eric Curry .15 .07
❑ 174 Hardy Nickerson .30 .14
❑ 175 Derek Brown RBK .15 .07
❑ 176 Jim Everett .30 .14
❑ 177 Michael Haynes .30 .14
❑ 178 Tyrone Hughes .30 .14
❑ 179 Wayne Martin .15 .07
❑ 180 Willie Roaf .15 .07
❑ 181 Irv Smith .15 .07
❑ 182 Jeff George .50 .23
❑ 183 Andre Rison .30 .14
❑ 184 Erric Pegram .15 .07
❑ 185 Bret Emanuel RC 1.50 .70
❑ 186 Chris Doleman .15 .07
❑ 187 Ron George .15 .07
❑ 188 Chris Miller .15 .07
❑ 189 Troy Drayton .15 .07
❑ 190 Chris Chandler .30 .14
❑ 191 Jerome Bettis .50 .23
❑ 192 Jimmie Jones .15 .07
❑ 193 Sean Gilbert .15 .07
❑ 194 Jerry Rice 2.00 .90
❑ 195 Brent Jones .30 .14
❑ 196 Deion Sanders 1.00 .45
❑ 197 Steve Young 1.50 .70
❑ 198 Ricky Watters .50 .23
❑ 199 Dana Stubblefield .50 .23
❑ 200 Ken Norton Jr. .30 .14
❑ RB1 Dan Marino 300 TDs 25.00 11.00
❑ RB2 Jerry Rice 127 TDs .. 25.00 11.00
❑ P16 Joe Montana Promo 4.00 1.80

1995 SP

	MINT	NRMT
COMPLETE SET (200)	70.00	32.00

❑ 1 Ki-Jana Carter PP RC 2.00 .90
❑ 2 Eric Zeier PP RC UER 2.00 .90
Height listed at 6'11"
❑ 3 Steve McNair PP RC 8.00 3.60
❑ 4 Michael Westbrook PP RC 5.00 2.20
❑ 5 Kerry Collins PP RC 6.00 2.70
❑ 6 Joey Galloway PP RC 6.00 2.70
❑ 7 Kevin Carter PP RC 2.00 .90
❑ 8 Mike Mamula PP RC .50 .23
❑ 9 Kyle Brady PP RC 1.00 .45
❑ 10 J.J. Stokes PP RC 2.00 .90
❑ 11 Tyrone Poole PP RC 1.00 .45
❑ 12 Rashaan Salaam PP RC 2.00 .90
❑ 13 Sherman Williams PP RC .50 .23
❑ 14 Luther Elliss PP RC .50 .23
❑ 15 James O. Stewart PP RC 6.00 2.70
❑ 16 Tamarick Vanover PP RC 2.00 .90
❑ 17 Napoleon Kaufman PP RC 5.00 2.20
❑ 18 Curtis Martin PP RC 8.00 3.60
❑ 19 Tyrone Wheatley PP RC 4.00 1.80
❑ 20 Frank Sanders PP RC 3.00 1.35
❑ 21 Devin Bush .20 .09
❑ 22 Terance Mathis .40 .18
❑ 23 Bert Emanuel .75 .35
❑ 24 Eric Metcalf .40 .18
❑ 25 Craig Heyward .40 .18
❑ 26 Jeff George .40 .18
❑ 27 Mark Carrier WR .40 .18
❑ 28 Pete Metzelaars .20 .09
❑ 29 Frank Reich .20 .09
❑ 30 Sam Mills .40 .18
❑ 31 John Kasay .20 .09

❑ 32 Willie Green .40 .18
❑ 33 Jeff Graham .20 .09
❑ 34 Curtis Conway .75 .35
❑ 35 Steve Walsh .20 .09
❑ 36 Erik Kramer .20 .09
❑ 37 Michael Timpson .20 .09
❑ 38 Mark Carrier .20 .09
❑ 39 Troy Aikman 2.00 .90
❑ 40 Michael Irvin .75 .35
❑ 41 Charles Haley .40 .18
❑ 42 Deion Sanders 1.25 .55
❑ 43 Jay Novacek .40 .18
❑ 44 Emmitt Smith 3.00 1.35
❑ 45 Herman Moore .75 .35
❑ 46 Scott Mitchell UER .40 .18
(Front reads Mitcehill)
❑ 47 Bennie Blades .20 .09
❑ 48 Johnnie Morton .40 .18
❑ 49 Chris Spielman .40 .18
❑ 50 Barry Sanders 4.00 1.80
❑ 51 Edgar Bennett .40 .18
❑ 52 Reggie White .75 .35
❑ 53 Sean Jones .20 .09
❑ 54 Mark Ingram .20 .09
❑ 55 Robert Brooks .75 .35
❑ 56 Brett Favre 4.00 1.80
❑ 57 Lovell Pinkney RC .50 .23
❑ 58 Chris Miller .20 .09
❑ 59 Isaac Bruce 1.25 .55
❑ 60 Roman Phifer .20 .09
❑ 61 Sean Gilbert .40 .18
❑ 62 Jerome Bettis .75 .35
❑ 63 Derrick Alexander DE RC .50 .23
❑ 64 Cris Carter .75 .35
❑ 65 Jake Reed .40 .18
❑ 66 Robert Smith .75 .35
❑ 67 David Palmer .40 .18
❑ 68 Warren Moon .40 .18
❑ 69 Ray Zellars RC 1.00 .45
❑ 70 Jim Everett .20 .09
❑ 71 Michael Haynes .40 .18
❑ 72 Quinn Early .40 .18
❑ 73 Willie Roaf .20 .09
❑ 74 Mario Bates .75 .35
❑ 75 Mike Sherrard .20 .09
❑ 76 Chris Calloway .20 .09
❑ 77 Dave Brown .40 .18
❑ 78 Thomas Lewis .40 .18
❑ 79 Herschel Walker .40 .18
❑ 80 Rodney Hampton .40 .18
❑ 81 Fred Barnett .40 .18
❑ 82 Calvin Williams .40 .18
❑ 83 Randall Cunningham .75 .35
❑ 84 Charlie Garner .40 .18
❑ 85 Bobby Taylor RC 2.00 .90
❑ 86 Ricky Watters .75 .35
❑ 87 Dave Krieg .20 .09
❑ 88 Rob Moore .20 .09
❑ 89 Eric Swann .40 .18
❑ 90 Clyde Simmons .20 .09
❑ 91 Seth Joyner .20 .09
❑ 92 Garrison Hearst .75 .35
❑ 93 Jerry Rice 2.00 .90
❑ 94 Bryant Young .40 .18
❑ 95 Brent Jones .20 .09
❑ 96 Ken Norton .40 .18
❑ 97 William Floyd .75 .35
❑ 98 Steve Young 1.50 .70
❑ 99 Warren Sapp RC 3.00 1.35
❑ 100 Trent Dilfer .75 .35
❑ 101 Alvin Harper .20 .09
❑ 102 Hardy Nickerson .20 .09
❑ 103 Derrick Brooks RC 2.00 .90
❑ 104 Errict Rhett .75 .35
❑ 105 Henry Ellard .40 .18
❑ 106 Ken Harvey .20 .09
❑ 107 Gus Frerotte .75 .35
❑ 108 Brian Mitchell .20 .09
❑ 109 Terry Allen .40 .18
❑ 110 Heath Shuler .75 .35
❑ 111 Jim Kelly .75 .35
❑ 112 Andre Reed .40 .18
❑ 113 Bruce Smith .75 .35
❑ 114 Darick Holmes RC 1.00 .45
❑ 115 Bryce Paup .75 .35
❑ 116 Cornelius Bennett .40 .18
❑ 117 Carl Pickens .75 .35
❑ 118 Darnay Scott .75 .35
❑ 119 Jeff Blake RC 3.00 1.35
❑ 120 Steve Tovar .20 .09
❑ 121 Tony McGee .20 .09
❑ 122 Dan Wilkinson .40 .18
❑ 123 Craig Powell .20 .09
❑ 124 Vinny Testaverde .40 .18
❑ 125 Eric Turner .20 .09
❑ 126 Leroy Hoard .20 .09
❑ 127 Lorenzo White .20 .09
❑ 128 Andre Rison .40 .18
❑ 129 Shannon Sharpe .40 .18
❑ 130 Terrell Davis RC 20.00 9.00
❑ 131 Anthony Miller .40 .18
❑ 132 Mike Pritchard .20 .09
❑ 133 Steve Atwater .20 .09
❑ 134 John Elway 4.00 1.80
❑ 135 Haywood Jeffires .20 .09
❑ 136 Gary Brown .20 .09
❑ 137 Al Smith .20 .09
❑ 138 Rodney Thomas RC 1.00 .45
❑ 139 Chris Chandler .40 .18
❑ 140 Mel Gray .20 .09
❑ 141 Craig Erickson .20 .09
❑ 142 Sean Dawkins .40 .18
❑ 143 Ken Dilger RC 1.00 .45
❑ 144 Ellis Johnson RC UER .50 .23
(Front reads Elliss)
❑ 145 Quentin Coryatt .40 .18
❑ 146 Marshall Faulk 1.25 .55
❑ 147 Tony Boselli RC 2.00 .90
❑ 148 Rob Johnson RC 6.00 2.70
❑ 149 Desmond Howard .40 .18
❑ 150 Steve Beuerlein .20 .09
❑ 151 Reggie Cobb .20 .09
❑ 152 Jeff Lageman .20 .09
❑ 153 Willie Davis .40 .18
❑ 154 Marcus Allen .75 .35
❑ 155 Neil Smith .40 .18
❑ 156 Greg Hill .40 .18
❑ 157 Steve Bono .40 .18
❑ 158 Derrick Thomas .40 .18
❑ 159 Jeff Hostetler .40 .18
❑ 160 Harvey Williams .20 .09
❑ 161 Rocket Ismail .40 .18
❑ 162 Chester McGlockton .40 .18
❑ 163 Terry McDaniel .20 .09
❑ 164 Tim Brown .75 .35
❑ 165 Terry Kirby .40 .18
❑ 166 Irving Fryar .40 .18
❑ 167 O.J. McDuffie .75 .35
❑ 168 Bryan Cox .20 .09
❑ 169 Eric Green .20 .09
❑ 170 Dan Marino 4.00 1.80
❑ 171 Ben Coates .40 .18
❑ 172 Vincent Brisby .20 .09
❑ 173 Chris Slade .40 .18
❑ 174 Ty Law .40 .18
❑ 175 Vincent Brown .20 .09
❑ 176 Drew Bledsoe 2.00 .90
❑ 177 Johnny Mitchell .20 .09
❑ 178 Boomer Esiason .40 .18
❑ 179 Wayne Chrebet RC 6.00 2.70
❑ 180 Mo Lewis .20 .09
❑ 181 Ronald Moore .20 .09
❑ 182 Aaron Glenn .20 .09
❑ 183 Mark Bruener RC 1.00 .45
❑ 184 Neil O'Donnell .40 .18
❑ 185 Charles Johnson .40 .18
❑ 186 Greg Lloyd .40 .18
❑ 187 Rod Woodson .40 .18
❑ 188 Byron Bam Morris .40 .18
❑ 189 Terrell Fletcher RC .50 .23
❑ 190 Terrance Shaw RC UER .50 .23
front reads Terrence
❑ 191 Stan Humphries .40 .18
❑ 192 Junior Seau .75 .35
❑ 193 Leslie O'Neal .40 .18
❑ 194 Natrone Means .75 .35
❑ 195 Christian Fauria RC 1.00 .45
❑ 196 Rick Mirer .75 .35
❑ 197 Sam Adams .20 .09
❑ 198 Cortez Kennedy .40 .18
❑ 199 Eugene Robinson .20 .09
❑ 200 Chris Warren .40 .18
❑ DM1 Dan Marino Tribute 20.00 9.00
❑ JM1 Joe Montana Salute 20.00 9.00
❑ NNO Dan Marino TRI Jumbo 25.00 11.00
Card measures 3 1/2" by 5"
Issued by Upper Deck Authenticated
Numbered of 10,000
❑ NNO J.Montana SAL Jumbo 25.00 11.00
Card meaures 3 1/2" by 5"
Issued by Upper Deck Authenticated
Numbered of 10,000
❑ P1 Joe Montana Promo 4.00 1.80
All-Pro Silver card
❑ P113 Dan Marino Promo 3.00 1.35

1995 SP Championship

	MINT	NRMT
COMPLETE SET (225)	60.00	27.00

❑ 1 Frank Sanders RC 2.00 .90
❑ 2 Stoney Case RC .75 .35
❑ 3 Lorenzo Styles RC .20 .09
❑ 4 Todd Collins RC .75 .35
❑ 5 Darick Holmes RC .40 .18
❑ 6 Brian DeMarco RC .20 .09
❑ 7 Tyrone Poole RC .40 .18
❑ 8 Kerry Collins RC 4.00 1.80
❑ 9 Rashaan Salaam RC .75 .35
❑ 10 Steve Stenstrom RC .20 .09
❑ 11 Ki-Jana Carter RC .75 .35
❑ 12 Eric Zeier RC .75 .35
❑ 13 Sherman Williams RC .20 .09
❑ 14 Terrell Davis RC 15.00 6.75
❑ 15 David Dunn RC .20 .09
❑ 16 Luther Elliss RC .20 .09
❑ 17 Craig Newsome RC .20 .09
❑ 18 Antonio Freeman RC 6.00 2.70
❑ 19 Steve McNair RC 6.00 2.70
❑ 20 Anthony Cook RC .20 .09
❑ 21 Rodney Thomas RC .40 .18
❑ 22 Ellis Johnson RC .20 .09
❑ 23 Ken Dilger RC .40 .18
❑ 24 James O. Stewart RC 5.00 2.20
❑ 25 Pete Mitchell RC .75 .35
❑ 26 Tamarick Vanover RC .75 .35
❑ 27 Orlando Thomas RC .20 .09
❑ 28 Corey Fuller RC .20 .09
❑ 29 Curtis Martin RC 6.00 2.70
❑ 30 Ty Law RC .40 .18
❑ 31 Roell Preston RC 1.00 .45
❑ 32 Mark Fields RC .20 .09
❑ 33 Tyrone Wheatley RC 2.50 1.10
❑ 34 Kyle Brady RC .40 .18
❑ 35 Napoleon Kaufman RC 4.00 1.80
❑ 36 Kordell Stewart RC 5.00 2.20
❑ 37 Mark Bruener RC .40 .18
❑ 38 Terrance Shaw RC .20 .09
❑ 39 Terrell Fletcher RC .20 .09
❑ 40 J.J. Stokes RC .75 .35
❑ 41 Christian Fauria RC .40 .18
❑ 42 Joey Galloway RC 5.00 2.20
❑ 43 Kevin Carter RC .75 .35
❑ 44 Warren Sapp RC 1.00 .45
❑ 45 Michael Westbrook RC 4.00 1.80
❑ 46 Clyde Simmons .15 .07
❑ 47 Rob Moore .15 .07
❑ 48 Seth Joyner .15 .07
❑ 49 Dave Krieg .15 .07

No.	Player	Mint	NrMt
❑ 50	Garrison Hearst	.50	.23
❑ 51	Aeneas Williams	.15	.07
❑ 52	Terance Mathis	.30	.14
❑ 53	Bert Emanuel UER Name spelled Emanual	.50	.23
❑ 54	Chris Doleman	.15	.07
❑ 55	Craig Heyward	.30	.14
❑ 56	Jeff George	.30	.14
❑ 57	Eric Metcalf	.30	.14
❑ 58	Jim Kelly	.50	.23
❑ 59	Andre Reed	.30	.14
❑ 60	Russell Copeland	.15	.07
❑ 61	Bruce Smith	.50	.23
❑ 62	Cornelius Bennett	.30	.14
❑ 63	Jeff Burris	.15	.07
❑ 64	Mark Carrier WR	.30	.14
❑ 65	Pete Metzelaars	.15	.07
❑ 66	Frank Reich	.15	.07
❑ 67	Sam Mills	.30	.14
❑ 68	John Kasay	.15	.07
❑ 69	Willie Green	.30	.14
❑ 70	Curtis Conway	.50	.23
❑ 71	Erik Kramer	.15	.07
❑ 72	Donnell Woolford	.15	.07
❑ 73	Mark Carrier	.15	.07
❑ 74	Jeff Graham	.15	.07
❑ 75	Raymont Harris	.15	.07
❑ 76	Carl Pickens	.50	.23
❑ 77	Darnay Scott	.50	.23
❑ 78	Jeff Blake RC	2.00	.90
❑ 79	Dan Wilkinson	.30	.14
❑ 80	Tony McGee	.15	.07
❑ 81	Eric Bieniemy	.15	.07
❑ 82	Vinny Testaverde	.30	.14
❑ 83	Eric Turner	.15	.07
❑ 84	Leroy Hoard	.15	.07
❑ 85	Lorenzo White	.15	.07
❑ 86	Antonio Langham	.15	.07
❑ 87	Andre Rison	.30	.14
❑ 88	Troy Aikman	1.50	.70
❑ 89	Michael Irvin	.50	.23
❑ 90	Charles Haley	.30	.14
❑ 91	Daryl Johnston	.30	.14
❑ 92	Jay Novacek	.30	.14
❑ 93	Emmitt Smith	2.50	1.10
❑ 94	Shannon Sharpe	.30	.14
❑ 95	Anthony Miller	.30	.14
❑ 96	Mike Pritchard	.15	.07
❑ 97	Glyn Milburn	.15	.07
❑ 98	Simon Fletcher	.15	.07
❑ 99	John Elway	3.00	1.35
❑ 100	Henry Thomas	.15	.07
❑ 101	Herman Moore	.50	.23
❑ 102	Scott Mitchell	.30	.14
❑ 103	Bennie Blades	.15	.07
❑ 104	Chris Spielman	.30	.14
❑ 105	Barry Sanders	3.00	1.35
❑ 106	Mark Ingram	.15	.07
❑ 107	Edgar Bennett	.30	.14
❑ 108	Reggie White	.50	.23
❑ 109	Sean Jones	.15	.07
❑ 110	Robert Brooks	.50	.23
❑ 111	Brett Favre	3.00	1.35
❑ 112	Chris Chandler	.30	.14
❑ 113	Haywood Jeffires	.15	.07
❑ 114	Gary Brown	.15	.07
❑ 115	Al Smith	.15	.07
❑ 116	Ray Childress	.15	.07
❑ 117	Mel Gray	.15	.07
❑ 118	Jim Harbaugh	.30	.14
❑ 119	Sean Dawkins	.30	.14
❑ 120	Roosevelt Potts	.15	.07
❑ 121	Marshall Faulk	.75	.35
❑ 122	Tony Bennett	.15	.07
❑ 123	Quentin Coryatt	.30	.14
❑ 124	Desmond Howard	.30	.14
❑ 125	Tony Boselli	.50	.23
❑ 126	Steve Beuerlein	.15	.07
❑ 127	Jeff Lageman	.15	.07
❑ 128	Rob Johnson RC	5.00	2.20
❑ 129	Ernest Givins	.15	.07
❑ 130	Willie Davis	.30	.14
❑ 131	Marcus Allen	.50	.23
❑ 132	Neil Smith	.30	.14
❑ 133	Greg Hill	.30	.14
❑ 134	Steve Bono	.30	.14

No.	Player	Mint	NrMt
❑ 135	Lake Dawson	.30	.14
❑ 136	Dan Marino	3.00	1.35
❑ 137	Terry Kirby	.30	.14
❑ 138	Irving Fryar	.30	.14
❑ 139	O.J. McDuffie	.50	.23
❑ 140	Bryan Cox	.15	.07
❑ 141	Eric Green	.15	.07
❑ 142	Cris Carter	.50	.23
❑ 143	Robert Smith	.50	.23
❑ 144	John Randle	.30	.14
❑ 145	Jake Reed	.30	.14
❑ 146	Dewayne Washington	.30	.14
❑ 147	Warren Moon	.30	.14
❑ 148	Dave Meggett	.15	.07
❑ 149	Ben Coates	.30	.14
❑ 150	Vincent Brisby	.15	.07
❑ 151	Willie McGinest	.30	.14
❑ 152	Chris Slade	.30	.14
❑ 153	Drew Bledsoe	1.50	.70
❑ 154	Eric Allen	.15	.07
❑ 155	Mario Bates	.50	.23
❑ 156	Jim Everett	.15	.07
❑ 157	Renaldo Turnbull	.15	.07
❑ 158	Tyrone Hughes	.30	.14
❑ 159	Michael Haynes	.30	.14
❑ 160	Mike Sherrard	.15	.07
❑ 161	Dave Brown	.30	.14
❑ 162	Chris Calloway	.15	.07
❑ 163	Keith Hamilton	.15	.07
❑ 164	Rodney Hampton	.30	.14
❑ 165	Herschel Walker	.30	.14
❑ 166	Adrian Murrell	.30	.14
❑ 167	Johnny Mitchell	.15	.07
❑ 168	Boomer Esiason	.30	.14
❑ 169	Mo Lewis	.15	.07
❑ 170	Brad Baxter	.15	.07
❑ 171	Aaron Glenn	.15	.07
❑ 172	Jeff Hostetler	.30	.14
❑ 173	Harvey Williams	.15	.07
❑ 174	Tim Brown	.50	.23
❑ 175	Terry McDaniel	.15	.07
❑ 176	Pat Swilling	.15	.07
❑ 177	Rocket Ismail	.30	.14
❑ 178	Randall Cunningham	.50	.23
❑ 179	Calvin Williams	.30	.14
❑ 180	Ricky Watters	.50	.23
❑ 181	Charlie Garner	.30	.14
❑ 182	Fred Barnett	.30	.14
❑ 183	Rodney Peete	.15	.07
❑ 184	Neil O'Donnell	.30	.14
❑ 185	Charles Johnson	.30	.14
❑ 186	Rod Woodson	.30	.14
❑ 187	Byron Bam Morris	.30	.14
❑ 188	Kevin Greene	.30	.14
❑ 189	Greg Lloyd	.30	.14
❑ 190	Chris Miller	.15	.07
❑ 191	Isaac Bruce	.75	.35
❑ 192	Roman Phifer	.15	.07
❑ 193	Jerome Bettis	.50	.23
❑ 194	Carlos Jenkins	.15	.07
❑ 195	Troy Drayton	.15	.07
❑ 196	Andre Coleman	.15	.07
❑ 197	Natrone Means	.50	.23
❑ 198	Leslie O'Neal	.30	.14
❑ 199	Junior Seau	.50	.23
❑ 200	Tony Martin	.30	.14
❑ 201	Stan Humphries	.30	.14
❑ 202	Steve Young	1.25	.55
❑ 203	Jerry Rice	1.50	.70
❑ 204	Brent Jones	.15	.07
❑ 205	Dana Stubblefield	.50	.23
❑ 206	Lee Woodall	.15	.07
❑ 207	Merton Hanks	.15	.07
❑ 208	Rick Mirer	.50	.23
❑ 209	Brian Blades	.30	.14
❑ 210	Chris Warren	.30	.14
❑ 211	Sam Adams	.15	.07
❑ 212	Cortez Kennedy	.30	.14
❑ 213	Eugene Robinson	.15	.07
❑ 214	Alvin Harper	.15	.07
❑ 215	Trent Dilfer	.50	.23
❑ 216	Hardy Nickerson	.15	.07
❑ 217	Errict Rhett	.50	.23
❑ 218	Eric Curry	.15	.07
❑ 219	Jackie Harris	.15	.07
❑ 220	Henry Ellard	.30	.14
❑ 221	Terry Allen	.30	.14
❑ 222	Brian Mitchell	.15	.07
❑ 223	Ken Harvey	.15	.07
❑ 224	Gus Frerotte	.50	.23
❑ 225	Heath Shuler	.50	.23
❑ P116	Joe Montana Promo (Numbered 116)	3.00	1.35

1996 SP

		MINT	NRMT
COMPLETE SET (188)		150.00	70.00
❑ 1	Keyshawn Johnson PP RC	12.00	5.50
❑ 2	Kevin Hardy PP RC	1.00	.45
❑ 3	Simeon Rice PP RC	1.00	.45
❑ 4	Jonathan Ogden PP RC	.50	.23
❑ 5	Eddie George PP RC	25.00	11.00
❑ 6	Terry Glenn PP RC	6.00	2.70
❑ 7	Terrell Owens PP RC	15.00	6.75
❑ 8	Tim Biakabutuka PP RC	5.00	2.20
❑ 9	Lawrence Phillips PP RC	1.00	.45
❑ 10	Alex Molden PP RC	.50	.23
❑ 11	Regan Upshaw PP RC	.50	.23
❑ 12	Rickey Dudley PP RC	1.50	.70
❑ 13	Duane Clemons PP RC	.50	.23
❑ 14	John Mobley PP RC	1.00	.45
❑ 15	Eddie Kennison RC	1.50	.70
❑ 16	K.Abdul-Jabbar PP RC	2.00	.90
❑ 17	Eric Moulds PP RC	10.00	4.50
❑ 18	Marvin Harrison PP RC	15.00	6.75
❑ 19	Stepfret Williams PP RC	.50	.23
❑ 20	Stephen Davis PP RC	20.00	9.00
❑ 21	Deion Sanders	1.25	.55
❑ 22	Emmitt Smith	3.00	1.35
❑ 23	Troy Aikman	2.00	.90
❑ 24	Michael Irvin	.75	.35
❑ 25	Herschel Walker	.40	.18
❑ 26	Kavika Pittman RC	.25	.11
❑ 27	Andre Hastings	.20	.09
❑ 28	Jerome Bettis	.75	.35
❑ 29	Mike Tomczak	.20	.09
❑ 30	Kordell Stewart	1.25	.55
❑ 31	Charles Johnson	.20	.09
❑ 32	Greg Lloyd	.40	.18
❑ 33	Brett Favre	4.00	1.80
❑ 34	Mark Chmura	.40	.18
❑ 35	Edgar Bennett	.40	.18
❑ 36	Robert Brooks	.40	.18
❑ 37	Craig Newsome	.20	.09
❑ 38	Reggie White	.75	.35
❑ 39	Jim Harbaugh	.40	.18
❑ 40	Marshall Faulk	.75	.35
❑ 41	Sean Dawkins	.20	.09
❑ 42	Quentin Coryatt	.20	.09
❑ 43	Ray Buchanan	.20	.09
❑ 44	Ken Dilger	.40	.18
❑ 45	Jerry Rice	2.00	.90
❑ 46	J.J. Stokes	.75	.35
❑ 47	Steve Young	1.50	.70
❑ 48	Derek Loville	.20	.09
❑ 49	Terry Kirby	.40	.18
❑ 50	Ken Norton	.20	.09
❑ 51	Tamarick Vanover	.40	.18
❑ 52	Marcus Allen	.75	.35
❑ 53	Steve Bono	.20	.09
❑ 54	Neil Smith	.20	.09
❑ 55	Derrick Thomas	.40	.18

❑ 56 Dale Carter .20 .09
❑ 57 Terance Mathis .20 .09
❑ 58 Eric Metcalf .20 .09
❑ 59 Jamal Anderson RC 15.00 6.75
❑ 60 Bert Emanuel .40 .18
❑ 61 Craig Heyward .20 .09
❑ 62 Cornelius Bennett .20 .09
❑ 63 Tony Martin .40 .18
❑ 64 Stan Humphries .40 .18
❑ 65 Andre Coleman .20 .09
❑ 66 Junior Seau .40 .18
❑ 67 Terrell Fletcher .20 .09
❑ 68 John Carney .20 .09
❑ 69 Charlie Jones RC .50 .23
❑ 70 Ricky Watters .40 .18
❑ 71 Charlie Garner .20 .09
❑ 72 Bobby Hoying RC 1.50 .70
❑ 73 Jason Dunn RC .50 .23
❑ 74 Bobby Taylor .20 .09
❑ 75 Irving Fryar .40 .18
❑ 76 Jim Kelly .75 .35
❑ 77 Thurman Thomas .75 .35
❑ 78 Bruce Smith .40 .18
❑ 79 Bryce Paup .20 .09
❑ 80 Darick Holmes .20 .09
❑ 81 Andre Reed .40 .18
❑ 82 Glyn Milburn .20 .09
❑ 83 Brett Perriman .20 .09
❑ 84 Herman Moore .75 .35
❑ 85 Scott Mitchell .40 .18
❑ 86 Barry Sanders 4.00 1.80
❑ 87 Johnnie Morton .40 .18
❑ 88 Dan Marino 4.00 1.80
❑ 89 O.J. McDuffie .40 .18
❑ 90 Stanley Pritchett RC .25 .11
❑ 91 Zach Thomas RC 5.00 2.20
❑ 92 Daryl Gardener RC .25 .11
❑ 93 Rashaan Salaam .75 .35
❑ 94 Erik Kramer .20 .09
❑ 95 Curtis Conway .75 .35
❑ 96 Bobby Engram RC 1.00 .45
❑ 97 Walt Harris RC .25 .11
❑ 98 Bryan Cox .20 .09
❑ 99 John Elway 4.00 1.80
❑ 100 Terrell Davis 4.00 1.80
❑ 101 Anthony Miller .40 .18
❑ 102 Shannon Sharpe .40 .18
❑ 103 Tory James .20 .09
❑ 104 Jeff Lewis RC 4.00 1.80
❑ 105 Joey Galloway 1.25 .55
❑ 106 Chris Warren .40 .18
❑ 107 Rick Mirer .40 .18
❑ 108 Cortez Kennedy .20 .09
❑ 109 Michael Sinclair .20 .09
❑ 110 John Friesz .20 .09
❑ 111 Warren Moon .40 .18
❑ 112 Cris Carter .75 .35
❑ 113 Jake Reed .40 .18
❑ 114 Robert Smith .40 .18
❑ 115 John Randle .40 .18
❑ 116 Orlando Thomas .20 .09
❑ 117 Jeff Hostetler .20 .09
❑ 118 Tim Brown .75 .35
❑ 119 Joe Aska .20 .09
❑ 120 Napoleon Kaufman .75 .35
❑ 121 Terry McDaniel .20 .09
❑ 122 Harvey Williams .20 .09
❑ 123 Trent Dilfer .75 .35
❑ 124 Reggie Brooks .20 .09
❑ 125 Alvin Harper .20 .09
❑ 126 Mike Alstott RC 8.00 3.60
❑ 127 Hardy Nickerson .20 .09
❑ 128 Mario Bates .40 .18
❑ 129 Jim Everett .20 .09
❑ 130 Tyrone Hughes .20 .09
❑ 131 Michael Haynes .20 .09
❑ 132 Eric Allen .20 .09
❑ 133 Isaac Bruce .75 .35
❑ 134 Kevin Carter .20 .09
❑ 135 Leslie O'Neal .20 .09
❑ 136 Tony Banks RC 10.00 4.50
❑ 137 Chris Chandler .40 .18
❑ 138 Steve McNair 1.50 .70
❑ 139 Chris Sanders .40 .18
❑ 140 Ronnie Harmon .20 .09
❑ 141 Willie Davis .20 .09
❑ 142 Michael Westbrook .75 .35
❑ 143 Terry Allen .40 .18
❑ 144 Brian Mitchell .20 .09
❑ 145 Henry Ellard .20 .09
❑ 146 Gus Frerotte .75 .35
❑ 147 Kerry Collins .75 .35
❑ 148 Sam Mills .20 .09
❑ 149 Wesley Walls .40 .18
❑ 150 Kevin Greene .40 .18
❑ 151 Muhsin Muhammad RC 6.00 2.70
❑ 152 Winslow Oliver .20 .09
❑ 153 Jeff Blake .75 .35
❑ 154 Carl Pickens .75 .35
❑ 155 Darnay Scott .40 .18
❑ 156 Garrison Hearst .40 .18
❑ 157 Marco Battaglia RC .25 .11
❑ 158 Drew Bledsoe 2.00 .90
❑ 159 Curtis Martin 1.50 .70
❑ 160 Shawn Jefferson .20 .09
❑ 161 Ben Coates .40 .18
❑ 162 Lawyer Milloy .20 .09
❑ 163 Tyrone Wheatley .40 .18
❑ 164 Rodney Hampton .40 .18
❑ 165 Chris Calloway .20 .09
❑ 166 Dave Brown .20 .09
❑ 167 Amani Toomer RC 4.00 1.80
❑ 168 Vinny Testaverde .40 .18
❑ 169 Michael Jackson .40 .18
❑ 170 Eric Turner .20 .09
❑ 171 DeRon Jenkins .20 .09
❑ 172 Jermaine Lewis RC 4.00 1.80
❑ 173 Frank Sanders .40 .18
❑ 174 Rob Moore .40 .18
❑ 175 Kent Graham .20 .09
❑ 176 Leeland McElroy RC 1.00 .45
❑ 177 Larry Centers .40 .18
❑ 178 Eric Swann .20 .09
❑ 179 Mark Brunell 2.00 .90
❑ 180 Willie Jackson .20 .09
❑ 181 James O. Stewart .40 .18
❑ 182 Natrone Means .75 .35
❑ 183 Tony Brackens RC 1.00 .45
❑ 184 Adrian Murrell .75 .35
❑ 185 Neil O'Donnell .40 .18
❑ 186 Hugh Douglas .40 .18
❑ 187 Wayne Chrebet 1.25 .55
❑ 188 Alex Van Dyke RC .50 .23
❑ SP13 Dan Marino Promo 3.00 1.35

1997 SP Authentic

	MINT	NRMT
COMPLETE SET (198)	150.00	70.00

❑ 1 Orlando Pace RC 2.00 .90
❑ 2 Darrell Russell RC .50 .23
❑ 3 Shawn Springs RC 1.00 .45
❑ 4 Peter Boulware RC 2.00 .90
❑ 5 Bryant Westbrook RC 1.00 .45
❑ 6 Walter Jones RC .50 .23
❑ 7 Ike Hilliard RC 5.00 2.20
❑ 8 James Farrior RC .50 .23
❑ 9 Tom Knight RC .50 .23
❑ 10 Warrick Dunn RC 20.00 9.00
❑ 11 Tony Gonzalez RC 20.00 9.00
❑ 12 Reinard Wilson RC .50 .23
❑ 13 Yatil Green RC 1.00 .45
❑ 14 Reidel Anthony RC 5.00 2.20
❑ 15 Kenny Holmes RC 2.00 .90
❑ 16 Dwayne Rudd RC 2.00 .90
❑ 17 Renaldo Wynn RC .50 .23
❑ 18 David LaFleur RC 2.50 1.10
❑ 19 Antowain Smith RC 10.00 4.50
❑ 20 Jim Druckenmiller RC 2.00 .90
❑ 21 Rae Carruth RC .50 .23
❑ 22 Byron Hanspard RC 2.00 .90
❑ 23 Jake Plummer RC 25.00 11.00
❑ 24 Joey Kent RC 1.00 .45
❑ 25 Corey Dillon RC 40.00 18.00
❑ 26 Danny Wuerffel RC 4.00 1.80
❑ 27 Will Blackwell RC 1.00 .45
❑ 28 Troy Davis RC 1.00 .45
❑ 29 Darnell Autry RC 2.00 .90
❑ 30 Pat Barnes RC 2.00 .90
❑ 31 Kent Graham .30 .14
❑ 32 Simeon Rice .50 .23
❑ 33 Frank Sanders .50 .23
❑ 34 Rob Moore .50 .23
❑ 35 Eric Swann .30 .14
❑ 36 Chris Chandler .50 .23
❑ 37 Jamal Anderson 1.50 .70
❑ 38 Terance Mathis .50 .23
❑ 39 Bert Emanuel .50 .23
❑ 40 Michael Booker .30 .14
❑ 41 Vinny Testaverde .50 .23
❑ 42 Byron Bam Morris .30 .14
❑ 43 Michael Jackson .50 .23
❑ 44 Derrick Alexander WR .50 .23
❑ 45 Jamie Sharper RC 2.00 .90
❑ 46 Kim Herring RC .50 .23
❑ 47 Todd Collins .30 .14
❑ 48 Thurman Thomas 1.00 .45
❑ 49 Andre Reed .50 .23
❑ 50 Quinn Early .30 .14
❑ 51 Bryce Paup .30 .14
❑ 52 Lonnie Johnson .30 .14
❑ 53 Kerry Collins .50 .23
❑ 54 Anthony Johnson .30 .14
❑ 55 Tim Biakabutuka .50 .23
❑ 56 Muhsin Muhammad .50 .23
❑ 57 Sam Mills .30 .14
❑ 58 Wesley Walls .50 .23
❑ 59 Rick Mirer .30 .14
❑ 60 Raymont Harris .30 .14
❑ 61 Curtis Conway .50 .23
❑ 62 Bobby Engram .50 .23
❑ 63 Bryan Cox .30 .14
❑ 64 John Allred RC .50 .23
❑ 65 Jeff Blake .50 .23
❑ 66 Ki-Jana Carter .30 .14
❑ 67 Darnay Scott .50 .23
❑ 68 Carl Pickens 1.00 .45
❑ 69 Dan Wilkinson .30 .14
❑ 70 Troy Aikman 2.50 1.10
❑ 71 Emmitt Smith 4.00 1.80
❑ 72 Michael Irvin 1.00 .45
❑ 73 Deion Sanders 1.00 .45
❑ 74 Anthony Miller .30 .14
❑ 75 Antonio Anderson RC .50 .23
❑ 76 John Elway 5.00 2.20
❑ 77 Terrell Davis 4.00 1.80
❑ 78 Rod Smith WR 1.00 .45
❑ 79 Shannon Sharpe .50 .23
❑ 80 Neil Smith .50 .23
❑ 81 Trevor Pryce RC .50 .23
❑ 82 Scott Mitchell .50 .23
❑ 83 Barry Sanders 5.00 2.20
❑ 84 Herman Moore 1.00 .45
❑ 85 Johnnie Morton .50 .23
❑ 86 Matt Russell RC .50 .23
❑ 87 Brett Favre 5.00 2.20
❑ 88 Edgar Bennett .50 .23
❑ 89 Robert Brooks .50 .23
❑ 90 Antonio Freeman 1.50 .70
❑ 91 Reggie White 1.00 .45
❑ 92 Craig Newsome .30 .14
❑ 93 Jim Harbaugh .50 .23
❑ 94 Marshall Faulk 1.00 .45
❑ 95 Sean Dawkins .30 .14
❑ 96 Marvin Harrison 1.00 .45
❑ 97 Quentin Coryatt .30 .14
❑ 98 Tarik Glenn RC .50 .23
❑ 99 Mark Brunell 2.50 1.10
❑ 100 Natrone Means 1.00 .45

Card		
❑ 101 Keenan McCardell	.50	.23
❑ 102 Jimmy Smith	.50	.23
❑ 103 Tony Brackens	.30	.14
❑ 104 Kevin Hardy	.30	.14
❑ 105 Elvis Grbac	.50	.23
❑ 106 Marcus Allen	1.00	.45
❑ 107 Greg Hill	.30	.14
❑ 108 Derrick Thomas	.50	.23
❑ 109 Dale Carter	.30	.14
❑ 110 Dan Marino	5.00	2.20
❑ 111 Karim Abdul-Jabbar	1.00	.45
❑ 112 Brian Manning RC	.50	.23
❑ 113 Daryl Gardener	.30	.14
❑ 114 Troy Drayton	.30	.14
❑ 115 Zach Thomas	.50	.23
❑ 116 Jason Taylor RC	.50	.23
❑ 117 Brad Johnson	1.25	.55
❑ 118 Robert Smith	.50	.23
❑ 119 John Randle	.50	.23
❑ 120 Cris Carter	1.00	.45
❑ 121 Jake Reed	.50	.23
❑ 122 Randall Cunningham	1.00	.45
❑ 123 Drew Bledsoe	2.50	1.10
❑ 124 Curtis Martin	1.50	.70
❑ 125 Terry Glenn	1.00	.45
❑ 126 Willie McGinest	.30	.14
❑ 127 Chris Canty RC	.50	.23
❑ 128 Sedrick Shaw RC	2.00	.90
❑ 129 Heath Shuler	.30	.14
❑ 130 Mario Bates	.30	.14
❑ 131 Ray Zellars	.30	.14
❑ 132 Andre Hastings	.30	.14
❑ 133 Dave Brown	.30	.14
❑ 134 Tyrone Wheatley	.50	.23
❑ 135 Rodney Hampton	.50	.23
❑ 136 Chris Calloway	.30	.14
❑ 137 Tiki Barber RC	20.00	9.00
❑ 138 Neil O'Donnell	.50	.23
❑ 139 Adrian Murrell	.50	.23
❑ 140 Wayne Chrebet	1.00	.45
❑ 141 Keyshawn Johnson	1.00	.45
❑ 142 Hugh Douglas	.30	.14
❑ 143 Jeff George	.50	.23
❑ 144 Napoleon Kaufman	1.00	.45
❑ 145 Tim Brown	1.00	.45
❑ 146 Desmond Howard	.50	.23
❑ 147 Rickey Dudley	.50	.23
❑ 148 Terry McDaniel	.30	.14
❑ 149 Ty Detmer	.50	.23
❑ 150 Ricky Watters	.50	.23
❑ 151 Chris T. Jones	.30	.14
❑ 152 Irving Fryar	.50	.23
❑ 153 Mike Mamula	.30	.14
❑ 154 Jon Harris RC	.50	.23
❑ 155 Kordell Stewart	1.25	.55
❑ 156 Jerome Bettis	1.00	.45
❑ 157 Charles Johnson	.50	.23
❑ 158 Greg Lloyd	.30	.14
❑ 159 George Jones RC	1.00	.45
❑ 160 Terrell Fletcher	.30	.14
❑ 161 Stan Humphries	.50	.23
❑ 162 Tony Martin	.50	.23
❑ 163 Eric Metcalf	.50	.23
❑ 164 Junior Seau	.50	.23
❑ 165 Rod Woodson	.50	.23
❑ 166 Steve Young	2.00	.90
❑ 167 Terry Kirby	.50	.23
❑ 168 Garrison Hearst	.50	.23
❑ 169 Jerry Rice	2.50	1.10
❑ 170 Ken Norton	.30	.14
❑ 171 Kevin Greene	.50	.23
❑ 172 Lamar Smith	1.00	.45
❑ 173 Warren Moon	1.00	.45
❑ 174 Chris Warren	.50	.23
❑ 175 Cortez Kennedy	.30	.14
❑ 176 Joey Galloway	1.25	.55
❑ 177 Tony Banks	.50	.23
❑ 178 Isaac Bruce	1.00	.45
❑ 179 Eddie Kennison	.50	.23
❑ 180 Kevin Carter	.30	.14
❑ 181 Craig Heyward	.30	.14
❑ 182 Trent Dilfer	1.00	.45
❑ 183 Errict Rhett	.30	.14
❑ 184 Mike Alstott	1.00	.45
❑ 185 Hardy Nickerson	.30	.14
❑ 186 Ronde Barber RC	1.00	.45
❑ 187 Steve McNair	1.50	.70
❑ 188 Eddie George	2.50	1.10
❑ 189 Chris Sanders	.30	.14
❑ 190 Blaine Bishop	.30	.14
❑ 191 Derrick Mason RC	20.00	9.00
❑ 192 Gus Frerotte	.30	.14
❑ 193 Terry Allen	1.00	.45
❑ 194 Brian Mitchell	.30	.14
❑ 195 Alvin Harper	.30	.14
❑ 196 Jeff Hostetler	.30	.14
❑ 197 Leslie Shepherd	.30	.14
❑ 198 Stephen Davis	2.50	1.10
❑ A1 Aikman Audio Blue	4.00	1.80
❑ A2 Aikman Audio Pro Bowl	10.00	4.50
❑ A3 Aikman Audio White	30.00	13.50

(500 cards made)

1998 SP Authentic

	MINT	NRMT
COMPLETE SET (126)	2400.00	1100.00
COMP.SET w/o SP's (84)	40.00	18.00

*HAND NUMBERED RCs: .5X TO .8X

Card	MINT	NRMT
❑ 1 Andre Wadsworth RC	20.00	9.00
❑ 2 Corey Chavous RC	15.00	6.75
❑ 3 Keith Brooking RC	20.00	9.00
❑ 4 Duane Starks RC	15.00	6.75
❑ 5 Pat Johnson RC	20.00	9.00
❑ 6 Jason Peter RC	15.00	6.75
❑ 7 Curtis Enis RC	50.00	22.00
❑ 8 Takeo Spikes RC	20.00	9.00
❑ 9 Greg Ellis RC	15.00	6.75
❑ 10 Marcus Nash RC	35.00	16.00
❑ 11 Brian Griese RC	300.00	135.00
❑ 12 Germane Crowell RC	75.00	34.00
❑ 13 Vonnie Holliday RC	20.00	9.00
❑ 14 Peyton Manning RC	750.00	350.00
❑ 15 Jerome Pathon RC	30.00	13.50
❑ 16 Fred Taylor RC	250.00	110.00
❑ 17 John Avery RC	20.00	9.00
❑ 18 Randy Moss RC	500.00	220.00
❑ 19 Robert Edwards RC	60.00	27.00
❑ 20 Tony Simmons RC	30.00	13.50
❑ 21 Shaun Williams RC	15.00	6.75
❑ 22 Joe Jurevicius RC	20.00	9.00
❑ 23 Charles Woodson RC	50.00	22.00
❑ 24 Tra Thomas RC	15.00	6.75
❑ 25 Grant Wistrom RC	15.00	6.75
❑ 26 Ryan Leaf RC	135.00	60.00
❑ 27 Ahman Green RC	100.00	45.00
❑ 28 Jacquez Green RC	50.00	22.00
❑ 29 Kevin Dyson RC	60.00	27.00
❑ 30 Stephen Alexander RC	20.00	9.00
❑ 31 John Elway TW	20.00	9.00
❑ 32 Jerry Rice TW	12.00	5.50
❑ 33 Emmitt Smith TW	20.00	9.00
❑ 34 Steve Young TW	8.00	3.60
❑ 35 Jerome Bettis TW	6.00	2.70
❑ 36 Deion Sanders TW	6.00	2.70
❑ 37 Andre Rison TW	4.00	1.80
❑ 38 Warren Moon TW	6.00	2.70
❑ 39 Mark Brunell TW	10.00	4.50
❑ 40 Ricky Watters TW	4.00	1.80
❑ 41 Dan Marino TW	25.00	11.00
❑ 42 Brett Favre TW	25.00	11.00
❑ 43 Jake Plummer	1.50	.70
❑ 44 Adrian Murrell	.40	.18
❑ 45 Eric Swann	.20	.09
❑ 46 Jamal Anderson	.75	.35
❑ 47 Chris Chandler	.40	.18
❑ 48 Jim Harbaugh	.40	.18
❑ 49 Michael Jackson	.20	.09
❑ 50 Jermaine Lewis	.40	.18
❑ 51 Rob Johnson	.40	.18
❑ 52 Antowain Smith	.75	.35
❑ 53 Thurman Thomas	.75	.35
❑ 54 Kerry Collins	.40	.18
❑ 55 Fred Lane	.40	.18
❑ 56 Rae Carruth	.40	.18
❑ 57 Erik Kramer	.20	.09
❑ 58 Curtis Conway	.40	.18
❑ 59 Corey Dillon	1.25	.55
❑ 60 Neil O'Donnell	.40	.18
❑ 61 Carl Pickens	.75	.35
❑ 62 Troy Aikman	2.00	.90
❑ 63 Emmitt Smith	3.00	1.35
❑ 64 Deion Sanders	.75	.35
❑ 65 Terrell Davis	3.00	1.35
❑ 66 John Elway	4.00	1.80
❑ 67 Rod Smith	.40	.18
❑ 68 Scott Mitchell	.40	.18
❑ 69 Barry Sanders	4.00	1.80
❑ 70 Herman Moore	.75	.35
❑ 71 Brett Favre	4.00	1.80
❑ 72 Dorsey Levens	.75	.35
❑ 73 Antonio Freeman	.75	.35
❑ 74 Marshall Faulk	.75	.35
❑ 75 Marvin Harrison	.40	.18
❑ 76 Mark Brunell	1.50	.70
❑ 77 Keenan McCardell	.40	.18
❑ 78 Jimmy Smith	.40	.18
❑ 79 Andre Rison	.40	.18
❑ 80 Elvis Grbac	.40	.18
❑ 81 Derrick Alexander	.40	.18
❑ 82 Dan Marino	4.00	1.80
❑ 83 Karim Abdul-Jabbar	.75	.35
❑ 84 O.J. McDuffie	.40	.18
❑ 85 Brad Johnson	.75	.35
❑ 86 Cris Carter	.75	.35
❑ 87 Robert Smith	.75	.35
❑ 88 Drew Bledsoe	1.50	.70
❑ 89 Terry Glenn	.75	.35
❑ 90 Ben Coates	.40	.18
❑ 91 Lamar Smith	.40	.18
❑ 92 Danny Wuerffel	.40	.18
❑ 93 Tiki Barber	.40	.18
❑ 94 Danny Kanell	.40	.18
❑ 95 Ike Hilliard	.40	.18
❑ 96 Curtis Martin	.75	.35
❑ 97 Keyshawn Johnson	.75	.35
❑ 98 Glenn Foley	.40	.18
❑ 99 Jeff George	.40	.18
❑ 100 Tim Brown	.75	.35
❑ 101 Napoleon Kaufman	.75	.35
❑ 102 Bobby Hoying	.40	.18
❑ 103 Charlie Garner	.20	.09
❑ 104 Irving Fryar	.40	.18
❑ 105 Kordell Stewart	.75	.35
❑ 106 Jerome Bettis	.75	.35
❑ 107 Charles Johnson	.20	.09
❑ 108 Tony Banks	.40	.18
❑ 109 Isaac Bruce	.75	.35
❑ 110 Natrone Means	.75	.35
❑ 111 Junior Seau	.40	.18
❑ 112 Steve Young	1.25	.55
❑ 113 Jerry Rice	2.00	.90
❑ 114 Garrison Hearst	.75	.35
❑ 115 Ricky Watters	.40	.18
❑ 116 Warren Moon	.75	.35
❑ 117 Joey Galloway	.75	.35
❑ 118 Trent Dilfer	.75	.35
❑ 119 Warrick Dunn	1.25	.55
❑ 120 Mike Alstott	.75	.35
❑ 121 Steve McNair	.75	.35
❑ 122 Eddie George	1.50	.70
❑ 123 Yancey Thigpen	.20	.09
❑ 124 Gus Frerotte	.20	.09
❑ 125 Terry Allen	.75	.35
❑ 126 Michael Westbrook	.40	.18
❑ AE13 Dan Marino SAMPLE	2.00	.90

1999 SP Authentic

	MINT	NRMT
COMPLETE SET (145)	2000.00	900.00
COMP.SET w/o SPs (90)	35.00	16.00

	Card	MINT	NRMT
❑ 1	Jake Plummer	1.50	.70
❑ 2	Adrian Murrell	.40	.18
❑ 3	Frank Sanders	.40	.18
❑ 4	Jamal Anderson	.75	.35
❑ 5	Chris Chandler	.40	.18
❑ 6	Terance Mathis	.40	.18
❑ 7	Priest Holmes	.75	.35
❑ 8	Jermaine Lewis	.40	.18
❑ 9	Antowain Smith	.75	.35
❑ 10	Doug Flutie	1.00	.45
❑ 11	Eric Moulds	.75	.35
❑ 12	Muhsin Muhammad	.40	.18
❑ 13	Tim Biakabutuka	.40	.18
❑ 14	Wesley Walls	.40	.18
❑ 15	Curtis Enis	.75	.35
❑ 16	Bobby Engram	.40	.18
❑ 17	Corey Dillon	.75	.35
❑ 18	Darnay Scott	.40	.18
❑ 19	Terry Kirby	.20	.09
❑ 20	Ty Detmer	.40	.18
❑ 21	Troy Aikman	2.00	.90
❑ 22	Michael Irvin	.40	.18
❑ 23	Emmitt Smith	2.00	.90
❑ 24	Terrell Davis	2.00	.90
❑ 25	Brian Griese	1.50	.70
❑ 26	Rod Smith	.40	.18
❑ 27	Shannon Sharpe	.40	.18
❑ 28	Barry Sanders	3.00	1.35
❑ 29	Charlie Batch	1.50	.70
❑ 30	Herman Moore	.75	.35
❑ 31	Johnnie Morton	.40	.18
❑ 32	Brett Favre	3.00	1.35
❑ 33	Antonio Freeman	.75	.35
❑ 34	Dorsey Levens	.75	.35
❑ 35	Mark Chmura	.40	.18
❑ 36	Peyton Manning	3.00	1.35
❑ 37	Marvin Harrison	.75	.35
❑ 38	Mark Brunell	1.25	.55
❑ 39	Fred Taylor	2.00	.90
❑ 40	Jimmy Smith	.40	.18
❑ 41	Elvis Grbac	.40	.18
❑ 42	Andre Rison	.40	.18
❑ 43	Dan Marino	3.00	1.35
❑ 44	O.J. McDuffie	.40	.18
❑ 45	Yatil Green	.20	.09
❑ 46	Randall Cunningham	.75	.35
❑ 47	Randy Moss	4.00	1.80
❑ 48	Robert Smith	.75	.35
❑ 49	Cris Carter	.75	.35
❑ 50	Drew Bledsoe	1.25	.55
❑ 51	Ben Coates	.20	.09
❑ 52	Terry Glenn	.75	.35
❑ 53	Eddie Kennison	.40	.18
❑ 54	Cam Cleeland	.20	.09
❑ 55	Ike Hilliard	.40	.18
❑ 56	Gary Brown	.20	.09
❑ 57	Kerry Collins	.40	.18
❑ 58	Vinny Testaverde	.40	.18
❑ 59	Keyshawn Johnson	.75	.35
❑ 60	Wayne Chrebet	.75	.35
❑ 61	Curtis Martin	.75	.35
❑ 62	Tim Brown	.75	.35
❑ 63	Napoleon Kaufman	.75	.35
❑ 64	Charles Woodson	.75	.35
❑ 65	Duce Staley	.75	.35
❑ 66	Charles Johnson	.40	.18
❑ 67	Kordell Stewart	.75	.35
❑ 68	Jerome Bettis	.75	.35
❑ 69	Marshall Faulk	.75	.35
❑ 70	Isaac Bruce	.75	.35
❑ 71	Trent Green	.40	.18
❑ 72	Jim Harbaugh	.40	.18
❑ 73	Junior Seau	.40	.18
❑ 74	Natrone Means	.40	.18
❑ 75	Steve Young	1.25	.55
❑ 76	Jerry Rice	2.00	.90
❑ 77	Terrell Owens	.75	.35
❑ 78	Lawrence Phillips	.40	.18
❑ 79	Joey Galloway	.75	.35
❑ 80	Ricky Watters	.40	.18
❑ 81	Jon Kitna	.75	.35
❑ 82	Warrick Dunn	.75	.35
❑ 83	Trent Dilfer	.40	.18
❑ 84	Mike Alstott	.75	.35
❑ 85	Eddie George	1.00	.45
❑ 86	Steve McNair	.75	.35
❑ 87	Yancey Thigpen	.20	.09
❑ 88	Brad Johnson	.75	.35
❑ 89	Skip Hicks	.40	.18
❑ 90	Michael Westbrook	.40	.18
❑ 91	Ricky Williams RC	250.00	110.00
❑ 92	Tim Couch RC	175.00	80.00
❑ 93	Akili Smith RC	80.00	36.00
❑ 94	Edgerrin James RC	400.00	180.00
❑ 95	Donovan McNabb RC	250.00	110.00
❑ 96	Torry Holt RC	100.00	45.00
❑ 97	Cade McNown RC	80.00	36.00
❑ 98	Shaun King RC	80.00	36.00
❑ 99	Daunte Culpepper RC	400.00	180.00
❑ 100	Brock Huard RC	40.00	18.00
❑ 101	Chris Claiborne RC	15.00	6.75
❑ 102	James Johnson RC	25.00	11.00
❑ 103	Rob Konrad RC	25.00	11.00
❑ 104	Peerless Price RC	40.00	18.00
❑ 105	Kevin Faulk RC	40.00	18.00
❑ 106	Andy Katzenmoyer RC	25.00	11.00
❑ 107	Troy Edwards RC	40.00	18.00
❑ 108	Kevin Johnson RC	40.00	18.00
❑ 109	Mike Cloud RC	25.00	11.00
❑ 110	David Boston RC	60.00	27.00
❑ 111	Champ Bailey RC	25.00	11.00
❑ 112	D'Wayne Bates RC	20.00	9.00
❑ 113	Joe Germaine RC	25.00	11.00
❑ 114	Antoine Winfield RC	20.00	9.00
❑ 115	Fernando Bryant RC	20.00	9.00
❑ 116	Jevon Kearse RC	60.00	27.00
❑ 117	Chris McAlister RC	20.00	9.00
❑ 118	Brandon Stokley RC	25.00	11.00
❑ 119	Karsten Bailey RC	20.00	9.00
❑ 120	Daylon McCutcheon RC	20.00	9.00
❑ 121	Jermaine Fazande RC	20.00	9.00
❑ 122	Joel Makovicka RC	25.00	11.00
❑ 123	Ebenezer Ekuban RC	20.00	9.00
❑ 124	Joe Montgomery RC	20.00	9.00
❑ 125	Sean Bennett RC	20.00	9.00
❑ 126	Na Brown RC	25.00	11.00
❑ 127	De'Mond Parker RC	20.00	9.00
❑ 128	Sedrick Irvin RC	15.00	6.75
❑ 129	Terry Jackson RC	20.00	9.00
❑ 130	Jeff Paulk RC	20.00	9.00
❑ 131	Cecil Collins RC	20.00	9.00
❑ 132	Bobby Collins RC	20.00	9.00
❑ 133	Amos Zereoue RC	20.00	9.00
❑ 134	Travis McGriff RC	20.00	9.00
❑ 135	Larry Parker RC	20.00	9.00
❑ 136	Wane McGarity RC	20.00	9.00
❑ 137	Cecil Martin RC	20.00	9.00
❑ 138	Al Wilson RC	20.00	9.00
❑ 139	Jim Kleinsasser RC	20.00	9.00
❑ 140	Dat Nguyen RC	20.00	9.00
❑ 141	Marty Booker RC	20.00	9.00
❑ 142	Reginald Kelly RC	15.00	6.75
❑ 143	Scott Covington RC	25.00	11.00
❑ 144	Antuan Edwards RC	20.00	9.00
❑ 145	Craig Yeast RC	20.00	9.00
❑ WPA	W.Payton AUTO/100	400.00	180.00
❑ WPSP	Walter Payton (Game Jersey AUTO/34)	2000.00	900.00

2000 SP Authentic

	MINT	NRMT
COMPLETE SET (150)	2000.00	900.00
COMP.SET w/o SP's (90)	15.00	6.75

	Card	MINT	NRMT
❑ 1	Jake Plummer	.60	.25
❑ 2	David Boston	.60	.25
❑ 3	Frank Sanders	.30	.14
❑ 4	Chris Chandler	.30	.14
❑ 5	Jamal Anderson	.60	.25
❑ 6	Shawn Jefferson	.15	.07
❑ 7	Tony Banks	.30	.14
❑ 8	Shannon Sharpe	.30	.14
❑ 9	Rob Johnson	.30	.14
❑ 10	Antowain Smith	.30	.14
❑ 11	Muhsin Muhammad	.30	.14
❑ 12	Steve Beuerlein	.30	.14
❑ 13	Cade McNown	.60	.25
❑ 14	Curtis Enis	.60	.25
❑ 15	Marcus Robinson	.60	.25
❑ 16	Akili Smith	.60	.25
❑ 17	Corey Dillon	.60	.25
❑ 18	Tim Couch	1.25	.55
❑ 19	Kevin Johnson	.60	.25
❑ 20	Errict Rhett	.15	.07
❑ 21	Troy Aikman	1.50	.70
❑ 22	Emmitt Smith	1.50	.70
❑ 23	Rocket Ismail	.30	.14
❑ 24	Joey Galloway	.60	.25
❑ 25	Terrell Davis	1.50	.70
❑ 26	Olandis Gary	.60	.25
❑ 27	Ed McCaffrey	.60	.25
❑ 28	Brian Griese	.75	.35
❑ 29	Charlie Batch	.60	.25
❑ 30	Germane Crowell	.30	.14
❑ 31	James O. Stewart	.30	.14
❑ 32	Brett Favre	2.50	1.10
❑ 33	Antonio Freeman	.60	.25
❑ 34	Dorsey Levens	.30	.14
❑ 35	Peyton Manning	2.00	.90
❑ 36	Edgerrin James	2.50	1.10
❑ 37	Marvin Harrison	.60	.25
❑ 38	Mark Brunell	1.00	.45
❑ 39	Fred Taylor	.75	.35
❑ 40	Jimmy Smith	.30	.14
❑ 41	Elvis Grbac	.30	.14
❑ 42	Tony Gonzalez	.30	.14
❑ 43	James Johnson	.30	.14
❑ 44	Oronde Gadsden	.30	.14
❑ 45	Damon Huard	.60	.25
❑ 46	Randy Moss	2.00	.90
❑ 47	Cris Carter	.60	.25
❑ 48	Daunte Culpepper	1.25	.55
❑ 49	Drew Bledsoe	1.00	.45
❑ 50	Terry Glenn	.30	.14
❑ 51	Ricky Williams	1.50	.70
❑ 52	Jeff Blake	.30	.14
❑ 53	Keith Poole	.15	.07
❑ 54	Kerry Collins	.30	.14
❑ 55	Amani Toomer	.30	.14
❑ 56	Ike Hilliard	.30	.14
❑ 57	Wayne Chrebet	.30	.14
❑ 58	Curtis Martin	.60	.25
❑ 59	Vinny Testaverde	.30	.14
❑ 60	Tim Brown	.60	.25
❑ 61	Rich Gannon	.30	.14
❑ 62	Tyrone Wheatley	.30	.14

	MINT	NRMT
❑ 63 Duce Staley	.60	.25
❑ 64 Donovan McNabb	1.00	.45
❑ 65 Troy Edwards	.30	.14
❑ 66 Jerome Bettis	.60	.25
❑ 67 Kordell Stewart	.60	.25
❑ 68 Marshall Faulk	.75	.35
❑ 69 Kurt Warner	2.50	1.10
❑ 70 Isaac Bruce	.60	.25
❑ 71 Torry Holt	.60	.25
❑ 72 Ryan Leaf	.60	.25
❑ 73 Jim Harbaugh	.30	.14
❑ 74 Jermaine Fazande	.15	.07
❑ 75 Jerry Rice	1.50	.70
❑ 76 Terrell Owens	.60	.25
❑ 77 Jeff Garcia	.60	.25
❑ 78 Ricky Watters	.15	.07
❑ 79 Jon Kitna	.60	.25
❑ 80 Derrick Mayes	.30	.14
❑ 81 Shaun King	1.00	.45
❑ 82 Mike Alstott	.60	.25
❑ 83 Keyshawn Johnson	.60	.25
❑ 84 Warrick Dunn	.60	.25
❑ 85 Eddie George	.75	.35
❑ 86 Steve McNair	.60	.25
❑ 87 Jevon Kearse	.60	.25
❑ 88 Brad Johnson	.60	.25
❑ 89 Stephen Davis	.60	.25
❑ 90 Michael Westbrook	.30	.14
❑ 91 Anthony Lucas RC	15.00	6.75
❑ 92 Avion Black RC	20.00	9.00
❑ 93 Dante Hall RC	20.00	9.00
❑ 94 Darrell Jackson RC	50.00	22.00
❑ 95 Deltha O'Neal RC	20.00	9.00
❑ 96 Erron Kinney RC	25.00	11.00
❑ 97 Doug Chapman RC	50.00	22.00
❑ 98 Frank Murphy RC	15.00	6.75
❑ 99 Gari Scott RC	20.00	9.00
❑ 100 Giovanni Carmazzi RC	40.00	18.00
❑ 101 JaJuan Dawson RC	25.00	11.00
❑ 102 Jarious Jackson RC	25.00	11.00
❑ 103 Rashard Anderson RC	20.00	9.00
❑ 104 Michael Wiley RC	25.00	11.00
❑ 105 Spergon Wynn RC	25.00	11.00
❑ 106 Muneer Moore RC	15.00	6.75
❑ 107 Ahmed Plummer RC	25.00	11.00
❑ 108 Chad Morton RC	25.00	11.00
❑ 109 Rob Morris RC	20.00	9.00
❑ 110 Ron Dixon RC	40.00	18.00
❑ 111 Rondell Mealey RC	15.00	6.75
❑ 112 Sebastian Janikowski RC	25.00	11.00
❑ 113 Shaun Ellis RC	20.00	9.00
❑ 114 Rogers Beckett RC	20.00	9.00
❑ 115 Shyrone Stith RC	20.00	9.00
❑ 116 Tim Rattay RC	50.00	22.00
❑ 117 Todd Husak RC	25.00	11.00
❑ 118 Tom Brady RC	25.00	11.00
❑ 119 Trevor Gaylor RC	20.00	9.00
❑ 120 Windrell Hayes RC	20.00	9.00
❑ 121 Anthony Becht RC	25.00	11.00
❑ 122 Brian Urlacher RC	120.00	55.00
❑ 123 Bubba Franks RC	40.00	18.00
❑ 124 Chad Pennington RC	150.00	70.00
❑ 125 Chris Redman RC	80.00	36.00
❑ 126 Corey Simon RC	30.00	13.50
❑ 127 Curtis Keaton RC	20.00	9.00
❑ 128 Danny Farmer RC	25.00	11.00
❑ 129 Dennis Northcutt RC	40.00	18.00
❑ 130 Dez White RC	20.00	9.00
❑ 131 J.R. Redmond RC	40.00	18.00
❑ 132 Jamal Lewis RC	350.00	160.00
❑ 133 Jerry Porter RC	25.00	11.00
❑ 134 Joe Hamilton RC	40.00	18.00
❑ 135 Laveranues Coles RC	50.00	22.00
❑ 136 R.Jay Soward RC	25.00	11.00
❑ 137 Reuben Droughns RC	25.00	11.00
❑ 138 Ron Dayne RC	150.00	70.00
❑ 139 Ron Dugans RC	20.00	9.00
❑ 140 Shaun Alexander RC	120.00	55.00
❑ 141 Sylvester Morris RC	60.00	27.00
❑ 142 Tee Martin RC	50.00	22.00
❑ 143 Thomas Jones RC	60.00	27.00
❑ 144 Todd Pinkston RC	25.00	11.00
❑ 145 Travis Prentice RC	60.00	27.00
❑ 146 Travis Taylor RC	50.00	22.00
❑ 147 Trung Canidate RC	25.00	11.00
❑ 148 Courtney Brown RC	40.00	18.00
❑ 149 Plaxico Burress RC	80.00	36.00
❑ 150 Peter Warrick RC	150.00	70.00
❑ 151 Billy Volek		
❑ 152 Bobby Shaw		
❑ 153 Brad Hoover		
❑ 154 Brian Finneran		
❑ 155 Charles Lee		
❑ 156 Chris Cole		
❑ 157 Clint Stoerner		
❑ 158 Doug Johnson		
❑ 159 Frank Moreau		
❑ 160 Jake Delhomme		
❑ 161 KaRon Coleman		
❑ 162 Kevin McDougal		
❑ 163 Larry Foster		
❑ 164 Mike Anderson		
❑ 165 Patrick Pass		
❑ 166 Reggie Jones		
❑ 167 Sammy Morris		
❑ 168 Shockmain Davis		
❑ 169 Terrelle Smith		
❑ 170 Ronney Jenkins		
❑ 171 Troy Walters		

1999 SP Signature

	MINT	NRMT
COMPLETE SET (180)	400.00	180.00
COMP.SET w/o SP's (170)	100.00	45.00
COMMON ROOKIE (171-180)	15.00	6.75
UNPRICED LEGENDARY CUTS #'d TO 1		

	MINT	NRMT
❑ 1 Jake Plummer	2.50	1.10
❑ 2 Mario Bates	.50	.23
❑ 3 Adrian Murrell	.75	.35
❑ 4 Jamal Anderson	1.25	.55
❑ 5 Chris Chandler	.75	.35
❑ 6 Bob Christian	.50	.23
❑ 7 O.J. Santiago	.50	.23
❑ 8 Jim Harbaugh	.75	.35
❑ 9 Priest Holmes	1.25	.55
❑ 10 Ray Lewis	.75	.35
❑ 11 Michael Jackson	.50	.23
❑ 12 Tony Siragusa	.50	.23
❑ 13 Doug Flutie	1.50	.70
❑ 14 Antowain Smith	1.25	.55
❑ 15 Eric Moulds	1.25	.55
❑ 16 William Floyd	.50	.23
❑ 17 Fred Lane	.50	.23
❑ 18 Muhsin Muhammad	.75	.35
❑ 19 Bobby Engram	.75	.35
❑ 20 Curtis Enis	1.25	.55
❑ 21 Curtis Conway	.75	.35
❑ 22 Corey Dillon	1.25	.55
❑ 23 Carl Pickens	.75	.35
❑ 24 Ashley Ambrose	.50	.23
❑ 25 Damay Scott	.50	.23
❑ 26 Troy Aikman	3.00	1.35
❑ 27 Jason Garrett	.50	.23
❑ 28 Emmitt Smith	3.00	1.35
❑ 29 Deion Sanders	1.25	.55
❑ 30 John Elway	5.00	2.20
❑ 31 Terrell Davis	3.00	1.35
❑ 32 Ed McCaffrey	.75	.35
❑ 33 John Mobley	.50	.23
❑ 34 Maa Tanuvasa	.50	.23
❑ 35 Ray Crockett	.50	.23
❑ 36 Barry Sanders	5.00	2.20
❑ 37 Herman Moore	1.25	.55
❑ 38 Charlie Batch	2.50	1.10
❑ 39 Robert Porcher	.50	.23
❑ 40 Tommy Vardell	.50	.23
❑ 41 Brett Favre	5.00	2.20
❑ 42 Antonio Freeman	1.25	.55
❑ 43 Darick Holmes	.50	.23
❑ 44 Robert Brooks	.75	.35
❑ 45 Peyton Manning	6.00	2.70
❑ 46 Marshall Faulk	1.25	.55
❑ 47 Torrance Small	.50	.23
❑ 48 Lamont Warren	.50	.23
❑ 49 Zack Crockett	.50	.23
❑ 50 Mark Brunell	2.00	.90
❑ 51 Pete Mitchell	.50	.23
❑ 52 Fred Taylor	3.00	1.35
❑ 53 Jimmy Smith	.75	.35
❑ 54 Andre Rison	.75	.35
❑ 55 Rich Gannon	.75	.35
❑ 56 Donnell Bennett	.50	.23
❑ 57 Dan Marino	5.00	2.20
❑ 58 Karim Abdul-Jabbar	.75	.35
❑ 59 Troy Drayton	.50	.23
❑ 60 Jason Taylor	.50	.23
❑ 61 Cris Carter	1.25	.55
❑ 62 Randy Moss	6.00	2.70
❑ 63 Robert Smith	1.25	.55
❑ 64 Leroy Hoard	.50	.23
❑ 65 Randall Cunningham	1.25	.55
❑ 66 Derrick Alexander DE	.50	.23
❑ 67 Drew Bledsoe	2.00	.90
❑ 68 Robert Edwards	.75	.35
❑ 69 Willie McGinest	.50	.23
❑ 70 Chris Slade	.50	.23
❑ 71 Terry Glenn	1.25	.55
❑ 72 Ty Law	.50	.23
❑ 73 Kerry Collins	.75	.35
❑ 74 Sean Dawkins	.50	.23
❑ 75 Cam Cleeland	.50	.23
❑ 76 Sammy Knight	.50	.23
❑ 77 Danny Kanell	.50	.23
❑ 78 Gary Brown	.50	.23
❑ 79 Chris Calloway	.75	.35
❑ 80 Curtis Martin	1.25	.55
❑ 81 Keyshawn Johnson	1.25	.55
❑ 82 Vinny Testaverde	.75	.35
❑ 83 Leon Johnson	.50	.23
❑ 84 Kyle Brady	.50	.23
❑ 85 Tim Brown	1.25	.55
❑ 86 Jeff George	.75	.35
❑ 87 Rickey Dudley	.50	.23
❑ 88 Napoleon Kaufman	1.25	.55
❑ 89 James Jett	.75	.35
❑ 90 Harvey Williams	.50	.23
❑ 91 Koy Detmer	.50	.23
❑ 92 Duce Staley	1.25	.55
❑ 93 Charlie Garner	.75	.35
❑ 94 Jerome Bettis	1.25	.55
❑ 95 Kordell Stewart	1.25	.55
❑ 96 Courtney Hawkins	.50	.23
❑ 97 Hines Ward	.50	.23
❑ 98 Isaac Bruce	1.25	.55
❑ 99 Tony Banks	.75	.35
❑ 100 Greg Hill	.50	.23
❑ 101 Keith Lyle	.50	.23
❑ 102 Ryan Leaf	1.25	.55
❑ 103 Craig Whelihan	.50	.23
❑ 104 Charlie Jones	.50	.23
❑ 105 Junior Seau	.75	.35
❑ 106 Natrone Means	.75	.35
❑ 107 Rodney Harrison	.50	.23
❑ 108 Steve Young	2.00	.90
❑ 109 Garrison Hearst	.75	.35
❑ 110 Jerry Rice	3.00	1.35
❑ 111 Chris Doleman	.50	.23
❑ 112 Roy Barker	.50	.23
❑ 113 Ricky Watters	.75	.35
❑ 114 Jon Kitna	1.25	.55
❑ 115 Joey Galloway	1.25	.55
❑ 116 Chad Brown	.50	.23
❑ 117 Michael Sinclair	.50	.23
❑ 118 Warrick Dunn	1.25	.55
❑ 119 Mike Alstott	1.25	.55
❑ 120 Bert Emanuel	.75	.35
❑ 121 Hardy Nickerson	.50	.23
❑ 122 Eddie George	1.50	.70

Card		
❑ 123 Steve McNair	1.25	.55
❑ 124 Yancey Thigpen	.50	.23
❑ 125 Frank Wycheck	.50	.23
❑ 126 Jackie Harris	.50	.23
❑ 127 Terry Allen	.75	.35
❑ 128 Trent Green	.75	.35
❑ 129 Jamie Asher	.50	.23
❑ 130 Brian Mitchell	.50	.23
❑ 131 Lance Alworth	1.25	.55
❑ 132 Fred Biletnikoff	1.25	.55
❑ 133 Mel Blount	.50	.23
❑ 134 Cliff Branch	.50	.23
❑ 135 Harold Carmichael	.50	.23
❑ 136 Larry Csonka	1.25	.55
❑ 137 Eric Dickerson	.50	.23
❑ 138 Randy Gradishar	.50	.23
❑ 139 Joe Greene	.75	.35
❑ 140 Jack Ham	.75	.35
❑ 141 Ted Hendricks	.50	.23
❑ 142 Charlie Joiner	.50	.23
❑ 143 Ed Jones	.50	.23
❑ 144 Billy Kilmer	.50	.23
❑ 145 Paul Krause	.50	.23
❑ 146 James Lofton	.50	.23
❑ 147 Archie Manning	.75	.35
❑ 148 Don Maynard	.50	.23
❑ 149 Ozzie Newsome	.50	.23
❑ 150 Jim Otto	.50	.23
❑ 151 Lee Roy Selmon	.50	.23
❑ 152 Billy Sims	.50	.23
❑ 153 Mike Singletary	.75	.35
❑ 154 Ken Stabler	1.50	.70
❑ 155 John Stallworth	.75	.35
❑ 156 Roger Staubach	2.00	.90
❑ 157 Charley Taylor	.50	.23
❑ 158 Paul Warfield	1.25	.55
❑ 159 Kellen Winslow	.50	.23
❑ 160 Jack Youngblood	.50	.23
❑ 161 Bill Bergey	.50	.23
❑ 162 Raymond Berry	.75	.35
❑ 163 Chuck Howley	.50	.23
❑ 164 Rocky Bleier	.75	.35
❑ 165 Russ Francis	.50	.23
❑ 166 Drew Pearson	.50	.23
❑ 167 Mercury Morris	.50	.23
❑ 168 Dick Anderson	.50	.23
❑ 169 Earl Morrall	.50	.23
❑ 170 Jim Hart	.50	.23
❑ 171 Ricky Williams RC	30.00	13.50
❑ 172 Cade McNown RC	20.00	9.00
❑ 173 Tim Couch RC	30.00	13.50
❑ 174 Daunte Culpepper RC	50.00	22.00
❑ 175 Akili Smith RC	25.00	11.00
❑ 176 Brock Huard RC	15.00	6.75
❑ 177 Donovan McNabb RC	30.00	13.50
❑ 178 Michael Bishop RC	15.00	6.75
❑ 179 Shaun King RC	20.00	9.00
❑ 180 Torry Holt RC	20.00	9.00

1994 Sportflics

	MINT	NRMT
COMPLETE SET (184)	25.00	11.00
❑ 1 Deion Sanders	.60	.25
❑ 2 Leslie O'Neal	.10	.05
❑ 3 Flipper Anderson	.10	.05
❑ 4 Anthony Carter	.20	.09
❑ 5 Thurman Thomas	.30	.14
❑ 6 Johnny Mitchell	.10	.05
❑ 7 Jeff Hostetler	.20	.09
❑ 8 Renaldo Turnbull	.10	.05
❑ 9 Chris Warren	.20	.09
❑ 10 Darrell Green	.10	.05
❑ 11 Randall Cunningham	.30	.14
❑ 12 Barry Sanders	2.50	1.10
❑ 13 Jeff Cross	.10	.05
❑ 14 Glyn Milburn	.20	.09
❑ 15 Willie Davis	.20	.09
❑ 16 Tony McGee	.10	.05
❑ 17 Gary Clark	.20	.09
❑ 18 Michael Jackson	.20	.09
❑ 19 Alvin Harper	.20	.09
❑ 20 Tim Worley	.10	.05
❑ 21 Quentin Coryatt	.10	.05
❑ 22 Michael Brooks	.10	.05
❑ 23 Boomer Esiason	.20	.09
❑ 24 Ricky Watters	.20	.09
❑ 25 Craig Erickson	.10	.05
❑ 26 Willie Green	.10	.05
❑ 27 Brett Favre	2.50	1.10
❑ 28 John Elway	2.50	1.10
❑ 29 Steve Beuerlein	.10	.05
❑ 30 Emmitt Smith	2.00	.90
❑ 31 Troy Aikman	1.25	.55
❑ 32 Cody Carlson	.10	.05
❑ 33 Brian Mitchell	.10	.05
❑ 34 Herschel Walker	.20	.09
❑ 35 Bruce Smith	.20	.09
❑ 36 Harold Green	.10	.05
❑ 37 Erric Pegram	.10	.05
❑ 38 Ronnie Harmon	.10	.05
❑ 39 Brian Blades	.20	.09
❑ 40 Sterling Sharpe	.20	.09
❑ 41 Leonard Russell	.10	.05
❑ 42 Cleveland Gary	.10	.05
❑ 43 Tom Waddle	.10	.05
❑ 44 Lawrence Dawsey	.10	.05
❑ 45 Jerry Rice	1.25	.55
❑ 46 Terry Allen	.20	.09
❑ 47 Reggie Langhorne	.10	.05
❑ 48 Derek Brown RBK	.10	.05
❑ 49 Terry Kirby	.20	.09
❑ 50 Reggie Brooks	.20	.09
❑ 51 Calvin Williams	.20	.09
❑ 52 Cornelius Bennett	.20	.09
❑ 53 Russell Maryland	.10	.05
❑ 54 Rob Moore	.20	.09
❑ 55 Dana Stubblefield	.20	.09
❑ 56 Rod Woodson	.30	.14
❑ 57 Rodney Hampton	.20	.09
❑ 58 Neil Smith	.20	.09
❑ 59 Anthony Smith	.10	.05
❑ 60 Neal Anderson	.10	.05
❑ 61 Drew Bledsoe	1.25	.55
❑ 62 John Copeland	.10	.05
❑ 63 David Klingler	.10	.05
❑ 64 Phil Simms	.20	.09
❑ 65 Vincent Brisby	.20	.09
❑ 66 Richard Dent	.20	.09
❑ 67 Eric Metcalf	.20	.09
❑ 68 Eric Curry	.10	.05
❑ 69 Victor Bailey	.10	.05
❑ 70 Herman Moore	.30	.14
❑ 71 Steve Jordan	.10	.05
❑ 72 Jerome Bettis	.30	.14
❑ 73 Natrone Means	.30	.14
❑ 74 Webster Slaughter	.10	.05
❑ 75 Jackie Harris	.10	.05
❑ 76 Michael Irvin	.30	.14
❑ 77 Steve Emtman	.10	.05
❑ 78 Eugene Robinson	.10	.05
❑ 79 Tim Brown	.30	.14
❑ 80 Derrick Thomas	.30	.14
❑ 81 Vinny Testaverde	.20	.09
❑ 82 Mark Jackson	.10	.05
❑ 83 Ricky Proehl	.10	.05
❑ 84 Stan Humphries	.20	.09
❑ 85 Garrison Hearst	.30	.14
❑ 86 Jim Kelly	.30	.14
❑ 87 Brent Jones	.20	.09
❑ 88 Eric Martin	.10	.05
❑ 89 Wilber Marshall	.10	.05
❑ 90 Chris Spielman	.20	.09
❑ 91 Eric Green	.10	.05
❑ 92 Andre Rison	.20	.09
❑ 93 Andre Reed	.20	.09
❑ 94 Carl Pickens	.30	.14
❑ 95 Junior Seau	.30	.14
❑ 96 Dwight Stone	.10	.05
❑ 97 Mike Sherrard	.10	.05
❑ 98 Vincent Brown	.10	.05
❑ 99 Cris Carter	.60	.25
❑ 100 Mark Higgs	.10	.05
❑ 101 Steve Young	.75	.35
❑ 102 Mark Carrier WR	.20	.09
❑ 103 Barry Foster	.10	.05
❑ 104 Tommy Vardell	.10	.05
❑ 105 Shannon Sharpe	.20	.09
❑ 106 Reggie White	.30	.14
❑ 107 Ernest Givins	.20	.09
❑ 108 Marcus Allen	.30	.14
❑ 109 James Jett	.10	.05
❑ 110 Keith Jackson	.10	.05
❑ 111 Irving Fryar	.20	.09
❑ 112 Ronnie Lott	.20	.09
❑ 113 Cortez Kennedy	.20	.09
❑ 114 Ronald Moore	.10	.05
❑ 115 Rick Mirer	.20	.09
❑ 116 Neil O'Donnell	.20	.09
❑ 117 Courtney Hawkins	.10	.05
❑ 118 Johnny Johnson	.10	.05
❑ 119 Ben Coates	.20	.09
❑ 120 Dan Marino	2.50	1.10
❑ 121 Sean Gilbert	.10	.05
❑ 122 Rocket Ismail	.20	.09
❑ 123 Joe Montana	2.50	1.10
❑ 124 Roosevelt Potts	.10	.05
❑ 125 Gary Brown	.10	.05
❑ 126 Reggie Cobb	.10	.05
❑ 127 Marion Butts	.10	.05
❑ 128 Scott Mitchell	.20	.09
❑ 129 John L. Williams	.10	.05
❑ 130 Jeff George	.20	.09
❑ 131 Bobby Hebert	.10	.05
❑ 132 John Friesz	.20	.09
❑ 133 Anthony Miller	.20	.09
❑ 134 Jim Harbaugh	.20	.09
❑ 135 Erik Kramer	.20	.09
❑ 136 Jim Everett	.20	.09
❑ 137 Michael Haynes	.20	.09
❑ 138 Rod Bernstine	.10	.05
❑ 139 Chris Miller	.10	.05
❑ 140 Henry Ellard	.20	.09
❑ 141 William Fuller	.10	.05
❑ 142 Warren Moon	.30	.14
❑ 143 Lamar Smith RC	2.00	.90
❑ 144 Charlie Garner RC	1.50	.70
❑ 145 Chuck Levy RC	.10	.05
❑ 146 Dan Wilkinson RC	.20	.09
❑ 147 Perry Klein RC	.10	.05
❑ 148 William Floyd RC	.20	.09
❑ 149 Lake Dawson RC	.30	.14
❑ 150 David Palmer RC	.75	.35
❑ 151 James Bostic RC	.20	.09
❑ 152 Marshall Faulk RC	4.00	1.80
❑ 153 Greg Hill RC	.30	.14
❑ 154 Heath Shuler RC	.30	.14
❑ 155 Errict Rhett RC	.75	.35
❑ 156 Sam Adams RC	.20	.09
❑ 157 Charles Johnson RC	.30	.14
❑ 158 Ryan Yarborough RC	.10	.05
❑ 159 Thomas Lewis RC	.20	.09
❑ 160 Willie McGinest RC	.30	.14
❑ 161 Jamir Miller RC	.10	.05
❑ 162 Calvin Jones RC	.10	.05
❑ 163 Donnell Bennett RC	.30	.14
❑ 164 Trev Alberts RC	.20	.09
❑ 165 LeShon Johnson RC	.20	.09
❑ 166 Johnnie Morton RC	.30	.14
❑ 167 Derrick Alexander WR RC	.30	.14
❑ 168 Jeff Cothran RC	.10	.05
❑ 169 Bucky Brooks RC	.10	.05
❑ 170 Bert Emanuel RC	.75	.35
❑ 171 Darnay Scott RC	1.00	.45
❑ 172 Kevin Lee RC	.10	.05
❑ 173 Mario Bates RC	.20	.09
❑ 174 Bryant Young RC	.20	.09
❑ 175 Trent Dilfer RC	1.50	.70
❑ 176 Joe Montana SF	1.25	.55
❑ 177 Emmitt Smith SF	1.00	.45
❑ 178 Troy Aikman SF	.60	.25
❑ 179 Steve Young SF	.30	.14
❑ 180 Jerome Bettis SF	.20	.09
❑ 181 John Elway SF	1.25	.55
❑ 182 Dan Marino SF	1.25	.55
❑ 183 Brett Favre SF	1.25	.55
❑ 184 Barry Sanders SF	1.25	.55
❑ FTF1 Terry Kirby Leonard Russell	4.00	1.80

1995 Sportflix

	MINT	NRMT
COMPLETE SET (175)	25.00	11.00
❑ 1 Troy Aikman	1.00	.45

❑ 2 Rodney Hampton .20 .09
❑ 3 Jerry Rice 1.00 .45
❑ 4 Reggie White .30 .14
❑ 5 Mark Ingram .10 .05
❑ 6 Chris Spielman .20 .09
❑ 7 Curtis Conway .30 .14
❑ 8 Erik Kramer .10 .05
❑ 9 Emmitt Smith 1.50 .70
❑ 10 Alvin Harper .10 .05
❑ 11 Junior Seau .30 .14
❑ 12 Mike Pritchard .10 .05
❑ 13 Ricky Ervins .10 .05
❑ 14 Jim Harbaugh .20 .09
❑ 15 Dan Marino 2.00 .90
❑ 16 Marshall Faulk .50 .23
❑ 17 Lorenzo White .10 .05
❑ 18 Cortez Kennedy .20 .09
❑ 19 Rocket Ismail .20 .09
❑ 20 Eric Metcalf .20 .09
❑ 21 Chris Chandler .20 .09
❑ 22 John Elway 2.00 .90
❑ 23 Boomer Esiason .20 .09
❑ 24 Herman Moore .30 .14
❑ 25 Deion Sanders .60 .25
❑ 26 Charles Johnson .20 .09
❑ 27 Daryl Johnston .20 .09
❑ 28 Dave Krieg .10 .05
❑ 29 Jim Kelly .30 .14
❑ 30 Warren Moon .20 .09
❑ 31 Lewis Tillman .10 .05
❑ 32 Bruce Smith .30 .14
❑ 33 Jake Reed .20 .09
❑ 34 Craig Heyward .20 .09
❑ 35 Frank Reich .10 .05
❑ 36 Stan Humphries .20 .09
❑ 37 Charles Haley .20 .09
❑ 38 Andre Rison .20 .09
❑ 39 James Jett .20 .09
❑ 40 Jay Novacek .20 .09
❑ 41 Gary Brown .10 .05
❑ 42 Steve Bono .20 .09
❑ 43 Cris Carter .30 .14
❑ 44 Steve Atwater .10 .05
❑ 45 Andre Reed .20 .09
❑ 46 Greg Lloyd .20 .09
❑ 47 Mark Seay .20 .09
❑ 48 Dave Meggett .10 .05
❑ 49 Steve Beuerlein .10 .05
❑ 50 Jeff Graham .10 .05
❑ 51 Barry Sanders 2.00 .90
❑ 52 Willie Davis .20 .09
❑ 53 Robert Smith .30 .14
❑ 54 Steve Walsh .10 .05
❑ 55 Michael Irvin .30 .14
❑ 56 Natrone Means .30 .14
❑ 57 Chris Warren .20 .09
❑ 58 Tim Brown .30 .14
❑ 59 Steve Young .75 .35
❑ 60 Jerome Bettis .30 .14
❑ 61 Shannon Sharpe .20 .09
❑ 62 Errict Rhett .30 .14
❑ 63 Scott Mitchell .20 .09
❑ 64 Leroy Hoard .10 .05
❑ 65 Garrison Hearst .30 .14
❑ 66 Terance Mathis .20 .09
❑ 67 Sean Gilbert .20 .09
❑ 68 Fred Barnett .20 .09
❑ 69 Hardy Nickerson .10 .05
❑ 70 Jim Everett .10 .05
❑ 71 Randall Cunningham .30 .14
❑ 72 Carl Pickens .30 .14
❑ 73 Jeff Hostetler .20 .09
❑ 74 Marcus Allen .30 .14
❑ 75 Jeff George .20 .09
❑ 76 Brett Favre 2.00 .90
❑ 77 Chris Miller .10 .05
❑ 78 Craig Erickson .10 .05
❑ 79 Herschel Walker .20 .09
❑ 80 Bert Emanuel .30 .14
❑ 81 Leonard Russell .10 .05
❑ 82 Ricky Watters .30 .14
❑ 83 Robert Brooks .30 .14
❑ 84 Dave Brown .20 .09
❑ 85 Henry Ellard .20 .09
❑ 86 Barry Foster .20 .09
❑ 87 Johnny Mitchell .10 .05
❑ 88 Eric Allen .10 .05
❑ 89 Darnay Scott .30 .14
❑ 90 Harvey Williams .10 .05
❑ 91 Neil O'Donnell .20 .09
❑ 92 Drew Bledsoe 1.00 .45
❑ 93 Ken Harvey .10 .05
❑ 94 Irving Fryar .20 .09
❑ 95 Rod Woodson .20 .09
❑ 96 Anthony Miller .20 .09
❑ 97 Mario Bates .30 .14
❑ 98 Jeff Blake RC 1.00 .45
❑ 99 Rick Mirer .30 .14
❑ 100 William Floyd .30 .14
❑ 101 Michael Haynes .20 .09
❑ 102 Flipper Anderson .10 .05
❑ 103 Greg Hill .20 .09
❑ 104 Mark Brunell 1.00 .45
❑ 105 Vinny Testaverde .20 .09
❑ 106 Heath Shuler .30 .14
❑ 107 Ronald Moore .10 .05
❑ 108 Ernest Givins .10 .05
❑ 109 Mike Sherrard .10 .05
❑ 110 Charlie Garner .20 .09
❑ 111 Trent Dilfer .30 .14
❑ 112 Byron Bam Morris .20 .09
❑ 113 Lake Dawson .20 .09
❑ 114 Brian Blades .20 .09
❑ 115 Brent Jones .10 .05
❑ 116 Ronnie Harmon .10 .05
❑ 117 Eric Green .10 .05
❑ 118 Ben Coates .20 .09
❑ 119 Ki-Jana Carter RC .30 .14
❑ 120 Steve McNair RC 2.50 1.10
❑ 121 Michael Westbrook RC 1.50 .70
❑ 122 Kerry Collins RC 1.50 .70
❑ 123 Joey Galloway RC 2.00 .90
❑ 124 Kyle Brady RC .30 .14
❑ 125 J.J. Stokes RC .30 .14
❑ 126 Tyrone Wheatley RC 1.25 .55
❑ 127 Rashaan Salaam RC .30 .14
❑ 128 Napoleon Kaufman RC 1.50 .70
❑ 129 Frank Sanders RC 1.00 .45
❑ 130 Stoney Case RC .30 .14
❑ 131 Todd Collins RC .30 .14
❑ 132 Lovell Pinkney RC .10 .05
❑ 133 Sherman Williams RC .10 .05
❑ 134 Rob Johnson RC 2.00 .90
❑ 135 Mark Bruener RC .20 .09
❑ 136 Lee DeRamus RC .10 .05
❑ 137 Chad May RC .10 .05
❑ 138 James A.Stewart RC .10 .05
❑ 139 Ray Zellars RC .20 .09
❑ 140 Dave Barr RC .10 .05
❑ 141 Kordell Stewart RC 2.00 .90
❑ 142 Jimmy Oliver RC .10 .05
❑ 143 Terrell Fletcher RC .10 .05
❑ 144 James O. Stewart RC 2.00 .90
❑ 145 Terrell Davis RC 10.00 4.50
❑ 146 Joe Aska RC .20 .09
❑ 147 John Walsh RC .10 .05
❑ 148 Tyrone Davis RC .10 .05
❑ 149 Emmitt Smith GW .75 .35
❑ 150 Barry Sanders GW 1.00 .45
❑ 151 Jerry Rice GW .50 .23
❑ 152 Steve Young GW .40 .18
❑ 153 Dan Marino GW 1.00 .45
❑ 154 Troy Aikman GW .50 .23
❑ 155 Drew Bledsoe GW .50 .23
❑ 156 John Elway GW 1.00 .45
❑ 157 Brett Favre GW 1.00 .45
❑ 158 Michael Irvin GW .20 .09
❑ 159 Heath Shuler GW .30 .14
❑ 160 Warren Moon GW .10 .05
❑ 161 Jim Kelly GW .30 .14
❑ 162 Randall Cunningham GW .20 .09
❑ 163 Jeff Hostetler GW .20 .09
❑ 164 Dave Brown GW .20 .09
❑ 165 Neil O'Donnell GW .20 .09
❑ 166 Rick Mirer GW .20 .09
❑ 167 Jim Everett GW .10 .05
❑ 168 Boomer Esiason GW .20 .09
❑ 169 Dan Marino CL .50 .23
❑ 170 Drew Bledsoe CL .30 .14
❑ 171 John Elway CL .30 .14
❑ 172 Emmitt Smith CL .40 .18
❑ 173 Steve Young CL .30 .14
❑ 174 Barry Sanders CL .30 .14
❑ 175 Jerry Rice CL .30 .14
Junior Seau CL
❑ P1 Troy Aikman Promo 1.25 .55
❑ P6 Jerry Rice Promo 1.25 .55
Lightning Card
❑ P92 Drew Bledsoe Promo 1.25 .55

1999 Sports Illustrated

	MINT	NRMT
COMPLETE SET (150)	75.00	34.00

❑ 1 Bart Starr MVP .60 .25
❑ 2 Bart Starr MVP .60 .25
❑ 3 Joe Namath MVP .60 .25
❑ 4 Len Dawson MVP .15 .07
❑ 5 Chuck Howley MVP .15 .07
❑ 6 Roger Staubach MVP .60 .25
❑ 7 Jake Scott MVP .15 .07
❑ 8 Larry Csonka MVP .30 .14
❑ 9 Franco Harris MVP .30 .14
❑ 10 Fred Biletnikoff MVP .30 .14
❑ 11 Harvey Martin MVP .15 .07
Randy White MVP
❑ 12 Terry Bradshaw MVP .60 .25
❑ 13 Terry Bradshaw MVP .60 .25
❑ 14 Jim Plunkett MVP .15 .07
❑ 15 Joe Montana MVP .75 .35
❑ 16 Marcus Allen MVP .30 .14
❑ 17 Joe Montana MVP .75 .35
❑ 18 Richard Dent MVP .30 .14
❑ 19 Phil Simms MVP .15 .07
❑ 20 Doug Williams MVP .15 .07
❑ 21 Jerry Rice MVP .75 .35
❑ 22 Joe Montana MVP .75 .35
❑ 23 Ottis Anderson MVP .15 .07
❑ 24 Mark Rypien MVP .15 .07
❑ 25 Troy Aikman MVP .75 .35
❑ 26 Emmitt Smith MVP 1.25 .55
❑ 27 Steve Young MVP .60 .25
❑ 28 Larry Brown MVP .15 .07
❑ 29 Desmond Howard MVP .30 .14
❑ 30 Terrell Davis MVP 1.25 .55
❑ 31 Y.A. Tittle .30 .14
❑ 32 Paul Hornung .30 .14
❑ 33 Gale Sayers .30 .14
❑ 34 Garo Yepremian .15 .07
❑ 35 Bert Jones .15 .07

❑ 36 Joe Washington .15 .07
❑ 37 Joe Theismann .15 .07
❑ 38 Roger Craig .15 .07
❑ 39 Mike Singletary .15 .07
❑ 40 Bobby Bell .15 .07
❑ 41 Ken Houston .15 .07
❑ 42 Lenny Moore .15 .07
❑ 43 Mark Moseley .15 .07
❑ 44 Chuck Bednarik .15 .07
❑ 45 Ted Hendricks .15 .07
❑ 46 Steve Largent .60 .25
❑ 47 Bob Lilly .15 .07
❑ 48 Don Maynard .15 .07
❑ 49 John Mackey .15 .07
❑ 50 Anthony Munoz .15 .07
❑ 51 Bobby Mitchell .15 .07
❑ 52 Jim Brown .60 .25
❑ 53 Otto Graham .30 .14
❑ 54 Earl Morrall .15 .07
❑ 55 Danny White .15 .07
❑ 56 Karim Abdul-Jabbar .30 .14
❑ 57 Charlie Garner .30 .14
❑ 58 Jeff Blake .30 .14
❑ 59 Reggie White .60 .25
❑ 60 Derrick Thomas .30 .14
❑ 61 Duce Staley .60 .25
❑ 62 Tim Brown .60 .25
❑ 63 Elvis Grbac .30 .14
❑ 64 Tony Banks .30 .14
❑ 65 Rob Johnson .30 .14
❑ 66 Danny Kanell .15 .07
❑ 67 Marshall Faulk .60 .25
❑ 68 Warrick Dunn .60 .25
❑ 69 Dan Marino 3.00 1.35
❑ 70 Jimmy Smith .30 .14
❑ 71 John Elway 3.00 1.35
❑ 72 Charles Way .15 .07
❑ 73 Ricky Watters .30 .14
❑ 74 Terry Glenn .60 .25
❑ 75 Bobby Hoying .30 .14
❑ 76 Curtis Martin .60 .25
❑ 77 Trent Dilfer .30 .14
❑ 78 Emmitt Smith 2.50 1.10
❑ 79 Irving Fryar .30 .14
❑ 80 Troy Aikman 1.50 .70
❑ 81 Barry Sanders 3.00 1.35
❑ 82 Brett Favre 3.00 1.35
❑ 83 Robert Smith .60 .25
❑ 84 Dorsey Levens .60 .25
❑ 85 Cris Carter .60 .25
❑ 86 Jeff George .30 .14
❑ 87 Jerome Bettis .60 .25
❑ 88 Warren Moon .60 .25
❑ 89 Steve Young 1.00 .45
❑ 90 Fred Lane .15 .07
❑ 91 Jerry Rice 1.50 .70
❑ 92 Natrone Means .30 .14
❑ 93 Mike Alstott .60 .25
❑ 94 Kordell Stewart .60 .25
❑ 95 Jake Plummer 2.00 .90
❑ 96 Jamal Anderson .60 .25
❑ 97 Corey Dillon 1.00 .45
❑ 98 Deion Sanders .60 .25
❑ 99 Mark Brunell 1.25 .55
❑ 100 Garrison Hearst .30 .14
❑ 101 Andre Rison .30 .14
❑ 102 Antowain Smith .60 .25
❑ 103 Drew Bledsoe 1.25 .55
❑ 104 Eddie George .75 .35
❑ 105 Keyshawn Johnson .60 .25
❑ 106 Isaac Bruce .60 .25
❑ 107 Rob Moore .30 .14
❑ 108 Steve McNair .60 .25
❑ 109 Terrell Davis 2.50 1.10
❑ 110 Carl Pickens .30 .14
❑ 111 Wayne Chrebet .30 .14
❑ 112 Kerry Collins .30 .14
❑ 113 Eric Metcalf .15 .07
❑ 114 Joey Galloway .60 .25
❑ 115 Shannon Sharpe .30 .14
❑ 116 Robert Brooks .30 .14
❑ 117 Glenn Foley .30 .14
❑ 118 Yancey Thigpen .15 .07
❑ 119 Frank Sanders .30 .14
❑ 120 Herman Moore .60 .25
❑ 121 Antonio Freeman .60 .25
❑ 122 Michael Irvin .30 .14
❑ 123 Brad Johnson .60 .25
❑ 124 James Stewart .30 .14
❑ 125 Jim Harbaugh .30 .14
❑ 126 Peyton Manning FF 10.00 4.50
❑ 127 Ryan Leaf FF .30 .14
❑ 128 Curtis Enis FF 2.00 .90
❑ 129 Fred Taylor FF 6.00 2.70
❑ 130 Randy Moss FF 10.00 4.50
❑ 131 John Avery FF 2.00 .90
❑ 132 Charles Woodson FF 2.00 .90
❑ 133 Robert Edwards FF 2.00 .90
❑ 134 Charlie Batch FF 5.00 2.20
❑ 135 Brian Griese FF 5.00 2.20
❑ 136 Skip Hicks FF .60 .25
❑ 137 Jacquez Green FF 2.00 .90
❑ 138 Robert Holcombe FF 2.00 .90
❑ 139 Kevin Dyson FF 2.00 .90
❑ 140 Rodney Williams FF .60 .25
❑ 141 Ahman Green FF 1.00 .45
❑ 142 Tavian Banks FF 2.00 .90
❑ 143 Donald Hayes FF 1.00 .45
❑ 144 Tony Simmons FF 2.00 .90
❑ 145 Pat Johnson FF 2.00 .90
❑ 146 Marcus Nash FF 2.00 .90
❑ 147 Germane Crowell FF 2.00 .90
❑ 148 R.W. McQuarters FF .60 .25
❑ 149 Jonathan Quinn FF 2.00 .90
❑ 150 Andre Wadsworth FF .60 .25
❑ P35 Gale Sayers Promo 3.00 1.35

1996 SPx

	MINT	NRMT
COMPLETE SET (50)	40.00	18.00

❑ 1 Frank Sanders 1.00 .45
❑ 2 Terance Mathis .50 .23
❑ 3 Todd Collins 1.00 .45
❑ 4 Kerry Collins 2.00 .90
❑ 5 Carl Pickens 2.00 .90
❑ 6 Darnay Scott 1.00 .45
❑ 7 Ki-Jana Carter 1.00 .45
❑ 8 Eric Zeier .50 .23
❑ 9 Andre Rison 1.00 .45
❑ 10 Sherman Williams .50 .23
❑ 11 Troy Aikman 4.00 1.80
❑ 12 Michael Irvin 2.00 .90
❑ 13 Emmitt Smith 6.00 2.70
❑ 14 Shannon Sharpe 1.00 .45
❑ 15 John Elway 8.00 3.60
❑ 16 Barry Sanders 8.00 3.60
❑ 17 Brett Favre 8.00 3.60
❑ 18 Rodney Thomas .50 .23
❑ 19 Marshall Faulk 2.00 .90
❑ 20 James O.Stewart 1.00 .45
❑ 21 Greg Hill 1.00 .45
❑ 22 Tamarick Vanover 1.00 .45
❑ 23 Dan Marino 8.00 3.60
❑ 24 Cris Carter 2.00 .90
❑ 25 Warren Moon 1.00 .45
❑ 26 Drew Bledsoe 4.00 1.80
❑ 27 Ben Coates 1.00 .45
❑ 28 Curtis Martin 4.00 1.80
❑ 29 Mario Bates 1.00 .45
❑ 30 Tyrone Wheatley 1.00 .45
❑ 31 Rodney Hampton 1.00 .45
❑ 32 Kyle Brady .50 .23
❑ 33 Jeff Hostetler .50 .23
❑ 34 Napoleon Kaufman 2.00 .90
❑ 35 Tim Brown 2.00 .90
❑ 36 Charles Johnson .50 .23
❑ 37 Rod Woodson UER 1.00 .45
Incorrect birth year
❑ 38 Natrone Means 2.00 .90
❑ 39 J.J. Stokes 2.00 .90
❑ 40 Steve Young 4.00 1.80
❑ 41 Brent Jones .50 .23
❑ 42 Jerry Rice 4.00 1.80
❑ 43 Joe Montana 8.00 3.60
❑ 44 Rick Mirer 1.00 .45
❑ 45 Chris Warren 1.00 .45
❑ 46 Joey Galloway 3.00 1.35
❑ 47 Isaac Bruce 2.00 .90
❑ 48 Jerome Bettis 2.00 .90
❑ 49 Errict Rhett 1.00 .45
❑ 50 Michael Westbrook 2.00 .90
❑ UDT13 Dan Marino 15.00 6.75
Record Breaker
❑ UDT13 Dan Marino AUTO 100.00 45.00
Record Breaker signed
❑ UDT19 Joe Montana Tribute 15.00 6.75
❑ UDT19 Joe Montana AUTO 120.00 55.00
Tribute card signed
❑ P1 Dan Marino Promo 5.00 2.20
❑ P2 Joe Montana Promo 5.00 2.20

1997 SPx

	MINT	NRMT
COMPLETE SET (50)	40.00	18.00

❑ 1 Jerry Rice 4.00 1.80
❑ 2 Steve Young 3.00 1.35
❑ 3 Karim Abdul-Jabbar 1.25 .55
❑ 4 Dan Marino 8.00 3.60
❑ 5 Bobby Engram .60 .25
❑ 6 Rashaan Salaam .30 .14
❑ 7 Marvin Harrison 1.25 .55
❑ 8 Jim Harbaugh .60 .25
❑ 9 Marshall Faulk 1.25 .55
❑ 10 Eric Moulds 1.25 .55
❑ 11 Thurman Thomas 1.25 .55
❑ 12 Tamarick Vanover .60 .25
❑ 13 Steve Bono .60 .25
❑ 14 Warren Moon 1.25 .55
❑ 15 Cris Carter 1.25 .55
❑ 16 Carl Pickens 1.25 .55
❑ 17 Ki-Jana Carter .30 .14
❑ 18 Jeff Blake .60 .25
❑ 19 Tim Biakabutuka .60 .25
❑ 20 Kerry Collins .60 .25
❑ 21 Leeland McElroy .30 .14
❑ 22 Simeon Rice .60 .25
❑ 23 John Elway 8.00 3.60
❑ 24 Terrell Davis 8.00 3.60
❑ 25 Jeff Lewis .30 .14
❑ 26 Terry Glenn 1.25 .55
❑ 27 Curtis Martin 2.00 .90
❑ 28 Drew Bledsoe 4.00 1.80
❑ 29 Lawrence Phillips .30 .14
❑ 30 Isaac Bruce 1.25 .55
❑ 31 Eddie Kennison .60 .25
❑ 32 Keyshawn Johnson 1.25 .55
❑ 33 Stepfret Williams .30 .14
❑ 34 Emmitt Smith 6.00 2.70

Card		
35 Troy Aikman	4.00	1.80
36 Deion Sanders	1.25	.55
37 Joey Galloway	1.50	.70
38 Rick Mirer	.30	.14
39 Rickey Dudley	.60	.25
40 Jeff Hostetler	.30	.14
41 Junior Seau	.60	.25
42 Derrick Mayes	.60	.25
43 Brett Favre	8.00	3.60
44 Edgar Bennett	.60	.25
45 Barry Sanders	8.00	3.60
46 Herman Moore	1.25	.55
47 Kordell Stewart	1.50	.70
48 Jerome Bettis	1.25	.55
49 Eddie George	4.00	1.80
50 Steve McNair	2.00	.90
P80 Jerry Rice Promo Numbered SPX80 (1996 on copyright line)	3.00	1.35

1998 SPx

	MINT	NRMT
COMPLETE SET (50)	80.00	36.00

Card	MINT	NRMT
1 Jake Plummer	4.00	1.80
2 Byron Hanspard	.75	.35
3 Vinny Testaverde	.75	.35
4 Antowain Smith	1.50	.70
5 Kerry Collins	.75	.35
6 Rae Carruth	.75	.35
7 Darnell Autry	.50	.23
8 Rick Mirer	.50	.23
9 Jeff Blake	.75	.35
10 Carl Pickens	1.50	.70
11 Troy Aikman	4.00	1.80
12 Emmitt Smith	6.00	2.70
13 Deion Sanders	1.50	.70
14 John Elway	8.00	3.60
15 Terrell Davis	6.00	2.70
16 Herman Moore	1.50	.70
17 Barry Sanders	8.00	3.60
18 Brett Favre	8.00	3.60
19 Reggie White	1.50	.70
20 Marshall Faulk	1.50	.70
21 Mark Brunell	3.00	1.35
22 Elvis Grbac	.75	.35
23 Marcus Allen	1.50	.70
24 Karim Abdul-Jabbar	1.50	.70
25 Dan Marino	8.00	3.60
26 Cris Carter	1.50	.70
27 Drew Bledsoe	3.00	1.35
28 Curtis Martin	1.50	.70
29 Heath Shuler	.50	.23
30 Ike Hilliard	.75	.35
31 Keyshawn Johnson	1.50	.70
32 Jeff George	.75	.35
33 Napoleon Kaufman	1.50	.70
34 Darrell Russell	.50	.23
35 Ricky Watters	.75	.35
36 Kordell Stewart	1.50	.70
37 Jerome Bettis	1.50	.70
38 Junior Seau	.75	.35
39 Steve Young	2.50	1.10
40 Jerry Rice	4.00	1.80
41 Joey Galloway	1.50	.70
42 Chris Warren	.75	.35
43 Orlando Pace	.50	.23
44 Isaac Bruce	1.50	.70
45 Tony Banks	.75	.35
46 Trent Dilfer	1.50	.70
47 Warrick Dunn	1.50	.70
48 Steve McNair	1.50	.70
49 Eddie George	3.00	1.35
50 Terry Allen	1.50	.70

1998 SPx Finite

	MINT	NRMT
COMPLETE SET (370)	2500.00	1100.00
COMP.SERIES 1 (190)	1200.00	550.00
COMP.SERIES 2 (180)	1400.00	650.00
COMMON CARD (1-90)	.75	.35
COMMON PM (91-120)	1.50	.70
COMMON YM (121-150)	1.50	.70
COMMON PE (151-170)	2.50	1.10
COMMON HG (171-180)	6.00	2.70
COMMON ROOKIE (181-190)	15.00	6.75
COMMON CARD (191-280)	.40	.18
COMMON ROOKIE (191-280)	1.25	.55
COMMON ET (281-310)	1.00	.45
COMMON NS (311-340)	1.50	.70
COMMON SS (341-360)	1.50	.70
COMMON UV (361-370)	5.00	2.20

Card	MINT	NRMT
1 Jake Plummer	4.00	1.80
2 Eric Swann	.75	.35
3 Rob Moore	1.25	.55
4 Jamal Anderson	2.00	.90
5 Byron Hanspard	1.25	.55
6 Cornelius Bennett	.75	.35
7 Michael Jackson	.75	.35
8 Peter Boulware	.75	.35
9 Jermaine Lewis	1.25	.55
10 Antowain Smith	2.00	.90
11 Bruce Smith	1.25	.55
12 Bryce Paup	.75	.35
13 Rae Carruth	1.25	.55
14 Michael Bates	.75	.35
15 Fred Lane	1.25	.55
16 Darnell Autry	1.25	.55
17 Curtis Conway	1.25	.55
18 Erik Kramer	.75	.35
19 Corey Dillon	3.00	1.35
20 Darnay Scott	1.25	.55
21 Reinard Wilson	.75	.35
22 Troy Aikman	5.00	2.20
23 David LaFleur	.75	.35
24 Emmitt Smith	8.00	3.60
25 John Elway	10.00	4.50
26 John Mobley	.75	.35
27 Terrell Davis	8.00	3.60
28 Rod Smith	1.25	.55
29 Bryant Westbrook	.75	.35
30 Scott Mitchell	1.25	.55
31 Barry Sanders	10.00	4.50
32 Dorsey Levens	2.00	.90
33 Antonio Freeman	2.00	.90
34 Reggie White	2.00	.90
35 Marshall Faulk	2.00	.90
36 Marvin Harrison	1.25	.55
37 Ken Dilger	.75	.35
38 Mark Brunell	4.00	1.80
39 Keenan McCardell	1.25	.55
40 Renaldo Wynn	.75	.35
41 Marcus Allen	2.00	.90
42 Elvis Grbac	1.25	.55
43 Andre Rison	1.25	.55
44 Yatil Green	.75	.35
45 Zach Thomas	1.25	.55
46 Karim Abdul-Jabbar (UER Karim Abdul front and back)	2.00	.90
47 John Randle	1.25	.55
48 Brad Johnson	2.00	.90
49 Jake Reed	1.25	.55
50 Danny Wuerffel	1.25	.55
51 Andre Hastings	.75	.35
52 Drew Bledsoe	4.00	1.80
53 Terry Glenn	2.00	.90
54 Ty Law	.75	.35
55 Danny Kanell	1.25	.55
56 Tiki Barber	1.25	.55
57 Jessie Armstead	.75	.35
58 Glenn Foley	1.25	.55
59 James Farrior	.75	.35
60 Wayne Chrebet	2.00	.90
61 Tim Brown	2.00	.90
62 Napoleon Kaufman	2.00	.90
63 Darrell Russell	.75	.35
64 Bobby Hoying	1.25	.55
65 Irving Fryar	1.25	.55
66 Charlie Garner	.75	.35
67 Will Blackwell	.75	.35
68 Kordell Stewart	2.00	.90
69 Levon Kirkland	.75	.35
70 Tony Banks	1.25	.55
71 Ryan McNeil	.75	.35
72 Isaac Bruce	2.00	.90
73 Tony Martin	1.25	.55
74 Junior Seau	1.25	.55
75 Natrone Means	2.00	.90
76 Jerry Rice	5.00	2.20
77 Garrison Hearst	2.00	.90
78 Terrell Owens	2.00	.90
79 Warren Moon	2.00	.90
80 Joey Galloway	2.00	.90
81 Chad Brown	.75	.35
82 Warrick Dunn	2.00	.90
83 Mike Alstott	2.00	.90
84 Hardy Nickerson	.75	.35
85 Steve McNair	2.00	.90
86 Chris Sanders	.75	.35
87 Darryll Lewis	.75	.35
88 Gus Frerotte	.75	.35
89 Terry Allen	2.00	.90
90 Chris Dishman	.75	.35
91 Kordell Stewart PM	3.00	1.35
92 Jerry Rice PM	6.00	2.70
93 Michael Irvin PM	3.00	1.35
94 Brett Favre PM	12.00	5.50
95 Jeff George PM	2.50	1.10
96 Joey Galloway PM	3.00	1.35
97 John Elway PM	12.00	5.50
98 Troy Aikman PM	6.00	2.70
99 Steve Young PM	4.00	1.80
100 Andre Rison PM	2.50	1.10
101 Ben Coates PM	2.50	1.10
102 Robert Brooks PM	2.50	1.10
103 Dan Marino PM	12.00	5.50
104 Isaac Bruce PM	3.00	1.35
105 Junior Seau PM	2.50	1.10
106 Jake Plummer PM	6.00	2.70
107 Curtis Conway PM	2.50	1.10
108 Jeff Blake PM	2.50	1.10
109 Rod Smith PM	2.50	1.10
110 Barry Sanders PM	12.00	5.50
111 Deion Sanders PM	3.00	1.35
112 Drew Bledsoe PM	5.00	2.20
113 Emmitt Smith PM	10.00	4.50
114 Herman Moore PM	3.00	1.35
115 Dorsey Levens PM	3.00	1.35
116 Jimmy Smith PM	2.50	1.10
117 Tony Martin PM	1.50	.70
118 Carl Pickens PM	3.00	1.35
119 Keyshawn Johnson PM	3.00	1.35
120 Cris Carter PM	3.00	1.35
121 Warrick Dunn YM	4.00	1.80
122 Marshall Faulk YM	4.00	1.80
123 Trent Dilfer YM	4.00	1.80
124 Napoleon Kaufman YM	4.00	1.80
125 Corey Dillon YM	6.00	2.70
126 Darrell Russell YM	1.50	.70

❑ 127 Danny Kanell YM 2.50 1.10
❑ 128 Reidel Anthony YM 4.00 1.80
❑ 129 Steve McNair YM 4.00 1.80
❑ 130 Ike Hilliard YM 2.50 1.10
❑ 131 Tony Banks YM 2.50 1.10
❑ 132 Yatil Green YM 1.50 .70
❑ 133 J.J. Stokes YM 2.50 1.10
❑ 134 Fred Lane YM 2.50 1.10
❑ 135 Bryant Westbrook YM 1.50 .70
❑ 136 Jake Plummer YM 10.00 4.50
❑ 137 Byron Hanspard YM 2.50 1.10
❑ 138 Rae Carruth YM 2.50 1.10
❑ 139 Keyshawn Johnson YM 4.00 1.80
❑ 140 Jim Druckenmiller YM 2.50 1.10
❑ 141 Amani Toomer YM 2.50 1.10
❑ 142 Troy Davis YM 1.50 .70
❑ 143 Antowain Smith YM 4.00 1.80
❑ 144 Shawn Springs YM 1.50 .70
❑ 145 Rickey Dudley YM 1.50 .70
❑ 146 Terry Glenn YM 4.00 1.80
❑ 147 Johnnie Morton YM 2.50 1.10
❑ 148 David LaFleur YM 1.50 .70
❑ 149 Eddie Kennison YM 2.50 1.10
❑ 150 Bobby Hoying YM 2.50 1.10
❑ 151 Junior Seau PE 4.00 1.80
❑ 152 Shannon Sharpe PE 4.00 1.80
❑ 153 Bruce Smith PE 4.00 1.80
❑ 154 Brett Favre PE 20.00 9.00
❑ 155 Emmitt Smith PE 15.00 6.75
❑ 156 Keenan McCardell PE 2.50 1.10
❑ 157 Kordell Stewart PE 5.00 2.20
❑ 158 Troy Aikman PE 10.00 4.50
❑ 159 Steve Young PE 6.00 2.70
❑ 160 Tim Brown PE 5.00 2.20
❑ 161 Eddie George PE 8.00 3.60
❑ 162 Herman Moore PE 5.00 2.20
❑ 163 Dan Marino PE 20.00 9.00
❑ 164 Dorsey Levens PE 5.00 2.20
❑ 165 Jerry Rice PE 10.00 4.50
❑ 166 Warren Sapp PE 4.00 1.80
❑ 167 Robert Smith PE 5.00 2.20
❑ 168 Mark Brunell PE 8.00 3.60
❑ 169 Terrell Davis PE 15.00 6.75
❑ 170 Jerome Bettis PE 5.00 2.20
❑ 171 Dan Marino HG 30.00 13.50
❑ 172 Barry Sanders HG 30.00 13.50
❑ 173 Marcus Allen HG 5.00 2.20
❑ 174 Brett Favre HG 30.00 13.50
❑ 175 Warrick Dunn HG 5.00 2.20
❑ 176 Eddie George HG 12.00 5.50
❑ 177 John Elway HG 30.00 13.50
❑ 178 Troy Aikman HG 15.00 6.75
❑ 179 Cris Carter HG 5.00 2.20
❑ 180 Terrell Davis HG 25.00 11.00
❑ 181 Peyton Manning RC 300.00 135.00
❑ 182 Ryan Leaf RC 60.00 27.00
❑ 183 Andre Wadsworth RC 20.00 9.00
❑ 184 Charles Woodson RC 30.00 13.50
❑ 185 Curtis Enis RC 40.00 18.00
❑ 186 Grant Wistrom RC 15.00 6.75
❑ 187 Fred Taylor RC 135.00 60.00
❑ 188 Takeo Spikes RC 20.00 9.00
❑ 189 Kevin Dyson RC 30.00 13.50
❑ 190 Robert Edwards RC 25.00 11.00
❑ 191 Adrian Murrell .75 .35
❑ 192 Simeon Rice .75 .35
❑ 193 Frank Sanders .75 .35
❑ 194 Chris Chandler .75 .35
❑ 195 Terance Mathis .75 .35
❑ 196 Keith Brooking RC .75 .35
❑ 197 Jim Harbaugh .75 .35
❑ 198 Errict Rhett .75 .35
❑ 199 Pat Johnson RC 2.50 1.10
❑ 200 Rob Johnson .75 .35
❑ 201 Andre Reed .75 .35
❑ 202 Thurman Thomas 1.25 .55
❑ 203 Kerry Collins .75 .35
❑ 204 William Floyd .40 .18
❑ 205 Sean Gilbert .40 .18
❑ 206 Bobby Engram .75 .35
❑ 207 Edgar Bennett .75 .35
❑ 208 Walt Harris .75 .35
❑ 209 Carl Pickens 1.25 .55
❑ 210 Neil O'Donnell .75 .35
❑ 211 Tony McGee .40 .18
❑ 212 Deion Sanders 1.25 .55
❑ 213 Michael Irvin 1.25 .55
❑ 214 Greg Ellis RC 1.25 .55
❑ 215 Shannon Sharpe .75 .35
❑ 216 Neil Smith .75 .35
❑ 217 Marcus Nash RC 2.50 1.10
❑ 218 Brian Griese RC 80.00 36.00
❑ 219 Johnnie Morton .75 .35
❑ 220 Herman Moore 1.25 .55
❑ 221 Charlie Batch RC 50.00 22.00
❑ 222 Robert Brooks .75 .35
❑ 223 Mark Chmura .75 .35
❑ 224 Brett Favre 6.00 2.70
❑ 225 Jerome Pathon RC 2.50 1.10
❑ 226 Zack Crockett .40 .18
❑ 227 Dan Footman .40 .18
❑ 228 Jimmy Smith .75 .35
❑ 229 Bryce Paup .40 .18
❑ 230 James Stewart .75 .35
❑ 231 Derrick Thomas .75 .35
❑ 232 Derrick Alexander .75 .35
❑ 233 Tony Gonzalez .40 .18
❑ 234 Dan Marino 6.00 2.70
❑ 235 O.J. McDuffie .75 .35
❑ 236 Troy Drayton .40 .18
❑ 237 Cris Carter 1.25 .55
❑ 238 Robert Smith 1.25 .55
❑ 239 Randy Moss RC 150.00 70.00
❑ 240 Lamar Smith .75 .35
❑ 241 Sean Dawkins .40 .18
❑ 242 Alex Molden .40 .18
❑ 243 Ben Coates .75 .35
❑ 244 Ted Johnson .40 .18
❑ 245 Sedrick Shaw .40 .18
❑ 246 Ike Hilliard .75 .35
❑ 247 Jason Sehorn .75 .35
❑ 248 Michael Strahan .40 .18
❑ 249 Keyshawn Johnson 1.25 .55
❑ 250 Curtis Martin 1.25 .55
❑ 251 Jeff George .75 .35
❑ 252 Rickey Dudley .40 .18
❑ 253 James Jett .75 .35
❑ 254 Bobby Taylor .75 .35
❑ 255 Rodney Peete .75 .35
❑ 256 William Thomas .75 .35
❑ 257 Jerome Bettis 1.25 .55
❑ 258 Charles Johnson .40 .18
❑ 259 C.Fuamatu-Ma'afala RC 2.50 1.10
❑ 260 Eddie Kennison .75 .35
❑ 261 Az-Zahir Hakim RC 5.00 2.20
❑ 262 Robert Holcombe RC 2.50 1.10
❑ 263 Bryan Still .40 .18
❑ 264 Mikhael Ricks RC 2.50 1.10
❑ 265 Charlie Jones .40 .18
❑ 266 J.J. Stokes .75 .35
❑ 267 Marc Edwards .40 .18
❑ 268 Steve Young 2.00 .90
❑ 269 Ricky Watters .75 .35
❑ 270 Cortez Kennedy .40 .18
❑ 271 Shawn Springs .40 .18
❑ 272 Trent Dilfer 1.25 .55
❑ 273 Warren Sapp .75 .35
❑ 274 Reidel Anthony .75 .35
❑ 275 Yancey Thigpen .40 .18
❑ 276 Chris Sanders .40 .18
❑ 277 Eddie George 2.50 1.10
❑ 278 Leslie Shepherd .40 .18
❑ 279 Skip Hicks RC 2.50 1.10
❑ 280 Dana Stubblefield .40 .18
❑ 281 John Elway ET 8.00 3.60
❑ 282 Brett Favre ET 8.00 3.60
❑ 283 Junior Seau ET 1.50 .70
❑ 284 Barry Sanders ET 8.00 3.60
❑ 285 Jerry Rice ET 4.00 1.80
❑ 286 Antonio Freeman ET 1.50 .70
❑ 287 Peyton Manning ET 25.00 11.00
❑ 288 Warrick Dunn ET 1.50 .70
❑ 289 Steve Young ET 2.50 1.10
❑ 290 Dan Marino ET 8.00 3.60
❑ 291 Jerome Bettis ET 1.50 .70
❑ 292 Ryan Leaf ET 8.00 3.60
❑ 293 Deion Sanders ET 1.50 .70
❑ 294 Eddie George ET 3.00 1.35
❑ 295 Joey Galloway ET 1.50 .70
❑ 296 Troy Aikman ET 4.00 1.80
❑ 297 Andre Wadsworth ET 1.00 .45
❑ 298 Terrell Davis ET 6.00 2.70
❑ 299 Steve McNair ET 1.50 .70
❑ 300 Jake Plummer ET 3.00 1.35
❑ 301 Emmitt Smith ET 6.00 2.70
❑ 302 Isaac Bruce ET 1.50 .70
❑ 303 Kordell Stewart ET 1.50 .70
❑ 304 Dorsey Levens ET 1.50 .70
❑ 305 Antowain Smith ET 1.50 .70
❑ 306 Drew Bledsoe ET 3.00 1.35
❑ 307 Marshall Faulk ET 1.50 .70
❑ 308 Herman Moore ET 1.50 .70
❑ 309 Mark Brunell ET 3.00 1.35
❑ 310 Charles Woodson ET 6.00 2.70
❑ 311 Peyton Manning NS 30.00 13.50
❑ 312 Curtis Enis NS 6.00 2.70
❑ 313 Terry Fair NS RC 5.00 2.20
❑ 314 Andre Wadsworth NS 2.50 1.10
❑ 315 A.Simmons NS RC 2.50 1.10
❑ 316 Jacquez Green NS RC 12.00 5.50
❑ 317 Takeo Spikes NS 2.50 1.10
❑ 318 Vonnie Holliday NS RC 8.00 3.60
❑ 319 Kyle Turley NS RC 2.50 1.10
❑ 320 Keith Brooking NS 2.50 1.10
❑ 321 Randy Moss NS 60.00 27.00
❑ 322 Shaun Williams NS RC 2.50 1.10
❑ 323 Greg Ellis NS 1.50 .70
❑ 324 Mikhael Ricks NS 2.50 1.10
❑ 325 Charles Woodson NS 8.00 3.60
❑ 326 Corey Chavous NS RC 2.50 1.10
❑ 327 S.Alexander NS RC 8.00 3.60
❑ 328 Marcus Nash NS 5.00 2.20
❑ 329 Tra Thomas NS RC 2.50 1.10
❑ 330 Duane Starks NS RC 5.00 2.20
❑ 331 John Avery NS RC 5.00 2.20
❑ 332 Kevin Dyson NS 8.00 3.60
❑ 333 Fred Taylor NS 12.00 5.50
❑ 334 Grant Wistrom NS 1.50 .70
❑ 335 Ryan Leaf NS 12.00 5.50
❑ 336 Robert Edwards NS 5.00 2.20
❑ 337 Jason Peter NS RC 2.50 1.10
❑ 338 Brian Griese NS 30.00 13.50
❑ 339 Charlie Batch NS 25.00 11.00
❑ 340 Pat Johnson NS 2.50 1.10
❑ 341 John Elway SS 15.00 6.75
❑ 342 Curtis Enis SS 6.00 2.70
❑ 343 Antonio Freeman SS 4.00 1.80
❑ 344 Mark Brunell SS 6.00 2.70
❑ 345 Robert Edwards SS 5.00 2.20
❑ 346 Ryan Leaf SS 12.00 5.50
❑ 347 Steve Young SS 5.00 2.20
❑ 348 Jerome Bettis SS 4.00 1.80
❑ 349 Antowain Smith SS 4.00 1.80
❑ 350 Tim Brown SS 4.00 1.80
❑ 351 Peyton Manning SS 30.00 13.50
❑ 352 Troy Aikman SS 8.00 3.60
❑ 353 Natrone Means SS 4.00 1.80
❑ 354 Dan Marino SS 15.00 6.75
❑ 355 Junior Seau SS 1.50 .70
❑ 356 Brad Johnson SS 4.00 1.80
❑ 357 Jerry Rice SS 8.00 3.60
❑ 358 Drew Bledsoe SS 6.00 2.70
❑ 359 Fred Taylor SS 12.00 5.50
❑ 360 Emmitt Smith SS 12.00 5.50
❑ 361 Terrell Davis UV 20.00 9.00
❑ 362 Kordell Stewart UV 5.00 2.20
❑ 363 Barry Sanders UV 25.00 11.00
❑ 364 Jake Plummer UV 10.00 4.50
❑ 365 Brett Favre UV 25.00 11.00
❑ 366 Curtis Enis UV 10.00 4.50
❑ 367 Eddie George UV 10.00 4.50
❑ 368 Napoleon Kaufman UV 8.00 3.60
❑ 369 Randy Moss UV 50.00 22.00
❑ 370 Warrick Dunn UV 8.00 3.60
❑ S8 Troy Aikman SAMPLE 1.00 .45
❑ S234 Dan Marino Sample 2.00 .90

1999 SPx

	MINT	NRMT
COMPLETE SET (135)	3500.00	1600.00
COMP.SET w/o SP's (90)	25.00	11.00

*HAND NUMBERED RCs: .5X TO .8X

❑ 1 Jake Plummer 2.50 1.10
❑ 2 Adrian Murrell .60 .25
❑ 3 Frank Sanders .60 .25
❑ 4 Jamal Anderson 1.25 .55

❑ 5 Chris Chandler .60 .25
❑ 6 Terance Mathis .60 .25
❑ 7 Tony Banks .60 .25
❑ 8 Priest Holmes 1.25 .55
❑ 9 Jermaine Lewis .60 .25
❑ 10 Antowain Smith 1.25 .55
❑ 11 Doug Flutie 1.50 .70
❑ 12 Eric Moulds 1.25 .55
❑ 13 Tim Biakabutuka .60 .25
❑ 14 Steve Beuerlein .60 .25
❑ 15 Muhsin Muhammad .60 .25
❑ 16 Bobby Engram .60 .25
❑ 17 Curtis Conway .60 .25
❑ 18 Curtis Enis 1.25 .55
❑ 19 Corey Dillon 1.25 .55
❑ 20 Jeff Blake .60 .25
❑ 21 Carl Pickens .60 .25
❑ 22 Ty Detmer .60 .25
❑ 23 Terry Kirby .30 .14
❑ 24 Leslie Shepherd .30 .14
❑ 25 Troy Aikman 3.00 1.35
❑ 26 Emmitt Smith 3.00 1.35
❑ 27 Deion Sanders 1.25 .55
❑ 28 Terrell Davis 3.00 1.35
❑ 29 Rod Smith .60 .25
❑ 30 Bubby Brister .60 .25
❑ 31 Barry Sanders 5.00 2.20
❑ 32 Herman Moore 1.25 .55
❑ 33 Charlie Batch 2.50 1.10
❑ 34 Brett Favre 5.00 2.20
❑ 35 Antonio Freeman 1.25 .55
❑ 36 Dorsey Levens 1.25 .55
❑ 37 Peyton Manning 5.00 2.20
❑ 38 Marvin Harrison 1.25 .55
❑ 39 Jerome Pathon .30 .14
❑ 40 Mark Brunell 2.00 .90
❑ 41 Jimmy Smith .60 .25
❑ 42 Fred Taylor 3.00 1.35
❑ 43 Elvis Grbac .60 .25
❑ 44 Andre Rison .60 .25
❑ 45 Warren Moon 1.25 .55
❑ 46 Dan Marino 5.00 2.20
❑ 47 Karim Abdul-Jabbar .60 .25
❑ 48 O.J. McDuffie .60 .25
❑ 49 Randall Cunningham 1.25 .55
❑ 50 Robert Smith 1.25 .55
❑ 51 Randy Moss 5.00 2.20
❑ 52 Drew Bledsoe 2.00 .90
❑ 53 Terry Glenn 1.25 .55
❑ 54 Tony Simmons .30 .14
❑ 55 Danny Wuerffel .30 .14
❑ 56 Cam Cleeland .30 .14
❑ 57 Kerry Collins .60 .25
❑ 58 Gary Brown .30 .14
❑ 59 Ike Hilliard .30 .14
❑ 60 Vinny Testaverde .60 .25
❑ 61 Curtis Martin 1.25 .55
❑ 62 Keyshawn Johnson 1.25 .55
❑ 63 Rich Gannon .60 .25
❑ 64 Napoleon Kaufman 1.25 .55
❑ 65 Tim Brown 1.25 .55
❑ 66 Duce Staley 1.25 .55
❑ 67 Doug Pederson .30 .14
❑ 68 Charles Johnson .30 .14
❑ 69 Kordell Stewart 1.25 .55
❑ 70 Jerome Bettis 1.25 .55
❑ 71 Trent Green .60 .25
❑ 72 Marshall Faulk 1.25 .55
❑ 73 Ryan Leaf 1.25 .55
❑ 74 Natrone Means .60 .25
❑ 75 Jim Harbaugh .60 .25
❑ 76 Steve Young 2.00 .90
❑ 77 Garrison Hearst .60 .25
❑ 78 Jerry Rice 3.00 1.35
❑ 79 Terrell Owens 1.25 .55
❑ 80 Ricky Watters .60 .25
❑ 81 Joey Galloway 1.25 .55
❑ 82 Jon Kitna 1.25 .55
❑ 83 Warrick Dunn 1.25 .55
❑ 84 Trent Dilfer .60 .25
❑ 85 Mike Alstott 1.25 .55
❑ 86 Steve McNair 1.25 .55
❑ 87 Eddie George 1.50 .70
❑ 88 Yancey Thigpen .30 .14
❑ 89 Skip Hicks 1.25 .55
❑ 90 Michael Westbrook .60 .25
❑ 91 Amos Zereoue RC 12.00 5.50
❑ 92 Chris Claiborne AUTO RC 20.00 9.00
❑ 93 Scott Covington RC 12.00 5.50
❑ 94 Jeff Paulk RC 12.00 5.50
❑ 95 Brandon Stokley AUTO RC 30.00 13.50
❑ 96 Antoine Winfield RC 12.00 5.50
❑ 97 Reginald Kelly RC 12.00 5.50
❑ 98 J.Fazande AUTO RC 25.00 11.00
❑ 99 Andy Katzenmoyer RC 12.00 5.50
❑ 100 Craig Yeast RC 12.00 5.50
❑ 101 Joe Montgomery RC 15.00 6.75
❑ 102 Darrin Chiaverini RC 15.00 6.75
❑ 103 Travis McGriff RC 12.00 5.50
❑ 104 Jevon Kearse RC 40.00 18.00
❑ 105 J.Makovicka AUTO RC 20.00 9.00
❑ 106 Aaron Brooks RC 100.00 45.00
❑ 107 Chris McAlister RC 15.00 6.75
❑ 108 Jim Kleinsasser RC 12.00 5.50
❑ 109 Ebenezer Ekuban RC 15.00 6.75
❑ 110 Karsten Bailey RC 12.00 5.50
❑ 111 Sedrick Irvin AUTO RC 20.00 9.00
❑ 112 D.Bates AUTO RC 20.00 9.00
❑ 113 Joe Germaine AUTO RC 35.00 16.00
❑ 114 Cecil Collins AUTO RC 20.00 9.00
❑ 115 Mike Cloud RC 15.00 6.75
❑ 116 James Johnson RC 15.00 6.75
❑ 117 Champ Bailey AUTO RC 35.00 16.00
❑ 118 Rob Konrad RC 12.00 5.50
❑ 119 Peerless Price AUTO RC 40.00 18.00
❑ 120 Kevin Faulk AUTO RC 30.00 13.50
❑ 121 Dameane Douglas RC 12.00 5.50
❑ 122 Kevin Johnson AUTO RC 40.00 18.00
❑ 123 Troy Edwards AUTO RC 30.00 13.50
❑ 124 E.James AUTO RC 350.00 160.00
❑ 125 David Boston AUTO RC 60.00 27.00
❑ 126 Michael Bishop AUTO RC 60.00 27.00
❑ 127 S.King AUTO SP RC 350.00 160.00
❑ 127X Shaun King EXCH 50.00 22.00
❑ 128 Brock Huard AUTO RC 50.00 22.00
❑ 129 Torry Holt AUTO RC 80.00 36.00
❑ 130 C.McNown AU/500 RC 200.00 90.00
❑ 131 Tim Couch AU/500 RC 400.00 180.00
❑ 132 D.McNabb AUTO RC 200.00 90.00
❑ 133 Akili Smith AU/500 RC 200.00 90.00
❑ 134 D.Culpepper AU/500 RC 800.00 350.00
❑ 135 R.Williams AU/500 RC 500.00 220.00
❑ S8 Troy Aikman Sample 2.00 .90

2000 SPx

	MINT	NRMT
❑ 1 Jake Plummer	.75	.35
❑ 2 David Boston	.75	.35
❑ 3 Frank Sanders	.50	.23
❑ 4 Chris Chandler	.50	.23
❑ 5 Jamal Anderson	.75	.35
❑ 6 Shawn Jefferson	.25	.11
❑ 7 Qadry Ismail	.50	.23
❑ 8 Tony Banks	.50	.23
❑ 9 Shannon Sharpe	.50	.23
❑ 10 Rob Johnson	.50	.23
❑ 11 Eric Moulds	.75	.35
❑ 12 Muhsin Muhammad	.50	.23
❑ 13 Steve Beuerlein	.25	.11
❑ 14 Cade McNown	.75	.35
❑ 15 Marcus Robinson	.75	.35
❑ 16 Akili Smith	.75	.35
❑ 17 Corey Dillon	.75	.35
❑ 18 Darnay Scott	.50	.23
❑ 19 Tim Couch	1.50	.70
❑ 20 Kevin Johnson	.75	.35
❑ 21 Errict Rhett	.25	.11
❑ 22 Troy Aikman	2.00	.90
❑ 23 Emmitt Smith	2.00	.90
❑ 24 Joey Galloway	.75	.35
❑ 25 Terrell Davis	2.00	.90
❑ 26 Olandis Gary	.75	.35
❑ 27 Brian Griese	1.00	.45
❑ 28 Charlie Batch	.75	.35
❑ 29 Germane Crowell	.50	.23
❑ 30 James Stewart	.50	.23
❑ 31 Brett Favre	3.00	1.35
❑ 32 Antonio Freeman	.75	.35
❑ 33 Dorsey Levens	.50	.23
❑ 34 Peyton Manning	2.50	1.10
❑ 35 Edgerrin James	2.50	1.10
❑ 36 Marvin Harrison	.75	.35
❑ 37 Mark Brunell	1.25	.55
❑ 38 Fred Taylor	1.00	.45
❑ 39 Jimmy Smith	.50	.23
❑ 40 Keenan McCardell	.50	.23
❑ 41 Elvis Grbac	.50	.23
❑ 42 Tony Gonzalez	.50	.23
❑ 43 Tony Martin	.50	.23
❑ 44 Jay Fiedler	.75	.35
❑ 45 Damon Huard	.75	.35
❑ 46 Randy Moss	2.50	1.10
❑ 47 Robert Smith	.75	.35
❑ 48 Cris Carter	.75	.35
❑ 49 Daunte Culpepper	1.50	.70
❑ 50 Drew Bledsoe	1.25	.55
❑ 51 Terry Glenn	.50	.23
❑ 52 Ricky Williams	2.00	.90
❑ 53 Jeff Blake	.50	.23
❑ 54 Keith Poole	.25	.11
❑ 55 Kerry Collins	.50	.23
❑ 56 Amani Toomer	.50	.23
❑ 57 Ike Hilliard	.50	.23
❑ 58 Ray Lucas	.75	.35
❑ 59 Curtis Martin	.75	.35
❑ 60 Vinny Testaverde	.50	.23
❑ 61 Tim Brown	.75	.35
❑ 62 Rich Gannon	.50	.23
❑ 63 Tyrone Wheatley	.50	.23
❑ 64 Napoleon Kaufman	.50	.23
❑ 65 Duce Staley	.75	.35
❑ 66 Donovan McNabb	1.25	.55
❑ 67 Troy Edwards	.50	.23
❑ 68 Jerome Bettis	.75	.35
❑ 69 Kordell Stewart	.75	.35
❑ 70 Marshall Faulk	1.00	.45
❑ 71 Kurt Warner	2.50	1.10
❑ 72 Isaac Bruce	.75	.35
❑ 73 Torry Holt	.75	.35
❑ 74 Ryan Leaf	.75	.35
❑ 75 Jim Harbaugh	.50	.23
❑ 76 Jerry Rice	2.00	.90
❑ 77 Terrell Owens	.75	.35
❑ 78 Jeff Garcia	.75	.35
❑ 79 Ricky Watters	.50	.23
❑ 80 Jon Kitna	.75	.35
❑ 81 Derrick Mayes	.50	.23
❑ 82 Shaun King	1.25	.55
❑ 83 Mike Alstott	.75	.35
❑ 84 Keyshawn Johnson	.75	.35
❑ 85 Eddie George	1.00	.45

	Card	Mint	NrMt
❑	86 Steve McNair	.75	.35
❑	87 Jevon Kearse	.75	.35
❑	88 Brad Johnson	.75	.35
❑	89 Stephen Davis	.75	.35
❑	90 Michael Westbrook	.50	.23
❑	91 Anthony Lucas RC	8.00	3.60
❑	92 Avion Black RC	12.00	5.50
❑	93 Corey Moore RC	12.00	5.50
❑	94 Chris Cole RC	12.00	5.50
❑	95 Chris Hovan RC	12.00	5.50
❑	96 Dante Hall RC	12.00	5.50
❑	97 Darrell Jackson RC	25.00	11.00
❑	98 Deltha O'Neal RC	12.00	5.50
❑	99 Doug Chapman RC	30.00	13.50
❑	100 Doug Johnson RC	15.00	6.75
❑	101 Erron Kinney RC	15.00	6.75
❑	102 Frank Moreau RC	15.00	6.75
❑	103 Patrick Pass RC	12.00	5.50
❑	104 Gari Scott RC	12.00	5.50
❑	105 Giovanni Carmazzi RC	20.00	9.00
❑	106 JaJuan Dawson RC	15.00	6.75
❑	107 James Williams RC	12.00	5.50
❑	108 Jarious Jackson RC	15.00	6.75
❑	109 John Abraham RC	12.00	5.50
❑	110 Keith Bulluck RC	12.00	5.50
❑	111 Jonas Lewis RC	12.00	5.50
❑	112 Mike Green RC	12.00	5.50
❑	113 Ronney Jenkins RC	12.00	5.50
❑	114 Michael Wiley RC	15.00	6.75
❑	115 Mike Anderson RC	150.00	70.00
❑	116 Mareno Philyaw RC	8.00	3.60
❑	117 Muneer Moore RC	8.00	3.60
❑	118 Paul Smith RC	12.00	5.50
❑	119 Raynoch Thompson RC	12.00	5.50
❑	120 Rob Morris RC	12.00	5.50
❑	121 Ron Dixon RC	20.00	9.00
❑	122 Rondell Mealey RC	8.00	3.60
❑	123 Sebastian Janikowski RC	15.00	6.75
❑	124 Shaun Ellis RC	12.00	5.50
❑	125 Charles Lee RC	12.00	5.50
❑	126 Shyrone Stith RC	12.00	5.50
❑	127 Thomas Hamner RC	12.00	5.50
❑	128 Tim Rattay RC	25.00	11.00
❑	129 Todd Husak RC	15.00	6.75
❑	130 Tom Brady RC	15.00	6.75
❑	131 Trevor Gaylor RC	12.00	5.50
❑	132 Windrell Hayes RC	12.00	5.50
❑	133 Anthony Becht RC	25.00	11.00
❑	134 Brian Urlacher RC	100.00	45.00
❑	135 Bubba Franks RC	30.00	13.50
❑	136 C.Pennington RC EXCH	150.00	70.00
❑	137 Chris Redman RC	90.00	40.00
❑	138 Corey Simon RC	40.00	18.00
❑	139 Curtis Keaton RC	25.00	11.00
❑	140 Danny Farmer RC	30.00	13.50
❑	141 Dennis Northcutt RC	40.00	18.00
❑	142 Dez White RC	25.00	11.00
❑	143 J.R. Redmond RC	40.00	18.00
❑	144 Jamal Lewis RC	200.00	90.00
❑	145 Jerry Porter RC	30.00	13.50
❑	146 Joe Hamilton RC	40.00	18.00
❑	147 Lavernues Coles RC	40.00	18.00
❑	148 R.Jay Soward RC	30.00	13.50
❑	149 R.Droughns RC EXCH	30.00	13.50
❑	150 Ron Dayne RC	120.00	55.00
❑	151 Ron Dugans RC	25.00	11.00
❑	152 Shaun Alexander RC	100.00	45.00
❑	153 Sylvester Morris RC	60.00	27.00
❑	154 Tee Martin RC	60.00	27.00
❑	155 Thomas Jones RC EXCH	60.00	27.00
❑	156 Todd Pinkston RC	30.00	13.50
❑	157 Travis Prentice RC	50.00	22.00
❑	158 Travis Taylor RC EXCH	60.00	27.00
❑	159 Trung Canidate RC	30.00	13.50
❑	160 Courtney Brown RC/500	120.00	55.00
❑	161 Pe Warrick RC/500	350.00	160.00
❑	162 Plaxico Burress RC/500	225.00	100.00

1991 Stadium Club

	MINT	NRMT
COMPLETE SET (500)	60.00	27.00

	Card	Mint	NrMt
❑	1 Pepper Johnson	.20	.09
❑	2 Emmitt Smith	6.00	2.70
❑	3 Deion Sanders	1.50	.70

	Card	Mint	NrMt
❑	4 Andre Collins	.20	.09
❑	5 Eric Metcalf	.40	.18
❑	6 Richard Dent	.40	.18
❑	7 Eric Martin	.20	.09
❑	8 Marcus Allen	.75	.35
❑	9 Gary Anderson K	.20	.09
❑	10 Joey Browner	.20	.09
❑	11 Lorenzo White	.20	.09
❑	12 Bruce Smith	.75	.35
❑	13 Mark Boyer	.20	.09
❑	14 Mike Piel	.20	.09
❑	15 Albert Bentley	.20	.09
❑	16 Bennie Blades	.20	.09
❑	17 Jason Staurovsky	.20	.09
❑	18 Anthony Toney	.20	.09
❑	19 Dave Krieg	.40	.18
❑	20 Harvey Williams RC	.75	.35
❑	21 Bubba Paris	.20	.09
❑	22 Tim McGee	.20	.09
❑	23 Brian Noble	.20	.09
❑	24 Vinny Testaverde	.40	.18
❑	25 Doug Widell	.20	.09
❑	26 John Jackson RC	.20	.09
❑	27 Marion Butts	.40	.18
❑	28 Deron Cherry	.20	.09
❑	29 Don Warren	.20	.09
❑	30 Rod Woodson	.75	.35
❑	31 Mike Baab	.20	.09
❑	32 Greg Jackson RC	.20	.09
❑	33 Jerry Robinson	.20	.09
❑	34 Dalton Hilliard	.20	.09
❑	35 Brian Jordan	.40	.18
❑	36 James Thornton UER (Misspelled Thorton on card back)	.20	.09
❑	37 Michael Irvin	.75	.35
❑	38 Billy Joe Tolliver	.20	.09
❑	39 Jeff Herrod	.20	.09
❑	40 Scott Norwood	.20	.09
❑	41 Ferrell Edmunds	.20	.09
❑	42 Andre Waters	.20	.09
❑	43 Kevin Glover	.20	.09
❑	44 Ray Berry	.20	.09
❑	45 Timm Rosenbach	.20	.09
❑	46 Reuben Davis	.20	.09
❑	47 Charles Wilson	.20	.09
❑	48 Todd Marinovich RC	.20	.09
❑	49 Harris Barton	.20	.09
❑	50 Jim Breech	.20	.09
❑	51 Ron Holmes	.20	.09
❑	52 Chris Singleton	.20	.09
❑	53 Pat Leahy	.20	.09
❑	54 Tom Newberry	.20	.09
❑	55 Greg Montgomery	.20	.09
❑	56 Robert Blackmon	.20	.09
❑	57 Jay Hilgenberg	.20	.09
❑	58 Rodney Hampton	.75	.35
❑	59 Brett Perriman	.75	.35
❑	60 Ricky Watters RC	6.00	2.70
❑	61 Howie Long	.40	.18
❑	62 Frank Cornish	.20	.09
❑	63 Chris Miller	.40	.18
❑	64 Keith Taylor	.20	.09
❑	65 Tony Paige	.20	.09
❑	66 Gary Zimmerman	.20	.09
❑	67 Mark Royals RC	.20	.09
❑	68 Ernie Jones	.20	.09
❑	69 David Grant	.20	.09
❑	70 Shane Conlan	.20	.09
❑	71 Jerry Rice	3.00	1.35
❑	72 Christian Okoye	.20	.09
❑	73 Eddie Murray	.20	.09
❑	74 Reggie White	.75	.35
❑	75 Jeff Graham RC	1.00	.45
❑	76 Mark Jackson	.20	.09
❑	77 David Grayson	.20	.09
❑	78 Dan Stryzinski	.20	.09
❑	79 Sterling Sharpe	.75	.35
❑	80 Cleveland Gary	.20	.09
❑	81 Johnny Meads	.20	.09
❑	82 Howard Cross	.20	.09
❑	83 Ken O'Brien	.20	.09
❑	84 Brian Blades	.40	.18
❑	85 Ethan Horton	.20	.09
❑	86 Bruce Armstrong	.20	.09
❑	87 James Washington RC	.20	.09
❑	88 Eugene Daniel	.20	.09
❑	89 James Lofton	.40	.18
❑	90 Louis Oliver	.20	.09
❑	91 Boomer Esiason	.40	.18
❑	92 Seth Joyner	.40	.18
❑	93 Mark Carrier WR	.75	.35
❑	94 Brett Favre RC UER (Favre misspelled as Farve)	50.00	22.00
❑	95 Lee Williams	.20	.09
❑	96 Neal Anderson	.40	.18
❑	97 Brent Jones	.75	.35
❑	98 John Alt	.20	.09
❑	99 Rodney Peete	.40	.18
❑	100 Steve Broussard	.20	.09
❑	101 Cedric Mack	.20	.09
❑	102 Pat Swilling	.40	.18
❑	103 Stan Humphries	.75	.35
❑	104 Darrell Thompson	.20	.09
❑	105 Reggie Langhorne	.20	.09
❑	106 Kenny Davidson	.20	.09
❑	107 Jim Everett	.40	.18
❑	108 Keith Millard	.20	.09
❑	109 Garry Lewis	.20	.09
❑	110 Jeff Hostetler	.40	.18
❑	111 Lamar Lathon	.20	.09
❑	112 Johnny Bailey	.20	.09
❑	113 Cornelius Bennett	.40	.18
❑	114 Travis McNeal	.20	.09
❑	115 Jeff Lageman	.20	.09
❑	116 Nick Bell RC	.20	.09
❑	117 Calvin Williams	.40	.18
❑	118 Shawn Lee RC	.20	.09
❑	119 Anthony Munoz	.40	.18
❑	120 Jay Novacek	.75	.35
❑	121 Kevin Fagan	.20	.09
❑	122 Leo Goeas	.20	.09
❑	123 Vance Johnson	.20	.09
❑	124 Brent Williams	.20	.09
❑	125 Clarence Verdin	.20	.09
❑	126 Luis Sharpe	.20	.09
❑	127 Darrell Green	.20	.09
❑	128 Barry Word	.20	.09
❑	129 Steve Walsh	.20	.09
❑	130 Bryan Hinkle	.20	.09
❑	131 Ed West	.20	.09
❑	132 Jeff Campbell	.20	.09
❑	133 Dennis Byrd	.20	.09
❑	134 Nate Odomes	.20	.09
❑	135 Trace Armstrong	.20	.09
❑	136 Jarvis Williams	.20	.09
❑	137 Warren Moon	.75	.35
❑	138 Eric Moten RC	.20	.09
❑	139 Tony Woods	.20	.09
❑	140 Phil Simms	.40	.18
❑	141 Ricky Reynolds	.20	.09
❑	142 Frank Stams	.20	.09
❑	143 Kevin Mack	.20	.09
❑	144 Wade Wilson	.40	.18
❑	145 Shawn Collins	.20	.09
❑	146 Roger Craig	.40	.18
❑	147 Jeff Feagles RC	.20	.09
❑	148 Norm Johnson	.20	.09
❑	149 Terance Mathis	.40	.18
❑	150 Reggie Cobb	.20	.09
❑	151 Chip Banks	.20	.09
❑	152 Darryl Pollard	.20	.09

❑ 153 Karl Mecklenburg .20 .09
❑ 154 Ricky Proehl .20 .09
❑ 155 Pete Stoyanovich .20 .09
❑ 156 John Stephens .20 .09
❑ 157 Ron Morris .20 .09
❑ 158 Steve DeBerg .20 .09
❑ 159 Mike Munchak .20 .09
❑ 160 Brett Maxie .20 .09
❑ 161 Don Beebe .20 .09
❑ 162 Martin Mayhew .20 .09
❑ 163 Merril Hoge .20 .09
❑ 164 Kelvin Pritchett RC .40 .18
❑ 165 Jim Jeffcoat .20 .09
❑ 166 Myron Guyton .20 .09
❑ 167 Ickey Woods .20 .09
❑ 168 Andre Ware .40 .18
❑ 169 Gary Plummer .20 .09
❑ 170 Henry Ellard .40 .18
❑ 171 Scott Davis .20 .09
❑ 172 Randall McDaniel .20 .09
❑ 173 Randal Hill RC .40 .18
❑ 174 Anthony Bell .20 .09
❑ 175 Gary Anderson RB .20 .09
❑ 176 Byron Evans .20 .09
❑ 177 Tony Mandarich .20 .09
❑ 178 Jeff George 1.25 .55
❑ 179 Art Monk .40 .18
❑ 180 Mike Kenn .20 .09
❑ 181 Sean Landeta .20 .09
❑ 182 Shaun Gayle .20 .09
❑ 183 Michael Carter .20 .09
❑ 184 Robb Thomas .20 .09
❑ 185 Richmond Webb .20 .09
❑ 186 Carnell Lake .20 .09
❑ 187 Rueben Mayes .20 .09
❑ 188 Issiac Holt .20 .09
❑ 189 Leon Seals .20 .09
❑ 190 Al Smith .20 .09
❑ 191 Steve Atwater .20 .09
❑ 192 Greg McMurtry .20 .09
❑ 193 Al Toon .40 .18
❑ 194 Cortez Kennedy .75 .35
❑ 195 Gill Byrd .20 .09
❑ 196 Carl Zander .20 .09
❑ 197 Robert Brown .20 .09
❑ 198 Buford McGee .20 .09
❑ 199 Mervyn Fernandez .20 .09
❑ 200 Mike Dumas RC .20 .09
❑ 201 Rob Burnett RC .40 .18
❑ 202 Brian Mitchell .40 .18
❑ 203 Randall Cunningham .75 .35
❑ 204 Sammie Smith .20 .09
❑ 205 Ken Clarke .20 .09
❑ 206 Floyd Dixon .20 .09
❑ 207 Ken Norton .75 .35
❑ 208 Tony Siragusa RC .40 .18
❑ 209 Louis Lipps .20 .09
❑ 210 Chris Martin .20 .09
❑ 211 Jamie Mueller .20 .09
❑ 212 Dave Waymer .20 .09
❑ 213 Donnell Woolford .20 .09
❑ 214 Paul Gruber .20 .09
❑ 215 Ken Harvey .40 .18
❑ 216 Henry Jones RC .40 .18
❑ 217 Tommy Barnhardt RC .20 .09
❑ 218 Arthur Cox .20 .09
❑ 219 Pat Terrell .20 .09
❑ 220 Curtis Duncan .20 .09
❑ 221 Jeff Jaeger .20 .09
❑ 222 Scott Stephen RC .20 .09
❑ 223 Rob Moore 1.25 .55
❑ 224 Chris Hinton .20 .09
❑ 225 Marv Cook .20 .09
❑ 226 Patrick Hunter RC .20 .09
❑ 227 Earnest Byner .20 .09
❑ 228 Troy Aikman 3.00 1.35
❑ 229 Kevin Walker RC .20 .09
❑ 230 Keith Jackson .40 .18
❑ 231 Russell Maryland RC .75 .35
(UER, Card back says
Dallas Cowboy)
❑ 232 Charles Haley .40 .18
❑ 233 Nick Lowery .20 .09
❑ 234 Erik Howard .20 .09
❑ 235 Leonard Smith .20 .09
❑ 236 Tim Irwin .20 .09
❑ 237 Simon Fletcher .20 .09
❑ 238 Thomas Everett .20 .09
❑ 239 Reggie Roby .20 .09
❑ 240 Leroy Hoard .40 .18
❑ 241 Wayne Haddix .20 .09
❑ 242 Gary Clark .75 .35
❑ 243 Eric Andolsek .20 .09
❑ 244 Jim Wahler RC .20 .09
❑ 245 Vaughan Johnson .20 .09
❑ 246 Kevin Butler .20 .09
❑ 247 Steve Tasker .40 .18
❑ 248 LeRoy Butler .40 .18
❑ 249 Darion Conner .20 .09
❑ 250 Eric Turner RC .40 .18
❑ 251 Kevin Ross .20 .09
❑ 252 Stephen Baker .20 .09
❑ 253 Harold Green .40 .18
❑ 254 Rohn Stark .20 .09
❑ 255 Joe Nash .20 .09
❑ 256 Jesse Sapolu .20 .09
❑ 257 Willie Gault .40 .18
❑ 258 Jerome Brown .20 .09
❑ 259 Ken Willis .20 .09
❑ 260 Courtney Hall .20 .09
❑ 261 Hart Lee Dykes .20 .09
❑ 262 William Fuller .40 .18
❑ 263 Stan Thomas .20 .09
❑ 264 Dan Marino 5.00 2.20
❑ 265 Ron Cox .20 .09
❑ 266 Eric Green .20 .09
❑ 267 Anthony Carter .40 .18
❑ 268 Jerry Ball .20 .09
❑ 269 Ron Hall .20 .09
❑ 270 Dennis Smith .20 .09
❑ 271 Eric Hill .20 .09
❑ 272 Dan McGwire RC .20 .09
❑ 273 Lewis Billups UER .20 .09
Louis on back
❑ 274 Rickey Jackson .20 .09
❑ 275 Jim Sweeney .20 .09
❑ 276 Pat Beach .20 .09
❑ 277 Kevin Porter .20 .09
❑ 278 Mike Sherrard .20 .09
❑ 279 Andy Heck .20 .09
❑ 280 Ron Brown .20 .09
❑ 281 Lawrence Taylor .75 .35
❑ 282 Anthony Pleasant .20 .09
❑ 283 Wes Hopkins .20 .09
❑ 284 Jim Lachey .20 .09
❑ 285 Tim Harris .20 .09
❑ 286 Tory Epps .20 .09
❑ 287 Wendell Davis .20 .09
❑ 288 Bubba McDowell .20 .09
❑ 289 Bubby Brister .20 .09
❑ 290 Chris Zorich RC .75 .35
❑ 291 Mike Merriweather .20 .09
❑ 292 Burt Grossman .20 .09
❑ 293 Erik McMillan .20 .09
❑ 294 John Elway 5.00 2.20
❑ 295 Toi Cook RC .20 .09
❑ 296 Tom Rathman .20 .09
❑ 297 Matt Bahr .20 .09
❑ 298 Chris Spielman .40 .18
❑ 299 Freddie Joe Nunn .40 .18
(Troy Aikman and
Emmitt Smith shown
in background)
❑ 300 Jim C. Jensen .20 .09
❑ 301 David Fulcher UER .20 .09
(Rookie card should
be '88, not '89)
❑ 302 Tommy Hodson .20 .09
❑ 303 Stephone Paige .20 .09
❑ 304 Greg Townsend .20 .09
❑ 305 Dean Biasucci .20 .09
❑ 306 Jimmie Jones .20 .09
❑ 307 Eugene Marve .20 .09
❑ 308 Flipper Anderson .20 .09
❑ 309 Darryl Talley .20 .09
❑ 310 Mike Croel RC .20 .09
❑ 311 Thane Gash .20 .09
❑ 312 Perry Kemp .20 .09
❑ 313 Heath Sherman .20 .09
❑ 314 Mike Singletary .40 .18
❑ 315 Chip Lohmiller .20 .09
❑ 316 Tunch Ilkin .20 .09
❑ 317 Junior Seau 1.25 .55
❑ 318 Mike Gann .20 .09
❑ 319 Tim McDonald .20 .09
❑ 320 Kyle Clifton .20 .09
❑ 321 Dan Owens .20 .09
❑ 322 Tim Grunhard .20 .09
❑ 323 Stan Brock .20 .09
❑ 324 Rodney Holman .20 .09
❑ 325 Mark Ingram .40 .18
❑ 326 Browning Nagle RC .20 .09
❑ 327 Joe Montana 5.00 2.20
❑ 328 Carl Lee .20 .09
❑ 329 John L. Williams .20 .09
❑ 330 David Griggs .20 .09
❑ 331 Clarence Kay .20 .09
❑ 332 Irving Fryar .40 .18
❑ 333 Doug Smith RC** .20 .09
❑ 334 Kent Hull .20 .09
❑ 335 Mike Wilcher .20 .09
❑ 336 Ray Donaldson .20 .09
❑ 337 Mark Carrier DB UER .20 .09
(Rookie card should
be '90, not '89)
❑ 338 Kelvin Martin .20 .09
❑ 339 Keith Byars .20 .09
❑ 340 Wilber Marshall .20 .09
❑ 341 Ronnie Lott .40 .18
❑ 342 Blair Thomas .20 .09
❑ 343 Ronnie Harmon .20 .09
❑ 344 Brian Brennan .20 .09
❑ 345 Charles McRae RC .20 .09
❑ 346 Michael Cofer .20 .09
❑ 347 Keith Willis .20 .09
❑ 348 Bruce Kozerski .20 .09
❑ 349 Dave Meggett .40 .18
❑ 350 John Taylor .40 .18
❑ 351 Johnny Holland .20 .09
❑ 352 Steve Christie .20 .09
❑ 353 Ricky Ervins RC .40 .18
❑ 354 Robert Massey .20 .09
❑ 355 Derrick Thomas .75 .35
❑ 356 Tommy Kane .20 .09
❑ 357 Melvin Bratton .20 .09
❑ 358 Bruce Matthews .40 .18
❑ 359 Mark Duper .40 .18
❑ 360 Jeff Wright RC .20 .09
❑ 361 Barry Sanders 5.00 2.20
❑ 362 Chuck Webb RC .20 .09
❑ 363 Darryl Grant .20 .09
❑ 364 William Roberts .20 .09
❑ 365 Reggie Rutland .20 .09
❑ 366 Clay Matthews .40 .18
❑ 367 Anthony Miller .40 .18
❑ 368 Mike Prior .20 .09
❑ 369 Jessie Tuggle .20 .09
❑ 370 Brad Muster .20 .09
❑ 371 Jay Schroeder .20 .09
❑ 372 Greg Lloyd .75 .35
❑ 373 Mike Cofer .20 .09
❑ 374 James Brooks .40 .18
❑ 375 Danny Noonan UER .20 .09
(Misspelled Noonen
on card back)
❑ 376 Latin Berry RC .20 .09
❑ 377 Brad Baxter .20 .09
❑ 378 Godfrey Myles RC .20 .09
❑ 379 Morten Andersen .20 .09
❑ 380 Keith Woodside .20 .09
❑ 381 Bobby Humphrey .20 .09
❑ 382 Mike Golic .20 .09
❑ 383 Keith McCants .20 .09
❑ 384 Anthony Thompson .20 .09
❑ 385 Mark Clayton .40 .18
❑ 386 Neil Smith .75 .35
❑ 387 Bryan Millard .20 .09
❑ 388 Mel Gray UER .40 .18
(Wrong Mel Gray
pictured on card back)
❑ 389 Ernest Givins .40 .18
❑ 390 Reyna Thompson .20 .09
❑ 391 Eric Bieniemy RC .20 .09
❑ 392 Jon Hand .20 .09
❑ 393 Mark Rypien .40 .18
❑ 394 Bill Romanowski .20 .09
❑ 395 Thurman Thomas .75 .35
❑ 396 Jim Harbaugh .75 .35

	Card	Mint	NrMt
❑	397 Don Mosebar	.20	.09
❑	398 Andre Rison	.40	.18
❑	399 Mike Johnson	.20	.09
❑	400 Dermontti Dawson	.20	.09
❑	401 Herschel Walker	.40	.18
❑	402 Joe Prokop	.20	.09
❑	403 Eddie Brown	.20	.09
❑	404 Nate Newton	.40	.18
❑	405 Damone Johnson RC	.20	.09
❑	406 Jessie Hester	.20	.09
❑	407 Jim Arnold	.20	.09
❑	408 Ray Agnew	.20	.09
❑	409 Michael Brooks	.20	.09
❑	410 Keith Sims	.20	.09
❑	411 Carl Banks	.20	.09
❑	412 Jonathan Hayes	.20	.09
❑	413 Richard Johnson RC	.20	.09
❑	414 Darryll Lewis RC	.40	.18
❑	415 Jeff Bryant	.20	.09
❑	416 Leslie O'Neal	.40	.18
❑	417 Andre Reed	.40	.18
❑	418 Charles Mann	.20	.09
❑	419 Keith DeLong	.20	.09
❑	420 Bruce Hill	.20	.09
❑	421 Matt Brock RC	.20	.09
❑	422 Johnny Johnson	.20	.09
❑	423 Mark Bortz	.20	.09
❑	424 Ben Smith	.20	.09
❑	425 Jeff Cross	.20	.09
❑	426 Irv Pankey	.20	.09
❑	427 Hassan Jones	.20	.09
❑	428 Andre Tippett	.20	.09
❑	429 Tim Worley	.20	.09
❑	430 Daniel Stubbs	.20	.09
❑	431 Max Montoya	.20	.09
❑	432 Jumbo Elliott	.20	.09
❑	433 Duane Bickett	.20	.09
❑	434 Nate Lewis RC	.20	.09
❑	435 Leonard Russell RC	.75	.35
❑	436 Hoby Brenner	.20	.09
❑	437 Ricky Sanders	.20	.09
❑	438 Pierce Holt	.20	.09
❑	439 Derrick Fenner	.20	.09
❑	440 Drew Hill	.20	.09
❑	441 Will Wolford	.20	.09
❑	442 Albert Lewis	.20	.09
❑	443 James Francis	.20	.09
❑	444 Chris Jacke	.20	.09
❑	445 Mike Farr	.20	.09
❑	446 Stephen Braggs	.20	.09
❑	447 Michael Haynes	.75	.35
❑	448 Freeman McNeil UER (2,008 Pounds for weight)	.20	.09
❑	449 Kevin Donnalley	.20	.09
❑	450 John Offerdahl	.20	.09
❑	451 Eric Allen	.20	.09
❑	452 Keith McKeller	.20	.09
❑	453 Kevin Greene	.75	.35
❑	454 Ronnie Lippett	.20	.09
❑	455 Ray Childress	.20	.09
❑	456 Mike Saxon	.20	.09
❑	457 Mark Robinson	.20	.09
❑	458 Greg Kragen	.20	.09
❑	459 Steve Jordan	.20	.09
❑	460 John Johnson RC	.20	.09
❑	461 Sam Mills	.20	.09
❑	462 Bo Jackson	1.00	.45
❑	463 Mark Collins	.20	.09
❑	464 Percy Snow	.20	.09
❑	465 Jeff Bostic	.20	.09
❑	466 Jacob Green	.20	.09
❑	467 Dexter Carter	.20	.09
❑	468 Rich Camarillo	.20	.09
❑	469 Bill Brooks	.20	.09
❑	470 John Carney	.20	.09
❑	471 Don Majkowski	.20	.09
❑	472 Ralph Tamm RC	.20	.09
❑	473 Fred Barnett	.75	.35
❑	474 Jim Covert	.20	.09
❑	475 Kenneth Davis	.20	.09
❑	476 Jerry Gray	.20	.09
❑	477 Broderick Thomas	.20	.09
❑	478 Chris Doleman	.20	.09
❑	479 Haywood Jeffires	.40	.18
❑	480 Craig Heyward	.40	.18
❑	481 Markus Koch	.20	.09
❑	482 Tim Krumrie	.20	.09
❑	483 Robert Clark	.20	.09
❑	484 Mike Rozier	.20	.09
❑	485 Danny Villa	.20	.09
❑	486 Gerald Williams	.20	.09
❑	487 Steve Wisniewski	.20	.09
❑	488 J.B. Brown	.20	.09
❑	489 Eugene Robinson	.20	.09
❑	490 Ottis Anderson	.40	.18
❑	491 Tony Stargell	.20	.09
❑	492 Jack Del Rio	.20	.09
❑	493 Lamar Rogers RC	.20	.09
❑	494 Ricky Nattiel	.20	.09
❑	495 Dan Saleaumua	.20	.09
❑	496 Checklist 1-100	.20	.09
❑	497 Checklist 101-200	.20	.09
❑	498 Checklist 201-300	.20	.09
❑	499 Checklist 301-400	.20	.09
❑	500 Checklist 401-500	.20	.09

1992 Stadium Club

	MINT	NRMT
COMPLETE SET (700)	150.00	70.00
COMP.SERIES 1 (300)	15.00	6.75
COMP.SERIES 2 (300)	15.00	6.75
COMP.HIGH SER.(100)	120.00	55.00
COMMON CARD (1-600)	.08	.04
COMMON CARD (601-700)	.50	.23

	Card	Mint	NrMt
❑	1 Mark Rypien	.08	.04
❑	2 Carlton Bailey RC	.15	.07
❑	3 Kevin Glover	.08	.04
❑	4 Vance Johnson	.08	.04
❑	5 Jim Jeffcoat	.08	.04
❑	6 Dan Saleaumua	.08	.04
❑	7 Darion Conner	.08	.04
❑	8 Don Maggs	.08	.04
❑	9 Richard Dent	.15	.07
❑	10 Mark Murphy	.08	.04
❑	11 Wesley Carroll	.08	.04
❑	12 Chris Burkett	.08	.04
❑	13 Steve Wallace	.08	.04
❑	14 Jacob Green	.08	.04
❑	15 Roger Ruzek	.08	.04
❑	16 J.B. Brown	.08	.04
❑	17 Dave Meggett	.15	.07
❑	18 D.J. Johnson	.08	.04
❑	19 Rich Gannon	.30	.14
❑	20 Kevin Mack	.08	.04
❑	21A Reggie Cobb ERR (Buccaneers upside down on card front)	.08	.04
❑	21B Reggie Cobb COR	.08	.04
❑	22 Nate Lewis	.08	.04
❑	23 Doug Smith	.08	.04
❑	24 Irving Fryar	.15	.07
❑	25 Anthony Thompson	.08	.04
❑	26 Duane Bickett	.08	.04
❑	27 Don Majkowski	.08	.04
❑	28 Mark Schlereth RC	.08	.04
❑	29 Melvin Jenkins	.08	.04
❑	30 Michael Haynes	.15	.07
❑	31 Greg Lewis	.08	.04
❑	32 Kenneth Davis	.08	.04
❑	33 Derrick Thomas	.30	.14
❑	34 David Williams	.08	.04
❑	35 Neal Anderson	.08	.04
❑	36 Andre Collins	.08	.04
❑	37 Jesse Solomon	.08	.04
❑	38 Barry Sanders	3.00	1.35
❑	39 Jeff Gossett	.08	.04
❑	40 Rickey Jackson	.08	.04
❑	41 Ray Berry	.08	.04
❑	42 Leroy Hoard	.15	.07
❑	43 Eric Thomas	.08	.04
❑	44 Brian Washington	.08	.04
❑	45 Pat Terrell	.08	.04
❑	46 Eugene Robinson	.08	.04
❑	47 Luis Sharpe	.08	.04
❑	48 Jerome Brown	.08	.04
❑	49 Mark Collins	.08	.04
❑	50 Johnny Holland	.08	.04
❑	51 Tony Paige	.08	.04
❑	52 Willie Green	.08	.04
❑	53 Steve Atwater	.08	.04
❑	54 Brad Muster	.08	.04
❑	55 Cris Dishman	.08	.04
❑	56 Eddie Anderson	.08	.04
❑	57 Sam Mills	.08	.04
❑	58 Donald Evans	.08	.04
❑	59 Jon Vaughn	.08	.04
❑	60 Marion Butts	.08	.04
❑	61 Rodney Holman	.08	.04
❑	62 Dwayne White RC	.08	.04
❑	63 Martin Mayhew	.08	.04
❑	64 Jonathan Hayes	.08	.04
❑	65 Andre Rison	.15	.07
❑	66 Calvin Williams	.15	.07
❑	67 James Washington	.08	.04
❑	68 Tim Harris	.08	.04
❑	69 Jim Ritcher	.08	.04
❑	70 Johnny Johnson	.08	.04
❑	71 John Offerdahl	.08	.04
❑	72 Herschel Walker	.15	.07
❑	73 Perry Kemp	.08	.04
❑	74 Erik Howard	.08	.04
❑	75 Lamar Lathon	.08	.04
❑	76 Greg Kragen	.08	.04
❑	77 Jay Schroeder	.08	.04
❑	78 Jim Arnold	.08	.04
❑	79 Chris Miller	.15	.07
❑	80 Deron Cherry	.08	.04
❑	81 Jim Harbaugh	.30	.14
❑	82 Gill Fenerty	.08	.04
❑	83 Fred Stokes	.08	.04
❑	84 Roman Phifer	.08	.04
❑	85 Clyde Simmons	.08	.04
❑	86 Vince Newsome	.08	.04
❑	87 Lawrence Dawsey	.15	.07
❑	88 Eddie Brown	.08	.04
❑	89 Greg Montgomery	.08	.04
❑	90 Jeff Lageman	.08	.04
❑	91 Terry Wooden	.08	.04
❑	92 Nate Newton	.15	.07
❑	93 David Richards	.08	.04
❑	94 Derek Russell	.08	.04
❑	95 Steve Jordan	.08	.04
❑	96 Hugh Millen	.08	.04
❑	97 Mark Duper	.08	.04
❑	98 Sean Landeta	.08	.04
❑	99 James Thornton	.08	.04
❑	100 Darrell Green	.08	.04
❑	101 Harris Barton	.08	.04
❑	102 John Alt	.08	.04
❑	103 Mike Farr	.08	.04
❑	104 Bob Golic	.08	.04
❑	105 Gene Atkins	.08	.04
❑	106 Gary Anderson K	.08	.04
❑	107 Norm Johnson	.08	.04
❑	108 Eugene Daniel	.08	.04
❑	109 Kent Hull	.08	.04
❑	110 John Elway	2.50	1.10
❑	111 Rich Camarillo	.08	.04
❑	112 Charles Wilson	.08	.04
❑	113 Matt Bahr	.08	.04
❑	114 Mark Carrier WR	.15	.07
❑	115 Richmond Webb	.08	.04
❑	116 Charles Mann	.08	.04
❑	117 Tim McGee	.08	.04
❑	118 Wes Hopkins	.08	.04
❑	119 Mo Lewis	.08	.04
❑	120 Warren Moon	.30	.14
❑	121 Damone Johnson	.08	.04

No.	Player		
❑ 122	Kevin Gogan	.08	.04
❑ 123	Joey Browner	.08	.04
❑ 124	Tommy Kane	.08	.04
❑ 125	Vincent Brown	.08	.04
❑ 126	Barry Word	.08	.04
❑ 127	Michael Brooks	.08	.04
❑ 128	Jumbo Elliott	.08	.04
❑ 129	Marcus Allen	.30	.14
❑ 130	Tom Waddle	.08	.04
❑ 131	Jim Dombrowski	.08	.04
❑ 132	Aeneas Williams	.15	.07
❑ 133	Clay Matthews	.15	.07
❑ 134	Thurman Thomas	.30	.14
❑ 135	Dean Biasucci	.08	.04
❑ 136	Moe Gardner	.08	.04
❑ 137	James Campen	.08	.04
❑ 138	Tim Johnson	.08	.04
❑ 139	Erik Kramer	.15	.07
❑ 140	Keith McCants	.08	.04
❑ 141	John Carney	.08	.04
❑ 142	Tunch Ilkin	.08	.04
❑ 143	Louis Oliver	.08	.04
❑ 144	Bill Maas	.08	.04
❑ 145	Wendell Davis	.08	.04
❑ 146	Pepper Johnson	.08	.04
❑ 147	Howie Long	.15	.07
❑ 148	Brett Maxie	.08	.04
❑ 149	Tony Casillas	.08	.04
❑ 150	Michael Carter	.08	.04
❑ 151	Byron Evans	.08	.04
❑ 152	Lorenzo White	.08	.04
❑ 153	Larry Kelm	.08	.04
❑ 154	Andy Heck	.08	.04
❑ 155	Harry Newsome	.08	.04
❑ 156	Chris Singleton	.08	.04
❑ 157	Mike Kenn	.08	.04
❑ 158	Jeff Faulkner	.08	.04
❑ 159	Ken Lanier	.08	.04
❑ 160	Darryl Talley	.08	.04
❑ 161	Louie Aguiar RC	.08	.04
❑ 162	Danny Copeland	.08	.04
❑ 163	Kevin Porter	.08	.04
❑ 164	Trace Armstrong	.08	.04
❑ 165	Dermontti Dawson	.08	.04
❑ 166	Fred McAfee RC	.08	.04
❑ 167	Ronnie Lott	.15	.07
❑ 168	Tony Mandarich	.08	.04
❑ 169	Howard Cross	.08	.04
❑ 170	Vestee Jackson	.08	.04
❑ 171	Jeff Herrod	.08	.04
❑ 172	Randy Hilliard RC	.08	.04
❑ 173	Robert Wilson	.08	.04
❑ 174	Joe Walter RC	.08	.04
❑ 175	Chris Spielman	.15	.07
❑ 176	Darryl Henley	.08	.04
❑ 177	Jay Hilgenberg	.08	.04
❑ 178	John Kidd	.08	.04
❑ 179	Doug Widell	.08	.04
❑ 180	Seth Joyner	.15	.07
❑ 181	Nick Bell	.08	.04
❑ 182	Don Griffin	.08	.04
❑ 183	Johnny Meads	.08	.04
❑ 184	Jeff Bostic	.08	.04
❑ 185	Johnny Hector	.08	.04
❑ 186	Jessie Tuggle	.08	.04
❑ 187	Robb Thomas	.08	.04
❑ 188	Shane Conlan	.08	.04
❑ 189	Michael Zordich RC	.08	.04
❑ 190	Emmitt Smith	3.00	1.35
❑ 191	Robert Blackmon	.08	.04
❑ 192	Carl Lee	.08	.04
❑ 193	Harry Galbreath	.08	.04
❑ 194	Ed King	.08	.04
❑ 195	Stan Thomas	.08	.04
❑ 196	Andre Waters	.08	.04
❑ 197	Pat Harlow	.08	.04
❑ 198	Zefross Moss	.08	.04
❑ 199	Bobby Hebert	.08	.04
❑ 200	Doug Riesenberg	.08	.04
❑ 201	Mike Croel	.08	.04
❑ 202	Jeff Jaeger	.08	.04
❑ 203	Gary Plummer	.08	.04
❑ 204	Chris Jacke	.08	.04
❑ 205	Neil O'Donnell	.30	.14
❑ 206	Mark Bortz	.08	.04
❑ 207	Tim Barnett	.08	.04
❑ 208	Jerry Ball	.08	.04
❑ 209	Chip Lohmiller	.08	.04
❑ 210	Jim Everett	.15	.07
❑ 211	Tim McKyer	.08	.04
❑ 212	Aaron Craver	.08	.04
❑ 213	John L. Williams	.08	.04
❑ 214	Simon Fletcher	.08	.04
❑ 215	Walter Reeves	.08	.04
❑ 216	Terance Mathis	.15	.07
❑ 217	Mike Pitts	.08	.04
❑ 218	Bruce Matthews	.08	.04
❑ 219	Howard Ballard	.08	.04
❑ 220	Leonard Russell	.15	.07
❑ 221	Michael Stewart	.08	.04
❑ 222	Mike Merriweather	.08	.04
❑ 223	Ricky Sanders	.08	.04
❑ 224	Ray Horton	.08	.04
❑ 225	Michael Jackson	.15	.07
❑ 226	Bill Romanowski	.08	.04
❑ 227	Steve McMichael UER (His wife is former Mrs. Illinois, not Miss Illinois)	.15	.07
❑ 228	Chris Martin	.08	.04
❑ 229	Tim Green	.08	.04
❑ 230	Karl Mecklenburg	.08	.04
❑ 231	Felix Wright	.08	.04
❑ 232	Charles McRae	.08	.04
❑ 233	Pete Stoyanovich	.08	.04
❑ 234	Stephen Baker	.08	.04
❑ 235	Herman Moore	1.00	.45
❑ 236	Terry McDaniel	.08	.04
❑ 237	Dalton Hilliard	.08	.04
❑ 238	Gill Byrd	.08	.04
❑ 239	Leon Seals	.08	.04
❑ 240	Rod Woodson	.30	.14
❑ 241	Curtis Duncan	.08	.04
❑ 242	Keith Jackson	.15	.07
❑ 243	Mark Stepnoski	.15	.07
❑ 244	Art Monk	.15	.07
❑ 245	Matt Stover	.08	.04
❑ 246	John Roper	.08	.04
❑ 247	Rodney Hampton	.30	.14
❑ 248	Steve Wisniewski	.08	.04
❑ 249	Bryan Millard	.08	.04
❑ 250	Todd Lyght	.08	.04
❑ 251	Marvin Washington	.08	.04
❑ 252	Eric Swann	.15	.07
❑ 253	Bruce Kozerski	.08	.04
❑ 254	Jon Hand	.08	.04
❑ 255	Scott Fulhage	.08	.04
❑ 256	Chuck Cecil	.08	.04
❑ 257	Eric Martin	.08	.04
❑ 258	Eric Metcalf	.15	.07
❑ 259	T.J. Turner	.08	.04
❑ 260	Kirk Lowdermilk	.08	.04
❑ 261	Keith McKeller	.08	.04
❑ 262	Wymon Henderson	.08	.04
❑ 263	David Alexander	.08	.04
❑ 264	George Jamison	.08	.04
❑ 265	Ken Norton Jr.	.30	.14
❑ 266	Jim Lachey	.08	.04
❑ 267	Bo Orlando RC	.08	.04
❑ 268	Nick Lowery	.08	.04
❑ 269	Keith Van Horne	.08	.04
❑ 270	Dwight Stone	.08	.04
❑ 271	Keith DeLong	.08	.04
❑ 272	James Francis	.08	.04
❑ 273	Greg McMurtry	.08	.04
❑ 274	Ethan Horton	.08	.04
❑ 275	Stan Brock	.08	.04
❑ 276	Ken Harvey	.08	.04
❑ 277	Ronnie Harmon	.08	.04
❑ 278	Mike Pritchard	.15	.07
❑ 279	Kyle Clifton	.08	.04
❑ 280	Anthony Johnson	.15	.07
❑ 281	Esera Tuaolo	.08	.04
❑ 282	Vernon Turner	.08	.04
❑ 283	David Griggs	.08	.04
❑ 284	Dino Hackett	.08	.04
❑ 285	Carwell Gardner	.08	.04
❑ 286	Ron Hall	.08	.04
❑ 287	Reggie White	.30	.14
❑ 288	Checklist 1-100	.08	.04
❑ 289	Checklist 101-200	.08	.04
❑ 290	Checklist 201-300	.08	.04
❑ 291	Mark Clayton MC	.08	.04
❑ 292	Pat Swilling MC	.08	.04
❑ 293	Ernest Givins MC	.08	.04
❑ 294	Broderick Thomas MC	.08	.04
❑ 295	John Friesz MC	.08	.04
❑ 296	Cornelius Bennett MC	.08	.04
❑ 297	Anthony Carter MC	.15	.07
❑ 298	Earnest Byner MC	.08	.04
❑ 299	Michael Irvin MC	.30	.14
❑ 300	Cortez Kennedy MC	.08	.04
❑ 301	Barry Sanders MC	1.50	.70
❑ 302	Mike Croel MC	.08	.04
❑ 303	Emmitt Smith MC	2.00	.90
❑ 304	Leonard Russell MC	.08	.04
❑ 305	Neal Anderson MC	.08	.04
❑ 306	Derrick Thomas MC	.15	.07
❑ 307	Mark Rypien MC	.08	.04
❑ 308	Reggie White MC	.15	.07
❑ 309	Rod Woodson MC	.15	.07
❑ 310	Rodney Hampton MC	.15	.07
❑ 311	Carnell Lake	.08	.04
❑ 312	Robert Delpino	.08	.04
❑ 313	Brian Blades	.15	.07
❑ 314	Marc Spindler	.08	.04
❑ 315	Scott Norwood	.08	.04
❑ 316	Frank Warren	.08	.04
❑ 317	David Treadwell	.08	.04
❑ 318	Steve Broussard	.08	.04
❑ 319	Lorenzo Lynch	.08	.04
❑ 320	Ray Agnew	.08	.04
❑ 321	Derrick Walker	.08	.04
❑ 322	Vinson Smith RC	.08	.04
❑ 323	Gary Clark	.30	.14
❑ 324	Charles Haley	.15	.07
❑ 325	Keith Byars	.08	.04
❑ 326	Winston Moss	.08	.04
❑ 327	Paul McJulien RC UER (Has Brett Perriman card back; see also 453)	.08	.04
❑ 328	Tony Covington	.08	.04
❑ 329	Mark Carrier DB	.08	.04
❑ 330	Mark Tuinei	.08	.04
❑ 331	Tracy Simien RC	.08	.04
❑ 332	Jeff Wright	.08	.04
❑ 333	Bryan Cox	.15	.07
❑ 334	Lonnie Young	.08	.04
❑ 335	Clarence Verdin	.08	.04
❑ 336	Dan Fike	.08	.04
❑ 337	Steve Sewell	.08	.04
❑ 338	Gary Zimmerman	.08	.04
❑ 339	Barney Bussey	.08	.04
❑ 340	William Perry	.15	.07
❑ 341	Jeff Hostetler	.15	.07
❑ 342	Doug Smith	.08	.04
❑ 343	Cleveland Gary	.08	.04
❑ 344	Todd Marinovich	.08	.04
❑ 345	Rich Moran	.08	.04
❑ 346	Tony Woods	.08	.04
❑ 347	Vaughan Johnson	.08	.04
❑ 348	Marv Cook	.08	.04
❑ 349	Pierce Holt	.08	.04
❑ 350	Gerald Williams	.08	.04
❑ 351	Kevin Butler	.08	.04
❑ 352	William White	.08	.04
❑ 353	Henry Rolling	.08	.04
❑ 354	James Joseph	.08	.04
❑ 355	Vinny Testaverde	.15	.07
❑ 356	Scott Radecic	.08	.04
❑ 357	Lee Johnson	.08	.04
❑ 358	Steve Tasker	.15	.07
❑ 359	David Lutz	.08	.04
❑ 360	Audray McMillian UER (Name on back misspelled Audrey)	.08	.04
❑ 361	Brad Baxter	.08	.04
❑ 362	Mark Dennis	.08	.04
❑ 363	Erric Pegram	.15	.07
❑ 364	Sean Jones	.15	.07
❑ 365	William Roberts	.08	.04
❑ 366	Steve Young	1.00	.45
❑ 367	Joe Jacoby	.08	.04
❑ 368	Richard Brown RC	.08	.04
❑ 369	Keith Kartz	.08	.04
❑ 370	Freddie Joe Nunn	.08	.04
❑ 371	Darren Comeaux	.08	.04
❑ 372	Larry Brown DB	.08	.04

❑ 373 Haywood Jeffires .15 .07
❑ 374 Tom Newberry .08 .04
❑ 375 Steve Bono RC .30 .14
❑ 376 Kevin Ross .08 .04
❑ 377 Kelvin Pritchett .08 .04
❑ 378 Jessie Hester .08 .04
❑ 379 Mitchell Price .08 .04
❑ 380 Barry Foster .15 .07
❑ 381 Reyna Thompson .08 .04
❑ 382 Cris Carter .75 .35
❑ 383 Lemuel Stinson .08 .04
❑ 384 Rod Bernstine .08 .04
❑ 385 James Lofton .15 .07
❑ 386 Kevin Murphy .08 .04
❑ 387 Greg Townsend .08 .04
❑ 388 Edgar Bennett RC .40 .18
❑ 389 Rob Moore .15 .07
❑ 390 Eugene Lockhart .08 .04
❑ 391 Bern Brostek .08 .04
❑ 392 Craig Heyward .15 .07
❑ 393 Ferrell Edmunds .08 .04
❑ 394 John Kasay .08 .04
❑ 395 Jesse Sapolu .08 .04
❑ 396 Jim Breech .08 .04
❑ 397 Neil Smith .30 .14
❑ 398 Bryce Paup .30 .14
❑ 399 Tony Tolbert .08 .04
❑ 400 Bubby Brister .08 .04
❑ 401 Dennis Smith .08 .04
❑ 402 Dan Owens .08 .04
❑ 403 Steve Beuerlein .08 .04
❑ 404 Rick Tuten .08 .04
❑ 405 Eric Allen .08 .04
❑ 406 Eric Hill .08 .04
❑ 407 Don Warren .08 .04
❑ 408 Greg Jackson .08 .04
❑ 409 Chris Doleman .08 .04
❑ 410 Anthony Munoz .15 .07
❑ 411 Michael Young .08 .04
❑ 412 Cornelius Bennett .15 .07
❑ 413 Ray Childress .08 .04
❑ 414 Kevin Call .08 .04
❑ 415 Burt Grossman .08 .04
❑ 416 Scott Miller .08 .04
❑ 417 Tim Newton .08 .04
❑ 418 Robert Young .08 .04
❑ 419 Tommy Vardell RC .15 .07
❑ 420 Michael Walter .08 .04
❑ 421 Chris Port RC .08 .04
❑ 422 Carlton Haselrig RC .08 .04
❑ 423 Rodney Peete .15 .07
❑ 424 Scott Stephen .08 .04
❑ 425 Chris Warren .30 .14
❑ 426 Scott Galbraith RC .08 .04
❑ 427 Fuad Reveiz UER .08 .04
(Born in Colombia, not Columbia)
❑ 428 Irv Eatman .08 .04
❑ 429 David Szott .08 .04
❑ 430 Brent Williams .08 .04
❑ 431 Mike Horan .08 .04
❑ 432 Brent Jones .15 .07
❑ 433 Paul Gruber .08 .04
❑ 434 Carlos Huerta .08 .04
❑ 435 Scott Case .08 .04
❑ 436 Greg Davis .08 .04
❑ 437 Ken Clarke .08 .04
❑ 438 Alfred Williams .08 .04
❑ 439 Jim C. Jensen .08 .04
❑ 440 Louis Lipps .08 .04
❑ 441 Larry Roberts .08 .04
❑ 442 James Jones .08 .04
❑ 443 Don Mosebar .08 .04
❑ 444 Quinn Early .15 .07
❑ 445 Robert Brown .08 .04
❑ 446 Tom Thayer .08 .04
❑ 447 Michael Irvin .30 .14
❑ 448 Jarrod Bunch .08 .04
❑ 449 Riki Ellison .08 .04
❑ 450 Joe Phillips .08 .04
❑ 451 Ernest Givins .15 .07
❑ 452 Glenn Parker .08 .04
❑ 453 Brett Perriman UER .30 .14
(Has Paul McJulien card back; see also 327)
❑ 454 Jayice Pearson RC .08 .04
❑ 455 Mark Jackson .08 .04
❑ 456 Siran Stacy RC .08 .04
❑ 457 Rufus Porter .08 .04
❑ 458 Michael Ball .08 .04
❑ 459 Craig Taylor .08 .04
❑ 460 George Thomas RC .08 .04
❑ 461 Alvin Wright .08 .04
❑ 462 Ron Hallstrom .08 .04
❑ 463 Mike Mooney RC .08 .04
❑ 464 Dexter Carter .08 .04
❑ 465 Marty Carter RC .08 .04
❑ 466 Pat Swilling .15 .07
❑ 467 Mike Golic .08 .04
❑ 468 Reggie Roby .08 .04
❑ 469 Randall McDaniel .08 .04
❑ 470 John Stephens .08 .04
❑ 471 Ricardo McDonald RC .08 .04
❑ 472 Wilber Marshall .08 .04
❑ 473 Jim Sweeney .08 .04
❑ 474 Ernie Jones .08 .04
❑ 475 Bennie Blades .08 .04
❑ 476 Don Beebe .08 .04
❑ 477 Grant Feasel .08 .04
❑ 478 Ernie Mills .08 .04
❑ 479 Tony Jones .08 .04
❑ 480 Jeff Uhlenhake .08 .04
❑ 481 Gaston Green .08 .04
❑ 482 John Taylor .15 .07
❑ 483 Anthony Smith .08 .04
❑ 484 Tony Bennett .08 .04
❑ 485 David Brandon RC .08 .04
❑ 486 Shawn Jefferson .08 .04
❑ 487 Christian Okoye .08 .04
❑ 488 Leonard Marshall .08 .04
❑ 489 Jay Novacek .15 .07
❑ 490 Harold Green .08 .04
❑ 491 Bubba McDowell .08 .04
❑ 492 Gary Anderson RB .08 .04
❑ 493 Terrell Buckley RC .08 .04
❑ 494 Jamie Dukes RC .08 .04
❑ 495 Morten Andersen .08 .04
❑ 496 Henry Thomas .08 .04
❑ 497 Bill Lewis .08 .04
❑ 498 Jeff Cross .08 .04
❑ 499 Hardy Nickerson .15 .07
❑ 500 Henry Ellard .15 .07
❑ 501 Joe Bowden RC .08 .04
❑ 502 Brian Noble .08 .04
❑ 503 Mike Cofer .08 .04
❑ 504 Jeff Bryant .08 .04
❑ 505 Lomas Brown .08 .04
❑ 506 Chip Banks .08 .04
❑ 507 Keith Traylor .08 .04
❑ 508 Mark Kelso .08 .04
❑ 509 Dexter McNabb RC .08 .04
❑ 510 Gene Chilton RC .08 .04
❑ 511 George Thornton .08 .04
❑ 512 Jeff Criswell .08 .04
❑ 513 Brad Edwards .08 .04
❑ 514 Ron Heller .08 .04
❑ 515 Tim Brown .30 .14
❑ 516 Keith Hamilton RC .15 .07
❑ 517 Mark Higgs .08 .04
❑ 518 Tommy Barnhardt .08 .04
❑ 519 Brian Jordan .15 .07
❑ 520 Ray Crockett .08 .04
❑ 521 Karl Wilson .08 .04
❑ 522 Ricky Reynolds .08 .04
❑ 523 Max Montoya .08 .04
❑ 524 David Little .08 .04
❑ 525 Alonzo Mitz RC .08 .04
❑ 526 Darryll Lewis .08 .04
❑ 527 Keith Henderson .08 .04
❑ 528 LeRoy Butler .08 .04
❑ 529 Rob Burnett .08 .04
❑ 530 Chris Chandler .30 .14
❑ 531 Maury Buford .08 .04
❑ 532 Mark Ingram .08 .04
❑ 533 Mike Saxon .08 .04
❑ 534 Bill Fralic .08 .04
❑ 535 Craig Patterson RC .08 .04
❑ 536 John Randle .15 .07
❑ 537 Dwayne Harper .08 .04
❑ 538 Chris Hakel RC .08 .04
❑ 539 Maurice Hurst .08 .04
❑ 540 Warren Powers UER .08 .04
(Front has photo of Ron Holmes)
❑ 541 Will Wolford .08 .04
❑ 542 Dennis Gibson .08 .04
❑ 543 Jackie Slater .08 .04
❑ 544 Floyd Turner .08 .04
❑ 545 Guy McIntyre .08 .04
❑ 546 Eric Green .08 .04
❑ 547 Rohn Stark .08 .04
❑ 548 William Fuller .15 .07
❑ 549 Alvin Harper .15 .07
❑ 550 Mark Clayton .15 .07
❑ 551 Natu Tuatagaloa RC .08 .04
❑ 552 Fred Barnett .30 .14
❑ 553 Bob Whitfield RC .08 .04
❑ 554 Courtney Hall .08 .04
❑ 555 Brian Mitchell .15 .07
❑ 556 Patrick Hunter .08 .04
❑ 557 Rick Bryan .08 .04
❑ 558 Anthony Carter .15 .07
❑ 559 Jim Wahler .08 .04
❑ 560 Joe Morris .08 .04
❑ 561 Tony Zendejas .08 .04
❑ 562 Mervyn Fernandez .08 .04
❑ 563 Jamie Williams .08 .04
❑ 564 Darrell Thompson .08 .04
❑ 565 Adrian Cooper .08 .04
❑ 566 Chris Goode .08 .04
❑ 567 Jeff Davidson RC .08 .04
❑ 568 James Hasty .08 .04
❑ 569 Chris Mims RC .15 .07
❑ 570 Ray Seals RC .08 .04
❑ 571 Myron Guyton .08 .04
❑ 572 Todd McNair .08 .04
❑ 573 Andre Tippett .08 .04
❑ 574 Kirby Jackson .08 .04
❑ 575 Mel Gray .15 .07
❑ 576 Stephone Paige .08 .04
❑ 577 Scott Davis .08 .04
❑ 578 John Gesek .08 .04
❑ 579 Earnest Byner .08 .04
❑ 580 John Friesz .15 .07
❑ 581 Al Smith .08 .04
❑ 582 Flipper Anderson .08 .04
❑ 583 Amp Lee RC .08 .04
❑ 584 Greg Lloyd .30 .14
❑ 585 Cortez Kennedy .15 .07
❑ 586 Keith Sims .08 .04
❑ 587 Terry Allen .30 .14
❑ 588 David Fulcher .08 .04
❑ 589 Chris Hinton .08 .04
❑ 590 Tim McDonald .08 .04
❑ 591 Bruce Armstrong .08 .04
❑ 592 Sterling Sharpe .30 .14
❑ 593 Tom Rathman .08 .04
❑ 594 Bill Brooks .08 .04
❑ 595 Broderick Thomas .08 .04
❑ 596 Jim Wilks .08 .04
❑ 597 Tyrone Braxton UER .08 .04
(Bio for Melvin Braxton)
❑ 598 Checklist 301-400 UER .08 .04
(Audray McMillian is misspelled Audrey)
❑ 599 Checklist 401-500 .08 .04
❑ 600 Checklist 501-600 .08 .04
❑ 601 Andre Reed MC .75 .35
❑ 602 Troy Aikman MC 4.00 1.80
❑ 603 Dan Marino MC 6.00 2.70
❑ 604 Randall Cunningham MC .75 .35
❑ 605 Jim Kelly MC 1.50 .70
❑ 606 Deion Sanders MC 2.00 .90
❑ 607 Junior Seau MC 1.50 .70
❑ 608 Jerry Rice MC 4.00 1.80
❑ 609 Bruce Smith MC .75 .35
❑ 610 Lawrence Taylor MC 1.50 .70
❑ 611 Todd Collins RC .50 .23
❑ 612 Ty Detmer 1.50 .70
❑ 613 Browning Nagle .50 .23
❑ 614 Tony Sacca RC UER .50 .23
(Reverse negative photo on back)
❑ 615 Boomer Esiason .75 .35
❑ 616 Billy Joe Tolliver .50 .23
❑ 617 Leslie O'Neal .75 .35
❑ 618 Mark Wheeler RC .50 .23
❑ 619 Eric Dickerson .75 .35

❑ 620 Phil Simms .75 .35
❑ 621 Troy Vincent RC .75 .35
❑ 622 Jason Hanson RC .75 .35
❑ 623 Andre Reed .75 .35
❑ 624 Russell Maryland .75 .35
❑ 625 Steve Emtman RC .50 .23
❑ 626 Sean Gilbert RC 1.50 .70
❑ 627 Dana Hall RC .75 .35
❑ 628 Dan McGwire .50 .23
❑ 629 Lewis Billups .50 .23
❑ 630 Darryl Williams RC .50 .23
❑ 631 Dwayne Sabb RC .50 .23
❑ 632 Mark Royals .50 .23
❑ 633 Cary Conklin .50 .23
❑ 634 Al Toon .75 .35
❑ 635 Junior Seau 1.50 .70
❑ 636 Greg Skrepenak RC UER .50 .23
(Card misnumbered 686)
❑ 637 Deion Sanders 3.00 1.35
❑ 638 Steve DeOssie .50 .23
❑ 639 Randall Cunningham 1.50 .70
❑ 640 Jim Kelly 1.50 .70
❑ 641 Michael Brandon RC .50 .23
❑ 642 Clayton Holmes RC .50 .23
❑ 643 Webster Slaughter .50 .23
❑ 644 Ricky Proehl .50 .23
❑ 645 Jerry Rice 5.00 2.20
❑ 646 Carl Banks .50 .23
❑ 647 J.J.Birden .50 .23
❑ 648 Tracy Scroggins RC .50 .23
❑ 649 Alonzo Spellman RC .75 .35
❑ 650 Joe Montana 8.00 3.60
❑ 651 Courtney Hawkins RC .75 .35
❑ 652 Corey Widmer RC .50 .23
❑ 653 Robert Brooks RC 6.00 2.70
❑ 654 Darren Woodson RC 1.50 .70
❑ 655 Derrick Fenner .50 .23
❑ 656 Steve Christie .50 .23
❑ 657 Chester McGlockton RC 1.50 .70
❑ 658 Steve Israel RC .50 .23
❑ 659 Robert Harris RC .50 .23
❑ 660 Dan Marino 8.00 3.60
❑ 661 Ed McCaffrey 5.00 2.20
❑ 662 Johnny Mitchell RC .50 .23
❑ 663 Timm Rosenbach .50 .23
❑ 664 Anthony Miller .75 .35
❑ 665 Merril Hoge .50 .23
❑ 666 Eugene Chung RC .50 .23
❑ 667 Rueben Mayes .50 .23
❑ 668 Martin Bayless .50 .23
❑ 669 Ashley Ambrose RC .75 .35
❑ 670 Michael Cofer UER .50 .23
(Back shows card for Mike Cofer, the kicker)
❑ 671 Shane Dronett RC .50 .23
❑ 672 Bernie Kosar .75 .35
❑ 673 Mike Singletary .75 .35
❑ 674 Mike Lodish RC .50 .23
❑ 675 Phillippi Sparks RC .50 .23
❑ 676 Joel Steed RC .50 .23
❑ 677 Kevin Fagan .50 .23
❑ 678 Randal Hill .50 .23
❑ 679 Ken O'Brien .50 .23
❑ 680 Lawrence Taylor 1.50 .70
❑ 681 Harvey Williams 1.50 .70
❑ 682 Quentin Coryatt RC 1.50 .70
❑ 683 Brett Favre 60.00 27.00
❑ 684 Robert Jones RC .50 .23
❑ 685 Michael Dean Perry .75 .35
❑ 686 Bruce Smith 1.50 .70
❑ 687 Troy Auzenne RC .50 .23
❑ 688 Thomas McLemore RC .50 .23
❑ 689 Dale Carter RC 1.50 .70
❑ 690 Marc Boutte RC .50 .23
❑ 691 Jeff George 1.50 .70
❑ 692 Dion Lambert RC UER .50 .23
(Birthdate is 2/12/19; should be 2/12/69)
❑ 693 Vaughn Dunbar RC .50 .23
❑ 694 Derek Brown TE RC .50 .23
❑ 695 Troy Aikman 5.00 2.20
❑ 696 John Fina RC .50 .23
❑ 697 Kevin Smith RC 1.50 .70
❑ 698 Corey Miller RC .50 .23
❑ 699 Lance Olberding RC .50 .23
❑ 700 Checklist 601-700 UER .50 .23
(Numbering sequence off from 616 to 636)
❑ P1 Promo Sheet blue 10.00 4.50
National July 10-12, 1992
Barry Sanders
Gene Atkins
Louis Oliver
Paul Gruber
Emmitt Smith
Steve Jordan
Warren Moon
Seth Joyner
Ronnie Lott
❑ P2 Promo Sheet red 12.00 5.50
National July 9, 1992
Barry Sanders
Gene Atkins
Louis Oliver
Paul Gruber
Emmitt Smith
Steve Jordan
Warren Moon
Seth Joyner
Ronnie Lott

1993 Stadium Club

	MINT	NRMT
COMPLETE SET (550)	50.00	22.00
COMP.SERIES 1 (250)	25.00	11.00
COMP.SERIES 2 (250)	18.00	8.00
COMP.HIGH SERIES (50)	8.00	3.60
COMP.HIGH FACT.SET (51)	12.00	5.50

❑ 1 Sterling Sharpe .20 .09
❑ 2 Chris Burkett .10 .05
❑ 3 Santana Dotson .20 .09
❑ 4 Michael Jackson .20 .09
❑ 5 Neal Anderson .10 .05
❑ 6 Bryan Cox .10 .05
❑ 7 Dennis Gibson .10 .05
❑ 8 Jeff Graham .20 .09
❑ 9 Roger Ruzek .10 .05
❑ 10 Duane Bickett .10 .05
❑ 11 Charles Mann .10 .05
❑ 12 Tommy Maddox .10 .05
❑ 13 Vaughn Dunbar .10 .05
❑ 14 Gary Plummer .10 .05
❑ 15 Chris Miller .20 .09
❑ 16 Chris Warren .20 .09
❑ 17 Alvin Harper .20 .09
❑ 18 Eric Dickerson .20 .09
❑ 19 Mike Jones .10 .05
❑ 20 Ernest Givins .20 .09
❑ 21 Natrone Means RC 1.00 .45
❑ 22 Doug Riesenberg .10 .05
❑ 23 Barry Word .10 .05
❑ 24 Sean Salisbury .10 .05
❑ 25 Derrick Fenner .10 .05
❑ 26 David Howard .10 .05
❑ 27 Mark Kelso .10 .05
❑ 28 Todd Lyght .10 .05
❑ 29 Dana Hall .10 .05
❑ 30 Eric Metcalf .20 .09
❑ 31 Jason Hanson .10 .05
❑ 32 Dwight Stone .10 .05
❑ 33 Johnny Mitchell .10 .05
❑ 34 Reggie Roby .10 .05
❑ 35 Terrell Buckley .10 .05
❑ 36 Steve McMichael .20 .09
❑ 37 Marty Carter .10 .05
❑ 38 Seth Joyner .10 .05
❑ 39 Rohn Stark .10 .05
❑ 40 Eric Curry RC .10 .05
❑ 41 Tommy Barnhardt .10 .05
❑ 42 Karl Mecklenburg .10 .05
❑ 43 Darion Conner .10 .05
❑ 44 Ronnie Harmon .10 .05
❑ 45 Cortez Kennedy .20 .09
❑ 46 Tim Brown .40 .18
❑ 47 Bill Lewis .10 .05
❑ 48 Randall McDaniel .10 .05
❑ 49 Curtis Duncan .10 .05
❑ 50 Troy Aikman 1.50 .70
❑ 51 David Klingler .10 .05
❑ 52 Brent Jones .20 .09
❑ 53 Dave Krieg .20 .09
❑ 54 Bruce Smith .40 .18
❑ 55 Vincent Brown .10 .05
❑ 56 O.J. McDuffie RC 1.25 .55
❑ 57 Cleveland Gary .10 .05
❑ 58 Larry Centers RC .40 .18
❑ 59 Pepper Johnson .10 .05
❑ 60 Dan Marino 3.00 1.35
❑ 61 Robert Porcher .10 .05
❑ 62 Jim Harbaugh .40 .18
❑ 63 Sam Mills .10 .05
❑ 64 Gary Anderson RB .10 .05
❑ 65 Neil O'Donnell .20 .09
❑ 66 Keith Byars .10 .05
❑ 67 Jeff Herrod .10 .05
❑ 68 Marion Butts .10 .05
❑ 69 Terry McDaniel .10 .05
❑ 70 John Elway 3.00 1.35
❑ 71 Steve Broussard .10 .05
❑ 72 Kelvin Martin .10 .05
❑ 73 Tom Carter RC .20 .09
❑ 74 Bryce Paup .40 .18
❑ 75 Jim Kelly UER .20 .09
(Back shows 1992 Topps card as RC)
❑ 76 Bill Romanowski .10 .05
❑ 77 Andre Collins .10 .05
❑ 78 Mike Farr .10 .05
❑ 79 Henry Ellard .20 .09
❑ 80 Dale Carter .10 .05
❑ 81 Johnny Bailey .10 .05
❑ 82 Garrison Hearst RC 1.25 .55
❑ 83 Brent Williams .10 .05
❑ 84 Ricardo McDonald .10 .05
❑ 85 Emmitt Smith 3.00 1.35
❑ 86 Vai Sikahema .10 .05
❑ 87 Jackie Harris .10 .05
❑ 88 Alonzo Spellman .10 .05
❑ 89 Mark Wheeler .10 .05
❑ 90 Dalton Hilliard .10 .05
❑ 91 Mark Higgs .10 .05
❑ 92 Aaron Wallace .10 .05
❑ 93 Earnest Byner .10 .05
❑ 94 Stanley Richard .10 .05
❑ 95 Cris Carter .75 .35
❑ 96 Bobby Houston RC .10 .05
❑ 97 Craig Heyward .20 .09
❑ 98 Bernie Kosar .20 .09
❑ 99 Mike Croel .10 .05
❑ 100 Deion Sanders 1.00 .45
❑ 101 Warren Moon .20 .09
❑ 102 Christian Okoye .10 .05
❑ 103 Ricky Watters .40 .18
❑ 104 Eric Swann .20 .09
❑ 105 Rodney Hampton .20 .09
❑ 106 Daryl Johnston .20 .09
❑ 107 Andre Reed .20 .09
❑ 108 Jerome Bettis RC 2.00 .90
❑ 109 Eugene Daniel .10 .05
❑ 110 Leonard Russell .20 .09
❑ 111 Darryl Williams .10 .05
❑ 112 Rod Woodson .20 .09
❑ 113 Boomer Esiason .20 .09
❑ 114 James Hasty .10 .05
❑ 115 Marc Boutte .10 .05
❑ 116 Tom Waddle .10 .05
❑ 117 Lawrence Dawsey .10 .05
❑ 118 Mark Collins .10 .05

❑ 119 Willie Gault .10 .05
❑ 120 Barry Sanders 3.00 1.35
❑ 121 Leroy Hoard .20 .09
❑ 122 Anthony Munoz .20 .09
❑ 123 Jesse Sapolu .10 .05
❑ 124 Art Monk .20 .09
❑ 125 Randal Hill .10 .05
❑ 126 John Offerdahl .10 .05
❑ 127 Carlos Jenkins .10 .05
❑ 128 Al Smith .10 .05
❑ 129 Michael Irvin .40 .18
❑ 130 Kenneth Davis .10 .05
❑ 131 Curtis Conway RC 1.00 .45
❑ 132 Steve Atwater .10 .05
❑ 133 Neil Smith .20 .09
❑ 134 Steve Everitt RC .10 .05
❑ 135 Chris Mims .10 .05
❑ 136 Rickey Jackson .10 .05
❑ 137 Edgar Bennett .40 .18
❑ 138 Mike Pritchard .20 .09
❑ 139 Richard Dent .20 .09
❑ 140 Barry Foster .20 .09
❑ 141 Eugene Robinson .10 .05
❑ 142 Jackie Slater .10 .05
❑ 143 Paul Gruber .10 .05
❑ 144 Rob Moore .20 .09
❑ 145 Robert Smith RC 4.00 1.80
❑ 146 Lorenzo White .10 .05
❑ 147 Tommy Vardell .10 .05
❑ 148 Dave Meggett .10 .05
❑ 149 Vince Workman .10 .05
❑ 150 Terry Allen .40 .18
❑ 151 Howie Long .20 .09
❑ 152 Charles Haley .20 .09
❑ 153 Pete Metzelaars .10 .05
❑ 154 John Copeland RC .20 .09
❑ 155 Aeneas Williams .10 .05
❑ 156 Ricky Sanders .10 .05
❑ 157 Andre Ware .10 .05
❑ 158 Tony Paige .10 .05
❑ 159 Jerome Henderson .10 .05
❑ 160 Harold Green .10 .05
❑ 161 Wymon Henderson .10 .05
❑ 162 Andre Rison .20 .09
❑ 163 Donald Evans .10 .05
❑ 164 Todd Scott .10 .05
❑ 165 Steve Emtman .10 .05
❑ 166 William Fuller .10 .05
❑ 167 Michael Dean Perry .20 .09
❑ 168 Randall Cunningham .40 .18
❑ 169 Toi Cook .10 .05
❑ 170 Browning Nagle .10 .05
❑ 171 Darryl Henley .10 .05
❑ 172 George Teague RC .20 .09
❑ 173 Derrick Thomas .20 .09
❑ 174 Jay Novacek .20 .09
❑ 175 Mark Carrier DB .10 .05
❑ 176 Kevin Fagan .10 .05
❑ 177 Nate Lewis .10 .05
❑ 178 Courtney Hawkins .10 .05
❑ 179 Robert Blackmon .10 .05
❑ 180 Rick Mirer RC .75 .35
❑ 181 Mike Lodish .10 .05
❑ 182 Jarrod Bunch .10 .05
❑ 183 Anthony Smith .10 .05
❑ 184 Brian Noble .10 .05
❑ 185 Eric Bieniemy .10 .05
❑ 186 Keith Jackson .20 .09
❑ 187 Eric Martin .10 .05
❑ 188 Vance Johnson .10 .05
❑ 189 Kevin Mack .10 .05
❑ 190 Rich Camarillo .10 .05
❑ 191 Ashley Ambrose .10 .05
❑ 192 Ray Childress .10 .05
❑ 193 Jim Arnold .10 .05
❑ 194 Ricky Ervins .10 .05
❑ 195 Gary Anderson K .10 .05
❑ 196 Eric Allen .10 .05
❑ 197 Roger Craig .20 .09
❑ 198 Jon Vaughn .10 .05
❑ 199 Tim McDonald .10 .05
❑ 200 Broderick Thomas .10 .05
❑ 201 Jessie Tuggle .10 .05
❑ 202 Alonzo Mitz .10 .05
❑ 203 Harvey Williams .20 .09
❑ 204 Russell Maryland .10 .05
❑ 205 Marvin Washington .10 .05
❑ 206 Jim Everett .20 .09
❑ 207 Trace Armstrong .10 .05
❑ 208 Steve Young 1.50 .70
❑ 209 Tony Woods .10 .05
❑ 210 Brett Favre 4.00 1.80
❑ 211 Nate Odomes .10 .05
❑ 212 Ricky Proehl .10 .05
❑ 213 Jim Dombrowski .10 .05
❑ 214 Anthony Carter .20 .09
❑ 215 Tracy Simien .10 .05
❑ 216 Clay Matthews .20 .09
❑ 217 Patrick Bates RC .10 .05
❑ 218 Jeff George .40 .18
❑ 219 David Fulcher .10 .05
❑ 220 Phil Simms .20 .09
❑ 221 Eugene Chung .10 .05
❑ 222 Reggie Cobb .10 .05
❑ 223 Jim Sweeney .10 .05
❑ 224 Greg Lloyd .40 .18
❑ 225 Sean Jones .10 .05
❑ 226 Marvin Jones RC .10 .05
❑ 227 Bill Brooks .10 .05
❑ 228 Moe Gardner .10 .05
❑ 229 Louis Oliver .10 .05
❑ 230 Flipper Anderson .10 .05
❑ 231 Marc Spindler .10 .05
❑ 232 Jerry Rice 2.00 .90
❑ 233 Chip Lohmiller .10 .05
❑ 234 Nolan Harrison .10 .05
❑ 235 Heath Sherman .10 .05
❑ 236 Reyna Thompson .10 .05
❑ 237 Derrick Walker .10 .05
❑ 238 Rufus Porter .10 .05
❑ 239 Checklist 1-125 .10 .05
❑ 240 Checklist 126-250 .10 .05
❑ 241 John Elway MC 1.50 .70
❑ 242 Troy Aikman MC .75 .35
❑ 243 Steve Emtman MC .10 .05
❑ 244 Ricky Watters MC .20 .09
❑ 245 Barry Foster MC .10 .05
❑ 246 Dan Marino MC 1.50 .70
❑ 247 Reggie White MC .20 .09
❑ 248 Thurman Thomas MC .20 .09
❑ 249 Broderick Thomas MC .10 .05
❑ 250 Joe Montana MC 1.50 .70
❑ 251 Tim Goad .10 .05
❑ 252 Joe Nash .10 .05
❑ 253 Anthony Johnson .20 .09
❑ 254 Carl Pickens .40 .18
❑ 255 Steve Beuerlein .10 .05
❑ 256 Anthony Newman .10 .05
❑ 257 Corey Miller .10 .05
❑ 258 Steve DeBerg .10 .05
❑ 259 Johnny Holland .10 .05
❑ 260 Jerry Ball .10 .05
❑ 261 Siupeli Malamala RC .10 .05
❑ 262 Steve Wisniewski .10 .05
❑ 263 Kelvin Pritchett .10 .05
❑ 264 Chris Gardocki .10 .05
❑ 265 Henry Thomas .10 .05
❑ 266 Arthur Marshall RC .10 .05
❑ 267 Quinn Early .20 .09
❑ 268 Jonathan Hayes .10 .05
❑ 269 Eric Pegram .20 .09
❑ 270 Clyde Simmons .10 .05
❑ 271 Eric Moten .10 .05
❑ 272 Brian Mitchell .20 .09
❑ 273 Adrian Cooper .10 .05
❑ 274 Gaston Green .10 .05
❑ 275 John Taylor .20 .09
❑ 276 Jeff Uhlenhake .10 .05
❑ 277 Phil Hansen .10 .05
❑ 278A K.Williams RC WR ERR .40 .18
(Missing draft pick logo on front)
❑ 278B K.Williams RC WR COR .40 .18
(With draft pick logo)
❑ 279 Robert Massey .10 .05
❑ 280A Drew Bledsoe RC ERR 8.00 3.60
(Missing draft pick logo on front)
❑ 280B Drew Bledsoe RC COR 4.00 1.80
(Draft pick logo on front)
❑ 281 Walter Reeves .10 .05
❑ 282A Carlton Gray RC ERR .25 .11
(Missing draft pick logo on front)
❑ 282B Carlton Gray RC COR .15 .07
(Draft pick logo on front)
❑ 283 Derek Brown TE .10 .05
❑ 284 Martin Mayhew .10 .05
❑ 285 Sean Gilbert .20 .09
❑ 286 Jessie Hester .10 .05
❑ 287 Mark Clayton .10 .05
❑ 288 Blair Thomas .10 .05
❑ 289 J.J. Birden .10 .05
❑ 290 Shannon Sharpe .40 .18
❑ 291 Richard Fain RC .10 .05
❑ 292 Gene Atkins .10 .05
❑ 293 Burt Grossman .10 .05
❑ 294 Chris Doleman .10 .05
❑ 295 Pat Swilling .10 .05
❑ 296 Mike Kenn .10 .05
❑ 297 Merril Hoge .10 .05
❑ 298 Don Mosebar .10 .05
❑ 299 Kevin Smith .20 .09
❑ 300 Darrell Green .10 .05
❑ 301A Dan Footman RC ERR .25 .11
(Missing draft pick logo on front)
❑ 301B Dan Footman RC COR .15 .07
(Draft pick logo on front)
❑ 302 Vestee Jackson .10 .05
❑ 303 Carwell Gardner .10 .05
❑ 304 Amp Lee .10 .05
❑ 305 Bruce Matthews .10 .05
❑ 306 Antone Davis .10 .05
❑ 307 Dean Biasucci .10 .05
❑ 308 Maurice Hurst .10 .05
❑ 309 John Kasay .10 .05
❑ 310 Lawrence Taylor .20 .09
❑ 311 Ken Harvey .10 .05
❑ 312 Willie Davis .20 .09
❑ 313 Tony Bennett .10 .05
❑ 314 Jay Schroeder .10 .05
❑ 315 Darren Perry .10 .05
❑ 316A Troy Drayton RC ERR .25 .11
(Missing draft pick logo on front)
❑ 316B Troy Drayton RC COR .15 .07
(Draft pick logo on front)
❑ 317A Dan Williams RC ERR .25 .11
(Missing draft pick logo on front)
❑ 317B Dan Williams RC COR .15 .07
(Draft pick logo on front)
❑ 318 Michael Haynes .20 .09
❑ 319 Renaldo Turnbull .10 .05
❑ 320 Junior Seau .20 .09
❑ 321 Ray Crockett .10 .05
❑ 322 Will Furrer .10 .05
❑ 323 Byron Evans .10 .05
❑ 324 Jim McMahon .10 .05
❑ 325 Robert Jones .10 .05
❑ 326 Eric Davis .10 .05
❑ 327 Jeff Cross .10 .05
❑ 328 Kyle Clifton .10 .05
❑ 329 Haywood Jeffires .20 .09
❑ 330 Jeff Hostetler .20 .09
❑ 331 Darryl Talley .10 .05
❑ 332 Keith McCants .10 .05
❑ 333 Mo Lewis .10 .05
❑ 334 Matt Stover .10 .05
❑ 335 Ferrell Edmunds .10 .05
❑ 336 Matt Brock .10 .05
❑ 337 Ernie Mills .10 .05
❑ 338 Shane Dronett .10 .05
❑ 339 Brad Muster .10 .05
❑ 340 Jesse Solomon .10 .05
❑ 341 John Randle .20 .09
❑ 342 Chris Spielman .20 .09
❑ 343 David Whitmore .10 .05
❑ 344 Glenn Parker .10 .05
❑ 345 Marco Coleman .10 .05
❑ 346 Kenneth Gant .10 .05
❑ 347 Cris Dishman .10 .05
❑ 348 Kenny Walker .10 .05
❑ 349A R.Potts RC ERR .25 .11
(Missing draft pick logo on front)
❑ 349B R.Potts RC COR .15 .07
(Draft pick logo on front)
❑ 350 Reggie White .40 .18
❑ 351 Gerald Robinson .10 .05
❑ 352 Mark Rypien .10 .05
❑ 353 Stan Humphries .20 .09
❑ 354 Chris Singleton .10 .05
❑ 355 Herschel Walker .20 .09

❑	356 Ron Hall	.10	.05
❑	357 Ethan Horton	.10	.05
❑	358 Anthony Pleasant	.10	.05
❑	359A Thomas Smith RC ERR	.25	.11
	(Missing draft pick logo on front)		
❑	359B Thomas Smith RC COR	.15	.07
	(Draft pick logo on front)		
❑	360 Audray McMillian	.10	.05
❑	361 D.J. Johnson	.10	.05
❑	362 Ron Heller	.10	.05
❑	363 Bern Brostek	.10	.05
❑	364 Ronnie Lott	.20	.09
❑	365 Reggie Johnson	.10	.05
❑	366 Lin Elliott	.10	.05
❑	367 Lemuel Stinson	.10	.05
❑	368 William White	.10	.05
❑	369 Ernie Jones	.10	.05
❑	370 Tom Rathman	.10	.05
❑	371 Tommy Kane	.10	.05
❑	372 David Brandon	.10	.05
❑	373 Lee Johnson	.10	.05
❑	374 Wade Wilson	.10	.05
❑	375 Nick Lowery	.10	.05
❑	376 Bubba McDowell	.10	.05
❑	377A W.Simmons RC ERR	.25	.11
	(Missing draft pick logo on fron)		
❑	377B W.Simmons RC COR	.15	.07
	(Draft pick logo on front)		
❑	378 Calvin Williams	.20	.09
❑	379 Courtney Hall	.10	.05
❑	380 Troy Vincent	.10	.05
❑	381 Tim McGee	.10	.05
❑	382 Russell Freeman RC	.10	.05
❑	383 Steve Tasker	.20	.09
❑	384A Michael Strahan RC ERR	.15	.07
	(Missing draft pick logo on front)		
❑	384B Michael Strahan RC COR	.15	.07
	(Draft pick logo on front)		
❑	385 Greg Skrepenak	.10	.05
❑	386 Jake Reed	.20	.09
❑	387 Pete Stoyanovich	.10	.05
❑	388 Levon Kirkland	.10	.05
❑	389 Mel Gray	.20	.09
❑	390 Brian Washington	.10	.05
❑	391 Don Griffin	.10	.05
❑	392 Desmond Howard	.20	.09
❑	393 Luis Sharpe	.10	.05
❑	394 Mike Johnson	.10	.05
❑	395 Andre Tippett	.10	.05
❑	396 Donnell Woolford	.10	.05
❑	397A D.DuBose RC ERR	.40	.18
	(Missing draft pick logo on front)		
❑	397B Demetrius DuBose RC COR	.30	.14
	(Draft pick logo on front)		
❑	398 Pat Terrell	.10	.05
❑	399 Todd McNair	.10	.05
❑	400 Ken Norton	.20	.09
❑	401 Keith Hamilton	.10	.05
❑	402 Andy Heck	.10	.05
❑	403 Jeff Gossett	.10	.05
❑	404 Dexter McNabb	.10	.05
❑	405 Richmond Webb	.10	.05
❑	406 Irving Fryar	.20	.09
❑	407 Brian Hansen	.10	.05
❑	408 David Little	.10	.05
❑	409A Glyn Milburn RC ERR	.40	.18
	(Missing draft pick logo on front)		
❑	409B Glyn Milburn RC COR	.20	.09
	(Draft pick logo on front)		
❑	410 Doug Dawson	.10	.05
❑	411 Scott Mersereau	.10	.05
❑	412 Don Beebe	.10	.05
❑	413 Vaughan Johnson	.10	.05
❑	414 Jack Del Rio	.10	.05
❑	415A D.Gordon RC ERR	.25	.11
	(Missing draft pick logo on front)		
❑	415B D.Gordon RC COR	.15	.07
	(Draft pick logo on front)		
❑	416 Mark Schlereth	.10	.05
❑	417 Lomas Brown	.10	.05
❑	418 William Thomas	.10	.05
❑	419 James Francis	.10	.05
❑	420 Quentin Coryatt	.20	.09
❑	421 Tyji Armstrong	.10	.05
❑	422 Hugh Millen	.10	.05
❑	423 Adrian White RC	.10	.05
❑	424 Eddie Anderson	.10	.05
❑	425 Mark Ingram	.10	.05
❑	426 Ken O'Brien	.10	.05
❑	427 Simon Fletcher	.10	.05
❑	428 Tim McKyer	.10	.05
❑	429 Leonard Marshall	.10	.05
❑	430 Eric Green	.10	.05
❑	431 Leonard Harris	.10	.05
❑	432 Darin Jordan RC	.10	.05
❑	433 Erik Howard	.10	.05
❑	434 David Lang	.10	.05
❑	435 Eric Turner	.10	.05
❑	436 Michael Cofer	.10	.05
❑	437 Jeff Bryant	.10	.05
❑	438 Charles McRae	.10	.05
❑	439 Henry Jones	.10	.05
❑	440 Joe Montana	3.00	1.35
❑	441 Morten Andersen	.10	.05
❑	442 Jeff Jaeger	.10	.05
❑	443 Leslie O'Neal	.20	.09
❑	444 LeRoy Butler	.10	.05
❑	445 Steve Jordan	.10	.05
❑	446 Brad Edwards	.10	.05
❑	447 J.B. Brown	.10	.05
❑	448 Kerry Cash	.10	.05
❑	449 Mark Tuinei	.10	.05
❑	450 Rodney Peete	.10	.05
❑	451 Sheldon White	.10	.05
❑	452 Wesley Carroll	.10	.05
❑	453 Brad Baxter	.10	.05
❑	454 Mike Pitts	.10	.05
❑	455 Greg Montgomery	.10	.05
❑	456 Kenny Davidson	.10	.05
❑	457 Scott Fulhage	.10	.05
❑	458 Greg Townsend	.10	.05
❑	459 Rod Bernstine	.10	.05
❑	460 Gary Clark	.20	.09
❑	461 Hardy Nickerson	.20	.09
❑	462 Sean Landeta	.10	.05
❑	463 Rob Burnett	.10	.05
❑	464 Fred Barnett	.20	.09
❑	465 John L. Williams	.10	.05
❑	466 Anthony Miller	.20	.09
❑	467 Roman Phifer	.10	.05
❑	468 Rich Moran	.10	.05
❑	469A Willie Roaf RC ERR	.25	.11
	(Missing draft pick logo on front)		
❑	469B Willie Roaf RC COR	.15	.07
	(Draft pick logo on front)		
❑	470 William Perry	.20	.09
❑	471 Marcus Allen	.40	.18
❑	472 Carl Lee	.10	.05
❑	473 Kurt Gouveia	.10	.05
❑	474 Jarvis Williams	.10	.05
❑	475 Alfred Williams	.10	.05
❑	476 Mark Stepnoski	.10	.05
❑	477 Steve Wallace	.10	.05
❑	478 Pat Harlow	.10	.05
❑	479 Chip Banks	.10	.05
❑	480 Cornelius Bennett	.20	.09
❑	481A Ryan McNeil RC ERR	.25	.11
	(Missing draft pick logo on front)		
❑	481B Ryan McNeil RC COR	.20	.09
	(Draft pick logo on front)		
❑	482 Norm Johnson	.10	.05
❑	483 Dermontti Dawson	.10	.05
❑	484 Dwayne White	.10	.05
❑	485 Derek Russell	.10	.05
❑	486 Lionel Washington	.10	.05
❑	487 Eric Hill	.10	.05
❑	488 Micheal Barrow RC	.20	.09
❑	489 Checklist 251-375 UER	.10	.05
	(No. 277 Hansen misspelled Hanson)		
❑	490 Checklist 376-500 UER	.10	.05
	(No. 488 Micheal Barrow misspelled Michael)		
❑	491 Emmitt Smith MC	1.50	.70
❑	492 Derrick Thomas MC	.20	.09
❑	493 Deion Sanders MC	.40	.18
❑	494 Randall Cunningham MC	.20	.09
❑	495 Sterling Sharpe MC	.20	.09
❑	496 Barry Sanders MC	1.50	.70
❑	497 Thurman Thomas MC	.20	.09
❑	498 Brett Favre MC	2.00	.90
❑	499 Vaughan Johnson MC	.10	.05
❑	500 Steve Young MC	.75	.35
❑	501 Marvin Jones MC	.10	.05
❑	502 Reggie Brooks RC MC	.20	.09
❑	503 Eric Curry MC	.10	.05
❑	504 Drew Bledsoe MC	2.00	.90
❑	505 Glyn Milburn MC	.20	.09
❑	506 Jerome Bettis MC	.75	.35
❑	507 Robert Smith MC	1.50	.70
❑	508 Dana Stubblefield RC MC	.20	.09
❑	509 Tom Carter MC	.20	.09
❑	510 Rick Mirer MC	.40	.18
❑	511 Russell Copeland RC	.20	.09
❑	512 Deon Figures RC	.10	.05
❑	513 Tony McGee RC	.20	.09
❑	514 Derrick Lassic RC	.10	.05
❑	515 Everett Lindsay RC	.10	.05
❑	516 Derek Brown RC RBK	.10	.05
❑	517 Harold Alexander RC	.10	.05
❑	518 Tom Scott RC	.10	.05
❑	519 Elvis Grbac RC	4.00	1.80
❑	520 Terry Kirby RC	.40	.18
❑	521 Doug Pelfrey RC	.10	.05
❑	522 Horace Copeland RC	.20	.09
❑	523 Irv Smith RC	.10	.05
❑	524 Lincoln Kennedy RC	.10	.05
❑	525 Jason Elam RC	.20	.09
❑	526 Qadry Ismail RC	1.25	.55
❑	527 Artie Smith RC	.10	.05
❑	528 Tyrone Hughes RC	.20	.09
❑	529 Lance Gunn RC	.10	.05
❑	530 Vincent Brisby RC	.40	.18
❑	531 Patrick Robinson RC	.10	.05
❑	532 Raghib Ismail	.20	.09
❑	533 Willie Beamon RC	.10	.05
❑	534 Vaughn Hebron RC	.10	.05
❑	535 Darren Drozdov RC	.40	.18
❑	536 James Jett RC	1.00	.45
❑	537 Michael Bates RC	.10	.05
❑	538 Tom Rouen RC	.10	.05
❑	539 Michael Husted RC	.10	.05
❑	540 Greg Robinson RC	.10	.05
❑	541 Carl Banks	.10	.05
❑	542 Kevin Greene	.40	.18
❑	543 Scott Mitchell	.40	.18
❑	544 Michael Brooks	.10	.05
❑	545 Shane Conlan	.10	.05
❑	546 Vinny Testaverde	.20	.09
❑	547 Robert Delpino	.10	.05
❑	548 Bill Fralic	.10	.05
❑	549 Carlton Bailey	.10	.05
❑	550 Johnny Johnson	.10	.05
❑	NNO Jerry Rice RB UER	10.00	4.50
	(Wrong date for record touchdown)		
❑	P1 Promo Sheet	5.00	2.20
	Johnny Bailey		
	Vai Sikahema		
	Richard Dent		
	Sterling Sharpe		
	Tommy Barnhardt		
	Cris Carter		
	Cortez Kennedy		
	Christian Okoye		
	Reggie Cobb		

1994 Stadium Club

	MINT	NRMT
COMPLETE SET (630)	60.00	27.00
COMP.SERIES 1 (270)	25.00	11.00
COMP.SERIES 2 (270)	25.00	11.00
COMP.HIGH SERIES (90)	10.00	4.50
❑ 1 Dan Wilkinson RC	.20	.09
❑ 2 Chip Lohmiller	.10	.05
❑ 3 Roosevelt Potts	.10	.05
❑ 4 Martin Mayhew	.10	.05
❑ 5 Shane Conlan	.10	.05
❑ 6 Sam Adams RC	.20	.09
❑ 7 Mike Kenn	.10	.05
❑ 8 Tim Goad	.10	.05
❑ 9 Tony Jones	.10	.05
❑ 10 Ronald Moore	.10	.05
❑ 11 Mark Bortz	.10	.05
❑ 12 Darren Carrington	.10	.05
❑ 13 Eric Martin	.10	.05
❑ 14 Eric Allen	.10	.05
❑ 15 Aaron Glenn RC	.20	.09
❑ 16 Bryan Cox	.10	.05
❑ 17 Levon Kirkland	.10	.05
❑ 18 Qadry Ismail	.40	.18
❑ 19 Shane Dronett	.10	.05
❑ 20 Chris Spielman	.20	.09
❑ 21 Rob Fredrickson RC	.20	.09
❑ 22 Wayne Simmons	.10	.05
❑ 23 Glenn Montgomery	.10	.05
❑ 24 Jason Sehorn RC	.50	.23
❑ 25 Nick Lowery	.10	.05
❑ 26 Dennis Brown	.10	.05
❑ 27 Kenneth Davis	.10	.05
❑ 28 Shante Carver RC	.10	.05
❑ 29 Ryan Yarborough RC	.10	.05
❑ 30 Cortez Kennedy	.20	.09
❑ 31 Anthony Pleasant	.10	.05
❑ 32 Jessie Tuggle	.10	.05
❑ 33 Herschel Walker	.20	.09
❑ 34 Andre Collins	.10	.05
❑ 35 William Floyd RC	.40	.18
❑ 36 Harold Green	.10	.05
❑ 37 Courtney Hawkins	.10	.05
❑ 38 Curtis Conway	.40	.18
❑ 39 Ben Coates	.40	.18
❑ 40 Natrone Means	.40	.18
❑ 41 Eric Hill	.10	.05
❑ 42 Keith Kartz	.10	.05
❑ 43 Alexander Wright	.10	.05
❑ 44 Willie Roaf	.10	.05
❑ 45 Vencie Glenn	.10	.05
❑ 46 Ronnie Lott	.20	.09
❑ 47 George Koonce	.10	.05
❑ 48 Rod Woodson	.40	.18
❑ 49 Tim Grunhard	.10	.05
❑ 50 Cody Carlson	.10	.05
❑ 51 Bryant Young RC	.40	.18
❑ 52 Jay Novacek	.20	.09
❑ 53 Darryl Talley	.10	.05
❑ 54 Harry Colon	.10	.05
❑ 55 Dave Meggett	.10	.05
❑ 56 Aubrey Beavers RC	.10	.05
❑ 57 James Folston	.10	.05
❑ 58 Willie Davis	.20	.09
❑ 59 Jason Elam	.10	.05
❑ 60 Eric Metcalf	.20	.09
❑ 61 Bruce Armstrong	.10	.05
❑ 62 Ron Heller	.10	.05
❑ 63 LeRoy Butler	.10	.05
❑ 64 Terry Obee	.10	.05
❑ 65 Kurt Gouveia	.10	.05
❑ 66 Pierce Holt	.10	.05
❑ 67 David Alexander	.10	.05
❑ 68 Deral Boykin	.10	.05
❑ 69 Carl Pickens	.40	.18
❑ 70 Broderick Thomas	.10	.05
❑ 71 Barry Sanders CT	1.50	.70
❑ 72 Qadry Ismail CT	.40	.18
❑ 73 Thurman Thomas CT	.40	.18
❑ 74 Junior Seau	.40	.18
❑ 75 Vinny Testaverde	.20	.09
❑ 76 Tyrone Hughes	.20	.09
❑ 77 Nate Newton	.10	.05
❑ 78 Eric Swann	.20	.09
❑ 79 Brad Baxter	.10	.05
❑ 80 Dana Stubblefield	.40	.18
❑ 81 Jumbo Elliott	.10	.05
❑ 82 Steve Wisniewski	.10	.05
❑ 83 Eddie Robinson	.10	.05
❑ 84 Isaac Davis	.10	.05
❑ 85 Cris Carter	.60	.25
❑ 86 Mel Gray	.10	.05
❑ 87 Cornelius Bennett	.20	.09
❑ 88 Neil O'Donnell	.40	.18
❑ 89 Jon Hand	.10	.05
❑ 90 John Elway	3.00	1.35
❑ 91 Bill Hitchcock	.10	.05
❑ 92 Neil Smith	.40	.18
❑ 93 Joe Johnson RC	.10	.05
❑ 94 Edgar Bennett	.40	.18
❑ 95 Vincent Brown	.10	.05
❑ 96 Tommy Vardell	.10	.05
❑ 97 Donnell Woolford	.10	.05
❑ 98 Lincoln Kennedy	.10	.05
❑ 99 O.J. McDuffie	.40	.18
❑ 100 Heath Shuler RC	.40	.18
❑ 101 Jerry Rice BO	.75	.35
❑ 102 Erik Williams BO	.10	.05
❑ 103 Randall McDaniel BO	.10	.05
❑ 104 Dermontti Dawson BO	.10	.05
❑ 105 Nate Newton BO	.10	.05
❑ 106 Harris Barton BO	.10	.05
❑ 107 Shannon Sharpe BO	.20	.09
❑ 108 Sterling Sharpe BO	.20	.09
❑ 109 Steve Young BO	.60	.25
❑ 110 Emmitt Smith BO	1.25	.55
❑ 111 Thurman Thomas BO	.40	.18
❑ 112 Kyle Clifton	.10	.05
❑ 113 Desmond Howard	.20	.09
❑ 114 Quinn Early	.20	.09
❑ 115 David Klingler	.10	.05
❑ 116 Bern Brostek	.10	.05
❑ 117 Gary Clark	.20	.09
❑ 118 Courtney Hall	.10	.05
❑ 119 Joe King	.10	.05
❑ 120 Quentin Coryatt	.10	.05
❑ 121 Johnnie Morton RC	1.50	.70
❑ 122 Andre Reed	.20	.09
❑ 123 Eric Davis	.10	.05
❑ 124 Jack Del Rio	.10	.05
❑ 125 Greg Lloyd	.40	.18
❑ 126 Bubba McDowell	.10	.05
❑ 127 Mark Jackson	.10	.05
❑ 128 Jeff Jaeger	.10	.05
❑ 129 Chris Warren	.20	.09
❑ 130 Tom Waddle	.10	.05
❑ 131 Tony Smith	.10	.05
❑ 132 Todd Collins	.10	.05
❑ 133 Mark Bavaro	.10	.05
❑ 134 Joe Phillips	.10	.05
❑ 135 Chris Jacke	.10	.05
❑ 136 Glyn Milburn	.20	.09
❑ 137 Keith Jackson	.10	.05
❑ 138 Steve Tovar	.10	.05
❑ 139 Tim Johnson	.10	.05
❑ 140 Brian Washington	.10	.05
❑ 141 Troy Drayton	.10	.05
❑ 142 Dewayne Washington RC	.20	.09
❑ 143 Erik Williams	.10	.05
❑ 144 Eric Turner	.10	.05
❑ 145 John Taylor	.20	.09
❑ 146 Richard Cooper	.10	.05
❑ 147 Van Malone	.10	.05
❑ 148 Tim Ruddy RC	.10	.05
❑ 149 Henry Jones	.10	.05
❑ 150 Tim Brown	.40	.18
❑ 151 Stan Humphries	.40	.18
❑ 152 Harry Newsome	.10	.05
❑ 153 Craig Erickson	.10	.05
❑ 154 Gary Anderson K	.10	.05
❑ 155 Ray Childress	.10	.05
❑ 156 Howard Cross	.10	.05
❑ 157 Heath Sherman	.10	.05
❑ 158 Terrell Buckley	.10	.05
❑ 159 J.B. Brown	.10	.05
❑ 160 Joe Montana	3.00	1.35
❑ 161 David Wyman	.10	.05
❑ 162 Norm Johnson	.10	.05
❑ 163 Rod Stephens	.10	.05
❑ 164 Willie McGinest RC	.40	.18
❑ 165 Barry Sanders	3.00	1.35
❑ 166 Marc Logan	.10	.05
❑ 167 Anthony Newman	.10	.05
❑ 168 Russell Maryland	.10	.05
❑ 169 Luis Sharpe	.10	.05
❑ 170 Jim Kelly	.40	.18
❑ 171 Tre Johnson RC	.10	.05
❑ 172 Johnny Mitchell	.10	.05
❑ 173 David Palmer RC	1.00	.45
❑ 174 Bob Dahl	.10	.05
❑ 175 Aaron Wallace	.10	.05
❑ 176 Chris Gardocki	.10	.05
❑ 177 Hardy Nickerson	.20	.09
❑ 178 Jeff Query	.10	.05
❑ 179 Leslie O'Neal	.10	.05
❑ 180 Kevin Greene	.40	.18
❑ 181 Alonzo Spellman	.10	.05
❑ 182 Reggie Brooks	.20	.09
❑ 183 Dana Stubblefield	.40	.18
❑ 184 Tyrone Hughes	.20	.09
❑ 185 Drew Bledsoe GE	1.00	.45
❑ 186 Ronald Moore GE	.10	.05
❑ 187 Jason Elam GE	.10	.05
❑ 188 Rick Mirer GE	.40	.18
❑ 189 Willie Roaf GE	.10	.05
❑ 190 Jerome Bettis GE	.40	.18
❑ 191 Brad Hopkins	.10	.05
❑ 192 Derek Brown RBK	.10	.05
❑ 193 Nolan Harrison	.10	.05
❑ 194 John Randle	.20	.09
❑ 195 Carlton Bailey	.10	.05
❑ 196 Kevin Williams	.20	.09
❑ 197 Greg Hill RC	.40	.18
❑ 198 Mark McMillian	.10	.05
❑ 199 Brad Edwards	.10	.05
❑ 200 Dan Marino	3.00	1.35
❑ 201 Ricky Watters	.40	.18
❑ 202 George Teague	.10	.05
❑ 203 Steve Beuerlein	.10	.05
❑ 204 Jeff Burris RC	.20	.09
❑ 205 Steve Atwater	.10	.05
❑ 206 John Thierry RC	.10	.05
❑ 207 Patrick Hunter	.10	.05
❑ 208 Wayne Gandy	.10	.05
❑ 209 Derrick Moore	.10	.05
❑ 210 Phil Simms	.20	.09
❑ 211 Kirk Lowdermilk	.10	.05
❑ 212 Patrick Robinson	.10	.05
❑ 213 Kevin Mitchell	.10	.05
❑ 214 Jonathan Hayes	.10	.05
❑ 215 Michael Dean Perry	.20	.09
❑ 216 John Fina	.10	.05
❑ 217 Anthony Smith	.10	.05
❑ 218 Paul Gruber	.10	.05
❑ 219 Carnell Lake	.10	.05
❑ 220 Carl Lee	.10	.05
❑ 221 Steve Christie	.10	.05
❑ 222 Greg Montgomery	.10	.05
❑ 223 Reggie Brooks	.20	.09
❑ 224 Derrick Thomas	.40	.18
❑ 225 Eric Metcalf	.20	.09
❑ 226 Michael Haynes	.20	.09
❑ 227 Bobby Hebert	.10	.05
❑ 228 Tyrone Hughes	.20	.09
❑ 229 Donald Frank	.10	.05
❑ 230 Vaughan Johnson	.10	.05
❑ 231 Eric Thomas	.10	.05
❑ 232 Ernest Givins	.20	.09
❑ 233 Charles Haley	.20	.09
❑ 234 Darrell Green	.10	.05
❑ 235 Harold Alexander	.10	.05
❑ 236 Dwayne Sabb	.10	.05
❑ 237 Harris Barton	.10	.05
❑ 238 Randall Cunningham	.40	.18
❑ 239 Ray Buchanan	.10	.05
❑ 240 Sterling Sharpe	.20	.09
❑ 241 Chris Mims	.10	.05
❑ 242 Mark Carrier DB	.10	.05
❑ 243 Ricky Proehl	.10	.05
❑ 244 Michael Brooks	.10	.05
❑ 245 Sean Gilbert	.10	.05
❑ 246 David Lutz	.10	.05
❑ 247 Kelvin Martin	.10	.05
❑ 248 Scottie Graham RC	.20	.09
❑ 249 Irving Fryar	.20	.09
❑ 250 Ricardo McDonald	.10	.05
❑ 251 Marvcus Patton	.10	.05
❑ 252 Errict Rhett RC	1.25	.55

❑ 253	Winston Moss	.10	.05
❑ 254	Rod Bernstine	.10	.05
❑ 255	Terry Wooden	.10	.05
❑ 256	Antonio Langham RC	.20	.09
❑ 257	Tommy Barnhardt	.10	.05
❑ 258	Marvin Washington	.10	.05
❑ 259	Bo Orlando	.10	.05
❑ 260	Marcus Allen	.40	.18
❑ 261	Mario Bates RC	.40	.18
❑ 262	Marco Coleman	.10	.05
❑ 263	Doug Riesenberg	.10	.05
❑ 264	Jesse Sapolu	.10	.05
❑ 265	Dermontti Dawson	.10	.05
❑ 266	Fernando Smith RC	.10	.05
❑ 267	David Szott	.10	.05
❑ 268	Steve Christie	.10	.05
❑ 269	Bruce Matthews	.10	.05
❑ 270	Michael Irvin	.40	.18
❑ 271	Seth Joyner	.10	.05
❑ 272	Santana Dotson	.20	.09
❑ 273	Vincent Brisby	.40	.18
❑ 274	Rohn Stark	.10	.05
❑ 275	John Copeland	.10	.05
❑ 276	Toby Wright	.10	.05
❑ 277	David Griggs	.10	.05
❑ 278	Aaron Taylor	.10	.05
❑ 279	Chris Doleman	.10	.05
❑ 280	Reggie Brooks	.20	.09
❑ 281	Flipper Anderson	.10	.05
❑ 282	Alvin Harper	.20	.09
❑ 283	Chris Hinton	.10	.05
❑ 284	Kelvin Pritchett	.10	.05
❑ 285	Russell Copeland	.10	.05
❑ 286	Dwight Stone	.10	.05
❑ 287	Jeff Gossett	.10	.05
❑ 288	Larry Allen RC	.20	.09
❑ 289	Kevin Mawae	.10	.05
❑ 290	Mark Collins	.10	.05
❑ 291	Chris Zorich	.10	.05
❑ 292	Vince Buck	.10	.05
❑ 293	Gene Atkins	.10	.05
❑ 294	Webster Slaughter	.10	.05
❑ 295	Steve Young	1.25	.55
❑ 296	Dan Williams	.10	.05
❑ 297	Jessie Armstead	.10	.05
❑ 298	Victor Bailey	.10	.05
❑ 299	John Carney	.10	.05
❑ 300	Emmitt Smith	2.50	1.10
❑ 301	Bucky Brooks RC	.10	.05
❑ 302	Mo Lewis	.10	.05
❑ 303	Eugene Daniel	.10	.05
❑ 304	Tyji Armstrong	.10	.05
❑ 305	Eugene Chung	.10	.05
❑ 306	Rocket Ismail	.20	.09
❑ 307	Sean Jones	.10	.05
❑ 308	Rick Cunningham	.10	.05
❑ 309	Ken Harvey	.10	.05
❑ 310	Jeff George	.40	.18
❑ 311	Jon Vaughn	.10	.05
❑ 312	Roy Barker RC	.10	.05
❑ 313	Micheal Barrow	.10	.05
❑ 314	Ryan McNeil	.10	.05
❑ 315	Pete Stoyanovich	.10	.05
❑ 316	Darryl Williams	.10	.05
❑ 317	Renaldo Turnbull	.10	.05
❑ 318	Eric Green	.10	.05
❑ 319	Nate Lewis	.10	.05
❑ 320	Mike Flores	.10	.05
❑ 321	Derek Russell	.10	.05
❑ 322	Marcus Spears	.10	.05
❑ 323	Corey Miller	.10	.05
❑ 324	Derrick Thomas	.40	.18
❑ 325	Steve Everitt	.10	.05
❑ 326	Brent Jones	.20	.09
❑ 327	Marshall Faulk RC	5.00	2.20
❑ 328	Don Beebe	.10	.05
❑ 329	Harry Swayne	.10	.05
❑ 330	Boomer Esiason	.20	.09
❑ 331	Don Mosebar	.10	.05
❑ 332	Isaac Bruce RC	5.00	2.20
❑ 333	Rickey Jackson	.10	.05
❑ 334	Daryl Johnston	.20	.09
❑ 335	Lorenzo Lynch	.10	.05
❑ 336	Brian Blades	.20	.09
❑ 337	Michael Timpson	.10	.05
❑ 338	Reggie Cobb	.10	.05
❑ 339	Joe Walter	.10	.05
❑ 340	Barry Foster	.10	.05
❑ 341	Richmond Webb	.10	.05
❑ 342	Pat Swilling	.10	.05
❑ 343	Shaun Gayle	.10	.05
❑ 344	Reggie Roby	.10	.05
❑ 345	Chris Calloway	.10	.05
❑ 346	Doug Dawson	.10	.05
❑ 347	Rob Burnett	.10	.05
❑ 348	Dana Hall	.10	.05
❑ 349	Horace Copeland	.10	.05
❑ 350	Shannon Sharpe	.20	.09
❑ 351	Rich Miano	.10	.05
❑ 352	Henry Thomas	.10	.05
❑ 353	Dan Saleaumua	.10	.05
❑ 354	Kevin Ross	.10	.05
❑ 355	Morten Andersen	.10	.05
❑ 356	Anthony Blaylock	.10	.05
❑ 357	Stanley Richard	.10	.05
❑ 358	Albert Lewis	.10	.05
❑ 359	Darren Woodson	.20	.09
❑ 360	Drew Bledsoe	1.50	.70
❑ 361	Eric Mahlum	.10	.05
❑ 362	Trent Dilfer RC	2.50	1.10
❑ 363	William Roberts	.10	.05
❑ 364	Robert Brooks	.40	.18
❑ 365	Jason Hanson	.10	.05
❑ 366	Troy Vincent	.10	.05
❑ 367	William Thomas	.10	.05
❑ 368	Lonnie Johnson RC	.10	.05
❑ 369	Jamir Miller RC	.10	.05
❑ 370	Michael Jackson	.20	.09
❑ 371	Charlie Ward CT RC	.40	.18
❑ 372	Shannon Sharpe CT	.20	.09
❑ 373	Jackie Slater CT	.10	.05
❑ 374	Steve Young CT	.60	.25
❑ 375	Bobby Wilson	.10	.05
❑ 376	Paul Frase	.10	.05
❑ 377	Dale Carter	.10	.05
❑ 378	Robert Delpino	.10	.05
❑ 379	Bert Emanuel RC	1.00	.45
❑ 380	Rick Mirer	.40	.18
❑ 381	Carlos Jenkins	.10	.05
❑ 382	Gary Brown	.10	.05
❑ 383	Doug Pelfrey	.10	.05
❑ 384	Dexter Carter	.10	.05
❑ 385	Chris Miller	.10	.05
❑ 386	Charles Johnson RC	.60	.25
❑ 387	James Joseph	.10	.05
❑ 388	Darrin Smith	.10	.05
❑ 389	James Jett	.10	.05
❑ 390	Junior Seau	.40	.18
❑ 391	Chris Slade	.10	.05
❑ 392	Jim Harbaugh	.40	.18
❑ 393	Herman Moore	.40	.18
❑ 394	Thomas Randolph RC	.10	.05
❑ 395	Lamar Thomas	.10	.05
❑ 396	Reggie Rivers	.10	.05
❑ 397	Larry Centers	.40	.18
❑ 398	Chad Brown	.10	.05
❑ 399	Terry Kirby	.40	.18
❑ 400	Bruce Smith	.40	.18
❑ 401	Keenan McCardell RC	2.00	.90
❑ 402	Tim McDonald	.10	.05
❑ 403	Robert Smith	.40	.18
❑ 404	Matt Brock	.10	.05
❑ 405	Tony McGee	.10	.05
❑ 406	Ethan Horton	.10	.05
❑ 407	Michael Haynes	.20	.09
❑ 408	Steve Jackson	.10	.05
❑ 409	Erik Kramer	.20	.09
❑ 410	Jerome Bettis	.40	.18
❑ 411	D.J. Johnson	.10	.05
❑ 412	John Alt	.10	.05
❑ 413	Jeff Lageman	.10	.05
❑ 414	Rick Tuten	.10	.05
❑ 415	Jeff Robinson	.10	.05
❑ 416	Kevin Lee RC	.10	.05
❑ 417	Thomas Lewis RC	.20	.09
❑ 418	Kerry Cash	.10	.05
❑ 419	Chuck Levy RC	.10	.05
❑ 420	Mark Ingram	.10	.05
❑ 421	Dennis Gibson	.10	.05
❑ 422	Tyronne Drakeford	.10	.05
❑ 423	James Washington	.10	.05
❑ 424	Dante Jones	.10	.05
❑ 425	Eugene Robinson	.10	.05
❑ 426	Johnny Johnson	.10	.05
❑ 427	Brian Mitchell	.10	.05
❑ 428	Charles Mincy	.10	.05
❑ 429	Mark Carrier WR	.20	.09
❑ 430	Vince Workman	.10	.05
❑ 431	James Francis	.10	.05
❑ 432	Clay Matthews	.10	.05
❑ 433	Randall McDaniel	.10	.05
❑ 434	Brad Ottis	.10	.05
❑ 435	Bruce Smith	.40	.18
❑ 436	Cortez Kennedy BD	.10	.05
❑ 437	John Randle BD	.20	.09
❑ 438	Neil Smith BD	.20	.09
❑ 439	Cornelius Bennett BD	.20	.09
❑ 440	Junior Seau BD	.20	.09
❑ 441	Derrick Thomas BD	.20	.09
❑ 442	Rod Woodson BD	.20	.09
❑ 443	Terry McDaniel BD	.10	.05
❑ 444	Tim McDonald BD	.10	.05
❑ 445	Mark Carrier DB BD	.10	.05
❑ 446	Irv Smith	.10	.05
❑ 447	Steve Wallace	.10	.05
❑ 448	Cris Dishman	.10	.05
❑ 449	Bill Brooks	.10	.05
❑ 450	Jeff Hostetler	.20	.09
❑ 451	Brenston Buckner RC	.10	.05
❑ 452	Ken Ruettgers	.10	.05
❑ 453	Marc Boutte	.10	.05
❑ 454	John Offerdahl	.10	.05
❑ 455	Allen Aldridge	.10	.05
❑ 456	Steve Emtman	.10	.05
❑ 457	Andre Rison	.20	.09
❑ 458	Shawn Jefferson	.10	.05
❑ 459	Todd Steussie RC	.20	.09
❑ 460	Scott Mitchell	.40	.18
❑ 461	Tom Carter	.10	.05
❑ 462	Donnell Bennett RC	.40	.18
❑ 463	James Jones	.10	.05
❑ 464	Antone Davis	.10	.05
❑ 465	Jim Everett	.20	.09
❑ 466	Tony Tolbert	.10	.05
❑ 467	Merril Hoge	.10	.05
❑ 468	Michael Bates	.10	.05
❑ 469	Phil Hansen	.10	.05
❑ 470	Rodney Hampton	.40	.18
❑ 471	Aeneas Williams	.10	.05
❑ 472	Al Del Greco	.10	.05
❑ 473	Todd Lyght	.10	.05
❑ 474	Joel Steed	.10	.05
❑ 475	Merton Hanks	.20	.09
❑ 476	Tony Stargell	.10	.05
❑ 477	Greg Robinson	.10	.05
❑ 478	Roger Duffy	.10	.05
❑ 479	Simon Fletcher	.10	.05
❑ 480	Reggie White	.40	.18
❑ 481	Lee Johnson	.10	.05
❑ 482	Wayne Martin	.10	.05
❑ 483	Thurman Thomas	.40	.18
❑ 484	Warren Moon	.40	.18
❑ 485	Sam Rogers RC	.10	.05
❑ 486	Erric Pegram	.10	.05
❑ 487	Will Wolford	.10	.05
❑ 488	Duane Young	.10	.05
❑ 489	Keith Hamilton	.10	.05
❑ 490	Haywood Jeffires	.20	.09
❑ 491	Trace Armstrong	.10	.05
❑ 492	J.J. Birden	.10	.05
❑ 493	Ricky Ervins	.10	.05
❑ 494	Robert Blackmon	.10	.05
❑ 495	William Perry	.20	.09
❑ 496	Robert Massey	.10	.05
❑ 497	Jim Jeffcoat	.10	.05
❑ 498	Pat Harlow	.10	.05
❑ 499	Jeff Cross	.10	.05
❑ 500	Jerry Rice	1.50	.70
❑ 501	Darnay Scott RC	1.50	.70
❑ 502	Clyde Simmons	.10	.05
❑ 503	Henry Rolling	.10	.05
❑ 504	James Hasty	.10	.05
❑ 505	Leroy Thompson	.10	.05
❑ 506	Darrell Thompson	.10	.05
❑ 507	Tim Bowens RC	.20	.09
❑ 508	Gerald Perry	.10	.05
❑ 509	Mike Croel	.10	.05
❑ 510	Sam Mills	.10	.05

No.	Player	Mint	Nrmt
511	Steve Young RZ	.60	.25
512	Hardy Nickerson RZ	.20	.09
513	Cris Carter RZ	.20	.09
514	Boomer Esiason RZ	.10	.05
515	Bruce Smith RZ	.20	.09
516	Emmitt Smith RZ	1.25	.55
517	Eugene Robinson RZ	.10	.05
518	Gary Brown RZ	.10	.05
519	Jerry Rice RZ	.75	.35
520	Troy Aikman RZ	.75	.35
521	Marcus Allen RZ	.20	.09
522	Junior Seau RZ	.20	.09
523	Sterling Sharpe RZ	.20	.09
524	Dana Stubblefield RZ	.20	.09
525	Tom Carter RZ	.10	.05
526	Pete Metzelaars	.10	.05
527	Russell Freeman	.10	.05
528	Keith Cash	.10	.05
529	Willie Drewrey	.10	.05
530	Randal Hill	.10	.05
531	Pepper Johnson	.10	.05
532	Rob Moore	.20	.09
533	Todd Kelly	.10	.05
534	Keith Byars	.10	.05
535	Mike Fox	.10	.05
536	Brett Favre	3.00	1.35
537	Terry McDaniel	.10	.05
538	Darren Perry	.10	.05
539	Maurice Hurst	.10	.05
540	Troy Aikman	1.50	.70
541	Junior Seau	.40	.18
542	Steve Broussard	.10	.05
543	Lorenzo White	.10	.05
544	Terry McDaniel	.10	.05
545	Henry Thomas	.10	.05
546	Tyrone Hughes	.20	.09
547	Mark Collins	.10	.05
548	Gary Anderson K	.10	.05
549	Darrell Green	.10	.05
550	Jerry Rice	1.25	.55
551	Cornelius Bennett	.20	.09
552	Aeneas Williams	.10	.05
553	Eric Metcalf	.20	.09
554	Jumbo Elliott	.10	.05
555	Mo Lewis	.10	.05
556	Darren Carrington	.10	.05
557	Kevin Greene	.40	.18
558	John Elway	2.50	1.10
559	Eugene Robinson	.10	.05
560	Drew Bledsoe	1.25	.55
561	Fred Barnett	.20	.09
562	Bernie Parmalee RC	.40	.18
563	Bryce Paup	.40	.18
564	Donnell Woolford	.10	.05
565	Terance Mathis	.20	.09
566	Santana Dotson	.20	.09
567	Randall McDaniel	.10	.05
568	Stanley Richard	.10	.05
569	Brian Blades	.20	.09
570	Jerome Bettis	.40	.18
571	Neil Smith	.40	.18
572	Andre Reed	.20	.09
573	Michael Bankston	.10	.05
574	Dana Stubblefield	.40	.18
575	Rod Woodson	.40	.18
576	Ken Harvey	.10	.05
577	Andre Rison	.20	.09
578	Darion Conner	.10	.05
579	Michael Strahan	.20	.09
580	Barry Sanders	2.50	1.10
581	Pepper Johnson	.10	.05
582	Lewis Tillman	.10	.05
583	Jeff George	.40	.18
584	Michael Haynes	.20	.09
585	Herschel Walker	.20	.09
586	Tim Brown	.40	.18
587	Jim Kelly	.40	.18
588	Ricky Watters	.40	.18
589	Randall Cunningham	.40	.18
590	Troy Aikman UER (Threw for 56, TD's in 93 season)	1.25	.55
591	Ken Norton Jr.	.20	.09
592	Cortez Kennedy	.20	.09
593	Ricky Ervins	.10	.05
594	Cris Carter	.50	.23
595	Sterling Sharpe	.20	.09
596	John Randle	.20	.09
597	Shannon Sharpe	.20	.09
598	Ray Crittenden RC	.10	.05
599	Barry Foster	.10	.05
600	Deion Sanders	.60	.25
601	Seth Joyner	.10	.05
602	Chris Warren	.20	.09
603	Tom Rathman	.10	.05
604	Brett Favre	2.50	1.10
605	Marshall Faulk	2.00	.90
606	Terry Allen	.20	.09
607	Ben Coates	.40	.18
608	Brian Washington	.10	.05
609	Henry Ellard	.20	.09
610	Dave Meggett	.10	.05
611	Stan Humphries	.40	.18
612	Warren Moon	.40	.18
613	Marcus Allen	.40	.18
614	Ed McDaniel	.10	.05
615	Joe Montana	2.50	1.10
616	Jeff Hostetler	.20	.09
617	Johnny Johnson	.10	.05
618	Andre Coleman RC	.10	.05
619	Willie Davis	.20	.09
620	Rick Mirer	.40	.18
621	Dan Marino	2.50	1.10
622	Rob Moore	.20	.09
623	Byron Bam Morris RC	.40	.18
624	Natrone Means	.40	.18
625	Steve Young	.75	.35
626	Jim Everett	.20	.09
627	Michael Brooks	.10	.05
628	Dermontti Dawson	.10	.05
629	Reggie White	.40	.18
630	Emmitt Smith	1.50	.70
O	Micheal Barrow TSC	4.00	1.80
NNO	Checklist Card 3	.10	.05
NNO	Checklist Card 1	.10	.05
NNO	Checklist Card 2	.10	.05

1995 Stadium Club

	MINT	NRMT
COMPLETE SET (450)	60.00	27.00
COMP.SERIES 1 (225)	30.00	13.50
COMP.SERIES 2 (225)	30.00	13.50

No.	Player	Mint	Nrmt
1	Steve Young	1.25	.55
2	Stan Humphries	.20	.09
3	Chris Boniol RC	.10	.05
4	Darren Perry	.10	.05
5	Vinny Testaverde	.20	.09
6	Aubrey Beavers	.10	.05
7	Dewayne Washington	.20	.09
8	Marion Butts	.10	.05
9	George Koonce	.10	.05
10	Joe Cain	.10	.05
11	Mike Johnson	.10	.05
12	Dale Carter	.20	.09
13	Greg Biekert	.10	.05
14	Aaron Pierce	.10	.05
15	Aeneas Williams	.10	.05
16	Stephen Grant RC	.10	.05
17	Henry Jones	.10	.05
18	James Williams	.10	.05
19	Andy Harmon	.10	.05
20	Anthony Miller	.20	.09
21	Kevin Ross	.10	.05
22	Erik Howard	.10	.05
23	Brian Blades	.20	.09
24	Trent Dilfer	.40	.18
25	Roman Phifer	.10	.05
26	Bruce Kozerski	.10	.05
27	Henry Ellard	.20	.09
28	Rich Camarillo	.10	.05
29	Richmond Webb	.10	.05
30	George Teague	.10	.05
31	Antonio Langham	.10	.05
32	Barry Foster	.20	.09
33	Bruce Armstrong	.10	.05
34	Tim McDonald	.10	.05
35	James Harris DE	.10	.05
36	Lomas Brown	.10	.05
37	Jay Novacek	.20	.09
38	John Thierry	.10	.05
39	John Elliott	.10	.05
40	Terry McDaniel	.10	.05
41	Shawn Lee	.10	.05
42	Shane Dronett	.10	.05
43	Cornelius Bennett	.20	.09
44	Steve Bono	.20	.09
45	Byron Evans	.10	.05
46	Eugene Robinson	.10	.05
47	Tony Bennett	.10	.05
48	Michael Bankston	.10	.05
49	Willie Roaf	.10	.05
50	Bobby Houston	.10	.05
51	Ken Harvey	.10	.05
52	Bruce Matthews	.10	.05
53	Lincoln Kennedy	.10	.05
54	Todd Lyght	.10	.05
55	Paul Gruber	.10	.05
56	Corey Sawyer	.10	.05
57	Myron Guyton	.10	.05
58	John Jackson	.10	.05
59	Sean Jones	.10	.05
60	Pepper Johnson	.10	.05
61	Steve Walsh	.10	.05
62	Corey Miller	.10	.05
63	Fuad Reveiz	.10	.05
64	Rickey Jackson	.10	.05
65	Scott Mitchell	.20	.09
66	Michael Irvin	.40	.18
67	Andre Reed	.20	.09
68	Mark Seay	.20	.09
69	Keith Byars	.10	.05
70	Marcus Allen	.40	.18
71	Shannon Sharpe	.20	.09
72	Eric Hill	.10	.05
73	James Washington	.10	.05
74	Greg Jackson	.10	.05
75	Chris Warren	.20	.09
76	Will Wolford	.10	.05
77	Anthony Smith	.10	.05
78	Cris Dishman	.10	.05
79	Carl Pickens	.40	.18
80	Tyrone Hughes	.20	.09
81	Chris Miller	.10	.05
82	Clay Matthews	.20	.09
83	Lonnie Marts	.10	.05
84	Jerome Henderson	.10	.05
85	Ben Coates	.20	.09
86	Deon Figures	.10	.05
87	Anthony Pleasant	.10	.05
88	Guy McIntyre	.10	.05
89	Jake Reed	.20	.09
90	Rodney Hampton	.20	.09
91	Santana Dotson	.10	.05
92	Jeff Blackshear	.10	.05
93	Willie Clay	.10	.05
94	Nate Newton	.20	.09
95	Bucky Brooks	.10	.05
96	Lamar Lathon	.10	.05
97	Tim Grunhard	.10	.05
98	Harris Barton	.10	.05
99	Brian Mitchell	.10	.05
100	Natrone Means	.40	.18
101	Sean Dawkins	.20	.09
102	Chris Slade	.20	.09
103	Tom Rathman	.10	.05
104	Fred Barnett	.20	.09
105	Gary Brown	.10	.05
106	Leonard Russell	.10	.05

❑ 107 Alfred Williams .10 .05
❑ 108 Kelvin Martin .10 .05
❑ 109 Alexander Wright .10 .05
❑ 110 O.J. McDuffie .40 .18
❑ 111 Mario Bates .40 .18
❑ 112 Tony Casillas .10 .05
❑ 113 Michael Timpson .10 .05
❑ 114 Robert Brooks .40 .18
❑ 115 Rob Burnett .10 .05
❑ 116 Mark Collins .10 .05
❑ 117 Chris Calloway .10 .05
❑ 118 Courtney Hawkins .10 .05
❑ 119 Marvcus Patton .10 .05
❑ 120 Greg Lloyd .20 .09
❑ 121 Ryan McNeil .10 .05
❑ 122 Gary Plummer .10 .05
❑ 123 Dwayne Sabb .10 .05
❑ 124 Jessie Hester .10 .05
❑ 125 Terance Mathis .20 .09
❑ 126 Steve Atwater .10 .05
❑ 127 Lorenzo Lynch .10 .05
❑ 128 James Francis .10 .05
❑ 129 John Fina .10 .05
❑ 130 Emmitt Smith 2.50 1.10
❑ 131 Bryan Cox .10 .05
❑ 132 Robert Blackmon .10 .05
❑ 133 Kenny Davidson .10 .05
❑ 134 Eugene Daniel .10 .05
❑ 135 Vince Buck .10 .05
❑ 136 Leslie O'Neal .20 .09
❑ 137 James Jett .20 .09
❑ 138 Johnny Johnson .10 .05
❑ 139 Michael Zordich .10 .05
❑ 140 Warren Moon .20 .09
❑ 141 William White .10 .05
❑ 142 Carl Banks .10 .05
❑ 143 Marty Carter .10 .05
❑ 144 Keith Hamilton .10 .05
❑ 145 Alvin Harper .10 .05
❑ 146 Corey Harris .10 .05
❑ 147 Elijah Alexander RC .10 .05
❑ 148 Darrell Green .10 .05
❑ 149 Yancey Thigpen RC .40 .18
❑ 150 Deion Sanders 1.00 .45
❑ 151 Burt Grossman .10 .05
❑ 152 J.B. Brown .10 .05
❑ 153 Johnny Bailey .10 .05
❑ 154 Harvey Williams .10 .05
❑ 155 Jeff Blake RC 1.25 .55
❑ 156 Al Smith .10 .05
❑ 157 Chris Doleman .10 .05
❑ 158 Garrison Hearst .40 .18
❑ 159 Bryce Paup .40 .18
❑ 160 Herman Moore .40 .18
❑ 161 Cortez Kennedy .20 .09
❑ 162 Marquez Pope .10 .05
❑ 163 Quinn Early .20 .09
❑ 164 Broderick Thomas .10 .05
❑ 165 Jeff Herrod .10 .05
❑ 166 Robert Jones .10 .05
❑ 167 Mo Lewis .10 .05
❑ 168 Ray Crittenden .10 .05
❑ 169 Raymont Harris .10 .05
❑ 170 Bruce Smith .40 .18
❑ 171 Dana Stubblefield .40 .18
❑ 172 Charles Haley .20 .09
❑ 173 Charles Johnson .20 .09
❑ 174 Shawn Jefferson .10 .05
❑ 175 Leroy Hoard .10 .05
❑ 176 Bernie Parmalee .20 .09
❑ 177 Scottie Graham .20 .09
❑ 178 Edgar Bennett .20 .09
❑ 179 Aubrey Matthews .10 .05
❑ 180 Don Beebe .10 .05
❑ 181 Eric Swann EC SP .30 .14
❑ 182 Jeff George EC SP .30 .14
❑ 183 Jim Kelly EC SP .60 .25
❑ 184 Sam Mills EC SP .30 .14
❑ 185 Mark Carrier DB EC SP .20 .09
❑ 186 Dan Wilkinson EC SP .30 .14
❑ 187 Eric Turner EC SP .20 .09
❑ 188 Troy Aikman EC SP 2.00 .90
❑ 189 John Elway EC SP 4.00 1.80
❑ 190 Barry Sanders EC SP 4.00 1.80
❑ 191 Brett Favre EC SP 4.00 1.80
❑ 192 Micheal Barrow EC SP .20 .09
❑ 193 Marshall Faulk EC SP 1.25 .55
❑ 194 Steve Beuerlein EC SP .20 .09
❑ 195 Neil Smith EC SP .30 .14
❑ 196 Jeff Hostetler EC SP .30 .14
❑ 197 Jerome Bettis EC SP .60 .25
❑ 198 Dan Marino EC SP 4.00 1.80
❑ 199 Cris Carter EC SP .60 .25
❑ 200 Drew Bledsoe EC SP 2.00 .90
❑ 201 Jim Everett EC SP .20 .09
❑ 202 Dave Brown EC SP .30 .14
❑ 203 Boomer Esiason EC SP .30 .14
❑ 204 R.Cunningham EC SP .30 .14
❑ 205 Rod Woodson EC SP .30 .14
❑ 206 Junior Seau EC SP .60 .25
❑ 207 Jerry Rice EC SP 2.00 .90
❑ 208 Rick Mirer EC SP .60 .25
❑ 209 Errict Rhett EC SP .60 .25
❑ 210 Heath Shuler EC SP .60 .25
❑ 211 Bobby Taylor DP SP RC .30 .14
❑ 212 Jesse James DP SP RC .20 .09
❑ 213 Devin Bush DP SP RC .20 .09
❑ 214 Luther Elliss DP SP RC .20 .09
❑ 215 Kerry Collins DP SP RC 2.00 .90
❑ 216 D.Alexander DE DP SP RC .20 .09
❑ 217 R.Salaam DP SP RC .30 .14
❑ 218 J.J. Stokes DP SP RC .60 .25
❑ 219 Todd Collins DP SP RC .30 .14
❑ 220 Ki-Jana Carter DP SP RC .30 .14
❑ 221 Kyle Brady DP SP RC .30 .14
❑ 222 Kevin Carter DP SP RC .20 .09
❑ 223 Tony Boselli DP SP RC .60 .25
❑ 224 Scott Gragg DP SP RC .20 .09
❑ 225 Warren Sapp DP SP RC 1.25 .55
❑ 226 Ricky Reynolds .10 .05
❑ 227 Roosevelt Potts .10 .05
❑ 228 Jessie Tuggle .10 .05
❑ 229 Anthony Newman .10 .05
❑ 230 Randall Cunningham .40 .18
❑ 231 Jason Elam .10 .05
❑ 232 Darnay Scott .40 .18
❑ 233 Tom Carter .10 .05
❑ 234 Micheal Barrow .10 .05
❑ 235 Steve Tasker .20 .09
❑ 236 Howard Cross .10 .05
❑ 237 Charles Wilson .10 .05
❑ 238 Rob Fredrickson .10 .05
❑ 239 Russell Maryland .10 .05
❑ 240 Dan Marino 3.00 1.35
❑ 241 Rafael Robinson .10 .05
❑ 242 Ed McDaniel .10 .05
❑ 243 Brett Perriman .20 .09
❑ 244 Chuck Levy .10 .05
❑ 245 Errict Rhett .40 .18
❑ 246 Tracy Simien .10 .05
❑ 247 Steve Everitt .10 .05
❑ 248 John Jurkovic .10 .05
❑ 249 Johnny Mitchell .10 .05
❑ 250 Mark Carrier .10 .05
❑ 251 Merton Hanks .10 .05
❑ 252 Joe Johnson .10 .05
❑ 253 Andre Coleman .10 .05
❑ 254 Ray Buchanan .10 .05
❑ 255 Jeff George .20 .09
❑ 256 Shane Conlan .10 .05
❑ 257 Gus Frerotte .40 .18
❑ 258 Doug Pelfrey .10 .05
❑ 259 Glenn Montgomery .10 .05
❑ 260 John Elway 3.00 1.35
❑ 261 Larry Centers .20 .09
❑ 262 Calvin Williams .20 .09
❑ 263 Gene Atkins .10 .05
❑ 264 Tim Brown .40 .18
❑ 265 Leon Lett .10 .05
❑ 266 Martin Mayhew .10 .05
❑ 267 Arthur Marshall .10 .05
❑ 268 Maurice Hurst .10 .05
❑ 269 Greg Hill .20 .09
❑ 270 Junior Seau .40 .18
❑ 271 Rick Mirer .40 .18
❑ 272 Jack Del Rio .10 .05
❑ 273 Lewis Tillman .10 .05
❑ 274 Renaldo Turnbull .10 .05
❑ 275 Dan Footman .10 .05
❑ 276 John Taylor .10 .05
❑ 277 Russell Copeland .10 .05
❑ 278 Tracy Scroggins .10 .05
❑ 279 Lou Benfatti .10 .05
❑ 280 Rod Woodson .20 .09
❑ 281 Troy Drayton .10 .05
❑ 282 Quentin Coryatt .20 .09
❑ 283 Craig Heyward .20 .09
❑ 284 Jeff Cross .10 .05
❑ 285 Hardy Nickerson .10 .05
❑ 286 Dorsey Levens .75 .35
❑ 287 Derek Russell .10 .05
❑ 288 Seth Joyner .10 .05
❑ 289 Kimble Anders .20 .09
❑ 290 Drew Bledsoe 1.50 .70
❑ 291 Bryant Young .20 .09
❑ 292 Chris Zorich .10 .05
❑ 293 Michael Strahan .20 .09
❑ 294 Kevin Greene .20 .09
❑ 295 Aaron Glenn .10 .05
❑ 296 Jimmy Spencer RC .10 .05
❑ 297 Eric Turner .10 .05
❑ 298 William Thomas .10 .05
❑ 299 Dan Wilkinson .20 .09
❑ 300 Troy Aikman 1.50 .70
❑ 301 Terry Wooden .10 .05
❑ 302 Heath Shuler .40 .18
❑ 303 Jeff Burris .10 .05
❑ 304 Mark Stepnoski .10 .05
❑ 305 Chris Mims .10 .05
❑ 306 Todd Steussie .10 .05
❑ 307 Johnnie Morton .20 .09
❑ 308 Darryl Talley .10 .05
❑ 309 Nolan Harrison .10 .05
❑ 310 Dave Brown .20 .09
❑ 311 Brent Jones .10 .05
❑ 312 Curtis Conway .40 .18
❑ 313 Ronald Humphrey .10 .05
❑ 314 Richie Anderson RC .40 .18
❑ 315 Jim Everett .10 .05
❑ 316 Willie Davis .20 .09
❑ 317 Ed Cunningham .10 .05
❑ 318 Willie McGinest .20 .09
❑ 319 Sean Gilbert .20 .09
❑ 320 Brett Favre 3.00 1.35
❑ 321 Bennie Thompson .10 .05
❑ 322 Neil O'Donnell .20 .09
❑ 323 Vince Workman .10 .05
❑ 324 Terry Kirby .20 .09
❑ 325 Simon Fletcher .10 .05
❑ 326 Ricardo McDonald .10 .05
❑ 327 Duane Young .10 .05
❑ 328 Jim Harbaugh .20 .09
❑ 329 D.J. Johnson .10 .05
❑ 330 Boomer Esiason .20 .09
❑ 331 Donnell Woolford .10 .05
❑ 332 Mike Sherrard .10 .05
❑ 333 Tyrone Legette .10 .05
❑ 334 Larry Brown DB .10 .05
❑ 335 William Floyd .40 .18
❑ 336 Reggie Brooks .20 .09
❑ 337 Patrick Bates .10 .05
❑ 338 Jim Jeffcoat .10 .05
❑ 339 Ray Childress .10 .05
❑ 340 Cris Carter .40 .18
❑ 341 Charlie Garner .20 .09
❑ 342 Bill Hitchcock .10 .05
❑ 343 Levon Kirkland .10 .05
❑ 344 Robert Porcher .10 .05
❑ 345 Darryl Williams .10 .05
❑ 346 Vincent Brisby .10 .05
❑ 347 Kenyon Rasheed .10 .05
❑ 348 Floyd Turner .10 .05
❑ 349 Bob Whitfield .10 .05
❑ 350 Jerome Bettis .40 .18
❑ 351 Brad Baxter .10 .05
❑ 352 Darrin Smith .10 .05
❑ 353 Lamar Thomas .10 .05
❑ 354 Lorenzo Neal .10 .05
❑ 355 Erik Kramer .10 .05
❑ 356 Dwayne Harper .10 .05
❑ 357 Doug Evans .10 .05
❑ 358 Jeff Feagles .10 .05
❑ 359 Ray Crockett .10 .05
❑ 360 Neil Smith .20 .09
❑ 361 Troy Vincent .10 .05
❑ 362 Don Griffin .10 .05
❑ 363 Michael Brooks .10 .05
❑ 364 Carlton Gray .10 .05

Card	Mint	Nrmt
❑ 365 Thomas Smith	.10	.05
❑ 366 Ken Norton	.20	.09
❑ 367 Tony McGee	.10	.05
❑ 368 Eric Metcalf	.20	.09
❑ 369 Mel Gray	.10	.05
❑ 370 Barry Sanders	3.00	1.35
❑ 371 Rocket Ismail	.20	.09
❑ 372 Chad Brown	.20	.09
❑ 373 Qadry Ismail	.20	.09
❑ 374 Anthony Prior	.10	.05
❑ 375 Kevin Lee	.10	.05
❑ 376 Robert Young	.10	.05
❑ 377 Kevin Williams WR	.20	.09
❑ 378 Tydus Winans	.10	.05
❑ 379 Ricky Watters	.40	.18
❑ 380 Jim Kelly	.40	.18
❑ 381 Eric Swann	.20	.09
❑ 382 Mike Pritchard	.10	.05
❑ 383 Derek Brown RBK	.10	.05
❑ 384 Dennis Gibson	.10	.05
❑ 385 Byron Bam Morris	.20	.09
❑ 386 Reggie White	.40	.18
❑ 387 Jeff Graham	.10	.05
❑ 388 Marshall Faulk	.75	.35
❑ 389 Joe Phillips	.10	.05
❑ 390 Jeff Hostetler	.20	.09
❑ 391 Irving Fryar	.20	.09
❑ 392 Stevon Moore	.10	.05
❑ 393 Bert Emanuel	.40	.18
❑ 394 Leon Searcy	.10	.05
❑ 395 Robert Smith	.40	.18
❑ 396 Michael Bates	.10	.05
❑ 397 Thomas Lewis	.20	.09
❑ 398 Joe Bowden	.10	.05
❑ 399 Steve Tovar	.10	.05
❑ 400 Jerry Rice	1.50	.70
❑ 401 Toby Wright	.10	.05
❑ 402 Daryl Johnston	.20	.09
❑ 403 Vincent Brown	.10	.05
❑ 404 Marvin Washington	.10	.05
❑ 405 Chris Spielman	.20	.09
❑ 406 Willie Jackson ET SP	.30	.14
❑ 407 Harry Boatswain ET SP	.20	.09
❑ 408 Kelvin Pritchett ET SP	.20	.09
❑ 409 Dave Widell ET SP	.20	.09
❑ 410 Frank Reich ET SP	.20	.09
❑ 411 Corey Mayfield ET SP	.20	.09
❑ 412 Pete Metzelaars ET SP	.20	.09
❑ 413 Keith Goganious ET SP	.20	.09
❑ 414 John Kasay ET SP	.20	.09
❑ 415 Ernest Givins ET SP	.20	.09
❑ 416 Randy Baldwin ET SP	.20	.09
❑ 417 Shawn Bouwens ET SP	.20	.09
❑ 418 Mike Fox ET SP	.20	.09
❑ 419 Mark Carrier WR ET SP	.30	.14
❑ 420 Steve Beuerlein ET SP	.20	.09
❑ 421 Steve Lofton ET SP	.20	.09
❑ 422 Jeff Lageman ET SP	.20	.09
❑ 423 Paul Butcher ET SP	.20	.09
❑ 424 Mark Brunell ET SP	2.00	.90
❑ 425 Vernon Turner ET SP	.20	.09
❑ 426 Tim McKyer ET SP	.20	.09
❑ 427 James Williams ET SP	.20	.09
❑ 428 Tommy Barnhardt ET SP	.20	.09
❑ 429 Rogerick Green ET SP	.20	.09
❑ 430 Desmond Howard ET SP	.30	.14
❑ 431 Darion Conner ET SP	.20	.09
❑ 432 Reggie Clark ET SP	.20	.09
❑ 433 Eric Guliford ET SP	.20	.09
❑ 434 Rob Johnson ET SP RC	3.00	1.35
❑ 435 Sam Mills ET SP	.30	.14
❑ 436 Kordell Stewart RC SP	4.00	1.80
❑ 437 James O. Stewart SP RC	3.00	1.35
❑ 438 Zach Wiegert SP	.20	.09
❑ 439 Ellis Johnson RC SP	.20	.09
❑ 440 Matt O'Dwyer RC SP	.20	.09
❑ 441 Anthony Cook RC SP	.20	.09
❑ 442 Ron Davis RC SP	.20	.09
❑ 443 Chris Hudson RC SP	.20	.09
❑ 444 Hugh Douglas RC SP	.60	.25
❑ 445 Tyrone Poole RC SP	.30	.14
❑ 446 Korey Stringer RC SP	.20	.09
❑ 447 Ruben Brown RC SP	.20	.09
❑ 448 Brian DeMarco RC SP	.20	.09
❑ 449 M.Westbrook RC SP	2.00	.90
❑ 450 Steve McNair RC SP	5.00	2.20

1996 Stadium Club

	MINT	NRMT
COMPLETE SET (360)	60.00	27.00
COMP.SERIES 1 (180)	30.00	13.50
COMP.SERIES 2 (180)	30.00	13.50

Card	Mint	Nrmt
❑ 1 Kyle Brady	.10	.05
❑ 2 Mickey Washington	.10	.05
❑ 3 Seth Joyner	.10	.05
❑ 4 Vinny Testaverde	.25	.11
❑ 5 Thomas Randolph	.10	.05
❑ 6 Heath Shuler	.25	.11
❑ 7 Ty Law	.10	.05
❑ 8 Blake Brockermeyer	.10	.05
❑ 9 Darryll Lewis	.10	.05
❑ 10 Jeff Blake	.50	.23
❑ 11 Tyrone Hughes	.10	.05
❑ 12 Horace Copeland	.10	.05
❑ 13 Roman Phifer	.10	.05
❑ 14 Eugene Robinson	.10	.05
❑ 15 Anthony Miller	.25	.11
❑ 16 Robert Smith	.25	.11
❑ 17 Chester McGlockton	.10	.05
❑ 18 Marty Carter	.10	.05
❑ 19 Scott Mitchell	.25	.11
❑ 20 O.J. McDuffie	.25	.11
❑ 21 Stan Humphries	.25	.11
❑ 22 Eugene Daniel	.10	.05
❑ 23 Devin Bush	.10	.05
❑ 24 Darick Holmes	.10	.05
❑ 25 Ricky Watters	.25	.11
❑ 26 J.J. Stokes	.50	.23
❑ 27 George Koonce	.10	.05
❑ 28 Tamarick Vanover	.25	.11
❑ 29 Yancey Thigpen	.25	.11
❑ 30 Troy Aikman	1.25	.55
❑ 31 Rashaan Salaam	.50	.23
❑ 32 Anthony Cook	.10	.05
❑ 33 Tim McKyer	.10	.05
❑ 34 Dale Carter	.10	.05
❑ 35 Marvin Washington	.10	.05
❑ 36 Terry Allen	.25	.11
❑ 37 Keith Goganious	.10	.05
❑ 38 Pepper Johnson	.10	.05
❑ 39 Dave Brown	.10	.05
❑ 40 Levon Kirkland	.10	.05
❑ 41 Ken Dilger	.25	.11
❑ 42 Harvey Williams	.10	.05
❑ 43 Robert Blackmon	.10	.05
❑ 44 Kevin Carter	.10	.05
❑ 45 Warren Moon	.25	.11
❑ 46 Allen Aldridge	.10	.05
❑ 47 Terance Mathis	.10	.05
❑ 48 Junior Seau	.25	.11
❑ 49 William Fuller	.10	.05
❑ 50 Lee Woodall	.10	.05
❑ 51 Aeneas Williams	.10	.05
❑ 52 Thomas Smith	.10	.05
❑ 53 Chris Slade	.10	.05
❑ 54 Eric Allen	.10	.05
❑ 55 David Sloan	.10	.05
❑ 56 Hardy Nickerson	.10	.05
❑ 57 Michael Irvin	.50	.23
❑ 58 Corey Sawyer	.10	.05
❑ 59 Eric Green	.10	.05
❑ 60 Reggie White	.50	.23
❑ 61 Isaac Bruce	.50	.23
❑ 62 Darrell Green	.10	.05
❑ 63 Aaron Glenn	.10	.05
❑ 64 Mark Brunell	1.25	.55
❑ 65 Mark Carrier WR	.10	.05
❑ 66 Mel Gray	.10	.05
❑ 67 Phillippi Sparks	.10	.05
❑ 68 Ernie Mills	.10	.05
❑ 69 Rick Mirer	.25	.11
❑ 70 Neil Smith	.10	.05
❑ 71 Terry McDaniel	.10	.05
❑ 72 Terrell Davis	3.00	1.35
❑ 73 Alonzo Spellman	.10	.05
❑ 74 Jessie Tuggle	.10	.05
❑ 75 Terry Kirby	.25	.11
❑ 76 David Palmer	.10	.05
❑ 77 Calvin Williams	.10	.05
❑ 78 Shaun Gayle	.10	.05
❑ 79 Bryant Young	.25	.11
❑ 80 Jim Harbaugh	.25	.11
❑ 81 Michael Jackson	.25	.11
❑ 82 Dave Meggett	.10	.05
❑ 83 Henry Thomas	.10	.05
❑ 84 Jim Kelly	.50	.23
❑ 85 Frank Sanders	.25	.11
❑ 86 Daryl Johnston	.25	.11
❑ 87 Alvin Harper	.10	.05
❑ 88 John Copeland	.10	.05
❑ 89 Mark Chmura	.25	.11
❑ 90 Jim Everett	.10	.05
❑ 91 Bobby Houston	.10	.05
❑ 92 Willie Jackson	.10	.05
❑ 93 Carlton Bailey	.10	.05
❑ 94 Todd Lyght	.10	.05
❑ 95 Ken Harvey	.10	.05
❑ 96 Erric Pegram	.10	.05
❑ 97 Anthony Smith	.10	.05
❑ 98 Kimble Anders	.25	.11
❑ 99 Steve McNair	1.00	.45
❑ 100 Jeff George	.25	.11
❑ 101 Michael Timpson	.10	.05
❑ 102 Brent Jones	.10	.05
❑ 103 Mike Mamula	.10	.05
❑ 104 Jeff Cross	.10	.05
❑ 105 Craig Newsome	.10	.05
❑ 106 Howard Cross	.10	.05
❑ 107 Terry Wooden	.10	.05
❑ 108 Randall McDaniel	.10	.05
❑ 109 Andre Reed	.25	.11
❑ 110 Steve Atwater	.10	.05
❑ 111 Larry Centers	.25	.11
❑ 112 Tony Bennett	.10	.05
❑ 113 Drew Bledsoe	1.25	.55
❑ 114 Terrell Fletcher	.10	.05
❑ 115 Warren Sapp	.10	.05
❑ 116 Deion Sanders	.75	.35
❑ 117 Bryce Paup	.10	.05
❑ 118 Mario Bates	.25	.11
❑ 119 Steve Tovar	.10	.05
❑ 120 Barry Sanders	2.50	1.10
❑ 121 Tony Boselli	.10	.05
❑ 122 Micheal Barrow	.10	.05
❑ 123 Sam Mills	.10	.05
❑ 124 Tim Brown	.50	.23
❑ 125 Darren Perry	.10	.05
❑ 126 Brian Blades	.10	.05
❑ 127 Tyrone Wheatley	.25	.11
❑ 128 Derrick Thomas	.25	.11
❑ 129 Edgar Bennett	.25	.11
❑ 130 Cris Carter	.50	.23
❑ 131 Stephen Grant	.10	.05
❑ 132 Kevin Williams	.10	.05
❑ 133 Darnay Scott	.25	.11
❑ 134 Rod Stephens	.10	.05
❑ 135 Ken Norton	.10	.05
❑ 136 Tim Biakabutuka RC	.75	.35
❑ 137 Willie Anderson RC	.10	.05
❑ 138 Lawrence Phillips RC	.50	.23
❑ 139 Jonathan Ogden RC	.10	.05
❑ 140 Simeon Rice RC	.50	.23
❑ 141 Alex Van Dyke RC	.25	.11
❑ 142 Jerome Woods RC	.10	.05
❑ 143 Eric Moulds RC	2.00	.90
❑ 144 Mike Alstott RC	1.50	.70
❑ 145 Marvin Harrison RC	3.00	1.35
❑ 146 Duane Clemons RC	.10	.05
❑ 147 Regan Upshaw RC	.10	.05

- ❑ 148 Eddie Kennison RC .50 .23
- ❑ 149 John Mobley RC .10 .05
- ❑ 150 Keyshawn Johnson RC 2.50 1.10
- ❑ 151 Marco Battaglia RC .10 .05
- ❑ 152 Rickey Dudley RC .50 .23
- ❑ 153 Kevin Hardy RC .50 .23
- ❑ 154 Curtis Martin SM 1.00 .45
- ❑ 155 Dan Marino SM 2.50 1.10
- ❑ 156 Rashaan Salaam SM .25 .11
- ❑ 157 Joey Galloway SM .75 .35
- ❑ 158 John Elway SM 2.50 1.10
- ❑ 159 Marshall Faulk SM .50 .23
- ❑ 160 Jerry Rice SM 1.25 .55
- ❑ 161 Darren Bennett SM .10 .05
- ❑ 162 Tamarick Vanover SM .25 .11
- ❑ 163 Orlando Thomas SM .10 .05
- ❑ 164 Jim Kelly SM .50 .23
- ❑ 165 Larry Brown SM .10 .05
- ❑ 166 Errict Rhett SM .25 .11
- ❑ 167 Warren Moon SM .10 .05
- ❑ 168 Hugh Douglas SM .10 .05
- ❑ 169 Jim Everett SM .10 .05
- ❑ 170 AFC Champ. Game .10 .05
  Colts vs. Steelers
  Hail Mary Pass
- ❑ 171 Larry Centers SM .25 .11
- ❑ 172 Marcus Allen GM .50 .23
- ❑ 173 Morten Andersen GM .10 .05
- ❑ 174 Brett Favre GM 2.50 1.10
- ❑ 175 Jerry Rice GM 1.25 .55
- ❑ 176 Glyn Milburn GM .10 .05
- ❑ 177 Thurman Thomas GM .25 .11
- ❑ 178 Michael Irvin GM .25 .11
- ❑ 179 Barry Sanders GM 2.50 1.10
- ❑ 180 Dan Marino GM 2.50 1.10
- ❑ 181 Joey Galloway .75 .35
- ❑ 182 Dwayne Harper .10 .05
- ❑ 183 Antonio Langham .10 .05
- ❑ 184 Chris Zorich .10 .05
- ❑ 185 Willie McGinest .10 .05
- ❑ 186 Wayne Chrebet .75 .35
- ❑ 187 Dermontti Dawson .10 .05
- ❑ 188 Charlie Garner .10 .05
- ❑ 189 Quentin Coryatt .10 .05
- ❑ 190 Rodney Hampton .25 .11
- ❑ 191 Kelvin Pritchett .10 .05
- ❑ 192 Willie Green .10 .05
- ❑ 193 Garrison Hearst .25 .11
- ❑ 194 Tracy Scroggins .10 .05
- ❑ 195 Rocket Ismail .10 .05
- ❑ 196 Michael Westbrook .50 .23
- ❑ 197 Troy Drayton .10 .05
- ❑ 198 Rob Fredrickson .10 .05
- ❑ 199 Sean Lumpkin .10 .05
- ❑ 200 John Elway 2.50 1.10
- ❑ 201 Bernie Parmalee .10 .05
- ❑ 202 Chris Chandler .25 .11
- ❑ 203 Lake Dawson .10 .05
- ❑ 204 Orlando Thomas .10 .05
- ❑ 205 Carl Pickens .50 .23
- ❑ 206 Kurt Schulz .10 .05
- ❑ 207 Clay Matthews .10 .05
- ❑ 208 Winston Moss .10 .05
- ❑ 209 Sean Dawkins .10 .05
- ❑ 210 Emmitt Smith 2.00 .90
- ❑ 211 Mark Carrier DB .10 .05
- ❑ 212 Clyde Simmons .10 .05
- ❑ 213 Derrick Brooks .10 .05
- ❑ 214 William Floyd .25 .11
- ❑ 215 Aaron Hayden .10 .05
- ❑ 216 Brian DeMarco .10 .05
- ❑ 217 Ben Coates .25 .11
- ❑ 218 Renaldo Turnbull .10 .05
- ❑ 219 Adrian Murrell .50 .23
- ❑ 220 Marcus Allen .50 .23
- ❑ 221 Brett Maxie .10 .05
- ❑ 222 Trev Alberts .10 .05
- ❑ 223 Darren Woodson .25 .11
- ❑ 224 Brian Mitchell .10 .05
- ❑ 225 Michael Haynes .10 .05
- ❑ 226 Sean Jones .10 .05
- ❑ 227 Eric Zeier .10 .05
- ❑ 228 Herman Moore .50 .23
- ❑ 229 Shane Conlan .10 .05
- ❑ 230 Chris Warren .25 .11
- ❑ 231 Dana Stubblefield .25 .11
- ❑ 232 Andre Coleman .10 .05
- ❑ 233 Kordell Stewart UER .75 .35
  (Card actually numbered 223)
- ❑ 234 Ray Crockett .10 .05
- ❑ 235 Craig Heyward .10 .05
- ❑ 236 Mike Fox .10 .05
- ❑ 237 Derek Brown RBK .10 .05
- ❑ 238 Thomas Lewis .10 .05
- ❑ 239 Hugh Douglas .25 .11
- ❑ 240 Tom Carter .10 .05
- ❑ 241 Toby Wright .10 .05
- ❑ 242 Jason Belser .10 .05
- ❑ 243 Rodney Peete .10 .05
- ❑ 244 Napoleon Kaufman .50 .23
- ❑ 245 Merton Hanks .10 .05
- ❑ 246 Harry Colon .10 .05
- ❑ 247 Greg Hill .25 .11
- ❑ 248 Vincent Brisby .10 .05
- ❑ 249 Eric Hill .10 .05
- ❑ 250 Brett Favre 2.50 1.10
- ❑ 251 Leroy Hoard .10 .05
- ❑ 252 Eric Guliford .10 .05
- ❑ 253 Stanley Richard .25 .11
- ❑ 254 Carlos Jenkins .10 .05
- ❑ 255 D'Marco Farr .10 .05
- ❑ 256 Carlton Gray .10 .05
- ❑ 257 Derek Loville .10 .05
- ❑ 258 Ray Buchanan .10 .05
- ❑ 259 Jake Reed .25 .11
- ❑ 260 Dan Marino 2.50 1.10
- ❑ 261 Brad Baxter .10 .05
- ❑ 262 Pat Swilling .10 .05
- ❑ 263 Andy Harmon .10 .05
- ❑ 264 Harold Green .10 .05
- ❑ 265 Shannon Sharpe .25 .11
- ❑ 266 Erik Kramer .10 .05
- ❑ 267 Lamar Lathon .10 .05
- ❑ 268 Stevon Moore .10 .05
- ❑ 269 Tony Martin .25 .11
- ❑ 270 Bruce Smith .25 .11
- ❑ 271 James Washington .10 .05
- ❑ 272 Tyrone Poole .10 .05
- ❑ 273 Eric Swann .10 .05
- ❑ 274 Dexter Carter .10 .05
- ❑ 275 Greg Lloyd .25 .11
- ❑ 276 Michael Zordich .10 .05
- ❑ 277 Steve Wisniewski .10 .05
- ❑ 278 Chris Calloway .10 .05
- ❑ 279 Irv Smith .10 .05
- ❑ 280 Steve Young 1.00 .45
- ❑ 281 James O.Stewart .25 .11
- ❑ 282 Blaine Bishop .10 .05
- ❑ 283 Rob Moore .25 .11
- ❑ 284 Eric Metcalf .10 .05
- ❑ 285 Kerry Collins .50 .23
- ❑ 286 Dan Wilkinson .10 .05
- ❑ 287 Curtis Conway .50 .23
- ❑ 288 Jay Novacek .10 .05
- ❑ 289 Henry Ellard .10 .05
- ❑ 290 Curtis Martin 1.00 .45
- ❑ 291 Brett Perriman .10 .05
- ❑ 292 Jeff Lageman .10 .05
- ❑ 293 Trent Dilfer .50 .23
- ❑ 294 Cortez Kennedy .10 .05
- ❑ 295 Jeff Hostetler .10 .05
- ❑ 296 Mark Fields .10 .05
- ❑ 297 Qadry Ismail .10 .05
- ❑ 298 Steve Bono .10 .05
- ❑ 299 Tony Tolbert .10 .05
- ❑ 300 Jerry Rice 1.25 .55
- ❑ 301 Marvcus Patton .10 .05
- ❑ 302 Robert Brooks .50 .23
- ❑ 303 Terry Ray .10 .05
- ❑ 304 John Thierry .10 .05
- ❑ 305 Errict Rhett .25 .11
- ❑ 306 Ricardo McDonald .10 .05
- ❑ 307 Antonio London .10 .05
- ❑ 308 Lonnie Johnson .10 .05
- ❑ 309 Mark Collins .10 .05
- ❑ 310 Marshall Faulk .50 .23
- ❑ 311 Anthony Pleasant .10 .05
- ❑ 312 Howard Griffith .10 .05
- ❑ 313 Roosevelt Potts .10 .05
- ❑ 314 Jim Flanigan .10 .05
- ❑ 315 'Omar Ellison RC .10 .05
- ❑ 316 Boomer Esiason SP .25 .11
- ❑ 317 Leslie O'Neal SP .10 .05
- ❑ 318 Jerome Bettis SP .50 .23
- ❑ 319 Larry Brown SP .10 .05
- ❑ 320 Neil O'Donnell SP .25 .11
- ❑ 321 Andre Rison SP .25 .11
- ❑ 322 Cornelius Bennett SP .10 .05
- ❑ 323 Quinn Early SP .10 .05
- ❑ 324 Bryan Cox SP .10 .05
- ❑ 325 Irving Fryar SP .25 .11
- ❑ 326 Eddie Robinson SP .10 .05
- ❑ 327 Chris Doleman SP .10 .05
- ❑ 328 Sean Gilbert SP .10 .05
- ❑ 329 Steve Walsh SP .10 .05
- ❑ 330 Kevin Greene SP .25 .11
- ❑ 331 Chris Spielman SP .10 .05
- ❑ 332 Jeff Graham SP .10 .05
- ❑ 333 Anthony Dorsett RC SP .10 .05
- ❑ 334 Amani Toomer RC SP 1.00 .45
- ❑ 335 Walt Harris RC SP .10 .05
- ❑ 336 Ray Mickens RC SP .10 .05
- ❑ 337 Danny Kanell RC SP .50 .23
- ❑ 338 Daryl Gardener RC SP .10 .05
- ❑ 339 Jonathan Ogden SP .10 .05
- ❑ 340 Eddie George RC SP 4.00 1.80
- ❑ 341 Jeff Lewis RC SP .60 .25
- ❑ 342 Terrell Owens RC SP 3.00 1.35
- ❑ 343 Brian Dawkins RC SP .10 .05
- ❑ 344 Tim Biakabutuka SP .50 .23
- ❑ 345 Marvin Harrison SP 1.25 .55
- ❑ 346 Lawyer Milloy RC SP .10 .05
- ❑ 347 Eric Moulds SP 1.00 .45
- ❑ 348 Alex Van Dyke SP .25 .11
- ❑ 349 John Mobley SP .10 .05
- ❑ 350 Kevin Hardy SP .50 .23
- ❑ 351 Ray Lewis RC SP 3.00 1.35
- ❑ 352 Lawrence Phillips SP .50 .23
- ❑ 353 Stepfret Williams RC SP .25 .11
- ❑ 354 Bobby Engram RC SP .50 .23
- ❑ 355 Leeland McElroy RC SP .50 .23
- ❑ 356 Marco Battaglia SP .10 .05
- ❑ 357 Rickey Dudley SP .50 .23
- ❑ 358 Bobby Hoying RC SP .75 .35
- ❑ 359 Cedric Jones RC SP .10 .05
- ❑ 360 Keyshawn Johnson SP 1.00 .45
- ❑ P19 Scott Mitchell Proto .50 .23
  (Team name on back
  not ghosted in white)
- ❑ P31 R.Salaam Proto .75 .35
  (Team name on back
  not ghosted in white)
- ❑ P56 H.Nickerson Proto .50 .23
  (Team name on back
  not ghosted in white)
- ❑ NNO Checklist Card .10 .05

1997 Stadium Club

	MINT	NRMT
COMPLETE SET (340)	60.00	27.00
COMP.SERIES 1 (170)	35.00	16.00
COMP.SERIES 2 (170)	35.00	16.00

- ❑ 1 Junior Seau .25 .11
- ❑ 2 Michael Irvin .50 .23
- ❑ 3 Marcus Allen .50 .23
- ❑ 4 Dale Carter .15 .07
- ❑ 5 Darnell Autry RC .25 .11
- ❑ 6 Isaac Bruce .50 .23

❑ 7 Darrell Green .25 .11
❑ 8 Joey Galloway .60 .25
❑ 9 Steve Atwater .15 .07
❑ 10 Kordell Stewart .60 .25
❑ 11 Tony Brackens .15 .07
❑ 12 Gus Frerotte .15 .07
❑ 13 Henry Ellard .15 .07
❑ 14 Charles Way .25 .11
❑ 15 Jim Druckenmiller RC .50 .23
❑ 16 Orlando Thomas .15 .07
❑ 17 Terrell Davis 2.50 1.10
❑ 18 Jim Schwantz .15 .07
❑ 19 Derrick Thomas .25 .11
❑ 20 Curtis Martin .75 .35
❑ 21 Deion Sanders .50 .23
❑ 22 Bruce Smith .25 .11
❑ 23 Jake Reed .25 .11
❑ 24 Leeland McElroy .15 .07
❑ 25 Jerome Bettis .50 .23
❑ 26 Neil Smith .25 .11
❑ 27 Terry Allen .50 .23
❑ 28 Gilbert Brown .15 .07
❑ 29 Steve McNair .75 .35
❑ 30 Kerry Collins .25 .11
❑ 31 Thurman Thomas .50 .23
❑ 32 Kenny Holmes RC .50 .23
❑ 33 Karim Abdul-Jabbar .50 .23
❑ 34 Steve Young 1.00 .45
❑ 35 Jerry Rice 1.50 .70
❑ 36 Jeff George .25 .11
❑ 37 Errict Rhett .15 .07
❑ 38 Mike Alstott .50 .23
❑ 39 Tim Brown .50 .23
❑ 40 Keyshawn Johnson .50 .23
❑ 41 Jim Harbaugh .25 .11
❑ 42 Kevin Hardy .15 .07
❑ 43 Kevin Greene .25 .11
❑ 44 Eric Metcalf .25 .11
❑ 45 Troy Aikman 1.50 .70
❑ 46 Marshall Faulk .50 .23
❑ 47 Shannon Sharpe .25 .11
❑ 48 Warren Moon .50 .23
❑ 49 Mark Brunell 1.50 .70
❑ 50 Dan Marino 3.00 1.35
❑ 51 Byron Hanspard RC .50 .23
❑ 52 Chris Chandler .25 .11
❑ 53 Wayne Chrebet .50 .23
❑ 54 Antonio Langham .15 .07
❑ 55 Barry Sanders 3.00 1.35
❑ 56 Curtis Conway .25 .11
❑ 57 Ricky Watters .25 .11
❑ 58 William Thomas .15 .07
❑ 59 Chris Warren .25 .11
❑ 60 Terry Glenn .50 .23
❑ 61 Peter Boulware RC .25 .11
❑ 62 Chad Cota .15 .07
❑ 63 Eddie Kennison .25 .11
❑ 64 Lamar Smith .50 .23
❑ 65 Brett Favre 3.00 1.35
❑ 66 Michael Westbrook .25 .11
❑ 67 Larry Centers .25 .11
❑ 68 Trent Dilfer .50 .23
❑ 69 Stevon Moore .15 .07
❑ 70 John Elway 3.00 1.35
❑ 71 Bryce Paup .15 .07
❑ 72 Quentin Coryatt .15 .07
❑ 73 Rashaan Salaam .15 .07
❑ 74 Thomas Lewis .15 .07
❑ 75 Drew Bledsoe 1.50 .70
❑ 76 Cris Carter .50 .23
❑ 77 Joe Bowden .15 .07
❑ 78 Allen Aldridge .15 .07
❑ 79 Zach Thomas .25 .11
❑ 80 Emmitt Smith 2.50 1.10
❑ 81 Daryl Johnston .25 .11
❑ 82 Vinny Testaverde .25 .11
❑ 83 James O.Stewart .25 .11
❑ 84 Edgar Bennett .25 .11
❑ 85 Shawn Springs RC .25 .11
❑ 86 Elvis Grbac .25 .11
❑ 87 Levon Kirkland .15 .07
❑ 88 Jeff Graham .15 .07
❑ 89 Terrell Fletcher .15 .07
❑ 90 Eddie George 1.50 .70
❑ 91 Jessie Tuggle .15 .07
❑ 92 Terrell Owens .50 .23
❑ 93 Wayne Martin .15 .07
❑ 94 Dwayne Harper .15 .07
❑ 95 Mark Collins .15 .07
❑ 96 Marvcus Patton .15 .07
❑ 97 Napoleon Kaufman .50 .23
❑ 98 Keenan McCardell .25 .11
❑ 99 Ty Detmer .25 .11
❑ 100 Reggie White .50 .23
❑ 101 William Floyd .25 .11
❑ 102 Scott Mitchell .25 .11
❑ 103 Robert Blackmon .15 .07
❑ 104 Dan Wilkinson .15 .07
❑ 105 Warren Sapp .25 .11
❑ 106 Dave Meggett .15 .07
❑ 107 Brian Mitchell .15 .07
❑ 108 Tyrone Poole .15 .07
❑ 109 Derrick Alexander WR .25 .11
❑ 110 David Palmer .15 .07
❑ 111 James Farrior RC .15 .07
❑ 112 Chad Brown .15 .07
❑ 113 Marty Carter .15 .07
❑ 114 Lawrence Phillips .15 .07
❑ 115 Wesley Walls .25 .11
❑ 116 John Friesz .15 .07
❑ 117 Roman Phifer .15 .07
❑ 118 Jason Sehorn .25 .11
❑ 119 Henry Thomas .15 .07
❑ 120 Natrone Means .50 .23
❑ 121 Ty Law .15 .07
❑ 122 Tony Gonzalez RC 2.50 1.10
❑ 123 Kevin Williams .15 .07
❑ 124 Regan Upshaw .15 .07
❑ 125 Antonio Freeman .75 .35
❑ 126 Jessie Armstead .15 .07
❑ 127 Pat Barnes RC .50 .23
❑ 128 Charlie Garner .15 .07
❑ 129 Irving Fryar .25 .11
❑ 130 Rickey Dudley .25 .11
❑ 131 Rodney Harrison .15 .07
❑ 132 Brent Jones .25 .11
❑ 133 Neil O'Donnell .25 .11
❑ 134 Darryll Lewis .15 .07
❑ 135 Jason Belser .15 .07
❑ 136 Mark Chmura .25 .11
❑ 137 Seth Joyner .15 .07
❑ 138 Herschel Walker .25 .11
❑ 139 Santana Dotson .15 .07
❑ 140 Carl Pickens .50 .23
❑ 141 Terance Mathis .25 .11
❑ 142 Walt Harris .15 .07
❑ 143 John Mobley .15 .07
❑ 144 Gabe Northern .15 .07
❑ 145 Herman Moore .50 .23
❑ 146 Michael Jackson .25 .11
❑ 147 Chris Sanders .15 .07
❑ 148 LeShon Johnson .15 .07
❑ 149 Darrell Russell RC .15 .07
❑ 150 Winslow Oliver .15 .07
❑ 151 Tamarick Vanover .25 .11
❑ 152 Tony Martin .25 .11
❑ 153 Lamar Lathon .15 .07
❑ 154 Ray Mickens .15 .07
❑ 155 Derrick Brooks .15 .07
❑ 156 Warrick Dunn RC 2.50 1.10
❑ 157 Tim McDonald .15 .07
❑ 158 Keith Lyle .15 .07
❑ 159 Terry McDaniel .15 .07
❑ 160 Andre Hastings .15 .07
❑ 161 Phillippi Sparks .15 .07
❑ 162 Tedy Bruschi .15 .07
❑ 163 Bryant Westbrook RC .15 .07
❑ 164 Victor Green .15 .07
❑ 165 Jimmy Smith .25 .11
❑ 166 Greg Biekert .15 .07
❑ 167 Frank Sanders .25 .11
❑ 168 Chris Doleman .15 .07
❑ 169 Phil Hansen .15 .07
❑ 170 Walter Jones RC .15 .07
❑ 171 Mark Carrier WR .15 .07
❑ 172 Greg Hill .15 .07
❑ 173 Erik Kramer .15 .07
❑ 174 Chris Spielman .15 .07
❑ 175 Tom Knight RC .15 .07
❑ 176 Sam Mills .15 .07
❑ 177 Robert Smith .25 .11
❑ 178 Dorsey Levens .50 .23
❑ 179 Chris Slade .15 .07
❑ 180 Troy Vincent .15 .07
❑ 181 Mario Bates .15 .07
❑ 182 Ed McCaffrey .25 .11
❑ 183 Mike Mamula .15 .07
❑ 184 Chad Hennings .15 .07
❑ 185 Stan Humphries .25 .11
❑ 186 Reinard Wilson .15 .07
❑ 187 Kevin Carter .15 .07
❑ 188 Qadry Ismail .25 .11
❑ 189 Cortez Kennedy .15 .07
❑ 190 Eric Swann .15 .07
❑ 191 Corey Dillon RC 5.00 2.20
❑ 192 Renaldo Wynn .15 .07
❑ 193 Bobby Hebert .15 .07
❑ 194 Fred Barnett .15 .07
❑ 195 Ray Lewis .60 .25
❑ 196 Robert Jones .15 .07
❑ 197 Brian Williams .15 .07
❑ 198 Willie McGinest .15 .07
❑ 199 Jake Plummer RC 5.00 2.20
❑ 200 Aeneas Williams .15 .07
❑ 201 Ashley Ambrose .15 .07
❑ 202 Cornelius Bennett .15 .07
❑ 203 Mo Lewis .15 .07
❑ 204 James Hasty .15 .07
❑ 205 Carnell Lake .15 .07
❑ 206 Heath Shuler .15 .07
❑ 207 Dana Stubblefield .15 .07
❑ 208 Corey Miller .15 .07
❑ 209 Ike Hilliard RC 1.50 .70
❑ 210 Bryant Young .15 .07
❑ 211 Hardy Nickerson .15 .07
❑ 212 Blaine Bishop .15 .07
❑ 213 Marcus Robertson .15 .07
❑ 214 Tony Bennett .15 .07
❑ 215 Kent Graham .15 .07
❑ 216 Steve Bono .25 .11
❑ 217 Will Blackwell RC .50 .23
❑ 218 Tyrone Braxton .15 .07
❑ 219 Eric Moulds .50 .23
❑ 220 Rod Woodson .25 .11
❑ 221 Anthony Johnson .15 .07
❑ 222 Willie Davis .15 .07
❑ 223 Darrin Smith .15 .07
❑ 224 Rick Mirer .15 .07
❑ 225 Marvin Harrison .50 .23
❑ 226 Terrell Buckley .15 .07
❑ 227 Joe Aska .15 .07
❑ 228 Yatil Green RC .25 .11
❑ 229 William Fuller .15 .07
❑ 230 Eddie Robinson .15 .07
❑ 231 Brian Blades .15 .07
❑ 232 Michael Sinclair .15 .07
❑ 233 Ken Harvey .15 .07
❑ 234 Harvey Williams .15 .07
❑ 235 Simeon Rice .25 .11
❑ 236 Chris T. Jones .15 .07
❑ 237 Bert Emanuel .25 .11
❑ 238 Corey Sawyer .15 .07
❑ 239 Chris Calloway .15 .07
❑ 240 Jeff Blake .25 .11
❑ 241 Alonzo Spellman .15 .07
❑ 242 Bryan Cox .15 .07
❑ 243 Antowain Smith RC 2.00 .90
❑ 244 Tim Biakabutuka .25 .11
❑ 245 Ray Crockett .15 .07
❑ 246 Dwayne Rudd .15 .07
❑ 247 Glyn Milburn .15 .07
❑ 248 Gary Plummer .15 .07
❑ 249 O.J. McDuffie .25 .11
❑ 250 Willie Clay .15 .07
❑ 251 Jim Everett .15 .07
❑ 252 Eugene Daniel .15 .07
❑ 253 Corey Widmer .15 .07
❑ 254 Mel Gray .15 .07
❑ 255 Ken Norton .15 .07
❑ 256 Johnnie Morton .25 .11
❑ 257 Courtney Hawkins .15 .07
❑ 258 Ricardo McDonald .15 .07
❑ 259 Todd Lyght .15 .07
❑ 260 Micheal Barrow .15 .07
❑ 261 Aaron Glenn .15 .07
❑ 262 Jeff Herrod .15 .07
❑ 263 Troy Davis RC .50 .23
❑ 264 Eric Hill .15 .07

❑ 265	Darrien Gordon	.15	.07
❑ 266	Lake Dawson	.15	.07
❑ 267	John Randle	.25	.11
❑ 268	Henry Jones	.15	.07
❑ 269	Mickey Washington	.15	.07
❑ 270	Amani Toomer	.25	.11
❑ 271	Steve Grant	.15	.07
❑ 272	Adrian Murrell	.25	.11
❑ 273	Derrick Witherspoon	.15	.07
❑ 274	Albert Lewis	.15	.07
❑ 275	Ben Coates	.25	.11
❑ 276	Reidel Anthony RC	1.50	.70
❑ 277	Jim Schwantz	.15	.07
❑ 278	Aaron Hayden	.15	.07
❑ 279	Ryan McNeil	.15	.07
❑ 280	LeRoy Butler	.15	.07
❑ 281	Craig Newsome	.15	.07
❑ 282	Bill Romanowski	.15	.07
❑ 283	Michael Bankston	.15	.07
❑ 284	Kevin Smith	.15	.07
❑ 285	Byron Bam Morris	.15	.07
❑ 286	Darnay Scott	.25	.11
❑ 287	David LaFleur RC	.25	.11
❑ 288	Randall Cunningham	.50	.23
❑ 289	Eric Davis	.15	.07
❑ 290	Todd Collins	.15	.07
❑ 291	Steve Tovar	.15	.07
❑ 292	Jermaine Lewis	.50	.23
❑ 293	Alfred Williams	.15	.07
❑ 294	Brad Johnson	.60	.25
❑ 295	Charles Johnson	.25	.11
❑ 296	Ted Johnson	.15	.07
❑ 297	Merton Hanks	.15	.07
❑ 298	Andre Coleman	.15	.07
❑ 299	Keith Jackson	.15	.07
❑ 300	Terry Kirby	.25	.11
❑ 301	Tony Banks	.25	.11
❑ 302	Terrance Shaw	.15	.07
❑ 303	Bobby Engram	.25	.11
❑ 304	Hugh Douglas	.15	.07
❑ 305	Lawyer Milloy	.15	.07
❑ 306	James Jett	.25	.11
❑ 307	Joey Kent RC	.50	.23
❑ 308	Rodney Hampton	.25	.11
❑ 309	Dewayne Washington	.15	.07
❑ 310	Kevin Lockett RC	.25	.11
❑ 311	Ki-Jana Carter	.15	.07
❑ 312	Jeff Lageman	.15	.07
❑ 313	Don Beebe	.15	.07
❑ 314	Willie Williams	.15	.07
❑ 315	Tyrone Wheatley	.25	.11
❑ 316	Leslie O'Neal	.15	.07
❑ 317	Quinn Early	.15	.07
❑ 318	Sean Gilbert	.15	.07
❑ 319	Tim Bowens	.15	.07
❑ 320	Sean Dawkins	.15	.07
❑ 321	Ken Dilger	.15	.07
❑ 322	George Koonce	.15	.07
❑ 323	Jevon Langford	.15	.07
❑ 324	Mike Caldwell	.15	.07
❑ 325	Orlando Pace RC	.50	.23
❑ 326	Garrison Hearst	.25	.11
❑ 327	Mike Tomczak	.15	.07
❑ 328	Rob Moore	.25	.11
❑ 329	Andre Reed	.25	.11
❑ 330	Kimble Anders	.25	.11
❑ 331	Qadry Ismail	.25	.11
❑ 332	Eric Allen	.15	.07
❑ 333	Dave Brown	.15	.07
❑ 334	Bennie Blades	.15	.07
❑ 335	Jamal Anderson	1.00	.45
❑ 336	John Lynch	.25	.11
❑ 337	Tyrone Hughes	.15	.07
❑ 338	Ronnie Harmon	.15	.07
❑ 339	Rae Carruth RC	.50	.23
❑ 340	Robert Brooks	.25	.11
❑ P1	Junior Seau Prototype (Line of text below copyrights)	.50	.23
❑ P20	Curtis Martin Prototype (Line of text below copyrights)	1.00	.45
❑ P21	Deion Sanders Prototype (Line of text below copyrights)	.50	.23
❑ P30	Kerry Collins Prototype (Line of text below copyrights)	.75	.35
❑ P47	Sh.Sharpe Prototype (Line of text below copyrights)	.50	.23
❑ P84	Edgar Bennett Prototype (Line of text below copyrights)	.50	.23

1998 Stadium Club

		MINT	NRMT
COMPLETE SET (195)		60.00	27.00
❑ 1	Barry Sanders	3.00	1.35
❑ 2	Tony Martin	.30	.14
❑ 3	Fred Lane	.30	.14
❑ 4	Darren Woodson	.15	.07
❑ 5	Andre Reed	.30	.14
❑ 6	Blaine Bishop	.15	.07
❑ 7	Robert Brooks	.30	.14
❑ 8	Tony Banks	.30	.14
❑ 9	Charles Way	.15	.07
❑ 10	Mark Brunell	1.25	.55
❑ 11	Darrell Green	.30	.14
❑ 12	Aeneas Williams	.15	.07
❑ 13	Rob Johnson	.30	.14
❑ 14	Deion Sanders	.60	.25
❑ 15	Marshall Faulk	.60	.25
❑ 16	Stephen Boyd	.15	.07
❑ 17	Adrian Murrell	.30	.14
❑ 18	Wayne Chrebet	.60	.25
❑ 19	Michael Sinclair	.15	.07
❑ 20	Dan Marino	3.00	1.35
❑ 21	Willie Davis	.15	.07
❑ 22	Chris Warren	.30	.14
❑ 23	John Mobley	.15	.07
❑ 24	Shannon Sharpe	.30	.14
❑ 25	Thurman Thomas	.60	.25
❑ 26	Corey Dillon	1.00	.45
❑ 27	Zach Thomas	.30	.14
❑ 28	James Jett	.30	.14
❑ 29	Eric Metcalf	.15	.07
❑ 30	Drew Bledsoe	1.25	.55
❑ 31	Scott Greene	.15	.07
❑ 32	Simeon Rice	.30	.14
❑ 33	Robert Smith	.60	.25
❑ 34	Keenan McCardell	.30	.14
❑ 35	Jessie Armstead	.15	.07
❑ 36	Jerry Rice	1.50	.70
❑ 37	Eric Green	.15	.07
❑ 38	Terrell Owens	.60	.25
❑ 39	Tim Brown	.60	.25
❑ 40	Vinny Testaverde	.30	.14
❑ 41	Brian Stablein	.15	.07
❑ 42	Bert Emanuel	.30	.14
❑ 43	Terry Glenn	.60	.25
❑ 44	Chad Cota	.15	.07
❑ 45	Jermaine Lewis	.30	.14
❑ 46	Derrick Thomas	.30	.14
❑ 47	O.J. McDuffie	.30	.14
❑ 48	Frank Wycheck	.15	.07
❑ 49	Steve Broussard	.15	.07
❑ 50	Terrell Davis	2.50	1.10
❑ 51	Eric Allen	.15	.07
❑ 52	Napoleon Kaufman	.60	.25
❑ 53	Dan Wilkinson	.15	.07
❑ 54	Kerry Collins	.30	.14
❑ 55	Frank Sanders	.30	.14
❑ 56	Jeff Burris	.15	.07
❑ 56	Ricky Proehl	.15	.07
❑ 57	Michael Westbrook	.30	.14
❑ 58	Michael McCrary	.15	.07
❑ 59	Bobby Hoying	.30	.14
❑ 60	Jerome Bettis	.60	.25
❑ 61	Amp Lee	.15	.07
❑ 62	Levon Kirkland	.15	.07
❑ 63	Dana Stubblefield	.15	.07
❑ 64	Terance Mathis	.30	.14
❑ 65	Mark Chmura	.30	.14
❑ 66	Bryant Westbrook	.15	.07
❑ 67	Rod Smith	.30	.14
❑ 68	Derrick Alexander	.30	.14
❑ 69	Jason Taylor	.15	.07
❑ 70	Eddie George	1.25	.55
❑ 71	Elvis Grbac	.30	.14
❑ 72	Junior Seau	.30	.14
❑ 73	Marvin Harrison	.30	.14
❑ 74	Neil O'Donnell	.30	.14
❑ 75	Johnnie Morton	.30	.14
❑ 76	John Randle	.30	.14
❑ 77	Danny Kanell	.30	.14
❑ 78	Charlie Garner	.15	.07
❑ 79	J.J. Stokes	.30	.14
❑ 80	Troy Aikman	1.50	.70
❑ 81	Gus Frerotte	.15	.07
❑ 82	Jake Plummer	1.25	.55
❑ 83	Andre Hastings	.15	.07
❑ 84	Steve Atwater	.15	.07
❑ 85	Larry Centers	.15	.07
❑ 86	Kevin Hardy	.15	.07
❑ 87	Willie McGinest	.15	.07
❑ 88	Joey Galloway	.60	.25
❑ 89	Charles Johnson	.15	.07
❑ 90	Warrick Dunn	.60	.25
❑ 91	Derrick Rodgers	.15	.07
❑ 92	Aaron Glenn	.15	.07
❑ 93	Shawn Jefferson	.15	.07
❑ 94	Antonio Freeman	.60	.25
❑ 95	Jake Reed	.30	.14
❑ 96	Reidel Anthony	.30	.14
❑ 97	Cris Dishman	.15	.07
❑ 98	Jason Sehorn	.30	.14
❑ 99	Herman Moore	.60	.25
❑ 100	John Elway	3.00	1.35
❑ 101	Brad Johnson	.60	.25
❑ 102	Jeff George	.30	.14
❑ 103	Emmitt Smith	2.50	1.10
❑ 104	Steve McNair	.60	.25
❑ 105	Ed McCaffrey	.30	.14
❑ 107	Dorsey Levens	.60	.25
❑ 108	Michael Jackson	.15	.07
❑ 109	Carl Pickens	.60	.25
❑ 110	James Stewart	.30	.14
❑ 111	Karim Abdul-Jabbar	.60	.25
❑ 112	Jim Harbaugh	.30	.14
❑ 113	Yancey Thigpen	.15	.07
❑ 114	Chad Brown	.15	.07
❑ 115	Chris Sanders	.15	.07
❑ 116	Cris Carter	.60	.25
❑ 117	Glenn Foley	.30	.14
❑ 118	Ben Coates	.30	.14
❑ 119	Jamal Anderson	.60	.25
❑ 120	Steve Young	1.00	.45
❑ 121	Scott Mitchell	.30	.14
❑ 122	Rob Moore	.30	.14
❑ 123	Bobby Engram	.30	.14
❑ 124	Rod Woodson	.30	.14
❑ 125	Terry Allen	.60	.25
❑ 126	Warren Sapp	.30	.14
❑ 127	Irving Fryar	.30	.14
❑ 128	Isaac Bruce	.60	.25
❑ 129	Rae Carruth	.30	.14
❑ 130	Sean Dawkins	.15	.07
❑ 131	Andre Rison	.30	.14
❑ 132	Kevin Greene	.30	.14
❑ 133	Warren Moon	.60	.25
❑ 134	Keyshawn Johnson	.60	.25
❑ 135	Jay Graham	.15	.07
❑ 136	Mike Alstott	.60	.25
❑ 137	Peter Boulware	.15	.07
❑ 138	Doug Evans	.15	.07
❑ 139	Jimmy Smith	.30	.14
❑ 140	Kordell Stewart	.60	.25
❑ 141	Tamarick Vanover	.15	.07
❑ 142	Chris Slade	.15	.07
❑ 143	Freddie Jones	.15	.07
❑ 144	Erik Kramer	.15	.07
❑ 145	Ricky Watters	.30	.14
❑ 146	Chris Chandler	.30	.14

	MINT	NRMT
❑ 147 Garrison Hearst	.60	.25
❑ 148 Trent Dilfer	.60	.25
❑ 149 Bruce Smith	.30	.14
❑ 150 Brett Favre	3.00	1.35
❑ 151 Will Blackwell	.15	.07
❑ 152 Rickey Dudley	.15	.07
❑ 153 Natrone Means	.60	.25
❑ 154 Curtis Conway	.30	.14
❑ 155 Tony Gonzalez	.15	.07
❑ 156 Jeff Blake	.30	.14
❑ 157 Michael Irvin	.60	.25
❑ 158 Curtis Martin	.60	.25
❑ 159 Tim McDonald	.15	.07
❑ 160 Wesley Walls	.30	.14
❑ 161 Michael Strahan	.15	.07
❑ 162 Reggie White	.60	.25
❑ 163 Jeff Graham	.15	.07
❑ 164 Ray Lewis	.60	.25
❑ 165 Antowain Smith	.60	.25
❑ 166 Ryan Leaf RC	6.00	2.70
❑ 167 Jerome Pathon RC	2.50	1.10
❑ 168 Duane Starks RC	2.00	.90
❑ 169 Brian Simmons RC	2.00	.90
❑ 170 Pat Johnson RC	2.50	1.10
❑ 171 Keith Brooking RC	2.50	1.10
❑ 172 Kevin Dyson RC	4.00	1.80
❑ 173 Robert Edwards RC	4.00	1.80
❑ 174 Grant Wistrom RC	2.00	.90
❑ 175 Curtis Enis RC	3.00	1.35
❑ 176 John Avery RC	3.00	1.35
❑ 177 Jason Peter RC	2.00	.90
❑ 178 Brian Griese RC	8.00	3.60
❑ 179 Tavian Banks RC	2.50	1.10
❑ 180 Andre Wadsworth RC	2.50	1.10
❑ 181 Skip Hicks RC	3.00	1.35
❑ 182 Hines Ward RC	2.50	1.10
❑ 183 Greg Ellis RC	2.00	.90
❑ 184 Robert Holcombe RC	3.00	1.35
❑ 185 Joe Jurevicius RC	2.50	1.10
❑ 186 Takeo Spikes RC	2.50	1.10
❑ 187 Ahman Green RC	6.00	2.70
❑ 188 Jacquez Green RC	4.00	1.80
❑ 189 Randy Moss RC	20.00	9.00
❑ 190 Charles Woodson RC	4.00	1.80
❑ 191 Fred Taylor RC	6.00	2.70
❑ 192 Marcus Nash RC	3.00	1.35
❑ 193 Germane Crowell RC	5.00	2.20
❑ 194 Tim Dwight RC	4.00	1.80
❑ 195 Peyton Manning RC	20.00	9.00

1999 Stadium Club

	MINT	NRMT
COMPLETE SET (200)	60.00	27.00
COMP.SET w/o SP's (175)	20.00	9.00

	MINT	NRMT
❑ 1 Dan Marino	2.50	1.10
❑ 2 Andre Reed	.30	.14
❑ 3 Michael Westbrook	.30	.14
❑ 4 Isaac Bruce	.60	.25
❑ 5 Curtis Martin	.60	.25
❑ 6 Courtney Hawkins	.15	.07
❑ 7 Charles Way	.15	.07
❑ 8 Terrell Owens	.60	.25
❑ 9 Warrick Dunn	.60	.25
❑ 10 Jake Plummer	1.25	.55
❑ 11 Chad Brown	.15	.07
❑ 12 Yancey Thigpen	.15	.07
❑ 13 Lamar Thomas	.15	.07
❑ 14 Keenan McCardell	.30	.14
❑ 15 Shannon Sharpe	.30	.14
❑ 16 Robert Brooks	.30	.14
❑ 17 Cameron Cleeland	.15	.07
❑ 18 Derrick Thomas	.30	.14
❑ 19 Mark Brunell	1.00	.45
❑ 20 Jamal Anderson	.60	.25
❑ 21 Germane Crowell	.30	.14
❑ 22 Rod Smith	.30	.14
❑ 23 Ty Law	.15	.07
❑ 24 Cris Carter	.60	.25
❑ 25 Terrell Davis	1.50	.70
❑ 26 Takeo Spikes	.15	.07
❑ 27 Tim Biakabutuka	.30	.14
❑ 28 Jermaine Lewis	.30	.14
❑ 29 Adrian Murrell	.30	.14
❑ 30 Doug Flutie	.75	.35
❑ 31 Curtis Enis	.60	.25
❑ 32 Skip Hicks	.60	.25
❑ 33 Steve McNair	.60	.25
❑ 34 Charles Woodson	.60	.25
❑ 35 Jessie Armstead	.15	.07
❑ 36 Shawn Springs	.15	.07
❑ 37 Levon Kirkland	.15	.07
❑ 38 Freddie Jones	.15	.07
❑ 39 Warren Sapp	.15	.07
❑ 40 Emmitt Smith	1.50	.70
❑ 41 Reidel Anthony	.30	.14
❑ 42 Tony Simmons	.15	.07
❑ 43 Andre Hastings	.15	.07
❑ 44 Byron Bam Morris	.15	.07
❑ 45 Jimmy Smith	.30	.14
❑ 46 Antonio Freeman	.60	.25
❑ 47 Herman Moore	.60	.25
❑ 48 Muhsin Muhammad	.30	.14
❑ 49 Chris Chandler	.30	.14
❑ 50 John Elway	2.50	1.10
❑ 51 Aeneas Williams	.15	.07
❑ 52 Bobby Engram	.30	.14
❑ 53 Keith Poole	.15	.07
❑ 54 Zach Thomas	.30	.14
❑ 55 Mike Alstott	.60	.25
❑ 56 Junior Seau	.30	.14
❑ 57 Aaron Glenn	.15	.07
❑ 58 Darrell Green	.15	.07
❑ 59 Thurman Thomas	.30	.14
❑ 60 Troy Aikman	1.50	.70
❑ 61 Bill Romanowski	.15	.07
❑ 62 Wesley Walls	.30	.14
❑ 63 Andre Wadsworth	.15	.07
❑ 64 Robert Smith	.60	.25
❑ 65 Elvis Grbac	.30	.14
❑ 66 Terry Fair	.15	.07
❑ 67 Ben Coates	.30	.14
❑ 68 Bert Emanuel	.30	.14
❑ 69 Jacquez Green	.30	.14
❑ 70 Barry Sanders	2.50	1.10
❑ 71 James Jett	.30	.14
❑ 72 Gary Brown	.15	.07
❑ 73 Stephen Alexander	.15	.07
❑ 74 Wayne Chrebet	.30	.14
❑ 75 Drew Bledsoe	1.00	.45
❑ 76 John Lynch	.15	.07
❑ 77 Jake Reed	.30	.14
❑ 78 Marvin Harrison	.60	.25
❑ 79 Johnnie Morton	.30	.14
❑ 80 Brett Favre	2.50	1.10
❑ 81 Charlie Batch	1.25	.55
❑ 82 Antowain Smith	.60	.25
❑ 83 Mikhael Ricks	.15	.07
❑ 84 Derrick Mayes	.15	.07
❑ 85 John Mobley	.15	.07
❑ 86 Ernie Mills	.15	.07
❑ 87 Jeff Blake	.30	.14
❑ 88 Curtis Conway	.30	.14
❑ 89 Bruce Smith	.30	.14
❑ 90 Peyton Manning	2.50	1.10
❑ 91 Tyrone Davis	.15	.07
❑ 92 Ray Buchanan	.15	.07
❑ 93 Tim Dwight	.60	.25
❑ 94 O.J. McDuffie	.30	.14
❑ 95 Vonnie Holliday	.15	.07
❑ 96 Jon Kitna	.60	.25
❑ 97 Trent Dilfer	.30	.14
❑ 98 Jerome Bettis	.60	.25
❑ 99 Dedric Ward	.15	.07
❑ 100 Fred Taylor	1.50	.70
❑ 101 Ike Hilliard	.15	.07
❑ 102 Frank Wycheck	.15	.07
❑ 103 Eric Moulds	.60	.25
❑ 104 Rob Moore	.30	.14
❑ 105 Ed McCaffrey	.30	.14
❑ 106 Carl Pickens	.30	.14
❑ 107 Priest Holmes	.60	.25
❑ 108 Kevin Hardy	.15	.07
❑ 109 Terry Glenn	.60	.25
❑ 110 Keyshawn Johnson	.60	.25
❑ 111 Karim Abdul-Jabbar	.30	.14
❑ 112 Stephen Boyd	.15	.07
❑ 113 Ahman Green	.30	.14
❑ 114 Duce Staley	.60	.25
❑ 115 Vinny Testaverde	.30	.14
❑ 116 Napoleon Kaufman	.60	.25
❑ 117 Frank Sanders	.30	.14
❑ 118 Peter Boulware	.15	.07
❑ 119 Kevin Greene	.15	.07
❑ 120 Steve Young	1.00	.45
❑ 121 Darnay Scott	.15	.07
❑ 122 Deion Sanders	.60	.25
❑ 123 Corey Dillon	.60	.25
❑ 124 Randall Cunningham	.60	.25
❑ 125 Eddie George	.75	.35
❑ 126 Derrick Alexander	.15	.07
❑ 127 Mark Chmura	.15	.07
❑ 128 Michael Sinclair	.15	.07
❑ 129 Rickey Dudley	.15	.07
❑ 130 Joey Galloway	.60	.25
❑ 131 Michael Strahan	.15	.07
❑ 132 Ricky Proehl	.15	.07
❑ 133 Natrone Means	.30	.14
❑ 134 Dorsey Levens	.60	.25
❑ 135 Andre Rison	.30	.14
❑ 136 Alonzo Mayes	.15	.07
❑ 137 John Randle	.30	.14
❑ 138 Terance Mathis	.30	.14
❑ 139 Rae Carruth	.30	.14
❑ 140 Jerry Rice	1.50	.70
❑ 141 Michael Irvin	.30	.14
❑ 142 Oronde Gadsden	.15	.07
❑ 143 Jerome Pathon	.15	.07
❑ 144 Ricky Watters	.30	.14
❑ 145 J.J. Stokes	.30	.14
❑ 146 Kordell Stewart	.60	.25
❑ 147 Tim Brown	.60	.25
❑ 148 Garrison Hearst	.30	.14
❑ 149 Tony Gonzalez	.30	.14
❑ 150 Randy Moss	2.50	1.10
❑ 151 Daunte Culpepper RC	10.00	4.50
❑ 152 Amos Zereoue RC	2.00	.90
❑ 153 Champ Bailey RC	2.50	1.10
❑ 154 Peerless Price RC	2.50	1.10
❑ 155 Edgerrin James RC	10.00	4.50
❑ 156 Joe Germaine RC	2.00	.90
❑ 157 David Boston RC	4.00	1.80
❑ 158 Kevin Faulk RC	3.00	1.35
❑ 159 Troy Edwards RC	2.50	1.10
❑ 160 Akili Smith RC	4.00	1.80
❑ 161 Kevin Johnson RC	4.00	1.80
❑ 162 Rob Konrad RC	1.25	.55
❑ 163 Shaun King RC	4.00	1.80
❑ 164 James Johnson RC	2.00	.90
❑ 165 Donovan McNabb RC	8.00	3.60
❑ 166 Torry Holt RC	5.00	2.20
❑ 167 Mike Cloud RC	1.25	.55
❑ 168 Sedrick Irvin RC	2.00	.90
❑ 169 Cade McNown RC	3.00	1.35
❑ 170 Ricky Williams RC	8.00	3.60
❑ 171 Karsten Bailey RC	1.25	.55
❑ 172 Cecil Collins RC	2.00	.90
❑ 173 Brock Huard RC	3.00	1.35
❑ 174 D'Wayne Bates RC	1.25	.55
❑ 175 Tim Couch RC	6.00	2.70
❑ 176 Torrance Small	.15	.07
❑ 177 Warren Moon	.60	.25
❑ 178 Rocket Ismail	.30	.14
❑ 179 Marshall Faulk	.60	.25
❑ 180 Trent Green	.30	.14
❑ 181 Sean Dawkins	.15	.07
❑ 182 Pete Mitchell	.15	.07
❑ 183 Jeff Graham	.15	.07
❑ 184 Eddie Kennison	.30	.14

❑ 185 Kerry Collins	.30	.14
❑ 186 Eric Green	.15	.07
❑ 187 Kyle Brady	.15	.07
❑ 188 Tony Martin	.30	.14
❑ 189 Jim Harbaugh	.30	.14
❑ 190 Erik Kramer	.15	.07
❑ 191 Steve Atwater	.15	.07
❑ 192 Chad Bratzke	.15	.07
❑ 193 Charles Johnson	.15	.07
❑ 194 Damon Gibson	.15	.07
❑ 195 Jeff George	.30	.14
❑ 196 Scott Mitchell	.15	.07
❑ 197 Terry Kirby	.15	.07
❑ 198 Rich Gannon	.30	.14
❑ 199 Chris Spielman	.15	.07
❑ 200 Brad Johnson	.60	.25

2000 Stadium Club

	MINT	NRMT
COMPLETE SET (175)	80.00	36.00
COMP.SET w/o SP's (150)	20.00	9.00
❑ 1 Peyton Manning	1.50	.70
❑ 2 Pete Mitchell	.15	.07
❑ 3 Napoleon Kaufman	.25	.11
❑ 4 Mikhael Ricks	.15	.07
❑ 5 Mike Alstott	.50	.23
❑ 6 Brad Johnson	.50	.23
❑ 7 Tony Gonzalez	.25	.11
❑ 8 Germane Crowell	.25	.11
❑ 9 Marcus Robinson	.50	.23
❑ 10 Stephen Davis	.50	.23
❑ 11 Terance Mathis	.25	.11
❑ 12 Jake Plummer	.50	.23
❑ 13 Qadry Ismail	.15	.07
❑ 14 Cade McNown	.50	.23
❑ 15 Zach Thomas	.25	.11
❑ 16 Curtis Martin	.50	.23
❑ 17 Torrance Small	.15	.07
❑ 18 Steve McNair	.50	.23
❑ 19 Jim Harbaugh	.25	.11
❑ 20 Keyshawn Johnson	.50	.23
❑ 21 Antonio Freeman	.50	.23
❑ 22 Ed McCaffrey	.50	.23
❑ 23 Elvis Grbac	.25	.11
❑ 24 Peerless Price	.50	.23
❑ 25 Jerome Bettis	.50	.23
❑ 26 Yancey Thigpen	.15	.07
❑ 27 Jake Delhomme RC	.50	.23
❑ 28 Keith Poole	.15	.07
❑ 29 Carl Pickens	.25	.11
❑ 30 Jerry Rice	1.25	.55
❑ 31 Rob Moore	.25	.11
❑ 32 Reidel Anthony	.15	.07
❑ 33 Jimmy Smith	.25	.11
❑ 34 Ray Lucas	.50	.23
❑ 35 Troy Aikman	1.25	.55
❑ 36 Steve Beuerlein	.25	.11
❑ 37 Charlie Batch	.50	.23
❑ 38 Derrick Mayes	.25	.11
❑ 39 Tim Brown	.50	.23
❑ 40 Eddie George	.60	.25
❑ 41 O.J. McDuffie	.25	.11
❑ 42 Ike Hilliard	.25	.11
❑ 43 Bill Schroeder	.25	.11
❑ 44 Jim Miller	.15	.07
❑ 45 Chris Chandler	.25	.11
❑ 46 Fred Taylor	.60	.25
❑ 47 Ricky Watters	.25	.11
❑ 48 Tyrone Wheatley	.25	.11
❑ 49 Bruce Smith	.25	.11
❑ 50 Marshall Faulk	.60	.25
❑ 51 Kevin Carter	.15	.07
❑ 52 Champ Bailey	.25	.11
❑ 53 Troy Edwards	.25	.11
❑ 54 Doug Flutie	.60	.25
❑ 55 Charles Johnson	.25	.11
❑ 56 Michael Westbrook	.25	.11
❑ 57 Frank Wycheck	.15	.07
❑ 58 Drew Bledsoe	.75	.35
❑ 59 Terrence Wilkins	.15	.07
❑ 60 Ricky Williams	1.25	.55
❑ 61 Rod Smith	.25	.11
❑ 62 Errict Rhett	.25	.11
❑ 63 Vinny Testaverde	.25	.11
❑ 64 Jacquez Green	.25	.11
❑ 65 Curtis Conway	.25	.11
❑ 66 Wayne Chrebet	.25	.11
❑ 67 Albert Connell	.15	.07
❑ 68 Kordell Stewart	.50	.23
❑ 69 Bert Emanuel	.15	.07
❑ 70 Randy Moss	1.50	.70
❑ 71 Akili Smith	.50	.23
❑ 72 Brian Griese	.60	.25
❑ 73 Frank Sanders	.25	.11
❑ 74 Wesley Walls	.15	.07
❑ 75 Michael Pittman	.15	.07
❑ 76 Steve Young	.75	.35
❑ 77 Jevon Kearse	.50	.23
❑ 78 Az-Zahir Hakim	.25	.11
❑ 79 James Stewart	.25	.11
❑ 80 Brett Favre	2.00	.90
❑ 81 Dan Marino	2.00	.90
❑ 82 Joe Horn	.25	.11
❑ 83 Mark Brunell	.75	.35
❑ 84 Eddie Kennison	.25	.11
❑ 85 Deion Sanders	.50	.23
❑ 86 Priest Holmes	.25	.11
❑ 87 Terry Glenn	.25	.11
❑ 88 Olandis Gary	.50	.23
❑ 89 Patrick Jeffers	.50	.23
❑ 90 Emmitt Smith	1.25	.55
❑ 91 J.J. Stokes	.25	.11
❑ 92 Warrick Dunn	.50	.23
❑ 93 Damon Huard	.50	.23
❑ 94 Herman Moore	.25	.11
❑ 95 Corey Dillon	.50	.23
❑ 96 Joey Galloway	.50	.23
❑ 97 Jamal Anderson	.50	.23
❑ 98 Junior Seau	.25	.11
❑ 99 Robert Smith	.50	.23
❑ 100 Edgerrin James	2.00	.90
❑ 101 Derrick Alexander	.25	.11
❑ 102 Johnnie Morton	.25	.11
❑ 103 Sean Dawkins	.15	.07
❑ 104 Derrick Brooks	.15	.07
❑ 105 Rickey Dudley	.15	.07
❑ 106 Keenan McCardell	.25	.11
❑ 107 Kerry Collins	.25	.11
❑ 108 Kevin Johnson	.50	.23
❑ 109 Eric Moulds	.50	.23
❑ 110 Terrell Davis	1.25	.55
❑ 111 Shawn Jefferson	.15	.07
❑ 112 Donovan McNabb	.75	.35
❑ 113 Torry Holt	.50	.23
❑ 114 Marvin Harrison	.50	.23
❑ 115 Amani Toomer	.25	.11
❑ 116 Tony Martin	.25	.11
❑ 117 Curtis Enis	.25	.11
❑ 118 Tiki Barber	.25	.11
❑ 119 Freddie Jones	.15	.07
❑ 120 Muhsin Muhammad	.25	.11
❑ 121 Shaun King	.75	.35
❑ 122 Isaac Bruce	.50	.23
❑ 123 Duce Staley	.50	.23
❑ 124 Hardy Nickerson	.15	.07
❑ 125 Corey Bradford	.25	.11
❑ 126 Kevin Hardy	.15	.07
❑ 127 Hines Ward	.15	.07
❑ 128 Charlie Garner	.25	.11
❑ 129 Warren Sapp	.25	.11
❑ 130 Tim Couch	1.00	.45
❑ 131 Kevin Dyson	.25	.11
❑ 132 Rocket Ismail	.25	.11
❑ 133 Tim Dwight	.50	.23
❑ 134 Darnay Scott	.25	.11
❑ 135 Jeff George	.25	.11
❑ 136 Dorsey Levens	.25	.11
❑ 137 Jeff Blake	.25	.11
❑ 138 Jon Kitna	.50	.23
❑ 139 Rich Gannon	.25	.11
❑ 140 Cris Carter	.50	.23
❑ 141 Jeff Graham	.15	.07
❑ 142 James Johnson	.25	.11
❑ 143 Tim Biakabutuka	.25	.11
❑ 144 Bobby Engram	.25	.11
❑ 145 Tony Banks	.25	.11
❑ 146 Shannon Sharpe	.25	.11
❑ 147 Antowain Smith	.25	.11
❑ 148 Terrell Owens	.50	.23
❑ 149 Rob Johnson	.25	.11
❑ 150 Kurt Warner	2.00	.90
❑ 151 Thomas Jones RC	4.00	1.80
❑ 152 Chad Pennington RC	8.00	3.60
❑ 153 Ron Dayne RC	8.00	3.60
❑ 154 Tee Martin RC	4.00	1.80
❑ 155 Reuben Droughns RC	2.50	1.10
❑ 156 Jerry Porter RC	2.50	1.10
❑ 157 R.Jay Soward RC	2.50	1.10
❑ 158 Sylvester Morris RC	5.00	2.20
❑ 159 Todd Pinkston RC	2.50	1.10
❑ 160 Courtney Brown RC	3.00	1.35
❑ 161 Travis Taylor RC	3.00	1.35
❑ 162 Ron Dugans RC	2.00	.90
❑ 163 Laveranues Coles RC	4.00	1.80
❑ 164 Joe Hamilton RC	3.00	1.35
❑ 165 Curtis Keaton RC	2.00	.90
❑ 166 Bubba Franks RC	3.00	1.35
❑ 167 Dennis Northcutt RC	3.00	1.35
❑ 168 Chris Redman RC	5.00	2.20
❑ 169 Travis Prentice RC	4.00	1.80
❑ 170 Shaun Alexander RC	6.00	2.70
❑ 171 Jamal Lewis RC	12.00	5.50
❑ 172 Peter Warrick RC	8.00	3.60
❑ 173 J.R. Redmond RC	3.00	1.35
❑ 174 Trung Canidate RC	2.50	1.10
❑ 175 Plaxico Burress RC	5.00	2.20

1999 Stadium Club Chrome

	MINT	NRMT
COMPLETE SET (150)	80.00	36.00
❑ 1 Dan Marino	4.00	1.80
❑ 2 Andre Reed	.50	.23
❑ 3 Michael Westbrook	.50	.23
❑ 4 Isaac Bruce	1.00	.45
❑ 5 Curtis Martin	1.00	.45
❑ 6 Terrell Owens	1.00	.45
❑ 7 Warrick Dunn	1.00	.45
❑ 8 Jake Plummer	2.00	.90
❑ 9 Chad Brown	.25	.11
❑ 10 Yancey Thigpen	.50	.23
❑ 11 Keenan McCardell	.50	.23
❑ 12 Shannon Sharpe	.50	.23
❑ 13 Cameron Cleeland	.25	.11
❑ 14 Mark Brunell	1.50	.70
❑ 15 Jamal Anderson	1.00	.45
❑ 16 Germane Crowell	.50	.23

	No.	Player	Mint	Nrmt
❑	17	Rod Smith	.50	.23
❑	18	Cris Carter	1.00	.45
❑	19	Terrell Davis	2.50	1.10
❑	20	Tim Biakabutuka	.50	.23
❑	21	Jermaine Lewis	.50	.23
❑	22	Adrian Murrell	.50	.23
❑	23	Doug Flutie	1.25	.55
❑	24	Curtis Enis	1.00	.45
❑	25	Skip Hicks	.50	.23
❑	26	Steve McNair	1.00	.45
❑	27	Charles Woodson	1.00	.45
❑	28	Freddie Jones	.25	.11
❑	29	Warren Sapp	.50	.23
❑	30	Emmitt Smith	2.50	1.10
❑	31	Reidel Anthony	.25	.11
❑	32	Tony Simmons	.25	.11
❑	33	Andre Hastings	.25	.11
❑	34	Byron Bam Morris	.25	.11
❑	35	Jimmy Smith	.50	.23
❑	36	Antonio Freeman	1.00	.45
❑	37	Herman Moore	1.00	.45
❑	38	Muhsin Muhammad	.50	.23
❑	39	Chris Chandler	.50	.23
❑	40	John Elway	4.00	1.80
❑	41	Bobby Engram	.50	.23
❑	42	Keith Poole	.25	.11
❑	43	Mike Alstott	1.00	.45
❑	44	Junior Seau	.50	.23
❑	45	Thurman Thomas	.50	.23
❑	46	Troy Aikman	2.50	1.10
❑	47	Wesley Walls	.50	.23
❑	48	Robert Smith	1.00	.45
❑	49	Elvis Grbac	.50	.23
❑	50	Ben Coates	.25	.11
❑	51	Bert Emanuel	.50	.23
❑	52	Jacquez Green	.25	.11
❑	53	Barry Sanders	4.00	1.80
❑	54	James Jett	.25	.11
❑	55	Gary Brown	.25	.11
❑	56	Stephen Alexander	.25	.11
❑	57	Wayne Chrebet	1.00	.45
❑	58	Drew Bledsoe	1.50	.70
❑	59	Jake Reed	.50	.23
❑	60	Marvin Harrison	1.00	.45
❑	61	Johnnie Morton	.50	.23
❑	62	Brett Favre	4.00	1.80
❑	63	Charlie Batch	2.00	.90
❑	64	Antowain Smith	1.00	.45
❑	65	Ernie Mills	.25	.11
❑	66	Jeff Blake	.50	.23
❑	67	Curtis Conway	.50	.23
❑	68	Bruce Smith	.50	.23
❑	69	Peyton Manning	4.00	1.80
❑	70	Tim Dwight	1.00	.45
❑	71	O.J. McDuffie	.50	.23
❑	72	Jon Kitna	1.00	.45
❑	73	Trent Dilfer	.50	.23
❑	74	Jerome Bettis	1.00	.45
❑	75	Dedric Ward	.25	.11
❑	76	Fred Taylor	2.50	1.10
❑	77	Ike Hilliard	.50	.23
❑	78	Frank Wycheck	.25	.11
❑	79	Eric Moulds	1.00	.45
❑	80	Rob Moore	.50	.23
❑	81	Ed McCaffrey	.50	.23
❑	82	Carl Pickens	.50	.23
❑	83	Priest Holmes	1.00	.45
❑	84	Terry Glenn	1.00	.45
❑	85	Keyshawn Johnson	1.00	.45
❑	86	Karim Abdul-Jabbar	.50	.23
❑	87	Ahman Green	.50	.23
❑	88	Duce Staley	1.00	.45
❑	89	Vinny Testaverde	.50	.23
❑	90	Napoleon Kaufman	1.00	.45
❑	91	Frank Sanders	.50	.23
❑	92	Steve Young	1.50	.70
❑	93	Darnay Scott	.50	.23
❑	94	Deion Sanders	1.00	.45
❑	95	Corey Dillon	1.00	.45
❑	96	Randall Cunningham	1.00	.45
❑	97	Eddie George	1.25	.55
❑	98	Derrick Alexander	.50	.23
❑	99	Mark Chmura	.50	.23
❑	100	Rickey Dudley	.25	.11
❑	101	Joey Galloway	1.00	.45
❑	102	Ricky Proehl	.25	.11
❑	103	Natrone Means	.50	.23
❑	104	Dorsey Levens	1.00	.45
❑	105	Andre Rison	.50	.23
❑	106	John Randle	.50	.23
❑	107	Terance Mathis	.50	.23
❑	108	Rae Carruth	.25	.11
❑	109	Jerry Rice	2.50	1.10
❑	110	Michael Irvin	.50	.23
❑	111	Oronde Gadsden	.25	.11
❑	112	Jerome Pathon	.25	.11
❑	113	Ricky Watters	.50	.23
❑	114	J.J. Stokes	.50	.23
❑	115	Kordell Stewart	1.00	.45
❑	116	Tim Brown	1.00	.45
❑	117	Tony Gonzalez	.50	.23
❑	118	Randy Moss	4.00	1.80
❑	119	Daunte Culpepper RC	12.00	5.50
❑	120	Amos Zereoue RC	3.00	1.35
❑	121	Champ Bailey RC	3.00	1.35
❑	122	Peerless Price RC	3.00	1.35
❑	123	Edgerrin James RC	12.00	5.50
❑	124	Joe Germaine RC	2.50	1.10
❑	125	David Boston RC	5.00	2.20
❑	126	Kevin Faulk RC	4.00	1.80
❑	127	Troy Edwards RC	3.00	1.35
❑	128	Akili Smith RC	5.00	2.20
❑	129	Kevin Johnson RC	5.00	2.20
❑	130	Rob Konrad RC	3.00	1.35
❑	131	Shaun King RC	5.00	2.20
❑	132	James Johnson RC	2.50	1.10
❑	133	Donovan McNabb RC	10.00	4.50
❑	134	Torry Holt RC	6.00	2.70
❑	135	Mike Cloud RC	3.00	1.35
❑	136	Sedrick Irvin RC	2.50	1.10
❑	137	Cade McNown RC	3.00	1.35
❑	138	Ricky Williams RC	10.00	4.50
❑	139	Karsten Bailey RC	2.00	.90
❑	140	Cecil Collins RC	3.00	1.35
❑	141	Brock Huard RC	4.00	1.80
❑	142	D'Wayne Bates RC	2.00	.90
❑	143	Tim Couch RC	8.00	3.60
❑	144	Rocket Ismail	.50	.23
❑	145	Marshall Faulk	1.00	.45
❑	146	Trent Green	.50	.23
❑	147	Tony Martin	.50	.23
❑	148	Jim Harbaugh	.50	.23
❑	149	Rich Gannon	.50	.23
❑	150	Brad Johnson	1.00	.45

1995 Summit

	No.	Player	MINT	NRMT
		COMPLETE SET (200)	15.00	6.75
❑	1	Neil O'Donnell	.20	.09
❑	2	Jim Everett	.10	.05
❑	3	Craig Heyward	.20	.09
❑	4	Jeff Blake RC	1.25	.55
❑	5	Alvin Harper	.10	.05
❑	6	Heath Shuler	.40	.18
❑	7	Rodney Hampton	.20	.09
❑	8	Dave Krieg	.10	.05
❑	9	Mark Brunell	1.00	.45
❑	10	Rob Moore	.10	.05
❑	11	Daryl Johnston	.20	.09
❑	12	Marcus Allen	.40	.18
❑	13	Terance Mathis	.20	.09
❑	14	Frank Reich	.10	.05
❑	15	Gus Frerotte	.40	.18
❑	16	John Elway	2.00	.90
❑	17	Amp Lee	.10	.05
❑	18	Chris Miller	.10	.05
❑	19	Leroy Hoard	.10	.05
❑	20	Stan Humphries	.20	.09
❑	21	Charlie Garner	.20	.09
❑	22	Jim Kelly	.40	.18
❑	23	Gary Brown	.10	.05
❑	24	Byron Bam Morris	.20	.09
❑	25	Edgar Bennett	.20	.09
❑	26	Erik Kramer	.10	.05
❑	27	Dan Marino	2.00	.90
❑	28	Michael Haynes	.20	.09
❑	29	Lake Dawson	.20	.09
❑	30	Ben Coates	.20	.09
❑	31	Michael Jackson	.20	.09
❑	32	Brett Favre	2.00	.90
❑	33	Calvin Williams	.20	.09
❑	34	Steve Young	.75	.35
❑	35	Troy Aikman	1.00	.45
❑	36	Greg Hill	.20	.09
❑	37	Leonard Russell	.10	.05
❑	38	Jeff George	.20	.09
❑	39	Herschel Walker	.20	.09
❑	40	Eric Green	.10	.05
❑	41	Haywood Jeffires	.10	.05
❑	42	Terry Kirby	.20	.09
❑	43	Darnay Scott	.40	.18
❑	44	Tim Brown	.40	.18
❑	45	Brian Mitchell	.10	.05
❑	46	Desmond Howard	.20	.09
❑	47	Warren Moon	.20	.09
❑	48	Andre Reed	.20	.09
❑	49	Adrian Murrell	.20	.09
❑	50	Marshall Faulk	.60	.25
❑	51	Lewis Tillman	.10	.05
❑	52	Don Beebe	.10	.05
❑	53	Jerome Bettis	.40	.18
❑	54	Brett Perriman	.20	.09
❑	55	Mario Bates	.40	.18
❑	56	Ronnie Harmon	.10	.05
❑	57	Isaac Bruce	.60	.25
❑	58	Jackie Harris	.10	.05
❑	59	Dexter Carter	.10	.05
❑	60	Charles Johnson	.20	.09
❑	61	Herman Moore	.40	.18
❑	62	Craig Erickson	.10	.05
❑	63	Tony Martin	.20	.09
❑	64	Emmitt Smith	1.50	.70
❑	65	Brent Jones	.10	.05
❑	66	Ricky Watters	.40	.18
❑	67	Henry Ellard	.20	.09
❑	68	Vinny Testaverde	.20	.09
❑	69	Mark Pike	.10	.05
❑	70	Curtis Conway	.40	.18
❑	71	Michael Irvin	.40	.18
❑	72	Jay Novacek	.20	.09
❑	73	Howard Cross	.10	.05
❑	74	Drew Bledsoe	1.00	.45
❑	75	Steve Beuerlein	.10	.05
❑	76	Andre Rison	.20	.09
❑	77	Morten Andersen	.10	.05
❑	78	Trent Dilfer	.40	.18
❑	79	Cris Carter	.40	.18
❑	80	Natrone Means	.40	.18
❑	81	Bernie Parmalee	.20	.09
❑	82	Randall Cunningham	.40	.18
❑	83	Eric Metcalf	.20	.09
❑	84	Rick Mirer	.40	.18
❑	85	Mark Ingram	.10	.05
❑	86	David Klingler	.20	.09
❑	87	Kevin Williams	.20	.09
❑	88	Erric Pegram	.20	.09
❑	89	Keith Byars	.10	.05
❑	90	Sean Dawkins	.20	.09
❑	91	Chris Warren	.20	.09
❑	92	William Floyd	.40	.18
❑	93	Jeff Hostetler	.20	.09
❑	94	Carl Pickens	.40	.18
❑	95	Flipper Anderson	.10	.05
❑	96	Johnny Mitchell	.10	.05
❑	97	Larry Centers	.20	.09
❑	98	Shannon Sharpe	.20	.09
❑	99	Erric Rhett	.40	.18
❑	100	Fred Barnett	.20	.09

❑ 101	Harold Green	.10	.05
❑ 102	Scott Mitchell	.20	.09
❑ 103	Jerry Rice	1.00	.45
❑ 104	Shawn Jefferson	.10	.05
❑ 105	Glyn Milburn	.10	.05
❑ 106	Garrison Hearst	.40	.18
❑ 107	John Taylor	.10	.05
❑ 108	Keith Cash	.10	.05
❑ 109	Robert Brooks	.40	.18
❑ 110	Barry Sanders	2.00	.90
❑ 111	Ernest Givins	.10	.05
❑ 112	Steve Tasker	.20	.09
❑ 113	Jeff Graham	.10	.05
❑ 114	Chris Chandler	.20	.09
❑ 115	Lorenzo Neal	.10	.05
❑ 116	Bert Emanuel	.40	.18
❑ 117	Mike Sherrard	.10	.05
❑ 118	Harvey Williams	.10	.05
❑ 119	Reggie Brooks	.20	.09
❑ 120	Steve Walsh	.10	.05
❑ 121	Leroy Thompson	.10	.05
❑ 122	Dave Brown	.20	.09
❑ 123	Lorenzo White	.10	.05
❑ 124	Steve Bono	.20	.09
❑ 125	Irving Fryar	.20	.09
❑ 126	Jake Reed	.20	.09
❑ 127	Boomer Esiason	.20	.09
❑ 128	Rocket Ismail	.20	.09
❑ 129	Vincent Brisby	.10	.05
❑ 130	Robert Smith	.40	.18
❑ 131	Anthony Miller	.20	.09
❑ 132	Roosevelt Potts	.10	.05
❑ 133	Dave Meggett	.10	.05
❑ 134	Junior Seau CC	.20	.09
❑ 135	Neil Smith CC	.20	.09
❑ 136	Charles Haley CC	.20	.09
❑ 137	Rod Woodson CC	.20	.09
❑ 138	Deion Sanders CC	.60	.25
❑ 139	Reggie White CC	.40	.18
❑ 140	John Randle CC	.20	.09
❑ 141	Greg Lloyd CC	.20	.09
❑ 142	Cortez Kennedy CC	.20	.09
❑ 143	Bruce Smith CC	.40	.18
❑ 144	J.J. Stokes CC RC	.40	.18
❑ 145	Kyle Brady CC RC	.40	.18
❑ 146	Frank Sanders RC	1.25	.55
❑ 147	Michael Westbrook RC	2.50	1.10
❑ 148	Rob Johnson RC	3.00	1.35
❑ 149	Tyrone Poole RC	.20	.09
❑ 150	Lovell Pinkney RC	.10	.05
❑ 151	Tyrone Wheatley RC	2.00	.90
❑ 152	Steve McNair RC	4.00	1.80
❑ 153	Napoleon Kaufman RC	2.50	1.10
❑ 154	Tamarick Vanover RC	.40	.18
❑ 155	Todd Collins RC	.40	.18
❑ 156	Kevin Carter RC	.40	.18
❑ 157	Rodney Thomas RC	.40	.18
❑ 158	Stoney Case RC	.40	.18
❑ 159	Kordell Stewart RC	3.00	1.35
❑ 160	Tony Boselli RC	.40	.18
❑ 161	Sherman Williams RC	.10	.05
❑ 162	Christian Fauria RC	.10	.05
❑ 163	Ray Zellars RC	.20	.09
❑ 164	Ki-Jana Carter RC	.40	.18
❑ 165	Terrell Fletcher RC	.10	.05
❑ 166	Curtis Martin RC	4.00	1.80
❑ 167	Eric Zeier RC	.40	.18
❑ 168	Joey Galloway RC	3.00	1.35
❑ 169	Warren Sapp RC	.75	.35
❑ 170	Kerry Collins RC	2.50	1.10
❑ 171	Mark Bruener RC	.20	.09
❑ 172	Chris Sanders RC	.40	.18
❑ 173	Rashaan Salaam RC	.40	.18
❑ 174	Jerry Rice OW	.50	.23
❑ 175	Marshall Faulk OW	.40	.18
❑ 176	Drew Bledsoe OW	.50	.23
❑ 177	Emmitt Smith OW	.75	.35
❑ 178	Tim Brown OW	.20	.09
❑ 179	Steve Young OW	.40	.18
❑ 180	Barry Sanders OW	1.00	.45
❑ 181	Michael Irvin OW	.20	.09
❑ 182	Dan Marino OW	1.00	.45
❑ 183	Jeff George OW	.20	.09
❑ 184	Chris Warren OW	.20	.09
❑ 185	Herman Moore OW	.40	.18
❑ 186	Andre Rison OW	.20	.09
❑ 187	Byron Bam Morris OW	.20	.09
❑ 188	Troy Aikman OW	.50	.23
❑ 189	Jim Kelly OW	.40	.18
❑ 190	John Elway OW	1.00	.45
❑ 191	Cris Carter OW	.40	.18
❑ 192	Shannon Sharpe OW	.10	.05
❑ 193	Brett Favre OW	1.00	.45
❑ 194	Drew Bledsoe CL	.40	.18
❑ 195	John Elway CL	.60	.25
❑ 196	Dan Marino CL	.60	.25
❑ 197	Brett Favre CL	.60	.25
❑ 198	Troy Aikman CL	.40	.18
❑ 199	Steve Young CL	.40	.18
❑ 200	Rick Mirer CL	.20	.09
❑ P1	Emmitt Smith Promo Backfield Stars	2.00	.90
❑ P34	Steve Young Promo	1.00	.45
❑ P74	Drew Bledsoe Promo	1.25	.55

1996 Summit

		MINT	NRMT
COMPLETE SET (200)		30.00	13.50
❑ 1	Troy Aikman	1.25	.55
❑ 2	Marshall Faulk	.50	.23
❑ 3	Bruce Smith	.25	.11
❑ 4	Jerome Bettis	.50	.23
❑ 5	Bryan Cox	.10	.05
❑ 6	Robert Brooks	.50	.23
❑ 7	Dan Marino	2.50	1.10
❑ 8	Irving Fryar	.25	.11
❑ 9	Jerry Rice	1.25	.55
❑ 10	Ki-Jana Carter	.25	.11
❑ 11	Herman Moore	.50	.23
❑ 12	Derrick Thomas	.25	.11
❑ 13	Curtis Martin	1.00	.45
❑ 14	Jeff Hostetler	.10	.05
❑ 15	Errict Rhett	.25	.11
❑ 16	Emmitt Smith	2.00	.90
❑ 17	Aaron Craver	.10	.05
❑ 18	Kyle Brady	.10	.05
❑ 19	Tony Martin	.25	.11
❑ 20	Vinny Testaverde	.25	.11
❑ 21	Charles Haley	.25	.11
❑ 22	Rodney Thomas	.10	.05
❑ 23	Jim Everett	.10	.05
❑ 24	Brian Blades	.10	.05
❑ 25	Frank Sanders	.25	.11
❑ 26	Bryce Paup	.10	.05
❑ 27	Anthony Miller	.25	.11
❑ 28	Ken Dilger	.25	.11
❑ 29	Orlando Thomas	.10	.05
❑ 30	Rodney Hampton	.25	.11
❑ 31	Ken Norton Jr.	.10	.05
❑ 32	Darren Woodson	.25	.11
❑ 33	Antonio Freeman	1.00	.45
❑ 34	Steve Bono	.10	.05
❑ 35	Ben Coates	.25	.11
❑ 36	Jeff George	.25	.11
❑ 37	Curtis Conway	.50	.23
❑ 38	Steve Atwater	.10	.05
❑ 39	Fred Barnett	.10	.05
❑ 40	Joey Galloway	.75	.35
❑ 41	Jim Kelly	.50	.23
❑ 42	Michael Irvin	.50	.23
❑ 43	Steve Tasker	.10	.05
❑ 44	Warren Moon	.25	.11
❑ 45	Hugh Douglas	.25	.11
❑ 46	Steve Walsh	.10	.05
❑ 47	Kerry Collins	.50	.23
❑ 48	Barry Sanders	2.50	1.10
❑ 49	Steve Young	1.00	.45
❑ 50	Jim Harbaugh	.25	.11
❑ 51	Tyrone Wheatley	.25	.11
❑ 52	Boomer Esiason	.25	.11
❑ 53	Deion Sanders	.75	.35
❑ 54	Steve McNair	1.00	.45
❑ 55	Willie McGinest	.10	.05
❑ 56	Adrian Murrell	.50	.23
❑ 57	Thurman Thomas	.50	.23
❑ 58	John Elway	2.50	1.10
❑ 59	William Floyd	.25	.11
❑ 60	Eric Zeier	.10	.05
❑ 61	Dave Krieg	.10	.05
❑ 62	Eric Bjornson	.10	.05
❑ 63	Brett Favre	2.50	1.10
❑ 64	Derrick Alexander DE	.10	.05
❑ 65	Charlie Garner	.10	.05
❑ 66	Stan Humphries	.25	.11
❑ 67	Bert Emanuel	.25	.11
❑ 68	Scott Mitchell	.25	.11
❑ 69	Quentin Coryatt	.10	.05
❑ 70	Eric Green	.10	.05
❑ 71	Jeff Graham	.10	.05
❑ 72	Ernie Mills	.10	.05
❑ 73	Trent Dilfer	.50	.23
❑ 74	Sherman Williams	.10	.05
❑ 75	Tamarick Vanover	.25	.11
❑ 76	Drew Bledsoe	1.25	.55
❑ 77	Jay Novacek	.10	.05
❑ 78	Edgar Bennett	.25	.11
❑ 79	Tim Brown	.50	.23
❑ 80	Greg Lloyd	.25	.11
❑ 81	Darick Holmes	.10	.05
❑ 82	Carl Pickens	.50	.23
❑ 83	Flipper Anderson	.10	.05
❑ 84	Bernie Kosar	.10	.05
❑ 85	Dave Brown	.10	.05
❑ 86	Calvin Williams	.10	.05
❑ 87	Michael Westbrook	.50	.23
❑ 88	Kevin Williams	.10	.05
❑ 89	Chris Sanders	.25	.11
❑ 90	Robert Smith	.25	.11
❑ 91	Cris Carter	.50	.23
❑ 92	Gus Frerotte	.50	.23
❑ 93	Larry Centers	.25	.11
❑ 94	Eric Metcalf	.10	.05
❑ 95	Isaac Bruce	.50	.23
❑ 96	Kordell Stewart	.75	.35
❑ 97	Ricky Watters	.25	.11
❑ 98	Terrell Fletcher	.10	.05
❑ 99	Bernie Parmalee	.10	.05
❑ 100	Harvey Williams	.10	.05
❑ 101	Hardy Nickerson	.10	.05
❑ 102	Jeff Blake	.50	.23
❑ 103	Terry Allen	.25	.11
❑ 104	Yancey Thigpen	.25	.11
❑ 105	Greg Hill	.25	.11
❑ 106	Chris Warren	.25	.11
❑ 107	Terrell Davis	3.00	1.35
❑ 108	Mark Brunell	1.25	.55
❑ 109	Alvin Harper	.10	.05
❑ 110	Marcus Allen	.50	.23
❑ 111	Garrison Hearst	.25	.11
❑ 112	Derek Loville	.10	.05
❑ 113	Craig Heyward	.10	.05
❑ 114	Kimble Anders	.25	.11
❑ 115	O.J. McDuffie	.25	.11
❑ 116	Junior Seau	.25	.11
❑ 117	Terry Kirby	.25	.11
❑ 118	Erric Pegram	.10	.05
❑ 119	Rick Mirer	.25	.11
❑ 120	Erik Kramer	.10	.05
❑ 121	Brett Perriman	.10	.05
❑ 122	Shawn Jefferson	.10	.05
❑ 123	J.J. Stokes	.50	.23
❑ 124	Kevin Greene	.25	.11
❑ 125	Daryl Johnston	.25	.11
❑ 126	Mark Chmura	.25	.11
❑ 127	James O.Stewart	.25	.11
❑ 128	Mario Bates	.25	.11
❑ 129	Rodney Peete	.10	.05
❑ 130	Quinn Early	.10	.05

❑ 131 Shannon Sharpe .25 .11
❑ 132 Neil Smith .10 .05
❑ 133 Herschel Walker .25 .11
❑ 134 Aaron Bailey .10 .05
❑ 135 Rashaan Salaam .50 .23
❑ 136 Kevin Smith .10 .05
❑ 137 Sean Dawkins .10 .05
❑ 138 Jake Reed .25 .11
❑ 139 Neil O'Donnell .25 .11
❑ 140 Reggie White .50 .23
❑ 141 Vincent Brisby .10 .05
❑ 142 Napoleon Kaufman .50 .23
❑ 143 Brent Jones .10 .05
❑ 144 Mark Seay .10 .05
❑ 145 Heath Shuler .25 .11
❑ 146 Wayne Chrebet .75 .35
❑ 147 Leeland McElroy RC .50 .23
❑ 148 Tim Biakabutuka RC .75 .35
❑ 149 John Mobley RC .10 .05
❑ 150 Tony Brackens RC .25 .11
❑ 151 Danny Kanell RC .50 .23
❑ 152 Eddie Kennison RC .50 .23
❑ 153 Jonathan Ogden RC .10 .05
❑ 154 Bobby Engram RC .50 .23
❑ 155 Chris Darkins RC .10 .05
❑ 156 Daryl Gardener RC .10 .05
❑ 157 Keyshawn Johnson RC 2.00 .90
❑ 158 Mike Alstott RC 1.50 .70
❑ 159 Simeon Rice RC .50 .23
❑ 160 Eric Moulds RC 2.00 .90
❑ 161 Stepfret Williams RC .25 .11
❑ 162 Eddie George RC 4.00 1.80
❑ 163 Duane Clemons RC .10 .05
❑ 164 Amani Toomer RC 1.00 .45
❑ 165 Rickey Dudley RC .50 .23
❑ 166 Bobby Hoying RC .60 .25
❑ 167 Lawrence Phillips RC .50 .23
❑ 168 Willie Anderson RC .10 .05
❑ 169 Derrick Mayes RC .75 .35
❑ 170 Kevin Hardy RC .50 .23
❑ 171 Terry Glenn RC 1.25 .55
❑ 172 Stephen Davis RC 4.00 1.80
❑ 173 Walt Harris RC .10 .05
❑ 174 Marvin Harrison RC 2.50 1.10
❑ 175 Karim Abdul-Jabbar RC .60 .25
❑ 176 Alex Molden RC .10 .05
❑ 177 Regan Upshaw RC .10 .05
❑ 178 Jerald Moore RC .50 .23
❑ 179 Alex Van Dyke RC .25 .11
❑ 180 Jeff Lewis RC .60 .25
❑ 181 Cedric Jones RC .10 .05
❑ 182 Jim Kelly QH .50 .23
❑ 183 Troy Aikman QH .60 .25
❑ 184 Jim Harbaugh QH .25 .11
❑ 185 Neil O'Donnell QH .25 .11
❑ 186 Steve Young QH .50 .23
❑ 187 Kerry Collins QH .50 .23
❑ 188 Scott Mitchell QH .10 .05
❑ 189 Drew Bledsoe QH .60 .25
❑ 190 Kordell Stewart QH .60 .25
❑ 191 Erik Kramer QH .10 .05
❑ 192 Brett Favre QH 1.25 .55
❑ 193 Warren Moon QH .10 .05
❑ 194 Jeff Blake QH .25 .11
❑ 195 Mark Brunell QH .60 .25
❑ 196 John Elway QH 1.25 .55
❑ 197 Emmitt Smith .50 .23
Checklist back
❑ 198 Dan Marino .60 .25
Checklist back
❑ 199 Brett Favre .60 .25
Checklist back
❑ 200 Jim Harbaugh .25 .11
Checklist back

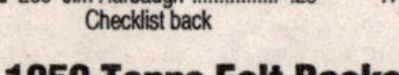

1950 Topps Felt Backs

	NRMT	VG-E
COMPLETE SET (100)	5500.00	2500.00
COMMON YEL. BOR.	60.00	27.00
WRAPPER (1-CENT)	500.00	220.00

❑ 1 Lou Allen 40.00 18.00
❑ 2 Morris Bailey 40.00 18.00
❑ 3 George Bell 40.00 18.00
❑ 4 Lindy Berry HOR 40.00 18.00

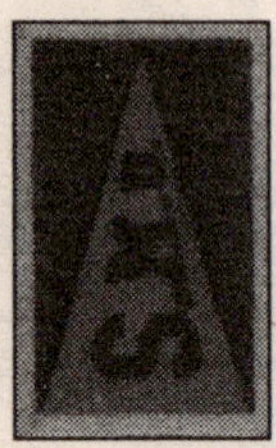

❑ 5A Mike Boldin 40.00 18.00
❑ 5B Mike Boldin 60.00 27.00
❑ 6A Bernie Botula 40.00 18.00
❑ 6B Bernie Botula 60.00 27.00
❑ 7 Bob Bowlby 40.00 18.00
❑ 8 Bob Bucher 40.00 18.00
❑ 9A Al Burnett 40.00 18.00
❑ 9B Al Burnett 60.00 27.00
❑ 10 Don Burson 40.00 18.00
❑ 11 Paul Campbell 40.00 18.00
❑ 12 Herb Carey 40.00 18.00
❑ 13A Bimbo Cecconi 40.00 18.00
❑ 13B Bimbo Cecconi 60.00 27.00
❑ 14 Bill Chauncey 40.00 18.00
❑ 15 Dick Clark 40.00 18.00
❑ 16 Tom Coleman 40.00 18.00
❑ 17 Billy Conn 40.00 18.00
❑ 18 John Cox 40.00 18.00
❑ 19 Lou Creekmur RC 90.00 40.00
❑ 20 Glen Davis RC 50.00 22.00
❑ 21 Warren Davis 40.00 18.00
❑ 22 Bob Deuber 40.00 18.00
❑ 23 Ray Dooney 40.00 18.00
❑ 24 Tom Dublinski 40.00 18.00
❑ 25 Jeff Fleischman 40.00 18.00
❑ 26 Jack Friedland 40.00 18.00
❑ 27 Bob Fuchs 40.00 18.00
❑ 28 Arnold Galiffa RC 50.00 22.00
❑ 29 Dick Gilman 40.00 18.00
❑ 30A Frank Gitschier 40.00 18.00
❑ 30B Frank Gitschier 60.00 27.00
❑ 31 Gene Glick 40.00 18.00
❑ 32 Bill Gregus 40.00 18.00
❑ 33 Harold Hagan 40.00 18.00
❑ 34 Charles Hall 40.00 18.00
❑ 35A Leon Hart 80.00 36.00
❑ 35B Leon Hart 120.00 55.00
❑ 36A Bob Hester 40.00 18.00
❑ 36B Bob Hester 60.00 27.00
❑ 37 George Hughes 40.00 18.00
❑ 38 Levi Jackson 50.00 22.00
❑ 39A Jackie Jensen 140.00 65.00
❑ 39B Jackie Jensen 250.00 110.00
❑ 40 Charlie Justice 150.00 70.00
❑ 41 Gary Kerkorian 40.00 18.00
❑ 42 Bernie Krueger 40.00 18.00
❑ 43 Bill Kuhn 40.00 18.00
❑ 44 Dean Laun 40.00 18.00
❑ 45 Chet Leach 40.00 18.00
❑ 46A Bobby Lee 40.00 18.00
❑ 46B Bobby Lee 60.00 27.00
❑ 47 Roger Lehew 40.00 18.00
❑ 48 Glenn Lippman 40.00 18.00
❑ 49 Melvin Lyle 40.00 18.00
❑ 50 Len Makowski 40.00 18.00
❑ 51A Al Malekoff 40.00 18.00
❑ 51B Al Malekoff 60.00 27.00
❑ 52A Jim Martin 50.00 22.00
❑ 52B Jim Martin 90.00 40.00
❑ 53 Frank Mataya 40.00 18.00
❑ 54A Ray Mathews RC 50.00 22.00
❑ 54B Ray Mathews RC 90.00 40.00
❑ 55A Dick McKissack 40.00 18.00
❑ 55B Dick McKissack 60.00 27.00
❑ 56 Frank Miller 40.00 18.00
❑ 57A John Miller 40.00 18.00
❑ 57B John Miller 60.00 27.00
❑ 58 Ed Modzelewski RC 50.00 22.00
❑ 59 Don Mouser 40.00 18.00
❑ 60 James Murphy 40.00 18.00
❑ 61A Ray Nagle 40.00 18.00
❑ 61B Ray Nagle 60.00 27.00
❑ 62 Leo Nomellini 200.00 90.00
❑ 63 James O'Day 40.00 18.00
❑ 64 Joe Paterno RC 1400.00 650.00
❑ 65 Andy Pavich 40.00 18.00
❑ 66A Pete Perini 40.00 18.00
❑ 66B Pete Perini 60.00 27.00
❑ 67 Jim Powers 40.00 18.00
❑ 68 Dave Rakestraw 40.00 18.00
❑ 69 Herb Rich 40.00 18.00
❑ 70 Fran Rogel RC 40.00 18.00
❑ 71A Darrell Royal RC 125.00 55.00
❑ 71B Darrell Royal RC 200.00 90.00
❑ 72 Steve Sawle 40.00 18.00
❑ 73 Nick Sebek 40.00 18.00
❑ 74 Herb Seidell 40.00 18.00
❑ 75A Charles Shaw 40.00 18.00
❑ 75B Charles Shaw 60.00 27.00
❑ 76A Emil Sitko RC 50.00 22.00
❑ 76B Emil Sitko RC 90.00 40.00
❑ 77 Ed(Butch) Songin RC 50.00 22.00
❑ 78A Mariano Stalloni 40.00 18.00
❑ 78B Mariano Stalloni 60.00 27.00
❑ 79 Ernie Stautner RC 200.00 90.00
❑ 80 Don Stehley 40.00 18.00
❑ 81 Gil Stevenson 40.00 18.00
❑ 82 Bishop Strickland 40.00 18.00
❑ 83 Harry Szulborski 40.00 18.00
❑ 84A Wally Teninga 40.00 18.00
❑ 84B Wally Teninga 60.00 27.00
❑ 85 Clayton Tonnemaker 40.00 18.00
❑ 86A Deacon Dan Towler RC 80.00 36.00
❑ 86B Deacon Dan Towler RC 120.00 55.00
❑ 87A Bert Turek 40.00 18.00
❑ 87B Bert Turek 60.00 27.00
❑ 88 Harry Ulinski 40.00 18.00
❑ 89 Leon Van Billingham 40.00 18.00
❑ 90 Langdon Viracola 40.00 18.00
❑ 91 Leo Wagner 40.00 18.00
❑ 92A Doak Walker 200.00 90.00
❑ 92B Doak Walker 375.00 170.00
❑ 93 Jim Ward 40.00 18.00
❑ 94 Art Weiner 40.00 18.00
❑ 95 Dick Weiss 40.00 18.00
❑ 96 Froggie Williams 40.00 18.00
❑ 97 Robert Red Wilson 40.00 18.00
❑ 98 Roger Red Wilson 40.00 18.00
❑ 99 Carl Wren 40.00 18.00
❑ 100A Pete Zinaich 40.00 18.00
❑ 100B Pete Zinaich 60.00 27.00

1951 Topps Magic

	NRMT	VG-E
COMPLETE SET (75)	1100.00	500.00
*BACK UNSCRATCHED: 1.5X TO 2.5X		
WRAPPER (1-CENT)	200.00	90.00
WRAPPER (5-CENT)	300.00	135.00

❑ 1 Jimmy Monahan RC 30.00 13.50
❑ 2 Bill Wade RC 50.00 22.00
❑ 3 Bill Reichardt 18.00 8.00
❑ 4 Babe Parilli RC 50.00 22.00
❑ 5 Billie Burkhalter 18.00 8.00

Card	NRMT	VG-E
❑ 6 Ed Weber	18.00	8.00
❑ 7 Tom Scott	25.00	11.00
❑ 8 Frank Guthridge	18.00	8.00
❑ 9 John Karras	18.00	8.00
❑ 10 Vic Janowicz RC	150.00	70.00
❑ 11 Lloyd Hill	18.00	8.00
❑ 12 Jim Weatherall RC	25.00	11.00
❑ 13 Howard Hansen	18.00	8.00
❑ 14 Lou D'Achille	18.00	8.00
❑ 15 Johnny Turco	18.00	8.00
❑ 16 Jerrell Price	18.00	8.00
❑ 17 John Coatta	18.00	8.00
❑ 18 Bruce Patton	18.00	8.00
❑ 19 Marion Campbell RC	35.00	16.00
❑ 20 Blaine Earon	18.00	8.00
❑ 21 Dewey McConnell	18.00	8.00
❑ 22 Ray Beck	18.00	8.00
❑ 23 Jim Prewett	18.00	8.00
❑ 24 Bob Steele	18.00	8.00
❑ 25 Art Betts	18.00	8.00
❑ 26 Walt Trillhaase	18.00	8.00
❑ 27 Gil Bartosh	18.00	8.00
❑ 28 Bob Bestwick	18.00	8.00
❑ 29 Tom Rushing	18.00	8.00
❑ 30 Bert Rechichar RC	35.00	16.00
❑ 31 Bill Owens	18.00	8.00
❑ 32 Mike Goggins	18.00	8.00
❑ 33 John Petitbon	18.00	8.00
❑ 34 Byron Townsend	18.00	8.00
❑ 35 Ed Rotticci	18.00	8.00
❑ 36 Steve Wadiak	18.00	8.00
❑ 37 Bobby Marlow RC	25.00	11.00
❑ 38 Bill Fuchs	18.00	8.00
❑ 39 Ralph Staub	18.00	8.00
❑ 40 Bill Vesprini	18.00	8.00
❑ 41 Zack Jordan	18.00	8.00
❑ 42 Bob Smith RC	25.00	11.00
❑ 43 Charles Hanson	18.00	8.00
❑ 44 Glenn Smith	18.00	8.00
❑ 45 Armand Kitto	18.00	8.00
❑ 46 Vinnie Drake	18.00	8.00
❑ 47 Bill Putich	18.00	8.00
❑ 48 George Young RC	40.00	18.00
❑ 49 Don McRae	18.00	8.00
❑ 50 Frank Smith	18.00	8.00
❑ 51 Dick Hightower	18.00	8.00
❑ 52 Clyde Pickard	18.00	8.00
❑ 53 Bob Reynolds	18.00	8.00
❑ 54 Dick Gregory	18.00	8.00
❑ 55 Dale Samuels	18.00	8.00
❑ 56 Gale Galloway	18.00	8.00
❑ 57 Vic Pujo	18.00	8.00
❑ 58 Dave Waters	18.00	8.00
❑ 59 Joe Ernest	18.00	8.00
❑ 60 Elmer Costa	18.00	8.00
❑ 61 Nick Liotta	18.00	8.00
❑ 62 John Dottley	18.00	8.00
❑ 63 Hi Faubion	18.00	8.00
❑ 64 David Harr	18.00	8.00
❑ 65 Bill Matthews	18.00	8.00
❑ 66 Carroll McDonald	18.00	8.00
❑ 67 Dick Dewing	18.00	8.00
❑ 68 Joe Johnson	18.00	8.00
❑ 69 Arnold Burwitz	18.00	8.00
❑ 70 Ed Dobrowolski	18.00	8.00
❑ 71 Joe Dudeck	18.00	8.00
❑ 72 Johnny Bright RC	25.00	11.00
❑ 73 Harold Loehlein	18.00	8.00
❑ 74 Lawrence Hairston	18.00	8.00
❑ 75 Bob Carey RC	25.00	11.00

1955 Topps All-American

	NRMT	VG-E
COMPLETE SET (100)	3600.00	1600.00
COMMON SP (93-100)	40.00	18.00
WRAPPER (1-CENT)	250.00	110.00
WRAPPER (5-CENT)	150.00	70.00

Card	NRMT	VG-E
❑ 1 Herman Hickman RC	125.00	31.00
❑ 2 John Kimbrough	16.00	7.25
❑ 3 Ed Weir	16.00	7.25
❑ 4 Erny Pinckert	16.00	7.25
❑ 5 Bobby Grayson	16.00	7.25

Card	NRMT	VG-E
❑ 6 Nile Kinnick RC UER (Spelled Niles)	100.00	45.00
❑ 7 Andy Bershak	16.00	7.25
❑ 8 George Cafego RC	16.00	7.25
❑ 9 Tom Hamilton SP	30.00	13.50
❑ 10 Bill Dudley	40.00	18.00
❑ 11 Bobby Dodd SP	30.00	13.50
❑ 12 Otto Graham	200.00	90.00
❑ 13 Aaron Rosenberg	16.00	7.25
❑ 14A Gaynell Tinsley RC ERR (With Whizzer White bio)	100.00	45.00
❑ 14B Gaynell Tinsley RC COR (Correct bio)	25.00	11.00
❑ 15 Ed Kaw SP	30.00	13.50
❑ 16 Knute Rockne	275.00	125.00
❑ 17 Bob Reynolds	16.00	7.25
❑ 18 Pudge Heffelfinger RC SP	40.00	18.00
❑ 19 Bruce Smith	35.00	16.00
❑ 20 Sammy Baugh	200.00	90.00
❑ 21A W.White RC SP ERR (With Gaynell Tinsley bio)	150.00	70.00
❑ 21B W.White RC SP COR (Correct bio)	80.00	36.00
❑ 22 Brick Muller	16.00	7.25
❑ 23 Dick Kazmaier RC	16.00	7.25
❑ 24 Ken Strong	40.00	18.00
❑ 25 Casimir Myslinski SP	30.00	13.50
❑ 26 Larry Kelley RC SP	40.00	18.00
❑ 27 Red Grange UER (Card says he was QB, should say halfback)	300.00	135.00
❑ 28 Mel Hein RC SP	40.00	18.00
❑ 29 Leo Nomellini SP	75.00	34.00
❑ 30 Wes Fesler	16.00	7.25
❑ 31 George Sauer Sr. RC	20.00	9.00
❑ 32 Hank Foldberg	16.00	7.25
❑ 33 Bob Higgins	16.00	7.25
❑ 34 Davey O'Brien RC	40.00	18.00
❑ 35 Tom Harmon RC SP	60.00	27.00
❑ 36 Turk Edwards SP	40.00	18.00
❑ 37 Jim Thorpe	400.00	180.00
❑ 38 Amos A. Stagg COR RC	60.00	27.00
❑ 38A Amos A. Stagg RC ERR (Wrong back 19)	100.00	45.00
❑ 39 Jerome Holland RC	20.00	9.00
❑ 40 Donn Moomaw	16.00	7.25
❑ 41 Joseph Alexander SP	30.00	13.50
❑ 42 Eddie Tryon RC SP	40.00	18.00
❑ 43 George Savitsky	16.00	7.25
❑ 44 Ed Garbisch	16.00	7.25
❑ 45 Elmer Oliphant	16.00	7.25
❑ 46 Arnold Lassman	16.00	7.25
❑ 47 Bo McMillin RC	20.00	9.00
❑ 48 Ed Widseth	16.00	7.25
❑ 49 Don Zimmerman	16.00	7.25
❑ 50 Ken Kavanaugh	20.00	9.00
❑ 51 Duane Purvis SP	30.00	13.50
❑ 52 John Lujack	50.00	22.00
❑ 53 John F. Green	16.00	7.25
❑ 54 Edwin Dooley SP	30.00	13.50
❑ 55 Frank Merritt SP	30.00	13.50
❑ 56 Ernie Nevers RC	70.00	32.00
❑ 57 Vic Hanson SP	30.00	13.50
❑ 58 Ed Franco	16.00	7.25
❑ 59 Doc Blanchard RC	50.00	22.00
❑ 60 Dan Hill	16.00	7.25
❑ 61 Charles Brickley SP	30.00	13.50
❑ 62 Harry Newman	16.00	7.25
❑ 63 Charlie Justice	35.00	16.00
❑ 64 Benny Friedman RC	20.00	9.00
❑ 65 Joe Donchess SP	30.00	13.50
❑ 66 Bruiser Kinard RC	35.00	16.00
❑ 67 Frankie Albert	20.00	9.00
❑ 68 Four Horsemen RC SP (Jim Crowley, Elmer Layden, Creighton Miller, Harry Stuhldreher)	500.00	220.00
❑ 69 Frank Sinkwich RC	20.00	9.00
❑ 70 Bill Daddio	16.00	7.25
❑ 71 Bobby Wilson	16.00	7.25
❑ 72 Chub Peabody	16.00	7.25
❑ 73 Paul Governali	20.00	9.00
❑ 74 Gene McEver	16.00	7.25
❑ 75 Hugh Gallarneau	16.00	7.25
❑ 76 Angelo Bertelli RC	20.00	9.00
❑ 77 Bowden Wyatt SP	30.00	13.50
❑ 78 Jay Berwanger RC	35.00	16.00
❑ 79 Pug Lund	16.00	7.25
❑ 80 Bennie Oosterbaan	16.00	7.25
❑ 81 Cotton Warburton	16.00	7.25
❑ 82 Alex Wojciechowicz	30.00	13.50
❑ 83 Ted Coy SP	30.00	13.50
❑ 84 Ace Parker RC SP	40.00	18.00
❑ 85 Sid Luckman	125.00	55.00
❑ 86 Albie Booth SP	30.00	13.50
❑ 87 Adolph Schultz SP	30.00	13.50
❑ 88 Ralph Kercheval	16.00	7.25
❑ 89 Marshall Goldberg	20.00	9.00
❑ 90 Charlie O'Rourke	16.00	7.25
❑ 91 Bob Odell UER (Photo actually Howard Odell)	16.00	7.25
❑ 92 Biggie Munn	16.00	7.25
❑ 93 Willie Heston SP	40.00	18.00
❑ 94 Joe Bernard SP	40.00	18.00
❑ 95 Chris(Red) Cagle SP	40.00	18.00
❑ 96 Bill Hollenback SP	40.00	18.00
❑ 97 Don Hutson RC SP	225.00	100.00
❑ 98 Beattie Feathers SP	80.00	36.00
❑ 99 Don Whitmire SP	40.00	18.00
❑ 100 Fats Henry SP RC	160.00	40.00

1956 Topps

	NRMT	VG-E
COMPLETE SET (120)	1400.00	650.00
WRAPPER (1-CENT)	250.00	110.00
WRAPPER (5-CENT)	50.00	22.00

Card	NRMT	VG-E
❑ 1 Johnny Carson SP	80.00	20.00
❑ 2 Gordy Soltau	6.00	2.70
❑ 3 Frank Varrichione	6.00	2.70
❑ 4 Eddie Bell	6.00	2.70
❑ 5 Alex Webster RC	12.00	5.50
❑ 6 Norm Van Brocklin	30.00	13.50
❑ 7 Green Bay Packers Team Card	18.00	8.00
❑ 8 Lou Creekmur	15.00	6.75
❑ 9 Lou Groza	25.00	11.00
❑ 10 Tom Bienemann SP	25.00	11.00
❑ 11 George Blanda	50.00	22.00
❑ 12 Alan Ameche	12.00	5.50
❑ 13 Vic Janowicz SP	45.00	20.00
❑ 14 Dick Moegle	8.00	3.60

❑ 15 Fran Rogel ... 6.00 2.70
❑ 16 Harold Giancanelli ... 6.00 2.70
❑ 17 Emlen Tunnell ... 15.00 6.75
❑ 18 Tank Younger ... 12.00 5.50
❑ 19 Billy Howton ... 8.00 3.60
❑ 20 Jack Christiansen ... 15.00 6.75
❑ 21 Darrel Brewster ... 6.00 2.70
❑ 22 Chicago Cardinals SP 100.00 45.00
Team Card
❑ 23 Ed Brown ... 8.00 3.60
❑ 24 Joe Campanella ... 6.00 2.70
❑ 25 Leon Heath SP ... 22.00 10.00
❑ 26 San Francisco 49ers ... 18.00 8.00
Team Card
❑ 27 Dick Flanagan ... 6.00 2.70
❑ 28 Chuck Bednarik ... 25.00 11.00
❑ 29 Kyle Rote ... 12.00 5.50
❑ 30 Les Richter ... 8.00 3.60
❑ 31 Howard Ferguson ... 6.00 2.70
❑ 32 Dorne Dibble ... 6.00 2.70
❑ 33 Kenny Konz ... 6.00 2.70
❑ 34 Dave Mann SP ... 25.00 11.00
❑ 35 Rick Casares ... 12.00 5.50
❑ 36 Art Donovan ... 30.00 13.50
❑ 37 Chuck Drazenovich SP 22.00 10.00
❑ 38 Joe Arenas ... 6.00 2.70
❑ 39 Lynn Chandnois ... 6.00 2.70
❑ 40 Philadelphia Eagles ... 18.00 8.00
Team Card
❑ 41 Roosevelt Brown RC ... 30.00 13.50
❑ 42 Tom Fears ... 25.00 11.00
❑ 43 Gary Knafelc ... 6.00 2.70
❑ 44 Joe Schmidt RC ... 45.00 20.00
❑ 45 Cleveland Browns ... 18.00 8.00
Team Card UER
(Card back does not
credit the Browns with
being Champs in 1955)
❑ 46 Len Teeuws RC SP ... 25.00 11.00
❑ 47 Bill George RC ... 30.00 13.50
❑ 48 Baltimore Colts ... 18.00 8.00
Team Card
❑ 49 Eddie LeBaron SP ... 45.00 20.00
❑ 50 Hugh McElhenny ... 25.00 11.00
❑ 51 Ted Marchibroda ... 12.00 5.50
❑ 52 Adrian Burk ... 6.00 2.70
❑ 53 Frank Gifford ... 75.00 34.00
❑ 54 Charley Toogood ... 6.00 2.70
❑ 55 Tobin Rote ... 8.00 3.60
❑ 56 Bill Stits ... 6.00 2.70
❑ 57 Don Colo ... 6.00 2.70
❑ 58 Ollie Matson SP ... 75.00 34.00
❑ 59 Harlon Hill ... 8.00 3.60
❑ 60 Lenny Moore RC ! ... 90.00 40.00
❑ 61 Washington Redskins SP 90.00 40.00
Team Card
❑ 62 Billy Wilson ... 6.00 2.70
❑ 63 Pittsburgh Steelers ... 18.00 8.00
Team Card
❑ 64 Bob Pellegrini ... 6.00 2.70
❑ 65 Ken MacAfee ... 6.00 2.70
❑ 66 Willard Sherman ... 6.00 2.70
❑ 67 Roger Zatkoff ... 6.00 2.70
❑ 68 Dave Middleton ... 6.00 2.70
❑ 69 Ray Renfro ... 8.00 3.60
❑ 70 Don Stonesifer SP ... 25.00 11.00
❑ 71 Stan Jones RC ... 30.00 13.50
❑ 72 Jim Mutscheller ... 6.00 2.70
❑ 73 Volney Peters SP ... 22.00 10.00
❑ 74 Leo Nomellini ... 20.00 9.00
❑ 75 Ray Mathews ... 6.00 2.70
❑ 76 Dick Bielski ... 6.00 2.70
❑ 77 Charley Conerly ... 25.00 11.00
❑ 78 Elroy Hirsch ... 25.00 11.00
❑ 79 Bill Forester RC ... 8.00 3.60
❑ 80 Jim Doran ... 6.00 2.70
❑ 81 Fred Morrison ... 6.00 2.70
❑ 82 Jack Simmons SP ... 25.00 11.00
❑ 83 Bill McColl ... 6.00 2.70
❑ 84 Bert Rechichar ... 6.00 2.70
❑ 85 Joe Scudero SP ... 22.00 10.00
❑ 86 Y.A. Tittle UER ... 50.00 22.00
(Misspelled Yelverton on back)
❑ 87 Ernie Stautner ... 20.00 9.00
❑ 88 Norm Willey ... 6.00 2.70
❑ 89 Bob Schnelker ... 6.00 2.70
❑ 90 Dan Towler ... 12.00 5.50
❑ 91 John Martinkovic ... 6.00 2.70
❑ 92 Detroit Lions ... 18.00 8.00
Team Card
❑ 93 George Ratterman ... 8.00 3.60
❑ 94 Chuck Ulrich SP ... 25.00 11.00
❑ 95 Bobby Watkins ... 6.00 2.70
❑ 96 Buddy Young ... 12.00 5.50
❑ 97 Billy Wells SP ... 22.00 10.00
❑ 98 Bob Toneff ... 6.00 2.70
❑ 99 Bill McPeak ... 6.00 2.70
❑ 100 Bobby Thomason ... 6.00 2.70
❑ 101 Roosevelt Grier RC ... 40.00 18.00
❑ 102 Ron Waller ... 6.00 2.70
❑ 103 Bobby Dillon ... 6.00 2.70
❑ 104 Leon Hart ... 12.00 5.50
❑ 105 Mike McCormack ... 15.00 6.75
❑ 106 John Olszewski SP ... 25.00 11.00
❑ 107 Bill Wightkin ... 6.00 2.70
❑ 108 George Shaw RC ... 8.00 3.60
❑ 109 Dale Atkeson SP ... 22.00 10.00
❑ 110 Joe Perry ... 25.00 11.00
❑ 111 Dale Dodrill ... 6.00 2.70
❑ 112 Tom Scott ... 6.00 2.70
❑ 113 New York Giants ... 18.00 8.00
Team Card
❑ 114 Los Angeles Rams ... 18.00 8.00
Team Card UER
(Back incorrect, Rams
were not 1955 champs)
❑ 115 Al Carmichael ... 6.00 2.70
❑ 116 Bobby Layne ... 50.00 22.00
❑ 117 Ed Modzelewski ... 6.00 2.70
❑ 118 Lamar McHan RC SP 25.00 11.00
❑ 119 Chicago Bears ... 18.00 8.00
Team Card
❑ 120 Billy Vessels RC ... 40.00 10.00
❑ AD1 Lou Groza ... 250.00 110.00
Don Colo
Darrel Brewster
(Ad back panel)
❑ NNO Checklist Card SP .. 400.00 100.00
(Unnumbered)
❑ C1 Contest Card ... 80.00 36.00
Sunday, October 14
Colts vs. Packers
Cards vs. Redskins
❑ C2 Contest Card ... 80.00 36.00
Sunday, October 14
Rams vs. Lions
Giants vs. Browns
❑ C3 Contest Card ... 80.00 36.00
Sunday, October 14
Eagles vs. Steelers
49ers vs. Bears
❑ CA Contest Card ... 90.00 40.00
Sunday, November 25
Bears vs. Giants
Rams vs. Colts
❑ CB Contest Card ... 110.00 50.00
Sunday, November 25
Steelers vs. Cards
49ers vs. Eagles

1957 Topps

	NRMT	VG-E
COMPLETE SET (154)	2200.00	1000.00
COMMON CARD (1-88)	4.00	1.80
COMMON CARD (89-154)	10.00	4.50
WRAPPER (1-CENT)	50.00	22.00
WRAPPER (5-CENT)	60.00	27.00

❑ 1 Eddie LeBaron ... 40.00 10.00
❑ 2 Pete Retzlaff RC ... 15.00 6.75
❑ 3 Mike McCormack ... 12.00 5.50
❑ 4 Lou Baldacci ... 4.00 1.80
❑ 5 Gino Marchetti ... 15.00 6.75
❑ 6 Leo Nomellini ... 20.00 9.00
❑ 7 Bobby Watkins ... 4.00 1.80
❑ 8 Dave Middleton ... 4.00 1.80
❑ 9 Bobby Dillon ... 4.00 1.80
❑ 10 Les Richter ... 6.00 2.70
❑ 11 Roosevelt Brown ... 20.00 9.00
❑ 12 Lavern Torgeson RC ... 4.00 1.80
❑ 13 Dick Bielski ... 4.00 1.80
❑ 14 Pat Summerall ... 20.00 9.00
❑ 15 Jack Butler RC ... 10.00 4.50
❑ 16 John Henry Johnson ... 15.00 6.75
❑ 17 Art Spinney ... 4.00 1.80
❑ 18 Bob St. Clair ... 12.00 5.50
❑ 19 Perry Jeter ... 4.00 1.80
❑ 20 Lou Creekmur ... 12.00 5.50
❑ 21 Dave Hanner ... 6.00 2.70
❑ 22 Norm Van Brocklin ... 30.00 13.50
❑ 23 Don Chandler RC ... 10.00 4.50
❑ 24 Al Dorow ... 4.00 1.80
❑ 25 Tom Scott ... 4.00 1.80
❑ 26 Ollie Matson ... 20.00 9.00
❑ 27 Fran Rogel ... 4.00 1.80
❑ 28 Lou Groza ... 25.00 11.00
❑ 29 Billy Vessels ... 6.00 2.70
❑ 30 Y.A. Tittle ... 40.00 18.00
❑ 31 George Blanda ... 40.00 18.00
❑ 32 Bobby Layne ... 40.00 18.00
❑ 33 Billy Howton ... 6.00 2.70
❑ 34 Bill Wade ... 10.00 4.50
❑ 35 Emlen Tunnell ... 15.00 6.75
❑ 36 Leo Elter ... 4.00 1.80
❑ 37 Clarence Peaks RC ... 6.00 2.70
❑ 38 Don Stonesifer ... 4.00 1.80
❑ 39 George Tarasovic ... 4.00 1.80
❑ 40 Darrel Brewster ... 4.00 1.80
❑ 41 Bert Rechichar ... 4.00 1.80
❑ 42 Billy Wilson ... 4.00 1.80
❑ 43 Ed Brown ... 6.00 2.70
❑ 44 Gene Gedman ... 4.00 1.80
❑ 45 Gary Knafelc ... 4.00 1.80
❑ 46 Elroy Hirsch ... 20.00 9.00
❑ 47 Don Heinrich ... 6.00 2.70
❑ 48 Gene Brito ... 4.00 1.80
❑ 49 Chuck Bednarik ... 25.00 11.00
❑ 50 Dave Mann ... 4.00 1.80
❑ 51 Bill McPeak ... 4.00 1.80
❑ 52 Kenny Konz ... 4.00 1.80
❑ 53 Alan Ameche ... 10.00 4.50
❑ 54 Gordy Soltau ... 4.00 1.80
❑ 55 Rick Casares ... 6.00 2.70
❑ 56 Charlie Ane ... 4.00 1.80
❑ 57 Al Carmichael ... 4.00 1.80
❑ 58A Willard Sherman ERR 300.00 135.00
(No team on front)
❑ 58B Willard Sherman COR 4.00 1.80
❑ 59 Kyle Rote ... 10.00 4.50
❑ 60 Chuck Drazenovich ... 4.00 1.80
❑ 61 Bobby Walston ... 4.00 1.80
❑ 62 John Olszewski ... 4.00 1.80
❑ 63 Ray Mathews ... 4.00 1.80
❑ 64 Maurice Bassett ... 4.00 1.80
❑ 65 Art Donovan ... 25.00 11.00
❑ 66 Joe Arenas ... 4.00 1.80
❑ 67 Harlon Hill ... 6.00 2.70
❑ 68 Yale Lary ... 12.00 5.50
❑ 69 Bill Forester ... 6.00 2.70
❑ 70 Bob Boyd ... 4.00 1.80
❑ 71 Andy Robustelli ... 20.00 9.00
❑ 72 Sam Baker RC ... 6.00 2.70
❑ 73 Bob Pellegrini ... 4.00 1.80
❑ 74 Leo Sanford ... 4.00 1.80
❑ 75 Sid Watson ... 4.00 1.80
❑ 76 Ray Renfro ... 6.00 2.70
❑ 77 Carl Taseff ... 4.00 1.80
❑ 78 Clyde Conner ... 4.00 1.80
❑ 79 J.C. Caroline ... 4.00 1.80
❑ 80 Howard Cassady RC ... 15.00 6.75

❑ 81	Tobin Rote	6.00	2.70
❑ 82	Ron Waller	4.00	1.80
❑ 83	Jim Patton RC	6.00	2.70
❑ 84	Volney Peters	4.00	1.80
❑ 85	Dick Lane RC	40.00	18.00
❑ 86	Royce Womble	4.00	1.80
❑ 87	Duane Putnam RC	6.00	2.70
❑ 88	Frank Gifford	90.00	40.00
❑ 89	Steve Meilinger	10.00	4.50
❑ 90	Buck Lansford	10.00	4.50
❑ 91	Lindon Crow DP	8.00	3.60
❑ 92	Ernie Stautner DP	20.00	9.00
❑ 93	Preston Carpenter DP RC	10.00	4.50
❑ 94	Raymond Berry RC	125.00	55.00
❑ 95	Hugh McElhenny	30.00	13.50
❑ 96	Stan Jones	20.00	9.00
❑ 97	Dorne Dibble	10.00	4.50
❑ 98	Joe Scudero DP	8.00	3.60
❑ 99	Eddie Bell	10.00	4.50
❑ 100	Joe Childress DP	8.00	3.60
❑ 101	Elbert Nickel	12.00	5.50
❑ 102	Walt Michaels	12.00	5.50
❑ 103	Jim Mutscheller DP	8.00	3.60
❑ 104	Earl Morrall RC	40.00	18.00
❑ 105	Larry Strickland	10.00	4.50
❑ 106	Jack Christiansen	15.00	6.75
❑ 107	Fred Cone DP	8.00	3.60
❑ 108	Bud McFadin RC	12.00	5.50
❑ 109	Charley Conerly	30.00	13.50
❑ 110	Tom Runnels DP	8.00	3.60
❑ 111	Ken Keller DP	8.00	3.60
❑ 112	James Root	10.00	4.50
❑ 113	Ted Marchibroda DP	10.00	4.50
❑ 114	Don Paul	10.00	4.50
❑ 115	George Shaw	12.00	5.50
❑ 116	Dick Moegle	12.00	5.50
❑ 117	Don Bingham	10.00	4.50
❑ 118	Leon Hart	14.00	6.25
❑ 119	Bart Starr RC	450.00	200.00
❑ 120	Paul Miller DP	8.00	3.60
❑ 121	Alex Webster	12.00	5.50
❑ 122	Ray Wietecha DP	8.00	3.60
❑ 123	Johnny Carson	10.00	4.50
❑ 124	Tommy McDonald DP RC	25.00	11.00
❑ 125	Jerry Tubbs RC	12.00	5.50
❑ 126	Jack Scarbath	10.00	4.50
❑ 127	Ed Modzelewski DP	8.00	3.60
❑ 128	Lenny Moore	50.00	22.00
❑ 129	Joe Perry DP	25.00	11.00
❑ 130	Bill Wightkin	10.00	4.50
❑ 131	Jim Doran	10.00	4.50
❑ 132	Howard Ferguson UER (Name misspelled Furgeson on front)	10.00	4.50
❑ 133	Tom Wilson	10.00	4.50
❑ 134	Dick James	10.00	4.50
❑ 135	Jimmy Harris	10.00	4.50
❑ 136	Chuck Ulrich	10.00	4.50
❑ 137	Lynn Chandnois	10.00	4.50
❑ 138	John Unitas DP RC	450.00	200.00
❑ 139	Jim Ridlon DP	8.00	3.60
❑ 140	Zeke Bratkowski DP	10.00	4.50
❑ 141	Ray Krouse	10.00	4.50
❑ 142	John Martinkovic	10.00	4.50
❑ 143	Jim Cason DP	8.00	3.60
❑ 144	Ken MacAfee	10.00	4.50
❑ 145	Sid Youngelman RC	12.00	5.50
❑ 146	Paul Larson	10.00	4.50
❑ 147	Len Ford	30.00	13.50
❑ 148	Bob Toneff DP	8.00	3.60
❑ 149	Ronnie Knox DP	8.00	3.60
❑ 150	Jim David RC	12.00	5.50
❑ 151	Paul Hornung RC	400.00	180.00
❑ 152	Tank Younger	14.00	6.25
❑ 153	Bill Svoboda DP	8.00	3.60
❑ 154	Fred Morrison	70.00	17.50
❑ AD1	Al Dorow / Harlon Hill / Bert Rechichar / (Ollie Matson back) / (Ad back panel)	175.00	80.00
❑ NNO	Checklist Card SP	750.00	190.00

1958 Topps

	NRMT	VG-E
COMPLETE SET (132)	1250.00	550.00
WRAPPER (1-CENT)	40.00	18.00
WRAPPER (5-CENT)	50.00	22.00

❑ 1	Gene Filipski RC	15.00	3.70
❑ 2	Bobby Layne	30.00	13.50
❑ 3	Joe Schmidt	12.00	5.50
❑ 4	Bill Barnes	4.00	1.80
❑ 5	Milt Plum RC	8.00	3.60
❑ 6	Billy Howton UER (Misspelled Billie on card front)	5.00	2.20
❑ 7	Howard Cassady	5.00	2.20
❑ 8	Jim Dooley	4.00	1.80
❑ 9	Cleveland Browns Team Card	6.00	2.70
❑ 10	Lenny Moore	20.00	9.00
❑ 11	Darrel Brewster	4.00	1.80
❑ 12	Alan Ameche	8.00	3.60
❑ 13	Jim David	4.00	1.80
❑ 14	Jim Mutscheller	4.00	1.80
❑ 15	Andy Robustelli UER (Never played for San Francisco)	10.00	4.50
❑ 16	Gino Marchetti	12.00	5.50
❑ 17	Ray Renfro	5.00	2.20
❑ 18	Yale Lary	8.00	3.60
❑ 19	Gary Glick	4.00	1.80
❑ 20	Jon Arnett RC	8.00	3.60
❑ 21	Bob Boyd	4.00	1.80
❑ 22	John Unitas UER (College: Pittsburgh should be Louisville)	125.00	55.00
❑ 23	Zeke Bratkowski	5.00	2.20
❑ 24	Sid Youngelman UER (Misspelled Youngleman on card back)	4.00	1.80
❑ 25	Leo Elter	4.00	1.80
❑ 26	Kenny Konz	4.00	1.80
❑ 27	Washington Redskins Team Card	6.00	2.70
❑ 28	Carl Brettschneider UER (Misspelled on back as Brettschnieder)	4.00	1.80
❑ 29	Chicago Bears Team Card	6.00	2.70
❑ 30	Alex Webster	5.00	2.20
❑ 31	Al Carmichael	4.00	1.80
❑ 32	Bobby Dillon	4.00	1.80
❑ 33	Steve Meilinger	4.00	1.80
❑ 34	Sam Baker	4.00	1.80
❑ 35	Chuck Bednarik UER (Misspelled Bednarick on card back)	15.00	6.75
❑ 36	Bert Vic Zucco	4.00	1.80
❑ 37	George Tarasovic	4.00	1.80
❑ 38	Bill Wade	8.00	3.60
❑ 39	Dick Stanfel	5.00	2.20
❑ 40	Jerry Norton	4.00	1.80
❑ 41	San Francisco 49ers Team Card	6.00	2.70
❑ 42	Emlen Tunnell	10.00	4.50
❑ 43	Jim Doran	4.00	1.80
❑ 44	Ted Marchibroda	8.00	3.60
❑ 45	Chet Hanulak	4.00	1.80
❑ 46	Dale Dodrill	4.00	1.80
❑ 47	Johnny Carson	4.00	1.80
❑ 48	Dick Deschaine	4.00	1.80
❑ 49	Billy Wells UER (College should be Michigan State)	4.00	1.80
❑ 50	Larry Morris	4.00	1.80
❑ 51	Jack McClairen	4.00	1.80
❑ 52	Lou Groza	15.00	6.75
❑ 53	Rick Casares	5.00	2.20
❑ 54	Don Chandler	5.00	2.20
❑ 55	Duane Putnam	4.00	1.80
❑ 56	Gary Knafelc	4.00	1.80
❑ 57	Earl Morrall UER (Misspelled Morall on card back)	10.00	4.50
❑ 58	Ron Kramer RC	5.00	2.20
❑ 59	Mike McCormack	8.00	3.60
❑ 60	Gern Nagler	4.00	1.80
❑ 61	New York Giants Team Card	6.00	2.70
❑ 62	Jim Brown RC	450.00	200.00
❑ 63	Joe Marconi RC UER (Avg. gain should be 4.4)	4.00	1.80
❑ 64	R.C. Owens RC UER (Photo actually Don Owens)	5.00	2.20
❑ 65	Jimmy Carr RC	5.00	2.20
❑ 66	Bart Starr UER (Life and year stats reversed)	100.00	45.00
❑ 67	Tom Wilson	4.00	1.80
❑ 68	Lamar McHan	4.00	1.80
❑ 69	Chicago Cardinals Team Card	6.00	2.70
❑ 70	Jack Christiansen	8.00	3.60
❑ 71	Don McIlhenny RC	4.00	1.80
❑ 72	Ron Waller	4.00	1.80
❑ 73	Frank Gifford	50.00	22.00
❑ 74	Bert Rechichar	4.00	1.80
❑ 75	John Henry Johnson	10.00	4.50
❑ 76	Jack Butler	5.00	2.20
❑ 77	Frank Varrichione	4.00	1.80
❑ 78	Ray Mathews	4.00	1.80
❑ 79	Marv Matuszak UER (Misspelled Matuzsak on card front)	4.00	1.80
❑ 80	Harlon Hill UER (Lifetime yards and Avg. gain incorrect)	4.00	1.80
❑ 81	Lou Creekmur	8.00	3.60
❑ 82	Woodley Lewis UER (Misspelled Woodly on front; end on front and halfback on back)	4.00	1.80
❑ 83	Don Heinrich	4.00	1.80
❑ 84	Charley Conerly UER (Misspelled Charlie on card back)	15.00	6.75
❑ 85	Los Angeles Rams Team Card	6.00	2.70
❑ 86	Y.A. Tittle	30.00	13.50
❑ 87	Bobby Walston	4.00	1.80
❑ 88	Earl Putman	4.00	1.80
❑ 89	Leo Nomellini	15.00	6.75
❑ 90	Sonny Jurgensen RC	100.00	45.00
❑ 91	Don Paul	4.00	1.80
❑ 92	Paige Cothren	4.00	1.80
❑ 93	Joe Perry	15.00	6.75
❑ 94	Tobin Rote	5.00	2.20
❑ 95	Billy Wilson	4.00	1.80
❑ 96	Green Bay Packers Team Card	6.00	2.70
❑ 97	Lavern Torgeson	4.00	1.80
❑ 98	Milt Davis	4.00	1.80
❑ 99	Larry Strickland	4.00	1.80
❑ 100	Matt Hazeltine RC	5.00	2.20
❑ 101	Walt Yowarsky	4.00	1.80
❑ 102	Roosevelt Brown	8.00	3.60
❑ 103	Jim Ringo	10.00	4.50
❑ 104	Joe Krupa	4.00	1.80
❑ 105	Les Richter	5.00	2.20
❑ 106	Art Donovan	20.00	9.00
❑ 107	John Olszewski	4.00	1.80
❑ 108	Ken Keller	4.00	1.80
❑ 109	Philadelphia Eagles Team Card	6.00	2.70
❑ 110	Baltimore Colts Team Card	6.00	2.70

No.	Card	NRMT	VG-E
❑ 111	Dick Bielski	4.00	1.80
❑ 112	Eddie LeBaron	8.00	3.60
❑ 113	Gene Brito	4.00	1.80
❑ 114	Willie Galimore RC	8.00	3.60
❑ 115	Detroit Lions	6.00	2.70
	Team Card		
❑ 116	Pittsburgh Steelers	6.00	2.70
	Team Card		
❑ 117	L.G. Dupre	5.00	2.20
❑ 118	Babe Parilli	5.00	2.20
❑ 119	Bill George	10.00	4.50
❑ 120	Raymond Berry	40.00	18.00
❑ 121	Jim Podoley UER	4.00	1.80
	(Photo actually		
	Volney Peters;		
	Podoly in cartoon)		
❑ 122	Hugh McElhenny	15.00	6.75
❑ 123	Ed Brown	5.00	2.20
❑ 124	Dick Moegle	5.00	2.20
❑ 125	Tom Scott	4.00	1.80
❑ 126	Tommy McDonald	10.00	4.50
❑ 127	Ollie Matson	20.00	9.00
❑ 128	Preston Carpenter	4.00	1.80
❑ 129	George Blanda	30.00	13.50
❑ 130	Gordy Soltau	4.00	1.80
❑ 131	Dick Nolan RC	5.00	2.20
❑ 132	Don Bosseler RC	20.00	5.00
❑ NNO	Free Felt Initial Card	25.00	11.00

1959 Topps

	NRMT	VG-E
COMPLETE SET (176)	900.00	400.00
COMMON CARD (1-88)	3.00	1.35
COMMON CARD (89-176)	2.00	.90
WRAPPER (1-CENT)	35.00	16.00
WRAPPER (1-CENT, REP)	50.00	22.00
WRAPPER (5-CENT)	50.00	22.00

No.	Card	NRMT	VG-E
❑ 1	Johnny Unitas	125.00	31.00
❑ 2	Gene Brito	3.00	1.35
❑ 3	Detroit Lions	6.00	2.70
	Team Card		
	(Checklist back)		
❑ 4	Max McGee RC	15.00	6.75
❑ 5	Hugh McElhenny	15.00	6.75
❑ 6	Joe Schmidt	8.00	3.60
❑ 7	Kyle Rote	6.00	2.70
❑ 8	Clarence Peaks	3.00	1.35
❑ 9	Pittsburgh Steelers	3.50	1.55
	Pennant Card		
❑ 10	Jim Brown	150.00	70.00
❑ 11	Ray Mathews	3.00	1.35
❑ 12	Bobby Dillon	3.00	1.35
❑ 13	Joe Childress	3.00	1.35
❑ 14	Terry Barr RC	3.00	1.35
❑ 15	Del Shofner RC	4.00	1.80
❑ 16	Bob Pellegrini UER	3.00	1.35
	(Misspelled Pellagrini		
	on card back)		
❑ 17	Baltimore Colts	6.00	2.70
	Team Card		
	(Checklist back)		
❑ 18	Preston Carpenter	3.00	1.35
❑ 19	Leo Nomellini	10.00	4.50
❑ 20	Frank Gifford	50.00	22.00
❑ 21	Charlie Ane	3.00	1.35
❑ 22	Jack Butler	3.00	1.35
❑ 23	Bart Starr	60.00	27.00
❑ 24	Chicago Cardinals	3.50	1.55
	Pennant Card		
❑ 25	Bill Barnes	3.00	1.35
❑ 26	Walt Michaels	4.00	1.80
❑ 27	Clyde Conner UER	3.00	1.35
	(Misspelled Connor		
	on card back)		
❑ 28	Paige Cothren	3.00	1.35
❑ 29	Roosevelt Grier	6.00	2.70
❑ 30	Alan Ameche	6.00	2.70
❑ 31	Philadelphia Eagles	6.00	2.70
	Team Card		
	(Checklist back)		
❑ 32	Dick Nolan	4.00	1.80
❑ 33	R.C. Owens	4.00	1.80
❑ 34	Dale Dodrill	3.00	1.35
❑ 35	Gene Gedman	3.00	1.35
❑ 36	Gene Lipscomb RC	10.00	4.50
❑ 37	Ray Renfro	4.00	1.80
❑ 38	Cleveland Browns	3.50	1.55
	Pennant Card		
❑ 39	Bill Forester	4.00	1.80
❑ 40	Bobby Layne	25.00	11.00
❑ 41	Pat Summerall	10.00	4.50
❑ 42	Jerry Mertens	3.00	1.35
❑ 43	Steve Myhra	3.00	1.35
❑ 44	John Henry Johnson	8.00	3.60
❑ 45	Woodley Lewis UER	3.00	1.35
	(Misspelled Woody)		
❑ 46	Green Bay Packers	8.00	3.60
	Team Card		
	(Checklist back)		
❑ 47	Don Owens UER	3.00	1.35
	(Def.Tackle on front,		
	Linebacker on back)		
❑ 48	Ed Beatty	3.00	1.35
❑ 49	Don Chandler	3.00	1.35
❑ 50	Ollie Matson	12.00	5.50
❑ 51	Sam Huff RC	50.00	22.00
❑ 52	Tom Miner	3.00	1.35
❑ 53	New York Giants	3.50	1.55
	Pennant Card		
❑ 54	Kenny Konz	3.00	1.35
❑ 55	Raymond Berry	20.00	9.00
❑ 56	Howard Ferguson UER	3.00	1.35
	(Misspelled Fergeson		
	on card back)		
❑ 57	Chuck Ulrich	3.00	1.35
❑ 58	Bob St. Clair	6.00	2.70
❑ 59	Don Burroughs RC	3.00	1.35
❑ 60	Lou Groza	12.00	5.50
❑ 61	San Francisco 49ers	6.00	2.70
	Team Card		
	(Checklist back)		
❑ 62	Andy Nelson	3.00	1.35
❑ 63	Harold Bradley	3.00	1.35
❑ 64	Dave Hanner	4.00	1.80
❑ 65	Charley Conerly	10.00	4.50
❑ 66	Gene Cronin	3.00	1.35
❑ 67	Duane Putnam	3.00	1.35
❑ 68	Baltimore Colts	3.50	1.55
	Pennant Card		
❑ 69	Ernie Stautner	8.00	3.60
❑ 70	Jon Arnett	4.00	1.80
❑ 71	Ken Panfil	3.00	1.35
❑ 72	Matt Hazeltine	3.00	1.35
❑ 73	Harley Sewell	3.00	1.35
❑ 74	Mike McCormack	6.00	2.70
❑ 75	Jim Ringo	8.00	3.60
❑ 76	Los Angeles Rams	6.00	2.70
	Team Card		
	(Checklist back)		
❑ 77	Bob Gain RC	3.00	1.35
❑ 78	Buzz Nutter	3.00	1.35
❑ 79	Jerry Norton	3.00	1.35
❑ 80	Joe Perry	12.00	5.50
❑ 81	Carl Brettschneider	3.00	1.35
❑ 82	Paul Hornung	60.00	27.00
❑ 83	Philadelphia Eagles	3.50	1.55
	Pennant Card		
❑ 84	Les Richter	4.00	1.80
❑ 85	Howard Cassady	4.00	1.80
❑ 86	Art Donovan	15.00	6.75
❑ 87	Jim Patton	4.00	1.80
❑ 88	Pete Retzlaff	4.00	1.80
❑ 89	Jim Mutscheller	2.00	.90
❑ 90	Zeke Bratkowski	3.00	1.35
❑ 91	Washington Redskins	4.00	1.80
	Team Card		
	(Checklist back)		
❑ 92	Art Hunter	2.00	.90
❑ 93	Gern Nagler	2.00	.90
❑ 94	Chuck Weber	2.00	.90
❑ 95	Lew Carpenter RC	3.00	1.35
❑ 96	Stan Jones	5.00	2.20
❑ 97	Ralph Guglielmi UER	3.00	1.35
	(Misspelled Gugliemi		
	on card front)		
❑ 98	Green Bay Packers	3.00	1.35
	Pennant Card		
❑ 99	Ray Wietecha	2.00	.90
❑ 100	Lenny Moore	12.00	5.50
❑ 101	Jim Ray Smith RC UER	3.00	1.35
	(Lions logo on front)		
❑ 102	Abe Woodson RC	3.00	1.35
❑ 103	Alex Karras RC	40.00	18.00
❑ 104	Chicago Bears	4.00	1.80
	Team Card		
	(Checklist back)		
❑ 105	John David Crow RC	12.00	5.50
❑ 106	Joe Fortunato RC	2.00	.90
❑ 107	Babe Parilli	3.00	1.35
❑ 108	Proverb Jacobs	2.00	.90
❑ 109	Gino Marchetti	8.00	3.60
❑ 110	Bill Wade	3.00	1.35
❑ 111	San Francisco 49ers	3.00	1.35
	Pennant Card		
❑ 112	Karl Rubke	2.00	.90
❑ 113	Dave Middleton UER	2.00	.90
	(Browns logo in		
	upper left corner)		
❑ 114	Roosevelt Brown	5.00	2.20
❑ 115	John Olszewski	2.00	.90
❑ 116	Jerry Kramer RC	30.00	13.50
❑ 117	King Hill RC	3.00	1.35
❑ 118	Chicago Cardinals	4.00	1.80
	Team Card		
	(Checklist back)		
❑ 119	Frank Varrichione	2.00	.90
❑ 120	Rick Casares	3.00	1.35
❑ 121	George Strugar	2.00	.90
❑ 122	Bill Glass RC UER	3.00	1.35
	(Center on front,		
	tackle on back)		
❑ 123	Don Bosseler	2.00	.90
❑ 124	John Reger	2.00	.90
❑ 125	Jim Ninowski RC	2.00	.90
❑ 126	Los Angeles Rams	3.00	1.35
	Pennant Card		
❑ 127	Willard Sherman	2.00	.90
❑ 128	Bob Schnelker	2.00	.90
❑ 129	Ollie Spencer	2.00	.90
❑ 130	Y.A. Tittle	25.00	11.00
❑ 131	Yale Lary	5.00	2.20
❑ 132	Jim Parker RC	20.00	9.00
❑ 133	New York Giants	4.00	1.80
	Team Card		
	(Checklist back)		
❑ 134	Jim Schrader	2.00	.90
❑ 135	M.C. Reynolds	2.00	.90
❑ 136	Mike Sandusky	2.00	.90
❑ 137	Ed Brown	3.00	1.35
❑ 138	Al Barry	2.00	.90
❑ 139	Detroit Lions	3.00	1.35
	Pennant Card		
❑ 140	Bobby Mitchell RC	35.00	16.00
❑ 141	Larry Morris	2.00	.90
❑ 142	Jim Phillips RC	3.00	1.35
❑ 143	Jim David	2.00	.90
❑ 144	Joe Krupa	2.00	.90
❑ 145	Willie Galimore	3.00	1.35
❑ 146	Pittsburgh Steelers	4.00	1.80
	Team Card		
	(Checklist back)		
❑ 147	Andy Robustelli	8.00	3.60
❑ 148	Billy Wilson	2.00	.90
❑ 149	Leo Sanford	2.00	.90
❑ 150	Eddie LeBaron	5.00	2.20
❑ 151	Bill McColl	2.00	.90
❑ 152	Buck Lansford UER	2.00	.90
	(Tackle on front,		

guard on back)
❑ 153 Chicago Bears 3.00 1.35
Pennant Card
❑ 154 Leo Sugar 2.00 .90
❑ 155 Jim Taylor RC UER 25.00 11.00
(Photo actually other Jim Taylor, Cardinal LB)
❑ 156 Lindon Crow 2.00 .90
❑ 157 Jack McClairen 2.00 .90
❑ 158 Vince Costello RC UER 2.00 .90
(Linebacker on front, Guard on back)
❑ 159 Stan Wallace 2.00 .90
❑ 160 Mel Triplett RC 2.00 .90
❑ 161 Cleveland Browns 4.00 1.80
Team Card (Checklist back)
❑ 162 Dan Currie 3.00 1.35
❑ 163 L.G. Dupre UER 3.00 1.35
(Misspelled DuPre on back)
❑ 164 John Morrow UER 2.00 .90
(Center on front, Linebacker on back)
❑ 165 Jim Podoley 2.00 .90
❑ 166 Bruce Bosley RC 2.00 .90
❑ 167 Harlon Hill 2.00 .90
❑ 168 Washington Redskins 3.00 1.35
Pennant Card
❑ 169 Junior Wren 2.00 .90
❑ 170 Tobin Rote 3.00 1.35
❑ 171 Art Spinney 2.00 .90
❑ 172 Chuck Drazenovich UER 2.00 .90
(Linebacker on front, Defensive Back on back)
❑ 173 Bobby Joe Conrad RC 3.00 1.35
❑ 174 Jesse Richardson 2.00 .90
❑ 175 Sam Baker 2.00 .90
❑ 176 Tom Tracy RC 8.00 2.00

1960 Topps

	NRMT	VG-E
COMPLETE SET (132)	600.00	275.00
WRAPPER (1-CENT)	40.00	18.00
WRAPPER (1-CENT, REP)	150.00	70.00
WRAPPER (5-CENT)	40.00	18.00

❑ 1 John Unitas 80.00 20.00
❑ 2 Alan Ameche 4.00 1.80
❑ 3 Lenny Moore 10.00 4.50
❑ 4 Raymond Berry 12.00 5.50
❑ 5 Jim Parker 8.00 3.60
❑ 6 George Preas 2.50 1.10
❑ 7 Art Spinney 2.50 1.10
❑ 8 Bill Pellington RC 3.00 1.35
❑ 9 John Sample RC 3.00 1.35
❑ 10 Gene Lipscomb UER 3.00 1.35
(Def. Tackle on front, Tackle on back)
❑ 11 Baltimore Colts 3.00 1.35
Team Card (Checklist 67-132)
❑ 12 Ed Brown 3.00 1.35
❑ 13 Rick Casares 3.00 1.35
❑ 14 Willie Galimore 3.00 1.35
❑ 15 Jim Dooley 2.50 1.10
❑ 16 Harlon Hill UER 2.50 1.10
(Lifetime yards and Avg. gain incorrect)
❑ 17 Stan Jones UER 4.00 1.80
(Defensive ... All-Star Team, should be Offensive)
❑ 18 Bill George 4.00 1.80
❑ 19 Erich Barnes RC 3.00 1.35
❑ 20 Doug Atkins UER 6.00 2.70
(Reversed negative)
❑ 21 Chicago Bears 3.00 1.35
Team Card (Checklist 1-66)
❑ 22 Milt Plum 3.00 1.35
❑ 23 Jim Brown 100.00 45.00
❑ 24 Sam Baker 2.50 1.10
❑ 25 Bobby Mitchell 10.00 4.50
❑ 26 Ray Renfro 3.00 1.35
❑ 27 Billy Howton 3.00 1.35
❑ 28 Jim Ray Smith 2.50 1.10
❑ 29 Jim Shofner RC 3.00 1.35
❑ 30 Bob Gain 2.50 1.10
❑ 31 Cleveland Browns 3.00 1.35
Team Card (Checklist 1-66)
❑ 32 Don Heinrich 2.50 1.10
❑ 33 Ed Modzelewski UER 2.50 1.10
(Lifetime yards and Avg. gain incorrect)
❑ 34 Fred Cone 2.50 1.10
❑ 35 L.G. Dupre 3.00 1.35
❑ 36 Dick Bielski 2.50 1.10
❑ 37 Charlie Ane UER 2.50 1.10
(Misspelled Charley)
❑ 38 Jerry Tubbs 3.00 1.35
❑ 39 Doyle Nix 2.50 1.10
❑ 40 Ray Krouse 2.50 1.10
❑ 41 Earl Morrall 4.00 1.80
❑ 42 Howard Cassady 3.00 1.35
❑ 43 Dave Middleton 2.50 1.10
❑ 44 Jim Gibbons RC 3.00 1.35
❑ 45 Darris McCord 2.50 1.10
❑ 46 Joe Schmidt 6.00 2.70
❑ 47 Terry Barr 2.50 1.10
❑ 48 Yale Lary UER 4.00 1.80
(Def.back on front, halfback on back)
❑ 49 Gil Mains 2.50 1.10
❑ 50 Detroit Lions 3.00 1.35
Team Card (Checklist 1-66)
❑ 51 Bart Starr 45.00 20.00
❑ 52 Jim Taylor UER 8.00 3.60
(photo actually Jim Taylor, Cardinal LB)
❑ 53 Lew Carpenter 3.00 1.35
❑ 54 Paul Hornung UER 45.00 20.00
(Halfback on front, fullback on back)
❑ 55 Max McGee 4.00 1.80
❑ 56 Forrest Gregg RC 35.00 16.00
❑ 57 Jim Ringo 5.00 2.20
❑ 58 Bill Forester 3.00 1.35
❑ 59 Dave Hanner 3.00 1.35
❑ 60 Green Bay Packers 8.00 3.60
Team Card (Checklist 67-132)
❑ 61 Bill Wade 3.00 1.35
❑ 62 Frank Ryan RC 4.00 1.80
❑ 63 Ollie Matson 10.00 4.50
❑ 64 Jon Arnett 3.00 1.35
❑ 65 Del Shofner 3.00 1.35
❑ 66 Jim Phillips 2.50 1.10
❑ 67 Art Hunter 2.50 1.10
❑ 68 Les Richter 3.00 1.35
❑ 69 Lou Michaels RC 3.00 1.35
❑ 70 John Baker 2.50 1.10
❑ 71 Los Angeles Rams 3.00 1.35
Team Card (Checklist 1-66)
❑ 72 Charley Conerly 8.00 3.60
❑ 73 Mel Triplett 2.50 1.10
❑ 74 Frank Gifford 35.00 16.00
❑ 75 Alex Webster 3.00 1.35
❑ 76 Bob Schnelker 2.50 1.10
❑ 77 Pat Summerall 8.00 3.60
❑ 78 Roosevelt Brown 4.00 1.80
❑ 79 Jim Patton 2.50 1.10
❑ 80 Sam Huff UER 20.00 9.00
(Def.tackle on front, linebacker on back)
❑ 81 Andy Robustelli 6.00 2.70
❑ 82 New York Giants 3.00 1.35
Team Card (Checklist 1-66)
❑ 83 Clarence Peaks 2.50 1.10
❑ 84 Bill Barnes 2.50 1.10
❑ 85 Pete Retzlaff 3.00 1.35
❑ 86 Bobby Walston 2.50 1.10
❑ 87 Chuck Bednarik UER 8.00 3.60
(Misspelled Bednarick on both sides of card)
❑ 88 Bob Pellegrini 2.50 1.10
(Misspelled Pellagrini on both sides)
❑ 89 Tom Brookshier RC 3.00 1.35
❑ 90 Marion Campbell 3.00 1.35
❑ 91 Jesse Richardson 2.50 1.10
❑ 92 Philadelphia Eagles 3.00 1.35
Team Card (Checklist 1-66)
❑ 93 Bobby Layne 30.00 13.50
❑ 94 John Henry Johnson 6.00 2.70
❑ 95 Tom Tracy UER 3.00 1.35
(Halfback on front, fullback on back)
❑ 96 Preston Carpenter 2.50 1.10
❑ 97 Frank Varrichione UER 2.50 1.10
(Reversed negative)
❑ 98 John Nisby 2.50 1.10
❑ 99 Dean Derby 2.50 1.10
❑ 100 George Tarasovic 2.50 1.10
❑ 101 Ernie Stautner 5.00 2.20
❑ 102 Pittsburgh Steelers 3.00 1.35
Team Card (Checklist 67-132)
❑ 103 King Hill 2.50 1.10
❑ 104 Mal Hammack 2.50 1.10
❑ 105 John David Crow 3.00 1.35
❑ 106 Bobby Joe Conrad 3.00 1.35
❑ 107 Woodley Lewis 2.50 1.10
❑ 108 Don Gillis 2.50 1.10
❑ 109 Carl Brettschneider 2.50 1.10
❑ 110 Leo Sugar 2.50 1.10
❑ 111 Frank Fuller 2.50 1.10
❑ 112 St. Louis Cardinals 3.00 1.35
Team Card (Checklist 67-132)
❑ 113 Y.A. Tittle 30.00 13.50
❑ 114 Joe Perry 8.00 3.60
❑ 115 J.D. Smith RC 3.00 1.35
❑ 116 Hugh McElhenny 8.00 3.60
❑ 117 Billy Wilson 2.50 1.10
❑ 118 Bob St. Clair 4.00 1.80
❑ 119 Matt Hazeltine 2.50 1.10
❑ 120 Abe Woodson 2.50 1.10
❑ 121 Leo Nomellini 5.00 2.20
❑ 122 San Francisco 49ers 3.00 1.35
Team Card (Checklist 67-132)
❑ 123 Ralph Guglielmi UER 2.50 1.10
(Misspelled Gugliemi on card front)
❑ 124 Don Bosseler 2.50 1.10
❑ 125 John Olszewski 2.50 1.10
❑ 126 Bill Anderson UER 2.50 1.10
(Walt on back)
❑ 127 Joe Walton RC 3.00 1.35
❑ 128 Jim Schrader 2.50 1.10
❑ 129 Ralph Felton 2.50 1.10
❑ 130 Gary Glick 2.50 1.10
❑ 131 Bob Toneff 2.50 1.10
❑ 132 Washington Redskins 35.00 8.75
Team Card (Checklist 67-132)
❑ AD1 Alan Ameche 125.00 55.00
Paul Hornung
Tom Tracy
(Gene Cronin back)
❑ AD2 Del Shofner 90.00 40.00

		NRMT	VG-E
	Milt Plum Jim Patton (Gene Cronin back)		
❑ AD3	Bob St.Clair Jim Shofner Gil Mains (Gene Cronin back)	100.00	45.00
❑ AD4	Tom Brookshier Packers Team George Preas (Gene Cronin back)	100.00	45.00

1961 Topps

	NRMT	VG-E
COMPLETE SET (198)	1000.00	450.00
COMMON CARD (1-132)	2.50	1.10
COMMON CARD (133-198)	3.00	1.35
WRAPPER (1-CENT)	275.00	125.00
WRAPPER (1-CENT, REP)	225.00	100.00
WRAPPER (5-CENT)	50.00	22.00

		NRMT	VG-E
❑ 1	Johnny Unitas	100.00	25.00
❑ 2	Lenny Moore	12.00	5.50
❑ 3	Alan Ameche	4.00	1.80
❑ 4	Raymond Berry	12.00	5.50
❑ 5	Jim Mutscheller	2.50	1.10
❑ 6	Jim Parker	5.00	2.20
❑ 7	Gino Marchetti	6.00	2.70
❑ 8	Gene Lipscomb	4.00	1.80
❑ 9	Baltimore Colts Team Card	3.00	1.35
❑ 10	Bill Wade	3.00	1.35
❑ 11	Johnny Morris RC UER (Years pro and return averages wrong)	6.00	2.70
❑ 12	Rick Casares	3.00	1.35
❑ 13	Harlon Hill	2.50	1.10
❑ 14	Stan Jones	4.00	1.80
❑ 15	Doug Atkins	5.00	2.20
❑ 16	Bill George	4.00	1.80
❑ 17	J.C. Caroline	2.50	1.10
❑ 18	Chicago Bears Team Card	3.00	1.35
❑ 19	Big Time Football Comes to Texas (Eddie LeBaron)	3.00	1.35
❑ 20	Eddie LeBaron	3.00	1.35
❑ 21	Don McIlhenny	2.50	1.10
❑ 22	L.G. Dupre	3.00	1.35
❑ 23	Jim Doran	2.50	1.10
❑ 24	Billy Howton	3.00	1.35
❑ 25	Buzz Guy	2.50	1.10
❑ 26	Jack Patera RC	2.50	1.10
❑ 27	Tom Franckhauser UER (Misspelled Frankhauser)	2.50	1.10
❑ 28	Dallas Cowboys Team Card	15.00	6.75
❑ 29	Jim Ninowski	2.50	1.10
❑ 30	Dan Lewis RC	2.50	1.10
❑ 31	Nick Pietrosante RC	3.00	1.35
❑ 32	Gail Cogdill RC	3.00	1.35
❑ 33	Jim Gibbons	2.50	1.10
❑ 34	Jim Martin	2.50	1.10
❑ 35	Alex Karras	15.00	6.75
❑ 36	Joe Schmidt	5.00	2.20
❑ 37	Detroit Lions Team Card	3.00	1.35
❑ 38	Packers' Hornung Sets NFL Scoring Record	18.00	8.00
❑ 39	Bart Starr	40.00	18.00
❑ 40	Paul Hornung	40.00	18.00
❑ 41	Jim Taylor	30.00	13.50
❑ 42	Max McGee	4.00	1.80
❑ 43	Boyd Dowler RC	8.00	3.60
❑ 44	Jim Ringo	5.00	2.20
❑ 45	Hank Jordan RC	20.00	9.00
❑ 46	Bill Forester	3.00	1.35
❑ 47	Green Bay Packers Team Card	8.00	3.60
❑ 48	Frank Ryan	3.00	1.35
❑ 49	Jon Arnett	3.00	1.35
❑ 50	Ollie Matson	8.00	3.60
❑ 51	Jim Phillips	2.50	1.10
❑ 52	Del Shofner	3.00	1.35
❑ 53	Art Hunter	2.50	1.10
❑ 54	Gene Brito	2.50	1.10
❑ 55	Lindon Crow	2.50	1.10
❑ 56	Los Angeles Rams Team Card	3.00	1.35
❑ 57	Colts' Unitas 25 TD Passes	25.00	11.00
❑ 58	Y.A. Tittle	30.00	13.50
❑ 59	John Brodie RC	40.00	18.00
❑ 60	J.D. Smith	2.50	1.10
❑ 61	R.C. Owens	3.00	1.35
❑ 62	Clyde Conner	2.50	1.10
❑ 63	Bob St. Clair	4.00	1.80
❑ 64	Leo Nomellini	6.00	2.70
❑ 65	Abe Woodson	2.50	1.10
❑ 66	San Francisco 49ers Team Card	3.00	1.35
❑ 67	Checklist Card	40.00	10.00
❑ 68	Milt Plum	3.00	1.35
❑ 69	Ray Renfro	3.00	1.35
❑ 70	Bobby Mitchell	8.00	3.60
❑ 71	Jim Brown	100.00	45.00
❑ 72	Mike McCormack	4.00	1.80
❑ 73	Jim Ray Smith	2.50	1.10
❑ 74	Sam Baker	2.50	1.10
❑ 75	Walt Michaels	3.00	1.35
❑ 76	Cleveland Browns Team Card	3.00	1.35
❑ 77	Jimmy Brown Gains 1257 Yards	35.00	16.00
❑ 78	George Shaw	2.50	1.10
❑ 79	Hugh McElhenny	8.00	3.60
❑ 80	Clancy Osborne	2.50	1.10
❑ 81	Dave Middleton	2.50	1.10
❑ 82	Frank Youso	2.50	1.10
❑ 83	Don Joyce	2.50	1.10
❑ 84	Ed Culpepper	2.50	1.10
❑ 85	Charley Conerly	8.00	3.60
❑ 86	Mel Triplett	2.50	1.10
❑ 87	Kyle Rote	3.00	1.35
❑ 88	Roosevelt Brown	4.00	1.80
❑ 89	Ray Wietecha	2.50	1.10
❑ 90	Andy Robustelli	5.00	2.20
❑ 91	Sam Huff	8.00	3.60
❑ 92	Jim Patton	2.50	1.10
❑ 93	New York Giants Team Card	3.00	1.35
❑ 94	Charley Conerly UER Leads Giants for 13th Year (Misspelled Charlie on card)	6.00	2.70
❑ 95	Sonny Jurgensen	25.00	11.00
❑ 96	Tommy McDonald	4.00	1.80
❑ 97	Bill Barnes	2.50	1.10
❑ 98	Bobby Walston	2.50	1.10
❑ 99	Pete Retzlaff	3.00	1.35
❑ 100	Jim McCusker	2.50	1.10
❑ 101	Chuck Bednarik	8.00	3.60
❑ 102	Tom Brookshier	3.00	1.35
❑ 103	Philadelphia Eagles Team Card	3.00	1.35
❑ 104	Bobby Layne	30.00	13.50
❑ 105	John Henry Johnson	4.00	1.80
❑ 106	Tom Tracy	3.00	1.35
❑ 107	Buddy Dial RC	2.50	1.10
❑ 108	Jimmy Orr RC	5.00	2.20
❑ 109	Mike Sandusky	2.50	1.10
❑ 110	John Reger	2.50	1.10
❑ 111	Junior Wren	2.50	1.10
❑ 112	Pittsburgh Steelers Team Card	3.00	1.35
❑ 113	Bobby Layne Sets New Passing Record	10.00	4.50
❑ 114	John Roach	2.50	1.10
❑ 115	Sam Etcheverry RC**/C	3.00	1.35
❑ 116	John David Crow	3.00	1.35
❑ 117	Mal Hammack	2.50	1.10
❑ 118	Sonny Randle RC	3.00	1.35
❑ 119	Leo Sugar	2.50	1.10
❑ 120	Jerry Norton	2.50	1.10
❑ 121	St. Louis Cardinals Team Card	3.00	1.35
❑ 122	Checklist Card	50.00	12.50
❑ 123	Ralph Guglielmi	2.50	1.10
❑ 124	Dick James	2.50	1.10
❑ 125	Don Bosseler	2.50	1.10
❑ 126	Joe Walton	2.50	1.10
❑ 127	Bill Anderson	2.50	1.10
❑ 128	Vince Promuto RC	2.50	1.10
❑ 129	Bob Toneff	2.50	1.10
❑ 130	John Paluck	2.50	1.10
❑ 131	Washington Redskins Team Card	3.00	1.35
❑ 132	Browns' Plum Wins NFL Passing Title	2.50	1.10
❑ 133	Abner Haynes	8.00	3.60
❑ 134	Mel Branch UER (Def. Tackle on front, Def. End on back)	4.00	1.80
❑ 135	Jerry Cornelison UER (Misspelled Cornielson)	3.00	1.35
❑ 136	Bill Krisher	3.00	1.35
❑ 137	Paul Miller	3.00	1.35
❑ 138	Jack Spikes	4.00	1.80
❑ 139	Johnny Robinson RC	8.00	3.60
❑ 140	Cotton Davidson RC	4.00	1.80
❑ 141	Dave Smith	3.00	1.35
❑ 142	Bill Groman	3.00	1.35
❑ 143	Rich Michael	3.00	1.35
❑ 144	Mike Dukes	3.00	1.35
❑ 145	George Blanda	25.00	11.00
❑ 146	Billy Cannon	6.00	2.70
❑ 147	Dennit Morris	3.00	1.35
❑ 148	Jacky Lee UER (Misspelled Jackie on card back)	4.00	1.80
❑ 149	Al Dorow	3.00	1.35
❑ 150	Don Maynard RC	60.00	27.00
❑ 151	Art Powell RC	8.00	3.60
❑ 152	Sid Youngelman	3.00	1.35
❑ 153	Bob Mischak	3.00	1.35
❑ 154	Larry Grantham	3.00	1.35
❑ 155	Tom Saidock	3.00	1.35
❑ 156	Roger Donnahoo	3.00	1.35
❑ 157	Laverne Torczon	3.00	1.35
❑ 158	Archie Matsos RC	4.00	1.80
❑ 159	Elbert Dubenion	4.00	1.80
❑ 160	Wray Carlton RC	4.00	1.80
❑ 161	Rich McCabe	3.00	1.35
❑ 162	Ken Rice	3.00	1.35
❑ 163	Art Baker	3.00	1.35
❑ 164	Tom Rychlec	3.00	1.35
❑ 165	Mack Yoho	3.00	1.35
❑ 166	Jack Kemp	125.00	55.00
❑ 167	Paul Lowe	6.00	2.70
❑ 168	Ron Mix	10.00	4.50
❑ 169	Paul Maguire	6.00	2.70
❑ 170	Volney Peters	3.00	1.35
❑ 171	Ernie Wright RC	4.00	1.80
❑ 172	Ron Nery RC	3.00	1.35
❑ 173	Dave Kocourek RC	4.00	1.80
❑ 174	Jim Colclough	3.00	1.35
❑ 175	Babe Parilli	4.00	1.80
❑ 176	Billy Lott	3.00	1.35
❑ 177	Fred Bruney	3.00	1.35
❑ 178	Ross O'Hanley	3.00	1.35
❑ 179	Walt Cudzik	3.00	1.35
❑ 180	Charley Leo	3.00	1.35
❑ 181	Bob Dee	3.00	1.35
❑ 182	Jim Otto RC	40.00	18.00
❑ 183	Eddie Macon	3.00	1.35
❑ 184	Dick Christy	3.00	1.35
❑ 185	Alan Miller	3.00	1.35

❑ 186 Tom Flores RC	20.00	9.00
❑ 187 Joe Cannavino	3.00	1.35
❑ 188 Don Manoukian	3.00	1.35
❑ 189 Bob Coolbaugh	3.00	1.35
❑ 190 Lionel Taylor RC	8.00	3.60
❑ 191 Bud McFadin	3.00	1.35
❑ 192 Goose Gonsoulin RC	6.00	2.70
❑ 193 Frank Tripucka	4.00	1.80
❑ 194 Gene Mingo RC	4.00	1.80
❑ 195 Eldon Danenhauer	3.00	1.35
❑ 196 Bob McNamara	3.00	1.35
❑ 197 Dave Rolle UER	3.00	1.35
(End on front,		
Fullback on back)		
❑ 198 Checklist Card UER !	100.00	25.00
(135 Cornielson)		
❑ AD1 Jim Martin	100.00	45.00
George Shaw		
Jim Ray Smith		

1962 Topps

	NRMT	VG-E
COMPLETE SET (176)	1800.00	800.00
WRAPPER (1-CENT)	250.00	110.00
WRAPPER (5-CENT)	25.00	11.00
WRAPPER (5-CENT, BUCK)	30.00	13.50
❑ 1 John Unitas	150.00	38.00
❑ 2 Lenny Moore	12.00	5.50
❑ 3 Alex Hawkins RC SP	10.00	4.50
❑ 4 Joe Perry	8.00	3.60
❑ 5 Raymond Berry SP	40.00	18.00
❑ 6 Steve Myhra	4.00	1.80
❑ 7 Tom Gilburg SP	8.00	3.60
❑ 8 Gino Marchetti	8.00	3.60
❑ 9 Bill Pellington	4.00	1.80
❑ 10 Andy Nelson	4.00	1.80
❑ 11 Wendell Harris SP	8.00	3.60
❑ 12 Baltimore Colts	6.00	2.70
Team Card		
❑ 13 Bill Wade SP	10.00	4.50
❑ 14 Willie Galimore	5.00	2.20
❑ 15 Johnny Morris SP	8.00	3.60
❑ 16 Rick Casares	5.00	2.20
❑ 17 Mike Ditka RC	200.00	90.00
❑ 18 Stan Jones	6.00	2.70
❑ 19 Roger LeClerc	4.00	1.80
❑ 20 Angelo Coia	4.00	1.80
❑ 21 Doug Atkins	7.00	3.10
❑ 22 Bill George	6.00	2.70
❑ 23 Richie Petitbon RC	5.00	2.20
❑ 24 Ron Bull RC SP	8.00	3.60
❑ 25 Chicago Bears	6.00	2.70
Team Card		
❑ 26 Howard Cassady	5.00	2.20
❑ 27 Ray Renfro SP	10.00	4.50
❑ 28 Jim Brown	150.00	70.00
❑ 29 Rich Kreitling	4.00	1.80
❑ 30 Jim Ray Smith	4.00	1.80
❑ 31 John Morrow	4.00	1.80
❑ 32 Lou Groza	10.00	4.50
❑ 33 Bob Gain	4.00	1.80
❑ 34 Bernie Parrish	4.00	1.80
❑ 35 Jim Shofner	4.00	1.80
❑ 36 Ernie Davis RC SP	150.00	70.00
❑ 37 Cleveland Browns	6.00	2.70
Team Card		
❑ 38 Eddie LeBaron	5.00	2.20
❑ 39 Don Meredith SP	100.00	45.00
❑ 40 J.W. Lockett SP	8.00	3.60
❑ 41 Don Perkins RC	10.00	4.50
❑ 42 Billy Howton	5.00	2.20
❑ 43 Dick Bielski	4.00	1.80
❑ 44 Mike Connelly RC	4.00	1.80
❑ 45 Jerry Tubbs SP	8.00	3.60
❑ 46 Don Bishop SP	8.00	3.60
❑ 47 Dick Moegle	4.00	1.80
❑ 48 Bobby Plummer SP	8.00	3.60
❑ 49 Dallas Cowboys	20.00	9.00
Team Card		
❑ 50 Milt Plum	5.00	2.20
❑ 51 Dan Lewis	4.00	1.80
❑ 52 Nick Pietrosante SP	8.00	3.60
❑ 53 Gail Cogdill	4.00	1.80
❑ 54 Jim Gibbons	4.00	1.80
❑ 55 Jim Martin	4.00	1.80
❑ 56 Yale Lary	6.00	2.70
❑ 57 Darris McCord	4.00	1.80
❑ 58 Alex Karras	15.00	6.75
❑ 59 Joe Schmidt	7.00	3.10
❑ 60 Dick Lane	6.00	2.70
❑ 61 John Lomakoski SP	8.00	3.60
❑ 62 Detroit Lions SP	18.00	8.00
Team Card		
❑ 63 Bart Starr SP	100.00	45.00
❑ 64 Paul Hornung SP	80.00	36.00
❑ 65 Tom Moore SP	12.00	5.50
❑ 66 Jim Taylor SP	50.00	22.00
❑ 67 Max McGee SP	12.00	5.50
❑ 68 Jim Ringo SP	15.00	6.75
❑ 69 Fuzzy Thurston RC SP	20.00	9.00
❑ 70 Forrest Gregg	7.00	3.10
❑ 71 Boyd Dowler	6.00	2.70
❑ 72 Hank Jordan SP	15.00	6.75
❑ 73 Bill Forester SP	10.00	4.50
❑ 74 Earl Gros SP	8.00	3.60
❑ 75 Green Bay Packers SP	35.00	16.00
Team Card		
❑ 76 Checklist SP	80.00	20.00
❑ 77 Zeke Bratkowski SP	10.00	4.50
(Inset photo is		
Johnny Unitas)		
❑ 78 Jon Arnett SP	10.00	4.50
❑ 79 Ollie Matson SP	35.00	16.00
❑ 80 Dick Bass SP	10.00	4.50
❑ 81 Jim Phillips	4.00	1.80
❑ 82 Carroll Dale RC	5.00	2.20
❑ 83 Frank Varrichione	4.00	1.80
❑ 84 Art Hunter	4.00	1.80
❑ 85 Danny Villanueva RC	4.00	1.80
❑ 86 Les Richter SP	8.00	3.60
❑ 87 Lindon Crow	4.00	1.80
❑ 88 Roman Gabriel RC SP	60.00	27.00
(Inset photo is		
Y.A. Tittle)		
❑ 89 Los Angeles Rams SP	18.00	8.00
Team Card		
❑ 90 F.Tarkenton SP RC UER	200.00	90.00
Small photo actually		
Sonny Jurgensen		
with airbrushed jersey		
❑ 91 Jerry Reichow SP	8.00	3.60
❑ 92 Hugh McElhenny SP	30.00	13.50
❑ 93 Mel Triplett SP	8.00	3.60
❑ 94 Tommy Mason RC SP	12.00	5.50
❑ 95 Dave Middleton SP	8.00	3.60
❑ 96 Frank Youso SP	8.00	3.60
❑ 97 Mike Mercer SP	8.00	3.60
❑ 98 Rip Hawkins SP	8.00	3.60
❑ 99 Cliff Livingston SP	8.00	3.60
❑ 100 Roy Winston RC SP	8.00	3.60
❑ 101 Minnesota Vikings SP	25.00	11.00
Team Card		
❑ 102 Y.A. Tittle	35.00	16.00
❑ 103 Joe Walton	4.00	1.80
❑ 104 Frank Gifford	40.00	18.00
❑ 105 Alex Webster	5.00	2.20
❑ 106 Del Shofner	5.00	2.20
❑ 107 Don Chandler	4.00	1.80
❑ 108 Andy Robustelli	7.00	3.10
❑ 109 Jim Katcavage RC	5.00	2.20
❑ 110 Sam Huff SP	40.00	18.00
❑ 111 Erich Barnes	4.00	1.80
❑ 112 Jim Patton	4.00	1.80
❑ 113 Jerry Hillebrand SP	8.00	3.60
❑ 114 New York Giants	6.00	2.70
Team Card		
❑ 115 Sonny Jurgensen	35.00	16.00
❑ 116 Tommy McDonald	6.00	2.70
❑ 117 Ted Dean SP	8.00	3.60
❑ 118 Clarence Peaks	4.00	1.80
❑ 119 Bobby Walston	4.00	1.80
❑ 120 Pete Retzlaff SP	10.00	4.50
❑ 121 Jim Schrader SP	8.00	3.60
❑ 122 J.D. Smith T	4.00	1.80
❑ 123 King Hill	4.00	1.80
❑ 124 Maxie Baughan	5.00	2.20
❑ 125 Pete Case SP	8.00	3.60
❑ 126 Philadelphia Eagles	6.00	2.70
Team Card		
❑ 127 Bobby Layne UER	35.00	16.00
(Bears until 1958,		
should be Lions)		
❑ 128 Tom Tracy	5.00	2.20
❑ 129 John Henry Johnson	6.00	2.70
❑ 130 Buddy Dial SP	10.00	4.50
❑ 131 Preston Carpenter	4.00	1.80
❑ 132 Lou Michaels SP	8.00	3.60
❑ 133 Gene Lipscomb SP	10.00	4.50
❑ 134 Ernie Stautner SP	20.00	9.00
❑ 135 John Reger SP	8.00	3.60
❑ 136 Myron Pottios RC	4.00	1.80
❑ 137 Bob Ferguson SP	8.00	3.60
❑ 138 Pittsburgh Steelers SP	18.00	8.00
Team Card		
❑ 139 Sam Etcheverry	5.00	2.20
❑ 140 John David Crow SP	10.00	4.50
❑ 141 Bobby Joe Conrad SP	10.00	4.50
❑ 142 Prentice Gautt RC SP	8.00	3.60
❑ 143 Frank Mestnick	4.00	1.80
❑ 144 Sonny Randle	5.00	2.20
❑ 145 Gerry Perry UER	4.00	1.80
(T-K on both sides,		
but Def. End in bio)		
❑ 146 Jerry Norton	4.00	1.80
❑ 147 Jimmy Hill	4.00	1.80
❑ 148 Bill Stacy	4.00	1.80
❑ 149 Fate Echols SP	8.00	3.60
❑ 150 St. Louis Cardinals	6.00	2.70
Team Card		
❑ 151 Bill Kilmer RC	25.00	11.00
❑ 152 John Brodie	18.00	8.00
❑ 153 J.D. Smith RB	5.00	2.20
❑ 154 C.R. Roberts SP	8.00	3.60
❑ 155 Monty Stickles	4.00	1.80
❑ 156 Clyde Conner UER	4.00	1.80
(Misspelled Connor		
on card back)		
❑ 157 Bob St. Clair	6.00	2.70
❑ 158 Tommy Davis RC	4.00	1.80
❑ 159 Leo Nomellini	8.00	3.60
❑ 160 Matt Hazeltine	4.00	1.80
❑ 161 Abe Woodson	4.00	1.80
❑ 162 Dave Baker	4.00	1.80
❑ 163 San Francisco 49ers	6.00	2.70
Team Card		
❑ 164 Norm Snead RC SP	25.00	11.00
❑ 165 Dick James	5.00	2.20
(Inset photo is		
Don Bosseler)		
❑ 166 Bobby Mitchell	8.00	3.60
❑ 167 Sam Horner	4.00	1.80
❑ 168 Bill Barnes	4.00	1.80
❑ 169 Bill Anderson	4.00	1.80
❑ 170 Fred Dugan	4.00	1.80
❑ 171 John Aveni SP	8.00	3.60
❑ 172 Bob Toneff	4.00	1.80
❑ 173 Jim Kerr	4.00	1.80
❑ 174 Leroy Jackson SP	8.00	3.60
❑ 175 Washington Redskins	6.00	2.70
Team Card		
❑ 176 Checklist !	100.00	25.00

1963 Topps

	NRMT	VG-E
COMPLETE SET (170)	1350.00	600.00
WRAPPER (1-CENT)	400.00	180.00
WRAPPER (5-CENT)	50.00	22.00

❑ 1 John Unitas 100.00 25.00
❑ 2 Lenny Moore 8.00 3.60
❑ 3 Jimmy Orr 2.50 1.10
❑ 4 Raymond Berry 8.00 3.60
❑ 5 Jim Parker 5.00 2.20
❑ 6 Alex Sandusky 2.50 1.10
❑ 7 Dick Szymanski 2.50 1.10
❑ 8 Gino Marchetti 6.00 2.70
❑ 9 Billy Ray Smith RC 3.00 1.35
❑ 10 Bill Pellington 2.50 1.10
❑ 11 Bob Boyd RC 2.50 1.10
❑ 12 Baltimore Colts SP 10.00 4.50
Team Card
❑ 13 Frank Ryan SP 8.00 3.60
❑ 14 Jim Brown SP 200.00 90.00
❑ 15 Ray Renfro SP 8.00 3.60
❑ 16 Rich Kreitling SP 6.00 2.70
❑ 17 Mike McCormack SP 10.00 4.50
❑ 18 Jim Ray Smith SP 6.00 2.70
❑ 19 Lou Groza SP 20.00 9.00
❑ 20 Bill Glass SP 6.00 2.70
❑ 21 Galen Fiss SP 6.00 2.70
❑ 22 Don Fleming RC SP 8.00 3.60
❑ 23 Bob Gain SP 6.00 2.70
❑ 24 Cleveland Browns SP 10.00 4.50
Team Card
❑ 25 Milt Plum 3.00 1.35
❑ 26 Dan Lewis 2.50 1.10
❑ 27 Nick Pietrosante 2.50 1.10
❑ 28 Gail Cogdill 2.50 1.10
❑ 29 Harley Sewell 2.50 1.10
❑ 30 Jim Gibbons 2.50 1.10
❑ 31 Carl Brettschneider 2.50 1.10
❑ 32 Dick Lane 5.00 2.20
❑ 33 Yale Lary 5.00 2.20
❑ 34 Roger Brown RC 3.00 1.35
❑ 35 Joe Schmidt 6.00 2.70
❑ 36 Detroit Lions SP 10.00 4.50
Team Card
❑ 37 Roman Gabriel 8.00 3.60
❑ 38 Zeke Bratkowski 3.00 1.35
❑ 39 Dick Bass 3.00 1.35
❑ 40 Jon Arnett 3.00 1.35
❑ 41 Jim Phillips 2.50 1.10
❑ 42 Frank Varrichione 2.50 1.10
❑ 43 Danny Villanueva 2.50 1.10
❑ 44 Deacon Jones RC 50.00 22.00
❑ 45 Lindon Crow 2.50 1.10
❑ 46 Marlin McKeever 2.50 1.10
❑ 47 Ed Meador RC 2.50 1.10
❑ 48 Los Angeles Rams 4.00 1.80
Team Card
❑ 49 Y.A. Tittle SP 50.00 22.00
❑ 50 Del Shofner SP 6.00 2.70
❑ 51 Alex Webster SP 8.00 3.60
❑ 52 Phil King SP 6.00 2.70
❑ 53 Jack Stroud SP 6.00 2.70
❑ 54 Darrell Dess SP 6.00 2.70
❑ 55 Jim Katcavage SP 6.00 2.70
❑ 56 Roosevelt Grier SP 10.00 4.50
❑ 57 Erich Barnes SP 6.00 2.70
❑ 58 Jim Patton SP 6.00 2.70
❑ 59 Sam Huff SP 20.00 9.00
❑ 60 New York Giants 4.00 1.80
Team Card
❑ 61 Bill Wade 3.00 1.35
❑ 62 Mike Ditka 60.00 27.00
❑ 63 Johnny Morris 2.50 1.10
❑ 64 Roger LeClerc 2.50 1.10
❑ 65 Roger Davis 2.50 1.10
❑ 66 Joe Marconi 2.50 1.10
❑ 67 Herman Lee 2.50 1.10
❑ 68 Doug Atkins 6.00 2.70
❑ 69 Joe Fortunato 2.50 1.10
❑ 70 Bill George 5.00 2.20
❑ 71 Richie Petitbon 3.00 1.35
❑ 72 Chicago Bears SP 10.00 4.50
Team Card
❑ 73 Eddie LeBaron SP 8.00 3.60
❑ 74 Don Meredith SP 60.00 27.00
❑ 75 Don Perkins SP 10.00 4.50
❑ 76 Amos Marsh SP 6.00 2.70
❑ 77 Billy Howton SP 8.00 3.60
❑ 78 Andy Cvercko SP 6.00 2.70
❑ 79 Sam Baker SP 6.00 2.70
❑ 80 Jerry Tubbs SP 6.00 2.70
❑ 81 Don Bishop SP 6.00 2.70
❑ 82 Bob Lilly RC SP 150.00 70.00
❑ 83 Jerry Norton SP 6.00 2.70
❑ 84 Dallas Cowboys SP 20.00 9.00
Team Card
❑ 85 Checklist Card 25.00 6.25
❑ 86 Bart Starr 50.00 22.00
❑ 87 Jim Taylor 25.00 11.00
❑ 88 Boyd Dowler 5.00 2.20
❑ 89 Forrest Gregg 6.00 2.70
❑ 90 Fuzzy Thurston 6.00 2.70
❑ 91 Jim Ringo 6.00 2.70
❑ 92 Ron Kramer 3.00 1.35
❑ 93 Hank Jordan 6.00 2.70
❑ 94 Bill Forester 3.00 1.35
❑ 95 Willie Wood RC 35.00 16.00
❑ 96 Ray Nitschke RC 90.00 40.00
❑ 97 Green Bay Packers 8.00 3.60
Team Card
❑ 98 Fran Tarkenton 60.00 27.00
❑ 99 Tommy Mason 3.00 1.35
❑ 100 Mel Triplett 2.50 1.10
❑ 101 Jerry Reichow 2.50 1.10
❑ 102 Frank Youso 2.50 1.10
❑ 103 Hugh McElhenny 8.00 3.60
❑ 104 Gerald Huth 2.50 1.10
❑ 105 Ed Sharockman 2.50 1.10
❑ 106 Rip Hawkins 2.50 1.10
❑ 107 Jim Marshall RC 30.00 13.50
❑ 108 Jim Prestel 2.50 1.10
❑ 109 Minnesota Vikings 4.00 1.80
Team Card
❑ 110 Sonny Jurgensen SP 25.00 11.00
❑ 111 Tim Brown SP RC 10.00 4.50
❑ 112 Tommy McDonald SP 10.00 4.50
❑ 113 Clarence Peaks SP 6.00 2.70
❑ 114 Pete Retzlaff SP 8.00 3.60
❑ 115 Jim Schrader SP 6.00 2.70
❑ 116 Jim McCusker SP 6.00 2.70
❑ 117 Don Burroughs SP 6.00 2.70
❑ 118 Maxie Baughan SP 6.00 2.70
❑ 119 Riley Gunnels SP 6.00 2.70
❑ 120 Jimmy Carr SP 6.00 2.70
❑ 121 Philadelphia Eagles SP 10.00 4.50
Team Card
❑ 122 Ed Brown SP 8.00 3.60
❑ 123 John Henry Johnson SP 15.00 6.75
❑ 124 Buddy Dial SP 6.00 2.70
❑ 125 Bill Red Mack SP 6.00 2.70
❑ 126 Preston Carpenter SP 6.00 2.70
❑ 127 Ray Lemek SP 6.00 2.70
❑ 128 Buzz Nutter SP 6.00 2.70
❑ 129 Ernie Stautner SP 15.00 6.75
❑ 130 Lou Michaels SP 6.00 2.70
❑ 131 Clendon Thomas RC SP 6.00 2.70
❑ 132 Tom Bettis SP 6.00 2.70
❑ 133 Pittsburgh Steelers SP 10.00 4.50
Team Card
❑ 134 John Brodie 8.00 3.60
❑ 135 J.D. Smith 2.50 1.10
❑ 136 Bill Kilmer UER 5.00 2.20
(College listed as
San Francisco 49ers)
❑ 137 Bernie Casey RC 3.00 1.35
❑ 138 Tommy Davis 2.50 1.10
❑ 139 Ted Connolly 2.50 1.10
❑ 140 Bob St. Clair 5.00 2.20
❑ 141 Abe Woodson 2.50 1.10
❑ 142 Matt Hazeltine 2.50 1.10
❑ 143 Leo Nomellini 6.00 2.70
❑ 144 Dan Colchico 2.50 1.10
❑ 145 San Francisco 49ers SP 10.00 4.50
Team Card
❑ 146 Charlie Johnson RC 8.00 3.60
❑ 147 John David Crow 3.00 1.35
❑ 148 Bobby Joe Conrad 3.00 1.35
❑ 149 Sonny Randle 2.50 1.10
❑ 150 Prentice Gautt 2.50 1.10
❑ 151 Taz Anderson 2.50 1.10
❑ 152 Ernie McMillan RC 3.00 1.35
❑ 153 Jimmy Hill 2.50 1.10
❑ 154 Bill Koman 2.50 1.10
❑ 155 Larry Wilson RC 20.00 9.00
❑ 156 Don Owens 2.50 1.10
❑ 157 St. Louis Cardinals SP 10.00 4.50
Team Card
❑ 158 Norm Snead SP 10.00 4.50
❑ 159 Bobby Mitchell SP 15.00 6.75
❑ 160 Bill Barnes SP 6.00 2.70
❑ 161 Fred Dugan SP 6.00 2.70
❑ 162 Don Bosseler SP 6.00 2.70
❑ 163 John Nisby SP 6.00 2.70
❑ 164 Riley Mattson SP 6.00 2.70
❑ 165 Bob Toneff SP 6.00 2.70
❑ 166 Rod Breedlove SP 6.00 2.70
❑ 167 Dick James SP 6.00 2.70
❑ 168 Claude Crabb SP UER 6.00 2.70
(Claud on front and back)
❑ 169 Washington Redskins SP 10.00 4.50
Team Card
❑ 170 Checklist Card UER 60.00 15.00
(108 Jim Prestal)
❑ AD1 Charlie Johnson 100.00 45.00
John David Crow
Bobby Joe Conrad
(Y.A. Tittle/ad back panel)

1964 Topps

	NRMT	VG-E
COMPLETE SET (176)	1500.00	700.00
WRAPPER (1-CENT)	40.00	18.00
WRAPPER (5-CENT)	40.00	18.00
WRAP. (5-CENT, 8-CARD)	75.00	34.00

❑ 1 Tommy Addison SP 30.00 7.50
❑ 2 Houston Antwine RC 4.00 1.80
❑ 3 Nick Buoniconti 15.00 6.75
❑ 4 Ron Burton SP 10.00 4.50
❑ 5 Gino Cappelletti UER 5.00 2.20
(Misspelled Cappalletti
on card front)
❑ 6 Jim Colclough SP 6.00 2.70
❑ 7 Bob Dee SP 6.00 2.70
❑ 8 Larry Eisenhauer 4.00 1.80
❑ 9 Dick Felt SP 6.00 2.70
❑ 10 Larry Garron 4.00 1.80
❑ 11 Art Graham 4.00 1.80
❑ 12 Ron Hall 4.00 1.80
❑ 13 Charles Long 4.00 1.80
❑ 14 Don McKinnon 4.00 1.80
❑ 15 Don Oakes SP 6.00 2.70
❑ 16 Ross O'Hanley SP 6.00 2.70
❑ 17 Babe Parilli SP 10.00 4.50
❑ 18 Jesse Richardson SP 6.00 2.70

❑ 19 Jack Rudolph SP 6.00 2.70
❑ 20 Don Webb RC 4.00 1.80
❑ 21 Boston Patriots 6.00 2.70
Team Card
❑ 22 Ray Abruzzese UER 4.00 1.80
(photo is Ed Rutkowski)
❑ 23 Stew Barber RC 4.00 1.80
❑ 24 Dave Behrman 4.00 1.80
❑ 25 Al Bemiller 4.00 1.80
❑ 26 Elbert Dubenion SP 10.00 4.50
❑ 27 Jim Dunaway RC SP 6.00 2.70
❑ 28 Booker Edgerson SP 6.00 2.70
❑ 29 Cookie Gilchrist SP 20.00 9.00
❑ 30 Jack Kemp SP 175.00 80.00
❑ 31 Daryle Lamonica RC 75.00 34.00
❑ 32 Bill Miller 4.00 1.80
❑ 33 Herb Paterra RC 4.00 1.80
❑ 34 Ken Rice SP 6.00 2.70
❑ 35 Ed Rutkowski UER 4.00 1.80
(photo is Ray Abruzzese)
❑ 36 George Saimes RC 4.00 1.80
❑ 37 Tom Sestak 4.00 1.80
❑ 38 Billy Shaw SP 15.00 6.75
❑ 39 Mike Stratton 5.00 2.20
❑ 40 Gene Sykes 4.00 1.80
❑ 41 John Tracey SP 6.00 2.70
❑ 42 Sid Youngelman SP 6.00 2.70
❑ 43 Buffalo Bills 6.00 2.70
Team Card
❑ 44 Eldon Danenhauer SP 6.00 2.70
❑ 45 Jim Fraser SP 6.00 2.70
❑ 46 Chuck Gavin SP 6.00 2.70
❑ 47 Goose Gonsoulin SP 10.00 4.50
❑ 48 Ernie Barnes RC 4.00 1.80
❑ 49 Tom Janik 4.00 1.80
❑ 50 Billy Joe RC 5.00 2.20
❑ 51 Ike Lassiter RC 4.00 1.80
❑ 52 John McCormick SP 6.00 2.70
❑ 53 Bud McFadin SP 6.00 2.70
❑ 54 Gene Mingo SP 6.00 2.70
❑ 55 Charlie Mitchell 4.00 1.80
❑ 56 John Nocera SP 6.00 2.70
❑ 57 Tom Nomina 4.00 1.80
❑ 58 Harold Olson SP 6.00 2.70
❑ 59 Bob Scarpitto 4.00 1.80
❑ 60 John Sklopan 4.00 1.80
❑ 61 Mickey Slaughter 4.00 1.80
❑ 62 Don Stone 4.00 1.80
❑ 63 Jerry Sturm 4.00 1.80
❑ 64 Lionel Taylor SP 12.00 5.50
❑ 65 Denver Broncos SP 20.00 9.00
Team Card
❑ 66 Scott Appleton RC 4.00 1.80
❑ 67 Tony Banfield SP 6.00 2.70
❑ 68 George Blanda SP 60.00 27.00
❑ 69 Billy Cannon 6.00 2.70
❑ 70 Doug Cline SP 6.00 2.70
❑ 71 Gary Cutsinger SP 6.00 2.70
❑ 72 Willard Dewveall SP 6.00 2.70
❑ 73 Don Floyd SP 6.00 2.70
❑ 74 Freddy Glick SP 6.00 2.70
❑ 75 Charlie Hennigan SP 10.00 4.50
❑ 76 Ed Husmann SP 6.00 2.70
❑ 77 Bobby Jancik SP 6.00 2.70
❑ 78 Jacky Lee SP 10.00 4.50
❑ 79 Bob McLeod SP 6.00 2.70
❑ 80 Rich Michael SP 6.00 2.70
❑ 81 Larry Onesti RC 4.00 1.80
❑ 82 Checklist Card UER 60.00 15.00
(16 Ross O'Hanldy)
❑ 83 Bob Schmidt SP 6.00 2.70
❑ 84 Walt Suggs SP 6.00 2.70
❑ 85 Bob Talamini SP 6.00 2.70
❑ 86 Charley Tolar SP 6.00 2.70
❑ 87 Don Trull RC 4.00 1.80
❑ 88 Houston Oilers 6.00 2.70
Team Card
❑ 89 Fred Arbanas 4.00 1.80
❑ 90 Bobby Bell RC 40.00 18.00
❑ 91 Mel Branch SP 10.00 4.50
❑ 92 Buck Buchanan RC 40.00 18.00
❑ 93 Ed Budde RC 4.00 1.80
❑ 94 Chris Burford SP 10.00 4.50
❑ 95 Walt Corey RC 5.00 2.20
❑ 96 Len Dawson SP 75.00 34.00
❑ 97 Dave Grayson RC 4.00 1.80
❑ 98 Abner Haynes 6.00 2.70
❑ 99 Sherrill Headrick SP 10.00 4.50
❑ 100 E.J. Holub 4.00 1.80
❑ 101 Bobby Hunt 4.00 1.80
❑ 102 Frank Jackson SP 6.00 2.70
❑ 103 Curtis McClinton 5.00 2.20
❑ 104 Jerry Mays SP 10.00 4.50
❑ 105 Johnny Robinson SP 10.00 4.50
❑ 106 Jack Spikes SP 6.00 2.70
❑ 107 Smokey Stover SP 6.00 2.70
❑ 108 Jim Tyrer RC 8.00 3.60
❑ 109 Duane Wood SP 6.00 2.70
❑ 110 Kansas City Chiefs 6.00 2.70
Team Card
❑ 111 Dick Christy SP 6.00 2.70
❑ 112 Dan Ficca SP 6.00 2.70
❑ 113 Larry Grantham 4.00 1.80
❑ 114 Curley Johnson SP 6.00 2.70
❑ 115 Gene Heeter 4.00 1.80
❑ 116 Jack Klotz 4.00 1.80
❑ 117 Pete Liske RC 5.00 2.20
❑ 118 Bob McAdam 4.00 1.80
❑ 119 Dee Mackey SP 6.00 2.70
❑ 120 Bill Mathis SP 10.00 4.50
❑ 121 Don Maynard 35.00 16.00
❑ 122 Dainard Paulson SP 6.00 2.70
❑ 123 Gerry Philbin RC 5.00 2.20
❑ 124 Mark Smolinski SP 6.00 2.70
❑ 125 Matt Snell RC 20.00 9.00
❑ 126 Mike Taliaferro 4.00 1.80
❑ 127 Bake Turner RC SP 10.00 4.50
❑ 128 Jeff Ware 4.00 1.80
❑ 129 Clyde Washington 4.00 1.80
❑ 130 Dick Wood RC 4.00 1.80
❑ 131 New York Jets 6.00 2.70
Team Card
❑ 132 Dalva Allen SP 6.00 2.70
❑ 133 Dan Birdwell 4.00 1.80
❑ 134 Dave Costa RC 4.00 1.80
❑ 135 Dobie Craig 4.00 1.80
❑ 136 Clem Daniels 5.00 2.20
❑ 137 Cotton Davidson SP 10.00 4.50
❑ 138 Claude Gibson 4.00 1.80
❑ 139 Tom Flores SP 15.00 6.75
❑ 140 Wayne Hawkins SP 6.00 2.70
❑ 141 Ken Herock 4.00 1.80
❑ 142 Jon Jelacic SP 6.00 2.70
❑ 143 Joe Krakoski 4.00 1.80
❑ 144 Archie Matsos SP 6.00 2.70
❑ 145 Mike Mercer 4.00 1.80
❑ 146 Alan Miller SP 6.00 2.70
❑ 147 Bob Mischak SP 6.00 2.70
❑ 148 Jim Otto SP 30.00 13.50
❑ 149 Clancy Osborne SP 6.00 2.70
❑ 150 Art Powell SP 12.00 5.50
❑ 151 Bo Roberson 4.00 1.80
(Raider helmet placed over his foot)
❑ 152 Fred Williamson SP 15.00 6.75
❑ 153 Oakland Raiders 6.00 2.70
Team Card
❑ 154 Chuck Allen RC SP 10.00 4.50
❑ 155 Lance Alworth 50.00 22.00
❑ 156 George Blair 4.00 1.80
❑ 157 Earl Faison 4.00 1.80
❑ 158 Sam Gruneisen 4.00 1.80
❑ 159 John Hadl RC 40.00 18.00
❑ 160 Dick Harris SP 6.00 2.70
❑ 161 Emil Karas SP 6.00 2.70
❑ 162 Dave Kocourek SP 6.00 2.70
❑ 163 Ernie Ladd 8.00 3.60
❑ 164 Keith Lincoln 6.00 2.70
❑ 165 Paul Lowe SP 12.00 5.50
❑ 166 Charley McNeil 4.00 1.80
❑ 167 Jacque MacKinnon SP 6.00 2.70
❑ 168 Ron Mix SP 20.00 9.00
❑ 169 Don Norton SP 6.00 2.70
❑ 170 Don Rogers SP 6.00 2.70
❑ 171 Tobin Rote SP 10.00 4.50
❑ 172 Henry Schmidt SP 6.00 2.70
❑ 173 Bud Whitehead 4.00 1.80
❑ 174 Ernie Wright SP 10.00 4.50
❑ 175 San Diego Chargers 6.00 2.70
Team Card
❑ 176 Checklist SP UER 160.00 40.00
(155 Lance Allworth)

1965 Topps

	NRMT	VG-E
COMPLETE SET (176)	4000.00	1800.00
WRAPPER (5-CENT)	30.00	13.50

❑ 1 Tommy Addison SP 35.00 8.75
❑ 2 Houston Antwine SP 12.00 5.50
❑ 3 Nick Buoniconti SP 30.00 13.50
❑ 4 Ron Burton SP 20.00 9.00
❑ 5 Gino Cappelletti SP 20.00 9.00
❑ 6 Jim Colclough 7.00 3.10
❑ 7 Bob Dee SP 12.00 5.50
❑ 8 Larry Eisenhauer 7.00 3.10
❑ 9 J.D. Garrett 7.00 3.10
❑ 10 Larry Garron 7.00 3.10
❑ 11 Art Graham SP 12.00 5.50
❑ 12 Ron Hall 7.00 3.10
❑ 13 Charles Long 7.00 3.10
❑ 14 Jon Morris RC 10.00 4.50
❑ 15 Billy Neighbors SP 12.00 5.50
❑ 16 Ross O'Hanley 7.00 3.10
❑ 17 Babe Parilli SP 20.00 9.00
❑ 18 Tony Romeo SP 12.00 5.50
❑ 19 Jack Rudolph SP 12.00 5.50
❑ 20 Bob Schmidt 7.00 3.10
❑ 21 Don Webb SP 12.00 5.50
❑ 22 Jim Whalen SP 12.00 5.50
❑ 23 Stew Barber 7.00 3.10
❑ 24 Glenn Bass SP 12.00 5.50
❑ 25 Al Bemiller SP 12.00 5.50
❑ 26 Wray Carlton SP 12.00 5.50
❑ 27 Tom Day 7.00 3.10
❑ 28 Elbert Dubenion SP 15.00 6.75
❑ 29 Jim Dunaway 7.00 3.10
❑ 30 Pete Gogolak RC SP 20.00 9.00
❑ 31 Dick Hudson SP 12.00 5.50
❑ 32 Harry Jacobs SP 12.00 5.50
❑ 33 Billy Joe SP 15.00 6.75
❑ 34 Tom Keating RC SP 12.00 5.50
❑ 35 Jack Kemp SP 200.00 90.00
❑ 36 Daryle Lamonica SP 45.00 20.00
❑ 37 Paul Maguire SP 20.00 9.00
❑ 38 Ron McDole RC SP 12.00 5.50
❑ 39 George Saimes SP 12.00 5.50
❑ 40 Tom Sestak SP 12.00 5.50
❑ 41 Billy Shaw SP 20.00 9.00
❑ 42 Mike Stratton SP 12.00 5.50
❑ 43 John Tracey SP 12.00 5.50
❑ 44 Ernie Warlick 7.00 3.10
❑ 45 Odell Barry 7.00 3.10
❑ 46 Willie Brown RC SP 90.00 40.00
❑ 47 Gerry Bussell SP 12.00 5.50
❑ 48 Eldon Danenhauer SP 12.00 5.50
❑ 49 Al Denson SP 12.00 5.50
❑ 50 Hewritt Dixon RC SP 15.00 6.75
❑ 51 Cookie Gilchrist SP 30.00 13.50
❑ 52 Goose Gonsoulin SP 15.00 6.75
❑ 53 Abner Haynes SP 20.00 9.00
❑ 54 Jerry Hopkins 7.00 3.10
❑ 55 Ray Jacobs SP 12.00 5.50
❑ 56 Jacky Lee SP 15.00 6.75
❑ 57 John McCormick 7.00 3.10
❑ 58 Bob McCullough SP 12.00 5.50
❑ 59 John McGeever 7.00 3.10
❑ 60 Charlie Mitchell SP 12.00 5.50
❑ 61 Jim Perkins SP 12.00 5.50
❑ 62 Bob Scarpitto SP 12.00 5.50

- ❑ 63 Mickey Slaughter SP 12.00 5.50
- ❑ 64 Jerry Sturm SP 12.00 5.50
- ❑ 65 Lionel Taylor SP 20.00 9.00
- ❑ 66 Scott Appleton SP 12.00 5.50
- ❑ 67 Johnny Baker SP 12.00 5.50
- ❑ 68 Sonny Bishop SP 12.00 5.50
- ❑ 69 George Blanda SP 100.00 45.00
- ❑ 70 Sid Blanks SP 12.00 5.50
- ❑ 71 Ode Burrell SP 12.00 5.50
- ❑ 72 Doug Cline SP 12.00 5.50
- ❑ 73 Willard Dewveall 7.00 3.10
- ❑ 74 Larry Elkins RC 7.00 3.10
- ❑ 75 Don Floyd SP 12.00 5.50
- ❑ 76 Freddy Glick 7.00 3.10
- ❑ 77 Tom Goode SP 12.00 5.50
- ❑ 78 Charlie Hennigan SP 20.00 9.00
- ❑ 79 Ed Husmann 7.00 3.10
- ❑ 80 Bobby Jancik SP 12.00 5.50
- ❑ 81 Bud McFadin SP 12.00 5.50
- ❑ 82 Bob McLeod SP 12.00 5.50
- ❑ 83 Jim Norton SP 12.00 5.50
- ❑ 84 Walt Suggs 7.00 3.10
- ❑ 85 Bob Talamini 7.00 3.10
- ❑ 86 Charley Tolar SP 12.00 5.50
- ❑ 87 Checklist SP 150.00 38.00
- ❑ 88 Don Trull SP 12.00 5.50
- ❑ 89 Fred Arbanas SP 12.00 5.50
- ❑ 90 Pete Beathard RC SP 12.00 5.50
- ❑ 91 Bobby Bell SP 35.00 16.00
- ❑ 92 Mel Branch SP 12.00 5.50
- ❑ 93 Tommy Brooker SP 12.00 5.50
- ❑ 94 Buck Buchanan SP 35.00 16.00
- ❑ 95 Ed Budde SP 12.00 5.50
- ❑ 96 Chris Burford SP 12.00 5.50
- ❑ 97 Walt Corey 7.00 3.10
- ❑ 98 Jerry Cornelison 7.00 3.10
- ❑ 99 Len Dawson SP 100.00 45.00
- ❑ 100 Jon Gilliam SP 12.00 5.50
- ❑ 101 Sherrill Headrick SP UER 12.00 5.50 (Name spelled Sherill on front)
- ❑ 102 Dave Hill SP 12.00 5.50
- ❑ 103 E.J. Holub SP 12.00 5.50
- ❑ 104 Bobby Hunt SP 12.00 5.50
- ❑ 105 Frank Jackson SP 12.00 5.50
- ❑ 106 Jerry Mays 10.00 4.50
- ❑ 107 Curtis McClinton SP 15.00 6.75
- ❑ 108 Bobby Ply SP 12.00 5.50
- ❑ 109 Johnny Robinson SP 15.00 6.75
- ❑ 110 Jim Tyrer SP 12.00 5.50
- ❑ 111 Bill Baird SP 12.00 5.50
- ❑ 112 Ralph Baker RC SP 12.00 5.50
- ❑ 113 Sam DeLuca SP 12.00 5.50
- ❑ 114 Larry Grantham SP 15.00 6.75
- ❑ 115 Gene Heeter SP 12.00 5.50
- ❑ 116 Winston Hill RC SP 20.00 9.00
- ❑ 117 John Huarte RC SP 30.00 13.50
- ❑ 118 Cosmo Iacavazzi SP 12.00 5.50
- ❑ 119 Curley Johnson SP 12.00 5.50
- ❑ 120 Dee Mackey UER 7.00 3.10 (College WVU, should be East Texas State)
- ❑ 121 Don Maynard 50.00 22.00
- ❑ 122 Joe Namath SP RC 1500.00 650.00
- ❑ 123 Dainard Paulson 7.00 3.10
- ❑ 124 Gerry Philbin SP 12.00 5.50
- ❑ 125 Sherman Plunkett RC SP 15.00 6.75
- ❑ 126 Mark Smolinski 7.00 3.10
- ❑ 127 Matt Snell SP 30.00 13.50
- ❑ 128 Mike Taliaferro SP 12.00 5.50
- ❑ 129 Bake Turner SP 12.00 5.50
- ❑ 130 Clyde Washington SP 12.00 5.50
- ❑ 131 Verlon Biggs RC SP 12.00 5.50
- ❑ 132 Dalva Allen 7.00 3.10
- ❑ 133 Fred Biletnikoff RC SP 225.00 100.00
- ❑ 134 Billy Cannon SP 20.00 9.00
- ❑ 135 Dave Costa SP 12.00 5.50
- ❑ 136 Clem Daniels SP 15.00 6.75
- ❑ 137 Ben Davidson RC SP 60.00 27.00
- ❑ 138 Cotton Davidson SP 15.00 6.75
- ❑ 139 Tom Flores SP 20.00 9.00
- ❑ 140 Claude Gibson 7.00 3.10
- ❑ 141 Wayne Hawkins 7.00 3.10
- ❑ 142 Archie Matsos SP 12.00 5.50
- ❑ 143 Mike Mercer SP 12.00 5.50
- ❑ 144 Bob Mischak SP 12.00 5.50
- ❑ 145 Jim Otto 30.00 13.50
- ❑ 146 Art Powell UER 10.00 4.50 (Photo actually Clem Daniels)
- ❑ 147 Warren Powers SP 12.00 5.50
- ❑ 148 Ken Rice SP 12.00 5.50
- ❑ 149 Bo Roberson SP 12.00 5.50
- ❑ 150 Harry Schuh RC 7.00 3.10
- ❑ 151 Larry Todd SP 12.00 5.50
- ❑ 152 Fred Williamson SP 20.00 9.00
- ❑ 153 J.R. Williamson 7.00 3.10
- ❑ 154 Chuck Allen 10.00 4.50
- ❑ 155 Lance Alworth 75.00 34.00
- ❑ 156 Frank Buncom 7.00 3.10
- ❑ 157 Steve DeLong RC SP 12.00 5.50
- ❑ 158 Earl Faison SP 15.00 6.75
- ❑ 159 Kenny Graham SP 12.00 5.50
- ❑ 160 George Gross SP 12.00 5.50
- ❑ 161 John Hadl SP 30.00 13.50
- ❑ 162 Emil Karas SP 12.00 5.50
- ❑ 163 Dave Kocourek SP 12.00 5.50
- ❑ 164 Ernie Ladd SP 20.00 9.00
- ❑ 165 Keith Lincoln SP 20.00 9.00
- ❑ 166 Paul Lowe SP 20.00 9.00
- ❑ 167 Jacque MacKinnon 7.00 3.10
- ❑ 168 Ron Mix 20.00 9.00
- ❑ 169 Don Norton SP 12.00 5.50
- ❑ 170 Bob Petrich 7.00 3.10
- ❑ 171 Rick Redman SP 12.00 5.50
- ❑ 172 Pat Shea 7.00 3.10
- ❑ 173 Walt Sweeney RC SP 15.00 6.75
- ❑ 174 Dick Westmoreland RC 7.00 3.10
- ❑ 175 Ernie Wright SP 20.00 9.00
- ❑ 176 Checklist SP 225.00 55.00

1966 Topps

	NRMT	VG-E
COMPLETE SET (132)	1500.00	700.00
WRAPPER (5-CENT)	20.00	9.00

- ❑ 1 Tommy Addison 20.00 5.00
- ❑ 2 Houston Antwine 5.00 2.20
- ❑ 3 Nick Buoniconti 10.00 4.50
- ❑ 4 Gino Cappelletti 7.00 3.10
- ❑ 5 Bob Dee 5.00 2.20
- ❑ 6 Larry Garron 5.00 2.20
- ❑ 7 Art Graham 5.00 2.20
- ❑ 8 Ron Hall 5.00 2.20
- ❑ 9 Charles Long 5.00 2.20
- ❑ 10 Jon Morris 5.00 2.20
- ❑ 11 Don Oakes 5.00 2.20
- ❑ 12 Babe Parilli 7.00 3.10
- ❑ 13 Don Webb 5.00 2.20
- ❑ 14 Jim Whalen 5.00 2.20
- ❑ 15 Funny Ring Checklist 300.00 75.00
- ❑ 16 Stew Barber 5.00 2.20
- ❑ 17 Glenn Bass 5.00 2.20
- ❑ 18 Dave Behrman 5.00 2.20
- ❑ 19 Al Bemiller 5.00 2.20
- ❑ 20 George Butch Byrd RC 7.00 3.10
- ❑ 21 Wray Carlton 5.00 2.20
- ❑ 22 Tom Day 5.00 2.20
- ❑ 23 Elbert Dubenion 7.00 3.10
- ❑ 24 Jim Dunaway 5.00 2.20
- ❑ 25 Dick Hudson 5.00 2.20
- ❑ 26 Jack Kemp 150.00 70.00
- ❑ 27 Daryle Lamonica 20.00 9.00
- ❑ 28 Tom Sestak 5.00 2.20
- ❑ 29 Billy Shaw 10.00 4.50
- ❑ 30 Mike Stratton 5.00 2.20
- ❑ 31 Eldon Danenhauer 5.00 2.20
- ❑ 32 Cookie Gilchrist 10.00 4.50
- ❑ 33 Goose Gonsoulin 7.00 3.10
- ❑ 34 Wendell Hayes RC 10.00 4.50
- ❑ 35 Abner Haynes 10.00 4.50
- ❑ 36 Jerry Hopkins 5.00 2.20
- ❑ 37 Ray Jacobs 5.00 2.20
- ❑ 38 Charlie Janerette 5.00 2.20
- ❑ 39 Ray Kubala 5.00 2.20
- ❑ 40 John McCormick 5.00 2.20
- ❑ 41 Leroy Moore 5.00 2.20
- ❑ 42 Bob Scarpitto 5.00 2.20
- ❑ 43 Mickey Slaughter 5.00 2.20
- ❑ 44 Jerry Sturm 5.00 2.20
- ❑ 45 Lionel Taylor 10.00 4.50
- ❑ 46 Scott Appleton 5.00 2.20
- ❑ 47 Johnny Baker 5.00 2.20
- ❑ 48 George Blanda 35.00 16.00
- ❑ 49 Sid Blanks 5.00 2.20
- ❑ 50 Danny Brabham 5.00 2.20
- ❑ 51 Ode Burrell 5.00 2.20
- ❑ 52 Gary Cutsinger 5.00 2.20
- ❑ 53 Larry Elkins 5.00 2.20
- ❑ 54 Don Floyd 5.00 2.20
- ❑ 55 Willie Frazier RC 7.00 3.10
- ❑ 56 Freddy Glick 5.00 2.20
- ❑ 57 Charlie Hennigan 7.00 3.10
- ❑ 58 Bobby Jancik 5.00 2.20
- ❑ 59 Rich Michael 5.00 2.20
- ❑ 60 Don Trull 5.00 2.20
- ❑ 61 Checklist Card 55.00 14.00
- ❑ 62 Fred Arbanas 5.00 2.20
- ❑ 63 Pete Beathard 5.00 2.20
- ❑ 64 Bobby Bell 10.00 4.50
- ❑ 65 Ed Budde 5.00 2.20
- ❑ 66 Chris Burford 5.00 2.20
- ❑ 67 Len Dawson 40.00 18.00
- ❑ 68 Jon Gilliam 5.00 2.20
- ❑ 69 Sherrill Headrick 5.00 2.20
- ❑ 70 E.J. Holub UER 5.00 2.20 (College: TCU, should be Texas Tech)
- ❑ 71 Bobby Hunt 5.00 2.20
- ❑ 72 Curtis McClinton 7.00 3.10
- ❑ 73 Jerry Mays 5.00 2.20
- ❑ 74 Johnny Robinson 7.00 3.10
- ❑ 75 Otis Taylor RC 25.00 11.00
- ❑ 76 Tom Erlandson 7.00 3.10
- ❑ 77 Norm Evans RC UER 10.00 4.50 (Flanker on front, tackle on back)
- ❑ 78 Tom Goode 7.00 3.10
- ❑ 79 Mike Hudock 7.00 3.10
- ❑ 80 Frank Jackson 7.00 3.10
- ❑ 81 Billy Joe 7.00 3.10
- ❑ 82 Dave Kocourek 7.00 3.10
- ❑ 83 Bo Roberson 7.00 3.10
- ❑ 84 Jack Spikes 7.00 3.10
- ❑ 85 Jim Warren RC 7.00 3.10
- ❑ 86 Willie West RC 7.00 3.10
- ❑ 87 Dick Westmoreland 7.00 3.10
- ❑ 88 Eddie Wilson 7.00 3.10
- ❑ 89 Dick Wood 7.00 3.10
- ❑ 90 Verlon Biggs 7.00 3.10
- ❑ 91 Sam DeLuca 5.00 2.20
- ❑ 92 Winston Hill 5.00 2.20
- ❑ 93 Dee Mackey 5.00 2.20
- ❑ 94 Bill Mathis 5.00 2.20
- ❑ 95 Don Maynard 30.00 13.50
- ❑ 96 Joe Namath 250.00 110.00
- ❑ 97 Dainard Paulson 5.00 2.20
- ❑ 98 Gerry Philbin 7.00 3.10
- ❑ 99 Sherman Plunkett 5.00 2.20
- ❑ 100 Paul Rochester 5.00 2.20
- ❑ 101 George Sauer Jr. RC 15.00 6.75
- ❑ 102 Matt Snell 10.00 4.50
- ❑ 103 Jim Turner RC 7.00 3.10
- ❑ 104 Fred Biletnikoff UER 50.00 22.00 (Misspelled on back as Bilentnikoff)
- ❑ 105 Bill Budness 5.00 2.20
- ❑ 106 Billy Cannon 10.00 4.50
- ❑ 107 Clem Daniels 7.00 3.10
- ❑ 108 Ben Davidson 15.00 6.75

	Card	NRMT	VG-E
❑	109 Cotton Davidson	7.00	3.10
❑	110 Claude Gibson	5.00	2.20
❑	111 Wayne Hawkins	5.00	2.20
❑	112 Ken Herock	5.00	2.20
❑	113 Bob Mischak	5.00	2.20
❑	114 Gus Otto	5.00	2.20
❑	115 Jim Otto	20.00	9.00
❑	116 Art Powell	10.00	4.50
❑	117 Harry Schuh	5.00	2.20
❑	118 Chuck Allen	5.00	2.20
❑	119 Lance Alworth	40.00	18.00
❑	120 Frank Buncom	5.00	2.20
❑	121 Steve DeLong	5.00	2.20
❑	122 John Farris	5.00	2.20
❑	123 Kenny Graham	5.00	2.20
❑	124 Sam Gruneisen	5.00	2.20
❑	125 John Hadl	10.00	4.50
❑	126 Walt Sweeney	5.00	2.20
❑	127 Keith Lincoln	10.00	4.50
❑	128 Ron Mix	10.00	4.50
❑	129 Don Norton	5.00	2.20
❑	130 Pat Shea	5.00	2.20
❑	131 Ernie Wright	10.00	4.50
❑	132 Checklist Card	100.00	25.00

1967 Topps

	NRMT	VG-E
COMPLETE SET (132)	700.00	325.00
WRAPPER (5-CENT)	20.00	9.00

	Card	NRMT	VG-E
❑	1 John Huarte	18.00	4.50
❑	2 Babe Parilli	4.00	1.80
❑	3 Gino Cappelletti	4.00	1.80
❑	4 Larry Garron	3.00	1.35
❑	5 Tommy Addison	3.00	1.35
❑	6 Jon Morris	3.00	1.35
❑	7 Houston Antwine	3.00	1.35
❑	8 Don Oakes	3.00	1.35
❑	9 Larry Eisenhauer	3.00	1.35
❑	10 Jim Hunt	3.00	1.35
❑	11 Jim Whalen	3.00	1.35
❑	12 Art Graham	3.00	1.35
❑	13 Nick Buoniconti	6.00	2.70
❑	14 Bob Dee	3.00	1.35
❑	15 Keith Lincoln	6.00	2.70
❑	16 Tom Flores	4.00	1.80
❑	17 Art Powell	4.00	1.80
❑	18 Stew Barber	3.00	1.35
❑	19 Wray Carlton	3.00	1.35
❑	20 Elbert Dubenion	4.00	1.80
❑	21 Jim Dunaway	3.00	1.35
❑	22 Dick Hudson	3.00	1.35
❑	23 Harry Jacobs	3.00	1.35
❑	24 Jack Kemp	90.00	40.00
❑	25 Ron McDole	3.00	1.35
❑	26 George Saimes	3.00	1.35
❑	27 Tom Sestak	3.00	1.35
❑	28 Billy Shaw	6.00	2.70
❑	29 Mike Stratton	3.00	1.35
❑	30 Nemiah Wilson RC	3.00	1.35
❑	31 John McCormick	3.00	1.35
❑	32 Rex Mirich	3.00	1.35
❑	33 Dave Costa	3.00	1.35
❑	34 Goose Gonsoulin	4.00	1.80
❑	35 Abner Haynes	6.00	2.70
❑	36 Wendell Hayes	4.00	1.80
❑	37 Archie Matsos	3.00	1.35
❑	38 John Bramlett	3.00	1.35
❑	39 Jerry Sturm	3.00	1.35
❑	40 Max Leetzow	3.00	1.35
❑	41 Bob Scarpitto	3.00	1.35
❑	42 Lionel Taylor	6.00	2.70
❑	43 Al Denson	3.00	1.35
❑	44 Miller Farr RC	3.00	1.35
❑	45 Don Trull	3.00	1.35
❑	46 Jacky Lee	4.00	1.80
❑	47 Bobby Jancik	3.00	1.35
❑	48 Ode Burrell	3.00	1.35
❑	49 Larry Elkins	3.00	1.35
❑	50 W.K. Hicks	3.00	1.35
❑	51 Sid Blanks	3.00	1.35
❑	52 Jim Norton	3.00	1.35
❑	53 Bobby Maples RC	3.00	1.35
❑	54 Bob Talamini	3.00	1.35
❑	55 Walt Suggs	3.00	1.35
❑	56 Gary Cutsinger	3.00	1.35
❑	57 Danny Brabham	3.00	1.35
❑	58 Ernie Ladd	6.00	2.70
❑	59 Checklist Card	50.00	22.00
❑	60 Pete Beathard	3.00	1.35
❑	61 Len Dawson	30.00	13.50
❑	62 Bobby Hunt	3.00	1.35
❑	63 Bert Coan	3.00	1.35
❑	64 Curtis McClinton	4.00	1.80
❑	65 Johnny Robinson	4.00	1.80
❑	66 E.J. Holub	3.00	1.35
❑	67 Jerry Mays	3.00	1.35
❑	68 Jim Tyrer	4.00	1.80
❑	69 Bobby Bell	6.00	2.70
❑	70 Fred Arbanas	3.00	1.35
❑	71 Buck Buchanan	6.00	2.70
❑	72 Chris Burford	3.00	1.35
❑	73 Otis Taylor	6.00	2.70
❑	74 Cookie Gilchrist	8.00	3.60
❑	75 Earl Faison	3.00	1.35
❑	76 George Wilson Jr.	4.00	1.80
❑	77 Rick Norton	3.00	1.35
❑	78 Frank Jackson	4.00	1.80
❑	79 Joe Auer	3.00	1.35
❑	80 Willie West	3.00	1.35
❑	81 Jim Warren	3.00	1.35
❑	82 Wahoo McDaniel RC	40.00	18.00
❑	83 Ernie Park	3.00	1.35
❑	84 Billy Neighbors	3.00	1.35
❑	85 Norm Evans	4.00	1.80
❑	86 Tom Nomina	3.00	1.35
❑	87 Rich Zecher	3.00	1.35
❑	88 Dave Kocourek	3.00	1.35
❑	89 Bill Baird	3.00	1.35
❑	90 Ralph Baker	3.00	1.35
❑	91 Verlon Biggs	3.00	1.35
❑	92 Sam DeLuca	3.00	1.35
❑	93 Larry Grantham	4.00	1.80
❑	94 Jim Harris	3.00	1.35
❑	95 Winston Hill	3.00	1.35
❑	96 Bill Mathis	3.00	1.35
❑	97 Don Maynard	20.00	9.00
❑	98 Joe Namath	150.00	70.00
❑	99 Gerry Philbin	4.00	1.80
❑	100 Paul Rochester	3.00	1.35
❑	101 George Sauer Jr.	4.00	1.80
❑	102 Matt Snell	6.00	2.70
❑	103 Daryle Lamonica	10.00	4.50
❑	104 Glenn Bass	3.00	1.35
❑	105 Jim Otto	6.00	2.70
❑	106 Fred Biletnikoff	30.00	13.50
❑	107 Cotton Davidson	4.00	1.80
❑	108 Larry Todd	3.00	1.35
❑	109 Billy Cannon	6.00	2.70
❑	110 Clem Daniels	4.00	1.80
❑	111 Dave Grayson	3.00	1.35
❑	112 Kent McCloughan RC	3.00	1.35
❑	113 Bob Svihus	3.00	1.35
❑	114 Ike Lassiter	3.00	1.35
❑	115 Harry Schuh	3.00	1.35
❑	116 Ben Davidson	8.00	3.60
❑	117 Tom Day	3.00	1.35
❑	118 Scott Appleton	3.00	1.35
❑	119 Steve Tensi RC	3.00	1.35
❑	120 John Hadl	6.00	2.70
❑	121 Paul Lowe	4.00	1.80
❑	122 Jim Allison	3.00	1.35
❑	123 Lance Alworth	30.00	13.50
❑	124 Jacque MacKinnon	3.00	1.35
❑	125 Ron Mix	6.00	2.70
❑	126 Bob Petrich	3.00	1.35
❑	127 Howard Kindig	3.00	1.35
❑	128 Steve DeLong	3.00	1.35
❑	129 Chuck Allen	3.00	1.35
❑	130 Frank Buncom	3.00	1.35
❑	131 Speedy Duncan RC	4.00	1.80
❑	132 Checklist Card	70.00	17.50

1968 Topps

	NRMT	VG-E
COMPLETE SET (219)	550.00	250.00
COMMON CARD (1-131)	1.50	.70
COMMON CARD (132-219)	2.00	.90
WRAPPER (5-CENT, SER.1)	15.00	6.75
WRAPPER (5-CENT, SER.2)	25.00	11.00

	Card	NRMT	VG-E
❑	1 Bart Starr	40.00	10.00
❑	2 Dick Bass	2.00	.90
❑	3 Grady Alderman	1.50	.70
❑	4 Obert Logan	1.50	.70
❑	5 Ernie Koy RC	2.00	.90
❑	6 Don Hultz	1.50	.70
❑	7 Earl Gros	1.50	.70
❑	8 Jim Bakken	1.50	.70
❑	9 George Mira	2.00	.90
❑	10 Carl Kammerer	1.50	.70
❑	11 Willie Frazier	1.50	.70
❑	12 Kent McCloughan UER (McCloughlan on card back)	1.50	.70
❑	13 George Sauer Jr.	2.00	.90
❑	14 Jack Clancy	1.50	.70
❑	15 Jim Tyrer	2.00	.90
❑	16 Bobby Maples	1.50	.70
❑	17 Bo Hickey	1.50	.70
❑	18 Frank Buncom	1.50	.70
❑	19 Keith Lincoln	2.00	.90
❑	20 Jim Whalen	1.50	.70
❑	21 Junior Coffey	1.50	.70
❑	22 Billy Ray Smith	1.50	.70
❑	23 Johnny Morris	1.50	.70
❑	24 Ernie Green	1.50	.70
❑	25 Don Meredith	25.00	11.00
❑	26 Wayne Walker	1.50	.70
❑	27 Carroll Dale	2.00	.90
❑	28 Bernie Casey	2.00	.90
❑	29 Dave Osborn RC	2.00	.90
❑	30 Ray Poage	1.50	.70
❑	31 Homer Jones	1.50	.70
❑	32 Sam Baker	1.50	.70
❑	33 Bill Saul	1.50	.70
❑	34 Ken Willard	2.00	.90
❑	35 Bobby Mitchell	4.00	1.80
❑	36 Gary Garrison RC	2.00	.90
❑	37 Billy Cannon	2.00	.90
❑	38 Ralph Baker	1.50	.70
❑	39 Howard Twilley RC	4.00	1.80
❑	40 Wendell Hayes	2.00	.90
❑	41 Jim Norton	1.50	.70
❑	42 Tom Beer	1.50	.70
❑	43 Chris Burford	1.50	.70
❑	44 Stew Barber	1.50	.70
❑	45 Leroy Mitchell UER (Lifetime Int. should be 3, not 2)	1.50	.70

❑ 46 Dan Grimm 1.50 .70
❑ 47 Jerry Logan 1.50 .70
❑ 48 Andy Livingston 1.50 .70
❑ 49 Paul Warfield 15.00 6.75
❑ 50 Don Perkins 3.00 1.35
❑ 51 Ron Kramer 1.50 .70
❑ 52 Bob Jeter RC**/C 2.00 .90
❑ 53 Les Josephson RC 2.00 .90
❑ 54 Bobby Walden 1.50 .70
❑ 55 Checklist Card 15.00 3.70
❑ 56 Walter Roberts 1.50 .70
❑ 57 Henry Carr 1.50 .70
❑ 58 Gary Ballman 1.50 .70
❑ 59 J.R. Wilburn 1.50 .70
❑ 60 Jim Hart RC 10.00 4.50
❑ 61 Jim Johnson 3.00 1.35
❑ 62 Chris Hanburger 2.00 .90
❑ 63 John Hadl 3.00 1.35
❑ 64 Hewritt Dixon 2.00 .90
❑ 65 Joe Namath 75.00 34.00
❑ 66 Jim Warren 1.50 .70
❑ 67 Curtis McClinton 2.00 .90
❑ 68 Bob Talamini 1.50 .70
❑ 69 Steve Tensi 1.50 .70
❑ 70 Dick Van Raaphorst UER 1.50 .70
(Van Raap Horst
on card back)
❑ 71 Art Powell 2.00 .90
❑ 72 Jim Nance RC 4.00 1.80
❑ 73 Bob Riggle 1.50 .70
❑ 74 John Mackey 5.00 2.20
❑ 75 Gale Sayers 40.00 18.00
❑ 76 Gene Hickerson 1.50 .70
❑ 77 Dan Reeves 10.00 4.50
❑ 78 Tom Nowatzke 1.50 .70
❑ 79 Elijah Pitts 3.00 1.35
❑ 80 Lamar Lundy 2.00 .90
❑ 81 Paul Flatley 1.50 .70
❑ 82 Dave Whitsell 1.50 .70
❑ 83 Spider Lockhart 2.00 .90
❑ 84 Dave Lloyd 1.50 .70
❑ 85 Roy Jefferson 2.00 .90
❑ 86 Jackie Smith 6.00 2.70
❑ 87 John David Crow 2.00 .90
❑ 88 Sonny Jurgensen 6.00 2.70
❑ 89 Ron Mix 3.00 1.35
❑ 90 Clem Daniels 2.00 .90
❑ 91 Cornell Gordon 1.50 .70
❑ 92 Tom Goode 1.50 .70
❑ 93 Bobby Bell 3.00 1.35
❑ 94 Walt Suggs 1.50 .70
❑ 95 Eric Crabtree 1.50 .70
❑ 96 Sherrill Headrick 1.50 .70
❑ 97 Wray Carlton 1.50 .70
❑ 98 Gino Cappelletti 2.00 .90
❑ 99 Tommy McDonald 3.00 1.35
❑ 100 John Unitas 25.00 11.00
❑ 101 Richie Petitbon 1.50 .70
❑ 102 Erich Barnes 1.50 .70
❑ 103 Bob Hayes 8.00 3.60
❑ 104 Milt Plum 2.00 .90
❑ 105 Boyd Dowler 2.00 .90
❑ 106 Ed Meador 1.50 .70
❑ 107 Fred Cox 1.50 .70
❑ 108 Steve Stonebreaker RC 1.50 .70
❑ 109 Aaron Thomas 1.50 .70
❑ 110 Norm Snead 2.00 .90
❑ 111 Paul Martha RC 1.50 .70
❑ 112 Jerry Stovall 1.50 .70
❑ 113 Kay McFarland 1.50 .70
❑ 114 Pat Richter 1.50 .70
❑ 115 Rick Redman 1.50 .70
❑ 116 Tom Keating 1.50 .70
❑ 117 Matt Snell 2.00 .90
❑ 118 Dick Westmoreland 1.50 .70
❑ 119 Jerry Mays 1.50 .70
❑ 120 Sid Blanks 1.50 .70
❑ 121 Al Denson 1.50 .70
❑ 122 Bobby Hunt 1.50 .70
❑ 123 Mike Mercer 1.50 .70
❑ 124 Nick Buoniconti 3.00 1.35
❑ 125 Ron Vanderkelen RC 1.50 .70
❑ 126 Ordell Braase 1.50 .70
❑ 127 Dick Butkus 45.00 20.00
❑ 128 Gary Collins 2.00 .90
❑ 129 Mel Renfro 6.00 2.70
❑ 130 Alex Karras 5.00 2.20
❑ 131 Herb Adderley 5.00 2.20
❑ 132 Roman Gabriel 4.00 1.80
❑ 133 Bill Brown 2.50 1.10
❑ 134 Kent Kramer 2.00 .90
❑ 135 Tucker Frederickson 2.50 1.10
❑ 136 Nate Ramsey 2.00 .90
❑ 137 Marv Woodson 2.00 .90
❑ 138 Ken Gray 2.00 .90
❑ 139 John Brodie 5.00 2.20
❑ 140 Jerry Smith 2.00 .90
❑ 141 Brad Hubbert 2.00 .90
❑ 142 George Blanda 20.00 9.00
❑ 143 Pete Lammons RC 2.00 .90
❑ 144 Doug Moreau 2.00 .90
❑ 145 E.J. Holub 2.00 .90
❑ 146 Ode Burrell 2.00 .90
❑ 147 Bob Scarpitto 2.00 .90
❑ 148 Andre White 2.00 .90
❑ 149 Jack Kemp 50.00 22.00
❑ 150 Art Graham 2.00 .90
❑ 151 Tommy Nobis 6.00 2.70
❑ 152 Willie Richardson RC 2.50 1.10
❑ 153 Jack Concannon 2.00 .90
❑ 154 Bill Glass 2.00 .90
❑ 155 Craig Morton RC 10.00 4.50
❑ 156 Pat Studstill 2.00 .90
❑ 157 Ray Nitschke 8.00 3.60
❑ 158 Roger Brown 2.00 .90
❑ 159 Joe Kapp RC**/C 5.00 2.20
❑ 160 Jim Taylor 15.00 5.50
(Shown in uniform of
Green Bay Packers)
❑ 161 Fran Tarkenton 20.00 9.00
❑ 162 Mike Ditka 30.00 11.00
❑ 163 Andy Russell RC 6.00 2.70
❑ 164 Larry Wilson 4.00 1.80
❑ 165 Tommy Davis 2.00 .90
❑ 166 Paul Krause 4.00 1.80
❑ 167 Speedy Duncan 2.00 .90
❑ 168 Fred Biletnikoff 15.00 5.50
❑ 169 Don Maynard 10.00 4.50
❑ 170 Frank Emanuel 2.00 .90
❑ 171 Len Dawson 15.00 6.75
❑ 172 Miller Farr 2.00 .90
❑ 173 Floyd Little RC 20.00 9.00
❑ 174 Lonnie Wright 2.00 .90
❑ 175 Paul Costa 2.00 .90
❑ 176 Don Trull 2.00 .90
❑ 177 Jerry Simmons 2.00 .90
❑ 178 Tom Matte 2.50 1.10
❑ 179 Bennie McRae 2.00 .90
❑ 180 Jim Kanicki 2.00 .90
❑ 181 Bob Lilly 15.00 5.50
❑ 182 Tom Watkins 2.00 .90
❑ 183 Jim Grabowski RC 4.00 1.80
❑ 184 Jack Snow RC 4.00 1.80
❑ 185 Gary Cuozzo RC 2.50 1.10
❑ 186 Bill Kilmer 4.00 1.80
❑ 187 Jim Katcavage 2.00 .90
❑ 188 Floyd Peters 2.00 .90
❑ 189 Bill Nelsen 2.50 1.10
❑ 190 Bobby Joe Conrad 2.50 1.10
❑ 191 Kermit Alexander 2.00 .90
❑ 192 Charley Taylor UER 6.00 2.70
(Called Charley
and Charlie on back)
❑ 193 Lance Alworth 20.00 9.00
❑ 194 Daryle Lamonica 5.00 2.20
❑ 195 Al Atkinson 2.00 .90
❑ 196 Bob Griese RC 80.00 36.00
❑ 197 Buck Buchanan 4.00 1.80
❑ 198 Pete Beathard 2.00 .90
❑ 199 Nemiah Wilson 2.00 .90
❑ 200 Ernie Wright 2.00 .90
❑ 201 George Saimes 2.00 .90
❑ 202 John Charles 2.00 .90
❑ 203 Randy Johnson 2.00 .90
❑ 204 Tony Lorick 2.00 .90
❑ 205 Dick Evey 2.00 .90
❑ 206 Leroy Kelly 10.00 4.50
❑ 207 Lee Roy Jordan 6.00 2.70
❑ 208 Jim Gibbons 2.00 .90
❑ 209 Donny Anderson RC 4.00 1.80
❑ 210 Maxie Baughan 2.00 .90
❑ 211 Joe Morrison 2.00 .90
❑ 212 Jim Snowden 2.00 .90
❑ 213 Lenny Lyles 2.00 .90
❑ 214 Bobby Joe Green 2.00 .90
❑ 215 Frank Ryan 2.50 1.10
❑ 216 Cornell Green 2.50 1.10
❑ 217 Karl Sweetan 2.00 .90
❑ 218 Dave Williams 2.00 .90
❑ 219A Checklist 132-218 18.00 4.50
(Green print on back)
❑ 219B Checklist 132-218 20.00 5.00
(Blue print on back)

1969 Topps

	NRMT	VG-E
COMPLETE SET (263)	550.00	250.00
COMMON CARD (1-132)	1.50	.70
COMMON CARD (133-263)	2.00	.90
WRAPPER (5-CENT)	15.00	6.75

❑ 1 Leroy Kelly 20.00 5.00
❑ 2 Paul Flatley 1.50 .70
❑ 3 Jim Cadile 1.50 .70
❑ 4 Erich Barnes 1.50 .70
❑ 5 Willie Richardson 1.50 .70
❑ 6 Bob Hayes 5.00 2.20
❑ 7 Bob Jeter 1.50 .70
❑ 8 Jim Colclough 1.50 .70
❑ 9 Sherrill Headrick 1.50 .70
❑ 10 Jim Dunaway 1.50 .70
❑ 11 Bill Munson 2.00 .90
❑ 12 Jack Pardee 2.00 .90
❑ 13 Jim Lindsey 1.50 .70
❑ 14 Dave Whitsell 1.50 .70
❑ 15 Tucker Frederickson 1.50 .70
❑ 16 Alvin Haymond 2.00 .90
❑ 17 Andy Russell 2.00 .90
❑ 18 Tom Beer 1.50 .70
❑ 19 Bobby Maples 1.50 .70
❑ 20 Len Dawson 8.00 3.60
❑ 21 Willis Crenshaw 1.50 .70
❑ 22 Tommy Davis 1.50 .70
❑ 23 Rickie Harris 1.50 .70
❑ 24 Jerry Simmons 1.50 .70
❑ 25 John Unitas 35.00 16.00
❑ 26 Brian Piccolo RC UER 80.00 36.00
(Misspelled Bryon on front
and Bryan on back)
❑ 27 Bob Matheson 1.50 .70
❑ 28 Howard Twilley 2.00 .90
❑ 29 Jim Turner 2.00 .90
❑ 30 Pete Banaszak RC 2.00 .90
❑ 31 Lance Rentzel RC 2.00 .90
❑ 32 Bill Triplett 1.50 .70
❑ 33 Boyd Dowler 2.00 .90
❑ 34 Merlin Olsen 5.00 2.20
❑ 35 Joe Kapp 3.00 1.35
❑ 36 Dan Abramowicz RC 4.00 1.80
❑ 37 Spider Lockhart 2.00 .90
❑ 38 Tom Day 1.50 .70
❑ 39 Art Graham 1.50 .70
❑ 40 Bob Cappadona 1.50 .70
❑ 41 Gary Ballman 1.50 .70
❑ 42 Clendon Thomas 1.50 .70
❑ 43 Jackie Smith 4.00 1.80
❑ 44 Dave Wilcox 3.00 1.35
❑ 45 Jerry Smith 1.50 .70
❑ 46 Dan Grimm 1.50 .70

❑ 47 Tom Matte 2.00 .90
❑ 48 John Stofa 1.50 .70
❑ 49 Rex Mirich 1.50 .70
❑ 50 Miller Farr 1.50 .70
❑ 51 Gale Sayers 40.00 18.00
❑ 52 Bill Nelsen 2.00 .90
❑ 53 Bob Lilly 6.00 2.70
❑ 54 Wayne Walker 1.50 .70
❑ 55 Ray Nitschke 5.00 2.20
❑ 56 Ed Meador 1.50 .70
❑ 57 Lonnie Warwick 1.50 .70
❑ 58 Wendell Hayes 1.50 .70
❑ 59 Dick Anderson RC 5.00 2.20
❑ 60 Don Maynard 6.00 2.70
❑ 61 Tony Lorick 1.50 .70
❑ 62 Pete Gogolak 1.50 .70
❑ 63 Nate Ramsey 1.50 .70
❑ 64 Dick Shiner 1.50 .70
❑ 65 Larry Wilson 3.00 1.35
❑ 66 Ken Willard 2.00 .90
❑ 67 Charley Taylor UER 5.00 2.20
(Led Redskins in
pass interceptions)
❑ 68 Billy Cannon 2.00 .90
❑ 69 Lance Alworth 8.00 3.60
❑ 70 Jim Nance 2.00 .90
❑ 71 Nick Rassas 1.50 .70
❑ 72 Lenny Lyles 1.50 .70
❑ 73 Bennie McRae 1.50 .70
❑ 74 Bill Glass 1.50 .70
❑ 75 Don Meredith 25.00 11.00
❑ 76 Dick LeBeau 1.50 .70
❑ 77 Carroll Dale 2.00 .90
❑ 78 Ron McDole 1.50 .70
❑ 79 Charley King 1.50 .70
❑ 80 Checklist 1-132 UER 15.00 3.70
(26 Bryon Piccolo)
❑ 81 Dick Bass 2.00 .90
❑ 82 Roy Winston 1.50 .70
❑ 83 Don McCall 1.50 .70
❑ 84 Jim Katcavage 2.00 .90
❑ 85 Norm Snead 2.00 .90
❑ 86 Earl Gros 1.50 .70
❑ 87 Don Brumm 1.50 .70
❑ 88 Sonny Bishop 1.50 .70
❑ 89 Fred Arbanas 1.50 .70
❑ 90 Karl Noonan 1.50 .70
❑ 91 Dick Witcher 1.50 .70
❑ 92 Vince Promuto 1.50 .70
❑ 93 Tommy Nobis 4.00 1.80
❑ 94 Jerry Hill 1.50 .70
❑ 95 Ed O'Bradovich RC 1.50 .70
❑ 96 Ernie Kellerman 1.50 .70
❑ 97 Chuck Howley 2.00 .90
❑ 98 Hewritt Dixon 1.50 .70
❑ 99 Ron Mix 3.00 1.35
❑ 100 Joe Namath 75.00 34.00
❑ 101 Billy Gambrell 1.50 .70
❑ 102 Elijah Pitts 2.00 .90
❑ 103 Billy Truax RC 2.00 .90
❑ 104 Ed Sharockman 1.50 .70
❑ 105 Doug Atkins 3.00 1.35
❑ 106 Greg Larson 1.50 .70
❑ 107 Israel Lang 1.50 .70
❑ 108 Houston Antwine 1.50 .70
❑ 109 Paul Guidry 1.50 .70
❑ 110 Al Denson 1.50 .70
❑ 111 Roy Jefferson 2.00 .90
❑ 112 Chuck Latourette 1.50 .70
❑ 113 Jim Johnson 3.00 1.35
❑ 114 Bobby Mitchell 4.00 1.80
❑ 115 Randy Johnson 1.50 .70
❑ 116 Lou Michaels 1.50 .70
❑ 117 Rudy Kuechenberg 1.50 .70
❑ 118 Walt Suggs 1.50 .70
❑ 119 Goldie Sellers 1.50 .70
❑ 120 Larry Csonka RC ! 75.00 34.00
❑ 121 Jim Houston 1.50 .70
❑ 122 Craig Baynham 1.50 .70
❑ 123 Alex Karras 5.00 2.20
❑ 124 Jim Grabowski 2.00 .90
❑ 125 Roman Gabriel 3.00 1.35
❑ 126 Larry Bowie 1.50 .70
❑ 127 Dave Parks 2.00 .90
❑ 128 Ben Davidson 3.00 1.35
❑ 129 Steve DeLong 1.50 .70
❑ 130 Fred Hill 1.50 .70
❑ 131 Ernie Koy 2.00 .90
❑ 132A Checklist 133-263 15.00 3.70
(no border)
❑ 132B Checklist 133-263 20.00 5.00
(Thin white border
like second series)
❑ 133 Dick Hoak 2.00 .90
❑ 134 Larry Stallings RC 2.00 .90
❑ 135 Clifton McNeil RC 2.00 .90
❑ 136 Walter Rock 2.00 .90
❑ 137 Billy Lothridge 2.00 .90
❑ 138 Bob Vogel 2.00 .90
❑ 139 Dick Butkus 40.00 18.00
❑ 140 Frank Ryan 2.50 1.10
❑ 141 Larry Garron 2.00 .90
❑ 142 George Saimes 2.00 .90
❑ 143 Frank Buncom 2.00 .90
❑ 144 Don Perkins 2.50 1.10
❑ 145 Johnnie Robinson UER 2.00 .90
(Misspelled Johnny)
❑ 146 Lee Roy Caffey 2.50 1.10
❑ 147 Bernie Casey 2.50 1.10
❑ 148 Billy Martin E 2.00 .90
❑ 149 Gene Howard 2.00 .90
❑ 150 Fran Tarkenton 20.00 6.75
❑ 151 Eric Crabtree 2.00 .90
❑ 152 W.K. Hicks 2.00 .90
❑ 153 Bobby Bell 4.00 1.80
❑ 154 Sam Baker 2.00 .90
❑ 155 Marv Woodson 2.00 .90
❑ 156 Dave Williams 2.00 .90
❑ 157 Bruce Bosley UER 2.00 .90
(Considered one of the
three centers in all
of pro football)
❑ 158 Carl Kammerer 2.00 .90
❑ 159 Jim Burson 2.00 .90
❑ 160 Roy Hilton 2.00 .90
❑ 161 Bob Griese 25.00 11.00
❑ 162 Bob Talamini 2.00 .90
❑ 163 Jim Otto 4.00 1.80
❑ 164 Ron Bull 2.00 .90
❑ 165 Walter Johnson RC 2.00 .90
❑ 166 Lee Roy Jordan 4.00 1.80
❑ 167 Mike Lucci 2.50 1.10
❑ 168 Willie Wood 4.00 1.80
❑ 169 Maxie Baughan 2.00 .90
❑ 170 Bill Brown 2.50 1.10
❑ 171 John Hadl 4.00 1.80
❑ 172 Gino Cappelletti 2.50 1.10
❑ 173 George Butch Byrd 2.50 1.10
❑ 174 Steve Stonebreaker 2.00 .90
❑ 175 Joe Morrison 2.00 .90
❑ 176 Joe Scarpati 2.00 .90
❑ 177 Bobby Walden 2.00 .90
❑ 178 Roy Shivers 2.00 .90
❑ 179 Kermit Alexander 2.00 .90
❑ 180 Pat Richter 2.00 .90
❑ 181 Pete Perreault 2.00 .90
❑ 182 Pete Duranko 2.00 .90
❑ 183 Leroy Mitchell 2.00 .90
❑ 184 Jim Simon 2.00 .90
❑ 185 Billy Ray Smith 2.00 .90
❑ 186 Jack Concannon 2.00 .90
❑ 187 Ben Davis 2.00 .90
❑ 188 Mike Clark 2.00 .90
❑ 189 Jim Gibbons 2.00 .90
❑ 190 Dave Robinson 2.50 1.10
❑ 191 Otis Taylor 2.50 1.10
❑ 192 Nick Buoniconti 4.00 1.80
❑ 193 Matt Snell 2.50 1.10
❑ 194 Bruce Gossett 2.00 .90
❑ 195 Mick Tingelhoff 2.50 1.10
❑ 196 Earl Leggett 2.00 .90
❑ 197 Pete Case 2.00 .90
❑ 198 Tom Woodeshick RC 2.00 .90
❑ 199 Ken Kortas 2.00 .90
❑ 200 Jim Hart 4.00 1.80
❑ 201 Fred Biletnikoff 10.00 4.50
❑ 202 Jacque MacKinnon 2.00 .90
❑ 203 Jim Whalen 2.00 .90
❑ 204 Matt Hazeltine 2.00 .90
❑ 205 Charlie Gogolak 2.00 .90
❑ 206 Ray Ogden 2.00 .90
❑ 207 John Mackey 4.00 1.80
❑ 208 Roosevelt Taylor 2.00 .90
❑ 209 Gene Hickerson 2.00 .90
❑ 210 Dave Edwards RC 2.50 1.10
❑ 211 Tom Sestak 2.00 .90
❑ 212 Ernie Wright 2.00 .90
❑ 213 Dave Costa 2.00 .90
❑ 214 Tom Vaughn 2.00 .90
❑ 215 Bart Starr 30.00 13.50
❑ 216 Les Josephson 2.00 .90
❑ 217 Fred Cox 2.00 .90
❑ 218 Mike Tilleman 2.00 .90
❑ 219 Darrell Dess 2.00 .90
❑ 220 Dave Lloyd 2.00 .90
❑ 221 Pete Beathard 2.00 .90
❑ 222 Buck Buchanan 4.00 1.80
❑ 223 Frank Emanuel 2.00 .90
❑ 224 Paul Martha 2.00 .90
❑ 225 Johnny Roland 2.00 .90
❑ 226 Gary Lewis 2.00 .90
❑ 227 Sonny Jurgensen UER 6.00 2.70
(Chiefs logo)
❑ 228 Jim Butler 2.00 .90
❑ 229 Mike Curtis RC 6.00 2.70
❑ 230 Richie Petitbon 2.00 .90
❑ 231 George Sauer Jr. 2.50 1.10
❑ 232 George Blanda 20.00 9.00
❑ 233 Gary Garrison 2.00 .90
❑ 234 Gary Collins 2.50 1.10
❑ 235 Craig Morton 4.00 1.80
❑ 236 Tom Nowatzke 2.00 .90
❑ 237 Donny Anderson 2.50 1.10
❑ 238 Deacon Jones 4.00 1.80
❑ 239 Grady Alderman 2.00 .90
❑ 240 Bill Kilmer 4.00 1.80
❑ 241 Mike Taliaferro 2.00 .90
❑ 242 Stew Barber 2.00 .90
❑ 243 Bobby Hunt 2.00 .90
❑ 244 Homer Jones 2.00 .90
❑ 245 Bob Brown OT 2.50 1.10
❑ 246 Bill Asbury 2.00 .90
❑ 247 Charlie Johnson UER 2.50 1.10
(Misspelled Charley
on both sides)
❑ 248 Chris Hanburger 2.50 1.10
❑ 249 John Brodie 6.00 2.70
❑ 250 Earl Morrall 2.50 1.10
❑ 251 Floyd Little 5.00 2.20
❑ 252 Jerrel Wilson RC 2.00 .90
❑ 253 Jim Keyes 2.00 .90
❑ 254 Mel Renfro 4.00 1.80
❑ 255 Herb Adderley 4.00 1.80
❑ 256 Jack Snow 2.50 1.10
❑ 257 Charlie Durkee 2.00 .90
❑ 258 Charlie Harper 2.00 .90
❑ 259 J.R. Wilburn 2.00 .90
❑ 260 Charlie Krueger 2.00 .90
❑ 261 Pete Jacques 2.00 .90
❑ 262 Gerry Philbin 2.00 .90
❑ 263 Daryle Lamonica 10.00 2.50

1970 Topps

	NRMT	VG-E
COMPLETE SET (263)	475.00	210.00
COMMON CARD (1-132)	1.00	.45
COMMON CARD (133-263)	1.25	.55
WRAPPER (10-CENT)	12.00	5.50

	No.	Player		
❑	1	Len Dawson UER (Cartoon caption says, "AFL AN NFL")	20.00	5.00
❑	2	Doug Hart	1.00	.45
❑	3	Verlon Biggs	1.00	.45
❑	4	Ralph Neely RC	1.50	.70
❑	5	Harmon Wages	1.00	.45
❑	6	Dan Conners	1.00	.45
❑	7	Gino Cappelletti	1.50	.70
❑	8	Erich Barnes	1.00	.45
❑	9	Checklist 1-132	10.00	2.50
❑	10	Bob Griese	15.00	6.75
❑	11	Ed Flanagan	1.00	.45
❑	12	George Seals	1.00	.45
❑	13	Harry Jacobs	1.00	.45
❑	14	Mike Haffner	1.00	.45
❑	15	Bob Vogel	1.00	.45
❑	16	Bill Peterson	1.00	.45
❑	17	Spider Lockhart	1.00	.45
❑	18	Billy Truax	1.00	.45
❑	19	Jim Beirne	1.00	.45
❑	20	Leroy Kelly	6.00	2.70
❑	21	Dave Lloyd	1.00	.45
❑	22	Mike Tilleman	1.00	.45
❑	23	Gary Garrison	1.00	.45
❑	24	Larry Brown RC	8.00	3.60
❑	25	Jan Stenerud RC	12.00	5.50
❑	26	Rolf Krueger	1.00	.45
❑	27	Roland Lakes	1.00	.45
❑	28	Dick Hoak	1.00	.45
❑	29	Gene Washington RC	2.50	1.10
❑	30	Bart Starr	20.00	9.00
❑	31	Dave Grayson	1.00	.45
❑	32	Jerry Rush	1.00	.45
❑	33	Len St. Jean	1.00	.45
❑	34	Randy Edmunds	1.00	.45
❑	35	Matt Snell	1.50	.70
❑	36	Paul Costa	1.00	.45
❑	37	Mike Pyle	1.00	.45
❑	38	Roy Hilton	1.00	.45
❑	39	Steve Tensi	1.00	.45
❑	40	Tommy Nobis	2.50	1.10
❑	41	Pete Case	1.00	.45
❑	42	Andy Rice	1.00	.45
❑	43	Elvin Bethea RC	2.50	1.10
❑	44	Jack Snow	1.50	.70
❑	45	Mel Renfro	2.50	1.10
❑	46	Andy Livingston	1.00	.45
❑	47	Gary Ballman	1.00	.45
❑	48	Bob DeMarco	1.00	.45
❑	49	Steve DeLong	1.00	.45
❑	50	Daryle Lamonica	4.00	1.80
❑	51	Jim Lynch RC	1.00	.45
❑	52	Mel Farr RC	1.00	.45
❑	53	Bob Long	1.00	.45
❑	54	John Elliott	1.00	.45
❑	55	Ray Nitschke	5.00	2.20
❑	56	Jim Shorter	1.00	.45
❑	57	Dave Wilcox	2.50	1.10
❑	58	Eric Crabtree	1.00	.45
❑	59	Alan Page RC	25.00	11.00
❑	60	Jim Nance	1.50	.70
❑	61	Glen Ray Hines	1.00	.45
❑	62	John Mackey	2.50	1.10
❑	63	Ron McDole	1.00	.45
❑	64	Tom Beier	1.00	.45
❑	65	Bill Nelsen	1.50	.70
❑	66	Paul Flatley	1.00	.45
❑	67	Sam Brunelli	1.00	.45
❑	68	Jack Pardee	1.50	.70
❑	69	Brig Owens	1.00	.45
❑	70	Gale Sayers	25.00	11.00
❑	71	Lee Roy Jordan	2.50	1.10
❑	72	Harold Jackson RC	5.00	2.20
❑	73	John Hadl	2.50	1.10
❑	74	Dave Parks	1.00	.45
❑	75	Lem Barney RC	14.00	6.25
❑	76	Johnny Roland	1.00	.45
❑	77	Ed Budde	1.00	.45
❑	78	Ben McGee	1.00	.45
❑	79	Ken Bowman	1.00	.45
❑	80	Fran Tarkenton	15.00	6.75
❑	81	Gene Washington RC	5.00	2.20
❑	82	Larry Grantham	1.00	.45
❑	83	Bill Brown	1.50	.70
❑	84	John Charles	1.00	.45
❑	85	Fred Biletnikoff	7.00	3.10
❑	86	Royce Berry	1.00	.45
❑	87	Bob Lilly	5.00	2.20
❑	88	Earl Morrall	1.50	.70
❑	89	Jerry LeVias RC	1.50	.70
❑	90	O.J. Simpson RC	70.00	32.00
❑	91	Mike Howell	1.00	.45
❑	92	Ken Gray	1.00	.45
❑	93	Chris Hanburger	1.00	.45
❑	94	Larry Seiple RC	1.00	.45
❑	95	Rich Jackson RC	1.00	.45
❑	96	Rockne Freitas	1.00	.45
❑	97	Dick Post RC	1.50	.70
❑	98	Ben Hawkins	1.00	.45
❑	99	Ken Reaves	1.00	.45
❑	100	Roman Gabriel	2.50	1.10
❑	101	Dave Rowe	1.00	.45
❑	102	Dave Robinson	1.00	.45
❑	103	Otis Taylor	1.50	.70
❑	104	Jim Turner	1.00	.45
❑	105	Joe Morrison	1.00	.45
❑	106	Dick Evey	1.00	.45
❑	107	Ray Mansfield	1.00	.45
❑	108	Grady Alderman	1.00	.45
❑	109	Bruce Gossett	1.00	.45
❑	110	Bob Trumpy RC	4.00	1.80
❑	111	Jim Hunt	1.00	.45
❑	112	Larry Stallings	1.00	.45
❑	113A	Lance Rentzel (name in red)	1.50	.70
❑	113B	Lance Rentzel (name in black)	1.50	.70
❑	114	Bubba Smith RC	25.00	11.00
❑	115	Norm Snead	1.50	.70
❑	116	Jim Otto	2.50	1.10
❑	117	Bo Scott RC**/C	1.00	.45
❑	118	Rick Redman	1.00	.45
❑	119	George Butch Byrd	1.00	.45
❑	120	George Webster RC	1.50	.70
❑	121	Chuck Walton	1.00	.45
❑	122	Dave Costa	1.00	.45
❑	123	Al Dodd	1.00	.45
❑	124	Len Hauss	1.00	.45
❑	125	Deacon Jones	2.50	1.10
❑	126	Randy Johnson	1.00	.45
❑	127	Ralph Heck	1.00	.45
❑	128	Emerson Boozer RC	1.50	.70
❑	129	Johnny Robinson	1.50	.70
❑	130	John Brodie	5.00	2.20
❑	131	Gale Gillingham RC	1.00	.45
❑	132	Checklist 133-263 DP UER (145 Charley Taylor misspelled Charlie)	6.00	1.50
❑	133	Chuck Walker	1.25	.55
❑	134	Bennie McRae	1.25	.55
❑	135	Paul Warfield	7.00	3.10
❑	136	Dan Darragh	1.25	.55
❑	137	Paul Robinson RC	1.25	.55
❑	138	Ed Philpott	1.25	.55
❑	139	Craig Morton	3.00	1.35
❑	140	Tom Dempsey RC	2.00	.90
❑	141	Al Nelson	1.25	.55
❑	142	Tom Matte	2.00	.90
❑	143	Dick Schafrath	1.25	.55
❑	144	Willie Brown	4.00	1.80
❑	145	Charley Taylor UER (Misspelled Charlie on both sides)	5.00	2.20
❑	146	John Huard	1.25	.55
❑	147	Dave Osborn	1.25	.55
❑	148	Gene Mingo	1.25	.55
❑	149	Larry Hand	1.25	.55
❑	150	Joe Namath	50.00	22.00
❑	151	Tom Mack RC	7.00	3.10
❑	152	Kenny Graham	1.25	.55
❑	153	Don Herrmann	1.25	.55
❑	154	Bobby Bell	3.00	1.35
❑	155	Hoyle Granger	1.25	.55
❑	156	Claude Humphrey RC	2.00	.90
❑	157	Clifton McNeil	1.25	.55
❑	158	Mick Tingelhoff	2.00	.90
❑	159	Don Horn RC	1.25	.55
❑	160	Larry Wilson	3.00	1.35
❑	161	Tom Neville	1.25	.55
❑	162	Larry Csonka	20.00	9.00
❑	163	Doug Buffone RC	1.25	.55
❑	164	Cornell Green	2.00	.90
❑	165	Haven Moses RC	2.00	.90
❑	166	Bill Kilmer	3.00	1.35
❑	167	Tim Rossovich RC	1.25	.55
❑	168	Bill Bergey RC	4.00	1.80
❑	169	Gary Collins	2.00	.90
❑	170	Floyd Little	3.00	1.35
❑	171	Tom Keating	1.25	.55
❑	172	Pat Fischer	1.25	.55
❑	173	Walt Sweeney	1.25	.55
❑	174	Greg Larson	1.25	.55
❑	175	Carl Eller	2.00	.90
❑	176	George Sauer Jr.	2.00	.90
❑	177	Jim Hart	3.00	1.35
❑	178	Bob Brown OT	1.25	.55
❑	179	Mike Garrett RC	2.00	.90
❑	180	John Unitas	25.00	11.00
❑	181	Tom Regner	1.25	.55
❑	182	Bob Jeter	1.25	.55
❑	183	Gail Cogdill	1.25	.55
❑	184	Earl Gros	1.25	.55
❑	185	Dennis Partee	1.25	.55
❑	186	Charlie Krueger	1.25	.55
❑	187	Martin Baccaglio	1.25	.55
❑	188	Charles Long	1.25	.55
❑	189	Bob Hayes	4.00	1.80
❑	190	Dick Butkus	25.00	11.00
❑	191	Al Bemiller	1.25	.55
❑	192	Dick Westmoreland	1.25	.55
❑	193	Joe Scarpati	1.25	.55
❑	194	Ron Snidow	1.25	.55
❑	195	Earl McCullouch RC	1.25	.55
❑	196	Jake Kupp	1.25	.55
❑	197	Bob Lurtsema	1.25	.55
❑	198	Mike Current	1.25	.55
❑	199	Charlie Smith	1.25	.55
❑	200	Sonny Jurgensen	6.00	2.70
❑	201	Mike Curtis	2.00	.90
❑	202	Aaron Brown	1.25	.55
❑	203	Richie Petitbon	1.25	.55
❑	204	Walt Suggs	1.25	.55
❑	205	Roy Jefferson	1.25	.55
❑	206	Russ Washington RC	1.25	.55
❑	207	Woody Peoples RC	1.25	.55
❑	208	Dave Williams	1.25	.55
❑	209	John Zook RC	1.25	.55
❑	210	Tom Woodeshick	1.25	.55
❑	211	Howard Fest	1.25	.55
❑	212	Jack Concannon	1.25	.55
❑	213	Jim Marshall	3.00	1.35
❑	214	Jon Morris	1.25	.55
❑	215	Dan Abramowicz	2.00	.90
❑	216	Paul Martha	1.25	.55
❑	217	Ken Willard	1.25	.55
❑	218	Walter Rock	1.25	.55
❑	219	Garland Boyette	1.25	.55
❑	220	Buck Buchanan	3.00	1.35
❑	221	Bill Munson	2.00	.90
❑	222	David Lee RC	1.25	.55
❑	223	Karl Noonan	1.25	.55
❑	224	Harry Schuh	1.25	.55
❑	225	Jackie Smith	3.00	1.35
❑	226	Gerry Philbin	1.25	.55
❑	227	Ernie Koy	1.25	.55
❑	228	Chuck Howley	2.00	.90
❑	229	Billy Shaw	3.00	1.35
❑	230	Jerry Hillebrand	1.25	.55
❑	231	Bill Thompson RC	2.00	.90
❑	232	Carroll Dale	2.00	.90
❑	233	Gene Hickerson	1.25	.55
❑	234	Jim Butler	1.25	.55
❑	235	Greg Cook RC	1.25	.55
❑	236	Lee Roy Caffey	1.25	.55
❑	237	Merlin Olsen	4.00	1.80
❑	238	Fred Cox	1.25	.55
❑	239	Nate Ramsey	1.25	.55
❑	240	Lance Alworth	7.00	3.10
❑	241	Chuck Hinton	1.25	.55
❑	242	Jerry Smith	1.25	.55
❑	243	Tony Baker	1.25	.55
❑	244	Nick Buoniconti	3.00	1.35
❑	245	Jim Johnson	3.00	1.35
❑	246	Willie Richardson	1.25	.55
❑	247	Fred Dryer RC	10.00	4.50
❑	248	Bobby Maples	1.25	.55
❑	249	Alex Karras	4.00	1.80

❑ 250 Joe Kapp .... 2.00 .90
❑ 251 Ben Davidson 3.00 1.35
❑ 252 Mike Stratton .... 1.25 .55
❑ 253 Les Josephson .... 1.25 .55
❑ 254 Don Maynard 6.00 2.70
❑ 255 Houston Antwine .... 1.25 .55
❑ 256 Mac Percival RC .... 1.25 .55
❑ 257 George Goeddeke .... 1.25 .55
❑ 258 Homer Jones .... 1.25 .55
❑ 259 Bob Berry .... 1.25 .55
❑ 260A Calvin Hill RC 15.00 6.75
(Name in red)
❑ 260B Calvin Hill RC 20.00 9.00
(Name in black)
❑ 261 Willie Wood 3.00 1.35
❑ 262 Ed Weisacosky .... 1.25 .55
❑ 263 Jim Tyrer .... 3.00 .75

1971 Topps

	NRMT	VG-E
COMPLETE SET (263)	500.00	220.00
COMMON CARD (1-132)	.75	.35
COMMON CARD (133-263)	1.00	.45

❑ 1 John Unitas 30.00 7.50
❑ 2 Jim Butler .... .75 .35
❑ 3 Marty Schottenheimer RC 12.00 5.50
❑ 4 Joe O'Donnell .... .75 .35
❑ 5 Tom Dempsey .... 1.25 .55
❑ 6 Chuck Allen .... .75 .35
❑ 7 Ernie Kellerman .... .75 .35
❑ 8 Walt Garrison RC .... 2.00 .90
❑ 9 Bill Van Heusen .... .75 .35
❑ 10 Lance Alworth 8.00 3.60
❑ 11 Greg Landry RC .... 2.00 .90
❑ 12 Larry Krause .... .75 .35
❑ 13 Buck Buchanan .... 2.00 .90
❑ 14 Roy Gerela RC .... 1.25 .55
❑ 15 Clifton McNeil .... .75 .35
❑ 16 Bob Brown OT .... .75 .35
❑ 17 Lloyd Mumphord .... .75 .35
❑ 18 Gary Cuozzo .... .75 .35
❑ 19 Don Maynard 5.00 2.20
❑ 20 Larry Wilson .... 2.00 .90
❑ 21 Charlie Smith .... .75 .35
❑ 22 Ken Avery .... .75 .35
❑ 23 Billy Walik .... .75 .35
❑ 24 Jim Johnson .... 2.00 .90
❑ 25 Dick Butkus 25.00 11.00
❑ 26 Charley Taylor UER 4.00 1.80
(Misspelled Charlie
on both sides)
❑ 27 Checklist 1-132 UER 8.00 2.00
(26 Charlie Taylor
should be Charley)
❑ 28 Lionel Aldridge RC .... .75 .35
❑ 29 Billy Lothridge .... .75 .35
❑ 30 Terry Hanratty RC .... 1.25 .55
❑ 31 Lee Roy Jordan .... 2.00 .90
❑ 32 Rick Volk RC .... .75 .35
❑ 33 Howard Kindig .... .75 .35
❑ 34 Carl Garrett RC .... .75 .35
❑ 35 Bobby Bell .... 2.00 .90
❑ 36 Gene Hickerson .... .75 .35
❑ 37 Dave Parks .... .75 .35
❑ 38 Paul Martha .... .75 .35
❑ 39 George Blanda 15.00 6.75
❑ 40 Tom Woodeshick .... .75 .35
❑ 41 Alex Karras 3.00 1.35
❑ 42 Rick Redman .... .75 .35
❑ 43 Zeke Moore .... .75 .35
❑ 44 Jack Snow .... 1.25 .55
❑ 45 Larry Csonka 15.00 6.75
❑ 46 Karl Kassulke .... .75 .35
❑ 47 Jim Hart .... 2.00 .90
❑ 48 Al Atkinson .... .75 .35
❑ 49 Horst Muhlmann RC .... .75 .35
❑ 50 Sonny Jurgensen 5.00 2.20
❑ 51 Ron Johnson RC .... 1.25 .55
❑ 52 Cas Banaszek .... .75 .35
❑ 53 Bubba Smith 8.00 3.60
❑ 54 Bobby Douglass RC .... 1.25 .55
❑ 55 Willie Wood .... 2.00 .90
❑ 56 Bake Turner .... .75 .35
❑ 57 Mike Morgan .... .75 .35
❑ 58 George Butch Byrd .... 1.25 .55
❑ 59 Don Horn .... .75 .35
❑ 60 Tommy Nobis .... 2.00 .90
❑ 61 Jan Stenerud 4.00 1.80
❑ 62 Altie Taylor RC .... .75 .35
❑ 63 Gary Pettigrew .... .75 .35
❑ 64 Spike Jones .... .75 .35
❑ 65 Duane Thomas RC .... 2.00 .90
❑ 66 Marty Domres RC .... .75 .35
❑ 67 Dick Anderson .... 1.25 .55
❑ 68 Ken Iman .... .75 .35
❑ 69 Miller Farr .... .75 .35
❑ 70 Daryle Lamonica 3.00 1.35
❑ 71 Alan Page 12.00 5.50
❑ 72 Pat Matson .... .75 .35
❑ 73 Emerson Boozer .... .75 .35
❑ 74 Pat Fischer .... .75 .35
❑ 75 Gary Collins .... 1.25 .55
❑ 76 John Fuqua RC .... 1.25 .55
❑ 77 Bruce Gossett .... .75 .35
❑ 78 Ed O'Bradovich .... .75 .35
❑ 79 Bob Tucker RC .... 1.25 .55
❑ 80 Mike Curtis .... 1.25 .55
❑ 81 Rich Jackson .... .75 .35
❑ 82 Tom Janik .... .75 .35
❑ 83 Gale Gillingham .... .75 .35
❑ 84 Jim Mitchell .... .75 .35
❑ 85 Charlie Johnson .... 1.25 .55
❑ 86 Edgar Chandler .... .75 .35
❑ 87 Cyril Pinder .... .75 .35
❑ 88 Johnny Robinson .... 1.25 .55
❑ 89 Ralph Neely .... .75 .35
❑ 90 Dan Abramowicz .... .75 .35
❑ 91 Mercury Morris RC 5.00 2.20
❑ 92 Steve DeLong .... .75 .35
❑ 93 Larry Stallings .... .75 .35
❑ 94 Tom Mack .... 2.00 .90
❑ 95 Hewritt Dixon .... .75 .35
❑ 96 Fred Cox .... .75 .35
❑ 97 Chris Hanburger .... .75 .35
❑ 98 Gerry Philbin .... .75 .35
❑ 99 Ernie Wright .... .75 .35
❑ 100 John Brodie 4.00 1.80
❑ 101 Tucker Frederickson .... .75 .35
❑ 102 Bobby Walden .... .75 .35
❑ 103 Dick Gordon .... .75 .35
❑ 104 Walter Johnson .... .75 .35
❑ 105 Mike Lucci .... 1.25 .55
❑ 106 Checklist 133-263 DP .. 6.00 1.50
❑ 107 Ron Berger .... .75 .35
❑ 108 Dan Sullivan .... .75 .35
❑ 109 George Kunz RC .... .75 .35
❑ 110 Floyd Little .... 2.00 .90
❑ 111 Zeke Bratkowski .... 1.25 .55
❑ 112 Haven Moses .... 1.25 .55
❑ 113 Ken Houston RC 15.00 6.75
❑ 114 Willie Lanier RC 15.00 6.75
❑ 115 Larry Brown .... 2.00 .90
❑ 116 Tim Rossovich .... .75 .35
❑ 117 Errol Linden .... .75 .35
❑ 118 Mel Renfro .... 2.00 .90
❑ 119 Mike Garrett .... .75 .35
❑ 120 Fran Tarkenton 15.00 6.75
❑ 121 Garo Yepremian RC .... 2.00 .90
❑ 122 Glen Condren .... .75 .35
❑ 123 Johnny Roland .... .75 .35
❑ 124 Dave Herman .... .75 .35
❑ 125 Merlin Olsen 3.00 1.35
❑ 126 Doug Buffone .... .75 .35
❑ 127 Earl McCullouch .... .75 .35
❑ 128 Spider Lockhart .... .75 .35
❑ 129 Ken Willard .... .75 .35
❑ 130 Gene Washington .... .75 .35
❑ 131 Mike Phipps RC .... 1.25 .55
❑ 132 Andy Russell .... 1.25 .55
❑ 133 Ray Nitschke 4.00 1.80
❑ 134 Jerry Logan .... 1.00 .45
❑ 135 MacArthur Lane RC .... 1.50 .70
❑ 136 Jim Turner .... 1.00 .45
❑ 137 Kent McCloughan .... 1.00 .45
❑ 138 Paul Guidry .... 1.00 .45
❑ 139 Otis Taylor .... 1.50 .70
❑ 140 Virgil Carter RC .... 1.00 .45
❑ 141 Joe Dawkins .... 1.00 .45
❑ 142 Steve Preece .... 1.00 .45
❑ 143 Mike Bragg RC .... 1.00 .45
❑ 144 Bob Lilly 5.00 2.20
❑ 145 Joe Kapp .... 1.50 .70
❑ 146 Al Dodd .... 1.00 .45
❑ 147 Nick Buoniconti 2.50 1.10
❑ 148 Speedy Duncan .... 1.00 .45
(Back mentions his
trade to Redskins)
❑ 149 Cedrick Hardman RC .. 1.00 .45
❑ 150 Gale Sayers 25.00 11.00
❑ 151 Jim Otto 2.50 1.10
❑ 152 Billy Truax .... 1.00 .45
❑ 153 John Elliott .... 1.00 .45
❑ 154 Dick LeBeau .... 1.00 .45
❑ 155 Bill Bergey .... 1.50 .70
❑ 156 Terry Bradshaw RC ! 150.00 70.00
❑ 157 Leroy Kelly 6.00 2.70
❑ 158 Paul Krause 2.50 1.10
❑ 159 Ted Vactor .... 1.00 .45
❑ 160 Bob Griese 15.00 6.75
❑ 161 Ernie McMillan .... 1.00 .45
❑ 162 Donny Anderson .... 1.50 .70
❑ 163 John Pitts .... 1.00 .45
❑ 164 Dave Costa .... 1.00 .45
❑ 165 Gene Washington .... 1.50 .70
❑ 166 John Zook .... 1.00 .45
❑ 167 Pete Gogolak .... 1.00 .45
❑ 168 Erich Barnes .... 1.00 .45
❑ 169 Alvin Reed .... 1.00 .45
❑ 170 Jim Nance .... 1.50 .70
❑ 171 Craig Morton 2.50 1.10
❑ 172 Gary Garrison .... 1.00 .45
❑ 173 Joe Scarpati .... 1.00 .45
❑ 174 Adrian Young UER .... 1.00 .45
(Photo actually
Rick Duncan)
❑ 175 John Mackey 2.50 1.10
❑ 176 Mac Percival .... 1.00 .45
❑ 177 Preston Pearson RC 4.00 1.80
❑ 178 Fred Biletnikoff 8.00 3.60
❑ 179 Mike Battle RC .... 1.00 .45
❑ 180 Len Dawson 8.00 3.60
❑ 181 Les Josephson .... 1.00 .45
❑ 182 Royce Berry .... 1.00 .45
❑ 183 Herman Weaver .... 1.00 .45
❑ 184 Norm Snead .... 1.50 .70
❑ 185 Sam Brunelli .... 1.00 .45
❑ 186 Jim Kiick RC 5.00 2.20
❑ 187 Austin Denney .... 1.00 .45
❑ 188 Roger Wehrli RC .... 1.50 .70
❑ 189 Dave Wilcox 2.50 1.10
❑ 190 Bob Hayes 2.50 1.10
❑ 191 Joe Morrison .... 1.00 .45
❑ 192 Manny Sistrunk .... 1.00 .45
❑ 193 Don Cockroft RC .... 1.00 .45
❑ 194 Lee Bouggess .... 1.00 .45
❑ 195 Bob Berry .... 1.00 .45
❑ 196 Ron Sellers .... 1.00 .45
❑ 197 George Webster .... 1.00 .45
❑ 198 Hoyle Granger .... 1.00 .45
❑ 199 Bob Vogel .... 1.00 .45
❑ 200 Bart Starr 20.00 9.00
❑ 201 Mike Mercer .... 1.00 .45
❑ 202 Dave Smith .... 1.00 .45
❑ 203 Lee Roy Caffey .... 1.00 .45
❑ 204 Mick Tingelhoff .... 1.50 .70
❑ 205 Matt Snell .... 1.50 .70
❑ 206 Jim Tyrer .... 1.00 .45
❑ 207 Willie Brown 2.50 1.10

❑ 208 Bob Johnson RC 1.00 .45
❑ 209 Deacon Jones 2.50 1.10
❑ 210 Charlie Sanders RC 1.50 .70
❑ 211 Jake Scott RC 6.00 2.70
❑ 212 Bob Anderson RC 1.00 .45
❑ 213 Charlie Krueger 1.00 .45
❑ 214 Jim Bakken 1.00 .45
❑ 215 Harold Jackson 1.50 .70
❑ 216 Bill Brundige 1.00 .45
❑ 217 Calvin Hill 5.00 2.20
❑ 218 Claude Humphrey 1.00 .45
❑ 219 Glen Ray Hines 1.00 .45
❑ 220 Bill Nelsen 1.50 .70
❑ 221 Roy Hilton 1.00 .45
❑ 222 Don Herrmann 1.00 .45
❑ 223 John Bramlett 1.00 .45
❑ 224 Ken Ellis 1.00 .45
❑ 225 Dave Osborn 1.50 .70
❑ 226 Edd Hargett RC 1.00 .45
❑ 227 Gene Mingo 1.00 .45
❑ 228 Larry Grantham 1.00 .45
❑ 229 Dick Post 1.00 .45
❑ 230 Roman Gabriel 2.50 1.10
❑ 231 Mike Eischeid 1.00 .45
❑ 232 Jim Lynch 1.00 .45
❑ 233 Lemar Parrish RC 1.50 .70
❑ 234 Cecil Turner 1.00 .45
❑ 235 Dennis Shaw RC 1.00 .45
❑ 236 Mel Farr 1.00 .45
❑ 237 Curt Knight 1.00 .45
❑ 238 Chuck Howley 1.50 .70
❑ 239 Bruce Taylor RC 1.00 .45
❑ 240 Jerry LeVias 1.00 .45
❑ 241 Bob Lurtsema 1.00 .45
❑ 242 Earl Morrall 1.50 .70
❑ 243 Kermit Alexander 1.00 .45
❑ 244 Jackie Smith 2.50 1.10
❑ 245 Joe Greene RC 40.00 18.00
❑ 246 Harmon Wages 1.00 .45
❑ 247 Errol Mann 1.00 .45
❑ 248 Mike McCoy 1.00 .45
❑ 249 Milt Morin RC 1.00 .45
❑ 250 Joe Namath UER 60.00 27.00
In 9th line, Joe is
spelled in small letters
❑ 251 Jackie Burkett 1.00 .45
❑ 252 Steve Chomyszak 1.00 .45
❑ 253 Ed Sharockman 1.00 .45
❑ 254 Robert Holmes RC 1.00 .45
❑ 255 John Hadl 2.50 1.10
❑ 256 Cornell Gordon 1.00 .45
❑ 257 Mark Moseley RC 1.50 .70
❑ 258 Gus Otto 1.00 .45
❑ 259 Mike Taliaferro 1.00 .45
❑ 260 O.J. Simpson 25.00 11.00
❑ 261 Paul Warfield 8.00 3.60
❑ 262 Jack Concannon 1.00 .45
❑ 263 Tom Matte 2.50 .60

1972 Topps

	NRMT	VG-E
COMPLETE SET (351)	2200.00	1000.00
COMMON CARD (1-132)	.50	.23
COMMON CARD (133-263)	.60	.25
COMMON CARD (264-351)	18.00	8.00
WRAPPER (10-CENT)	10.00	4.50
WRAPPER SER.3 (10-CENT)	20.00	9.00

❑ 1 AFC Rushing Leaders 4.00 1.80
Floyd Little
Larry Csonka
Marv Hubbard
❑ 2 NFC Rushing Leaders .50 .23
John Brockington
Steve Owens
Willie Ellison
❑ 3 AFC Passing Leaders 2.00 .90
Bob Griese
Len Dawson
Virgil Carter
❑ 4 NFC Passing Leaders 5.00 2.20
Roger Staubach
Greg Landry
Bill Kilmer
❑ 5 AFC Receiving Leaders 1.00 .45
Fred Biletnikoff
Otis Taylor
Randy Vataha
❑ 6 NFC Receiving Leaders .50 .23
Bob Tucker
Ted Kwalick
Harold Jackson
Roy Jefferson
❑ 7 AFC Scoring Leaders .50 .23
Garo Yepremian
Jan Stenerud
Jim O'Brien
❑ 8 NFC Scoring Leaders .50 .23
Curt Knight
Errol Mann
Bruce Gossett
❑ 9 Jim Kiick 2.00 .90
❑ 10 Otis Taylor 1.00 .45
❑ 11 Bobby Joe Green .50 .23
❑ 12 Ken Ellis .50 .23
❑ 13 John Riggins RC 20.00 9.00
❑ 14 Dave Parks .50 .23
❑ 15 John Hadl 2.00 .90
❑ 16 Ron Hornsby .50 .23
❑ 17 Chip Myers RC .50 .23
❑ 18 Bill Kilmer 2.00 .90
❑ 19 Fred Hoaglin .50 .23
❑ 20 Carl Eller 2.00 .90
❑ 21 Steve Zabel .50 .23
❑ 22 Vic Washington RC .50 .23
❑ 23 Len St. Jean .50 .23
❑ 24 Bill Thompson .50 .23
❑ 25 Steve Owens RC 2.00 .90
❑ 26 Ken Burrough RC 1.00 .45
❑ 27 Mike Clark .50 .23
❑ 28 Willie Brown 2.00 .90
❑ 29 Checklist 1-132 6.00 1.50
❑ 30 Marlin Briscoe RC .50 .23
❑ 31 Jerry Logan .50 .23
❑ 32 Donny Anderson 1.00 .45
❑ 33 Rich McGeorge .50 .23
❑ 34 Charlie Durkee .50 .23
❑ 35 Willie Lanier 4.00 1.80
❑ 36 Chris Farasopoulos .50 .23
❑ 37 Ron Shanklin RC .50 .23
❑ 38 Forrest Blue RC .50 .23
❑ 39 Ken Reaves .50 .23
❑ 40 Roman Gabriel 2.00 .90
❑ 41 Mac Percival .50 .23
❑ 42 Lem Barney 3.00 1.35
❑ 43 Nick Buoniconti 2.00 .90
❑ 44 Charlie Gogolak .50 .23
❑ 45 Bill Bradley RC 1.00 .45
❑ 46 Joe Jones .50 .23
❑ 47 Dave Williams .50 .23
❑ 48 Pete Athas .50 .23
❑ 49 Virgil Carter .50 .23
❑ 50 Floyd Little 2.00 .90
❑ 51 Curt Knight .50 .23
❑ 52 Bobby Maples .50 .23
❑ 53 Charlie West .50 .23
❑ 54 Marv Hubbard RC 1.00 .45
❑ 55 Archie Manning RC 20.00 9.00
❑ 56 Jim O'Brien RC 1.00 .45
❑ 57 Wayne Patrick .50 .23
❑ 58 Ken Bowman .50 .23
❑ 59 Roger Wehrli .50 .23
❑ 60 Charlie Sanders UER .50 .23
(Front WR, back TE)
❑ 61 Jan Stenerud 2.00 .90
❑ 62 Willie Ellison .50 .23
❑ 63 Walt Sweeney .50 .23
❑ 64 Ron Smith .50 .23
❑ 65 Jim Plunkett RC 20.00 9.00
❑ 66 Herb Adderley UER 2.00 .90
(misspelled Adderly)
❑ 67 Mike Reid RC 2.00 .90
❑ 68 Richard Caster RC 1.00 .45
❑ 69 Dave Wilcox 2.00 .90
❑ 70 Leroy Kelly 3.00 1.35
❑ 71 Bob Lee RC .50 .23
❑ 72 Verlon Biggs .50 .23
❑ 73 Henry Allison .50 .23
❑ 74 Steve Ramsey .50 .23
❑ 75 Claude Humphrey 1.00 .45
❑ 76 Bob Grim RC .50 .23
❑ 77 John Fuqua 1.00 .45
❑ 78 Ken Houston 4.00 1.80
❑ 79 Checklist 133-263 DP 5.00 1.25
❑ 80 Bob Griese 8.00 3.60
❑ 81 Lance Rentzel 1.00 .45
❑ 82 Ed Podolak RC 1.00 .45
❑ 83 Ike Hill .50 .23
❑ 84 George Farmer .50 .23
❑ 85 John Brockington RC 2.00 .90
❑ 86 Jim Otto 2.00 .90
❑ 87 Richard Neal .50 .23
❑ 88 Jim Hart 2.00 .90
❑ 89 Bob Babich .50 .23
❑ 90 Gene Washington 1.00 .45
❑ 91 John Zook .50 .23
❑ 92 Bobby Duhon .50 .23
❑ 93 Ted Hendricks RC 15.00 6.75
❑ 94 Rockne Freitas .50 .23
❑ 95 Larry Brown 2.00 .90
❑ 96 Mike Phipps 1.00 .45
❑ 97 Julius Adams .50 .23
❑ 98 Dick Anderson 1.00 .45
❑ 99 Fred Willis .50 .23
❑ 100 Joe Namath 30.00 13.50
❑ 101 L.C. Greenwood RC 15.00 6.75
❑ 102 Mark Nordquist .50 .23
❑ 103 Robert Holmes .50 .23
❑ 104 Ron Yary RC 3.00 1.35
❑ 105 Bob Hayes 2.00 .90
❑ 106 Lyle Alzado RC 15.00 6.75
❑ 107 Bob Berry .50 .23
❑ 108 Phil Villapiano RC 1.00 .45
❑ 109 Dave Elmendorf .50 .23
❑ 110 Gale Sayers 20.00 9.00
❑ 111 Jim Tyrer .50 .23
❑ 112 Mel Gray RC 2.00 .90
❑ 113 Gerry Philbin .50 .23
❑ 114 Bob James .50 .23
❑ 115 Garo Yepremian 1.00 .45
❑ 116 Dave Robinson 1.00 .45
❑ 117 Jeff Queen .50 .23
❑ 118 Norm Snead 1.00 .45
❑ 119 Jim Nance IA 1.00 .45
❑ 120 Terry Bradshaw IA 15.00 6.75
❑ 121 Jim Kiick IA 1.00 .45
❑ 122 Roger Staubach IA 20.00 9.00
❑ 123 Bo Scott IA .50 .23
❑ 124 John Brodie IA 2.00 .90
❑ 125 Rick Volk IA .50 .23
❑ 126 John Riggins IA 6.00 2.70
❑ 127 Bubba Smith IA 2.00 .90
❑ 128 Roman Gabriel IA 1.00 .45
❑ 129 Calvin Hill IA 1.00 .45
❑ 130 Bill Nelsen IA .50 .23
❑ 131 Tom Matte IA 1.00 .45
❑ 132 Bob Griese IA 4.00 1.80
❑ 133 AFC Semi-Final 1.00 .45
Dolphins 27,
Chiefs 24
❑ 134 NFC Semi-Final 1.00 .45
Cowboys 20,
Vikings 12
(Duane Thomas
getting tackled)
❑ 135 AFC Semi-Final 1.00 .45
Colts 20,
Browns 3
(Don Nottingham)

❑ 136 NFC Semi-Final .... 1.00 .45
49ers 24,
Redskins 20
❑ 137 AFC Title Game 3.00 1.35
Dolphins 21,
Colts 0
(Johnny Unitas
getting tackled)
❑ 138 NFC Title Game .... 2.00 .90
Cowboys 14,
49ers 3
(Bob Lilly
making tackle)
❑ 139 Super Bowl 5.00 2.20
Cowboys 24,
Dolphins 3
(Roger Staubach
rolling out)
❑ 140 Larry Csonka 8.00 3.60
❑ 141 Rick Volk .... .60 .25
❑ 142 Roy Jefferson .... 1.00 .45
❑ 143 Raymond Chester RC .. 1.00 .45
❑ 144 Bobby Douglass .... .60 .25
❑ 145 Bob Lilly 4.00 1.80
❑ 146 Harold Jackson .... 1.00 .45
❑ 147 Pete Gogolak .... .60 .25
❑ 148 Art Malone .... .60 .25
❑ 149 Ed Flanagan .... .60 .25
❑ 150 Terry Bradshaw 40.00 18.00
❑ 151 MacArthur Lane .... 1.00 .45
❑ 152 Jack Snow .... 1.00 .45
❑ 153 Al Beauchamp .... .60 .25
❑ 154 Bob Anderson .... .60 .25
❑ 155 Ted Kwalick RC .... .60 .25
❑ 156 Dan Pastorini RC .... 2.00 .90
❑ 157 Emmitt Thomas RC ...... 1.00 .45
❑ 158 Randy Vataha RC .... .60 .25
❑ 159 Al Atkinson .... .60 .25
❑ 160 O.J. Simpson 15.00 6.75
❑ 161 Jackie Smith .... 2.00 .90
❑ 162 Ernie Kellerman .... .60 .25
❑ 163 Dennis Partee .... .60 .25
❑ 164 Jake Kupp .... .60 .25
❑ 165 John Unitas 20.00 9.00
❑ 166 Clint Jones RC .... .60 .25
❑ 167 Paul Warfield 6.00 2.70
❑ 168 Roland McDole .... .60 .25
❑ 169 Daryle Lamonica .... 2.00 .90
❑ 170 Dick Butkus 15.00 6.75
❑ 171 Jim Butler .... .60 .25
❑ 172 Mike McCoy .... .60 .25
❑ 173 Dave Smith .... .60 .25
❑ 174 Greg Landry .... 1.00 .45
❑ 175 Tom Dempsey .... 1.00 .45
❑ 176 John Charles .... .60 .25
❑ 177 Bobby Bell .... 2.00 .90
❑ 178 Don Horn .... .60 .25
❑ 179 Bob Trumpy .... 2.00 .90
❑ 180 Duane Thomas .... 1.00 .45
❑ 181 Merlin Olsen 3.00 1.35
❑ 182 Dave Herman .... .60 .25
❑ 183 Jim Nance .... 1.00 .45
❑ 184 Pete Beathard .... .60 .25
❑ 185 Bob Tucker .... .60 .25
❑ 186 Gene Upshaw RC 15.00 6.75
❑ 187 Bo Scott .... .60 .25
❑ 188 J.D. Hill RC .... .60 .25
❑ 189 Bruce Gossett .... .60 .25
❑ 190 Bubba Smith 4.00 1.80
❑ 191 Edd Hargett .... .60 .25
❑ 192 Gary Garrison .... .60 .25
❑ 193 Jake Scott .... 1.00 .45
❑ 194 Fred Cox .... .60 .25
❑ 195 Sonny Jurgensen 4.00 1.80
❑ 196 Greg Brezina RC .... .60 .25
❑ 197 Ed O'Bradovich .... .60 .25
❑ 198 John Rowser .... .60 .25
❑ 199 Altie Taylor UER .... .60 .25
(Taylor misspelled as
Tayor on front)
❑ 200 Roger Staubach RC 150.00 70.00
❑ 201 Leroy Keyes RC .... .60 .25
❑ 202 Garland Boyette .... .60 .25
❑ 203 Tom Beer .... .60 .25
❑ 204 Buck Buchanan .... 2.00 .90
❑ 205 Larry Wilson .... 2.00 .90
❑ 206 Scott Hunter RC .... .60 .25
❑ 207 Ron Johnson .... .60 .25
❑ 208 Sam Brunelli .... .60 .25
❑ 209 Deacon Jones .... 2.00 .90
❑ 210 Fred Biletnikoff 6.00 2.70
❑ 211 Bill Nelsen .... 1.00 .45
❑ 212 George Nock .... .60 .25
❑ 213 Dan Abramowicz .... 1.00 .45
❑ 214 Irv Goode .... .60 .25
❑ 215 Isiah Robertson RC ...... 1.00 .45
❑ 216 Tom Matte .... 1.00 .45
❑ 217 Pat Fischer .... .60 .25
❑ 218 Gene Washington .... .60 .25
❑ 219 Paul Robinson .... .60 .25
❑ 220 John Brodie 4.00 1.80
❑ 221 Manny Fernandez RC .. 1.00 .45
❑ 222 Errol Mann .... .60 .25
❑ 223 Dick Gordon .... .60 .25
❑ 224 Calvin Hill .... 2.00 .90
❑ 225 Fran Tarkenton UER .. 12.00 5.50
(Plays in the Masters
each spring)
❑ 226 Jim Turner .... .60 .25
❑ 227 Jim Mitchell .... .60 .25
❑ 228 Pete Liske .... .60 .25
❑ 229 Carl Garrett .... .60 .25
❑ 230 Joe Greene 20.00 9.00
❑ 231 Gale Gillingham .... .60 .25
❑ 232 Norm Bulaich RC .... 1.00 .45
❑ 233 Spider Lockhart .... .60 .25
❑ 234 Ken Willard .... .60 .25
❑ 235 George Blanda 12.00 5.50
❑ 236 Wayne Mulligan .... .60 .25
❑ 237 Dave Lewis .... .60 .25
❑ 238 Dennis Shaw .... .60 .25
❑ 239 Fair Hooker .... .60 .25
❑ 240 Larry Little RC 15.00 6.75
❑ 241 Mike Garrett .... .60 .25
❑ 242 Glen Ray Hines .... .60 .25
❑ 243 Myron Pottios .... .60 .25
❑ 244 Charlie Joiner RC 20.00 9.00
❑ 245 Len Dawson 6.00 2.70
❑ 246 W.K. Hicks .... .60 .25
❑ 247 Les Josephson .... .60 .25
❑ 248 Lance Alworth UER...... 6.00 2.70
(Front TE, back WR)
❑ 249 Frank Nunley .... .60 .25
❑ 250 Mel Farr IA .... .60 .25
❑ 251 Johnny Unitas IA 8.00 3.60
❑ 252 George Farmer IA .... .60 .25
❑ 253 Duane Thomas IA .... 1.00 .45
❑ 254 John Hadl IA .... 2.00 .90
❑ 255 Vic Washington IA .... .60 .25
❑ 256 Don Horn IA .... .60 .25
❑ 257 L.C. Greenwood IA ...... 2.00 .90
❑ 258 Bob Lee IA .... .60 .25
❑ 259 Larry Csonka IA 4.00 1.80
❑ 260 Mike McCoy IA .... .60 .25
❑ 261 Greg Landry IA .... 1.00 .45
❑ 262 Ray May IA .... .60 .25
❑ 263 Bobby Douglass IA .... .60 .25
❑ 264 Charlie Sanders AP.... 30.00 13.50
❑ 265 Ron Yary AP 30.00 13.50
❑ 266 Rayfield Wright AP 30.00 13.50
❑ 267 Larry Little AP 35.00 16.00
❑ 268 John Niland AP 30.00 13.50
❑ 269 Forrest Blue AP 30.00 13.50
❑ 270 Otis Taylor AP 30.00 13.50
❑ 271 Paul Warfield AP 50.00 22.00
❑ 272 Bob Griese AP 70.00 32.00
❑ 273 John Brockington AP.. 30.00 13.50
❑ 274 Floyd Little AP 30.00 13.50
❑ 275 Garo Yepremian AP .. 30.00 13.50
❑ 276 Jerrel Wilson AP 18.00 8.00
❑ 277 Carl Eller AP 30.00 13.50
❑ 278 Bubba Smith AP 40.00 18.00
❑ 279 Alan Page AP 40.00 18.00
❑ 280 Bob Lilly AP 60.00 27.00
❑ 281 Ted Hendricks AP 50.00 22.00
❑ 282 Dave Wilcox AP 30.00 13.50
❑ 283 Willie Lanier AP 35.00 16.00
❑ 284 Jim Johnson AP 30.00 13.50
❑ 285 Willie Brown AP 35.00 16.00
❑ 286 Bill Bradley AP 30.00 13.50
❑ 287 Ken Houston AP 35.00 16.00
❑ 288 Mel Farr 18.00 8.00
❑ 289 Kermit Alexander 18.00 8.00
❑ 290 John Gilliam RC 25.00 11.00
❑ 291 Steve Spurrier RC 100.00 45.00
❑ 292 Walter Johnson 18.00 8.00
❑ 293 Jack Pardee 25.00 11.00
❑ 294 Checklist 264-351 UER 80.00 20.00
(334 Charlie Taylor
should be Charley)
❑ 295 Winston Hill 18.00 8.00
❑ 296 Hugo Hollas 18.00 8.00
❑ 297 Ray May RC 18.00 8.00
❑ 298 Jim Bakken 18.00 8.00
❑ 299 Larry Carwell 18.00 8.00
❑ 300 Alan Page 50.00 22.00
❑ 301 Walt Garrison 25.00 11.00
❑ 302 Mike Lucci 25.00 11.00
❑ 303 Nemiah Wilson 18.00 8.00
❑ 304 Carroll Dale 25.00 11.00
❑ 305 Jim Kanicki 18.00 8.00
❑ 306 Preston Pearson 30.00 13.50
❑ 307 Lemar Parrish 25.00 11.00
❑ 308 Earl Morrall 25.00 11.00
❑ 309 Tommy Nobis 25.00 11.00
❑ 310 Rich Jackson 18.00 8.00
❑ 311 Doug Cunningham 18.00 8.00
❑ 312 Jim Marsalis 18.00 8.00
❑ 313 Jim Beirne 18.00 8.00
❑ 314 Tom McNeill 18.00 8.00
❑ 315 Milt Morin 18.00 8.00
❑ 316 Rayfield Wright RC 25.00 11.00
❑ 317 Jerry LeVias 25.00 11.00
❑ 318 Travis Williams RC 25.00 11.00
❑ 319 Edgar Chandler 18.00 8.00
❑ 320 Bob Wallace 18.00 8.00
❑ 321 Delles Howell 18.00 8.00
❑ 322 Emerson Boozer 25.00 11.00
❑ 323 George Atkinson RC .. 25.00 11.00
❑ 324 Mike Montler 18.00 8.00
❑ 325 Randy Johnson 18.00 8.00
❑ 326 Mike Curtis UER 25.00 11.00
(Text on back states he was
named Super Bowl MVP in 1972.
Chuck Howley won the award)
❑ 327 Miller Farr 18.00 8.00
❑ 328 Horst Muhlmann 18.00 8.00
❑ 329 John Niland RC 25.00 11.00
❑ 330 Andy Russell 25.00 11.00
❑ 331 Mercury Morris 35.00 16.00
❑ 332 Jim Johnson 30.00 13.50
❑ 333 Jerrel Wilson 18.00 8.00
❑ 334 Charley Taylor UER .. 40.00 18.00
(Misspelled Charlie
on both sides)
❑ 335 Dick LeBeau 18.00 8.00
❑ 336 Jim Marshall 30.00 13.50
❑ 337 Tom Mack 30.00 13.50
❑ 338 Steve Spurrier IA 60.00 27.00
❑ 339 Floyd Little IA 25.00 11.00
❑ 340 Len Dawson IA 40.00 18.00
❑ 341 Dick Butkus IA 70.00 32.00
❑ 342 Larry Brown IA 25.00 11.00
❑ 343 Joe Namath IA 250.00 110.00
❑ 344 Jim Turner IA 18.00 8.00
❑ 345 Doug Cunningham IA 18.00 8.00
❑ 346 Edd Hargett IA 18.00 8.00
❑ 347 Steve Owens IA 18.00 8.00
❑ 348 George Blanda IA 50.00 22.00
❑ 349 Ed Podolak IA 18.00 8.00
❑ 350 Rich Jackson IA 18.00 8.00
❑ 351 Ken Willard IA 40.00 18.00

1973 Topps

NRMT-MT EXC
COMPLETE SET (528) 400.00 180.00

❑ 1 Rushing Leaders 8.00 2.00
Larry Brown
O.J. Simpson
❑ 2 Passing Leaders .... 1.00 .45
Norm Snead
Earl Morrall
❑ 3 Receiving Leaders UER .. 1.50 .70
Harold Jackson
Fred Biletnikoff
(Charley Taylor mis-

spelled as Charlie)
❑ 4 Scoring Leaders .50 .23
Chester Marcol
Bobby Howfield
❑ 5 Interception Leaders .50 .23
Bill Bradley
Mike Sensibaugh
❑ 6 Punting Leaders .50 .23
Dave Chapple
Jerrel Wilson
❑ 7 Bob Trumpy 1.50 .70
❑ 8 Mel Tom .50 .23
❑ 9 Clarence Ellis .50 .23
❑ 10 John Niland .50 .23
❑ 11 Randy Jackson .50 .23
❑ 12 Greg Landry 1.50 .70
❑ 13 Cid Edwards .50 .23
❑ 14 Phil Olsen .50 .23
❑ 15 Terry Bradshaw 25.00 11.00
❑ 16 Al Cowlings RC 1.50 .70
❑ 17 Walker Gillette .50 .23
❑ 18 Bob Atkins .50 .23
❑ 19 Diron Talbert RC .50 .23
❑ 20 Jim Johnson 1.50 .70
❑ 21 Howard Twilley 1.00 .45
❑ 22 Dick Enderle .50 .23
❑ 23 Wayne Colman .50 .23
❑ 24 John Schmitt .50 .23
❑ 25 George Blanda 10.00 4.50
❑ 26 Milt Morin .50 .23
❑ 27 Mike Current .50 .23
❑ 28 Rex Kern RC .50 .23
❑ 29 MacArthur Lane 1.00 .45
❑ 30 Alan Page 3.00 1.35
❑ 31 Randy Vataha .50 .23
❑ 32 Jim Kearney .50 .23
❑ 33 Steve Smith .50 .23
❑ 34 Ken Anderson RC 15.00 6.75
❑ 35 Calvin Hill 1.50 .70
❑ 36 Andy Maurer .50 .23
❑ 37 Joe Taylor .50 .23
❑ 38 Deacon Jones 1.50 .70
❑ 39 Mike Weger .50 .23
❑ 40 Roy Gerela 1.00 .45
❑ 41 Les Josephson .50 .23
❑ 42 Dave Washington .50 .23
❑ 43 Bill Curry RC 1.00 .45
❑ 44 Fred Heron .50 .23
❑ 45 John Brodie 3.00 1.35
❑ 46 Roy Winston .50 .23
❑ 47 Mike Bragg .50 .23
❑ 48 Mercury Morris 1.50 .70
❑ 49 Jim Files .50 .23
❑ 50 Gene Upshaw 3.00 1.35
❑ 51 Hugo Hollas .50 .23
❑ 52 Rod Sherman .50 .23
❑ 53 Ron Snidow .50 .23
❑ 54 Steve Tannen RC .50 .23
❑ 55 Jim Carter .50 .23
❑ 56 Lydell Mitchell RC 1.50 .70
❑ 57 Jack Rudnay RC .50 .23
❑ 58 Halvor Hagen .50 .23
❑ 59 Tom Dempsey 1.00 .45
❑ 60 Fran Tarkenton 10.00 4.50
❑ 61 Lance Alworth 5.00 2.20
❑ 62 Vern Holland .50 .23
❑ 63 Steve DeLong .50 .23
❑ 64 Art Malone .50 .23
❑ 65 Isiah Robertson 1.00 .45
❑ 66 Jerry Rush .50 .23
❑ 67 Bryant Salter .50 .23
❑ 68 Checklist 1-132 5.00 1.25
❑ 69 J.D. Hill .50 .23
❑ 70 Forrest Blue .50 .23
❑ 71 Myron Pottios .50 .23
❑ 72 Norm Thompson RC .50 .23
❑ 73 Paul Robinson .50 .23
❑ 74 Larry Grantham .50 .23
❑ 75 Manny Fernandez 1.00 .45
❑ 76 Kent Nix .50 .23
❑ 77 Art Shell RC 15.00 6.75
❑ 78 George Saimes .50 .23
❑ 79 Don Cockroft .50 .23
❑ 80 Bob Tucker 1.00 .45
❑ 81 Don McCauley RC .50 .23
❑ 82 Bob Brown DT .50 .23
❑ 83 Larry Carwell .50 .23
❑ 84 Mo Moorman .50 .23
❑ 85 John Gilliam 1.00 .45
❑ 86 Wade Key .50 .23
❑ 87 Ross Brupbacher .50 .23
❑ 88 Dave Lewis .50 .23
❑ 89 Franco Harris RC 50.00 22.00
❑ 90 Tom Mack 1.50 .70
❑ 91 Mike Tilleman .50 .23
❑ 92 Carl Mauck .50 .23
❑ 93 Larry Hand .50 .23
❑ 94 Dave Foley .50 .23
❑ 95 Frank Nunley .50 .23
❑ 96 John Charles .50 .23
❑ 97 Jim Bakken .50 .23
❑ 98 Pat Fischer 1.00 .45
❑ 99 Randy Rasmussen .50 .23
❑ 100 Larry Csonka 6.00 2.70
❑ 101 Mike Siani RC .50 .23
❑ 102 Tom Roussel .50 .23
❑ 103 Clarence Scott RC 1.00 .45
❑ 104 Charlie Johnson 1.00 .45
❑ 105 Rick Volk .50 .23
❑ 106 Willie Young .50 .23
❑ 107 Emmitt Thomas 1.00 .45
❑ 108 Jon Morris .50 .23
❑ 109 Clarence Williams .50 .23
❑ 110 Rayfield Wright 1.00 .45
❑ 111 Norm Bulaich .50 .23
❑ 112 Mike Eischeid .50 .23
❑ 113 Speedy Thomas .50 .23
❑ 114 Glen Holloway .50 .23
❑ 115 Jack Ham RC 30.00 13.50
❑ 116 Jim Nettles .50 .23
❑ 117 Errol Mann .50 .23
❑ 118 John Mackey 1.50 .70
❑ 119 George Kunz .50 .23
❑ 120 Bob James .50 .23
❑ 121 Garland Boyette .50 .23
❑ 122 Mel Phillips .50 .23
❑ 123 Johnny Roland .50 .23
❑ 124 Doug Swift .50 .23
❑ 125 Archie Manning 4.00 1.80
❑ 126 Dave Herman .50 .23
❑ 127 Carleton Oats .50 .23
❑ 128 Bill Van Heusen .50 .23
❑ 129 Rich Jackson .50 .23
❑ 130 Len Hauss 1.00 .45
❑ 131 Billy Parks RC .50 .23
❑ 132 Ray May .50 .23
❑ 133 NFC Semi-Final 5.00 2.20
(Cowboys 30, 49ers 28:
Roger Staubach dropping back)
❑ 134 AFC Semi-Final 2.50 1.10
(Steelers 13, Raiders 7:
Immaculate Reception Game)
❑ 135 NFC Semi-Final 1.00 .45
(Redskins 16, Packers 3:
Redskins defense)
❑ 136 AFC Semi-Final 2.00 .90
(Dolphins 20, Browns 14:
Bob Griese handing
off to Larry Csonka)
❑ 137 NFC Title Game 1.50 .70
(Redskins 26, Cowboys 3:
Billy Kilmer handing
off to Larry Brown)
❑ 138 AFC Title Game 1.00 .45
(Dolphins 21, Steelers 17:
Miami stops John Fuqua)
❑ 139 Super Bowl 1.50 .70
(Dolphins 14, Redskins 7:
Miami defense)
❑ 140 Dwight White RC UER 3.00 1.35
(College North Texas
State, should be
East Texas State)
❑ 141 Jim Marsalis .50 .23
❑ 142 Doug Van Horn .50 .23
❑ 143 Al Matthews .50 .23
❑ 144 Bob Windsor .50 .23
❑ 145 Dave Hampton RC .50 .23
❑ 146 Horst Muhlmann .50 .23
❑ 147 Wally Hilgenberg RC .50 .23
❑ 148 Ron Smith .50 .23
❑ 149 Coy Bacon RC 1.00 .45
❑ 150 Winston Hill .50 .23
❑ 151 Ron Jessie RC 1.00 .45
❑ 152 Ken Iman .50 .23
❑ 153 Ron Saul .50 .23
❑ 154 Jim Braxton RC 1.00 .45
❑ 155 Bubba Smith 2.50 1.10
❑ 156 Gary Cuozzo 1.00 .45
❑ 157 Charlie Krueger 1.00 .45
❑ 158 Tim Foley RC 1.00 .45
❑ 159 Lee Roy Jordan 1.50 .70
❑ 160 Bob Brown OT 1.00 .45
❑ 161 Margene Adkins .50 .23
❑ 162 Ron Widby .50 .23
❑ 163 Jim Houston .50 .23
❑ 164 Joe Dawkins .50 .23
❑ 165 L.C. Greenwood 4.00 1.80
❑ 166 Richmond Flowers RC .50 .23
❑ 167 Curley Culp RC 1.50 .70
❑ 168 Len St. Jean .50 .23
❑ 169 Walter Rock .50 .23
❑ 170 Bill Bradley 1.00 .45
❑ 171 Ken Riley RC 1.50 .70
❑ 172 Rich Coady .50 .23
❑ 173 Don Hansen .50 .23
❑ 174 Lionel Aldridge .50 .23
❑ 175 Don Maynard 4.00 1.80
❑ 176 Dave Osborn 1.00 .45
❑ 177 Jim Bailey .50 .23
❑ 178 John Pitts .50 .23
❑ 179 Dave Parks .50 .23
❑ 180 Chester Marcol RC .50 .23
❑ 181 Len Rohde .50 .23
❑ 182 Jeff Staggs .50 .23
❑ 183 Gene Hickerson .50 .23
❑ 184 Charlie Evans .50 .23
❑ 185 Mel Renfro 1.50 .70
❑ 186 Marvin Upshaw .50 .23
❑ 187 George Atkinson 1.00 .45
❑ 188 Norm Evans 1.00 .45
❑ 189 Steve Ramsey .50 .23
❑ 190 Dave Chapple .50 .23
❑ 191 Gerry Mullins .50 .23
❑ 192 John Didion .50 .23
❑ 193 Bob Gladieux .50 .23
❑ 194 Don Hultz .50 .23
❑ 195 Mike Lucci .50 .23
❑ 196 John Wilbur .50 .23
❑ 197 George Farmer .50 .23
❑ 198 Tommy Casanova RC 1.00 .45
❑ 199 Russ Washington .50 .23
❑ 200 Claude Humphrey 1.50 .70
(Tackling Roger Staubach)
❑ 201 Pat Hughes .50 .23
❑ 202 Zeke Moore .50 .23
❑ 203 Chip Glass .50 .23
❑ 204 Glenn Ressler .50 .23
❑ 205 Willie Ellison 1.00 .45
❑ 206 John Leypoldt .50 .23
❑ 207 Johnny Fuller .50 .23
❑ 208 Bill Hayhoe .50 .23
❑ 209 Ed Bell .50 .23
❑ 210 Willie Brown 1.50 .70
❑ 211 Carl Eller 1.50 .70
❑ 212 Mark Nordquist .50 .23
❑ 213 Larry Willingham .50 .23
❑ 214 Nick Buoniconti 1.50 .70
❑ 215 John Hadl 1.50 .70

❑ 216 Jethro Pugh RC 1.50 .70
❑ 217 Leroy Mitchell .50 .23
❑ 218 Billy Newsome .50 .23
❑ 219 John McMakin .50 .23
❑ 220 Larry Brown 1.50 .70
❑ 221 Clarence Scott .50 .23
❑ 222 Paul Naumoff .50 .23
❑ 223 Ted Fritsch Jr. .50 .23
❑ 224 Checklist 133-264 5.00 1.25
❑ 225 Dan Pastorini 1.50 .70
❑ 226 Joe Beauchamp UER .50 .23
(Safety on front,
Cornerback on back)
❑ 227 Pat Matson .50 .23
❑ 228 Tony McGee .50 .23
❑ 229 Mike Phipps 1.00 .45
❑ 230 Harold Jackson 1.50 .70
❑ 231 Willie Williams .50 .23
❑ 232 Spike Jones .50 .23
❑ 233 Jim Tyrer .50 .23
❑ 234 Roy Hilton .50 .23
❑ 235 Phil Villapiano 1.00 .45
❑ 236 Charley Taylor UER 3.00 1.35
(Misspelled Charlie
on both sides)
❑ 237 Malcolm Snider .50 .23
❑ 238 Vic Washington .50 .23
❑ 239 Grady Alderman .50 .23
❑ 240 Dick Anderson 1.00 .45
❑ 241 Ron Yankowski .50 .23
❑ 242 Billy Masters .50 .23
❑ 243 Herb Adderley 1.50 .70
❑ 244 David Ray .50 .23
❑ 245 John Riggins 8.00 3.60
❑ 246 Mike Wagner RC 1.50 .70
❑ 247 Don Morrison .50 .23
❑ 248 Earl McCullouch .50 .23
❑ 249 Dennis Wirgowski .50 .23
❑ 250 Chris Hanburger 1.00 .45
❑ 251 Pat Sullivan RC 1.50 .70
❑ 252 Walt Sweeney .50 .23
❑ 253 Willie Alexander .50 .23
❑ 254 Doug Dressler .50 .23
❑ 255 Walter Johnson .50 .23
❑ 256 Ron Hornsby .50 .23
❑ 257 Ben Hawkins .50 .23
❑ 258 Donnie Green .50 .23
❑ 259 Fred Hoaglin .50 .23
❑ 260 Jerrel Wilson .50 .23
❑ 261 Horace Jones .50 .23
❑ 262 Woody Peoples .50 .23
❑ 263 Jim Hill RC .50 .23
❑ 264 John Fuqua .50 .23
❑ 265 Donny Anderson KP 1.00 .45
❑ 266 Roman Gabriel KP 1.50 .70
❑ 267 Mike Garrett KP 1.00 .45
❑ 268 Rufus Mayes RC .50 .23
❑ 269 Chip Myrtle .50 .23
❑ 270 Bill Stanfill RC 1.00 .45
❑ 271 Clint Jones .50 .23
❑ 272 Miller Farr .50 .23
❑ 273 Harry Schuh .50 .23
❑ 274 Bob Hayes 1.50 .70
❑ 275 Bobby Douglass 1.00 .45
❑ 276 Gus Hollomon .50 .23
❑ 277 Del Williams .50 .23
❑ 278 Julius Adams .50 .23
❑ 279 Herman Weaver .50 .23
❑ 280 Joe Greene 8.00 3.60
❑ 281 Wes Chesson .50 .23
❑ 282 Charlie Harraway .50 .23
❑ 283 Paul Guidry .50 .23
❑ 284 Terry Owens .50 .23
❑ 285 Jan Stenerud 1.50 .70
❑ 286 Pete Athas .50 .23
❑ 287 Dale Lindsey .50 .23
❑ 288 Jack Tatum RC 10.00 4.50
❑ 289 Floyd Little 1.50 .70
❑ 290 Bob Johnson .50 .23
❑ 291 Tommy Hart RC .50 .23
❑ 292 Tom Mitchell .50 .23
❑ 293 Walt Patulski RC .50 .23
❑ 294 Jim Skaggs .50 .23
❑ 295 Bob Griese 6.00 2.70
❑ 296 Mike McCoy .50 .23
❑ 297 Mel Gray 1.00 .45
❑ 298 Bobby Bryant .50 .23
❑ 299 Blaine Nye RC .50 .23
❑ 300 Dick Butkus 12.00 5.50
❑ 301 Charlie Cowan RC .50 .23
❑ 302 Mark Lomas .50 .23
❑ 303 Josh Ashton .50 .23
❑ 304 Happy Feller .50 .23
❑ 305 Ron Shanklin .50 .23
❑ 306 Wayne Rasmussen .50 .23
❑ 307 Jerry Smith .50 .23
❑ 308 Ken Reaves .50 .23
❑ 309 Ron East .50 .23
❑ 310 Otis Taylor 1.50 .70
❑ 311 John Garlington .50 .23
❑ 312 Lyle Alzado 4.00 1.80
❑ 313 Remi Prudhomme .50 .23
❑ 314 Cornelius Johnson .50 .23
❑ 315 Lemar Parrish 1.00 .45
❑ 316 Jim Kiick 1.50 .70
❑ 317 Steve Zabel .50 .23
❑ 318 Alden Roche .50 .23
❑ 319 Tom Blanchard .50 .23
❑ 320 Fred Biletnikoff 4.00 1.80
❑ 321 Ralph Neely 1.00 .45
❑ 322 Dan Dierdorf RC 20.00 9.00
❑ 323 Richard Caster 1.00 .45
❑ 324 Gene Howard .50 .23
❑ 325 Elvin Bethea 1.00 .45
❑ 326 Carl Garrett 1.00 .45
❑ 327 Ron Billingsley .50 .23
❑ 328 Charlie West .50 .23
❑ 329 Tom Neville .50 .23
❑ 330 Ted Kwalick 1.00 .45
❑ 331 Rudy Redmond .50 .23
❑ 332 Henry Davis .50 .23
❑ 333 John Zook .50 .23
❑ 334 Jim Turner .50 .23
❑ 335 Len Dawson 5.00 2.20
❑ 336 Bob Chandler RC 1.00 .45
❑ 337 Al Beauchamp .50 .23
❑ 338 Tom Matte 1.00 .45
❑ 339 Paul Laaveg .50 .23
❑ 340 Ken Ellis .50 .23
❑ 341 Jim Langer RC 10.00 4.50
❑ 342 Ron Porter .50 .23
❑ 343 Jack Youngblood RC 15.00 6.75
❑ 344 Cornell Green 1.50 .70
❑ 345 Marv Hubbard 1.00 .45
❑ 346 Bruce Taylor .50 .23
❑ 347 Sam Havrilak .50 .23
❑ 348 Walt Sumner .50 .23
❑ 349 Steve O'Neal .50 .23
❑ 350 Ron Johnson 1.00 .45
❑ 351 Rockne Freitas .50 .23
❑ 352 Larry Stallings .50 .23
❑ 353 Jim Cadile .50 .23
❑ 354 Ken Burrough 1.00 .45
❑ 355 Jim Plunkett 4.00 1.80
❑ 356 Dave Long .50 .23
❑ 357 Ralph Anderson .50 .23
❑ 358 Checklist 265-396 5.00 1.25
❑ 359 Gene Washington 1.00 .45
❑ 360 Dave Wilcox 1.00 .45
❑ 361 Paul Smith .50 .23
❑ 362 Alvin Wyatt .50 .23
❑ 363 Charlie Smith .50 .23
❑ 364 Royce Berry .50 .23
❑ 365 Dave Elmendorf .50 .23
❑ 366 Scott Hunter 1.00 .45
❑ 367 Bob Kuechenberg RC 3.00 1.35
❑ 368 Pete Gogolak .50 .23
❑ 369 Dave Edwards .50 .23
❑ 370 Lem Barney 2.50 1.10
❑ 371 Verlon Biggs .50 .23
❑ 372 John Reaves RC .50 .23
❑ 373 Ed Podolak 1.00 .45
❑ 374 Chris Farasopoulos .50 .23
❑ 375 Gary Garrison .50 .23
❑ 376 Tom Funchess .50 .23
❑ 377 Bobby Joe Green .50 .23
❑ 378 Don Brumm .50 .23
❑ 379 Jim O'Brien .50 .23
❑ 380 Paul Krause 1.50 .70
❑ 381 Leroy Kelly 2.50 1.10
❑ 382 Ray Mansfield .50 .23
❑ 383 Dan Abramowicz 1.00 .45
❑ 384 John Outlaw RC .50 .23
❑ 385 Tommy Nobis 1.50 .70
❑ 386 Tom Domres .50 .23
❑ 387 Ken Willard .50 .23
❑ 388 Mike Stratton .50 .23
❑ 389 Fred Dryer 2.50 1.10
❑ 390 Jake Scott 1.50 .70
❑ 391 Rich Houston .50 .23
❑ 392 Virgil Carter .50 .23
❑ 393 Tody Smith .50 .23
❑ 394 Ernie Calloway .50 .23
❑ 395 Charlie Sanders 1.00 .45
❑ 396 Fred Willis .50 .23
❑ 397 Curt Knight .50 .23
❑ 398 Nemiah Wilson .50 .23
❑ 399 Carroll Dale 1.00 .45
❑ 400 Joe Namath 30.00 13.50
❑ 401 Wayne Mulligan .50 .23
❑ 402 Jim Harrison .50 .23
❑ 403 Tim Rossovich .50 .23
❑ 404 David Lee .50 .23
❑ 405 Frank Pitts .50 .23
❑ 406 Jim Marshall 1.50 .70
❑ 407 Bob Brown TE .50 .23
❑ 408 John Rowser .50 .23
❑ 409 Mike Montler .50 .23
❑ 410 Willie Lanier 1.50 .70
❑ 411 Bill Bell .50 .23
❑ 412 Cedrick Hardman .50 .23
❑ 413 Bob Anderson .50 .23
❑ 414 Earl Morrall 1.50 .70
❑ 415 Ken Houston 1.50 .70
❑ 416 Jack Snow 1.00 .45
❑ 417 Dick Cunningham .50 .23
❑ 418 Greg Larson .50 .23
❑ 419 Mike Bass 1.00 .45
❑ 420 Mike Reid 1.50 .70
❑ 421 Walt Garrison 1.50 .70
❑ 422 Pete Liske .50 .23
❑ 423 Jim Yarbrough .50 .23
❑ 424 Rich McGeorge .50 .23
❑ 425 Bobby Howfield .50 .23
❑ 426 Pete Banaszak .50 .23
❑ 427 Willie Holman .50 .23
❑ 428 Dale Hackbart .50 .23
❑ 429 Fair Hooker .50 .23
❑ 430 Ted Hendricks 5.00 2.20
❑ 431 Mike Garrett 1.00 .45
❑ 432 Glen Ray Hines .50 .23
❑ 433 Fred Cox .50 .23
❑ 434 Bobby Walden .50 .23
❑ 435 Bobby Bell 1.50 .70
❑ 436 Dave Rowe .50 .23
❑ 437 Bob Berry .50 .23
❑ 438 Bill Thompson .50 .23
❑ 439 Jim Beirne .50 .23
❑ 440 Larry Little 3.00 1.35
❑ 441 Rocky Thompson .50 .23
❑ 442 Brig Owens .50 .23
❑ 443 Richard Neal .50 .23
❑ 444 Al Nelson .50 .23
❑ 445 Chip Myers .50 .23
❑ 446 Ken Bowman .50 .23
❑ 447 Jim Purnell .50 .23
❑ 448 Altie Taylor .50 .23
❑ 449 Linzy Cole .50 .23
❑ 450 Bob Lilly 4.00 1.80
❑ 451 Charlie Ford .50 .23
❑ 452 Milt Sunde .50 .23
❑ 453 Doug Wyatt .50 .23
❑ 454 Don Nottingham RC 1.00 .45
❑ 455 John Unitas 15.00 6.75
❑ 456 Frank Lewis RC 1.00 .45
❑ 457 Roger Wehrli 1.00 .45
❑ 458 Jim Cheyunski .50 .23
❑ 459 Jerry Sherk RC 1.00 .45
❑ 460 Gene Washington 1.00 .45
❑ 461 Jim Otto 1.50 .70
❑ 462 Ed Budde .50 .23
❑ 463 Jim Mitchell 1.00 .45
❑ 464 Emerson Boozer 1.00 .45
❑ 465 Garo Yepremian 1.50 .70
❑ 466 Pete Duranko .50 .23
❑ 467 Charlie Joiner 8.00 3.60
❑ 468 Spider Lockhart 1.00 .45
❑ 469 Marty Domres .50 .23

❑ 470 John Brockington 1.50 .70
❑ 471 Ed Flanagan .50 .23
❑ 472 Roy Jefferson 1.00 .45
❑ 473 Julian Fagan .50 .23
❑ 474 Bill Brown 1.00 .45
❑ 475 Roger Staubach 30.00 13.50
❑ 476 Jan White .50 .23
❑ 477 Pat Holmes .50 .23
❑ 478 Bob DeMarco .50 .23
❑ 479 Merlin Olsen 2.50 1.10
❑ 480 Andy Russell 1.50 .70
❑ 481 Steve Spurrier 20.00 9.00
❑ 482 Nate Ramsey .50 .23
❑ 483 Dennis Partee .50 .23
❑ 484 Jerry Simmons .50 .23
❑ 485 Donny Anderson 1.50 .70
❑ 486 Ralph Baker .50 .23
❑ 487 Ken Stabler RC 60.00 27.00
❑ 488 Ernie McMillan .50 .23
❑ 489 Ken Burrow .50 .23
❑ 490 Jack Gregory RC .50 .23
❑ 491 Larry Seiple 1.00 .45
❑ 492 Mick Tingelhoff 1.00 .45
❑ 493 Craig Morton 1.50 .70
❑ 494 Cecil Turner .50 .23
❑ 495 Steve Owens 1.50 .70
❑ 496 Rickie Harris .50 .23
❑ 497 Buck Buchanan 1.50 .70
❑ 498 Checklist 397-528 5.00 1.25
❑ 499 Billy Kilmer 1.50 .70
❑ 500 O.J. Simpson 15.00 6.75
❑ 501 Bruce Gossett .50 .23
❑ 502 Art Thoms .50 .23
❑ 503 Larry Kaminski .50 .23
❑ 504 Larry Smith .50 .23
❑ 505 Bruce Van Dyke .50 .23
❑ 506 Alvin Reed .50 .23
❑ 507 Delles Howell .50 .23
❑ 508 Leroy Keyes .50 .23
❑ 509 Bo Scott 1.00 .45
❑ 510 Ron Yary 1.00 .45
❑ 511 Paul Warfield 5.00 2.20
❑ 512 Mac Percival .50 .23
❑ 513 Essex Johnson .50 .23
❑ 514 Jackie Smith 1.50 .70
❑ 515 Norm Snead 1.50 .70
❑ 516 Charlie Stukes .50 .23
❑ 517 Reggie Rucker RC 1.00 .45
❑ 518 Bill Sandeman UER .50 .23
(Should be a period between run and he instead of a comma)
❑ 519 Mel Farr 1.00 .45
❑ 520 Raymond Chester 1.00 .45
❑ 521 Fred Carr RC 1.00 .45
❑ 522 Jerry LeVias 1.00 .45
❑ 523 Jim Strong .50 .23
❑ 524 Roland McDole .50 .23
❑ 525 Dennis Shaw .50 .23
❑ 526 Dave Manders .50 .23
❑ 527 Skip Vanderbundt .50 .23
❑ 528 Mike Sensibaugh RC 1.50 .35

1974 Topps

NRMT-MT EXC
COMPLETE SET (528) 300.00 135.00

❑ 1 O.J. Simpson RB UER 20.00 5.00
(Text on back says 100 years, should say 100 yards)
❑ 2 Blaine Nye .40 .18
❑ 3 Don Hansen .40 .18
❑ 4 Ken Bowman .40 .18
❑ 5 Carl Eller 1.50 .70
❑ 6 Jerry Smith .40 .18
❑ 7 Ed Podolak .40 .18
❑ 8 Mel Gray 1.50 .70
❑ 9 Pat Matson .40 .18
❑ 10 Floyd Little 1.50 .70
❑ 11 Frank Pitts .40 .18
❑ 12 Vern Den Herder RC .75 .35
❑ 13 John Fuqua .75 .35
❑ 14 Jack Tatum 2.00 .90
❑ 15 Winston Hill .40 .18
❑ 16 John Beasley .40 .18
❑ 17 David Lee .40 .18
❑ 18 Rich Coady .40 .18
❑ 19 Ken Willard .40 .18
❑ 20 Coy Bacon .75 .35
❑ 21 Ben Hawkins .40 .18
❑ 22 Paul Guidry .40 .18
❑ 23A Norm Snead 5.00 2.20
(Vertical pose; 1973 stats; one asterisk before TCG on back)
❑ 23B Norm Snead HOR .75 .35
❑ 24 Jim Yarbrough .40 .18
❑ 25 Jack Reynolds RC 3.00 1.35
❑ 26 Josh Ashton .40 .18
❑ 27 Donnie Green .40 .18
❑ 28 Bob Hayes 1.50 .70
❑ 29 John Zook .40 .18
❑ 30 Bobby Bryant .40 .18
❑ 31 Scott Hunter .75 .35
❑ 32 Dan Dierdorf 6.00 2.70
❑ 33 Curt Knight .40 .18
❑ 34 Elmo Wright RC .40 .18
❑ 35 Essex Johnson .40 .18
❑ 36 Walt Sumner .40 .18
❑ 37 Marv Montgomery .40 .18
❑ 38 Tim Foley .75 .35
❑ 39 Mike Siani .40 .18
❑ 40 Joe Greene 6.00 2.70
❑ 41 Bobby Howfield .40 .18
❑ 42 Del Williams .40 .18
❑ 43 Don McCauley .40 .18
❑ 44 Randy Jackson .40 .18
❑ 45 Ron Smith .40 .18
❑ 46 Gene Washington .75 .35
❑ 47 Po James .40 .18
❑ 48 Solomon Freelon .40 .18
❑ 49A Bob Windsor 3.00 1.35
(Vertical pose; 1973 stats; one asterisk before TCG on back)
❑ 49B Bob Windsor HOR .40 .18
❑ 50 John Hadl 1.50 .70
❑ 51 Greg Larson .40 .18
❑ 52 Steve Owens .75 .35
❑ 53 Jim Cheyunski .40 .18
❑ 54 Rayfield Wright .75 .35
❑ 55 Dave Hampton .40 .18
❑ 56 Ron Widby .40 .18
❑ 57 Milt Sunde .40 .18
❑ 58 Billy Kilmer 1.50 .70
❑ 59 Bobby Bell 1.50 .70
❑ 60 Jim Bakken .40 .18
❑ 61 Rufus Mayes .40 .18
❑ 62 Vic Washington .40 .18
❑ 63 Gene Washington .75 .35
❑ 64 Clarence Scott .40 .18
❑ 65 Gene Upshaw 2.00 .90
❑ 66 Larry Seiple .75 .35
❑ 67 John McMakin .40 .18
❑ 68 Ralph Baker .40 .18
❑ 69 Lydell Mitchell .75 .35
❑ 70 Archie Manning 2.50 1.10
❑ 71 George Farmer .40 .18
❑ 72 Ron East .40 .18
❑ 73 Al Nelson .40 .18
❑ 74 Pat Hughes .40 .18
❑ 75 Fred Willis .40 .18
❑ 76 Larry Walton .40 .18
❑ 77 Tom Neville .40 .18
❑ 78 Ted Kwalick .40 .18
❑ 79 Walt Patulski .40 .18
❑ 80 John Niland .40 .18
❑ 81 Ted Fritsch Jr. .40 .18
❑ 82 Paul Krause 1.50 .70
❑ 83 Jack Snow .75 .35
❑ 84 Mike Bass .40 .18
❑ 85 Jim Tyrer .40 .18
❑ 86 Ron Yankowski .40 .18
❑ 87 Mike Phipps .75 .35
❑ 88 Al Beauchamp .40 .18
❑ 89 Riley Odoms RC 1.50 .70
❑ 90 MacArthur Lane .40 .18
❑ 91 Art Thoms .40 .18
❑ 92 Marlin Briscoe .40 .18
❑ 93 Bruce Van Dyke .40 .18
❑ 94 Tom Myers RC .40 .18
❑ 95 Calvin Hill 1.50 .70
❑ 96 Bruce Laird .40 .18
❑ 97 Tony McGee .40 .18
❑ 98 Len Rohde .40 .18
❑ 99 Tom McNeill .40 .18
❑ 100 Delles Howell .40 .18
❑ 101 Gary Garrison .40 .18
❑ 102 Dan Goich .40 .18
❑ 103 Len St. Jean .40 .18
❑ 104 Zeke Moore .40 .18
❑ 105 Ahmad Rashad RC 15.00 6.75
❑ 106 Mel Renfro 1.50 .70
❑ 107 Jim Mitchell .40 .18
❑ 108 Ed Budde .40 .18
❑ 109 Harry Schuh .40 .18
❑ 110 Greg Pruitt RC 4.00 1.80
❑ 111 Ed Flanagan .40 .18
❑ 112 Larry Stallings .40 .18
❑ 113 Chuck Foreman RC 4.00 1.80
❑ 114 Royce Berry .40 .18
❑ 115 Gale Gillingham .40 .18
❑ 116A Charlie Johnson 5.00 2.20
(Vertical pose; 1973 stats; one asterisk before TCG on back)
❑ 116B Charlie Johnson HOR 1.50 .70
❑ 117 Checklist 1-132 UER 4.00 1.00
(345 Hamburger)
❑ 118 Bill Butler .40 .18
❑ 119 Roy Jefferson .75 .35
❑ 120 Bobby Douglass .75 .35
❑ 121 Harold Carmichael 12.00 5.50
AP RC
❑ 122 George Kunz AP .40 .18
❑ 123 Larry Little AP 2.00 .90
❑ 124A Forrest Blue AP 3.00 1.35
(Not All-Pro style; 1973 stats; one asterisk before TCG on back)
❑ 124B Forrest Blue AP .40 .18
❑ 125 Ron Yary AP .75 .35
❑ 126A Tom Mack 3.00 1.35
(Not All-Pro style; 1973 stats; one asterisk before TCG on back)
❑ 126B Tom Mack AP 1.50 .70
❑ 127A Bob Tucker 3.00 1.35
(Not All-Pro style; 1973 stats; one asterisk before TCG on back)
❑ 127B Bob Tucker AP .75 .35
❑ 128 Paul Warfield AP 4.00 1.80
❑ 129 Fran Tarkenton AP 10.00 4.50
❑ 130 O.J. Simpson AP 12.00 5.50
❑ 131 Larry Csonka AP 6.00 2.70
❑ 132 Bruce Gossett AP .40 .18
❑ 133 Bill Stanfill AP .75 .35
❑ 134 Alan Page AP 2.50 1.10
❑ 135 Paul Smith AP .40 .18
❑ 136 Claude Humphrey AP .75 .35
❑ 137 Jack Ham AP 10.00 4.50
❑ 138 Lee Roy Jordan AP 1.50 .70
❑ 139 Phil Villapiano AP .75 .35
❑ 140 Ken Ellis AP .40 .18
❑ 141 Willie Brown AP 1.50 .70
❑ 142 Dick Anderson AP .75 .35
❑ 143 Bill Bradley AP .75 .35

❑ 144 Jerrel Wilson AP .40 .18
❑ 145 Reggie Rucker .75 .35
❑ 146 Marty Domres .40 .18
❑ 147 Bob Kowalkowski .40 .18
❑ 148 John Matuszak RC 6.00 2.70
❑ 149 Mike Adamle RC .75 .35
❑ 150 John Unitas 15.00 6.75
❑ 151 Charlie Ford .40 .18
❑ 152 Bob Klein RC .40 .18
❑ 153 Jim Merlo .40 .18
❑ 154 Willie Young .40 .18
❑ 155 Donny Anderson .75 .35
❑ 156 Brig Owens .40 .18
❑ 157 Bruce Jarvis .40 .18
❑ 158 Ron Carpenter .40 .18
❑ 159 Don Cockroft .40 .18
❑ 160 Tommy Nobis 1.50 .70
❑ 161 Craig Morton 1.50 .70
❑ 162 Jon Staggers .40 .18
❑ 163 Mike Eischeid .40 .18
❑ 164 Jerry Sisemore RC .40 .18
❑ 165 Cedrick Hardman .40 .18
❑ 166 Bill Thompson .75 .35
❑ 167 Jim Lynch .75 .35
❑ 168 Bob Moore .40 .18
❑ 169 Glen Edwards .40 .18
❑ 170 Mercury Morris 1.50 .70
❑ 171 Julius Adams .40 .18
❑ 172 Cotton Speyrer .40 .18
❑ 173 Bill Munson .75 .35
❑ 174 Benny Johnson .40 .18
❑ 175 Burgess Owens RC .40 .18
❑ 176 Cid Edwards .40 .18
❑ 177 Doug Buffone .40 .18
❑ 178 Charlie Cowan .40 .18
❑ 179 Bob Newland .40 .18
❑ 180 Ron Johnson .75 .35
❑ 181 Bob Rowe .40 .18
❑ 182 Len Hauss .40 .18
❑ 183 Joe DeLamielleure RC 1.50 .70
❑ 184 Sherman White RC .40 .18
❑ 185 Fair Hooker .40 .18
❑ 186 Nick Mike-Mayer .40 .18
❑ 187 Ralph Neely .40 .18
❑ 188 Rich McGeorge .40 .18
❑ 189 Ed Marinaro RC 4.00 1.80
❑ 190 Dave Wilcox .75 .35
❑ 191 Joe Owens .40 .18
❑ 192 Bill Van Heusen .40 .18
❑ 193 Jim Kearney .40 .18
❑ 194 Otis Sistrunk RC 1.50 .70
❑ 195 Ron Shanklin .40 .18
❑ 196 Bill Lenkaitis .40 .18
❑ 197 Tom Drougas .40 .18
❑ 198 Larry Hand .40 .18
❑ 199 Mack Alston .40 .18
❑ 200 Bob Griese 6.00 2.70
❑ 201 Earlie Thomas .40 .18
❑ 202 Carl Gersbach .40 .18
❑ 203 Jim Harrison .40 .18
❑ 204 Jake Kupp .40 .18
❑ 205 Merlin Olsen 2.00 .90
❑ 206 Spider Lockhart .75 .35
❑ 207 Walker Gillette .40 .18
❑ 208 Verlon Biggs .40 .18
❑ 209 Bob James .40 .18
❑ 210 Bob Trumpy 1.50 .70
❑ 211 Jerry Sherk HOR .40 .18
❑ 212 Andy Maurer .40 .18
❑ 213 Fred Carr .40 .18
❑ 214 Mick Tingelhoff .75 .35
❑ 215 Steve Spurrier 15.00 6.75
❑ 216 Richard Harris .40 .18
❑ 217 Charlie Greer .40 .18
❑ 218 Buck Buchanan 1.50 .70
❑ 219 Ray Guy RC 10.00 4.50
❑ 220 Franco Harris 12.00 5.50
❑ 221 Darryl Stingley RC 1.50 .70
❑ 222 Rex Kern .40 .18
❑ 223 Toni Fritsch .75 .35
❑ 224 Levi Johnson .40 .18
❑ 225 Bob Kuechenberg .75 .35
❑ 226 Elvin Bethea .75 .35
❑ 227 Al Woodall RC .75 .35
❑ 228 Terry Owens .40 .18
❑ 229 Bivian Lee .40 .18
❑ 230 Dick Butkus 10.00 4.50
❑ 231 Jim Bertelsen RC .75 .35
❑ 232 John Mendenhall RC .40 .18
❑ 233 Conrad Dobler RC 1.50 .70
❑ 234 J.D. Hill .75 .35
❑ 235 Ken Houston 1.50 .70
❑ 236 Dave Lewis .40 .18
❑ 237 John Garlington .40 .18
❑ 238 Bill Sandeman .40 .18
❑ 239 Alden Roche .40 .18
❑ 240 John Gilliam .75 .35
❑ 241 Bruce Taylor .40 .18
❑ 242 Vern Winfield .40 .18
❑ 243 Bobby Maples .40 .18
❑ 244 Wendell Hayes .40 .18
❑ 245 George Blanda 8.00 3.60
❑ 246 Dwight White .75 .35
❑ 247 Sandy Durko .40 .18
❑ 248 Tom Mitchell .40 .18
❑ 249 Chuck Walton .40 .18
❑ 250 Bob Lilly 3.00 1.35
❑ 251 Doug Swift .40 .18
❑ 252 Lynn Dickey RC 1.50 .70
❑ 253 Jerome Barkum RC .40 .18
❑ 254 Clint Jones .40 .18
❑ 255 Billy Newsome .40 .18
❑ 256 Bob Asher .40 .18
❑ 257 Joe Scibelli .40 .18
❑ 258 Tom Blanchard .40 .18
❑ 259 Norm Thompson .40 .18
❑ 260 Larry Brown 1.50 .70
❑ 261 Paul Seymour .40 .18
❑ 262 Checklist 133-264 4.00 1.00
❑ 263 Doug Dieken RC .40 .18
❑ 264 Lemar Parrish .75 .35
❑ 265 Bob Lee UER .40 .18
(Listed as Atlanta
Hawks on card back)
❑ 266 Bob Brown DT .40 .18
❑ 267 Roy Winston .40 .18
❑ 268 Randy Beisler .40 .18
❑ 269 Joe Dawkins .40 .18
❑ 270 Tom Dempsey .75 .35
❑ 271 Jack Rudnay .40 .18
❑ 272 Art Shell 5.00 2.20
❑ 273 Mike Wagner .75 .35
❑ 274 Rick Cash .40 .18
❑ 275 Greg Landry 1.50 .70
❑ 276 Glenn Ressler .40 .18
❑ 277 Billy Joe DuPree RC 3.00 1.35
❑ 278 Norm Evans .40 .18
❑ 279 Billy Parks .40 .18
❑ 280 John Riggins 6.00 2.70
❑ 281 Lionel Aldridge .40 .18
❑ 282 Steve O'Neal .40 .18
❑ 283 Craig Clemons .40 .18
❑ 284 Willie Williams .40 .18
❑ 285 Isiah Robertson .75 .35
❑ 286 Dennis Shaw .40 .18
❑ 287 Bill Brundige .40 .18
❑ 288 John Leypoldt .40 .18
❑ 289 John DeMarie .40 .18
❑ 290 Mike Reid 1.50 .70
❑ 291 Greg Brezina .40 .18
❑ 292 Willie Buchanon RC .40 .18
❑ 293 Dave Osborn .75 .35
❑ 294 Mel Phillips .40 .18
❑ 295 Haven Moses .75 .35
❑ 296 Wade Key .40 .18
❑ 297 Marvin Upshaw .40 .18
❑ 298 Ray Mansfield .40 .18
❑ 299 Edgar Chandler .40 .18
❑ 300 Marv Hubbard .75 .35
❑ 301 Herman Weaver .40 .18
❑ 302 Jim Bailey .40 .18
❑ 303 D.D. Lewis RC 1.50 .70
❑ 304 Ken Burrough .75 .35
❑ 305 Jake Scott 1.50 .70
❑ 306 Randy Rasmussen .40 .18
❑ 307 Pettis Norman .40 .18
❑ 308 Carl Johnson .40 .18
❑ 309 Joe Taylor .40 .18
❑ 310 Pete Gogolak .40 .18
❑ 311 Tony Baker .40 .18
❑ 312 John Richardson .40 .18
❑ 313 Dave Robinson .75 .35
❑ 314 Reggie McKenzie RC 1.50 .70
❑ 315 Isaac Curtis RC 1.50 .70
❑ 316 Thom Darden .40 .18
❑ 317 Ken Reaves .40 .18
❑ 318 Malcolm Snider .40 .18
❑ 319 Jeff Siemon RC .75 .35
❑ 320 Dan Abramowicz .75 .35
❑ 321 Lyle Alzado 2.00 .90
❑ 322 John Reaves .40 .18
❑ 323 Morris Stroud .40 .18
❑ 324 Bobby Walden .40 .18
❑ 325 Randy Vataha .40 .18
❑ 326 Nemiah Wilson .40 .18
❑ 327 Paul Naumoff .40 .18
❑ 328 Rushing Leaders 3.00 1.35
O.J. Simpson
John Brockington
❑ 329 Passing Leaders 5.00 2.20
Ken Stabler
Roger Staubach
❑ 330 Receiving Leaders 1.50 .70
Fred Willis
Harold Carmichael
❑ 331 Scoring Leaders .75 .35
Roy Gerela
David Ray
❑ 332 Interception Leaders .75 .35
Dick Anderson
Mike Wagner
Bobby Bryant
❑ 333 Punting Leaders .75 .35
Jerrel Wilson
Tom Wittum
❑ 334 Dennis Nelson .40 .18
❑ 335 Walt Garrison .75 .35
❑ 336 Tody Smith .40 .18
❑ 337 Ed Bell .40 .18
❑ 338 Bryant Salter .40 .18
❑ 339 Wayne Colman .40 .18
❑ 340 Garo Yepremian .75 .35
❑ 341 Bob Newton .40 .18
❑ 342 Vince Clements RC .40 .18
❑ 343 Ken Iman .40 .18
❑ 344 Jim Tolbert .40 .18
❑ 345 Chris Hanburger .75 .35
❑ 346 Dave Foley .40 .18
❑ 347 Tommy Casanova .75 .35
❑ 348 John James .40 .18
❑ 349 Clarence Williams .40 .18
❑ 350 Leroy Kelly 1.50 .70
❑ 351 Stu Voigt RC .75 .35
❑ 352 Skip Vanderbundt .40 .18
❑ 353 Pete Duranko .40 .18
❑ 354 John Outlaw .40 .18
❑ 355 Jan Stenerud 1.50 .70
❑ 356 Barry Pearson .40 .18
❑ 357 Brian Dowling RC .40 .18
❑ 358 Dan Conners .40 .18
❑ 359 Bob Bell .40 .18
❑ 360 Rick Volk .40 .18
❑ 361 Pat Toomay .75 .35
❑ 362 Bob Gresham .40 .18
❑ 363 John Schmitt .40 .18
❑ 364 Mel Rogers .40 .18
❑ 365 Manny Fernandez .75 .35
❑ 366 Ernie Jackson .40 .18
❑ 367 Gary Huff RC .75 .35
❑ 368 Bob Grim .40 .18
❑ 369 Ernie McMillan .40 .18
❑ 370 Dave Elmendorf .40 .18
❑ 371 Mike Bragg .40 .18
❑ 372 John Skorupan .40 .18
❑ 373 Howard Fest .40 .18
❑ 374 Jerry Tagge RC .75 .35
❑ 375 Art Malone .40 .18
❑ 376 Bob Babich .40 .18
❑ 377 Jim Marshall 1.50 .70
❑ 378 Bob Hoskins .40 .18
❑ 379 Don Zimmerman .40 .18
❑ 380 Ray May .40 .18
❑ 381 Emmitt Thomas .75 .35
❑ 382 Terry Hanratty .75 .35
❑ 383 John Hannah RC 15.00 6.75
❑ 384 George Atkinson .40 .18
❑ 385 Ted Hendricks 3.00 1.35
❑ 386 Jim O'Brien .40 .18

❑ 387 Jethro Pugh .75 .35
❑ 388 Elbert Drungo .40 .18
❑ 389 Richard Caster .75 .35
❑ 390 Deacon Jones 1.50 .70
❑ 391 Checklist 265-396 4.00 1.00
❑ 392 Jess Phillips .40 .18
❑ 393 Garry Lyle UER .40 .18
(Misspelled Gary
on card front)
❑ 394 Jim Files .40 .18
❑ 395 Jim Hart 1.50 .70
❑ 396 Dave Chapple .40 .18
❑ 397 Jim Langer 2.00 .90
❑ 398 John Wilbur .40 .18
❑ 399 Dwight Harrison .40 .18
❑ 400 John Brockington .75 .35
❑ 401 Ken Anderson 6.00 2.70
❑ 402 Mike Tilleman .40 .18
❑ 403 Charlie Hall .40 .18
❑ 404 Tommy Hart .40 .18
❑ 405 Norm Bulaich .75 .35
❑ 406 Jim Turner .40 .18
❑ 407 Mo Moorman .40 .18
❑ 408 Ralph Anderson .40 .18
❑ 409 Jim Otto 1.50 .70
❑ 410 Andy Russell 1.50 .70
❑ 411 Glenn Doughty .40 .18
❑ 412 Altie Taylor .40 .18
❑ 413 Marv Bateman .40 .18
❑ 414 Willie Alexander .40 .18
❑ 415 Bill Zapalac RC .40 .18
❑ 416 Russ Washington .40 .18
❑ 417 Joe Federspiel .40 .18
❑ 418 Craig Cotton .40 .18
❑ 419 Randy Johnson .40 .18
❑ 420 Harold Jackson 1.50 .70
❑ 421 Roger Wehrli .75 .35
❑ 422 Charlie Harraway .40 .18
❑ 423 Spike Jones .40 .18
❑ 424 Bob Johnson .40 .18
❑ 425 Mike McCoy .40 .18
❑ 426 Dennis Havig HOR .40 .18
❑ 427 Bob McKay .40 .18
❑ 428 Steve Zabel .40 .18
❑ 429 Horace Jones .40 .18
❑ 430 Jim Johnson 1.50 .70
❑ 431 Roy Gerela .75 .35
❑ 432 Tom Graham .40 .18
❑ 433 Curley Culp .75 .35
❑ 434 Ken Mendenhall .40 .18
❑ 435 Jim Plunkett 2.50 1.10
❑ 436 Julian Fagan .40 .18
❑ 437 Mike Garrett .75 .35
❑ 438 Bobby Joe Green .40 .18
❑ 439 Jack Gregory HOR .40 .18
❑ 440 Charlie Sanders .75 .35
❑ 441 Bill Curry .75 .35
❑ 442 Bob Pollard .40 .18
❑ 443 David Ray .40 .18
❑ 444 Terry Metcalf RC 3.00 1.35
❑ 445 Pat Fischer .75 .35
❑ 446 Bob Chandler .75 .35
❑ 447 Bill Bergey .75 .35
❑ 448 Walter Johnson .40 .18
❑ 449 Charlie Young RC 1.50 .70
❑ 450 Chester Marcol .40 .18
❑ 451 Ken Stabler 20.00 9.00
❑ 452 Preston Pearson 1.50 .70
❑ 453 Mike Current .40 .18
❑ 454 Ron Bolton .40 .18
❑ 455 Mark Lomas .40 .18
❑ 456 Raymond Chester .75 .35
❑ 457 Jerry LeVias .75 .35
❑ 458 Skip Butler .40 .18
❑ 459 Mike Livingston RC .40 .18
❑ 460 AFC Semi-Finals .75 .35
Raiders 33,
Steelers 14 and
Dolphins 34,
Bengals 16
❑ 461 NFC Semi-Finals 4.00 1.80
Vikings 27,
Redskins 20 and
Cowboys 27,
Rams 16
(Staubach)
❑ 462 Playoff Championship 3.00 1.35
Dolphins 27,
Raiders 10 and
Vikings 27,
Cowboys 10
(Ken Stabler and
Fran Tarkenton)
❑ 463 Super Bowl 2.00 .90
Dolphins 24,
Vikings 7
❑ 464 Wayne Mulligan .40 .18
❑ 465 Horst Muhlmann .40 .18
❑ 466 Milt Morin .40 .18
❑ 467 Don Parish .40 .18
❑ 468 Richard Neal .40 .18
❑ 469 Ron Jessie .75 .35
❑ 470 Terry Bradshaw 20.00 9.00
❑ 471 Fred Dryer 1.50 .70
❑ 472 Jim Carter .40 .18
❑ 473 Ken Burrow .40 .18
❑ 474 Wally Chambers RC .75 .35
❑ 475 Dan Pastorini 1.50 .70
❑ 476 Don Morrison .40 .18
❑ 477 Carl Mauck .40 .18
❑ 478 Larry Cole RC .75 .35
❑ 479 Jim Kiick 1.50 .70
❑ 480 Willie Lanier 1.50 .70
❑ 481 Don Herrmann .75 .35
❑ 482 George Hunt .40 .18
❑ 483 Bob Howard .40 .18
❑ 484 Myron Pottios .40 .18
❑ 485 Jackie Smith 1.50 .70
❑ 486 Vern Holland .40 .18
❑ 487 Jim Braxton .40 .18
❑ 488 Joe Reed .40 .18
❑ 489 Wally Hilgenberg .40 .18
❑ 490 Fred Biletnikoff 4.00 1.80
❑ 491 Bob DeMarco HOR .40 .18
❑ 492 Mark Nordquist .40 .18
❑ 493 Larry Brooks .40 .18
❑ 494 Pete Athas .40 .18
❑ 495 Emerson Boozer .75 .35
❑ 496 L.C. Greenwood 2.00 .90
❑ 497 Rockne Freitas .40 .18
❑ 498 Checklist 397-528 UER 4.00 1.00
(510 Charlie Taylor
should be Charley)
❑ 499 Joe Schmiesing .40 .18
❑ 500 Roger Staubach 25.00 11.00
❑ 501 Al Cowlings UER .75 .35
(Def. tackle on front,
Def. End on back)
❑ 502 Sam Cunningham RC 1.50 .70
❑ 503 Dennis Partee .40 .18
❑ 504 John Didion .40 .18
❑ 505 Nick Buoniconti 1.50 .70
❑ 506 Carl Garrett .75 .35
❑ 507 Doug Van Horn .40 .18
❑ 508 Jamie Rivers .40 .18
❑ 509 Jack Youngblood 4.00 1.80
❑ 510 Charley Taylor UER 2.50 1.10
(Misspelled Charlie
on both sides)
❑ 511 Ken Riley 1.50 .70
❑ 512 Joe Ferguson RC 2.00 .90
❑ 513 Bill Lueck .40 .18
❑ 514 Ray Brown .40 .18
❑ 515 Fred Cox .40 .18
❑ 516 Joe Jones .40 .18
❑ 517 Larry Schreiber .40 .18
❑ 518 Dennis Wirgowski .40 .18
❑ 519 Leroy Mitchell .40 .18
❑ 520 Otis Taylor 1.50 .70
❑ 521 Henry Davis .40 .18
❑ 522 Bruce Barnes .40 .18
❑ 523 Charlie Smith .40 .18
❑ 524 Bert Jones RC 5.00 2.20
❑ 525 Lem Barney 2.00 .90
❑ 526 John Fitzgerald RC .40 .18
❑ 527 Tom Funchess .40 .18
❑ 528 Steve Tannen 1.50 .70

1975 Topps

NRMT-MT EXC
COMPLETE SET (528) 300.00 135.00

❑ 1 Rushing Leaders 1.50 .35
Lawrence McCutcheon
Otis Armstrong
❑ 2 Passing Leaders 1.50 .70
Sonny Jurgensen
Ken Anderson
❑ 3 Receiving Leaders 1.50 .70
Charlie Young
Lydell Mitchell
❑ 4 Scoring Leaders .75 .35
Chester Marcol
Roy Gerela
❑ 5 Interception Leaders .75 .35
Ray Brown
Emmitt Thomas
❑ 6 Punting Leaders 1.50 .70
Tom Blanchard
Ray Guy
❑ 7 George Blanda 5.00 2.20
(Black jersey;
highlights on back)
❑ 8 George Blanda 5.00 2.20
(White jersey;
career record on back)
❑ 9 Ralph Baker .30 .14
❑ 10 Don Woods .30 .14
❑ 11 Bob Asher .30 .14
❑ 12 Mel Blount RC 20.00 9.00
❑ 13 Sam Cunningham .75 .35
❑ 14 Jackie Smith 1.50 .70
❑ 15 Greg Landry .75 .35
❑ 16 Buck Buchanan 1.50 .70
❑ 17 Haven Moses .75 .35
❑ 18 Clarence Ellis .30 .14
❑ 19 Jim Carter .30 .14
❑ 20 Charley Taylor UER 2.00 .90
(Misspelled Charlie
on card front)
❑ 21 Jess Phillips .30 .14
❑ 22 Larry Seiple .30 .14
❑ 23 Doug Dieken .30 .14
❑ 24 Ron Saul .30 .14
❑ 25 Isaac Curtis UER 1.50 .70
(Misspelled Issac
on card front)
❑ 26 Gary Larsen RC .30 .14
❑ 27 Bruce Jarvis .30 .14
❑ 28 Steve Zabel .30 .14
❑ 29 John Mendenhall .30 .14
❑ 30 Rick Volk .30 .14
❑ 31 Checklist 1-132 4.00 1.00
❑ 32 Dan Abramowicz .75 .35
❑ 33 Bubba Smith 1.50 .70
❑ 34 David Ray .30 .14
❑ 35 Dan Dierdorf 4.00 1.80
❑ 36 Randy Rasmussen .30 .14
❑ 37 Bob Howard .30 .14
❑ 38 Gary Huff .75 .35
❑ 39 Rocky Bleier RC 20.00 9.00
❑ 40 Mel Gray .75 .35
❑ 41 Tony McGee .30 .14
❑ 42 Larry Hand .30 .14
❑ 43 Wendell Hayes .30 .14
❑ 44 Doug Wilkerson RC .30 .14
❑ 45 Paul Smith .30 .14
❑ 46 Dave Robinson .75 .35
❑ 47 Bivian Lee .30 .14

- ❑ 48 Jim Mandich RC .75 .35
- ❑ 49 Greg Pruitt 1.50 .70
- ❑ 50 Dan Pastorini UER 1.50 .70
  (5/26/39 birthdate incorrect)
- ❑ 51 Ron Pritchard .30 .14
- ❑ 52 Dan Conners .30 .14
- ❑ 53 Fred Cox .30 .14
- ❑ 54 Tony Greene .30 .14
- ❑ 55 Craig Morton 1.50 .70
- ❑ 56 Jerry Sisemore .30 .14
- ❑ 57 Glenn Doughty .30 .14
- ❑ 58 Larry Schreiber .30 .14
- ❑ 59 Charlie Waters RC 4.00 1.80
- ❑ 60 Jack Youngblood 1.50 .70
- ❑ 61 Bill Lenkaitis .30 .14
- ❑ 62 Greg Brezina .30 .14
- ❑ 63 Bob Pollard .30 .14
- ❑ 64 Mack Alston .30 .14
- ❑ 65 Drew Pearson RC 20.00 9.00
- ❑ 66 Charlie Stukes .30 .14
- ❑ 67 Emerson Boozer .75 .35
- ❑ 68 Dennis Partee .30 .14
- ❑ 69 Bob Newton .30 .14
- ❑ 70 Jack Tatum 1.50 .70
- ❑ 71 Frank Lewis .30 .14
- ❑ 72 Bob Young .30 .14
- ❑ 73 Julius Adams .30 .14
- ❑ 74 Paul Naumoff .30 .14
- ❑ 75 Otis Taylor 1.50 .70
- ❑ 76 Dave Hampton .30 .14
- ❑ 77 Mike Current .30 .14
- ❑ 78 Brig Owens .30 .14
- ❑ 79 Bobby Scott .30 .14
- ❑ 80 Harold Carmichael 3.00 1.35
- ❑ 81 Bill Stanfill .30 .14
- ❑ 82 Bob Babich .30 .14
- ❑ 83 Vic Washington .30 .14
- ❑ 84 Mick Tingelhoff .75 .35
- ❑ 85 Bob Trumpy 1.50 .70
- ❑ 86 Earl Edwards .30 .14
- ❑ 87 Ron Hornsby .30 .14
- ❑ 88 Don McCauley .30 .14
- ❑ 89 Jim Johnson 1.50 .70
- ❑ 90 Andy Russell .75 .35
- ❑ 91 Cornell Green 1.50 .70
- ❑ 92 Charlie Cowan .30 .14
- ❑ 93 Jon Staggers .30 .14
- ❑ 94 Billy Newsome .30 .14
- ❑ 95 Willie Brown 1.50 .70
- ❑ 96 Carl Mauck .30 .14
- ❑ 97 Doug Buffone .30 .14
- ❑ 98 Preston Pearson .75 .35
- ❑ 99 Jim Bakken .30 .14
- ❑ 100 Bob Griese 5.00 2.20
- ❑ 101 Bob Windsor .30 .14
- ❑ 102 Rockne Freitas .30 .14
- ❑ 103 Jim Marsalis .30 .14
- ❑ 104 Bill Thompson .75 .35
- ❑ 105 Ken Burrow .30 .14
- ❑ 106 Diron Talbert .30 .14
- ❑ 107 Joe Federspiel .30 .14
- ❑ 108 Norm Bulaich .75 .35
- ❑ 109 Bob DeMarco .30 .14
- ❑ 110 Tom Wittum .30 .14
- ❑ 111 Larry Hefner .30 .14
- ❑ 112 Tody Smith .30 .14
- ❑ 113 Stu Voigt .30 .14
- ❑ 114 Horst Muhlmann .30 .14
- ❑ 115 Ahmad Rashad 6.00 2.70
- ❑ 116 Joe Dawkins .30 .14
- ❑ 117 George Kunz .30 .14
- ❑ 118 D.D. Lewis .75 .35
- ❑ 119 Levi Johnson .30 .14
- ❑ 120 Len Dawson 4.00 1.80
- ❑ 121 Jim Bertelsen .30 .14
- ❑ 122 Ed Bell .30 .14
- ❑ 123 Art Thoms .30 .14
- ❑ 124 Joe Beauchamp .30 .14
- ❑ 125 Jack Ham 6.00 2.70
- ❑ 126 Carl Garrett .30 .14
- ❑ 127 Roger Finnie .30 .14
- ❑ 128 Howard Twilley .75 .35
- ❑ 129 Bruce Barnes .30 .14
- ❑ 130 Nate Wright .30 .14
- ❑ 131 Jerry Tagge .30 .14
- ❑ 132 Floyd Little 1.50 .70
- ❑ 133 John Zook .30 .14
- ❑ 134 Len Hauss .30 .14
- ❑ 135 Archie Manning 1.50 .70
- ❑ 136 Po James .30 .14
- ❑ 137 Walt Sumner .30 .14
- ❑ 138 Randy Beisler .30 .14
- ❑ 139 Willie Alexander .30 .14
- ❑ 140 Garo Yepremian .75 .35
- ❑ 141 Chip Myers .30 .14
- ❑ 142 Jim Braxton .30 .14
- ❑ 143 Doug Van Horn .30 .14
- ❑ 144 Stan White .30 .14
- ❑ 145 Roger Staubach 25.00 11.00
- ❑ 146 Herman Weaver .30 .14
- ❑ 147 Marvin Upshaw .30 .14
- ❑ 148 Bob Klein .30 .14
- ❑ 149 Earlie Thomas .30 .14
- ❑ 150 John Brockington .75 .35
- ❑ 151 Mike Siani .30 .14
- ❑ 152 Sam Davis .30 .14
- ❑ 153 Mike Wagner .75 .35
- ❑ 154 Larry Stallings .30 .14
- ❑ 155 Wally Chambers .30 .14
- ❑ 156 Randy Vataha .30 .14
- ❑ 157 Jim Marshall 1.50 .70
- ❑ 158 Jim Turner .30 .14
- ❑ 159 Walt Sweeney .30 .14
- ❑ 160 Ken Anderson 4.00 1.80
- ❑ 161 Ray Brown .30 .14
- ❑ 162 John Didion .30 .14
- ❑ 163 Tom Dempsey .30 .14
- ❑ 164 Clarence Scott .30 .14
- ❑ 165 Gene Washington .75 .35
- ❑ 166 Willie Rogers .30 .14
- ❑ 167 Doug Swift .30 .14
- ❑ 168 Rufus Mayes .30 .14
- ❑ 169 Marv Bateman .30 .14
- ❑ 170 Lydell Mitchell .75 .35
- ❑ 171 Ron Smith .30 .14
- ❑ 172 Bill Munson .75 .35
- ❑ 173 Bob Grim .30 .14
- ❑ 174 Ed Budde .30 .14
- ❑ 175 Bob Lilly UER 3.00 1.35
  (Was first draft, not first player)
- ❑ 176 Jim Youngblood RC 1.50 .70
- ❑ 177 Steve Tannen .30 .14
- ❑ 178 Rich McGeorge .30 .14
- ❑ 179 Jim Tyrer .30 .14
- ❑ 180 Forrest Blue .30 .14
- ❑ 181 Jerry LeVias .75 .35
- ❑ 182 Joe Gilliam RC .30 .14
- ❑ 183 Jim Otis RC .75 .35
- ❑ 184 Mel Tom .30 .14
- ❑ 185 Paul Seymour .30 .14
- ❑ 186 George Webster .30 .14
- ❑ 187 Pete Duranko .30 .14
- ❑ 188 Essex Johnson .30 .14
- ❑ 189 Bob Lee .75 .35
- ❑ 190 Gene Upshaw 1.50 .70
- ❑ 191 Tom Myers .30 .14
- ❑ 192 Don Zimmerman .30 .14
- ❑ 193 John Garlington .30 .14
- ❑ 194 Skip Butler .30 .14
- ❑ 195 Tom Mitchell .30 .14
- ❑ 196 Jim Langer 1.50 .70
- ❑ 197 Ron Carpenter .30 .14
- ❑ 198 Dave Foley .30 .14
- ❑ 199 Bert Jones 1.50 .70
- ❑ 200 Larry Brown .75 .35
- ❑ 201 All Pro Receivers 2.00 .90
  Charley Taylor
  Fred Biletnikoff
- ❑ 202 All Pro Tackles .30 .14
  Rayfield Wright
  Russ Washington
- ❑ 203 All Pro Guards 1.50 .70
  Tom Mack
  Larry Little
- ❑ 204 All Pro Centers .30 .14
  Jeff Van Note
  Jack Rudnay
- ❑ 205 All Pro Guards 1.50 .70
  Gale Gillingham
  John Hannah
- ❑ 206 All Pro Tackles 1.50 .70
  Dan Dierdorf
  Winston Hill
- ❑ 207 All Pro Tight Ends .75 .35
  Charlie Young
  Riley Odoms
- ❑ 208 All Pro Quarterbacks 4.00 1.80
  Fran Tarkenton
  Ken Stabler
- ❑ 209 All Pro Backs 3.00 1.35
  Lawrence McCutcheon
  O.J. Simpson
- ❑ 210 All Pro Backs .75 .35
  Terry Metcalf
  Otis Armstrong
- ❑ 211 All Pro Receivers .75 .35
  Mel Gray
  Isaac Curtis
- ❑ 212 All Pro Kickers .30 .14
  Chester Marcol
  Roy Gerela
- ❑ 213 All Pro Ends .75 .35
  Jack Youngblood
  Elvin Bethea
- ❑ 214 All Pro Tackles .75 .35
  Alan Page
  Otis Sistrunk
- ❑ 215 All Pro Tackles 1.50 .70
  Merlin Olsen
  Mike Reid
- ❑ 216 All Pro Ends 1.50 .70
  Carl Eller
  Lyle Alzado
- ❑ 217 All Pro Linebackers 1.50 .70
  Ted Hendricks
  Phil Villapiano
- ❑ 218 All Pro Linebackers 1.50 .70
  Lee Roy Jordan
  Willie Lanier
- ❑ 219 All Pro Linebackers .75 .35
  Isiah Robertson
  Andy Russell
- ❑ 220 All Pro Cornerbacks .30 .14
  Nate Wright
  Emmitt Thomas
- ❑ 221 All Pro Cornerbacks .30 .14
  Willie Buchanon
  Lemar Parrish
- ❑ 222 All Pro Safeties .75 .35
  Ken Houston
  Dick Anderson
- ❑ 223 All Pro Safeties 1.50 .70
  Cliff Harris
  Jack Tatum
- ❑ 224 All Pro Punters .75 .35
  Tom Wittum
  Ray Guy
- ❑ 225 All Pro Returners .75 .35
  Terry Metcalf
  Greg Pruitt
- ❑ 226 Ted Kwalick .30 .14
- ❑ 227 Spider Lockhart .75 .35
- ❑ 228 Mike Livingston .30 .14
- ❑ 229 Larry Cole .30 .14
- ❑ 230 Gary Garrison .30 .14
- ❑ 231 Larry Brooks .30 .14
- ❑ 232 Bobby Howfield .30 .14
- ❑ 233 Fred Carr .30 .14
- ❑ 234 Norm Evans .30 .14
- ❑ 235 Dwight White .75 .35
- ❑ 236 Conrad Dobler .75 .35
- ❑ 237 Garry Lyle .30 .14
- ❑ 238 Darryl Stingley 1.50 .70
- ❑ 239 Tom Graham .30 .14
- ❑ 240 Chuck Foreman 1.50 .70
- ❑ 241 Ken Riley .75 .35
- ❑ 242 Don Morrison .30 .14
- ❑ 243 Lynn Dickey .75 .35
- ❑ 244 Don Cockroft .30 .14
- ❑ 245 Claude Humphrey .75 .35
- ❑ 246 John Skorupan .30 .14
- ❑ 247 Raymond Chester .75 .35
- ❑ 248 Cas Banaszek .30 .14
- ❑ 249 Art Malone .30 .14
- ❑ 250 Ed Flanagan .30 .14
- ❑ 251 Checklist 133-264 4.00 1.00

❑ 252 Nemiah Wilson .30 .14
❑ 253 Ron Jessie .30 .14
❑ 254 Jim Lynch .30 .14
❑ 255 Bob Tucker .75 .35
❑ 256 Terry Owens .30 .14
❑ 257 John Fitzgerald .30 .14
❑ 258 Jack Snow .75 .35
❑ 259 Garry Puetz .30 .14
❑ 260 Mike Phipps .75 .35
❑ 261 Al Matthews .30 .14
❑ 262 Bob Kuechenberg .30 .14
❑ 263 Ron Yankowski .30 .14
❑ 264 Ron Shanklin .30 .14
❑ 265 Bobby Douglass .75 .35
❑ 266 Josh Ashton .30 .14
❑ 267 Bill Van Heusen .30 .14
❑ 268 Jeff Siemon .30 .14
❑ 269 Bob Newland .30 .14
❑ 270 Gale Gillingham .30 .14
❑ 271 Zeke Moore .30 .14
❑ 272 Mike Tilleman .30 .14
❑ 273 John Leypoldt .30 .14
❑ 274 Ken Mendenhall .30 .14
❑ 275 Norm Snead .75 .35
❑ 276 Bill Bradley .75 .35
❑ 277 Jerry Smith .30 .14
❑ 278 Clarence Davis .30 .14
❑ 279 Jim Yarbrough .30 .14
❑ 280 Lemar Parrish .30 .14
❑ 281 Bobby Bell 1.50 .70
❑ 282 Lynn Swann RC UER 60.00 27.00
(Wide Reciever on front)
❑ 283 John Hicks .30 .14
❑ 284 Coy Bacon .75 .35
❑ 285 Lee Roy Jordan 1.50 .70
❑ 286 Willie Buchanon .30 .14
❑ 287 Al Woodall .30 .14
❑ 288 Reggie Rucker .75 .35
❑ 289 John Schmitt .30 .14
❑ 290 Carl Eller 1.50 .70
❑ 291 Jake Scott .75 .35
❑ 292 Donny Anderson .75 .35
❑ 293 Charley Wade .30 .14
❑ 294 John Tanner .30 .14
❑ 295 Charlie Johnson .75 .35
(Misspelled Charley
on both sides)
❑ 296 Tom Blanchard .30 .14
❑ 297 Curley Culp .75 .35
❑ 298 Jeff Van Note RC .75 .35
❑ 299 Bob James .30 .14
❑ 300 Franco Harris 8.00 3.60
❑ 301 Tim Berra .75 .35
❑ 302 Bruce Gossett .30 .14
❑ 303 Verlon Biggs .30 .14
❑ 304 Bob Kowalkowski .30 .14
❑ 305 Marv Hubbard .30 .14
❑ 306 Ken Avery .30 .14
❑ 307 Mike Adamle .30 .14
❑ 308 Don Herrmann .30 .14
❑ 309 Chris Fletcher .30 .14
❑ 310 Roman Gabriel 1.50 .70
❑ 311 Billy Joe DuPree 1.50 .70
❑ 312 Fred Dryer 1.50 .70
❑ 313 John Riggins 5.00 2.20
❑ 314 Bob McKay .30 .14
❑ 315 Ted Hendricks 1.50 .70
❑ 316 Bobby Bryant .30 .14
❑ 317 Don Nottingham .30 .14
❑ 318 John Hannah 4.00 1.80
❑ 319 Rich Coady .30 .14
❑ 320 Phil Villapiano .75 .35
❑ 321 Jim Plunkett 1.50 .70
❑ 322 Lyle Alzado 1.50 .70
❑ 323 Ernie Jackson .30 .14
❑ 324 Billy Parks .30 .14
❑ 325 Willie Lanier 1.50 .70
❑ 326 John James .30 .14
❑ 327 Joe Ferguson .75 .35
❑ 328 Ernie Holmes RC 1.50 .70
❑ 329 Bruce Laird .30 .14
❑ 330 Chester Marcol .30 .14
❑ 331 Dave Wilcox .75 .35
❑ 332 Pat Fischer .75 .35
❑ 333 Steve Owens .75 .35
❑ 334 Royce Berry .30 .14

❑ 335 Russ Washington .30 .14
❑ 336 Walker Gillette .30 .14
❑ 337 Mark Nordquist .30 .14
❑ 338 James Harris RC 1.50 .70
❑ 339 Warren Koegel .30 .14
❑ 340 Emmitt Thomas .75 .35
❑ 341 Walt Garrison .75 .35
❑ 342 Thom Darden .30 .14
❑ 343 Mike Eischeid .30 .14
❑ 344 Ernie McMillan .30 .14
❑ 345 Nick Buoniconti 1.50 .70
❑ 346 George Farmer .30 .14
❑ 347 Sam Adams .30 .14
❑ 348 Larry Cipa .30 .14
❑ 349 Bob Moore .30 .14
❑ 350 Otis Armstrong RC 1.50 .70
❑ 351 George Blanda RB 3.00 1.35
All Time Scoring
Leader
❑ 352 Fred Cox RB .75 .35
151 Straight PAT's
❑ 353 Tom Dempsey RB .75 .35
63 Yard FG
❑ 354 Ken Houston RB 1.50 .70
9th Int. for TD
(Shown as Oiler,
should be Redskin)
❑ 355 O.J. Simpson RB 5.00 2.20
2003 Yard Season
❑ 356 Ron Smith RB .75 .35
All Time Return
Yardage Mark
❑ 357 Bob Atkins .30 .14
❑ 358 Pat Sullivan .75 .35
❑ 359 Joe DeLamielleure .75 .35
❑ 360 L.McCutcheon RC 1.50 .70
❑ 361 David Lee .30 .14
❑ 362 Mike McCoy .30 .14
❑ 363 Skip Vanderbundt .30 .14
❑ 364 Mark Moseley .75 .35
❑ 365 Lem Barney 1.50 .70
❑ 366 Doug Dressler .30 .14
❑ 367 Dan Fouts RC 45.00 20.00
❑ 368 Bob Hyland .30 .14
❑ 369 John Outlaw .30 .14
❑ 370 Roy Gerela .30 .14
❑ 371 Isiah Robertson .75 .35
❑ 372 Jerome Barkum .30 .14
❑ 373 Ed Podolak .30 .14
❑ 374 Milt Morin .30 .14
❑ 375 John Niland .30 .14
❑ 376 Checklist 265-396 UER 4.00 1.00
(295 Charlie Johnson
missppelled as Charley)
❑ 377 Ken Iman .30 .14
❑ 378 Manny Fernandez .75 .35
❑ 379 Dave Gallagher .30 .14
❑ 380 Ken Stabler 15.00 6.75
❑ 381 Mack Herron .30 .14
❑ 382 Bill McClard .30 .14
❑ 383 Ray May .30 .14
❑ 384 Don Hansen .30 .14
❑ 385 Elvin Bethea .75 .35
❑ 386 Joe Scibelli .30 .14
❑ 387 Neal Craig .30 .14
❑ 388 Marty Domres .30 .14
❑ 389 Ken Ellis .30 .14
❑ 390 Charlie Young .75 .35
❑ 391 Tommy Hart .30 .14
❑ 392 Moses Denson .30 .14
❑ 393 Larry Walton .30 .14
❑ 394 Dave Green .30 .14
❑ 395 Ron Johnson .75 .35
❑ 396 Ed Bradley .30 .14
❑ 397 J.T. Thomas .30 .14
❑ 398 Jim Bailey .30 .14
❑ 399 Barry Pearson .30 .14
❑ 400 Fran Tarkenton 8.00 3.60
❑ 401 Jack Rudnay .30 .14
❑ 402 Rayfield Wright .75 .35
❑ 403 Roger Wehrli .75 .35
❑ 404 Vern Den Herder .30 .14
❑ 405 Fred Biletnikoff 3.00 1.35
❑ 406 Ken Grandberry .30 .14
❑ 407 Bob Adams .30 .14
❑ 408 Jim Merlo .30 .14

❑ 409 John Pitts .30 .14
❑ 410 Dave Osborn .75 .35
❑ 411 Dennis Havig .30 .14
❑ 412 Bob Johnson .30 .14
❑ 413 Ken Burrough UER .75 .35
(Misspelled Burrow
on card front)
❑ 414 Jim Cheyunski .30 .14
❑ 415 MacArthur Lane .30 .14
❑ 416 Joe Theismann RC**/C 25.00 11.00
❑ 417 Mike Boryla RC .30 .14
❑ 418 Bruce Taylor .30 .14
❑ 419 Chris Hanburger .75 .35
❑ 420 Tom Mack .75 .35
❑ 421 Errol Mann .30 .14
❑ 422 Jack Gregory .30 .14
❑ 423 Harrison Davis .30 .14
❑ 424 Burgess Owens .30 .14
❑ 425 Joe Greene 5.00 2.20
❑ 426 Morris Stroud .30 .14
❑ 427 John DeMarie .30 .14
❑ 428 Mel Renfro 1.50 .70
❑ 429 Cid Edwards .30 .14
❑ 430 Mike Reid 1.50 .70
❑ 431 Jack Mildren .30 .14
❑ 432 Jerry Simmons .30 .14
❑ 433 Ron Yary .75 .35
❑ 434 Howard Stevens .30 .14
❑ 435 Ray Guy 2.00 .90
❑ 436 Tommy Nobis 1.50 .70
❑ 437 Solomon Freelon .30 .14
❑ 438 J.D. Hill .75 .35
❑ 439 Toni Linhart .30 .14
❑ 440 Dick Anderson .75 .35
❑ 441 Guy Morriss .30 .14
❑ 442 Bob Hoskins .30 .14
❑ 443 John Hadl 1.50 .70
❑ 444 Roy Jefferson .30 .14
❑ 445 Charlie Sanders .75 .35
❑ 446 Pat Curran .30 .14
❑ 447 David Knight .30 .14
❑ 448 Bob Brown DT .30 .14
❑ 449 Pete Gogolak .30 .14
❑ 450 Terry Metcalf 1.50 .70
❑ 451 Bill Bergey 1.50 .70
❑ 452 Dan Abramowicz HL .75 .35
105 Straight Games
❑ 453 Otis Armstrong HL .75 .35
183 Yard Game
❑ 454 Cliff Branch HL 1.50 .70
13 TD Passes
❑ 455 John James HL .30 .14
Record 96 Punts
❑ 456 Lydell Mitchell HL .75 .35
13 Passes in Game
❑ 457 Lemar Parrish HL .75 .35
3 TD Punt Returns
❑ 458 Ken Stabler HL 5.00 2.20
26 TD Passes
in One Season
❑ 459 Lynn Swann HL 8.00 3.60
577 Yards in
Punt Returns
❑ 460 Emmitt Thomas HL .30 .14
73 Yd. Interception
❑ 461 Terry Bradshaw 20.00 9.00
❑ 462 Jerrel Wilson .30 .14
❑ 463 Walter Johnson .30 .14
❑ 464 Golden Richards .75 .35
❑ 465 Tommy Casanova .75 .35
❑ 466 Randy Jackson .30 .14
❑ 467 Ron Bolton .30 .14
❑ 468 Joe Owens .30 .14
❑ 469 Wally Hilgenberg .30 .14
❑ 470 Riley Odoms .75 .35
❑ 471 Otis Sistrunk .75 .35
❑ 472 Eddie Ray .30 .14
❑ 473 Reggie McKenzie .75 .35
❑ 474 Elbert Drungo .30 .14
❑ 475 Mercury Morris 1.50 .70
❑ 476 Dan Dickel .30 .14
❑ 477 Merritt Kersey .30 .14
❑ 478 Mike Holmes .30 .14
❑ 479 Clarence Williams .30 .14
❑ 480 Billy Kilmer 1.50 .70
❑ 481 Altie Taylor .30 .14

	Player	NRMT-MT	EXC
❑ 482	Dave Elmendorf	.30	.14
❑ 483	Bob Rowe	.30	.14
❑ 484	Pete Athas	.30	.14
❑ 485	Winston Hill	.30	.14
❑ 486	Bo Matthews	.30	.14
❑ 487	Earl Thomas	.30	.14
❑ 488	Jan Stenerud	1.50	.70
❑ 489	Steve Holden	.30	.14
❑ 490	Cliff Harris RC	4.00	1.80
❑ 491	Boobie Clark RC	.75	.35
❑ 492	Joe Taylor	.30	.14
❑ 493	Tom Neville	.30	.14
❑ 494	Wayne Colman	.30	.14
❑ 495	Jim Mitchell	.30	.14
❑ 496	Paul Krause	1.50	.70
❑ 497	Jim Otto	1.50	.70
❑ 498	John Rowser	.30	.14
❑ 499	Larry Little	1.50	.70
❑ 500	O.J. Simpson	10.00	4.50
❑ 501	John Dutton RC	1.50	.70
❑ 502	Pat Hughes	.30	.14
❑ 503	Malcolm Snider	.30	.14
❑ 504	Fred Willis	.30	.14
❑ 505	Harold Jackson	1.50	.70
❑ 506	Mike Bragg	.30	.14
❑ 507	Jerry Sherk	.75	.35
❑ 508	Mirro Roder	.30	.14
❑ 509	Tom Sullivan	.30	.14
❑ 510	Jim Hart	1.50	.70
❑ 511	Cedrick Hardman	.30	.14
❑ 512	Blaine Nye	.30	.14
❑ 513	Elmo Wright	.30	.14
❑ 514	Herb Orvis	.30	.14
❑ 515	Richard Caster	.75	.35
❑ 516	Doug Kotar RC	.30	.14
❑ 517	Checklist 397-528	4.00	1.00
❑ 518	Jesse Freitas	.30	.14
❑ 519	Ken Houston	1.50	.70
❑ 520	Alan Page	1.50	.70
❑ 521	Tim Foley	.75	.35
❑ 522	Bill Olds	.30	.14
❑ 523	Bobby Maples	.30	.14
❑ 524	Cliff Branch RC	15.00	6.75
❑ 525	Merlin Olsen	1.50	.70
❑ 526	AFC Champs. Pittsburgh 24, Oakland 13 (Bradshaw and Franco Harris)	4.00	1.80
❑ 527	NFC Champs Minnesota 14, Los Angeles 10 (C.Foreman tackled)	1.50	.70
❑ 528	Super Bowl IX Steelers 16, Vikings 6 (Bradshaw watching pass)	5.00	1.25

1976 Topps

		NRMT-MT	EXC
	COMPLETE SET (528)	350.00	160.00
❑ 1	George Blanda RB First to Score 2000 Points	5.00	1.25
❑ 2	Neal Colzie RB Punt Returns	.75	.35
❑ 3	Chuck Foreman RB Catches 73 Passes	.75	.35
❑ 4	Jim Marshall RB 26th Fumble Recovery	.75	.35
❑ 5	Terry Metcalf RB Most all-purpose yards; season	.75	.35
❑ 6	O.J. Simpson RB 23 Touchdowns	3.00	1.35
❑ 7	Fran Tarkenton RB Most Attempts;Season	3.00	1.35
❑ 8	Charley Taylor RB Career Receptions	1.50	.70
❑ 9	Ernie Holmes	.75	.35
❑ 10	Ken Anderson AP	1.50	.70
❑ 11	Bobby Bryant	.30	.14
❑ 12	Jerry Smith	.75	.35
❑ 13	David Lee	.30	.14
❑ 14	Robert Newhouse RC	1.50	.70
❑ 15	Vern Den Herder	.30	.14
❑ 16	John Hannah	1.50	.70
❑ 17	J.D. Hill	.75	.35
❑ 18	James Harris	.75	.35
❑ 19	Willie Buchanon	.30	.14
❑ 20	Charlie Young AP	.75	.35
❑ 21	Jim Yarbrough	.30	.14
❑ 22	Ronnie Coleman	.30	.14
❑ 23	Don Cockroft	.30	.14
❑ 24	Willie Lanier	1.50	.70
❑ 25	Fred Biletnikoff	3.00	1.35
❑ 26	Ron Yankowski	.30	.14
❑ 27	Spider Lockhart	.30	.14
❑ 28	Bob Johnson	.30	.14
❑ 29	J.T. Thomas	.30	.14
❑ 30	Ron Yary AP	.75	.35
❑ 31	Brad Dusek RC	.30	.14
❑ 32	Raymond Chester	.75	.35
❑ 33	Larry Little	1.50	.70
❑ 34	Pat Leahy RC	1.50	.70
❑ 35	Steve Bartkowski RC	4.00	1.80
❑ 36	Tom Myers	.30	.14
❑ 37	Bill Van Heusen	.30	.14
❑ 38	Russ Washington	.30	.14
❑ 39	Tom Sullivan	.30	.14
❑ 40	Curley Culp AP	.75	.35
❑ 41	Johnnie Gray	.30	.14
❑ 42	Bob Klein	.30	.14
❑ 43	Lem Barney	1.50	.70
❑ 44	Harvey Martin RC	5.00	2.20
❑ 45	Reggie Rucker	.75	.35
❑ 46	Neil Clabo	.30	.14
❑ 47	Ray Hamilton	.30	.14
❑ 48	Joe Ferguson	.75	.35
❑ 49	Ed Podolak	.30	.14
❑ 50	Ray Guy AP	1.50	.70
❑ 51	Glen Edwards	.30	.14
❑ 52	Jim LeClair	.30	.14
❑ 53	Mike Barnes	.30	.14
❑ 54	Nat Moore RC	1.50	.70
❑ 55	Billy Kilmer	1.50	.70
❑ 56	Larry Stallings	.30	.14
❑ 57	Jack Gregory	.30	.14
❑ 58	Steve Mike-Mayer	.30	.14
❑ 59	Virgil Livers	.30	.14
❑ 60	Jerry Sherk AP	.75	.35
❑ 61	Guy Morriss	.30	.14
❑ 62	Barty Smith	.30	.14
❑ 63	Jerome Barkum	.30	.14
❑ 64	Ira Gordon	.30	.14
❑ 65	Paul Krause	1.50	.70
❑ 66	John McMakin	.30	.14
❑ 67	Checklist 1-132	3.00	.75
❑ 68	Charlie Johnson UER (Misspelled Charley on both sides)	.75	.35
❑ 69	Tommy Nobis	1.50	.70
❑ 70	Lydell Mitchell	.75	.35
❑ 71	Vern Holland	.30	.14
❑ 72	Tim Foley	.75	.35
❑ 73	Golden Richards	.75	.35
❑ 74	Bryant Salter	.30	.14
❑ 75	Terry Bradshaw	20.00	9.00
❑ 76	Ted Hendricks	1.50	.70
❑ 77	Rich Saul RC	.30	.14
❑ 78	John Smith RC	.30	.14
❑ 79	Altie Taylor	.30	.14
❑ 80	Cedrick Hardman AP	.30	.14
❑ 81	Ken Payne	.30	.14
❑ 82	Zeke Moore	.30	.14
❑ 83	Alvin Maxson	.30	.14
❑ 84	Wally Hilgenberg	.30	.14
❑ 85	John Niland	.30	.14
❑ 86	Mike Sensibaugh	.30	.14
❑ 87	Ron Johnson	.75	.35
❑ 88	Winston Hill	.30	.14
❑ 89	Charlie Joiner	4.00	1.80
❑ 90	Roger Wehrli AP	.75	.35
❑ 91	Mike Bragg	.30	.14
❑ 92	Dan Dickel	.30	.14
❑ 93	Earl Morrall	.75	.35
❑ 94	Pat Toomay	.30	.14
❑ 95	Gary Garrison	.30	.14
❑ 96	Ken Geddes	.30	.14
❑ 97	Mike Current	.30	.14
❑ 98	Bob Avellini RC	.75	.35
❑ 99	Dave Pureifory	.30	.14
❑ 100	Franco Harris AP	8.00	3.60
❑ 101	Randy Logan	.30	.14
❑ 102	John Fitzgerald	.30	.14
❑ 103	Gregg Bingham RC	.75	.35
❑ 104	Jim Plunkett	1.50	.70
❑ 105	Carl Eller	1.50	.70
❑ 106	Larry Walton	.30	.14
❑ 107	Clarence Scott	.30	.14
❑ 108	Skip Vanderbundt	.30	.14
❑ 109	Boobie Clark	.75	.35
❑ 110	Tom Mack AP	.75	.35
❑ 111	Bruce Laird	.30	.14
❑ 112	Dave Dalby RC	.30	.14
❑ 113	John Leypoldt	.30	.14
❑ 114	Barry Pearson	.30	.14
❑ 115	Larry Brown	.75	.35
❑ 116	Jackie Smith	1.50	.70
❑ 117	Pat Hughes	.30	.14
❑ 118	Al Woodall	.30	.14
❑ 119	John Zook	.30	.14
❑ 120	Jake Scott AP	.75	.35
❑ 121	Rich Glover	.30	.14
❑ 122	Ernie Jackson	.30	.14
❑ 123	Otis Armstrong	1.50	.70
❑ 124	Bob Grim	.30	.14
❑ 125	Jeff Siemon	.75	.35
❑ 126	Harold Hart	.30	.14
❑ 127	John DeMarie	.30	.14
❑ 128	Dan Fouts	12.00	5.50
❑ 129	Jim Kearney	.30	.14
❑ 130	John Dutton AP	.75	.35
❑ 131	Calvin Hill	1.50	.70
❑ 132	Toni Fritsch	.30	.14
❑ 133	Ron Jessie	.30	.14
❑ 134	Don Nottingham	.30	.14
❑ 135	Lemar Parrish	.30	.14
❑ 136	Russ Francis RC	1.50	.70
❑ 137	Joe Reed	.30	.14
❑ 138	C.L. Whittington	.30	.14
❑ 139	Otis Sistrunk	.75	.35
❑ 140	Lynn Swann AP	20.00	9.00
❑ 141	Jim Carter	.30	.14
❑ 142	Mike Montler	.30	.14
❑ 143	Walter Johnson	.30	.14
❑ 144	Doug Kotar	.30	.14
❑ 145	Roman Gabriel	1.50	.70
❑ 146	Billy Newsome	.30	.14
❑ 147	Ed Bradley	.30	.14
❑ 148	Walter Payton RC	250.00	110.00
❑ 149	Johnny Fuller	.30	.14
❑ 150	Alan Page AP	1.50	.70
❑ 151	Frank Grant	.30	.14
❑ 152	Dave Green	.30	.14
❑ 153	Nelson Munsey	.30	.14
❑ 154	Jim Mandich	.30	.14
❑ 155	Lawrence McCutcheon	1.50	.70
❑ 156	Steve Ramsey	.30	.14
❑ 157	Ed Flanagan	.30	.14
❑ 158	Randy White RC	20.00	9.00
❑ 159	Gerry Mullins	.30	.14
❑ 160	Jan Stenerud AP	1.50	.70
❑ 161	Steve Odom	.30	.14
❑ 162	Roger Finnie	.30	.14
❑ 163	Norm Snead	.75	.35
❑ 164	Jeff Van Note	.75	.35

❑ 165 Bill Bergey 1.50 .70
❑ 166 Allen Carter .30 .14
❑ 167 Steve Holden .30 .14
❑ 168 Sherman White .30 .14
❑ 169 Bob Berry .30 .14
❑ 170 Ken Houston AP 1.50 .70
❑ 171 Bill Olds .30 .14
❑ 172 Larry Seiple .30 .14
❑ 173 Cliff Branch 4.00 1.80
❑ 174 Reggie McKenzie .75 .35
❑ 175 Dan Pastorini 1.50 .70
❑ 176 Paul Naumoff .30 .14
❑ 177 Checklist 133-264 3.00 .75
❑ 178 Durwood Keeton .30 .14
❑ 179 Earl Thomas .30 .14
❑ 180 L.C. Greenwood AP 1.50 .70
❑ 181 John Outlaw .30 .14
❑ 182 Frank Nunley .30 .14
❑ 183 Dave Jennings RC .75 .35
❑ 184 MacArthur Lane .30 .14
❑ 185 Chester Marcol .30 .14
❑ 186 J.J. Jones .30 .14
❑ 187 Tom DeLeone .30 .14
❑ 188 Steve Zabel .30 .14
❑ 189 Ken Johnson .30 .14
❑ 190 Rayfield Wright AP .75 .35
❑ 191 Brent McClanahan .30 .14
❑ 192 Pat Fischer .75 .35
❑ 193 Roger Carr RC .75 .35
❑ 194 Manny Fernandez .75 .35
❑ 195 Roy Gerela .30 .14
❑ 196 Dave Elmendorf .30 .14
❑ 197 Bob Kowalkowski .30 .14
❑ 198 Phil Villapiano .75 .35
❑ 199 Will Wynn .30 .14
❑ 200 Terry Metcalf 1.50 .70
❑ 201 Passing Leaders 2.00 .90
Ken Anderson
Fran Tarkenton
❑ 202 Receiving Leaders .75 .35
Reggie Rucker
Lydell Mitchell
Chuck Foreman
❑ 203 Rushing Leaders 2.50 1.10
O.J. Simpson
Jim Otis
❑ 204 Scoring Leaders 2.50 1.10
O.J. Simpson
Chuck Foreman
❑ 205 Interception Leaders 1.50 .70
Mel Blount
Paul Krause
❑ 206 Punting Leaders .75 .35
Ray Guy
Herman Weaver
❑ 207 Ken Ellis .30 .14
❑ 208 Ron Saul .30 .14
❑ 209 Toni Linhart .30 .14
❑ 210 Jim Langer AP 1.50 .70
❑ 211 Jeff Wright .30 .14
❑ 212 Moses Denson .30 .14
❑ 213 Earl Edwards .30 .14
❑ 214 Walker Gillette .30 .14
❑ 215 Bob Trumpy .75 .35
❑ 216 Emmitt Thomas .75 .35
❑ 217 Lyle Alzado 1.50 .70
❑ 218 Carl Garrett .75 .35
❑ 219 Van Green .30 .14
❑ 220 Jack Lambert AP RC 30.00 13.50
❑ 221 Spike Jones .30 .14
❑ 222 John Hadl 1.50 .70
❑ 223 Billy Johnson RC 1.50 .70
❑ 224 Tony McGee .30 .14
❑ 225 Preston Pearson .75 .35
❑ 226 Isiah Robertson .75 .35
❑ 227 Errol Mann .30 .14
❑ 228 Paul Seal .30 .14
❑ 229 Roland Harper RC .30 .14
❑ 230 Ed White AP RC .75 .35
❑ 231 Joe Theismann 6.00 2.70
❑ 232 Jim Cheyunski .30 .14
❑ 233 Bill Stanfill .75 .35
❑ 234 Marv Hubbard .30 .14
❑ 235 Tommy Casanova .75 .35
❑ 236 Bob Hyland .30 .14
❑ 237 Jesse Freitas .30 .14
❑ 238 Norm Thompson .30 .14
❑ 239 Charlie Smith .30 .14
❑ 240 John James AP .30 .14
❑ 241 Alden Roche .30 .14
❑ 242 Gordon Jolley .30 .14
❑ 243 Larry Ely .30 .14
❑ 244 Richard Caster .30 .14
❑ 245 Joe Greene 5.00 2.20
❑ 246 Larry Schreiber .30 .14
❑ 247 Terry Schmidt .30 .14
❑ 248 Jerrel Wilson .30 .14
❑ 249 Marty Domres .30 .14
❑ 250 Isaac Curtis AP .75 .35
❑ 251 Harold McLinton .30 .14
❑ 252 Fred Dryer 1.50 .70
❑ 253 Bill Lenkaitis .30 .14
❑ 254 Don Hardeman .30 .14
❑ 255 Bob Griese 4.00 1.80
❑ 256 Oscar Roan RC .30 .14
❑ 257 Randy Gradishar RC 2.50 1.10
❑ 258 Bob Thomas RC .30 .14
❑ 259 Joe Owens .30 .14
❑ 260 Cliff Harris AP 1.50 .70
❑ 261 Frank Lewis .30 .14
❑ 262 Mike McCoy .30 .14
❑ 263 Rickey Young RC .30 .14
❑ 264 Brian Kelley RC .30 .14
❑ 265 Charlie Sanders .75 .35
❑ 266 Jim Hart 1.50 .70
❑ 267 Greg Gantt .30 .14
❑ 268 John Ward .30 .14
❑ 269 Al Beauchamp .30 .14
❑ 270 Jack Tatum AP 1.50 .70
❑ 271 Jim Lash .30 .14
❑ 272 Diron Talbert .30 .14
❑ 273 Checklist 265-396 3.00 .75
❑ 274 Steve Spurrier 8.00 3.60
❑ 275 Greg Pruitt 1.50 .70
❑ 276 Jim Mitchell .30 .14
❑ 277 Jack Rudnay .30 .14
❑ 278 Freddie Solomon RC .75 .35
❑ 279 Frank LeMaster .30 .14
❑ 280 Wally Chambers AP .30 .14
❑ 281 Mike Collier .30 .14
❑ 282 Clarence Williams .30 .14
❑ 283 Mitch Hoopes .30 .14
❑ 284 Ron Bolton .30 .14
❑ 285 Harold Jackson 1.50 .70
❑ 286 Greg Landry .75 .35
❑ 287 Tony Greene .30 .14
❑ 288 Howard Stevens .30 .14
❑ 289 Roy Jefferson .30 .14
❑ 290 Jim Bakken AP .30 .14
❑ 291 Doug Sutherland .30 .14
❑ 292 Marvin Cobb .30 .14
❑ 293 Mack Alston .30 .14
❑ 294 Rod McNeill .30 .14
❑ 295 Gene Upshaw 1.50 .70
❑ 296 Dave Gallagher .30 .14
❑ 297 Larry Ball .30 .14
❑ 298 Ron Howard .30 .14
❑ 299 Don Strock RC 1.50 .70
❑ 300 O.J. Simpson AP 8.00 3.60
❑ 301 Ray Mansfield .30 .14
❑ 302 Larry Marshall .30 .14
❑ 303 Dick Himes .30 .14
❑ 304 Ray Wersching RC .30 .14
❑ 305 John Riggins 4.00 1.80
❑ 306 Bob Parsons .30 .14
❑ 307 Ray Brown .30 .14
❑ 308 Len Dawson 3.00 1.35
❑ 309 Andy Maurer .30 .14
❑ 310 Jack Youngblood AP 1.50 .70
❑ 311 Essex Johnson .30 .14
❑ 312 Stan White .30 .14
❑ 313 Drew Pearson 5.00 2.20
❑ 314 Rockne Freitas .30 .14
❑ 315 Mercury Morris 1.50 .70
❑ 316 Willie Alexander .30 .14
❑ 317 Paul Warfield 3.00 1.35
❑ 318 Bob Chandler .75 .35
❑ 319 Bobby Walden .30 .14
❑ 320 Riley Odoms AP .75 .35
❑ 321 Mike Boryla .30 .14
❑ 322 Bruce Van Dyke .30 .14
❑ 323 Pete Banaszak .30 .14
❑ 324 Darryl Stingley 1.50 .70
❑ 325 John Mendenhall .30 .14
❑ 326 Dan Dierdorf 2.00 .90
❑ 327 Bruce Taylor .30 .14
❑ 328 Don McCauley .30 .14
❑ 329 John Reaves UER .30 .14
(24 attempts in '72; should be 224)
❑ 330 Chris Hanburger AP .75 .35
❑ 331 NFC Champions 3.00 1.35
Cowboys 37,
Rams 7
(Roger Staubach)
❑ 332 AFC Champions 2.00 .90
Steelers 16,
Raiders 10
(Franco Harris)
❑ 333 Super Bowl X 2.50 1.10
Steelers 21,
Cowboys 17
(Terry Bradshaw)
❑ 334 Godwin Turk .30 .14
❑ 335 Dick Anderson .75 .35
❑ 336 Woody Green .30 .14
❑ 337 Pat Curran .30 .14
❑ 338 Council Rudolph .30 .14
❑ 339 Joe Lavender .30 .14
❑ 340 John Gilliam AP .75 .35
❑ 341 Steve Furness RC .75 .35
❑ 342 D.D. Lewis .75 .35
❑ 343 Duane Carrell .30 .14
❑ 344 Jon Morris .30 .14
❑ 345 John Brockington .75 .35
❑ 346 Mike Phipps .75 .35
❑ 347 Lyle Blackwood RC .30 .14
❑ 348 Julius Adams .30 .14
❑ 349 Terry Hermeling .30 .14
❑ 350 R.Lawrence AP RC .30 .14
❑ 351 Glenn Doughty .30 .14
❑ 352 Doug Swift .30 .14
❑ 353 Mike Strachan .30 .14
❑ 354 Craig Morton 1.50 .70
❑ 355 George Blanda 5.00 2.20
❑ 356 Garry Puetz .30 .14
❑ 357 Carl Mauck .30 .14
❑ 358 Walt Patulski .30 .14
❑ 359 Stu Voigt .30 .14
❑ 360 Fred Carr AP .30 .14
❑ 361 Po James .30 .14
❑ 362 Otis Taylor 1.50 .70
❑ 363 Jeff West .30 .14
❑ 364 Gary Huff .75 .35
❑ 365 Dwight White .75 .35
❑ 366 Dan Ryczek .30 .14
❑ 367 Jon Keyworth RC .30 .14
❑ 368 Mel Renfro 1.50 .70
❑ 369 Bruce Coslet RC 1.50 .70
❑ 370 Len Hauss AP .30 .14
❑ 371 Rick Volk .30 .14
❑ 372 Howard Twilley .75 .35
❑ 373 Cullen Bryant RC .75 .35
❑ 374 Bob Babich .30 .14
❑ 375 Herman Weaver .30 .14
❑ 376 Steve Grogan RC 3.00 1.35
❑ 377 Bubba Smith 1.50 .70
❑ 378 Burgess Owens .30 .14
❑ 379 Al Matthews .30 .14
❑ 380 Art Shell 1.50 .70
❑ 381 Larry Brown .30 .14
❑ 382 Horst Muhlmann .30 .14
❑ 383 Ahmad Rashad 2.50 1.10
❑ 384 Bobby Maples .30 .14
❑ 385 Jim Marshall 1.50 .70
❑ 386 Joe Dawkins .30 .14
❑ 387 Dennis Partee .30 .14
❑ 388 Eddie McMillan .30 .14
❑ 389 Randy Johnson .30 .14
❑ 390 Bob Kuechenberg AP .30 .14
❑ 391 Rufus Mayes .30 .14
❑ 392 Lloyd Mumphord .30 .14
❑ 393 Ike Harris .30 .14
❑ 394 Dave Hampton .30 .14
❑ 395 Roger Staubach 20.00 9.00
❑ 396 Doug Buffone .30 .14
❑ 397 Howard Fest .30 .14
❑ 398 Wayne Mulligan .30 .14
❑ 399 Bill Bradley .75 .35

❑ 400 Chuck Foreman AP 1.50 .70
❑ 401 Jack Snow .75 .35
❑ 402 Bob Howard .30 .14
❑ 403 John Matuszak 1.50 .70
❑ 404 Bill Munson .75 .35
❑ 405 Andy Russell .75 .35
❑ 406 Skip Butler .30 .14
❑ 407 Hugh McKinnis .30 .14
❑ 408 Bob Penchion .30 .14
❑ 409 Mike Bass .30 .14
❑ 410 George Kunz AP .30 .14
❑ 411 Ron Pritchard .30 .14
❑ 412 Barry Smith .30 .14
❑ 413 Norm Bulaich .30 .14
❑ 414 Marv Bateman .30 .14
❑ 415 Ken Stabler 12.00 5.50
❑ 416 Conrad Dobler .75 .35
❑ 417 Bob Tucker .75 .35
❑ 418 Gene Washington .75 .35
❑ 419 Ed Marinaro 1.50 .70
❑ 420 Jack Ham AP 4.00 1.80
❑ 421 Jim Turner .30 .14
❑ 422 Chris Fletcher .30 .14
❑ 423 Carl Barzilauskas .30 .14
❑ 424 Robert Brazile RC 1.50 .70
❑ 425 Harold Carmichael 2.00 .90
❑ 426 Ron Jaworski RC 5.00 2.20
❑ 427 Ed Too Tall Jones RC 20.00 9.00
❑ 428 Larry McCarren .30 .14
❑ 429 Mike Thomas RC .30 .14
❑ 430 Joe DeLamielleure AP .30 .14
❑ 431 Tom Blanchard .30 .14
❑ 432 Ron Carpenter .30 .14
❑ 433 Levi Johnson .30 .14
❑ 434 Sam Cunningham .75 .35
❑ 435 Garo Yepremian .75 .35
❑ 436 Mike Livingston .30 .14
❑ 437 Larry Csonka 4.00 1.80
❑ 438 Doug Dieken .75 .35
❑ 439 Bill Lueck .30 .14
❑ 440 Tom MacLeod AP .30 .14
❑ 441 Mick Tingelhoff .75 .35
❑ 442 Terry Hanratty .75 .35
❑ 443 Mike Siani .30 .14
❑ 444 Dwight Harrison .30 .14
❑ 445 Jim Otis .75 .35
❑ 446 Jack Reynolds .75 .35
❑ 447 Jean Fugett RC .75 .35
❑ 448 Dave Beverly .30 .14
❑ 449 Bernard Jackson RC .30 .14
❑ 450 Charley Taylor 2.00 .90
❑ 451 Atlanta Falcons 2.00 .50
Team Checklist
❑ 452 Baltimore Colts 2.00 .50
Team Checklist
❑ 453 Buffalo Bills 2.00 .50
Team Checklist
❑ 454 Chicago Bears 2.00 .50
Team Checklist
❑ 455 Cincinnati Bengals 2.00 .50
Team Checklist
❑ 456 Cleveland Browns 2.00 .50
Team Checklist
❑ 457 Dallas Cowboys 2.00 .50
Team Checklist
❑ 458 Denver Broncos UER 2.00 .50
Team Checklist
(Charlie Johnson
spelled Charley)
❑ 459 Detroit Lions 2.00 .50
Team Checklist
❑ 460 Green Bay Packers 2.00 .50
Team Checklist
❑ 461 Houston Oilers 2.00 .50
Team Checklist
❑ 462 Kansas City Chiefs 2.00 .50
Team Checklist
❑ 463 Los Angeles Rams 2.00 .50
Team Checklist
❑ 464 Miami Dolphins 2.00 .50
Team Checklist
❑ 465 Minnesota Vikings 2.00 .50
Team Checklist
❑ 466 New England Patriots 2.00 .50
Team Checklist
❑ 467 New Orleans Saints 2.00 .50
Team Checklist
❑ 468 New York Giants 2.00 .50
Team Checklist
❑ 469 New York Jets 2.00 .50
Team Checklist
❑ 470 Oakland Raiders 2.00 .50
Team Checklist
❑ 471 Philadelphia Eagles 2.00 .50
Team Checklist
❑ 472 Pittsburgh Steelers 2.00 .50
Team Checklist
❑ 473 St. Louis Cardinals 2.00 .50
Team Checklist
❑ 474 San Diego Chargers 2.00 .50
Team Checklist
❑ 475 San Francisco 49ers 2.00 .50
Team Checklist
❑ 476 Seattle Seahawks 2.00 .50
Team Checklist
❑ 477 Tampa Bay Buccaneers 2.00 .50
Team Checklist
❑ 478 Washington Redskins 2.00 .50
Team Checklist
❑ 479 Fred Cox .30 .14
❑ 480 Mel Blount AP 6.00 2.70
❑ 481 John Bunting .30 .14
❑ 482 Ken Mendenhall .30 .14
❑ 483 Will Harrell .30 .14
❑ 484 Marlin Briscoe .30 .14
❑ 485 Archie Manning 1.50 .70
❑ 486 Tody Smith .30 .14
❑ 487 George Hunt .30 .14
❑ 488 Roscoe Word .30 .14
❑ 489 Paul Seymour .30 .14
❑ 490 Lee Roy Jordan AP 1.50 .70
❑ 491 Chip Myers .30 .14
❑ 492 Norm Evans .30 .14
❑ 493 Jim Bertelsen .30 .14
❑ 494 Mark Moseley .75 .35
❑ 495 George Buehler .30 .14
❑ 496 Charlie Hall .30 .14
❑ 497 Marvin Upshaw .30 .14
❑ 498 Tom Banks RC .30 .14
❑ 499 Randy Vataha .30 .14
❑ 500 Fran Tarkenton AP 6.00 2.70
❑ 501 Mike Wagner .75 .35
❑ 502 Art Malone .30 .14
❑ 503 Fred Cook .30 .14
❑ 504 Rich McGeorge .30 .14
❑ 505 Ken Burrough .75 .35
❑ 506 Nick Mike-Mayer .30 .14
❑ 507 Checklist 397-528 3.00 .75
❑ 508 Steve Owens .75 .35
❑ 509 Brad Van Pelt RC .30 .14
❑ 510 Ken Riley AP .75 .35
❑ 511 Art Thoms .30 .14
❑ 512 Ed Bell .30 .14
❑ 513 Tom Wittum .30 .14
❑ 514 Jim Braxton .30 .14
❑ 515 Nick Buoniconti 1.50 .70
❑ 516 Brian Sipe RC 6.00 2.70
❑ 517 Jim Lynch .30 .14
❑ 518 Prentice McCray .30 .14
❑ 519 Tom Dempsey .30 .14
❑ 520 Mel Gray AP .75 .35
❑ 521 Nate Wright .30 .14
❑ 522 Rocky Bleier 6.00 2.70
❑ 523 Dennis Johnson .30 .14
❑ 524 Jerry Sisemore .30 .14
❑ 525 Bert Jones .30 .14
❑ 526 Perry Smith .30 .14
❑ 527 Blaine Nye .30 .14
❑ 528 Bob Moore 1.50 .35

1977 Topps

NRMT-MT EXC
COMPLETE SET (528) 200.00 90.00

❑ 1 Passing Leaders 2.50 .60
James Harris
Ken Stabler
❑ 2 Receiving Leaders 1.00 .45
Drew Pearson
MacArthur Lane
❑ 3 Rushing Leaders 10.00 4.50

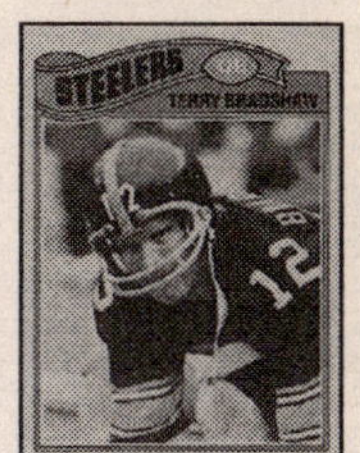

Walter Payton
O.J. Simpson
❑ 4 Scoring Leaders .50 .23
Mark Moseley
Toni Linhart
❑ 5 Interception Leaders .50 .23
Monte Jackson
Ken Riley
❑ 6 Punting Leaders .25 .11
John James
Marv Bateman
❑ 7 Mike Phipps .50 .23
❑ 8 Rick Volk .25 .11
❑ 9 Steve Furness .50 .23
❑ 10 Isaac Curtis .50 .23
❑ 11 Nate Wright .50 .23
❑ 12 Jean Fugett .25 .11
❑ 13 Ken Mendenhall .25 .11
❑ 14 Sam Adams .25 .11
❑ 15 Charlie Waters 1.00 .45
❑ 16 Bill Stanfill .25 .11
❑ 17 John Holland .25 .11
❑ 18 Pat Haden RC 2.00 .90
❑ 19 Bob Young .25 .11
❑ 20 Wally Chambers AP .25 .11
❑ 21 Lawrence Gaines .25 .11
❑ 22 Larry McCarren .25 .11
❑ 23 Horst Muhlmann .25 .11
❑ 24 Phil Villapiano .50 .23
❑ 25 Greg Pruitt .50 .23
❑ 26 Ron Howard .25 .11
❑ 27 Craig Morton 1.00 .45
❑ 28 Rufus Mayes .25 .11
❑ 29 Lee Roy Selmon RC UER 10.00 4.50
(Misspelled Leroy)
❑ 30 Ed White AP .50 .23
❑ 31 Harold McLinton .25 .11
❑ 32 Glenn Doughty .25 .11
❑ 33 Bob Kuechenberg 1.00 .45
❑ 34 Duane Carrell .25 .11
❑ 35 Riley Odoms .25 .11
❑ 36 Bobby Scott .25 .11
❑ 37 Nick Mike-Mayer .25 .11
❑ 38 Bill Lenkaitis .25 .11
❑ 39 Roland Harper .50 .23
❑ 40 Tommy Hart AP .25 .11
❑ 41 Mike Sensibaugh .25 .11
❑ 42 Rusty Jackson .25 .11
❑ 43 Levi Johnson .25 .11
❑ 44 Mike McCoy .25 .11
❑ 45 Roger Staubach 15.00 6.75
❑ 46 Fred Cox .25 .11
❑ 47 Bob Babich .25 .11
❑ 48 Reggie McKenzie .50 .23
❑ 49 Dave Jennings .25 .11
❑ 50 Mike Haynes AP RC 6.00 2.70
❑ 51 Larry Brown .50 .23
❑ 52 Marvin Cobb .25 .11
❑ 53 Fred Cook .25 .11
❑ 54 Freddie Solomon .50 .23
❑ 55 John Riggins 2.50 1.10
❑ 56 John Bunting .25 .11
❑ 57 Ray Wersching .50 .23
❑ 58 Mike Livingston .25 .11
❑ 59 Billy Johnson .50 .23
❑ 60 Mike Wagner AP .25 .11
❑ 61 Waymond Bryant .25 .11

❑ 62 Jim Otis .50 .23
❑ 63 Ed Galigher .25 .11
❑ 64 Randy Vataha .25 .11
❑ 65 Jim Zorn RC 4.00 1.80
❑ 66 Jon Keyworth .25 .11
❑ 67 Checklist 1-132 2.00 .50
❑ 68 Henry Childs .25 .11
❑ 69 Thom Darden .25 .11
❑ 70 George Kunz AP .25 .11
❑ 71 Lenvil Elliott .25 .11
❑ 72 Curtis Johnson .25 .11
❑ 73 Doug Van Horn .25 .11
❑ 74 Joe Theismann 4.00 1.80
❑ 75 Dwight White .50 .23
❑ 76 Scott Laidlaw .25 .11
❑ 77 Monte Johnson .25 .11
❑ 78 Dave Beverly .25 .11
❑ 79 Jim Mitchell .25 .11
❑ 80 Jack Youngblood AP 1.00 .45
❑ 81 Mel Gray .50 .23
❑ 82 Dwight Harrison .25 .11
❑ 83 John Hadl .50 .23
❑ 84 Matt Blair RC 1.00 .45
❑ 85 Charlie Sanders .25 .11
❑ 86 Noah Jackson .25 .11
❑ 87 Ed Marinaro .50 .23
❑ 88 Bob Howard .25 .11
❑ 89 John McDaniel .25 .11
❑ 90 Dan Dierdorf AP 1.50 .70
❑ 91 Mark Moseley .50 .23
❑ 92 Cleo Miller .25 .11
❑ 93 Andre Tillman .25 .11
❑ 94 Bruce Taylor .25 .11
❑ 95 Bert Jones 1.00 .45
❑ 96 Anthony Davis RC 1.00 .45
❑ 97 Don Goode .25 .11
❑ 98 Ray Rhodes RC 6.00 2.70
❑ 99 Mike Webster RC 10.00 4.50
❑ 100 O.J. Simpson AP 5.00 2.20
❑ 101 Doug Plank RC .25 .11
❑ 102 Efren Herrera .50 .23
❑ 103 Charlie Smith .25 .11
❑ 104 Carlos Brown .25 .11
❑ 105 Jim Marshall 1.00 .45
❑ 106 Paul Naumoff .25 .11
❑ 107 Walter White .25 .11
❑ 108 John Cappelletti RC 3.00 1.35
❑ 109 Chip Myers .25 .11
❑ 110 Ken Stabler AP 10.00 4.50
❑ 111 Joe Ehrmann .25 .11
❑ 112 Rick Engles .25 .11
❑ 113 Jack Dolbin RC .25 .11
❑ 114 Ron Bolton .25 .11
❑ 115 Mike Thomas .25 .11
❑ 116 Mike Fuller .25 .11
❑ 117 John Hill .25 .11
❑ 118 Richard Todd RC 1.00 .45
❑ 119 Duriel Harris RC .50 .23
❑ 120 John James AP .25 .11
❑ 121 Lionel Antoine .25 .11
❑ 122 John Skorupan .25 .11
❑ 123 Skip Butler .25 .11
❑ 124 Bob Tucker .25 .11
❑ 125 Paul Krause .50 .23
❑ 126 Dave Hampton .25 .11
❑ 127 Tom Wittum .25 .11
❑ 128 Gary Huff .50 .23
❑ 129 Emmitt Thomas .25 .11
❑ 130 Drew Pearson AP 2.00 .90
❑ 131 Ron Saul .25 .11
❑ 132 Steve Niehaus .25 .11
❑ 133 Fred Carr 1.00 .45
❑ 134 Norm Bulaich .25 .11
❑ 135 Bob Trumpy .50 .23
❑ 136 Greg Landry .50 .23
❑ 137 George Buehler .25 .11
❑ 138 Reggie Rucker .50 .23
❑ 139 Julius Adams .25 .11
❑ 140 Jack Ham AP 2.50 1.10
❑ 141 Wayne Morris RC .25 .11
❑ 142 Marv Bateman .25 .11
❑ 143 Bobby Maples .25 .11
❑ 144 Harold Carmichael 1.00 .45
❑ 145 Bob Avellini .50 .23
❑ 146 Harry Carson RC 3.00 1.35
❑ 147 Lawrence Pillers .25 .11
❑ 148 Ed Williams .25 .11
❑ 149 Dan Pastorini .50 .23
❑ 150 Ron Yary AP .50 .23
❑ 151 Joe Lavender .25 .11
❑ 152 Pat McInally RC .50 .23
❑ 153 Lloyd Mumphord .25 .11
❑ 154 Cullen Bryant .50 .23
❑ 155 Willie Lanier 1.00 .45
❑ 156 Gene Washington .50 .23
❑ 157 Scott Hunter .25 .11
❑ 158 Jim Merlo .25 .11
❑ 159 Randy Grossman .50 .23
❑ 160 Blaine Nye AP .25 .11
❑ 161 Ike Harris .25 .11
❑ 162 Doug Dieken .25 .11
❑ 163 Guy Morriss .25 .11
❑ 164 Bob Parsons .25 .11
❑ 165 Steve Grogan 1.00 .45
❑ 166 John Brockington .50 .23
❑ 167 Charlie Joiner 2.50 1.10
❑ 168 Ron Carpenter .25 .11
❑ 169 Jeff Wright .25 .11
❑ 170 Chris Hanburger AP .25 .11
❑ 171 Roosevelt Leaks RC .50 .23
❑ 172 Larry Little 1.00 .45
❑ 173 John Matuszak .50 .23
❑ 174 Joe Ferguson .50 .23
❑ 175 Brad Van Pelt .50 .23
❑ 176 Dexter Bussey RC .50 .23
❑ 177 Steve Largent RC 40.00 18.00
❑ 178 Dewey Selmon .50 .23
❑ 179 Randy Gradishar 1.00 .45
❑ 180 Mel Blount AP 3.00 1.35
❑ 181 Dan Neal .25 .11
❑ 182 Rich Szaro .25 .11
❑ 183 Mike Boryla .25 .11
❑ 184 Steve Jones .25 .11
❑ 185 Paul Warfield 2.50 1.10
❑ 186 Greg Buttle RC .25 .11
❑ 187 Rich McGeorge .25 .11
❑ 188 Leon Gray RC .50 .23
❑ 189 John Shinners .25 .11
❑ 190 Toni Linhart AP .25 .11
❑ 191 Robert Miller .25 .11
❑ 192 Jake Scott .25 .11
❑ 193 Jon Morris .25 .11
❑ 194 Randy Crowder .25 .11
❑ 195 Lynn Swann UER 15.00 6.75
(Interception Record
on card back)
❑ 196 Marsh White .25 .11
❑ 197 Rod Perry RC .25 .11
❑ 198 Willie Hall .25 .11
❑ 199 Mike Hartenstine .25 .11
❑ 200 Jim Bakken AP .25 .11
❑ 201 Atlanta Falcons UER 1.25 .30
Team Checklist
(79 Jim Mitchell
is not listed)
❑ 202 Baltimore Colts 1.25 .30
Team Checklist
❑ 203 Buffalo Bills 1.25 .30
Team Checklist
❑ 204 Chicago Bears 1.25 .30
Team Checklist
❑ 205 Cincinnati Bengals 1.25 .30
Team Checklist
❑ 206 Cleveland Browns 1.25 .30
Team Checklist
❑ 207 Dallas Cowboys 1.25 .30
Team Checklist
❑ 208 Denver Broncos 1.25 .30
Team Checklist
❑ 209 Detroit Lions 1.25 .30
Team Checklist
❑ 210 Green Bay Packers 1.25 .30
Team Checklist
❑ 211 Houston Oilers 1.25 .30
Team Checklist
❑ 212 Kansas City Chiefs 1.25 .30
Team Checklist
❑ 213 Los Angeles Rams 1.25 .30
Team Checklist
❑ 214 Miami Dolphins 1.25 .30
Team Checklist
❑ 215 Minnesota Vikings 1.25 .30
Team Checklist
❑ 216 New England Patriots 1.25 .30
Team Checklist
❑ 217 New Orleans Saints 1.25 .30
Team Checklist
❑ 218 New York Giants 1.25 .30
Team Checklist
❑ 219 New York Jets 1.25 .30
Team Checklist
❑ 220 Oakland Raiders 1.25 .30
Team Checklist
❑ 221 Philadelphia Eagles 1.25 .30
Team Checklist
❑ 222 Pittsburgh Steelers 1.25 .30
Team Checklist
❑ 223 St. Louis Cardinals 1.25 .30
Team Checklist
❑ 224 San Diego Chargers 1.25 .30
Team Checklist
❑ 225 San Francisco 49ers 1.25 .30
Team Checklist
❑ 226 Seattle Seahawks 1.25 .30
Team Checklist
❑ 227 Tampa Bay Buccaneers 1.25 .30
Team Checklist UER
(Lee Roy Selmon mis-
spelled as Leroy)
❑ 228 Washington Redskins 1.25 .30
Team Checklist
❑ 229 Sam Cunningham .50 .23
❑ 230 Alan Page AP 1.00 .45
❑ 231 Eddie Brown .25 .11
❑ 232 Stan White .25 .11
❑ 233 Vern Den Herder .25 .11
❑ 234 Clarence Davis .25 .11
❑ 235 Ken Anderson 1.00 .45
❑ 236 Karl Chandler .25 .11
❑ 237 Will Harrell .25 .11
❑ 238 Clarence Scott .25 .11
❑ 239 Bo Rather .25 .11
❑ 240 Robert Brazile AP .50 .23
❑ 241 Bob Bell .25 .11
❑ 242 Rolland Lawrence .25 .11
❑ 243 Tom Sullivan .25 .11
❑ 244 Larry Brunson .25 .11
❑ 245 Terry Bradshaw 12.00 5.50
❑ 246 Rich Saul .25 .11
❑ 247 Cleveland Elam .25 .11
❑ 248 Don Woods .25 .11
❑ 249 Bruce Laird .25 .11
❑ 250 Coy Bacon AP .50 .23
❑ 251 Russ Francis 1.00 .45
❑ 252 Jim Braxton .25 .11
❑ 253 Perry Smith .25 .11
❑ 254 Jerome Barkum .25 .11
❑ 255 Garo Yepremian .50 .23
❑ 256 Checklist 133-264 2.00 .50
❑ 257 Tony Galbreath RC .50 .23
❑ 258 Troy Archer .25 .11
❑ 259 Brian Sipe 1.00 .45
❑ 260 Billy Joe DuPree AP .50 .23
❑ 261 Bobby Walden .25 .11
❑ 262 Larry Marshall .25 .11
❑ 263 Ted Fritsch Jr. .25 .11
❑ 264 Larry Hand .25 .11
❑ 265 Tom Mack .50 .23
❑ 266 Ed Bradley .25 .11
❑ 267 Pat Leahy .50 .23
❑ 268 Louis Carter .25 .11
❑ 269 Archie Griffin RC 6.00 2.70
❑ 270 Art Shell AP 1.00 .45
❑ 271 Stu Voigt .25 .11
❑ 272 Prentice McCray .25 .11
❑ 273 MacArthur Lane .25 .11
❑ 274 Dan Fouts 6.00 2.70
❑ 275 Charlie Young .50 .23
❑ 276 Wilbur Jackson RC .25 .11
❑ 277 John Hicks .25 .11
❑ 278 Nat Moore 1.00 .45
❑ 279 Virgil Livers .25 .11
❑ 280 Curley Culp AP .50 .23
❑ 281 Rocky Bleier 2.50 1.10
❑ 282 John Zook .25 .11
❑ 283 Tom DeLeone .25 .11
❑ 284 Danny White RC 8.00 3.60
❑ 285 Otis Armstrong .50 .23

No.	Player		
286	Larry Walton	.25	.11
287	Jim Carter	.25	.11
288	Don McCauley	.25	.11
289	Frank Grant	.25	.11
290	Roger Wehrli AP	.50	.23
291	Mick Tingelhoff	.50	.23
292	Bernard Jackson	.25	.11
293	Tom Owen RC	.25	.11
294	Mike Esposito	.25	.11
295	Fred Biletnikoff	2.50	1.10
296	Revie Sorey RC	.25	.11
297	John McMakin	.25	.11
298	Dan Ryczek	.25	.11
299	Wayne Moore	.25	.11
300	Franco Harris AP	4.00	1.80
301	Rick Upchurch RC	1.00	.45
302	Jim Stienke	.25	.11
303	Charlie Davis	.25	.11
304	Don Cockroft	.25	.11
305	Ken Burrough	.50	.23
306	Clark Gaines	.25	.11
307	Bobby Douglass	.25	.11
308	Ralph Perretta	.25	.11
309	Wally Hilgenberg	.25	.11
310	Monte Jackson AP RC	.50	.23
311	Chris Bahr RC	.50	.23
312	Jim Cheyunski	.25	.11
313	Mike Patrick	.25	.11
314	Ed Too Tall Jones	5.00	2.20
315	Bill Bradley	.25	.11
316	Benny Malone	.25	.11
317	Paul Seymour	.25	.11
318	Jim Laslavic	.25	.11
319	Frank Lewis	.50	.23
320	Ray Guy AP	1.00	.45
321	Allan Ellis	.25	.11
322	Conrad Dobler	.50	.23
323	Chester Marcol	.25	.11
324	Doug Kotar	.25	.11
325	Lemar Parrish	.50	.23
326	Steve Holden	.25	.11
327	Jeff Van Note	.50	.23
328	Howard Stevens	.25	.11
329	Brad Dusek	.50	.23
330	Joe DeLamielleure AP	.25	.11
331	Jim Plunkett	1.00	.45
332	Checklist 265-396	2.00	.50
333	Lou Piccone	.25	.11
334	Ray Hamilton	.25	.11
335	Jan Stenerud	.50	.23
336	Jeris White	.25	.11
337	Sherman Smith RC	.25	.11
338	Dave Green	.25	.11
339	Terry Schmidt	.25	.11
340	Sammie White AP RC	1.00	.45
341	Jon Kolb RC	.25	.11
342	Randy White	8.00	3.60
343	Bob Klein	.25	.11
344	Bob Kowalkowski	.25	.11
345	Terry Metcalf	.50	.23
346	Joe Danelo	.25	.11
347	Ken Payne	.25	.11
348	Neal Craig	.25	.11
349	Dennis Johnson	.25	.11
350	Bill Bergey AP	.50	.23
351	Raymond Chester	.25	.11
352	Bob Matheson	.25	.11
353	Mike Kadish	.25	.11
354	Mark Van Eeghen RC	1.00	.45
355	L.C. Greenwood	1.00	.45
356	Sam Hunt	.25	.11
357	Darrell Austin	.25	.11
358	Jim Turner	.25	.11
359	Ahmad Rashad	2.00	.90
360	Walter Payton AP	40.00	18.00
361	Mark Arneson	.25	.11
362	Jerrel Wilson	.25	.11
363	Steve Bartkowski	1.00	.45
364	John Watson	.25	.11
365	Ken Riley	.50	.23
366	Gregg Bingham	.25	.11
367	Golden Richards	.50	.23
368	Clyde Powers	.25	.11
369	Diron Talbert	.25	.11
370	Lydell Mitchell	.50	.23
371	Bob Jackson	.25	.11
372	Jim Mandich	.25	.11
373	Frank LeMaster	.25	.11
374	Benny Ricardo	.25	.11
375	Lawrence McCutcheon	.50	.23
376	Lynn Dickey	.50	.23
377	Phil Wise	.25	.11
378	Tony McGee	.25	.11
379	Norm Thompson	.25	.11
380	Dave Casper AP RC	4.00	1.80
381	Glen Edwards	.25	.11
382	Bob Thomas	.25	.11
383	Bob Chandler	.50	.23
384	Rickey Young	.50	.23
385	Carl Eller	1.00	.45
386	Lyle Alzado	1.00	.45
387	John Leypoldt	.25	.11
388	Gordon Bell	.25	.11
389	Mike Bragg	.25	.11
390	Jim Langer AP	1.00	.45
391	Vern Holland	.25	.11
392	Nelson Munsey	.25	.11
393	Mack Mitchell	.25	.11
394	Tony Adams	.25	.11
395	Preston Pearson	.50	.23
396	Emanuel Zanders	.25	.11
397	Vince Papale	.25	.11
398	Joe Fields RC	.50	.23
399	Craig Clemons	.25	.11
400	Fran Tarkenton AP	5.00	2.20
401	Andy Johnson	.25	.11
402	Willie Buchanon	.25	.11
403	Pat Curran	.25	.11
404	Ray Jarvis	.25	.11
405	Joe Greene	2.50	1.10
406	Bill Simpson	.25	.11
407	Ronnie Coleman	.25	.11
408	J.K. McKay	.50	.23
409	Pat Fischer	.50	.23
410	John Dutton AP	.50	.23
411	Boobie Clark	.25	.11
412	Pat Tilley RC	1.00	.45
413	Don Strock	.50	.23
414	Brian Kelley	.25	.11
415	Gene Upshaw	1.00	.45
416	Mike Montler	.25	.11
417	Checklist 397-528	2.00	.50
418	John Gilliam	.25	.11
419	Brent McClanahan	.25	.11
420	Jerry Sherk AP	.25	.11
421	Roy Gerela	.25	.11
422	Tim Fox	.50	.23
423	John Ebersole	.25	.11
424	James Scott	.25	.11
425	Delvin Williams RC	.50	.23
426	Spike Jones	.25	.11
427	Harvey Martin	1.00	.45
428	Don Herrmann	.25	.11
429	Calvin Hill	.50	.23
430	Isiah Robertson AP	.25	.11
431	Tony Greene	.25	.11
432	Bob Johnson	.25	.11
433	Lem Barney	1.00	.45
434	Eric Torkelson	.25	.11
435	John Mendenhall	.25	.11
436	Larry Seiple	.50	.23
437	Art Kuehn	.25	.11
438	John Vella	.25	.11
439	Greg Latta	.25	.11
440	Roger Carr AP	.50	.23
441	Doug Sutherland	.25	.11
442	Mike Kruczek	.25	.11
443	Steve Zabel	.25	.11
444	Mike Pruitt RC	1.00	.45
445	Harold Jackson	.50	.23
446	George Jakowenko	.25	.11
447	John Fitzgerald	.25	.11
448	Carey Joyce	.25	.11
449	Jim LeClair	.25	.11
450	Ken Houston AP	1.00	.45
451	Steve Grogan RB Most Touchdowns Rushing by QB, Season	.50	.23
452	Jim Marshall RB Most Games Played, Lifetime	.50	.23
453	O.J. Simpson RB Most Yardage, Rushing, Game	2.50	1.10
454	Fran Tarkenton RB Most Yardage, Passing, Lifetime	3.00	1.35
455	Jim Zorn RB Most Passing Yards Season, Rookie	.50	.23
456	Robert Pratt	.25	.11
457	Walker Gillette	.25	.11
458	Charlie Hall	.25	.11
459	Robert Newhouse	.50	.23
460	John Hannah AP	1.00	.45
461	Ken Reaves	.25	.11
462	Herman Weaver	.25	.11
463	James Harris	.50	.23
464	Howard Twilley	.50	.23
465	Jeff Siemon	.50	.23
466	John Outlaw	.25	.11
467	Chuck Muncie RC	1.00	.45
468	Bob Moore	.25	.11
469	Robert Woods	.25	.11
470	Cliff Branch AP	2.00	.90
471	Johnnie Gray	.25	.11
472	Don Hardeman	.25	.11
473	Steve Ramsey	.25	.11
474	Steve Mike-Mayer	.25	.11
475	Gary Garrison	.25	.11
476	Walter Johnson	.25	.11
477	Neil Clabo	.25	.11
478	Len Hauss	.25	.11
479	Darryl Stingley	.50	.23
480	Jack Lambert AP	8.00	3.60
481	Mike Adamle	.50	.23
482	David Lee	.25	.11
483	Tom Mullen	.25	.11
484	Claude Humphrey	.25	.11
485	Jim Hart	1.00	.45
486	Bobby Thompson RB	.25	.11
487	Jack Rudnay	.25	.11
488	Rich Sowells	.25	.11
489	Reuben Gant	.25	.11
490	Cliff Harris AP	1.00	.45
491	Bob Brown DT	.25	.11
492	Don Nottingham	.25	.11
493	Ron Jessie	.25	.11
494	Otis Sistrunk	.50	.23
495	Billy Kilmer	.50	.23
496	Oscar Roan	.25	.11
497	Bill Van Heusen	.25	.11
498	Randy Logan	.25	.11
499	John Smith	.25	.11
500	Chuck Foreman AP	.50	.23
501	J.T. Thomas	.25	.11
502	Steve Schubert	.25	.11
503	Mike Barnes	.25	.11
504	J.V. Cain	.25	.11
505	Larry Csonka	3.00	1.35
506	Elvin Bethea	.50	.23
507	Ray Easterling	.25	.11
508	Joe Reed	.25	.11
509	Steve Odom	.25	.11
510	Tommy Casanova AP	.25	.11
511	Dave Dalby	.25	.11
512	Richard Caster	.25	.11
513	Fred Dryer	1.00	.45
514	Jeff Kinney	.25	.11
515	Bob Griese	3.00	1.35
516	Butch Johnson RC	1.00	.45
517	Gerald Irons	.25	.11
518	Don Calhoun	.25	.11
519	Jack Gregory	.25	.11
520	Tom Banks AP	.25	.11
521	Bobby Bryant	.25	.11
522	Reggie Harrison	.25	.11
523	Terry Hermeling	.25	.11
524	David Taylor	.25	.11
525	Brian Baschnagel RC	.50	.23
526	AFC Championship Raiders 24, Steelers 7 (Stabler)	1.00	.45
527	NFC Championship Vikings 24, Rams 13	.50	.23

	NRMT-MT	EXC
❑ 528 Super Bowl XI Raiders 32, Vikings 14 (Line play)	1.00	.25

1978 Topps

	NRMT-MT	EXC
COMPLETE SET (528)	150.00	70.00
❑ 1 Gary Huff HL Huff Leads Bucs to First Win	1.00	.25
❑ 2 Craig Morton HL Morton Passes Broncos to Super Bowl	1.00	.45
❑ 3 Walter Payton HL Rushes for 275 Yards	8.00	3.60
❑ 4 O.J. Simpson HL Reaches 10,000 Yards	2.00	.90
❑ 5 Fran Tarkenton HL Completes 17 of 18	2.00	.90
❑ 6 Bob Thomas HL Thomas' FG Sends Bears to Playoffs	.20	.09
❑ 7 Joe Pisarcik	.50	.23
❑ 8 Skip Thomas	.20	.09
❑ 9 Roosevelt Leaks	.20	.09
❑ 10 Ken Houston AP	1.00	.45
❑ 11 Tom Blanchard	.20	.09
❑ 12 Jim Turner	.20	.09
❑ 13 Tom DeLeone	.20	.09
❑ 14 Jim LeClair	.20	.09
❑ 15 Bob Avellini	.50	.23
❑ 16 Tony McGee	.20	.09
❑ 17 James Harris	.50	.23
❑ 18 Terry Nelson	.20	.09
❑ 19 Rocky Bleier	2.00	.90
❑ 20 Joe DeLamielleure AP	.50	.23
❑ 21 Richard Caster	.20	.09
❑ 22 A.J. Duhe RC	1.00	.45
❑ 23 John Outlaw	.20	.09
❑ 24 Danny White	1.25	.55
❑ 25 Larry Csonka	2.50	1.10
❑ 26 David Hill	.50	.23
❑ 27 Mark Arneson	.20	.09
❑ 28 Jack Tatum	.50	.23
❑ 29 Norm Thompson	.20	.09
❑ 30 Sammie White	.50	.23
❑ 31 Dennis Johnson	.20	.09
❑ 32 Robin Earl	.20	.09
❑ 33 Don Cockroft	.20	.09
❑ 34 Bob Johnson	.20	.09
❑ 35 John Hannah	1.00	.45
❑ 36 Scott Hunter	.20	.09
❑ 37 Ken Burrough	.50	.23
❑ 38 Wilbur Jackson	.50	.23
❑ 39 Rich McGeorge	.20	.09
❑ 40 Lyle Alzado AP	1.00	.45
❑ 41 John Ebersole	.20	.09
❑ 42 Gary Green RC	.20	.09
❑ 43 Art Kuehn	.20	.09
❑ 44 Glen Edwards	.50	.23
❑ 45 Lawrence McCutcheon	.50	.23
❑ 46 Duriel Harris	.20	.09
❑ 47 Rich Szaro	.20	.09
❑ 48 Mike Washington	.20	.09
❑ 49 Stan White	.20	.09
❑ 50 Dave Casper AP	1.00	.45
❑ 51 Len Hauss	.20	.09
❑ 52 James Scott	.20	.09
❑ 53 Brian Sipe	1.00	.45
❑ 54 Gary Shirk	.20	.09
❑ 55 Archie Griffin	1.00	.45
❑ 56 Mike Patrick	.20	.09
❑ 57 Mario Clark	.20	.09
❑ 58 Jeff Siemon	.20	.09
❑ 59 Steve Mike-Mayer	.20	.09
❑ 60 Randy White AP	4.00	1.80
❑ 61 Darrell Austin	.20	.09
❑ 62 Tom Sullivan	.20	.09
❑ 63 Johnny Rodgers RC	1.00	.45
❑ 64 Ken Reaves	.20	.09
❑ 65 Terry Bradshaw	10.00	4.50
❑ 66 Fred Steinfort	.20	.09
❑ 67 Curley Culp	.50	.23
❑ 68 Ted Hendricks	1.00	.45
❑ 69 Raymond Chester	.20	.09
❑ 70 Jim Langer AP	1.00	.45
❑ 71 Calvin Hill	.50	.23
❑ 72 Mike Hartenstine	.20	.09
❑ 73 Gerald Irons	.20	.09
❑ 74 Billy Brooks	.50	.23
❑ 75 John Mendenhall	.20	.09
❑ 76 Andy Johnson	.20	.09
❑ 77 Tom Wittum	.20	.09
❑ 78 Lynn Dickey	.50	.23
❑ 79 Carl Eller	1.00	.45
❑ 80 Tom Mack	.50	.23
❑ 81 Clark Gaines	.20	.09
❑ 82 Lem Barney	1.00	.45
❑ 83 Mike Montler	.20	.09
❑ 84 Jon Kolb	.20	.09
❑ 85 Bob Chandler	.50	.23
❑ 86 Robert Newhouse	.50	.23
❑ 87 Frank LeMaster	.20	.09
❑ 88 Jeff West	.20	.09
❑ 89 Lyle Blackwood	.50	.23
❑ 90 Gene Upshaw AP	1.00	.45
❑ 91 Frank Grant	.20	.09
❑ 92 Tom Hicks	.20	.09
❑ 93 Mike Pruitt	.50	.23
❑ 94 Chris Bahr	.20	.09
❑ 95 Russ Francis	.50	.23
❑ 96 Norris Thomas	.20	.09
❑ 97 Gary Barbaro RC	.50	.23
❑ 98 Jim Merlo	.20	.09
❑ 99 Karl Chandler	.20	.09
❑ 100 Fran Tarkenton	4.00	1.80
❑ 101 Abdul Salaam	.20	.09
❑ 102 Marv Kellum	.20	.09
❑ 103 Herman Weaver	.20	.09
❑ 104 Roy Gerela	.20	.09
❑ 105 Harold Jackson	.50	.23
❑ 106 Dewey Selmon	.50	.23
❑ 107 Checklist 1-132	1.00	.25
❑ 108 Clarence Davis	.20	.09
❑ 109 Robert Pratt	.20	.09
❑ 110 Harvey Martin AP	1.00	.45
❑ 111 Brad Dusek	.20	.09
❑ 112 Greg Latta	.20	.09
❑ 113 Tony Peters	.20	.09
❑ 114 Jim Braxton	.20	.09
❑ 115 Ken Riley	.50	.23
❑ 116 Steve Nelson	.20	.09
❑ 117 Rick Upchurch	.50	.23
❑ 118 Spike Jones	.20	.09
❑ 119 Doug Kotar	.20	.09
❑ 120 Bob Griese AP	2.50	1.10
❑ 121 Burgess Owens	.20	.09
❑ 122 Rolf Benirschke RC	.50	.23
❑ 123 Haskel Stanback RC	.20	.09
❑ 124 J.T. Thomas	.20	.09
❑ 125 Ahmad Rashad	1.50	.70
❑ 126 Rick Kane	.20	.09
❑ 127 Elvin Bethea	.20	.09
❑ 128 Dave Dalby	.20	.09
❑ 129 Mike Barnes	.20	.09
❑ 130 Isiah Robertson	.20	.09
❑ 131 Jim Plunkett	1.00	.45
❑ 132 Allan Ellis	.20	.09
❑ 133 Mike Bragg	.20	.09
❑ 134 Bob Jackson	.20	.09
❑ 135 Coy Bacon	.20	.09
❑ 136 John Smith	.20	.09
❑ 137 Chuck Muncie	.50	.23
❑ 138 Johnnie Gray	.20	.09
❑ 139 Jimmy Robinson	.20	.09
❑ 140 Tom Banks	.20	.09
❑ 141 Marvin Powell RC	.20	.09
❑ 142 Jerrel Wilson	.20	.09
❑ 143 Ron Howard	.20	.09
❑ 144 Rob Lytle RC	.50	.23
❑ 145 L.C. Greenwood	1.00	.45
❑ 146 Morris Owens	.20	.09
❑ 147 Joe Reed	.20	.09
❑ 148 Mike Kadish	.20	.09
❑ 149 Phil Villapiano	.50	.23
❑ 150 Lydell Mitchell	.50	.23
❑ 151 Randy Logan	.20	.09
❑ 152 Mike Williams	.20	.09
❑ 153 Jeff Van Note	.50	.23
❑ 154 Steve Schubert	.20	.09
❑ 155 Billy Kilmer	.50	.23
❑ 156 Boobie Clark	.20	.09
❑ 157 Charlie Hall	.20	.09
❑ 158 Raymond Clayborn RC	1.00	.45
❑ 159 Jack Gregory	.20	.09
❑ 160 Cliff Harris AP	1.00	.45
❑ 161 Joe Fields	.20	.09
❑ 162 Don Nottingham	.20	.09
❑ 163 Ed White	.50	.23
❑ 164 Toni Fritsch	.20	.09
❑ 165 Jack Lambert	4.00	1.80
❑ 166 NFC Champions Cowboys 23, Vikings 6 (Roger Staubach)	1.50	.70
❑ 167 AFC Champions Broncos 20, Raiders 17 (Lytle running)	.50	.23
❑ 168 Super Bowl XII Cowboys 27, Broncos 10 (Tony Dorsett)	3.00	1.35
❑ 169 Neal Colzie RC	.20	.09
❑ 170 Cleveland Elam AP	.20	.09
❑ 171 David Lee	.20	.09
❑ 172 Jim Otis	.20	.09
❑ 173 Archie Manning	1.00	.45
❑ 174 Jim Carter	.20	.09
❑ 175 Jean Fugett	.20	.09
❑ 176 Willie Parker	.20	.09
❑ 177 Haven Moses	.50	.23
❑ 178 Horace King	.20	.09
❑ 179 Bob Thomas	.20	.09
❑ 180 Monte Jackson	.20	.09
❑ 181 Steve Zabel	.20	.09
❑ 182 John Fitzgerald	.20	.09
❑ 183 Mike Livingston	.20	.09
❑ 184 Larry Poole	.20	.09
❑ 185 Isaac Curtis	.50	.23
❑ 186 Chuck Ramsey	.20	.09
❑ 187 Bob Klein	.20	.09
❑ 188 Ray Rhodes	1.00	.45
❑ 189 Otis Sistrunk	.50	.23
❑ 190 Bill Bergey	.50	.23
❑ 191 Sherman Smith	.50	.23
❑ 192 Dave Green	.20	.09
❑ 193 Carl Mauck	.20	.09
❑ 194 Reggie Harrison	.20	.09
❑ 195 Roger Carr	.50	.23
❑ 196 Steve Bartkowski	1.00	.45
❑ 197 Ray Wersching	.20	.09
❑ 198 Willie Buchanon	.20	.09
❑ 199 Neil Clabo	.20	.09
❑ 200 Walter Payton AP UER (Born 7/5/54, should be 7/25/54)	25.00	11.00
❑ 201 Sam Adams	.20	.09
❑ 202 Larry Gordon	.20	.09
❑ 203 Pat Tilley	.50	.23
❑ 204 Mack Mitchell	.20	.09
❑ 205 Ken Anderson	1.00	.45
❑ 206 Scott Dierking	.20	.09
❑ 207 Jack Rudnay	.20	.09
❑ 208 Jim Stienke	.20	.09
❑ 209 Bill Simpson	.20	.09
❑ 210 Errol Mann	.20	.09

❑ 211 Bucky Dilts .20 .09
❑ 212 Reuben Gant .20 .09
❑ 213 Thomas Henderson RC 1.50 .70
❑ 214 Steve Furness .50 .23
❑ 215 John Riggins 2.00 .90
❑ 216 Keith Krepfle RC .20 .09
❑ 217 Fred Dean RC .50 .23
❑ 218 Emanuel Zanders .20 .09
❑ 219 Don Testerman .20 .09
❑ 220 George Kunz .20 .09
❑ 221 Darryl Stingley .50 .23
❑ 222 Ken Sanders .20 .09
❑ 223 Gary Huff .20 .09
❑ 224 Gregg Bingham .20 .09
❑ 225 Jerry Sherk .20 .09
❑ 226 Doug Plank .20 .09
❑ 227 Ed Taylor .20 .09
❑ 228 Emery Moorehead .20 .09
❑ 229 Reggie Williams RC 1.00 .45
❑ 230 Claude Humphrey .20 .09
❑ 231 Randy Cross RC 2.00 .90
❑ 232 Jim Hart 1.00 .45
❑ 233 Bobby Bryant .20 .09
❑ 234 Larry Brown .20 .09
❑ 235 Mark Van Eeghen .50 .23
❑ 236 Terry Hermeling .20 .09
❑ 237 Steve Odom .20 .09
❑ 238 Jan Stenerud 1.00 .45
❑ 239 Andre Tillman .20 .09
❑ 240 Tom Jackson AP RC 5.00 2.20
❑ 241 Ken Mendenhall .20 .09
❑ 242 Tim Fox .20 .09
❑ 243 Don Herrmann .20 .09
❑ 244 Eddie McMillan .20 .09
❑ 245 Greg Pruitt .50 .23
❑ 246 J.K. McKay .20 .09
❑ 247 Larry Keller .20 .09
❑ 248 Dave Jennings .50 .23
❑ 249 Bo Harris .20 .09
❑ 250 Revie Sorey .20 .09
❑ 251 Tony Greene .20 .09
❑ 252 Butch Johnson .50 .23
❑ 253 Paul Naumoff .20 .09
❑ 254 Rickey Young .50 .23
❑ 255 Dwight White .50 .23
❑ 256 Joe Lavender .20 .09
❑ 257 Checklist 133-264 1.00 .25
❑ 258 Ronnie Coleman .20 .09
❑ 259 Charlie Smith .20 .09
❑ 260 Ray Guy AP 1.00 .45
❑ 261 David Taylor .20 .09
❑ 262 Bill Lenkaitis .20 .09
❑ 263 Jim Mitchell .20 .09
❑ 264 Delvin Williams .20 .09
❑ 265 Jack Youngblood 1.00 .45
❑ 266 Chuck Crist .20 .09
❑ 267 Richard Todd .50 .23
❑ 268 Dave Logan RC .50 .23
❑ 269 Rufus Mayes .20 .09
❑ 270 Brad Van Pelt .20 .09
❑ 271 Chester Marcol .20 .09
❑ 272 J.V. Cain .20 .09
❑ 273 Larry Seiple .20 .09
❑ 274 Brent McClanahan .20 .09
❑ 275 Mike Wagner .20 .09
❑ 276 Diron Talbert .20 .09
❑ 277 Brian Baschnagel .20 .09
❑ 278 Ed Podolak .20 .09
❑ 279 Don Goode .20 .09
❑ 280 John Dutton .50 .23
❑ 281 Don Calhoun .20 .09
❑ 282 Monte Johnson .20 .09
❑ 283 Ron Jessie .20 .09
❑ 284 Jon Morris .20 .09
❑ 285 Riley Odoms .20 .09
❑ 286 Marv Bateman .20 .09
❑ 287 Joe Klecko RC 1.00 .45
❑ 288 Oliver Davis .20 .09
❑ 289 John McDaniel .20 .09
❑ 290 Roger Staubach 12.00 5.50
❑ 291 Brian Kelley .20 .09
❑ 292 Mike Hogan .20 .09
❑ 293 John Leypoldt .20 .09
❑ 294 Jack Novak .20 .09
❑ 295 Joe Greene 2.00 .90
❑ 296 John Hill .20 .09
❑ 297 Danny Buggs .20 .09
❑ 298 Ted Albrecht .20 .09
❑ 299 Nelson Munsey .20 .09
❑ 300 Chuck Foreman .50 .23
❑ 301 Dan Pastorini .50 .23
❑ 302 Tommy Hart .20 .09
❑ 303 Dave Beverly .20 .09
❑ 304 Tony Reed RC .50 .23
❑ 305 Cliff Branch 1.50 .70
❑ 306 Clarence Duren .20 .09
❑ 307 Randy Rasmussen .20 .09
❑ 308 Oscar Roan .20 .09
❑ 309 Lenvil Elliott .20 .09
❑ 310 Dan Dierdorf AP 1.00 .45
❑ 311 Johnny Perkins .20 .09
❑ 312 Rafael Septien RC .50 .23
❑ 313 Terry Beeson .20 .09
❑ 314 Lee Roy Selmon 2.00 .90
❑ 315 Tony Dorsett RC 30.00 13.50
❑ 316 Greg Landry .50 .23
❑ 317 Jake Scott .20 .09
❑ 318 Dan Peiffer .20 .09
❑ 319 John Bunting .20 .09
❑ 320 John Stallworth RC 15.00 6.75
❑ 321 Bob Howard .20 .09
❑ 322 Larry Little 1.00 .45
❑ 323 Reggie McKenzie .50 .23
❑ 324 Duane Carrell .20 .09
❑ 325 Ed Simonini .20 .09
❑ 326 John Vella .20 .09
❑ 327 Wesley Walker RC 3.00 1.35
❑ 328 Jon Keyworth .20 .09
❑ 329 Ron Bolton .20 .09
❑ 330 Tommy Casanova .20 .09
❑ 331 Passing Leaders 4.00 1.80
    Bob Griese
    Roger Staubach
❑ 332 Receiving Leaders 1.00 .45
    Lydell Mitchell
    Ahmad Rashad
❑ 333 Rushing Leaders 3.00 1.35
    Mark Van Eeghen
    Walter Payton
❑ 334 Scoring Leaders 3.00 1.35
    Errol Mann
    Walter Payton
❑ 335 Interception Leaders .20 .09
    Lyle Blackwood
    Rolland Lawrence
❑ 336 Punting Leaders .50 .23
    Ray Guy
    Tom Blanchard
❑ 337 Robert Brazile .50 .23
❑ 338 Charlie Joiner 1.50 .70
❑ 339 Joe Ferguson .50 .23
❑ 340 Bill Thompson .20 .09
❑ 341 Sam Cunningham .50 .23
❑ 342 Curtis Johnson .20 .09
❑ 343 Jim Marshall 1.00 .45
❑ 344 Charlie Sanders .20 .09
❑ 345 Willie Hall .20 .09
❑ 346 Pat Haden 1.00 .45
❑ 347 Jim Bakken .20 .09
❑ 348 Bruce Taylor .20 .09
❑ 349 Barty Smith .20 .09
❑ 350 Drew Pearson AP 1.50 .70
❑ 351 Mike Webster 2.50 1.10
❑ 352 Bobby Hammond .20 .09
❑ 353 Dave Mays .20 .09
❑ 354 Pat McInally .20 .09
❑ 355 Toni Linhart .20 .09
❑ 356 Larry Hand .20 .09
❑ 357 Ted Fritsch Jr. .20 .09
❑ 358 Larry Marshall .20 .09
❑ 359 Waymond Bryant .20 .09
❑ 360 Louie Kelcher RC .50 .23
❑ 361 Stanley Morgan RC 2.00 .90
❑ 362 Bruce Harper RC .50 .23
❑ 363 Bernard Jackson .20 .09
❑ 364 Walter White .20 .09
❑ 365 Ken Stabler 8.00 3.60
❑ 366 Fred Dryer 1.00 .45
❑ 367 Ike Harris .20 .09
❑ 368 Norm Bulaich .20 .09
❑ 369 Merv Krakau .20 .09
❑ 370 John James .20 .09
❑ 371 Bennie Cunningham RC .20 .09
❑ 372 Doug Van Horn .20 .09
❑ 373 Thom Darden .20 .09
❑ 374 Eddie Edwards RC .20 .09
❑ 375 Mike Thomas .20 .09
❑ 376 Fred Cook .20 .09
❑ 377 Mike Phipps .50 .23
❑ 378 Paul Krause 1.00 .45
❑ 379 Harold Carmichael 1.00 .45
❑ 380 Mike Haynes AP 1.00 .45
❑ 381 Wayne Morris .20 .09
❑ 382 Greg Buttle .20 .09
❑ 383 Jim Zorn 1.00 .45
❑ 384 Jack Dolbin .20 .09
❑ 385 Charlie Waters 1.00 .45
❑ 386 Dan Ryczek .20 .09
❑ 387 Joe Washington RC 1.00 .45
❑ 388 Checklist 265-396 1.00 .25
❑ 389 James Hunter .20 .09
❑ 390 Billy Johnson .50 .23
❑ 391 Jim Allen .20 .09
❑ 392 George Buehler .20 .09
❑ 393 Harry Carson .20 .09
❑ 394 Cleo Miller .20 .09
❑ 395 Gary Burley .20 .09
❑ 396 Mark Moseley .50 .23
❑ 397 Virgil Livers .20 .09
❑ 398 Joe Ehrmann .20 .09
❑ 399 Freddie Solomon .20 .09
❑ 400 O.J. Simpson 4.00 1.80
❑ 401 Julius Adams .20 .09
❑ 402 Artimus Parker .20 .09
❑ 403 Gene Washington .50 .23
❑ 404 Herman Edwards .20 .09
❑ 405 Craig Morton 1.00 .45
❑ 406 Alan Page 1.00 .45
❑ 407 Larry McCarren .20 .09
❑ 408 Tony Galbreath .50 .23
❑ 409 Roman Gabriel 1.00 .45
❑ 410 Efren Herrera AP .20 .09
❑ 411 Jim Smith RC 1.00 .45
❑ 412 Bill Bryant .20 .09
❑ 413 Doug Dieken .20 .09
❑ 414 Marvin Cobb .20 .09
❑ 415 Fred Biletnikoff 2.00 .90
❑ 416 Joe Theismann 2.50 1.10
❑ 417 Roland Harper .20 .09
❑ 418 Derrel Luce .20 .09
❑ 419 Ralph Perretta .20 .09
❑ 420 Louis Wright RC 1.00 .45
❑ 421 Prentice McCray .20 .09
❑ 422 Garry Puetz .20 .09
❑ 423 Alfred Jenkins RC 1.00 .45
❑ 424 Paul Seymour .20 .09
❑ 425 Garo Yepremian .50 .23
❑ 426 Emmitt Thomas .20 .09
❑ 427 Dexter Bussey .20 .09
❑ 428 John Sanders .20 .09
❑ 429 Ed Too Tall Jones 2.00 .90
❑ 430 Ron Yary .50 .23
❑ 431 Frank Lewis .50 .23
❑ 432 Jerry Golsteyn .20 .09
❑ 433 Clarence Scott .20 .09
❑ 434 Pete Johnson RC 1.00 .45
❑ 435 Charlie Young .50 .23
❑ 436 Harold McLinton .20 .09
❑ 437 Noah Jackson .20 .09
❑ 438 Bruce Laird .20 .09
❑ 439 John Matuszak .50 .23
❑ 440 Nat Moore AP .50 .23
❑ 441 Leon Gray .20 .09
❑ 442 Jerome Barkum .20 .09
❑ 443 Steve Largent 12.00 5.50
❑ 444 John Zook .20 .09
❑ 445 Preston Pearson .50 .23
❑ 446 Conrad Dobler .50 .23
❑ 447 Wilbur Summers .20 .09
❑ 448 Lou Piccone .20 .09
❑ 449 Ron Jaworski 1.00 .45
❑ 450 Jack Ham AP 1.50 .70
❑ 451 Mick Tingelhoff .50 .23
❑ 452 Clyde Powers .20 .09
❑ 453 John Cappelletti 1.00 .45
❑ 454 Dick Ambrose .20 .09
❑ 455 Lemar Parrish .20 .09
❑ 456 Ron Saul .20 .09

❑ 457 Bob Parsons .20 .09
❑ 458 Glenn Doughty .20 .09
❑ 459 Don Woods .20 .09
❑ 460 Art Shell AP 1.00 .45
❑ 461 Sam Hunt .20 .09
❑ 462 Lawrence Pillers .20 .09
❑ 463 Henry Childs .20 .09
❑ 464 Roger Wehrli .20 .09
❑ 465 Otis Armstrong .50 .23
❑ 466 Bob Baumhower RC 1.00 .45
❑ 467 Ray Jarvis .20 .09
❑ 468 Guy Morriss .20 .09
❑ 469 Matt Blair .50 .23
❑ 470 Billy Joe DuPree .50 .23
❑ 471 Roland Hooks .20 .09
❑ 472 Joe Danelo .20 .09
❑ 473 Reggie Rucker .50 .23
❑ 474 Vern Holland .20 .09
❑ 475 Mel Blount 1.50 .70
❑ 476 Eddie Brown .20 .09
❑ 477 Bo Rather .20 .09
❑ 478 Don McCauley .20 .09
❑ 479 Glen Walker .20 .09
❑ 480 Randy Gradishar AP 1.00 .45
❑ 481 Dave Rowe .20 .09
❑ 482 Pat Leahy .50 .23
❑ 483 Mike Fuller .20 .09
❑ 484 David Lewis .20 .09
❑ 485 Steve Grogan 1.00 .45
❑ 486 Mel Gray .50 .23
❑ 487 Eddie Payton RC .50 .23
❑ 488 Checklist 397-528 1.00 .25
❑ 489 Stu Voigt .20 .09
❑ 490 Rolland Lawrence AP .20 .09
❑ 491 Nick Mike-Mayer .20 .09
❑ 492 Troy Archer .20 .09
❑ 493 Benny Malone .20 .09
❑ 494 Golden Richards .50 .23
❑ 495 Chris Hanburger .20 .09
❑ 496 Dwight Harrison .20 .09
❑ 497 Gary Fencik RC 1.00 .45
❑ 498 Rich Saul .20 .09
❑ 499 Dan Fouts 4.00 1.80
❑ 500 Franco Harris AP 4.00 1.80
❑ 501 Atlanta Falcons TL .60 .15
Haskel Stanback
Alfred Jenkins
Claude Humphrey
Jeff Merrow
Rolland Lawrence
(checklist back)
❑ 502 Baltimore Colts TL .60 .15
Lydell Mitchell
Lydell Mitchell
Lyle Blackwood
Fred Cook
(checklist back)
❑ 503 Buffalo Bills TL .60 .15
O.J. Simpson
Bob Chandler
Tony Greene
Sherman White
(checklist back)
❑ 504 Chicago Bears TL 2.00 .50
Walter Payton
James Scott
Allan Ellis
Ron Rydalch
(checklist back)
❑ 505 Cincinnati Bengals TL .60 .15
Pete Johnson
Billy Brooks
Lemar Parrish
Reggie Williams
Gary Burley
(checklist back)
❑ 506 Cleveland Browns TL .60 .15
Greg Pruitt
Reggie Rucker
Thom Darden
Mack Mitchell
(checklist back)
❑ 507 Dallas Cowboys TL 2.50 .60
Tony Dorsett
Drew Pearson
Cliff Harris
Harvey Martin
(checklist back)
❑ 508 Denver Broncos TL .60 .15
Otis Armstrong
Haven Moses
Bill Thompson
Rick Upchurch
(checklist back)
❑ 509 Detroit Lions TL .60 .15
Horace King
David Hill
James Hunter
Ken Sanders
(checklist back)
❑ 510 Green Bay Packers TL .60 .15
Barty Smith
Steve Odom
Steve Luke
Mike C. McCoy
Dave Pureifory
Dave Roller
(checklist back)
❑ 511 Houston Oilers TL .60 .15
Ronnie Coleman
Ken Burrough
Mike Reinfeldt
James Young
(checklist back)
❑ 512 Kansas City Chiefs TL .60 .15
Ed Podolak
Walter White
Gary Barbaro
Wilbur Young
(checklist back)
❑ 513 Los Angeles Rams TL .60 .15
Lawrence McCutcheon
Harold Jackson
Bill Simpson
Jack Youngblood
(checklist back)
❑ 514 Miami Dolphins TL .60 .15
Benny Malone
Nat Moore
Curtis Johnson
A.J. Duhe
(checklist back)
❑ 515 Minnesota Vikings TL .60 .15
Chuck Foreman
Sammie White
Bobby Bryant
Carl Eller
(checklist back)
❑ 516 New England Patriots TL .60 .15
Sam Cunningham
Darryl Stingley
Mike Haynes
Tony McGee
(checklist back)
❑ 517 New Orleans Saints TL .60 .15
Chuck Muncie
Don Herrmann
Chuck Crist
Elois Grooms
(checklist back)
❑ 518 New York Giants TL .60 .15
Bobby Hammond
Jimmy Robinson
Bill Bryant
John Mendenhall
(checklist back)
❑ 519 New York Jets TL .60 .15
Clark Gaines
Wesley Walker
Burgess Owens
Joe Klecko
(checklist back)
❑ 520 Oakland Raiders TL .60 .15
Mark Van Eeghen
Dave Casper
Jack Tatum
Neal Colzie
(checklist back)
❑ 521 Philadelphia Eagles TL .60 .15
Mike Hogan
Harold Carmichael
Herman Edwards
John Sanders
Lem Burnham
(checklist back)
❑ 522 Pittsburgh Steelers TL .60 .15
Franco Harris
Jim Smith
Mel Blount
Steve Furness
(checklist back)
❑ 523 St.Louis Cardinals TL .60 .15
Terry Metcalf
Mel Gray
Roger Wehrli
Mike Dawson
(checklist back)
❑ 524 San Diego Chargers TL .60 .15
Rickey Young
Charlie Joiner
Mike Fuller
Gary Johnson
(checklist back)
❑ 525 San Francisco 49ers TL .60 .15
Delvin Williams
Gene Washington
Mel Phillips
Dave Washington
Cleveland Elam
(checklist back)
❑ 526 Seattle Seahawks TL 1.50 .35
Sherman Smith
Steve Largent
Autry Beamon
Walter Packer
(checklist back)
❑ 527 Tampa Bay Bucs TL .20 .05
Morris Owens
Isaac Hagins
Mike Washington
Lee Roy Selmon
(checklist back)
❑ 528 Wash. Redskins TL .60 .15
Mike Thomas
Jean Fugett
Ken Houston
Dennis Johnson
(checklist back)

1979 Topps

	NRMT-MT	EXC
COMPLETE SET (528)	150.00	70.00

❑ 1 Passing Leaders 8.00 2.00
Roger Staubach
Terry Bradshaw
❑ 2 Receiving Leaders 1.00 .45
Rickey Young
Steve Largent
❑ 3 Rushing Leaders 8.00 3.60
Walter Payton
Earl Campbell
❑ 4 Scoring Leaders .20 .09
Frank Corral
Pat Leahy
❑ 5 Interception Leaders .20 .09
Willie Buchanon
Ken Stone
Thom Darden

❑ 6 Punting Leaders .20 .09
Tom Skladany
Pat McInally
❑ 7 Johnny Perkins .20 .09
❑ 8 Charles Phillips .20 .09
❑ 9 Derrel Luce .20 .09
❑ 10 John Riggins 1.25 .55
❑ 11 Chester Marcol .20 .09
❑ 12 Bernard Jackson .20 .09
❑ 13 Dave Logan .20 .09
❑ 14 Bo Harris .20 .09
❑ 15 Alan Page 1.00 .45
❑ 16 John Smith .20 .09
❑ 17 Dwight McDonald .20 .09
❑ 18 John Cappelletti .50 .23
❑ 19 Pittsburgh Steelers TL 1.00 .45
Franco Harris
Larry Anderson
Tony Dungy
L.C. Greenwood
(checklist back)
❑ 20 Bill Bergey AP .50 .23
❑ 21 Jerome Barkum .20 .09
❑ 22 Larry Csonka 2.50 1.10
❑ 23 Joe Ferguson .50 .23
❑ 24 Ed Too Tall Jones 1.25 .55
❑ 25 Dave Jennings .50 .23
❑ 26 Horace King .20 .09
❑ 27 Steve Little .50 .23
❑ 28 Morris Bradshaw .20 .09
❑ 29 Joe Ehrmann .20 .09
❑ 30 Ahmad Rashad AP 1.00 .45
❑ 31 Joe Lavender .20 .09
❑ 32 Dan Neal .20 .09
❑ 33 Johnny Evans .20 .09
❑ 34 Pete Johnson .50 .23
❑ 35 Mike Haynes AP 1.00 .45
❑ 36 Tim Mazzetti .20 .09
❑ 37 Mike Barber RC .20 .09
❑ 38 San Francisco 49ers TL 1.00 .45
O.J. Simpson
Freddie Solomon
Chuck Crist
Cedrick Hardman
(checklist back)
❑ 39 Bill Gregory .20 .09
❑ 40 Randy Gradishar AP 1.00 .45
❑ 41 Richard Todd .50 .23
❑ 42 Henry Marshall .20 .09
❑ 43 John Hill .20 .09
❑ 44 Sidney Thornton .20 .09
❑ 45 Ron Jessie .20 .09
❑ 46 Bob Baumhower .50 .23
❑ 47 Johnnie Gray .20 .09
❑ 48 Doug Williams RC 6.00 2.70
❑ 49 Don McCauley .20 .09
❑ 50 Ray Guy AP .50 .23
❑ 51 Bob Klein .20 .09
❑ 52 Golden Richards .20 .09
❑ 53 Mark Miller .20 .09
❑ 54 John Sanders .20 .09
❑ 55 Gary Burley .20 .09
❑ 56 Steve Nelson .20 .09
❑ 57 Buffalo Bills TL .75 .35
Terry Miller
Frank Lewis
Mario Clark
Lucius Sanford
(checklist back)
❑ 58 Bobby Bryant .20 .09
❑ 59 Rick Kane .20 .09
❑ 60 Larry Little 1.00 .45
❑ 61 Ted Fritsch Jr. .20 .09
❑ 62 Larry Mallory .20 .09
❑ 63 Marvin Powell .20 .09
❑ 64 Jim Hart 1.00 .45
❑ 65 Joe Greene AP 1.50 .70
❑ 66 Walter White .20 .09
❑ 67 Gregg Bingham .20 .09
❑ 68 Errol Mann .20 .09
❑ 69 Bruce Laird .20 .09
❑ 70 Drew Pearson 1.00 .45
❑ 71 Steve Bartkowski 1.00 .45
❑ 72 Ted Albrecht .20 .09
❑ 73 Charlie Hall .20 .09
❑ 74 Pat McInally .20 .09
❑ 75 Al(Bubba) Baker AP RC 1.00 .45
❑ 76 New England Pats TL .75 .35
Sam Cunningham
Stanley Morgan
Mike Haynes
Tony McGee
(checklist back)
❑ 77 Steve DeBerg RC 2.00 .90
❑ 78 John Yarno .20 .09
❑ 79 Stu Voigt .20 .09
❑ 80 Frank Corral AP .20 .09
❑ 81 Troy Archer .20 .09
❑ 82 Bruce Harper .20 .09
❑ 83 Tom Jackson 1.50 .70
❑ 84 Larry Brown .50 .23
❑ 85 Wilbert Montgomery AP RC 1.00 .45
❑ 86 Butch Johnson .50 .23
❑ 87 Mike Kadish .20 .09
❑ 88 Ralph Perretta .20 .09
❑ 89 David Lee .20 .09
❑ 90 Mark Van Eeghen .50 .23
❑ 91 John McDaniel .20 .09
❑ 92 Gary Fencik .50 .23
❑ 93 Mack Mitchell .20 .09
❑ 94 Cincinnati Bengals TL .75 .35
Pete Johnson
Isaac Curtis
Dick Jauron
Ross Browner
(Checklist back)
❑ 95 Steve Grogan 1.00 .45
❑ 96 Garo Yepremian .50 .23
❑ 97 Barty Smith .20 .09
❑ 98 Frank Reed .20 .09
❑ 99 Jim Clack .20 .09
❑ 100 Chuck Foreman .50 .23
❑ 101 Joe Klecko 1.00 .45
❑ 102 Pat Tilley .50 .23
❑ 103 Conrad Dobler .50 .23
❑ 104 Craig Colquitt .20 .09
❑ 105 Dan Pastorini .50 .23
❑ 106 Rod Perry AP .20 .09
❑ 107 Nick Mike-Mayer .20 .09
❑ 108 John Matuszak .50 .23
❑ 109 David Taylor .20 .09
❑ 110 Billy Joe DuPree AP .50 .23
❑ 111 Harold McLinton .20 .09
❑ 112 Virgil Livers .20 .09
❑ 113 Cleveland Browns TL .75 .35
Greg Pruitt
Reggie Rucker
Thom Darden
Mack Mitchell
(checklist back)
❑ 114 Checklist 1-132 1.00 .25
❑ 115 Ken Anderson 1.00 .45
❑ 116 Bill Lenkaitis .20 .09
❑ 117 Bucky Dilts .20 .09
❑ 118 Tony Greene .20 .09
❑ 119 Bobby Hammond .20 .09
❑ 120 Nat Moore .50 .23
❑ 121 Pat Leahy AP .50 .23
❑ 122 James Harris .50 .23
❑ 123 Lee Roy Selmon 1.25 .55
❑ 124 Bennie Cunningham .50 .23
❑ 125 Matt Blair AP .50 .23
❑ 126 Jim Allen .20 .09
❑ 127 Alfred Jenkins .50 .23
❑ 128 Arthur Whittington .20 .09
❑ 129 Norm Thompson .20 .09
❑ 130 Pat Haden 1.00 .45
❑ 131 Freddie Solomon .20 .09
❑ 132 Chicago Bears TL 2.00 .90
Walter Payton
James Scott
Gary Fencik
Alan Page
(checklist back)
❑ 133 Mark Moseley .20 .09
❑ 134 Cleo Miller .20 .09
❑ 135 Ross Browner RC .50 .23
❑ 136 Don Calhoun .20 .09
❑ 137 David Whitehurst .20 .09
❑ 138 Terry Beeson .20 .09
❑ 139 Ken Stone .20 .09
❑ 140 Brad Van Pelt AP .20 .09
❑ 141 Wesley Walker AP 1.00 .45
❑ 142 Jan Stenerud 1.00 .45
❑ 143 Henry Childs .20 .09
❑ 144 Otis Armstrong 1.00 .45
❑ 145 Dwight White .50 .23
❑ 146 Steve Wilson .20 .09
❑ 147 Tom Skladany AP RC .20 .09
❑ 148 Lou Piccone .20 .09
❑ 149 Monte Johnson .20 .09
❑ 150 Joe Washington .50 .23
❑ 151 Philadelphia Eagles TL .75 .35
Wilbert Montgomery
Harold Carmichael
Herman Edwards
Dennis Harrison
(checklist back)
❑ 152 Fred Dean .20 .09
❑ 153 Rolland Lawrence .20 .09
❑ 154 Brian Baschnagel .20 .09
❑ 155 Joe Theismann 2.00 .90
❑ 156 Marvin Cobb .20 .09
❑ 157 Dick Ambrose .20 .09
❑ 158 Mike Patrick .20 .09
❑ 159 Gary Shirk .20 .09
❑ 160 Tony Dorsett 12.00 5.50
❑ 161 Greg Buttle .20 .09
❑ 162 A.J. Duhe .50 .23
❑ 163 Mick Tingelhoff .50 .23
❑ 164 Ken Burrough .50 .23
❑ 165 Mike Wagner .20 .09
❑ 166 AFC Championship 1.00 .45
Steelers 34,
Oilers 5
(Franco Harris)
❑ 167 NFC Championship .50 .23
Cowboys 28,
Rams 0
(line of scrimmage)
❑ 168 Super Bowl XIII 1.25 .55
Steelers 35,
Cowboys 31
(Franco Harris)
❑ 169 Oakland Raiders TL .75 .35
Mark Van Eeghen
Dave Casper
Charles Phillips
Ted Hendricks
(checklist back)
❑ 170 O.J. Simpson 4.00 1.80
❑ 171 Doug Nettles .20 .09
❑ 172 Dan Dierdorf AP 1.00 .45
❑ 173 Dave Beverly .20 .09
❑ 174 Jim Zorn 1.00 .45
❑ 175 Mike Thomas .20 .09
❑ 176 John Outlaw .20 .09
❑ 177 Jim Turner .20 .09
❑ 178 Freddie Scott .20 .09
❑ 179 Mike Phipps .50 .23
❑ 180 Jack Youngblood AP 1.00 .45
❑ 181 Sam Hunt .20 .09
❑ 182 Tony Hill RC 1.00 .45
❑ 183 Gary Barbaro .20 .09
❑ 184 Archie Griffin .50 .23
❑ 185 Jerry Sherk .20 .09
❑ 186 Bobby Jackson .20 .09
❑ 187 Don Woods .20 .09
❑ 188 New York Giants TL .75 .35
Doug Kotar
Jimmy Robinson
Terry Jackson
George Martin
(checklist back)
❑ 189 Raymond Chester .20 .09
❑ 190 Joe DeLamielleure AP .20 .09
❑ 191 Tony Galbreath .50 .23
❑ 192 Robert Brazile AP .50 .23
❑ 193 Neil O'Donoghue .20 .09
❑ 194 Mike Webster AP 1.00 .45
❑ 195 Ed Simonini .20 .09
❑ 196 Benny Malone .20 .09
❑ 197 Tom Wittum .20 .09
❑ 198 Steve Largent AP 8.00 3.60
❑ 199 Tommy Hart .20 .09
❑ 200 Fran Tarkenton 3.00 1.35
❑ 201 Leon Gray AP .20 .09

❑ 202 Leroy Harris .20 .09
❑ 203 Eric Williams .20 .09
❑ 204 Thom Darden AP .20 .09
❑ 205 Ken Riley .50 .23
❑ 206 Clark Gaines .20 .09
❑ 207 Kansas City Chiefs TL .75 .35
Tony Reed
Tony Reed
Tim Gray
Art Still
(checklist back)
❑ 208 Joe Danelo .20 .09
❑ 209 Glen Walker .20 .09
❑ 210 Art Shell 1.00 .45
❑ 211 Jon Keyworth .20 .09
❑ 212 Herman Edwards .20 .09
❑ 213 John Fitzgerald .20 .09
❑ 214 Jim Smith .50 .23
❑ 215 Coy Bacon .50 .23
❑ 216 Dennis Johnson .20 .09
❑ 217 John Jefferson RC 3.00 1.35
(Charlie Joiner
in background)
❑ 218 Gary Weaver .20 .09
❑ 219 Tom Blanchard .20 .09
❑ 220 Bert Jones 1.00 .45
❑ 221 Stanley Morgan 1.00 .45
❑ 222 James Hunter .20 .09
❑ 223 Jim O'Bradovich .20 .09
❑ 224 Carl Mauck .20 .09
❑ 225 Chris Bahr .20 .09
❑ 226 New York Jets TL .75 .35
Kevin Long
Wesley Walker
Bobby Jackson
Burgess Owens
Joe Klecko
(checklist back)
❑ 227 Roland Harper .20 .09
❑ 228 Randy Dean .20 .09
❑ 229 Bob Jackson .20 .09
❑ 230 Sammie White .50 .23
❑ 231 Mike Dawson .20 .09
❑ 232 Checklist 133-264 1.00 .25
❑ 233 Ken MacAfee .20 .09
❑ 234 Jon Kolb AP .20 .09
❑ 235 Willie Hall .20 .09
❑ 236 Ron Saul AP .20 .09
❑ 237 Haskel Stanback .20 .09
❑ 238 Zenon Andrusyshyn .20 .09
❑ 239 Norris Thomas .20 .09
❑ 240 Rick Upchurch .50 .23
❑ 241 Robert Pratt .20 .09
❑ 242 Julius Adams .20 .09
❑ 243 Rich McGeorge .20 .09
❑ 244 Seattle Seahawks TL 1.25 .55
Sherman Smith
Steve Largent
Cornell Webster
Bill Gregory
(checklist back)
❑ 245 Blair Bush RC .20 .09
❑ 246 Billy Johnson .50 .23
❑ 247 Randy Rasmussen .20 .09
❑ 248 Brian Kelley .20 .09
❑ 249 Mike Pruitt .50 .23
❑ 250 Harold Carmichael AP 1.00 .45
❑ 251 Mike Hartenstine .20 .09
❑ 252 Robert Newhouse .50 .23
❑ 253 Gary Danielson RC 1.00 .45
❑ 254 Mike Fuller .20 .09
❑ 255 L.C. Greenwood AP 1.00 .45
❑ 256 Lemar Parrish .20 .09
❑ 257 Ike Harris .20 .09
❑ 258 Ricky Bell RC 1.00 .45
❑ 259 Willie Parker .20 .09
❑ 260 Gene Upshaw 1.00 .45
❑ 261 Glenn Doughty .20 .09
❑ 262 Steve Zabel .20 .09
❑ 263 Atlanta Falcons TL .75 .35
Bubba Bean
Wallace Francis
Rolland Lawrence
Greg Brezina
(checklist back)
❑ 264 Ray Wersching .20 .09
❑ 265 Lawrence McCutcheon .50 .23
❑ 266 Willie Buchanon AP .20 .09
❑ 267 Matt Robinson .20 .09
❑ 268 Reggie Rucker .50 .23
❑ 269 Doug Van Horn .20 .09
❑ 270 Lydell Mitchell .50 .23
❑ 271 Vern Holland .20 .09
❑ 272 Eason Ramson .20 .09
❑ 273 Steve Towle .20 .09
❑ 274 Jim Marshall 1.00 .45
❑ 275 Mel Blount 1.25 .55
❑ 276 Bob Kuziel .20 .09
❑ 277 James Scott .20 .09
❑ 278 Tony Reed .20 .09
❑ 279 Dave Green .20 .09
❑ 280 Toni Linhart .20 .09
❑ 281 Andy Johnson .20 .09
❑ 282 Los Angeles Rams TL .75 .35
Cullen Bryant
Willie Miller
Rod Perry
Pat Thomas
Larry Brooks
(checklist back)
❑ 283 Phil Villapiano .50 .23
❑ 284 Dexter Bussey .20 .09
❑ 285 Craig Morton 1.00 .45
❑ 286 Guy Morriss .20 .09
❑ 287 Lawrence Pillers .20 .09
❑ 288 Gerald Irons .20 .09
❑ 289 Scott Perry .20 .09
❑ 290 Randy White AP 2.00 .90
❑ 291 Jack Gregory .20 .09
❑ 292 Bob Chandler .20 .09
❑ 293 Rich Szaro .20 .09
❑ 294 Sherman Smith .20 .09
❑ 295 Tom Banks AP .20 .09
❑ 296 Revie Sorey AP .20 .09
❑ 297 Ricky Thompson .20 .09
❑ 298 Ron Yary .50 .23
❑ 299 Lyle Blackwood .20 .09
❑ 300 Franco Harris 2.50 1.10
❑ 301 Houston Oilers TL 3.00 1.35
Earl Campbell
Ken Burrough
Willie Alexander
Elvin Bethea
(checklist back)
❑ 302 Scott Bull .20 .09
❑ 303 Dewey Selmon .50 .23
❑ 304 Jack Rudnay .20 .09
❑ 305 Fred Biletnikoff 2.00 .90
❑ 306 Jeff West .20 .09
❑ 307 Shafer Suggs .20 .09
❑ 308 Ozzie Newsome RC 15.00 6.75
❑ 309 Boobie Clark .20 .09
❑ 310 James Lofton RC 15.00 6.75
❑ 311 Joe Pisarcik .20 .09
❑ 312 Bill Simpson AP .20 .09
❑ 313 Haven Moses .50 .23
❑ 314 Jim Merlo .20 .09
❑ 315 Preston Pearson .50 .23
❑ 316 Larry Tearry .20 .09
❑ 317 Tom Dempsey .20 .09
❑ 318 Greg Latta .20 .09
❑ 319 Wash. Redskins TL .75 .35
John Riggins
John McDaniel
Jake Scott
Coy Bacon
(checklist back)
❑ 320 Jack Ham AP 1.25 .55
❑ 321 Harold Jackson .50 .23
❑ 322 George Roberts .20 .09
❑ 323 Ron Jaworski 1.00 .45
❑ 324 Jim Otis .20 .09
❑ 325 Roger Carr .50 .23
❑ 326 Jack Tatum .50 .23
❑ 327 Derrick Gaffney .20 .09
❑ 328 Reggie Williams 1.00 .45
❑ 329 Doug Dieken .20 .09
❑ 330 Efren Herrera .20 .09
❑ 331 Earl Campbell RB 6.00 2.70
Most Yards
Rushing, Rookie
❑ 332 Tony Galbreath RB .20 .09
Most Receptions,
Running Back, Game
❑ 333 Bruce Harper RB .20 .09
Most Combined Kick
Return Yards, Season
❑ 334 John James RB .20 .09
Most Punts, Season
❑ 335 Walter Payton RB 4.00 1.80
Most Combined
Attempts, Season
❑ 336 Rickey Young RB .20 .09
Most Receptions,
Running Back, Season
❑ 337 Jeff Van Note .50 .23
❑ 338 San Diego Chargers TL .75 .35
Lydell Mitchell
John Jefferson
Mike Fuller
Fred Dean
(checklist back)
❑ 339 Stan Walters AP RC .20 .09
❑ 340 Louis Wright AP .50 .23
❑ 341 Horace Ivory .20 .09
❑ 342 Andre Tillman .20 .09
❑ 343 Greg Coleman RC .20 .09
❑ 344 Doug English AP RC 1.00 .45
❑ 345 Ted Hendricks 1.00 .45
❑ 346 Rich Saul .20 .09
❑ 347 Mel Gray .50 .23
❑ 348 Toni Fritsch .20 .09
❑ 349 Cornell Webster .20 .09
❑ 350 Ken Houston 1.00 .45
❑ 351 Ron Johnson .50 .23
❑ 352 Doug Kotar .20 .09
❑ 353 Brian Sipe 1.00 .45
❑ 354 Billy Brooks .20 .09
❑ 355 John Dutton .50 .23
❑ 356 Don Goode .20 .09
❑ 357 Detroit Lions TL .75 .35
Dexter Bussey
David Hill
Jim Allen
Al(Bubba) Baker
(checklist back)
❑ 358 Reuben Gant .20 .09
❑ 359 Bob Parsons .20 .09
❑ 360 Cliff Harris AP 1.00 .45
❑ 361 Raymond Clayborn .50 .23
❑ 362 Scott Dierking .20 .09
❑ 363 Bill Bryan .20 .09
❑ 364 Mike Livingston .20 .09
❑ 365 Otis Sistrunk .50 .23
❑ 366 Charlie Young .50 .23
❑ 367 Keith Wortman .20 .09
❑ 368 Checklist 265-396 1.00 .25
❑ 369 Mike Michel .20 .09
❑ 370 Delvin Williams AP .20 .09
❑ 371 Steve Furness .50 .23
❑ 372 Emery Moorehead .20 .09
❑ 373 Clarence Scott .20 .09
❑ 374 Rufus Mayes .20 .09
❑ 375 Chris Hanburger .20 .09
❑ 376 Baltimore Colts TL .75 .35
Joe Washington
Roger Carr
Norm Thompson
John Dutton
(checklist back)
❑ 377 Bob Avellini .50 .23
❑ 378 Jeff Siemon .20 .09
❑ 379 Roland Hooks .20 .09
❑ 380 Russ Francis .50 .23
❑ 381 Roger Wehrli .20 .09
❑ 382 Joe Fields .20 .09
❑ 383 Archie Manning 1.00 .45
❑ 384 Rob Lytle .20 .09
❑ 385 Thomas Henderson .50 .23
❑ 386 Morris Owens .20 .09
❑ 387 Dan Fouts 3.00 1.35
❑ 388 Chuck Crist .20 .09
❑ 389 Ed O'Neil .20 .09
❑ 390 Earl Campbell AP RC 30.00 13.50
❑ 391 Randy Grossman .20 .09
❑ 392 Monte Jackson .20 .09
❑ 393 John Mendenhall .20 .09
❑ 394 Miami Dolphins TL .75 .35

Delvin Williams
Duriel Harris
Tim Foley
Vern Den Herder
(checklist back)

❑ 395 Isaac Curtis .50 .23
❑ 396 Mike Bragg .20 .09
❑ 397 Doug Plank .20 .09
❑ 398 Mike Barnes .20 .09
❑ 399 Calvin Hill .50 .23
❑ 400 Roger Staubach AP .. 10.00 4.50
❑ 401 Doug Beaudoin .20 .09
❑ 402 Chuck Ramsey .20 .09
❑ 403 Mike Hogan .20 .09
❑ 404 Mario Clark .20 .09
❑ 405 Riley Odoms .20 .09
❑ 406 Carl Eller .50 .23
❑ 407 Green Bay Packers TL 2.00 .90
Terdell Middleton
James Lofton
Willie Buchanon
Ezra Johnson
(checklist back)
❑ 408 Mark Arneson .20 .09
❑ 409 Vince Ferragamo RC .. 1.00 .45
❑ 410 Cleveland Elam .20 .09
❑ 411 Donnie Shell RC 4.00 1.80
❑ 412 Ray Rhodes 1.00 .45
❑ 413 Don Cockroft .20 .09
❑ 414 Don Bass .50 .23
❑ 415 Cliff Branch 1.00 .45
❑ 416 Diron Talbert .20 .09
❑ 417 Tom Hicks .20 .09
❑ 418 Roosevelt Leaks .20 .09
❑ 419 Charlie Joiner 1.00 .45
❑ 420 Lyle Alzado AP 1.00 .45
❑ 421 Sam Cunningham .50 .23
❑ 422 Larry Keller .20 .09
❑ 423 Jim Mitchell .20 .09
❑ 424 Randy Logan .20 .09
❑ 425 Jim Langer 1.00 .45
❑ 426 Gary Green .20 .09
❑ 427 Luther Blue .20 .09
❑ 428 Dennis Johnson .20 .09
❑ 429 Danny White 1.00 .45
❑ 430 Roy Gerela .20 .09
❑ 431 Jimmy Robinson .20 .09
❑ 432 Minnesota Vikings TL .... .75 .35
Chuck Foreman
Ahmad Rashad
Bobby Bryant
Mark Mullaney
(checklist back)
❑ 433 Oliver Davis .20 .09
❑ 434 Lenvil Elliott .20 .09
❑ 435 Willie Miller RC .20 .09
❑ 436 Brad Dusek .20 .09
❑ 437 Bob Thomas .20 .09
❑ 438 Ken Mendenhall .20 .09
❑ 439 Clarence Davis .20 .09
❑ 440 Bob Griese 2.50 1.10
❑ 441 Tony McGee .20 .09
❑ 442 Ed Taylor .20 .09
❑ 443 Ron Howard .20 .09
❑ 444 Wayne Morris .20 .09
❑ 445 Charlie Waters 1.00 .45
❑ 446 Rick Danmeier .20 .09
❑ 447 Paul Naumoff .20 .09
❑ 448 Keith Krepfle .20 .09
❑ 449 Rusty Jackson .20 .09
❑ 450 John Stallworth 4.00 1.80
❑ 451 New Orleans Saints TL .. .75 .35
Tony Galbreath
Henry Childs
Tom Myers
Elex Price
(checklist back)
❑ 452 Ron Mikolajczyk .20 .09
❑ 453 Fred Dryer 1.00 .45
❑ 454 Jim LeClair .20 .09
❑ 455 Greg Pruitt .50 .23
❑ 456 Jake Scott .20 .09
❑ 457 Steve Schubert .20 .09
❑ 458 George Kunz .20 .09
❑ 459 Mike Williams .20 .09
❑ 460 Dave Casper AP .50 .23
❑ 461 Sam Adams .20 .09
❑ 462 Abdul Salaam .20 .09
❑ 463 Terdell Middleton .50 .23
❑ 464 Mike Wood .20 .09
❑ 465 Bill Thompson AP .20 .09
❑ 466 Larry Gordon .20 .09
❑ 467 Benny Ricardo .20 .09
❑ 468 Reggie McKenzie .50 .23
❑ 469 Dallas Cowboys TL ...... 1.25 .55
Tony Dorsett
Tony Hill
Benny Barnes
Harvey Martin
Randy White
(checklist back)
❑ 470 Rickey Young .50 .23
❑ 471 Charlie Smith .20 .09
❑ 472 Al Dixon .20 .09
❑ 473 Tom DeLeone .20 .09
❑ 474 Louis Breeden .50 .23
❑ 475 Jack Lambert 2.00 .90
❑ 476 Terry Hermeling .20 .09
❑ 477 J.K. McKay .20 .09
❑ 478 Stan White .20 .09
❑ 479 Terry Nelson .20 .09
❑ 480 Walter Payton AP 20.00 9.00
❑ 481 Dave Dalby .20 .09
❑ 482 Burgess Owens .20 .09
❑ 483 Rolf Benirschke .20 .09
❑ 484 Jack Dolbin .20 .09
❑ 485 John Hannah AP 1.00 .45
❑ 486 Checklist 397-528 1.00 .25
❑ 487 Greg Landry .50 .23
❑ 488 St. Louis Cardinals TL.... .75 .35
Jim Otis
Pat Tilley
Ken Stone
Mike Dawson
(checklist back)
❑ 489 Paul Krause .50 .23
❑ 490 John James .20 .09
❑ 491 Merv Krakau .20 .09
❑ 492 Dan Doornink .20 .09
❑ 493 Curtis Johnson .20 .09
❑ 494 Rafael Septien .20 .09
❑ 495 Jean Fugett .20 .09
❑ 496 Frank LeMaster .20 .09
❑ 497 Allan Ellis .20 .09
❑ 498 Billy Waddy RC .50 .23
❑ 499 Hank Bauer .20 .09
❑ 500 Terry Bradshaw AP UER 8.00 3.60
(Stat headers on back
are for a runner)
❑ 501 Larry McCarren .20 .09
❑ 502 Fred Cook .20 .09
❑ 503 Chuck Muncie .50 .23
❑ 504 Herman Weaver .20 .09
❑ 505 Eddie Edwards .20 .09
❑ 506 Tony Peters .20 .09
❑ 507 Denver Broncos TL .... .75 .35
Lonnie Perrin
Riley Odoms
Steve Foley
Bernard Jackson
Lyle Alzado
(checklist back)
❑ 508 Jimbo Elrod .20 .09
❑ 509 David Hill .20 .09
❑ 510 Harvey Martin 1.00 .45
❑ 511 Terry Miller .50 .23
❑ 512 June Jones RC .50 .23
❑ 513 Randy Cross 1.00 .45
❑ 514 Duriel Harris .20 .09
❑ 515 Harry Carson 1.00 .45
❑ 516 Tim Fox .20 .09
❑ 517 John Zook .20 .09
❑ 518 Bob Tucker .20 .09
❑ 519 Kevin Long .20 .09
❑ 520 Ken Stabler 6.00 2.70
❑ 521 John Bunting .20 .09
❑ 522 Rocky Bleier 1.25 .55
❑ 523 Noah Jackson .20 .09
❑ 524 Cliff Parsley .20 .09
❑ 525 Louie Kelcher AP .50 .23
❑ 526 Tampa Bay Bucs TL ...... .75 .35
Ricky Bell
Morris Owens
Cedric Brown
Lee Roy Selmon
(checklist back)
❑ 527 Bob Brudzinski .20 .09
❑ 528 Danny Buggs .20 .09

1980 Topps

	NRMT-MT	EXC
COMPLETE SET (528)	60.00	27.00

❑ 1 Ottis Anderson RB 1.00 .45
Most Yardage,
Rushing, Rookie
❑ 2 Harold Carmichael RB .... 1.00 .45
Most Consec. Games,
One or More Receptions
❑ 3 Dan Fouts RB 1.00 .45
Most Yardage,
Passing, Season
❑ 4 Paul Krause RB .50 .23
Most Interceptions,
Lifetime
❑ 5 Rick Upchurch RB .50 .23
Most Punt Return
Yards, Lifetime
❑ 6 Garo Yepremian RB .15 .07
Most Consecutive
Field Goals
❑ 7 Harold Jackson .50 .23
❑ 8 Mike Williams .15 .07
❑ 9 Calvin Hill .50 .23
❑ 10 Jack Ham AP 1.00 .45
❑ 11 Dan Melville .15 .07
❑ 12 Matt Robinson .15 .07
❑ 13 Billy Campfield .15 .07
❑ 14 Phil Tabor .15 .07
❑ 15 Randy Hughes UER .15 .07
(Cowboys didn't play
in SB VII)
❑ 16 Andre Tillman .15 .07
❑ 17 Isaac Curtis .50 .23
❑ 18 Charley Hannah .15 .07
❑ 19 Wash. Redskins TL........ 1.00 .45
John Riggins
Danny Buggs
Joe Lavender
Coy Bacon
(checklist back)
❑ 20 Jim Zorn .50 .23
❑ 21 Brian Baschnagel .15 .07
❑ 22 Jon Keyworth .15 .07
❑ 23 Phil Villapiano .15 .07
❑ 24 Richard Osborne .15 .07
❑ 25 Rich Saul AP .15 .07
❑ 26 Doug Beaudoin .15 .07
❑ 27 Cleveland Elam .15 .07
❑ 28 Charlie Joiner 1.00 .45
❑ 29 Dick Ambrose .15 .07
❑ 30 Mike Reinfeldt AP RC .... .15 .07
❑ 31 Matt Bahr RC 1.00 .45
❑ 32 Keith Krepfle .15 .07
❑ 33 Herb Scott .15 .07
❑ 34 Doug Kotar .15 .07
❑ 35 Bob Griese 1.50 .70
❑ 36 Jerry Butler RC .15 .07
❑ 37 Rolland Lawrence .15 .07

❑ 38	Gary Weaver	.15	.07
❑ 39	Kansas City Chiefs TL	.50	.23
	Ted McKnight		
	J.T. Smith		
	Gary Barbaro		
	Art Still		
	(checklist back)		
❑ 40	Chuck Muncie	.50	.23
❑ 41	Mike Hartenstine	.15	.07
❑ 42	Sammie White	.50	.23
❑ 43	Ken Clark	.15	.07
❑ 44	Clarence Harmon	.15	.07
❑ 45	Bert Jones	1.00	.45
❑ 46	Mike Washington	.15	.07
❑ 47	Joe Fields	.15	.07
❑ 48	Mike Wood	.15	.07
❑ 49	Oliver Davis	.15	.07
❑ 50	Stan Walters AP	.15	.07
❑ 51	Riley Odoms	.15	.07
❑ 52	Steve Pisarkiewicz	.15	.07
❑ 53	Tony Hill	1.00	.45
❑ 54	Scott Perry	.15	.07
❑ 55	George Martin RC	.15	.07
❑ 56	George Roberts	.15	.07
❑ 57	Seattle Seahawks TL	1.00	.45
	Sherman Smith		
	Steve Largent		
	Dave Brown		
	Manu Tuiasosopo		
	(checklist back)		
❑ 58	Billy Johnson	.50	.23
❑ 59	Reuben Gant	.15	.07
❑ 60	Dennis Harrah AP RC	.15	.07
❑ 61	Rocky Bleier	1.00	.45
❑ 62	Sam Hunt	.15	.07
❑ 63	Allan Ellis	.15	.07
❑ 64	Ricky Thompson	.15	.07
❑ 65	Ken Stabler	4.00	1.80
❑ 66	Dexter Bussey	.15	.07
❑ 67	Ken Mendenhall	.15	.07
❑ 68	Woodrow Lowe	.15	.07
❑ 69	Thom Darden	.15	.07
❑ 70	Randy White AP	1.50	.70
❑ 71	Ken MacAfee	.15	.07
❑ 72	Ron Jaworski	1.00	.45
❑ 73	William Andrews RC	1.00	.45
❑ 74	Jimmy Robinson	.15	.07
❑ 75	Roger Wehrli AP	.15	.07
❑ 76	Miami Dolphins TL	1.00	.45
	Larry Csonka		
	Nat Moore		
	Neal Colzie		
	Gerald Small		
	Vern Den Herder		
	(checklist back)		
❑ 77	Jack Rudnay	.15	.07
❑ 78	James Lofton	2.00	.90
❑ 79	Robert Brazile	.50	.23
❑ 80	Russ Francis	.50	.23
❑ 81	Ricky Bell	1.00	.45
❑ 82	Bob Avellini	.50	.23
❑ 83	Bobby Jackson	.15	.07
❑ 84	Mike Bragg	.15	.07
❑ 85	Cliff Branch	1.00	.45
❑ 86	Blair Bush	.15	.07
❑ 87	Sherman Smith	.15	.07
❑ 88	Glen Edwards	.15	.07
❑ 89	Don Cockroft	.15	.07
❑ 90	Louis Wright AP	.50	.23
❑ 91	Randy Grossman	.15	.07
❑ 92	Carl Hairston RC	1.00	.45
❑ 93	Archie Manning	1.00	.45
❑ 94	New York Giants TL	.50	.23
	Billy Taylor		
	Earnest Gray		
	George Martin		
	(checklist back)		
❑ 95	Preston Pearson	.50	.23
❑ 96	Rusty Chambers	.15	.07
❑ 97	Greg Coleman	.15	.07
❑ 98	Charlie Young	.15	.07
❑ 99	Matt Cavanaugh RC	.50	.23
❑ 100	Jesse Baker	.15	.07
❑ 101	Doug Plank	.15	.07
❑ 102	Checklist 1-132	.60	.15
❑ 103	Luther Bradley RC	.15	.07
❑ 104	Bob Kuziel	.15	.07
❑ 105	Craig Morton	.50	.23
❑ 106	Sherman White	.15	.07
❑ 107	Jim Breech RC	.50	.23
❑ 108	Hank Bauer	.15	.07
❑ 109	Tom Blanchard	.15	.07
❑ 110	Ozzie Newsome AP	2.00	.90
❑ 111	Steve Furness	.15	.07
❑ 112	Frank LeMaster	.15	.07
❑ 113	Dallas Cowboys TL	1.00	.45
	Tony Dorsett		
	Tony Hill		
	Harvey Martin		
	(checklist back)		
❑ 114	Doug Van Horn	.15	.07
❑ 115	Delvin Williams	.15	.07
❑ 116	Lyle Blackwood	.15	.07
❑ 117	Derrick Gaffney	.15	.07
❑ 118	Cornell Webster	.15	.07
❑ 119	Sam Cunningham	.50	.23
❑ 120	Jim Youngblood AP	.50	.23
❑ 121	Bob Thomas	.15	.07
❑ 122	Jack Thompson RC	.50	.23
❑ 123	Randy Cross	1.00	.45
❑ 124	Karl Lorch	.15	.07
❑ 125	Mel Gray	.15	.07
❑ 126	John James	.15	.07
❑ 127	Terdell Middleton	.15	.07
❑ 128	Leroy Jones	.15	.07
❑ 129	Tom DeLeone	.15	.07
❑ 130	John Stallworth AP	1.50	.70
❑ 131	Jimmie Giles RC	.50	.23
❑ 132	Philadelphia Eagles TL	1.00	.45
	Wilbert Montgomery		
	Harold Carmichael		
	Brenard Wilson		
	Carl Hairston		
	(checklist back)		
❑ 133	Gary Green	.15	.07
❑ 134	John Dutton	.50	.23
❑ 135	Harry Carson AP	1.00	.45
❑ 136	Bob Kuechenberg	.50	.23
❑ 137	Ike Harris	.15	.07
❑ 138	Tommy Kramer RC	1.00	.45
❑ 139	Sam Adams	.15	.07
❑ 140	Doug English AP	.50	.23
❑ 141	Steve Schubert	.15	.07
❑ 142	Rusty Jackson	.15	.07
❑ 143	Reese McCall	.15	.07
❑ 144	Scott Dierking	.15	.07
❑ 145	Ken Houston AP	1.00	.45
❑ 146	Bob Martin	.15	.07
❑ 147	Sam McCullum	.15	.07
❑ 148	Tom Banks	.15	.07
❑ 149	Willie Buchanon	.15	.07
❑ 150	Greg Pruitt	.50	.23
❑ 151	Denver Broncos TL	1.00	.45
	Otis Armstrong		
	Rick Upchurch		
	Steve Foley		
	Brison Manor		
	(checklist back)		
❑ 152	Don Smith	.15	.07
❑ 153	Pete Johnson	.50	.23
❑ 154	Charlie Smith	.15	.07
❑ 155	Mel Blount	1.00	.45
❑ 156	John Mendenhall	.15	.07
❑ 157	Danny White	1.00	.45
❑ 158	Jimmy Cefalo RC	.50	.23
❑ 159	Richard Bishop AP	.15	.07
❑ 160	Walter Payton AP	10.00	4.50
❑ 161	Dave Dalby	.15	.07
❑ 162	Preston Dennard	.15	.07
❑ 163	Johnnie Gray	.15	.07
❑ 164	Russell Erxleben	.15	.07
❑ 165	Toni Fritsch AP	.15	.07
❑ 166	Terry Hermeling	.15	.07
❑ 167	Roland Hooks	.15	.07
❑ 168	Roger Carr	.15	.07
❑ 169	San Diego Chargers TL	1.00	.45
	Clarence Williams		
	John Jefferson		
	Woodrow Lowe		
	Ray Preston		
	Wilbur Young		
	(checklist back)		
❑ 170	Ottis Anderson AP RC	4.00	1.80
❑ 171	Brian Sipe	1.00	.45
❑ 172	Leonard Thompson	.15	.07
❑ 173	Tony Reed	.15	.07
❑ 174	Bob Tucker	.15	.07
❑ 175	Joe Greene	1.00	.45
❑ 176	Jack Dolbin	.15	.07
❑ 177	Chuck Ramsey	.15	.07
❑ 178	Paul Hofer	.15	.07
❑ 179	Randy Logan	.15	.07
❑ 180	David Lewis AP	.15	.07
❑ 181	Duriel Harris	.15	.07
❑ 182	June Jones	.50	.23
❑ 183	Larry McCarren	.15	.07
❑ 184	Ken Johnson	.15	.07
❑ 185	Charlie Waters	1.00	.45
❑ 186	Noah Jackson	.15	.07
❑ 187	Reggie Williams	.50	.23
❑ 188	New England Patriots TL	.50	.23
	Sam Cunningham		
	Harold Jackson		
	Raymond Clayborn		
	Tony McGee		
	(checklist back)		
❑ 189	Carl Eller	.50	.23
❑ 190	Ed White AP	.15	.07
❑ 191	Mario Clark	.15	.07
❑ 192	Roosevelt Leaks	.15	.07
❑ 193	Ted McKnight	.15	.07
❑ 194	Danny Buggs	.15	.07
❑ 195	Lester Hayes RC	1.25	.55
❑ 196	Clarence Scott	.15	.07
❑ 197	New Orleans Saints TL	.50	.23
	Chuck Muncie		
	Wes Chandler		
	Tom Myers		
	Elois Grooms		
	Don Reese		
	(checklist back)		
❑ 198	Richard Caster	.15	.07
❑ 199	Louie Giammona	.15	.07
❑ 200	Terry Bradshaw	5.00	2.20
❑ 201	Ed Newman	.15	.07
❑ 202	Fred Dryer	1.00	.45
❑ 203	Dennis Franks	.15	.07
❑ 204	Bob Breunig RC	.50	.23
❑ 205	Alan Page	1.00	.45
❑ 206	Earnest Gray RC	.15	.07
❑ 207	Minnesota Vikings TL	1.00	.45
	Rickey Young		
	Ahmad Rashad		
	Tom Hannon		
	Nate Wright		
	Mark Mullaney		
	(checklist back)		
❑ 208	Horace Ivory	.15	.07
❑ 209	Isaac Hagins	.15	.07
❑ 210	Gary Johnson AP	.15	.07
❑ 211	Kevin Long	.15	.07
❑ 212	Bill Thompson	.15	.07
❑ 213	Don Bass	.15	.07
❑ 214	George Starke RC	.15	.07
❑ 215	Efren Herrera	.15	.07
❑ 216	Theo Bell	.15	.07
❑ 217	Monte Jackson	.15	.07
❑ 218	Reggie McKenzie	.15	.07
❑ 219	Bucky Dilts	.15	.07
❑ 220	Lyle Alzado	1.00	.45
❑ 221	Tim Foley	.15	.07
❑ 222	Mark Arneson	.15	.07
❑ 223	Fred Quillan	.15	.07
❑ 224	Benny Ricardo	.15	.07
❑ 225	Phil Simms RC	12.00	5.50
❑ 226	Chicago Bears TL	1.25	.55
	Walter Payton		
	Brian Baschnagel		
	Gary Fencik		
	Terry Schmidt		
	Jim Osborne		
	(checklist back)		
❑ 227	Max Runager	.15	.07
❑ 228	Barty Smith	.15	.07
❑ 229	Jay Saldi	.50	.23
❑ 230	John Hannah AP	1.00	.45
❑ 231	Tim Wilson	.15	.07
❑ 232	Jeff Van Note	.15	.07

❑ 233 Henry Marshall .15 .07
❑ 234 Diron Talbert .15 .07
❑ 235 Garo Yepremian .50 .23
❑ 236 Larry Brown .15 .07
❑ 237 Clarence Williams .15 .07
❑ 238 Burgess Owens .15 .07
❑ 239 Vince Ferragamo .50 .23
❑ 240 Rickey Young .15 .07
❑ 241 Dave Logan .15 .07
❑ 242 Larry Gordon .15 .07
❑ 243 Terry Miller .15 .07
❑ 244 Baltimore Colts TL 1.00 .45
Joe Washington
Joe Washington
Fred Cook
(checklist back)
❑ 245 Steve DeBerg 1.00 .45
❑ 246 Checklist 133-264 .60 .15
❑ 247 Greg Latta .15 .07
❑ 248 Raymond Clayborn .50 .23
❑ 249 Jim Clack .15 .07
❑ 250 Drew Pearson 1.00 .45
❑ 251 John Bunting .15 .07
❑ 252 Rob Lytle .15 .07
❑ 253 Jim Hart 1.00 .45
❑ 254 John McDaniel .15 .07
❑ 255 Dave Pear AP .15 .07
❑ 256 Donnie Shell 1.00 .45
❑ 257 Dan Doornink .15 .07
❑ 258 Wallace Francis RC 1.00 .45
❑ 259 Dave Beverly .15 .07
❑ 260 Lee Roy Selmon AP 1.00 .45
❑ 261 Doug Dieken .15 .07
❑ 262 Gary Davis .15 .07
❑ 263 Bob Rush .15 .07
❑ 264 Buffalo Bills TL .50 .23
Curtis Brown
Frank Lewis
Keith Moody
Sherman White
(checklist back)
❑ 265 Greg Landry .50 .23
❑ 266 Jan Stenerud .50 .23
❑ 267 Tom Hicks .15 .07
❑ 268 Pat McInally .15 .07
❑ 269 Tim Fox .15 .07
❑ 270 Harvey Martin 1.00 .45
❑ 271 Dan Lloyd .15 .07
❑ 272 Mike Barber .15 .07
❑ 273 Wendell Tyler RC 1.00 .45
❑ 274 Jeff Komlo .15 .07
❑ 275 Wes Chandler RC 1.00 .45
❑ 276 Brad Dusek .15 .07
❑ 277 Charlie Johnson .15 .07
❑ 278 Dennis Swilley .15 .07
❑ 279 Johnny Evans .15 .07
❑ 280 Jack Lambert AP 1.50 .70
❑ 281 Vern Den Herder .15 .07
❑ 282 Tampa Bay Bucs TL 1.00 .45
Ricky Bell
Isaac Hagins
Lee Roy Selmon
(checklist back)
❑ 283 Bob Klein .15 .07
❑ 284 Jim Turner .15 .07
❑ 285 Marvin Powell AP .50 .23
❑ 286 Aaron Kyle .15 .07
❑ 287 Dan Neal .15 .07
❑ 288 Wayne Morris .15 .07
❑ 289 Steve Bartkowski .50 .23
❑ 290 Dave Jennings AP .50 .23
❑ 291 John Smith .15 .07
❑ 292 Bill Gregory .15 .07
❑ 293 Frank Lewis .15 .07
❑ 294 Fred Cook .15 .07
❑ 295 David Hill AP .15 .07
❑ 296 Wade Key .15 .07
❑ 297 Sidney Thornton .15 .07
❑ 298 Charlie Hall .15 .07
❑ 299 Joe Lavender .15 .07
❑ 300 Tom Rafferty RC .15 .07
❑ 301 Mike Renfro RC .50 .23
❑ 302 Wilbur Jackson .50 .23
❑ 303 Green Bay Packers TL 1.00 .45
Terdell Middleton
James Lofton
Johnnie Gray
Robert Barber
Ezra Johnson
(checklist back)
❑ 304 Henry Childs .15 .07
❑ 305 Russ Washington AP .15 .07
❑ 306 Jim LeClair .15 .07
❑ 307 Tommy Hart .15 .07
❑ 308 Gary Barbaro .15 .07
❑ 309 Billy Taylor .15 .07
❑ 310 Ray Guy .50 .23
❑ 311 Don Hasselbeck .15 .07
❑ 312 Doug Williams 1.00 .45
❑ 313 Nick Mike-Mayer .15 .07
❑ 314 Don McCauley .15 .07
❑ 315 Wesley Walker 1.00 .45
❑ 316 Dan Dierdorf 1.00 .45
❑ 317 Dave Brown RC .50 .23
❑ 318 Leroy Harris .15 .07
❑ 319 Pittsburgh Steelers TL 1.00 .45
Franco Harris
John Stallworth
Jack Lambert
Steve Furness
L.C. Greenwood
(checklist back)
❑ 320 Mark Moseley AP UER .15 .07
(Bio on back refers
to him as Mike)
❑ 321 Mark Dennard .15 .07
❑ 322 Terry Nelson .15 .07
❑ 323 Tom Jackson 1.00 .45
❑ 324 Rick Kane .15 .07
❑ 325 Jerry Sherk .15 .07
❑ 326 Ray Preston .15 .07
❑ 327 Golden Richards .15 .07
❑ 328 Randy Dean .15 .07
❑ 329 Rick Danmeier .15 .07
❑ 330 Tony Dorsett 6.00 2.70
❑ 331 Passing Leaders 3.00 1.35
Dan Fouts
Roger Staubach
❑ 332 Receiving Leaders .50 .23
Joe Washington
Ahmad Rashad
❑ 333 Sacks Leaders 1.00 .45
Jesse Baker
Al(Bubba) Baker
Jack Youngblood
❑ 334 Scoring Leaders 1.00 .45
John Smith
Mark Moseley
❑ 335 Interception Leaders 1.00 .45
Mike Reinfeldt
Lemar Parrish
❑ 336 Punting Leaders 1.00 .45
Bob Grupp
Dave Jennings
❑ 337 Freddie Solomon .15 .07
❑ 338 Cincinnati Bengals TL .50 .23
Pete Johnson
Don Bass
Dick Jauron
Gary Burley
(checklist back)
❑ 339 Ken Stone .15 .07
❑ 340 Greg Buttle AP .15 .07
❑ 341 Bob Baumhower .50 .23
❑ 342 Billy Waddy .15 .07
❑ 343 Cliff Parsley .15 .07
❑ 344 Walter White .15 .07
❑ 345 Mike Thomas .15 .07
❑ 346 Neil O'Donoghue .15 .07
❑ 347 Freddie Scott .15 .07
❑ 348 Joe Ferguson .50 .23
❑ 349 Doug Nettles .15 .07
❑ 350 Mike Webster AP 1.00 .45
❑ 351 Ron Saul .15 .07
❑ 352 Julius Adams .15 .07
❑ 353 Rafael Septien .15 .07
❑ 354 Cleo Miller .15 .07
❑ 355 Keith Simpson AP .15 .07
❑ 356 Johnny Perkins .15 .07
❑ 357 Jerry Sisemore .15 .07
❑ 358 Arthur Whittington .15 .07
❑ 359 St. Louis Cardinals TL 1.00 .45
Ottis Anderson
Pat Tilley
Ken Stone
Bob Pollard
(checklist back)
❑ 360 Rick Upchurch .50 .23
❑ 361 Kim Bokamper RC .15 .07
❑ 362 Roland Harper .15 .07
❑ 363 Pat Leahy .15 .07
❑ 364 Louis Breeden .15 .07
❑ 365 John Jefferson 1.00 .45
❑ 366 Jerry Eckwood .15 .07
❑ 367 David Whitehurst .15 .07
❑ 368 Willie Parker .15 .07
❑ 369 Ed Simonini .15 .07
❑ 370 Jack Youngblood AP 1.00 .45
❑ 371 Don Warren RC 1.00 .45
❑ 372 Andy Johnson .15 .07
❑ 373 D.D. Lewis .50 .23
❑ 374A Beasley Reece RC ERR 1.00 .45
(No S in position
on front of card)
❑ 374B B.Reece COR RC .50 .23
❑ 375 L.C. Greenwood 1.00 .45
❑ 376 Cleveland Browns TL .50 .23
Mike Pruitt
Dave Logan
Thom Darden
Jerry Sherk
(checklist back)
❑ 377 Herman Edwards .15 .07
❑ 378 Rob Carpenter RC .15 .07
❑ 379 Herman Weaver .15 .07
❑ 380 Gary Fencik AP .15 .07
❑ 381 Don Strock .50 .23
❑ 382 Art Shell 1.00 .45
❑ 383 Tim Mazzetti .15 .07
❑ 384 Bruce Harper .15 .07
❑ 385 Al(Bubba) Baker .50 .23
❑ 386 Conrad Dobler .15 .07
❑ 387 Stu Voigt .15 .07
❑ 388 Ken Anderson 1.00 .45
❑ 389 Pat Tilley .15 .07
❑ 390 John Riggins 1.00 .45
❑ 391 Checklist 265-396 .60 .15
❑ 392 Fred Dean AP .15 .07
❑ 393 Benny Barnes RC .15 .07
❑ 394 Los Angeles Rams TL .50 .23
Wendell Tyler
Preston Dennard
Nolan Cromwell
Jim Youngblood
Jack Youngblood
(checklist back)
❑ 395 Brad Van Pelt .15 .07
❑ 396 Eddie Hare .15 .07
❑ 397 John Sciarra RC .15 .07
❑ 398 Bob Jackson .15 .07
❑ 399 John Yarno .15 .07
❑ 400 Franco Harris AP 2.00 .90
❑ 401 Ray Wersching .15 .07
❑ 402 Virgil Livers .15 .07
❑ 403 Raymond Chester .15 .07
❑ 404 Leon Gray .15 .07
❑ 405 Richard Todd .50 .23
❑ 406 Larry Little 1.00 .45
❑ 407 Ted Fritsch Jr. .15 .07
❑ 408 Larry Mucker .15 .07
❑ 409 Jim Allen .15 .07
❑ 410 Randy Gradishar 1.00 .45
❑ 411 Atlanta Falcons TL 1.00 .45
William Andrews
Wallace Francis
Rolland Lawrence
Don Smith
(checklist back)
❑ 412 Louie Kelcher .50 .23
❑ 413 Robert Newhouse .50 .23
❑ 414 Gary Shirk .15 .07
❑ 415 Mike Haynes AP 1.00 .45
❑ 416 Craig Colquitt .15 .07
❑ 417 Lou Piccone .15 .07
❑ 418 Clay Matthews RC 2.00 .90
❑ 419 Marvin Cobb .15 .07
❑ 420 Harold Carmichael AP 1.00 .45
❑ 421 Uwe Von Schamann .50 .23

❑ 422 Mike Phipps .50 .23
❑ 423 Nolan Cromwell RC 1.00 .45
❑ 424 Glenn Doughty .15 .07
❑ 425 Bob Young AP .15 .07
❑ 426 Tony Galbreath .15 .07
❑ 427 Luke Prestridge .15 .07
❑ 428 Terry Beeson .15 .07
❑ 429 Jack Tatum .50 .23
❑ 430 Lemar Parrish AP .15 .07
❑ 431 Chester Marcol .15 .07
❑ 432 Houston Oilers TL 1.00 .45
Dan Pastorini
Ken Burrough
Mike Reinfeldt
Jesse Baker
(checklist back)
❑ 433 John Fitzgerald .15 .07
❑ 434 Gary Jeter RC .50 .23
❑ 435 Steve Grogan 1.00 .45
❑ 436 Jon Kolb UER .15 .07
John on front
❑ 437 Jim O'Bradovich UER .15 .07
(Neil O'Donoghue's bio)
❑ 438 Gerald Irons .15 .07
❑ 439 Jeff West .15 .07
❑ 440 Wilbert Montgomery .50 .23
❑ 441 Norris Thomas .15 .07
❑ 442 James Scott .15 .07
❑ 443 Curtis Brown .15 .07
❑ 444 Ken Fantetti .15 .07
❑ 445 Pat Haden 1.00 .45
❑ 446 Carl Mauck .15 .07
❑ 447 Bruce Laird .15 .07
❑ 448 Otis Armstrong .15 .07
❑ 449 Gene Upshaw 1.00 .45
❑ 450 Steve Largent AP 6.00 2.70
❑ 451 Benny Malone .15 .07
❑ 452 Steve Nelson .15 .07
❑ 453 Mark Cotney .15 .07
❑ 454 Joe Danelo .15 .07
❑ 455 Billy Joe DuPree .50 .23
❑ 456 Ron Johnson .15 .07
❑ 457 Archie Griffin .50 .23
❑ 458 Reggie Rucker .15 .07
❑ 459 Claude Humphrey .15 .07
❑ 460 Lydell Mitchell .50 .23
❑ 461 Steve Towle .15 .07
❑ 462 Revie Sorey .15 .07
❑ 463 Tom Skladany .15 .07
❑ 464 Clark Gaines .15 .07
❑ 465 Frank Corral .15 .07
❑ 466 Steve Fuller RC .50 .23
❑ 467 Ahmad Rashad AP 1.00 .45
❑ 468 Oakland Raiders TL 1.00 .45
Mark Van Eeghen
Cliff Branch
Lester Hayes
Willie Jones
(Checklist back)
❑ 469 Brian Peets .15 .07
❑ 470 Pat Donovan AP RC .50 .23
❑ 471 Ken Burrough .15 .07
❑ 472 Don Calhoun .15 .07
❑ 473 Bill Bryan .15 .07
❑ 474 Terry Jackson .15 .07
❑ 475 Joe Theismann 1.25 .55
❑ 476 Jim Smith .50 .23
❑ 477 Joe DeLamielleure .15 .07
❑ 478 Mike Pruitt AP .50 .23
❑ 479 Steve Mike-Mayer .15 .07
❑ 480 Bill Bergey .50 .23
❑ 481 Mike Fuller .15 .07
❑ 482 Bob Parsons .15 .07
❑ 483 Billy Brooks .15 .07
❑ 484 Jerome Barkum .15 .07
❑ 485 Larry Csonka 1.50 .70
❑ 486 John Hill .15 .07
❑ 487 Mike Dawson .15 .07
❑ 488 Detroit Lions TL .50 .23
Dexter Bussey
Freddie Scott
Jim Allen
Luther Bradley
Al (Bubba) Baker
(Checklist back)
❑ 489 Ted Hendricks 1.00 .45
❑ 490 Dan Pastorini .50 .23
❑ 491 Stanley Morgan 1.00 .45
❑ 492 AFC Championship 1.00 .45
Steelers 27,
Oilers 13
(Rocky Bleier running)
❑ 493 NFC Championship .50 .23
Rams 9,
Buccaneers 0
(Vince Ferragamo)
❑ 494 Super Bowl XIV 1.00 .45
Steelers 31,
Rams 19
(Line play)
❑ 495 Dwight White .50 .23
❑ 496 Haven Moses .15 .07
❑ 497 Guy Morriss .15 .07
❑ 498 Dewey Selmon .50 .23
❑ 499 Dave Butz RC 1.00 .45
❑ 500 Chuck Foreman .50 .23
❑ 501 Chris Bahr .15 .07
❑ 502 Mark Miller .15 .07
❑ 503 Tony Greene .15 .07
❑ 504 Brian Kelley .15 .07
❑ 505 Joe Washington .50 .23
❑ 506 Butch Johnson .50 .23
❑ 507 New York Jets TL .50 .23
Clark Gaines
Wesley Walker
Burgess Owens
Joe Klecko
(checklist back0
❑ 508 Steve Little .15 .07
❑ 509 Checklist 397-528 .60 .15
❑ 510 Mark Van Eeghen .15 .07
❑ 511 Gary Danielson .50 .23
❑ 512 Manu Tuiasosopo .15 .07
❑ 513 Paul Coffman RC .50 .23
❑ 514 Cullen Bryant .15 .07
❑ 515 Nat Moore .50 .23
❑ 516 Bill Lenkaitis .15 .07
❑ 517 Lynn Cain RC .15 .07
❑ 518 Gregg Bingham .15 .07
❑ 519 Ted Albrecht .15 .07
❑ 520 Dan Fouts AP 2.00 .90
❑ 521 Bernard Jackson .15 .07
❑ 522 Coy Bacon .15 .07
❑ 523 Tony Franklin RC .50 .23
❑ 524 Bo Harris .15 .07
❑ 525 Bob Grupp AP .15 .07
❑ 526 San Francisco 49ers TL 1.00 .45
Paul Hofer
Freddie Solomon
James Owens
Dwaine Board
(checklist back)
❑ 527 Steve Wilson .15 .07
❑ 528 Bennie Cunningham .50 .23

1981 Topps

	NRMT-MT	EXC
COMPLETE SET (528)	225.00	100.00

❑ 1 Passing Leaders .75 .35
Ron Jaworski
Brian Sipe
❑ 2 Receiving Leaders .75 .35
Earl Cooper
Kellen Winslow
❑ 3 Sack Leaders .40 .18
Al (Bubba) Baker
Gary Johnson
❑ 4 Scoring Leaders .15 .07
Eddie Murray
John Smith
❑ 5 Interception Leaders .40 .18
Nolan Cromwell
Lester Hayes
❑ 6 Punting Leaders .15 .07
Dave Jennings
Luke Prestridge
❑ 7 Don Calhoun .15 .07
❑ 8 Jack Tatum .40 .18
❑ 9 Reggie Rucker .15 .07
❑ 10 Mike Webster AP .75 .35
❑ 11 Vince Evans RC .75 .35
❑ 12 Ottis Anderson SA .75 .35
❑ 13 Leroy Harris .15 .07
❑ 14 Gordon King .15 .07
❑ 15 Harvey Martin .75 .35
❑ 16 Johnny Lam Jones RC .40 .18
❑ 17 Ken Greene .15 .07
❑ 18 Frank Lewis .15 .07
❑ 19 Seattle Seahawks TL .75 .35
Jim Jodat
Dave Brown
John Harris
Steve Largent
Jacob Green
(checklist back)
❑ 20 Lester Hayes AP .75 .35
❑ 21 Uwe Von Schamann .15 .07
❑ 22 Joe Washington .15 .07
❑ 23 Louie Kelcher .15 .07
❑ 24 Willie Miller .15 .07
❑ 25 Steve Grogan .75 .35
❑ 26 John Hill .15 .07
❑ 27 Stan White .15 .07
❑ 28 William Andrews SA .40 .18
❑ 29 Clarence Scott .15 .07
❑ 30 Leon Gray AP .15 .07
❑ 31 Craig Colquitt .15 .07
❑ 32 Doug Williams .75 .35
❑ 33 Bob Breunig .40 .18
❑ 34 Billy Taylor .15 .07
❑ 35 Harold Carmichael .75 .35
❑ 36 Ray Wersching .15 .07
❑ 37 Dennis Johnson .15 .07
❑ 38 Archie Griffin .40 .18
❑ 39 Los Angeles Rams TL .40 .18
Cullen Bryant
Billy Waddy
Nolan Cromwell
Jack Youngblood
(checklist back)
❑ 40 Gary Fencik AP .40 .18
❑ 41 Lynn Dickey .15 .07
❑ 42 Steve Bartkowski SA .40 .18
❑ 43 Art Shell .75 .35
❑ 44 Wilbur Jackson .15 .07
❑ 45 Frank Corral .15 .07
❑ 46 Ted McKnight .15 .07
❑ 47 Joe Klecko .40 .18
❑ 48 Dan Doornink .15 .07
❑ 49 Doug Dieken .15 .07
❑ 50 Jerry Robinson AP RC .40 .18
❑ 51 Wallace Francis .15 .07
❑ 52 Dave Preston RC .15 .07
❑ 53 Jay Saldi .15 .07
❑ 54 Rush Brown .15 .07
❑ 55 Phil Simms 3.00 1.35
❑ 56 Nick Mike-Mayer .15 .07
❑ 57 Wash. Redskins TL 2.00 .90
Wilbur Jackson
Art Monk
Lemar Parrish
Coy Bacon
(checklist back)
❑ 58 Mike Renfro .15 .07
❑ 59 Ted Brown SA .15 .07
❑ 60 Steve Nelson AP .15 .07
❑ 61 Sidney Thornton .15 .07
❑ 62 Kent Hill .15 .07

❑ 63 Don Bessillieu .15 .07
❑ 64 Fred Cook .15 .07
❑ 65 Raymond Chester .15 .07
❑ 66 Rick Kane .15 .07
❑ 67 Mike Fuller .15 .07
❑ 68 Dewey Selmon .40 .18
❑ 69 Charles White RC .75 .35
❑ 70 Jeff Van Note AP .15 .07
❑ 71 Robert Newhouse .40 .18
❑ 72 Roynell Young RC .15 .07
❑ 73 Lynn Cain SA .15 .07
❑ 74 Mike Friede .15 .07
❑ 75 Earl Cooper RC .15 .07
❑ 76 New Orleans Saints TL .40 .18
Jimmy Rogers
Wes Chandler
Tom Myers
Elois Grooms
Derland Moore
(checklist back)
❑ 77 Rick Danmeier .15 .07
❑ 78 Darrol Ray .15 .07
❑ 79 Gregg Bingham .15 .07
❑ 80 John Hannah AP .75 .35
❑ 81 Jack Thompson .40 .18
❑ 82 Rick Upchurch .40 .18
❑ 83 Mike Butler .15 .07
❑ 84 Don Warren .15 .07
❑ 85 Mark Van Eeghen .15 .07
❑ 86 J.T. Smith RC .75 .35
❑ 87 Herman Weaver .15 .07
❑ 88 Terry Bradshaw SA 2.00 .90
❑ 89 Charlie Hall .15 .07
❑ 90 Donnie Shell .75 .35
❑ 91 Ike Harris .15 .07
❑ 92 Charlie Johnson .15 .07
❑ 93 Rickey Watts .15 .07
❑ 94 New England Patriots TL .75 .35
Vagas Ferguson
Stanley Morgan
Raymond Clayborn
Julius Adams
(checklist back)
❑ 95 Drew Pearson .75 .35
❑ 96 Neil O'Donoghue .15 .07
❑ 97 Conrad Dobler .15 .07
❑ 98 Jewerl Thomas RC .15 .07
❑ 99 Mike Barber .15 .07
❑ 100 Billy Sims AP RC 2.00 .90
❑ 101 Vern Den Herder .15 .07
❑ 102 Greg Landry .40 .18
❑ 103 Joe Cribbs SA .40 .18
❑ 104 Mark Murphy RC .15 .07
❑ 105 Chuck Muncie .40 .18
❑ 106 Alfred Jackson .40 .18
❑ 107 Chris Bahr .15 .07
❑ 108 Gordon Jones .15 .07
❑ 109 Willie Harper RC .15 .07
❑ 110 Dave Jennings AP .15 .07
❑ 111 Bennie Cunningham .15 .07
❑ 112 Jerry Sisemore .15 .07
❑ 113 Cleveland Browns TL .75 .35
Mike Pruitt
Dave Logan
Ron Bolton
Lyle Alzado
(checklist back)
❑ 114 Rickey Young .15 .07
❑ 115 Ken Anderson .75 .35
❑ 116 Randy Gradishar .75 .35
❑ 117 Eddie Lee Ivery RC .15 .07
❑ 118 Wesley Walker .75 .35
❑ 119 Chuck Foreman .40 .18
❑ 120 Nolan Cromwell AP .40 .18
UER (Rushing TD's
added wrong)
❑ 121 Curtis Dickey SA .15 .07
❑ 122 Wayne Morris .15 .07
❑ 123 Greg Stemrick .15 .07
❑ 124 Coy Bacon .15 .07
❑ 125 Jim Zorn .40 .18
(Steve Largent
in background)
❑ 126 Henry Childs .15 .07
❑ 127 Checklist 1-132 .50 .23
❑ 128 Len Walterscheid .15 .07
❑ 129 Johnny Evans .15 .07
❑ 130 Gary Barbaro AP .15 .07
❑ 131 Jim Smith .15 .07
❑ 132 New York Jets TL .40 .18
Scott Dierking
Bruce Harper
Ken Schroy
Mark Gastineau
(checklist back)
❑ 133 Curtis Brown .15 .07
❑ 134 D.D. Lewis .15 .07
❑ 135 Jim Plunkett .75 .35
❑ 136 Nat Moore .40 .18
❑ 137 Don McCauley .15 .07
❑ 138 Tony Dorsett SA .75 .35
❑ 139 Julius Adams .15 .07
❑ 140 Ahmad Rashad AP .75 .35
❑ 141 Rich Saul .15 .07
❑ 142 Ken Fantetti .15 .07
❑ 143 Kenny Johnson .15 .07
❑ 144 Clark Gaines .15 .07
❑ 145 Mark Moseley .15 .07
❑ 146 Vernon Perry RC .15 .07
❑ 147 Jerry Eckwood .15 .07
❑ 148 Freddie Solomon .15 .07
❑ 149 Jerry Sherk .15 .07
❑ 150 Kellen Winslow AP RC 8.00 3.60
❑ 151 Green Bay Packers TL .75 .35
Eddie Lee Ivery
James Lofton
Johnnie Gray
Mike Butler
(checklist back)
❑ 152 Ross Browner .15 .07
❑ 153 Dan Fouts SA .75 .35
❑ 154 Woody Peoples .15 .07
❑ 155 Jack Lambert 1.00 .45
❑ 156 Mike Dennis .15 .07
❑ 157 Rafael Septien .15 .07
❑ 158 Archie Manning .75 .35
❑ 159 Don Hasselbeck .15 .07
❑ 160 Alan Page AP .75 .35
❑ 161 Arthur Whittington .15 .07
❑ 162 Billy Waddy .15 .07
❑ 163 Horace Belton .15 .07
❑ 164 Luke Prestridge .15 .07
❑ 165 Joe Theismann .75 .35
❑ 166 Morris Towns .15 .07
❑ 167 Dave Brown .15 .07
❑ 168 Ezra Johnson .15 .07
❑ 169 Tampa Bay Bucs TL .15 .07
Ricky Bell
Gordon Jones
Mike Washington
Lee Roy Selmon
(checklist back)
❑ 170 Joe DeLamielleure AP .15 .07
❑ 171 Earnest Gray SA .15 .07
❑ 172 Mike Thomas .15 .07
❑ 173 Jim Haslett RC 2.00 .90
❑ 174 David Woodley RC .40 .18
❑ 175 Al(Bubba) Baker .40 .18
❑ 176 Nesby Glasgow RC .15 .07
❑ 177 Pat Leahy .15 .07
❑ 178 Tom Brahaney .15 .07
❑ 179 Herman Edwards .15 .07
❑ 180 Junior Miller AP RC .15 .07
❑ 181 Richard Wood RC .15 .07
❑ 182 Lenvil Elliott .15 .07
❑ 183 Sammie White .40 .18
❑ 184 Russell Erxleben .15 .07
❑ 185 Ed Too Tall Jones .75 .35
❑ 186 Ray Guy SA .40 .18
❑ 187 Haven Moses .15 .07
❑ 188 New York Giants TL .40 .18
Billy Taylor
Earnest Gray
Mike Dennis
Gary Jeter
(checklist back)
❑ 189 David Whitehurst .15 .07
❑ 190 John Jefferson AP .75 .35
❑ 191 Terry Beeson .15 .07
❑ 192 Dan Ross RC .40 .18
❑ 193 Dave Williams .15 .07
❑ 194 Art Monk RC 10.00 4.50
❑ 195 Roger Wehrli .15 .07
❑ 196 Ricky Feacher .15 .07
❑ 197 Miami Dolphins TL .75 .35
Delvin Williams
Tony Nathan
Gerald Small
Kim Bokamper
A.J. Duhe
(checklist back)
❑ 198 Carl Roaches RC .15 .07
❑ 199 Billy Campfield .15 .07
❑ 200 Ted Hendricks AP .75 .35
❑ 201 Fred Smerlas RC .75 .35
❑ 202 Walter Payton SA 3.00 1.35
❑ 203 Luther Bradley .15 .07
❑ 204 Herb Scott .15 .07
❑ 205 Jack Youngblood .75 .35
❑ 206 Danny Pittman .15 .07
❑ 207 Houston Oilers TL .40 .18
Carl Roaches
Mike Barber
Jack Tatum
Jesse Baker
Robert Brazile
(checklist back)
❑ 208 Vagas Ferguson RC .40 .18
❑ 209 Mark Dennard .15 .07
❑ 210 Lemar Parrish AP .15 .07
❑ 211 Bruce Harper .15 .07
❑ 212 Ed Simonini .15 .07
❑ 213 Nick Lowery RC .75 .35
❑ 214 Kevin House RC .40 .18
❑ 215 Mike Kenn RC .75 .35
❑ 216 Joe Montana RC 200.00 90.00
❑ 217 Joe Senser .15 .07
❑ 218 Lester Hayes SA .40 .18
❑ 219 Gene Upshaw .75 .35
❑ 220 Franco Harris 1.25 .55
❑ 221 Ron Bolton .15 .07
❑ 222 Charles Alexander RC .40 .18
❑ 223 Matt Robinson .15 .07
❑ 224 Ray Oldham .15 .07
❑ 225 George Martin .15 .07
❑ 226 Buffalo Bills TL .75 .35
Joe Cribbs
Jerry Butler
Steve Freeman
Ben Williams
(checklist back)
❑ 227 Tony Franklin .15 .07
❑ 228 George Cumby .15 .07
❑ 229 Butch Johnson .40 .18
❑ 230 Mike Haynes AP .75 .35
❑ 231 Rob Carpenter .40 .18
❑ 232 Steve Fuller .40 .18
❑ 233 John Sawyer .15 .07
❑ 234 Kenny King SA .15 .07
❑ 235 Jack Ham .75 .35
❑ 236 Jimmy Rogers .15 .07
❑ 237 Bob Parsons .15 .07
❑ 238 Marty Lyons RC .75 .35
❑ 239 Pat Tilley .15 .07
❑ 240 Dennis Harrah AP .15 .07
❑ 241 Thom Darden .15 .07
❑ 242 Rolf Benirschke .15 .07
❑ 243 Gerald Small .15 .07
❑ 244 Atlanta Falcons TL .75 .35
William Andrews
Alfred Jenkins
Al Richardson
Joel Williams
(checklist back)
❑ 245 Roger Carr .15 .07
❑ 246 Sherman White .15 .07
❑ 247 Ted Brown .15 .07
❑ 248 Matt Cavanaugh .40 .18
❑ 249 John Dutton .15 .07
❑ 250 Bill Bergey AP .40 .18
❑ 251 Jim Allen .15 .07
❑ 252 Mike Nelms SA .15 .07
❑ 253 Tom Blanchard .15 .07
❑ 254 Ricky Thompson .15 .07
❑ 255 John Matuszak .40 .18
❑ 256 Randy Grossman .15 .07
❑ 257 Ray Griffin .15 .07
❑ 258 Lynn Cain .15 .07

❑ 259 Checklist 133-264 .50 .23
❑ 260 Mike Pruitt AP .40 .18
❑ 261 Chris Ward .15 .07
❑ 262 Fred Steinfort .15 .07
❑ 263 James Owens .15 .07
❑ 264 Chicago Bears TL 1.50 .70
Walter Payton
James Scott
Len Walterscheid
Dan Hampton
(checklist back)
❑ 265 Dan Fouts 1.50 .70
❑ 266 Arnold Morgado .15 .07
❑ 267 John Jefferson SA .75 .35
❑ 268 Bill Lenkaitis .15 .07
❑ 269 James Jones .15 .07
❑ 270 Brad Van Pelt .15 .07
❑ 271 Steve Largent 2.50 1.10
❑ 272 Elvin Bethea .15 .07
❑ 273 Cullen Bryant .15 .07
❑ 274 Gary Danielson .40 .18
❑ 275 Tony Galbreath .15 .07
❑ 276 Dave Butz .15 .07
❑ 277 Steve Mike-Mayer .15 .07
❑ 278 Ron Johnson .15 .07
❑ 279 Tom DeLeone .15 .07
❑ 280 Ron Jaworski .75 .35
❑ 281 Mel Gray .15 .07
❑ 282 San Diego Chargers TL .75 .35
Chuck Muncie
John Jefferson
Glen Edwards
Gary Johnson
(checklist back)
❑ 283 Mark Brammer .15 .07
❑ 284 Alfred Jenkins SA .40 .18
❑ 285 Greg Buttle .15 .07
❑ 286 Randy Hughes .15 .07
❑ 287 Delvin Williams .15 .07
❑ 288 Brian Baschnagel .15 .07
❑ 289 Gary Jeter .15 .07
❑ 290 Stanley Morgan AP .75 .35
❑ 291 Gerry Ellis .15 .07
❑ 292 Al Richardson .15 .07
❑ 293 Jimmie Giles .40 .18
❑ 294 Dave Jennings SA .15 .07
❑ 295 Wilbert Montgomery .40 .18
❑ 296 Dave Pureifory .15 .07
❑ 297 Greg Hawthorne .15 .07
❑ 298 Dick Ambrose .15 .07
❑ 299 Terry Hermeling .15 .07
❑ 300 Danny White .75 .35
❑ 301 Ken Burrough .15 .07
❑ 302 Paul Hofer .15 .07
❑ 303 Denver Broncos TL .75 .35
Jim Jensen
Haven Moses
Steve Foley
Rulon Jones
(checklist back)
❑ 304 Eddie Payton .40 .18
❑ 305 Isaac Curtis .40 .18
❑ 306 Benny Ricardo .15 .07
❑ 307 Riley Odoms .15 .07
❑ 308 Bob Chandler .15 .07
❑ 309 Larry Heater .15 .07
❑ 310 Art Still AP RC .75 .35
❑ 311 Harold Jackson .40 .18
❑ 312 Charlie Joiner SA .75 .35
❑ 313 Jeff Nixon .15 .07
❑ 314 Aundra Thompson .15 .07
❑ 315 Richard Todd .40 .18
❑ 316 Dan Hampton RC 3.00 1.35
❑ 317 Doug Marsh .15 .07
❑ 318 Louie Giammona .15 .07
❑ 319 San Francisco 49ers TL .75 .35
Earl Cooper
Dwight Clark
Ricky Churchman
Dwight Hicks
Jim Stuckey
(checklist back)
❑ 320 Manu Tuiasosopo .15 .07
❑ 321 Rich Milot .15 .07
❑ 322 Mike Guman .15 .07
❑ 323 Bob Kuechenberg .40 .18
❑ 324 Tom Skladany .15 .07
❑ 325 Dave Logan .15 .07
❑ 326 Bruce Laird .15 .07
❑ 327 James Jones SA .15 .07
❑ 328 Joe Danelo .15 .07
❑ 329 Kenny King RC .40 .18
❑ 330 Pat Donovan AP .15 .07
❑ 331 Earl Cooper RB .40 .18
Most Receptions,
Running Back,
Season, Rookie
❑ 332 John Jefferson RB .75 .35
Most Cons. Seasons,
1000 Yards Receiving,
Start of Career
❑ 333 Kenny King RB .40 .18
Longest Pass Caught,
Super Bowl History
❑ 334 Rod Martin RB .40 .18
Most Interceptions
Super Bowl Game
❑ 335 Jim Plunkett RB .75 .35
Longest Pass,
Super Bowl History
❑ 336 Bill Thompson RB .40 .18
Most Touchdowns,
Fumble Recoveries,
Lifetime
❑ 337 John Cappelletti .40 .18
❑ 338 Detroit Lions TL .75 .35
Billy Sims
Freddie Scott
Jim Allen
James Hunter
Al(Bubba) Baker
(checklist back)
❑ 339 Don Smith .15 .07
❑ 340 Rod Perry AP .15 .07
❑ 341 David Lewis .15 .07
❑ 342 Mark Gastineau RC .75 .35
❑ 343 Steve Largent SA .75 .35
❑ 344 Charlie Young .15 .07
❑ 345 Toni Fritsch .15 .07
❑ 346 Matt Blair .40 .18
❑ 347 Don Bass .15 .07
❑ 348 Jim Jensen RC .40 .18
❑ 349 Karl Lorch .15 .07
❑ 350 Brian Sipe AP .40 .18
❑ 351 Theo Bell .15 .07
❑ 352 Sam Adams .15 .07
❑ 353 Paul Coffman .15 .07
❑ 354 Eric Harris .15 .07
❑ 355 Tony Hill .40 .18
❑ 356 J.T. Turner .15 .07
❑ 357 Frank LeMaster .15 .07
❑ 358 Jim Jodat .15 .07
❑ 359 Oakland Raiders TL .75 .35
Mark Van Eeghen
Cliff Branch
Lester Hayes
Cedrick Hardman
Ted Hendricks
(checklist back)
❑ 360 Joe Cribbs AP RC .75 .35
❑ 361 James Lofton SA .75 .35
❑ 362 Dexter Bussey .15 .07
❑ 363 Bobby Jackson .15 .07
❑ 364 Steve DeBerg .75 .35
❑ 365 Ottis Anderson 1.00 .45
❑ 366 Tom Myers .15 .07
❑ 367 John James .15 .07
❑ 368 Reese McCall .15 .07
❑ 369 Jack Reynolds .40 .18
❑ 370 Gary Johnson AP .15 .07
❑ 371 Jimmy Cefalo .15 .07
❑ 372 Horace Ivory .15 .07
❑ 373 Garo Yepremian .15 .07
❑ 374 Brian Kelley .15 .07
❑ 375 Terry Bradshaw 4.00 1.80
❑ 376 Dallas Cowboys TL .75 .35
Tony Dorsett
Tony Hill
Dennis Thurman
Charlie Waters
Harvey Martin
(checklist back)
❑ 377 Randy Logan .15 .07
❑ 378 Tim Wilson .15 .07
❑ 379 Archie Manning SA .75 .35
❑ 380 Revie Sorey AP .15 .07
❑ 381 Randy Holloway .15 .07
❑ 382 Henry Lawrence .15 .07
❑ 383 Pat McInally .15 .07
❑ 384 Kevin Long .15 .07
❑ 385 Louis Wright .40 .18
❑ 386 Leonard Thompson .15 .07
❑ 387 Jan Stenerud .40 .18
❑ 388 Raymond Butler RC .15 .07
❑ 389 Checklist 265-396 .50 .23
❑ 390 Steve Bartkowski AP .40 .18
❑ 391 Clarence Harmon .15 .07
❑ 392 Wilbert Montgomery SA .40 .18
❑ 393 Billy Joe DuPree .40 .18
❑ 394 Kansas City Chiefs TL .40 .18
Ted McKnight
Henry Marshall
Gary Barbaro
Art Still
(checklist back)
❑ 395 Earnest Gray .15 .07
❑ 396 Ray Hamilton .15 .07
❑ 397 Brenard Wilson .15 .07
❑ 398 Calvin Hill .75 .35
❑ 399 Robin Cole .15 .07
❑ 400 Walter Payton AP 8.00 3.60
❑ 401 Jim Hart .75 .35
❑ 402 Ron Yary .40 .18
❑ 403 Cliff Branch .75 .35
❑ 404 Roland Hooks .15 .07
❑ 405 Ken Stabler 3.00 1.35
❑ 406 Chuck Ramsey .15 .07
❑ 407 Mike Nelms RC .15 .07
❑ 408 Ron Jaworski SA .40 .18
❑ 409 James Hunter .15 .07
❑ 410 Lee Roy Selmon AP .75 .35
❑ 411 Baltimore Colts TL .40 .18
Curtis Dickey
Roger Carr
Bruce Laird
Mike Barnes
(checklist back)
❑ 412 Henry Marshall .15 .07
❑ 413 Preston Pearson .40 .18
❑ 414 Richard Bishop .15 .07
❑ 415 Greg Pruitt .40 .18
❑ 416 Matt Bahr .40 .18
❑ 417 Tom Mullady .15 .07
❑ 418 Glen Edwards .15 .07
❑ 419 Sam McCullum .15 .07
❑ 420 Stan Walters AP .15 .07
❑ 421 George Roberts .15 .07
❑ 422 Dwight Clark RC 4.00 1.80
❑ 423 Pat Thomas RC .15 .07
❑ 424 Bruce Harper SA .15 .07
❑ 425 Craig Morton .40 .18
❑ 426 Derrick Gaffney .15 .07
❑ 427 Pete Johnson .15 .07
❑ 428 Wes Chandler .75 .35
❑ 429 Burgess Owens .15 .07
❑ 430 James Lofton AP 2.00 .90
❑ 431 Tony Reed .15 .07
❑ 432 Minnesota Vikings TL .75 .35
Ted Brown
Ahmad Rashad
John Turner
Doug Sutherland
(checklist back)
❑ 433 Ron Springs RC .40 .18
❑ 434 Tim Fox .15 .07
❑ 435 Ozzie Newsome 2.00 .90
❑ 436 Steve Furness .15 .07
❑ 437 Will Lewis .15 .07
❑ 438 Mike Hartenstine .15 .07
❑ 439 John Bunting .15 .07
❑ 440 Eddie Murray RC .75 .35
❑ 441 Mike Pruitt SA .40 .18
❑ 442 Larry Swider .15 .07
❑ 443 Steve Freeman .15 .07
❑ 444 Bruce Hardy RC .15 .07
❑ 445 Pat Haden .40 .18
❑ 446 Curtis Dickey RC .15 .07
❑ 447 Doug Wilkerson .15 .07

❑ 448 Alfred Jenkins .40 .18
❑ 449 Dave Dalby .15 .07
❑ 450 Robert Brazile AP .15 .07
❑ 451 Bobby Hammond .15 .07
❑ 452 Raymond Clayborn .15 .07
❑ 453 Jim Miller .15 .07
❑ 454 Roy Simmons .15 .07
❑ 455 Charlie Waters .75 .35
❑ 456 Ricky Bell .75 .35
❑ 457 Ahmad Rashad SA .75 .35
❑ 458 Don Cockroft .15 .07
❑ 459 Keith Krepfle .15 .07
❑ 460 Marvin Powell AP .15 .07
❑ 461 Tommy Kramer .75 .35
❑ 462 Jim LeClair .15 .07
❑ 463 Freddie Scott .15 .07
❑ 464 Rob Lytle .15 .07
❑ 465 Johnnie Gray .15 .07
❑ 466 Doug France RC .15 .07
❑ 467 Carlos Carson RC .40 .18
❑ 468 St. Louis Cardinals TL .75 .35
Ottis Anderson
Pat Tilley
Ken Stone
Curtis Greer
Steve Neils
(checklist back)
❑ 469 Efren Herrera .15 .07
❑ 470 Randy White AP 1.00 .45
❑ 471 Richard Caster .15 .07
❑ 472 Andy Johnson .15 .07
❑ 473 Billy Sims SA .75 .35
❑ 474 Joe Lavender .15 .07
❑ 475 Harry Carson .40 .18
❑ 476 John Stallworth 1.00 .45
❑ 477 Bob Thomas .15 .07
❑ 478 Keith Wright .15 .07
❑ 479 Ken Stone .15 .07
❑ 480 Carl Hairston AP .40 .18
❑ 481 Reggie McKenzie .15 .07
❑ 482 Bob Griese 1.50 .70
❑ 483 Mike Bragg .15 .07
❑ 484 Scott Dierking .15 .07
❑ 485 David Hill .15 .07
❑ 486 Brian Sipe SA .40 .18
❑ 487 Rod Martin RC .40 .18
❑ 488 Cincinnati Bengals TL .40 .18
Pete Johnson
Dan Ross
Louis Breeden
Eddie Edwards
(checklist back)
❑ 489 Preston Dennard .15 .07
❑ 490 John Smith AP .15 .07
❑ 491 Mike Reinfeldt .15 .07
❑ 492 1980 NFC Champions .75 .35
Eagles 20,
Cowboys 7
(Ron Jaworski)
❑ 493 1980 AFC Champions .75 .35
Raiders 34,
Chargers 27
(Jim Plunkett)
❑ 494 Super Bowl XV .75 .35
Raiders 27,
Eagles 10
(Plunkett handing
off to Kenny King)
❑ 495 Joe Greene .75 .35
❑ 496 Charlie Joiner .75 .35
❑ 497 Rolland Lawrence .15 .07
❑ 498 Al(Bubba) Baker SA .40 .18
❑ 499 Brad Dusek .15 .07
❑ 500 Tony Dorsett 4.00 1.80
❑ 501 Robin Earl .15 .07
❑ 502 Theotis Brown RC .15 .07
❑ 503 Joe Ferguson .40 .18
❑ 504 Beasley Reece .15 .07
❑ 505 Lyle Alzado .75 .35
❑ 506 Tony Nathan RC .75 .35
❑ 507 Philadelphia Eagles TL .40 .18
Wilbert Montgomery
Charlie Smith
Brenard Wilson
Claude Humphrey
(checklist back)
❑ 508 Herb Orvis .15 .07
❑ 509 Clarence Williams .15 .07
❑ 510 Ray Guy AP .40 .18
❑ 511 Jeff Komlo .15 .07
❑ 512 Freddie Solomon SA .15 .07
❑ 513 Tim Mazzetti .15 .07
❑ 514 Elvis Peacock RC .15 .07
❑ 515 Russ Francis .40 .18
❑ 516 Roland Harper .15 .07
❑ 517 Checklist 397-528 .50 .23
❑ 518 Billy Johnson .40 .18
❑ 519 Dan Dierdorf .75 .35
❑ 520 Fred Dean AP .15 .07
❑ 521 Jerry Butler .15 .07
❑ 522 Ron Saul .15 .07
❑ 523 Charlie Smith .15 .07
❑ 524 Kellen Winslow SA 3.00 1.35
❑ 525 Bert Jones .75 .35
❑ 526 Pittsburgh Steelers TL .75 .35
Franco Harris
Theo Bell
Donnie Shell
L.C. Greenwood
(checklist back)
❑ 527 Duriel Harris .15 .07
❑ 528 William Andrews .75 .35

1982 Topps

	NRMT-MT	EXC
COMPLETE SET (528)	80.00	36.00

❑ 1 Ken Anderson RB .75 .35
Most Completions,
Super Bowl Game
❑ 2 Dan Fouts RB .75 .35
Most Passing Yards,
Playoff Game
❑ 3 LeRoy Irvin RB .15 .07
Most Punt Return
Yardage, Game
❑ 4 Stump Mitchell RB .15 .07
Most Return
Yardage, Season
❑ 5 George Rogers RB .75 .35
Most Rushing Yards,
Rookie Season
❑ 6 Dan Ross RB .15 .07
Most Receptions,
Super Bowl Game
❑ 7 AFC Championship .75 .35
Bengals 27,
Chargers 7
(Ken Anderson
handing off to
Pete Johnson)
❑ 8 NFC Championship .75 .35
49ers 28,
Cowboys 27
(Earl Cooper)
❑ 9 Super Bowl XVI .75 .35
49ers 26,
Bengals 7
(Anthony Munoz
blocking)
❑ 10 Baltimore Colts TL .15 .07
Curtis Dickey
Raymond Butler
Larry Braziel
Bruce Laird
❑ 11 Raymond Butler .15 .07
❑ 12 Roger Carr .15 .07
❑ 13 Curtis Dickey .40 .18
❑ 14 Zachary Dixon .15 .07
❑ 15 Nesby Glasgow .15 .07
❑ 16 Bert Jones .75 .35
❑ 17 Bruce Laird .15 .07
❑ 18 Reese McCall .15 .07
❑ 19 Randy McMillan .15 .07
❑ 20 Ed Simonini .15 .07
❑ 21 Buffalo Bills TL .40 .18
Joe Cribbs
Frank Lewis
Mario Clark
Fred Smerlas
❑ 22 Mark Brammer .15 .07
❑ 23 Curtis Brown .15 .07
❑ 24 Jerry Butler .15 .07
❑ 25 Mario Clark .15 .07
❑ 26 Joe Cribbs .40 .18
❑ 27 Joe Cribbs IA .40 .18
❑ 28 Joe Ferguson .40 .18
❑ 29 Jim Haslett .75 .35
❑ 30 Frank Lewis AP .15 .07
❑ 31 Frank Lewis IA .15 .07
❑ 32 Shane Nelson .15 .07
❑ 33 Charles Romes .15 .07
❑ 34 Bill Simpson .15 .07
❑ 35 Fred Smerlas .15 .07
❑ 36 Cincinnati Bengals TL .40 .18
Pete Johnson
Cris Collinsworth
Ken Riley
Reggie Williams
❑ 37 Charles Alexander .15 .07
❑ 38 Ken Anderson AP .75 .35
❑ 39 Ken Anderson IA .75 .35
❑ 40 Jim Breech .15 .07
❑ 41 Jim Breech IA .15 .07
❑ 42 Louis Breeden .15 .07
❑ 43 Ross Browner .15 .07
❑ 44 Cris Collinsworth RC 1.50 .70
❑ 45 Cris Collinsworth IA .75 .35
❑ 46 Isaac Curtis .15 .07
❑ 47 Pete Johnson .15 .07
❑ 48 Pete Johnson IA .15 .07
❑ 49 Steve Kreider .15 .07
❑ 50 Pat McInally AP .15 .07
❑ 51 Anthony Munoz AP RC 8.00 3.60
❑ 52 Dan Ross .15 .07
❑ 53 David Verser RC .15 .07
❑ 54 Reggie Williams .40 .18
❑ 55 Cleveland Browns TL .40 .18
Mike Pruitt
Ozzie Newsome
Clarence Scott
Lyle Alzado
❑ 56 Lyle Alzado .75 .35
❑ 57 Dick Ambrose .15 .07
❑ 58 Ron Bolton .15 .07
❑ 59 Steve Cox .15 .07
❑ 60 Joe DeLamielleure .15 .07
❑ 61 Tom DeLeone .15 .07
❑ 62 Doug Dieken .15 .07
❑ 63 Ricky Feacher .15 .07
❑ 64 Don Goode .15 .07
❑ 65 Robert L. Jackson RC .15 .07
❑ 66 Dave Logan .15 .07
❑ 67 Ozzie Newsome 1.00 .45
❑ 68 Ozzie Newsome IA .75 .35
❑ 69 Greg Pruitt .40 .18
❑ 70 Mike Pruitt .40 .18
❑ 71 Mike Pruitt IA .40 .18
❑ 72 Reggie Rucker .15 .07
❑ 73 Clarence Scott .15 .07
❑ 74 Brian Sipe .40 .18
❑ 75 Charles White .40 .18
❑ 76 Denver Broncos TL .40 .18
Rick Parros
Steve Watson
Steve Foley
Rulon Jones
❑ 77 Rubin Carter .15 .07
❑ 78 Steve Foley .15 .07

No.	Card		
79	Randy Gradishar	.40	.18
80	Tom Jackson	.75	.35
81	Craig Morton	.40	.18
82	Craig Morton IA	.40	.18
83	Riley Odoms	.15	.07
84	Rick Parros	.15	.07
85	Dave Preston	.15	.07
86	Tony Reed	.15	.07
87	Bob Swenson RC	.15	.07
88	Bill Thompson	.15	.07
89	Rick Upchurch	.40	.18
90	Steve Watson AP RC	.40	.18
91	Steve Watson IA	.15	.07
92	Houston Oilers TL	.15	.07
	Carl Roaches		
	Ken Burrough		
	Carter Hartwig		
	Greg Stemrick		
	Jesse Baker		
93	Mike Barber	.15	.07
94	Elvin Bethea	.15	.07
95	Gregg Bingham	.15	.07
96	Robert Brazile AP	.15	.07
97	Ken Burrough	.15	.07
98	Toni Fritsch	.15	.07
99	Leon Gray	.15	.07
100	Gifford Nielsen RC	.40	.18
101	Vernon Perry	.15	.07
102	Mike Reinfeldt	.15	.07
103	Mike Renfro	.15	.07
104	Carl Roaches AP	.15	.07
105	Ken Stabler	2.00	.90
106	Greg Stemrick	.15	.07
107	J.C. Wilson	.15	.07
108	Tim Wilson	.15	.07
109	Kansas City Chiefs TL	.15	.07
	Joe Delaney		
	J.T. Smith		
	Eric Harris		
	Ken Kremer		
110	Gary Barbaro AP	.15	.07
111	Brad Budde	.15	.07
112	Joe Delaney AP RC	.75	.35
113	Joe Delaney IA	.40	.18
114	Steve Fuller	.15	.07
115	Gary Green	.15	.07
116	James Hadnot	.15	.07
117	Eric Harris	.15	.07
118	Billy Jackson	.15	.07
119	Bill Kenney RC	.15	.07
120	Nick Lowery AP	.75	.35
121	Nick Lowery IA	.40	.18
122	Henry Marshall	.15	.07
123	J.T. Smith	.40	.18
124	Art Still	.15	.07
125	Miami Dolphins TL	.40	.18
	Tony Nathan		
	Duriel Harris		
	Glenn Blackwood		
	Bob Baumhower		
126	Bob Baumhower AP	.40	.18
127	Glenn Blackwood	.15	.07
128	Jimmy Cefalo	.15	.07
129	A.J. Duhe	.40	.18
130	Andra Franklin RC	.15	.07
131	Duriel Harris	.15	.07
132	Nat Moore	.40	.18
133	Tony Nathan	.40	.18
134	Ed Newman	.15	.07
135	Earnie Rhone	.15	.07
136	Don Strock	.15	.07
137	Tommy Vigorito	.15	.07
138	Uwe Von Schamann	.15	.07
139	Uwe Von Schamann IA	.15	.07
140	David Woodley	.40	.18
141	New England Pats TL	.40	.18
	Tony Collins		
	Stanley Morgan		
	Tim Fox		
	Rick Sanford		
	Tony McGee		
142	Julius Adams	.15	.07
143	Richard Bishop	.15	.07
144	Matt Cavanaugh	.15	.07
145	Raymond Clayborn	.15	.07
146	Tony Collins RC	.15	.07
147	Vagas Ferguson	.15	.07
148	Tim Fox	.15	.07
149	Steve Grogan	.40	.18
150	John Hannah AP	.75	.35
151	John Hannah IA	.40	.18
152	Don Hasselbeck	.15	.07
153	Mike Haynes	.40	.18
154	Harold Jackson	.40	.18
155	Andy Johnson	.15	.07
156	Stanley Morgan	.40	.18
157	Stanley Morgan IA	.40	.18
158	Steve Nelson	.15	.07
159	Rod Shoate	.15	.07
160	New York Jets TL	.40	.18
	Freeman McNeil		
	Wesley Walker		
	Darrol Ray		
	Joe Klecko		
161	Dan Alexander RC	.15	.07
162	Mike Augustyniak	.15	.07
163	Jerome Barkum	.15	.07
164	Greg Buttle	.15	.07
165	Scott Dierking	.15	.07
166	Joe Fields	.15	.07
167	Mark Gastineau AP	.40	.18
168	Mark Gastineau IA	.40	.18
169	Bruce Harper	.15	.07
170	Johnny Lam Jones	.15	.07
171	Joe Klecko AP	.40	.18
172	Joe Klecko IA	.40	.18
173	Pat Leahy	.40	.18
174	Pat Leahy IA	.15	.07
175	Marty Lyons	.40	.18
176	Freeman McNeil RC	.75	.35
177	Marvin Powell AP	.15	.07
178	Chuck Ramsey	.15	.07
179	Darrol Ray	.15	.07
180	Abdul Salaam	.15	.07
181	Richard Todd	.40	.18
182	Richard Todd IA	.40	.18
183	Wesley Walker	.40	.18
184	Chris Ward	.15	.07
185	Oakland Raiders TL	.40	.18
	Kenny King		
	Derrick Ramsey		
	Lester Hayes		
	Odis McKinney		
	Rod Martin		
186	Cliff Branch	.75	.35
187	Bob Chandler	.15	.07
188	Ray Guy	.40	.18
189	Lester Hayes AP	.40	.18
190	Ted Hendricks AP	.75	.35
191	Monte Jackson	.15	.07
192	Derrick Jensen	.15	.07
193	Kenny King	.15	.07
194	Rod Martin	.15	.07
195	John Matuszak	.40	.18
196	Matt Millen RC	1.50	.70
197	Derrick Ramsey	.15	.07
198	Art Shell	.75	.35
199	Mark Van Eeghen	.15	.07
200	Arthur Whittington	.15	.07
201	Marc Wilson RC	.40	.18
202	Pittsburgh Steelers TL	.75	.35
	Franco Harris		
	John Stallworth		
	Mel Blount		
	Jack Lambert		
	Gary Dunn		
203	Mel Blount AP	.75	.35
204	Terry Bradshaw	3.00	1.35
205	Terry Bradshaw IA	1.25	.55
206	Craig Colquitt	.15	.07
207	Bennie Cunningham	.15	.07
208	Russell Davis	.15	.07
209	Gary Dunn	.15	.07
210	Jack Ham	.75	.35
211	Franco Harris	1.00	.45
212	Franco Harris IA	.75	.35
213	Jack Lambert AP	.75	.35
214	Jack Lambert IA	.75	.35
215	Mark Malone RC	.75	.35
216	Frank Pollard RC	.15	.07
217	Donnie Shell AP	.75	.35
218	Jim Smith	.15	.07
219	John Stallworth	.75	.35
220	John Stallworth IA	.75	.35
221	David Trout	.15	.07
222	Mike Webster AP	.75	.35
223	San Diego Chargers TL	.75	.35
	Chuck Muncie		
	Charlie Joiner		
	Willie Buchanon		
	Gary Johnson		
224	Rolf Benirschke	.15	.07
225	Rolf Benirschke IA	.15	.07
226	James Brooks RC	.75	.35
227	Willie Buchanon	.15	.07
228	Wes Chandler	.75	.35
229	Wes Chandler IA	.40	.18
230	Dan Fouts	1.00	.45
231	Dan Fouts IA	.75	.35
232	Gary Johnson AP	.15	.07
233	Charlie Joiner	.75	.35
234	Charlie Joiner IA	.75	.35
235	Louie Kelcher	.15	.07
236	Chuck Muncie AP	.40	.18
237	Chuck Muncie IA	.15	.07
238	George Roberts	.15	.07
239	Ed White	.15	.07
240	Doug Wilkerson AP	.15	.07
241	Kellen Winslow AP	2.00	.90
242	Kellen Winslow IA	.75	.35
243	Seattle Seahawks TL	.75	.35
	Theotis Brown		
	Steve Largent		
	John Harris		
	Jacob Green		
244	Theotis Brown	.15	.07
245	Dan Doornink	.15	.07
246	John Harris	.15	.07
247	Efren Herrera	.15	.07
248	David Hughes	.15	.07
249	Steve Largent	2.00	.90
250	Steve Largent IA	.75	.35
251	Sam McCullum	.15	.07
252	Sherman Smith	.15	.07
253	Manu Tuiasosopo	.15	.07
254	John Yarno	.15	.07
255	Jim Zorn	.40	.18
	(Sitting with Dave Krieg)		
256	Jim Zorn IA	.40	.18
257	Passing Leaders	4.00	1.80
	Ken Anderson		
	Joe Montana		
258	Receiving Leaders	.75	.35
	Kellen Winslow		
	Dwight Clark		
259	QB Sack Leaders	.15	.07
	Joe Klecko		
	Curtis Greer		
260	Scoring Leaders	.40	.18
	Jim Breech		
	Nick Lowery		
	Eddie Murray		
	Rafael Septien		
261	Interception Leaders	.40	.18
	John Harris		
	Everson Walls		
262	Punting Leaders	.15	.07
	Pat McInally		
	Tom Skladany		
263	Brothers: Bahr	.15	.07
	Chris and Matt		
264	Brothers: Blackwood	.40	.18
	Lyle and Glenn		
265	Brothers: Brock	.15	.07
	Pete and Stan		
266	Brothers: Griffin	.40	.18
	Archie and Ray		
267	Brothers: Hannah	.75	.35
	John and Charley		
268	Brothers: Jackson	.15	.07
	Monte and Terry		
269	Brothers: Payton	1.00	.45
	Eddie and Walter		
270	Brothers: Selmon	.75	.35
	Dewey and Lee Roy		
271	Atlanta Falcons TL	.40	.18
	William Andrews		
	Alfred Jenkins		

Tom Pridemore
Al Richardson
❑ 272 William Andrews .40 .18
❑ 273 William Andrews IA .40 .18
❑ 274 Steve Bartkowski .40 .18
❑ 275 Steve Bartkowski IA .40 .18
❑ 276 Bobby Butler .15 .07
❑ 277 Lynn Cain .15 .07
❑ 278 Wallace Francis .15 .07
❑ 279 Alfred Jackson .15 .07
❑ 280 John James .15 .07
❑ 281 Alfred Jenkins AP .15 .07
❑ 282 Alfred Jenkins IA .15 .07
❑ 283 Kenny Johnson .15 .07
❑ 284 Mike Kenn AP .75 .35
❑ 285 Fulton Kuykendall .15 .07
❑ 286 Mick Luckhurst RC .15 .07
❑ 287 Mick Luckhurst IA .15 .07
❑ 288 Junior Miller .15 .07
❑ 289 Al Richardson .15 .07
❑ 290 R.C. Thielemann RC .15 .07
❑ 291 Jeff Van Note .15 .07
❑ 292 Chicago Bears TL .75 .35
Walter Payton
Ken Margerum
Gary Fencik
Dan Hampton
Alan Page
❑ 293 Brian Baschnagel .15 .07
❑ 294 Robin Earl .15 .07
❑ 295 Vince Evans .40 .18
❑ 296 Gary Fencik AP .15 .07
❑ 297 Dan Hampton .75 .35
❑ 298 Noah Jackson .15 .07
❑ 299 Ken Margerum .15 .07
❑ 300 Jim Osborne .15 .07
❑ 301 Bob Parsons .15 .07
❑ 302 Walter Payton 6.00 2.70
❑ 303 Walter Payton IA 2.50 1.10
❑ 304 Revie Sorey .15 .07
❑ 305 Matt Suhey RC .75 .35
(Walter Payton
in background)
❑ 306 Rickey Watts .15 .07
❑ 307 Dallas Cowboys TL .75 .35
Tony Dorsett
Tony Hill
Everson Walls
Harvey Martin
❑ 308 Bob Breunig .15 .07
❑ 309 Doug Cosbie RC .15 .07
❑ 310 Pat Donovan AP .15 .07
❑ 311 Tony Dorsett AP 1.50 .70
❑ 312 Tony Dorsett IA .75 .35
❑ 313 Michael Downs RC .15 .07
❑ 314 Billy Joe DuPree .40 .18
❑ 315 John Dutton .15 .07
❑ 316 Tony Hill .40 .18
❑ 317 Butch Johnson .40 .18
❑ 318 Ed Too Tall Jones AP .75 .35
❑ 319 James Jones .15 .07
❑ 320 Harvey Martin .75 .35
❑ 321 Drew Pearson .75 .35
❑ 322 Herb Scott AP .15 .07
❑ 323 Rafael Septien AP .15 .07
❑ 324 Rafael Septien IA .15 .07
❑ 325 Ron Springs .40 .18
❑ 326 Dennis Thurman RC .15 .07
❑ 327 Everson Walls RC .75 .35
❑ 328 Everson Walls IA .75 .35
❑ 329 Danny White .75 .35
❑ 330 Danny White IA .40 .18
❑ 331 Randy White AP .75 .35
❑ 332 Randy White IA .75 .35
❑ 333 Detroit Lions TL .40 .18
Billy Sims
Freddie Scott
Jim Allen
Dave Pureifory
❑ 334 Jim Allen .15 .07
❑ 335 Al(Bubba) Baker .40 .18
❑ 336 Dexter Bussey .15 .07
❑ 337 Doug English AP .40 .18
❑ 338 Ken Fantetti .15 .07
❑ 339 William Gay .15 .07
❑ 340 David Hill .15 .07
❑ 341 Eric Hipple RC .15 .07
❑ 342 Rick Kane .15 .07
❑ 343 Ed Murray .75 .35
❑ 344 Ed Murray IA .40 .18
❑ 345 Ray Oldham .15 .07
❑ 346 Dave Pureifory .15 .07
❑ 347 Freddie Scott .15 .07
❑ 348 Freddie Scott IA .15 .07
❑ 349 Billy Sims AP .75 .35
❑ 350 Billy Sims IA .75 .35
❑ 351 Tom Skladany AP .15 .07
❑ 352 Leonard Thompson .15 .07
❑ 353 Stan White .15 .07
❑ 354 Green Bay Packers TL .75 .35
Gerry Ellis
James Lofton
Maurice Harvey
Mark Lee
Mike Butler
❑ 355 Paul Coffman .15 .07
❑ 356 George Cumby .15 .07
❑ 357 Lynn Dickey .15 .07
❑ 358 Lynn Dickey IA .15 .07
❑ 359 Gerry Ellis .15 .07
❑ 360 Maurice Harvey .15 .07
❑ 361 Harlan Huckleby .15 .07
❑ 362 John Jefferson .75 .35
❑ 363 Mark Lee RC .15 .07
❑ 364 James Lofton AP 1.00 .45
❑ 365 James Lofton IA .75 .35
❑ 366 Jan Stenerud .40 .18
❑ 367 Jan Stenerud IA .40 .18
❑ 368 Rich Wingo .15 .07
❑ 369 Los Angeles Rams TL .40 .18
Wendell Tyler
Preston Dennard
Nolan Cromwell
Jack Youngblood
❑ 370 Frank Corral .15 .07
❑ 371 Nolan Cromwell AP .40 .18
❑ 372 Nolan Cromwell IA .40 .18
❑ 373 Preston Dennard .15 .07
❑ 374 Mike Fanning .15 .07
❑ 375 Doug France .15 .07
❑ 376 Mike Guman .15 .07
❑ 377 Pat Haden .40 .18
❑ 378 Dennis Harrah .15 .07
❑ 379 Drew Hill RC .75 .35
❑ 380 LeRoy Irvin RC .15 .07
❑ 381 Cody Jones .15 .07
❑ 382 Rod Perry .15 .07
❑ 383 Rich Saul AP .15 .07
❑ 384 Pat Thomas .15 .07
❑ 385 Wendell Tyler .40 .18
❑ 386 Wendell Tyler IA .40 .18
❑ 387 Billy Waddy .15 .07
❑ 388 Jack Youngblood .75 .35
❑ 389 Minnesota Vikings TL .15 .07
Ted Brown
Joe Senser
Tom Hannon
Willie Teal
Matt Blair
❑ 390 Matt Blair AP .15 .07
❑ 391 Ted Brown .15 .07
❑ 392 Ted Brown IA .15 .07
❑ 393 Rick Danmeier .15 .07
❑ 394 Tommy Kramer .40 .18
❑ 395 Mark Mullaney .15 .07
❑ 396 Eddie Payton .15 .07
❑ 397 Ahmad Rashad .75 .35
❑ 398 Joe Senser .15 .07
❑ 399 Joe Senser IA .15 .07
❑ 400 Sammie White .40 .18
❑ 401 Sammie White IA .15 .07
❑ 402 Ron Yary .15 .07
❑ 403 Rickey Young .15 .07
❑ 404 New Orleans Saints TL .40 .18
George Rogers
Guido Merkens
Dave Waymer
Rickey Jackson
❑ 405 Russell Erxleben .15 .07
❑ 406 Elois Grooms .15 .07
❑ 407 Jack Holmes .15 .07
❑ 408 Archie Manning .75 .35
❑ 409 Derland Moore .15 .07
❑ 410 George Rogers RC .75 .35
❑ 411 George Rogers IA .75 .35
❑ 412 Toussaint Tyler .15 .07
❑ 413 Dave Waymer RC .15 .07
❑ 414 Wayne Wilson .15 .07
❑ 415 New York Giants TL .15 .07
Rob Carpenter
Johnny Perkins
Beasley Reece
George Martin
❑ 416 Scott Brunner RC .15 .07
❑ 417 Rob Carpenter .15 .07
❑ 418 Harry Carson AP .40 .18
❑ 419 Bill Currier .15 .07
❑ 420 Joe Danelo .15 .07
❑ 421 Joe Danelo IA .15 .07
❑ 422 Mark Haynes RC .15 .07
❑ 423 Terry Jackson .15 .07
❑ 424 Dave Jennings .15 .07
❑ 425 Gary Jeter .15 .07
❑ 426 Brian Kelley .15 .07
❑ 427 George Martin .15 .07
❑ 428 Curtis McGriff .15 .07
❑ 429 Bill Neill .15 .07
❑ 430 Johnny Perkins .15 .07
❑ 431 Beasley Reece .15 .07
❑ 432 Gary Shirk .15 .07
❑ 433 Phil Simms 2.00 .90
❑ 434 Lawrence Taylor AP RC 20.00 9.00
❑ 435 Lawrence Taylor IA 10.00 4.50
❑ 436 Brad Van Pelt .15 .07
❑ 437 Philadelphia Eagles TL .40 .18
Wilbert Montgomery
Harold Carmichael
Brenard Wilson
Carl Hairston
❑ 438 John Bunting .15 .07
❑ 439 Billy Campfield .15 .07
❑ 440 Harold Carmichael .75 .35
❑ 441 Harold Carmichael IA .75 .35
❑ 442 Herman Edwards .15 .07
❑ 443 Tony Franklin .15 .07
❑ 444 Tony Franklin IA .15 .07
❑ 445 Carl Hairston .15 .07
❑ 446 Dennis Harrison .15 .07
❑ 447 Ron Jaworski .75 .35
❑ 448 Charlie Johnson .15 .07
❑ 449 Keith Krepfle .15 .07
❑ 450 Frank LeMaster .15 .07
❑ 451 Randy Logan .15 .07
❑ 452 Wilbert Montgomery .40 .18
❑ 453 Wilbert Montgomery IA .40 .18
❑ 454 Hubie Oliver .15 .07
❑ 455 Jerry Robinson .15 .07
❑ 456 Jerry Robinson IA .15 .07
❑ 457 Jerry Sisemore .15 .07
❑ 458 Charlie Smith .15 .07
❑ 459 Stan Walters .15 .07
❑ 460 Brenard Wilson .15 .07
❑ 461 Roynell Young AP .15 .07
❑ 462 St. Louis Cardinals TL .40 .18
Ottis Anderson
Pat Tilley
Ken Greene
Curtis Greer
❑ 463 Ottis Anderson .75 .35
❑ 464 Ottis Anderson IA .75 .35
❑ 465 Carl Birdsong .15 .07
❑ 466 Rush Brown .15 .07
❑ 467 Mel Gray .40 .18
❑ 468 Ken Greene .15 .07
❑ 469 Jim Hart .75 .35
❑ 470 E.J. Junior RC .40 .18
❑ 471 Neil Lomax RC .75 .35
❑ 472 Stump Mitchell RC .75 .35
❑ 473 Wayne Morris .15 .07
❑ 474 Neil O'Donoghue .15 .07
❑ 475 Pat Tilley .15 .07
❑ 476 Pat Tilley IA .15 .07
❑ 477 San Francisco 49ers TL .40 .18
Ricky Patton
Dwight Clark
Dwight Hicks
Fred Dean
❑ 478 Dwight Clark .75 .35

❑ 479 Dwight Clark IA .75 .35
❑ 480 Earl Cooper .15 .07
❑ 481 Randy Cross AP .40 .18
❑ 482 Johnny Davis .15 .07
❑ 483 Fred Dean .15 .07
❑ 484 Fred Dean IA .15 .07
❑ 485 Dwight Hicks RC .75 .35
❑ 486 Ronnie Lott AP RC 20.00 9.00
❑ 487 Ronnie Lott IA 6.00 2.70
❑ 488 Joe Montana AP 20.00 9.00
❑ 489 Joe Montana IA 12.00 5.50
❑ 490 Ricky Patton .15 .07
❑ 491 Jack Reynolds .40 .18
❑ 492 Freddie Solomon .15 .07
❑ 493 Ray Wersching .15 .07
❑ 494 Charlie Young .15 .07
❑ 495 Tampa Bay Bucs TL .40 .18
Jerry Eckwood
Kevin House
Cedric Brown
Lee Roy Selmon
❑ 496 Cedric Brown .15 .07
❑ 497 Neal Colzie .15 .07
❑ 498 Jerry Eckwood .15 .07
❑ 499 Jimmie Giles AP .40 .18
❑ 500 Hugh Green RC .75 .35
❑ 501 Kevin House .15 .07
❑ 502 Kevin House IA .15 .07
❑ 503 Cecil Johnson .15 .07
❑ 504 James Owens .15 .07
❑ 505 Lee Roy Selmon AP .75 .35
❑ 506 Mike Washington .15 .07
❑ 507 James Wilder RC .40 .18
❑ 508 Doug Williams .40 .18
❑ 509 Wash. Redskins TL .75 .35
Joe Washington
Art Monk
Mark Murphy
Perry Brooks
❑ 510 Perry Brooks .15 .07
❑ 511 Dave Butz .40 .18
❑ 512 Wilbur Jackson .15 .07
❑ 513 Joe Lavender .15 .07
❑ 514 Terry Metcalf .40 .18
❑ 515 Art Monk 3.00 1.35
❑ 516 Mark Moseley .15 .07
❑ 517 Mark Murphy .15 .07
❑ 518 Mike Nelms AP .15 .07
❑ 519 Lemar Parrish .15 .07
❑ 520 John Riggins .75 .35
❑ 521 Joe Theismann .75 .35
❑ 522 Ricky Thompson .15 .07
❑ 523 Don Warren UER .15 .07
(Photo actually
Ricky Thompson)
❑ 524 Joe Washington .40 .18
❑ 525 Checklist 1-132 .40 .18
❑ 526 Checklist 133-264 .40 .18
❑ 527 Checklist 265-396 .40 .18
❑ 528 Checklist 397-528 .40 .18

1983 Topps

	NRMT-MT	EXC
COMPLETE SET (396)	50.00	22.00

❑ 1 Ken Anderson RB .60 .25
20 Consecutive
Pass Completions
❑ 2 Tony Dorsett RB .60 .25
99 Yard Run
❑ 3 Dan Fouts RB .60 .25
30 Games Over
300 Yards Passing
❑ 4 Joe Montana RB 3.00 1.35
Five Straight
300 Yard Games
❑ 5 Mark Moseley RB .30 .14
21 Straight
Field Goals
❑ 6 Mike Nelms RB .10 .05
Most Yards,
Punt Returns,
Super Bowl Game
❑ 7 Darrol Ray RB .10 .05
Longest Interception
Return, Playoff Game
❑ 8 John Riggins RB .60 .25
Most Yards Rushing,
Super Bowl Game
❑ 9 Fulton Walker RB .10 .05
Most Yards,
Kickoff Returns,
Super Bowl Game
❑ 10 NFC Championship .60 .25
Redskins 31,
Cowboys 17
(John Riggins tackled)
❑ 11 AFC Championship .30 .14
Dolphins 14,
Jets 0
❑ 12 Super Bowl XVII .10 .05
Redskins 27,
Dolphins 17
(John Riggins running)
❑ 13 Atlanta Falcons TL .30 .14
William Andrews
❑ 14 William Andrews DP PB .30 .14
❑ 15 Steve Bartkowski .30 .14
❑ 16 Bobby Butler .10 .05
❑ 17 Buddy Curry .10 .05
❑ 18 Alfred Jackson DP .10 .05
❑ 19 Alfred Jenkins .10 .05
❑ 20 Kenny Johnson .10 .05
❑ 21 Mike Kenn PB .10 .05
❑ 22 Mick Luckhurst .10 .05
❑ 23 Junior Miller .10 .05
❑ 24 Al Richardson .10 .05
❑ 25 Gerald Riggs DP RC .30 .14
❑ 26 R.C. Thielemann PB .10 .05
❑ 27 Jeff Van Note PB .10 .05
❑ 28 Chicago Bears TL 1.00 .45
Walter Payton
❑ 29 Brian Baschnagel .10 .05
❑ 30 Dan Hampton PB .60 .25
❑ 31 Mike Hartenstine .10 .05
❑ 32 Noah Jackson .10 .05
❑ 33 Jim McMahon RC 8.00 3.60
❑ 34 Emery Moorehead DP .10 .05
❑ 35 Bob Parsons .10 .05
❑ 36 Walter Payton 6.00 2.70
❑ 37 Terry Schmidt .10 .05
❑ 38 Mike Singletary RC 8.00 3.60
❑ 39 Matt Suhey DP .30 .14
❑ 40 Rickey Watts DP .10 .05
❑ 41 Otis Wilson DP RC .30 .14
❑ 42 Dallas Cowboys TL .60 .25
Tony Dorsett
❑ 43 Bob Breunig PB .30 .14
❑ 44 Doug Cosbie .10 .05
❑ 45 Pat Donovan PB .10 .05
❑ 46 Tony Dorsett DP PB 1.00 .45
❑ 47 Tony Hill .30 .14
❑ 48 Butch Johnson DP .30 .14
❑ 49 Ed Jones DP PB .60 .25
❑ 50 Harvey Martin DP .30 .14
❑ 51 Drew Pearson .60 .25
❑ 52 Rafael Septien .10 .05
❑ 53 Ron Springs DP .10 .05
❑ 54 Dennis Thurman .10 .05
❑ 55 Everson Walls PB .30 .14
❑ 56 Danny White DP PB .60 .25
❑ 57 Randy White PB .60 .25
❑ 58 Detroit Lions TL .30 .14
Billy Sims
❑ 59 Al(Bubba) Baker DP .30 .14
❑ 60 Dexter Bussey DP .10 .05
❑ 61 Gary Danielson DP .10 .05
❑ 62 Keith Dorney DP PB .10 .05
❑ 63 Doug English PB .10 .05
❑ 64 Ken Fantetti DP .10 .05
❑ 65 Alvin Hall DP .10 .05
❑ 66 David Hill DP .10 .05
❑ 67 Eric Hipple .10 .05
❑ 68 Ed Murray DP .30 .14
❑ 69 Freddie Scott .10 .05
❑ 70 Billy Sims DP PB .30 .14
❑ 71 Tom Skladany DP .10 .05
❑ 72 Leonard Thompson DP .10 .05
❑ 73 Bobby Watkins .10 .05
❑ 74 Green Bay Packers TL .10 .05
Eddie Lee Ivery
❑ 75 John Anderson .10 .05
❑ 76 Paul Coffman PB .10 .05
❑ 77 Lynn Dickey .10 .05
❑ 78 Mike Douglass DP .10 .05
❑ 79 Eddie Lee Ivery .10 .05
❑ 80 John Jefferson DP PB .60 .25
❑ 81 Ezra Johnson .10 .05
❑ 82 Mark Lee .10 .05
❑ 83 James Lofton PB .60 .25
❑ 84 Larry McCarren PB .10 .05
❑ 85 Jan Stenerud DP .30 .14
❑ 86 Los Angeles Rams TL .10 .05
Wendell Tyler
❑ 87 Bill Bain DP .10 .05
❑ 88 Nolan Cromwell PB .30 .14
❑ 89 Preston Dennard .10 .05
❑ 90 Vince Ferragamo DP .30 .14
❑ 91 Mike Guman .10 .05
❑ 92 Kent Hill PB .10 .05
❑ 93 Mike Lansford DP RC .10 .05
❑ 94 Rod Perry .10 .05
❑ 95 Pat Thomas DP .10 .05
❑ 96 Jack Youngblood .60 .25
❑ 97 Minnesota Vikings TL .10 .05
Ted Brown
❑ 98 Matt Blair PB .10 .05
❑ 99 Ted Brown .10 .05
❑ 100 Greg Coleman .10 .05
❑ 101 Randy Holloway .10 .05
❑ 102 Tommy Kramer .30 .14
❑ 103 Doug Martin DP .10 .05
❑ 104 Mark Mullaney .10 .05
❑ 105 Joe Senser .10 .05
❑ 106 Willie Teal DP .10 .05
❑ 107 Sammie White .30 .14
❑ 108 Rickey Young .10 .05
❑ 109 New Orleans Saints TL .30 .14
George Rogers
❑ 110 Stan Brock RC .10 .05
❑ 111 Bruce Clark RC .10 .05
❑ 112 Russell Erxleben DP .10 .05
❑ 113 Russell Gary .10 .05
❑ 114 Jeff Groth DP .10 .05
❑ 115 John Hill DP .10 .05
❑ 116 Derland Moore .10 .05
❑ 117 George Rogers PB .30 .14
❑ 118 Ken Stabler 1.50 .70
❑ 119 Wayne Wilson .10 .05
❑ 120 New York Giants TL .10 .05
Butch Woolfolk
❑ 121 Scott Brunner .10 .05
❑ 122 Rob Carpenter .10 .05
❑ 123 Harry Carson PB .30 .14
❑ 124 Joe Danelo DP .10 .05
❑ 125 Earnest Gray .10 .05
❑ 126 Mark Haynes DP PB .30 .14
❑ 127 Terry Jackson .10 .05
❑ 128 Dave Jennings PB .10 .05
❑ 129 Brian Kelley .10 .05
❑ 130 George Martin .10 .05
❑ 131 Tom Mullady .10 .05
❑ 132 Johnny Perkins .10 .05
❑ 133 Lawrence Taylor PB 5.00 2.20
❑ 134 Brad Van Pelt .10 .05
❑ 135 Butch Woolfolk DP .10 .05
❑ 136 Philadelphia Eagles TL .30 .14
Wilbert Montgomery
❑ 137 Harold Carmichael .60 .25

❑ 138 Herman Edwards .... .10 .05
❑ 139 Tony Franklin DP .... .10 .05
❑ 140 Carl Hairston DP .... .10 .05
❑ 141 Dennis Harrison DP PB.. .10 .05
❑ 142 Ron Jaworski DP............ .30 .14
❑ 143 Frank LeMaster.............. .10 .05
❑ 144 Wilbert Montgomery DP .30 .14
❑ 145 Guy Morriss..................... .10 .05
❑ 146 Jerry Robinson .... .10 .05
(TD stats don't match)
❑ 147 Max Runager................... .10 .05
❑ 148 Ron Smith DP.................. .10 .05
❑ 149 John Spagnola .... .10 .05
❑ 150 Stan Walters DP .... .10 .05
❑ 151 Roynell Young DP.......... .10 .05
❑ 152 St. Louis Cardinals TL..... .30 .14
Ottis Anderson
❑ 153 Ottis Anderson .... .60 .25
❑ 154 Carl Birdsong .... .10 .05
❑ 155 Dan Dierdorf DP .... .60 .25
❑ 156 Roy Green RC................ .60 .25
❑ 157 Elois Grooms.................. .10 .05
❑ 158 Neil Lomax DP .... .30 .14
❑ 159 Wayne Morris .... .10 .05
❑ 160 Tootie Robbins RC .... .10 .05
❑ 161 Luis Sharpe RC.............. .10 .05
❑ 162 Pat Tilley .... .10 .05
❑ 163 San Francisco 49ers TL .10 .05
Jeff Moore
❑ 164 Dwight Clark PB .... .60 .25
❑ 165 Randy Cross PB .... .30 .14
❑ 166 Russ Francis.................. .30 .14
❑ 167 Dwight Hicks PB .... .10 .05
❑ 168 Ronnie Lott PB 2.50 1.10
❑ 169 Joe Montana DP 10.00 4.50
❑ 170 Jeff Moore...................... .10 .05
❑ 171 R.Nehemiah DP RC ...... .60 .25
❑ 172 Freddie Solomon............ .10 .05
❑ 173 Ray Wersching DP .... .10 .05
❑ 174 Tampa Bay Bucs TL ...... .10 .05
James Wilder
❑ 175 Cedric Brown.................. .10 .05
❑ 176 Bill Capece .... .10 .05
❑ 177 Neal Colzie .... .10 .05
❑ 178 Jimmie Giles PB .... .10 .05
❑ 179 Hugh Green PB.............. .30 .14
❑ 180 Kevin House DP .... .10 .05
❑ 181 James Owens .... .10 .05
❑ 182 Lee Roy Selmon PB ...... .60 .25
❑ 183 Mike Washington............ .10 .05
❑ 184 James Wilder .... .10 .05
❑ 185 Doug Williams DP .... .30 .14
❑ 186 Wash. Redskins TL........ .60 .25
John Riggins
❑ 187 Jeff Bostic DP RC .... 1.00 .45
❑ 188 Charlie Brown PB RC..... .30 .14
❑ 189 Vernon Dean DP............ .10 .05
❑ 190 Joe Jacoby RC .... 1.00 .45
❑ 191 Dexter Manley RC.......... .30 .14
❑ 192 Rich Milot .... .10 .05
❑ 193 Art Monk DP .... 1.00 .45
❑ 194 Mark Moseley DP PB ..... .10 .05
❑ 195 Mike Nelms PB .... .10 .05
❑ 196 Neal Olkewicz DP .... .10 .05
❑ 197 Tony Peters PB.............. .10 .05
❑ 198 John Riggins DP............ .60 .25
❑ 199 Joe Theismann PB .... .60 .25
❑ 200 Don Warren..................... .10 .05
❑ 201 Jeris White DP .... .10 .05
❑ 202 Passing Leaders .... .60 .25
Joe Theismann
Ken Anderson
❑ 203 Receiving Leaders .... .30 .14
Dwight Clark
Kellen Winslow
❑ 204 Rushing Leaders............ .60 .25
Tony Dorsett
Freeman McNeil
❑ 205 Scoring Leaders .... 1.25 .55
Wendell Tyler
Marcus Allen
❑ 206 Interception Leaders ...... .30 .14
Everson Walls
AFC Tie (Four)
❑ 207 Punting Leaders .... .10 .05
Carl Birdsong
Luke Prestridge
❑ 208 Baltimore Colts TL.......... .10 .05
Randy McMillan
❑ 209 Matt Bouza .... .10 .05
❑ 210 Johnie Cooks DP RC ..... .10 .05
❑ 211 Curtis Dickey.................. .10 .05
❑ 212 Nesby Glasgow DP........ .10 .05
❑ 213 Derrick Hatchett .... .10 .05
❑ 214 Randy McMillan.............. .10 .05
❑ 215 Mike Pagel RC .... .30 .14
❑ 216 Rohn Stark DP RC .... .30 .14
❑ 217 D.Thompson DP RC ...... .10 .05
❑ 218 Leo Wisniewski DP .... .10 .05
❑ 219 Buffalo Bills TL .... .30 .14
Joe Cribbs
❑ 220 Curtis Brown .... .10 .05
❑ 221 Jerry Butler .... .10 .05
❑ 222 Greg Cater DP .... .10 .05
❑ 223 Joe Cribbs...................... .30 .14
❑ 224 Joe Ferguson .... .30 .14
❑ 225 Roosevelt Leaks .... .10 .05
❑ 226 Frank Lewis.................... .10 .05
❑ 227 Eugene Marve RC.......... .10 .05
❑ 228 Fred Smerlas DP PB...... .10 .05
❑ 229 Ben Williams DP PB ...... .10 .05
❑ 230 Cincinnati Bengals TL .... .10 .05
Pete Johnson
❑ 231 Charles Alexander.......... .10 .05
❑ 232 Ken Anderson DP PB .... .60 .25
❑ 233 Jim Breech DP .... .10 .05
❑ 234 Ross Browner .... .10 .05
❑ 235 Cris Collinsworth .... .60 .25
DP PB
❑ 236 Isaac Curtis.................... .10 .05
❑ 237 Pete Johnson .... .10 .05
❑ 238 Steve Kreider DP .... .10 .05
❑ 239 Max Montoya DP RC .... .10 .05
❑ 240 Anthony Munoz PB ...... 1.00 .45
❑ 241 Ken Riley........................ .10 .05
❑ 242 Dan Ross PB.................. .10 .05
❑ 243 Reggie Williams .... .30 .14
❑ 244 Cleveland Browns TL .... .30 .14
Mike Pruitt
❑ 245 Chip Banks DP PB RC .. .30 .14
❑ 246 Tom Cousineau DP RC.. .30 .14
❑ 247 Joe DeLamielleure DP .. .10 .05
❑ 248 Doug Dieken DP .... .10 .05
❑ 249 Hanford Dixon RC.......... .10 .05
❑ 250 Ricky Feacher DP.......... .10 .05
❑ 251 Lawrence Johnson DP .. .10 .05
❑ 252 Dave Logan DP.............. .10 .05
❑ 253 Paul McDonald DP .... .10 .05
❑ 254 Ozzie Newsome DP ...... .60 .25
❑ 255 Mike Pruitt...................... .30 .14
❑ 256 Clarence Scott DP.......... .10 .05
❑ 257 Brian Sipe DP .... .30 .14
❑ 258 Dwight Walker DP.......... .10 .05
❑ 259 Charles White .... .30 .14
❑ 260 Denver Broncos TL........ .10 .05
Gerald Willhite
❑ 261 Steve DeBerg DP .... .30 .14
❑ 262 Randy Gradishar DP PB .30 .14
❑ 263 Rulon Jones DP RC ...... .10 .05
❑ 264 Rich Karlis DP................ .10 .05
❑ 265 Don Latimer.................... .10 .05
❑ 266 Rick Parros DP .... .10 .05
❑ 267 Luke Prestridge PB........ .10 .05
❑ 268 Rick Upchurch PB.......... .30 .14
❑ 269 Steve Watson DP .... .10 .05
❑ 270 Gerald Willhite DP.......... .10 .05
❑ 271 Houston Oilers TL.......... .10 .05
Gifford Nielsen
❑ 272 Harold Bailey.................. .10 .05
❑ 273 Jesse Baker DP .... .10 .05
❑ 274 Gregg Bingham DP........ .10 .05
❑ 275 Robert Brazile DP PB .... .10 .05
❑ 276 Donnie Craft .... .10 .05
❑ 277 Daryl Hunt...................... .10 .05
❑ 278 Archie Manning DP........ .30 .14
❑ 279 Gifford Nielsen .... .10 .05
❑ 280 Mike Renfro.................... .10 .05
❑ 281 Carl Roaches DP .... .10 .05
❑ 282 Kansas City Chiefs TL.... .30 .14
Joe Delaney
❑ 283 Gary Barbaro PB............ .10 .05
❑ 284 Joe Delaney .... .10 .05
❑ 285 Jeff Gossett RC.............. .60 .25
❑ 286 Gary Green DP PB .... .10 .05
❑ 287 Eric Harris DP .... .10 .05
❑ 288 Billy Jackson DP .... .10 .05
❑ 289 Bill Kenney DP .... .10 .05
❑ 290 Nick Lowery.................... .60 .25
❑ 291 Henry Marshall .... .10 .05
❑ 292 Art Still DP PB................ .10 .05
❑ 293 Los Angeles Raiders TL 2.00 .90
Marcus Allen
❑ 294 Marcus Allen DP PB RC 20.00 9.00
❑ 295 Lyle Alzado .... .60 .25
❑ 296 Chris Bahr DP .... .10 .05
❑ 297 Cliff Branch .... .60 .25
❑ 298 Todd Christensen RC .... .75 .35
❑ 299 Ray Guy .... .30 .14
❑ 300 Frank Hawkins DP .... .10 .05
❑ 301 Lester Hayes DP PB...... .10 .05
❑ 302 Ted Hendricks DP PB.... .60 .25
❑ 303 Kenny King DP .... .10 .05
❑ 304 Rod Martin...................... .10 .05
❑ 305 Matt Millen DP................ .60 .25
❑ 306 Burgess Owens.............. .10 .05
❑ 307 Jim Plunkett.................... .60 .25
❑ 308 Miami Dolphins TL .... .30 .14
Andra Franklin
❑ 309 Bob Baumhower PB ...... .10 .05
❑ 310 Glenn Blackwood .... .10 .05
❑ 311 Lyle Blackwood DP........ .10 .05
❑ 312 A.J. Duhe .... .10 .05
❑ 313 Andra Franklin PB.......... .10 .05
❑ 314 Duriel Harris .... .10 .05
❑ 315 Bob Kuechenberg DP PB .30 .14
❑ 316 Don McNeal .... .10 .05
❑ 317 Tony Nathan .... .30 .14
❑ 318 Ed Newman PB.............. .10 .05
❑ 319 Earnie Rhone DP .... .10 .05
❑ 320 Joe Rose DP.................. .10 .05
❑ 321 Don Strock DP .... .10 .05
❑ 322 Uwe Von Schamann ...... .10 .05
❑ 323 David Woodley DP .... .30 .14
❑ 324 New England Pats TL .... .10 .05
Tony Collins
❑ 325 Julius Adams.................. .10 .05
❑ 326 Pete Brock...................... .10 .05
❑ 327 Rich Camarillo DP RC.... .10 .05
❑ 328 Tony Collins DP .... .10 .05
❑ 329 Steve Grogan .... .30 .14
❑ 330 John Hannah PB............ .60 .25
❑ 331 Don Hasselbeck .... .10 .05
❑ 332 Mike Haynes PB .... .30 .14
❑ 333 Roland James RC.......... .10 .05
❑ 334A Stanley Morgan ERR .. .60 .25
(Inside Linebacker-
printed upside down
on card back)
❑ 334B Stanley Morgan COR .. .30 .14
❑ 335 Steve Nelson.................. .10 .05
❑ 336 Kenneth Sims DP .... .10 .05
❑ 337 Mark Van Eeghen .... .30 .14
❑ 338 New York Jets TL .... .30 .14
Freeman McNeil
❑ 339 Greg Buttle .... .10 .05
❑ 340 Joe Fields PB .... .10 .05
❑ 341 Mark Gastineau DP PB.. .30 .14
❑ 342 Bruce Harper.................. .10 .05
❑ 343 Bobby Jackson .... .10 .05
❑ 344 Bobby Jones .... .10 .05
❑ 345 Johnny Lam Jones DP .. .10 .05
❑ 346 Joe Klecko...................... .30 .14
❑ 347 Marty Lyons.................... .10 .05
❑ 348 Freeman McNeil PB ...... .60 .25
❑ 349 Lance Mehl RC .... .10 .05
❑ 350 Marvin Powell DP PB .... .10 .05
❑ 351 Darrol Ray DP................ .10 .05
❑ 352 Abdul Salaam .... .10 .05
❑ 353 Richard Todd.................. .30 .14
❑ 354 Wesley Walker PB .... .30 .14
❑ 355 Pittsburgh Steelers TL.... .60 .25
Franco Harris
❑ 356 Gary Anderson K DP RC 8.00 3.60
❑ 357 Mel Blount DP................ .60 .25
❑ 358 Terry Bradshaw DP...... 1.50 .70
❑ 359 Larry Brown PB.............. .10 .05
❑ 360 Bennie Cunningham ...... .10 .05
❑ 361 Gary Dunn...................... .10 .05

	No.	Player	NRMT-MT	EXC
❑	362	Franco Harris	.75	.35
❑	363	Jack Lambert PB	.60	.25
❑	364	Frank Pollard	.10	.05
❑	365	Donnie Shell PB	.30	.14
❑	366	John Stallworth PB	.60	.25
❑	367	Loren Toews	.10	.05
❑	368	Mike Webster DP PB	.60	.25
❑	369	Dwayne Woodruff RC	.10	.05
❑	370	San Diego Chargers TL Chuck Muncie	.30	.14
❑	371	Rolf Benirschke DP PB	.10	.05
❑	372	James Brooks	.60	.25
❑	373	Wes Chandler PB	.30	.14
❑	374	Dan Fouts DP PB	.60	.25
❑	375	Tim Fox	.10	.05
❑	376	Gary Johnson PB	.10	.05
❑	377	Charlie Joiner DP	.60	.25
❑	378	Louie Kelcher	.10	.05
❑	379	Chuck Muncie PB	.10	.05
❑	380	Cliff Thrift	.10	.05
❑	381	Doug Wilkerson PB	.10	.05
❑	382	Kellen Winslow PB	.75	.35
❑	383	Seattle Seahawks TL Sherman Smith	.10	.05
❑	384	Kenny Easley PB RC	.60	.25
❑	385	Jacob Green RC	.30	.14
❑	386	John Harris	.10	.05
❑	387	Michael Jackson	.10	.05
❑	388	Norm Johnson RC	.10	.05
❑	389	Steve Largent	1.25	.55
❑	390	Keith Simpson	.10	.05
❑	391	Sherman Smith	.10	.05
❑	392	Jeff West DP	.10	.05
❑	393	Jim Zorn DP	.30	.14
❑	394	Checklist 1-132	.20	.09
❑	395	Checklist 133-264	.20	.09
❑	396	Checklist 265-396	.20	.09

1984 Topps

	NRMT-MT	EXC
COMPLETE SET (396)	200.00	90.00
COMP.FACT.SET (396)	275.00	125.00

	No.	Player	NRMT-MT	EXC
❑	1	Eric Dickerson RB Sets Rookie Mark With 1808 Yards	.50	.23
❑	2	Ali Haji-Sheikh RB Sets Field Goal Mark as a Rookie	.25	.11
❑	3	Franco Harris RB Records Eighth 1000 Yard Year	.50	.23
❑	4	Mark Moseley RB 161 Points Sets Mark for Kickers	.25	.11
❑	5	John Riggins RB 24 Rushing TD's	.50	.23
❑	6	Jan Stenerud RB 338th Career FG	.25	.11
❑	7	AFC Championship Raiders 30, Seahawks 14 (Marcus Allen running)	.50	.23
❑	8	NFC Championship Redskins 24, 49ers 21 (John Riggins running)	.25	.11
❑	9	Super Bowl XVIII UER Raiders 38, Redskins 9 (Hand-off to Marcus Allen; score wrong, 28-9 on card front)	.50	.23
❑	10	Indianapolis Colts TL Curtis Dickey	.10	.05
❑	11	Raul Allegre RC	.10	.05
❑	12	Curtis Dickey	.25	.11
❑	13	Ray Donaldson RC	.25	.11
❑	14	Nesby Glasgow	.10	.05
❑	15	Chris Hinton PB RC	.50	.23
❑	16	Vernon Maxwell RC	.10	.05
❑	17	Randy McMillan	.10	.05
❑	18	Mike Pagel	.25	.11
❑	19	Rohn Stark	.25	.11
❑	20	Leo Wisniewski	.10	.05
❑	21	Buffalo Bills TL Joe Cribbs	.25	.11
❑	22	Jerry Butler	.10	.05
❑	23	Joe Danelo	.10	.05
❑	24	Joe Ferguson	.25	.11
❑	25	Steve Freeman	.10	.05
❑	26	Roosevelt Leaks	.25	.11
❑	27	Frank Lewis	.10	.05
❑	28	Eugene Marve	.10	.05
❑	29	Booker Moore	.10	.05
❑	30	Fred Smerlas PB	.10	.05
❑	31	Ben Williams	.25	.11
❑	32	Cincinnati Bengals TL Cris Collinsworth	.25	.11
❑	33	Charles Alexander	.10	.05
❑	34	Ken Anderson	.50	.23
❑	35	Ken Anderson IR	.50	.23
❑	36	Jim Breech	.10	.05
❑	37	Cris Collinsworth PB	.50	.23
❑	38	Cris Collinsworth IR	.50	.23
❑	39	Isaac Curtis	.25	.11
❑	40	Eddie Edwards	.10	.05
❑	41	Ray Horton RC	.10	.05
❑	42	Pete Johnson	.25	.11
❑	43	Steve Kreider	.10	.05
❑	44	Max Montoya	.10	.05
❑	45	Anthony Munoz PB	.50	.23
❑	46	Reggie Williams	.25	.11
❑	47	Cleveland Browns TL Mike Pruitt	.25	.11
❑	48	Matt Bahr	.25	.11
❑	49	Chip Banks PB	.10	.05
❑	50	Tom Cousineau	.10	.05
❑	51	Joe DeLamielleure	.10	.05
❑	52	Doug Dieken	.10	.05
❑	53	Bob Golic RC	.50	.23
❑	54	Bobby Jones	.10	.05
❑	55	Dave Logan	.10	.05
❑	56	Clay Matthews	.50	.23
❑	57	Paul McDonald	.10	.05
❑	58	Ozzie Newsome	.50	.23
❑	59	Ozzie Newsome IR	.50	.23
❑	60	Mike Pruitt	.25	.11
❑	61	Denver Broncos TL Steve Watson	.25	.11
❑	62	Barney Chavous RC	.10	.05
❑	63	John Elway RC	100.00	45.00
❑	64	Steve Foley	.10	.05
❑	65	Tom Jackson	.50	.23
❑	66	Rich Karlis	.10	.05
❑	67	Luke Prestridge	.10	.05
❑	68	Zach Thomas	.10	.05
❑	69	Rick Upchurch	.25	.11
❑	70	Steve Watson	.25	.11
❑	71	Sammy Winder RC	.25	.11
❑	72	Louis Wright PB	.25	.11
❑	73	Houston Oilers TL Tim Smith	.10	.05
❑	74	Jesse Baker	.10	.05
❑	75	Gregg Bingham	.10	.05
❑	76	Robert Brazile	.25	.11
❑	77	Steve Brown	.10	.05
❑	78	Chris Dressel	.10	.05
❑	79	Doug France	.10	.05
❑	80	Florian Kempf	.10	.05
❑	81	Carl Roaches	.25	.11
❑	82	Tim Smith RC	.25	.11
❑	83	Willie Tullis	.10	.05
❑	84	Kansas City Chiefs TL Carlos Carson	.10	.05
❑	85	Mike Bell	.10	.05
❑	86	Theotis Brown	.10	.05
❑	87	Carlos Carson PB	.50	.23
❑	88	Carlos Carson IR	.25	.11
❑	89	Deron Cherry PB RC	.25	.11
❑	90	Gary Green PB	.10	.05
❑	91	Billy Jackson	.10	.05
❑	92	Bill Kenney	.25	.11
❑	93	Bill Kenney IR	.25	.11
❑	94	Nick Lowery	.50	.23
❑	95	Henry Marshall	.10	.05
❑	96	Art Still	.10	.05
❑	97	Los Angeles Raiders TL Todd Christensen	.25	.11
❑	98	Marcus Allen	5.00	2.20
❑	99	Marcus Allen IR	2.50	1.10
❑	100	Lyle Alzado	.25	.11
❑	101	Lyle Alzado IR	.25	.11
❑	102	Chris Bahr	.10	.05
❑	103	Malcolm Barnwell RC	.10	.05
❑	104	Cliff Branch	.50	.23
❑	105	Todd Christensen PB	.50	.23
❑	106	Todd Christensen IR	.50	.23
❑	107	Ray Guy	.50	.23
❑	108	Frank Hawkins	.10	.05
❑	109	Lester Hayes PB	.25	.11
❑	110	Ted Hendricks PB	.50	.23
❑	111	Howie Long PB RC	15.00	6.75
❑	112	Rod Martin PB	.25	.11
❑	113	Vann McElroy PB RC	.10	.05
❑	114	Jim Plunkett	.50	.23
❑	115	Greg Pruitt PB	.25	.11
❑	116	Miami Dolphins TL Mark Duper	.50	.23
❑	117	Bob Baumhower PB	.10	.05
❑	118	Doug Betters PB RC	.10	.05
❑	119	A.J. Duhe	.10	.05
❑	120	Mark Duper PB RC	.50	.23
❑	121	Andra Franklin	.10	.05
❑	122	William Judson	.10	.05
❑	123	Dan Marino PB RC UER (Quaterback on back)	100.00	45.00
❑	124	Dan Marino IR	12.00	5.50
❑	125	Nat Moore	.25	.11
❑	126	Ed Newman PB	.10	.05
❑	127	Reggie Roby RC	.25	.11
❑	128	Gerald Small	.10	.05
❑	129	Dwight Stephenson RC	1.25	.55
❑	130	Uwe Von Schamann	.10	.05
❑	131	New England Pats TL Tony Collins	.10	.05
❑	132	Rich Camarillo PB	.25	.11
❑	133	Tony Collins PB	.25	.11
❑	134	Tony Collins IR	.10	.05
❑	135	Bob Cryder	.10	.05
❑	136	Steve Grogan	.25	.11
❑	137	John Hannah PB	.50	.23
❑	138	Brian Holloway PB RC	.10	.05
❑	139	Roland James	.10	.05
❑	140	Stanley Morgan	.25	.11
❑	141	Rick Sanford	.10	.05
❑	142	Mosi Tatupu RC	.10	.05
❑	143	Andre Tippett RC	.50	.23
❑	144	New York Jets TL Wesley Walker	.25	.11
❑	145	Jerome Barkum	.10	.05
❑	146	Mark Gastineau PB	.25	.11
❑	147	Mark Gastineau IR	.25	.11
❑	148	Bruce Harper	.10	.05
❑	149	Johnny Lam Jones	.10	.05
❑	150	Joe Klecko PB	.25	.11
❑	151	Pat Leahy	.10	.05
❑	152	Freeman McNeil	.25	.11
❑	153	Lance Mehl	.10	.05
❑	154	Marvin Powell PB	.25	.11
❑	155	Darrol Ray	.10	.05
❑	156	Pat Ryan RC	.10	.05
❑	157	Kirk Springs	.10	.05
❑	158	Wesley Walker	.25	.11
❑	159	Pittsburgh Steelers TL Franco Harris	.50	.23
❑	160	Walter Abercrombie RC	.25	.11
❑	161	Gary Anderson K PB	.50	.23
❑	162	Terry Bradshaw	2.00	.90

	No.	Card	Price	Price
❑	163	Craig Colquitt	.10	.05
❑	164	Bennie Cunningham	.10	.05
❑	165	Franco Harris	.50	.23
❑	166	Franco Harris IR	.50	.23
❑	167	Jack Lambert PB	.50	.23
❑	168	Jack Lambert IR	.50	.23
❑	169	Frank Pollard	.10	.05
❑	170	Donnie Shell	.25	.11
❑	171	Mike Webster PB	.25	.11
❑	172	Keith Willis RC	.10	.05
❑	173	Rick Woods	.10	.05
❑	174	San Diego Chargers TL	.50	.23
		Kellen Winslow		
❑	175	Rolf Benirschke	.10	.05
❑	176	James Brooks	.25	.11
❑	177	Maury Buford	.10	.05
❑	178	Wes Chandler PB	.25	.11
❑	179	Dan Fouts PB	.60	.25
❑	180	Dan Fouts IR	.50	.23
❑	181	Charlie Joiner	.50	.23
❑	182	Linden King	.10	.05
❑	183	Chuck Muncie	.25	.11
❑	184	Billy Ray Smith RC	.50	.23
❑	185	Danny Walters RC	.10	.05
❑	186	Kellen Winslow PB	.60	.25
❑	187	Kellen Winslow IR	.50	.23
❑	188	Seattle Seahawks TL	.50	.23
		Curt Warner		
❑	189	Steve August	.10	.05
❑	190	Dave Brown	.10	.05
❑	191	Zachary Dixon	.10	.05
❑	192	Kenny Easley	.25	.11
❑	193	Jacob Green	.10	.05
❑	194	Norm Johnson	.25	.11
❑	195	Dave Krieg RC	1.50	.70
❑	196	Steve Largent	1.00	.45
❑	197	Steve Largent IR	.50	.23
❑	198	Curt Warner PB RC	.50	.23
❑	199	Curt Warner IR	.50	.23
❑	200	Jeff West	.10	.05
❑	201	Charlie Young	.10	.05
❑	202	Passing Leaders	6.00	2.70
		Dan Marino		
		Steve Bartkowski		
❑	203	Receiving Leaders	.25	.11
		Todd Christensen		
		Charlie Brown		
		Earnest Gray		
		Roy Green		
❑	204	Rushing Leaders	.50	.23
		Curt Warner		
		Eric Dickerson		
❑	205	Scoring Leaders	.10	.05
		Gary Anderson K		
		Mark Moseley		
❑	206	Interception Leaders	.10	.05
		Vann McElroy		
		Ken Riley		
		Mark Murphy		
❑	207	Punting Leaders	.10	.05
		Rich Camarillo		
		Greg Coleman		
❑	208	Atlanta Falcons TL	.25	.11
		William Andrews		
❑	209	William Andrews PB	.25	.11
❑	210	William Andrews IR	.25	.11
❑	211	Stacey Bailey RC	.10	.05
❑	212	Steve Bartkowski	.50	.23
❑	213	Steve Bartkowski IR	.25	.11
❑	214	Ralph Giacomarro	.10	.05
❑	215	Billy Johnson PB	.25	.11
❑	216	Mike Kenn PB	.25	.11
❑	217	Mick Luckhurst	.10	.05
❑	218	Gerald Riggs	.50	.23
❑	219	R.C. Thielemann PB	.10	.05
❑	220	Jeff Van Note	.25	.11
❑	221	Chicago Bears TL	.75	.35
		Walter Payton		
❑	222	Jim Covert RC	.50	.23
❑	223	Leslie Frazier	.10	.05
❑	224	Willie Gault RC	.50	.23
❑	225	Mike Hartenstine	.10	.05
❑	226	Noah Jackson UER	.10	.05
		(photo actually		
		Jim Osborne)		
❑	227	Jim McMahon	1.25	.55
❑	228	Walter Payton PB	4.00	1.80
❑	229	Walter Payton IR	1.25	.55
❑	230	Mike Richardson RC	.10	.05
❑	231	Terry Schmidt	.10	.05
❑	232	Mike Singletary PB	1.25	.55
❑	233	Matt Suhey	.25	.11
❑	234	Bob Thomas	.10	.05
❑	235	Dallas Cowboys TL	.50	.23
		Tony Dorsett		
❑	236	Bob Breunig	.10	.05
❑	237	Doug Cosbie PB	.25	.11
❑	238	Tony Dorsett PB	1.00	.45
❑	239	Tony Dorsett IR	.50	.23
❑	240	John Dutton	.10	.05
❑	241	Tony Hill	.25	.11
❑	242	Ed Jones PB	.50	.23
❑	243	Drew Pearson	.50	.23
❑	244	Rafael Septien	.10	.05
❑	245	Ron Springs	.25	.11
❑	246	Dennis Thurman	.10	.05
❑	247	Everson Walls PB	.10	.05
❑	248	Danny White	.50	.23
❑	249	Randy White PB	.50	.23
❑	250	Detroit Lions TL	.25	.11
		Billy Sims		
❑	251	Jeff Chadwick RC	.25	.11
❑	252	Garry Cobb	.10	.05
❑	253	Doug English PB	.25	.11
❑	254	William Gay	.10	.05
❑	255	Eric Hipple	.25	.11
❑	256	James Jones RC	.25	.11
❑	257	Bruce McNorton	.10	.05
❑	258	Eddie Murray	.25	.11
❑	259	Ulysses Norris	.10	.05
❑	260	Billy Sims	.50	.23
❑	261	Billy Sims IR	.25	.11
❑	262	Leonard Thompson	.10	.05
❑	263	Green Bay Packers TL	.50	.23
		James Lofton		
❑	264	John Anderson	.10	.05
❑	265	Paul Coffman PB	.25	.11
❑	266	Lynn Dickey	.25	.11
❑	267	Gerry Ellis	.10	.05
❑	268	John Jefferson	.50	.23
❑	269	John Jefferson IR	.50	.23
❑	270	Ezra Johnson	.10	.05
❑	271	Tim Lewis	.10	.05
❑	272	James Lofton PB	.50	.23
❑	273	James Lofton IR	.50	.23
❑	274	Larry McCarren PB	.10	.05
❑	275	Jan Stenerud	.25	.11
❑	276	Los Angeles Rams TL	.50	.23
		Eric Dickerson		
❑	277	Mike Barber	.10	.05
❑	278	Jim Collins	.10	.05
❑	279	Nolan Cromwell PB	.25	.11
❑	280	Eric Dickerson PB RC	12.00	5.50
❑	281	Eric Dickerson IR	2.00	.90
❑	282	George Farmer	.10	.05
❑	283	Vince Ferragamo	.25	.11
❑	284	Kent Hill PB	.10	.05
❑	285	John Misko	.10	.05
❑	286	Jackie Slater PB RC	4.00	1.80
❑	287	Jack Youngblood	.25	.11
❑	288	Minnesota Vikings TL	.10	.05
		Darrin Nelson		
❑	289	Ted Brown	.25	.11
❑	290	Greg Coleman	.10	.05
❑	291	Steve Dils	.10	.05
❑	292	Tony Galbreath	.10	.05
❑	293	Tommy Kramer	.25	.11
❑	294	Doug Martin	.10	.05
❑	295	Darrin Nelson RC	.25	.11
❑	296	Benny Ricardo	.10	.05
❑	297	John Swain	.10	.05
❑	298	John Turner	.10	.05
❑	299	New Orleans Saints TL	.25	.11
		George Rogers		
❑	300	Morten Andersen RC	1.50	.70
❑	301	Russell Erxleben	.10	.05
❑	302	Jeff Groth	.10	.05
❑	303	Rickey Jackson PB RC	.50	.23
❑	304	Johnnie Poe	.10	.05
❑	305	George Rogers	.25	.11
❑	306	Richard Todd	.25	.11
❑	307	Jim Wilks RC	.10	.05
❑	308	Dave Wilson RC	.10	.05
❑	309	Wayne Wilson	.10	.05
❑	310	New York Giants TL	.10	.05
		Earnest Gray		
❑	311	Leon Bright	.10	.05
❑	312	Scott Brunner	.10	.05
❑	313	Rob Carpenter	.10	.05
❑	314	Harry Carson PB	.25	.11
❑	315	Earnest Gray	.10	.05
❑	316	Ali Haji-Sheikh PB RC	.10	.05
❑	317	Mark Haynes PB	.25	.11
❑	318	Dave Jennings	.10	.05
❑	319	Brian Kelley	.10	.05
❑	320	Phil Simms	.75	.35
❑	321	Lawrence Taylor PB	3.00	1.35
❑	322	Lawrence Taylor IR	1.50	.70
❑	323	Brad Van Pelt	.10	.05
❑	324	Butch Woolfolk	.10	.05
❑	325	Philadelphia Eagles TL	.25	.11
		Mike Quick		
❑	326	Harold Carmichael	.25	.11
❑	327	Herman Edwards	.10	.05
❑	328	Michael Haddix RC	.10	.05
❑	329	Dennis Harrison	.10	.05
❑	330	Ron Jaworski	.25	.11
❑	331	Wilbert Montgomery	.25	.11
❑	332	Hubie Oliver	.10	.05
❑	333	Mike Quick PB RC	.50	.23
❑	334	Jerry Robinson	.10	.05
❑	335	Max Runager	.10	.05
❑	336	Michael Williams	.10	.05
❑	337	St. Louis Cardinals TL	.25	.11
		Ottis Anderson		
❑	338	Ottis Anderson	.50	.23
❑	339	Al(Bubba) Baker	.25	.11
❑	340	Carl Birdsong PB	.10	.05
❑	341	David Galloway	.10	.05
❑	342	Roy Green PB	.25	.11
❑	343	Roy Green IR	.25	.11
❑	344	Curtis Greer RC	.10	.05
❑	345	Neil Lomax	.25	.11
❑	346	Doug Marsh	.10	.05
❑	347	Stump Mitchell	.25	.11
❑	348	Lionel Washington RC	.25	.11
❑	349	San Francisco 49ers TL	.25	.11
		Dwight Clark		
❑	350	Dwaine Board	.10	.05
❑	351	Dwight Clark	.50	.23
❑	352	Dwight Clark IR	.25	.11
❑	353	Roger Craig RC !	3.00	1.35
❑	354	Fred Dean	.25	.11
❑	355	Fred Dean IR	.50	.23
		Marino in background		
❑	356	Dwight Hicks PB	.25	.11
❑	357	Ronnie Lott PB	1.50	.70
❑	358	Joe Montana PB	10.00	4.50
❑	359	Joe Montana IR	3.00	1.35
❑	360	Freddie Solomon	.10	.05
❑	361	Wendell Tyler	.10	.05
❑	362	Ray Wersching	.10	.05
❑	363	Eric Wright RC	.25	.11
❑	364	Tampa Bay Bucs TL	.10	.05
		Kevin House		
❑	365	Gerald Carter	.10	.05
❑	366	Hugh Green PB	.25	.11
❑	367	Kevin House	.25	.11
❑	368	Michael Morton RC	.10	.05
❑	369	James Owens	.10	.05
❑	370	Booker Reese	.10	.05
❑	371	Lee Roy Selmon PB	.50	.23
❑	372	Jack Thompson	.25	.11
❑	373	James Wilder	.25	.11
❑	374	Steve Wilson	.10	.05
❑	375	Wash. Redskins TL	.50	.23
		John Riggins		
❑	376	Jeff Bostic PB	.10	.05
❑	377	Charlie Brown PB	.50	.23
❑	378	Charlie Brown IR	.25	.11
❑	379	Dave Butz PB	.25	.11
❑	380	Darrell Green RC	10.00	4.50
❑	381	Russ Grimm PB RC	.50	.23
❑	382	Joe Jacoby PB	.25	.11
❑	383	Dexter Manley	.25	.11
❑	384	Art Monk	1.00	.45
❑	385	Mark Moseley	.25	.11
❑	386	Mark Murphy PB	.10	.05

❑ 387 Mike Nelms	.10	.05
❑ 388 John Riggins	.50	.23
❑ 389 John Riggins IR	.50	.23
❑ 390 Joe Theismann PB	.50	.23
❑ 391 Joe Theismann IR	.50	.23
❑ 392 Don Warren	.25	.11
❑ 393 Joe Washington	.25	.11
❑ 394 Checklist 1-132	.20	.09
❑ 395 Checklist 133-264	.20	.09
❑ 396 Checklist 265-396	.20	.09

1984 Topps USFL

	NRMT-MT	EXC
COMP.FACT.SET (132)	350.00	160.00
❑ 1 Luther Bradley	2.00	.90
❑ 2 Frank Corral	2.00	.90
❑ 3 Trumaine Johnson	2.00	.90
❑ 4 Greg Landry	2.50	1.10
❑ 5 Kit Lathrop	2.00	.90
❑ 6 Kevin Long	2.00	.90
❑ 7 Tim Spencer	2.00	.90
❑ 8 Stan White	2.00	.90
❑ 9 Buddy Aydelette	2.00	.90
❑ 10 Tom Banks	2.00	.90
❑ 11 Fred Bohannon	2.00	.90
❑ 12 Joe Cribbs	4.00	1.80
❑ 13 Joey Jones	2.00	.90
❑ 14 Scott Norwood XRC	2.50	1.10
❑ 15 Jim Smith	2.50	1.10
❑ 16 Cliff Stoudt	4.00	1.80
❑ 17 Vince Evans	4.00	1.80
❑ 18 Vagas Ferguson	2.00	.90
❑ 19 John Gillen	2.00	.90
❑ 20 Kris Haines	2.00	.90
❑ 21 Glenn Hyde	2.00	.90
❑ 22 Mark Keel	2.00	.90
❑ 23 Gary Lewis	2.00	.90
❑ 24 Doug Plank	2.00	.90
❑ 25 Neil Balholm	2.00	.90
❑ 26 David Dumars	2.00	.90
❑ 27 David Martin	2.00	.90
❑ 28 Craig Penrose	2.00	.90
❑ 29 Dave Stalls	2.00	.90
❑ 30 Harry Sydney XRC	2.00	.90
❑ 31 Vincent White	2.00	.90
❑ 32 George Yarno	2.00	.90
❑ 33 Kiki DeAyala	2.00	.90
❑ 34 Sam Harrell	2.00	.90
❑ 35 Mike Hawkins	2.00	.90
❑ 36 Jim Kelly XRC !	80.00	36.00
❑ 37 Mark Rush	2.00	.90
❑ 38 Ricky Sanders XRC	6.00	2.70
❑ 39 Paul Bergmann	2.00	.90
❑ 40 Tom Dinkel	2.00	.90
❑ 41 Wyatt Henderson	2.00	.90
❑ 42 Vaughan Johnson XRC	2.50	1.10
❑ 43 Willie McClendon	2.00	.90
❑ 44 Matt Robinson	2.00	.90
❑ 45 George Achica	2.00	.90
❑ 46 Mark Adickes	2.00	.90
❑ 47 Howard Carson	2.00	.90
❑ 48 Kevin Nelson	2.00	.90
❑ 49 Jeff Partridge	2.00	.90
❑ 50 Jo Jo Townsell	2.50	1.10
❑ 51 Eddie Weaver	2.00	.90
❑ 52 Steve Young XRC !	175.00	80.00
❑ 53 Derrick Crawford	2.00	.90
❑ 54 Walter Lewis	2.00	.90
❑ 55 Phil McKinnely	2.00	.90
❑ 56 Vic Minore	2.00	.90
❑ 57 Gary Shirk	2.00	.90
❑ 58 Reggie White XRC	70.00	32.00
❑ 59 Anthony Carter XRC UER (College stats are wrong)	12.00	5.50
❑ 60 John Corker	2.00	.90
❑ 61 David Greenwood	2.00	.90
❑ 62 Bobby Hebert XRC	4.00	1.80
❑ 63 Derek Holloway	2.00	.90
❑ 64 Ken Lacy	2.00	.90
❑ 65 Tyrone McGriff	2.00	.90
❑ 66 Ray Pinney	2.00	.90
❑ 67 Gary Barbaro	2.00	.90
❑ 68 Sam Bowers	2.00	.90
❑ 69 Clarence Collins	2.00	.90
❑ 70 Willie Harper	2.00	.90
❑ 71 Jim LeClair	2.00	.90
❑ 72 Bobby Leopold RC	2.00	.90
❑ 73 Brian Sipe	4.00	1.80
❑ 74 Herschel Walker XRC	25.00	11.00
❑ 75 Junior Ah You RC	2.00	.90
❑ 76 Marcus Dupree XRC	4.00	1.80
❑ 77 Marcus Marek	2.00	.90
❑ 78 Tim Mazzetti	2.00	.90
❑ 79 Mike Robinson	2.00	.90
❑ 80 Dan Ross	4.00	1.80
❑ 81 Mark Schellen	2.00	.90
❑ 82 Johnnie Walton	2.00	.90
❑ 83 Gordon Banks	2.00	.90
❑ 84 Fred Besana	2.00	.90
❑ 85 Dave Browning	2.00	.90
❑ 86 Eric Jordan	2.00	.90
❑ 87 Frank Manumaleuga	2.00	.90
❑ 88 Gary Plummer XRC	6.00	2.70
❑ 89 Stan Talley	2.00	.90
❑ 90 Arthur Whittington	2.00	.90
❑ 91 Terry Beeson	2.00	.90
❑ 92 Mel Gray	4.00	1.80
❑ 93 Mike Katolin	2.00	.90
❑ 94 Dewey McClain	2.00	.90
❑ 95 Sidney Thornton	2.00	.90
❑ 96 Doug Williams	4.00	1.80
❑ 97 Kelvin Bryant XRC	4.00	1.80
❑ 98 John Bunting	2.00	.90
❑ 99 Irv Eatman XRC	2.50	1.10
❑ 100 Scott Fitzkee	2.00	.90
❑ 101 Chuck Fusina	2.00	.90
❑ 102 Sean Landeta XRC	2.50	1.10
❑ 103 David Trout	2.00	.90
❑ 104 Scott Woerner	2.00	.90
❑ 105 Glenn Carano	2.00	.90
❑ 106 Ron Crosby	2.00	.90
❑ 107 Jerry Holmes	2.00	.90
❑ 108 Bruce Huther	2.00	.90
❑ 109 Mike Rozier XRC	4.00	1.80
❑ 110 Larry Swider	2.00	.90
❑ 111 Danny Buggs	2.00	.90
❑ 112 Putt Choate	2.00	.90
❑ 113 Rich Garza	2.00	.90
❑ 114 Joey Hackett	2.00	.90
❑ 115 Rick Neuheisel XRC	4.00	1.80
❑ 116 Mike St. Clair	2.00	.90
❑ 117 Gary Anderson XRC	4.00	1.80
❑ 118 Zenon Andrusyshyn	2.00	.90
❑ 119 Doug Beaudoin	2.00	.90
❑ 120 Mike Butler	2.00	.90
❑ 121 Willie Gillespie	2.00	.90
❑ 122 Fred Nordgren	2.00	.90
❑ 123 John Reaves	2.00	.90
❑ 124 Eric Truvillion	2.00	.90
❑ 125 Reggie Collier	2.00	.90
❑ 126 Mike Guess	2.00	.90
❑ 127 Mike Hohensee	2.00	.90
❑ 128 Craig James XRC	6.00	2.70
❑ 129 Eric Robinson	2.00	.90
❑ 130 Billy Taylor	2.00	.90
❑ 131 Joey Walters	2.00	.90
❑ 132 Checklist 1-132	2.50	1.10

1985 Topps

	NRMT-MT	EXC
COMPLETE SET (396)	60.00	27.00
COMP.FACT.SET (396)	75.00	34.00
❑ 1 Mark Clayton RB Most Touchdown Receptions, Season	.50	.23
❑ 2 Eric Dickerson RB Most Yards Rushing, Season	.50	.23
❑ 3 Charlie Joiner RB Most Receptions, Career	.50	.23
❑ 4 Dan Marino RB UER Most Touchdown Passes, Season (Dolphins misspelled as Dophins)	6.00	2.70
❑ 5 Art Monk RB Most Receptions, Season	.50	.23
❑ 6 Walter Payton RB Most Yards Rushing, Career	1.00	.45
❑ 7 NFC Championship 49ers 23, Bears 0 (Matt Suhey tackled)	.25	.11
❑ 8 AFC Championship Dolphins 45, Steelers 28 (Woody Bennett over)	.25	.11
❑ 9 Super Bowl XIX 49ers 38, Dolphins 16 (Wendell Tyler)	.25	.11
❑ 10 Atlanta Falcons TL Stretching For The First Down (Gerald Riggs)	.10	.05
❑ 11 William Andrews	.25	.11
❑ 12 Stacey Bailey	.10	.05
❑ 13 Steve Bartkowski	.50	.23
❑ 14 Rick Bryan RC	.10	.05
❑ 15 Alfred Jackson	.10	.05
❑ 16 Kenny Johnson	.10	.05
❑ 17 Mike Kenn AP	.10	.05
❑ 18 Mike Pitts RC	.10	.05
❑ 19 Gerald Riggs	.25	.11
❑ 20 Sylvester Stamps	.10	.05
❑ 21 R.C. Thielemann	.10	.05
❑ 22 Chicago Bears TL Sweetness Sets Record Straight (Walter Payton)	.75	.35
❑ 23 Todd Bell AP RC	.10	.05
❑ 24 Richard Dent AP RC	4.00	1.80
❑ 25 Gary Fencik	.25	.11
❑ 26 Dave Finzer	.10	.05
❑ 27 Leslie Frazier	.10	.05
❑ 28 Steve Fuller	.25	.11
❑ 29 Willie Gault	.50	.23
❑ 30 Dan Hampton AP	.50	.23
❑ 31 Jim McMahon	.75	.35
❑ 32 Steve McMichael RC	.50	.23
❑ 33 Walter Payton AP	3.00	1.35
❑ 34 Mike Singletary	.75	.35
❑ 35 Matt Suhey	.10	.05
❑ 36 Bob Thomas	.10	.05
❑ 37 Dallas Cowboys TL	.50	.23

Busting Through
The Defense
(Tony Dorsett)
❑ 38 Bill Bates RC .... 1.00 .45
❑ 39 Doug Cosbie .... .25 .11
❑ 40 Tony Dorsett .... .75 .35
❑ 41 Michael Downs .... .10 .05
❑ 42 Mike Hegman RC UER .... .10 .05
(Reference to SB VIII,
should be SB XIII)
❑ 43 Tony Hill .... .25 .11
❑ 44 Gary Hogeboom RC .... .10 .05
❑ 45 Jim Jeffcoat RC .... .50 .23
❑ 46 Ed Too Tall Jones .... .50 .23
❑ 47 Mike Renfro .... .10 .05
❑ 48 Rafael Septien .... .10 .05
❑ 49 Dennis Thurman .... .10 .05
❑ 50 Everson Walls .... .25 .11
❑ 51 Danny White .... .50 .23
❑ 52 Randy White .... .50 .23
❑ 53 Detroit Lions TL .... .10 .05
Popping One Loose
(Lions' Defense)
❑ 54 Jeff Chadwick .... .10 .05
❑ 55 Mike Cofer RC .... .10 .05
❑ 56 Gary Danielson .... .10 .05
❑ 57 Keith Dorney .... .10 .05
❑ 58 Doug English .... .25 .11
❑ 59 William Gay .... .10 .05
❑ 60 Ken Jenkins .... .10 .05
❑ 61 James Jones .... .25 .11
❑ 62 Eddie Murray .... .25 .11
❑ 63 Billy Sims .... .50 .23
❑ 64 Leonard Thompson .... .10 .05
❑ 65 Bobby Watkins .... .10 .05
❑ 66 Green Bay Packers TL .... .25 .11
Spotting His
Deep Receiver
(Lynn Dickey)
❑ 67 Paul Coffman .... .10 .05
❑ 68 Lynn Dickey .... .25 .11
❑ 69 Mike Douglass .... .10 .05
❑ 70 Tom Flynn RC .... .10 .05
❑ 71 Eddie Lee Ivery .... .10 .05
❑ 72 Ezra Johnson .... .10 .05
❑ 73 Mark Lee .... .10 .05
❑ 74 Tim Lewis .... .10 .05
❑ 75 James Lofton .... .50 .23
❑ 76 Bucky Scribner .... .10 .05
❑ 77 Los Angeles Rams TL .... .50 .23
Record-Setting
Ground Attack
(Eric Dickerson)
❑ 78 Nolan Cromwell .... .25 .11
❑ 79 Eric Dickerson AP .... 1.25 .55
❑ 80 Henry Ellard RC 2.50 1.10
❑ 81 Kent Hill .... .10 .05
❑ 82 LeRoy Irvin .... .25 .11
❑ 83 Jeff Kemp RC .... .25 .11
❑ 84 Mike Lansford .... .10 .05
❑ 85 Barry Redden .... .10 .05
❑ 86 Jackie Slater .... .50 .23
❑ 87 Doug Smith RC C .... .25 .11
❑ 88 Jack Youngblood .... .25 .11
❑ 89 Minnesota Vikings TL .... .10 .05
Smothering The
Opposition
(Vikings' Defense)
❑ 90 Alfred Anderson RC .... .10 .05
❑ 91 Ted Brown .... .25 .11
❑ 92 Greg Coleman .... .10 .05
❑ 93 Tommy Hannon .... .10 .05
❑ 94 Tommy Kramer .... .25 .11
❑ 95 Leo Lewis RC .... .25 .11
❑ 96 Doug Martin .... .10 .05
❑ 97 Darrin Nelson .... .25 .11
❑ 98 Jan Stenerud AP .... .25 .11
❑ 99 Sammie White .... .25 .11
❑ 100 New Orleans Saints TL .... .10 .05
Hurdling Over
Front Line
❑ 101 Morten Andersen .... .50 .23
❑ 102 Hoby Brenner RC .... .25 .11
❑ 103 Bruce Clark .... .10 .05
❑ 104 Hokie Gajan .... .10 .05
❑ 105 Brian Hansen RC .... .10 .05
❑ 106 Rickey Jackson .... .50 .23
❑ 107 George Rogers .... .25 .11
❑ 108 Dave Wilson .... .10 .05
❑ 109 Tyrone Young .... .10 .05
❑ 110 New York Giants TL .... .10 .05
Engulfing The
Quarterback
(Giants' Defense)
❑ 111 Carl Banks RC .... .50 .23
❑ 112 Jim Burt RC .... .25 .11
❑ 113 Rob Carpenter .... .10 .05
❑ 114 Harry Carson .... .25 .11
❑ 115 Earnest Gray .... .10 .05
❑ 116 Ali Haji-Sheikh .... .10 .05
❑ 117 Mark Haynes AP .... .25 .11
❑ 118 Bobby Johnson .... .10 .05
❑ 119 Lionel Manuel RC .... .25 .11
❑ 120 Joe Morris RC .... .50 .23
❑ 121 Zeke Mowatt RC .... .25 .11
❑ 122 Jeff Rutledge RC .... .10 .05
❑ 123 Phil Simms .... .50 .23
❑ 124 Lawrence Taylor AP .... 1.50 .70
❑ 125 Philadelphia Eagles TL .... .10 .05
Finding The Wide
Open Spaces
(Wilbert Montgomery)
❑ 126 Greg Brown .... .10 .05
❑ 127 Ray Ellis .... .10 .05
❑ 128 Dennis Harrison .... .10 .05
❑ 129 Wes Hopkins RC .... .25 .11
❑ 130 Mike Horan .... .10 .05
❑ 131 Kenny Jackson RC .... .10 .05
❑ 132 Ron Jaworski .... .25 .11
❑ 133 Paul McFadden .... .10 .05
❑ 134 Wilbert Montgomery .... .25 .11
❑ 135 Mike Quick .... .50 .23
❑ 136 John Spagnola .... .10 .05
❑ 137 St.Louis Cardinals TL .... .10 .05
Exploiting The
Air Route
(Neil Lomax)
❑ 138 Ottis Anderson .... .50 .23
❑ 139 Al(Bubba) Baker .... .25 .11
❑ 140 Roy Green .... .25 .11
❑ 141 Curtis Greer .... .10 .05
❑ 142 E.J. Junior AP .... .10 .05
❑ 143 Neil Lomax .... .25 .11
❑ 144 Stump Mitchell .... .25 .11
❑ 145 Neil O'Donoghue .... .10 .05
❑ 146 Pat Tilley .... .10 .05
❑ 147 Lionel Washington .... .10 .05
❑ 148 San Francisco 49ers TL 1.25 .55
The Road To
Super Bowl XIX
(Joe Montana)
❑ 149 Dwaine Board .... .10 .05
❑ 150 Dwight Clark .... .50 .23
❑ 151 Roger Craig .... 1.00 .45
❑ 152 Randy Cross AP .... .25 .11
❑ 153 Fred Dean .... .25 .11
❑ 154 Keith Fahnhorst RC .... .10 .05
❑ 155 Dwight Hicks .... .10 .05
❑ 156 Ronnie Lott .... .50 .23
❑ 157 Joe Montana 10.00 4.50
❑ 158 Renaldo Nehemiah .... .25 .11
❑ 159 Fred Quillan .... .10 .05
❑ 160 Jack Reynolds .... .10 .05
❑ 161 Freddie Solomon .... .10 .05
❑ 162 Keena Turner RC .... .10 .05
❑ 163 Wendell Tyler .... .10 .05
❑ 164 Ray Wersching .... .10 .05
❑ 165 Carlton Williamson .... .10 .05
❑ 166 Tampa Bay Bucs TL .... .25 .11
Protecting The
Quarterback
(Steve DeBerg)
❑ 167 Gerald Carter .... .10 .05
❑ 168 Mark Cotney .... .10 .05
❑ 169 Steve DeBerg .... .50 .23
❑ 170 Sean Farrell RC .... .10 .05
❑ 171 Hugh Green .... .25 .11
❑ 172 Kevin House .... .25 .11
❑ 173 David Logan .... .10 .05
❑ 174 Michael Morton .... .10 .05
❑ 175 Lee Roy Selmon .... .50 .23
❑ 176 James Wilder .... .10 .05
❑ 177 Wash. Redskins TL .... .50 .23
Diesel Named Desire
(John Riggins)
❑ 178 Charlie Brown .... .10 .05
❑ 179 Monte Coleman RC .... .25 .11
❑ 180 Vernon Dean .... .10 .05
❑ 181 Darrell Green .... .50 .23
❑ 182 Russ Grimm .... .25 .11
❑ 183 Joe Jacoby .... .25 .11
❑ 184 Dexter Manley .... .25 .11
❑ 185 Art Monk AP .... .50 .23
❑ 186 Mark Moseley .... .25 .11
❑ 187 Calvin Muhammad .... .10 .05
❑ 188 Mike Nelms .... .10 .05
❑ 189 John Riggins .... .50 .23
❑ 190 Joe Theismann .... .50 .23
❑ 191 Joe Washington .... .25 .11
❑ 192 Passing Leaders 10.00 4.50
Dan Marino
Joe Montana
❑ 193 Receiving Leaders .... .25 .11
Ozzie Newsome
Art Monk
❑ 194 Rushing Leaders .... .50 .23
Earnest Jackson
Eric Dickerson
❑ 195 Scoring Leaders .... .10 .05
Gary Anderson K
Ray Wersching
❑ 196 Interception Leaders .... .10 .05
Kenny Easley
Tom Flynn
❑ 197 Punting Leaders .... .10 .05
Jim Arnold
Brian Hansen
❑ 198 Buffalo Bills TL .... .10 .05
Rushing Toward
Rookie Stardom
(Greg Bell)
❑ 199 Greg Bell RC .... .25 .11
❑ 200 Preston Dennard .... .10 .05
❑ 201 Joe Ferguson .... .25 .11
❑ 202 Byron Franklin .... .10 .05
❑ 203 Steve Freeman .... .10 .05
❑ 204 Jim Haslett .... .25 .11
❑ 205 Charles Romes .... .10 .05
❑ 206 Fred Smerlas .... .10 .05
❑ 207 Darryl Talley RC .... .50 .23
❑ 208 Van Williams .... .10 .05
❑ 209 Cincinnati Bengals TL .... .25 .11
Advancing The
Ball Downfield
(Ken Anderson and
Larry Kinnebrew)
❑ 210 Ken Anderson .... .50 .23
❑ 211 Jim Breech .... .10 .05
❑ 212 Louis Breeden .... .10 .05
❑ 213 James Brooks .... .25 .11
❑ 214 Ross Browner .... .25 .11
❑ 215 Eddie Edwards .... .10 .05
❑ 216 M.L. Harris .... .10 .05
❑ 217 Bobby Kemp .... .10 .05
❑ 218 Larry Kinnebrew RC .... .10 .05
❑ 219 Anthony Munoz AP .... .50 .23
❑ 220 Reggie Williams .... .25 .11
❑ 221 Cleveland Browns TL .... .10 .05
Evading The
Defensive Pursuit
(Boyce Green)
❑ 222 Matt Bahr .... .25 .11
❑ 223 Chip Banks .... .10 .05
❑ 224 Reggie Camp .... .10 .05
❑ 225 Tom Cousineau .... .10 .05
❑ 226 Joe DeLamielleure .... .10 .05
❑ 227 Ricky Feacher .... .10 .05
❑ 228 Boyce Green RC .... .10 .05
❑ 229 Al Gross .... .10 .05
❑ 230 Clay Matthews .... .50 .23
❑ 231 Paul McDonald .... .10 .05
❑ 232 Ozzie Newsome AP .... .50 .23
❑ 233 Mike Pruitt .... .25 .11
❑ 234 Don Rogers .... .10 .05
❑ 235 Denver Broncos TL 2.50 1.10
Thousand Yarder
Gets The Ball
(Sammy Winder and

John Elway)
❑ 236 Rubin Carter .10 .05
❑ 237 Barney Chavous .10 .05
❑ 238 John Elway 15.00 6.75
❑ 239 Steve Foley .10 .05
❑ 240 Mike Harden RC .10 .05
❑ 241 Tom Jackson .50 .23
❑ 242 Butch Johnson .10 .05
❑ 243 Rulon Jones .10 .05
❑ 244 Rich Karlis .10 .05
❑ 245 Steve Watson .25 .11
❑ 246 Gerald Willhite .10 .05
❑ 247 Sammy Winder .25 .11
❑ 248 Houston Oilers TL .10 .05
Eluding A
Traffic Jam
(Larry Moriarty)
❑ 249 Jesse Baker .10 .05
❑ 250 Carter Hartwig .10 .05
❑ 251 Warren Moon RC**/C 15.00 6.75
❑ 252 Larry Moriarty RC .10 .05
❑ 253 Mike Munchak RC .50 .23
❑ 254 Carl Roaches .10 .05
❑ 255 Tim Smith .25 .11
❑ 256 Willie Tullis .10 .05
❑ 257 Jamie Williams RC .10 .05
❑ 258 Indianapolis Colts TL .10 .05
Start Of A
Long Gainer
(Art Schlichter)
❑ 259 Raymond Butler .10 .05
❑ 260 Johnie Cooks .10 .05
❑ 261 Eugene Daniel .10 .05
❑ 262 Curtis Dickey .25 .11
❑ 263 Chris Hinton .25 .11
❑ 264 Vernon Maxwell .10 .05
❑ 265 Randy McMillan .10 .05
❑ 266 Art Schlichter RC .25 .11
❑ 267 Rohn Stark .25 .11
❑ 268 Leo Wisniewski .10 .05
❑ 269 Kansas City Chiefs TL .10 .05
Pigskin About To
Soar Upward
(Bill Kenney)
❑ 270 Jim Arnold .10 .05
❑ 271 Mike Bell .10 .05
❑ 272 Todd Blackledge RC .25 .11
❑ 273 Carlos Carson .25 .11
❑ 274 Deron Cherry .25 .11
❑ 275 Herman Heard RC .10 .05
❑ 276 Bill Kenney .25 .11
❑ 277 Nick Lowery .50 .23
❑ 278 Bill Maas RC .10 .05
❑ 279 Henry Marshall .10 .05
❑ 280 Art Still .10 .05
❑ 281 Los Angeles Raiders TL .50 .23
Diving For The
Goal Line
(Marcus Allen)
❑ 282 Marcus Allen 2.50 1.10
❑ 283 Lyle Alzado .25 .11
❑ 284 Chris Bahr .10 .05
❑ 285 Malcolm Barnwell .10 .05
❑ 286 Cliff Branch .50 .23
❑ 287 Todd Christensen .50 .23
❑ 288 Ray Guy .50 .23
❑ 289 Lester Hayes .25 .11
❑ 290 Mike Haynes AP .25 .11
❑ 291 Henry Lawrence .10 .05
❑ 292 Howie Long 2.00 .90
❑ 293 Rod Martin AP .25 .11
❑ 294 Vann McElroy .10 .05
❑ 295 Matt Millen .25 .11
❑ 296 Bill Pickel RC .10 .05
❑ 297 Jim Plunkett .50 .23
❑ 298 Dokie Williams RC .10 .05
❑ 299 Marc Wilson .25 .11
❑ 300 Miami Dolphins TL .25 .11
Super Duper
Performance
(Mark Duper)
❑ 301 Bob Baumhower .10 .05
❑ 302 Doug Betters .10 .05
❑ 303 Glenn Blackwood .25 .11
❑ 304 Lyle Blackwood .25 .11
❑ 305 Kim Bokamper .10 .05
❑ 306 Charles Bowser .10 .05
❑ 307 Jimmy Cefalo .10 .05
❑ 308 Mark Clayton AP RC .75 .35
❑ 309 A.J. Duhe .10 .05
❑ 310 Mark Duper .50 .23
❑ 311 Andra Franklin .10 .05
❑ 312 Bruce Hardy .10 .05
❑ 313 Pete Johnson .25 .11
❑ 314 Dan Marino AP UER 15.00 6.75
(Fouts 4802 yards in
1981, should be 4082)
❑ 315 Tony Nathan .25 .11
❑ 316 Ed Newman .10 .05
❑ 317 Reggie Roby AP .50 .23
❑ 318 Dwight Stephenson AP .25 .11
❑ 319 Uwe Von Schamann .10 .05
❑ 320 New England Pats TL .10 .05
Refusing To
Be Denied
(Tony Collins)
❑ 321 Raymond Clayborn .25 .11
❑ 322 Tony Collins .25 .11
❑ 323 Tony Eason RC .50 .23
❑ 324 Tony Franklin .10 .05
❑ 325 Irving Fryar RC 5.00 2.20
❑ 326 John Hannah AP .50 .23
❑ 327 Brian Holloway .10 .05
❑ 328 Craig James RC* .75 .35
❑ 329 Stanley Morgan .25 .11
❑ 330 Steve Nelson AP .10 .05
❑ 331 Derrick Ramsey .10 .05
❑ 332 Stephen Starring .25 .11
❑ 333 Mosi Tatupu .10 .05
❑ 334 Andre Tippett .50 .23
❑ 335 New York Jets TL .25 .11
Thwarting The
Passing Game
(Mark Gastineau
and Joe Ferguson)
❑ 336 Russell Carter RC .10 .05
❑ 337 Mark Gastineau AP .25 .11
❑ 338 Bruce Harper .10 .05
❑ 339 Bobby Humphery RC .10 .05
❑ 340 Johnny Lam Jones .10 .05
❑ 341 Joe Klecko .25 .11
❑ 342 Pat Leahy .10 .05
❑ 343 Marty Lyons .25 .11
❑ 344 Freeman McNeil .25 .11
❑ 345 Lance Mehl .10 .05
❑ 346 Ken O'Brien RC .50 .23
❑ 347 Marvin Powell .10 .05
❑ 348 Pat Ryan .10 .05
❑ 349 Mickey Shuler RC .10 .05
❑ 350 Wesley Walker .25 .11
❑ 351 Pittsburgh Steelers TL .25 .11
Testing Defensive
Pass Coverage
(Mark Malone)
❑ 352 Walter Abercrombie .10 .05
❑ 353 Gary Anderson K .25 .11
❑ 354 Robin Cole .10 .05
❑ 355 Bennie Cunningham .10 .05
❑ 356 Rich Erenberg .10 .05
❑ 357 Jack Lambert .50 .23
❑ 358 Louis Lipps RC .50 .23
❑ 359 Mark Malone .25 .11
❑ 360 Mike Merriweather RC .10 .05
❑ 361 Frank Pollard .10 .05
❑ 362 Donnie Shell .25 .11
❑ 363 John Stallworth .50 .23
❑ 364 Sam Washington .10 .05
❑ 365 Mike Webster .25 .11
❑ 366 Dwayne Woodruff .10 .05
❑ 367 San Diego Chargers TL .10 .05
Jarring The
Ball Loose
(Chargers' Defense)
❑ 368 Rolf Benirschke .10 .05
❑ 369 Gill Byrd RC .50 .23
❑ 370 Wes Chandler .25 .11
❑ 371 Bobby Duckworth .10 .05
❑ 372 Dan Fouts .50 .23
❑ 373 Mike Green .10 .05
❑ 374 Pete Holohan RC .10 .05
❑ 375 Earnest Jackson RC .25 .11
❑ 376 Lionel James RC .25 .11
❑ 377 Charlie Joiner .50 .23
❑ 378 Billy Ray Smith .25 .11
❑ 379 Kellen Winslow .50 .23
❑ 380 Seattle Seahawks TL .25 .11
Setting Up For
The Air Attack
(Dave Krieg)
❑ 381 Dave Brown .10 .05
❑ 382 Jeff Bryant .10 .05
❑ 383 Dan Doornink .10 .05
❑ 384 Kenny Easley AP .25 .11
❑ 385 Jacob Green .25 .11
❑ 386 David Hughes .10 .05
❑ 387 Norm Johnson .10 .05
❑ 388 Dave Krieg .50 .23
❑ 389 Steve Largent 1.00 .45
❑ 390 Joe Nash RC .10 .05
❑ 391 Daryl Turner RC .10 .05
❑ 392 Curt Warner .50 .23
❑ 393 Fredd Young RC .25 .11
❑ 394 Checklist 1-132 .15 .07
❑ 395 Checklist 133-264 .15 .07
❑ 396 Checklist 265-396 .15 .07

1985 Topps USFL

	NRMT-MT	EXC
COMP.FACT.SET (132)	135.00	60.00

❑ 1 Case DeBruijn .50 .23
❑ 2 Mike Katolin .50 .23
❑ 3 Bruce Laird .50 .23
❑ 4 Kit Lathrop .50 .23
❑ 5 Kevin Long .50 .23
❑ 6 Karl Lorch .50 .23
❑ 7 Dave Tipton .50 .23
❑ 8 Doug Williams 2.00 .90
❑ 9 Luis Zendejas XRC .50 .23
❑ 10 Kelvin Bryant 1.00 .45
❑ 11 Willie Collier .50 .23
❑ 12 Irv Eatman .50 .23
❑ 13 Scott Fitzkee .50 .23
❑ 14 William Fuller XRC 4.00 1.80
❑ 15 Chuck Fusina .50 .23
❑ 16 Pete Kugler .50 .23
❑ 17 Garcia Lane .50 .23
❑ 18 Mike Lush .50 .23
❑ 19 Sam Mills XRC 5.00 2.20
❑ 20 Buddy Aydelette .50 .23
❑ 21 Joe Cribbs 2.00 .90
❑ 22 David Dumars .50 .23
❑ 23 Robin Earl .50 .23
❑ 24 Joey Jones .50 .23
❑ 25 Leon Perry .50 .23
❑ 26 Dave Pureifory .50 .23
❑ 27 Bill Roe .50 .23
❑ 28 Doug Smith XRC ! DT 2.00 .90
❑ 29 Cliff Stoudt 1.00 .45
❑ 30 Jeff Delaney .50 .23
❑ 31 Vince Evans 1.00 .45
❑ 32 Leonard Harris XRC .50 .23
❑ 33 Bill Johnson .50 .23
❑ 34 Marc Lewis .50 .23
❑ 35 David Martin .50 .23
❑ 36 Bruce Thornton .50 .23
❑ 37 Craig Walls .50 .23
❑ 38 Vincent White .50 .23
❑ 39 Luther Bradley .50 .23

Card	MINT	NRMT
❑ 40 Pete Catan	.50	.23
❑ 41 Kiki DeAyala	.50	.23
❑ 42 Toni Fritsch	.50	.23
❑ 43 Sam Harrell	.50	.23
❑ 44 Richard Johnson XRC	1.00	.45
❑ 45 Jim Kelly	25.00	11.00
❑ 46 Gerald McNeil XRC	.50	.23
❑ 47 Clarence Verdin XRC	2.00	.90
❑ 48 Dale Walters	.50	.23
❑ 49 Gary Clark XRC	10.00	4.50
❑ 50 Tom Dinkel	.50	.23
❑ 51 Mike Edwards	.50	.23
❑ 52 Brian Franco	.50	.23
❑ 53 Bob Gruber	.50	.23
❑ 54 Robbie Mahfouz	.50	.23
❑ 55 Mike Rozier	2.00	.90
❑ 56 Brian Sipe	1.00	.45
❑ 57 J.T. Turner	.50	.23
❑ 58 Howard Carson	.50	.23
❑ 59 Wymon Henderson XRC	.50	.23
❑ 60 Kevin Nelson	.50	.23
❑ 61 Jeff Partridge	.50	.23
❑ 62 Ben Rudolph	.50	.23
❑ 63 Jo Jo Townsell	1.00	.45
❑ 64 Eddie Weaver	.50	.23
❑ 65 Steve Young	50.00	22.00
❑ 66 Tony Zendejas XRC	1.00	.45
❑ 67 Mossy Cade	.50	.23
❑ 68 Leonard Coleman XRC	.50	.23
❑ 69 John Corker	.50	.23
❑ 70 Derrick Crawford	.50	.23
❑ 71 Art Kuehn	.50	.23
❑ 72 Walter Lewis	.50	.23
❑ 73 Tyrone McGriff	.50	.23
❑ 74 Tim Spencer	1.00	.45
❑ 75 Reggie White	20.00	9.00
❑ 76 Gizmo Williams XRC	2.00	.90
❑ 77 Sam Bowers	.50	.23
❑ 78 Maurice Carthon XRC	1.00	.45
❑ 79 Clarence Collins	.50	.23
❑ 80 Doug Flutie XRC	60.00	27.00
❑ 81 Freddie Gilbert	.50	.23
❑ 82 Kerry Justin	.50	.23
❑ 83 Dave Lapham	.50	.23
❑ 84 Rick Partridge	.50	.23
❑ 85 Roger Ruzek XRC	1.00	.45
❑ 86 Herschel Walker	10.00	4.50
❑ 87 Gordon Banks	.50	.23
❑ 88 Monte Bennett	.50	.23
❑ 89 Albert Bentley XRC	1.00	.45
❑ 90 Novo Bojovic	.50	.23
❑ 91 Dave Browning	.50	.23
❑ 92 Anthony Carter	2.00	.90
❑ 93 Bobby Hebert	2.00	.90
❑ 94 Ray Pinney	.50	.23
❑ 95 Stan Talley	.50	.23
❑ 96 Ruben Vaughan	.50	.23
❑ 97 Curtis Bledsoe	.50	.23
❑ 98 Reggie Collier	.50	.23
❑ 99 Jerry Doerger	.50	.23
❑ 100 Jerry Golsteyn	.50	.23
❑ 101 Bob Niziolek	.50	.23
❑ 102 Joel Patten	.50	.23
❑ 103 Ricky Simmons	.50	.23
❑ 104 Joey Walters	.50	.23
❑ 105 Marcus Dupree	1.00	.45
❑ 106 Jeff Gossett	1.00	.45
❑ 107 Frank Lockett	.50	.23
❑ 108 Marcus Marek	.50	.23
❑ 109 Kenny Neil	.50	.23
❑ 110 Robert Pennywell	.50	.23
❑ 111 Matt Robinson	.50	.23
❑ 112 Dan Ross	1.00	.45
❑ 113 Doug Woodward	.50	.23
❑ 114 Danny Buggs	.50	.23
❑ 115 Putt Choate	.50	.23
❑ 116 Greg Fields	.50	.23
❑ 117 Ken Hartley	.50	.23
❑ 118 Nick Mike-Mayer	.50	.23
❑ 119 Rick Neuheisel	2.00	.90
❑ 120 Peter Raeford	.50	.23
❑ 121 Gary Worthy	.50	.23
❑ 122 Gary Anderson RB	1.00	.45
❑ 123 Zenon Andrusyshyn	.50	.23
❑ 124 Greg Boone	.50	.23
❑ 125 Mike Butler	.50	.23
❑ 126 Mike Clark	.50	.23
❑ 127 Willie Gillespie	.50	.23
❑ 128 James Harrell	.50	.23
❑ 129 Marvin Harvey	.50	.23
❑ 130 John Reaves	1.00	.45
❑ 131 Eric Truvillion	.50	.23
❑ 132 Checklist 1-132	1.00	.45

1986 Topps

	MINT	NRMT
COMPLETE SET (396)	120.00	55.00
COMP.FACT.SET (396)	200.00	90.00
❑ 1 Marcus Allen RB Most Yards From Scrimmage, Season	.75	.35
❑ 2 Eric Dickerson RB Most Yards Rushing, Playoff Game	.50	.23
❑ 3 Lionel James RB Most All-Purpose Yards, Season	.10	.05
❑ 4 Steve Largent RB Most Seasons, 50 or More Receptions	.50	.23
❑ 5 George Martin RB Most Touchdowns, Def. Lineman, Career	.10	.05
❑ 6 Stephone Paige RB Most Yards Receiving, Game	.10	.05
❑ 7 Walter Payton RB Most Consecutive Games, 100 or More Yards Rushing	.75	.35
❑ 8 Super Bowl XX Bears 46, Patriots 10 (Jim McMahon handing off)	.25	.11
❑ 9 Bears TL (Walter Payton in Motion)	.60	.25
❑ 10 Jim McMahon	.50	.23
❑ 11 Walter Payton AP	3.00	1.35
❑ 12 Matt Suhey	.10	.05
❑ 13 Willie Gault	.25	.11
❑ 14 Dennis McKinnon RC	.10	.05
❑ 15 Emery Moorehead	.10	.05
❑ 16 Jim Covert AP	.25	.11
❑ 17 Jay Hilgenberg AP RC	.50	.23
❑ 18 Kevin Butler RC	.25	.11
❑ 19 Richard Dent AP	.75	.35
❑ 20 William Perry RC	.50	.23
❑ 21 Steve McMichael	.50	.23
❑ 22 Dan Hampton	.50	.23
❑ 23 Otis Wilson	.10	.05
❑ 24 Mike Singletary	.60	.25
❑ 25 Wilber Marshall RC	.50	.23
❑ 26 Leslie Frazier	.10	.05
❑ 27 Dave Duerson RC	.10	.05
❑ 28 Gary Fencik	.10	.05
❑ 29 Patriots TL (Craig James on the Run)	.50	.23
❑ 30 Tony Eason	.10	.05
❑ 31 Steve Grogan	.25	.11
❑ 32 Craig James	.50	.23
❑ 33 Tony Collins	.10	.05
❑ 34 Irving Fryar	1.25	.55
❑ 35 Brian Holloway AP	.10	.05
❑ 36 John Hannah AP	.50	.23
❑ 37 Tony Franklin	.10	.05
❑ 38 Garin Veris RC	.10	.05
❑ 39 Andre Tippett AP	.25	.11
❑ 40 Steve Nelson	.10	.05
❑ 41 Raymond Clayborn	.10	.05
❑ 42 Fred Marion RC	.10	.05
❑ 43 Rich Camarillo	.10	.05
❑ 44 Dolphins TL (Dan Marino Sets Up)	2.00	.90
❑ 45 Dan Marino AP	8.00	3.60
❑ 46 Tony Nathan	.25	.11
❑ 47 Ron Davenport RC	.10	.05
❑ 48 Mark Duper	.50	.23
❑ 49 Mark Clayton	.50	.23
❑ 50 Nat Moore	.25	.11
❑ 51 Bruce Hardy	.10	.05
❑ 52 Roy Foster	.10	.05
❑ 53 Dwight Stephenson	.25	.11
❑ 54 Fuad Reveiz RC	.25	.11
❑ 55 Bob Baumhower	.10	.05
❑ 56 Mike Charles	.10	.05
❑ 57 Hugh Green	.25	.11
❑ 58 Glenn Blackwood	.10	.05
❑ 59 Reggie Roby	.25	.11
❑ 60 Raiders TL (Marcus Allen Cuts Upfield)	.50	.23
❑ 61 Marc Wilson	.10	.05
❑ 62 Marcus Allen AP	1.50	.70
❑ 63 Dokie Williams	.10	.05
❑ 64 Todd Christensen	.50	.23
❑ 65 Chris Bahr	.10	.05
❑ 66 Fulton Walker	.10	.05
❑ 67 Howie Long	1.25	.55
❑ 68 Bill Pickel	.10	.05
❑ 69 Ray Guy	.50	.23
❑ 70 Greg Townsend RC	.50	.23
❑ 71 Rod Martin	.25	.11
❑ 72 Matt Millen	.25	.11
❑ 73 Mike Haynes AP	.25	.11
❑ 74 Lester Hayes	.25	.11
❑ 75 Vann McElroy	.10	.05
❑ 76 Rams TL (Eric Dickerson Stiff-Arm)	.50	.23
❑ 77 Dieter Brock RC**/C	.25	.11
❑ 78 Eric Dickerson	.75	.35
❑ 79 Henry Ellard	1.00	.45
❑ 80 Ron Brown RC	.25	.11
❑ 81 Tony Hunter RC	.10	.05
❑ 82 Kent Hill AP	.10	.05
❑ 83 Doug Smith	.10	.05
❑ 84 Dennis Harrah	.10	.05
❑ 85 Jackie Slater	.50	.23
❑ 86 Mike Lansford	.10	.05
❑ 87 Gary Jeter	.10	.05
❑ 88 Mike Wilcher	.10	.05
❑ 89 Jim Collins	.10	.05
❑ 90 LeRoy Irvin	.25	.11
❑ 91 Gary Green	.10	.05
❑ 92 Nolan Cromwell	.25	.11
❑ 93 Dale Hatcher RC	.10	.05
❑ 94 Jets TL (Freeman McNeil Powers)	.25	.11
❑ 95 Ken O'Brien	.50	.23
❑ 96 Freeman McNeil	.25	.11
❑ 97 Tony Paige RC	.10	.05
❑ 98 Johnny Lam Jones	.10	.05
❑ 99 Wesley Walker	.25	.11
❑ 100 Kurt Sohn	.10	.05
❑ 101 Al Toon RC	.50	.23
❑ 102 Mickey Shuler	.10	.05
❑ 103 Marvin Powell	.10	.05
❑ 104 Pat Leahy	.10	.05
❑ 105 Mark Gastineau	.25	.11
❑ 106 Joe Klecko AP	.25	.11
❑ 107 Marty Lyons	.10	.05
❑ 108 Lance Mehl	.10	.05
❑ 109 Bobby Jackson	.10	.05
❑ 110 Dave Jennings	.10	.05
❑ 111 Broncos TL (Sammy Winder Up Middle)	.25	.11
❑ 112 John Elway	8.00	3.60
❑ 113 Sammy Winder	.25	.11
❑ 114 Gerald Willhite	.10	.05
❑ 115 Steve Watson	.10	.05

No.	Card	Price	Price
❑ 116	Vance Johnson RC	.50	.23
❑ 117	Rich Karlis	.10	.05
❑ 118	Rulon Jones	.10	.05
❑ 119	Karl Mecklenburg AP RC	.50	.23
❑ 120	Louis Wright	.10	.05
❑ 121	Mike Harden	.10	.05
❑ 122	Dennis Smith RC	.50	.23
❑ 123	Steve Foley	.10	.05
❑ 124	Cowboys TL	.25	.11
	(Tony Hill Evades Defender)		
❑ 125	Danny White	.50	.23
❑ 126	Tony Dorsett	.60	.25
❑ 127	Timmy Newsome	.10	.05
❑ 128	Mike Renfro	.10	.05
❑ 129	Tony Hill	.25	.11
❑ 130	Doug Cosbie AP	.25	.11
❑ 131	Rafael Septien	.10	.05
❑ 132	Ed Too Tall Jones	.50	.23
❑ 133	Randy White	.50	.23
❑ 134	Jim Jeffcoat	.50	.23
❑ 135	Everson Walls AP	.25	.11
❑ 136	Dennis Thurman	.10	.05
❑ 137	Giants TL	.25	.11
	(Joe Morris Opening)		
❑ 138	Phil Simms	.50	.23
❑ 139	Joe Morris	.50	.23
❑ 140	George Adams RC	.10	.05
❑ 141	Lionel Manuel	.25	.11
❑ 142	Bobby Johnson	.10	.05
❑ 143	Phil McConkey RC	.25	.11
❑ 144	Mark Bavaro RC	.50	.23
❑ 145	Zeke Mowatt	.10	.05
❑ 146	Brad Benson RC	.10	.05
❑ 147	Bart Oates RC	.25	.11
❑ 148	Leonard Marshall AP RC	.50	.23
❑ 149	Jim Burt	.25	.11
❑ 150	George Martin	.10	.05
❑ 151	Lawrence Taylor AP	1.25	.55
❑ 152	Harry Carson AP	.25	.11
❑ 153	Elvis Patterson RC	.10	.05
❑ 154	Sean Landeta RC*	.25	.11
❑ 155	49ers TL	.50	.23
	(Roger Craig Scampers)		
❑ 156	Joe Montana	8.00	3.60
❑ 157	Roger Craig	.50	.23
❑ 158	Wendell Tyler	.10	.05
❑ 159	Carl Monroe	.10	.05
❑ 160	Dwight Clark	.25	.11
❑ 161	Jerry Rice RC !	80.00	36.00
❑ 162	Randy Cross	.25	.11
❑ 163	Keith Fahnhorst	.10	.05
❑ 164	Jeff Stover	.10	.05
❑ 165	Michael Carter RC	.10	.05
❑ 166	Dwaine Board	.10	.05
❑ 167	Eric Wright	.25	.11
❑ 168	Ronnie Lott	.75	.35
❑ 169	Carlton Williamson	.10	.05
❑ 170	Redskins TL	.25	.11
	(Dave Butz Gets His Man)		
❑ 171	Joe Theismann	.50	.23
❑ 172	Jay Schroeder RC	.50	.23
❑ 173	George Rogers	.25	.11
❑ 174	Ken Jenkins	.10	.05
❑ 175	Art Monk AP	.50	.23
❑ 176	Gary Clark RC*	2.00	.90
❑ 177	Joe Jacoby	.25	.11
❑ 178	Russ Grimm	.25	.11
❑ 179	Mark Moseley	.10	.05
❑ 180	Dexter Manley	.25	.11
❑ 181	Charles Mann RC	.50	.23
❑ 182	Vernon Dean	.10	.05
❑ 183	Raphel Cherry RC	.10	.05
❑ 184	Curtis Jordan	.10	.05
❑ 185	Browns TL	.50	.23
	(Bernie Kosar Fakes Handoff)		
❑ 186	Gary Danielson	.25	.11
❑ 187	Bernie Kosar RC	3.00	1.35
❑ 188	Kevin Mack RC	.50	.23
❑ 189	Earnest Byner RC	.75	.35
❑ 190	Glen Young	.10	.05
❑ 191	Ozzie Newsome	.50	.23
❑ 192	Mike Baab	.10	.05
❑ 193	Cody Risien	.25	.11
❑ 194	Bob Golic	.25	.11
❑ 195	Reggie Camp	.10	.05
❑ 196	Chip Banks	.25	.11
❑ 197	Tom Cousineau	.10	.05
❑ 198	Frank Minnifield RC	.10	.05
❑ 199	Al Gross	.10	.05
❑ 200	Seahawks TL	.25	.11
	(Curt Warner Breaks Free)		
❑ 201	Dave Krieg	.50	.23
❑ 202	Curt Warner	.25	.11
❑ 203	Steve Largent AP	.60	.25
❑ 204	Norm Johnson	.10	.05
❑ 205	Daryl Turner	.10	.05
❑ 206	Jacob Green	.10	.05
❑ 207	Joe Nash	.10	.05
❑ 208	Jeff Bryant	.10	.05
❑ 209	Randy Edwards	.10	.05
❑ 210	Fredd Young	.10	.05
❑ 211	Kenny Easley	.10	.05
❑ 212	John Harris	.10	.05
❑ 213	Packers TL	.10	.05
	(Paul Coffman Conquers)		
❑ 214	Lynn Dickey	.25	.11
❑ 215	Gerry Ellis	.10	.05
❑ 216	Eddie Lee Ivery	.10	.05
❑ 217	Jessie Clark	.10	.05
❑ 218	James Lofton	.50	.23
❑ 219	Paul Coffman	.10	.05
❑ 220	Alphonso Carreker	.10	.05
❑ 221	Ezra Johnson	.10	.05
❑ 222	Mike Douglass	.10	.05
❑ 223	Tim Lewis	.10	.05
❑ 224	Mark Murphy RC	.10	.05
❑ 225	Passing Leaders:	1.00	.45
	Ken O'Brien AFC		
	Joe Montana NFC		
❑ 226	Receiving Leaders:	.25	.11
	Lionel James AFC		
	Roger Craig NFC		
❑ 227	Rushing Leaders:	.50	.23
	Marcus Allen AFC		
	Gerald Riggs NFC		
❑ 228	Scoring Leaders:	.25	.11
	Gary Anderson K AFC		
	Kevin Butler NFC		
❑ 229	Interception Leaders:	.10	.05
	Eugene Daniel AFC		
	Albert Lewis AFC		
	Everson Walls NFC		
❑ 230	Chargers TL	.50	.23
	(Dan Fouts Over Top)		
❑ 231	Dan Fouts	.50	.23
❑ 232	Lionel James	.10	.05
❑ 233	Gary Anderson RB RC	.50	.23
❑ 234	Tim Spencer RC*	.25	.11
❑ 235	Wes Chandler	.25	.11
❑ 236	Charlie Joiner	.50	.23
❑ 237	Kellen Winslow	.50	.23
❑ 238	Jim Lachey RC	.50	.23
❑ 239	Bob Thomas	.10	.05
❑ 240	Jeffery Dale	.10	.05
❑ 241	Ralf Mojsiejenko	.10	.05
❑ 242	Lions TL	.10	.05
	(Eric Hipple Spots Receiver)		
❑ 243	Eric Hipple	.10	.05
❑ 244	Billy Sims	.25	.11
❑ 245	James Jones	.10	.05
❑ 246	Pete Mandley RC	.10	.05
❑ 247	Leonard Thompson	.10	.05
❑ 248	Lomas Brown RC	.25	.11
❑ 249	Eddie Murray	.25	.11
❑ 250	Curtis Green	.10	.05
❑ 251	William Gay	.10	.05
❑ 252	Jimmy Williams	.10	.05
❑ 253	Bobby Watkins	.10	.05
❑ 254	Bengals TL	.50	.23
	(Boomer Esiason Zeroes In)		
❑ 255	Boomer Esiason RC	5.00	2.20
❑ 256	James Brooks	.25	.11
❑ 257	Larry Kinnebrew	.10	.05
❑ 258	Cris Collinsworth	.25	.11
❑ 259	Mike Martin	.10	.05
❑ 260	Eddie Brown RC	.50	.23
❑ 261	Anthony Munoz	.50	.23
❑ 262	Jim Breech	.10	.05
❑ 263	Ross Browner	.25	.11
❑ 264	Carl Zander	.10	.05
❑ 265	James Griffin	.10	.05
❑ 266	Robert Jackson	.10	.05
❑ 267	Pat McInally	.10	.05
❑ 268	Eagles TL	.50	.23
	(Ron Jaworski Surveys)		
❑ 269	Ron Jaworski	.25	.11
❑ 270	Earnest Jackson	.25	.11
❑ 271	Mike Quick	.25	.11
❑ 272	John Spagnola	.10	.05
❑ 273	Mark Dennard	.10	.05
❑ 274	Paul McFadden	.10	.05
❑ 275	Reggie White RC*	10.00	4.50
❑ 276	Greg Brown	.10	.05
❑ 277	Herman Edwards	.10	.05
❑ 278	Roynell Young	.10	.05
❑ 279	Wes Hopkins AP	.10	.05
❑ 280	Steelers TL	.25	.11
	(Walter Abercrombie Inches)		
❑ 281	Mark Malone	.25	.11
❑ 282	Frank Pollard	.10	.05
❑ 283	Walter Abercrombie	.10	.05
❑ 284	Louis Lipps	.50	.23
❑ 285	John Stallworth	.50	.23
❑ 286	Mike Webster	.25	.11
❑ 287	Gary Anderson K AP	.25	.11
❑ 288	Keith Willis	.10	.05
❑ 289	Mike Merriweather	.10	.05
❑ 290	Dwayne Woodruff	.10	.05
❑ 291	Donnie Shell	.25	.11
❑ 292	Vikings TL	.25	.11
	(Tommy Kramer Audible)		
❑ 293	Tommy Kramer	.25	.11
❑ 294	Darrin Nelson	.10	.05
❑ 295	Ted Brown	.25	.11
❑ 296	Buster Rhymes	.10	.05
❑ 297	Anthony Carter RC*	1.00	.45
❑ 298	Steve Jordan RC	.50	.23
❑ 299	Keith Millard RC	.50	.23
❑ 300	Joey Browner RC	.50	.23
❑ 301	John Turner	.10	.05
❑ 302	Greg Coleman	.10	.05
❑ 303	Chiefs TL	.10	.05
	(Todd Blackledge)		
❑ 304	Bill Kenney	.10	.05
❑ 305	Herman Heard	.10	.05
❑ 306	Stephone Paige RC	.50	.23
❑ 307	Carlos Carson	.25	.11
❑ 308	Nick Lowery	.25	.11
❑ 309	Mike Bell	.10	.05
❑ 310	Bill Maas	.10	.05
❑ 311	Art Still	.10	.05
❑ 312	Albert Lewis RC	.50	.23
❑ 313	Deron Cherry AP	.25	.11
❑ 314	Colts TL	.10	.05
	(Rohn Stark Booms It)		
❑ 315	Mike Pagel	.10	.05
❑ 316	Randy McMillan	.10	.05
❑ 317	Albert Bentley RC*	.25	.11
❑ 318	George Wonsley RC	.10	.05
❑ 319	Robbie Martin	.10	.05
❑ 320	Pat Beach	.10	.05
❑ 321	Chris Hinton	.25	.11
❑ 322	Duane Bickett RC	.50	.23
❑ 323	Eugene Daniel	.10	.05
❑ 324	Cliff Odom RC	.10	.05
❑ 325	Rohn Stark AP	.25	.11
❑ 326	Cardinals TL	.10	.05
	(Stump Mitchell Outside)		
❑ 327	Neil Lomax	.25	.11
❑ 328	Stump Mitchell	.25	.11
❑ 329	Ottis Anderson	.50	.23
❑ 330	J.T. Smith	.25	.11
❑ 331	Pat Tilley	.10	.05
❑ 332	Roy Green	.25	.11
❑ 333	Lance Smith RC	.10	.05
❑ 334	Curtis Greer	.10	.05
❑ 335	Freddie Joe Nunn RC	.25	.11
❑ 336	E.J. Junior	.25	.11
❑ 337	Lonnie Young RC	.10	.05
❑ 338	Saints TL	.10	.05
	(Wayne Wilson running)		
❑ 339	Bobby Hebert RC*	.50	.23
❑ 340	Dave Wilson	.10	.05
❑ 341	Wayne Wilson	.10	.05
❑ 342	Hoby Brenner	.10	.05
❑ 343	Stan Brock	.25	.11
❑ 344	Morten Andersen	.50	.23
❑ 345	Bruce Clark	.10	.05

Card	Mint	NRMT
❑ 346 Rickey Jackson	.50	.23
❑ 347 Dave Waymer	.10	.05
❑ 348 Brian Hansen	.10	.05
❑ 349 Oilers TL	.50	.23
(Warren Moon Throws Bomb)		
❑ 350 Warren Moon	3.00	1.35
❑ 351 Mike Rozier RC*	.50	.23
❑ 352 Butch Woolfolk	.10	.05
❑ 353 Drew Hill	.50	.23
❑ 354 Willie Drewrey RC	.10	.05
❑ 355 Tim Smith	.25	.11
❑ 356 Mike Munchak	.25	.11
❑ 357 Ray Childress RC	.50	.23
❑ 358 Frank Bush	.10	.05
❑ 359 Steve Brown	.10	.05
❑ 360 Falcons TL	.10	.05
(Gerald Riggs Around End)		
❑ 361 David Archer RC	.50	.23
❑ 362 Gerald Riggs	.25	.11
❑ 363 William Andrews	.25	.11
❑ 364 Billy Johnson	.25	.11
❑ 365 Arthur Cox	.10	.05
❑ 366 Mike Kenn	.10	.05
❑ 367 Bill Fralic RC	.25	.11
❑ 368 Mick Luckhurst	.10	.05
❑ 369 Rick Bryan	.10	.05
❑ 370 Bobby Butler	.10	.05
❑ 371 Rick Donnelly RC	.10	.05
❑ 372 Buccaneers TL	.10	.05
(James Wilder Sweeps Left)		
❑ 373 Steve DeBerg	.50	.23
❑ 374 Steve Young RC*	20.00	9.00
❑ 375 James Wilder	.10	.05
❑ 376 Kevin House	.10	.05
❑ 377 Gerald Carter	.10	.05
❑ 378 Jimmie Giles	.25	.11
❑ 379 Sean Farrell	.10	.05
❑ 380 Donald Igwebuike	.10	.05
❑ 381 David Logan	.10	.05
❑ 382 Jeremiah Castille RC	.10	.05
❑ 383 Bills TL	.10	.05
(Greg Bell Sees Daylight)		
❑ 384 Bruce Mathison RC	.10	.05
❑ 385 Joe Cribbs	.25	.11
❑ 386 Greg Bell	.25	.11
❑ 387 Jerry Butler	.10	.05
❑ 388 Andre Reed RC	6.00	2.70
❑ 389 Bruce Smith RC	5.00	2.20
❑ 390 Fred Smerlas	.10	.05
❑ 391 Darryl Talley	.50	.23
❑ 392 Jim Haslett	.25	.11
❑ 393 Charles Romes	.10	.05
❑ 394 Checklist 1-132	.12	.05
❑ 395 Checklist 133-264	.12	.05
❑ 396 Checklist 265-396	.12	.05

1987 Topps

	MINT	NRMT
COMPLETE SET (396)	30.00	13.50
COMP.FACT.SET (396)	40.00	18.00

Card	Mint	NRMT
❑ 1 Super Bowl XXI	.50	.23
Giants 39,		
Broncos 20		
(Line play shown)		
❑ 2 Todd Christensen RB	.25	.11
Most Seasons,		
80 or More Receptions		
❑ 3 Dave Jennings RB	.10	.05
Most Punts, Career		
❑ 4 Charlie Joiner RB	.50	.23
Most Receiving		
Yards, Career		
❑ 5 Steve Largent RB	.50	.23
Most Cons. Games		
With a Reception		
❑ 6 Dan Marino RB	2.00	.90
Most Cons. Seasons,		
30 or More TD Passes		
❑ 7 Donnie Shell RB	.25	.11
Most Interceptions,		
Strong Safety, Career		
❑ 8 Phil Simms RB	.50	.23
Highest Completion		
Percentage, Super Bowl		
❑ 9 New York Giants TL	.25	.11
(Mark Bavaro Pulls Free)		
❑ 10 Phil Simms	.50	.23
❑ 11 Joe Morris AP	.25	.11
❑ 12 Maurice Carthon RC**	.10	.05
❑ 13 Lee Rouson	.10	.05
❑ 14 Bobby Johnson	.10	.05
❑ 15 Lionel Manuel	.10	.05
❑ 16 Phil McConkey	.10	.05
❑ 17 Mark Bavaro AP	.50	.23
❑ 18 Zeke Mowatt	.10	.05
❑ 19 Raul Allegre	.10	.05
❑ 20 Sean Landeta	.10	.05
❑ 21 Brad Benson	.10	.05
❑ 22 Jim Burt	.10	.05
❑ 23 Leonard Marshall	.50	.23
❑ 24 Carl Banks	.50	.23
❑ 25 Harry Carson	.10	.05
❑ 26 Lawrence Taylor AP	.75	.35
❑ 27 Terry Kinard RC	.10	.05
❑ 28 Pepper Johnson RC	.50	.23
❑ 29 Erik Howard RC	.10	.05
❑ 30 Broncos TL	.10	.05
(Gerald Willhite Dives)		
❑ 31 John Elway	6.00	2.70
❑ 32 Gerald Willhite	.10	.05
❑ 33 Sammy Winder	.25	.11
❑ 34 Ken Bell	.10	.05
❑ 35 Steve Watson	.10	.05
❑ 36 Rich Karlis	.10	.05
❑ 37 Keith Bishop	.10	.05
❑ 38 Rulon Jones	.10	.05
❑ 39 Karl Mecklenburg AP	.50	.23
❑ 40 Louis Wright	.10	.05
❑ 41 Mike Harden	.10	.05
❑ 42 Dennis Smith	.25	.11
❑ 43 Bears TL	.50	.23
(Walter Payton Barrels)		
❑ 44 Jim McMahon	.50	.23
❑ 45 Doug Flutie RC**	10.00	4.50
❑ 46 Walter Payton	2.00	.90
❑ 47 Matt Suhey	.10	.05
❑ 48 Willie Gault	.25	.11
❑ 49 Dennis Gentry RC	.10	.05
❑ 50 Kevin Butler	.10	.05
❑ 51 Jim Covert AP	.10	.05
❑ 52 Jay Hilgenberg	.25	.11
❑ 53 Dan Hampton	.25	.11
❑ 54 Steve McMichael	.50	.23
❑ 55 William Perry	.50	.23
❑ 56 Richard Dent	.50	.23
❑ 57 Otis Wilson	.10	.05
❑ 58 Mike Singletary AP	.50	.23
❑ 59 Wilber Marshall	.50	.23
❑ 60 Mike Richardson	.10	.05
❑ 61 Dave Duerson	.10	.05
❑ 62 Gary Fencik	.10	.05
❑ 63 Redskins TL	.25	.11
(George Rogers Plunges)		
❑ 64 Jay Schroeder	.25	.11
❑ 65 George Rogers	.25	.11
❑ 66 Kelvin Bryant RC**	.25	.11
❑ 67 Ken Jenkins	.10	.05
❑ 68 Gary Clark	.50	.23
❑ 69 Art Monk	.50	.23
❑ 70 Clint Didier RC	.10	.05
❑ 71 Steve Cox	.10	.05
❑ 72 Joe Jacoby	.10	.05
❑ 73 Russ Grimm	.10	.05
❑ 74 Charles Mann	.25	.11
❑ 75 Dave Butz	.10	.05
❑ 76 Dexter Manley AP	.25	.11
❑ 77 Darrell Green AP	.50	.23
❑ 78 Curtis Jordan	.10	.05
❑ 79 Browns TL	.10	.05
(Harry Holt Sees Daylight)		
❑ 80 Bernie Kosar	.50	.23
❑ 81 Curtis Dickey	.10	.05
❑ 82 Kevin Mack	.25	.11
❑ 83 Herman Fontenot	.10	.05
❑ 84 Brian Brennan RC	.10	.05
❑ 85 Ozzie Newsome	.50	.23
❑ 86 Jeff Gossett	.25	.11
❑ 87 Cody Risien AP	.10	.05
❑ 88 Reggie Camp	.10	.05
❑ 89 Bob Golic	.10	.05
❑ 90 Carl Hairston	.10	.05
❑ 91 Chip Banks	.10	.05
❑ 92 Frank Minnifield	.10	.05
❑ 93 Hanford Dixon AP	.10	.05
❑ 94 Gerald McNeil RC**	.10	.05
❑ 95 Dave Puzzuoli	.10	.05
❑ 96 Patriots TL	.10	.05
(Andre Tippett Gets		
His Man (Marcus Allen))		
❑ 97 Tony Eason	.25	.11
❑ 98 Craig James	.25	.11
❑ 99 Tony Collins	.25	.11
❑ 100 Mosi Tatupu	.10	.05
❑ 101 Stanley Morgan	.25	.11
❑ 102 Irving Fryar	.50	.23
❑ 103 Stephen Starring	.10	.05
❑ 104 Tony Franklin AP	.10	.05
❑ 105 Rich Camarillo	.10	.05
❑ 106 Garin Veris	.10	.05
❑ 107 Andre Tippett AP	.25	.11
❑ 108 Don Blackmon	.10	.05
❑ 109 Ronnie Lippett RC	.10	.05
❑ 110 Raymond Clayborn	.10	.05
❑ 111 49ers TL	.25	.11
(Roger Craig Up the Middle)		
❑ 112 Joe Montana	6.00	2.70
❑ 113 Roger Craig	.50	.23
❑ 114 Joe Cribbs	.25	.11
❑ 115 Jerry Rice AP	6.00	2.70
❑ 116 Dwight Clark	.25	.11
❑ 117 Ray Wersching	.10	.05
❑ 118 Max Runager	.10	.05
❑ 119 Jeff Stover	.10	.05
❑ 120 Dwaine Board	.10	.05
❑ 121 Tim McKyer RC	.25	.11
❑ 122 Don Griffin RC	.25	.11
❑ 123 Ronnie Lott AP	.50	.23
❑ 124 Tom Holmoe	.10	.05
❑ 125 Charles Haley RC	1.25	.55
❑ 126 Jets TL	.10	.05
(Mark Gastineau Seeks)		
❑ 127 Ken O'Brien	.25	.11
❑ 128 Pat Ryan	.10	.05
❑ 129 Freeman McNeil	.25	.11
❑ 130 Johnny Hector RC	.10	.05
❑ 131 Al Toon AP	.50	.23
❑ 132 Wesley Walker	.25	.11
❑ 133 Mickey Shuler	.10	.05
❑ 134 Pat Leahy	.10	.05
❑ 135 Mark Gastineau	.25	.11
❑ 136 Joe Klecko	.25	.11
❑ 137 Marty Lyons	.10	.05
❑ 138 Bob Crable	.10	.05
❑ 139 Lance Mehl	.10	.05
❑ 140 Dave Jennings	.10	.05
❑ 141 Harry Hamilton RC	.10	.05
❑ 142 Lester Lyles	.10	.05
❑ 143 Bobby Humphery UER	.10	.05
(Misspelled Humphrey		
on card front)		
❑ 144 Rams TL	.50	.23
(Eric Dickerson		
Through the Line)		
❑ 145 Jim Everett RC	2.00	.90
❑ 146 Eric Dickerson AP	.50	.23
❑ 147 Barry Redden	.10	.05
❑ 148 Ron Brown	.25	.11
❑ 149 Kevin House	.10	.05

❑ 150 Henry Ellard .50 .23
❑ 151 Doug Smith .10 .05
❑ 152 Dennis Harrah AP .10 .05
❑ 153 Jackie Slater .25 .11
❑ 154 Gary Jeter .10 .05
❑ 155 Carl Ekern .10 .05
❑ 156 Mike Wilcher .10 .05
❑ 157 Jerry Gray RC .10 .05
❑ 158 LeRoy Irvin .10 .05
❑ 159 Nolan Cromwell .25 .11
❑ 160 Chiefs TL .10 .05
(Todd Blackledge Hands Off)
❑ 161 Bill Kenney .10 .05
❑ 162 Stephone Paige .25 .11
❑ 163 Henry Marshall .10 .05
❑ 164 Carlos Carson .10 .05
❑ 165 Nick Lowery .25 .11
❑ 166 Irv Eatman RC** .10 .05
❑ 167 Brad Budde .10 .05
❑ 168 Art Still .10 .05
❑ 169 Bill Maas AP .10 .05
❑ 170 Lloyd Burruss RC .10 .05
❑ 171 Deron Cherry AP .10 .05
❑ 172 Seahawks TL .25 .11
(Curt Warner Finds Opening)
❑ 173 Dave Krieg .50 .23
❑ 174 Curt Warner .25 .11
❑ 175 John L. Williams RC .50 .23
❑ 176 Bobby Joe Edmonds RC .25 .11
❑ 177 Steve Largent .60 .25
❑ 178 Bruce Scholtz .10 .05
❑ 179 Norm Johnson .10 .05
❑ 180 Jacob Green .10 .05
❑ 181 Fredd Young .10 .05
❑ 182 Dave Brown .10 .05
❑ 183 Kenny Easley .10 .05
❑ 184 Bengals TL .25 .11
(James Brooks Stiff-Arm)
❑ 185 Boomer Esiason .50 .23
❑ 186 James Brooks .25 .11
❑ 187 Larry Kinnebrew .10 .05
❑ 188 Cris Collinsworth .25 .11
❑ 189 Eddie Brown .50 .23
❑ 190 Tim McGee RC .50 .23
❑ 191 Jim Breech .10 .05
❑ 192 Anthony Munoz .50 .23
❑ 193 Max Montoya .10 .05
❑ 194 Eddie Edwards .10 .05
❑ 195 Ross Browner .25 .11
❑ 196 Emanuel King .10 .05
❑ 197 Louis Breeden .10 .05
❑ 198 Vikings TL .10 .05
(Darrin Nelson In Motion)
❑ 199 Tommy Kramer .25 .11
❑ 200 Darrin Nelson .10 .05
❑ 201 Allen Rice .10 .05
❑ 202 Anthony Carter .50 .23
❑ 203 Leo Lewis .10 .05
❑ 204 Steve Jordan .50 .23
❑ 205 Chuck Nelson RC .10 .05
❑ 206 Greg Coleman .10 .05
❑ 207 Gary Zimmerman RC .25 .11
❑ 208 Doug Martin .10 .05
❑ 209 Keith Millard .10 .05
❑ 210 Issiac Holt RC .10 .05
❑ 211 Joey Browner .25 .11
❑ 212 Rufus Bess .10 .05
❑ 213 Raiders TL .50 .23
(Marcus Allen Quick Feet)
❑ 214 Jim Plunkett .50 .23
❑ 215 Marcus Allen 1.00 .45
❑ 216 Napoleon McCallum RC .25 .11
❑ 217 Dokie Williams .10 .05
❑ 218 Todd Christensen .50 .23
❑ 219 Chris Bahr .10 .05
❑ 220 Howie Long .60 .25
❑ 221 Bill Pickel .10 .05
❑ 222 Sean Jones RC .75 .35
❑ 223 Lester Hayes .25 .11
❑ 224 Mike Haynes .25 .11
❑ 225 Vann McElroy .10 .05
❑ 226 Fulton Walker .10 .05
❑ 227 Passing Leaders 1.25 .55
Tommy Kramer,
Minnesota Vikings
Dan Marino,
❑ 228 Receiving Leaders 1.25 .55
Jerry Rice,
San Francisco 49ers
Todd Christensen,
❑ 229 Rushing Leaders .50 .23
Eric Dickerson,
Los Angeles Rams
Curt Warner,
❑ 230 Scoring Leaders .10 .05
Kevin Butler,
Chicago Bears
Tony Franklin,
❑ 231 Interception Leaders .50 .23
Ronnie Lott,
San Francisco 49ers
Deron Cherry,
❑ 232 Dolphins TL .25 .11
(Reggie Roby Booms It)
❑ 233 Dan Marino AP 6.00 2.70
❑ 234 Lorenzo Hampton RC .10 .05
❑ 235 Tony Nathan .25 .11
❑ 236 Mark Duper .50 .23
❑ 237 Mark Clayton .50 .23
❑ 238 Nat Moore .25 .11
❑ 239 Bruce Hardy .10 .05
❑ 240 Reggie Roby .25 .11
❑ 241 Roy Foster .10 .05
❑ 242 Dwight Stephenson AP .25 .11
❑ 243 Hugh Green .10 .05
❑ 244 John Offerdahl RC .50 .23
❑ 245 Mark Brown .10 .05
❑ 246 Doug Betters .10 .05
❑ 247 Bob Baumhower .10 .05
❑ 248 Falcons TL .10 .05
(Gerald Riggs Uses Blockers)
❑ 249 David Archer .50 .23
❑ 250 Gerald Riggs .25 .11
❑ 251 William Andrews .25 .11
❑ 252 Charlie Brown .10 .05
❑ 253 Arthur Cox .10 .05
❑ 254 Rick Donnelly .10 .05
❑ 255 Bill Fralic AP .10 .05
❑ 256 Mike Gann RC .10 .05
❑ 257 Rick Bryan .10 .05
❑ 258 Bret Clark .10 .05
❑ 259 Mike Pitts .10 .05
❑ 260 Cowboys TL .50 .23
(Tony Dorsett Cuts)
❑ 261 Danny White .50 .23
❑ 262 Steve Pelluer RC .10 .05
❑ 263 Tony Dorsett .50 .23
❑ 264 Herschel Walker RC UER 2.50 1.10
(Stats show 12 TD's
in '86, text says 14)
❑ 265 Timmy Newsome .10 .05
❑ 266 Tony Hill .25 .11
❑ 267 Mike Sherrard RC .50 .23
❑ 268 Jim Jeffcoat .50 .23
❑ 269 Ron Fellows .10 .05
❑ 270 Bill Bates .50 .23
❑ 271 Michael Downs .10 .05
❑ 272 Saints TL .25 .11
(Bobby Hebert Fakes)
❑ 273 Dave Wilson .10 .05
❑ 274 Rueben Mayes RC UER .10 .05
(Stats show 1353 completions, should be yards)
❑ 275 Hoby Brenner .10 .05
❑ 276 Eric Martin RC .50 .23
❑ 277 Morten Andersen .25 .11
❑ 278 Brian Hansen .10 .05
❑ 279 Rickey Jackson .50 .23
❑ 280 Dave Waymer .10 .05
❑ 281 Bruce Clark .10 .05
❑ 282 James Geathers RC .25 .11
❑ 283 Steelers TL .25 .11
(Walter Abercrombie Resists)
❑ 284 Mark Malone .25 .11
❑ 285 Earnest Jackson .10 .05
❑ 286 Walter Abercrombie .10 .05
❑ 287 Louis Lipps .25 .11
❑ 288 John Stallworth UER .50 .23
(Stats only go up
through 1981)
❑ 289 Gary Anderson K .10 .05
❑ 290 Keith Willis .10 .05
❑ 291 Mike Merriweather .10 .05
❑ 292 Lupe Sanchez .10 .05
❑ 293 Donnie Shell .25 .11
❑ 294 Eagles TL .50 .23
(Keith Byars Inches Ahead)
❑ 295 Mike Reichenbach .10 .05
❑ 296 R.Cunningham RC ! 8.00 3.60
❑ 297 Keith Byars RC .75 .35
❑ 298 Mike Quick .25 .11
❑ 299 Kenny Jackson .10 .05
❑ 300 John Teltschik RC .10 .05
❑ 301 Reggie White AP 3.00 1.35
❑ 302 Ken Clarke .10 .05
❑ 303 Greg Brown .10 .05
❑ 304 Roynell Young .10 .05
❑ 305 Andre Waters RC .50 .23
❑ 306 Oilers TL .50 .23
(Warren Moon Plots Play)
❑ 307 Warren Moon 1.50 .70
❑ 308 Mike Rozier .25 .11
❑ 309 Drew Hill .25 .11
❑ 310 Ernest Givins RC .50 .23
❑ 311 Lee Johnson RC .10 .05
❑ 312 Kent Hill .10 .05
❑ 313 Dean Steinkuhler RC .25 .11
❑ 314 Ray Childress .50 .23
❑ 315 John Grimsley RC .10 .05
❑ 316 Jesse Baker .10 .05
❑ 317 Lions TL .10 .05
(Eric Hipple Surveys)
❑ 318 Chuck Long RC .25 .11
❑ 319 James Jones .10 .05
❑ 320 Garry James .10 .05
❑ 321 Jeff Chadwick .10 .05
❑ 322 Leonard Thompson .10 .05
❑ 323 Pete Mandley .10 .05
❑ 324 Jimmie Giles .25 .11
❑ 325 Herman Hunter .10 .05
❑ 326 Keith Ferguson .10 .05
❑ 327 Devon Mitchell .10 .05
❑ 328 Cardinals TL .10 .05
(Neil Lomax Audible)
❑ 329 Neil Lomax .25 .11
❑ 330 Stump Mitchell .10 .05
❑ 331 Earl Ferrell .10 .05
❑ 332 Vai Sikahema RC .25 .11
❑ 333 Ron Wolfley RC .10 .05
❑ 334 J.T. Smith .25 .11
❑ 335 Roy Green .25 .11
❑ 336 Al(Bubba) Baker .10 .05
❑ 337 Freddie Joe Nunn .10 .05
❑ 338 Cedric Mack .10 .05
❑ 339 Chargers TL .25 .11
(Gary Anderson Evades)
❑ 340 Dan Fouts .50 .23
❑ 341 Gary Anderson UER .50 .23
(Two Topps logos
on card front)
❑ 342 Wes Chandler .25 .11
❑ 343 Kellen Winslow .50 .23
❑ 344 Ralf Mojsiejenko .10 .05
❑ 345 Rolf Benirschke .10 .05
❑ 346 Lee Williams RC .25 .11
❑ 347 Leslie O'Neal RC 1.00 .45
❑ 348 Billy Ray Smith .25 .11
❑ 349 Gill Byrd .25 .11
❑ 350 Packers TL .10 .05
(Paul Ott Carruth Around End)
❑ 351 Randy Wright .10 .05
❑ 352 Kenneth Davis RC .50 .23
❑ 353 Gerry Ellis .10 .05
❑ 354 James Lofton .50 .23
❑ 355 Phillip Epps RC .10 .05
❑ 356 Walter Stanley RC .10 .05
❑ 357 Eddie Lee Ivery .10 .05
❑ 358 Tim Harris RC .50 .23
❑ 359 Mark Lee UER .10 .05
(Red flag, rest of
Packers have yellow)
❑ 360 Mossy Cade .10 .05
❑ 361 Bills TL 1.00 .45
(Jim Kelly Works Ground)
❑ 362 Jim Kelly RC** 8.00 3.60
❑ 363 Robb Riddick RC .10 .05
❑ 364 Greg Bell .10 .05
❑ 365 Andre Reed 1.25 .55

❑ 366 Pete Metzelaars RC .50 .23
❑ 367 Sean McNanie .10 .05
❑ 368 Fred Smerlas .10 .05
❑ 369 Bruce Smith 2.00 .90
❑ 370 Darryl Talley .25 .11
❑ 371 Charles Romes .10 .05
❑ 372 Colts TL .10 .05
(Rohn Stark High and Far)
❑ 373 Jack Trudeau RC .25 .11
❑ 374 Gary Hogeboom .10 .05
❑ 375 Randy McMillan .10 .05
❑ 376 Albert Bentley .10 .05
❑ 377 Matt Bouza .10 .05
❑ 378 Bill Brooks RC 1.00 .45
❑ 379 Rohn Stark AP .10 .05
❑ 380 Chris Hinton .10 .05
❑ 381 Ray Donaldson .10 .05
❑ 382 Jon Hand RC .10 .05
❑ 383 Buccaneers TL .10 .05
(James Wilder Braces)
❑ 384 Steve Young 5.00 2.20
❑ 385 James Wilder .10 .05
❑ 386 Frank Garcia .10 .05
❑ 387 Gerald Carter .10 .05
❑ 388 Phil Freeman .10 .05
❑ 389 Calvin Magee .10 .05
❑ 390 Donald Igwebuike .10 .05
❑ 391 David Logan .10 .05
❑ 392 Jeff Davis .10 .05
❑ 393 Chris Washington .10 .05
❑ 394 Checklist 1-132 .10 .05
❑ 395 Checklist 133-264 .10 .05
❑ 396 Checklist 265-396 .10 .05

1988 Topps

	MINT	NRMT
COMPLETE SET (396)	15.00	6.75
COMP.FACT.SET (396)	20.00	9.00

❑ 1 Super Bowl XXII .20 .09
Redskins 42,
Broncos 10
(Redskins celebrating)
❑ 2 Vencie Glenn RB .05 .02
Longest Interception
Return
❑ 3 Steve Largent RB .40 .18
Most Receptions,
Career
❑ 4 Joe Montana RB .75 .35
Most Consecutive
Pass Completions
❑ 5 Walter Payton RB .40 .18
Most Rushing
Touchdowns, Career
❑ 6 Jerry Rice RB .75 .35
Most Touchdown
Receptions, Season
❑ 7 Redskins TL .20 .09
(Kelvin Bryant Sees Daylight)
❑ 8 Doug Williams .20 .09
❑ 9 George Rogers .20 .09
❑ 10 Kelvin Bryant .20 .09
❑ 11 Timmy Smith SR .20 .09
❑ 12 Art Monk .40 .18
❑ 13 Gary Clark .40 .18
❑ 14 Ricky Sanders RC** .40 .18
❑ 15 Steve Cox .05 .02
❑ 16 Joe Jacoby .05 .02
❑ 17 Charles Mann .20 .09
❑ 18 Dave Butz .05 .02
❑ 19 Darrell Green AP .20 .09
❑ 20 Dexter Manley .05 .02
❑ 21 Barry Wilburn .05 .02
❑ 22 Broncos TL .05 .02
(Sammy Winder Winds
Through)
❑ 23 John Elway AP 2.00 .90
❑ 24 Sammy Winder .05 .02
❑ 25 Vance Johnson .20 .09
❑ 26 Mark Jackson RC .40 .18
❑ 27 Ricky Nattiel SR RC .05 .02
❑ 28 Clarence Kay .05 .02
❑ 29 Rich Karlis .05 .02
❑ 30 Keith Bishop .05 .02
❑ 31 Mike Horan .05 .02
❑ 32 Rulon Jones .05 .02
❑ 33 Karl Mecklenburg .20 .09
❑ 34 Jim Ryan .05 .02
❑ 35 Mark Haynes .20 .09
❑ 36 Mike Harden .05 .02
❑ 37 49ers TL .40 .18
(Roger Craig Gallops
For Yardage)
❑ 38 Joe Montana 2.00 .90
❑ 39 Steve Young 1.00 .45
❑ 40 Roger Craig .20 .09
❑ 41 Tom Rathman RC .40 .18
❑ 42 Joe Cribbs .20 .09
❑ 43 Jerry Rice AP 2.00 .90
❑ 44 Mike Wilson RC .05 .02
❑ 45 Ron Heller RC .05 .02
❑ 46 Ray Wersching .05 .02
❑ 47 Michael Carter .05 .02
❑ 48 Dwaine Board .05 .02
❑ 49 Michael Walter .05 .02
❑ 50 Don Griffin .05 .02
❑ 51 Ronnie Lott .40 .18
❑ 52 Charles Haley .40 .18
❑ 53 Dana McLemore .05 .02
❑ 54 Saints TL .20 .09
(Bobby Hebert Hands Off)
❑ 55 Bobby Hebert .20 .09
❑ 56 Rueben Mayes .05 .02
❑ 57 Dalton Hilliard RC .05 .02
❑ 58 Eric Martin .20 .09
❑ 59 John Tice RC .05 .02
❑ 60 Brad Edelman .05 .02
❑ 61 Morten Andersen AP .20 .09
❑ 62 Brian Hansen .05 .02
❑ 63 Mel Gray RC .40 .18
❑ 64 Rickey Jackson .20 .09
❑ 65 Sam Mills RC** .40 .18
❑ 66 Pat Swilling RC .40 .18
❑ 67 Dave Waymer .05 .02
❑ 68 Bears TL .20 .09
(Willie Gault Powers
Forward)
❑ 69 Jim McMahon .40 .18
❑ 70 Mike Tomczak RC .05 .02
❑ 71 Neal Anderson RC .40 .18
❑ 72 Willie Gault .20 .09
❑ 73 Dennis Gentry .05 .02
❑ 74 Dennis McKinnon .05 .02
❑ 75 Kevin Butler .05 .02
❑ 76 Jim Covert .05 .02
❑ 77 Jay Hilgenberg .05 .02
❑ 78 Steve McMichael .20 .09
❑ 79 William Perry .20 .09
❑ 80 Richard Dent .40 .18
❑ 81 Ron Rivera RC .05 .02
❑ 82 Mike Singletary AP .40 .18
❑ 83 Dan Hampton .20 .09
❑ 84 Dave Duerson .05 .02
❑ 85 Browns TL .20 .09
(Bernie Kosar Lets
It Go)
❑ 86 Bernie Kosar .40 .18
❑ 87 Earnest Byner .40 .18
❑ 88 Kevin Mack .20 .09
❑ 89 Webster Slaughter RC .40 .18
❑ 90 Gerald McNeil .05 .02
❑ 91 Brian Brennan .05 .02
❑ 92 Ozzie Newsome .40 .18
❑ 93 Cody Risien .05 .02
❑ 94 Bob Golic .05 .02
❑ 95 Carl Hairston .05 .02
❑ 96 Mike Johnson RC .05 .02
❑ 97 Clay Matthews .20 .09
❑ 98 Frank Minnifield .05 .02
❑ 99 Hanford Dixon AP .05 .02
❑ 100 Dave Puzzuoli .05 .02
❑ 101 Felix Wright RC**/C .05 .02
❑ 102 Oilers TL .40 .18
(Warren Moon Over The Top)
❑ 103 Warren Moon .50 .23
❑ 104 Mike Rozier .05 .02
❑ 105 Alonzo Highsmith SR RC .20 .09
❑ 106 Drew Hill .20 .09
❑ 107 Ernest Givins .40 .18
❑ 108 Curtis Duncan RC .40 .18
❑ 109 Tony Zendejas RC** .05 .02
❑ 110 Mike Munchak AP .05 .02
❑ 111 Kent Hill .05 .02
❑ 112 Ray Childress .20 .09
❑ 113 Al Smith RC .20 .09
❑ 114 Keith Bostic RC .05 .02
❑ 115 Jeff Donaldson .05 .02
❑ 116 Colts TL .40 .18
(Eric Dickerson Finds Opening)
❑ 117 Jack Trudeau .05 .02
❑ 118 Eric Dickerson AP .40 .18
❑ 119 Albert Bentley .05 .02
❑ 120 Matt Bouza .05 .02
❑ 121 Bill Brooks .40 .18
❑ 122 Dean Biasucci RC .05 .02
❑ 123 Chris Hinton .05 .02
❑ 124 Ray Donaldson .05 .02
❑ 125 Ron Solt RC .05 .02
❑ 126 Donnell Thompson .05 .02
❑ 127 Barry Krauss RC .05 .02
❑ 128 Duane Bickett .05 .02
❑ 129 Mike Prior RC .05 .02
❑ 130 Seahawks TL .20 .09
(Curt Warner Follows Blocking)
❑ 131 Dave Krieg .20 .09
❑ 132 Curt Warner .20 .09
❑ 133 John L. Williams .40 .18
❑ 134 Bobby Joe Edmonds .05 .02
❑ 135 Steve Largent .40 .18
❑ 136 Raymond Butler .05 .02
❑ 137 Norm Johnson .05 .02
❑ 138 Ruben Rodriguez .05 .02
❑ 139 Blair Bush .05 .02
❑ 140 Jacob Green .05 .02
❑ 141 Joe Nash .05 .02
❑ 142 Jeff Bryant .05 .02
❑ 143 Fredd Young AP .05 .02
❑ 144 Brian Bosworth SR RC 1.00 .45
❑ 145 Kenny Easley AP .05 .02
❑ 146 Vikings TL .20 .09
(Tommy Kramer Spots His Man)
❑ 147 Wade Wilson RC .40 .18
❑ 148 Tommy Kramer .20 .09
❑ 149 Darrin Nelson .05 .02
❑ 150 D.J. Dozier SR RC .20 .09
❑ 151 Anthony Carter .20 .09
❑ 152 Leo Lewis .05 .02
❑ 153 Steve Jordan .20 .09
❑ 154 Gary Zimmerman .05 .02
❑ 155 Chuck Nelson .05 .02
❑ 156 Henry Thomas SR RC .40 .18
❑ 157 Chris Doleman RC .40 .18
❑ 158 Scott Studwell RC .05 .02
❑ 159 Jesse Solomon RC .05 .02
❑ 160 Joey Browner AP .05 .02
❑ 161 Neal Guggemos .05 .02
❑ 162 Steelers TL .20 .09
(Louis Lipps In a Crowd)
❑ 163 Mark Malone .05 .02
❑ 164 Walter Abercrombie .05 .02
❑ 165 Earnest Jackson .05 .02
❑ 166 Frank Pollard .05 .02
❑ 167 Dwight Stone RC .20 .09
❑ 168 Gary Anderson K .05 .02
❑ 169 Harry Newsome RC .05 .02
❑ 170 Keith Willis .05 .02
❑ 171 Keith Gary .05 .02
❑ 172 David Little RC .05 .02
❑ 173 Mike Merriweather .05 .02

- ❑ 174 Dwayne Woodruff .05 .02
- ❑ 175 Patriots TL .40 .18
  (Irving Fryar One on One)
- ❑ 176 Steve Grogan .20 .09
- ❑ 177 Tony Eason .20 .09
- ❑ 178 Tony Collins .20 .09
- ❑ 179 Mosi Tatupu .05 .02
- ❑ 180 Stanley Morgan .20 .09
- ❑ 181 Irving Fryar .40 .18
- ❑ 182 Stephen Starring .05 .02
- ❑ 183 Tony Franklin .05 .02
- ❑ 184 Rich Camarillo .05 .02
- ❑ 185 Garin Veris .05 .02
- ❑ 186 Andre Tippett AP .20 .09
- ❑ 187 Ronnie Lippett .05 .02
- ❑ 188 Fred Marion .05 .02
- ❑ 189 Dolphins TL .75 .35
  (Dan Marino Play-
  Action Pass)
- ❑ 190 Dan Marino 2.00 .90
- ❑ 191 Troy Stradford SR RC .05 .02
- ❑ 192 Lorenzo Hampton .05 .02
- ❑ 193 Mark Duper .20 .09
- ❑ 194 Mark Clayton .20 .09
- ❑ 195 Reggie Roby .20 .09
- ❑ 196 Dwight Stephenson AP .05 .02
- ❑ 197 T.J. Turner .05 .02
- ❑ 198 John Bosa SR .05 .02
- ❑ 199 Jackie Shipp .05 .02
- ❑ 200 John Offerdahl .20 .09
- ❑ 201 Mark Brown .05 .02
- ❑ 202 Paul Lankford .05 .02
- ❑ 203 Chargers TL .40 .18
  (Kellen Winslow Sure Hands)
- ❑ 204 Tim Spencer .05 .02
- ❑ 205 Gary Anderson RB .20 .09
- ❑ 206 Curtis Adams .05 .02
- ❑ 207 Lionel James .05 .02
- ❑ 208 Chip Banks .05 .02
- ❑ 209 Kellen Winslow .40 .18
- ❑ 210 Ralf Mojsiejenko .05 .02
- ❑ 211 Jim Lachey .20 .09
- ❑ 212 Lee Williams .05 .02
- ❑ 213 Billy Ray Smith .05 .02
- ❑ 214 Vencie Glenn RC .20 .09
- ❑ 215 Passing Leaders .50 .23
  Bernie Kosar
  Joe Montana
- ❑ 216 Receiving Leaders .20 .09
  Al Toon
  J.T. Smith
- ❑ 217 Rushing Leaders .20 .09
  Charles White
  Eric Dickerson
- ❑ 218 Scoring Leaders .40 .18
  Jim Breech
  Jerry Rice
- ❑ 219 Interception Leaders .05 .02
  Keith Bostic
  Mark Kelso
  Mike Prior
  Barry Wilburn
- ❑ 220 Bills TL .40 .18
  (Jim Kelly Plots His Course)
- ❑ 221 Jim Kelly .75 .35
- ❑ 222 Ronnie Harmon RC .40 .18
- ❑ 223 Robb Riddick .05 .02
- ❑ 224 Andre Reed .40 .18
- ❑ 225 Chris Burkett RC .05 .02
- ❑ 226 Pete Metzelaars .40 .18
- ❑ 227 Bruce Smith AP .50 .23
- ❑ 228 Darryl Talley .20 .09
- ❑ 229 Eugene Marve .05 .02
- ❑ 230 Cornelius Bennett SR RC .75 .35
- ❑ 231 Mark Kelso RC .05 .02
- ❑ 232 Shane Conlan SR RC .40 .18
- ❑ 233 Eagles TL .40 .18
  (Randall Cunningham
  QB Keeper)
- ❑ 234 Randall Cunningham 1.00 .45
- ❑ 235 Keith Byars .40 .18
- ❑ 236 Anthony Toney RC .05 .02
- ❑ 237 Mike Quick .20 .09
- ❑ 238 Kenny Jackson .05 .02
- ❑ 239 John Spagnola .05 .02
- ❑ 240 Paul McFadden .05 .02
- ❑ 241 Reggie White AP .60 .25
- ❑ 242 Ken Clarke .05 .02
- ❑ 243 Mike Pitts .05 .02
- ❑ 244 Clyde Simmons RC .40 .18
- ❑ 245 Seth Joyner RC .40 .18
- ❑ 246 Andre Waters .40 .18
- ❑ 247 Jerome Brown SR RC .40 .18
- ❑ 248 Cardinals TL .05 .02
  (Stump Mitchell On the Run)
- ❑ 249 Neil Lomax .20 .09
- ❑ 250 Stump Mitchell .05 .02
- ❑ 251 Earl Ferrell .05 .02
- ❑ 252 Vai Sikahema .05 .02
- ❑ 253 J.T. Smith AP .20 .09
- ❑ 254 Roy Green .20 .09
- ❑ 255 Robert Awalt SR .20 .09
- ❑ 256 Freddie Joe Nunn .05 .02
- ❑ 257 Leonard Smith RC .05 .02
- ❑ 258 Travis Curtis .05 .02
- ❑ 259 Cowboys TL .40 .18
  (Herschel Walker Around End)
- ❑ 260 Danny White .40 .18
- ❑ 261 Herschel Walker .40 .18
- ❑ 262 Tony Dorsett .40 .18
- ❑ 263 Doug Cosbie .05 .02
- ❑ 264 Roger Ruzek RC** .20 .09
- ❑ 265 Darryl Clack .05 .02
- ❑ 266 Ed Too Tall Jones .40 .18
- ❑ 267 Jim Jeffcoat .05 .02
- ❑ 268 Everson Walls .05 .02
- ❑ 269 Bill Bates .20 .09
- ❑ 270 Michael Downs .05 .02
- ❑ 271 Giants TL .20 .09
  (Mark Bavaro Drives Ahead)
- ❑ 272 Phil Simms .40 .18
- ❑ 273 Joe Morris .20 .09
- ❑ 274 Lee Rouson .05 .02
- ❑ 275 George Adams .05 .02
- ❑ 276 Lionel Manuel .05 .02
- ❑ 277 Mark Bavaro AP .20 .09
- ❑ 278 Raul Allegre .05 .02
- ❑ 279 Sean Landeta .05 .02
- ❑ 280 Erik Howard .05 .02
- ❑ 281 Leonard Marshall .20 .09
- ❑ 282 Carl Banks AP .20 .09
- ❑ 283 Pepper Johnson .20 .09
- ❑ 284 Harry Carson .20 .09
- ❑ 285 Lawrence Taylor .40 .18
- ❑ 286 Terry Kinard .05 .02
- ❑ 287 Rams TL .40 .18
  (Jim Everett Races Downfield)
- ❑ 288 Jim Everett .40 .18
- ❑ 289 Charles White AP .20 .09
- ❑ 290 Ron Brown .20 .09
- ❑ 291 Henry Ellard .40 .18
- ❑ 292 Mike Lansford .05 .02
- ❑ 293 Dale Hatcher .05 .02
- ❑ 294 Doug Smith .05 .02
- ❑ 295 Jackie Slater AP .20 .09
- ❑ 296 Jim Collins .05 .02
- ❑ 297 Jerry Gray .05 .02
- ❑ 298 LeRoy Irvin .05 .02
- ❑ 299 Nolan Cromwell .20 .09
- ❑ 300 Kevin Greene RC 1.25 .55
- ❑ 301 Jets TL .20 .09
  (Ken O'Brien Reads Defense)
- ❑ 302 Ken O'Brien .20 .09
- ❑ 303 Freeman McNeil .20 .09
- ❑ 304 Johnny Hector .05 .02
- ❑ 305 Al Toon .20 .09
- ❑ 306 Jo Jo Townsell RC .20 .09
- ❑ 307 Mickey Shuler .05 .02
- ❑ 308 Pat Leahy .05 .02
- ❑ 309 Roger Vick .05 .02
- ❑ 310 Alex Gordon RC .05 .02
- ❑ 311 Troy Benson .05 .02
- ❑ 312 Bob Crable .05 .02
- ❑ 313 Harry Hamilton .05 .02
- ❑ 314 Packers TL .05 .02
  (Phillip Epps Ready
  for Contact)
- ❑ 315 Randy Wright .05 .02
- ❑ 316 Kenneth Davis .20 .09
- ❑ 317 Phillip Epps .05 .02
- ❑ 318 Walter Stanley .05 .02
- ❑ 319 Frankie Neal .05 .02
- ❑ 320 Don Bracken .05 .02
- ❑ 321 Brian Noble RC .20 .09
- ❑ 322 Johnny Holland SR RC .20 .09
- ❑ 323 Tim Harris .20 .09
- ❑ 324 Mark Murphy .05 .02
- ❑ 325 Raiders TL .50 .23
  (Bo Jackson All Alone)
- ❑ 326 Marc Wilson .05 .02
- ❑ 327 Bo Jackson SR RC 4.00 1.80
- ❑ 328 Marcus Allen .40 .18
- ❑ 329 James Lofton .40 .18
- ❑ 330 Todd Christensen .20 .09
- ❑ 331 Chris Bahr .05 .02
- ❑ 332 Stan Talley .05 .02
- ❑ 333 Howie Long .40 .18
- ❑ 334 Sean Jones .40 .18
- ❑ 335 Matt Millen .20 .09
- ❑ 336 Stacey Toran .05 .02
- ❑ 337 Vann McElroy .05 .02
- ❑ 338 Greg Townsend .20 .09
- ❑ 339 Bengals TL .40 .18
  (Boomer Esiason Calls Signals)
- ❑ 340 Boomer Esiason .40 .18
- ❑ 341 Larry Kinnebrew .05 .02
- ❑ 342 Stanford Jennings RC .05 .02
- ❑ 343 Eddie Brown .20 .09
- ❑ 344 Jim Breech .05 .02
- ❑ 345 Anthony Munoz AP .40 .18
- ❑ 346 Scott Fulhage RC .05 .02
- ❑ 347 Tim Krumrie RC .05 .02
- ❑ 348 Reggie Williams .20 .09
- ❑ 349 David Fulcher RC .05 .02
- ❑ 350 Buccaneers TL .05 .02
  (James Wilder Free
  and Clear)
- ❑ 351 Frank Garcia .05 .02
- ❑ 352 Vinny Testaverde SR RC 4.00 1.80
- ❑ 353 James Wilder .05 .02
- ❑ 354 Jeff Smith .05 .02
- ❑ 355 Gerald Carter .05 .02
- ❑ 356 Calvin Magee .05 .02
- ❑ 357 Donald Igwebuike .05 .02
- ❑ 358 Ron Holmes RC .05 .02
- ❑ 359 Chris Washington .05 .02
- ❑ 360 Ervin Randle .05 .02
- ❑ 361 Chiefs TL .05 .02
  (Bill Kenney Ground Attack)
- ❑ 362 Bill Kenney .05 .02
- ❑ 363 Christian Okoye SR RC .40 .18
- ❑ 364 Paul Palmer .05 .02
- ❑ 365 Stephone Paige .20 .09
- ❑ 366 Carlos Carson .05 .02
- ❑ 367 Kelly Goodburn RC .05 .02
- ❑ 368 Bill Maas AP .05 .02
- ❑ 369 Mike Bell .05 .02
- ❑ 370 Dino Hackett RC .05 .02
- ❑ 371 Deron Cherry .05 .02
- ❑ 372 Lions TL .05 .02
  (James Jones Stretches
  For More)
- ❑ 373 Chuck Long .20 .09
- ❑ 374 Garry James .05 .02
- ❑ 375 James Jones .05 .02
- ❑ 376 Pete Mandley .05 .02
- ❑ 377 Gary Lee SR .05 .02
- ❑ 378 Eddie Murray .05 .02
- ❑ 379 Jim Arnold .05 .02
- ❑ 380 Dennis Gibson SR RC .05 .02
- ❑ 381 Mike Cofer .05 .02
- ❑ 382 James Griffin .05 .02
- ❑ 383 Falcons TL .05 .02
  (Gerald Riggs Carries
  Heavy Load)
- ❑ 384 Scott Campbell .05 .02
- ❑ 385 Gerald Riggs .20 .09
- ❑ 386 Floyd Dixon RC .05 .02
- ❑ 387 Rick Donnelly AP .05 .02
- ❑ 388 Bill Fralic AP .20 .09
- ❑ 389 Major Everett .05 .02
- ❑ 390 Mike Gann .05 .02
- ❑ 391 Tony Casillas RC .20 .09
- ❑ 392 Rick Bryan .05 .02
- ❑ 393 John Rade RC .05 .02
- ❑ 394 Checklist 1-132 .05 .02
- ❑ 395 Checklist 133-264 .05 .02
- ❑ 396 Checklist 265-396 .05 .02

1989 Topps

	MINT	NRMT
COMPLETE SET (396)	12.00	5.50
COMP.FACT.SET (396)	20.00	9.00

Card	MINT	NRMT
❑ 1 Super Bowl XXIII (Joe Montana back to pass)	.50	.23
❑ 2 Tim Brown RB Most Combined Net Yards Gained, Rookie Season	.50	.23
❑ 3 Eric Dickerson RB Most Consecutive Seasons, Start of Career, 1000 or More Yards Rushing	.10	.05
❑ 4 Steve Largent RB Most Yards Receiving, Career	.25	.11
❑ 5 Dan Marino RB Most Seasons 4000 or More Yards Passing	.75	.35
❑ 6 49ers Team Joe Montana On The Run	.50	.23
❑ 7 Jerry Rice	1.50	.70
❑ 8 Roger Craig	.25	.11
❑ 9 Ronnie Lott	.10	.05
❑ 10 Michael Carter	.05	.02
❑ 11 Charles Haley	.25	.11
❑ 12 Joe Montana	2.00	.90
❑ 13 John Taylor RC	.10	.05
❑ 14 Michael Walter	.05	.02
❑ 15 Mike Cofer K RC	.05	.02
❑ 16 Tom Rathman	.05	.02
❑ 17 Daniel Stubbs RC	.05	.02
❑ 18 Keena Turner	.05	.02
❑ 19 Tim McKyer	.05	.02
❑ 20 Larry Roberts	.05	.02
❑ 21 Jeff Fuller	.05	.02
❑ 22 Bubba Paris	.05	.02
❑ 23 Bengals Team UER (Boomer Esiason Measures Up; Should be versus Steelers in week three)	.10	.05
❑ 24 Eddie Brown	.05	.02
❑ 25 Boomer Esiason	.10	.05
❑ 26 Tim Krumrie	.05	.02
❑ 27 Ickey Woods RC	.10	.05
❑ 28 Anthony Munoz	.10	.05
❑ 29 Tim McGee	.05	.02
❑ 30 Max Montoya	.05	.02
❑ 31 David Grant	.05	.02
❑ 32 Rodney Holman RC (Cincinnati Bengals on card front is subject to various printing errors)	.05	.02
❑ 33 David Fulcher	.10	.05
❑ 34 Jim Skow	.05	.02
❑ 35 James Brooks	.10	.05
❑ 36 Reggie Williams	.05	.02
❑ 37 Eric Thomas RC	.05	.02
❑ 38 Stanford Jennings	.05	.02
❑ 39 Jim Breech	.05	.02
❑ 40 Bills Team (Jim Kelly Reads Defense)	.25	.11
❑ 41 Shane Conlan	.05	.02
❑ 42 Scott Norwood RC**	.05	.02
❑ 43 Cornelius Bennett	.10	.05
❑ 44 Bruce Smith	.25	.11
❑ 45 Thurman Thomas RC	1.00	.45
❑ 46 Jim Kelly	.50	.23
❑ 47 John Kidd	.05	.02
❑ 48 Kent Hull RC	.05	.02
❑ 49 Art Still	.05	.02
❑ 50 Fred Smerlas	.05	.02
❑ 51A Derrick Burroughs (White name plate)	.05	.02
❑ 51B Derrick Burroughs (Yellow name plate)	.05	.02
❑ 52 Andre Reed	.25	.11
❑ 53 Robb Riddick	.05	.02
❑ 54 Chris Burkett	.05	.02
❑ 55 Ronnie Harmon	.10	.05
❑ 56 Mark Kelso UER (Team shown as Buffalo Bill)	.05	.02
❑ 57 Bears Team Thomas Sanders Changes Pace	.05	.02
❑ 58 Mike Singletary	.10	.05
❑ 59 Jay Hilgenberg UER (Lettering is missing from Chicago)	.05	.02
❑ 60 Richard Dent	.10	.05
❑ 61 Ron Rivera	.05	.02
❑ 62 Jim McMahon	.10	.05
❑ 63 Mike Tomczak	.10	.05
❑ 64 Neal Anderson	.10	.05
❑ 65 Dennis Gentry	.05	.02
❑ 66 Dan Hampton	.10	.05
❑ 67 David Tate	.05	.02
❑ 68 Thomas Sanders RC	.05	.02
❑ 69 Steve McMichael	.10	.05
❑ 70 Dennis McKinnon	.05	.02
❑ 71 Brad Muster RC	.05	.02
❑ 72 Vestee Jackson RC	.05	.02
❑ 73 Dave Duerson	.05	.02
❑ 74 Vikings Team (Millard Gets His Man)	.05	.02
❑ 75 Joey Browner	.05	.02
❑ 76 Carl Lee RC	.05	.02
❑ 77 Gary Zimmerman	.05	.02
❑ 78 Hassan Jones RC	.05	.02
❑ 79 Anthony Carter	.10	.05
❑ 80 Ray Berry	.05	.02
❑ 81 Steve Jordan	.05	.02
❑ 82 Issiac Holt	.05	.02
❑ 83 Wade Wilson	.10	.05
❑ 84 Chris Doleman	.10	.05
❑ 85 Alfred Anderson	.05	.02
❑ 86 Keith Millard	.05	.02
❑ 87 Darrin Nelson	.05	.02
❑ 88 D.J. Dozier	.05	.02
❑ 89 Scott Studwell	.05	.02
❑ 90 Oilers Team (Tony Zendejas Big Boot)	.05	.02
❑ 91 Bruce Matthews RC	.50	.23
❑ 92 Curtis Duncan	.05	.02
❑ 93 Warren Moon	.25	.11
❑ 94 Johnny Meads RC	.05	.02
❑ 95 Drew Hill	.05	.02
❑ 96 Alonzo Highsmith	.05	.02
❑ 97 Mike Munchak	.05	.02
❑ 98 Mike Rozier	.05	.02
❑ 99 Tony Zendejas	.05	.02
❑ 100 Jeff Donaldson	.05	.02
❑ 101 Ray Childress	.05	.02
❑ 102 Sean Jones	.10	.05
❑ 103 Ernest Givins	.10	.05
❑ 104 William Fuller RC**	.25	.11
❑ 105 Allen Pinkett RC	.05	.02
❑ 106 Eagles Team (Randall Cunningham Takes Field)	.10	.05
❑ 107 Keith Jackson RC	.25	.11
❑ 108 Reggie White	.25	.11
❑ 109 Clyde Simmons	.10	.05
❑ 110 John Teltschik	.05	.02
❑ 111 Wes Hopkins	.05	.02
❑ 112 Keith Byars	.10	.05
❑ 113 Jerome Brown	.10	.05
❑ 114 Mike Quick	.05	.02
❑ 115 Randall Cunningham	.40	.18
❑ 116 Anthony Toney	.05	.02
❑ 117 Ron Johnson	.05	.02
❑ 118 Terry Hoage	.05	.02
❑ 119 Seth Joyner	.10	.05
❑ 120 Eric Allen RC	.25	.11
❑ 121 Cris Carter RC	2.50	1.10
❑ 122 Rams Team (Greg Bell Runs To Glory)	.05	.02
❑ 123 Tom Newberry RC	.05	.02
❑ 124 Pete Holohan	.05	.02
❑ 125 Robert Delpino RC UER (Listed as Raider on card back)	.05	.02
❑ 126 Carl Ekern	.05	.02
❑ 127 Greg Bell	.05	.02
❑ 128 Mike Lansford	.05	.02
❑ 129 Jim Everett	.10	.05
❑ 130 Mike Wilcher	.05	.02
❑ 131 Jerry Gray	.05	.02
❑ 132 Dale Hatcher	.05	.02
❑ 133 Doug Smith	.05	.02
❑ 134 Kevin Greene	.25	.11
❑ 135 Jackie Slater	.05	.02
❑ 136 Aaron Cox RC	.05	.02
❑ 137 Henry Ellard	.25	.11
❑ 138 Browns Team (Bernie Kosar Quick Release)	.10	.05
❑ 139 Frank Minnifield	.05	.02
❑ 140 Webster Slaughter	.10	.05
❑ 141 Bernie Kosar	.10	.05
❑ 142 Charles Buchanan	.05	.02
❑ 143 Clay Matthews	.10	.05
❑ 144 Reggie Langhorne RC	.05	.02
❑ 145 Hanford Dixon	.05	.02
❑ 146 Brian Brennan	.05	.02
❑ 147 Earnest Byner	.05	.02
❑ 148 Michael Dean Perry RC	.10	.05
❑ 149 Kevin Mack	.05	.02
❑ 150 Matt Bahr	.05	.02
❑ 151 Ozzie Newsome	.10	.05
❑ 152 Saints Team (Craig Heyward Motors Forward)	.10	.05
❑ 153 Morten Andersen	.05	.02
❑ 154 Pat Swilling	.10	.05
❑ 155 Sam Mills	.10	.05
❑ 156 Lonzell Hill	.05	.02
❑ 157 Dalton Hilliard	.05	.02
❑ 158 Craig Heyward RC	.10	.05
❑ 159 Vaughan Johnson RC**	.05	.02
❑ 160 Rueben Mayes	.05	.02
❑ 161 Gene Atkins RC	.05	.02
❑ 162 Bobby Hebert	.10	.05
❑ 163 Rickey Jackson	.10	.05
❑ 164 Eric Martin	.05	.02
❑ 165 Giants Team (Joe Morris Up The Middle)	.05	.02
❑ 166 Lawrence Taylor	.25	.11
❑ 167 Bart Oates	.05	.02
❑ 168 Carl Banks	.05	.02
❑ 169 Eric Moore	.05	.02
❑ 170 Sheldon White RC	.05	.02
❑ 171 Mark Collins RC	.05	.02
❑ 172 Phil Simms	.10	.05
❑ 173 Jim Burt	.05	.02
❑ 174 Stephen Baker RC	.10	.05
❑ 175 Mark Bavaro	.10	.05
❑ 176 Pepper Johnson	.05	.02
❑ 177 Lionel Manuel	.05	.02
❑ 178 Joe Morris	.05	.02
❑ 179 John Elliott RC	.05	.02
❑ 180 Gary Reasons RC	.05	.02
❑ 181 Seahawks Team (Dave Krieg Winds Up)	.10	.05
❑ 182 Brian Blades RC	.25	.11
❑ 183 Steve Largent	.25	.11
❑ 184 Rufus Porter RC	.05	.02
❑ 185 Ruben Rodriguez	.05	.02
❑ 186 Curt Warner	.05	.02
❑ 187 Paul Moyer	.05	.02
❑ 188 Dave Krieg	.10	.05
❑ 189 Jacob Green	.05	.02
❑ 190 John L. Williams	.05	.02

❑ 191 Eugene Robinson RC .05 .02
❑ 192 Brian Bosworth .10 .05
❑ 193 Patriots Team .05 .02
(Tony Eason Behind Blocking)
❑ 194 John Stephens RC .05 .02
❑ 195 Robert Perryman RC .05 .02
❑ 196 Andre Tippett .05 .02
❑ 197 Fred Marion .05 .02
❑ 198 Doug Flutie 1.00 .45
❑ 199 Stanley Morgan .05 .02
❑ 200 Johnny Rembert RC .05 .02
❑ 201 Tony Eason .05 .02
❑ 202 Marvin Allen .05 .02
❑ 203 Raymond Clayborn .05 .02
❑ 204 Irving Fryar .25 .11
❑ 205 Colts Team .05 .02
(Chris Chandler All Alone)
❑ 206 Eric Dickerson .10 .05
❑ 207 Chris Hinton .05 .02
❑ 208 Duane Bickett .05 .02
❑ 209 Chris Chandler RC 1.00 .45
❑ 210 Jon Hand .05 .02
❑ 211 Ray Donaldson .05 .02
❑ 212 Dean Biasucci .05 .02
❑ 213 Bill Brooks .10 .05
❑ 214 Chris Goode RC .05 .02
❑ 215 Clarence Verdin RC** .05 .02
❑ 216 Albert Bentley .05 .02
❑ 217 Passing Leaders .10 .05
Wade Wilson
Boomer Esiason
❑ 218 Receiving Leaders .10 .05
Henry Ellard
Al Toon
❑ 219 Rushing Leaders .10 .05
Herschel Walker
Eric Dickerson
❑ 220 Scoring Leaders .05 .02
Mike Cofer
Scott Norwood
❑ 221 Intercept Leaders .05 .02
Scott Case
Erik McMillan
❑ 222 Jets Team .05 .02
(Ken O'Brien Surveys Scene)
❑ 223 Erik McMillan RC .05 .02
❑ 224 James Hasty RC .05 .02
❑ 225 Al Toon .10 .05
❑ 226 John Booty RC .05 .02
❑ 227 Johnny Hector .05 .02
❑ 228 Ken O'Brien .05 .02
❑ 229 Marty Lyons .05 .02
❑ 230 Mickey Shuler .05 .02
❑ 231 Robin Cole .05 .02
❑ 232 Freeman McNeil .05 .02
❑ 233 Marion Barber .05 .02
❑ 234 Jo Jo Townsell .05 .02
❑ 235 Wesley Walker .05 .02
❑ 236 Roger Vick .05 .02
❑ 237 Pat Leahy .05 .02
❑ 238 Broncos Team UER .50 .23
(John Elway Ground Attack)
(Score of week 15 says 42-21, should be 42-14)
❑ 239 Mike Horan .05 .02
❑ 240 Tony Dorsett .25 .11
❑ 241 John Elway 2.00 .90
❑ 242 Mark Jackson .05 .02
❑ 243 Sammy Winder .05 .02
❑ 244 Rich Karlis .05 .02
❑ 245 Vance Johnson .10 .05
❑ 246 Steve Sewell RC .05 .02
❑ 247 Karl Mecklenburg UER .05 .02
(Drafted 2, should be 12)
❑ 248 Rulon Jones .05 .02
❑ 249 Simon Fletcher RC .05 .02
❑ 250 Redskins Team .10 .05
Doug Williams Sets Up
❑ 251 Chip Lohmiller RC .05 .02
❑ 252 Jamie Morris .05 .02
❑ 253 Mark Rypien RC UER .10 .05
(14 1988 completions, should be 114)
❑ 254 Barry Wilburn .05 .02
❑ 255 Mark May RC .05 .02
❑ 256 Wilber Marshall .05 .02
❑ 257 Charles Mann .05 .02
❑ 258 Gary Clark .25 .11
❑ 259 Doug Williams .10 .05
❑ 260 Art Monk .10 .05
❑ 261 Kelvin Bryant .05 .02
❑ 262 Dexter Manley .05 .02
❑ 263 Ricky Sanders .05 .02
❑ 264 Raiders Team .25 .11
(Marcus Allen Through the Line)
❑ 265 Tim Brown RC 1.50 .70
❑ 266 Jay Schroeder .05 .02
❑ 267 Marcus Allen .25 .11
❑ 268 Mike Haynes .10 .05
❑ 269 Bo Jackson .30 .14
❑ 270 Steve Beuerlein RC .60 .25
❑ 271 Vann McElroy .05 .02
❑ 272 Willie Gault .10 .05
❑ 273 Howie Long .10 .05
❑ 274 Greg Townsend .05 .02
❑ 275 Mike Wise .05 .02
❑ 276 Cardinals Team .05 .02
(Neil Lomax Looks Long)
❑ 277 Luis Sharpe .05 .02
❑ 278 Scott Dill .05 .02
❑ 279 Vai Sikahema .05 .02
❑ 280 Ron Wolfley .05 .02
❑ 281 David Galloway .05 .02
❑ 282 Jay Novacek RC .25 .11
❑ 283 Neil Lomax .05 .02
❑ 284 Robert Awalt .05 .02
❑ 285 Cedric Mack .05 .02
❑ 286 Freddie Joe Nunn .05 .02
❑ 287 J.T. Smith .05 .02
❑ 288 Stump Mitchell .05 .02
❑ 289 Roy Green .10 .05
❑ 290 Dolphins Team .50 .23
(Dan Marino High and Far)
❑ 291 Jarvis Williams RC .05 .02
❑ 292 Troy Stradford .05 .02
❑ 293 Dan Marino 2.00 .90
❑ 294 T.J. Turner .05 .02
❑ 295 John Offerdahl .05 .02
❑ 296 Ferrell Edmunds RC .05 .02
❑ 297 Scott Schwedes .05 .02
❑ 298 Lorenzo Hampton .05 .02
❑ 299 Jim C.Jensen RC .05 .02
❑ 300 Brian Sochia .05 .02
❑ 301 Reggie Roby .05 .02
❑ 302 Mark Clayton .10 .05
❑ 303 Chargers Team .05 .02
(Tim Spencer Leads the Way)
❑ 304 Lee Williams .05 .02
❑ 305 Gary Plummer RC** .05 .02
❑ 306 Gary Anderson RB .05 .02
❑ 307 Gill Byrd .05 .02
❑ 308 Jamie Holland RC .05 .02
❑ 309 Billy Ray Smith .05 .02
❑ 310 Lionel James .05 .02
❑ 311 Mark Vlasic RC .05 .02
❑ 312 Curtis Adams .05 .02
❑ 313 Anthony Miller RC .25 .11
❑ 314 Steelers Team .05 .02
(Frank Pollard Set for Action)
❑ 315 Bubby Brister RC .50 .23
❑ 316 David Little .05 .02
❑ 317 Tunch Ilkin RC .05 .02
❑ 318 Louis Lipps .10 .05
❑ 319 Warren Williams RC .05 .02
❑ 320 Dwight Stone .10 .05
❑ 321 Merril Hoge RC .05 .02
❑ 322 Thomas Everett RC .05 .02
❑ 323 Rod Woodson RC .50 .23
❑ 324 Gary Anderson K .05 .02
❑ 325 Buccaneers Team .05 .02
(Ron Hall in Pursuit)
❑ 326 Donnie Elder .05 .02
❑ 327 Vinny Testaverde .30 .14
❑ 328 Harry Hamilton .05 .02
❑ 329 James Wilder .05 .02
❑ 330 Lars Tate .05 .02
❑ 331 Mark Carrier WR RC .25 .11
❑ 332 Bruce Hill RC .05 .02
❑ 333 Paul Gruber RC .05 .02
❑ 334 Ricky Reynolds .05 .02
❑ 335 Eugene Marve .05 .02
❑ 336 Falcons Team .05 .02
(Joel Williams Holds On)
❑ 337 Aundray Bruce RC .05 .02
❑ 338 John Rade .05 .02
❑ 339 Scott Case RC .05 .02
❑ 340 Robert Moore .05 .02
❑ 341 Chris Miller RC .25 .11
❑ 342 Gerald Riggs .10 .05
❑ 343 Gene Lang .05 .02
❑ 344 Marcus Cotton .05 .02
❑ 345 Rick Donnelly .05 .02
❑ 346 John Settle RC .05 .02
❑ 347 Bill Fralic .05 .02
❑ 348 Chiefs Team .05 .02
(Dino Hackett Zeros In)
❑ 349 Steve DeBerg .05 .02
❑ 350 Mike Stensrud .05 .02
❑ 351 Dino Hackett .05 .02
❑ 352 Deron Cherry .10 .05
❑ 353 Christian Okoye .05 .02
❑ 354 Bill Maas .05 .02
❑ 355 Carlos Carson .05 .02
❑ 356 Albert Lewis .05 .02
❑ 357 Paul Palmer .05 .02
❑ 358 Nick Lowery .05 .02
❑ 359 Stephone Paige .05 .02
❑ 360 Lions Team .05 .02
(Chuck Long Gets the Snap)
❑ 361 Chris Spielman RC .25 .11
❑ 362 Jim Arnold .05 .02
❑ 363 Devon Mitchell .05 .02
❑ 364 Mike Cofer .05 .02
❑ 365 Bennie Blades RC .05 .02
❑ 366 James Jones .05 .02
❑ 367 Garry James .05 .02
❑ 368 Pete Mandley .05 .02
❑ 369 Keith Ferguson .05 .02
❑ 370 Dennis Gibson .05 .02
❑ 371 Packers Team UER .05 .02
(Johnny Holland Over the Top) (Week 16 has vs. Vikings, but they played Bears)
❑ 372 Brent Fullwood RC .05 .02
❑ 373 Don Majkowski RC UER .10 .05
(3 TD's in 1987, should be 5)
❑ 374 Tim Harris .05 .02
❑ 375 Keith Woodside RC .05 .02
❑ 376 Mark Murphy .05 .02
❑ 377 Dave Brown DB .05 .02
❑ 378 Perry Kemp RC .05 .02
❑ 379 Sterling Sharpe RC .75 .35
❑ 380 Chuck Cecil RC .05 .02
❑ 381 Walter Stanley .05 .02
❑ 382 Cowboys Team .05 .02
(Steve Pelluer Lets It Go)
❑ 383 Michael Irvin RC 1.25 .55
❑ 384 Bill Bates .10 .05
❑ 385 Herschel Walker .25 .11
❑ 386 Darryl Clack .05 .02
❑ 387 Danny Noonan .05 .02
❑ 388 Eugene Lockhart RC .05 .02
❑ 389 Ed Too Tall Jones .10 .05
❑ 390 Steve Pelluer .05 .02
❑ 391 Ray Alexander .05 .02
❑ 392 Nate Newton RC .10 .05
❑ 393 Garry Cobb .05 .02
❑ 394 Checklist 1-132 .05 .02
❑ 395 Checklist 133-264 .05 .02
❑ 396 Checklist 265-396 .05 .02

1989 Topps Traded

	MINT	NRMT
COMP.FACT.SET (132)	15.00	6.75
❑ 1T Eric Ball RC	.05	.02
❑ 2T Tony Mandarich RC	.05	.02

❑ 3T Shawn Collins RC	.05	.02
❑ 4T Ray Bentley RC	.05	.02
❑ 5T Tony Casillas	.05	.02
❑ 6T Al Del Greco RC	.05	.02
❑ 7T Dan Saleaumua RC	.10	.05
❑ 8T Keith Bishop	.05	.02
❑ 9T Rodney Peete RC	.25	.11
❑ 10T Lorenzo White RC	.25	.11
❑ 11T Steve Smith RC	.10	.05
❑ 12T Pete Mandley	.05	.02
❑ 13T M.Fernandez RC**/C	.05	.02
❑ 14T Flipper Anderson RC	.25	.11
❑ 15T Louis Oliver RC	.10	.05
❑ 16T Rick Fenney	.05	.02
❑ 17T Gary Jeter	.05	.02
❑ 18T Greg Cox	.05	.02
❑ 19T Bubba McDowell RC	.10	.05
❑ 20T Ron Heller	.05	.02
❑ 21T Tim McDonald RC	.05	.02
❑ 22T Jerrol Williams RC	.05	.02
❑ 23T Marion Butts RC	.10	.05
❑ 24T Steve Young	.75	.35
❑ 25T Mike Merriweather	.05	.02
❑ 26T Richard Johnson	.05	.02
❑ 27T Gerald Riggs	.10	.05
❑ 28T Dave Waymer	.05	.02
❑ 29T Issiac Holt	.05	.02
❑ 30T Deion Sanders RC	1.50	.70
❑ 31T Todd Blackledge	.05	.02
❑ 32T Jeff Cross RC	.05	.02
❑ 33T Steve Wisniewski RC	.10	.05
❑ 34T Ron Brown	.10	.05
❑ 35T Rod Bernstine RC	.05	.02
❑ 36T Jeff Uhlenhake RC	.05	.02
❑ 37T Donnell Woolford RC	.25	.11
❑ 38T Bob Gagliano RC	.05	.02
❑ 39T Ezra Johnson	.05	.02
❑ 40T Ron Jaworski	.05	.02
❑ 41T Lawyer Tillman RC	.05	.02
❑ 42T Lorenzo Lynch RC	.05	.02
❑ 43T Mike Alexander	.05	.02
❑ 44T Tim Worley RC	.05	.02
❑ 45T Guy Bingham	.05	.02
❑ 46T Cleveland Gary RC	.05	.02
❑ 47T Danny Peebles	.05	.02
❑ 48T Clarence Weathers RC	.05	.02
❑ 49T Jeff Lageman RC	.25	.11
❑ 50T Eric Metcalf RC	.25	.11
❑ 51T Myron Guyton RC	.05	.02
❑ 52T Steve Atwater RC	.05	.02
❑ 53T John Fourcade RC	.05	.02
❑ 54T Randall McDaniel RC	.25	.11
❑ 55T Al Noga RC	.05	.02
❑ 56T Sammie Smith RC	.10	.05
❑ 57T Jesse Solomon	.05	.02
❑ 58T Greg Kragen RC	.05	.02
❑ 59T Don Beebe RC	.25	.11
❑ 60T Hart Lee Dykes RC	.10	.05
❑ 61T Trace Armstrong RC	.10	.05
❑ 62T Steve Pelluer	.05	.02
❑ 63T Barry Krauss	.05	.02
❑ 64T Kevin Murphy RC	.05	.02
❑ 65T Steve Tasker RC	.25	.11
❑ 66T Jessie Small RC	.05	.02
❑ 67T Dave Meggett RC	.25	.11
❑ 68T Dean Hamel	.05	.02
❑ 69T Jim Covert	.05	.02
❑ 70T Troy Aikman RC	5.00	2.20
❑ 71T Raul Allegre	.05	.02
❑ 72T Chris Jacke RC	.10	.05
❑ 73T Leslie O'Neal	.10	.05
❑ 74T Keith Taylor RC	.05	.02
❑ 75T Steve Walsh RC	.25	.11
❑ 76T Tracy Rocker	.05	.02
❑ 77T Robert Massey RC	.10	.05
❑ 78T Bryan Wagner	.05	.02
❑ 79T Steve DeOssie	.05	.02
❑ 80T Carnell Lake RC	.25	.11
❑ 81T Frank Reich RC	.25	.11
❑ 82T Tyrone Braxton RC	.05	.02
❑ 83T Barry Sanders RC	10.00	4.50
❑ 84T Pete Stoyanovich RC	.10	.05
❑ 85T Paul Palmer	.05	.02
❑ 86T Billy Joe Tolliver RC	.05	.02
❑ 87T Eric Hill RC	.10	.05
❑ 88T Gerald McNeil	.05	.02
❑ 89T Bill Hawkins RC	.05	.02
❑ 90T Derrick Thomas RC	1.25	.55
❑ 91T Jim Harbaugh RC	.75	.35
❑ 92T Brian Williams OL	.05	.02
❑ 93T Jack Trudeau	.05	.02
❑ 94T Leonard Smith	.05	.02
❑ 95T Gary Hogeboom	.05	.02
❑ 96T A.J. Johnson RC	.05	.02
❑ 97T Jim McMahon	.10	.05
❑ 98T David Williams RC	.05	.02
❑ 99T Rohn Stark	.05	.02
❑ 100T Sean Landeta	.05	.02
❑ 101T Tim Johnson RC	.05	.02
❑ 102T Andre Rison RC	.75	.35
❑ 103T Earnest Byner	.10	.05
❑ 104T Don McPherson RC	.05	.02
❑ 105T Zefross Moss RC	.05	.02
❑ 106T Frank Stams RC	.05	.02
❑ 107T Courtney Hall RC	.10	.05
❑ 108T Marc Logan RC	.05	.02
❑ 109T James Lofton	.25	.11
❑ 110T Lewis Tillman RC	.10	.05
❑ 111T Irv Pankey RC	.05	.02
❑ 112T Ralf Mojsiejenko	.05	.02
❑ 113T Bobby Humphrey RC	.05	.02
❑ 114T Chris Burkett	.05	.02
❑ 115T Greg Lloyd RC	.25	.11
❑ 116T Matt Millen	.10	.05
❑ 117T Carl Zander	.05	.02
❑ 118T Wayne Martin RC	.25	.11
❑ 119T Mike Saxon	.05	.02
❑ 120T Herschel Walker	.10	.05
❑ 121T Andy Heck RC	.05	.02
❑ 122T Mark Robinson	.05	.02
❑ 123T Keith Van Horne RC	.05	.02
❑ 124T Ricky Hunley	.05	.02
❑ 125T Timm Rosenbach RC	.10	.05
❑ 126T Steve Grogan	.10	.05
❑ 127T Stephen Braggs RC	.05	.02
❑ 128T Terry Long	.05	.02
❑ 129T Evan Cooper	.05	.02
❑ 130T Robert Lyles	.05	.02
❑ 131T Mike Webster	.10	.05
❑ 132T Checklist 1-132	.05	.02

1990 Topps

	MINT	NRMT
COMPLETE SET (528)	10.00	4.50
COMP.FACT.SET (528)	12.00	5.50
❑ 1 Joe Montana RB	.50	.23
Most TD Passes,		
Super Bowl		
❑ 2 Flipper Anderson RB	.04	.02
Most Receiving		
Yards, Game		
❑ 3 Troy Aikman RB	.40	.18
Most Passing Yards,		
Game, Rookie		
❑ 4 Kevin Butler RB	.04	.02
Most Consecutive		
Field Goals		
❑ 5 Super Bowl XXIV	.04	.02
49ers 55		
Broncos 10		
(Line of scrimmage)		
❑ 6 Dexter Carter RC	.04	.02
❑ 7 Matt Millen	.10	.05
❑ 8 Jerry Rice	.75	.35
❑ 9 Ronnie Lott	.10	.05
❑ 10 John Taylor	.10	.05
❑ 11 Guy McIntyre	.04	.02
❑ 12 Roger Craig	.10	.05
❑ 13 Joe Montana	1.25	.55
❑ 14 Brent Jones RC	.25	.11
❑ 15 Tom Rathman	.04	.02
❑ 16 Harris Barton	.04	.02
❑ 17 Charles Haley	.10	.05
❑ 18 Pierce Holt RC	.04	.02
❑ 19 Michael Carter	.04	.02
❑ 20 Chet Brooks	.04	.02
❑ 21 Eric Wright	.04	.02
❑ 22 Mike Cofer	.04	.02
❑ 23 Jim Fahnhorst	.04	.02
❑ 24 Keena Turner	.04	.02
❑ 25 Don Griffin	.04	.02
❑ 26 Kevin Fagan RC	.04	.02
❑ 27 Bubba Paris	.04	.02
❑ 28 Rushing Leaders	.50	.23
Barry Sanders		
Christian Okoye		
❑ 29 Steve Atwater	.04	.02
❑ 30 Tyrone Braxton	.04	.02
❑ 31 Ron Holmes	.04	.02
❑ 32 Bobby Humphrey	.04	.02
❑ 33 Greg Kragen	.04	.02
❑ 34 David Treadwell	.04	.02
❑ 35 Karl Mecklenburg	.04	.02
❑ 36 Dennis Smith	.04	.02
❑ 37 John Elway	1.25	.55
❑ 38 Vance Johnson	.04	.02
❑ 39 Simon Fletcher UER	.04	.02
(Front DL, back LB)		
❑ 40 Jim Juriga	.04	.02
❑ 41 Mark Jackson	.04	.02
❑ 42 Melvin Bratton RC	.04	.02
❑ 43 Wymon Henderson RC**	.04	.02
❑ 44 Ken Bell	.04	.02
❑ 45 Sammy Winder	.04	.02
❑ 46 Alphonso Carreker	.04	.02
❑ 47 Orson Mobley RC	.04	.02
❑ 48 Rodney Hampton RC	.40	.18
❑ 49 Dave Meggett	.10	.05
❑ 50 Myron Guyton	.04	.02
❑ 51 Phil Simms	.10	.05
❑ 52 Lawrence Taylor	.25	.11
❑ 53 Carl Banks	.04	.02
❑ 54 Pepper Johnson	.04	.02
❑ 55 Leonard Marshall	.04	.02
❑ 56 Mark Collins	.04	.02
❑ 57 Erik Howard	.04	.02
❑ 58 Eric Dorsey RC	.04	.02
❑ 59 Ottis Anderson	.10	.05
❑ 60 Mark Bavaro	.04	.02
❑ 61 Odessa Turner RC	.04	.02
❑ 62 Gary Reasons	.04	.02
❑ 63 Maurice Carthon	.04	.02
❑ 64 Lionel Manuel	.04	.02
❑ 65 Sean Landeta	.04	.02
❑ 66 Perry Williams	.04	.02
❑ 67 Pat Terrell RC	.04	.02
❑ 68 Flipper Anderson	.04	.02
❑ 69 Jackie Slater	.04	.02
❑ 70 Tom Newberry	.04	.02

- ❑ 71 Jerry Gray .04 .02
- ❑ 72 Henry Ellard .10 .05
- ❑ 73 Doug Smith .04 .02
- ❑ 74 Kevin Greene .25 .11
- ❑ 75 Jim Everett .10 .05
- ❑ 76 Mike Lansford .04 .02
- ❑ 77 Greg Bell .04 .02
- ❑ 78 Pete Holohan .04 .02
- ❑ 79 Robert Delpino .04 .02
- ❑ 80 Mike Wilcher .04 .02
- ❑ 81 Mike Piel .04 .02
- ❑ 82 Mel Owens .04 .02
- ❑ 83 Michael Stewart RC .04 .02
- ❑ 84 Ben Smith RC .04 .02
- ❑ 85 Keith Jackson .10 .05
- ❑ 86 Reggie White .25 .11
- ❑ 87 Eric Allen .04 .02
- ❑ 88 Jerome Brown .04 .02
- ❑ 89 Robert Drummond .04 .02
- ❑ 90 Anthony Toney .04 .02
- ❑ 91 Keith Byars .04 .02
- ❑ 92 Cris Carter .50 .23
- ❑ 93 Randall Cunningham .25 .11
- ❑ 94 Ron Johnson .04 .02
- ❑ 95 Mike Quick .04 .02
- ❑ 96 Clyde Simmons .04 .02
- ❑ 97 Mike Pitts .04 .02
- ❑ 98 Izel Jenkins RC .04 .02
- ❑ 99 Seth Joyner .10 .05
- ❑ 100 Mike Schad .04 .02
- ❑ 101 Wes Hopkins .04 .02
- ❑ 102 Kirk Lowdermilk .04 .02
- ❑ 103 Rick Fenney .04 .02
- ❑ 104 Randall McDaniel .10 .05
- ❑ 105 Herschel Walker .10 .05
- ❑ 106 Al Noga .04 .02
- ❑ 107 Gary Zimmerman .04 .02
- ❑ 108 Chris Doleman .04 .02
- ❑ 109 Keith Millard .04 .02
- ❑ 110 Carl Lee .04 .02
- ❑ 111 Joey Browner .04 .02
- ❑ 112 Steve Jordan .04 .02
- ❑ 113 Reggie Rutland RC .04 .02
- ❑ 114 Wade Wilson .10 .05
- ❑ 115 Anthony Carter .10 .05
- ❑ 116 Rich Karlis .04 .02
- ❑ 117 Hassan Jones .04 .02
- ❑ 118 Henry Thomas .04 .02
- ❑ 119 Scott Studwell .04 .02
- ❑ 120 Ralf Mojsiejenko .04 .02
- ❑ 121 Earnest Byner .04 .02
- ❑ 122 Gerald Riggs .10 .05
- ❑ 123 Tracy Rocker .04 .02
- ❑ 124 A.J. Johnson .04 .02
- ❑ 125 Charles Mann .04 .02
- ❑ 126 Art Monk .10 .05
- ❑ 127 Ricky Sanders .04 .02
- ❑ 128 Gary Clark .25 .11
- ❑ 129 Jim Lachey .04 .02
- ❑ 130 Martin Mayhew RC .04 .02
- ❑ 131 Ravin Caldwell .04 .02
- ❑ 132 Don Warren .04 .02
- ❑ 133 Mark Rypien .10 .05
- ❑ 134 Ed Simmons RC .04 .02
- ❑ 135 Darryl Grant .04 .02
- ❑ 136 Darrell Green .10 .05
- ❑ 137 Chip Lohmiller .04 .02
- ❑ 138 Tony Bennett RC .25 .11
- ❑ 139 Tony Mandarich .04 .02
- ❑ 140 Sterling Sharpe .25 .11
- ❑ 141 Tim Harris .04 .02
- ❑ 142 Don Majkowski .04 .02
- ❑ 143 Rich Moran RC .04 .02
- ❑ 144 Jeff Query .04 .02
- ❑ 145 Brent Fullwood .04 .02
- ❑ 146 Chris Jacke .04 .02
- ❑ 147 Keith Woodside .04 .02
- ❑ 148 Perry Kemp .04 .02
- ❑ 149 Herman Fontenot .04 .02
- ❑ 150 Dave Brown DB .04 .02
- ❑ 151 Brian Noble .04 .02
- ❑ 152 Johnny Holland .04 .02
- ❑ 153 Mark Murphy .04 .02
- ❑ 154 Bob Nelson .04 .02
- ❑ 155 Darrell Thompson RC .04 .02
- ❑ 156 Lawyer Tillman .04 .02
- ❑ 157 Eric Metcalf .25 .11
- ❑ 158 Webster Slaughter .10 .05
- ❑ 159 Frank Minnifield .04 .02
- ❑ 160 Brian Brennan .04 .02
- ❑ 161 Thane Gash RC .04 .02
- ❑ 162 Robert Banks DE .04 .02
- ❑ 163 Bernie Kosar .10 .05
- ❑ 164 David Grayson .04 .02
- ❑ 165 Kevin Mack .04 .02
- ❑ 166 Mike Johnson .04 .02
- ❑ 167 Tim Manoa .04 .02
- ❑ 168 Ozzie Newsome .10 .05
- ❑ 169 Felix Wright .04 .02
- ❑ 170 Al(Bubba) Baker .10 .05
- ❑ 171 Reggie Langhorne .04 .02
- ❑ 172 Clay Matthews .10 .05
- ❑ 173 Andrew Stewart .04 .02
- ❑ 174 Barry Foster RC .25 .11
- ❑ 175 Tim Worley .04 .02
- ❑ 176 Tim Johnson .04 .02
- ❑ 177 Carnell Lake .04 .02
- ❑ 178 Greg Lloyd .25 .11
- ❑ 179 Rod Woodson .25 .11
- ❑ 180 Tunch Ilkin .04 .02
- ❑ 181 Dermontti Dawson .10 .05
- ❑ 182 Gary Anderson K .04 .02
- ❑ 183 Bubby Brister .04 .02
- ❑ 184 Louis Lipps .10 .05
- ❑ 185 Merril Hoge .04 .02
- ❑ 186 Mike Mularkey .04 .02
- ❑ 187 Derek Hill .04 .02
- ❑ 188 Rodney Carter .04 .02
- ❑ 189 Dwayne Woodruff .04 .02
- ❑ 190 Keith Willis .04 .02
- ❑ 191 Jerry Olsavsky .04 .02
- ❑ 192 Mark Stock .04 .02
- ❑ 193 Sacks Leaders .04 .02
  Chris Doleman
  Lee Williams
- ❑ 194 Leonard Smith .04 .02
- ❑ 195 Darryl Talley .04 .02
- ❑ 196 Mark Kelso .04 .02
- ❑ 197 Kent Hull .04 .02
- ❑ 198 Nate Odomes RC .10 .05
- ❑ 199 Pete Metzelaars .04 .02
- ❑ 200 Don Beebe .10 .05
- ❑ 201 Ray Bentley .04 .02
- ❑ 202 Steve Tasker .10 .05
- ❑ 203 Scott Norwood .04 .02
- ❑ 204 Andre Reed .25 .11
- ❑ 205 Bruce Smith .25 .11
- ❑ 206 Thurman Thomas .25 .11
- ❑ 207 Jim Kelly .25 .11
- ❑ 208 Cornelius Bennett .10 .05
- ❑ 209 Shane Conlan .04 .02
- ❑ 210 Larry Kinnebrew .04 .02
- ❑ 211 Jeff Alm RC .04 .02
- ❑ 212 Robert Lyles .04 .02
- ❑ 213 Bubba McDowell .04 .02
- ❑ 214 Mike Munchak .04 .02
- ❑ 215 Bruce Matthews .10 .05
- ❑ 216 Warren Moon .25 .11
- ❑ 217 Drew Hill .04 .02
- ❑ 218 Ray Childress .04 .02
- ❑ 219 Steve Brown .04 .02
- ❑ 220 Alonzo Highsmith .04 .02
- ❑ 221 Allen Pinkett .04 .02
- ❑ 222 Sean Jones .10 .05
- ❑ 223 Johnny Meads .04 .02
- ❑ 224 John Grimsley .04 .02
- ❑ 225 Haywood Jeffires RC .25 .11
- ❑ 226 Curtis Duncan .04 .02
- ❑ 227 Greg Montgomery RC .04 .02
- ❑ 228 Ernest Givins .10 .05
- ❑ 229 Passing Leaders .30 .14
  Joe Montana
  Boomer Esiason
- ❑ 230 Robert Massey .04 .02
- ❑ 231 John Fourcade .04 .02
- ❑ 232 Dalton Hilliard .04 .02
- ❑ 233 Vaughan Johnson .04 .02
- ❑ 234 Hoby Brenner .04 .02
- ❑ 235 Pat Swilling .10 .05
- ❑ 236 Kevin Haverdink .04 .02
- ❑ 237 Bobby Hebert .04 .02
- ❑ 238 Sam Mills .10 .05
- ❑ 239 Eric Martin .04 .02
- ❑ 240 Lonzell Hill .04 .02
- ❑ 241 Steve Trapilo .04 .02
- ❑ 242 Rickey Jackson .10 .05
- ❑ 243 Craig Heyward .10 .05
- ❑ 244 Rueben Mayes .04 .02
- ❑ 245 Morten Andersen .04 .02
- ❑ 246 Percy Snow RC .04 .02
- ❑ 247 Pete Mandley .04 .02
- ❑ 248 Derrick Thomas .25 .11
- ❑ 249 Dan Saleaumua .04 .02
- ❑ 250 Todd McNair RC .04 .02
- ❑ 251 Leonard Griffin .04 .02
- ❑ 252 Jonathan Hayes .04 .02
- ❑ 253 Christian Okoye .04 .02
- ❑ 254 Albert Lewis .04 .02
- ❑ 255 Nick Lowery .04 .02
- ❑ 256 Kevin Ross .04 .02
- ❑ 257 Steve DeBerg UER .04 .02
  (Total 45,046,
  should be 25,046)
- ❑ 258 Stephone Paige .04 .02
- ❑ 259 James Saxon RC .04 .02
- ❑ 260 Herman Heard .04 .02
- ❑ 261 Deron Cherry .04 .02
- ❑ 262 Dino Hackett .04 .02
- ❑ 263 Neil Smith .25 .11
- ❑ 264 Steve Pelluer .04 .02
- ❑ 265 Eric Thomas .04 .02
- ❑ 266 Eric Ball .04 .02
- ❑ 267 Leon White .04 .02
- ❑ 268 Tim Krumrie .04 .02
- ❑ 269 Jason Buck .04 .02
- ❑ 270 Boomer Esiason .10 .05
- ❑ 271 Carl Zander .04 .02
- ❑ 272 Eddie Brown .04 .02
- ❑ 273 David Fulcher .04 .02
- ❑ 274 Tim McGee .04 .02
- ❑ 275 James Brooks .10 .05
- ❑ 276 Rickey Dixon RC .04 .02
- ❑ 277 Ickey Woods .04 .02
- ❑ 278 Anthony Munoz .10 .05
- ❑ 279 Rodney Holman .04 .02
- ❑ 280 Mike Alexander .04 .02
- ❑ 281 Mervyn Fernandez .04 .02
- ❑ 282 Steve Wisniewski .10 .05
- ❑ 283 Steve Smith .04 .02
- ❑ 284 Howie Long .10 .05
- ❑ 285 Bo Jackson .30 .14
- ❑ 286 Mike Dyal .04 .02
- ❑ 287 Thomas Benson .04 .02
- ❑ 288 Willie Gault .10 .05
- ❑ 289 Marcus Allen .25 .11
- ❑ 290 Greg Townsend .04 .02
- ❑ 291 Steve Beuerlein .10 .05
- ❑ 292 Scott Davis .04 .02
- ❑ 293 Eddie Anderson RC .04 .02
- ❑ 294 Terry McDaniel .04 .02
- ❑ 295 Tim Brown .25 .11
- ❑ 296 Bob Golic .04 .02
- ❑ 297 Jeff Jaeger RC .04 .02
- ❑ 298 Jeff George RC 1.00 .45
- ❑ 299 Chip Banks .04 .02
- ❑ 300 Andre Rison UER .25 .11
  (Photo actually
  Clarence Weathers)
- ❑ 301 Rohn Stark .04 .02
- ❑ 302 Keith Taylor .04 .02
- ❑ 303 Jack Trudeau .04 .02
- ❑ 304 Chris Hinton .04 .02
- ❑ 305 Ray Donaldson .04 .02
- ❑ 306 Jeff Herrod RC .04 .02
- ❑ 307 Clarence Verdin .04 .02
- ❑ 308 Jon Hand .04 .02
- ❑ 309 Bill Brooks .04 .02
- ❑ 310 Albert Bentley .04 .02
- ❑ 311 Mike Prior .04 .02
- ❑ 312 Pat Beach .04 .02
- ❑ 313 Eugene Daniel .04 .02
- ❑ 314 Duane Bickett .04 .02
- ❑ 315 Dean Biasucci .04 .02
- ❑ 316 Richmond Webb RC .04 .02
- ❑ 317 Jeff Cross .04 .02
- ❑ 318 Louis Oliver .04 .02
- ❑ 319 Sammie Smith .04 .02
- ❑ 320 Pete Stoyanovich .04 .02

❑ 321 John Offerdahl .04 .02
❑ 322 Ferrell Edmunds .04 .02
❑ 323 Dan Marino 1.25 .55
❑ 324 Andre Brown .04 .02
❑ 325 Reggie Roby .04 .02
❑ 326 Jarvis Williams .04 .02
❑ 327 Roy Foster .04 .02
❑ 328 Mark Clayton .10 .05
❑ 329 Brian Sochia .04 .02
❑ 330 Mark Duper .10 .05
❑ 331 T.J. Turner .04 .02
❑ 332 Jeff Uhlenhake .04 .02
❑ 333 Jim C.Jensen .04 .02
❑ 334 Cortez Kennedy RC .25 .11
❑ 335 Andy Heck .04 .02
❑ 336 Rufus Porter .04 .02
❑ 337 Brian Blades .10 .05
❑ 338 Dave Krieg .10 .05
❑ 339 John L. Williams .04 .02
❑ 340 David Wyman .04 .02
❑ 341 Paul Skansi RC .04 .02
❑ 342 Eugene Robinson .04 .02
❑ 343 Joe Nash .04 .02
❑ 344 Jacob Green .04 .02
❑ 345 Jeff Bryant .04 .02
❑ 346 Ruben Rodriguez .04 .02
❑ 347 Norm Johnson .04 .02
❑ 348 Darren Comeaux .04 .02
❑ 349 Andre Ware RC .10 .05
❑ 350 Richard Johnson .04 .02
❑ 351 Rodney Peete .10 .05
❑ 352 Barry Sanders 1.50 .70
❑ 353 Chris Spielman .25 .11
❑ 354 Eddie Murray .04 .02
❑ 355 Jerry Ball .04 .02
❑ 356 Mel Gray .10 .05
❑ 357 Eric Williams RC .04 .02
❑ 358 Robert Clark RC .04 .02
❑ 359 Jason Phillips .04 .02
❑ 360 Terry Taylor RC .04 .02
❑ 361 Bennie Blades .04 .02
❑ 362 Michael Cofer .04 .02
❑ 363 Jim Arnold .04 .02
❑ 364 Marc Spindler RC .04 .02
❑ 365 Jim Covert .04 .02
❑ 366 Jim Harbaugh .25 .11
❑ 367 Neal Anderson .10 .05
❑ 368 Mike Singletary .10 .05
❑ 369 John Roper .04 .02
❑ 370 Steve McMichael .10 .05
❑ 371 Dennis Gentry .04 .02
❑ 372 Brad Muster .04 .02
❑ 373 Ron Morris .04 .02
❑ 374 James Thornton .04 .02
❑ 375 Kevin Butler .04 .02
❑ 376 Richard Dent .10 .05
❑ 377 Dan Hampton .10 .05
❑ 378 Jay Hilgenberg .04 .02
❑ 379 Donnell Woolford .04 .02
❑ 380 Trace Armstrong .04 .02
❑ 381 Junior Seau RC 1.00 .45
❑ 382 Rod Bernstine .04 .02
❑ 383 Marion Butts .10 .05
❑ 384 Burt Grossman .04 .02
❑ 385 Darrin Nelson .04 .02
❑ 386 Leslie O'Neal .10 .05
❑ 387 Billy Joe Tolliver .04 .02
❑ 388 Courtney Hall .04 .02
❑ 389 Lee Williams .04 .02
❑ 390 Anthony Miller .25 .11
❑ 391 Gill Byrd .04 .02
❑ 392 Wayne Walker .04 .02
❑ 393 Billy Ray Smith .04 .02
❑ 394 Vencie Glenn .04 .02
❑ 395 Tim Spencer .04 .02
❑ 396 Gary Plummer .04 .02
❑ 397 Arthur Cox .04 .02
❑ 398 Jamie Holland .04 .02
❑ 399 Keith McCants RC .04 .02
❑ 400 Kevin Murphy .04 .02
❑ 401 Danny Peebles .04 .02
❑ 402 Mark Robinson .04 .02
❑ 403 Broderick Thomas .04 .02
❑ 404 Ron Hall .04 .02
❑ 405 Mark Carrier WR .25 .11
❑ 406 Paul Gruber .04 .02
❑ 407 Vinny Testaverde .10 .05
❑ 408 Bruce Hill .04 .02
❑ 409 Lars Tate .04 .02
❑ 410 Harry Hamilton .04 .02
❑ 411 Ricky Reynolds .04 .02
❑ 412 Donald Igwebuike .04 .02
❑ 413 Reuben Davis .04 .02
❑ 414 William Howard .04 .02
❑ 415 Winston Moss RC .04 .02
❑ 416 Chris Singleton RC .04 .02
❑ 417 Hart Lee Dykes .04 .02
❑ 418 Steve Grogan .10 .05
❑ 419 Bruce Armstrong .04 .02
❑ 420 Robert Perryman .04 .02
❑ 421 Andre Tippett .04 .02
❑ 422 Sammy Martin .04 .02
❑ 423 Stanley Morgan .04 .02
❑ 424 Cedric Jones .04 .02
❑ 425 Sean Farrell .04 .02
❑ 426 Marc Wilson .04 .02
❑ 427 John Stephens .04 .02
❑ 428 Eric Sievers RC .04 .02
❑ 429 Maurice Hurst RC .04 .02
❑ 430 Johnny Rembert .04 .02
❑ 431 Receiving Leaders .30 .14
Jerry Rice
Andre Reed
❑ 432 Eric Hill .04 .02
❑ 433 Gary Hogeboom .04 .02
❑ 434 Timm Rosenbach UER .04 .02
(Born 1967 in Everett,
Wa., should be 1966
in Missoula, Mont.)
❑ 435 Tim McDonald .04 .02
❑ 436 Rich Camarillo .04 .02
❑ 437 Luis Sharpe .04 .02
❑ 438 J.T. Smith .04 .02
❑ 439 Roy Green .10 .05
❑ 440 Ernie Jones RC .04 .02
❑ 441 Robert Awalt .04 .02
❑ 442 Vai Sikahema .04 .02
❑ 443 Joe Wolf .04 .02
❑ 444 Stump Mitchell .04 .02
❑ 445 David Galloway .04 .02
❑ 446 Ron Wolfley .04 .02
❑ 447 Freddie Joe Nunn .04 .02
❑ 448 Blair Thomas RC .10 .05
❑ 449 Jeff Lageman .04 .02
❑ 450 Tony Eason .04 .02
❑ 451 Erik McMillan .04 .02
❑ 452 Jim Sweeney .04 .02
❑ 453 Ken O'Brien .04 .02
❑ 454 Johnny Hector .04 .02
❑ 455 Jo Jo Townsell .04 .02
❑ 456 Roger Vick .04 .02
❑ 457 James Hasty .04 .02
❑ 458 Dennis Byrd RC .10 .05
❑ 459 Ron Stallworth .04 .02
❑ 460 Mickey Shuler .04 .02
❑ 461 Bobby Humphery .04 .02
❑ 462 Kyle Clifton .04 .02
❑ 463 Al Toon .10 .05
❑ 464 Freeman McNeil .04 .02
❑ 465 Pat Leahy .04 .02
❑ 466 Scott Case .04 .02
❑ 467 Shawn Collins .04 .02
❑ 468 Floyd Dixon .04 .02
❑ 469 Deion Sanders .50 .23
❑ 470 Tony Casillas .04 .02
❑ 471 Michael Haynes RC .25 .11
❑ 472 Chris Miller .25 .11
❑ 473 John Settle .04 .02
❑ 474 Aundray Bruce .04 .02
❑ 475 Gene Lang .04 .02
❑ 476 Tim Gordon RC .04 .02
❑ 477 Scott Fulhage .04 .02
❑ 478 Bill Fralic .04 .02
❑ 479 Jessie Tuggle RC .04 .02
❑ 480 Marcus Cotton .04 .02
❑ 481 Steve Walsh .10 .05
❑ 482 Troy Aikman .75 .35
❑ 483 Ray Horton .04 .02
❑ 484 Tony Tolbert RC .10 .05
❑ 485 Steve Folsom .04 .02
❑ 486 Ken Norton RC .25 .11
❑ 487 Kelvin Martin RC .04 .02
❑ 488 Jack Del Rio .04 .02
❑ 489 Daryl Johnston RC 1.00 .45
❑ 490 Bill Bates .10 .05
❑ 491 Jim Jeffcoat .04 .02
❑ 492 Vince Albritton .04 .02
❑ 493 Eugene Lockhart .04 .02
❑ 494 Mike Saxon .04 .02
❑ 495 James Dixon .04 .02
❑ 496 Willie Broughton .04 .02
❑ 497 Checklist 1-132 .04 .02
❑ 498 Checklist 133-264 .04 .02
❑ 499 Checklist 265-396 .04 .02
❑ 500 Checklist 397-528 .04 .02
❑ 501 Bears Team .10 .05
(Jim) Harbaugh
Eludes the Pursuit
❑ 502 Bengals Team .04 .02
Boomer (Esiason)
Studies the Defense
❑ 503 Bills Team .04 .02
(Shane) Conlan Calls
Defensive Scheme
❑ 504 Broncos Team .04 .02
(Melvin) Bratton
Breaks Away
❑ 505 Browns Team .04 .02
(Bernie) Kosar
Calls the Play
❑ 506 Buccaneers Team .04 .02
(Winston) Moss Assists
in Squeeze Play
❑ 507 Cardinals Team .04 .02
(Michael) Zordich
Saves the Day
❑ 508 Chargers Team .04 .02
(Lee) Williams
Plugs the Hole
❑ 509 Chiefs Team .04 .02
(Deron) Cherry
Applies The %%D~
❑ 510 Colts Team .04 .02
(Jack) Trudeau
Begins a Reverse
❑ 511 Cowboys Team .30 .14
(Troy) Aikman Directs
Ground Attack
❑ 512 Dolphins Team .04 .02
Double-Decker By
(Louis) Oliver
and (Jarvis) Williams
❑ 513 Eagles Team .04 .02
(Anthony) Toney
Bangs into the Line
❑ 514 Falcons Team .04 .02
(Jessie) Tuggle
Falls on Fumble
❑ 515 49ers Team .30 .14
(Joe) Montana To
(Roger) Craig,
A Winning Duo
❑ 516 Giants Team .04 .02
(Phil) Simms Likes
His O.J. (Anderson)
❑ 517 Jets Team .04 .02
A (James) Hasty Return
❑ 518 Lions Team .04 .02
(Bob) Gagliano Orchestrates
The Offense
❑ 519 Oilers Team .10 .05
(Warren) Moon
Scrambles to Daylight
❑ 520 Packers Team .04 .02
A Bit Of Packer "Majik"
❑ 521 Patriots Team .04 .02
(John) Stephens
Steams Ahead
❑ 522 Raiders Team .10 .05
Bo (Jackson)
Knows Yardage
❑ 523 Rams Team .04 .02
(Jim) Everett
Rolls Right
❑ 524 Redskins Team .04 .02
(Gerald) Riggs
Rumbles Downfield
❑ 525 Saints Team .04 .02

		MINT	NRMT
	(Sam) Mills Takes A Stand		
❑ 526	Seahawks Team (Grant) Feasel Sets To Snap	.04	.02
❑ 527	Steelers Team (Bubby) Brister Has a Clear Lane	.04	.02
❑ 528	Vikings Team (Rick) Fenney Spots Opening	.04	.02

1990 Topps Traded

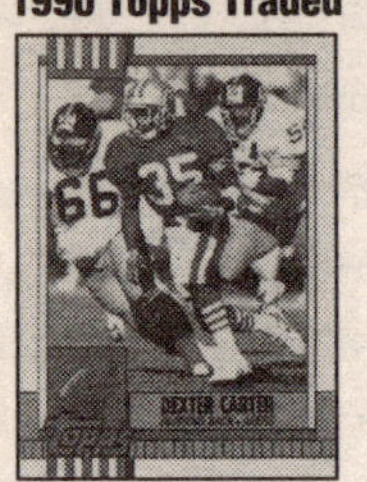

		MINT	NRMT
	COMP.FACT.SET (132)	15.00	6.75
❑ 1T	Gerald McNeil	.05	.02
❑ 2T	Andre Rison	.25	.11
❑ 3T	Steve Walsh	.25	.11
❑ 4T	Lorenzo White	.10	.05
❑ 5T	Max Montoya	.05	.02
❑ 6T	William Roberts RC	.05	.02
❑ 7T	Alonzo Highsmith	.05	.02
❑ 8T	Chris Hinton	.10	.05
❑ 9T	Stanley Morgan	.10	.05
❑ 10T	Mickey Shuler	.05	.02
❑ 11T	Bobby Humphery	.05	.02
❑ 12T	Gary Anderson RB	.05	.02
❑ 13T	Mike Tomczak	.10	.05
❑ 14T	Anthony Pleasant RC	.10	.05
❑ 15T	Walter Stanley	.05	.02
❑ 16T	Greg Bell	.05	.02
❑ 17T	Tony Martin RC	1.50	.70
❑ 18T	Terry Kinard	.05	.02
❑ 19T	Cris Carter	.50	.23
❑ 20T	James Wilder	.05	.02
❑ 21T	Jerry Kauric	.05	.02
❑ 22T	Irving Fryar	.25	.11
❑ 23T	Ken Harvey RC	.25	.11
❑ 24T	James Williams RC	.05	.02
❑ 25T	Ron Cox RC	.05	.02
❑ 26T	Andre Ware	.25	.11
❑ 27T	Emmitt Smith RC	10.00	4.50
❑ 28T	Junior Seau	.60	.25
❑ 29T	Mark Carrier RC	.25	.11
❑ 30T	Rodney Hampton	.25	.11
❑ 31T	Rob Moore RC	1.25	.55
❑ 32T	Bern Brostek RC	.05	.02
❑ 33T	Dexter Carter	.10	.05
❑ 34T	Blair Thomas	.10	.05
❑ 35T	Harold Green RC	.25	.11
❑ 36T	Darrell Thompson	.05	.02
❑ 37T	Eric Green RC	.25	.11
❑ 38T	Renaldo Turnbull RC	.25	.11
❑ 39T	Leroy Hoard RC	.50	.23
❑ 40T	Anthony Thompson RC	.10	.05
❑ 41T	Jeff George	.60	.25
❑ 42T	Alexander Wright RC	.05	.02
❑ 43T	Richmond Webb	.05	.02
❑ 44T	Cortez Kennedy	.25	.11
❑ 45T	Ray Agnew RC	.05	.02
❑ 46T	Percy Snow	.05	.02
❑ 47T	Chris Singleton	.05	.02
❑ 48T	James Francis RC	.10	.05
❑ 49T	Tony Bennett	.10	.05
❑ 50T	Reggie Cobb RC	.10	.05
❑ 51T	Barry Foster	.25	.11
❑ 52T	Ben Smith	.05	.02
❑ 53T	Anthony Smith RC	.25	.11
❑ 54T	Steve Christie RC	.05	.02
❑ 55T	Johnny Bailey RC	.10	.05
❑ 56T	Alan Grant RC	.05	.02
❑ 57T	Eric Floyd RC	.05	.02
❑ 58T	Robert Blackmon RC	.05	.02
❑ 59T	Brent Williams	.05	.02
❑ 60T	Raymond Clayborn	.05	.02
❑ 61T	Dave Duerson	.05	.02
❑ 62T	Derrick Fenner RC	.10	.05
❑ 63T	Ken Willis	.05	.02
❑ 64T	Brad Baxter RC	.10	.05
❑ 65T	Tony Paige	.05	.02
❑ 66T	Jay Schroeder	.05	.02
❑ 67T	Jim Breech	.05	.02
❑ 68T	Barry Word RC	.10	.05
❑ 69T	Anthony Dilweg	.05	.02
❑ 70T	Rich Gannon RC	5.00	2.20
❑ 71T	Stan Humphries RC	.25	.11
❑ 72T	Jay Novacek	.25	.11
❑ 73T	Tommy Kane RC	.05	.02
❑ 74T	Everson Walls	.05	.02
❑ 75T	Mike Rozier	.10	.05
❑ 76T	Robb Thomas	.05	.02
❑ 77T	Terance Mathis RC	2.00	.90
❑ 78T	LeRoy Irvin	.05	.02
❑ 79T	Jeff Donaldson	.05	.02
❑ 80T	Ethan Horton RC	.10	.05
❑ 81T	J.B. Brown RC	.05	.02
❑ 82T	Joe Kelly	.05	.02
❑ 83T	John Carney RC	.05	.02
❑ 84T	Dan Stryzinski RC	.05	.02
❑ 85T	John Kidd	.05	.02
❑ 86T	Al Smith	.10	.05
❑ 87T	Travis McNeal	.05	.02
❑ 88T	Reyna Thompson RC	.05	.02
❑ 89T	Rick Donnelly	.05	.02
❑ 90T	Marv Cook RC	.10	.05
❑ 91T	Mike Farr RC	.05	.02
❑ 92T	Daniel Stubbs	.05	.02
❑ 93T	Jeff Campbell RC	.05	.02
❑ 94T	Tim McKyer	.05	.02
❑ 95T	Ian Beckles RC	.05	.02
❑ 96T	Lemuel Stinson	.05	.02
❑ 97T	Frank Cornish	.05	.02
❑ 98T	Riki Ellison	.05	.02
❑ 99T	Jamie Mueller RC	.05	.02
❑ 100T	Brian Hansen	.05	.02
❑ 101T	Warren Powers RC	.05	.02
❑ 102T	Howard Cross RC	.05	.02
❑ 103T	Tim Grunhard RC	.05	.02
❑ 104T	Johnny Johnson RC	.25	.11
❑ 105T	Calvin Williams RC	.25	.11
❑ 106T	Keith McCants	.05	.02
❑ 107T	Lamar Lathon RC	.10	.05
❑ 108T	Steve Broussard RC	.10	.05
❑ 109T	Glenn Parker RC	.05	.02
❑ 110T	Alton Montgomery RC	.05	.02
❑ 111T	Jim McMahon	.10	.05
❑ 112T	Aaron Wallace RC	.05	.02
❑ 113T	Keith Sims RC	.05	.02
❑ 114T	Ervin Randle	.05	.02
❑ 115T	Walter Wilson	.05	.02
❑ 116T	Terry Wooden RC	.05	.02
❑ 117T	Bernard Clark	.05	.02
❑ 118T	Tony Stargell RC	.05	.02
❑ 119T	Jimmie Jones RC	.05	.02
❑ 120T	Andre Collins RC	.10	.05
❑ 121T	Ricky Proehl RC	.10	.05
❑ 122T	Darion Conner RC	.10	.05
❑ 123T	Jeff Rutledge	.05	.02
❑ 124T	Heath Sherman RC	.10	.05
❑ 125T	Tommie Agee RC	.05	.02
❑ 126T	Tory Epps RC	.05	.02
❑ 127T	Tommy Hodson RC	.05	.02
❑ 128T	Jessie Hester RC	.05	.02
❑ 129T	Alfred Oglesby RC	.05	.02
❑ 130T	Chris Chandler	.25	.11
❑ 131T	Fred Barnett RC	.25	.11
❑ 132T	Checklist 1-132	.05	.02

1991 Topps

		MINT	NRMT
	COMPLETE SET (660)	15.00	6.75
	COMP.FACT.SET (660)	15.00	6.75
❑ 1	Super Bowl XXV	.04	.02
❑ 2	Roger Craig HL	.10	.05
❑ 3	Derrick Thomas HL	.10	.05
❑ 4	Pete Stoyanovich HL	.04	.02
❑ 5	Ottis Anderson HL	.10	.05
❑ 6	Jerry Rice HL	.50	.23
❑ 7	Warren Moon HL	.10	.05
❑ 8	Leaders Passing Yards Warren Moon Jim Everett	.10	.05
❑ 9	Leaders Rushing Barry Sanders Thurman Thomas	.50	.23
❑ 10	Leaders Receiving Jerry Rice Haywood Jeffires	.30	.14
❑ 11	Leaders Interceptions Mark Carrier DB Richard Johnson	.04	.02
❑ 12	Leaders Sacks Derrick Thomas Charles Haley	.10	.05
❑ 13	Jumbo Elliott	.04	.02
❑ 14	Leonard Marshall	.04	.02
❑ 15	William Roberts	.04	.02
❑ 16	Lawrence Taylor	.25	.11
❑ 17	Mark Ingram	.10	.05
❑ 18	Rodney Hampton	.25	.11
❑ 19	Carl Banks	.04	.02
❑ 20	Ottis Anderson	.10	.05
❑ 21	Mark Collins	.04	.02
❑ 22	Pepper Johnson	.04	.02
❑ 23	Dave Meggett	.10	.05
❑ 24	Reyna Thompson	.04	.02
❑ 25	Stephen Baker	.04	.02
❑ 26	Mike Fox	.04	.02
❑ 27	Maurice Carthon UER (Herschel Walker mis- spelled as Herschell)	.04	.02
❑ 28	Jeff Hostetler	.25	.11
❑ 29	Greg Jackson RC	.04	.02
❑ 30	Sean Landeta	.04	.02
❑ 31	Bart Oates	.04	.02
❑ 32	Phil Simms	.10	.05
❑ 33	Erik Howard	.04	.02
❑ 34	Myron Guyton	.04	.02
❑ 35	Mark Bavaro	.04	.02
❑ 36	Jarrod Bunch RC	.04	.02
❑ 37	Will Wolford	.04	.02
❑ 38	Ray Bentley	.04	.02
❑ 39	Nate Odomes	.04	.02
❑ 40	Scott Norwood	.04	.02
❑ 41	Darryl Talley	.04	.02
❑ 42	Carwell Gardner	.04	.02
❑ 43	James Lofton	.10	.05
❑ 44	Shane Conlan	.04	.02
❑ 45	Steve Tasker	.10	.05
❑ 46	James Williams	.04	.02
❑ 47	Kent Hull	.04	.02
❑ 48	Al Edwards	.04	.02
❑ 49	Frank Reich	.10	.05
❑ 50	Leon Seals	.04	.02
❑ 51	Keith McKeller	.04	.02
❑ 52	Thurman Thomas	.25	.11
❑ 53	Leonard Smith	.04	.02

❑ 54 Andre Reed .10 .05
❑ 55 Kenneth Davis .04 .02
❑ 56 Jeff Wright RC .04 .02
❑ 57 Jamie Mueller .04 .02
❑ 58 Jim Ritcher .04 .02
❑ 59 Bruce Smith .25 .11
❑ 60 Ted Washington RC .04 .02
❑ 61 Guy McIntyre .04 .02
❑ 62 Michael Carter .04 .02
❑ 63 Pierce Holt .04 .02
❑ 64 Darryl Pollard .04 .02
❑ 65 Mike Sherrard .04 .02
❑ 66 Dexter Carter .04 .02
❑ 67 Bubba Paris .04 .02
❑ 68 Harry Sydney .04 .02
❑ 69 Tom Rathman .04 .02
❑ 70 Jesse Sapolu .04 .02
❑ 71 Mike Cofer .04 .02
❑ 72 Keith DeLong .04 .02
❑ 73 Joe Montana 1.25 .55
❑ 74 Bill Romanowski .04 .02
❑ 75 John Taylor .10 .05
❑ 76 Brent Jones .25 .11
❑ 77 Harris Barton .04 .02
❑ 78 Charles Haley .10 .05
❑ 79 Eric Davis .04 .02
❑ 80 Kevin Fagan .04 .02
❑ 81 Jerry Rice .75 .35
❑ 82 Dave Waymer .04 .02
❑ 83 Todd Marinovich RC .04 .02
❑ 84 Steve Smith .04 .02
❑ 85 Tim Brown .25 .11
❑ 86 Ethan Horton .04 .02
❑ 87 Marcus Allen .25 .11
❑ 88 Terry McDaniel .04 .02
❑ 89 Thomas Benson .04 .02
❑ 90 Roger Craig .10 .05
❑ 91 Don Mosebar .04 .02
❑ 92 Aaron Wallace .04 .02
❑ 93 Eddie Anderson .04 .02
❑ 94 Willie Gault .10 .05
❑ 95 Howie Long .10 .05
❑ 96 Jay Schroeder .04 .02
❑ 97 Ronnie Lott .10 .05
❑ 98 Bob Golic .04 .02
❑ 99 Bo Jackson .30 .14
❑ 100 Max Montoya .04 .02
❑ 101 Scott Davis .04 .02
❑ 102 Greg Townsend .04 .02
❑ 103 Garry Lewis .04 .02
❑ 104 Mervyn Fernandez .04 .02
❑ 105 Steve Wisniewski UER .04 .02
(Back has drafted, should be traded to)
❑ 106 Jeff Jaeger .04 .02
❑ 107 Nick Bell RC .04 .02
❑ 108 Mark Dennis RC .04 .02
❑ 109 Jarvis Williams .04 .02
❑ 110 Mark Clayton .10 .05
❑ 111 Harry Galbreath .04 .02
❑ 112 Dan Marino 1.25 .55
❑ 113 Louis Oliver .04 .02
❑ 114 Pete Stoyanovich .04 .02
❑ 115 Ferrell Edmunds .04 .02
❑ 116 Jeff Cross .04 .02
❑ 117 Richmond Webb .04 .02
❑ 118 Jim C. Jensen .04 .02
❑ 119 Keith Sims .04 .02
❑ 120 Mark Duper .10 .05
❑ 121 Shawn Lee RC .04 .02
❑ 122 Reggie Roby .04 .02
❑ 123 Jeff Uhlenhake .04 .02
❑ 124 Sammie Smith .04 .02
❑ 125 John Offerdahl .04 .02
❑ 126 Hugh Green .04 .02
❑ 127 Tony Paige .04 .02
❑ 128 David Griggs .04 .02
❑ 129 J.B. Brown .04 .02
❑ 130 Harvey Williams RC .25 .11
❑ 131 John Alt .04 .02
❑ 132 Albert Lewis .04 .02
❑ 133 Robb Thomas .04 .02
❑ 134 Neil Smith .25 .11
❑ 135 Stephone Paige .04 .02
❑ 136 Nick Lowery .04 .02
❑ 137 Steve DeBerg .04 .02
❑ 138 Rich Baldinger RC .04 .02
❑ 139 Percy Snow .04 .02
❑ 140 Kevin Porter .04 .02
❑ 141 Chris Martin .04 .02
❑ 142 Deron Cherry .04 .02
❑ 143 Derrick Thomas .25 .11
❑ 144 Tim Grunhard .04 .02
❑ 145 Todd McNair .04 .02
❑ 146 David Szott .04 .02
❑ 147 Dan Saleaumua .04 .02
❑ 148 Jonathan Hayes .04 .02
❑ 149 Christian Okoye .04 .02
❑ 150 Dino Hackett .04 .02
❑ 151 Bryan Barker RC .04 .02
❑ 152 Kevin Ross .04 .02
❑ 153 Barry Word .04 .02
❑ 154 Stan Thomas .04 .02
❑ 155 Brad Muster .04 .02
❑ 156 Donnell Woolford .04 .02
❑ 157 Neal Anderson .10 .05
❑ 158 Jim Covert .04 .02
❑ 159 Jim Harbaugh .25 .11
❑ 160 Shaun Gayle .04 .02
❑ 161 William Perry .10 .05
❑ 162 Ron Morris .04 .02
❑ 163 Mark Bortz .04 .02
❑ 164 James Thornton .04 .02
❑ 165 Ron Rivera .04 .02
❑ 166 Kevin Butler .04 .02
❑ 167 Jay Hilgenberg .04 .02
❑ 168 Peter Tom Willis .04 .02
❑ 169 Johnny Bailey .04 .02
❑ 170 Ron Cox .04 .02
❑ 171 Keith Van Horne .04 .02
❑ 172 Mark Carrier DB .10 .05
❑ 173 Richard Dent .10 .05
❑ 174 Wendell Davis .04 .02
❑ 175 Trace Armstrong .04 .02
❑ 176 Mike Singletary .10 .05
❑ 177 Chris Zorich RC .25 .11
❑ 178 Gerald Riggs .04 .02
❑ 179 Jeff Bostic .04 .02
❑ 180 Kurt Gouveia RC .04 .02
❑ 181 Stan Humphries .25 .11
❑ 182 Chip Lohmiller .04 .02
❑ 183 Raleigh McKenzie RC .04 .02
❑ 184 Alvin Walton .04 .02
❑ 185 Earnest Byner .04 .02
❑ 186 Markus Koch .04 .02
❑ 187 Art Monk .10 .05
❑ 188 Ed Simmons .04 .02
❑ 189 Bobby Wilson RC .04 .02
❑ 190 Charles Mann .04 .02
❑ 191 Darrell Green .04 .02
❑ 192 Mark Rypien .10 .05
❑ 193 Ricky Sanders .04 .02
❑ 194 Jim Lachey .04 .02
❑ 195 Martin Mayhew .04 .02
❑ 196 Gary Clark .25 .11
❑ 197 Wilber Marshall .04 .02
❑ 198 Darryl Grant .04 .02
❑ 199 Don Warren .04 .02
❑ 200 Ricky Ervins RC UER .10 .05
(Front has Chiefs, back has Redskins)
❑ 201 Eric Allen .04 .02
❑ 202 Anthony Toney .04 .02
❑ 203 Ben Smith UER .04 .02
(Front CB, back S)
❑ 204 David Alexander .04 .02
❑ 205 Jerome Brown .04 .02
❑ 206 Mike Golic .04 .02
❑ 207 Roger Ruzek .04 .02
❑ 208 Andre Waters .04 .02
❑ 209 Fred Barnett .25 .11
❑ 210 Randall Cunningham .25 .11
❑ 211 Mike Schad .04 .02
❑ 212 Reggie White .25 .11
❑ 213 Mike Bellamy .04 .02
❑ 214 Jeff Feagles RC .04 .02
❑ 215 Wes Hopkins .04 .02
❑ 216 Clyde Simmons .04 .02
❑ 217 Keith Byars .04 .02
❑ 218 Seth Joyner .10 .05
❑ 219 Byron Evans .04 .02
❑ 220 Keith Jackson .10 .05
❑ 221 Calvin Williams .10 .05
❑ 222 Mike Dumas RC .04 .02
❑ 223 Ray Childress .04 .02
❑ 224 Ernest Givins .10 .05
❑ 225 Lamar Lathon .04 .02
❑ 226 Greg Montgomery .04 .02
❑ 227 Mike Munchak .04 .02
❑ 228 Al Smith .04 .02
❑ 229 Bubba McDowell .04 .02
❑ 230 Haywood Jeffires .10 .05
❑ 231 Drew Hill .04 .02
❑ 232 William Fuller .10 .05
❑ 233 Warren Moon .25 .11
❑ 234 Doug Smith RC** .04 .02
❑ 235 Cris Dishman RC .04 .02
❑ 236 Teddy Garcia RC .04 .02
❑ 237 Richard Johnson RC .04 .02
❑ 238 Bruce Matthews .10 .05
❑ 239 Gerald McNeil .04 .02
❑ 240 Johnny Meads .04 .02
❑ 241 Curtis Duncan .04 .02
❑ 242 Sean Jones .10 .05
❑ 243 Lorenzo White .04 .02
❑ 244 Rob Carpenter RC .04 .02
❑ 245 Bruce Reimers .04 .02
❑ 246 Ickey Woods .04 .02
❑ 247 Lewis Billups .04 .02
❑ 248 Boomer Esiason .10 .05
❑ 249 Tim Krumrie .04 .02
❑ 250 David Fulcher .04 .02
❑ 251 Jim Breech .04 .02
❑ 252 Mitchell Price RC .04 .02
❑ 253 Carl Zander .04 .02
❑ 254 Barney Bussey RC .04 .02
❑ 255 Leon White .04 .02
❑ 256 Eddie Brown .04 .02
❑ 257 James Francis .04 .02
❑ 258 Harold Green .10 .05
❑ 259 Anthony Munoz .10 .05
❑ 260 James Brooks .10 .05
❑ 261 Kevin Walker RC UER .04 .02
(Hometown should be West Milford Township)
❑ 262 Bruce Kozerski .04 .02
❑ 263 David Grant .04 .02
❑ 264 Tim McGee .04 .02
❑ 265 Rodney Holman .04 .02
❑ 266 Dan McGwire RC .04 .02
❑ 267 Andy Heck .04 .02
❑ 268 Dave Krieg .10 .05
❑ 269 David Wyman .04 .02
❑ 270 Robert Blackmon .04 .02
❑ 271 Grant Feasel .04 .02
❑ 272 Patrick Hunter RC .04 .02
❑ 273 Travis McNeal .04 .02
❑ 274 John L. Williams .04 .02
❑ 275 Tony Woods .04 .02
❑ 276 Derrick Fenner .04 .02
❑ 277 Jacob Green .04 .02
❑ 278 Brian Blades .10 .05
❑ 279 Eugene Robinson .04 .02
❑ 280 Terry Wooden .04 .02
❑ 281 Jeff Bryant .04 .02
❑ 282 Norm Johnson .04 .02
❑ 283 Joe Nash UER .04 .02
Front DT, Back NT)
❑ 284 Rick Donnelly .04 .02
❑ 285 Chris Warren .25 .11
❑ 286 Tommy Kane .04 .02
❑ 287 Cortez Kennedy .25 .11
❑ 288 Ernie Mills RC .10 .05
❑ 289 Dermontti Dawson .04 .02
❑ 290 Tunch Ilkin .04 .02
❑ 291 Tim Worley .04 .02
❑ 292 David Little .04 .02
❑ 293 Gary Anderson K .04 .02
❑ 294 Chris Calloway .04 .02
❑ 295 Carnell Lake .04 .02
❑ 296 Dan Stryzinski .04 .02
❑ 297 Rod Woodson .25 .11
❑ 298 John Jackson RC .04 .02
❑ 299 Bubby Brister .04 .02
❑ 300 Thomas Everett .04 .02
❑ 301 Merril Hoge .04 .02
❑ 302 Eric Green .04 .02
❑ 303 Greg Lloyd .25 .11

❑ 304 Gerald Williams .04 .02
❑ 305 Bryan Hinkle .04 .02
❑ 306 Keith Willis .04 .02
❑ 307 Louis Lipps .04 .02
❑ 308 Donald Evans .04 .02
❑ 309 D.J. Johnson .04 .02
❑ 310 Wesley Carroll RC .04 .02
❑ 311 Eric Martin .04 .02
❑ 312 Brett Maxie .04 .02
❑ 313 Rickey Jackson .04 .02
❑ 314 Robert Massey .04 .02
❑ 315 Pat Swilling .10 .05
❑ 316 Morten Andersen .04 .02
❑ 317 Toi Cook RC .04 .02
❑ 318 Sam Mills .04 .02
❑ 319 Steve Walsh .04 .02
❑ 320 Tommy Barnhardt RC .04 .02
❑ 321 Vince Buck .04 .02
❑ 322 Joel Hilgenberg .04 .02
❑ 323 Rueben Mayes .04 .02
❑ 324 Renaldo Turnbull .04 .02
❑ 325 Brett Perriman .25 .11
❑ 326 Vaughan Johnson .04 .02
❑ 327 Gill Fenerty .04 .02
❑ 328 Stan Brock .04 .02
❑ 329 Dalton Hilliard .04 .02
❑ 330 Hoby Brenner .04 .02
❑ 331 Craig Heyward .10 .05
❑ 332 Jon Hand .04 .02
❑ 333 Duane Bickett .04 .02
❑ 334 Jessie Hester .04 .02
❑ 335 Rohn Stark .04 .02
❑ 336 Zefross Moss .04 .02
❑ 337 Bill Brooks .04 .02
❑ 338 Clarence Verdin .04 .02
❑ 339 Mike Prior .04 .02
❑ 340 Chip Banks .04 .02
❑ 341 Dean Biasucci .04 .02
❑ 342 Ray Donaldson .04 .02
❑ 343 Jeff Herrod .04 .02
❑ 344 Donnell Thompson .04 .02
❑ 345 Chris Goode .04 .02
❑ 346 Eugene Daniel .04 .02
❑ 347 Pat Beach .04 .02
❑ 348 Keith Taylor .04 .02
❑ 349 Jeff George .25 .11
❑ 350 Tony Siragusa RC .10 .05
❑ 351 Randy Dixon .04 .02
❑ 352 Albert Bentley .04 .02
❑ 353 Russell Maryland RC .25 .11
❑ 354 Mike Saxon .04 .02
❑ 355 Godfrey Myles RC UER .04 .02
(Misspelled Miles
on card front)
❑ 356 Mark Stepnoski RC .10 .05
❑ 357 James Washington RC .04 .02
❑ 358 Jay Novacek .25 .11
❑ 359 Kelvin Martin .04 .02
❑ 360 Emmitt Smith UER 2.00 .90
(Played for Florida,
not Florida State)
❑ 361 Jim Jeffcoat .04 .02
❑ 362 Alexander Wright .04 .02
❑ 363 James Dixon UER .04 .02
(Photo is not Dixon
on card front)
❑ 364 Alonzo Highsmith .04 .02
❑ 365 Daniel Stubbs .04 .02
❑ 366 Jack Del Rio .04 .02
❑ 367 Mark Tuinei RC .04 .02
❑ 368 Michael Irvin .25 .11
❑ 369 John Gesek RC .04 .02
❑ 370 Ken Willis .04 .02
❑ 371 Troy Aikman .75 .35
❑ 372 Jimmie Jones .04 .02
❑ 373 Nate Newton .10 .05
❑ 374 Issiac Holt .04 .02
❑ 375 Alvin Harper RC .25 .11
❑ 376 Todd Kalis .04 .02
❑ 377 Wade Wilson .10 .05
❑ 378 Joey Browner .04 .02
❑ 379 Chris Doleman .04 .02
❑ 380 Hassan Jones .04 .02
❑ 381 Henry Thomas .04 .02
❑ 382 Darrell Fullington .04 .02
❑ 383 Steve Jordan .04 .02
❑ 384 Gary Zimmerman .04 .02
❑ 385 Ray Berry .04 .02
❑ 386 Cris Carter .50 .23
❑ 387 Mike Merriweather .04 .02
❑ 388 Carl Lee .04 .02
❑ 389 Keith Millard .04 .02
❑ 390 Reggie Rutland .04 .02
❑ 391 Anthony Carter .10 .05
❑ 392 Mark Dusbabek .04 .02
❑ 393 Kirk Lowdermilk .04 .02
❑ 394 Al Noga UER .04 .02
(Card says DT,
should be DE)
❑ 395 Herschel Walker .10 .05
❑ 396 Randall McDaniel .04 .02
❑ 397 Herman Moore RC 2.00 .90
❑ 398 Eddie Murray .04 .02
❑ 399 Lomas Brown .04 .02
❑ 400 Marc Spindler .04 .02
❑ 401 Bennie Blades .04 .02
❑ 402 Kevin Glover .04 .02
❑ 403 Aubrey Matthews RC .04 .02
❑ 404 Michael Cofer .04 .02
❑ 405 Robert Clark .04 .02
❑ 406 Eric Andolsek .04 .02
❑ 407 William White .04 .02
❑ 408 Rodney Peete .10 .05
❑ 409 Mel Gray .10 .05
❑ 410 Jim Arnold .04 .02
❑ 411 Jeff Campbell .04 .02
❑ 412 Chris Spielman .10 .05
❑ 413 Jerry Ball .04 .02
❑ 414 Dan Owens .04 .02
❑ 415 Barry Sanders 1.50 .70
❑ 416 Andre Ware .10 .05
❑ 417 Stanley Richard RC .04 .02
❑ 418 Gill Byrd .04 .02
❑ 419 John Kidd .04 .02
❑ 420 Sam Seale .04 .02
❑ 421 Gary Plummer .04 .02
❑ 422 Anthony Miller .10 .05
❑ 423 Ronnie Harmon .04 .02
❑ 424 Frank Cornish .04 .02
❑ 425 Marion Butts .10 .05
❑ 426 Leo Goeas .04 .02
❑ 427 Junior Seau .25 .11
❑ 428 Courtney Hall .04 .02
❑ 429 Leslie O'Neal .10 .05
❑ 430 Martin Bayless .04 .02
❑ 431 John Carney .04 .02
❑ 432 Lee Williams .04 .02
❑ 433 Arthur Cox .04 .02
❑ 434 Burt Grossman .04 .02
❑ 435 Nate Lewis RC .04 .02
❑ 436 Rod Bernstine .04 .02
❑ 437 Henry Rolling RC .04 .02
❑ 438 Billy Joe Tolliver .04 .02
❑ 439 Vinnie Clark RC .04 .02
❑ 440 Brian Noble .04 .02
❑ 441 Charles Wilson .04 .02
❑ 442 Don Majkowski .04 .02
❑ 443 Tim Harris .04 .02
❑ 444 Scott Stephen RC .04 .02
❑ 445 Perry Kemp .04 .02
❑ 446 Darrell Thompson .04 .02
❑ 447 Chris Jacke .04 .02
❑ 448 Mark Murphy .04 .02
❑ 449 Ed West .04 .02
❑ 450 LeRoy Butler .10 .05
❑ 451 Keith Woodside .04 .02
❑ 452 Tony Bennett .10 .05
❑ 453 Mark Lee .04 .02
❑ 454 James Campen RC .04 .02
❑ 455 Robert Brown .04 .02
❑ 456 Sterling Sharpe .25 .11
❑ 457A Tony Mandarich ERR 2.50 1.10
(Broncos listed as team)
❑ 457B Tony Mandarich COR .04 .02
(Packers listed as team)
❑ 458 Johnny Holland .04 .02
❑ 459 Matt Brock RC .04 .02
❑ 460A Esera Tuaolo RC ERR .04 .02
(See also 462; no 1991
NFL Draft Pick logo)
❑ 460B Esera Tuaolo RC COR .04 .02
(See also 462; 1991 NFL
Draft Pick logo on front)
❑ 461 Freeman McNeil .04 .02
❑ 462 Terance Mathis UER .25 .11
(Card numbered in-
correctly as 460)
❑ 463 Rob Moore .25 .11
❑ 464 Darrell Davis RC .04 .02
❑ 465 Chris Burkett .04 .02
❑ 466 Jeff Criswell .04 .02
❑ 467 Tony Stargell .04 .02
❑ 468 Ken O'Brien .04 .02
❑ 469 Erik McMillan .04 .02
❑ 470 Jeff Lageman UER .04 .02
(Front DE, back LB)
❑ 471 Pat Leahy .04 .02
❑ 472 Dennis Byrd .04 .02
❑ 473 Jim Sweeney .04 .02
❑ 474 Brad Baxter .04 .02
❑ 475 Joe Kelly .04 .02
❑ 476 Al Toon .10 .05
❑ 477 Joe Prokop .04 .02
❑ 478 Mark Boyer .04 .02
❑ 479 Kyle Clifton .04 .02
❑ 480 James Hasty .04 .02
❑ 481 Browning Nagle RC .04 .02
❑ 482 Gary Anderson RB .04 .02
❑ 483 Mark Carrier WR .25 .11
❑ 484 Ricky Reynolds .04 .02
❑ 485 Bruce Hill .04 .02
❑ 486 Steve Christie .04 .02
❑ 487 Paul Gruber .04 .02
❑ 488 Jesse Anderson .04 .02
❑ 489 Reggie Cobb .04 .02
❑ 490 Harry Hamilton .04 .02
❑ 491 Vinny Testaverde .10 .05
❑ 492 Mark Royals RC .04 .02
❑ 493 Keith McCants .04 .02
❑ 494 Ron Hall .04 .02
❑ 495 Ian Beckles .04 .02
❑ 496 Mark Robinson .04 .02
❑ 497 Reuben Davis .04 .02
❑ 498 Wayne Haddix .04 .02
❑ 499 Kevin Murphy .04 .02
❑ 500 Eugene Marve .04 .02
❑ 501 Broderick Thomas .04 .02
❑ 502 Eric Swann RC UER .25 .11
(Draft pick logo miss-
ing from card front)
❑ 503 Ernie Jones .04 .02
❑ 504 Rich Camarillo .04 .02
❑ 505 Tim McDonald .04 .02
❑ 506 Freddie Joe Nunn .04 .02
❑ 507 Tim Jorden RC .04 .02
❑ 508 Johnny Johnson .04 .02
❑ 509 Eric Hill .04 .02
❑ 510 Derek Kennard .04 .02
❑ 511 Ricky Proehl .04 .02
❑ 512 Bill Lewis .04 .02
❑ 513 Roy Green .04 .02
❑ 514 Anthony Bell .04 .02
❑ 515 Timm Rosenbach .04 .02
❑ 516 Jim Wahler RC .04 .02
❑ 517 Anthony Thompson .04 .02
❑ 518 Ken Harvey .10 .05
❑ 519 Luis Sharpe .04 .02
❑ 520 Walter Reeves .04 .02
❑ 521 Lonnie Young .04 .02
❑ 522 Rod Saddler .04 .02
❑ 523 Todd Lyght RC .04 .02
❑ 524 Alvin Wright .04 .02
❑ 525 Flipper Anderson .04 .02
❑ 526 Jackie Slater .04 .02
❑ 527 Damone Johnson RC .04 .02
❑ 528 Cleveland Gary .04 .02
❑ 529 Mike Piel .04 .02
❑ 530 Buford McGee .04 .02
❑ 531 Michael Stewart .04 .02
❑ 532 Jim Everett .10 .05
❑ 533 Mike Wilcher .04 .02
❑ 534 Irv Pankey .04 .02
❑ 535 Bern Brostek .04 .02
❑ 536 Henry Ellard .10 .05
❑ 537 Doug Smith .04 .02
❑ 538 Larry Kelm .04 .02
❑ 539 Pat Terrell .04 .02
❑ 540 Tom Newberry .04 .02

❑ 541	Jerry Gray	.04	.02
❑ 542	Kevin Greene	.25	.11
❑ 543	Duval Love RC	.04	.02
❑ 544	Frank Stams	.04	.02
❑ 545	Mike Croel RC	.04	.02
❑ 546	Mark Jackson	.04	.02
❑ 547	Greg Kragen	.04	.02
❑ 548	Karl Mecklenburg	.04	.02
❑ 549	Simon Fletcher	.04	.02
❑ 550	Bobby Humphrey	.04	.02
❑ 551	Ken Lanier	.04	.02
❑ 552	Vance Johnson	.04	.02
❑ 553	Ron Holmes	.04	.02
❑ 554	John Elway	1.25	.55
❑ 555	Melvin Bratton	.04	.02
❑ 556	Dennis Smith	.04	.02
❑ 557	Ricky Nattiel	.04	.02
❑ 558	Clarence Kay	.04	.02
❑ 559	Michael Brooks	.04	.02
❑ 560	Mike Horan	.04	.02
❑ 561	Warren Powers	.04	.02
❑ 562	Keith Kartz	.04	.02
❑ 563	Shannon Sharpe	.50	.23
❑ 564	Wymon Henderson	.04	.02
❑ 565	Steve Atwater	.04	.02
❑ 566	David Treadwell	.04	.02
❑ 567	Bruce Pickens RC	.04	.02
❑ 568	Jessie Tuggle	.04	.02
❑ 569	Chris Hinton	.04	.02
❑ 570	Keith Jones	.04	.02
❑ 571	Bill Fralic	.04	.02
❑ 572	Mike Rozier	.04	.02
❑ 573	Scott Fulhage	.04	.02
❑ 574	Floyd Dixon	.04	.02
❑ 575	Andre Rison	.10	.05
❑ 576	Darion Conner	.04	.02
❑ 577	Brian Jordan	.10	.05
❑ 578	Michael Haynes	.25	.11
❑ 579	Oliver Barnett	.04	.02
❑ 580	Shawn Collins	.04	.02
❑ 581	Tim Green	.04	.02
❑ 582	Deion Sanders	.40	.18
❑ 583	Mike Kenn	.04	.02
❑ 584	Mike Gann	.04	.02
❑ 585	Chris Miller	.10	.05
❑ 586	Tory Epps	.04	.02
❑ 587	Steve Broussard	.04	.02
❑ 588	Gary Wilkins	.04	.02
❑ 589	Eric Turner RC	.10	.05
❑ 590	Thane Gash	.04	.02
❑ 591	Clay Matthews	.10	.05
❑ 592	Mike Johnson	.04	.02
❑ 593	Raymond Clayborn	.04	.02
❑ 594	Leroy Hoard	.10	.05
❑ 595	Reggie Langhorne	.04	.02
❑ 596	Mike Baab	.04	.02
❑ 597	Anthony Pleasant	.04	.02
❑ 598	David Grayson	.04	.02
❑ 599	Rob Burnett RC	.10	.05
❑ 600	Frank Minnifield	.04	.02
❑ 601	Gregg Rakoczy	.04	.02
❑ 602	Eric Metcalf UER (1989 stats given twice)	.25	.11
❑ 603	Paul Farren	.04	.02
❑ 604	Brian Brennan	.04	.02
❑ 605	Tony Jones	.04	.02
❑ 606	Stephen Braggs	.04	.02
❑ 607	Kevin Mack	.04	.02
❑ 608	Pat Harlow RC	.04	.02
❑ 609	Marv Cook	.04	.02
❑ 610	John Stephens	.04	.02
❑ 611	Ed Reynolds	.04	.02
❑ 612	Tim Goad	.04	.02
❑ 613	Chris Singleton	.04	.02
❑ 614	Bruce Armstrong	.04	.02
❑ 615	Tommy Hodson	.04	.02
❑ 616	Sammy Martin	.04	.02
❑ 617	Andre Tippett	.04	.02
❑ 618	Johnny Rembert	.04	.02
❑ 619	Maurice Hurst	.04	.02
❑ 620	Vincent Brown	.04	.02
❑ 621	Ray Agnew	.04	.02
❑ 622	Ronnie Lippett	.04	.02
❑ 623	Greg McMurtry	.04	.02
❑ 624	Brent Williams	.04	.02
❑ 625	Jason Staurovsky	.04	.02
❑ 626	Marvin Allen	.04	.02
❑ 627	Hart Lee Dykes	.04	.02
❑ 628	Atlanta Falcons Team: (Keith) Jones Jumps for Yardage	.04	.02
❑ 629	Buffalo Bills Team: (Jeff) Wright Goes for a Block	.04	.02
❑ 630	Chicago Bears Team: (Jim) Harbaugh Makes Like a Halfback	.10	.05
❑ 631	Cincinnati Bengals Team: (Stanford) Jennings Cuts Through Hole	.04	.02
❑ 632	Cleveland Browns Team: (Eric) Metcalf Makes a Return	.04	.02
❑ 633	Dallas Cowboys Team: (Kelvin) Martin Makes a Move	.04	.02
❑ 634	Denver Broncos Team: (Shannon) Sharpe Into the Wedge	.04	.02
❑ 635	Detroit Lions Team: (Rodney) Peete Hunted by a Bear (Mike Singletary)	.04	.02
❑ 636	Green Bay Packers Team: (Don) Majkowski Orchestrates Some Magic	.04	.02
❑ 637	Houston Oilers Team: (Warren) Moon Monitors the Action	.10	.05
❑ 638	Indianapolis Colts Team: (Jeff) George Releases Just in Time	.04	.02
❑ 639	Kansas City Chiefs Team: (Christian) Okoye Powers Ahead	.04	.02
❑ 640	Los Angeles Raiders Team: (Marcus) Allen Crosses the Plane	.10	.05
❑ 641	Los Angeles Rams Team: (Jim) Everett Connects With Soft Touch	.04	.02
❑ 642	Miami Dolphins Team: (Pete) Stoyanovich Kicks It Through	.04	.02
❑ 643	Minnesota Vikings Team: (Rich) Gannon Loads Cannon	.10	.05
❑ 644	New Eng. Patriots Team: (John) Stephens Gets Stood Up	.04	.02
❑ 645	New Orleans Saints Team: (Gill) Fenerty Finds Opening	.04	.02
❑ 646	New York Giants Team: (Maurice) Carthon Inches Ahead	.04	.02
❑ 647	New York Jets Team: (Pat) Leahy Perfect on Extra Point	.04	.02
❑ 648	Philadelphia Eagles Team: (Randall) Cunningham Calls Own Play for TD	.04	.02
❑ 649	Phoenix Cardinals Team: (Bill) Lewis Provides the Protection	.04	.02
❑ 650	Pittsburgh Steelers Team: (Bubby) Brister Eyes Downfield Attack	.04	.02
❑ 651	San Diego Chargers Team: (John) Friesz Finds the Passing Lane	.04	.02
❑ 652	San Francisco 49ers Team: (Dexter) Carter Follows Rathman's Block	.04	.02
❑ 653	Seattle Seahawks Team: (Derrick) Fenner With Fancy Footwork	.04	.02
❑ 654	Tampa Bay Buccaneers Team: (Reggie) Cobb Hurdles His Way to First Down	.04	.02
❑ 655	Washington Redskins Team: (Earnest) Byner Cuts Back to Follow Block	.04	.02
❑ 656	Checklist 1-132	.04	.02
❑ 657	Checklist 132-264	.04	.02
❑ 658	Checklist 265-396	.04	.02
❑ 659	Checklist 397-528	.04	.02
❑ 660	Checklist 529-660	.04	.02

1992 Topps

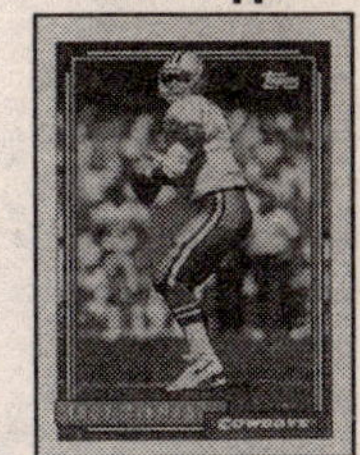

	MINT	NRMT
COMPLETE SET (759)	40.00	18.00
COMP.FACT.SET (680)	35.00	16.00
COMP.SERIES 1 (330)	15.00	6.75
COMP.SERIES 2 (330)	15.00	6.75
COMP.HIGH SER.(99)	10.00	4.50
COMP.FACT.HIGH SET (113)	10.00	4.50

❑ 1	Tim McGee	.05	.02
❑ 2	Rich Camarillo	.05	.02
❑ 3	Anthony Johnson	.10	.05
❑ 4	Larry Kelm	.05	.02
❑ 5	Irving Fryar	.10	.05
❑ 6	Joey Browner	.05	.02
❑ 7	Michael Walter	.05	.02
❑ 8	Cortez Kennedy	.10	.05
❑ 9	Reyna Thompson	.05	.02
❑ 10	John Friesz	.10	.05
❑ 11	Leroy Hoard	.10	.05
❑ 12	Steve McMichael	.10	.05
❑ 13	Marvin Washington	.05	.02
❑ 14	Clyde Simmons	.05	.02
❑ 15	Stephone Paige	.05	.02
❑ 16	Mike Utley	.10	.05
❑ 17	Tunch Ilkin	.05	.02
❑ 18	Lawrence Dawsey	.10	.05
❑ 19	Vance Johnson	.05	.02
❑ 20	Bryce Paup	.25	.11
❑ 21	Jeff Wright	.05	.02
❑ 22	Gill Fenerty	.05	.02
❑ 23	Lamar Lathon	.05	.02
❑ 24	Danny Copeland	.05	.02
❑ 25	Marcus Allen	.25	.11
❑ 26	Tim Green	.05	.02
❑ 27	Pete Stoyanovich	.05	.02
❑ 28	Alvin Harper	.10	.05
❑ 29	Roy Foster	.05	.02
❑ 30	Eugene Daniel	.05	.02
❑ 31	Luis Sharpe	.05	.02
❑ 32	Terry Wooden	.05	.02
❑ 33	Jim Breech	.05	.02
❑ 34	Randy Hilliard RC	.05	.02
❑ 35	Roman Phifer	.05	.02
❑ 36	Erik Howard	.05	.02
❑ 37	Chris Singleton	.05	.02
❑ 38	Matt Stover	.05	.02
❑ 39	Tim Irwin	.05	.02
❑ 40	Karl Mecklenburg	.05	.02
❑ 41	Joe Phillips	.05	.02
❑ 42	Bill Jones RC	.05	.02
❑ 43	Mark Carrier DB	.05	.02
❑ 44	George Jamison	.05	.02
❑ 45	Rob Taylor	.05	.02
❑ 46	Jeff Jaeger	.05	.02
❑ 47	Don Majkowski	.05	.02
❑ 48	Al Edwards	.05	.02
❑ 49	Curtis Duncan	.05	.02

❑ 50 Sam Mills .05 .02
❑ 51 Terance Mathis .10 .05
❑ 52 Brian Mitchell .10 .05
❑ 53 Mike Pritchard .10 .05
❑ 54 Calvin Williams .10 .05
❑ 55 Hardy Nickerson .10 .05
❑ 56 Nate Newton .10 .05
❑ 57 Steve Wallace .05 .02
❑ 58 John Offerdahl .05 .02
❑ 59 Aeneas Williams .10 .05
❑ 60 Lee Johnson .05 .02
❑ 61 Ricardo McDonald RC .05 .02
❑ 62 David Richards .05 .02
❑ 63 Paul Gruber .05 .02
❑ 64 Greg McMurtry .05 .02
❑ 65 Jay Hilgenberg .05 .02
❑ 66 Tim Grunhard .05 .02
❑ 67 Dwayne White RC .05 .02
❑ 68 Don Beebe .05 .02
❑ 69 Simon Fletcher .05 .02
❑ 70 Warren Moon .25 .11
❑ 71 Chris Jacke .05 .02
❑ 72 Steve Wisniewski UER .05 .02
(Traded to Raiders, not drafted by them)
❑ 73 Mike Cofer .05 .02
❑ 74 Tim Johnson UER .05 .02
(No position listed on back)
❑ 75 T.J. Turner .05 .02
❑ 76 Scott Case .05 .02
❑ 77 Michael Jackson .10 .05
❑ 78 Jon Hand .05 .02
❑ 79 Stan Brock .05 .02
❑ 80 Robert Blackmon .05 .02
❑ 81 D.J. Johnson .05 .02
❑ 82 Damone Johnson .05 .02
❑ 83 Marc Spindler .05 .02
❑ 84 Larry Brown DB .05 .02
❑ 85 Ray Berry .05 .02
❑ 86 Andre Waters .05 .02
❑ 87 Carlos Huerta .05 .02
❑ 88 Brad Muster .05 .02
❑ 89 Chuck Cecil .05 .02
❑ 90 Nick Lowery .05 .02
❑ 91 Cornelius Bennett .10 .05
❑ 92 Jessie Tuggle .05 .02
❑ 93 Mark Schlereth RC .05 .02
❑ 94 Vestee Jackson .05 .02
❑ 95 Eric Bieniemy .05 .02
❑ 96 Jeff Hostetler .10 .05
❑ 97 Ken Lanier .05 .02
❑ 98 Wayne Haddix .05 .02
❑ 99 Lorenzo White .05 .02
❑ 100 Mervyn Fernandez .05 .02
❑ 101 Brent Williams .05 .02
❑ 102 Ian Beckles .05 .02
❑ 103 Harris Barton .05 .02
❑ 104 Edgar Bennett RC .25 .11
❑ 105 Mike Pitts .05 .02
❑ 106 Fuad Reveiz .05 .02
❑ 107 Vernon Turner .05 .02
❑ 108 Tracy Hayworth RC .05 .02
❑ 109 Checklist 1-110 .05 .02
❑ 110 Tom Waddle .05 .02
❑ 111 Fred Stokes .05 .02
❑ 112 Howard Ballard .05 .02
❑ 113 David Szott .05 .02
❑ 114 Tim McKyer .05 .02
❑ 115 Kyle Clifton .05 .02
❑ 116 Tony Bennett .05 .02
❑ 117 Joel Hilgenberg .05 .02
❑ 118 Dwayne Harper .05 .02
❑ 119 Mike Baab .05 .02
❑ 120 Mark Clayton .10 .05
❑ 121 Eric Swann .10 .05
❑ 122 Neil O'Donnell .25 .11
❑ 123 Mike Munchak .05 .02
❑ 124 Howie Long .10 .05
❑ 125 John Elway UER 1.25 .55
(Card says 6-year vet, should be 9)
❑ 126 Joe Prokop .05 .02
❑ 127 Pepper Johnson .05 .02
❑ 128 Richard Dent .10 .05
❑ 129 Robert Porcher RC .10 .05
❑ 130 Earnest Byner .05 .02
❑ 131 Kent Hull .05 .02
❑ 132 Mike Merriweather .05 .02
❑ 133 Scott Fulhage .05 .02
❑ 134 Kevin Porter .05 .02
❑ 135 Tony Casillas .05 .02
❑ 136 Dean Biasucci .05 .02
❑ 137 Ben Smith .05 .02
❑ 138 Bruce Kozerski .05 .02
❑ 139 Jeff Campbell .05 .02
❑ 140 Kevin Greene .25 .11
❑ 141 Gary Plummer .05 .02
❑ 142 Vincent Brown .05 .02
❑ 143 Ron Hall .05 .02
❑ 144 Louie Aguiar RC .05 .02
❑ 145 Mark Duper .05 .02
❑ 146 Jesse Sapolu .05 .02
❑ 147 Jeff Gossett .05 .02
❑ 148 Brian Noble .05 .02
❑ 149 Derek Russell .05 .02
❑ 150 Carlton Bailey RC .10 .05
❑ 151 Kelly Goodburn .05 .02
❑ 152 Audray McMillian UER .05 .02
(Misspelled Audrey)
❑ 153 Neal Anderson .05 .02
❑ 154 Bill Maas .05 .02
❑ 155 Rickey Jackson .05 .02
❑ 156 Chris Miller .10 .05
❑ 157 Darren Comeaux .05 .02
❑ 158 David Williams .05 .02
❑ 159 Rich Gannon .25 .11
❑ 160 Kevin Mack .05 .02
❑ 161 Jim Arnold .05 .02
❑ 162 Reggie White .25 .11
❑ 163 Leonard Russell .10 .05
❑ 164 Doug Smith .05 .02
❑ 165 Tony Mandarich .05 .02
❑ 166 Greg Lloyd .25 .11
❑ 167 Jumbo Elliott .05 .02
❑ 168 Jonathan Hayes .05 .02
❑ 169 Jim Ritcher .05 .02
❑ 170 Mike Kenn .05 .02
❑ 171 James Washington .05 .02
❑ 172 Tim Harris .05 .02
❑ 173 James Thornton .05 .02
❑ 174 John Brandes RC .05 .02
❑ 175 Fred McAfee RC .05 .02
❑ 176 Henry Rolling .05 .02
❑ 177 Tony Paige .05 .02
❑ 178 Jay Schroeder .05 .02
❑ 179 Jeff Herrod .05 .02
❑ 180 Emmitt Smith 1.50 .70
❑ 181 Wymon Henderson .05 .02
❑ 182 Rob Moore .10 .05
❑ 183 Robert Wilson .05 .02
❑ 184 Michael Zordich RC .05 .02
❑ 185 Jim Harbaugh .25 .11
❑ 186 Vince Workman .10 .05
❑ 187 Ernest Givins .10 .05
❑ 188 Herschel Walker .10 .05
❑ 189 Dan Fike .05 .02
❑ 190 Seth Joyner .10 .05
❑ 191 Steve Young .60 .25
❑ 192 Dennis Gibson .05 .02
❑ 193 Darryl Talley .05 .02
❑ 194 Emile Harry .05 .02
❑ 195 Bill Fralic .05 .02
❑ 196 Michael Stewart .05 .02
❑ 197 James Francis .05 .02
❑ 198 Jerome Henderson .05 .02
❑ 199 John L. Williams .05 .02
❑ 200 Rod Woodson .25 .11
❑ 201 Mike Farr .05 .02
❑ 202 Greg Montgomery .05 .02
❑ 203 Andre Collins .05 .02
❑ 204 Scott Miller .05 .02
❑ 205 Clay Matthews .10 .05
❑ 206 Ethan Horton .05 .02
❑ 207 Rich Miano .05 .02
❑ 208 Chris Mims RC .10 .05
❑ 209 Anthony Morgan .05 .02
❑ 210 Rodney Hampton .25 .11
❑ 211 Chris Hinton .05 .02
❑ 212 Esera Tuaolo .05 .02
❑ 213 Shane Conlan .05 .02
❑ 214 John Carney .05 .02
❑ 215 Kenny Walker .05 .02
❑ 216 Scott Radecic .05 .02
❑ 217 Chris Martin .05 .02
❑ 218 Checklist 111-220 UER .05 .02
(152 Audray McMillian misspelled Audrey)
❑ 219 Wesley Carroll UER .05 .02
(Stats say 1st round pick, bio correctly has 2nd)
❑ 220 Bill Romanowski .05 .02
❑ 221 Reggie Cobb .05 .02
❑ 222 Alfred Anderson .05 .02
❑ 223 Cleveland Gary .05 .02
❑ 224 Eddie Blake RC .05 .02
❑ 225 Chris Spielman .10 .05
❑ 226 John Roper .05 .02
❑ 227 George Thomas RC .05 .02
❑ 228 Jeff Faulkner .05 .02
❑ 229 Chip Lohmiller UER .05 .02
(RFK Stadium not identified on back)
❑ 230 Hugh Millen .05 .02
❑ 231 Ray Horton .05 .02
❑ 232 James Campen .05 .02
❑ 233 Howard Cross .05 .02
❑ 234 Keith McKeller .05 .02
❑ 235 Dino Hackett .05 .02
❑ 236 Jerome Brown .05 .02
❑ 237 Andy Heck .05 .02
❑ 238 Rodney Holman .05 .02
❑ 239 Bruce Matthews .05 .02
❑ 240 Jeff Lageman .05 .02
❑ 241 Bobby Hebert .05 .02
❑ 242 Gary Anderson K .05 .02
❑ 243 Mark Bortz .05 .02
❑ 244 Rich Moran .05 .02
❑ 245 Jeff Uhlenhake .05 .02
❑ 246 Ricky Sanders .05 .02
❑ 247 Clarence Kay .05 .02
❑ 248 Ed King .05 .02
❑ 249 Eddie Anderson .05 .02
❑ 250 Amp Lee RC .05 .02
❑ 251 Norm Johnson .05 .02
❑ 252 Michael Carter .05 .02
❑ 253 Felix Wright .05 .02
❑ 254 Leon Seals .05 .02
❑ 255 Nate Lewis .05 .02
❑ 256 Kevin Call .05 .02
❑ 257 Darryl Henley .05 .02
❑ 258 Jon Vaughn .05 .02
❑ 259 Matt Bahr .05 .02
❑ 260 Johnny Johnson .05 .02
❑ 261 Ken Norton .25 .11
❑ 262 Wendell Davis .05 .02
❑ 263 Eugene Robinson .05 .02
❑ 264 David Treadwell .05 .02
❑ 265 Michael Haynes .10 .05
❑ 266 Robb Thomas .05 .02
❑ 267 Nate Odomes .05 .02
❑ 268 Martin Mayhew .05 .02
❑ 269 Perry Kemp .05 .02
❑ 270 Jerry Ball .05 .02
❑ 271 Tommy Vardell RC .10 .05
❑ 272 Ernie Mills .05 .02
❑ 273 Mo Lewis .05 .02
❑ 274 Roger Ruzek .05 .02
❑ 275 Steve Smith .05 .02
❑ 276 Bo Orlando RC .05 .02
❑ 277 Louis Oliver .05 .02
❑ 278 Toi Cook .05 .02
❑ 279 Eddie Brown .05 .02
❑ 280 Keith McCants .05 .02
❑ 281 Rob Burnett .05 .02
❑ 282 Keith DeLong .05 .02
❑ 283 Stan Thomas UER .05 .02
(9th line bio notes, the word of is in caps)
❑ 284 Robert Brown .05 .02
❑ 285 John Alt .05 .02
❑ 286 Randy Dixon .05 .02
❑ 287 Siran Stacy RC .05 .02
❑ 288 Ray Agnew .05 .02
❑ 289 Darion Conner .05 .02
❑ 290 Kirk Lowdermilk .05 .02
❑ 291 Greg Jackson .05 .02

❑ 292 Ken Harvey .05 .02
❑ 293 Jacob Green .05 .02
❑ 294 Mark Tuinei .05 .02
❑ 295 Mark Rypien .05 .02
❑ 296 Gerald Robinson RC .05 .02
❑ 297 Broderick Thompson .05 .02
❑ 298 Doug Widell .05 .02
❑ 299 Carwell Gardner .05 .02
❑ 300 Barry Sanders 1.50 .70
❑ 301 Eric Metcalf .10 .05
❑ 302 Eric Thomas .05 .02
❑ 303 Terrell Buckley RC .05 .02
❑ 304 Byron Evans .05 .02
❑ 305 Johnny Hector .05 .02
❑ 306 Steve Broussard .05 .02
❑ 307 Gene Atkins .05 .02
❑ 308 Terry McDaniel .05 .02
❑ 309 Charles McRae .05 .02
❑ 310 Jim Lachey .05 .02
❑ 311 Pat Harlow .05 .02
❑ 312 Kevin Butler .05 .02
❑ 313 Scott Stephen .05 .02
❑ 314 Dermontti Dawson .05 .02
❑ 315 Johnny Meads .05 .02
❑ 316 Checklist 221-330 .05 .02
❑ 317 Aaron Craver .05 .02
❑ 318 Michael Brooks .05 .02
❑ 319 Guy McIntyre .05 .02
❑ 320 Thurman Thomas .25 .11
❑ 321 Courtney Hall .05 .02
❑ 322 Dan Saleaumua .05 .02
❑ 323 Vinson Smith RC .05 .02
❑ 324 Steve Jordan .05 .02
❑ 325 Walter Reeves .05 .02
❑ 326 Erik Kramer .10 .05
❑ 327 Duane Bickett .05 .02
❑ 328 Tom Newberry .05 .02
❑ 329 John Kasay .05 .02
❑ 330 Dave Meggett .10 .05
❑ 331 Kevin Ross .05 .02
❑ 332 Keith Hamilton RC .10 .05
❑ 333 Dwight Stone .05 .02
❑ 334 Mel Gray .10 .05
❑ 335 Harry Galbreath .05 .02
❑ 336 William Perry .10 .05
❑ 337 Brian Blades .10 .05
❑ 338 Randall McDaniel .05 .02
❑ 339 Pat Coleman RC .05 .02
❑ 340 Michael Irvin .25 .11
❑ 341 Checklist 331-440 .05 .02
❑ 342 Chris Mohr .05 .02
❑ 343 Greg Davis .05 .02
❑ 344 Dave Cadigan .05 .02
❑ 345 Art Monk .10 .05
❑ 346 Tim Goad .05 .02
❑ 347 Vinnie Clark .05 .02
❑ 348 David Fulcher .05 .02
❑ 349 Craig Heyward .10 .05
❑ 350 Ronnie Lott .10 .05
❑ 351 Dexter Carter .05 .02
❑ 352 Mark Jackson .05 .02
❑ 353 Brian Jordan .10 .05
❑ 354 Ray Donaldson .05 .02
❑ 355 Jim Price .05 .02
❑ 356 Rod Bernstine .05 .02
❑ 357 Tony Mayberry RC .05 .02
❑ 358 Richard Brown RC .05 .02
❑ 359 David Alexander .05 .02
❑ 360 Haywood Jeffires .10 .05
❑ 361 Henry Thomas .05 .02
❑ 362 Jeff Graham .25 .11
❑ 363 Don Warren .05 .02
❑ 364 Scott Davis .05 .02
❑ 365 Harlon Barnett .05 .02
❑ 366 Mark Collins .05 .02
❑ 367 Rick Tuten .05 .02
❑ 368 Lonnie Marts RC UER .05 .02
(Injured Reserved should be Reserve)
❑ 369 Dennis Smith .05 .02
❑ 370 Steve Tasker .10 .05
❑ 371 Robert Massey .05 .02
❑ 372 Ricky Reynolds .05 .02
❑ 373 Alvin Wright .05 .02
❑ 374 Kelvin Martin .05 .02
❑ 375 Vince Buck .05 .02
❑ 376 John Kidd .05 .02
❑ 377 William White .05 .02
❑ 378 Bryan Cox .10 .05
❑ 379 Jamie Dukes RC .05 .02
❑ 380 Anthony Munoz .10 .05
❑ 381 Mark Gunn RC .05 .02
❑ 382 Keith Henderson .05 .02
❑ 383 Charles Wilson .05 .02
❑ 384 Shawn McCarthy RC .05 .02
❑ 385 Ernie Jones .05 .02
❑ 386 Nick Bell .05 .02
❑ 387 Derrick Walker .05 .02
❑ 388 Mark Stepnoski .10 .05
❑ 389 Broderick Thomas .05 .02
❑ 390 Reggie Roby .05 .02
❑ 391 Bubba McDowell .05 .02
❑ 392 Eric Martin .05 .02
❑ 393 Toby Caston RC .05 .02
❑ 394 Bern Brostek .05 .02
❑ 395 Christian Okoye .05 .02
❑ 396 Frank Minnifield .05 .02
❑ 397 Mike Golic .05 .02
❑ 398 Grant Feasel .05 .02
❑ 399 Michael Ball .05 .02
❑ 400 Mike Croel .05 .02
❑ 401 Maury Buford .05 .02
❑ 402 Jeff Bostic UER .05 .02
(Signed as free agent in 1980, not 1984)
❑ 403 Sean Landeta .05 .02
❑ 404 Terry Allen .25 .11
❑ 405 Donald Evans .05 .02
❑ 406 Don Mosebar .05 .02
❑ 407 D.J. Dozier .05 .02
❑ 408 Bruce Pickens .05 .02
❑ 409 Jim Dombrowski .05 .02
❑ 410 Deron Cherry .05 .02
❑ 411 Richard Johnson .05 .02
❑ 412 Alexander Wright .05 .02
❑ 413 Tom Rathman .05 .02
❑ 414 Mark Dennis .05 .02
❑ 415 Phil Hansen .05 .02
❑ 416 Lonnie Young .05 .02
❑ 417 Burt Grossman .05 .02
❑ 418 Tony Covington .05 .02
❑ 419 John Stephens .05 .02
❑ 420 Jim Everett .10 .05
❑ 421 Johnny Holland .05 .02
❑ 422 Mike Barber RC .05 .02
❑ 423 Carl Lee .05 .02
❑ 424 Craig Patterson RC .05 .02
❑ 425 Greg Townsend .05 .02
❑ 426 Brett Perriman .25 .11
❑ 427 Morten Andersen .05 .02
❑ 428 John Gesek .05 .02
❑ 429 Bryan Barker .05 .02
❑ 430 John Taylor .10 .05
❑ 431 Donnell Woolford .05 .02
❑ 432 Ron Holmes .05 .02
❑ 433 Lee Williams .05 .02
❑ 434 Alfred Oglesby .05 .02
❑ 435 Jarrod Bunch .05 .02
❑ 436 Carlton Haselrig RC .05 .02
❑ 437 Rufus Porter .05 .02
❑ 438 Rohn Stark .05 .02
❑ 439 Tony Jones .05 .02
❑ 440 Andre Rison .10 .05
❑ 441 Eric Hill .05 .02
❑ 442 Jesse Solomon .05 .02
❑ 443 Jackie Slater .05 .02
❑ 444 Donnie Elder .05 .02
❑ 445 Brett Maxie .05 .02
❑ 446 Max Montoya .05 .02
❑ 447 Will Wolford .05 .02
❑ 448 Craig Taylor .05 .02
❑ 449 Jimmie Jones .05 .02
❑ 450 Anthony Carter .10 .05
❑ 451 Brian Bollinger RC .05 .02
❑ 452 Checklist 441-550 .05 .02
❑ 453 Brad Edwards .05 .02
❑ 454 Gene Chilton RC .05 .02
❑ 455 Eric Allen .05 .02
❑ 456 William Roberts .05 .02
❑ 457 Eric Green .05 .02
❑ 458 Irv Eatman .05 .02
❑ 459 Derrick Thomas .25 .11
❑ 460 Tommy Kane .05 .02
❑ 461 LeRoy Butler .05 .02
❑ 462 Oliver Barnett .05 .02
❑ 463 Anthony Smith .05 .02
❑ 464 Cris Dishman .05 .02
❑ 465 Pat Terrell .05 .02
❑ 466 Greg Kragen .05 .02
❑ 467 Rodney Peete .10 .05
❑ 468 Willie Drewrey .05 .02
❑ 469 Jim Wilks .05 .02
❑ 470 Vince Newsome .05 .02
❑ 471 Chris Gardocki .05 .02
❑ 472 Chris Chandler .25 .11
❑ 473 George Thornton .05 .02
❑ 474 Albert Lewis .05 .02
❑ 475 Kevin Glover .05 .02
❑ 476 Joe Bowden RC .05 .02
❑ 477 Harry Sydney .05 .02
❑ 478 Bob Golic .05 .02
❑ 479 Tony Zendejas .05 .02
❑ 480 Brad Baxter .05 .02
❑ 481 Steve Beuerlein .05 .02
❑ 482 Mark Higgs .05 .02
❑ 483 Drew Hill .05 .02
❑ 484 Bryan Millard .05 .02
❑ 485 Mark Kelso .05 .02
❑ 486 David Grant .05 .02
❑ 487 Gary Zimmerman .05 .02
❑ 488 Leonard Marshall .05 .02
❑ 489 Keith Jackson .10 .05
❑ 490 Sterling Sharpe .25 .11
❑ 491 Ferrell Edmunds .05 .02
❑ 492 Wilber Marshall .05 .02
❑ 493 Charles Haley .10 .05
❑ 494 Riki Ellison .05 .02
❑ 495 Bill Brooks .05 .02
❑ 496 Bill Hawkins .05 .02
❑ 497 Erik Williams .05 .02
❑ 498 Leon Searcy RC .10 .05
❑ 499 Mike Horan .05 .02
❑ 500 Pat Swilling .10 .05
❑ 501 Maurice Hurst .05 .02
❑ 502 William Fuller .10 .05
❑ 503 Tim Newton .05 .02
❑ 504 Lorenzo Lynch .05 .02
❑ 505 Tim Barnett .05 .02
❑ 506 Tom Thayer .05 .02
❑ 507 Chris Burkett .05 .02
❑ 508 Ronnie Harmon .05 .02
❑ 509 James Brooks .10 .05
❑ 510 Bennie Blades .05 .02
❑ 511 Roger Craig .10 .05
❑ 512 Tony Woods .05 .02
❑ 513 Greg Lewis .05 .02
❑ 514 Erric Pegram .10 .05
❑ 515 Elvis Patterson .05 .02
❑ 516 Jeff Cross .05 .02
❑ 517 Myron Guyton .05 .02
❑ 518 Jay Novacek .10 .05
❑ 519 Leo Barker RC .05 .02
❑ 520 Keith Byars .05 .02
❑ 521 Dalton Hilliard .05 .02
❑ 522 Ted Washington .05 .02
❑ 523 Dexter McNabb RC .05 .02
❑ 524 Frank Reich .10 .05
❑ 525 Henry Ellard .10 .05
❑ 526 Barry Foster .10 .05
❑ 527 Barry Word .05 .02
❑ 528 Gary Anderson RB .05 .02
❑ 529 Reggie Rutland .05 .02
❑ 530 Stephen Baker .05 .02
❑ 531 John Flannery .05 .02
❑ 532 Steve Wright .05 .02
❑ 533 Eric Sanders .05 .02
❑ 534 Bob Whitfield RC .05 .02
❑ 535 Gaston Green .05 .02
❑ 536 Anthony Pleasant .05 .02
❑ 537 Jeff Bryant .05 .02
❑ 538 Jarvis Williams .05 .02
❑ 539 Jim Morrissey .05 .02
❑ 540 Andre Tippett .05 .02
❑ 541 Gill Byrd .05 .02
❑ 542 Raleigh McKenzie .05 .02
❑ 543 Jim Sweeney .05 .02
❑ 544 David Lutz .05 .02
❑ 545 Wayne Martin .05 .02

	No.	Player	Mint	Nrmt
❑	546	Karl Wilson	.05	.02
❑	547	Pierce Holt	.05	.02
❑	548	Doug Smith	.05	.02
❑	549	Nolan Harrison RC	.05	.02
❑	550	Freddie Joe Nunn	.05	.02
❑	551	Eric Moore	.05	.02
❑	552	Cris Carter	.50	.23
❑	553	Kevin Gogan	.05	.02
❑	554	Harold Green	.05	.02
❑	555	Kenneth Davis	.05	.02
❑	556	Travis McNeal	.05	.02
❑	557	Jim C. Jensen	.05	.02
❑	558	Willie Green	.05	.02
❑	559	Scott Galbraith RC UER (Drafted in 1990, not 1989)	.05	.02
❑	560	Louis Lipps	.05	.02
❑	561	Matt Brock	.05	.02
❑	562	Mike Prior	.05	.02
❑	563	Checklist 551-660	.05	.02
❑	564	Robert Delpino	.05	.02
❑	565	Vinny Testaverde	.10	.05
❑	566	Willie Gault	.10	.05
❑	567	Quinn Early	.10	.05
❑	568	Eric Moten	.05	.02
❑	569	Lance Smith	.05	.02
❑	570	Darrell Green	.05	.02
❑	571	Moe Gardner	.05	.02
❑	572	Steve Atwater	.05	.02
❑	573	Ray Childress	.05	.02
❑	574	Dave Krieg	.10	.05
❑	575	Bruce Armstrong	.05	.02
❑	576	Fred Barnett	.25	.11
❑	577	Don Griffin	.05	.02
❑	578	David Brandon RC	.05	.02
❑	579	Robert Young	.05	.02
❑	580	Keith Van Horne	.05	.02
❑	581	Jeff Criswell	.05	.02
❑	582	Lewis Tillman	.05	.02
❑	583	Bubby Brister	.05	.02
❑	584	Aaron Wallace	.05	.02
❑	585	Chris Doleman	.05	.02
❑	586	Marty Carter RC	.05	.02
❑	587	Chris Warren	.25	.11
❑	588	David Griggs	.05	.02
❑	589	Darrell Thompson	.05	.02
❑	590	Marion Butts	.05	.02
❑	591	Scott Norwood	.05	.02
❑	592	Lomas Brown	.05	.02
❑	593	Daryl Johnston	.25	.11
❑	594	Alonzo Mitz RC	.05	.02
❑	595	Tommy Barnhardt	.05	.02
❑	596	Tim Jorden	.05	.02
❑	597	Neil Smith	.25	.11
❑	598	Todd Marinovich	.05	.02
❑	599	Sean Jones	.10	.05
❑	600	Clarence Verdin	.05	.02
❑	601	Trace Armstrong	.05	.02
❑	602	Steve Bono RC	.25	.11
❑	603	Mark Ingram	.05	.02
❑	604	Flipper Anderson	.05	.02
❑	605	James Jones	.05	.02
❑	606	Al Noga	.05	.02
❑	607	Rick Bryan	.05	.02
❑	608	Eugene Lockhart	.05	.02
❑	609	Charles Mann	.05	.02
❑	610	James Hasty	.05	.02
❑	611	Jeff Feagles	.05	.02
❑	612	Tim Brown	.25	.11
❑	613	David Little	.05	.02
❑	614	Keith Sims	.05	.02
❑	615	Kevin Murphy	.05	.02
❑	616	Ray Crockett	.05	.02
❑	617	Jim Jeffcoat	.05	.02
❑	618	Patrick Hunter	.05	.02
❑	619	Keith Kartz	.05	.02
❑	620	Peter Tom Willis	.05	.02
❑	621	Vaughan Johnson	.05	.02
❑	622	Shawn Jefferson	.05	.02
❑	623	Anthony Thompson	.05	.02
❑	624	John Rienstra	.05	.02
❑	625	Don Maggs	.05	.02
❑	626	Todd Lyght	.05	.02
❑	627	Brent Jones	.10	.05
❑	628	Todd McNair	.05	.02
❑	629	Winston Moss	.05	.02
❑	630	Mark Carrier WR	.10	.05
❑	631	Dan Owens	.05	.02
❑	632	Sammie Smith UER (Old team front, correct new team back; acquired via trade, not draft)	.05	.02
❑	633	James Lofton	.10	.05
❑	634	Paul McJulien RC	.05	.02
❑	635	Tony Tolbert	.05	.02
❑	636	Carnell Lake	.05	.02
❑	637	Gary Clark	.25	.11
❑	638	Brian Washington	.05	.02
❑	639	Jessie Hester	.05	.02
❑	640	Doug Riesenberg	.05	.02
❑	641	Joe Walter RC	.05	.02
❑	642	John Rade	.05	.02
❑	643	Wes Hopkins	.05	.02
❑	644	Kelly Stouffer	.05	.02
❑	645	Marv Cook	.05	.02
❑	646	Ken Clarke	.05	.02
❑	647	Bobby Humphrey UER (Old team front, correct new team back; acquired via trade, not draft)	.05	.02
❑	648	Tim McDonald	.05	.02
❑	649	Donald Frank RC	.05	.02
❑	650	Richmond Webb	.05	.02
❑	651	Lemuel Stinson	.05	.02
❑	652	Merton Hanks	.10	.05
❑	653	Frank Warren	.05	.02
❑	654	Thomas Benson	.05	.02
❑	655	Al Smith	.05	.02
❑	656	Steve DeBerg	.05	.02
❑	657	Jayice Pearson RC	.05	.02
❑	658	Joe Morris	.05	.02
❑	659	Fred Strickland	.05	.02
❑	660	Kelvin Pritchett	.05	.02
❑	661	Lewis Billups	.05	.02
❑	662	Todd Collins RC	.05	.02
❑	663	Corey Miller RC	.05	.02
❑	664	Levon Kirkland RC	.05	.02
❑	665	Jerry Rice	.75	.35
❑	666	Mike Lodish RC	.05	.02
❑	667	Chuck Smith RC	.05	.02
❑	668	Lance Olberding RC	.05	.02
❑	669	Kevin Smith RC	.25	.11
❑	670	Dale Carter RC	.25	.11
❑	671	Sean Gilbert RC	.25	.11
❑	672	Ken O'Brien	.05	.02
❑	673	Ricky Proehl	.05	.02
❑	674	Junior Seau	.25	.11
❑	675	Courtney Hawkins RC	.10	.05
❑	676	Eddie Robinson RC	.05	.02
❑	677	Tom Jeter RC	.05	.02
❑	678	Jeff George	.25	.11
❑	679	Cary Conklin	.05	.02
❑	680	Rueben Mayes	.05	.02
❑	681	Sean Lumpkin RC	.05	.02
❑	682	Dan Marino	1.25	.55
❑	683	Ed McDaniel RC	.05	.02
❑	684	Greg Skrepenak RC	.05	.02
❑	685	Tracy Scroggins RC	.05	.02
❑	686	Tommy Maddox RC	.05	.02
❑	687	Mike Singletary	.10	.05
❑	688	Patrick Rowe RC	.05	.02
❑	689	Phillippi Sparks RC	.05	.02
❑	690	Joel Steed RC	.05	.02
❑	691	Kevin Fagan	.05	.02
❑	692	Deion Sanders	.50	.23
❑	693	Bruce Smith	.25	.11
❑	694	David Klingler RC	.10	.05
❑	695	Clayton Holmes RC	.05	.02
❑	696	Brett Favre	2.50	1.10
❑	697	Marc Boutte RC	.05	.02
❑	698	Dwayne Sabb RC	.05	.02
❑	699	Ed McCaffrey	.30	.14
❑	700	Randall Cunningham	.25	.11
❑	701	Quentin Coryatt RC	.25	.11
❑	702	Bernie Kosar	.10	.05
❑	703	Vaughn Dunbar RC	.05	.02
❑	704	Browning Nagle	.05	.02
❑	705	Mark Wheeler RC	.05	.02
❑	706	Paul Siever RC	.05	.02
❑	707	Anthony Miller	.10	.05
❑	708	Corey Widmer RC	.05	.02
❑	709	Eric Dickerson	.10	.05
❑	710	Martin Bayless	.05	.02
❑	711	Jason Hanson RC	.10	.05
❑	712	Michael Dean Perry	.10	.05
❑	713	Billy Joe Tolliver UER (Stats say 1991 Chargers, should be Falcons)	.05	.02
❑	714	Chad Hennings RC	.10	.05
❑	715	Bucky Richardson RC	.05	.02
❑	716	Steve Israel RC	.05	.02
❑	717	Robert Harris RC	.05	.02
❑	718	Timm Rosenbach	.05	.02
❑	719	Joe Montana	1.25	.55
❑	720	Derek Brown TE RC	.05	.02
❑	721	Robert Brooks RC	1.00	.45
❑	722	Boomer Esiason	.10	.05
❑	723	Troy Auzenne RC	.05	.02
❑	724	John Fina RC	.05	.02
❑	725	Chris Crooms RC	.05	.02
❑	726	Eugene Chung RC	.05	.02
❑	727	Darren Woodson RC	.25	.11
❑	728	Leslie O'Neal	.10	.05
❑	729	Dan McGwire	.05	.02
❑	730	Al Toon	.10	.05
❑	731	Michael Brandon RC	.05	.02
❑	732	Steve DeOssie	.05	.02
❑	733	Jim Kelly	.25	.11
❑	734	Webster Slaughter	.05	.02
❑	735	Tony Smith RC	.05	.02
❑	736	Shane Collins RC	.05	.02
❑	737	Randal Hill	.05	.02
❑	738	Chris Holder RC	.05	.02
❑	739	Russell Maryland	.10	.05
❑	740	Carl Pickens RC	.60	.25
❑	741	Andre Reed	.10	.05
❑	742	Steve Emtman RC	.05	.02
❑	743	Carl Banks	.05	.02
❑	744	Troy Aikman	.75	.35
❑	745	Mark Royals	.05	.02
❑	746	J.J. Birden	.05	.02
❑	747	Michael Cofer	.05	.02
❑	748	Darryl Ashmore RC	.05	.02
❑	749	Dion Lambert RC	.05	.02
❑	750	Phil Simms	.10	.05
❑	751	Reggie E. White RC	.05	.02
❑	752	Harvey Williams	.25	.11
❑	753	Ty Detmer	.25	.11
❑	754	Tony Brooks RC	.05	.02
❑	755	Steve Christie	.05	.02
❑	756	Lawrence Taylor	.25	.11
❑	757	Merril Hoge	.05	.02
❑	758	Robert Jones RC	.05	.02
❑	759	Checklist 661-759	.05	.02

1993 Topps

	MINT	NRMT
COMPLETE SET (660)	25.00	11.00
COMP.FACT.SET (673)	50.00	22.00
COMP.SERIES 1 (330)	15.00	6.75
COMP.SERIES 2 (330)	10.00	4.50

	No.	Player	Mint	Nrmt
❑	1	Art Monk RB	.05	.02
❑	2	Jerry Rice RB	.50	.23
❑	3	Stanley Richard	.05	.02
❑	4	Ron Hall	.05	.02
❑	5	Daryl Johnston	.25	.11

❑ 6 Wendell Davis .05 .02
❑ 7 Vaughn Dunbar .05 .02
❑ 8 Mike Jones .05 .02
❑ 9 Anthony Johnson .10 .05
❑ 10 Chris Miller .10 .05
❑ 11 Kyle Clifton .05 .02
❑ 12 Curtis Conway RC .40 .18
❑ 13 Lionel Washington .05 .02
❑ 14 Reggie Johnson .05 .02
❑ 15 David Little .05 .02
❑ 16 Nick Lowery .05 .02
❑ 17 Darryl Williams .05 .02
❑ 18 Brent Jones .10 .05
❑ 19 Bruce Matthews .05 .02
❑ 20 Heath Sherman .05 .02
❑ 21 John Kasay UER .05 .02
(Text on back states he did not attempt any FG's over 50 yds. but made 8)
❑ 22 Troy Drayton RC .10 .05
❑ 23 Eric Metcalf .10 .05
❑ 24 Andre Tippett .05 .02
❑ 25 Rodney Hampton .25 .11
❑ 26 Henry Jones .05 .02
❑ 27 Jim Everett .10 .05
❑ 28 Steve Jordan .05 .02
❑ 29 LeRoy Butler .05 .02
❑ 30 Troy Vincent .05 .02
❑ 31 Nate Lewis .05 .02
❑ 32 Rickey Jackson .05 .02
❑ 33 Darion Conner .05 .02
❑ 34 Tom Carter RC .10 .05
❑ 35 Jeff George .25 .11
❑ 36 Larry Centers RC .25 .11
❑ 37 Reggie Cobb .05 .02
❑ 38 Mike Saxon .05 .02
❑ 39 Brad Baxter .05 .02
❑ 40 Reggie White .25 .11
❑ 41 Haywood Jeffires .10 .05
❑ 42 Alfred Williams .05 .02
❑ 43 Aaron Wallace .05 .02
❑ 44 Tracy Simien .05 .02
❑ 45 Pat Harlow .05 .02
❑ 46 D.J. Johnson .05 .02
❑ 47 Don Griffin .05 .02
❑ 48 Flipper Anderson .05 .02
❑ 49 Keith Kartz .05 .02
❑ 50 Bernie Kosar .10 .05
❑ 51 Kent Hull .05 .02
❑ 52 Erik Howard .05 .02
❑ 53 Pierce Holt .05 .02
❑ 54 Dwayne Harper .05 .02
❑ 55 Bennie Blades .05 .02
❑ 56 Mark Duper .05 .02
❑ 57 Brian Noble .05 .02
❑ 58 Jeff Feagles .05 .02
❑ 59 Michael Haynes .10 .05
❑ 60 Junior Seau .25 .11
❑ 61 Gary Anderson RB .05 .02
❑ 62 Jon Hand .05 .02
❑ 63 Lin Elliott RC .05 .02
❑ 64 Dana Stubblefield RC .25 .11
❑ 65 Vaughan Johnson .05 .02
❑ 66 Mo Lewis .05 .02
❑ 67 Aeneas Williams .05 .02
❑ 68 David Fulcher .05 .02
❑ 69 Chip Lohmiller .05 .02
❑ 70 Greg Townsend .05 .02
❑ 71 Simon Fletcher .05 .02
❑ 72 Sean Salisbury .05 .02
❑ 73 Christian Okoye .05 .02
❑ 74 Jim Arnold .05 .02
❑ 75 Bruce Smith .25 .11
❑ 76 Fred Barnett .10 .05
❑ 77 Bill Romanowski .05 .02
❑ 78 Dermontti Dawson .05 .02
❑ 79 Bern Brostek .05 .02
❑ 80 Warren Moon .25 .11
❑ 81 Bill Fralic .05 .02
❑ 82 Lomas Brown FP .05 .02
❑ 83 Duane Bickett FP .05 .02
❑ 84 Neil Smith FP .10 .05
❑ 85 Reggie White FP .10 .05
❑ 86 Tim McDonald FP .05 .02
❑ 87 Leslie O'Neal FP .05 .02
❑ 88 Steve Young FP .40 .18
❑ 89 Paul Gruber FP .05 .02
❑ 90 Wilber Marshall FP .05 .02
❑ 91 Trace Armstrong .05 .02
❑ 92 Bobby Houston RC .05 .02
❑ 93 George Thornton .05 .02
❑ 94 Keith McCants .05 .02
❑ 95 Ricky Sanders .05 .02
❑ 96 Jackie Harris .05 .02
❑ 97 Todd Marinovich .05 .02
❑ 98 Henry Thomas .05 .02
❑ 99 Jeff Wright .05 .02
❑ 100 John Elway 1.50 .70
❑ 101 Garrison Hearst RC .50 .23
❑ 102 Roy Foster .05 .02
❑ 103 David Lang .05 .02
❑ 104 Matt Stover .05 .02
❑ 105 Lawrence Taylor .25 .11
❑ 106 Pete Stoyanovich .05 .02
❑ 107 Jessie Tuggle .05 .02
❑ 108 William White .05 .02
❑ 109 Andy Harmon RC .10 .05
❑ 110 John L. Williams .05 .02
❑ 111 Jon Vaughn .05 .02
❑ 112 John Alt .05 .02
❑ 113 Chris Jacke .05 .02
❑ 114 Jim Breech .05 .02
❑ 115 Eric Martin .05 .02
❑ 116 Derrick Walker .05 .02
❑ 117 Ricky Ervins .05 .02
❑ 118 Roger Craig .10 .05
❑ 119 Jeff Gossett .05 .02
❑ 120 Emmitt Smith 1.50 .70
❑ 121 Bob Whitfield .05 .02
❑ 122 Alonzo Spellman .05 .02
❑ 123 David Klingler .05 .02
❑ 124 Tommy Maddox .05 .02
❑ 125 Robert Porcher .05 .02
❑ 126 Edgar Bennett .25 .11
❑ 127 Harvey Williams .10 .05
❑ 128 Dave Brown RC .25 .11
❑ 129 Johnny Mitchell .05 .02
❑ 130 Drew Bledsoe RC 2.00 .90
❑ 131 Zefross Moss .05 .02
❑ 132 Nate Odomes .05 .02
❑ 133 Rufus Porter .05 .02
❑ 134 Jackie Slater .05 .02
❑ 135 Steve Young .75 .35
❑ 136 Chris Calloway .05 .02
❑ 137 Steve Atwater .05 .02
❑ 138 Mark Carrier DB .05 .02
❑ 139 Marvin Washington .05 .02
❑ 140 Barry Foster .10 .05
❑ 141 Ricky Reynolds .05 .02
❑ 142 Bubba McDowell .05 .02
❑ 143 Dan Footman RC .05 .02
❑ 144 Richmond Webb .05 .02
❑ 145 Mike Pritchard .10 .05
❑ 146 Chris Spielman .10 .05
❑ 147 Dave Krieg .10 .05
❑ 148 Nick Bell .05 .02
❑ 149 Vincent Brown .05 .02
❑ 150 Seth Joyner .05 .02
❑ 151 Tommy Kane .05 .02
❑ 152 Carlton Gray RC .05 .02
❑ 153 Harry Newsome .05 .02
❑ 154 Rohn Stark .05 .02
❑ 155 Shannon Sharpe .25 .11
❑ 156 Charles Haley .10 .05
❑ 157 Cornelius Bennett .10 .05
❑ 158 Doug Riesenberg .05 .02
❑ 159 Amp Lee .05 .02
❑ 160 Sterling Sharpe UER .25 .11
(Card front pictures Edgar Bennett)
❑ 161 Alonzo Mitz .05 .02
❑ 162 Pat Terrell .05 .02
❑ 163 Mark Schlereth .05 .02
❑ 164 Gary Anderson K .05 .02
❑ 165 Quinn Early .10 .05
❑ 166 Jerome Bettis RC .75 .35
❑ 167 Lawrence Dawsey .05 .02
❑ 168 Derrick Thomas .25 .11
❑ 169 Rodney Peete .05 .02
❑ 170 Jim Kelly .25 .11
❑ 171 Deion Sanders TL .25 .11
❑ 172 Richard Dent TL .05 .02
❑ 173 Emmitt Smith TL .75 .35
❑ 174 Barry Sanders TL .75 .35
❑ 175 Sterling Sharpe TL .05 .02
❑ 176 Cleveland Gary TL .05 .02
❑ 177 Terry Allen TL .10 .05
❑ 178 Vaughan Johnson TL .05 .02
❑ 179 Rodney Hampton TL .05 .02
❑ 180 Randall Cunningham TL .10 .05
❑ 181 Ricky Proehl TL .05 .02
❑ 182 Jerry Rice TL .50 .23
❑ 183 Reggie Cobb TL .05 .02
❑ 184 Earnest Byner TL .05 .02
❑ 185 Jeff Lageman .05 .02
❑ 186 Carlos Jenkins .05 .02
❑ 187 Cardinals Draft Picks .40 .18
Ernest Dye RC
Ronald Moore RC
Garrison Hearst
Ben Coleman RC
❑ 188 Todd Lyght .05 .02
❑ 189 Carl Simpson RC .05 .02
❑ 190 Barry Sanders 1.50 .70
❑ 191 Jim Harbaugh .25 .11
❑ 192 Roger Ruzek .05 .02
❑ 193 Brent Williams .05 .02
❑ 194 Chip Banks .05 .02
❑ 195 Mike Croel .05 .02
❑ 196 Marion Butts .05 .02
❑ 197 James Washington .05 .02
❑ 198 John Offerdahl .05 .02
❑ 199 Tom Rathman .05 .02
❑ 200 Joe Montana 1.50 .70
❑ 201 Pepper Johnson .05 .02
❑ 202 Cris Dishman .05 .02
❑ 203 Adrian White RC .05 .02
❑ 204 Reggie Brooks RC .10 .05
❑ 205 Cortez Kennedy .10 .05
❑ 206 Robert Massey .05 .02
❑ 207 Toi Cook .05 .02
❑ 208 Harry Sydney .05 .02
❑ 209 Lincoln Kennedy RC .05 .02
❑ 210 Randall McDaniel .05 .02
❑ 211 Eugene Daniel .05 .02
❑ 212 Rob Burnett .05 .02
❑ 213 Steve Broussard .05 .02
❑ 214 Brian Washington .05 .02
❑ 215 Leonard Renfro RC .05 .02
❑ 216 Audray McMillian LL .05 .02
Henry Jones
❑ 217 Sterling Sharpe LL .05 .02
Anthony Miller
❑ 218 Clyde Simmons LL .05 .02
Leslie O'Neal
❑ 219 Emmitt Smith LL .40 .18
Barry Foster
❑ 220 Steve Young LL .25 .11
Warren Moon
❑ 221 Mel Gray .10 .05
❑ 222 Luis Sharpe .05 .02
❑ 223 Eric Moten .05 .02
❑ 224 Albert Lewis .05 .02
❑ 225 Alvin Harper .10 .05
❑ 226 Steve Wallace .05 .02
❑ 227 Mark Higgs .05 .02
❑ 228 Eugene Lockhart .05 .02
❑ 229 Sean Jones .05 .02
❑ 230 Buccaneers Draft Picks .40 .18
Eric Curry
Lamar Thomas RC
Demetrious DuBose
John Lynch RC
❑ 231 Jimmy Williams .05 .02
(Text states drafted in 1992; he was drafted in 1982)
❑ 232 Demetrius DuBose RC .05 .02
❑ 233 John Roper .05 .02
❑ 234 Keith Hamilton .05 .02
❑ 235 Donald Evans .05 .02
❑ 236 Kenneth Davis .05 .02
❑ 237 John Copeland RC .10 .05
❑ 238 Leonard Russell .10 .05
❑ 239 Ken Harvey .05 .02
❑ 240 Dale Carter .05 .02
❑ 241 Anthony Pleasant .05 .02
❑ 242 Darrell Green .05 .02
❑ 243 Natrone Means RC .40 .18

❑ 244 Rob Moore .10 .05
❑ 245 Chris Doleman .05 .02
❑ 246 J.B. Brown .05 .02
❑ 247 Ray Crockett .05 .02
❑ 248 John Taylor .10 .05
❑ 249 Russell Maryland .05 .02
❑ 250 Brett Favre 2.00 .90
❑ 251 Carl Pickens .25 .11
❑ 252 Andy Heck .05 .02
❑ 253 Jerome Henderson .05 .02
❑ 254 Deion Sanders .50 .23
❑ 255 Steve Emtman .05 .02
❑ 256 Calvin Williams .10 .05
❑ 257 Sean Gilbert .10 .05
❑ 258 Don Beebe .05 .02
❑ 259 Robert Smith RC 1.50 .70
❑ 260 Robert Blackmon .05 .02
❑ 261 Jim Kelly TL .10 .05
❑ 262 Harold Green TL UER .05 .02
(Harold Green is identified as Gaston Green)
❑ 263 Clay Matthews TL .05 .02
❑ 264 John Elway TL .75 .35
❑ 265 Warren Moon TL .10 .05
❑ 266 Jeff George TL .10 .05
❑ 267 Derrick Thomas TL .05 .02
❑ 268 Howie Long TL .05 .02
❑ 269 Dan Marino TL .75 .35
❑ 270 Jon Vaughn TL .05 .02
❑ 271 Chris Burkett TL .05 .02
❑ 272 Barry Foster TL .05 .02
❑ 273 Marion Butts TL .05 .02
❑ 274 Chris Warren TL .05 .02
❑ 275 Michael Strahan RC .25 .11
Marcus Buckley RC
(Giants Draft Picks)
❑ 276 Tony Casillas .05 .02
❑ 277 Jarrod Bunch .05 .02
❑ 278 Eric Green .05 .02
❑ 279 Stan Brock .05 .02
❑ 280 Chester McGlockton .10 .05
❑ 281 Ricky Watters .25 .11
❑ 282 Dan Saleaumua .05 .02
❑ 283 Rich Camarillo .05 .02
❑ 284 Cris Carter .50 .23
❑ 285 Rick Mirer RC .30 .14
❑ 286 Matt Brock .05 .02
❑ 287 Burt Grossman .05 .02
❑ 288 Andre Collins .05 .02
❑ 289 Mark Jackson .05 .02
❑ 290 Dan Marino 1.50 .70
❑ 291 Cornelius Bennett FG .05 .02
❑ 292 Steve Atwater FG .05 .02
❑ 293 Bryan Cox FG .05 .02
❑ 294 Sam Mills FG .05 .02
❑ 295 Pepper Johnson FG .05 .02
❑ 296 Seth Joyner FG .05 .02
❑ 297 Chris Spielman FG .05 .02
❑ 298 Junior Seau FG .10 .05
❑ 299 Cortez Kennedy FG .05 .02
❑ 300 Broderick Thomas FG .05 .02
❑ 301 Todd McNair .05 .02
❑ 302 Nate Newton .10 .05
❑ 303 Michael Walter .05 .02
❑ 304 Clyde Simmons .05 .02
❑ 305 Ernie Mills .05 .02
❑ 306 Steve Wisniewski .05 .02
❑ 307 Coleman Rudolph RC .05 .02
❑ 308 Thurman Thomas .25 .11
❑ 309 Reggie Roby .05 .02
❑ 310 Eric Swann .10 .05
❑ 311 Mark Wheeler .05 .02
❑ 312 Jeff Herrod .05 .02
❑ 313 Leroy Hoard .10 .05
❑ 314 Patrick Bates RC .05 .02
❑ 315 Earnest Byner .05 .02
❑ 316 Dave Meggett .05 .02
❑ 317 George Teague RC .10 .05
❑ 318 Ray Childress .05 .02
❑ 319 Mike Kenn .05 .02
❑ 320 Jason Hanson .05 .02
❑ 321 Gary Clark .10 .05
❑ 322 Chris Gardocki .05 .02
❑ 323 Ken Norton .10 .05
❑ 324 Eric Curry RC .05 .02
❑ 325 Byron Evans .05 .02
❑ 326 O.J. McDuffie RC .50 .23
❑ 327 Dwight Stone .05 .02
❑ 328 Tommy Barnhardt .05 .02
❑ 329 Checklist 1-165 .05 .02
❑ 330 Checklist 166-329 .05 .02
❑ 331 Erik Williams .05 .02
❑ 332 Phil Hansen .05 .02
❑ 333 Martin Harrison RC .05 .02
❑ 334 Mark Ingram .05 .02
❑ 335 Mark Rypien .05 .02
❑ 336 Anthony Miller .10 .05
❑ 337 Antone Davis .05 .02
❑ 338 Mike Munchak .05 .02
❑ 339 Wayne Martin .05 .02
❑ 340 Joe Montana 1.50 .70
❑ 341 Deon Figures RC .10 .05
❑ 342 Ed McDaniel .05 .02
❑ 343 Chris Burkett .05 .02
❑ 344 Tony Smith .05 .02
❑ 345 James Lofton .10 .05
❑ 346 Courtney Hawkins .05 .02
❑ 347 Dennis Smith .05 .02
❑ 348 Anthony Morgan .05 .02
❑ 349 Chris Goode .05 .02
❑ 350 Phil Simms .10 .05
❑ 351 Patrick Hunter .05 .02
❑ 352 Brett Perriman .25 .11
❑ 353 Corey Miller .05 .02
❑ 354 Harry Galbreath .05 .02
❑ 355 Mark Carrier WR .10 .05
❑ 356 Troy Drayton .10 .05
❑ 357 Greg Davis .05 .02
❑ 358 Tim Krumrie .05 .02
❑ 359 Tim McDonald .05 .02
❑ 360 Webster Slaughter .05 .02
❑ 361 Steve Christie .05 .02
❑ 362 Courtney Hall .05 .02
❑ 363 Charles Mann .05 .02
❑ 364 Vestee Jackson .05 .02
❑ 365 Robert Jones .05 .02
❑ 366 Rich Miano .05 .02
❑ 367 Morten Andersen .05 .02
❑ 368 Jeff Graham .10 .05
❑ 369 Martin Mayhew .05 .02
❑ 370 Anthony Carter .10 .05
❑ 371 Greg Kragen .05 .02
❑ 372 Ron Cox .05 .02
❑ 373 Perry Williams .05 .02
❑ 374 Willie Gault .05 .02
❑ 375 Chris Warren .10 .05
❑ 376 Reyna Thompson .05 .02
❑ 377 Bennie Thompson .05 .02
❑ 378 Kevin Mack .05 .02
❑ 379 Clarence Verdin .05 .02
❑ 380 Marc Boutte .05 .02
❑ 381 Marvin Jones RC .05 .02
❑ 382 Greg Jackson .05 .02
❑ 383 Steve Bono .25 .11
❑ 384 Terrell Buckley .05 .02
❑ 385 Garrison Hearst .25 .11
❑ 386 Mike Brim .05 .02
❑ 387 Jesse Sapolu .05 .02
❑ 388 Carl Lee .05 .02
❑ 389 Jeff Cross .05 .02
❑ 390 Karl Mecklenburg .05 .02
❑ 391 Chad Hennings .05 .02
❑ 392 Oliver Barnett .05 .02
❑ 393 Dalton Hilliard .05 .02
❑ 394 Broderick Thompson .05 .02
❑ 395 Raghib Ismail .10 .05
❑ 396 John Kidd .05 .02
❑ 397 Eddie Anderson .05 .02
❑ 398 Lamar Lathon .05 .02
❑ 399 Darren Perry .05 .02
❑ 400 Drew Bledsoe 1.00 .45
❑ 401 Ferrell Edmunds .05 .02
❑ 402 Lomas Brown .05 .02
❑ 403 Drew Hill .05 .02
❑ 404 David Whitmore .05 .02
❑ 405 Mike Johnson .05 .02
❑ 406 Paul Gruber .05 .02
❑ 407 Kirk Lowdermilk .05 .02
❑ 408 Curtis Conway .25 .11
❑ 409 Bryce Paup .25 .11
❑ 410 Boomer Esiason .10 .05
❑ 411 Jay Schroeder .05 .02
❑ 412 Anthony Newman .05 .02
❑ 413 Ernie Jones .05 .02
❑ 414 Carlton Bailey .05 .02
❑ 415 Kenneth Gant .05 .02
❑ 416 Todd Scott .05 .02
❑ 417 Anthony Smith .05 .02
❑ 418 Erik McMillan .05 .02
❑ 419 Ronnie Harmon .05 .02
❑ 420 Andre Reed .10 .05
❑ 421 Wymon Henderson .05 .02
❑ 422 Carnell Lake .05 .02
❑ 423 Al Noga .05 .02
❑ 424 Curtis Duncan .05 .02
❑ 425 Mike Gann .05 .02
❑ 426 Eugene Robinson .05 .02
❑ 427 Scott Mersereau .05 .02
❑ 428 Chris Singleton .05 .02
❑ 429 Gerald Robinson .05 .02
❑ 430 Pat Swilling .05 .02
❑ 431 Ed McCaffrey .10 .05
❑ 432 Neal Anderson .05 .02
❑ 433 Joe Phillips .05 .02
❑ 434 Jerry Ball .05 .02
❑ 435 Tyronne Stowe .05 .02
❑ 436 Dana Stubblefield .25 .11
❑ 437 Eric Curry .05 .02
❑ 438 Derrick Fenner .05 .02
❑ 439 Mark Clayton .05 .02
❑ 440 Quentin Coryatt .10 .05
❑ 441 Willie Roaf RC .10 .05
❑ 442 Ernest Dye .05 .02
❑ 443 Jeff Jaeger .05 .02
❑ 444 Stan Humphries .25 .11
❑ 445 Johnny Johnson .05 .02
❑ 446 Larry Brown DB .05 .02
❑ 447 Kurt Gouveia .05 .02
❑ 448 Qadry Ismail RC .50 .23
❑ 449 Dan Footman .05 .02
❑ 450 Tom Waddle .05 .02
❑ 451 Kelvin Martin .05 .02
❑ 452 Kanavis McGhee .05 .02
❑ 453 Herman Moore .50 .23
❑ 454 Jesse Solomon .05 .02
❑ 455 Shane Conlan .05 .02
❑ 456 Joel Steed .05 .02
❑ 457 Charles Arbuckle .05 .02
❑ 458 Shane Dronett .05 .02
❑ 459 Steve Tasker .10 .05
❑ 460 Herschel Walker .10 .05
❑ 461 Willie Davis .25 .11
❑ 462 Al Smith .05 .02
❑ 463 O.J. McDuffie .25 .11
❑ 464 Kevin Fagan .05 .02
❑ 465 Hardy Nickerson .10 .05
❑ 466 Leonard Marshall .05 .02
❑ 467 John Baylor .05 .02
❑ 468 Jay Novacek .10 .05
❑ 469 Wayne Simmons RC .05 .02
❑ 470 Tommy Vardell .05 .02
❑ 471 Cleveland Gary .05 .02
❑ 472 Mark Collins .05 .02
❑ 473 Craig Heyward .10 .05
❑ 474 John Copeland UER .10 .05
(Bio states he was born 0-29-70 instead of 9-29-70)
❑ 475 Jeff Hostetler .10 .05
❑ 476 Brian Mitchell .10 .05
❑ 477 Natrone Means .25 .11
❑ 478 Brad Muster .05 .02
❑ 479 David Lutz .05 .02
❑ 480 Andre Rison .10 .05
❑ 481 Michael Zordich .05 .02
❑ 482 Jim McMahon .05 .02
❑ 483 Carlton Gray .05 .02
❑ 484 Chris Mohr .05 .02
❑ 485 Ernest Givins .10 .05
❑ 486 Tony Tolbert .05 .02
❑ 487 Vai Sikahema .05 .02
❑ 488 Larry Webster .05 .02
❑ 489 James Hasty .05 .02
❑ 490 Reggie White .25 .11
❑ 491 Reggie Rivers RC .05 .02
❑ 492 Roman Phifer .05 .02
❑ 493 Levon Kirkland .05 .02
❑ 494 Demetrius DuBose .05 .02
❑ 495 William Perry .10 .05

❑ 496 Clay Matthews .10 .05
❑ 497 Aaron Jones .05 .02
❑ 498 Jack Trudeau .05 .02
❑ 499 Michael Brooks .05 .02
❑ 500 Jerry Rice 1.00 .45
❑ 501 Lonnie Marts .05 .02
❑ 502 Tim McGee .05 .02
❑ 503 Kelvin Pritchett .05 .02
❑ 504 Bobby Hebert .05 .02
❑ 505 Audray McMillian .05 .02
❑ 506 Chuck Cecil .05 .02
❑ 507 Leonard Renfro .05 .02
❑ 508 Ethan Horton .05 .02
❑ 509 Kevin Smith .10 .05
❑ 510 Louis Oliver .05 .02
❑ 511 John Stephens .05 .02
❑ 512 Browning Nagle .05 .02
❑ 513 Ricardo McDonald .05 .02
❑ 514 Leslie O'Neal .10 .05
❑ 515 Lorenzo White .05 .02
❑ 516 Thomas Smith RC .10 .05
❑ 517 Tony Woods .05 .02
❑ 518 Darryl Henley .05 .02
❑ 519 Robert Delpino .05 .02
❑ 520 Rod Woodson .25 .11
❑ 521 Phillippi Sparks .05 .02
❑ 522 Jessie Hester .05 .02
❑ 523 Shaun Gayle .05 .02
❑ 524 Brad Edwards .05 .02
❑ 525 Randall Cunningham .25 .11
❑ 526 Marv Cook .05 .02
❑ 527 Dennis Gibson .05 .02
❑ 528 Erric Pegram .10 .05
❑ 529 Terry McDaniel .05 .02
❑ 530 Troy Aikman .75 .35
❑ 531 Irving Fryar .10 .05
❑ 532 Blair Thomas .05 .02
❑ 533 Jim Wilks .05 .02
❑ 534 Michael Jackson .10 .05
❑ 535 Eric Davis .05 .02
❑ 536 James Campen .05 .02
❑ 537 Steve Beuerlein .05 .02
❑ 538 Robert Smith .60 .25
❑ 539 J.J. Birden .05 .02
❑ 540 Broderick Thomas .05 .02
❑ 541 Darryl Talley .05 .02
❑ 542 Russell Freeman RC .05 .02
❑ 543 David Alexander .05 .02
❑ 544 Chris Mims .05 .02
❑ 545 Coleman Rudolph .05 .02
❑ 546 Steve McMichael .10 .05
❑ 547 David Williams .05 .02
❑ 548 Chris Hinton .05 .02
❑ 549 Jim Jeffcoat .05 .02
❑ 550 Howie Long .10 .05
❑ 551 Roosevelt Potts RC .05 .02
❑ 552 Bryan Cox .05 .02
❑ 553 David Richards UER .05 .02
(Photo on front is Stanley Richards)
❑ 554 Reggie Brooks .10 .05
❑ 555 Neil O'Donnell .25 .11
❑ 556 Irv Smith RC .05 .02
❑ 557 Henry Ellard .10 .05
❑ 558 Steve DeBerg .05 .02
❑ 559 Jim Sweeney .05 .02
❑ 560 Harold Green .05 .02
❑ 561 Darrell Thompson .05 .02
❑ 562 Vinny Testaverde .10 .05
❑ 563 Bubby Brister .05 .02
❑ 564 Sean Landeta .05 .02
❑ 565 Neil Smith .25 .11
❑ 566 Craig Erickson .10 .05
❑ 567 Jim Ritcher .05 .02
❑ 568 Don Mosebar .05 .02
❑ 569 John Gesek .05 .02
❑ 570 Gary Plummer .05 .02
❑ 571 Norm Johnson .05 .02
❑ 572 Ron Heller .05 .02
❑ 573 Carl Simpson .05 .02
❑ 574 Greg Montgomery .05 .02
❑ 575 Dana Hall .05 .02
❑ 576 Vencie Glenn .05 .02
❑ 577 Dean Biasucci .05 .02
❑ 578 Rod Bernstine UER .05 .02
(Name spelled Bemstein on front)
❑ 579 Randal Hill .05 .02
❑ 580 Sam Mills .05 .02
❑ 581 Santana Dotson .10 .05
❑ 582 Greg Lloyd .25 .11
❑ 583 Eric Thomas .05 .02
❑ 584 Henry Rolling .05 .02
❑ 585 Tony Bennett .05 .02
❑ 586 Sheldon White .05 .02
❑ 587 Mark Kelso .05 .02
❑ 588 Marc Spindler .05 .02
❑ 589 Greg McMurtry .05 .02
❑ 590 Art Monk .10 .05
❑ 591 Marco Coleman .05 .02
❑ 592 Tony Jones .05 .02
❑ 593 Melvin Jenkins .05 .02
❑ 594 Kevin Ross .05 .02
❑ 595 William Fuller .05 .02
❑ 596 James Joseph .05 .02
❑ 597 Lamar McGriggs RC .05 .02
❑ 598 Gill Byrd .05 .02
❑ 599 Alexander Wright .05 .02
❑ 600 Rick Mirer .25 .11
❑ 601 Richard Dent .10 .05
❑ 602 Thomas Everett .05 .02
❑ 603 Jack Del Rio .05 .02
❑ 604 Jerome Bettis .40 .18
❑ 605 Ronnie Lott .10 .05
❑ 606 Marty Carter .05 .02
❑ 607 Arthur Marshall RC .05 .02
❑ 608 Lee Johnson .05 .02
❑ 609 Bruce Armstrong .05 .02
❑ 610 Ricky Proehl .05 .02
❑ 611 Will Wolford .05 .02
❑ 612 Mike Prior .05 .02
❑ 613 George Jamison .05 .02
❑ 614 Gene Atkins .05 .02
❑ 615 Merril Hoge .05 .02
❑ 616 Desmond Howard UER .10 .05
(Stats indicate 8 TD's receiving; he had 0)
❑ 617 Jarvis Williams .05 .02
❑ 618 Marcus Allen .25 .11
❑ 619 Gary Brown .05 .02
❑ 620 Bill Brooks .05 .02
❑ 621 Eric Allen .05 .02
❑ 622 Todd Kelly .05 .02
❑ 623 Michael Dean Perry .10 .05
❑ 624 David Braxton .05 .02
❑ 625 Mike Sherrard .05 .02
❑ 626 Jeff Bryant .05 .02
❑ 627 Eric Bieniemy .05 .02
❑ 628 Tim Brown .25 .11
❑ 629 Troy Auzenne .05 .02
❑ 630 Michael Irvin .25 .11
❑ 631 Maurice Hurst .05 .02
❑ 632 Duane Bickett .05 .02
❑ 633 George Teague .10 .05
❑ 634 Vince Workman .05 .02
❑ 635 Renaldo Turnbull .05 .02
❑ 636 Johnny Bailey .05 .02
❑ 637 Dan Williams RC .05 .02
❑ 638 James Thornton .05 .02
❑ 639 Terry Allen .25 .11
❑ 640 Kevin Greene .25 .11
❑ 641 Tony Zendejas .05 .02
❑ 642 Scott Kowalkowski RC .05 .02
❑ 643 Jeff Query UER .05 .02
(Text states he played for Packers in '92; he played for Bengals)
❑ 644 Brian Blades .10 .05
❑ 645 Keith Jackson .10 .05
❑ 646 Monte Coleman .05 .02
❑ 647 Guy McIntyre .05 .02
❑ 648 Barry Word .05 .02
❑ 649 Steve Everitt RC .05 .02
❑ 650 Patrick Bates .05 .02
❑ 651 Marcus Robertson RC .05 .02
❑ 652 John Carney .05 .02
❑ 653 Derek Brown TE .05 .02
❑ 654 Carwell Gardner .05 .02
❑ 655 Moe Gardner .05 .02
❑ 656 Andre Ware .05 .02
❑ 657 Keith Van Horne .05 .02
❑ 658 Hugh Millen .05 .02
❑ 659 Checklist 330-495 .05 .02
❑ 660 Checklist 496-660 .05 .02

1994 Topps

	MINT	NRMT
COMPLETE SET (660)	50.00	22.00
COMP.FACT.SET	60.00	27.00
COMP.SERIES 1 (330)	25.00	11.00
COMP.SERIES 2 (330)	25.00	11.00

❑ 1 Emmitt Smith 1.50 .70
❑ 2 Russell Copeland .05 .02
❑ 3 Jesse Sapolu .05 .02
❑ 4 David Szott .05 .02
❑ 5 Rodney Hampton .25 .11
❑ 6 Bubba McDowell .05 .02
❑ 7 Bryce Paup .25 .11
❑ 8 Winston Moss .05 .02
❑ 9 Brett Perriman .10 .05
❑ 10 Rod Woodson .25 .11
❑ 11 John Randle .10 .05
❑ 12 David Wyman .05 .02
❑ 13 Jeff Cross .05 .02
❑ 14 Richard Cooper .05 .02
❑ 15 Johnny Mitchell .05 .02
❑ 16 David Alexander .05 .02
❑ 17 Ronnie Harmon .05 .02
❑ 18 Tyronne Stowe UER .05 .02
(Tyrone on both sides)
❑ 19 Chris Zorich .05 .02
❑ 20 Rob Burnett .05 .02
❑ 21 Harold Alexander .05 .02
❑ 22 Rod Stephens .05 .02
❑ 23 Mark Wheeler .05 .02
❑ 24 Dwayne Sabb .05 .02
❑ 25 Troy Drayton .05 .02
❑ 26 Kurt Gouveia .05 .02
❑ 27 Warren Moon .25 .11
❑ 28 Jeff Query .05 .02
❑ 29 Chuck Levy RC .05 .02
❑ 30 Bruce Smith .25 .11
❑ 31 Doug Riesenberg .05 .02
❑ 32 Willie Drewrey .05 .02
❑ 33 Nate Newton UER .05 .02
(Listed as Defensive End; should be Guard)
❑ 34 James Jett .05 .02
❑ 35 George Teague .05 .02
❑ 36 Marc Spindler .05 .02
❑ 37 Jack Del Rio .05 .02
❑ 38 Dale Carter .05 .02
❑ 39 Steve Atwater .05 .02
❑ 40 Herschel Walker .10 .05
❑ 41 James Hasty .05 .02
❑ 42 Seth Joyner .05 .02
❑ 43 Keith Jackson .05 .02
❑ 44 Tommy Vardell .05 .02
❑ 45 Antonio Langham RC .10 .05
❑ 46 Derek Brown RBK .05 .02
❑ 47 John Wojciechowski .05 .02
❑ 48 Horace Copeland .05 .02
❑ 49 Luis Sharpe .05 .02
❑ 50 Pat Harlow .05 .02
❑ 51 David Palmer RC .50 .23
❑ 52 Tony Smith .05 .02
❑ 53 Tim Johnson .05 .02
❑ 54 Anthony Newman .05 .02
❑ 55 Terry Wooden .05 .02
❑ 56 Derrick Fenner .05 .02
❑ 57 Mike Fox .05 .02

	No.	Player		
❑	58	Brad Hopkins	.05	.02
❑	59	Daryl Johnston UER	.10	.05
		(Johnson on front)		
❑	60	Steve Young	.75	.35
❑	61	Scottie Graham RC	.10	.05
❑	62	Nolan Harrison	.05	.02
❑	63	David Richards	.05	.02
❑	64	Chris Mohr	.05	.02
❑	65	Hardy Nickerson	.10	.05
❑	66	Heath Sherman	.05	.02
❑	67	Irving Fryar	.10	.05
❑	68	Ray Buchanan UER	.05	.02
		(Buchannan on front)		
❑	69	Jay Taylor	.05	.02
❑	70	Shannon Sharpe	.10	.05
❑	71	Vinny Testaverde	.10	.05
❑	72	Renaldo Turnbull	.05	.02
❑	73	Dwight Stone	.05	.02
❑	74	Willie McGinest RC	.25	.11
❑	75	Darrell Green	.05	.02
❑	76	Kyle Clifton	.05	.02
❑	77	Leo Goeas	.05	.02
❑	78	Ken Ruettgers	.05	.02
❑	79	Craig Heyward	.10	.05
❑	80	Andre Rison	.10	.05
❑	81	Chris Mims	.05	.02
❑	82	Gary Clark	.10	.05
❑	83	Ricardo McDonald	.05	.02
❑	84	Patrick Hunter	.05	.02
❑	85	Bruce Matthews	.05	.02
❑	86	Russell Maryland	.05	.02
❑	87	Gary Anderson K	.05	.02
❑	88	Brad Edwards	.05	.02
❑	89	Carlton Bailey	.05	.02
❑	90	Qadry Ismail	.25	.11
❑	91	Terry McDaniel	.05	.02
❑	92	Willie Green	.05	.02
❑	93	Cornelius Bennett	.10	.05
❑	94	Paul Gruber	.05	.02
❑	95	Pete Stoyanovich	.05	.02
❑	96	Merton Hanks	.10	.05
❑	97	Tre Johnson RC	.05	.02
❑	98	Jonathan Hayes	.05	.02
❑	99	Jason Elam	.05	.02
❑	100	Jerome Bettis	.25	.11
❑	101	Ronnie Lott	.10	.05
❑	102	Maurice Hurst	.05	.02
❑	103	Kirk Lowdermilk	.05	.02
❑	104	Tony Jones	.05	.02
❑	105	Steve Beuerlein	.05	.02
❑	106	Isaac Davis RC	.05	.02
❑	107	Vaughan Johnson	.05	.02
❑	108	Terrell Buckley	.05	.02
❑	109	Pierce Holt	.05	.02
❑	110	Alonzo Spellman	.05	.02
❑	111	Patrick Robinson	.05	.02
❑	112	Cortez Kennedy	.10	.05
❑	113	Kevin Williams	.10	.05
❑	114	Danny Copeland	.05	.02
❑	115	Chris Doleman	.05	.02
❑	116	Jerry Rice LL	.50	.23
❑	117	Neil Smith LL	.10	.05
❑	118	Emmitt Smith LL	.75	.35
❑	119	Eugene Robinson LL	.05	.02
		Nate Odomes		
❑	120	Steve Young LL	.25	.11
❑	121	Carnell Lake	.05	.02
❑	122	Ernest Givins UER	.10	.05
		(Givens on front)		
❑	123	Henry Jones	.05	.02
❑	124	Michael Brooks	.05	.02
❑	125	Jason Hanson	.05	.02
❑	126	Andy Harmon	.05	.02
❑	127	Errict Rhett RC	.75	.35
❑	128	Harris Barton	.05	.02
❑	129	Greg Robinson	.05	.02
❑	130	Derrick Thomas	.25	.11
❑	131	Keith Kartz	.05	.02
❑	132	Lincoln Kennedy	.05	.02
❑	133	Leslie O'Neal	.05	.02
❑	134	Tim Goad	.05	.02
❑	135	Rohn Stark	.05	.02
❑	136	O.J. McDuffie	.25	.11
❑	137	Donnell Woolford	.05	.02
❑	138	Jamir Miller RC	.05	.02
❑	139	Eric Thomas UER	.05	.02
		(Listed as tight end; he		
		is a cornerback)		
❑	140	Willie Roaf	.05	.02
❑	141	Wayne Gandy RC	.05	.02
❑	142	Mike Brim	.05	.02
❑	143	Kelvin Martin	.05	.02
❑	144	Edgar Bennett	.25	.11
❑	145	Michael Dean Perry	.10	.05
❑	146	Shante Carver RC	.05	.02
❑	147	Jessie Armstead UER	.05	.02
		(Jesse on both sides)		
❑	148	Mo Elewonibi	.05	.02
❑	149	Dana Stubblefield	.25	.11
❑	150	Cody Carlson	.05	.02
❑	151	Vencie Glenn	.05	.02
❑	152	Levon Kirkland	.05	.02
❑	153	Derrick Moore	.05	.02
❑	154	John Fina	.05	.02
❑	155	Jeff Hostetler	.10	.05
❑	156	Courtney Hawkins	.05	.02
❑	157	Todd Collins	.05	.02
❑	158	Neil Smith	.25	.11
❑	159	Simon Fletcher	.05	.02
❑	160	Dan Marino	2.00	.90
❑	161	Sam Adams RC	.10	.05
❑	162	Marvin Washington	.05	.02
❑	163	John Copeland	.05	.02
❑	164	Eugene Robinson	.05	.02
❑	165	Mark Carrier DB	.05	.02
❑	166	Mike Kenn	.05	.02
❑	167	Tyrone Hughes	.10	.05
❑	168	Darren Carrington	.05	.02
❑	169	Shane Conlan	.05	.02
❑	170	Ricky Proehl	.05	.02
❑	171	Jeff Herrod	.05	.02
❑	172	Mark Carrier WR	.10	.05
❑	173	George Koonce	.05	.02
❑	174	Desmond Howard	.10	.05
❑	175	Dave Meggett	.05	.02
❑	176	Charles Haley	.10	.05
❑	177	Steve Wisniewski	.05	.02
❑	178	Dermontti Dawson	.05	.02
❑	179	Tim McDonald	.05	.02
❑	180	Broderick Thomas	.05	.02
❑	181	Bernard Dafney	.05	.02
❑	182	Bo Orlando	.05	.02
❑	183	Andre Reed	.10	.05
❑	184	Randall Cunningham	.25	.11
❑	185	Chris Spielman	.10	.05
❑	186	Keith Byars	.05	.02
❑	187	Ben Coates	.25	.11
❑	188	Tracy Simien	.05	.02
❑	189	Carl Pickens	.25	.11
❑	190	Reggie White	.25	.11
❑	191	Norm Johnson	.05	.02
❑	192	Brian Washington	.05	.02
❑	193	Stan Humphries	.25	.11
❑	194	Fred Stokes	.05	.02
❑	195	Dan Williams	.05	.02
❑	196	John Elway TOG	.75	.35
❑	197	Eric Allen TOG	.05	.02
❑	198	Hardy Nickerson TOG	.10	.05
❑	199	Jerome Bettis TOG	.10	.05
❑	200	Troy Aikman TOG	.50	.23
❑	201	Thurman Thomas TOG	.10	.05
❑	202	Cornelius Bennett TOG	.10	.05
❑	203	Michael Irvin TOG	.10	.05
❑	204	Jim Kelly TOG	.10	.05
❑	205	Junior Seau TOG	.10	.05
❑	206	Heath Shuler RC UER	.25	.11
		(Rifle spelled rife on back)		
❑	207	Howard Cross UER	.05	.02
		(Listed as linebacker; he		
		he plays tight end)		
❑	208	Pat Swilling	.05	.02
❑	209	Pete Metzelaars	.05	.02
❑	210	Tony McGee	.05	.02
❑	211	Neil O'Donnell	.25	.11
❑	212	Eugene Chung	.05	.02
❑	213	J.B. Brown	.05	.02
❑	214	Marcus Allen	.25	.11
❑	215	Harry Newsome	.05	.02
❑	216	Greg Hill RC	.25	.11
❑	217	Ryan Yarborough	.05	.02
❑	218	Marty Carter	.05	.02
❑	219	Bern Brostek	.05	.02
❑	220	Boomer Esiason	.10	.05
❑	221	Vince Buck	.05	.02
❑	222	Jim Jeffcoat	.05	.02
❑	223	Bob Dahl	.05	.02
❑	224	Marion Butts	.05	.02
❑	225	Ronald Moore	.05	.02
❑	226	Robert Blackmon	.05	.02
❑	227	Curtis Conway	.25	.11
❑	228	Jon Hand	.05	.02
❑	229	Shane Dronett	.05	.02
❑	230	Erik Williams UER	.05	.02
		(Misspelled Eric on front)		
❑	231	Dennis Brown	.05	.02
❑	232	Ray Childress	.05	.02
❑	233	Johnnie Morton RC	.25	.11
❑	234	Kent Hull	.05	.02
❑	235	John Elliott	.05	.02
❑	236	Ron Heller	.05	.02
❑	237	J.J. Birden	.05	.02
❑	238	Thomas Randolph RC	.05	.02
❑	239	Chip Lohmiller	.05	.02
❑	240	Tim Brown	.25	.11
❑	241	Steve Tovar	.05	.02
❑	242	Moe Gardner	.05	.02
❑	243	Vincent Brown	.05	.02
❑	244	Tony Zendejas	.05	.02
❑	245	Eric Allen	.05	.02
❑	246	Joe King RC	.05	.02
❑	247	Mo Lewis	.05	.02
❑	248	Rod Bernstine	.05	.02
❑	249	Tom Waddle	.05	.02
❑	250	Junior Seau	.25	.11
❑	251	Eric Metcalf	.10	.05
❑	252	Cris Carter	.50	.23
❑	253	Bill Hitchcock	.05	.02
❑	254	Zefross Moss	.05	.02
❑	255	Morten Andersen	.05	.02
❑	256	Keith Rucker RC	.05	.02
❑	257	Chris Jacke	.05	.02
❑	258	Richmond Webb	.05	.02
❑	259	Herman Moore	.25	.11
❑	260	Phil Simms	.10	.05
❑	261	Mark Tuinei	.05	.02
❑	262	Don Beebe	.05	.02
❑	263	Marc Logan	.05	.02
❑	264	Willie Davis	.10	.05
❑	265	David Klingler	.05	.02
❑	266	Martin Mayhew UER	.05	.02
		(Listed as wide receiver; he		
		is a cornerback)		
❑	267	Mark Bavaro	.05	.02
❑	268	Greg Lloyd	.25	.11
❑	269	Al Del Greco	.05	.02
❑	270	Reggie Brooks	.10	.05
❑	271	Greg Townsend	.05	.02
❑	272	Rohn Stark CAL	.05	.02
❑	273	Marcus Allen CAL	.10	.05
❑	274	Ronnie Lott CAL	.10	.05
❑	275	Dan Marino CAL	.75	.35
❑	276	Sean Gilbert	.05	.02
❑	277	LeRoy Butler	.05	.02
❑	278	Troy Auzenne	.05	.02
❑	279	Eric Swann	.10	.05
❑	280	Quentin Coryatt	.05	.02
❑	281	Anthony Pleasant	.05	.02
❑	282	Brad Baxter	.05	.02
❑	283	Carl Lee	.05	.02
❑	284	Courtney Hall	.05	.02
❑	285	Quinn Early	.10	.05
❑	286	Eddie Robinson	.05	.02
❑	287	Marco Coleman	.05	.02
❑	288	Harold Green	.05	.02
❑	289	Santana Dotson	.10	.05
❑	290	Robert Porcher	.05	.02
❑	291	Joe Phillips	.05	.02
❑	292	Mark McMillian	.05	.02
❑	293	Eric Davis	.05	.02
❑	294	Mark Jackson	.05	.02
❑	295	Darryl Talley	.05	.02
❑	296	Curtis Duncan	.05	.02
❑	297	Bruce Armstrong	.05	.02
❑	298	Eric Hill	.05	.02
❑	299	Andre Collins	.05	.02
❑	300	Jay Novacek	.10	.05
❑	301	Roosevelt Potts	.05	.02
❑	302	Eric Martin	.05	.02

❑ 303 Chris Warren .10 .05
❑ 304 Deral Boykin RC .05 .02
❑ 305 Jessie Tuggle .05 .02
❑ 306 Glyn Milburn .10 .05
❑ 307 Terry Obee .05 .02
❑ 308 Eric Turner .05 .02
❑ 309 Dewayne Washington RC .10 .05
❑ 310 Sterling Sharpe .10 .05
❑ 311 Jeff Gossett .05 .02
❑ 312 John Carney .05 .02
❑ 313 Aaron Glenn RC .10 .05
❑ 314 Nick Lowery .05 .02
❑ 315 Thurman Thomas .25 .11
❑ 316 Troy Aikman MG .50 .23
❑ 317 Thurman Thomas MG .10 .05
❑ 318 Michael Irvin MG .10 .05
❑ 319 Steve Beuerlein MG .05 .02
❑ 320 Jerry Rice 1.00 .45
❑ 321 Alexander Wright .05 .02
❑ 322 Michael Bates .05 .02
❑ 323 Greg Davis .05 .02
❑ 324 Mark Bortz .05 .02
❑ 325 Kevin Greene .25 .11
❑ 326 Wayne Simmons .05 .02
❑ 327 Wayne Martin .05 .02
❑ 328 Michael Irvin UER .25 .11
(Stats on back have three career touchdowns; should be 34)
❑ 329 Checklist Card .05 .02
❑ 330 Checklist Card .05 .02
❑ 331 Doug Pelfrey .05 .02
❑ 332 Myron Guyton .05 .02
❑ 333 Howard Ballard .05 .02
❑ 334 Ricky Ervins .05 .02
❑ 335 Steve Emtman .05 .02
❑ 336 Eric Curry .05 .02
❑ 337 Bert Emanuel RC .50 .23
❑ 338 Darryl Ashmore .05 .02
❑ 339 Stevon Moore .05 .02
❑ 340 Garrison Hearst .25 .11
❑ 341 Vance Johnson .05 .02
❑ 342 Anthony Johnson .10 .05
❑ 343 Merril Hoge .05 .02
❑ 344 William Thomas .05 .02
❑ 345 Scott Mitchell .25 .11
❑ 346 Jim Everett .10 .05
❑ 347 Ray Crockett .05 .02
❑ 348 Bryan Cox .05 .02
❑ 349 Charles Johnson RC .40 .18
❑ 350 Randall McDaniel .05 .02
❑ 351 Micheal Barrow .05 .02
❑ 352 Darrell Thompson .05 .02
❑ 353 Kevin Gogan .05 .02
❑ 354 Brad Daluiso .05 .02
❑ 355 Mark Collins .05 .02
❑ 356 Bryant Young RC .25 .11
❑ 357 Steve Christie .05 .02
❑ 358 Derek Kennard .05 .02
❑ 359 Jon Vaughn .05 .02
❑ 360 Drew Bledsoe 1.25 .55
❑ 361 Randy Baldwin .05 .02
❑ 362 Kevin Ross .05 .02
❑ 363 Reuben Davis .05 .02
❑ 364 Chris Miller .05 .02
❑ 365 Tim McGee .05 .02
❑ 366 Tony Woods .05 .02
❑ 367 Dean Biasucci .05 .02
❑ 368 George Jamison .05 .02
❑ 369 Lorenzo Lynch .05 .02
❑ 370 Johnny Johnson .05 .02
❑ 371 Greg Kragen .05 .02
❑ 372 Vinson Smith .05 .02
❑ 373 Vince Workman .05 .02
❑ 374 Allen Aldridge .05 .02
❑ 375 Terry Kirby .25 .11
❑ 376 Mario Bates RC .25 .11
❑ 377 Dixon Edwards .05 .02
❑ 378 Leon Searcy .05 .02
❑ 379 Eric Guliford RC .05 .02
❑ 380 Gary Brown .05 .02
❑ 381 Phil Hansen .05 .02
❑ 382 Keith Hamilton .05 .02
❑ 383 John Alt .05 .02
❑ 384 John Taylor .10 .05
❑ 385 Reggie Cobb .05 .02
❑ 386 Rob Fredrickson RC .10 .05
❑ 387 Pepper Johnson .05 .02
❑ 388 Kevin Lee RC .05 .02
❑ 389 Stanley Richard .05 .02
❑ 390 Jackie Slater .05 .02
❑ 391 Darrick Brilz .05 .02
❑ 392 John Gesek .05 .02
❑ 393 Kelvin Pritchett .05 .02
❑ 394 Aeneas Williams .05 .02
❑ 395 Henry Ford .05 .02
❑ 396 Eric Mahlum .05 .02
❑ 397 Tom Rouen .05 .02
❑ 398 Vinnie Clark .05 .02
❑ 399 Jim Sweeney .05 .02
❑ 400 Troy Aikman UER 1.00 .45
(Threw for 56 TD's in 1993)
❑ 401 Toi Cook .05 .02
❑ 402 Dan Saleaumua .05 .02
❑ 403 Andy Heck .05 .02
❑ 404 Deon Figures .05 .02
❑ 405 Henry Thomas .05 .02
❑ 406 Glenn Montgomery .05 .02
❑ 407 Trent Dilfer RC 1.50 .70
❑ 408 Eddie Murray .05 .02
❑ 409 Gene Atkins .05 .02
❑ 410 Mike Sherrard .05 .02
❑ 411 Don Mosebar .05 .02
❑ 412 Thomas Smith .05 .02
❑ 413 Ken Norton Jr. .10 .05
❑ 414 Robert Brooks .25 .11
❑ 415 Jeff Lageman .05 .02
❑ 416 Tony Siragusa .05 .02
❑ 417 Brian Blades .10 .05
❑ 418 Matt Stover .05 .02
❑ 419 Jesse Solomon .05 .02
❑ 420 Reggie Roby .05 .02
❑ 421 Shawn Jefferson .05 .02
❑ 422 Marc Boutte .05 .02
❑ 423 William White .05 .02
❑ 424 Clyde Simmons .05 .02
❑ 425 Anthony Miller .10 .05
❑ 426 Brent Jones .10 .05
❑ 427 Tim Grunhard .05 .02
❑ 428 Alfred Williams .05 .02
❑ 429 Roy Barker RC .05 .02
❑ 430 Dante Jones .05 .02
❑ 431 Leroy Thompson .05 .02
❑ 432 Marcus Robertson .05 .02
❑ 433 Thomas Lewis RC .10 .05
❑ 434 Sean Jones .05 .02
❑ 435 Michael Haynes .10 .05
❑ 436 Albert Lewis .05 .02
❑ 437 Tim Bowens RC .10 .05
❑ 438 Marvcus Patton .05 .02
❑ 439 Rich Miano .05 .02
❑ 440 Craig Erickson .05 .02
❑ 441 Larry Allen RC .10 .05
❑ 442 Fernando Smith .05 .02
❑ 443 D.J. Johnson .05 .02
❑ 444 Leonard Russell .05 .02
❑ 445 Marshall Faulk RC 4.00 1.80
❑ 446 Najee Mustafaa .05 .02
❑ 447 Brian Hansen .05 .02
❑ 448 Isaac Bruce RC 4.00 1.80
❑ 449 Kevin Scott .05 .02
❑ 450 Natrone Means .25 .11
❑ 451 Tracy Rogers RC .05 .02
❑ 452 Mike Croel .05 .02
❑ 453 Anthony Edwards .05 .02
❑ 454 Brenston Buckner RC .05 .02
❑ 455 Tom Carter .05 .02
❑ 456 Burt Grossman .05 .02
❑ 457 Jimmy Spencer RC .05 .02
❑ 458 Rocket Ismail .10 .05
❑ 459 Fred Strickland .05 .02
❑ 460 Jeff Burris RC .10 .05
❑ 461 Adrian Hardy .05 .02
❑ 462 Lamar McGriggs .05 .02
❑ 463 Webster Slaughter .05 .02
❑ 464 Demetrius DuBose .05 .02
❑ 465 Dave Brown .10 .05
❑ 466 Kenneth Gant .05 .02
❑ 467 Erik Kramer .10 .05
❑ 468 Mark Ingram .05 .02
❑ 469 Roman Phifer .05 .02
❑ 470 Steve Young .50 .23
❑ 471 Nick Lowery .05 .02
❑ 472 Irving Fryar .10 .05
❑ 473 Art Monk .10 .05
❑ 474 Mel Gray .05 .02
❑ 475 Reggie White .25 .11
❑ 476 Eric Ball .05 .02
❑ 477 Dwayne Harper .05 .02
❑ 478 Will Shields .05 .02
❑ 479 Roger Harper .05 .02
❑ 480 Rick Mirer .25 .11
❑ 481 Vincent Brisby .25 .11
❑ 482 John Jurkovic RC .10 .05
❑ 483 Michael Jackson .10 .05
❑ 484 Ed Cunningham .05 .02
❑ 485 Brad Ottis .05 .02
❑ 486 Sterling Palmer RC .05 .02
❑ 487 Tony Bennett .05 .02
❑ 488 Mike Pritchard .05 .02
❑ 489 Bucky Brooks RC .05 .02
❑ 490 Troy Vincent .05 .02
❑ 491 Eric Green .05 .02
❑ 492 Van Malone .05 .02
❑ 493 Marcus Spears .05 .02
❑ 494 Brian Williams OL .05 .02
❑ 495 Robert Smith .25 .11
❑ 496 Haywood Jeffires .10 .05
❑ 497 Darrin Smith .05 .02
❑ 498 Tommy Barnhardt .05 .02
❑ 499 Anthony Smith .05 .02
❑ 500 Ricky Watters .25 .11
❑ 501 Antone Davis .05 .02
❑ 502 David Braxton .05 .02
❑ 503 Donnell Bennett RC .25 .11
❑ 504 Donald Evans .05 .02
❑ 505 Lewis Tillman .05 .02
❑ 506 Lance Smith .05 .02
❑ 507 Aaron Taylor .05 .02
❑ 508 Ricky Sanders .05 .02
❑ 509 Dennis Smith .05 .02
❑ 510 Barry Foster .05 .02
❑ 511 Stan Brock .05 .02
❑ 512 Henry Rolling .05 .02
❑ 513 Walter Reeves .05 .02
❑ 514 John Booty .05 .02
❑ 515 Kenneth Davis .05 .02
❑ 516 Cris Dishman .05 .02
❑ 517 Bill Lewis .05 .02
❑ 518 Jeff Bryant .05 .02
❑ 519 Brian Mitchell .05 .02
❑ 520 Joe Montana 2.00 .90
❑ 521 Keith Sims .05 .02
❑ 522 Harry Colon .05 .02
❑ 523 Leon Lett .05 .02
❑ 524 Carlos Jenkins .05 .02
❑ 525 Victor Bailey .05 .02
❑ 526 Harvey Williams .10 .05
❑ 527 Irv Smith .05 .02
❑ 528 Jason Sehorn RC .30 .14
❑ 529 John Thierry RC .05 .02
❑ 530 Brett Favre 2.00 .90
❑ 531 Sean Dawkins RC .25 .11
❑ 532 Erric Pegram .05 .02
❑ 533 Jimmy Williams .05 .02
❑ 534 Michael Timpson .05 .02
❑ 535 Flipper Anderson .05 .02
❑ 536 John Parrella .05 .02
❑ 537 Freddie Joe Nunn .05 .02
❑ 538 Doug Dawson .05 .02
❑ 539 Michael Stewart .05 .02
❑ 540 John Elway 2.00 .90
❑ 541 Ronnie Lott .10 .05
❑ 542 Barry Sanders .75 .35
❑ 543 Andre Reed .10 .05
❑ 544 Deion Sanders .25 .11
❑ 545 Dan Marino .75 .35
❑ 546 Carlton Bailey .05 .02
❑ 547 Emmitt Smith .75 .35
❑ 548 Alvin Harper .10 .05
❑ 549 Eric Metcalf .10 .05
❑ 550 Jerry Rice .50 .23
❑ 551 Derrick Thomas .25 .11
❑ 552 Mark Collins .05 .02
❑ 553 Eric Turner .05 .02
❑ 554 Sterling Sharpe .25 .11
❑ 555 Steve Young .25 .11
❑ 556 Darnay Scott RC .75 .35
❑ 557 Joel Steed .05 .02

	#	Player	Mint	NrMt
❑	558	Dennis Gibson	.05	.02
❑	559	Charles Mincy	.05	.02
❑	560	Rickey Jackson	.05	.02
❑	561	Dave Cadigan	.05	.02
❑	562	Rick Tuten	.05	.02
❑	563	Mike Caldwell	.05	.02
❑	564	Todd Steussie RC	.10	.05
❑	565	Kevin Smith	.05	.02
❑	566	Arthur Marshall	.05	.02
❑	567	Aaron Wallace	.05	.02
❑	568	Calvin Williams	.10	.05
❑	569	Todd Kelly	.05	.02
❑	570	Barry Sanders	2.00	.90
❑	571	Shaun Gayle	.05	.02
❑	572	Will Wolford	.05	.02
❑	573	Ethan Horton	.05	.02
❑	574	Chris Slade	.05	.02
❑	575	Jeff Wright	.05	.02
❑	576	Toby Wright	.05	.02
❑	577	Lamar Thomas	.05	.02
❑	578	Chris Singleton	.05	.02
❑	579	Ed West	.05	.02
❑	580	Jeff George	.25	.11
❑	581	Kevin Mitchell	.05	.02
❑	582	Chad Brown	.05	.02
❑	583	Rich Camarillo	.05	.02
❑	584	Gary Zimmerman	.05	.02
❑	585	Randal Hill	.05	.02
❑	586	Keith Cash	.05	.02
❑	587	Sam Mills	.05	.02
❑	588	Shawn Lee	.05	.02
❑	589	Kent Graham	.10	.05
❑	590	Steve Everitt	.05	.02
❑	591	Rob Moore	.10	.05
❑	592	Kevin Mawae	.05	.02
❑	593	Jerry Ball	.05	.02
❑	594	Larry Brown DB	.05	.02
❑	595	Tim Krumrie	.05	.02
❑	596	Aubrey Beavers RC	.05	.02
❑	597	Chris Hinton	.05	.02
❑	598	Greg Montgomery	.05	.02
❑	599	Jimmie Jones	.05	.02
❑	600	Jim Kelly	.25	.11
❑	601	Joe Johnson RC	.05	.02
❑	602	Tim Irwin	.05	.02
❑	603	Steve Jackson	.05	.02
❑	604	James Williams RC	.05	.02
❑	605	Blair Thomas	.05	.02
❑	606	Danan Hughes	.05	.02
❑	607	Russell Freeman	.05	.02
❑	608	Andre Hastings	.10	.05
❑	609	Ken Harvey	.05	.02
❑	610	Jim Harbaugh	.25	.11
❑	611	Emmitt Smith MG	.75	.35
❑	612	Andre Rison MG	.10	.05
❑	613	Steve Young MG	.25	.11
❑	614	Anthony Miller MG	.05	.02
❑	615	Barry Sanders MG	1.00	.45
❑	616	Bernie Kosar	.10	.05
❑	617	Chris Gardocki	.05	.02
❑	618	William Floyd RC	.25	.11
❑	619	Matt Brock	.05	.02
❑	620	Dan Wilkinson RC	.10	.05
❑	621	Tony Meola RC	.10	.05
❑	622	Tony Tolbert	.05	.02
❑	623	Mike Zandofsky	.05	.02
❑	624	William Fuller	.05	.02
❑	625	Steve Jordan	.05	.02
❑	626	Mike Johnson	.05	.02
❑	627	Ferrell Edmunds	.05	.02
❑	628	Gene Williams	.05	.02
❑	629	Willie Beamon	.05	.02
❑	630	Gerald Perry	.05	.02
❑	631	John Baylor	.05	.02
❑	632	Carwell Gardner	.05	.02
❑	633	Thomas Everett	.05	.02
❑	634	Lamar Lathon	.05	.02
❑	635	Michael Bankston	.05	.02
❑	636	Ray Crittenden RC	.05	.02
❑	637	Kimble Anders	.10	.05
❑	638	Robert Delpino	.05	.02
❑	639	Darren Perry	.05	.02
❑	640	Byron Evans	.05	.02
❑	641	Mark Higgs	.05	.02
❑	642	Lorenzo Neal	.05	.02
❑	643	Henry Ellard	.10	.05
❑	644	Trace Armstrong	.05	.02
❑	645	Greg McMurtry	.05	.02
❑	646	Steve McMichael	.10	.05
❑	647	Terance Mathis	.10	.05
❑	648	Eric Bieniemy	.05	.02
❑	649	Bobby Houston	.05	.02
❑	650	Alvin Harper	.10	.05
❑	651	James Folston	.05	.02
❑	652	Mel Gray	.05	.02
❑	653	Adrian Cooper	.05	.02
❑	654	Dexter Carter	.05	.02
❑	655	Don Griffin	.05	.02
❑	656	Corey Widmer	.05	.02
❑	657	Lee Johnson	.05	.02
❑	658	Nate Odomes	.05	.02
❑	659	Checklist Card	.05	.02
❑	660	Checklist Card	.05	.02
❑	P1	Promo Sheet Stan Humphries Darryl Talley Rodney Hampton Jerome Bettis Chris Zorich Harry Newsome Tyrone Hughes Rod Woodson Chris Spielman	4.00	1.80
❑	P2	Promo Sheet Spec. Eff. Jerome Bettis Chris Zorich Harry Newsome	4.00	1.80

1995 Topps

	MINT	NRMT
COMPLETE SET (468)	40.00	18.00
COMP.FACT.SET (478)	50.00	22.00
COMP.SERIES 1 (248)	20.00	9.00
COMP.SERIES 2 (220)	20.00	9.00

	#	Player	Mint	NrMt
❑	1	Barry Sanders	1.00	.45
❑	2	Chris Warren	.20	.09
❑	3	Jerry Rice	.50	.23
❑	4	Emmitt Smith	.75	.35
❑	5	Henry Ellard	.20	.09
❑	6	Natrone Means TYC	.30	.14
❑	7	Terance Mathis	.20	.09
❑	8	Tim Brown TYC	.20	.09
❑	9	Andre Reed	.20	.09
❑	10	Marshall Faulk	.30	.14
❑	11	Irving Fryar	.20	.09
❑	12	Cris Carter	.30	.14
❑	13	Michael Irvin	.30	.14
❑	14	Jake Reed	.20	.09
❑	15	Ben Coates	.20	.09
❑	16	Herman Moore	.30	.14
❑	17	Carl Pickens	.30	.14
❑	18	Fred Barnett	.20	.09
❑	19	Sterling Sharpe	.20	.09
❑	20	Anthony Miller	.20	.09
❑	21	Thurman Thomas	.30	.14
❑	22	Andre Rison	.20	.09
❑	23	Brian Blades	.20	.09
❑	24	Rodney Hampton	.20	.09
❑	25	Terry Allen	.20	.09
❑	26	Jerome Bettis	.30	.14
❑	27	Errict Rhett	.30	.14
❑	28	Rob Moore	.10	.05
❑	29	Shannon Sharpe	.20	.09
❑	30	Drew Bledsoe	.50	.23
❑	31	Dan Marino	1.00	.45
❑	32	Warren Moon	.20	.09
❑	33	Steve Young	.40	.18
❑	34	Brett Favre	1.00	.45
❑	35	Jim Everett	.10	.05
❑	36	Jeff George	.20	.09
❑	37	John Elway	1.00	.45
❑	38	Jeff Hostetler	.20	.09
❑	39	Randall Cunningham	.30	.14
❑	40	Stan Humphries	.20	.09
❑	41	Jim Kelly	.30	.14
❑	42	Tommy Barnhardt	.10	.05
❑	43	Bob Whitfield	.10	.05
❑	44	William Thomas	.10	.05
❑	45	Glyn Milburn	.10	.05
❑	46	Steve Christie	.10	.05
❑	47	Kevin Mawae	.10	.05
❑	48	Vencie Glenn	.10	.05
❑	49	Eric Curry	.10	.05
❑	50	Jeff Hostetler	.20	.09
❑	51	Tyronne Stowe	.10	.05
❑	52	Steve Jackson	.10	.05
❑	53	Ben Coleman	.10	.05
❑	54	Brad Baxter	.10	.05
❑	55	Darryl Williams	.10	.05
❑	56	Troy Drayton	.10	.05
❑	57	George Teague	.10	.05
❑	58	Calvin Williams	.20	.09
❑	59	Jeff Cross	.10	.05
❑	60	Leroy Hoard	.10	.05
❑	61	John Carney	.10	.05
❑	62	Daryl Johnston	.20	.09
❑	63	Jim Jeffcoat	.10	.05
❑	64	Matt Stover	.10	.05
❑	65	LeRoy Butler	.10	.05
❑	66	Curtis Conway	.30	.14
❑	67	O.J. McDuffie	.30	.14
❑	68	Robert Massey	.10	.05
❑	69	Ed McDaniel	.10	.05
❑	70	William Floyd	.30	.14
❑	71	Willie Davis	.20	.09
❑	72	William Roberts	.10	.05
❑	73	Chester McGlockton	.20	.09
❑	74	D.J. Johnson	.10	.05
❑	75	Rondell Jones	.10	.05
❑	76	Morten Andersen	.10	.05
❑	77	Glenn Parker	.10	.05
❑	78	William Fuller	.10	.05
❑	79	Ray Buchanan	.10	.05
❑	80	Maurice Hurst	.10	.05
❑	81	Wayne Gandy	.10	.05
❑	82	Marcus Turner	.10	.05
❑	83	Greg Davis	.10	.05
❑	84	Terry Wooden	.10	.05
❑	85	Thomas Everett	.10	.05
❑	86	Steve Broussard	.10	.05
❑	87	Tom Carter	.10	.05
❑	88	Glenn Montgomery	.10	.05
❑	89	Larry Allen	.20	.09
❑	90	Donnell Woolford	.10	.05
❑	91	John Alt	.10	.05
❑	92	Phil Hansen	.10	.05
❑	93	Seth Joyner	.10	.05
❑	94	Michael Brooks	.10	.05
❑	95	Randall McDaniel	.10	.05
❑	96	Tydus Winans	.10	.05
❑	97	Rob Fredrickson	.10	.05
❑	98	Ray Crockett	.10	.05
❑	99	Courtney Hall	.10	.05
❑	100	Merton Hanks	.10	.05
❑	101	Aaron Glenn	.10	.05
❑	102	Roosevelt Potts	.10	.05
❑	103	Leon Lett	.10	.05
❑	104	Jessie Tuggle	.10	.05
❑	105	Martin Mayhew	.10	.05
❑	106	Willie Roaf	.10	.05
❑	107	Todd Lyght	.10	.05
❑	108	Ernest Givins	.10	.05
❑	109	Tony McGee	.10	.05
❑	110	Barry Sanders	2.00	.90
❑	111	Dermontti Dawson	.20	.09
❑	112	Rick Tuten	.10	.05
❑	113	Vincent Brisby	.10	.05
❑	114	Charlie Garner	.20	.09

❑ 115 Irving Fryar .20 .09
❑ 116 Stevon Moore .10 .05
❑ 117 Matt Darby .10 .05
❑ 118 Howard Cross .10 .05
❑ 119 John Gesek .10 .05
❑ 120 Jack Del Rio .10 .05
❑ 121 Marcus Allen .30 .14
❑ 122 Torrance Small .10 .05
❑ 123 Chris Mims .10 .05
❑ 124 Don Mosebar .10 .05
❑ 125 Carl Pickens .30 .14
❑ 126 Tom Rouen .10 .05
❑ 127 Garrison Hearst .30 .14
❑ 128 Charles Johnson .20 .09
❑ 129 Derek Brown RBK .10 .05
❑ 130 Troy Aikman 1.00 .45
❑ 131 Troy Vincent .10 .05
❑ 132 Ken Ruettgers .10 .05
❑ 133 Michael Jackson .20 .09
❑ 134 Dennis Gibson .10 .05
❑ 135 Brett Perriman .20 .09
❑ 136 Jeff Graham .10 .05
❑ 137 Chad Brown .20 .09
❑ 138 Ken Norton Jr. .20 .09
❑ 139 Chris Slade .20 .09
❑ 140 Dave Brown .20 .09
❑ 141 Bert Emanuel .30 .14
❑ 142 Renaldo Turnbull .10 .05
❑ 143 Jim Harbaugh .20 .09
❑ 144 Micheal Barrow .10 .05
❑ 145 Vincent Brown .10 .05
❑ 146 Bryant Young .20 .09
❑ 147 Boomer Esiason .20 .09
❑ 148 Sean Gilbert .20 .09
❑ 149 Greg Truitt .10 .05
❑ 150 Rod Woodson .20 .09
❑ 151 Robert Porcher .10 .05
❑ 152 Joe Phillips .10 .05
❑ 153 Gary Zimmerman .10 .05
❑ 154 Bruce Smith .30 .14
❑ 155 Randall Cunningham .30 .14
❑ 156 Fred Strickland .10 .05
❑ 157 Derrick Alexander WR .30 .14
❑ 158 James Williams .10 .05
❑ 159 Scott Dill .10 .05
❑ 160 Tim Bowens .10 .05
❑ 161 Floyd Turner .10 .05
❑ 162 Ronnie Harmon .10 .05
❑ 163 Wayne Martin .10 .05
❑ 164 John Randle .20 .09
❑ 165 Larry Centers .20 .09
❑ 166 Larry Brown DB .10 .05
❑ 167 Albert Lewis .10 .05
❑ 168 Michael Strahan .20 .09
❑ 169 Reggie Brooks .20 .09
❑ 170 Craig Heyward .20 .09
❑ 171 Pat Harlow .10 .05
❑ 172 Eugene Robinson .10 .05
❑ 173 Shane Conlan .10 .05
❑ 174 Bennie Blades .10 .05
❑ 175 Neil O'Donnell .20 .09
❑ 176 Steve Tovar .10 .05
❑ 177 Donald Evans .10 .05
❑ 178 Brent Jones .10 .05
❑ 179 Ray Childress .10 .05
❑ 180 Reggie White .30 .14
❑ 181 David Alexander .10 .05
❑ 182 Greg Hill .20 .09
❑ 183 Vinny Testaverde .20 .09
❑ 184 Jeff Burris .10 .05
❑ 185 Hardy Nickerson .10 .05
❑ 186 Terry Kirby .20 .09
❑ 187 Kirk Lowdermilk .10 .05
❑ 188 Eric Swann .20 .09
❑ 189 Chris Zorich .10 .05
❑ 190 Simon Fletcher .10 .05
❑ 191 Qadry Ismail .20 .09
❑ 192 Heath Shuler .30 .14
❑ 193 Michael Haynes .20 .09
❑ 194 Mike Sherrard .10 .05
❑ 195 Nolan Harrison .10 .05
❑ 196 Marcus Robertson .10 .05
❑ 197 Kevin Williams WR .20 .09
❑ 198 Moe Gardner .10 .05
❑ 199 Rick Mirer .30 .14
❑ 200 Junior Seau .30 .14
❑ 201 Byron Bam Morris .20 .09
❑ 202 Willie McGinest .20 .09
❑ 203 Chris Spielman .20 .09
❑ 204 Darnay Scott .30 .14
❑ 205 Jesse Sapolu .10 .05
❑ 206 Marvin Washington .10 .05
❑ 207 Anthony Newman .10 .05
❑ 208 Cortez Kennedy .20 .09
❑ 209 Quentin Coryatt .20 .09
❑ 210 Neil Smith .20 .09
❑ 211 Keith Sims .10 .05
❑ 212 Sean Jones .10 .05
❑ 213 Tony Jones .10 .05
❑ 214 Lewis Tillman .10 .05
❑ 215 Darren Woodson .20 .09
❑ 216 Jason Hanson .10 .05
❑ 217 John Taylor .10 .05
❑ 218 Shawn Lee .10 .05
❑ 219 Kevin Greene .20 .09
❑ 220 Jerry Rice 1.00 .45
❑ 221 Ki-Jana Carter RC .30 .14
❑ 222 Tony Boselli RC .30 .14
❑ 223 Michael Westbrook RC 1.50 .70
❑ 224 Kerry Collins RC 1.25 .55
❑ 225 Kevin Carter RC .30 .14
❑ 226 Kyle Brady RC .30 .14
❑ 227 J.J. Stokes RC .30 .14
❑ 228 Der. Alexander DE RC .10 .05
❑ 229 Warren Sapp RC .60 .25
❑ 230 Ruben Brown RC .10 .05
❑ 231 Hugh Douglas RC .30 .14
❑ 232 Luther Elliss RC .10 .05
❑ 233 Rashaan Salaam RC .30 .14
❑ 234 Tyrone Poole RC .20 .09
❑ 235 Korey Stringer .10 .05
❑ 236 Devin Bush RC .10 .05
❑ 237 Cory Raymer .10 .05
❑ 238 Zach Wiegert RC .10 .05
❑ 239 Ron Davis RC .10 .05
❑ 240 Todd Collins QB RC .30 .14
❑ 241 Bobby Taylor RC .20 .09
❑ 242 Patrick Riley RC .10 .05
❑ 243 Scott Gragg .10 .05
❑ 244 Marvcus Patton .10 .05
❑ 245 Alvin Harper .10 .05
❑ 246 Ricky Watters .30 .14
❑ 247 Checklist 1 .10 .05
❑ 248 Checklist 2 .10 .05
❑ 249 Terance Mathis .20 .09
❑ 250 Mark Carrier DB .10 .05
❑ 251 Elijah Alexander .10 .05
❑ 252 George Koonce .10 .05
❑ 253 Tony Bennett .10 .05
❑ 254 Steve Wisniewski .10 .05
❑ 255 Bernie Parmalee .20 .09
❑ 256 Dwayne Sabb .10 .05
❑ 257 Lorenzo Neal .10 .05
❑ 258 Corey Miller .10 .05
❑ 259 Fred Barnett .20 .09
❑ 260 Greg Lloyd .20 .09
❑ 261 Robert Blackmon .10 .05
❑ 262 Ken Harvey .10 .05
❑ 263 Eric Hill .10 .05
❑ 264 Russell Copeland .10 .05
❑ 265 Jeff Blake RC 1.00 .45
❑ 266 Carl Banks .10 .05
❑ 267 Jay Novacek .20 .09
❑ 268 Mel Gray .10 .05
❑ 269 Kimble Anders .20 .09
❑ 270 Cris Carter .30 .14
❑ 271 Johnny Mitchell .10 .05
❑ 272 Shawn Jefferson .10 .05
❑ 273 Doug Brien .10 .05
❑ 274 Sean Landeta .10 .05
❑ 275 Scott Mitchell .20 .09
❑ 276 Charles Wilson .10 .05
❑ 277 Anthony Smith .10 .05
❑ 278 Anthony Miller .20 .09
❑ 279 Steve Walsh .10 .05
❑ 280 Drew Bledsoe 1.00 .45
❑ 281 Jamir Miller .10 .05
❑ 282 Robert Brooks UER .30 .14
(Rushing and receiving totals are reversed)
❑ 283 Sean Lumpkin .10 .05
❑ 284 Bryan Cox .10 .05
❑ 285 Byron Evans .10 .05
❑ 286 Chris Doleman .10 .05
❑ 287 Anthony Pleasant .10 .05
❑ 288 Stephen Grant RC .10 .05
❑ 289 Doug Riesenberg .10 .05
❑ 290 Natrone Means .30 .14
❑ 291 Henry Thomas .10 .05
❑ 292 Mike Pritchard .10 .05
❑ 293 Courtney Hawkins .10 .05
❑ 294 Bill Bates .20 .09
❑ 295 Jerome Bettis .30 .14
❑ 296 Russell Maryland .10 .05
❑ 297 Stanley Richard .10 .05
❑ 298 William White .10 .05
❑ 299 Dan Wilkinson .20 .09
❑ 300 Steve Young .75 .35
❑ 301 Gary Brown .10 .05
❑ 302 Jake Reed .20 .09
❑ 303 Carlton Gray .10 .05
❑ 304 Levon Kirkland .10 .05
❑ 305 Shannon Sharpe .20 .09
❑ 306 Luis Sharpe .10 .05
❑ 307 Marshall Faulk .40 .18
❑ 308 Stan Humphries .20 .09
❑ 309 Chris Calloway .10 .05
❑ 310 Tim Brown .30 .14
❑ 311 Steve Everitt .10 .05
❑ 312 Raymont Harris .10 .05
❑ 313 Tim McDonald .10 .05
❑ 314 Trent Dilfer .30 .14
❑ 315 Jim Everett .10 .05
❑ 316 Ray Crittenden .10 .05
❑ 317 Jim Kelly .30 .14
❑ 318 Andre Reed .20 .09
❑ 319 Chris Miller .10 .05
❑ 320 Bobby Houston .10 .05
❑ 321 Charles Haley .20 .09
❑ 322 James Francis .10 .05
❑ 323 Bernard Williams .10 .05
❑ 324 Michael Bates .10 .05
❑ 325 Brian Mitchell .10 .05
❑ 326 Mike Johnson .10 .05
❑ 327 Eric Bieniemy .10 .05
❑ 328 Aubrey Beavers .10 .05
❑ 329 Dale Carter .20 .09
❑ 330 Emmitt Smith 1.50 .70
❑ 331 Darren Perry .10 .05
❑ 332 Marquez Pope .10 .05
❑ 333 Clyde Simmons .10 .05
❑ 334 Corey Croom .10 .05
❑ 335 Thomas Randolph .10 .05
❑ 336 Harvey Williams .10 .05
❑ 337 Michael Timpson .10 .05
❑ 338 Eugene Daniel .10 .05
❑ 339 Shane Dronett .10 .05
❑ 340 Eric Turner .10 .05
❑ 341 Eric Metcalf .20 .09
❑ 342 Leslie O'Neal .20 .09
❑ 343 Mark Wheeler .10 .05
❑ 344 Mark Pike .10 .05
❑ 345 Brett Favre 2.00 .90
❑ 346 Johnny Bailey .10 .05
❑ 347 Henry Ellard .20 .09
❑ 348 Chris Gardocki .10 .05
❑ 349 Henry Jones .10 .05
❑ 350 Dan Marino 2.00 .90
❑ 351 Lake Dawson .20 .09
❑ 352 Mark McMillian .10 .05
❑ 353 Deion Sanders .60 .25
❑ 354 Antonio London .10 .05
❑ 355 Cris Dishman .10 .05
❑ 356 Ricardo McDonald .10 .05
❑ 357 Dexter Carter .10 .05
❑ 358 Kevin Smith .10 .05
❑ 359 Yancey Thigpen RC .30 .14
❑ 360 Chris Warren .20 .09
❑ 361 Quinn Early .20 .09
❑ 362 John Mangum .10 .05
❑ 363 Santana Dotson .10 .05
❑ 364 Rocket Ismail .20 .09
❑ 365 Aeneas Williams .10 .05
❑ 366 Dan Williams .10 .05
❑ 367 Sean Dawkins .20 .09
❑ 368 Pepper Johnson .10 .05
❑ 369 Roman Phifer .10 .05
❑ 370 Rodney Hampton .20 .09

❑ 371 Darrell Green .10 .05
❑ 372 Michael Zordich .10 .05
❑ 373 Andre Coleman .10 .05
❑ 374 Wayne Simmons .10 .05
❑ 375 Michael Irvin .30 .14
❑ 376 Clay Matthews .20 .09
❑ 377 Dewayne Washington .20 .09
❑ 378 Keith Byars .10 .05
❑ 379 Todd Collins LB .30 .14
❑ 380 Mark Collins .10 .05
❑ 381 Joel Steed .10 .05
❑ 382 Bart Oates .10 .05
❑ 383 Al Smith .10 .05
❑ 384 Rafael Robinson .10 .05
❑ 385 Mo Lewis .10 .05
❑ 386 Aubrey Matthews .10 .05
❑ 387 Corey Sawyer .10 .05
❑ 388 Bucky Brooks .10 .05
❑ 389 Erik Kramer .10 .05
❑ 390 Tyrone Hughes .20 .09
❑ 391 Terry McDaniel .10 .05
❑ 392 Craig Erickson .10 .05
❑ 393 Mike Flores .10 .05
❑ 394 Harry Swayne .10 .05
❑ 395 Irving Spikes .20 .09
❑ 396 Lorenzo Lynch .10 .05
❑ 397 Antonio Langham .10 .05
❑ 398 Edgar Bennett .20 .09
❑ 399 Thomas Lewis .20 .09
❑ 400 John Elway 2.00 .90
❑ 401 Jeff George .20 .09
❑ 402 Errict Rhett .30 .14
❑ 403 Bill Romanowski .10 .05
❑ 404 Alexander Wright .10 .05
❑ 405 Warren Moon .20 .09
❑ 406 Eddie Robinson .10 .05
❑ 407 John Copeland .10 .05
❑ 408 Robert Jones .10 .05
❑ 409 Steve Bono .20 .09
❑ 410 Cornelius Bennett .20 .09
❑ 411 Ben Coates .20 .09
❑ 412 Dana Stubblefield .30 .14
❑ 413 Darryl Talley .10 .05
❑ 414 Brian Blades .20 .09
❑ 415 Herman Moore .30 .14
❑ 416 Nick Lowery .10 .05
❑ 417 Donnell Bennett .20 .09
❑ 418 Van Malone .10 .05
❑ 419 Pete Stoyanovich .10 .05
❑ 420 Joe Montana 2.00 .90
❑ 421 Steve Young .50 .23
Super Bowl XXIX MVP
❑ 422 Steve Young .50 .23
Quarterback Rating Leaders
❑ 423 Steve Young .50 .23
Super Bowl Touchdown Record
❑ 424 Steve Young .50 .23
NFL League MVP
❑ 425 Steve Young .50 .23
Pro Bowl
❑ 426 Rod Stephens .10 .05
❑ 427 Ellis Johnson RC UER .10 .05
(Card is numbered 436)
❑ 428 Kordell Stewart RC 2.00 .90
❑ 429 James O. Stewart RC 2.00 .90
❑ 430 Steve McNair RC 2.50 1.10
❑ 431 Brian DeMarco .20 .09
❑ 432 Matt O'Dwyer .10 .05
❑ 433 Lorenzo Styles RC .10 .05
❑ 434 Anthony Cook RC .10 .05
❑ 435 Jesse James .10 .05
❑ 436 Darryl Pounds .10 .05
❑ 437 Derrick Graham .10 .05
❑ 438 Vernon Turner .10 .05
❑ 439 Carlton Bailey .10 .05
❑ 440 Darion Conner .10 .05
❑ 441 Randy Baldwin .10 .05
❑ 442 Tim McKyer .10 .05
❑ 443 Sam Mills .20 .09
❑ 444 Bob Christian .10 .05
❑ 445 Steve Lofton .10 .05
❑ 446 Lamar Lathon .10 .05
❑ 447 Tony Smith .10 .05
❑ 448 Don Beebe .10 .05
❑ 449 Barry Foster .20 .09
❑ 450 Frank Reich .10 .05
❑ 451 Pete Metzelaars .10 .05
❑ 452 Reggie Cobb .10 .05
❑ 453 Jeff Lageman .10 .05
❑ 454 Derek Brown TE .10 .05
❑ 455 Desmond Howard .20 .09
❑ 456 Vinnie Clark .10 .05
❑ 457 Keith Goganious .10 .05
❑ 458 Shawn Bouwens .10 .05
❑ 459 Rob Johnson RC 2.00 .90
❑ 460 Steve Beuerlein .10 .05
❑ 461 Mark Brunell 1.00 .45
❑ 462 Harry Colon .10 .05
❑ 463 Chris Hudson .10 .05
❑ 464 Darren Carrington .10 .05
❑ 465 Ernest Givins .10 .05
❑ 466 Kelvin Pritchett .10 .05
❑ 467 Checklist (249-358) .10 .05
❑ 468 Checklist (358-468) .10 .05

1996 Topps

	MINT	NRMT
COMPLETE SET (440)	35.00	16.00
COMP.FACT.SET (448)	50.00	22.00
COMP.CER.FACT.SET (445)	40.00	18.00

❑ 1 Troy Aikman 1.00 .45
❑ 2 Kevin Greene .20 .09
❑ 3 Robert Brooks .30 .14
❑ 4 Eugene Daniel .10 .05
❑ 5 Rodney Peete .10 .05
❑ 6 James Hasty .10 .05
❑ 7 Tim McDonald .10 .05
❑ 8 Darick Holmes .10 .05
❑ 9 Morten Andersen .10 .05
❑ 10 Junior Seau .20 .09
❑ 11 Brett Perriman .10 .05
❑ 12 Eric Green .10 .05
❑ 13 Jim Flanigan .10 .05
❑ 14 Cortez Kennedy .10 .05
❑ 15 Orlando Thomas .10 .05
❑ 16 Anthony Miller .20 .09
❑ 17 Sean Gilbert .10 .05
❑ 18 Rob Fredrickson .10 .05
❑ 19 Willie Green .10 .05
❑ 20 Jeff Blake .30 .14
❑ 21 Trent Dilfer .30 .14
❑ 22 Chris Chandler .20 .09
❑ 23 Renaldo Turnbull .10 .05
❑ 24 Dave Meggett .10 .05
❑ 25 Heath Shuler .20 .09
❑ 26 Michael Jackson .20 .09
❑ 27 Thomas Randolph .10 .05
❑ 28 Keith Goganious .10 .05
❑ 29 Seth Joyner .10 .05
❑ 30 Wayne Chrebet .60 .25
❑ 31 Craig Newsome .10 .05
❑ 32 William Fuller .10 .05
❑ 33 Merton Hanks .10 .05
❑ 34 Dale Carter .10 .05
❑ 35 Quentin Coryatt .10 .05
❑ 36 Robert Jones .10 .05
❑ 37 Eric Metcalf .10 .05
❑ 38 Byron Bam Morris .20 .09
❑ 39 Bill Brooks .10 .05
❑ 40 Barry Sanders 2.00 .90
❑ 41 Michael Haynes .10 .05
❑ 42 Joey Galloway .60 .25
❑ 43 Robert Smith .20 .09
❑ 44 John Thierry .10 .05
❑ 45 Bryan Cox .10 .05
❑ 46 Anthony Parker .10 .05
❑ 47 Harvey Williams .10 .05
❑ 48 Terrell Davis 2.50 1.10
❑ 49 Darnay Scott .20 .09
❑ 50 Kerry Collins .30 .14
❑ 51 Cris Dishman .10 .05
❑ 52 Dwayne Harper .10 .05
❑ 53 Warren Sapp .10 .05
❑ 54 Will Moore .10 .05
❑ 55 Earnest Byner .10 .05
❑ 56 Aaron Glenn .10 .05
❑ 57 Michael Westbrook .30 .14
❑ 58 Vencie Glenn .10 .05
❑ 59 Rob Moore .20 .09
❑ 60 Mark Brunell 1.00 .45
❑ 61 Craig Heyward .10 .05
❑ 62 Eric Allen .10 .05
❑ 63 Bill Romanowski .10 .05
❑ 64 Dana Stubblefield .20 .09
❑ 65 Steve Bono .10 .05
❑ 66 George Koonce .10 .05
❑ 67 Larry Brown .10 .05
❑ 68 Warren Moon .20 .09
❑ 69 Erric Pegram .10 .05
❑ 70 Jim Kelly .30 .14
❑ 71 Jason Belser .10 .05
❑ 72 Henry Thomas .10 .05
❑ 73 Mark Carrier DB .10 .05
❑ 74 Terry Wooden .10 .05
❑ 75 Terry McDaniel .10 .05
❑ 76 O.J. McDuffie .20 .09
❑ 77 Dan Wilkinson .10 .05
❑ 78 Blake Brockermeyer .10 .05
❑ 79 Micheal Barrow .10 .05
❑ 80 Dave Brown .10 .05
❑ 81 Todd Lyght .10 .05
❑ 82 Henry Ellard .10 .05
❑ 83 Jeff Lageman .10 .05
❑ 84 Anthony Pleasant .10 .05
❑ 85 Aeneas Williams .10 .05
❑ 86 Vincent Brisby .10 .05
❑ 87 Terrell Fletcher .10 .05
❑ 88 Brad Baxter .10 .05
❑ 89 Shannon Sharpe .20 .09
❑ 90 Errict Rhett .20 .09
❑ 91 Michael Zordich .10 .05
❑ 92 Dan Saleaumua .10 .05
❑ 93 Devin Bush .10 .05
❑ 94 Wayne Simmons .10 .05
❑ 95 Tyrone Hughes .10 .05
❑ 96 John Randle .20 .09
❑ 97 Tony Tolbert .10 .05
❑ 98 Yancey Thigpen .20 .09
❑ 99 J.J. Stokes .30 .14
❑ 100 Marshall Faulk .30 .14
❑ 101 Barry Minter .10 .05
❑ 102 Glenn Foley .20 .09
❑ 103 Chester McGlockton .10 .05
❑ 104 Carlton Gray .10 .05
❑ 105 Terry Kirby .20 .09
❑ 106 Darryll Lewis .10 .05
❑ 107 Thomas Smith .10 .05
❑ 108 Mike Fox .10 .05
❑ 109 Antonio Langham .10 .05
❑ 110 Drew Bledsoe 1.00 .45
❑ 111 Troy Drayton .10 .05
❑ 112 Marvcus Patton .10 .05
❑ 113 Tyrone Wheatley .20 .09
❑ 114 Desmond Howard .20 .09
❑ 115 Johnny Mitchell .10 .05
❑ 116 Dave Krieg .10 .05
❑ 117 Natrone Means .30 .14
❑ 118 Herman Moore .30 .14
❑ 119 Darren Woodson .20 .09
❑ 120 Ricky Watters .20 .09
❑ 121 Emmitt Smith TYC .75 .35
❑ 122 Barry Sanders TYC 1.00 .45
❑ 123 Curtis Martin TYC .30 .14
❑ 124 Chris Warren TYC .20 .09
❑ 125 Terry Allen TYC .20 .09
❑ 126 Ricky Watters TYC .20 .09
❑ 127 Errict Rhett TYC .20 .09
❑ 128 Rodney Hampton TYC .10 .05

❑ 129 Terrell Davis TYC .... 1.25 .55
❑ 130 Harvey Williams TYC ..... .10 .05
❑ 131 Craig Heyward TYC ...... .10 .05
❑ 132 Marshall Faulk TYC........ .20 .09
❑ 133 Rashaan Salaam TYC .. .20 .09
❑ 134 Garrison Hearst TYC...... .20 .09
❑ 135 Edgar Bennett TYC........ .20 .09
❑ 136 Thurman Thomas TYC .. .20 .09
❑ 137 Brian Washington .... .10 .05
❑ 138 Derek Loville .... .10 .05
❑ 139 Curtis Conway................ .30 .14
❑ 140 Isaac Bruce.................... .30 .14
❑ 141 Ricardo McDonald.......... .10 .05
❑ 142 Bruce Armstrong............ .10 .05
❑ 143 Will Wolford.................... .10 .05
❑ 144 Thurman Thomas .... .30 .14
❑ 145 Mel Gray .... .10 .05
❑ 146 Napoleon Kaufman .... .30 .14
❑ 147 Terry Allen...................... .20 .09
❑ 148 Chris Calloway .... .10 .05
❑ 149 Harry Colon.................... .10 .05
❑ 150 Pepper Johnson .... .10 .05
❑ 151 Marco Coleman.............. .10 .05
❑ 152 Shawn Jefferson .... .10 .05
❑ 153 Larry Centers .... .20 .09
❑ 154 Lamar Lathon .... .10 .05
❑ 155 Mark Chmura .... .20 .09
❑ 156 Dermontti Dawson.......... .10 .05
❑ 157 Alvin Harper .... .10 .05
❑ 158 Randall McDaniel .... .10 .05
❑ 159 Allen Aldridge .... .10 .05
❑ 160 Chris Warren.................. .20 .09
❑ 161 Jessie Tuggle .... .10 .05
❑ 162 Sean Lumpkin................ .10 .05
❑ 163 Bobby Houston .... .10 .05
❑ 164 Dexter Carter.................. .10 .05
❑ 165 Erik Kramer.................... .10 .05
❑ 166 Brock Marion.................. .10 .05
❑ 167 Toby Wright.................... .10 .05
❑ 168 John Copeland .... .10 .05
❑ 169 Sean Dawkins................ .10 .05
❑ 170 Tim Brown...................... .30 .14
❑ 171 Darion Conner................ .10 .05
❑ 172 Aaron Hayden RC.......... .10 .05
❑ 173 Charlie Garner................ .10 .05
❑ 174 Anthony Cook .... .10 .05
❑ 175 Derrick Thomas.............. .20 .09
❑ 176 Willie McGinest .... .10 .05
❑ 177 Thomas Lewis................ .10 .05
❑ 178 Sherman Williams .... .10 .05
❑ 179 Cornelius Bennett .... .10 .05
❑ 180 Frank Sanders................ .30 .14
❑ 181 Leroy Hoard .... .10 .05
❑ 182 Bernie Parmalee .... .10 .05
❑ 183 Sterling Palmer .... .10 .05
❑ 184 Kelvin Pritchett .... .10 .05
❑ 185 Kordell Stewart .... .60 .25
❑ 186 Brent Jones.................... .10 .05
❑ 187 Robert Blackmon............ .10 .05
❑ 188 Adrian Murrell .... .30 .14
❑ 189 Edgar Bennett................ .20 .09
❑ 190 Rashaan Salaam............ .30 .14
❑ 191 Ellis Johnson.................. .10 .05
❑ 192 Andre Coleman.............. .10 .05
❑ 193 Will Shields .... .10 .05
❑ 194 Derrick Brooks................ .10 .05
❑ 195 Carl Pickens .... .30 .14
❑ 196 Carlton Bailey .... .10 .05
❑ 197 Terance Mathis .... .20 .09
❑ 198 Carlos Jenkins................ .10 .05
❑ 199 Derrick Alexander DE ..... .10 .05
❑ 200 Deion Sanders .... .60 .25
❑ 201 Glyn Milburn .... .10 .05
❑ 202 Chris Sanders .... .20 .09
❑ 203 Rocket Ismail.................. .10 .05
❑ 204 Fred Barnett .... .10 .05
❑ 205 Quinn Early.................... .10 .05
❑ 206 Henry Jones .... .10 .05
❑ 207 Herschel Walker .... .20 .09
❑ 208 James Washington .... .10 .05
❑ 209 Lee Woodall .... .10 .05
❑ 210 Neil Smith...................... .10 .05
❑ 211 Tony Bennett.................. .10 .05
❑ 212 Ernie Mills .... .10 .05
❑ 213 Clyde Simmons.............. .10 .05
❑ 214 Chris Slade .... .10 .05
❑ 215 Tony Boselli.................... .10 .05
❑ 216 Ryan McNeil .... .10 .05
❑ 217 Rob Burnett.................... .10 .05
❑ 218 Stan Humphries .... .20 .09
❑ 219 Rick Mirer .... .20 .09
❑ 220 Troy Vincent .... .10 .05
❑ 221 Sean Jones .... .10 .05
❑ 222 Marty Carter .... .10 .05
❑ 223 Boomer Esiason .... .20 .09
❑ 224 Charles Haley .... .20 .09
❑ 225 Sam Mills........................ .10 .05
❑ 226 Greg Biekert .... .10 .05
❑ 227 Bryant Young .... .20 .09
❑ 228 Ken Dilger...................... .20 .09
❑ 229 Levon Kirkland .... .10 .05
❑ 230 Brian Mitchell.................. .10 .05
❑ 231 Hardy Nickerson .... .10 .05
❑ 232 Elvis Grbac .... .20 .09
❑ 233 Kurt Schulz .... .10 .05
❑ 234 Chris Doleman .... .10 .05
❑ 235 Tamarick Vanover.......... .20 .09
❑ 236 Jesse Campbell.............. .10 .05
❑ 237 William Thomas.............. .10 .05
❑ 238 Shane Conlan .... .10 .05
❑ 239 Jason Elam .... .10 .05
❑ 240 Steve McNair.................. .75 .35
❑ 241 Jerry Rice TYC .... .50 .23
❑ 242 Isaac Bruce TYC............ .30 .14
❑ 243 Herman Moore TYC ...... .30 .14
❑ 244 Michael Irvin TYC .... .20 .09
❑ 245 Robert Brooks TYC........ .30 .14
❑ 246 Brett Perriman TYC........ .10 .05
❑ 247 Cris Carter TYC.............. .30 .14
❑ 248 Tim Brown TYC.............. .20 .09
❑ 249 Yancey Thigpen TYC .... .20 .09
❑ 250 Jeff Graham TYC .... .10 .05
❑ 251 Carl Pickens TYC .... .30 .14
❑ 252 Tony Martin TYC............ .10 .05
❑ 253 Eric Metcalf TYC............ .10 .05
❑ 254 Jake Reed TYC.............. .20 .09
❑ 255 Quinn Early TYC............ .10 .05
❑ 256 Anthony Miller TYC........ .20 .09
❑ 257 Joey Galloway TYC........ .30 .14
❑ 258 Bert Emanuel TYC .... .20 .09
❑ 259 Terance Mathis TYC ...... .10 .05
❑ 260 Curtis Conway TYC........ .20 .09
❑ 261 Henry Ellard TYC .... .10 .05
❑ 262 Mark Carrier WR TYC .... .10 .05
❑ 263 Brian Blades TYC .... .10 .05
❑ 264 William Roaf .... .10 .05
❑ 265 Ed McDaniel .... .10 .05
❑ 266 Nate Newton .... .10 .05
❑ 267 Brett Maxie .... .10 .05
❑ 268 Anthony Smith................ .10 .05
❑ 269 Mickey Washington........ .10 .05
❑ 270 Jerry Rice .... 1.00 .45
❑ 271 Shaun Gayle .... .10 .05
❑ 272 Gilbert Brown .... .20 .09
❑ 273 Mark Bruener .... .10 .05
❑ 274 Eugene Robinson .... .10 .05
❑ 275 Marvin Washington .... .10 .05
❑ 276 Keith Sims...................... .10 .05
❑ 277 Ashley Ambrose .... .10 .05
❑ 278 Garrison Hearst.............. .20 .09
❑ 279 Donnell Woolford............ .10 .05
❑ 280 Cris Carter...................... .30 .14
❑ 281 Curtis Martin .... .75 .35
❑ 282 Scott Mitchell.................. .20 .09
❑ 283 Stevon Moore .... .10 .05
❑ 284 Roman Phifer .... .10 .05
❑ 285 Ken Harvey .... .10 .05
❑ 286 Rodney Hampton .... .20 .09
❑ 287 Willie Davis .... .10 .05
❑ 288 Yonel Jourdain .... .10 .05
❑ 289 Brian DeMarco .... .10 .05
❑ 290 Reggie White.................. .30 .14
❑ 291 Kevin Williams................ .10 .05
❑ 292 Gary Plummer................ .10 .05
❑ 293 Terrance Shaw .... .10 .05
❑ 294 Calvin Williams .... .10 .05
❑ 295 Eddie Robinson.............. .10 .05
❑ 296 Tony McGee .... .10 .05
❑ 297 Clay Matthews................ .10 .05
❑ 298 Joe Cain .... .10 .05
❑ 299 Tim McKyer.................... .10 .05
❑ 300 Greg Lloyd...................... .20 .09
❑ 301 Steve Wisniewski .... .10 .05
❑ 302 Ray Buchanan................ .10 .05
❑ 303 Lake Dawson .... .10 .05
❑ 304 Kevin Carter .... .10 .05
❑ 305 Phillippi Sparks .... .10 .05
❑ 306 Emmitt Smith................ 1.50 .70
❑ 307 Ruben Brown .... .10 .05
❑ 308 Tom Carter .... .10 .05
❑ 309 William Floyd.................. .20 .09
❑ 310 Jim Everett .... .10 .05
❑ 311 Vincent Brown................ .10 .05
❑ 312 Dennis Gibson................ .10 .05
❑ 313 Lorenzo Lynch................ .10 .05
❑ 314 Corey Harris .... .10 .05
❑ 315 James O.Stewart............ .20 .09
❑ 316 Kyle Brady...................... .10 .05
❑ 317 Irving Fryar .... .20 .09
❑ 318 Jake Reed...................... .20 .09
❑ 319 Vinny Testaverde .... .20 .09
❑ 320 John Elway .... 2.00 .90
❑ 321 Tracy Scroggins .... .10 .05
❑ 322 Chris Spielman .... .10 .05
❑ 323 Horace Copeland .... .10 .05
❑ 324 Chris Zorich.................... .10 .05
❑ 325 Mike Mamula.................. .10 .05
❑ 326 Henry Ford .... .10 .05
❑ 327 Steve Walsh .... .10 .05
❑ 328 Stanley Richard.............. .20 .09
❑ 329 Mike Jones .... .10 .05
❑ 330 Jim Harbaugh .... .20 .09
❑ 331 Darren Perry .... .10 .05
❑ 332 Ken Norton .... .10 .05
❑ 333 Kimble Anders................ .20 .09
❑ 334 Harold Green.................. .10 .05
❑ 335 Tyrone Poole.................. .10 .05
❑ 336 Mark Fields .... .10 .05
❑ 337 Darren Bennett .... .10 .05
❑ 338 Mike Sherrard .... .10 .05
❑ 339 Terry Ray .... .10 .05
❑ 340 Bruce Smith.................... .20 .09
❑ 341 Daryl Johnston .... .20 .09
❑ 342 Vinnie Clark.................... .10 .05
❑ 343 Mike Caldwell .... .10 .05
❑ 344 Vinson Smith.................. .10 .05
❑ 345 Mo Lewis........................ .10 .05
❑ 346 Brian Blades .... .10 .05
❑ 347 Rod Stephens .... .10 .05
❑ 348 David Palmer.................. .10 .05
❑ 349 Blaine Bishop .... .10 .05
❑ 350 Jeff George .... .20 .09
❑ 351 George Teague.............. .10 .05
❑ 352 Jeff Hostetler.................. .10 .05
❑ 353 Michael Strahan .... .10 .05
❑ 354 Eric Davis .... .10 .05
❑ 355 Jerome Bettis .... .30 .14
❑ 356 Irv Smith .... .10 .05
❑ 357 Jeff Herrod .... .10 .05
❑ 358 Jay Novacek .... .10 .05
❑ 359 Bryce Paup .... .10 .05
❑ 360 Neil O'Donnell................ .20 .09
❑ 361 Eric Swann .... .10 .05
❑ 362 Corey Sawyer .... .10 .05
❑ 363 Ty Law............................ .10 .05
❑ 364 Bo Orlando .... .10 .05
❑ 365 Marcus Allen .... .30 .14
❑ 366 Mark McMillian .... .10 .05
❑ 367 Mark Carrier WR............ .10 .05
❑ 368 Jackie Harris .... .10 .05
❑ 369 Steve Atwater .... .10 .05
❑ 370 Steve Young .... .75 .35
❑ 371 Brett Favre TYC .... 1.00 .45
❑ 372 Scott Mitchell TYC.......... .10 .05
❑ 373 Warren Moon TYC .... .10 .05
❑ 374 Jeff George TYC............ .20 .09
❑ 375 Jim Everett TYC .... .10 .05
❑ 376 John Elway TYC .... 1.00 .45
❑ 377 Erik Kramer TYC............ .10 .05
❑ 378 Jeff Blake TYC .... .20 .09
❑ 379 Dan Marino TYC .... 1.00 .45
❑ 380 Dave Krieg TYC .... .10 .05
❑ 381 Drew Bledsoe TYC .... .50 .23
❑ 382 Stan Humphries TYC .... .10 .05
❑ 383 Troy Aikman TYC .... .50 .23
❑ 384 Steve Young TYC .... .35 .16
❑ 385 Jim Kelly TYC .... .30 .14
❑ 386 Steve Bono TYC .... .10 .05

❑ 387 David Sloan .10 .05
❑ 388 Jeff Graham .10 .05
❑ 389 Hugh Douglas .20 .09
❑ 390 Dan Marino 2.00 .90
❑ 391 Winston Moss .10 .05
❑ 392 Darrell Green .10 .05
❑ 393 Mark Stepnoski .10 .05
❑ 394 Bert Emanuel .20 .09
❑ 395 Eric Zeier .10 .05
❑ 396 Willie Jackson .10 .05
❑ 397 Qadry Ismail .10 .05
❑ 398 Michael Brooks .10 .05
❑ 399 D'Marco Farr .10 .05
❑ 400 Brett Favre 2.00 .90
❑ 401 Carnell Lake .10 .05
❑ 402 Pat Swilling .10 .05
❑ 403 Stephen Grant .10 .05
❑ 404 Steve Tasker .10 .05
❑ 405 Ben Coates .20 .09
❑ 406 Steve Tovar .10 .05
❑ 407 Tony Martin .20 .09
❑ 408 Greg Hill .20 .09
❑ 409 Eric Guliford .10 .05
❑ 410 Michael Irvin .30 .14
❑ 411 Eric Hill .10 .05
❑ 412 Mario Bates .20 .09
❑ 413 Brian Stablein RC .10 .05
❑ 414 Marcus Jones RC .10 .05
❑ 415 Reggie Brown LB RC .10 .05
❑ 416 Lawrence Phillips RC .30 .14
❑ 417 Alex Van Dyke RC .20 .09
❑ 418 Daryl Gardener RC .10 .05
❑ 419 Mike Alstott RC 1.25 .55
❑ 420 Kevin Hardy RC .30 .14
❑ 421 Rickey Dudley RC .30 .14
❑ 422 Jerome Woods RC .10 .05
❑ 423 Eric Moulds RC 1.50 .70
❑ 424 Cedric Jones RC .10 .05
❑ 425 Simeon Rice RC .30 .14
❑ 426 Marvin Harrison RC 2.00 .90
❑ 427 Tim Biakabutuka RC .60 .25
❑ 428 Duane Clemons RC .10 .05
❑ 429 Alex Molden RC .10 .05
❑ 430 Keyshawn Johnson RC 1.50 .70
❑ 431 Willie Anderson RC .10 .05
❑ 432 John Mobley RC .10 .05
❑ 433 Leeland McElroy RC .30 .14
❑ 434 Regan Upshaw RC .10 .05
❑ 435 Eddie George RC 3.00 1.35
❑ 436 Jonathan Ogden RC .10 .05
❑ 437 Eddie Kennison RC .30 .14
❑ 438 Jermane Mayberry RC .10 .05
❑ 439 Checklist 1 of 2 .10 .05
❑ 440 Checklist 2 of 2 .10 .05
❑ P1 Joe Namath Promo 15.00 6.75
Steve Young
❑ P1R Joe Namath Promo 20.00 9.00
Steve Young
(Refractor version)

1997 Topps

	MINT	NRMT
COMPLETE SET (415)	40.00	18.00
COMP.FACT.SET (424)	60.00	27.00

❑ 1 Brett Favre 2.00 .90
❑ 2 Lawyer Milloy .10 .05
❑ 3 Tim Biakabutuka .20 .09
❑ 4 Clyde Simmons .10 .05
❑ 5 Deion Sanders .40 .18
❑ 6 Anthony Miller .10 .05
❑ 7 Marquez Pope .10 .05
❑ 8 Mike Tomczak .10 .05
❑ 9 William Thomas .10 .05
❑ 10 Marshall Faulk .40 .18
❑ 11 John Randle .20 .09
❑ 12 Jim Kelly .40 .18
❑ 13 Steve Bono .20 .09
❑ 14 Rod Stephens .10 .05
❑ 15 Stan Humphries .20 .09
❑ 16 Terrell Buckley .10 .05
❑ 17 Ki-Jana Carter .10 .05
❑ 18 Marcus Robertson .10 .05
❑ 19 Corey Harris .10 .05
❑ 20 Rashaan Salaam .10 .05
❑ 21 Rickey Dudley .20 .09
❑ 22 Jamir Miller .10 .05
❑ 23 Martin Mayhew .10 .05
❑ 24 Jason Sehorn .20 .09
❑ 25 Isaac Bruce .40 .18
❑ 26 Johnnie Morton .20 .09
❑ 27 Antonio Langham .10 .05
❑ 28 Cornelius Bennett .10 .05
❑ 29 Joe Johnson .10 .05
❑ 30 Keyshawn Johnson .40 .18
❑ 31 Willie Green .10 .05
❑ 32 Craig Newsome .10 .05
❑ 33 Brock Marion .10 .05
❑ 34 Corey Fuller .10 .05
❑ 35 Ben Coates .20 .09
❑ 36 Ty Detmer .20 .09
❑ 37 Charles Johnson .20 .09
❑ 38 Willie Jackson .10 .05
❑ 39 Tyronne Drakeford .10 .05
❑ 40 Gus Frerotte .10 .05
❑ 41 Robert Blackmon .10 .05
❑ 42 Andre Coleman .10 .05
❑ 43 Mario Bates .10 .05
❑ 44 Chris Calloway .10 .05
❑ 45 Terry McDaniel .10 .05
❑ 46 Anthony Davis .10 .05
❑ 47 Stanley Pritchett .10 .05
❑ 48 Ray Buchanan .10 .05
❑ 49 Chris Chandler .20 .09
❑ 50 Ashley Ambrose .10 .05
❑ 51 Tyrone Braxton .10 .05
❑ 52 Pepper Johnson .10 .05
❑ 53 Frank Sanders .20 .09
❑ 54 Clay Matthews .10 .05
❑ 55 Bruce Smith .20 .09
❑ 56 Jermaine Lewis .40 .18
❑ 57 Mark Carrier WR UER .10 .05
(Features the cardback
for Mark Carrier DB)
❑ 58 Jeff Graham .10 .05
❑ 59 Keith Lyle .10 .05
❑ 60 Trent Dilfer .40 .18
❑ 61 Trace Armstrong .10 .05
❑ 62 Jeff Herrod .10 .05
❑ 63 Tyrone Wheatley .20 .09
❑ 64 Torrance Small .10 .05
❑ 65 Chris Warren .20 .09
❑ 66 Terry Kirby .20 .09
❑ 67 Erric Pegram .10 .05
❑ 68 Sean Gilbert .10 .05
❑ 69 Greg Biekert .10 .05
❑ 70 Ricky Watters .20 .09
❑ 71 Chris Hudson .10 .05
❑ 72 Tamarick Vanover .20 .09
❑ 73 Orlando Thomas .10 .05
❑ 74 Jimmy Spencer .10 .05
❑ 75 John Mobley .10 .05
❑ 76 Henry Thomas .10 .05
❑ 77 Santana Dotson .10 .05
❑ 78 Boomer Esiason .20 .09
❑ 79 Bobby Hebert .10 .05
❑ 80 Kerry Collins .20 .09
❑ 81 Bobby Engram .20 .09
❑ 82 Kevin Smith .10 .05
❑ 83 Rick Mirer .10 .05
❑ 84 Ted Johnson .10 .05
❑ 85 Derrick Alexander WR .20 .09
❑ 86 Hugh Douglas .10 .05
❑ 87 Rodney Harrison .10 .05
❑ 88 Roman Phifer .10 .05
❑ 89 Warren Moon .40 .18
❑ 90 Thurman Thomas .40 .18
❑ 91 Michael McCrary .10 .05
❑ 92 Dana Stubblefield .10 .05
❑ 93 Andre Hastings UER .10 .05
front reads Hasting
❑ 94 William Fuller .10 .05
❑ 95 Jeff Hostetler .10 .05
❑ 96 Danny Kanell .20 .09
❑ 97 Mark Fields .10 .05
❑ 98 Eddie Robinson .10 .05
❑ 99 Daryl Gardener .10 .05
❑ 100 Drew Bledsoe 1.00 .45
❑ 101 Winslow Oliver .10 .05
❑ 102 Raymont Harris .10 .05
❑ 103 LeShon Johnson .10 .05
❑ 104 Byron Bam Morris .10 .05
❑ 105 Herman Moore .40 .18
❑ 106 Keith Jackson .10 .05
❑ 107 Chris Penn .10 .05
❑ 108 Robert Griffith RC .10 .05
❑ 109 Jeff Burris .10 .05
❑ 110 Troy Aikman 1.00 .45
❑ 111 Allen Aldridge .10 .05
❑ 112 Mel Gray .10 .05
❑ 113 Aaron Bailey .10 .05
❑ 114 Michael Strahan .10 .05
❑ 115 Adrian Murrell .20 .09
❑ 116 Chris Mims .10 .05
❑ 117 Robert Jones .10 .05
❑ 118 Derrick Brooks .10 .05
❑ 119 Tom Carter .10 .05
❑ 120 Carl Pickens .40 .18
❑ 121 Tony Brackens .10 .05
❑ 122 O.J. McDuffie .20 .09
❑ 123 Napoleon Kaufman .40 .18
❑ 124 Chris T. Jones .10 .05
❑ 125 Kordell Stewart .50 .23
❑ 126 Ray Zellars .10 .05
❑ 127 Jessie Tuggle .10 .05
❑ 128 Greg Kragen .10 .05
❑ 129 Brett Perriman .10 .05
❑ 130 Steve Young .60 .25
❑ 131 Willie Clay .10 .05
❑ 132 Kimble Anders .20 .09
❑ 133 Eugene Daniel .10 .05
❑ 134 Jevon Langford .10 .05
❑ 135 Shannon Sharpe .20 .09
❑ 136 Wayne Simmons .10 .05
❑ 137 Leeland McElroy .10 .05
❑ 138 Mike Caldwell .10 .05
❑ 139 Eric Moulds .40 .18
❑ 140 Eddie George 1.00 .45
❑ 141 Jamal Anderson .60 .25
❑ 142 Michael Timpson .10 .05
❑ 143 Tony Tolbert .10 .05
❑ 144 Robert Smith .20 .09
❑ 145 Mike Alstott .40 .18
❑ 146 Gary Jones .10 .05
❑ 147 Terrance Shaw .10 .05
❑ 148 Carlton Gray .10 .05
❑ 149 Kevin Carter .10 .05
❑ 150 Darrell Green .20 .09
❑ 151 David Dunn .10 .05
❑ 152 Ken Norton .10 .05
❑ 153 Chad Brown .10 .05
❑ 154 Pat Swilling .10 .05
❑ 155 Irving Fryar .20 .09
❑ 156 Michael Haynes .10 .05
❑ 157 Shawn Jefferson .10 .05
❑ 158 Stephen Grant .10 .05
❑ 159 James O.Stewart .20 .09
❑ 160 Derrick Thomas .20 .09
❑ 161 Tim Bowens .10 .05
❑ 162 Dixon Edwards .10 .05
❑ 163 Micheal Barrow .10 .05
❑ 164 Antonio Freeman .50 .23
❑ 165 Terrell Davis 1.50 .70
❑ 166 Henry Ellard .10 .05
❑ 167 Daryl Johnston .20 .09
❑ 168 Bryan Cox .10 .05
❑ 169 Chad Cota .10 .05
❑ 170 Vinny Testaverde .20 .09
❑ 171 Andre Reed .20 .09

❑ 172 Larry Centers .20 .09
❑ 173 Craig Heyward .10 .05
❑ 174 Glyn Milburn .10 .05
❑ 175 Hardy Nickerson .10 .05
❑ 176 Corey Miller .10 .05
❑ 177 Bobby Houston .10 .05
❑ 178 Marco Coleman .10 .05
❑ 179 Winston Moss .10 .05
❑ 180 Tony Banks .20 .09
❑ 181 Jeff Lageman .10 .05
❑ 182 Jason Belser .10 .05
❑ 183 James Jett .20 .09
❑ 184 Wayne Martin .10 .05
❑ 185 Dave Meggett .10 .05
❑ 186 Terrell Owens .40 .18
❑ 187 Willie Williams .10 .05
❑ 188 Eric Turner .10 .05
❑ 189 Chuck Smith .10 .05
❑ 190 Simeon Rice .20 .09
❑ 191 Kevin Greene .20 .09
❑ 192 Lance Johnstone .10 .05
❑ 193 Marty Carter .10 .05
❑ 194 Ricardo McDonald .10 .05
❑ 195 Michael Irvin .40 .18
❑ 196 George Koonce .10 .05
❑ 197 Robert Porcher .10 .05
❑ 198 Mark Collins .10 .05
❑ 199 Louis Oliver .10 .05
❑ 200 John Elway 2.00 .90
❑ 201 Jake Reed .20 .09
❑ 202 Rodney Hampton .20 .09
❑ 203 Aaron Glenn .10 .05
❑ 204 Mike Mamula .10 .05
❑ 205 Terry Allen .40 .18
❑ 206 John Lynch .20 .09
❑ 207 Todd Lyght .10 .05
❑ 208 Dean Wells .10 .05
❑ 209 Aaron Hayden .10 .05
❑ 210 Blaine Bishop .10 .05
❑ 211 Bert Emanuel .20 .09
❑ 212 Mark Carrier DB UER .10 .05
(Features the cardback for Mark Carrier WR)
❑ 213 Dale Carter .10 .05
❑ 214 Jimmy Smith .20 .09
❑ 215 Jim Harbaugh .20 .09
❑ 216 Jeff George .20 .09
❑ 217 Anthony Newman .10 .05
❑ 218 Ty Law .10 .05
❑ 219 Brent Jones .20 .09
❑ 220 Emmitt Smith 1.50 .70
❑ 221 Bennie Blades .10 .05
❑ 222 Alfred Williams .10 .05
❑ 223 Eugene Robinson .10 .05
❑ 224 Fred Barnett .10 .05
❑ 225 Errict Rhett .10 .05
❑ 226 Leslie O'Neal .10 .05
❑ 227 Michael Sinclair .10 .05
❑ 228 Marvcus Patton .10 .05
❑ 229 Darrien Gordon .10 .05
❑ 230 Jerome Bettis .40 .18
❑ 231 Troy Vincent .10 .05
❑ 232 Ray Mickens .10 .05
❑ 233 Lonnie Johnson .10 .05
❑ 234 Charles Way .20 .09
❑ 235 Chris Sanders .10 .05
❑ 236 Bracey Walker .10 .05
❑ 237 Dave Krieg UER .10 .05
(Front has Bears logo)
❑ 238 Kent Graham .10 .05
❑ 239 Ray Lewis .50 .23
❑ 240 Cris Carter .40 .18
❑ 241 Elvis Grbac .20 .09
❑ 242 Eric Davis .10 .05
❑ 243 Harvey Williams .10 .05
❑ 244 Eric Allen .10 .05
❑ 245 Bryant Young .10 .05
❑ 246 Terrell Fletcher .10 .05
❑ 247 Darren Perry .10 .05
❑ 248 Ken Harvey .10 .05
❑ 249 Marvin Washington .10 .05
❑ 250 Marcus Allen .40 .18
❑ 251 Darrin Smith .10 .05
❑ 252 James Francis .10 .05
❑ 253 Michael Jackson .20 .09
❑ 254 Ryan McNeil .10 .05
❑ 255 Mark Chmura .20 .09
❑ 256 Keenan McCardell .20 .09
❑ 257 Tony Bennett .10 .05
❑ 258 Irving Spikes .10 .05
❑ 259 Jason Dunn .10 .05
❑ 260 Joey Galloway .50 .23
❑ 261 Eddie Kennison .20 .09
❑ 262 Lonnie Marts .10 .05
❑ 263 Thomas Lewis .10 .05
❑ 264 Tedy Bruschi .10 .05
❑ 265 Steve Atwater .10 .05
❑ 266 Dorsey Levens .40 .18
❑ 267 Kurt Schulz .10 .05
❑ 268 Rob Moore .20 .09
❑ 269 Walt Harris .10 .05
❑ 270 Steve McNair .50 .23
❑ 271 Bill Romanowski .10 .05
❑ 272 Sean Dawkins .10 .05
❑ 273 Don Beebe .10 .05
❑ 274 Fernando Smith .10 .05
❑ 275 Willie McGinest .10 .05
❑ 276 Levon Kirkland .10 .05
❑ 277 Tony Martin .20 .09
❑ 278 Warren Sapp .20 .09
❑ 279 Lamar Smith .40 .18
❑ 280 Mark Brunell 1.00 .45
❑ 281 Jim Everett .10 .05
❑ 282 Victor Green .10 .05
❑ 283 Mike Jones .10 .05
❑ 284 Charlie Garner .10 .05
❑ 285 Karim Abdul-Jabbar .40 .18
❑ 286 Michael Westbrook .20 .09
❑ 287 Lawrence Phillips .10 .05
❑ 288 Amani Toomer .20 .09
❑ 289 Neil Smith .20 .09
❑ 290 Barry Sanders 2.00 .90
❑ 291 Willie Davis .10 .05
❑ 292 Bo Orlando .10 .05
❑ 293 Alonzo Spellman .10 .05
❑ 294 Eric Hill .10 .05
❑ 295 Wesley Walls .20 .09
❑ 296 Todd Collins .10 .05
❑ 297 Stevon Moore .10 .05
❑ 298 Eric Metcalf .20 .09
❑ 299 Darren Woodson .10 .05
❑ 300 Jerry Rice 1.00 .45
❑ 301 Scott Mitchell .20 .09
❑ 302 Ray Crockett .10 .05
❑ 303 Jim Schwantz RC UER .10 .05
(Back reads Schwartz)
❑ 304 Steve Tovar .10 .05
❑ 305 Terance Mathis .20 .09
❑ 306 Earnest Byner .10 .05
❑ 307 Chris Spielman .10 .05
❑ 308 Curtis Conway .20 .09
❑ 309 Cris Dishman .10 .05
❑ 310 Marvin Harrison .40 .18
❑ 311 Sam Mills .10 .05
❑ 312 Brent Alexander RC .10 .05
❑ 313 Shawn Wooden .10 .05
❑ 314 Dewayne Washington .10 .05
❑ 315 Terry Glenn .40 .18
❑ 316 Winfred Tubbs .10 .05
❑ 317 Dave Brown .10 .05
❑ 318 Neil O'Donnell .20 .09
❑ 319 Anthony Parker .10 .05
❑ 320 Junior Seau .20 .09
❑ 321 Brian Mitchell .10 .05
❑ 322 Regan Upshaw .10 .05
❑ 323 Darryl Williams .10 .05
❑ 324 Chris Doleman .10 .05
❑ 325 Rod Woodson .20 .09
❑ 326 Derrick Witherspoon .10 .05
❑ 327 Chester McGlockton .10 .05
❑ 328 Mickey Washington .10 .05
❑ 329 Greg Hill .10 .05
❑ 330 Reggie White .40 .18
❑ 331 John Copeland .10 .05
❑ 332 Doug Evans .10 .05
❑ 333 Lamar Lathon .10 .05
❑ 334 Mark Maddox .10 .05
❑ 335 Natrone Means .40 .18
❑ 336 Corey Widmer .10 .05
❑ 337 Terry Wooden .10 .05
❑ 338 Merton Hanks .10 .05
❑ 339 Cortez Kennedy .10 .05
❑ 340 Tyrone Hughes .10 .05
❑ 341 Tim Brown .40 .18
❑ 342 John Jurkovic .10 .05
❑ 343 Carnell Lake .10 .05
❑ 344 Stanley Richard .10 .05
❑ 345 Darryll Lewis .10 .05
❑ 346 Dan Wilkinson .10 .05
❑ 347 Broderick Thomas .10 .05
❑ 348 Brian Williams .10 .05
❑ 349 Eric Swann .10 .05
❑ 350 Dan Marino 2.00 .90
❑ 351 Anthony Johnson .10 .05
❑ 352 Joe Cain .10 .05
❑ 353 Quinn Early .10 .05
❑ 354 Seth Joyner .10 .05
❑ 355 Garrison Hearst .20 .09
❑ 356 Edgar Bennett .20 .09
❑ 357 Brian Washington .10 .05
❑ 358 Kevin Hardy .10 .05
❑ 359 Quentin Coryatt .10 .05
❑ 360 Tim McDonald .10 .05
❑ 361 Brian Blades .10 .05
❑ 362 Courtney Hawkins .10 .05
❑ 363 Ray Farmer .10 .05
❑ 364 Jessie Armstead .10 .05
❑ 365 Curtis Martin .50 .23
❑ 366 Zach Thomas .20 .09
❑ 367 Frank Wycheck .10 .05
❑ 368 Darnay Scott .20 .09
❑ 369 Percy Ellsworth .10 .05
❑ 370 Desmond Howard .20 .09
❑ 371 Aeneas Williams .10 .05
❑ 372 Bryce Paup .10 .05
❑ 373 Michael Bates .10 .05
❑ 374 Brad Johnson .50 .23
❑ 375 Jeff Blake .20 .09
❑ 376 Donnell Woolford UER .10 .05
(Front photo incorrect)
❑ 377 Mo Lewis .10 .05
❑ 378 Phillippi Sparks .10 .05
❑ 379 Michael Bankston .10 .05
❑ 380 LeRoy Butler .10 .05
❑ 381 Tyrone Poole .10 .05
❑ 382 Wayne Chrebet .40 .18
❑ 383 Chris Slade .10 .05
❑ 384 Checklist 1 (1-208) .10 .05
❑ 385 Checklist 2 (209-415) .10 .05
❑ 386 Will Blackwell RC SP .40 .18
❑ 387 Tom Knight RC SP .10 .05
❑ 388 Darnell Autry RC SP .50 .23
❑ 389 Bryant Westbrook RC SP .10 .05
❑ 390 David LaFleur RC SP .50 .23
❑ 391 Antowain Smith RC SP 2.00 .90
❑ 392 Kevin Lockett RC SP .50 .23
❑ 393 Rae Carruth RC SP .75 .35
❑ 394 Renaldo Wynn RC SP .30 .14
❑ 395 Jim Druckenmiller RC SP .75 .35
❑ 396 Kenny Holmes RC SP .75 .35
❑ 397 Shawn Springs RC SP .50 .23
❑ 398 Troy Davis RC SP .75 .35
❑ 399 Dwayne Rudd RC SP .75 .35
❑ 400 Orlando Pace RC SP .75 .35
❑ 401 Byron Hanspard RC SP .75 .35
❑ 402 Corey Dillon RC SP 6.00 2.70
❑ 403 Walter Jones RC SP .30 .14
❑ 404 Reidel Anthony RC SP 1.50 .70
❑ 405 Peter Boulware RC SP .50 .23
❑ 406 Reinard Wilson RC SP .30 .14
❑ 407 Pat Barnes RC SP .75 .35
❑ 408 Yatil Green RC SP .75 .35
❑ 409 Joey Kent RC SP .75 .35
❑ 410 Ike Hilliard RC SP 1.50 .70
❑ 411 Jake Plummer RC SP 6.00 2.70
❑ 412 Darrell Russell RC SP .30 .14
❑ 413 James Farrior RC SP .30 .14
❑ 414 Tony Gonzalez RC SP 3.00 1.35
❑ 415 Warrick Dunn RC SP 3.00 1.35
❑ P40 Gus Frerotte Promo .25 .11
(Green border on back)
❑ P170 V.Testaverde Promo .25 .11
(Green border on back)
❑ P240 Cris Carter Promo .40 .18
(Green border on back)
❑ P250 Marcus Allen Promo .40 .18
(Green border on back)

❑ P285 K.Abdul-Jabbar Promo .25 .11
(Green border on bac)
❑ P356 Edgar Bennett Promo .. .25 .11
(Green border on back)

1998 Topps

	MINT	NRMT
COMPLETE SET (360)	60.00	27.00
COMP.FACT.SET (365)..........	70.00	32.00

❑ 1 Barry Sanders .... 2.00 .90
❑ 2 Derrick Rodgers .... .10 .05
❑ 3 Chris Calloway .... .10 .05
❑ 4 Bruce Armstrong .... .10 .05
❑ 5 Horace Copeland .... .10 .05
❑ 6 Chad Brown .... .10 .05
❑ 7 Ken Harvey .... .10 .05
❑ 8 Levon Kirkland .... .10 .05
❑ 9 Glenn Foley .... .20 .09
❑ 10 Corey Dillon .... .50 .23
❑ 11 Sean Dawkins .... .10 .05
❑ 12 Curtis Conway .20 .09
❑ 13 Chris Chandler .20
❑ 14 Kerry Collins .20 .09
❑ 15 Jonathan Ogden .10
❑ 16 Sam Shade .10 .05
❑ 17 Vaughn Hebron .10
❑ 18 Quentin Coryatt .10
❑ 19 Jerris McPhail .10 .05
❑ 20 Warrick Dunn .40 .18
❑ 21 Wayne Martin .10 .05
❑ 22 Chad Lewis .10 .05
❑ 23 Danny Kanell .20 .09
❑ 24 Shawn Springs .10
❑ 25 Emmitt Smith 1.50 .70
❑ 26 Todd Lyght .10 .05
❑ 27 Donnie Edwards .10
❑ 28 Charlie Jones .10 .05
❑ 29 Willie McGinest .10
❑ 30 Steve Young .50 .23
❑ 31 Darrell Russell .10 .05
❑ 32 Gary Anderson .10
❑ 33 Stanley Richard .10
❑ 34 Leslie O'Neal .10 .05
❑ 35 Dermontti Dawson .10
❑ 36 Jeff Brady .10 .05
❑ 37 Kimble Anders .20 .09
❑ 38 Glyn Milburn .10 .05
❑ 39 Greg Hill .10 .05
❑ 40 Freddie Jones .10 .05
❑ 41 Bobby Engram .20
❑ 42 Aeneas Williams .10
❑ 43 Antowain Smith .40
❑ 44 Reggie White .40 .18
❑ 45 Rae Carruth .20 .09
❑ 46 Leon Johnson .10 .05
❑ 47 Bryant Young .10 .05
❑ 48 Jamie Asher .10 .05
❑ 49 Hardy Nickerson .10
❑ 50 Jerome Bettis .40 .18
❑ 51 Michael Strahan .10
❑ 52 John Randle .20 .09
❑ 53 Kevin Hardy .10 .05
❑ 54 Eric Bjornson .10 .05
❑ 55 Morten Andersen UER .10
(Misspelled Anderson)
❑ 56 Larry Centers .... .10 .05
❑ 57 Bryce Paup .... .10 .05
❑ 58 John Mobley .... .10 .05
❑ 59 Michael Bates .... .10 .05
❑ 60 Tim Brown .... .40 .18
❑ 61 Doug Evans .... .10 .05
❑ 62 Will Shields .... .10 .05
❑ 63 Jeff Graham .... .10 .05
❑ 64 Henry Jones .... .10 .05
❑ 65 Steve Broussard .... .10 .05
❑ 66 Blaine Bishop .... .10 .05
❑ 67 Ernie Conwell .... .10 .05
❑ 68 Heath Shuler .... .10 .05
❑ 69 Eric Metcalf .... .10 .05
❑ 70 Terry Glenn .... .40 .18
❑ 71 James Hasty .... .10 .05
❑ 72 Robert Porcher .... .10 .05
❑ 73 Keenan McCardell .... .20 .09
❑ 74 Tyrone Hughes .... .10 .05
❑ 75 Troy Aikman .... 1.00 .45
❑ 76 Peter Boulware .... .10 .05
❑ 77 Rob Johnson .... .20 .09
❑ 78 Erik Kramer .... .10 .05
❑ 79 Kevin Smith .... .10 .05
❑ 80 Andre Rison .... .20 .09
❑ 81 Jim Harbaugh .... .20 .09
❑ 82 Chris Hudson .... .10 .05
❑ 83 Ray Zellars .... .10 .05
❑ 84 Jeff George .... .20 .09
❑ 85 Willie Davis .... .10 .05
❑ 86 Jason Gildon .... .10 .05
❑ 87 Robert Brooks .... .20 .09
❑ 88 Chad Cota .... .10 .05
❑ 89 Simeon Rice .... .20 .09
❑ 90 Mark Brunell .... .75 .35
❑ 91 Jay Graham .... .10 .05
❑ 92 Scott Greene .... .10 .05
❑ 93 Jeff Blake .... .20 .09
❑ 94 Jason Belser .... .10 .05
❑ 95 Derrick Alexander DE ...... .10 .05
❑ 96 Ty Law .... .10 .05
❑ 97 Charles Johnson .... .10 .05
❑ 98 James Jett .... .20 .09
❑ 99 Darrell Green .... .20 .09
❑ 100 Brett Favre .... 2.00 .90
❑ 101 George Jones .... .10 .05
❑ 102 Derrick Mason .... .20 .09
❑ 103 Sam Adams .... .10 .05
❑ 104 Lawrence Phillips .... .10 .05
❑ 105 Randal Hill .... .10 .05
❑ 106 John Mangum .... .10 .05
❑ 107 Natrone Means .... .40 .18
❑ 108 Bill Romanowski .... .10 .05
❑ 109 Terance Mathis .... .20 .09
❑ 110 Bruce Smith .... .20 .09
❑ 111 Pete Mitchell .... .10 .05
❑ 112 Duane Clemons .... .10 .05
❑ 113 Willie Clay .... .10 .05
❑ 114 Eric Allen .... .10 .05
❑ 115 Troy Drayton .... .10 .05
❑ 116 Derrick Thomas .... .20 .09
❑ 117 Charles Way .... .10 .05
❑ 118 Wayne Chrebet .... .40 .18
❑ 119 Bobby Hoying .... .20 .09
❑ 120 Michael Jackson .... .10 .05
❑ 121 Gary Zimmerman .... .10 .05
❑ 122 Yancey Thigpen .... .10 .05
❑ 123 Dana Stubblefield .... .10 .05
❑ 124 Keith Lyle .... .10 .05
❑ 125 Marco Coleman .... .10 .05
❑ 126 Karl Williams .... .10 .05
❑ 127 Stephen Davis .... .10 .05
❑ 128 Chris Sanders .... .10 .05
❑ 129 Cris Dishman .... .10 .05
❑ 130 Jake Plummer .... .60 .25
❑ 131 Darryl Williams .... .10 .05
❑ 132 Merton Hanks .... .10 .05
❑ 133 Torrance Small .... .10 .05
❑ 134 Aaron Glenn .... .10 .05
❑ 135 Chester McGlockton ...... .10 .05
❑ 136 William Thomas .... .10 .05
❑ 137 Kordell Stewart .... .40 .18
❑ 138 Jason Taylor .... .10 .05
❑ 139 Lake Dawson .... .10 .05
❑ 140 Carl Pickens .... .40 .18
❑ 141 Eugene Robinson .... .10 .05
❑ 142 Ed McCaffrey .... .20 .09
❑ 143 Lamar Lathon .... .10 .05
❑ 144 Ray Buchanan .... .10 .05
❑ 145 Thurman Thomas .... .40 .18
❑ 146 Andre Reed .... .20 .09
❑ 147 Wesley Walls .... .20 .09
❑ 148 Rob Moore .... .20 .09
❑ 149 Darren Woodson .... .10 .05
❑ 150 Eddie George .... .75 .35
❑ 151 Michael Irvin .... .40 .18
❑ 152 Johnnie Morton .... .20 .09
❑ 153 Ken Dilger .... .10 .05
❑ 154 Tony Boselli .... .10 .05
❑ 155 Randall McDaniel .... .10 .05
❑ 156 Mark Fields .... .10 .05
❑ 157 Phillippi Sparks .... .10 .05
❑ 158 Troy Davis .... .10 .05
❑ 159 Troy Vincent .... .10 .05
❑ 160 Cris Carter .... .40 .18
❑ 161 Amp Lee .... .10 .05
❑ 162 Will Blackwell .... .10 .05
❑ 163 Chad Scott .... .10 .05
❑ 164 Henry Ellard .... .20 .09
❑ 165 Robert Jones .... .10 .05
❑ 166 Garrison Hearst .... .40 .18
❑ 167 James McKnight .... .10 .05
❑ 168 Rodney Harrison .... .20 .09
❑ 169 Adrian Murrell .... .20 .09
❑ 170 Rod Smith WR .... .20 .09
❑ 171 Desmond Howard .... .20 .09
❑ 172 Ben Coates .... .20 .09
❑ 173 David Palmer .... .10 .05
❑ 174 Zach Thomas .... .20 .09
❑ 175 Dale Carter .... .10 .05
❑ 176 Mark Chmura .... .20 .09
❑ 177 Elvis Grbac .... .20 .09
❑ 178 Jason Hanson .... .10 .05
❑ 179 Walt Harris .... .10 .05
❑ 180 Ricky Watters .... .20 .09
❑ 181 Ray Lewis .... .40 .18
❑ 182 Lonnie Johnson .... .10 .05
❑ 183 Marvin Harrison .... .20 .09
❑ 184 Dorsey Levens .... .40 .18
❑ 185 Tony Gonzalez .... .10 .05
❑ 186 Andre Hastings .... .10 .05
❑ 187 Kevin Turner .... .10 .05
❑ 188 Mo Lewis .... .10 .05
❑ 189 Jason Sehorn .... .20 .09
❑ 190 Drew Bledsoe .... .75 .35
❑ 191 Michael Sinclair .... .10 .05
❑ 192 William Floyd .... .10 .05
❑ 193 Kenny Holmes .... .10 .05
❑ 194 Marvcus Patton .... .10 .05
❑ 195 Warren Sapp .... .20 .09
❑ 196 Junior Seau .... .20 .09
❑ 197 Ryan McNeil .... .10 .05
❑ 198 Tyrone Wheatley .... .20 .09
❑ 199 Robert Smith .... .40 .18
❑ 200 Terrell Davis .... 1.50 .70
❑ 201 Brett Perriman .... .10 .05
❑ 202 Tamarick Vanover .... .10 .05
❑ 203 Stephen Boyd .... .10 .05
❑ 204 Zack Crockett .... .10 .05
❑ 205 Sherman Williams .... .10 .05
❑ 206 Neil Smith .... .20 .09
❑ 207 Jermaine Lewis .... .20 .09
❑ 208 Kevin Williams .... .10 .05
❑ 209 Byron Hanspard .... .20 .09
❑ 210 Warren Moon .... .40 .18
❑ 211 Tony McGee .... .10 .05
❑ 212 Raymont Harris .... .10 .05
❑ 213 Eric Davis .... .10 .05
❑ 214 Darrien Gordon .... .10 .05
❑ 215 James Stewart .... .20 .09
❑ 216 Derrick Mayes .... .20 .09
❑ 217 Brad Johnson .... .40 .18
❑ 218 Karim Abdul-Jabbar UER .40 .18
(Jabbar missing from name)
❑ 219 Hugh Douglas .... .10 .05
❑ 220 Terry Allen .... .40 .18
❑ 221 Rhett Hall .... .10 .05
❑ 222 Terrell Fletcher .... .10 .05
❑ 223 Carnell Lake .... .10 .05
❑ 224 Darryll Lewis .... .10 .05
❑ 225 Chris Slade .... .10 .05
❑ 226 Michael Westbrook .... .20 .09
❑ 227 Willie Williams .... .10 .05

❑ 228 Tony Banks .20 .09
❑ 229 Keyshawn Johnson .40 .18
❑ 230 Mike Alstott .40 .18
❑ 231 Tiki Barber .20 .09
❑ 232 Jake Reed .20 .09
❑ 233 Eric Swann .10 .05
❑ 234 Eric Moulds .40 .18
❑ 235 Vinny Testaverde .20 .09
❑ 236 Jessie Tuggle .10 .05
❑ 237 Ryan Wetnight RC .10 .05
❑ 238 Tyrone Poole .10 .05
❑ 239 Bryant Westbrook .10 .05
❑ 240 Steve McNair .40 .18
❑ 241 Jimmy Smith .20 .09
❑ 242 Dewayne Washington .10 .05
❑ 243 Robert Harris .10 .05
❑ 244 Rod Woodson .20 .09
❑ 245 Reidel Anthony .20 .09
❑ 246 Jessie Armstead .10 .05
❑ 247 O.J. McDuffie .20 .09
❑ 248 Carlton Gray .10 .05
❑ 249 LeRoy Butler .10 .05
❑ 250 Jerry Rice 1.00 .45
❑ 251 Frank Sanders .20 .09
❑ 252 Todd Collins .10 .05
❑ 253 Fred Lane .20 .09
❑ 254 David Dunn .10 .05
❑ 255 Micheal Barrow .10 .05
❑ 256 Luther Elliss .10 .05
❑ 257 Scott Mitchell .20 .09
❑ 258 Dave Meggett .10 .05
❑ 259 Rickey Dudley .10 .05
❑ 260 Isaac Bruce .40 .18
❑ 261 Tony Martin .20 .09
❑ 262 Leslie Shepherd .10 .05
❑ 263 Derrick Brooks .10 .05
❑ 264 Greg Lloyd .10 .05
❑ 265 Terrell Buckley .10 .05
❑ 266 Antonio Freeman .40 .18
❑ 267 Tony Brackens .10 .05
❑ 268 Mark McMillian .10 .05
❑ 269 Dexter Coakley .10 .05
❑ 270 Dan Marino 2.00 .90
❑ 271 Bryan Cox .10 .05
❑ 272 Leeland McElroy .10 .05
❑ 273 Jeff Burris .10 .05
❑ 274 Eric Green .10 .05
❑ 275 Darnay Scott .20 .09
❑ 276 Greg Clark .10 .05
❑ 277 Mario Bates .20 .09
❑ 278 Eric Turner .10 .05
❑ 279 Neil O'Donnell .20 .09
❑ 280 Herman Moore .40 .18
❑ 281 Gary Brown .10 .05
❑ 282 Terrell Owens .40 .18
❑ 283 Frank Wycheck .10 .05
❑ 284 Trent Dilfer .40 .18
❑ 285 Curtis Martin .40 .18
❑ 286 Ricky Proehl .10 .05
❑ 287 Steve Atwater .10 .05
❑ 288 Aaron Bailey .10 .05
❑ 289 William Henderson .10 .05
❑ 290 Marcus Allen .40 .18
❑ 291 Tom Knight .10 .05
❑ 292 Quinn Early .10 .05
❑ 293 Michael McCrary .10 .05
❑ 294 Bert Emanuel .20 .09
❑ 295 Tom Carter .10 .05
❑ 296 Kevin Glover .10 .05
❑ 297 Marshall Faulk .40 .18
❑ 298 Harvey Williams .10 .05
❑ 299 Chris Warren .20 .09
❑ 300 John Elway 2.00 .90
❑ 301 Eddie Kennison .20 .09
❑ 302 Gus Frerotte .10 .05
❑ 303 Regan Upshaw .10 .05
❑ 304 Kevin Gogan .10 .05
❑ 305 Napoleon Kaufman .40 .18
❑ 306 Charlie Garner .10 .05
❑ 307 Shawn Jefferson .10 .05
❑ 308 Tommy Vardell .10 .05
❑ 309 Mike Hollis .10 .05
❑ 310 Irving Fryar .20 .09
❑ 311 Shannon Sharpe .20 .09
❑ 312 Byron Bam Morris .10 .05
❑ 313 Jamal Anderson .40 .18
❑ 314 Chris Gedney .10 .05
❑ 315 Chris Spielman .10 .05
❑ 316 Derrick Alexander WR .20 .09
❑ 317 O.J. Santiago .10 .05
❑ 318 Anthony Miller .10 .05
❑ 319 Ki-Jana Carter .10 .05
❑ 320 Deion Sanders .40 .18
❑ 321 Joey Galloway .40 .18
❑ 322 J.J. Stokes .20 .09
❑ 323 Rodney Thomas .10 .05
❑ 324 John Lynch .20 .09
❑ 325 Mike Pritchard .10 .05
❑ 326 Terrance Shaw .10 .05
❑ 327 Ted Johnson .10 .05
❑ 328 Ashley Ambrose .10 .05
❑ 329 Checklist 1 .10 .05
❑ 330 Checklist 2 .10 .05
❑ 331 Jerome Pathon RC 2.00 .90
❑ 332 Ryan Leaf RC 5.00 2.20
❑ 333 Duane Starks RC 1.25 .55
❑ 334 Brian Simmons RC 1.25 .55
❑ 335 Keith Brooking RC 2.00 .90
❑ 336 Robert Edwards RC 3.00 1.35
❑ 337 Curtis Enis RC 2.50 1.10
❑ 338 John Avery RC 2.50 1.10
❑ 339 Fred Taylor RC 6.00 2.70
❑ 340 Germane Crowell RC 5.00 2.20
❑ 341 Hines Ward RC 2.00 .90
❑ 342 Marcus Nash RC 2.50 1.10
❑ 343 Jacquez Green RC 3.00 1.35
❑ 344 Joe Jurevicius RC 2.00 .90
❑ 345 Greg Ellis RC 1.25 .55
❑ 346 Brian Griese RC 8.00 3.60
❑ 347 Tavian Banks RC 2.00 .90
❑ 348 Robert Holcombe RC 2.50 1.10
❑ 349 Skip Hicks RC 2.50 1.10
❑ 350 Ahman Green RC 5.00 2.20
❑ 351 Takeo Spikes RC 2.00 .90
❑ 352 Randy Moss RC 20.00 9.00
❑ 353 Andre Wadsworth RC 2.00 .90
❑ 354 Jason Peter RC 1.25 .55
❑ 355 Grant Wistrom RC 1.25 .55
❑ 356 Charles Woodson RC 3.00 1.35
❑ 357 Kevin Dyson RC 3.00 1.35
❑ 358 Pat Johnson RC 2.00 .90
❑ 359 Tim Dwight RC 3.00 1.35
❑ 360 Peyton Manning RC 20.00 9.00
❑ P1 Robert Tisch 5.00 2.20
(Promo card of Giants' owner)

1999 Topps

	MINT	NRMT
COMPLETE SET (357)	60.00	27.00
COMP.SET w/o SP's (330)	20.00	9.00

❑ 1 Terrell Davis 1.25 .55
❑ 2 Adrian Murrell .25 .11
❑ 3 Ernie Mills .15 .07
❑ 4 Jimmy Hitchcock .15 .07
❑ 5 Charlie Garner .25 .11
❑ 6 Blaine Bishop .15 .07
❑ 7 Junior Seau .25 .11
❑ 8 Andre Rison .25 .11
❑ 9 Jake Reed .25 .11
❑ 10 Cris Carter .50 .23
❑ 11 Torrance Small .15 .07
❑ 12 Ronald McKinnon .15 .07
❑ 13 Tyrone Davis .15 .07
❑ 14 Warren Moon .50 .23
❑ 15 Joe Johnson .15 .07
❑ 16 Bert Emanuel .25 .11
❑ 17 Brad Culpepper .15 .07
❑ 18 Henry Jones .15 .07
❑ 19 Jonathan Ogden .15 .07
❑ 20 Terrell Owens .50 .23
❑ 21 Derrick Mason .25 .11
❑ 22 Jon Ritchie .15 .07
❑ 23 Eric Metcalf .15 .07
❑ 24 Kevin Carter .15 .07
❑ 25 Fred Taylor 1.25 .55
❑ 26 DeWayne Washington .15 .07
❑ 27 William Thomas .15 .07
❑ 28 Rocket Ismail .25 .11
❑ 29 Jason Taylor .15 .07
❑ 30 Doug Flutie .60 .25
❑ 31 Michael Sinclair .15 .07
❑ 32 Yancey Thigpen .15 .07
❑ 33 Darnay Scott .15 .07
❑ 34 Amani Toomer .15 .07
❑ 35 Edgar Bennett .15 .07
❑ 36 LeRoy Butler .15 .07
❑ 37 Jessie Tuggle .15 .07
❑ 38 Andrew Glover .15 .07
❑ 39 Tim McDonald .15 .07
❑ 40 Marshall Faulk .50 .23
❑ 41 Ray Mickens .15 .07
❑ 42 Kimble Anders .25 .11
❑ 43 Trent Green .25 .11
❑ 44 Dermontti Dawson .15 .07
❑ 45 Greg Ellis .15 .07
❑ 46 Hugh Douglas .15 .07
❑ 47 Amp Lee .15 .07
❑ 48 Lamar Thomas .15 .07
❑ 49 Curtis Conway .25 .11
❑ 50 Emmitt Smith 1.25 .55
❑ 51 Elvis Grbac .25 .11
❑ 52 Tony Simmons .15 .07
❑ 53 Darrin Smith .15 .07
❑ 54 Donovin Darius .15 .07
❑ 55 Corey Chavous .15 .07
❑ 56 Phillippi Sparks .15 .07
❑ 57 Luther Elliss .15 .07
❑ 58 Tim Dwight .50 .23
❑ 59 Andre Hastings .15 .07
❑ 60 Dan Marino 2.00 .90
❑ 61 Micheal Barrow .15 .07
❑ 62 Corey Fuller .15 .07
❑ 63 Bill Romanowski .15 .07
❑ 64 Derrick Rodgers .25 .11
❑ 65 Natrone Means .25 .11
❑ 66 Peter Boulware .15 .07
❑ 67 Brian Mitchell .15 .07
❑ 68 Cornelius Bennett .15 .07
❑ 69 Dedric Ward .15 .07
❑ 70 Drew Bledsoe .75 .35
❑ 71 Freddie Jones .15 .07
❑ 72 Derrick Thomas .25 .11
❑ 73 Willie Davis .15 .07
❑ 74 Larry Centers .15 .07
❑ 75 Mark Brunell .75 .35
❑ 76 Chuck Smith .15 .07
❑ 77 Desmond Howard .25 .11
❑ 78 Sedrick Shaw .15 .07
❑ 79 Tiki Barber .15 .07
❑ 80 Curtis Martin .50 .23
❑ 81 Barry Minter .15 .07
❑ 82 Skip Hicks .50 .23
❑ 83 O.J. Santiago .15 .07
❑ 84 Ed McCaffrey .25 .11
❑ 85 Terrell Buckley .15 .07
❑ 86 Charlie Jones .15 .07
❑ 87 Pete Mitchell .15 .07
❑ 88 La'Roi Glover .15 .07
❑ 89 Eric Davis .15 .07
❑ 90 John Elway 2.00 .90
❑ 91 Kavika Pittman .15 .07
❑ 92 Fred Lane .25 .11
❑ 93 Warren Sapp .15 .07
❑ 94 Lorenzo Bromell .15 .07
❑ 95 Lawyer Milloy .15 .07
❑ 96 Aeneas Williams .15 .07
❑ 97 Michael McCrary .15 .07
❑ 98 Rickey Dudley .15 .07
❑ 99 Bryce Paup .15 .07

	#	Card		
❑	100	Jamal Anderson	.50	.23
❑	101	D'Marco Farr	.15	.07
❑	102	Johnnie Morton	.25	.11
❑	103	Jeff Graham	.15	.07
❑	104	Sam Cowart	.15	.07
❑	105	Bryant Young	.15	.07
❑	106	Jermaine Lewis	.25	.11
❑	107	Chad Bratzke	.15	.07
❑	108	Jeff Burris	.15	.07
❑	109	Roell Preston	.15	.07
❑	110	Vinny Testaverde	.25	.11
❑	111	Ruben Brown	.15	.07
❑	112	Darryll Lewis	.15	.07
❑	113	Billy Davis	.15	.07
❑	114	Bryant Westbrook	.15	.07
❑	115	Stephen Alexander	.15	.07
❑	116	Terrell Fletcher	.15	.07
❑	117	Terry Glenn	.50	.23
❑	118	Rod Smith	.25	.11
❑	119	Carl Pickens	.25	.11
❑	120	Tim Brown	.50	.23
❑	121	Mikhael Ricks	.15	.07
❑	122	Jason Gildon	.15	.07
❑	123	Charles Way	.15	.07
❑	124	Rob Moore	.25	.11
❑	125	Jerome Bettis	.50	.23
❑	126	Kerry Collins	.25	.11
❑	127	Bruce Smith	.25	.11
❑	128	James Hasty	.15	.07
❑	129	Ken Norton Jr.	.15	.07
❑	130	Charles Woodson	.50	.23
❑	131	Tony McGee	.15	.07
❑	132	Kevin Turner	.15	.07
❑	133	Jerome Pathon	.15	.07
❑	134	Garrison Hearst	.25	.11
❑	135	Craig Newsome	.15	.07
❑	136	Hardy Nickerson	.15	.07
❑	137	Ray Lewis	.25	.11
❑	138	Derrick Alexander	.15	.07
❑	139	Phil Hansen	.15	.07
❑	140	Joey Galloway	.50	.23
❑	141	Oronde Gadsden	.15	.07
❑	142	Herman Moore	.50	.23
❑	143	Bobby Taylor	.15	.07
❑	144	Mario Bates	.15	.07
❑	145	Kevin Dyson	.25	.11
❑	146	Aaron Glenn	.15	.07
❑	147	Ed McDaniel	.15	.07
❑	148	Terry Allen	.25	.11
❑	149	Ike Hilliard	.15	.07
❑	150	Steve Young	.75	.35
❑	151	Eugene Robinson	.15	.07
❑	152	John Mobley	.15	.07
❑	153	Kevin Hardy	.15	.07
❑	154	Lance Johnstone	.15	.07
❑	155	Willie McGinest	.15	.07
❑	156	Gary Anderson	.15	.07
❑	157	Dexter Coakley	.15	.07
❑	158	Mark Fields	.15	.07
❑	159	Steve McNair	.50	.23
❑	160	Corey Dillon	.50	.23
❑	161	Zach Thomas	.25	.11
❑	162	Kent Graham	.15	.07
❑	163	Tony Parrish	.15	.07
❑	164	Sam Gash	.15	.07
❑	165	Kyle Brady	.15	.07
❑	166	Donnell Bennett	.15	.07
❑	167	Tony Martin	.25	.11
❑	168	Michael Bates	.15	.07
❑	169	Bobby Engram	.25	.11
❑	170	Jimmy Smith	.25	.11
❑	171	Vonnie Holliday	.15	.07
❑	172	Simeon Rice	.15	.07
❑	173	Kevin Greene	.15	.07
❑	174	Mike Alstott	.50	.23
❑	175	Eddie George	.60	.25
❑	176	Michael Jackson	.15	.07
❑	177	Neil O'Donnell	.25	.11
❑	178	Sean Dawkins	.15	.07
❑	179	Courtney Hawkins	.15	.07
❑	180	Michael Irvin	.25	.11
❑	181	Thurman Thomas	.25	.11
❑	182	Cam Cleeland	.15	.07
❑	183	Ellis Johnson	.15	.07
❑	184	Will Blackwell	.15	.07
❑	185	Ty Law	.15	.07
❑	186	Merton Hanks	.15	.07
❑	187	Dan Wilkinson	.15	.07
❑	188	Andre Wadsworth	.15	.07
❑	189	Troy Vincent	.15	.07
❑	190	Frank Sanders	.25	.11
❑	191	Stephen Boyd	.15	.07
❑	192	Jason Elam	.15	.07
❑	193	Kordell Stewart	.50	.23
❑	194	Ted Johnson	.15	.07
❑	195	Glyn Milburn	.15	.07
❑	196	Gary Brown	.15	.07
❑	197	Travis Hall	.15	.07
❑	198	John Randle	.25	.11
❑	199	Jay Riemersma	.15	.07
❑	200	Barry Sanders	2.00	.90
❑	201	Chris Spielman	.15	.07
❑	202	Rod Woodson	.25	.11
❑	203	Darrell Russell	.15	.07
❑	204	Tony Boselli	.15	.07
❑	205	Darren Woodson	.15	.07
❑	206	Muhsin Muhammad	.25	.11
❑	207	Jim Harbaugh	.25	.11
❑	208	Isaac Bruce	.50	.23
❑	209	Mo Lewis	.15	.07
❑	210	Dorsey Levens	.50	.23
❑	211	Frank Wycheck	.15	.07
❑	212	Napoleon Kaufman	.50	.23
❑	213	Walt Harris	.15	.07
❑	214	Leon Lett	.15	.07
❑	215	Karim Abdul-Jabbar	.25	.11
❑	216	Carnell Lake	.15	.07
❑	217	Byron Bam Morris	.15	.07
❑	218	John Avery	.25	.11
❑	219	Chris Slade	.15	.07
❑	220	Robert Smith	.50	.23
❑	221	Mike Pritchard	.15	.07
❑	222	Ty Detmer	.25	.11
❑	223	Randall Cunningham	.50	.23
❑	224	Alonzo Mayes	.15	.07
❑	225	Jake Plummer	1.00	.45
❑	226	Derrick Mayes	.15	.07
❑	227	Jeff Brady	.15	.07
❑	228	John Lynch	.15	.07
❑	229	Steve Atwater	.15	.07
❑	230	Warrick Dunn	.50	.23
❑	231	Shawn Jefferson	.15	.07
❑	232	Erik Kramer	.15	.07
❑	233	Ken Dilger	.15	.07
❑	234	Ryan Leaf	.50	.23
❑	235	Ray Buchanan	.15	.07
❑	236	Kevin Williams	.15	.07
❑	237	Ricky Watters	.25	.11
❑	238	Dwayne Rudd	.15	.07
❑	239	Duce Staley	.50	.23
❑	240	Charlie Batch	1.00	.45
❑	241	Tim Biakabutuka	.25	.11
❑	242	Tony Gonzalez	.25	.11
❑	243	Bryan Still	.15	.07
❑	244	Donnie Edwards	.15	.07
❑	245	Troy Aikman	1.25	.55
❑	246	Tony Banks	.25	.11
❑	247	Curtis Enis	.50	.23
❑	248	Chris Chandler	.25	.11
❑	249	James Jett	.25	.11
❑	250	Brett Favre	2.00	.90
❑	251	Keith Poole	.15	.07
❑	252	Ricky Proehl	.15	.07
❑	253	Shannon Sharpe	.25	.11
❑	254	Robert Jones	.15	.07
❑	255	Chad Brown	.15	.07
❑	256	Ben Coates	.25	.11
❑	257	Jacquez Green	.25	.11
❑	258	Jessie Armstead	.15	.07
❑	259	Dale Carter	.15	.07
❑	260	Antowain Smith	.50	.23
❑	261	Mark Chmura	.15	.07
❑	262	Michael Westbrook	.25	.11
❑	263	Marvin Harrison	.50	.23
❑	264	Darrien Gordon	.15	.07
❑	265	Rodney Harrison	.15	.07
❑	266	Charles Johnson	.15	.07
❑	267	Roman Phifer	.15	.07
❑	268	Reidel Anthony	.25	.11
❑	269	Jerry Rice	1.25	.55
❑	270	Eric Moulds	.50	.23
❑	271	Robert Porcher	.15	.07
❑	272	Deion Sanders	.50	.23
❑	273	Germane Crowell	.25	.11
❑	274	Randy Moss	2.00	.90
❑	275	Antonio Freeman	.50	.23
❑	276	Trent Dilfer	.25	.11
❑	277	Eric Turner	.15	.07
❑	278	Jeff George	.25	.11
❑	279	Levon Kirkland	.15	.07
❑	280	O.J. McDuffie	.25	.11
❑	281	Takeo Spikes	.15	.07
❑	282	Jim Flanigan	.15	.07
❑	283	Chris Warren	.15	.07
❑	284	J.J. Stokes	.25	.11
❑	285	Bryan Cox	.15	.07
❑	286	Sam Madison	.15	.07
❑	287	Priest Holmes	.50	.23
❑	288	Keenan McCardell	.25	.11
❑	289	Michael Strahan	.15	.07
❑	290	Robert Edwards	.25	.11
❑	291	Tommy Vardell	.15	.07
❑	292	Wayne Chrebet	.25	.11
❑	293	Chris Calloway	.15	.07
❑	294	Wesley Walls	.25	.11
❑	295	Derrick Brooks	.15	.07
❑	296	Trace Armstrong	.15	.07
❑	297	Brian Simmons	.15	.07
❑	298	Darrell Green	.15	.07
❑	299	Robert Brooks	.25	.11
❑	300	Peyton Manning	2.00	.90
❑	301	Dana Stubblefield	.15	.07
❑	302	Shawn Springs	.15	.07
❑	303	Leslie Shepherd	.15	.07
❑	304	Ken Harvey	.15	.07
❑	305	Jon Kitna	.50	.23
❑	306	Terance Mathis	.25	.11
❑	307	Andre Reed	.25	.11
❑	308	Jackie Harris	.15	.07
❑	309	Rich Gannon	.25	.11
❑	310	Keyshawn Johnson	.50	.23
❑	311	Victor Green	.15	.07
❑	312	Eric Allen	.15	.07
❑	313	Terry Fair	.15	.07
❑	314	Jason Elam SH	.15	.07
❑	315	Garrison Hearst SH	.25	.11
❑	316	Jake Plummer SH	.60	.25
❑	317	Randall Cunningham SH	.50	.23
❑	318	Randy Moss SH	1.00	.45
❑	319	Jamal Anderson SH	.50	.23
❑	320	John Elway SH	1.00	.45
❑	321	Doug Flutie SH	.50	.23
❑	322	Emmitt Smith SH	.75	.35
❑	323	Terrell Davis SH	.75	.35
❑	324	Jerris McPhail	.15	.07
❑	325	Damon Gibson	.15	.07
❑	326	Jim Pyne	.15	.07
❑	327	Antonio Langham	.15	.07
❑	328	Freddie Solomon	.15	.07
❑	329	Ricky Williams RC	10.00	4.50
❑	330	Daunte Culpepper RC	12.00	5.50
❑	331	Chris Claiborne RC	2.00	.90
❑	332	Amos Zereoue RC	2.50	1.10
❑	333	Chris McAlister RC	2.00	.90
❑	334	Kevin Faulk RC	4.00	1.80
❑	335	James Johnson RC	2.50	1.10
❑	336	Mike Cloud RC	2.00	.90
❑	337	Jevon Kearse RC	5.00	2.20
❑	338	Akili Smith RC	5.00	2.20
❑	339	Edgerrin James RC	12.00	5.50
❑	340	Cecil Collins RC	2.50	1.10
❑	341	Donovan McNabb RC	10.00	4.50
❑	342	Kevin Johnson RC	5.00	2.20
❑	343	Torry Holt RC	6.00	2.70
❑	344	Rob Konrad RC	2.00	.90
❑	345	Tim Couch RC	8.00	3.60
❑	346	David Boston RC	5.00	2.20
❑	347	Karsten Bailey RC	2.00	.90
❑	348	Troy Edwards RC	3.00	1.35
❑	349	Sedrick Irvin RC	2.50	1.10
❑	350	Shaun King RC	5.00	2.20
❑	351	Peerless Price RC	3.00	1.35
❑	352	Brock Huard RC	4.00	1.80
❑	353	Cade McNown RC	3.00	1.35
❑	354	Champ Bailey RC	3.00	1.35
❑	355	D'Wayne Bates RC	2.00	.90
❑	356	Checklist Card	.15	.07
❑	357	Checklist Card	.15	.07

2000 Topps

	MINT	NRMT
COMPLETE SET (400)	120.00	55.00
COMP.SET w/o SP's (360)	20.00	9.00

Card	MINT	NRMT
❑ 1 Kurt Warner	2.00	.90
❑ 2 Darrell Russell	.15	.07
❑ 3 Courtney Hawkins	.15	.07
❑ 4 Bryant Young	.15	.07
❑ 5 Kent Graham	.15	.07
❑ 6 Shawn Jefferson	.15	.07
❑ 7 Wesley Walls	.15	.07
❑ 8 Jessie Armstead	.15	.07
❑ 9 Dedric Ward	.15	.07
❑ 10 Emmitt Smith	1.25	.55
❑ 11 James Stewart	.25	.11
❑ 12 Frank Sanders	.15	.07
❑ 13 Ray Buchanan	.15	.07
❑ 14 Olindo Mare	.15	.07
❑ 15 Andre Reed	.25	.11
❑ 16 Curtis Conway	.25	.11
❑ 17 Patrick Jeffers	.50	.23
❑ 18 Greg Hill	.15	.07
❑ 19 John Unitas	.50	.23
❑ 20 Brett Favre	2.00	.90
❑ 21 Jerome Pathon	.25	.11
❑ 22 Jason Tucker	.25	.11
❑ 23 Charles Johnson	.25	.11
❑ 24 Brian Mitchell	.15	.07
❑ 25 Billy Miller	.15	.07
❑ 26 Jay Fiedler	.50	.23
❑ 27 Marcus Pollard	.15	.07
❑ 28 De'Mond Parker	.15	.07
❑ 29 Leslie Shepherd	.15	.07
❑ 30 Fred Taylor	.60	.25
❑ 31 Michael Pittman	.15	.07
❑ 32 Ricky Watters	.15	.07
❑ 33 Derrick Brooks	.15	.07
❑ 34 Junior Seau	.25	.11
❑ 35 Troy Vincent	.15	.07
❑ 36 Eric Allen	.15	.07
❑ 37 Pete Mitchell	.15	.07
❑ 38 Tony Simmons	.15	.07
❑ 39 Az-Zahir Hakim	.25	.11
❑ 40 Dan Marino	2.00	.90
❑ 41 Mac Cody	.15	.07
❑ 42 Scott Dreisbach	.15	.07
❑ 43 Al Wilson	.15	.07
❑ 44 Luther Broughton RC	.25	.11
❑ 45 Wane McGarity	.15	.07
❑ 46 Stephen Boyd	.15	.07
❑ 47 Michael Strahan	.15	.07
❑ 48 Chris Chandler	.25	.11
❑ 49 Tony Martin	.25	.11
❑ 50 Edgerrin James	2.00	.90
❑ 51 John Randle	.25	.11
❑ 52 Warrick Dunn	.50	.23
❑ 53 Elvis Grbac	.25	.11
❑ 54 Champ Bailey	.25	.11
❑ 55 Kyle Brady	.15	.07
❑ 56 John Lynch	.15	.07
❑ 57 Kevin Carter	.15	.07
❑ 58 Mike Pritchard	.15	.07
❑ 59 Deon Mitchell RC	.25	.11
❑ 60 Randy Moss	1.50	.70
❑ 61 Jermaine Fazande	.15	.07
❑ 62 Donovan McNabb	.75	.35
❑ 63 Richard Huntley	.15	.07
❑ 64 Rich Gannon	.25	.11
❑ 65 Aaron Glenn	.15	.07
❑ 66 Amani Toomer	.15	.07
❑ 67 Andre Hastings	.15	.07
❑ 68 Ricky Williams	1.25	.55
❑ 69 Sam Madison	.15	.07
❑ 70 Drew Bledsoe	.75	.35
❑ 71 Eric Moulds	.50	.23
❑ 72 Justin Armour	.15	.07
❑ 73 Jamal Anderson	.50	.23
❑ 74 Mario Bates	.15	.07
❑ 75 Sam Gash	.15	.07
❑ 76 Macey Brooks	.15	.07
❑ 77 Tremain Mack	.15	.07
❑ 78 David LaFleur	.15	.07
❑ 79 Dexter Coakley	.15	.07
❑ 80 Cris Carter	.50	.23
❑ 81 Byron Chamberlain	.15	.07
❑ 82 David Sloan	.15	.07
❑ 83 Mike Devlin	.15	.07
❑ 84 Jimmy Smith	.25	.11
❑ 85 Derrick Alexander	.25	.11
❑ 86 Damon Huard	.50	.23
❑ 87 Jake Reed	.25	.11
❑ 88 Darrell Green	.15	.07
❑ 89 Derrick Mason	.25	.11
❑ 90 Curtis Martin	.50	.23
❑ 91 Donnie Abraham	.15	.07
❑ 92 D'Marco Farr	.15	.07
❑ 93 Ahman Green	.25	.11
❑ 94 Shane Matthews	.25	.11
❑ 95 Torrance Small	.15	.07
❑ 96 Duce Staley	.50	.23
❑ 97 Jon Ritchie	.15	.07
❑ 98 Victor Green	.15	.07
❑ 99 Kerry Collins	.25	.11
❑ 100 Peyton Manning	1.50	.70
❑ 101 Ben Coates	.15	.07
❑ 102 Thurman Thomas	.25	.11
❑ 103 Cornelius Bennett	.15	.07
❑ 104 Terance Mathis	.15	.07
❑ 105 Adrian Murrell	.25	.11
❑ 106 Donald Hayes	.15	.07
❑ 107 Terry Kirby	.15	.07
❑ 108 James Allen	.25	.11
❑ 109 Ty Law	.15	.07
❑ 110 Tim Brown	.50	.23
❑ 111 Chad Bratzke	.15	.07
❑ 112 Deion Sanders	.50	.23
❑ 113 James Johnson	.25	.11
❑ 114 Tony Richardson RC	.25	.11
❑ 115 Tony Brackens	.15	.07
❑ 116 Ken Dilger	.15	.07
❑ 117 Albert Connell	.15	.07
❑ 118 Neil O'Donnell	.15	.07
❑ 119 Selucio Sanford EP RC	.60	.25
❑ 120 Steve Young	.75	.35
❑ 121 Tony Horne	.15	.07
❑ 122 Charlie Rogers	.15	.07
❑ 123 J.J. Stokes	.25	.11
❑ 124 Kenny Bynum	.15	.07
❑ 125 Jeff Graham	.15	.07
❑ 126 Ike Hilliard	.25	.11
❑ 127 Ray Lucas	.50	.23
❑ 128 Terry Glenn	.25	.11
❑ 129 Rickey Dudley	.15	.07
❑ 130 Joey Galloway	.50	.23
❑ 131 Brian Dawkins	.15	.07
❑ 132 Rob Moore	.25	.11
❑ 133 Bob Christian	.15	.07
❑ 134 Anthony Wright RC	3.00	1.35
❑ 135 Antowain Smith	.25	.11
❑ 136 Kevin Johnson	.50	.23
❑ 137 Scott Covington	.15	.07
❑ 138 D'Wayne Bates	.15	.07
❑ 139 Sam Cowart	.15	.07
❑ 140 Isaac Bruce	.50	.23
❑ 141 Tony McGee	.15	.07
❑ 142 Dale Carter	.15	.07
❑ 143 Matt Hasselbeck	.25	.11
❑ 144 Torry Holt	.50	.23
❑ 145 Daunte Culpepper	1.00	.45
❑ 146 Yatil Green	.15	.07
❑ 147 Chris Howard	.15	.07
❑ 148 Irving Fryar	.15	.07
❑ 149 Derrick Mayes	.25	.11
❑ 150 Warren Sapp	.25	.11
❑ 151 Ricky Proehl	.15	.07
❑ 152 Eric Kresser EP	.50	.23
❑ 153 Jeff Garcia	.50	.23
❑ 154 Freddie Jones	.15	.07
❑ 155 Mike Cloud	.15	.07
❑ 156 Wayne Chrebet	.25	.11
❑ 157 Joe Montgomery	.15	.07
❑ 158 Shannon Sharpe	.25	.11
❑ 159 Eddie Kennison	.15	.07
❑ 160 Eddie George	.60	.25
❑ 161 Jay Riemersma	.15	.07
❑ 162 Peter Boulware	.15	.07
❑ 163 Aeneas Williams	.15	.07
❑ 164 Jim Miller	.15	.07
❑ 165 Jamir Miller	.15	.07
❑ 166 Tim Biakabutuka	.25	.11
❑ 167 Kordell Stewart	.50	.23
❑ 168 Charlie Garner	.25	.11
❑ 169 Germane Crowell	.25	.11
❑ 170 Stephen Davis	.50	.23
❑ 171 Jeff George	.25	.11
❑ 172 Mark Brunell	.75	.35
❑ 173 Stephen Alexander	.15	.07
❑ 174 Mike Alstott	.50	.23
❑ 175 Terry Allen	.25	.11
❑ 176 Ed McCaffrey	.50	.23
❑ 177 Bobby Engram	.15	.07
❑ 178 Andre Cooper	.15	.07
❑ 179 Kevin Faulk	.15	.07
❑ 180 Errict Rhett	.25	.11
❑ 181 Jammi German	.15	.07
❑ 182 Oronde Gadsden	.25	.11
❑ 183 Jevon Kearse	.50	.23
❑ 184 Herman Moore	.25	.11
❑ 185 Terrence Wilkins	.50	.23
❑ 186 Rocket Ismail	.25	.11
❑ 187 Patrick Johnson	.15	.07
❑ 188 Simeon Rice	.15	.07
❑ 189 Mo Lewis	.15	.07
❑ 190 Qadry Ismail	.15	.07
❑ 191 Terry Jackson	.15	.07
❑ 192 Rashaan Shehee	.15	.07
❑ 193 Charles Woodson	.25	.11
❑ 194 Akili Smith	.50	.23
❑ 195 Yancey Thigpen	.15	.07
❑ 196 Michael Westbrook	.25	.11
❑ 197 Donnell Bennett	.15	.07
❑ 198 Sedrick Irvin	.15	.07
❑ 199 Keenan McCardell	.25	.11
❑ 200 Marshall Faulk	.60	.25
❑ 201 Jeff Blake	.25	.11
❑ 202 Rob Johnson	.25	.11
❑ 203 Vinny Testaverde	.25	.11
❑ 204 Andy Katzenmoyer	.15	.07
❑ 205 Michael Basnight	.15	.07
❑ 206 Lance Schulters	.15	.07
❑ 207 Shaun King	.75	.35
❑ 208 Bill Schroeder	.25	.11
❑ 209 Skip Hicks	.25	.11
❑ 210 Jake Plummer	.50	.23
❑ 211 Leroy Hoard	.15	.07
❑ 212 Reggie Barlow	.15	.07
❑ 213 E.G. Green	.15	.07
❑ 214 Fred Lane	.15	.07
❑ 215 Antonio Freeman	.50	.23
❑ 216 Grant Wistrom	.15	.07
❑ 217 Kevin Dyson	.25	.11
❑ 218 Mikhael Ricks	.15	.07
❑ 219 Rod Woodson	.25	.11
❑ 220 Tim Dwight	.50	.23
❑ 221 Darnay Scott	.25	.11
❑ 222 Curtis Enis	.25	.11
❑ 223 Sean Bennett	.15	.07
❑ 224 Napoleon Kaufman	.25	.11
❑ 225 Jonathan Linton	.15	.07
❑ 226 Jim Harbaugh	.25	.11
❑ 227 Hardy Nickerson	.15	.07
❑ 228 Todd Lyght	.15	.07
❑ 229 Dorsey Levens	.25	.11
❑ 230 Steve Beuerlein	.25	.11
❑ 231 Marty Booker	.15	.07
❑ 232 Shawn Bryson	.15	.07
❑ 233 James Hasty	.15	.07
❑ 234 Shawn Bryson	.15	.07
❑ 235 Larry Centers	.15	.07
❑ 236 Charlie Batch	.50	.23
❑ 237 Steve McNair	.50	.23
❑ 238 Darrin Chiaverini	.15	.07
❑ 239 Jerome Bettis	.50	.23
❑ 240 Muhsin Muhammad	.25	.11
❑ 241 Terrell Fletcher	.15	.07
❑ 242 Jon Kitna	.50	.23
❑ 243 Frank Wycheck	.15	.07
❑ 244 Tony Gonzalez	.25	.11
❑ 245 Ron Rivers	.15	.07
❑ 246 Olandis Gary	.50	.23
❑ 247 Jermaine Lewis	.15	.07
❑ 248 Joe Jurevicius	.15	.07
❑ 249 Richie Anderson	.25	.11
❑ 250 Marcus Robinson	.50	.23
❑ 251 Shawn Springs	.15	.07

❑ 252	William Floyd	.15	.07
❑ 253	Bobby Shaw RC	.60	.25
❑ 254	Glyn Milburn	.15	.07
❑ 255	Brian Griese	.60	.25
❑ 256	Donnie Edwards	.15	.07
❑ 257	Joe Horn	.25	.11
❑ 258	Cameron Cleeland	.15	.07
❑ 259	Glenn Foley	.15	.07
❑ 260	Corey Dillon	.50	.23
❑ 261	Troy Brown	.15	.07
❑ 262	Stoney Case	.15	.07
❑ 263	Kevin Williams	.15	.07
❑ 264	London Fletcher RC	.25	.11
❑ 265	O.J. McDuffie	.25	.11
❑ 266	Jonathan Quinn	.15	.07
❑ 267	Trent Dilfer	.25	.11
❑ 268	Dameyune Craig	.15	.07
❑ 269	Terrell Owens	.50	.23
❑ 270	Tim Couch	1.00	.45
❑ 271	Dameane Douglas	.15	.07
❑ 272	Moses Moreno	.15	.07
❑ 273	Bruce Smith	.25	.11
❑ 274	Peerless Price	.50	.23
❑ 275	Sam Games	.15	.07
❑ 276	Natrone Means	.15	.07
❑ 277	Na Brown	.15	.07
❑ 278	Dave Moore	.15	.07
❑ 279	Chris Sanders	.15	.07
❑ 280	Troy Aikman	1.25	.55
❑ 281	Cecil Collins	.15	.07
❑ 282	Matthew Hatchette	.25	.11
❑ 283	Bill Romanowski	.15	.07
❑ 284	Basil Mitchell	.15	.07
❑ 285	Tony Banks	.25	.11
❑ 286	Jake Delhomme RC	.50	.23
❑ 287	Keyshawn Johnson	.50	.23
❑ 288	Dexter McLeon	.15	.07
❑ 289	Corey Bradford	.25	.11
❑ 290	Terrell Davis	1.25	.55
❑ 291	Johnnie Morton	.25	.11
❑ 292	Kevin Lockett	.15	.07
❑ 293	Robert Smith	.50	.23
❑ 294	Jeff Lewis	.15	.07
❑ 295	Wali Rainer	.15	.07
❑ 296	Troy Edwards	.25	.11
❑ 297	Keith Poole	.15	.07
❑ 298	Priest Holmes	.25	.11
❑ 299	David Boston	.50	.23
❑ 300	Marvin Harrison	.50	.23
❑ 301	Levon Kirkland	.15	.07
❑ 302	Robert Holcombe	.15	.07
❑ 303	Autry Denson	.15	.07
❑ 304	Kevin Hardy	.15	.07
❑ 305	Rod Smith	.25	.11
❑ 306	Robert Porcher	.15	.07
❑ 307	Cade McNown	.50	.23
❑ 308	Craig Yeast	.15	.07
❑ 309	Doug Flutie	.60	.25
❑ 310	Jerry Rice	1.25	.55
❑ 311	Brad Johnson	.50	.23
❑ 312	Tiki Barber	.25	.11
❑ 313	Will Blackwell	.15	.07
❑ 314	Sean Dawkins	.15	.07
❑ 315	Jacquez Green	.25	.11
❑ 316	Zach Thomas	.25	.11
❑ 317	Gus Frerotte	.15	.07
❑ 318	Chris Warren	.15	.07
❑ 319	Carl Pickens	.25	.11
❑ 320	Tyrone Wheatley HL	.15	.07
❑ 321	Kurt Warner HL	1.00	.45
❑ 322	Dan Marino HL	1.00	.45
❑ 323	Cris Carter HL	.25	.11
❑ 324	Brett Favre HL	1.00	.45
❑ 325	Marshall Faulk HL	.25	.11
❑ 326	Jevon Kearse HL	.25	.11
❑ 327	Edgerrin James HL	1.00	.45
❑ 328	Emmitt Smith HL	.60	.25
❑ 329	Andre Reed HL	.15	.07
❑ 330	Kevin Dyson Frank Wycheck	.15	.07
❑ 331	Olindo Mare MM	.15	.07
❑ 332	Marcus Coleman MM	.15	.07
❑ 333	James Johnson MM	.15	.07
❑ 334	Ray Lucas MM	.25	.11
❑ 335	Dedric Ward MM	.15	.07
❑ 336	Richie Cunningham MM	.15	.07
❑ 337	James Hasty MM	.15	.07
❑ 338	Sedrick Shaw MM	.15	.07
❑ 339	Kurt Warner MM	1.00	.45
❑ 340	Marshall Faulk MM	.25	.11
❑ 341	Brian Shay EP	.50	.23
❑ 342	L.C. Stevens EP	.50	.23
❑ 343	Corey Thomas EP	.50	.23
❑ 344	Scott Milanovich EP	.60	.25
❑ 345	Pat Barnes EP	.60	.25
❑ 346	Danny Wuerffel EP	.60	.25
❑ 347	Kevin Daft EP	.50	.23
❑ 348	Ron Powlus EP RC	1.50	.70
❑ 349	Tony Graziani EP	.60	.25
❑ 350	Norman Miller EP RC	.50	.23
❑ 351	Cory Sauter EP	.50	.23
❑ 352	Marcus Crandell EP RC	.50	.23
❑ 353	Sean Morey EP RC	.60	.25
❑ 354	Jeff Ogden EP	.60	.25
❑ 355	Ted White EP	.50	.23
❑ 356	Jim Kubiak EP RC	.60	.25
❑ 357	Aaron Stecker EP RC	1.00	.45
❑ 358	Ronnie Powell EP	.50	.23
❑ 359	Matt Lytle EP RC	.60	.25
❑ 360	Kendrick Nord EP RC	.50	.23
❑ 361	Tim Rattay RC	4.00	1.80
❑ 362	Rob Morris RC	2.50	1.10
❑ 363	Chris Samuels RC	2.00	.90
❑ 364	Todd Husak RC	2.50	1.10
❑ 365	Ahmed Plummer RC	2.50	1.10
❑ 366	Frank Murphy RC	2.00	.90
❑ 367	Michael Wiley RC	2.50	1.10
❑ 368	Giovanni Carmazzi RC	3.00	1.35
❑ 369	Anthony Becht RC	2.50	1.10
❑ 370	John Abraham RC	2.50	1.10
❑ 371	Shaun Alexander RC	6.00	2.70
❑ 372	Thomas Jones RC	4.00	1.80
❑ 373	Courtney Brown RC	3.00	1.35
❑ 374	Curtis Keaton RC	2.00	.90
❑ 375	Jerry Porter RC	2.50	1.10
❑ 376	Corey Simon RC	3.00	1.35
❑ 377	Dez White RC	2.50	1.10
❑ 378	Jamal Lewis RC	12.00	5.50
❑ 379	Ron Dayne RC	8.00	3.60
❑ 380	R.Jay Soward RC	2.50	1.10
❑ 381	Tee Martin RC	4.00	1.80
❑ 382	Shaun Ellis RC	2.00	.90
❑ 383	Brian Urlacher RC	8.00	3.60
❑ 384	Reuben Droughns RC	2.50	1.10
❑ 385	Travis Taylor RC	3.00	1.35
❑ 386	Plaxico Burress RC	5.00	2.20
❑ 387	Chad Pennington RC	8.00	3.60
❑ 388	Sylvester Morris RC	5.00	2.20
❑ 389	Ron Dugans RC	2.50	1.10
❑ 390	Joe Hamilton RC	3.00	1.35
❑ 391	Chris Redman RC	5.00	2.20
❑ 392	Trung Canidate RC	2.50	1.10
❑ 393	J.R. Redmond RC	3.00	1.35
❑ 394	Danny Farmer RC	2.50	1.10
❑ 395	Todd Pinkston RC	2.50	1.10
❑ 396	Dennis Northcutt RC	3.00	1.35
❑ 397	Laveranues Coles RC	4.00	1.80
❑ 398	Bubba Franks RC	3.00	1.35
❑ 399	Travis Prentice RC	4.00	1.80
❑ 400	Peter Warrick RC	8.00	3.60

1996 Topps Chrome

	MINT	NRMT
COMPLETE SET (165)	250.00	110.00

❑ 1	Troy Aikman	2.50	1.10
❑ 2	Kevin Greene	.50	.23
❑ 3	Robert Brooks	1.00	.45
❑ 4	Junior Seau	.50	.23
❑ 5	Brett Perriman	.20	.09
❑ 6	Cortez Kennedy	.20	.09
❑ 7	Orlando Thomas	.20	.09
❑ 8	Anthony Miller	.50	.23
❑ 9	Jeff Blake	1.00	.45
❑ 10	Trent Dilfer	1.00	.45
❑ 11	Heath Shuler	.50	.23
❑ 12	Michael Jackson	.50	.23
❑ 13	Merton Hanks	.20	.09
❑ 14	Dale Carter	.20	.09
❑ 15	Eric Metcalf	.20	.09
❑ 16	Barry Sanders	5.00	2.20
❑ 17	Joey Galloway	1.25	.55
❑ 18	Bryan Cox	.20	.09
❑ 19	Harvey Williams	.20	.09
❑ 20	Terrell Davis	5.00	2.20
❑ 21	Darnay Scott	.50	.23
❑ 22	Kerry Collins	1.00	.45
❑ 23	Warren Sapp	.20	.09
❑ 24	Michael Westbrook	1.00	.45
❑ 25	Mark Brunell	2.50	1.10
❑ 26	Craig Heyward	.20	.09
❑ 27	Eric Allen	.20	.09
❑ 28	Dana Stubblefield	.50	.23
❑ 29	Steve Bono	.20	.09
❑ 30	Larry Brown	.20	.09
❑ 31	Warren Moon	.50	.23
❑ 32	Jim Kelly	1.00	.45
❑ 33	Terry McDaniel	.20	.09
❑ 34	Dan Wilkinson	.20	.09
❑ 35	Dave Brown	.20	.09
❑ 36	Todd Lyght	.20	.09
❑ 37	Aeneas Williams	.20	.09
❑ 38	Shannon Sharpe	.50	.23
❑ 39	Errict Rhett	.50	.23
❑ 40	Yancey Thigpen	.50	.23
❑ 41	J.J. Stokes	1.00	.45
❑ 42	Marshall Faulk	1.00	.45
❑ 43	Chester McGlockton	.20	.09
❑ 44	Darryll Lewis	.20	.09
❑ 45	Drew Bledsoe	2.50	1.10
❑ 46	Tyrone Wheatley	.50	.23
❑ 47	Herman Moore	1.00	.45
❑ 48	Darren Woodson	.50	.23
❑ 49	Ricky Watters	.50	.23
❑ 50	Emmitt Smith TYC	1.50	.70
❑ 51	Barry Sanders TYC	2.00	.90
❑ 52	Curtis Martin TYC	1.00	.45
❑ 53	Chris Warren TYC	.50	.23
❑ 54	Errict Rhett TYC	.50	.23
❑ 55	Rodney Hampton TYC	.20	.09
❑ 56	Terrell Davis TYC	2.50	1.10
❑ 57	Marshall Faulk TYC	.50	.23
❑ 58	Rashaan Salaam TYC	.50	.23
❑ 59	Curtis Conway	1.00	.45
❑ 60	Isaac Bruce	1.00	.45
❑ 61	Thurman Thomas	1.00	.45
❑ 62	Terry Allen	.50	.23
❑ 63	Lamar Lathon	.20	.09
❑ 64	Mark Chmura	.50	.23
❑ 65	Chris Warren	.50	.23
❑ 66	Jessie Tuggle	.20	.09
❑ 67	Erik Kramer	.20	.09
❑ 68	Tim Brown	1.00	.45
❑ 69	Derrick Thomas	.50	.23
❑ 70	Willie McGinest	.20	.09
❑ 71	Frank Sanders	.50	.23
❑ 72	Bernie Parmalee	.20	.09
❑ 73	Kordell Stewart	1.25	.55
❑ 74	Brent Jones	.20	.09
❑ 75	Edgar Bennett	.50	.23
❑ 76	Rashaan Salaam	1.00	.45
❑ 77	Carl Pickens	1.00	.45
❑ 78	Terance Mathis	.20	.09
❑ 79	Deion Sanders	1.25	.55
❑ 80	Glyn Milburn	.20	.09
❑ 81	Lee Woodall	.20	.09
❑ 82	Neil Smith	.20	.09
❑ 83	Stan Humphries	.50	.23
❑ 84	Rick Mirer	.50	.23
❑ 85	Troy Vincent	.20	.09

❑ 86 Sam Mills	.20	.09
❑ 87 Brian Mitchell	.20	.09
❑ 88 Hardy Nickerson	.20	.09
❑ 89 Tamarick Vanover	.50	.23
❑ 90 Steve McNair	1.50	.70
❑ 91 Jerry Rice TYC	1.00	.45
❑ 92 Isaac Bruce TYC	1.00	.45
❑ 93 Herman Moore TYC	1.00	.45
❑ 94 Cris Carter TYC	1.00	.45
❑ 95 Tim Brown TYC	.50	.23
❑ 96 Carl Pickens TYC	1.00	.45
❑ 97 Joey Galloway TYC	1.00	.45
❑ 98 Jerry Rice	2.50	1.10
❑ 99 Cris Carter	1.00	.45
❑ 100 Curtis Martin	1.50	.70
❑ 101 Scott Mitchell	.50	.23
❑ 102 Ken Harvey	.20	.09
❑ 103 Rodney Hampton	.50	.23
❑ 104 Reggie White	1.00	.45
❑ 105 Eddie Robinson	.20	.09
❑ 106 Greg Lloyd	.50	.23
❑ 107 Phillippi Sparks	.20	.09
❑ 108 Emmitt Smith	4.00	1.80
❑ 109 Tom Carter	.20	.09
❑ 110 Jim Everett	.20	.09
❑ 111 James O.Stewart	.50	.23
❑ 112 Kyle Brady	.20	.09
❑ 113 Irving Fryar	.50	.23
❑ 114 Vinny Testaverde	.50	.23
❑ 115 John Elway	5.00	2.20
❑ 116 Chris Spielman	.20	.09
❑ 117 Mike Mamula	.20	.09
❑ 118 Jim Harbaugh	.50	.23
❑ 119 Ken Norton	.20	.09
❑ 120 Bruce Smith	.50	.23
❑ 121 Daryl Johnston	.50	.23
❑ 122 Blaine Bishop	.20	.09
❑ 123 Jeff George	.50	.23
❑ 124 Jeff Hostetler	.20	.09
❑ 125 Jerome Bettis	1.00	.45
❑ 126 Jay Novacek	.20	.09
❑ 127 Bryce Paup	.20	.09
❑ 128 Neil O'Donnell	.50	.23
❑ 129 Marcus Allen	1.00	.45
❑ 130 Steve Young	1.50	.70
❑ 131 Brett Favre TYC	2.00	.90
❑ 132 Scott Mitchell TYC	.20	.09
❑ 133 John Elway TYC	2.00	.90
❑ 134 Jeff Blake TYC	.50	.23
❑ 135 Dan Marino TYC	2.00	.90
❑ 136 Drew Bledsoe TYC	1.00	.45
❑ 137 Troy Aikman TYC	1.00	.45
❑ 138 Steve Young TYC	1.00	.45
❑ 139 Jim Kelly TYC	1.00	.45
❑ 140 Jeff Graham	.20	.09
❑ 141 Hugh Douglas	.50	.23
❑ 142 Dan Marino	5.00	2.20
❑ 143 Darrell Green	.20	.09
❑ 144 Eric Zeier	.20	.09
❑ 145 Brett Favre	5.00	2.20
❑ 146 Carnell Lake	.20	.09
❑ 147 Ben Coates	.50	.23
❑ 148 Tony Martin	.50	.23
❑ 149 Michael Irvin	1.00	.45
❑ 150 Lawrence Phillips RC	1.00	.45
❑ 151 Alex Van Dyke RC	2.00	.90
❑ 152 Kevin Hardy RC	2.00	.90
❑ 153 Rickey Dudley RC	6.00	2.70
❑ 154 Eric Moulds RC	20.00	9.00
❑ 155 Simeon Rice RC	2.00	.90
❑ 156 Marvin Harrison RC	40.00	18.00
❑ 157 Tim Biakabutuka RC	12.00	5.50
❑ 158 Duane Clemons RC	1.25	.55
❑ 159 Keyshawn Johnson RC	25.00	11.00
❑ 160 John Mobley RC	2.00	.90
❑ 161 Leeland McElroy RC	2.00	.90
❑ 162 Eddie George RC	60.00	27.00
❑ 163 Jonathan Ogden RC	1.25	.55
❑ 164 Eddie Kennison RC	10.00	4.50
❑ 165 Checklist	.20	.09

1997 Topps Chrome

	MINT	NRMT
COMPLETE SET (165)	100.00	45.00

❑ 1 Brett Favre	6.00	2.70
❑ 2 Tim Biakabutuka	.60	.25
❑ 3 Deion Sanders	1.25	.55
❑ 4 Marshall Faulk	1.25	.55
❑ 5 John Randle	.60	.25
❑ 6 Stan Humphries	.60	.25
❑ 7 Ki-Jana Carter	.30	.14
❑ 8 Rashaan Salaam	.30	.14
❑ 9 Rickey Dudley	.60	.25
❑ 10 Isaac Bruce	1.25	.55
❑ 11 Keyshawn Johnson	1.25	.55
❑ 12 Ben Coates	.60	.25
❑ 13 Ty Detmer	.60	.25
❑ 14 Gus Frerotte	.30	.14
❑ 15 Mario Bates	.30	.14
❑ 16 Chris Calloway	.30	.14
❑ 17 Frank Sanders	.60	.25
❑ 18 Bruce Smith	.60	.25
❑ 19 Jeff Graham	.30	.14
❑ 20 Trent Dilfer	1.25	.55
❑ 21 Tyrone Wheatley	.60	.25
❑ 22 Chris Warren	.60	.25
❑ 23 Terry Kirby	.60	.25
❑ 24 Tony Gonzalez RC	15.00	6.75
❑ 25 Ricky Watters	.60	.25
❑ 26 Tamarick Vanover	.60	.25
❑ 27 Kerry Collins	.60	.25
❑ 28 Bobby Engram	.60	.25
❑ 29 Derrick Alexander WR	.60	.25
❑ 30 Hugh Douglas	.30	.14
❑ 31 Thurman Thomas	1.25	.55
❑ 32 Drew Bledsoe	3.00	1.35
❑ 33 LeShon Johnson	.30	.14
❑ 34 Byron Bam Morris	.30	.14
❑ 35 Herman Moore	1.25	.55
❑ 36 Troy Aikman	3.00	1.35
❑ 37 Mel Gray	.30	.14
❑ 38 Adrian Murrell	.60	.25
❑ 39 Carl Pickens	1.25	.55
❑ 40 Tony Brackens	.30	.14
❑ 41 O.J. McDuffie	.60	.25
❑ 42 Napoleon Kaufman	1.25	.55
❑ 43 Chris T. Jones	.30	.14
❑ 44 Kordell Stewart	1.50	.70
❑ 45 Steve Young	2.00	.90
❑ 46 Shannon Sharpe	.60	.25
❑ 47 Leeland McElroy	.30	.14
❑ 48 Eric Moulds	1.25	.55
❑ 49 Eddie George	3.00	1.35
❑ 50 Jamal Anderson	2.00	.90
❑ 51 Robert Smith	.60	.25
❑ 52 Mike Alstott	1.25	.55
❑ 53 Darrell Green	.60	.25
❑ 54 Irving Fryar	.60	.25
❑ 55 Derrick Thomas	.60	.25
❑ 56 Antonio Freeman	1.50	.70
❑ 57 Terrell Davis	5.00	2.20
❑ 58 Henry Ellard	.30	.14
❑ 59 Daryl Johnston	.60	.25
❑ 60 Bryan Cox	.30	.14
❑ 61 Vinny Testaverde	.60	.25
❑ 62 Andre Reed	.60	.25
❑ 63 Larry Centers	.60	.25
❑ 64 Hardy Nickerson	.30	.14
❑ 65 Tony Banks	.60	.25
❑ 66 Dave Meggett	.30	.14
❑ 67 Simeon Rice	.60	.25
❑ 68 Warrick Dunn RC	20.00	9.00
❑ 69 Michael Irvin	1.25	.55
❑ 70 John Elway	6.00	2.70
❑ 71 Jake Reed	.60	.25
❑ 72 Rodney Hampton	.60	.25
❑ 73 Aaron Glenn	.30	.14
❑ 74 Terry Allen	1.25	.55
❑ 75 Blaine Bishop	.30	.14
❑ 76 Bert Emanuel	.60	.25
❑ 77 Mark Carrier WR	.30	.14
❑ 78 Jimmy Smith	.60	.25
❑ 79 Jim Harbaugh	.60	.25
❑ 80 Brent Jones	.60	.25
❑ 81 Emmitt Smith	5.00	2.20
❑ 82 Fred Barnett	.30	.14
❑ 83 Errict Rhett	.30	.14
❑ 84 Michael Sinclair	.30	.14
❑ 85 Jerome Bettis	1.25	.55
❑ 86 Chris Sanders	.30	.14
❑ 87 Kent Graham	.30	.14
❑ 88 Cris Carter	1.25	.55
❑ 89 Harvey Williams	.30	.14
❑ 90 Eric Allen	.30	.14
❑ 91 Bryant Young	.30	.14
❑ 92 Marcus Allen	1.25	.55
❑ 93 Michael Jackson	.60	.25
❑ 94 Mark Chmura	.60	.25
❑ 95 Keenan McCardell	.60	.25
❑ 96 Joey Galloway	1.50	.70
❑ 97 Eddie Kennison	.60	.25
❑ 98 Steve Atwater	.30	.14
❑ 99 Dorsey Levens	1.25	.55
❑ 100 Rob Moore	.60	.25
❑ 101 Steve McNair	1.50	.70
❑ 102 Sean Dawkins	.30	.14
❑ 103 Don Beebe	.30	.14
❑ 104 Willie McGinest	.30	.14
❑ 105 Tony Martin	.60	.25
❑ 106 Mark Brunell	3.00	1.35
❑ 107 Karim Abdul-Jabbar	1.25	.55
❑ 108 Michael Westbrook	.60	.25
❑ 109 Lawrence Phillips	.30	.14
❑ 110 Barry Sanders	6.00	2.70
❑ 111 Willie Davis	.30	.14
❑ 112 Wesley Walls	.60	.25
❑ 113 Todd Collins	.30	.14
❑ 114 Jerry Rice	3.00	1.35
❑ 115 Scott Mitchell	.60	.25
❑ 116 Terance Mathis	.60	.25
❑ 117 Chris Spielman	.30	.14
❑ 118 Curtis Conway	.60	.25
❑ 119 Marvin Harrison	1.25	.55
❑ 120 Terry Glenn	1.25	.55
❑ 121 Dave Brown	.30	.14
❑ 122 Neil O'Donnell	.60	.25
❑ 123 Junior Seau	.60	.25
❑ 124 Reggie White	1.25	.55
❑ 125 Lamar Lathon	.30	.14
❑ 126 Natrone Means	1.25	.55
❑ 127 Tim Brown	1.25	.55
❑ 128 Eric Swann	.30	.14
❑ 129 Dan Marino	6.00	2.70
❑ 130 Anthony Johnson	.30	.14
❑ 131 Edgar Bennett	.60	.25
❑ 132 Kevin Hardy	.30	.14
❑ 133 Brian Blades	.30	.14
❑ 134 Curtis Martin	1.50	.70
❑ 135 Zach Thomas	.60	.25
❑ 136 Darnay Scott	.60	.25
❑ 137 Desmond Howard	.60	.25
❑ 138 Aeneas Williams	.30	.14
❑ 139 Bryce Paup	.30	.14
❑ 140 Brad Johnson	1.25	.55
❑ 141 Jeff Blake	.60	.25
❑ 142 Wayne Chrebet	1.25	.55
❑ 143 Will Blackwell RC	2.50	1.10
❑ 144 Tom Knight RC	.30	.14
❑ 145 Darnell Autry RC	.60	.25
❑ 146 Bryant Westbrook RC	.30	.14
❑ 147 David LaFleur RC	4.00	1.80
❑ 148 Antowain Smith RC	10.00	4.50
❑ 149 Rae Carruth RC	2.50	1.10
❑ 150 Jim Druckenmiller RC	1.25	.55
❑ 151 Shawn Springs RC	1.50	.70
❑ 152 Troy Davis RC	3.00	1.35
❑ 153 Orlando Pace RC	3.00	1.35

❑ 154 Byron Hanspard RC	3.00	1.35
❑ 155 Corey Dillon RC	25.00	11.00
❑ 156 Reidel Anthony RC	6.00	2.70
❑ 157 Peter Boulware RC	3.00	1.35
❑ 158 Reinard Wilson RC	1.50	.70
❑ 159 Pat Barnes RC	3.00	1.35
❑ 160 Joey Kent RC	3.00	1.35
❑ 161 Ike Hilliard RC	6.00	2.70
❑ 162 Jake Plummer RC	20.00	9.00
❑ 163 Darrell Russell RC	1.50	.70
❑ 164 Checklist Card	.30	.14
❑ 165 Checklist Card	.30	.14

1998 Topps Chrome

	MINT	NRMT
COMPLETE SET (165)	200.00	90.00
❑ 1 Barry Sanders	5.00	2.20
❑ 2 Duane Starks RC	4.00	1.80
❑ 3 J.J. Stokes	.50	.23
❑ 4 Joey Galloway	1.00	.45
❑ 5 Deion Sanders	1.00	.45
❑ 6 Anthony Miller	.25	.11
❑ 7 Jamal Anderson	1.00	.45
❑ 8 Shannon Sharpe	.50	.23
❑ 9 Irving Fryar	.50	.23
❑ 10 Curtis Martin	1.00	.45
❑ 11 Shawn Jefferson	.25	.11
❑ 12 Charlie Garner	.25	.11
❑ 13 Robert Edwards RC	10.00	4.50
❑ 14 Napoleon Kaufman	1.00	.45
❑ 15 Gus Frerotte	.25	.11
❑ 16 John Elway	5.00	2.20
❑ 17 Jerome Pathon RC	6.00	2.70
❑ 18 Marshall Faulk	1.00	.45
❑ 19 Michael McCrary	.25	.11
❑ 20 Marcus Allen	1.00	.45
❑ 21 Trent Dilfer	1.00	.45
❑ 22 Frank Wycheck	.25	.11
❑ 23 Terrell Owens	1.00	.45
❑ 24 Herman Moore	1.00	.45
❑ 25 Neil O'Donnell	.50	.23
❑ 26 Darnay Scott	.50	.23
❑ 27 Keith Brooking RC	6.00	2.70
❑ 28 Eric Green	.25	.11
❑ 29 Dan Marino	5.00	2.20
❑ 30 Antonio Freeman	1.00	.45
❑ 31 Tony Martin	.50	.23
❑ 32 Isaac Bruce	1.00	.45
❑ 33 Rickey Dudley	.25	.11
❑ 34 Scott Mitchell	.50	.23
❑ 35 Randy Moss RC	60.00	27.00
❑ 36 Fred Lane	.50	.23
❑ 37 Frank Sanders	.50	.23
❑ 38 Jerry Rice	2.50	1.10
❑ 39 O.J. McDuffie	.50	.23
❑ 40 Jessie Armstead	.25	.11
❑ 41 Reidel Anthony	.50	.23
❑ 42 Steve McNair	1.00	.45
❑ 43 Jake Reed	.50	.23
❑ 44 Charles Woodson RC	12.00	5.50
❑ 45 Tiki Barber	.50	.23
❑ 46 Mike Alstott	1.00	.45
❑ 47 Keyshawn Johnson	1.00	.45
❑ 48 Tony Banks	.50	.23
❑ 49 Michael Westbrook	.50	.23
❑ 50 Chris Slade	.25	.11
❑ 51 Terry Allen	1.00	.45
❑ 52 Karim Abdul-Jabbar	1.00	.45
❑ 53 Brad Johnson	1.00	.45
❑ 54 Tony McGee	.25	.11
❑ 55 Kevin Dyson RC	12.00	5.50
❑ 56 Warren Moon	1.00	.45
❑ 57 Byron Hanspard	.50	.23
❑ 58 Jermaine Lewis	.50	.23
❑ 59 Neil Smith	.50	.23
❑ 60 Tamarick Vanover	.25	.11
❑ 61 Terrell Davis	4.00	1.80
❑ 62 Robert Smith	1.00	.45
❑ 63 Junior Seau	.50	.23
❑ 64 Warren Sapp	.50	.23
❑ 65 Michael Sinclair	.25	.11
❑ 66 Ryan Leaf RC	15.00	6.75
❑ 67 Drew Bledsoe	2.00	.90
❑ 68 Jason Sehorn	.50	.23
❑ 69 Andre Hastings	.25	.11
❑ 70 Tony Gonzalez	.25	.11
❑ 71 Dorsey Levens	1.00	.45
❑ 72 Ray Lewis	1.00	.45
❑ 73 Grant Wistrom RC	4.00	1.80
❑ 74 Elvis Grbac	.50	.23
❑ 75 Mark Chmura	.50	.23
❑ 76 Zach Thomas	.50	.23
❑ 77 Ben Coates	.50	.23
❑ 78 Rod Smith WR	.50	.23
❑ 79 Andre Wadsworth RC	6.00	2.70
❑ 80 Garrison Hearst	1.00	.45
❑ 81 Will Blackwell	.25	.11
❑ 82 Cris Carter	1.00	.45
❑ 83 Mark Fields	.25	.11
❑ 84 Ken Dilger	.25	.11
❑ 85 Johnnie Morton	.50	.23
❑ 86 Michael Irvin	1.00	.45
❑ 87 Eddie George	2.00	.90
❑ 88 Rob Moore	.50	.23
❑ 89 Takeo Spikes RC	6.00	2.70
❑ 90 Wesley Walls	.50	.23
❑ 91 Andre Reed	.50	.23
❑ 92 Thurman Thomas	1.00	.45
❑ 93 Ed McCaffrey	.50	.23
❑ 94 Carl Pickens	1.00	.45
❑ 95 Jason Taylor	.25	.11
❑ 96 Kordell Stewart	1.00	.45
❑ 97 Greg Ellis RC	4.00	1.80
❑ 98 Aaron Glenn	.25	.11
❑ 99 Jake Plummer	2.00	.90
❑ 100 Checklist	.25	.11
❑ 101 Chris Sanders	.25	.11
❑ 102 Michael Jackson	.25	.11
❑ 103 Bobby Hoying	.50	.23
❑ 104 Wayne Chrebet	1.00	.45
❑ 105 Charles Way	.25	.11
❑ 106 Derrick Thomas	.50	.23
❑ 107 Troy Drayton	.25	.11
❑ 108 Robert Holcombe RC	6.00	2.70
❑ 109 Pete Mitchell	.25	.11
❑ 110 Bruce Smith	.50	.23
❑ 111 Terance Mathis	.50	.23
❑ 112 Lawrence Phillips	.25	.11
❑ 113 Brett Favre	5.00	2.20
❑ 114 Darrell Green	.50	.23
❑ 115 Charles Johnson	.25	.11
❑ 116 Jeff Blake	.50	.23
❑ 117 Mark Brunell	2.00	.90
❑ 118 Simeon Rice	.50	.23
❑ 119 Robert Brooks	.50	.23
❑ 120 Jacquez Green RC	12.00	5.50
❑ 121 Willie Davis	.25	.11
❑ 122 Jeff George	.50	.23
❑ 123 Andre Rison	.50	.23
❑ 124 Erik Kramer	.25	.11
❑ 125 Peter Boulware	.25	.11
❑ 126 Marcus Nash RC		
❑ 127 Troy Aikman	2.50	1.10
❑ 128 Keenan McCardell	.50	.23
❑ 129 Bryant Westbrook	.25	.11
❑ 130 Terry Glenn	1.00	.45
❑ 131 Blaine Bishop	.25	.11
❑ 132 Tim Brown	1.00	.45
❑ 133 Brian Griese RC	30.00	13.50
❑ 134 John Mobley	.25	.11
❑ 135 Larry Centers	.25	.11
❑ 136 Eric Bjornson	.25	.11
❑ 137 Kevin Hardy	.25	.11
❑ 138 John Randle	.50	.23
❑ 139 Michael Strahan	.25	.11
❑ 140 Jerome Bettis	1.00	.45
❑ 141 Rae Carruth	.50	.23
❑ 142 Reggie White	1.00	.45
❑ 143 Antowain Smith	1.00	.45
❑ 144 Aeneas Williams	.25	.11
❑ 145 Bobby Engram	.50	.23
❑ 146 Germane Crowell RC	15.00	6.75
❑ 147 Freddie Jones	.25	.11
❑ 148 Kimble Anders	.50	.23
❑ 149 Steve Young	1.50	.70
❑ 150 Willie McGinest	.25	.11
❑ 151 Emmitt Smith	4.00	1.80
❑ 152 Fred Taylor RC	25.00	11.00
❑ 153 Danny Kanell	.50	.23
❑ 154 Warrick Dunn	1.00	.45
❑ 155 Kerry Collins	.50	.23
❑ 156 Chris Chandler	.50	.23
❑ 157 Curtis Conway	.50	.23
❑ 158 Curtis Enis RC	10.00	4.50
❑ 159 Corey Dillon	1.50	.70
❑ 160 Glenn Foley	.50	.23
❑ 161 Marvin Harrison	.50	.23
❑ 162 Chad Brown	.25	.11
❑ 163 Derrick Rodgers	.25	.11
❑ 164 Levon Kirkland	.25	.11
❑ 165 Peyton Manning RC	60.00	27.00

1999 Topps Chrome

	MINT	NRMT
COMPLETE SET (165)	300.00	135.00
COMP.SET w/o SP's (135)	50.00	22.00
❑ 1 Randy Moss	4.00	1.80
❑ 2 Keyshawn Johnson	1.00	.45
❑ 3 Priest Holmes	1.00	.45
❑ 4 Warren Moon	1.00	.45
❑ 5 Joey Galloway	1.00	.45
❑ 6 Zach Thomas	.50	.23
❑ 7 Cam Cleeland	.25	.11
❑ 8 Jim Harbaugh	.50	.23
❑ 9 Napoleon Kaufman	1.00	.45
❑ 10 Fred Taylor	2.50	1.10
❑ 11 Mark Brunell	1.50	.70
❑ 12 Shannon Sharpe	.50	.23
❑ 13 Jacquez Green	.50	.23
❑ 14 Adrian Murrell	.50	.23
❑ 15 Cris Carter	1.00	.45
❑ 16 Jerome Pathon	.25	.11
❑ 17 Drew Bledsoe	1.50	.70
❑ 18 Curtis Martin	1.00	.45
❑ 19 Johnnie Morton	.50	.23
❑ 20 Doug Flutie	1.25	.55
❑ 21 Carl Pickens	.50	.23
❑ 22 Jerome Bettis	1.00	.45
❑ 23 Derrick Alexander	.25	.11
❑ 24 Antowain Smith	1.00	.45
❑ 25 Barry Sanders	4.00	1.80
❑ 26 Reidel Anthony	.50	.23
❑ 27 Wayne Chrebet	.50	.23
❑ 28 Terance Mathis	.50	.23
❑ 29 Shawn Springs	.25	.11
❑ 30 Emmitt Smith	2.50	1.10
❑ 31 Robert Smith	1.00	.45
❑ 32 Charles Johnson	.25	.11

	MINT	NRMT
❑ 33 Mike Alstott	1.00	.45
❑ 34 Ike Hilliard	.25	.11
❑ 35 Ricky Watters	.50	.23
❑ 36 Charles Woodson	1.00	.45
❑ 37 Rod Smith	.50	.23
❑ 38 Pete Mitchell	.25	.11
❑ 39 Derrick Thomas	.50	.23
❑ 40 Dan Marino	4.00	1.80
❑ 41 Darnay Scott	.25	.11
❑ 42 Jake Reed	.50	.23
❑ 43 Chris Chandler	.50	.23
❑ 44 Dorsey Levens	1.00	.45
❑ 45 Kordell Stewart	1.00	.45
❑ 46 Eddie George	1.25	.55
❑ 47 Corey Dillon	1.00	.45
❑ 48 Rich Gannon	.50	.23
❑ 49 Chris Spielman	.25	.11
❑ 50 Jerry Rice	2.50	1.10
❑ 51 Trent Dilfer	.50	.23
❑ 52 Mark Chmura	.25	.11
❑ 53 Jimmy Smith	.50	.23
❑ 54 Isaac Bruce	1.00	.45
❑ 55 Karim Abdul-Jabbar	.50	.23
❑ 56 Sedrick Shaw	.25	.11
❑ 57 Jake Plummer	2.00	.90
❑ 58 Tony Gonzalez	.50	.23
❑ 59 Ben Coates	.50	.23
❑ 60 John Elway	4.00	1.80
❑ 61 Bruce Smith	.50	.23
❑ 62 Tim Brown	1.00	.45
❑ 63 Tim Dwight	1.00	.45
❑ 64 Yancey Thigpen	.25	.11
❑ 65 Terrell Owens	1.00	.45
❑ 66 Kyle Brady	.25	.11
❑ 67 Tony Martin	.50	.23
❑ 68 Michael Strahan	.25	.11
❑ 69 Deion Sanders	1.00	.45
❑ 70 Steve Young	1.50	.70
❑ 71 Dale Carter	.25	.11
❑ 72 Ty Law	.25	.11
❑ 73 Frank Wycheck	.25	.11
❑ 74 Marshall Faulk	1.00	.45
❑ 75 Vinny Testaverde	.50	.23
❑ 76 Chad Brown	.25	.11
❑ 77 Natrone Means	.50	.23
❑ 78 Bert Emanuel	.50	.23
❑ 79 Kerry Collins	.50	.23
❑ 80 Randall Cunningham	1.00	.45
❑ 81 Garrison Hearst	.50	.23
❑ 82 Curtis Enis	1.00	.45
❑ 83 Steve Atwater	.25	.11
❑ 84 Kevin Greene	.25	.11
❑ 85 Steve McNair	1.00	.45
❑ 86 Andre Reed	.50	.23
❑ 87 J.J. Stokes	.50	.23
❑ 88 Eric Moulds	1.00	.45
❑ 89 Marvin Harrison	1.00	.45
❑ 90 Troy Aikman	2.50	1.10
❑ 91 Herman Moore	1.00	.45
❑ 92 Michael Irvin	.50	.23
❑ 93 Frank Sanders	.50	.23
❑ 94 Duce Staley	1.00	.45
❑ 95 James Jett	.50	.23
❑ 96 Ricky Proehl	.25	.11
❑ 97 Andre Rison	.50	.23
❑ 98 Leslie Shepherd	.25	.11
❑ 99 Trent Green	.50	.23
❑ 100 Terrell Davis	2.50	1.10
❑ 101 Freddie Jones	.25	.11
❑ 102 Skip Hicks	1.00	.45
❑ 103 Jeff Graham	.25	.11
❑ 104 Rob Moore	.50	.23
❑ 105 Torrance Small	.25	.11
❑ 106 Antonio Freeman	1.00	.45
❑ 107 Robert Brooks	.50	.23
❑ 108 Jon Kitna	1.00	.45
❑ 109 Curtis Conway	.50	.23
❑ 110 Brett Favre	4.00	1.80
❑ 111 Warrick Dunn	1.00	.45
❑ 112 Elvis Grbac	.50	.23
❑ 113 Corey Fuller	.25	.11
❑ 114 Rickey Dudley	.25	.11
❑ 115 Jamal Anderson	1.00	.45
❑ 116 Terry Glenn	1.00	.45
❑ 117 Rocket Ismail	.50	.23
❑ 118 John Randle	.50	.23
❑ 119 Chris Calloway	.25	.11
❑ 120 Peyton Manning	4.00	1.80
❑ 121 Keenan McCardell	.50	.23
❑ 122 O.J. McDuffie	.50	.23
❑ 123 Ed McCaffrey	.50	.23
❑ 124 Charlie Batch	2.00	.90
❑ 125 Jason Elam SH	.25	.11
❑ 126 Randy Moss SH	2.00	.90
❑ 127 John Elway SH	2.00	.90
❑ 128 Emmitt Smith SH	1.25	.55
❑ 129 Terrell Davis SH	1.25	.55
❑ 130 Jerris McPhail	.25	.11
❑ 131 Damon Gibson	.25	.11
❑ 132 Jim Pyne	.25	.11
❑ 133 Antonio Langham	.25	.11
❑ 134 Freddie Solomon	.25	.11
❑ 135 Ricky Williams RC	50.00	22.00
❑ 136 Daunte Culpepper RC	60.00	27.00
❑ 137 Chris Claiborne RC	8.00	3.60
❑ 138 Amos Zereoue RC	10.00	4.50
❑ 139 Chris McAlister RC	8.00	3.60
❑ 140 Kevin Faulk RC	15.00	6.75
❑ 141 James Johnson RC	10.00	4.50
❑ 142 Mike Cloud RC	10.00	4.50
❑ 143 Jevon Kearse RC	20.00	9.00
❑ 144 Akili Smith RC	20.00	9.00
❑ 145 Edgerrin James RC	60.00	27.00
❑ 146 Cecil Collins RC	10.00	4.50
❑ 147 Donovan McNabb RC	40.00	18.00
❑ 148 Kevin Johnson RC	20.00	9.00
❑ 149 Torry Holt RC	20.00	9.00
❑ 150 Rob Konrad RC	10.00	4.50
❑ 151 Tim Couch RC	40.00	18.00
❑ 152 David Boston RC	20.00	9.00
❑ 153 Karsten Bailey RC	8.00	3.60
❑ 154 Troy Edwards RC	15.00	6.75
❑ 155 Sedrick Irvin RC	10.00	4.50
❑ 156 Shaun King RC	20.00	9.00
❑ 157 Peerless Price RC	15.00	6.75
❑ 158 Brock Huard RC	20.00	9.00
❑ 159 Cade McNown RC	15.00	6.75
❑ 160 Champ Bailey RC	15.00	6.75
❑ 161 D'Wayne Bates RC	8.00	3.60
❑ 162 Joe Germaine RC	10.00	4.50
❑ 163 Andy Katzenmoyer RC	10.00	4.50
❑ 164 Antoine Winfield RC	8.00	3.60
❑ 165 Checklist Card	.25	.11

2000 Topps Chrome

	MINT	NRMT
COMPLETE SET (270)	1000.00	450.00
COMP.SET w/o SPs (180)	50.00	22.00
❑ 1 Daunte Culpepper	2.00	.90
❑ 2 Troy Edwards	.50	.23
❑ 3 Terrell Owens	1.00	.45
❑ 4 Ricky Proehl	.25	.11
❑ 5 Shaun King	1.50	.70
❑ 6 Jeff George	.50	.23
❑ 7 Champ Bailey	.50	.23
❑ 8 Amani Toomer	.25	.11
❑ 9 Stephen Boyd	.25	.11
❑ 10 Thurman Thomas	.50	.23
❑ 11 Patrick Jeffers	1.00	.45
❑ 12 Jake Plummer	1.00	.45
❑ 13 Peter Boulware	.25	.11
❑ 14 Darrin Chiaverini	.25	.11
❑ 15 Olandis Gary	1.00	.45
❑ 16 Peyton Manning	3.00	1.35
❑ 17 Joe Horn	.50	.23
❑ 18 Wayne Chrebet	.50	.23
❑ 19 Freddie Jones	.25	.11
❑ 20 Kurt Warner	4.00	1.80
❑ 21 Mike Alstott	1.00	.45
❑ 22 Stephen Davis	1.00	.45
❑ 23 Tim Brown	1.00	.45
❑ 24 Damon Huard	1.00	.45
❑ 25 Terry Glenn	.50	.23
❑ 26 Ricky Williams	2.50	1.10
❑ 27 Tim Dwight	1.00	.45
❑ 28 Jay Riemersma	.25	.11
❑ 29 Carl Pickens	.50	.23
❑ 30 Brett Favre	4.00	1.80
❑ 31 Oronde Gadsden	.50	.23
❑ 32 Steve McNair	1.00	.45
❑ 33 Michael Pittman	.25	.11
❑ 34 Emmitt Smith	2.50	1.10
❑ 35 Mark Brunell	1.50	.70
❑ 36 Ed McCaffrey	1.00	.45
❑ 37 Tyrone Wheatley	.50	.23
❑ 38 Sean Dawkins	.25	.11
❑ 39 Jevon Kearse	1.00	.45
❑ 40 Tai Streets	.25	.11
❑ 41 Keyshawn Johnson	1.00	.45
❑ 42 Germane Crowell	.50	.23
❑ 43 Yatil Green	.25	.11
❑ 44 Anthony Wright RC	10.00	4.50
❑ 45 Jerry Rice	2.50	1.10
❑ 46 Az-Zahir Hakim	.50	.23
❑ 47 Stephen Alexander	.25	.11
❑ 48 Zach Thomas	.50	.23
❑ 49 Tony Simmons	.25	.11
❑ 50 Jessie Armstead	.25	.11
❑ 51 Kordell Stewart	1.00	.45
❑ 52 Cade McNown	1.00	.45
❑ 53 Tony Gonzalez	.50	.23
❑ 54 John Randle	.50	.23
❑ 55 Donovan McNabb	1.50	.70
❑ 56 Warrick Dunn	1.00	.45
❑ 57 Dorsey Levens	.50	.23
❑ 58 Errict Rhett	.50	.23
❑ 59 Priest Holmes	.50	.23
❑ 60 Terrell Davis	2.50	1.10
❑ 61 Natrone Means	.25	.11
❑ 62 Brad Johnson	1.00	.45
❑ 63 Rickey Dudley	.25	.11
❑ 64 Moses Moreno	.25	.11
❑ 65 Randy Moss	3.00	1.35
❑ 66 Joe Montgomery	.25	.11
❑ 67 Johnnie Morton	.50	.23
❑ 68 Peerless Price	1.00	.45
❑ 69 Rocket Ismail	.50	.23
❑ 70 David Boston	1.00	.45
❑ 71 Fred Taylor	1.25	.55
❑ 72 Jermaine Fazande	.25	.11
❑ 73 Elvis Grbac	.50	.23
❑ 74 Derrick Mayes	.50	.23
❑ 75 Yancey Thigpen	.25	.11
❑ 76 Ike Hilliard	.50	.23
❑ 77 Muhsin Muhammad	.50	.23
❑ 78 Shawn Jefferson	.25	.11
❑ 79 Rod Smith	.50	.23
❑ 80 Darnay Scott	.50	.23
❑ 81 Cam Cleeland	.25	.11
❑ 82 Steve Young	1.50	.70
❑ 83 E.G. Green	.25	.11
❑ 84 Robert Smith	1.00	.45
❑ 85 Jermaine Lewis	.50	.23
❑ 86 Tim Biakabutuka	.50	.23
❑ 87 Jerome Pathon	.50	.23
❑ 88 Kent Graham	.25	.11
❑ 89 Bruce Smith	.50	.23
❑ 90 Isaac Bruce	1.00	.45
❑ 91 Curtis Enis	.50	.23
❑ 92 Bert Emanuel	.25	.11
❑ 93 Keith Poole	.25	.11
❑ 94 Troy Aikman	2.50	1.10
❑ 95 Rich Gannon	.50	.23
❑ 96 Michael Westbrook	.50	.23
❑ 97 Albert Connell	.25	.11
❑ 98 James Johnson	.50	.23
❑ 99 Jeff Blake	.50	.23

❑	100 Joey Galloway	1.00	.45
❑	101 Rob Moore	.50	.23
❑	102 Chris Chandler	.50	.23
❑	103 Fred Lane	.25	.11
❑	104 Eddie Kennison	.50	.23
❑	105 Kevin Hardy	.25	.11
❑	106 Napoleon Kaufman	.50	.23
❑	107 Kevin Dyson	.50	.23
❑	108 Keenan McCardell	.50	.23
❑	109 Drew Bledsoe	1.50	.70
❑	110 Kevin Johnson	1.00	.45
❑	111 Terance Mathis	.50	.23
❑	112 Gus Frerotte	.25	.11
❑	113 Matthew Hatchette	.50	.23
❑	114 Herman Moore	.50	.23
❑	115 Curtis Martin	1.00	.45
❑	116 Jacquez Green	.50	.23
❑	117 Jake Reed	.50	.23
❑	118 Antonio Freeman	1.00	.45
❑	119 Jim Miller	.25	.11
❑	120 Frank Sanders	.50	.23
❑	121 Brian Griese	1.00	.45
❑	122 Troy Brown	.25	.11
❑	123 Jeff Graham	.25	.11
❑	124 Marshall Faulk	1.25	.55
❑	125 Vinny Testaverde	.50	.23
❑	126 Frank Wycheck	.25	.11
❑	127 Kerry Collins	.50	.23
❑	128 Jay Fiedler	1.00	.45
❑	129 Cris Carter	1.00	.45
❑	130 Jason Tucker	.25	.11
❑	131 Antowain Smith	.50	.23
❑	132 Tony Banks	.50	.23
❑	133 Terrence Wilkins	1.00	.45
❑	134 Tony Martin	.50	.23
❑	135 Richard Huntley	.25	.11
❑	136 J.J. Stokes	.50	.23
❑	137 Ricky Watters	.50	.23
❑	138 Pete Mitchell	.25	.11
❑	139 Jimmy Smith	.50	.23
❑	140 Doug Flutie	1.25	.55
❑	141 Corey Bradford	.50	.23
❑	142 Curtis Conway	.50	.23
❑	143 Pete Mitchell	.25	.11
❑	144 Torry Holt	1.00	.45
❑	145 Warren Sapp	.50	.23
❑	146 Duce Staley	1.00	.45
❑	147 Mikhael Ricks	.25	.11
❑	148 Edgerrin James	4.00	1.80
❑	149 Charlie Batch	1.00	.45
❑	150 Rob Johnson	.50	.23
❑	151 Jamal Anderson	1.00	.45
❑	152 Tim Couch	2.00	.90
❑	153 O.J. McDuffie	.50	.23
❑	154 Charles Woodson	.50	.23
❑	155 Jake Delhomme RC	1.00	.45
❑	156 Eddie George	1.25	.55
❑	157 Jim Harbaugh	.50	.23
❑	158 Jon Kitna	1.00	.45
❑	159 Derrick Alexander	.50	.23
❑	160 Marvin Harrison	1.00	.45
❑	161 James Stewart	.50	.23
❑	162 Qadry Ismail	.25	.11
❑	163 Wesley Walls	.25	.11
❑	164 Steve Beuerlein	.50	.23
❑	165 Marcus Robinson	1.00	.45
❑	166 Bill Schroeder	.50	.23
❑	167 Charles Johnson	.50	.23
❑	168 Charlie Garner	.50	.23
❑	169 Eric Moulds	1.00	.45
❑	170 Jerome Bettis	1.00	.45
❑	171 Tai Streets	.25	.11
❑	172 Akili Smith	1.00	.45
❑	173 Jonathan Linton	.25	.11
❑	174 Corey Dillon	1.00	.45
❑	175 Junior Seau	.50	.23
❑	176 Jonathan Quinn	.25	.11
❑	177 Bobby Engram	.25	.11
❑	178 Shannon Sharpe	.50	.23
❑	179 Michael Basnight	.25	.11
❑	180 Sedrick Irvin	.25	.11
❑	181 Sammy Morris RC	25.00	11.00
❑	182 Ron Dixon RC	25.00	11.00
❑	183 Trevor Gaylor RC	12.00	5.50
❑	184 Chris Cole RC	10.00	4.50
❑	185 Deltha O'Neal RC	12.00	5.50
❑	186 Sebastian Janikowski RC	15.00	6.75
❑	187 Kwame Cavil RC	12.00	5.50
❑	188 Chad Morton RC	15.00	6.75
❑	189 Terrelle Smith RC	12.00	5.50
❑	190 Frank Moreau RC	15.00	6.75
❑	191 Kurt Warner HL	2.50	1.10
❑	192 Dan Marino HL	2.50	1.10
❑	193 Cris Carter HL	.50	.23
❑	194 Brett Favre HL	2.50	1.10
❑	195 Marshall Faulk HL	.50	.23
❑	196 Jevon Kearse HL	.50	.23
❑	197 Edgerrin James HL	2.00	.90
❑	198 Emmitt Smith HL	1.50	.70
❑	199 Andre Reed HL	.25	.11
❑	200 Kevin Dyson HL Frank Wycheck HL	.25	.11
❑	201 Olindo Mare MM	.25	.11
❑	202 Marcus Coleman MM	.25	.11
❑	203 James Johnson MM	.25	.11
❑	204 Ray Lucas MM	.50	.23
❑	205 Dedric Ward MM	.25	.11
❑	206 Richie Cunningham MM	.25	.11
❑	207 James Hasty MM	.25	.11
❑	208 Sedrick Shaw MM	.25	.11
❑	209 Kurt Warner MM	2.50	1.10
❑	210 Marshall Faulk MM	.50	.23
❑	211 Brian Shay EP	1.00	.45
❑	212 L.C. Stevens EP	1.00	.45
❑	213 Corey Thomas EP	1.00	.45
❑	214 Scott Milanovich EP	1.50	.70
❑	215 Pat Barnes EP	1.50	.70
❑	216 Danny Wuerffel EP	1.50	.70
❑	217 Kevin Daft EP	1.00	.45
❑	218 Ron Powlus EP RC	3.00	1.35
❑	219 Eric Kresser EP	1.00	.45
❑	220 Norman Miller EP RC	1.00	.45
❑	221 Cory Sauter EP	1.00	.45
❑	222 Marcus Crandell EP RC	1.00	.45
❑	223 Sean Morey EP RC	1.50	.70
❑	224 Jeff Ogden EP	1.50	.70
❑	225 Ted White EP	1.00	.45
❑	226 Jim Kubiak EP RC	1.50	.70
❑	227 Aaron Stecker EP RC	2.00	.90
❑	228 Ronnie Powell EP	1.00	.45
❑	229 Matt Lytle EP RC	1.50	.70
❑	230 Kendrick Nord EP RC	1.00	.45
❑	231 Tim Rattay RC	30.00	13.50
❑	232 Rob Morris RC	12.00	5.50
❑	233 Chris Samuels RC	12.00	5.50
❑	234 Todd Husak RC	15.00	6.75
❑	235 Ahmed Plummer RC	15.00	6.75
❑	236 Frank Murphy RC	10.00	4.50
❑	237 Michael Wiley RC	15.00	6.75
❑	238 Giovanni Carmazzi RC	25.00	11.00
❑	239 Anthony Becht RC	15.00	6.75
❑	240 John Abraham RC	12.00	5.50
❑	241 Shaun Alexander RC	60.00	27.00
❑	242 Thomas Jones RC	30.00	13.50
❑	243 Courtney Brown RC	25.00	11.00
❑	244 Curtis Keaton RC	12.00	5.50
❑	245 Jerry Porter RC	15.00	6.75
❑	246 Corey Simon RC	25.00	11.00
❑	247 Dez White RC	12.00	5.50
❑	248 Jamal Lewis RC	120.00	55.00
❑	249 Ron Dayne RC	80.00	36.00
❑	250 R.Jay Soward RC	15.00	6.75
❑	251 Tee Martin RC	30.00	13.50
❑	252 Shaun Ellis RC	12.00	5.50
❑	253 Brian Urlacher RC	80.00	36.00
❑	254 Reuben Droughns RC	15.00	6.75
❑	255 Travis Taylor RC	25.00	11.00
❑	256 Plaxico Burress RC	50.00	22.00
❑	257 Chad Pennington RC	80.00	36.00
❑	258 Sylvester Morris RC	50.00	22.00
❑	259 Ron Dugans RC	12.00	5.50
❑	260 Joe Hamilton RC	25.00	11.00
❑	261 Chris Redman RC	30.00	13.50
❑	262 Trung Canidate RC	15.00	6.75
❑	263 J.R. Redmond RC	25.00	11.00
❑	264 Danny Farmer RC	15.00	6.75
❑	265 Todd Pinkston RC	15.00	6.75
❑	266 Dennis Northcutt RC	25.00	11.00
❑	267 Laveranues Coles RC	30.00	13.50
❑	268 Bubba Franks RC	25.00	11.00
❑	269 Travis Prentice RC	30.00	13.50
❑	270 Peter Warrick RC	80.00	36.00

1997 Topps Gallery

		MINT	NRMT
	COMPLETE SET (135)	30.00	13.50
❑	1 Orlando Pace RC	.50	.23
❑	2 Darrell Russell RC	.15	.07
❑	3 Shawn Springs RC	.25	.11
❑	4 Peter Boulware RC	.25	.11
❑	5 Bryant Westbrook RC	.15	.07
❑	6 Walter Jones RC	.15	.07
❑	7 Ike Hilliard RC	2.00	.90
❑	8 James Farrior RC	.15	.07
❑	9 Tom Knight RC	.15	.07
❑	10 Warrick Dunn RC	4.00	1.80
❑	11 Tony Gonzalez RC	4.00	1.80
❑	12 Reinard Wilson RC	.15	.07
❑	13 Yatil Green RC	.25	.11
❑	14 Reidel Anthony RC	2.00	.90
❑	15 Kenny Holmes RC	.50	.23
❑	16 Dwayne Rudd RC	.50	.23
❑	17 Renaldo Wynn RC	.15	.07
❑	18 David LaFleur RC	1.00	.45
❑	19 Antowain Smith RC	2.50	1.10
❑	20 Jim Druckenmiller RC	.50	.23
❑	21 Rae Carruth RC	.50	.23
❑	22 Byron Hanspard RC	.50	.23
❑	23 Jake Plummer RC	8.00	3.60
❑	24 Corey Dillon RC	8.00	3.60
❑	25 Darnell Autry RC	.25	.11
❑	26 Kevin Lockett RC	.50	.23
❑	27 Troy Davis RC	.50	.23
❑	28 Mike Alstott	.50	.23
❑	29 Napoleon Kaufman	.50	.23
❑	30 Terrell Davis	2.00	.90
❑	31 Byron Bam Morris	.15	.07
❑	32 Dana Stubblefield	.15	.07
❑	33 Ki-Jana Carter	.15	.07
❑	34 Hugh Douglas	.15	.07
❑	35 Natrone Means	.50	.23
❑	36 Marshall Faulk	.50	.23
❑	37 Tyrone Wheatley	.25	.11
❑	38 Tony Banks	.25	.11
❑	39 Marvin Harrison	.50	.23
❑	40 Eddie George	1.25	.55
❑	41 Eddie Kennison	.25	.11
❑	42 Ray Mickens	.15	.07
❑	43 Mike Mamula	.15	.07
❑	44 Tamarick Vanover	.25	.11
❑	45 Rashaan Salaam	.15	.07
❑	46 Trent Dilfer	.50	.23
❑	47 John Mobley	.15	.07
❑	48 Gus Frerotte	.15	.07
❑	49 Isaac Bruce	.50	.23
❑	50 Mark Brunell	1.25	.55
❑	51 Jamal Anderson	.75	.35
❑	52 Keyshawn Johnson	.50	.23
❑	53 Curtis Conway	.25	.11
❑	54 Zach Thomas	.25	.11
❑	55 Simeon Rice	.25	.11
❑	56 Lawrence Phillips	.15	.07
❑	57 Ty Detmer	.25	.11
❑	58 Bobby Engram	.25	.11
❑	59 Joey Galloway	.60	.25
❑	60 Curtis Martin	.60	.25
❑	61 Kevin Hardy	.15	.07
❑	62 Eric Moulds	.50	.23
❑	63 Michael Westbrook	.25	.11

❑ 64 Robert Smith .25 .11
❑ 65 Karim Abdul-Jabbar .50 .23
❑ 66 Errict Rhett .15 .07
❑ 67 Ray Lewis .60 .25
❑ 68 Terry Glenn .50 .23
❑ 69 Leeland McElroy .15 .07
❑ 70 Kerry Collins .25 .11
❑ 71 Steve McNair .60 .25
❑ 72 Kordell Stewart .60 .25
❑ 73 Terry Allen .50 .23
❑ 74 Michael Irvin .50 .23
❑ 75 John Elway 2.50 1.10
❑ 76 Lamar Lathon .15 .07
❑ 77 Rob Moore .25 .11
❑ 78 Irving Fryar .25 .11
❑ 79 Jim Everett .15 .07
❑ 80 Steve Young .75 .35
❑ 81 Bryan Cox .15 .07
❑ 82 Dale Carter .15 .07
❑ 83 Chris Warren .25 .11
❑ 84 Shannon Sharpe .25 .11
❑ 85 Reggie White .50 .23
❑ 86 Deion Sanders .50 .23
❑ 87 Hardy Nickerson .15 .07
❑ 88 Edgar Bennett .25 .11
❑ 89 Kent Graham .15 .07
❑ 90 Dan Marino 2.50 1.10
❑ 91 Kevin Greene .25 .11
❑ 92 Derrick Thomas .25 .11
❑ 93 Carl Pickens .50 .23
❑ 94 Neil O'Donnell .25 .11
❑ 95 Drew Bledsoe 1.25 .55
❑ 96 Michael Haynes .15 .07
❑ 97 Tony Martin .25 .11
❑ 98 Scott Mitchell .25 .11
❑ 99 Rodney Hampton .25 .11
❑ 100 Brett Favre 2.50 1.10
❑ 101 Darrell Green .25 .11
❑ 102 Rod Woodson .25 .11
❑ 103 Chris Spielman .15 .07
❑ 104 Jake Reed .25 .11
❑ 105 Jerry Rice 1.25 .55
❑ 106 Jeff Hostetler .15 .07
❑ 107 Anthony Johnson .15 .07
❑ 108 Keenan McCardell .25 .11
❑ 109 Ben Coates .25 .11
❑ 110 Emmitt Smith 2.00 .90
❑ 111 LeRoy Butler .15 .07
❑ 112 Steve Atwater .15 .07
❑ 113 Ricky Watters .25 .11
❑ 114 Jim Harbaugh .25 .11
❑ 115 Marcus Allen .50 .23
❑ 116 Levon Kirkland .15 .07
❑ 117 Jessie Tuggle .15 .07
❑ 118 Ken Norton .15 .07
❑ 119 Thurman Thomas .50 .23
❑ 120 Junior Seau .25 .11
❑ 121 Tim Brown .50 .23
❑ 122 Michael Jackson .25 .11
❑ 123 Eric Metcalf .25 .11
❑ 124 Herman Moore .50 .23
❑ 125 Bruce Smith .25 .11
❑ 126 Cris Carter .50 .23
❑ 127 Dave Brown .15 .07
❑ 128 Jeff Blake .25 .11
❑ 129 Robert Blackmon .15 .07
❑ 130 Barry Sanders 2.50 1.10
❑ 131 Blaine Bishop .15 .07
❑ 132 Jerome Bettis .50 .23
❑ 133 Stan Humphries .25 .11
❑ 134 Vinny Testaverde .25 .11
❑ 135 Troy Aikman 1.25 .55
❑ P54 Zach Thomas Promo .. 1.00 .45
(On back HT/WT in yellow box instead of team name)

2000 Topps Gallery

	MINT	NRMT
COMPLETE SET (175)	60.00	27.00
COMP.SET w/o SP's (125)	20.00	9.00
COMMON CARD (1-125)	.15	.07
COMMON CARD (126-150)	.75	.35
COMMON ROOKIE (151-175)	1.50	.70

❑ 1 Marshall Faulk .75 .35

❑ 2 Kordell Stewart .60 .25
❑ 3 Priest Holmes .30 .14
❑ 4 James Johnson .30 .14
❑ 5 Charlie Garner .30 .14
❑ 6 Jeff Blake .30 .14
❑ 7 Joey Galloway .60 .25
❑ 8 Terrell Davis 1.50 .70
❑ 9 Jerome Bettis .60 .25
❑ 10 Bobby Engram .30 .14
❑ 11 Muhsin Muhammad .30 .14
❑ 12 Marcus Robinson .60 .25
❑ 13 Kerry Collins .30 .14
❑ 14 Jake Plummer .60 .25
❑ 15 J.J. Stokes .30 .14
❑ 16 Tim Couch 1.25 .55
❑ 17 Napoleon Kaufman .30 .14
❑ 18 Az-Zahir Hakim .30 .14
❑ 19 Jimmy Smith .30 .14
❑ 20 Eddie George .75 .35
❑ 21 Jacquez Green .30 .14
❑ 22 Champ Bailey .30 .14
❑ 23 Wesley Walls .15 .07
❑ 24 Eric Moulds .60 .25
❑ 25 Corey Dillon .60 .25
❑ 26 Freddie Jones .15 .07
❑ 27 Jevon Kearse .60 .25
❑ 28 Ray Lucas .60 .25
❑ 29 Germane Crowell .30 .14
❑ 30 Randy Moss 2.00 .90
❑ 31 Patrick Jeffers .60 .25
❑ 32 Zach Thomas .30 .14
❑ 33 Shannon Sharpe .30 .14
❑ 34 Derrick Mayes .30 .14
❑ 35 Antonio Freeman .60 .25
❑ 36 Terance Mathis .30 .14
❑ 37 Herman Moore .30 .14
❑ 38 Tony Banks .30 .14
❑ 39 Jerry Rice 1.50 .70
❑ 40 Troy Aikman 1.50 .70
❑ 41 Rickey Dudley .15 .07
❑ 42 Troy Edwards .30 .14
❑ 43 Curtis Martin .60 .25
❑ 44 Eddie Kennison .30 .14
❑ 45 Mark Brunell 1.00 .45
❑ 46 Shaun King 1.00 .45
❑ 47 Duce Staley .60 .25
❑ 48 Darnay Scott .30 .14
❑ 49 Sean Dawkins .15 .07
❑ 50 Edgerrin James 2.50 1.10
❑ 51 Olandis Gary .60 .25
❑ 52 Peerless Price .60 .25
❑ 53 Akili Smith .60 .25
❑ 54 Charlie Batch .60 .25
❑ 55 Tim Biakabutuka .30 .14
❑ 56 Rob Moore .30 .14
❑ 57 Keenan McCardell .30 .14
❑ 58 Dan Marino 2.50 1.10
❑ 59 Tony Gonzalez .30 .14
❑ 60 Stephen Davis .60 .25
❑ 61 Ricky Watters .30 .14
❑ 62 Frank Wycheck .15 .07
❑ 63 Kevin Johnson .60 .25
❑ 64 Isaac Bruce .60 .25
❑ 65 Andre Reed .30 .14
❑ 66 Jamal Anderson .60 .25
❑ 67 Dorsey Levens .30 .14
❑ 68 Rocket Ismail .30 .14
❑ 69 Albert Connell .15 .07
❑ 70 Brett Favre 2.50 1.10
❑ 71 Wayne Chrebet .30 .14
❑ 72 Jon Kitna .60 .25
❑ 73 Brian Griese .75 .35
❑ 74 Rob Johnson .30 .14
❑ 75 Qadry Ismail .15 .07
❑ 76 Derrick Alexander .30 .14
❑ 77 Tim Dwight .60 .25
❑ 78 Ike Hilliard .30 .14
❑ 79 Frank Sanders .30 .14
❑ 80 Fred Taylor .75 .35
❑ 81 Robert Smith .60 .25
❑ 82 Vinny Testaverde .30 .14
❑ 83 Steve Young 1.00 .45
❑ 84 Tyrone Wheatley .30 .14
❑ 85 Mikhael Ricks .15 .07
❑ 86 Tony Martin .30 .14
❑ 87 Carl Pickens .30 .14
❑ 88 Warrick Dunn .60 .25
❑ 89 Emmitt Smith 1.50 .70
❑ 90 Keyshawn Johnson .60 .25
❑ 91 James Stewart .30 .14
❑ 92 Doug Flutie .75 .35
❑ 93 Torry Holt .60 .25
❑ 94 Jeff Graham .15 .07
❑ 95 Steve McNair .60 .25
❑ 96 Errict Rhett .30 .14
❑ 97 Terrell Owens .60 .25
❑ 98 Terry Glenn .30 .14
❑ 99 Steve Beuerlein .30 .14
❑ 100 Kurt Warner 2.50 1.10
❑ 101 Jeff George .30 .14
❑ 102 Deion Sanders .60 .25
❑ 103 Johnnie Morton .30 .14
❑ 104 Antowain Smith .30 .14
❑ 105 O.J. McDuffie .30 .14
❑ 106 Rod Smith .30 .14
❑ 107 Jim Harbaugh .30 .14
❑ 108 Marvin Harrison .60 .25
❑ 109 Curtis Enis .30 .14
❑ 110 Drew Bledsoe 1.00 .45
❑ 111 Mike Alstott .60 .25
❑ 112 Amani Toomer .30 .14
❑ 113 Elvis Grbac .30 .14
❑ 114 Tim Brown .60 .25
❑ 115 Cris Carter .60 .25
❑ 116 Donovan McNabb 1.00 .45
❑ 117 Chris Chandler .30 .14
❑ 118 Kevin Dyson .30 .14
❑ 119 Rich Gannon .30 .14
❑ 120 Ricky Williams 1.50 .70
❑ 121 Brad Johnson .60 .25
❑ 122 Cade McNown .60 .25
❑ 123 Ed McCaffrey .60 .25
❑ 124 Michael Westbrook .30 .14
❑ 125 Peyton Manning 2.00 .90
❑ 126 Brett Favre MAS 4.00 1.80
❑ 127 Emmitt Smith MAS 2.50 1.10
❑ 128 Tim Brown MAS 1.00 .45
❑ 129 Troy Aikman MAS 2.50 1.10
❑ 130 Jimmy Smith MAS .75 .35
❑ 131 Dan Marino MAS 4.00 1.80
❑ 132 Cris Carter MAS 1.00 .45
❑ 133 Jerry Rice MAS 2.50 1.10
❑ 134 Steve Young MAS 1.50 .70
❑ 135 Marshall Faulk MAS 1.25 .55
❑ 136 Eddie George MAS 1.25 .55
❑ 137 Drew Bledsoe MAS 1.50 .70
❑ 138 Randy Moss ART 3.00 1.35
❑ 139 Germane Crowell ART .. .75 .35
❑ 140 Akili Smith ART 1.00 .45
❑ 141 Tim Couch ART 2.00 .90
❑ 142 Marcus Robinson ART 1.00 .45
❑ 143 Daunte Culpepper ART 2.00 .90
❑ 144 Jevon Kearse ART 1.00 .45
❑ 145 Edgerrin James ART 4.00 1.80
❑ 146 Tony Gonzalez ART .75 .35
❑ 147 Cade McNown ART 1.00 .45
❑ 148 Fred Taylor ART 1.25 .55
❑ 149 Donovan McNabb ART 1.50 .70
❑ 150 Ricky Williams ART 2.50 1.10
❑ 151 Jamal Lewis RC 10.00 4.50
❑ 152 Tee Martin RC 3.00 1.35
❑ 153 Plaxico Burress RC 4.00 1.80
❑ 154 Chad Pennington RC .. 6.00 2.70

❑ 155 Curtis Keaton RC	1.50	.70
❑ 156 Thomas Jones RC	3.00	1.35
❑ 157 Courtney Brown RC	2.50	1.10
❑ 158 Ron Dayne RC	6.00	2.70
❑ 159 Shaun Alexander RC	5.00	2.20
❑ 160 Travis Taylor RC	2.50	1.10
❑ 161 Sylvester Morris RC	4.00	1.80
❑ 162 Giovanni Carmazzi RC	2.50	1.10
❑ 163 Laveranues Coles RC	3.00	1.35
❑ 164 Chris Redman RC	4.00	1.80
❑ 165 Bubba Franks RC	2.50	1.10
❑ 166 R.Jay Soward RC	2.00	.90
❑ 167 Reuben Droughns RC	2.00	.90
❑ 168 Todd Pinkston RC	2.00	.90
❑ 169 Trung Canidate RC	2.00	.90
❑ 170 Danny Farmer RC	2.00	.90
❑ 171 Ron Dugans RC	1.50	.70
❑ 172 Dennis Northcutt RC	2.50	1.10
❑ 173 J.R. Redmond RC	2.50	1.10
❑ 174 Travis Prentice RC	3.00	1.35
❑ 175 Peter Warrick RC	6.00	2.70

1998 Topps Gold Label Class 1

	MINT	NRMT
COMP.GOLD CLASS 1 (100)	60.00	27.00
❑ 1 John Elway	5.00	2.20
❑ 2 Rob Moore	.50	.23
❑ 3 Jamal Anderson	1.00	.45
❑ 4 Pat Johnson RC	4.00	1.80
❑ 5 Troy Aikman	2.50	1.10
❑ 6 Antowain Smith	1.00	.45
❑ 7 Wesley Walls	.50	.23
❑ 8 Curtis Enis RC	4.00	1.80
❑ 9 Jimmy Smith	.50	.23
❑ 10 Terrell Davis	4.00	1.80
❑ 11 Marshall Faulk	1.00	.45
❑ 12 Germane Crowell RC	6.00	2.70
❑ 13 Marcus Nash RC	4.00	1.80
❑ 14 Deion Sanders	1.00	.45
❑ 15 Dorsey Levens	1.00	.45
❑ 16 Corey Dillon	1.50	.70
❑ 17 Fred Taylor RC	10.00	4.50
❑ 18 Derrick Thomas	.50	.23
❑ 19 Kevin Dyson RC	5.00	2.20
❑ 20 Peyton Manning RC	20.00	9.00
❑ 21 Warren Sapp	.50	.23
❑ 22 Robert Holcombe RC	4.00	1.80
❑ 23 Joey Galloway	1.00	.45
❑ 24 Garrison Hearst	1.00	.45
❑ 25 Brett Favre	5.00	2.20
❑ 26 Aeneas Williams	.25	.11
❑ 27 Danny Kanell	.50	.23
❑ 28 Robert Smith	1.00	.45
❑ 29 Brad Johnson	1.00	.45
❑ 30 Dan Marino	5.00	2.20
❑ 31 Elvis Grbac	.50	.23
❑ 32 Terry Allen	1.00	.45
❑ 33 Frank Sanders	.50	.23
❑ 34 Peter Boulware	.25	.11
❑ 35 Tim Brown	1.00	.45
❑ 36 Keyshawn Johnson	1.00	.45
❑ 37 Rae Carruth	.50	.23
❑ 38 Michael Irvin	1.00	.45
❑ 39 Brian Griese RC	12.00	5.50
❑ 40 Kordell Stewart	1.00	.45
❑ 41 Johnnie Morton	.50	.23
❑ 42 Robert Brooks	.50	.23
❑ 43 Keenan McCardell	.50	.23
❑ 44 Ben Coates	.50	.23
❑ 45 Jerry Rice	2.50	1.10
❑ 46 Tony Simmons RC	4.00	1.80
❑ 47 Irving Fryar	.50	.23
❑ 48 Jerome Pathon RC	4.00	1.80
❑ 49 Steve McNair	1.00	.45
❑ 50 Warrick Dunn	1.00	.45
❑ 51 Skip Hicks RC	4.00	1.80
❑ 52 Andre Wadsworth RC	4.00	1.80
❑ 53 Chris Chandler	.50	.23
❑ 54 Curtis Conway	.50	.23
❑ 55 Eddie George	2.00	.90
❑ 56 Jeff Blake	.50	.23
❑ 57 Greg Ellis RC	2.00	.90
❑ 58 Scott Mitchell	.50	.23
❑ 59 Antonio Freeman	1.00	.45
❑ 60 Drew Bledsoe	2.00	.90
❑ 61 Mark Brunell	2.00	.90
❑ 62 Andre Rison	.50	.23
❑ 63 Cris Carter	1.00	.45
❑ 64 Jake Reed	.50	.23
❑ 65 Napoleon Kaufman	1.00	.45
❑ 66 Terry Glenn	1.00	.45
❑ 67 Jason Sehorn	.50	.23
❑ 68 Rickey Dudley	.25	.11
❑ 69 Junior Seau	.50	.23
❑ 70 Jerome Bettis	1.00	.45
❑ 71 Curtis Martin	1.00	.45
❑ 72 Warren Moon	1.00	.45
❑ 73 Isaac Bruce	1.00	.45
❑ 74 Mike Alstott	1.00	.45
❑ 75 Steve Young	1.50	.70
❑ 76 Jacquez Green RC	5.00	2.20
❑ 77 Gus Frerotte	.25	.11
❑ 78 Michael Jackson	.25	.11
❑ 79 Carl Pickens	1.00	.45
❑ 80 Bruce Smith	.50	.23
❑ 81 Shannon Sharpe	.50	.23
❑ 82 Herman Moore	1.00	.45
❑ 83 Reggie White	1.00	.45
❑ 84 Marvin Harrison	.50	.23
❑ 85 Jake Plummer	1.50	.70
❑ 86 Karim Abdul-Jabbar	1.00	.45
❑ 87 John Randle	.50	.23
❑ 88 Robert Edwards RC	5.00	2.20
❑ 89 Jeff George	.50	.23
❑ 90 Emmitt Smith	4.00	1.80
❑ 91 Terrell Owens	1.00	.45
❑ 92 Trent Dilfer	1.00	.45
❑ 93 Darrell Green	.50	.23
❑ 94 Andre Reed	.50	.23
❑ 95 Ryan Leaf RC	8.00	3.60
❑ 96 Rod Smith WR	.50	.23
❑ 97 O.J. McDuffie	.50	.23
❑ 98 John Avery RC	4.00	1.80
❑ 99 Charles Way	.25	.11
❑ 100 Barry Sanders	5.00	2.20

1999 Topps Gold Label Class 1

	MINT	NRMT
COMPLETE SET (100)	80.00	36.00
❑ 1 Terrell Davis	2.50	1.10
❑ 2 Jake Plummer	2.00	.90
❑ 3 Mike Cloud RC	1.25	.55
❑ 4 D'Wayne Bates RC	1.25	.55
❑ 5 Jamal Anderson	1.00	.45
❑ 6 Cecil Collins RC	2.00	.90
❑ 7 Keyshawn Johnson	1.00	.45
❑ 8 Jerome Bettis	1.00	.45
❑ 9 Ricky Watters	.50	.23
❑ 10 Brett Favre	4.00	1.80
❑ 11 Joe Germaine RC	2.00	.90
❑ 12 Eddie George	1.25	.55
❑ 13 Jevon Kearse RC	4.00	1.80
❑ 14 Skip Hicks	1.00	.45
❑ 15 James Johnson RC	2.00	.90
❑ 16 Terry Glenn	1.00	.45
❑ 17 Troy Edwards RC	2.50	1.10
❑ 18 Karsten Bailey RC	1.25	.55
❑ 19 Trent Dilfer	.50	.23
❑ 20 Barry Sanders	4.00	1.80
❑ 21 Vinny Testaverde	.50	.23
❑ 22 Ed McCaffrey	.50	.23
❑ 23 Shannon Sharpe	.50	.23
❑ 24 Robert Smith	1.00	.45
❑ 25 Emmitt Smith	2.50	1.10
❑ 26 Rob Moore	.50	.23
❑ 27 J.J. Stokes	.50	.23
❑ 28 Champ Bailey RC	2.50	1.10
❑ 29 Napoleon Kaufman	1.00	.45
❑ 30 Fred Taylor	2.50	1.10
❑ 31 Corey Dillon	1.00	.45
❑ 32 Sedrick Irvin RC	2.00	.90
❑ 33 Chris McAlister RC	1.25	.55
❑ 34 Warrick Dunn	1.00	.45
❑ 35 Isaac Bruce	1.00	.45
❑ 36 Peerless Price RC	2.50	1.10
❑ 37 Dorsey Levens	1.00	.45
❑ 38 Wayne Chrebet	.50	.23
❑ 39 Randall Cunningham	1.00	.45
❑ 40 Dan Marino	4.00	1.80
❑ 41 Chris Chandler	.50	.23
❑ 42 Mark Brunell	1.50	.70
❑ 43 Kevin Johnson RC	4.00	1.80
❑ 44 Natrone Means	.50	.23
❑ 45 Jerome Pathon	.25	.11
❑ 46 Daunte Culpepper RC	10.00	4.50
❑ 47 Akili Smith RC	4.00	1.80
❑ 48 Keenan McCardell	.50	.23
❑ 49 Steve McNair	1.00	.45
❑ 50 Randy Moss	4.00	1.80
❑ 51 Terance Mathis	.50	.23
❑ 52 Eric Moulds	1.00	.45
❑ 53 Rocket Ismail	.50	.23
❑ 54 Cade McNown RC	2.50	1.10
❑ 55 Kordell Stewart	1.00	.45
❑ 56 Rob Konrad RC	2.00	.90
❑ 57 Andre Rison	.50	.23
❑ 58 Curtis Conway	.50	.23
❑ 59 Chris Claiborne RC	1.25	.55
❑ 60 Jerry Rice	2.50	1.10
❑ 61 Peyton Manning	4.00	1.80
❑ 62 Jimmy Smith	.50	.23
❑ 63 Doug Flutie	1.25	.55
❑ 64 Frank Sanders	.50	.23
❑ 65 Antowain Smith	1.00	.45
❑ 66 Curtis Enis	1.00	.45
❑ 67 Charlie Batch	2.00	.90
❑ 68 Marvin Harrison	1.00	.45
❑ 69 Garrison Hearst	.50	.23
❑ 70 Ricky Williams RC	8.00	3.60
❑ 71 Torry Holt RC	5.00	2.20
❑ 72 Mike Alstott	1.00	.45
❑ 73 Drew Bledsoe	1.50	.70
❑ 74 O.J. McDuffie	.50	.23
❑ 75 Donovan McNabb RC	8.00	3.60
❑ 76 Curtis Martin	1.00	.45
❑ 77 Priest Holmes	1.00	.45
❑ 78 Antonio Freeman	1.00	.45
❑ 79 Herman Moore	1.00	.45
❑ 80 Tim Couch RC	6.00	2.70
❑ 81 Troy Aikman	2.50	1.10
❑ 82 David Boston RC	4.00	1.80
❑ 83 Tim Brown	1.00	.45
❑ 84 Kevin Faulk RC	3.00	1.35
❑ 85 Cris Carter	1.00	.45
❑ 86 Marshall Faulk	1.00	.45
❑ 87 Shaun King RC	4.00	1.80

		MINT	NRMT
❑ 88	Terrell Owens	1.00	.45
❑ 89	Carl Pickens	.50	.23
❑ 90	Steve Young	1.50	.70
❑ 91	Rod Smith	.50	.23
❑ 92	Michael Irvin	.50	.23
❑ 93	Ike Hilliard	.25	.11
❑ 94	Jon Kitna	1.00	.45
❑ 95	Brock Huard RC	3.00	1.35
❑ 96	Joey Galloway	1.00	.45
❑ 97	Amos Zereoue RC	2.00	.90
❑ 98	Duce Staley	1.00	.45
❑ 99	John Elway	4.00	1.80
❑ 100	Edgerrin James RC	10.00	4.50

2000 Topps Gold Label Class 1

		MINT	NRMT
COMPLETE SET (100)		40.00	18.00
❑ 1	Eric Moulds	.60	.25
❑ 2	Muhsin Muhammad	.30	.14
❑ 3	Patrick Jeffers	.60	.25
❑ 4	Joey Galloway	.60	.25
❑ 5	Edgerrin James	2.00	.90
❑ 6	Germane Crowell	.30	.14
❑ 7	Ed McCaffrey	.60	.25
❑ 8	Dorsey Levens	.30	.14
❑ 9	Marcus Robinson	.60	.25
❑ 10	Tony Gonzalez	.30	.14
❑ 11	Robert Smith	.30	.14
❑ 12	Rich Gannon	.30	.14
❑ 13	Jerry Rice	1.50	.70
❑ 14	Mike Alstott	.60	.25
❑ 15	Brad Johnson	.60	.25
❑ 16	Emmitt Smith	1.50	.70
❑ 17	Marvin Harrison	.60	.25
❑ 18	Duce Staley	.60	.25
❑ 19	Terry Glenn	.30	.14
❑ 20	Terrell Owens	.60	.25
❑ 21	Antonio Freeman	.60	.25
❑ 22	Curtis Enis	.30	.14
❑ 23	Michael Westbrook	.30	.14
❑ 24	Cris Carter	.60	.25
❑ 25	Tim Brown	.60	.25
❑ 26	Terrell Davis	1.50	.70
❑ 27	Fred Taylor	.75	.35
❑ 28	Amani Toomer	.15	.07
❑ 29	Donovan McNabb	1.00	.45
❑ 30	Charlie Garner	.30	.14
❑ 31	Kurt Warner	2.50	1.10
❑ 32	Antowain Smith	.30	.14
❑ 33	Torry Holt	.60	.25
❑ 34	Jake Plummer	.60	.25
❑ 35	Steve Beuerlein	.30	.14
❑ 36	Rocket Ismail	.30	.14
❑ 37	Brett Favre	2.00	.90
❑ 38	Mark Brunell	1.00	.45
❑ 39	Qadry Ismail	.30	.14
❑ 40	Carl Pickens	.30	.14
❑ 41	James Stewart	.30	.14
❑ 42	Drew Bledsoe	1.00	.45
❑ 43	Keenan McCardell	.30	.14
❑ 44	Jerome Bettis	.60	.25
❑ 45	Jon Kitna	.60	.25
❑ 46	Warrick Dunn	.60	.25
❑ 47	Jevon Kearse	.60	.25
❑ 48	Jamal Anderson	.60	.25
❑ 49	Shaun King	1.00	.45
❑ 50	Ricky Williams	1.50	.70
❑ 51	Elvis Grbac	.30	.14
❑ 52	Corey Dillon	.60	.25
❑ 53	Brian Griese	.75	.35
❑ 54	Steve Young	1.00	.45
❑ 55	Tyrone Wheatley	.30	.14
❑ 56	Daunte Culpepper	1.25	.55
❑ 57	Troy Aikman	1.50	.70
❑ 58	Peyton Manning	2.00	.90
❑ 59	Stephen Davis	.60	.25
❑ 60	Keyshawn Johnson	.60	.25
❑ 61	Doug Flutie	.75	.35
❑ 62	Yancey Thigpen	.15	.07
❑ 63	Jeff Blake	.30	.14
❑ 64	Tony Banks	.30	.14
❑ 65	Tim Couch	1.25	.55
❑ 66	Charlie Batch	.60	.25
❑ 67	Rob Johnson	.30	.14
❑ 68	Cade McNown	.60	.25
❑ 69	Steve McNair	.60	.25
❑ 70	Eddie George	.75	.35
❑ 71	Isaac Bruce	.60	.25
❑ 72	Ricky Watters	.30	.14
❑ 73	Kordell Stewart	.60	.25
❑ 74	Wayne Chrebet	.30	.14
❑ 75	Curtis Martin	.60	.25
❑ 76	Jimmy Smith	.30	.14
❑ 77	Randy Moss	2.00	.90
❑ 78	Akili Smith	.60	.25
❑ 79	Marshall Faulk	.75	.35
❑ 80	Kerry Collins	.30	.14
❑ 81	Ron Dayne RC	4.00	1.80
❑ 82	Chad Pennington RC	4.00	1.80
❑ 83	Sylvester Morris RC	2.50	1.10
❑ 84	Thomas Jones RC	2.00	.90
❑ 85	Shaun Alexander RC	3.00	1.35
❑ 86	Chris Redman RC	2.50	1.10
❑ 87	Courtney Brown RC	1.50	.70
❑ 88	Jerry Porter RC	1.25	.55
❑ 89	Ron Dugans RC	1.25	.55
❑ 90	Jamal Lewis RC	6.00	2.70
❑ 91	Travis Prentice RC	2.00	.90
❑ 92	Travis Taylor RC	1.50	.70
❑ 93	R.Jay Soward RC	1.25	.55
❑ 94	Peter Warrick RC	4.00	1.80
❑ 95	Trung Canidate RC	1.25	.55
❑ 96	Tee Martin RC	2.00	.90
❑ 97	Bubba Franks RC	1.50	.70
❑ 98	Plaxico Burress RC	2.50	1.10
❑ 99	J.R. Redmond RC	1.50	.70
❑ 100	Dennis Northcutt RC	1.50	.70

1998 Topps Season Opener

		MINT	NRMT
COMPLETE SET (165)		120.00	55.00
❑ 1	Peyton Manning RC	25.00	11.00
❑ 2	Jerome Pathon RC	4.00	1.80
❑ 3	Duane Starks RC	2.00	.90
❑ 4	Brian Simmons RC	2.00	.90
❑ 5	Keith Brooking RC	2.00	.90
❑ 6	Robert Edwards RC	5.00	2.20
❑ 7	Curtis Enis RC	4.00	1.80
❑ 8	John Avery RC	3.00	1.35
❑ 9	Fred Taylor RC	10.00	4.50
❑ 10	Germane Crowell RC	6.00	2.70
❑ 11	Hines Ward RC	4.00	1.80
❑ 12	Marcus Nash RC	4.00	1.80
❑ 13	Jacquez Green RC	5.00	2.20
❑ 14	Joe Jurevicius RC	3.00	1.35
❑ 15	Greg Ellis RC	3.00	1.35
❑ 16	Brian Griese RC	12.00	5.50
❑ 17	Tavian Banks RC	4.00	1.80
❑ 18	Robert Holcombe RC	3.00	1.35
❑ 19	Skip Hicks RC	4.00	1.80
❑ 20	Ahman Green RC	8.00	3.60
❑ 21	Takeo Spikes RC	3.00	1.35
❑ 22	Randy Moss RC	25.00	11.00
❑ 23	Andre Wadsworth RC	3.00	1.35
❑ 24	Jason Peter RC	2.00	.90
❑ 25	Grant Wistrom RC	2.00	.90
❑ 26	Charles Woodson RC	5.00	2.20
❑ 27	Kevin Dyson RC	5.00	2.20
❑ 28	Pat Johnson RC	3.00	1.35
❑ 29	Tim Dwight RC	5.00	2.20
❑ 30	Ryan Leaf RC	8.00	3.60
❑ 31	Chad Brown	.10	.05
❑ 32	Levon Kirkland	.10	.05
❑ 33	Corey Dillon	.10	.05
❑ 34	Curtis Conway	.10	.05
❑ 35	Chris Chandler	.10	.05
❑ 36	Warrick Dunn	.10	.05
❑ 37	Danny Kanell	.10	.05
❑ 38	Emmitt Smith	.10	.05
❑ 39	Steve Young	.10	.05
❑ 40	Kimble Anders	.10	.05
❑ 41	Freddie Jones	.10	.05
❑ 42	Bobby Engram	.10	.05
❑ 43	Aeneas Williams	.10	.05
❑ 44	Antowain Smith	.10	.05
❑ 45	Reggie White	.10	.05
❑ 46	Rae Carruth	.10	.05
❑ 47	Jamie Asher	.10	.05
❑ 48	Hardy Nickerson	.10	.05
❑ 49	Jerome Bettis	.10	.05
❑ 50	Michael Strahan	.10	.05
❑ 51	John Randle	.10	.05
❑ 52	Larry Centers	.10	.05
❑ 53	Tim Brown	.10	.05
❑ 54	Terry Glenn	.10	.05
❑ 55	Keenan McCardell	.10	.05
❑ 56	Troy Aikman	.10	.05
❑ 57	Peter Boulware	.10	.05
❑ 58	Erik Kramer	.10	.05
❑ 59	Andre Rison	.10	.05
❑ 60	Jeff George	.10	.05
❑ 61	Robert Brooks	.10	.05
❑ 62	Simeon Rice	.10	.05
❑ 63	Mark Brunell	.10	.05
❑ 64	Jeff Blake	.10	.05
❑ 65	Brett Favre	.10	.05
❑ 66	Lawrence Phillips	.10	.05
❑ 67	Randal Hill	.10	.05
❑ 68	Terance Mathis	.10	.05
❑ 69	Bruce Smith	.10	.05
❑ 70	Troy Drayton	.10	.05
❑ 71	Derrick Thomas	.10	.05
❑ 72	Charles Way	.10	.05
❑ 73	Bobby Hoying	.10	.05
❑ 74	Michael Jackson	.10	.05
❑ 75	Chris Sanders	.10	.05
❑ 76	Cris Dishman	.10	.05
❑ 77	Jake Plummer	.10	.05
❑ 78	Kordell Stewart	.10	.05
❑ 79	Carl Pickens	.10	.05
❑ 80	Ed McCaffrey	.10	.05
❑ 81	Ray Buchanan	.10	.05
❑ 82	Thurman Thomas	.10	.05
❑ 83	Andre Reed	.10	.05
❑ 84	Wesley Walls	.10	.05
❑ 85	Rob Moore	.10	.05
❑ 86	Eddie George	.10	.05
❑ 87	Michael Irvin	.10	.05
❑ 88	Johnnie Morton	.10	.05
❑ 89	Cris Carter	.10	.05
❑ 90	Garrison Hearst	.10	.05
❑ 91	Rod Smith	.10	.05
❑ 92	Ben Coates	.10	.05
❑ 93	Zach Thomas	.10	.05
❑ 94	Dale Carter	.10	.05
❑ 95	Mark Chmura	.10	.05

❑ 96 Elvis Grbac .10 .05
❑ 97 Ray Lewis .10 .05
❑ 98 Lonnie Johnson .10 .05
❑ 99 Darrell Green .10 .05
❑ 100 Marvin Harrison .10 .05
❑ 101 Dorsey Levens .10 .05
❑ 102 Tony Gonzalez .10 .05
❑ 103 Andre Hastings .10 .05
❑ 104 Jason Sehorn .10 .05
❑ 105 Drew Bledsoe .10 .05
❑ 106 Junior Seau .10 .05
❑ 107 Robert Smith .10 .05
❑ 108 Terrell Davis .10 .05
❑ 109 Neil Smith .10 .05
❑ 110 Jermaine Lewis .10 .05
❑ 111 Warren Moon .10 .05
❑ 112 Brad Johnson .10 .05
❑ 113 Karim Abdul-Jabbar .10 .05
❑ 114 Terry Allen .10 .05
❑ 115 Chris Slade .10 .05
❑ 116 Michael Westbrook .10 .05
❑ 117 Tony Banks .10 .05
❑ 118 Mike Alstott .10 .05
❑ 119 Jake Reed .10 .05
❑ 120 Bryant Westbrook .10 .05
❑ 121 Steve McNair .10 .05
❑ 122 Jimmy Smith .10 .05
❑ 123 Reidel Anthony .10 .05
❑ 124 Jessie Armstead .10 .05
❑ 125 O.J. McDuffie .10 .05
❑ 126 Jerry Rice .10 .05
❑ 127 Frank Sanders .10 .05
❑ 128 Fred Lane .10 .05
❑ 129 Scott Mitchell .10 .05
❑ 130 Rickey Dudley .10 .05
❑ 131 Isaac Bruce .10 .05
❑ 132 Tony Martin .10 .05
❑ 133 Leslie Shepherd .10 .05
❑ 134 Derrick Brooks .10 .05
❑ 135 Antonio Freeman .10 .05
❑ 136 Dan Marino .10 .05
❑ 137 Eric Green .10 .05
❑ 138 Darnay Scott .10 .05
❑ 139 Herman Moore .10 .05
❑ 140 Terrell Owens .10 .05
❑ 141 Trent Dilfer .10 .05
❑ 142 Marshall Faulk .10 .05
❑ 143 John Elway .10 .05
❑ 144 Gus Frerotte .10 .05
❑ 145 Napoleon Kaufman .10 .05
❑ 146 Charlie Garner .10 .05
❑ 147 Irving Fryar .10 .05
❑ 148 Shannon Sharpe .10 .05
❑ 149 Jamal Anderson .10 .05
❑ 150 Chris Spielman .10 .05
❑ 151 Deion Sanders .10 .05
❑ 152 Joey Galloway .10 .05
❑ 153 J.J. Stokes .10 .05
❑ 154 Quinn Early .10 .05
❑ 155 Michael McCrary .10 .05
❑ 156 Willie McGinest .10 .05
❑ 157 Kevin Hardy .10 .05
❑ 158 Micheal Barrow .10 .05
❑ 159 John Mobley .10 .05
❑ 160 Michael Sinclair .10 .05
❑ 161 Warren Sapp .10 .05
❑ 162 Michael Bates .10 .05
❑ 163 Pete Mitchell .10 .05
❑ 164 Barry Sanders .10 .05
❑ 165 Checklist .10 .05

1999 Topps Season Opener

	MINT	NRMT
COMPLETE SET (165)	40.00	18.00

❑ 1 Jerry Rice 1.00 .45
❑ 2 Emmitt Smith 1.00 .45
❑ 3 Curtis Martin .40 .18
❑ 4 Ed McCaffrey .20 .09
❑ 5 Oronde Gadsden .10 .05
❑ 6 Byron Bam Morris .10 .05
❑ 7 Michael Irvin .20 .09

❑ 8 Shannon Sharpe .20 .09
❑ 9 Levon Kirkland .10 .05
❑ 10 Fred Taylor 1.00 .45
❑ 11 Andre Reed .20 .09
❑ 12 Chad Brown .10 .05
❑ 13 Skip Hicks .40 .18
❑ 14 Tim Dwight .40 .18
❑ 15 Michael Sinclair .10 .05
❑ 16 Carl Pickens .20 .09
❑ 17 Derrick Alexander WR .20 .09
❑ 18 Kevin Greene .10 .05
❑ 19 Duce Staley .40 .18
❑ 20 Dan Marino 1.50 .70
❑ 21 Frank Sanders .20 .09
❑ 22 Ricky Proehl .10 .05
❑ 23 Frank Wycheck .10 .05
❑ 24 Andre Rison .20 .09
❑ 25 Natrone Means .20 .09
❑ 26 Steve McNair .40 .18
❑ 27 Vonnie Holliday .10 .05
❑ 28 Charles Woodson .40 .18
❑ 29 Rob Moore .20 .09
❑ 30 John Elway 1.50 .70
❑ 31 Derrick Thomas .20 .09
❑ 32 Jake Plummer .75 .35
❑ 33 Mike Alstott .40 .18
❑ 34 Keenan McCardell .20 .09
❑ 35 Mark Chmura .10 .05
❑ 36 Keyshawn Johnson .40 .18
❑ 37 Priest Holmes .40 .18
❑ 38 Antonio Freeman .40 .18
❑ 39 Ty Law .10 .05
❑ 40 Jamal Anderson .40 .18
❑ 41 Courtney Hawkins .10 .05
❑ 42 James Jett .20 .09
❑ 43 Aaron Glenn .10 .05
❑ 44 Jimmy Smith .20 .09
❑ 45 Michael McCrary .10 .05
❑ 46 Junior Seau .20 .09
❑ 47 Bill Romanowski .10 .05
❑ 48 Mark Brunell .60 .25
❑ 49 Yancey Thigpen .10 .05
❑ 50 Steve Young .60 .25
❑ 51 Cris Carter .40 .18
❑ 52 Vinny Testaverde .20 .09
❑ 53 Zach Thomas .20 .09
❑ 54 Kordell Stewart .40 .18
❑ 55 Tim Biakabutuka .20 .09
❑ 56 J.J. Stokes .20 .09
❑ 57 Jon Kitna .40 .18
❑ 58 Jacquez Green .20 .09
❑ 59 Marvin Harrison .40 .18
❑ 60 Barry Sanders 1.50 .70
❑ 61 Darrell Green .10 .05
❑ 62 Terance Mathis .20 .09
❑ 63 Ricky Watters .20 .09
❑ 64 Chris Chandler .20 .09
❑ 65 Cameron Cleeland .10 .05
❑ 66 Rod Smith .20 .09
❑ 67 Freddie Jones .10 .05
❑ 68 Adrian Murrell .20 .09
❑ 69 Terrell Owens .40 .18
❑ 70 Troy Aikman 1.00 .45
❑ 71 John Mobley .10 .05
❑ 72 Corey Dillon .40 .18
❑ 73 Rickey Dudley .10 .05
❑ 74 Randall Cunningham .40 .18
❑ 75 Muhsin Muhammad .20 .09
❑ 76 Stephen Boyd .10 .05
❑ 77 Tony Gonzalez .20 .09
❑ 78 Deion Sanders .40 .18
❑ 79 Ben Coates .20 .09
❑ 80 Brett Favre 1.50 .70
❑ 81 Shawn Springs .10 .05
❑ 82 Dorsey Levens .40 .18
❑ 83 Ray Buchanan .10 .05
❑ 84 Charlie Batch .75 .35
❑ 85 John Randle .20 .09
❑ 86 Eddie George .50 .23
❑ 87 Ray Lewis .20 .09
❑ 88 Johnnie Morton .20 .09
❑ 89 Kevin Hardy .10 .05
❑ 90 O.J. McDuffie .20 .09
❑ 91 Herman Moore .40 .18
❑ 92 Tim Brown .40 .18
❑ 93 Bert Emanuel .20 .09
❑ 94 Elvis Grbac .20 .09
❑ 95 Peter Boulware .10 .05
❑ 96 Curtis Conway .20 .09
❑ 97 Doug Flutie .50 .23
❑ 98 Jake Reed .20 .09
❑ 99 Ike Hilliard .10 .05
❑ 100 Randy Moss 1.50 .70
❑ 101 Warren Sapp .10 .05
❑ 102 Bruce Smith .20 .09
❑ 103 Joey Galloway .40 .18
❑ 104 Napoleon Kaufman .40 .18
❑ 105 Warrick Dunn .40 .18
❑ 106 Wayne Chrebet .20 .09
❑ 107 Robert Brooks .20 .09
❑ 108 Antowain Smith .40 .18
❑ 109 Trent Dilfer .20 .09
❑ 110 Peyton Manning 1.50 .70
❑ 111 Isaac Bruce .40 .18
❑ 112 John Lynch .10 .05
❑ 113 Terry Glenn .40 .18
❑ 114 Garrison Hearst .20 .09
❑ 115 Jerome Bettis .40 .18
❑ 116 Darnay Scott .10 .05
❑ 117 Lamar Thomas .10 .05
❑ 118 Chris Spielman .10 .05
❑ 119 Robert Smith .40 .18
❑ 120 Drew Bledsoe .60 .25
❑ 121 Reidel Anthony .20 .09
❑ 122 Wesley Walls .20 .09
❑ 123 Eric Moulds .40 .18
❑ 124 Terrell Davis 1.00 .45
❑ 125 Dale Carter .10 .05
❑ 126 Charles Johnson .10 .05
❑ 127 Steve Atwater .10 .05
❑ 128 Jim Harbaugh .20 .09
❑ 129 Tony Martin .20 .09
❑ 130 Kerry Collins .20 .09
❑ 131 Trent Green .20 .09
❑ 132 Marshall Faulk .40 .18
❑ 133 Rocket Ismail .20 .09
❑ 134 Warren Moon .40 .18
❑ 135 Jerris McPhail .10 .05
❑ 136 Damon Gibson .10 .05
❑ 137 Jim Pyne .10 .05
❑ 138 Antonio Langham .10 .05
❑ 139 Freddie Solomon .10 .05
❑ 140 Randy Moss SH .75 .35
❑ 141 John Elway SH .75 .35
❑ 142 Doug Flutie SH .40 .18
❑ 143 Emmitt Smith SH .50 .23
❑ 144 Terrell Davis SH .50 .23
❑ 145 Troy Edwards RC 2.50 1.10
❑ 146 Torry Holt RC 5.00 2.20
❑ 147 Tim Couch RC 6.00 2.70
❑ 148 Sedrick Irvin RC 2.00 .90
❑ 149 Ricky Williams RC 8.00 3.60
❑ 150 Peerless Price RC 2.50 1.10
❑ 151 Mike Cloud RC 2.00 .90
❑ 152 Kevin Faulk RC 3.00 1.35
❑ 153 Kevin Johnson RC 4.00 1.80
❑ 154 James Johnson RC 2.00 .90
❑ 155 Edgerrin James RC 12.00 5.50
❑ 156 D'Wayne Bates RC 1.50 .70
❑ 157 Donovan McNabb RC 8.00 3.60
❑ 158 David Boston RC 4.00 1.80
❑ 159 Daunte Culpepper RC 12.00 5.50
❑ 160 Champ Bailey RC 2.50 1.10

❑ 161 Cecil Collins RC	2.00	.90
❑ 162 Cade McNown RC	2.50	1.10
❑ 163 Brock Huard RC	3.00	1.35
❑ 164 Akili Smith RC	4.00	1.80
❑ 165 Checklist Card	.10	.05

2000 Topps Season Opener

	MINT	NRMT
COMPLETE SET (220)	40.00	18.00

❑ 1 Tyrone Wheatley	.15	.07
❑ 2 Carl Pickens	.15	.07
❑ 3 Zach Thomas	.15	.07
❑ 4 Jacquez Green	.15	.07
❑ 5 Sean Dawkins	.10	.05
❑ 6 Brad Johnson	.30	.14
❑ 7 Jerry Rice	.75	.35
❑ 8 Doug Flutie	.40	.18
❑ 9 Cade McNown	.30	.14
❑ 10 Rod Smith	.15	.07
❑ 11 Kevin Hardy	.10	.05
❑ 12 Marvin Harrison	.30	.14
❑ 13 David Boston	.30	.14
❑ 14 Priest Holmes	.15	.07
❑ 15 Keith Poole	.10	.05
❑ 16 Troy Edwards	.15	.07
❑ 17 Robert Smith	.30	.14
❑ 18 Kevin Lockett	.10	.05
❑ 19 Johnnie Morton	.15	.07
❑ 20 Terrell Davis	.75	.35
❑ 21 Corey Bradford	.15	.07
❑ 22 Keyshawn Johnson	.30	.14
❑ 23 Tony Banks	.15	.07
❑ 24 Matthew Hatchette	.15	.07
❑ 25 Troy Aikman	.75	.35
❑ 26 Natrone Means	.10	.05
❑ 27 Peerless Price	.30	.14
❑ 28 Bruce Smith	.15	.07
❑ 29 Tim Couch	.60	.25
❑ 30 Terrell Owens	.30	.14
❑ 31 O.J. McDuffie	.15	.07
❑ 32 Troy Brown	.10	.05
❑ 33 Corey Dillon	.30	.14
❑ 34 Cam Cleeland	.10	.05
❑ 35 Brian Griese	.40	.18
❑ 36 Shawn Springs	.10	.05
❑ 37 Marcus Robinson	.30	.14
❑ 38 Jermaine Lewis	.15	.07
❑ 39 Olandis Gary	.30	.14
❑ 40 Tony Gonzalez	.15	.07
❑ 41 Frank Wycheck	.10	.05
❑ 42 Jon Kitna	.30	.14
❑ 43 Muhsin Muhammad	.15	.07
❑ 44 Jerome Bettis	.30	.14
❑ 45 Darrin Chiaverini	.10	.05
❑ 46 Steve McNair	.30	.14
❑ 47 Charlie Batch	.30	.14
❑ 48 Steve Beuerlein	.15	.07
❑ 49 Dorsey Levens	.15	.07
❑ 50 Jim Harbaugh	.15	.07
❑ 51 Jonathan Linton	.10	.05
❑ 52 Napoleon Kaufman	.15	.07
❑ 53 Curtis Enis	.15	.07
❑ 54 Darnay Scott	.15	.07
❑ 55 Tim Dwight	.30	.14
❑ 56 Mikhael Ricks	.10	.05
❑ 57 Kevin Dyson	.15	.07
❑ 58 Antonio Freeman	.30	.14
❑ 59 E.G. Green	.10	.05
❑ 60 Jake Plummer	.30	.14
❑ 61 Bill Schroeder	.15	.07
❑ 62 Shaun King	.50	.23
❑ 63 Michael Basnight	.10	.05
❑ 64 Vinny Testaverde	.15	.07
❑ 65 Rob Johnson	.15	.07
❑ 66 Jeff Blake	.15	.07
❑ 67 Marshall Faulk	.40	.18
❑ 68 Keenan McCardell	.15	.07
❑ 69 Michael Westbrook	.15	.07
❑ 70 Yancey Thigpen	.10	.05
❑ 71 Akili Smith	.30	.14
❑ 72 Charles Woodson	.15	.07
❑ 73 Qadry Ismail	.10	.05
❑ 74 Pat Johnson	.10	.05
❑ 75 Rocket Ismail	.15	.07
❑ 76 Terrence Wilkins	.30	.14
❑ 77 Herman Moore	.15	.07
❑ 78 Jevon Kearse	.30	.14
❑ 79 Oronde Gadsden	.15	.07
❑ 80 Errict Rhett	.15	.07
❑ 81 Ed McCaffrey	.30	.14
❑ 82 Mike Alstott	.30	.14
❑ 83 Stephen Alexander	.10	.05
❑ 84 Mark Brunell	.50	.23
❑ 85 Jeff George	.15	.07
❑ 86 Stephen Davis	.30	.14
❑ 87 Germane Crowell	.15	.07
❑ 88 Charlie Garner	.15	.07
❑ 89 Kordell Stewart	.30	.14
❑ 90 Tim Biakabutuka	.15	.07
❑ 91 Jim Miller	.10	.05
❑ 92 Eddie George	.40	.18
❑ 93 Joe Montgomery	.10	.05
❑ 94 Wayne Chrebet	.15	.07
❑ 95 Freddie Jones	.10	.05
❑ 96 Ricky Proehl	.10	.05
❑ 97 Warren Sapp	.15	.07
❑ 98 Derrick Mayes	.15	.07
❑ 99 Daunte Culpepper	.60	.25
❑ 100 Torry Holt	.30	.14
❑ 101 Isaac Bruce	.30	.14
❑ 102 Kevin Johnson	.30	.14
❑ 103 Antowain Smith	.15	.07
❑ 104 Rob Moore	.15	.07
❑ 105 Joey Galloway	.30	.14
❑ 106 Rickey Dudley	.10	.05
❑ 107 Terry Glenn	.15	.07
❑ 108 Ike Hilliard	.15	.07
❑ 109 Jeff Graham	.10	.05
❑ 110 J.J. Stokes	.15	.07
❑ 111 Steve Young	.50	.23
❑ 112 Albert Connell	.10	.05
❑ 113 Tony Brackens	.10	.05
❑ 114 James Johnson	.15	.07
❑ 115 Tim Brown	.30	.14
❑ 116 Terance Mathis	.15	.07
❑ 117 Peyton Manning	1.00	.45
❑ 118 Kerry Collins	.15	.07
❑ 119 Duce Staley	.30	.14
❑ 120 Torrance Small	.10	.05
❑ 121 Curtis Martin	.30	.14
❑ 122 Damon Huard	.30	.14
❑ 123 Derrick Alexander	.15	.07
❑ 124 Jimmy Smith	.15	.07
❑ 125 Cris Carter	.30	.14
❑ 126 Jamal Anderson	.30	.14
❑ 127 Eric Moulds	.30	.14
❑ 128 Drew Bledsoe	.50	.23
❑ 129 Ricky Williams	.75	.35
❑ 130 Andre Hastings	.10	.05
❑ 131 Amani Toomer	.10	.05
❑ 132 Rich Gannon	.15	.07
❑ 133 Richard Huntley	.10	.05
❑ 134 Donovan McNabb	.50	.23
❑ 135 Jermaine Fazande	.10	.05
❑ 136 Randy Moss	1.00	.45
❑ 137 Champ Bailey	.15	.07
❑ 138 Elvis Grbac	.15	.07
❑ 139 Warrick Dunn	.30	.14
❑ 140 John Randle	.15	.07
❑ 141 Edgerrin James	1.25	.55
❑ 142 Tony Martin	.15	.07
❑ 143 Chris Chandler	.15	.07
❑ 144 Stephen Boyd	.10	.05
❑ 145 Az-Zahir Hakim	.15	.07
❑ 146 Tony Simmons	.10	.05
❑ 147 Pete Mitchell	.10	.05
❑ 148 Junior Seau	.15	.07
❑ 149 Ricky Watters	.15	.07
❑ 150 Michael Pittman	.10	.05
❑ 151 Fred Taylor	.40	.18
❑ 152 Charles Johnson	.15	.07
❑ 153 Jason Tucker	.10	.05
❑ 154 Brett Favre	1.25	.55
❑ 155 Patrick Jeffers	.30	.14
❑ 156 Curtis Conway	.15	.07
❑ 157 Frank Sanders	.15	.07
❑ 158 James Stewart	.15	.07
❑ 159 Emmitt Smith	.75	.35
❑ 161 Wesley Walls	.10	.05
❑ 162 Kent Graham	.10	.05
❑ 163 Kurt Warner	1.25	.55
❑ 164 Shawn Jefferson	.10	.05
❑ 165 Jammi German	.10	.05
❑ 166 Jay Riemersma	.10	.05
❑ 167 Fred Lane	.10	.05
❑ 168 Jamir Miller	.10	.05
❑ 169 David LaFleur	.10	.05
❑ 170 David Sloan	.10	.05
❑ 171 Jerome Pathon	.15	.07
❑ 172 Sam Madison	.10	.05
❑ 173 Tiki Barber	.15	.07
❑ 174 Yatil Green	.10	.05
❑ 175 Checklist	.10	.05
❑ 176 Kurt Warner HL	.60	.25
❑ 177 Brett Favre HL	.60	.25
❑ 178 Marshall Faulk HL	.15	.07
❑ 179 Jevon Kearse HL	.15	.07
❑ 180 Edgerrin James CL	.60	.25
❑ 181 Troy Aikman CS	.40	.18
❑ 182 Terrell Davis CS	.40	.18
❑ 183 Steve Beuerlein CS	.10	.05
❑ 184 Tim Brown CS	.15	.07
❑ 185 Randy Moss CS	.50	.23
❑ 186 Drew Bledsoe CS	.30	.14
❑ 187 Curtis Martin CS	.15	.07
❑ 188 Shannon Sharpe CS	.10	.05
❑ 189 Brett Favre CS	.60	.25
❑ 190 Brad Johnson CS	.15	.07
❑ 191 Tony Gonzalez CS	.10	.05
❑ 192 Jon Kitna CS	.15	.07
❑ 193 Peyton Manning CS	.50	.23
❑ 194 Mark Brunell CS	.30	.14
❑ 195 Cade McNown CS	.30	.14
❑ 196 Jim Harbaugh CS	.10	.05
❑ 197 Shaun King CS	.30	.14
❑ 198 Kurt Warner CS	.60	.25
❑ 199 Eddie George CS	.15	.07
❑ 200 Ricky Williams CS	.40	.18
❑ 201 Curtis Keaton RC	.75	.35
❑ 202 Tee Martin RC	1.50	.70
❑ 203 Thomas Jones RC	1.50	.70
❑ 204 Giovanni Carmazzi RC	1.25	.55
❑ 205 Courtney Brown RC	1.25	.55
❑ 206 Shaun Alexander RC	2.50	1.10
❑ 207 Travis Taylor RC	1.25	.55
❑ 208 Dennis Northcutt RC	1.25	.55
❑ 209 Trung Canidate RC	.75	.35
❑ 210 Jamal Lewis RC	5.00	2.20
❑ 211 R.Jay Soward RC	1.00	.45
❑ 212 Sylvester Morris RC	2.00	.90
❑ 213 Ron Dugans RC	.75	.35
❑ 214 Chris Redman RC	2.00	.90
❑ 215 Plaxico Burress RC	2.00	.90
❑ 216 Peter Warrick RC	3.00	1.35
❑ 217 Travis Prentice RC	1.50	.70
❑ 218 Ron Dayne RC	3.00	1.35
❑ 219 J.R. Redmond RC	1.25	.55
❑ 220 Chad Pennington RC	3.00	1.35

1997 Topps Stars

	MINT	NRMT
COMPLETE SET (125)	25.00	11.00

❑ 1 Brett Favre	2.50	1.10
❑ 2 Michael Jackson	.25	.11
❑ 3 Simeon Rice	.25	.11

Card	Player	Mint	Nrmt
❑ 4	Thurman Thomas	.50	.23
❑ 5	Karim Abdul-Jabbar	.50	.23
❑ 6	Marvin Harrison	.50	.23
❑ 7	John Elway	2.50	1.10
❑ 8	Carl Pickens	.50	.23
❑ 9	Rod Woodson	.25	.11
❑ 10	Kerry Collins	.25	.11
❑ 11	Cortez Kennedy	.15	.07
❑ 12	William Fuller	.15	.07
❑ 13	Michael Irvin	.50	.23
❑ 14	Tyrone Braxton	.15	.07
❑ 15	Steve Young	.75	.35
❑ 16	Keith Lyle	.15	.07
❑ 17	Blaine Bishop	.15	.07
❑ 18	Jeff Hostetler	.15	.07
❑ 19	Levon Kirkland	.15	.07
❑ 20	Barry Sanders	2.50	1.10
❑ 21	Deion Sanders	.50	.23
❑ 22	Jamal Anderson	.75	.35
❑ 23	Eric Davis	.15	.07
❑ 24	Hardy Nickerson	.15	.07
❑ 25	LeRoy Butler	.15	.07
❑ 26	Mark Brunell	1.25	.55
❑ 27	Aeneas Williams	.15	.07
❑ 28	Curtis Martin	.60	.25
❑ 29	Wayne Chrebet	.50	.23
❑ 30	Jerry Rice	1.25	.55
❑ 31	Jake Reed	.25	.11
❑ 32	Wayne Martin	.15	.07
❑ 33	Derrick Alexander WR	.25	.11
❑ 34	Isaac Bruce	.50	.23
❑ 35	Terrell Davis	2.00	.90
❑ 36	Jerome Bettis	.50	.23
❑ 37	Keenan McCardell	.25	.11
❑ 38	Derrick Thomas	.25	.11
❑ 39	Jason Sehorn	.25	.11
❑ 40	Keyshawn Johnson	.50	.23
❑ 41	Jeff Blake	.25	.11
❑ 42	Terry Allen	.50	.23
❑ 43	Ben Coates	.25	.11
❑ 44	William Thomas	.15	.07
❑ 45	Bryce Paup	.15	.07
❑ 46	Bryant Young	.15	.07
❑ 47	Eric Swann	.15	.07
❑ 48	Tim Brown	.50	.23
❑ 49	Tony Martin	.25	.11
❑ 50	Eddie George	1.50	.70
❑ 51	Sam Mills	.15	.07
❑ 52	Terry McDaniel	.15	.07
❑ 53	Darren Woodson	.15	.07
❑ 54	Ashley Ambrose	.15	.07
❑ 55	Drew Bledsoe	1.25	.55
❑ 56	Larry Centers	.25	.11
❑ 57	Ty Detmer	.25	.11
❑ 58	Merton Hanks	.15	.07
❑ 59	Charles Johnson	.25	.11
❑ 60	Dan Marino	2.50	1.10
❑ 61	Joey Galloway	.60	.25
❑ 62	Junior Seau	.25	.11
❑ 63	Brett Perriman	.15	.07
❑ 64	Wesley Walls	.25	.11
❑ 65	Chad Brown	.15	.07
❑ 66	Henry Ellard	.15	.07
❑ 67	Keith Jackson	.15	.07
❑ 68	John Randle	.25	.11
❑ 69	Chester McGlockton	.15	.07
❑ 70	Emmitt Smith	2.00	.90
❑ 71	Vinny Testaverde	.25	.11
❑ 72	Steve Atwater	.15	.07
❑ 73	Irving Fryar	.25	.11
❑ 74	Gus Frerotte	.15	.07
❑ 75	Terry Glenn	.50	.23
❑ 76	Anthony Johnson	.15	.07
❑ 77	Jimmy Smith	.25	.11
❑ 78	Terrell Buckley	.15	.07
❑ 79	Kimble Anders	.25	.11
❑ 80	Cris Carter	.50	.23
❑ 81	Dave Meggett	.15	.07
❑ 82	Shannon Sharpe	.25	.11
❑ 83	Adrian Murrell	.25	.11
❑ 84	Herman Moore	.50	.23
❑ 85	Bruce Smith	.25	.11
❑ 86	Lamar Lathon	.15	.07
❑ 87	Ken Harvey	.15	.07
❑ 88	Curtis Conway	.25	.11
❑ 89	Alfred Williams	.15	.07
❑ 90	Troy Aikman	1.25	.55
❑ 91	Carnell Lake	.15	.07
❑ 92	Michael Sinclair	.15	.07
❑ 93	Ricky Watters	.25	.11
❑ 94	Kevin Greene	.25	.11
❑ 95	Reggie White	.50	.23
❑ 96	Tyrone Hughes	.15	.07
❑ 97	Dale Carter	.15	.07
❑ 98	Rob Moore	.25	.11
❑ 99	Tony Tolbert	.15	.07
❑ 100	Willie McGinest	.15	.07
❑ 101	Orlando Pace RC	1.00	.45
❑ 102	Yatil Green RC	.50	.23
❑ 103	Antowain Smith RC	2.50	1.10
❑ 104	David LaFleur RC	1.00	.45
❑ 105	Jake Plummer RC	10.00	4.50
❑ 106	Will Blackwell RC	.50	.23
❑ 107	Dwayne Rudd RC	1.00	.45
❑ 108	Corey Dillon RC	8.00	3.60
❑ 109	Pat Barnes RC	1.00	.45
❑ 110	Peter Boulware RC	1.00	.45
❑ 111	Tony Gonzalez RC	4.00	1.80
❑ 112	Renaldo Wynn RC	.25	.11
❑ 113	Darrell Russell RC	.25	.11
❑ 114	Bryant Westbrook RC	.25	.11
❑ 115	James Farrior RC	.25	.11
❑ 116	Joey Kent RC	.50	.23
❑ 117	Rae Carruth RC	.50	.23
❑ 118	Jim Druckenmiller RC	1.00	.45
❑ 119	Byron Hanspard RC	.50	.23
❑ 120	Ike Hilliard RC	2.00	.90
❑ 121	Kevin Lockett RC	.50	.23
❑ 122	Tom Knight RC	.25	.11
❑ 123	Shawn Springs RC	.50	.23
❑ 124	Troy Davis RC	.50	.23
❑ 125	Darnell Autry RC	.50	.23
❑ NNO	Checklist Card	.15	.07
❑ PP36	Jerome Bettis Promo	1.50	.70

1998 Topps Stars

Card	Player	MINT	NRMT
	COMP.RED SET (150)	100.00	45.00
❑ 1	John Elway	5.00	2.20
❑ 2	Duane Starks RC	1.50	.70
❑ 3	Bruce Smith	.50	.23
❑ 4	Jeff Blake	.50	.23
❑ 5	Carl Pickens	1.00	.45
❑ 6	Shannon Sharpe	.50	.23
❑ 7	Jerome Pathon RC	2.50	1.10
❑ 8	Jimmy Smith	.50	.23
❑ 9	Elvis Grbac	.50	.23
❑ 10	Mark Brunell	2.00	.90
❑ 11	Karim Abdul-Jabbar	1.00	.45
❑ 12	Terry Glenn	1.00	.45
❑ 13	Larry Centers	.25	.11
❑ 14	Jeff George	.50	.23
❑ 15	Terry Allen	1.00	.45
❑ 16	Charles Johnson	.25	.11
❑ 17	Chris Spielman	.25	.11
❑ 18	Ahman Green RC	5.00	2.20
❑ 19	Kevin Dyson RC	4.00	1.80
❑ 20	Dan Marino	5.00	2.20
❑ 21	Andre Wadsworth RC	2.50	1.10
❑ 22	Chris Chandler	.50	.23
❑ 23	Kerry Collins	.50	.23
❑ 24	Erik Kramer	.25	.11
❑ 25	Warrick Dunn	1.00	.45
❑ 26	Michael Irvin	1.00	.45
❑ 27	Herman Moore	1.00	.45
❑ 28	Dorsey Levens	1.00	.45
❑ 29	Cris Carter	1.00	.45
❑ 30	Drew Bledsoe	2.00	.90
❑ 31	Kevin Greene	.50	.23
❑ 32	Charles Way	.25	.11
❑ 33	Bobby Hoying	.50	.23
❑ 34	Tony Banks	.50	.23
❑ 35	Steve Young	1.50	.70
❑ 36	Trent Dilfer	1.00	.45
❑ 37	Warren Sapp	.50	.23
❑ 38	Skip Hicks RC	3.00	1.35
❑ 39	Michael Jackson	.25	.11
❑ 40	Curtis Martin	1.00	.45
❑ 41	Thurman Thomas	1.00	.45
❑ 42	Corey Dillon	1.50	.70
❑ 43	Brian Griese RC	10.00	4.50
❑ 44	Marshall Faulk	1.00	.45
❑ 45	Isaac Bruce	1.00	.45
❑ 46	Fred Taylor RC	8.00	3.60
❑ 47	Andre Rison	.50	.23
❑ 48	O.J. McDuffie	.50	.23
❑ 49	John Avery RC	3.00	1.35
❑ 50	Terrell Davis	4.00	1.80
❑ 51	Robert Edwards RC	4.00	1.80
❑ 52	Keyshawn Johnson	1.00	.45
❑ 53	Rickey Dudley	.25	.11
❑ 54	Hines Ward RC	2.50	1.10
❑ 55	Irving Fryar	.50	.23
❑ 56	Freddie Jones	.25	.11
❑ 57	Michael Sinclair	.25	.11
❑ 58	Darnay Scott	.50	.23
❑ 59	Tim Dwight RC	4.00	1.80
❑ 60	Tim Brown	1.00	.45
❑ 61	Ray Lewis	1.00	.45
❑ 62	Curtis Enis RC	3.00	1.35
❑ 63	Emmitt Smith	4.00	1.80
❑ 64	Scott Mitchell	.50	.23
❑ 65	Antonio Freeman	1.00	.45
❑ 66	Randy Moss RC	15.00	6.75
❑ 67	Peyton Manning RC	15.00	6.75
❑ 68	Danny Kanell	.50	.23
❑ 69	Charlie Garner	.25	.11
❑ 70	Mike Alstott	1.00	.45
❑ 71	Grant Wistrom RC	1.50	.70
❑ 72	Jacquez Green RC	4.00	1.80
❑ 73	Gus Frerotte	.25	.11
❑ 74	Peter Boulware	.25	.11
❑ 75	Jerry Rice	2.50	1.10
❑ 76	Antowain Smith	1.00	.45
❑ 77	Brian Simmons RC	1.50	.70
❑ 78	Rod Smith	.50	.23
❑ 79	Marvin Harrison	.50	.23
❑ 80	Ryan Leaf RC	5.00	2.20
❑ 81	Keenan McCardell	.50	.23
❑ 82	Derrick Thomas	.50	.23
❑ 83	Zach Thomas	.50	.23
❑ 84	Ben Coates	.50	.23
❑ 85	Rob Moore	.50	.23
❑ 86	Wayne Chrebet	1.00	.45
❑ 87	Napoleon Kaufman	1.00	.45
❑ 88	Levon Kirkland	.25	.11
❑ 89	Junior Seau	.50	.23
❑ 90	Eddie George	2.00	.90
❑ 91	Warren Moon	1.00	.45

❑ 92 Anthony Simmons RC .... 1.50 .70
❑ 93 Steve McNair .... 1.00 .45
❑ 94 Frank Sanders .... .50 .23
❑ 95 Joey Galloway .... 1.00 .45
❑ 96 Jamal Anderson .... 1.00 .45
❑ 97 Rae Carruth .... .50 .23
❑ 98 Curtis Conway .... .50 .23
❑ 99 Greg Ellis RC .... 1.50 .70
❑ 100 Kordell Stewart .... 1.00 .45
❑ 101 Germane Crowell RC .. 5.00 2.20
❑ 102 Mark Chmura .... .50 .23
❑ 103 Robert Smith .... 1.00 .45
❑ 104 Andre Hastings .... .25 .11
❑ 105 Reggie White .... 1.00 .45
❑ 106 Jessie Armstead .... .25 .11
❑ 107 Kevin Hardy .... .25 .11
❑ 108 Robert Holcombe RC .. 3.00 1.35
❑ 109 Garrison Hearst .... 1.00 .45
❑ 110 Jerome Bettis .... 1.00 .45
❑ 111 Reidel Anthony .... .50 .23
❑ 112 Michael Westbrook .... .50 .23
❑ 113 Pat Johnson RC 2.50 1.10
❑ 114 Andre Reed .... .50 .23
❑ 115 Charles Woodson RC .. 4.00 1.80
❑ 116 Takeo Spikes RC 2.50 1.10
❑ 117 Marcus Nash RC 3.00 1.35
❑ 118 Tavian Banks RC .... .50 .23
❑ 119 Tony Gonzalez .... .25 .11
❑ 120 Jake Plummer .... 1.50 .70
❑ 121 Tony Simmons RC 2.50 1.10
❑ 122 Aaron Glenn .... .25 .11
❑ 123 Ricky Watters .... .50 .23
❑ 124 Kimble Anders .... .50 .23
❑ 125 Barry Sanders 5.00 2.20
❑ 126 Terance Mathis .... .50 .23
❑ 127 Wesley Walls .... .50 .23
❑ 128 Bobby Engram .... .50 .23
❑ 129 Johnnie Morton .... .50 .23
❑ 130 Brett Favre 5.00 2.20
❑ 131 Brad Johnson .... 1.00 .45
❑ 132 John Randle .... .50 .23
❑ 133 Chris Sanders .... .25 .11
❑ 134 Joe Jurevicius RC 2.50 1.10
❑ 135 Deion Sanders .... 1.00 .45
❑ 136 Terrell Owens .... 1.00 .45
❑ 137 Darrell Green .... .50 .23
❑ 138 Jermaine Lewis .... .50 .23
❑ 139 James Stewart .... .50 .23
❑ 140 Troy Aikman 2.50 1.10
❑ 141 Hardy Nickerson .... .25 .11
❑ 142 Blaine Bishop .... .25 .11
❑ 143 Keith Brooking RC 3.00 1.35
❑ 144 Jason Peter RC .... 1.50 .70
❑ 145 Jake Reed .... .50 .23
❑ 146 Jason Sehorn .... .50 .23
❑ 147 Robert Brooks .... .50 .23
❑ 148 J.J. Stokes .... .50 .23
❑ 149 Michael Strahan .... .25 .11
❑ 150 Glenn Foley .... .50 .23
❑ NNO Checklist Card .... .25 .11

1999 Topps Stars

	MINT	NRMT
COMPLETE SET (140)	50.00	22.00

❑ 1 Champ Bailey RC .... 1.50 .70
❑ 2 Akili Smith RC 2.50 1.10
❑ 3 Randy Moss 3.00 1.35
❑ 4 Cade McNown RC .... 1.50 .70
❑ 5 Torry Holt RC 3.00 1.35
❑ 6 Troy Edwards RC .... 1.50 .70
❑ 7 David Boston RC 2.50 1.10
❑ 8 Edgerrin James RC 8.00 3.60
❑ 9 Daunte Culpepper RC 8.00 3.60
❑ 10 Tim Couch RC 4.00 1.80
❑ 11 Ricky Williams RC 5.00 2.20
❑ 12 Fred Taylor .... 2.00 .90
❑ 13 Barry Sanders 3.00 1.35
❑ 14 Emmitt Smith .... 2.00 .90
❑ 15 Jerry Rice .... 2.00 .90
❑ 16 Jake Plummer .... 1.50 .70
❑ 17 Terrell Owens .... .75 .35
❑ 18 Eric Moulds .... .75 .35
❑ 19 Dan Marino 3.00 1.35
❑ 20 Steve McNair .... .75 .35
❑ 21 Donovan McNabb RC 5.00 2.20
❑ 22 Curtis Martin .... .75 .35
❑ 23 Peyton Manning 3.00 1.35
❑ 24 Garrison Hearst .... .40 .18
❑ 25 Eddie George .... 1.00 .45
❑ 26 Antonio Freeman .... .75 .35
❑ 27 Doug Flutie .... 1.00 .45
❑ 28 Kevin Faulk RC .... 2.00 .90
❑ 29 Brett Favre 3.00 1.35
❑ 30 Randall Cunningham .... .75 .35
❑ 31 Mark Brunell .... 1.25 .55
❑ 32 Keyshawn Johnson .... .75 .35
❑ 33 Terrell Davis .... 2.00 .90
❑ 34 Drew Bledsoe .... 1.25 .55
❑ 35 Jerome Bettis .... .75 .35
❑ 36 Charlie Batch .... 1.50 .70
❑ 37 Steve Young .... 1.25 .55
❑ 38 Jamal Anderson .... .75 .35
❑ 39 Troy Aikman .... 2.00 .90
❑ 40 John Elway 3.00 1.35
❑ 41 Amos Zereoue RC .... 1.00 .45
❑ 42 J.J. Stokes .... .40 .18
❑ 43 Antowain Smith .... .75 .35
❑ 44 Jimmy Smith .... .40 .18
❑ 45 Shaun King RC 2.50 1.10
❑ 46 Jevon Kearse RC 2.50 1.10
❑ 47 Sedrick Irvin RC .... 1.25 .55
❑ 48 Rod Smith .... .40 .18
❑ 49 Kevin Johnson RC 2.50 1.10
❑ 50 Joey Galloway .... .75 .35
❑ 51 Mike Cloud RC .... 1.00 .45
❑ 52 D'Wayne Bates RC .... 1.00 .45
❑ 53 Peerless Price RC .... 1.50 .70
❑ 54 Herman Moore .... .75 .35
❑ 55 Rob Konrad RC .... 1.00 .45
❑ 56 James Johnson RC .... 1.25 .55
❑ 57 Cecil Collins RC .... 1.25 .55
❑ 58 Wayne Chrebet .... .75 .35
❑ 59 Cris Carter .... .75 .35
❑ 60 Tim Brown .... .75 .35
❑ 61 Frank Wycheck .... .40 .18
❑ 62 Charles Woodson .... .75 .35
❑ 63 Antoine Winfield RC .... 1.00 .45
❑ 64 Ryan Leaf .... .75 .35
❑ 65 Ricky Watters .... .40 .18
❑ 66 Yancey Thigpen .... .20 .09
❑ 67 Michael Westbrook .... .40 .18
❑ 68 Vinny Testaverde .... .40 .18
❑ 69 Kordell Stewart .... .75 .35
❑ 70 Duce Staley .... .75 .35
❑ 71 Shannon Sharpe .... .40 .18
❑ 72 Junior Seau .... .40 .18
❑ 73 Bruce Smith .... .40 .18
❑ 74 Frank Sanders .... .40 .18
❑ 75 Lawrence Phillips .... .40 .18
❑ 76 Robert Smith .... .75 .35
❑ 77 Andre Reed .... .40 .18
❑ 78 Darnay Scott .... .40 .18
❑ 79 Adrian Murrell .... .40 .18
❑ 80 Ricky Proehl .... .20 .09
❑ 81 Zach Thomas .... .40 .18
❑ 82 Deion Sanders .... .75 .35
❑ 83 Andre Rison .... .40 .18
❑ 84 Jake Reed .... .40 .18
❑ 85 Carl Pickens .... .40 .18
❑ 86 John Randle .... .40 .18
❑ 87 Jerome Pathon .... .20 .09
❑ 88 Brock Huard RC .... 2.00 .90
❑ 89 Elvis Grbac .... .40 .18
❑ 90 Curtis Enis .... .75 .35
❑ 91 Rickey Dudley .... .20 .09
❑ 92 Amani Toomer .... .20 .09
❑ 93 Robert Brooks .... .20 .09
❑ 94 Derrick Alexander .... .40 .18
❑ 95 Reidel Anthony .... .20 .09
❑ 96 Mark Chmura .... .20 .09
❑ 97 Trent Dilfer .... .40 .18
❑ 98 Ebenezer Ekuban RC .... 1.00 .45
❑ 99 Tony Banks .... .40 .18
❑ 100 Terry Glenn .... .75 .35
❑ 101 Andre Hastings .... .20 .09
❑ 102 Ike Hilliard .... .40 .18
❑ 103 Michael Irvin .... .40 .18
❑ 104 Napoleon Kaufman .... .75 .35
❑ 105 Dorsey Levens .... .75 .35
❑ 106 Ed McCaffrey .... .40 .18
❑ 107 Natrone Means .... .40 .18
❑ 108 Skip Hicks .... .40 .18
❑ 109 James Jett .... .20 .09
❑ 110 Priest Holmes .... .75 .35
❑ 111 Tim Dwight .... .75 .35
❑ 112 Curtis Conway .... .40 .18
❑ 113 Jeff Blake .... .40 .18
❑ 114 Karim Abdul-Jabbar .... .40 .18
❑ 115 Karsten Bailey RC .... 1.00 .45
❑ 116 Chris Chandler .... .40 .18
❑ 117 Germane Crowell .... .40 .18
❑ 118 Warrick Dunn .... .75 .35
❑ 119 Bert Emanuel .... .40 .18
❑ 120 Jermaine Fazande RC 1.25 .55
❑ 121 Joe Germaine RC .... 1.25 .55
❑ 122 Tony Gonzalez .... .40 .18
❑ 123 Jacquez Green .... .20 .09
❑ 124 Marvin Harrison .... .75 .35
❑ 125 Corey Dillon .... .75 .35
❑ 126 Ben Coates .... .20 .09
❑ 127 Chris Claiborne RC .... 1.00 .45
❑ 128 Isaac Bruce .... .75 .35
❑ 129 Mike Alstott .... .75 .35
❑ 130 Andy Katzenmoyer RC 1.00 .45
❑ 131 Jon Kitna .... .75 .35
❑ 132 Keenan McCardell .... .40 .18
❑ 133 Johnnie Morton .... .40 .18
❑ 134 O.J. McDuffie .... .40 .18
❑ 135 Chris McAlister .... 1.00 .45
❑ 136 Terance Mathis .... .40 .18
❑ 137 Thurman Thomas .... .40 .18
❑ 138 Jermaine Lewis .... .40 .18
❑ 139 Rob Moore .... .40 .18
❑ 140 Brad Johnson .... .75 .35
❑ P1 Pro Bowl Jersey EXCH.. 1.00 .45

2000 Topps Stars

	MINT	NRMT
COMPLETE SET (175)	50.00	22.00

❑ 1 Keyshawn Johnson .... .60 .25
❑ 2 Marcus Robinson .... .60 .25
❑ 3 Antonio Freeman .... .60 .25
❑ 4 Jake Plummer .... .60 .25
❑ 5 Zach Thomas .... .30 .14
❑ 6 Kordell Stewart .... .60 .25
❑ 7 Mike Alstott .... .60 .25
❑ 8 Fred Taylor .... .75 .35
❑ 9 J.J. Stokes .... .30 .14

❑ 10 Emmitt Smith 1.50 .70
❑ 11 Derrick Mayes .30 .14
❑ 12 Stephen Davis .60 .25
❑ 13 Jamal Anderson .60 .25
❑ 14 Antowain Smith .30 .14
❑ 15 Steve Beuerlein .30 .14
❑ 16 Olandis Gary .60 .25
❑ 17 Rickey Dudley .15 .07
❑ 18 Sean Dawkins .15 .07
❑ 19 Mark Brunell 1.00 .45
❑ 20 Brett Favre 2.50 1.10
❑ 21 Jim Harbaugh .30 .14
❑ 22 Darnay Scott .30 .14
❑ 23 Herman Moore .30 .14
❑ 24 Drew Bledsoe 1.00 .45
❑ 25 Priest Holmes .30 .14
❑ 26 Albert Connell .15 .07
❑ 27 Ike Hilliard .30 .14
❑ 28 Charlie Garner .30 .14
❑ 29 Jimmy Smith .30 .14
❑ 30 Randy Moss 2.00 .90
❑ 31 Peerless Price .60 .25
❑ 32 Terrell Davis 1.50 .70
❑ 33 Troy Edwards .30 .14
❑ 34 Kevin Dyson .30 .14
❑ 35 O.J. McDuffie .30 .14
❑ 36 Troy Aikman 1.50 .70
❑ 37 Frank Sanders .30 .14
❑ 38 Bobby Engram .15 .07
❑ 39 Tyrone Wheatley .30 .14
❑ 40 Ricky Williams 1.50 .70
❑ 41 Warrick Dunn .60 .25
❑ 42 Elvis Grbac .30 .14
❑ 43 Dorsey Levens .30 .14
❑ 44 Curtis Conway .30 .14
❑ 45 Johnnie Morton .30 .14
❑ 46 Ed McCaffrey .60 .25
❑ 47 Kevin Johnson .60 .25
❑ 48 Muhsin Muhammad .30 .14
❑ 49 Terance Mathis .30 .14
❑ 50 Eddie George .75 .35
❑ 51 Daunte Culpepper 1.25 .55
❑ 52 Jeff Graham .15 .07
❑ 53 Jon Kitna .60 .25
❑ 54 Marvin Harrison .60 .25
❑ 55 Steve McNair .60 .25
❑ 56 Jeff Blake .30 .14
❑ 57 Carl Pickens .30 .14
❑ 58 Germane Crowell .30 .14
❑ 59 Rob Moore .30 .14
❑ 60 Marshall Faulk .75 .35
❑ 61 Jerome Bettis .60 .25
❑ 62 Michael Westbrook .30 .14
❑ 63 Keenan McCardell .30 .14
❑ 64 Shannon Sharpe .30 .14
❑ 65 Rod Smith .30 .14
❑ 66 Curtis Enis .30 .14
❑ 67 Vinny Testaverde .30 .14
❑ 68 Freddie Jones .15 .07
❑ 69 Jevon Kearse .60 .25
❑ 70 Jerry Rice 1.50 .70
❑ 71 Champ Bailey .30 .14
❑ 72 Peyton Manning 2.00 .90
❑ 73 Rich Gannon .30 .14
❑ 74 Cris Carter .60 .25
❑ 75 Doug Flutie .75 .35
❑ 76 Corey Dillon .60 .25
❑ 77 Tony Gonzalez .30 .14
❑ 78 Shaun King 1.00 .45
❑ 79 Terrell Owens .60 .25
❑ 80 Dan Marino 2.50 1.10
❑ 81 Curtis Martin .60 .25
❑ 82 Patrick Jeffers .60 .25
❑ 83 Brian Griese .75 .35
❑ 84 Akili Smith .60 .25
❑ 85 Charlie Batch .60 .25
❑ 86 Tim Dwight .60 .25
❑ 87 Robert Smith .60 .25
❑ 88 Duce Staley .60 .25
❑ 89 Jacquez Green .30 .14
❑ 90 Steve Young 1.00 .45
❑ 91 Tony Martin .30 .14
❑ 92 Az-Zahir Hakim .30 .14
❑ 93 Tim Brown .60 .25
❑ 94 Donovan McNabb 1.00 .45
❑ 95 Chris Chandler .30 .14
❑ 96 Tim Couch 1.25 .55
❑ 97 Tim Biakabutuka .30 .14
❑ 98 Terry Glenn .30 .14
❑ 99 Wayne Chrebet .30 .14
❑ 100 Kurt Warner 2.50 1.10
❑ 101 Qadry Ismail .15 .07
❑ 102 Torry Holt .60 .25
❑ 103 Ray Lucas .60 .25
❑ 104 James Johnson .30 .14
❑ 105 Errict Rhett .30 .14
❑ 106 James Stewart .30 .14
❑ 107 Tony Banks .30 .14
❑ 108 Amani Toomer .15 .07
❑ 109 Isaac Bruce .60 .25
❑ 110 Brad Johnson .60 .25
❑ 111 Kerry Collins .30 .14
❑ 112 Eric Moulds .60 .25
❑ 113 Rocket Ismail .30 .14
❑ 114 Keith Poole .15 .07
❑ 115 Rob Johnson .30 .14
❑ 116 Deion Sanders .60 .25
❑ 117 Ricky Watters .30 .14
❑ 118 Cade McNown .60 .25
❑ 119 Joey Galloway .60 .25
❑ 120 Edgerrin James 2.50 1.10
❑ 121 Franco Harris 1.00 .45
❑ 122 Steve Largent 1.00 .45
❑ 123 Joe Montana 4.00 1.80
❑ 124 Deacon Jones .60 .25
❑ 125 Ronnie Lott .60 .25
❑ 126 Mark Brunell HH .60 .25
❑ 127 Rich Gannon HH .15 .07
❑ 128 Tony Gonzalez HH .15 .07
❑ 129 Randy Moss HH 1.25 .55
❑ 130 Kurt Warner HH 1.50 .70
❑ 131 Marvin Harrison HH .30 .14
❑ 132 Jimmy Smith HH .15 .07
❑ 133 Edgerrin James HH 1.50 .70
❑ 134 Corey Dillon HH .30 .14
❑ 135 Peyton Manning HH 1.25 .55
❑ 136 Brad Johnson HH .30 .14
❑ 137 Steve Beuerlein HH .15 .07
❑ 138 Emmitt Smith HH 1.00 .45
❑ 139 Marshall Faulk HH .30 .14
❑ 140 Mike Alstott HH .30 .14
❑ 141 Deacon Jones HH .30 .14
❑ 142 Joe Montana HH 3.00 1.35
❑ 143 Jim Brown HH .60 .25
❑ 144 Steve Largent HH .60 .25
❑ 145 Ronnie Lott HH .30 .14
❑ 146 Chad Pennington HF 2.00 .90
❑ 147 Peter Warrick HF 2.00 .90
❑ 148 Plaxico Burress HF 1.25 .55
❑ 149 Thomas Jones HF 1.00 .45
❑ 150 Jamal Lewis HF 3.00 1.35
❑ 151 Travis Taylor RC 1.00 .45
❑ 152 Shaun Alexander RC 2.00 .90
❑ 153 Dez White RC .60 .25
❑ 154 Thomas Jones RC 1.25 .55
❑ 155 Curtis Keaton RC .50 .23
❑ 156 Courtney Brown RC 1.00 .45
❑ 157 Danny Farmer RC .75 .35
❑ 158 Trung Canidate RC .75 .35
❑ 159 R.Jay Soward RC .75 .35
❑ 160 Jamal Lewis RC 4.00 1.80
❑ 161 Todd Pinkston RC .75 .35
❑ 162 Reuben Droughns RC .75 .35
❑ 163 Ron Dugans RC .60 .25
❑ 164 Ron Dayne RC 2.50 1.10
❑ 165 Laveranues Coles RC 1.25 .55
❑ 166 Sylvester Morris RC 1.50 .70
❑ 167 Peter Warrick RC 2.50 1.10
❑ 168 Dennis Northcutt RC 1.00 .45
❑ 169 Tee Martin RC 1.25 .55
❑ 170 Brian Urlacher RC 2.50 1.10
❑ 171 Chris Redman RC 1.50 .70
❑ 172 Chad Pennington RC 2.50 1.10
❑ 173 J.R. Redmond RC 1.00 .45
❑ 174 Travis Prentice RC 1.25 .55
❑ 175 Plaxico Burress RC 1.50 .70

2001 Topps XFL

	MINT	NRMT
COMPLETE SET (100)	30.00	13.50

❑ 1 Mike Pawlawski 2.00 .90
❑ 2 Todd Doxzon .30 .14
❑ 3 James Bostic 1.00 .45
❑ 4 Jim Druckenmiller 1.00 .45
❑ 5 Mario Bailey .30 .14
❑ 6 Mike Cawley .50 .23
❑ 7 Dino Philyaw .30 .14
❑ 8 Aaron Bailey .50 .23
❑ 9 Juan Johnson 1.00 .45
❑ 10 Kaipo McGuire .30 .14
❑ 11 Toya Jones .30 .14
❑ 12 Todd Floyd .30 .14
❑ 13 Jamie Baisley .30 .14
❑ 14 Brian Shay 1.00 .45
❑ 15 Eric England .30 .14
❑ 16 Curtis Alexander .30 .14
❑ 17 Tim Lester 1.00 .45
❑ 18 Dialleo Burks 1.00 .45
❑ 19 Charles Puleri 1.00 .45
❑ 20 Zechariah Lord .30 .14
❑ 21 Chrys Chukwuma .30 .14
❑ 22 Rickey Brady .50 .23
❑ 23 Rashaan Salaam 2.00 .90
❑ 24 Jermaine Copeland .50 .23
❑ 25 Butler B'Ynot'e .30 .14
❑ 26 Tommy Maddox 2.00 .90
❑ 27 Mike Furrey .50 .23
❑ 28 Ed Smith .30 .14
❑ 29 Pat Barnes 1.00 .45
❑ 30 James Hundon .50 .23
❑ 31 John Avery 2.00 .90
❑ 32 James Willis .30 .14
❑ 33 Larry Ryans .30 .14
❑ 34 Vaughn Dunbar .30 .14
❑ 35 John Williams .30 .14
❑ 36 Casey Weldon 1.00 .45
❑ 37 Roell Preston .50 .23
❑ 38 Jeff Brohm 1.00 .45
❑ 39 Rashaan Shehee .50 .23
❑ 40 Kevin Swayne .50 .23
❑ 41 Ben Snell .30 .14
❑ 42 James Williams UER .30 .14
(College listed as NC)
❑ 43 Corte McGuffey .50 .23
❑ 44 Charles Jordan .50 .23
❑ 45 Frank Leatherwood .30 .14
❑ 46 Dwayne Sabb .30 .14
❑ 47 Shannon Culver .30 .14
❑ 48 Brent Moss .50 .23
❑ 49 Zola Davis .30 .14
❑ 50 Ryan Clement 1.00 .45
❑ 51 Tyji Armstrong .30 .14
❑ 52 Paul Failla .30 .14
❑ 53 Michael Blair .50 .23
❑ 54 Corey Ivy .30 .14
❑ 55 Daryl Hobbs .50 .23
❑ 56 Paul Lacoste .30 .14
❑ 57 Damon Gourdine .30 .14
❑ 58 Wendell Davis .30 .14
❑ 59 Joe Cummings .30 .14
❑ 60 Stephen Fisher .30 .14
❑ 61 Stepfret Williams 1.00 .45
❑ 62 Brandon Sanders .30 .14
❑ 63 Michael Black .50 .23
❑ 64 Scott Milanovich 1.00 .45
❑ 65 Brian Roche .30 .14
❑ 66 Darnell McDonald .50 .23

❑ 67 Marcus Hinton	.30	.14
❑ 68 Quincy Jackson	.50	.23
❑ 69 Roosevelt Potts	.50	.23
❑ 70 Rod Smart	2.00	.90
❑ 71 Keith Elias	.30	.14
❑ 72 Latario Rachal	.30	.14
❑ 73 Mike Sutton	.30	.14
❑ 74 Kirby DarDar	.50	.23
❑ 75 Derrick Clark	.50	.23
❑ 76 Antonio Edwards	.30	.14
❑ 77 Marcus Crandell	.50	.23
❑ 78 Jerry Crafts	.30	.14
❑ 79 Brian Roberson	.50	.23
❑ 80 Las Vegas vs New York LB	.30	.14
❑ 81 Orlando vs Chicago LB	.30	.14
❑ 82 S.F. vs L.A. LB	.30	.14
❑ 83 Memp. vs Birm. LB	.30	.14
❑ 84 Kat GF	.30	.14
❑ 85 Rose GF	.30	.14
❑ 86 Dana GF	.30	.14
❑ 87 Lisa Michelle GF	.30	.14
❑ 88 Kiushin GF	.30	.14
❑ 89 Youn GF	.30	.14
❑ 90 Sunni GF	.30	.14
❑ 91 Cicely GF	.30	.14
❑ 92 Tanisha GF	.30	.14
❑ 93 Krissy GF	.30	.14
❑ 94 TK GF	.30	.14
❑ 95 Jensi GF	.30	.14
❑ 96 Jenny GF	.30	.14
❑ 97 Karla GF	.30	.14
❑ 98 Jenny GF	.30	.14
❑ 99 Susanne GF	.30	.14
❑ 100 Checklist	.30	.14

1997 UD3

	MINT	NRMT
COMPLETE SET (90)	50.00	22.00
❑ 1 Orlando Pace RC	1.00	.45
❑ 2 Walter Jones RC	.30	.14
❑ 3 Tony Gonzalez RC	3.00	1.35
❑ 4 David LaFleur RC	.60	.25
❑ 5 Jim Druckenmiller RC	1.00	.45
❑ 6 Jake Plummer RC	6.00	2.70
❑ 7 Pat Barnes RC	.60	.25
❑ 8 Ike Hilliard RC	1.50	.70
❑ 9 Reidel Anthony RC	1.50	.70
❑ 10 Rae Carruth RC	1.00	.45
❑ 11 Yatil Green RC	.60	.25
❑ 12 Joey Kent RC	1.00	.45
❑ 13 Will Blackwell RC	1.00	.45
❑ 14 Kevin Lockett RC	.60	.25
❑ 15 Warrick Dunn RC	3.00	1.35
❑ 16 Antowain Smith RC	2.00	.90
❑ 17 Troy Davis RC	1.00	.45
❑ 18 Byron Hanspard RC	1.00	.45
❑ 19 Corey Dillon RC	6.00	2.70
❑ 20 Darnell Autry RC	.60	.25
❑ 21 Peter Boulware RC	.60	.25
❑ 22 Darrell Russell RC	.30	.14
❑ 23 Kenny Holmes RC	1.00	.45
❑ 24 Reinard Wilson RC	.30	.14
❑ 25 Renaldo Wynn RC	.30	.14
❑ 26 Dwayne Rudd RC	1.00	.45
❑ 27 James Farrior RC	.30	.14
❑ 28 Shawn Springs RC	.60	.25
❑ 29 Bryant Westbrook RC	.30	.14
❑ 30 Tom Knight RC	.30	.14
❑ 31 Barry Sanders EC	5.00	2.20
❑ 32 Brett Favre EC	5.00	2.20
❑ 33 Brian Mitchell EC	.30	.14
❑ 34 Curtis Martin EC	1.50	.70
❑ 35 Dan Marino EC	5.00	2.20
❑ 36 Deion Sanders EC	1.00	.45
❑ 37 Drew Bledsoe EC	2.50	1.10
❑ 38 Eddie George EC	2.50	1.10
❑ 39 Edgar Bennett EC	.30	.14
❑ 40 Emmitt Smith EC	4.00	1.80
❑ 41 Isaac Bruce EC	1.00	.45
❑ 42 Jerome Bettis EC	1.00	.45
❑ 43 Jerry Rice EC	2.50	1.10
❑ 44 John Elway EC	5.00	2.20
❑ 45 Junior Seau EC	.60	.25
❑ 46 Karim Abdul-Jabbar EC	1.00	.45
❑ 47 Kerry Collins EC	.60	.25
❑ 48 Marshall Faulk EC	1.00	.45
❑ 49 Marvin Harrison EC	1.00	.45
❑ 50 Michael Irvin EC	1.00	.45
❑ 51 Natrone Means EC	1.00	.45
❑ 52 Reggie White EC	1.00	.45
❑ 53 Ricky Watters EC	.60	.25
❑ 54 Stan Humphries EC	.60	.25
❑ 55 Steve Young EC	1.50	.70
❑ 56 Terry Glenn EC	1.00	.45
❑ 57 Thurman Thomas EC	1.00	.45
❑ 58 Tony Martin EC	.60	.25
❑ 59 Troy Aikman EC	2.50	1.10
❑ 60 Vinny Testaverde EC	.60	.25
❑ 61 Anthony Johnson PH	.30	.14
❑ 62 Bobby Engram EC	.60	.25
❑ 63 Carl Pickens PH	.60	.25
❑ 64 Cris Carter PH	.60	.25
❑ 65 Derrick Witherspoon PH	.30	.14
❑ 66 Eddie Kennison PH	.60	.25
❑ 67 Eric Swann PH	.30	.14
❑ 68 Gus Frerotte PH	.60	.25
❑ 69 Herman Moore PH	1.00	.45
❑ 70 Irving Fryar PH	.60	.25
❑ 71 Jamal Anderson PH	1.50	.70
❑ 72 Jeff Blake PH	1.00	.45
❑ 73 Jim Harbaugh PH	.60	.25
❑ 74 Joey Galloway PH	1.25	.55
❑ 76 Kevin Greene PH	.60	.25
❑ 77 Keyshawn Johnson PH	1.00	.45
❑ 78 Kordell Stewart PH	1.25	.55
❑ 79 Marcus Allen PH	1.00	.45
❑ 80 Mario Bates PH	.30	.14
❑ 81 Mark Brunell PH	2.50	1.10
❑ 82 Michael Jackson PH	.60	.25
❑ 83 Mike Alstott PH	1.00	.45
❑ 84 Scott Mitchell PH	.60	.25
❑ 85 Shannon Sharpe PH	.60	.25
❑ 86 Steve McNair PH	1.50	.70
❑ 87 Terrell Davis PH	5.00	2.20
❑ 87 Keenan McCardell PH	.60	.25
❑ 88 Tim Brown PH	1.00	.45
❑ 89 Ty Detmer PH	.60	.25
❑ 90 Tyrone Wheatley PH	.60	.25

1998 UD3

	MINT	NRMT
COMPLETE SET (270)	800.00	350.00
COMP.FS EMB.(30)	150.00	70.00
COMMON FS EMB.(1-30)	2.50	1.10
COMP.NW EMB.(30)	30.00	13.50
COMMON NW EMB.(31-60)	1.50	.70
COMP.UR EMB.(30)	40.00	18.00
COMMON UR EMB.(61-90)	.75	.35
COMP.FS FX (30)	250.00	110.00
COMMON FS FX (91-120)	4.00	1.80
COMP.NW FX (30)	15.00	6.75
COMMON NW FX (121-150)	.75	.35
COMP.UR FX (30)	100.00	45.00
COMMON UR FX (151-180)	2.00	.90
COMP.FS RBW.(30)	60.00	27.00
COMMON FS RBW.(181-210)	1.00	.45
COMP.NW RBW.(30)	60.00	27.00
COMMON NW RBW.(211-240)	3.00	1.35
COMP.UR RBW.(30)	200.00	90.00
COMMON UR RBW.(241-270)	4.00	1.80
❑ 1 Peyton Manning FE	25.00	11.00
❑ 2 Ryan Leaf FE	8.00	3.60
❑ 3 Andre Wadsworth FE	4.00	1.80
❑ 4 Charles Woodson FE	6.00	2.70
❑ 5 Curtis Enis FE	5.00	2.20
❑ 6 Grant Wistrom FE	4.00	1.80
❑ 7 Greg Ellis FE	2.50	1.10
❑ 8 Fred Taylor FE	10.00	4.50
❑ 9 Duane Starks FE	2.50	1.10
❑ 10 Keith Brooking FE	4.00	1.80
❑ 11 Takeo Spikes FE	4.00	1.80
❑ 12 Jason Peter FE	2.50	1.10
❑ 13 Anthony Simmons FE	2.50	1.10
❑ 14 Kevin Dyson FE	6.00	2.70
❑ 15 Brian Simmons FE	2.50	1.10
❑ 16 Robert Edwards FE	5.00	2.20
❑ 17 Randy Moss FE	25.00	11.00
❑ 18 John Avery FE	5.00	2.20
❑ 19 Marcus Nash FE	5.00	2.20
❑ 20 Jerome Pathon FE	4.00	1.80
❑ 21 Jacquez Green FE	6.00	2.70
❑ 22 Robert Holcombe FE	5.00	2.20
❑ 23 Pat Johnson FE	4.00	1.80
❑ 24 Germane Crowell FE	8.00	3.60
❑ 25 Joe Jurevicius FE	4.00	1.80
❑ 26 Skip Hicks FE	4.00	1.80
❑ 27 Ahman Green FE	8.00	3.60
❑ 28 Brian Griese FE	12.00	5.50
❑ 29 Hines Ward FE	4.00	1.80
❑ 30 Tavian Banks FE	5.00	2.20
❑ 31 Warrick Dunn NE	3.00	1.35
❑ 32 Jake Plummer NE	10.00	4.50
❑ 33 Derrick Mayes NE	3.00	1.35
❑ 34 Napoleon Kaufman NE	3.00	1.35
❑ 35 Jamal Anderson NE	3.00	1.35
❑ 36 Marvin Harrison NE	3.00	1.35
❑ 37 Jermaine Lewis NE	3.00	1.35
❑ 38 Corey Dillon NE	5.00	2.20
❑ 39 Keyshawn Johnson NE	3.00	1.35
❑ 40 Mike Alstott NE	3.00	1.35
❑ 41 Bobby Hoying NE	3.00	1.35
❑ 42 Keenan McCardell NE	3.00	1.35
❑ 43 Will Blackwell NE	1.50	.70
❑ 44 Peter Boulware NE	1.50	.70
❑ 45 Tony Banks NE	3.00	1.35
❑ 46 Rod Smith WR NE	3.00	1.35
❑ 47 Tony Gonzalez NE	3.00	1.35
❑ 48 Antowain Smith NE	3.00	1.35
❑ 49 Rae Carruth NE	3.00	1.35
❑ 50 J.J. Stokes NE	3.00	1.35
❑ 51 Brad Johnson NE	3.00	1.35
❑ 52 Shawn Springs NE	1.50	.70
❑ 53 Elvis Grbac NE	1.50	.70
❑ 54 Jimmy Smith NE	3.00	1.35
❑ 55 Terry Glenn NE	3.00	1.35
❑ 56 Tiki Barber NE	3.00	1.35
❑ 57 Gus Frerotte NE	1.50	.70
❑ 58 Danny Wuerffel NE	3.00	1.35
❑ 59 Fred Lane NE	3.00	1.35
❑ 60 Todd Collins NE	1.50	.70
❑ 61 Barry Sanders UE	8.00	3.60
❑ 62 Troy Aikman UE	4.00	1.80
❑ 63 Dan Marino UE	8.00	3.60
❑ 64 Drew Bledsoe UE	3.00	1.35
❑ 65 Dorsey Levens UE	1.50	.70
❑ 66 Jerome Bettis UE	1.50	.70
❑ 67 John Elway UE	8.00	3.60
❑ 68 Steve Young UE	2.50	1.10

❑ 69 Terrell Davis UE 6.00 2.70
❑ 70 Kordell Stewart UE 1.50 .70
❑ 71 Jeff George UE 1.50 .70
❑ 72 Emmitt Smith UE 6.00 2.70
❑ 73 Irving Fryar UE .75 .35
❑ 74 Brett Favre UE 8.00 3.60
❑ 75 Eddie George UE 3.00 1.35
❑ 76 Terry Allen UE 1.50 .70
❑ 77 Warren Moon UE 1.50 .70
❑ 78 Mark Brunell UE 3.00 1.35
❑ 79 Robert Smith UE 1.50 .70
❑ 80 Jerry Rice UE 4.00 1.80
❑ 81 Tim Brown UE 1.50 .70
❑ 82 Carl Pickens UE 1.50 .70
❑ 83 Joey Galloway UE 1.50 .70
❑ 84 Herman Moore UE 1.50 .70
❑ 85 Adrian Murrell UE 1.50 .70
❑ 86 Thurman Thomas UE 1.50 .70
❑ 87 Robert Brooks UE 1.50 .70
❑ 88 Michael Irvin UE 1.50 .70
❑ 89 Andre Rison UE 1.50 .70
❑ 90 Marshall Faulk UE 1.50 .70
❑ 91 Peyton Manning FF 40.00 18.00
❑ 92 Ryan Leaf FF 12.00 5.50
❑ 93 Andre Wadsworth FF 5.00 2.20
❑ 94 Charles Woodson FF 8.00 3.60
❑ 95 Curtis Enis FF 6.00 2.70
❑ 96 Grant Wistrom FF 4.00 1.80
❑ 97 Greg Ellis FF 4.00 1.80
❑ 98 Fred Taylor FF 15.00 6.75
❑ 99 Duane Starks FF 4.00 1.80
❑ 100 Keith Brooking FF 5.00 2.20
❑ 101 Takeo Spikes FF 5.00 2.20
❑ 102 Jason Peter FF 4.00 1.80
❑ 103 Anthony Simmons FF 4.00 1.80
❑ 104 Kevin Dyson FF 8.00 3.60
❑ 105 Brian Simmons FF 4.00 1.80
❑ 106 Robert Edwards FF 6.00 2.70
❑ 107 Randy Moss FF 40.00 18.00
❑ 108 John Avery FF 6.00 2.70
❑ 109 Marcus Nash FF 6.00 2.70
❑ 110 Jerome Pathon FF 5.00 2.20
❑ 111 Jacquez Green FF 8.00 3.60
❑ 112 Robert Holcombe FF 6.00 2.70
❑ 113 Pat Johnson FF 5.00 2.20
❑ 114 Germane Crowell FF 10.00 4.50
❑ 115 Joe Jurevicius FF 5.00 2.20
❑ 116 Skip Hicks FF 5.00 2.20
❑ 117 Ahman Green FF 12.00 5.50
❑ 118 Brian Griese FF 20.00 9.00
❑ 119 Hines Ward FF 5.00 2.20
❑ 120 Tavian Banks FF 5.00 2.20
❑ 121 Warrick Dunn NF 1.50 .70
❑ 122 Jake Plummer NF 5.00 2.20
❑ 123 Derrick Mayes NF 1.50 .70
❑ 124 Napoleon Kaufman NF 1.50 .70
❑ 125 Jamal Anderson NF 1.50 .70
❑ 126 Marvin Harrison NF 1.50 .70
❑ 127 Jermaine Lewis NF 1.50 .70
❑ 128 Corey Dillon NF 2.50 1.10
❑ 129 Keyshawn Johnson NF 1.50 .70
❑ 130 Mike Alstott NF 1.50 .70
❑ 131 Bobby Hoying NF 1.50 .70
❑ 132 Keenan McCardell NF 1.50 .70
❑ 133 Will Blackwell NF .75 .35
❑ 134 Peter Boulware NF .75 .35
❑ 135 Tony Banks NF 1.50 .70
❑ 136 Rod Smith NF 1.50 .70
❑ 137 Tony Gonzalez NF 1.50 .70
❑ 138 Antowain Smith NF 1.50 .70
❑ 139 Rae Carruth NF 1.50 .70
❑ 140 J.J. Stokes NF 1.50 .70
❑ 141 Brad Johnson NF 1.50 .70
❑ 142 Shawn Springs NF .75 .35
❑ 143 Elvis Grbac NF .75 .35
❑ 144 Jimmy Smith NF 1.50 .70
❑ 145 Terry Glenn NF 1.50 .70
❑ 146 Tiki Barber NF 1.50 .70
❑ 147 Gus Frerotte NF .75 .35
❑ 148 Danny Wuerffel NF 1.50 .70
❑ 149 Fred Lane NF 1.50 .70
❑ 150 Todd Collins NF .75 .35
❑ 151 Barry Sanders UF 20.00 9.00
❑ 152 Troy Aikman UF 10.00 4.50
❑ 153 Dan Marino UF 20.00 9.00
❑ 154 Drew Bledsoe UF 8.00 3.60
❑ 155 Dorsey Levens UF 4.00 1.80
❑ 156 Jerome Bettis UF 4.00 1.80
❑ 157 John Elway UF 20.00 9.00
❑ 158 Steve Young UF 6.00 2.70
❑ 159 Terrell Davis UF 15.00 6.75
❑ 160 Kordell Stewart UF 4.00 1.80
❑ 161 Jeff George UF 4.00 1.80
❑ 162 Emmitt Smith UF 15.00 6.75
❑ 163 Irving Fryar UF 2.00 .90
❑ 164 Brett Favre UF 20.00 9.00
❑ 165 Eddie George UF 8.00 3.60
❑ 166 Terry Allen UF 4.00 1.80
❑ 167 Warren Moon UF 4.00 1.80
❑ 168 Mark Brunell UF 8.00 3.60
❑ 169 Robert Smith UF 4.00 1.80
❑ 170 Jerry Rice UF 10.00 4.50
❑ 171 Tim Brown UF 4.00 1.80
❑ 172 Carl Pickens UF 4.00 1.80
❑ 173 Joey Galloway UF 4.00 1.80
❑ 174 Herman Moore UF 4.00 1.80
❑ 175 Adrian Murrell UF 4.00 1.80
❑ 176 Thurman Thomas UF 4.00 1.80
❑ 177 Robert Brooks UF 4.00 1.80
❑ 178 Michael Irvin UF 4.00 1.80
❑ 179 Andre Rison UF 4.00 1.80
❑ 180 Marshall Faulk UF 4.00 1.80
❑ 181 Peyton Manning FR RC 15.00 6.75
❑ 182 Ryan Leaf FR RC 4.00 1.80
❑ 183 Andre Wadsworth FR RC 1.50 .70
❑ 184 Charles Woodson FR RC 3.00 1.35
❑ 185 Curtis Enis FR RC 2.00 .90
❑ 186 Grant Wistrom FR RC 1.00 .45
❑ 187 Greg Ellis FR RC 1.00 .45
❑ 188 Fred Taylor FR RC 5.00 2.20
❑ 189 Duane Starks FR RC 1.00 .45
❑ 190 Keith Brooking FR RC 1.50 .70
❑ 191 Takeo Spikes FR RC 1.50 .70
❑ 192 Jason Peter FR RC 1.00 .45
❑ 193 Anthony Simmons FR RC 1.00 .45
❑ 194 Kevin Dyson FR RC 3.00 1.35
❑ 195 Brian Simmons FR RC 1.00 .45
❑ 196 Robert Edwards FR RC 2.50 1.10
❑ 197 Randy Moss FR RC 15.00 6.75
❑ 198 John Avery FR RC 2.00 .90
❑ 199 Marcus Nash FR RC 2.00 .90
❑ 200 Jerome Pathon FR RC 1.50 .70
❑ 201 Jacquez Green FR RC 3.00 1.35
❑ 202 Robert Holcombe FR RC 2.00 .90
❑ 203 Pat Johnson FR RC 1.50 .70
❑ 204 Germane Crowell FR RC 5.00 2.20
❑ 205 Joe Jurevicius FR RC 1.50 .70
❑ 206 Skip Hicks FR RC 1.50 .70
❑ 207 Ahman Green FR RC 4.00 1.80
❑ 208 Brian Griese FR RC 6.00 2.70
❑ 209 Hines Ward FR RC 1.50 .70
❑ 210 Tavian Banks FR RC 1.50 .70
❑ 211 Warrick Dunn NR 6.00 2.70
❑ 212 Jake Plummer NR 20.00 9.00
❑ 213 Derrick Mayes NR 6.00 2.70
❑ 214 Napoleon Kaufman NR 6.00 2.70
❑ 215 Jamal Anderson NR 6.00 2.70
❑ 216 Marvin Harrison NR 6.00 2.70
❑ 217 Jermaine Lewis NR 6.00 2.70
❑ 218 Corey Dillon NR 10.00 4.50
❑ 219 Keyshawn Johnson NR 6.00 2.70
❑ 220 Mike Alstott NR 6.00 2.70
❑ 221 Bobby Hoying NR 6.00 2.70
❑ 222 Keenan McCardell NR 6.00 2.70
❑ 223 Will Blackwell NR 3.00 1.35
❑ 224 Peter Boulware NR 3.00 1.35
❑ 225 Tony Banks NR 6.00 2.70
❑ 226 Rod Smith NR 6.00 2.70
❑ 227 Tony Gonzalez NR 6.00 2.70
❑ 228 Antowain Smith NR 3.00 1.35
❑ 229 Rae Carruth NR 6.00 2.70
❑ 230 J.J. Stokes NR 6.00 2.70
❑ 231 Brad Johnson NR 6.00 2.70
❑ 232 Shawn Springs NR 3.00 1.35
❑ 233 Elvis Grbac NR 3.00 1.35
❑ 234 Jimmy Smith NR 6.00 2.70
❑ 235 Terry Glenn NR 6.00 2.70
❑ 236 Tiki Barber NR 6.00 2.70
❑ 237 Gus Frerotte NR 3.00 1.35
❑ 238 Danny Wuerffel NR 6.00 2.70
❑ 239 Fred Lane NR 6.00 2.70
❑ 240 Todd Collins NR 3.00 1.35
❑ 241 Barry Sanders UR 40.00 18.00
❑ 242 Troy Aikman UR 20.00 9.00
❑ 243 Dan Marino UR 40.00 18.00
❑ 244 Drew Bledsoe UR 15.00 6.75
❑ 245 Dorsey Levens UR 8.00 3.60
❑ 246 Jerome Bettis UR 8.00 3.60
❑ 247 John Elway UR 40.00 18.00
❑ 248 Steve Young UR 12.00 5.50
❑ 249 Terrell Davis UR 30.00 13.50
❑ 250 Kordell Stewart UR 8.00 3.60
❑ 251 Jeff George UR 8.00 3.60
❑ 252 Emmitt Smith UR 30.00 13.50
❑ 253 Irving Fryar UR 4.00 1.80
❑ 254 Brett Favre UR 40.00 18.00
❑ 255 Eddie George UR 15.00 6.75
❑ 256 Terry Allen UR 8.00 3.60
❑ 257 Warren Moon UR 8.00 3.60
❑ 258 Mark Brunell UR 15.00 6.75
❑ 259 Robert Smith UR 8.00 3.60
❑ 260 Jerry Rice UR 20.00 9.00
❑ 261 Tim Brown UR 8.00 3.60
❑ 262 Carl Pickens UR 8.00 3.60
❑ 263 Joey Galloway UR 8.00 3.60
❑ 264 Herman Moore UR 8.00 3.60
❑ 265 Adrian Murrell UR 8.00 3.60
❑ 266 Thurman Thomas UR 8.00 3.60
❑ 267 Robert Brooks UR 8.00 3.60
❑ 268 Michael Irvin UR 8.00 3.60
❑ 269 Andre Rison UR 8.00 3.60
❑ 270 Marshall Faulk UR 8.00 3.60
❑ P243 Dan Marino UR Promo 3.00 1.35

1998 UD Choice

	MINT	NRMT
COMPLETE SET (438)	70.00	32.00
COMP.SERIES 1 (255)	35.00	16.00
COMP.SERIES 2 (183)	40.00	18.00
COMP.FACT.SER.1 (275)	40.00	18.00

❑ 1 Jake Plummer .60 .25
❑ 2 Rob Moore .20 .09
❑ 3 Simeon Rice .20 .09
❑ 4 Larry Centers .10 .05
❑ 5 Aeneas Williams .10 .05
❑ 6 Chris Gedney .10 .05
❑ 7 Jamal Anderson .40 .18
❑ 8 Michael Booker .10 .05
❑ 9 Ronnie Bradford .10 .05
❑ 10 Cornelius Bennett .10 .05
❑ 11 Terance Mathis .20 .09
❑ 12 Byron Hanspard .20 .09
❑ 13 Peter Boulware .10 .05
❑ 14 Jonathan Ogden .10 .05
❑ 15 Jermaine Lewis .20 .09
❑ 16 Tony Siragusa .10 .05
❑ 17 Brian Kinchen .10 .05
❑ 18 Michael Jackson .10 .05
❑ 19 Doug Flutie .50 .23
❑ 20 Eric Moulds .40 .18
❑ 21 Antowain Smith .40 .18
❑ 22 Bruce Smith .20 .09
❑ 23 Jay Riemersma .10 .05
❑ 24 Ruben Brown .10 .05
❑ 25 Fred Lane .20 .09
❑ 26 Rae Carruth .20 .09
❑ 27 Wesley Walls .20 .09
❑ 28 Winslow Oliver .10 .05

❑ 29 Tyrone Poole .10 .05
❑ 30 Lamar Lathon .10 .05
❑ 31 Anthony Johnson .10 .05
❑ 32 Erik Kramer .10 .05
❑ 33 Darnell Autry .10 .05
❑ 34 Bobby Engram .20 .09
❑ 35 Curtis Conway .20 .09
❑ 36 Jeff Jaeger .10 .05
❑ 37 Chris Penn .10 .05
❑ 38 Corey Dillon .50 .23
❑ 39 Jeff Blake .20 .09
❑ 40 Carl Pickens .40 .18
❑ 41 Ki-Jana Carter .10 .05
❑ 42 Reinard Wilson .10 .05
❑ 43 Tremain Mack .10 .05
❑ 44 Troy Aikman 1.00 .45
❑ 45 Larry Allen .10 .05
❑ 46 Darren Woodson .10 .05
❑ 47 Anthony Miller .10 .05
❑ 48 Erik Williams .10 .05
❑ 49 Deion Sanders .40 .18
❑ 50 Richie Cunningham .10 .05
❑ 51 John Elway 2.00 .90
❑ 52 Steve Atwater .10 .05
❑ 53 Ed McCaffrey .20 .09
❑ 54 Maa Tanuvasa .10 .05
❑ 55 John Mobley .10 .05
❑ 56 Bill Romanowski .10 .05
❑ 57 Shannon Sharpe .20 .09
❑ 58 Scott Mitchell .20 .09
❑ 59 Jason Hanson .10 .05
❑ 60 Herman Moore .40 .18
❑ 61 Luther Elliss .10 .05
❑ 62 Bryant Westbrook .10 .05
❑ 63 Kevin Abrams RC .20 .09
❑ 64 Brett Favre 2.00 .90
❑ 65 Gilbert Brown .10 .05
❑ 66 Antonio Freeman .40 .18
❑ 67 Reggie White .40 .18
❑ 68 Mark Chmura .20 .09
❑ 69 Seth Joyner .10 .05
❑ 70 LeRoy Butler .10 .05
❑ 71 Marvin Harrison .20 .09
❑ 72 Marshall Faulk .40 .18
❑ 73 Ken Dilger .10 .05
❑ 74 Steve Morrison .10 .05
❑ 75 Zack Crockett .10 .05
❑ 76 Quentin Coryatt .10 .05
❑ 77 Keenan McCardell .20 .09
❑ 78 Mark Brunell .75 .35
❑ 79 Renaldo Wynn .10 .05
❑ 80 Jimmy Smith .20 .09
❑ 81 James O. Stewart .20 .09
❑ 82 Kevin Hardy .10 .05
❑ 83 Marcus Allen .40 .18
❑ 84 Andre Rison .20 .09
❑ 85 Pete Stoyanovich .10 .05
❑ 86 Tony Gonzalez .10 .05
❑ 87 Derrick Thomas .20 .09
❑ 88 Rich Gannon .20 .09
❑ 89 Elvis Grbac .20 .09
❑ 90 Dan Marino 2.00 .90
❑ 91 Lawrence Phillips .10 .05
❑ 92 Yatil Green .10 .05
❑ 93 Zach Thomas .20 .09
❑ 94 Olindo Mare RC .10 .05
❑ 95 Charles Jordan .10 .05
❑ 96 Brad Johnson .40 .18
❑ 97 Cris Carter .40 .18
❑ 98 Jake Reed .20 .09
❑ 99 Ed McDaniel .10 .05
❑ 100 Dwayne Rudd .10 .05
❑ 101 Leroy Hoard .10 .05
❑ 102 Danny Wuerffel .20 .09
❑ 103 Troy Davis .10 .05
❑ 104 Andre Hastings .10 .05
❑ 105 Nicky Savoie .10 .05
❑ 106 Willie Roaf .10 .05
❑ 107 Ray Zellars .10 .05
❑ 108 Tedy Bruschi .10 .05
❑ 109 Drew Bledsoe .75 .35
❑ 110 Terry Glenn .40 .18
❑ 111 Ben Coates .20 .09
❑ 112 Willie Clay .10 .05
❑ 113 Chris Slade .10 .05
❑ 114 Larry Whigham .10 .05
❑ 115 Danny Kanell .20 .09
❑ 116 Jessie Armstead .10 .05
❑ 117 Phillippi Sparks .10 .05
❑ 118 Michael Strahan .10 .05
❑ 119 Tiki Barber .20 .09
❑ 120 Charles Way .10 .05
❑ 121 Chris Calloway .10 .05
❑ 122 Glenn Foley .20 .09
❑ 123 Wayne Chrebet .40 .18
❑ 124 Kyle Brady .10 .05
❑ 125 Keyshawn Johnson .40 .18
❑ 126 Aaron Glenn .10 .05
❑ 127 James Farrior .10 .05
❑ 128 Victor Green .10 .05
❑ 129 Jeff George .20 .09
❑ 130 Rickey Dudley .10 .05
❑ 131 Darrell Russell .10 .05
❑ 132 Tim Brown .40 .18
❑ 133 James Trapp .10 .05
❑ 134 Napoleon Kaufman .40 .18
❑ 135 Bobby Hoying .20 .09
❑ 136 Irving Fryar .20 .09
❑ 137 Mike Mamula .10 .05
❑ 138 Troy Vincent .10 .05
❑ 139 Bobby Taylor .10 .05
❑ 140 Chris Boniol .10 .05
❑ 141 Jerome Bettis .40 .18
❑ 142 Charles Johnson .10 .05
❑ 143 Levon Kirkland .10 .05
❑ 144 Carnell Lake .10 .05
❑ 145 Will Blackwell .10 .05
❑ 146 Tim Lester .10 .05
❑ 147 Greg Lloyd .10 .05
❑ 148 Tony Banks .20 .09
❑ 149 Ryan McNeil .10 .05
❑ 150 Orlando Pace .10 .05
❑ 151 Isaac Bruce .40 .18
❑ 152 Eddie Kennison .20 .09
❑ 153 Leslie O'Neal .10 .05
❑ 154 Darren Bennett .10 .05
❑ 155 Natrone Means .40 .18
❑ 156 Junior Seau .20 .09
❑ 157 Tony Martin .20 .09
❑ 158 Rodney Harrison .20 .09
❑ 159 Freddie Jones .10 .05
❑ 160 Terrell Owens .40 .18
❑ 161 Merton Hanks .10 .05
❑ 162 Chris Doleman .10 .05
❑ 163 Steve Young .50 .23
❑ 164 Chuck Levy .10 .05
❑ 165 J.J. Stokes .20 .09
❑ 166 Ken Norton .10 .05
❑ 167 Bennie Blades .10 .05
❑ 168 Chad Brown .10 .05
❑ 169 Warren Moon .40 .18
❑ 170 Cortez Kennedy .10 .05
❑ 171 Darryl Williams .10 .05
❑ 172 Michael Sinclair .10 .05
❑ 173 Trent Dilfer .40 .18
❑ 174 Mike Alstott .40 .18
❑ 175 Warren Sapp .20 .09
❑ 176 Reidel Anthony .20 .09
❑ 177 Derrick Brooks .10 .05
❑ 178 Horace Copeland .10 .05
❑ 179 Hardy Nickerson .10 .05
❑ 180 Steve McNair .40 .18
❑ 181 Anthony Dorsett .10 .05
❑ 182 Chris Sanders .10 .05
❑ 183 Derrick Mason .20 .09
❑ 184 Eddie George .75 .35
❑ 185 Blaine Bishop .10 .05
❑ 186 Gus Frerotte .10 .05
❑ 187 Terry Allen .40 .18
❑ 188 Darrell Green .20 .09
❑ 189 Ken Harvey .10 .05
❑ 190 Matt Turk .10 .05
❑ 191 Cris Dishman .10 .05
❑ 192 Keith Thibodeaux RC .10 .05
❑ 193 Peyton Manning RC 10.00 4.50
❑ 194 Ryan Leaf RC 2.00 .90
❑ 195 Charles Woodson RC 1.50 .70
❑ 196 Andre Wadsworth RC .60 .25
❑ 197 Keith Brooking RC 1.00 .45
❑ 198 Jason Peter RC .40 .18
❑ 199 Curtis Enis RC 1.00 .45
❑ 200 Randy Moss RC 10.00 4.50
❑ 201 Tra Thomas RC .40 .18
❑ 202 Robert Edwards RC 1.25 .55
❑ 203 Kevin Dyson RC 1.50 .70
❑ 204 Fred Taylor RC 2.50 1.10
❑ 205 Corey Chavous RC .40 .18
❑ 206 Grant Wistrom RC .40 .18
❑ 207 Vonnie Holliday RC .60 .25
❑ 208 Brian Simmons RC .40 .18
❑ 209 Jeremy Staat RC .40 .18
❑ 210 Alonzo Mayes RC .40 .18
❑ 211 Anthony Simmons RC .40 .18
❑ 212 Sam Cowart RC .40 .18
❑ 213 Flozell Adams RC .40 .18
❑ 214 Terry Fair RC .60 .25
❑ 215 Germane Crowell RC 2.00 .90
❑ 216 Robert Holcombe RC 1.00 .45
❑ 217 Jacquez Green RC 1.50 .70
❑ 218 Skip Hicks RC 1.00 .45
❑ 219 Takeo Spikes RC .60 .25
❑ 220 Az-Zahir Hakim RC 1.00 .45
❑ 221 Ahman Green RC 2.00 .90
❑ 222 C.Fuamatu-Ma'afala RC .60 .25
❑ 223 Darnell Autry DYOC .10 .05
❑ 224 John Randle DYOC .20 .09
❑ 225 Scott Mitchell DYOC .10 .05
❑ 226 Troy Aikman DYOC .40 .18
❑ 227 Terrell Davis DYOC .40 .18
❑ 228 Kordell Stewart DYOC .40 .18
❑ 229 Warrick Dunn DYOC .40 .18
❑ 230 Craig Newsome DYOC .10 .05
❑ 231 Brett Favre DYOC .50 .23
❑ 232 Kordell Stewart DYOC .40 .18
❑ 233 Barry Sanders DYOC .50 .23
❑ 234 Dan Marino DYOC .50 .23
❑ 235 Dan Marino DYOC .50 .23
❑ 236 Tamarick Vanover DYOC .10 .05
❑ 237 Warrick Dunn DYOC .40 .18
❑ 238 Andre Rison DYOC .10 .05
❑ 239 Dan Marino DYOC .50 .23
❑ 240 Reggie White DYOC .40 .18
❑ 241 Tim Brown DYOC .40 .18
❑ 242 Joe Montana DYOC .50 .23
❑ 243 Robert Brooks DYOC .20 .09
❑ 244 Danny Kanell DYOC .10 .05
❑ 245 Emmitt Smith DYOC .60 .25
❑ 246 Barry Sanders DYOC .75 .35
❑ 247 Brett Favre DYOC .75 .35
❑ 248 Brett Favre DYOC .75 .35
❑ 249 Jerome Bettis DYOC .10 .05
❑ 250 Kordell Stewart DYOC .40 .18
❑ 251 Terrell Davis DYOC .75 .35
❑ 252 Drew Bledsoe DYOC .40 .18
❑ 253 Troy Aikman CL .40 .18
❑ 254 Dan Marino CL .75 .35
❑ 255 Warrick Dunn CL .40 .18
❑ 256 Peyton Manning DN 10.00 4.50
❑ 257 Ryan Leaf DN 2.50 1.10
❑ 258 Andre Wadsworth DN 1.50 .70
❑ 259 Charles Woodson DN 2.00 .90
❑ 260 Curtis Enis DN 2.00 .90
❑ 261 Grant Wistrom DN 1.00 .45
❑ 262 Greg Ellis DN RC 1.00 .45
❑ 263 Fred Taylor DN 2.50 1.10
❑ 264 Duane Starks DN RC 1.00 .45
❑ 265 Keith Brooking DN 1.50 .70
❑ 266 Takeo Spikes DN 1.50 .70
❑ 267 Anthony Simmons DN 1.00 .45
❑ 268 Kevin Dyson DN 2.00 .90
❑ 269 Robert Edwards DN 2.00 .90
❑ 270 Randy Moss DN 10.00 4.50
❑ 271 John Avery DN RC 2.00 .90
❑ 272 Marcus Nash DN RC 2.00 .90
❑ 273 Jerome Pathon DN RC 1.50 .70
❑ 274 Jacquez Green DN 2.00 .90
❑ 275 Robert Holcombe DN 2.00 .90
❑ 276 Pat Johnson DN RC 1.50 .70
❑ 277 Germane Crowell DN 2.50 1.10
❑ 278 Tony Simmons DN RC 1.50 .70
❑ 279 Joe Jurevicius DN RC 1.50 .70
❑ 280 Skip Hicks DN 1.50 .70
❑ 281 Sam Cowart DN 1.00 .45
❑ 282 Rashaan Shehee DN RC 1.50 .70
❑ 283 Brian Griese DN RC 8.00 3.60
❑ 284 Tim Dwight DN RC 4.00 1.80
❑ 285 Ahman Green DN 2.50 1.10
❑ 286 Adrian Murrell .20 .09

❑ 287	Corey Chavous	.20	.09
❑ 288	Eric Swann	.10	.05
❑ 289	Frank Sanders	.20	.09
❑ 290	Eric Metcalf	.10	.05
❑ 291	Jammi German RC	.40	.18
❑ 292	Eugene Robinson	.10	.05
❑ 293	Chris Chandler	.20	.09
❑ 294	Tony Martin	.20	.09
❑ 295	Jessie Tuggle	.10	.05
❑ 296	Errict Rhett	.20	.09
❑ 297	Jim Harbaugh	.20	.09
❑ 298	Eric Green	.20	.09
❑ 299	Ray Lewis	.40	.18
❑ 300	Jamie Sharper	.10	.05
❑ 301	Fred Coleman RC	.40	.18
❑ 302	Rob Johnson	.20	.09
❑ 303	Quinn Early	.10	.05
❑ 304	Thurman Thomas	.40	.18
❑ 305	Andre Reed	.20	.09
❑ 306	Sean Gilbert	.10	.05
❑ 307	Kerry Collins	.20	.09
❑ 308	Jason Peter	.10	.05
❑ 309	Michael Bates	.10	.05
❑ 310	William Floyd	.20	.09
❑ 311	Alonzo Mayes RC	.40	.18
❑ 312	Tony Parrish RC	.40	.18
❑ 313	Walt Harris	.10	.05
❑ 314	Edgar Bennett	.10	.05
❑ 315	Jeff Jaeger	.10	.05
❑ 316	Brian Simmons	.20	.09
❑ 317	David Dunn	.10	.05
❑ 318	Ashley Ambrose	.10	.05
❑ 319	Darnay Scott	.20	.09
❑ 320	Neil O'Donnell	.20	.09
❑ 321	Flozell Adams	.20	.09
❑ 322	Stepfret Williams	.10	.05
❑ 323	Emmitt Smith	1.50	.70
❑ 324	Michael Irvin	.40	.18
❑ 325	Chris Warren	.20	.09
❑ 326	Eric Brown RC	.40	.18
❑ 327	Rod Smith WR	.20	.09
❑ 328	Terrell Davis	1.50	.70
❑ 329	Neil Smith	.20	.09
❑ 330	Darrien Gordon	.10	.05
❑ 331	Curtis Alexander RC	.40	.18
❑ 332	Barry Sanders	2.00	.90
❑ 333	David Sloan	.10	.05
❑ 334	Johnnie Morton	.20	.09
❑ 335	Robert Porcher	.10	.05
❑ 336	Tommy Vardell	.10	.05
❑ 337	Vonnie Holliday	.20	.09
❑ 338	Dorsey Levens	.40	.18
❑ 339	Derrick Mayes	.20	.09
❑ 340	Robert Brooks	.20	.09
❑ 341	Raymont Harris	.10	.05
❑ 342	E.G. Green RC	.60	.25
❑ 343	Carlton Gray	.10	.05
❑ 344	Albert Fontenot	.10	.05
❑ 345	Aaron Bailey	.10	.05
❑ 346	Jeff Burris	.10	.05
❑ 347	Donovin Darius RC	.40	.18
❑ 348	Tavian Banks RC	.20	.09
❑ 349	Aaron Beasley RC	.40	.18
❑ 350	Tony Brackens	.10	.05
❑ 351	Bryce Paup	.10	.05
❑ 352	Chester McGlockton	.10	.05
❑ 353	Leslie O'Neal	.10	.05
❑ 354	Derrick Alexander WR	.20	.09
❑ 355	Kimble Anders	.20	.09
❑ 356	Tamarick Vanover	.10	.05
❑ 357	Brock Marion	.10	.05
❑ 358	Larry Shannon RC	.40	.18
❑ 359	Karim Abdul-Jabbar	.40	.18
❑ 360	Troy Drayton	.10	.05
❑ 361	O.J. McDuffie	.20	.09
❑ 362	John Randle	.20	.09
❑ 363	David Palmer	.10	.05
❑ 364	Robert Smith	.40	.18
❑ 365	Kailee Wong RC	.40	.18
❑ 366	Duane Clemons	.10	.05
❑ 367	Kyle Turley RC	.40	.18
❑ 368	Sean Dawkins	.10	.05
❑ 369	Lamar Smith	.20	.09
❑ 370	Cameron Cleeland RC	.60	.25
❑ 371	Keith Poole	.10	.05
❑ 372	Tebucky Jones RC	.40	.18
❑ 373	Willie McGinest	.10	.05
❑ 374	Ty Law	.10	.05
❑ 375	Lawyer Milloy	.10	.05
❑ 376	Tony Carter	.10	.05
❑ 377	Shaun Williams RC	.40	.18
❑ 378	Brian Alford RC	.60	.25
❑ 379	Tyrone Wheatley	.20	.09
❑ 380	Jason Sehorn	.20	.09
❑ 381	David Patten RC	1.00	.45
❑ 382	Scott Frost RC	.60	.25
❑ 383	Mo Lewis	.10	.05
❑ 384	Kevin Williams DB RC	.40	.18
❑ 385	Curtis Martin	.40	.18
❑ 386	Vinny Testaverde	.20	.09
❑ 387	Mo Collins RC	.40	.18
❑ 388	James Jett	.20	.09
❑ 389	Eric Allen	.10	.05
❑ 390	Jon Ritchie RC UER (John on back)	.60	.25
❑ 391	Harvey Williams	.10	.05
❑ 392	Tra Thomas	.10	.05
❑ 393	Rodney Peete	.10	.05
❑ 394	Hugh Douglas UER (card #395 on back)	.10	.05
❑ 395	Charlie Garner	.10	.05
❑ 396	Karl Hankton RC	.40	.18
❑ 397	Kordell Stewart	.40	.18
❑ 398	George Jones	.10	.05
❑ 399	Earl Holmes	.10	.05
❑ 400	Hines Ward RC	.60	.25
❑ 401	Jason Gildon	.10	.05
❑ 402	Ricky Proehl	.10	.05
❑ 403	Az-Zahir Hakim	.10	.05
❑ 404	Amp Lee	.10	.05
❑ 405	Eric Hill	.10	.05
❑ 406	Leonard Little RC	.40	.18
❑ 407	Charlie Jones	.10	.05
❑ 408	Craig Whelihan RC	.10	.05
❑ 409	Terrell Fletcher	.10	.05
❑ 410	Kenny Bynum RC	.40	.18
❑ 411	Mikhael Ricks RC	.60	.25
❑ 412	R.W. McQuarters RC	.40	.18
❑ 413	Jerry Rice	1.00	.45
❑ 414	Garrison Hearst	.40	.18
❑ 415	Ty Detmer	.20	.09
❑ 416	Gabe Wilkins	.10	.05
❑ 417	Michael Black RC	1.00	.45
❑ 418	James McKnight	.10	.05
❑ 419	Darrin Smith	.10	.05
❑ 420	Joey Galloway	.40	.18
❑ 421	Ricky Watters	.20	.09
❑ 422	Warrick Dunn	.40	.18
❑ 423	Brian Kelly	.10	.05
❑ 424	Bert Emanuel	.20	.09
❑ 425	John Lynch	.20	.09
❑ 426	Regan Upshaw	.10	.05
❑ 427	Yancey Thigpen	.10	.05
❑ 428	Kenny Holmes	.10	.05
❑ 429	Frank Wycheck	.10	.05
❑ 430	Samari Rolle RC	.40	.18
❑ 431	Brian Mitchell	.10	.05
❑ 432	Stephen Alexander	.10	.05
❑ 433	Jamie Asher	.10	.05
❑ 434	Michael Westbrook	.20	.09
❑ 435	Dana Stubblefield	.10	.05
❑ 436	Dan Wilkinson	.10	.05
❑ 437	Dan Marino CL	.60	.25
❑ 438	Jerry Rice CL	.40	.18

2000 UD Graded

		MINT	NRMT
❑ 1	Jake Plummer	3.00	1.35
❑ 2	David Boston	3.00	1.35
❑ 3	Jamal Anderson	3.00	1.35
❑ 4	Shawn Jefferson	1.50	.70
❑ 5	Qadry Ismail	2.00	.90
❑ 6	Tony Banks	2.00	.90
❑ 7	Priest Holmes	2.00	.90
❑ 8	Rob Johnson	2.00	.90
❑ 9	Eric Moulds	3.00	1.35
❑ 10	Steve Beuerlein	2.00	.90
❑ 11	Muhsin Muhammad	2.00	.90
❑ 12	Donald Hayes	1.50	.70
❑ 13	Tim Biakabutuka	2.00	.90
❑ 14	Cade McNown	3.00	1.35

❑ 15	Marcus Robinson	3.00	1.35
❑ 16	James Allen	1.50	.70
❑ 17	Akili Smith	3.00	1.35
❑ 18	Corey Dillon	3.00	1.35
❑ 19	Tim Couch	6.00	2.70
❑ 20	Kevin Johnson	3.00	1.35
❑ 21	Troy Aikman	8.00	3.60
❑ 22	Emmitt Smith	8.00	3.60
❑ 23	Rocket Ismail	2.00	.90
❑ 24	Terrell Davis	8.00	3.60
❑ 25	Rod Smith	2.00	.90
❑ 26	Brian Griese	4.00	1.80
❑ 27	Charlie Batch	3.00	1.35
❑ 28	James Stewart	2.00	.90
❑ 29	Germane Crowell	2.00	.90
❑ 30	Brett Favre	12.00	5.50
❑ 31	Antonio Freeman	3.00	1.35
❑ 32	Dorsey Levens	2.00	.90
❑ 33	Peyton Manning	10.00	4.50
❑ 34	Edgerrin James	12.00	5.50
❑ 35	Marvin Harrison	3.00	1.35
❑ 36	Mark Brunell	5.00	2.20
❑ 37	Jimmy Smith	2.00	.90
❑ 38	Fred Taylor	4.00	1.80
❑ 39	Elvis Grbac	2.00	.90
❑ 40	Tony Gonzalez	2.00	.90
❑ 41	Lamar Smith	2.00	.90
❑ 42	Jay Fiedler	3.00	1.35
❑ 43	Randy Moss	10.00	4.50
❑ 44	Daunte Culpepper	6.00	2.70
❑ 45	Robert Smith	3.00	1.35
❑ 46	Cris Carter	3.00	1.35
❑ 47	Drew Bledsoe	5.00	2.20
❑ 48	Kevin Faulk	2.00	.90
❑ 49	Terry Glenn	3.00	1.35
❑ 50	Ricky Williams	8.00	3.60
❑ 51	Jeff Blake	2.00	.90
❑ 52	Joe Horn	3.00	1.35
❑ 53	Kerry Collins	2.00	.90
❑ 54	Amani Toomer	2.00	.90
❑ 55	Tiki Barber	2.00	.90
❑ 56	Wayne Chrebet	2.00	.90
❑ 57	Curtis Martin	3.00	1.35
❑ 58	Vinny Testaverde	2.00	.90
❑ 59	Tyrone Wheatley	2.00	.90
❑ 60	Tim Brown	3.00	1.35
❑ 61	Rich Gannon	2.00	.90
❑ 62	Duce Staley	3.00	1.35
❑ 63	Charles Johnson	2.00	.90
❑ 64	Donovan McNabb	5.00	2.20
❑ 65	Bobby Shaw RC	1.25	.55
❑ 66	Kordell Stewart	3.00	1.35
❑ 67	Jerome Bettis	3.00	1.35
❑ 68	Marshall Faulk	4.00	1.80
❑ 69	Isaac Bruce	3.00	1.35
❑ 70	Torry Holt	3.00	1.35
❑ 71	Kurt Warner	12.00	5.50
❑ 72	Neil Smith	1.50	.70
❑ 73	Ryan Leaf	3.00	1.35
❑ 74	Curtis Conway	2.00	.90
❑ 75	Jeff Garcia	3.00	1.35
❑ 76	Charlie Garner	2.00	.90
❑ 77	Jerry Rice	8.00	3.60
❑ 78	Ricky Watters	1.50	.70
❑ 79	Brock Huard	2.00	.90
❑ 80	Jon Kitna	3.00	1.35
❑ 81	Keyshawn Johnson	3.00	1.35

Card	MINT	NRMT
❑ 82 Jacquez Green	2.00	.90
❑ 83 Mike Alstott	3.00	1.35
❑ 84 Shaun King	5.00	2.20
❑ 85 Eddie George	4.00	1.80
❑ 86 Kevin Dyson	2.00	.90
❑ 87 Steve McNair	3.00	1.35
❑ 88 Brad Johnson	3.00	1.35
❑ 89 Stephen Davis	3.00	1.35
❑ 90 Jeff George	2.00	.90
❑ 91 Ron Dixon RC	10.00	4.50
❑ 92 Avion Black RC	8.00	3.60
❑ 93 Hank Poteat RC	8.00	3.60
❑ 94 Doug Chapman RC	20.00	9.00
❑ 95 Drew Haddad RC	6.00	2.70
❑ 96 Rondell Mealey RC	6.00	2.70
❑ 97 Spergon Wynn RC	10.00	4.50
❑ 98 Keith Bulluck RC	8.00	3.60
❑ 99 John Abraham RC	8.00	3.60
❑ 100 Rob Morris RC	8.00	3.60
❑ 101 Jerry Porter RC	10.00	4.50
❑ 102 Laveranues Coles RC	15.00	6.75
❑ 103 Jarious Jackson RC	10.00	4.50
❑ 104 Tom Brady RC	10.00	4.50
❑ 105 Jonas Lewis RC	6.00	2.70
❑ 106 Todd Husak RC	10.00	4.50
❑ 107 Shyrone Stith RC	8.00	3.60
❑ 108 Sammy Morris RC	12.00	5.50
❑ 109 Corey Simon RC	12.00	5.50
❑ 110 Chad Morton RC	10.00	4.50
❑ 111 Brian Urlacher RC	30.00	13.50
❑ 112 Anthony Becht RC	10.00	4.50
❑ 113 Chris Cole RC	8.00	3.60
❑ 114 Anthony Lucas RC	6.00	2.70
❑ 115 Charles Lee RC	6.00	2.70
❑ 116 JaJuan Dawson RC	12.00	5.50
❑ 117 Darrell Jackson RC	15.00	6.75
❑ 118 Gari Scott RC	8.00	3.60
❑ 119 Windrell Hayes RC	8.00	3.60
❑ 120 Paul Smith RC	8.00	3.60
❑ 121 Mareno Philyaw RC	6.00	2.70
❑ 122 Trevor Gaylor RC	8.00	3.60
❑ 123 Muneer Moore RC	6.00	2.70
❑ 124 Michael Wiley RC	10.00	4.50
❑ 125 Ronney Jenkins RC	8.00	3.60
❑ 126 Frank Moreau RC	10.00	4.50
❑ 127 Dante Hall RC	8.00	3.60
❑ 128 Darren Howard RC	8.00	3.60
❑ 129 Todd Pinkston RC	10.00	4.50
❑ 130 Mike Anderson RC	60.00	27.00
❑ 131 Doug Johnson RC	10.00	4.50
❑ 132 Shaun Ellis RC	8.00	3.60
❑ 133 James Williams RC	8.00	3.60
❑ 134 Ron Dugans RC	10.00	4.50
❑ 135 Frank Murphy RC	6.00	2.70
❑ 136 Dez White RC	30.00	13.50
❑ 137 Danny Farmer RC	30.00	13.50
❑ 140 Reuben Droughns RC	30.00	13.50
❑ 141 Jamal Lewis RC	250.00	110.00
❑ 142 J.R. Redmond RC	40.00	18.00
❑ 143 Tee Martin RC	50.00	22.00
❑ 144 Giovanni Carmazzi RC	40.00	18.00
❑ 145 Tim Rattay RC	50.00	22.00
❑ 146 Trung Canidate RC	30.00	13.50
❑ 149 Chris Coleman RC	20.00	9.00
❑ 150 Corey Moore RC	25.00	11.00
❑ 151 Troy Walters RC	30.00	13.50
❑ 152 Joe Hamilton RC	40.00	18.00
❑ 153 Kwame Cavil RC	25.00	11.00
❑ 154 Dennis Northcutt RC	40.00	18.00
❑ 155 Travis Taylor RC	40.00	18.00
❑ 156 Curtis Keaton RC	30.00	13.50
❑ 157 Shaun Alexander RC	150.00	70.00
❑ 158 Chad Pennington RC	200.00	90.00
❑ 159 Sylvester Morris RC	80.00	36.00
❑ 160 Plaxico Burress RC	80.00	36.00
❑ 161 Ron Dayne RC	200.00	90.00
❑ 162 Courtney Brown RC	50.00	22.00
❑ 164 Peter Warrick RC	200.00	90.00
❑ 165 Chris Redman RC	120.00	55.00

1999 UD Ionix

	MINT	NRMT
COMPLETE SET (90)	120.00	55.00
COMP.SET w/o SP's (60)	25.00	11.00
COMMON ROOKIE (61-90)	2.00	.90

Card	MINT	NRMT
❑ 1 Jake Plummer	2.00	.90
❑ 2 Adrian Murrell	.50	.23
❑ 3 Jamal Anderson	1.00	.45
❑ 4 Chris Chandler	.50	.23
❑ 5 Priest Holmes	1.00	.45
❑ 6 Michael Jackson	.25	.11
❑ 7 Antowain Smith	1.00	.45
❑ 8 Doug Flutie	1.25	.55
❑ 9 Tim Biakabutuka	.50	.23
❑ 10 Muhsin Muhammad	.50	.23
❑ 11 Erik Kramer	.25	.11
❑ 12 Curtis Enis	1.00	.45
❑ 13 Corey Dillon	1.00	.45
❑ 14 Ty Detmer	.50	.23
❑ 15 Justin Armour	.25	.11
❑ 16 Troy Aikman	2.50	1.10
❑ 17 Emmitt Smith	2.50	1.10
❑ 18 John Elway	4.00	1.80
❑ 19 Terrell Davis	2.50	1.10
❑ 20 Barry Sanders	4.00	1.80
❑ 21 Charlie Batch	2.00	.90
❑ 22 Brett Favre	4.00	1.80
❑ 23 Dorsey Levens	1.00	.45
❑ 24 Marshall Faulk	1.00	.45
❑ 25 Peyton Manning	4.00	1.80
❑ 26 Mark Brunell	1.50	.70
❑ 27 Fred Taylor	2.50	1.10
❑ 28 Elvis Grbac	.50	.23
❑ 29 Andre Rison	.50	.23
❑ 30 Dan Marino	4.00	1.80
❑ 31 Karim Abdul-Jabbar	.50	.23
❑ 32 Randall Cunningham	1.00	.45
❑ 33 Randy Moss	4.00	1.80
❑ 34 Drew Bledsoe	1.50	.70
❑ 35 Terry Glenn	1.00	.45
❑ 36 Danny Wuerffel	.25	.11
❑ 37 Kent Graham	.25	.11
❑ 38 Gary Brown	.25	.11
❑ 39 Vinny Testaverde	.50	.23
❑ 40 Keyshawn Johnson	1.00	.45
❑ 41 Napoleon Kaufman	1.00	.45
❑ 42 Tim Brown	1.00	.45
❑ 43 Koy Detmer	.25	.11
❑ 44 Duce Staley	1.00	.45
❑ 45 Kordell Stewart	1.00	.45
❑ 46 Jerome Bettis	1.00	.45
❑ 47 Isaac Bruce	1.00	.45
❑ 48 Robert Holcombe	.50	.23
❑ 49 Jim Harbaugh	.50	.23
❑ 50 Natrone Means	.50	.23
❑ 51 Steve Young	1.50	.70
❑ 52 Jerry Rice	2.50	1.10
❑ 53 Jon Kitna	1.00	.45
❑ 54 Joey Galloway	1.00	.45
❑ 55 Warrick Dunn	1.00	.45
❑ 56 Trent Dilfer	.50	.23
❑ 57 Steve McNair	1.00	.45
❑ 58 Eddie George	1.25	.55
❑ 59 Skip Hicks	1.00	.45
❑ 60 Michael Westbrook	.50	.23
❑ 61 Tim Couch RC	10.00	4.50
❑ 62 Ricky Williams RC	12.00	5.50
❑ 63 Daunte Culpepper RC	15.00	6.75
❑ 64 Akili Smith RC	5.00	2.20
❑ 65 Donovan McNabb RC	12.00	5.50
❑ 66 Michael Bishop RC	3.00	1.35
❑ 67 Brock Huard RC	4.00	1.80
❑ 68 Torry Holt RC	6.00	2.70
❑ 69 Cade McNown RC	3.00	1.35
❑ 70 Shaun King RC	5.00	2.20
❑ 71 Champ Bailey RC	3.00	1.35
❑ 72 Chris Claiborne RC	2.00	.90
❑ 73 Jevon Kearse RC	5.00	2.20
❑ 74 D'Wayne Bates RC	2.00	.90
❑ 75 David Boston RC	5.00	2.20
❑ 76 Edgerrin James RC	15.00	6.75
❑ 77 Sedrick Irvin RC	4.00	1.80
❑ 78 Dameane Douglas RC	2.00	.90
❑ 79 Troy Edwards RC	3.00	1.35
❑ 80 Ebenezer Ekuban RC	2.00	.90
❑ 81 Kevin Faulk RC	4.00	1.80
❑ 82 Joe Germaine RC	4.00	1.80
❑ 83 Kevin Johnson RC	5.00	2.20
❑ 84 Andy Katzenmoyer RC	4.00	1.80
❑ 85 Rob Konrad RC	4.00	1.80
❑ 86 Chris McAlister RC	2.50	1.10
❑ 87 Peerless Price RC	3.00	1.35
❑ 88 Tai Streets RC	4.00	1.80
❑ 89 Autry Denson RC	4.00	1.80
❑ 90 Amos Zereoue RC	4.00	1.80

2000 UD Ionix

	MINT	NRMT
COMPLETE SET (120)	500.00	220.00
❑ 1 Jake Plummer	.40	.18
❑ 2 Jamal Anderson	.40	.18
❑ 3 Qadry Ismail	.10	.05
❑ 4 Rob Johnson	.20	.09
❑ 5 Eric Moulds	.40	.18
❑ 6 Muhsin Muhammad	.20	.09
❑ 7 Patrick Jeffers	.40	.18
❑ 8 Cade McNown	.40	.18
❑ 9 Marcus Robinson	.40	.18
❑ 10 Akili Smith	.40	.18
❑ 11 Corey Dillon	.40	.18
❑ 12 Tim Couch	.75	.35
❑ 13 Kevin Johnson	.40	.18
❑ 14 Troy Aikman	1.00	.45
❑ 15 Emmitt Smith	1.00	.45
❑ 16 Rocket Ismail	.20	.09
❑ 17 Terrell Davis	1.00	.45
❑ 18 Olandis Gary	.40	.18
❑ 19 Charlie Batch	.40	.18
❑ 20 James Stewart	.20	.09
❑ 21 Brett Favre	1.50	.70
❑ 22 Antonio Freeman	.40	.18
❑ 23 Peyton Manning	1.25	.55
❑ 24 Edgerrin James	1.50	.70
❑ 25 Marvin Harrison	.40	.18
❑ 26 Mark Brunell	.60	.25
❑ 27 Fred Taylor	.50	.23
❑ 28 Elvis Grbac	.20	.09
❑ 29 Tony Gonzalez	.20	.09
❑ 30 O.J. McDuffie	.20	.09
❑ 31 Damon Huard	.40	.18
❑ 32 Randy Moss	1.25	.55
❑ 33 Cris Carter	.40	.18
❑ 34 Drew Bledsoe	.60	.25
❑ 35 Terry Glenn	.20	.09
❑ 36 Ricky Williams	1.00	.45
❑ 37 Kerry Collins	.20	.09
❑ 38 Amani Toomer	.20	.09

❑ 39 Keyshawn Johnson	.40	.18
❑ 40 Vinny Testaverde	.20	.09
❑ 41 Tim Brown	.40	.18
❑ 42 Rich Gannon	.20	.09
❑ 43 Duce Staley	.40	.18
❑ 44 Donovan McNabb	.60	.25
❑ 45 Troy Edwards	.20	.09
❑ 46 Jerome Bettis	.40	.18
❑ 47 Marshall Faulk	.50	.23
❑ 48 Kurt Warner	1.50	.70
❑ 49 Junior Seau	.20	.09
❑ 50 Jeff Graham	.10	.05
❑ 51 Charlie Garner	.20	.09
❑ 52 Jerry Rice	1.00	.45
❑ 53 Ricky Watters	.20	.09
❑ 54 Jon Kitna	.40	.18
❑ 55 Mike Alstott	.40	.18
❑ 56 Shaun King	.60	.25
❑ 57 Eddie George	.50	.23
❑ 58 Steve McNair	.40	.18
❑ 59 Brad Johnson	.40	.18
❑ 60 Stephen Davis	.40	.18
❑ 61 Ahmed Plummer RC	8.00	3.60
❑ 62 Courtney Brown RC	10.00	4.50
❑ 63 Deltha O'Neal RC	6.00	2.70
❑ 64 Chad Morton RC	8.00	3.60
❑ 65 Corey Simon RC	10.00	4.50
❑ 66 Hank Poteat RC	6.00	2.70
❑ 67 Raynoch Thompson RC	6.00	2.70
❑ 68 Darren Howard RC	6.00	2.70
❑ 69 Rondell Mealey RC	4.00	1.80
❑ 70 Marcus Knight RC	4.00	1.80
❑ 71 Keith Bulluck RC UER Name spelled Bullock on card	6.00	2.70
❑ 72 John Abraham RC	6.00	2.70
❑ 73 Rob Morris RC	8.00	3.60
❑ 74 Chris Redman RC	15.00	6.75
❑ 75 Joe Hamilton RC	10.00	4.50
❑ 76 Jarious Jackson RC	8.00	3.60
❑ 77 Tom Brady RC	8.00	3.60
❑ 78 Chad Pennington RC	25.00	11.00
❑ 79 Tee Martin RC	12.00	5.50
❑ 80 Giovanni Carmazzi RC	10.00	4.50
❑ 81 Tim Rattay RC	12.00	5.50
❑ 82 Marc Bulger RC	8.00	3.60
❑ 83 Todd Husak RC	8.00	3.60
❑ 84 Curtis Keaton RC	6.00	2.70
❑ 85 Ron Dayne RC	25.00	11.00
❑ 86 Shaun Alexander RC	20.00	9.00
❑ 87 Thomas Jones RC	12.00	5.50
❑ 88 Reuben Droughns RC	8.00	3.60
❑ 89 Jamal Lewis RC	40.00	18.00
❑ 90 J.R. Redmond RC	10.00	4.50
❑ 91 Travis Prentice RC	12.00	5.50
❑ 92 Shyrone Stith RC	6.00	2.70
❑ 93 Chris Hovan RC	6.00	2.70
❑ 94 Michael Wiley RC	8.00	3.60
❑ 95 Trung Canidate RC	8.00	3.60
❑ 96 Sebastian Janikowski RC	8.00	3.60
❑ 97 Brian Urlacher RC	25.00	11.00
❑ 98 Bubba Franks RC	10.00	4.50
❑ 99 Anthony Becht RC	8.00	3.60
❑ 100 Chris Cole RC	6.00	2.70
❑ 101 R.Jay Soward RC	8.00	3.60
❑ 102 Peter Warrick RC	25.00	11.00
❑ 103 Plaxico Burress RC	15.00	6.75
❑ 104 Sylvester Morris RC	15.00	6.75
❑ 105 Dez White RC	6.00	2.70
❑ 106 Travis Taylor RC	10.00	4.50
❑ 107 Trevor Gaylor RC	6.00	2.70
❑ 108 Anthony Lucas RC	4.00	1.80
❑ 109 Sherrod Gideon RC	4.00	1.80
❑ 110 Todd Pinkston RC	8.00	3.60
❑ 111 Dennis Northcutt RC	10.00	4.50
❑ 112 Jerry Porter RC	8.00	3.60
❑ 113 Ron Dugans RC	6.00	2.70
❑ 114 Laveranues Coles RC	12.00	5.50
❑ 115 Darrell Jackson RC	12.00	5.50
❑ 116 Danny Farmer RC	8.00	3.60
❑ 117 Gari Scott RC	6.00	2.70
❑ 118 JaJuan Dawson RC	8.00	3.60
❑ 119 Troy Walters RC	8.00	3.60
❑ 120 Quinton Spotwood RC	4.00	1.80

1991 Ultra

	MINT	NRMT
COMPLETE SET (300)	12.00	5.50
❑ 1 Don Beebe	.05	.02
❑ 2 Shane Conlan	.05	.02
❑ 3 Pete Metzelaars	.05	.02
❑ 4 Jamie Mueller	.05	.02
❑ 5 Scott Norwood	.05	.02
❑ 6 Andre Reed	.10	.05
❑ 7 Leon Seals	.05	.02
❑ 8 Bruce Smith	.25	.11
❑ 9 Leonard Smith	.05	.02
❑ 10 Thurman Thomas	.25	.11
❑ 11 Lewis Billups	.05	.02
❑ 12 Jim Breech	.05	.02
❑ 13 James Brooks	.10	.05
❑ 14 Eddie Brown	.05	.02
❑ 15 Boomer Esiason	.10	.05
❑ 16 David Fulcher	.05	.02
❑ 17 Rodney Holman	.05	.02
❑ 18 Bruce Kozerski	.05	.02
❑ 19 Tim Krumrie	.05	.02
❑ 20 Tim McGee	.05	.02
❑ 21 Anthony Munoz	.10	.05
❑ 22 Leon White	.05	.02
❑ 23 Ickey Woods	.05	.02
❑ 24 Carl Zander	.05	.02
❑ 25 Brian Brennan	.05	.02
❑ 26 Thane Gash	.05	.02
❑ 27 Leroy Hoard	.10	.05
❑ 28 Mike Johnson	.05	.02
❑ 29 Reggie Langhorne	.05	.02
❑ 30 Kevin Mack	.05	.02
❑ 31 Clay Matthews	.10	.05
❑ 32 Eric Metcalf	.10	.05
❑ 33 Steve Atwater	.05	.02
❑ 34 Melvin Bratton	.05	.02
❑ 35 John Elway	1.25	.55
❑ 36 Bobby Humphrey	.05	.02
❑ 37 Mark Jackson	.05	.02
❑ 38 Vance Johnson	.05	.02
❑ 39 Ricky Nattiel	.05	.02
❑ 40 Steve Sewell	.05	.02
❑ 41 Dennis Smith	.05	.02
❑ 42 David Treadwell	.05	.02
❑ 43 Michael Young	.05	.02
❑ 44 Ray Childress	.05	.02
❑ 45 Cris Dishman RC	.05	.02
❑ 46 William Fuller	.10	.05
❑ 47 Ernest Givins	.10	.05
❑ 48 John Grimsley UER (Acquired line should be Trade '91, not Draft 6-'84)	.05	.02
❑ 49 Drew Hill	.05	.02
❑ 50 Haywood Jeffires	.10	.05
❑ 51 Sean Jones	.10	.05
❑ 52 Johnny Meads	.05	.02
❑ 53 Warren Moon	.25	.11
❑ 54 Al Smith	.05	.02
❑ 55 Lorenzo White	.05	.02
❑ 56 Albert Bentley	.05	.02
❑ 57 Duane Bickett	.05	.02
❑ 58 Bill Brooks	.05	.02
❑ 59 Jeff George	.25	.11
❑ 60 Mike Prior	.05	.02
❑ 61 Rohn Stark	.05	.02
❑ 62 Jack Trudeau	.05	.02
❑ 63 Clarence Verdin	.05	.02
❑ 64 Steve DeBerg	.05	.02
❑ 65 Emile Harry	.05	.02
❑ 66 Albert Lewis	.05	.02
❑ 67 Nick Lowery UER (NFL Exp. has 12 years, should be 13)	.05	.02
❑ 68 Todd McNair	.05	.02
❑ 69 Christian Okoye	.05	.02
❑ 70 Stephone Paige	.05	.02
❑ 71 Kevin Porter UER (Front has traded logo, but he has been a Chief all career)	.05	.02
❑ 72 Derrick Thomas	.25	.11
❑ 73 Robb Thomas	.05	.02
❑ 74 Barry Word	.05	.02
❑ 75 Marcus Allen	.25	.11
❑ 76 Eddie Anderson	.05	.02
❑ 77 Tim Brown	.25	.11
❑ 78 Mervyn Fernandez	.05	.02
❑ 79 Willie Gault	.10	.05
❑ 80 Ethan Horton	.05	.02
❑ 81 Howie Long	.10	.05
❑ 82 Vance Mueller	.05	.02
❑ 83 Jay Schroeder	.05	.02
❑ 84 Steve Smith	.05	.02
❑ 85 Greg Townsend	.05	.02
❑ 86 Mark Clayton	.10	.05
❑ 87 Jim C. Jensen	.05	.02
❑ 88 Dan Marino	1.25	.55
❑ 89 Tim McKyer UER (Acquired line should be Trade '91, not Trade '90)	.05	.02
❑ 90 John Offerdahl	.05	.02
❑ 91 Louis Oliver	.05	.02
❑ 92 Reggie Roby	.05	.02
❑ 93 Sammie Smith	.05	.02
❑ 94 Hart Lee Dykes	.05	.02
❑ 95 Irving Fryar	.10	.05
❑ 96 Tommy Hodson	.05	.02
❑ 97 Maurice Hurst	.05	.02
❑ 98 John Stephens	.05	.02
❑ 99 Andre Tippett	.05	.02
❑ 100 Mark Boyer	.05	.02
❑ 101 Kyle Clifton	.05	.02
❑ 102 James Hasty	.05	.02
❑ 103 Erik McMillan	.05	.02
❑ 104 Rob Moore	.25	.11
❑ 105 Joe Mott	.05	.02
❑ 106 Ken O'Brien	.05	.02
❑ 107 Ron Stallworth UER (Acquired line should be Trade '91, not Draft 4-'89)	.05	.02
❑ 108 Al Toon	.10	.05
❑ 109 Gary Anderson K	.05	.02
❑ 110 Bubby Brister	.05	.02
❑ 111 Thomas Everett	.05	.02
❑ 112 Merril Hoge	.05	.02
❑ 113 Louis Lipps	.05	.02
❑ 114 Greg Lloyd	.25	.11
❑ 115 Hardy Nickerson	.10	.05
❑ 116 Dwight Stone	.05	.02
❑ 117 Rod Woodson	.25	.11
❑ 118 Tim Worley	.05	.02
❑ 119 Rod Bernstine	.05	.02
❑ 120 Marion Butts	.10	.05
❑ 121 Gill Byrd	.05	.02
❑ 122 Arthur Cox	.05	.02
❑ 123 Burt Grossman	.05	.02
❑ 124 Ronnie Harmon	.05	.02
❑ 125 Anthony Miller	.10	.05
❑ 126 Leslie O'Neal	.10	.05
❑ 127 Gary Plummer	.05	.02
❑ 128 Sam Seale	.05	.02
❑ 129 Junior Seau	.25	.11
❑ 130 Broderick Thompson	.05	.02
❑ 131 Billy Joe Tolliver	.05	.02
❑ 132 Brian Blades	.10	.05
❑ 133 Jeff Bryant	.05	.02
❑ 134 Derrick Fenner	.05	.02
❑ 135 Jacob Green	.05	.02

❑ 136 Andy Heck .05 .02
❑ 137 Patrick Hunter RC UER .05 .02
(Photos on back show 23 and 27)
❑ 138 Norm Johnson .05 .02
❑ 139 Tommy Kane .05 .02
❑ 140 Dave Krieg .10 .05
❑ 141 John L. Williams .05 .02
❑ 142 Terry Wooden .05 .02
❑ 143 Steve Broussard .05 .02
❑ 144 Keith Jones .05 .02
❑ 145 Brian Jordan .10 .05
❑ 146 Chris Miller .10 .05
❑ 147 John Rade .05 .02
❑ 148 Andre Rison .10 .05
❑ 149 Mike Rozier .05 .02
❑ 150 Deion Sanders .40 .18
❑ 151 Neal Anderson .10 .05
❑ 152 Trace Armstrong .05 .02
❑ 153 Kevin Butler .05 .02
❑ 154 Mark Carrier DB .10 .05
❑ 155 Richard Dent .10 .05
❑ 156 Dennis Gentry .05 .02
❑ 157 Jim Harbaugh .25 .11
❑ 158 Brad Muster .05 .02
❑ 159 William Perry .10 .05
❑ 160 Mike Singletary .10 .05
❑ 161 Lemuel Stinson .05 .02
❑ 162 Troy Aikman .75 .35
❑ 163 Michael Irvin .25 .11
❑ 164 Mike Saxon .05 .02
❑ 165 Emmitt Smith 2.00 .90
❑ 166 Jerry Ball .05 .02
❑ 167 Michael Cofer .05 .02
❑ 168 Rodney Peete .10 .05
❑ 169 Barry Sanders 1.50 .70
❑ 170 Robert Brown .05 .02
❑ 171 Anthony Dilweg .05 .02
❑ 172 Tim Harris .05 .02
❑ 173 Johnny Holland .05 .02
❑ 174 Perry Kemp .05 .02
❑ 175 Don Majkowski .05 .02
❑ 176 Brian Noble .05 .02
❑ 177 Jeff Query .05 .02
❑ 178 Sterling Sharpe .25 .11
❑ 179 Charles Wilson .05 .02
❑ 180 Keith Woodside .05 .02
❑ 181 Flipper Anderson UER .05 .02
(Back photo not him)
❑ 182 Bern Brostek .05 .02
❑ 183 Pat Carter RC .05 .02
❑ 184 Aaron Cox .05 .02
❑ 185 Henry Ellard .10 .05
❑ 186 Jim Everett .10 .05
❑ 187 Cleveland Gary .05 .02
❑ 188 Jerry Gray .05 .02
❑ 189 Kevin Greene .25 .11
❑ 190 Mike Wilcher .05 .02
❑ 191 Alfred Anderson .05 .02
❑ 192 Joey Browner .05 .02
❑ 193 Anthony Carter .10 .05
❑ 194 Chris Doleman .05 .02
❑ 195 Rick Fenney .05 .02
❑ 196 Darrell Fullington .05 .02
❑ 197 Rich Gannon .25 .11
❑ 198 Hassan Jones .05 .02
❑ 199 Steve Jordan .05 .02
❑ 200 Mike Merriweather .05 .02
❑ 201 Al Noga .05 .02
❑ 202 Herschel Walker .10 .05
❑ 203 Wade Wilson .10 .05
❑ 204 Morten Andersen .05 .02
❑ 205 Gene Atkins .05 .02
❑ 206 Toi Cook RC .05 .02
❑ 207 Craig Heyward .10 .05
❑ 208 Dalton Hilliard .05 .02
❑ 209 Vaughan Johnson .05 .02
❑ 210 Eric Martin .05 .02
❑ 211 Brett Perriman .25 .11
❑ 212 Pat Swilling .10 .05
❑ 213 Steve Walsh .05 .02
❑ 214 Ottis Anderson .10 .05
❑ 215 Carl Banks .05 .02
❑ 216 Maurice Carthon .05 .02
❑ 217 Mark Collins .05 .02
❑ 218 Rodney Hampton .25 .11
❑ 219 Erik Howard .05 .02
❑ 220 Mark Ingram .10 .05
❑ 221 Pepper Johnson .05 .02
❑ 222 Dave Meggett .10 .05
❑ 223 Phil Simms .10 .05
❑ 224 Lawrence Taylor .25 .11
❑ 225 Lewis Tillman .05 .02
❑ 226 Everson Walls .05 .02
❑ 227 Fred Barnett .25 .11
❑ 228 Jerome Brown .05 .02
❑ 229 Keith Byars .05 .02
❑ 230 Randall Cunningham .25 .11
❑ 231 Byron Evans .05 .02
❑ 232 Wes Hopkins .05 .02
❑ 233 Keith Jackson .10 .05
❑ 234 Heath Sherman .05 .02
❑ 235 Anthony Toney .05 .02
❑ 236 Reggie White .25 .11
❑ 237 Rich Camarillo .05 .02
❑ 238 Ken Harvey .10 .05
❑ 239 Eric Hill .05 .02
❑ 240 Johnny Johnson .05 .02
❑ 241 Ernie Jones .05 .02
❑ 242 Tim McDonald .05 .02
❑ 243 Timm Rosenbach .05 .02
❑ 244 Jay Taylor .05 .02
❑ 245 Dexter Carter .05 .02
❑ 246 Mike Cofer .05 .02
❑ 247 Kevin Fagan .05 .02
❑ 248 Don Griffin .05 .02
❑ 249 Charles Haley .10 .05
❑ 250 Brent Jones .25 .11
❑ 251 Joe Montana UER 1.25 .55
(Born: Monongahela, not New Eagle)
❑ 252 Darryl Pollard .05 .02
❑ 253 Tom Rathman .05 .02
❑ 254 Jerry Rice .75 .35
❑ 255 John Taylor .10 .05
❑ 256 Steve Young .75 .35
❑ 257 Gary Anderson RB .05 .02
❑ 258 Mark Carrier WR .25 .11
❑ 259 Chris Chandler .25 .11
❑ 260 Reggie Cobb .05 .02
❑ 261 Reuben Davis .05 .02
❑ 262 Willie Drewrey .05 .02
❑ 263 Ron Hall .05 .02
❑ 264 Eugene Marve .05 .02
❑ 265 Winston Moss UER .05 .02
(Acquired line should be Trade '91, not Draft 2-'87)
❑ 266 Vinny Testaverde .10 .05
❑ 267 Broderick Thomas .05 .02
❑ 268 Jeff Bostic .05 .02
❑ 269 Earnest Byner .05 .02
❑ 270 Gary Clark .25 .11
❑ 271 Darrell Green .05 .02
❑ 272 Jim Lachey .05 .02
❑ 273 Wilber Marshall .05 .02
❑ 274 Art Monk .10 .05
❑ 275 Gerald Riggs .05 .02
❑ 276 Mark Rypien .10 .05
❑ 277 Ricky Sanders .05 .02
❑ 278 Alvin Walton .05 .02
❑ 279 Nick Bell RC .05 .02
❑ 280 Eric Bieniemy RC .05 .02
❑ 281 Jarrod Bunch RC .05 .02
❑ 282 Mike Croel RC .05 .02
❑ 283 Brett Favre RC 5.00 2.20
❑ 284 Moe Gardner RC .05 .02
❑ 285 Pat Harlow RC .05 .02
❑ 286 Randal Hill RC .10 .05
❑ 287 Todd Marinovich RC .05 .02
❑ 288 Russell Maryland RC .25 .11
❑ 289 Dan McGwire RC .05 .02
❑ 290 Ernie Mills RC UER .10 .05
(Patterns misspelled as patternsn in first sentence)
❑ 291 Herman Moore RC 2.00 .90
❑ 292 Godfrey Myles RC .05 .02
❑ 293 Browning Nagle RC .05 .02
❑ 294 Mike Pritchard RC .25 .11
❑ 295 Esera Tuaolo RC .05 .02
❑ 296 Mark Vander Poel RC .05 .02
❑ 297 Ricky Watters RC UER 1.50 .70
(Photo on back actually Ray Griggs)
❑ 298 Chris Zorich RC .25 .11
❑ 299 Checklist Card .10 .05
(Randall Cunningham and Emmitt Smith)
❑ 300 Checklist Card .10 .05
(Randall Cunningham and Emmitt Smith)

1991 Ultra Update

	MINT	NRMT
COMP.FACT.SET (100)	20.00	9.00

❑ U1 Brett Favre 15.00 6.75
❑ U2 Moe Gardner .10 .05
❑ U3 Tim McKyer .10 .05
❑ U4 Bruce Pickens RC .10 .05
❑ U5 Mike Pritchard .40 .18
❑ U6 Cornelius Bennett .20 .09
❑ U7 Phil Hansen RC .10 .05
❑ U8 Henry Jones RC .20 .09
❑ U9 Mark Kelso .10 .05
❑ U10 James Lofton .20 .09
❑ U11 Anthony Morgan RC .10 .05
❑ U12 Stan Thomas .10 .05
❑ U13 Chris Zorich .20 .09
❑ U14 Reggie Rembert .10 .05
❑ U15 Alfred Williams RC .10 .05
❑ U16 Michael Jackson RC .75 .35
❑ U17 Ed King RC .10 .05
❑ U18 Joe Morris .10 .05
❑ U19 Vince Newsome .10 .05
❑ U20 Tony Casillas .10 .05
❑ U21 Russell Maryland .40 .18
❑ U22 Jay Novacek .40 .18
❑ U23 Mike Croel .10 .05
❑ U24 Gaston Green .10 .05
❑ U25 Kenny Walker RC .10 .05
❑ U26 Melvin Jenkins RC .10 .05
❑ U27 Herman Moore 4.00 1.80
❑ U28 Kelvin Pritchett RC .20 .09
❑ U29 Chris Spielman .20 .09
❑ U30 Vinnie Clark RC .10 .05
❑ U31 Allen Rice .10 .05
❑ U32 Vai Sikahema .10 .05
❑ U33 Esera Tuaolo .10 .05
❑ U34 Mike Dumas RC .10 .05
❑ U35 John Flannery RC .10 .05
❑ U36 Allen Pinkett .10 .05
❑ U37 Tim Barnett RC .10 .05
❑ U38 Dan Saleaumua .10 .05
❑ U39 Harvey Williams RC .40 .18
❑ U40 Nick Bell .10 .05
❑ U41 Roger Craig .20 .09
❑ U42 Ronnie Lott .20 .09
❑ U43 Todd Marinovich .10 .05
❑ U44 Robert Delpino .10 .05
❑ U45 Todd Lyght RC .10 .05
❑ U46 Robert Young RC .20 .09
❑ U47 Aaron Craver RC .10 .05
❑ U48 Mark Higgs RC .10 .05
❑ U49 Vestee Jackson .10 .05
❑ U50 Carl Lee .10 .05
❑ U51 Felix Wright .10 .05
❑ U52 Darrell Fullington .10 .05

❑ U53 Pat Harlow .10 .05
❑ U54 Eugene Lockhart .10 .05
❑ U55 Hugh Millen RC .10 .05
❑ U56 Leonard Russell RC .40 .18
❑ U57 Jon Vaughn RC .10 .05
❑ U58 Quinn Early .20 .09
❑ U59 Bobby Hebert .10 .05
❑ U60 Rickey Jackson .10 .05
❑ U61 Sam Mills .20 .09
❑ U62 Jarrod Bunch .10 .05
❑ U63 John Elliott .10 .05
❑ U64 Jeff Hostetler .20 .09
❑ U65 Ed McCaffrey RC 10.00 4.50
❑ U66 Kanavis McGhee RC .10 .05
❑ U67 Mo Lewis RC .20 .09
❑ U68 Browning Nagle .10 .05
❑ U69 Blair Thomas .10 .05
❑ U70 Antone Davis RC .10 .05
❑ U71 Brad Goebel RC .10 .05
(See card U74)
❑ U72 Jim McMahon .20 .09
❑ U73 Clyde Simmons .10 .05
❑ U74 Randal Hill UER .20 .09
(Card number on back U71 instead of U74)
❑ U75 Eric Swann RC .40 .18
❑ U76 Tom Tupa .10 .05
❑ U77 Jeff Graham RC .40 .18
❑ U78 Eric Green .10 .05
❑ U79 Neil O'Donnell RC 2.00 .90
❑ U80 Huey Richardson RC .10 .05
❑ U81 Eric Bieniemy .10 .05
❑ U82 John Friesz .40 .18
❑ U83 Eric Moten RC .10 .05
❑ U84 Stanley Richard RC .10 .05
❑ U85 Todd Bowles .10 .05
❑ U86 Merton Hanks RC .40 .18
❑ U87 Tim Harris .10 .05
❑ U88 Pierce Holt .10 .05
❑ U89 Ted Washington RC .10 .05
❑ U90 John Kasay RC .20 .09
❑ U91 Dan McGwire .10 .05
❑ U92 Lawrence Dawsey RC .20 .09
❑ U93 Charles McRae RC .10 .05
❑ U94 Jesse Solomon .10 .05
❑ U95 Robert Wilson RC .10 .05
❑ U96 Ricky Ervins RC .20 .09
❑ U97 Charles Mann .10 .05
❑ U98 Bobby Wilson RC .10 .05
❑ U99 Jerry Rice 1.50 .70
Pro-Visions
❑ U100 Checklist 1-100 .10 .05
(Nick Bell and Jim McMahon)

1992 Ultra

	MINT	NRMT
COMPLETE SET (450)	15.00	6.75

❑ 1 Steve Broussard .10 .05
❑ 2 Rick Bryan .10 .05
❑ 3 Scott Case .10 .05
❑ 4 Darion Conner .10 .05
❑ 5 Bill Fralic .10 .05
❑ 6 Moe Gardner .10 .05
❑ 7 Tim Green .10 .05
❑ 8 Michael Haynes .20 .09
❑ 9 Chris Hinton .10 .05
❑ 10 Mike Kenn .10 .05
❑ 11 Tim McKyer .10 .05
❑ 12 Chris Miller .20 .09
❑ 13 Erric Pegram .20 .09
❑ 14 Mike Pritchard .20 .09
❑ 15 Andre Rison .20 .09
❑ 16 Jessie Tuggle .10 .05
❑ 17 Carlton Bailey RC .20 .09
❑ 18 Howard Ballard .10 .05
❑ 19 Cornelius Bennett .20 .09
❑ 20 Shane Conlan .10 .05
❑ 21 Kenneth Davis .10 .05
❑ 22 Kent Hull .10 .05
❑ 23 Mark Kelso .10 .05
❑ 24 James Lofton .20 .09
❑ 25 Keith McKeller .10 .05
❑ 26 Nate Odomes .10 .05
❑ 27 Jim Ritcher .10 .05
❑ 28 Leon Seals .10 .05
❑ 29 Darryl Talley .10 .05
❑ 30 Steve Tasker .20 .09
❑ 31 Thurman Thomas .40 .18
❑ 32 Will Wolford .10 .05
❑ 33 Jeff Wright .10 .05
❑ 34 Neal Anderson .10 .05
❑ 35 Trace Armstrong .10 .05
❑ 36 Mark Carrier DB .10 .05
❑ 37 Wendell Davis .10 .05
❑ 38 Richard Dent .20 .09
❑ 39 Shaun Gayle .10 .05
❑ 40 Jim Harbaugh .40 .18
❑ 41 Jay Hilgenberg .10 .05
❑ 42 Darren Lewis .10 .05
❑ 43 Steve McMichael .20 .09
❑ 44 Anthony Morgan .10 .05
❑ 45 Brad Muster .10 .05
❑ 46 William Perry .20 .09
❑ 47 John Roper .10 .05
❑ 48 Lemuel Stinson .10 .05
❑ 49 Tom Waddle .10 .05
❑ 50 Donnell Woolford .10 .05
❑ 51 Leo Barker RC .10 .05
❑ 52 Eddie Brown .10 .05
❑ 53 James Francis .10 .05
❑ 54 David Fulcher UER .10 .05
(Photo on back actually Eddie Brown)
❑ 55 David Grant .10 .05
❑ 56 Harold Green .10 .05
❑ 57 Rodney Holman .10 .05
❑ 58 Lee Johnson .10 .05
❑ 59 Tim Krumrie .10 .05
❑ 60 Tim McGee .10 .05
❑ 61 Alonzo Mitz RC .10 .05
❑ 62 Anthony Munoz .20 .09
❑ 63 Alfred Williams .10 .05
❑ 64 Stephen Braggs .10 .05
❑ 65 Richard Brown RC .10 .05
❑ 66 Randy Hilliard RC .10 .05
❑ 67 Leroy Hoard .20 .09
❑ 68 Michael Jackson .20 .09
❑ 69 Mike Johnson .10 .05
❑ 70 James Jones .10 .05
❑ 71 Tony Jones .10 .05
❑ 72 Ed King .10 .05
❑ 73 Kevin Mack .10 .05
❑ 74 Clay Matthews .20 .09
❑ 75 Eric Metcalf .20 .09
❑ 76 Vince Newsome .10 .05
❑ 77 Steve Beuerlein .10 .05
❑ 78 Larry Brown DB .10 .05
❑ 79 Tony Casillas .10 .05
❑ 80 Alvin Harper .20 .09
❑ 81 Issiac Holt .10 .05
❑ 82 Ray Horton .10 .05
❑ 83 Michael Irvin .40 .18
❑ 84 Daryl Johnston .40 .18
❑ 85 Kelvin Martin .10 .05
❑ 86 Ken Norton .40 .18
❑ 87 Jay Novacek .20 .09
❑ 88 Emmitt Smith 3.00 1.35
❑ 89 Vinson Smith RC .10 .05
❑ 90 Mark Stepnoski .20 .09
❑ 91 Tony Tolbert .10 .05
❑ 92 Alexander Wright .10 .05
❑ 93 Steve Atwater .10 .05
❑ 94 Tyrone Braxton .10 .05
❑ 95 Michael Brooks .10 .05
❑ 96 Mike Croel .10 .05
❑ 97 John Elway 2.50 1.10
❑ 98 Simon Fletcher .10 .05
❑ 99 Gaston Green .10 .05
❑ 100 Mark Jackson .10 .05
❑ 101 Keith Kartz .10 .05
❑ 102 Greg Kragen .10 .05
❑ 103 Greg Lewis .10 .05
❑ 104 Karl Mecklenburg .10 .05
❑ 105 Derek Russell .10 .05
❑ 106 Steve Sewell .10 .05
❑ 107 Dennis Smith .10 .05
❑ 108 David Treadwell .10 .05
❑ 109 Kenny Walker .10 .05
❑ 110 Michael Young .10 .05
❑ 111 Jerry Ball .10 .05
❑ 112 Bennie Blades .10 .05
❑ 113 Lomas Brown .10 .05
❑ 114 Scott Conover RC .10 .05
❑ 115 Ray Crockett .10 .05
❑ 116 Mel Gray .20 .09
❑ 117 Willie Green .10 .05
❑ 118 Erik Kramer .20 .09
❑ 119 Dan Owens .10 .05
❑ 120 Rodney Peete .20 .09
❑ 121 Brett Perriman .40 .18
❑ 122 Barry Sanders 3.00 1.35
❑ 123 Chris Spielman .20 .09
❑ 124 Marc Spindler .10 .05
❑ 125 William White .10 .05
❑ 126 Tony Bennett .10 .05
❑ 127 Matt Brock .10 .05
❑ 128 LeRoy Butler .10 .05
❑ 129 Chuck Cecil .10 .05
❑ 130 Johnny Holland .10 .05
❑ 131 Perry Kemp .10 .05
❑ 132 Don Majkowski .10 .05
❑ 133 Tony Mandarich .10 .05
❑ 134 Brian Noble .10 .05
❑ 135 Bryce Paup .40 .18
❑ 136 Sterling Sharpe .40 .18
❑ 137 Darrell Thompson .10 .05
❑ 138 Mike Tomczak .10 .05
❑ 139 Vince Workman .20 .09
❑ 140 Ray Childress .10 .05
❑ 141 Cris Dishman .10 .05
❑ 142 Curtis Duncan .10 .05
❑ 143 William Fuller .20 .09
❑ 144 Ernest Givins .20 .09
❑ 145 Haywood Jeffires .20 .09
❑ 146 Sean Jones .20 .09
❑ 147 Lamar Lathon .10 .05
❑ 148 Bruce Matthews .10 .05
❑ 149 Bubba McDowell .10 .05
❑ 150 Johnny Meads .10 .05
❑ 151 Warren Moon .40 .18
❑ 152 Mike Munchak .10 .05
❑ 153 Bo Orlando RC .10 .05
❑ 154 Al Smith .10 .05
❑ 155 Doug Smith .10 .05
❑ 156 Lorenzo White .10 .05
❑ 157 Chip Banks .10 .05
❑ 158 Duane Bickett .10 .05
❑ 159 Bill Brooks .10 .05
❑ 160 Eugene Daniel .10 .05
❑ 161 Jon Hand .10 .05
❑ 162 Jeff Herrod .10 .05
❑ 163 Jessie Hester .10 .05
❑ 164 Scott Radecic .10 .05
❑ 165 Rohn Stark .10 .05
❑ 166 Clarence Verdin .10 .05
❑ 167 John Alt .10 .05
❑ 168 Tim Barnett .10 .05
❑ 169 Tim Grunhard .10 .05
❑ 170 Dino Hackett .10 .05
❑ 171 Jonathan Hayes .10 .05
❑ 172 Bill Maas .10 .05
❑ 173 Chris Martin .10 .05
❑ 174 Christian Okoye .10 .05
❑ 175 Stephone Paige .10 .05
❑ 176 Jayice Pearson RC .10 .05
❑ 177 Kevin Porter .10 .05
❑ 178 Kevin Ross .10 .05

	No.	Player		
❑	179	Dan Saleaumua	.10	.05
❑	180	Tracy Simien RC	.10	.05
❑	181	Neil Smith	.40	.18
❑	182	Derrick Thomas	.40	.18
❑	183	Robb Thomas	.10	.05
❑	184	Barry Word	.10	.05
❑	185	Marcus Allen	.40	.18
❑	186	Eddie Anderson	.10	.05
❑	187	Nick Bell	.10	.05
❑	188	Tim Brown	.40	.18
❑	189	Mervyn Fernandez	.10	.05
❑	190	Willie Gault	.20	.09
❑	191	Jeff Gossett	.10	.05
❑	192	Ethan Horton	.10	.05
❑	193	Jeff Jaeger	.10	.05
❑	194	Howie Long	.20	.09
❑	195	Ronnie Lott	.20	.09
❑	196	Todd Marinovich	.10	.05
❑	197	Don Mosebar	.10	.05
❑	198	Jay Schroeder	.10	.05
❑	199	Anthony Smith	.10	.05
❑	200	Greg Townsend	.10	.05
❑	201	Lionel Washington	.10	.05
❑	202	Steve Wisniewski	.10	.05
❑	203	Flipper Anderson	.10	.05
❑	204	Robert Delpino	.10	.05
❑	205	Henry Ellard	.20	.09
❑	206	Jim Everett	.20	.09
❑	207	Kevin Greene	.40	.18
❑	208	Darryl Henley	.10	.05
❑	209	Damone Johnson	.10	.05
❑	210	Larry Kelm	.10	.05
❑	211	Todd Lyght	.10	.05
❑	212	Jackie Slater	.10	.05
❑	213	Michael Stewart	.10	.05
❑	214	Pat Terrell	.10	.05
❑	215	Robert Young	.10	.05
❑	216	Mark Clayton	.20	.09
❑	217	Bryan Cox	.20	.09
❑	218	Jeff Cross	.10	.05
❑	219	Mark Duper	.10	.05
❑	220	Harry Galbreath	.10	.05
❑	221	David Griggs	.10	.05
❑	222	Mark Higgs	.10	.05
❑	223	Vestee Jackson	.10	.05
❑	224	John Offerdahl	.10	.05
❑	225	Louis Oliver	.10	.05
❑	226	Tony Paige	.10	.05
❑	227	Reggie Roby	.10	.05
❑	228	Pete Stoyanovich	.10	.05
❑	229	Richmond Webb	.10	.05
❑	230	Terry Allen	.40	.18
❑	231	Ray Berry	.10	.05
❑	232	Anthony Carter	.20	.09
❑	233	Cris Carter	.75	.35
❑	234	Chris Doleman	.10	.05
❑	235	Rich Gannon	.40	.18
❑	236	Steve Jordan	.10	.05
❑	237	Carl Lee	.10	.05
❑	238	Randall McDaniel	.10	.05
❑	239	Mike Merriweather	.10	.05
❑	240	Harry Newsome	.10	.05
❑	241	John Randle	.20	.09
❑	242	Henry Thomas	.10	.05
❑	243	Bruce Armstrong	.10	.05
❑	244	Vincent Brown	.10	.05
❑	245	Marv Cook	.10	.05
❑	246	Irving Fryar	.20	.09
❑	247	Pat Harlow	.10	.05
❑	248	Maurice Hurst	.10	.05
❑	249	Eugene Lockhart	.10	.05
❑	250	Greg McMurtry	.10	.05
❑	251	Hugh Millen	.10	.05
❑	252	Leonard Russell	.20	.09
❑	253	Chris Singleton	.10	.05
❑	254	Andre Tippett	.10	.05
❑	255	Jon Vaughn	.10	.05
❑	256	Morten Andersen	.10	.05
❑	257	Gene Atkins	.10	.05
❑	258	Wesley Caroll	.10	.05
❑	259	Jim Dombrowski	.10	.05
❑	260	Quinn Early	.20	.09
❑	261	Bobby Hebert	.10	.05
❑	262	Joel Hilgenberg	.10	.05
❑	263	Rickey Jackson	.10	.05
❑	264	Vaughan Johnson	.10	.05
❑	265	Eric Martin	.10	.05
❑	266	Brett Maxie	.10	.05
❑	267	Fred McAfee RC	.10	.05
❑	268	Sam Mills	.10	.05
❑	269	Pat Swilling	.20	.09
❑	270	Floyd Turner	.10	.05
❑	271	Steve Walsh	.10	.05
❑	272	Stephen Baker	.10	.05
❑	273	Jarrod Bunch	.10	.05
❑	274	Mark Collins	.10	.05
❑	275	John Elliott	.10	.05
❑	276	Myron Guyton	.10	.05
❑	277	Rodney Hampton	.40	.18
❑	278	Jeff Hostetler	.20	.09
❑	279	Mark Ingram	.10	.05
❑	280	Pepper Johnson	.10	.05
❑	281	Sean Landeta	.10	.05
❑	282	Leonard Marshall	.10	.05
❑	283	Kanavis McGhee	.10	.05
❑	284	Dave Meggett	.20	.09
❑	285	Bart Oates	.10	.05
❑	286	Phil Simms	.20	.09
❑	287	Reyna Thompson	.10	.05
❑	288	Lewis Tillman	.10	.05
❑	289	Brad Baxter	.10	.05
❑	290	Mike Brim RC	.10	.05
❑	291	Chris Burkett	.10	.05
❑	292	Kyle Clifton	.10	.05
❑	293	James Hasty	.10	.05
❑	294	Joe Kelly	.10	.05
❑	295	Jeff Lageman	.10	.05
❑	296	Mo Lewis	.10	.05
❑	297	Erik McMillan	.10	.05
❑	298	Scott Mersereau	.10	.05
❑	299	Rob Moore	.20	.09
❑	300	Tony Stargell	.10	.05
❑	301	Jim Sweeney	.10	.05
❑	302	Marvin Washington	.10	.05
❑	303	Lonnie Young	.10	.05
❑	304	Eric Allen	.10	.05
❑	305	Fred Barnett	.40	.18
❑	306	Keith Byars	.10	.05
❑	307	Byron Evans	.10	.05
❑	308	Wes Hopkins	.10	.05
❑	309	Keith Jackson	.20	.09
❑	310	James Joseph	.10	.05
❑	311	Seth Joyner	.20	.09
❑	312	Roger Ruzek	.10	.05
❑	313	Clyde Simmons	.10	.05
❑	314	William Thomas	.10	.05
❑	315	Reggie White	.40	.18
❑	316	Calvin Williams	.20	.09
❑	317	Rich Camarillo	.10	.05
❑	318	Jeff Faulkner	.10	.05
❑	319	Ken Harvey	.10	.05
❑	320	Eric Hill	.10	.05
❑	321	Johnny Johnson	.10	.05
❑	322	Ernie Jones	.10	.05
❑	323	Tim McDonald	.10	.05
❑	324	Freddie Joe Nunn	.10	.05
❑	325	Luis Sharpe	.10	.05
❑	326	Eric Swann	.20	.09
❑	327	Aeneas Williams	.20	.09
❑	328	Michael Zordich RC	.10	.05
❑	329	Gary Anderson K	.10	.05
❑	330	Bubby Brister	.10	.05
❑	331	Barry Foster	.20	.09
❑	332	Eric Green	.10	.05
❑	333	Bryan Hinkle	.10	.05
❑	334	Tunch Ilkin	.10	.05
❑	335	Carnell Lake	.10	.05
❑	336	Louis Lipps	.10	.05
❑	337	David Little	.10	.05
❑	338	Greg Lloyd	.40	.18
❑	339	Neil O'Donnell	.40	.18
❑	340	Rod Woodson	.40	.18
❑	341	Rod Bernstine	.10	.05
❑	342	Marion Butts	.10	.05
❑	343	Gill Byrd	.10	.05
❑	344	John Friesz	.20	.09
❑	345	Burt Grossman	.10	.05
❑	346	Courtney Hall	.10	.05
❑	347	Ronnie Harmon	.10	.05
❑	348	Shawn Jefferson	.10	.05
❑	349	Nate Lewis	.10	.05
❑	350	Craig McEwen RC	.10	.05
❑	351	Eric Moten	.10	.05
❑	352	Gary Plummer	.10	.05
❑	353	Henry Rolling	.10	.05
❑	354	Broderick Thompson	.10	.05
❑	355	Derrick Walker	.10	.05
❑	356	Harris Barton	.10	.05
❑	357	Steve Bono RC	.40	.18
❑	358	Todd Bowles	.10	.05
❑	359	Dexter Carter	.10	.05
❑	360	Michael Carter	.10	.05
❑	361	Keith DeLong	.10	.05
❑	362	Charles Haley	.20	.09
❑	363	Merton Hanks	.20	.09
❑	364	Tim Harris	.10	.05
❑	365	Brent Jones	.20	.09
❑	366	Guy McIntyre	.10	.05
❑	367	Tom Rathman	.10	.05
❑	368	Bill Romanowski	.10	.05
❑	369	Jesse Sapolu	.10	.05
❑	370	John Taylor	.20	.09
❑	371	Steve Young	1.50	.70
❑	372	Robert Blackmon	.10	.05
❑	373	Brian Blades	.20	.09
❑	374	Jacob Green	.10	.05
❑	375	Dwayne Harper	.10	.05
❑	376	Andy Heck	.10	.05
❑	377	Tommy Kane	.10	.05
❑	378	John Kasay	.10	.05
❑	379	Cortez Kennedy	.20	.09
❑	380	Bryan Millard	.10	.05
❑	381	Rufus Porter	.10	.05
❑	382	Eugene Robinson	.10	.05
❑	383	John L. Williams	.10	.05
❑	384	Terry Wooden	.10	.05
❑	385	Gary Anderson RB	.10	.05
❑	386	Ian Beckles	.10	.05
❑	387	Mark Carrier WR	.20	.09
❑	388	Reggie Cobb	.10	.05
❑	389	Tony Covington	.10	.05
❑	390	Lawrence Dawsey	.20	.09
❑	391	Ron Hall	.10	.05
❑	392	Keith McCants	.10	.05
❑	393	Charles McRae	.10	.05
❑	394	Tim Newton	.10	.05
❑	395	Jesse Solomon	.10	.05
❑	396	Vinny Testaverde	.20	.09
❑	397	Broderick Thomas	.10	.05
❑	398	Robert Wilson	.10	.05
❑	399	Earnest Byner	.10	.05
❑	400	Gary Clark	.40	.18
❑	401	Andre Collins	.10	.05
❑	402	Brad Edwards	.10	.05
❑	403	Kurt Gouveia	.10	.05
❑	404	Darrell Green	.10	.05
❑	405	Joe Jacoby	.10	.05
❑	406	Jim Lachey	.10	.05
❑	407	Chip Lohmiller	.10	.05
❑	408	Charles Mann	.10	.05
❑	409	Wilber Marshall	.10	.05
❑	410	Brian Mitchell	.20	.09
❑	411	Art Monk	.20	.09
❑	412	Mark Rypien	.10	.05
❑	413	Ricky Sanders	.10	.05
❑	414	Mark Schlereth RC	.10	.05
❑	415	Fred Stokes	.10	.05
❑	416	Bobby Wilson	.10	.05
❑	417	Corey Barlow RC	.10	.05
❑	418	Edgar Bennett RC	.50	.23
❑	419	Eddie Blake RC	.10	.05
❑	420	Terrell Buckley RC	.10	.05
❑	421	Willie Clay RC	.10	.05
❑	422	Rodney Culver RC	.10	.05
❑	423	Ed Cunningham RC	.10	.05
❑	424	Mark D'Onofrio RC	.10	.05
❑	425	Matt Darby RC	.10	.05
❑	426	Charles Davenport RC	.10	.05
❑	427	Will Furrer RC	.10	.05
❑	428	Keith Goganious RC	.10	.05
❑	429	Mario Bailey RC	.20	.09
❑	430	Chris Hakel RC	.10	.05
❑	431	Keith Hamilton RC	.20	.09
❑	432	Aaron Pierce RC	.10	.05
❑	433	Amp Lee RC	.10	.05
❑	434	Scott Lockwood RC	.10	.05
❑	435	Ricardo McDonald RC	.10	.05
❑	436	Dexter McNabb RC	.10	.05

❑	437 Chris Mims RC	.20	.09
❑	438 Mike Mooney RC	.10	.05
❑	439 Ray Roberts RC	.10	.05
❑	440 Patrick Rowe RC	.10	.05
❑	441 Leon Searcy RC	.20	.09
❑	442 Siran Stacy RC	.10	.05
❑	443 Kevin Turner RC	.10	.05
❑	444 Tommy Vardell RC	.20	.09
❑	445 Bob Whitfield RC	.10	.05
❑	446 Darryl Williams RC	.10	.05
❑	447 Checklist 1-110	.10	.05
❑	448 Checklist 111-224	.10	.05
❑	449 Checklist 230-340 UER (Missing 225-229)	.10	.05
❑	450 Checklist 341-450	.10	.05

1993 Ultra

		MINT	NRMT
	COMPLETE SET (500)	25.00	11.00
❑	1 Vinnie Clark	.10	.05
❑	2 Darion Conner	.10	.05
❑	3 Eric Dickerson	.20	.09
❑	4 Moe Gardner	.10	.05
❑	5 Tim Green	.10	.05
❑	6 Roger Harper RC	.10	.05
❑	7 Michael Haynes	.20	.09
❑	8 Bobby Hebert	.10	.05
❑	9 Chris Hinton	.10	.05
❑	10 Pierce Holt	.10	.05
❑	11 Mike Kenn	.10	.05
❑	12 Lincoln Kennedy RC	.10	.05
❑	13 Chris Miller	.20	.09
❑	14 Mike Pritchard	.20	.09
❑	15 Andre Rison	.20	.09
❑	16 Deion Sanders	.75	.35
❑	17 Tony Smith	.10	.05
❑	18 Jessie Tuggle	.10	.05
❑	19 Howard Ballard	.10	.05
❑	20 Don Beebe	.10	.05
❑	21 Cornelius Bennett	.20	.09
❑	22 Bill Brooks	.10	.05
❑	23 Kenneth Davis	.10	.05
❑	24 Phil Hansen	.10	.05
❑	25 Henry Jones	.10	.05
❑	26 Jim Kelly	.40	.18
❑	27 Nate Odomes	.10	.05
❑	28 John Parrella RC	.10	.05
❑	29 Andre Reed	.20	.09
❑	30 Frank Reich	.20	.09
❑	31 Jim Ritcher	.10	.05
❑	32 Bruce Smith	.40	.18
❑	33 Thomas Smith RC	.20	.09
❑	34 Darryl Talley	.10	.05
❑	35 Steve Tasker	.20	.09
❑	36 Thurman Thomas	.40	.18
❑	37 Jeff Wright	.10	.05
❑	38 Neal Anderson	.10	.05
❑	39 Trace Armstrong	.10	.05
❑	40 Mark Carrier DB	.10	.05
❑	41 Curtis Conway RC	.75	.35
❑	42 Wendell Davis	.10	.05
❑	43 Richard Dent	.20	.09
❑	44 Shaun Gayle	.10	.05
❑	45 Jim Harbaugh	.40	.18
❑	46 Craig Heyward	.20	.09
❑	47 Darren Lewis	.10	.05
❑	48 Steve McMichael	.20	.09
❑	49 William Perry	.20	.09
❑	50 Carl Simpson RC	.10	.05
❑	51 Alonzo Spellman	.10	.05
❑	52 Keith Van Horne	.10	.05
❑	53 Tom Waddle	.10	.05
❑	54 Donnell Woolford	.10	.05
❑	55 John Copeland RC	.20	.09
❑	56 Derrick Fenner	.10	.05
❑	57 James Francis	.10	.05
❑	58 Harold Green	.10	.05
❑	59 David Klingler	.10	.05
❑	60 Tim Krumrie	.10	.05
❑	61 Ricardo McDonald	.10	.05
❑	62 Tony McGee RC	.20	.09
❑	63 Carl Pickens	.40	.18
❑	64 Lamar Rogers	.10	.05
❑	65 Jay Schroeder	.10	.05
❑	66 Daniel Stubbs	.10	.05
❑	67 Steve Tovar RC	.10	.05
❑	68 Alfred Williams	.10	.05
❑	69 Darryl Williams	.10	.05
❑	70 Jerry Ball	.10	.05
❑	71 David Brandon	.10	.05
❑	72 Rob Burnett	.10	.05
❑	73 Mark Carrier WR	.20	.09
❑	74 Steve Everitt RC	.10	.05
❑	75 Dan Footman RC	.10	.05
❑	76 Leroy Hoard	.20	.09
❑	77 Michael Jackson	.20	.09
❑	78 Mike Johnson	.10	.05
❑	79 Bernie Kosar	.20	.09
❑	80 Clay Matthews	.20	.09
❑	81 Eric Metcalf	.20	.09
❑	82 Michael Dean Perry	.20	.09
❑	83 Vinny Testaverde	.20	.09
❑	84 Tommy Vardell	.10	.05
❑	85 Troy Aikman	1.50	.70
❑	86 Larry Brown DB	.10	.05
❑	87 Tony Casillas	.10	.05
❑	88 Thomas Everett	.10	.05
❑	89 Charles Haley	.20	.09
❑	90 Alvin Harper	.20	.09
❑	91 Michael Irvin	.40	.18
❑	92 Jim Jeffcoat	.10	.05
❑	93 Daryl Johnston	.40	.18
❑	94 Robert Jones	.10	.05
❑	95 Leon Lett RC	.20	.09
❑	96 Russell Maryland	.10	.05
❑	97 Nate Newton	.20	.09
❑	98 Ken Norton	.20	.09
❑	99 Jay Novacek	.20	.09
❑	100 Darrin Smith RC	.20	.09
❑	101 Emmitt Smith	3.00	1.35
❑	102 Kevin Smith	.20	.09
❑	103 Mark Stepnoski	.10	.05
❑	104 Tony Tolbert	.10	.05
❑	105 Kevin Williams RC	.40	.18
❑	106 Steve Atwater	.10	.05
❑	107 Rod Bernstine	.10	.05
❑	108 Mike Croel	.10	.05
❑	109 Robert Delpino	.10	.05
❑	110 Shane Dronett	.10	.05
❑	111 John Elway	3.00	1.35
❑	112 Simon Fletcher	.10	.05
❑	113 Greg Kragen	.10	.05
❑	114 Tommy Maddox	.10	.05
❑	115 Arthur Marshall RC	.10	.05
❑	116 Karl Mecklenburg	.10	.05
❑	117 Glyn Milburn RC	.40	.18
❑	118 Reggie Rivers RC	.10	.05
❑	119 Shannon Sharpe	.40	.18
❑	120 Dennis Smith	.10	.05
❑	121 Kenny Walker	.10	.05
❑	122 Dan Williams RC	.10	.05
❑	123 Bennie Blades	.10	.05
❑	124 Lomas Brown	.10	.05
❑	125 Bill Fralic	.10	.05
❑	126 Mel Gray	.20	.09
❑	127 Willie Green	.10	.05
❑	128 Jason Hanson	.10	.05
❑	129 Antonio London RC	.10	.05
❑	130 Ryan McNeil RC	.10	.05
❑	131 Herman Moore	1.00	.45
❑	132 Rodney Peete	.10	.05
❑	133 Brett Perriman	.40	.18
❑	134 Kelvin Pritchett	.10	.05
❑	135 Barry Sanders	3.00	1.35
❑	136 Tracy Scroggins	.10	.05
❑	137 Chris Spielman	.20	.09
❑	138 Pat Swilling	.10	.05
❑	139 Andre Ware	.10	.05
❑	140 Edgar Bennett	.40	.18
❑	141 Tony Bennett	.10	.05
❑	142 Matt Brock	.10	.05
❑	143 Terrell Buckley	.10	.05
❑	144 LeRoy Butler	.10	.05
❑	145 Mark Clayton	.10	.05
❑	146 Brett Favre	4.00	1.80
❑	147 Jackie Harris	.10	.05
❑	148 Johnny Holland	.10	.05
❑	149 Bill Maas	.10	.05
❑	150 Brian Noble	.10	.05
❑	151 Bryce Paup	.40	.18
❑	152 Ken Ruettgers	.10	.05
❑	153 Sterling Sharpe	.40	.18
❑	154 Wayne Simmons RC	.10	.05
❑	155 John Stephens	.10	.05
❑	156 George Teague RC	.20	.09
❑	157 Reggie White	.40	.18
❑	158 Micheal Barrow RC	.20	.09
❑	159 Cody Carlson	.10	.05
❑	160 Ray Childress	.10	.05
❑	161 Cris Dishman	.10	.05
❑	162 Curtis Duncan	.10	.05
❑	163 William Fuller	.10	.05
❑	164 Ernest Givins	.20	.09
❑	165 Brad Hopkins RC	.10	.05
❑	166 Haywood Jeffires	.20	.09
❑	167 Lamar Lathon	.10	.05
❑	168 Wilber Marshall	.10	.05
❑	169 Bruce Matthews	.10	.05
❑	170 Bubba McDowell	.10	.05
❑	171 Warren Moon	.40	.18
❑	172 Mike Munchak	.10	.05
❑	173 Eddie Robinson	.10	.05
❑	174 Al Smith	.10	.05
❑	175 Lorenzo White	.10	.05
❑	176 Lee Williams	.10	.05
❑	177 Chip Banks	.10	.05
❑	178 John Baylor	.10	.05
❑	179 Duane Bickett	.10	.05
❑	180 Kerry Cash	.10	.05
❑	181 Quentin Coryatt	.20	.09
❑	182 Rodney Culver	.10	.05
❑	183 Steve Emtman	.10	.05
❑	184 Jeff George	.40	.18
❑	185 Jeff Herrod	.10	.05
❑	186 Jessie Hester	.10	.05
❑	187 Anthony Johnson	.20	.09
❑	188 Reggie Langhorne	.10	.05
❑	189 Roosevelt Potts RC	.10	.05
❑	190 Rohn Stark	.10	.05
❑	191 Clarence Verdin	.10	.05
❑	192 Will Wolford	.10	.05
❑	193 Marcus Allen	.40	.18
❑	194 John Alt	.10	.05
❑	195 Tim Barnett	.10	.05
❑	196 J.J.Birden	.10	.05
❑	197 Dale Carter	.10	.05
❑	198 Willie Davis	.40	.18
❑	199 Jaime Fields RC	.10	.05
❑	200 Dave Krieg	.20	.09
❑	201 Nick Lowery	.10	.05
❑	202 Charles Mincy RC	.10	.05
❑	203 Joe Montana	3.00	1.35
❑	204 Christian Okoye	.10	.05
❑	205 Dan Saleaumua	.10	.05
❑	206 Will Shields RC	.10	.05
❑	207 Tracy Simien	.10	.05
❑	208 Neil Smith	.40	.18
❑	209 Derrick Thomas	.40	.18
❑	210 Harvey Williams	.20	.09
❑	211 Barry Word	.10	.05
❑	212 Eddie Anderson	.10	.05
❑	213 Patrick Bates RC	.10	.05
❑	214 Nick Bell	.10	.05
❑	215 Tim Brown	.40	.18
❑	216 Willie Gault	.10	.05
❑	217 Gaston Green	.10	.05
❑	218 Billy Joe Hobert RC	.40	.18
❑	219 Ethan Horton	.10	.05

❑ 220 Jeff Hostetler .20 .09
❑ 221 James Lofton .20 .09
❑ 222 Howie Long .20 .09
❑ 223 Todd Marinovich .10 .05
❑ 224 Terry McDaniel .10 .05
❑ 225 Winston Moss .10 .05
❑ 226 Anthony Smith .10 .05
❑ 227 Greg Townsend .10 .05
❑ 228 Aaron Wallace .10 .05
❑ 229 Lionel Washington .10 .05
❑ 230 Steve Wisniewski .10 .05
❑ 231 Flipper Anderson .10 .05
❑ 232 Jerome Bettis RC 1.50 .70
❑ 233 Marc Boutte .10 .05
❑ 234 Shane Conlan .10 .05
❑ 235 Troy Drayton RC .20 .09
❑ 236 Henry Ellard .20 .09
❑ 237 Jim Everett .20 .09
❑ 238 Cleveland Gary .10 .05
❑ 239 Sean Gilbert .20 .09
❑ 240 Darryl Henley .10 .05
❑ 241 David Lang .10 .05
❑ 242 Todd Lyght .10 .05
❑ 243 Anthony Newman .10 .05
❑ 244 Roman Phifer .10 .05
❑ 245 Gerald Robinson .10 .05
❑ 246 Henry Rolling .10 .05
❑ 247 Jackie Slater .10 .05
❑ 248 Keith Byars .10 .05
❑ 249 Marco Coleman .10 .05
❑ 250 Bryan Cox .10 .05
❑ 251 Jeff Cross .10 .05
❑ 252 Irving Fryar .20 .09
❑ 253 Mark Higgs .10 .05
❑ 254 Dwight Hollier RC .10 .05
❑ 255 Mark Ingram .10 .05
❑ 256 Keith Jackson .20 .09
❑ 257 Terry Kirby RC .40 .18
❑ 258 Dan Marino 3.00 1.35
❑ 259 O.J.McDuffie RC 1.00 .45
❑ 260 John Offerdahl .10 .05
❑ 261 Louis Oliver .10 .05
❑ 262 Pete Stoyanovich .10 .05
❑ 263 Troy Vincent .10 .05
❑ 264 Richmond Webb .10 .05
❑ 265 Jarvis Williams .10 .05
❑ 266 Terry Allen .40 .18
❑ 267 Anthony Carter .20 .09
❑ 268 Cris Carter .75 .35
❑ 269 Roger Craig .20 .09
❑ 270 Jack Del Rio .10 .05
❑ 271 Chris Doleman .10 .05
❑ 272 Qadry Ismail RC 1.00 .45
❑ 273 Steve Jordan .10 .05
❑ 274 Randall McDaniel .10 .05
❑ 275 Audray McMillian .10 .05
❑ 276 John Randle .20 .09
❑ 277 Sean Salisbury .10 .05
❑ 278 Todd Scott .10 .05
❑ 279 Robert Smith RC 3.00 1.35
❑ 280 Henry Thomas .10 .05
❑ 281 Ray Agnew .10 .05
❑ 282 Bruce Armstrong .10 .05
❑ 283 Drew Bledsoe RC 4.00 1.80
❑ 284 Vincent Brisby RC .40 .18
❑ 285 Vincent Brown .10 .05
❑ 286 Eugene Chung .10 .05
❑ 287 Marv Cook .10 .05
❑ 288 Pat Harlow .10 .05
❑ 289 Jerome Henderson .10 .05
❑ 290 Greg McMurtry .10 .05
❑ 291 Leonard Russell .20 .09
❑ 292 Chris Singleton .10 .05
❑ 293 Chris Slade RC .20 .09
❑ 294 Andre Tippett .10 .05
❑ 295 Brent Williams .10 .05
❑ 296 Scott Zolak .10 .05
❑ 297 Morten Andersen .10 .05
❑ 298 Gene Atkins .10 .05
❑ 299 Mike Buck .10 .05
❑ 300 Toi Cook .10 .05
❑ 301 Jim Dombrowski .10 .05
❑ 302 Vaughn Dunbar .10 .05
❑ 303 Quinn Early .20 .09
❑ 304 Joel Hilgenberg .10 .05
❑ 305 Dalton Hilliard .10 .05
❑ 306 Rickey Jackson .10 .05
❑ 307 Vaughan Johnson .10 .05
❑ 308 Reginald Jones .10 .05
❑ 309 Eric Martin .10 .05
❑ 310 Wayne Martin .10 .05
❑ 311 Sam Mills .10 .05
❑ 312 Brad Muster .10 .05
❑ 313 Willie Roaf RC .20 .09
❑ 314 Irv Smith RC .10 .05
❑ 315 Wade Wilson .10 .05
❑ 316 Carlton Bailey .10 .05
❑ 317 Michael Brooks .10 .05
❑ 318 Derek Brown TE .10 .05
❑ 319 Marcus Buckley RC .10 .05
❑ 320 Jarrod Bunch .10 .05
❑ 321 Mark Collins .10 .05
❑ 322 Eric Dorsey .10 .05
❑ 323 Rodney Hampton .40 .18
❑ 324 Mark Jackson .10 .05
❑ 325 Pepper Johnson .10 .05
❑ 326 Ed McCaffrey .20 .09
❑ 327 Dave Meggett .10 .05
❑ 328 Bart Oates .10 .05
❑ 329 Mike Sherrard .10 .05
❑ 330 Phil Simms .20 .09
❑ 331 Michael Strahan RC .40 .18
❑ 332 Lawrence Taylor .40 .18
❑ 333 Brad Baxter .10 .05
❑ 334 Chris Burkett .10 .05
❑ 335 Kyle Clifton .10 .05
❑ 336 Boomer Esiason .20 .09
❑ 337 James Hasty .10 .05
❑ 338 Johnny Johnson .10 .05
❑ 339 Marvin Jones RC .10 .05
❑ 340 Jeff Lageman .10 .05
❑ 341 Mo Lewis .10 .05
❑ 342 Ronnie Lott .20 .09
❑ 343 Leonard Marshall .10 .05
❑ 344 Johnny Mitchell .10 .05
❑ 345 Rob Moore .20 .09
❑ 346 Browning Nagle .10 .05
❑ 347 Coleman Rudolph RC .10 .05
❑ 348 Blair Thomas .10 .05
❑ 349 Eric Thomas .10 .05
❑ 350 Brian Washington .10 .05
❑ 351 Marvin Washington .10 .05
❑ 352 Eric Allen .10 .05
❑ 353 Victor Bailey RC .10 .05
❑ 354 Fred Barnett .20 .09
❑ 355 Mark Bavaro .10 .05
❑ 356 Randall Cunningham .40 .18
❑ 357 Byron Evans .10 .05
❑ 358 Andy Harmon .20 .09
❑ 359 Tim Harris .10 .05
❑ 360 Lester Holmes .10 .05
❑ 361 Seth Joyner .10 .05
❑ 362 Keith Millard .10 .05
❑ 363 Leonard Renfro RC .10 .05
❑ 364 Heath Sherman .10 .05
❑ 365 Vai Sikahema .10 .05
❑ 366 Clyde Simmons .10 .05
❑ 367 William Thomas .10 .05
❑ 368 Herschel Walker .20 .09
❑ 369 Andre Waters .10 .05
❑ 370 Calvin Williams .20 .09
❑ 371 Johnny Bailey .10 .05
❑ 372 Steve Beuerlein .10 .05
❑ 373 Rich Camarillo .10 .05
❑ 374 Chuck Cecil .10 .05
❑ 375 Chris Chandler .20 .09
❑ 376 Gary Clark .20 .09
❑ 377 Ben Coleman RC .10 .05
❑ 378 Ernest Dye RC .10 .05
❑ 379 Ken Harvey .10 .05
❑ 380 Garrison Hearst RC 1.00 .45
❑ 381 Randal Hill .10 .05
❑ 382 Robert Massey .10 .05
❑ 383 Freddie Joe Nunn .10 .05
❑ 384 Ricky Proehl .10 .05
❑ 385 Luis Sharpe .10 .05
❑ 386 Tyronne Stowe .10 .05
❑ 387 Eric Swann .20 .09
❑ 388 Aeneas Williams .10 .05
❑ 389 Chad Brown RC .20 .09
❑ 390 Dermontti Dawson .10 .05
❑ 391 Donald Evans .10 .05
❑ 392 Deon Figures RC .20 .09
❑ 393 Barry Foster .20 .09
❑ 394 Jeff Graham .20 .09
❑ 395 Eric Green .10 .05
❑ 396 Kevin Greene .40 .18
❑ 397 Carlton Haselrig .10 .05
❑ 398 Andre Hastings RC .40 .18
❑ 399 D.J. Johnson .10 .05
❑ 400 Carnell Lake .10 .05
❑ 401 Greg Lloyd .40 .18
❑ 402 Neil O'Donnell .40 .18
❑ 403 Darren Perry .10 .05
❑ 404 Mike Tomczak .10 .05
❑ 405 Rod Woodson .40 .18
❑ 406 Eric Bieniemy .10 .05
❑ 407 Marion Butts .10 .05
❑ 408 Gill Byrd .10 .05
❑ 409 Darren Carrington RC .10 .05
❑ 410 Darrien Gordon RC .10 .05
❑ 411 Burt Grossman .10 .05
❑ 412 Courtney Hall .10 .05
❑ 413 Ronnie Harmon .10 .05
❑ 414 Stan Humphries .40 .18
❑ 415 Nate Lewis .10 .05
❑ 416 Natrone Means RC .75 .35
❑ 417 Anthony Miller .20 .09
❑ 418 Chris Mims .10 .05
❑ 419 Leslie O'Neal .20 .09
❑ 420 Gary Plummer .10 .05
❑ 421 Stanley Richard .10 .05
❑ 422 Junior Seau .40 .18
❑ 423 Harry Swayne .10 .05
❑ 424 Jerrol Williams .10 .05
❑ 425 Harris Barton .10 .05
❑ 426 Steve Bono .40 .18
❑ 427 Kevin Fagan .10 .05
❑ 428 Don Griffin .10 .05
❑ 429 Dana Hall .10 .05
❑ 430 Adrian Hardy .10 .05
❑ 431 Brent Jones .20 .09
❑ 432 Todd Kelly RC .10 .05
❑ 433 Amp Lee .10 .05
❑ 434 Tim McDonald .10 .05
❑ 435 Guy McIntyre .10 .05
❑ 436 Tom Rathman .10 .05
❑ 437 Jerry Rice 2.00 .90
❑ 438 Bill Romanowski .10 .05
❑ 439 Dana Stubblefield RC .40 .18
❑ 440 John Taylor .20 .09
❑ 441 Steve Wallace .10 .05
❑ 442 Michael Walter .10 .05
❑ 443 Ricky Watters .40 .18
❑ 444 Steve Young 1.50 .70
❑ 445 Robert Blackmon .10 .05
❑ 446 Brian Blades .20 .09
❑ 447 Jeff Bryant .10 .05
❑ 448 Ferrell Edmunds .10 .05
❑ 449 Carlton Gray RC .10 .05
❑ 450 Dwayne Harper .10 .05
❑ 451 Andy Heck .10 .05
❑ 452 Tommy Kane .10 .05
❑ 453 Cortez Kennedy .20 .09
❑ 454 Kelvin Martin .10 .05
❑ 455 Dan McGwire .10 .05
❑ 456 Rick Mirer RC .60 .25
❑ 457 Rufus Porter .10 .05
❑ 458 Ray Roberts .10 .05
❑ 459 Eugene Robinson .10 .05
❑ 460 Chris Warren .20 .09
❑ 461 John L. Williams .10 .05
❑ 462 Gary Anderson RB .10 .05
❑ 463 Tyji Armstrong .10 .05
❑ 464 Reggie Cobb .10 .05
❑ 465 Eric Curry RC .10 .05
❑ 466 Lawrence Dawsey .10 .05
❑ 467 Steve DeBerg .10 .05
❑ 468 Santana Dotson .20 .09
❑ 469 Demetrius DuBose RC .10 .05
❑ 470 Paul Gruber .10 .05
❑ 471 Ron Hall .10 .05
❑ 472 Courtney Hawkins .10 .05
❑ 473 Hardy Nickerson .20 .09
❑ 474 Ricky Reynolds .10 .05
❑ 475 Broderick Thomas .10 .05
❑ 476 Mark Wheeler .10 .05
❑ 477 Jimmy Williams .10 .05

	MINT	NRMT
❑ 478 Carl Banks	.10	.05
❑ 479 Reggie Brooks RC	.20	.09
❑ 480 Earnest Byner	.10	.05
❑ 481 Tom Carter RC	.20	.09
❑ 482 Andre Collins	.10	.05
❑ 483 Brad Edwards	.10	.05
❑ 484 Ricky Ervins	.10	.05
❑ 485 Kurt Gouveia	.10	.05
❑ 486 Darrell Green	.10	.05
❑ 487 Desmond Howard	.20	.09
❑ 488 Jim Lachey	.10	.05
❑ 489 Chip Lohmiller	.10	.05
❑ 490 Charles Mann	.10	.05
❑ 491 Tim McGee	.10	.05
❑ 492 Brian Mitchell	.20	.09
❑ 493 Art Monk	.20	.09
❑ 494 Mark Rypien	.10	.05
❑ 495 Ricky Sanders	.10	.05
❑ 496 Checklist 1-126 Chip Lohmiller	.10	.05
❑ 497 Checklist 127-254 Ricky Proehl	.10	.05
❑ 498 Checklist 255-382 Randall Cunningham	.10	.05
❑ 499 Checklist 383-500 Dave Meggett	.10	.05
❑ 500 Inserts Checklist William Perry	.10	.05

1994 Ultra

	MINT	NRMT
COMPLETE SET (525)	25.00	11.00
COMP.SERIES 1 (325)	12.00	5.50
COMP.SERIES 2 (200)	12.00	5.50

	MINT	NRMT
❑ 1 Steve Beuerlein	.10	.05
❑ 2 Gary Clark	.20	.09
❑ 3 Randal Hill	.10	.05
❑ 4 Seth Joyner	.10	.05
❑ 5 Jamir Miller RC	.10	.05
❑ 6 Ronald Moore	.10	.05
❑ 7 Luis Sharpe	.10	.05
❑ 8 Clyde Simmons	.10	.05
❑ 9 Eric Swann	.20	.09
❑ 10 Aeneas Williams	.10	.05
❑ 11 Chris Doleman	.10	.05
❑ 12 Bert Emanuel RC	1.00	.45
❑ 13 Moe Gardner	.10	.05
❑ 14 Jeff George	.40	.18
❑ 15 Roger Harper	.10	.05
❑ 16 Pierce Holt	.10	.05
❑ 17 Lincoln Kennedy	.10	.05
❑ 18 Erric Pegram	.10	.05
❑ 19 Andre Rison	.20	.09
❑ 20 Deion Sanders	.75	.35
❑ 21 Jessie Tuggle	.10	.05
❑ 22 Cornelius Bennett	.20	.09
❑ 23 Bill Brooks	.10	.05
❑ 24 Jeff Burris RC	.20	.09
❑ 25 Kent Hull	.10	.05
❑ 26 Henry Jones	.10	.05
❑ 27 Jim Kelly	.40	.18
❑ 28 Marvcus Patton	.10	.05
❑ 29 Andre Reed	.20	.09
❑ 30 Bruce Smith	.40	.18
❑ 31 Thomas Smith	.10	.05
❑ 32 Thurman Thomas	.40	.18
❑ 33 Jeff Wright	.10	.05
❑ 34 Trace Armstrong	.10	.05
❑ 35 Mark Carrier DB	.10	.05
❑ 36 Dante Jones	.10	.05
❑ 37 Erik Kramer	.20	.09
❑ 38 Terry Obee	.10	.05
❑ 39 Alonzo Spellman	.10	.05
❑ 40 John Thierry RC	.10	.05
❑ 41 Tom Waddle	.10	.05
❑ 42 Donnell Woolford	.10	.05
❑ 43 Tim Worley	.10	.05
❑ 44 Chris Zorich	.10	.05
❑ 45 John Copeland	.10	.05
❑ 46 Harold Green	.10	.05
❑ 47 David Klingler	.10	.05
❑ 48 Ricardo McDonald	.10	.05
❑ 49 Tony McGee	.10	.05
❑ 50 Louis Oliver	.10	.05
❑ 51 Carl Pickens	.40	.18
❑ 52 Darnay Scott RC	1.25	.55
❑ 53 Steve Tovar	.10	.05
❑ 54 Dan Wilkinson RC	.20	.09
❑ 55 Darryl Williams	.10	.05
❑ 56 Derrick Alexander WR RC	1.00	.45
❑ 57 Michael Jackson	.20	.09
❑ 58 Tony Jones	.10	.05
❑ 59 Antonio Langham RC	.20	.09
❑ 60 Eric Metcalf	.20	.09
❑ 61 Stevon Moore	.10	.05
❑ 62 Michael Dean Perry	.20	.09
❑ 63 Anthony Pleasant	.10	.05
❑ 64 Vinny Testaverde	.20	.09
❑ 65 Eric Turner	.10	.05
❑ 66 Tommy Vardell	.10	.05
❑ 67 Troy Aikman	1.50	.70
❑ 68 Larry Brown DB	.10	.05
❑ 69 Shante Carver RC	.10	.05
❑ 70 Charles Haley	.20	.09
❑ 71 Michael Irvin	.40	.18
❑ 72 Leon Lett	.10	.05
❑ 73 Nate Newton	.10	.05
❑ 74 Jay Novacek	.20	.09
❑ 75 Darrin Smith	.10	.05
❑ 76 Emmitt Smith	2.50	1.10
❑ 77 Tony Tolbert	.10	.05
❑ 78 Erik Williams	.10	.05
❑ 79 Kevin Williams WR	.20	.09
❑ 80 Steve Atwater	.10	.05
❑ 81 Rod Bernstine	.10	.05
❑ 82 Ray Crockett	.10	.05
❑ 83 Mike Croel	.10	.05
❑ 84 Shane Dronett	.10	.05
❑ 85 Jason Elam	.10	.05
❑ 86 John Elway	3.00	1.35
❑ 87 Simon Fletcher	.10	.05
❑ 88 Glyn Milburn	.20	.09
❑ 89 Anthony Miller	.20	.09
❑ 90 Shannon Sharpe	.20	.09
❑ 91 Gary Zimmerman	.10	.05
❑ 92 Bennie Blades	.10	.05
❑ 93 Lomas Brown	.10	.05
❑ 94 Mel Gray	.10	.05
❑ 95 Jason Hanson	.10	.05
❑ 96 Ryan McNeil	.10	.05
❑ 97 Scott Mitchell	.40	.18
❑ 98 Herman Moore	.40	.18
❑ 99 Johnnie Morton RC	1.25	.55
❑ 100 Robert Porcher	.10	.05
❑ 101 Barry Sanders	3.00	1.35
❑ 102 Chris Spielman	.20	.09
❑ 103 Pat Swilling	.10	.05
❑ 104 Edgar Bennett	.40	.18
❑ 105 Terrell Buckley	.10	.05
❑ 106 Reggie Cobb	.10	.05
❑ 107 Brett Favre	3.00	1.35
❑ 108 Sean Jones	.10	.05
❑ 109 Ken Ruettgers	.10	.05
❑ 110 Sterling Sharpe	.20	.09
❑ 111 Wayne Simmons	.10	.05
❑ 112 Aaron Taylor RC	.10	.05
❑ 113 George Teague	.10	.05
❑ 114 Reggie White	.40	.18
❑ 115 Micheal Barrow	.10	.05
❑ 116 Gary Brown	.10	.05
❑ 117 Cody Carlson	.10	.05
❑ 118 Ray Childress	.10	.05
❑ 119 Cris Dishman	.10	.05
❑ 120 Henry Ford RC	.10	.05
❑ 121 Haywood Jeffires	.20	.09
❑ 122 Bruce Matthews	.10	.05
❑ 123 Bubba McDowell	.10	.05
❑ 124 Marcus Robertson	.10	.05
❑ 125 Eddie Robinson	.10	.05
❑ 126 Webster Slaughter	.10	.05
❑ 127 Trev Alberts RC	.20	.09
❑ 128 Tony Bennett	.10	.05
❑ 129 Ray Buchanan	.10	.05
❑ 130 Quentin Coryatt	.10	.05
❑ 131 Eugene Daniel	.10	.05
❑ 132 Steve Emtman	.10	.05
❑ 133 Marshall Faulk RC	5.00	2.20
❑ 134 Jim Harbaugh	.40	.18
❑ 135 Roosevelt Potts	.10	.05
❑ 136 Rohn Stark	.10	.05
❑ 137 Marcus Allen	.40	.18
❑ 138 Donnell Bennett RC	.40	.18
❑ 139 Dale Carter	.10	.05
❑ 140 Tony Casillas	.10	.05
❑ 141 Mark Collins	.10	.05
❑ 142 Willie Davis	.20	.09
❑ 143 Tim Grunhard	.10	.05
❑ 144 Greg Hill RC	.40	.18
❑ 145 Joe Montana	3.00	1.35
❑ 146 Tracy Simien	.10	.05
❑ 147 Neil Smith	.40	.18
❑ 148 Derrick Thomas	.40	.18
❑ 149 Tim Brown	.40	.18
❑ 150 James Folston RC	.10	.05
❑ 151 Rob Fredrickson RC	.20	.09
❑ 152 Jeff Hostetler	.20	.09
❑ 153 Rocket Ismail	.20	.09
❑ 154 James Jett	.10	.05
❑ 155 Terry McDaniel	.10	.05
❑ 156 Winston Moss	.10	.05
❑ 157 Greg Robinson	.10	.05
❑ 158 Anthony Smith	.10	.05
❑ 159 Steve Wisniewski	.10	.05
❑ 160 Flipper Anderson	.10	.05
❑ 161 Jerome Bettis	.40	.18
❑ 162 Isaac Bruce RC	4.00	1.80
❑ 163 Shane Conlan	.10	.05
❑ 164 Wayne Gandy RC	.10	.05
❑ 165 Sean Gilbert	.10	.05
❑ 166 Todd Lyght	.10	.05
❑ 167 Chris Miller	.10	.05
❑ 168 Anthony Newman	.10	.05
❑ 169 Roman Phifer	.10	.05
❑ 170 Jackie Slater	.10	.05
❑ 171 Gene Atkins	.10	.05
❑ 172 Aubrey Beavers RC	.10	.05
❑ 173 Tim Bowens RC	.20	.09
❑ 174 J.B. Brown	.10	.05
❑ 175 Marco Coleman	.10	.05
❑ 176 Bryan Cox	.10	.05
❑ 177 Irving Fryar	.20	.09
❑ 178 Terry Kirby	.40	.18
❑ 179 Dan Marino	3.00	1.35
❑ 180 Troy Vincent	.10	.05
❑ 181 Richmond Webb	.10	.05
❑ 182 Terry Allen	.20	.09
❑ 183 Cris Carter	.75	.35
❑ 184 Jack Del Rio	.10	.05
❑ 185 Vencie Glenn	.10	.05
❑ 186 Randall McDaniel	.10	.05
❑ 187 Warren Moon	.40	.18
❑ 188 David Palmer RC	1.00	.45
❑ 189 John Randle	.20	.09
❑ 190 Todd Scott	.10	.05
❑ 191 Todd Steussie RC	.20	.09
❑ 192 Henry Thomas	.10	.05
❑ 193 Dewayne Washington RC	.20	.09
❑ 194 Bruce Armstrong	.10	.05
❑ 195 Harlon Barnett	.10	.05
❑ 196 Drew Bledsoe	1.50	.70
❑ 197 Vincent Brisby	.40	.18
❑ 198 Vincent Brown	.10	.05
❑ 199 Marion Butts	.10	.05
❑ 200 Ben Coates	.40	.18
❑ 201 Todd Collins	.10	.05
❑ 202 Maurice Hurst	.10	.05
❑ 203 Willie McGinest RC	.40	.18
❑ 204 Ricky Reynolds	.10	.05

❑ 205 Chris Slade .10 .05
❑ 206 Mario Bates RC .40 .18
❑ 207 Derek Brown RBK .10 .05
❑ 208 Vince Buck .10 .05
❑ 209 Quinn Early .20 .09
❑ 210 Jim Everett .20 .09
❑ 211 Michael Haynes .20 .09
❑ 212 Tyrone Hughes .20 .09
❑ 213 Joe Johnson RC .10 .05
❑ 214 Vaughan Johnson .10 .05
❑ 215 Willie Roaf .10 .05
❑ 216 Renaldo Turnbull .10 .05
❑ 217 Michael Brooks .10 .05
❑ 218 Dave Brown .20 .09
❑ 219 Howard Cross .10 .05
❑ 220 Stacey Dillard .10 .05
❑ 221 Jumbo Elliott .10 .05
❑ 222 Keith Hamilton .10 .05
❑ 223 Rodney Hampton .40 .18
❑ 224 Thomas Lewis RC .20 .09
❑ 225 Dave Meggett .10 .05
❑ 226 Corey Miller .10 .05
❑ 227 Thomas Randolph RC .10 .05
❑ 228 Mike Sherrard .10 .05
❑ 229 Kyle Clifton .10 .05
❑ 230 Boomer Esiason .20 .09
❑ 231 Aaron Glenn RC .20 .09
❑ 232 James Hasty .10 .05
❑ 233 Bobby Houston .10 .05
❑ 234 Johnny Johnson .10 .05
❑ 235 Mo Lewis .10 .05
❑ 236 Ronnie Lott .20 .09
❑ 237 Rob Moore .20 .09
❑ 238 Marvin Washington .10 .05
❑ 239 Ryan Yarborough RC .10 .05
❑ 240 Eric Allen .10 .05
❑ 241 Victor Bailey .10 .05
❑ 242 Fred Barnett .20 .09
❑ 243 Mark Bavaro .10 .05
❑ 244 Randall Cunningham .40 .18
❑ 245 Byron Evans .10 .05
❑ 246 William Fuller .10 .05
❑ 247 Andy Harmon .10 .05
❑ 248 William Perry .20 .09
❑ 249 Herschel Walker .20 .09
❑ 250 Bernard Williams RC .10 .05
❑ 251 Dermontti Dawson .10 .05
❑ 252 Deon Figures .10 .05
❑ 253 Barry Foster .10 .05
❑ 254 Kevin Greene .40 .18
❑ 255 Charles Johnson RC 1.00 .45
❑ 256 Levon Kirkland .10 .05
❑ 257 Greg Lloyd .40 .18
❑ 258 Neil O'Donnell .40 .18
❑ 259 Darren Perry .10 .05
❑ 260 Dwight Stone .10 .05
❑ 261 Rod Woodson .40 .18
❑ 262 John Carney .10 .05
❑ 263 Issac Davis RC .10 .05
❑ 264 Courtney Hall .10 .05
❑ 265 Ronnie Harmon .10 .05
❑ 266 Stan Humphries .40 .18
❑ 267 Vance Johnson .10 .05
❑ 268 Natrone Means .40 .18
❑ 269 Chris Mims .10 .05
❑ 270 Leslie O'Neal .10 .05
❑ 271 Stanley Richard .10 .05
❑ 272 Junior Seau .40 .18
❑ 273 Harris Barton .10 .05
❑ 274 Dennis Brown .10 .05
❑ 275 Eric Davis .10 .05
❑ 276 William Floyd RC .40 .18
❑ 277 John Johnson .10 .05
❑ 278 Tim McDonald .10 .05
❑ 279 Ken Norton Jr. .20 .09
❑ 280 Jerry Rice 1.50 .70
❑ 281 Jesse Sapolu .10 .05
❑ 282 Dana Stubblefield .40 .18
❑ 283 Ricky Watters .40 .18
❑ 284 Bryant Young RC .40 .18
❑ 285 Steve Young 1.00 .45
❑ 286 Sam Adams RC .20 .09
❑ 287 Brian Blades .20 .09
❑ 288 Ferrell Edmunds .10 .05
❑ 289 Patrick Hunter .10 .05
❑ 290 Cortez Kennedy .20 .09
❑ 291 Rick Mirer .40 .18
❑ 292 Nate Odomes .10 .05
❑ 293 Ray Roberts .10 .05
❑ 294 Eugene Robinson .10 .05
❑ 295 Rod Stephens .10 .05
❑ 296 Chris Warren .20 .09
❑ 297 Marty Carter .10 .05
❑ 298 Horace Copeland .10 .05
❑ 299 Eric Curry .10 .05
❑ 300 Santana Dotson .20 .09
❑ 301 Craig Erickson .10 .05
❑ 302 Paul Gruber .10 .05
❑ 303 Courtney Hawkins .10 .05
❑ 304 Martin Mayhew .10 .05
❑ 305 Hardy Nickerson .20 .09
❑ 306 Errict Rhett RC 1.00 .45
❑ 307 Vince Workman .10 .05
❑ 308 Reggie Brooks .20 .09
❑ 309 Tom Carter .10 .05
❑ 310 Andre Collins .10 .05
❑ 311 Brad Edwards .10 .05
❑ 312 Kurt Gouveia .10 .05
❑ 313 Darrell Green .10 .05
❑ 314 Ethan Horton .10 .05
❑ 315 Desmond Howard .20 .09
❑ 316 Tre Johnson RC .10 .05
❑ 317 Sterling Palmer RC .10 .05
❑ 318 Heath Shuler RC .40 .18
❑ 319 Tyronne Stowe .10 .05
❑ 320 NFL 75th Anniversary .10 .05
❑ 321 Checklist .10 .05
❑ 322 Checklist .10 .05
❑ 323 Checklist .10 .05
❑ 324 Checklist .10 .05
❑ 325 Checklist .10 .05
❑ 326 Garrison Hearst .40 .18
❑ 327 Eric Hill .10 .05
❑ 328 Seth Joyner .10 .05
❑ 329 Jim McMahon .10 .05
❑ 330 Jamir Miller .10 .05
❑ 331 Ricky Proehl .10 .05
❑ 332 Clyde Simmons .10 .05
❑ 333 Chris Doleman .10 .05
❑ 334 Bert Emanuel .40 .18
❑ 335 Jeff George .40 .18
❑ 336 D.J. Johnson .10 .05
❑ 337 Terance Mathis .20 .09
❑ 338 Clay Matthews .10 .05
❑ 339 Tony Smith .10 .05
❑ 340 Don Beebe .10 .05
❑ 341 Bucky Brooks RC .10 .05
❑ 342 Jeff Burris .20 .09
❑ 343 Kenneth Davis .10 .05
❑ 344 Phil Hansen .10 .05
❑ 345 Pete Metzelaars .10 .05
❑ 346 Darryl Talley .10 .05
❑ 347 Joe Cain .10 .05
❑ 348 Curtis Conway .40 .18
❑ 349 Shaun Gayle .10 .05
❑ 350 Chris Gedney .10 .05
❑ 351 Erik Kramer .20 .09
❑ 352 Vinson Smith .10 .05
❑ 353 John Thierry .10 .05
❑ 354 Lewis Tillman .10 .05
❑ 355 Mike Brim .10 .05
❑ 356 Derrick Fenner .10 .05
❑ 357 James Francis .10 .05
❑ 358 Louis Oliver .10 .05
❑ 359 Darnay Scott .50 .23
❑ 360 Dan Wilkinson .20 .09
❑ 361 Alfred Williams .10 .05
❑ 362 Derrick Alexander WR .40 .18
❑ 363 Rob Burnett .10 .05
❑ 364 Mark Carrier WR .20 .09
❑ 365 Steve Everitt .10 .05
❑ 366 Leroy Hoard .10 .05
❑ 367 Pepper Johnson .10 .05
❑ 368 Antonio Langham .20 .09
❑ 369 Shante Carver .10 .05
❑ 370 Alvin Harper .20 .09
❑ 371 Daryl Johnston .20 .09
❑ 372 Russell Maryland .10 .05
❑ 373 Kevin Smith .10 .05
❑ 374 Mark Stepnoski .10 .05
❑ 375 Darren Woodson .20 .09
❑ 376 Allen Aldridge RC .10 .05
❑ 377 Ray Crockett .10 .05
❑ 378 Karl Mecklenburg .10 .05
❑ 379 Anthony Miller .20 .09
❑ 380 Mike Pritchard .10 .05
❑ 381 Leonard Russell .10 .05
❑ 382 Dennis Smith .10 .05
❑ 383 Anthony Carter .20 .09
❑ 384 Van Malone RC .10 .05
❑ 385 Robert Massey .10 .05
❑ 386 Scott Mitchell .40 .18
❑ 387 Johnnie Morton .40 .18
❑ 388 Brett Perriman .20 .09
❑ 389 Tracy Scroggins .10 .05
❑ 390 Robert Brooks .40 .18
❑ 391 LeRoy Butler .10 .05
❑ 392 Reggie Cobb .10 .05
❑ 393 Sean Jones .10 .05
❑ 394 George Koonce .10 .05
❑ 395 Steve McMichael .20 .09
❑ 396 Bryce Paup .40 .18
❑ 397 Aaron Taylor .10 .05
❑ 398 Henry Ford .10 .05
❑ 399 Ernest Givins .20 .09
❑ 400 Jeremy Nunley RC .10 .05
❑ 401 Bo Orlando .10 .05
❑ 402 Al Smith .10 .05
❑ 403 Barron Wortham RC .10 .05
❑ 404 Trev Alberts .20 .09
❑ 405 Tony Bennett .10 .05
❑ 406 Kerry Cash .10 .05
❑ 407 Sean Dawkins RC .40 .18
❑ 408 Marshall Faulk 2.00 .90
❑ 409 Jim Harbaugh .40 .18
❑ 410 Jeff Herrod .10 .05
❑ 411 Kimble Anders .20 .09
❑ 412 Donnell Bennett .20 .09
❑ 413 J.J. Birden .10 .05
❑ 414 Mark Collins .10 .05
❑ 415 Lake Dawson RC .40 .18
❑ 416 Greg Hill .40 .18
❑ 417 Charles Mincy .10 .05
❑ 418 Greg Biekert .10 .05
❑ 419 Rob Fredrickson .20 .09
❑ 420 Nolan Harrison .10 .05
❑ 421 Jeff Jaeger .10 .05
❑ 422 Albert Lewis .10 .05
❑ 423 Chester McGlockton .10 .05
❑ 424 Tom Rathman .10 .05
❑ 425 Harvey Williams .20 .09
❑ 426 Isaac Bruce 1.50 .70
❑ 427 Troy Drayton .10 .05
❑ 428 Wayne Gandy .10 .05
❑ 429 Fred Stokes .10 .05
❑ 430 Robert Young .10 .05
❑ 431 Gene Atkins .10 .05
❑ 432 Aubrey Beavers .10 .05
❑ 433 Tim Bowens .20 .09
❑ 434 Keith Byars .10 .05
❑ 435 Jeff Cross .10 .05
❑ 436 Mark Ingram .10 .05
❑ 437 Keith Jackson .10 .05
❑ 438 Michael Stewart .10 .05
❑ 439 Chris Hinton .10 .05
❑ 440 Qadry Ismail .40 .18
❑ 441 Carlos Jenkins .10 .05
❑ 442 Warren Moon .40 .18
❑ 443 David Palmer .20 .09
❑ 444 Jake Reed .20 .09
❑ 445 Robert Smith .40 .18
❑ 446 Todd Steussie .20 .09
❑ 447 Dewayne Washington .20 .09
❑ 448 Marion Butts .10 .05
❑ 449 Tim Goad .10 .05
❑ 450 Myron Guyton .10 .05
❑ 451 Kevin Lee RC .10 .05
❑ 452 Willie McGinest .40 .18
❑ 453 Ricky Reynolds .10 .05
❑ 454 Michael Timpson .10 .05
❑ 455 Morten Andersen .10 .05
❑ 456 Jim Everett .20 .09
❑ 457 Michael Haynes .20 .09
❑ 458 Joe Johnson .10 .05
❑ 459 Wayne Martin .10 .05
❑ 460 Sam Mills .10 .05
❑ 461 Irv Smith .10 .05
❑ 462 Carlton Bailey .10 .05

❑ 463 Chris Calloway .10 .05
❑ 464 Mark Jackson .10 .05
❑ 465 Thomas Lewis .20 .09
❑ 466 Thomas Randolph .10 .05
❑ 467 Stevie Anderson RC .10 .05
❑ 468 Brad Baxter .10 .05
❑ 469 Aaron Glenn .20 .09
❑ 470 Jeff Lageman .10 .05
❑ 471 Johnny Mitchell .10 .05
❑ 472 Art Monk .20 .09
❑ 473 William Fuller .10 .05
❑ 474 Charlie Garner RC 1.50 .70
❑ 475 Vaughn Hebron .10 .05
❑ 476 Bill Romanowski .10 .05
❑ 477 William Thomas .10 .05
❑ 478 Greg Townsend .10 .05
❑ 479 Bernard Williams .10 .05
❑ 480 Calvin Williams .20 .09
❑ 481 Eric Green .10 .05
❑ 482 Charles Johnson .40 .18
❑ 483 Carnell Lake .10 .05
❑ 484 Byron Bam Morris RC .40 .18
❑ 485 John L. Williams .10 .05
❑ 486 Darren Carrington .10 .05
❑ 487 Andre Coleman RC .10 .05
❑ 488 Isaac Davis .10 .05
❑ 489 Dwayne Harper .10 .05
❑ 490 Tony Martin .40 .18
❑ 491 Mark Seay RC .40 .18
❑ 492 Richard Dent .20 .09
❑ 493 William Floyd .40 .18
❑ 494 Rickey Jackson .10 .05
❑ 495 Brent Jones .20 .09
❑ 496 Ken Norton Jr. .20 .09
❑ 497 Gary Plummer .10 .05
❑ 498 Deion Sanders .75 .35
❑ 499 John Taylor .20 .09
❑ 500 Lee Woodall RC .10 .05
❑ 501 Bryant Young .40 .18
❑ 502 Sam Adams .20 .09
❑ 503 Howard Ballard .10 .05
❑ 504 Michael Bates .10 .05
❑ 505 Robert Blackmon .10 .05
❑ 506 John Kasay .10 .05
❑ 507 Kelvin Martin .10 .05
❑ 508 Kevin Mawae RC .10 .05
❑ 509 Rufus Porter .10 .05
❑ 510 Lawrence Dawsey .10 .05
❑ 511 Trent Dilfer RC 2.00 .90
❑ 512 Thomas Everett .10 .05
❑ 513 Jackie Harris .10 .05
❑ 514 Errict Rhett .20 .09
❑ 515 Henry Ellard .20 .09
❑ 516 John Friesz .20 .09
❑ 517 Ken Harvey .10 .05
❑ 518 Ethan Horton .10 .05
❑ 519 Tre Johnson .10 .05
❑ 520 Jim Lachey .10 .05
❑ 521 Heath Shuler .40 .18
❑ 522 Tony Woods .10 .05
❑ 523 Checklist .10 .05
❑ 524 Checklist .10 .05
❑ 525 Checklist .10 .05

1995 Ultra

	MINT	NRMT
COMPLETE SET (550)	60.00	27.00
COMP.SERIES 1 (350)	30.00	13.50
COMP.SERIES 2 (200)	30.00	13.50

❑ 1 Michael Bankston .10 .05
❑ 2 Larry Centers .20 .09
❑ 3 Garrison Hearst .40 .18
❑ 4 Eric Hill .10 .05
❑ 5 Seth Joyner .10 .05
❑ 6 Lorenzo Lynch .10 .05
❑ 7 Jamir Miller .10 .05
❑ 8 Clyde Simmons .10 .05
❑ 9 Eric Swann .20 .09
❑ 10 Aeneas Williams .10 .05
❑ 11 Devin Bush RC .10 .05
❑ 12 Ron Davis RC .10 .05
❑ 13 Chris Doleman .10 .05
❑ 14 Bert Emanuel .40 .18
❑ 15 Jeff George .20 .09
❑ 16 Roger Harper .10 .05
❑ 17 Craig Heyward .20 .09
❑ 18 Pierce Holt .10 .05
❑ 19 D.J. Johnson .10 .05
❑ 20 Terance Mathis .20 .09
❑ 21 Chuck Smith .10 .05
❑ 22 Jessie Tuggle .10 .05
❑ 23 Cornelius Bennett .20 .09
❑ 24 Ruben Brown RC .10 .05
❑ 25 Jeff Burris .10 .05
❑ 26 Matt Darby .10 .05
❑ 27 Phil Hansen .10 .05
❑ 28 Henry Jones .10 .05
❑ 29 Jim Kelly .40 .18
❑ 30 Mark Maddox RC .10 .05
❑ 31 Andre Reed .20 .09
❑ 32 Bruce Smith .40 .18
❑ 33 Don Beebe .10 .05
❑ 34 Kerry Collins RC 2.00 .90
❑ 35 Darion Conner .10 .05
❑ 36 Pete Metzelaars .10 .05
❑ 37 Sam Mills .20 .09
❑ 38 Tyrone Poole RC .20 .09
❑ 39 Joe Cain .10 .05
❑ 40 Mark Carrier DB .10 .05
❑ 41 Curtis Conway .40 .18
❑ 42 Jeff Graham .10 .05
❑ 43 Raymont Harris .10 .05
❑ 44 Erik Kramer .10 .05
❑ 45 Rashaan Salaam RC .40 .18
❑ 46 Lewis Tillman .10 .05
❑ 47 Donnell Woolford .10 .05
❑ 48 Chris Zorich .10 .05
❑ 49 Jeff Blake RC 1.25 .55
❑ 50 Mike Brim .10 .05
❑ 51 Ki-Jana Carter RC .40 .18
❑ 52 James Francis .10 .05
❑ 53 Carl Pickens .40 .18
❑ 54 Darnay Scott .40 .18
❑ 55 Steve Tovar .10 .05
❑ 56 Dan Wilkinson .20 .09
❑ 57 Alfred Williams .10 .05
❑ 58 Darryl Williams .10 .05
❑ 59 Derrick Alexander WR .40 .18
❑ 60 Rob Burnett .10 .05
❑ 61 Steve Everitt .10 .05
❑ 62 Leroy Hoard .10 .05
❑ 63 Michael Jackson .20 .09
❑ 64 Pepper Johnson .10 .05
❑ 65 Tony Jones .10 .05
❑ 66 Antonio Langham .10 .05
❑ 67 Anthony Pleasant .10 .05
❑ 68 Craig Powell RC .10 .05
❑ 69 Vinny Testaverde .20 .09
❑ 70 Eric Turner .10 .05
❑ 71 Troy Aikman 1.50 .70
❑ 72 Charles Haley .20 .09
❑ 73 Michael Irvin .40 .18
❑ 74 Daryl Johnston .20 .09
❑ 75 Robert Jones .10 .05
❑ 76 Leon Lett .10 .05
❑ 77 Russell Maryland .10 .05
❑ 78 Jay Novacek .20 .09
❑ 79 Darrin Smith .10 .05
❑ 80 Emmitt Smith 2.50 1.10
❑ 81 Kevin Smith .10 .05
❑ 82 Erik Williams .10 .05
❑ 83 Kevin Williams WR .20 .09
❑ 84 Sherman Williams RC .10 .05
❑ 85 Darren Woodson .20 .09
❑ 86 Elijah Alexander RC .10 .05
❑ 87 Steve Atwater .10 .05
❑ 88 Ray Crockett .10 .05
❑ 89 Shane Dronett .10 .05
❑ 90 Jason Elam .10 .05
❑ 91 John Elway 3.00 1.35
❑ 92 Simon Fletcher .10 .05
❑ 93 Glyn Milburn .10 .05
❑ 94 Anthony Miller .20 .09
❑ 95 Leonard Russell .10 .05
❑ 96 Shannon Sharpe .20 .09
❑ 97 Bennie Blades .10 .05
❑ 98 Lomas Brown .10 .05
❑ 99 Willie Clay .10 .05
❑ 100 Luther Elliss RC .10 .05
❑ 101 Mike Johnson .10 .05
❑ 102 Robert Massey .10 .05
❑ 103 Scott Mitchell .20 .09
❑ 104 Herman Moore .40 .18
❑ 105 Brett Perriman .20 .09
❑ 106 Robert Porcher .10 .05
❑ 107 Barry Sanders 3.00 1.35
❑ 108 Chris Spielman .20 .09
❑ 109 Edgar Bennett .20 .09
❑ 110 Robert Brooks .40 .18
❑ 111 LeRoy Butler .10 .05
❑ 112 Brett Favre 3.00 1.35
❑ 113 Sean Jones .10 .05
❑ 114 John Jurkovic .10 .05
❑ 115 George Koonce .10 .05
❑ 116 Wayne Simmons .10 .05
❑ 117 George Teague .10 .05
❑ 118 Reggie White .40 .18
❑ 119 Micheal Barrow .10 .05
❑ 120 Gary Brown .10 .05
❑ 121 Cody Carlson .10 .05
❑ 122 Ray Childress .10 .05
❑ 123 Cris Dishman .10 .05
❑ 124 Bruce Matthews .10 .05
❑ 125 Steve McNair RC 3.00 1.35
❑ 126 Marcus Robertson .10 .05
❑ 127 Webster Slaughter .10 .05
❑ 128 Al Smith .10 .05
❑ 129 Tony Bennett .10 .05
❑ 130 Ray Buchanan .10 .05
❑ 131 Quentin Coryatt .20 .09
❑ 132 Sean Dawkins .20 .09
❑ 133 Marshall Faulk .75 .35
❑ 134 Stephen Grant RC .10 .05
❑ 135 Jim Harbaugh .20 .09
❑ 136 Jeff Herrod .10 .05
❑ 137 Ellis Johnson RC .10 .05
❑ 138 Tony Siragusa .10 .05
❑ 139 Steve Beuerlein .10 .05
❑ 140 Tony Boselli RC .40 .18
❑ 141 Darren Carrington .10 .05
❑ 142 Reggie Cobb .10 .05
❑ 143 Kelvin Martin .10 .05
❑ 144 Kelvin Pritchett .10 .05
❑ 145 Joel Smeenge .10 .05
❑ 146 James O. Stewart RC 2.50 1.10
❑ 147 Marcus Allen .40 .18
❑ 148 Kimble Anders .20 .09
❑ 149 Dale Carter .20 .09
❑ 150 Mark Collins .10 .05
❑ 151 Willie Davis .20 .09
❑ 152 Lake Dawson .20 .09
❑ 153 Greg Hill .20 .09
❑ 154 Trezelle Jenkins RC .10 .05
❑ 155 Darren Mickell .10 .05
❑ 156 Tracy Simien .10 .05
❑ 157 Neil Smith .20 .09
❑ 158 William White .10 .05
❑ 159 Joe Aska RC .20 .09
❑ 160 Greg Biekert .10 .05
❑ 161 Tim Brown .40 .18
❑ 162 Rob Fredrickson .10 .05
❑ 163 Andrew Glover RC .10 .05
❑ 164 Jeff Hostetler .20 .09
❑ 165 Rocket Ismail .20 .09
❑ 166 Napoleon Kaufman RC 2.00 .90
❑ 167 Terry McDaniel .10 .05
❑ 168 Chester McGlockton .20 .09
❑ 169 Anthony Smith .10 .05

❑ 170 Harvey Williams .10 .05
❑ 171 Steve Wisniewski .10 .05
❑ 172 Gene Atkins .10 .05
❑ 173 Aubrey Beavers .10 .05
❑ 174 Tim Bowens .10 .05
❑ 175 Bryan Cox .10 .05
❑ 176 Jeff Cross .10 .05
❑ 177 Irving Fryar .20 .09
❑ 178 Dan Marino 3.00 1.35
❑ 179 O.J. McDuffie .40 .18
❑ 180 Billy Milner .10 .05
❑ 181 Bernie Parmalee .20 .09
❑ 182 Troy Vincent .10 .05
❑ 183 Richmond Webb .10 .05
❑ 184 De. Alexander DE RC .10 .05
❑ 185 Cris Carter .40 .18
❑ 186 Jack Del Rio .10 .05
❑ 187 Qadry Ismail .20 .09
❑ 188 Ed McDaniel .10 .05
❑ 189 Randall McDaniel .10 .05
❑ 190 Warren Moon .20 .09
❑ 191 John Randle .20 .09
❑ 192 Jake Reed .20 .09
❑ 193 Fuad Reveiz .10 .05
❑ 194 Korey Stringer RC .10 .05
❑ 195 Dewayne Washington .20 .09
❑ 196 Bruce Armstrong .10 .05
❑ 197 Drew Bledsoe 1.50 .70
❑ 198 Vincent Brisby .10 .05
❑ 199 Vincent Brown .10 .05
❑ 200 Marion Butts .10 .05
❑ 201 Ben Coates .20 .09
❑ 202 Myron Guyton .10 .05
❑ 203 Maurice Hurst .10 .05
❑ 204 Mike Jones .10 .05
❑ 205 Ty Law RC .20 .09
❑ 206 Willie McGinest .20 .09
❑ 207 Chris Slade .20 .09
❑ 208 Mario Bates .40 .18
❑ 209 Quinn Early .20 .09
❑ 210 Jim Everett .10 .05
❑ 211 Mark Fields RC .10 .05
❑ 212 Michael Haynes .20 .09
❑ 213 Tyrone Hughes .20 .09
❑ 214 Joe Johnson .10 .05
❑ 215 Wayne Martin .10 .05
❑ 216 Willie Roaf .10 .05
❑ 217 Irv Smith .10 .05
❑ 218 Jimmy Spencer .10 .05
❑ 219 Winfred Tubbs .10 .05
❑ 220 Renaldo Turnbull .10 .05
❑ 221 Michael Brooks .10 .05
❑ 222 Dave Brown .20 .09
❑ 223 Chris Calloway .10 .05
❑ 224 Howard Cross .10 .05
❑ 225 John Elliott .10 .05
❑ 226 Keith Hamilton .10 .05
❑ 227 Rodney Hampton .20 .09
❑ 228 Thomas Lewis .20 .09
❑ 229 Thomas Randolph .10 .05
❑ 230 Mike Sherrard .10 .05
❑ 231 Michael Strahan .20 .09
❑ 232 Tyrone Wheatley RC 1.50 .70
❑ 233 Brad Baxter .10 .05
❑ 234 Kyle Brady RC .40 .18
❑ 235 Kyle Clifton .10 .05
❑ 236 Hugh Douglas RC .40 .18
❑ 237 Boomer Esiason .20 .09
❑ 238 Aaron Glenn .10 .05
❑ 239 Bobby Houston .10 .05
❑ 240 Johnny Johnson .10 .05
❑ 241 Mo Lewis .10 .05
❑ 242 Johnny Mitchell .10 .05
❑ 243 Marvin Washington .10 .05
❑ 244 Fred Barnett .20 .09
❑ 245 Randall Cunningham .40 .18
❑ 246 William Fuller .10 .05
❑ 247 Charlie Garner .20 .09
❑ 248 Andy Harmon .10 .05
❑ 249 Greg Jackson .10 .05
❑ 250 Mike Mamula RC .20 .09
❑ 251 Bill Romanowski .10 .05
❑ 252 Bobby Taylor RC .20 .09
❑ 253 William Thomas .10 .05
❑ 254 Calvin Williams .20 .09
❑ 255 Michael Zordich .10 .05
❑ 256 Chad Brown .20 .09
❑ 257 Mark Bruener RC .20 .09
❑ 258 Dermontti Dawson .20 .09
❑ 259 Barry Foster .20 .09
❑ 260 Kevin Greene .20 .09
❑ 261 Charles Johnson .20 .09
❑ 262 Carnell Lake .10 .05
❑ 263 Greg Lloyd .20 .09
❑ 264 Byron Bam Morris .20 .09
❑ 265 Neil O'Donnell .20 .09
❑ 266 Darren Perry .10 .05
❑ 267 Ray Seals .10 .05
❑ 268 Kordell Stewart RC 2.50 1.10
❑ 269 John L. Williams .10 .05
❑ 270 Rod Woodson .20 .09
❑ 271 Jerome Bettis .40 .18
❑ 272 Isaac Bruce .75 .35
❑ 273 Kevin Carter RC .40 .18
❑ 274 Shane Conlan .10 .05
❑ 275 Troy Drayton .10 .05
❑ 276 Sean Gilbert .20 .09
❑ 277 Todd Lyght .10 .05
❑ 278 Chris Miller .10 .05
❑ 279 Anthony Newman .10 .05
❑ 280 Roman Phifer .10 .05
❑ 281 Robert Young .10 .05
❑ 282 John Carney .10 .05
❑ 283 Andre Coleman .10 .05
❑ 284 Courtney Hall .10 .05
❑ 285 Ronnie Harmon .10 .05
❑ 286 Dwayne Harper .10 .05
❑ 287 Stan Humphries .20 .09
❑ 288 Shawn Jefferson .10 .05
❑ 289 Tony Martin .20 .09
❑ 290 Natrone Means .40 .18
❑ 291 Chris Mims .10 .05
❑ 292 Leslie O'Neal .20 .09
❑ 293 Junior Seau .40 .18
❑ 294 Mark Seay .20 .09
❑ 295 Eric Davis .10 .05
❑ 296 William Floyd .40 .18
❑ 297 Merton Hanks .10 .05
❑ 298 Brent Jones .10 .05
❑ 299 Ken Norton Jr. .20 .09
❑ 300 Gary Plummer .10 .05
❑ 301 Jerry Rice 1.50 .70
❑ 302 Deion Sanders 1.00 .45
❑ 303 Jesse Sapolu .10 .05
❑ 304 J.J. Stokes RC .40 .18
❑ 305 Dana Stubblefield .40 .18
❑ 306 John Taylor .10 .05
❑ 307 Steve Wallace .10 .05
❑ 308 Lee Woodall .10 .05
❑ 309 Bryant Young .20 .09
❑ 310 Steve Young 1.25 .55
❑ 311 Sam Adams .10 .05
❑ 312 Howard Ballard .10 .05
❑ 313 Robert Blackmon .10 .05
❑ 314 Brian Blades .20 .09
❑ 315 Joey Galloway RC 2.50 1.10
❑ 316 Carlton Gray .10 .05
❑ 317 Cortez Kennedy .20 .09
❑ 318 Rick Mirer .40 .18
❑ 319 Eugene Robinson .10 .05
❑ 320 Chris Warren .20 .09
❑ 321 Terry Wooden .10 .05
❑ 322 Derrick Brooks RC .40 .18
❑ 323 Lawrence Dawsey .10 .05
❑ 324 Trent Dilfer .40 .18
❑ 325 Santana Dotson .10 .05
❑ 326 Thomas Everett .10 .05
❑ 327 Paul Gruber .10 .05
❑ 328 Jackie Harris .10 .05
❑ 329 Courtney Hawkins .10 .05
❑ 330 Martin Mayhew .10 .05
❑ 331 Hardy Nickerson .10 .05
❑ 332 Errict Rhett .40 .18
❑ 333 Warren Sapp RC .75 .35
❑ 334 Charles Wilson .10 .05
❑ 335 Reggie Brooks .20 .09
❑ 336 Tom Carter .10 .05
❑ 337 Henry Ellard .20 .09
❑ 338 Ricky Ervins .10 .05
❑ 339 Darrell Green .10 .05
❑ 340 Ken Harvey .10 .05
❑ 341 Brian Mitchell .10 .05
❑ 342 Cory Raymer RC .10 .05
❑ 343 Heath Shuler .40 .18
❑ 344 Michael Westbrook RC 2.00 .90
❑ 345 Tony Woods .10 .05
❑ 346 Checklist .10 .05
❑ 347 Checklist .10 .05
❑ 348 Checklist .10 .05
❑ 349 Checklist .10 .05
❑ 350 Checklist .10 .05
❑ 351 Checklist .10 .05
❑ 352 Checklist .10 .05
❑ 353 Dave Krieg .10 .05
❑ 354 Rob Moore .10 .05
❑ 355 J.J. Birden .10 .05
❑ 356 Eric Metcalf .20 .09
❑ 357 Bryce Paup .40 .18
❑ 358 Willie Green .20 .09
❑ 359 Derrick Moore .10 .05
❑ 360 Michael Timpson .10 .05
❑ 361 Eric Bieniemy .10 .05
❑ 362 Keenan McCardell .40 .18
❑ 363 Andre Rison .20 .09
❑ 364 Lorenzo White .10 .05
❑ 365 Deion Sanders 1.00 .45
❑ 366 Wade Wilson .10 .05
❑ 367 Aaron Craver .10 .05
❑ 368 Michael Dean Perry .10 .05
❑ 369 Rod Smith WR RC 12.00 5.50
❑ 370 Henry Thomas .10 .05
❑ 371 Mark Ingram .10 .05
❑ 372 Chris Chandler .20 .09
❑ 373 Mel Gray .10 .05
❑ 374 Flipper Anderson .10 .05
❑ 375 Craig Erickson .10 .05
❑ 376 Mark Brunell 1.50 .70
❑ 377 Ernest Givins .10 .05
❑ 378 Randy Jordan .10 .05
❑ 379 Webster Slaughter .10 .05
❑ 380 Tamarick Vanover RC .40 .18
❑ 381 Gary Clark .10 .05
❑ 382 Steve Emtman .10 .05
❑ 383 Eric Green .10 .05
❑ 384 Louis Oliver .10 .05
❑ 385 Robert Smith .40 .18
❑ 386 Dave Meggett .10 .05
❑ 387 Eric Allen .10 .05
❑ 388 Wesley Walls .20 .09
❑ 389 Herschel Walker .20 .09
❑ 390 Ronald Moore .10 .05
❑ 391 Adrian Murrell .20 .09
❑ 392 Charles Wilson .10 .05
❑ 393 Derrick Fenner .10 .05
❑ 394 Pat Swilling .10 .05
❑ 395 Kelvin Martin .10 .05
❑ 396 Rodney Peete .10 .05
❑ 397 Ricky Watters .40 .18
❑ 398 Erric Pegram .20 .09
❑ 399 Leonard Russell .10 .05
❑ 400 Alexander Wright .10 .05
❑ 401 Darrien Gordon .10 .05
❑ 402 Alfred Pupunu .10 .05
❑ 403 Elvis Grbac .40 .18
❑ 404 Derek Loville .10 .05
❑ 405 Steve Broussard .10 .05
❑ 406 Ricky Proehl .10 .05
❑ 407 Bobby Joe Edmonds .10 .05
❑ 408 Alvin Harper .10 .05
❑ 409 Dave Moore .10 .05
❑ 410 Terry Allen .20 .09
❑ 411 Gus Frerotte .40 .18
❑ 412 Leslie Shepherd RC .20 .09
❑ 413 Stoney Case RC .40 .18
❑ 414 Frank Sanders RC 1.25 .55
❑ 415 Roell Preston RC .10 .05
❑ 416 Lorenzo Styles RC .10 .05
❑ 417 Justin Armour RC .10 .05
❑ 418 Todd Collins RC .40 .18
❑ 419 Darick Holmes RC .20 .09
❑ 420 Kerry Collins .75 .35
❑ 421 Tyrone Poole .10 .05
❑ 422 Rashaan Salaam .20 .09
❑ 423 Todd Sauerbrun RC .10 .05
❑ 424 Ki-Jana Carter .40 .18
❑ 425 David Dunn RC .10 .05
❑ 426 Ernest Hunter RC .10 .05
❑ 427 Eric Zeier RC .40 .18

	Card	Mint	Nrmt
❑	428 Eric Bjornson RC	.20	.09
❑	429 Sherman Williams	.10	.05
❑	430 Terrell Davis RC	12.00	5.50
❑	431 Luther Elliss	.10	.05
❑	432 Kez McCorvey RC	.10	.05
❑	433 Antonio Freeman RC	3.00	1.35
❑	434 Craig Newsome RC	.10	.05
❑	435 Steve McNair	1.50	.70
❑	436 Chris Sanders RC	.40	.18
❑	437 Zack Crockett RC	.10	.05
❑	438 Ellis Johnson	.10	.05
❑	439 Tony Boselli	.40	.18
❑	440 James O. Stewart	1.25	.55
❑	441 Trezelle Jenkins	.10	.05
❑	442 Tamarick Vanover	.40	.18
❑	443 Derrick Alexander DE	.10	.05
❑	444 Chad May RC	.10	.05
❑	445 James A.Stewart RC	.10	.05
❑	446 Ty Law	.10	.05
❑	447 Curtis Martin RC	3.00	1.35
❑	448 Will Moore RC	.10	.05
❑	449 Mark Fields	.10	.05
❑	450 Ray Zellars RC	.20	.09
❑	451 Charles Way RC	.10	.05
❑	452 Tyrone Wheatley	.40	.18
❑	453 Kyle Brady	.40	.18
❑	454 Wayne Chrebet RC	2.50	1.10
❑	455 Hugh Douglas	.20	.09
❑	456 Chris T.Jones RC	.40	.18
❑	457 Mike Mamula	.10	.05
❑	458 Fred McCrary RC	.10	.05
❑	459 Bobby Taylor	.20	.09
❑	460 Mark Bruener	.20	.09
❑	461 Kordell Stewart	1.25	.55
❑	462 Kevin Carter	.40	.18
❑	463 Lovell Pinkney RC	.10	.05
❑	464 Johnny Thomas RC	.10	.05
❑	465 Terrell Fletcher RC	.10	.05
❑	466 Jimmy Oliver RC	.10	.05
❑	467 J.J. Stokes	.40	.18
❑	468 Christian Fauria RC	.10	.05
❑	469 Joey Galloway	1.25	.55
❑	470 Derrick Brooks	.10	.05
❑	471 Warren Sapp	.20	.09
❑	472 Michael Westbrook	.75	.35
❑	473 Garrison Hearst	.40	.18
❑	474 Jeff George	.20	.09
❑	475 Terance Mathis	.20	.09
❑	476 Andre Reed	.20	.09
❑	477 Bruce Smith	.40	.18
❑	478 Lamar Lathon	.10	.05
❑	479 Curtis Conway	.40	.18
❑	480 Jeff Blake	.40	.18
❑	481 Carl Pickens	.40	.18
❑	482 Eric Turner	.10	.05
❑	483 Troy Aikman	.75	.35
❑	484 Michael Irvin	.40	.18
❑	485 Emmitt Smith	1.25	.55
❑	486 John Elway	1.50	.70
❑	487 Shannon Sharpe	.20	.09
❑	488 Herman Moore	.40	.18
❑	489 Barry Sanders	1.50	.70
❑	490 Brett Favre	1.50	.70
❑	491 Reggie White	.40	.18
❑	492 Haywood Jeffires	.10	.05
❑	493 Sean Dawkins	.10	.05
❑	494 Marshall Faulk	.40	.18
❑	495 Desmond Howard	.20	.09
❑	496 Steve Bono	.20	.09
❑	497 Derrick Thomas	.20	.09
❑	498 Irving Fryar	.20	.09
❑	499 Terry Kirby	.20	.09
❑	500 Dan Marino	1.50	.70
❑	501 O.J. McDuffie	.40	.18
❑	502 Cris Carter	.40	.18
❑	503 Warren Moon	.20	.09
❑	504 Jake Reed	.20	.09
❑	505 Drew Bledsoe	.75	.35
❑	506 Ben Coates	.20	.09
❑	507 Jim Everett	.10	.05
❑	508 Rodney Hampton	.20	.09
❑	509 Mo Lewis	.10	.05
❑	510 Tim Brown	.40	.18
❑	511 Jeff Hostetler	.20	.09
❑	512 Rocket Ismail	.20	.09
❑	513 Chester McGlockton	.20	.09
❑	514 Fred Barnett	.20	.09
❑	515 Greg Lloyd	.20	.09
❑	516 Byron Bam Morris	.20	.09
❑	517 Rod Woodson	.20	.09
❑	518 Jerome Bettis	.40	.18
❑	519 Isaac Bruce	.40	.18
❑	520 Stan Humphries	.20	.09
❑	521 Natrone Means	.40	.18
❑	522 Junior Seau	.40	.18
❑	523 William Floyd	.20	.09
❑	524 Jerry Rice	.75	.35
❑	525 Steve Young	.60	.25
❑	526 Cortez Kennedy	.20	.09
❑	527 Rick Mirer	.40	.18
❑	528 Chris Warren	.20	.09
❑	529 Trent Dilfer	.40	.18
❑	530 Errict Rhett	.40	.18
❑	531 Darrell Green	.10	.05
❑	532 Heath Shuler	.40	.18
❑	533 Stoney Case RO	.10	.05
❑	534 Eric Zeier RO	.40	.18
❑	535 Kerry Collins RO	.40	.18
❑	536 Steve McNair RO	1.00	.45
❑	537 Kordell Stewart RO	1.25	.55
❑	538 Rob Johnson RO RC	2.50	1.10
❑	539 Eric Ball EE	.10	.05
❑	540 Darrick Brownlow EE	.10	.05
❑	541 Paul Butcher EE	.10	.05
❑	542 Carlester Crumpler EE	.10	.05
❑	543 Maurice Douglas EE	.10	.05
❑	544 Keith Elias EE RC	.10	.05
❑	545 Kenneth Gant EE	.10	.05
❑	546 Corey Harris EE	.10	.05
❑	547 Andre Hastings EE	.20	.09
❑	548 Thomas Homco EE	.10	.05
❑	549 Lenny McGill EE	.10	.05
❑	550 Mark Pike EE	.10	.05
❑	P1 Promo Sheet Dave Meggett Justin Armour Brett Favre William Floyd	2.00	.90
❑	P264 Byron Bam Morris Prototype Card back includes "1994 Steelers" in stat information	1.00	.45

1996 Ultra

		MINT	NRMT
	COMPLETE SET (200)	25.00	11.00
❑	1 Larry Centers	.25	.11
❑	2 Garrison Hearst	.25	.11
❑	3 Rob Moore	.25	.11
❑	4 Eric Swann	.10	.05
❑	5 Aeneas Williams	.10	.05
❑	6 Bert Emanuel	.25	.11
❑	7 Jeff George	.25	.11
❑	8 Craig Heyward	.10	.05
❑	9 Terance Mathis	.10	.05
❑	10 Eric Metcalf	.10	.05
❑	11 Cornelius Bennett	.10	.05
❑	12 Darick Holmes	.10	.05
❑	13 Jim Kelly	.50	.23
❑	14 Bryce Paup	.10	.05
❑	15 Bruce Smith	.25	.11
❑	16 Mark Carrier WR	.10	.05
❑	17 Kerry Collins	.50	.23
❑	18 Lamar Lathon	.10	.05
❑	19 Derrick Moore	.10	.05
❑	20 Tyrone Poole	.10	.05
❑	21 Curtis Conway	.50	.23
❑	22 Jeff Graham	.10	.05
❑	23 Raymont Harris	.25	.11
❑	24 Erik Kramer	.10	.05
❑	25 Rashaan Salaam	.50	.23
❑	26 Jeff Blake	.50	.23
❑	27 Ki-Jana Carter	.25	.11
❑	28 Carl Pickens	.50	.23
❑	29 Darnay Scott	.25	.11
❑	30 Dan Wilkinson	.10	.05
❑	31 Leroy Hoard	.10	.05
❑	32 Michael Jackson	.25	.11
❑	33 Andre Rison	.25	.11
❑	34 Vinny Testaverde	.25	.11
❑	35 Eric Turner	.10	.05
❑	36 Troy Aikman	1.25	.55
❑	37 Charles Haley	.25	.11
❑	38 Michael Irvin	.50	.23
❑	39 Daryl Johnston	.25	.11
❑	40 Jay Novacek	.10	.05
❑	41 Deion Sanders	.75	.35
❑	42 Emmitt Smith	2.00	.90
❑	43 Steve Atwater	.10	.05
❑	44 Terrell Davis	3.00	1.35
❑	45 John Elway	2.50	1.10
❑	46 Anthony Miller	.25	.11
❑	47 Shannon Sharpe	.25	.11
❑	48 Scott Mitchell	.25	.11
❑	49 Herman Moore	.50	.23
❑	50 Johnnie Morton	.25	.11
❑	51 Brett Perriman	.10	.05
❑	52 Barry Sanders	2.50	1.10
❑	53 Chris Spielman	.10	.05
❑	54 Edgar Bennett	.25	.11
❑	55 Robert Brooks	.50	.23
❑	56 Mark Chmura	.25	.11
❑	57 Brett Favre	2.50	1.10
❑	58 Reggie White	.50	.23
❑	59 Mel Gray	.10	.05
❑	60 Haywood Jeffires	.10	.05
❑	61 Steve McNair	1.00	.45
❑	62 Chris Sanders	.25	.11
❑	63 Rodney Thomas	.10	.05
❑	64 Quentin Coryatt	.10	.05
❑	65 Sean Dawkins	.10	.05
❑	66 Ken Dilger	.25	.11
❑	67 Marshall Faulk	.50	.23
❑	68 Jim Harbaugh	.25	.11
❑	69 Tony Boselli	.10	.05
❑	70 Mark Brunell	1.25	.55
❑	71 Desmond Howard	.25	.11
❑	72 Jimmy Smith	.25	.11
❑	73 James O. Stewart	.25	.11
❑	74 Marcus Allen	.50	.23
❑	75 Steve Bono	.10	.05
❑	76 Lake Dawson	.10	.05
❑	77 Neil Smith	.10	.05
❑	78 Derrick Thomas	.25	.11
❑	79 Tamarick Vanover	.25	.11
❑	80 Bryan Cox	.10	.05
❑	81 Irving Fryar	.25	.11
❑	82 Eric Green	.10	.05
❑	83 Dan Marino	2.50	1.10
❑	84 O.J. McDuffie	.25	.11
❑	85 Bernie Parmalee	.10	.05
❑	86 Cris Carter	.50	.23
❑	87 Qadry Ismail	.10	.05
❑	88 Warren Moon	.25	.11
❑	89 Jake Reed	.25	.11
❑	90 Robert Smith	.25	.11
❑	91 Drew Bledsoe	1.25	.55
❑	92 Vincent Brisby	.10	.05
❑	93 Ben Coates	.25	.11
❑	94 Curtis Martin	1.00	.45
❑	95 Willie McGinest	.10	.05
❑	96 Dave Meggett	.10	.05
❑	97 Mario Bates	.25	.11
❑	98 Quinn Early	.10	.05
❑	99 Jim Everett	.10	.05
❑	100 Michael Haynes	.10	.05
❑	101 Renaldo Turnbull	.10	.05
❑	102 Dave Brown	.10	.05

❑ 103	Rodney Hampton	.25	.11
❑ 104	Mike Sherrard	.10	.05
❑ 105	Phillippi Sparks	.10	.05
❑ 106	Tyrone Wheatley	.25	.11
❑ 107	Hugh Douglas	.25	.11
❑ 108	Boomer Esiason	.25	.11
❑ 109	Aaron Glenn	.10	.05
❑ 110	Mo Lewis	.10	.05
❑ 111	Johnny Mitchell	.10	.05
❑ 112	Tim Brown	.50	.23
❑ 113	Jeff Hostetler	.10	.05
❑ 114	Rocket Ismail	.10	.05
❑ 115	Chester McGlockton	.10	.05
❑ 116	Harvey Williams	.10	.05
❑ 117	Fred Barnett	.10	.05
❑ 118	William Fuller	.10	.05
❑ 119	Charlie Garner	.10	.05
❑ 120	Ricky Watters	.25	.11
❑ 121	Calvin Williams	.10	.05
❑ 122	Kevin Greene	.25	.11
❑ 123	Greg Lloyd	.25	.11
❑ 124	Byron Bam Morris	.25	.11
❑ 125	Neil O'Donnell	.25	.11
❑ 126	Erric Pegram	.10	.05
❑ 127	Kordell Stewart	.75	.35
❑ 128	Yancey Thigpen	.25	.11
❑ 129	Rod Woodson	.25	.11
❑ 130	Jerome Bettis	.50	.23
❑ 131	Isaac Bruce	.50	.23
❑ 132	Troy Drayton	.10	.05
❑ 133	Sean Gilbert	.10	.05
❑ 134	Chris Miller	.10	.05
❑ 135	Andre Coleman	.10	.05
❑ 136	Ronnie Harmon	.10	.05
❑ 137	Aaron Hayden RC	.10	.05
❑ 138	Stan Humphries	.25	.11
❑ 139	Natrone Means	.50	.23
❑ 140	Junior Seau	.25	.11
❑ 141	William Floyd	.25	.11
❑ 142	Merton Hanks	.10	.05
❑ 143	Brent Jones	.10	.05
❑ 144	Derek Loville	.10	.05
❑ 145	Jerry Rice	1.25	.55
❑ 146	J.J. Stokes	.50	.23
❑ 147	Steve Young	1.00	.45
❑ 148	Brian Blades	.10	.05
❑ 149	Joey Galloway	.75	.35
❑ 150	Cortez Kennedy	.10	.05
❑ 151	Rick Mirer	.25	.11
❑ 152	Chris Warren	.25	.11
❑ 153	Derrick Brooks	.10	.05
❑ 154	Trent Dilfer	.50	.23
❑ 155	Alvin Harper	.10	.05
❑ 156	Jackie Harris	.10	.05
❑ 157	Hardy Nickerson	.10	.05
❑ 158	Errict Rhett	.25	.11
❑ 159	Terry Allen	.25	.11
❑ 160	Henry Ellard	.10	.05
❑ 161	Brian Mitchell	.10	.05
❑ 162	Heath Shuler	.25	.11
❑ 163	Michael Westbrook	.50	.23
❑ 164	Tim Biakabutuka RC	.75	.35
❑ 165	Tony Brackens RC	.25	.11
❑ 166	Rickey Dudley RC	.50	.23
❑ 167	Bobby Engram RC	.50	.23
❑ 168	Daryl Gardener RC	.10	.05
❑ 169	Eddie George RC	4.00	1.80
❑ 170	Terry Glenn RC	1.25	.55
❑ 171	Kevin Hardy RC	.50	.23
❑ 172	Keyshawn Johnson RC	2.00	.90
❑ 173	Cedric Jones RC	.10	.05
❑ 174	Leeland McElroy RC	.50	.23
❑ 175	Jonathan Ogden RC	.10	.05
❑ 176	Lawrence Phillips RC	.50	.23
❑ 177	Simeon Rice RC	.50	.23
❑ 178	Regan Upshaw RC	.10	.05
❑ 179	Justin Armour FI	.10	.05
❑ 180	Kyle Brady FI	.10	.05
❑ 181	Devin Bush FI	.10	.05
❑ 182	Kevin Carter FI	.10	.05
❑ 183	Wayne Chrebet FI	.75	.35
❑ 184	Napoleon Kaufman FI	.50	.23
❑ 185	Frank Sanders FI	.25	.11
❑ 186	Warren Sapp FI	.10	.05
❑ 187	Eric Zeier FI	.10	.05
❑ 188	Ray Zellars FI	.10	.05
❑ 189	Bill Brooks SW	.10	.05
❑ 190	Chris Calloway SW	.10	.05
❑ 191	Zack Crockett SW	.10	.05
❑ 192	Antonio Freeman SW	1.00	.45
❑ 193	Tyrone Hughes SW	.10	.05
❑ 194	Daryl Johnston SW	.25	.11
❑ 195	Tony Martin SW	.10	.05
❑ 196	Keenan McCardell SW	.50	.23
❑ 197	Glyn Milburn SW	.10	.05
❑ 198	David Palmer SW	.10	.05
❑ 199	Checklist	.10	.05
❑ 200	Checklist	.10	.05
❑ P1	Promo Sheet Trent Dilfer Brett Favre Mr.Momentum Daryl Johnston Secret Weapon	2.00	.90

1997 Ultra

	MINT	NRMT
COMPLETE SET (350)	100.00	45.00
COMP.SERIES 1 (200)	30.00	13.50
COMP.SERIES 2 (150)	70.00	32.00

❑ 1	Brett Favre	2.50	1.10
❑ 2	Ricky Watters	.25	.11
❑ 3	Dan Marino	2.50	1.10
❑ 4	Bryan Still	.15	.07
❑ 5	Chester McGlockton	.15	.07
❑ 6	Tim Biakabutuka	.25	.11
❑ 7	Dave Brown	.15	.07
❑ 8	Mike Alstott	.50	.23
❑ 9	O.J. McDuffie	.25	.11
❑ 10	Mark Brunell	1.25	.55
❑ 11	Michael Bates	.15	.07
❑ 12	Tyrone Wheatley	.25	.11
❑ 13	Eddie George	1.25	.55
❑ 14	Kevin Greene	.25	.11
❑ 15	Jerris McPhail	.15	.07
❑ 16	Harvey Williams	.15	.07
❑ 17	Eric Swann	.15	.07
❑ 18	Carl Pickens	.50	.23
❑ 19	Terrell Davis	2.00	.90
❑ 20	Charles Way	.25	.11
❑ 21	Jamie Asher	.15	.07
❑ 22	Qadry Ismail	.25	.11
❑ 23	Lawrence Phillips	.15	.07
❑ 24	John Friesz	.15	.07
❑ 25	Dorsey Levens	.50	.23
❑ 26	Willie McGinest	.15	.07
❑ 27	Chris T. Jones	.15	.07
❑ 28	Cortez Kennedy	.15	.07
❑ 29	Raymont Harris	.15	.07
❑ 30	William Roaf	.15	.07
❑ 31	Ted Johnson	.15	.07
❑ 32	Tony Martin	.25	.11
❑ 33	Jim Everett	.15	.07
❑ 34	Ray Zellars	.15	.07
❑ 35	Derrick Alexander WR	.25	.11
❑ 36	Leonard Russell	.15	.07
❑ 37	William Thomas	.15	.07
❑ 38	Karim Abdul-Jabbar	.50	.23
❑ 39	Kevin Turner	.15	.07
❑ 40	Robert Brooks	.25	.11
❑ 41	Kent Graham	.15	.07
❑ 42	Tony Brackens	.15	.07
❑ 43	Rodney Hampton	.25	.11
❑ 44	Drew Bledsoe	1.25	.55
❑ 45	Barry Sanders	2.50	1.10
❑ 46	Tim Brown	.50	.23
❑ 47	Reggie White	.50	.23
❑ 48	Terry Allen	.50	.23
❑ 49	Jim Harbaugh	.25	.11
❑ 50	John Elway	2.50	1.10
❑ 51	William Floyd	.25	.11
❑ 52	Michael Jackson	.25	.11
❑ 53	Larry Centers	.25	.11
❑ 54	Emmitt Smith	2.00	.90
❑ 55	Bruce Smith	.25	.11
❑ 56	Terrell Owens	.50	.23
❑ 57	Deion Sanders	.50	.23
❑ 58	Neil O'Donnell	.25	.11
❑ 59	Kordell Stewart	.60	.25
❑ 60	Bobby Engram	.25	.11
❑ 61	Keenan McCardell	.25	.11
❑ 62	Ben Coates	.25	.11
❑ 63	Curtis Martin	.75	.35
❑ 64	Hugh Douglas	.15	.07
❑ 65	Eric Moulds	.50	.23
❑ 66	Derrick Thomas	.25	.11
❑ 67	Byron Bam Morris	.15	.07
❑ 68	Bryan Cox	.15	.07
❑ 69	Rob Moore	.25	.11
❑ 70	Michael Haynes	.15	.07
❑ 71	Brian Mitchell	.15	.07
❑ 72	Alex Molden	.15	.07
❑ 73	Steve Young	.75	.35
❑ 74	Andre Reed	.25	.11
❑ 75	Michael Westbrook	.25	.11
❑ 76	Eric Metcalf	.25	.11
❑ 77	Tony Banks	.25	.11
❑ 78	Ken Dilger	.15	.07
❑ 79	John Henry Mills RC	.15	.07
❑ 80	Ashley Ambrose	.15	.07
❑ 81	Jason Dunn	.15	.07
❑ 82	Trent Dilfer	.50	.23
❑ 83	Wayne Chrebet	.50	.23
❑ 84	Ty Detmer	.25	.11
❑ 85	Aeneas Williams	.15	.07
❑ 86	Frank Wycheck	.15	.07
❑ 87	Jessie Tuggle	.15	.07
❑ 88	Steve McNair	.75	.35
❑ 89	Chris Slade	.15	.07
❑ 90	Anthony Johnson	.15	.07
❑ 91	Simeon Rice	.25	.11
❑ 92	Mike Tomczak	.15	.07
❑ 93	Sean Jones	.15	.07
❑ 94	Wesley Walls	.25	.11
❑ 95	Thurman Thomas	.50	.23
❑ 96	Scott Mitchell	.25	.11
❑ 97	Desmond Howard	.25	.11
❑ 98	Chris Warren	.25	.11
❑ 99	Glyn Milburn	.15	.07
❑ 100	Vinny Testaverde	.25	.11
❑ 101	James O.Stewart	.25	.11
❑ 102	Iheanyi Uwaezuoke	.25	.11
❑ 103	Stan Humphries	.25	.11
❑ 104	Terance Mathis	.25	.11
❑ 105	Thomas Lewis	.15	.07
❑ 106	Eddie Kennison	.25	.11
❑ 107	Rashaan Salaam	.15	.07
❑ 108	Curtis Conway	.25	.11
❑ 109	Chris Sanders	.15	.07
❑ 110	Marcus Allen	.50	.23
❑ 111	Gilbert Brown	.15	.07
❑ 112	Jason Sehorn	.25	.11
❑ 113	Zach Thomas	.25	.11
❑ 114	Bobby Hebert	.15	.07
❑ 115	Herman Moore	.50	.23
❑ 116	Ray Lewis	.60	.25
❑ 117	Darnay Scott	.25	.11
❑ 118	Jamal Anderson	.75	.35
❑ 119	Keyshawn Johnson	.50	.23
❑ 120	Adrian Murrell	.25	.11
❑ 121	Sam Mills	.15	.07
❑ 122	Irving Fryar	.25	.11
❑ 123	Ki-Jana Carter	.15	.07
❑ 124	Gus Frerotte	.15	.07
❑ 125	Terry Glenn	.50	.23
❑ 126	Quentin Coryatt	.15	.07
❑ 127	Robert Smith	.25	.11
❑ 128	Jeff Blake	.25	.11
❑ 129	Natrone Means	.50	.23
❑ 130	Isaac Bruce	.50	.23

❑ 131 Lamar Lathon .15 .07
❑ 132 Johnnie Morton .25 .11
❑ 133 Jerry Rice 1.25 .55
❑ 134 Errict Rhett .15 .07
❑ 135 Junior Seau .25 .11
❑ 136 Joey Galloway .60 .25
❑ 137 Napoleon Kaufman .50 .23
❑ 138 Troy Aikman 1.25 .55
❑ 139 Kevin Hardy .15 .07
❑ 140 Jimmy Smith .25 .11
❑ 141 Edgar Bennett .25 .11
❑ 142 Hardy Nickerson .15 .07
❑ 143 Greg Lloyd .15 .07
❑ 144 Dale Carter .15 .07
❑ 145 Jake Reed .25 .11
❑ 146 Cris Carter .50 .23
❑ 147 Todd Collins .15 .07
❑ 148 Mel Gray .15 .07
❑ 149 Lawyer Milloy .15 .07
❑ 150 Kimble Anders .25 .11
❑ 151 Darick Holmes .15 .07
❑ 152 Bert Emanuel .25 .11
❑ 153 Marshall Faulk .50 .23
❑ 154 Frank Sanders .25 .11
❑ 155 Leeland McElroy .15 .07
❑ 156 Rickey Dudley .25 .11
❑ 157 Tamarick Vanover .25 .11
❑ 158 Kerry Collins .25 .11
❑ 159 Jeff Graham .15 .07
❑ 160 Jerome Bettis .50 .23
❑ 161 Greg Hill .15 .07
❑ 162 John Mobley .15 .07
❑ 163 Michael Irvin .50 .23
❑ 164 Marvin Harrison .50 .23
❑ 165 Jim Schwantz RC .15 .07
❑ 166 Jermaine Lewis .50 .23
❑ 167 Levon Kirkland .15 .07
❑ 168 Nilo Silvan .15 .07
❑ 169 Ken Norton .15 .07
❑ 170 Yancey Thigpen .25 .11
❑ 171 Antonio Freeman .75 .35
❑ 172 Terry Kirby .25 .11
❑ 173 Brad Johnson .60 .25
❑ 174 Reidel Anthony RC 1.25 .55
❑ 175 Tiki Barber RC 2.00 .90
❑ 176 Pat Barnes RC .50 .23
❑ 177 Michael Booker RC .15 .07
❑ 178 Peter Boulware RC .25 .11
❑ 179 Rae Carruth RC .50 .23
❑ 180 Troy Davis RC .50 .23
❑ 181 Corey Dillon RC 4.00 1.80
❑ 182 Jim Druckenmiller RC .50 .23
❑ 183 Warrick Dunn RC 2.00 .90
❑ 184 James Farrior RC .15 .07
❑ 185 Yatil Green RC .25 .11
❑ 186 Walter Jones RC .15 .07
❑ 187 Tom Knight RC .15 .07
❑ 188 Sam Madison RC .50 .23
❑ 189 Tyrus McCloud RC .15 .07
❑ 190 Orlando Pace RC .50 .23
❑ 191 Jake Plummer RC 4.00 1.80
❑ 192 Dwayne Rudd RC .50 .23
❑ 193 Darrell Russell RC .15 .07
❑ 194 Sedrick Shaw RC .50 .23
❑ 195 Shawn Springs RC .25 .11
❑ 196 Bryant Westbrook RC .15 .07
❑ 197 Danny Wuerffel RC 1.00 .45
❑ 198 Reinard Wilson RC .15 .07
❑ 199 Checklist .15 .07
Rodney Hampton
❑ 200 Checklist .50 .23
John Elway
❑ 201 Rick Mirer .15 .07
❑ 202 Torrance Small .15 .07
❑ 203 Ricky Proehl .15 .07
❑ 204 Will Blackwell RC .50 .23
❑ 205 Warrick Dunn 1.00 .45
❑ 206 Rob Johnson .50 .23
❑ 207 Jim Schwantz .15 .07
❑ 208 Ike Hilliard RC 1.25 .55
❑ 209 Chris Canty RC .15 .07
❑ 210 Chris Boniol .15 .07
❑ 211 Jim Druckenmiller .50 .23
❑ 212 Tony Gonzalez RC 2.00 .90
❑ 213 Scottie Graham .15 .07
❑ 214 Byron Hanspard RC .50 .23
❑ 215 Gary Brown .15 .07
❑ 216 Darrell Russell .15 .07
❑ 217 Sedrick Shaw .50 .23
❑ 218 Boomer Esiason .25 .11
❑ 219 Peter Boulware .25 .11
❑ 220 Willie Green .15 .07
❑ 221 Dietrich Jells .15 .07
❑ 222 Freddie Jones RC .25 .11
❑ 223 Eric Metcalf .25 .11
❑ 224 John Henry Mills .15 .07
❑ 225 Michael Timpson .15 .07
❑ 226 Danny Wuerffel .25 .11
❑ 227 Daimon Shelton RC .15 .07
❑ 228 Henry Ellard .15 .07
❑ 229 Flipper Anderson .15 .07
❑ 230 Hunter Goodwin RC .15 .07
❑ 231 Jay Graham RC .50 .23
❑ 232 Duce Staley RC 15.00 6.75
❑ 233 Lamar Thomas .15 .07
❑ 234 Rod Woodson .25 .11
❑ 235 Zack Crockett .15 .07
❑ 236 Ernie Mills .15 .07
❑ 237 Kyle Brady .15 .07
❑ 238 Jesse Campbell .15 .07
❑ 239 Anthony Miller .15 .07
❑ 240 Michael Haynes .15 .07
❑ 241 Qadry Ismail .25 .11
❑ 242 Tom Knight .15 .07
❑ 243 Brian Manning RC .15 .07
❑ 244 Derrick Mayes .25 .11
❑ 245 Jamie Sharper RC .25 .11
❑ 246 Sherman Williams .15 .07
❑ 247 Yatil Green .25 .11
❑ 248 Howard Griffith .15 .07
❑ 249 Brian Blades .15 .07
❑ 250 Mark Chmura .25 .11
❑ 251 Chris Darkins .15 .07
❑ 252 Willie Davis .15 .07
❑ 253 Quinn Early .15 .07
❑ 254 Marc Edwards RC .15 .07
❑ 255 Charlie Jones .25 .11
❑ 256 Jake Plummer 2.00 .90
❑ 257 Heath Shuler .15 .07
❑ 258 Fred Barnett .15 .07
❑ 259 William Henderson .25 .11
❑ 260 Michael Booker .15 .07
❑ 261 Chad Brown .15 .07
❑ 262 Garrison Hearst .25 .11
❑ 263 Leon Johnson RC .15 .07
❑ 264 Antowain Smith RC 1.50 .70
❑ 265 Darnell Autry RC .25 .11
❑ 266 Craig Heyward .15 .07
❑ 267 Walter Jones .15 .07
❑ 268 Dexter Coakley RC .15 .07
❑ 269 Mercury Hayes .15 .07
❑ 270 Brett Perriman .15 .07
❑ 271 Chris Spielman .15 .07
❑ 272 Kevin Greene .25 .11
❑ 273 Kevin Lockett RC .25 .11
❑ 274 Troy Davis .50 .23
❑ 275 Brent Jones .25 .11
❑ 276 Chris Chandler .25 .11
❑ 277 Bryant Westbrook .15 .07
❑ 278 Desmond Howard .25 .11
❑ 279 Tyrone Hughes .15 .07
❑ 280 Kez McCorvey .15 .07
❑ 281 Stephen Davis 1.25 .55
❑ 282 Steve Everitt .15 .07
❑ 283 Andre Hastings .15 .07
❑ 284 Marcus Robinson RC 20.00 9.00
❑ 285 Donnell Woolford .15 .07
❑ 286 Mario Bates .15 .07
❑ 287 Corey Dillon 2.00 .90
❑ 288 Jackie Harris .15 .07
❑ 289 Lorenzo Neal .15 .07
❑ 290 Anthony Pleasant .15 .07
❑ 291 Andre Rison .25 .11
❑ 292 Amani Toomer .25 .11
❑ 293 Eric Turner .15 .07
❑ 294 Elvis Grbac .25 .11
❑ 295 Cris Dishman .15 .07
❑ 296 Tom Carter .15 .07
❑ 297 Mark Carrier DB .15 .07
❑ 298 Orlando Pace .15 .07
❑ 299 Jay Riemersma RC .15 .07
❑ 300 Daryl Johnston .25 .11
❑ 301 Joey Kent RC .50 .23
❑ 302 Ronnie Harmon .15 .07
❑ 303 Rocket Ismail .25 .11
❑ 304 Terrell Davis 2.00 .90
❑ 305 Sean Dawkins .15 .07
❑ 306 Jeff George .25 .11
❑ 307 David Palmer .15 .07
❑ 308 Dwayne Rudd .15 .07
❑ 309 J.J. Stokes .25 .11
❑ 310 James Farrior .15 .07
❑ 311 William Fuller .15 .07
❑ 312 George Jones RC .25 .11
❑ 313 John Allred RC .15 .07
❑ 314 Tony Graziani RC .50 .23
❑ 315 Jeff Hostetler .15 .07
❑ 316 Keith Poole RC .50 .23
❑ 317 Neil Smith .25 .11
❑ 318 Steve Tasker .15 .07
❑ 319 Mike Vrabel RC .15 .07
❑ 320 Pat Barnes .50 .23
❑ 321 James Hundon RC .50 .23
❑ 322 O.J. Santiago RC .50 .23
❑ 323 Billy Davis RC .15 .07
❑ 324 Shawn Springs .25 .11
❑ 325 Reinard Wilson RC .15 .07
❑ 326 Charles Johnson .25 .11
❑ 327 Micheal Barrow .15 .07
❑ 328 Derrick Mason RC 3.00 1.35
❑ 329 Muhsin Muhammad .25 .11
❑ 330 David LaFleur RC .25 .11
❑ 331 Reidel Anthony .50 .23
❑ 332 Tiki Barber .50 .23
❑ 333 Ray Buchanan .15 .07
❑ 334 John Elway 2.50 1.10
❑ 335 Alvin Harper .15 .07
❑ 336 Damon Jones RC .15 .07
❑ 337 Dedric Ward RC 2.50 1.10
❑ 338 Jim Everett .15 .07
❑ 339 Jon Harris .15 .07
❑ 340 Warren Moon .50 .23
❑ 341 Rae Carruth .25 .11
❑ 342 John Mobley .15 .07
❑ 343 Tyrone Poole .15 .07
❑ 344 Mike Cherry RC .15 .07
❑ 345 Horace Copeland .15 .07
❑ 346 Deon Figures .15 .07
❑ 347 Antwuan Wyatt RC .15 .07
❑ 348 Tommy Vardell .15 .07
❑ 349 Checklist (201-324) .15 .07
❑ 350 Checklist .15 .07
325-350/inserts
❑ S1A Terrell Davis 120.00 55.00
(Sample Auto)
❑ AU3 Dan Marino AUTO .. 200.00 90.00
(Reportedly 100 were signed)
❑ S1 Terrell Davis Sample 3.00 1.35

1998 Ultra

	MINT	NRMT
COMPLETE SET (425)	200.00	90.00
COMP.SERIES 1 (225)	120.00	55.00
COMP.SERIES 2 (200)	80.00	36.00

❑ 1 Barry Sanders 3.00 1.35
❑ 2 Brett Favre 3.00 1.35
❑ 3 Napoleon Kaufman .60 .25
❑ 4 Robert Smith .60 .25

No.	Player		
❑ 5	Terry Allen	.60	.25
❑ 6	Vinny Testaverde	.30	.14
❑ 7	William Floyd	.15	.07
❑ 8	Carl Pickens	.60	.25
❑ 9	Antonio Freeman	.60	.25
❑ 10	Ben Coates	.30	.14
❑ 11	Elvis Grbac	.30	.14
❑ 12	Kerry Collins	.30	.14
❑ 13	Orlando Pace	.15	.07
❑ 14	Steve Broussard	.15	.07
❑ 15	Terance Mathis	.30	.14
❑ 16	Tiki Barber	.30	.14
❑ 17	Cris Carter	.60	.25
❑ 18	Eric Green	.15	.07
❑ 19	Eric Metcalf	.15	.07
❑ 20	Jeff George	.30	.14
❑ 21	Leslie Shepherd	.15	.07
❑ 22	Natrone Means	.60	.25
❑ 23	Scott Mitchell	.30	.14
❑ 24	Adrian Murrell	.30	.14
❑ 25	Gilbert Brown	.15	.07
❑ 26	Jimmy Smith	.30	.14
❑ 27	Mark Bruener	.15	.07
❑ 28	Troy Aikman	1.50	.70
❑ 29	Warrick Dunn	.60	.25
❑ 30	Jay Graham	.15	.07
❑ 31	Craig Whelihan RC	.15	.07
❑ 32	Ed McCaffrey	.30	.14
❑ 33	Jamie Asher	.15	.07
❑ 34	John Randle	.30	.14
❑ 35	Michael Jackson	.15	.07
❑ 36	Rickey Dudley	.15	.07
❑ 37	Sean Dawkins	.15	.07
❑ 38	Andre Rison	.30	.14
❑ 39	Bert Emanuel	.30	.14
❑ 40	Jeff Blake	.30	.14
❑ 41	Curtis Conway	.30	.14
❑ 42	Eddie Kennison	.30	.14
❑ 43	James McKnight	.15	.07
❑ 44	Rae Carruth	.30	.14
❑ 45	Tito Wooten RC	.15	.07
❑ 46	Cris Dishman	.15	.07
❑ 47	Ernie Conwell	.15	.07
❑ 48	Fred Lane	.30	.14
❑ 49	Jamal Anderson	.60	.25
❑ 50	Lake Dawson	.15	.07
❑ 51	Michael Strahan	.15	.07
❑ 52	Reggie White	.60	.25
❑ 53	Trent Dilfer	.60	.25
❑ 54	Troy Brown	.15	.07
❑ 55	Wesley Walls	.30	.14
❑ 56	Chidi Ahanotu	.15	.07
❑ 57	Dwayne Rudd	.15	.07
❑ 58	Jerry Rice	1.50	.70
❑ 59	Johnnie Morton	.30	.14
❑ 60	Sherman Williams	.15	.07
❑ 61	Steve McNair	.60	.25
❑ 62	Will Blackwell	.15	.07
❑ 63	Chris Chandler	.30	.14
❑ 64	Dexter Coakley	.15	.07
❑ 65	Horace Copeland	.15	.07
❑ 66	Jerald Moore	.15	.07
❑ 67	Leon Johnson	.15	.07
❑ 68	Mark Chmura	.30	.14
❑ 69	Micheal Barrow	.15	.07
❑ 70	Muhsin Muhammad	.30	.14
❑ 71	Terry Glenn	.60	.25
❑ 72	Tony Brackens	.15	.07
❑ 73	Chad Scott	.15	.07
❑ 74	Glenn Foley	.30	.14
❑ 75	Keenan McCardell	.30	.14
❑ 76	Peter Boulware	.15	.07
❑ 77	Reidel Anthony	.30	.14
❑ 78	William Henderson	.15	.07
❑ 79	Tony Martin	.30	.14
❑ 80	Tony Gonzalez	.15	.07
❑ 81	Charlie Jones	.15	.07
❑ 82	Chris Gedney	.15	.07
❑ 83	Chris Calloway	.15	.07
❑ 84	Dale Carter	.15	.07
❑ 85	Ki-Jana Carter	.15	.07
❑ 86	Shawn Springs	.15	.07
❑ 87	Antowain Smith	.60	.25
❑ 88	Eric Turner	.15	.07
❑ 89	John Mobley	.15	.07
❑ 90	Ken Dilger	.15	.07
❑ 91	Bobby Hoying	.30	.14
❑ 92	Curtis Martin	.60	.25
❑ 93	Drew Bledsoe	1.25	.55
❑ 94	Gary Brown	.15	.07
❑ 95	Marvin Harrison	.30	.14
❑ 96	Todd Collins	.15	.07
❑ 97	Chris Warren	.30	.14
❑ 98	Danny Kanell	.30	.14
❑ 99	Tony McGee	.15	.07
❑ 100	Rod Smith	.30	.14
❑ 101	Frank Sanders	.30	.14
❑ 102	Irving Fryar	.30	.14
❑ 103	Marcus Allen	.60	.25
❑ 104	Marshall Faulk	.60	.25
❑ 105	Bruce Smith	.30	.14
❑ 106	Charlie Garner	.15	.07
❑ 107	Paul Justin	.15	.07
❑ 108	Randal Hill	.15	.07
❑ 109	Erik Kramer	.15	.07
❑ 110	Rob Moore	.30	.14
❑ 111	Shannon Sharpe	.30	.14
❑ 112	Warren Moon	.60	.25
❑ 113	Zach Thomas	.30	.14
❑ 114	Dan Marino	3.00	1.35
❑ 115	Duce Staley	1.25	.55
❑ 116	Eric Swann	.15	.07
❑ 117	Kenny Holmes	.15	.07
❑ 118	Merton Hanks	.15	.07
❑ 119	Raymont Harris	.15	.07
❑ 120	Terrell Davis	2.50	1.10
❑ 121	Thurman Thomas	.60	.25
❑ 122	Wayne Martin	.15	.07
❑ 123	Charles Way	.15	.07
❑ 124	Chuck Smith	.15	.07
❑ 125	Corey Dillon	1.00	.45
❑ 126	Darnell Autry	.15	.07
❑ 127	Isaac Bruce	.60	.25
❑ 128	Joey Galloway	.60	.25
❑ 129	Kimble Anders	.30	.14
❑ 130	Aeneas Williams	.15	.07
❑ 131	Andre Hastings	.15	.07
❑ 132	Chad Lewis	.15	.07
❑ 133	J.J. Stokes	.30	.14
❑ 134	John Elway	3.00	1.35
❑ 135	Karim Abdul-Jabbar	.60	.25
❑ 136	Ken Harvey	.15	.07
❑ 137	Robert Brooks	.30	.14
❑ 138	Rodney Thomas	.15	.07
❑ 139	James Stewart	.30	.14
❑ 140	Billy Joe Hobert	.15	.07
❑ 141	Frank Wycheck	.15	.07
❑ 142	Jake Plummer	1.25	.55
❑ 143	Jerris McPhail	.15	.07
❑ 144	Kordell Stewart	.60	.25
❑ 145	Terrell Owens	.60	.25
❑ 146	Willie Green	.15	.07
❑ 147	Anthony Miller	.15	.07
❑ 148	Courtney Hawkins	.15	.07
❑ 149	Larry Centers	.15	.07
❑ 150	Gus Frerotte	.15	.07
❑ 151	O.J. McDuffie	.30	.14
❑ 152	Ray Zellars	.15	.07
❑ 153	Terry Kirby	.15	.07
❑ 154	Tommy Vardell	.15	.07
❑ 155	Willie Davis	.15	.07
❑ 156	Chris Canty	.15	.07
❑ 157	Byron Hanspard	.30	.14
❑ 158	Chris Penn	.15	.07
❑ 159	Damon Jones	.15	.07
❑ 160	Derrick Mayes	.30	.14
❑ 161	Emmitt Smith	2.50	1.10
❑ 162	Keyshawn Johnson	.60	.25
❑ 163	Mike Alstott	.60	.25
❑ 164	Tom Carter	.15	.07
❑ 165	Tony Banks	.30	.14
❑ 166	Bryant Westbrook	.15	.07
❑ 167	Chris Sanders	.15	.07
❑ 168	Deion Sanders	.60	.25
❑ 169	Garrison Hearst	.60	.25
❑ 170	Jason Taylor	.15	.07
❑ 171	Jerome Bettis	.60	.25
❑ 172	John Lynch	.30	.14
❑ 173	Troy Davis	.15	.07
❑ 174	Freddie Jones	.15	.07
❑ 175	Herman Moore	.60	.25
❑ 176	Jake Reed	.30	.14
❑ 177	Mark Brunell	1.25	.55
❑ 178	Ray Lewis	.60	.25
❑ 179	Stephen Davis	.15	.07
❑ 180	Tim Brown	.60	.25
❑ 181	Willie McGinest	.15	.07
❑ 182	Andre Reed	.30	.14
❑ 183	Darrien Gordon	.15	.07
❑ 184	David Palmer	.15	.07
❑ 185	James Jett	.30	.14
❑ 186	Junior Seau	.30	.14
❑ 187	Zack Crockett	.15	.07
❑ 188	Brad Johnson	.60	.25
❑ 189	Charles Johnson	.15	.07
❑ 190	Eddie George	1.25	.55
❑ 191	Jermaine Lewis	.30	.14
❑ 192	Michael Irvin	.60	.25
❑ 193	Reggie Brown LB	.15	.07
❑ 194	Steve Young	1.00	.45
❑ 195	Warren Sapp	.30	.14
❑ 196	Wayne Chrebet	.60	.25
❑ 197	David Dunn	.15	.07
❑ 198	Dorsey Levens CL	.30	.14
❑ 199	Troy Aikman CL	.60	.25
❑ 200	John Elway CL	.75	.35
❑ 201	Peyton Manning RC	30.00	13.50
❑ 202	Ryan Leaf RC	10.00	4.50
❑ 203	Charles Woodson RC	6.00	2.70
❑ 204	Andre Wadsworth RC	3.00	1.35
❑ 205	Brian Simmons RC	2.00	.90
❑ 206	Curtis Enis RC	5.00	2.20
❑ 207	Randy Moss RC	30.00	13.50
❑ 208	Germane Crowell RC	6.00	2.70
❑ 209	Greg Ellis RC	2.00	.90
❑ 210	Kevin Dyson RC	6.00	2.70
❑ 211	Skip Hicks RC	4.00	1.80
❑ 212	Alonzo Mayes RC	2.00	.90
❑ 213	Robert Edwards RC	5.00	2.20
❑ 214	Fred Taylor RC	12.00	5.50
❑ 215	Robert Holcombe RC	4.00	1.80
❑ 216	John Dutton RC	2.00	.90
❑ 217	Vonnie Holliday RC	3.00	1.35
❑ 218	Tim Dwight RC	6.00	2.70
❑ 219	Tavian Banks RC	3.00	1.35
❑ 220	Marcus Nash RC	4.00	1.80
❑ 221	Jason Peter RC	2.00	.90
❑ 222	Michael Myers RC	2.00	.90
❑ 223	Takeo Spikes RC	3.00	1.35
❑ 224	Kivuusama Mays RC	2.00	.90
❑ 225	Jacquez Green RC	6.00	2.70
❑ 226	Doug Flutie	.60	.25
❑ 227	Ike Hilliard	.30	.14
❑ 228	Craig Heyward	.15	.07
❑ 229	Kevin Hardy	.15	.07
❑ 230	Jason Dunn	.15	.07
❑ 231	Billy Davis	.15	.07
❑ 232	Chester McGlockton	.15	.07
❑ 233	Sean Gilbert	.15	.07
❑ 234	Bert Emanuel	.30	.14
❑ 235	Keith Byars	.15	.07
❑ 236	Tyrone Wheatley	.30	.14
❑ 237	Ricky Proehl	.15	.07
❑ 238	Michael Bates	.15	.07
❑ 239	Derrick Alexander	.30	.14
❑ 240	Harvey Williams	.15	.07
❑ 241	Mike Pritchard	.15	.07
❑ 242	Paul Justin	.15	.07
❑ 243	Jeff Hostetler	.15	.07
❑ 244	Eric Moulds	.60	.25
❑ 245	Jeff Burris	.15	.07
❑ 246	Gary Brown	.15	.07
❑ 247	Anthony Johnson	.15	.07
❑ 248	Dan Wilkinson	.15	.07
❑ 249	Chris Warren	.30	.14
❑ 250	Chris Darkins	.15	.07
❑ 251	Eric Metcalf	.15	.07
❑ 252	Pat Swilling	.15	.07
❑ 253	Lamar Smith	.30	.14
❑ 254	Quinn Early	.15	.07
❑ 255	Carlester Crumpler	.15	.07
❑ 256	Eric Bieniemy	.15	.07
❑ 257	Aaron Bailey	.15	.07
❑ 258	Neil O'Donnell	.30	.14
❑ 259	Rod Woodson	.30	.14
❑ 260	Ricky Whittle	.15	.07
❑ 261	Iheanyi Uwaezuoke	.15	.07
❑ 262	Heath Shuler	.15	.07

❑ 263	Darren Sharper	.15	.07
❑ 264	John Henry Mills	.15	.07
❑ 265	Marco Battaglia	.15	.07
❑ 266	Yancey Thigpen	.15	.07
❑ 267	Irv Smith	.15	.07
❑ 268	Jamie Sharper	.15	.07
❑ 269	Marcus Robinson	5.00	2.20
❑ 270	Dorsey Levens	.60	.25
❑ 271	Qadry Ismail	.15	.07
❑ 272	Desmond Howard	.30	.14
❑ 273	Webster Slaughter	.15	.07
❑ 274	Eugene Robinson	.15	.07
❑ 275	Bill Romanowski	.15	.07
❑ 276	Vincent Brisby	.15	.07
❑ 277	Errict Rhett	.30	.14
❑ 278	Albert Connell	.15	.07
❑ 279	Thomas Lewis	.15	.07
❑ 280	John Farquhar RC	.15	.07
❑ 281	Marc Edwards	.15	.07
❑ 282	Tyrone Davis	.15	.07
❑ 283	Eric Allen	.15	.07
❑ 284	Aaron Glenn	.15	.07
❑ 285	Roosevelt Potts	.15	.07
❑ 286	Kez McCorvey	.15	.07
❑ 287	Joey Kent	.30	.14
❑ 288	Jim Druckenmiller	.30	.14
❑ 289	Sean Dawkins	.15	.07
❑ 290	Edgar Bennett	.15	.07
❑ 291	Vinny Testaverde	.30	.14
❑ 292	Chris Slade	.15	.07
❑ 293	Lamar Lathon	.15	.07
❑ 294	Jackie Harris	.15	.07
❑ 295	Jim Harbaugh	.30	.14
❑ 296	Rob Fredrickson	.15	.07
❑ 297	Ty Detmer	.30	.14
❑ 298	Karl Williams	.15	.07
❑ 299	Troy Drayton	.15	.07
❑ 300	Curtis Martin	.60	.25
❑ 301	Tamarick Vanover	.15	.07
❑ 302	Lorenzo Neal	.15	.07
❑ 303	John Hall	.15	.07
❑ 304	Kevin Greene	.30	.14
❑ 305	Bryan Still	.15	.07
❑ 306	Neil Smith	.30	.14
❑ 307	Greg Lloyd	.15	.07
❑ 308	Shawn Jefferson	.15	.07
❑ 309	Aaron Taylor	.15	.07
❑ 310	Sedrick Shaw	.15	.07
❑ 311	O.J. Santiago	.15	.07
❑ 312	Kevin Abrams	.15	.07
❑ 313	Dana Stubblefield	.15	.07
❑ 314	Daryl Johnston	.30	.14
❑ 315	Bryan Cox	.15	.07
❑ 316	Jeff Graham	.15	.07
❑ 317	Mario Bates	.30	.14
❑ 318	Adrian Murrell	.30	.14
❑ 319	Greg Hill	.15	.07
❑ 320	Jahine Arnold	.15	.07
❑ 321	Justin Armour	.15	.07
❑ 322	Ricky Watters	.30	.14
❑ 323	Lamont Warren	.15	.07
❑ 324	Mack Strong	.15	.07
❑ 325	Darnay Scott	.30	.14
❑ 326	Brian Mitchell	.15	.07
❑ 327	Rob Johnson	.30	.14
❑ 328	Kent Graham	.15	.07
❑ 329	Hugh Douglas	.15	.07
❑ 330	Simeon Rice	.30	.14
❑ 331	Rick Mirer	.15	.07
❑ 332	Randall Cunningham	.60	.25
❑ 333	Steve Atwater	.15	.07
❑ 334	Latario Rachal	.15	.07
❑ 335	Tony Martin	.30	.14
❑ 336	Leroy Hoard	.15	.07
❑ 337	Howard Griffith	.15	.07
❑ 338	Kevin Lockett	.15	.07
❑ 339	William Floyd	.15	.07
❑ 340	Jerry Ellison	.15	.07
❑ 341	Kyle Brady	.15	.07
❑ 342	Michael Westbrook	.30	.14
❑ 343	Kevin Turner	.15	.07
❑ 344	David LaFleur	.15	.07
❑ 345	Robert Jones	.15	.07
❑ 346	Dave Brown	.15	.07
❑ 347	Kevin Williams	.15	.07
❑ 348	Amani Toomer	.30	.14
❑ 349	Amp Lee	.15	.07
❑ 350	Bryce Paup	.15	.07
❑ 351	Dewayne Washington	.15	.07
❑ 352	Mercury Hayes	.15	.07
❑ 353	Tim Biakabutuka	.30	.14
❑ 354	Ray Crockett	.15	.07
❑ 355	Ted Washington	.15	.07
❑ 356	Pete Mitchell	.15	.07
❑ 357	Billy Jenkins RC	.15	.07
❑ 358	Troy Aikman CL	.60	.25
❑ 359	Drew Bledsoe CL	.60	.25
❑ 360	Steve Young CL	.60	.25
❑ 361	Antonio Freeman NG	.30	.14
❑ 362	Antowain Smith NG	.30	.14
❑ 363	Barry Sanders NG	2.00	.90
❑ 364	Bobby Hoying NG	.15	.07
❑ 365	Brett Favre NG	2.00	.90
❑ 366	Corey Dillon NG	.30	.14
❑ 367	Dan Marino NG	2.00	.90
❑ 368	Drew Bledsoe NG	.75	.35
❑ 369	Eddie George NG	.75	.35
❑ 370	Emmitt Smith NG	1.50	.70
❑ 371	Herman Moore NG	.30	.14
❑ 372	Jake Plummer NG	.75	.35
❑ 373	Jerome Bettis NG	.30	.14
❑ 374	Jerry Rice NG	1.00	.45
❑ 375	Joey Galloway NG	.30	.14
❑ 376	John Elway NG	2.00	.90
❑ 377	Kordell Stewart NG	.30	.14
❑ 378	Mark Brunell NG	.75	.35
❑ 379	Keyshawn Johnson NG	.30	.14
❑ 380	Steve Young NG	.60	.25
❑ 381	Steve McNair NG	.30	.14
❑ 382	Terrell Davis NG	1.50	.70
❑ 383	Tim Brown NG	.30	.14
❑ 384	Troy Aikman NG	1.00	.45
❑ 385	Warrick Dunn NG	.60	.25
❑ 386	Ryan Leaf	8.00	3.60
❑ 387	Tony Simmons RC	2.50	1.10
❑ 388	Rodney Williams RC	1.50	.70
❑ 389	John Avery RC	4.00	1.80
❑ 390	Shaun Williams RC	1.50	.70
❑ 391	Anthony Simmons RC	1.50	.70
❑ 392	Rashaan Shehee RC	2.50	1.10
❑ 393	Robert Holcombe	1.50	.70
❑ 394	Larry Shannon RC	1.50	.70
❑ 395	Skip Hicks	4.00	1.80
❑ 396	Rod Rutledge RC	1.50	.70
❑ 397	Donald Hayes RC	4.00	1.80
❑ 398	Curtis Enis	5.00	2.20
❑ 399	Mikhael Ricks RC	2.50	1.10
❑ 400	Brian Griese RC	15.00	6.75
❑ 401	Michael Pittman RC	4.00	1.80
❑ 402	Jacquez Green	4.00	1.80
❑ 403	Jerome Pathon RC	2.50	1.10
❑ 404	Ahman Green RC	10.00	4.50
❑ 405	Marcus Nash	4.00	1.80
❑ 406	Randy Moss	20.00	9.00
❑ 407	Terry Fair RC	2.50	1.10
❑ 408	Jammi German RC	1.50	.70
❑ 409	Stephen Alexander RC	2.50	1.10
❑ 410	Grant Wistrom RC	1.50	.70
❑ 411	Charlie Batch RC	12.00	5.50
❑ 412	Fred Taylor	10.00	4.50
❑ 413	Pat Johnson RC	2.50	1.10
❑ 414	Robert Edwards	4.00	1.80
❑ 415	Keith Brooking RC	2.50	1.10
❑ 416	Peyton Manning	20.00	9.00
❑ 417	Duane Starks RC	1.50	.70
❑ 418	Andre Wadsworth	2.50	1.10
❑ 419	Brian Alford RC	4.00	1.80
❑ 420	Brian Kelly RC	1.50	.70
❑ 421	Joe Jurevicius RC	2.50	1.10
❑ 422	Tebucky Jones RC	1.50	.70
❑ 423	R.W. McQuarters RC	1.50	.70
❑ 424	Kevin Dyson	4.00	1.80
❑ 425	Charles Woodson	5.00	2.20
❑ R1	Reggie White COMM	.60	.25
❑ P20	Jeff George Promo	.75	.35

1999 Ultra

	MINT	NRMT
COMPLETE SET (300)	200.00	90.00
COMP.SET w/o SP's (250)	20.00	9.00

❑ 1	Terrell Davis	1.50	.70
❑ 2	Courtney Hawkins	.15	.07
❑ 3	Cris Carter	.60	.25
❑ 4	Darnay Scott	.15	.07
❑ 5	Darrell Green	.30	.14
❑ 6	Jimmy Smith	.30	.14
❑ 7	Doug Flutie	.75	.35
❑ 8	Michael Jackson	.15	.07
❑ 9	Warren Sapp	.30	.14
❑ 10	Greg Hill	.15	.07
❑ 11	Karim Abdul-Jabbar	.30	.14
❑ 12	Greg Ellis	.15	.07
❑ 13	Dan Marino	2.50	1.10
❑ 14	Napoleon Kaufman	.60	.25
❑ 15	Peyton Manning	2.50	1.10
❑ 16	Simeon Rice	.30	.14
❑ 17	Tony Simmons	.15	.07
❑ 18	Carlester Crumpler	.15	.07
❑ 19	Charles Johnson	.15	.07
❑ 20	Derrick Alexander	.15	.07
❑ 21	Kent Graham	.15	.07
❑ 22	Randall Cunningham	.60	.25
❑ 23	Trent Green	.30	.14
❑ 24	Chris Spielman	.15	.07
❑ 25	Carl Pickens	.30	.14
❑ 26	Bill Romanowski	.15	.07
❑ 27	Jermaine Lewis	.30	.14
❑ 28	Ahman Green	.30	.14
❑ 29	Bryan Still	.15	.07
❑ 30	Dorsey Levens	.60	.25
❑ 31	Frank Wycheck	.15	.07
❑ 32	Jerome Bettis	.60	.25
❑ 33	Reidel Anthony	.30	.14
❑ 34	Robert Jones	.15	.07
❑ 35	Terry Glenn	.60	.25
❑ 36	Tim Brown	.60	.25
❑ 37	Eric Metcalf	.15	.07
❑ 38	Kevin Greene	.30	.14
❑ 39	Takeo Spikes	.15	.07
❑ 40	Brian Mitchell	.15	.07
❑ 41	Duane Starks	.15	.07
❑ 42	Eddie George	.75	.35
❑ 43	Joe Jurevicius	.15	.07
❑ 44	Kimble Anders	.30	.14
❑ 45	Kordell Stewart	.60	.25
❑ 46	Leroy Hoard	.15	.07
❑ 47	Rod Smith	.30	.14
❑ 48	Terrell Owens	.60	.25
❑ 49	Ty Detmer	.30	.14
❑ 50	Charles Woodson	.60	.25
❑ 51	Andre Rison	.30	.14
❑ 52	Chris Slade	.15	.07
❑ 53	Frank Sanders	.30	.14
❑ 54	Michael Irvin	.30	.14
❑ 55	Jerome Pathon	.15	.07
❑ 56	Desmond Howard	.30	.14
❑ 57	Billy Davis	.15	.07
❑ 58	Anthony Simmons	.15	.07
❑ 59	James Jett	.30	.14
❑ 60	Jake Plummer	1.25	.55
❑ 61	John Avery	.30	.14
❑ 62	Marvin Harrison	.60	.25
❑ 63	Merton Hanks	.15	.07
❑ 64	Ricky Proehl	.15	.07
❑ 65	Steve Beuerlein	.15	.07
❑ 66	Willie McGinest	.15	.07
❑ 67	Bryce Paup	.15	.07

❑ 68	Brett Favre	2.50	1.10
❑ 69	Brian Griese	1.25	.55
❑ 70	Curtis Martin	.60	.25
❑ 71	Drew Bledsoe	1.00	.45
❑ 72	Jim Harbaugh	.30	.14
❑ 73	Joey Galloway	.60	.25
❑ 74	Natrone Means	.30	.14
❑ 75	O.J. McDuffie	.30	.14
❑ 76	Tiki Barber	.30	.14
❑ 77	Wesley Walls	.30	.14
❑ 78	Will Blackwell	.15	.07
❑ 79	Bert Emanuel	.30	.14
❑ 80	J.J. Stokes	.30	.14
❑ 81	Steve McNair	.60	.25
❑ 82	Adrian Murrell	.30	.14
❑ 83	Dexter Coakley	.15	.07
❑ 84	Jeff George	.30	.14
❑ 85	Marshall Faulk	.60	.25
❑ 86	Tim Biakabutuka	.30	.14
❑ 87	Troy Drayton	.15	.07
❑ 88	Ty Law	.15	.07
❑ 89	Brian Simmons	.15	.07
❑ 90	Eric Allen	.15	.07
❑ 91	Jon Kitna	.60	.25
❑ 92	Junior Seau	.30	.14
❑ 93	Kevin Turner	.15	.07
❑ 94	Larry Centers	.15	.07
❑ 95	Robert Edwards	.30	.14
❑ 96	Rocket Ismail	.30	.14
❑ 97	Sam Madison	.15	.07
❑ 98	Stephen Alexander	.15	.07
❑ 99	Trent Dilfer	.30	.14
❑ 100	Vonnie Holliday	.15	.07
❑ 101	Charlie Garner	.30	.14
❑ 102	Deion Sanders	.60	.25
❑ 103	Jamal Anderson	.60	.25
❑ 104	Mike Vanderjagt	.15	.07
❑ 105	Aeneas Williams	.15	.07
❑ 106	Daryl Johnston	.30	.14
❑ 107	Hugh Douglas	.15	.07
❑ 108	Torrance Small	.15	.07
❑ 109	Amani Toomer	.15	.07
❑ 110	Amp Lee	.15	.07
❑ 111	Germane Crowell	.30	.14
❑ 112	Marco Battaglia	.15	.07
❑ 113	Michael Westbrook	.30	.14
❑ 114	Randy Moss	2.50	1.10
❑ 115	Ricky Watters	.30	.14
❑ 116	Rob Johnson	.30	.14
❑ 117	Tony Gonzalez	.30	.14
❑ 118	Charles Way	.15	.07
❑ 119	Chris Penn	.15	.07
❑ 120	Eddie Kennison	.30	.14
❑ 121	Elvis Grbac	.30	.14
❑ 122	Eric Moulds	.60	.25
❑ 123	Terry Fair	.15	.07
❑ 124	Tony Banks	.30	.14
❑ 125	Chris Chandler	.30	.14
❑ 126	Emmitt Smith	1.50	.70
❑ 127	Herman Moore	.60	.25
❑ 128	Irv Smith	.15	.07
❑ 129	Kyle Brady	.15	.07
❑ 130	Lamont Warren	.15	.07
❑ 131	Troy Davis	.15	.07
❑ 132	Andre Reed	.30	.14
❑ 133	Justin Armour	.15	.07
❑ 134	James Hasty	.15	.07
❑ 135	Johnnie Morton	.30	.14
❑ 136	Reggie Barlow	.15	.07
❑ 137	Robert Holcombe	.30	.14
❑ 138	Sean Dawkins	.15	.07
❑ 139	Steve Atwater	.15	.07
❑ 140	Tim Dwight	.60	.25
❑ 141	Wayne Chrebet	.30	.14
❑ 142	Alonzo Mayes	.15	.07
❑ 143	Mark Brunell	1.00	.45
❑ 144	Antowain Smith	.60	.25
❑ 145	Byron Bam Morris	.15	.07
❑ 146	Isaac Bruce	.60	.25
❑ 147	Bryan Cox	.15	.07
❑ 148	Bryant Westbrook	.15	.07
❑ 149	Duce Staley	.60	.25
❑ 150	Barry Sanders	2.50	1.10
❑ 151	La'Roi Glover RC	.15	.07
❑ 152	Ray Crockett	.15	.07
❑ 153	Tony Brackens	.15	.07
❑ 154	Roy Barker	.15	.07
❑ 155	Kerry Collins	.30	.14
❑ 156	Andre Wadsworth	.15	.07
❑ 157	Cameron Cleeland	.15	.07
❑ 158	Koy Detmer	.15	.07
❑ 159	Marcus Pollard	.15	.07
❑ 160	Patrick Jeffers RC	6.00	2.70
❑ 161	Aaron Glenn	.15	.07
❑ 162	Andre Hastings	.15	.07
❑ 163	Bruce Smith	.30	.14
❑ 164	David Palmer	.15	.07
❑ 165	Erik Kramer	.30	.14
❑ 166	Orlando Pace	.15	.07
❑ 167	Robert Brooks	.30	.14
❑ 168	Shawn Springs	.15	.07
❑ 169	Terance Mathis	.30	.14
❑ 170	Chris Calloway	.15	.07
❑ 171	Gilbert Brown	.15	.07
❑ 172	Charlie Jones	.15	.07
❑ 173	Curtis Enis	.60	.25
❑ 174	Eugene Robinson	.15	.07
❑ 175	Garrison Hearst	.30	.14
❑ 176	Jason Elam	.15	.07
❑ 177	John Randle	.30	.14
❑ 178	Keith Poole	.15	.07
❑ 179	Kevin Hardy	.15	.07
❑ 180	Keyshawn Johnson	.60	.25
❑ 181	O.J. Santiago	.15	.07
❑ 182	Jacquez Green	.30	.14
❑ 183	Bobby Engram	.30	.14
❑ 184	Damon Jones	.15	.07
❑ 185	Freddie Jones	.15	.07
❑ 186	Jake Reed	.30	.14
❑ 187	Jerry Rice	1.50	.70
❑ 188	Joey Kent	.15	.07
❑ 189	Lamar Smith	.30	.14
❑ 190	John Elway	2.50	1.10
❑ 191	Leon Johnson	.15	.07
❑ 192	Mark Chmura	.30	.14
❑ 193	Peter Boulware	.15	.07
❑ 194	Zach Thomas	.30	.14
❑ 195	Marc Edwards	.15	.07
❑ 196	Mike Alstott	.60	.25
❑ 197	Yancey Thigpen	.15	.07
❑ 198	Oronde Gadsden	.15	.07
❑ 199	Rae Carruth	.30	.14
❑ 200	Troy Aikman	1.50	.70
❑ 201	Shawn Jefferson	.15	.07
❑ 202	Rob Moore	.30	.14
❑ 203	Rickey Dudley	.15	.07
❑ 204	Jason Taylor	.15	.07
❑ 205	Curtis Conway	.30	.14
❑ 206	Darrien Gordon	.15	.07
❑ 207	Eric Green	.15	.07
❑ 208	Jessie Armstead	.15	.07
❑ 209	Keenan McCardell	.30	.14
❑ 210	Robert Smith	.60	.25
❑ 211	Mo Lewis	.15	.07
❑ 212	Ryan Leaf	.60	.25
❑ 213	Steve Young	1.00	.45
❑ 214	Tyrone Davis	.15	.07
❑ 215	Chad Brown	.15	.07
❑ 216	Ike Hilliard	.15	.07
❑ 217	Jimmy Hitchcock	.15	.07
❑ 218	Kevin Dyson	.30	.14
❑ 219	Levon Kirkland	.15	.07
❑ 220	Neil O'Donnell	.30	.14
❑ 221	Ray Lewis	.30	.14
❑ 222	Shannon Sharpe	.30	.14
❑ 223	Skip Hicks	.60	.25
❑ 224	Brad Johnson	.60	.25
❑ 225	Charlie Batch	1.25	.55
❑ 226	Corey Dillon	.60	.25
❑ 227	Dale Carter	.15	.07
❑ 228	John Mobley	.15	.07
❑ 229	Hines Ward	.15	.07
❑ 230	Leslie Shepherd	.15	.07
❑ 231	Michael Strahan	.15	.07
❑ 232	R.W. McQuarters	.15	.07
❑ 233	Mike Pritchard	.15	.07
❑ 234	Antonio Freeman	.60	.25
❑ 235	Ben Coates	.30	.14
❑ 236	Michael Bates	.15	.07
❑ 237	Ed McCaffrey	.30	.14
❑ 238	Gary Brown	.15	.07
❑ 239	Mark Bruener	.15	.07
❑ 240	Mikhael Ricks	.15	.07
❑ 241	Muhsin Muhammad	.15	.07
❑ 242	Priest Holmes	.60	.25
❑ 243	Stephen Davis	.60	.25
❑ 244	Vinny Testaverde	.30	.14
❑ 245	Warrick Dunn	.60	.25
❑ 246	Derrick Mayes	.15	.07
❑ 247	Fred Taylor	1.50	.70
❑ 248	Drew Bledsoe CL	.30	.14
❑ 249	Eddie George CL	.30	.14
❑ 250	Steve Young CL	.30	.14
❑ 251	Jamal Anderson BB	1.25	.55
❑ 252	Darrien Gordon BB Bill Romanowski BB	.30	.14
❑ 253	Shannon Sharpe BB	.30	.14
❑ 254	Terrell Davis BB	3.00	1.35
❑ 255	Rod Smith BB	.30	.14
❑ 256	Rod Smith BB	.30	.14
❑ 257	John Elway BB	5.00	2.20
❑ 258	Tim Dwight BB	1.25	.55
❑ 259	John Elway BB Ed McCaffrey BB Howard Griffith BB Terrell Davis BB	4.00	1.80
❑ 260	John Elway BB	5.00	2.20
❑ 261	Ricky Williams RC	12.00	5.50
❑ 262	Tim Couch RC	12.00	5.50
❑ 263	Chris Claiborne RC	1.50	.70
❑ 264	Champ Bailey RC	5.00	2.20
❑ 265	Torry Holt RC	10.00	4.50
❑ 266	Donovan McNabb RC	12.00	5.50
❑ 267	David Boston RC	8.00	3.60
❑ 268	Chris McAlister RC	2.50	1.10
❑ 269	Brock Huard RC	6.00	2.70
❑ 270	Daunte Culpepper RC	15.00	6.75
❑ 271	Matt Stinchcomb RC	1.50	.70
❑ 272	Edgerrin James RC	15.00	6.75
❑ 273	Jevon Kearse RC	8.00	3.60
❑ 274	Ebenezer Ekuban RC	2.50	1.10
❑ 275	Kris Farris RC	1.50	.70
❑ 276	Chris Terry RC	1.50	.70
❑ 277	Jerame Tuman RC	2.50	1.10
❑ 278	Akili Smith RC	8.00	3.60
❑ 279	Aaron Gibson RC	1.50	.70
❑ 280	Rahim Abdullah RC	2.50	1.10
❑ 281	Peerless Price RC	5.00	2.20
❑ 282	Antoine Winfield RC	2.50	1.10
❑ 283	Antuan Edwards RC	1.50	.70
❑ 284	Rob Konrad RC	3.00	1.35
❑ 285	Troy Edwards RC	5.00	2.20
❑ 286	John Thornton RC	1.50	.70
❑ 287	James Johnson RC	3.00	1.35
❑ 288	Gary Stills RC	1.50	.70
❑ 289	Mike Peterson RC	2.50	1.10
❑ 290	Kevin Faulk RC	6.00	2.70
❑ 291	Jared DeVries RC	1.50	.70
❑ 292	Martin Gramatica RC	1.50	.70
❑ 293	Montae Reagor RC	1.50	.70
❑ 294	Andy Katzenmoyer RC	3.00	1.35
❑ 295	Sedrick Irvin RC	3.00	1.35
❑ 296	D'Wayne Bates RC	2.50	1.10
❑ 297	Amos Zereoue RC	3.00	1.35
❑ 298	Dre' Bly RC	2.50	1.10
❑ 299	Kevin Johnson RC	6.00	2.70
❑ 300	Cade McNown RC	5.00	2.20
❑ P247	Fred Taylor Promo	2.00	.90

2000 Ultra

	MINT	NRMT
COMPLETE SET (249)	120.00	55.00
COMP.SET w/o SP's (220)	20.00	9.00
❑ 1 Kurt Warner	2.50	1.10
❑ 2 Derrick Alexander	.30	.14
❑ 3 Aaron Craver	.15	.07
❑ 4 Kevin Faulk	.30	.14
❑ 5 Marcus Robinson	.60	.25
❑ 6 Tony Banks	.30	.14
❑ 7 Jon Ritchie	.15	.07
❑ 8 Torry Holt	.60	.25
❑ 9 Joe Horn	.30	.14
❑ 10 Eddie George	.75	.35
❑ 11 Michael Westbrook	.30	.14
❑ 12 Gus Frerotte	.15	.07
❑ 13 Tim Brown	.60	.25
❑ 14 Tamarick Vanover	.15	.07
❑ 15 David Sloan	.15	.07
❑ 16 Darnay Scott	.15	.07
❑ 17 Junior Seau	.30	.14
❑ 18 Warren Sapp	.30	.14
❑ 19 Priest Holmes	.30	.14
❑ 20 Jerry Rice	1.50	.70
❑ 21 Cade McNown	.60	.25
❑ 22 Johnnie Morton	.30	.14
❑ 23 Vinny Testaverde	.30	.14
❑ 24 James Jett	.15	.07
❑ 25 Tony Gonzalez	.30	.14
❑ 26 Charlie Batch	.60	.25
❑ 27 Tony Simmons	.15	.07
❑ 28 James Stewart	.30	.14
❑ 29 Corey Dillon	.60	.25
❑ 30 Ricky Williams	1.50	.70
❑ 31 Ryan Leaf	.60	.25
❑ 32 Terry Allen	.30	.14
❑ 33 Freddie Jones	.15	.07
❑ 34 Terry Kirby	.15	.07
❑ 35 Charles Johnson	.30	.14
❑ 36 William Henderson	.15	.07
❑ 37 Stephen Alexander	.15	.07
❑ 38 Moe Williams	.15	.07
❑ 39 David Boston	.60	.25
❑ 40 Emmitt Smith	1.50	.70
❑ 41 Ken Oxendine	.15	.07
❑ 42 Byron Hanspard	.15	.07
❑ 43 Dwight Stone	.15	.07
❑ 44 Jim Harbaugh	.30	.14
❑ 45 Curtis Enis	.30	.14
❑ 46 Peerless Price	.60	.25
❑ 47 Terance Mathis	.15	.07
❑ 48 Mike Alstott	.60	.25
❑ 49 Rod Smith	.30	.14
❑ 50 Marshall Faulk	.75	.35
❑ 51 Derrick Mayes	.30	.14
❑ 52 Keenan McCardell	.30	.14
❑ 53 Curtis Martin	.60	.25
❑ 54 Bobby Engram	.15	.07
❑ 55 Carl Pickens	.30	.14
❑ 56 Robert Smith	.60	.25
❑ 57 Ike Hilliard	.30	.14
❑ 58 Reidel Anthony	.30	.14
❑ 59 Jeff Graham	.15	.07
❑ 60 Mark Brunell	1.00	.45
❑ 61 Joe Montgomery	.15	.07
❑ 62 Ed McCaffrey	.60	.25
❑ 63 Kenny Bynum	.15	.07
❑ 64 Curtis Conway	.30	.14
❑ 65 Trent Dilfer	.30	.14
❑ 66 Jake Reed	.30	.14
❑ 67 Jake Plummer	.60	.25
❑ 68 Tony Martin	.30	.14
❑ 69 Yatil Green	.15	.07
❑ 70 Keyshawn Johnson	.60	.25
❑ 71 Leroy Hoard	.15	.07
❑ 72 Skip Hicks	.30	.14
❑ 73 Marvin Harrison	.60	.25
❑ 74 Steve Beuerlein	.30	.14
❑ 75 Will Blackwell	.15	.07
❑ 76 Derek Loville	.15	.07
❑ 77 Warrick Dunn	.60	.25
❑ 78 Amos Zereoue	.15	.07
❑ 79 Ray Lucas	.60	.25
❑ 80 Randy Moss	2.00	.90
❑ 81 Wesley Walls	.15	.07
❑ 82 Jimmy Smith	.30	.14
❑ 83 Kordell Stewart	.60	.25
❑ 84 Brian Griese	.75	.35
❑ 85 Martin Gramatica	.15	.07
❑ 86 Chris Chandler	.30	.14
❑ 87 Reggie Barlow	.15	.07
❑ 88 Jeff George	.30	.14
❑ 89 Tavian Banks	.15	.07
❑ 90 Mushin Muhammad	.30	.14
❑ 91 Steve McNair	.60	.25
❑ 92 Hines Ward	.15	.07
❑ 93 Brian Mitchell	.15	.07
❑ 94 Daunte Culpepper	1.25	.55
❑ 95 Tim Dwight	.60	.25
❑ 96 Terrence Wilkins	.60	.25
❑ 97 Fred Lane	.15	.07
❑ 98 Brett Favre	2.50	1.10
❑ 99 Richie Anderson	.30	.14
❑ 100 Jamal Anderson	.60	.25
❑ 101 Doug Flutie	.75	.35
❑ 102 Charles Woodson	.30	.14
❑ 103 Jacquez Green	.30	.14
❑ 104 Olandis Gary	.60	.25
❑ 105 Steve Young	1.00	.45
❑ 106 Wayne Chrebet	.30	.14
❑ 107 Karim Abdul-Jabbar	.30	.14
❑ 108 Andre Rison	.30	.14
❑ 109 Eddie Kennison	.15	.07
❑ 110 Jevon Kearse	.60	.25
❑ 111 Tony Richardson RC	.30	.14
❑ 112 Jake Delhomme RC	.60	.25
❑ 113 Errict Rhett	.30	.14
❑ 114 Akili Smith	.60	.25
❑ 115 Tyrone Wheatley	.30	.14
❑ 116 Corey Bradford	.30	.14
❑ 117 J.J. Stokes	.30	.14
❑ 118 Simeon Rice	.15	.07
❑ 119 Brad Johnson	.60	.25
❑ 120 Edgerrin James	2.50	1.10
❑ 121 Amani Toomer	.15	.07
❑ 122 O.J. McDuffie	.30	.14
❑ 123 Az-Zahir Hakim	.30	.14
❑ 124 Troy Edwards	.30	.14
❑ 125 Tim Biakabutuka	.30	.14
❑ 126 Jason Tucker	.30	.14
❑ 127 Charles Way	.15	.07
❑ 128 Terrell Davis	1.50	.70
❑ 129 Garrison Hearst	.30	.14
❑ 130 Fred Taylor	.75	.35
❑ 131 Robert Holcombe	.15	.07
❑ 132 Frank Sanders	.30	.14
❑ 133 Morten Andersen	.15	.07
❑ 134 Cris Carter	.60	.25
❑ 135 Patrick Jeffers	.60	.25
❑ 136 Antonio Freeman	.60	.25
❑ 137 Jonathan Linton	.15	.07
❑ 138 Rashaan Shehee	.15	.07
❑ 139 Luther Broughton RC	.30	.14
❑ 140 Tim Couch	1.25	.55
❑ 141 Keith Poole	.15	.07
❑ 142 Champ Bailey	.30	.14
❑ 143 Yancey Thigpen	.15	.07
❑ 144 Joey Galloway	.60	.25
❑ 145 Mac Cody	.15	.07
❑ 146 Damon Huard	.60	.25
❑ 147 Dorsey Levens	.30	.14
❑ 148 Donovan McNabb	1.00	.45
❑ 149 Jamie Asher	.15	.07
❑ 150 Peyton Manning	2.00	.90
❑ 151 Leslie Shepherd	.15	.07
❑ 152 Charlie Rogers	.15	.07
❑ 153 Tony Home	.15	.07
❑ 154 Jim Miller	.15	.07
❑ 155 Richard Huntley	.15	.07
❑ 156 Germane Crowell	.30	.14
❑ 157 Natrone Means	.15	.07
❑ 158 Justin Armour	.15	.07
❑ 159 Drew Bledsoe	1.00	.45
❑ 160 Dedric Ward	.15	.07
❑ 161 Allen Rossum	.15	.07
❑ 162 Ricky Watters	.30	.14
❑ 163 Kerry Collins	.30	.14
❑ 164 James Johnson	.30	.14
❑ 165 Elvis Grbac	.30	.14
❑ 166 Larry Centers	.15	.07
❑ 167 Rob Moore	.30	.14
❑ 168 Jay Riemersma	.15	.07
❑ 169 Bill Schroeder	.30	.14
❑ 170 Deion Sanders	.60	.25
❑ 171 Jerome Bettis	.60	.25
❑ 172 Dan Marino	2.50	1.10
❑ 173 Terrell Owens	.60	.25
❑ 174 Kevin Carter	.15	.07
❑ 175 Lamar Smith	.30	.14
❑ 176 Ken Dilger	.15	.07
❑ 177 Napoleon Kaufman	.30	.14
❑ 178 Kevin Williams	.15	.07
❑ 179 Tremain Mack	.15	.07
❑ 180 Troy Aikman	1.50	.70
❑ 181 Glyn Milburn	.15	.07
❑ 182 Pete Mitchell	.15	.07
❑ 183 Cameron Cleeland	.15	.07
❑ 184 Qadry Ismail	.15	.07
❑ 185 Michael Pittman	.15	.07
❑ 186 Kevin Dyson	.30	.14
❑ 187 Matt Hasselbeck	.30	.14
❑ 188 Kevin Johnson	.60	.25
❑ 189 Rich Gannon	.30	.14
❑ 190 Stephen Davis	.60	.25
❑ 191 Frank Wycheck	.15	.07
❑ 192 Eric Moulds	.60	.25
❑ 193 Jon Kitna	.60	.25
❑ 194 Mario Bates	.15	.07
❑ 195 Na Brown	.15	.07
❑ 196 Jeff Blake	.30	.14
❑ 197 Charles Evans	.15	.07
❑ 198 Oronde Gadsden	.30	.14
❑ 199 Donnell Bennett	.15	.07
❑ 200 Isaac Bruce	.60	.25
❑ 201 Olindo Mare	.15	.07
❑ 202 Darnell McDonald	.15	.07
❑ 203 Charlie Garner	.30	.14
❑ 204 Shawn Jefferson	.15	.07
❑ 205 Adrian Murrell	.30	.14
❑ 206 Peter Boulware	.15	.07
❑ 207 LeShon Johnson	.15	.07
❑ 208 Herman Moore	.30	.14
❑ 209 Duce Staley	.60	.25
❑ 210 Sean Dawkins	.15	.07
❑ 211 Antowain Smith	.30	.14
❑ 212 Albert Connell	.15	.07
❑ 213 Jeff Garcia	.60	.25
❑ 214 Kimble Anders	.15	.07
❑ 215 Shaun King	1.00	.45
❑ 216 Rocket Ismail	.30	.14
❑ 217 Andrew Glover	.15	.07
❑ 218 Rickey Dudley	.15	.07
❑ 219 Michael Basnight	.15	.07
❑ 220 Terry Glenn	.30	.14
❑ 221 Peter Warrick RC	10.00	4.50
❑ 222 Ron Dayne RC	10.00	4.50
❑ 223 Thomas Jones RC	5.00	2.20
❑ 224 Joe Hamilton RC	4.00	1.80
❑ 225 Tim Rattay RC	5.00	2.20
❑ 226 Chad Pennington RC	10.00	4.50
❑ 227 Dennis Northcutt RC	4.00	1.80
❑ 228 Troy Walters RC	3.00	1.35
❑ 229 Travis Prentice RC	5.00	2.20
❑ 230 Shaun Alexander RC	8.00	3.60
❑ 231 J.R. Redmond RC	4.00	1.80
❑ 232 Chris Redman RC	6.00	2.70
❑ 233 Tee Martin RC	5.00	2.20
❑ 234 Tom Brady RC	3.00	1.35
❑ 235 Travis Taylor RC	4.00	1.80
❑ 236 R.Jay Soward RC	3.00	1.35
❑ 237 Jamal Lewis RC	15.00	6.75
❑ 238 Giovanni Carmazzi RC	4.00	1.80
❑ 239 Dez White RC	2.50	1.10
❑ 240 LaVar Arrington RC SP	200.00	90.00
❑ 241 Laveranues Coles RC	5.00	2.20
❑ 242 Sherrod Gideon RC	2.00	.90
❑ 243 Trung Canidate RC	3.00	1.35
❑ 244 Michael Wiley RC	3.00	1.35
❑ 245 Anthony Lucas RC	2.00	.90
❑ 246 Darrell Jackson RC	5.00	2.20
❑ 247 Plaxico Burress RC	6.00	2.70
❑ 248 Reuben Droughns RC	3.00	1.35
❑ 249 Marc Bulger RC	3.00	1.35
❑ 250 Danny Farmer RC	3.00	1.35

1996 Ultra Sensations

	MINT	NRMT
COMPLETE GOLD SET (101)	15.00	6.75
❑ 1 Leeland McElroy RC	.40	.18
❑ 2 Frank Sanders	.20	.09
❑ 3 Eric Swann	.10	.05
❑ 4 Jeff George	.20	.09
❑ 5 Terance Mathis	.10	.05
❑ 6 Eric Metcalf	.10	.05
❑ 7 Michael Jackson	.20	.09
❑ 8 Eric Turner	.10	.05
❑ 9 Jim Kelly	.40	.18
❑ 10 Bryce Paup	.10	.05
❑ 11 Bruce Smith	.20	.09
❑ 12 Thurman Thomas	.40	.18
❑ 13 Tim Biakabutuka RC	.75	.35
❑ 14 Kerry Collins	.40	.18
❑ 15 Muhsin Muhammad RC	.75	.35
❑ 16 Winslow Oliver RC	.10	.05
❑ 17 Curtis Conway	.40	.18
❑ 18 Bryan Cox	.10	.05
❑ 19 Bobby Engram RC	.40	.18
❑ 20 Erik Kramer	.10	.05
❑ 21 Rashaan Salaam	.40	.18
❑ 22 Jeff Blake	.40	.18
❑ 23 Ki-Jana Carter	.20	.09
❑ 24 Carl Pickens	.40	.18
❑ 25 Troy Aikman	1.00	.45
❑ 26 Michael Irvin	.40	.18
❑ 27 Daryl Johnston	.20	.09
❑ 28 Deion Sanders	.75	.35
❑ 29 Emmitt Smith	1.50	.70
❑ 30 Terrell Davis	2.50	1.10
❑ 31 John Elway	2.00	.90
❑ 32 Anthony Miller	.20	.09
❑ 33 John Mobley RC	.10	.05
❑ 34 Scott Mitchell	.20	.09
❑ 35 Herman Moore	.40	.18
❑ 36 Barry Sanders	2.00	.90
❑ 37 Edgar Bennett	.20	.09
❑ 38 Robert Brooks	.40	.18
❑ 39 Brett Favre	2.00	.90
❑ 40 Reggie White	.40	.18
❑ 41 Eddie George RC	2.50	1.10
❑ 42 Steve McNair	.75	.35
❑ 43 Chris Sanders	.20	.09
❑ 44 Quentin Coryatt	.10	.05
❑ 45 Marshall Faulk	.40	.18
❑ 46 Jim Harbaugh	.20	.09
❑ 47 Marvin Harrison RC	2.00	.90
❑ 48 Mark Brunell	1.00	.45
❑ 49 Natrone Means	.40	.18
❑ 50 Andre Rison	.20	.09
❑ 51 Marcus Allen	.40	.18
❑ 52 Steve Bono	.10	.05
❑ 53 Greg Hill	.20	.09
❑ 54 Tamarick Vanover	.20	.09
❑ 55 Karim Abdul-Jabbar RC	.50	.23
❑ 56 Dan Marino	2.00	.90
❑ 57 O.J. McDuffie	.20	.09
❑ 58 Zach Thomas RC	.75	.35
❑ 59 Cris Carter	.40	.18
❑ 60 Warren Moon	.20	.09
❑ 61 Jake Reed	.20	.09
❑ 62 Drew Bledsoe	1.00	.45
❑ 63 Ben Coates	.20	.09
❑ 64 Terry Glenn RC	1.00	.45
❑ 65 Curtis Martin	.75	.35
❑ 66 Mario Bates	.20	.09
❑ 67 Michael Haynes	.10	.05
❑ 68 Dave Brown	.10	.05
❑ 69 Rodney Hampton	.20	.09
❑ 70 Amani Toomer RC	.75	.35
❑ 71 Tyrone Wheatley	.20	.09
❑ 72 Keyshawn Johnson RC	1.50	.70
❑ 73 Neil O'Donnell	.20	.09
❑ 74 Tim Brown	.40	.18
❑ 75 Rickey Dudley RC	.40	.18
❑ 76 Napoleon Kaufman	.40	.18
❑ 77 Chester McGlockton	.10	.05
❑ 78 Charlie Garner	.10	.05
❑ 79 Chris T. Jones	.20	.09
❑ 80 Ricky Watters	.20	.09
❑ 81 Jerome Bettis	.40	.18
❑ 82 Kordell Stewart	.60	.25
❑ 83 Rod Woodson	.20	.09
❑ 84 Aaron Hayden	.10	.05
❑ 85 Stan Humphries	.20	.09
❑ 86 Junior Seau	.20	.09
❑ 87 Tony Banks RC	1.00	.45
❑ 88 Isaac Bruce	.40	.18
❑ 89 Lawrence Phillips RC	.40	.18
❑ 90 Derek Loville	.10	.05
❑ 91 Jerry Rice	1.00	.45
❑ 92 J.J. Stokes	.40	.18
❑ 93 Steve Young	.75	.35
❑ 94 Joey Galloway	.60	.25
❑ 95 Rick Mirer	.20	.09
❑ 96 Chris Warren	.20	.09
❑ 97 Trent Dilfer	.40	.18
❑ 98 Errict Rhett	.20	.09
❑ 99 Terry Allen	.20	.09
❑ 100 Michael Westbrook	.40	.18
❑ NNO Brett Favre Checklist Card	2.50	1.10
❑ NNO Promo Sheet Brett Favre Gold, Blue, and Marble Gold cards	2.50	1.10

1991 Upper Deck

	MINT	NRMT
COMPLETE SET (700)	12.00	5.50
COMP.FACT.SET (700)	15.00	6.75
COMP.SERIES 1 SET (500)	8.00	3.60
COMP.SERIES 2 SET (200)	4.00	1.80
COMP.FACT.SERIES 2 (200)	4.00	1.80
❑ 1 Star Rookie Checklist Dan McGwire	.04	.02
❑ 2 Eric Bieniemy RC	.04	.02
❑ 3 Mike Dumas RC	.04	.02
❑ 4 Mike Croel RC	.04	.02
❑ 5 Russell Maryland RC	.25	.11
❑ 6 Charles McRae RC	.04	.02
❑ 7 Dan McGwire RC	.04	.02
❑ 8 Mike Pritchard RC	.25	.11
❑ 9 Ricky Watters RC	1.50	.70
❑ 10 Chris Zorich RC	.25	.11
❑ 11 Browning Nagle RC	.04	.02
❑ 12 Wesley Carroll RC	.04	.02
❑ 13 Brett Favre RC	6.00	2.70
❑ 14 Rob Carpenter RC	.04	.02
❑ 15 Eric Swann RC	.25	.11
❑ 16 Stanley Richard RC	.04	.02
❑ 17 Herman Moore RC	2.00	.90
❑ 18 Todd Marinovich RC	.04	.02
❑ 19 Aaron Craver RC	.04	.02
❑ 20 Chuck Webb RC	.04	.02
❑ 21 Todd Lyght RC	.04	.02
❑ 22 Greg Lewis RC	.04	.02
❑ 23 Eric Turner RC	.10	.05
❑ 24 Alvin Harper RC	.25	.11
❑ 25 Jarrod Bunch RC	.04	.02
❑ 26 Bruce Pickens RC	.04	.02
❑ 27 Harvey Williams RC	.25	.11
❑ 28 Randal Hill RC	.10	.05
❑ 29 Nick Bell RC	.04	.02
❑ 30 Jim Everett AT Henry Ellard	.10	.05
❑ 31 Randall Cunningham AT Keith Jackson	.04	.02
❑ 32 Steve DeBerg AT Stephone Paige	.04	.02
❑ 33 Warren Moon AT Drew Hill	.10	.05
❑ 34 Dan Marino AT Mark Clayton	.50	.23
❑ 35 Joe Montana AT Jerry Rice	.50	.23
❑ 36 Percy Snow	.04	.02
❑ 37 Kelvin Martin	.04	.02
❑ 38 Scott Case	.04	.02
❑ 39 John Gesek RC	.04	.02
❑ 40 Barry Word	.04	.02
❑ 41 Cornelius Bennett	.10	.05
❑ 42 Mike Kenn	.04	.02
❑ 43 Andre Reed	.10	.05
❑ 44 Bobby Hebert	.04	.02
❑ 45 William Perry	.10	.05
❑ 46 Dennis Byrd	.04	.02
❑ 47 Martin Mayhew	.04	.02
❑ 48 Issiac Holt	.04	.02
❑ 49 William White	.04	.02
❑ 50 JoJo Townsell	.04	.02
❑ 51 Jarvis Williams	.04	.02
❑ 52 Joey Browner	.04	.02
❑ 53 Pat Terrell	.04	.02
❑ 54 Joe Montana UER (Born Monongahela, not New Eagle)	1.25	.55
❑ 55 Jeff Herrod	.04	.02
❑ 56 Cris Carter	.50	.23
❑ 57 Jerry Rice	.75	.35
❑ 58 Brett Perriman	.25	.11
❑ 59 Kevin Fagan	.04	.02
❑ 60 Wayne Haddix	.04	.02
❑ 61 Tommy Kane	.04	.02
❑ 62 Pat Beach	.04	.02
❑ 63 Jeff Lageman	.04	.02
❑ 64 Hassan Jones	.04	.02
❑ 65 Bennie Blades	.04	.02
❑ 66 Tim McGee	.04	.02
❑ 67 Robert Blackmon	.04	.02
❑ 68 Fred Stokes RC	.04	.02
❑ 69 Barney Bussey RC	.04	.02
❑ 70 Eric Metcalf	.10	.05
❑ 71 Mark Kelso	.04	.02
❑ 72 Neal Anderson TC	.04	.02
❑ 73 Boomer Esiason TC	.04	.02
❑ 74 Thurman Thomas TC	.25	.11
❑ 75 John Elway TC	.50	.23
❑ 76 Eric Metcalf TC	.10	.05
❑ 77 Vinny Testaverde TC	.10	.05
❑ 78 Johnny Johnson TC	.04	.02
❑ 79 Anthony Miller TC	.10	.05
❑ 80 Derrick Thomas TC	.10	.05
❑ 81 Jeff George TC	.10	.05
❑ 82 Troy Aikman TC	.40	.18
❑ 83 Dan Marino TC	.50	.23
❑ 84 Randall Cunningham TC	.10	.05
❑ 85 Deion Sanders TC	.04	.02
❑ 86 Jerry Rice TC	.40	.18
❑ 87 Lawrence Taylor TC	.10	.05
❑ 88 Al Toon TC	.04	.02
❑ 89 Barry Sanders TC	.60	.25
❑ 90 Warren Moon TC	.10	.05
❑ 91 Don Majkowski TC	.04	.02
❑ 92 Andre Tippett TC	.04	.02
❑ 93 Bo Jackson TC	.30	.14

❑ 94	Jim Everett TC	.10	.05
❑ 95	Art Monk TC	.10	.05
❑ 96	Morten Andersen TC	.04	.02
❑ 97	John L. Williams TC	.04	.02
❑ 98	Rod Woodson TC	.10	.05
❑ 99	Herschel Walker TC	.10	.05
❑ 100	Checklist 1-100	.04	.02
❑ 101	Steve Young	.75	.35
❑ 102	Jim Lachey	.04	.02
❑ 103	Tom Rathman	.04	.02
❑ 104	Earnest Byner	.04	.02
❑ 105	Karl Mecklenburg	.04	.02
❑ 106	Wes Hopkins	.04	.02
❑ 107	Michael Irvin	.25	.11
❑ 108	Burt Grossman	.04	.02
❑ 109	Jay Novacek UER (Wearing 82, but card says he wears 84)	.25	.11
❑ 110	Ben Smith	.04	.02
❑ 111	Rod Woodson	.25	.11
❑ 112	Ernie Jones	.04	.02
❑ 113	Bryan Hinkle	.04	.02
❑ 114	Vai Sikahema	.04	.02
❑ 115	Bubby Brister	.04	.02
❑ 116	Brian Blades	.10	.05
❑ 117	Don Majkowski	.04	.02
❑ 118	Rod Bernstine	.04	.02
❑ 119	Brian Noble	.04	.02
❑ 120	Eugene Robinson	.04	.02
❑ 121	John Taylor	.10	.05
❑ 122	Vance Johnson	.04	.02
❑ 123	Art Monk	.10	.05
❑ 124	John Elway	1.25	.55
❑ 125	Dexter Carter	.04	.02
❑ 126	Anthony Miller	.10	.05
❑ 127	Keith Jackson	.10	.05
❑ 128	Albert Lewis	.04	.02
❑ 129	Billy Ray Smith	.04	.02
❑ 130	Clyde Simmons	.04	.02
❑ 131	Merril Hoge	.04	.02
❑ 132	Ricky Proehl	.04	.02
❑ 133	Tim McDonald	.04	.02
❑ 134	Louis Lipps	.04	.02
❑ 135	Ken Harvey	.10	.05
❑ 136	Sterling Sharpe	.10	.05
❑ 137	Gill Byrd	.04	.02
❑ 138	Tim Harris	.04	.02
❑ 139	Derrick Fenner	.04	.02
❑ 140	Johnny Holland	.04	.02
❑ 141	Ricky Sanders	.04	.02
❑ 142	Bobby Humphrey	.04	.02
❑ 143	Roger Craig	.10	.05
❑ 144	Steve Atwater	.04	.02
❑ 145	Ickey Woods	.04	.02
❑ 146	Randall Cunningham	.25	.11
❑ 147	Marion Butts	.10	.05
❑ 148	Reggie White	.25	.11
❑ 149	Ronnie Harmon	.04	.02
❑ 150	Mike Saxon	.04	.02
❑ 151	Greg Townsend	.04	.02
❑ 152	Troy Aikman	.75	.35
❑ 153	Shane Conlan	.04	.02
❑ 154	Deion Sanders	.40	.18
❑ 155	Bo Jackson	.30	.14
❑ 156	Jeff Hostetler	.10	.05
❑ 157	Albert Bentley	.04	.02
❑ 158	James Williams	.04	.02
❑ 159	Bill Brooks	.04	.02
❑ 160	Nick Lowery	.04	.02
❑ 161	Ottis Anderson	.10	.05
❑ 162	Kevin Greene	.25	.11
❑ 163	Neil Smith	.25	.11
❑ 164	Jim Everett	.10	.05
❑ 165	Derrick Thomas	.25	.11
❑ 166	John L. Williams	.04	.02
❑ 167	Timm Rosenbach	.04	.02
❑ 168	Leslie O'Neal	.10	.05
❑ 169	Clarence Verdin	.04	.02
❑ 170	Dave Krieg	.10	.05
❑ 171	Steve Broussard	.04	.02
❑ 172	Emmitt Smith	2.00	.90
❑ 173	Andre Rison	.10	.05
❑ 174	Bruce Smith	.25	.11
❑ 175	Mark Clayton	.10	.05
❑ 176	Christian Okoye	.04	.02
❑ 177	Duane Bickett	.04	.02
❑ 178	Stephone Paige	.04	.02
❑ 179	Fredd Young	.04	.02
❑ 180	Mervyn Fernandez	.04	.02
❑ 181	Phil Simms	.10	.05
❑ 182	Pete Holohan	.04	.02
❑ 183	Pepper Johnson	.04	.02
❑ 184	Jackie Slater	.04	.02
❑ 185	Stephen Baker	.04	.02
❑ 186	Frank Cornish	.04	.02
❑ 187	Dave Waymer	.04	.02
❑ 188	Terance Mathis	.10	.05
❑ 189	Darryl Talley	.04	.02
❑ 190	James Hasty	.04	.02
❑ 191	Jay Schroeder	.04	.02
❑ 192	Kenneth Davis	.04	.02
❑ 193	Chris Miller	.10	.05
❑ 194	Scott Davis	.04	.02
❑ 195	Tim Green	.04	.02
❑ 196	Dan Saleaumua	.04	.02
❑ 197	Rohn Stark	.04	.02
❑ 198	John Alt	.04	.02
❑ 199	Steve Tasker	.10	.05
❑ 200	Checklist 101-200	.04	.02
❑ 201	Freddie Joe Nunn	.04	.02
❑ 202	Jim Breech	.04	.02
❑ 203	Roy Green	.04	.02
❑ 204	Gary Anderson RB	.04	.02
❑ 205	Rich Camarillo	.04	.02
❑ 206	Mark Bortz	.04	.02
❑ 207	Eddie Brown	.04	.02
❑ 208	Brad Muster	.04	.02
❑ 209	Anthony Munoz	.10	.05
❑ 210	Dalton Hilliard	.04	.02
❑ 211	Erik McMillan	.04	.02
❑ 212	Perry Kemp	.04	.02
❑ 213	Jim Thornton	.04	.02
❑ 214	Anthony Dilweg	.04	.02
❑ 215	Cleveland Gary	.04	.02
❑ 216	Leo Goeas	.04	.02
❑ 217	Mike Merriweather	.04	.02
❑ 218	Courtney Hall	.04	.02
❑ 219	Wade Wilson	.10	.05
❑ 220	Billy Joe Tolliver	.04	.02
❑ 221	Harold Green	.10	.05
❑ 222	Al(Bubba) Baker	.10	.05
❑ 223	Carl Zander	.04	.02
❑ 224	Thane Gash	.04	.02
❑ 225	Kevin Mack	.04	.02
❑ 226	Morten Andersen	.04	.02
❑ 227	Dennis Gentry	.04	.02
❑ 228	Vince Buck	.04	.02
❑ 229	Mike Singletary	.10	.05
❑ 230	Rueben Mayes	.04	.02
❑ 231	Mark Carrier WR	.25	.11
❑ 232	Tony Mandarich	.04	.02
❑ 233	Al Toon	.10	.05
❑ 234	Renaldo Turnbull	.04	.02
❑ 235	Broderick Thomas	.04	.02
❑ 236	Anthony Carter	.10	.05
❑ 237	Flipper Anderson	.04	.02
❑ 238	Jerry Robinson	.04	.02
❑ 239	Vince Newsome	.04	.02
❑ 240	Keith Millard	.04	.02
❑ 241	Reggie Langhorne	.04	.02
❑ 242	James Francis	.04	.02
❑ 243	Felix Wright	.04	.02
❑ 244	Neal Anderson	.10	.05
❑ 245	Boomer Esiason	.10	.05
❑ 246	Pat Swilling	.10	.05
❑ 247	Richard Dent	.10	.05
❑ 248	Craig Heyward	.10	.05
❑ 249	Ron Morris	.04	.02
❑ 250	Eric Martin	.04	.02
❑ 251	Jim C. Jensen	.04	.02
❑ 252	Anthony Toney	.04	.02
❑ 253	Sammie Smith	.04	.02
❑ 254	Calvin Williams	.10	.05
❑ 255	Dan Marino	1.25	.55
❑ 256	Warren Moon	.25	.11
❑ 257	Tommie Agee	.04	.02
❑ 258	Haywood Jeffires	.10	.05
❑ 259	Eugene Lockhart	.04	.02
❑ 260	Drew Hill	.04	.02
❑ 261	Vinny Testaverde	.10	.05
❑ 262	Jim Arnold	.04	.02
❑ 263	Steve Christie	.04	.02
❑ 264	Chris Spielman	.10	.05
❑ 265	Reggie Cobb	.04	.02
❑ 266	John Stephens	.04	.02
❑ 267	Jay Hilgenberg	.04	.02
❑ 268	Brent Williams	.04	.02
❑ 269	Rodney Hampton	.25	.11
❑ 270	Irving Fryar	.10	.05
❑ 271	Terry McDaniel	.04	.02
❑ 272	Reggie Roby	.04	.02
❑ 273	Allen Pinkett	.04	.02
❑ 274	Tim McKyer	.04	.02
❑ 275	Bob Golic	.04	.02
❑ 276	Wilber Marshall	.04	.02
❑ 277	Ray Childress	.04	.02
❑ 278	Charles Mann	.04	.02
❑ 279	Cris Dishman RC	.04	.02
❑ 280	Mark Rypien	.10	.05
❑ 281	Michael Cofer	.04	.02
❑ 282	Keith Byars	.04	.02
❑ 283	Mike Rozier	.04	.02
❑ 284	Seth Joyner	.10	.05
❑ 285	Jessie Tuggle	.04	.02
❑ 286	Mark Bavaro	.04	.02
❑ 287	Eddie Anderson	.04	.02
❑ 288	Sean Landeta	.04	.02
❑ 289	Howie Long (With George Brett)	.10	.05
❑ 290	Reyna Thompson	.04	.02
❑ 291	Ferrell Edmunds	.04	.02
❑ 292	Willie Gault	.10	.05
❑ 293	John Offerdahl	.04	.02
❑ 294	Tim Brown	.25	.11
❑ 295	Bruce Matthews	.10	.05
❑ 296	Kevin Ross	.04	.02
❑ 297	Lorenzo White	.04	.02
❑ 298	Dino Hackett	.04	.02
❑ 299	Curtis Duncan	.04	.02
❑ 300	Checklist 201-300	.04	.02
❑ 301	Andre Ware	.10	.05
❑ 302	David Little	.04	.02
❑ 303	Jerry Ball	.04	.02
❑ 304	Dwight Stone UER (He's a WR, not RB)	.04	.02
❑ 305	Rodney Peete	.10	.05
❑ 306	Mike Baab	.04	.02
❑ 307	Tim Worley	.04	.02
❑ 308	Paul Farren	.04	.02
❑ 309	Carnell Lake	.04	.02
❑ 310	Clay Matthews	.10	.05
❑ 311	Alton Montgomery	.04	.02
❑ 312	Ernest Givins	.10	.05
❑ 313	Mike Horan	.04	.02
❑ 314	Sean Jones	.10	.05
❑ 315	Leonard Smith	.04	.02
❑ 316	Carl Banks	.04	.02
❑ 317	Jerome Brown	.04	.02
❑ 318	Everson Walls	.04	.02
❑ 319	Ron Heller	.04	.02
❑ 320	Mark Collins	.04	.02
❑ 321	Eddie Murray	.04	.02
❑ 322	Jim Harbaugh	.25	.11
❑ 323	Mel Gray	.10	.05
❑ 324	Keith Van Horne	.04	.02
❑ 325	Lomas Brown	.04	.02
❑ 326	Carl Lee	.04	.02
❑ 327	Ken O'Brien	.04	.02
❑ 328	Dermontti Dawson	.04	.02
❑ 329	Brad Baxter	.04	.02
❑ 330	Chris Doleman	.04	.02
❑ 331	Louis Oliver	.04	.02
❑ 332	Frank Stams	.04	.02
❑ 333	Mike Munchak	.04	.02
❑ 334	Fred Strickland	.04	.02
❑ 335	Mark Duper	.10	.05
❑ 336	Jacob Green	.04	.02
❑ 337	Tony Paige	.04	.02
❑ 338	Jeff Bryant	.04	.02
❑ 339	Lemuel Stinson	.04	.02
❑ 340	David Wyman	.04	.02
❑ 341	Lee Williams	.04	.02
❑ 342	Trace Armstrong	.04	.02
❑ 343	Junior Seau	.25	.11
❑ 344	John Roper	.04	.02
❑ 345	Jeff George	.25	.11
❑ 346	Herschel Walker	.10	.05
❑ 347	Sam Clancy	.04	.02

❑ 348 Steve Jordan	.04	.02
❑ 349 Nate Odomes	.04	.02
❑ 350 Martin Bayless	.04	.02
❑ 351 Brent Jones	.25	.11
❑ 352 Ray Agnew	.04	.02
❑ 353 Charles Haley	.10	.05
❑ 354 Andre Tippett	.04	.02
❑ 355 Ronnie Lott	.10	.05
❑ 356 Thurman Thomas	.25	.11
❑ 357 Fred Barnett	.25	.11
❑ 358 James Lofton	.10	.05
❑ 359 William Frizzell RC	.04	.02
❑ 360 Keith McKeller	.04	.02
❑ 361 Rodney Holman	.04	.02
❑ 362 Henry Ellard	.10	.05
❑ 363 David Fulcher	.04	.02
❑ 364 Jerry Gray	.04	.02
❑ 365 James Brooks	.10	.05
❑ 366 Tony Stargell	.04	.02
❑ 367 Keith McCants	.04	.02
❑ 368 Lewis Billups	.04	.02
❑ 369 Ervin Randle	.04	.02
❑ 370 Pat Leahy	.04	.02
❑ 371 Bruce Armstrong	.04	.02
❑ 372 Steve DeBerg	.04	.02
❑ 373 Guy McIntyre	.04	.02
❑ 374 Deron Cherry	.04	.02
❑ 375 Fred Marion	.04	.02
❑ 376 Michael Haddix	.04	.02
❑ 377 Kent Hull	.04	.02
❑ 378 Jerry Holmes	.04	.02
❑ 379 Jim Ritcher	.04	.02
❑ 380 Ed West	.04	.02
❑ 381 Richmond Webb	.04	.02
❑ 382 Mark Jackson	.04	.02
❑ 383 Tom Newberry	.04	.02
❑ 384 Ricky Nattiel	.04	.02
❑ 385 Keith Sims	.04	.02
❑ 386 Ron Hall	.04	.02
❑ 387 Ken Norton	.25	.11
❑ 388 Paul Gruber	.04	.02
❑ 389 Daniel Stubbs	.04	.02
❑ 390 Ian Beckles	.04	.02
❑ 391 Hoby Brenner	.04	.02
❑ 392 Tory Epps	.04	.02
❑ 393 Sam Mills	.04	.02
❑ 394 Chris Hinton	.04	.02
❑ 395 Steve Walsh	.04	.02
❑ 396 Simon Fletcher	.04	.02
❑ 397 Tony Bennett	.10	.05
❑ 398 Aundray Bruce	.04	.02
❑ 399 Mark Murphy	.04	.02
❑ 400 Checklist 301-400	.04	.02
❑ 401 Barry Sanders LL	.60	.25
❑ 402 Jerry Rice LL	.40	.18
❑ 403 Warren Moon LL	.10	.05
❑ 404 Derrick Thomas LL	.10	.05
❑ 405 Nick Lowery LL	.04	.02
❑ 406 Mark Carrier DB LL	.10	.05
❑ 407 Michael Carter	.04	.02
❑ 408 Chris Singleton	.04	.02
❑ 409 Matt Millen	.10	.05
❑ 410 Ronnie Lippett	.04	.02
❑ 411 E.J. Junior	.04	.02
❑ 412 Ray Donaldson	.04	.02
❑ 413 Keith Willis	.04	.02
❑ 414 Jessie Hester	.04	.02
❑ 415 Jeff Cross	.04	.02
❑ 416 Greg Jackson RC	.04	.02
❑ 417 Alvin Walton	.04	.02
❑ 418 Bart Oates	.04	.02
❑ 419 Chip Lohmiller	.04	.02
❑ 420 John Elliott	.04	.02
❑ 421 Randall McDaniel	.04	.02
❑ 422 Richard Johnson RC	.04	.02
❑ 423 Al Noga	.04	.02
❑ 424 Lamar Lathon	.04	.02
❑ 425 Rick Fenney	.04	.02
❑ 426 Jack Del Rio	.04	.02
❑ 427 Don Mosebar	.04	.02
❑ 428 Luis Sharpe	.04	.02
❑ 429 Steve Wisniewski	.04	.02
❑ 430 Jimmie Jones	.04	.02
❑ 431 Freeman McNeil	.04	.02
❑ 432 Ron Rivera	.04	.02
❑ 433 Hart Lee Dykes	.04	.02
❑ 434 Mark Carrier DB	.10	.05
❑ 435 Rob Moore	.25	.11
❑ 436 Gary Clark	.25	.11
❑ 437 Heath Sherman	.04	.02
❑ 438 Darrell Green	.04	.02
❑ 439 Jessie Small	.04	.02
❑ 440 Monte Coleman	.04	.02
❑ 441 Leonard Marshall	.04	.02
❑ 442 Richard Johnson	.04	.02
❑ 443 Dave Meggett	.10	.05
❑ 444 Barry Sanders	1.50	.70
❑ 445 Lawrence Taylor	.25	.11
❑ 446 Marcus Allen	.25	.11
❑ 447 Johnny Johnson	.04	.02
❑ 448 Aaron Wallace	.04	.02
❑ 449 Anthony Thompson	.04	.02
❑ 450 Steve DeBerg Dan Marino Team MVP CL 453-473	.40	.18
❑ 451 Andre Rison MVP	.10	.05
❑ 452 Thurman Thomas MVP	.10	.05
❑ 453 Neal Anderson MVP	.04	.02
❑ 454 Boomer Esiason MVP	.04	.02
❑ 455 Eric Metcalf MVP	.10	.05
❑ 456 Emmitt Smith MVP	1.00	.45
❑ 457 Bobby Humphrey MVP	.04	.02
❑ 458 Barry Sanders MVP	.60	.25
❑ 459 Sterling Sharpe MVP	.10	.05
❑ 460 Warren Moon MVP	.10	.05
❑ 461 Albert Bentley MVP	.04	.02
❑ 462 Steve DeBerg MVP	.04	.02
❑ 463 Greg Townsend MVP	.04	.02
❑ 464 Henry Ellard MVP	.10	.05
❑ 465 Dan Marino MVP	.50	.23
❑ 466 Anthony Carter MVP	.10	.05
❑ 467 John Stephens MVP	.04	.02
❑ 468 Pat Swilling MVP	.04	.02
❑ 469 Ottis Anderson MVP	.10	.05
❑ 470 Dennis Byrd MVP	.04	.02
❑ 471 Randall Cunningham MVP	.10	.05
❑ 472 Johnny Johnson MVP	.04	.02
❑ 473 Rod Woodson MVP	.10	.05
❑ 474 Anthony Miller MVP	.10	.05
❑ 475 Jerry Rice MVP	.40	.18
❑ 476 John L.Williams MVP	.04	.02
❑ 477 Wayne Haddix MVP	.04	.02
❑ 478 Earnest Byner MVP	.04	.02
❑ 479 Doug Widell	.04	.02
❑ 480 Tommy Hodson	.04	.02
❑ 481 Shawn Collins	.04	.02
❑ 482 Rickey Jackson	.04	.02
❑ 483 Tony Casillas	.04	.02
❑ 484 Vaughan Johnson	.04	.02
❑ 485 Floyd Dixon	.04	.02
❑ 486 Eric Green	.04	.02
❑ 487 Harry Hamilton	.04	.02
❑ 488 Gary Anderson K	.04	.02
❑ 489 Bruce Hill	.04	.02
❑ 490 Gerald Williams	.04	.02
❑ 491 Cortez Kennedy	.25	.11
❑ 492 Chet Brooks	.04	.02
❑ 493 Dwayne Harper RC	.04	.02
❑ 494 Don Griffin	.04	.02
❑ 495 Andy Heck	.04	.02
❑ 496 David Treadwell	.04	.02
❑ 497 Irv Pankey	.04	.02
❑ 498 Dennis Smith	.04	.02
❑ 499 Marcus Dupree	.04	.02
❑ 500 Checklist 401-500	.04	.02
❑ 501 Wendell Davis	.04	.02
❑ 502 Matt Bahr	.04	.02
❑ 503 Rob Burnett RC	.10	.05
❑ 504 Maurice Carthon	.04	.02
❑ 505 Donnell Woolford	.04	.02
❑ 506 Howard Ballard	.04	.02
❑ 507 Mark Boyer	.04	.02
❑ 508 Eugene Marve	.04	.02
❑ 509 Joe Kelly	.04	.02
❑ 510 Will Wolford	.04	.02
❑ 511 Robert Clark	.04	.02
❑ 512 Matt Brock RC	.04	.02
❑ 513 Chris Warren	.25	.11
❑ 514 Ken Willis	.04	.02
❑ 515 George Jamison RC	.04	.02
❑ 516 Rufus Porter	.04	.02
❑ 517 Mark Higgs RC	.04	.02
❑ 518 Thomas Everett	.04	.02
❑ 519 Robert Brown	.04	.02
❑ 520 Gene Atkins	.04	.02
❑ 521 Hardy Nickerson	.10	.05
❑ 522 Johnny Bailey	.04	.02
❑ 523 William Frizzell	.04	.02
❑ 524 Steve McMichael	.10	.05
❑ 525 Kevin Porter	.04	.02
❑ 526 Carwell Gardner	.04	.02
❑ 527 Eugene Daniel	.04	.02
❑ 528 Vestee Jackson	.04	.02
❑ 529 Chris Goode	.04	.02
❑ 530 Leon Seals	.04	.02
❑ 531 Darion Conner	.04	.02
❑ 532 Stan Brock	.04	.02
❑ 533 Kirby Jackson RC	.04	.02
❑ 534 Marv Cook	.04	.02
❑ 535 Bill Fralic	.04	.02
❑ 536 Keith Woodside	.04	.02
❑ 537 Hugh Green	.04	.02
❑ 538 Grant Feasel	.04	.02
❑ 539 Bubba McDowell	.04	.02
❑ 540 Vai Sikahema	.04	.02
❑ 541 Aaron Cox	.04	.02
❑ 542 Roger Craig	.10	.05
❑ 543 Robb Thomas	.04	.02
❑ 544 Ronnie Lott	.10	.05
❑ 545 Robert Delpino	.04	.02
❑ 546 Greg McMurtry	.04	.02
❑ 547 Jim Morrissey RC	.04	.02
❑ 548 Johnny Rembert	.04	.02
❑ 549 Markus Paul RC	.04	.02
❑ 550 Karl Wilson RC	.04	.02
❑ 551 Gaston Green	.04	.02
❑ 552 Willie Drewrey	.04	.02
❑ 553 Michael Young	.04	.02
❑ 554 Tom Tupa	.04	.02
❑ 555 John Friesz	.25	.11
❑ 556 Cody Carlson RC	.04	.02
❑ 557 Eric Allen	.04	.02
❑ 558 Thomas Benson	.04	.02
❑ 559 Scott Mersereau RC	.04	.02
❑ 560 Lionel Washington	.04	.02
❑ 561 Brian Brennan	.04	.02
❑ 562 Jim Jeffcoat	.04	.02
❑ 563 Jeff Jaeger	.04	.02
❑ 564 D.J. Johnson	.04	.02
❑ 565 Danny Villa	.04	.02
❑ 566 Don Beebe	.04	.02
❑ 567 Michael Haynes	.25	.11
❑ 568 Brett Faryniarz RC	.04	.02
❑ 569 Mike Prior	.04	.02
❑ 570 John Davis RC	.04	.02
❑ 571 Vernon Turner RC	.04	.02
❑ 572 Michael Brooks	.04	.02
❑ 573 Mike Gann	.04	.02
❑ 574 Ron Holmes	.04	.02
❑ 575 Gary Plummer	.04	.02
❑ 576 Bill Romanowski	.04	.02
❑ 577 Chris Jacke	.04	.02
❑ 578 Gary Reasons	.04	.02
❑ 579 Tim Jorden RC	.04	.02
❑ 580 Tim McKyer	.04	.02
❑ 581 Johnnie Jackson RC	.04	.02
❑ 582 Ethan Horton	.04	.02
❑ 583 Pete Stoyanovich	.04	.02
❑ 584 Jeff Query	.04	.02
❑ 585 Frank Reich	.10	.05
❑ 586 Riki Ellison	.04	.02
❑ 587 Eric Hill	.04	.02
❑ 588 Anthony Shelton RC	.04	.02
❑ 589 Steve Smith	.04	.02
❑ 590 Garth Jax RC	.04	.02
❑ 591 Greg Davis RC	.04	.02
❑ 592 Bill Maas	.04	.02
❑ 593 Henry Rolling RC	.04	.02
❑ 594 Keith Jones	.04	.02
❑ 595 Tootie Robbins	.04	.02
❑ 596 Brian Jordan	.10	.05
❑ 597 Derrick Walker RC	.04	.02
❑ 598 Jonathan Hayes	.04	.02
❑ 599 Nate Lewis RC	.04	.02
❑ 600 Checklist 501-600	.04	.02
❑ 601 AFC Checklist RF Mike Croel	.04	.02

Greg Lewis
Keith Traylor
Kenny Walker
❑ 602 James Jones RF RC .04 .02
❑ 603 Tim Barnett RF RC .04 .02
❑ 604 Ed King RF RC .04 .02
❑ 605 Shane Curry RF .04 .02
❑ 606 Mike Croel RF .04 .02
❑ 607 Bryan Cox RF RC .25 .11
❑ 608 Shawn Jefferson RF RC .10 .05
❑ 609 Kenny Walker RF RC .04 .02
❑ 610 Michael Jackson RF RC .25 .11
❑ 611 Jon Vaughn RF RC .04 .02
❑ 612 Greg Lewis RF .04 .02
❑ 613 Joe Valerio RF .04 .02
❑ 614 Pat Harlow RF RC .04 .02
❑ 615 Henry Jones RF RC .10 .05
❑ 616 Jeff Graham RF RC .25 .11
❑ 617 Darryll Lewis RF RC .10 .05
❑ 618 Keith Traylor RF RC UER .04 .02
(Bronchos on back)
❑ 619 Scott Miller RF .04 .02
❑ 620 Nick Bell RF .04 .02
❑ 621 John Flannery RF RC .04 .02
❑ 622 Leonard Russell RF RC .10 .05
❑ 623 Alfred Williams RF RC .04 .02
❑ 624 Browning Nagle RF .04 .02
❑ 625 Harvey Williams RF .10 .05
❑ 626 Dan McGwire RF .04 .02
❑ 627 NFC Checklist RF .50 .23
Brett Favre
Moe Gardner
Erric Pegram
Bruce Pickens
Mike Pritchard
❑ 628 William Thomas RF RC .04 .02
❑ 629 L.Dawsey RF RC .10 .05
❑ 630 Aeneas Williams RF RC .10 .05
❑ 631 Stan Thomas RF .04 .02
❑ 632 Randal Hill RF .04 .02
❑ 633 Moe Gardner RF RC .04 .02
❑ 634 Alvin Harper RF .10 .05
❑ 635 Esera Tuaolo RF RC .04 .02
❑ 636 Russell Maryland RF .10 .05
❑ 637 Anthony Morgan RF RC .04 .02
❑ 638 Erric Pegram RF RC .25 .11
❑ 639 Herman Moore RF 1.00 .45
❑ 640 Ricky Ervins RF RC .10 .05
❑ 641 Kelvin Pritchett RF RC .10 .05
❑ 642 Roman Phifer RF RC .04 .02
❑ 643 Antone Davis RF RC .04 .02
❑ 644 Mike Pritchard RF .10 .05
❑ 645 Vinnie Clark RF RC .04 .02
❑ 646 Jake Reed RF RC .75 .35
❑ 647 Brett Favre RF 2.50 1.10
❑ 648 Todd Lyght RF .04 .02
❑ 649 Bruce Pickens RF .04 .02
❑ 650 Darren Lewis RF RC .04 .02
❑ 651 Wesley Carroll RF .04 .02
❑ 652 James Joseph RF RC .10 .05
❑ 653 Robert Delpino AR .04 .02
Tim McDonald
❑ 654 Vencie Glenn AR .04 .02
Deion Sanders
❑ 655 Jerry Rice AR .30 .14
Terry McDaniel
❑ 656 Barry Sanders AR .50 .23
Derrick Thomas
❑ 657 Ken Tippins AR .04 .02
Lorenzo White
❑ 658 Christian Okoye AR .04 .02
Jacob Green
❑ 659 Rich Gannon .25 .11
❑ 660 Johnny Meads .04 .02
❑ 661 J.J. Birden RC .10 .05
❑ 662 Bruce Kozerski .04 .02
❑ 663 Felix Wright .04 .02
❑ 664 Al Smith .04 .02
❑ 665 Stan Humphries .25 .11
❑ 666 Alfred Anderson .04 .02
❑ 667 Nate Newton .10 .05
❑ 668 Vince Workman RC .10 .05
❑ 669 Ricky Reynolds .04 .02
❑ 670 Bryce Paup RC .25 .11
❑ 671 Gill Fenerty .04 .02
❑ 672 Darrell Thompson .04 .02
❑ 673 Anthony Smith .04 .02
❑ 674 Darryl Henley RC .04 .02
❑ 675 Brett Maxie .04 .02
❑ 676 Craig Taylor RC .04 .02
❑ 677 Steve Wallace .10 .05
❑ 678 Jeff Feagles RC .04 .02
❑ 679 James Washington RC .04 .02
❑ 680 Tim Harris .04 .02
❑ 681 Dennis Gibson .04 .02
❑ 682 Toi Cook RC .04 .02
❑ 683 Lorenzo Lynch .04 .02
❑ 684 Brad Edwards RC .04 .02
❑ 685 Ray Crockett RC .04 .02
❑ 686 Harris Barton .04 .02
❑ 687 Byron Evans .04 .02
❑ 688 Eric Thomas .04 .02
❑ 689 Jeff Criswell .04 .02
❑ 690 Eric Ball .04 .02
❑ 691 Brian Mitchell .10 .05
❑ 692 Quinn Early .10 .05
❑ 693 Aaron Jones .04 .02
❑ 694 Jim Dombrowski .04 .02
❑ 695 Jeff Bostic .04 .02
❑ 696 Tony Casillas .04 .02
❑ 697 Ken Lanier .04 .02
❑ 698 Henry Thomas .04 .02
❑ 699 Steve Beuerlein .04 .02
❑ 700 Checklist 601-700 .04 .02
❑ P1 Joe Montana Promo 2.50 1.10
Numbered 1
❑ P2 Barry Sanders Promo 2.00 .90
Numbered 500
❑ SP1 Darrell Green .50 .23
NFL's Fastest Man
❑ SP2 Don Shula CO 2.00 .90
300th Victory

1992 Upper Deck

	MINT	NRMT
COMPLETE SET (620)	15.00	6.75
COMP.SERIES 1 (400)	10.00	4.50
COMP.SERIES 2 (220)	5.00	2.20

❑ 1 Star Rookie Checklist .10 .05
Edgar Bennett
Terrell Buckley
Dexter McNabb
❑ 2 Edgar Bennett RC .25 .11
❑ 3 Eddie Blake RC .05 .02
❑ 4 Brian Bollinger RC .05 .02
❑ 5 Joe Bowden RC .05 .02
❑ 6 Terrell Buckley RC .05 .02
❑ 7 Willie Clay RC .05 .02
❑ 8 Ed Cunningham RC .05 .02
❑ 9 Matt Darby RC .05 .02
❑ 10 Will Furrer RC .05 .02
❑ 11 Chris Hakel RC .05 .02
❑ 12 Carlos Huerta .05 .02
❑ 13 Amp Lee RC .05 .02
❑ 14 Ricardo McDonald RC .05 .02
❑ 15 Dexter McNabb RC .05 .02
❑ 16 Chris Mims RC .10 .05
❑ 17 Derrick Moore RC .10 .05
❑ 18 Mark D'Onofrio RC .05 .02
❑ 19 Patrick Rowe RC .05 .02
❑ 20 Leon Searcy RC .10 .05
❑ 21 Torrance Small RC .25 .11
❑ 22 Jimmy Smith RC 3.00 1.35
❑ 23 Tony Smith RC .05 .02
❑ 24 Siran Stacy RC .05 .02
❑ 25 Kevin Turner RC .05 .02
❑ 26 Tommy Vardell RC .10 .05
❑ 27 Bob Whitfield RC .05 .02
❑ 28 Darryl Williams RC .05 .02
❑ 29 Jeff Sydner RC .05 .02
❑ 30 All-Rookie Checklist .05 .02
Mike Croel
Leonard Russell
❑ 31 Todd Marinovich AR .05 .02
❑ 32 Leonard Russell AR .05 .02
❑ 33 Nick Bell AR .05 .02
❑ 34 Alvin Harper AR .05 .02
❑ 35 Mike Pritchard AR .05 .02
❑ 36 Lawrence Dawsey AR .05 .02
❑ 37 Tim Barnett AR .05 .02
❑ 38 John Flannery AR .05 .02
❑ 39 Stan Thomas AR .05 .02
❑ 40 Ed King AR .05 .02
❑ 41 Charles McRae AR .05 .02
❑ 42 Eric Moten AR .05 .02
❑ 43 Moe Gardner AR .05 .02
❑ 44 Kenny Walker AR .05 .02
❑ 45 Esera Tuaolo AR .05 .02
❑ 46 Alfred Williams AR .05 .02
❑ 47 Bryan Cox AR .05 .02
❑ 48 Mo Lewis AR .05 .02
❑ 49 Mike Croel AR .05 .02
❑ 50 Stanley Richard AR .05 .02
❑ 51 Tony Covington AR .05 .02
❑ 52 Larry Brown DB AR .05 .02
❑ 53 Aeneas Williams AR .05 .02
❑ 54 John Kasay AR .05 .02
❑ 55 Jon Vaughn AR .05 .02
❑ 56 David Fulcher .05 .02
❑ 57 Barry Foster .10 .05
❑ 58 Terry Wooden .05 .02
❑ 59 Gary Anderson K .05 .02
❑ 60 Alfred Williams .05 .02
❑ 61 Robert Blackmon .05 .02
❑ 62 Brian Noble .05 .02
❑ 63 Terry Allen .25 .11
❑ 64 Darrell Green .05 .02
❑ 65 Darren Comeaux .05 .02
❑ 66 Rob Burnett .05 .02
❑ 67 Jarrod Bunch .05 .02
❑ 68 Michael Jackson .10 .05
❑ 69 Greg Lloyd .25 .11
❑ 70 Richard Brown RC .05 .02
❑ 71 Harold Green .05 .02
❑ 72 William Fuller .10 .05
❑ 73 Mark Carrier DB TC .05 .02
❑ 74 David Fulcher TC .05 .02
❑ 75 Cornelius Bennett TC .05 .02
❑ 76 Steve Atwater TC .05 .02
❑ 77 Kevin Mack TC .05 .02
❑ 78 Mark Carrier WR TC .05 .02
❑ 79 Tim McDonald TC .05 .02
❑ 80 Marion Butts TC .05 .02
❑ 81 Christian Okoye TC .05 .02
❑ 82 Jeff Herrod TC .05 .02
❑ 83 Emmitt Smith TC .60 .25
❑ 84 Mark Duper TC .05 .02
❑ 85 Keith Jackson TC .05 .02
❑ 86 Andre Rison TC .10 .05
❑ 87 John Taylor TC .05 .02
❑ 88 Rodney Hampton TC .10 .05
❑ 89 Rob Moore TC .05 .02
❑ 90 Chris Spielman TC .05 .02
❑ 91 Haywood Jeffires TC .05 .02
❑ 92 Sterling Sharpe TC .10 .05
❑ 93 Irving Fryar TC .10 .05
❑ 94 Marcus Allen TC .10 .05
❑ 95 Henry Ellard TC .05 .02
❑ 96 Mark Rypien TC .05 .02
❑ 97 Pat Swilling TC .05 .02
❑ 98 Brian Blades TC .05 .02
❑ 99 Eric Green TC .05 .02
❑ 100 Anthony Carter TC .05 .02
❑ 101 Burt Grossman .05 .02
❑ 102 Gary Anderson RB .05 .02
❑ 103 Neil Smith .25 .11
❑ 104 Jeff Feagles .05 .02
❑ 105 Shane Conlan .05 .02

❑ 106 Jay Novacek .10 .05
❑ 107 Bill Brooks .05 .02
❑ 108 Mark Ingram .05 .02
❑ 109 Anthony Munoz .10 .05
❑ 110 Wendell Davis .05 .02
❑ 111 Jim Everett .10 .05
❑ 112 Bruce Matthews .05 .02
❑ 113 Mark Higgs .05 .02
❑ 114 Chris Warren .25 .11
❑ 115 Brad Baxter .05 .02
❑ 116 Greg Townsend .05 .02
❑ 117 Al Smith .05 .02
❑ 118 Jeff Cross .05 .02
❑ 119 Terry McDaniel .05 .02
❑ 120 Ernest Givins .10 .05
❑ 121 Fred Barnett .25 .11
❑ 122 Flipper Anderson .05 .02
❑ 123 Floyd Turner .05 .02
❑ 124 Stephen Baker .05 .02
❑ 125 Tim Johnson .05 .02
❑ 126 Brent Jones .10 .05
❑ 127 Leonard Marshall .05 .02
❑ 128 Jim Price .05 .02
❑ 129 Jessie Hester .05 .02
❑ 130 Mark Carrier WR .10 .05
❑ 131 Bubba McDowell .05 .02
❑ 132 Andre Tippett .05 .02
❑ 133 James Hasty .05 .02
❑ 134 Mel Gray .10 .05
❑ 135 Christian Okoye .05 .02
❑ 136 Earnest Byner .05 .02
❑ 137 Ferrell Edmunds .05 .02
❑ 138 Henry Ellard .10 .05
❑ 139 Rob Moore .10 .05
❑ 140 Brian Jordan .10 .05
❑ 141 Clarence Verdin .05 .02
❑ 142 Cornelius Bennett .10 .05
❑ 143 John Taylor .10 .05
❑ 144 Derrick Thomas .25 .11
❑ 145 Thurman Thomas .25 .11
❑ 146 Warren Moon .25 .11
❑ 147 Vinny Testaverde .10 .05
❑ 148 Steve Bono RC .25 .11
❑ 149 Robb Thomas .05 .02
❑ 150 John Friesz .10 .05
❑ 151 Richard Dent .10 .05
❑ 152 Eddie Anderson .05 .02
❑ 153 Kevin Greene .25 .11
❑ 154 Marion Butts .05 .02
❑ 155 Barry Sanders 1.50 .70
❑ 156 Andre Rison .10 .05
❑ 157 Ronnie Lott .10 .05
❑ 158 Eric Allen .05 .02
❑ 159 Mark Clayton .10 .05
❑ 160 Terance Mathis .10 .05
❑ 161 Darryl Talley .05 .02
❑ 162 Eric Metcalf .10 .05
❑ 163 Reggie Cobb .05 .02
❑ 164 Ernie Jones .05 .02
❑ 165 David Griggs .05 .02
❑ 166 Tom Rathman .05 .02
❑ 167 Bubby Brister .05 .02
❑ 168 Broderick Thomas .05 .02
❑ 169 Chris Doleman .05 .02
❑ 170 Charles Haley .10 .05
❑ 171 Michael Haynes .10 .05
❑ 172 Rodney Hampton .25 .11
❑ 173 Nick Bell .05 .02
❑ 174 Gene Atkins .05 .02
❑ 175 Mike Merriweather .05 .02
❑ 176 Reggie Roby .05 .02
❑ 177 Bennie Blades .05 .02
❑ 178 John L. Williams .05 .02
❑ 179 Rodney Peete .10 .05
❑ 180 Greg Montgomery .05 .02
❑ 181 Vince Newsome .05 .02
❑ 182 Andre Collins .05 .02
❑ 183 Erik Kramer .10 .05
❑ 184 Bryan Hinkle .05 .02
❑ 185 Reggie White .25 .11
❑ 186 Bruce Armstrong .05 .02
❑ 187 Anthony Carter .10 .05
❑ 188 Pat Swilling .10 .05
❑ 189 Robert Delpino .05 .02
❑ 190 Brent Williams .05 .02
❑ 191 Johnny Johnson .05 .02
❑ 192 Aaron Craver .05 .02
❑ 193 Vincent Brown .05 .02
❑ 194 Herschel Walker .10 .05
❑ 195 Tim McDonald .05 .02
❑ 196 Gaston Green .05 .02
❑ 197 Brian Blades .10 .05
❑ 198 Rod Bernstine .05 .02
❑ 199 Brett Perriman .25 .11
❑ 200 John Elway 1.25 .55
❑ 201 Michael Carter .05 .02
❑ 202 Mark Carrier DB .05 .02
❑ 203 Cris Carter .50 .23
❑ 204 Kyle Clifton .05 .02
❑ 205 Alvin Wright .05 .02
❑ 206 Andre Ware .05 .02
❑ 207 Dave Waymer .05 .02
❑ 208 Darren Lewis .05 .02
❑ 209 Joey Browner .05 .02
❑ 210 Rich Miano .05 .02
❑ 211 Marcus Allen .25 .11
❑ 212 Steve Broussard .05 .02
❑ 213 Joel Hilgenberg .05 .02
❑ 214 Bo Orlando RC .05 .02
❑ 215 Clay Matthews .10 .05
❑ 216 Chris Hinton .05 .02
❑ 217 Al Edwards .05 .02
❑ 218 Tim Brown .25 .11
❑ 219 Sam Mills .05 .02
❑ 220 Don Majkowski .05 .02
❑ 221 James Francis .05 .02
❑ 222 Steve Hendrickson RC .05 .02
❑ 223 James Thornton .05 .02
❑ 224 Byron Evans .05 .02
❑ 225 Pepper Johnson .05 .02
❑ 226 Darryl Henley .05 .02
❑ 227 Simon Fletcher .05 .02
❑ 228 Hugh Millen .05 .02
❑ 229 Tim McGee .05 .02
❑ 230 Richmond Webb .05 .02
❑ 231 Tony Bennett .05 .02
❑ 232 Nate Odomes .05 .02
❑ 233 Scott Case .05 .02
❑ 234 Dalton Hilliard .05 .02
❑ 235 Paul Gruber .05 .02
❑ 236 Jeff Lageman .05 .02
❑ 237 Tony Mandarich .05 .02
❑ 238 Cris Dishman .05 .02
❑ 239 Steve Walsh .05 .02
❑ 240 Moe Gardner .05 .02
❑ 241 Bill Romanowski .05 .02
❑ 242 Chris Zorich .10 .05
❑ 243 Stephone Paige .05 .02
❑ 244 Mike Croel .05 .02
❑ 245 Leonard Russell .10 .05
❑ 246 Mark Rypien .05 .02
❑ 247 Aeneas Williams .10 .05
❑ 248 Steve Atwater .05 .02
❑ 249 Michael Stewart .05 .02
❑ 250 Pierce Holt .05 .02
❑ 251 Kevin Mack .05 .02
❑ 252 Sterling Sharpe .25 .11
❑ 253 Lawrence Dawsey .10 .05
❑ 254 Emmitt Smith 1.50 .70
❑ 255 Todd Marinovich .05 .02
❑ 256 Neal Anderson .05 .02
❑ 257 Mo Lewis .05 .02
❑ 258 Vance Johnson .05 .02
❑ 259 Rickey Jackson .05 .02
❑ 260 Esera Tuaolo .05 .02
❑ 261 Wilber Marshall .05 .02
❑ 262 Keith Henderson .05 .02
❑ 263 William Thomas .05 .02
❑ 264 Rickey Dixon .05 .02
❑ 265 Dave Meggett .10 .05
❑ 266 Gerald Riggs .05 .02
❑ 267 Tim Harris .05 .02
❑ 268 Ken Harvey .05 .02
❑ 269 Clyde Simmons .05 .02
❑ 270 Irving Fryar .10 .05
❑ 271 Darion Conner .05 .02
❑ 272 Vince Workman .10 .05
❑ 273 Jim Harbaugh .25 .11
❑ 274 Lorenzo White .05 .02
❑ 275 Bobby Hebert .05 .02
❑ 276 Duane Bickett .05 .02
❑ 277 Jeff Bryant .05 .02
❑ 278 Scott Stephen .05 .02
❑ 279 Bob Golic .05 .02
❑ 280 Steve McMichael .10 .05
❑ 281 Jeff Graham .25 .11
❑ 282 Keith Jackson .10 .05
❑ 283 Howard Ballard .05 .02
❑ 284 Michael Brooks .05 .02
❑ 285 Freeman McNeil .05 .02
❑ 286 Rodney Holman .05 .02
❑ 287 Eric Bieniemy .05 .02
❑ 288 Seth Joyner .10 .05
❑ 289 Carwell Gardner .05 .02
❑ 290 Brian Mitchell .10 .05
❑ 291 Chris Miller .10 .05
❑ 292 Ray Berry .05 .02
❑ 293 Matt Brock .05 .02
❑ 294 Eric Thomas .05 .02
❑ 295 John Kasay .05 .02
❑ 296 Jay Hilgenberg .05 .02
❑ 297 Darrell Thompson .05 .02
❑ 298 Rich Gannon .25 .11
❑ 299 Steve Young .60 .25
❑ 300 Mike Kenn .05 .02
❑ 301 Emmitt Smith SL .60 .25
❑ 302 Haywood Jeffires SL .05 .02
❑ 303 Michael Irvin SL .25 .11
❑ 304 Warren Moon SL .10 .05
❑ 305 Chip Lohmiller SL .05 .02
❑ 306 Barry Sanders SL .60 .25
❑ 307 Ronnie Lott SL .10 .05
❑ 308 Pat Swilling SL .05 .02
❑ 309 Thurman Thomas SL .10 .05
❑ 310 Reggie Roby SL .05 .02
❑ 311 Season Leader CL .10 .05
Warren Moon
Michael Irvin
Thurman Thomas
❑ 312 Jacob Green .05 .02
❑ 313 Stephen Braggs .05 .02
❑ 314 Haywood Jeffires .10 .05
❑ 315 Freddie Joe Nunn .05 .02
❑ 316 Gary Clark .25 .11
❑ 317 Tim Barnett .05 .02
❑ 318 Mark Duper .05 .02
❑ 319 Eric Green .05 .02
❑ 320 Robert Wilson .05 .02
❑ 321 Michael Ball .05 .02
❑ 322 Eric Martin .05 .02
❑ 323 Alexander Wright .05 .02
❑ 324 Jessie Tuggle .05 .02
❑ 325 Ronnie Harmon .05 .02
❑ 326 Jeff Hostetler .10 .05
❑ 327 Eugene Daniel .05 .02
❑ 328 Ken Norton Jr. .25 .11
❑ 329 Reyna Thompson .05 .02
❑ 330 Jerry Ball .05 .02
❑ 331 Leroy Hoard .10 .05
❑ 332 Chris Martin .05 .02
❑ 333 Keith McKeller .05 .02
❑ 334 Brian Washington .05 .02
❑ 335 Eugene Robinson .05 .02
❑ 336 Maurice Hurst .05 .02
❑ 337 Dan Saleaumua .05 .02
❑ 338 Neil O'Donnell .25 .11
❑ 339 Dexter Davis .05 .02
❑ 340 Keith McCants .05 .02
❑ 341 Steve Beuerlein .05 .02
❑ 342 Roman Phifer .05 .02
❑ 343 Bryan Cox .10 .05
❑ 344 Art Monk .10 .05
❑ 345 Michael Irvin .25 .11
❑ 346 Vaughan Johnson .05 .02
❑ 347 Jeff Herrod .05 .02
❑ 348 Stanley Richard .05 .02
❑ 349 Michael Young .05 .02
❑ 350 Team MVP Checklist .10 .05
Rodney Hampton
Reggie Cobb
❑ 351 Jim Harbaugh MVP .10 .05
❑ 352 David Fulcher MVP .05 .02
❑ 353 Thurman Thomas MVP .10 .05
❑ 354 Gaston Green MVP .05 .02
❑ 355 Leroy Hoard MVP .05 .02
❑ 356 Reggie Cobb MVP .05 .02
❑ 357 Tim McDonald MVP .05 .02
❑ 358 R.Harmon MVP UER .05 .02

	No.	Card		
		(Bernstine misspelled as Bernstein)		
❑	359	Derrick Thomas MVP	.10	.05
❑	360	Jeff Herrod MVP	.05	.02
❑	361	Michael Irvin MVP	.25	.11
❑	362	Mark Higgs MVP	.05	.02
❑	363	Reggie White MVP	.10	.05
❑	364	Chris Miller MVP	.05	.02
❑	365	Steve Young MVP	.30	.14
❑	366	Rodney Hampton MVP	.10	.05
❑	367	Jeff Lageman MVP	.05	.02
❑	368	Barry Sanders MVP	.60	.25
❑	369	Haywood Jeffires MVP	.05	.02
❑	370	Tony Bennett MVP	.05	.02
❑	371	Leonard Russell MVP	.05	.02
❑	372	Jeff Jaeger MVP	.05	.02
❑	373	Robert Delpino MVP	.05	.02
❑	374	Mark Rypien MVP	.05	.02
❑	375	Pat Swilling MVP	.05	.02
❑	376	Cortez Kennedy MVP	.10	.05
❑	377	Eric Green MVP	.05	.02
❑	378	Cris Carter MVP	.10	.05
❑	379	John Roper	.05	.02
❑	380	Barry Word	.05	.02
❑	381	Shawn Jefferson	.05	.02
❑	382	Tony Casillas	.05	.02
❑	383	John Baylor RC	.05	.02
❑	384	Al Noga	.05	.02
❑	385	Charles Mann	.05	.02
❑	386	Gill Byrd	.05	.02
❑	387	Chris Singleton	.05	.02
❑	388	James Joseph	.05	.02
❑	389	Larry Brown DB	.05	.02
❑	390	Chris Spielman	.10	.05
❑	391	Anthony Thompson	.05	.02
❑	392	Karl Mecklenburg	.05	.02
❑	393	Joe Kelly	.05	.02
❑	394	Kanavis McGhee	.05	.02
❑	395	Bill Maas	.05	.02
❑	396	Marv Cook	.05	.02
❑	397	Louis Lipps	.05	.02
❑	398	Marty Carter RC	.05	.02
❑	399	Louis Oliver	.05	.02
❑	400	Eric Swann	.10	.05
❑	401	Troy Auzenne RC	.05	.02
❑	402	Kurt Barber	.05	.02
❑	403	Marc Boutte RC	.05	.02
❑	404	Dale Carter	.10	.05
❑	405	Marco Coleman	.10	.05
❑	406	Quentin Coryatt	.25	.11
❑	407	Shane Dronett RC	.05	.02
❑	408	Vaughn Dunbar	.05	.02
❑	409	Steve Emtman	.05	.02
❑	410	Dana Hall RC	.10	.05
❑	411	Jason Hansen RC	.10	.05
❑	412	Courtney Hawkins RC	.10	.05
❑	413	Terrell Buckley	.05	.02
❑	414	Robert Jones RC	.05	.02
❑	415	David Klingler	.05	.02
❑	416	Tommy Maddox	.05	.02
❑	417	Johnny Mitchell RC	.05	.02
❑	418	Carl Pickens	.25	.11
❑	419	Tracy Scroggins	.05	.02
❑	420	Tony Sacca RC	.05	.02
❑	421	Kevin Smith	.25	.11
❑	422	Alonzo Spellman	.10	.05
❑	423	Troy Vincent RC	.10	.05
❑	424	Sean Gilbert RC	.25	.11
❑	425	Larry Webster RC	.05	.02
❑	426	Rookie Force Checklist	.25	.11
		Carl Pickens		
		David Klingler		
❑	427	Bill Fralic	.05	.02
❑	428	Kevin Murphy	.05	.02
❑	429	Lemuel Stinson	.05	.02
❑	430	Harris Barton	.05	.02
❑	431	Dino Hackett	.05	.02
❑	432	John Stephens	.05	.02
❑	433	Keith Jennings RC	.05	.02
❑	434	Derrick Fenner	.05	.02
❑	435	Kenneth Gant RC	.05	.02
❑	436	Willie Gault	.10	.05
❑	437	Steve Jordan	.05	.02
❑	438	Charles Haley	.10	.05
❑	439	Keith Kartz	.05	.02
❑	440	Nate Lewis	.05	.02
❑	441	Doug Widell	.05	.02
❑	442	William White	.05	.02
❑	443	Eric Hill	.05	.02
❑	444	Melvin Jenkins	.05	.02
❑	445	David Wyman	.05	.02
❑	446	Ed West	.05	.02
❑	447	Brad Muster	.05	.02
❑	448	Ray Childress	.05	.02
❑	449	Kevin Ross	.05	.02
❑	450	Johnnie Jackson	.05	.02
❑	451	Tracy Simien RC	.05	.02
❑	452	Don Mosebar	.05	.02
❑	453	Jay Hilgenberg	.05	.02
❑	454	Wes Hopkins	.05	.02
❑	455	Jay Schroeder	.05	.02
❑	456	Jeff Bostic	.05	.02
❑	457	Bryce Paup	.25	.11
❑	458	Dave Waymer	.05	.02
❑	459	Toi Cook	.05	.02
❑	460	Anthony Smith	.05	.02
❑	461	Don Griffin	.05	.02
❑	462	Bill Hawkins	.05	.02
❑	463	Courtney Hall	.05	.02
❑	464	Jeff Uhlenhake	.05	.02
❑	465	Mike Sherrard	.05	.02
❑	466	James Jones	.05	.02
❑	467	Jerrol Williams	.05	.02
❑	468	Eric Ball	.05	.02
❑	469	Randall McDaniel	.05	.02
❑	470	Alvin Harper	.10	.05
❑	471	Tom Waddle	.05	.02
❑	472	Tony Woods	.05	.02
❑	473	Kelvin Martin	.05	.02
❑	474	Jon Vaughn	.05	.02
❑	475	Gill Fenerty	.05	.02
❑	476	Aundray Bruce	.05	.02
❑	477	Morten Andersen	.05	.02
❑	478	Lamar Lathon	.05	.02
❑	479	Steve DeOssie	.05	.02
❑	480	Marvin Washington	.05	.02
❑	481	Herschel Walker	.10	.05
❑	482	Howie Long	.10	.05
❑	483	Calvin Williams	.10	.05
❑	484	Brett Favre	2.50	1.10
❑	485	Johnny Bailey	.05	.02
❑	486	Jeff Gossett	.05	.02
❑	487	Carnell Lake	.05	.02
❑	488	Michael Zordich RC	.05	.02
❑	489	Henry Rolling	.05	.02
❑	490	Steve Smith	.05	.02
❑	491	Vestee Jackson	.05	.02
❑	492	Ray Crockett	.05	.02
❑	493	Dexter Carter	.05	.02
❑	494	Nick Lowery	.05	.02
❑	495	Cortez Kennedy	.10	.05
❑	496	Cleveland Gary	.05	.02
❑	497	Kelly Stouffer	.05	.02
❑	498	Carl Carter	.05	.02
❑	499	Shannon Sharpe	.25	.11
❑	500	Roger Craig	.10	.05
❑	501	Willie Drewrey	.05	.02
❑	502	Mark Schlereth RC	.05	.02
❑	503	Tony Martin	.25	.11
❑	504	Tom Newberry	.05	.02
❑	505	Ron Hall	.05	.02
❑	506	Scott Miller	.05	.02
❑	507	Donnell Woolford	.05	.02
❑	508	Dave Krieg	.10	.05
❑	509	Eric Pegram	.10	.05
❑	510	Checklist 401-510	.05	.02
❑	511	Barry Sanders SBK	.60	.25
❑	512	Thurman Thomas SBK	.10	.05
❑	513	Warren Moon SBK	.10	.05
❑	514	John Elway SBK	.50	.23
❑	515	Ronnie Lott SBK	.10	.05
❑	516	Emmitt Smith SBK	.60	.25
❑	517	Andre Rison SBK	.10	.05
❑	518	Steve Atwater SBK	.05	.02
❑	519	Steve Young SBK	.30	.14
❑	520	Mark Rypien SBK	.05	.02
❑	521	Rich Camarillo	.05	.02
❑	522	Mark Bavaro	.05	.02
❑	523	Brad Edwards	.05	.02
❑	524	Chad Hennings RC	.10	.05
❑	525	Tony Paige	.05	.02
❑	526	Shawn Moore	.05	.02
❑	527	Sidney Johnson RC	.05	.02
❑	528	Sanjay Beach RC	.05	.02
❑	529	Kelvin Pritchett	.05	.02
❑	530	Jerry Holmes	.05	.02
❑	531	Al Del Greco	.05	.02
❑	532	Bob Gagliano	.05	.02
❑	533	Drew Hill	.05	.02
❑	534	Donald Frank RC	.05	.02
❑	535	Pio Sagapolutele RC	.05	.02
❑	536	Jackie Slater	.05	.02
❑	537	Vernon Turner	.05	.02
❑	538	Bobby Humphrey	.05	.02
❑	539	Audray McMillian	.05	.02
❑	540	Gary Brown RC	.25	.11
❑	541	Wesley Carroll	.05	.02
❑	542	Nate Newton	.10	.05
❑	543	Vai Sikahema	.05	.02
❑	544	Chris Chandler	.25	.11
❑	545	Nolan Harrison RC	.05	.02
❑	546	Mark Green	.05	.02
❑	547	Ricky Watters	.25	.11
❑	548	J.J. Birden	.05	.02
❑	549	Cody Carlson	.05	.02
❑	550	Tim Green	.05	.02
❑	551	Mark Jackson	.05	.02
❑	552	Vince Buck	.05	.02
❑	553	George Jamison	.05	.02
❑	554	Anthony Pleasant	.05	.02
❑	555	Reggie Johnson	.05	.02
❑	556	John Jackson	.05	.02
❑	557	Ian Beckles	.05	.02
❑	558	Buford McGee	.05	.02
❑	559	Fuad Reveiz UER	.05	.02
		(Born in Colombia, not Columbia)		
❑	560	Joe Montana	1.25	.55
❑	561	Phil Simms	.10	.05
❑	562	Greg McMurtry	.05	.02
❑	563	Gerald Williams	.05	.02
❑	564	Dave Cadigan	.05	.02
❑	565	Rufus Porter	.05	.02
❑	566	Jim Kelly	.25	.11
❑	567	Deion Sanders	.50	.23
❑	568	Mike Singletary	.10	.05
❑	569	Boomer Esiason	.10	.05
❑	570	Andre Reed	.10	.05
❑	571	James Washington	.05	.02
❑	572	Jack Del Rio	.05	.02
❑	573	Gerald Perry	.05	.02
❑	574	Vinnie Clark	.05	.02
❑	575	Mike Piel	.05	.02
❑	576	Michael Dean Perry	.10	.05
❑	577	Ricky Proehl	.05	.02
❑	578	Leslie O'Neal	.10	.05
❑	579	Russell Maryland	.10	.05
❑	580	Eric Dickerson	.10	.05
❑	581	Fred Strickland	.05	.02
❑	582	Nick Lowery	.05	.02
❑	583	Joe Milinichik RC	.05	.02
❑	584	Mark Vlasic	.05	.02
❑	585	James Lofton	.10	.05
❑	586	Bruce Smith	.25	.11
❑	587	Harvey Williams	.25	.11
❑	588	Bernie Kosar	.10	.05
❑	589	Carl Banks	.05	.02
❑	590	Jeff George	.25	.11
❑	591	Fred Jones RC	.05	.02
❑	592	Todd Scott	.05	.02
❑	593	Keith Jones	.05	.02
❑	594A	Tootie Robbins ERR	.05	.02
		(Card has him as a Denver Bronco)		
❑	594B	Tootie Robbins COR	.05	.02
❑	595	Todd Philcox RC	.05	.02
❑	596	Browning Nagle	.05	.02
❑	597	Troy Aikman	.75	.35
❑	598	Dan Marino	1.25	.55
❑	599	Lawrence Taylor	.25	.11
❑	600	Webster Slaughter	.05	.02
❑	601	Aaron Cox	.05	.02
❑	602	Matt Stover	.05	.02
❑	603	Keith Sims	.05	.02
❑	604	Dennis Smith	.05	.02
❑	605	Kevin Porter	.05	.02
❑	606	Anthony Miller	.10	.05
❑	607	Ken O'Brien	.05	.02

❑ 608 Randall Cunningham...... .25 .11
❑ 609 Timm Rosenbach .... .05 .02
❑ 610 Junior Seau.................... .25 .11
❑ 611 Johnny Rembert .... .05 .02
❑ 612 Rick Tuten .... .05 .02
❑ 613 Willie Green..................... .05 .02
❑ 614 Sean Salisbury RC UER .05 .02
(He is listed with Lions in 1990 and Chargers in 1991; he was with Vikings both years)
❑ 615 Martin Bayless................ .05 .02
❑ 616 Jerry Rice .... .75 .35
❑ 617 Randal Hill...................... .05 .02
❑ 618 Dan McGwire .... .05 .02
❑ 619 Merril Hoge .... .05 .02
❑ 620 Checklist 571-620 .... .05 .02
❑ A560 Joe Montana Blowup 15.00 6.75
Available only through Upper Deck Authenticated Card measures 8 1/2" by 11"
❑ A598 Dan Marino Blowup 15.00 6.75
Available only through Upper Deck Authenticated Card measures 8 1/2" by 11"
❑ SP3 James Lofton Yardage .. .75 .35
❑ SP4 Art Monk Catches.......... .50 .23

1993 Upper Deck

	MINT	NRMT
COMPLETE SET (530)	25.00	11.00

❑ 1 Star Rookie Checklist .... .25 .11
Rick Mirer
Garrison Hearst
Curtis Conway
Lincoln Kennedy
❑ 2 Eric Curry SR RC .... .05 .02
❑ 3 Rick Mirer SR RC .... .30 .14
❑ 4 Dan Williams SR RC........... .05 .02
❑ 5 Marvin Jones SR RC.......... .05 .02
❑ 6 Willie Roaf SR RC.............. .05 .02
❑ 7 Reggie Brooks SR RC .... .10 .05
❑ 8 Horace Copeland SR RC .. .10 .05
❑ 9 Lincoln Kennedy SR RC .... .05 .02
❑ 10 Curtis Conway SR RC...... .40 .18
❑ 11 Drew Bledsoe SR RC .... 2.00 .90
❑ 12 Patrick Bates SR RC......... .05 .02
❑ 13 Wayne Simmons SR RC.. .05 .02
❑ 14 Irv Smith SR RC .... .05 .02
❑ 15 Robert Smith SR RC...... 1.50 .70
❑ 16 O.J. McDuffie SR RC .... .50 .23
❑ 17 Darrien Gordon SR RC..... .05 .02
❑ 18 John Copeland SR RC ..... .10 .05
❑ 19 Derek Brown RBK SR RC .05 .02
❑ 20 Jerome Bettis SR RC .... .75 .35
❑ 21 Deon Figures SR RC .... .05 .02
❑ 22 Glyn Milburn SR RC .... .25 .11
❑ 23 Garrison Hearst SR RC.... .50 .23
❑ 24 Qadry Ismail SR RC .... .50 .23
❑ 25 Terry Kirby SR RC .... .25 .11
❑ 26 Lamar Thomas SR RC ..... .05 .02
❑ 27 Tom Carter SR RC .... .10 .05
❑ 28 Andre Hastings SR RC ..... .25 .11
❑ 29 George Teague SR RC..... .10 .05
❑ 30 All-Rookie Team CL .... .25 .11
Tommy Maddox
❑ 31 David Klingler ART .... .05 .02
❑ 32 Tommy Maddox ART .... .05 .02
❑ 33 Vaughn Dunbar ART........ .05 .02
❑ 34 Rodney Culver ART .... .05 .02
❑ 35 Carl Pickens ART .... .25 .11
❑ 36 Courtney Hawkins ART..... .05 .02
❑ 37 Tyji Armstrong ART.......... .05 .02
❑ 38 Ray Roberts ART .... .05 .02
❑ 39 Troy Auzenne ART .... .05 .02
❑ 40 Shane Dronett ART.......... .05 .02
❑ 41 Chris Mims ART .... .05 .02
❑ 42 Sean Gilbert ART .... .05 .02
❑ 43 Steve Emtman ART .... .05 .02
❑ 44 Robert Jones ART............ .05 .02
❑ 45 Marco Coleman ART........ .05 .02
❑ 46 Ricardo McDonald ART .. .05 .02
❑ 47 Quentin Coryatt ART........ .10 .05
❑ 48 Dana Hall ART .... .05 .02
❑ 49 Darren Perry ART .... .05 .02
❑ 50 Darryl Williams ART .... .05 .02
❑ 51 Kevin Smith ART.............. .05 .02
❑ 52 Terrell Buckley ART .... .05 .02
❑ 53 Troy Vincent ART .... .05 .02
❑ 54 Lin Elliott ART .... .05 .02
❑ 55 Dale Carter ART .... .05 .02
❑ 56 Steve Atwater HIT............ .05 .02
❑ 57 Junior Seau HIT .... .10 .05
❑ 58 Ronnie Lott HIT................ .05 .02
❑ 59 Louis Oliver HIT .... .05 .02
❑ 60 Cortez Kennedy HIT .... .05 .02
❑ 61 Pat Swilling HIT................ .05 .02
❑ 62 Hitmen Checklist .... .05 .02
❑ 63 Curtis Conway TC............ .25 .11
❑ 64 Alfred Williams TC........... .05 .02
❑ 65 Jim Kelly TC .... .10 .05
❑ 66 Simon Fletcher TC .... .05 .02
❑ 67 Eric Metcalf TC .... .05 .02
❑ 68 Lawrence Dawsey TC...... .05 .02
❑ 69 Garrison Hearst TC.......... .25 .11
❑ 70 Anthony Miller TC .... .05 .02
❑ 71 Neil Smith TC .... .05 .02
❑ 72 Jeff George TC .... .10 .05
❑ 73 Emmitt Smith TC.............. .75 .35
❑ 74 Dan Marino TC .... .75 .35
❑ 75 Clyde Simmons TC.......... .05 .02
❑ 76 Deion Sanders TC............ .25 .11
❑ 77 Ricky Watters TC .... .10 .05
❑ 78 Rodney Hampton TC ...... .10 .05
❑ 79 Brad Baxter TC .... .05 .02
❑ 80 Barry Sanders TC .... .75 .35
❑ 81 Warren Moon TC.............. .10 .05
❑ 82 Brett Favre TC............... 1.00 .45
❑ 83 Drew Bledsoe TC .... 1.00 .45
❑ 84 Eric Dickerson TC .... .10 .05
❑ 85 Cleveland Gary TC .... .05 .02
❑ 86 Earnest Byner TC .... .05 .02
❑ 87 Wayne Martin TC .... .05 .02
❑ 88 Rick Mirer TC .... .25 .11
❑ 89 Barry Foster TC............... .05 .02
❑ 90 Terry Allen TC.................. .10 .05
❑ 91 Vinnie Clark...................... .05 .02
❑ 92 Howard Ballard .... .05 .02
❑ 93 Eric Ball........................... .05 .02
❑ 94 Marc Boutte...................... .05 .02
❑ 95 Larry Centers RC .... .25 .11
❑ 96 Gary Brown .... .05 .02
❑ 97 Hugh Millen .... .05 .02
❑ 98 Anthony Newman RC ...... .05 .02
❑ 99 Darrell Thompson .... .05 .02
❑ 100 George Jamison .... .05 .02
❑ 101 James Francis................ .05 .02
❑ 102 Leonard Harris .... .05 .02
❑ 103 Lomas Brown .... .05 .02
❑ 104 James Lofton.................. .10 .05
❑ 105 Jamie Dukes .... .05 .02
❑ 106 Quinn Early .... .10 .05
❑ 107 Ernie Jones..................... .05 .02
❑ 108 Torrance Small .... .05 .02
❑ 109 Michael Carter................ .05 .02
❑ 110 Aeneas Williams .... .05 .02
❑ 111 Renaldo Turnbull............ .05 .02
❑ 112 Al Smith........................... .05 .02
❑ 113 Troy Auzenne .... .05 .02
❑ 114 Stephen Baker .... .05 .02
❑ 115 Daniel Stubbs .... .05 .02
❑ 116 Dana Hall .... .05 .02
❑ 117 Lawrence Taylor .... .25 .11
❑ 118 Ron Hall .... .05 .02
❑ 119 Derrick Fenner .... .05 .02
❑ 120 Martin Mayhew .... .05 .02
❑ 121 Jay Schroeder................ .05 .02
❑ 122 Michael Zordich.............. .05 .02
❑ 123 Ed McCaffrey .... .10 .05
❑ 124 John Stephens .... .05 .02
❑ 125 Brad Edwards .... .05 .02
❑ 126 Don Griffin....................... .05 .02
❑ 127 Broderick Thomas.......... .05 .02
❑ 128 Ted Washington .... .05 .02
❑ 129 Haywood Jeffires............ .10 .05
❑ 130 Gary Plummer................ .05 .02
❑ 131 Mark Wheeler .... .05 .02
❑ 132 Ty Detmer .... .25 .11
❑ 133 Derrick Walker................ .05 .02
❑ 134 Henry Ellard .... .10 .05
❑ 135 Neal Anderson .... .05 .02
❑ 136 Bruce Smith.................... .25 .11
❑ 137 Cris Carter...................... .50 .23
❑ 138 Vaughn Dunbar.............. .05 .02
❑ 139 Dan Marino .... 1.50 .70
❑ 140 Troy Aikman .... .75 .35
❑ 141 Randall Cunningham...... .25 .11
❑ 142 Daryl Johnston .... .25 .11
❑ 143 Mark Clayton.................. .05 .02
❑ 144 Rich Gannon................... .25 .11
❑ 145 Nate Newton .... .10 .05
❑ 146 Willie Gault .... .05 .02
❑ 147 Brian Washington .... .05 .02
❑ 148 Fred Barnett .... .10 .05
❑ 149 Gill Byrd.......................... .05 .02
❑ 150 Art Monk .... .10 .05
❑ 151 Stan Humphries .... .25 .11
❑ 152 Charles Mann .... .05 .02
❑ 153 Greg Lloyd...................... .25 .11
❑ 154 Marvin Washington .... .05 .02
❑ 155 Bernie Kosar .... .10 .05
❑ 156 Pete Metzelaars .... .05 .02
❑ 157 Chris Hinton .... .05 .02
❑ 158 Jim Harbaugh .... .25 .11
❑ 159 Willie Davis .... .25 .11
❑ 160 Leroy Thompson .... .05 .02
❑ 161 Scott Miller .... .05 .02
❑ 162 Eugene Robinson .... .05 .02
❑ 163 David Little .... .05 .02
❑ 164 Pierce Holt...................... .05 .02
❑ 165 James Hasty .... .05 .02
❑ 166 Dave Krieg .... .10 .05
❑ 167 Gerald Williams.............. .05 .02
❑ 168 Kyle Clifton .... .05 .02
❑ 169 Bill Brooks...................... .05 .02
❑ 170 Vance Johnson .... .05 .02
❑ 171 Greg Townsend.............. .05 .02
❑ 172 Jason Belser .... .05 .02
❑ 173 Brett Perriman................. .25 .11
❑ 174 Steve Jordan................... .05 .02
❑ 175 Kelvin Martin .... .05 .02
❑ 176 Greg Kragen .... .05 .02
❑ 177 Kerry Cash .... .05 .02
❑ 178 Chester McGlockton ...... .10 .05
❑ 179 Jim Kelly .... .25 .11
❑ 180 Todd McNair .... .05 .02
❑ 181 Leroy Hoard .... .10 .05
❑ 182 Seth Joyner.................... .05 .02
❑ 183 Sam Gash RC................. .10 .05
❑ 184 Joe Nash......................... .05 .02
❑ 185 Lin Elliott RC .... .05 .02
❑ 186 Robert Porcher .... .05 .02
❑ 187 Tommy Hodson.............. .05 .02
❑ 188 Greg Lewis .... .05 .02
❑ 189 Dan Saleaumua .... .05 .02
❑ 190 Chris Goode .... .05 .02
❑ 191 Henry Thomas................ .05 .02
❑ 192 Bobby Hebert .... .05 .02
❑ 193 Clay Matthews................ .10 .05
❑ 194 Mark Carrier WR............ .10 .05
❑ 195 Anthony Pleasant .... .05 .02
❑ 196 Eric Dorsey .... .05 .02
❑ 197 Clarence Verdin .... .05 .02
❑ 198 Marc Spindler .... .05 .02
❑ 199 Tommy Maddox .... .05 .02
❑ 200 Wendell Davis................ .05 .02
❑ 201 John Fina .... .05 .02
❑ 202 Alonzo Spellman .... .05 .02
❑ 203 Darryl Williams .... .05 .02

❑ 204 Mike Croel .05 .02
❑ 205 Ken Norton Jr. .10 .05
❑ 206 Mel Gray .10 .05
❑ 207 Chuck Cecil .05 .02
❑ 208 John Flannery .05 .02
❑ 209 Chip Banks .05 .02
❑ 210 Chris Martin .05 .02
❑ 211 Dennis Brown .05 .02
❑ 212 Vinny Testaverde .10 .05
❑ 213 Nick Bell .05 .02
❑ 214 Robert Delpino .05 .02
❑ 215 Mark Higgs .05 .02
❑ 216 Al Noga .05 .02
❑ 217 Andre Tippett .05 .02
❑ 218 Pat Swilling .05 .02
❑ 219 Phil Simms .10 .05
❑ 220 Ricky Proehl .05 .02
❑ 221 William Thomas .05 .02
❑ 222 Jeff Graham .10 .05
❑ 223 Darion Conner .05 .02
❑ 224 Mark Carrier DB .05 .02
❑ 225 Willie Green .05 .02
❑ 226 Reggie Rivers RC .05 .02
❑ 227 Andre Reed .10 .05
❑ 228 Deion Sanders .50 .23
❑ 229 Chris Doleman .05 .02
❑ 230 Jerry Ball .05 .02
❑ 231 Eric Dickerson .10 .05
❑ 232 Carlos Jenkins .05 .02
❑ 233 Mike Johnson .05 .02
❑ 234 Marco Coleman .05 .02
❑ 235 Leslie O'Neal .10 .05
❑ 236 Browning Nagle .05 .02
❑ 237 Carl Pickens .25 .11
❑ 238 Steve Emtman .05 .02
❑ 239 Alvin Harper .10 .05
❑ 240 Keith Jackson .10 .05
❑ 241 Jerry Rice 1.00 .45
❑ 242 Cortez Kennedy .10 .05
❑ 243 Tyji Armstrong .05 .02
❑ 244 Troy Vincent .05 .02
❑ 245 Randal Hill .05 .02
❑ 246 Robert Blackmon .05 .02
❑ 247 Junior Seau .25 .11
❑ 248 Sterling Sharpe .25 .11
❑ 249 Thurman Thomas .25 .11
❑ 250 David Klingler .05 .02
❑ 251 Jeff George .25 .11
❑ 252 Anthony Miller .10 .05
❑ 253 Earnest Byner .05 .02
❑ 254 Eric Swann .10 .05
❑ 255 Jeff Herrod .05 .02
❑ 256 Eddie Robinson .05 .02
❑ 257 Eric Allen .05 .02
❑ 258 John Taylor .10 .05
❑ 259 Sean Gilbert .10 .05
❑ 260 Ray Childress .05 .02
❑ 261 Michael Haynes .10 .05
❑ 262 Greg McMurtry .05 .02
❑ 263 Bill Romanowski .05 .02
❑ 264 Todd Lyght .05 .02
❑ 265 Clyde Simmons .05 .02
❑ 266 Webster Slaughter .05 .02
❑ 267 J.J. Birden .05 .02
❑ 268 Aaron Wallace .05 .02
❑ 269 Carl Banks .05 .02
❑ 270 Ricardo McDonald .05 .02
❑ 271 Michael Brooks .05 .02
❑ 272 Dale Carter .05 .02
❑ 273 Mike Pritchard .10 .05
❑ 274 Derek Brown TE .05 .02
❑ 275 Burt Grossman .05 .02
❑ 276 Mark Schlereth .05 .02
❑ 277 Karl Mecklenburg .05 .02
❑ 278 Rickey Jackson .05 .02
❑ 279 Ricky Ervins .05 .02
❑ 280 Jeff Bryant .05 .02
❑ 281 Eric Martin .05 .02
❑ 282 Carlton Haselrig .05 .02
❑ 283 Kevin Mack .05 .02
❑ 284 Brad Muster .05 .02
❑ 285 Kelvin Pritchett .05 .02
❑ 286 Courtney Hawkins .05 .02
❑ 287 Levon Kirkland .05 .02
❑ 288 Steve DeBerg .05 .02
❑ 289 Edgar Bennett .25 .11
❑ 290 Michael Dean Perry .10 .05
❑ 291 Richard Dent .10 .05
❑ 292 Howie Long .10 .05
❑ 293 Chris Mims .05 .02
❑ 294 Kurt Barber .05 .02
❑ 295 Wilber Marshall .05 .02
❑ 296 Ethan Horton .05 .02
❑ 297 Tony Bennett .05 .02
❑ 298 Johnny Johnson .05 .02
❑ 299 Craig Heyward .10 .05
❑ 300 Steve Israel .05 .02
❑ 301 Kenneth Gant .05 .02
❑ 302 Eugene Chung .05 .02
❑ 303 Harvey Williams .10 .05
❑ 304 Jarrod Bunch .05 .02
❑ 305 Darren Perry .05 .02
❑ 306 Steve Christie .05 .02
❑ 307 John Randle .10 .05
❑ 308 Warren Moon .25 .11
❑ 309 Charles Haley .10 .05
❑ 310 Tony Smith .05 .02
❑ 311 Steve Broussard .05 .02
❑ 312 Alfred Williams .05 .02
❑ 313 Terrell Buckley .05 .02
❑ 314 Trace Armstrong .05 .02
❑ 315 Brian Mitchell .10 .05
❑ 316 Steve Atwater .05 .02
❑ 317 Nate Lewis .05 .02
❑ 318 Richard Brown .05 .02
❑ 319 Rufus Porter .05 .02
❑ 320 Pat Harlow .05 .02
❑ 321 Anthony Smith .05 .02
❑ 322 Jack Del Rio .05 .02
❑ 323 Darryl Talley .05 .02
❑ 324 Sam Mills .05 .02
❑ 325 Chris Miller .10 .05
❑ 326 Ken Harvey .05 .02
❑ 327 Rod Woodson .25 .11
❑ 328 Tony Tolbert .05 .02
❑ 329 Todd Kinchen .05 .02
❑ 330 Brian Noble .05 .02
❑ 331 Dave Meggett .05 .02
❑ 332 Chris Spielman .10 .05
❑ 333 Barry Word .05 .02
❑ 334 Jessie Hester .05 .02
❑ 335 Michael Jackson .10 .05
❑ 336 Mitchell Price .05 .02
❑ 337 Michael Irvin .25 .11
❑ 338 Simon Fletcher .05 .02
❑ 339 Keith Jennings .05 .02
❑ 340 Vai Sikahema .05 .02
❑ 341 Roger Craig .10 .05
❑ 342 Ricky Watters .25 .11
❑ 343 Reggie Cobb .05 .02
❑ 344 Kanavis McGhee .05 .02
❑ 345 Barry Foster .10 .05
❑ 346 Marion Butts .05 .02
❑ 347 Bryan Cox .05 .02
❑ 348 Wayne Martin .05 .02
❑ 349 Jim Everett .10 .05
❑ 350 Nate Odomes .05 .02
❑ 351 Anthony Johnson .10 .05
❑ 352 Rodney Hampton .25 .11
❑ 353 Terry Allen .25 .11
❑ 354 Derrick Thomas .25 .11
❑ 355 Calvin Williams .10 .05
❑ 356 Pepper Johnson .05 .02
❑ 357 John Elway 1.50 .70
❑ 358 Steve Young .75 .35
❑ 359 Emmitt Smith 1.50 .70
❑ 360 Brett Favre 2.00 .90
❑ 361 Cody Carlson .05 .02
❑ 362 Vincent Brown .05 .02
❑ 363 Gary Anderson RB .05 .02
❑ 364 Jon Vaughn .05 .02
❑ 365 Todd Marinovich .05 .02
❑ 366 Carnell Lake .05 .02
❑ 367 Kurt Gouveia .05 .02
❑ 368 Lawrence Dawsey .05 .02
❑ 369 Neil O'Donnell .25 .11
❑ 370 Duane Bickett .05 .02
❑ 371 Ronnie Harmon .05 .02
❑ 372 Rodney Peete .05 .02
❑ 373 Cornelius Bennett .10 .05
❑ 374 Brad Baxter .05 .02
❑ 375 Ernest Givins .10 .05
❑ 376 Keith Byars .05 .02
❑ 377 Eric Bieniemy .05 .02
❑ 378 Mike Brim .05 .02
❑ 379 Darren Lewis .05 .02
❑ 380 Heath Sherman .05 .02
❑ 381 Leonard Russell .10 .05
❑ 382 Brent Jones .10 .05
❑ 383 David Whitmore .05 .02
❑ 384 Ray Roberts .05 .02
❑ 385 John Offerdahl .05 .02
❑ 386 Keith McCants .05 .02
❑ 387 John Baylor .05 .02
❑ 388 Amp Lee .05 .02
❑ 389 Chris Warren .10 .05
❑ 390 Herman Moore .50 .23
❑ 391 Johnny Bailey .05 .02
❑ 392 Tim Johnson .05 .02
❑ 393 Eric Metcalf .10 .05
❑ 394 Chris Chandler .10 .05
❑ 395 Mark Rypien .05 .02
❑ 396 Christian Okoye .05 .02
❑ 397 Shannon Sharpe .25 .11
❑ 398 Eric Hill .05 .02
❑ 399 David Lang .05 .02
❑ 400 Bruce Matthews .05 .02
❑ 401 Harold Green .05 .02
❑ 402 Mo Lewis .05 .02
❑ 403 Terry McDaniel .05 .02
❑ 404 Wesley Carroll .05 .02
❑ 405 Richmond Webb .05 .02
❑ 406 Andre Rison .10 .05
❑ 407 Lonnie Young .05 .02
❑ 408 Tommy Vardell .05 .02
❑ 409 Gene Atkins .05 .02
❑ 410 Sean Salisbury .05 .02
❑ 411 Kenneth Davis .05 .02
❑ 412 John L. Williams .05 .02
❑ 413 Roman Phifer .05 .02
❑ 414 Bennie Blades .05 .02
❑ 415 Tim Brown .25 .11
❑ 416 Lorenzo White .05 .02
❑ 417 Tony Casillas .05 .02
❑ 418 Tom Waddle .05 .02
❑ 419 David Fulcher .05 .02
❑ 420 Jessie Tuggle .05 .02
❑ 421 Emmitt Smith SL .75 .35
❑ 422 Clyde Simmons SL .05 .02
❑ 423 Sterling Sharpe SL .10 .05
❑ 424 Sterling Sharpe SL .10 .05
❑ 425 Emmitt Smith SL .75 .35
❑ 426 Dan Marino SL .75 .35
❑ 427 Henry Jones SL .05 .02
Audray McMillian
❑ 428 Thurman Thomas SL .10 .05
❑ 429 Greg Montgomery SL .05 .02
❑ 430 Pete Stoyanovich SL .05 .02
❑ 431 Season Leaders CL .40 .18
Emmitt Smith
❑ 432 Steve Young BB .40 .18
❑ 433 Jerry Rice BB .50 .23
❑ 434 Ricky Watters BB .10 .05
❑ 435 Barry Foster BB .05 .02
❑ 436 Cortez Kennedy BB .05 .02
❑ 437 Warren Moon BB .10 .05
❑ 438 Thurman Thomas BB .10 .05
❑ 439 Brett Favre BB 1.00 .45
❑ 440 Andre Rison BB .10 .05
❑ 441 Barry Sanders BB .75 .35
❑ 442 Berman's Best RC CL .05 .02
Chris Berman
❑ 443 Moe Gardner .05 .02
❑ 444 Robert Jones .05 .02
❑ 445 Reggie Langhorne .05 .02
❑ 446 Flipper Anderson .05 .02
❑ 447 James Washington .05 .02
❑ 448 Aaron Craver .05 .02
❑ 449 Jack Trudeau .05 .02
❑ 450 Neil Smith .25 .11
❑ 451 Chris Burkett .05 .02
❑ 452 Russell Maryland .05 .02
❑ 453 Drew Hill .05 .02
❑ 454 Barry Sanders 1.50 .70
❑ 455 Jeff Cross .05 .02
❑ 456 Bennie Thompson .05 .02
❑ 457 Marcus Allen .25 .11
❑ 458 Tracy Scroggins .05 .02

❑ 459 LeRoy Butler .05 .02
❑ 460 Joe Montana 1.50 .70
❑ 461 Eddie Anderson .05 .02
❑ 462 Tim McDonald .05 .02
❑ 463 Ronnie Lott .10 .05
❑ 464 Gaston Green .05 .02
❑ 465 Shane Conlan .05 .02
❑ 466 Leonard Marshall .05 .02
❑ 467 Melvin Jenkins .05 .02
❑ 468 Don Beebe .05 .02
❑ 469 Johnny Mitchell .05 .02
❑ 470 Darryl Henley .05 .02
❑ 471 Boomer Esiason .10 .05
❑ 472 Mark Kelso .05 .02
❑ 473 John Booty .05 .02
❑ 474 Pete Stoyanovich .05 .02
❑ 475 Thomas Smith RC .10 .05
❑ 476 Carlton Gray RC .05 .02
❑ 477 Dana Stubblefield RC .25 .11
❑ 478 Ryan McNeil RC .05 .02
❑ 479 Natrone Means RC .40 .18
❑ 480 Carl Simpson RC .05 .02
❑ 481 Robert O'Neal RC .05 .02
❑ 482 Demetrius DuBose RC .05 .02
❑ 483 Darrin Smith RC .10 .05
❑ 484 Micheal Barrow RC .10 .05
❑ 485 Chris Slade RC .10 .05
❑ 486 Steve Tovar RC .05 .02
❑ 487 Ron George RC .05 .02
❑ 488 Steve Tasker .10 .05
❑ 489 Will Furrer .05 .02
❑ 490 Reggie White .25 .11
❑ 491 Sean Jones .05 .02
❑ 492 Gary Clark .10 .05
❑ 493 Donnell Woolford .05 .02
❑ 494 Steve Beuerlein .05 .02
❑ 495 Anthony Carter .10 .05
❑ 496 Louis Oliver .05 .02
❑ 497 Chris Zorich .05 .02
❑ 498 David Brandon .05 .02
❑ 499 Bubba McDowell .05 .02
❑ 500 Adrian Cooper .05 .02
❑ 501 Bill Johnson .05 .02
❑ 502 Shawn Jefferson .05 .02
❑ 503 Siran Stacy .05 .02
❑ 504 James Jones .05 .02
❑ 505 Tom Rathman .05 .02
❑ 506 Vince Buck .05 .02
❑ 507 Kent Graham RC .25 .11
❑ 508 Darren Carrington RC .05 .02
❑ 509 Rickey Dixon .05 .02
❑ 510 Toi Cook .05 .02
❑ 511 Steve Smith .05 .02
❑ 512 Eric Green .05 .02
❑ 513 Phillippi Sparks .05 .02
❑ 514 Lee Williams .05 .02
❑ 515 Gary Reasons .05 .02
❑ 516 Shane Dronett .05 .02
❑ 517 Jay Novacek .10 .05
❑ 518 Kevin Greene .25 .11
❑ 519 Derek Russell .05 .02
❑ 520 Quentin Coryatt .10 .05
❑ 521 Santana Dotson .10 .05
❑ 522 Donald Frank .05 .02
❑ 523 Mike Prior .05 .02
❑ 524 Dwight Hollier RC .05 .02
❑ 525 Eric Davis .05 .02
❑ 526 Dalton Hilliard .05 .02
❑ 527 Rodney Culver .05 .02
❑ 528 Jeff Hostetler .10 .05
❑ 529 Ernie Mills .05 .02
❑ 530 Craig Erickson .10 .05
❑ A139 Dan Marino Blowup 15.00 6.75
Available from Upper Deck Authenticated Card Measures 8 1/2" by 11"
❑ A140 Troy Aikman Blowup 12.00 5.50
Issued by Upper Deck Authenticated Card Measures 8 1/2" by 11";
❑ A460 Joe Montana Blowup 15.00 6.75
Card measures 8 1/2" by 11"; Card available from Upper Deck Authenticated
❑ P1 Eric Dickerson Promo 1.25 .55
Numbered 231

1994 Upper Deck

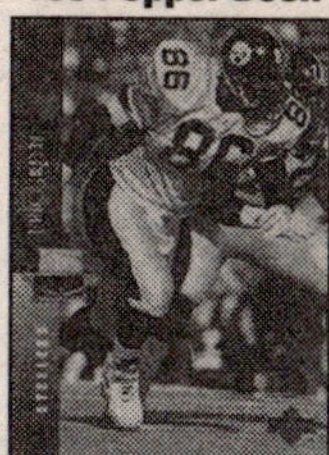

	MINT	NRMT
COMPLETE SET (330)	25.00	11.00

❑ 1 Dan Wilkinson RC .20 .09
❑ 2 Antonio Langham RC .20 .09
❑ 3 Derrick Alexander WR RC 1.00 .45
❑ 4 Charles Johnson RC 1.00 .45
❑ 5 Bucky Brooks RC .10 .05
❑ 6 Trev Alberts RC .20 .09
❑ 7 Marshall Faulk RC 5.00 2.20
❑ 8 Willie McGinest RC .40 .18
❑ 9 Aaron Glenn RC .20 .09
❑ 10 Ryan Yarborough RC .10 .05
❑ 11 Greg Hill RC .40 .18
❑ 12 Sam Adams RC .20 .09
❑ 13 John Thierry RC .10 .05
❑ 14 Johnnie Morton RC 1.25 .55
❑ 15 LeShon Johnson RC .20 .09
❑ 16 David Palmer RC 1.00 .45
❑ 17 Trent Dilfer RC 2.00 .90
❑ 18 Jamir Miller RC .10 .05
❑ 19 Thomas Lewis RC .20 .09
❑ 20 Heath Shuler RC .40 .18
❑ 21 Wayne Gandy .10 .05
❑ 22 Isaac Bruce RC 4.00 1.80
❑ 23 Joe Johnson RC .10 .05
❑ 24 Mario Bates RC .40 .18
❑ 25 Bryant Young RC .40 .18
❑ 26 William Floyd RC .40 .18
❑ 27 Errict Rhett RC 1.00 .45
❑ 28 Chuck Levy RC .10 .05
❑ 29 Darnay Scott RC 1.25 .55
❑ 30 Rob Fredrickson RC .20 .09
❑ 31 Jamir Miller HW .10 .05
❑ 32 Thomas Lewis HW .10 .05
❑ 33 John Thierry HW .10 .05
❑ 34 Sam Adams HW .10 .05
❑ 35 Joe Johnson HW .10 .05
❑ 36 Bryant Young HW .20 .09
❑ 37 Wayne Gandy HW .10 .05
❑ 38 LeShon Johnson HW .10 .05
❑ 39 Mario Bates HW .20 .09
❑ 40 Greg Hill HW .20 .09
❑ 41 Andy Heck .10 .05
❑ 42 Warren Moon .40 .18
❑ 43 Jim Everett .20 .09
❑ 44 Bill Romanowski .10 .05
❑ 45 Michael Haynes .20 .09
❑ 46 Chris Doleman .10 .05
❑ 47 Merril Hoge .10 .05
❑ 48 Chris Miller .10 .05
❑ 49 Clyde Simmons .10 .05
❑ 50 Jeff George .40 .18
❑ 51 Jeff Burris RC .20 .09
❑ 52 Ethan Horton .10 .05
❑ 53 Scott Mitchell .40 .18
❑ 54 Howard Ballard .10 .05
❑ 55 Lewis Tillman .10 .05
❑ 56 Marion Butts .10 .05
❑ 57 Erik Kramer .20 .09
❑ 58 Ken Norton Jr. .20 .09
❑ 59 Anthony Miller .20 .09
❑ 60 Chris Hinton .10 .05
❑ 61 Ricky Proehl .10 .05
❑ 62 Craig Heyward .20 .09
❑ 63 Darryl Talley .10 .05
❑ 64 Tim Worley .10 .05
❑ 65 Derrick Fenner .10 .05
❑ 66 Jerry Ball .10 .05
❑ 67 Darrin Smith .10 .05
❑ 68 Mike Croel .10 .05
❑ 69 Ray Crockett .10 .05
❑ 70 Tony Bennett .10 .05
❑ 71 Webster Slaughter .10 .05
❑ 72 Anthony Johnson .20 .09
❑ 73 Charles Mincy .10 .05
❑ 74 Calvin Jones RC .10 .05
❑ 75 Henry Ellard .20 .09
❑ 76 Troy Vincent .10 .05
❑ 77 Sean Salisbury .10 .05
❑ 78 Pat Harlow .10 .05
❑ 79 James Williams RC .10 .05
❑ 80 Dave Brown .20 .09
❑ 81 Kent Graham .20 .09
❑ 82 Seth Joyner .10 .05
❑ 83 Deon Figures .10 .05
❑ 84 Stanley Richard .10 .05
❑ 85 Tom Rathman .10 .05
❑ 86 Rod Stephens .10 .05
❑ 87 Ray Seals .10 .05
❑ 88 Andre Collins .10 .05
❑ 89 Cornelius Bennett .20 .09
❑ 90 Richard Dent .20 .09
❑ 91 Louis Oliver .10 .05
❑ 92 Rodney Peete .10 .05
❑ 93 Jackie Harris .10 .05
❑ 94 Tracy Simien .10 .05
❑ 95 Greg Townsend .10 .05
❑ 96 Michael Stewart .10 .05
❑ 97 Irving Fryar .20 .09
❑ 98 Todd Collins .10 .05
❑ 99 Irv Smith .10 .05
❑ 100 Chris Calloway .10 .05
❑ 101 Kevin Greene .40 .18
❑ 102 John Friesz .20 .09
❑ 103 Steve Bono .20 .09
❑ 104 Brian Blades .20 .09
❑ 105 Reggie Cobb .10 .05
❑ 106 Eric Swann .20 .09
❑ 107 Mike Pritchard .10 .05
❑ 108 Bill Brooks .10 .05
❑ 109 Jim Harbaugh .40 .18
❑ 110 David Whitmore .10 .05
❑ 111 Eddie Anderson .10 .05
❑ 112 Ray Crittenden RC .10 .05
❑ 113 Mark Collins .10 .05
❑ 114 Brian Washington .10 .05
❑ 115 Barry Foster .10 .05
❑ 116 Gary Plummer .10 .05
❑ 117 Marc Logan .10 .05
❑ 118 John L. Williams .10 .05
❑ 119 Marty Carter .10 .05
❑ 120 Kurt Gouveia .10 .05
❑ 121 Ronald Moore .10 .05
❑ 122 Pierce Holt .10 .05
❑ 123 Henry Jones .10 .05
❑ 124 Donnell Woolford .10 .05
❑ 125 Steve Tovar .10 .05
❑ 126 Anthony Pleasant .10 .05
❑ 127 Jay Novacek .20 .09
❑ 128 Dan Williams .10 .05
❑ 129 Barry Sanders 3.00 1.35
❑ 130 Robert Brooks .40 .18
❑ 131 Lorenzo White .10 .05
❑ 132 Kerry Cash .10 .05
❑ 133 Joe Montana 3.00 1.35
❑ 134 Jeff Hostetler .20 .09
❑ 135 Jerome Bettis .40 .18
❑ 136 Dan Marino 3.00 1.35
❑ 137 Vencie Glenn .10 .05
❑ 138 Vincent Brown .10 .05
❑ 139 Rickey Jackson .10 .05
❑ 140 Carlton Bailey .10 .05
❑ 141 Jeff Lageman .10 .05
❑ 142 William Thomas .10 .05
❑ 143 Neil O'Donnell .40 .18
❑ 144 Shawn Jefferson .10 .05
❑ 145 Steve Young 1.00 .45
❑ 146 Chris Warren .20 .09
❑ 147 Courtney Hawkins .10 .05
❑ 148 Brad Edwards .10 .05
❑ 149 O.J. McDuffie .40 .18

❑ 150 David Lang .10 .05
❑ 151 Chuck Cecil .10 .05
❑ 152 Norm Johnson .10 .05
❑ 153 Pete Metzelaars .10 .05
❑ 154 Shaun Gayle .10 .05
❑ 155 Alfred Williams .10 .05
❑ 156 Eric Turner .10 .05
❑ 157A Emmitt Smith ERR 2.50 1.10
(Incorrect stat total)
❑ 157B Emmitt Smith COR 2.50 1.10
(Corrected stats)
❑ 158 Steve Atwater .10 .05
❑ 159 Robert Porcher .10 .05
❑ 160 Edgar Bennett .40 .18
❑ 161 Bubba McDowell .10 .05
❑ 162 Jeff Herrod .10 .05
❑ 163 Keith Cash .10 .05
❑ 164 Patrick Bates .10 .05
❑ 165 Todd Lyght .10 .05
❑ 166 Mark Higgs .10 .05
❑ 167 Carlos Jenkins .10 .05
❑ 168 Drew Bledsoe 1.50 .70
❑ 169 Wayne Martin .10 .05
❑ 170 Mike Sherrard .10 .05
❑ 171 Ronnie Lott .20 .09
❑ 172 Fred Barnett .20 .09
❑ 173 Eric Green .10 .05
❑ 174 Leslie O'Neal .10 .05
❑ 175 Brent Jones .20 .09
❑ 176 Jon Vaughn .10 .05
❑ 177 Vince Workman .10 .05
❑ 178 Ron Middleton .10 .05
❑ 179 Terry McDaniel .10 .05
❑ 180 Willie Davis .20 .09
❑ 181 Gary Clark .20 .09
❑ 182 Bobby Hebert .10 .05
❑ 183 Russell Copeland .10 .05
❑ 184 Chris Gedney .10 .05
❑ 185 Tony McGee .10 .05
❑ 186 Rob Burnett .10 .05
❑ 187 Charles Haley .20 .09
❑ 188 Shannon Sharpe .20 .09
❑ 189 Mel Gray .10 .05
❑ 190 George Teague .10 .05
❑ 191 Ernest Givins .20 .09
❑ 192 Ray Buchanan .10 .05
❑ 193 J.J. Birden .10 .05
❑ 194 Tim Brown .40 .18
❑ 195 Tim Lester .10 .05
❑ 196 Marco Coleman .10 .05
❑ 197 Randall McDaniel .10 .05
❑ 198 Bruce Armstrong .10 .05
❑ 199 Willie Roaf .10 .05
❑ 200 Greg Jackson .10 .05
❑ 201 Johnny Mitchell .10 .05
❑ 202 Calvin Williams .20 .09
❑ 203 Jeff Graham .10 .05
❑ 204 Darren Carrington .10 .05
❑ 205 Jerry Rice 1.50 .70
❑ 206 Cortez Kennedy .20 .09
❑ 207 Charles Wilson .10 .05
❑ 208 James Jenkins RC .10 .05
❑ 209 Ray Childress .10 .05
❑ 210 LeRoy Butler .10 .05
❑ 211 Randal Hill .10 .05
❑ 212 Lincoln Kennedy .10 .05
❑ 213 Kenneth Davis .10 .05
❑ 214 Terry Obee .10 .05
❑ 215 Ricardo McDonald .10 .05
❑ 216 Pepper Johnson .10 .05
❑ 217 Alvin Harper .20 .09
❑ 218 John Elway 3.00 1.35
❑ 219 Derrick Moore .10 .05
❑ 220 Terrell Buckley .10 .05
❑ 221 Haywood Jeffires .20 .09
❑ 222 Jessie Hester .10 .05
❑ 223 Kimble Anders .20 .09
❑ 224 Rocket Ismail .20 .09
❑ 225 Roman Phifer .10 .05
❑ 226 Bryan Cox .10 .05
❑ 227 Cris Carter .75 .35
❑ 228 Sam Gash .10 .05
❑ 229 Renaldo Turnbull .10 .05
❑ 230 Rodney Hampton .40 .18
❑ 231 Johnny Johnson .10 .05
❑ 232 Tim Harris .10 .05
❑ 233 Leroy Thompson .10 .05
❑ 234 Junior Seau .40 .18
❑ 235 Tim McDonald .10 .05
❑ 236 Eugene Robinson .10 .05
❑ 237 Lawrence Dawsey .10 .05
❑ 238 Tim Johnson .10 .05
❑ 239 Jason Elam .10 .05
❑ 240 Willie Green .10 .05
❑ 241 Larry Centers .40 .18
❑ 242 Erric Pegram .10 .05
❑ 243 Bruce Smith .40 .18
❑ 244 Alonzo Spellman .10 .05
❑ 245 Carl Pickens .40 .18
❑ 246 Michael Jackson .20 .09
❑ 247 Kevin Williams .20 .09
❑ 248 Glyn Milburn .20 .09
❑ 249 Herman Moore .40 .18
❑ 250 Brett Favre 3.00 1.35
❑ 251 Al Smith .10 .05
❑ 252 Roosevelt Potts .10 .05
❑ 253 Marcus Allen .40 .18
❑ 254 Anthony Smith .10 .05
❑ 255 Sean Gilbert .10 .05
❑ 256 Keith Byars .10 .05
❑ 257 Scottie Graham RC .20 .09
❑ 258 Leonard Russell .10 .05
❑ 259 Eric Martin .10 .05
❑ 260 Jarrod Bunch .10 .05
❑ 261 Rob Moore .20 .09
❑ 262 Herschel Walker .20 .09
❑ 263 Levon Kirkland .10 .05
❑ 264 Chris Mims .10 .05
❑ 265 Ricky Watters .40 .18
❑ 266 Rick Mirer .40 .18
❑ 267 Santana Dotson .20 .09
❑ 268 Reggie Brooks .20 .09
❑ 269 Garrison Hearst .40 .18
❑ 270 Thurman Thomas .40 .18
❑ 271 Johnny Bailey .10 .05
❑ 272 Andre Rison .20 .09
❑ 273 Jim Kelly .40 .18
❑ 274 Mark Carrier DB .10 .05
❑ 275 David Klingler .10 .05
❑ 276 Eric Metcalf .20 .09
❑ 277 Troy Aikman 1.50 .70
❑ 278 Simon Fletcher .10 .05
❑ 279 Pat Swilling .10 .05
❑ 280 Sterling Sharpe .20 .09
❑ 281 Cody Carlson .10 .05
❑ 282 Steve Emtman .10 .05
❑ 283 Neil Smith .20 .09
❑ 284 James Jett .10 .05
❑ 285 Shane Conlan .10 .05
❑ 286 Keith Jackson .10 .05
❑ 287 Qadry Ismail .40 .18
❑ 288 Chris Slade .10 .05
❑ 289 Derek Brown RBK .10 .05
❑ 290 Phil Simms .20 .09
❑ 291 Boomer Esiason .20 .09
❑ 292 Eric Allen .10 .05
❑ 293 Rod Woodson .40 .18
❑ 294 Ronnie Harmon .10 .05
❑ 295 John Taylor .20 .09
❑ 296 Ferrell Edmunds .10 .05
❑ 297 Craig Erickson .10 .05
❑ 298 Brian Mitchell .10 .05
❑ 299 Dante Jones .10 .05
❑ 300 John Copeland .10 .05
❑ 301 Steve Beuerlein .10 .05
❑ 302 Deion Sanders .75 .35
❑ 303 Andre Reed .20 .09
❑ 304 Curtis Conway .40 .18
❑ 305 Harold Green .10 .05
❑ 306 Vinny Testaverde .20 .09
❑ 307 Michael Irvin .40 .18
❑ 308 Rod Bernstine .10 .05
❑ 309 Chris Spielman .20 .09
❑ 310 Reggie White .40 .18
❑ 311 Gary Brown .10 .05
❑ 312 Quentin Coryatt .10 .05
❑ 313 Derrick Thomas .40 .18
❑ 314 Greg Robinson .10 .05
❑ 315 Troy Drayton .10 .05
❑ 316 Terry Kirby .40 .18
❑ 317 John Randle .20 .09
❑ 318 Ben Coates .40 .18
❑ 319 Tyrone Hughes .20 .09
❑ 320 Corey Miller .10 .05
❑ 321 Brad Baxter .10 .05
❑ 322 Randall Cunningham .40 .18
❑ 323 Greg Lloyd .40 .18
❑ 324 Stan Humphries .40 .18
❑ 325 Dana Stubblefield .40 .18
❑ 326 Kelvin Martin .10 .05
❑ 327 Hardy Nickerson .20 .09
❑ 328 Desmond Howard .20 .09
❑ 329 Mark Carrier WR .20 .09
❑ 330 Daryl Johnston .20 .09
❑ A133 Joe Montana Blowup 15.00 6.75
Card measures 8 1/2" by 11";
Available from Upper Deck
Authenticated
❑ A136 Dan Marino Blowup 15.00 6.75
Card measures 8 1/2" by 11";
Available from Upper Deck
Authenticated
❑ P19 Joe Montana Promo 2.50 1.10

1995 Upper Deck

	MINT	NRMT
COMPLETE SET (300)	30.00	13.50

❑ 1 Ki-Jana Carter RC .40 .18
❑ 2 Tony Boselli RC .40 .18
❑ 3 Steve McNair RC 4.00 1.80
❑ 4 Michael Westbrook RC 2.50 1.10
❑ 5 Kerry Collins RC 2.50 1.10
❑ 6 Kevin Carter RC .40 .18
❑ 7 James A.Stewart RC .10 .05
❑ 8 Joey Galloway RC 3.00 1.35
❑ 9 Kyle Brady RC .40 .18
❑ 10 J.J. Stokes RC .40 .18
❑ 11 Derrick Alexander DE RC .10 .05
❑ 12 Warren Sapp RC .75 .35
❑ 13 Mark Fields RC UER .10 .05
(Linebacker on front, running back on back)
❑ 14 Tyrone Wheatley RC 2.00 .90
❑ 15 Napoleon Kaufman RC 2.50 1.10
❑ 16 James O. Stewart RC 3.00 1.35
❑ 17 Luther Elliss RC .10 .05
❑ 18 Rashaan Salaam RC .40 .18
❑ 19 Jimmy Oliver RC .10 .05
❑ 20 Mark Bruener RC .20 .09
❑ 21 Derrick Brooks RC .40 .18
❑ 22 Christian Fauria RC .10 .05
❑ 23 Ray Zellars RC .20 .09
❑ 24 Todd Collins RC .40 .18
❑ 25 Sherman Williams RC .10 .05
❑ 26 Frank Sanders RC 1.25 .55
❑ 27 Rodney Thomas RC .40 .18
❑ 28 Rob Johnson RC 3.00 1.35
❑ 29 Steve Stenstrom RC .10 .05
❑ 30 Curtis Martin RC 4.00 1.80
❑ 31 Gary Clark .10 .05
❑ 32 Troy Aikman 1.50 .70
❑ 33 Mike Sherrard .10 .05
❑ 34 Fred Barnett .20 .09
❑ 35 Henry Ellard .20 .09
❑ 36 Terry Allen .20 .09
❑ 37 Jeff Graham .10 .05
❑ 38 Herman Moore .40 .18
❑ 39 Brett Favre 3.00 1.35

	No.	Player		
❑	40	Trent Dilfer	.40	.18
❑	41	Derek Brown RBK	.10	.05
❑	42	Andre Rison	.20	.09
❑	43	Flipper Anderson	.10	.05
❑	44	Jerry Rice	1.50	.70
❑	45	Andre Reed	.20	.09
❑	46	Sean Dawkins	.20	.09
❑	47	Irving Fryar	.20	.09
❑	48	Vincent Brisby	.10	.05
❑	49	Rob Moore	.10	.05
❑	50	Carl Pickens	.40	.18
❑	51	Vinny Testaverde	.20	.09
❑	52	Ray Childress	.10	.05
❑	53	Eric Green	.10	.05
❑	54	Anthony Miller	.20	.09
❑	55	Lake Dawson	.20	.09
❑	56	Tim Brown	.40	.18
❑	57	Stan Humphries	.20	.09
❑	58	Rick Mirer	.40	.18
❑	59	Randal Hill	.10	.05
❑	60	Charles Haley	.20	.09
❑	61	Chris Calloway	.10	.05
❑	62	Calvin Williams	.20	.09
❑	63	Ethan Horton	.10	.05
❑	64	Cris Carter	.40	.18
❑	65	Curtis Conway	.40	.18
❑	66	Scott Mitchell	.20	.09
❑	67	Edgar Bennett	.20	.09
❑	68	Craig Erickson	.10	.05
❑	69	Jim Everett	.10	.05
❑	70	Terance Mathis	.20	.09
❑	71	Robert Young	.10	.05
❑	72	Brent Jones	.10	.05
❑	73	Thurman Thomas	.40	.18
❑	74	Marshall Faulk	.75	.35
❑	75	O.J. McDuffie	.40	.18
❑	76	Ben Coates	.20	.09
❑	77	Johnny Mitchell	.10	.05
❑	78	Darnay Scott	.40	.18
❑	79	Derrick Alexander WR	.40	.18
❑	80	Lorenzo White	.10	.05
❑	81	Charles Johnson	.20	.09
❑	82	John Elway	3.00	1.35
❑	83	Willie Davis	.20	.09
❑	84	James Jett	.20	.09
❑	85	Mark Seay	.20	.09
❑	86	Brian Blades	.20	.09
❑	87	Ronald Moore	.10	.05
❑	88	Alvin Harper	.10	.05
❑	89	Dave Brown	.20	.09
❑	90	Randall Cunningham	.40	.18
❑	91	Heath Shuler	.40	.18
❑	92	Jake Reed	.20	.09
❑	93	Donnell Woolford	.10	.05
❑	94	Barry Sanders	3.00	1.35
❑	95	Reggie White	.40	.18
❑	96	Lawrence Dawsey	.10	.05
❑	97	Michael Haynes	.20	.09
❑	98	Bert Emanuel	.40	.18
❑	99	Troy Drayton	.10	.05
❑	100	Steve Young	1.25	.55
❑	101	Bruce Smith	.40	.18
❑	102	Roosevelt Potts	.10	.05
❑	103	Dan Marino	3.00	1.35
❑	104	Michael Timpson	.10	.05
❑	105	Boomer Esiason	.20	.09
❑	106	David Klingler	.20	.09
❑	107	Eric Metcalf	.20	.09
❑	108	Gary Brown	.10	.05
❑	109	Neil O'Donnell	.20	.09
❑	110	Shannon Sharpe	.20	.09
❑	111	Joe Montana	3.00	1.35
❑	112	Jeff Hostetler	.20	.09
❑	113	Ronnie Harmon	.10	.05
❑	114	Chris Warren	.20	.09
❑	115	Larry Centers	.20	.09
❑	116	Michael Irvin	.40	.18
❑	117	Rodney Hampton	.20	.09
❑	118	Herschel Walker	.20	.09
❑	119	Reggie Brooks	.20	.09
❑	120	Qadry Ismail	.20	.09
❑	121	Chris Zorich	.10	.05
❑	122	Chris Spielman	.20	.09
❑	123	Sean Jones	.10	.05
❑	124	Errict Rhett	.40	.18
❑	125	Tyrone Hughes	.20	.09
❑	126	Jeff George	.20	.09
❑	127	Chris Miller	.10	.05
❑	128	Ricky Watters	.40	.18
❑	129	Jim Kelly	.40	.18
❑	130	Tony Bennett	.10	.05
❑	131	Terry Kirby	.20	.09
❑	132	Drew Bledsoe	1.50	.70
❑	133	Johnny Johnson	.10	.05
❑	134	Dan Wilkinson	.20	.09
❑	135	Leroy Hoard	.10	.05
❑	136	Darryll Lewis	.10	.05
❑	137	Barry Foster	.20	.09
❑	138	Shane Dronett	.10	.05
❑	139	Marcus Allen	.40	.18
❑	140	Harvey Williams	.10	.05
❑	141	Tony Martin	.20	.09
❑	142	Rod Stephens	.10	.05
❑	143	Eric Swann	.20	.09
❑	144	Daryl Johnston	.20	.09
❑	145	Dave Meggett	.10	.05
❑	146	Charlie Garner	.20	.09
❑	147	Ken Harvey	.10	.05
❑	148	Warren Moon	.20	.09
❑	149	Steve Walsh	.10	.05
❑	150	Pat Swilling	.10	.05
❑	151	Terrell Buckley	.10	.05
❑	152	Courtney Hawkins	.10	.05
❑	153	Willie Roaf	.10	.05
❑	154	Chris Doleman	.10	.05
❑	155	Jerome Bettis	.40	.18
❑	156	Dana Stubblefield	.40	.18
❑	157	Cornelius Bennett	.20	.09
❑	158	Quentin Coryatt	.20	.09
❑	159	Bryan Cox	.10	.05
❑	160	Marion Butts	.10	.05
❑	161	Aaron Glenn	.10	.05
❑	162	Louis Oliver	.10	.05
❑	163	Eric Turner	.10	.05
❑	164	Cris Dishman	.10	.05
❑	165	John L. Williams	.10	.05
❑	166	Simon Fletcher	.10	.05
❑	167	Neil Smith	.20	.09
❑	168	Chester McGlockton	.20	.09
❑	169	Natrone Means	.40	.18
❑	170	Sam Adams	.10	.05
❑	171	Clyde Simmons	.10	.05
❑	172	Jay Novacek	.20	.09
❑	173	Keith Hamilton	.10	.05
❑	174	William Fuller	.10	.05
❑	175	Tom Carter	.10	.05
❑	176	John Randle	.20	.09
❑	177	Lewis Tillman	.10	.05
❑	178	Mel Gray	.10	.05
❑	179	George Teague	.10	.05
❑	180	Hardy Nickerson	.10	.05
❑	181	Mario Bates	.40	.18
❑	182	D.J. Johnson	.10	.05
❑	183	Sean Gilbert	.20	.09
❑	184	Bryant Young	.20	.09
❑	185	Jeff Burris	.10	.05
❑	186	Floyd Turner	.10	.05
❑	187	Troy Vincent	.10	.05
❑	188	Willie McGinest	.20	.09
❑	189	James Hasty	.10	.05
❑	190	Jeff Blake RC	1.25	.55
❑	191	Stevon Moore	.10	.05
❑	192	Ernest Givins	.10	.05
❑	193	Byron Bam Morris	.20	.09
❑	194	Ray Crockett	.10	.05
❑	195	Dale Carter	.20	.09
❑	196	Terry McDaniel	.10	.05
❑	197	Leslie O'Neal	.20	.09
❑	198	Cortez Kennedy	.20	.09
❑	199	Seth Joyner	.10	.05
❑	200	Emmitt Smith	2.50	1.10
❑	201	Thomas Lewis	.20	.09
❑	202	Andy Harmon	.10	.05
❑	203	Ricky Ervins	.10	.05
❑	204	Fuad Reveiz	.10	.05
❑	205	John Thierry	.10	.05
❑	206	Bennie Blades	.10	.05
❑	207	LeShon Johnson	.20	.09
❑	208	Charles Wilson	.10	.05
❑	209	Joe Johnson	.10	.05
❑	210	Chuck Smith	.10	.05
❑	211	Roman Phifer	.10	.05
❑	212	Ken Norton Jr.	.20	.09
❑	213	Bucky Brooks	.10	.05
❑	214	Ray Buchanan	.10	.05
❑	215	Tim Bowens	.10	.05
❑	216	Vincent Brown	.10	.05
❑	217	Marcus Turner	.10	.05
❑	218	Derrick Fenner	.10	.05
❑	219	Antonio Langham	.10	.05
❑	220	Cody Carlson	.10	.05
❑	221	Greg Lloyd	.20	.09
❑	222	Steve Atwater	.10	.05
❑	223	Donnell Bennett	.20	.09
❑	224	Rocket Ismail	.20	.09
❑	225	John Carney	.10	.05
❑	226	Eugene Robinson	.10	.05
❑	227	Aeneas Williams	.10	.05
❑	228	Darrin Smith	.10	.05
❑	229	Phillippi Sparks	.10	.05
❑	230	Eric Allen	.10	.05
❑	231	Brian Mitchell	.10	.05
❑	232	David Palmer	.20	.09
❑	233	Mark Carrier DB	.10	.05
❑	234	Dave Krieg	.10	.05
❑	235	Robert Brooks	.40	.18
❑	236	Eric Curry	.10	.05
❑	237	Wayne Martin	.10	.05
❑	238	Craig Heyward	.20	.09
❑	239	Isaac Bruce	.75	.35
❑	240	Deion Sanders	1.00	.45
❑	241	Steve Tasker	.20	.09
❑	242	Jim Harbaugh	.20	.09
❑	243	Aubrey Beavers	.10	.05
❑	244	Chris Slade	.20	.09
❑	245	Mo Lewis	.10	.05
❑	246	Alfred Williams	.10	.05
❑	247	Michael Dean Perry	.10	.05
❑	248	Marcus Robertson	.10	.05
❑	249	Kevin Greene	.20	.09
❑	250	Leonard Russell	.10	.05
❑	251	Greg Hill	.20	.09
❑	252	Rob Fredrickson	.10	.05
❑	253	Junior Seau	.40	.18
❑	254	Rick Tuten	.10	.05
❑	255	Garrison Hearst	.40	.18
❑	256	Russell Maryland	.10	.05
❑	257	Michael Brooks	.10	.05
❑	258	Bernard Williams	.10	.05
❑	259	Reggie Roby	.10	.05
❑	260	Dewayne Washington	.20	.09
❑	261	Raymont Harris	.10	.05
❑	262	Brett Perriman	.20	.09
❑	263	LeRoy Butler	.10	.05
❑	264	Santana Dotson	.10	.05
❑	265	Irv Smith	.10	.05
❑	266	Ron George	.10	.05
❑	267	Marquez Pope	.10	.05
❑	268	William Floyd	.40	.18
❑	269	Matt Darby	.10	.05
❑	270	Jeff Herrod	.10	.05
❑	271	Bernie Parmalee	.20	.09
❑	272	Leroy Thompson	.10	.05
❑	273	Ronnie Lott	.20	.09
❑	274	Steve Tovar	.10	.05
❑	275	Michael Jackson	.20	.09
❑	276	Al Smith	.10	.05
❑	277	Rod Woodson	.20	.09
❑	278	Glyn Milburn	.10	.05
❑	279	Kimble Anders	.20	.09
❑	280	Anthony Smith	.10	.05
❑	281	Andre Coleman	.10	.05
❑	282	Terry Wooden	.10	.05
❑	283	Mickey Washington	.10	.05
❑	284	Steve Beuerlein	.10	.05
❑	285	Mark Brunell	1.50	.70
❑	286	Keith Goganious	.10	.05
❑	287	Desmond Howard	.20	.09
❑	288	Darren Carrington	.10	.05
❑	289	Derek Brown TE	.10	.05
❑	290	Reggie Cobb	.10	.05
❑	291	Jeff Lageman	.10	.05
❑	292	Lamar Lathon	.10	.05
❑	293	Sam Mills	.20	.09
❑	294	Carlton Bailey	.10	.05
❑	295	Mark Carrier WR	.20	.09
❑	296	Willie Green	.20	.09
❑	297	Frank Reich	.10	.05

❑ 298 Don Beebe .10 .05
❑ 299 Tim McKyer .10 .05
❑ 300 Pete Metzelaars .10 .05
❑ A19 Joe Montana Blowup 15.00 6.75
Card Numbered #19,
Card Measures 8 1/2" by 11",
Upper Deck Authenticated
❑ A103 Dan Marino Blowup 15.00 6.75
Card measures 8 1/2" by 11",
Upper Deck Authenticated
❑ P1 Joe Montana Promo 2.00 .90
Base brand card
Numbered 19
❑ P2 Joe Montana Promo 2.00 .90
Predictor card
Numbered 19
❑ P3 Marshall Faulk Promo 1.00 .45
Pro Bowl hologram card
Numbered PB95

1996 Upper Deck

	MINT	NRMT
COMPLETE SET (300)	30.00	13.50

❑ 1 Keyshawn Johnson RC 2.00 .90
❑ 2 Kevin Hardy RC .50 .23
❑ 3 Simeon Rice RC .50 .23
❑ 4 Jonathan Ogden RC .10 .05
❑ 5 Cedric Jones RC .10 .05
❑ 6 Lawrence Phillips RC .50 .23
❑ 7 Tim Biakabutuka RC .75 .35
❑ 8 Terry Glenn RC 1.25 .55
❑ 9 Rickey Dudley RC .50 .23
❑ 10 Willie Anderson RC .10 .05
❑ 11 Alex Molden RC .10 .05
❑ 12 Regan Upshaw RC .10 .05
❑ 13 Walt Harris RC .10 .05
❑ 14 Eddie George RC 4.00 1.80
❑ 15 John Mobley RC .10 .05
❑ 16 Duane Clemons RC .10 .05
❑ 17 Eddie Kennison RC .50 .23
❑ 18 Marvin Harrison RC 2.50 1.10
❑ 19 Daryl Gardener RC .10 .05
❑ 20 Leeland McElroy RC .50 .23
❑ 21 Eric Moulds RC 2.00 .90
❑ 22 Alex Van Dyke RC .25 .11
❑ 23 Mike Alstott RC 1.50 .70
❑ 24 Jeff Lewis RC .60 .25
❑ 25 Bobby Engram RC .50 .23
❑ 26 Derrick Mayes RC 1.00 .45
❑ 27 Karim Abdul-Jabbar RC .60 .25
❑ 28 Bobby Hoying RC .60 .25
❑ 29 Stepfret Williams RC .25 .11
❑ 30 Chris Darkins RC .10 .05
❑ 31 Stephen Davis RC 4.00 1.80
❑ 32 Danny Kanell RC .50 .23
❑ 33 Tony Brackens RC .25 .11
❑ 34 Leslie O'Neal .10 .05
❑ 35 Chris Doleman .10 .05
❑ 36 Larry Brown .10 .05
❑ 37 Ronnie Harmon .10 .05
❑ 38 Chris Spielman .10 .05
❑ 39 John Jurkovic .10 .05
❑ 40 Shawn Jefferson .10 .05
❑ 41 William Floyd .25 .11
❑ 42 Eric Davis .10 .05
❑ 43 Willie Clay .10 .05
❑ 44 Marco Coleman .10 .05
❑ 45 Lorenzo White .10 .05
❑ 46 Neil O'Donnell .25 .11
❑ 47 Natrone Means .50 .23
❑ 48 Cornelius Bennett .10 .05
❑ 49 Steve Walsh .10 .05
❑ 50 Jerome Bettis .50 .23
❑ 51 Boomer Esiason .25 .11
❑ 52 Glyn Milburn .10 .05
❑ 53 Kevin Greene .25 .11
❑ 54 Seth Joyner .10 .05
❑ 55 Jeff Graham .10 .05
❑ 56 Darren Woodson .25 .11
❑ 57 Dale Carter .10 .05
❑ 58 Lorenzo Lynch .10 .05
❑ 59 Tim Brown .50 .23
❑ 60 Jerry Rice 1.25 .55
❑ 61 Garrison Hearst .25 .11
❑ 62 Eric Metcalf .10 .05
❑ 63 Leroy Hoard .10 .05
❑ 64 Thurman Thomas .50 .23
❑ 65 Sam Mills .10 .05
❑ 66 Curtis Conway .50 .23
❑ 67 Carl Pickens .50 .23
❑ 68 Deion Sanders .75 .35
❑ 69 Shannon Sharpe .25 .11
❑ 70 Herman Moore .50 .23
❑ 71 Robert Brooks .50 .23
❑ 72 Rodney Thomas .10 .05
❑ 73 Ken Dilger .25 .11
❑ 74 Mark Brunell 1.25 .55
❑ 75 Marcus Allen .50 .23
❑ 76 Dan Marino 2.50 1.10
❑ 77 Robert Smith .25 .11
❑ 78 Drew Bledsoe 1.25 .55
❑ 79 Jim Everett .10 .05
❑ 80 Rodney Hampton .25 .11
❑ 81 Adrian Murrell .50 .23
❑ 82 Daryl Hobbs RC .10 .05
❑ 83 Ricky Watters .25 .11
❑ 84 Yancey Thigpen .25 .11
❑ 85 Roman Phifer .10 .05
❑ 86 Tony Martin .25 .11
❑ 87 Dana Stubblefield .25 .11
❑ 88 Joey Galloway .75 .35
❑ 89 Errict Rhett .25 .11
❑ 90 Terry Allen .25 .11
❑ 91 Aeneas Williams .10 .05
❑ 92 Craig Heyward .10 .05
❑ 93 Vinny Testaverde .25 .11
❑ 94 Bryce Paup .10 .05
❑ 95 Kerry Collins .50 .23
❑ 96 Rashaan Salaam .50 .23
❑ 97 Dan Wilkinson .10 .05
❑ 98 Jay Novacek .10 .05
❑ 99 John Elway 2.50 1.10
❑ 100 Bennie Blades .10 .05
❑ 101 Edgar Bennett .25 .11
❑ 102 Darryll Lewis .10 .05
❑ 103 Marshall Faulk .50 .23
❑ 104 Bryan Schwartz .10 .05
❑ 105 Tamarick Vanover .25 .11
❑ 106 Terry Kirby .25 .11
❑ 107 John Randle .25 .11
❑ 108 Ted Johnson RC .10 .05
❑ 109 Mario Bates .25 .11
❑ 110 Phillippi Sparks .10 .05
❑ 111 Marvin Washington .10 .05
❑ 112 Terry McDaniel .10 .05
❑ 113 Bobby Taylor .10 .05
❑ 114 Carnell Lake .10 .05
❑ 115 Troy Drayton .10 .05
❑ 116 Darren Bennett .10 .05
❑ 117 J.J. Stokes .50 .23
❑ 118 Rick Mirer .25 .11
❑ 119 Jackie Harris .10 .05
❑ 120 Ken Harvey .10 .05
❑ 121 Rob Moore .25 .11
❑ 122 Jeff George .25 .11
❑ 123 Andre Rison .25 .11
❑ 124 Darick Holmes .10 .05
❑ 125 Tim McKyer .10 .05
❑ 126 Alonzo Spellman .10 .05
❑ 127 Jeff Blake .50 .23
❑ 128 Kevin Williams .10 .05
❑ 129 Anthony Miller .25 .11
❑ 130 Barry Sanders 2.50 1.10
❑ 131 Brett Favre 2.50 1.10
❑ 132 Steve McNair 1.00 .45
❑ 133 Jim Harbaugh .25 .11
❑ 134 Desmond Howard .25 .11
❑ 135 Steve Bono .10 .05
❑ 136 Bernie Parmalee .10 .05
❑ 137 Warren Moon .25 .11
❑ 138 Curtis Martin 1.00 .45
❑ 139 Irv Smith .10 .05
❑ 140 Thomas Lewis .10 .05
❑ 141 Kyle Brady .10 .05
❑ 142 Napoleon Kaufman .50 .23
❑ 143 Mike Mamula .10 .05
❑ 144 Erric Pegram .10 .05
❑ 145 Isaac Bruce .50 .23
❑ 146 Andre Coleman .10 .05
❑ 147 Merton Hanks .10 .05
❑ 148 Brian Blades .10 .05
❑ 149 Hardy Nickerson .10 .05
❑ 150 Michael Westbrook .50 .23
❑ 151 Larry Centers .25 .11
❑ 152 Morten Andersen .10 .05
❑ 153 Michael Jackson .25 .11
❑ 154 Bruce Smith .25 .11
❑ 155 Derrick Moore .10 .05
❑ 156 Mark Carrier DB .10 .05
❑ 157 John Copeland .10 .05
❑ 158 Emmitt Smith 2.00 .90
❑ 159 Jason Elam .10 .05
❑ 160 Scott Mitchell .25 .11
❑ 161 Mark Chmura .25 .11
❑ 162 Blaine Bishop .10 .05
❑ 163 Tony Bennett .10 .05
❑ 164 Pete Mitchell .25 .11
❑ 165 Dan Saleaumua .10 .05
❑ 166 Pete Stoyanovich .10 .05
❑ 167 Cris Carter .50 .23
❑ 168 Vince Brisby .10 .05
❑ 169 Wayne Martin .10 .05
❑ 170 Tyrone Wheatley .25 .11
❑ 171 Mo Lewis .10 .05
❑ 172 Harvey Williams .10 .05
❑ 173 Calvin Williams .10 .05
❑ 174 Norm Johnson .10 .05
❑ 175 Mark Rypien .10 .05
❑ 176 Stan Humphries .25 .11
❑ 177 Derek Loville .10 .05
❑ 178 Christian Fauria .10 .05
❑ 179 Warren Sapp .10 .05
❑ 180 Henry Ellard .10 .05
❑ 181 Jamir Miller .10 .05
❑ 182 Jessie Tuggle .10 .05
❑ 183 Stevon Moore .10 .05
❑ 184 Jim Kelly .50 .23
❑ 185 Mark Carrier WR .10 .05
❑ 186 Chris Zorich .10 .05
❑ 187 Harold Green .10 .05
❑ 188 Chris Boniol .10 .05
❑ 189 Allen Aldridge .10 .05
❑ 190 Brett Perriman .10 .05
❑ 191 Chris Jacke .10 .05
❑ 192 Todd McNair .10 .05
❑ 193 Floyd Turner .10 .05
❑ 194 Jeff Lageman .10 .05
❑ 195 Derrick Thomas .25 .11
❑ 196 Eric Green .10 .05
❑ 197 Orlando Thomas .10 .05
❑ 198 Ben Coates .25 .11
❑ 199 Tyrone Hughes .10 .05
❑ 200 Dave Brown .10 .05
❑ 201 Brad Baxter .10 .05
❑ 202 Chester McGlockton .10 .05
❑ 203 Rodney Peete .10 .05
❑ 204 Willie Williams .10 .05
❑ 205 Kevin Carter .10 .05
❑ 206 Aaron Hayden RC .10 .05
❑ 207 Steve Young 1.00 .45
❑ 208 Chris Warren .25 .11
❑ 209 Eric Curry .10 .05
❑ 210 Brian Mitchell .10 .05
❑ 211 Frank Sanders .25 .11
❑ 212 Terance Mathis UER .10 .05
name misspelled Terence
❑ 213 Eric Turner .10 .05
❑ 214 Bill Brooks .10 .05

❑ 215 John Kasay .10 .05
❑ 216 Erik Kramer .10 .05
❑ 217 Darnay Scott .25 .11
❑ 218 Charles Haley .25 .11
❑ 219 Steve Atwater .10 .05
❑ 220 Jason Hanson .10 .05
❑ 221 LeRoy Butler .10 .05
❑ 222 Cris Dishman .10 .05
❑ 223 Sean Dawkins .10 .05
❑ 224 James O. Stewart .25 .11
❑ 225 Greg Hill .25 .11
❑ 226 Jeff Cross .10 .05
❑ 227 Qadry Ismail .10 .05
❑ 228 Dave Meggett .10 .05
❑ 229 Eric Allen .10 .05
❑ 230 Chris Calloway .10 .05
❑ 231 Wayne Chrebet .75 .35
❑ 232 Jeff Hostetler .10 .05
❑ 233 Andy Harmon .10 .05
❑ 234 Greg Lloyd .25 .11
❑ 235 Toby Wright .10 .05
❑ 236 Junior Seau .25 .11
❑ 237 Bryant Young .25 .11
❑ 238 Robert Blackmon .10 .05
❑ 239 Trent Dilfer .50 .23
❑ 240 Leslie Shepherd .10 .05
❑ 241 Eric Swann .10 .05
❑ 242 Bert Emanuel .25 .11
❑ 243 Antonio Langham .10 .05
❑ 244 Steve Christie .10 .05
❑ 245 Tyrone Poole .10 .05
❑ 246 Jim Flanigan .10 .05
❑ 247 Tony McGee .10 .05
❑ 248 Michael Irvin .50 .23
❑ 249 Byron Bam Morris .25 .11
❑ 250 Terrell Davis 3.00 1.35
❑ 251 Johnnie Morton .25 .11
❑ 252 Sean Jones .10 .05
❑ 253 Chris Sanders .25 .11
❑ 254 Quentin Coryatt .10 .05
❑ 255 Willie Jackson .10 .05
❑ 256 Mark Collins .10 .05
❑ 257 Randal Hill .10 .05
❑ 258 David Palmer .10 .05
❑ 259 Will Moore .10 .05
❑ 260 Michael Haynes .10 .05
❑ 261 Mike Sherrard .10 .05
❑ 262 William Thomas .10 .05
❑ 263 Kordell Stewart .75 .35
❑ 264 D'Marco Farr .10 .05
❑ 265 Terrell Fletcher .10 .05
❑ 266 Lee Woodall .10 .05
❑ 267 Eugene Robinson .10 .05
❑ 268 Alvin Harper .10 .05
❑ 269 Gus Frerotte .50 .23
❑ 270 Antonio Freeman 1.00 .45
❑ 271 Clyde Simmons .10 .05
❑ 272 Chuck Smith .10 .05
❑ 273 Steve Tasker .10 .05
❑ 274 Kevin Butler .10 .05
❑ 275 Steve Tovar .10 .05
❑ 276 Troy Aikman 1.25 .55
❑ 277 Aaron Craver .10 .05
❑ 278 Henry Thomas .10 .05
❑ 279 Craig Newsome .10 .05
❑ 280 Brent Jones .10 .05
❑ 281 Micheal Barrow .10 .05
❑ 282 Ray Buchanan .10 .05
❑ 283 Jimmy Smith .25 .11
❑ 284 Neil Smith .10 .05
❑ 285 O.J. McDuffie .25 .11
❑ 286 Jake Reed .25 .11
❑ 287 Ty Law .10 .05
❑ 288 Torrance Small .10 .05
❑ 289 Hugh Douglas .25 .11
❑ 290 Pat Swilling .10 .05
❑ 291 Charlie Garner .10 .05
❑ 292 Ernie Mills .10 .05
❑ 293 John Carney .10 .05
❑ 294 Ken Norton .10 .05
❑ 295 Cortez Kennedy .10 .05
❑ 296 Derrick Brooks .10 .05
❑ 297 Heath Shuler .25 .11
❑ 298 Reggie White .50 .23
❑ 299 Kimble Anders .25 .11
❑ 300 Willie McGinest .10 .05

❑ P96 Dan Marino Promo 2.00 .90
(Predictor Promo Card)
❑ MS1 Dan Marino 5.00 2.20
Dynamic Debut
Meet the Stars Prize
❑ MS2 Dan Marino 5.00 2.20
Magic Memories
Meet the Stars Prize
❑ P13 Dan Marino Promo 2.50 1.10
(Numbered 1996 on back)

1997 Upper Deck

	MINT	NRMT
COMPLETE SET (300)	40.00	18.00

❑ 1 Orlando Pace RC .50 .23
❑ 2 Darrell Russell RC .15 .07
❑ 3 Shawn Springs RC .25 .11
❑ 4 Bryant Westbrook RC .15 .07
❑ 5 Ike Hilliard RC 1.25 .55
❑ 6 Peter Boulware RC .25 .11
❑ 7 Tom Knight RC .15 .07
❑ 8 Yatil Green RC .25 .11
❑ 9 Tony Gonzalez RC 2.00 .90
❑ 10 Reidel Anthony RC 1.25 .55
❑ 11 Warrick Dunn RC 2.00 .90
❑ 12 Kenny Holmes RC .50 .23
❑ 13 Jim Druckenmiller RC .50 .23
❑ 14 James Farrior RC .15 .07
❑ 15 David LaFleur RC .25 .11
❑ 16 Antowain Smith RC 1.50 .70
❑ 17 Rae Carruth RC .50 .23
❑ 18 Dwayne Rudd RC .50 .23
❑ 19 Jake Plummer RC 4.00 1.80
❑ 20 Reinard Wilson RC .15 .07
❑ 21 Byron Hanspard RC .50 .23
❑ 22 Will Blackwell RC .50 .23
❑ 23 Troy Davis RC .50 .23
❑ 24 Corey Dillon RC 4.00 1.80
❑ 25 Joey Kent RC .50 .23
❑ 26 Renaldo Wynn RC .15 .07
❑ 27 Pat Barnes RC .50 .23
❑ 28 Kevin Lockett RC .25 .11
❑ 29 Darnell Autry RC .25 .11
❑ 30 Walter Jones RC .15 .07
❑ 31 Trevor Pryce RC .15 .07
❑ 32 Dan Marino SRF 1.25 .55
❑ 33 Steve Young SRF .50 .23
❑ 34 John Elway SRF 1.25 .55
❑ 35 Jerry Rice SRF .60 .25
❑ 36 Tim Brown SRF .50 .23
❑ 37 Deion Sanders SRF .50 .23
❑ 38 Troy Aikman SRF .60 .25
❑ 39 Barry Sanders SRF 1.25 .55
❑ 40 Emmitt Smith SRF 1.00 .45
❑ 41 Junior Seau SRF .25 .11
❑ 42 Neil Smith .25 .11
❑ 43 Brett Perriman .15 .07
❑ 44 Jim Everett .15 .07
❑ 45 Qadry Ismail .25 .11
❑ 46 Dana Stubblefield .15 .07
❑ 47 Bryant Young .15 .07
❑ 48 Ken Norton Jr. .15 .07
❑ 49 Terrell Owens .50 .23
❑ 50 Jerry Rice 1.25 .55
❑ 51 Steve Young .75 .35
❑ 52 Terry Kirby .25 .11

❑ 53 Chris Doleman .15 .07
❑ 54 Lee Woodall .15 .07
❑ 55 Merton Hanks .15 .07
❑ 56 Garrison Hearst .25 .11
❑ 57 Rashaan Salaam .15 .07
❑ 58 Raymont Harris .15 .07
❑ 59 Curtis Conway .25 .11
❑ 60 Bobby Engram .25 .11
❑ 61 Bryan Cox .15 .07
❑ 62 Walt Harris .15 .07
❑ 63 Tyrone Hughes .15 .07
❑ 64 Rick Mirer .15 .07
❑ 65 Jeff Blake .25 .11
❑ 66 Carl Pickens .50 .23
❑ 67 Darnay Scott .25 .11
❑ 68 Tony McGee .15 .07
❑ 69 Ki-Jana Carter .15 .07
❑ 70 Ashley Ambrose .15 .07
❑ 71 Dan Wilkinson .15 .07
❑ 72 Chris Spielman .15 .07
❑ 73 Todd Collins .15 .07
❑ 74 Andre Reed .25 .11
❑ 75 Quinn Early .15 .07
❑ 76 Eric Moulds .50 .23
❑ 77 Darick Holmes .15 .07
❑ 78 Thurman Thomas .50 .23
❑ 79 Bruce Smith .25 .11
❑ 80 Bryce Paup .15 .07
❑ 81 John Elway 2.50 1.10
❑ 82 Terrell Davis 2.00 .90
❑ 83 Anthony Miller .15 .07
❑ 84 Shannon Sharpe .25 .11
❑ 85 Alfred Williams .15 .07
❑ 86 John Mobley .15 .07
❑ 87 Tory James .15 .07
❑ 88 Steve Atwater .15 .07
❑ 89 Darrien Gordon .15 .07
❑ 90 Mike Alstott .50 .23
❑ 91 Errict Rhett .15 .07
❑ 92 Trent Dilfer .50 .23
❑ 93 Courtney Hawkins .15 .07
❑ 94 Warren Sapp .25 .11
❑ 95 Regan Upshaw .15 .07
❑ 96 Hardy Nickerson .15 .07
❑ 97 Donnie Abraham RC .50 .23
❑ 98 Larry Centers .25 .11
❑ 99 Aeneas Williams .15 .07
❑ 100 Kent Graham .15 .07
❑ 101 Rob Moore .25 .11
❑ 102 Frank Sanders .25 .11
❑ 103 Leeland McElroy .15 .07
❑ 104 Eric Swann .15 .07
❑ 105 Simeon Rice .25 .11
❑ 106 Seth Joyner .15 .07
❑ 107 Stan Humphries .25 .11
❑ 108 Tony Martin .25 .11
❑ 109 Charlie Jones .25 .11
❑ 110 Andre Coleman UER .15 .07
(Card mistakenly #103)
❑ 111 Terrell Fletcher .15 .07
❑ 112 Junior Seau .25 .11
❑ 113 Eric Metcalf .25 .11
❑ 114 Chris Penn .15 .07
❑ 115 Marcus Allen .50 .23
❑ 116 Greg Hill .15 .07
❑ 117 Tamarick Vanover .25 .11
❑ 118 Lake Dawson .15 .07
❑ 119 Derrick Thomas .25 .11
❑ 120 Dale Carter .15 .07
❑ 121 Elvis Grbac .25 .11
❑ 122 Aaron Bailey .15 .07
❑ 123 Jim Harbaugh .25 .11
❑ 124 Marshall Faulk .50 .23
❑ 125 Sean Dawkins .15 .07
❑ 126 Marvin Harrison .50 .23
❑ 127 Ken Dilger .15 .07
❑ 128 Tony Bennett .15 .07
❑ 129 Jeff Herrod .15 .07
❑ 130 Chris Gardocki .15 .07
❑ 131 Cary Blanchard .15 .07
❑ 132 Troy Aikman 1.25 .55
❑ 133 Emmitt Smith 2.00 .90
❑ 134 Sherman Williams .15 .07
❑ 135 Michael Irvin .50 .23
❑ 136 Eric Bjornson .15 .07
❑ 137 Herschel Walker .25 .11

No.	Player		
138	Tony Tolbert	.15	.07
139	Deion Sanders	.50	.23
140	Daryl Johnston	.25	.11
141	Dan Marino	2.50	1.10
142	O.J. McDuffie	.25	.11
143	Troy Drayton	.15	.07
144	Karim Abdul-Jabbar	.50	.23
145	Stanley Pritchett	.15	.07
146	Fred Barnett	.15	.07
147	Zach Thomas	.25	.11
148	Shawn Wooden	.15	.07
149	Ty Detmer	.25	.11
150	Derrick Witherspoon	.15	.07
151	Ricky Watters	.25	.11
152	Charlie Garner	.15	.07
153	Chris T. Jones	.15	.07
154	Irving Fryar	.25	.11
155	Mike Mamula	.15	.07
156	Troy Vincent	.15	.07
157	Bobby Taylor	.15	.07
158	Chris Boniol	.15	.07
159	Devin Bush	.15	.07
160	Bert Emanuel	.25	.11
161	Jamal Anderson	.75	.35
162	Terance Mathis	.25	.11
163	Cornelius Bennett	.15	.07
164	Ray Buchanan	.15	.07
165	Chris Chandler	.25	.11
166	Dave Brown	.15	.07
167	Danny Kanell	.25	.11
168	Rodney Hampton	.25	.11
169	Tyrone Wheatley	.25	.11
170	Amani Toomer	.25	.11
171	Chris Calloway	.15	.07
172	Thomas Lewis	.15	.07
173	Phillippi Sparks	.15	.07
174	Mark Brunell	1.25	.55
175	Keenan McCardell	.25	.11
176	Willie Jackson	.15	.07
177	Jimmy Smith	.25	.11
178	Pete Mitchell	.15	.07
179	Natrone Means	.50	.23
180	Kevin Hardy	.15	.07
181	Tony Brackens	.15	.07
182	James O. Stewart	.25	.11
183	Wayne Chrebet	.50	.23
184	Keyshawn Johnson	.50	.23
185	Adrian Murrell	.25	.11
186	Neil O'Donnell	.25	.11
187	Hugh Douglas	.15	.07
188	Mo Lewis	.15	.07
189	Marvin Washington	.15	.07
190	Aaron Glenn	.15	.07
191	Barry Sanders	2.50	1.10
192	Scott Mitchell	.25	.11
193	Herman Moore	.50	.23
194	Johnnie Morton	.25	.11
195	Glyn Milburn	.15	.07
196	Reggie Brown LB	.25	.11
197	Jason Hanson	.15	.07
198	Steve McNair	.60	.25
199	Eddie George	1.25	.55
200	Ronnie Harmon	.15	.07
201	Chris Sanders	.15	.07
202	Willie Davis	.15	.07
203	Frank Wycheck	.15	.07
204	Darryll Lewis	.15	.07
205	Blaine Bishop	.15	.07
206	Robert Brooks	.25	.11
207	Brett Favre	2.50	1.10
208	Edgar Bennett	.25	.11
209	Dorsey Levens	.50	.23
210	Derrick Mayes	.25	.11
211	Antonio Freeman	.60	.25
212	Mark Chmura	.25	.11
213	Reggie White	.50	.23
214	Gilbert Brown	.15	.07
215	LeRoy Butler	.15	.07
216	Craig Newsome	.15	.07
217	Kerry Collins	.25	.11
218	Wesley Walls	.25	.11
219	Muhsin Muhammad	.25	.11
220	Anthony Johnson	.15	.07
221	Tim Biakabutuka	.25	.11
222	Kevin Greene	.25	.11
223	Sam Mills	.15	.07

No.	Player		
224	John Kasay	.15	.07
225	Micheal Barrow	.15	.07
226	Drew Bledsoe	1.25	.55
227	Curtis Martin	.60	.25
228	Terry Glenn	.50	.23
229	Ben Coates	.25	.11
230	Shawn Jefferson	.15	.07
231	Willie McGinest	.15	.07
232	Ted Johnson	.15	.07
233	Lawyer Milloy	.15	.07
234	Ty Law	.15	.07
235	Willie Clay	.15	.07
236	Tim Brown	.50	.23
237	Rickey Dudley	.25	.11
238	Napoleon Kaufman	.50	.23
239	Chester McGlockton	.15	.07
240	Rob Fredrickson	.15	.07
241	Terry McDaniel	.15	.07
242	Desmond Howard	.25	.11
243	Jeff George	.25	.11
244	Isaac Bruce	.50	.23
245	Tony Banks	.25	.11
246	Lawrence Phillips UER (Card mistakenly #247)	.15	.07
247	Kevin Carter	.15	.07
248	Roman Phifer	.15	.07
249	Keith Lyle	.15	.07
250	Eddie Kennison	.25	.11
251	Craig Heyward	.15	.07
252	Vinny Testaverde	.25	.11
253	Derrick Alexander WR	.25	.11
254	Michael Jackson	.25	.11
255	Byron Bam Morris	.15	.07
256	Eric Green	.15	.07
257	Ray Lewis	.60	.25
258	Antonio Langham	.15	.07
259	Michael McCrary	.15	.07
260	Gus Frerotte	.15	.07
261	Terry Allen	.50	.23
262	Brian Mitchell	.15	.07
263	Michael Westbrook	.25	.11
264	Sean Gilbert	.15	.07
265	Rich Owens	.15	.07
266	Ken Harvey	.15	.07
267	Jeff Hostetler	.15	.07
268	Michael Haynes	.15	.07
269	Mario Bates	.15	.07
270	Renaldo Turnbull UER (Card mistakenly #273)	.15	.07
271	Ray Zellars	.15	.07
272	Joe Johnson	.15	.07
273	Eric Allen	.15	.07
274	Heath Shuler	.15	.07
275	Daryl Hobbs	.15	.07
276	John Friesz	.15	.07
277	Brian Blades	.15	.07
278	Joey Galloway	.60	.25
279	Chris Warren	.25	.11
280	Lamar Smith	.50	.23
281	Cortez Kennedy	.15	.07
282	Chad Brown	.15	.07
283	Warren Moon	.50	.23
284	Jerome Bettis	.50	.23
285	Charles Johnson	.25	.11
286	Kordell Stewart	.60	.25
287	Erric Pegram	.15	.07
288	Norm Johnson	.15	.07
289	Levon Kirkland	.15	.07
290	Greg Lloyd	.15	.07
291	Carnell Lake	.15	.07
292	Brad Johnson	.60	.25
293	Cris Carter	.50	.23
294	Jake Reed	.25	.11
295	Robert Smith	.25	.11
296	Derrick Alexander DE	.15	.07
297	John Randle	.25	.11
298	Dixon Edwards	.15	.07
299	Orlanda Thomas	.15	.07
300	Dewayne Washington	.15	.07

1998 Upper Deck

	MINT	NRMT
COMPLETE SET (255)	250.00	110.00
COMP.SET w/o SP's (213)	25.00	11.00

No.	Player		
1	Peyton Manning RC	40.00	18.00
2	Ryan Leaf RC	12.00	5.50
3	Andre Wadsworth RC	3.00	1.35
4	Charles Woodson RC	10.00	4.50
5	Curtis Enis RC	8.00	3.60
6	Grant Wistrom RC	2.50	1.10
7	Greg Ellis RC	2.50	1.10
8	Fred Taylor RC	15.00	6.75
9	Duane Starks RC	2.50	1.10
10	Keith Brooking RC	3.00	1.35
11	Takeo Spikes RC	3.00	1.35
12	Jason Peter RC	2.50	1.10
13	Anthony Simmons RC	2.50	1.10
14	Kevin Dyson RC	10.00	4.50
15	Brian Simmons RC	2.50	1.10
16	Robert Edwards RC	5.00	2.20
17	Randy Moss RC	40.00	18.00
18	John Avery RC	4.00	1.80
19	Marcus Nash RC	4.00	1.80
20	Jerome Pathon RC	3.00	1.35
21	Jacquez Green RC	10.00	4.50
22	Robert Holcombe RC	4.00	1.80
23	Pat Johnson RC	3.00	1.35
24	Germane Crowell RC	12.00	5.50
25	Joe Jurevicius RC	3.00	1.35
26	Skip Hicks RC	4.00	1.80
27	Ahman Green RC	12.00	5.50
28	Brian Griese RC	20.00	9.00
29	Hines Ward RC	3.00	1.35
30	Tavian Banks RC	3.00	1.35
31	Tony Simmons RC	3.00	1.35
32	Victor Riley RC	2.50	1.10
33	Rashaan Shehee RC	3.00	1.35
34	R.W. McQuarters RC	2.50	1.10
35	Flozell Adams RC	2.50	1.10
36	Tra Thomas RC	2.50	1.10
37	Greg Favors RC	2.50	1.10
38	Jon Ritchie RC	3.00	1.35
39	Jesse Haynes RC	2.50	1.10
40	Ryan Sutter RC	2.50	1.10
41	Mo Collins RC	2.50	1.10
42	Tim Dwight RC	10.00	4.50
43	Chris Chandler	.25	.11
44	Byron Hanspard	.25	.11
45	Jessie Tuggle	.15	.07
46	Jamal Anderson	.50	.23
47	Terance Mathis	.25	.11
48	Morten Andersen	.15	.07
49	Jake Plummer	1.00	.45
50	Mario Bates	.25	.11
51	Frank Sanders	.25	.11
52	Adrian Murrell	.25	.11
53	Simeon Rice	.25	.11
54	Aeneas Williams	.15	.07
55	Eric Swann UER (Number on back 98)	.15	.07
56	Jim Harbaugh	.25	.11
57	Michael Jackson	.15	.07
58	Peter Boulware	.15	.07
59	Errict Rhett	.25	.11
60	Jermaine Lewis	.25	.11
61	Eric Zeier	.25	.11
62	Rod Woodson	.25	.11
63	Rob Johnson	.50	.23
64	Antowain Smith	.50	.23
65	Bruce Smith	.25	.11
66	Eric Moulds	.50	.23

❑ 67	Andre Reed	.25	.11
❑ 68	Thurman Thomas	.50	.23
❑ 69	Lonnie Johnson	.15	.07
❑ 70	Kerry Collins	.25	.11
❑ 71	Kevin Greene	.25	.11
❑ 72	Fred Lane	.25	.11
❑ 73	Rae Carruth	.25	.11
❑ 74	Michael Bates	.15	.07
❑ 75	William Floyd	.15	.07
❑ 76	Sean Gilbert	.15	.07
❑ 77	Erik Kramer	.15	.07
❑ 78	Edgar Bennett	.15	.07
❑ 79	Curtis Conway	.25	.11
❑ 80	Darnell Autry	.15	.07
❑ 81	Ryan Wetnight RC	.15	.07
❑ 82	Walt Harris	.15	.07
❑ 83	Bobby Engram	.25	.11
❑ 84	Jeff Blake	.25	.11
❑ 85	Carl Pickens	.50	.23
❑ 86	Darnay Scott	.25	.11
❑ 87	Corey Dillon	.75	.35
❑ 88	Reinard Wilson	.15	.07
❑ 89	Ashley Ambrose	.15	.07
❑ 90	Troy Aikman	1.25	.55
❑ 91	Michael Irvin	.50	.23
❑ 92	Emmitt Smith	2.00	.90
❑ 93	Deion Sanders	.50	.23
❑ 94	David LaFleur	.15	.07
❑ 95	Chris Warren	.25	.11
❑ 96	Darren Woodson	.15	.07
❑ 97	John Elway	2.50	1.10
❑ 98	Terrell Davis	2.00	.90
❑ 99	Rod Smith	.25	.11
❑ 100	Shannon Sharpe	.25	.11
❑ 101	Ed McCaffrey	.25	.11
❑ 102	Steve Atwater	.15	.07
❑ 103	John Mobley	.15	.07
❑ 104	Darrien Gordon	.15	.07
❑ 105	Barry Sanders	2.50	1.10
❑ 106	Scott Mitchell	.25	.11
❑ 107	Herman Moore	.50	.23
❑ 108	Johnnie Morton	.25	.11
❑ 109	Robert Porcher	.15	.07
❑ 110	Bryant Westbrook	.15	.07
❑ 111	Tommy Vardell	.15	.07
❑ 112	Brett Favre	2.50	1.10
❑ 113	Dorsey Levens	.50	.23
❑ 114	Reggie White	.50	.23
❑ 115	Antonio Freeman	.50	.23
❑ 116	Robert Brooks	.25	.11
❑ 117	Mark Chmura	.25	.11
❑ 118	Derrick Mayes	.25	.11
❑ 119	Gilbert Brown	.15	.07
❑ 120	Marshall Faulk	.50	.23
❑ 121	Jeff Burris	.15	.07
❑ 122	Marvin Harrison	.25	.11
❑ 123	Quentin Coryatt	.15	.07
❑ 124	Ken Dilger	.15	.07
❑ 125	Zack Crockett	.15	.07
❑ 126	Mark Brunell	1.00	.45
❑ 127	Bryce Paup	.15	.07
❑ 128	Tony Brackens	.15	.07
❑ 129	Renaldo Wynn	.15	.07
❑ 130	Keenan McCardell	.25	.11
❑ 131	Jimmy Smith	.25	.11
❑ 132	Kevin Hardy	.15	.07
❑ 133	Elvis Grbac	.25	.11
❑ 134	Tamarick Vanover	.15	.07
❑ 135	Chester McGlockton	.15	.07
❑ 136	Andre Rison	.25	.11
❑ 137	Derrick Alexander	.25	.11
❑ 138	Tony Gonzalez	.15	.07
❑ 139	Derrick Thomas	.25	.11
❑ 140	Dan Marino	2.50	1.10
❑ 141	Karim Abdul-Jabbar	.50	.23
❑ 142	O.J. McDuffie	.25	.11
❑ 143	Yatil Green	.15	.07
❑ 144	Charles Jordan	.15	.07
❑ 145	Brock Marion	.15	.07
❑ 146	Zach Thomas	.25	.11
❑ 147	Brad Johnson	.50	.23
❑ 148	Cris Carter	.50	.23
❑ 149	Jake Reed	.25	.11
❑ 150	Robert Smith	.50	.23
❑ 151	John Randle	.25	.11
❑ 152	Dwayne Rudd	.15	.07
❑ 153	Randall Cunningham	.50	.23
❑ 154	Drew Bledsoe	1.00	.45
❑ 155	Terry Glenn	.50	.23
❑ 156	Ben Coates	.25	.11
❑ 157	Willie Clay	.15	.07
❑ 158	Chris Slade	.15	.07
❑ 159	Derrick Cullors RC	.25	.11
❑ 160	Ty Law	.15	.07
❑ 161	Danny Wuerffel	.25	.11
❑ 162	Andre Hastings	.15	.07
❑ 163	Troy Davis	.15	.07
❑ 164	Billy Joe Hobert	.15	.07
❑ 165	Eric Guliford	.15	.07
❑ 166	Mark Fields	.15	.07
❑ 167	Alex Molden	.15	.07
❑ 168	Danny Kanell	.25	.11
❑ 169	Tiki Barber	.25	.11
❑ 170	Charles Way	.15	.07
❑ 171	Amani Toomer	.25	.11
❑ 172	Michael Strahan	.15	.07
❑ 173	Jessie Armstead	.15	.07
❑ 174	Jason Sehorn	.25	.11
❑ 175	Glenn Foley	.25	.11
❑ 176	Curtis Martin	.50	.23
❑ 177	Aaron Glenn	.15	.07
❑ 178	Keyshawn Johnson	.50	.23
❑ 179	James Farrior	.15	.07
❑ 180	Wayne Chrebet	.50	.23
❑ 181	Keith Byars	.15	.07
❑ 182	Jeff George	.25	.11
❑ 183	Napoleon Kaufman	.50	.23
❑ 184	Tim Brown	.50	.23
❑ 185	Darrell Russell	.15	.07
❑ 186	Rickey Dudley	.15	.07
❑ 187	James Jett	.25	.11
❑ 188	Desmond Howard	.25	.11
❑ 189	Bobby Hoying	.25	.11
❑ 190	Charlie Garner	.15	.07
❑ 191	Irving Fryar	.25	.11
❑ 192	Chris T. Jones	.15	.07
❑ 193	Mike Mamula	.15	.07
❑ 194	Troy Vincent	.15	.07
❑ 195	Kordell Stewart	.50	.23
❑ 196	Jerome Bettis	.50	.23
❑ 197	Will Blackwell	.15	.07
❑ 198	Levon Kirkland	.15	.07
❑ 199	Carnell Lake	.15	.07
❑ 200	Charles Johnson	.15	.07
❑ 201	Greg Lloyd	.15	.07
❑ 202	Donnell Woolford	.15	.07
❑ 203	Tony Banks	.25	.11
❑ 204	Amp Lee	.15	.07
❑ 205	Isaac Bruce	.50	.23
❑ 206	Eddie Kennison	.25	.11
❑ 207	Ryan McNeil	.15	.07
❑ 208	Mike Jones	.15	.07
❑ 209	Ernie Conwell	.15	.07
❑ 210	Natrone Means	.50	.23
❑ 211	Junior Seau	.25	.11
❑ 212	Tony Martin	.25	.11
❑ 213	Freddie Jones	.15	.07
❑ 214	Bryan Still	.15	.07
❑ 215	Rodney Harrison	.25	.11
❑ 216	Steve Young	.75	.35
❑ 217	Jerry Rice	1.25	.55
❑ 218	Garrison Hearst	.50	.23
❑ 219	J.J. Stokes	.25	.11
❑ 220	Ken Norton	.15	.07
❑ 221	Greg Clark	.15	.07
❑ 222	Terrell Owens	.50	.23
❑ 223	Bryant Young	.15	.07
❑ 224	Warren Moon	.50	.23
❑ 225	Jon Kitna	.75	.35
❑ 226	Ricky Watters	.25	.11
❑ 227	Chad Brown	.15	.07
❑ 228	Joey Galloway	.50	.23
❑ 229	Shawn Springs	.15	.07
❑ 230	Cortez Kennedy	.15	.07
❑ 231	Trent Dilfer	.50	.23
❑ 232	Warrick Dunn	.50	.23
❑ 233	Mike Alstott	.50	.23
❑ 234	Warren Sapp	.25	.11
❑ 235	Bert Emanuel	.25	.11
❑ 236	Reidel Anthony	.25	.11
❑ 237	Hardy Nickerson	.15	.07
❑ 238	Derrick Brooks	.15	.07
❑ 239	Steve McNair	.50	.23
❑ 240	Yancey Thigpen	.15	.07
❑ 241	Anthony Dorsett	.15	.07
❑ 242	Blaine Bishop	.15	.07
❑ 243	Kenny Holmes	.15	.07
❑ 244	Eddie George	1.00	.45
❑ 245	Chris Sanders	.15	.07
❑ 246	Gus Frerotte	.15	.07
❑ 247	Terry Allen	.50	.23
❑ 248	Dana Stubblefield	.15	.07
❑ 249	Michael Westbrook	.25	.11
❑ 250	Darrell Green	.25	.11
❑ 251	Brian Mitchell	.15	.07
❑ 252	Ken Harvey	.15	.07
❑ CL1	Troy Aikman CL	.50	.23
❑ CL2	Dan Marino CL	.75	.35
❑ CL3	Herman Moore CL	.25	.11

1999 Upper Deck

		MINT	NRMT
COMPLETE SET (270)		150.00	70.00
COMP.SET w/o SP's (225)		25.00	11.00
❑ 1	Jake Plummer	1.25	.55
❑ 2	Adrian Murrell	.30	.14
❑ 3	Rob Moore	.30	.14
❑ 4	Larry Centers	.15	.07
❑ 5	Simeon Rice	.15	.07
❑ 6	Andre Wadsworth	.15	.07
❑ 7	Frank Sanders	.30	.14
❑ 8	Tim Dwight	.60	.25
❑ 9	Ray Buchanan	.15	.07
❑ 10	Chris Chandler	.30	.14
❑ 11	Jamal Anderson	.60	.25
❑ 12	O.J. Santiago	.15	.07
❑ 13	Danny Kanell	.15	.07
❑ 14	Terance Mathis	.30	.14
❑ 15	Priest Holmes	.60	.25
❑ 16	Tony Banks	.30	.14
❑ 17	Ray Lewis	.30	.14
❑ 18	Patrick Johnson	.15	.07
❑ 19	Michael Jackson	.15	.07
❑ 20	Michael McCrary	.15	.07
❑ 21	Jermaine Lewis	.30	.14
❑ 22	Eric Moulds	.60	.25
❑ 23	Doug Flutie	.75	.35
❑ 24	Antowain Smith	.60	.25
❑ 25	Rob Johnson	.30	.14
❑ 26	Bruce Smith	.30	.14
❑ 27	Andre Reed	.30	.14
❑ 28	Thurman Thomas	.30	.14
❑ 29	Fred Lane	.30	.14
❑ 30	Wesley Walls	.30	.14
❑ 31	Tim Biakabutuka	.30	.14
❑ 32	Kevin Greene	.15	.07
❑ 33	Steve Beuerlein	.15	.07
❑ 34	Muhsin Muhammad	.30	.14
❑ 35	Rae Carruth	.30	.14
❑ 36	Bobby Engram	.30	.14
❑ 37	Curtis Enis	.60	.25
❑ 38	Edgar Bennett	.15	.07
❑ 39	Erik Kramer	.15	.07
❑ 40	Steve Stenstrom	.15	.07
❑ 41	Alonzo Mayes	.15	.07
❑ 42	Curtis Conway	.30	.14
❑ 43	Tony McGee	.15	.07
❑ 44	Darnay Scott	.15	.07

❑ 45	Jeff Blake	.30	.14
❑ 46	Corey Dillon	.60	.25
❑ 47	Ki-Jana Carter	.15	.07
❑ 48	Takeo Spikes	.15	.07
❑ 49	Carl Pickens	.30	.14
❑ 50	Ty Detmer	.30	.14
❑ 51	Leslie Shepherd	.15	.07
❑ 52	Terry Kirby	.15	.07
❑ 53	Marquez Pope	.15	.07
❑ 54	Antonio Langham	.15	.07
❑ 55	Jamir Miller	.15	.07
❑ 56	Derrick Alexander DT	.15	.07
❑ 57	Troy Aikman	1.50	.70
❑ 58	Rocket Ismail	.30	.14
❑ 59	Emmitt Smith	1.50	.70
❑ 60	Michael Irvin	.30	.14
❑ 61	David LaFleur	.15	.07
❑ 62	Chris Warren	.15	.07
❑ 63	Deion Sanders	.60	.25
❑ 64	Greg Ellis	.15	.07
❑ 65	John Elway	2.50	1.10
❑ 66	Bubby Brister	.15	.07
❑ 67	Terrell Davis	1.50	.70
❑ 68	Ed McCaffrey	.30	.14
❑ 69	John Mobley	.15	.07
❑ 70	Bill Romanowski	.15	.07
❑ 71	Rod Smith	.30	.14
❑ 72	Shannon Sharpe	.30	.14
❑ 73	Charlie Batch	1.25	.55
❑ 74	Germane Crowell	.30	.14
❑ 75	Johnnie Morton	.15	.07
❑ 76	Barry Sanders	2.50	1.10
❑ 77	Robert Porcher	.15	.07
❑ 78	Stephen Boyd	.15	.07
❑ 79	Herman Moore	.60	.25
❑ 80	Brett Favre	2.50	1.10
❑ 81	Mark Chmura	.15	.07
❑ 82	Antonio Freeman	.60	.25
❑ 83	Robert Brooks	.30	.14
❑ 84	Vonnie Holliday	.15	.07
❑ 85	Bill Schroeder	.60	.25
❑ 86	Dorsey Levens	.60	.25
❑ 87	Santana Dotson	.15	.07
❑ 88	Peyton Manning	2.50	1.10
❑ 89	Jerome Pathon	.15	.07
❑ 90	Marvin Harrison	.60	.25
❑ 91	Ellis Johnson	.15	.07
❑ 92	Ken Dilger	.15	.07
❑ 93	E.G. Green	.15	.07
❑ 94	Jeff Burris	.15	.07
❑ 95	Mark Brunell	1.00	.45
❑ 96	Fred Taylor	1.50	.70
❑ 97	Jimmy Smith	.30	.14
❑ 98	James Stewart	.30	.14
❑ 99	Kyle Brady	.15	.07
❑ 100	Dave Thomas RC	.15	.07
❑ 101	Keenan McCardell	.30	.14
❑ 102	Elvis Grbac	.30	.14
❑ 103	Tony Gonzalez	.30	.14
❑ 104	Andre Rison	.30	.14
❑ 105	Donnell Bennett	.15	.07
❑ 106	Derrick Thomas	.30	.14
❑ 107	Warren Moon	.60	.25
❑ 108	Derrick Alexander WR	.30	.14
❑ 109	Dan Marino	2.50	1.10
❑ 110	O.J. McDuffie	.30	.14
❑ 111	Karim Abdul-Jabbar	.30	.14
❑ 112	John Avery	.30	.14
❑ 113	Sam Madison	.15	.07
❑ 114	Jason Taylor	.15	.07
❑ 115	Zach Thomas	.30	.14
❑ 116	Randall Cunningham	.60	.25
❑ 117	Randy Moss	2.50	1.10
❑ 118	Cris Carter	.60	.25
❑ 119	Jake Reed	.30	.14
❑ 120	Matthew Hatchette	.15	.07
❑ 121	John Randle	.30	.14
❑ 122	Robert Smith	.60	.25
❑ 123	Drew Bledsoe	1.00	.45
❑ 124	Ben Coates	.30	.14
❑ 125	Terry Glenn	.60	.25
❑ 126	Ty Law	.15	.07
❑ 127	Tony Simmons	.15	.07
❑ 128	Ted Johnson	.15	.07
❑ 129	Tony Carter	.15	.07
❑ 130	Willie McGinest	.15	.07
❑ 131	Danny Wuerffel	.15	.07
❑ 132	Cameron Cleeland	.15	.07
❑ 133	Eddie Kennison	.30	.14
❑ 134	Joe Johnson	.15	.07
❑ 135	Andre Hastings	.15	.07
❑ 136	La'Roi Glover	.15	.07
❑ 137	Kent Graham	.15	.07
❑ 138	Tiki Barber	.15	.07
❑ 139	Gary Brown	.15	.07
❑ 140	Ike Hilliard	.15	.07
❑ 141	Jason Sehorn	.15	.07
❑ 142	Michael Strahan	.15	.07
❑ 143	Amani Toomer	.15	.07
❑ 144	Kerry Collins	.30	.14
❑ 145	Vinny Testaverde	.30	.14
❑ 146	Wayne Chrebet	.30	.14
❑ 147	Curtis Martin	.60	.25
❑ 148	Mo Lewis	.15	.07
❑ 149	Aaron Glenn	.15	.07
❑ 150	Steve Atwater	.15	.07
❑ 151	Keyshawn Johnson	.60	.25
❑ 152	James Farrior	.15	.07
❑ 153	Rich Gannon	.30	.14
❑ 154	Tim Brown	.60	.25
❑ 155	Darrell Russell	.15	.07
❑ 156	Rickey Dudley	.15	.07
❑ 157	Charles Woodson	.60	.25
❑ 158	James Jett	.30	.14
❑ 159	Napoleon Kaufman	.60	.25
❑ 160	Duce Staley	.60	.25
❑ 161	Doug Pederson	.15	.07
❑ 162	Bobby Hoying	.30	.14
❑ 163	Koy Detmer	.15	.07
❑ 164	Kevin Turner	.15	.07
❑ 165	Charles Johnson	.15	.07
❑ 166	Mike Mamula	.15	.07
❑ 167	Jerome Bettis	.60	.25
❑ 168	Courtney Hawkins	.15	.07
❑ 169	Will Blackwell	.15	.07
❑ 170	Kordell Stewart	.60	.25
❑ 171	Richard Huntley	.60	.25
❑ 172	Levon Kirkland	.15	.07
❑ 173	Hines Ward	.15	.07
❑ 174	Trent Green	.30	.14
❑ 175	Marshall Faulk	.60	.25
❑ 176	Az-Zahir Hakim	.15	.07
❑ 177	Amp Lee	.15	.07
❑ 178	Robert Holcombe	.30	.14
❑ 179	Isaac Bruce	.60	.25
❑ 180	Kevin Carter	.15	.07
❑ 181	Jim Harbaugh	.30	.14
❑ 182	Junior Seau	.30	.14
❑ 183	Natrone Means	.30	.14
❑ 184	Ryan Leaf	.60	.25
❑ 185	Charlie Jones	.15	.07
❑ 186	Rodney Harrison	.15	.07
❑ 187	Mikhael Ricks	.15	.07
❑ 188	Steve Young	1.00	.45
❑ 189	Terrell Owens	.60	.25
❑ 190	Jerry Rice	1.50	.70
❑ 191	J.J. Stokes	.30	.14
❑ 192	Irv Smith	.15	.07
❑ 193	Bryant Young	.15	.07
❑ 194	Garrison Hearst	.30	.14
❑ 195	Jon Kitna	.60	.25
❑ 196	Ahman Green	.30	.14
❑ 197	Joey Galloway	.60	.25
❑ 198	Ricky Watters	.30	.14
❑ 199	Chad Brown	.15	.07
❑ 200	Shawn Springs	.15	.07
❑ 201	Mike Pritchard	.15	.07
❑ 202	Trent Dilfer	.30	.14
❑ 203	Reidel Anthony	.30	.14
❑ 204	Bert Emanuel	.30	.14
❑ 205	Warrick Dunn	.60	.25
❑ 206	Jacquez Green	.30	.14
❑ 207	Hardy Nickerson	.15	.07
❑ 208	Mike Alstott	.60	.25
❑ 209	Eddie George	.75	.35
❑ 210	Steve McNair	.60	.25
❑ 211	Kevin Dyson	.30	.14
❑ 212	Frank Wycheck	.15	.07
❑ 213	Jackie Harris	.15	.07
❑ 214	Blaine Bishop	.15	.07
❑ 215	Yancey Thigpen	.15	.07
❑ 216	Brad Johnson	.60	.25
❑ 217	Rodney Peete	.15	.07
❑ 218	Michael Westbrook	.30	.14
❑ 219	Skip Hicks	.60	.25
❑ 220	Brian Mitchell	.15	.07
❑ 221	Dan Wilkinson	.15	.07
❑ 222	Dana Stubblefield	.15	.07
❑ 223	Kordell Stewart CL	.30	.14
❑ 224	Fred Taylor CL	.60	.25
❑ 225	Warrick Dunn CL	.30	.14
❑ 226	Champ Bailey RC	5.00	2.20
❑ 227	Chris McAlister RC	2.50	1.10
❑ 228	Jevon Kearse RC	8.00	3.60
❑ 229	Ebenezer Ekuban RC	2.50	1.10
❑ 230	Chris Claiborne RC	1.50	.70
❑ 231	Andy Katzenmoyer RC	3.00	1.35
❑ 232	Tim Couch RC	12.00	5.50
❑ 233	Daunte Culpepper RC	20.00	9.00
❑ 234	Akili Smith RC	8.00	3.60
❑ 235	Donovan McNabb RC	15.00	6.75
❑ 236	Sean Bennett RC	3.00	1.35
❑ 237	Brock Huard RC	6.00	2.70
❑ 238	Cade McNown RC	5.00	2.20
❑ 239	Shaun King RC	8.00	3.60
❑ 240	Joe Germaine RC	3.00	1.35
❑ 241	Ricky Williams RC	15.00	6.75
❑ 242	Edgerrin James RC	20.00	9.00
❑ 243	Sedrick Irvin RC	3.00	1.35
❑ 244	Kevin Faulk RC	6.00	2.70
❑ 245	Rob Konrad RC	3.00	1.35
❑ 246	James Johnson RC	3.00	1.35
❑ 247	Amos Zereoue RC	3.00	1.35
❑ 248	Torry Holt RC	10.00	4.50
❑ 249	D'Wayne Bates RC	3.00	1.35
❑ 250	David Boston RC	8.00	3.60
❑ 251	Dameane Douglas RC	3.00	1.35
❑ 252	Troy Edwards RC	5.00	2.20
❑ 253	Kevin Johnson RC	6.00	2.70
❑ 254	Peerless Price RC	5.00	2.20
❑ 255	Antoine Winfield RC	2.50	1.10
❑ 256	Mike Cloud RC	3.00	1.35
❑ 257	Joe Montgomery RC	3.00	1.35
❑ 258	Jermaine Fazande RC	3.00	1.35
❑ 259	Scott Covington RC	3.00	1.35
❑ 260	Aaron Brooks RC	15.00	6.75
❑ 261	Patrick Kerney RC	1.50	.70
❑ 262	Cecil Collins RC	3.00	1.35
❑ 263	Chris Greisen RC	3.00	1.35
❑ 264	Craig Yeast RC	2.50	1.10
❑ 265	Karsten Bailey RC	2.50	1.10
❑ 266	Reginald Kelly RC	1.50	.70
❑ 267	Al Wilson RC	2.50	1.10
❑ 268	Jeff Paulk RC	3.00	1.35
❑ 269	Jim Kleinsasser RC	3.00	1.35
❑ 270	Darrin Chiaverini RC	2.50	1.10

2000 Upper Deck

	MINT	NRMT
COMPLETE SET (1-270)	150.00	70.00
COMP.SET w/o SPs (222)	20.00	9.00

❑ 1	Jake Plummer	.60	.25
❑ 2	Michael Pittman	.15	.07
❑ 3	Rob Moore	.30	.14
❑ 4	David Boston	.60	.25
❑ 5	Frank Sanders	.30	.14
❑ 6	Aeneas Williams	.15	.07
❑ 7	Kwamie Lassiter	.15	.07

❑	8 Rob Fredrickson	.15	.07
❑	9 Tim Dwight	.60	.25
❑	10 Chris Chandler	.30	.14
❑	11 Jamal Anderson	.60	.25
❑	12 Shawn Jefferson	.15	.07
❑	13 Ken Oxendine	.15	.07
❑	14 Terance Mathis	.30	.14
❑	15 Bob Christian	.15	.07
❑	16 Qadry Ismail	.15	.07
❑	17 Jermaine Lewis	.30	.14
❑	18 Rod Woodson	.30	.14
❑	19 Michael McCrary	.15	.07
❑	20 Tony Banks	.30	.14
❑	21 Peter Boulware	.15	.07
❑	22 Shannon Sharpe	.30	.14
❑	23 Peerless Price	.60	.25
❑	24 Rob Johnson	.30	.14
❑	25 Eric Moulds	.60	.25
❑	26 Doug Flutie	.75	.35
❑	27 Jay Riemersma	.15	.07
❑	28 Antowain Smith	.30	.14
❑	29 Jonathan Linton	.15	.07
❑	30 Muhsin Muhammad	.30	.14
❑	31 Patrick Jeffers	.60	.25
❑	32 Steve Beuerlein	.30	.14
❑	33 Natrone Means	.15	.07
❑	34 Tim Biakabutuka	.30	.14
❑	35 Michael Bates	.15	.07
❑	36 Chuck Smith	.15	.07
❑	37 Wesley Walls	.15	.07
❑	38 Cade McNown	.60	.25
❑	39 Curtis Enis	.30	.14
❑	40 Marcus Robinson	.60	.25
❑	41 Eddie Kennison	.30	.14
❑	42 Bobby Engram	.30	.14
❑	43 Glyn Milburn	.15	.07
❑	44 Marty Booker	.15	.07
❑	45 Akili Smith	.60	.25
❑	46 Corey Dillon	.60	.25
❑	47 Darnay Scott	.30	.14
❑	48 Tremain Mack	.15	.07
❑	49 Damon Griffin	.15	.07
❑	50 Takeo Spikes	.15	.07
❑	51 Tony McGee	.15	.07
❑	52 Tim Couch	1.25	.55
❑	53 Kevin Johnson	.60	.25
❑	54 Darrin Chiaverini	.15	.07
❑	55 Jamir Miller	.15	.07
❑	56 Errict Rhett	.30	.14
❑	57 Terry Kirby	.15	.07
❑	58 Marc Edwards	.15	.07
❑	59 Troy Aikman	1.50	.70
❑	60 Emmitt Smith	1.50	.70
❑	61 Rocket Ismail	.30	.14
❑	62 Jason Tucker	.30	.14
❑	63 Dexter Coakley	.15	.07
❑	64 Joey Galloway	.60	.25
❑	65 Wane McGarity	.15	.07
❑	66 Terrell Davis	1.50	.70
❑	67 Olandis Gary	.60	.25
❑	68 Brian Griese	.75	.35
❑	69 Gus Frerotte	.15	.07
❑	70 Byron Chamberlain	.15	.07
❑	71 Ed McCaffrey	.60	.25
❑	72 Rod Smith	.30	.14
❑	73 Al Wilson	.15	.07
❑	74 Charlie Batch	.60	.25
❑	75 Germane Crowell	.30	.14
❑	76 Sedrick Irvin	.15	.07
❑	77 Johnnie Morton	.30	.14
❑	78 Robert Porcher	.15	.07
❑	79 Herman Moore	.30	.14
❑	80 James Stewart	.30	.14
❑	81 Brett Favre	2.50	1.10
❑	82 Antonio Freeman	.60	.25
❑	83 Bill Schroeder	.30	.14
❑	84 Dorsey Levens	.30	.14
❑	85 Corey Bradford	.30	.14
❑	86 De'Mond Parker	.15	.07
❑	87 Vonnie Holliday	.15	.07
❑	88 Peyton Manning	2.00	.90
❑	89 Edgerrin James	2.00	.90
❑	90 Marvin Harrison	.60	.25
❑	91 Ken Dilger	.15	.07
❑	92 Terrence Wilkins	.60	.25
❑	93 Marcus Pollard	.15	.07
❑	94 Fred Lane	.15	.07
❑	95 Mark Brunell	1.00	.45
❑	96 Fred Taylor	.75	.35
❑	97 Jimmy Smith	.30	.14
❑	98 Keenan McCardell	.30	.14
❑	99 Carnell Lake	.15	.07
❑	100 Tavian Banks	.15	.07
❑	101 Kyle Brady	.15	.07
❑	102 Hardy Nickerson	.15	.07
❑	103 Elvis Grbac	.30	.14
❑	104 Tony Gonzalez	.30	.14
❑	105 Derrick Alexander WR	.30	.14
❑	106 Donnell Bennett	.15	.07
❑	107 Mike Cloud	.15	.07
❑	108 Donnie Edwards	.15	.07
❑	109 Jay Fiedler	.60	.25
❑	110 James Johnson	.30	.14
❑	111 Tony Martin	.30	.14
❑	112 Damon Huard	.60	.25
❑	113 O.J. McDuffie	.30	.14
❑	114 Thurman Thomas	.30	.14
❑	115 Zach Thomas	.30	.14
❑	116 Oronde Gadsden	.30	.14
❑	117 Randy Moss	2.00	.90
❑	118 Robert Smith	.60	.25
❑	119 Cris Carter	.60	.25
❑	120 Matthew Hatchette	.30	.14
❑	121 Daunte Culpepper	1.25	.55
❑	122 Leroy Hoard	.15	.07
❑	123 Drew Bledsoe	1.00	.45
❑	124 Terry Glenn	.30	.14
❑	125 Troy Brown	.15	.07
❑	126 Kevin Faulk	.15	.07
❑	127 Lawyer Milloy	.15	.07
❑	128 Ricky Williams	1.50	.70
❑	129 Keith Poole	.15	.07
❑	130 Jake Reed	.30	.14
❑	131 Cam Cleeland	.15	.07
❑	132 Jeff Blake	.30	.14
❑	133 Andrew Glover	.15	.07
❑	134 Kerry Collins	.30	.14
❑	135 Amani Toomer	.30	.14
❑	136 Joe Montgomery	.15	.07
❑	137 Ike Hilliard	.30	.14
❑	138 Tiki Barber	.30	.14
❑	139 Pete Mitchell	.15	.07
❑	140 Ray Lucas	.60	.25
❑	141 Mo Lewis	.15	.07
❑	142 Curtis Martin	.60	.25
❑	143 Vinny Testaverde	.30	.14
❑	144 Wayne Chrebet	.30	.14
❑	145 Dedric Ward	.30	.14
❑	146 Tim Brown	.60	.25
❑	147 Rich Gannon	.30	.14
❑	148 Tyrone Wheatley	.30	.14
❑	149 Napoleon Kaufman	.30	.14
❑	150 Charles Woodson	.30	.14
❑	151 Darrell Russell	.15	.07
❑	152 James Jett	.15	.07
❑	153 Rickey Dudley	.15	.07
❑	154 Jon Ritchie	.15	.07
❑	155 Duce Staley	.60	.25
❑	156 Donovan McNabb	1.00	.45
❑	157 Torrance Small	.15	.07
❑	158 Allen Rossum	.15	.07
❑	159 Mike Mamula	.15	.07
❑	160 Na Brown	.15	.07
❑	161 Charles Johnson	.30	.14
❑	162 Kent Graham	.15	.07
❑	163 Troy Edwards	.30	.14
❑	164 Jerome Bettis	.60	.25
❑	165 Hines Ward	.15	.07
❑	166 Kordell Stewart	.60	.25
❑	167 Levon Kirkland	.15	.07
❑	168 Richard Huntley	.15	.07
❑	169 Marshall Faulk	.75	.35
❑	170 Kurt Warner	2.50	1.10
❑	171 Torry Holt	.60	.25
❑	172 Isaac Bruce	.60	.25
❑	173 Kevin Carter	.15	.07
❑	174 Az-Zahir Hakim	.30	.14
❑	175 Ricky Proehl	.15	.07
❑	176 Jermaine Fazande	.15	.07
❑	177 Curtis Conway	.30	.14
❑	178 Freddie Jones	.15	.07
❑	179 Junior Seau	.30	.14
❑	180 Jeff Graham	.15	.07
❑	181 Jim Harbaugh	.30	.14
❑	182 Rodney Harrison	.15	.07
❑	183 Steve Young	1.00	.45
❑	184 Jerry Rice	1.50	.70
❑	185 Charlie Garner	.30	.14
❑	186 Terrell Owens	.60	.25
❑	187 Jeff Garcia	.60	.25
❑	188 Fred Beasley	.15	.07
❑	189 J.J. Stokes	.30	.14
❑	190 Ricky Watters	.30	.14
❑	191 Jon Kitna	.60	.25
❑	192 Derrick Mayes	.30	.14
❑	193 Sean Dawkins	.15	.07
❑	194 Charlie Rogers	.15	.07
❑	195 Mike Pritchard	.15	.07
❑	196 Cortez Kennedy	.15	.07
❑	197 Christian Fauria	.15	.07
❑	198 Warrick Dunn	.60	.25
❑	199 Shaun King	1.00	.45
❑	200 Mike Alstott	.60	.25
❑	201 Warren Sapp	.30	.14
❑	202 Jacquez Green	.30	.14
❑	203 Reidel Anthony	.15	.07
❑	204 Dave Moore	.15	.07
❑	205 Keyshawn Johnson	.60	.25
❑	206 Eddie George	.75	.35
❑	207 Steve McNair	.60	.25
❑	208 Kevin Dyson	.30	.14
❑	209 Jevon Kearse	.60	.25
❑	210 Yancey Thigpen	.15	.07
❑	211 Frank Wycheck	.15	.07
❑	212 Isaac Byrd	.15	.07
❑	213 Neil O'Donnell	.15	.07
❑	214 Brad Johnson	.60	.25
❑	215 Stephen Davis	.60	.25
❑	216 Michael Westbrook	.30	.14
❑	217 Albert Connell	.15	.07
❑	218 Brian Mitchell	.15	.07
❑	219 Bruce Smith	.30	.14
❑	220 Stephen Alexander	.15	.07
❑	221 Jeff George	.30	.14
❑	222 Adrian Murrell	.15	.07
❑	223 Courtney Brown RC	5.00	2.20
❑	224 John Engelberger RC	2.50	1.10
❑	225 Deltha O'Neal RC	2.50	1.10
❑	226 Corey Simon RC	5.00	2.20
❑	227 R.Jay Soward RC	4.00	1.80
❑	228 Marc Bulger RC	4.00	1.80
❑	229 Raynoch Thompson RC	2.50	1.10
❑	230 Deon Grant RC	2.00	.90
❑	231 Darrell Jackson RC	6.00	2.70
❑	232 Chris Cole RC	2.50	1.10
❑	233 Trevor Gaylor RC	2.50	1.10
❑	234 John Abraham RC	2.50	1.10
❑	235 Chris Redman RC	8.00	3.60
❑	236 Joe Hamilton RC	5.00	2.20
❑	237 Chad Pennington RC	12.00	5.50
❑	238 Tee Martin RC	8.00	3.60
❑	239 Giovanni Carmazzi RC	5.00	2.20
❑	240 Tim Rattay RC	6.00	2.70
❑	241 Ron Dayne RC	12.00	5.50
❑	242 Shaun Alexander RC	10.00	4.50
❑	243 Thomas Jones RC	8.00	3.60
❑	244 Reuben Droughns RC	4.00	1.80
❑	245 Jamal Lewis RC	20.00	9.00
❑	246 Michael Wiley RC	4.00	1.80
❑	247 J.R. Redmond RC	5.00	2.20
❑	248 Travis Prentice RC	6.00	2.70
❑	249 Todd Husak RC	4.00	1.80
❑	250 Trung Canidate RC	4.00	1.80
❑	251 Brian Urlacher RC	12.00	5.50
❑	252 Anthony Becht RC	4.00	1.80
❑	253 Bubba Franks RC	5.00	2.20
❑	254 Tom Brady RC	4.00	1.80
❑	255 Peter Warrick RC	12.00	5.50
❑	256 Plaxico Burress RC	8.00	3.60
❑	257 Sylvester Morris RC	8.00	3.60
❑	258 Dez White RC	2.50	1.10
❑	259 Travis Taylor RC	5.00	2.20
❑	260 Todd Pinkston RC	4.00	1.80
❑	261 Dennis Northcutt RC	5.00	2.20
❑	262 Jerry Porter RC	4.00	1.80
❑	263 Laveranues Coles RC	6.00	2.70
❑	264 Danny Farmer RC	4.00	1.80
❑	265 Curtis Keaton RC	2.50	1.10

Card	MINT	NRMT
❑ 266 Sherrod Gideon RC	2.00	.90
❑ 267 Ron Dugans RC	2.50	1.10
❑ 268 Steve McNair CL	.30	.14
❑ 269 Jake Plummer CL	.30	.14
❑ 270 Antonio Freeman CL	.30	.14

1999 Upper Deck Century Legends

	MINT	NRMT
COMPLETE SET (173)	50.00	22.00

CARDS 4/6/14/26/31/38/43 NOT RELEASED

Card	MINT	NRMT
❑ 1 Jim Brown	2.00	.90
❑ 2 Jerry Rice	1.25	.55
❑ 3 Joe Montana	3.00	1.35
❑ 5 Johnny Unitas	1.25	.55
❑ 7 Otto Graham	.50	.23
❑ 8 Walter Payton	3.00	1.35
❑ 9 Dick Butkus	1.00	.45
❑ 10 Bob Lilly	.30	.14
❑ 11 Sammy Baugh	.50	.23
❑ 12 Barry Sanders	2.00	.90
❑ 13 Deacon Jones	.30	.14
❑ 15 Gino Marchetti	.15	.07
❑ 16 John Elway	2.00	.90
❑ 17 Anthony Munoz	.15	.07
❑ 18 Ray Nitschke	.30	.14
❑ 19 Dick Lane	.15	.07
❑ 20 John Hannah	.15	.07
❑ 21 Gale Sayers	1.00	.45
❑ 22 Reggie White	.30	.14
❑ 23 Ronnie Lott	.30	.14
❑ 24 Jim Parker	.15	.07
❑ 25 Merlin Olsen	.30	.14
❑ 27 Dan Marino	2.00	.90
❑ 28 Forrest Gregg	.30	.14
❑ 29 Roger Staubach	1.50	.70
❑ 30 Jack Lambert	.30	.14
❑ 32 Marion Motley	.15	.07
❑ 33 Earl Campbell	.50	.23
❑ 34 Alan Page	.15	.07
❑ 35 Bronko Nagurski	.30	.14
❑ 36 Mel Blount	.15	.07
❑ 37 Deion Sanders	.50	.23
❑ 39 Sid Luckman	.30	.14
❑ 40 Raymond Berry	.30	.14
❑ 41 Bart Starr	1.25	.55
❑ 42 Willie Lanier	.15	.07
❑ 44 Terry Bradshaw	1.50	.70
❑ 45 Herb Adderley	.30	.14
❑ 46 Steve Largent	.30	.14
❑ 47 Jack Ham	.30	.14
❑ 48 John Mackey	.15	.07
❑ 49 Bill George	.15	.07
❑ 50 Willie Brown	.15	.07
❑ 51 Jerry Rice	1.25	.55
❑ 52 Barry Sanders	2.00	.90
❑ 53 John Elway	2.00	.90
❑ 54 Reggie White	.30	.14
❑ 55 Dan Marino	2.00	.90
❑ 56 Deion Sanders	.50	.23
❑ 57 Bruce Smith	.30	.14
❑ 58 Steve Young	.75	.35
❑ 59 Emmitt Smith	1.25	.55
❑ 60 Brett Favre	2.00	.90
❑ 61 Rod Woodson	.30	.14
❑ 62 Troy Aikman	1.25	.55
❑ 63 Terrell Davis	1.25	.55
❑ 64 Michael Irvin	.30	.14
❑ 65 Andre Rison	.30	.14
❑ 66 Warren Moon	.50	.23
❑ 67 Thurman Thomas	.30	.14
❑ 68 Randall Cunningham	.50	.23
❑ 69 Jerome Bettis	.50	.23
❑ 70 Junior Seau	.30	.14
❑ 71 Drew Bledsoe	.75	.35
❑ 72 Andre Reed	.30	.14
❑ 73 Tim Brown	.50	.23
❑ 74 Derrick Thomas	.30	.14
❑ 75 Jake Plummer	1.00	.45
❑ 76 Kordell Stewart	.50	.23
❑ 77 Herman Moore	.50	.23
❑ 78 Shannon Sharpe	.30	.14
❑ 79 Antonio Freeman	.50	.23
❑ 80 Ricky Watters	.30	.14
❑ 81 Warrick Dunn	.50	.23
❑ 82 Mark Brunell	.75	.35
❑ 83 Randy Moss	2.00	.90
❑ 84 Fred Taylor	1.25	.55
❑ 85 Curtis Martin	.50	.23
❑ 86 Keyshawn Johnson	.50	.23
❑ 87 Eddie George	.60	.25
❑ 88 Marshall Faulk	.50	.23
❑ 89 Joey Galloway	.50	.23
❑ 90 Vinny Testaverde	.30	.14
❑ 91 Garrison Hearst	.30	.14
❑ 92 Jimmy Smith	.30	.14
❑ 93 Doug Flutie	.60	.25
❑ 94 Napoleon Kaufman	.50	.23
❑ 95 Natrone Means	.30	.14
❑ 96 Peyton Manning	2.00	.90
❑ 97 Steve McNair	.50	.23
❑ 98 Corey Dillon	.50	.23
❑ 99 Terrell Owens	.50	.23
❑ 100 Charlie Batch	1.00	.45
❑ 101 Brett Favre APR	1.50	.70
❑ 102 Terrell Davis APR	1.00	.45
❑ 103 Roger Staubach APR	1.25	.55
❑ 104 Terry Bradshaw APR	1.25	.55
❑ 105 Fran Tarkenton APR	.60	.25
❑ 106 Walter Payton APR	2.50	1.10
❑ 107 Mark Brunell APR	.60	.25
❑ 108 Jim Brown APR	1.50	.70
❑ 109 Kordell Stewart APR	.50	.23
❑ 110 Bart Starr APR	1.00	.45
❑ 111 Steve Largent APR	.30	.14
❑ 112 Raymond Berry APR	.15	.07
❑ 113 Emmitt Smith APR	1.00	.45
❑ 114 Forrest Gregg APR	.15	.07
❑ 115 Drew Bledsoe APR	.60	.25
❑ 116 Dick Butkus APR	.60	.25
❑ 117 Johnny Unitas APR	1.00	.45
❑ 118 Joe Montana APR	2.50	1.10
❑ 119 Deacon Jones APR	.15	.07
❑ 120 Steve Young APR	.60	.25
❑ 121 Bob Lilly APR	.15	.07
❑ 122 Troy Aikman APR	1.00	.45
❑ 123 Alan Page APR	.15	.07
❑ 124 Earl Campbell APR	.60	.25
❑ 125 Deion Sanders APR	.50	.23
❑ 126 Ronnie Lott APR	.30	.14
❑ 127 Reggie White APR	.30	.14
❑ 128 Marshall Faulk APR	.50	.23
❑ 129 Gale Sayers APR	.75	.35
❑ 130 Dick Lane APR	.15	.07
❑ 131 Ricky Williams RC	5.00	2.20
❑ 132 Tim Couch RC	5.00	2.20
❑ 133 Donovan McNabb RC	5.00	2.20
❑ 134 Daunte Culpepper RC	8.00	3.60
❑ 135 Edgerrin James RC	8.00	3.60
❑ 136 Cade McNown RC	1.50	.70
❑ 137 Torry Holt RC	3.00	1.35
❑ 138 David Boston RC	2.50	1.10
❑ 139 Champ Bailey RC	2.00	.90
❑ 140 Peerless Price RC	2.00	.90
❑ 141 D'Wayne Bates RC	.75	.35
❑ 142 Joe Germaine RC	1.25	.55
❑ 143 Brock Huard RC	2.00	.90
❑ 144 Chris Claiborne RC	.75	.35
❑ 145 Jevon Kearse RC	2.50	1.10
❑ 146 Troy Edwards RC	2.00	.90
❑ 147 Amos Zereoue RC	1.25	.55
❑ 148 Aaron Brooks RC	5.00	2.20
❑ 149 Andy Katzenmoyer RC	1.25	.55
❑ 150 Kevin Faulk RC	2.00	.90
❑ 151 Shaun King RC	2.50	1.10
❑ 152 Kevin Johnson RC	2.50	1.10
❑ 153 Dameane Douglas RC	.75	.35
❑ 154 Mike Cloud RC	1.25	.55
❑ 155 Sedrick Irvin RC	1.25	.55
❑ 156 Akili Smith RC	2.50	1.10
❑ 157 Rob Konrad RC	1.25	.55
❑ 158 Scott Covington RC	1.25	.55
❑ 159 Jeff Paulk RC	.75	.35
❑ 160 Shawn Bryson RC	1.25	.55
❑ 161 Joe Montana CM	2.50	1.10
❑ 162 John Elway CM	1.50	.70
❑ 163 Joe Namath CM	1.50	.70
❑ 164 Jerry Rice CM	1.00	.45
❑ 165 Terry Bradshaw CM	1.25	.55
❑ 166 Jim Brown CM	1.50	.70
❑ 167 Paul Warfield CM	.30	.14
❑ 168 Herman Moore CM	.50	.23
❑ 169 Walter Payton CM	2.50	1.10
❑ 170 Roger Staubach CM	1.25	.55
❑ 171 Ken Stabler CM	1.00	.45
❑ 172A Steve Young CM	.60	.25
❑ 172B John Riggins CM ERR (Card is partially embossed)	80.00	36.00
❑ 173 Troy Aikman CM	1.00	.45
❑ 174 Fran Tarkenton CM	.60	.25
❑ 175 Doug Williams CM	.15	.07
❑ 176 Steve Largent CM	.30	.14
❑ 177 Marcus Allen CM	.30	.14
❑ 178 Mike Singletary CM	.15	.07
❑ 179 Earl Campbell CM	.30	.14
❑ 180 Dan Fouts CM	.30	.14
❑ WPAC W.Payton AUTO/50	600.00	275.00
❑ WPCL W.Payton AUTO/34 signed Jersey card	2000.00	900.00

1998 Upper Deck Encore

	MINT	NRMT
COMPLETE SET (150)	250.00	110.00

Card	MINT	NRMT
❑ 1 Peyton Manning RC	30.00	13.50
❑ 2 Ryan Leaf RC	12.00	5.50
❑ 3 Andre Wadsworth RC	4.00	1.80
❑ 4 Charles Woodson RC	10.00	4.50
❑ 5 Curtis Enis RC	8.00	3.60
❑ 6 Fred Taylor RC	15.00	6.75
❑ 7 Duane Starks RC	2.50	1.10
❑ 8 Keith Brooking RC	4.00	1.80
❑ 9 Takeo Spikes RC	4.00	1.80
❑ 10 Kevin Dyson RC	10.00	4.50
❑ 11 Robert Edwards RC	8.00	3.60
❑ 12 Randy Moss RC	30.00	13.50
❑ 13 John Avery RC	4.00	1.80
❑ 14 Marcus Nash RC	6.00	2.70
❑ 15 Jerome Pathon RC	4.00	1.80
❑ 16 Jacquez Green RC	10.00	4.50
❑ 17 Robert Holcombe RC	4.00	1.80
❑ 18 Pat Johnson RC	4.00	1.80
❑ 19 Skip Hicks RC	6.00	2.70
❑ 20 Ahman Green RC	12.00	5.50
❑ 21 Brian Griese RC	15.00	6.75
❑ 22 Hines Ward RC	4.00	1.80
❑ 23 Tavian Banks RC	4.00	1.80

❑ 24 Tony Simmons RC 4.00 1.80
❑ 25 Rashaan Shehee RC 4.00 1.80
❑ 26 R.W. McQuarters RC 2.50 1.10
❑ 27 Jon Ritchie RC 4.00 1.80
❑ 28 Ryan Sutter RC 2.50 1.10
❑ 29 Tim Dwight RC 10.00 4.50
❑ 30 Charlie Batch RC 15.00 6.75
❑ 31 Chris Chandler .40 .18
❑ 32 Jamal Anderson .75 .35
❑ 33 Terance Mathis .40 .18
❑ 34 Jake Plummer 1.50 .70
❑ 35 Mario Bates .40 .18
❑ 36 Frank Sanders .40 .18
❑ 37 Adrian Murrell .40 .18
❑ 38 Jim Harbaugh .40 .18
❑ 39 Michael Jackson .25 .11
❑ 40 Jermaine Lewis .40 .18
❑ 41 Doug Flutie 1.00 .45
❑ 42 Rob Johnson .40 .18
❑ 43 Antowain Smith .75 .35
❑ 44 Eric Moulds .75 .35
❑ 45 Thurman Thomas .75 .35
❑ 46 Kevin Greene .25 .11
❑ 47 Fred Lane .40 .18
❑ 48 Rae Carruth .40 .18
❑ 49 William Floyd .25 .11
❑ 50 Erik Kramer .25 .11
❑ 51 Edgar Bennett .25 .11
❑ 52 Curtis Conway .40 .18
❑ 53 Bobby Engram .40 .18
❑ 54 Jeff Blake .40 .18
❑ 55 Carl Pickens .75 .35
❑ 56 Darnay Scott .25 .11
❑ 57 Corey Dillon 1.00 .45
❑ 58 Troy Aikman 2.00 .90
❑ 59 Michael Irvin .75 .35
❑ 60 Emmitt Smith 3.00 1.35
❑ 61 Deion Sanders .75 .35
❑ 62 John Elway 4.00 1.80
❑ 63 Terrell Davis 3.00 1.35
❑ 64 Rod Smith WR .40 .18
❑ 65 Shannon Sharpe .40 .18
❑ 66 Ed McCaffrey .40 .18
❑ 67 Barry Sanders 4.00 1.80
❑ 68 Scott Mitchell .25 .11
❑ 69 Herman Moore .75 .35
❑ 70 Johnnie Morton .40 .18
❑ 71 Brett Favre 4.00 1.80
❑ 72 Dorsey Levens .75 .35
❑ 73 Reggie White .75 .35
❑ 74 Antonio Freeman .75 .35
❑ 75 Robert Brooks .40 .18
❑ 76 Marshall Faulk .75 .35
❑ 77 Marvin Harrison .40 .18
❑ 78 Mark Brunell 1.50 .70
❑ 79 Keenan McCardell .40 .18
❑ 80 Jimmy Smith .40 .18
❑ 81 Elvis Grbac .40 .18
❑ 82 Andre Rison .40 .18
❑ 83 Tony Gonzalez .25 .11
❑ 84 Derrick Thomas .40 .18
❑ 85 Dan Marino 4.00 1.80
❑ 86 Karim Abdul-Jabbar .75 .35
❑ 87 O.J. McDuffie .40 .18
❑ 88 Zach Thomas .40 .18
❑ 89 Brad Johnson .75 .35
❑ 90 Cris Carter .75 .35
❑ 91 Jake Reed .40 .18
❑ 92 Robert Smith .75 .35
❑ 93 John Randle .40 .18
❑ 94 Randall Cunningham .75 .35
❑ 95 Drew Bledsoe 1.50 .70
❑ 96 Terry Glenn .75 .35
❑ 97 Ben Coates .40 .18
❑ 98 Danny Wuerffel .40 .18
❑ 99 Andre Hastings .25 .11
❑ 100 Troy Davis .25 .11
❑ 101 Danny Kanell .40 .18
❑ 102 Tiki Barber .40 .18
❑ 103 Amani Toomer .40 .18
❑ 104 Vinny Testaverde .40 .18
❑ 105 Glenn Foley .40 .18
❑ 106 Curtis Martin .75 .35
❑ 107 Keyshawn Johnson .75 .35
❑ 108 Wayne Chrebet .75 .35
❑ 109 Jeff George .40 .18
❑ 110 Napoleon Kaufman .75 .35
❑ 111 Tim Brown .75 .35
❑ 112 James Jett .25 .11
❑ 113 Bobby Hoying .40 .18
❑ 114 Charlie Garner .25 .11
❑ 115 Irving Fryar .40 .18
❑ 116 Kordell Stewart .75 .35
❑ 117 Jerome Bettis .75 .35
❑ 118 Will Blackwell .25 .11
❑ 119 Charles Johnson .25 .11
❑ 120 Tony Banks .40 .18
❑ 121 Amp Lee .25 .11
❑ 122 Isaac Bruce .75 .35
❑ 123 Eddie Kennison .40 .18
❑ 124 Natrone Means .75 .35
❑ 125 Junior Seau .40 .18
❑ 126 Bryan Still .25 .11
❑ 127 Steve Young 1.00 .45
❑ 128 Jerry Rice 2.00 .90
❑ 129 Garrison Hearst .75 .35
❑ 130 J.J. Stokes .40 .18
❑ 131 Terrell Owens .75 .35
❑ 132 Warren Moon .25 .11
❑ 133 Jon Kitna 1.00 .45
❑ 134 Ricky Watters .40 .18
❑ 135 Joey Galloway .75 .35
❑ 136 Trent Dilfer .75 .35
❑ 137 Warrick Dunn .75 .35
❑ 138 Mike Alstott .75 .35
❑ 139 Bert Emanuel .40 .18
❑ 140 Reidel Anthony .40 .18
❑ 141 Steve McNair .75 .35
❑ 142 Yancey Thigpen .25 .11
❑ 143 Eddie George 1.50 .70
❑ 144 Chris Sanders .25 .11
❑ 145 Gus Frerotte .25 .11
❑ 146 Terry Allen .75 .35
❑ 147 Michael Westbrook .40 .18
❑ 148 Troy Aikman CL .75 .35
❑ 149 Dan Marino CL 1.00 .45
❑ 150 Randy Moss CL 8.00 3.60

1999 Upper Deck Encore

	MINT	NRMT
COMPLETE SET (225)	250.00	110.00
COMP.SET w/o SP's (180)	50.00	22.00

❑ 1 Jake Plummer 1.25 .55
❑ 2 Adrian Murrell .40 .18
❑ 3 Rob Moore .40 .18
❑ 4 Simeon Rice .20 .09
❑ 5 Andre Wadsworth .20 .09
❑ 6 Frank Sanders .40 .18
❑ 7 Tim Dwight .75 .35
❑ 8 Chris Chandler .40 .18
❑ 9 Jamal Anderson .75 .35
❑ 10 O.J. Santiago .40 .18
❑ 11 Tony Graziani .20 .09
❑ 12 Terance Mathis .40 .18
❑ 13 Priest Holmes .75 .35
❑ 14 Stoney Case .20 .09
❑ 15 Ray Lewis .40 .18
❑ 16 Peter Boulware .20 .09
❑ 17 Errict Rhett .40 .18
❑ 18 Jermaine Lewis .40 .18
❑ 19 Eric Moulds .75 .35
❑ 20 Doug Flutie 1.00 .45
❑ 21 Antowain Smith .75 .35
❑ 22 Rob Johnson .40 .18
❑ 23 Bruce Smith .40 .18
❑ 24 Andre Reed .40 .18
❑ 25 Wesley Walls .40 .18
❑ 26 Tim Biakabutuka .40 .18
❑ 27 Fred Lane .40 .18
❑ 28 Steve Beuerlein .40 .18
❑ 29 Muhsin Muhammad .40 .18
❑ 30 Rae Carruth .20 .09
❑ 31 Bobby Engram .40 .18
❑ 32 Curtis Enis .75 .35
❑ 33 Edgar Bennett .20 .09
❑ 34 Curtis Conway .40 .18
❑ 35 Shane Matthews .75 .35
❑ 36 Tony McGee .20 .09
❑ 37 Darnay Scott .40 .18
❑ 38 Jeff Blake .40 .18
❑ 39 Corey Dillon .75 .35
❑ 40 Ki-Jana Carter .20 .09
❑ 41 Ty Detmer .40 .18
❑ 42 Leslie Shepherd .20 .09
❑ 43 Terry Kirby .40 .18
❑ 44 Antonio Langham .20 .09
❑ 45 Jamir Miller .20 .09
❑ 46 Marc Edwards .20 .09
❑ 47 Troy Aikman 2.00 .90
❑ 48 Rocket Ismail .40 .18
❑ 49 Emmitt Smith 2.00 .90
❑ 50 Michael Irvin .40 .18
❑ 51 Deion Sanders .75 .35
❑ 52 Greg Ellis .20 .09
❑ 53 Bubby Brister .40 .18
❑ 54 Terrell Davis 2.00 .90
❑ 55 Ed McCaffrey .40 .18
❑ 56 Rod Smith .40 .18
❑ 57 Shannon Sharpe .40 .18
❑ 58 Brian Griese 1.50 .70
❑ 59 Charlie Batch 1.50 .70
❑ 60 Germane Crowell .40 .18
❑ 61 Johnnie Morton .40 .18
❑ 62 Robert Porcher .20 .09
❑ 63 Ron Rivers .20 .09
❑ 64 Herman Moore .75 .35
❑ 65 Brett Favre 3.00 1.35
❑ 66 Bill Schroeder .75 .35
❑ 67 Antonio Freeman .75 .35
❑ 68 Dorsey Levens .75 .35
❑ 69 Desmond Howard .40 .18
❑ 70 Vonnie Holliday .40 .18
❑ 71 Peyton Manning 2.50 1.10
❑ 72 Jerome Pathon .40 .18
❑ 73 Marvin Harrison .75 .35
❑ 74 Ken Dilger .40 .18
❑ 75 E.G. Green .20 .09
❑ 76 Cornelius Bennett .20 .09
❑ 77 Mark Brunell 1.25 .55
❑ 78 Fred Taylor 2.00 .90
❑ 79 Jimmy Smith .40 .18
❑ 80 James Stewart .40 .18
❑ 81 Keenan McCardell .40 .18
❑ 82 Carnell Lake .20 .09
❑ 83 Elvis Grbac .40 .18
❑ 84 Tony Gonzalez .40 .18
❑ 85 Andre Rison .40 .18
❑ 86 Derrick Thomas .40 .18
❑ 87 Warren Moon .75 .35
❑ 88 Derrick Alexander WR .40 .18
❑ 89 Dan Marino 3.00 1.35
❑ 90 O.J. McDuffie .40 .18
❑ 91 Karim Abdul-Jabbar .40 .18
❑ 92 Sam Madison .20 .09
❑ 93 Zach Thomas .40 .18
❑ 94 Tony Martin .40 .18
❑ 95 Randall Cunningham .75 .35
❑ 96 Randy Moss 2.50 1.10
❑ 97 Cris Carter .75 .35
❑ 98 Jake Reed .40 .18
❑ 99 John Randle .40 .18
❑ 100 Robert Smith .75 .35
❑ 101 Drew Bledsoe 1.25 .55
❑ 102 Ben Coates .40 .18
❑ 103 Terry Glenn .40 .18
❑ 104 Tony Simmons .20 .09

❑ 105 Terry Allen .40 .18
❑ 106 Danny Wuerffel .20 .09
❑ 107 Cameron Cleeland .20 .09
❑ 108 Eddie Kennison .40 .18
❑ 109 Billy Joe Hobert .20 .09
❑ 110 Andre Hastings .20 .09
❑ 111 Kent Graham .20 .09
❑ 112 Tiki Barber .40 .18
❑ 113 Gary Brown .20 .09
❑ 114 Ike Hilliard .40 .18
❑ 115 Jason Sehorn .20 .09
❑ 116 Kerry Collins .40 .18
❑ 117 Vinny Testaverde .40 .18
❑ 118 Wayne Chrebet .75 .35
❑ 119 Curtis Martin .75 .35
❑ 120 Rick Mirer .40 .18
❑ 121 Aaron Glenn .20 .09
❑ 122 Keyshawn Johnson .75 .35
❑ 123 Rich Gannon .40 .18
❑ 124 Tim Brown .75 .35
❑ 125 Darrell Russell .20 .09
❑ 126 Tyrone Wheatley .75 .35
❑ 127 Charles Woodson .75 .35
❑ 128 Napoleon Kaufman .75 .35
❑ 129 Duce Staley .75 .35
❑ 130 Doug Pederson .20 .09
❑ 131 Kevin Turner .20 .09
❑ 132 Charles Johnson .20 .09
❑ 133 Jerome Bettis .75 .35
❑ 134 Courtney Hawkins .20 .09
❑ 135 Kordell Stewart .75 .35
❑ 136 Richard Huntley .75 .35
❑ 137 Levon Kirkland .20 .09
❑ 138 Hines Ward .20 .09
❑ 139 Kurt Warner RC 20.00 9.00
❑ 140 Marshall Faulk .75 .35
❑ 141 Az-Zahir Hakim .40 .18
❑ 142 Amp Lee .20 .09
❑ 143 Isaac Bruce .75 .35
❑ 144 Kevin Carter .20 .09
❑ 145 Jim Harbaugh .40 .18
❑ 146 Junior Seau .20 .09
❑ 147 Natrone Means .40 .18
❑ 148 Rodney Harrison .20 .09
❑ 149 Mikhael Ricks .20 .09
❑ 150 Erik Kramer .20 .09
❑ 151 Steve Young 1.25 .55
❑ 152 Terrell Owens .75 .35
❑ 153 Jerry Rice 2.00 .90
❑ 154 J.J. Stokes .40 .18
❑ 155 Jeff Garcia RC 15.00 6.75
❑ 156 Lawrence Phillips .40 .18
❑ 157 Jon Kitna .75 .35
❑ 158 Derrick Mayes .40 .18
❑ 159 Ricky Watters .40 .18
❑ 160 Chad Brown .20 .09
❑ 161 Shawn Springs .20 .09
❑ 162 Sean Dawkins .20 .09
❑ 163 Trent Dilfer .40 .18
❑ 164 Reidel Anthony .40 .18
❑ 165 Bert Emanuel .40 .18
❑ 166 Warrick Dunn .75 .35
❑ 167 Jacquez Green .20 .09
❑ 168 Mike Alstott .75 .35
❑ 169 Eddie George 1.00 .45
❑ 170 Steve McNair .75 .35
❑ 171 Kevin Dyson .40 .18
❑ 172 Frank Wycheck .20 .09
❑ 173 Blaine Bishop .20 .09
❑ 174 Yancey Thigpen .40 .18
❑ 175 Brad Johnson .75 .35
❑ 176 Michael Westbrook .40 .18
❑ 177 Skip Hicks .40 .18
❑ 178 Brian Mitchell .20 .09
❑ 179 Dana Stubblefield .20 .09
❑ 180 Stephen Davis .75 .35
❑ 181 Champ Bailey RC 5.00 2.20
❑ 182 Chris McAlister RC 3.00 1.35
❑ 183 Jevon Kearse RC 8.00 3.60
❑ 184 Ebenezer Ekuban RC 3.00 1.35
❑ 185 Chris Claiborne RC 3.00 1.35
❑ 186 Andy Katzenmoyer RC 4.00 1.80
❑ 187 Tim Couch RC 12.00 5.50
❑ 188 Daunte Culpepper RC 20.00 9.00
❑ 189 Akili Smith RC 8.00 3.60
❑ 190 Donovan McNabb RC 15.00 6.75
❑ 191 Sean Bennett RC 4.00 1.80
❑ 192 Brock Huard RC 6.00 2.70
❑ 193 Cade McNown RC 5.00 2.20
❑ 194 Shaun King RC 8.00 3.60
❑ 195 Joe Germaine RC 4.00 1.80
❑ 196 Ricky Williams RC 15.00 6.75
❑ 197 Edgerrin James RC 20.00 9.00
❑ 198 Sedrick Irvin RC 4.00 1.80
❑ 199 Kevin Faulk RC 6.00 2.70
❑ 200 Rob Konrad RC 4.00 1.80
❑ 201 James Johnson RC 4.00 1.80
❑ 202 Amos Zereoue RC 4.00 1.80
❑ 203 Torry Holt RC 10.00 4.50
❑ 204 D'Wayne Bates RC 3.00 1.35
❑ 205 David Boston RC 8.00 3.60
❑ 206 Dameane Douglas RC 3.00 1.35
❑ 207 Troy Edwards RC 5.00 2.20
❑ 208 Kevin Johnson RC 8.00 3.60
❑ 209 Peerless Price RC 5.00 2.20
❑ 210 Antoine Winfield RC 3.00 1.35
❑ 211 Mike Cloud RC 4.00 1.80
❑ 212 Joe Montgomery RC 4.00 1.80
❑ 213 Jermaine Fazande RC 4.00 1.80
❑ 214 Scott Covington RC 4.00 1.80
❑ 215 Aaron Brooks RC 15.00 6.75
❑ 216 Terry Jackson RC 3.00 1.35
❑ 217 Cecil Collins RC 4.00 1.80
❑ 218 Olandis Gary RC 8.00 3.60
❑ 219 Craig Yeast RC 3.00 1.35
❑ 220 Karsten Bailey RC 3.00 1.35
❑ 221 Reginald Kelly RC 3.00 1.35
❑ 222 Travis McGriff RC 3.00 1.35
❑ 223 Jeff Paulk RC 3.00 1.35
❑ 224 Jim Kleinsasser RC 4.00 1.80
❑ 225 Jason Tucker RC 5.00 2.20
❑ WPE Walter Payton 2000.00 900.00
Jersey AUTO/34

2000 Upper Deck Encore

	MINT	NRMT
COMPLETE SET (270)	150.00	70.00
COMP.SET w/o SP's (225)	15.00	6.75

❑ 1 Jake Plummer .50 .23
❑ 2 Michael Pittman .15 .07
❑ 3 Rob Moore .25 .11
❑ 4 David Boston .25 .11
❑ 5 Frank Sanders .25 .11
❑ 6 Aeneas Williams .15 .07
❑ 7 Kwamie Lassiter .15 .07
❑ 8 Rob Fredrickson .15 .07
❑ 9 Tim Dwight .50 .23
❑ 10 Chris Chandler .25 .11
❑ 11 Jamal Anderson .50 .23
❑ 12 Shawn Jefferson .15 .07
❑ 13 Brian Finneran RC 2.50 1.10
❑ 14 Terance Mathis .25 .11
❑ 15 Bob Christian .15 .07
❑ 16 Qadry Ismail .25 .11
❑ 17 Jermaine Lewis .25 .11
❑ 18 Rod Woodson .25 .11
❑ 19 Michael McCrary .15 .07
❑ 20 Tony Banks .25 .11
❑ 21 Peter Boulware .15 .07
❑ 22 Shannon Sharpe .25 .11
❑ 23 Peerless Price .50 .23
❑ 24 Rob Johnson .25 .11
❑ 25 Eric Moulds .50 .23
❑ 26 Doug Flutie .60 .25
❑ 27 Jeremy McDaniel .25 .11
❑ 28 Antowain Smith .25 .11
❑ 29 Shawn Bryson .15 .07
❑ 30 Muhsin Muhammad .25 .11
❑ 31 Donald Hayes .15 .07
❑ 32 Steve Beuerlein .25 .11
❑ 33 Reggie White .50 .23
❑ 34 Tim Biakabutuka .25 .11
❑ 35 Michael Bates .15 .07
❑ 36 Chuck Smith .15 .07
❑ 37 Wesley Walls .15 .07
❑ 38 Cade McNown .50 .23
❑ 39 Curtis Enis .25 .11
❑ 40 Marcus Robinson .50 .23
❑ 41 Eddie Kennison .25 .11
❑ 42 Bobby Engram .15 .07
❑ 43 Glyn Milburn .15 .07
❑ 44 Marty Booker .15 .07
❑ 45 Akili Smith .50 .23
❑ 46 Corey Dillon .50 .23
❑ 47 James Allen .25 .11
❑ 48 Tremain Mack .15 .07
❑ 49 Damon Griffin .15 .07
❑ 50 Takeo Spikes .15 .07
❑ 51 Tony McGee .15 .07
❑ 52 Tim Couch 1.00 .45
❑ 53 Kevin Johnson .50 .23
❑ 54 Darrin Chiaverini .15 .07
❑ 55 Jamir Miller .15 .07
❑ 56 Errict Rhett .15 .07
❑ 57 Aaron Shea RC 2.50 1.10
❑ 58 Kevin Thompson RC .50 .23
❑ 59 Troy Aikman 1.25 .55
❑ 60 Emmitt Smith 1.25 .55
❑ 61 Rocket Ismail .25 .11
❑ 62 Jason Tucker .25 .11
❑ 63 Chris Brazzell RC .25 .11
❑ 64 Joey Galloway .50 .23
❑ 65 Wane McGarity .15 .07
❑ 66 Terrell Davis 1.25 .55
❑ 67 Olandis Gary .50 .23
❑ 68 Brian Griese .60 .25
❑ 69 Gus Frerotte .25 .11
❑ 70 Byron Chamberlain .15 .07
❑ 71 Ed McCaffrey .50 .23
❑ 72 Rod Smith .25 .11
❑ 73 Al Wilson .15 .07
❑ 74 Charlie Batch .50 .23
❑ 75 Germane Crowell .25 .11
❑ 76 Sedrick Irvin .15 .07
❑ 77 Johnnie Morton .25 .11
❑ 78 Robert Porcher .15 .07
❑ 79 Herman Moore .25 .11
❑ 80 James Stewart .25 .11
❑ 81 Brett Favre 2.00 .90
❑ 82 Antonio Freeman .50 .23
❑ 83 Bill Schroeder .25 .11
❑ 84 Dorsey Levens .25 .11
❑ 85 Herbert Goodman RC .25 .11
❑ 86 Ahman Green .25 .11
❑ 87 Matt Hasselbeck .25 .11
❑ 88 Peyton Manning 1.50 .70
❑ 89 Edgerrin James 2.00 .90
❑ 90 Marvin Harrison .50 .23
❑ 91 Basil Mitchell .15 .07
❑ 92 Terrence Wilkins .50 .23
❑ 93 Abdul-Karim Al-Jabbar .25 .11
❑ 94 Ken Dilger .15 .07
❑ 95 Mark Brunell .75 .35
❑ 96 Fred Taylor .60 .25
❑ 97 Jimmy Smith .25 .11
❑ 98 Keenan McCardell .25 .11
❑ 99 Stacey Mack .15 .07
❑ 100 Jonathan Quinn .15 .07
❑ 101 Kyle Brady .15 .07
❑ 102 Hardy Nickerson .15 .07
❑ 103 Elvis Grbac .25 .11
❑ 104 Tony Gonzalez .25 .11
❑ 105 Derrick Alexander WR .25 .11
❑ 106 Tony Richardson RC .15 .07
❑ 107 Michael Cloud .15 .07
❑ 108 Donnie Edwards .15 .07
❑ 109 Jay Fiedler .50 .23

Card	MINT	NRMT
❑ 110 James Johnson	.25	.11
❑ 111 Tony Martin	.25	.11
❑ 112 Damon Huard	.50	.23
❑ 113 Lamar Smith	.25	.11
❑ 114 Thurman Thomas	.25	.11
❑ 115 Mike Quinn	.15	.07
❑ 116 Oronde Gadsden	.25	.11
❑ 117 Randy Moss	1.50	.70
❑ 118 Robert Smith	.50	.23
❑ 119 Cris Carter	.50	.23
❑ 120 Matthew Hatchette	.25	.11
❑ 121 Daunte Culpepper	1.00	.45
❑ 122 Moe Williams	.15	.07
❑ 123 Drew Bledsoe	.75	.35
❑ 124 Terry Glenn	.25	.11
❑ 125 Troy Brown	.15	.07
❑ 126 Kevin Faulk	.25	.11
❑ 127 Lawyer Milloy	.15	.07
❑ 128 Ricky Williams	1.25	.55
❑ 129 Keith Poole	.15	.07
❑ 130 Jake Reed	.25	.11
❑ 131 Jake Delhomme RC	.50	.23
❑ 132 Jeff Blake	.25	.11
❑ 133 Andrew Glover	.15	.07
❑ 134 Kerry Collins	.25	.11
❑ 135 Amani Toomer	.15	.07
❑ 136 Joe Montgomery	.15	.07
❑ 137 Ike Hilliard	.25	.11
❑ 138 Tiki Barber	.25	.11
❑ 139 Pete Mitchell	.15	.07
❑ 140 Ray Lucas	.50	.23
❑ 141 Mo Lewis	.15	.07
❑ 142 Curtis Martin	.50	.23
❑ 143 Vinny Testaverde	.25	.11
❑ 144 Wayne Chrebet	.25	.11
❑ 145 Dedric Ward	.15	.07
❑ 146 Tim Brown	.50	.23
❑ 147 Rich Gannon	.25	.11
❑ 148 Tyrone Wheatley	.25	.11
❑ 149 Napoleon Kaufman	.25	.11
❑ 150 Charles Woodson	.25	.11
❑ 151 Darrell Russell	.15	.07
❑ 152 James Jett	.15	.07
❑ 153 Rickey Dudley	.15	.07
❑ 154 Jon Ritchie	.15	.07
❑ 155 Duce Staley	.50	.23
❑ 156 Donovan McNabb	.75	.35
❑ 157 Torrance Small	.15	.07
❑ 158 Ron Powlus RC	3.00	1.35
❑ 159 Mike Mamula	.15	.07
❑ 160 Dameane Douglas	.15	.07
❑ 161 Charles Johnson	.25	.11
❑ 162 Kent Graham	.15	.07
❑ 163 Troy Edwards	.25	.11
❑ 164 Jerome Bettis	.50	.23
❑ 165 Hines Ward	.15	.07
❑ 166 Kordell Stewart	.50	.23
❑ 167 Levon Kirkland	.15	.07
❑ 168 Bobby Shaw RC	.50	.23
❑ 169 Marshall Faulk	.60	.25
❑ 170 Kurt Warner	2.00	.90
❑ 171 Torry Holt	.50	.23
❑ 172 Isaac Bruce	.50	.23
❑ 173 Kevin Carter	.15	.07
❑ 174 Az-Zahir Hakim	.15	.07
❑ 175 Ricky Proehl	.15	.07
❑ 176 Robert Chancey	.15	.07
❑ 177 Curtis Conway	.25	.11
❑ 178 Freddie Jones	.15	.07
❑ 179 Junior Seau	.25	.11
❑ 180 Jeff Graham	.15	.07
❑ 181 Reggie Jones RC	.50	.23
❑ 182 Rodney Harrison	.15	.07
❑ 183 Rick Mirer	.25	.11
❑ 184 Jerry Rice	1.25	.55
❑ 185 Charlie Garner	.15	.07
❑ 186 Terrell Owens	.50	.23
❑ 187 Jeff Garcia	.50	.23
❑ 188 Fred Beasley	.15	.07
❑ 189 J.J. Stokes	.25	.11
❑ 190 Ricky Watters	.25	.11
❑ 191 Jon Kitna	.50	.23
❑ 192 Derrick Mayes	.25	.11
❑ 193 Sean Dawkins	.15	.07
❑ 194 Charlie Rogers	.15	.07
❑ 195 Brock Huard	.25	.11
❑ 196 Cortez Kennedy	.15	.07
❑ 197 Christian Fauria	.15	.07
❑ 198 Warrick Dunn	.50	.23
❑ 199 Shaun King	.75	.35
❑ 200 Mike Alstott	.50	.23
❑ 201 Warren Sapp	.25	.11
❑ 202 Jacquez Green	.25	.11
❑ 203 Reidel Anthony	.15	.07
❑ 204 Dave Moore	.15	.07
❑ 205 Keyshawn Johnson	.50	.23
❑ 206 Eddie George	.60	.25
❑ 207 Steve McNair	.50	.23
❑ 208 Billy Volek RC	.25	.11
❑ 209 Jevon Kearse	.50	.23
❑ 210 Yancey Thigpen	.15	.07
❑ 211 Frank Wycheck	.15	.07
❑ 212 Carl Pickens	.25	.11
❑ 213 Neil O'Donnell	.15	.07
❑ 214 Brad Johnson	.50	.23
❑ 215 Stephen Davis	.50	.23
❑ 216 Michael Westbrook	.25	.11
❑ 217 Albert Connell	.15	.07
❑ 218 Aaron Stecker RC	3.00	1.35
❑ 219 Bruce Smith	.25	.11
❑ 220 Stephen Alexander	.15	.07
❑ 221 Jeff George	.25	.11
❑ 222 Adrian Murrell	.15	.07
❑ 223 Courtney Brown RC	4.00	1.80
❑ 224 John Engelberger RC	2.50	1.10
❑ 225 Deltha O'Neal RC	2.50	1.10
❑ 226 Corey Simon RC	4.00	1.80
❑ 227 R.Jay Soward RC	3.00	1.35
❑ 228 Chris Samuels RC	2.50	1.10
❑ 229 Avion Black RC	2.50	1.10
❑ 230 Doug Chapman RC	6.00	2.70
❑ 231 Darrell Jackson RC	4.00	1.80
❑ 232 Chris Cole RC	2.50	1.10
❑ 233 Trevor Gaylor RC	3.00	1.35
❑ 234 Chad Morton RC	3.00	1.35
❑ 235 Chris Redman RC	6.00	2.70
❑ 236 Joe Hamilton RC	4.00	1.80
❑ 237 Chad Pennington RC	10.00	4.50
❑ 238 Tee Martin RC	5.00	2.20
❑ 239 Giovanni Carmazzi RC	4.00	1.80
❑ 240 Tim Rattay RC	5.00	2.20
❑ 241 Ron Dayne RC	10.00	4.50
❑ 242 Shaun Alexander RC	8.00	3.60
❑ 243 Thomas Jones RC	5.00	2.20
❑ 244 Reuben Droughns RC	3.00	1.35
❑ 245 Jamal Lewis RC	15.00	6.75
❑ 246 Michael Wiley RC	3.00	1.35
❑ 247 J.R. Redmond RC	4.00	1.80
❑ 248 Travis Prentice RC	5.00	2.20
❑ 249 Todd Husak RC	3.00	1.35
❑ 250 Trung Canidate RC	3.00	1.35
❑ 251 Brian Urlacher RC	10.00	4.50
❑ 252 Anthony Becht RC	3.00	1.35
❑ 253 Bubba Franks RC	4.00	1.80
❑ 254 Tom Brady RC	3.00	1.35
❑ 255 Peter Warrick RC	10.00	4.50
❑ 256 Plaxico Burress RC	6.00	2.70
❑ 257 Sylvester Morris RC	6.00	2.70
❑ 258 Dez White RC	2.50	1.10
❑ 259 Travis Taylor RC	4.00	1.80
❑ 260 Todd Pinkston RC	3.00	1.35
❑ 261 Dennis Northcutt RC	4.00	1.80
❑ 262 Jerry Porter RC	3.00	1.35
❑ 263 Laveranues Coles RC	5.00	2.20
❑ 264 Danny Farmer RC	3.00	1.35
❑ 265 Curtis Keaton RC	2.50	1.10
❑ 266 Windrell Hayes RC	2.50	1.10
❑ 267 Ron Dugans RC	2.50	1.10
❑ 268 Steve McNair CL	.25	.11
❑ 269 Jake Plummer CL	.25	.11
❑ 270 Antonio Freeman CL	.25	.11
❑ 271 Brad Hoover		
❑ 272 Charles Lee		
❑ 273 Deon Dyer		
❑ 274 Doug Johnson		
❑ 275 JaJuan Dawson		
❑ 276 Jarious Jackson		
❑ 277 Larry Foster		
❑ 278 Mike Anderson		
❑ 279 Ron Dixon		
❑ 280 Sammy Morris		
❑ 281 Shyrone Stith		
❑ 282 Spergon Wynn		
❑ 283 Troy Walters		

2000 Upper Deck Gold Reserve

	MINT	NRMT
COMP.SET w/o SP's	25.00	11.00
❑ 1 Jake Plummer	.60	.25
❑ 2 Rob Moore	.30	.14
❑ 3 David Boston	.60	.25
❑ 4 Frank Sanders	.30	.14
❑ 5 Chris Chandler	.30	.14
❑ 6 Jamal Anderson	.60	.25
❑ 7 Shawn Jefferson	.15	.07
❑ 8 Terance Mathis	.30	.14
❑ 9 Qadry Ismail	.30	.14
❑ 10 Jermaine Lewis	.30	.14
❑ 11 Tony Banks	.30	.14
❑ 12 Peter Boulware	.15	.07
❑ 13 Shannon Sharpe	.30	.14
❑ 14 Peerless Price	.60	.25
❑ 15 Rob Johnson	.30	.14
❑ 16 Eric Moulds	.60	.25
❑ 17 Doug Flutie	.75	.35
❑ 18 Antowain Smith	.30	.14
❑ 19 Muhsin Muhammad	.30	.14
❑ 20 Patrick Jeffers	.60	.25
❑ 21 Steve Beuerlein	.30	.14
❑ 22 Natrone Means	.30	.14
❑ 23 Tim Biakabutuka	.30	.14
❑ 24 Wesley Walls	.15	.07
❑ 25 Cade McNown	.60	.25
❑ 26 Curtis Enis	.60	.25
❑ 27 Marcus Robinson	.60	.25
❑ 28 Eddie Kennison	.30	.14
❑ 29 Bobby Engram	.30	.14
❑ 30 Akili Smith	.60	.25
❑ 31 Corey Dillon	.60	.25
❑ 32 Damon Griffin	.15	.07
❑ 33 Takeo Spikes	.15	.07
❑ 34 Tony McGee	.15	.07
❑ 35 Tim Couch	1.25	.55
❑ 36 Kevin Johnson	.60	.25
❑ 37 Darrin Chiaverini	.15	.07
❑ 38 Errict Rhett	.30	.14
❑ 39 Troy Aikman	1.50	.70
❑ 40 Emmitt Smith	1.50	.70
❑ 41 Rocket Ismail	.30	.14
❑ 42 Jason Tucker	.30	.14
❑ 43 Joey Galloway	.60	.25
❑ 44 Wane McGarity	.15	.07
❑ 45 Terrell Davis	1.50	.70
❑ 46 Olandis Gary	.60	.25
❑ 47 Brian Griese	.75	.35
❑ 48 Gus Frerotte	.15	.07
❑ 49 Ed McCaffrey	.60	.25
❑ 50 Rod Smith	.30	.14
❑ 51 Charlie Batch	.60	.25
❑ 52 Germane Crowell	.30	.14
❑ 53 Johnnie Morton	.30	.14
❑ 54 Robert Porcher	.15	.07
❑ 55 Herman Moore	.30	.14
❑ 56 James Stewart	.30	.14
❑ 57 Brett Favre	2.50	1.10
❑ 58 Antonio Freeman	.60	.25
❑ 59 Bill Schroeder	.15	.07

❑ 60 Dorsey Levens .30 .14
❑ 61 Corey Bradford .15 .07
❑ 62 Vonnie Holliday .15 .07
❑ 63 Peyton Manning 2.00 .90
❑ 64 Edgerrin James 2.50 1.10
❑ 65 Marvin Harrison .60 .25
❑ 66 Ken Dilger .15 .07
❑ 67 Terrence Wilkins .60 .25
❑ 68 Marcus Pollard .15 .07
❑ 69 Mark Brunell 1.00 .45
❑ 70 Fred Taylor .75 .35
❑ 71 Jimmy Smith .30 .14
❑ 72 Keenan McCardell .30 .14
❑ 73 Carnell Lake .15 .07
❑ 74 Kyle Brady .15 .07
❑ 75 Hardy Nickerson .15 .07
❑ 76 Elvis Grbac .30 .14
❑ 77 Tony Gonzalez .30 .14
❑ 78 Derrick Alexander .30 .14
❑ 79 Donnell Bennett .15 .07
❑ 80 Mike Cloud .15 .07
❑ 81 Donnie Edwards .15 .07
❑ 82 Jay Fiedler .60 .25
❑ 83 James Johnson .30 .14
❑ 84 Tony Martin .30 .14
❑ 85 Damon Huard .60 .25
❑ 86 O.J. McDuffie .30 .14
❑ 87 Thurman Thomas .30 .14
❑ 88 Oronde Gadsden .30 .14
❑ 89 Randy Moss 2.00 .90
❑ 90 Robert Smith .60 .25
❑ 91 Cris Carter .60 .25
❑ 92 Daunte Culpepper 1.25 .55
❑ 93 Matthew Hatchette .15 .07
❑ 94 Drew Bledsoe 1.00 .45
❑ 95 Terry Glenn .30 .14
❑ 96 Troy Brown .15 .07
❑ 97 Kevin Faulk .30 .14
❑ 98 Lawyer Milloy .15 .07
❑ 99 Ricky Williams 1.50 .70
❑ 100 Keith Poole .30 .14
❑ 101 Jake Reed .30 .14
❑ 102 Jeff Blake .30 .14
❑ 103 Andrew Glover .15 .07
❑ 104 Kerry Collins .30 .14
❑ 105 Amani Toomer .30 .14
❑ 106 Joe Montgomery .15 .07
❑ 107 Ike Hilliard .30 .14
❑ 108 Tiki Barber .30 .14
❑ 109 Ray Lucas .60 .25
❑ 110 Mo Lewis .15 .07
❑ 111 Curtis Martin .60 .25
❑ 112 Vinny Testaverde .30 .14
❑ 113 Wayne Chrebet .30 .14
❑ 114 Dedric Ward .15 .07
❑ 115 Tim Brown .60 .25
❑ 116 Rich Gannon .30 .14
❑ 117 Tyrone Wheatley .30 .14
❑ 118 Napoleon Kaufman .30 .14
❑ 119 Charles Woodson .30 .14
❑ 120 James Jett .15 .07
❑ 121 Rickey Dudley .15 .07
❑ 122 Duce Staley .60 .25
❑ 123 Donovan McNabb 1.00 .45
❑ 124 Torrance Small .15 .07
❑ 125 Allen Rossum .15 .07
❑ 126 Na Brown .15 .07
❑ 127 Charles Johnson .30 .14
❑ 128 Kent Graham .15 .07
❑ 129 Troy Edwards .30 .14
❑ 130 Jerome Bettis .60 .25
❑ 131 Hines Ward .15 .07
❑ 132 Kordell Stewart .60 .25
❑ 133 Richard Huntley .15 .07
❑ 134 Marshall Faulk .75 .35
❑ 135 Kurt Warner 2.50 1.10
❑ 136 Torry Holt .60 .25
❑ 137 Isaac Bruce .60 .25
❑ 138 Kevin Carter .15 .07
❑ 139 Az-Zahir Hakim .15 .07
❑ 140 Jermaine Fazande .15 .07
❑ 141 Curtis Conway .30 .14
❑ 142 Freddie Jones .15 .07
❑ 143 Junior Seau .30 .14
❑ 144 Jeff Graham .15 .07
❑ 145 Jim Harbaugh .30 .14
❑ 146 Jerry Rice 1.50 .70
❑ 147 Charlie Garner .30 .14
❑ 148 Terrell Owens .60 .25
❑ 149 Jeff Garcia .60 .25
❑ 150 J.J. Stokes .30 .14
❑ 151 Ricky Watters .15 .07
❑ 152 Jon Kitna .60 .25
❑ 153 Derrick Mayes .30 .14
❑ 154 Sean Dawkins .15 .07
❑ 155 Charlie Rogers .15 .07
❑ 156 Cortez Kennedy .15 .07
❑ 157 Warrick Dunn .60 .25
❑ 158 Shaun King 1.00 .45
❑ 159 Mike Alstott .60 .25
❑ 160 Warren Sapp .30 .14
❑ 161 Jacquez Green .30 .14
❑ 162 Reidel Anthony .15 .07
❑ 163 Keyshawn Johnson .60 .25
❑ 164 Eddie George .75 .35
❑ 165 Steve McNair .60 .25
❑ 166 Kevin Dyson .30 .14
❑ 167 Jevon Kearse .60 .25
❑ 168 Yancey Thigpen .15 .07
❑ 169 Isaac Byrd .15 .07
❑ 170 Neil O'Donnell .15 .07
❑ 171 Brad Johnson .60 .25
❑ 172 Stephen Davis .60 .25
❑ 173 Michael Westbrook .30 .14
❑ 174 Albert Connell .15 .07
❑ 175 Bruce Smith .30 .14
❑ 176 Stephen Alexander .30 .14
❑ 177 Jeff George .30 .14
❑ 178 Bubba Franks RC 6.00 2.70
❑ 179 Brian Urlacher RC 15.00 6.75
❑ 180 Chad Pennington RC 15.00 6.75
❑ 181 Tim Rattay RC 8.00 3.60
❑ 182 Chris Redman RC 10.00 4.50
❑ 183 Corey Simon RC 6.00 2.70
❑ 184 Courtney Brown RC 6.00 2.70
❑ 185 Curtis Keaton RC 4.00 1.80
❑ 186 Danny Farmer RC 5.00 2.20
❑ 187 Erron Kinney RC 5.00 2.20
❑ 188 Deltha O'Neal RC 4.00 1.80
❑ 189 Dennis Northcutt RC 6.00 2.70
❑ 190 Dez White RC 4.00 1.80
❑ 191 Frank Murphy RC 2.50 1.10
❑ 192 Gari Scott RC 4.00 1.80
❑ 193 Giovanni Carmazzi RC 6.00 2.70
❑ 194 J.R. Redmond RC 6.00 2.70
❑ 195 JaJuan Dawson RC 5.00 2.20
❑ 196 Jamal Lewis RC 25.00 11.00
❑ 197 Jerry Porter RC 5.00 2.20
❑ 198 Joe Hamilton RC 6.00 2.70
❑ 199 Laveranues Coles RC 8.00 3.60
❑ 200 Michael Wiley RC 5.00 2.20
❑ 201 Peter Warrick RC 15.00 6.75
❑ 202 Plaxico Burress RC 10.00 4.50
❑ 203 R.Jay Soward RC 5.00 2.20
❑ 204 Reuben Droughns RC 5.00 2.20
❑ 205 Rob Morris RC 4.00 1.80
❑ 206 Ron Dayne RC 15.00 6.75
❑ 207 Ron Dugans RC 4.00 1.80
❑ 208 Sebastian Janikowski RC 5.00 2.20
❑ 209 Shaun Alexander RC 12.00 5.50
❑ 210 Sylvester Morris RC 10.00 4.50
❑ 211 Tee Martin RC 8.00 3.60
❑ 212 Thomas Jones RC 8.00 3.60
❑ 213 Todd Husak RC 5.00 2.20
❑ 214 Todd Pinkston RC 5.00 2.20
❑ 215 Tom Brady RC 5.00 2.20
❑ 216 Travis Prentice RC 8.00 3.60
❑ 217 Travis Taylor RC 6.00 2.70
❑ 218 Trevor Gaylor RC 4.00 1.80
❑ 219 Trung Canidate RC 5.00 2.20
❑ 223 Peyton Manning CL 1.00 .45
❑ 224 Randy Moss CL 1.00 .45
❑ 225 Kurt Warner CL 1.25 .55

1999 Upper Deck HoloGrFX

	MINT	NRMT
COMPLETE SET (89)	60.00	27.00

❑ 1 Jake Plummer 1.50 .70

❑ 2 Jamal Anderson .50 .23
❑ 3 Priest Holmes .50 .23
❑ 4 Antowain Smith .50 .23
❑ 5 Doug Flutie .75 .35
❑ 6 Tim Biakabutuka .40 .18
❑ 7 Curtis Enis .50 .23
❑ 8 Corey Dillon .50 .23
❑ 9 Darnay Scott .20 .09
❑ 10 Leslie Shepherd .20 .09
❑ 11 Troy Aikman 2.00 .90
❑ 12 Emmitt Smith 2.00 .90
❑ 13 Michael Irvin .40 .18
❑ 14 Terrell Davis 2.00 .90
❑ 15 Shannon Sharpe .40 .18
❑ 16 Rod Smith .40 .18
❑ 17 Barry Sanders 3.00 1.35
❑ 18 Charlie Batch 1.50 .70
❑ 19 Herman Moore .50 .23
❑ 20 Brett Favre 3.00 1.35
❑ 21 Dorsey Levens .50 .23
❑ 22 Antonio Freeman .50 .23
❑ 23 Peyton Manning 3.00 1.35
❑ 24 Mark Brunell 1.25 .55
❑ 25 Fred Taylor 2.00 .90
❑ 26 Jimmy Smith .40 .18
❑ 27 Andre Rison .40 .18
❑ 28 Tony Gonzalez .40 .18
❑ 29 Dan Marino 3.00 1.35
❑ 30 Karim Abdul-Jabbar .40 .18
❑ 31 Randy Moss 3.00 1.35
❑ 32 Randall Cunningham .50 .23
❑ 33 Drew Bledsoe 1.25 .55
❑ 34 Terry Glenn .50 .23
❑ 35 Cameron Cleeland .20 .09
❑ 36 Andre Hastings .20 .09
❑ 37 Amani Toomer .20 .09
❑ 38 Kent Graham .20 .09
❑ 39 Curtis Martin .50 .23
❑ 40 Keyshawn Johnson .50 .23
❑ 41 Vinny Testaverde .40 .18
❑ 42 Napoleon Kaufman .50 .23
❑ 43 Tim Brown .50 .23
❑ 44 Duce Staley .50 .23
❑ 45 Kordell Stewart .50 .23
❑ 46 Jerome Bettis .50 .23
❑ 47 Marshall Faulk .50 .23
❑ 48 Natrone Means .40 .18
❑ 49 Ryan Leaf .20 .09
❑ 50 Steve Young 1.25 .55
❑ 51 Jerry Rice 2.00 .90
❑ 52 Terrell Owens .50 .23
❑ 53 Joey Galloway .50 .23
❑ 54 Ricky Watters .40 .18
❑ 55 Jon Kitna .50 .23
❑ 56 Warrick Dunn .50 .23
❑ 57 Trent Dilfer .40 .18
❑ 58 Steve McNair .50 .23
❑ 59 Eddie George .75 .35
❑ 60 Brad Johnson .50 .23
❑ 61 Tim Couch RC 5.00 2.20
❑ 62 Donovan McNabb RC 6.00 2.70
❑ 63 Akili Smith RC 2.50 1.10
❑ 64 Edgerrin James RC 10.00 4.50
❑ 65 Ricky Williams RC 6.00 2.70
❑ 66 Torry Holt RC 4.00 1.80
❑ 67 Champ Bailey RC 1.50 .70
❑ 68 David Boston RC 2.50 1.10

	MINT	NRMT
❑ 69 Daunte Culpepper RC	10.00	4.50
❑ 70 Cade McNown RC	1.50	.70
❑ 71 Troy Edwards RC	1.50	.70
❑ 72 Kevin Johnson RC	2.50	1.10
❑ 73 James Johnson RC	1.25	.55
❑ 74 Rob Konrad RC	1.25	.55
❑ 75 Kevin Faulk RC	2.00	.90
❑ 76 Shaun King RC	3.00	1.35
❑ 77 Peerless Price RC	1.50	.70
❑ 78 Mike Cloud RC	1.25	.55
❑ 79 Jermaine Fazande RC	1.25	.55
❑ 80 D'Wayne Bates RC	.75	.35
❑ 81 Brock Huard RC	2.00	.90
❑ 82 Marty Booker RC	1.25	.55
❑ 83 Karsten Bailey RC	.75	.35
❑ 84 Al Wilson RC	1.25	.55
❑ 85 Joe Germaine RC	1.25	.55
❑ 86 Dameane Douglas RC	.75	.35
❑ 87 Sedrick Irvin RC	1.25	.55
❑ 88 Aaron Brooks RC	6.00	2.70
❑ 89 Cecil Collins RC	1.25	.55

2000 Upper Deck Legends

	MINT	NRMT
COMPLETE SET (132)	500.00	220.00
❑ 1 Jake Plummer	.50	.23
❑ 2 Jamal Anderson	.50	.23
❑ 3 Doug Flutie	.60	.25
❑ 4 Jim Kelly	.50	.23
❑ 5 Dick Butkus	.75	.35
❑ 6 Mike Singletary	.25	.11
❑ 7 Gale Sayers	.75	.35
❑ 8 Boomer Esiason	.25	.11
❑ 9 Anthony Munoz	.15	.07
❑ 10 Otto Graham	.50	.23
❑ 11 Jim Brown	1.25	.55
❑ 12 Ozzie Newsome	.25	.11
❑ 13 Bob Lilly	.25	.11
❑ 14 Troy Aikman	1.25	.55
❑ 15 Emmitt Smith	1.25	.55
❑ 16 Roger Staubach	1.50	.70
❑ 17 Deion Sanders	.50	.23
❑ 18 Tony Dorsett	.50	.23
❑ 19 Terrell Davis	1.25	.55
❑ 20 John Elway	2.00	.90
❑ 21 Charlie Batch	.50	.23
❑ 22 Brett Favre	2.00	.90
❑ 23 Bart Starr	1.50	.70
❑ 24 Reggie White	.25	.11
❑ 25 Earl Campbell	.50	.23
❑ 26 Peyton Manning	1.50	.70
❑ 27 Edgerrin James	2.00	.90
❑ 28 Johnny Unitas	1.50	.70
❑ 29 Marvin Harrison	.50	.23
❑ 30 Mark Brunell	.75	.35
❑ 31 Fred Taylor	.60	.25
❑ 32 Len Dawson	.50	.23
❑ 33 Dan Marino	2.00	.90
❑ 34 Bob Griese	.50	.23
❑ 35 Mark Duper	.15	.07
❑ 36 Thurman Thomas	.25	.11
❑ 37 Fran Tarkenton	.75	.35
❑ 38 Randy Moss	1.50	.70
❑ 39 Cris Carter	.50	.23
❑ 40 Gary Anderson	.15	.07
❑ 41 John Randle	.25	.11
❑ 42 Drew Bledsoe	.75	.35
❑ 43 Archie Manning	.25	.11
❑ 44 Ricky Williams	1.25	.55
❑ 45 Frank Gifford	.50	.23
❑ 46 Kerry Collins	.25	.11
❑ 47 Phil Simms	.25	.11
❑ 48 Vinny Testaverde	.25	.11
❑ 49 Curtis Martin	.50	.23
❑ 50 Keyshawn Johnson	.50	.23
❑ 51 Joe Namath	2.00	.90
❑ 52 Marcus Allen	.50	.23
❑ 53 Bruce Smith	.25	.11
❑ 54 Ken Stabler	.75	.35
❑ 55 Fred Biletnikoff	.25	.11
❑ 56 Howie Long	.25	.11
❑ 57 Ron Jaworski	.15	.07
❑ 58 Harold Carmichael	.15	.07
❑ 59 Kordell Stewart	.50	.23
❑ 60 Levon Kirkland	.15	.07
❑ 61 Mel Blount	.15	.07
❑ 62 Jerome Bettis	.50	.23
❑ 63 John Stallworth	.25	.11
❑ 64 Franco Harris	.50	.23
❑ 65 Jim Harbaugh	.25	.11
❑ 66 Kellen Winslow	.25	.11
❑ 67 Charlie Joiner	.15	.07
❑ 68 Junior Seau	.25	.11
❑ 69 Jerry Rice	1.25	.55
❑ 70 Steve Young	.75	.35
❑ 71 Joe Montana	2.50	1.10
❑ 72 Roger Craig	.25	.11
❑ 73 Ronnie Lott	.25	.11
❑ 74 Jon Kitna	.50	.23
❑ 75 Steve Largent	.50	.23
❑ 76 Ricky Watters	.25	.11
❑ 77 Kurt Warner	2.00	.90
❑ 78 Marshall Faulk	.60	.25
❑ 79 Isaac Bruce	.50	.23
❑ 80 Merlin Olsen	.25	.11
❑ 81 Lee Roy Selmon	.15	.07
❑ 82 Tim Brown	.50	.23
❑ 83 Tim Couch	1.00	.45
❑ 84 Mike Alstott	.50	.23
❑ 85 Eddie George	.60	.25
❑ 86 Steve McNair	.50	.23
❑ 87 Brad Johnson	.50	.23
❑ 88 Sonny Jurgensen	.50	.23
❑ 89 Art Monk	.25	.11
❑ 90 Joe Theismann	.25	.11
❑ 91 Ray Nitschke TCL	10.00	4.50
❑ 92 Doak Walker TCL	10.00	4.50
❑ 93 Thurman Thomas TCL	10.00	4.50
❑ 94 Jim Brown TCL	12.00	5.50
❑ 95 Sammy Baugh TCL	15.00	6.75
❑ 96 Reggie White TCL	10.00	4.50
❑ 97 Eric Dickerson TCL	10.00	4.50
❑ 98 Paul Hornung TCL	10.00	4.50
❑ 99 Deion Sanders TCL	12.00	5.50
❑ 100 Bronko Nagurski TCL	10.00	4.50
❑ 101 Walter Payton TCL	25.00	11.00
❑ 102 Jim Thorpe TCL	12.00	5.50
❑ 103 Ron Dayne RC	20.00	9.00
❑ 104 Tim Rattay RC	10.00	4.50
❑ 105 Brian Urlacher RC	20.00	9.00
❑ 106 Bubba Franks RC	8.00	3.60
❑ 107 Chad Pennington RC	20.00	9.00
❑ 108 Chris Cole RC	5.00	2.20
❑ 109 Chris Redman RC	12.00	5.50
❑ 110 Courtney Brown RC	8.00	3.60
❑ 111 Curtis Keaton RC	5.00	2.20
❑ 112 Dennis Northcutt RC	8.00	3.60
❑ 113 Dez White RC	5.00	2.20
❑ 114 Giovanni Carmazzi RC	8.00	3.60
❑ 115 J.R. Redmond RC	8.00	3.60
❑ 116 JaJuan Dawson RC	10.00	4.50
❑ 117 Jamal Lewis RC	30.00	13.50
❑ 118 Jerry Porter RC	6.00	2.70
❑ 119 Laveranues Coles RC	10.00	4.50
❑ 120 Peter Warrick RC	20.00	9.00
❑ 121 Plaxico Burress RC	12.00	5.50
❑ 122 R.Jay Soward RC	6.00	2.70
❑ 123 Reuben Droughns RC	6.00	2.70
❑ 124 Ron Dixon RC	8.00	3.60
❑ 125 Ron Dugans RC	10.00	4.50
❑ 126 Shaun Alexander RC	15.00	6.75
❑ 127 Sylvester Morris RC	12.00	5.50
❑ 128 Thomas Jones RC	10.00	4.50
❑ 129 Todd Pinkston RC	6.00	2.70
❑ 130 Travis Prentice RC	10.00	4.50
❑ 131 Travis Taylor RC	8.00	3.60
❑ 132 Trung Canidate RC	6.00	2.70

1999 Upper Deck MVP

	MINT	NRMT
COMPLETE SET (220)	30.00	13.50
❑ 1 Jake Plummer	.75	.35
❑ 2 Adrian Murrell	.20	.09
❑ 3 Larry Centers	.10	.05
❑ 4 Frank Sanders	.20	.09
❑ 5 Andre Wadsworth	.10	.05
❑ 6 Rob Moore	.20	.09
❑ 7 Simeon Rice	.10	.05
❑ 8 Jamal Anderson	.40	.18
❑ 9 Chris Chandler	.20	.09
❑ 10 Chuck Smith	.10	.05
❑ 11 Terance Mathis	.20	.09
❑ 12 Tim Dwight	.40	.18
❑ 13 Ray Buchanan	.10	.05
❑ 14 O.J. Santiago	.10	.05
❑ 15 Eric Zeier	.20	.09
❑ 16 Priest Holmes	.40	.18
❑ 17 Michael Jackson	.10	.05
❑ 18 Jermaine Lewis	.20	.09
❑ 19 Michael McCrary	.10	.05
❑ 20 Rob Johnson	.20	.09
❑ 21 Antowain Smith	.40	.18
❑ 22 Thurman Thomas	.20	.09
❑ 23 Doug Flutie	.50	.23
❑ 24 Eric Moulds	.40	.18
❑ 25 Bruce Smith	.20	.09
❑ 26 Andre Reed	.20	.09
❑ 27 Fred Lane	.10	.05
❑ 28 Tim Biakabutuka	.20	.09
❑ 29 Rae Carruth	.20	.09
❑ 30 Wesley Walls	.20	.09
❑ 31 Steve Beuerlein	.10	.05
❑ 32 Muhsin Muhammad	.20	.09
❑ 33 Erik Kramer	.10	.05
❑ 34 Edgar Bennett	.10	.05
❑ 35 Curtis Conway	.20	.09
❑ 36 Curtis Enis	.40	.18
❑ 37 Bobby Engram	.20	.09
❑ 38 Alonzo Mayes	.10	.05
❑ 39 Corey Dillon	.40	.18
❑ 40 Jeff Blake	.20	.09
❑ 41 Carl Pickens	.20	.09
❑ 42 Darnay Scott	.10	.05
❑ 43 Tony McGee	.10	.05
❑ 44 Ki-Jana Carter	.10	.05
❑ 45 Ty Detmer	.20	.09
❑ 46 Terry Kirby	.10	.05
❑ 47 Justin Armour	.10	.05
❑ 48 Freddie Solomon	.10	.05
❑ 49 Marquez Pope	.10	.05
❑ 50 Antonio Langham	.10	.05
❑ 51 Troy Aikman	1.00	.45
❑ 52 Emmitt Smith	1.00	.45
❑ 53 Deion Sanders	.40	.18
❑ 54 Rocket Ismail	.20	.09
❑ 55 Michael Irvin	.20	.09
❑ 56 Chris Warren	.10	.05

- ❑ 57 Greg Ellis .10 .05
- ❑ 58 John Elway 1.50 .70
- ❑ 59 Terrell Davis 1.00 .45
- ❑ 60 Rod Smith .20 .09
- ❑ 61 Shannon Sharpe .20 .09
- ❑ 62 Ed McCaffrey .20 .09
- ❑ 63 John Mobley .10 .05
- ❑ 64 Bill Romanowski .10 .05
- ❑ 65 Barry Sanders 1.50 .70
- ❑ 66 Johnnie Morton .20 .09
- ❑ 67 Herman Moore .40 .18
- ❑ 68 Charlie Batch .75 .35
- ❑ 69 Germane Crowell .20 .09
- ❑ 70 Robert Porcher .10 .05
- ❑ 71 Brett Favre 1.50 .70
- ❑ 72 Antonio Freeman .40 .18
- ❑ 73 Dorsey Levens .40 .18
- ❑ 74 Mark Chmura .20 .09
- ❑ 75 Vonnie Holliday .10 .05
- ❑ 76 Bill Schroeder .40 .18
- ❑ 77 Marshall Faulk .40 .18
- ❑ 78 Marvin Harrison .40 .18
- ❑ 79 Peyton Manning 1.50 .70
- ❑ 80 Jerome Pathon .10 .05
- ❑ 81 E.G. Green .10 .05
- ❑ 82 Ellis Johnson .10 .05
- ❑ 83 Mark Brunell .60 .25
- ❑ 84 Jimmy Smith .20 .09
- ❑ 85 Keenan McCardell .20 .09
- ❑ 86 Fred Taylor 1.00 .45
- ❑ 87 James Stewart .20 .09
- ❑ 88 Kevin Hardy .10 .05
- ❑ 89 Elvis Grbac .20 .09
- ❑ 90 Andre Rison .20 .09
- ❑ 91 Derrick Alexander WR .20 .09
- ❑ 92 Tony Gonzalez .20 .09
- ❑ 93 Donnell Bennett .10 .05
- ❑ 94 Derrick Thomas .20 .09
- ❑ 95 Tamarick Vanover .10 .05
- ❑ 96 Dan Marino 1.50 .70
- ❑ 97 Karim Abdul-Jabbar .20 .09
- ❑ 98 Zach Thomas .20 .09
- ❑ 99 O.J. McDuffie .20 .09
- ❑ 100 John Avery .20 .09
- ❑ 101 Sam Madison .10 .05
- ❑ 102 Randall Cunningham .40 .18
- ❑ 103 Cris Carter .40 .18
- ❑ 104 Robert Smith .40 .18
- ❑ 105 Randy Moss 1.50 .70
- ❑ 106 Jake Reed .20 .09
- ❑ 107 Matthew Hatchette .10 .05
- ❑ 108 John Randle .20 .09
- ❑ 109 Drew Bledsoe .60 .25
- ❑ 110 Terry Glenn .40 .18
- ❑ 111 Ben Coates .20 .09
- ❑ 112 Ty Law .10 .05
- ❑ 113 Tony Simmons .10 .05
- ❑ 114 Ted Johnson .10 .05
- ❑ 115 Danny Wuerffel .10 .05
- ❑ 116 Lamar Smith .20 .09
- ❑ 117 Sean Dawkins .10 .05
- ❑ 118 Cameron Cleeland .10 .05
- ❑ 119 Joe Johnson .10 .05
- ❑ 120 Andre Hastings .10 .05
- ❑ 121 Kent Graham .10 .05
- ❑ 122 Gary Brown .10 .05
- ❑ 123 Amani Toomer .10 .05
- ❑ 124 Tiki Barber .10 .05
- ❑ 125 Ike Hilliard .10 .05
- ❑ 126 Jason Sehorn .10 .05
- ❑ 127 Vinny Testaverde .20 .09
- ❑ 128 Curtis Martin .40 .18
- ❑ 129 Keyshawn Johnson .40 .18
- ❑ 130 Wayne Chrebet .20 .09
- ❑ 131 Mo Lewis .10 .05
- ❑ 132 Steve Atwater .10 .05
- ❑ 133 Donald Hollas .10 .05
- ❑ 134 Napoleon Kaufman .40 .18
- ❑ 135 Tim Brown .40 .18
- ❑ 136 Darrell Russell .10 .05
- ❑ 137 Rickey Dudley .10 .05
- ❑ 138 Charles Woodson .40 .18
- ❑ 139 Koy Detmer .10 .05
- ❑ 140 Duce Staley .40 .18
- ❑ 141 Charlie Garner .20 .09
- ❑ 142 Doug Pederson .10 .05
- ❑ 143 Jeff Graham .10 .05
- ❑ 144 Charles Johnson .10 .05
- ❑ 145 Kordell Stewart .40 .18
- ❑ 146 Jerome Bettis .40 .18
- ❑ 147 Hines Ward .10 .05
- ❑ 148 Courtney Hawkins .10 .05
- ❑ 149 Will Blackwell .10 .05
- ❑ 150 Richard Huntley .40 .18
- ❑ 151 Levon Kirkland .10 .05
- ❑ 152 Trent Green .20 .09
- ❑ 153 Tony Banks .20 .09
- ❑ 154 Isaac Bruce .40 .18
- ❑ 155 Eddie Kennison .20 .09
- ❑ 156 Az-Zahir Hakim .10 .05
- ❑ 157 Amp Lee .10 .05
- ❑ 158 Robert Holcombe .20 .09
- ❑ 159 Ryan Leaf .40 .18
- ❑ 160 Natrone Means .20 .09
- ❑ 161 Jim Harbaugh .20 .09
- ❑ 162 Junior Seau .20 .09
- ❑ 163 Charlie Jones .10 .05
- ❑ 164 Rodney Harrison .10 .05
- ❑ 165 Steve Young .60 .25
- ❑ 166 Jerry Rice 1.00 .45
- ❑ 167 Garrison Hearst .20 .09
- ❑ 168 Terrell Owens .40 .18
- ❑ 169 J.J. Stokes .20 .09
- ❑ 170 Bryant Young .10 .05
- ❑ 171 Ricky Watters .20 .09
- ❑ 172 Joey Galloway .40 .18
- ❑ 173 Jon Kitna .40 .18
- ❑ 174 Ahman Green .20 .09
- ❑ 175 Mike Pritchard .10 .05
- ❑ 176 Chad Brown .10 .05
- ❑ 177 Warrick Dunn .40 .18
- ❑ 178 Trent Dilfer .20 .09
- ❑ 179 Mike Alstott .40 .18
- ❑ 180 Reidel Anthony .20 .09
- ❑ 181 Bert Emanuel .20 .09
- ❑ 182 Jacquez Green .20 .09
- ❑ 183 Hardy Nickerson .10 .05
- ❑ 184 Steve McNair .40 .18
- ❑ 185 Eddie George .50 .23
- ❑ 186 Yancey Thigpen .10 .05
- ❑ 187 Frank Wycheck .10 .05
- ❑ 188 Kevin Dyson .20 .09
- ❑ 189 Jackie Harris .10 .05
- ❑ 190 Blaine Bishop .10 .05
- ❑ 191 Skip Hicks .40 .18
- ❑ 192 Michael Westbrook .20 .09
- ❑ 193 Stephen Alexander .10 .05
- ❑ 194 Leslie Shepherd .10 .05
- ❑ 195 Casey Weldon .10 .05
- ❑ 196 Brian Mitchell .10 .05
- ❑ 197 Dan Wilkinson .10 .05
- ❑ 198 Terrell Davis CL .50 .23
- ❑ 199 Troy Aikman CL .40 .18
- ❑ 200 Tim Couch CL 2.00 .90
- ❑ 201 Ricky Williams RC 4.00 1.80
- ❑ 202 Tim Couch RC 4.00 1.80
- ❑ 203 Akili Smith RC 2.00 .90
- ❑ 204 Daunte Culpepper RC 8.00 3.60
- ❑ 205 Torry Holt RC 2.50 1.10
- ❑ 206 Edgerrin James RC 8.00 3.60
- ❑ 207 David Boston RC 2.00 .90
- ❑ 208 Peerless Price RC 1.25 .55
- ❑ 209 Chris Claiborne RC .75 .35
- ❑ 210 Champ Bailey RC 1.25 .55
- ❑ 211 Cade McNown RC 1.25 .55
- ❑ 212 Jevon Kearse RC 2.00 .90
- ❑ 213 Joe Germaine RC 1.00 .45
- ❑ 214 D'Wayne Bates RC .75 .35
- ❑ 215 Dameane Douglas RC .75 .35
- ❑ 216 Troy Edwards RC 1.25 .55
- ❑ 217 Sedrick Irvin RC 1.00 .45
- ❑ 218 Brock Huard RC 1.50 .70
- ❑ 219 Amos Zereoue RC 1.00 .45
- ❑ 220 Donovan McNabb RC 4.00 1.80

2000 Upper Deck MVP

	MINT	NRMT
COMPLETE SET (218)	25.00	11.00

- ❑ 1 Jake Plummer .40 .18
- ❑ 2 Michael Pittman .10 .05

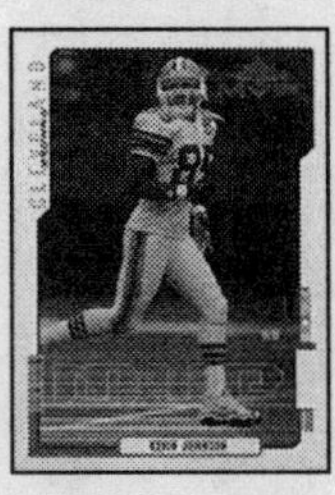

- ❑ 3 Rob Moore .20 .09
- ❑ 4 David Boston .40 .18
- ❑ 5 Frank Sanders .20 .09
- ❑ 6 Aeneas Williams .10 .05
- ❑ 7 Kwamie Lassiter .10 .05
- ❑ 8 Tim Dwight .40 .18
- ❑ 9 Chris Chandler .20 .09
- ❑ 10 Jamal Anderson .40 .18
- ❑ 11 Shawn Jefferson .10 .05
- ❑ 12 Qadry Ismail .10 .05
- ❑ 13 Jermaine Lewis .10 .05
- ❑ 14 Rod Woodson .20 .09
- ❑ 15 Michael McCrary .10 .05
- ❑ 16 Tony Banks .20 .09
- ❑ 17 Peter Boulware .10 .05
- ❑ 18 Shannon Sharpe .20 .09
- ❑ 19 Peerless Price .40 .18
- ❑ 20 Rob Johnson .20 .09
- ❑ 21 Eric Moulds .40 .18
- ❑ 22 Doug Flutie .50 .23
- ❑ 23 Muhsin Muhammad .20 .09
- ❑ 24 Patrick Jeffers .40 .18
- ❑ 25 Steve Beuerlein .20 .09
- ❑ 26 Tim Biakabutuka .20 .09
- ❑ 27 Michael Bates .10 .05
- ❑ 28 Cade McNown .40 .18
- ❑ 29 Curtis Enis .20 .09
- ❑ 30 Marcus Robinson .40 .18
- ❑ 31 Shane Matthews .20 .09
- ❑ 32 Bobby Engram .20 .09
- ❑ 33 Glyn Milburn .10 .05
- ❑ 34 Akili Smith .40 .18
- ❑ 35 Corey Dillon .40 .18
- ❑ 36 Darnay Scott .20 .09
- ❑ 37 Tremain Mack .10 .05
- ❑ 38 Tim Couch .75 .35
- ❑ 39 Kevin Johnson .40 .18
- ❑ 40 Darrin Chiaverini .10 .05
- ❑ 41 Jamir Miller .10 .05
- ❑ 42 Errict Rhett .20 .09
- ❑ 43 Troy Aikman 1.00 .45
- ❑ 44 Emmitt Smith 1.00 .45
- ❑ 45 Rocket Ismail .20 .09
- ❑ 46 Jason Tucker .20 .09
- ❑ 47 Dexter Coakley .10 .05
- ❑ 48 Joey Galloway .40 .18
- ❑ 49 Greg Ellis .10 .05
- ❑ 50 Terrell Davis 1.00 .45
- ❑ 51 Olandis Gary .40 .18
- ❑ 52 Brian Griese .50 .23
- ❑ 53 Ed McCaffrey .40 .18
- ❑ 54 Rod Smith .20 .09
- ❑ 55 Trevor Pryce .10 .05
- ❑ 56 Charlie Batch .40 .18
- ❑ 57 Germane Crowell .20 .09
- ❑ 58 Johnnie Morton .20 .09
- ❑ 59 Robert Porcher .10 .05
- ❑ 60 Luther Elliss .10 .05
- ❑ 61 James Stewart .20 .09
- ❑ 62 Brett Favre 1.50 .70
- ❑ 63 Antonio Freeman .40 .18
- ❑ 64 Bill Schroeder .20 .09
- ❑ 65 Dorsey Levens .20 .09
- ❑ 66 Peyton Manning 1.25 .55
- ❑ 67 Edgerrin James 1.50 .70
- ❑ 68 Marvin Harrison .40 .18
- ❑ 69 Ken Dilger .10 .05

❑ 70 Terrence Wilkins .40 .18
❑ 71 Mark Brunell .60 .25
❑ 72 Fred Taylor .50 .23
❑ 73 Jimmy Smith .20 .09
❑ 74 Keenan McCardell .20 .09
❑ 75 Carnell Lake .10 .05
❑ 76 Tony Brackens .10 .05
❑ 77 Kevin Hardy .10 .05
❑ 78 Hardy Nickerson .10 .05
❑ 79 Elvis Grbac .20 .09
❑ 80 Tony Gonzalez .20 .09
❑ 81 Derrick Alexander .20 .09
❑ 82 Donnell Bennett .10 .05
❑ 83 James Hasty .10 .05
❑ 84 Jay Fiedler .40 .18
❑ 85 James Johnson .20 .09
❑ 86 Tony Martin .20 .09
❑ 87 Damon Huard .40 .18
❑ 88 O.J. McDuffie .20 .09
❑ 89 Oronde Gadsden .20 .09
❑ 90 Zach Thomas .20 .09
❑ 91 Sam Madison .10 .05
❑ 92 Jeff George .20 .09
❑ 93 Randy Moss 1.25 .55
❑ 94 Robert Smith .40 .18
❑ 95 Cris Carter .40 .18
❑ 96 Matthew Hatchette .20 .09
❑ 97 Drew Bledsoe .60 .25
❑ 98 Terry Glenn .20 .09
❑ 99 Troy Brown .10 .05
❑ 100 Kevin Faulk .20 .09
❑ 101 Lawyer Milloy .10 .05
❑ 102 Ricky Williams 1.00 .45
❑ 103 Keith Poole .10 .05
❑ 104 Jake Reed .20 .09
❑ 105 Cam Cleeland .10 .05
❑ 106 Jeff Blake .20 .09
❑ 107 Andrew Glover .10 .05
❑ 108 Kerry Collins .20 .09
❑ 109 Amani Toomer .10 .05
❑ 110 Joe Montgomery .10 .05
❑ 111 Ike Hilliard .20 .09
❑ 112 Michael Strahan .10 .05
❑ 113 Jessie Armstead .10 .05
❑ 114 Ray Lucas .40 .18
❑ 115 Keyshawn Johnson .40 .18
❑ 116 Curtis Martin .40 .18
❑ 117 Vinny Testaverde .20 .09
❑ 118 Wayne Chrebet .20 .09
❑ 119 Dedric Ward .10 .05
❑ 120 Tim Brown .40 .18
❑ 121 Rich Gannon .20 .09
❑ 122 Tyrone Wheatley .20 .09
❑ 123 Napoleon Kaufman .20 .09
❑ 124 Charles Woodson .20 .09
❑ 125 Darrell Russell .10 .05
❑ 126 Duce Staley .40 .18
❑ 127 Donovan McNabb .60 .25
❑ 128 Torrance Small .10 .05
❑ 129 Allen Rossum .10 .05
❑ 130 Brian Dawkins .10 .05
❑ 131 Troy Vincent .10 .05
❑ 132 Troy Edwards .20 .09
❑ 133 Jerome Bettis .40 .18
❑ 134 Hines Ward .10 .05
❑ 135 Kordell Stewart .40 .18
❑ 136 Levon Kirkland .10 .05
❑ 137 Kent Graham .10 .05
❑ 138 Marshall Faulk .50 .23
❑ 139 Kurt Warner 1.50 .70
❑ 140 Torry Holt .40 .18
❑ 141 Isaac Bruce .40 .18
❑ 142 Kevin Carter .10 .05
❑ 143 Az-Zahir Hakim .20 .09
❑ 144 Todd Lyght .10 .05
❑ 145 Jermaine Fazande .10 .05
❑ 146 Curtis Conway .20 .09
❑ 147 Freddie Jones .10 .05
❑ 148 Junior Seau .20 .09
❑ 149 Jeff Graham .10 .05
❑ 150 Ryan Leaf .40 .18
❑ 151 Rodney Harrison .10 .05
❑ 152 Steve Young .60 .25
❑ 153 Jerry Rice 1.00 .45
❑ 154 Charlie Garner .20 .09
❑ 155 Terrell Owens .40 .18
❑ 156 Jeff Garcia .40 .18
❑ 157 Bryant Young .10 .05
❑ 158 Lance Schulters .10 .05
❑ 159 Ricky Watters .10 .05
❑ 160 Jon Kitna .40 .18
❑ 161 Derrick Mayes .20 .09
❑ 162 Sean Dawkins .10 .05
❑ 163 Cortez Kennedy .10 .05
❑ 164 Chad Brown .10 .05
❑ 165 Warrick Dunn .40 .18
❑ 166 Shaun King .60 .25
❑ 167 Mike Alstott .40 .18
❑ 168 Warren Sapp .20 .09
❑ 169 Jacquez Green .20 .09
❑ 170 Derrick Brooks .10 .05
❑ 171 John Lynch .10 .05
❑ 172 Donnie Abraham .10 .05
❑ 173 Eddie George .50 .23
❑ 174 Steve McNair .40 .18
❑ 175 Kevin Dyson .20 .09
❑ 176 Jevon Kearse .40 .18
❑ 177 Yancey Thigpen .10 .05
❑ 178 Frank Wycheck .10 .05
❑ 179 Eddie Robinson .10 .05
❑ 180 Samari Rolle .10 .05
❑ 181 Brad Johnson .40 .18
❑ 182 Stephen Davis .40 .18
❑ 183 Michael Westbrook .20 .09
❑ 184 Albert Connell .10 .05
❑ 185 Brian Mitchell .10 .05
❑ 186 Bruce Smith .20 .09
❑ 187 Stephen Alexander .10 .05
❑ 188 Peter Warrick RC 2.00 .90
❑ 189 Cutout Card/Arrington 25.00 11.00
❑ 190 Chris Redman RC 1.25 .55
❑ 191 Courtney Brown RC .75 .35
❑ 192 Brian Urlacher RC 2.00 .90
❑ 193 Plaxico Burress RC 1.25 .55
❑ 194 Corey Simon RC 1.00 .45
❑ 195 Bubba Franks RC .75 .35
❑ 196 Deon Grant RC .40 .18
❑ 197 Michael Wiley RC .60 .25
❑ 198 Tim Rattay RC 1.00 .45
❑ 199 Ron Dayne RC 2.00 .90
❑ 200 Sylvester Morris RC 1.25 .55
❑ 201 Shaun Alexander RC 1.50 .70
❑ 202 Dez White RC .50 .23
❑ 203 Thomas Jones RC 1.00 .45
❑ 204 Reuben Droughns RC .60 .25
❑ 205 Travis Taylor RC .75 .35
❑ 206 Trevor Gaylor RC .40 .18
❑ 207 Jamal Lewis RC 3.00 1.35
❑ 208 Chad Pennington RC 2.00 .90
❑ 209 J.R. Redmond RC .75 .35
❑ 210 Laveranues Coles RC 1.00 .45
❑ 211 Travis Prentice RC 1.00 .45
❑ 212 R.Jay Soward RC .60 .25
❑ 213 Todd Pinkston RC .50 .23
❑ 214 Dennis Northcutt RC .75 .35
❑ 215 Shyrone Stith RC .40 .18
❑ 216 Tee Martin RC 1.00 .45
❑ 217 Giovanni Carmazzi RC .75 .35
❑ 218 Drew Bledsoe CL .20 .09
❑ 219 Steve Young CL .20 .09
❑ 220 Donovan McNabb CL SP 30.00 13.50

1999 Upper Deck Ovation

	MINT	NRMT
COMPLETE SET (90)	120.00	55.00

❑ 1 Jake Plummer 1.50 .70
❑ 2 Adrian Murrell .40 .18
❑ 3 Jamal Anderson .75 .35
❑ 4 Chris Chandler .40 .18
❑ 5 Tony Banks .40 .18
❑ 6 Antowain Smith .75 .35
❑ 7 Doug Flutie 1.00 .45
❑ 8 Tim Biakabutuka .40 .18
❑ 9 Steve Beuerlein .20 .09
❑ 10 Curtis Conway .40 .18
❑ 11 Curtis Enis .75 .35
❑ 12 Corey Dillon .75 .35

❑ 13 Jeff Blake .40 .18
❑ 14 Ty Detmer .40 .18
❑ 15 Troy Aikman 2.00 .90
❑ 16 Emmitt Smith 2.00 .90
❑ 17 Terrell Davis 2.00 .90
❑ 18 Bubby Brister .20 .09
❑ 19 Barry Sanders 3.00 1.35
❑ 20 Charlie Batch 1.50 .70
❑ 21 Brett Favre 3.00 1.35
❑ 22 Dorsey Levens .75 .35
❑ 23 Peyton Manning 3.00 1.35
❑ 24 Marvin Harrison .75 .35
❑ 25 Mark Brunell 1.25 .55
❑ 26 Fred Taylor 2.00 .90
❑ 27 Elvis Grbac .40 .18
❑ 28 Andre Rison .40 .18
❑ 29 Dan Marino 3.00 1.35
❑ 30 Karim Abdul-Jabbar .40 .18
❑ 31 Randall Cunningham .75 .35
❑ 32 Randy Moss 3.00 1.35
❑ 33 Drew Bledsoe 1.25 .55
❑ 34 Terry Glenn .75 .35
❑ 35 Danny Wuerffel .20 .09
❑ 36 Cam Cleeland .20 .09
❑ 37 Kerry Collins .40 .18
❑ 38 Amani Toomer .20 .09
❑ 39 Curtis Martin .75 .35
❑ 40 Keyshawn Johnson .75 .35
❑ 41 Napoleon Kaufman .75 .35
❑ 42 Tim Brown .75 .35
❑ 43 Doug Pederson .20 .09
❑ 44 Charles Johnson .20 .09
❑ 45 Kordell Stewart .75 .35
❑ 46 Jerome Bettis .75 .35
❑ 47 Trent Green .40 .18
❑ 48 Marshall Faulk .75 .35
❑ 49 Natrone Means .40 .18
❑ 50 Jim Harbaugh .40 .18
❑ 51 Steve Young 1.25 .55
❑ 52 Jerry Rice 2.00 .90
❑ 53 Joey Galloway .75 .35
❑ 54 Jon Kitna .75 .35
❑ 55 Warrick Dunn .75 .35
❑ 56 Trent Dilfer .40 .18
❑ 57 Steve McNair .75 .35
❑ 58 Eddie George 1.00 .45
❑ 59 Brad Johnson .75 .35
❑ 60 Skip Hicks .75 .35
❑ 61 Tim Couch RC 10.00 4.50
❑ 62 Donovan McNabb RC 10.00 4.50
❑ 63 Akili Smith RC 5.00 2.20
❑ 64 Edgerrin James RC 12.00 5.50
❑ 65 Ricky Williams RC 10.00 4.50
❑ 66 Torry Holt RC 6.00 2.70
❑ 67 Champ Bailey RC 3.00 1.35
❑ 68 David Boston RC 5.00 2.20
❑ 69 Daunte Culpepper RC 12.00 5.50
❑ 70 Cade McNown RC 3.00 1.35
❑ 71 Troy Edwards RC 3.00 1.35
❑ 72 Kevin Johnson RC 5.00 2.20
❑ 73 James Johnson RC 2.50 1.10
❑ 74 Rob Konrad RC 1.50 .70
❑ 75 Kevin Faulk RC 4.00 1.80
❑ 76 Shaun King RC 5.00 2.20
❑ 77 Peerless Price RC 3.00 1.35
❑ 78 Mike Cloud RC 1.50 .70
❑ 79 Jermaine Fazande RC 2.50 1.10

		MINT	NRMT
❑ 80	D'Wayne Bates RC	1.50	.70
❑ 81	Brock Huard RC	4.00	1.80
❑ 82	Marty Booker RC	2.50	1.10
❑ 83	Karsten Bailey RC	1.50	.70
❑ 84	Al Wilson RC	1.50	.70
❑ 85	Joe Germaine RC	2.50	1.10
❑ 86	Dameane Douglas RC	1.50	.70
❑ 87	Sedrick Irvin RC	2.50	1.10
❑ 88	Amos Zereoue RC	1.50	.70
❑ 89	Cecil Collins RC	1.50	.70
❑ 90	Ebenezer Ekuban RC	1.50	.70
❑ WPO	Walter Payton Jersey AUTO/34	2000.00	900.00

2000 Upper Deck Ovation

		MINT	NRMT
	COMPLETE SET (90)	250.00	110.00
❑ 1	Jake Plummer	.50	.23
❑ 2	Frank Sanders	.25	.11
❑ 3	Chris Chandler	.25	.11
❑ 4	Jamal Anderson	.50	.23
❑ 5	Qadry Ismail	.15	.07
❑ 6	Eric Moulds	.50	.23
❑ 7	Muhsin Muhammad	.25	.11
❑ 8	Steve Beuerlein	.25	.11
❑ 9	Cade McNown	.50	.23
❑ 10	Marcus Robinson	.50	.23
❑ 11	Akili Smith	.60	.23
❑ 12	Corey Dillon	.50	.23
❑ 13	Tim Couch	1.00	.45
❑ 14	Kevin Johnson	.50	.23
❑ 15	Troy Aikman	1.25	.55
❑ 16	Emmitt Smith	1.25	.55
❑ 17	Terrell Davis	1.25	.55
❑ 18	Olandis Gary	.50	.23
❑ 19	Charlie Batch	.50	.23
❑ 20	Germane Crowell	.25	.11
❑ 21	Brett Favre	2.00	.90
❑ 22	Antonio Freeman	.50	.23
❑ 23	Peyton Manning	1.50	.70
❑ 24	Edgerrin James	2.00	.90
❑ 25	Mark Brunell	.75	.35
❑ 26	Fred Taylor	.60	.25
❑ 27	Elvis Grbac	.25	.11
❑ 28	Tony Gonzalez	.25	.11
❑ 29	Tony Martin	.25	.11
❑ 30	Damon Huard	.50	.23
❑ 31	Randy Moss	1.50	.70
❑ 32	Daunte Culpepper	1.00	.45
❑ 33	Drew Bledsoe	.75	.35
❑ 34	Terry Glenn	.25	.11
❑ 35	Ricky Williams	1.25	.55
❑ 36	Jeff Blake	.25	.11
❑ 37	Kerry Collins	.25	.11
❑ 38	Amani Toomer	.25	.11
❑ 39	Curtis Martin	.50	.23
❑ 40	Vinny Testaverde	.25	.11
❑ 41	Tim Brown	.50	.23
❑ 42	Rickey Dudley	.15	.07
❑ 43	Duce Staley	.50	.23
❑ 44	Donovan McNabb	.75	.35
❑ 45	Troy Edwards	.25	.11
❑ 46	Jerome Bettis	.50	.23
❑ 47	Marshall Faulk	.60	.25
❑ 48	Kurt Warner	2.00	.90
❑ 49	Freddie Jones	.15	.07
❑ 50	Junior Seau	.25	.11
❑ 51	Jerry Rice	1.25	.55
❑ 52	Steve Young	.75	.35
❑ 53	Ricky Watters	.25	.11
❑ 54	Jon Kitna	.50	.23
❑ 55	Shaun King	.75	.35
❑ 56	Keyshawn Johnson	.50	.23
❑ 57	Eddie George	.60	.25
❑ 58	Steve McNair	.50	.23
❑ 59	Brad Johnson	.50	.23
❑ 60	Stephen Davis	.50	.23
❑ 61	Courtney Brown RC	6.00	2.70
❑ 62	Corey Simon RC	6.00	2.70
❑ 63	R.Jay Soward RC	5.00	2.20
❑ 64	Anthony Becht RC	5.00	2.20
❑ 65	Chris Redman RC	10.00	4.50
❑ 66	Chad Pennington RC	15.00	6.75
❑ 67	Tee Martin RC	8.00	3.60
❑ 68	Giovanni Carmazzi RC	6.00	2.70
❑ 69	Ron Dayne RC	15.00	6.75
❑ 70	Shaun Alexander RC	12.00	5.50
❑ 71	Thomas Jones RC	8.00	3.60
❑ 72	Reuben Droughns RC	5.00	2.20
❑ 73	Jamal Lewis RC	25.00	11.00
❑ 74	J.R. Redmond RC	6.00	2.70
❑ 75	Travis Prentice RC	8.00	3.60
❑ 76	Trung Canidate RC	5.00	2.20
❑ 77	Brian Urlacher RC	15.00	6.75
❑ 78	Bubba Franks RC	6.00	2.70
❑ 79	Peter Warrick RC	15.00	6.75
❑ 80	Plaxico Burress RC	10.00	4.50
❑ 81	Sylvester Morris RC	10.00	4.50
❑ 82	Dez White RC	4.00	1.80
❑ 83	Travis Taylor RC	6.00	2.70
❑ 84	Todd Pinkston RC	5.00	2.20
❑ 85	Dennis Northcutt RC	6.00	2.70
❑ 86	Jerry Porter RC	5.00	2.20
❑ 87	Laveranues Coles RC	8.00	3.60
❑ 88	Danny Farmer RC	5.00	2.20
❑ 89	Curtis Keaton RC	4.00	1.80
❑ 90	Ron Dugans RC	4.00	1.80

1999 Upper Deck PowerDeck

		MINT	NRMT
	COMPLETE SET (30)	100.00	45.00
❑ PD1	Troy Aikman	6.00	2.70
❑ PD2	Drew Bledsoe	4.00	1.80
❑ PD3	Randy Moss	10.00	4.50
❑ PD4	Barry Sanders	10.00	4.50
❑ PD5	Brett Favre	10.00	4.50
❑ PD6	Terrell Davis	6.00	2.70
❑ PD7	Peyton Manning	10.00	4.50
❑ PD8	Emmitt Smith	6.00	2.70
❑ PD9	Dan Marino	10.00	4.50
❑ PD10	Jake Plummer	4.00	1.80
❑ PD11	Eddie George	3.00	1.35
❑ PD12	Jerry Rice	6.00	2.70
❑ PD13	Steve Young	4.00	1.80
❑ PD14	Mark Brunell	4.00	1.80
❑ PD15	Kordell Stewart	2.50	1.10
❑ PD16	Keyshawn Johnson	2.50	1.10
❑ PD17	Fred Taylor	6.00	2.70
❑ PD18	Jamal Anderson	2.50	1.10
❑ PD19	Cecil Collins	2.50	1.10
❑ PD20	Ricky Williams	8.00	3.60
❑ PD21	Tim Couch	10.00	4.50
❑ PD22	Donovan McNabb	8.00	3.60
❑ PD23	Akili Smith	5.00	2.20
❑ PD24	Edgerrin James	12.00	5.50
❑ PD25	Daunte Culpepper	12.00	5.50
❑ PD26	Brock Huard	4.00	1.80
❑ PD27	Torry Holt	5.00	2.20
❑ PD28	David Boston	5.00	2.20
❑ PD29	Cade McNown	4.00	1.80
❑ PD30	Champ Bailey	3.00	1.35
❑ WPPD	Walter Payton Jersey AUTO/34	2000.00	900.00

2000 Upper Deck Pros and Prospects

		MINT	NRMT
	COMPLETE SET (126)	1200.00	550.00
	COMP.SET w/o SP's (84)	12.00	5.50
❑ 1	Jake Plummer	.40	.18
❑ 2	Michael Pittman	.10	.05
❑ 3	Tim Dwight	.40	.18
❑ 4	Chris Chandler	.20	.09
❑ 5	Qadry Ismail	.10	.05
❑ 6	Shannon Sharpe	.20	.09
❑ 7	Peerless Price	.40	.18
❑ 8	Rob Johnson	.20	.09
❑ 9	Eric Moulds	.40	.18
❑ 10	Muhoin Muhammad	.20	.00
❑ 11	Patrick Jeffers	.40	.18
❑ 12	Steve Beuerlein	.20	.09
❑ 13	Cade McNown	.40	.18
❑ 14	Curtis Enis	.20	.09
❑ 15	Marcus Robinson	.40	.18
❑ 16	Akili Smith	.40	.18
❑ 17	Corey Dillon	.40	.18
❑ 18	Tim Couch	.75	.35
❑ 19	Kevin Johnson	.40	.18
❑ 20	Errict Rhett	.20	.09
❑ 21	Troy Aikman	1.00	.45
❑ 22	Emmitt Smith	1.00	.45
❑ 23	Rocket Ismail	.20	.09
❑ 24	Terrell Davis	1.00	.45
❑ 25	Olandis Gary	.40	.18
❑ 26	Brian Griese	.50	.23
❑ 27	Ed McCaffrey	.40	.18
❑ 28	Charlie Batch	.40	.18
❑ 29	Germane Crowell	.20	.09
❑ 30	James O. Stewart	.20	.09
❑ 31	Brett Favre	1.50	.70
❑ 32	Antonio Freeman	.40	.18
❑ 33	Dorsey Levens	.20	.09
❑ 34	Peyton Manning	1.25	.55
❑ 35	Edgerrin James	1.50	.70
❑ 36	Marvin Harrison	.40	.18
❑ 37	Mark Brunell	.60	.25
❑ 38	Fred Taylor	.50	.23
❑ 39	Jimmy Smith	.20	.09
❑ 40	Elvis Grbac	.20	.09
❑ 41	Tony Gonzalez	.20	.09
❑ 42	Damon Huard	.40	.18
❑ 43	James Johnson	.20	.09
❑ 44	Jay Fiedler	.40	.18
❑ 45	Randy Moss	1.25	.55
❑ 46	Robert Smith	.40	.18
❑ 47	Cris Carter	.40	.18

❑ 48 Drew Bledsoe .60 .25
❑ 49 Terry Glenn .20 .09
❑ 50 Ricky Williams 1.00 .45
❑ 51 Jeff Blake .20 .09
❑ 52 Keith Poole .10 .05
❑ 53 Kerry Collins .20 .09
❑ 54 Amani Toomer .10 .05
❑ 55 Vinny Testaverde .20 .09
❑ 56 Keyshawn Johnson .40 .18
❑ 57 Curtis Martin .40 .18
❑ 58 Tim Brown .40 .18
❑ 59 Rich Gannon .20 .09
❑ 60 Tyrone Wheatley .20 .09
❑ 61 Duce Staley .40 .18
❑ 62 Donovan McNabb .60 .25
❑ 63 Troy Edwards .20 .09
❑ 64 Jerome Bettis .40 .18
❑ 65 Marshall Faulk .50 .23
❑ 66 Kurt Warner 1.50 .70
❑ 67 Torry Holt .40 .18
❑ 68 Isaac Bruce .40 .18
❑ 69 Junior Seau .20 .09
❑ 70 Jeff Graham .10 .05
❑ 71 Steve Young .60 .25
❑ 72 Jerry Rice 1.00 .45
❑ 73 Charlie Garner .20 .09
❑ 74 Ricky Watters .20 .09
❑ 75 Jon Kitna .40 .18
❑ 76 Warrick Dunn .40 .18
❑ 77 Shaun King .60 .25
❑ 78 Mike Alstott .40 .18
❑ 79 Eddie George .50 .23
❑ 80 Steve McNair .40 .18
❑ 81 Kevin Dyson .20 .09
❑ 82 Brad Johnson .40 .18
❑ 83 Stephen Davis .40 .18
❑ 84 Michael Westbrook .20 .09
❑ 85 Peter Warrick RC 100.00 45.00
❑ 86 LaVar Arrington RC 100.00 45.00
❑ 87 Chris Redman RC 60.00 27.00
❑ 88 Courtney Brown RC 40.00 18.00
❑ 89 Plaxico Burress RC 60.00 27.00
❑ 90 Corey Simon RC 40.00 18.00
❑ 91 Bubba Franks RC 40.00 18.00
❑ 92 Deon Grant RC 15.00 6.75
❑ 93 Brian Urlacher RC 100.00 45.00
❑ 94 Ron Dayne RC 100.00 45.00
❑ 95 Sylvester Morris RC 60.00 27.00
❑ 96 Shaun Alexander RC 80.00 36.00
❑ 97 Dez White RC .20 .09
❑ 98 Thomas Jones RC 50.00 22.00
❑ 99 Travis Taylor RC 40.00 18.00
❑ 100 Kwame Cavil RC 20.00 9.00
❑ 101 Jamal Lewis RC 150.00 70.00
❑ 102 Chad Pennington RC 100.00 45.00
❑ 103 J.R. Redmond RC 40.00 18.00
❑ 104 Sebastian Janikowski RC 25.00 11.00
❑ 105 Anthony Lucas RC 15.00 6.75
❑ 106 Travis Prentice RC 50.00 22.00
❑ 107 Danny Farmer RC 25.00 11.00
❑ 108 Sherrod Gideon RC 15.00 6.75
❑ 109 Todd Pinkston RC 25.00 11.00
❑ 110 Dennis Northcutt RC 40.00 18.00
❑ 111 Tim Rattay RC 40.00 18.00
❑ 112 Troy Walters RC 25.00 11.00
❑ 113 Michael Wiley RC 25.00 11.00
❑ 114 R.Jay Soward RC 25.00 11.00
❑ 115 Trung Canidate RC 25.00 11.00
❑ 116 Reuben Droughns RC 25.00 11.00
❑ 117 Rondell Mealey RC 15.00 6.75
❑ 118 Chris Coleman RC 25.00 11.00
❑ 119 Giovanni Carmazzi RC 40.00 18.00
❑ 120 Trevor Insley RC 20.00 9.00
❑ 121 Shyrone Stith RC 20.00 9.00
❑ 122 Gari Scott RC 20.00 9.00
❑ 123 Tee Martin RC 50.00 22.00
❑ 124 Tom Brady RC 25.00 11.00
❑ 125 Marcus Knight RC 15.00 6.75
❑ 126 Jerry Porter RC 25.00 11.00
❑ 127 Brad Hoover
❑ 128 Chad Morton
❑ 129 Charles Lee
❑ 130 Damon Hodge
❑ 131 Darrell Jackson
❑ 132 Doug Johnson
❑ 133 Frank Moreau
❑ 134 JaJuan Dawson
❑ 135 Jake Delhomme
❑ 136 Jarious Jackson
❑ 137 Joe Hamilton
❑ 138 Larry Foster
❑ 139 Laveranues Coles
❑ 140 Aaron Shea
❑ 141 Matt Lytle
❑ 142 Mike Anderson
❑ 143 Ron Dixon
❑ 144 Ronney Jenkins
❑ 145 Sammy Morris
❑ 146 Shockmain Davis
❑ 147 Spergon Wynn
❑ 148 Todd Husak
❑ 149 Trevor Gaylor
❑ 150 Tywan Mitchell
❑ 151 Windrell Hayes
❑ 152 Bobby Shaw

1999 Upper Deck Retro

	MINT	NRMT
COMPLETE SET (165)	50.00	22.00

❑ 1 Jake Plummer 1.25 .55
❑ 2 Adrian Murrell .30 .14
❑ 3 Rob Moore .30 .14
❑ 4 Frank Sanders .30 .14
❑ 5 David Boston RC 2.50 1.10
❑ 6 Tim Dwight .60 .25
❑ 7 Chris Chandler .30 .14
❑ 8 Jamal Anderson .60 .25
❑ 9 O.J. Santiago .15 .07
❑ 10 Terance Mathis .30 .14
❑ 11 Priest Holmes .60 .25
❑ 12 Tony Banks .30 .14
❑ 13 Patrick Johnson .15 .07
❑ 14 Scott Mitchell .15 .07
❑ 15 Jermaine Lewis .30 .14
❑ 16 Eric Moulds .60 .25
❑ 17 Doug Flutie .75 .35
❑ 18 Antowain Smith .60 .25
❑ 19 Thurman Thomas .30 .14
❑ 20 Peerless Price RC 1.50 .70
❑ 21 Fred Lane .30 .14
❑ 22 Tim Biakabutuka .30 .14
❑ 23 Steve Beuerlein .15 .07
❑ 24 Muhsin Muhammad .30 .14
❑ 25 Rae Carruth .30 .14
❑ 26 Curtis Enis .60 .25
❑ 27 Walter Payton 5.00 2.20
❑ 28 Bobby Engram .30 .14
❑ 29 Cade McNown RC 1.50 .70
❑ 30 Curtis Conway .30 .14
❑ 31 Darnay Scott .15 .07
❑ 32 Jeff Blake .30 .14
❑ 33 Corey Dillon .60 .25
❑ 34 Akili Smith RC 2.50 1.10
❑ 35 Carl Pickens .30 .14
❑ 36 Tim Couch RC 5.00 2.20
❑ 37 Ty Detmer .30 .14
❑ 38 Jim Brown UER 2.50 1.10
(Photo is Terry Kirby)
❑ 39 Kevin Johnson RC 2.50 1.10
❑ 40 Ozzie Newsome .15 .07
❑ 41 Troy Aikman 1.50 .70
❑ 42 Rocket Ismail .30 .14
❑ 43 Emmitt Smith 1.50 .70
❑ 44 Michael Irvin .30 .14
❑ 45 Deion Sanders .60 .25
❑ 46 Roger Staubach 2.00 .90
❑ 47 John Elway 2.50 1.10
❑ 48 Bubby Brister .15 .07
❑ 49 Terrell Davis 1.50 .70
❑ 50 Ed McCaffrey .30 .14
❑ 51 Rod Smith .30 .14
❑ 52 Shannon Sharpe .30 .14
❑ 53 Charlie Batch 1.25 .55
❑ 54 Johnnie Morton .30 .14
❑ 55 Barry Sanders 2.50 1.10
❑ 56 Sedrick Irvin RC 1.00 .45
❑ 57 Herman Moore .60 .25
❑ 58 Brett Favre 2.50 1.10
❑ 59 Mark Chmura .15 .07
❑ 60 Antonio Freeman .60 .25
❑ 61 Robert Brooks .30 .14
❑ 62 Dorsey Levens .60 .25
❑ 63 Peyton Manning 2.50 1.10
❑ 64 Jerome Pathon .15 .07
❑ 65 Marvin Harrison .60 .25
❑ 66 Edgerrin James RC 8.00 3.60
❑ 67 Ken Dilger .15 .07
❑ 68 Mark Brunell 1.00 .45
❑ 69 Fred Taylor 1.50 .70
❑ 70 Jimmy Smith .30 .14
❑ 71 James Stewart .30 .14
❑ 72 Keenan McCardell .30 .14
❑ 73 Elvis Grbac .30 .14
❑ 74 Mike Cloud RC 1.00 .45
❑ 75 Andre Rison .30 .14
❑ 76 Tony Gonzalez .30 .14
❑ 77 Warren Moon .60 .25
❑ 78 Derrick Alexander WR .30 .14
❑ 79 Dan Marino 2.50 1.10
❑ 80 O.J. McDuffie .30 .14
❑ 81 James Johnson RC 1.00 .45
❑ 82 Paul Warfield .15 .07
❑ 83 Cecil Collins RC 1.00 .45
❑ 84 Randall Cunningham .60 .25
❑ 85 Randy Moss 2.50 1.10
❑ 86 Cris Carter .60 .25
❑ 87 Fran Tarkenton 1.00 .45
❑ 88 Daunte Culpepper RC 8.00 3.60
❑ 89 Robert Smith .60 .25
❑ 90 Drew Bledsoe 1.00 .45
❑ 91 Terry Glenn .60 .25
❑ 92 Kevin Faulk RC 2.00 .90
❑ 93 Tony Simmons .15 .07
❑ 94 Ben Coates .30 .14
❑ 95 Billy Joe Hobert .15 .07
❑ 96 Cameron Cleeland .15 .07
❑ 97 Eddie Kennison .30 .14
❑ 98 Andre Hastings .15 .07
❑ 99 Ricky Williams RC 5.00 2.20
❑ 100 Kerry Collins .30 .14
❑ 101 Joe Montgomery RC 1.00 .45
❑ 102 Gary Brown .15 .07
❑ 103 Ike Hilliard .15 .07
❑ 104 Amani Toomer .15 .07
❑ 105 Vinny Testaverde .30 .14
❑ 106 Wayne Chrebet .30 .14
❑ 107 Curtis Martin .60 .25
❑ 108 Joe Namath 2.50 1.10
❑ 109 Keyshawn Johnson .60 .25
❑ 110 Don Maynard .15 .07
❑ 111 Rich Gannon .30 .14
❑ 112 Tim Brown .60 .25
❑ 113 Charles Woodson .60 .25
❑ 114 Rickey Dudley .15 .07
❑ 115 Darrell Russell .15 .07
❑ 116 Napoleon Kaufman .60 .25
❑ 117 Donovan McNabb RC 5.00 2.20
❑ 118 Doug Pederson .15 .07
❑ 119 Duce Staley .60 .25
❑ 120 Torrance Small .15 .07
❑ 121 Charles Johnson .15 .07
❑ 122 Jerome Bettis .60 .25
❑ 123 Courtney Hawkins .15 .07
❑ 124 Kordell Stewart .60 .25
❑ 125 Troy Edwards RC 1.50 .70
❑ 126 Amos Zereoue RC 1.00 .45
❑ 127 Trent Green .30 .14
❑ 128 Marshall Faulk .60 .25

No.	Player		
129	Az-Zahir Hakim	.15	.07
130	Joe Germaine RC	1.00	.45
131	Torry Holt RC	3.00	1.35
132	Isaac Bruce	.60	.25
133	Jim Harbaugh	.30	.14
134	Junior Seau	.30	.14
135	Natrone Means	.30	.14
136	Ryan Leaf	.60	.25
137	Dan Fouts	.60	.25
138	Mikhael Ricks	.15	.07
139	Steve Young	1.00	.45
140	Terrell Owens	.60	.25
141	Jerry Rice	1.50	.70
142	J.J. Stokes	.30	.14
143	Lawrence Phillips	.30	.14
144	Joe Montana	4.00	1.80
145	Jon Kitna	.60	.25
146	Ahman Green	.30	.14
147	Joey Galloway	.60	.25
148	Ricky Watters	.30	.14
149	Brock Huard RC	2.00	.90
150	Steve Largent	.60	.25
151	Trent Dilfer	.30	.14
152	Reidel Anthony	.30	.14
153	Warrick Dunn	.60	.25
154	Mike Alstott	.60	.25
155	Shaun King RC	2.50	1.10
156	Eddie George	.75	.35
157	Steve McNair	.60	.25
158	Kevin Dyson	.30	.14
159	Frank Wycheck	.15	.07
160	Yancey Thigpen	.15	.07
161	Brad Johnson	.60	.25
162	Rodney Peete	.15	.07
163	Michael Westbrook	.30	.14
164	Skip Hicks	.60	.25
165	Champ Bailey RC	1.50	.70
WP1	Walter Payton AUTO	300.00	135.00
WPR	Walter Payton Jersey AUTO/34	2000.00	900.00

1996 Upper Deck Silver

		MINT	NRMT
COMPLETE SET (225)		20.00	9.00
1	Larry Centers	.20	.09
2	Terance Mathis	.10	.05
3	Justin Armour	.10	.05
4	Kerry Collins	.40	.18
5	Jim Flanigan UER (Mike on front)	.10	.05
6	Dan Wilkinson	.10	.05
7	Eric Zeier	.10	.05
8	Deion Sanders	.50	.23
9	Steve Atwater	.10	.05
10	Johnnie Morton	.20	.09
11	Craig Newsome	.10	.05
12	Broncos Offensive Line	.10	.05
13	Ken Dilger	.20	.09
14	Mark Brunell	1.00	.45
15	Tamarick Vanover	.20	.09
16	Bernie Parmalee	.10	.05
17	Orlando Thomas	.10	.05
18	Will Moore	.10	.05
19	Mark Fields	.10	.05
20	Tyrone Wheatley	.20	.09
21	Kyle Brady	.10	.05
22	Napoleon Kaufman	.40	.18
23	Mike Mamula	.10	.05
24	Erric Pegram	.10	.05
25	Brent Jones	.10	.05
26	Aaron Hayden RC	.10	.05
27	Christian Fauria	.10	.05
28	Cowboys Offensive Line with Troy Aikman	.20	.09
29	Derrick Brooks	.10	.05
30	Brian Mitchell	.10	.05
31	Garrison Hearst	.20	.09
32	Devin Bush	.10	.05
33	Andre Reed	.20	.09
34	Derrick Moore	.10	.05
35	Erik Kramer	.10	.05
36	Jeff Blake	.40	.18
37	Andre Rison	.20	.09
38	Troy Aikman	1.00	.45
39	Anthony Miller	.20	.09
40	Scott Mitchell	.20	.09
41	Reggie White	.40	.18
42	Chris Sanders	.20	.09
43	Ellis Johnson	.10	.05
44	Willie Jackson	.10	.05
45	Steve Bono	.10	.05
46	Terry Kirby	.20	.09
47	Jake Reed	.20	.09
48	Vincent Brisby	.10	.05
49	Quinn Early	.10	.05
50	Thomas Lewis	.10	.05
51	Wayne Chrebet	.60	.25
52	Pat Swilling	.10	.05
53	Bobby Taylor	.10	.05
54	Mark Bruener	.10	.05
55	Jerry Rice	1.00	.45
56	Natrone Means	.40	.18
57	Rick Mirer	.20	.09
58	Kevin Carter	.10	.05
59	Hardy Nickerson	.10	.05
60	Lions Offensive Line with Scott Mitchell	.10	.05
61	Eric Swann	.10	.05
62	Eric Metcalf	.10	.05
63	Russell Copeland	.10	.05
64	Pete Metzelaars	.10	.05
65	Curtis Conway	.40	.18
66	Darnay Scott	.20	.09
67	Leroy Hoard	.10	.05
68	Darron Woodcon	.20	.09
69	John Elway	2.00	.90
70	Brett Perriman	.10	.05
71	Mark Chmura	.20	.09
72	Chris Chandler	.20	.09
73	Marshall Faulk	.40	.18
74	Pete Mitchell	.20	.09
75	Willie Davis	.10	.05
76	Irving Fryar	.20	.09
77	Robert Smith	.20	.09
78	Drew Bledsoe	1.00	.45
79	Mario Bates	.20	.09
80	Chris Calloway	.10	.05
81	Boomer Esiason	.20	.09
82	Harvey Williams	.10	.05
83	Fred Barnett	.10	.05
84	Neil O'Donnell	.20	.09
85	Lee Woodall	.10	.05
86	Junior Seau	.20	.09
87	Brian Blades	.10	.05
88	Chris Miller	.10	.05
89	Warren Sapp	.10	.05
90	Terry Allen	.20	.09
91	Dave Krieg	.10	.05
92	Bert Emanuel	.20	.09
93	Jim Kelly	.40	.18
94	Mark Carrier WR	.10	.05
95	Jeff Graham	.10	.05
96	Tony McGee	.10	.05
97	Vinny Testaverde	.20	.09
98	Michael Irvin	.40	.18
99	Shannon Sharpe	.20	.09
100	Chris Spielman	.10	.05
101	Edgar Bennett	.20	.09
102	Haywood Jeffires	.10	.05
103	Quentin Coryatt	.10	.05
104	Jeff Lageman	.10	.05
105	Neil Smith	.10	.05
106	O.J. McDuffie	.20	.09
107	Warren Moon	.20	.09
108	Ben Coates	.20	.09
109	Michael Haynes	.10	.05
110	Mike Sherrard	.10	.05
111	Adrian Murrell	.40	.18
112	Jeff Hostetler	.10	.05
113	Charlie Garner	.10	.05
114	Yancey Thigpen	.20	.09
115	Steve Young	.60	.25
116	Tony Martin	.20	.09
117	49ers Offensive Line	.10	.05
118	Jerome Bettis	.40	.18
119	Alvin Harper	.10	.05
120	Heath Shuler	.20	.09
121	Rob Moore	.20	.09
122	Chris Doleman	.10	.05
123	Bruce Smith	.20	.09
124	Sam Mills	.10	.05
125	Donnell Woolford	.10	.05
126	Harold Green	.10	.05
127	Antonio Langham	.10	.05
128	Charles Haley	.20	.09
129	Aaron Craver	.10	.05
130	Barry Sanders	2.00	.90
131	Sean Jones	.10	.05
132	Steve McNair	.75	.35
133	Tony Bennett	.10	.05
134	Dolphins Offensive Line with Dan Marino	.40	.18
135	Greg Hill	.20	.09
136	Eric Green	.10	.05
137	John Randle	.20	.09
138	Dave Meggett	.10	.05
139	Irv Smith	.10	.05
140	Dave Brown	.10	.05
141	Raiders Offensive Line	.10	.05
142	Rocket Ismail	.10	.05
143	Rodney Peete	.10	.05
144	Kevin Greene	.20	.09
145	Derek Loville	.10	.05
146	Leslie O'Neal	.10	.05
147	Cortez Kennedy	.10	.05
148	Sean Gilbert	.10	.05
149	Jackie Harris	.10	.05
150	Henry Ellard	.10	.05
151	Frank Sanders	.20	.09
152	Jeff George	.20	.09
153	Darick Holmes	.10	.05
154	Tyrone Poole	.10	.05
155	Rashaan Salaam	.40	.18
156	Carl Pickens	.40	.18
157	Eric Turner	.10	.05
158	Jay Novacek	.10	.05
159	Terrell Davis	2.50	1.10
160	Herman Moore	.40	.18
161	Robert Brooks	.40	.18
162	Rodney Thomas	.10	.05
163	Sean Dawkins	.10	.05
164	James O. Stewart	.20	.09
165	Marcus Allen	.40	.18
166	Dan Marino	2.00	.90
167	Cris Carter	.40	.18
168	Curtis Martin	.75	.35
169	Tyrone Hughes	.10	.05
170	Rodney Hampton	.20	.09
171	Hugh Douglas	.20	.09
172	Tim Brown	.40	.18
173	Ricky Watters	.20	.09
174	Kordell Stewart	.60	.25
175	Stan Humphries	.20	.09
176	J.J. Stokes	.40	.18
177	Joey Galloway	.60	.25
178	Isaac Bruce	.40	.18
179	Errict Rhett	.20	.09
180	Michael Westbrook	.40	.18
181	Steelers Offensive Line	.10	.05
182	Craig Heyward	.10	.05
183	Bryce Paup	.10	.05
184	Brett Maxie	.10	.05
185	Kevin Butler	.10	.05
186	John Copeland	.10	.05
187	Keenan McCardell	.40	.18
188	Emmitt Smith	1.50	.70
189	Glyn Milburn	.10	.05
190	Jason Hanson	.10	.05

❑ 191 Brett Favre	2.00	.90
❑ 192 Darryll Lewis UER	.10	.05
(Name spelled Darryl on front)		
❑ 193 Jim Harbaugh	.20	.09
❑ 194 Desmond Howard	.20	.09
❑ 195 Derrick Thomas	.20	.09
❑ 196 Bryan Cox	.10	.05
❑ 197 Amp Lee	.10	.05
❑ 198 Ty Law	.10	.05
❑ 199 Jim Everett	.10	.05
❑ 200 Vencie Glenn	.10	.05
❑ 201 Charles Wilson	.10	.05
❑ 202 Terry McDaniel	.10	.05
❑ 203 Calvin Williams	.10	.05
❑ 204 Greg Lloyd	.20	.09
❑ 205 Merton Hanks	.10	.05
❑ 206 Andre Coleman	.10	.05
❑ 207 Chris Warren	.20	.09
❑ 208 D'Marco Farr	.10	.05
❑ 209 Trent Dilfer	.40	.18
❑ 210 Ken Harvey	.10	.05
❑ 211 Jim Harbaugh SL	.20	.09
❑ 212 Brett Favre SL	1.00	.45
❑ 213 Curtis Martin SL	.40	.18
❑ 214 Carl Pickens SL	.40	.18
❑ 215 Norm Johnson SL	.10	.05
❑ 216 Bryce Paup SL	.10	.05
❑ 217 Herman Moore SL	.40	.18
❑ 218 Jerry Rice SL	.50	.23
❑ 219 Orlando Thomas SL	.10	.05
❑ 220 Emmitt Smith SL	.75	.35
❑ 221 Tyrone Hughes SL	.10	.05
❑ 222 Tamarick Vanover SL	.20	.09
❑ 223 Rick Tuten SL	.10	.05
❑ 224 49ers Defense SL	.10	.05
❑ 225 Lions Offensive Line SL	.10	.05

2000 Upper Deck Ultimate Victory

	MINT	NRMT
COMPLETE SET (150)	300.00	135.00
❑ 1 Jake Plummer	.40	.18
❑ 2 David Boston	.40	.18
❑ 3 Frank Sanders	.20	.09
❑ 4 Chris Chandler	.20	.09
❑ 5 Jamal Anderson	.40	.18
❑ 6 Shawn Jefferson	.15	.07
❑ 7 Qadry Ismail	.15	.07
❑ 8 Tony Banks	.20	.09
❑ 9 Shannon Sharpe	.20	.09
❑ 10 Peerless Price	.40	.18
❑ 11 Rob Johnson	.20	.09
❑ 12 Eric Moulds	.40	.18
❑ 13 Muhsin Muhammad	.20	.09
❑ 14 Steve Beuerlein	.20	.09
❑ 15 Tim Biakabutuka	.20	.09
❑ 16 Cade McNown	.40	.18
❑ 17 Curtis Enis	.20	.09
❑ 18 Marcus Robinson	.40	.18
❑ 19 Akili Smith	.40	.18
❑ 20 Corey Dillon	.40	.18
❑ 21 Darnay Scott	.20	.09
❑ 22 Tim Couch	.75	.35
❑ 23 Kevin Johnson	.40	.18
❑ 24 Errict Rhett	.20	.09
❑ 25 Troy Aikman	1.00	.45
❑ 26 Emmitt Smith	1.00	.45
❑ 27 Rocket Ismail	.20	.09
❑ 28 Joey Galloway	.40	.18
❑ 29 Terrell Davis	1.00	.45
❑ 30 Olandis Gary	.40	.18
❑ 31 Ed McCaffrey	.40	.18
❑ 32 Charlie Batch	.40	.18
❑ 33 Germane Crowell	.20	.09
❑ 34 James Stewart	.20	.09
❑ 35 Brett Favre	1.50	.70
❑ 36 Antonio Freeman	.40	.18
❑ 37 Dorsey Levens	.20	.09
❑ 38 Peyton Manning	1.25	.55
❑ 39 Edgerrin James	1.50	.70
❑ 40 Marvin Harrison	.40	.18
❑ 41 Mark Brunell	.60	.25
❑ 42 Fred Taylor	.50	.23
❑ 43 Jimmy Smith	.20	.09
❑ 44 Elvis Grbac	.20	.09
❑ 45 Tony Gonzalez	.20	.09
❑ 46 Derrick Alexander	.20	.09
❑ 47 Tony Martin	1.50	.70
❑ 48 Damon Huard	.40	.18
❑ 49 O.J. McDuffie	.20	.09
❑ 50 Randy Moss	1.25	.55
❑ 51 Robert Smith	.40	.18
❑ 52 Daunte Culpepper	.75	.35
❑ 53 Drew Bledsoe	.60	.25
❑ 54 Terry Glenn	.20	.09
❑ 55 Ricky Williams	1.00	.45
❑ 56 Jake Reed	.20	.09
❑ 57 Jeff Blake	.20	.09
❑ 58 Kerry Collins	.20	.09
❑ 59 Amani Toomer	.20	.09
❑ 60 Ike Hilliard	.20	.09
❑ 61 Ray Lucas	.40	.18
❑ 62 Curtis Martin	.40	.18
❑ 63 Vinny Testaverde	.20	.09
❑ 64 Tim Brown	.40	.18
❑ 65 Rich Gannon	.20	.09
❑ 66 Tyrone Wheatley	.20	.09
❑ 67 Duce Staley	.40	.18
❑ 68 Donovan McNabb	.60	.25
❑ 69 Troy Edwards	.20	.09
❑ 70 Jerome Bettis	.40	.18
❑ 71 Marshall Faulk	.50	.23
❑ 72 Kurt Warner	1.50	.70
❑ 73 Isaac Bruce	.40	.18
❑ 74 Curtis Conway	.20	.09
❑ 75 Freddie Jones	.15	.07
❑ 76 Jeff Graham	.15	.07
❑ 77 Jeff Garcia	.40	.18
❑ 78 Jerry Rice	1.00	.45
❑ 79 Ricky Watters	.20	.09
❑ 80 Jon Kitna	.40	.18
❑ 81 Derrick Mayes	.20	.09
❑ 82 Keyshawn Johnson	.40	.18
❑ 83 Shaun King	.60	.25
❑ 84 Mike Alstott	.40	.18
❑ 85 Eddie George	.50	.23
❑ 86 Steve McNair	.40	.18
❑ 87 Jevon Kearse	.40	.18
❑ 88 Brad Johnson	.40	.18
❑ 89 Stephen Davis	.40	.18
❑ 90 Michael Westbrook	.20	.09
❑ 91 Anthony Becht RC	5.00	2.20
❑ 92 Anthony Lucas RC	2.50	1.10
❑ 93 Bashir Yamini RC	4.00	1.80
❑ 94 Brian Urlacher RC	15.00	6.75
❑ 95 Chad Morton RC	5.00	2.20
❑ 96 Chad Pennington RC	15.00	6.75
❑ 97 Chris Cole RC	4.00	1.80
❑ 98 Chris Hovan RC	4.00	1.80
❑ 99 Tim Rattay RC	8.00	3.60
❑ 100 Chris Redman RC	10.00	4.50
❑ 101 Chris Samuels RC	4.00	1.80
❑ 102 Corey Simon RC	6.00	2.70
❑ 103 Courtney Brown RC	6.00	2.70
❑ 104 Curtis Keaton RC	4.00	1.80
❑ 105 Danny Farmer RC	5.00	2.20
❑ 106 Erron Kinney RC	5.00	2.20
❑ 107 Darren Howard RC	4.00	1.80
❑ 108 Deltha O'Neal RC	4.00	1.80
❑ 109 Dennis Northcutt RC	6.00	2.70
❑ 110 Demario Brown RC	4.00	1.80
❑ 111 Dez White RC	4.00	1.80
❑ 112 Frank Murphy RC	2.50	1.10
❑ 113 Gari Scott RC	4.00	1.80
❑ 114 Giovanni Carmazzi RC	6.00	2.70
❑ 115 J.R. Redmond RC	6.00	2.70
❑ 116 JaJuan Dawson RC	5.00	2.20
❑ 117 Jamal Lewis RC	25.00	11.00
❑ 118 Leon Murray RC	2.50	1.10
❑ 119 Jerry Porter RC	5.00	2.20
❑ 120 Joe Hamilton RC	6.00	2.70
❑ 121 John Abraham RC	4.00	1.80
❑ 122 John Engelberger RC	4.00	1.80
❑ 123 Keith Bulluck RC	4.00	1.80
❑ 124 Kwame Cavil RC	4.00	1.80
❑ 125 Laveranues Coles RC	8.00	3.60
❑ 126 Marc Bulger RC	5.00	2.20
❑ 127 Marcus Knight RC	2.50	1.10
❑ 128 Mareno Philyaw RC	2.50	1.10
❑ 129 Michael Wiley RC	5.00	2.20
❑ 130 Na'il Diggs RC	5.00	2.20
❑ 131 Peter Warrick RC	15.00	6.75
❑ 132 Plaxico Burress RC	10.00	4.50
❑ 133 Raynoch Thompson RC	4.00	1.80
❑ 134 Reuben Droughns RC	5.00	2.20
❑ 135 Rob Morris RC	4.00	1.80
❑ 136 Ron Dayne RC	15.00	6.75
❑ 137 Ron Dugans RC	4.00	1.80
❑ 138 Sebastian Janikowski RC	5.00	2.20
❑ 139 Shaun Alexander RC	12.00	5.50
❑ 140 Sherrod Gideon RC	2.50	1.10
❑ 141 Sylvester Morris RC	10.00	4.50
❑ 142 Tee Martin RC	8.00	3.60
❑ 143 Thomas Jones RC	8.00	3.60
❑ 144 Todd Husak RC	5.00	2.20
❑ 145 Todd Pinkston RC	5.00	2.20
❑ 146 Tom Brady RC	5.00	2.20
❑ 147 Travis Prentice RC	8.00	3.60
❑ 148 Travis Taylor RC	6.00	2.70
❑ 149 Trevor Gaylor RC	4.00	1.80
❑ 150 Trung Canidate RC	5.00	2.20

1999 Upper Deck Victory

	MINT	NRMT
COMPLETE SET (440)	60.00	27.00
COMP. SET w/o SP's (380)	10.00	4.50
❑ 1 Checklist Card	.10	.05
❑ 2 Jake Plummer	.75	.35
❑ 3 Adrian Murrell	.20	.09
❑ 4 Michael Pittman	.10	.05
❑ 5 Frank Sanders	.20	.09
❑ 6 Andre Wadsworth	.10	.05
❑ 7 Rob Moore	.20	.09
❑ 8 Simeon Rice	.10	.05
❑ 9 Kwamie Lassiter RC	.10	.05
❑ 10 Mario Bates	.10	.05
❑ 11 Checklist Card	.10	.05
❑ 12 Jamal Anderson	.40	.18
❑ 13 Chris Chandler	.20	.09
❑ 14 Chuck Smith	.10	.05
❑ 15 Terance Mathis	.20	.09
❑ 16 Tim Dwight	.40	.18
❑ 17 Ray Buchanan	.10	.05
❑ 18 O.J. Santiago	.10	.05
❑ 19 Lester Archambeau	.10	.05
❑ 20 Checklist Card	.10	.05
❑ 21 Tony Banks	.20	.09

❑ 22 Priest Holmes .40 .18
❑ 23 Michael Jackson .10 .05
❑ 24 Jermaine Lewis .20 .09
❑ 25 Michael McCrary .10 .05
❑ 26 Rod Woodson .20 .09
❑ 27 Checklist Card .10 .05
❑ 28 Rob Johnson .20 .09
❑ 29 Antowain Smith .40 .18
❑ 30 Thurman Thomas .20 .09
❑ 31 Doug Flutie .50 .23
❑ 32 Eric Moulds .40 .18
❑ 33 Bruce Smith .20 .09
❑ 34 Andre Reed .20 .09
❑ 35 Phil Hansen .10 .05
❑ 36 Checklist Card .10 .05
❑ 37 Fred Lane .20 .09
❑ 38 Tim Biakabutuka .20 .09
❑ 39 Rae Carruth .20 .09
❑ 40 Wesley Walls .20 .09
❑ 41 Steve Beuerlein .10 .05
❑ 42 Muhsin Muhammad .20 .09
❑ 43 Kevin Greene .10 .05
❑ 44 Checklist Card .10 .05
❑ 45 Erik Kramer .10 .05
❑ 46 Edgar Bennett .10 .05
❑ 47 Curtis Conway .20 .09
❑ 48 Curtis Enis .40 .18
❑ 49 Bobby Engram .20 .09
❑ 50 Alonzo Mayes .10 .05
❑ 51 Tony Parrish .10 .05
❑ 52 Glyn Milburn .10 .05
❑ 53 Checklist Card .10 .05
❑ 54 Corey Dillon .40 .18
❑ 55 Jeff Blake .20 .09
❑ 56 Carl Pickens .20 .09
❑ 57 Darnay Scott .10 .05
❑ 58 Tony McGee .10 .05
❑ 59 Ki-Jana Carter .10 .05
❑ 60 Takeo Spikes .10 .05
❑ 61 Checklist Card .10 .05
❑ 62 Ty Detmer .20 .09
❑ 63 Terry Kirby .10 .05
❑ 64 Derrick Alexander DT .10 .05
❑ 65 Leslie Shepherd .10 .05
❑ 66 Marquez Pope .10 .05
❑ 67 Antonio Langham .10 .05
❑ 68 Marc Edwards .10 .05
❑ 69 Checklist Card .10 .05
❑ 70 Troy Aikman 1.00 .45
❑ 71 Emmitt Smith 1.00 .45
❑ 72 Deion Sanders .40 .18
❑ 73 Rocket Ismail .20 .09
❑ 74 Michael Irvin .20 .09
❑ 75 Chris Warren .10 .05
❑ 76 Greg Ellis .10 .05
❑ 77 Kavika Pittman .10 .05
❑ 78 David LaFleur .10 .05
❑ 79 Checklist Card .10 .05
❑ 80 John Elway 1.50 .70
❑ 81 Terrell Davis 1.00 .45
❑ 82 Rod Smith .20 .09
❑ 83 Shannon Sharpe .20 .09
❑ 84 Ed McCaffrey .20 .09
❑ 85 John Mobley .10 .05
❑ 86 Bill Romanowski .10 .05
❑ 87 Jason Elam .10 .05
❑ 88 Howard Griffith .10 .05
❑ 89 Checklist Card .10 .05
❑ 90 Barry Sanders 1.50 .70
❑ 91 Johnnie Morton .20 .09
❑ 92 Herman Moore .40 .18
❑ 93 Charlie Batch .75 .35
❑ 94 Germane Crowell .20 .09
❑ 95 Robert Porcher .10 .05
❑ 96 Stephen Boyd .10 .05
❑ 97 Checklist Card .10 .05
❑ 98 Brett Favre 1.50 .70
❑ 99 Antonio Freeman .40 .18
❑ 100 Dorsey Levens .40 .18
❑ 101 Mark Chmura .10 .05
❑ 102 Vonnie Holliday .10 .05
❑ 103 Bill Schroeder .40 .18
❑ 104 LeRoy Butler .10 .05
❑ 105 William Henderson .10 .05
❑ 106 Checklist Card .10 .05
❑ 107 Peyton Manning 1.50 .70
❑ 108 Marvin Harrison .40 .18
❑ 109 Ken Dilger .10 .05
❑ 110 Jerome Pathon .10 .05
❑ 111 E.G. Green .10 .05
❑ 112 Ellis Johnson .10 .05
❑ 113 Jeff Burris .10 .05
❑ 114 Checklist Card .10 .05
❑ 115 Mark Brunell .60 .25
❑ 116 Jimmy Smith .20 .09
❑ 117 Keenan McCardell .20 .09
❑ 118 Fred Taylor 1.00 .45
❑ 119 James Stewart .20 .09
❑ 120 Dave Thomas .10 .05
❑ 121 Kyle Brady .10 .05
❑ 122 Bryce Paup .10 .05
❑ 123 Checklist Card .10 .05
❑ 124 Elvis Grbac .20 .09
❑ 125 Andre Rison .20 .09
❑ 126 Derrick Alexander WR .20 .09
❑ 127 Tony Gonzalez .20 .09
❑ 128 Donnell Bennett .10 .05
❑ 129 Derrick Thomas .20 .09
❑ 130 Tamarick Vanover .10 .05
❑ 131 Donnie Edwards .10 .05
❑ 132 Checklist Card .10 .05
❑ 133 Dan Marino 1.50 .70
❑ 134 Karim Abdul-Jabbar .20 .09
❑ 135 Zach Thomas .20 .09
❑ 136 O.J. McDuffie .20 .09
❑ 137 John Avery .20 .09
❑ 138 Sam Madison .10 .05
❑ 139 Terrell Buckley .10 .05
❑ 140 Jason Taylor .10 .05
❑ 141 Oronde Gadsden .10 .05
❑ 142 Checklist Card .10 .05
❑ 143 Randall Cunningham .40 .18
❑ 144 Cris Carter .40 .18
❑ 145 Robert Smith .40 .18
❑ 146 Randy Moss 1.50 .70
❑ 147 Jake Reed .20 .09
❑ 148 Leroy Hoard .10 .05
❑ 149 Matthew Hatchette .10 .05
❑ 150 John Randle .20 .09
❑ 151 Gary Anderson .10 .05
❑ 152 Checklist Card .10 .05
❑ 153 Drew Bledsoe .60 .25
❑ 154 Terry Glenn .40 .18
❑ 155 Ben Coates .20 .09
❑ 156 Ty Law .10 .05
❑ 157 Tony Simmons .10 .05
❑ 158 Ted Johnson .10 .05
❑ 159 Willie McGinest .10 .05
❑ 160 Tony Carter .10 .05
❑ 161 Shawn Jefferson .10 .05
❑ 162 Checklist Card .10 .05
❑ 163 Danny Wuerffel .10 .05
❑ 164 Lamar Smith .20 .09
❑ 165 Keith Poole .10 .05
❑ 166 Cameron Cleeland .10 .05
❑ 167 Joe Johnson .10 .05
❑ 168 Andre Hastings .10 .05
❑ 169 La'Roi Glover .10 .05
❑ 170 Aaron Craver .10 .05
❑ 171 Checklist Card .10 .05
❑ 172 Kent Graham .10 .05
❑ 173 Gary Brown .10 .05
❑ 174 Amani Toomer .10 .05
❑ 175 Tiki Barber .10 .05
❑ 176 Ike Hilliard .10 .05
❑ 177 Jason Sehorn .10 .05
❑ 178 Michael Strahan .10 .05
❑ 179 Charles Way .10 .05
❑ 180 Checklist Card .10 .05
❑ 181 Vinny Testaverde .20 .09
❑ 182 Curtis Martin .40 .18
❑ 183 Keyshawn Johnson .40 .18
❑ 184 Wayne Chrebet .20 .09
❑ 185 Mo Lewis .10 .05
❑ 186 Steve Atwater .10 .05
❑ 187 Leon Johnson .10 .05
❑ 188 Bryan Cox .10 .05
❑ 189 Checklist Card .10 .05
❑ 190 Rich Gannon .20 .09
❑ 191 Napoleon Kaufman .40 .18
❑ 192 Tim Brown .40 .18
❑ 193 Darrell Russell .10 .05
❑ 194 Rickey Dudley .10 .05
❑ 195 Charles Woodson .40 .18
❑ 196 Harvey Williams .10 .05
❑ 197 James Jett .20 .09
❑ 198 Checklist Card .10 .05
❑ 199 Koy Detmer .10 .05
❑ 200 Duce Staley .40 .18
❑ 201 Bobby Taylor .10 .05
❑ 202 Doug Pederson .10 .05
❑ 203 Karl Hankton .10 .05
❑ 204 Charles Johnson .10 .05
❑ 205 Kevin Turner .10 .05
❑ 206 Hugh Douglas .10 .05
❑ 207 Checklist Card .10 .05
❑ 208 Kordell Stewart .40 .18
❑ 209 Jerome Bettis .40 .18
❑ 210 Hines Ward .10 .05
❑ 211 Courtney Hawkins .10 .05
❑ 212 Will Blackwell .10 .05
❑ 213 Richard Huntley .40 .18
❑ 214 Levon Kirkland .10 .05
❑ 215 Jason Gildon .10 .05
❑ 216 Checklist Card .10 .05
❑ 217 Trent Green .20 .09
❑ 218 Isaac Bruce .40 .18
❑ 219 Az-Zahir Hakim .10 .05
❑ 220 Amp Lee .10 .05
❑ 221 Robert Holcombe .20 .09
❑ 222 Ricky Proehl .10 .05
❑ 223 Kevin Carter .10 .05
❑ 224 Marshall Faulk .40 .18
❑ 225 Checklist Card .10 .05
❑ 226 Ryan Leaf .40 .18
❑ 227 Natrone Means .20 .09
❑ 228 Jim Harbaugh .20 .09
❑ 229 Junior Seau .20 .09
❑ 230 Charlie Jones .10 .05
❑ 231 Rodney Harrison .10 .05
❑ 232 Terrell Fletcher .10 .05
❑ 233 Tremayne Stephens .10 .05
❑ 234 Checklist Card .10 .05
❑ 235 Steve Young .60 .25
❑ 236 Jerry Rice 1.00 .45
❑ 237 Garrison Hearst .20 .09
❑ 238 Terrell Owens .40 .18
❑ 239 J.J. Stokes .20 .09
❑ 240 Bryant Young .10 .05
❑ 241 Tim McDonald .10 .05
❑ 242 Merton Hanks .10 .05
❑ 243 Travis Jervey .10 .05
❑ 244 Checklist Card .10 .05
❑ 245 Ricky Watters .20 .09
❑ 246 Joey Galloway .40 .18
❑ 247 Jon Kitna .40 .18
❑ 248 Ahman Green .20 .09
❑ 249 Mike Pritchard .10 .05
❑ 250 Chad Brown .10 .05
❑ 251 Christian Fauria .10 .05
❑ 252 Michael Sinclair .10 .05
❑ 253 Checklist Card .10 .05
❑ 254 Warrick Dunn .40 .18
❑ 255 Trent Dilfer .20 .09
❑ 256 Mike Alstott .40 .18
❑ 257 Reidel Anthony .20 .09
❑ 258 Bert Emanuel .20 .09
❑ 259 Jacquez Green .20 .09
❑ 260 Hardy Nickerson .10 .05
❑ 261 Derrick Brooks .10 .05
❑ 262 Dave Moore .10 .05
❑ 263 Checklist Card .10 .05
❑ 264 Steve McNair .40 .18
❑ 265 Eddie George .50 .23
❑ 266 Yancey Thigpen .10 .05
❑ 267 Frank Wycheck .10 .05
❑ 268 Kevin Dyson .20 .09
❑ 269 Jackie Harris .10 .05
❑ 270 Blaine Bishop .10 .05
❑ 271 Willie Davis .10 .05
❑ 272 Checklist Card .10 .05
❑ 273 Skip Hicks .40 .18
❑ 274 Michael Westbrook .20 .09
❑ 275 Stephen Alexander .10 .05
❑ 276 Dana Stubblefield .10 .05
❑ 277 Brad Johnson .40 .18
❑ 278 Brian Mitchell .10 .05
❑ 279 Dan Wilkinson .10 .05

Card	MINT	NRMT
❑ 280 Stephen Davis	.40	.18
❑ 281 John Elway AV	.60	.25
❑ 282 Dan Marino AV	.60	.25
❑ 283 Troy Aikman AV	.40	.18
❑ 284 Vinny Testaverde AV	.20	.09
❑ 285 Corey Dillon AV	.40	.18
❑ 286 Steve Young AV	.20	.09
❑ 287 Randy Moss AV	.60	.25
❑ 288 Drew Bledsoe AV	.20	.09
❑ 289 Jerome Bettis AV	.40	.18
❑ 290 Antonio Freeman AV	.40	.18
❑ 291 Fred Taylor AV	.40	.18
❑ 292 Doug Flutie AV	.40	.18
❑ 293 Jerry Rice AV	.40	.18
❑ 294 Peyton Manning AV	.60	.25
❑ 295 Brett Favre AV	.60	.25
❑ 296 Barry Sanders AV	.60	.25
❑ 297 Keyshawn Johnson AV	.40	.18
❑ 298 Mark Brunell AV	.20	.09
❑ 299 Jamal Anderson AV	.40	.18
❑ 300 Terrell Davis AV	.40	.18
❑ 301 Randall Cunningham AV	.40	.18
❑ 302 Kordell Stewart AV	.40	.18
❑ 303 Warrick Dunn AV	.40	.18
❑ 304 Jake Plummer AV	.20	.09
❑ 305 Junior Seau AV	.20	.09
❑ 306 Antowain Smith AV	.40	.18
❑ 307 Charlie Batch AV	.20	.09
❑ 308 Eddie George AV	.20	.09
❑ 309 Michael Irvin AV	.20	.09
❑ 310 Joey Galloway AV	.40	.18
❑ 311 Randall Cunningham SL	.40	.18
❑ 312 Vinny Testaverde SL	.20	.09
❑ 313 Steve Young SL	.20	.09
❑ 314 Chris Chandler SL	.20	.09
❑ 315 John Elway SL	.60	.25
❑ 316 Steve Young SL	.20	.09
❑ 317 Randall Cunningham SL	.40	.18
❑ 318 Brett Favre SL	.60	.25
❑ 319 Vinny Testaverde SL	.20	.09
❑ 320 Peyton Manning SL	.50	.23
❑ 321 Terrell Davis SL	.40	.18
❑ 322 Jamal Anderson SL	.40	.18
❑ 323 Garrison Hearst SL	.20	.09
❑ 324 Barry Sanders SL	.60	.25
❑ 325 Emmitt Smith SL	.40	.18
❑ 326 Terrell Davis SL	.40	.18
❑ 327 Fred Taylor SL	.40	.18
❑ 328 Jamal Anderson SL	.40	.18
❑ 329 Emmitt Smith SL	.40	.18
❑ 330 Ricky Watters SL	.20	.09
❑ 331 O.J. McDuffie SL	.20	.09
❑ 332 Frank Sanders SL	.20	.09
❑ 333 Rod Smith SL	.20	.09
❑ 334 Marshall Faulk SL	.40	.18
❑ 335 Antonio Freeman SL	.40	.18
❑ 336 Randy Moss SL	.60	.25
❑ 337 Antonio Freeman SL	.40	.18
❑ 338 Terrell Owens SL	.40	.18
❑ 339 Cris Carter SL	.40	.18
❑ 340 Terance Mathis SL	.20	.09
❑ 341 Jake Plummer VP	.20	.09
❑ 342 Steve McNair VP	.40	.18
❑ 343 Randy Moss VP	.60	.25
❑ 344 Peyton Manning VP	.60	.25
❑ 345 Mark Brunell VP	.20	.09
❑ 346 Terrell Owens VP	.40	.18
❑ 347 Antowain Smith VP	.40	.18
❑ 348 Jerry Rice VP	.40	.18
❑ 349 Troy Aikman VP	.40	.18
❑ 350 Fred Taylor VP	.40	.18
❑ 351 Charlie Batch VP	.20	.09
❑ 352 Dan Marino VP	.60	.25
❑ 353 Eddie George VP	.20	.09
❑ 354 Drew Bledsoe VP	.20	.09
❑ 355 Kordell Stewart VP	.40	.18
❑ 356 Doug Flutie VP	.40	.18
❑ 357 Deion Sanders VP	.40	.18
❑ 358 Keyshawn Johnson VP	.40	.18
❑ 359 Jerome Bettis VP	.40	.18
❑ 360 Warrick Dunn VP	.40	.18
❑ 361 John Elway RF	.60	.25
❑ 362 Dan Marino RF	.60	.25
❑ 363 Brett Favre RF	.60	.25
❑ 364 Andre Rison RF	.20	.09
❑ 365 Rod Woodson RF	.20	.09
❑ 366 Jerry Rice RF	.40	.18
❑ 367 Barry Sanders RF	.60	.25
❑ 368 Thurman Thomas RF	.20	.09
❑ 369 Troy Aikman RF	.40	.18
❑ 370 Ricky Watters RF	.20	.09
❑ 371 Jerome Bettis RF	.40	.18
❑ 372 Reggie White RF	.10	.05
❑ 373 Junior Seau RF	.20	.09
❑ 374 Deion Sanders RF	.40	.18
❑ 375 Chris Chandler RF	.20	.09
❑ 376 Curtis Martin RF	.40	.18
❑ 377 Kordell Stewart RF	.40	.18
❑ 378 Mark Brunell RF	.20	.09
❑ 379 Cris Carter RF	.40	.18
❑ 380 Emmitt Smith RF	.40	.18
❑ 381 Tim Couch RC	5.00	2.20
❑ 382 Donovan McNabb RC	6.00	2.70
❑ 383 Akili Smith RC	3.00	1.35
❑ 384 Edgerrin James RC	10.00	4.50
❑ 385 Ricky Williams RC	6.00	2.70
❑ 386 Torry Holt RC	4.00	1.80
❑ 387 Champ Bailey RC	2.00	.90
❑ 388 David Boston RC	3.00	1.35
❑ 389 Chris Claiborne RC	.50	.23
❑ 390 Chris McAlister RC	1.00	.45
❑ 391 Daunte Culpepper RC	10.00	4.50
❑ 392 Cade McNown RC	2.00	.90
❑ 393 Troy Edwards RC	2.00	.90
❑ 394 John Tait RC	.50	.23
❑ 395 Anthony McFarland RC	1.50	.70
❑ 396 Jevon Kearse RC	3.00	1.35
❑ 397 Damien Woody RC	.50	.23
❑ 398 Matt Stinchcomb RC	.50	.23
❑ 399 Luke Petitgout RC	.50	.23
❑ 400 Ebenezer Ekuban RC	1.00	.45
❑ 401 L.J. Shelton RC	.50	.23
❑ 402 Daylon McCutcheon RC	.50	.23
❑ 403 Antoine Winfield RC	1.00	.45
❑ 404 Scott Covington RC	1.50	.70
❑ 405 Antuan Edwards RC	.50	.23
❑ 406 Fernando Bryant RC	1.00	.45
❑ 407 Aaron Gibson RC	.50	.23
❑ 408 Andy Katzenmoyer RC	1.50	.70
❑ 409 Dimitrius Underwood RC	1.00	.45
❑ 410 Patrick Kerney RC	1.00	.45
❑ 411 Al Wilson RC	1.50	.70
❑ 412 Kevin Johnson RC	2.50	1.10
❑ 413 Joel Makovicka RC	1.50	.70
❑ 414 Reginald Kelly RC	.50	.23
❑ 415 Jeff Paulk RC	1.00	.45
❑ 416 Brandon Stokley RC	1.50	.70
❑ 417 Peerless Price RC	2.00	.90
❑ 418 D'Wayne Bates RC	1.00	.45
❑ 419 Travis McGriff RC	1.50	.70
❑ 420 Sedrick Irvin RC	1.50	.70
❑ 421 Aaron Brooks RC	6.00	2.70
❑ 422 Mike Cloud RC	1.50	.70
❑ 423 Joe Montgomery RC	1.50	.70
❑ 424 Shaun King RC	3.00	1.35
❑ 425 Dameane Douglas RC	1.50	.70
❑ 426 Joe Germaine RC	1.50	.70
❑ 427 James Johnson RC	1.50	.70
❑ 428 Michael Bishop RC	2.00	.90
❑ 429 Karsten Bailey RC	1.00	.45
❑ 430 Craig Yeast RC	1.00	.45
❑ 431 Jim Kleinsasser RC	1.50	.70
❑ 432 Martin Gramatica RC	.50	.23
❑ 433 Jermaine Fazande RC	1.50	.70
❑ 434 Dre'Bly RC	1.00	.45
❑ 435 Brock Huard RC	2.50	1.10
❑ 436 Rob Konrad RC	1.50	.70
❑ 437 Tony Bryant RC	1.00	.45
❑ 438 Sean Bennett RC	1.50	.70
❑ 439 Kevin Faulk RC	2.50	1.10
❑ 440 Amos Zereoue RC	1.50	.70

2000 Upper Deck Victory

	MINT	NRMT
COMPLETE SET (330)	50.00	22.00
❑ 1 Jake Plummer	.30	.14
❑ 2 Michael Pittman	.10	.05
❑ 3 Rob Moore	.15	.07

Card	MINT	NRMT
❑ 4 David Boston	.30	.14
❑ 5 Frank Sanders	.15	.07
❑ 6 Aeneas Williams	.10	.05
❑ 7 Tim Dwight	.30	.14
❑ 8 Chris Chandler	.15	.07
❑ 9 Jamal Anderson	.30	.14
❑ 10 Shawn Jefferson	.10	.05
❑ 11 Ken Oxendine	.10	.05
❑ 12 Terance Mathis	.15	.07
❑ 13 Qadry Ismail	.10	.05
❑ 14 Jermaine Lewis	.15	.07
❑ 15 Rod Woodson	.15	.07
❑ 16 Michael McCrary	.10	.05
❑ 17 Tony Banks	.15	.07
❑ 18 Peter Boulware	.10	.05
❑ 19 Shannon Sharpe	.15	.07
❑ 20 Peerless Price	.30	.14
❑ 21 Rob Johnson	.15	.07
❑ 22 Eric Moulds	.30	.14
❑ 23 Doug Flutie	.40	.18
❑ 24 Jay Riemersma	.10	.05
❑ 25 Antowain Smith	.15	.07
❑ 26 Sam Cowart	.10	.05
❑ 27 Muhsin Muhammad	.15	.07
❑ 28 Patrick Jeffers	.30	.14
❑ 29 Steve Beuerlein	.15	.07
❑ 30 Natrone Means	.10	.05
❑ 31 Tim Biakabutuka	.15	.07
❑ 32 Michael Bates	.10	.05
❑ 33 Wesley Walls	.10	.05
❑ 34 Cade McNown	.30	.14
❑ 35 Curtis Enis	.15	.07
❑ 36 Marcus Robinson	.30	.14
❑ 37 Bobby Engram	.10	.05
❑ 38 Glyn Milburn	.10	.05
❑ 39 Marty Booker	.10	.05
❑ 40 Akili Smith	.30	.14
❑ 41 Corey Dillon	.30	.14
❑ 42 Darnay Scott	.15	.07
❑ 43 Tremain Mack	.10	.05
❑ 44 Michael Bankston	.10	.05
❑ 45 Tony McGee	.10	.05
❑ 46 Tim Couch	.60	.25
❑ 47 Kevin Johnson	.30	.14
❑ 48 Darrin Chiaverini	.10	.05
❑ 49 Jamir Miller	.10	.05
❑ 50 Errict Rhett	.15	.07
❑ 51 Ty Detmer	.10	.05
❑ 52 Terry Kirby	.10	.05
❑ 53 Troy Aikman	.75	.35
❑ 54 Emmitt Smith	.75	.35
❑ 55 Rocket Ismail	.15	.07
❑ 56 Chris Warren	.10	.05
❑ 57 Joey Galloway	.30	.14
❑ 58 Terrell Davis	.75	.35
❑ 59 Olandis Gary	.30	.14
❑ 60 Brian Griese	.40	.18
❑ 61 Gus Frerotte	.10	.05
❑ 62 Glenn Cadrez	.10	.05
❑ 63 Ed McCaffrey	.30	.14
❑ 64 Rod Smith	.15	.07
❑ 65 Charlie Batch	.30	.14
❑ 66 Germane Crowell	.15	.07
❑ 67 Stephen Boyd	.10	.05
❑ 68 Johnnie Morton	.15	.07
❑ 69 Robert Porcher	.10	.05
❑ 70 James Stewart	.15	.07

	No.	Card		
❑	71	Brett Favre	1.25	.55
❑	72	Antonio Freeman	.30	.14
❑	73	Bill Schroeder	.15	.07
❑	74	Dorsey Levens	.15	.07
❑	75	Darren Sharper	.10	.05
❑	76	Peyton Manning	1.00	.45
❑	77	Edgerrin James	1.25	.55
❑	78	Marvin Harrison	.30	.14
❑	79	Ken Dilger	.10	.05
❑	80	Terrence Wilkins	.30	.14
❑	81	Cornelius Bennett	.10	.05
❑	82	E.G. Green	.10	.05
❑	83	Mark Brunell	.50	.23
❑	84	Fred Taylor	.40	.18
❑	85	Jimmy Smith	.15	.07
❑	86	Keenan McCardell	.15	.07
❑	87	Carnell Lake	.10	.05
❑	88	Kevin Hardy	.10	.05
❑	89	Elvis Grbac	.15	.07
❑	90	Tony Gonzalez	.15	.07
❑	91	Derrick Alexander	.15	.07
❑	92	Donnell Bennett	.10	.05
❑	93	James Hasty	.10	.05
❑	94	Kevin Lockett	.10	.05
❑	95	Trace Armstrong	.10	.05
❑	96	Terrell Buckley	.10	.05
❑	97	Tony Martin	.15	.07
❑	98	Damon Huard	.30	.14
❑	99	O.J. McDuffie	.15	.07
❑	100	Brock Marion	.10	.05
❑	101	Zach Thomas	.15	.07
❑	102	Randy Moss	1.00	.45
❑	103	Robert Smith	.30	.14
❑	104	Cris Carter	.30	.14
❑	105	Bubby Brister	.10	.05
❑	106	Daunte Culpepper	.60	.25
❑	107	John Randle	.15	.07
❑	108	Drew Bledsoe	.50	.23
❑	109	Terry Glenn	.15	.07
❑	110	Willie McGinest	.10	.05
❑	111	Kevin Faulk	.15	.07
❑	112	Tedy Bruschi	.10	.05
❑	113	Ricky Williams	.75	.35
❑	114	Keith Poole	.10	.05
❑	115	Jake Reed	.15	.07
❑	116	Mark Fields	.10	.05
❑	117	Jeff Blake	.15	.07
❑	118	Andrew Glover	.10	.05
❑	119	Kerry Collins	.15	.07
❑	120	Amani Toomer	.10	.05
❑	121	Jessie Armstead	.10	.05
❑	122	Ike Hilliard	.15	.07
❑	123	Ray Lucas	.30	.14
❑	124	Curtis Martin	.30	.14
❑	125	Vinny Testaverde	.15	.07
❑	126	Wayne Chrebet	.15	.07
❑	127	Dedric Ward	.10	.05
❑	128	Tim Brown	.30	.14
❑	129	Rich Gannon	.15	.07
❑	130	Tyrone Wheatley	.15	.07
❑	131	Napoleon Kaufman	.15	.07
❑	132	Charles Woodson	.15	.07
❑	133	Greg Biekert	.10	.05
❑	134	Rickey Dudley	.10	.05
❑	135	Duce Staley	.30	.14
❑	136	Donovan McNabb	.50	.23
❑	137	Torrance Small	.10	.05
❑	138	Mike Mamula	.10	.05
❑	139	Brian Dawkins	.10	.05
❑	140	Troy Vincent	.10	.05
❑	141	Kent Graham	.10	.05
❑	142	Troy Edwards	.15	.07
❑	143	Jerome Bettis	.30	.14
❑	144	Hines Ward	.10	.05
❑	145	Kordell Stewart	.30	.14
❑	146	Levon Kirkland	.10	.05
❑	147	Richard Huntley	.10	.05
❑	148	Marshall Faulk	.40	.18
❑	149	Kurt Warner	1.25	.55
❑	150	Torry Holt	.30	.14
❑	151	Isaac Bruce	.30	.14
❑	152	Kevin Carter	.10	.05
❑	153	Az-Zahir Hakim	.15	.07
❑	154	Todd Lyght	.10	.05
❑	155	Jermaine Fazande	.10	.05
❑	156	Curtis Conway	.15	.07
❑	157	Freddie Jones	.10	.05
❑	158	Junior Seau	.15	.07
❑	159	Jeff Graham	.10	.05
❑	160	Moses Moreno	.10	.05
❑	161	Rodney Harrison	.10	.05
❑	162	Steve Young	.50	.23
❑	163	Jerry Rice	.75	.35
❑	164	Ken Norton	.10	.05
❑	165	Terrell Owens	.30	.14
❑	166	Jeff Garcia	.30	.14
❑	167	Ricky Watters	.15	.07
❑	168	Jon Kitna	.30	.14
❑	169	Derrick Mayes	.15	.07
❑	170	Sean Dawkins	.10	.05
❑	171	Chad Brown	.10	.05
❑	172	Warrick Dunn	.30	.14
❑	173	Keyshawn Johnson	.30	.14
❑	174	Shaun King	.50	.23
❑	175	Mike Alstott	.30	.14
❑	176	Warren Sapp	.15	.07
❑	177	Jacquez Green	.15	.07
❑	178	Derrick Brooks	.10	.05
❑	179	John Lynch	.10	.05
❑	180	Eddie George	.40	.18
❑	181	Steve McNair	.30	.14
❑	182	Kevin Dyson	.15	.07
❑	183	Jevon Kearse	.30	.14
❑	184	Yancey Thigpen	.10	.05
❑	185	Frank Wycheck	.10	.05
❑	186	Eddie Robinson	.15	.07
❑	187	Jeff George	.15	.07
❑	188	Brad Johnson	.30	.14
❑	189	Stephen Davis	.30	.14
❑	190	Michael Westbrook	.15	.07
❑	191	Albert Connell	.10	.05
❑	192	Brian Mitchell	.10	.05
❑	193	Bruce Smith	.15	.07
❑	194	Champ Bailey	.15	.07
❑	195	Sam Shade	.10	.05
❑	196	Marvin Harrison SL	.15	.07
❑	197	Jimmy Smith SL	.10	.05
❑	198	Randy Moss SL	.50	.23
❑	199	Marcus Robinson SL	.10	.05
❑	200	Tim Brown SL	.15	.07
❑	201	Jimmy Smith SL	.10	.05
❑	202	Marvin Harrison SL	.15	.07
❑	203	Muhsin Muhammad SL	.10	.05
❑	204	Tim Brown SL	.15	.07
❑	205	Cris Carter SL	.15	.07
❑	206	Edgerrin James SL	.60	.25
❑	207	Curtis Martin SL	.15	.07
❑	208	Stephen Davis SL	.15	.07
❑	209	Emmitt Smith SL	.40	.18
❑	210	Marshall Faulk SL	.15	.07
❑	211	Kurt Warner SL	.60	.25
❑	212	Steve Beuerlein SL	.10	.05
❑	213	Jeff George SL	.10	.05
❑	214	Peyton Manning SL	.50	.23
❑	215	Brad Johnson SL	.15	.07
❑	216	Kurt Warner CL	.60	.25
❑	217	Peyton Manning CL	.50	.23
❑	218	Edgerrin James CL	.60	.25
❑	219	Marshall Faulk CL	.15	.07
❑	220	Randy Moss CL	.50	.23
❑	221	Jimmy Smith CL	.10	.05
❑	222	Tony Gonzalez CL	.10	.05
❑	223	Tony Boselli CL	.10	.05
❑	224	Orlando Pace CL	.10	.05
❑	225	Larry Allen CL	.10	.05
❑	226	Randall McDaniel CL	.10	.05
❑	227	Tom Nalen CL	.10	.05
❑	228	Kevin Carter CL	.10	.05
❑	229	Jevon Kearse CL	.15	.07
❑	230	Warren Sapp CL	.10	.05
❑	231	Darrell Russell CL	.10	.05
❑	232	Derrick Brooks CL	.10	.05
❑	233	Peter Boulware CL	.10	.05
❑	234	Junior Seau CL	.10	.05
❑	235	Sam Madison CL	.10	.05
❑	236	Charles Woodson CL	.10	.05
❑	237	John Lynch CL	.10	.05
❑	238	Carnell Lake CL	.10	.05
❑	239	Mitch Berger CL	.10	.05
❑	240	Jason Hanson CL	.10	.05
❑	241	Randy Moss PM	.50	.23
❑	242	Kurt Warner PM	.60	.25
❑	243	Peyton Manning PM	.50	.23
❑	244	Marshall Faulk PM	.15	.07
❑	245	Edgerrin James PM	.60	.25
❑	246	Eddie George PM	.15	.07
❑	247	Stephen Davis PM	.15	.07
❑	248	Keyshawn Johnson PM	.15	.07
❑	249	Brad Johnson PM	.15	.07
❑	250	Ricky Williams PM	.40	.18
❑	251	Jimmy Smith PM	.10	.05
❑	252	Isaac Bruce PM	.15	.07
❑	253	Muhsin Muhammad PM	.10	.05
❑	254	Marcus Robinson PM	.10	.05
❑	255	Kevin Johnson PM	.15	.07
❑	256	Tim Couch PM	.30	.14
❑	257	Curtis Martin PM	.15	.07
❑	258	Charlie Batch PM	.15	.07
❑	259	Tim Brown PM	.15	.07
❑	260	Jerry Rice PM	.40	.18
❑	261	Drew Bledsoe PM	.30	.14
❑	262	Brett Favre PM	.60	.25
❑	263	Mark Brunell PM	.30	.14
❑	264	Fred Taylor PM	.30	.14
❑	265	Troy Edwards PM	.10	.05
❑	266	Marvin Harrison PM	.15	.07
❑	267	Germane Crowell PM	.10	.05
❑	268	Terry Glenn PM	.15	.07
❑	269	Qadry Ismail PM	.10	.05
❑	270	Jake Plummer PM	.15	.07
❑	271	Anthony Becht RC	.75	.35
❑	272	Anthony Lucas RC	.75	.35
❑	273	Bashir Yamini RC	.60	.25
❑	274	Brian Urlacher RC	2.50	1.10
❑	275	Chad Morton RC	.75	.35
❑	276	Chad Pennington RC	2.50	1.10
❑	277	Chris Cole RC	.60	.25
❑	278	Chris Hovan RC	.60	.25
❑	279	Tim Rattay RC	1.25	.55
❑	280	Chris Redman RC	1.50	.70
❑	281	Chris Samuels RC	.60	.25
❑	282	Corey Simon RC	1.00	.45
❑	283	Courtney Brown RC	1.00	.45
❑	284	Curtis Keaton RC	.60	.25
❑	285	Danny Farmer RC	.75	.35
❑	286	Erron Kinney RC	.75	.35
❑	287	Darren Howard RC	.60	.25
❑	288	Deltha O'Neal RC	.60	.25
❑	289	Dennis Northcutt RC	1.00	.45
❑	290	Demario Brown RC	.60	.25
❑	291	Dez White RC	.60	.25
❑	292	Frank Murphy RC	.40	.18
❑	293	Gari Scott RC	.75	.35
❑	294	Giovanni Carmazzi RC	1.00	.45
❑	295	J.R. Redmond RC	1.00	.45
❑	296	JaJuan Dawson RC	.75	.35
❑	297	Jamal Lewis RC	4.00	1.80
❑	298	Leon Murray RC	.40	.18
❑	299	Jerry Porter RC	.75	.35
❑	300	Joe Hamilton RC	1.00	.45
❑	301	John Abraham RC	.60	.25
❑	302	John Engelberger RC	.60	.25
❑	303	Keith Bulluck RC	.60	.25
❑	304	Kwame Cavil RC	.60	.25
❑	305	Laveranues Coles RC	1.25	.55
❑	306	Marc Bulger RC	.75	.35
❑	307	Marcus Knight RC	.40	.18
❑	308	Mareno Philyaw RC	.60	.25
❑	309	Michael Wiley RC	.75	.35
❑	310	Na'il Diggs RC	.60	.25
❑	311	Peter Warrick RC	2.50	1.10
❑	312	Plaxico Burress RC	1.50	.70
❑	313	Raynoch Thompson RC	.60	.25
❑	314	Reuben Droughns RC	.75	.35
❑	315	Rob Morris RC	.75	.35
❑	316	Ron Dayne RC	2.50	1.10
❑	317	Ron Dugans RC	.60	.25
❑	318	Sebastian Janikowski RC	.75	.35
❑	319	Shaun Alexander RC	2.00	.90
❑	320	Sherrod Gideon RC	.60	.25
❑	321	Sylvester Morris RC	1.50	.70
❑	322	Tee Martin RC	1.25	.55
❑	323	Thomas Jones RC	1.25	.55
❑	324	Todd Husak RC	.75	.35
❑	325	Todd Pinkston RC	.75	.35
❑	326	Tom Brady RC	.75	.35
❑	327	Travis Prentice RC	1.25	.55
❑	328	Travis Taylor RC	1.00	.45

❑ 329	Trevor Gaylor RC	.60	.25
❑ 330	Trung Canidate RC	.75	.35

2000 Upper Deck Vintage Previews

		MINT	NRMT
❑ 1	Jamal Lewis	60.00	27.00
❑ 2	Sammy Morris	15.00	6.75
❑ 3	Peter Warrick	40.00	18.00
❑ 4	Travis Prentice	20.00	9.00
❑ 5	Mike Anderson	60.00	27.00
❑ 6	Sylvester Morris	25.00	11.00
❑ 7	Ron Dayne	40.00	18.00
❑ 8	Chad Pennington	40.00	18.00
❑ 9	Plaxico Burress	25.00	11.00
❑ 10	Laveranues Coles	20.00	9.00
❑ 11	Spergon Wynn Dennis Northcutt	6.00	2.70
❑ 12	Courtney Brown JaJuan Dawson	8.00	3.60
❑ 13	Raynoch Thompson Thomas Jones	10.00	4.50
❑ 14	Tom Brady J.R. Redmond	8.00	3.60
❑ 15	John Abraham Windrell Hayes	5.00	2.20
❑ 16	Todd Husak Chris Samuels	6.00	2.70
❑ 17	Giovanni Carmazzi Tim Rattay	10.00	4.50
❑ 18	Shaun Alexander Darrell Jackson	15.00	6.75
❑ 19	Rob Morris Kevin McDougle	5.00	2.20
❑ 20	Brian Urlacher Dez White	20.00	9.00
❑ 21	Doug Johnson Darrick Vaughn Mark Simoneau	5.00	2.20
❑ 22	Chris Redman John Jones Travis Taylor	10.00	4.50
❑ 23	Kwame Cavil Corey Moore Erik Flowers	5.00	2.20
❑ 24	Ray Green Lester Towns Brad Hoover	10.00	4.50
❑ 25	Curtis Keaton Danny Farmer Ron Dugans	5.00	2.20
❑ 26	Scottie Montgomery KaRon Coleman Deltha O'Neal	4.00	1.80
❑ 27	Bubba Franks Na'il Diggs Charles Lee	6.00	2.70
❑ 28	Troy Walters Chris Hovan Doug Chapman	10.00	4.50
❑ 29	Chad Morton Darren Howard Terrelle Smith	5.00	2.20
❑ 30	Gari Scott Todd Pinkston Corey Simon	5.00	2.20
❑ 31	Chris Coleman Keith Bulluck Erron Kinney	5.00	2.20
❑ 32	Peter Sirmon Billy Volek Bashir Yamini	4.00	1.80
❑ 33	Jason Webster Ahmed Plummer Julian Peterson	4.00	1.80
❑ 34	Shockmain Davis Patrick Pass Antwan Harris	5.00	2.20
❑ 35	R.Jay Soward Shyrone Stith T.J. Slaughter	5.00	2.20
❑ 36	Trevor Gaylor Ronney Jenkins Rogers Beckett	4.00	1.80
❑ 37	Martin/Hamilton/J.Jackson	5.00	2.20
❑ 38	Chris Cole Ron Dixon James Williams	6.00	2.70
❑ 39	Reuben Droughns Trung Canidate Frank Moreau	5.00	2.20
❑ 40	Mike Brown Jerry Porter Michael Wiley	5.00	2.20
❑ 41	Jake Plummer	2.00	.90
❑ 42	Jamal Anderson	2.00	.90
❑ 43	Qadry Ismail	15.00	6.75
❑ 44	Doug Flutie	2.50	1.10
❑ 45	Rob Johnson	15.00	6.75
❑ 46	Steve Beuerlein	15.00	6.75
❑ 47	Marcus Robinson	2.00	.90
❑ 48	Cade McNown	2.00	.90
❑ 49	Tim Couch	4.00	1.80
❑ 50	Corey Dillon	2.00	.90
❑ 51	Troy Aikman	5.00	2.20
❑ 52	Emmitt Smith	5.00	2.20
❑ 53	Charlie Batch	2.00	.90
❑ 54	Brian Griese	2.50	1.10
❑ 55	Terrell Davis	5.00	2.20
❑ 56	Brett Favre	8.00	3.60
❑ 57	Antonio Freeman	2.00	.90
❑ 58	Peyton Manning	6.00	2.70
❑ 59	Edgerrin James	6.00	2.70
❑ 60	Marvin Harrison	2.00	.90
❑ 61	Mark Brunell	3.00	1.35
❑ 62	Fred Taylor	2.50	1.10
❑ 63	Elvis Grbac	15.00	6.75
❑ 64	Derrick Alexander	15.00	6.75
❑ 65	Lamar Smith	15.00	6.75
❑ 66	Daunte Culpepper	4.00	1.80
❑ 67	Randy Moss	6.00	2.70
❑ 68	Drew Bledsoe	3.00	1.35
❑ 69	Vinny Testaverde	15.00	6.75
❑ 70	Curtis Martin	2.00	.90
❑ 71	Kerry Collins	15.00	6.75
❑ 72	Amani Toomer	15.00	6.75
❑ 73	Jeff Blake	15.00	6.75
❑ 74	Ricky Williams	4.00	1.80
❑ 75	Rich Gannon	15.00	6.75
❑ 76	Tim Brown	2.00	.90
❑ 77	Jerome Bettis	2.00	.90
❑ 78	Kurt Warner	8.00	3.60
❑ 79	Marshall Faulk	2.50	1.10
❑ 80	Junior Seau	15.00	6.75
❑ 81	Jeff Garcia	2.00	.90
❑ 82	Terrell Owens	2.00	.90
❑ 83	Jerry Rice	5.00	2.20
❑ 84	Ricky Watters	15.00	6.75
❑ 85	Shaun King	2.50	1.10
❑ 86	Keyshawn Johnson	2.00	.90
❑ 87	Steve McNair	2.00	.90
❑ 88	Eddie George	2.50	1.10
❑ 89	Stephen Davis	2.00	.90
❑ 90	Brad Johnson	2.00	.90

1991 Wild Card

	MINT	NRMT
COMPLETE SET (160)	6.00	2.70

*5 STRIPES: 1X TO 2.5X BASIC CARDS
*10 STRIPES: 1.5X TO 3.5X BASIC CARDS
*20 STRIPES: 2X TO 5X BASIC CARDS
*50 STRIPES: 4X TO 10X BASIC CARDS

*100 STRIPE VETS: 10X TO 25X BASIC CARDS
*100 STRIPE RCs: 8X TO 20X BASIC CARDS
*1000 STRIPE VETS: 75X TO 150X BASIC CARDS
*1000 STRIPE RCs: 30X TO 80X BASIC CARDS

❑ 1	Jeff George	.10	.05
❑ 2	Sean Jones	.10	.05
❑ 3	Duane Bickett	.04	.02
❑ 4	John Elway	1.00	.45
❑ 5	Christian Okoye	.10	.05
❑ 6	Steve Atwater	.04	.02
❑ 7	Anthony Munoz	.10	.05
❑ 8	Dave Krieg	.10	.05
❑ 9	Nick Lowery	.04	.02
❑ 10	Albert Bentley	.04	.02
❑ 11	Mark Jackson	.04	.02
❑ 12	Jeff Bryant	.04	.02
❑ 13	Johnny Hector	.04	.02
❑ 14	John L. Williams	.04	.02
❑ 15	Jim Everett	.10	.05
❑ 16	Mark Duper	.10	.05
❑ 17	Drew Hill UER (Reversed negative on card front)	.10	.05
❑ 18	Randal Hill RC	.10	.05
❑ 19	Ernest Givins	.10	.05
❑ 20	Ken O'Brien	.04	.02
❑ 21	Blair Thomas UER (Says he caught 204 passes in 1990)	.10	.05
❑ 22	Derrick Thomas	.10	.05
❑ 23	Harvey Williams RC	.10	.05
❑ 24	Simon Fletcher	.04	.02
❑ 25	Stephone Paige	.04	.02
❑ 26	Barry Word	.04	.02
❑ 27	Warren Moon	.10	.05
❑ 28	Derrick Fenner	.04	.02
❑ 29	Shane Conlan	.04	.02
❑ 30	Karl Mecklenburg	.04	.02
❑ 31	Gary Anderson RB	.04	.02
❑ 32	Sammie Smith	.04	.02
❑ 33	Steve DeBerg	.10	.05
❑ 34	Dan McGwire RC UER (TD stats say 29, should be 27)	.04	.02
❑ 35	Roger Craig	.10	.05
❑ 36	Tom Tupa	.04	.02
❑ 37	Rod Woodson	.10	.05
❑ 38	Junior Seau	.20	.09
❑ 39	Bruce Pickens RC	.04	.02
❑ 40	Greg Townsend	.04	.02
❑ 41	Gary Clark	.10	.05
❑ 42	Broderick Thomas	.04	.02
❑ 43	Charles Mann	.10	.05
❑ 44	Browning Nagle RC	.04	.02
❑ 45	James Joseph RC	.10	.05
❑ 46	Emmitt Smith UER (Scoring 1 TD, should be 11)	1.50	.70
❑ 47	Cornelius Bennett	.10	.05
❑ 48	Maurice Hurst	.04	.02
❑ 49	Art Monk	.10	.05
❑ 50	Louis Lipps	.10	.05
❑ 51	Mark Rypien	.10	.05
❑ 52	Bubby Brister	.10	.05
❑ 53	John Stephens	.04	.02
❑ 54	Merril Hoge	.04	.02

❑ 55 Kevin Mack .04 .02
❑ 56 Al Toon .10 .05
❑ 57 Ronnie Lott .10 .05
❑ 58 Eric Metcalf .10 .05
❑ 59 Vinny Testaverde .10 .05
❑ 60 Darrell Green .04 .02
❑ 61 Randall Cunningham .20 .09
❑ 62 Charles Haley .10 .05
❑ 63 Mark Carrier .10 .05
❑ 64 Jim Harbaugh .10 .05
❑ 65 Richard Dent .10 .05
❑ 66 Stan Thomas .04 .02
❑ 67 Neal Anderson .10 .05
❑ 68 Troy Aikman .50 .23
❑ 69 Mike Pritchard RC .10 .05
❑ 70 Deion Sanders .30 .14
❑ 71 Andre Rison .10 .05
❑ 72 Keith Millard .04 .02
❑ 73 Jerry Rice .50 .23
❑ 74 Johnny Johnson .04 .02
❑ 75 Tim McDonald .04 .02
❑ 76 Leonard Russell RC .10 .05
❑ 77 Keith Jackson .10 .05
❑ 78 Keith Byars .10 .05
❑ 79 Ricky Proehl .04 .02
❑ 80 Dexter Carter .04 .02
❑ 81 Alvin Harper RC .10 .05
❑ 82 Irving Fryar .10 .05
❑ 83 Marion Butts .10 .05
❑ 84 Alfred Williams RC .04 .02
❑ 85 Timm Rosenbach .04 .02
❑ 86 Steve Young .50 .23
❑ 87 Albert Lewis .04 .02
❑ 88 Rodney Peete .10 .05
❑ 89 Barry Sanders 1.50 .70
❑ 90 Bennie Blades .04 .02
❑ 91 Chris Spielman .10 .05
❑ 92 John Friesz .10 .05
❑ 93 Jerome Brown .10 .05
❑ 94 Reggie White .20 .09
❑ 95 Michael Irvin .20 .09
❑ 96 Keith McCants .04 .02
❑ 97 Vinnie Clark RC .10 .05
❑ 98 Louis Oliver .04 .02
❑ 99 Mark Clayton .10 .05
❑ 100 John Offerdahl .04 .02
❑ 101 Michael Carter .04 .02
❑ 102 John Taylor .10 .05
❑ 103 William Perry .10 .05
❑ 104 Gill Byrd .04 .02
❑ 105 Burt Grossman .04 .02
❑ 106 Herman Moore RC 1.50 .70
❑ 107 Howie Long .10 .05
❑ 108 Bo Jackson .25 .11
❑ 109 Kelvin Pritchett RC .04 .02
❑ 110 Jacob Green .04 .02
❑ 111 Chris Doleman .10 .05
❑ 112 Herschel Walker .10 .05
❑ 113 Russell Maryland RC .10 .05
❑ 114 Anthony Carter .10 .05
❑ 115 Joey Browner .04 .02
❑ 116 Tony Mandarich .04 .02
❑ 117 Don Majkowski .04 .02
❑ 118 Ricky Ervins RC .10 .05
❑ 119 Sterling Sharpe .10 .05
❑ 120 Tim Harris .04 .02
❑ 121 Hugh Millen RC .04 .02
❑ 122 Mike Rozier .04 .02
❑ 123 Chris Miller .10 .05
❑ 124 Morten Andersen .04 .02
❑ 125 Neil O'Donnell RC 1.00 .45
❑ 126 Surprise Wild Card .04 .02
(Exchangeable for ten-card NFL Experience set)
❑ 127 Eddie Brown .04 .02
❑ 128 James Francis .04 .02
❑ 129 James Brooks .04 .02
❑ 130 David Fulcher .04 .02
❑ 131 Michael Jackson RC .20 .09
❑ 132 Clay Matthews .10 .05
❑ 133 Scott Norwood .04 .02
❑ 134 Wesley Carroll RC .04 .02
❑ 135 Thurman Thomas .20 .09
❑ 136 Mark Ingram .10 .05
❑ 137 Bobby Hebert .10 .05
❑ 138 Bobby Wilson RC .04 .02
❑ 139 Craig Heyward .04 .02
❑ 140 Dalton Hilliard .04 .02
❑ 141 Jeff Hostetler .10 .05
❑ 142 Dave Meggett .10 .05
❑ 143 Cris Dishman RC .04 .02
❑ 144 Lawrence Taylor .10 .05
❑ 145 Leonard Marshall .04 .02
❑ 146 Pepper Johnson .04 .02
❑ 147 Todd Marinovich RC .04 .02
❑ 148 Mike Croel RC .04 .02
❑ 149 Erik McMillan .04 .02
❑ 150 Flipper Anderson .04 .02
❑ 151 Cleveland Gary .04 .02
❑ 152 Henry Ellard .10 .05
❑ 153 Kevin Greene .10 .05
❑ 154 Michael Cofer .04 .02
❑ 155 Todd Lyght RC .10 .05
❑ 156 Bruce Smith .10 .05
❑ 157 Checklist 1 .04 .02
❑ 158 Checklist 2 .04 .02
❑ 159 Checklist 3 .04 .02
❑ 160 Checklist 4 .04 .02

1992 Wild Card

	MINT	NRMT
COMPLETE SET (460)	25.00	11.00
COMP.SERIES 1 (250)	5.00	2.20
COMP.SERIES 2 (210)	20.00	9.00

*5 STRIPES: 1X TO 2.5X HI COL.
*10 STRIPES: 1.5X TO 3.5X HI COL.
*20 STRIPE VETS: 2X TO 5X HI COL.
*20 STRIPE RCs: 1.2X TO 3X HI COL.
*50 STRIPE VETS: 4X TO 10X HI COL.
*50 STRIPE RCs: 2.5X TO 6X HI COL.
*100 STRIPE VETS: 10X TO 25X HI COL.
*1000 STRIPE VETS: 50X TO 120X HI COL.

❑ 1 Surprise Card .04 .02
❑ 2 Marcus Dupree .04 .02
❑ 3 Jackie Slater .04 .02
❑ 4 Robert Delpino .04 .02
❑ 5 Jerry Gray .04 .02
❑ 6 Jim Everett .10 .05
❑ 7 Roman Phifer .04 .02
❑ 8 Alvin Wright .04 .02
❑ 9 Todd Lyght .04 .02
❑ 10 Reggie White .25 .11
❑ 11 Randal Hill .04 .02
❑ 12 Keith Byars .04 .02
❑ 13 Clyde Simmons .04 .02
❑ 14 Keith Jackson .10 .05
❑ 15 Seth Joyner .04 .02
❑ 16 James Joseph .04 .02
❑ 17 Eric Allen .04 .02
❑ 18 Sammie Smith .04 .02
❑ 19 Mark Clayton .04 .02
❑ 20 Aaron Craver .04 .02
❑ 21 Hugh Green .04 .02
❑ 22 John Offerdahl .04 .02
❑ 23 Jeff Cross .04 .02
❑ 24 Ferrell Edmunds .04 .02
❑ 25 Mark Duper .10 .05
❑ 26 Ronnie Harmon .04 .02
❑ 27 Derrick Walker .04 .02
❑ 28 Gary Plummer .04 .02
❑ 29 Rod Bernstine .04 .02
❑ 30 Burt Grossman .04 .02
❑ 31 Donnie Elder .04 .02
❑ 32 John Friesz .10 .05
❑ 33 Billy Ray Smith .04 .02
❑ 34 Luis Sharpe .04 .02
❑ 35 Aeneas Williams .10 .05
❑ 36 Ken Harvey .04 .02
❑ 37 Johnny Johnson UER .04 .02
(1990 rushing stats are wrong)
❑ 38 Eric Swann .10 .05
❑ 39 Tom Tupa .04 .02
❑ 40 Anthony Thompson .04 .02
❑ 41 Broderick Thomas .04 .02
❑ 42 Vinny Testaverde .10 .05
❑ 43 Mark Carrier WR .10 .05
❑ 44 Gary Anderson RB .04 .02
❑ 45 Keith McCants .04 .02
❑ 46 Reggie Cobb .04 .02
❑ 47 Lawrence Dawsey .04 .02
❑ 48 Kevin Murphy .04 .02
❑ 49 Keith Woodside .04 .02
❑ 50 Darrell Thompson .04 .02
❑ 51 Vinnie Clark .04 .02
❑ 52 Sterling Sharpe .10 .05
❑ 53 Mike Tomczak .04 .02
❑ 54A Don Majkowski ERR .10 .05
(Listed as Dan)
❑ 54B Don Majikowski COR .10 .05
❑ 55 Tony Mandarich .04 .02
❑ 56 Mark Murphy .04 .02
❑ 57 Dexter McNabb RC .04 .02
❑ 58 Rick Fenney .04 .02
❑ 59 Cris Carter .25 .11
❑ 60 Wade Wilson .04 .02
❑ 61 Mike Merriweather .04 .02
❑ 62 Rich Gannon .25 .11
❑ 63 Herschel Walker .10 .05
❑ 64 Chris Doleman .10 .05
❑ 65 Al Noga UER .04 .02
(On front, he's a DE; (on back, he's a DT)
❑ 66 Chris Mims RC .04 .02
❑ 67 Ed Cunningham RC .04 .02
❑ 68 Marcus Allen .25 .11
❑ 69 Kevin Turner RC .04 .02
❑ 70 Howie Long .10 .05
❑ 71 Tim Brown .25 .11
❑ 72 Nick Bell .04 .02
❑ 73 Todd Marinovich .04 .02
❑ 74 Jay Schroeder .04 .02
❑ 75 Mervyn Fernandez .04 .02
❑ 76 Tony Smith RC .04 .02
❑ 77 John Alt .04 .02
❑ 78 Christian Okoye .04 .02
❑ 79 Nick Lowery .04 .02
❑ 80 Derrick Thomas .10 .05
❑ 81 Bill Maas .04 .02
❑ 82 Dino Hackett .04 .02
❑ 83 Deron Cherry .04 .02
❑ 84 Barry Word .04 .02
❑ 85 Mike Mooney RC .04 .02
❑ 86 Cris Dishman .04 .02
❑ 87 Bruce Matthews .04 .02
❑ 88 Tony Jones .04 .02
❑ 89 William Fuller .04 .02
❑ 90 Ray Childress .04 .02
❑ 91 Warren Moon .25 .11
❑ 92 Lorenzo White .04 .02
❑ 93 Joe Bowden RC .04 .02
❑ 94 Tom Rathman .04 .02
❑ 95 Keith Henderson .04 .02
❑ 96 Jesse Sapolu .04 .02
❑ 97 Charles Haley .10 .05
❑ 98 Steve Young .60 .25
❑ 99 John Taylor .10 .05
❑ 100 Tim Harris .04 .02
❑ 101 Scott Davis .04 .02
❑ 102 Steve Bono RC .25 .11
❑ 103 Mike Kenn .04 .02
❑ 104 Mike Farr .04 .02
❑ 105 Rodney Peete .10 .05
❑ 106 Jerry Ball .04 .02
❑ 107 Chris Spielman .10 .05
❑ 108 Barry Sanders 1.50 .70
❑ 109 Bennie Blades .04 .02

❑ 110	Herman Moore	.50	.23
❑ 111	Erik Kramer	.10	.05
❑ 112	Vance Johnson	.04	.02
❑ 113	Mike Croel	.04	.02
❑ 114	Mark Jackson	.04	.02
❑ 115	Steve Atwater	.04	.02
❑ 116	Gaston Green	.04	.02
❑ 117	John Elway	1.25	.55
❑ 118	Simon Fletcher	.04	.02
❑ 119	Karl Mecklenburg	.04	.02
❑ 120	Hart Lee Dykes	.04	.02
❑ 121	Jerome Henderson	.04	.02
❑ 122	Chris Singleton	.04	.02
❑ 123	Marv Cook	.04	.02
❑ 124	Leonard Russell	.04	.02
❑ 125	Hugh Millen	.04	.02
❑ 126	Pat Harlow	.04	.02
❑ 127	Andre Tippett	.04	.02
❑ 128	Bruce Armstrong	.04	.02
❑ 129	Gary Clark	.10	.05
❑ 130	Art Monk	.10	.05
❑ 131	Darrell Green	.04	.02
❑ 132	Wilber Marshall	.04	.02
❑ 133	Jim Lachey	.04	.02
❑ 134	Earnest Byner	.04	.02
❑ 135	Chip Lohmiller	.04	.02
❑ 136	Mark Rypien	.04	.02
❑ 137	Ricky Sanders	.04	.02
❑ 138	Stan Thomas	.04	.02
❑ 139	Neal Anderson	.10	.05
❑ 140	Trace Armstrong	.04	.02
❑ 141	Kevin Butler	.04	.02
❑ 142	Mark Carrier DB	.04	.02
❑ 143	Dennis Gentry	.04	.02
❑ 144	Jim Harbaugh	.10	.05
❑ 145	Richard Dent	.10	.05
❑ 146	Andre Rison	.10	.05
❑ 147	Bruce Pickens	.04	.02
❑ 148	Chris Hinton UER (Dealt to Falcons in 1990, not 1989)	.04	.02
❑ 149	Brian Jordan	.10	.05
❑ 150	Chris Miller	.04	.02
❑ 151	Moe Gardner	.04	.02
❑ 152	Bill Fralic	.04	.02
❑ 153	Michael Haynes	.10	.05
❑ 154	Mike Pritchard	.10	.05
❑ 155	Dean Biasucci	.04	.02
❑ 156	Clarence Verdin	.04	.02
❑ 157	Donnell Thompson	.04	.02
❑ 158	Duane Bickett	.04	.02
❑ 159	Jon Hand	.04	.02
❑ 160	Sam Graddy RC	.04	.02
❑ 161	Emmitt Smith	1.50	.70
❑ 162	Michael Irvin	.25	.11
❑ 163	Danny Noonan	.04	.02
❑ 164	Jack Del Rio	.04	.02
❑ 165	Jim Jeffcoat	.04	.02
❑ 166	Alexander Wright	.04	.02
❑ 167	Frank Minnifield	.04	.02
❑ 168	Ed King	.04	.02
❑ 169	Reggie Langhorne	.04	.02
❑ 170	Mike Baab	.04	.02
❑ 171	Eric Metcalf	.10	.05
❑ 172	Clay Matthews	.04	.02
❑ 173	Kevin Mack	.04	.02
❑ 174	Mike Johnson	.04	.02
❑ 175	Jeff Lageman	.04	.02
❑ 176	Freeman McNeil	.10	.05
❑ 177	Erik McMillan	.04	.02
❑ 178	James Hasty	.04	.02
❑ 179	Kyle Clifton	.04	.02
❑ 180	Joe Kelly	.04	.02
❑ 181	Phil Simms	.10	.05
❑ 182	Everson Walls	.04	.02
❑ 183	Jeff Hostetler	.10	.05
❑ 184	Dave Meggett	.10	.05
❑ 185	Matt Bahr	.04	.02
❑ 186	Mark Ingram	.04	.02
❑ 187	Rodney Hampton	.10	.05
❑ 188	Kanavis McGhee	.04	.02
❑ 189	Tim McGee	.04	.02
❑ 190	Eddie Brown	.04	.02
❑ 191	Rodney Holman	.04	.02
❑ 192	Harold Green	.04	.02
❑ 193	James Francis	.04	.02
❑ 194	Anthony Munoz	.10	.05
❑ 195	David Fulcher	.04	.02
❑ 196	Tim Krumrie	.04	.02
❑ 197	Bubby Brister	.10	.05
❑ 198	Rod Woodson	.10	.05
❑ 199	Louis Lipps	.04	.02
❑ 200	Carnell Lake	.04	.02
❑ 201	Don Beebe	.04	.02
❑ 202	Thurman Thomas	.25	.11
❑ 203	Cornelius Bennett	.10	.05
❑ 204	Mark Kelso	.04	.02
❑ 205	James Lofton	.10	.05
❑ 206	Darryl Talley	.04	.02
❑ 207	Morten Andersen	.04	.02
❑ 208	Vince Buck	.04	.02
❑ 209	Wesley Carroll	.04	.02
❑ 210	Bobby Hebert	.04	.02
❑ 211	Craig Heyward	.10	.05
❑ 212	Dalton Hilliard	.04	.02
❑ 213	Rickey Jackson	.04	.02
❑ 214	Eric Martin	.04	.02
❑ 215	Pat Swilling	.10	.05
❑ 216	Steve Walsh	.04	.02
❑ 217	Torrance Small RC	.04	.02
❑ 218	Jacob Green	.04	.02
❑ 219	Cortez Kennedy	.10	.05
❑ 220	John L. Williams	.04	.02
❑ 221	Terry Wooden	.04	.02
❑ 222	Grant Feasel	.04	.02
❑ 223	Siran Stacy RC	.04	.02
❑ 224	Chris Hakel RC	.04	.02
❑ 225	Todd Harrison RC	.04	.02
❑ 226	Bob Whitfield RC	.04	.02
❑ 227	Eddie Blake RC	.04	.02
❑ 228	Keith Hamilton RC	.10	.05
❑ 229	Darryl Williams RC	.04	.02
❑ 230	Ricardo McDonald RC	.04	.02
❑ 231	Alan Haller RC	.04	.02
❑ 232	Leon Searcy RC	.04	.02
❑ 233	Patrick Rowe RC	.04	.02
❑ 234	Edgar Bennett RC	.25	.11
❑ 235	Terrell Buckley RC	.04	.02
❑ 236	Will Furrer RC	.04	.02
❑ 237	Amp Lee RC UER (Front photo actually Edgar Bennett)	.04	.02
❑ 238	Jimmy Smith RC	3.00	1.35
❑ 239	Tommy Vardell RC	.10	.05
❑ 240	Leonard Russell '91 Offensive ROY	.04	.02
❑ 241	Mike Croel '91 Defensive ROY	.04	.02
❑ 242	Warren Moon '91 AFC Passing Leader	.10	.05
❑ 243	Mark Rypien '91 NFC Passing Leader	.04	.02
❑ 244	Thurman Thomas '91 AFC Rushing Leader	.10	.05
❑ 245	Emmitt Smith '91 NFC Rushing Leader	.75	.35
❑ 246	Checklist 1-50	.04	.02
❑ 247	Checklist 51-100	.04	.02
❑ 248	Checklist 101-150	.04	.02
❑ 249	Checklist 151-200	.04	.02
❑ 250	Checklist 201-250	.04	.02
❑ 251	Surprise Card	.04	.02
❑ 252	Eric Pegram	.10	.05
❑ 253	Anthony Carter	.10	.05
❑ 254	Roger Craig	.10	.05
❑ 255	Hassan Jones	.04	.02
❑ 256	Steve Jordan	.04	.02
❑ 257	Randall McDaniel	.04	.02
❑ 258	Henry Thomas	.04	.02
❑ 259	Carl Lee	.04	.02
❑ 260	Ray Agnew	.04	.02
❑ 261	Irving Fryar	.10	.05
❑ 262	Tom Waddle	.04	.02
❑ 263	Greg McMurtry	.04	.02
❑ 264	Stephen Baker	.04	.02
❑ 265	Mark Collins	.04	.02
❑ 266	Howard Cross	.04	.02
❑ 267	Pepper Johnson	.04	.02
❑ 268	Fred Barnett	.10	.05
❑ 269	Heath Sherman	.04	.02
❑ 270	William Thomas	.04	.02
❑ 271	Bill Bates	.10	.05
❑ 272	Issiac Holt	.04	.02
❑ 273	Emmitt Smith	1.50	.70
❑ 274	Eric Bieniemy	.04	.02
❑ 275	Marion Butts	.04	.02
❑ 276	Gill Byrd	.04	.02
❑ 277	Robert Blackmon	.04	.02
❑ 278	Brian Blades	.10	.05
❑ 279	Joe Nash	.04	.02
❑ 280	Bill Brooks	.04	.02
❑ 281	Mel Gray	.04	.02
❑ 282	Andre Ware	.10	.05
❑ 283	Steve McMichael	.04	.02
❑ 284	Brad Muster	.04	.02
❑ 285	Ron Rivera	.04	.02
❑ 286	Chris Zorich	.10	.05
❑ 287	Chris Burkett	.04	.02
❑ 288	Irv Eatman	.04	.02
❑ 289	Rob Moore	.10	.05
❑ 290	Joe Mott	.04	.02
❑ 291	Brian Washington	.04	.02
❑ 292	Michael Carter	.04	.02
❑ 293	Dexter Carter	.04	.02
❑ 294	Don Griffin	.04	.02
❑ 295	John Taylor	.10	.05
❑ 296	Ted Washington	.04	.02
❑ 297	Monte Coleman	.04	.02
❑ 298	Andre Collins	.04	.02
❑ 299	Charles Mann	.04	.02
❑ 300	Shane Conlan	.04	.02
❑ 301	Keith McKeller	.04	.02
❑ 302	Nate Odomes	.04	.02
❑ 303	Riki Ellison	.04	.02
❑ 304	Willie Gault	.04	.02
❑ 305	Bob Golic	.04	.02
❑ 306	Ethan Horton	.04	.02
❑ 307	Ronnie Lott	.10	.05
❑ 308	Don Mosebar	.04	.02
❑ 309	Aaron Wallace	.04	.02
❑ 310	Wymon Henderson	.04	.02
❑ 311	Vance Johnson	.04	.02
❑ 312	Ken Lanier	.04	.02
❑ 313	Steve Sewell	.04	.02
❑ 314	Dennis Smith	.04	.02
❑ 315	Kenny Walker	.04	.02
❑ 316	Chris Martin	.04	.02
❑ 317	Albert Lewis	.04	.02
❑ 318	Todd McNair	.04	.02
❑ 319	Tracy Simien RC	.04	.02
❑ 320	Percy Snow	.04	.02
❑ 321	Mark Rypien	.04	.02
❑ 322	Bryan Hinkle	.04	.02
❑ 323	David Little	.04	.02
❑ 324	Dwight Stone	.04	.02
❑ 325	Van Waiters RC	.04	.02
❑ 326	Pio Sagapolutele RC	.04	.02
❑ 327	Michael Jackson	.10	.05
❑ 328	Vestee Jackson	.04	.02
❑ 329	Tony Paige	.04	.02
❑ 330	Reggie Roby	.04	.02
❑ 331	Haywood Jeffires	.10	.05
❑ 332	Lamar Lathon	.04	.02
❑ 333	Bubba McDowell	.04	.02
❑ 334	Doug Smith	.04	.02
❑ 335	Dean Steinkuhler	.04	.02
❑ 336	Jessie Tuggle	.04	.02
❑ 337	Freddie Joe Nunn	.04	.02
❑ 338	Pat Terrell	.04	.02
❑ 339	Tom McHale RC	.04	.02
❑ 340	Sam Mills	.10	.05
❑ 341	John Tice	.04	.02
❑ 342	Brent Jones	.10	.05
❑ 343	Robert Porcher RC	.04	.02
❑ 344	Mark D'Onofrio RC	.04	.02
❑ 345	David Tate	.04	.02
❑ 346	Courtney Hawkins RC	.10	.05
❑ 347	Ricky Watters	.10	.05
❑ 348	Amp Lee	.04	.02
❑ 349	Steve Young	.60	.25
❑ 350	Natu Tuatagaloa RC	.04	.02
❑ 351	Alfred Williams	.04	.02
❑ 352	Derek Brown TE RC	.04	.02
❑ 353	Marco Coleman RC UER (Back photo actually a Denver Bronco)	.10	.05
❑ 354	Tommy Maddox RC	.04	.02
❑ 355	Siran Stacy	.04	.02

- ❑ 356 Greg Lewis .04 .02
- ❑ 357 Paul Gruber .04 .02
- ❑ 358 Troy Vincent RC .10 .05
- ❑ 359 Robert Wilson .04 .02
- ❑ 360 Jessie Hester .04 .02
- ❑ 361 Shaun Gayle .04 .02
- ❑ 362 Deron Cherry .04 .02
- ❑ 363 Wendell Davis .04 .02
- ❑ 364 David Klingler RC UER .10 .05
  (Bio misspells his name as Klinger)
- ❑ 365 Jason Hanson RC .10 .05
- ❑ 366 Marquez Pope RC .04 .02
- ❑ 367 Robert Williams RC .04 .02
- ❑ 368 Kelvin Pritchett .04 .02
- ❑ 369 Dana Hall RC .10 .05
- ❑ 370 David Brandon RC .04 .02
- ❑ 371 Tim McKyer .04 .02
- ❑ 372 Darion Conner .04 .02
- ❑ 373 Derrick Fenner .04 .02
- ❑ 374 Hugh Millen .04 .02
- ❑ 375 Bill Jones RC .04 .02
- ❑ 376 J.J. Birden .04 .02
- ❑ 377 Ty Detmer .25 .11
- ❑ 378 Alonzo Spellman RC .04 .02
- ❑ 379 Sammie Smith .04 .02
- ❑ 380 Al Smith .04 .02
- ❑ 381 Louis Clark RC .04 .02
- ❑ 382 Vernice Smith RC .04 .02
- ❑ 383 Tony Martin .10 .05
- ❑ 384 Willie Green .04 .02
- ❑ 385 Sean Gilbert RC .10 .05
- ❑ 386 Eugene Chung RC .04 .02
- ❑ 387 Toi Cook .04 .02
- ❑ 388 Brett Maxie .04 .02
- ❑ 389 Steve Israel RC .04 .02
- ❑ 390 Mike Mularkey .04 .02
- ❑ 391 Barry Foster .10 .05
- ❑ 392 Hardy Nickerson .10 .05
- ❑ 393 Johnny Mitchell RC .04 .02
- ❑ 394 Thurman Thomas .25 .11
- ❑ 395 Tony Smith RC .04 .02
- ❑ 396 Keith Goganious RC .04 .02
- ❑ 397 Matt Darby RC .04 .02
- ❑ 398 Nate Turner RC .04 .02
- ❑ 399 Keith Jennings RC .04 .02
- ❑ 400 Mitchell Benson RC .04 .02
- ❑ 401 Kurt Barber RC .04 .02
- ❑ 402 Tony Sacca RC .04 .02
- ❑ 403 Steve Hendrickson RC .04 .02
- ❑ 404 Johnny Johnson .04 .02
- ❑ 405 Lorenzo Lynch .04 .02
- ❑ 406 Luis Sharpe .04 .02
- ❑ 407 Jim Everett .10 .05
- ❑ 408 Neal Anderson .10 .05
- ❑ 409 Ashley Ambrose RC .04 .02
- ❑ 410 George Williams RC .04 .02
- ❑ 411 Clarence Kay .04 .02
- ❑ 412 Dave Krieg .10 .05
- ❑ 413 Terrell Buckley .04 .02
- ❑ 414 Ricardo McDonald .04 .02
- ❑ 415 Kelly Stouffer .04 .02
- ❑ 416 Barney Bussey .04 .02
- ❑ 417 Ray Roberts RC .04 .02
- ❑ 418 Fred McAfee RC .04 .02
- ❑ 419 Fred Banks .04 .02
- ❑ 420 Tim McDonald .04 .02
- ❑ 421 Darryl Williams .04 .02
- ❑ 422 Bobby Abrams RC .04 .02
- ❑ 423 Tommy Vardell .10 .05
- ❑ 424 William White .04 .02
- ❑ 425 Billy Ray Smith .04 .02
- ❑ 426 Lemuel Stinson .04 .02
- ❑ 427 Brad Johnson RC 15.00 6.75
- ❑ 428 Herschel Walker .10 .05
- ❑ 429 Eric Thomas .04 .02
- ❑ 430 Anthony Thompson .04 .02
- ❑ 431 Ed West .04 .02
- ❑ 432 Edgar Bennett .25 .11
- ❑ 433 Warren Powers .04 .02
- ❑ 434 Byron Evans .04 .02
- ❑ 435 Rodney Culver RC .04 .02
- ❑ 436 Ray Horton .04 .02
- ❑ 437 Richmond Webb .04 .02
- ❑ 438 Mark McMillian RC .04 .02
- ❑ 439 Subset Checklist .04 .02
- ❑ 440 Lawrence Pete RC .04 .02
- ❑ 441 Rod Smith DB RC .04 .02
- ❑ 442 Mark Rodenhauser RC .04 .02
- ❑ 443 Scott Lockwood RC .04 .02
- ❑ 444 Charles Davenport RC .04 .02
- ❑ 445 Terry McDaniel .04 .02
- ❑ 446 Darren Perry RC .04 .02
- ❑ 447 Darrick Owens RC .04 .02
- ❑ 448 Alvin Wright .04 .02
- ❑ 449 Frank Stams .04 .02
- ❑ 450 Santana Dotson RC .10 .05
- ❑ 451 Mark Carrier DB .04 .02
- ❑ 452 Kevin Murphy .04 .02
- ❑ 453 Jeff Bryant .04 .02
- ❑ 454 Eric Allen .04 .02
- ❑ 455 Brian Bollinger RC .04 .02
- ❑ 456 Elston Ridgle RC .04 .02
- ❑ 457 Jim Riggs RC .04 .02
- ❑ 458 Checklist 251-320 .04 .02
- ❑ 459 Checklist 321-391 .04 .02
- ❑ 460 Checklist 392-460 .04 .02
- ❑ P1 Barry Sanders 1.00 .45
  National Promo
- ❑ P2 Barry Sanders 2.00 .90
  (5-card National Promo sheet)

1993 Wild Card

	MINT	NRMT
COMPLETE SET (260)	10.00	4.50
COMP.SERIES 1 (200)	6.00	2.70
COMP.SERIES 2 (60)	4.00	1.80

*5 STRIPES: 1X TO 2.5X HI COL.
*10 STRIPES: 1.5X TO 3.5X HI COL.
*20 STRIPES: 2X TO 5X HI COL.
*50 STRIPE VETS: 4X TO 10X HI COL.
*50 STRIPE RCs: 3X TO 8X HI COL.
*100 STRIPE VETS: 10X TO 25X HI COL.
*100 STRIPE RCs: 8X TO 20X HI COL.
*1000 STRIPE VETS: 50X TO 120X HI COL.
*1000 STRIPE RCs: 50X TO 120X HI COL.

- ❑ 1 Surprise Card .05 .02
- ❑ 2 Steve Young .75 .35
- ❑ 3 John Taylor .10 .05
- ❑ 4 Jerry Rice 1.00 .45
- ❑ 5 Brent Jones .10 .05
- ❑ 6 Ricky Watters .10 .05
- ❑ 7 Elvis Grbac RC 1.50 .70
- ❑ 8 Amp Lee .05 .02
- ❑ 9 Steve Bono .10 .05
- ❑ 10 Wendell Davis .05 .02
- ❑ 11 Mark Carrier DB .05 .02
- ❑ 12 Jim Harbaugh .10 .05
- ❑ 13 Curtis Conway RC .40 .18
- ❑ 14 Neal Anderson .05 .02
- ❑ 15 Tom Waddle .05 .02
- ❑ 16 Jeff Query .05 .02
- ❑ 17 David Klingler .05 .02
- ❑ 18 Eric Ball .05 .02
- ❑ 19 Derrick Fenner .05 .02
- ❑ 20 Steve Tovar RC .05 .02
- ❑ 21 Carl Pickens .10 .05
- ❑ 22 Ricardo McDonald .05 .02
- ❑ 23 Harold Green .05 .02
- ❑ 24 Keith McKeller .05 .02
- ❑ 25 Steve Christie .05 .02
- ❑ 26 Andre Reed .10 .05
- ❑ 27 Kenneth Davis .05 .02
- ❑ 28 Frank Reich .05 .02
- ❑ 29 Jim Kelly .25 .11
- ❑ 30 Bruce Smith .10 .05
- ❑ 31 Thurman Thomas .25 .11
- ❑ 32 Glyn Milburn RC .10 .05
- ❑ 33 John Elway 1.50 .70
- ❑ 34 Vance Johnson .05 .02
- ❑ 35 Greg Lewis .05 .02
- ❑ 36 Steve Atwater .05 .02
- ❑ 37 Shannon Sharpe .10 .05
- ❑ 38 Mike Croel .05 .02
- ❑ 39 Kevin Mack .05 .02
- ❑ 40 Lawyer Tillman .05 .02
- ❑ 41 Tommy Vardell .05 .02
- ❑ 42 Bernie Kosar .10 .05
- ❑ 43 Eric Metcalf .10 .05
- ❑ 44 Clay Matthews .05 .02
- ❑ 45 Keith McCants .05 .02
- ❑ 46 Broderick Thomas .05 .02
- ❑ 47 Lawrence Dawsey .05 .02
- ❑ 48 Reggie Cobb .05 .02
- ❑ 49 Lamar Thomas RC .05 .02
- ❑ 50 Courtney Hawkins .10 .05
- ❑ 51 Ivory Lee Brown RC .05 .02
- ❑ 52 Ernie Jones .05 .02
- ❑ 53 Freddie Joe Nunn .05 .02
- ❑ 54 Chris Chandler .10 .05
- ❑ 55 Randal Hill .05 .02
- ❑ 56 Lorenzo Lynch .05 .02
- ❑ 57 Garrison Hearst RC .50 .23
- ❑ 58 Marion Butts .05 .02
- ❑ 59 Anthony Miller .10 .05
- ❑ 60 Eric Bieniemy .05 .02
- ❑ 61 Ronnie Harmon .05 .02
- ❑ 62 Junior Seau .10 .05
- ❑ 63 Gill Byrd .05 .02
- ❑ 64 Stan Humphries .10 .05
- ❑ 65 John Friesz .05 .02
- ❑ 66 J.J. Birden .10 .05
- ❑ 67 Joe Montana 1.50 .70
- ❑ 68 Christian Okoye .10 .05
- ❑ 69 Dale Carter .05 .02
- ❑ 70 Barry Word .05 .02
- ❑ 71 Derrick Thomas .10 .05
- ❑ 72 Todd McNair .05 .02
- ❑ 73 Harvey Williams .05 .02
- ❑ 74 Jack Trudeau .05 .02
- ❑ 75 Rodney Culver .05 .02
- ❑ 76 Anthony Johnson .05 .02
- ❑ 77 Steve Emtman .05 .02
- ❑ 78 Quentin Coryatt .10 .05
- ❑ 79 Kerry Cash .05 .02
- ❑ 80 Jeff George .10 .05
- ❑ 81 Darrin Smith RC .05 .02
- ❑ 82 Jay Novacek .10 .05
- ❑ 83 Michael Irvin .25 .11
- ❑ 84 Alvin Harper .10 .05
- ❑ 85 Kevin Williams RC .10 .05
- ❑ 86 Troy Aikman .75 .35
- ❑ 87 Emmitt Smith 1.50 .70
- ❑ 88 O.J. McDuffie RC .50 .23
- ❑ 89 Mike Williams RC .05 .02
- ❑ 90 Dan Marino 1.50 .70
- ❑ 91 Aaron Craver .05 .02
- ❑ 92 Troy Vincent .05 .02
- ❑ 93 Keith Jackson .10 .05
- ❑ 94 Marco Coleman .05 .02
- ❑ 95 Mark Higgs .05 .02
- ❑ 96 Fred Barnett .10 .05
- ❑ 97 Wes Hopkins .05 .02
- ❑ 98 Randall Cunningham .25 .11
- ❑ 99 Heath Sherman .05 .02
- ❑ 100 Vai Sikahema .05 .02
- ❑ 101 Tony Smith .05 .02
- ❑ 102 Andre Rison .10 .05
- ❑ 103 Chris Miller .05 .02
- ❑ 104 Deion Sanders .50 .23
- ❑ 105 Mike Pritchard .10 .05
- ❑ 106 Steve Broussard .05 .02
- ❑ 107 Stephen Baker .05 .02
- ❑ 108 Carl Banks .05 .02
- ❑ 109 Jarrod Bunch .05 .02
- ❑ 110 Phil Simms .10 .05
- ❑ 111 Rodney Hampton .10 .05

❑ 112 Dave Meggett .05 .02
❑ 113 Pepper Johnson .05 .02
❑ 114 Coleman Rudolph RC .05 .02
❑ 115 Boomer Esiason .10 .05
❑ 116 Browning Nagle .05 .02
❑ 117 Rob Moore .10 .05
❑ 118 Marvin Jones RC .05 .02
❑ 119 Herman Moore .50 .23
❑ 120 Bennie Blades .05 .02
❑ 121 Erik Kramer .05 .02
❑ 122 Mel Gray .05 .02
❑ 123 Rodney Peete .05 .02
❑ 124 Barry Sanders 1.50 .70
❑ 125 Chris Spielman .05 .02
❑ 126 Lamar Lathon .05 .02
❑ 127 Ernest Givins .10 .05
❑ 128 Lorenzo White .10 .05
❑ 129 Micheal Barrow RC .10 .05
❑ 130 Warren Moon .10 .05
❑ 131 Cody Carlson .05 .02
❑ 132 Reggie White .25 .11
❑ 133 Terrell Buckley .05 .02
❑ 134 Ed West .05 .02
❑ 135 Mark Brunell RC 2.50 1.10
❑ 136 Brett Favre 2.00 .90
❑ 137 Edgar Bennett .10 .05
❑ 138 Sterling Sharpe .10 .05
❑ 139 George Teague RC .05 .02
❑ 140 Leonard Russell .10 .05
❑ 141 Drew Bledsoe RC 2.00 .90
❑ 142 Eugene Chung .05 .02
❑ 143 Walter Stanley .05 .02
❑ 144 Scott Zolak .05 .02
❑ 145 Jon Vaughn .05 .02
❑ 146 Andre Tippett .05 .02
❑ 147 Alexander Wright .05 .02
❑ 148 Billy Joe Hobert RC .25 .11
❑ 149 Terry McDaniel .05 .02
❑ 150 Tim Brown .10 .05
❑ 151 Willie Gault .05 .02
❑ 152 Howie Long .10 .05
❑ 153 Todd Marinovich .05 .02
❑ 154 Jim Everett .10 .05
❑ 155 David Lang .05 .02
❑ 156 Henry Ellard .10 .05
❑ 157 Cleveland Gary .05 .02
❑ 158 Steve Israel .05 .02
❑ 159 Jerome Bettis RC .75 .35
❑ 160 Jackie Slater .05 .02
❑ 161 Art Monk .10 .05
❑ 162 Ricky Sanders .05 .02
❑ 163 Brian Mitchell .05 .02
❑ 164 Reggie Brooks RC .05 .02
❑ 165 Mark Rypien .05 .02
❑ 166 Earnest Byner .05 .02
❑ 167 Andre Collins .05 .02
❑ 168 Quinn Early .10 .05
❑ 169 Fred McAfee .05 .02
❑ 170 Wesley Carroll .05 .02
❑ 171 Gene Atkins .05 .02
❑ 172 Derek Brown RBK RC .10 .05
(UER, Name spelled Derrek)
❑ 173 Vaughn Dunbar .05 .02
❑ 174 Rickey Jackson UER .05 .02
(Name spelled Ricky on front)
❑ 175 John L. Williams .05 .02
❑ 176 Carlton Gray RC .05 .02
❑ 177 Cortez Kennedy .10 .05
❑ 178 Kelly Stouffer .05 .02
❑ 179 Rick Mirer RC .30 .14
❑ 180 Dan McGwire .05 .02
❑ 181 Chris Warren .10 .05
❑ 182 Barry Foster .10 .05
❑ 183 Merril Hoge .05 .02
❑ 184 Darren Perry .05 .02
❑ 185 Deon Figures RC .10 .05
❑ 186A Jeff Graham ERR .10 .05
(Name misspelled Grahm on front)
❑ 186B Jeff Graham COR .10 .05
(Name spelled correctly)
❑ 187 Dwight Stone .05 .02
❑ 188 Neil O'Donnell .10 .05
❑ 189 Rod Woodson .10 .05
❑ 190 Alex Van Pelt RC .05 .02
❑ 191 Steve Jordan .05 .02
❑ 192 Roger Craig .10 .05
❑ 193 Qadry Ismail RC UER .50 .23
(Misspelled Quadry on card front)
❑ 194 Robert Smith RC 1.50 .70
❑ 195 Gino Torretta RC .10 .05
❑ 196 Anthony Carter .10 .05
❑ 197 Terry Allen .10 .05
❑ 198 Rich Gannon .25 .11
❑ 199 Checklist 1-100 .05 .02
❑ 200 Checklist 101-200 .05 .02
❑ 201 Victor Bailey RC .05 .02
❑ 202 Micheal Barrow .05 .02
❑ 203 Patrick Bates RC .05 .02
❑ 204 Jerome Bettis .40 .18
❑ 205 Drew Bledsoe 1.00 .45
❑ 206 Vincent Brisby RC .10 .05
❑ 207 Reggie Brooks .10 .05
❑ 208 Derek Brown RBK .10 .05
❑ 209 Keith Byars .05 .02
❑ 210 Tom Carter RC .05 .02
❑ 211 Curtis Conway .25 .11
❑ 212 Russell Copeland RC .10 .05
❑ 213 John Copeland RC .10 .05
❑ 214 Eric Curry RC .10 .05
❑ 215 Troy Drayton RC .10 .05
❑ 216 Jason Elam RC .10 .05
❑ 217 Steve Everitt RC .05 .02
❑ 218 Deon Figures .10 .05
❑ 219 Irving Fryar .10 .05
❑ 220 Darrien Gordon RC .05 .02
❑ 221 Carlton Gray .05 .02
❑ 222 Kevin Greene .10 .05
❑ 223 Andre Hastings RC .10 .05
❑ 224 Michael Haynes .10 .05
❑ 225 Garrison Hearst .25 .11
❑ 226 Bobby Hebert .05 .02
❑ 227 Lester Holmes .05 .02
❑ 228 Jeff Hostetler .10 .05
❑ 229 Desmond Howard .10 .05
❑ 230 Tyrone Hughes RC .10 .05
❑ 231 Qadry Ismail .10 .05
❑ 232 Rocket Ismail .10 .05
❑ 233 James Jett RC .50 .23
❑ 234 Marvin Jones .05 .02
❑ 235 Todd Kelly RC .05 .02
❑ 236 Lincoln Kennedy RC .05 .02
❑ 237 Terry Kirby RC .10 .05
❑ 238 Bernie Kosar .10 .05
❑ 239 Derrick Lassic RC .05 .02
❑ 240 Wilber Marshall .05 .02
❑ 241 O.J. McDuffie .25 .11
❑ 242 Ryan McNeil RC .05 .02
❑ 243 Natrone Means RC .40 .18
❑ 244 Glyn Milburn .10 .05
❑ 245 Rick Mirer .25 .11
❑ 246 Scott Mitchell .25 .11
❑ 247 Ronald Moore RC .10 .05
❑ 248 Lorenzo Neal RC .05 .02
❑ 249 Erric Pegram .10 .05
❑ 250 Roosevelt Potts RC .05 .02
❑ 251 Leonard Renfro RC .05 .02
❑ 252 Greg Robinson RC .05 .02
❑ 253 Wayne Simmons RC .05 .02
❑ 254 Chris Slade RC .10 .05
❑ 255 Irv Smith RC .10 .05
❑ 256 Robert Smith .75 .35
❑ 257 Dana Stubblefield RC .25 .11
❑ 258 George Teague .05 .02
❑ 259 Kevin Williams WR .10 .05
❑ 260 Checklist 201-260 .05 .02

1995 Zenith

	MINT	NRMT
COMPLETE SET (150)	20.00	9.00

❑ Z1 Emmitt Smith 2.00 .90
❑ Z2 Chris Spielman .15 .07
❑ Z3 Johnny Mitchell .05 .02
❑ Z4 Boomer Esiason .15 .07
❑ Z5 Jackie Harris .05 .02
❑ Z6 Warren Moon .15 .07
❑ Z7 Harvey Williams .05 .02
❑ Z8 Steve Walsh .05 .02
❑ Z9 Cris Carter .30 .14

❑ Z10 Natrone Means .30 .14
❑ Z11 Art Monk .15 .07
❑ Z12 Leslie O'Neal .15 .07
❑ Z13 Adrian Murrell .30 .14
❑ Z14 John Elway 2.50 1.10
❑ Z15 Larry Centers .15 .07
❑ Z16 Ricky Ervins .05 .02
❑ Z17 Jeff Graham .05 .02
❑ Z18 Ricky Watters .30 .14
❑ Z19 Eric Green .05 .02
❑ Z20 Curtis Conway .30 .14
❑ Z21 Jake Reed .15 .07
❑ Z22 Michael Timpson .05 .02
❑ Z23 Marcus Allen .30 .14
❑ Z24 Andre Rison .15 .07
❑ Z25 Terry Kirby .15 .07
❑ Z26 Reggie White .30 .14
❑ Z27 Randall Cunningham .30 .14
❑ Z28 Jim Kelly .30 .14
❑ Z29 Robert Brooks .30 .14
❑ Z30 Terance Mathis .15 .07
❑ Z31 Anthony Miller .15 .07
❑ Z32 Neil O'Donnell .15 .07
❑ Z33 Jeff Hostetler .15 .07
❑ Z34 Drew Bledsoe 1.25 .55
❑ Z35 Irving Spikes .15 .07
❑ Z36 Keith Byars .05 .02
❑ Z37 Rod Woodson .15 .07
❑ Z38 Rob Moore .15 .07
❑ Z39 Scott Mitchell .15 .07
❑ Z40 Cody Carlson .05 .02
❑ Z41 Alvin Harper .05 .02
❑ Z42 Chris Warren .15 .07
❑ Z43 Ben Coates .15 .07
❑ Z44 Jim Everett .05 .02
❑ Z45 Vinny Testaverde .15 .07
❑ Z46 Glyn Milburn .05 .02
❑ Z47 Calvin Williams .15 .07
❑ Z48 Fred Barnett .15 .07
❑ Z49 Tim Brown .30 .14
❑ Z50 Lorenzo White .05 .02
❑ Z51 Brent Jones .05 .02
❑ Z52 Henry Ellard .15 .07
❑ Z53 Rick Mirer .30 .14
❑ Z54 Junior Seau .30 .14
❑ Z55 Jeff Blake RC 1.25 .55
❑ Z56 Desmond Howard .15 .07
❑ Z57 Jerry Rice 1.25 .55
❑ Z58 Lewis Tillman .05 .02
❑ Z59 Roosevelt Potts .05 .02
❑ Z60 Rocket Ismail .15 .07
❑ Z61 Eric Hill .05 .02
❑ Z62 Brett Favre 2.50 1.10
❑ Z63 Haywood Jeffires .05 .02
❑ Z64 Barry Foster .15 .07
❑ Z65 Flipper Anderson .05 .02
❑ Z66 Troy Aikman 1.25 .55
❑ Z67 Herschel Walker .15 .07
❑ Z68 Sean Dawkins .15 .07
❑ Z69 Erric Pegram .15 .07
❑ Z70 Irving Fryar .15 .07
❑ Z71 Thurman Thomas .30 .14
❑ Z72 Eric Metcalf .15 .07
❑ Z73 John Taylor .05 .02
❑ Z74 Jeff George .15 .07
❑ Z75 Courtney Hawkins .05 .02
❑ Z76 Carl Pickens .30 .14

❑ Z77 Mike Sherrard .05 .02
❑ Z78 Rodney Hampton .15 .07
❑ Z79 Joe Montana 2.50 1.10
❑ Z80 Willie Davis .15 .07
❑ Z81 Chris Penn .05 .02
❑ Z82 Dave Brown .15 .07
❑ Z83 Gary Brown .05 .02
❑ Z84 Andre Reed .15 .07
❑ Z85 Michael Irvin .30 .14
❑ Z86 Vincent Brisby .05 .02
❑ Z87 Barry Sanders 2.50 1.10
❑ Z88 Qadry Ismail .15 .07
❑ Z89 Reggie Brooks .15 .07
❑ Z90 Bruce Smith .30 .14
❑ Z91 David Klingler .15 .07
❑ Z92 Michael Haynes .15 .07
❑ Z93 Derek Russell .05 .02
❑ Z94 Steve Young 1.00 .45
❑ Z95 Terry Allen .15 .07
❑ Z96 Mark Seay .15 .07
❑ Z97 Dan Marino 2.50 1.10
❑ Z98 Jerry Rice 1.25 .55
1994 Record Wrecker
❑ Z99 Cris Carter .30 .14
1994 Record Wrecker
❑ Z100 Art Monk .15 .07
Record Wrecker
❑ Z102 Stan Humphries .15 .07
❑ Z103 Herman Moore .30 .14
❑ Z104 Ronald Moore .05 .02
❑ Z105 Greg Lloyd .15 .07
❑ Z106 Jerome Bettis .30 .14
❑ Z107 Craig Erickson .05 .02
❑ Z108 Keith Jackson .05 .02
❑ Z109 Sterling Sharpe .15 .07
❑ Z110 Ronnie Harmon .05 .02
❑ Z111 Deion Sanders .75 .35
❑ Z112 Charles Haley .15 .07
❑ Z113 Bernie Parmalee .15 .07
❑ Z114 Leroy Hoard .05 .02
❑ Z115 O.J. McDuffie .30 .14
❑ Z116 Garrison Hearst .30 .14
❑ Z117 Kevin Greene .15 .07
❑ Z118 Derek Brown .05 .02
❑ Z119 Mark Brunell 1.25 .55
❑ Z120 Kevin Williams .15 .07
❑ Z121 Dan Wilkinson .15 .07
❑ Z122 Chuck Levy .05 .02
❑ Z123 Derrick Alexander .30 .14
❑ Z124 Aaron Bailey RC .05 .02
❑ Z125 Thomas Lewis .15 .07
❑ Z126 Antonio Langham .05 .02
❑ Z127 Bryan Reeves .05 .02
❑ Z128 William Floyd .30 .14
❑ Z129 Lake Dawson .15 .07
❑ Z130 Bert Emanuel .30 .14
❑ Z131 Marshall Faulk .60 .25
❑ Z132 Heath Shuler .30 .14
❑ Z133 David Palmer .15 .07
❑ Z134 Willie McGinest .15 .07
❑ Z135 Mario Bates .30 .14
❑ Z136 Byron Bam Morris .15 .07
❑ Z137 Tim Bowens .05 .02
❑ Z138 Errict Rhett .30 .14
❑ Z139 Charlie Garner .15 .07
❑ Z140 Darnay Scott .30 .14
❑ Z141 Greg Hill .15 .07
❑ Z142 LeShon Johnson .15 .07
❑ Z143 Charles Johnson .15 .07
❑ Z144 Trent Dilfer .30 .14
❑ Z145 Gus Frerotte .30 .14
❑ Z146 Johnnie Morton .15 .07
❑ Z147 Glenn Foley .05 .02
❑ Z148 Perry Klein .05 .02
❑ Z149 Ryan Yarborough .15 .07
❑ Z150 Tydus Winans .05 .02

1996 Zenith

	MINT	NRMT
COMPLETE SET (150)	25.00	11.00

❑ 1 Dan Marino 3.00 1.35
❑ 2 Yancey Thigpen .25 .11
❑ 3 Marcus Allen .50 .23
❑ 4 Curtis Conway .50 .23

❑ 5 Troy Aikman 1.50 .70
❑ 6 William Floyd .25 .11
❑ 7 Ricky Watters .25 .11
❑ 8 Herman Moore .50 .23
❑ 9 Jim Harbaugh .25 .11
❑ 10 Isaac Bruce .50 .23
❑ 11 Drew Bledsoe 1.50 .70
❑ 12 Jeff Blake .50 .23
❑ 13 Tim Brown .50 .23
❑ 14 Deion Sanders 1.00 .45
❑ 15 Greg Hill .25 .11
❑ 16 Ben Coates .25 .11
❑ 17 Errict Rhett .25 .11
❑ 18 Barry Sanders 3.00 1.35
❑ 19 Erik Kramer .10 .05
❑ 20 Emmitt Smith 2.50 1.10
❑ 21 Brett Favre 3.00 1.35
❑ 22 Jerome Bettis .50 .23
❑ 23 Garrison Hearst .25 .11
❑ 24 Michael Irvin .50 .23
❑ 25 Chris Warren .25 .11
❑ 26 Steve Young 1.25 .55
❑ 27 Cris Carter .50 .23
❑ 28 Carl Pickens .50 .23
❑ 29 Lake Dawson .10 .05
❑ 30 Marshall Faulk .50 .23
❑ 31 Vincent Brisby .10 .05
❑ 32 Jerry Rice 1.50 .70
❑ 33 Eric Metcalf .10 .05
❑ 34 Natrone Means .50 .23
❑ 35 Steve Bono .10 .05
❑ 36 John Elway 3.00 1.35
❑ 37 Jeff Hostetler .10 .05
❑ 38 Scott Mitchell .25 .11
❑ 39 Andre Rison .25 .11
❑ 40 Daryl Johnston .25 .11
❑ 41 Mark Brunell 1.50 .70
❑ 42 Jeff George .25 .11
❑ 43 Mario Bates .25 .11
❑ 44 Erric Pegram .10 .05
❑ 45 Brent Jones .10 .05
❑ 46 Trent Dilfer .50 .23
❑ 47 Larry Centers .25 .11
❑ 48 Anthony Miller .25 .11
❑ 49 Reggie White .50 .23
❑ 50 Bill Brooks .10 .05
❑ 51 Chris Zorich .10 .05
❑ 52 Jim Kelly .50 .23
❑ 53 Junior Seau .25 .11
❑ 54 Chris Miller .10 .05
❑ 55 Gus Frerotte .50 .23
❑ 56 Andre Reed .25 .11
❑ 57 Darnay Scott .25 .11
❑ 58 Brett Perriman .10 .05
❑ 59 Edgar Bennett .25 .11
❑ 60 Warren Moon .25 .11
❑ 61 Neil O'Donnell .25 .11
❑ 62 Jay Novacek .10 .05
❑ 63 Byron Bam Morris .25 .11
❑ 64 Jim Everett .10 .05
❑ 65 Ken Norton, Jr. .10 .05
❑ 66 Tony Martin .25 .11
❑ 67 Steve Atwater .10 .05
❑ 68 Henry Ellard .10 .05
❑ 69 Rodney Hampton .25 .11
❑ 70 Derrick Thomas .25 .11
❑ 71 Stan Humphries .25 .11
❑ 72 Harvey Williams .10 .05
❑ 73 Greg Lloyd .25 .11
❑ 74 Jake Reed .25 .11
❑ 75 Charles Haley .25 .11
❑ 76 Quinn Early .10 .05
❑ 77 Rodney Peete .10 .05
❑ 78 Brian Blades .10 .05
❑ 79 Robert Brooks .50 .23
❑ 80 Terry Allen .25 .11
❑ 81 Dave Brown .10 .05
❑ 82 Derrick Alexander WR .25 .11
❑ 83 Terance Mathis .10 .05
❑ 84 Rick Mirer .25 .11
❑ 85 Herschel Walker .25 .11
❑ 86 Charlie Garner .10 .05
❑ 87 Jeff Graham .10 .05
❑ 88 Bruce Smith .25 .11
❑ 89 Terry Kirby .25 .11
❑ 90 Craig Heyward .10 .05
❑ 91 Bernie Parmalee .10 .05
❑ 92 Adrian Murrell .50 .23
❑ 93 Derek Loville .10 .05
❑ 94 Heath Shuler .25 .11
❑ 95 Shannon Sharpe .25 .11
❑ 96 Bert Emanuel .25 .11
❑ 97 Hugh Douglas .25 .11
❑ 98 Lovell Pinkney .10 .05
❑ 99 Sherman Williams .10 .05
❑ 100 Tony Boselli .10 .05
❑ 101 Wayne Chrebet .75 .35
❑ 102 Orlando Thomas .10 .05
❑ 103 Darick Holmes .10 .05
❑ 104 Tyrone Wheatley .25 .11
❑ 105 Christian Fauria .10 .05
❑ 106 Frank Sanders .25 .11
❑ 107 Chad May .10 .05
❑ 108 James O. Stewart .25 .11
❑ 109 Ken Dilger .25 .11
❑ 110 Kyle Brady .10 .05
❑ 111 Todd Collins .25 .11
❑ 112 Terrell Fletcher .10 .05
❑ 113 Eric Bjornson .10 .05
❑ 114 Justin Armour .10 .05
❑ 115 Rob Johnson .50 .23
❑ 116 Terrell Davis 4.00 1.80
❑ 117 J.J. Stokes .50 .23
❑ 118 Rashaan Salaam .50 .23
❑ 119 Chris Sanders .25 .11
❑ 120 Kerry Collins .50 .23
❑ 121 Michael Westbrook .50 .23
❑ 122 Eric Zeier .10 .05
❑ 123 Curtis Martin 1.00 .45
❑ 124 Rodney Thomas .10 .05
❑ 125 Kordell Stewart .75 .35
❑ 126 Joey Galloway .75 .35
❑ 127 Steve McNair 1.00 .45
❑ 128 Napoleon Kaufman .50 .23
❑ 129 Tamarick Vanover .25 .11
❑ 130 Stoney Case .10 .05
❑ 131 James A. Stewart .10 .05
❑ 132 Carl Pickens PP .50 .23
❑ 133 Jim Harbaugh PP .25 .11
❑ 134 Yancey Thigpen PP .25 .11
❑ 135 Ricky Watters PP .25 .11
❑ 136 Isaac Bruce PP .50 .23
❑ 137 Kordell Stewart PP .50 .23
❑ 138 Jeff Blake PP .25 .11
❑ 139 Terrell Davis PP 2.00 .90
❑ 140 Scott Mitchell PP .10 .05
❑ 141 Rodney Thomas PP .10 .05
❑ 142 Robert Brooks PP .50 .23
❑ 143 Joey Galloway PP .50 .23
❑ 144 Brett Favre PP 1.50 .70
❑ 145 Kerry Collins PP .50 .23
❑ 146 Herman Moore PP .50 .23
❑ 147 Michael Irvin 1.50 .70
Emmitt Smith
Troy Aikman
❑ 148 Dan Marino .50 .23
Checklist
❑ 149 Jerry Rice .50 .23
Checklist
❑ 150 Emmitt Smith .50 .23
Checklist

1997 Zenith

	MINT	NRMT
COMPLETE SET (150)	25.00	11.00
❑ 1 Brett Favre	3.00	1.35
❑ 2 Jerry Rice	1.50	.70
❑ 3 Shannon Sharpe	.25	.11
❑ 4 Dan Marino	3.00	1.35
❑ 5 James O.Stewart	.25	.11
❑ 6 Warren Moon	.50	.23
❑ 7 Emmitt Smith	2.50	1.10
❑ 8 Kordell Stewart	.60	.25
❑ 9 Kerry Collins	.25	.11
❑ 10 Ricky Watters	.25	.11
❑ 11 Gus Frerotte	.15	.07
❑ 12 Barry Sanders	3.00	1.35
❑ 13 Joey Galloway	.60	.25
❑ 14 Marshall Faulk	.50	.23
❑ 15 Todd Collins	.15	.07
❑ 16 Steve McNair	.75	.35
❑ 17 Tyrone Wheatley	.25	.11
❑ 18 Isaac Bruce	.50	.23
❑ 19 Troy Aikman	1.50	.70
❑ 20 Larry Centers	.25	.11
❑ 21 Alvin Harper	.15	.07
❑ 22 Rashaan Salaam	.15	.07
❑ 23 Eric Metcalf	.25	.11
❑ 24 Jim Everett	.15	.07
❑ 25 Ken Dilger	.15	.07
❑ 26 Curtis Martin	.75	.35
❑ 27 Neil O'Donnell	.25	.11
❑ 28 Thurman Thomas	.50	.23
❑ 29 Andre Rison	.25	.11
❑ 30 Steve Bono	.25	.11
❑ 31 Garrison Hearst	.25	.11
❑ 32 Junior Seau	.25	.11
❑ 33 Napoleon Kaufman	.50	.23
❑ 34 Jerome Bettis	.50	.23
❑ 35 Frank Wycheck	.15	.07
❑ 36 Lamar Smith	.50	.23
❑ 37 Derrick Alexander WR	.25	.11
❑ 38 Steve Young	1.00	.45
❑ 39 Cris Carter	.50	.23
❑ 40 O.J. McDuffie	.25	.11
❑ 41 Deion Sanders	.50	.23
❑ 42 Robert Brooks	.25	.11
❑ 43 Jeff Blake	.25	.11
❑ 44 Marcus Allen	.50	.23
❑ 45 Herman Moore	.50	.23
❑ 46 Ray Zellars	.15	.07
❑ 47 Tim Brown	.50	.23
❑ 48 John Elway	3.00	1.35
❑ 49 Charles Johnson	.25	.11
❑ 50 Rodney Peete	.15	.07
❑ 51 Curtis Conway	.25	.11
❑ 52 Kevin Greene	.25	.11
❑ 53 Andre Reed	.25	.11
❑ 54 Mark Brunell	1.50	.70
❑ 55 Tony Martin	.25	.11
❑ 56 Elvis Grbac	.25	.11
❑ 57 Wayne Chrebet	.50	.23
❑ 58 Vinny Testaverde	.25	.11
❑ 59 Terry Allen	.50	.23
❑ 60 Dave Brown	.15	.07
❑ 61 LeShon Johnson	.15	.07
❑ 62 Trent Dilfer	.50	.23
❑ 63 Chris Warren	.25	.11
❑ 64 Chris Sanders	.15	.07
❑ 65 Kevin Carter	.15	.07
❑ 66 Jim Harbaugh	.25	.11
❑ 67 Terance Mathis	.25	.11
❑ 68 Ben Coates	.25	.11
❑ 69 Robert Smith	.25	.11
❑ 70 Drew Bledsoe	1.50	.70
❑ 71 Henry Ellard	.15	.07
❑ 72 Scott Mitchell	.25	.11
❑ 73 Andre Hastings	.15	.07
❑ 74 Rodney Hampton	.25	.11
❑ 75 Michael Jackson	.25	.11
❑ 76 Jeff Hostetler	.15	.07
❑ 77 Reggie White	.50	.23
❑ 78 Desmond Howard	.25	.11
❑ 79 Adrian Murrell	.25	.11
❑ 80 Carl Pickens	.50	.23
❑ 81 Erik Kramer	.15	.07
❑ 82 Terrell Davis	2.50	1.10
❑ 83 Sean Dawkins	.15	.07
❑ 84 Jamal Anderson	1.00	.45
❑ 85 Stan Humphries	.25	.11
❑ 86 Chris T. Jones	.15	.07
❑ 87 Hardy Nickerson	.15	.07
❑ 88 Anthony Johnson	.15	.07
❑ 89 Michael Haynes	.15	.07
❑ 90 Irving Spikes	.15	.07
❑ 91 Bruce Smith	.25	.11
❑ 92 Keenan McCardell	.25	.11
❑ 93 Chris Chandler	.25	.11
❑ 94 Tamarick Vanover	.25	.11
❑ 95 Dorsey Levens	.50	.23
❑ 96 Roman Phifer	.15	.07
❑ 97 Michael Irvin	.50	.23
❑ 98 Tim Biakabutuka	.25	.11
❑ 99 Stepfret Williams	.15	.07
❑ 100 Eddie George	1.50	.70
❑ 101 Karim Abdul-Jabbar	.50	.23
❑ 102 Amani Toomer	.25	.11
❑ 103 Tony Banks	.25	.11
❑ 104 Regan Upshaw	.15	.07
❑ 105 Leeland McElroy	.15	.07
❑ 106 Jason Dunn	.15	.07
❑ 107 Keyshawn Johnson	.50	.23
❑ 108 Winslow Oliver	.15	.07
❑ 109 Walt Harris	.15	.07
❑ 110 Stanley Pritchett	.15	.07
❑ 111 Eddie Kennison	.25	.11
❑ 112 Terrell Owens	.50	.23
❑ 113 Duane Clemons	.15	.07
❑ 114 John Mobley	.15	.07
❑ 115 Simeon Rice	.25	.11
❑ 116 Tony Brackens	.15	.07
❑ 117 Eric Moulds	.50	.23
❑ 118 Marvin Harrison	.50	.23
❑ 119 Rickey Dudley	.25	.11
❑ 120 Mike Alstott	.50	.23
❑ 121 Terry Glenn	.50	.23
❑ 122 Brian Dawkins	.15	.07
❑ 123 Kevin Hardy	.15	.07
❑ 124 Bobby Engram	.25	.11
❑ 125 Alex Van Dyke	.15	.07
❑ 126 Zach Thomas	.25	.11
❑ 127 Bryan Still	.15	.07
❑ 128 Detron Smith	.15	.07
❑ 129 Jerome Woods	.15	.07
❑ 130 Muhsin Muhammad	.25	.11
❑ 131 Lawrence Phillips	.15	.07
❑ 132 Alex Molden	.15	.07
❑ 133 Steve Young SH	.60	.25
❑ 134 Troy Aikman SH	.75	.35
❑ 135 Junior Seau SH	.15	.07
❑ 136 John Elway SH	1.50	.70
❑ 137 Dan Marino SH	1.50	.70
❑ 138 Desmond Howard SH	.25	.11
❑ 139 Brett Favre SH	1.50	.70
❑ 140 Jerry Rice SH	.75	.35
❑ 141 Kerry Collins SH	.25	.11
❑ 142 Barry Sanders SH	1.50	.70
❑ 143 Mark Brunell SH	.75	.35
❑ 144 Drew Bledsoe SH	.75	.35
❑ 145 Eddie Kennison SH	.25	.11
❑ 146 Marvin Harrison SH	.50	.23
❑ 147 Emmitt Smith SH	1.25	.55
❑ 148 Eddie George Terry Glenn Rickey Dudley Bobby Hoying Awesome Foursome	.75	.35
❑ 149 Emmitt Smith Checklist back	.60	.25
❑ 150 Dan Marino Checklist back	.75	.35

1991 Classic

	MINT	NRMT
COMPLETE SET (50)	4.00	1.80
❑ 1 Rocket Ismail	.40	.18
❑ 2 Russell Maryland	.05	.02
❑ 3 Eric Turner	.10	.05
❑ 4 Bruce Pickens	.05	.02
❑ 5 Mike Croel	.05	.02
❑ 6 Todd Lyght	.05	.02
❑ 7 Eric Swann	.10	.05
❑ 8 Antone Davis	.05	.02
❑ 9 Stanley Richard	.05	.02
❑ 10 Pat Harlow	.05	.02
❑ 11 Alvin Harper	.05	.02
❑ 12 Mike Pritchard	.10	.05
❑ 13 Leonard Russell	.10	.05
❑ 14 Dan McGwire	.05	.02
❑ 15 Bobby Wilson	.05	.02
❑ 16 Alfred Williams	.05	.02
❑ 17 Vinnie Clark	.05	.02
❑ 18 Kelvin Pritchett	.05	.02
❑ 19 Harvey Williams	.10	.05
❑ 20 Stan Thomas	.05	.02
❑ 21 Randal Hill	.10	.05
❑ 22 Todd Marinovich	.05	.02
❑ 23 Henry Jones	.05	.02
❑ 24 Jarrod Bunch	.10	.05
❑ 25 Mike Dumas	.05	.02
❑ 26 Ed King	.05	.02
❑ 27 Reggie Johnson	.05	.02
❑ 28 Roman Phifer	.05	.02
❑ 29 Mike Jones	.05	.02
❑ 30 Brett Favre	2.50	1.10
❑ 31 Browning Nagle	.05	.02
❑ 32 Esera Tuaolo	.05	.02
❑ 33 George Thornton	.05	.02
❑ 34 Dixon Edwards	.05	.02
❑ 35 Darryl Lewis	.05	.02
❑ 36 Eric Bieniemy	.05	.02
❑ 37 Shane Curry	.05	.02
❑ 38 Jerome Henderson	.05	.02
❑ 39 Wesley Carroll	.10	.05
❑ 40 Nick Bell	.05	.02
❑ 41 John Flannery	.05	.02
❑ 42 Ricky Watters	.60	.25
❑ 43 Jeff Graham	.25	.11
❑ 44 Eric Moten	.05	.02
❑ 45 Jesse Campbell	.05	.02
❑ 46 Chris Zorich	.10	.05
❑ 47 Doug Thomas	.05	.02
❑ 48 Phil Hansen	.10	.05
❑ 49 Kanavis McGhee	.10	.05
❑ 50 Reggie Barrett	.05	.02

1993 Classic

	MINT	NRMT
COMPLETE SET (100)	6.00	2.70

Card	MINT	EXC
❑ 1 Drew Bledsoe	2.00	.90
❑ 2 Rick Mirer	.25	.11
❑ 3 Garrison Hearst	.25	.11
❑ 4 Marvin Jones	.05	.02
❑ 5 John Copeland	.05	.02
❑ 6 Eric Curry	.05	.02
❑ 7 Curtis Conway	.25	.11
❑ 8 Willie Roaf	.05	.02
❑ 9 Lincoln Kennedy	.05	.02
❑ 10 Jerome Bettis	.50	.23
❑ 11 Mike Compton	.05	.02
❑ 12 John Gerak	.05	.02
❑ 13 Will Shields	.05	.02
❑ 14 Ben Coleman	.05	.02
❑ 15 Ernest Dye	.05	.02
❑ 16 Lester Holmes	.05	.02
❑ 17 Brad Hopkins	.05	.02
❑ 18 Everett Lindsay	.05	.02
❑ 19 Todd Rucci	.05	.02
❑ 20 Lance Gunn	.05	.02
❑ 21 Elvis Grbac	.60	.25
❑ 22 Shane Matthews	.60	.25
❑ 23 Rudy Harris	.05	.02
❑ 24 Richie Anderson	.25	.11
❑ 25 Derek Brown RB	.05	.02
❑ 26 Roger Harper	.05	.02
❑ 27 Terry Kirby	.25	.11
❑ 28 Natrone Means	.25	.11
❑ 29 Glyn Milburn	.10	.05
❑ 30 Adrian Murrell	.25	.11
❑ 31 Lorenzo Neal	.05	.02
❑ 32 Roosevelt Potts	.10	.05
❑ 33 Kevin Williams RB	.05	.02
❑ 34 Russell Copeland	.05	.02
❑ 35 Fred Baxter	.05	.02
❑ 36 Troy Drayton	.10	.05
❑ 37 Chris Gedney	.05	.02
❑ 38 Irv Smith	.05	.02
❑ 39 Olanda Truitt	.05	.02
❑ 40 Victor Bailey	.05	.02
❑ 41 Horace Copeland	.05	.02
❑ 42 Ron Dickerson Jr.	.05	.02
❑ 43 Willie Harris	.05	.02
❑ 44 Tyrone Hughes	.05	.02
❑ 45 Qadry Ismail	.40	.18
❑ 46 Reggie Brooks	.10	.05
❑ 47 Sean LaChapelle	.05	.02
❑ 48 O.J.McDuffie UER	.40	.18
❑ 49 Larry Ryans	.05	.02
❑ 50 Kenny Shedd	.10	.05
❑ 51 Brian Stablein	.05	.02
❑ 52 Lamar Thomas	.05	.02
❑ 53 Kevin Williams WR	.10	.05
❑ 54 Othello Henderson	.05	.02
❑ 55 Kevin Henry	.05	.02
❑ 56 Todd Kelly	.05	.02
❑ 57 Devon McDonald	.05	.02
❑ 58 Michael Strahan	.25	.11
❑ 59 Dan Williams	.05	.02
❑ 60 Gilbert Brown	.10	.05
❑ 61 Mark Caesar	.05	.02
❑ 62 Ronnie Dixon	.05	.02
❑ 63 John Parrella	.05	.02
❑ 64 Leonard Renfro	.05	.02
❑ 65 Coleman Rudolph	.05	.02
❑ 66 Ronnie Bradford	.05	.02
❑ 67 Tom Carter	.05	.02
❑ 68 Deon Figures	.10	.05
❑ 69 Derrick Frazier	.05	.02
❑ 70 Darrien Gordon	.10	.05
❑ 71 Carlton Gray	.05	.02
❑ 72 Adrian Hardy	.05	.02
❑ 73 Mike Reid	.05	.02
❑ 74 Thomas Smith	.05	.02
❑ 75 Robert O'Neal	.05	.02
❑ 76 Chad Brown	.05	.02
❑ 77 Demetrius DuBose	.05	.02
❑ 78 Reggie Givens	.05	.02
❑ 79 Travis Hill	.05	.02
❑ 80 Rich McKenzie	.05	.02
❑ 81 Barry Minter	.05	.02
❑ 82 Darrin Smith	.05	.02
❑ 83 Steve Tovar	.05	.02
❑ 84 Patrick Bates	.05	.02
❑ 85 Dan Footman	.05	.02
❑ 86 Ryan McNeil	.05	.02
❑ 87 Danan Hughes	.05	.02
❑ 88 Mark Brunell	2.00	.90
❑ 89 Ron Moore	.10	.05
❑ 90 Antonio London	.05	.02
❑ 91 Steve Everitt	.05	.02
❑ 92 Wayne Simmons	.05	.02
❑ 93 Robert Smith	1.00	.45
❑ 94 Dana Stubblefield	.10	.05
❑ 95 George Teague	.05	.02
❑ 96 Carl Simpson	.05	.02
❑ 97 Billy Joe Hobert	.10	.05
❑ 98 Gino Torretta	.10	.05
❑ 99 Checklist 1	.05	.02
❑ 100 Checklist 2	.05	.02
❑ AU1 Troy Aikman AU/1000	80.00	36.00
❑ AU2 Drew Bledsoe AU/5000	40.00	18.00
❑ AU3 Rick Mirer AU/5000	25.00	11.00
❑ PR1A Drew Bledsoe Promo	2.50	1.10
❑ PR1B Drew Bledsoe Promo Vince's June '93 gold foil logo	2.00	.90
❑ P2 Rick Mirer Promo National Convention logo on back	1.50	.70

1994 Classic

	MINT	EXC
COMPLETE SET (105)	6.00	2.70
❑ 1 Heath Shuler	.10	.05
❑ 2 Trent Dilfer	.75	.35
❑ 3 Marshall Faulk	2.00	.90
❑ 4 Errict Rhett	.60	.25
❑ 5 Charlie Garner	1.00	.45
❑ 6 Sam Adams	.05	.02
❑ 7 Shante Carver	.05	.02
❑ 8 Dwayne Chandler	.05	.02
❑ 9 Andre Coleman	.05	.02
❑ 10 Carlester Crumpler	.05	.02
❑ 11 Charles Johnson	.25	.11
❑ 12 David Palmer	.10	.05
❑ 13 Dan Wilkinson	.10	.05
❑ 14 LeShon Johnson	.05	.02
❑ 15 Mario Bates	.10	.05
❑ 16 Glenn Foley	.05	.02
❑ 17 William Gaines	.05	.02
❑ 18 Wayne Gandy	.05	.02
❑ 19 Jason Gildon	.05	.02
❑ 20 Eric Gant	.05	.02
❑ 21 Tre Johnson	.05	.02
❑ 22 Calvin Jones	.05	.02
❑ 23 Jake Kelchner	.05	.02
❑ 24 Perry Klein	.05	.02
❑ 25 Chuck Levy	.05	.02
❑ 26 Corey Louchiey	.05	.02
❑ 27 Chris Maumalanga	.05	.02
❑ 28 Jamir Miller	.10	.05
❑ 29 Jim Miller	.10	.05
❑ 30 Johnnie Morton	.25	.11
❑ 31 Doug Nussmeier	.10	.05
❑ 32 Vaughn Parker	.05	.02
❑ 33 Darnay Scott	.25	.11
❑ 34 Fernando Smith	.05	.02
❑ 35 Lamar Smith	1.00	.45
❑ 36 Marcus Spears	.05	.02
❑ 37 Irving Spikes	.05	.02
❑ 38 Todd Steussie	.05	.02
❑ 39 Aaron Taylor	.05	.02
❑ 40 John Thierry	.05	.02
❑ 41 Dewayne Washington	.05	.02
❑ 42 Jason Winrow	.05	.02
❑ 43 Ronnie Woolfork	.05	.02
❑ 44 Bryant Young	.10	.05
❑ 45 Arthur Bussie	.05	.02
❑ 46 Derrick Alexander WR	.25	.11
❑ 47 Larry Allen	.05	.02
❑ 48 Aubrey Beavers	.05	.02
❑ 49 James Bostic	.05	.02
❑ 50 Jeff Burris	.05	.02
❑ 51 Lindsey Chapman	.05	.02
❑ 52 Isaac Davis	.05	.02
❑ 53 Lake Dawson	.10	.05
❑ 54 Tyronne Drakeford	.05	.02
❑ 55 William Floyd	.10	.05
❑ 56 Henry Ford	.05	.02
❑ 57 Rob Fredrickson	.05	.02
❑ 58 Aaron Glenn	.10	.05
❑ 59 Shelby Hill	.05	.02
❑ 60 Willie Jackson	.25	.11
❑ 61 Joe Johnson	.05	.02
❑ 62 Aaron Laing	.05	.02
❑ 63 Kevin Lee	.05	.02
❑ 64 Eric Mahlum	.05	.02
❑ 65 Steve Matthews	.05	.02
❑ 66 Willie McGinest	.10	.05
❑ 67 Kevin Mitchell	.05	.02
❑ 68 Byron Bam Morris	.10	.05
❑ 69 Thomas Randolph	.05	.02
❑ 70 Tony Richardson	.10	.05
❑ 71 Corey Sawyer	.05	.02
❑ 72 Jason Sehorn	.25	.11
❑ 73 Rob Waldrop	.05	.02
❑ 74 Jay Walker	.05	.02
❑ 75 Bernard Williams	.05	.02
❑ 76 Marvin Goodwin	.05	.02
❑ 77 Romeo Bandison	.05	.02
❑ 78 Bucky Brooks	.05	.02
❑ 79 James Folston	.05	.02
❑ 80 Donnell Bennett	.10	.05
❑ 81 Charlie Ward	.25	.11
❑ 82 Antonio Langham	.05	.02
❑ 83 Greg Hill	.10	.05
❑ 84 Anthony Phillips	.05	.02
❑ 85 Winfred Tubbs	.05	.02
❑ 86 Trev Alberts	.05	.02
❑ 87 Tim Bowens	.05	.02
❑ 88 Thomas Lewis	.05	.02
❑ 89 Allen Aldridge	.05	.02
❑ 90 Bert Emanuel	.25	.11
❑ 91 Ryan Yarborough	.05	.02
❑ 92 Lonnie Johnson	.05	.02
❑ 93 Isaac Bruce	2.00	.90
❑ 94 Checklist 1	.05	.02
❑ 95 Checklist 2	.05	.02
❑ 96 Troy Aikman FLB	.50	.23
❑ 97 Steve Young FLB	.25	.11
❑ 98 Rick Mirer FLB	.10	.05
❑ 99 Drew Bledsoe FLB	.50	.23
❑ 100 Jerry Rice FLB	.50	.23
❑ 101 Heath Shuler COMIC SP	.10	.05
❑ 102 M.Faulk COMIC SP	.75	.35
❑ 103 Trent Dilfer COMIC SP	.25	.11
❑ 104 D.Wilkinson COMIC SP	.10	.05
❑ 105 David Palmer COMIC SP	.10	.05
❑ FD2 Marshall Faulk AUTO/10,000	20.00	9.00

(1994 Draft Day card)

❑ JR1 Jerry Rice Special	15.00	6.75
❑ NNO Jerry Rice AUTO/1994	120.00	55.00
❑ NNO Marshall Faulk Promo	1.25	.55

(International Expo back)

1995 Classic NFL Rookies

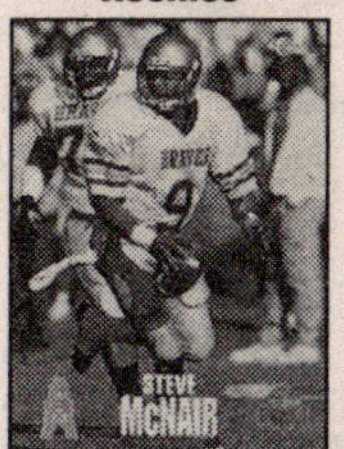

	MINT	EXC
COMPLETE SET (110)	12.00	5.50
❑ 1 Ki-Jana Carter	.25	.11
❑ 2 Tony Boselli	.10	.05
❑ 3 Steve McNair	1.25	.55
❑ 4 Michael Westbrook	.50	.23
❑ 5 Kerry Collins	.50	.23
❑ 6 Kevin Carter	.10	.05
❑ 7 Mike Mamula	.05	.02
❑ 8 Joey Galloway	1.00	.45
❑ 9 Kyle Brady	.05	.02
❑ 10 J.J. Stokes	.25	.11
❑ 11 Derrick Alexander	.05	.02
❑ 12 Warren Sapp	.10	.05
❑ 13 Mark Fields	.05	.02
❑ 14 Ruben Brown	.05	.02
❑ 15 Ellis Johnson	.05	.02
❑ 16 Hugh Douglas	.25	.11
❑ 17 Tyrone Wheatley	.25	.11
❑ 18 Napoleon Kaufman	.50	.23
❑ 19 James O. Stewart	1.00	.45
❑ 20 Luther Elliss	.05	.02
❑ 21 Rashaan Salaam	.10	.05
❑ 22 Tyrone Poole	.05	.02
❑ 23 Ty Law	.05	.02
❑ 24 Korey Stringer	.05	.02
❑ 25 Billy Milner	.05	.02
❑ 26 Devin Bush	.05	.02
❑ 27 Mark Bruener	.05	.02
❑ 28 Derrick Brooks	.25	.11
❑ 29 Blake Brockermeyer	.05	.02
❑ 30 Craig Powell	.05	.02
❑ 31 Trezelle Jenkins	.05	.02
❑ 32 Craig Newsome	.05	.02
❑ 33 Thomas Bailey	.05	.02
❑ 34 Chad May	.05	.02
❑ 35 J.J. Smith	.05	.02
❑ 36 Lorenzo Styles	.05	.02
❑ 37 Brian Williams	.05	.02
❑ 38 Damien Covington	.05	.02
❑ 39 Steve Stenstrom	.05	.02
❑ 40 Darius Holland	.05	.02
❑ 41 Pete Mitchell	.05	.02
❑ 42 Todd Collins	.10	.05
❑ 43 Kordell Stewart	1.00	.45
❑ 44 Eric Zeier	.10	.05
❑ 45 Frank Sanders	.75	.35
❑ 46 Ben Talley	.05	.02
❑ 47 Billy Williams	.05	.02
❑ 48 Chris T. Jones	.05	.02
❑ 49 Tamarick Vanover	.10	.05
❑ 50 Jimmy Hitchcock	.05	.02
❑ 51 Chris Hudson	.05	.02
❑ 52 Terrell Fletcher	.05	.02
❑ 53 Brent Moss	.05	.02
❑ 54 Terrell Davis	6.00	2.70
❑ 55 Rodney Thomas	.05	.02
❑ 56 Larry Jones	.05	.02
❑ 57 Ray Zellars	.05	.02
❑ 58 David Sloan	.05	.02
❑ 59 Brandon Bennett	.05	.02
❑ 60 Brian DeMarco	.05	.02
❑ 61 Bryan Schwartz	.05	.02
❑ 62 Jack Jackson	.05	.02
❑ 63 Bobby Taylor	.10	.05
❑ 64 Kevin Hickman	.05	.02
❑ 65 Matt O'Dwyer	.05	.02
❑ 66 Patrick Riley	.05	.02
❑ 67 Ki-Jana Carter	.10	.05
❑ 68 Kerry Collins	.25	.11
❑ 69 Steve McNair	1.25	.55
❑ 70 Tyrone Wheatley	.25	.11
❑ 71 Antonio Freeman	1.25	.55
❑ 72 Clifton Abraham	.05	.02
❑ 73 Kez McCorvey	.05	.02
❑ 74 Lovell Pinkney	.05	.02
❑ 75 Lee DeRamus	.05	.02
❑ 76 John Walsh	.05	.02
❑ 77 Cory Raymer	.05	.02
❑ 78 Corey Fuller	.05	.02
❑ 79 Tyrone Davis	.05	.02
❑ 80 David Dunn	.05	.02
❑ 81 Dana Howard	.05	.02
❑ 82 Melvin Johnson	.05	.02
❑ 83 Robert Baldwin	.05	.02
❑ 84 Curtis Martin	1.25	.55
❑ 85 Zack Crockett	.05	.02
❑ 86 Jay Barker	.05	.02
❑ 87 Christian Fauria	.05	.02
❑ 88 Zach Wiegert	.05	.02
❑ 89 Barrett Brooks	.05	.02
❑ 90 Ken Dilger	.10	.05
❑ 91 James A. Stewart	.05	.02
❑ 92 Ed Hervey	.05	.02
❑ 93 Torey Hunter	.05	.02
❑ 94 Sherman Williams	.05	.02
❑ 95 Shawn King	.05	.02
❑ 96 Dave Barr	.05	.02
❑ 97 Rob Johnson	1.00	.45
❑ 98 Stoney Case	.10	.05
❑ 99 Ki-Jana Carter CL	.05	.02
❑ 100 Steve McNair CL	.25	.11
❑ 101 Rashaan Salaam AW	.05	.02
❑ 102 Kerry Collins AW	.10	.05
❑ 103 Rashaan Salaam AW	.05	.02
❑ 104 Kerry Collins AW	.10	.05
❑ 105 Jay Barker	.05	.02
❑ 106 Drew Bledsoe	.50	.23
❑ 107 Marshall Faulk	.40	.18
❑ 108 Steve Young	.25	.11
❑ 109 Troy Aikman	.40	.18
❑ 110 Emmitt Smith	.75	.35
❑ MF1 Marshall Faulk	6.00	2.70

1996 Classic NFL Rookies

	MINT	NRMT
COMPLETE SET (100)	8.00	3.60
❑ 1 Keyshawn Johnson	1.50	.70
❑ 2 Jonathan Ogden	.05	.02
❑ 3 Kevin Hardy	.20	.09
❑ 4 Leeland McElroy	.20	.09
❑ 5 Terry Glenn	1.00	.45
❑ 6 Tim Biakabutuka	.60	.25
❑ 7 Tony Brackens	.20	.09
❑ 8 Duane Clemons	.05	.02
❑ 9 Willie Anderson	.05	.02
❑ 10 Karim Abdul-Jabbar	.50	.23
❑ 11 Daryl Gardener	.05	.02
❑ 12 Simeon Rice	.20	.09
❑ 13 Eddie George	2.00	.90
❑ 14 Andre Johnson	.05	.02
❑ 15 Jon Runyan	.05	.02
❑ 16 Jevon Langford	.05	.02
❑ 17 Derrick Mayes	.40	.18
❑ 18 Stephen Davis	2.00	.90
❑ 19 Ray Farmer	.05	.02
❑ 20 Chris Doering	.05	.02
❑ 21 Jimmy Herndon	.05	.02
❑ 22 Jerome Woods	.05	.02
❑ 23 Scott Greene	.05	.02
❑ 24 Jamain Stephens	.05	.02
❑ 25 Tommie Frazier	.40	.18
❑ 26 Dusty Zeigler	.05	.02
❑ 27 Alex Molden	.05	.02
❑ 28 Dietrich Jells	.05	.02
❑ 29 Brian Roche	.05	.02
❑ 30 Danny Kanell	.40	.18
❑ 31 Roman Oben	.05	.02
❑ 32 Chris Darkins	.05	.02
❑ 33 Christian Peter	.05	.02
❑ 34 Jeff Hartings	.05	.02
❑ 35 Bobby Hoying	.40	.18
❑ 36 Steve Taneyhill	.05	.02
❑ 37 Lance Johnstone	.05	.02
❑ 38 Zach Thomas	.60	.25
❑ 39 Donnie Edwards	.05	.02
❑ 40 Eric Moulds	1.25	.55
❑ 41 Amani Toomer	.75	.35
❑ 42 Scott Slutzker	.05	.02
❑ 43 Matt Stevens	.05	.02
❑ 44 Randall Godfrey	.05	.02
❑ 45 Orpheus Roye	.05	.02
❑ 46 Jason Odom	.05	.02
❑ 47 Je'Rod Cherry	.05	.02
❑ 48 Jeff Lewis	.20	.09
❑ 49 Mike Alstott	1.00	.45
❑ 50 Tony Banks	1.00	.45
❑ 51 Stepfret Williams	.20	.09
❑ 52 Michael Cheever	.05	.02
❑ 53 Bryant Mix	.05	.02
❑ 54 James Ritchey	.05	.02
❑ 55 Marcus Coleman	.05	.02
❑ 56 Sedric Clark	.05	.02
❑ 57 Kyle Wachholtz	.05	.02
❑ 58 Johnny McWilliams	.05	.02
❑ 59 Lawyer Milloy	.05	.02
❑ 60 Alex Van Dyke	.20	.09
❑ 61 Stanley Pritchett	.05	.02
❑ 62 Ray Mickens	.05	.02
❑ 63 Toraino Singleton	.05	.02
❑ 64 Richard Huntley	.50	.23
❑ 65 Eddie George AA	1.00	.45
❑ 66 Terry Glenn AA	.20	.09
❑ 67 Keyshawn Johnson AA	.40	.18
❑ 68 Jonathan Ogden AA	.05	.02
❑ 69 Tommie Frazier AA	.20	.09
❑ 70 Kevin Hardy AA	.05	.02
❑ 71 Zach Thomas AA	.20	.09
❑ 72 Tony Brackens AA	.05	.02
❑ 73 Lawyer Milloy AA	.05	.02
❑ 74 Leeland McElroy AA	.05	.02
❑ 75 Emmitt Smith	.75	.35
❑ 76 Steve McNair	.40	.18
❑ 77 Kerry Collins	.20	.09
❑ 78 Drew Bledsoe	.40	.18
❑ 79 Marshall Faulk	.40	.18
❑ 80 Pete Kendall	.05	.02
❑ 81 Regan Upshaw	.05	.02
❑ 82 Mercury Hayes	.05	.02
❑ 83 Dou Innocent	.05	.02
❑ 84 DeRon Jenkins	.05	.02
❑ 85 Marco Battaglia	.05	.02
❑ 86 John Mobley	.05	.02
❑ 87 Cedric Jones	.05	.02
❑ 88 Marvin Harrison	1.50	.70
❑ 89 Israel Ifeanyi	.05	.02
❑ 90 Reggie Brown	.05	.02
❑ 91 Jermane Mayberry	.05	.02
❑ 92 Brian Dawkins	.05	.02

Card	MINT	NRMT
❑ 93 Tedy Bruschi	.05	.02
❑ 94 Terrell Owens	1.50	.70
❑ 95 Jermaine Lewis	.20	.09
❑ 96 Sean Boyd	.05	.02
❑ 97 Phillip Daniels	.05	.02
❑ 98 Lawrence Phillips	.05	.02
❑ 99 Keyshawn Johnson CL	.20	.09
❑ 100 Terry Glenn CL	.20	.09
❑ P1 Keyshawn Johnson Promo	1.25	.55

1996 Press Pass

	MINT	NRMT
COMPLETE SET (55)	15.00	6.75
❑ 1 Keyshawn Johnson	2.50	1.10
❑ 2 Jonathan Ogden	.10	.05
❑ 3 Duane Clemons	.10	.05
❑ 4 Kevin Hardy	.10	.05
❑ 5 Eddie George	4.00	1.80
❑ 6 Karim Abdul-Jabbar	1.00	.45
❑ 7 Terry Glenn	1.25	.55
❑ 8 Leeland McElroy	.30	.14
❑ 9 Simeon Rice	.30	.14
❑ 10 Roman Oben	.10	.05
❑ 11 Daryl Gardener	.10	.05
❑ 12 Marcus Coleman	.10	.05
❑ 13 Christian Peter	.10	.05
❑ 14 Tim Biakabutuka	1.25	.55
❑ 15 Eric Moulds	2.00	.90
❑ 16 Chris Darkins	.10	.05
❑ 17 Andre Johnson	.10	.05
❑ 18 Lawyer Milloy	.10	.05
❑ 19 Jon Runyan	.10	.05
❑ 20 Mike Alstott	1.50	.70
❑ 21 Jeff Hartings	.10	.05
❑ 22 Amani Toomer	1.25	.55
❑ 23 Danny Kanell	.75	.35
❑ 24 Marco Battaglia	.10	.05
❑ 25 Stephen Davis	4.00	1.80
❑ 26 Johnny McWilliams	.10	.05
❑ 27 Israel Ifeanyi	.10	.05
❑ 28 Scott Slutzker	.10	.05
❑ 29 Bryant Mix	.10	.05
❑ 30 Brian Roche	.10	.05
❑ 31 Stanley Pritchett	.10	.05
❑ 32 Jerome Woods	.10	.05
❑ 33 Tommie Frazier	.30	.14
❑ 34 Stepfret Williams	.10	.05
❑ 35 Ray Mickens	.10	.05
❑ 36 Alex Van Dyke	.10	.05
❑ 37 Bobby Hoying	.75	.35
❑ 38 Tony Brackens	.30	.14
❑ 39 Dietrich Jells	.10	.05
❑ 40 Jason Odom	.10	.05
❑ 41 Randall Godfrey	.10	.05
❑ 42 Willie Anderson	.10	.05
❑ 43 Tony Banks	1.25	.55
❑ 44 Michael Cheever	.10	.05
❑ 45 Je'Rod Cherry	.10	.05
❑ 46 Chris Doering	.10	.05
❑ 47 Steve Taneyhill	.10	.05
❑ 48 Kyle Wachholtz	.10	.05
❑ 49 Dusty Zeigler	.10	.05
❑ 50 Derrick Mayes	.30	.14
❑ 51 Orpheus Roye	.10	.05
❑ 52 Sedric Clark	.10	.05
❑ 53 Richard Huntley	1.00	.45
❑ 54 Donnie Edwards	.10	.05
❑ 55 Zach Thomas CL	.30	.14
❑ RED Lawrence Phillips	6.00	2.70
❑ P1 Tim Biakabutuka Promo	1.00	.45

1996 Press Pass Paydirt

	MINT	NRMT
COMPLETE SET (75)	25.00	11.00
❑ 1 Keyshawn Johnson	2.50	1.10
❑ 2 Jonathan Ogden	.10	.05
❑ 3 Duane Clemons	.10	.05
❑ 4 Kevin Hardy	.30	.14
❑ 5 Eddie George	4.00	1.80
❑ 6 Karim Abdul-Jabbar	1.00	.45
❑ 7 Terry Glenn	1.25	.55
❑ 8 Leeland McElroy	.30	.14
❑ 9 Simeon Rice	.30	.14
❑ 10 Roman Oben	.10	.05
❑ 11 Daryl Gardener	.10	.05
❑ 12 Marcus Coleman	.10	.05
❑ 13 Christian Peter UER (Chris Doering stamp on front)	.10	.05
❑ 14 Tim Biakabutuka	1.25	.55
❑ 15 Eric Moulds	.75	.35
❑ 16 Chris Darkins	.10	.05
❑ 17 Andre Johnson	.10	.05
❑ 18 Lawyer Milloy	.10	.05
❑ 19 Jon Runyan	.10	.05
❑ 20 Mike Alstott	1.50	.70
❑ 21 Jeff Hartings	.10	.05
❑ 22 Amani Toomer	1.25	.55
❑ 23 Danny Kanell	.75	.35
❑ 24 Marco Battaglia	.10	.05
❑ 25 Stephen Davis	4.00	1.80
❑ 26 Johnny McWilliams	.10	.05
❑ 27 Israel Ifeanyi	.10	.05
❑ 28 Scott Slutzker	.10	.05
❑ 29 Bryant Mix	.10	.05
❑ 30 Brian Roche	.10	.05
❑ 31 Stanley Pritchett	.10	.05
❑ 32 Jerome Woods	.10	.05
❑ 33 Tommie Frazier	.30	.14
❑ 34 Stepfret Williams	.10	.05
❑ 35 Ray Mickens	.10	.05
❑ 36 Alex Van Dyke	.10	.05
❑ 37 Bobby Hoying	.75	.35
❑ 38 Tony Brackens	.30	.14
❑ 39 Dietrich Jells	.10	.05
❑ 40 Jason Odom	.10	.05
❑ 41 Randall Godfrey	.10	.05
❑ 42 Willie Anderson	.10	.05
❑ 43 Tony Banks	1.25	.55
❑ 44 Michael Cheever	.10	.05
❑ 45 Je'Rod Cherry	.10	.05
❑ 46 Chris Doering	.10	.05
❑ 47 Steve Taneyhill	.10	.05
❑ 48 Kyle Wachholtz	.10	.05
❑ 49 Dusty Zeigler	.10	.05
❑ 50 Derrick Mayes	.30	.14
❑ 51 Orpheus Roye	.10	.05
❑ 52 Sedric Clark	.10	.05
❑ 53 Richard Huntley	1.00	.45
❑ 54 Donnie Edwards	.10	.05
❑ 55 Zach Thomas	1.25	.55
❑ 56 Alex Molden	.10	.05
❑ 57 Jimmy Herndon	.10	.05
❑ 58 Mike Alstott	1.50	.70
❑ 59 Scott Greene	.10	.05
❑ 60 Danny Kanell	.75	.35
❑ 61 Jonathan Ogden	.10	.05
❑ 62 Simeon Rice	.30	.14
❑ 63 Kevin Hardy	.30	.14
❑ 64 Jon Runyan	.10	.05
❑ 65 Stephen Davis	4.00	1.80
❑ 66 Tim Biakabutuka	1.25	.55
❑ 67 Terry Glenn	1.25	.55
❑ 68 Leeland McElroy	.30	.14
❑ 69 Eric Moulds	2.00	.90
❑ 70 Karim Abdul-Jabbar	1.00	.45
❑ 71 Lawyer Milloy	.10	.05
❑ 72 Derrick Mayes	.75	.35
❑ 73 Tommie Frazier	.30	.14
❑ 74 Bobby Hoying	.75	.35
❑ 75 Kyle Wachholtz CL	.10	.05
❑ RED Lawrence Phillips	6.00	2.70

1997 Press Pass

	MINT	NRMT
COMPLETE SET (49)	15.00	6.75
❑ 1 Orlando Pace	.20	.09
❑ 2 Warrick Dunn	1.00	.45
❑ 3 Danny Wuerffel	.50	.23
❑ 4 Darnell Autry	.10	.05
❑ 5 Troy Davis	.10	.05
❑ 6 Jake Plummer	2.50	1.10
❑ 7 Corey Dillon	2.50	1.10
❑ 8 Reidel Anthony	.75	.35
❑ 9 Byron Hanspard	.60	.25
❑ 10 Tiki Barber	1.00	.45
❑ 11 Ike Hilliard	.75	.35
❑ 12 Rae Carruth	.10	.05
❑ 13 Yatil Green	.20	.09
❑ 14 Peter Boulware	.20	.09
❑ 15 Jim Druckenmiller	.50	.23
❑ 16 Pat Barnes	.20	.09
❑ 17 Trevor Pryce	.10	.05
❑ 18 Kevin Lockett	.10	.05
❑ 19 Koy Detmer	.20	.09
❑ 20 Bryant Westbrook	.10	.05
❑ 21 Darrell Russell	.10	.05
❑ 22 Tony Gonzalez	1.00	.45
❑ 23 Shawn Springs	.20	.09
❑ 24 Chris Canty	.10	.05
❑ 25 David LaFleur	.20	.09
❑ 26 Dwayne Rudd	.10	.05
❑ 27 Bob Sapp	.10	.05
❑ 28 Mike Vrabel	.10	.05
❑ 29 Antowain Smith	1.25	.55
❑ 30 Keith Poole	.10	.05
❑ 31 Sedrick Shaw	.20	.09
❑ 32 Tremain Mack	.10	.05
❑ 33 Matt Russell	.10	.05
❑ 34 Reinard Wilson	.10	.05
❑ 35 Marc Edwards	.20	.09
❑ 36 Greg Jones	.10	.05
❑ 37 Michael Booker	.10	.05
❑ 38 James Farrior	.10	.05
❑ 39 Danny Wuerffel HL	.20	.09
❑ 40 Troy Davis HL	.10	.05
❑ 41 Corey Dillon HL	1.25	.55

❑ 42 Jake Plummer HL	1.25	.55
❑ 43 Peter Boulware HL	.20	.09
❑ 44 Eddie Robinson CO	.50	.23
❑ 45 Bobby Bowden CO	.75	.35
❑ 46 Steve Spurrier CO	1.25	.55
❑ 47 Gary Barnett CO	.10	.05
❑ 48 Joe Paterno CO SP	50.00	22.00
❑ 49 Tom Osborne CO	1.25	.55
❑ 50 Jarrett Irons CL	.10	.05

1998 Press Pass

	MINT	NRMT
COMPLETE SET (50)	20.00	9.00
❑ 1 Peyton Manning	4.00	1.80
❑ 2 Ryan Leaf	1.00	.45
❑ 3 Charles Woodson	.75	.35
❑ 4 Andre Wadsworth	.50	.23
❑ 5 Randy Moss	4.00	1.80
❑ 6 Curtis Enis	.60	.25
❑ 7 Tra Thomas	.10	.05
❑ 8 Flozell Adams	.10	.05
❑ 9 Jason Peter	.10	.05
❑ 10 Brian Simmons	.10	.05
❑ 11 Takeo Spikes	.25	.11
❑ 12 Michael Myers	.10	.05
❑ 13 Kevin Dyson	.75	.35
❑ 14 Grant Wistrom	.25	.11
❑ 15 Fred Taylor	1.50	.70
❑ 16 Germane Crowell	1.00	.45
❑ 17 Sam Cowart	.10	.05
❑ 18 Anthony Simmons LB	.10	.05
❑ 19 Robert Edwards	.50	.23
❑ 20 Shaun Williams	.10	.05
❑ 21 Phil Savoy	.10	.05
❑ 22 Leonard Little	.10	.05
❑ 23 Saladin McCullough	.10	.05
❑ 24 Duane Starks	.10	.05
❑ 25 John Avery	.50	.23
❑ 26 Vonnie Holliday	.50	.23
❑ 27 Tim Dwight	1.00	.45
❑ 28 Donovin Darius	.10	.05
❑ 29 Alonzo Mayes	.10	.05
❑ 30 Jerome Pathon	.50	.23
❑ 31 Brian Kelly	.10	.05
❑ 32 Hines Ward	.25	.11
❑ 33 Jacquez Green	.75	.35
❑ 34 Marcus Nash	.25	.11
❑ 35 Ahman Green	1.00	.45
❑ 36 Joe Jurevicius	.25	.11
❑ 37 Tavian Banks	.25	.11
❑ 38 Donald Hayes	.50	.23
❑ 39 Robert Holcombe	.50	.23
❑ 40 E.G. Green	.25	.11
❑ 41 John Dutton	.10	.05
❑ 42 Skip Hicks	.50	.23
❑ 43 Pat Johnson	.25	.11
❑ 44 Keith Brooking	.25	.11
❑ 45 Alan Faneca	.10	.05
❑ 46 Steve Spurrier CO	1.00	.45
❑ 47 Mike Price CO	.10	.05
❑ 48 Bobby Bowden CO	.25	.11
❑ 49 Tom Osborne CO	1.00	.45
❑ 50 Peyton Manning CL	1.25	.55
❑ P1 Randy Moss Promo	3.00	1.35

1999 Press Pass

	MINT	NRMT
COMPLETE SET (45)	20.00	9.00
❑ 1 Ricky Williams	2.50	1.10
❑ 2 Tim Couch	2.50	1.10
❑ 3 Champ Bailey	.60	.25
❑ 4 Chris Claiborne	.20	.09
❑ 5 Donovan McNabb	2.00	.90
❑ 6 Edgerrin James	5.00	2.20
❑ 7 Akili Smith	1.25	.55
❑ 8 John Tait	.20	.09
❑ 9 Jevon Kearse	1.25	.55
❑ 10 Torry Holt	1.50	.70
❑ 11 Troy Edwards	.60	.25
❑ 12 Chris McAlister	.30	.14
❑ 13 Daunte Culpepper	3.00	1.35
❑ 14 Andy Katzenmoyer	.50	.23
❑ 15 David Boston	1.25	.55
❑ 16 Ebenezer Ekuban	.30	.14
❑ 17 Peerless Price	.60	.25
❑ 18 Shaun King	2.00	.90
❑ 19 Joe Germaine	.50	.23
❑ 20 Brock Huard	1.00	.45
❑ 21 Michael Bishop	.60	.25
❑ 22 Amos Zereoue	.50	.23
❑ 23 Sedrick Irvin	.50	.23
❑ 24 Autry Denson	.30	.14
❑ 25 Kevin Faulk	1.00	.45
❑ 26 James Johnson	.50	.23
❑ 27 D'Wayne Bates	.30	.14
❑ 28 Kevin Johnson	1.25	.55
❑ 29 Tai Streets	.50	.23
❑ 30 Craig Yeast	.30	.14
❑ 31 Dre' Bly	.20	.09
❑ 32 Anthony Poindexter	.20	.09
❑ 33 Jared DeVries	.20	.09
❑ 34 Rob Konrad	.50	.23
❑ 35 Dat Nguyen	.50	.23
❑ 36 Cade McNown	1.25	.55
❑ 37 Scott Covington	.50	.23
❑ 38 Jon Jansen	.20	.09
❑ 39 Rufus French	.20	.09
❑ 40 Mike Rucker	.20	.09
❑ 41 Aaron Gibson	.20	.09
❑ 42 Kris Farris	.20	.09
❑ 43 Anthony McFarland	.20	.09
❑ 44 Matt Stinchcomb	.30	.14
❑ 45 Dee Miller CL	.30	.14

2000 Press Pass

	MINT	NRMT
COMPLETE SET (45)	20.00	9.00
❑ 1 Peter Warrick	1.50	.70
❑ 2 Travis Claridge	.25	.11
❑ 3 Courtney Brown	.60	.25
❑ 4 Plaxico Burress	1.00	.45
❑ 5 Chad Pennington	1.50	.70
❑ 6 Thomas Jones	.75	.35
❑ 7 Ron Dayne	1.50	.70
❑ 8 Brian Urlacher	1.50	.70
❑ 9 Corey Simon	.60	.25
❑ 10 Chris Samuels	.40	.18
❑ 11 Stockar McDougle	.25	.11
❑ 12 Deon Grant	.25	.11
❑ 13 Cosey Coleman	.25	.11
❑ 14 Sylvester Morris	1.00	.45
❑ 15 Shyrone Stith	.40	.18
❑ 16 Shaun Alexander	1.25	.55
❑ 17 Dez White	.40	.18
❑ 18 John Engelberger	.40	.18
❑ 19 Tim Rattay	.75	.35
❑ 20 Todd Pinkston	.50	.23
❑ 21 John Abraham	.40	.18
❑ 22 R.Jay Soward	.50	.23
❑ 23 Shaun Ellis	.40	.18
❑ 24 Keith Bulluck	.40	.18
❑ 25 Jerry Porter	.50	.23
❑ 26 Darren Howard	.40	.18
❑ 27 Joe Hamilton	.60	.25
❑ 28 Deltha O'Neal	.40	.18
❑ 29 Chris Redman	1.00	.45
❑ 30 Deon Dyer	.40	.18
❑ 31 Jamal Lewis	2.50	1.10
❑ 32 Chris Hovan	.40	.18
❑ 33 Raynoch Thompson	.40	.18
❑ 34 Travis Taylor	.60	.25
❑ 35 Sebastian Janikowski	.50	.23
❑ 36 Travis Prentice	.75	.35
❑ 37 Tom Brady	.50	.23
❑ 38 Tee Martin	.75	.35
❑ 39 J.R. Redmond	.60	.25
❑ 40 Dennis Northcutt	.60	.25
❑ 41 Laveranues Coles	.75	.35
❑ 42 Danny Farmer	.50	.23
❑ 43 Darrell Jackson	.75	.35
❑ 44 Chris McIntosh	.25	.11
❑ 45 Peter Warrick CL	.60	.25
❑ P1 Peter Warrick Promo	2.00	.90

1999 Sage

	MINT	NRMT
COMPLETE SET (50)	40.00	18.00
❑ 1 Rahim Abdullah	.50	.23
❑ 2 Jerry Azumah	.50	.23
❑ 3 Champ Bailey	1.00	.45
❑ 4 D'Wayne Bates	.50	.23
❑ 5 Michael Bishop	1.00	.45
❑ 6 David Boston	2.00	.90
❑ 7 Fernando Bryant	.50	.23
❑ 8 Tony Bryant	.50	.23
❑ 9 Chris Claiborne	.40	.18
❑ 10 Mike Cloud	.75	.35

	Player	MINT	NRMT
❑ 11	Cecil Collins	.75	.35
❑ 12	Tim Couch	4.00	1.80
❑ 13	Daunte Culpepper	5.00	2.20
❑ 14	Jared DeVries	.50	.23
❑ 15	Adrian Dingle	.50	.23
❑ 16	Antuan Edwards	.50	.23
❑ 17	Troy Edwards	1.00	.45
❑ 18	Kevin Faulk	1.25	.55
❑ 19	Rufus French	.40	.18
❑ 20	Martin Gramatica	.40	.18
❑ 21	Torry Holt	2.50	1.10
❑ 22	Sedrick Irvin	.75	.35
❑ 23	Edgerrin James	10.00	4.50
❑ 24	Jon Jansen	.50	.23
❑ 25	Andy Katzenmoyer	.75	.35
❑ 26	Jevon Kearse	2.00	.90
❑ 27	Patrick Kerney	.40	.18
❑ 28	Lamar King	.50	.23
❑ 29	Shaun King	3.00	1.35
❑ 30	Jim Kleinsasser	.75	.35
❑ 31	Rob Konrad	.75	.35
❑ 32	Brian Kuklick	.50	.23
❑ 33	Chris McAlister	.50	.23
❑ 34	Darnell McDonald	.75	.35
❑ 35	Reggie McGrew	.50	.23
❑ 36	Donovan McNabb	3.00	1.35
❑ 37	Cade McNown	2.00	.90
❑ 38	Dat Nguyen	.75	.35
❑ 39	Solomon Page	.40	.18
❑ 40	Mike Peterson	.75	.35
❑ 41	Anthony Poindexter	.50	.23
❑ 42	Peerless Price	1.00	.45
❑ 43	Michael Rucker	.50	.23
❑ 44	L.J. Shelton	.40	.18
❑ 45	Akili Smith	2.00	.90
❑ 46	John Tait	.40	.18
❑ 47	Fred Vinson	.50	.23
❑ 48	Al Wilson	.75	.35
❑ 49	Antoine Winfield	.50	.23
❑ 50	Damien Woody	.50	.23

2000 Sage

		MINT	NRMT
COMPLETE SET (50)		10.00	4.50
❑ 1	John Abraham	.60	.25
❑ 2	Shaun Alexander	2.00	.90
❑ 3	LaVar Arrington	3.00	1.35
❑ 4	Courtney Brown	1.00	.45
❑ 5	Keith Bulluck	.60	.25
❑ 6	Plaxico Burress	1.50	.70
❑ 7	Giovanni Carmazzi	1.00	.45
❑ 8	Kwame Cavil	.60	.25
❑ 9	Cosey Coleman	.40	.18
❑ 10	Laveranues Coles	1.25	.55
❑ 11	Tim Couch	1.50	.70
❑ 12	Ron Dayne	2.50	1.10
❑ 13	Reuben Droughns	.75	.35
❑ 14	Shaun Ellis	.60	.25
❑ 15	John Engelberger	.60	.25
❑ 16	Danny Farmer	.75	.35
❑ 17	Dwayne Goodrich	.75	.35
❑ 18	Deon Grant	.40	.18
❑ 19	Chris Hovan	.60	.25
❑ 20	Darren Howard	.60	.25
❑ 21	Todd Husak	.75	.35
❑ 22	Thomas Jones	1.25	.55
❑ 23	Curtis Keaton	.60	.25
❑ 24	Jamal Lewis	4.00	1.80
❑ 25	Anthony Lucas	.40	.18
❑ 26	Tee Martin	1.25	.55
❑ 27	Stockar McDougle	.40	.18
❑ 28	Corey Moore	.60	.25
❑ 29	Rob Morris	.60	.25
❑ 30	Sammy Morris	1.00	.45
❑ 31	Sylvester Morris	1.50	.70
❑ 32	Chad Pennington	2.50	1.10
❑ 33	Todd Pinkston	.75	.35
❑ 34	Ahmed Plummer	.75	.35
❑ 35	Jerry Porter	.75	.35
❑ 36	Travis Prentice	1.25	.55
❑ 37	Tim Rattay	1.25	.55
❑ 38	Chris Redman	1.50	.70
❑ 39	J.R. Redmond	1.00	.45
❑ 40	Chris Samuels	.60	.25
❑ 41	Brandon Short	.60	.25
❑ 42	Corey Simon	1.00	.45
❑ 43	R.Jay Soward	.75	.35
❑ 44	Shyrone Stith	.60	.25
❑ 45	Raynoch Thompson	.60	.25
❑ 46	Brian Urlacher	2.50	1.10
❑ 47	Todd Wade	.40	.18
❑ 48	Troy Walters	.75	.35
❑ 49	Dez White	.60	.25
❑ 50	Michael Wiley	.75	.35

2000 Sage HIT

		MINT	NRMT
COMPLETE SET (50)		25.00	11.00
❑ 1	Jerry Porter	.75	.35
❑ 2	Tim Couch	1.50	.70
❑ 3	Chris Samuels	.60	.25
❑ 4	Plaxico Burress	1.50	.70
❑ 5	Michael Wiley	.75	.35
❑ 6	Thomas Jones	1.25	.55
❑ 7	Chris Redman	1.50	.70
❑ 8	Anthony Lucas	.40	.18
❑ 9	Kwame Cavil	.60	.25
❑ 10	Chad Pennington	2.50	1.10
❑ 11	LaVar Arrington	4.00	1.80
❑ 12	Giovanni Carmazzi	1.00	.45
❑ 13	Tim Rattay	1.25	.55
❑ 14	Laveranues Coles	1.25	.55
❑ 15	Mario Edwards	.40	.18
❑ 16	John Engelberger	.60	.25
❑ 17	Tee Martin	1.25	.55
❑ 18	R.Jay Soward	.75	.35
❑ 19	Ahmed Plummer	.75	.35
❑ 20	Na'il Diggs	.75	.35
❑ 21	J.R. Redmond	1.00	.45
❑ 22	Dez White	.60	.25
❑ 23	Reuben Droughns	.75	.35
❑ 24	Sylvester Morris	1.50	.70
❑ 25	Cosey Coleman	.40	.18
❑ 26	Corey Moore	.60	.25
❑ 27	Curtis Keaton	.60	.25
❑ 28	Danny Farmer	.75	.35
❑ 29	Travis Claridge	.40	.18
❑ 30	Troy Walters	.75	.35
❑ 31	Jamal Lewis	4.00	1.80
❑ 32	Shaun King	1.25	.55
❑ 33	Ron Dayne	2.50	1.10
❑ 34	Keith Bulluck	.60	.25
❑ 35	Corey Simon	1.00	.45
❑ 36	Deon Dyer	.60	.25
❑ 37	Shaun Alexander	2.00	.90
❑ 38	Shyrone Stith	.60	.25
❑ 39	Shaun Ellis	.60	.25
❑ 40	Todd Pinkston	.75	.35
❑ 41	Travis Prentice	1.25	.55
❑ 42	Chris Hovan	.60	.25
❑ 43	Brandon Short	.60	.25
❑ 44	Brian Urlacher	2.50	1.10
❑ 45	Rob Morris	.75	.35
❑ 46	Raynoch Thompson	.60	.25
❑ 47	Deon Grant	.40	.18
❑ 48	Stockar McDougle	.40	.18
❑ 49	Darren Howard	.60	.25
❑ 50	Courtney Brown	1.00	.45

1997 Score Board NFL Rookies

		MINT	NRMT
COMPLETE SET (100)		10.00	4.50
❑ 1	Jake Plummer	2.00	.90
❑ 2	Tony Gonzalez	.75	.35
❑ 3	Trevor Pryce	.05	.02
❑ 4	Greg Jones	.05	.02
❑ 5	Koy Detmer	.10	.05
❑ 6	Rae Carruth	.25	.11
❑ 7	Peter Boulware	.10	.05
❑ 8	Warrick Dunn	.75	.35
❑ 9	Antowain Smith	.75	.35
❑ 10	Troy Davis	.05	.02
❑ 11	David LaFleur	.10	.05
❑ 12	Yatil Green	.25	.11
❑ 13	Michael Booker	.05	.02
❑ 14	Shawn Springs	.10	.05
❑ 15	Bryant Westbrook	.10	.05
❑ 16	Byron Hanspard	.40	.18
❑ 17	Darrell Russell	.05	.02
❑ 18	Corey Dillon	2.00	.90
❑ 19	Tyrus McCloud	.05	.02
❑ 20	Reinard Wilson	.10	.05
❑ 21	Adam Meadows	.05	.02
❑ 22	Tremain Mack	.05	.02
❑ 23	Ricky Parker	.05	.02
❑ 24	George Jones	.05	.02
❑ 25	Terry Battle	.05	.02
❑ 26	Will Blackwell	.10	.05
❑ 27	Jerald Sowell	.05	.02
❑ 28	Isaac Byrd	.25	.11
❑ 29	Chris Naeole	.05	.02
❑ 30	Kevin Lockett	.10	.05
❑ 31	Freddie Jones	.05	.02
❑ 32	Pat Barnes	.10	.05
❑ 33	Torrian Gray	.05	.02
❑ 34	Brian Manning	.05	.02
❑ 35	Dedric Ward	.75	.35
❑ 36	Pete Monty	.05	.02
❑ 37	Sam Madison	.10	.05
❑ 38	Sedrick Shaw	.25	.11
❑ 39	Mike Logan	.05	.02
❑ 40	Albert Connell	.75	.35
❑ 41	Canute Curtis	.05	.02
❑ 42	Ronde Barber	.05	.02
❑ 43	Orlando Pace	.10	.05
❑ 44	Edward Perry	.05	.02
❑ 45	Tiki Barber	.75	.35
❑ 46	Kevin Jackson	.05	.02
❑ 47	Jerry Wunsch	.05	.02
❑ 48	Michael Hamilton	.05	.02
❑ 49	Darnell Autry	.10	.05
❑ 50	Jim Druckenmiller	.25	.11
❑ 51	James Farrior	.05	.02
❑ 52	Derrick Mason	.25	.11
❑ 53	Ty Howard	.05	.02
❑ 54	Jason Taylor	.05	.02
❑ 55	Reidel Anthony	.50	.23
❑ 56	Bert Berry	.05	.02
❑ 57	Marc Edwards	.10	.05
❑ 58	James Hamilton	.05	.02
❑ 59	Ike Hilliard	.50	.23
❑ 60	Tommy Knight	.05	.02
❑ 61	Walter Jones	.05	.02
❑ 62	Chad Levitt	.05	.02

❑ 63 Pratt Lyons .05 .02
❑ 64 Greg Clark .05 .02
❑ 65 Ryan Phillips .05 .02
❑ 66 Jason Martin .05 .02
❑ 67 Scott Sanderson .05 .02
❑ 68 Alshermond Singleton .05 .02
❑ 69 Duce Staley 2.00 .90
❑ 70 Jared Tomich .05 .02
❑ 71 Ross Verba .05 .02
❑ 72 Derrick Rodgers .05 .02
❑ 73 Mike Vrabel .05 .02
❑ 74 John Allred .05 .02
❑ 75 Bob Sapp .05 .02
❑ 76 Brad Otton .05 .02
❑ 77 Tarik Glenn .05 .02
❑ 78 Chad Scott .05 .02
❑ 79 Nathan Davis .05 .02
❑ 80 Henri Crockett .05 .02
❑ 81 Tarek Saleh .05 .02
❑ 82 Seth Payne .05 .02
❑ 83 Pete Chryplewicz .05 .02
❑ 84 Reidel Anthony AA .05 .02
❑ 85 Reinard Wilson AA .05 .02
❑ 86 Byron Hanspard AA .25 .11
❑ 87 Shawn Springs AA .05 .02
❑ 88 David LaFleur AA .05 .02
❑ 89 Troy Davis AA .05 .02
❑ 90 Warrick Dunn AA .40 .18
❑ 91 Peter Boulware AA .10 .05
❑ 92 Rae Carruth AA .05 .02
❑ 93 Tony Gonzalez AA .25 .11
❑ 94 Jake Plummer AA 1.00 .45
❑ 95 Orlando Pace AA .05 .02
❑ 96 Ike Hilliard AA .25 .11
❑ 97 Kevin Jackson AA .05 .02
❑ 98 Jim Druckenmiller AA .25 .11
❑ 99 Shawn Springs CL .05 .02
❑ 100 Warrick Dunn CL .40 .18

1995 SR Draft Preview

	MINT	EXC
COMPLETE SET (80)	10.00	4.50

❑ 1 Derrick Alexander DE .05 .02
❑ 2 Kelvin Anderson .05 .02
❑ 3 Antonio Armstrong .05 .02
❑ 4 Jamie Asher .10 .05
❑ 5 Joe Aska .05 .02
❑ 6 Dave Barr .05 .02
❑ 7 Brandon Bennett .05 .02
❑ 8 Tony Berti .05 .02
❑ 9 Mark Birchmeier .05 .02
❑ 10 Tony Boselli .10 .05
❑ 11 Derrick Brooks .25 .11
❑ 12 Anthony Brown .05 .02
❑ 13 Ruben Brown .05 .02
❑ 14 Mark Bruener .05 .02
❑ 15 Ontiwaun Carter .05 .02
❑ 16 Stoney Case .10 .05
❑ 17 Byron Chamberlain .50 .23
❑ 18 Shannon Clavelle .05 .02
❑ 19 Jamal Cox .05 .02
❑ 20 Zack Crockett .05 .02
❑ 21 Terrell Davis 5.00 2.20
❑ 22 Tyrone Davis .05 .02
❑ 23 Lee DeRamus .05 .02
❑ 24 Ken Dilger .10 .05
❑ 25 Hugh Douglas .25 .11
❑ 26 David Dunn .05 .02
❑ 27 Chad Eaton .05 .02
❑ 28 Hicham El-Mashtoub .05 .02
❑ 29 Christian Fauria .05 .02
❑ 30 Terrell Fletcher .05 .02
❑ 31 Antonio Freeman 1.25 .55
❑ 32 Eddie Goines .05 .02
❑ 33 Roger Graham .05 .02
❑ 34 Carl Greenwood .05 .02
❑ 35 Ed Hervey .05 .02
❑ 36 Jimmy Hitchcock .05 .02
❑ 37 Darius Holland .05 .02
❑ 38 Torey Hunter .05 .02
❑ 39 Steve Ingram .05 .02
❑ 40 Jack Jackson .05 .02
❑ 41 Trezelle Jenkins .05 .02
❑ 42 Ellis Johnson .05 .02
❑ 43 Eric Johnson .05 .02
❑ 44 Rob Johnson .75 .35
❑ 45 Chris T. Jones .05 .02
❑ 46 Larry Jones .05 .02
❑ 47 Shawn King .05 .02
❑ 48 Scotty Lewis .05 .02
❑ 49 Curtis Martin 1.25 .55
❑ 50 Oscar McBride .05 .02
❑ 51 Kez McCorvey .05 .02
❑ 52 Bronzell Miller .05 .02
❑ 53 Pete Mitchell .05 .02
❑ 54 Brent Moss .05 .02
❑ 55 Craig Newsome .05 .02
❑ 56 Herman O'Berry .05 .02
❑ 57 Matt O'Dwyer .05 .02
❑ 58 Tyrone Poole .10 .05
❑ 59 Brian Pruitt .05 .02
❑ 60 Cory Raymer .05 .02
❑ 61 John Sacca .05 .02
❑ 62 Frank Sanders .50 .23
❑ 63 J.J. Smith .05 .02
❑ 64 Brendan Stai .05 .02
❑ 65 Steve Stenstrom .10 .05
❑ 66 James O. Stewart .75 .35
❑ 67 Kordell Stewart 1.00 .45
❑ 68 Ben Talley .05 .02
❑ 69 Bobby Taylor .05 .02
❑ 70 Johnny Thomas .05 .02
❑ 71 Orlando Thomas .05 .02
❑ 72 Rodney Thomas .10 .05
❑ 73 Zach Wiegert .05 .02
❑ 74 Jerrott Willard .05 .02
❑ 75 Billy Williams .05 .02
❑ 76 Sherman Williams .05 .02
❑ 77 Jamal Willis .05 .02
❑ 78 Dave Wohlabaugh .05 .02
❑ 79 Eric Zeier .10 .05
❑ 80 Checklist .05 .02

1995 SR Signature Prime

	MINT	EXC
COMPLETE SET (50)	15.00	6.75

❑ 1 Justin Armour .10 .05
❑ 2 Joe Aska .10 .05
❑ 3 Henry Bailey .10 .05
❑ 4 Jay Barker .10 .05
❑ 5 Dave Barr .10 .05
❑ 6 Kevin Bouie .10 .05
❑ 7 Mark Bruener .20 .09
❑ 8 Stoney Case .20 .09
❑ 9 Curtis Ceaser .10 .05
❑ 10 Todd Collins .20 .09
❑ 11 Jerry Colquitt .10 .05
❑ 12 Terrell Davis 8.00 3.60
❑ 13 David Dunn .10 .05
❑ 14 Omar Ellison .10 .05
❑ 15 Christian Fauria .10 .05
❑ 16 Antonio Freeman 2.00 .90
❑ 17 Eddie Goines .10 .05
❑ 18 Aaron Hayden .10 .05
❑ 19 William Henderson .10 .05
❑ 20 Kevin Hickman .10 .05
❑ 21 Jack Jackson .10 .05
❑ 22 Travis Jervey .10 .05
❑ 23 Rob Johnson 1.25 .55
❑ 24 Chris T. Jones .10 .05
❑ 25 Larry Jones .10 .05
❑ 26 Curtis Marsh .10 .05
❑ 27 Curtis Martin 2.00 .90
❑ 28 Fred McCrary .10 .05
❑ 29 Mike Miller .10 .05
❑ 30 Shannon Myers .10 .05
❑ 31 Jimmy Oliver .10 .05
❑ 32 Dino Philyaw .10 .05
❑ 33 Lovell Pinkney .10 .05
❑ 34 Michael Roan .10 .05
❑ 35 Chris Sanders .20 .09
❑ 36 Frank Sanders 1.00 .45
❑ 37 Cory Schlesinger .10 .05
❑ 38 Charlie Simmons .10 .05
❑ 39 David Sloan .10 .05
❑ 40 Steve Stenstrom .10 .05
❑ 41 James A. Stewart .10 .05
❑ 42 Rodney Thomas .10 .05
❑ 43 A.C. Tellison .10 .05
❑ 44 Tamarick Vanover .20 .09
❑ 45 John Walsh .10 .05
❑ 46 Kendell Watkins .10 .05
❑ 47 Charles Way .20 .09
❑ 48 Craig Whelihan .20 .09
❑ 49 Eric Zeier .20 .09
❑ 50 Ray Zellars .20 .09
❑ NNO Checklist Card .10 .05
❑ P1 J.J. Stokes Promo .50 .23

1991 Star Pics

	MINT	EXC
COMP.FACT.SET (113)	5.00	2.20

❑ 1 1991 NFL Draft Overview .05 .02
❑ 2 Barry Sanders FLB 1.00 .45
❑ 3 Nick Bell .05 .02
❑ 4 Kelvin Pritchett .05 .02
❑ 5 Huey Richardson .05 .02
❑ 6 Mike Croel .05 .02
❑ 7 Paul Justin .10 .05
❑ 8 Ivory Lee Brown .05 .02
❑ 9 Herman Moore .75 .35
❑ 10 Derrick Thomas FLB .25 .11
❑ 11 Keith Traylor .05 .02
❑ 12 Joe Johnson .05 .02
❑ 13 Dan McGwire .05 .02
❑ 14 Harvey Williams .10 .05
❑ 15 Eric Moten .05 .02

		MINT	EXC
☐ 16	Steve Zucker	.05	.02
☐ 17	Randal Hill	.05	.02
☐ 18	Browning Nagle	.05	.02
☐ 19	Stan Thomas	.05	.02
☐ 20	Emmitt Smith FLB	.75	.35
☐ 21	Ted Washington	.05	.02
☐ 22	Lamar Rogers	.05	.02
☐ 23	Kenny Walker	.05	.02
☐ 24	Howard Griffith	.05	.02
☐ 25	Reggie Johnson	.05	.02
☐ 26	Lawrence Dawsey	.05	.02
☐ 27	Joe Garten	.05	.02
☐ 28	Moe Gardner	.05	.02
☐ 29	Michael Stonebreaker	.05	.02
☐ 30	Jeff George FLB	.10	.05
☐ 31	Leigh Steinberg	.05	.02
☐ 32	John Flannery	.05	.02
☐ 33	Pat Harlow	.05	.02
☐ 34	Kanavis McGhee	.05	.02
☐ 35	Mike Dumas	.05	.02
☐ 36	Godfrey Myles	.05	.02
☐ 37	Shawn Moore	.05	.02
☐ 38	Jeff Graham	.10	.05
☐ 39	Ricky Watters	.60	.25
☐ 40	Andre Ware	.10	.05
☐ 41	Henry Jones	.05	.02
☐ 42	Eric Turner	.05	.02
☐ 43	Bob Woolf	.05	.02
☐ 44	Randy Baldwin	.05	.02
☐ 45	Mo Lewis	.05	.02
☐ 46	Jerry Evans	.05	.02
☐ 47	Derek Russell	.05	.02
☐ 48	Merton Hanks	.10	.05
☐ 49	Kevin Donnalley	.05	.02
☐ 50	Troy Aikman FLB	.50	.23
☐ 51	William Thomas	.10	.05
☐ 52	Chris Thome	.05	.02
☐ 53	Ricky Ervins	.05	.02
☐ 54	Jake Reed	.25	.11
☐ 55	Jerome Henderson	.05	.02
☐ 56	Mark Vander Poel	.05	.02
☐ 57	Bernard Ellison	.05	.02
☐ 58	Jack Mills	.05	.02
☐ 59	Jarrod Bunch	.05	.02
☐ 60	Mark Carrier DB	.05	.02
☐ 61	Rocen Keeton	.05	.02
☐ 62	Louis Riddick	.05	.02
☐ 63	Bobby Wilson	.05	.02
☐ 64	Steve Jackson	.05	.02
☐ 65	Brett Favre	2.50	1.10
☐ 66	Ernie Mills	.10	.05
☐ 67	Joe Valerio	.05	.02
☐ 68	Chris Smith	.05	.02
☐ 69	Ralph Cindrich	.05	.02
☐ 70	Christian Okoye	.10	.05
☐ 71	Charles McRae	.05	.02
☐ 72	Jon Vaughn	.05	.02
☐ 73	Eric Swann	.10	.05
☐ 74	Bill Musgrave	.05	.02
☐ 75	Eric Bieniemy	.05	.02
☐ 76	Pat Tyrance	.05	.02
☐ 77	Vinnie Clark	.05	.02
☐ 78	Eugene Williams	.05	.02
☐ 79	Rob Carpenter	.05	.02
☐ 80	Deion Sanders FLB	.25	.11
☐ 81	Roman Phifer	.05	.02
☐ 82	Greg Lewis	.05	.02
☐ 83	John Johnson	.05	.02
☐ 84	Richard Howell	.05	.02
☐ 85	Jesse Campbell	.05	.02
☐ 86	Stanley Richard	.05	.02
☐ 87	Alfred Williams	.05	.02
☐ 88	Mike Pritchard	.10	.05
☐ 89	Mel Agee	.05	.02
☐ 90	Aaron Craver	.05	.02
☐ 91	Tim Barnett	.05	.02
☐ 92	Wesley Carroll	.10	.05
☐ 93	Kevin Scott	.05	.02
☐ 94	Darren Lewis	.05	.02
☐ 95	Tim Bruton	.05	.02
☐ 96	Tim James	.05	.02
☐ 97	Darryll Lewis	.05	.02
☐ 98	Shawn Jefferson	.25	.11
☐ 99	Mitch Donahue	.05	.02
☐ 100	Marvin Demoff	.05	.02
☐ 101	Adrian Cooper	.05	.02
☐ 102	Bruce Pickens	.05	.02
☐ 103	Scott Zolak	.05	.02
☐ 104	Phil Hansen	.05	.02
☐ 105	Ed King	.05	.02
☐ 106	Mike Jones	.05	.02
☐ 107	Alvin Harper	.10	.05
☐ 108	Robert Young	.05	.02
☐ 109	Offensive Prospects Nick Bell Brett Favre Alvin Harper Charles McRae	1.00	.45
☐ 110	Defensive Prospects Mike Croel Eric Swann Eric Turner	.10	.05
☐ 111	Checklist 1	.05	.02
☐ 112	Checklist 2	.05	.02
☐ NNO	Salute/Advertisement American Flag background	.05	.02

1995 Superior Pix

		MINT	EXC
COMPLETE SET (110)		12.00	5.50
☐ 1	Ki-Jana Carter	.10	.05
☐ 2	Tony Boselli	.10	.05
☐ 3	Steve McNair	1.25	.55
☐ 4	Michael Westbrook	.50	.23
☐ 5	Kerry Collins	.50	.23
☐ 6	Terrell Davis	6.00	2.70
☐ 7	Kevin Bouie	.05	.02
☐ 8	Brian Williams	.05	.02
☐ 9	Kez McCorvey	.05	.02
☐ 10	Kyle Brady	.05	.02
☐ 11	Rob Johnson	.75	.35
☐ 12	Carl Greenwood	.05	.02
☐ 13	Mark Fields	.05	.02
☐ 14	Andrew Greene	.05	.02
☐ 15	Orlando Thomas	.05	.02
☐ 16	Don Sasa	.05	.02
☐ 17	Brent Moss	.05	.02
☐ 18	Jamal Willis	.05	.02
☐ 19	Michael Hendricks	.05	.02
☐ 20	Rashaan Salaam	.10	.05
☐ 21	John Sacca	.05	.02
☐ 22	Cory Raymer	.05	.02
☐ 23	Kirby Dar Dar	.10	.05
☐ 24	Lee DeRamus	.05	.02
☐ 25	Joey Galloway	1.00	.45
☐ 26	Mike Frederick	.05	.02
☐ 27	Todd Collins	.10	.05
☐ 28	Stoney Case	.10	.05
☐ 29	Devin Bush	.05	.02
☐ 30	Chad May	.05	.02
☐ 31	Darick Holmes	.10	.05
☐ 32	Johnny Thomas	.05	.02
☐ 33	Luther Elliss	.05	.02
☐ 34	Tyrone Wheatley	.25	.11
☐ 35	Terry Connealy	.05	.02
☐ 36	Ruben Brown	.05	.02
☐ 37	Kelvin Anderson	.05	.02
☐ 38	Tony Berti	.05	.02
☐ 39	Steve Ingram	.05	.02
☐ 40	Kevin Carter	.05	.02
☐ 41	Dave Wohlabaugh	.05	.02
☐ 42	Mike Morton	.05	.02
☐ 43	Steve Stenstrom	.05	.02
☐ 44	Zach Wiegert	.05	.02
☐ 45	Rodney Thomas	.05	.02
☐ 46	Eddie Goines	.05	.02
☐ 47	Kenny Gales	.05	.02
☐ 48	Jamal Ellis	.05	.02
☐ 49	Demetrius Edwards	.05	.02
☐ 50	Justin Armour	.05	.02
☐ 51	Billy Williams	.05	.02
☐ 52	Ed Hervey	.05	.02
☐ 53	Antonio Armstrong	.05	.02
☐ 54	Oliver Gibson	.05	.02
☐ 55	David Dunn	.10	.05
☐ 56	Tyrone Davis	.05	.02
☐ 57	Craig Newsome	.05	.02
☐ 58	William Strong	.05	.02
☐ 59	Sherman Williams	.05	.02
☐ 60	James O. Stewart	.75	.35
☐ 61	Bryan Schwartz	.05	.02
☐ 62	Frank Sanders	.25	.11
☐ 63	Barrett Robbins	.05	.02
☐ 64	Bronzell Miller	.05	.02
☐ 65	Curtis Martin	1.25	.55
☐ 66	Chris T. Jones	.10	.05
☐ 67	Dave Barr	.05	.02
☐ 68	Anthony Brown	.05	.02
☐ 69	Ken Dilger	.05	.02
☐ 70	Warren Sapp	.10	.05
☐ 71	James A. Stewart	.05	.02
☐ 72	Corey Fuller	.05	.02
☐ 73	Christian Fauria	.10	.05
☐ 74	Brian DeMarco	.05	.02
☐ 75	J.J. Stokes	.25	.11
☐ 76	Hicham El-Mashtoub	.05	.02
☐ 77	Anthony Cook	.05	.02
☐ 78	Mark Bruener	.10	.05
☐ 79	Blake Brockermeyer	.05	.02
☐ 80	Derrick Brooks	.25	.11
☐ 81	Joe Aska	.05	.02
☐ 82	Lance Brown	.05	.02
☐ 83	Pete Mitchell	.05	.02
☐ 84	Kordell Stewart	1.00	.45
☐ 85	Bobby Taylor	.10	.05
☐ 86	Jimmy Hitchcock	.05	.02
☐ 87	Jack Jackson	.05	.02
☐ 88	Ray Zellars	.05	.02
☐ 89	Darius Holland	.05	.02
☐ 90	Derrick Alexander	.10	.05
☐ 91	Torey Hunter	.05	.02
☐ 92	Scotty Lewis	.05	.02
☐ 93	Carl Reeves	.05	.02
☐ 94	Terrell Fletcher	.05	.02
☐ 95	Ontiwaun Carter	.05	.02
☐ 96	Trezelle Jenkins	.05	.02
☐ 97	Mark Birchmeier	.05	.02
☐ 98	Len Raney	.05	.02
☐ 99	Ronald Cherry	.05	.02
☐ 100	Tyrone Wheatley	.25	.11
☐ 101	John Jones	.05	.02
☐ 102	Zack Crockett	.05	.02
☐ 103	Larry Jones	.05	.02
☐ 104	Michael McCoy	.05	.02
☐ 105	Ellis Johnson	.05	.02
☐ 106	Jerrott Willard	.05	.02
☐ 107	Jason James	.05	.02
☐ 108	J.J. Smith	.05	.02
☐ 109	Mike Mamula	.05	.02
☐ 110	Checklist	.05	.02

1991 Wild Card Draft

		MINT	NRMT
COMPLETE SET (160)		6.00	2.70

*5 STRIPES: 1X TO 2.5X BASIC CARDS
*10 STRIPES: 1.5X TO 3.5X BASIC CARDS
*20 STRIPES: 2X TO 5X BASIC CARDS
*50 STRIPES: 4X TO 10X BASIC CARDS
*100 STRIPES: 10X TO 25X BASIC CARDS
*1000 STRIPES: 50X TO 120X BASIC CARDS

		MINT	NRMT
☐ 1A	Wild Card 1	.05	.02
☐ 1B	Todd Lyght	.05	.02
☐ 2	Kelvin Pritchett	.05	.02
☐ 3	Robert Young	.05	.02

❑ 4 Reggie Johnson .05 .02
❑ 5 Eric Turner .10 .05
❑ 6 Pat Tyrance .05 .02
❑ 7 Curvin Richards .05 .02
❑ 8 Calvin Stephens .05 .02
❑ 9 Corey Miller .05 .02
❑ 10 Michael Jackson .10 .05
❑ 11 Simmie Carter .05 .02
❑ 12 Roland Smith .05 .02
❑ 13 Pat O'Hara .05 .02
❑ 14 Scott Conover .05 .02
❑ 15A Wild Card 2 .05 .02
❑ 15B Russell Maryland .05 .02
❑ 16 Greg Amsler .05 .02
❑ 17 Moe Gardner .05 .02
❑ 18 Howard Griffith .05 .02
❑ 19 David Daniels .05 .02
❑ 20 Henry Jones .05 .02
❑ 21 Don Davey .05 .02
❑ 22A Wild Card 3 .05 .02
❑ 22B Rocket Ismail .40 .18
❑ 23 Richie Andrews .05 .02
❑ 24 Shawn Moore .05 .02
❑ 25 Anthony Moss .05 .02
❑ 26 Vince Moore .05 .02
❑ 27 Leroy Thompson .05 .02
❑ 28 Darrick Brown .05 .02
❑ 29 Mel Agee .05 .02
❑ 30 Darryll Lewis .05 .02
❑ 31 Hyland Hickson .05 .02
❑ 32 Leonard Russell .05 .02
❑ 33 Floyd Fields .05 .02
❑ 34 Esera Tuaolo .05 .02
❑ 35 Todd Marinovich .05 .02
❑ 36 Gary Wellman .05 .02
❑ 37 Ricky Ervins .05 .02
❑ 38 Pat Harlow .05 .02
❑ 39 Mo Lewis .05 .02
❑ 40 John Kasay .05 .02
❑ 41 Phil Hansen .05 .02
❑ 42 Kevin Donnalley .05 .02
❑ 43 Dexter Davis .05 .02
❑ 44 Vance Hammond .05 .02
❑ 45 Chris Gardocki .05 .02
❑ 46 Bruce Pickens .05 .02
❑ 47 Godfrey Myles .05 .02
❑ 48 Ernie Mills .10 .05
❑ 49 Derek Russell .05 .02
❑ 50 Chris Zorich .05 .02
❑ 51 Alfred Williams .05 .02
❑ 52 Jon Vaughn .05 .02
❑ 53 Adrian Cooper .05 .02
❑ 54 Eric Bieniemy .05 .02
❑ 55 Robert Bailey .05 .02
❑ 56 Ricky Watters .60 .25
❑ 57 Mark Vander Poel .05 .02
❑ 58 James Joseph .05 .02
❑ 59 Darren Lewis .05 .02
❑ 60 Wesley Carroll .10 .05
❑ 61 Dave Key .05 .02
❑ 62 Mike Pritchard .10 .05
❑ 63 Craig Erickson .10 .05
❑ 64 Browning Nagle .05 .02
❑ 65 Mike Dumas .05 .02
❑ 66 Andre Jones .05 .02
❑ 67 Herman Moore .75 .35
❑ 68 Greg Lewis .05 .02
❑ 69 James Goode .05 .02
❑ 70 Stan Thomas .05 .02
❑ 71 Jerome Henderson .05 .02
❑ 72 Doug Thomas .05 .02
❑ 73 Tony Covington .05 .02
❑ 74 Charles Mincy .05 .02
❑ 75 Kanavis McGhee .05 .02
❑ 76 Tom Backes .05 .02
❑ 77 Fernandus Vinson .05 .02
❑ 78 Marcus Robertson .05 .02
❑ 79 Eric Harmon .05 .02
❑ 80 Rob Selby .05 .02
❑ 81 Ed King .05 .02
❑ 82 William Thomas .05 .02
❑ 83 Mike Jones .05 .02
❑ 84 Paul Justin .05 .02
❑ 85 Robert Wilson .05 .02
❑ 86 Jesse Campbell .05 .02
❑ 87 Hayward Haynes .05 .02
❑ 88 Mike Croel .05 .02
❑ 89 Jeff Graham .10 .05
❑ 90 Vinnie Clark .05 .02
❑ 91 Keith Cash .05 .02
❑ 92 Tim Ryan .05 .02
❑ 93 Jarrod Bunch .05 .02
❑ 94 Stanley Richard .05 .02
❑ 95 Alvin Harper .05 .02
❑ 96 Bob Dahl .05 .02
❑ 97 Mark Gunn .05 .02
❑ 98 Frank Blevins .05 .02
❑ 99 Harvey Williams .10 .05
❑ 100 Dixon Edwards .05 .02
❑ 101 Blake Miller .05 .02
❑ 102 Bobby Wilson .05 .02
❑ 103 Chuck Webb .05 .02
❑ 104 Randal Hill .10 .05
❑ 105 Shane Curry .05 .02
❑ 106 Barry Sanders 1.00 .45
❑ 107 Richard Fain .05 .02
❑ 108 Joe Garten .05 .02
❑ 109 Dean Dingman .05 .02
❑ 110 Mark Tucker .05 .02
❑ 111 Dan McGwire .05 .02
❑ 112 Paul Glonek .05 .02
❑ 113 Tom Dohring .05 .02
❑ 114 Joe Sims .05 .02
❑ 115 Bryan Cox .05 .02
❑ 116 Bobby Olive .05 .02
❑ 117 Blaise Bryant .05 .02
❑ 118 Charles Johnson .05 .02
❑ 119 Brett Favre 2.50 1.10
❑ 120 Luis Cristobal .05 .02
❑ 121 Don Gibson .05 .02
❑ 122 Scott Ross .05 .02
❑ 123 Huey Richardson .05 .02
❑ 124 Chris Smith .05 .02
❑ 125 Duane Young .05 .02
❑ 126 Eric Swann .10 .05
❑ 127 Jeff Fite .05 .02
❑ 128 Eugene Williams .05 .02
❑ 129 Harlan Davis .05 .02
❑ 130 James Bradley .05 .02
❑ 131 Rob Carpenter .05 .02
❑ 132 Dennis Ransom .05 .02
❑ 133 Mike Arthur .05 .02
❑ 134 Chuck Weatherspoon .05 .02
❑ 135 Darrell Malone .05 .02
❑ 136 George Thornton .05 .02
❑ 137 Lamar McGriggs .05 .02
❑ 138 Alex Johnson .05 .02
❑ 139 Eric Moten .05 .02
❑ 140 Joe Valerio .05 .02
❑ 141 Jake Reed .25 .11
❑ 142 Ernie Thompson .05 .02
❑ 143 Roland Poles .05 .02
❑ 144 Randy Bethel .05 .02
❑ 145 Terry Bagsby .05 .02
❑ 146 Tim James .05 .02
❑ 147 Kenny Walker .05 .02
❑ 148 Nolan Harrison .05 .02
❑ 149 Keith Traylor .05 .02
❑ 150 Nick Subis .05 .02
❑ 151 Scott Zolak .05 .02
❑ 152 Pio Sagapolutele .05 .02
❑ 153 James Jones .05 .02
❑ 154 Mike Sullivan .05 .02
❑ 155 Joe Johnson .05 .02
❑ 156 Todd Scott .05 .02
❑ 157 Checklist 1 .05 .02
❑ 158 Checklist 2 .05 .02
❑ 159 Checklist 3 .05 .02
❑ 160 Checklist 4 .05 .02

Acknowledgments

A great deal of diligence, hard work, and dedicated effort went into this First Edition. The high standards to which we hold ourselves, however, could not have been met without the expert input and generous amount of time contributed by many people. Our sincere thanks are extended to each and every one of you.

Each year we refine the process of developing the most accurate and up-to-date information for this book. Thanks again to all of the contributors nationwide (listed below) as well as our staff here in Dallas.

Those who have worked closely with us on this and many other books have again proven themselves invaluable — Action Sports Cards, Mike Aronstein, Jerry Bell, Bubba Bennett, Chuck Bennett (Clubhouse), Mike Blaisdell, Bill Bossert (Mid-Atlantic Sports Cards), John Bradley (JOGO), Ralph Ciarlo, Mike Caffey, Don Chubey, Joe Colabella, Alan Custer, Robert Der, Bill and Diane Dodge, Rick Donohoo, John Douglas, John Durkos, Fleer/SkyBox (Rich Bradley), Gervise Ford, Steve Freedman, Larry and Jeff Fritsch, Mike Gallella, Steven Galletta, Dick Gilkeson, Steve Gold (AU Sports), Mike and Howard Gordon, George Grauer, Jerry and Etta Hersh, Mike Hersh, Gary Hlady, Ed Kabala, Wayne Kleman, Carl Lamendola, Lew Lipset, Michael McDonald, Pat Mills, Michael Moretto, Jeff Morris, Pacific (Mike Mosier), Playoff (Tracy Hackler and Rob Springs), NFL Properties (Bill Barron), Don Niemi, Lawrence Nyeste, Mike O'Brien, Richard Ochoa, Oldies and Goodies (Nigel Spill), Pacific Trading Cards (Mike Cramer and Mike Monson), Michael Perrotta, Jack Pollard, Gavin Riley, Greg Rosen, Rotman Productions, John Rumierz, San Diego Sport Collectibles, Barry Sanders, Kevin Savage, Mike Schechter (MSA), Rick Smith, Gerry Sobie, John Spalding, Pat Quinn, Murvin Sterling, Richard Tattoli, Paul S. Taylor, Lee Temanson, Topps (Clay Luraschi), Upper Deck (Justin Kanoya), U-Trading Cards (Mike Livingston), Rob Veres (Burbank Sportscards), Brian Wentz, Dale Wesolewski, Bill Wesslund, Kit Young and Bob Ivanjack (Kit Young Cards), Robert Zanze, Steve Zeller, Dean Zindler, and Tim Zwick.

Many people have provided checklist verifications, errata, and/or background information. At the risk of inadvertently overlooking or omitting these many contributors, we would like to individually thank A & J Cards, Jerry Adamic, Aliso Hills Stamp and Coin, Rich Altman, Neil Armstrong (World Series Cards), Tom Barborich, Red Barnes, Bob Bawiel, William E. Baxendale, Dean Bedell, Patrick Benes, Carl Berg, Eric Berger, Kevin Bergson, Skip Bertman, Beulah Sports (Jeff Blatt), Brian L. Bigelow, David Bitar, Virgil Burns, Danny Cariseo, Dale Carlson, Bud Carter, Sally Carves, Dwight Chapin, Howard Churchill, Ralph H. Ciarlo, Orr Cihlar, Craig Coddling, Jon Cohen, Matt Collett, Taylor Crane, Jim Curie, Paul Czuchna, Samuel Davis, Tony Wayne Davis,Cliff Dolgins, Joseph Drelich, E and R Galleries, Ed Emmitt, The End Zone, Darrell Ereth, Doak Ewing, Rodney Faciane, Bob Farmer, Terry Faulkner, Fleischman and Walsh, Craig Frank, Mark Franke, Richard Freiburghouse, Brian Froehlich, Gallagher Archives, Tony Galovich, Tom Giacchino, Michael R. Gionet, David Giove, Todd Goldenberg, Jeff Goldstein, Gregg Gornes, Joseph Griffin, Robert G. Gross, Hall's Nostalgia, Steve Hart, Michael Hattley, Rod Heffern, Kevin Heffner, Dennis Heitland, Clay Hill, Russ Hoover, Nelson Hu, Don Hurry, Jeff Issler, Bob Ivanjack, Robert R. Jackson, Dan Jaskula, Terry Johnson, Craig Jones, Stewart Jones, Larry Jordon, Chuck Juliana, Loyd Jungling, Jay and Mary Kasper, Frank Katen, Jack Kemps (Triple Play), Rick Keplinger, John Kilian, Ron Klassnik, Don Knutsen, Bob and Bryan Kornfield, Terry Kreider, George Kruk, Thomas Kunnecke, Dan Lavin, Walter Ledzki, Marc Lefkowitz (Baseball Card Baron), Tom Leon (Unisource Collectibles), Irv Lerner, Ed Lim, Frank Lopez, Neil Lopez, Frank Lucito, Kevin Lynch, Bud Lyle, Jim Macie, Gary Madrack, Paul Marchant, Adam Martin, Alex

McCollum, Bob McDonald, Steve McHenry, Carlos Medina, Fernando Mercado, Chris Merrill, Blake Meyer, Lee Milazzo, Dick Millerd, Ron Moermond, Morgan Moore, John Morales, Brian Morris, Rusty Morse, Dick Mueller, Bob Nappe, Roger Neufeldt, Raymond Ng, John O'Hara, Glenn Olsen, Mike Orth, Andrew Pak, Clay Pasternack, Paul and Judy's, John Peavy, Mark Perna, Steve Peters, Ira Petsrillo, Tom Pfirrmann, Chris Pomerleau, Jeff Porter, Jeff Prillaman, Jonathan Pullano, Loran Pulver, Phil Regli, Tom Reid, Owen Ricker, Evelyn Roberts, Jim Roberts, Mark Rose, Chip Rosenberg, Blake and Sheldon Rudman, George Rusnak, Terry Ryan, Terry Sack, Joe Sak, Nathan Schank, R.J. Schulhof, Perry Schwartzberg, Patrick W. Scoggin, Dan Scolman, Rick Scruggs, Charlie Seaver, Burns Searfoss, Eric Shillito, Shinder's Cards, Bob Singer, John Smith, Keith Smith, Carl Specht, Don Spagnolo, Sportcards Etc., Vic Stanley, Bill Steinberg, Cary Stephenson, Dan Stickney, Jack Stowe, Del Stracke, Richard Strobino, Kevin Struss, Bob Swick, George Tahinos, Jeff Thomas (Koinz and Kardz), D. Tisdale, Bud Tompkins, Greg Tranter, John Tumazos, Eric Valkys, Wayne Varner, Kevin M. VanderKelen, Bill Vizas, Tom Wall, Mike Wasserman, Keith Watson, Mark Watson, Rick Wilson, Jay Wolt (Cavalcade of Sports), Paul Wright, Darryl Yee, Sheraton Yee, and Eugene Zalewski.

Every year we make active solicitations for expert input. We are particularly appreciative of the help (however extensive or cursory) provided for this volume. We receive many inquiries, comments and questions regarding material within this book. In fact, each and every one is read and digested. Time constraints, however, prevent us from personally replying. But keep sharing your knowledge. Even though we cannot respond to each letter, you are making significant contributions to the hobby through your interest and comments.

The effort to continually refine and improve our books also involves a growing number of people and types of expertise on our home team. Our company boasts a substantial Sports Data Publishing team, which strengthens our ability to provide comprehensive analysis of the marketplace.

Our football analysts played a major part in compiling this year's book, traveling thousands of miles during the past year to attend sports card shows and visit card shops around the United States and Canada. The Beckett Football specialists are Jim Churilla, Dan Hitt (Manager of SDP as well as Football Price Guide Editor), David Porter, Bill Sutherland and Joe White.

Dan Hitt's coordination of input as BFCM editor helped immeasurably; Rich Klein as research analyst and primary proofer also added many hours of painstaking work.

The effort was ably assisted by the rest of the Analytical Team: Wayne Grove, Clint Hall, Keith Hower, Tony Joseph, Denny Parsons, Grant Sandground (Senior Price Guide Editor) and Brad Grmela.

The price-gathering and analytical talents of this fine group of hobbyists have helped make our Beckett team stronger, while making this guide and its companion monthly Price Guide more widely recognized as the hobby's most reliable and relied-upon source of pricing information.

In addition, Regina McGill contributed many programming improvements to make this process smoother while Gean Paul Figari is responsible for the typesetting and general preparation of this volume.

BECKETT GRADING SERVICES

$4 OFF *one card grading*

Cut out coupon and attach to BGS submission form. No photocopies or other reproductions accepted. Offer is good at any BGS service level. To receive discount on multiple submissions, one coupon must accompany each card submitted. Offer expires May 15, 2002. Cannot be combined with any other promotional offer. For a submission form, complete submission instructions or more information about Beckett Grading Services, visit our web site at www.beckett.com.

HOCF01

B

BECKETT GRADING SERVICES

$4 OFF *one card grading*

Cut out coupon and attach to BGS submission form. No photocopies or other reproductions accepted. Offer is good at any BGS service level. To receive discount on multiple submissions, one coupon must accompany each card submitted. Offer expires May 15, 2002. Cannot be combined with any other promotional offer. For a submission form, complete submission instructions or more information about Beckett Grading Services, visit our web site at www.beckett.com.

HOCF01

notes